INTRODUCTION

In December 2003 more albums were sold in the UK than in any previous month in history, with 32 million of them crossing the counters of record stores and supermarkets throughout the land. With internet shopping contributing to this figure, British album sales are, for the first time, 10 times those of singles.

What better time, then, to update our British Hit Albums information, which is, for the first time, included in this one volume with British Hit Singles? Guinness World Records last published its albums book in 1996, and a lot of troubled water has flowed under the bridge since then. Illegal downloading has plagued the record industry in recent years, but still UK album sales (discounted quite heavily if you're a customer) buck the trend of depression elsewhere in the world. The official album chart is receiving more recognition than ever: it gets a brief airing on Top of the Pops and it has its own show on BBC Radio 2. In fact, many chart-watchers believe it gives a more accurate picture of what's happening in music these days than the singles market.

Don't write off the single, though. The format may well hit back when the legal downloading of individual songs really takes off. The technology that makes this possible is the perfect partner to create a new listing of the most popular songs alongside the physical CD and vinyl purchaser.

Because we last published British Hit Albums in 1996 you would be expecting eight years of updates in this book, right? Wrong, it's 10. An extra two years have been excavated by chartologists from the archives dating back to 1956, not 1958, which all previous editions of British Hit Albums used as an albums chart start date. For this we can thank chart researchers Alan Smith and Keith Badman, together with assistance from our own chart consultant Dave McAleer and the support of the Official UK Chart Company.

So enjoy the results and continue your feedback on the singles chart data (printed in black), album data (printed in red) and the many new features dotted throughout the 768 pages.

David Roberts
Editor: British Hit Singles & Albums

The seven editions of British Hit Albums
Paul Gambaccini, Tim Rice, Jo Rice and Mike Read introduced the first edition of British Hit Albums in 1983 to a growing army of fans with a keen interest in LP history thus: 'Should you enjoy it, we hope to present updated volumes on a regular basis. Should you not like it, we will flagellate ourselves with wet strands of spaghetti and find some other way to express our passion for the charts. These books are, after all, a socially approved form of madness, and they allow us to be crazy together.'

CONTENTS

The main A-Z listing of every act to have made the singles and album charts starts on page 9. The song title index can be found on page 627. You can also navigate your way around the book with this easy-to-find run-down of the feature articles dotted throughout the 768 pages.

CHART MILESTONES

What follows is a history of the charts used to compile this book and some significant changes to the way in which we have listened to music over the years.

1952 – First UK singles chart launched by New Musical Express. No.1 in the first Top 12 on Friday 14 November 1952 was Al Martino with 'Here in My Heart'.

1953 – Seven-inch vinyl 45rpm pop singles introduced.

1954 – The singles chart became a Top 20 on 1 October.

1956 – Top 30 singles chart established on 13 April and the albums chart used by this book began with a Record Mirror Top 5 on 28 July.

1958 – Albums chart extended to a Top 10 using Melody Maker on 8 November.

1959 – Sales of vinyl 45s overtook 78s. Newspaper strike prevented album chart publication between 27 June and 8 August with the 20 June chart repeated during this period.

1960 – For the purposes of this book a larger Top 50 Record Retailer chart data replaced NME singles listings on 5 March, and a Record Retailer Top 20 albums chart replaced the Melody Maker version on 26 March. On 10 March the date of the chart changed to a Thursday.

1963 – Singles chart was independently audited for Record Retailer.

1966 – Albums chart became a Top 30 on 14 April and Top 40 on 8 December.

1967 – On 5 July the date of the chart changed to a Wednesday.

1969 – Date of the chart changed to a Saturday on 9 August. Albums chart decreased to a Top 15 on 12 February, rose to a Top 20 on 11 June, back up to a Top 40 on 25 June, a Top 32 for one week on 9 August and dropped to a Top 25 on 11 October. Then it varied from a Top 20 to Top 24 until January 1970. Singles Top 50 now compiled for Record Retailer and BBC by the British Market Research Bureau.

Brian Epstein's 'stable' of stars, Beatles, Gerry and The Pacemakers, Billy J Kramer and The Dakotas, pose for the camera in 1963

Ring in the changes: Edison recorded sound for the first time on his phonograph in 1877. Today's Apple iPod is capable of storing 10,000 songs

CHART MILESTONES CONTINUED

1970 – Albums chart list varied from a list totalling 47 to 77 entries from 31 January to 9 January 1971.

1971 – Record Retailer became Record and Tape Retailer. Album chart stabilised as a Top 50 on 16 January. Postal strike resulted in no Record and Tape Retailer album chart from 6 February to 3 April and, as a result, this book returned to Melody Maker chart listings for this eight-week period. On 7 August the Record and Tape Retailer Full Price Chart was combined with the previously separate Budget Chart.

1972 – Album chart reverted to a Full Price listing only on 8 January. Record and Tape Retailer changed its name to Music Week.

1973 – First year of BPI trade delivery figures which showed 54.6 million singles sold compared to 96.5 million LPs. Album chart was a Top 24 for one week on 13 January.

1974 – Album chart was a Top 42 for one week on 5 January.

1975 – Album chart became a Top 60 on 5 July.

1977 – The first edition of The Guinness Book of British Hit Singles was published. Singles sold in the year totalled 62.1 million.

1978 – Singles chart expanded to a Top 75. Album chart was a Top 30 for one week on 14 January. Singles sold in the year totalled 88.1 million.

1979 – Highest yearly figure for singles sales to date: 89.1 million. Two consecutive weeks' album charts were published simultaneously as a result of a new faster chart compilation system which enabled Music Week to catch up a week.

1980 – First cassette single released: 'C-30, C-60, C-90' by Bow Wow Wow. Singles sales dropped by 10 million.

1981 – Album chart became a Top 100.

1983 – Chart compilation taken over by Gallup with 500 record stores used. The first edition of The Guinness Book of British Hit Albums was published.

1986 – Sales of singles totalled 67.4 million, the first dip below 70 million in nine years.

1987 – First CD singles released. Singles chart announcement day changed from Tuesday lunchtime to Sunday teatime on 4 October.

1989 – Albums chart split in two with an Artists Top 75 and a Compilations Top 20.

1992 – CD singles outsold vinyl and cassette for the first time with sales dropping to 52.9 million. The chart in association with the BPI and Bard became the copyright of Chart Information Network Co Ltd (CIN).

1994 – Millward Brown took over the chart compilation from Gallup using a sample of 1,000 record stores.

1995 – Singles sales rose to more than 70 million for the year.

1996 – Album sales topped the 200-million mark for the first time.

1997 – Total sales of singles for the year totalled 87 million boosted by the UK's biggest best-seller, 'Candle in the Wind 1997' by Elton John.

2000 – Sales of singles dropped to 66.1 million.

2001 – CIN changed its name to The Official UK Charts Company.

2003 – Plans for the official UK singles and album charts to be sponsored by Coca-Cola were announced. Albums shipped to the trade reached an all-time high of 237 million.

TODAY'S CHART

The Official UK Charts Company is responsible for the commissioning, marketing, distribution and management of the UK's official music charts. Sales information is supplied by more than 5,600 retailers including all the major high street music retail chains, supermarkets, a number of internet retailers and approximately 600 independent record stores. This market research sample equates to 99 per cent of the total UK singles market. The week's sales which contribute to the official charts are collated after the close of business on Saturday for release from noon the following day. The chart rundown at 4pm on Sundays is still the most listened-to programme on BBC Radio 1.

A-Z BY ARTIST

Here begins the alphabetical listing of every group, solo singer, duo, trio, orchestra, glove puppet, cartoon character, choir, marching band, brass band, comedian, actor, rapper, pop idol, footballer, etc that has achieved the distinction of at least one week at the lowest position in the UK singles and albums charts

Elvis Presley, quite simply the most successful chart act of all time

HOW TO USE THE A-Z

This contrived entry (below) illustrates how to navigate your way through the mountain of information in this A-Z by Artist section of the book. We have used one of the most entertaining new acts around for this purpose. They had not charted at time of going to press but they kept us hugely entertained during the production of this book. Check out these Welsh rappers and watch them get listed for real in the next edition.

Alphabetical ordering

Note that **all hit singles are printed in black** and **all hit albums are printed in red.** In keeping with traditional alphabetical ordering, artist names consisting of initials (eg AC/DC, KLF) are dealt with at the beginning of each letter's section, except when the names have become acronyms (ie pronounceable as one word such as for Abba). The only exceptions to this rule are for acts appearing as DJs and MCs where their actual names are listed in alphabetical order.

Re-entries

All singles that have re-entered the chart at some point are indicated by (re) which shows that the single has re-entered once and (2re), (3re), etc for twice and three times. Where a re-entry on the chart has outperformed the original hit, you will find the relevant information as an act's footnote. All the weeks on chart for re-entries are added together with those of the one listing for that single. There is no re-entry data in the albums listings. Albums re-entries are too numerous to record and all re-entry weeks on chart are given with the one original chart entry.

Biographies

Abbreviations: b. – born, d. – died, b – bass guitar, d – drums, fl – flute, g – guitar, k – keyboard, prc – percussion, prog – programming, s – saxophone, syn – synthesizer, t – trumpet, v – vocals. The act biographies include real names (if the act has a different surname) of all solo artists and duos scoring a Top 40 hit single or album and the death date of deceased soloists and duo members.

Act name ›

GOLDIE LOOKIN' CHAIN 398 *Top 500*

‹ Indicates position of an act within the list of Top 500 acts of all time, calculated by weeks on chart totals at the end of the biographies

UK, male rap / production / DJ group, the 'Welsh Wu-Tang' put Newport firmly on the map with their distinctive vocal style. The leisurewear-clad collective was finally recognised as future stars in 2004. Members include 2hats (v), Adam Hussein (v), Mike Balls (v), Billy Web (v), Mr Loveeggs (v), the Maggot (v), Mystical (v), P.Xain (v) and DJ Shopmobility (prog). Their varied output includes heavy metal and electro but is centred around hip hop. Best-selling single: 'The Maggot' 1,306,422 (Singles: 53 weeks, Albums: 184 weeks)

Selected acts now have their best-selling single listed at the end of their biographies ›

‹ Peak position / weeks on chart

Dates indicate date record first entered the chart, not date of reaching peak postion ›

New listing for re-entries: › (3re) here denotes that MONKEY LOVE re-entered the Top 75 three times

‹ Label / catalogue numbers *Knowzit Records 013* generally taken from the seven-inch vinyl single before Jan 1993 and CD single after this

Date		Title / Label	pos	wks
19 Mar 01		**GLC PARENTAL WARNING** *Knowzit Records 002* [1]	14	5
24 Dec 01	●	**I WANT MY GLC (EP)** *Knowzit Records 006*	4	12
2 Feb 02	★	**THE MAGGOT** *Knowzit Records 09* ◆	1	22
30 Sep 02	●	**TAXI (ENTER THE DRAGON)** *Knowzit Records 010* ▲	8	8
1 Apr 03		**MONKEY LOVE (3re)** *Knowzit Records 011*	16	5
27 Dec 03		**SELF SUICIDE** *Knowzit Records 012*	52	1+
22 Oct 01	●	**DON'T BLAIM THE CHAIN** *Knowzit Records CD013*	6	55
3 Dec 01	★	**CHAIN'S ADDICTION** *Knowzit Records CD014* ■	1	102
13 Mar 02		**RETURN OF THE REDEYE** *Knowzit Records CD015*	26	8
11 Sep 02	★	**THE PARTY ALBUM** *Knowzit Records CD016*	1	14
30 Nov 03		**THE MANIFESTO** *Knowzit Records CD017*	11	5+

[1] [2] etc refers to a footnote › indicating a change to the name of the act for a particular single/album or a collaboration with another artist

[1] GLC featuring Ice T

Tracks on I Want My GLC (EP): Holiday / Shotgun Surgeon / Professor Doppelganger / Sexy Ladies

‹ EP track titles

Cross-reference linking › act to associated act

See also Adam HUSSEIN; DJ SHOPMOBILITY

UK No.1 ★★ UK Top 10 ●● Still on chart ++ UK entry at No.1 ■■ US No.1 ▲▲ UK million seller ◆

A *UK, male vocal / instrumental group (Singles: 18 weeks, Albums: 10 weeks)*

Date		Title / Label	pos	wks
7 Feb 98		**FOGHORN** *Tycoon TYCD 5*	63	1
11 Apr 98		**NUMBER ONE** *Tycoon TYCD 6*	47	1
27 Jun 98		**SING-A-LONG** *Tycoon TYCD 7*	57	1
24 Oct 98		**SUMMER ON THE UNDERGROUND** *Tycoon TYCD 8*	72	1
5 Jun 99		**OLD FOLKS** *Tycoon TYCD 9*	54	1
21 Aug 99		**I LOVE LAKE TAHOE** *Tycoon TYCD 10*	59	1
2 Mar 02	●	**NOTHING** *London LONCD 463*	9	6
1 Jun 02		**STARBUCKS** *London LONCD 467*	20	3
30 Nov 02		**SOMETHING'S GOING ON** *London LONCD 471*	51	1
13 Sep 03		**GOOD TIME** *London LONCD 480*	23	2
28 Aug 99		**MONKEY KONG** *Tycoon 3984276952*	62	1
16 Mar 02		**HI-FI SERIOUS** *London 927447762*	18	9

ABC (356 Top 500) *Glossy but witty pop group formed 1980 in Sheffield, South Yorkshire, UK. Led by stylish vocalist Martin Fry b. 9 Mar 1959. First UK group of the 1980s to prise four Top 20 hits off debut album (1982's 'The Lexicon of Love') and were equally successful Stateside (Singles: 93 weeks, Albums: 91 weeks)*

Date		Title / Label	pos	wks
31 Oct 81		**TEARS ARE NOT ENOUGH** *Neutron NT 101*	19	8
20 Feb 82	●	**POISON ARROW** *Neutron NT 102*	6	11
15 May 82	●	**THE LOOK OF LOVE (re)** *Neutron NT 103*	4	12
4 Sep 82	●	**ALL OF MY HEART** *Neutron NT 104*	5	8
5 Nov 83		**THAT WAS THEN THIS IS NOW** *Neutron NT 105*	18	4
21 Jan 84		**S.O.S.** *Neutron NT 106*	39	5
10 Nov 84		**HOW TO BE A MILLIONAIRE** *Neutron NT 107*	49	4
6 Apr 85		**BE NEAR ME** *Neutron NT 108*	26	4
15 Jun 85		**VANITY KILLS** *Neutron NT 109*	70	1
16 Jan 86		**OCEAN BLUE** *Neutron NT 110*	51	3
6 Jun 87		**WHEN SMOKEY SINGS** *Neutron NT 111*	11	10
5 Sep 87		**THE NIGHT YOU MURDERED LOVE** *Neutron NT 112*	31	8
28 Nov 87		**KING WITHOUT A CROWN** *Neutron NT 113*	44	3
27 May 89		**ONE BETTER WORLD** *Neutron NT 114*	32	4
23 Sep 89		**THE REAL THING** *Neutron NT 115*	68	1
14 Apr 90		**THE LOOK OF LOVE (re-mix)** *Neutron NT 116*	68	1
27 Jul 91		**LOVE CONQUERS ALL** *Parlophone R 6292*	47	2
11 Jan 92		**SAY IT** *Parlophone R 6298*	42	3
22 Mar 97		**STRANGER THINGS** *Blatant / Deconstruction 453632*	57	1
3 Jul 82	★	**THE LEXICON OF LOVE** *Neutron NTRS 1* ■	1	50
26 Nov 83		**BEAUTY STAB** *Neutron NTRL 2*	12	13
26 Oct 85		**HOW TO BE A ZILLIONAIRE** *Neutron NTRH 3*	28	3
24 Oct 87	●	**ALPHABET CITY** *Neutron NTRH 4*	7	10
28 Oct 89		**UP** *Neutron 838646 1*	58	1
21 Apr 90	●	**ABSOLUTELY** *Neutron 8429671*	7	12
24 Aug 91		**ABRACADABRA** *Parlophone PCS 7355*	50	1
4 Aug 01		**LOOK OF LOVE – THE VERY BEST OF ABC** *Mercury 5862372*	69	1

The act was a UK, male vocal / instrumental group for first six hits, and a UK / US, male / female vocal / instrumental group for the next four; male duo 87-92 and Martin Fry alone for 'Stranger Things'

A.B.'S *Japan, instrumental group (Albums: 2 weeks)*

Date		Title / Label	pos	wks
14 Apr 84		**DÉJÀ VU** *Street Sounds XKHAN 503*	80	2

AC/DC (124 Top 500)

Internationally acclaimed Australia-based quintet: Angus Young (g), Malcolm Young (g), Bon Scott (v) (d. 1980), Cliff Williams (b), Phillip Rudd (d). Brian Johnson (ex-Geordie) replaced Scott in 1980. No act has had more hit singles (28) without a Top 10 than AC/DC. Inducted into the Rock and Roll Hall of Fame in 2003 (Singles: 126 weeks, Albums: 255 weeks)

Date		Title / Label	pos	wks
10 Jun 78		**ROCK 'N' ROLL DAMNATION** *Atlantic K 11142*	24	9
1 Sep 79		**HIGHWAY TO HELL** *Atlantic K 11321*	56	4
2 Feb 80		**TOUCH TOO MUCH** *Atlantic K 11435*	29	9
28 Jun 80		**DIRTY DEEDS DONE DIRT CHEAP** *Atlantic HM 2*	47	3
28 Jun 80		**HIGH VOLTAGE (LIVE VERSION)** *Atlantic HM 1*	48	3
28 Jun 80		**IT'S A LONG WAY TO THE TOP (IF YOU WANNA ROCK 'N' ROLL)** *Atlantic HM 3*	55	3
28 Jun 80		**WHOLE LOTTA ROSIE** *Atlantic HM 4*	36	8
13 Sep 80		**YOU SHOOK ME ALL NIGHT LONG** *Atlantic K 11600*	38	6
29 Nov 80		**ROCK 'N' ROLL AIN'T NOISE POLLUTION** *Atlantic K 11630*	15	8
6 Feb 82		**LET'S GET IT UP** *Atlantic K 11706*	13	6
3 Jul 82		**FOR THOSE ABOUT TO ROCK (WE SALUTE YOU)** *Atlantic K 11721*	15	6
29 Oct 83		**GUNS FOR HIRE** *Atlantic A 9774*	37	4
4 Aug 84		**NERVOUS SHAKEDOWN** *Atlantic A 9651*	35	5
6 Jul 85		**DANGER** *Atlantic A 9532*	48	4
18 Jan 86		**SHAKE YOUR FOUNDATIONS** *Atlantic A 9474*	24	5
24 May 86		**WHO MADE WHO** *Atlantic A 9425*	16	5
30 Aug 86		**YOU SHOOK ME ALL NIGHT LONG (re-issue)** *Atlantic A 9377*	46	4
16 Jan 88		**HEATSEEKER** *Atlantic A 9136*	12	6
2 Apr 88		**THAT'S THE WAY I WANNA ROCK 'N' ROLL** *Atlantic A 9098*	22	5
22 Sep 90		**THUNDERSTRUCK** *Atco B 8907*	13	5
24 Nov 90		**MONEYTALKS** *Atco B 8886*	36	3
27 Apr 91		**ARE YOU READY** *Atco B 8830*	34	3
17 Oct 92		**HIGHWAY TO HELL (LIVE)** *Atco B 8479*	14	4
6 Mar 93		**DIRTY DEEDS DONE DIRT CHEAP (LIVE)** *Atco B 6073CD*	68	1
10 Jul 93		**BIG GUN** *Atco B 8396CD*	23	3
30 Sep 95		**HARD AS A ROCK** *Atlantic A 4368CD*	33	2
11 May 96		**HAIL CAESAR** *East West 7559660512*	56	1
15 Apr 00		**STIFF UPPER LIP** *EMI CDSTIFF 100*	65	1
5 Nov 77		**LET THERE BE ROCK** *Atlantic K 50366*	17	5
20 May 78		**POWERAGE** *Atlantic K 50483*	26	9
28 Oct 78		**IF YOU WANT BLOOD YOU'VE GOT IT** *Atlantic K 50532*	13	58
18 Aug 79	●	**HIGHWAY TO HELL** *Atlantic K 50628*	8	32
9 Aug 80	★	**BACK IN BLACK** *Atlantic K 50735* ■	1	40
5 Dec 81	●	**FOR THOSE ABOUT TO ROCK (WE SALUTE YOU)** *Atlantic K 50851* ▲	3	29
3 Sep 83	●	**FLICK OF THE SWITCH** *Atlantic 7801001*	4	9
13 Jul 85	●	**FLY ON THE WALL** *Atlantic 781263*	7	10
7 Jun 86		**WHO MADE WHO** *Atlantic WX 57*	11	12
13 Feb 88	●	**BLOW UP YOUR VIDEO** *Atlantic WX 144*	2	14
6 Oct 90	●	**THE RAZOR'S EDGE** *Atco WX 364*	4	18
7 Nov 92	●	**AC/DC LIVE** *Atco 7567922152*	5	7
7 Oct 95	●	**BALLBREAKER** *East West 7559617802*	6	8
11 Mar 00		**STIFF UPPER LIP** *EMI 5256672*	12	4

A CAMP *Sweden / US, female / male vocal / instrumental group – leader – Nina Persson (Singles: 1 week)*

Date		Title / Label	pos	wks
1 Sep 01		**I CAN BUY YOU** *Stockholm 0152162*	46	1

A CERTAIN RATIO, A FLOCK OF SEAGULLS, A GUY CALLED GERALD, A HOME BOY A HIPPIE AND A FUNKY DREDD, A LOVE SUPREME, A TASTE OF HONEY, A TRIBE CALLED QUEST, A VERY GOOD FRIEND OF MINE, A WAY OF LIFE, ETC

– See SECOND LETTER OF EACH ACT NAME TO LOCATE THESE ENTRIES

A.D.A.M. featuring AMY

France, male / female vocal / instrumental duo (Singles: 11 weeks)

Date		Title / Label	pos	wks
1 Jul 95		**ZOMBIE** *Eternal YZ 951CD*	16	11

AFI *US, male vocal / instrumental group (Singles: 4 weeks, Albums: 1 week)*

		pos	wks
21 Jun 03	**GIRL'S NOT GREY** *Dreamworks / Polydor 4504600*	**22**	3
20 Sep 03	**THE LEAVING SONG PT.2** *Dreamworks / Polydor 4504625*	**43**	1
22 Mar 03	**SING THE SORROW** *Dreamworks / Polydor 04504482*	**52**	1

AFX *UK, male instrumentalist / producer – Richard James (Singles: 1 week)*

		pos	wks
11 Aug 01	**2 REMIXES BY AFX** *MEN1 MEN1CD*	**69**	1

See also APHEX TWIN; POLYGON WINDOW

A FLUX OF PINK INDIANS
UK, male vocal / instrumental group (Albums: 2 weeks)

		pos	wks
5 Feb 83	**STRIVE TO SURVIVE CAUSING LEAST SUFFERING POSSIBLE** *Spiderleg SDL 8*	**79**	2

A HOUSE
Ireland, male vocal / instrumental group (Singles: 8 weeks)

		pos	wks
13 Jun 92	**ENDLESS ART** *Setanta AHOU 1*	**46**	3
8 Aug 92	**TAKE IT EASY ON ME** *Setanta AHOU 2*	**55**	2
25 Jun 94	**WHY ME** *Setanta CDAHOU 4*	**52**	1
1 Oct 94	**HERE COME THE GOOD TIMES** *Setanta CDAHOUS 5*	**37**	2

AKA *UK, male vocal group (Singles: 2 weeks)*

		pos	wks
12 Oct 96	**WARNING** *RCA 74321360662*	**43**	2

a1 *UK, male vocal group (Singles: 91 weeks, Albums: 19 weeks)*

		pos	wks
3 Jul 99	● **BE THE FIRST TO BELIEVE** *Columbia 6674222*	**6**	9
11 Sep 99	● **SUMMERTIME OF OUR LIVES (re)** *Columbia 6678322*	**5**	8
20 Nov 99	● **EVERYTIME / READY OR NOT** *Columbia 6681872*	**3**	11
4 Mar 00	● **LIKE A ROSE** *Columbia 6689032*	**6**	12
9 Sep 00	★ **TAKE ON ME (re)** *Columbia 6695902* ■	**1**	11
18 Nov 00	★ **SAME OLD BRAND NEW YOU** *Columbia 6705202* ■	**1**	10
3 Mar 01	● **NO MORE (re)** *Columbia 6708742*	**6**	13
2 Feb 02	● **CAUGHT IN THE MIDDLE** *Columbia 6722322*	**2**	12
25 May 02	**MAKE IT GOOD (re)** *Columbia 6726182*	**11**	5
4 Dec 99	**HERE WE COME** *Columbia 4961362*	**20**	8
2 Dec 00	**THE A LIST** *Columbia 5011952*	**14**	9
8 Jun 02	**MAKE IT GOOD** *Columbia 5082212*	**15**	2

A PERFECT CIRCLE *US, male vocal / instrumental group (Singles: 2 weeks, Albums: 2 weeks)*

		pos	wks
18 Nov 00	**THE HOLLOW** *Virgin VUSCD 181*	**72**	1
13 Jan 01	**3 LIBRAS** *Virgin VUSCD 184*	**49**	1
3 Jun 00	**MER DE NOMS** *Virgin CDVUS 173*	**55**	1
27 Sep 03	**THIRTEENTH STEP** *Virgin CDVUS247*	**37**	1

A+ *US, male rapper – Andre Levins (Singles: 9 weeks)*

		pos	wks
13 Feb 99	● **ENJOY YOURSELF** *Universal UND 56230*	**5**	9

A.R.E. WEAPONS
US, male vocal / insrumental group (Singles: 1 week)

		pos	wks
4 Aug 01	**STREET GANG** *Rough Trade RTRADESCD 022*	**72**	1

ASAP *UK, male vocal / instrumental group (Singles: 4 weeks, Albums: 1 week)*

		pos	wks
14 Oct 89	**SILVER AND GOLD** *EMI EM 107*	**60**	2
3 Feb 90	**DOWN THE WIRE** *EMI EM 131*	**67**	2
4 Nov 89	**SILVER AND GOLD** *EMI EMC 3566*	**70**	1

ATB *Germany, male producer – Andre Tanneberger (Singles: 52 weeks, Albums: 3 weeks)*

		pos	wks
13 Mar 99	**(9PM) TILL I COME** *Ministry of Sound DATA 1*	**68**	1
22 May 99	**(9PM) TILL I COME (German import) (re)** *Club Tools CLU 66066*	**47**	5
19 Jun 99	**(9PM) TILL I COME (Australian import)** *Dancenet DNET 131*	**63**	1
3 Jul 99	★ **9PM (TILL I COME)** *Sound of Ministry MOSCDS 132* ■	**1**	15
9 Oct 99	**DON'T STOP (import)** *Club Tools CLU 66406*	**61**	2
23 Oct 99	● **DON'T STOP (re)** *Sound of Ministry MOSCDS 134*	**3**	13
25 Mar 00	● **KILLER (re)** *Sound of Ministry MOSCDS 138*	**4**	9
27 Jan 01	**THE FIELDS OF LOVE** *Club Tools / Edel 0124095 CLU* [1]	**16**	4
30 Jun 01	**LET U GO** *Kontour 0117335 KTR*	**34**	2
8 Apr 00	**MOVIN MELODIES** *Sound of Ministry ATBCDZ 1*	**32**	3

[1] ATB featuring York

ATC *Italy / New Zealand / UK / Australia, male / female vocal group (Singles: 4 weeks)*

		pos	wks
17 Aug 02	**AROUND THE WORLD (LA LA LA LA LA)** *EMI / Liberty CDATC 001*	**15**	4

A.T.F.C. presents ONEPHATDEEVA
UK, male producer – Aydin Hasirci (Singles: 10 weeks)

		pos	wks
30 Oct 99	**IN AND OUT OF MY LIFE** *Defected DEFECT 8CDS*	**11**	5
16 Sep 00	**BAD HABIT** *Defected DFECT 19CDS* [1]	**17**	3
9 Feb 02	**SLEEP TALK** *Defected DFECT 43CDS* [2]	**33**	2

[1] A.T.F.C. presents Onephatdeeva featuring Lisa Millett [2] A.T.F.C. featuring Lisa Millett

A.T.G.O.C. *Italy, male instrumentalist / producer – Andrea Mazzali (Singles: 2 weeks)*

		pos	wks
21 Nov 98	**REPEATED LOVE** *Wonderboy WBOYD 012*	**38**	2

A*TEENS *Sweden, male / female vocal group (Singles: 19 weeks)*

		pos	wks
4 Sep 99	**MAMMA MIA** *Stockholm 5613432*	**12**	5
11 Dec 99	**SUPER TROUPER** *Stockholm 5615002*	**21**	5
26 May 01	● **UPSIDE DOWN** *Stockholm 1588492*	**10**	7
27 Oct 01	**HALFWAY AROUND THE WORLD** *Stockholm 0153612*	**30**	2

A vs B *UK, male production duo (Singles: 1 week)*

		pos	wks
9 May 98	**RIPPED IN 2 MINUTES** *Positiva CDTIV 89*	**49**	1

AALIYAH *US, female vocalist – Aaliyah Haughton, d. 25 Aug 2001 (Singles: 72 weeks, Albums: 56 weeks)*

		pos	wks
2 Jul 94	**BACK AND FORTH** *Jive JIVECD 357*	**16**	5
15 Oct 94	**(AT YOUR BEST) YOU ARE LOVE** *Jive JIVECD 359*	**27**	2
11 Mar 95	**AGE AIN'T NOTHING BUT A NUMBER** *Jive JIVECD 369*	**32**	2
13 May 95	**DOWN WITH THE CLIQUE** *Jive JIVECD 377*	**33**	2
9 Sep 95	**THE THING I LIKE** *Jive JIVECD 382*	**33**	2
3 Feb 96	**I NEED YOU TONIGHT** *Big Beat A 8130CD* [1]	**66**	1
24 Aug 96	**IF YOUR GIRL ONLY KNEW** *Atlantic A 5669CD*	**21**	2
23 Nov 96	**GOT TO GIVE IT UP** *Atlantic A 5632CD*	**37**	2
24 May 97	**IF YOUR GIRL ONLY KNEW / ONE IN A MILLION (re-issue)** *Atlantic A 5610CD*	**15**	3
30 Aug 97	**4 PAGE LETTER** *Atlantic AT 0010CD1*	**24**	2
22 Nov 97	**THE ONE I GAVE MY HEART TO / HOT LIKE FIRE** *Atlantic AT 0017CD*	**30**	2
18 Apr 98	**JOURNEY TO THE PAST** *Atlantic AT 0026CD*	**22**	3
12 Sep 98	**ARE YOU THAT SOMEBODY?** *Atlantic AT 0047CD*	**11**	4
22 Jul 00	● **TRY AGAIN (re)** *Virgin VUSCD 167* ▲	**5**	12
21 Jul 01	**WE NEED A RESOLUTION (re)** *Blackground VUSCD 206* [2]	**20**	6
19 Jan 02	★ **MORE THAN A WOMAN** *Blackgound / Virgin VUSCD 230* ■	**1**	12
18 May 02	**ROCK THE BOAT** *Blackground / Virgin VUSCD 243*	**12**	7
26 Apr 03	**DON'T KNOW WHAT TO TELL YA** *Independiente / Blackgroud / Unique ISOM 73MS*	**22**	3
23 Jul 94	**AGE AIN'T NOTHING BUT A NUMBER** *Jive CHIP 149*	**23**	6
7 Sep 96	**ONE IN A MILLION** *Atlantic 7567927152*	**33**	3
28 Jul 01	● **AALIYAH** *Virgin CDVUS 199* ▲	**5**	31
15 Feb 03	● **I CARE 4 U** *Independiente / Blackground / Unique ISOM37CDL*	**4**	16

[1] Junior M.A.F.I.A. featuring Aaliyah [2] Aaliyah featuring Timbaland

ABBA (17 Top 500)
The most successful Swedish recording act ever amassed 10,004,039 UK single sales, nine No.1 singles and eight successive chart-topping albums: Bjorn Ulvaeus (g/v), Benny Andersson (k/v), Agnetha Faltskog (v), Anni-Frid

*(Frida) Lyngstad (v). The video-genic quartet's 'Waterloo' was the first No.1 by a Scandinavian act in the UK and the biggest ever Eurovision Song Contest hit in the US. Their 'Gold – Greatest Hits' topped the chart on two separate occasions – six years apart – selling one million copies in 1999 alone. It returned to the top on its 218th chart week – a longevity record – and was the only album in the UK's Top 100 sellers every year between 1992 and 2000. Long after the group split in 1982 (following the divorces of Bjorn and Agnetha and Benny and Frida) they continued to collect awards and gold records on every continent, and their influence is still heard in countless acts around the globe. They have sold more than 300 million records, the vast majority being self-penned, and many feature in the Abba-based hit musical 'Mamma Mia'. They were given a star-studded tribute at the 1999 Brit awards, which resulted in the hit single 'Thank Abba for the Music' by Steps, Tina Cousins, Cleopatra, B*Witched and Billie. They were the first act from mainland Europe to become chart regulars in both the UK and US, opening doors to many later European artists (Singles: 252 weeks, Albums: 867 weeks)* pos/wks

Date		Title / Label	pos	wks
20 Apr 74	★	**WATERLOO** *Epic EPC 2240*	1	9
13 Jul 74		**RING RING** *Epic EPC 2452*	32	5
12 Jul 75		**I DO, I DO, I DO, I DO, I DO** *Epic EPC 3229*	38	6
20 Sep 75	●	**S.O.S.** *Epic EPC 3576*	6	10
13 Dec 75	★	**MAMMA MIA** *Epic EPC 3790*	1	14
27 Mar 76	★	**FERNANDO** *Epic EPC 4036*	1	15
21 Aug 76	★	**DANCING QUEEN** *Epic EPC 4499* ▲	1	15
20 Nov 76	●	**MONEY, MONEY, MONEY** *Epic EPC 4713*	3	12
26 Feb 77	★	**KNOWING ME, KNOWING YOU** *Epic EPC 4955*	1	13
22 Oct 77	★	**THE NAME OF THE GAME** *Epic EPC 5750*	1	12
4 Feb 78	★	**TAKE A CHANCE ON ME** *Epic EPC 5950*	1	10
16 Sep 78	●	**SUMMER NIGHT CITY** *Epic EPC 6595*	5	9
3 Feb 79	●	**CHIQUITITA** *Epic EPC 7030*	2	9
5 May 79	●	**DOES YOUR MOTHER KNOW** *Epic EPC 7316*	4	9
14 Jul 79	●	**ANGELEYES / VOULEZ-VOUS** *Epic EPC 7499*	3	11
20 Oct 79	●	**GIMME, GIMME, GIMME (A MAN AFTER MIDNIGHT)** *Epic EPC 7914*	3	12
15 Dec 79	●	**I HAVE A DREAM** *Epic EPC 8088*	2	10
2 Aug 80	★	**THE WINNER TAKES IT ALL** *Epic EPC 8835*	1	10
15 Nov 80	★	**SUPER TROUPER** *Epic EPC 9089*	1	12
18 Jul 81	●	**LAY ALL YOUR LOVE ON ME** *Epic EPC A13 1456*	7	7
12 Dec 81	●	**ONE OF US** *Epic EPC A 1740*	3	10
20 Feb 82		**HEAD OVER HEELS** *Epic EPC A 2037*	25	7
23 Oct 82		**THE DAY BEFORE YOU CAME** *Epic EPC A 2847*	32	6
11 Dec 82		**UNDER ATTACK** *Epic EPC A 2971*	26	8
12 Nov 83		**THANK YOU FOR THE MUSIC** *CBS A 3894*	33	6
5 Sep 92		**DANCING QUEEN (re-issue)** *Polydor PO 231*	16	5
8 Jun 74		WATERLOO *Epic EPC 80179*	28	2
31 Jan 76		ABBA *Epic EPC 80835*	13	10
10 Apr 76	★	GREATEST HITS *Epic EPC 69218*	1	130
27 Nov 76	★	ARRIVAL *Epic EPC 86018*	1	92
4 Feb 78	★	THE ALBUM *Epic EPC 86052* ■	1	61
19 May 79	★	VOULEZ-VOUS *Epic EPC 86086* ■	1	43
10 Nov 79	★	GREATEST HITS VOLUME 2 *Epic EPC 10017*	1	63
22 Nov 80	★	SUPER TROUPER *Epic EPC 10022* ■	1	43
19 Dec 81	★	THE VISITORS *Epic EPC 10032* ■	1	21
20 Nov 82	★	THE SINGLES – THE FIRST TEN YEARS *Epic ABBA 10*	1	22
19 Nov 83		THANK YOU FOR THE MUSIC *Epic EPC 10043*	17	12
19 Nov 88		ABSOLUTE ABBA *Telstar STAR 2329*	70	7
3 Oct 92	★	GOLD – GREATEST HITS *Polydor 5170072* ■	1	328
5 Jun 93		MORE ABBA GOLD – MORE ABBA HITS *Polydor 5193532*	13	23
7 Nov 98		LOVE STORIES *Polydor 5592212*	51	2
10 Nov 01		THE DEFINITIVE COLLECTION *Polydor 5499742*	17	8

'Lay All Your Love on Me' was available only on 12-inch vinyl in the UK

ABBACADABRA

UK, male / female vocal / instrumental group (Singles: 1 week) pos/wks

Date		Title / Label	pos	wks
5 Sep 92		**DANCING QUEEN** *PWL International PWL 246*	57	1

Russ ABBOT *UK, male comedian / vocalist – Russell Roberts (Singles: 22 weeks, Albums: 16 weeks)* pos/wks

Date		Title / Label	pos	wks
6 Feb 82		**A DAY IN THE LIFE OF VINCE PRINCE (re)** *EMI 5249*	61	2
29 Dec 84	●	**ATMOSPHERE** *Spirit FIRE 4*	7	13
13 Jul 85		**ALL NIGHT HOLIDAY** *Spirit FIRE 6*	20	7
5 Nov 83		RUSS ABBOT'S MADHOUSE *Ronco RTL 2096*	41	7
23 Nov 85		I LOVE A PARTY *K-Tel ONE 1313*	12	9

Gregory ABBOTT

US, male vocalist (Singles: 13 weeks, Albums: 5 weeks) pos/wks

Date		Title / Label	pos	wks
22 Nov 86	●	**SHAKE YOU DOWN** *CBS A 7326* ▲	6	13
10 Jan 87		SHAKE YOU DOWN *CBS 4500611*	53	5

Paula ABDUL

US, female vocalist (Singles: 67 weeks, Albums: 51 weeks) pos/wks

Date		Title / Label	pos	wks
4 Mar 89	●	**STRAIGHT UP** *Siren SRN 111* ▲	3	13
3 Jun 89		**FOREVER YOUR GIRL** *Siren SRN 112* ▲	24	6
19 Aug 89		**KNOCKED OUT** *Siren SRN 92*	45	3
2 Dec 89		**(IT'S JUST) THE WAY THAT YOU LOVE ME** *Siren SRN 101*	74	1
7 Apr 90	●	**OPPOSITES ATTRACT** *Siren SRN 124* [1] ▲	2	13
21 Jul 90		**KNOCKED OUT (re-mix)** *Virgin America VUS 23*	21	5
29 Sep 90		**COLD HEARTED** *Virgin America VUS 27* ▲	46	3
22 Jun 91	●	**RUSH RUSH** *Virgin America VUS 38* ▲	6	11
31 Aug 91		**THE PROMISE OF A NEW DAY** *Virgin America VUS 44* ▲	52	2
18 Jan 92		**VIBEOLOGY** *Virgin America VUS 53*	19	6
8 Aug 92		**WILL YOU MARRY ME** *Virgin America VUS 58*	73	1
17 Jun 95		**MY LOVE IS FOR REAL** *Virgin America VUSCD 91* [2]	28	3
15 Apr 89	●	FOREVER YOUR GIRL *Siren SRNLP 19* ▲	3	39
10 Nov 90		SHUT UP AND DANCE (THE DANCE MIXES) *Virgin America VUSLP 28*	40	2
27 Jul 91	●	SPELLBOUND *Virgin America VUSLP 33* ▲	4	9
1 Jul 95		HEAD OVER HEELS *Virgin America CDVUS 90*	61	1

[1] Paula Abdul with the Wild Pair [2] Paula Abdul featuring Ofra Haza

ABI *UK, male vocalist (Singles: 2 weeks)* pos/wks

Date		Title / Label	pos	wks
13 Jun 98		**COUNTING THE DAYS** *Kuku CDKUKU 1*	44	2

ABIGAIL

UK, female vocalist – Gayle Zsigmond (Singles: 4 weeks) pos/wks

Date		Title / Label	pos	wks
16 Jul 94		**SMELLS LIKE TEEN SPIRIT** *Klone CDKLONE 25*	29	4

ABNEA – *See Johan GIELEN presents ABNEA*

Colonel ABRAMS

US, male vocalist (Singles: 35 weeks) pos/wks

Date		Title / Label	pos	wks
17 Aug 85	●	**TRAPPED** *MCA MCA 997*	3	23
7 Dec 85		**THE TRUTH** *MCA MCA 1022*	53	3
8 Feb 86		**I'M NOT GONNA LET YOU** *MCA MCA 1031*	24	7
15 Aug 87		**HOW SOON WE FORGET** *MCA MCA 1179*	75	2

ABS *UK, male vocalist / rapper – Richard Breen (Singles: 24 weeks, Albums: 2 weeks)* pos/wks

Date		Title / Label	pos	wks
31 Aug 02	●	**WHAT YOU GOT** *S 74321957192*	4	8
7 Jun 03	●	**STOP SIGN** *BMG 82876530392*	10	9
6 Sep 03	●	**MISS PERFECT** *BMG 82876556742* [1]	5	7
13 Sep 03		ABSTRACT THEORY *BMG 82876538802*	29	3

[1] Abs featuring Nodesha

See also FIVE

ABSOLUTE *US, male production / instrumental duo – Mark Picchiotti and Craig Snider (Singles: 3 weeks)* pos/wks

Date		Title / Label	pos	wks
18 Jan 97		**I BELIEVE** *AM:PM 5820752* [1]	38	2
14 Mar 98		**CATCH ME** *AM:PM 5825032*	69	1

[1] Absolute featuring Suzanne Palmer

ABSOLUTELY FABULOUS – *See PET SHOP BOYS*

ACADEMY OF ST MARTIN IN THE FIELDS – *See Neville MARRINER and the ACADEMY OF ST MARTIN IN THE FIELDS; Christopher HOGWOOD*

Marc ACARDIPANE – *See SCOOTER*

ACCEPT

Germany, male vocal / instrumental group (Albums: 5 weeks) pos/wks

Date		Title / Label	pos	wks
7 May 83		RESTLESS AND WILD *Heavy Metal Worldwide HMILP 6*	98	2

Date		Title / Label	Pos	Wks
30 Mar 85		**METAL HEART** *Portrait PRT 26358*	50	1
15 Feb 86		**KAIZOKU-BAN** *Portrait PRT 5916*	91	1
3 May 86		**RUSSIAN ROULETTE** *Portrait PRT 26893*	80	1

ACE *UK, male vocal / instrumental group – includes Paul Carrack (Singles: 10 weeks)* pos/wks

Date		Title / Label	Pos	Wks
9 Nov 74		**HOW LONG** *Anchor ANC 1002*	20	10

Richard ACE *Jamaica, male vocalist (Singles: 2 weeks)* pos/wks

Date		Title / Label	Pos	Wks
2 Dec 78		**STAYIN' ALIVE** *Blue Inc. INC 2*	66	2

ACE OF BASE (474 Top 500)
Swedish pop-reggae outfit comprising three Berggren family members, Linn (v), Jenny (v), Jonas 'Joker' (k) and Ulf 'Buddha' Ekberg (k) all from Gothenburg. Only Swedish act to top the US album chart with 'The Sign' (titled 'Happy Nation' outside US) in 1994. Best-selling single: 'All That She Wants' 603,900 (Singles: 100 weeks, Albums: 45 weeks) pos/wks

Date		Title / Label	Pos	Wks
8 May 93	★	**ALL THAT SHE WANTS** *London 8612702*	1	16
28 Aug 93		**WHEEL OF FORTUNE** *London 8615452*	20	6
13 Nov 93		**HAPPY NATION** *London 8619272*	42	3
26 Feb 94	●	**THE SIGN** *London ACECD 1* ▲	2	16
11 Jun 94	●	**DON'T TURN AROUND** *London ACECD 2*	5	11
15 Oct 94		**HAPPY NATION (re-issue)** *London 8610972*	40	3
14 Jan 95		**LIVING IN DANGER** *London ACECD 3*	18	4
11 Nov 95		**LUCKY LOVE** *London ACECD 4*	20	5
27 Jan 96		**BEAUTIFUL LIFE** *London ACECD 5*	15	6
25 Jul 98	●	**LIFE IS A FLOWER** *London ACECD 7*	5	11
10 Oct 98	●	**CRUEL SUMMER** *London ACECD 8*	8	5
19 Dec 98		**ALWAYS HAVE, ALWAYS WILL** *London ACECD 9*	12	10
17 Apr 99		**EVERYTIME IT RAINS** *London ACECD 10*	22	4
19 Jun 93	★	**HAPPY NATION** *London 5177492* ▲	1	38
2 Dec 95		**THE BRIDGE** *London 5296552*	66	1
22 Aug 98		**FLOWERS** *London 5576912*	15	5
27 Nov 99		**SINGLES OF THE 90'S** *Polydor 5432272*	62	1

'Happy Nation' changed its catalogue number to 5214722 during its chart run

ACEN *UK, male producer – Syed Ahsen Razvi (Singles: 4 weeks)* pos/wks

Date		Title / Label	Pos	Wks
8 Aug 92		**TRIP II THE MOON** *Production House PNT 042*	38	3
10 Oct 92		**TRIP II THE MOON (re-mix)** *Production House PNT 042RX*	71	1

ACES – *See Desmond DEKKER and the ACES*

Tracy ACKERMAN – *See Q*

ACT *UK / Germany, male / female vocal / instrumental group (Singles: 2 weeks)* pos/wks

Date		Title / Label	Pos	Wks
23 May 87		**SNOBBERY AND DECAY** *ZTT ZTAS 28*	60	2

ACT ONE *US, male / female vocal / instrumental group (Singles: 6 weeks)* pos/wks

Date		Title / Label	Pos	Wks
18 May 74		**TOM THE PEEPER** *Mercury 6008 005*	40	6

ACZESS *UK, male producer (Singles: 1 week)* pos/wks

Date		Title / Label	Pos	Wks
27 Oct 01		**DO WHAT WE WOULD** *INCredible 6719782*	65	1

ADAM and the ANTS (248 Top 500)
Warpaint-wearing, colourfully costumed 'Antmusic' innovators: included Stuart (Adam Ant) Goddard (v) and Marco Pirroni (g). The London-based act was 1981's top chart act with nine hits. Also in that year, they amassed 91 chart weeks – a total not bettered until 1996. Best-selling single: 'Stand and Deliver' 985,000 (Singles: 130 weeks, Albums: 118 weeks) pos/wks

Date		Title / Label	Pos	Wks
2 Aug 80	●	**KINGS OF THE WILD FRONTIER (re)** *CBS 8877*	2	18
11 Oct 80	●	**DOG EAT DOG** *CBS 9039*	4	16
6 Dec 80	●	**ANTMUSIC** *CBS 9352*	2	18
27 Dec 80	●	**YOUNG PARISIANS** *Decca F13803*	9	13
24 Jan 81		**CARTROUBLE** *Do It DUN 10*	33	9
24 Jan 81		**ZEROX** *Do It DUN 8*	45	9
9 May 81	★	**STAND AND DELIVER** *CBS A 1065* ■	1	15
12 Sep 81	★	**PRINCE CHARMING** *CBS A 1408*	1	12
12 Dec 81	●	**ANT RAP** *CBS A 1738*	3	10
27 Feb 82		**DEUTSCHER GIRLS** *Ego 5*	13	6
13 Mar 82		**THE ANTMUSIC EP (THE B-SIDES)** *Do It DUN 20*	46	4
15 Nov 80	★	**KINGS OF THE WILD FRONTIER** *CBS 84549*	1	66
17 Jan 81		**DIRK WEARS WHITE SOX** *Do It RIDE 3*	16	29
14 Nov 81	●	**PRINCE CHARMING** *CBS 85268*	2	21
3 Apr 99		**THE VERY BEST OF ADAM AND THE ANTS** *Columbia 4942292*	56	2

'Kings of the Wild Frontier' reached No.48 on its first visit to the chart, peaking at No.2 as a re-entry in Feb 1981. Tracks on The Antmusic EP (The B-sides): Friends / Kick / Physical

See also Adam ANT

Arthur ADAMS *US, male vocalist (Singles: 5 weeks)* pos/wks

Date		Title / Label	Pos	Wks
24 Oct 81		**YOU GOT THE FLOOR** *RCA 146*	38	5

Bryan ADAMS (51 Top 500) *Globally successful rock singer / songwriter / guitarist, b. 5 Nov 1959, Kingston, Ontario. He has had more UK hits than any other Canadian artist and was the biggest-selling singles artist in the UK in 1991 when he hogged the No.1 spot for a record 16 consecutive weeks. Biggest-selling single: '(Everything I Do) I Do It for You' 1,527,824 (Singles: 243 weeks, Albums: 398 weeks)* pos/wks

Date		Title / Label	Pos	Wks
12 Jan 85		**RUN TO YOU** *A&M AM 224*	11	12
16 Mar 85		**SOMEBODY** *A&M AM 236*	35	7
25 May 85		**HEAVEN** *A&M AM 256* ▲	38	5
10 Aug 85		**SUMMER OF '69** *A&M AM 267*	42	7
2 Nov 85		**IT'S ONLY LOVE** *A&M 285* [1]	29	6
21 Dec 85		**CHRISTMAS TIME** *A&M AM 297*	55	2
22 Feb 86		**THIS TIME** *A&M AM 295*	41	7
12 Jul 86		**STRAIGHT FROM THE HEART** *A&M AM 322*	51	3
28 Mar 87		**HEAT OF THE NIGHT** *A&M ADAM 2*	50	2
20 Jun 87		**HEARTS ON FIRE** *A&M ADAM 3*	57	3
17 Oct 87		**VICTIM OF LOVE** *A&M AM 407*	68	2
29 Jun 91	★	**(EVERYTHING I DO) I DO IT FOR YOU (re)** *A&M AM 789* ◆ ▲	1	25
14 Sep 91		**CAN'T STOP THIS THING WE STARTED** *A&M AM 612*	12	6
23 Nov 91		**THERE WILL NEVER BE ANOTHER TONIGHT** *A&M AM 838*	32	3
22 Feb 92	●	**THOUGHT I'D DIED AND GONE TO HEAVEN** *A&M AM 848*	8	7
18 Jul 92		**ALL I WANT IS YOU** *A&M AM 879*	22	5
26 Sep 92		**DO I HAVE TO SAY THE WORDS** *A&M AM 0068*	30	3
30 Oct 93	●	**PLEASE FORGIVE ME** *A&M 5804232*	2	16
15 Jan 94	●	**ALL FOR LOVE** *A&M 5804772* [2] ▲	2	13
22 Apr 95	●	**HAVE YOU EVER REALLY LOVED A WOMAN** *A&M 5810282* ▲	4	9
11 Nov 95		**ROCK STEADY** *Capitol CDCL 763* [3]	50	2
1 Jun 96	●	**THE ONLY THING THAT LOOKS GOOD ON ME IS YOU** *A&M 5813692*	6	7
24 Aug 96	●	**LET'S MAKE A NIGHT TO REMEMBER** *A&M 5815672*	10	8
23 Nov 96		**STAR** *A&M 5820252*	13	4
8 Feb 97	●	**I FINALLY FOUND SOMEONE** *A&M 5820832* [4]	10	7
19 Apr 97		**18 TIL I DIE** *A&M 5821852*	22	3
20 Dec 97		**BACK TO YOU** *A&M 5824752*	18	7
21 Mar 98		**I'M READY** *A&M 5825352*	20	4
10 Oct 98		**ON A DAY LIKE TODAY** *Mercury MERCD 516*	13	5
12 Dec 98	●	**WHEN YOU'RE GONE** *A&M 5828212* [5]	3	19
15 May 99	●	**CLOUD NUMBER 9** *A&M / Mercury 5828492*	6	9
18 Dec 99		**THE BEST OF ME (re)** *Mercury / A&M 4971952*	47	3
18 Mar 00	★	**DON'T GIVE UP** *Xtravaganza XTRAV 9CDS* [6] ■	1	14
20 Jul 02	●	**HERE I AM** *A&M 4977442*	5	8
2 Mar 85	●	**RECKLESS** *A&M AMA 5013* ▲	7	115
24 Aug 85		**YOU WANT IT YOU GOT IT** *A&M AMLH 64864*	78	5
15 Mar 86		**CUTS LIKE A KNIFE** *A&M AMLH 64919*	21	6
11 Apr 87	●	**INTO THE FIRE** *A&M AMA 3907*	10	21
5 Oct 91	★	**WAKING UP THE NEIGHBOURS** *A&M 3971641* ■	1	54
20 Nov 93	★	**SO FAR SO GOOD** *A&M 5401572*	1	55
6 Aug 94		**LIVE! LIVE! LIVE!** *A&M 3970942*	17	4
22 Jun 96	★	**18 TIL I DIE** *A&M 5405512* ■	1	40
13 Dec 97		**UNPLUGGED** *A&M 5408312*	19	19
31 Oct 98		**ON A DAY LIKE TODAY** *Mercury / A&M 5410162*	11	35
27 Nov 99		**THE BEST OF ME** *Mercury / A&M 4905222*	12	39

		pos	wks
27 Jul 02 ●	SPIRIT – STALLION OF THE CIMARRON (FILM SOUNDTRACK) *A&M 4933042*	8	5

[1] Bryan Adams and Tina Turner [2] Bryan Adams, Rod Stewart and Sting [3] Bonnie Raitt and Bryan Adams [4] Barbra Streisand and Bryan Adams [5] Bryan Adams featuring Melanie C [6] Chicane featuring Bryan Adams

Gayle ADAMS *US, female vocalist (1 WEEK)* pos/wks

		pos	wks
26 Jul 80	STRETCHIN' OUT *Epic EPC 8791*	64	1

Marie ADAMS – *See Johnny OTIS SHOW*

Oleta ADAMS *US, female vocalist / instrumentalist – keyboards (Singles: 36 weeks, Albums: 34 weeks)* pos/wks

		pos	wks
24 Mar 90	RHYTHM OF LIFE (re) *Fontana OLETA 1*	52	5
12 Jan 91 ●	GET HERE *Fontana OLETA 3*	4	12
13 Apr 91	YOU'VE GOT TO GIVE ME ROOM / RHYTHM OF LIFE (re-issue) *Fontana OLETA 4*	49	3
29 Jun 91	CIRCLE OF ONE *Fontana OLETA 5*	73	1
28 Sep 91	DON'T LET THE SUN GO DOWN ON ME *Fontana TRIBO 1*	33	5
25 Apr 92	WOMAN IN CHAINS (re-issue) *Fontana IDEA 16* [1]	57	1
10 Jul 93	I JUST HAD TO HEAR YOUR VOICE *Fontana OLECD 6*	42	3
7 Oct 95	NEVER KNEW LOVE *Fontana OLECD 9*	22	3
16 Dec 95	RHYTHM OF LIFE (re-mix) *Fontana OLECD 10*	38	2
10 Feb 96	WE WILL MEET AGAIN *Mercury OLECD 11*	51	1
26 May 90 ★	CIRCLE OF ONE *Fontana 8427441*	1	26
7 Aug 93 ●	EVOLUTION *Fontana 5149652*	10	7
4 Nov 95	MOVING ON *Fontana 5285302*	59	1

[1] Tears for Fears featuring Oleta Adams

The original release of 'Woman in Chains' credited Tears for Fears only

Ryan ADAMS *US, male vocalist (Singles: 4 weeks, Albums: 13 weeks)* pos/wks

		pos	wks
8 Dec 01	NEW YORK NEW YORK *Lost Highway 1722232*	53	1
20 Apr 02	ANSWERING BELL *Lost Highway 1722392*	39	2
28 Sep 02	NUCLEAR *Lost Highway 1722592*	37	1
6 Oct 01	GOLD *Lost Highway 1702622*	20	9
5 Oct 02	DEMOLITION *Lost Highway 1703332*	22	2
15 Nov 03	ROCK N ROLL *Lost Highway 9861324*	41	1
15 Nov 03	LOVE IS HELL PT 1 *Lost Highway 9813666*	62	1

Cliff ADAMS SINGERS *UK, male / female vocal group (Singles: 2 weeks, Albums: 20 weeks)* pos/wks

		pos	wks
28 Apr 60	THE LONELY MAN THEME *Pye International 7N 25056* [1]	39	2
16 Apr 60	SING SOMETHING SIMPLE *Pye MPL 28013*	15	4
24 Nov 62	SING SOMETHING SIMPLE *Pye Golden Guinea GGL 0150*	15	2
20 Nov 76	SING SOMETHING SIMPLE '76 *Warwick WW 5016/17*	23	8
25 Dec 82	SING SOMETHING SIMPLE *Ronco RTD 2087*	39	6

[1] Cliff Adams Orchestra

ADAMSKI *UK, male instrumentalist / producer – Adam Tinley (Singles: 39 weeks, Albums: 16 weeks)* pos/wks

		pos	wks
20 Jan 90	N-R-G *MCA MCA 1386*	12	6
7 Apr 90 ★	KILLER *MCA MCA 1400*	1	18
8 Sep 90 ●	THE SPACE JUNGLE *MCA MCA 1435*	7	8
17 Nov 90	FLASHBACK JACK *MCA MCA 1459*	46	2
9 Nov 91	NEVER GOIN' DOWN / BORN TO BE ALIVE *MCA MCS 1578* [1]	51	2
4 Apr 92	GET YOUR BODY *MCA MCS 1613* [2]	68	1
4 Jul 92	BACK TO FRONT *MCA MCS 1644*	63	1
11 Jul 98	ONE OF THE PEOPLE *ZTT ZTT 101CD* [3]	56	1
9 Dec 89	LIVEANDIRECT *MCA MCL 1900*	47	11
13 Oct 90 ●	DOCTOR ADAMSKI'S MUSICAL PHARMACY *MCA MCG 6107*	8	5

[1] Adamski featuring Jimi Polo / Adamski featuring Soho [2] Adamski featuring Nina Hagen [3] Adamski's Thing

Featured vocalist on 'Killer' was Seal

Barry ADAMSON *UK, male vocal / instrumental (Albums: 1 week)* pos/wks

		pos	wks
10 Aug 96	OEDIPUS SCHMOEDIPUS *Mute CDSTUMM 134*	51	1

ADDAMS and GEE *UK, male instrumental duo (Singles: 1 week)* pos/wks

		pos	wks
20 Apr 91	CHUNG KUO (REVISITED) *Debut DEBT 3108*	72	1

ADDIS BLACK WIDOW *US, male rap duo (Singles: 2 weeks)* pos/wks

		pos	wks
3 Feb 96	INNOCENT *Mercury Black Vinyl MBVCD 1*	42	2

ADDRISI BROTHERS *US, male vocal duo – Don Addrisi d. 13 Nov 1984 (Singles: 3 weeks)* pos/wks

		pos	wks
6 Oct 79	GHOST DANCER *Scotti Brothers K 11361*	57	3

King Sunny ADE and his AFRICAN BEATS *Nigeria, male vocalist and male vocal / instrumental group (Albums: 1 week)* pos/wks

		pos	wks
9 Jul 83	SYNCHRO SYSTEM *Island ILPS 9737*	93	1

ADEMA *US, male vocal / instrumental group (Singles: 3 weeks)* pos/wks

		pos	wks
16 Mar 02	GIVING IN *Arista 74321924022*	62	1
10 Aug 02	THE WAY YOU LIKE IT *Arista 74321954712*	61	1
23 Aug 03	UNSTABLE *Arista 82876534512*	46	1

ADEVA *US, female vocalist – Patricia Daniels (Singles: 66 weeks, Albums: 24 weeks)* pos/wks

		pos	wks
14 Jan 89	RESPECT *Cooltempo COOL 179*	17	9
25 Mar 89	MUSICAL FREEDOM (MOVING ON UP) *Cooltempo COOL 182* [1]	22	8
12 Aug 89	WARNING *Cooltempo COOL 185*	17	8
21 Oct 89	I THANK YOU *Cooltempo COOL 192*	17	7
16 Dec 89	BEAUTIFUL LOVE *Cooltempo COOL 195*	57	5
28 Apr 90	TREAT ME RIGHT *Cooltempo COOL 200*	62	2
6 Apr 91	RING MY BELL *Cooltempo COOL 224* [2]	20	5
19 Oct 91	IT SHOULD'VE BEEN ME *Cooltempo COOL 236*	48	3
29 Feb 92	DON'T LET IT SHOW ON YOUR FACE *Cooltempo COOL 248*	34	4
6 Jun 92	UNTIL YOU COME BACK TO ME *Cooltempo COOL 254*	45	3
17 Oct 92	I'M THE ONE FOR YOU *Cooltempo COOL 264*	51	2
11 Dec 93	RESPECT (re-mix) *Network NWKCD 79*	65	1
27 May 95	TOO MANY FISH *Virgin America VUSCD 89* [3]	34	2
18 Nov 95	WHADDA U WANT (FROM ME) *Virgin America VUSCD 98* [3]	36	2
6 Apr 96	DO WATCHA DO *Avex UK AVEXCD 24* [4]	54	1
4 May 96	I THANK YOU (re-mix) *Cooltempo CDCOOLS 318*	37	2
12 Apr 97	DO WATCHA DO (re-mix) *Distinctive DISNCD 28* [4]	60	1
26 Jul 97	WHERE IS THE LOVE? / THE WAY THAT YOU FEEL *Distinctive DISNCD 31*	54	1
9 Sep 89 ●	ADEVA *Cooltempo ICTLP 13*	6	24

[1] Paul Simpson featuring Adeva [2] Monie Love vs Adeva [3] Frankie Knuckles featuring Adeva [4] Hyper Go Go and Adeva

ADICTS *UK, male vocal / instrumental group (Singles: 1 week, Albums: 1 week)* pos/wks

		pos	wks
14 May 83	BAD BOY *Razor RZS 104*	75	1
4 Dec 82	SOUND OF MUSIC *Razor RAZ 2*	99	1

ADIEMUS *UK, male instrumental duo – Karl Jenkins and Mark Ratledge (Singles: 2 weeks, Albums: 23 weeks)* pos/wks

		pos	wks
14 Oct 95	ADIEMUS *Venture VEND 4*	48	2
1 Jul 95	SONGS OF SANCTUARY *Virgin CDVE 925*	35	13
1 Mar 97	ADIEMUS II: CANTATA MUNDI *Venture CDVE 932*	15	9
24 Oct 98	ADIEMUS II: DANCES OF TIME *Venture CDVE 940*	58	1

Larry ADLER *US, male instrumentalist - harmonica (Albums: 18 weeks)* pos/wks

		pos	wks
6 Aug 94 ●	THE GLORY OF GERSHWIN *Mercury 5227272*	2	18

See also Kate BUSH

ADONIS featuring 2 PUERTO RICANS, A BLACK MAN AND A DOMINICAN *US, male vocal / instrumental group (Singles: 4 weeks)* pos/wks

		pos	wks
13 Jun 87	DO IT PROPERLY ('NO WAY BACK') / NO WAY BACK *London LON 136*	47	4

ADORABLE *UK, male vocal / instrumental band (Albums: 1 week)* pos/wks

		pos	wks
13 Mar 93	AGAINST PERFECTION *Creation CRECD 138*	70	1

ADRENALIN M.O.D.
UK, male instrumental / production group (Singles: 5 weeks)

		pos	wks
8 Oct 88	**O-O-O** *MCA RAGAT 2*	49	5

ADULT NET *UK / US, male / female vocal / instrumental group (Singles: 2 weeks)*

		pos	wks
10 Jun 89	**WHERE WERE YOU** *Fontana BRX 2*	66	2

ADVENTURES *UK, male vocal / instrumental group (Singles: 24 weeks, Albums: 11 weeks)*

		pos	wks
15 Sep 84	**ANOTHER SILENT DAY** *Chrysalis CHS 2000*	71	2
1 Dec 84	**SEND MY HEART** *Chrysalis CHS 2001*	62	4
13 Jul 85	**FEEL THE RAINDROPS** *Chrysalis AD 1*	58	3
9 Apr 88	**BROKEN LAND** *Elektra EKR 69*	20	10
2 Jul 88	**DROWNING IN THE SEA OF LOVE** *Elektra EKR 76*	44	4
13 Jun 92	**RAINING ALL OVER THE WORLD** *Polydor PO 211*	68	1
21 May 88	**THE SEA OF LOVE** *Elektra EKT 45*	30	10
17 Mar 90	**TRADING SECRETS WITH THE MOON** *Elektra EKT 63*	64	1

ADVENTURES OF STEVIE V
UK, male / female vocal / production group (Singles: 22 weeks)

		pos	wks
21 Apr 90 ●	**DIRTY CASH** *Mercury MER 311*	2	13
29 Sep 90	**BODY LANGUAGE** *Mercury MER 331*	29	5
2 Mar 91	**JEALOUSY** *Mercury MER 337*	58	3
27 Sep 97	**DIRTY CASH (re-mix)** *Avex Trax AVEXCDX 57*	69	1

ADVERTS *UK, male / female vocal / instrumental group (Singles: 11 weeks, Albums: 1 week)*

		pos	wks
27 Aug 77	**GARY GILMORE'S EYES** *Anchor ANC 1043*	18	7
4 Feb 78	**NO TIME TO BE 21** *Bright BR 1*	34	4
11 Mar 78	**CROSSING THE RED SEA WITH THE ADVERTS** *Bright BRL 201*	38	1

AEROSMITH 283 Top 500
Godfathers of contemporary heavy rock scene, formed 1970, New Hampshire, US. Multi-platinum album act's UK success came only after front men Steven Tyler (v) and Joe Perry (g) teamed with rappers Run-DMC on 'Walk This Way' (1986). Group's first US No.1 single (1998) came 25 years after chart debut. Best-selling single: 'I Don't Want to Miss a Thing' 572,900 (Singles: 92 weeks, Albums: 134 weeks)

		pos	wks
17 Oct 87	**DUDE (LOOKS LIKE A LADY)** *Geffen GEF 29*	45	5
16 Apr 88	**ANGEL** *Geffen GEF 34*	69	2
9 Sep 89	**LOVE IN AN ELEVATOR** *Geffen GEF 63*	13	8
24 Feb 90	**DUDE (LOOKS LIKE A LADY) (re-issue)** *Geffen GEF 72*	20	5
14 Apr 90	**RAG DOLL** *Geffen GEF 76*	42	4
1 Sep 90	**THE OTHER SIDE** *Geffen GEF 79*	46	2
10 Apr 93	**LIVIN' ON THE EDGE** *Geffen GFSTD 35*	19	4
3 Jul 93	**EAT THE RICH** *Geffen GFSTD 46*	34	3
30 Oct 93	**CRYIN'** *Geffen GFSTD 56*	17	6
18 Dec 93	**AMAZING** *Geffen GFSTD 63*	57	3
2 Jul 94	**SHUT UP AND DANCE** *Geffen GFSTD 75*	24	4
20 Aug 94	**SWEET EMOTION** *Columbia 6604492*	74	1
5 Nov 94	**CRAZY / BLIND MAN** *Geffen GFSTD 80*	23	4
8 Mar 97	**FALLING IN LOVE (IS HARD ON THE KNEES)** *Columbia 6640752*	22	4
21 Jun 97	**HOLE IN MY SOUL** *Columbia 66645012*	29	2
27 Dec 97	**PINK** *Columbia 6648722*	38	2
12 Sep 98 ●	**I DON'T WANT TO MISS A THING** *Columbia 6664082* ▲	4	20
26 Jun 99	**PINK (re-issue)** *Columbia 6675342*	13	6
17 Mar 01	**JADED** *Columbia 6709312*	13	7
5 Sep 87	**PERMANENT VACATION** *Geffen WX 126*	37	14
23 Sep 89 ●	**PUMP** *Geffen WX 304*	3	26
1 May 93 ●	**GET A GRIP** *Geffen GED 24444* ▲	2	38
12 Nov 94 ●	**BIG ONES** *Geffen GED 24546*	7	16
22 Mar 97 ●	**NINE LIVES** *Columbia 4850206* ▲	4	11
31 Oct 98	**A LITTLE SOUTH OF SANITY** *Geffen GED 25221*	36	2
24 Mar 01 ●	**JUST PUSH PLAY** *Columbia 5015352*	7	5
8 Dec 01	**YOUNG LUST – THE AEROSMITH ANTHOLOGY** *UMTV 4931192*	32	14
3 Aug 02 ●	**O YEAH! – ULTIMATE HITS** *Columbia / UMTV 5084672*	6	8

'Pump' changed its catalogue number to GEF 24245 during its chart run

AFGHAN WHIGS
US, male vocal / instrumental group (Albums: 3 weeks)

		pos	wks
16 Oct 93	**GENTLEMEN** *Blast First BFFP 90CD*	58	1
23 Mar 96	**BLACK LOVE** *Mute CDSTUMM 143*	41	2

AFRICAN BEATS – See King Sunny ADE and his AFRICAN BEATS

AFRICAN BUSINESS
Italy, male vocal / instrumental group (Singles: 1 week)

		pos	wks
17 Nov 90	**IN ZAIRE** *Urban URB 64*	73	1

AFRO CELT SOUND SYSTEM *UK / Ireland / France / Guinea, male vocal / instrumental group (Singles: 1 week, Albums: 5 weeks)*

		pos	wks
29 Apr 00	**RELEASE** *Realworld RWSCD 10*	71	1
27 Jul 96	**VOLUME 1 – SOUND MAGIC** *Realworld CDRW 61*	59	2
8 May 99	**VOLUME 2: RELEASE** *Realworld CDRW 76*	38	3

AFRO MEDUSA *UK, male production duo – Patrick Cole and Nick Benneti and Spain, female vocalist – Isabel Fructuoso (Singles: 2 weeks)*

		pos	wks
28 Oct 00	**PASILDA** *Rulin RULIN 6CDS*	31	2

AFROMAN *US, male vocalist – Joseph Foreman (Singles: 30 weeks)*

		pos	wks
6 Oct 01	**BECAUSE I GOT HIGH (import)** *Universal 0152822*	45	3
27 Oct 01 ★	**BECAUSE I GOT HIGH (re)** *Universal MCSTD 40266* ■	1	19
2 Feb 02 ●	**CRAZY RAP** *Universal MCSTD 40273*	10	8

AFTER DARK *UK, male instrumentalist – Mornington Lockett – saxophone (Albums: 5 weeks)*

		pos	wks
3 Feb 96	**LATE NIGHT SAX** *EMI TV CDEMTV 108*	18	5

AFTER 7 *US, male vocal group (Singles: 3 weeks)*

		pos	wks
3 Nov 90	**CAN'T STOP** *Virgin America VUS 31*	54	3

AFTER THE FIRE *UK, male vocal / instrumental group (Singles: 12 weeks, Albums: 4 weeks)*

		pos	wks
9 Jun 79	**ONE RULE FOR YOU** *CBS 7025*	40	6
8 Sep 79	**LASER LOVE** *CBS 7769*	62	2
9 Apr 83	**DER KOMMISSAR** *CBS A 2399*	47	4
13 Oct 79	**LASER LOVE** *CBS 83795*	57	1
1 Nov 80	**80 F** *Epic 84545*	69	1
3 Apr 82	**BATTERIES NOT INCLUDED** *CBS 85566*	82	2

AFTERNOON BOYS – See Steve WRIGHT

AFTERSHOCK *US, male vocal / instrumental duo – Frost Rivera and Guy Routte (Singles: 8 weeks)*

		pos	wks
21 Aug 93	**SLAVE TO THE VIBE** *Virgin America VUSCD 75*	11	8

AGE OF CHANCE
UK, male / female vocal / instrumental group (Singles: 13 weeks)

		pos	wks
17 Jan 87	**KISS** *Fon AGE 5*	50	6
30 May 87	**WHO'S AFRAID OF THE BIG BAD NOISE!** *Fon VS 962*	65	2
20 Jan 90	**HIGHER THAN HEAVEN** *Virgin VS 1228*	53	5

AGE OF LOVE
Italy, male instrumental / production trio (Singles: 6 weeks)

		pos	wks
5 Jul 97	**THE AGE OF LOVE – THE REMIXES** *React CDREACT 100*	17	4
19 Sep 98	**AGE OF LOVE** *React CDREACT 135*	38	2

AGENT 00 *UK, male production duo (Singles: 1 week)*

		pos	wks
7 Mar 98	**THE MAGNIFICENT** *Inferno CDFERN 002*	65	1

AGENT PROVOCATEUR
UK, male / female vocal / production group (Singles: 1 week)

		pos	wks
22 Mar 97	**AGENT DAN** *Epic AGENT 3CD*	49	1

AGENT SUMO *UK, male production duo (Singles: 4 weeks)*

		pos	wks
9 Jun 01	**24 HOURS** *Virgin VSCDT 1806*	44	2
20 Apr 02	**WHY** *Virgin VSCDT 1819*	40	2

AGNELLI & NELSON *UK, male DJ duo – Chris Agnelli and Robbie Nelson (Singles: 15 weeks)*

		pos	wks
15 Aug 98	**EL NINO** *Xtravaganza 0091575 EXT*	21	4
11 Sep 99	**EVERYDAY** *Xtravaganza XTRAV 2CDS*	17	4
17 Jun 00	**EMBRACE** *Xtravaganza XTRAV 11CDS*	35	2
9 Sep 00	**HUDSON STREET** *Xtravaganza XTRAV 13CDS*	29	2
7 Apr 01	**VEGAS** *Xtravaganza XTRAV 23CDS*	48	1
15 Jun 02	**EVERYDAY (re-mix)** *Xtravaganza XTRAV 31CDS*	33	2

Christina AGUILERA (311 Top 500)
Internationally successful, photogenic pop vocalist, b. 18 Dec 1980, New York. Four US chart-toppers and the winner of 1999 Best New Artist Grammy and World Music Awards in 2000 and 2001. Best-selling single: 'Genie in a Bottle' 608,100 (Singles: 124 weeks, Albums: 85 weeks)

		pos	wks
11 Sep 99	**GENIE IN A BOTTLE (import)** *RCA 701062*	50	5
16 Oct 99 ★	**GENIE IN A BOTTLE** *RCA 74321705482* ■ ▲	1	19
26 Feb 00 ●	**WHAT A GIRL WANTS** *RCA 74321737522* ▲	3	13
22 Jul 00	**I TURN TO YOU** *RCA 74321765472*	19	6
11 Nov 00 ●	**COME ON OVER BABY (ALL I WANT IS YOU) (re)** *RCA 74321799912* ▲	8	8
10 Mar 01 ●	**NOBODY WANTS TO BE LONELY** *Columbia 6709462* [1]	4	12
30 Jun 01 ★	**LADY MARMALADE** *Interscope / Polydor 4975612* [2] ■ ▲	1	16
23 Nov 02 ★	**DIRRTY** *RCA 74321962722* [3] ■	1	9
22 Feb 03	**BEAUTIFUL (import)** *Arista 74321983642*	51	2
8 Mar 03 ★	**BEAUTIFUL** *RCA 82876502462* ■	1	10
21 Jun 03 ●	**FIGHTER** *RCA 82876524292*	3	13
20 Sep 03 ●	**CAN'T HOLD US DOWN** *RCA 87876556332* [4]	6	9
20 Dec 03 ●	**THE VOICE WITHIN** *RCA 82876584292*	9	2+
30 Oct 99	**CHRISTINA AGUILERA** *RCA 7863676902* ▲	14	25
9 Nov 02 ●	**STRIPPED** *RCA 74321961252*	2	60+

[1] Ricky Martin and Christina Aguilera [2] Christina Aguilera, Lil' Kim, Mya and Pink [3] Christina Aguilera featuring Redman [4] Christina Aguilera featuring Lil' Kim

A-HA (214 Top 500) *Norway's biggest-selling act: Morten Harket (v), Pal Waaktaar (g), Magna Furuholmen (k). This globally popular teen-targeted trio was noted for its innovative videos and stage shows (Singles: 133 weeks, Albums: 148 weeks)*

		pos	wks
28 Sep 85 ●	**TAKE ON ME** *Warner Bros. W 9006* ▲	2	19
28 Dec 85 ★	**THE SUN ALWAYS SHINES ON TV** *Warner Bros. W 8846*	1	12
5 Apr 86 ●	**TRAIN OF THOUGHT** *Warner Bros. W 8736*	8	8
14 Jun 86 ●	**HUNTING HIGH AND LOW** *Warner Bros. W 6663*	5	10
4 Oct 86 ●	**I'VE BEEN LOSING YOU** *Warner Bros. W 8594*	8	7
6 Dec 86 ●	**CRY WOLF** *Warner Bros. W 8500*	5	9
28 Feb 87	**MANHATTAN SKYLINE** *Warner Bros. W 8405*	13	6
4 Jul 87 ●	**THE LIVING DAYLIGHTS** *Warner Bros. W 8305*	5	9
26 Mar 88 ●	**STAY ON THESE ROADS** *Warner Bros. W 7936*	5	6
18 Jun 88	**THE BLOOD THAT MOVES THE BODY** *Warner Bros. W 7840*	25	4
27 Aug 88	**TOUCHY!** *Warner Bros. W 7749*	11	7
3 Dec 88	**YOU ARE THE ONE** *Warner Bros. W 7636*	13	10
13 Oct 90	**CRYING IN THE RAIN** *Warner Bros. W 9547*	13	7
15 Dec 90	**I CALL YOUR NAME** *Warner Bros. W 9462*	44	5
26 Oct 91	**MOVE TO MEMPHIS** *Warner Bros. W 0070*	47	2
5 Jun 93	**DARK IS THE NIGHT** *Warner Bros. W 0175CD*	19	4
18 Sep 93	**ANGEL** *Warner Bros. W 0195CD*	41	3
26 Mar 94	**SHAPES THAT GO TOGETHER** *Warner Bros. W 0236CD*	27	3
3 Jun 00	**SUMMER MOVED ON** *WEA WEA 275CD*	33	2
9 Nov 85 ●	**HUNTING HIGH AND LOW** *Warner Bros. WX 30*	2	78
18 Oct 86 ●	**SCOUNDREL DAYS** *Warner Bros. WX 62*	2	29
14 May 88 ●	**STAY ON THESE ROADS** *Warner Bros. WX 166*	2	19
2 Nov 90	**EAST OF THE SUN WEST OF THE MOON** *Warner Bros. WX 378*	12	4
16 Nov 91	**HEADLINES AND DEADLINES – THE HITS OF A-HA** *Warner Bros. WX 450*	12	12
26 Jun 93	**MEMORIAL BEACH** *Warner Bros. 9362452292*	17	3
17 Jun 00	**MINOR EARTH MAJOR SKY** *WEA 8573821832*	27	2
22 Jun 02	**LIFELINES** *WEA 927448492*	67	1

AHMAD *US, male rapper (Singles: 2 weeks)*

		pos	wks
9 Jul 94	**BACK IN THE DAY** *Giant 74321212042*	64	2

AIDA *Holland, male production duo (Singles: 1 week)*

		pos	wks
19 Feb 00	**FAR AND AWAY** *48K / Perfecto SPECT 03CDS*	58	1

AIM *UK, male DJ / producer (Albums: 1 week)*

		pos	wks
9 Mar 02	**HINTERLAND** *Grand Central GCCD 112*	47	1

AIR *France, male instrumental / production duo – Jean -Benôit Dunckel and Nicolas Godin (Singles: 14 weeks, Albums: 78 weeks)*

		pos	wks
21 Feb 98	**SEXY BOY** *Virgin VSCDT 1672*	13	4
16 May 98	**KELLY WATCH THE STARS** *Virgin VSCDT 1690*	18	3
21 Nov 98	**ALL I NEED** *Virgin VSCDT 1702*	29	3
26 Feb 00	**PLAYGROUND LOVE** *Virgin VSCDT 1764* [1]	25	2
2 Jun 01	**RADIO #1** *Virgin VSCDT 1803*	31	2
31 Jan 98 ●	**MOON SAFARI** *Virgin CDV 2848*	6	61
18 Sep 99	**PREMIERS SYMPTOMES** *Virgin CDV 2895*	12	7
11 Mar 00	**THE VIRGIN SUICIDES (FILM SOUNDTRACK)** *Virgin CDV 2910*	14	4
9 Jun 01 ●	**10,000 HZ LEGEND** *Virgin CDV 2945*	7	5
2 Mar 02	**EVERYBODY HERTZ** *Virgin CDV 2956*	67	1

[1] Sung by Gordon Tracks

AIR SUPPLY
UK / Australia, male vocal / instrumental group – Russell Hitchcock and Graham Russell (Singles: 17 weeks)

		pos	wks
27 Sep 80	**ALL OUT OF LOVE** *Arista ARIST 362*	11	11
2 Oct 82	**EVEN THE NIGHTS ARE BETTER** *Arista ARIST 474*	44	4
20 Nov 93	**GOODBYE** *Giant 74321153462*	66	2

AIRHEAD *UK, male vocal / instrumental group (Singles: 10 weeks, Albums: 7 weeks)*

		pos	wks
5 Oct 91	**FUNNY HOW** *Korova KOW 47*	57	3
21 Dec 91	**COUNTING SHEEP** *Korova KOW 48*	35	5
7 Mar 92	**RIGHT NOW** *Korova KOW 49*	50	2
1 Feb 92	**BOING!** *Korova 9031746792*	29	7

AIRHEADZ *UK, male DJ / production duo – Leigh Guest and Andrew Peach (Singles: 2 weeks)*

		pos	wks
28 Apr 01	**STANLEY (HERE I AM)** *AM:PM CDAMPM 145*	36	2

See also DOUBLE TROUBLE

AIRSCAPE *Belgium / Holland, male instrumental / production duo – Johann Gielen and Sven Maes (Singles: 5 weeks)*

		pos	wks
9 Aug 97	**PACIFIC MELODY** *Xtravaganza 0091165*	27	2
29 Aug 98	**AMAZON CHANT** *Xtravaganza 0091605 EXT*	46	1
4 Dec 99	**L'ESPERANZA** *Xtravaganza EXTRAV 7CD*	33	2

See also BLUE BAMBOO; CUBIC 22; TRANSFORMER 2; BALEARIC BILL; Johan GIELEN *presents* ABNEA; SVENSON *and* GIELEN

Laurel AITKEN and the UNITONE
Jamaica / Cuba, male vocal / instrumental group (Singles: 3 weeks)

		pos	wks
17 May 80	**RUDI GOT MARRIED** *I-Spy SEE 6*	60	3

AKABU featuring Linda CLIFFORD *UK, male producer – Dave Lee and US, female vocalist (Singles: 1 week)*

		pos	wks
15 Sep 01	**RIDE THE STORM** *NRK Sound Division NRKCD 053*	69	1

See also HED BOYS; Li KWAN; RAVEN MAIZE; Joey NEGRO; Z FACTOR; JAKATTA; PHASE II; IL PADRINOS *featuring* Jocelyn BROWN

Jewel AKENS *US, male vocalist (Singles: 8 weeks)*

		pos	wks
25 Mar 65	**THE BIRDS AND THE BEES** *London HLN 9954*	29	8

AKIL – *See* JURASSIC 5; DJ FORMAT *featuring* Chali 2NA & AKIL

AKIN *UK, female vocal duo (Singles: 1 week)* pos/wks

14 Jun 97 **STAY RIGHT HERE** *WEA WEA 117CD* 60 1

ALABAMA 3
UK, male vocal / instrumental group (Singles: 3 weeks) pos/wks

22 Nov 97 **SPEED AT THE SOUND OF LONELINESS** *Elemental ELM 42CDS 1721* 72 1
11 Apr 98 **AIN'T GOIN' TO GOA** *Elemental ELM 45CDS1* 40 2

Roberto ALAGNA / Angela GHEORGIU
France / Romania, male / female vocal duo (Albums: 5 weeks) pos/wks

18 May 96 **DUETS & ARIAS** *EMI Classics CDC 5561172* 42 5

ALANA – *See MK*

ALARM *UK, male vocal / instrumental group (Singles: 64 weeks, Albums: 29 weeks)* pos/wks

24 Sep 83 **68 GUNS** *IRS PFP 1023* 17 7
21 Jan 84 **WHERE WERE YOU HIDING WHEN THE STORM BROKE** *IRS IRS 101* 22 6
31 Mar 84 **THE DECEIVER** *IRS IRS 103* 51 4
3 Nov 84 **THE CHANT HAS JUST BEGUN** *IRS IRS 104* 48 4
2 Mar 85 **ABSOLUTE REALITY** *IRS ALARM 1* 35 6
28 Sep 85 **STRENGTH** *IRS IRM 104* 40 4
18 Jan 86 **SPIRIT OF '76** *IRS IRM 109* 22 5
26 Apr 86 **KNIFE EDGE** *IRS IRM 112* 43 3
17 Oct 87 **RAIN IN THE SUMMERTIME** *IRS IRM 144* 18 5
12 Dec 87 **RESCUE ME** *IRS IRM 150* 48 2
20 Feb 88 **PRESENCE OF LOVE** *IRS IRM 155* 44 3
16 Sep 89 **SOLD ME DOWN THE RIVER** *IRS EIRS 123* 43 3
4 Nov 89 **A NEW SOUTH WALES / THE ROCK** *IRS EIRS 129* 31 5
3 Feb 90 **LOVE DON'T COME EASY** *IRS EIRS 134* 48 3
27 Oct 90 **UNSAFE BUILDING 1990** *IRS ALARM 2* 54 2
13 Apr 91 **RAW** *IRS ALARM 3* 51 2
25 Feb 84 ● **DECLARATION** *IRS IRSA 7044* 6 11
26 Oct 85 **STRENGTH** *IRS MIRF 1004* 18 6
14 Nov 87 **EYE OF THE HURRICANE** *IRS MIRG 1023* 23 4
5 Nov 88 **ELECTRIC FOLKLORE LIVE** *IRS MIRMC 5001* 62 2
30 Sep 89 **CHANGE** *IRS EIRSAX 1020* 13 3
24 Nov 90 **STANDARDS** *IRS EIRSA 1043* 47 1
4 May 91 **RAW** *IRS EIRSA 1055* 33 2

'A New South Wales' features Morriston Orpheus Male Voice Choir. 'Sold Me Down the River' was joined by 'Yn Gymreag' for the first week on chart

Morris ALBERT
Brazil, male vocalist – Morris Kaisermann (Singles: 10 weeks) pos/wks

27 Sep 75 ● **FEELINGS** *Decca F 13591* 4 10

ALBERTA *Sierra Leone, female vocalist (Singles: 3 weeks)* pos/wks

26 Dec 98 **YOYO BOY** *RCA 74321640602* 48 3

ALBERTO Y LOS TRIOS PARANOIAS
UK, male vocal / instrumental group (Singles: 5 weeks) pos/wks

23 Sep 78 **HEADS DOWN NO NONSENSE MINDLESS BOOGIE** *Logo GO 323* 47 5

Al ALBERTS – *See FOUR ACES*

ALBION
Holland, male producer – Ferry Corsten (Singles: 1 week) pos/wks

3 Jun 00 **AIR 2000** *Platipus PLATCD 73* 59 1

See also MOONMAN; SYSTEM F; VERACOCHA; GOURYELLA; STARPARTY; Ferry CORSTEN

ALCATRAZ *US, male instrumental / production duo – Jean-Philippe Aviance and Victor Imbres (Singles: 4 weeks)* pos/wks

17 Feb 96 **GIV ME LUV** *AM:PM 5814332* 12 4

ALCAZAR *Sweden, male / female vocal trio (Singles: 13 weeks)* pos/wks

8 Dec 01 **CRYING AT THE DISCOTEQUE** *Arista 74321893432* 13 11
16 Mar 02 **SEXUAL GUARANTEE** *Arista 74321920252* 30 2

ALDA
Iceland, female vocalist – Alda Olafsdottir (Singles: 14 weeks) pos/wks

29 Aug 98 ● **REAL GOOD TIME** *Wildstar CDWILD 7* 7 7
26 Dec 98 **GIRLS NIGHT OUT** *Wildstar CDWILD 10* 20 7

John ALDISS – *See LONDON PHILHARMONIC CHOIR*

Cali ALEMAN – *See Tito PUENTE Jr and The LATIN RHYTHM featuring Tito PUENTE, INDIA and Cali ALEMAN*

ALENA *Jamaica, female vocalist (Singles: 5 weeks)* pos/wks

13 Nov 99 **TURN IT AROUND** *Wonderboy WBOYD 16* 14 5

Hannah ALETHEA – *See SODA CLUB*

ALESSI
US, male vocal duo – Billy and Bobby Alessi (Singles: 11 weeks) pos/wks

11 Jun 77 ● **OH, LORI** *A&M AMS 7289* 8 11

ALEX PARTY *Italy / UK, male / female vocal / instrumental group – leader – Paolo Visnadi (Singles: 28 weeks)* pos/wks

18 Dec 93 **SATURDAY NIGHT PARTY (READ MY LIPS) (re)** *Cleveland City Imports CCICD 17000* 29 10
18 Feb 95 ● **DON'T GIVE ME YOUR LIFE** *Systematic SYSCD 7* 2 13
18 Nov 95 **WRAP ME UP** *Systematic SYSCD 22* 17 3
19 Oct 96 **READ MY LIPS (re-mix)** *Systematic SYSCD 30* 28 2

'Read My Lips' in 1996 is a remix of the first hit with added vocals

See also LIVIN' JOY

ALEXANDER BROTHERS
UK, male vocal duo – Tom and Jack Alexander (Albums: 1 week) pos/wks

10 Dec 66 **THESE ARE MY MOUNTAINS** *Pye GGL 0375* 29 1

ALEXIA
Italy, female vocalist – Alessia Aquilani (Singles: 15 weeks) pos/wks

21 Mar 98 ● **UH LA LA LA** *Dance Pool ALEX 1CD* 10 9
13 Jun 98 **GIMME LOVE** *Dance Pool ALEX 2CDZ* 17 4
10 Oct 98 **THE MUSIC I LIKE** *Dance Pool ALEX 3CD* 31 2

ALEXIA *UK, female vocalist (Singles: 1 week)* pos/wks

22 Feb 03 **RING** *Virgin VSCDT 1836* 48 1

ALFI and HARRY
US, male vocalist / instumentalist – David Seville (d. 16 Jan 1972) under two false names (Singles: 5 weeks) pos/wks

23 Mar 56 **THE TROUBLE WITH HARRY** *London HLU 8242* 15 5

See also CHIPMUNKS; David SEVILLE

ALFIE *UK, male vocal / instrumental group (Singles: 4 weeks, Albums: 1 week)* pos/wks

8 Sep 01 **YOU MAKE NO BONES** *Twisted Nerve TN 033CD* 61 1
16 Mar 02 **A WORD IN YOUR EAR** *Twisted Nerve TN 037CD* 66 1
21 Jun 03 **PEOPLE** *Regal REG 84CD* 53 1
13 Sep 03 **STUNTMAN** *Regal REG 87CDS* 51 1
7 Apr 01 **IF YOU HAPPY WITH YOU NEED DO NOTHING** *Twisted Nerve TN 026CD* 62 1

John ALFORD *UK, male actor / vocalist (Singles: 12 weeks)* pos/wks

17 Feb 96 **SMOKE GETS IN YOUR EYES** *Love This LUVTHISCD 7* 13 5
25 May 96 ● **BLUE MOON / ONLY YOU** *Love This LUVTHISCD 9* 9 4
23 Nov 96 **IF / KEEP ON RUNNING** *Love This LUVTHISCD 15* 24 3

ALI *UK, male vocalist (Singles: 2 weeks)* pos/wks

23 May 98	**LOVE LETTERS** *Wild Card 5698092*	63	1
24 Oct 98	**FEELIN' YOU** *Wild Card 5676992*	63	1

Tatyana ALI
US, female vocalist (Singles: 18 weeks, Albums: 4 weeks) pos/wks

14 Nov 98 ●	**DAYDREAMIN'** *Epic 6665462*	6	5
13 Feb 99 ●	**BOY YOU KNOCK ME OUT (re)** *MJJ / Epic 6669372* [1]	3	9
19 Jun 99	**EVERYTIME** *Epic / MJJ 674742*	20	4
20 Feb 99	**KISS THE SKY** *Epic 4916519*	41	4

[1] Tatyana Ali featuring Will Smith

ALI and FRAZIER *UK, female vocal duo – Kirsty Ali and Natasha Frazier (Singles: 4 weeks)* pos/wks

7 Aug 93	**UPTOWN TOP RANKING** *Arista 74321158842*	33	4

ALIBI *UK, male vocal duo (Singles: 2 weeks)* pos/wks

15 Feb 97	**I'M NOT TO BLAME** *Urgent 74321434762*	51	1
7 Feb 98	**HOW MUCH I FEEL** *Urgent 74321548472*	58	1

ALICE BAND *UK / Ireland / US, female vocal / instrumental group (Singles: 2 weeks, Albums: 1 week)* pos/wks

23 Jun 01	**ONE DAY AT A TIME** *Instant Karma KARMA 5CD*	52	1
27 Apr 02	**NOW THAT YOU LOVE ME** *Instant Karma KARMA 17CD*	44	1
25 May 02	**THE LOVE JUNK STORE** *Instant Karma KARMACD 4*	55	1

ALICE DEEJAY
Holland, male / female production / vocal group (Singles: 50 weeks, Albums: 11 weeks) pos/wks

31 Jul 99 ●	**BETTER OFF ALONE** *Positiva CDTIV 113* [1]	2	16
4 Dec 99 ●	**BACK IN MY LIFE** *Positiva CDTIV 121*	4	15
15 Jul 00 ●	**WILL I EVER** *Positiva CDTIV 134*	7	10
21 Oct 00	**THE LONELY ONE** *Positiva CDTIV 145*	16	5
10 Feb 01	**CELEBRATE OUR LOVE** *Positiva CDTIV 149*	17	4
29 Jul 00 ●	**WHO NEEDS GUITARS ANYWAY?** *Positiva 5270010*	8	11

[1] DJ Jurgen presents Alice Deejay

ALICE IN CHAINS *US, male vocal / instrumental group (Singles: 14 weeks, Albums: 22 weeks)* pos/wks

23 Jan 93	**WOULD** *Columbia 6588882*	19	3
20 Mar 93	**THEM BONES** *Columbia 6590902*	26	3
5 Jun 93	**ANGRY CHAIR** *Columbia 6593652*	33	2
23 Oct 93	**DOWN IN A HOLE** *Columbia 6597512*	36	2
11 Nov 95	**GRIND** *Columbia 6626232*	23	2
10 Feb 96	**HEAVEN BESIDE YOU** *Columbia 6628935*	35	2
24 Oct 92	**DIRT** *Columbia 4723302*	42	13
5 Feb 94 ●	**JAR OF FLIES / SAP** *Columbia 4757132* ▲	4	5
18 Nov 95	**ALICE IN CHAINS** *Columbia 4811149* ▲	37	2
10 Aug 96	**MTV UNPLUGGED** *Columbia 4843002*	20	2

ALIEN ANT FARM *US, male vocal / instrumental group (Singles: 25 weeks, Albums: 24 weeks)* pos/wks

30 Jun 01	**MOVIES** *Dreamworks / Polydor 4508992*	53	1
8 Sep 01	**SMOOTH CRIMINAL (import)** *Dreamworks / Polydor 4508852*	74	2
29 Sep 01 ●	**SMOOTH CRIMINAL (re)** *Dreamworks / Polydor DRMDM 50887*	3	13
16 Feb 02 ●	**MOVIES** *Dreamworks / Polydor 4508492*	5	8
25 May 02	**ATTITUDE** *Dreamworks / New Noize 4508292*	66	1
18 Aug 01	**ANTHOLOGY** *Dreamworks 4502932*	11	23
30 Aug 03	**TRUANT** *Dreamworks / Polydor 4505014*	68	1

ALIEN SEX FIEND
UK, male / female vocal / instrumental group (Albums: 1 week) pos/wks

12 Oct 85	**MAXIMUM SECURITY** *Anagram GRAM 24*	100	1

ALIEN VOICES featuring The THREE DEGREES
UK, male producer – Andros Georgiou featuring US, female vocal trio (Singles: 2 weeks) pos/wks

26 Dec 98	**LAST CHRISTMAS** *Wildstar CDWILD 15*	54	2

See also BOOGIE BOX HIGH; Andy G's STARSKY and HUTCH ALL STARS

ALISHA *US, female vocalist (Singles: 2 weeks)* pos/wks

25 Jan 86	**BABY TALK** *Total Control TOCO 6*	67	2

ALISHA'S ATTIC *UK, female vocal duo – Shellie and Karen Poole (Singles: 47 weeks, Albums: 47 weeks)* pos/wks

3 Aug 96	**I AM I FEEL** *Mercury AATCD 1*	14	10
2 Nov 96	**ALISHA RULES THE WORLD** *Mercury AATCD 2*	12	6
15 Mar 97	**INDESTRUCTIBLE** *Mercury AATCD 3*	12	6
12 Jul 97	**AIR WE BREATHE** *Mercury AATCD 4*	12	6
19 Sep 98	**THE INCIDENTALS** *Mercury AATCD 5*	13	7
9 Jan 99	**WISH I WERE YOU** *Mercury AATCD 6*	29	5
17 Apr 99	**BARBARELLA** *Mercury AATCD 7*	34	2
24 Mar 01	**PUSH IT ALL ASIDE** *Mercury AATCD 8*	24	4
28 Jul 01	**PRETENDER GOT MY HEART** *Mercury AATCD 9*	43	1
23 Nov 96	**ALISHA RULES THE WORLD** *Mercury 5340272*	14	43
17 Oct 98	**ILLUMINA** *Mercury 5589912*	15	3
4 Aug 01	**THE HOUSE WE BUILT** *Mercury 5428542*	55	1

ALIVE featuring D.D. KLEIN *Italy, male production trio and Antigua, female vocalist (Singles: 1 week)* pos/wks

27 Jul 02	**ALIVE** *Serious / Universal CDAMPM 153*	49	1

ALIZÉE
France, female vocalist (Singles: 9 weeks) pos/wks

23 Feb 02 ●	**MOI ...LOLITA** *Polydor 5705952*	9	9

ALKALINE TRIO *US, male vocal / instrumental trio (Singles: 4 weeks, Albums: 1 week)* pos/wks

2 Feb 02	**PRIVATE EYE** *B Unique / Vagrant BUN 013CDS*	51	1
30 Mar 02	**STUPID KID** *B Unique / Vagrant BUN 016CD*	53	1
26 Jul 03	**WE'VE HAD ENOUGH** *Vagrant 9809023*	50	1
18 Oct 03	**ALL ON BLACK** *Interscope 9811506*	60	1
24 May 03	**GOOD MOURNING** *Vagrant 9801238*	32	1

ALL ABOUT EVE *UK, female / male vocal / instrumental group (Singles: 47 weeks, Albums: 37 weeks)* pos/wks

31 Oct 87	**IN THE CLOUDS** *Mercury EVEN 5*	47	5
23 Jan 88	**WILD HEARTED WOMAN** *Mercury EVEN 6*	33	4
9 Apr 88	**EVERY ANGEL** *Mercury EVEN 7*	30	5
30 Jul 88 ●	**MARTHA'S HARBOUR** *Mercury EVEN 8*	10	8
12 Nov 88	**WHAT KIND OF FOOL** *Mercury EVEN 9*	29	4
30 Sep 89	**ROAD TO YOUR SOUL** *Mercury EVEN 10*	37	4
16 Dec 89	**DECEMBER** *Mercury EVEN 11*	34	5
28 Apr 90	**SCARLET** *Mercury EVEN 12*	34	2
15 Jun 91	**FAREWELL MR SORROW** *Mercury EVEN 14*	36	2
10 Aug 91	**STRANGE WAY** *Vertigo EVEN 15*	50	3
19 Oct 91	**THE DREAMER** *Vertigo EVEN 16*	41	2
10 Oct 92	**PHASED (EP)** *MCA MCS 1688*	38	2
28 Nov 92	**SOME FINER DAY** *MCA MCS 1706*	57	1
27 Feb 88 ●	**ALL ABOUT EVE** *Mercury MERH 119*	7	29
28 Oct 89 ●	**SCARLET AND OTHER STORIES** *Mercury 838965 1*	9	4
7 Sep 91	**TOUCHED BY JESUS** *Vertigo 510461*	17	3
7 Nov 92	**ULTRAVIOLET** *MCA MCD 10712*	46	1

Tracks on Phased (EP): Phased / Mine / Infra Red / Ascent-Descent

ALL-AMERICAN REJECTS *US, male vocal / instrumental group (Singles: 6 weeks, Albums: 5 weeks)* pos/wks

2 Aug 03	**SWING, SWING** *Dreamworks 4504616*	13	5
22 Nov 03	**THE LAST SONG** *Dreamworks 4504641*	69	1
9 Aug 03	**THE ALL-AMERICAN REJECTS** *Dreamworks / Polydor 4504606*	50	5

ALL BLUE *UK, male vocal duo (Singles: 1 week)*

		pos/wks	
21 Aug 99	**PRISONER** *WEA WEA 213CD1*	**73**	1

ALL-4-ONE
US, male vocal group (Singles: 23 weeks, Albums: 5 weeks)

		pos/wks	
2 Apr 94	**SO MUCH IN LOVE** *Atlantic A 7261CD*	**60**	1
18 Jun 94 ●	**I SWEAR** *Atlantic A 7255CD* ▲	**2**	18
19 Nov 94	**SO MUCH IN LOVE (re-mix)** *Atlantic A 7216CD*	**49**	2
15 Jul 95	**I CAN LOVE YOU LIKE THAT** *Atlantic A 8193CD*	**33**	2
23 Jul 94	ALL-4-ONE *Atlantic 7567825882*	25	5

ALL SAINTS (317 Top 500)
From All Saints Road, London, a cooler, R&B-motivated vocal girl group in the wake of The Spice Girls. Melanie Blatt, London, Shaznay Lewis, London, Nicole Appleton, Canada, Natalie Appleton, Canada. Crowned Best Breakthrough Artists in the 1998 MTV Europe Music Awards. Group split in 2001. Biggest-selling single: 'Never Ever' 1,254,604 (Singles: 109 weeks, Albums: 96 weeks)

		pos/wks	
6 Sep 97 ●	**I KNOW WHERE IT'S AT** *London LONCD 398*	**4**	8
22 Nov 97 ★	**NEVER EVER** *London LONCD 407* ◆	**1**	24
9 May 98 ★	**UNDER THE BRIDGE / LADY MARMALADE** *London LONCD 408* ■	**1**	14
12 Sep 98 ★	**BOOTIE CALL** *London LONCD 415* ■	**1**	11
5 Dec 98 ●	**WAR OF NERVES** *London LONCD 421*	**7**	11
26 Feb 00 ★	**PURE SHORES** *London LONCD 444* ■	**1**	16
14 Oct 00 ★	**BLACK COFFEE (2re)** *London LONCD 454* ■	**1**	18
27 Jan 01 ●	**ALL HOOKED UP (re)** *London LONCD 456*	**7**	7
6 Dec 97 ●	ALL SAINTS *London 8289792*	2	71
28 Oct 00 ★	SAINTS & SINNERS *London 8573852952* ■	1	21
17 Nov 01	ALL HITS *London 927421522*	18	4

From 29 Apr 00 'All Saints' changed catalogue number to London 3984291362

See also APPLETON

ALL SEEING I *UK, male vocal / instrumental group (Singles: 17 weeks, Albums: 1 week)*

		pos/wks	
28 Mar 98	**BEAT GOES ON** *ffrr FCD 334*	**11**	7
23 Jan 99 ●	**WALK LIKE A PANTHER '98** *ffrr FCD 351* [1]	**10**	7
18 Sep 99	**1ST MAN IN SPACE** *ffrr FCD 370* [2]	**28**	3
2 Oct 99	PICKLED EGGS & SHERBET *ffrr 3984292412*	45	1

[1] The All Seeing I featuring Tony Christie [2] The All Seeing I featuring Phil Oakey

ALL STAR CHOIR – *See Donna SUMMER*

ALL-STARS – *See Louis ARMSTRONG*

ALL-STARS – *See Jr WALKER & The ALL-STARS*

ALL SYSTEMS GO
UK, male vocal / instrumental group (Singles: 2 weeks)

		pos/wks	
18 Jun 88	**POP MUZIK** *Unique NIQ 03*	**63**	2

Richard ALLAN *UK, male vocalist (Singles: 1 week)*

		pos/wks	
24 Mar 60	**AS TIME GOES BY** *Parlophone R 4634*	**43**	1

Steve ALLAN *UK, male vocalist (Singles: 2 weeks)*

		pos/wks	
27 Jan 79	**TOGETHER WE ARE BEAUTIFUL (re)** *Creole CR 164*	**67**	2

ALLEN – *See FOSTER and ALLEN*

Donna ALLEN *US, female vocalist (Singles: 27 weeks)*

		pos/wks	
18 Apr 87 ●	**SERIOUS** *Portrait 650744 7*	**8**	12
3 Jun 89 ●	**JOY AND PAIN** *BCM BCM 257*	**10**	10
21 Jan 95	**REAL** *Epic 6610992*	**34**	2
11 Oct 97	**SATURDAY** *AM:PM 5823752* [1]	**29**	3

[1] East 57th Street featuring Donna Allen

Keith ALLEN – *See BLACK GRAPE; FAT LES; Joe STRUMMER; ENGLANDNEWORDER*

Ed ALLEYNE-JOHNSON
UK, male instrumentalist – violin (Albums: 1 week)

		pos/wks	
18 Jun 94	ULTRAVIOLET *Equation EQCD 002*	68	1

Dot ALLISON *UK, female vocalist (Singles: 1 week)*

		pos/wks	
17 Aug 02	**STRUNG OUT** *Mantra MNT 74CD*	**67**	1

See also ONE DOVE

Mose ALLISON
US, male vocalist / instrumentalist – piano (Albums: 1 week)

		pos/wks	
4 Jun 66	MOSE ALIVE *Atlantic 587007*	30	1

ALLISONS *UK, male vocal / Instrumental duo – John Allison (Brian Alford) and Bob Allison (Colin Day) (Singles: 27 weeks)*

		pos/wks	
23 Feb 61 ●	**ARE YOU SURE** *Fontana H 294*	**2**	16
18 May 61	**WORDS** *Fontana H 304*	**34**	5
15 Feb 62	**LESSONS IN LOVE** *Fontana H 362*	**30**	6

ALLMAN BROTHERS BAND
US, male vocal / instrumental group (Albums: 4 weeks)

		pos/wks	
6 Oct 73	BROTHERS AND SISTERS *Warner Bros. K 47507* ▲	42	3
6 Mar 76	THE ROAD GOES ON FOREVER *Capricorn 2637 101*	54	1

ALLNIGHT BAND
UK, male instrumental group (Singles: 3 weeks)

		pos/wks	
3 Feb 79	**THE JOKER (THE WIGAN JOKER)** *Casino Classics CC 6*	**50**	3

ALLSTARS *UK, male / female vocal group (Singles: 22 weeks, Albums: 2 weeks)*

		pos/wks	
23 Jun 01	**BEST FRIENDS (re)** *Islands CID 775*	**20**	7
22 Sep 01	**THINGS THAT GO BUMP IN THE NIGHT / IS THERE SOMETHING I SHOULD KNOW** *Island CID 783*	**12**	4
26 Jan 02 ●	**THE LAND OF MAKE BELIEVE (re)** *Island CID 791*	**9**	8
11 May 02	**BACK WHEN / GOING ALL THE WAY** *Island CID 796*	**19**	3
25 May 02	ALLSTARS *Island CID 8116*	43	2

ALLURE *US, female vocal group (Singles: 8 weeks)*

		pos/wks	
14 Jun 97	**HEAD OVER HEELS** *Epic 6645942* [1]	**18**	3
10 Jan 98	**ALL CRIED OUT** *Epic 6652715* [2]	**12**	5

[1] Allure featuring NAS [2] Allure featuring 112

ALMIGHTY *UK, male vocal / instrumental group (Singles: 22 weeks, Albums: 13 weeks)*

		pos/wks	
30 Jun 90	**WILD AND WONDERFUL** *Polydor PO 75*	**50**	2
2 Mar 91	**FREE 'N' EASY** *Polydor PO 127*	**35**	2
11 May 91	**DEVIL'S TOY** *Polydor PO 144*	**36**	2
29 Jun 91	**LITTLE LOST SOMETIMES** *Polydor PO 151*	**42**	2
3 Apr 93	**ADDICTION** *Polydor PZCD 261*	**38**	2
29 May 93	**OUT OF SEASON** *Polydor PZCD 266*	**41**	2
30 Oct 93	**OVER THE EDGE** *Polydor PZCD 298*	**38**	2
24 Sep 94	**WRENCH** *Chrysalis CDCHS 5014*	**26**	2
14 Jan 95	**JONESTOWN MIND** *Chrysalis CDCHS 5017*	**26**	3
16 Mar 96	**ALL SUSSED OUT** *Chrysalis CDCHS 5030*	**28**	2
25 May 96	**DO YOU UNDERSTAND** *Raw Power RAWX 1022*	**38**	1
20 Oct 90	BLOOD FIRE AND LIVE *Polydor 8471071*	62	1
30 Mar 91	SOUL DESTRUCTION *Polydor 8479611*	22	4
17 Apr 93 ●	POWERTRIPPIN' *Polydor 5191042*	5	4
8 Oct 94	CRANK *Chrysalis CDCHRZ 6086*	15	2
30 Mar 96	JUST ADD LIFE *Chrysalis CDCHR 6112*	34	2

Marc ALMOND
UK, male vocalist (Singles: 112 weeks, Albums: 26 weeks)

		pos/wks	
2 Jul 83	**BLACK HEART** *Some Bizzare BZS 19* [1]	**49**	3
2 Jun 84	**THE BOY WHO CAME BACK** *Some Bizzare BZS 23*	**52**	5
1 Sep 84	**YOU HAVE** *Some Bizzare BZS 24*	**57**	3
20 Apr 85 ●	**I FEEL LOVE (MEDLEY)** *Forbidden Fruit BITE 4* [2]	**3**	12
24 Aug 85	**STORIES OF JOHNNY** *Some Bizzare BONK 1*	**23**	5

26 Oct 85 **LOVE LETTER** *Some Bizzare BONK 2* 68 3
4 Jan 86 **THE HOUSE IS HAUNTED (BY THE ECHO OF YOUR LAST GOODBYE)** *Some Bizzare GLOW 1* 55 3
7 Jun 86 **A WOMAN'S STORY** *Some Bizzare GLOW 2* [3] 41 5
18 Oct 86 **RUBY RED** *Some Bizzare GLOW 3* 47 3
14 Feb 87 **MELANCHOLY ROSE** *Some Bizzare GLOW 4* 71 1
3 Sep 88 **TEARS RUN RINGS** *Parlophone R 6186* 26 7
5 Nov 88 **BITTER SWEET** *Some Bizzare R 6194* 40 3
14 Jan 89 ★ **SOMETHING'S GOTTEN HOLD OF MY HEART** *Parlophone R 6201* [4] 1 12
8 Apr 89 **ONLY THE MOMENT** *Parlophone R 6210* 45 2
3 Mar 90 **A LOVER SPURNED** *Some Bizzare R 6229* 29 4
19 May 90 **THE DESPERATE HOURS** *Some Bizzare R 6252* 45 2
23 Mar 91 **SAY HELLO WAVE GOODBYE '91 (re-recording)** *Mercury SOFT 1* [5] 38 3
18 May 91 ● **TAINTED LOVE (re-issue)** *Mercury SOFT 2* [5] 5 8
28 Sep 91 **JACKY** *Some Bizzare YZ 610* 17 6
11 Jan 92 **MY HAND OVER MY HEART** *Some Bizzare YZ 633* 33 5
25 Apr 92 ● **THE DAYS OF PEARLY SPENCER** *Some Bizzare YZ 638* 4 7
27 Mar 93 **WHAT MAKES A MAN A MAN (LIVE)** *Some Bizzare YZ 720CD* 60 2
13 May 95 **ADORED AND EXPLORED** *Some Bizarre MERCD 431* 25 3
29 Jul 95 **THE IDOL** *Some Bizarre MERCD 437* 44 2
30 Dec 95 **CHILD STAR** *Some Bizarre MERCD 450* 41 1
28 Dec 96 **YESTERDAY HAS GONE (re)** *EMI Premier CDPRESX 13* [6] 58 2
16 Oct 82 **UNTITLED** *Some Bizzare BZA 13* [1] 42 4
20 Aug 83 **TORMENT & TOREROS** *Some Bizzare BIZL 4* [1] 28 5
10 Nov 84 **VERMIN IN ERMINE** *Some Bizzare BIZL 8* 36 2
5 Oct 85 **STORIES OF JOHNNY** *Some Bizzare FAITH 1* 22 3
18 Apr 87 **MOTHER FIST AND HER FIVE DAUGHTERS** *Some Bizzare FAITH 2* [2] 41 2
8 Oct 88 **THE STARS WE ARE** *Parlophone PCS 7324* 41 5
16 Jun 90 **ENCHANTED** *Some Bizzare PCS 7344* 52 1
26 Oct 91 **TENEMENT SYMPHONY** *Some Bizzare WX 442* 39 3
9 Mar 96 **FANTASTIC STAR** *Some Bizarre 5286592* 54 1

[1] Marc and the Mambas [2] Bronski Beat and Marc Almond [3] Marc Almond and the Willing Sinners [4] Marc Almond featuring special guest star Gene Pitney [5] Soft Cell / Marc Almond [6] PJ Proby and Marc Almond featuring the My Life Story Orchestra [1] Marc and the Mambas [2] Marc Almond and the Willing Sinners

I Feel Love medley comprises: I Feel Love / Love to Love You Baby / Johnny Remember Me. Original hit versions of 'Tainted Love' (1981) and 'Say Hello Wave Goodbye' (1982) credited to Soft Cell alone

ALOOF *UK, male vocal / instrumental group (Singles: 6 weeks)* pos/wks

19 Sep 92 **ON A MISSION** *Cowboy RODEO 5* 64 1
18 May 96 **WISH YOU WERE HERE ...** *East West EW 038CD* 61 1
30 Nov 96 **ONE NIGHT STAND** *East West EW 067CD* 30 2
1 Mar 97 **WISH YOU WERE HERE ... (re-mix)** *East West EW 083CD1* 43 1
29 Aug 98 **WHAT I MISS THE MOST** *East West EW 179CD1* 70 1

Herb ALPERT and the TIJUANA BRASS *106 Top 500*

Leader of the US's biggest-selling instrumental act, The Tijuana Brass, b. 31 Mar 1935, Los Angeles. The multi-talented trumpet-toting star's band had four albums simultaneously in the US Top 10 in the mid-1960s. He sold his A&M label for $300m in 1989 and his publishing company for $350m in 2000 (Singles: 106 weeks, Albums: 312 weeks) pos/wks

3 Jan 63 **THE LONELY BULL (EL SOLO TORRO)** *Stateside SS 138* [1] ..22 9
9 Dec 65 ● **SPANISH FLEA** *Pye International 7N 25335* 3 20
24 Mar 66 **TIJUANA TAXI** *Pye International 7N 25352* 37 4
27 Apr 67 **CASINO ROYALE** *A&M AMS 700* 27 14
3 Jul 68 ● **THIS GUY'S IN LOVE WITH YOU (3re)** *A&M AMS 727* [2] ▲ 3 19
18 Jun 69 **WITHOUT HER** *A&M AMS 755* 36 5
12 Dec 70 **JERUSALEM (re)** *A&M AMS 810* 42 3
13 Oct 79 **RISE** *A&M AMS 7465* [2] ▲ 13 13
19 Jan 80 **ROTATION** *A&M AMS 7500* [2] 46 3
21 Mar 87 **KEEP YOUR EYE ON ME** *Breakout USA 602* [2] 19 9
6 Jun 87 **DIAMONDS** *Breakout USA 605* [2] 27 7
29 Jan 66 ● **GOING PLACES** *Pye NPL 28065* ▲ 4 138
23 Apr 66 ● **WHIPPED CREAM AND OTHER DELIGHTS** *Pye NPL 28058* ▲ 2 42
28 May 66 **WHAT NOW MY LOVE** *Pye NPL 28077* ▲ 18 17
11 Feb 67 ● **SRO** *Pye NSPL 28088* 5 26
15 Jul 67 **SOUNDS LIKE** *A&M AMLS 900* ▲ 21 10
3 Feb 68 **NINTH** *A&M AMLS 905* 26 9
29 Jun 68 ● **BEAT OF THE BRASS** *A&M AMLS 916* ▲ 4 21
9 Aug 69 **WARM** *A&M AMLS 937* 30 4
14 Mar 70 **THE BRASS ARE COMIN'** *A&M AMLS 962* 40 1
30 May 70 ● **GREATEST HITS** *A&M AMLS 980* 8 27
27 Jun 70 **DOWN MEXICO WAY** *A&M AMLS 974* 64 1
13 Nov 71 **AMERICA** *A&M AMLB 1000* 45 1
12 Nov 77 **40 GREATEST** *K-Tel NE 1005* 45 2
17 Nov 79 **RISE** *A&M AMLH 64790* [1] 37 7
4 Apr 87 **KEEP YOUR EYE ON ME** *Breakout AMA 5125* [1] 79 3
28 Sep 91 **THE VERY BEST OF HERB ALPERT** *A&M 3971651* [1] 34 3

[1] Tijuana Brass [2] Herb Alpert [1] Herb Alpert

Alpert provides vocals on 'This Guy's in Love with You' and 'Without Her'. Janet Jackson and Lisa Keith provide uncredited vocals on 'Diamonds' On 29 Jun 67 'Going Places' and 'What Now My Love' changed labels and numbers to A&M AMLS 965 and AMLS 977 respectively

ALPHA-BETA – *See Izhar COHEN and the ALPHA-BETA*

ALPHAVILLE *Germany, male vocal / instrumental group (Singles: 13 weeks)* pos/wks

18 Aug 84 ● **BIG IN JAPAN** *WEA Int. X9505* 8 13

ALPINESTARS featuring Brian MOLKO *UK, male production duo and US, male vocalist (Singles: 1 week)* pos/wks

22 Jun 02 **CARBON KID** *Riverman RMR 11CDS* 63 1

ALSOU *Russia, female vocalist – Alsou Tenisheva (Singles: 3 weeks)* pos/wks

12 May 01 **BEFORE YOU LOVE ME** *Mercury 1589142* 27 3

Gerald ALSTON *US, male vocalist (Singles: 1 week)* pos/wks

15 Apr 89 **ACTIVATED** *RCA ZB 42681* 73 1

ALT *Ireland / New Zealand / UK, male vocal / instrumental band (Albums: 1 week)* pos/wks

24 Jun 95 **ALTITUDE** *Parlophone CDPCS 7377* 67 1

ALTERED IMAGES *UK, male / female vocal / instrumental group (Singles: 60 weeks, Albums: 40 weeks)* pos/wks

28 Mar 81 **DEAD POP STARS** *Epic EPC A 1023* 67 2
26 Sep 81 ● **HAPPY BIRTHDAY** *Epic EPC A 1522* 2 17
12 Dec 81 ● **I COULD BE HAPPY** *Epic EPC A 1834* 7 12
27 Mar 82 **SEE THOSE EYES** *Epic EPC A 2198* 11 7
22 May 82 **PINKY BLUE** *Epic EPC A 2426* 35 6
19 Mar 83 ● **DON'T TALK TO ME ABOUT LOVE** *Epic EPC A 3083* 7 7
28 May 83 **BRING ME CLOSER** *Epic EPC A 3398* 29 6
16 Jul 83 **LOVE TO STAY** *Epic EPC A 3582* 46 3
19 Sep 81 **HAPPY BIRTHDAY** *Epic EPC 84893* 26 21
15 May 82 **PINKY BLUE** *Epic EPC 85665* 12 10
25 Jun 83 **BITE** *Epic EPC 25413* 16 9

ALTERN 8 *UK, male instrumental / production duo – Mark Archer and Chris Peat (Singles: 34 weeks, Albums: 4 weeks)* pos/wks

13 Jul 91 **INFILTRATE 202** *Network NWK 24* 28 7
16 Nov 91 ● **ACTIV 8 (COME WITH ME)** *Network NWK 34* 3 9
8 Feb 92 **FREQUENCY** *Network NWKT 37* 41 1
11 Apr 92 ● **EVAPOR 8** *Network NWK 38* [1] 6 6
4 Jul 92 **HYPNOTIC ST-8** *Network NWK 49* 16 4
10 Oct 92 **SHAME** *Network NWKTEN 56* [2] 74 1
12 Dec 92 **BRUTAL-8-E** *Network NWK 59* 43 5
3 Jul 93 **EVERYBODY** *Network NWKCD 73* 58 1
25 Jul 92 **FULL ON ... MASK HYSTERIA** *Network TOPCD 1* 11 4

[1] Altern 8, guest vocal PP Arnold [2] Altern 8 vs Evelyn King

ALTHIA and DONNA *Jamaica, female vocal duo – Althea Forrest and Donna Reid (Singles: 11 weeks)* pos/wks

24 Dec 77 ★ **UPTOWN TOP RANKING** *Lightning LIG 506* 1 11

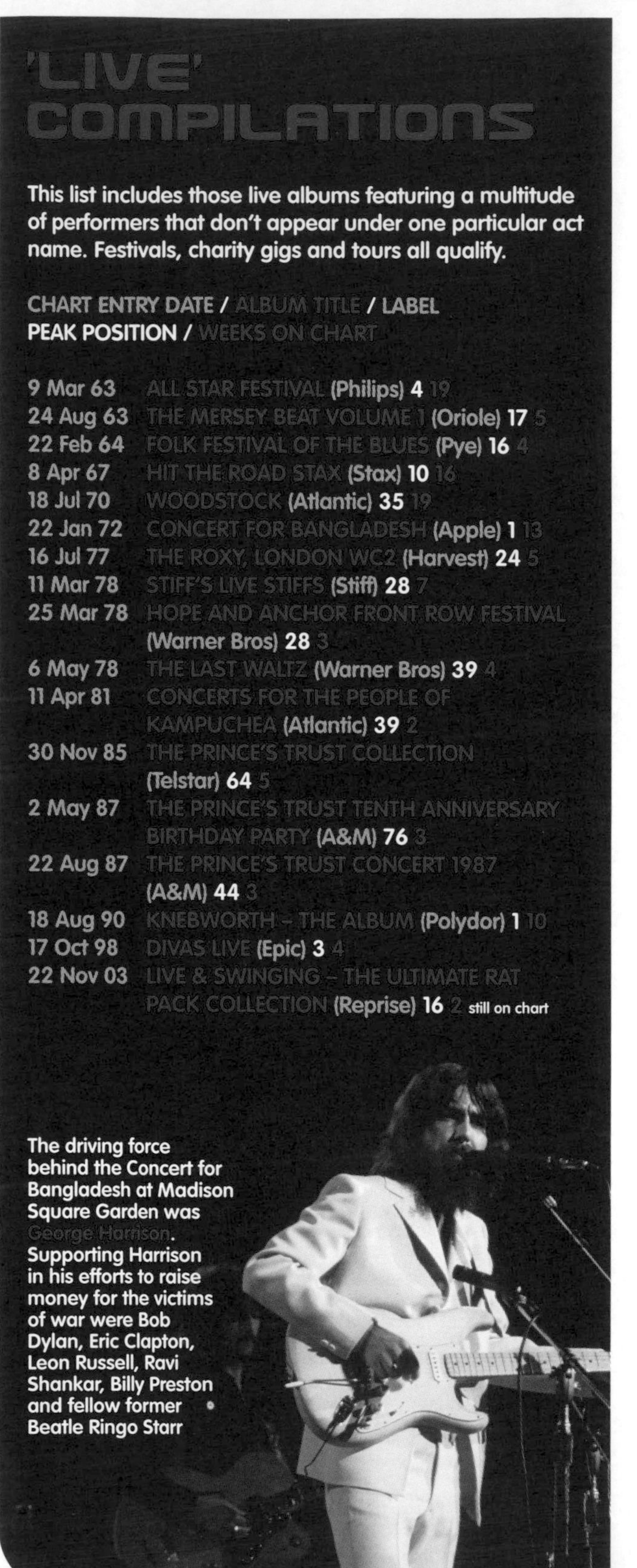

'LIVE' COMPILATIONS

This list includes those live albums featuring a multitude of performers that don't appear under one particular act name. Festivals, charity gigs and tours all qualify.

CHART ENTRY DATE / ALBUM TITLE / LABEL
PEAK POSITION / WEEKS ON CHART

9 Mar 63	ALL STAR FESTIVAL (Philips) **4** 19
24 Aug 63	THE MERSEY BEAT VOLUME 1 (Oriole) **17** 5
22 Feb 64	FOLK FESTIVAL OF THE BLUES (Pye) **16** 4
8 Apr 67	HIT THE ROAD STAX (Stax) **10** 16
18 Jul 70	WOODSTOCK (Atlantic) **35** 19
22 Jan 72	CONCERT FOR BANGLADESH (Apple) **1** 13
16 Jul 77	THE ROXY, LONDON WC2 (Harvest) **24** 5
11 Mar 78	STIFF'S LIVE STIFFS (Stiff) **28** 7
25 Mar 78	HOPE AND ANCHOR FRONT ROW FESTIVAL (Warner Bros) **28** 3
6 May 78	THE LAST WALTZ (Warner Bros) **39** 4
11 Apr 81	CONCERTS FOR THE PEOPLE OF KAMPUCHEA (Atlantic) **39** 2
30 Nov 85	THE PRINCE'S TRUST COLLECTION (Telstar) **64** 5
2 May 87	THE PRINCE'S TRUST TENTH ANNIVERSARY BIRTHDAY PARTY (A&M) **76** 3
22 Aug 87	THE PRINCE'S TRUST CONCERT 1987 (A&M) **44** 3
18 Aug 90	KNEBWORTH – THE ALBUM (Polydor) **1** 10
17 Oct 98	DIVAS LIVE (Epic) **3** 4
22 Nov 03	LIVE & SWINGING – THE ULTIMATE RAT PACK COLLECTION (Reprise) **16** 2 still on chart

The driving force behind the Concert for Bangladesh at Madison Square Garden was George Harrison. Supporting Harrison in his efforts to raise money for the victims of war were Bob Dylan, Eric Clapton, Leon Russell, Ravi Shankar, Billy Preston and fellow former Beatle Ringo Starr

ALVIN and the CHIPMUNKS – *See CHIPMUNKS*

ALY-US *US, male vocal / instrumental group (Singles: 3 weeks)* pos/wks

		pos	wks
21 Nov 92	FOLLOW ME *Cooltempo COOL 266*	**43**	2
25 May 02	FOLLOW ME (re-mix) *Strictly Rhythm SRUKCD 05*	**54**	1

Shola AMA *UK, female vocalist – Mathurin Campbell (Singles: 50 weeks, Albums: 32 weeks)* pos/wks

		pos	wks
19 Apr 97 ●	YOU MIGHT NEED SOMEBODY *WEA WEA 097CD1*	**4**	14
30 Aug 97 ●	YOU'RE THE ONE I LOVE *WEA WEA 121CD1*	**3**	8
29 Nov 97	WHO'S LOVING MY BABY *WEA WEA 145CD1*	**13**	7
21 Feb 98	MUCH LOVE *WEA WEA 154CD1*	**17**	3
11 Apr 98	SOMEDAY I'LL FIND YOU / I'VE BEEN TO A MARVELLOUS PARTY *EMI CDTCB 001* [1]	**28**	3
17 Apr 99 ●	TABOO *WEA WEA 203CD* [2]	**10**	8
6 Nov 99	STILL BELIEVE *WEA WEA 239CD1*	**26**	3
29 Apr 00	IMAGINE *WEA WEA 252 CD*	**24**	4
13 Sep 97 ●	MUCH LOVE *WEA 3984200202*	**6**	32

[1] Shola Ama and Craig Armstrong / Divine Comedy [2] Glamma Kid featuring Shola Ama

Eddie AMADOR *US, male DJ / producer (Singles: 5 weeks)* pos/wks

		pos	wks
24 Oct 98	HOUSE MUSIC *Pukka CDPUKKA 18*	**37**	2
22 Jan 00	RISE *Defected DEFECT 9CDS*	**19**	3

Ruby AMANFU *US, female vocalist (Singles: 2 weeks)* pos/wks

		pos	wks
15 Mar 03	SUGAH *Polydor 0658302*	**32**	2

AMAR *UK, female vocalist / instrumentalist – Amar Nagi (Singles: 1 week)* pos/wks

		pos	wks
9 Sep 00	SOMETIMES IT SNOWS IN APRIL *Blanco Y Negro NEG 129CD*	**48**	1

AMAZULU *UK, female / male vocal / instrumental group (Singles: 57 weeks, Albums: 1 week)* pos/wks

		pos	wks
6 Jul 85	EXCITABLE *Island IS 201*	**12**	13
23 Nov 85	DON'T YOU JUST KNOW IT *Island IS 233*	**15**	11
15 Mar 86	THE THINGS THE LONELY DO *Island IS 267*	**43**	6
31 May 86 ●	TOO GOOD TO BE FORGOTTEN *Island IS 284*	**5**	13
13 Sep 86	MONTEGO BAY *Island IS 293*	**16**	9
10 Oct 87	MONY MONY *EMI EM 32*	**38**	5
6 Dec 88	AMAZULU *Island ILPS 9851*	**97**	1

AMBASSADOR *Holland, male DJ / production group (Singles: 1 week)* pos/wks

		pos	wks
12 Feb 00	ONE OF THESE DAYS *Platipus PLATCD 69*	**67**	1

AMBASSADORS OF FUNK featuring MC MARIO *UK, male DJ and rapper – Simon Harris and Einstein (Singles: 8 weeks)* pos/wks

		pos	wks
31 Oct 92 ●	SUPERMARIOLAND *Living Beat SMASH 23*	**8**	8

See also Simon HARRIS

AMBER *Holland, female vocalist – Marie Cremers (Singles: 2 weeks)* pos/wks

		pos	wks
24 Jun 00	SEXUAL *Substance SUBS 2CDS*	**34**	2

AMEN *US, male vocal / instrumental group (Singles: 2 weeks)* pos/wks

		pos	wks
17 Feb 01	TOO HARD TO BE FREE *Virgin VUSCD 191*	**72**	1
21 Jul 01	THE WAITING 18 *Virgin VUSCD 207*	**61**	1

AMEN CORNER *UK, male vocal / instrumental group – lead vocal Andy Fairweather-Low (Singles: 67 weeks, Albums: 8 weeks)* pos/wks

		pos	wks
26 Jul 67	GIN HOUSE BLUES *Deram DM 136*	**12**	10

		pos	wks
11 Oct 67	**THE WORLD OF BROKEN HEARTS** *Deram DM 151*	24	6
17 Jan 68 ●	**BEND ME, SHAPE ME** *Deram DM 172*	3	12
31 Jul 68 ●	**HIGH IN THE SKY** *Deram DM 197*	6	13
29 Jan 69 ★	**(IF PARADISE IS) HALF AS NICE** *Immediate IM 073*	1	11
25 Jun 69 ●	**HELLO SUZIE** *Immediate IM 081*	4	10
14 Feb 76	**(IF PARADISE IS) HALF AS NICE (re-issue)** *Immediate IMS 103*	34	5
30 Mar 68	**ROUND AMEN CORNER** *Deram SML 1021*	26	7
1 Nov 69	**EXPLOSIVE COMPANY** *Immediate IMSP 023*	19	1

See also FAIR WEATHER; Andy FAIRWEATHER-LOW

AMEN UK

UK, male / female vocal / production group (Singles: 8 weeks)

		pos	wks
8 Feb 97	**PASSION** *Feverpitch CDFVR 1015*	15	4
28 Jun 97	**PEOPLE OF LOVE** *Feverpitch CDFVR 18*	36	2
6 Sep 03	**PASSION (re-mix)** *Positiva CDTIV 195* [1]	40	2

[1] Amen! UK

AMERICA

US, male vocal / instrumental group (Singles: 20 weeks, Albums: 22 weeks)

		pos	wks
18 Dec 71 ●	**A HORSE WITH NO NAME (re)** *Warner Bros. K 16128* ▲	3	13
25 Nov 72	**VENTURA HIGHWAY** *Warner Bros. K 16219*	43	4
6 Nov 82	**YOU CAN DO MAGIC** *Capitol CL 264*	59	3
22 Jan 72	**AMERICA** *Warner Bros. K 46093* ▲	14	13
9 Dec 72	**HOMECOMING** *Warner Bros. K 46180*	21	5
10 Nov 73	**HAT TRICK** *Warner Bros. K 56016*	41	3
7 Feb 76	**HISTORY – AMERICA'S GREATEST HITS** *Warner Bros. K 56169*	60	1

AMERICAN BREED

US, male vocal / instrumental group (Singles: 6 weeks)

		pos	wks
7 Feb 68	**BEND ME SHAPE ME** *Stateside SS 2078*	24	6

AMERICAN HEAD CHARGE

US, male vocal / instrumental group (Singles: 1 week)

		pos	wks
8 Jun 02	**JUST SO YOU KNOW** *Mercury 5829622*	52	1

AMERICAN HI-FI

US, male vocal / instrumental group (Singles: 4 weeks)

		pos	wks
8 Sep 01	**FLAVOR OF THE WEAK** *Mercury 5886722*	31	3
26 Apr 03	**THE ART OF LOSING** *Mercury 0779152*	75	1

AMERICAN MUSIC CLUB

US, male vocal / instrumental group (Singles: 4 weeks, Albums: 3 weeks)

		pos	wks
24 Apr 93	**JOHNNY MATHIS' FEET** *Virgin VSCDG 1445*	58	2
10 Sep 94	**WISH THE WORLD AWAY** *Virgin VSCDX 1512*	46	2
27 Mar 93	**MERCURY** *Virgin CDV 2708*	41	2
24 Sep 94	**SAN FRANCISCO** *Virgin CDV 2752*	72	1

AMERIE

US, female vocalist – Amerie Rogers (Singles: 7 weeks)

		pos	wks
9 Nov 02	**WHY DON'T WE FALL IN LOVE** *Columbia 6732212* [1]	40	2
22 Feb 03	**PARADISE** *Def Jam 0637032* [2]	18	5

[1] Amerie featuring Ludacris [2] LL Cool J featuring Amerie

AMES BROTHERS

US, male vocal group (Singles: 6 weeks)

		pos	wks
4 Feb 55 ●	**THE NAUGHTY LADY OF SHADY LANE** *HMV B 10800*	6	6

With Hugo Winterhalter and his Orchestra

AMICI FOREVER

UK / South Africa / New Zealand, male / female vocal group (Albums: 9 weeks)

		pos	wks
27 Sep 03	**THE OPERA BAND** *Victor / Arista Assoc 828765822*	39	9

AMIL – *See JAY-Z*

AMILLIONSONS

UK, male production trio (Singles: 2 weeks)

		pos	wks
24 Aug 02	**MISTI BLU** *London LONCD 468*	39	2

Includes vocal by Taka Boom

AMIRA

US, female vocalist – Amira McNeil (Singles: 7 weeks)

		pos	wks
13 Dec 97	**MY DESIRE** *VC VCRD 27*	51	1
8 Aug 98	**MY DESIRE (re-mix)** *VC Recordings VCRD 36*	46	2
10 Feb 01	**MY DESIRE (2nd re-mix)** *VC Recordings VCRD 71*	20	4

AMNESIA – *See Frank'o MOIRAGHI featuring AMNESIA*

Cherie AMORE

France, female vocalist (Singles: 2 weeks)

		pos	wks
15 Apr 00	**I DON'T WANT NOBODY (TELLIN' ME WHAT TO DO)** *Eternal / WEA WEA 262CD*	33	2

Vanessa AMOROSI

Australia, female vocalist (Singles: 10 weeks)

		pos	wks
23 Sep 00 ●	**ABSOLUTELY EVERYBODY** *Mercury 1582972*	7	10

AMORPHOUS ANDROGYNOUS

UK, male instrumental / production duo – Brian Dougans and Gary Cobain (Albums: 1 week)

		pos	wks
17 Aug 02	**FSOL PRESENTS AMORPHOUS ANDROGYNOUS: THE ISNESS** *Artful FSOLCD 101*	68	1

See also FUTURE SOUND OF LONDON

AMOS

UK, male vocalist / rapper / producer – Amos Pizzey (Singles: 12 weeks)

		pos	wks
3 Sep 94	**ONLY SAW TODAY – INSTANT KARMA** *Positiva CDTIV 16*	48	2
25 Mar 95	**LET LOVE SHINE** *Positiva CDTIV 24*	31	2
7 Oct 95	**CHURCH OF FREEDOM** *Positiva CDTIV 38*	54	1
12 Oct 96	**STAMP!** *Positiva CDTIV 65* [1]	11	5
31 May 97	**ARGENTINA** *Positiva CDTIV 74* [1]	30	2

[1] Jeremy Healy & Amos

Tori AMOS

US, female vocalist / instrumentalist – piano (Singles: 66 weeks, Albums: 53 weeks)

		pos	wks
23 Nov 91	**SILENT ALL THESE YEARS** *East West YZ 618*	51	3
1 Feb 92	**CHINA** *East West YZ 7531*	51	2
21 Mar 92	**WINTER** *East West A 7504*	25	4
20 Jun 92	**CRUCIFY** *East West A 7479*	15	6
22 Aug 92	**SILENT ALL THESE YEARS (re-issue)** *East West A 7433*	26	4
22 Jan 94 ●	**CORNFLAKE GIRL** *East West A 7281CD*	4	6
19 Mar 94 ●	**PRETTY GOOD YEAR** *East West A 7263CD*	7	4
28 May 94	**PAST THE MISSION** *East West YZ 7257CD*	31	3
15 Oct 94	**GOD** *East West A 7251CD*	44	2
13 Jan 96	**CAUGHT A LITE SNEEZE** *East West A 5524CD1*	20	3
23 Mar 96	**TALULA** *East West A 8512CD1*	22	2
3 Aug 96	**HEY JUPITER / PROFESSIONAL WIDOW** *East West A 5494CD*	20	9
9 Nov 96	**BLUE SKIES** *Perfecto PERF 130CD1* [1]	26	2
11 Jan 97 ★	**PROFESSIONAL WIDOW (IT'S GOT TO BE BIG) (re-mix)** *East West A 5450CD*	1	10
2 May 98	**SPARK** *Atlantic AT 0031CD*	16	3
13 Nov 99	**GLORY OF THE 80'S** *Atlantic AT 0077CD1*	46	1
26 Oct 02	**A SORTA FAIRYTALE** *Epic 6730432*	41	2
18 Jan 92	**LITTLE EARTHQUAKES** *East West 7567823582*	14	23
12 Feb 94 ★	**UNDER THE PINK** *East West 7567825672* ■	1	13
3 Feb 96 ●	**BOYS FOR PELE** *East West 7567828622*	2	6
16 May 98 ●	**FROM THE CHOIRGIRL HOTEL** *Atlantic 7567830952*	6	5
2 Oct 99	**TO VENUS AND BACK** *Atlantic 7567832422*	22	2
29 Sep 01	**STRANGE LITTLE GIRLS** *Atlantic 7567834862*	16	2
9 Nov 02	**SCARLET'S WALK** *Epic 5087829*	26	1
29 Nov 03	**TALES OF A LIBRARIAN** *Atlantic 7567932232*	74	1

[1] BT featuring Tori Amos

AMOURE

UK, male production duo – Rod Edwards and Nick Magnus (Singles: 2 weeks)

		pos	wks
27 May 00	**IS THAT YOUR FINAL ANSWER? (WHO WANTS TO BE A MILLIONAIRE – THE SINGLE)** *Celador MILLION 2*	33	2

AMPS *US, male / female vocal / instrumental group (Singles: 1 week, Albums: 1 week)* pos/wks

21 Oct 95	**TIPP CITY** *4AD BAD 5015CD*	**61**	1
11 Nov 95	**PACER** *4AD CAD 5016CD*	**60**	1

AMY – *See A.D.A.M. featuring AMY*

AN EMOTIONAL FISH *Ireland, male vocal / instrumental group (Singles: 5 weeks, Albums: 3 weeks)* pos/wks

23 Jun 90	**CELEBRATE** *East West YZ 489*	**46**	5
25 Aug 90	**AN EMOTIONAL FISH** *East West WX 359*	**40**	3

ANASTACIA *405 Top 500*
Unique, powerhouse vocalist who has sold more than six million albums in Europe but remains little known in her homeland, b. Anastacia Newkirk, 17 Sep 1975, Chicago. Her first two albums went double-platinum in the UK (Singles: 59 weeks, Albums: 107 weeks) pos/wks

30 Sep 00 ●	**I'M OUTTA LOVE** *Epic 6695782*	**6**	17
3 Feb 01	**NOT THAT KIND (re)** *Epic 6707632*	**11**	8
2 Jun 01	**COWBOYS & KISSES** *Epic 6712622*	**28**	5
25 Aug 01	**MADE FOR LOVIN' YOU** *Epic 6717172*	**27**	3
1 Dec 01	**PAID MY DUES** *Epic 6721252*	**14**	9
6 Apr 02	**ONE DAY IN YOUR LIFE** *Epic 6724562*	**11**	9
21 Sep 02	**WHY'D YOU LIE TO ME (re)** *Epic 6731112*	**25**	5
7 Dec 02	**YOU'LL NEVER BE ALONE** *Epic 6733802*	**31**	3
14 Oct 00 ●	**NOT THAT KIND** *Epic 4974122*	**2**	65
8 Dec 01 ●	**FREAK OF NATURE** *Epic 5047572*	**4**	42

Andrea ANATOLA – *See SODA CLUB*

AND WHY NOT? *UK, male vocal / instrumental group (Singles: 18 weeks, Albums: 3 weeks)* pos/wks

14 Oct 89	**RESTLESS DAYS (SHE CRIES OUT LOUD)** *Island IS 426*	**38**	7
13 Jan 90	**THE FACE** *Island IS 444*	**13**	8
21 Apr 90	**SOMETHING YOU GOT** *Island IS 452*	**39**	3
10 Mar 90	**MOVE YOUR SKIN** *Island ILPS 9935*	**24**	3

... AND YOU WILL KNOW US BY THE TRAIL OF DEAD *US, male vocal / instrumental group (Singles: 2 weeks, Albums: 1 week)* pos/wks

11 Nov 00	**MISTAKES AND REGRETS** *Domino RUG 114CD*	**69**	1
11 May 02	**ANOTHER MORNING STONER** *Interscope / Polydor 4977162*	**54**	1
16 Mar 02	**SOURCE TAGS AND CODES** *Interscope 4932492*	**73**	1

Angry ANDERSON *Australia, male vocalist (Singles: 13 weeks)* pos/wks

19 Nov 88 ●	**SUDDENLY** *Food For Thought YUM 113*	**3**	13

Carl ANDERSON *US, male vocalist (Singles: 4 weeks)* pos/wks

8 Jun 85	**BUTTERCUP** *Streetwave KHAN 45*	**49**	4

Carleen ANDERSON
US, female vocalist (Singles: 17 weeks, Albums: 7 weeks) pos/wks

12 Feb 94	**NERVOUS BREAKDOWN** *Circa YRCDG 112*	**27**	4
28 May 94	**MAMA SAID** *Circa YRCD 114*	**26**	4
13 Aug 94	**TRUE SPIRIT** *Circa YRCD 118*	**24**	3
14 Jan 95	**LET IT LAST** *Circa YRCD 119*	**16**	3
7 Feb 98	**MAYBE I'M AMAZED** *Circa YRCD 128*	**24**	2
25 Apr 98	**WOMAN IN ME** *Circa YRCD 129*	**74**	1
13 Nov 93	**DUSKY SAPPHO (EP)** *Circa YRCDG 108*	**38**	1
18 Jun 94	**TRUE SPIRIT** *Circa CIRCDX 30*	**12**	4
2 May 98	**BLESSED BURDEN** *Circa CIRCD 35*	**51**	2

See also BRAND NEW HEAVIES; Paul WELLER

Gillian ANDERSON – *See HAL featuring Gillian ANDERSON*

Ian ANDERSON
UK, male vocalist / instrumentalist – flute (Albums: 1 week) pos/wks

26 Nov 83	**WALK INTO LIGHT** *Chrysalis CDL 1443*	**78**	1

See also JETHRO TULL

John ANDERSON BIG BAND *UK, big band (Singles: 5 weeks)* pos/wks

21 Dec 85	**GLENN MILLER MEDLEY (re)** *Modern GLEN 1*	**61**	5

Glenn Miller Medley comprises the following tracks: In the Mood / American Patrol / Little Brown Jug / Pennsylvania 65000

Jon ANDERSON *UK, male vocalist (Albums: 19 weeks)* pos/wks

24 Jul 76 ●	**OLIAS OF SUNHILLOW** *Atlantic K 50261*	**8**	10
15 Nov 80	**SONG OF SEVEN** *Atlantic K 50756*	**38**	3
5 Jun 82	**ANIMATION** *Polydor POLD 5044*	**43**	6

See also YES; JON and VANGELIS; ANDERSON BRUFORD WAKEMAN HOWE

Laurie ANDERSON
US, female vocalist / multi-instrumentalist (Singles: 6 weeks, Albums: 8 weeks) pos/wks

17 Oct 81 ●	**O SUPERMAN** *Warner Bros. K 17870*	**2**	6
1 May 82	**BIG SCIENCE** *Warner Bros. K 57002*	**29**	6
10 Mar 84	**MISTER HEARTBREAK** *Warner Bros. 9250771*	**93**	2

LC ANDERSON vs PSYCHO RADIO
UK, male vocalist and Italy, male production duo (Singles: 2 weeks) pos/wks

26 Jul 03	**RIGHT STUFF** *Faith & Hope FHCD 039*	**45**	2

Leroy ANDERSON and his POP CONCERT ORCHESTRA
US, orchestra, leader d. 18 May 1975 (Singles: 4 weeks) pos/wks

28 Jun 57	**FORGOTTEN DREAMS (2re)** *Brunswick 05485*	**24**	4

Lynn ANDERSON
US, female vocalist (Singles: 20 weeks, Albums: 1 week) pos/wks

20 Feb 71 ●	**ROSE GARDEN** *CBS 5360*	**3**	20
17 Apr 71	**ROSE GARDEN** *CBS 64333*	**45**	1

Moira ANDERSON
UK, female vocalist (Singles: 2 weeks, Albums: 6 weeks) pos/wks

27 Dec 69	**THE HOLY CITY** *Decca F 12989*	**43**	2
20 Jun 70	**THESE ARE MY SONGS** *Decca SKL 5016*	**50**	1
5 Dec 81	**GOLDEN MEMORIES** *Warwick WW 5107* [1]	**46**	5

[1] Harry Secombe and Moira Anderson

Sunshine ANDERSON
US, female vocalist (Singles: 8 weeks, Albums: 6 weeks) pos/wks

2 Jun 01 ●	**HEARD IT ALL BEFORE** *Atlantic AT 0100CD*	**9**	7
22 Sep 01	**LUNCH OR DINNER** *Atlantic AT 0109CD*	**57**	1
26 May 01	**YOUR WOMAN** *Atlantic 7567930112*	**39**	6

ANDERSON BRUFORD WAKEMAN HOWE
UK, male vocal / instrumental group (Singles: 2 weeks, Albums: 6 weeks) pos/wks

24 Jun 89	**BROTHER OF MINE** *Arista 112379*	**63**	2
8 Jul 89	**ANDERSON BRUFORD WAKEMAN HOWE** *Arista 209970*	**14**	6

See also YES; Jon ANDERSON; Rick WAKEMAN; Steve HOWE

John ANDERSON ORCHESTRA
Ireland, orchestra (Albums: 5 weeks) pos/wks

25 Nov 95	**PAN PIPES – ROMANCE OF IRELAND** *MCA MCD 60004*	**56**	5

Peter ANDRE
UK, male vocalist (Singles: 83 weeks, Albums: 27 weeks) pos/wks

10 Jun 95	**TURN IT UP** *Mushroom D 1000*	**64**	1
16 Sep 95	**MYSTERIOUS GIRL** *Mushroom D 11921*	**53**	2
16 Mar 96	**ONLY ONE (re)** *Mushroom D 1307*	**16**	4
1 Jun 96 ●	**MYSTERIOUS GIRL (re-issue)** *Mushroom D 2000* [1]	**2**	18
14 Sep 96 ★	**FLAVA** *Mushroom D 2003* ■	**1**	9
7 Dec 96 ★	**I FEEL YOU (2re)** *Mushroom D 1521* ■	**1**	11
8 Mar 97 ●	**NATURAL (2re)** *Mushroom DX 1577*	**6**	11
9 Aug 97 ●	**ALL ABOUT US (re)** *Mushroom MUSH 5CD*	**3**	9

8 Nov 97 ● **LONELY (re)** *Mushroom MUSH 16CD* 6 9
24 Jan 98 **ALL NIGHT ALL RIGHT** *Mushroom MUSH 21CD* [2] 16 4
25 Jul 98 ● **KISS THE GIRL** *Mushroom MUSH 34CDSX* 9 5
12 Oct 96 ★ **NATURAL** *Mushroom D 2005* ■ 1 23
29 Nov 97 **TIME** *Mushroom MUSH 18CD* 28 4

[1] Peter Andre featuring Bubbler Ranx [2] Peter Andre featuring Warren G

Chris ANDREWS
UK, male vocalist (Singles: 36 weeks) pos/wks

7 Oct 65 ● **YESTERDAY MAN** *Decca F 12236* 3 15
2 Dec 65 **TO WHOM IT CONCERNS** *Decca F 22285* 13 10
14 Apr 66 **SOMETHING ON MY MIND (re)** *Decca F 22365* 41 3
2 Jun 66 **WHAT'CHA GONNA DO NOW?** *Decca F 22404* 40 4
25 Aug 66 **STOP THAT GIRL** *Decca F 22472* 36 4

Eamonn ANDREWS
Ireland, male vocalist, d. 5 Nov 1987 (Singles: 3 weeks) pos/wks

20 Jan 56 **THE SHIFTING WHISPERING SANDS (PARTS 1 & 2)** *Parlophone R 4106* 18 3

Hit is credited: 'with Ron Goodwin and his Orchestra and Chorus'

Julie ANDREWS
UK, female vocalist (Albums: 5 weeks) pos/wks

16 Jul 83 **LOVE ME TENDER** *Peach River JULIE 1* 63 5

Michael ANDREWS featuring Gary JULES
US, male producer and male vocalist (Singles: 1 week) pos/wks

27 Dec 03 ★ **MAD WORLD** *Adventures in Music / Sanctuary SANXD 250* ■ ....1 1+

ANDROIDS
Australia, male vocal / instrumental group (Singles: 5 weeks) pos/wks

17 May 03 **DO IT WITH MADONNA** *Universal MCSTD 40321* 15 5

ANEKA *UK, female vocalist – Mary Sandeman (Singles: 16 weeks)* pos/wks

8 Aug 81 ★ **JAPANESE BOY** *Hansa HANSA 5* 1 12
7 Nov 81 **LITTLE LADY** *Hansa HANSA 8* 50 4

Dave ANGEL
UK, male DJ / producer (Singles: 1 week) pos/wks

2 Aug 97 **TOKYO STEALTH FIGHTER** *Fourth & Broadway BRCD 355* 58 1

Simone ANGEL *Holland, female vocalist (Singles: 1 week)* pos/wks

13 Nov 93 **LET THIS FEELING** *A&M 5803652* 60 1

ANGEL CITY featuring Lara McALLEN
UK, male production duo and female vocalist (Singles: 7 weeks) pos/wks

8 Nov 03 **LOVE ME RIGHT (OH SHEILA)** *Data DATA 59CDS* 11 7

ANGELETTES *UK, female vocal group (Singles: 5 weeks)* pos/wks

13 May 72 **DON'T LET HIM TOUCH YOU** *Decca F 13284* 35 5

ANGELHEART *UK, female producer (Singles: 2 weeks)* pos/wks

6 Apr 96 **COME BACK TO ME** *Hi-Life 5776312* [1] 68 1
22 Mar 97 **I'M STILL WAITING** *Hi-Life 5735452* [2] 74 1

[1] Angelheart featuring Rochelle Harris [2] Angelheart featuring Aletia Bourne

ANGELIC *UK, male / female production / vocal duo – Amanda O'Riordan and Darren Tate (Singles: 16 weeks)* pos/wks

17 Jun 00 **IT'S MY TURN** *Serious MCSTD 40235* 11 10
24 Feb 01 **CAN'T KEEP ME SILENT** *Serious SERR 023CD* 12 4
10 Nov 01 **STAY WITH ME** *Serious SERR 35CD* 36 2

See also CITIZEN CANED; Jurgen VRIES

ANGELIC UPSTARTS *UK, male vocal / instrumental group (Singles: 30 weeks, Albums: 20 weeks)* pos/wks

21 Apr 79 **I'M AN UPSTART** *Warner Bros. K 17354* 31 8
11 Aug 79 **TEENAGE WARNING** *Warner Bros. K 17426* 29 6
3 Nov 79 **NEVER 'AD NOTHIN'** *Warner Bros. K 17476* 52 4
9 Feb 80 **OUT OF CONTROL** *Warner Bros. K 17558* 58 3
22 Mar 80 **WE GOTTA GET OUT OF THIS PLACE** *Warner Bros. K 17576* ..65 2
2 Aug 80 **LAST NIGHT ANOTHER SOLDIER** *Zonophone Z 7* 51 4
7 Feb 81 **KIDS ON THE STREET** *Zonophone Z 16* 57 3
18 Aug 79 **TEENAGE WARNING** *Warner Bros. K 50634* 29 7
12 Apr 80 **WE'VE GOTTA GET OUT OF THIS PLACE** *Warner Bros. K 56806* 54 3
7 Jun 81 **2000000 VOICES** *Zonophone ZONO 104* 32 3
26 Sep 81 **ANGELIC UPSTARTS** *Zonophone ZEM 102* 27 7

ANGELLE *UK, female vocalist (Singles: 1 week)* pos/wks

17 Aug 02 **JOY AND PAIN** *Innovation CDINNOV 1* 43 1

Bobby ANGELO and the TUXEDOS
UK, male vocal / instrumental group (Singles: 6 weeks) pos/wks

10 Aug 61 **BABY SITTIN'** *HMV POP 892* 30 6

ANGELS *US, female vocal group (Singles: 1 week)* pos/wks

3 Oct 63 **MY BOYFRIEND'S BACK** *Mercury AMT 1211* ▲ 50 1

ANGELS OF LIGHT – *See PSYCHIC TV*

ANGELS REVERSE
Germany, male production duo (Singles: 1 week) pos/wks

31 Aug 02 **DON'T CARE** *Inferno CDFERN 46* 71 1

ANGELWITCH
UK, male vocal / instrumental group (Singles: 1 week) pos/wks

7 Jun 80 **SWEET DANGER** *EMI 5064* 75 1

ANIMAL *US, male puppet vocalist / instrumentalist – drums (Singles: 3 weeks)* pos/wks

23 Jul 94 **WIPE OUT** *BMG Kidz 74321219532* 38 3

ANIMAL NIGHTLIFE *UK, male / female vocal / instrumental group (Singles: 22 weeks, Albums: 6 weeks)* pos/wks

13 Aug 83 **NATIVE BOY (UPTOWN)** *Innervision A3584* 60 3
18 Aug 84 **MR SOLITAIRE** *Island IS 193* 25 12
6 Jul 85 **LOVE IS JUST THE GREAT PRETENDER** *Island IS 200* 28 6
5 Oct 85 **PREACHER, PREACHER** *Island IS 245* 67 1
24 Aug 85 **SHANGRI-LA** *Island ILPS 9830* 36 6

ANIMALHOUSE
UK, male vocal / instrumental group (Singles: 1 week) pos/wks

15 Jul 00 **READY TO RECEIVE** *Boilerhouse / Arista 74321771072* 61 1

ANIMALS 269 Top 500
Ground-breaking Newcastle band: Eric Burdon (v), Alan Price (k), Brian 'Chas' Chandler (b) (d. 1996), Hilton Valentine (g), John Steel (d). They were the first hit act produced by Mickie Most who reportedly helped them to record 'The House of the Rising Sun' in 15 minutes at a cost of £1 10 shillings. After The Tornados and The Beatles, they were the third UK group to top the US singles chart (Singles: 147 weeks, Albums: 86 weeks) pos/wks

16 Apr 64 **BABY LET ME TAKE YOU HOME** *Columbia DB 7247* 21 8
25 Jun 64 ★ **THE HOUSE OF THE RISING SUN** *Columbia DB 7301* ▲ 1 12
17 Sep 64 ● **I'M CRYING** *Columbia DB 7354* 8 10
4 Feb 65 ● **DON'T LET ME BE MISUNDERSTOOD** *Columbia DB 7445* 3 9
8 Apr 65 ● **BRING IT ON HOME TO ME** *Columbia DB 7539* 7 11
15 Jul 65 ● **WE'VE GOTTA GET OUT OF THIS PLACE** *Columbia DB 7639* 2 12
28 Oct 65 ● **IT'S MY LIFE** *Columbia DB 7741* 7 11
17 Feb 66 **INSIDE – LOOKING OUT** *Decca F 12332* 12 8
2 Jun 66 ● **DON'T BRING ME DOWN** *Decca F 12407* 6 8

27 Oct 66 **HELP ME GIRL** *Decca F 12502* [1] 14 10
15 Jun 67 **WHEN I WAS YOUNG** *MGM 1340* [2] 45 3
6 Sep 67 **GOOD TIMES** *MGM 1344* [2] 20 11
18 Oct 67 ● **SAN FRANCISCAN NIGHTS** *MGM 1359* [2] 7 10
14 Feb 68 **SKY PILOT** *MGM 1373* [2] 40 3
15 Jan 69 **RING OF FIRE** *MGM 1461* [2] 35 5
7 Oct 72 **THE HOUSE OF THE RISING SUN (re) (re-issue)** *RAK RR 1* 11 16
14 Nov 64 ● **THE ANIMALS** *Columbia 33SX 1669* 6 20
22 May 65 ● **ANIMAL TRACKS** *Columbia 33SX 1708* 6 26
16 Apr 66 ● **THE MOST OF THE ANIMALS** *Columbia 33SX 6035* 4 20
28 May 66 ● **ANIMALISMS** *Decca LK 4797* 4 17
25 Sep 71 **MOST OF THE ANIMALS (re-issue)** *MFP 5218* 18 3

[1] Eric Burdon and session musicians billed as The Animals [2] Eric Burdon and The Animals

'The House of the Rising Sun' (re-issue) peaked at No.11 as a re-entry in 1982

ANIMOTION *US / UK, male / female vocal / instrumental group (Singles: 12 weeks)* pos/wks

11 May 85 ● **OBSESSION** *Mercury PH 34* 5 12

Paul ANKA *Canada, male vocalist (Singles: 134 weeks)* pos/wks

9 Aug 57 ★ **DIANA** *Columbia DB 3980* ◆ ▲ 1 25
8 Nov 57 ● **I LOVE YOU, BABY** *Columbia DB 4022* 3 15
8 Nov 57 **TELL ME THAT YOU LOVE ME** *Columbia DB 4022* 25 2
31 Jan 58 ● **YOU ARE MY DESTINY** *Columbia DB 4063* 6 13
30 May 58 **CRAZY LOVE** *Columbia DB 4110* 26 1
26 Sep 58 **MIDNIGHT** *Columbia DB 4172* 26 1
30 Jan 59 ● **(ALL OF A SUDDEN) MY HEART SINGS** *Columbia DB 4241* 10 13
10 Jul 59 ● **LONELY BOY** *Columbia DB 4324* ▲ 3 17
30 Oct 59 ● **PUT YOUR HEAD ON MY SHOULDER** *Columbia DB 4355* 7 12
26 Feb 60 **IT'S TIME TO CRY (re)** *Columbia DB 4390* 28 2
31 Mar 60 **PUPPY LOVE (re)** *Columbia DB 4434* 33 7
15 Sep 60 **HELLO YOUNG LOVERS** *Columbia DB 4504* 44 1
15 Mar 62 **LOVE ME WARM AND TENDER** *RCA 1276* 19 11
26 Jul 62 **A STEEL GUITAR AND A GLASS OF WINE** *RCA 1292* 41 4
28 Sep 74 ● **(YOU'RE) HAVING MY BABY** *United Artists UP 35713* [1] ▲ 6 10

[1] Paul Anka featuring Odia Coates

Ana ANN *UK, female vocalist – Ana Petrovic (Singles: 2 weeks)* pos/wks

23 Feb 02 **RIDE** *LL RIDELLR 100* 24 2

ANNIA – *See XTM & DJ CHUCKY presents ANNIA*

ANNIHILATOR *Canada, male vocal / instrumental group (Albums: 1 week)* pos/wks

11 Aug 90 **NEVER NEVERLAND** *Roadrunner RR 93741* 48 1

ANOTHER LEVEL *UK, male vocal group (Singles: 81 weeks, Albums: 40 weeks)* pos/wks

28 Feb 98 ● **BE ALONE NO MORE** *Northwestside 74321551982* 6 9
18 Jul 98 ★ **FREAK ME** *Northwestside 74321582362* ■ 1 12
7 Nov 98 ● **GUESS I WAS A FOOL** *Northwestside 74321621202* 5 13
23 Jan 99 ● **I WANT YOU FOR MYSELF** *Northwestside 7432164632* [1] 2 8
10 Apr 99 **BE ALONE NO MORE** *Northwestside 74321658472* [2] 11 9
12 Jun 99 ● **FROM THE HEART (re)** *Northwestside 74321673012* 6 11
4 Sep 99 ● **SUMMERTIME** *Northwestside 74321694672* [3] 7 7
13 Nov 99 ● **BOMB DIGGY** *Northwestside 74321712212* 6 12
21 Nov 98 **ANOTHER LEVEL** *Northwestside 74321582412* 13 25
25 Sep 99 ● **NEXUS ...** *Northwestside 74321694572* 7 15

[1] Another Level / Ghostface Killah [2] Another Level featuring Jay-Z [3] Another Level featuring TQ

ANOTHERSIDE *UK, female duo – Alani Gibbon and Celena Cherry (Singles: 1 week)* pos/wks

5 Jul 03 **THIS IS YOUR NIGHT** *V2 / J-Did JAD 5023293* 41 1

See also HONEYZ

ANOUCHKA – *See Terry HALL*

Adam ANT *UK, male vocalist - Stuart Goddard (Singles: 69 weeks, Albums: 39 weeks)* pos/wks

22 May 82 ★ **GOODY TWO SHOES** *CBS A 2367* 1 11
18 Sep 82 ● **FRIEND OR FOE** *CBS A 2736* 9 8
27 Nov 82 **DESPERATE BUT NOT SERIOUS** *CBS A 2892* 33 7
29 Oct 83 ● **PUSS 'N BOOTS** *CBS A 3614* 5 11
10 Dec 83 **STRIP** *CBS A 3589* 41 6
22 Sep 84 **APOLLO 9** *CBS A 4719* 13 8
13 Jul 85 **VIVE LE ROCK** *CBS A 6367* 50 4
17 Feb 90 **ROOM AT THE TOP** *MCA MCA 1387* 13 7
28 Apr 90 **CANT SET RULES ABOUT LOVE** *MCA MCA 1404* 47 2
11 Feb 95 **WONDERFUL** *EMI CDEMS 366* 32 3
3 Jun 95 **GOTTA BE A SIN** *EMI CDEMS 379* 48 2
23 Oct 82 ● **FRIEND OR FOE** *CBS 25040* 5 12
19 Nov 83 **STRIP** *CBS 25705* 20 8
14 Sep 85 **VIVE LE ROCK** *CBS 26583* 42 3
24 Mar 90 **MANNERS AND PHYSIQUE** *MCA MCG 6068* 19 3
28 Aug 93 ● **ANTMUSIC – THE VERY BEST OF ADAM ANT** *Arcade ARC 3100052* 6 11
15 Apr 95 **WONDERFUL** *EMI CDEMC 3687* 24 2

See also ADAM and the ANTS

ANT & DEC *UK, male vocal duo – Anthony McPartlin and Declan Donnelly (aka PJ & Duncan) (Singles: 92 weeks, Albums: 31 weeks)* pos/wks

18 Dec 93 **TONIGHT I'M FREE** *Telstar CDSTAS 2706* 62 3
23 Apr 94 **WHY ME** *Telstar CDSTAS 2719* 27 4
23 Jul 94 ● **LET'S GET READY TO RHUMBLE** *XSrhythm CDANT 1* 9 11
8 Oct 94 **IF I GIVE YOU MY NUMBER** *XSrhythm CDANT 2* 15 7
3 Dec 94 **ETERNAL LOVE** *XSrhythm CDANT 3* 12 9
25 Feb 95 **OUR RADIO ROCKS** *XSrhythm CDANT 4* 15 5
29 Jul 95 **STUCK ON U** *XSrhythm CDANT 5* 12 5
14 Oct 95 **U KRAZY KATZ** *XSrhythm CDANT 6* 15 4
2 Dec 95 **PERFECT** *Telstar CDANT 7* 16 7
20 Mar 96 **STEPPING STONE** *Telstar CDANT 8* 11 5
24 Aug 96 ● **BETTER WATCH OUT** *Telstar CDANT 9* 10 4
23 Nov 96 **WHEN I FALL IN LOVE** *Telstar CDANT 10* 12 8
15 Mar 97 ● **SHOUT** *Telstar CDDEC 11* 10 5
10 May 97 **FALLING** *Telstar CDDEC 12* 14 4
8 Jun 02 ● **WE'RE ON THE BALL** *Columbia 6727312* 3 11
19Nov 94 ● **PSYCHE - THE ALBUM** *Xsrhythm TCD 2746* 5 20
18 Nov 95 **TOP KATZ - THE ALBUM** *Xsrhythm TCD 2793* 46 8
24 May 97 **THE CULT OF ANT & DEC** *Telstar TCD 2887* 15 3

All hit singles and albums up to and including 20 Mar 96 credited to PJ & Duncan

ANTARCTICA *Australia, male producer – Steve Gibbs (Singles: 2 weeks)* pos/wks

29 Jan 00 **RETURN TO REALITY** *React CDREACT 173* 53 1
8 Jul 00 **ADRIFT (CAST YOUR MIND)** *React CDREACT 172* 72 1

Mark ANTHONI – *See FIRE ISLAND*

Billie ANTHONY *UK, female vocalist – Philomena Brown d. 1991 (Singles: 16 weeks)* pos/wks

15 Oct 54 ● **THIS OLE HOUSE** *Columbia DB 3519* 4 16

This release was 'With Eric Jupp and his Orchestra'

Marc ANTHONY *US, male vocalist – Marco Antonio Muniz (Singles: 3 weeks)* pos/wks

13 Nov 99 **I NEED TO KNOW** *Columbia 6683612* 28 3

See also Louie VEGA

Miki ANTHONY *UK, male vocalist (Singles: 7 weeks)* pos/wks

3 Feb 73 **IF IT WASN'T FOR THE REASON THAT I LOVE YOU** *Bell 1275* 27 7

Ray ANTHONY & His ORCHESTRA *US, orchestra (Singles: 2 weeks)* pos/wks

4 Dec 53 ● **DRAGNET (re)** *Capitol CL 13983* 7 2

Richard ANTHONY

France, male vocalist – Richard Anthony Btesh (Singles: 15 weeks) pos/wks

		pos	wks
12 Dec 63	**WALKING ALONE** *Columbia DB 7133*	37	5
2 Apr 64	**IF I LOVED YOU (re)** *Columbia DB 7235*	18	10

ANTHRAX *US, male vocal / instrumental group (Singles: 37 weeks, Albums: 23 weeks)*

pos/wks

		pos	wks
28 Feb 87	**I AM THE LAW** *Island IS LAW 1*	32	5
27 Jun 87	**INDIANS** *Island IS 325*	44	4
5 Dec 87	**I'M THE MAN** *Island IS 338*	20	6
10 Sep 88	**MAKE ME LAUGH** *Island IS 379*	26	3
18 Mar 89	**ANTI-SOCIAL** *Island IS 409*	44	3
1 Sep 90	**IN MY WORLD** *Island IS 470*	29	2
5 Jan 91	**GOT THE TIME** *Island IS 476*	16	4
6 Jul 91	**BRING THE NOISE** *Island IS 490* [1]	14	5
8 May 93	**ONLY** *Elektra EKR 166CD*	36	3
11 Sep 93	**BLACK LODGE** *Elektra EKR 171CD*	53	2
18 Apr 87	AMONG THE LIVING *Island ILPS 9865*	18	5
24 Sep 88	STATE OF EUPHORIA *Island ILPS 9916*	12	4
8 Sep 90	PERSISTENCE OF TIME *Island ILPS 9967*	13	5
20 Jul 91	ATTACK OF THE KILLER B'S *Island ILPS 9980*	13	5
29 May 93	SOUND OF WHITE NOISE *Elektra 7559614302*	14	3
1 Aug 98	VOLUME 8 – THE THREAT IS REAL! *Ignition IGN 740343*	73	1

[1] Anthrax featuring Chuck D

ANTI-NOWHERE LEAGUE *UK, male vocal / instrumental group (Singles: 10 weeks, Albums: 12 weeks)*

pos/wks

		pos	wks
23 Jan 82	**STREETS OF LONDON** *WXYZ ABCD 1*	48	5
20 Mar 82	**I HATE . . . PEOPLE** *WXYZ ABCD 2*	46	3
3 Jul 82	**WOMAN** *WXYZ ABCD 4*	72	2
22 May 82	WE ARE ... THE LEAGUE *WXYZ LMNOP 1*	24	11
5 Nov 83	LIVE IN YUGOSLAVIA *I.D. NOSE 3*	88	1

ANTI-PASTI *UK, male vocal / instrumental group (Albums: 7 weeks)*

pos/wks

		pos	wks
15 Aug 81	THE LAST CALL *Rondelet ABOUT 5*	31	7

See also EXPLOITED

ANTICAPPELLA *Italy / UK, male / female vocal / instrumental group (Singles: 12 weeks)*

pos/wks

		pos	wks
16 Nov 91	**THE SQUARE ROOT OF 231** *PWL Continental PWL 205*	24	4
18 Apr 92	**EVERY DAY** *PWL Continental PWL 220*	45	2
25 Jun 94	**MOVE YOUR BODY** *Media MCSTD 1980* [1]	21	3
1 Apr 95	**EXPRESS YOUR FREEDOM** *Media MCSTD 2048*	31	2
25 May 96	**THE SQUARE ROOT OF 231 / MOVE YOUR BODY (re-mix)** *Media MCSTD 40037*	54	1

[1] Anticappella featuring MC Fixx It

ANTONIA – *See BOMB THE BASS*

ANTS – *See ADAM and the ANTS*

ANUNA – *See Bill WHELAN*

APACHE INDIAN *UK, male vocalist – Steven Kapur (Singles: 33 weeks, Albums: 2 weeks)*

pos/wks

		pos	wks
28 Nov 92	**FE' REAL** *Ten TEN 416* [1]	33	3
2 Jan 93	**ARRANGED MARRIAGE** *Island CID 544*	16	6
27 Mar 93	**CHOK THERE** *Island CID 555*	30	4
14 Aug 93 ●	**NUFF VIBES (EP)** *Island CID 560*	5	10
22 Oct 93	**MOVIN' ON** *Island CID 580*	48	2
7 May 94	**WRECKX SHOP** *MCA MCSTD 1969* [2]	26	2
11 Feb 95	**MAKE WAY FOR THE INDIAN** *Island CID 586* [3]	29	2
22 Apr 95	**RAGGAMUFFIN GIRL** *Island CID 606* [4]	31	2
29 Mar 97	**LOVIN' (LET ME LOVE YOU)** *Coalition COLA 002CD*	53	1
18 Oct 97	**REAL PEOPLE** *Coalition COLA 019CD*	66	1
6 Feb 93	NO RESERVATIONS *Island CID 8001*	36	2

[1] Maxi Priest featuring Apache Indian [2] Wreckx-N-Effect featuring Apache Indian [3] Apache Indian and Tim Dog [4] Apache Indian with Frankie Paul

The listed flip side of 'Fe' Real' was 'Just Wanna Know' by Maxi Priest. Tracks on Nuff Vibes (EP): Boom Shack a Lak / Fun / Caste System / Warning

APHEX TWIN *UK, male instrumentalist / producer – Richard James (Singles: 12 weeks, Albums: 11 weeks)*

pos/wks

		pos	wks
9 May 92	**DIGERIDOO** *R&S RSUK 12*	55	2
27 Nov 93	**ON** *Warp WAP 39CD*	32	3
8 Apr 95	**VENTOLIN** *Warp WAP 60CD*	49	1
26 Oct 96	**GIRL / BOY (EP)** *Warp WAP 78CD*	64	1
18 Oct 97	**COME TO DADDY** *Warp WAP 94CD*	36	2
3 Apr 99	**WINDOWLICKER** *Warp WAP 105CD*	16	3
19 Mar 94	SELECTED AMBIENT WORKS VOLUME II *Warp WARPCD 21*	11	3
11 Feb 95	CLASSICS *R & S RS 94035CD*	24	2
6 May 95	... I CARE BECAUSE YOU DO *Warp WARPCD 30*	24	2
16 Nov 96	RICHARD D JAMES ALBUM *Warp WARPCD43*	62	1
3 Nov 01	DRUKQS *Warp WARPCD2*	22	2
5 Apr 03	26 MIXES FOR CASH *Warp WARPCD102*	63	1

Tracks on Girl / Boy (EP): Girl / Boy Song / Milkman / Inkey $ / Beatles Under My Carpet. The EP was incorrectly listed in the chart and, because of its length, should have been considered an album

See also POLYGON WINDOW; AFX

APHRODITE featuring WILDFLOWER

UK, male producer and female rapper / vocalist (Singles: 1 week) pos/wks

		pos	wks
16 Nov 02	**SEE THRU IT** *V2 VVR 5020983*	68	1

APHRODITE'S CHILD *Greece, male vocal / instrumental group – includes Demis Roussos and Vangelis (Singles: 7 weeks)*

pos/wks

		pos	wks
6 Nov 68	**RAIN AND TEARS** *Mercury MF 1039*	29	7

APOLLO presents HOUSE OF VIRGINISM *Sweden, male instrumentalist and vocal / instrumental group (Singles: 1 week)*

pos/wks

		pos	wks
17 Feb 96	**EXCLUSIVE** *Logic 74321324102*	67	1

APOLLO FOUR FORTY *UK, male instrumental / production group (Singles: 53 weeks, Albums: 4 weeks)*

pos/wks

		pos	wks
22 Jan 94	**ASTRAL AMERICA** *Stealth Sonic SSXCD 2* [1]	36	2
5 Nov 94	**LIQUID COOL** *Stealth Sonic SSXCD 3* [1]	35	2
25 Mar 95	**(DON'T FEAR) THE REAPER** *Stealth Sonic SSXCD 4* [1]	35	2
27 Jul 96	**KRUPA (re)** *Stealth Sonic SSXCD 5*	23	8
15 Feb 97 ●	**AIN'T TALKIN' 'BOUT DUB** *Stealth Sonic SSXCDX 6*	7	7
5 Jul 97	**RAW POWER** *Stealth Sonic SSXCD 7*	32	3
11 Jul 98	**RENDEZ-VOUS '98** *Epic 6661102* [2]	12	6
8 Aug 98 ●	**LOST IN SPACE** *Stealth Sonic SSX 9CD*	4	9
28 Aug 99 ●	**STOP THE ROCK** *Epic SSX 10CD*	10	6
27 Nov 99	**HEART GO BOOM** *Epic SSX 11CD*	57	1
9 Dec 00	**CHARLIE'S ANGELS 2000** *Epic SSX 13CD*	29	6
21 Jun 03	**DUDE DESCENDING A STAIRCASE** *Stealth/SONY SSX 14CD* [3]	58	1
15 Mar 97	ELECTRO GLIDE IN BLUE *Stealth Sonic SSX 2440CD*	62	1
18 Sep 99	GETTIN' HIGH ON YOUR OWN SUPPLY *Epic SSX 3440CD*	20	3

[1] Apollo 440 [2] Jean-Michel Jarre and Apollo 440
[3] Apollo Four Forty featuring The Beatnuts

APOLLO 2000

UK, male instrumentalist / producer (Albums: 3 weeks) pos/wks

		pos	wks
27 Apr 96	OUT OF THIS WORLD *Telstar TCD 2816*	43	3

Carmine APPICE – *See Jeff BECK and Tim BOGERT*

Fiona APPLE *US, female vocalist – Fiona Apple Maggart (Singles: 2 weeks, Albums: 1 week)*

pos/wks

		pos	wks
26 Feb 00	**FAST AS YOU CAN** *Columbia 6689962*	33	2
11 Mar 00	WHEN THE PAWN HITS THE CONFLICTS HE THINKSLIKE A KING WHAT HE KNOWS THROWS THE BLOWS WHEN HE GOES TO THE FIGHT AND HE'LL WIN THE WHOLE THING 'FORE HE ENTERS THE RING THERE'S NOBODY TO BATTER WHEN YOUR MIND IS YOUR MIGHT SO WHEN YOU GO SOLO, YOU HOLD YOUR OWN HAND AND REMEMBER THAT DEPTH IS THE GREATEST OF HEIGHTS AND IF YOU KNOW WHERE YOU STAND, THEN YOU KNOW WHERE TO		

			pos	wks
		LAND AND IF YOU FALL IT WON'T MATTER, CUZ YOU'LL KNOW THAT YOU'RE RIGHT *Columbia 4964282*	**46**	1

Kim APPLEBY

UK, female vocalist (Singles: 31 weeks, Albums: 13 weeks)

			pos	wks
3 Nov 90	●	**DON'T WORRY** *Parlophone R 6272*	**2**	10
9 Feb 91	●	**G.L.A.D.** *Parlophone R 6281*	**10**	6
29 Jun 91		**MAMA** *Parlophone R 6291*	**19**	8
19 Oct 91		**IF YOU CARED** *Parlophone R 6297*	**44**	3
31 Jul 93		**LIGHT OF THE WORLD** *Parlophone CDR 6352*	**41**	2
13 Nov 93		**BREAKAWAY** *Parlophone CDR 6362*	**56**	1
12 Nov 94		**FREE SPIRIT** *Parlophone CDR 6397*	**51**	1
8 Dec 90		**KIM APPLEBY** *Parlophone PCS 7348*	**23**	13

See also MEL and KIM

APPLEJACKS

UK, male / female vocal / instrumental group (Singles: 29 weeks)

			pos	wks
5 Mar 64	●	**TELL ME WHEN** *Decca F 11833*	**7**	13
11 Jun 64		**LIKE DREAMERS DO** *Decca F 11916*	**20**	11
15 Oct 64		**THREE LITTLE WORDS (I LOVE YOU)** *Decca F 11981*	**23**	5

APPLES *UK, male vocal / instrumental group (Singles: 1 week)*

			pos	wks
23 Mar 91		**EYE WONDER** *Epic 6566717*	**75**	1

APPLETON

Canada, female vocal duo (Singles: 22 weeks, Albums: 6 weeks)

			pos	wks
14 Sep 02	●	**FANTASY** *Polydor 5709842*	**2**	10
22 Feb 03	●	**DON'T WORRY** *Polydor 0658182*	**5**	10
26 Jul 03		**EVERYTHING EVENTUALLY** *Polydor 9808278*	**38**	2
8 Mar 03	●	**EVERYTHING'S EVENTUAL** *Polydor 0651992*	**9**	6

See also ALL SAINTS

Charlie APPLEWHITE with Victor YOUNG and CHORUS

US, male vocalist, d. 27 Apr 2001 (Singles: 1 week)

			pos	wks
23 Sep 55		**BLUE STAR** *Brunswick 05416*	**20**	1

Helen APRIL – *See John DUMMER and Helen APRIL*

APRIL WINE *Canada, male vocal / instrumental group (Singles: 9 weeks, Albums: 8 weeks)*

			pos	wks
15 Mar 80		**I LIKE TO ROCK** *Capitol CL 16121*	**41**	5
11 Apr 81		**JUST BETWEEN YOU AND ME** *Capitol CL 16184*	**52**	4
15 Mar 80		**HARDER ... FASTER** *Capitol EST 12013*	**34**	5
24 Jan 81		**THE NATURE OF THE BEAST** *Capitol EST 12125*	**48**	3

AQUA *Denmark / Norway, male / female vocal / production quartet – Claus Noreen, Soren Rasted, Lene Nystrom, Rene Dif (Singles: 85 weeks, Albums: 49 weeks)*

			pos	wks
25 Oct 97	★	**BARBIE GIRL (re)** *Universal UMD 80413* ◆	**1**	26
7 Feb 98	★	**DOCTOR JONES** *Universal UMD 80457* ■	**1**	14
16 May 98	★	**TURN BACK TIME** *Universal UMD 80490* ■	**1**	10
1 Aug 98	●	**MY OH MY (re)** *Universal UMD 85058*	**6**	11
26 Dec 98		**GOOD MORNING SUNSHINE** *Universal UMD 85086*	**18**	7
26 Feb 00	●	**CARTOON HEROES (re)** *Universal MCSTD 40226*	**7**	11
10 Jun 00		**AROUND THE WORLD** *Universal MCSTD 40234*	**26**	6
15 Nov 97	●	**AQUARIUM** *Universal UMD 85020*	**6**	47
11 Mar 00		**AQUARIUS** *Universal 1538102*	**24**	2

AQUA MARINA – *See FAB*

AQUAGEN *Germany, male production duo – Olaf Dieckman and Gino Montesano (Singles: 11 weeks)*

			pos	wks
9 Dec 00	●	**PHATT BASS** *Nulife / Arista 74321817102* [1]	**9**	8
1 Mar 03		**HARD TO SAY I'M SORRY** *All Around the World CDGLOBE 265*	**33**	3

[1] Warp Brothers vs Aquagen

AQUALUNG *UK, male vocalist / instrumentalist / producer – Matt Hales (Singles: 9 weeks, Albums: 6 weeks)*

			pos	wks
28 Sep 02	●	**STRANGE AND BEAUTIFUL (I'LL PUT A SPELL ON YOU)** *B Unique BUN 032CDS*	**7**	6
14 Dec 02		**GOOD TIMES GONNA COME** *B Unique BUN 043CDS*	**71**	1
25 Oct 03		**BRIGHTER THAN SUNSHINE** *B Unique BUN 072CDS*	**37**	2
12 Oct 02		**AQUALUNG** *B Unique 5046606982*	**15**	6

AQUANUTS

US / Argentina, male production / instrumental duo (Singles: 1 week)

			pos	wks
4 May 02		**DEEP SEA** *Data DATA 34T*	**74**	1

AQUARIAN DREAM

US, male / female vocal / instrumental group (Singles: 1 week)

			pos	wks
24 Feb 79		**YOU'RE A STAR** *Elektra LV 7*	**67**	1

ARAB STRAP *UK, male vocal / instrumental duo – Aiden Moffat and Malcolm Middleton (Singles: 4 weeks, Albums: 2 weeks)*

			pos	wks
13 Sep 97		**THE GIRLS OF SUMMER (EP)** *Chemikal Underground CHEM 017CD*	**74**	1
4 Apr 98		**HERE WE GO / TRIPPY** *Chemikal Underground CHEM 20CD*	**48**	1
10 Oct 98		**(AFTERNOON) SOAPS** *Chemikal Underground CHEM 27CD*	**74**	1
10 Feb 01		**LOVE DETECTIVE** *Chemikal Underground CHEM 049CD*	**66**	1
2 May 98		**PHILOPHOBIA** *Chemikal Underground CHEM 21CD*	**37**	2

Tracks on The Girls of Summer (EP): Hey! Fever / Girls of Summer / The Beautiful Barmaids of Dundee / One Day After School

ARCADIA *UK, male vocal / instrumental group (Singles: 13 weeks, Albums: 10 weeks)*

			pos	wks
26 Oct 85	●	**ELECTION DAY** *Odeon NSR 1*	**7**	7
25 Jan 86		**THE PROMISE** *Odeon NSR 2*	**37**	4
26 Jul 86		**THE FLAME** *Odeon NSR 3*	**58**	2
7 Dec 85		**SO RED THE ROSE** *Parlophone Odeon PCSD 101*	**30**	10

Arcadia was Duran Duran sideline band featuring Simon Le Bon, Nick Rhodes and Roger Taylor

See also DURAN DURAN

Tasmin ARCHER

UK, female vocalist (Singles: 37 weeks, Albums: 42 weeks)

			pos	wks
12 Sep 92	★	**SLEEPING SATELLITE (re)** *EMI EM 233*	**1**	17
20 Feb 93		**IN YOUR CARE** *EMI CDEMS 260*	**16**	6
29 May 93		**LORDS OF THE NEW CHURCH** *EMI CDEM 266*	**26**	4
21 Aug 93		**ARIENNE** *EMI CDEM 275*	**30**	4
8 Jan 94		**SHIPBUILDING** *EMI CDEM 302*	**40**	4
23 Mar 96		**ONE MORE GOOD NIGHT WITH THE BOYS** *EMI CDEM 401*	**45**	2
31 Oct 92	●	**GREAT EXPECTATIONS** *EMI CDEMC 3624*	**8**	42

ARCHIES *US, male / female cartoon vocal group – lead vocal Ron Dante (Singles: 26 weeks)*

			pos	wks
11 Oct 69	★	**SUGAR, SUGAR** *RCA 1872* ▲	**1**	26

See also CUFFLINKS

ARCHITECHS

UK, male production duo and female vocalist (Singles: 19 weeks)

			pos	wks
7 Oct 00	●	**BODY GROOVE** *Go. Beat / Polydor GOBCD33* [1]	**3**	14
7 Apr 01		**SHOW ME THE MONEY (re)** *Go. Beat GOBCD 38*	**20**	5

[1] Architechs featuring Nana

Jann ARDEN

Canada, female vocalist – Jann Arden Richards (Singles: 2 weeks)

			pos	wks
13 Jul 96		**INSENSITIVE** *A&M 5812652*	**40**	2

Tina ARENA

Australia, female vocalist (Singles: 33 weeks, Albums: 15 weeks)

			pos	wks
15 Apr 95	●	**CHAINS** *Columbia 6611255*	**6**	11
12 Aug 95		**HEAVEN HELP MY HEART** *Columbia 6620975*	**25**	5
2 Dec 95		**SHOW ME HEAVEN** *Columbia 6626975*	**29**	3
3 Aug 96		**SORRENTO MOON (I REMEMBER)** *Columbia 6635435*	**22**	4
27 Jun 98		**WHISTLE DOWN THE WIND** *Really Useful 5672192*	**24**	5
24 Oct 98		**IF I WAS A RIVER** *Columbia 6665605*	**43**	2
13 Mar 99		**BURN** *Columbia 6667442*	**47**	1

Date	Title / Label	Pos	Wks
20 May 00	**LIVE FOR THE ONE I LOVE** *Columbia 6691332*	63	1
12 Apr 03	**NEVER (PAST TENSE)** *Illustrious CDILL 010* [1]	42	1
20 May 95	**DON'T ASK** *Columbia 4778862*	11	15

[1] ROC Project featuring Tina Arena

ARGENT *UK, male vocal / instrumental group (Singles: 27 weeks, Albums: 9 weeks)* pos/wks

Date	Title / Label	Pos	Wks
4 Mar 72 ●	**HOLD YOUR HEAD UP** *Epic EPC 7786*	5	12
10 Jun 72	**TRAGEDY** *Epic EPC 8115*	34	7
24 Mar 73	**GOD GAVE ROCK AND ROLL TO YOU** *Epic EPC 1243*	18	8
29 Apr 72	**ALL TOGETHER NOW** *Epic EPC 64962*	13	8
31 Mar 73	**IN DEEP** *Epic EPC 65475*	49	1

See also SAN JOSE featuring Rodriguez ARGENTINA; SILSOE; ZOMBIES

india.arie *US, female vocalist – India.Arie Simpson (Singles: 6 weeks, Albums: 3 weeks)* pos/wks

Date	Title / Label	Pos	Wks
30 Jun 01	**VIDEO** *Motown TMGCD 1505*	32	3
20 Oct 01	**BROWN SKIN** *Motown TMGCD 1507*	29	2
12 Apr 03	**LITTLE THINGS** *Motown TMGCD 1509*	62	1
7 Jul 01	**ACOUSTIC SOUL** *Motown 137702*	55	3

ARIEL *UK, male production group (Singles: 2 weeks)* pos/wks

Date	Title / Label	Pos	Wks
27 Mar 93	**LET IT SLIDE** *Deconstruction 74321134512*	57	2

ARIEL *Argentina, male DJ producer - Ariel Belloso (Singles: 4 weeks)* pos/wks

Date	Title / Label	Pos	Wks
21 Jun 97	**DEEP (I'M FALLING DEEPER)** *Wonderboy WBOYD 005*	47	1
17 Jun 00	**A9** *Essential Recordings ESCD 15*	28	3

ARIZONA featuring ZEITIA *UK, male production / instrumental duo and female vocalist (Singles: 1 week)* pos/wks

Date	Title / Label	Pos	Wks
12 Mar 94	**I SPECIALIZE IN LOVE** *Union City UCRCD 27*	74	1

Ship's Company and Royal Marine Band of HMS ARK ROYAL *UK, male choir and marine band (Singles: 6 weeks)* pos/wks

Date	Title / Label	Pos	Wks
23 Dec 78	**THE LAST FAREWELL** *BBC RESL 61*	46	6

ARKARNA *UK, male vocal / instrumental / production group (Singles: 3 weeks)* pos/wks

Date	Title / Label	Pos	Wks
25 Jan 97	**HOUSE ON FIRE** *WEA WEA 088CD1*	33	2
2 Aug 97	**SO LITTLE TIME** *WEA WEA 108CD1*	46	1

Joan ARMATRADING (252 Top 500) *Highly acclaimed singer / songwriter / instrumentalist – guitar, b. 9 Dec 1950, St. Kitts, West Indies. Raised in Birmingham, UK, her debut album was issued in 1972. Twice nominated at both Brit and Grammy Awards, and won an Ivor Novello award in 1996 (Singles: 53 weeks, Albums: 193 weeks)* pos/wks

Date	Title / Label	Pos	Wks
16 Oct 76 ●	**LOVE AND AFFECTION** *A&M AMS 7249*	10	9
23 Feb 80	**ROSIE** *A&M AMS 7506*	49	5
14 Jun 80	**ME MYSELF I** *A&M AMS 7527*	21	11
6 Sep 80	**ALL THE WAY FROM AMERICA** *A&M AMS 7552*	54	3
12 Sep 81	**I'M LUCKY** *A&M AMS 8163*	46	5
16 Jan 82	**NO LOVE** *A&M AMS 8179*	50	5
19 Feb 83	**DROP THE PILOT** *A&M AMS 8306*	11	10
16 Mar 85	**TEMPTATION** *A&M AM 238*	65	2
26 May 90	**MORE THAN ONE KIND OF LOVE** *A&M AM 561*	75	1
23 May 92	**WRAPPED AROUND HER** *A&M AM 877*	56	2
4 Sep 76	**JOAN ARMATRADING** *A&M AMLH 64588*	12	27
1 Oct 77 ●	**SHOW SOME EMOTION** *A&M AMLH 68433*	6	11
14 Oct 78	**TO THE LIMIT** *A&M AMLH 64732*	13	10
24 May 80 ●	**ME MYSELF I** *A&M AMLH 64809*	5	23
12 Sep 81 ●	**WALK UNDER LADDERS** *A&M AMLH 64876*	6	29
12 Mar 83 ●	**THE KEY** *A&M AMLX 64912*	10	14
26 Nov 83	**TRACK RECORD** *A&M JA 2001*	18	32
16 Feb 85	**SECRET SECRETS** *A&M AMA 5040*	14	12
24 May 86	**SLEIGHT OF HAND** *A&M AMA 5130*	34	6
16 Jul 88	**THE SHOUTING STAGE** *A&M AMA 5211*	28	10
16 Jun 90	**HEARTS AND FLOWERS** *A&M 3952981*	29	4
16 Mar 91 ●	**THE VERY BEST OF JOAN ARMATRADING** *A&M 3971221*	9	11
20 Jun 92	**SQUARE THE CIRCLE** *A&M 3953882*	34	2
10 Jun 95	**WHAT'S INSIDE** *RCA 74321272692*	48	2

ARMIN *Holland, male DJ / producer – Armin van Buuren (Singles: 4 weeks)* pos/wks

Date	Title / Label	Pos	Wks
14 Feb 98	**BLUE FEAR** *Xtravaganza 0091485 EXT*	45	1
12 Feb 00	**COMMUNICATION** *AM:PM CDAMPM 129*	18	3

ARMOURY SHOW *UK, male vocal / instrumental group (Singles: 6 weeks, Albums: 1 week)* pos/wks

Date	Title / Label	Pos	Wks
25 Aug 84	**CASTLES IN SPAIN** *Parlophone R 6079*	69	2
26 Jan 85	**WE CAN BE BRAVE AGAIN** *Parlophone R 6087*	66	1
17 Jan 87	**LOVE IN ANGER** *Parlophone R 6149*	63	3
21 Sep 85	**WAITING FOR THE FLOODS** *Parlophone ARM 1*	57	1

Craig ARMSTRONG *UK, male musical director (Albums: 1 week)* pos/wks

Date	Title / Label	Pos	Wks
27 Apr 02	**AS IF TO NOTHING** *Melankolic CDSAD 13*	61	1

See also Shola AMA

Louis ARMSTRONG *US, male vocalist / instrumentalist – trumpet, b. 4 Aug 1901, d. Jul 6 1971 (Singles: 93 weeks, Albums: 31 weeks)* pos/wks

Date	Title / Label	Pos	Wks
19 Dec 52 ●	**TAKES TWO TO TANGO** *Brunswick 04995*	6	10
13 Apr 56 ●	**A THEME FROM THE THREEPENNY OPERA (MACK THE KNIFE)** *Philips PB 574* [1]	8	11
15 Jun 56	**TAKE IT SATCH (EP)** *Philips BBE 12035* [1]	29	1
13 Jul 56	**THE FAITHFUL HUSSAR** *Philips PB 604* [1]	27	2
6 Nov 59	**MACK THE KNIFE (A THEME FROM THE THREEPENNY OPERA)** *Philips PB 967* [1]	24	1
4 Jun 64 ●	**HELLO, DOLLY!** *London HLR 9878* [2] ▲	4	14
7 Feb 68 ★	**WHAT A WONDERFUL WORLD / CABARET** *HMV POP 1615* [3]	1	29
26 Jun 68	**THE SUNSHINE OF LOVE** *Stateside SS 2116*	41	7
16 Apr 88	**WHAT A WONDERFUL WORLD (re-issue)** *A&M AM 435* [3]	53	5
19 Nov 94 ●	**WE HAVE ALL THE TIME IN THE WORLD (re)** *EMI CDEM 357*	3	13
28 Jul 56 ●	**AT THE CRESCENDO** *Brunswick LAT 8084*	4	1
22 Oct 60	**SATCHMO PLAYS KING OLIVER** *Audio Fidelity AFLP 1930*	20	1
28 Oct 61	**JAZZ CLASSICS** *Ace of Hearts AH 7*	20	1
27 Jun 64	**HELLO, DOLLY!** *London HAR 8190* ▲	11	6
16 Nov 68	**WHAT A WONDERFUL WORLD** *Stateside SSL 10247*	37	3
20 Feb 82	**THE VERY BEST OF LOUIS ARMSTRONG** *Warwick WW 5112*	30	3
21 May 94	**THE ULTIMATE COLLECTION** *Bluebird 74321197062*	48	3
17 Dec 94 ●	**WE HAVE ALL THE TIME IN THE WORLD – THE VERY BEST OF LOUIS ARMSTRONG** *EMI CDEMTV 89*	10	12
25 Oct 03	**AT HIS VERY BEST** *UCJ 9812425*	75	1

[1] Louis Armstrong and his All-Stars [2] Louis Armstrong and the All Stars [3] Louis Armstrong Orchestra & Chorus

Take It Satch (EP) tracks: Tiger Rag / Mack the Knife / The Faithful Hussar / Back O'Town Blues. 'Mack the Knife' is a re-issue of 'Theme from The Threepenny Opera' under a different title. 'Cabaret' was not listed with 'What a Wonderful World' until 14 Feb 1968

ARMY OF LOVERS *Sweden / France, male / female vocal / group (Singles: 12 weeks)* pos/wks

Date	Title / Label	Pos	Wks
17 Aug 91	**CRUCIFIED** *Ton Son Ton WOK 2007*	47	5
28 Dec 91	**OBSESSION** *Ton Son Ton WOK 2009*	67	1
15 Feb 92	**CRUCIFIED (re-issue)** *Ton Son Ton WOK 2017*	31	5
18 Apr 92	**RIDE THE BULLET** *Ton Son Ton WOK 2018*	67	1

ARNEE and the TERMINATERS *UK, male vocal / instrumental group (Singles: 7 weeks)* pos/wks

Date	Title / Label	Pos	Wks
24 Aug 91 ●	**I'LL BE BACK** *Epic 6574177*	5	7

ARNIE'S LOVE *US, male / female vocal / instrumental group (Singles: 3 weeks)* pos/wks

Date	Title / Label	Pos	Wks
26 Nov 83	**I'M OUT OF YOUR LIFE** *Streetwave WAVE 9*	67	3

David ARNOLD *UK, male composer (Albums: 10 weeks)* pos/wks

Date	Title / Label	Pos	Wks
17 Aug 96	**INDEPENDENCE DAY (FILM SOUNDTRACK)** *RCA Victor 9026685642*	71	1
1 Nov 97	**SHAKEN AND STIRRED** *East West 3984207382*	11	9

See also BJÖRK; David McALMONT; PROPELLERHEADS; Nina PERSSON

Eddy ARNOLD *US, male vocalist (Singles: 21 weeks)* pos/wks

17 Feb 66 ● **MAKE THE WORLD GO AWAY** *RCA 1496* 8 17
26 May 66 **I WANT TO GO WITH YOU (re)** *RCA 1519* 46 3
28 Jul 66 **IF YOU WERE MINE MARY** *RCA 1529* 49 1

PP ARNOLD *US, female vocalist (Singles: 37 weeks)* pos/wks

4 May 67 **THE FIRST CUT IS THE DEEPEST** *Immediate IM 047* 18 10
2 Aug 67 **THE TIME HAS COME** *Immediate IM 055* 47 2
24 Jan 68 **(IF YOU THINK YOU'RE) GROOVY** *Immediate IM 061* 41 4
10 Jul 68 **ANGEL OF THE MORNING** *Immediate IM 067* 29 11
24 Sep 88 **BURN IT UP** *Rhythm King LEFT 27* [1] 14 10

[1] Beatmasters with PP Arnold

ARPEGGIO *US, male / female vocal group (Singles: 3 weeks)* pos/wks

31 Mar 79 **LOVE AND DESIRE (PART 1)** *Polydor POSP 40* 63 3

ARRESTED DEVELOPMENT *US, male / female vocal / instrumental / rap group (Singles: 39 weeks, Albums: 40 weeks)* pos/wks

16 May 92 **TENNESSEE (re)** *Cooltempo COOL 253* 46 7
24 Oct 92 ● **PEOPLE EVERYDAY** *Cooltempo COOL 265* 2 14
9 Jan 93 ● **MR WENDAL / REVOLUTION** *Cooltempo CDCOOL 268* 4 9
3 Apr 93 **TENNESSEE (re-issue)** *Cooltempo CDCOOL 270* 18 6
28 May 94 **EASE MY MIND** *Cooltempo CDCOOL 293* 33 3
31 Oct 92 ● 3 YEARS 5 MONTHS AND 2 DAYS IN THE LIFE OF ... *Cooltempo CCD 1929* 3 34
10 Apr 93 UNPLUGGED *Cooltempo CTCD 33* 40 3
18 Jun 94 ZINGALAMDUNI *Cooltempo CTCD 42* 16 3

Steve ARRINGTON
US, male vocalist (Singles: 19 weeks, Albums: 11 weeks) pos/wks

27 Apr 85 ● **FEEL SO REAL** *Atlantic A 9576* 5 10
6 Jul 85 **DANCIN' IN THE KEY OF LIFE (re)** *Atlantic A 9534* 21 9
13 Apr 85 DANCIN' IN THE KEY OF LIFE *Atlantic 781245* 41 11

ARRIVAL
UK, male / female vocal / instrumental group (Singles: 20 weeks) pos/wks

10 Jan 70 ● **FRIENDS** *Decca F 12986* 8 9
6 Jun 70 **I WILL SURVIVE** *Decca F 13026* 16 11

ARROLA – *See RUFF DRIVERZ*

ARROW
Montserrat, male vocalist – Alphonsus Cassell (Singles: 15 weeks) pos/wks

28 Jul 84 **HOT HOT HOT** *Cooltempo ARROW 1* 59 5
13 Jul 85 **LONG TIME** *London LON 70* 30 7
3 Sep 94 **HOT HOT HOT (re-mix)** *The Hit Label HLC 7* 38 3

ARROWS
US / UK, male vocal / instrumental group (Singles: 16 weeks) pos/wks

25 May 74 ● **A TOUCH TOO MUCH** *RAK 171* 8 9
1 Feb 75 **MY LAST NIGHT WITH YOU** *RAK 189* 25 7

ARSENAL FC
UK, male football team vocal group (Singles: 16 weeks) pos/wks

8 May 71 **GOOD OLD ARSENAL** *Pye 7N 45067* [1] 16 7
15 May 93 **SHOUTING FOR THE GUNNERS** *London LONCD 342* [2] 34 3
23 May 98 ● **HOT STUFF** *Grapevine AFCCD 1* 9 5
3 Jun 00 **ARSENAL NUMBER ONE / OUR GOAL** *Grapevine CDGPS280* 46 1

[1] Arsenal FC First Team Squad [2] Arsenal FA Cup Squad featuring Tippa Irie and Peter Hunnigale

ART COMPANY
Holland, male vocal / instrumental group (Singles: 11 weeks) pos/wks

26 May 84 **SUSANNA** *Epic A 4174* 12 11

ART OF NOISE *UK, male / female instrumental / production group (Singles: 65 weeks, Albums: 37 weeks)* pos/wks

24 Nov 84 ● **CLOSE (TO THE EDIT)** *ZTT ZTPS 01* 8 19
13 Apr 85 **MOMENTS IN LOVE / BEAT BOX** *ZTT ZTPS 02* 51 4
9 Nov 85 **LEGS** *China WOK 5* 69 1
22 Mar 86 ● **PETER GUNN (re-recording)** *China WOK 6* [1] 8 9
21 Jun 86 **PARANOIMIA** *China WOK 9* [2] 12 9
18 Jul 87 **DRAGNET** *China WOK 14* 60 4
29 Oct 88 ● **KISS** *China CHINA 11* [3] 5 7
12 Aug 89 **YEBO** *China CHINA 18* [4] 63 3
16 Jun 90 **ART OF LOVE** *China CHINA 23* 67 1
11 Jan 92 **INSTRUMENTS OF DARKNESS (ALL OF US ARE ONE PEOPLE)** *China WOK 2012* 45 5
29 Feb 92 **SHADES OF PARANOIMIA** *China WOK 2014* 53 2
26 Jun 99 **METAFORCE** *ZTT ZTT 129CD* 53 1
3 Nov 84 (WHO'S AFRAID OF?) THE ART OF NOISE! *ZTT ZTTIQ 2* 27 17
26 Apr 86 IN VISIBLE SILENCE *Chrysalis WOL 2* 18 15
10 Oct 87 IN NO SENSE / NONSENSE *China WOL 4* 55 2
3 Dec 88 THE BEST OF THE ART OF NOISE *China 837 367 1* 55 3

[1] Art of Noise featuring Duane Eddy [2] Art of Noise featuring Max Headroom [3] Art of Noise featuring Tom Jones [4] Art of Noise featuring Mahlathini and the Mahotella Queens

ART OF TRANCE
UK, male instrumentalist / producer (Singles: 6 weeks) pos/wks

31 Oct 98 **MADAGASCAR** *Platipus PLAT 43CD* 69 1
7 Aug 99 **MADAGASCAR (re-mix)** *Platipus PLAT 58CD* 48 2
15 Jun 02 **MADAGASCAR (2nd re-mix)** *Platipus PLATCD 102* 41 2
10 Aug 02 **LOVE WASHES OVER** *Platipus PLATCD 98* 60 1

ARTEMESIA
Holland, male producer – Patrick Prinz (Singles: 4 weeks) pos/wks

15 Apr 95 **BITS + PIECES (re)** *Hooj Choons HOOJ 31CD* 46 3
12 Aug 00 **BITS AND PIECES (re-mix)** *Tidy Trax TIDT 141CD* 51 1

See also ETHICS; MOVIN' MELODIES; SUBLIMINAL CUTS

ARTFUL DODGER
UK, male production / instrumental duo – Mark Hill and Peter Devereux (Singles: 71 weeks, Albums: 27 weeks) pos/wks

11 Dec 99 ● **RE-REWIND THE CROWD SAY BO SELECTA** *Public Demand / Relentless RELENT 1CDS* [1] 2 17
4 Mar 00 ● **MOVIN TOO FAST (re)** *Locked On XL LOX 117CD* [2] 2 12
15 Jul 00 ● **WOMAN TROUBLE** *Public Demand / ffrr FCD 380* [3] 6 10
25 Nov 00 ● **PLEASE DON'T TURN ME ON** *Public Demand / ffrr FCD 388* [4] 4 10
17 Mar 01 **THINK ABOUT ME** *ffrr FCD 394* [5] 11 8
15 Sep 01 ● **TWENTYFOURSEVEN** *ffrr / Public Demand FCD 400* [6] 6 9
15 Dec 01 **IT AIN'T ENOUGH** *ffrr / Public Demand FCD 401* [7] 20 5
2 Dec 00 IT'S ALL ABOUT THE STRAGGLERS *ffrr 8573859092* 18 27

[1] Artful Dodger featuring Craig David [2] Artful Dodger and Romina Johnson [3] Artful Dodger and Robbie Craig featuring Craig David [4] Artful Dodger featuring Lifford [5] Artful Dodger featuring Michelle Escoffery [6] Artful Dodger featuring Melanie Blatt [7] Dreem Teem vs Artful Dodger featuring MZ May and MC Alistair

Davey ARTHUR – *See FUREYS with Davey Arthur*

Neil ARTHUR *UK, male vocalist (Singles: 2 weeks)* pos/wks

5 Feb 94 **I LOVE I HATE** *Chrysalis CDCHSS 5005* 50 2

ARTIFICIAL FUNK featuring Nellie ETTISON *Denmark, male producer – Rune Kolsch and female vocalist (Singles: 1 week)* pos/wks

22 Mar 03 **TOGETHER** *Skint SKINT 82CD* 40 2

ARTIST – *See PRINCE*

ARTISTS AGAINST AIDS WORLDWIDE *US / Ireland, all-star male / female vocal ensemble (Singles: 12 weeks)* pos/wks

17 Nov 01 ● **WHAT'S GOING ON** *Columbia 6721172* 6 12

ARTISTS UNITED AGAINST APARTHEID *International, male / female vocal / instrumental charity assembly (Singles: 8 weeks)* pos/wks

23 Nov 85 **SUN CITY** *Manhattan MT 7* 21 8

ASCENSION *UK, male production duo – Ricky Simmons and Steve Jones (Singles: 4 weeks)*

Date		Title / Label	pos	wks
5 Jul 97		**SOMEONE** *Perfecto PERF 141CD*	55	1
15 Jul 00		**SOMEONE (re-mix)** *Code Blue BLU 011CD1*	43	2
23 Mar 02		**FOR A LIFETIME** *Xtravaganza XTRAV 20CDS* [1]	45	1

[1] Ascension featuring Erin Lordan

See also CHAKRA; ESSENCE; LUSTRAL; SPACE BROTHERS; OXYGEN featuring Andrea BRITTON

ASH *UK, male / female, vocal / instrumental group (Singles: 58 weeks, Albums: 65 weeks)*

Date		Title / Label	pos	wks
1 Apr 95		**KUNG FU** *Infectious INFECT 21CD*	57	1
12 Aug 95		**GIRL FROM MARS** *Infectious INFECT 24CD*	11	5
21 Oct 95		**ANGEL INTERCEPTOR** *Infectious INFECT 27CD*	14	4
27 Apr 96	●	**GOLDFINGER** *Infectious INFECT 39CD*	5	5
6 Jul 96	●	**OH YEAH (re)** *Infectious INFECT 41CD*	6	8
25 Oct 97	●	**A LIFE LESS ORDINARY** *Infectious INFECT 50CD*	10	5
3 Oct 98		**JESUS SAYS** *Infectious INFECT 59CD*	15	4
5 Dec 98		**WILD SURF** *Infectious INFECT 61CDS*	31	2
10 Feb 01	●	**SHINING LIGHT** *Infectious INFECT 98CD*	8	4
14 Apr 01		**BURN BABY BURN** *Infectious INFECT 99CDS*	13	6
21 Jul 01		**SOMETIMES** *Infectious INFECT 101CDS*	21	6
13 Oct 01		**CANDY** *Infectious INFECT 106CDS*	20	3
12 Jan 02		**THERE'S A STAR** *Infectious INFECT 112CDS*	13	3
7 Sep 02		**ENVY** *Infectious INFECT 119CDS*	21	2
18 May 96	★	**1977** *Infectious INFECT 40CD* ■	1	27
17 Oct 98	●	**NU-CLEAR SOUNDS** *Infectious INFECT 60CD*	7	4
5 May 01	★	**FREE ALL ANGELS** *Infectious INFECT 100CD* ■	1	28
21 Sep 02	●	**INTERGALACTIC SONIC 7"S** *Infectious INFEC 120CDB*	3	6

Act was a male trio before 1997 hit

ASH – *See QUENTIN and ASH*

ASHA *Italy, female vocalist (Singles: 2 weeks)*

Date		Title / Label	pos	wks
8 Jul 95		**JJ TRIBUTE** *Ffrreedom TABCD 228*	38	2

ASHANTI *US, female vocalist – Ashanti Douglas (Singles: 74 weeks, Albums: 44 weeks)*

Date		Title / Label	pos	wks
2 Feb 02	●	**ALWAYS ON TIME** *Def Jam 5889462* [1] ▲	6	13
25 May 02	●	**WHAT'S LUV?** *Atlantic AT 0128CD* [2]	4	8
8 Jun 02		**FOOLISH (import) (re)** *Mercury 5829362*	64	3
20 Jul 02	●	**FOOLISH** *Murder Inc. / Mercury 0639942* ▲	4	10
12 Oct 02	●	**DOWN 4 U (2re)** *Murder Inc 0639002* [3]	4	10
23 Nov 02		**HAPPY** *Murder Inc / Mercury 0638242*	13	8
29 Mar 03		**MESMERIZE** *Murder Inc / Mercury 0779582* [1]	12	8
28 Jun 03	●	**ROCK WIT U (AWWW BABY)** *Murder Inc / Mercy 9808431*	7	10
1 Nov 03		**RAIN ON ME** *Murder Inc / Mercury 9813176*	19	4
20 Apr 02	●	**ASHANTI** *Mercury 5868302* ▲	3	36
12 Jul 03	●	**CHAPTER II** *Murder Inc. / Mercury 9808434* ▲	5	8

[1] Ja Rule featuring Ashanti [2] Fat Joe featuring Ashanti [3] Irv Gotti presents Ja Rule, Ashanti, Charli Baltimore and Vita

ASHAYE *UK, male vocalist (Singles: 3 weeks)*

Date		Title / Label	pos	wks
15 Oct 83		**MICHAEL JACKSON MEDLEY** *Record Shack SOHO 10*	45	3

Tracks on medley: Don't Stop Til You Get Enough / Wanna Be Startin' Something / Shake Your Body Down to the Ground / Blame It on the Boogie

Richard ASHCROFT *UK, male vocalist (Singles: 30 weeks, Albums: 30 weeks)*

Date		Title / Label	pos	wks
15 Apr 00	●	**A SONG FOR THE LOVERS (re)** *Hut / Virgin HUTCD 128*	3	11
24 Jun 00		**MONEY TO BURN** *Hut / Virgin HUTCD 136*	17	4
23 Sep 00		**C'MON PEOPLE (WE'RE MAKING IT NOW)** *Hut / Virgin HUTCD 138*	21	3
19 Oct 02		**CHECK THE MEANING (re)** *Hut / Virgin HUTCD 161*	11	6
18 Jan 03		**SCIENCE OF SILENCE** *Hut / Virgin HUTCD 163*	14	4
19 Apr 03		**BUY IT IN BOTTLES** *Hut / Virgin HUTCD 167*	26	2
8 Jul 00	★	**ALONE WITH EVERYBODY** *Hut / Virgin CDHUTX 63* ■	1	20
2 Nov 02	●	**HUMAN CONDITIONS** *Hut / Virgin CDHUT 77*	3	10

See also VERVE

John ASHER *UK, male vocalist (Singles: 6 weeks)*

Date		Title / Label	pos	wks
15 Nov 75		**LET'S TWIST AGAIN** *Creole CR 112*	14	6

ASHFORD and SIMPSON *US, male / female vocal duo – Nickolas Ashford and Valerie Simpson (Singles: 22 weeks, Albums: 6 weeks)*

Date		Title / Label	pos	wks
18 Nov 78		**IT SEEMS TO HANG ON** *Warner Bros. K 17237*	48	4
5 Jan 85	●	**SOLID** *Capitol CL 345*	3	15
20 Apr 85		**BABIES** *Capitol CL 355*	56	3
16 Feb 85		**SOLID** *Capitol SASH 1*	42	6

ASHTON, GARDNER AND DYKE *UK, male vocal / instrumental group (Singles: 14 weeks)*

Date		Title / Label	pos	wks
16 Jan 71	●	**THE RESURRECTION SHUFFLE** *Capitol CL 15665*	3	14

ASIA *UK, male vocal / instrumental group (Singles: 13 weeks, Albums: 50 weeks)*

Date		Title / Label	pos	wks
3 Jul 82		**HEAT OF THE MOMENT** *Geffen GEF A2494*	46	5
18 Sep 82		**ONLY TIME WILL TELL** *Geffen GEF A2228*	54	3
13 Aug 83		**DON'T CRY** *Geffen A 3580*	33	5
10 Apr 82		**ASIA** *Geffen GEF 85577* ▲	11	38
20 Aug 83	●	**ALPHA** *Geffen GEF 25508*	5	11
14 Dec 85		**ASTRA** *Geffen GEF 26413*	68	1

See also Steve HOWE

ASIA BLUE *UK, female vocal group (Singles: 2 weeks)*

Date		Title / Label	pos	wks
27 Jun 92		**ESCAPING** *Atomic WNR 882*	50	2

ASIAN DUB FOUNDATION *UK, male vocal / instrumental group (Singles: 8 weeks, Albums: 6 weeks)*

Date		Title / Label	pos	wks
21 Feb 98		**FREE SATPAL RAM** *ffrr FCD 326*	56	1
2 May 98		**BUZZIN'** *ffrr FCD 335*	31	2
4 Jul 98		**BLACK WHITE** *ffrr FCD 337*	52	1
18 Mar 00		**REAL GREAT BRITAIN** *ffrr FCD 376*	41	2
3 Jun 00		**NEW WAY, NEW LIFE** *ffrr FCD 378*	49	1
1 Feb 03		**FORTRESS EUROPE** *Virgin DINSDX 253*	57	1
23 May 98		**RAFI'S REVENGE** *ffrr 5560062*	20	3
1 Apr 00		**COMMUNITY MUSIC** *ffrr 8573820422*	20	3

ASSEMBLY *UK, male vocal / instrumental group – includes Fergal Sharkey and Vince Clarke (Singles: 10 weeks)*

Date		Title / Label	pos	wks
12 Nov 83	●	**NEVER NEVER** *Mute TINY 1*	4	10

See also ERASURE; UNDERTONES; Feargal SHARKEY; YAZOO

ASSOCIATES *UK, male vocal / instrumental group (Singles: 47 weeks, Albums: 28 weeks)*

Date		Title / Label	pos	wks
20 Feb 82	●	**PARTY FEARS TWO** *Associates ASC 1*	9	10
8 May 82		**CLUB COUNTRY** *Associates ASC 2*	13	10
7 Aug 82		**LOVE HANGOVER / 18 CARAT LOVE AFFAIR** *Associates ASC 3*	21	8
16 Jun 84		**THOSE FIRST IMPRESSIONS** *WEA YZ 6*	43	6
1 Sep 84		**WAITING FOR THE LOVEBOAT** *WEA YZ 16*	53	4
19 Jan 85		**BREAKFAST** *WEA YZ 28*	49	6
17 Sep 88		**HEART OF GLASS** *WEA YZ 310*	56	3
22 May 82	●	**SULK** *Associates ASCL 1*	10	20
16 Feb 85		**PERHAPS** *WEA WX 9*	23	7
31 Mar 90		**WILD AND LONELY** *Circa CIRCA 11*	71	1

'18 Carat Love Affair' listed until 28 Aug only. Act was duo on 1982 hits Act was a duo for the first album

See also Billy MacKENZIE

ASSOCIATION *US, male vocal / instrumental group (Singles: 8 weeks)*

Date		Title / Label	pos	wks
22 May 68		**TIME FOR LIVIN'** *Warner Bros. WB 7195*	23	8

Rick ASTLEY 427 Top 500 *Soulful-voiced pop vocalist, b. 6 Feb 1966, Warrington, UK. Brit award-winning, US chart-topping debut hit was 1987's best-selling UK single. No British solo male can match his seven consecutive (mostly Stock Aitken Waterman produced) Top 10 hits in the 1980s (Singles: 91 weeks, Albums: 66 weeks)* pos/wks

8 Aug 87 ★	**NEVER GONNA GIVE YOU UP** *RCA PB 41447* ▲	1	18
31 Oct 87 ●	**WHENEVER YOU NEED SOMEBODY** *RCA PB 41567*	3	12
12 Dec 87 ●	**WHEN I FALL IN LOVE / MY ARMS KEEP MISSING YOU** *RCA PB 41683*	2	10
27 Feb 88 ●	**TOGETHER FOREVER** *RCA PB 41817* ▲	2	9
24 Sep 88 ●	**SHE WANTS TO DANCE WITH ME** *RCA PB 42189*	6	10
26 Nov 88 ●	**TAKE ME TO YOUR HEART** *RCA PB 42573*	8	10
11 Feb 89 ●	**HOLD ME IN YOUR ARMS** *RCA PB 42615*	10	8
26 Jan 91 ●	**CRY FOR HELP** *RCA PB 44247*	7	7
30 Mar 91	**MOVE RIGHT OUT** *RCA PB 44407*	58	2
29 Jun 91	**NEVER KNEW LOVE** *RCA PB 44737*	70	1
4 Sep 93	**THE ONES YOU LOVE** *RCA 74321160142*	48	2
13 Nov 93	**HOPELESSLY** *RCA 74321175642*	33	2
28 Nov 87 ★	**WHENEVER YOU NEED SOMEBODY** *RCA PL 71529* ■	1	34
10 Dec 88 ●	**HOLD ME IN YOUR ARMS** *RCA PL 71932*	8	19
2 Mar 91 ●	**FREE** *RCA PL 74896*	9	9
14 Sep 02	**GREATEST HITS** *BMG 74321955122*	16	4

Before 9 Jan 1988, 'When I Fall in Love' was listed by itself. After that date 'My Arms Keep Missing You' was the side listed

ASTRO TRAX
UK, male / female vocal / production trio (Singles: 1 week) pos/wks

24 Oct 98	**THE ENERGY (FEEL THE VIBE)** *Satellite 74321622052*	74	1

ASWAD 482 Top 500
Seminal reggae outfit formed 1975, London, UK. Featured former child actor Brinsley Forde (v), b. 1952, Guyana. They signed to Island in 1976, topped the chart with an old Tina Turner B-side and followed it into the Top 20 with a Bucks Fizz B-side (Singles: 81 weeks, Albums: 61 weeks) pos/wks

3 Mar 84	**CHASING FOR THE BREEZE** *Island IS 160*	51	3
6 Oct 84	**54-46 (WAS MY NUMBER)** *Island IS 170*	70	3
27 Feb 88 ★	**DON'T TURN AROUND** *Mango IS 341*	1	12
21 May 88	**GIVE A LITTLE LOVE** *Mango IS 358*	11	8
24 Sep 88	**SET THEM FREE** *Mango IS 383*	70	2
1 Apr 89	**BEAUTY'S ONLY SKIN DEEP** *Mango MNG 105*	31	6
22 Jul 89	**ON AND ON** *Mango MNG 708*	25	8
18 Aug 90	**NEXT TO YOU** *Mango MNG 753*	24	6
17 Nov 90	**SMILE** *Mango MNG 767* [1]	53	2
30 Mar 91	**TOO WICKED (EP)** *Mango MNG 771*	61	2
31 Jul 93	**HOW LONG** *Polydor PZCD 252* [2]	31	5
9 Oct 93	**DANCEHALL MOOD** *Bubblin' CDBUBB 1*	48	2
18 Jun 94 ●	**SHINE** *Bubblin' CDBUBB 3*	5	14
17 Sep 94	**WARRIORS** *Bubblin' CDBUBB 4*	33	3
18 Feb 95	**YOU'RE NO GOOD** *Bubblin' CDBUBB 5*	35	3
5 Aug 95	**IF I WAS** *Bubblin' CDBUBB 6*	58	1
31 Aug 02	**SHY GUY** *Universal TV 0192632* [3]	62	1
24 Jul 82	**NOT SATISFIED** *CBS 85666*	50	6
10 Dec 83	**LIVE AND DIRECT** *Island IMA 6*	57	16
3 Nov 84	**REBEL SOULS** *Island ILPS 9780*	48	2
28 Jun 86	**TO THE TOP** *Simba SIMBALP 2*	71	3
9 Apr 88 ●	**DISTANT THUNDER** *Mango ILPS 9895*	10	15
3 Dec 88	**RENAISSANCE** *Stylus SMR 866*	52	8
22 Sep 90	**TOO WICKED** *Mango MLPS 1054*	51	2
9 Jul 94	**RISE AND SHINE** *Bubblin' BUBBCD 1*	38	5
12 Aug 95	**GREATEST HITS** *Bubblin' BUBBCD 4*	20	3
24 Aug 02	**COOL SUMMER REGGAE** *UMTV 643762*	54	1

[1] Aswad featuring Sweetie Irie [2] Yazz & Aswad
[3] Aswad featuring Easther Bennett

Tracks on Too Wicked (EP): Best of My Love / Warrior Re-Charge / Fire / I Shot the Sheriff

AT THE DRIVE-IN
US, male vocal / instrumental group (Singles: 3 weeks, Albums: 2 weeks) pos/wks

19 Aug 00	**ONE ARMED SCISSOR** *Grand Royal GR 091CD*	64	1
16 Dec 00	**ROLODEX PROPAGANDA** *Grand Royal / Virgin VUSCD 189*	54	1
24 Mar 01	**INVALID LITTER DEPT** *Grand Royal / Virgin VUSCD 193*	50	1
30 Sep 00	**RELATIONSHIP OF COMMAND** *Grand Royal CDVUS 184*	33	2

Gali ATARI – *See MILK AND HONEY featuring Gali ATARI*

ATARIS *US, male vocal / instrumental group (Singles: 1 week)* pos/wks

11 Oct 03	**THE BOYS OF SUMMER** *Columbia 6743402*	49	1

ATEED *Germany, female vocalist (Singles: 1 week)* pos/wks

4 Oct 03	**COME TO ME** *Better the Devil BTD 4CD*	56	1

ATHLETE *UK, male vocal / instrumental group (Singles: 7 weeks, Albums: 21 weeks)* pos/wks

29 Jun 02	**YOU GOT THE STYLE** *Parlophone CDATH 001*	37	2
16 Nov 02	**BEAUTIFUL** *Parlophone CDATH 002*	41	1
5 Apr 03	**EL SALVADOR** *Parlophone CDATHS 003*	31	2
5 Jul 03	**WESTSIDE** *Parlophone CDATHS 005*	42	1
4 Oct 03	**YOU GOT THE STYLE** *Parlophone CDATH 006*	42	1
19 Apr 03	**VEHICLES & ANIMALS** *Parlophone 5822912*	19	21

ATHLETICO SPIZZ 80
UK, male vocal / instrumental group (Albums: 5 weeks) pos/wks

26 Jul 80	**DO A RUNNER** *A&M AMLE 68514*	27	5

Chet ATKINS *US, male instrumentalist – guitar, d. 30 Jun 2001 (Singles: 2 weeks, Albums: 16 weeks)* pos/wks

17 Mar 60	**TEENSVILLE (re)** *RCA 1174*	46	2
18 Mar 61	**THE OTHER CHET ATKINS** *RCA RD 27194*	20	1
17 Jun 61	**CHET ATKINS' WORKSHOP** *RCA RD 27214*	19	1
20 Feb 63	**CARIBBEAN GUITAR** *RCA RD 7519*	17	3
24 Nov 90	**NECK AND NECK** *CBS 4674351* [1]	41	11

[1] Chet Atkins and Mark Knopfler

Rowan ATKINSON *UK, male comedian (Albums: 9 weeks)* pos/wks

7 Feb 81	**LIVE IN BELFAST** *Arista SPART 1150*	44	9

See also NOT THE NINE O'CLOCK NEWS; MR BEAN

ATLANTA RHYTHM SECTION
US, male vocal / instrumental group (Singles: 4 weeks) pos/wks

27 Oct 79	**SPOOKY** *Polydor POSP 74*	48	4

ATLANTIC OCEAN *Holland, male instrumental duo – Rene van der Weyde and Lex van Coeverden (Singles: 14 weeks)* pos/wks

19 Feb 94	**WATERFALL** *Eastern Bloc BLOCCD 001*	22	6
2 Jul 94	**BODY IN MOTION** *Eastern Bloc BLOCCD 009*	15	4
26 Nov 94	**MUSIC IS A PASSION** *Eastern Bloc BLOCCDX 017*	59	1
30 Nov 96	**WATERFALL (re-mix)** *Eastern Bloc BLOC 104CD*	21	3

ATLANTIC STARR *US, male / female vocal / instrumental group (Singles: 48 weeks, Albums: 15 weeks)* pos/wks

9 Sep 78	**GIMME YOUR LUVIN'** *A&M AMS 7380*	66	3
29 Jun 85	**SILVER SHADOW** *A&M AM 260*	41	6
7 Sep 85	**ONE LOVE** *A&M AM 273*	58	4
15 Mar 86 ●	**SECRET LOVERS** *A&M AM 307*	10	12
24 May 86	**IF YOUR HEART ISN'T IN IT** *A&M AM 319*	48	4
13 Jun 87 ●	**ALWAYS** *Warner Bros. W 8455* ▲	3	14
12 Sep 87	**ONE LOVER AT A TIME** *Warner Bros. W 8327*	57	3
27 Aug 94	**EVERYBODY'S GOT SUMMER** *Arista 74321228072*	36	2
15 Jun 85	**AS THE BAND TURNS** *A&M AMA 5019*	64	3
11 Jul 87	**ALL IN THE NAME OF LOVE** *WEA WX 115*	48	12

ATLANTIS vs AVATAR *UK, male production group featuring female vocalist – Miriam Stockley (Singles: 2 weeks)* pos/wks

28 Oct 00	**FIJI** *Inferno CDFERN 34*	52	2

Natacha ATLAS – *See Jean-Michel JARRE*

ATMOSFEAR

UK, male instrumental group (Singles: 7 weeks) pos/wks

17 Nov 79 **DANCING IN OUTER SPACE** *MCA 543* 46 7

ATOMIC KITTEN

342 Top 500 *The Liverpool ladies were the first female trio to amass three No.1 singles. Line-up is Natasha Hamilton, Elizabeth McClarnon and Jenny Frost (who replaced Kerry Katona in 2001). 'Eternal Flame' and 'The Tide Is High' are the only songs to top the chart twice by two different female-fronted acts. Best-selling single: 'Whole Again' 940,000 (Singles: 124 weeks, Albums: 70 weeks)* pos/wks

11 Dec 99 ● **RIGHT NOW** *Innocent SINCD 15* 10 9
8 Apr 00 ● **SEE YA (re)** *Innocent SINCD 17* 6 7
15 Jul 00 ● **I WANT YOUR LOVE** *Innocent SINCD 18* 10 5
21 Oct 00 **FOLLOW ME** *Innocent SINCD 22* 20 5
10 Feb 01 ★ **WHOLE AGAIN (re)** *Innocent SINDX24* ■ 1 23
4 Aug 01 ★ **ETERNAL FLAME (re)** *Innocent SINCD 27* ■ 1 15
1 Jun 02 ● **IT'S OK!** *Innocent SINCD 36* 3 13
7 Sep 02 ★ **THE TIDE IS HIGH (GET THE FEELING)** *Innocent SINCD 38* ■ ..1 16
7 Dec 02 ● **THE LAST GOODBYE / BE WITH YOU** *Innocent SINDX 42* 2 12
12 Apr 03 ● **LOVE DOESN'T HAVE TO HURT** *Innocent SINCD 45* 4 10
8 Nov 03 ● **IF YOU COME TO ME** *Innocent SINCD 50* ....3 8+
27 Dec 03 ● **LADIES NIGHT** *Innocent SINCD 53* [1] ....8 1+
4 Nov 00 **RIGHT NOW** *Innocent CDSIN 6* 39 4
18Aug 01 ★ **RIGHT NOW (re-issue)** *Innocent CDSIN 6* ■ 1 37
21 Sep 02 ★ **FEELS SO GOOD** *Innocent CDSIN 10* ■ 1 27
22 Nov 03 ● **LADIES NIGHT** *Innocent CDSIN14* ....5 6+

[1] Atomic Kitten featuring Kool and the Gang

ATOMIC ROOSTER

UK, male vocal / instrumental group (Singles: 25 weeks, Albums: 13 weeks) pos/wks

6 Feb 71 **TOMORROW NIGHT** *B & C CB 131* 11 12
10 Jul 71 ● **DEVIL'S ANSWER** *B & C CB 157* 4 13
13 Jun 70 **ATOMIC ROOSTER** *B & C CAS 1010* 49 1
16 Jan 71 **DEATH WALKS BEHIND YOU** *Charisma CAS 1026* 12 8
21 Aug 71 **IN HEARING OF ATOMIC ROOSTER** *Pegasus PEG 1* 18 4

ATTRACTIONS – *See Elvis COSTELLO*

Winifred ATWELL

Trinidad, female instrumentalist – piano, d. 28 Feb 1983 (Singles: 117 weeks) pos/wks

12 Dec 52 ● **BRITANNIA RAG (re)** *Decca F 10015* 5 6
15 May 53 ● **CORONATION RAG (re)** *Decca F 10110* 5 6
25 Sep 53 ● **FLIRTATION WALTZ (2re)** *Decca F 10161* 10 3
4 Dec 53 ● **LET'S HAVE A PARTY (re)** *Philips PB 213* 2 15
23 Jul 54 ● **RACHMANINOFF'S 18TH VARIATION ON A THEME BY PAGANINI (THE STORY OF THREE LOVES) (re)** *Philips PB 234* 9 9
26 Nov 54 ★ **LET'S HAVE ANOTHER PARTY** *Philips PB 268* 1 8
4 Nov 55 ● **LET'S HAVE A DING DONG** *Decca F 10634* 3 10
16 Mar 56 ★ **THE POOR PEOPLE OF PARIS** *Decca F 10681* 1 16
18 May 56 **PORT-AU-PRINCE** *Decca F 10727* [1] 18 6
20 Jul 56 **LEFT BANK (C'EST À HAMBOURG)** *Decca F 10762* 14 7
26 Oct 56 ● **MAKE IT A PARTY** *Decca F 10796* 7 12
22 Feb 57 **LET'S ROCK 'N' ROLL (re)** *Decca F 10852* 24 4
6 Dec 57 ● **LET'S HAVE A BALL** *Decca F 10956* 4 6
7 Aug 59 **THE SUMMER OF THE SEVENTEENTH DOLL** *Decca F 11143* 24 2
27 Nov 59 ● **PIANO PARTY** *Decca F 11183* 10 7

[1] Winifred Atwell and Frank Chacksfield

Various hits listed above were medleys as follows: Let's Have a Party: If You Knew Suzie / The More We Are Together / That's My Weakness Now / Knees Up Mother Brown / Daisy Bell / Boomps a Daisy / She Was One of the Early Birds / Three O'Clock in the Morning. Let's Have Another Party: Somebody Stole My Gal / I Wonder Where My Baby Is Tonight / When the Red Red Robin / Bye Bye Blackbird / Sheik of Araby / Another Little Drink / Lilly of Laguna / Honeysuckle and the Bee / Broken Doll / Nellie Dean. Let's Have a Ding Dong: Ain't She Sweet / Oh Johnny Oh Johnny Oh / Oh You Beautiful Doll / Yes We Have No Bananas / Happy Days Are Here Again / I'm Forever Blowing Bubbles / I'll Be Your Sweetheart / If These Lips Could Only Speak / Who's Taking You Home Tonight. Make It a Party: Who Were You with Last Night / Hello Hello Who's Your Lady Friend / Yes Sir That's My Baby / Don't Dilly Dally on the Way / Beer Barrel Polka / After the Ball / Peggy O'Neil / Meet Me Tonight in Dreamland / I Belong to Glasgow / Down at the Old Bull and Bush. Let's Rock 'n' Roll: Singin' the Blues / Green Door / See You Later Alligator / Shake Rattle and Roll / Rock Around the Clock / Razzle Dazzle. Let's Have a Ball: Music Music Music / This Ole House / Heartbreaker / Woody Woodpecker / Last Train to San Fernando / Bring a Little Water Sylvie / Puttin' on the Style / Don't You Rock Me Daddy-O. Piano Party: Baby Face / Comin' Thru' the Rye / Annie Laurie / Little Brown Jug / Let Him Go Let Him Tarry / Put Your Arms Around Me Honey / I'll Be With You in Apple Blossom Time / Shine on Harvest Moon / Blue Skies / I'll Never Say 'Never Again' Again / I'll See You in My Dreams. 'Let's Have a Party' re-entered for a second visit peaking at No.14 in Nov 1954

AU PAIRS

UK, female / male vocal / instrumental group (Albums: 10 weeks) pos/wks

6 Jun 81 **PLAYING WITH A DIFFERENT SEX** *Human HUMAN 1* 33 7
4 Sep 82 **SENSE AND SENSUALITY** *Kamera KAM 010* 79 3

AUDIO BULLYS

UK, male vocal / production group (Singles: 6 weeks, Albums: 3 weeks) pos/wks

18 Jan 03 **WE DON'T CARE** *Source SOURCD 061* 15 3
31 May 03 **THE THINGS / TURNED AWAY** *Source SOURCD 084* 22 3
14 Jun 03 **EGO WAR** *Source CDSOUR073* 19 3

AUDIOSLAVE

US, male vocal / instrumental group (Singles: 3 weeks, Albums: 20 weeks) pos/wks

1 Feb 03 **COCHISE** *Epic / Interscope 6732762* 24 3
30 Nov 02 **AUDIOSLAVE** *Epic / Interscope 5101302* 19 20

AUDIOWEB

UK, male vocal / instrumental group (Singles: 12 weeks, Albums: 1 week) pos/wks

14 Oct 95 **SLEEPER** *Mother MUMCD 69* 74 1
9 Mar 96 **YEAH** *Mother MUMCD 72* 73 1
15 Jun 96 **INTO MY WORLD** *Mother MUMCD 76* 42 1
19 Oct 96 **SLEEPER (re-mix)** *Mother MUMCD 78* 50 2
15 Feb 97 **BANKROBBER** *Mother MUMCD 85* 19 2
24 May 97 **FAKER** *Mother MUMCD 91* 70 1
25 Apr 98 **POLICEMAN SKANK ... (THE STORY OF MY LIFE)** *Mother MUMCD 100* 21 2
4 Jul 98 **PERSONAL FEELING** *Mother MUMCD 104* 65 1
20 Feb 99 **TEST THE THEORY** *Mother MUMCD 110* 56 1
9 Nov 96 **AUDIOWEB** *Mother MUMXD 9604* 70 1

Brian AUGER / Brian AUGER TRINITY – *See Julie DRISCOLL, Brian AUGER and the TRINITY*

AURA – *See POPPERS presents AURA*

AURORA

UK, male production duo (Singles: 19 weeks) pos/wks

5 Jun 99 **HEAR YOU CALLING** *Additive 12AD 040* 71 1
5 Feb 00 **HEAR YOU CALLING (re-issue)** *Positiva CDTIV 124* 17 4
23 Sep 00 ● **ORDINARY WORLD** *Positiva CDTIV 139* [1] 5 7
13 Apr 02 **DREAMING** *EMI CDEM 611* 24 4
6 Jul 02 **THE DAY IT RAINED FOREVER** *EMI CDEMS 613* 29 3

[1] Aurora featuring Naimee Coleman

See also DIVE

AURRA

US, male / female vocal / instrumental group (Singles: 18 weeks) pos/wks

4 May 85 **LIKE I LIKE IT** *10 TEN 45* 51 5
19 Apr 86 **YOU AND ME TONIGHT** *10 TEN 71* 12 8
21 Jun 86 **LIKE I LIKE IT (re-issue)** *10 TEN 126* 43 5

Adam AUSTIN

UK, male vocalist (Singles: 1 week) pos/wks

13 Feb 99 **CENTERFOLD** *Media PSRCA 0107* 41 1

David AUSTIN

UK, male vocalist (Singles: 3 weeks) pos/wks

21 Jul 84 **TURN TO GOLD** *Parlophone R 6068* 68 3

DOUBLE TOPPERS

Here is the complete list of every act ever to have had a UK No.1 single and album at the same time. A measure of The Beatles' complete chart domination in the 1960s can be seen by the record number of times they achieved this simultaneous feat. They held the top spot on both charts in the same week on 45 occasions with 15 combinations of a top single and album.

DATE OF ENTRY – **WEEKS AT THE TOP** – **ARTIST** – SINGLE/ALBUM

26 Jan 61 4 **ELVIS PRESLEY** Are You Lonesome Tonight/GI Blues
23 Mar 61 1 **ELVIS PRESLEY** Wooden Heart/GI Blues
5 Oct 61 1 **SHADOWS** Kon-Tiki/The Shadows
11 Jan 62 6 **CLIFF RICHARD AND THE SHADOWS** The Young Ones/The Young Ones
22 Feb 62 4 **ELVIS PRESLEY** Rock-a-Hula Baby – Can't Help Falling in Love/Blue Hawaii
24 May 62 4 **ELVIS PRESLEY** Good Luck Charm/ Blue Hawaii
14 Mar 63 2 **CLIFF RICHARD AND THE SHADOWS** Summer Holiday/Summer Holiday
4 Apr 63 1 **CLIFF RICHARD AND THE SHADOWS** Summer Holiday/Summer Holiday
9 May 63 6 **BEATLES** From Me to You/Please Please Me
12 Sep 63 4 **BEATLES** She Loves You/Please Please Me
28 Nov 63 1 **BEATLES** She Loves You/Please Please Me
5 Dec 63 1 **BEATLES** She Loves You/With the Beatles
12 Dec 63 5 **BEATLES** I Want to Hold Your Hand/With the Beatles
2 Apr 64 3 **BEATLES** Can't Buy Me Love/With the Beatles
16 Jul 64 1 **ROLLING STONES** It's All Over Now/Rolling Stones
23 Jul 64 3 **BEATLES** A Hard Day's Night/A Hard Day's Night
10 Dec 64 1 **BEATLES** I Feel Fine/A Hard Day's Night
17 Dec 64 4 **BEATLES** Feel Fine/Beatles for Sale
18 Mar 65 3 **ROLLING STONES** The Last Time/Rolling Stones No.2
29 Apr 65 2 **BEATLES** Ticket to Ride/Beatles for Sale
12 Aug 65 2 **BEATLES** Help!/Help!
23 Dec 65 4 **BEATLES** Day Tripper – We Can Work It Out/Rubber Soul
26 May 66 1 **ROLLING STONES** Paint It Black/Aftermath
18 Aug 66 4 **BEATLES** Yellow Submarine/Revolver
2 Feb 67 2 **MONKEES** I'm a Believer/The Monkees
19 Jul 67 3 **BEATLES** All You Need Is Love/Sgt. Pepper's Lonely Hearts Club Band
20 Dec 67 2 **BEATLES** Hello Goodbye/Sgt. Pepper's Lonely Hearts Club Band
28 Mar 70 3 **SIMON AND GARFUNKEL** Bridge Over Troubled Water/Bridge Over Troubled Water
6 Feb 71 4 **GEORGE HARRISON** My Sweet Lord/All Things Must Pass
9 Oct 71 3 **ROD STEWART** Maggie May/Every Picture Tells a Story
5 Feb 72 2 **T. REX** Telegram Sam/Electric Warrior
20 May 72 3 **T. REX** Metal Guru/Bolan Boogie
16 Aug 75 2 **STYLISTICS** Can't Give You Anything (But My Love)/Best of the Stylistics
6 Sep 75 4 **ROD STEWART** Sailing/Atlantic Crossing
27 Dec 75 2 **QUEEN** Bohemian Rhapsody/A Night at the Opera
17 Jan 76 2 **QUEEN** Bohemian Rhapsody/A Night at the Opera
8 May 76 4 **ABBA** Fernando/Greatest Hits
16 Apr 77 3 **ABBA** Knowing Me, Knowing You/Arrival
10 Sep 77 1 **ELVIS PRESLEY** Way Down/40 Greatest Hits
18 Feb 78 3 **ABBA** Take a Chance on Me/The Album
7 Oct 78 6 **JOHN TRAVOLTA AND OLIVIA NEWTON-JOHN** Summer Nights/Grease
17 Feb 79 2 **BLONDIE** Heart of Glass/Parallel Lines
21 Jul 79 1 **TUBEWAY ARMY** Are 'Friends' Electric?/Replicas
22 Sep 79 1 **GARY NUMAN** Cars/The Pleasure Principle
19 Jan 80 2 **PRETENDERS** Brass in Pocket/Pretenders
11 Oct 80 2 **POLICE** Don't Stand So Close to Me/Zenyatta Mondatta
8 Nov 80 1 **BARBRA STREISAND** Woman in Love/Guilty
29 Nov 80 3 **ABBA** Super Trouper/Super Trouper
7 Feb 81 2 **JOHN LENNON** Woman/Double Fantasy
9 May 81 2 **ADAM AND THE ANTS** Stand and Deliver/Kings of the Wild Frontier
21 Nov 81 2 **QUEEN** Under Pressure (Queen and David Bowie)/Greatest Hits
9 Jan 82 1 **HUMAN LEAGUE** Don't You Want Me/Dare
20 Feb 82 1 **JAM** Town Called Malice/The Gift
8 May 82 1 **PAUL McCARTNEY** Ebony and Ivory (Paul McCartney and Stevie Wonder)/Tug of War
29 May 82 1 **MADNESS** House of Fun/Complete Madness
29 Jan 83 3 **MEN AT WORK** Down Under/Business As Usual
23 Apr 83 1 **DAVID BOWIE** Let's Dance/Let's Dance
14 May 83 1 **SPANDAU BALLET** True/True
25 Jun 83 1 **POLICE** Every Breath You Take/Synchronicity
22 Oct 83 1 **CULTURE CLUB** Karma Chameleon/Colour by Numbers
31 Mar 84 2 **LIONEL RICHIE** Hello/Can't Slow Down
26 Jan 85 2 **FOREIGNER** I Want to Know What Love Is/Agent Provocateur
16 Mar 85 2 **PHIL COLLINS** Easy Lover (Phil Collins and Philip Bailey)/No Jacket Required

Beyoncé, the youngest solo artist to have simultaneous single and album chart-toppers

12 Jul 86 3 **MADONNA** Papa Don't Preach/True Blue
13 Jun 87 1 **WHITNEY HOUSTON** I Wanna Dance with Somebody (Who Loves Me)/Whitney
24 Dec 88 2 **CLIFF RICHARD** Mistletoe and Wine/Private Collection
1 Apr 89 2 **MADONNA** Like a Prayer/Like a Prayer
10 Jun 89 2 **JASON DONOVAN** Sealed with a Kiss/Ten Good Reasons
15 Jul 89 1 **SOUL II SOUL** Back to Life (However Do You Want Me)/Club Classics Volume 1
5 Oct 91 1 **BRYAN ADAMS** (Everything I Do) I Do It for You/Waking Up the Neighbours
21 Dec 91 2 **QUEEN** Bohemian Rhapsody – These Are the Days of Our Lives/Greatest Hits II
8 Feb 92 1 **WET WET WET** Goodnight Girl/High on the Happy Side
25 Apr 92 1 **RIGHT SAID FRED** Deeply Dippy/Up
30 Oct 93 3 **MEAT LOAF** I'd Do Anything for Love (But I Won't Do That)/Bat Out of Hell II
26 Feb 94 3 **MARIAH CAREY** Without You/Music Box
30 Jul 94 4 **WET WET WET** Love Is All Around/End of Part One (Their Greatest Hits)
3 Sep 94 1 **WET WET WET** Love Is All Around/End of Part One (Their Greatest Hits)
4 Feb 95 5 **CELINE DION** Think Twice/The Colour of My Love
25 Nov 95 2 **ROBSON & JEROME** I Believe – Up on the Roof/Robson & Jerome
2 Mar 96 1 **OASIS** Don't Look Back in Anger/(What's the Story) Morning Glory
11 Jan 97 3 **SPICE GIRLS** 2 Become 1/Spice
22 Mar 97 2 **SPICE GIRLS** Mama – Who Do You Think You Are?/Spice
21 Jun 1 **HANSON** Mmmbop/Middle of Nowhere
7 Apr 01 1 **HEAR'SAY** Pure and Simple/Popstars
23 Jun 01 1 **SHAGGY** Angel (Shaggy featuring Rayvon)/Hot Shot
13 Oct 01 2 **KYLIE MINOGUE** Can't Get You Out of My Head/Fever
22 Dec 01 3 **ROBBIE WILLIAMS** Somethin' Stupid (Robbie Williams and Nicole Kidman)/Swing When You're Winning
16 Feb 02 2 **ENRIQUE** Hero/Escape
21 Sep 02 1 **ATOMIC KITTEN** The Tide Is High/Feels So Good
12 Jul 03 3 **BEYONCÉ** Crazy in Love/Dangerously in Love
13 Dec 03 1 **WILL YOUNG** Leave Right Now/Friday's Child

Patti AUSTIN *US, female vocalist (Singles: 11 weeks, Albums: 1 week)*

		pos	wks
12 Feb 83	BABY COME TO ME *Qwest K 15005* [1] ▲	11	10
5 Sep 92	I'LL KEEP YOUR DREAMS ALIVE *Ammi AMMI 101* [2]	68	1
26 Sep 81	EVERY HOME SHOULD HAVE ONE *Qwest K 56931*	99	1

[1] Patti Austin and James Ingram [2] George Benson and Patti Austin

AUTECHRE *UK, male instrumental duo (Singles: 1 week)*

		pos	wks
7 May 94	BASSCAD *Warp WAP 44CD*	56	1

AUTEURS *UK, male / female vocal / instrumental group (Singles: 9 weeks, Albums: 4 weeks)*

		pos	wks
27 Nov 93	LENNY VALENTINO *Hut HUTCD 36*	41	2
23 Apr 94	CHINESE BAKERY *Hut HUTDX 41*	42	2
6 Jan 96	BACK WITH THE KILLER AGAIN *Hut HUTCD 65*	45	3
24 Feb 96	LIGHT AIRCRAFT ON FIRE *Hut HUTCD 66*	58	1
3 Jul 99	THE RUBETTES *Hut HUTCD 113*	66	1
6 Mar 93	NEW WAVE *Hut CDHUT 7*	35	2
21 May 94	NOW I'M A COWBOY *Hut CDHUT 16*	27	1
16 Mar 96	AFTER MURDER PARK *Hut CDHUT 33*	53	1

AUTUMN *UK, male vocal / instrumental group (Singles: 6 weeks)*

		pos	wks
16 Oct 71	MY LITTLE GIRL *Pye 7N 45090*	37	6

Peter AUTY and the SINFONIA OF LONDON conducted by Howard BLAKE *UK, male vocalist with orchestra (Singles: 9 weeks)*

		pos	wks
14 Dec 85	WALKING IN THE AIR *Stiff LAD 1*	42	5
19 Dec 87	WALKING IN THE AIR (re-issue) *CBS GA 3950*	37	4

See also DIGITAL DREAM BABY

AVALANCHES *Australia, male production group (Singles: 12 weeks, Albums: 25 weeks)*

		pos	wks
7 Apr 01	SINCE I LEFT YOU *XL Recordings XLS 128CD*	16	7
21 Jul 01	FRONTIER PSYCHIATRIST *XL Recordings XLS 134CD*	18	5
28 Apr 01 ●	SINCE I LEFT YOU *XL Recordings XLCD 138*	8	25

Frankie AVALON *US, male vocalist – Francis Avallone (Singles: 15 weeks)*

		pos	wks
10 Oct 58	GINGERBREAD *HMV POP 517*	30	1
24 Apr 59	VENUS *HMV POP 603* ▲	16	6
22 Jan 60	WHY *HMV POP 688* ▲	20	4
28 Apr 60	DON'T THROW AWAY ALL THOSE TEARDROPS *HMV POP 727*	37	4

AVALON BOYS – *See LAUREL and HARDY with the AVALON BOYS featuring Chill WILLS*

AVERAGE WHITE BAND *UK, male vocal / instrumental group (Singles: 47 weeks, Albums: 50 weeks)*

		pos	wks
22 Feb 75 ●	PICK UP THE PIECES *Atlantic K 10489* ▲	6	9
26 Apr 75	CUT THE CAKE *Atlantic K 10605*	31	4
9 Oct 76	QUEEN OF MY SOUL *Atlantic K 10825*	23	7
28 Apr 79	WALK ON BY *RCA XC 1087*	46	5
25 Aug 79	WHEN WILL YOU BE MINE *RCA XB 1096*	49	5
26 Apr 80	LET'S GO ROUND AGAIN PT.1 *RCA AWB 1*	12	11
26 Jul 80	FOR YOU FOR LOVE *RCA AWB 2*	46	4
26 Mar 94	LET'S GO ROUND AGAIN (re-mix) *The Hit Label HLC 5*	56	2
1 Mar 75 ●	AVERAGE WHITE BAND *Atlantic K 50058* ▲	6	14
5 Jul 75	CUT THE CAKE *Atlantic K 50146*	28	4
31 Jul 76	SOUL SEARCHING TIME *Atlantic K 50272*	60	1
10 Mar 79	I FEEL NO FRET *RCA XL 13063*	15	15
31 May 80	SHINE *RCA XL 13123*	14	13
2 Apr 94	LET'S GO ROUND AGAIN – THE BEST OF THE AVERAGE WHITE BAND *The Hit Label AHLCD 15*	38	3

Kevin AVIANCE *US, male vocalist (Singles: 1 week)*

		pos	wks
13 Jun 98	DIN DA DA *Distinctive DISNCD 42*	65	1

AVONS *UK, male / female vocal trio (Singles: 22 weeks)*

		pos	wks
13 Nov 59 ●	SEVEN LITTLE GIRLS SITTING IN THE BACK SEAT *Columbia DB 4363*	3	13
7 Jul 60	WE'RE ONLY YOUNG ONCE (re) *Columbia DB 4461*	45	2
27 Oct 60	FOUR LITTLE HEELS (re) *Columbia DB 4522*	45	3
26 Jan 61	RUBBER BALL *Columbia DB 4569*	30	4

AWESOME *UK, male vocal group (Singles: 2 weeks)*

		pos	wks
8 Nov 97	RUMOURS *Universal MCSTD 40145*	58	1
21 Mar 98	CRAZY *Universal MCSTD 40195*	63	1

AWESOME 3 *UK, male / female vocal / instrumental group (Singles: 8 weeks)*

		pos	wks
8 Sep 90	HARD UP *A&M AM 591*	55	3
3 Oct 92	DON'T GO *Citybeat CBE 1271*	75	1
4 Jun 94	DON'T GO (re-mix) *XL Recordings CBX 771CD*	45	2
26 Oct 96	DON'T GO (2nd re-mix) *XL Recordings XLS 78CD* [1]	27	2

[1] Awesome 3 featuring Julie McDermott

Hoyt AXTON *US, male vocalist, d. 26 Oct 1999 (Singles: 4 weeks)*

		pos	wks
7 Jun 80	DELLA AND THE DEALER *Young Blood YB 82*	48	4

AXUS *UK, male / female vocal / production duo (Singles: 1 week)*

		pos	wks
26 Sep 98	ABACUS (WHEN I FALL IN LOVE) *INCcredible INCRL 8CD*	62	1

Roy AYERS *US, male vocalist / instrumentalist – vibraphone (Singles: 13 weeks, Albums: 2 weeks)*

		pos	wks
21 Oct 78	GET ON UP, GET ON DOWN *Polydor AYERS 7*	41	4
13 Jan 79	HEAT OF THE BEAT *Polydor POSP 16* [1]	43	5
2 Feb 80	DON'T STOP THE FEELING *Polydor STEP 6*	56	3
16 May 98	EXPANSIONS *Soma Recordings SOMA 65CDS* [2]	68	1
26 Oct 85	YOU MIGHT BE SURPRISED *CBS 26653*	91	2

[1] Roy Ayers and Wayne Henderson [2] Scott Grooves featuring Roy Ayers

AYLA *Germany, male producer – Ingo Kunzi (Singles: 3 weeks)*

		pos	wks
4 Sep 99	AYLA *Positiva CDTIV 117*	22	3

Pam AYRES *UK, female vocalist (Albums: 29 weeks)*

		pos	wks
27 Mar 76	SOME OF ME POEMS AND SONGS *Galaxy GAL 6003*	13	23
11 Dec 76	SOME MORE OF ME POEMS AND SONGS *Galaxy GAL 6010*	23	6

AZ *US, male rapper – Anthony Cruz (Singles: 1 week)*

		pos	wks
30 Mar 96	SUGARHILL *Cooltempo CDCOOL 315*	67	1

AZ YET *US, male vocal group (Singles: 10 weeks)*

		pos	wks
1 Mar 97	LAST NIGHT *LaFace 74321423202*	21	3
21 Jun 97 ●	HARD TO SAY I'M SORRY *LaFace 74321481482* [1]	7	7

[1] Az Yet featuring Peter Cetera

Charles AZNAVOUR *France, male vocalist – Shanaur Aznavourian (Singles: 29 weeks, Albums: 21 weeks)*

		pos	wks
22 Sep 73	THE OLD FASHIONED WAY (LES PLAISIRS DÉMODÉS) (2re) *Barclay BAR 20*	38	15
22 Jun 74 ★	SHE *Barclay BAR 26*	1	14
29 Jun 74	AZNAVOUR SINGS AZNAVOUR VOLUME 3 *Barclay 80472*	23	7
7 Sep 74 ●	A TAPESTRY OF DREAMS *Barclay 90003*	9	13
2 Aug 80	HIS GREATEST LOVE SONGS *K-Tel NE 1078*	73	1

'The Old Fashioned Way' re-entered the chart in Oct 1973 (at its peak position) and Jul 1974

AZTEC CAMERA *445* **Top 500**

Sensitive, tuneful pop band formed 1980, and centred around teenage singer / songwriter Roddy Frame, b. 29 Jan 1964, East Kilbride, Scotland.

Album 'Love' was among nominations for Best British Album at 1989 Brit awards (Singles: 74 weeks, Albums: 80 weeks) pos/wks

19 Feb 83	**OBLIVIOUS** *Rough Trade RT 122*	47	6
4 Jun 83	**WALK OUT TO WINTER** *Rough Trade RT 132*	64	4
5 Nov 83	**OBLIVIOUS (re-issue)** *WEA AZTEC 1*	18	11
1 Sep 84	**ALL I NEED IS EVERYTHING / JUMP** *WEA AC 1*	34	6
13 Feb 88	**HOW MEN ARE** *WEA YZ 168*	25	9
23 Apr 88 ●	**SOMEWHERE IN MY HEART** *WEA YZ 181*	3	14
6 Aug 88	**WORKING IN A GOLDMINE** *WEA YZ 199*	31	5
8 Oct 88	**DEEP AND WIDE AND TALL** *WEA YZ 154*	55	3
7 Jul 90	**THE CRYING SCENE** *WEA YZ 492*	70	3
6 Oct 90	**GOOD MORNING BRITAIN** *WEA YZ 521* [1]	19	8
18 Jul 92	**SPANISH HORSES** *WEA YZ 688*	52	3
1 May 93	**DREAM SWEET DREAMS** *WEA YZ 740CD1*	67	2
23 Apr 83	**HIGH LAND HARD RAIN** *Rough Trade ROUGH 47*	22	18
29 Sep 84	**KNIFE** *WEA WX 8*	14	6
21 Nov 87 ●	**LOVE** *WEA WX 128*	10	43
16 Jun 90	**STRAY** *WEA WX 350*	22	7
29 May 93	**DREAMLAND** *WEA 4509924922*	21	2
7 Aug 99	**THE BEST OF AZTEC CAMERA** *Warner.ESP 3984289842*	36	4

[1] Aztec Camera and Mick Jones

'Jump' listed only from 22 Sep 1984 to end of chart run

AZTEC MYSTIC – *See DJ ROLANDO AKA AZTEC MYSTIC*

AZURE *Italy / US, male / female vocal / DJ duo (Singles: 1 week)* pos/wks

25 Apr 98	**MAMA USED TO SAY** *Inferno CDFERN 005*	56	1

AZYMUTH

Brazil, male instrumental group (Singles: 8 weeks) pos/wks

12 Jan 80	**JAZZ CARNIVAL** *Milestone MRC 101*	19	8

Bob AZZAM and His ORCHESTRA and CHORUS

Egypt, bandleader and his orchestra (Singles: 14 weeks) pos/wks

26 May 60	**MUSTAPHA** *Decca F 21235*	23	14

Derek B *UK, male rapper – Derek Boland (Singles: 15 weeks, Albums: 9 weeks)* pos/wks

27 Feb 88	**GOODGROOVE** *Music of Life 7NOTE 12*	16	6
7 May 88	**BAD YOUNG BROTHER** *Tuff Audio DRKB 1*	16	6
2 Jul 88	**WE'VE GOT THE JUICE** *Tuff Audio DRKB 2*	56	3
28 May 88	**BULLET FROM A GUN** *Tuff Audio DRKLP 1*	11	9

Emma B – *See NU CIRCLES featuring Emma B*

Eric B and RAKIM *US, male DJ / rap duo – Eric Barrier and William Griffin Jr (Singles: 26 weeks, Albums: 10 weeks)* pos/wks

7 Nov 87	**PAID IN FULL** *Fourth & Broadway BRW 78*	15	6
20 Feb 88	**MOVE THE CROWD** *Fourth & Broadway BRW 88*	53	2
12 Mar 88	**I KNOW YOU GOT SOUL** *Cooltempo COOL 146*	13	6
2 Jul 88	**FOLLOW THE LEADER** *MCA MCA 1256*	21	5
19 Nov 88	**THE MICROPHONE FIEND** *MCA MCA 1300*	74	1
12 Aug 89	**FRIENDS** *MCA MCA 1352* [1]	21	6
12 Sep 87	**PAID IN FULL** *Fourth & Broadway BRLP 514*	85	4
6 Aug 88	**FOLLOW THE LEADER** *MCA MCG 6031*	25	4
7 Jul 90	**LET THE RHYTHM HIT 'EM** *MCA MCG 6097*	58	1
11 Jul 92	**DON'T SWEAT THE TECHNIQUE** *MCA MCAD 10594*	73	1

[1] Jody Watley with Eric B and Rakim

Howie B *UK, male instrumentalist / producer – Howard Bernstein (Singles: 4 weeks, Albums: 1 week)* pos/wks

19 Jul 97	**ANGELS GO BALD: TOO** *Polydor 5711672*	36	2
18 Oct 97	**SWITCH** *Polydor 5717112*	62	1
11 Apr 98	**TAKE YOUR PARTNER BY THE HAND** *Polydor 5693272* [1]	74	1
9 Aug 97	**TURN THE DARK OFF** *Polydor 5379342*	58	1

[1] Howie B featuring Robbie Robertson

Jazzie B – *See Maxi PRIEST; SOUL II SOUL*

John B *UK, male producer – John B Williams (Singles: 1 week)* pos/wks

22 Jun 02	**UP ALL NIGHT / TAKE CONTROL** *Metalheadz METH 041CD*	58	1

Jon B *US, male vocalist – Jonathan Buck (Singles: 5 weeks)* pos/wks

17 Oct 98	**THEY DON'T KNOW** *Epic 6663975*	32	2
26 May 01	**DON'T TALK** *Epic 6712792*	29	3

Lisa B *US, female vocalist – Lisa Barbuscia (Singles: 9 weeks)* pos/wks

12 Jun 93	**GLAM** *ffrr FCD 210*	49	2
25 Sep 93	**FASCINATED** *ffrr FCD 218*	35	3
8 Jan 94	**YOU AND ME** *ffrr FCD 226*	39	4

Lorna B *UK, female vocalist (Singles: 6 weeks)* pos/wks

28 Jan 95	**DO YOU WANNA PARTY** *Steppin' Out SPONCD 2* [1]	36	3
1 Apr 95	**SWEET DREAMS** *Steppin' Out SPONCD 3* [1]	37	2
15 Mar 97	**FEELS SO GOOD** *Avex UK AVEXCD 53*	69	1

[1] DJ Scott featuring Lorna B

Mark B & BLADE *UK, male rap / production duo – Mark Barnes and Vanik Torosian (Singles: 4 weeks)* pos/wks

10 Feb 01	**THE UNKNOWN** *Wordplay WORDCDS 011*	49	1
26 May 01	**YA DON'T SEE THE SIGNS** *Wordplay WORDCDSE 019*	23	3

Melanie B *UK, female vocalist – Melanie Brown (Singles: 36 weeks, Albums: 2 weeks)* pos/wks

26 Sep 98 ★	**I WANT YOU BACK** *Virgin VSCDT 1716* [1] ■	1	9
10 Jul 99	**WORD UP (re)** *Virgin VSCDT 1735* [2]	14	8
7 Oct 00 ●	**TELL ME** *Virgin VSCDT 1777*	4	7
3 Mar 01 ●	**FEELS SO GOOD** *Virgin VSCDT 1787*	5	8
16 Jun 01	**LULLABY** *Virgin VSCDT 1798*	13	4
21 Oct 00	**HOT** *Virgin CDVX 2918*	28	2

[1] Melanie B featuring Missy 'Misdemeanor' Elliott [2] Melanie G

See also SPICE GIRLS

Sandy B *US, female vocalist (Singles: 8 weeks)* pos/wks

20 Feb 93	**FEEL LIKE SINGIN'** *Nervous SANCD 1*	60	1
18 May 96	**MAKE THE WORLD GO ROUND** *Champion CHAMPCD 322*	73	1
24 May 97	**MAKE THE WORLD GO ROUND (re-mix)** *Champion CHAMPCD 327*	35	2
8 Nov 97	**AIN'T NO NEED TO HIDE** *Champion CHAMPCD 331*	60	1
28 Feb 98	**MAKE THE WORLD GO ROUND (2nd re-mix)** *Champion CHAMPCD 333*	20	3

Stevie B *US, male vocalist – Steven Hill (Singles: 9 weeks)* pos/wks

Date		Title	pos	wks
23 Feb 91	●	**BECAUSE I LOVE YOU (THE POSTMAN SONG)** *Polydor PO 126* ▲	6	9

Tairrie B *US, female rapper (Singles: 2 weeks)* pos/wks

Date		Title	pos	wks
1 Dec 90		**MURDER SHE WROTE** *MCA MCA 1455*	71	2

B B and Q BAND
US, male vocal / instrumental group (Singles: 15 weeks) pos/wks

Date		Title	pos	wks
18 Jul 81		**ON THE BEAT** *Capitol CL 202*	41	5
6 Jul 85		**GENIE** *Cooltempo COOL 110* [1]	40	4
20 Sep 86		**(I'M A) DREAMER** *Cooltempo COOL 132*	35	5
17 Oct 87		**RICOCHET** *Cooltempo COOL 154*	71	1

[1] Brooklyn Bronx and Queens

BBC CONCERT ORCHESTRA, BBC SYMPHONY CHORUS cond. Stephen JACKSON
UK, orchestra, chorus and conductor (Singles: 3 weeks) pos/wks

Date		Title	pos	wks
22 Jun 96		**ODE TO JOY (FROM BEETHOVEN'S SYMPHONY NO.9)** *Virgin VSCDT 1591*	36	3

BBC SYMPHONY ORCHESTRA SINGERS and CHORUS
UK, orchestra / choir and audience (Albums: 7 weeks) pos/wks

Date		Title	pos	wks
4 Oct 69		**LAST NIGHT OF THE PROMS** *Philips SFM 23033* [1]	36	1
11 Dec 82		**HIGHLIGHTS – LAST NIGHT OF THE PROMS '82** *K-Tel NE 1198* [2]	69	5
28 Feb 98		**ELGAR / PAYNE – SYMPHONY NO.3** *NMCD 053* [3]	44	1

[1] BBC Symphony Orchestra Singers and Chorus conducted by Colin Davis [2] BBC Symphony Orchestra Singers and Symphony Chorus conducted by James Loughran [3] BBC Symphony Orchestra conducted by Andrew Davis

BBC WELSH CHORUS – *See Aled JONES*

BBE *France / Italy, male instrumental group (Singles: 20 weeks, Albums: 2 weeks)* pos/wks

Date		Title	pos	wks
28 Sep 96	●	**SEVEN DAYS AND ONE WEEK** *Positiva CDTIV 67*	3	9
29 Mar 97	●	**FLASH** *Positiva CDTIV 73*	5	5
14 Feb 98		**DESIRE** *Positiva CDTIV 87*	19	3
30 May 98		**DEEPER LOVE (SYMPHONIC PARADISE)** *Positiva CDTIV 93*	19	3
28 Feb 98		GAMES *Positiva 4934932*	60	2

BBG *UK, male vocal / instrumental group (Singles: 10 weeks)* pos/wks

Date		Title	pos	wks
28 Apr 90		**SNAPPINESS** *Urban URB 54* [1]	28	5
11 Aug 90		**SOME KIND OF HEAVEN** *Urban URB 59*	65	2
23 Mar 96		**LET THE MUSIC PLAY** *MCA MCSTD 40029* [2]	46	1
18 May 96		**SNAPPINESS (re-mix)** *Hi-Life 5762972*	50	1
5 Jul 97		**JUST BE TONIGHT** *Hi-Life 5738972* [2]	45	1

[1] BBG featuring Dina Taylor [2] BBG featuring Erin

BBM *UK, male vocal / instrumental group (Singles: 2 weeks, Albums: 4 weeks)* pos/wks

Date		Title	pos	wks
6 Aug 94		**WHERE IN THE WORLD** *Virgin VSCD 1495*	57	2
18 Jun 94	●	AROUND THE NEXT DREAM *Virgin CDV 2745*	9	4

See also Ginger BAKER'S AIR FORCE; BAKER-GURVITZ ARMY; Gary MOORE

BBMAK
UK, male vocal group (Singles: 18 weeks, Albums: 3 weeks) pos/wks

Date		Title	pos	wks
28 Aug 99		**BACK HERE** *Telstar CDSTAS 3053*	37	2
24 Feb 01	●	**BACK HERE (re-issue)** *Telstar CDSTAS 3166*	5	10
26 May 01	●	**STILL ON YOUR SIDE** *Telstar CDSTAS 3185*	8	4
16 Nov 02		**OUT OF MY HEART** *Telstar CDSTAS 3281*	36	2
9 Jun 01		SOONER OR LATER *Telstar TCD 3179*	16	3

B BOYS *US, male vocal / instrumental group (Albums: 1 week)* pos/wks

Date		Title	pos	wks
28 Jan 84		CUTTIN' HERBIE *Streetwave X KHAN 501*	90	1

BEF featuring Lalah HATHAWAY *UK, male production duo – Martyn Ware and Ian Craig Marsh and US, female vocalist (Singles: 5 weeks)* pos/wks

Date		Title	pos	wks
27 Jul 91		**FAMILY AFFAIR** *Ten TEN 369*	37	5

B-15 PROJECT featuring Crissy D and Lady G *UK / Jamaica, male production duo and female vocalists (Singles: 10 weeks)* pos/wks

Date		Title	pos	wks
17 Jun 00	●	**GIRLS LIKE US (re)** *Ministry of Sound RELENT 3CDS*	7	10

B-52's *US, male / female vocal / instrumental group (Singles: 61 weeks, Albums: 69 weeks)* pos/wks

Date		Title	pos	wks
11 Aug 79		**ROCK LOBSTER** *Island WIP 6506*	37	5
9 Aug 80		**GIVE ME BACK MY MAN** *Island WIP 6579*	61	3
7 May 83		**(SONG FOR A) FUTURE GENERATION** *Island IS 107*	63	2
10 May 86		**ROCK LOBSTER / PLANET CLAIRE (re-issue)** *Island BFT 1*	12	7
3 Mar 90	●	**LOVE SHACK** *Reprise W 9917*	2	13
19 May 90		**ROAM** *Reprise W 9827*	17	7
18 Aug 90		**CHANNEL Z** *Reprise W 9737*	61	2
20 Jun 92		**GOOD STUFF** *Reprise W 0109*	21	6
12 Sep 92		**TELL IT LIKE IT T-I-IS** *Reprise W 0130*	61	3
9 Jul 94	●	**(MEET) THE FLINTSTONES** *MCA MCSTD 1986* [1]	3	12
30 Jan 99		**LOVE SHACK 99** *Reprise W 0461CD*	66	1
4 Aug 79		B-52'S *Island ILPS 9580*	22	12
13 Sep 80		WILD PLANET *Island ILPS 9622*	18	4
11 Jul 81		THE PARTY MIX ALBUM *Island IPM 1001*	36	5
27 Feb 82		MESOPOTAMIA *EMI ISSP 4006*	18	6
21 May 83		WHAMMY! *Island ILPS 9759*	33	4
8 Aug 87		BOUNCING OFF THE SATELLITES *Island ILPS 9871*	74	2
29 Jul 89	●	COSMIC THING *Reprise WX 283*	8	27
14 Jul 90		THE BEST OF THE B-52'S – DANCE THIS MESS AROUND *Island ILPS 9959*	36	3
11 Jul 92	●	GOOD STUFF *Reprise 7599269432*	8	6

[1] BC-52's

'Planet Claire' listed only from 17 May 1986

BG THE PRINCE OF RAP
Germany, male rapper (Singles: 2 weeks) pos/wks

Date		Title	pos	wks
18 Jan 92		**TAKE CONTROL OF THE PARTY** *Columbia 6576330*	71	2

BK *UK, male producer – Ben Keen (Singles: 9 weeks)* pos/wks

Date		Title	pos	wks
25 Nov 00		**HOOVERS AND HORNS** *Nukleuz NUKC 0185* [1]	57	2
8 Dec 01		**FLASH** *Nukleuz NUKP 0361* [2]	67	1
26 Jan 02		**ERECTION (TAKE IT TO THE TOP)** *Nukleuz NUKC 0352* [3]	48	1
9 Feb 02		**FLASH (re-mix)** *Nukleuz NUKC 0361* [2]	61	1
7 Dec 02		**REVOLUTION** *Nukleuz NUKC 0437*	42	2
16 Aug 03		**KLUB KOLLABORATIONS** *Nukleuz 0524 FNUK*	43	2

[1] Fergie and BK [2] BK and Nick Sentience [3] Cortina featuring BK and Madam Friction

BM DUBS present MR RUMBLE featuring BRASSTOOTH and KEE *UK, male production group (Singles: 2 weeks)* pos/wks

Date		Title	pos	wks
17 Mar 01		**WHOOMP THERE IT IS** *Incentive CENT 16CDS*	32	2

B M EX
UK, male production / instrumental group (Albums: 2 weeks) pos/wks

Date		Title	pos	wks
30 Jan 93		APPOLONIA *Union City UCRCD 14*	17	2

B.M.R. featuring FELICIA *Germany, male producer – Michi Lange featuring female vocalist (Singles: 2 weeks)* pos/wks

Date		Title	pos	wks
1 May 99		**CHECK IT OUT (EVERYBODY)** *AM:PM CDAMPM 120*	29	2

B.M.U. *US / UK, male vocal group (Singles: 2 weeks)* pos/wks

Date		Title	pos	wks
18 Feb 95		**U WILL KNOW** *Mercury MERCD 420*	23	2

B REAL / BUSTA RHYMES / COOLIO / LL COOL J / METHOD MAN
US, male rappers (Singles: 6 weeks) pos/wks

Date		Title	pos	wks
5 Apr 97	●	**HIT 'EM HIGH (MONSTARS' ANTHEM)** *Atlantic A 5449CD*	8	6

BT *US, male producer – Brian Transeau (Singles: 26 weeks, Albums: 5 weeks)* pos/wks

Date		Title / Label	pos	wks
18 Mar 95		**EMBRACING THE SUNSHINE** *East West YZ 895CD*	34	2
16 Sep 95		**LOVING YOU MORE** *Perfecto PERF 110CD* [1]	28	2
10 Feb 96		**LOVING YOU MORE (re-mix)** *Perfecto PERF 117CD* [1]	14	3
9 Nov 96		**BLUE SKIES** *Perfecto PERF 130CD1* [2]	26	2
19 Jul 97		**FLAMING JUNE** *Perfecto PERF 145CD1*	19	4
29 Nov 97		**LOVE, PEACE & GREASE** *Perfecto PERF 153CD1*	41	1
10 Jan 98		**FLAMING JUNE (re-mix)** *Perfecto PERF 157CD1*	28	4
18 Apr 98		**REMEMBER** *Perfecto PERF 160CD1*	27	2
21 Nov 98		**GODSPEED** *Renaissance RENCD 002*	54	1
9 Oct 99		**MERCURY AND SOLACE** *Headspace HEDSCD 001*	38	2
24 Jun 00		**DREAMING** *Headspace HEDSCD 002* [3]	38	2
23 Jun 01		**NEVER GONNA COME BACK DOWN** *Ministry of Sound MOSBT CDS1*	51	1
21 Oct 95		**IMA** *Perfecto 0630123452*	45	4
4 Oct 97		**ESCM** *Perfecto 3984200652*	35	1

[1] BT featuring Vincent Covello [2] BT featuring Tori Amos [3] BT featuring Kirsty Hawkshaw

BT EXPRESS *US, male instrumental / vocal group (Singles: 11 weeks)* pos/wks

Date		Title / Label	pos	wks
29 Mar 75		**EXPRESS** *Pye International 7N 25674*	34	6
26 Jul 80		**DOES IT FEEL GOOD / GIVE UP THE FUNK (LET'S DANCE)** *Calibre CAB 503*	52	4
23 Apr 94		**EXPRESS (re-mix)** *PWL International PWCD 285*	67	1

B BUMBLE and the STINGERS *US, male instrumental group (Singles: 26 weeks)* pos/wks

Date		Title / Label	pos	wks
19 Apr 62	★	**NUT ROCKER** *Top Rank JAR 611*	1	15
3 Jun 72		**NUT ROCKER (re-issue)** *Stateside SS 2203*	19	11

BC-52's – *See B-52's*

B-CREW *US, female vocal group (Singles: 1 week)* pos/wks

Date		Title / Label	pos	wks
20 Sep 97		**PARTAY FEELING** *Positiva CDTIV 78*	45	1

B-MOVIE *UK, male vocal / instrumental group (Singles: 7 weeks)* pos/wks

Date		Title / Label	pos	wks
18 Apr 81		**REMEMBRANCE DAY** *Deram DM 437*	61	3
27 Mar 82		**NOWHERE GIRL** *Some Bizzare B258*	67	4

B-TRIBE *Spain, male / female vocal / instrumental group (Singles: 4 weeks)* pos/wks

Date		Title / Label	pos	wks
25 Sep 93		**!FIESTA FATAL!** *East West YZ 770CD*	64	4

B2K *US, male vocal group (Singles: 15 weeks, Albums: 12 weeks)* pos/wks

Date		Title / Label	pos	wks
24 Aug 02		**UH HUH** *Epic 6729512*	35	2
29 Mar 03		**BUMP, BUMP, BUMP** *Epic 6736452* [1] ▲	11	8
21 Jun 03	●	**GIRLFRIEND** *Epic 6739332*	10	8
18 Oct 03		**UH HUH 2003 (re-mix)** *Epic 6744012*	31	2
5 Apr 03		**PANDEMONIUM** *Epic 5105342*	35	12

[1] B2K featuring P. Diddy

BVSMP *US, male rap / vocal group (Singles: 12 weeks)* pos/wks

Date		Title / Label	pos	wks
23 Jul 88	●	**I NEED YOU** *Debut DEBT 3044*	3	12

B*WITCHED (471 Top 500)

Ireland's most successful female group, Edele and Keavy Lynch, Sinead O'Carroll and Lindsay Armaou. Youngest girl group to top the chart. They sold more than one million copies of their debut album in the US and were the first act to enter at No.1 with their first four singles. Group split in Sept 2002. Best-selling single: 'C'est la vie' 850,500 (Singles: 98 weeks, Albums: 48 weeks) pos/wks

Date		Title / Label	pos	wks
6 Jun 98	★	**C'EST LA VIE** *Glow Worm / Epic 6660532* ■	1	19
3 Oct 98	★	**ROLLERCOASTER** *Glow Worm / Epic 6664752* ■	1	15
19 Dec 98	★	**TO YOU I BELONG (re)** *Glow Worm / Epic 6667712* ■	1	14
27 Mar 99	★	**BLAME IT ON THE WEATHERMAN** *Glow Worm / Epic 6670335* ■	1	9
10 Apr 99	●	**THANK ABBA FOR THE MUSIC** *Epic ABCD 1* [1]	4	13
16 Oct 99	●	**JESSE HOLD ON (re)** *Glow Worm / Epic 6679612*	4	12
18 Dec 99		**I SHALL BE THERE** *Glow Worm / Epic 683332* [2]	13	9
8 Apr 00		**JUMP DOWN (re)** *Glow Worm / Epic 6691282*	16	7
24 Oct 98	●	**B*WITCHED** *Epic 4917042*	3	36
30 Oct 99	●	**AWAKE AND BREATHE** *Epic 4960792*	5	12

[1] Steps, Tina Cousins, Cleopatra, B*Witched, Billie [2] B*Witched featuring Ladysmith Black Mambazo

BABE INSTINCT *UK, female vocal group (Singles: 2 weeks)* pos/wks

Date		Title / Label	pos	wks
16 Jan 99		**DISCO BABES FROM OUTER SPACE** *Positiva CDTIV 103*	21	2

BABE TEAM *UK, female vocal group (Singles: 2 weeks)* pos/wks

Date		Title / Label	pos	wks
8 Jun 02		**OVER THERE** *Edel 0140655ERE*	45	2

BABES IN TOYLAND *US, female vocal / instrumental group (Albums: 3 weeks)* pos/wks

Date		Title / Label	pos	wks
5 Sep 92		**FONTANELLE** *Southern 185012*	24	2
3 Jul 93		**PAINKILLERS** *Southern 185122*	53	1

Alice BABS *Sweden, female vocalist (Singles: 1 week)* pos/wks

Date		Title / Label	pos	wks
15 Aug 63		**AFTER YOU'VE GONE** *Fontana TF 409*	43	1

BABY ANIMALS *Australia, male vocal / instrumental group (Albums: 1 week)* pos/wks

Date		Title / Label	pos	wks
14 Mar 92		**BABY ANIMALS** *Imago PD 90580*	70	1

BABY BUMPS *UK, male / female vocal / instrumental duo – Sean Casey and Lisa Millett (Singles: 6 weeks)* pos/wks

Date		Title / Label	pos	wks
8 Aug 98		**BURNING** *Delirious DELICD 10*	17	4
26 Feb 00		**I GOT THIS FEELING** *Sound of Ministry MOSCDS 137*	22	2

BABY D *UK, male / female vocal / instrumental group (Singles: 45 weeks, Albums: 5 weeks)* pos/wks

Date		Title / Label	pos	wks
18 Dec 93		**DESTINY** *Production House PNC 057*	69	1
23 Jul 94		**CASANOVA** *Production House PNC 065*	67	1
19 Nov 94	★	**LET ME BE YOUR FANTASY** *Systematic SYSCD 4*	1	14
3 Jun 95	●	**(EVERYBODY'S GOT TO LEARN SOMETIME) I NEED YOUR LOVING** *Systematic SYSCD 11*	3	12
13 Jan 96	●	**SO PURE** *Systematic SYSCD 21*	3	7
6 Apr 96		**TAKE ME TO HEAVEN** *Systematic SYSCD 26*	15	5
2 Sep 00		**LET ME BE YOUR FANTASY (re-mix)** *Systematic SYSCD 35*	16	5
10 Feb 96	●	**DELIVERANCE** *Systematic 8287202*	5	5

BABY DC featuring IMAJIN *US, male rapper – Derrick Coleman Jr and vocal group (Singles: 1 week)* pos/wks

Date		Title / Label	pos	wks
24 Apr 99		**BOUNCE, ROCK, SKATE, ROLL** *Jive 0522142*	45	1

BABY FORD *UK, male instrumentalist – keyboards (Singles: 16 weeks)* pos/wks

Date		Title / Label	pos	wks
10 Sep 88		**OOCHY KOOCHY (F.U. BABY YEAH YEAH)** *Rhythm King 7BFORD 1*	58	6
24 Dec 88		**CHIKKI CHIKKI AHH AHH (re)** *Rhythm King 7BFORD 2*	54	4
17 Jun 89		**CHILDREN OF THE REVOLUTION** *Rhythm King 7BFORD 4*	53	4
17 Feb 90		**BEACH BUMP** *Rhythm King 7BFORD 6*	68	2

BABY JUNE *UK, male vocalist – Tim Hegarty (Singles: 1 week)* pos/wks

Date		Title / Label	pos	wks
15 Aug 92		**HEY! WHAT'S YOUR NAME** *Arista 115271*	75	1

BABY O *US, male / female vocal / instrumental group (Singles: 5 weeks)* pos/wks

Date		Title / Label	pos	wks
26 Jul 80		**IN THE FOREST** *Calibre CAB 505*	46	5

BABY ROOTS *UK, male vocalist (Singles: 1 week)* pos/wks

Date		Title / Label	pos	wks
1 Aug 92		**ROCK ME BABY** *ZYX ZYX 68027*	71	1

BABYBIRD *UK, male vocalist / instrumentalist (Singles: 35 weeks, Albums: 14 weeks)*

Date	Title / Label	pos	wks
10 Aug 96	**GOODNIGHT** *Echo ECSCD 24*	**28**	2
12 Oct 96	● **YOU'RE GORGEOUS** *Echo ECSD 26*	**3**	16
1 Feb 97	**CANDY GIRL** *Echo ECSCD 31*	**14**	3
17 May 97	**CORNERSHOP** *Echo ECSCD 33*	**37**	2
9 May 98	**BAD OLD MAN** *Echo ECSCD 60*	**31**	2
22 Aug 98	**IF YOU'LL BE MINE** *Echo ECSCX 65*	**28**	4
27 Feb 99	**BACK TOGETHER** *Echo ECSCD 73*	**22**	3
25 Mar 00	**THE F-WORD** *Echo ECSCD 92*	**35**	2
3 Jun 00	**OUT OF SIGHT** *Echo ECSCD 97*	**58**	1
2 Nov 96	● **UGLY BEAUTIFUL** *Echo ECHCD 11*	**9**	12
5 Sep 98	**THERE'S SOMETHING GOING ON** *Echo ECHCD 24*	**28**	2

BABYFACE *US, male vocalist – Kenneth Edmonds (Singles: 23 weeks, Albums: 5 weeks)*

Date	Title / Label	pos	wks
9 Jul 94	**ROCK BOTTOM** *Epic 6601832*	**50**	4
1 Oct 94	**WHEN CAN I SEE YOU** *Epic 6606592*	**35**	3
9 Nov 96	**THIS IS FOR THE LOVER IN YOU** *Epic 6639352*	**12**	5
8 Mar 97	**EVERYTIME I CLOSE MY EYES** *Epic 6642492*	**13**	4
19 Jul 97	● **HOW COME, HOW LONG** *Epic 6646202* [1]	**10**	5
25 Oct 97	**SUNSHINE** *Northwestside 74321528702* [2]	**25**	2
16 Nov 96	**THE DAY** *Epic 4853682*	**34**	5

[1] Babyface featuring Stevie Wonder [2] Jay-Z featuring Babyface and Foxy Brown

BABYLON ZOO *UK, male vocalist / multi-instrumentalist – Jas Mann (Singles: 20 weeks, Albums: 5 weeks)*

Date	Title / Label	pos	wks
27 Jan 96	★ **SPACEMAN** *EMI CDEM 416* ◆ ■	**1**	14
27 Apr 96	**ANIMAL ARMY** *EMI CDEM 425*	**17**	3
5 Oct 96	**THE BOY WITH THE X-RAY EYES** *EMI CDEMS 440*	**32**	2
6 Feb 99	**ALL THE MONEY'S GONE** *EMI CDEM 519*	**46**	1
17 Feb 96	● **THE BOY WITH THE X-RAY EYES** *EMI CDEMC 3742*	**6**	5

BABYS *US / UK, male vocal / instrumental group – includes John Waite (Singles: 3 weeks)*

Date	Title / Label	pos	wks
21 Jan 78	**ISN'T IT TIME** *Chrysalis CHS 2173*	**45**	3

See also John WAITE

BACCARA *Spain, female vocal duo – Maria Mendiola and Mayte Mateos (Singles: 25 weeks, Albums: 6 weeks)*

Date	Title / Label	pos	wks
17 Sep 77	★ **YES SIR, I CAN BOOGIE** *RCA PB 5526*	**1**	16
14 Jan 78	● **SORRY I'M A LADY** *RCA PB 5555*	**8**	9
4 Mar 78	**BACCARA** *RCA PL 28316*	**26**	6

Burt BACHARACH *US, male instrumentalist – piano (Singles: 12 weeks, Albums: 46 weeks)*

Date	Title / Label	pos	wks
20 May 65	● **TRAINS AND BOATS AND PLANES** *London HL 9968* [1]	**4**	11
1 May 99	**TOLEDO** *Mercury 8709652* [2]	**72**	1
22 May 65	● **HIT MAKER – BURT BACHARACH** *London HAR 8233*	**3**	18
28 Nov 70	**REACH OUT** *A&M AMLS 908*	**52**	3
27 Mar 71	● **PORTRAIT IN MUSIC** *A&M AMLS 2010*	**5**	23
10 Oct 98	**PAINTED FROM MEMORY** *Mercury 5380022* [1]	**32**	2

[1] Burt Bacharach, His Orchestra and Chorus [2] Elvis Costello / Burt Bacharach
[1] Elvis Costello with Burt Bacharach

BACHELORS (203 Top 500) *Irish vocal / instrumental trio from Dublin who were one of the few popular non-rock groups of the 1960s: brothers Declan and Con Cluskey and John Stokes. The first trio to top the UK singles chart, they had hits on both sides of the Atlantic with revivals of popular pre-rock ballads (Singles: 187 weeks, Albums: 102 weeks)*

Date	Title / Label	pos	wks
24 Jan 63	● **CHARMAINE** *Decca F 11559*	**6**	19
4 Jul 63	**FARAWAY PLACES** *Decca F 11666*	**36**	3
29 Aug 63	**WHISPERING** *Decca F 11712*	**18**	10
23 Jan 64	★ **DIANE** *Decca F 11799*	**1**	19
19 Mar 64	● **I BELIEVE** *Decca F 11857*	**2**	17
4 Jun 64	● **RAMONA** *Decca F 11910*	**4**	13
13 Aug 64	● **I WOULDN'T TRADE YOU FOR THE WORLD** *Decca F 11949*	**4**	16
3 Dec 64	● **NO ARMS CAN EVER HOLD YOU** *Decca F 12034*	**7**	12
1 Apr 65	**TRUE LOVE FOR EVER MORE** *Decca F 12108*	**34**	6
20 May 65	● **MARIE** *Decca F 12156*	**9**	12
28 Oct 65	**IN THE CHAPEL IN THE MOONLIGHT** *Decca F 12256*	**27**	10
6 Jan 66	**HELLO, DOLLY!** *Decca F 12309*	**38**	4
17 Mar 66	● **THE SOUND OF SILENCE** *Decca F 12351*	**3**	13
7 Jul 66	**CAN I TRUST YOU** *Decca F 12417*	**26**	7
1 Dec 66	**WALK WITH FAITH IN YOUR HEART** *Decca F 22523*	**21**	9
6 Apr 67	**OH HOW I MISS YOU** *Decca F 22592*	**30**	8
5 Jul 67	**MARTA** *Decca F 22634*	**20**	9
27 Jun 64	● **THE BACHELORS AND 16 GREAT SONGS** *Decca LK 4614*	**2**	44
9 Oct 65	**MORE GREAT SONG HITS FROM THE BACHELORS** *Decca LK 4721*	**15**	6
9 Jul 66	**HITS OF THE SIXTIES** *Decca TXL 102*	**12**	9
5 Nov 66	**BACHELORS' GIRLS** *Decca LK 4827*	**24**	7
1 Jul 67	**GOLDEN ALL TIME HITS** *Decca SKL 4849*	**19**	7
14 Jun 69	● **WORLD OF THE BACHELORS** *Decca SPA 2*	**8**	18
23 Aug 69	**WORLD OF THE BACHELORS VOLUME 2** *Decca SPA 22*	**11**	7
22 Dec 79	**25 GOLDEN GREATS** *Warwick WW 5068*	**38**	4

Randy BACHMAN – *See BACHMAN-TURNER OVERDRIVE; BUS STOP; IRONHORSE*

Tal BACHMAN *Canada, male vocalist / guitarist (Singles: 2 weeks)*

Date	Title / Label	pos	wks
30 Oct 99	**SHE'S SO HIGH** *Columbia 6679932*	**30**	2

BACHMAN-TURNER OVERDRIVE *Canada, male vocal / instrumental group (Singles: 18 weeks, Albums: 13 weeks)*

Date	Title / Label	pos	wks
16 Nov 74	● **YOU AIN'T SEEN NOTHING YET** *Mercury 6167 025* ▲	**2**	12
1 Feb 75	**ROLL ON DOWN THE HIGHWAY** *Mercury 6167 071*	**22**	6
14 Dec 74	**NOT FRAGILE** *Mercury 9100 007* ▲	**12**	13

BACK TO THE PLANET *UK, male / female vocal / instrumental group (Singles: 2 weeks, Albums: 2 weeks)*

Date	Title / Label	pos	wks
10 Apr 93	**TEENAGE TURTLES** *Parallel LLLCD 3*	**52**	1
4 Sep 93	**DAYDREAM** *Parallel LLLCD 8*	**52**	1
18 Sep 93	**MIND AND SOUL COLLABORATORS** *Parallel ALLCD 2*	**32**	2

BACKBEAT BAND *US, male vocal / instrumental group (Singles: 5 weeks, Albums: 2 weeks)*

Date	Title / Label	pos	wks
26 Mar 94	**MONEY (re)** *Virgin VSCDX 1489*	**48**	4
14 May 94	**PLEASE MR POSTMAN** *Virgin VSCDX 1502*	**69**	1
16 Apr 94	**BACKBEAT (FILM SOUNDTRACK)** *Virgin CDV 2729*	**39**	2

BACKBEAT DISCIPLES – *See Arthur BAKER*

BACKROOM BOYS – *See Frank IFIELD*

BACKSTREET BOYS (181 Top 500) *American boy band vocal quintet (Brian Littrell, Nick Carter, A J McLean, Howie Dorough, Kevin Richardson) created teen hysteria in Europe before becoming 1999's top-selling act in their homeland. Their 13 consecutive UK Top 10 entries are a record for a US group (Singles: 161 weeks, Albums: 146 weeks)*

Date	Title / Label	pos	wks
28 Oct 95	**WE'VE GOT IT GOIN' ON** *Jive JIVECD 386*	**54**	1
16 Dec 95	**I'LL NEVER BREAK YOUR HEART** *Jive JIVECD 389*	**42**	3
1 Jun 96	**GET DOWN (YOU'RE THE ONE FOR ME)** *Jive JIVECD 394*	**14**	8
24 Aug 96	● **WE'VE GOT IT GOIN' ON (re-issue)** *Jive JIVECD 400*	**3**	7
16 Nov 96	● **I'LL NEVER BREAK YOUR HEART (re-issue)** *Jive JIVERCD 406*	**8**	8
18 Jan 97	● **QUIT PLAYING GAMES (WITH MY HEART)** *Jive JIVECD 409*	**2**	10
29 Mar 97	● **ANYWHERE FOR YOU (2re)** *Jive JIVECD 416*	**4**	8
2 Aug 97	● **EVERYBODY (BACKSTREET'S BACK)** *Jive JIVECD 426*	**3**	11
11 Oct 97	● **AS LONG AS YOU LOVE ME** *Jive JIVECD 434*	**3**	19
14 Feb 98	● **ALL I HAVE TO GIVE** *Jive JIVECD 445*	**2**	12
15 May 99	★ **I WANT IT THAT WAY** *Jive 0523392* ■	**1**	14
30 Oct 99	● **LARGER THAN LIFE** *Jive 0550562*	**5**	14
26 Feb 00	**SHOW ME THE MEANING OF BEING LONELY (import)** *Jive IMPORT 9250082*	**66**	1
4 Mar 00	● **SHOW ME THE MEANING OF BEING LONELY (re)** *Jive 9250082*	**3**	11
24 Jun 00	● **THE ONE (re)** *Jive 9250662*	**8**	8

18 Nov 00 ● **SHAPE OF MY HEART** *Jive 9251442* 4 9
24 Feb 01 ● **THE CALL** *Jive 9251702* 8 5
7 Jul 01 **MORE THAN THAT** *Jive 9252342* 12 5
12 Jan 02 ● **DROWNING** *Jive 9252882* 4 7
21 Sep 96 **BACKSTREET BOYS** *Jive CHIP 169* 12 19
23 Aug 97 ● **BACKSTREET'S BACK** *Jive CHIP 186* 2 44
29 May 99 ● **MILLENNIUM** *Jive 523222* ▲....2 56
2 Dec 00 **BLACK & BLUE** *Jive 9221172* ▲ 13 9
10 Nov 01 ● **GREATEST HITS – CHAPTER ONE** *Jive 9222672* 5 18

BACKYARD DOG

UK, male vocal / production group (Singles: 6 weeks) pos/wks

7 Jul 01 **BADDEST RUFFEST (re)** *East West EW 233CD* 15 6

BAD ANGEL – *See BOOTH and the BAD ANGEL*

BAD BOYS INC

UK, male vocal group (Singles: 31 weeks, Albums: 6 weeks) pos/wks

14 Aug 93 **DON'T TALK ABOUT LOVE** *A&M 5803412* 19 5
2 Oct 93 **WHENEVER YOU NEED SOMEONE** *A&M 5804032* 26 3
11 Dec 93 **WALKING ON AIR** *A&M 5804692* 24 6
21 May 94 ● **MORE TO THIS WORLD** *A&M 5806072* 8 7
23 Jul 94 **TAKE ME AWAY (I'LL FOLLOW YOU)** *A&M 5806912* 15 6
17 Sep 94 **LOVE HERE I COME** *A&M 5807752* 26 4
18 Jun 94 **BAD BOYS INC** *A&M 5402002*....13 6

BAD COMPANY *UK, male vocal / instrumental group (Singles: 23 weeks, Albums: 87 weeks)* pos/wks

1 Jun 74 **CAN'T GET ENOUGH** *Island WIP 6191* 15 8
22 Mar 75 **GOOD LOVIN' GONE BAD** *Island WIP 6223* 31 6
30 Aug 75 **FEEL LIKE MAKIN' LOVE** *Island WIP 6242* 20 9
15 Jun 74 ● **BAD COMPANY** *Island ILPS 9279* ▲....3 25
12 Apr 75 ● **STRAIGHT SHOOTER** *Island ILPS 9304*....3 27
21 Feb 76 ● **RUN WITH THE PACK** *Island ILPS 9346* 4 12
19 Mar 77 **BURNIN' SKY** *Island ILPS 9441* 17 8
17 Mar 79 ● **DESOLATION ANGELS** *Swansong SSK 59408*....10 9
28 Aug 82 **ROUGH DIAMONDS** *Swansong SSK 59419*....15 6

BAD COMPANY *UK, male production group (Singles: 5 weeks)* pos/wks

9 Mar 02 **SPACEHOPPER / TONIGHT** *Ram RAMM 37* 56 1
4 May 02 **RUSH HOUR / BLIND** *BC Recordings BCRUK 002CD* 59 1
15 Mar 03 **MO' FIRE** *BC Recordings BCRUK 003CD* 24 3

See also DJ FRESH; FRESH BC

BAD ENGLISH *UK / US, male vocal / instrumental group (Singles: 3 weeks, Albums: 2 weeks)* pos/wks

25 Nov 89 **WHEN I SEE YOU SMILE** *Epic 655347 1* ▲ 61 3
16 Sep 89 **BAD ENGLISH** *Epic 4634471*....74 1
19 Oct 91 **BACKLASH** *Epic 4685691* 64 1

BAD HABIT BOYS

Germany, male production duo (Singles: 1 week) pos/wks

1 Jul 00 **WEEKEND** *Inferno CDFERN 28* 41 1

BAD MANNERS 437 Top 500

Good-time ska band fronted by shaven-headed Buster Bloodvessel (b. Douglas Trendle, 6 Sep 1958, London). Spent more weeks on UK chart in 1980 (45) than anyone bar Madness. Even after the hits, they remained a popular live attraction (Singles: 111 weeks, Albums: 44 weeks) pos/wks

1 Mar 80 **NE-NE NA-NA NA-NA NU-NU** *Magnet MAG 164* 28 14
14 Jun 80 **LIP UP FATTY** *Magnet MAG 175* 15 14
27 Sep 80 ● **SPECIAL BREW** *Magnet MAG 180* 3 13
6 Dec 80 **LORRAINE** *Magnet MAG 181* 21 12
28 Mar 81 **JUST A FEELING** *Magnet MAG 187* 13 9
27 Jun 81 ● **CAN CAN** *Magnet MAG 190* 3 13
26 Sep 81 ● **WALKING IN THE SUNSHINE** *Magnet MAG 197* 10 9
21 Nov 81 **BUONA SERA** *Magnet MAG 211* 34 9
1 May 82 **GOT NO BRAINS** *Magnet MAG 216* 44 5
31 Jul 82 ● **MY GIRL LOLLIPOP (MY BOY LOLLIPOP)** *Magnet MAG 232* 9 7
30 Oct 82 **SAMSON AND DELILAH** *Magnet MAG 236* 58 3
14 May 83 **THAT'LL DO NICELY** *Magnet MAG 243* 49 3
26 Apr 80 **SKA 'N' B** *Magnet MAG 5033* 34 13
29 Nov 80 **LOONEE TUNES** *Magnet MAG 5038*....36 12
24 Oct 81 **GOSH IT'S BAD MANNERS** *Magnet MAGL 5043*....18 12
27 Nov 82 **FORGING AHEAD** *Magnet MAGL 5050*....78 1
7 May 83 **THE HEIGHT OF BAD MANNERS** *Telstar STAR 2229*....23 6

BAD MEETS EVIL featuring EMINEM & ROYCE DA 5'9

US, male producer and male rappers (Singles: 1 week) pos/wks

1 Sep 01 **SCARY MOVIES** *Mole UK MOLEUK 045* 63 1

See also EMINEM

BAD NEWS

UK, male vocal group (Singles: 5 weeks, Albums: 1 week) pos/wks

12 Sep 87 **BOHEMIAN RHAPSODY** *EMI EM 24* 44 5
24 Oct 87 **BAD NEWS** *EMI EMC 3535*....69 1

BAD RELIGION

US, male vocal / instrumental group (Singles: 2 weeks) pos/wks

11 Feb 95 **21ST CENTURY (DIGITAL BOY)** *Columbia 6611435* 41 2

BAD SEEDS – *See Nick CAVE and the BAD SEEDS*

BAD YARD CLUB – *See David MORALES*

Angelo BADALAMENTI with Julee CRUISE and VARIOUS ARTISTS

US, male composer and female vocalist (Albums: 25 weeks) pos/wks

17 Nov 90 **MUSIC FROM 'TWIN PEAKS'** *Warner Bros. 7599263161* 27 25

See also BOOTH and the BAD ANGEL; ORBITAL

Wally BADAROU

France, male instrumentalist – keyboards (Singles: 6 weeks) pos/wks

19 Oct 85 **CHIEF INSPECTOR** *Fourth & Broadway BRW 37*....46 6

BADDIEL and SKINNER and THE LIGHTNING SEEDS

UK, male vocal group – David Baddiel, Frank Skinner (aka Christopher Collins) and The Lightning Seeds (Singles: 34 weeks) pos/wks

1 Jun 96 ★ **THREE LIONS (THE OFFICIAL SONG OF THE ENGLAND FOOTBALL TEAM)** *Epic 6632732* [1] ■ 1 15
20 Jun 98 ★ **THREE LIONS '98** *Epic 6660982* [1] ■ 1 13
15 Jun 02 **THREE LIONS '98 (re) (re-issue)** *Epic 6728152* [2] 16 6

[1] Baddiel and Skinner and the Lightning Seeds [2] Baddiel, Skinner and The Lightning Seeds

BADFELLAS featuring CK

UK, production group and Kenya, female vocalist (Singles: 1 week) pos/wks

15 Feb 03 **SOC IT TO ME** *Serious SER 053CD* 55 1

BADFINGER

UK, male vocal / instrumental group (Singles: 34 weeks) pos/wks

10 Jan 70 ● **COME AND GET IT** *Apple 20*....4 11
9 Jan 71 ● **NO MATTER WHAT** *Apple 31* 5 12
29 Jan 72 ● **DAY AFTER DAY** *Apple 40* 10 11

BADLANDS

UK, male vocal / instrumental group (Albums: 3 weeks) pos/wks

24 Jun 89 **BADLANDS** *WEA 7819661* 39 2
22 Jun 91 **VOODOO HIGHWAY** *Atlantic 7567822511* 74 1

BADLY DRAWN BOY *UK, male vocalist / producer / instrumentalist – Damon Gough (Singles: 26 weeks, Albums: 85 weeks)* pos/wks

4 Sep 99 **ONCE AROUND THE BLOCK** *Twisted Nerve / XL Recordings TNXL 003CD* 46 2
17 Jun 00 **ANOTHER PEARL** *Twisted Nerve / XL Recordings TNXL 004CD* 41 1

16 Sep 00 DISILLUSION *Twisted Nerve / XL Recordings TNXL 005CD* 26 2
25 Nov 00 ONCE AROUND THE BLOCK (re-issue) *Twisted Nerve / XL Recordings TNXL 009CD* 27 2
19 May 01 PISSING IN THE WIND *Twisted Nerve / XL Recordings TNXL 010CD* 22 2
6 Apr 02 SILENT SIGH *Twisted Nerve / XL Recordings TNXL 012CD* 16 7
22 Jun 02 SOMETHING TO TALK ABOUT *Twisted Nerve / XL Recordings TNXL 014CD* 28 2
26 Oct 02 ● YOU WERE RIGHT *Twisted Nerve / XL Recordings TNXL 015CD* 9 3
18 Jan 03 BORN AGAIN *Twisted Nerve / XL Recordings TNXL 016CD* 16 3
3 May 03 ALL POSSIBILITIES *Twisted Nerve / XL Recordings TNXL 017CD* 24 2
8 Jul 00 THE HOUR OF BEWILDERBEAST *XL Recordings TNXLCD 133* 13 47
20 Apr 02 ● ABOUT A BOY (FILM SOUNDTRACK) *Twisted Nerve TNXLCD 152* 6 18
16 Nov 02 ● HAVE YOU FED THE FISH? *Twisted Nerve TNXLCD 156* 10 20

BADMAN *UK, male producer – Julian Brettle (Singles: 3 weeks)* pos/wks

2 Feb 91 MAGIC STYLE *Citybeat CBE 759* 61 3

Erykah BADU *US, female vocalist – Erica Wright (Singles: 17 weeks, Albums: 25 weeks)* pos/wks

19 Apr 97 ON & ON *Universal UND 561117* 12 4
14 Jun 97 NEXT LIFETIME *Universal UND 56132* 30 3
29 Nov 97 APPLE TREE *Universal UND 56150* 47 1
11 Jul 98 ONE *Elektra E 3833CD1* [1] 23 3
6 Mar 99 YOU GOT ME *MCA MCSTD 48110* [2] 31 2
15 Sep 01 SWEET BABY *Epic 6718822* [3] 23 4
1 Mar 97 BADUIZM *MCA UND 53027* 17 25

[1] Busta Rhymes featuring Erykah Badu [2] Roots featuring Erykah Badu [3] Macy Gray featuring Erykah Badu

Joan BAEZ *US, female vocalist / instrumentalist – guitar (Singles: 47 weeks, Albums: 88 weeks)* pos/wks

6 May 65 WE SHALL OVERCOME *Fontana TF 564* 26 10
8 Jul 65 ● THERE BUT FOR FORTUNE *Fontana TF 587* 8 12
2 Sep 65 IT'S ALL OVER NOW, BABY BLUE *Fontana TF 604* 22 8
23 Dec 65 FAREWELL ANGELINA (re) *Fontana TF 639* 35 4
28 Jul 66 PACK UP YOUR SORROWS *Fontana TF 727* 50 1
9 Oct 71 ● THE NIGHT THEY DROVE OLD DIXIE DOWN *Vanguard VS 35138* 6 12
18 Jul 64 ● JOAN BAEZ IN CONCERT VOLUME 2 *Fontana TFL 6033* 8 19
15 May 65 ● JOAN BAEZ 5 *Fontana TFL 6043* 3 27
19 Jun 65 ● JOAN BAEZ *Fontana TFL 6002* 9 13
27 Nov 65 ● FAREWELL ANGELINA *Fontana TFL 6058* 5 23
19 Jul 69 JOAN BAEZ ON VANGUARD *Vanguard SVXL 100* 15 5
3 Apr 71 FIRST TEN YEARS *Vanguard 6635 003* 41 1

BAHA MEN *Bahamas, male vocal group (Singles: 35 weeks)* pos/wks

14 Oct 00 ● WHO LET THE DOGS OUT *Edel 0115425 ERE* 2 23
3 Feb 01 YOU ALL DAT *Edel 0124855 ERE* 14 5
13 Jul 02 MOVE IT LIKE THIS *S-Curve / EMI CDEM 615* 16 7

'You All Dat' features vocal by Imani Coppola

Carol BAILEY *UK, female vocalist (Singles: 2 weeks)* pos/wks

25 Feb 95 FEEL IT *Multiply CDMULTY 3* 41 2

Imogen BAILEY – *See Michael WOODS featuring Imogen BAILEY*

Philip BAILEY *US, male vocalist (Singles: 20 weeks, Albums: 17 weeks)* pos/wks

9 Mar 85 ★ EASY LOVER *CBS A 4915* [1] 1 12
18 May 85 WALKING ON THE CHINESE WALL *CBS A 6202* 34 8
30 Mar 85 CHINESE WALL *CBS 26161* 29 17

[1] Philip Bailey (duet with Phil Collins)

See also EARTH WIND AND FIRE

Merril BAINBRIDGE *Australia, female vocalist (Singles: 1 week)* pos/wks

7 Dec 96 MOUTH *Gotham 74321431012* 51 1

Adrian BAKER and the TONICS *UK, male vocalist (Singles: 8 weeks)* pos/wks

19 Jul 75 ● SHERRY *Magnet MAG 34* 10 8

See also GIDEA PARK

Anita BAKER *US, female vocalist (Singles: 22 weeks, Albums: 83 weeks)* pos/wks

15 Nov 86 SWEET LOVE *Elektra EKR 44* 13 10
31 Jan 87 CAUGHT UP IN THE RAPTURE *Elektra EKR 49* 51 5
8 Oct 88 GIVING YOU THE BEST THAT I GOT *Elektra EKR 79* 55 3
30 Jun 90 TALK TO ME *Elektra EKR 111* 68 2
17 Sep 94 BODY & SOUL *Elektra EKR 190CD* 48 2
3 May 86 RAPTURE *Elektra EKT 37* 13 47
29 Oct 88 ● GIVING YOU THE BEST THAT I GOT *Elektra EKT 49* ▲ 9 20
14 Jul 90 ● COMPOSITIONS *Elektra EKT 72* 7 9
24 Sep 94 RHYTHM OF LOVE *Elektra 7559615552* 14 5
1 Jun 02 SWEET LOVE – THE VERY BEST OF ANITA BAKER *Atlantic 8122736032* 49 2

Arthur BAKER *US, male producer / multi-instrumentalist (Singles: 8 weeks)* pos/wks

20 May 89 IT'S YOUR TIME *Breakout USA 654* [1] 64 2
21 Oct 89 THE MESSAGE IS LOVE *Breakout USA 668* [2] 38 5
30 Nov 02 CONFUSION (RE-MIX) *Whacked WACKT 002CD* [3] 64 1

[1] Arthur Baker featuring Shirley Lewis [2] Arthur Baker and the Backbeat Disciples featuring Al Green [3] Arthur Baker vs New Order

See also Wally JUMP Jr and the CRIMINAL ELEMENT

Hylda BAKER and Arthur MULLARD *UK, female / male actors / vocal duo (Singles: 6 weeks)* pos/wks

9 Sep 78 YOU'RE THE ONE THAT I WANT *Pye 7N 46121* 22 6

George BAKER SELECTION *Holland, male / female vocal / instrumental group (Singles: 10 weeks)* pos/wks

6 Sep 75 ● PALOMA BLANCA *Warner Bros. K 16541* 10 10

Ginger BAKER'S AIR FORCE *UK male vocal / instrumental band (Albums: 1 week)* pos/wks

13 Jun 70 GINGER BAKER'S AIR FORCE *Polydor 266 2001* 37 1

See also BAKER-GURVITZ ARMY; BBM; BLIND FAITH

BAKER-GURVITZ ARMY *UK, male vocal / instrumental group (Albums: 5 weeks)* pos/wks

22 Feb 75 BAKER-GURVITZ ARMY *Vertigo 9103 201* 22 5

See also BBM; BLIND FAITH, Ginger BAKER'S AIR FORCE

BAKSHELF DOG *UK, male bulldog vocalist – Churchill (Singles: 2 weeks)* pos/wks

21 Dec 02 NO LIMITS *WVC CDCHURCH 1* 51 2

BALAAM AND THE ANGEL *UK, male vocal / instrumental group (Singles: 2 weeks, Albums: 2 weeks)* pos/wks

29 Mar 86 SHE KNOWS *Virgin VS 842* 70 2
16 Aug 86 THE GREATEST STORY EVER TOLD *Virgin V 2377* 67 2

Long John BALDRY *UK, male vocalist (Singles: 36 weeks)* pos/wks

8 Nov 67 ★ LET THE HEARTACHES BEGIN *Pye 7N 17385* 1 13
28 Aug 68 WHEN THE SUN COMES SHINING THRU *Pye 7N 17593* 29 7
23 Oct 68 MEXICO *Pye 7N 17563* 15 8
29 Jan 69 IT'S TOO LATE NOW *Pye 7N 17664* 21 8

BALEARIC BILL *Belgium / Holland, male production duo – Johan Gielen and Sven Maes (Singles: 2 weeks)* pos/wks

2 Oct 99 DESTINATION SUNSHINE *Xtravaganza XTRAV 3CDS* 36 2

See also AIRSCAPE; BLUE BAMBOO; CUBIC 22; TRANSFORMER 2; SVENSON and GIELEN

Edward BALL

UK, male vocalist (Singles: 2 weeks) pos/wks

20 Jul 96	**THE MILL HILL SELF HATE CLUB** *Creation CRESCD 233*	57	1
22 Feb 97	**LOVE IS BLUE** *Creation CRESCD 244*	59	1

Kenny BALL and his JAZZMEN (352 Top 500)

Top UK trad jazz bandleader, b. 22 May 1930, Essex. His Dixieland band was at the forefront of the early 1960s jazz revival. Their biggest hit, 'Midnight in Moscow', reached runner-up spot on both sides of the Atlantic. (Singles: 136 weeks, Albums: 50 weeks) pos/wks

23 Feb 61	**SAMANTHA** *Pye Jazz Today 7NJ 2040* [1]	13	15
11 May 61	**I STILL LOVE YOU ALL** *Pye Jazz 7NJ 2042*	24	6
31 Aug 61	**SOMEDAY (YOU'LL BE SORRY)** *Pye Jazz 7NJ 2047*	28	6
9 Nov 61 ●	**MIDNIGHT IN MOSCOW** *Pye Jazz 7NJ 2049*	2	21
15 Feb 62 ●	**MARCH OF THE SIAMESE CHILDREN** *Pye Jazz 7NJ 2051*	4	13
17 May 62 ●	**THE GREEN LEAVES OF SUMMER** *Pye Jazz 7NJ 2054*	7	14
23 Aug 62	**SO DO I** *Pye Jazz 7NJ 2056*	14	8
18 Oct 62	**THE PAY-OFF (AMOI DE PAYER)** *Pye Jazz 7NJ 2061* [2]	23	6
17 Jan 63 ●	**SUKIYAKI** *Pye Jazz 7NJ 2062*	10	13
25 Apr 63	**CASABLANCA** *Pye Jazz 7NJ 2064*	21	11
13 Jun 63	**RONDO** *Pye Jazz 7NJ 2065*	24	8
22 Aug 63	**ACAPULCO 1922** *Pye Jazz 7NJ 2067*	27	6
11 Jun 64	**HELLO, DOLLY!** *Pye Jazz 7NJ 2071*	30	7
19 Jul 67	**WHEN I'M SIXTY FOUR** *Pye 7N 17348*	43	2
25 Aug 62 ★	**THE BEST OF BALL BARBER AND BILK** *Pye Golden Guinea GGL 0131* [1]	1	24
7 Sep 63 ●	**KENNY BALL'S GOLDEN HITS** *Pye Golden Guinea GGL 0209* [2]	4	26

[1] Lonnie Donegan presents Kenny Ball and His Jazz Band [2] Kenny Ball and his Jazzmen Clarinet – Dave Jones [1] Kenny Ball Chris Barber and Acker Bilk [2] Kenny Ball

Michael BALL

UK, male actor / vocalist (Singles: 39 weeks, Albums: 90 weeks) pos/wks

28 Jan 89 ●	**LOVE CHANGES EVERYTHING** *Really Useful RUR 3*	2	14
28 Oct 89	**THE FIRST MAN YOU REMEMBER** *Really Useful RUR 6* [1]	68	2
10 Aug 91	**IT'S STILL YOU** *Polydor PO 160*	58	2
25 Apr 92	**ONE STEP OUT OF TIME** *Polydor PO 206*	20	7
12 Dec 92	**IF I CAN DREAM (EP) (re)** *Polydor PO 248*	51	2
11 Sep 93	**SUNSET BOULEVARD** *Polydor PZCD 293*	72	1
30 Jul 94	**FROM HERE TO ETERNITY** *Columbia 6606905*	36	3
17 Sep 94	**THE LOVERS WE WERE** *Columbia 6607972*	63	2
9 Dec 95	**THE ROSE** *Columbia 6614535*	42	4
17 Feb 96	**(SOMETHING INSIDE) SO STRONG** *Columbia 6629005*	40	2
30 May 92 ★	**MICHAEL BALL** *Polydor 5113302* ■	1	10
17 Jul 93 ●	**ALWAYS** *Polydor 5196662*	3	11
13 Aug 94 ●	**ONE CAREFUL OWNER** *Columbia 4772802*	7	6
19 Nov 94	**THE BEST OF MICHAEL BALL** *PolyGram TV 5238912*	25	7
27 Jan 96 ●	**FIRST LOVE** *Columbia 4835992*	4	6
16 Nov 96	**THE MUSICALS** *PolyGram TV 5338922*	20	10
7 Nov 98	**THE MOVIES** *PolyGram TV 5592412*	13	17
20 Nov 99	**THE VERY BEST OF MICHAEL BALL – IN CONCERT AT THE ROYAL ALBERT HALL / CHRISTMAS** *Universal Music TV 5421952*	18	7
11 Nov 00	**THIS TIME ... IT'S PERSONAL** *Universal Music TV 1597282*	20	8
29 Sep 01	**CENTRE STAGE** *Universal Music TV 160712*	11	7
1 Nov 03	**A LOVE STORY** *Liberty 5919492*	41	1

[1] Michael Ball and Diana Morrison

Tracks on If I Can Dream (EP): If I Can Dream / You Don't Have to Say You Love Me / Always on My Mind / Tell Me There's a Heaven

Steve BALSAMO

UK, male vocalist (Singles: 2 weeks) pos/wks

16 Mar 02	**SUGAR FOR THE SOUL** *Columbia 6718552*	32	2

BALTIMORA *Ireland, male vocalist – Jimmy McShane, d. 14 Dec 2002 (Singles: 12 weeks)*

pos/wks

10 Aug 85 ●	**TARZAN BOY** *Columbia DB 9102*	3	12

Charli BALTIMORE

US, female rapper (Singles: 14 weeks) pos/wks

1 Aug 98	**MONEY** *Epic 6662272*	12	4
12 Oct 02 ●	**DOWN 4 U (2re)** *Murder Inc 0639002* [1]	4	10

[1] Irv Gotti presents Ja Rule, Ashanti, Charli Baltimore and Vita

BAM BAM

US, male vocalist / instrumentalist (Singles: 2 weeks) pos/wks

19 Mar 88	**GIVE IT TO ME** *Serious 7OUS 10*	65	2

Afrika BAMBAATAA *US, male DJ / producer / rapper – Kevin Donovan (Singles: 33 weeks)*

pos/wks

28 Aug 82	**PLANET ROCK** *21 POSP 497* [1]	53	3
10 Mar 84	**RENEGADES OF FUNK** *Tommy Boy AFR 1* [1]	30	4
1 Sep 84	**UNITY (PART 1 – THE THIRD COMING)** *Tommy Boy AFR 2* [2]	49	5
27 Feb 88	**RECKLESS** *EMI EM 41* [3]	17	8
12 Oct 91	**JUST GET UP AND DANCE** *EMI USA MT 100*	45	3
17 Oct 98	**GOT TO GET UP** *Multiply CDMULTY 42*	22	4
18 Sep 99 ●	**AFRIKA SHOX** *Hard Hands HAND 057CD1* [4]	7	5
25 Aug 01	**PLANET ROCK** *Tommy Boy TBCD 2266* [5]	47	1

[1] Afrika Bambaataa and the Soul Sonic Force [2] Afrika Bambaataa and James Brown [3] Afrika Bambaataa and Family featuring UB40 [4] Leftfield / Bambaataa [5] Paul Oakenfold presents Afrika Bambaataa and Soulsonic Force

BAMBOO

UK, male producer – Andrew Livingstone (Singles: 12 weeks) pos/wks

17 Jan 98 ●	**BAMBOOGIE** *VC Recordings VCRD 29*	2	10
4 Jul 98	**THE STRUTT** *VC Recordings VCRD 35*	36	2

BANANARAMA (191 Top 500)

Britain's most charted female group: Sarah Dallin, Keren Woodward, Siobhan Fahey. The London-based trio was also a best-selling act in the US, where 'Venus' topped the chart. Fahey, who married Eurythmic Dave Stewart, left in 1988 to form Shakespear's Sister and was replaced by Jacqui O'Sullivan (Singles: 202 weeks, Albums: 99 weeks) pos/wks

13 Feb 82 ●	**IT AIN'T WHAT YOU DO IT'S THE WAY THAT YOU DO IT** *Chrysalis CHS 2570* [1]	4	10
10 Apr 82 ●	**REALLY SAYING SOMETHING** *Deram NANA 1* [2]	5	10
3 Jul 82 ●	**SHY BOY** *London NANA 2*	4	11
4 Dec 82	**CHEERS THEN** *London NANA 3*	45	7
26 Feb 83 ●	**NA NA HEY HEY KISS HIM GOODBYE** *London NANA 4*	5	10
9 Jul 83 ●	**CRUEL SUMMER** *London NANA 5*	8	10
3 Mar 84 ●	**ROBERT DE NIRO'S WAITING** *London NANA 6*	3	11
26 May 84	**ROUGH JUSTICE** *London NANA 7*	23	7
24 Nov 84	**HOTLINE TO HEAVEN** *London NANA 8*	58	2
24 Aug 85	**DO NOT DISTURB** *London NANA 9*	31	6
31 May 86 ●	**VENUS** *London NANA 10* ▲	8	13
16 Aug 86	**MORE THAN PHYSICAL** *London NANA 11*	41	5
14 Feb 87	**TRICK OF THE NIGHT** *London NANA 12*	32	5
11 Jul 87	**I HEARD A RUMOUR** *London NANA 13*	14	9
10 Oct 87 ●	**LOVE IN THE FIRST DEGREE** *London NANA 14*	3	12
9 Jan 88	**I CAN'T HELP IT** *London NANA 15*	20	6
9 Apr 88 ●	**I WANT YOU BACK** *London NANA 16*	5	10
24 Sep 88	**LOVE, TRUTH AND HONESTY** *London NANA 17*	23	8
19 Nov 88	**NATHAN JONES** *London NANA 18*	15	9
25 Feb 89 ●	**HELP** *London LON 222* [3]	3	9
10 Jun 89	**CRUEL SUMMER (re-mix)** *London NANA 19*	19	6
28 Jul 90	**ONLY YOUR LOVE** *London NANA 21*	27	4
5 Jan 91	**PREACHER MAN** *London NANA 23*	20	6
20 Apr 91	**LONG TRAIN RUNNING** *London NANA 24*	30	5
29 Aug 92	**MOVIN' ON** *London NANA 25*	24	5
28 Nov 92	**LAST THING ON MY MIND** *London NANA 26*	71	2
20 Mar 93	**MORE MORE MORE** *London NACPD 27*	24	4
19 Mar 83 ●	**DEEP SEA SKIVING** *London RAMA 1*	7	16
28 Apr 84	**BANANARAMA** *London RAMA 2*	16	11
19 Jul 86	**TRUE CONFESSIONS** *London RAMA 3*	46	5
19 Sep 87	**WOW!** *London RAMA 4*	26	26
22 Oct 88 ●	**THE GREATEST HITS COLLECTION** *London RAMA 5*	3	37
25 May 91	**POP LIFE** *London 8282461*	42	1

10 Apr 93	**PLEASE YOURSELF** *London 8283572*	**46**	1
10Nov 01	**THE VERY BEST OF BANANARAMA** *London 927414992*	**43**	2

1 Fun Boy Three and Bananarama 2 Bananarama with Fun Boy Three 3 Bananarama / La Na Nee Nee Noo Noo

The listed flip side of 'Love in the First Degree' was 'Mr Sleaze' by Stock Aitken Waterman. Act was a duo for all 1992 and 1993 releases

BANCO DE GAIA

UK, male multi-instrumentalist – Toby Marks (Albums: 4 weeks) pos/wks

12 Mar 94	**MAYA** *Planet Dog BARKCD 3*	**34**	2
13 May 95	**LAST TRAIN TO LHASA** *Planet Dog BARKCD 0115*	**31**	2

BAND *Canada / US, male vocal / instrumental group (Singles: 18 weeks, Albums: 19 weeks)*

pos/wks

18 Sep 68	**THE WEIGHT** *Capitol CL 15559*	**21**	9
4 Apr 70	**RAG MAMA RAG** *Capitol CL 15629*	**16**	9
31 Jan 70	**THE BAND** *Capitol EST 132*	**25**	11
3 Oct 70	**STAGE FRIGHT** *Capitol EA SW 425*	**15**	6
27 Nov 71	**CAHOOTS** *Capitol EAST 651*	**41**	1
30 Aug 97	**THE BAND** *Capitol CDP7464932*	**41**	1

See also Robbie ROBERTSON; Bob DYLAN

BAND AID *International, male / female vocal / instrumental charity assembly (Singles: 26 weeks)*

pos/wks

15 Dec 84 ★	**DO THEY KNOW IT'S CHRISTMAS? (re)** *Mercury FEED 1* ◆ ■	**1**	20
23 Dec 89 ★	**DO THEY KNOW IT'S CHRISTMAS?** *PWL / Polydor FEED 2* 1 ■	**1**	6

1 Band Aid II

BAND AID: Adam Clayton, Bono (U2); Bob Geldof, Johnny Fingers, Simon Crowe, Peter Briquette (Boomtown Rats); David Bowie; Paul McCartney; Holly Johnson (Frankie Goes to Hollywood); Midge Ure, Chris Cross (Ultravox); Simon Le Bon, Nick Rhodes, Andy Taylor, John Taylor, Roger Taylor (Duran Duran); Paul Young; Tony Hadley, Martin Kemp, John Keeble, Gary Kemp, Steve Norman (Spandau Ballet); Martyn Ware, Glenn Gregory (Heaven 17); Francis Rossi, Rick Parfitt (Status Quo); Sting; Boy George, Jon Moss (Culture Club); Marilyn; Keren Woodward, Sarah Dallin, Siobhan Fahey (Bananarama); Jody Watley (Shalamar); Paul Weller; Robert 'Kool' Bell, James Taylor, Dennis Thomas (Kool and the Gang); George Michael and Phil Collins. Band Aid's 1984 'Do They Know It's Christmas?' re-entered the chart and peaked at No.3 in Dec 1985.

BAND AID II: Bananarama, Big Fun, Bros, Cathy Dennis, D Mob, Jason Donovan, Kevin Godley, Glen Goldsmith, Kylie Minogue, The Pasadenas, Chris Rea, Cliff Richard, Jimmy Somerville, Sonia, Lisa Stansfield, Technotronic, Wet Wet Wet

BAND AKA

US, male vocal / instrumental group (Singles: 12 weeks) pos/wks

15 May 82	**GRACE** *Epic EPC A 2376*	**41**	5
5 Mar 83	**JOY** *Epic EPC A 3145*	**24**	7

BAND OF GOLD *Holland, male / female vocal / instrumental group (Singles: 11 weeks)*

pos/wks

14 Jul 84	**LOVE SONGS ARE BACK AGAIN (MEDLEY)** *RCA 428*	**24**	11

BAND OF THIEVES – *See Luke GOSS and the BAND OF THIEVES*

BANDA SONORA

UK, male producer – Gerald Elms (Singles: 3 weeks) pos/wks

6 Oct 01	**GUITARRA G** *Defected DFECT 36CDS*	**50**	2
19 Oct 02	**PRESSURE COOKER** *Defected DFTD 060CDS*	**46**	1

BANDERAS *UK, female vocal / instrumental duo – Sally Herbert and Caroline Buckley (Singles: 16 weeks, Albums: 3 weeks)*

pos/wks

23 Feb 91	**THIS IS YOUR LIFE** *London LON 290*	**16**	10
15 Jun 91	**SHE SELLS** *London LON 298*	**41**	6
13 Apr 91	**RIPE** *London 8282471*	**40**	3

The BANDITS

UK, male vocal / instrumental group (Singles: 2 weeks) pos/wks

28 Jun 02	**TAKE IT AND RUN** *B Unique BUN 055CDS*	**32**	1
20 Sep 03	**2 STEP ROCK** *B Unique BUN 065CDS*	**35**	1

BANDWAGON – *See Johnny JOHNSON and the BANDWAGON*

Honey BANE

UK, female vocalist – Donna Boylan (Singles: 8 weeks) pos/wks

24 Jan 81	**TURN ME ON TURN ME OFF** *Zonophone Z 15*	**37**	5
18 Apr 81	**BABY LOVE** *Zonophone Z 19*	**58**	3

BANG *UK, male vocal duo (Singles: 2 weeks)*

pos/wks

6 May 89	**YOU'RE THE ONE** *RCA PB 42715*	**74**	2

BANGLES 327 Top 500

Originally named The Supersonic Bangs, then Bangs, melodic pop-rock quartet formed 1981, Los Angeles, California, US. Comprised Susanna Hoffs (v), sisters Vicki (g) and Debbi Peterson (d) and Michael Steele (b). Split 1989, having become the most successful all-female band in chart history, then reformed for a tour in 2000. 'Eternal Flame' returned to the top in 2001 by Atomic Kitten (Singles: 96 weeks, Albums: 105 weeks) pos/wks

15 Feb 86 ●	**MANIC MONDAY** *CBS A 6796*	**2**	12
26 Apr 86	**IF SHE KNEW WHAT SHE WANTS** *CBS A 7062*	**31**	7
5 Jul 86	**GOING DOWN TO LIVERPOOL** *CBS A 7255*	**56**	3
13 Sep 86 ●	**WALK LIKE AN EGYPTIAN** *CBS 650071 7* ▲	**3**	19
10 Jan 87	**WALKING DOWN YOUR STREET** *CBS BANGS 1*	**16**	6
18 Apr 87	**FOLLOWING** *CBS BANGS 2*	**55**	3
6 Feb 88	**HAZY SHADE OF WINTER** *Def Jam BANGS 3*	**11**	10
5 Nov 88	**IN YOUR ROOM** *CBS BANGS 4*	**35**	6
18 Feb 89 ★	**ETERNAL FLAME** *CBS BANGS 5* ▲	**1**	18
10 Jun 89	**BE WITH YOU** *CBS BANGS 6*	**23**	8
14 Oct 89	**I'LL SET YOU FREE** *CBS BANGS 7*	**74**	1
9 Jun 90	**WALK LIKE AN EGYPTIAN (re-issue)** *CBS BANGS 8*	**73**	1
15 Mar 03	**SOMETHING THAT YOU SAID** *Down Kiddie / EMI / Liberty BANGLES 003*	**38**	2
16 Mar 85	**ALL OVER THE PLACE** *CBS 26015*	**86**	1
15 Mar 86 ●	**DIFFERENT LIGHT** *CBS 26659*	**3**	47
10 Dec 88 ●	**EVERYTHING** *CBS 4629791*	**5**	26
9 Jun 90 ●	**GREATEST HITS** *CBS 4667691*	**4**	23
4 Aug 01	**ETERNAL FLAME – THE BEST OF THE BANGLES** *Columbia STVCD 121*	**15**	7
29 Mar 03	**DOLL REVOLUTION** *EMI / Liberty 5815102*	**62**	1

Tony BANKS *UK, male vocal / instrumentalist – keyboards (Singles: 1 week, Albums: 7 weeks)*

pos/wks

18 Oct 86	**SHORT CUT TO SOMEWHERE** *Charisma CB 426* 1	**75**	1
20 Oct 79	**A CURIOUS FEELING** *Charisma CAS 1148*	**21**	5
25 Jun 83	**THE FUGITIVE** *Charisma TBLP 1*	**50**	2

1 Fish and Tony Banks

See also FISH; GENESIS

BANNED *UK, male vocal / instrumental group (Singles: 6 weeks)*

pos/wks

17 Dec 77	**LITTLE GIRL** *Harvest HAR 5145*	**36**	6

BANSHEES – *See SIOUXSIE and the BANSHEES*

Buju BANTON *Jamaica, male vocalist (Singles: 1 week)*

pos/wks

7 Aug 93	**MAKE MY DAY** *Mercury BUJCD 2*	**72**	1

Pato BANTON

UK, male vocalist – Patrick Murray (Singles: 37 weeks) pos/wks

1 Oct 94 ★	**BABY COME BACK** *Virgin VSCDT 1522*	**1**	18
11 Feb 95	**THIS COWBOY SONG** *A&M 5809652* 1	**15**	6
8 Apr 95	**BUBBLING HOT** *Virgin VSCDT 1530* 2	**15**	7
20 Jan 96	**SPIRITS IN THE MATERIAL WORLD** *MCA MCSTD 2113* 3	**36**	2
27 Jul 96	**GROOVIN'** *IRS CDEIRS 195* 4	**14**	4

1 Sting featuring Pato Banton 2 Pato Banton with Ranking Roger 3 Pato Banton with Sting 4 Pato Banton and the Reggae Revolution

The sleeve of 'Baby Come Back' credits Ali and Robin Campbell

The 706 No.1 Albums

NO.1 ALBUMS OF THE 50S

Here is the complete chronological list of every UK chart-topping album stretching back to 1956. All dates given are for an album's first week at No.1, not its first entry into the chart.

The run at the top of the chart in weeks follows in brackets, followed by the US peak position of the album.

1956

28 Jul SONGS FOR SWINGIN' LOVERS **Frank Sinatra** (2 weeks) US 2
11 Aug CAROUSEL **Soundtrack** (2 weeks) US 2
25 Aug SONGS FOR SWINGIN' LOVERS **Frank Sinatra** (1 week) US 2
1 Sep CAROUSEL **Soundtrack** (4 weeks) US 2
29 Sep OKLAHOMA! **Soundtrack** (2 weeks) US 1
13 Oct THE KING AND I **Soundtrack** (2 weeks) US 1
27 Oct ROCK 'N' ROLL STAGE SHOW **Bill Haley** (1 week) US 18
3 Nov THE KING AND I **Soundtrack** (1 week) US 1
10 Nov ROCK 'N' ROLL **Elvis Presley** (1 week) US 1
17 Nov THE KING AND I **Soundtrack** (14 weeks) US 1

1957

2 Mar THIS IS SINATRA **Frank Sinatra** (1 week) US 8
9 Mar THE KING AND I **Soundtrack** (1 week) US 1
16 Mar THIS IS SINATRA **Frank Sinatra** (1 week) US 8
23 Mar THE KING AND I **Soundtrack** (1 week) US 1
30 Mar THIS IS SINATRA **Frank Sinatra** (1 week) US 8
6 Apr THE KING AND I **Soundtrack** (3 weeks) US 1
27 Apr THIS IS SINATRA **Frank Sinatra** (1 week) US 8
4 May THE KING AND I **Soundtrack** (6 weeks) US 1
15 Jun OKLAHOMA! **Soundtrack** (1 week) US 1
22 Jun THE KING AND I **Soundtrack** (4 weeks) US 1
20 July THE TOMMY STEELE STORY **Tommy Steele** (3 weeks)
10 Aug THE KING AND I **Soundtrack** (3 weeks) US 1
31 Aug THE TOMMY STEELE STORY **Tommy Steele** (1 week)
7 Sep LOVIN' YOU **Elvis Presley/Soundtrack** (2 weeks) US 1
21 Sep A SWINGIN' AFFAIR **Frank Sinatra** (7 weeks) US 2
9 Nov LOVIN' YOU **Elvis Presley/Soundtrack** (1 week) US 1
16 Nov THE KING AND I **Soundtrack** (11 weeks) US 1

1958

1 Feb PAL JOEY **Soundtrack** (7 weeks) US 2
22 Mar THE KING AND I **Soundtrack** (1 week) US 1
29 Mar PAL JOEY **Soundtrack** (4 weeks) US 2
26 Apr THE DUKE WORE JEANS **Tommy Steele** (2 weeks)
10 May MY FAIR LADY **Original London Cast** (19 weeks) US 1
20 Sep KING CREOLE **Elvis Presley** (7 weeks) US 2
8 Nov SOUTH PACIFIC **Soundtrack** (70 weeks) US 1

1959

SOUTH PACIFIC continues its run through to 1960

1956: CAROUSEL This Rodgers and Hammerstein soundtrack album contains the original version of the Liverpool FC football hymn 'You'll Never Walk Alone'

Record collector Rob Bayston **proudly displays a copy of the UK's first chart-topping album, 'Songs for Swingin' Lovers', by Frank Sinatra. Rob, from Hull, owns every No.1 album and single and a large number of releases peaking at No.2.**

BAR CODES featuring Alison BROWN
UK, male / female vocal group (Singles: 1 week) pos/wks

17 Dec 94 **SUPERMARKET SWEEP** *Blanca Casa BC 101CD* 72 1

Chris BARBER *UK, male jazz band, led by Chris Barber – trombone (Singles: 30 weeks, Albums: 91 weeks)* pos/wks

13 Feb 59 ● **PETITE FLEUR (re)** *Pye Nixa NJ 2026* [1] 3 24
9 Oct 59 **LONESOME (SI TU VOIS MA MÈRE)** *Columbia DB 4333* [2] 27 2
4 Jan 62 **REVIVAL (re)** *Columbia SCD 2166* [3] 43 4
24 Sep 60 **CHRIS BARBER BAND BOX NO. 2** *Columbia 33SCX 3277* 17 1
5 Nov 60 **ELITE SYNCOPATIONS** *Columbia 33SX 1245* 18 1
12 Nov 60 **THE BEST OF CHRIS BARBER** *Ace Of Clubs ACL 1037* 17 1
27 May 61 ● **THE BEST OF BARBER AND BILK VOLUME 1** *Pye Golden Guinea GGL 0075* [1] 4 43
11 Nov 61 ● **THE BEST OF BARBER AND BILK VOLUME 2** *Pye Golden Guinea GGL 0096* [1] 8 18
25 Aug 62 ★ **THE BEST OF BALL BARBER AND BILK** *Pye Golden Guinea GGL 0131* [2] 1 24
29 Jan 00 **THE SKIFFLE SESSIONS – LIVE IN BELFAST** *Venture CDVE 945* [3] 14 3

[1] Clarinet solo – Monty Sunshine [2] Chris Barber featuring Monty Sunshine [3] Chris Barber's Jazz Band [1] Chris Barber and Acker Bilk [2] Kenny Ball, Chris Barber and Acker Bilk [3] Van Morrison / Lonnie Donegan / Chris Barber

BARBRA and NEIL – *See Neil DIAMOND; Barbra STREISAND*

BARCLAY JAMES HARVEST *UK, male vocal / instrumental group (Singles: 9 weeks, Albums: 42 weeks)* pos/wks

2 Apr 77 **LIVE (EP) (re)** *Polydor 2229 198* 49 2
26 Jan 80 **LOVE ON THE LINE** *Polydor POSP 97* 63 2
22 Nov 80 **LIFE IS FOR LIVING** *Polydor POSP 195* 61 3
21 May 83 **JUST A DAY AWAY** *Polydor POSP 585* 68 2
14 Dec 74 **BARCLAY JAMES HARVEST LIVE** *Polydor 2683 052* 40 2
18 Oct 75 **TIME HONOURED GHOST** *Polydor 2383 361* 32 3
23 Oct 76 **OCTOBERON** *Polydor 2442 144* 19 4
1 Oct 77 **GONE TO EARTH** *Polydor 2442 148* 30 7
21 Oct 78 **BARCLAY JAMES HARVEST XII** *Polydor POLD 5006* 31 2
23 May 81 **TURN OF THE TIDE** *Polydor POLD 5040* 55 2
24 Jul 82 **A CONCERT FOR THE PEOPLE (BERLIN)** *Polydor POLD 5052* 15 11
28 May 83 **RING OF CHANGES** *Polydor POLH 3* 36 4
14 Apr 84 **VICTIMS OF CIRCUMSTANCE** *Polydor POLD 5135* 33 6
14 Feb 87 **FACE TO FACE** *Polydor POLD 5209* 65 1

Tracks on Live (EP): Rock 'n' Roll Star / Medicine Man (Parts 1 & 2)

BARDO *UK, male / female vocal duo – Sally Ann Triplett and Stephen Fischer (Singles: 8 weeks)* pos/wks

10 Apr 82 ● **ONE STEP FURTHER** *Epic EPC A2265* 2 8

BARDOT
Australia, female vocal group (Singles: 1 week) pos/wks

14 Apr 01 **POISON** *East West EW 229CD* 45 1

BAREFOOT MAN
Germany, male vocalist – George Nowak (Singles: 7 weeks) pos/wks

5 Dec 98 **BIG PANTY WOMAN** *Plaza PZACD 082* 21 7

BARENAKED LADIES *Canada, male vocal / instrumental group (Singles: 12 weeks, Albums: 19 weeks)* pos/wks

20 Feb 99 ● **ONE WEEK** *Reprise W 468CD* ▲ 5 8
15 May 99 **IT'S ALL BEEN DONE** *Reprise W 476CD* 28 2
24 Jul 99 **CALL AND ANSWER** *Reprise W498CD1* 52 1
11 Dec 99 **BRIAN WILSON** *Reprise W 511CD1* 73 1
27 Aug 94 **MAYBE YOU SHOULD DRIVE** *Reprise 9362457092* 57 1
6 Mar 99 **STUNT** *Reprise 9362469632* 20 17
30 Sep 00 **MAROON** *Reprise 9362478912* 64 1

Daniel BARENBOIM – *See John WILLIAMS*

BAR-KAYS
US, male vocal / instrumental group (Singles: 15 weeks) pos/wks

23 Aug 67 **SOUL FINGER** *Stax 601 014* 33 7
22 Jan 77 **SHAKE YOUR RUMP TO THE FUNK** *Mercury 6167 417* 41 4
12 Jan 85 **SEXOMATIC** *Club JAB 10* 51 4

BARKIN BROTHERS featuring Johnnie FIORI
UK, male production group and US, female vocalist (Singles: 2 weeks) pos/wks

15 Apr 00 **GONNA CATCH YOU** *Brothers Organisation BRUVCD 15* 51 2

Gary BARLOW
UK, male vocalist (Singles: 47 weeks, Albums: 27 weeks) pos/wks

20 Jul 96 ★ **FOREVER LOVE** *RCA 74321397922* ■ 1 16
10 May 97 ★ **LOVE WON'T WAIT (2re)** *RCA 74321470842* ■ 1 9
26 Jul 97 **SO HELP ME GIRL (re)** *RCA 74321501202* 11 11
15 Nov 97 ● **OPEN ROAD** *RCA 74321518292* 7 5
17 Jul 99 **STRONGER** *RCA 74321682002* 16 4
9 Oct 99 **FOR ALL THAT YOU WANT** *RCA 74321701012* 24 2
7 Jun 97 ★ **OPEN ROAD** *RCA 74321417202* ■ 1 26
23 Oct 99 **TWELVE MONTHS ELEVEN DAYS** *RCA 74321707662* 35 1

See also TAKE THAT

Gary BARNACLE – *See BIG FUN; SONIA*

BARNBRACK
UK, male vocal / instrumental group (Singles: 7 weeks) pos/wks

16 Mar 85 **BELFAST** *Homespun HS 092* 45 7

BARNDANCE BOYS *UK, male production duo – John Matthews and Darren Simpson (Singles: 2 weeks)* pos/wks

13 Sep 03 **YIPPIE-I-OH** *Concept CDCON 41* 32 2

Jimmy BARNES and INXS *Australia, male vocalist and vocal / instrumental group (Singles: 8 weeks)* pos/wks

26 Jan 91 **GOOD TIMES** *Atlantic A 7751* 18 8

Richard BARNES *UK, male vocalist (Singles: 10 weeks)* pos/wks

23 May 70 **TAKE TO THE MOUNTAINS** *Philips BF 1840* 35 6
24 Oct 70 **GO NORTH (re)** *Philips 6006 039* 38 4

BARRACUDAS
UK / US, male vocal / instrumental group (Singles: 6 weeks) pos/wks

16 Aug 80 **SUMMER FUN** *Zonophone Z 5* 37 6

Syd BARRETT
UK, male vocalist / instrumentalist – guitar (Albums: 1 week) pos/wks

7 Feb 70 **THE MADCAP LAUGHS** *Harvest SHVL 765* 40 1

See also PINK FLOYD

Wild Willy BARRETT – *See John OTWAY and Wild Willy BARRETT*

Amanda BARRIE and Johnny BRIGGS
UK, female / male vocal duo (Singles: 3 weeks) pos/wks

16 Dec 95 **SOMETHING STUPID** *EMI Premier CDEMS 411* 35 3

The listed flip side of 'Something Stupid' was 'Always Look on the Bright Side of Life' by the Coronation Street Cast

JJ BARRIE
Canada, male vocalist – Barrie Authors (Singles: 11 weeks) pos/wks

24 Apr 76 ★ **NO CHARGE** *Power Exchange PX 209* 1 11

Featured vocalist is Vicki Brown

Ken BARRIE *UK, male vocalist (Singles: 15 weeks)* pos/wks

10 Jul 82 **POSTMAN PAT (2re)** *Post Music PP 001* 44 15

Re-entries at Christmas 1982 and 1983

BARRON KNIGHTS *UK, male vocal / instrumental group – leader – Duke D'Mond (b. Richard Palmer) (Singles: 94 weeks, Albums: 22 weeks)* pos/wks

9 Jul 64 ●	**CALL UP THE GROUPS** *Columbia DB 7317* [1]	3	13
22 Oct 64	**COME TO THE DANCE** *Columbia DB 7375* [1]	42	2
25 Mar 65 ●	**POP GO THE WORKERS** *Columbia DB 7525* [1]	5	13
16 Dec 65 ●	**MERRY GENTLE POPS** *Columbia DB 7780* [1]	9	7
1 Dec 66	**UNDER NEW MANAGEMENT** *Columbia DB 8071* [1]	15	9
23 Oct 68	**AN OLYMPIC RECORD** *Columbia DB 8485*	35	4
29 Oct 77 ●	**LIVE IN TROUBLE** *Epic EPC 5752*	7	10
2 Dec 78 ●	**A TASTE OF AGGRO** *Epic EPC 6829*	3	10
8 Dec 79	**FOOD FOR THOUGHT** *Epic EPC 8011*	46	6
4 Oct 80	**THE SIT SONG** *Epic EPC 8994*	44	4
6 Dec 80	**NEVER MIND THE PRESENTS** *Epic EPC 9070*	17	8
5 Dec 81	**BLACKBOARD JUMBLE** *CBS A 1795*	52	5
19 Mar 83	**BUFFALO BILL'S LAST SCRATCH** *Epic EPC A 3208*	49	3
2 Dec 78	**NIGHT GALLERY** *Epic EPC 83221*	15	13
1 Dec 79	**TEACH THE WORLD TO LAUGH** *Epic EPC 83891*	51	4
13 Dec 80	**JUST A GIGGLE** *Epic EPC 84550*	45	5

[1] The Barron Knights with Duke D'Mond

Joe BARRY *US, male vocalist (Singles: 1 week)* pos/wks

24 Aug 61	**I'M A FOOL TO CARE** *Mercury AMT 1149*	49	1

John BARRY
UK, male composer (Singles: 79 weeks, Albums: 18 weeks) pos/wks

4 Mar 60 ●	**HIT AND MISS (re)** *Columbia DB 4414* [1]	10	14
28 Apr 60	**BEAT FOR BEATNIKS** *Columbia DB 4446* [2]	40	2
14 Jul 60	**NEVER LET GO** *Columbia DB 4480.* [2]	49	1
18 Aug 60	**BLUEBERRY HILL** *Columbia DB 4480* [2]	34	3
8 Sep 60	**WALK DON'T RUN (re)** *Columbia DB 4505* [3]	11	14
8 Dec 60	**BLACK STOCKINGS** *Columbia DB 4554* [3]	27	9
2 Mar 61	**THE MAGNIFICENT SEVEN (3re)** *Columbia DB 4598* [3]	45	5
26 Apr 62	**CUTTY SARK** *Columbia DB 4806* [3]	35	2
1 Nov 62	**THE JAMES BOND THEME** *Columbia DB 4898* [2]	13	11
21 Nov 63	**FROM RUSSIA WITH LOVE (re)** *Ember S 181* [2]	39	3
11 Dec 71	**THEME FROM 'THE PERSUADERS'** *CBS 7469*	13	15
29 Jan 72	**THE PERSUADERS** *CBS 64816*	18	9
20 Apr 91	**DANCES WITH WOLVES (FILM SOUNDTRACK)** *Epic 4675911*	45	8
8 May 99	**THE BEYONDNESS OF THINGS** *Decca 4600092* [1]	67	1

[1] John Barry Seven plus Four [2] John Barry Orchestra [3] John Barry Seven
[1] English Chamber Orchestra conducted by John Barry

Len BARRY
US, male vocalist – Leonard Borisoff (Singles: 24 weeks) pos/wks

4 Nov 65 ●	**1-2-3** *Brunswick 05942*	3	14
13 Jan 66 ●	**LIKE A BABY** *Brunswick 05949*	10	10

Michael BARRYMORE
UK, male vocalist / comedian – Michael Parker (Singles: 4 weeks) pos/wks

16 Dec 95	**TOO MUCH FOR ONE HEART** *EMI CDEM 412*	25	4

Lionel BART *UK, male vocalist, d. 3 Apr 1999 (Singles: 3 weeks)* pos/wks

25 Nov 89	**HAPPY ENDINGS (GIVE YOURSELF A PINCH) (re)** *EMI EM 121*	68	3

BART & HOMER – *See SIMPSONS*

BARTHEZZ
Holland, male producer – Bart Claessen (Singles: 8 weeks) pos/wks

22 Sep 01	**ON THE MOVE** *Positiva CDTIV 158*	18	4
20 Apr 02	**INFECTED** *Positiva CDTIVS 168*	25	4

BAS NOIR *US, female vocal duo (Singles: 1 week)* pos/wks

11 Feb 89	**MY LOVE IS MAGIC** *10 TEN 257*	73	1

Rob BASE and DJ E-Z ROCK *US, male rap / DJ duo – Robert Ginyard and Rodney Bryce (Singles: 19 weeks)* pos/wks

16 Apr 88	**IT TAKES TWO (re)** *Citybeat CBE 724*	24	9
14 Jan 89	**GET ON THE DANCE FLOOR** *Supreme SUPE 139*	14	7
22 Apr 89	**JOY AND PAIN** *Supreme SUPE 143*	47	3

The BASEMENT
UK, male vocal / instrumental group (Singles: 1 week) pos/wks

14 Jun 03	**SLAIN THE TRUTH (AT THE ROADHOUSE)** *Deltasonic DLTCD 012*	48	1

BASEMENT BOYS present Ultra NATÉ
US, male production group and female vocalist (Singles: 1 week) pos/wks

23 Feb 91	**IS IT LOVE?** *Eternal YZ 509*	71	1

BASEMENT JAXX *UK, male DJ / producer duo – Simon Ratcliffe and Felix Buxton (Singles: 59 weeks, Albums: 74 weeks)* pos/wks

31 May 97	**FLY LIFE** *Multiply CDMULTY 21*	19	3
1 May 99 ●	**RED ALERT** *XL Recordings XLS 100CD*	5	10
14 Aug 99 ●	**RENDEZ-VU** *XL Recordings XLS 110CD*	4	8
6 Nov 99	**JUMP 'N SHOUT** *XL Recordings XLS 116CD*	12	5
15 Apr 00	**BINGO BANGO** *XL Recordings XLS 120CD*	13	4
16 Jun 01 ●	**ROMEO** *XL Recordings XLS 132CD*	6	10
6 Oct 01	**JUS 1 KISS (re)** *XL Recordings XLS 136CD*	23	4
8 Dec 01 ●	**WHERE'S YOUR HEAD AT?** *XL Recordings XLS 140CD*	9	8
29 Jun 02	**GET ME OFF** *XL Recordings XLS 146CD*	22	3
22 Nov 03	**LUCKY STAR** *XL Recordings XLS 172CD* [1]	23	4
22 May 99 ●	**REMEDY** *XL Recordings XLCD 129*	4	45
7 Jul 01 ●	**ROOTY** *XL Recordings XLCD 143*	5	26
1 Nov 03	**KISH KASH** *XL Recordings XLCD174*	17	3

[1] Basement Jaxx featuring Dizzee Rascal

BASIA
Poland, female vocalist (Singles: 9 weeks, Albums: 4 weeks) pos/wks

23 Jan 88	**PROMISES** *Epic BASH 4*	48	4
28 May 88	**TIME AND TIDE** *Epic BASH 5*	61	3
14 Jan 95	**DRUNK ON LOVE** *Epic 6611582*	41	2
13 Feb 88	**TIME AND TIDE** *Portrait 4502631*	61	3
3 Mar 90	**LONDON WARSAW NEW YORK** *Epic 4632821*	68	1

See also MATT BIANCO

Count BASIE *US, orchestra leader – William Basie, d. 26 Mar 1984 (Albums: 24 weeks)* pos/wks

16 Apr 60	**CHAIRMAN OF THE BOARD** *Columbia 33SX 1209*	17	1
23 Feb 63 ●	**SINATRA – BASIE** *Reprise R 1008* [1]	2	23

[1] Frank Sinatra and Count Basie

Toni BASIL *US, female vocalist – Antonia Basilotta (Singles: 16 weeks, Albums: 16 weeks)* pos/wks

6 Feb 82 ●	**MICKEY** *Radialchoice TIC 4* ▲	2	12
1 May 82	**NOBODY** *Radialchoice TIC 2*	52	4
6 Feb 82	**WORD OF MOUTH** *Radialchoice BASIL 1*	15	16

Olav BASOSKI
Holland, male producer (Singles: 1 week) pos/wks

26 Aug 00	**OPIUM SCUMBAGZ** *Defected DFECT 20CDS*	56	1

Alfie BASS – *See Michael MEDWIN, Bernard BRESSLAW, Alfie BASS and Leslie FYSON*

Fontella BASS
US, female vocalist (Singles: 15 weeks) pos/wks

2 Dec 65	**RESCUE ME** *Chess CRS 8023*	11	10
20 Jan 66	**RECOVERY** *Chess CRS 8027*	32	5

Norman BASS *Germany, male producer (Singles: 4 weeks)* pos/wks

21 Apr 01	**HOW U LIKE BASS** *Substance SUBS 10CDS*	17	4

BASS BOYZ
UK, male producer – James Sammon (Singles: 1 week) pos/wks

28 Sep 96	**GUNZ AND PIANOZ** *Polydor 5753432*	74	1

See also PIANOMAN

BASS BUMPERS *Germany / UK, male / female vocal / instrumental group (Singles: 4 weeks)* pos/wks

		pos	wks
25 Sep 93	RUNNIN' *Vertigo VERCD 78*	68	1
5 Feb 94	THE MUSIC'S GOT ME *Vertigo VERCD 84*	25	3

BASS JUMPERS

Holland, male producer and female vocalist (Singles: 1 week) pos/wks

		pos	wks
13 Feb 99	MAKE UP YOUR MIND *Pepper 0530112*	44	1

Shirley BASSEY (55 Top 500) *Internationally acclaimed vocalist and cabaret entertainer, b. 8 Jan 1937, Cardiff, Wales. With 31 hit singles (spanning a record 42-year period for a female) and 36 hit albums, she is Britain's most successful female chart artist. Honoured with a damehood in 2000 (Singles: 326 weeks, Albums: 294 weeks)* pos/wks

		pos	wks
15 Feb 57 ●	THE BANANA BOAT SONG *Philips PB 668*	8	10
23 Aug 57	FIRE DOWN BELOW *Philips PB 723*	30	1
6 Sep 57	YOU YOU ROMEO *Philips PB 723*	29	2
19 Dec 58 ★	AS I LOVE YOU (re) *Philips PB 845*	1	19
26 Dec 58 ●	KISS ME, HONEY HONEY, KISS ME *Philips PB 860*	3	17
31 Mar 60	WITH THESE HANDS (2re) *Columbia DB 4421*	38	6
4 Aug 60 ●	AS LONG AS HE NEEDS ME *Columbia DB 4490*	2	30
11 May 61 ●	YOU'LL NEVER KNOW *Columbia DB 4643*	6	17
27 Jul 61 ★	REACH FOR THE STARS / CLIMB EV'RY MOUNTAIN (re) *Columbia DB 4685*	1	18
23 Nov 61 ●	I'LL GET BY (AS LONG AS I HAVE YOU) *Columbia DB 4737*	10	8
15 Feb 62	TONIGHT *Columbia DB 4777*	21	8
26 Apr 62	AVE MARIA *Columbia DB 4816*	31	4
31 May 62	FAR AWAY *Columbia DB 4836*	24	13
30 Aug 62 ●	WHAT NOW MY LOVE? *Columbia DB 4882*	5	17
28 Feb 63	WHAT KIND OF FOOL AM I? *Columbia DB 4974*	47	2
26 Sep 63 ●	I (WHO HAVE NOTHING) *Columbia DB 7113*	6	20
23 Jan 64	MY SPECIAL DREAM *Columbia DB 7185*	32	7
9 Apr 64	GONE *Columbia DB 7248*	36	5
15 Oct 64	GOLDFINGER *Columbia DB 7360*	21	9
20 May 65	NO REGRETS *Columbia DB 7535*	39	4
11 Oct 67	BIG SPENDER *United Artists UP 1192*	21	15
20 Jun 70 ●	SOMETHING (re) *United Artists UP 35125*	4	22
2 Jan 71	THE FOOL ON THE HILL *United Artists UP 35156*	48	1
27 Mar 71	(WHERE DO I BEGIN) LOVE STORY *United Artists UP 35194*	34	9
7 Aug 71 ●	FOR ALL WE KNOW (re) *United Artists UP 35267*	6	24
15 Jan 72	DIAMONDS ARE FOREVER *United Artists UP 35293*	38	6
3 Mar 73 ●	NEVER, NEVER, NEVER (GRANDE, GRANDE, GRANDE) (re) *United Artists UP 35490*	8	19
22 Aug 87	THE RHYTHM DIVINE *Mercury MER 253* [1]	54	2
16 Nov 96	'DISCO' LA PASSIONE *East West EW 072CD* [2]	41	1
20 Dec 97	HISTORY REPEATING *Wall of Sound WALLD 036* [3]	19	7
23 Oct 99	WORLD IN UNION *Universal TV 4669402* [4]	35	3
28 Jan 61	FABULOUS SHIRLEY BASSEY *Columbia 33SX 1178*	12	2
25 Feb 61 ●	SHIRLEY *Columbia 33SX 1286*	9	10
17 Feb 62	SHIRLEY BASSEY *Columbia 33SX 1382*	14	11
15 Dec 62	LET'S FACE THE MUSIC *Columbia 33SX 1454* [1]	12	7
4 Dec 65	SHIRLEY BASSEY AT THE PIGALLE *Columbia 33SX 1787*	15	7
27 Aug 66	I'VE GOT A SONG FOR YOU *United Artists ULP 1142*	26	1
17 Feb 68	TWELVE OF THOSE SONGS *Columbia SCX 6204*	38	3
7 Dec 68	GOLDEN HITS OF SHIRLEY BASSEY *Columbia SCX 6294*	28	40
11 Jul 70	LIVE AT THE TALK OF THE TOWN *United Artists UAS 29095*	38	6
29 Aug 70 ●	SOMETHING *United Artists UAS 29100*	5	20
15 May 71 ●	SOMETHING ELSE *United Artists UAG 29149*	7	9
2 Oct 71	BIG SPENDER *Sunset SLS 50262*	27	8
30 Oct 71	IT'S MAGIC *Starline SRS 5082*	32	1
6 Nov 71	THE FABULOUS SHIRLEY BASSEY *MFP 1398*	48	1
4 Dec 71	WHAT NOW MY LOVE *MFP 5230*	17	5
8 Jan 72	THE SHIRLEY BASSEY COLLECTION *United Artists UAD 60013/4*	37	1
19 Feb 72	I CAPRICORN *United Artists UAS 29246*	13	11
29 Nov 72	AND I LOVE YOU SO *United Artists UAS 29385*	24	9
2 Jun 73 ●	NEVER NEVER NEVER *United Artists UAG 29471*	10	10
15 Mar 75 ●	THE SHIRLEY BASSEY SINGLES ALBUM *United Artists UAS 29728*	2	23
1 Nov 75	GOOD BAD BUT BEAUTIFUL *United Artists UAS 29881*	13	7
15 May 76	LOVE LIFE AND FEELINGS *United Artists UAS 29944*	13	5
4 Dec 76	THOUGHTS OF LOVE *United Artists UAS 30011*	15	9
25 Jun 77	YOU TAKE MY HEART AWAY *United Artists UAS 30037*	34	5
4 Nov 78 ●	25TH ANNIVERSARY ALBUM *United Artists SBTV 601 4748*	3	12
12 May 79	THE MAGIC IS YOU *United Artists UATV 30230*	40	5
17 Jul 82	LOVE SONGS *Applause APKL 1163*	48	5
20 Oct 84	I AM WHAT I AM *Towerbell TOWLP 7*	25	18
18 May 91	KEEP THE MUSIC PLAYING *Dino DINTV 21*	25	7
5 Dec 92	THE BEST OF SHIRLEY BASSEY *Dino DINCD 49*	27	5
4 Dec 93	SHIRLEY BASSEY SINGS ANDREW LLOYD WEBBER *Premier CDDPR 114*	34	5
11 Nov 95	SHIRLEY BASSEY SINGS THE MOVIES *PolyGram TV 5293992*	24	9
9 Nov 96	THE SHOW MUST GO ON *PolyGram TV 5337122*	47	8
9 Sep 00	THE REMIX ALBUM ... DIAMONDS ARE FOREVER *EMI 5258732*	62	1
25 Nov 00	THIS IS MY LIFE – GREATEST HITS *Liberty 5258742*	54	4
7 Jun 03	THANK YOU FOR THE YEARS *Citrus 5122722*	19	4

[1] Yello featuring Shirley Bassey [2] Chris Rea and Shirley Bassey [3] Propellerheads featuring Miss Shirley Bassey [4] Shirley Bassey / Bryn Terfel [1] Shirley Bassey with the Nelson Riddle Orchestra

BASSHEADS

UK, male / female vocal / instrumental group (Singles: 19 weeks) pos/wks

		pos	wks
16 Nov 91 ●	IS THERE ANYBODY OUT THERE? *Deconstruction R 6303*	5	8
30 May 92	BACK TO THE OLD SCHOOL *Deconstruction R 6310*	12	4
28 Nov 92	WHO CAN MAKE ME FEEL GOOD *Deconstruction R 6326*	38	2
28 Aug 93	START A BRAND NEW LIFE (SAVE ME) *Deconstruction CDR 6353*	49	2
15 Jul 95	IS THERE ANYBODY OUT THERE? (re-mix) *Deconstruction 74321293882*	24	3

BASS-O-MATIC *UK, male multi-instrumentalist / producer – William Orbit (Singles: 19 weeks, Albums: 2 weeks)* pos/wks

		pos	wks
12 May 90	IN THE REALM OF THE SENSES *Virgin VS 1265*	66	3
1 Sep 90 ●	FASCINATING RHYTHM *Virgin VS 1274*	9	11
22 Dec 90	EASE ON BY *Virgin VS 1295*	61	4
3 Aug 91	FUNKY LOVE VIBRATIONS *Virgin VS 1355*	71	1
13 Oct 90	SET THE CONTROLS FOR THE HEART OF THE BASS *Virgin V 2641*	57	2

See also William ORBIT

BASSTOY

US, male / female vocal / production duo (Singles: 6 weeks) pos/wks

		pos	wks
27 May 00	RUNNIN *Neo NEOCD 029*	62	1
19 Jan 02	RUNNIN' (re-mix) *Black & White NEOCD 073* [1]	13	5

[1] Mark Pichiotti presents Basstoy featuring Dana

BATES

Germany, male vocal / instrumental group (Singles: 1 week) pos/wks

		pos	wks
3 Feb 96	BILLIE JEAN *Virgin International DINSD 151*	67	1

Mike BATT with NEW EDITION *UK, male vocalist with male / female vocal group (Singles: 8 weeks, Albums: 7 weeks)* pos/wks

		pos	wks
16 Aug 75 ●	SUMMERTIME CITY *Epic EPC 3460*	4	8
28 Oct 89	CLASSIC BLUE *Trax MODEM 1040* [1]	47	7

[1] Justin Hayward Mike Batt and the London Philharmonic Orchestra

BAUHAUS *UK, male vocal / instrumental group (Singles: 35 weeks, Albums: 24 weeks)* pos/wks

		pos	wks
18 Apr 81	KICK IN THE EYE *Beggars Banquet BEG 54*	59	3
4 Jul 81	THE PASSION OF LOVERS *Beggars Banquet BEG 59*	56	2
6 Mar 82	KICK IN THE EYE (EP) *Beggars Banquet BEG 74*	45	4
19 Jun 82	SPIRIT *Beggars Banquet BEG 79*	42	5
9 Oct 82	ZIGGY STARDUST *Beggars Banquet BEG 83*	15	7
22 Jan 83	LAGARTIJA NICK *Beggars Banquet BEG 88*	44	4
9 Apr 83	SHE'S IN PARTIES *Beggars Banquet BEG 91*	26	6
29 Oct 83	THE SINGLES 1981-83 *Beggars Banquet BEG 100E*	52	4
15 Nov 80	IN THE FLAT FIELD *4AD CAD 13*	72	1
24 Oct 81	MASK *Beggars Banquet BEGA 29*	30	5
30 Oct 82 ●	THE SKY'S GONE OUT *Beggars Banquet BEGA 42*	4	6

Date		Title	Label	Pos	Wks
23 Jul 83		**BURNING FROM THE INSIDE**	*Beggars Banquet BEGA 45*	**13**	10
30 Nov 85		**1979-1983**	*Beggars Banquet BEGA 64*	**36**	2

Tracks on Kick in the Eye (EP): Kick in the Eye (Searching for Satori) / Harry / Earwax. The Singles 1981-83 was an EP: The Passion of Lovers / Kick in the Eye / Spirit / Ziggy Stardust / Lagartija Nick / She's in Parties

See also Peter MURPHY

Les BAXTER his Chorus and Orchestra

US, orchestra and chorus, leader d. 15 Jan 1996 (Singles: 9 weeks) pos/wks

Date		Title	Label	Pos	Wks
13 May 55	●	**UNCHAINED MELODY**	*Capitol CL 14257*	**10**	9

Tasha BAXTER – *See Roger GOODE featuring Tasha BAXTER*

BAY CITY ROLLERS (257 Top 500)

Tartan teen sensations from Edinburgh: Leslie McKeown (v), Eric Faulkner (g), Stuart Wood (g), Alan Longmuir (b), Derek Longmuir (d). They were the first of many acts heralded as 'Biggest Group Since The Beatles' and one of the most screamed-at teeny-bopper acts of the 1970s (Singles: 116 weeks, Albums: 127 weeks) pos/wks

Date		Title	Label	Pos	Wks
18 Sep 71	●	**KEEP ON DANCING**	*Bell 1164*	**9**	13
9 Feb 74	●	**REMEMBER (SHA-LA-LA)**	*Bell 1338*	**6**	12
27 Apr 74	●	**SHANG-A-LANG**	*Bell 1355*	**2**	10
27 Jul 74	●	**SUMMERLOVE SENSATION**	*Bell 1369*	**3**	10
12 Oct 74	●	**ALL OF ME LOVES ALL OF YOU**	*Bell 1382*	**4**	10
8 Mar 75	★	**BYE BYE BABY**	*Bell 1409*	**1**	16
12 Jul 75	★	**GIVE A LITTLE LOVE**	*Bell 1425*	**1**	9
22 Nov 75	●	**MONEY HONEY**	*Bell 1461*	**3**	9
10 Apr 76	●	**LOVE ME LIKE I LOVE YOU**	*Bell 1477*	**4**	9
11 Sep 76	●	**I ONLY WANNA BE WITH YOU**	*Bell 1493*	**4**	9
7 May 77		**IT'S A GAME**	*Arista 108*	**16**	6
30 Jul 77		**YOU MADE ME BELIEVE IN MAGIC**	*Arista 127*	**34**	3
12 Oct 74	★	**ROLLIN'**	*Bell BELLS 244* ■	**1**	62
3 May 75	★	**ONCE UPON A STAR**	*Bell SYBEL 8001* ■	**1**	37
13 Dec 75	●	**WOULDN'T YOU LIKE IT**	*Bell SYBEL 8002*	**3**	12
25 Sep 76	●	**DEDICATION**	*Bell SYBEL 8005*	**4**	12
13 Aug 77		**IT'S A GAME**	*Arista SPARTY 1009*	**18**	4

Duke BAYSEE

UK, male vocalist – Kevin Rowe (Singles: 6 weeks) pos/wks

Date		Title	Label	Pos	Wks
3 Sep 94		**SUGAR SUGAR**	*Bell 74321228702*	**30**	4
21 Jan 95		**DO YOU LOVE ME**	*Double Dekker CDDEK 1*	**46**	2

BAZ

UK, female vocalist – Baz Gooden (Singles: 3 weeks) pos/wks

Date		Title	Label	Pos	Wks
15 Dec 01		**BELIEVERS**	*One Little Indian 313 TP7CD1*	**36**	2
30 Mar 02		**SMILE TO SHINE**	*One Little Indian 316 TP7CD*	**58**	1

BE BOP DELUXE

UK, male vocal / instrumental group (Singles: 13 weeks, Albums: 28 weeks) pos/wks

Date		Title	Label	Pos	Wks
21 Feb 76		**SHIPS IN THE NIGHT**	*Harvest HAR 5104*	**23**	8
13 Nov 76		**HOT VALVES (EP)**	*Harvest HAR 5117*	**36**	5
31 Jan 76		**SUNBURST FINISH**	*Harvest SHSP 4053*	**17**	12
25 Sep 76		**MODERN MUSIC**	*Harvest SHSP 4058*	**12**	6
6 Aug 77	●	**LIVE! IN THE AIR AGE**	*Harvest SHVL 816*	**10**	5
25 Feb 78		**DRASTIC PLASTIC**	*Harvest SHSP 4091*	**22**	5

Tracks on Hot Valves (EP): Maid in Heaven / Blazing Apostles / Jet Silver and the Dolls of Venus / Bring Back the Spark

See also Bill NELSON

BEACH BOYS (26 Top 500)

California family band famous for their harmonies. The most successful and consistently popular US group of the rock era: Brian Wilson (b/k/v), Mike Love (v), Carl Wilson (g/v) (d. 1998), Al Jardine (g/v), Dennis Wilson (d/v) (d. 1983) (Singles: 281 weeks, Albums: 563 weeks) pos/wks

Date		Title	Label	Pos	Wks
1 Aug 63		**SURFIN' U.S.A.**	*Capitol CL 15305*	**34**	7
9 Jul 64	●	**I GET AROUND**	*Capitol CL 15350* ▲	**7**	13
29 Oct 64		**WHEN I GROW UP (TO BE A MAN) (re)**	*Capitol CL 15361*	**27**	7
21 Jan 65		**DANCE, DANCE, DANCE**	*Capitol CL 15370*	**24**	6
3 Jun 65		**HELP ME, RHONDA**	*Capitol CL 15392* ▲	**27**	10
2 Sep 65		**CALIFORNIA GIRLS**	*Capitol CL 15409*	**26**	8
17 Feb 66	●	**BARBARA ANN**	*Capitol CL 15432*	**3**	10
21 Apr 66	●	**SLOOP JOHN B**	*Capitol CL 15441*	**2**	15
28 Jul 66	●	**GOD ONLY KNOWS**	*Capitol CL 15459*	**2**	14
3 Nov 66	★	**GOOD VIBRATIONS**	*Capitol CL 15475* ▲	**1**	13
4 May 67	●	**THEN I KISSED HER**	*Capitol CL 15502*	**4**	11
23 Aug 67	●	**HEROES AND VILLAINS**	*Capitol CL 15510*	**8**	9
22 Nov 67		**WILD HONEY**	*Capitol CL 15521*	**29**	6
17 Jan 68		**DARLIN'**	*Capitol CL 15527*	**11**	14
8 May 68		**FRIENDS**	*Capitol CL 15545*	**25**	7
24 Jul 68	★	**DO IT AGAIN**	*Capitol CL 15554*	**1**	14
25 Dec 68		**BLUEBIRDS OVER THE MOUNTAIN**	*Capitol CL 15572*	**33**	5
26 Feb 69	●	**I CAN HEAR MUSIC**	*Capitol CL 15584*	**10**	13
11 Jun 69	●	**BREAK AWAY**	*Capitol CL 15598*	**6**	11
16 May 70	●	**COTTONFIELDS**	*Capitol CL 15640*	**5**	17
3 Mar 73		**CALIFORNIA SAGA – CALIFORNIA**	*Reprise K 14232*	**37**	5
3 Jul 76		**GOOD VIBRATIONS (re-issue)**	*Capitol CL 15875*	**18**	7
10 Jul 76		**ROCK AND ROLL MUSIC**	*Reprise K 14440*	**36**	4
31 Mar 79		**HERE COMES THE NIGHT**	*Caribou CRB 7204*	**37**	8
16 Jun 79	●	**LADY LYNDA**	*Caribou CRB 7427*	**6**	11
29 Sep 79		**SUMAHAMA**	*Caribou CRB 7846*	**45**	4
29 Aug 81		**THE BEACH BOYS MEDLEY**	*Capitol CL 213*	**47**	4
22 Aug 87	●	**WIPEOUT**	*Urban URB 5* [1]	**2**	12
19 Nov 88		**KOKOMO**	*Elektra EKR 85* ▲	**25**	9
2 Jun 90		**WOULDN'T IT BE NICE**	*Capitol CL 579*	**58**	1
29 Jun 91		**DO IT AGAIN (re-issue)**	*Capitol EMCT 1*	**61**	2
2 Mar 96		**FUN FUN FUN**	*PolyGram TV 5762972* [2]	**24**	4
25 Sep 65		**SURFIN' USA**	*Capitol T 1890*	**17**	7
19 Feb 66	●	**BEACH BOYS PARTY**	*Capitol T 2398*	**3**	14
16 Apr 66	●	**BEACH BOYS TODAY**	*Capitol T 2269*	**6**	25
9 Jul 66	●	**PET SOUNDS**	*Capitol T 2458*	**2**	39
16 Jul 66	●	**SUMMER DAYS (AND SUMMER NIGHTS!!)**	*Capitol T 2354*	**4**	22
12 Nov 66	●	**BEST OF THE BEACH BOYS**	*Capitol T 20865*	**2**	142
11 Mar 67		**SURFER GIRL**	*Capitol T 1981*	**13**	14
21 Oct 67	●	**BEST OF THE BEACH BOYS VOLUME 2**	*Capitol ST 20956*	**3**	39
18 Nov 67	●	**SMILEY SMILE**	*Capitol ST 9001*	**9**	8
16 Mar 68	●	**WILD HONEY**	*Capitol ST 2859*	**7**	15
21 Sep 68		**FRIENDS**	*Capitol ST 2895*	**13**	8
23 Nov 68	●	**BEST OF THE BEACH BOYS VOLUME 3**	*Capitol ST 21142*	**9**	12
29 Mar 69	●	**20 / 20**	*Capitol EST 133*	**3**	10
19 Sep 70	●	**GREATEST HITS**	*Capitol T 21628*	**5**	22
5 Dec 70		**SUNFLOWER**	*Stateside SSL 8251*	**29**	6
27 Nov 71		**SURF'S UP**	*Stateside SLS 10313*	**15**	7
24 Jun 72		**CARL AND THE PASSIONS / SO TOUGH**	*Reprise K 44184*	**25**	1
17 Feb 73		**HOLLAND**	*Reprise K 54008*	**20**	7
10 Jul 76	★	**20 GOLDEN GREATS**	*Capitol EMTV 1*	**1**	86
24 Jul 76		**15 BIG ONES**	*Reprise K 54079*	**31**	3
7 May 77		**THE BEACH BOYS LOVE YOU**	*Reprise K 54087*	**28**	1
21 Apr 79		**LA (LIGHT ALBUM)**	*Caribou CRB 86081*	**32**	6
12 Apr 80		**KEEPING THE SUMMER ALIVE**	*Caribou CRB 86109*	**54**	3
30 Jul 83	★	**THE VERY BEST OF THE BEACH BOYS**	*Capitol BBTV 1867193*	**1**	17
22 Jun 85		**THE BEACH BOYS**	*Caribou CRB 26378*	**60**	2
23 Jun 90	●	**SUMMER DREAMS – 28 CLASSIC TRACKS**	*Capitol EMTVD 51*	**2**	27
1 Jul 95		**THE BEST OF THE BEACH BOYS**	*Capitol CDESTVD 3*	**25**	6
16 Sep 95		**PET SOUNDS (re-issue)**	*Fame CDFA 3298*	**59**	4
11 Jul 98		**GREATEST HITS**	*EMI 4956962*	**28**	4
19 Sep 98		**ENDLESS HARMONY SOUNDTRACK**	*Capitol 4963912*	**56**	1
21 Jul 01		**THE VERY BEST OF THE BEACH BOYS**	*Capitol 5326152*	**31**	5

[1] Fat Boys and the Beach Boys [2] Status Quo with the Beach Boys

The Beach Boys Medley comprised Good Vibrations / Help Me, Rhonda / I Get Around / Shut Down / Surfin' Safari / Barbara Ann / Surfin' USA / Fun, Fun, Fun The two 'Best of the Beach Boys' 'Greatest Hits' and 'The Very Best of the Beach Boys' albums are different

See also Brian WILSON

BEAR WHO? – *See DJ SNEAK featuring BEAR WHO?*

Walter BEASLEY

US, male vocalist (Singles: 3 weeks) pos/wks

Date		Title	Label	Pos	Wks
23 Jan 88		**I'M SO HAPPY**	*Urban URB 14*	**70**	3

BEASTIE BOYS (468 Top 500)

Scourge of the tabloids in the late 1980s: MCA (Adam Yauch, v/b), Mike D (Michael Diamond, v/d) and Ad-Rock (Adam Horowitz, v/g). This New York rap trio turned their backs on their early image

to become dedicated campaigners for a free Tibet. Known for their innovative videos, they founded a record label and magazine, both called Grand Royal (Singles: 59 weeks, Albums: 88 weeks) pos/wks

28 Feb 87		**(YOU GOTTA) FIGHT FOR YOUR RIGHT (TO PARTY)** *Def Jam 650418 7*	11 11
30 May 87		**NO SLEEP TILL BROOKLYN** *Def Jam BEAST 1*	14 7
18 Jul 87	●	**SHE'S ON IT** *Def Jam BEAST 2*	10 8
3 Oct 87		**GIRLS / SHE'S CRAFTY** *Def Jam BEAST 3*	34 4
11 Apr 92		**PASS THE MIC** *Capitol 12CL 653*	47 2
4 Jul 92		**FROZEN METAL HEAD (EP)** *Capitol 12CL 665*	55 1
9 Jul 94		**GET IT TOGETHER / SABOTAGE** *Capitol CDCL 716*	19 4
26 Nov 94		**SURE SHOT** *Capitol CDCL 726*	27 3
4 Jul 98	●	**INTERGALACTIC** *Grand Royal CDCL 803*	5 7
7 Nov 98		**BODY MOVIN' (re)** *Grand Royal CDCL 809*	15 5
29 May 99		**REMOTE CONTROL / 3 MCS & 1 DJ** *Grand Royal CDCL 812*	21 3
18 Dec 99		**ALIVE** *Grand Royal CDCL 818*	28 4
31 Jan 87	●	**LICENSED TO ILL** *Def Jam 450062* ▲	7 40
5 Aug 89		**PAUL'S BOUTIQUE** *Capitol EST 2102*	44 2
4 Jun 94	●	**ILL COMMUNICATION** *Capitol CDEST 2229* ▲	10 15
10 Jun 95		**ROOT DOWN EP** *Capitol CDEST 2262*	23 2
6 Apr 96		**THE IN SOUND FROM WAY OUT!** *Grand Royal CDEST 2281*	45 1
18 Jul 98	★	**HELLO NASTY** *Grand Royal 4957232* ■ ▲	1 21
4 Dec 99		**ANTHOLOGY – THE SOUNDS OF SCIENCE** *Grand Royal 5236642*	36 7

Tracks on Frozen Metal Head (EP): Jimmy James / Jimmy James (Original) / Drinkin' Wine / The Blue Nun

BEAT (409 Top 500)

Birmingham, UK-based band that married ska and new wave influences, formed 1978: Dave Wakeling (v/g), Ranking Roger (v), Andy Cox (g) and David Steele (b). After 1983 break-up, former two launched General Public and latter pair formed Fine Young Cannibals (Singles: 92 weeks, Albums: 73 weeks) pos/wks

8 Dec 79	●	**TEARS OF A CLOWN / RANKING FULL STOP** *2 Tone CHSTT 6*	6 11
23 Feb 80	●	**HANDS OFF – SHE'S MINE** *Go Feet FEET 1*	9 9
3 May 80	●	**MIRROR IN THE BATHROOM** *Go Feet FEET 2*	4 9
16 Aug 80		**BEST FRIEND / STAND DOWN MARGARET (DUB)** *Go Feet FEET 3*	22 9
13 Dec 80	●	**TOO NICE TO TALK TO** *Go Feet FEET 4*	7 11
18 Apr 81		**DROWNING / ALL OUT TO GET YOU** *Go Feet FEET 6*	22 8
20 Jun 81		**DOORS OF YOUR HEART** *Go Feet FEET 9*	33 6
5 Dec 81		**HIT IT** *Go Feet FEET 11*	70 2
17 Apr 82		**SAVE IT FOR LATER** *Go Feet FEET 333*	47 4
18 Sep 82		**JEANETTE** *Go Feet FEET 15*	45 3
4 Dec 82		**I CONFESS** *Go Feet FEET 16*	54 3
30 Apr 83	●	**CAN'T GET USED TO LOSING YOU** *Go Feet FEET 17*	3 11
2 Jul 83		**ACKEE 1-2-3** *Go Feet FEET 18*	54 4
27 Jan 96		**MIRROR IN THE BATHROOM (re-mix)** *Go Feet 74321232062*	44 2
31 May 80	●	**JUST CAN'T STOP IT** *Go-Feet BEAT 001*	3 32
16 May 81	●	**WHA'PPEN** *Go-Feet BEAT 3*	3 18
9 Oct 82		**SPECIAL BEAT SERVICE** *Go-Feet BEAT 5*	21 6
11 Jun 83	●	**WHAT IS BEAT? (THE BEST OF THE BEAT)** *Go-Feet BEAT 6*	10 13
10 Feb 96		**B.P.M.... THE VERY BEST OF THE BEAT** *Go-Feet 74321231952*	13 4

BEAT BOYS – *See Gene VINCENT*

BEAT RENEGADES

UK, male production duo – Ian Bland and Paul Fitzpatrick (Singles: 1 week) pos/wks

19 May 01		**AUTOMATIK** *Slinky Music SLINKY 014CD*	73 1

See also DREAM FREQUENCY; RED

BEAT SYSTEM

UK, male vocal / instrumental group (Singles: 3 weeks) pos/wks

3 Mar 90		**WALK ON THE WILD SIDE** *Fourth & Broadway BRW 163*	63 2
18 Sep 93		**TO A BRIGHTER DAY (O' HAPPY DAY)** *ffrr FCD 217*	70 1

BEATCHUGGERS featuring Eric CLAPTON

Denmark, male producer – Michael Linde and UK, male vocalist / instrumentalist (Singles: 2 weeks) pos/wks

18 Nov 00		**FOREVER MAN (HOW MANY TIMES)** *ffrr FCD 386* [1]	26 2

[1] Beatchuggers featuring Eric Clapton

BEATINGS

UK, male vocal / instrumental group (Singles: 1 week) pos/wks

26 Oct 02		**BAD FEELING** *Fantastic Plastic FPS 034*	68 1

BEATLES (3 Top 500)

World's most successful group: John Lennon (v/g) b. 9 Oct 1940, Liverpool, d. 8 Dec 1980, New York, Paul McCartney (v/b) b. 18 Jun 1942, Liverpool, George Harrison (v/g) b. 24 Feb 1943, Liverpool, d. 29 Nov 2001, Ringo Starr (Richard Starkey) (v/d) b. 7 Jul 1940, Liverpool. This legendary group changed the face of popular music. Achievements include more UK singles sold than any other group (20,799,632) and most No.1 albums in the UK and US. Within three months of their US chart debut in 1964, they held all the Top 5 single chart places, had a record 14 simultaneous entries in Billboard Top 100 and had the two top-selling albums. During those 12 weeks they earned six gold singles and sold four million albums. Their album 'Sgt. Pepper's Lonely Hearts Club Band' is the biggest seller ever in the UK, and the group is the No.1 all-time US best-selling album act. They split in 1970, since when Lennon, McCartney and Harrison have all had No.1 singles. (Starr reached No.2.) Their '1' collection (2000) is the world's fastest selling album with 23 million copies shipped in the first month and was the top-selling album of 2000 in the UK. The Beatles, who were made MBEs in 1965, have sold an estimated one billion records. Best-selling single in UK: 'She Loves You' 1,890,000 (Singles: 456 weeks, Albums: 1,284 weeks) pos/wks

11 Oct 62	●	**LOVE ME DO (2re)** *Parlophone R 4949* ▲	4 26
17 Jan 63	●	**PLEASE PLEASE ME (re)** *Parlophone R 4983*	2 22
18 Apr 63	★	**FROM ME TO YOU (re)** *Parlophone R 5015*	1 25
6 Jun 63		**MY BONNIE** *Polydor NH 66833* [1]	48 1
29 Aug 63	★	**SHE LOVES YOU (2re)** *Parlophone R 5055* ◆ ▲	1 36
5 Dec 63	★	**I WANT TO HOLD YOUR HAND (2re)** *Parlophone R 5084* ◆ ▲	1 24
26 Mar 64	★	**CAN'T BUY ME LOVE (2re)** *Parlophone R 5114* ◆ ▲	1 17
11 Jun 64		**AIN'T SHE SWEET** *Polydor 52 317*	29 6
16 Jul 64	★	**A HARD DAY'S NIGHT (re)** *Parlophone R 5160* ▲	1 15
3 Dec 64	★	**I FEEL FINE (re)** *Parlophone R 5200* ◆ ▲	1 14
15 Apr 65	★	**TICKET TO RIDE (re)** *Parlophone R 5265* ▲	1 14
29 Jul 65	★	**HELP! (re)** *Parlophone R 5305* ▲	1 17
9 Dec 65	★	**DAY TRIPPER / WE CAN WORK IT OUT** *Parlophone R 5389* ◆ ▲	1 12
16 Jun 66	★	**PAPERBACK WRITER (re)** *Parlophone R 5452* ▲	1 16
11 Aug 66	★	**YELLOW SUBMARINE / ELEANOR RIGBY (re)** *Parlophone R 5493*	1 14
23 Feb 67	●	**PENNY LANE / STRAWBERRY FIELDS FOREVER (2re)** *Parlophone R 5570* ▲	2 16
12 Jul 67	★	**ALL YOU NEED IS LOVE (re)** *Parlophone R 5620* ▲	1 16
29 Nov 67	★	**HELLO, GOODBYE (re)** *Parlophone R 5655* ▲	1 13
13 Dec 67	●	**MAGICAL MYSTERY TOUR (DOUBLE EP)** *Parlophone SMMT/MMT 1*	2 12
20 Mar 68	★	**LADY MADONNA (re)** *Parlophone R 5675*	1 9
4 Sep 68	★	**HEY JUDE (2re)** *Apple R 5722* ▲	1 25
23 Apr 69	★	**GET BACK (2re)** *Apple R 5777* [2] ■ ▲	1 23
4 Jun 69	★	**THE BALLAD OF JOHN AND YOKO** *Apple R 5786*	1 14
8 Nov 69	●	**SOMETHING / COME TOGETHER** *Apple R 5814* ▲	4 12
14 Mar 70	●	**LET IT BE (re)** *Apple R 5833* ▲	2 10
13 Mar 76	●	**YESTERDAY** *Apple R 6013* ▲	8 7
10 Jul 76		**BACK IN THE U.S.S.R.** *Parlophone R 6016*	19 6
7 Oct 78		**SGT. PEPPER'S LONELY HEARTS CLUB BAND – WITH A LITTLE HELP FROM MY FRIENDS** *Parlophone R 6022*	63 3
5 Jun 82	●	**BEATLES MOVIE MEDLEY** *Parlophone R 6055*	10 9
1 Apr 95	●	**BABY IT'S YOU (re)** *Apple CDR 6406*	7 7
16 Dec 95	●	**FREE AS A BIRD** *Apple CDR 6422*	2 8
16 Mar 96	●	**REAL LOVE** *Apple CDR 6425*	4 7
6 Apr 63	★	**PLEASE PLEASE ME** *Parlophone PMC 1202*	1 70
30 Nov 63	★	**WITH THE BEATLES** *Parlophone PMC 1206*	1 51
18 Jul 64	★	**A HARD DAY'S NIGHT** *Parlophone PMC 1230* ▲	1 38
12 Dec 64	★	**BEATLES FOR SALE** *Parlophone PMC 1240* ▲	1 46
14 Aug 65	★	**HELP!** *Parlophone PMC 1255* ■ ▲	1 37
11 Dec 65	★	**RUBBER SOUL** *Parlophone PMC 1267* ▲	1 42
13 Aug 66	★	**REVOLVER** *Parlophone PMC 7009* ■ ▲	1 34
10 Dec 66	●	**A COLLECTION OF BEATLES OLDIES** *Parlophone PMC 7016*	7 34
3 Jun 67	★	**SGT. PEPPER'S LONELY HEARTS CLUB BAND** *Parlophone PCS 7027* ▲	1 149
13 Jan 68		**MAGICAL MYSTERY TOUR (import)** *Capitol SMAL 2835* ▲	31 2

7 Dec 68 ★ **THE BEATLES** *Apple PCS 7067/8* ■ ▲ 1 22
1 Feb 69 ● **YELLOW SUBMARINE** *Apple PCS 7070*....................3 10
4 Oct 69 ★ **ABBEY ROAD** *Apple PCS 7088* ■ ▲ 1 81
23 May 70 ★ **LET IT BE** *Apple PXS 1* ■ ▲ 1 52
16 Jan 71 **A HARD DAY'S NIGHT (re-issue)** *Parlophone PCS 3058*....................30 1
24 Jul 71 **HELP! (re-issue)** *Parlophone PCS 3071* 33 2
5 May 73 ● **THE BEATLES 1962-1966** *Apple PCSP 717* 3 148
5 May 73 ● **THE BEATLES 1967-1970** *Apple PCSP 718* ▲ 2 115
26 Jun 76 **ROCK 'N' ROLL MUSIC** *Parlophone PCSP 719*....................11 15
21 Aug 76 **THE BEATLES TAPES** *Polydor 2683 068*....................45 1
21 May 77 ★ **THE BEATLES AT THE HOLLYWOOD BOWL** *Parlophone EMTV 4* 1 17
17 Dec 77 ● **LOVE SONGS** *Parlophone PCSP 721*....................7 17
3 Nov 79 **RARITIES** *Parlophone PCM 1001* 71 1
15 Nov 80 **BEATLES BALLADS** *Parlophone PCS 7214* 17 16
30 Oct 82 ● **20 GREATEST HITS** *Parlophone PCTC 260* 10 30
7 Mar 87 **A HARD DAY'S NIGHT (2nd re-issue)** *Parlophone CDP 746 4372* 30 4
7 Mar 87 **PLEASE PLEASE ME (re-issue)** *Parlophone CDP 746 4352*......32 4
7 Mar 87 **WITH THE BEATLES (re-issue)** *Parlophone CDP 746 4362*.......40 3
7 Mar 87 **BEATLES FOR SALE (re-issue)** *Parlophone CDP 746 4382* 45 2
9 May 87 **REVOLVER (re-issue)** *Parlophone CDP 746 4412* 46 12
9 May 87 **RUBBER SOUL (re-issue)** *Parlophone CDP 746 4402* 60 6
9 May 87 **HELP! (2nd re-issue)** *Parlophone CDP 746 4392*....................61 2
6 Jun 87 ● **SGT. PEPPER'S LONELY HEARTS CLUB BAND (re-issue)** *Parlophone CDP 746 4422* 3 49
5 Sep 87 **THE BEATLES (re-issue)** *Parlophone CDS 746 4439*....................18 2
5 Sep 87 **YELLOW SUBMARINE (re-issue)** *Parlophone CDP 746 4452*....................60 1
3 Oct 87 **MAGICAL MYSTERY TOUR (re-issue)** *Parlophone PCTC 255* 52 1
31 Oct 87 **ABBEY ROAD (re-issue)** *Parlophone CDP 746 4462* 30 11
31 Oct 87 **LET IT BE (re-issue)** *Parlophone CDP 746 4472*....................50 1
19 Mar 88 **PAST MASTERS VOLUME 2** *Parlophone CDBPM 2* 46 1
19 Mar 88 **PAST MASTERS VOLUME 1** *Parlophone CDBPM 1* 49 1
2 Oct 93 ● **THE BEATLES 1962-1966 (re-issue)** *Parlophone BEACD 2511* 3 23
2 Oct 93 ● **THE BEATLES 1967-1970 (re-issue)** *Parlophone BEACD 2512*.....4 21
10 Dec 94 ★ **LIVE AT THE BBC** *Apple CDS 8317962* ■ 1 20
2 Dec 95 ● **ANTHOLOGY 1** *Apple CDPCSP 727* ▲ 2 10
30 Mar 96 ★ **ANTHOLOGY 2** *Apple CDPCSP 728* ■ ▲ 1 12
9 Nov 96 ● **ANTHOLOGY 3** *Apple CDPCSP 729* ▲ 4 11
25 Sep 99 ● **YELLOW SUBMARINE – SONGTRACK (FILM SOUNDTRACK)** *Parlophone 5214812* 8 5
25 Nov 00 ★ **1** *Apple 5299702* ■ ▲....................1 46
29 Nov 03 ● **LET IT BE – NAKED** *Apple 5957132*....................7 5+

[1] Tony Sheridan and The Beatles [2] Beatles with Billy Preston

Tracks on Magical Mystery Tour (EP): Magical Mystery Tour / Your Mother Should Know / I Am the Walrus / Fool on the Hill / Flying / Blue Jay Way. 'We Can Work It Out', 'Come Together' and 'Penny Lane' were the tracks from the double A-sides that topped the US chart. The 1982 'Beatles Movie Medley' comprised (A-side) Magical Mystery Tour / All You Need Is Love / You've Got to Hide Your Love Away / I Should Have Known Better / A Hard Day's Night / Ticket To Ride / Get Back and (B-side) I'm Happy Just to Dance with You. Many Beatles hits re-entered the charts including a large number on the original Parlophone label between 1982 and 1992. The best performing re-entry was 'Love Me Do', which made No.4 in 1982 but peaked only at No.17 on its release in 1962

See also George HARRISON; John LENNON; Paul McCARTNEY; Ringo STARR

BEATMASTERS *UK, male / female production group (Singles: 47 weeks, Albums: 10 weeks)* pos/wks

9 Jan 88 ● **ROK DA HOUSE** *Rhythm King LEFT 11* [1] 5 11
24 Sep 88 **BURN IT UP** *Rhythm King LEFT 27* [2] 14 10
22 Apr 89 ● **WHO'S IN THE HOUSE** *Rhythm King LEFT 31* [3] 8 9
12 Aug 89 ● **HEY DJ – I CAN'T DANCE (TO THAT MUSIC YOU'RE PLAYING) / SKA TRAIN** *Rhythm King LEFT 34* [4] 7 11
2 Dec 89 **WARM LOVE** *Rhythm King LEFT 37* [5] 51 2
21 Sep 91 **BOULEVARD OF BROKEN DREAMS** *Rhythm King 6573617* 62 1
16 May 92 **DUNNO WHAT IT IS (ABOUT YOU)** *Rhythm King 6580017* [6] ..43 3
1 Jul 89 **ANYWAYAWANNA** *Rhythm King LEFTLP 10*....................30 10

[1] Beatmasters featuring the Cookie Crew [2] Beatmasters with PP Arnold
[3] The Beatmasters with Merlin [4] Beatmasters featuring Betty Boo
[5] Beatmasters featuring Claudia Fontaine [6] Beatmasters featuring Elaine Vassell

BEATNUTS *US, male rap duo (Singles: 2 weeks)* pos/wks

14 Jul 01 **NO ESCAPIN' THIS** *Epic 6713412* 47 1
21 Jun 03 **DUDE DESCENDING A STAIRCASE** *Stealth / SONY SSX 14CD* [1] 58 1

[1] Apollo Four Forty featuring The Beatnuts

BEATRICE – *See Mike KOGLIN*

BEATS INTERNATIONAL *UK, male / female vocal / instrumental group, leader – Norman Cook (Singles: 30 weeks, Albums: 15 weeks)* pos/wks

10 Feb 90 ★ **DUB BE GOOD TO ME** *Go.Beat GOD 39* [1] 1 13
12 May 90 ● **WON'T TALK ABOUT IT** *Go.Beat GOD 43* 9 7
15 Sep 90 **BURUNDI BLUES** *Go.Beat GOD 45* 51 3
2 Mar 91 **ECHO CHAMBER** *Go.Beat GOD 51* 60 2
21 Sep 91 **THE SUN DOESN'T SHINE** *Go.Beat GOD 59* 66 2
23 Nov 91 **IN THE GHETTO** *Go.Beat GOD 64* 44 3
14 Apr 90 **LET THEM EAT BINGO** *Go! Beat 8421961* 17 15

[1] Beats International featuring Lindy Layton

See also Norman COOK; FATBOY SLIM; FREAKPOWER; HOUSEMARTINS; MIGHTY DUB KATZ; PIZZAMAN

India BEAU – *See Basil BRUSH featuring India BEAU*

BEAUTIFUL PEOPLE

UK, male instrumental / production group (Singles: 1 week) pos/wks

28 May 94 **IF 60S WERE 90S** *Essential ESSX 2037* 74 1

BEAUTIFUL SOUTH (95 Top 500)

Ex-Housemartins Paul Heaton (v/g) and Dave Hemingway (v) (from the beautiful north of England) formed the band that featured Briana Corrigan (v) (replaced by Jacqui Abbot 1994-2000). Heaton and Dave Rotheray (g) write the witty and ironic songs (Singles: 155 weeks, Albums: 288 weeks) pos/wks

3 Jun 89 ● **SONG FOR WHOEVER** *Go! Discs GOD 32* 2 11
23 Sep 89 ● **YOU KEEP IT ALL IN** *Go! Discs GOD 35* 8 8
2 Dec 89 **I'LL SAIL THIS SHIP ALONE** *Go! Discs GOD 38*....................31 8
6 Oct 90 ★ **A LITTLE TIME** *Go! Discs GOD 47* 1 14
8 Dec 90 **MY BOOK** *Go! Discs GOD 48*....................43 6
16 Mar 91 **LET LOVE SPEAK UP ITSELF** *Go! Discs GOD 53* 51 2
11 Jan 92 **OLD RED EYES IS BACK** *Go! Discs GOD 66* 22 6
14 Mar 92 **WE ARE EACH OTHER** *Go! Discs GOD 71* 30 3
13 Jun 92 **BELL BOTTOMED TEAR** *Go! Discs GOD 78* 16 5
26 Sep 92 **36D** *Go! Discs GOD 88*....................46 2
12 Mar 94 **GOOD AS GOLD** *Go! Discs GODCD 110* 23 5
4 Jun 94 **EVERYBODY'S TALKIN'** *Go! Discs GODCD 113* 12 8
3 Sep 94 **PRETTIEST EYES** *Go! Discs GODCD 119*....................37 3
12 Nov 94 **ONE LAST LOVE SONG** *Go! Discs GODCD 122* 14 5
18 Nov 95 **PRETENDERS TO THE THRONE** *Go! Discs GODCD 134* 18 4
12 Oct 96 ● **ROTTERDAM** *Go! Discs GODCD 155* 5 9
14 Dec 96 ● **DON'T MARRY HER** *Go! Discs GODCD 158*....................8 10
29 Mar 97 **BLACKBIRD ON THE WIRE** *Go! Discs 5821252* 23 5
5 Jul 97 **LIARS' BAR** *Go! Discs 5822492* 43 1
3 Oct 98 ● **PERFECT 10** *Go! Discs 5664832*....................2 14
19 Dec 98 **DUMB (re)** *Go! Discs 5667532* 16 8
20 Mar 99 **HOW LONG'S A TEAR TAKE TO DRY?** *Go! Discs 8708212* 12 6
10 Jul 99 **THE TABLE** *Go! Discs 5621652* 47 2
7 Oct 00 **CLOSER THAN MOST** *Go! Discs / Mercury 5629672* 22 4
23 Dec 00 **THE RIVER / JUST CHECKIN'** *Go! Discs / Mercury 5727552* 59 1
17 Nov 01 **THE ROOT OF ALL EVIL** *Go! Discs / Mercury 5888702* 50 1
25 Oct 03 **JUST A FEW THINGS THAT I AIN'T** *Go! Discs / Mercury 9813038*....................30 2
13 Dec 03 **LET GO WITH THE FLOW** *Go! Discs / Mercury 9815083* 47 2
4 Nov 89 ● **WELCOME TO THE BEAUTIFUL SOUTH** *Go! Discs AGOLP 16*.....2 26
10 Nov 90 ● **CHOKE** *Go! Discs 8282331* 2 22
11 Apr 92 ● **0898 BEAUTIFUL SOUTH** *Go! Discs 8283102* 4 17
9 Apr 94 ● **MIAOW** *Go! Discs 8285072* 6 24
19 Nov 94 ★ **CARRY ON UP THE CHARTS – THE BEST OF THE BEAUTIFUL SOUTH** *Go! Discs 8285722*....................1 89
2 Nov 96 ★ **BLUE IS THE COLOUR** *Go! Discs 8288452* ■ 1 46
24 Oct 98 ★ **QUENCH** *Go! Discs / Mercury 5381662* ■....................1 37
21 Oct 00 ● **PAINTING IT RED** *Go! Discs / Mercury 5483352*....................2 11

24 Nov 01 ● SOLID BRONZE – GREAT HITS *Go! Discs / Mercury 5864442* 10 13
8 Nov 03 GAZE *Go! Discs / Mercury 9865694* 14 3

BEAVIS and BUTT-HEAD – *See CHER*

Gilbert BÉCAUD

France, male vocalist, d. 18 Dec 2001 (Singles: 12 weeks) pos/wks

29 Mar 75 ● **A LITTLE LOVE AND UNDERSTANDING** *Decca F 13537* 10 12

BECK *US, male vocalist – David Campbell*

(Singles: 27 weeks, Albums: 78 weeks) pos/wks

5 Mar 94 **LOSER** *Geffen GFSTD 67* 15 6
29 Jun 96 **WHERE IT'S AT** *Geffen GFSTD 22156* 35 2
16 Nov 96 **DEVIL'S HAIRCUT** *Geffen GFSTD 22183* 22 2
8 Mar 97 **THE NEW POLLUTION** *Geffen GFSTD 22205* 14 5
24 May 97 **SISSYNECK** *Geffen GFSTD 22253* 30 2
8 Nov 97 **DEADWEIGHT** *Geffen GFSTD 22293* 23 3
19 Dec 98 **TROPICALIA** *Geffen GFSTD 22365* 39 2
20 Nov 99 **SEXX LAWS** *Geffen 4971812* 27 3
8 Apr 00 **MIXED BIZNESS** *Geffen 4973002* 34 2
2 Apr 94 MELLOW GOLD *Geffen GED 24634* 41 4
6 Jul 96 ODELAY *Geffen GED 24926* 17 51
14 Nov 98 MUTATIONS *Geffen GED 25184* 24 6
4 Dec 99 MIDNITE VULTURES *Geffen 4905272* 19 14
5 Oct 02 SEA CHANGE *Geffen / Polydor 4933932* 20 3

Jeff BECK *UK, male vocalist / instrumentalist – guitar (Singles: 57 weeks, Albums: 15 weeks)* pos/wks

23 Mar 67 **HI-HO SILVER LINING** *Columbia DB 8151* 14 14
2 Aug 67 **TALLYMAN** *Columbia DB 8227* 30 3
28 Feb 68 **LOVE IS BLUE (L'AMOUR EST BLEU)** *Columbia DB 8359* 23 7
9 Jul 69 **GOO GOO BARABAJAGAL (LOVE IS HOT)** *Pye 7N 17778* [1] 12 9
4 Nov 72 **HI-HO SILVER LINING (re) (re-issue)** *RAK RR 3* 17 15
5 May 73 **I'VE BEEN DRINKING** *RAK RR 4* [2] 27 6
7 Mar 92 **PEOPLE GET READY** *Epic 6577567* [2] 49 3
13 Sep 69 BECK-OLA *Columbia SCX 6351* 39 1
28 Apr 73 JEFF BECK TIM BOGERT AND CARMINE APPICE *Epic EPC 65455* [1] 28 3
24 Jul 76 WIRED *CBS 86012* 38 5
19 Jul 80 THERE AND BACK *Epic EPC 83288* 38 4
17 Aug 85 FLASH *Epic EPC 26112* 83 1
27 Mar 99 WHO ELSE! *Epic 4930412* 74 1

[1] Donovan with the Jeff Beck Group [2] Jeff Beck and Rod Stewart [1] Jeff Beck Tim Bogert and Carmine Appice

See also YARDBIRDS

Robin BECK *US, female vocalist (Singles: 13 weeks)* pos/wks

22 Oct 88 ★ **THE FIRST TIME** *Mercury MER 270* 1 13

Peter BECKETT – *See Barry GRAY ORCHESTRA*

Victoria BECKHAM

UK, female vocalist (Singles: 38 weeks, Albums: 3 weeks) pos/wks

26 Aug 00 ● **OUT OF YOUR MIND (re)** *Nulife 74321782942* [1] 2 20
29 Sep 01 ● **NOT SUCH AN INNOCENT GIRL (2re)** *Virgin VSCDT 1816* 6 11
23 Feb 02 ● **A MIND OF ITS OWN** *Virgin VSCDT 1824* 6 7
13 Oct 01 ● VICTORIA BECKHAM *Virgin CDV 2942* 10 3

[1] True Steppers and Dane Bowers featuring Victoria Beckham

See also SPICE GIRLS

BEDAZZLED

UK, male vocal / instrumental group (Singles: 1 week) pos/wks

4 Jul 92 **SUMMER SONG** *Columbia 6581627* 73 1

Daniel BEDINGFIELD *New Zealand, male vocalist / producer (Singles: 71 weeks, Albums: 60 weeks)* pos/wks

8 Dec 01 ★ **GOTTA GET THRU THIS** *Relentless RELENT 27CD* ■ 1 18
24 Aug 02 ● **JAMES DEAN (I WANNA KNOW)** *Polydor 5709342* 4 8
7 Dec 02 ★ **IF YOU'RE NOT THE ONE** *Polydor 0658632* ■ 1 21
19 Apr 03 ● **I CAN'T READ YOU** *Polydor 0657132* 6 11
2 Aug 03 ★ **NEVER GONNA LEAVE YOUR SIDE** *Polydor 9809364* ■ 1 11
1 Nov 03 **FRIDAY** *Polydor 9812919* 28 2
7 Sep 02 ● GOTTA GET THRU THIS *Polydor 651252* 2 60+

BEDLAM *UK, male DJ / production duo – Alan Thomson and Richard 'Diddy' Dearlove (Singles: 1 week)* pos/wks

6 Feb 99 **DA-FORCE** *Playola 0091695 PLA* 68 1

See also DIDDY

BEDLAM AGO GO

UK, male vocal / instrumental group (Singles: 1 week) pos/wks

4 Apr 98 **SEASON NO.5** *Sony S2 BDLM 2CD* 57 1

BEDROCK *UK, male vocal / instrumental duo – John Digweed and Nick Muir (Singles: 9 weeks)* pos/wks

1 Jun 96 **FOR WHAT YOU DREAM OF** *Stress CDSTR 23* [1] 25 3
12 Jul 97 **SET IN STONE / FORBIDDEN ZONE** *Stress CDSTR 80* 71 1
6 Nov 99 **HEAVEN SCENT** *Bedrock BEDRCDS 001* 35 3
8 Jul 00 **VOICES** *Bedrock BEDRCDS 005* 44 2

[1] Bedrock featuring KYO

BEDROCKS

UK, male vocal / instrumental group (Singles: 7 weeks) pos/wks

18 Dec 68 **OB-LA-DI, OB-LA-DA** *Columbia DB 8516* 20 7

Celi BEE and the BUZZY BUNCH

US, male / female vocal / instrumental group (Singles: 1 week) pos/wks

17 Jun 78 **HOLD YOUR HORSES, BABE** *TK TKR 6032* 72 1

BEE GEES (31 Top 500)

All-time top family recording act, who are members of the exclusive 100 million-plus sales club, are Isle of Man, UK, born and Australian-raised Barry, Robin and Maurice Gibb (d. 12 Jan 2003). As composers, they have penned hits for many top acts and had 10 UK No.1s. In 1978 they wrote four consecutive US chart-toppers (three of which they also produced). Their 'Saturday Night Fever' album is the world's biggest selling soundtrack and they were the first group to have UK Top 20s in five decades. Distinctive trio has won countless trophies including the World Music Legend Award (1997) and Brits Outstanding Contribution to British Music (1997) (Singles: 354 weeks, Albums: 406 weeks) pos/wks

27 Apr 67 **NEW YORK MINING DISASTER 1941** *Polydor 56 161* 12 10
12 Jul 67 **TO LOVE SOMEBODY (re)** *Polydor 56 178* 41 5
20 Sep 67 ★ **(THE NIGHT THE LIGHTS WENT OUT IN) MASSACHUSETTS** *Polydor 56 192* 1 17
22 Nov 67 ● **WORLD** *Polydor 56 220* 9 16
31 Jan 68 ● **WORDS** *Polydor 56 229* 8 10
27 Mar 68 **JUMBO / THE SINGER SANG HIS SONG** *Polydor 56 242* 25 7
7 Aug 68 ★ **I'VE GOTTA GET A MESSAGE TO YOU** *Polydor 56 273* 1 15
19 Feb 69 ● **FIRST OF MAY** *Polydor 56 304* 6 11
4 Jun 69 **TOMORROW, TOMORROW** *Polydor 56 331* 23 8
16 Aug 69 ● **DON'T FORGET TO REMEMBER** *Polydor 56 343* 2 15
28 Mar 70 **I.O.I.O.** *Polydor 56 377* 49 1
5 Dec 70 **LONELY DAYS** *Polydor 2001 104* 33 9
29 Jan 72 **MY WORLD** *Polydor 2058 185* 16 9
22 Jul 72 ● **RUN TO ME** *Polydor 2058 255* 9 10
28 Jun 75 ● **JIVE TALKIN'** *RSO 2090 160* ▲ 5 11
31 Jul 76 ● **YOU SHOULD BE DANCING** *RSO 2090 195* ▲ 5 10
13 Nov 76 **LOVE SO RIGHT** *RSO 2090 207* 41 4
29 Oct 77 ● **HOW DEEP IS YOUR LOVE** *RSO 2090 259* ▲ 3 15
4 Feb 78 ● **STAYIN' ALIVE (re)** *RSO 2090 267* ▲ 4 18
15 Apr 78 ★ **NIGHT FEVER** *RSO 002* ▲ 1 20
25 Nov 78 ● **TOO MUCH HEAVEN** *RSO 25* ▲ 3 13
17 Feb 79 ★ **TRAGEDY** *RSO 27* ▲ 1 10
14 Apr 79 **LOVE YOU INSIDE OUT** *RSO 31* ▲ 13 9
5 Jan 80 **SPIRITS (HAVING FLOWN)** *RSO 52* 16 7
17 Sep 83 **SOMEONE BELONGING TO SOMEONE** *RSO 96* 49 4
26 Sep 87 ★ **YOU WIN AGAIN** *Warner Bros. W 8351* 1 15

Date		Title	pos	wks
12 Dec 87		**E.S.P.** *Warner Bros. W 8139*	51	5
15 Apr 89		**ORDINARY LIVES** *Warner Bros. W 7523*	54	3
24 Jun 89		**ONE** *Warner Bros. W 2916*	71	1
2 Mar 91	●	**SECRET LOVE** *Warner Bros. W 0014*	5	11
21 Aug 93		**PAYING THE PRICE OF LOVE** *Polydor PZCD 284*	23	5
27 Nov 93	●	**FOR WHOM THE BELL TOLLS** *Polydor PZCD 299*	4	14
16 Apr 94		**HOW TO FALL IN LOVE PART 1** *Polydor PZDD 311*	30	4
1 Mar 97	●	**ALONE** *Polydor 5735272*	5	9
21 Jun 97		**I COULD NOT LOVE YOU MORE** *Polydor 5712232*	14	3
8 Nov 97		**STILL WATERS (RUN DEEP)** *Polydor 5718892*	18	3
18 Jul 98	●	**IMMORTALITY** *Epic 6661682* [1]	5	12
7 Apr 01		**THIS IS WHERE I CAME IN** *Polydor 5879772*	18	5
12 Aug 67	●	**BEE GEES FIRST** *Polydor 583012*	8	27
24 Feb 68		**HORIZONTAL** *Polydor 582020*	16	15
28 Sep 68	●	**IDEA** *Polydor 583036*	4	18
5 Apr 69	●	**ODESSA** *Polydor 583049/50*	10	1
8 Nov 69	●	**BEST OF THE BEE GEES** *Polydor 583063*	7	22
9 May 70		**CUCUMBER CASTLE** *Polydor 2383010*	57	2
17 Feb 79	★	**SPIRITS HAVING FLOWN** *RSO RSBG 001* ▲	1	33
10 Nov 79	●	**BEE GEES GREATEST** *RSO RSDX 001* ▲	6	25
7 Nov 81		**LIVING EYES** *RSO RSBG 002*	73	8
3 Oct 87	●	**E.S.P.** *Warner Bros. WX 83*	5	24
29 Apr 89		**ONE** *Warner Bros. WX 252*	29	3
17 Nov 90	●	**THE VERY BEST OF THE BEE GEES** *Polydor 8473391*	6	108
6 Apr 91		**HIGH CIVILISATION** *Warner Bros. WX 417*	24	5
25 Sep 93		**SIZE ISN'T EVERYTHING** *Polydor 5199452*	23	13
22 Mar 97	●	**STILL WATERS** *Polydor 5373022*	2	19
19 Sep 98	●	**LIVE ONE NIGHT ONLY** *Polydor 5592202*	4	44
14 Apr 01	●	**THIS IS WHERE I CAME IN** *Polydor 5494582*	6	6
24 Nov 01	●	**THEIR GREATEST HITS – THE RECORD** *Polydor 5894492*	5	33

[1] Celine Dion with special guests The Bee Gees

See also Barry GIBB; Robin GIBB

Sir Thomas BEECHAM

UK, conductor, d. 8 Mar 1961 (Albums: 2 weeks) pos/wks

Date		Title	pos	wks
26 Mar 60		**CARMEN** *HMV ALP 1762/4*	18	2

Full credit on sleeve reads 'Orchestre National de la Radio Diffusion Française conducted by Sir Thomas Beecham'

BEENIE MAN *Jamaica, male vocalist / toaster / rapper – Anthony Moses David (Singles: 35 weeks)*

pos/wks

Date		Title	pos	wks
20 Sep 97		**DANCEHALL QUEEN** *Island Jamaica IJCD 2018* [1]	70	1
7 Mar 98	●	**WHO AM I** *Greensleeves GRECD 588*	10	5
8 Aug 98		**FOUNDATION** *Shocking Vibes SVJCDS1*	69	1
4 Mar 00	●	**MONEY** *Parlophone Rhythm Series CDRHYTHM 27* [2]	5	9
24 Mar 01		**GIRLS DEM SUGAR** *Virgin VUSCD 173* [3]	13	5
28 Sep 02	●	**FEEL IT BOY (re)** *Virgin VUSCD 258* [4]	9	7
14 Dec 02		**DIRTY HARRY'S REVENGE** *Kaos KAOS 004* [5]	50	2
8 Feb 03		**STREET LIFE** *Virgin VUSCD 260*	13	5

[1] Chevelle Franklyn / Beenie Man [2] Jamelia featuring Beenie Man [3] Beenie Man featuring Mya [4] Beenie Man featuring Janet [5] Adam F featuring Beenie Man

Lou BEGA *Germany, male vocalist – David Lubega (Singles: 21 weeks, Albums: 2 weeks)*

pos/wks

Date		Title	pos	wks
7 Aug 99		**MAMBO NO.5 (A LITTLE BIT OF ...) (import)** *Ariola 74321658012*	31	4
4 Sep 99	★	**MAMBO NO.5 (A LITTLE BIT OF ...)** *RCA 74321696722* ■	1	15
18 Dec 99		**I GOT A GIRL** *RCA 74321720642*	55	2
18 Sep 99		**A LITTLE BIT OF MAMBO** *RCA 74321688612*	50	2

BEGGAR and CO

UK, male vocal / instrumental group (Singles: 15 weeks) pos/wks

Date		Title	pos	wks
7 Feb 81		**(SOMEBODY) HELP ME OUT** *Ensign ENY 201*	15	10
12 Sep 81		**MULE (CHANT NO.2)** *RCA 130*	37	5

BEGINERZ *UK, male production duo – Ibi Tijani and Euen MacNeil (Singles: 3 weeks)*

pos/wks

Date		Title	pos	wks
13 Jul 02		**RECKLESS GIRL** *Cheeky / Arista 74321942232*	28	3

BEGINNING OF THE END

US, male vocal / instrumental group (Singles: 6 weeks) pos/wks

Date		Title	pos	wks
23 Feb 74		**FUNKY NASSAU** *Atlantic K 10021*	31	6

BEIJING SPRING *UK, female vocal duo (Singles: 5 weeks)*

pos/wks

Date		Title	pos	wks
23 Jan 93		**I WANNA BE IN LOVE AGAIN** *MCA MCSTD 1709*	43	3
8 May 93		**SUMMERLANDS** *MCA MCSTD 1761*	53	2

BEJAY – *See 56K featuring BEJAY*

BEL AMOUR

France, male / female vocal / production trio (Singles: 3 weeks) pos/wks

Date		Title	pos	wks
12 May 01		**BEL AMOUR** *Credence CDCRED 010*	23	3

BEL CANTO

UK, male vocal / instrumental group (Singles: 1 week) pos/wks

Date		Title	pos	wks
14 Oct 95		**WE'VE GOT TO WORK IT OUT** *Good Groove CDGG 2*	65	1

Harry BELAFONTE

US, male vocalist / actor (Singles: 87 weeks) pos/wks

Date		Title	pos	wks
1 Mar 57	●	**BANANA BOAT SONG (DAY-O)** *HMV POP 308* [1]	2	18
14 Jun 57	●	**ISLAND IN THE SUN** *RCA 1007*	3	25
6 Sep 57		**SCARLET RIBBONS** *HMV POP 360* [2]	18	6
1 Nov 57	★	**MARY'S BOY CHILD (2re)** *RCA 1022* ◆	1	19
22 Aug 58		**LITTLE BERNADETTE** *RCA 1072* [3]	16	7
12 Dec 58		**THE SON OF MARY** *RCA 1084*	18	4
21 Sep 61		**THERE'S A HOLE IN MY BUCKET (re)** *RCA 1247* [4]	32	8

[1] Harry Belafonte with Tony Scott's Orchestra and Chorus and Millard Thomas, Guitar [2] Harry Belafonte and Millard Thomas [3] Belafonte [4] Harry Belafonte and Odetta

'Mary's Boy Child' re-entered twice peaking at No.10 in 1958 and at No.30 in 1959

Archie BELL and the DRELLS

US, male vocal / instrumental group (Singles: 33 weeks) pos/wks

Date		Title	pos	wks
7 Oct 72		**HERE I GO AGAIN** *Atlantic K 10210*	11	10
27 Jan 73		**(THERE'S GONNA BE A) SHOWDOWN** *Atlantic K 10263*	36	5
8 May 76		**THE SOUL CITY WALK** *Philadelphia International PIR 4250*	13	10
11 Jun 77		**EVERYBODY HAVE A GOOD TIME** *Philadelphia International PIR 5179*	43	4
28 Jun 86		**DON'T LET LOVE GET YOU DOWN** *Portrait A 7254*	49	4

Freddie BELL and the BELLBOYS

US, male vocal / instrumental group (Singles: 10 weeks) pos/wks

Date		Title	pos	wks
28 Sep 56	●	**GIDDY-UP-A DING DONG** *Mercury MT 122*	4	10

Maggie BELL *UK, female vocalist (Singles: 12 weeks)*

pos/wks

Date		Title	pos	wks
15 Apr 78		**HAZELL (re)** *Swansong SSK 19412*	37	4
17 Oct 81		**HOLD ME** *Swansong BAM 1* [1]	11	8

[1] B A Robertson and Maggie Bell

See also STONE THE CROWS

William BELL

US, male vocalist – William Yarborough (Singles: 22 weeks) pos/wks

Date		Title	pos	wks
29 May 68		**A TRIBUTE TO A KING** *Stax 601 038*	31	7
20 Nov 68	●	**PRIVATE NUMBER** *Stax 101* [1]	8	14
26 Apr 86		**HEADLINE NEWS** *Absolute LUTE 1*	70	1

[1] Judy Clay and William Bell

BELL and JAMES *US, male vocal duo (Singles: 3 weeks)*

pos/wks

Date		Title	pos	wks
31 Mar 79		**LIVIN' IT UP (FRIDAY NIGHT) (re)** *A&M AMS 7424*	59	3

BELL & SPURLING *UK, male vocal duo – Martin Bellamy and John Spurling (Singles: 10 weeks)*

pos/wks

Date		Title	pos	wks
13 Oct 01	●	**SVEN SVEN SVEN** *Eternal WEA 336CD*	7	6
8 Jun 02		**GOLDENBALLS (MR BECKHAM TO YOU)** *Eternal WEA 350CD*	25	4

BELL BIV DEVOE

US, male vocal group (Singles: 29 weeks, Albums: 5 weeks) pos/wks

		pos	wks
30 Jun 90	**POISON** *MCA MCA 1414*	19	11
22 Sep 90	**DO ME** *MCA MCA 1440*	56	3
15 Aug 92	● **THE BEST THINGS IN LIFE ARE FREE** *Perspective PERSS 7400* [1]	2	13
9 Oct 93	**SOMETHING IN YOUR EYES** *MCA MCSTD 1934*	60	2
1 Sep 90	**POISON** *MCA MCG 6094*	35	5

[1] Luther Vandross and Janet Jackson with special guests BBD and Ralph Tresvant

BELL BOOK & CANDLE

Germany, male / female vocal / instrumental group (Singles: 1 week) pos/wks

		pos	wks
17 Oct 98	**RESCUE ME** *Logic 74321616882*	63	1

BELLAMY BROTHERS *US, male vocal duo – Howard and David Bellamy (Singles: 29 weeks, Albums: 6 weeks)* pos/wks

		pos	wks
17 Apr 76	● **LET YOUR LOVE FLOW** *Warner Bros. / Curb K 16690* ▲	7	12
21 Aug 76	**SATIN SHEETS** *Warner Bros. / Curb K 16775*	43	3
11 Aug 79	● **IF I SAID YOU HAVE A BEAUTIFUL BODY WOULD YOU HOLD IT AGAINST ME** *Warner Bros. / Curb K 17405*	3	14
19 Jun 76	**BELLAMY BROTHERS** *Warner Bros. K 56242*	21	6

BELLATRIX

Iceland, male / female vocal / instrumental group (Singles: 1 week) pos/wks

		pos	wks
16 Sep 00	**JEDI WANNABE** *Fierce Panda NING 101CD*	65	1

BELLBOYS – *See Freddie BELL and the BELLBOYS*

Regina BELLE

US, female vocalist (Singles: 13 weeks, Albums: 5 weeks) pos/wks

		pos	wks
21 Oct 89	**GOOD LOVIN'** *CBS 655230*	73	1
11 Dec 93	**A WHOLE NEW WORLD (ALADDIN'S THEME)** *Columbia 6599002* [1] ▲	12	12
1 Aug 87	**ALL BY MYSELF** *CBS 450 9981*	53	4
16 Sep 89	**STAY WITH ME** *CBS 465132 1*	62	1

[1] Regina Belle and Peabo Bryson

BELLE & SEBASTIAN *UK, male / female vocal / instrumental group (Singles: 14 weeks, Albums: 18 weeks)* pos/wks

		pos	wks
24 May 97	**DOG ON WHEELS** *Jeepster JPRCDS 001*	59	1
9 Aug 97	**LAZY LINE PAINTER JANE** *Jeepster JPRCDS 002*	41	2
25 Oct 97	**3... 6... 9 SECONDS OF LIGHT (EP)** *Jeepster JPRCDS 003*	32	2
3 Jun 00	**LEGAL MAN** *Jeepster JPRCD 018*	15	3
30 Jun 01	**JONATHAN DAVID** *Jeepster JPRCDS 022*	31	2
8 Dec 01	**I'M WAKING UP TO US** *Jeepster JPRCDS 023*	39	2
29 Nov 03	**STEP INTO MY OFFICE BABY** *Rough Trade RTRADESCD 128*	32	2
19 Sep 98	**THE BOY WITH THE ARAB STRAP** *Jeepster JPRCD 003*	12	6
24 Jul 99	**TIGERMILK** *Jeepster JPRCD 007*	13	4
17 Jun 00	● **FOLD YOUR HANDS CHILD, YOU WALK LIKE A PEASANT** *Jeepster JPRMD 010*	10	3
15 Jun 02	**STORYTELLING** *Jeepster JPRCD 014*	26	2
18 Oct 03	**DEAR CATASTROPHE WAITRESS** *Rough Trade RTRADECD080*	21	3

Tracks on 3... 6... 9 Seconds of Light (EP): A Century of Fakers / Le Pastie de la Bourgeoisie / Beautiful / Put the Book Back on the Shelf

BELLE and the DEVOTIONS

UK, female vocal group (Singles: 8 weeks) pos/wks

		pos	wks
21 Apr 84	**LOVE GAMES** *CBS A 4332*	11	8

BELLE STARS *UK, female vocal / instrumental group (Singles: 42 weeks, Albums: 12 weeks)* pos/wks

		pos	wks
5 Jun 82	**IKO IKO** *Stiff BUY 150*	35	6
17 Jul 82	**THE CLAPPING SONG** *Stiff BUY 155*	11	9
16 Oct 82	**MOCKINGBIRD** *Stiff BUY 159*	51	3
15 Jan 83	● **SIGN OF THE TIMES** *Stiff BUY 167*	3	11
16 Apr 83	**SWEET MEMORY** *Stiff BUY 174*	22	9
13 Aug 83	**INDIAN SUMMER** *Stiff BUY 185*	52	3
14 Jul 84	**80S ROMANCE** *Stiff BUY 200*	71	1
5 Feb 83	**THE BELLE STARS** *Stiff SEEZ 45*	15	12

BELLEFIRE

Ireland, female vocal group (Singles: 8 weeks) pos/wks

		pos	wks
14 Jul 01	**PERFECT BLISS** *Virgin VSCDT 1807*	18	4
18 May 02	**ALL I WANT IS YOU** *Virgin VSCDT 1820*	18	4

BELLINI

Germany, male vocal / production group (Singles: 7 weeks) pos/wks

		pos	wks
27 Sep 97	● **SAMBA DE JANEIRO** *Virgin DINSD 165*	8	7

BELLRAYS *US, male / female vocal / instrumental group (Singles: 1 week, Albums: 1 week)* pos/wks

		pos	wks
20 Jul 02	**THEY GLUED YOUR HEAD ON UPSIDE DOWN** *Poptones MC 5073SCD*	75	1
18 May 02	**MEET THE BELLRAYS** *Poptones MC 5069CD*	73	1

Louis BELLSON – *See Duke ELLINGTON*

BELLY *US, male / female vocal / instrumental group (Singles: 9 weeks, Albums: 13 weeks)* pos/wks

		pos	wks
23 Jan 93	**FEED THE TREE** *4AD BAD 3001CD*	32	3
10 Apr 93	**GEPETTO** *4AD BAD 2018CD*	49	2
4 Feb 95	**NOW THEY'LL SLEEP** *4AD BAD 5003CD*	28	2
22 Jul 95	**SEAL MY FATE** *4AD BAD 5007CD*	35	2
13 Feb 93	● **STAR** *4AD 3002CD*	2	10
25 Feb 95	● **KING** *4AD CADD 5004CD*	6	3

See also Tanya DONELLY

Pierre BELMONDE *France, male instrumentalist – panpipes – Jeff Jarrett (Albums: 10 weeks)* pos/wks

		pos	wks
7 Jun 80	**THEMES FOR DREAMS** *K-Tel ONE 1077*	13	10

See also Jeff JARRATT and Don REEDMAN

BELMONTS – *See DION*

BELOVED *UK, male / female vocal / instrumental duo (Singles: 47 weeks, Albums: 31 weeks)* pos/wks

		pos	wks
21 Oct 89	**THE SUN RISING** *WEA YZ 414*	26	7
27 Jan 90	**HELLO** *WEA YZ 426*	19	7
24 Mar 90	**YOUR LOVE TAKES ME HIGHER** *East West YZ 463*	39	3
9 Jun 90	**TIME AFTER TIME** *East West YZ 482*	46	4
10 Nov 90	**IT'S ALRIGHT NOW** *East West YZ 541*	48	3
23 Jan 93	● **SWEET HARMONY** *East West YZ 709CD*	8	10
10 Apr 93	**YOU'VE GOT ME THINKING** *East West YZ 738CD*	23	4
14 Aug 93	**OUTERSPACE GIRL** *East West YZ 726CD*	38	2
30 Mar 96	**SATELLITE** *East West EW 034CD*	19	3
10 Aug 96	**EASE THE PRESSURE** *East West EW 058CD*	43	2
30 Aug 97	**THE SUN RISING (re-issue)** *East West EW 122CD1*	31	2
3 Mar 90	**HAPPINESS** *East West WX 299*	14	14
1 Dec 90	**BLISSED OUT** *East West WX 383*	38	2
20 Feb 93	● **CONSCIENCE** *East West 4509914832*	2	12
20 Apr 96	**X** *East West 630133162*	25	3

Act was male only before 1993

BELTRAM

US, male producer – Joey Beltram (Singles: 4 weeks) pos/wks

		pos	wks
28 Sep 91	**ENERGY FLASH (EP)** *R&S RSUK 3*	52	2
7 Dec 91	**THE OMEN** *R&S RSUK 7* [1]	53	2

[1] Program 2 Beltram

Tracks on Energy Flash (EP): Energy Flash / Psycho Bass / My Sound / Sub-Base Experience

Benny BENASSI presents The BIZ

Italy, male producer (Singles: 11 weeks) pos/wks

		pos	wks
26 Jul 03	● **SATISFACTION** *Data / MoS DATA 58CDS*	2	11

Pat BENATAR *US, female vocalist – Patricia Andrzejewski (Singles: 53 weeks, Albums: 84 weeks)*

Date	Title / Label	pos	wks
21 Jan 84	**LOVE IS A BATTLEFIELD** *Chrysalis CHS 2747*	49	5
12 Jan 85	**WE BELONG** *Chrysalis CHS 2821*	22	9
23 Mar 85	**LOVE IS A BATTLEFIELD (re-issue)** *Chrysalis PAT 1*	17	10
15 Jun 85	**SHADOWS OF THE NIGHT** *Chrysalis PAT 2*	50	4
19 Oct 85	**INVINCIBLE (THEME FROM 'THE LEGEND OF BILLIE JEAN')** *Chrysalis PAT 3*	53	3
15 Feb 86	**SEX AS A WEAPON** *Chrysalis PAT 4*	67	3
2 Jul 88	**ALL FIRED UP** *Chrysalis PAT 5*	19	10
1 Oct 88	**DON'T WALK AWAY** *Chrysalis PAT 6*	42	5
14 Jan 89	**ONE LOVE** *Chrysalis PAT 7*	59	3
30 Oct 93	**SOMEBODY'S BABY** *Chrysalis CDCHS 5001*	48	1
25 Jul 81	**PRECIOUS TIME** *Chrysalis CHR 1346* ▲	30	7
13 Nov 82	**GET NERVOUS** *Chrysalis CHR 1396*	73	6
15 Oct 83	**LIVE FROM EARTH** *Chrysalis CHR 1451*	60	5
17 Nov 84	**TROPICO** *Chrysalis CHR 1471*	31	25
24 Aug 85	**IN THE HEAT OF THE NIGHT** *Chrysalis CHR 1236*	98	1
7 Dec 85	**SEVEN THE HARD WAY** *Chrysalis CHR 1507*	69	4
7 Nov 87 ●	**BEST SHOTS** *Chrysalis PATV 1*	6	19
16 Jul 88	**WIDE AWAKE IN DREAMLAND** *Chrysalis CDL 1628*	11	14
4 May 91	**TRUE LOVE** *Chrysalis CHR 1805*	40	3

David BENDETH *Canada, male vocalist and multi-instrumentalist (Singles: 5 weeks)*

Date	Title / Label	pos	wks
8 Sep 79	**FEEL THE REAL** *Sidewalk SID 113*	44	5

BENELUX and Nancy DEE *Belgium / Holland / Luxembourg, female vocal group (Singles: 4 weeks)*

Date	Title / Label	pos	wks
25 Aug 79	**SWITCH** *Scope SC 4*	52	4

Eric BENET *US, male vocalist – Eric Bennet Jordan (Singles: 5 weeks, Albums: 1 week)*

Date	Title / Label	pos	wks
22 Mar 97	**SPIRITUAL THANG** *Warner Bros. W 0390CD*	62	1
1 May 99	**GEORGY PORGY** *Warner Bros. W478CD2* [1]	28	3
5 Feb 00	**WHY YOU FOLLOW ME** *Warner Bros. W491CD*	48	1
15 May 99	**A DAY IN THE LIFE** *Warner Bros. 9362473702*	67	1

[1] Eric Benet featuring Faith Evans

Nigel BENN – *See PACK featuring Nigel BENN*

Simone BENN – *See VOLATILE AGENTS featuring Simone BENN*

BENNET *UK, male vocal / instrumental group (Singles: 3 weeks)*

Date	Title / Label	pos	wks
22 Feb 97	**MUM'S GONE TO ICELAND** *Roadrunner RR 22853*	34	2
3 May 97	**SOMEONE ALWAYS GETS THERE FIRST** *Roadrunner RR 22983*	69	1

Boyd BENNETT and his ROCKETS *US, male vocalist, d. 2 Jun 2002 and male vocal / instrumental group (Singles: 2 weeks)*

Date	Title / Label	pos	wks
23 Dec 55	**SEVENTEEN** *Parlophone R 4063*	16	2

Chris BENNETT – *See MUNICH MACHINE*

Cliff BENNETT and the REBEL ROUSERS *UK, male vocal / instrumental group (Singles: 23 weeks, Albums: 3 weeks)*

Date	Title / Label	pos	wks
1 Oct 64 ●	**ONE WAY LOVE** *Parlophone R 5173*	9	9
4 Feb 65	**I'LL TAKE YOU HOME** *Parlophone R 5229*	42	3
11 Aug 66 ●	**GOT TO GET YOU INTO MY LIFE** *Parlophone R 5489*	6	11
22 Oct 66	**DRIVIN' ME WILD** *MFP 1121*	25	3

Easther BENNETT – *See ASWAD; ETERNAL*

Peter E BENNETT with the CO-OPERATION CHOIR *UK, male vocalist and choir (Singles: 1 week)*

Date	Title / Label	pos	wks
7 Nov 70	**THE SEAGULL'S NAME WAS NELSON** *RCA 1991*	45	1

Tony BENNETT *US, male vocalist – Anthony Benedetto (Singles: 61 weeks, Albums: 70 weeks)*

Date	Title / Label	pos	wks
15 Apr 55 ★	**STRANGER IN PARADISE** *Philips PB 420*	1	16
16 Sep 55	**CLOSE YOUR EYES** *Philips PB 445*	18	1
13 Apr 56	**COME NEXT SPRING** *Philips PB 537*	29	1
5 Jan 61	**TILL** *Philips PB 1079*	35	2
18 Jul 63	**THE GOOD LIFE** *CBS AAG 153*	27	13
6 May 65	**IF I RULED THE WORLD** *CBS 201735*	40	5
27 May 65	**(I LEFT MY HEART) IN SAN FRANCISCO (2re)** *CBS 201730*	25	14
23 Dec 65	**THE VERY THOUGHT OF YOU** *CBS 202021*	21	9
29 May 65	**I LEFT MY HEART IN SAN FRANCISCO** *CBS BPG 62201*	13	14
19 Feb 66 ●	**A STRING OF TONY'S HITS** *CBS DP 66010*	9	13
10 Jun 67	**TONY'S GREATEST HITS** *CBS SBPG 62821*	14	24
23 Sep 67	**TONY MAKES IT HAPPEN** *CBS SBPG 63055*	31	3
23 Mar 68	**FOR ONCE IN MY LIFE** *CBS SBPG 63166*	29	5
26 Feb 77	**THE VERY BEST OF TONY BENNETT – 20 GREATEST HITS** *Warwick PA 5021*	23	4
28 Nov 98	**THE ESSENTIAL TONY BENNETT** *Columbia 4928222*	49	4
5 Jul 03	**A WONDERFUL WORLD** *Columbia 5098702* [1]	33	3

[1] Tony Bennett & kd lang

Gary BENSON *UK, male vocalist – Harry Hyams (Singles: 8 weeks)*

Date	Title / Label	pos	wks
9 Aug 75	**DON'T THROW IT ALL AWAY** *State STAT 10*	20	8

George BENSON (96 Top 500)

Grammy-winning guitarist / vocalist, b. 22 Mar 1943, Pennsylvania, US. This one-time child prodigy topped the US chart in 1976 with the triple-platinum album 'Breezin''. He was also a major live attraction in Britain during the 1980s (Singles: 143 weeks, Albums: 298 weeks)

Date	Title / Label	pos	wks
25 Oct 75	**SUPERSHIP** *CTI CTSP 002* [1]	30	6
4 Jun 77	**NATURE BOY** *Warner Bros. K 16921*	26	6
24 Sep 77	**THE GREATEST LOVE OF ALL** *Arista 133*	27	7
31 Mar 79	**LOVE BALLAD** *Warner Bros. K 17333*	29	9
26 Jul 80 ●	**GIVE ME THE NIGHT** *Warner Bros. K 17673*	7	10
4 Oct 80 ●	**LOVE X LOVE** *Warner Bros. K 17699*	10	8
7 Feb 81	**WHAT'S ON YOUR MIND** *Warner Bros. K 17748*	45	5
19 Sep 81	**LOVE ALL THE HURT AWAY** *Arista ARIST 428* [2]	49	3
14 Nov 81	**TURN YOUR LOVE AROUND** *Warner Bros. K 17877*	29	11
23 Jan 82	**NEVER GIVE UP ON A GOOD THING** *Warner Bros. K 17902*	14	10
21 May 83	**LADY LOVE ME (ONE MORE TIME)** *Warner Bros. W 9614*	11	10
16 Jul 83	**FEEL LIKE MAKIN' LOVE** *Warner Bros. W 9551*	28	7
24 Sep 83 ●	**IN YOUR EYES** *Warner Bros. W 9487*	7	10
17 Dec 83	**INSIDE LOVE (SO PERSONAL)** *WEA Int. W 9427*	57	5
19 Jan 85	**20 / 20** *Warner Bros. W 9120*	29	9
20 Apr 85	**BEYOND THE SEA (LA MER)** *Warner Bros. W 9014*	60	3
16 Aug 86	**KISSES IN THE MOONLIGHT** *Warner Bros. W 8640*	60	4
29 Nov 86	**SHIVER** *Warner Bros. W 8523*	19	9
14 Feb 87	**TEASER** *Warner Bros. W 8437*	45	4
27 Aug 88	**LET'S DO IT AGAIN** *Warner Bros. W 7780*	56	3
5 Sep 92	**I'LL KEEP YOUR DREAMS ALIVE** *Ammi AMMI 101* [3]	68	1
11 Jul 98	**SEVEN DAYS** *MCA MCSTD 48083* [4]	22	3
19 Mar 77	**IN FLIGHT** *Warner Bros. K 56237*	19	23
18 Feb 78	**WEEKEND IN L.A.** *Warner Bros. K 66074*	47	1
24 Mar 79	**LIVING INSIDE YOUR LOVE** *Warner Bros. K 66085*	24	14
26 Jul 80 ●	**GIVE ME THE NIGHT** *Warner Bros. K 56823*	3	40
14 Nov 81	**THE GEORGE BENSON COLLECTION** *Warner Bros. K 66107*	19	35
11 Jun 83 ●	**IN YOUR EYES** *Warner Bros. 9237441*	3	53
26 Jan 85 ●	**20 / 20** *Warner Bros. 9251781*	9	19
19 Oct 85 ★	**THE LOVE SONGS** *K-Tel NE 1308*	1	26
6 Sep 86	**WHILE THE CITY SLEEPS ...** *Warner Bros. WX 55*	13	27
11 Jul 87	**COLLABORATION** *Warner Bros. WX 91* [1]	47	6
10 Sep 88	**TWICE THE LOVE** *Warner Bros. WX 160*	16	10
8 Jul 89	**TENDERLY** *Warner Bros. WX 263*	52	3
26 Oct 91	**MIDNIGHT MOODS – THE LOVE COLLECTION** *Telstar STAR 2450*	25	12
29 Jun 96	**THAT'S RIGHT** *GRP GRP 98242*	61	1
25 Apr 98 ●	**ESSENTIALS ... THE VERY BEST OF GEORGE BENSON** *Warner.ESP / Jive 9548362292*	8	10

5 Jul 03 ● **THE VERY BEST OF – THE GREATEST HITS OF GEORGE BENSON** *WSM 8122736932* 4 18

[1] George 'Bad' Benson [2] Aretha Franklin and George Benson [3] George Benson and Patti Austin [4] Mary J Blige featuring George Benson [1] George Benson and Earl Klugh

BENT
UK, male production duo (Singles: 1 week) pos/wks

12 Jul 03 **STAY THE SAME** *Sport SPORT 9CDS* 59 1

BENTLEY RHYTHM ACE *UK, male instrumental duo – Mike Stokes and Richard March (Singles: 7 weeks, Albums: 6 weeks)* pos/wks

6 Sep 97 **BENTLEY'S GONNA SORT YOU OUT!** *Parlophone CDRS 6476* ..17 4
27 May 00 **THEME FROM GUTBUSTER** *Parlophone CDRS 6537* 29 2
2 Sep 00 **HOW'D I DO DAT** *Parlophone CDRS 6543* 57 1
24 May 97 **BENTLEY RHYTHM ACE** *Skint BRASSIC 5CD* 13 5
10 Jun 00 **FOR YOUR EARS ONLY** *Parlophone 5257322* 48 1

Brook BENTON
US, male vocalist – Benjamin Peay, d. 9 Apr 1988 (Singles: 18 weeks) pos/wks

10 Jul 59 **ENDLESSLY** *Mercury AMT 1043* 28 2
6 Oct 60 **KIDDIO (re)** *Mercury AMT 1109* 41 6
16 Feb 61 **FOOLS RUSH IN** *Mercury AMT 1121* 50 1
13 Jul 61 **THE BOLL WEEVIL SONG** *Mercury AMT 1148* 30 9

BENZ *UK, male rap / vocal group (Singles: 9 weeks)* pos/wks

16 Dec 95 **BOOM ROCK SOUL** *Hacktown 74321329652* 62 2
16 Mar 96 **URBAN CITY GIRL** *Hacktown 74321348732* 31 3
25 May 96 **MISS PARKER** *Hacktown 74321377292* 35 2
29 Mar 97 **IF I REMEMBER** *Hendricks CDBENZ 1* 59 1
9 Aug 97 **ON A SUN-DAY** *Hendricks CDBENZ 2* 73 1

Ingrid BERGMAN – *See Dooley WILSON*

BERLIN *US, male / female vocal / instrumental group – lead vocal Terri Nunn (Singles: 39 weeks, Albums: 11 weeks)* pos/wks

25 Oct 86 ★ **TAKE MY BREATH AWAY (LOVE THEME FROM 'TOP GUN') (re)** *CBS A 7320* ▲ 1 18
17 Jan 87 **YOU DON'T KNOW** *Mercury MER 237* 39 6
14 Mar 87 **LIKE FLAMES** *Mercury MER 240* 47 3
13 Oct 90 ● **TAKE MY BREATH AWAY (re-issue)** *CBS 656361 7* 3 12
17 Jan 87 **COUNT THREE AND PRAY** *Mercury MER 101* 32 11

The original 'Take My Breath Away' peaked at No.52 in 1988

BERLIN PHILHARMONIC ORCHESTRA / Herbert von KARAJAN
Germany, orchestra and Austria, male conductor (Albums: 1 week) pos/wks

13 Apr 96 **ADAGIO 2** *Deutsche Grammophon 4495152* [1] 63 1

Shelley BERMAN *US, male comedian (Albums: 4 weeks)* pos/wks

19 Nov 60 **INSIDE SHELLEY BERMAN** *Capitol CLP 1300* 12 4

Elmer BERNSTEIN *US, orchestra (Singles: 11 weeks)* pos/wks

18 Dec 59 ● **STACCATO'S THEME (re)** *Capitol CL 15101* 4 11

Leonard BERNSTEIN *US, orchestra and chorus leader d. 14 Oct 1990 (Singles: 4 weeks, Albums: 2 weeks)* pos/wks

2 Jul 94 **AMERICA – WORLD CUP THEME 1994** *Deutsche Grammophon USACD 1* [1] 44 4
10 Feb 90 **BERNSTEIN IN BERLIN – BEETHOVEN'S 9TH** *Deutsche Grammophon* 54 2

[1] Leonard Bernstein, Orchestra and Chorus

Leonard BERNSTEIN'S WEST SIDE STORY – *See STUDIO CAST RECORDINGS*

BERRI *UK, female vocalist – Beverley Sleight (Singles: 22 weeks)* pos/wks

26 Nov 94 **THE SUNSHINE AFTER THE RAIN** *Ffrreedom TABCD 223* [1] 26 6
2 Sep 95 ● **THE SUNSHINE AFTER THE RAIN (re-mix)** *Ffrreedom TABCD 232* 4 11
2 Dec 95 **SHINE LIKE A STAR** *Ffrreedom TABCD 239* 20 5

[1] New Atlantic / U4EA featuring Berri

LaKiesha BERRI
US, female vocalist (Singles: 1 week) pos/wks

5 Jul 97 **LIKE THIS AND LIKE THAT** *Adept ADPTCD 7* 54 1

Chuck BERRY (479 Top 500)
First guitar-playing rock star, b. 18 Oct 1926, Missouri, US. Often called rock 'n' roll's premier poet and most influential instrumentalist. 'Duck walking' legend was among the first acts inducted into the Rock and Roll Hall of Fame (Singles: 91 weeks, Albums: 53 weeks) pos/wks

21 Jun 57 **SCHOOL DAY (re)** *Columbia DB 3951* 24 4
25 Apr 58 **SWEET LITTLE SIXTEEN** *London HLM 8585* 16 5
11 Jul 63 **GO GO GO** *Pye International 7N 25209* 38 6
10 Oct 63 ● **LET IT ROCK / MEMPHIS TENNESSEE** *Pye International 7N 25218* 6 13
19 Dec 63 **RUN RUDOLPH RUN** *Pye International 7N 25228* 36 6
13 Feb 64 **NADINE (IS IT YOU) (re)** *Pye International 7N 25236* 27 7
7 May 64 ● **NO PARTICULAR PLACE TO GO** *Pye International 7N 25242* 3 12
20 Aug 64 **YOU NEVER CAN TELL** *Pye International 7N 25257* 23 8
14 Jan 65 **THE PROMISED LAND** *Pye International 7N 25285* 26 6
28 Oct 72 ★ **MY DING-A-LING** *Chess 6145 019* ▲ 1 17
3 Feb 73 **REELIN' AND ROCKIN'** *Chess 6145 020* 18 7
25 May 63 **CHUCK BERRY** *Pye International NPL 28024* 12 16
5 Oct 63 ● **CHUCK BERRY ON STAGE** *Pye International NPL 28027* 6 11
7 Dec 63 ● **MORE CHUCK BERRY** *Pye International NPL 28028* 9 8
30 May 64 ● **THE LATEST AND THE GREATEST** *Pye NPL 28037* 8 7
3 Oct 64 **YOU NEVER CAN TELL** *Pye NPL 29039* 18 2
12 Feb 77 ● **MOTORVATIN'** *Chess 9288 690* 7 9

Dave BERRY *UK, male vocalist – Dave Grundy (Singles: 77 weeks)* pos/wks

19 Sep 63 **MEMPHIS TENNESSEE** *Decca F 11734* [1] 19 13
9 Jan 64 **MY BABY LEFT ME (re)** *Decca F 11803* [1] 37 9
30 Apr 64 **BABY IT'S YOU** *Decca F 11876* 24 6
6 Aug 64 ● **THE CRYING GAME** *Decca F 11937* 5 12
26 Nov 64 **ONE HEART BETWEEN TWO (re)** *Decca F 12020* 41 3
25 Mar 65 ● **LITTLE THINGS** *Decca F 12103* 5 12
22 Jul 65 **THIS STRANGE EFFECT** *Decca F 12188* 37 6
30 Jun 66 ● **MAMA** *Decca F 12435* 5 16

[1] Dave Berry and the Cruisers

Mike BERRY *UK, male vocalist – Michael Bourne (Singles: 51 weeks, Albums: 3 weeks)* pos/wks

12 Oct 61 **TRIBUTE TO BUDDY HOLLY** *HMV POP 912* [1] 24 6
3 Jan 63 ● **DON'T YOU THINK IT'S TIME** *HMV POP 1105* [2] 6 12
11 Apr 63 **MY LITTLE BABY** *HMV POP 1142* [2] 34 7
2 Aug 80 ● **THE SUNSHINE OF YOUR SMILE** *Polydor 2059 261* 9 12
29 Nov 80 **IF I COULD ONLY MAKE YOU CARE** *Polydor POSP 202* 37 9
5 Sep 81 **MEMORIES** *Polydor POSP 287* 55 5
24 Jan 81 **THE SUNSHINE OF YOUR SMILE** *Polydor 2383 592* 63 3

[1] Mike Berry and the Outlaws [2] Mike Berry & the Outlaws

Nick BERRY
UK, male actor / vocalist (Singles: 24 weeks, Albums: 8 weeks) pos/wks

4 Oct 86 ★ **EVERY LOSER WINS (re)** *BBC RESL 204* 1 13
13 Jun 92 ● **HEARTBEAT** *Columbia 6581517* 2 8
31 Oct 92 **LONG LIVE LOVE** *Columbia 6587597* 47 3
20 Dec 86 **NICK BERRY** *BBC REB 618* 99 1
21 Nov 92 **NICK BERRY** *Columbia 4727182* 28 7

The two identically titled albums are different

Adele BERTEI – *See JELLYBEAN*

BEST COMPANY *UK, male vocal duo (Singles: 1 week)* pos/wks

27 Mar 93 **DON'T YOU FORGET ABOUT ME** *ZYX ZYX 69468* 65 1

BEST SHOT *UK, male rap group (Singles: 2 weeks)* pos/wks

5 Feb 94 **UNITED COLOURS** *East West YZ 795CD* 64 2

BETA BAND *UK, male vocal / instrumental group (Singles: 4 weeks, Albums: 6 weeks)* pos/wks

14 Jul 01 **BROKE / WON** *Regal Recordings REG 60CD* 30 2
27 Oct 01 **HUMAN BEING** *Regal Recordings REG 65CD* 57 1
16 Feb 02 **SQUARES** *Regal Recordings REG 69CD* 42 1
10 Oct 98 **THE THREE EP'S** *Regal Recordings 4973852* 35 1
3 Jul 99 **THE BETA BAND** *Regal Recordings REG 30CD* 18 2
28 Jul 01 **HOT SHOTS II** *Regal Recordings REG 59CD* 13 3

Martin BETTINGHAUS – *See Timo MAAS*

Frankie BEVERLY – *See MAZE featuring Frankie BEVERLY*

BEVERLEY SISTERS *UK, female vocal trio (Singles: 34 weeks)* pos/wks

27 Nov 53 ● **I SAW MOMMY KISSING SANTA CLAUS (re)** *Philips PB 188* 6 5
13 Apr 56 **WILLIE CAN** *Decca F 10705* 23 4
1 Feb 57 **I DREAMED** *Decca F 10832* 24 2
13 Feb 59 ● **LITTLE DRUMMER BOY** *Decca F 11107* 6 13
20 Nov 59 **LITTLE DONKEY** *Decca F 11172* 14 7
23 Jun 60 **GREEN FIELDS (re)** *Columbia DB 4444* 29 3

BEVERLEY-PHILLIPS ORCHESTRA *UK, orchestra (Albums: 9 weeks)* pos/wks

9 Oct 76 **GOLD ON SILVER** *Warwick WW 5018* 22 9

BEYONCÉ *US, female vocalist – Beyoncé Knowles (Singles: 48 weeks, Albums: 26 weeks)* pos/wks

27 Jul 02 ● **WORK IT OUT (re)** *Columbia 6729822* 7 11
1 Feb 03 ● **'03 BONNIE & CLYDE** *Roc-A-Fella 0770102* [1] 2 12
12 Jul 03 ★ **CRAZY IN LOVE** *Columbia 6740672* ■ ▲ 1 15
18 Oct 03 ● **BABY BOY** *Columbia 6744082* [2] ▲ 2 10
5 Jul 03 ★ **DANGEROUSLY IN LOVE** *Columbia 5093952* ■ ▲ 1 26+

[1] Jay-Z featuring Beyoncé Knowles [2] Beyoncé featuring Sean Paul

See also DESTINY'S CHILD

BEYOND *UK, male vocal / instrumental group (Singles: 1 week)* pos/wks

21 Sep 91 **RAGING (EP)** *Harvest HARS 530* 68 1

Tracks on Raging (EP): Great Indifference / Nail / Eve of My Release

BHANGRA KNIGHTS vs HUSAN *UK, male production duo and Holland, male production duo (Singles: 7 weeks)* pos/wks

17 May 03 ● **HUSAN** *Positiva CDTIV 188* 7 7

BIBLE *UK, male vocal / instrumental group (Singles: 8 weeks, Albums: 2 weeks)* pos/wks

20 May 89 **GRACELAND** *Chrysalis BIB 4* 51 4
26 Aug 89 **HONEY BE GOOD** *Ensign BIB 5* 54 4
2 Jan 88 **EUREKA** *Cooltempo CHR 1646* 71 1
7 Oct 89 **THE BIBLE** *Ensign CHEN 12* 67 1

BIBLE OF DREAMS – *See Johnny PANIC and the BIBLE OF DREAMS*

BIDDU ORCHESTRA *UK, orchestra – leader Biddu Appaiah (Singles: 13 weeks)* pos/wks

2 Aug 75 **SUMMER OF '42** *Epic EPC 3318* 14 8
17 Apr 76 **RAIN FOREST** *Epic EPC 4084* 39 4
11 Feb 78 **JOURNEY TO THE MOON** *Epic EPC 5910* 41 1

BIFFY CLYRO *UK, male vocal / instrumental trio (Singles: 4 weeks, Albums: 1 week)* pos/wks

16 Feb 02 **57** *Beggars Banquet BBQ 358CD* 61 1
5 Apr 03 **THE IDEAL HEIGHT** *Beggars Banquet BBQ 365CD* 46 1
7 Jun 03 **QUESTIONS & ANSWERS** *Beggars Banquet BBQ 368CD* 26 2
28 Jun 03 **THE VERTIGO OF BLISS** *Beggars Banquet BBQCD 233* 48 1

BIG APPLE BAND – *See Walter MURPHY and the BIG APPLE BAND*

BIG AUDIO DYNAMITE *UK / US, male vocal / instrumental group (Singles: 27 weeks, Albums: 43 weeks)* pos/wks

22 Mar 86 **E=MC2** *CBS A 6963* 11 9
7 Jun 86 **MEDICINE SHOW** *CBS A 7181* 29 5
18 Oct 86 **C'MON EVERY BEATBOX** *CBS 650147* 51 3
21 Feb 87 **V THIRTEEN** *CBS BAAD 2* 49 5
28 May 88 **JUST PLAY MUSIC** *CBS BAAD 4* 51 3
12 Nov 94 **LOOKING FOR A SONG** *Columbia 6610182* [1] 68 2
16 Nov 85 **THIS IS BIG AUDIO DYNAMITE** *CBS 26714* 27 27
8 Nov 86 **NO. 10 UPPING STREET** *CBS 450 1371* 11 8
9 Jul 88 **TIGHTEN UP VOL. 88** *CBS 4611991* 33 3
16 Sep 89 **MEGATOP PHOENIX** *CBS 4657901* 26 3
2 Nov 90 **KOOL-AID** *CBS 4674661* 55 1
17 Aug 91 **THE GLOBE** *Columbia 4677061* 63 1

[1] Big Audio

BIG BAD HORNS – *See LITTLE ANGELS*

BIG BAM BOO *UK / Canada, male vocal / instrumental duo (Singles: 2 weeks)* pos/wks

28 Jan 89 **SHOOTING FROM MY HEART** *MCA MCA 1281* 61 2

BIG BAND *UK, male instrumental group (Albums: 1 week)* pos/wks

16 Nov 02 **SWINGIN' WITH THE BIG BAND** *Columbia STVCD 157* 62 1

BIG BANG THEORY *UK, male producer – Seamus Haji (Singles: 1 week)* pos/wks

2 Mar 02 **GOD'S CHILD** *Defected DFECT 45CDS* 51 1

BIG BASS vs Michelle NARINE *Canada, male production group and female vocalist (Singles: 1 week)* pos/wks

2 Sep 00 **WHAT YOU DO** *Stonebridge / Edel 0110965ERE* 67 1

BIG BEN *UK, clock (Singles: 2 weeks)* pos/wks

1 Jan 00 **MILLENNIUM CHIMES** *London BIGONE 2000* 53 2

BIG BEN BANJO BAND *UK, male instrumental group – leader Norrie Paramor (Singles: 6 weeks, Albums: 1 week)* pos/wks

10 Dec 54 ● **LET'S GET TOGETHER NO.1** *Columbia DB 3549* 6 4
9 Dec 55 **LET'S GET TOGETHER AGAIN NO.1** *Columbia DB 3676* 18 2
17 Dec 60 **MORE MINSTREL MELODIES** *Columbia 33SX 1254* 20 1

These hits were both medleys as follows: Let's Get Together No.1: I'm Just Wild About Harry / April Showers / Rock-a-Bye Your Baby / Swanee / Darktown Strutters Ball / For Me and My Gal / Oh You Beautiful Doll / Yes Sir That's My Baby / Let's Get Together

BIG BOI – *See KILLER MIKE featuring BIG BOI*

BIG BOPPER *US, male vocalist – J P Richardson, d. 3 Feb 1959 (Singles: 8 weeks)* pos/wks

26 Dec 58 **CHANTILLY LACE (re)** *Mercury AMT 1002* 12 8

BIG BOSS STYLUS presents RED VENOM *UK, male production duo and male rapper – Mike Neilson (Singles: 1 week)* pos/wks

31 Jul 99 **LET'S GET IT ON** *All Around the World CDGLOBE 195* 72 1

BIG BROVAZ *UK, male / female vocal / rap / production group (Singles: 52 weeks, Albums: 35 weeks)* pos/wks

26 Oct 02 ● **NU FLOW (re)** *Epic 6730282* 3 18
15 Feb 03 ● **OK** *Epic 6735212* 7 9
17 May 03 ● **FAVOURITE THINGS** *Epic 6738072* 2 11

13 Sep 03 ●	**BABY BOY** *Epic 6743092*	4 12
20 Dec 03	**AIN'T WHAT YOU DO** *Epic 6745102*	15 2+
16 Nov 02 ●	**NU FLOW** *Epic 5099402*	6 35

BIG C – *See Alex WHITCOMBE & BIG C*

BIG COUNTRY 243 Top 500

Scottish-sounding rock quartet from Dunfermline, UK: Stuart Adamson b. 11 Apr 1958, d. 16 Dec 2001 (v / g, ex-Skids), Bruce Watson (g), Tony Butler (b), Mark Brzezicki (d). Their distinctive sound was created by Watson's bagpipe-like guitar playing (Singles: 103 weeks, Albums: 149 weeks) pos/wks

26 Feb 83 ●	**FIELDS OF FIRE (400 MILES)** *Mercury COUNT 2*	10 12
28 May 83	**IN A BIG COUNTRY** *Mercury COUNT 3*	17 7
3 Sep 83 ●	**CHANCE** *Mercury COUNT 4*	9 9
21 Jan 84 ●	**WONDERLAND** *Mercury COUNT 5*	8 8
29 Sep 84	**EAST OF EDEN** *Mercury MER 175*	17 6
1 Dec 84	**WHERE THE ROSE IS SOWN** *Mercury MER 185*	29 7
19 Jan 85	**JUST A SHADOW** *Mercury BCO 8*	26 4
12 Apr 86 ●	**LOOK AWAY** *Mercury BIGC 1*	7 8
21 Jun 86	**THE TEACHER** *Mercury BIGC 2*	28 4
20 Sep 86	**ONE GREAT THING** *Mercury BIGC 3*	19 6
29 Nov 86	**HOLD THE HEART** *Mercury BIGC 4*	55 2
20 Aug 88	**KING OF EMOTION (re)** *Mercury BIGC 5*	16 6
5 Nov 88	**BROKEN HEART (THIRTEEN VALLEYS)** *Mercury BIGC 6*	47 4
4 Feb 89	**PEACE IN OUR TIME** *Mercury BIGC 7*	39 3
12 May 90	**SAVE ME** *Mercury BIGC 8*	41 3
21 Jul 90	**HEART OF THE WORLD** *Mercury BIGC 9*	50 2
31 Aug 91	**REPUBLICAN PARTY REPTILE (EP)** *Vertigo BIC 1*	37 2
19 Oct 91	**BEAUTIFUL PEOPLE** *Vertigo BIC 2*	72 1
13 Mar 93	**ALONE** *Compulsion CDPULSS 4*	24 3
1 May 93	**SHIPS (WHERE WERE YOU)** *Compulsion CDPULSS 6*	29 3
10 Jun 95	**I'M NOT ASHAMED** *Transatlantic TRAX 1009*	69 1
9 Sep 95	**YOU DREAMER** *Transatlantic TRAD 1012*	68 1
21 Aug 99	**FRAGILE THING** *Track TRACK 0004A* 1	69 1
6 Aug 83 ●	**THE CROSSING** *Mercury MERH 27*	3 80
27 Oct 84 ★	**STEELTOWN** *Mercury MERH 49* ■	1 21
12 Jul 86 ●	**THE SEER** *Mercury MERH 87*	2 16
8 Oct 88 ●	**PEACE IN OUR TIME** *Mercury MERH 130*	9 6
26 May 90 ●	**THROUGH A BIG COUNTRY – GREATEST HITS** *Mercury 8460221*	2 17
28 Sep 91	**NO PLACE LIKE HOME** *Vertigo 5102301*	28 2
3 Apr 93	**THE BUFFALO SKINNERS** *Compulsion CDNOIS 2*	25 2
18 Jun 94	**WITHOUT THE AID OF A SAFETY NET (LIVE)** *Compulsion CDNOIS 5*	35 1
24 Jun 95	**WHY THE LONG FACE** *Transatlantic TRACD 109*	48 2
24 Aug 96	**ECLECTIC** *Transatlantic TRACD 234*	41 1
8 Jun 02	**THE GREATEST HITS OF BIG COUNTRY AND THE SKIDS – THE BEST OF STUART ADAMSON** *UMTV 5869892* 1	71 1

1 Big Country featuring Eddi Reader 1 Big Country and the Skids

Tracks on Republican Party Reptile (EP): Republican Party Reptile / Comes a Time / You Me and the Truth

BIG DADDY

US, male vocal group (Singles: 8 weeks) pos/wks

9 Mar 85	**DANCING IN THE DARK** *Making Waves SURF 1033*	21 8

BIG DADDY KANE

US, male rapper (Singles: 6 weeks, Albums: 3 weeks) pos/wks

13 May 89	**RAP SUMMARY / WRATH OF KANE** *Cold Chillin' W 2973*	52 2
26 Aug 89	**SMOOTH OPERATOR** *Cold Chillin' W 2804*	65 1
13 Jan 90	**AIN'T NO STOPPIN' US NOW** *Cold Chillin' W 2635*	44 3
30 Sep 89	**IT'S A BIG DADDY THING** *Cold Chillin' WX 305*	37 3

BIG DISH *UK, male vocal / instrumental group (Singles: 5 weeks, Albums: 3 weeks)* pos/wks

12 Jan 91	**MISS AMERICA** *East West YZ 529*	37 5
11 Oct 86	**SWIMMER** *Virgin V 2374*	85 1
23 Feb 91	**SATELLITES** *East West WX 400*	43 2

BIG FAMILY – *See JT and the BIG FAMILY*

BIG FUN

UK, male vocal group (Singles: 33 weeks, Albums: 11 weeks) pos/wks

12 Aug 89 ●	**BLAME IT ON THE BOOGIE** *Jive JIVE 217*	4 11
25 Nov 89 ●	**CAN'T SHAKE THE FEELING** *Jive JIVE 234*	8 9
17 Mar 90	**HANDFUL OF PROMISES** *Jive JIVE 243*	21 6
23 Jun 90	**YOU'VE GOT A FRIEND** *Jive CHILD 90* 1	14 6
4 Aug 90	**HEY THERE LONELY GIRL** *Jive JIVE 251*	62 1
12 May 90 ●	**A POCKETFUL OF DREAMS** *Jive FUN 1*	7 11

1 Big Fun and Sonia featuring Gary Barnacle

BIG MOUNTAIN

US, male / female vocal / instrumental group (Singles: 15 weeks) pos/wks

4 Jun 94 ●	**BABY I LOVE YOUR WAY** *RCA 74321198062*	2 14
24 Sep 94	**SWEET SENSUAL LOVE** *Giant 74321234642*	51 1

BIG PUN – *See Jennifer LOPEZ*

BIG ROLL BAND – *See Zoot MONEY and the BIG ROLL BAND*

BIG RON

UK, male producer – Aaron Gilbert (aka Jules Verne) (Singles: 1 week) pos/wks

11 Mar 00	**LET THE FREAK** *48k SPECT 06CDS*	57 1

BIG ROOM GIRL featuring Darryl PANDY

UK, male production / instrumental duo – Robert Chetcutti and Steve McGuinness – and US, male vocalist (Singles: 2 weeks) pos/wks

20 Feb 99	**RAISE YOUR HANDS** *VC Recordings VCRD 44*	40 2

See also RHYTHM MASTERS

BIG SOUND – *See Simon DUPREE and the BIG SOUND*

BIG SOUND AUTHORITY

UK, male / female vocal / instrumental group (Singles: 12 weeks) pos/wks

19 Jan 85	**THIS HOUSE (IS WHERE YOUR LOVE STANDS)** *Source BSA 1*	21 9
8 Jun 85	**A BAD TOWN** *Source BSA 2*	54 3

BIG SUPREME *UK, male vocal group (Singles: 5 weeks)* pos/wks

20 Sep 86	**DON'T WALK** *Polydor POSP 809*	58 3
14 Mar 87	**PLEASE YOURSELF** *Polydor POSP 840*	64 2

BIG THREE *UK, vocal / instrumental group (Singles: 17 weeks)* pos/wks

11 Apr 63	**SOME OTHER GUY** *Decca F 11614*	37 7
11 Jul 63	**BY THE WAY** *Decca F 11689*	22 10

BIG TIGGER – *See R KELLY*

BIG TIME CHARLIE *UK, male DJ / production duo – Aaron Gilbert and Les Sharma (Singles: 4 weeks)* pos/wks

23 Oct 99	**ON THE RUN** *Inferno CDFERN 18*	22 2
18 Mar 00	**MR DEVIL** *Inferno CDFERN 24* 1	39 2

1 Big Time Charlie featuring Soozy Q

See also BIG RON

BIGFELLA featuring Noel McCALLA

US, male rapper and UK, male vocalist (Singles: 1 week) pos/wks

17 Aug 02	**BEAUTIFUL** *Nulife 74321942282*	52 1

Barry BIGGS *Jamaica, male vocalist (Singles: 46 weeks)* pos/wks

28 Aug 76	**WORK ALL DAY** *Dynamic DYN 101*	38 5
4 Dec 76 ●	**SIDESHOW** *Dynamic DYN 118*	3 16
23 Apr 77	**YOU'RE MY LIFE** *Dynamic DYN 127*	36 4
9 Jul 77	**THREE RING CIRCUS** *Dynamic DYN 128*	22 8
15 Dec 79	**WHAT'S YOUR SIGN GIRL** *Dynamic DYN 150*	55 7
20 Jun 81	**WIDE AWAKE IN A DREAM** *Dynamic DYN 10*	44 6

Ronald BIGGS – *See SEX PISTOLS*

Ivor BIGGUN *UK, male vocalist – Doc Cox (Singles: 15 weeks)* pos/wks

		pos	wks
2 Sep 78	**THE WINKER'S SONG (MISPRINT)** *Beggars Banquet BOP 1* [1]	22	12
12 Sep 81	**BRAS ON 45 (FAMILY VERSION)** *Dead Badger BOP 6* [2]	50	3

[1] Ivor Biggun & the Red-Nosed Burglars [2] Ivor Biggun and the D Cups

BILBO *UK, male vocal / instrumental group (Singles: 7 weeks)* pos/wks

		pos	wks
26 Aug 78	**SHE'S GONNA WIN** *Lightning LIG 548*	42	7

Acker BILK 161 Top 500

First UK act to top US chart in 1960s, b. 28 Jan 1929, Somerset, UK. Band leader / clarinettist / vocalist was at the forefront of the UK trad-jazz revival. 'Stranger on the Shore' spent more than one year on chart, selling 1,130,000, and was voted No.1 instrumental of 1962 in the US. Made an MBE in the 2001 honours list (Singles: 172 weeks, Albums: 161 weeks) pos/wks

		pos	wks
22 Jan 60 ●	**SUMMER SET** *Columbia DB 4382* [1]	5	20
9 Jun 60	**GOODNIGHT SWEET PRINCE** *Melodisc MEL 1547* [1]	50	1
18 Aug 60	**WHITE CLIFFS OF DOVER** *Columbia DB 4492* [1]	30	9
8 Dec 60 ●	**BUONA SERA** *Columbia DB 4544* [1]	7	18
13 Jul 61 ●	**THAT'S MY HOME** *Columbia DB 4673* [1]	7	17
2 Nov 61	**STARS AND STRIPES FOREVER / CREOLE JAZZ** *Columbia SCD 2155* [1]	22	10
30 Nov 61 ●	**STRANGER ON THE SHORE** *Columbia DB 4750* [2] ◆ ▲	2	55
15 Mar 62	**FRANKIE AND JOHNNY** *Columbia DB 4795* [1]	42	2
26 Jul 62	**GOTTA SEE BABY TONIGHT** *Columbia SCD 2176* [1]	24	9
27 Sep 62	**LONELY** *Columbia DB 4897* [2]	14	11
24 Jan 63	**A TASTE OF HONEY** *Columbia DB 4949* [2]	16	9
21 Aug 76 ●	**ARIA** *Pye 7N 45607* [3]	5	11
19 Mar 60 ●	SEVEN AGES OF ACKER *Columbia 33SX 1205*	6	6
9 Apr 60	ACKER BILK'S OMNIBUS *Pye NJL 22*	14	3
4 Mar 61	ACKER *Columbia 33SX 1248*	17	1
1 Apr 61	GOLDEN TREASURY OF BILK *Columbia 33SX 1304*	11	6
27 May 61 ●	THE BEST OF BARBER AND BILK VOLUME 1 *Pye Golden Guinea GGL 0075* [1]	4	43
11 Nov 61 ●	THE BEST OF BARBER AND BILK VOLUME 2 *Pye Golden Guinea GGL 0096* [1]	8	18
26 May 62 ●	STRANGER ON THE SHORE *Columbia 33SX 1407*	6	28
25 Aug 62 ★	THE BEST OF BALL, BARBER AND BILK *Pye Golden Guinea GGL 0131* [2]	1	24
4 May 63	A TASTE OF HONEY *Columbia 33SX 1493*	17	4
9 Oct 76	THE ONE FOR ME *Pye NSPX 41052*	38	6
4 Jun 77 ●	SHEER MAGIC *Warwick WW 5028*	5	8
11 Nov 78	EVERGREEN *Warwick PW 5045*	17	14

[1] Mr Acker Bilk and his Paramount Jazz Band [2] Mr Acker Bilk with the Leon Young String Chorale [3] Acker Bilk, his Clarinet and Strings [1] Chris Barber and Acker Bilk [2] Kenny Ball, Chris Barber and Acker Bilk

BILL *UK, male vocalist (Singles: 1 week)* pos/wks

		pos	wks
23 Oct 93	**CAR BOOT SALE** *Mercury MINCD 1*	73	1

BILL & BEN *UK, male flowerpot-dwelling vocalists – voiced by John Thomson (Singles: 4 weeks)* pos/wks

		pos	wks
13 Jul 02	**FLOBBADANCE** *BBC Music WMSS 60552*	23	4

BILLIE – *See Billie PIPER*

BILLY TALENT

Canada, male vocal / instrumental group (Singles: 1 week) pos/wks

		pos	wks
13 Sep 03	**TRY HONESTLY** *Atlantic AT 0160CD*	68	1

BIMBO JET

France, male / female vocal / instrumental group (Singles: 10 weeks) pos/wks

		pos	wks
26 Jul 75	**EL BIMBO** *EMI 2317*	12	10

BINARY FINARY *UK, male production duo – Matt Lawes and Ricky Grant (Singles: 9 weeks)* pos/wks

		pos	wks
10 Oct 98	**1998** *Positiva CDTIV 98*	24	3
28 Aug 99	**1999** *Positiva CDTIV 118*	11	6

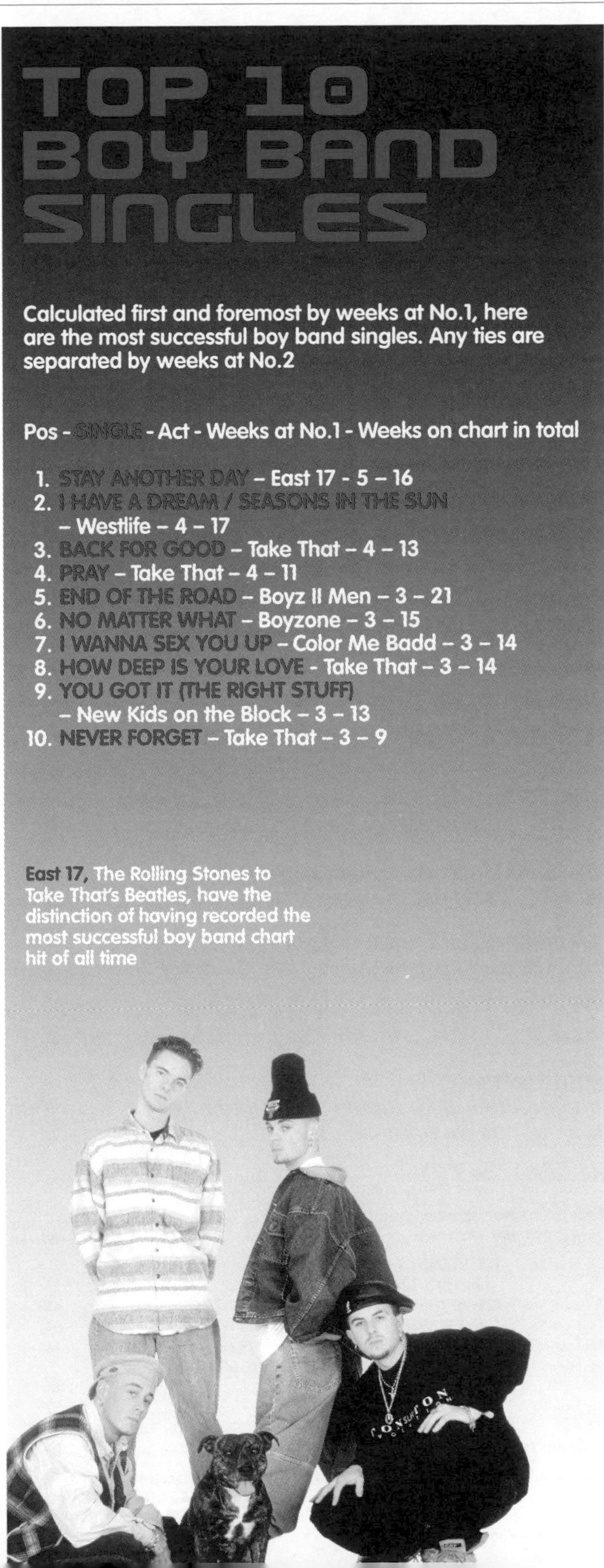

TOP 10 BOY BAND SINGLES
Calculated first and foremost by weeks at No.1, here are the most successful boy band singles. Any ties are separated by weeks at No.2
Pos - SINGLE - Act - Weeks at No.1 - Weeks on chart in total
1. STAY ANOTHER DAY – East 17 - 5 – 16
2. I HAVE A DREAM / SEASONS IN THE SUN – Westlife – 4 – 17
3. BACK FOR GOOD – Take That – 4 – 13
4. PRAY – Take That – 4 – 11
5. END OF THE ROAD – Boyz II Men – 3 – 21
6. NO MATTER WHAT – Boyzone – 3 – 15
7. I WANNA SEX YOU UP – Color Me Badd – 3 – 14
8. HOW DEEP IS YOUR LOVE – Take That – 3 – 14
9. YOU GOT IT (THE RIGHT STUFF) – New Kids on the Block – 3 – 13
10. NEVER FORGET – Take That – 3 – 9
East 17, The Rolling Stones to Take That's Beatles, have the distinction of having recorded the most successful boy band chart hit of all time

Umberto BINDI *Italy, male vocalist (Singles: 1 week)*

		pos/wks	
10 Nov 60	**IL NOSTRO CONCERTO** *Oriole CB 1577*	**47**	1

BINI & MARTINI
Italy, male production duo (Singles: 2 weeks)

		pos/wks	
4 Mar 00	**HAPPINESS (MY VISION IS CLEAR)** *Azuli AZNYCDX 113*	**53**	1
10 Mar 01	**BURNING UP** *Azuli AZNY 137*	**65**	1

See also ECLIPSE; HOUSE OF GLASS; GOODFELLAS featuring Lisa MILLETT

BIOHAZARD *US, male vocal / instrumental group (Singles: 4 weeks, Albums: 2 weeks)*

		pos/wks	
9 Jul 94	**TALES FROM THE HARD SIDE** *Warner Bros. W 0254CD*	**47**	2
20 Aug 94	**HOW IT IS** *Warner Bros. W 0259CD*	**62**	2
14 May 94	**STATE OF THE WORLD ADDRESS** *Warner Bros. 9362455952*	**72**	1
8 Jun 96	**MATA LEAO** *Warner Bros. 9362462082*	**72**	1

La BIONDA *Italy, male / female vocal group (Singles: 4 weeks)*

		pos/wks	
7 Oct 78	**ONE FOR YOU ONE FOR ME** *Philips 6198 227*	**54**	4

BIOSPHERE *Norway, male instrumentalist – Ger Jenssen, keyboards (Singles: 2 weeks, Albums: 1 week)*

		pos/wks	
29 Apr 95	**NOVELTY WAVES** *Apollo APOLLO 20CDX*	**51**	2
5 Mar 94	**PATASHNIK** *Apollo AMB 3927CDX*	**50**	1

BIRDLAND *UK, male vocal / instrumental group (Singles: 7 weeks, Albums: 1 week)*

		pos/wks	
1 Apr 89	**HOLLOW HEART** *Lazy LAZY 13*	**70**	1
8 Jul 89	**PARADISE** *Lazy LAZY 14*	**70**	1
3 Feb 90	**SLEEP WITH ME** *Lazy LAZY 17*	**32**	3
22 Sep 90	**ROCK 'N' ROLL NIGGER** *Lazy LAZY 20*	**47**	1
2 Feb 91	**EVERYBODY NEEDS SOMEBODY** *Lazy LAZY 24*	**44**	1
2 Mar 91	**BIRDLAND** *Lazy LAZY 25*	**44**	1

BIRDS *UK, male vocal / instrumental group (Singles: 1 week)*

		pos/wks	
27 May 65	**LEAVING HERE** *Decca F 12140*	**45**	1

Zoe BIRKETT *UK, female vocalist (Singles: 4 weeks)*

		pos/wks	
25 Jan 03	**TREAT ME LIKE A LADY** *19 / Universal 0196822*	**12**	6

Jane BIRKIN and Serge GAINSBOURG *UK / France, female / male vocal duo, Serge Gainsbourg d. 2 Mar 1991 (Singles: 34 weeks)*

		pos/wks	
30 Jul 69 ●	**JE T'AIME . . . MOI NON PLUS** *Fontana TF 1042*	**2**	11
4 Oct 69 ★	**JE T'AIME . . . MOI NON PLUS (re-issue)** *Major Minor MM 645*	**1**	14
7 Dec 74	**JE T'AIME . . . MOI NON PLUS (2nd re-issue)** *Antic K 11511*	**31**	9

BIRTHDAY PARTY
Australia, male vocal / instrumental group (Albums: 3 weeks)

		pos/wks	
24 Jul 82	**JUNKYARD** *4AD CAD 207*	**73**	3

See also Nick CAVE

BIS *UK, male / female vocal / instrumental group (Singles: 9 weeks, Albums: 1 week)*

		pos/wks	
30 Mar 96	**THE SECRET VAMPIRE SOUNDTRACK (EP)** *Chemikal Underground CHEM 003CD*	**25**	2
22 Jun 96	**BIS VS THE DIY CORPS (EP)** *Teen-C SKETCH 001CD*	**45**	1
9 Nov 96	**ATOM POWERED ACTION (EP)** *Wiiija WIJ 55CD*	**54**	1
15 Mar 97	**SWEET SHOP AVENGERZ** *Wiiija WIJ 67CD*	**46**	1
10 May 97	**EVERYBODY THINKS THAT THEY'RE GOING TO GET THEIRS** *Wiiija WIJ 69CD*	**64**	1
14 Nov 98	**EURODISCO** *Wiiija WIJ 86CD*	**37**	2
27 Feb 99	**ACTION AND DRAMA** *Wiiija WIJ 95CD*	**50**	1
19 Apr 97	**THE NEW TRANSISTOR HEROES** *Wiiija WIJCD 1064*	**55**	1

Tracks on The Secret Vampire Soundtrack (EP): Kandy Pop / Secret Vampires / Teen-C Power / Diska. Tracks on Bis vs the DIY Corps (EP): This Is Fake DIY / Burn the Suit / Dance to the Disco Beat. Tracks on Atom Powered Action (EP): Starbright Boy / Wee Love / Team Theme / Cliquesuck

BISCUIT BOY
UK, male vocal / instrumental trio (Singles: 1 week)

		pos/wks	
15 Sep 01	**MITCH** *Mercury 5887582*	**75**	1

Elvin BISHOP *US, male instrumentalist – guitar (Singles: 4 weeks)*

		pos/wks	
15 May 76	**FOOLED AROUND AND FELL IN LOVE** *Capricorn 2089 024*	**34**	4

Hit has uncredited vocal by Mickey Thomas of Starship

Stephen BISHOP
US, male instrumentalist – piano (Albums: 3 weeks)

		pos/wks	
1 Apr 72	**GRIEG AND SCHUMANN PIANO CONCERTOS** *Philips 6500 166*	**34**	3

BITI – *See DEGREES OF MOTION featuring BITI*

The BIZ – *See Benny BENASSI presents The BIZ*

BIZARRE INC *UK, male / female vocal / instrumental group (Singles: 49 weeks, Albums: 2 weeks)*

		pos/wks	
16 Mar 91	**PLAYING WITH KNIVES** *Vinyl Solution STORM 25R*	**43**	5
14 Sep 91	**SUCH A FEELING** *Vinyl Solution STORM 32S*	**13**	9
23 Nov 91 ●	**PLAYING WITH KNIVES (re-issue)** *Vinyl Solution STORM 38S*	**4**	8
3 Oct 92 ●	**I'M GONNA GET YOU (re)** *Vinyl Solution STORM 46S* [1]	**3**	13
27 Feb 93	**TOOK MY LOVE** *Vinyl Solution STORM 60CD* [1]	**19**	5
23 Mar 96	**KEEP THE MUSIC STRONG** *Some Bizarre MERCD 451*	**33**	2
6 Jul 96	**SURPRISE** *Some Bizarre MERCD 462*	**21**	3
14 Sep 96	**GET UP SUNSHINE STREET** *Some Bizarre MERCD 471*	**45**	2
13 Mar 99	**PLAYING WITH KNIVES (re-mix)** *Vinyl Solution VC01CD1*	**30**	2
7 Nov 92	**ENERGIQUE** *Vinyl Solution STEAM 47CD*	**41**	2

[1] Bizarre Inc featuring Angie Brown

BIZZ NIZZ *US / Belgium, male / female vocal / instrumental group (Singles: 11 weeks)*

		pos/wks	
31 Mar 90 ●	**DON'T MISS THE PARTYLINE** *Cooltempo COOL 203*	**7**	11

BIZZI *UK, male vocalist (Singles: 1 week)*

		pos/wks	
6 Dec 97	**BIZZI'S PARTY** *Parlophone Rhythm CDRHYTHM 7*	**62**	1

BJÖRK (322 Top 500) *Captivating, eccentric, uncompromising, female singer / songwriter, b. Björk Gudmundsdottir, 21 Nov 1965, Reykjavik, Iceland. Formerly a member of The Sugarcubes, she was a double Brits winner in 1994 (Best International Female and Best International Newcomer) (Singles: 77 weeks, Albums: 127 weeks)*

		pos/wks	
27 Apr 91	**OOOPS** *ZTT ZANG 19* [1]	**42**	3
19 Jun 93	**HUMAN BEHAVIOUR** *One Little Indian 112 TP7CD*	**36**	2
4 Sep 93	**VENUS AS A BOY** *One Little Indian 122 TP7CD*	**29**	4
23 Oct 93	**PLAY DEAD** *Island CID 573* [2]	**12**	6
4 Dec 93	**BIG TIME SENSUALITY** *One Little Indian 132 TP7CD*	**17**	8
19 Mar 94	**VIOLENTLY HAPPY** *One Little Indian 142 TP7CD*	**13**	4
6 May 95 ●	**ARMY OF ME** *One Little Indian 162 TP7CD*	**10**	5
26 Aug 95	**ISOBEL** *One Little Indian 172 TP7CD*	**23**	3
25 Nov 95 ●	**IT'S OH SO QUIET** *One Little Indian 182 TP7CD*	**4**	15
24 Feb 96 ●	**HYPERBALLAD** *One Little Indian 192 TP7CD*	**8**	4
9 Nov 96	**POSSIBLY MAYBE** *One Little Indian 193 TP7CD*	**13**	3
1 Mar 97	**I MISS YOU** *One Little Indian 194 TP7CDL*	**36**	2
20 Dec 97	**BACHELORETTE** *One Little Indian 212 TP7CD*	**21**	5
17 Oct 98	**HUNTER** *One Little Indian 222 TP7CD*	**44**	1
12 Dec 98	**ALARM CALL** *One Little Indian 232 TP7CDL*	**33**	2
19 Jun 99	**ALL IS FULL OF LOVE** *One Little Indian 242 TP7CD*	**24**	2
18 Aug 01	**HIDDEN PLACE** *One Little Indian 332 TP7CD*	**21**	2
17 Nov 01	**PAGAN POETRY** *One Little Indian 352 TP7CD*	**38**	2
23 Mar 02	**COCOON** *One Little Indian 322 TP7CD*	**35**	2
7 Dec 02	**IT'S IN OUR HANDS** *One Little Indian 366 TP7CD*	**37**	2
17 Jul 93 ●	**DEBUT** *One Little Indian TPLP 31CD*	**3**	69
24 Jun 95 ●	**POST / TELEGRAM** *One Little Indian TPLP 51CD*	**2**	38
4 Oct 97 ●	**HOMOGENIC** *One Little Indian TPLP 71CD*	**4**	13
30 Sep 00	**SELMA SONGS (FILM SOUNDTRACK)** *One Little Indian TPLP 151CD*	**34**	1
8 Sep 01 ●	**VESPERTINE** *One Little Indian TPLP 101CD*	**8**	4

16 Nov 02 GREATEST HITS *One Little Indian TPLP 359CD* ... 53 2

[1] 808 State featuring Björk [2] Björk and David Arnold

'Telegram', a remix album, was listed with 'Post' from 7 Dec 96 and sales were combined

BJORN AGAIN *Australia, male / female vocal / instrumental group (Singles: 8 weeks)* pos/wks

24 Oct 92 ERASURE-ISH (A LITTLE RESPECT / STOP! *M & G MAGS 32* .. 25 3
12 Dec 92 SANTA CLAUS IS COMING TO TOWN *M & G MAGS 35* ... 55 4
27 Nov 93 FLASHDANCE ... WHAT A FEELING *M & G MAGCD 50* ... 65 1

BLACK *UK, male vocalist – Colin Vearncombe (Singles: 35 weeks, Albums: 29 weeks)* pos/wks

27 Sep 86 WONDERFUL LIFE *Ugly Man JACK 71* ... 72 1
27 Jun 87 ● SWEETEST SMILE *A&M AM 394* ... 8 10
22 Aug 87 ● WONDERFUL LIFE *A&M AM 402* ... 8 9
16 Jan 88 PARADISE *A&M AM 422* ... 38 3
24 Sep 88 THE BIG ONE *A&M AM 468* ... 54 4
21 Jan 89 NOW YOU'RE GONE *A&M AM 491* ... 66 2
4 May 91 FEEL LIKE CHANGE *A&M AM 780* ... 56 2
15 Jun 91 HERE IT COMES AGAIN *A&M AM 753* ... 70 1
5 Mar 94 WONDERFUL LIFE (re-issue) *PolyGram TV 5805552* ... 42 3
26 Sep 87 ● WONDERFUL LIFE *A&M AMA 5165* ... 3 23
29 Oct 88 COMEDY *A&M AMA 5222* ... 32 4
1 Jun 91 BLACK *A&M 3971261* ... 42 2

'Wonderful Life' on A&M is a re-recording. It was re-issued on PolyGram TV in 1994

Cilla BLACK (235 Top 500)
Undoubtedly one of Britain's favourite female vocalists / entertainers of the past 50 years, b. Priscilla White, 27 May 1943, Liverpool. After handing in her Top 20 season ticket, she has become an award-winning and extremely popular TV presenter (Singles: 194 weeks, Albums: 64 weeks) pos/wks

17 Oct 63 LOVE OF THE LOVED *Parlophone R 5065* ... 35 6
6 Feb 64 ★ ANYONE WHO HAD A HEART *Parlophone R 5101* ... 1 17
7 May 64 ★ YOU'RE MY WORLD *Parlophone R 5133* ... 1 17
6 Aug 64 ● IT'S FOR YOU *Parlophone R 5162* ... 7 10
14 Jan 65 ● YOU'VE LOST THAT LOVIN' FEELIN' *Parlophone R 5225* ... 2 9
22 Apr 65 I'VE BEEN WRONG BEFORE *Parlophone R 5269* ... 17 8
13 Jan 66 ● LOVE'S JUST A BROKEN HEART *Parlophone R 5395* ... 5 11
31 Mar 66 ● ALFIE *Parlophone R 5427* ... 9 12
9 Jun 66 ● DON'T ANSWER ME *Parlophone R 5463* ... 6 10
20 Oct 66 A FOOL AM I (DIMMELO PARLAME) *Parlophone R 5515* ... 13 9
8 Jun 67 WHAT GOOD AM I? *Parlophone R 5608* ... 24 7
29 Nov 67 I ONLY LIVE TO LOVE YOU *Parlophone R 5652* ... 26 11
13 Mar 68 ● STEP INSIDE LOVE *Parlophone R 5674* ... 8 9
12 Jun 68 WHERE IS TOMORROW *Parlophone R 5706* ... 39 3
12 Feb 69 ● SURROUND YOURSELF WITH SORROW *Parlophone R 5759* ... 3 12
9 Jul 69 ● CONVERSATIONS *Parlophone R 5785* ... 7 12
13 Dec 69 IF I THOUGHT YOU'D EVER CHANGE YOUR MIND *Parlophone R 5820* ... 20 9
20 Nov 71 ● SOMETHING TELLS ME (SOMETHING IS GONNA HAPPEN TONIGHT) *Parlophone R 5924* ... 3 14
2 Feb 74 BABY WE CAN'T GO WRONG *EMI 2107* ... 36 6
18 Sep 93 THROUGH THE YEARS *Columbia 6596982* ... 54 1
30 Oct 93 HEART AND SOUL *Columbia 6598562* [1] ... 75 1
13 Feb 65 ● CILLA *Parlophone PMC 1243* ... 5 11
14 May 66 ● CILLA SINGS A RAINBOW *Parlophone PMC 7004* ... 4 15
13 Apr 68 ● SHER-OO *Parlophone PCS 7041* ... 7 11
30 Nov 68 THE BEST OF CILLA BLACK *Parlophone PCS 7065* ... 21 11
25 Jul 70 SWEET INSPIRATION *Parlophone PCS 7103* ... 42 4
29 Jan 83 THE VERY BEST OF CILLA BLACK *Parlophone EMTV 38* ... 20 9
2 Oct 93 THROUGH THE YEARS *Columbia 4746502* ... 41 2
4 Oct 03 BEGINNINGS ... GREATEST HITS AND NEW SONGS *EMI 5931812* ... 68 1

[1] Cilla Black with Dusty Springfield

Frank BLACK *US, male vocalist – Charles Thompson (Singles: 4 weeks, Albums: 8 weeks)* pos/wks

21 May 94 HEADACHE *4AD BAD 4007CD* ... 53 1
20 Jan 96 MEN IN BLACK *Dragnet 6627862* ... 37 2
27 Jul 96 I DON'T WANT TO HURT YOU (EVERY SINGLE TIME) *Dragnet 6634635* ... 63 1
20 Mar 93 ● FRANK BLACK *4AD CAD 3004CD* ... 9 3
4 Jun 94 TEENAGER OF THE YEAR *4AD CAD 4009CD* ... 21 2
3 Feb 96 THE CULT OF RAY *Dragnet 4816472* ... 39 2
16 May 98 FRANK BLACK AND THE CATHOLICS *Play It Again Sam BIAS 370CD* [1] ... 61 1

[1] Frank Black and the Catholics

Jeanne BLACK *US, female vocalist (Singles: 4 weeks)* pos/wks

23 Jun 60 HE'LL HAVE TO STAY *Capitol CL 15131* ... 41 4

Mary BLACK *Ireland, female vocalist (Albums: 10 weeks)* pos/wks

3 Jul 93 THE HOLY GROUND *Grapevine GRACD 11* ... 58 2
16 Sep 95 CIRCUS *Grapevine GRACD 014* ... 16 4
29 Mar 97 SHINE *Grapevine GRACD 015* ... 33 3
28 Aug 99 SPEAKING WITH THE ANGEL *Grapevine GRACD 264* ... 63 1

BLACK & WHITE ARMY
UK, 250 Newcastle United football fan vocalists (Singles: 2 weeks) pos/wks

23 May 98 BLACK & WHITE ARMY *Toon TOON 1CD* ... 26 2

BLACK BOX *Italy, male / female vocal / instrumental / production group (Singles: 74 weeks, Albums: 30 weeks)* pos/wks

12 Aug 89 ★ RIDE ON TIME *Deconstruction PB 43055* ... 1 22
17 Feb 90 ● I DON'T KNOW ANYBODY ELSE *Deconstruction PB 43479* ... 4 8
2 Jun 90 EVERYBODY EVERYBODY *Deconstruction PB 43715* ... 16 5
3 Nov 90 ● FANTASY *Deconstruction PB 43895* ... 5 11
15 Dec 90 THE TOTAL MIX *Deconstruction PB 44235* ... 12 8
6 Apr 91 STRIKE IT UP *Deconstruction PB 44459* ... 16 8
14 Dec 91 OPEN YOUR EYES *Deconstruction PB 45053* ... 48 4
14 Aug 93 ROCKIN' TO THE MUSIC *Deconstruction 74321158122* ... 39 2
24 Jun 95 NOT ANYONE *Mercury MERCD 434* ... 31 2
20 Apr 96 I GOT THE VIBRATION / A POSITIVE VIBRATION *Manifesto MERCD 459* [1] ... 21 3
22 Feb 97 NATIVE NEW YORKER *Manifesto FESCD 18* [1] ... 46 1
5 May 90 DREAMLAND *Deconstruction PL 74572* ... 14 30

[1] Blackbox

BLACK BOX RECORDER *UK, male / female vocal / instrumental group (Singles: 4 weeks, Albums: 1 week)* pos/wks

22 Apr 00 THE FACTS OF LIFE *Nude NUD 48CD1* ... 20 3
15 Jul 00 THE ART OF DRIVING *Nude NUD 51CD1* ... 53 1
13 May 00 THE FACTS OF LIFE *Nude NUDE 16CD* ... 37 1

BLACK CONNECTION
Italy, male / female vocal / production group (Singles: 3 weeks) pos/wks

14 Mar 98 GIVE ME RHYTHM *Xtravaganza / Edel 0091465 EXT* ... 32 2
24 Oct 98 I'M GONNA GET YA BABY *Xtravaganza 0091615 EXT* ... 62 1

BLACK CROWES *US, male vocal / instrumental group (Singles: 28 weeks, Albums: 33 weeks)* pos/wks

1 Sep 90 HARD TO HANDLE *Def American DEFA 6* ... 45 5
12 Jan 91 TWICE AS HARD *Def American DEFA 7* ... 47 3
22 Jun 91 JEALOUS AGAIN / SHE TALKS TO ANGELS *Def American DEFA 8* ... 70 1
24 Aug 91 HARD TO HANDLE (re-issue) *Def American DEFA 10* ... 39 4
26 Oct 91 SEEING THINGS *Def American DEFA 13* ... 72 1
2 May 92 REMEDY *Def American DEFA 16* ... 24 3
26 Sep 92 STING ME *Def American DEFA 21* ... 42 2
28 Nov 92 HOTEL ILLNESS *Def American DEFA 23* ... 47 3
11 Feb 95 HIGH HEAD BLUES / A CONSPIRACY *American 74321258492* 25 2
22 Jul 95 WISER TIME *American 74321298272* ... 34 2
27 Jul 96 ONE MIRROR TOO MANY *American 74321398572* ... 51 1
7 Nov 98 KICKING MY HEART AROUND *American Recordings 6666665* 55 1
24 Aug 91 SHAKE YOUR MONEY MAKER *Def American 8425151* ... 36 11
23 May 92 ● THE SOUTHERN HARMONY AND MUSICAL COMPANION *Def American 5122632* ▲ ... 2 7
12 Nov 94 ● AMORICA *American 74321241942* ... 8 4

3 Aug 96 **THREE SNAKES AND ONE CHARM** *American Recordings 74321384842* 17 3
23 Jan 99 **BY YOUR SIDE** *Columbia 4916992* 34 2
22 Jul 00 **LIVE AT THE GREEK** *SPV Recordings SPV 09172022* [1] 39 4
19 May 01 **LIONS** *V2 VVR 1015672* 37 2

[1] Jimmy Page and the Black Crowes

BLACK DIAMOND *US, male vocalist (Singles: 1 week)* pos/wks

17 Sep 94 **LET ME BE** *Systematic SYSCD 1* 56 1

BLACK DOG *UK, male instrumentalist / producer – Ken Downie (Singles: 1 week, Albums: 2 weeks)* pos/wks

3 Apr 99 **BABYLON** *Warner Esp. WESP 006 CD1* [1] 65 1
28 Jan 95 **SPANNERS** *Warp PUPCD 1* 30 2

[1] Black Dog featuring Ofra Haza

BLACK DUCK
UK, male rapper (Singles: 5 weeks) pos/wks

17 Dec 94 **WHIGGLE IN LINE** *Flying South CDDUCK 1* 33 5

BLACK EYED PEAS *US, male / female rap / DJ / vocal group (Singles: 23 weeks, Albums: 18 weeks)* pos/wks

10 Oct 98 **JOINTS & JAMS** *Interscope IND 95604* 53 1
12 May 01 **REQUEST LINE** *Interscope 4970532* [1] 31 3
13 Sep 03 ★ **WHERE IS THE LOVE?** *A&M 9810996* ■ ....1 16+
13 Dec 03 ● **SHUT UP** *A&M 9814501* ....2 3+
30 Aug 03 ● **ELEPHUNK** *A&M / Mercury 9860365* ....4 18+

[1] Black Eyed Peas featuring Macy Gray

BLACK GORILLA
UK, male / female vocal / instrumental group (Singles: 6 weeks) pos/wks

27 Aug 77 **GIMME DAT BANANA** *Response SR 502* 29 6

BLACK GRAPE *UK, male vocal / instrumental group (Singles: 25 weeks, Albums: 46 weeks)* pos/wks

10 Jun 95 ● **REVEREND BLACK GRAPE** *Radioactive RAXTD 16* 9 5
5 Aug 95 ● **IN THE NAME OF THE FATHER** *Radioactive RAXTD 19* 8 4
2 Dec 95 **KELLY'S HEROES** *Radioactive RAXTD 22* 17 5
25 May 96 ● **FAT NECK** *Radioactive RAXTD 24* 10 3
29 Jun 96 ● **ENGLAND'S IRIE** *Radioactive RAXTD 25* [1] 6 4
1 Nov 97 **GET HIGHER** *Radioactive RAXTD 32* 24 3
7 Mar 98 **MARBLES** *Radioactive RAXTD 33* 46 1
19 Aug 95 ★ **IT'S GREAT WHEN YOU'RE STRAIGHT ... YEAH** *Radioactive RAD 11224* ■ 1 39
22 Nov 97 **STUPID STUPID STUPID** *Radioactive RARD 11716* 11 7

[1] Black Grape featuring Joe Strummer and Keith Allen

BLACK LACE *UK, male vocal / instrumental group, Alan Barton d. 23 Mar 1995 (Singles: 83 weeks, Albums: 26 weeks)* pos/wks

31 Mar 79 **MARY ANN** *EMI 2919* 42 4
24 Sep 83 ● **SUPERMAN (GIOCA JOUER)** *Flair FLA 105* 9 18
30 Jun 84 ● **AGADOO** *Flair FLA 107* 2 30
24 Nov 84 ● **DO THE CONGA** *Flair FLA 108* 10 9
1 Jun 85 **EL VINO COLLAPSO** *Flair LACE 1* 42 5
7 Sep 85 **I SPEAKA DA LINGO** *Flair LACE 2* 49 4
7 Dec 85 **HOKEY COKEY** *Flair LACE 3* 31 6
20 Sep 86 **WIG WAM BAM** *Flair LACE 5* 63 3
26 Aug 89 **I AM THE MUSIC MAN** *Flair LACE 10* 52 3
22 Aug 98 **AGADOO (re-recording)** *NOW CDWAG 260* 64 1
8 Dec 84 ● **PARTY PARTY – 16 GREAT PARTY ICEBREAKERS** *Telstar STAR 2250* 4 14
7 Dec 85 **PARTY PARTY 2** *Telstar STAR 2266* 18 6
6 Dec 86 **PARTY CRAZY** *Telstar STAR 2288* 58 6

BLACK LEGEND
Italy, male production duo (Singles: 22 weeks) pos/wks

20 May 00 **YOU SEE THE TROUBLE WITH ME (import)** *Rise RISECD 072* ..52 5
24 Jun 00 ★ **YOU SEE THE TROUBLE WITH ME** *Eternal WEA 282CD* ■ 1 15
4 Aug 01 **SOMEBODY** *WEA WEA 328CD* [1] 37 2

[1] Shortie vs Black Legend

No.1 version features a 'karaoke' re-recording of the original Barry White vocal by UK vocalist Spoonface

BLACK MACHINE *France / Nigeria, male vocal / instrumental duo – Herry Iyere Innocent and Alasson Wat (Singles: 5 weeks)* pos/wks

9 Apr 94 **HOW GEE** *London LONCD 348* 17 5

BLACK MAGIC
US, male producer – Marvin Burns (Singles: 2 weeks) pos/wks

1 Jun 96 **FREEDOM (MAKE IT FUNKY)** *Positiva CDTIV 51* 41 2

See also LIL' LOUIS

BLACK REBEL MOTORCYCLE CLUB *US, male vocal / instrumental group (Singles: 10 weeks, Albums: 21 weeks)* pos/wks

2 Feb 02 **LOVE BURNS** *Virgin VUSCD 234* 37 2
1 Jun 02 **SPREAD YOUR LOVE** *Virgin VUSCD 245* 27 2
28 Sep 02 **WHATEVER HAPPENED TO MY ROCK 'N' ROLL (PUNK SONG)** *Virgin VUSCD 257* 46 2
30 Aug 03 **STOP** *Virgin VUSCD 273* 19 3
29 Nov 03 **WE'RE ALL IN LOVE** *Virgin VUSCDX 279* 45 1
26 Jan 02 **BLACK REBEL MOTORCYCLE CLUB** *Virgin CDVUS 207* 25 17
6 Sep 03 ● **TAKE THEM ON, ON YOUR OWN** *Virgin CDVUS 245* 3 4

BLACK RIOT *US, male producer (Singles: 3 weeks)* pos/wks

3 Dec 88 **WARLOCK / A DAY IN THE LIFE** *Champion CHAMP 75* 68 3

'A Day in the Life' listed only from 17 Dec 1988

BLACK ROB *US, male rapper – Robert Ross (Singles: 8 weeks)* pos/wks

12 Aug 00 **WHOA** *Puff Daddy / Arista 74321782732* 44 2
6 Oct 01 **BAD BOY FOR LIFE** *Bad Boy / Arista 74321889982* [1] 13 6

[1] P Diddy, Black Rob and Mark Curry

BLACK ROCK and RON *US, male rap group (Albums: 1 week)* pos/wks

22 Apr 89 **STOP THE WORLD** *Supreme SU 5* 72 1

BLACK SABBATH (208 Top 500) *Macabre Birmingham, UK-based seminal heavy metal outfit first fronted by Ozzy (John) Osbourne (v) and Tommy Iommi (g). Later vocalists include Ronnie James Dio and Ian Gillan. Voted Best Band in the World and Act of the Millennium by Kerrang! in 1999 (Singles: 70 weeks, Albums: 214 weeks)* pos/wks

29 Aug 70 ● **PARANOID** *Vertigo 6059 010* 4 18
3 Jun 78 **NEVER SAY DIE** *Vertigo SAB 001* 21 8
14 Oct 78 **HARD ROAD** *Vertigo SAB 002* 33 4
5 Jul 80 **NEON KNIGHTS** *Vertigo SAB 3* 22 9
16 Aug 80 **PARANOID (re-issue)** *Nems BSS 101* 14 12
6 Dec 80 **DIE YOUNG** *Vertigo SAB 4* 41 7
7 Nov 81 **MOB RULES** *Vertigo SAB 5* 46 4
13 Feb 82 **TURN UP THE NIGHT** *Vertigo SAB 6* 37 5
15 Apr 89 **HEADLESS CROSS** *IRS EIRS 107* 62 1
13 Jun 92 **TV CRIMES** *IRS EIRSP 178* 33 2
7 Mar 70 ● **BLACK SABBATH** *Vertigo VO 6* 8 42
26 Sep 70 ★ **PARANOID** *Vertigo 6360 011* 1 20
21 Aug 71 ● **MASTER OF REALITY** *Vertigo 6360 050* 5 13
30 Sep 72 ● **BLACK SABBATH VOLUME 4** *Vertigo 6360 071* 8 10
8 Dec 73 ● **SABBATH BLOODY SABBATH** *WWA WWA 005* 4 11
27 Sep 75 ● **SABOTAGE** *NEMS 9119 001* 7 7
7 Feb 76 **WE SOLD OUR SOUL FOR ROCK 'N' ROLL** *NEMS 6641 335* 35 5
6 Nov 76 **TECHNICAL ECSTASY** *Vertigo 9102 750* 13 6
14 Oct 78 **NEVER SAY DIE** *Vertigo 9102 751* 12 6
26 Apr 80 ● **HEAVEN AND HELL** *Vertigo 9102 752* 9 22
5 Jul 80 ● **BLACK SABBATH LIVE AT LAST** *NEMS BS 001* 5 15
27 Sep 80 **PARANOID (re-issue)** *NEMS NEL 6003* 54 2
14 Nov 81 **MOB RULES** *Mercury 6V02119* 12 14
22 Jan 83 **LIVE EVIL** *Vertigo SAB 10* 13 11
24 Sep 83 ● **BORN AGAIN** *Vertigo VERL 8* 4 7

		pos	wks
1 Mar 86	**SEVENTH STAR** *Vertigo VERH 29* [1]	27	5
28 Nov 87	**THE ETERNAL IDOL** *Vertigo VERH 51*	66	1
29 Apr 89	**HEADLESS CROSS** *IRS EIRSA 1002*	31	2
1 Sep 90	**TYR** *IRS EIRSA 1038*	24	3
4 Jul 92	**DEHUMANIZER** *IRS EIRSCD 1064*	28	2
12 Feb 94	**CROSS PURPOSES** *IRS EIRSCD 1067*	41	1
17 Jun 95	**FORBIDDEN** *IRS EIRSCD 1072*	71	1
31 Oct 98	**REUNION** *Epic 4919549*	41	1
17 Jun 00	**THE BEST OF BLACK SABBATH** *Metal Is RAWDD 145*	24	6
6 Jul 02	**PARANOID (2nd re-issue)** *Castle Music CMTCD 004*	63	1

[1] Black Sabbath featuring Tony Iommi

Group UK only for first three hits and re-issue of 'Paranoid'

See also Tony IOMMI; Ozzy OSBOURNE; GILLAN

BLACK SCIENCE ORCHESTRA

UK, male production group (Albums: 1 week) pos/wks

		pos	wks
3 Aug 96	**WALTERS ROOM** *Junior Boy's Own JBOCD 5*	68	1

BLACK SHEEP *US, male rap duo (Singles: 1 week)* pos/wks

		pos	wks
19 Nov 94	**WITHOUT A DOUBT** *Mercury MERCD 417*	60	1

BLACK SLATE

UK / Jamaica, male vocal / instrumental group (Singles: 15 weeks) pos/wks

		pos	wks
20 Sep 80 ●	**AMIGO** *Ensign ENY 42*	9	9
6 Dec 80	**BOOM BOOM** *Ensign ENY 47*	51	6

BLACK STAR LINER *UK, male / female vocal / instrumental group (Albums: 1 week)* pos/wks

		pos	wks
7 Sep 96	**YEMEN CUTTA CONNECTION** *EXP EXPCD 006*	66	1

BLACK UHURU *Jamaica, male vocal / instrumental group (Singles: 9 weeks, Albums: 22 weeks)* pos/wks

		pos	wks
8 Sep 84	**WHAT IS LIFE?** *Island IS 150*	56	6
31 May 86	**THE GREAT TRAIN ROBBERY** *Real Authentic Sound RAS 7018*	62	3
13 Jun 81	**RED** *Island ILPS 9625*	28	13
22 Aug 81	**BLACK UHURU** *Virgin VX 1004*	81	2
19 Jun 82	**CHILL OUT** *Island ILPS 9701*	38	6
25 Aug 84	**ANTHEM** *Island ILPS 9773*	90	1

Band of the BLACK WATCH

UK, military band (Singles: 22 weeks, Albums: 13 weeks) pos/wks

		pos	wks
30 Aug 75 ●	**SCOTCH ON THE ROCKS** *Spark SRL 1128*	8	14
13 Dec 75	**DANCE OF THE CUCKOOS (THE 'LAUREL AND HARDY' THEME)** *Spark SRL 1135*	37	8
7 Feb 76	**SCOTCH ON THE ROCKS** *Spark SRLM 503*	11	13

BLACK WIDOW

UK, male vocal / instrumental group (Albums: 2 weeks) pos/wks

		pos	wks
4 Apr 70	**SACRIFICE** *CBS 63948*	32	2

Tony BLACKBURN *UK, male vocalist (Singles: 7 weeks)* pos/wks

		pos	wks
24 Jan 68	**SO MUCH LOVE** *MGM 1375*	31	4
26 Mar 69	**IT'S ONLY LOVE** *MGM 1467*	42	3

BLACKBYRDS

US, male vocal / instrumental group (Singles: 6 weeks) pos/wks

		pos	wks
31 May 75	**WALKING IN RHYTHM** *Fantasy FTC 114*	23	6

BLACKFOOT *US, male vocal / instrumental group (Singles: 5 weeks, Albums: 22 weeks)* pos/wks

		pos	wks
6 Mar 82	**DRY COUNTY** *Atco K 11686*	43	4
18 Jun 83	**SEND ME AN ANGEL** *Atco B 9880*	66	1
18 Jul 81	**MARAUDER** *Atco K 50799*	38	12
11 Sep 82	**HIGHWAY SONG BLACKFOOT LIVE** *Atco K 50910*	14	6
21 May 83	**SIOGO** *Atco 7900801*	28	3
29 Sep 84	**VERTICAL SMILES** *Atco 790218*	82	1

J BLACKFOOT *US, male vocalist (Singles: 4 weeks)* pos/wks

		pos	wks
17 Mar 84	**TAXI** *Allegiance ALES 2*	48	4

BLACKFOOT SUE

UK, male vocal / instrumental group (Singles: 15 weeks) pos/wks

		pos	wks
12 Aug 72 ●	**STANDING IN THE ROAD** *Jam 13*	4	10
16 Dec 72	**SING DON'T SPEAK** *Jam 29*	36	5

BLACKGIRL *US, female vocal group (Singles: 3 weeks)* pos/wks

		pos	wks
16 Jul 94	**90S GIRL** *RCA 74321217882*	23	3

BLACKHEARTS – *See Joan JETT and the BLACKHEARTS*

Honor BLACKMAN – *See Patrick MacNEE and Honor BLACKMAN*

Ritchie BLACKMORE'S RAINBOW – *See RAINBOW*

BLACKNUSS

Sweden, male / female vocal / instrumental group (Singles: 1 week) pos/wks

		pos	wks
28 Jun 97	**DINAH** *Arista 74321479762*	56	1

BLACKOUT *UK, male production / instrumental duo – Marc Dillon and Pat Dickins (Singles: 1 week)* pos/wks

		pos	wks
27 Mar 99	**GOTTA HAVE HOPE** *Multiply CDMULTY 47*	46	1

BLACKOUT *UK, male / female vocal / rap group (Singles: 8 weeks)* pos/wks

		pos	wks
31 Mar 01	**MR DJ** *Independiente ISOM 48MS*	19	7
6 Oct 01	**GET UP** *Independiente ISOM 52MS*	67	1

Bill BLACK'S COMBO

US, male instrumental group, leader d. 21 Oct 1965 (Singles: 8 weeks) pos/wks

		pos	wks
8 Sep 60	**WHITE SILVER SANDS** *London HLU 9090*	50	1
3 Nov 60	**DON'T BE CRUEL** *London HLU 9212*	32	7

BLACKSTREET *US, male vocal group – includes Terry Riley (Singles: 78 weeks, Albums: 36 weeks)* pos/wks

		pos	wks
19 Jun 93	**BABY BE MINE** *MCA MCSTD 1772* [1]	37	3
13 Aug 94	**BOOTI CALL** *Interscope A 8250CD*	56	1
11 Feb 95	**U BLOW MY MIND** *Interscope A 8222CD*	39	2
27 May 95	**JOY** *Interscope A 8195CD*	56	2
19 Oct 96 ●	**NO DIGGITY** *Interscope IND 95003* [2] ▲	9	7
8 Mar 97	**GET ME HOME** *Def Jam DEFCD 32* [3]	11	5
26 Apr 97 ●	**DON'T LEAVE ME** *Interscope IND 95534*	6	10
27 Sep 97 ●	**FIX** *Interscope IND 97521*	7	5
13 Dec 97	**(MONEY CAN'T) BUY ME LOVE** *Interscope IND 95563*	18	6
4 Apr 98 ●	**I GET LONELY** *Virgin VSCDT 1683* [4]	5	7
27 Jun 98	**THE CITY IS MINE** *Northwestside 74321588012* [5]	38	2
12 Dec 98 ●	**TAKE ME THERE** *Interscope IND 95620* [6]	7	9
17 Apr 99	**GIRLFRIEND / BOYFRIEND** *Interscope IND 95640* [7]	11	7
10 Jul 99	**GET READY** *Puff Daddy / Arista 74321682602* [8]	32	4
8 Feb 03 ●	**WIZZY WOW** *Dreamworks 4507902*	37	2
9 Jul 94	**BLACKSTREET** *Interscope 6544923512*	35	6
21 Sep 96	**ANOTHER LEVEL** *Interscope INTD 90071*	26	9
3 Apr 99	**FINALLY** *Interscope IND 90323*	27	4

[1] BLACKstreet featuring Teddy Riley [2] BLACKstreet featuring Dr Dre [3] Foxy Brown featuring BLACKstreet [4] Janet featuring BLACKstreet [5] Jay-Z featuring BLACKstreet [6] BLACKstreet and Mya featuring Mase and Blinky Blink [7] BLACKstreet with Janet [8] Mase featuring BLACKstreet

BLACKWELLS *US, male vocal group (Singles: 2 weeks)* pos/wks

		pos	wks
18 May 61	**LOVE OR MONEY** *London HLW 9334*	46	2

Richard BLACKWOOD

UK, male comedian / rapper (Singles: 16 weeks, Albums: 2 weeks) pos/wks

		pos	wks
17 Jun 00 ●	**MAMA – WHO DA MAN?** *East West MICKY 01CD1*	3	7
16 Sep 00 ●	**1.2.3.4. GET WITH THE WICKED** *East West MICKY 05CD1*	10	6
25 Nov 00	**SOMEONE THERE FOR ME** *Hopefield / East West MICKY 06CD*	23	3
30 Sep 00	**YOU'LL LOVE TO HATE THIS** *Hopefield / East West 8573844882*	35	2

BLADE – *See Mark B & BLADE*

BLAGGERS I.T.A.

UK, male vocal / instrumental group (Singles: 7 weeks)

Date	Title / Label	pos	wks
12 Jun 93	**STRESS** *Parlophone CDITA 1*	**56**	2
9 Oct 93	**OXYGEN** *Parlophone CDITA 2*	**51**	2
8 Jan 94	**ABANDON SHIP** *Parlophone CDITA 3*	**48**	3

BLAHZAY BLAHZAY *US, male rap duo (Singles: 1 week)*

Date	Title / Label	pos	wks
2 Mar 96	**DANGER** *Mercury Black Vinyl MBVCD 2*	**56**	1

Vivian BLAINE *US, female actor / vocalist – Vivienne Stapleton, d. 13 Dec 1995 (Singles: 1 week)*

Date	Title / Label	pos	wks
10 Jul 53	**BUSHEL AND A PECK** *Brunswick 05100*	**12**	1

BLAIR *UK, male vocalist – Blair Mackichan (Singles: 5 weeks)*

Date	Title / Label	pos	wks
2 Sep 95	**HAVE FUN GO MAD** *Mercury MERCD 443*	**37**	3
6 Jan 96	**LIFE** *Mercury MERCD 447*	**44**	2

BLAIR – *See Terry HALL*

BLAK TWANG

UK, male rapper and female rapper / vocalist (Singles: 2 weeks)

Date	Title / Label	pos	wks
29 Jun 02	**TRIXSTAR** *Bad Magic MAGICD 24* [1]	**54**	1
26 Oct 02	**SO ROTTEN** *Bad Magic MAGICD 25* [2]	**48**	1

[1] Blak Twang featuring Est'Elle [2] Blak Twang featuring Jahmali

Howard BLAKE conducting the SINFONIA OF LONDON

UK, conductor and orchestra (Albums: 12 weeks)

Date	Title / Label	pos	wks
22 Dec 84	**THE SNOWMAN** *CBS 71116*	**54**	12

Narration by Bernard Cribbins

Peter BLAKE *UK, male vocalist (Singles: 4 weeks)*

Date	Title / Label	pos	wks
8 Oct 77	**LIPSMACKIN' ROCK 'N' ROLLIN'** *Pepper UP 36295*	**40**	4

BLAME

UK, male instrumental / production duo (Singles: 2 weeks)

Date	Title / Label	pos	wks
11 Apr 92	**MUSIC TAKES YOU** *Moving Shadow SHADOW 11*	**48**	2

BLAMELESS

UK, male vocal / instrumental group (Singles: 5 weeks)

Date	Title / Label	pos	wks
4 Nov 95	**TOWN CLOWNS** *China WOKCD 2046*	**56**	1
23 Mar 96	**BREATHE (A LITTLE DEEPER)** *China WOKCD 2070*	**27**	3
1 Jun 96	**SIGNS...** *China WOKCD 2077*	**49**	1

BLANCMANGE

UK, vocal / instrumental duo (Singles: 71 weeks, Albums: 57 weeks)

Date	Title / Label	pos	wks
17 Apr 82	**GOD'S KITCHEN / I'VE SEEN THE WORD** *London BLANC 1*	**65**	2
31 Jul 82	**FEEL ME** *London BLANC 2*	**46**	5
30 Oct 82 ●	**LIVING ON THE CEILING** *London BLANC 3*	**7**	14
19 Feb 83	**WAVES** *London BLANC 4*	**19**	9
7 May 83 ●	**BLIND VISION** *London BLANC 5*	**10**	8
26 Nov 83	**THAT'S LOVE, THAT IT IS** *London BLANC 6*	**33**	8
14 Apr 84 ●	**DON'T TELL ME** *London BLANC 7*	**8**	10
21 Jul 84	**THE DAY BEFORE YOU CAME** *London BLANC 8*	**22**	8
7 Sep 85	**WHAT'S YOUR PROBLEM** *London BLANC 9*	**40**	5
10 May 86	**I CAN SEE IT** *London BLANC 11*	**71**	2
9 Oct 82	**HAPPY FAMILIES** *London SH 8552*	**30**	38
26 May 84 ●	**MANGE TOUT** *London SH 8554*	**8**	17
26 Oct 85	**BELIEVE YOU ME** *London LONLP 10*	**54**	2

Billy BLAND

US, male vocalist (Singles: 10 weeks)

Date	Title / Label	pos	wks
19 May 60	**LET THE LITTLE GIRL DANCE** *London HL 9096*	**15**	10

TOP 10 MUSIC DVDS

Here are the Top 10 DVD best-sellers of 2003, which are dominated by some less than current legendary rock acts. With DVD players among the most popular Christmas presents in 2003, and with prices of equipment almost as low as the DVD music releases themselves, this comparatively new format is now established as a real growth area for the music industry.

Two new DVD rock releases in 2003: Rolling Stones, Four Flicks (extras highlight: sharing a stage with AC/DC) and Led Zeppelin (extras highlight: wonderfully nostalgic Old Grey Whistle Test interview with Robert Plant)

POS / DVD TITLE / ACT / LABEL / TOTAL SALES IN 2003

1. WHAT WE DID LAST SUMMER
   Robbie Williams Chrysalis 263,178
2. LED ZEPPELIN
   Led Zeppelin Warner Music Vision 151,834
3. LIVE AT WEMBLEY STADIUM
   Queen Parlophone 137,200
4. LIVE 2003
   Westlife BMG Video 86,972
5. GREATEST VIDEO HITS 2
   Queen Parlophone 76,618
6. LIVE 2003
   Coldplay Parlophone 73,249
7. THE BEATLES ANTHOLOGY BOX SET
   Beatles Apple 71,910
8. GO HOME – LIVE FROM SLANE CASTLE
   U2 Island 61,141
9. LIVE AT SLANE CASTLE
   Red Hot Chili Peppers Warner Music Vision 60,361
10. THE WORLD TOUR
    Cliff Richard VCI 57,600

BLANK & JONES *Germany, production duo – Piet Blank and Jaspa Jones (Singles: 9 weeks)*

Date	Title	pos	wks
26 Jun 99	**CREAM** *Devia DVNT 31CDS*	**24**	3
27 May 00	**AFTER LOVE** *Nebula NEBCDS 3*	**57**	1
30 Sep 00	**THE NIGHTFLY** *Nebula NEBCD 010*	**55**	1
3 Mar 01	**BEYOND TIME** *Gang Go / Edel 01245115 GAG*	**53**	2
29 Jun 02	**DJS FANS & FREAKS** *Incentive CENT 42CDS*	**45**	2

BLAQUE IVORY *US, female vocal group (Singles: 3 weeks)*

Date	Title	pos	wks
3 Jul 99	**808** *Columbia 6674962*	**31**	3

BLAST featuring VDC *Italy, male / female vocal / instrumental group (Singles: 5 weeks)*

Date	Title	pos	wks
18 Jun 94	**CRAYZY MAN** *UMM MCSTD 1982*	**22**	3
12 Nov 94	**PRINCES OF THE NIGHT** *UMM MCSTD 2011*	**40**	2

Mel BLATT *UK, female vocalist (Singles: 3 weeks)*

Date	Title	pos	wks
6 Sep 03	**DO ME WRONG** *London LONCD 479*	**18**	3

See also ALL SAINTS; ARTFUL DODGER; OUTSIDAZ featuring Rah DIGGA and Melanie BLATT

BLAZE featuring Palmer BROWN *US, male production duo, and male vocalist (Singles: 3 weeks)*

Date	Title	pos	wks
10 Mar 01	**MY BEAT** *Black & Blue / Kickin' NEOCD 053*	**53**	2
21 Sep 02	**DO YOU REMEMBER HOUSE** *Slip'n'Slide SLIPCD 151*	**55**	1

BLAZIN' SQUAD *UK, male vocal / rap group (Singles: 50 weeks, Albums: 8 weeks)*

Date	Title	pos	wks
31 Aug 02 ★	**CROSSROADS** *East West SQUAD 01CD* ■	**1**	13
23 Nov 02 ●	**LOVE ON THE LINE** *East West SQUAD 02CD1*	**6**	13
8 Feb 03 ●	**REMINISCE / WHERE THE STORY ENDS** *East West SQUAD 003CD1*	**8**	8
5 Jul 03 ●	**WE JUST BE DREAMIN'** *East West SQUAD 04CD*	**3**	9
15 Nov 03 ●	**FLIP REVERSE** *East West SQUAD 05CD1*	**2**	7+
7 Dec 02	**IN THE BEGINNING** *East West 50466 10792*	**33**	6
29 Nov 03	**NOW OR NEVER** *East West 5046703662*	**37**	2

BLEACHIN' *UK, male vocal / instrumental group (Singles: 4 weeks)*

Date	Title	pos	wks
22 Jul 00	**PEAKIN' (re)** *Boiler House / Arista 74321774812*	**32**	4

BLESSID UNION OF SOULS *US, male vocal / instrumental group (Singles: 6 weeks)*

Date	Title	pos	wks
27 May 95	**I BELIEVE** *EMI CDEM 374*	**29**	5
23 Mar 96	**LET ME BE THE ONE** *EMI CDEM 387*	**74**	1

BLESSING *UK, male vocal / instrumental group (Singles: 13 weeks)*

Date	Title	pos	wks
11 May 91	**HIGHWAY 5** *MCA MCS 1509*	**42**	6
18 Jan 92	**HIGHWAY 5 (re-mix)** *MCA MCS 1603*	**30**	6
19 Feb 94	**SOUL LOVE** *MCA MCSTD 1940*	**73**	1

Mary J BLIGE (261 Top 500)

Original queen of hip hop and soul, b. 11 Jan 1971, the Bronx, New York, US. Transatlantic chart regular since platinum-selling debut album 'What's the 411?' (1992). Recorded with numerous top acts including Elton John, Puff Daddy, Eric Clapton, Lauryn Hill, Bono, R Kelly, Wyclef Jean, Aretha Franklin and Ja Rule (Singles: 135 weeks, Albums: 104 weeks)

Date	Title	pos	wks
28 Nov 92	**REAL LOVE** *Uptown MCS 1721*	**68**	2
27 Feb 93	**REMINISCE** *Uptown MCSTD 1731*	**31**	4
12 Jun 93	**YOU REMIND ME** *Uptown MCSTD 1770*	**48**	3
28 Aug 93	**REAL LOVE (re-mix)** *Uptown MCSTD 1922*	**26**	4
4 Dec 93	**YOU DON'T HAVE TO WORRY** *Uptown MCSTD 1948*	**36**	2
14 May 94	**MY LOVE** *Uptown MCSTD 1972*	**29**	3
10 Dec 94	**BE HAPPY** *Uptown MCSTD 2033*	**30**	4
15 Apr 95	**I'M GOIN' DOWN** *Uptown MCSTD 2053*	**12**	4
29 Jul 95 ●	**I'LL BE THERE FOR YOU – YOU'RE ALL I NEED TO GET BY** *Def Jam DEFDX 11* [1]	**10**	5
30 Sep 95	**MARY JANE (ALL NIGHT LONG)** *Uptown MCSTD 2088*	**17**	4
16 Dec 95	**(YOU MAKE ME FEEL LIKE A) NATURAL WOMAN** *Uptown MCSTD 2108*	**23**	3
30 Mar 96	**NOT GON' CRY** *Arista 74321358252*	**39**	2
1 Mar 97	**CAN'T KNOCK THE HUSTLE** *Northwestside 74321447192* [2]	**30**	2
17 May 97	**LOVE IS ALL WE NEED** *Uptown MCSTD 48053*	**15**	4
16 Aug 97 ●	**EVERYTHING** *MCA MCSTD 48059*	**6**	9
29 Nov 97	**MISSING YOU (2re)** *MCA MCSTD 48071*	**19**	5
11 Jul 98	**SEVEN DAYS** *MCA MCSTD 48083* [3]	**22**	3
13 Mar 99 ●	**AS** *Epic 6670122* [4]	**4**	10
21 Aug 99	**ALL THAT I CAN SAY** *MCA MCSTD 40215*	**29**	3
11 Dec 99	**DEEP INSIDE** *MCA MCSTD 40224*	**42**	2
29 Apr 00	**GIVE ME YOU** *MCA MCSTD 40230*	**19**	4
16 Dec 00 ●	**911** *Columbia 6706122* [5]	**9**	10
6 Oct 01 ●	**FAMILY AFFAIR** *MCA MCSTD 40267* ▲	**8**	16
9 Feb 02	**DANCE FOR ME** *MCA MCSTD 40274* [6]	**13**	7
11 May 02 ●	**NO MORE DRAMA** *MCA MCSTD 40281*	**9**	7
24 Aug 02	**RAINY DAYZ** *MCA MCSTD 40288* [7]	**17**	5
27 Sep 03	**LOVE @ 1ST SIGHT** *Geffen / Island MCSTD 40338* [8]	**18**	5
6 Dec 03	**NOT TODAY** *Geffen MCSTD 40349* [9]	**40**	2
20 Dec 03	**WHENEVER I SAY YOUR NAME** *A&M 9815394* [10]	**60**	1
20 Mar 93	**WHAT'S THE 411?** *Uptown UPTD 10681*	**53**	1
17 Dec 94	**MY LIFE** *Uptown UPTD 11156*	**59**	3
26 Apr 97 ●	**SHARE MY WORLD** *MCA MCD 11619* ▲	**8**	32
28 Aug 99 ●	**MARY** *MCA MCD 11976*	**5**	6
8 Sep 01 ●	**NO MORE DRAMA** *MCA 1126322*	**4**	58
6 Sep 03 ●	**LOVE & LIFE** *Geffen / Island 9860700* ▲	**8**	5

[1] Method Man featuring Mary J Blige [2] Jay-Z featuring Mary J Blige [3] Mary J Blige featuring George Benson [4] George Michael and Mary J Blige [5] Wyclef Jean featuring Mary J Blige [6] Mary J Blige featuring Common [7] Mary J Blige featuring Ja Rule [8] Mary J Blige featuring Method Man [9] Mary J Blige featuring Eve [10] Sting and Mary J Blige

BLIND FAITH *UK, male vocal / instrumental group (Albums: 10 weeks)*

Date	Title	pos	wks
13 Sep 69 ★	**BLIND FAITH** *Polydor 583059* ▲	**1**	10

See also Eric CLAPTON; Steve WINWOOD; Ginger BAKER

BLIND MELON *US, male vocal / instrumental group (Singles: 13 weeks, Albums: 4 weeks)*

Date	Title	pos	wks
12 Jun 93	**TONES OF HOME** *Capitol CDCL 687*	**62**	2
11 Dec 93	**NO RAIN** *Capitol CDCL 699*	**17**	6
9 Jul 94	**CHANGE** *Capitol CDCL 717*	**35**	3
5 Aug 95	**GALAXIE** *Capitol CDCLS 755*	**37**	2
22 Jan 94	**BLIND MELON** *Capitol CDEST 2188*	**53**	3
19 Aug 95	**SOUP** *Capitol CDEST 2261*	**48**	1

BLINK *Ireland, male vocal / instrumental group (Singles: 1 week)*

Date	Title	pos	wks
16 Jul 94	**HAPPY DAY** *Lime CDR 6385*	**57**	1

BLINK-182 *US, male vocal / instrumental group (Singles: 33 weeks, Albums: 62 weeks)*

Date	Title	pos	wks
2 Oct 99	**WHAT'S MY AGE AGAIN?** *MCA MCSTD 40219*	**38**	2
25 Mar 00 ●	**ALL THE SMALL THINGS** *MCA MCSTD 40223*	**2**	10
8 Jul 00	**WHAT'S MY AGE AGAIN? (re-issue)** *MCA MCSZD 40219*	**17**	6
14 Jul 01	**THE ROCK SHOW** *MCA MCSTD 40259*	**14**	7
6 Oct 01	**FIRST DATE (re)** *MCA MCSTD 40264*	**31**	4
6 Dec 03	**FEELING THIS** *Geffen MCSTD 40347*	**15**	4+
11 Mar 00	**ENEMA OF THE STATE** *MCA MCD 11950*	**15**	32
18 Nov 00	**THE MARK TOM & TRAVIS SHOW – THE ENEMA STRIKES BACK** *MCA 1123792*	**69**	1
23 Jun 01 ●	**TAKE OFF YOUR PANTS AND JACKET** *MCA 1126712* ▲	**4**	24
29 Nov 03	**BLINK-182** *Geffen / Polydor 9861408*	**22**	5+

BLINKY BLINK – *See BLACKSTREET*

BLITZ *UK, male vocal / instrumental group (Albums: 3 weeks)*

Date	Title	pos	wks
6 Nov 82	**VOICE OF A GENERATION** *No Future PUNK 1*	**27**	3

BLIZZARD OF OZZ – *See Ozzy OSBOURNE*

BLOCKHEADS

UK, male vocal / instrumental group (Albums: 3 weeks) pos/wks

21 Apr 01 **BRAND NEW BOOTS AND PANTIES** *East Central One NEWBOOTS 2CD* 44 3

See also Ian DURY and the BLOCKHEADS

BLOCKSTER *UK / Italy, male production group (Singles: 11 weeks)* pos/wks

16 Jan 99 ● **YOU SHOULD BE ...** *Sound of Ministry MOSCDS 128* 3 9
24 Jul 99 **GROOVELINE** *Sound of Ministry MOSCDS 131* 18 2

BLODWYN PIG

UK, male vocal / instrumental group (Albums: 11 weeks) pos/wks

16 Aug 69 ● **AHEAD RINGS OUT** *Island ILPS 9101* 9 4
25 Apr 70 ● **GETTING TO THIS** *Island ILPS 9122* 8 7

BLOKES – *See Billy BRAGG*

Kristine BLOND *Denmark, female vocalist (Singles: 7 weeks)* pos/wks

11 Apr 98 **LOVE SHY** *Reverb BNOISE 1CD* 22 3
11 Nov 00 **LOVE SHY (re-mix)** *Relentless RELENT 4CDS* 28 2
4 May 02 **YOU MAKE ME GO OOOH** *WEA WEA 343CD* 35 2

BLONDIE (73 Top 500) *Influential New York-based quintet, fronted by ex-Bunny Girl Deborah Harry (v) (b. 1 Jul 1945, Miami) and fiancé Chris Stein (g). Few acts can match their 20-year span of No.1 hits. Best-selling single: 'Heart of Glass' 1,180,000 (Singles: 172 weeks, Albums: 349 weeks)* pos/wks

18 Feb 78 ● **DENIS (DENEE)** *Chrysalis CHS 2204* 2 14
6 May 78 ● **(I'M ALWAYS TOUCHED BY YOUR) PRESENCE DEAR** *Chrysalis CHS 2217* 10 9
26 Aug 78 **PICTURE THIS** *Chrysalis CHS 2242* 12 11
11 Nov 78 ● **HANGING ON THE TELEPHONE** *Chrysalis CHS 2266* 5 12
27 Jan 79 ★ **HEART OF GLASS** *Chrysalis CHS 2275* ◆ ▲ 1 12
19 May 79 ★ **SUNDAY GIRL** *Chrysalis CHS 2320* 1 13
29 Sep 79 ● **DREAMING** *Chrysalis CHS 2350* 2 8
24 Nov 79 **UNION CITY BLUE** *Chrysalis CHS 2400* 13 10
23 Feb 80 ★ **ATOMIC** *Chrysalis CHS 2410* 1 9
12 Apr 80 ★ **CALL ME** *Chrysalis CHS 2414* ▲ 1 9
8 Nov 80 ★ **THE TIDE IS HIGH** *Chrysalis CHS 2465* ▲ 1 12
24 Jan 81 ● **RAPTURE** *Chrysalis CHS 2485* ▲ 5 8
8 May 82 **ISLAND OF LOST SOULS** *Chrysalis CHS 2608* 11 9
24 Jul 82 **WAR CHILD** *Chrysalis CHS 2624* 39 4
3 Dec 88 **DENIS (re-mix)** *Chrysalis CHS 3328* 50 3
11 Feb 89 **CALL ME (re-mix)** *Chrysalis CHS 3342* 61 2
10 Sep 94 **ATOMIC (re-mix)** *Chrysalis CDCHS 5013* 19 4
8 Jul 95 **HEART OF GLASS (re-mix)** *Chrysalis CSCHS 5023* 15 3
28 Oct 95 **UNION CITY BLUE (re-mix)** *Chrysalis CDCHS 5027* 31 2
13 Feb 99 ★ **MARIA** *Beyond 74321645632* ■ 1 12
12 Jun 99 **NOTHING IS REAL BUT THE GIRL** *Beyond 74321669472* 26 3
18 Oct 03 **GOOD BOYS** *Epic 6743992* 12 3
4 Mar 78 ● **PLASTIC LETTERS** *Chrysalis CHR 1166* 10 54
23 Sep 78 ★ **PARALLEL LINES** *Chrysalis CDL 1192* 1 106
10 Mar 79 **BLONDIE** *Chrysalis CHR 1165* 75 1
13 Oct 79 ★ **EAT TO THE BEAT** *Chrysalis CDL 1225* ■ 1 38
29 Nov 80 ● **AUTOAMERICAN** *Chrysalis CDL 1290* 3 16
31 Oct 81 ● **THE BEST OF BLONDIE** *Chrysalis CDLTV 1* 4 40
5 Jun 82 ● **THE HUNTER** *Chrysalis CDL 1384* 9 12
17 Dec 88 **ONCE MORE INTO THE BLEACH** *Chrysalis CJB 2* [1] 50 4
16 Mar 91 ● **THE COMPLETE PICTURE – THE VERY BEST OF DEBORAH HARRY AND BLONDIE** *Chrysalis CHR 1817* [1] 3 22
29 Jul 95 **BEAUTIFUL – THE REMIX ALBUM** *Chrysalis CDCHR 6105* 25 2
25 Jul 98 **ATOMIC / ATOMIX – THE VERY BEST OF BLONDIE** *EMI 4949962* 12 34
27 Feb 99 ● **NO EXIT** *Beyond Music 74321641142* 3 15
2 Nov 02 **GREATEST HITS** *Chrysalis 5431052* 38 4
25 Oct 03 **CURSE OF BLONDIE** *Epic 5119219* 36 1

[1] Deborah Harry and Blondie

The remix album 'Atomix' was listed with 'Atomic – The Very Best of Blondie' from 20 Feb 99

See also Deborah HARRY

BLOOD SWEAT & TEARS *US / Canada, male vocal / instrumental group (Singles: 6 weeks, Albums: 21 weeks)* pos/wks

30 Apr 69 **YOU'VE MADE ME SO VERY HAPPY** *CBS 4116* 35 6
13 Jul 68 **CHILD IS FATHER TO THE MAN** *CBS 63296* 40 1
12 Apr 69 **BLOOD SWEAT & TEARS** *CBS 63504* ▲ 15 8
8 Aug 70 **BLOOD SWEAT & TEARS 3** *CBS 64024* ▲ 14 12

BLOODHOUND GANG *US, male vocal / instrumental group (Singles: 21 weeks, Albums: 7 weeks)* pos/wks

23 Aug 97 **WHY'S EVERYBODY ALWAYS PICKIN' ON ME?** *Geffen GFSTD 22252* 56 1
15 Apr 00 ● **THE BAD TOUCH** *Geffen 4972672* 4 14
2 Sep 00 **THE BALLAD OF CHASEY LAIN** *Geffen 4973812* 15 6
6 May 00 **HOORAY FOR BOOBIES** *Geffen 4904552* 37 7

Male / female act for 1997 debut hit

BLOODSTONE

US, male vocal / instrumental group (Singles: 4 weeks) pos/wks

18 Aug 73 **NATURAL HIGH** *Decca F 13382* 40 4

Bobby BLOOM *US, male vocalist, d. 28 Feb 1974 (Singles: 24 weeks)* pos/wks

29 Aug 70 ● **MONTEGO BAY (2re)** *Polydor 2058 051* 3 19
9 Jan 71 **HEAVY MAKES YOU HAPPY** *Polydor 2001 122* 31 5

BLOOMSBURY SET

UK, male vocal / instrumental group (Singles: 3 weeks) pos/wks

25 Jun 83 **HANGING AROUND WITH THE BIG BOYS** *Stiletto STL 13* 56 3

Tanya BLOUNT *US, female vocalist (Singles: 1 week)* pos/wks

11 Jun 94 **I'M GONNA MAKE YOU MINE** *Polydor PZCD 315* 69 1

Kurtis BLOW *US, male rapper – Kurtis Walker (Singles: 23 weeks)* pos/wks

15 Dec 79 **CHRISTMAS RAPPIN'** *Mercury BLOW 7* 30 6
11 Oct 80 **THE BREAKS** *Mercury BLOW 8* 47 4
16 Mar 85 **PARTY TIME (THE GO-GO EDIT)** *Club JAB 12* 67 1
15 Jun 85 **SAVE YOUR LOVE (FOR NUMBER 1)** *Club JAB 14* [1] 66 2
18 Jan 86 **IF I RULED THE WORLD** *Club JAB 26* 24 8
8 Nov 86 **I'M CHILLIN'** *Club JAB 42* 64 2

[1] René and Angela featuring Kurtis Blow

BLOW MONKEYS *UK, male vocal / instrumental group (Singles: 46 weeks, Albums: 27 weeks)* pos/wks

1 Mar 86 **DIGGING YOUR SCENE** *RCA PB 40599* 12 10
17 May 86 **WICKED WAYS** *RCA MONK 2* 60 2
31 Jan 87 ● **IT DOESN'T HAVE TO BE THIS WAY** *RCA MONK 4* 5 8
28 Mar 87 **OUT WITH HER** *RCA MONK 5* 30 6
30 May 87 **(CELEBRATE) THE DAY AFTER YOU** *RCA MONK 6* [1] 52 2
15 Aug 87 **SOME KIND OF WONDERFUL** *RCA MONK 7* 67 1
6 Aug 88 **THIS IS YOUR LIFE** *RCA PB 42149* 70 2
8 Apr 89 **THIS IS YOUR LIFE (re-mix)** *RCA PB 42695* 32 5
15 Jul 89 **CHOICE?** *RCA PB 42885* [2] 22 6
14 Oct 89 **SLAVES NO MORE** *RCA PB 43201* [2] 73 2
26 May 90 **SPRINGTIME FOR THE WORLD** *RCA PB 43623* 69 2
19 Apr 86 **ANIMAL MAGIC** *RCA PL 70910* 21 8
25 Apr 87 **SHE WAS ONLY A GROCER'S DAUGHTER** *RCA PL 71245* 20 8
11 Feb 89 **WHOOPS! THERE GOES THE NEIGHBOURHOOD** *RCA PL 71858* 46 2
26 Aug 89 ● **CHOICES – THE SINGLES COLLECTION** *RCA PL 74191* 5 9

[1] Blow Monkeys with Curtis Mayfield [2] Blow Monkeys featuring Sylvia Tella

BLOWING FREE *UK, male instrumental duo – Stewart and Bradley Palmer (Albums: 14 weeks)* pos/wks

29 Jul 95 ● **SAX MOODS** *Dino DINCD 106* 6 13
30 Nov 96 **SAX MOODS – VOLUME 2** *Dino DINCD 118* 70 1

See also HYPNOSIS; HARMONIUM; IN TUNE; JAMES BOYS; RAINDANCE; SCHOOL OF EXCELLENCE

Angel BLU – *See JAIMESON*

BLU PETER
UK, male DJ / producer (Singles: 1 week) pos/wks

21 Mar 98 **TELL ME WHAT YOU WANT / JAMES HAS KITTENS** *React CDREACT 285* 70 1

BLUE
UK, male vocal / instrumental group (Singles: 8 weeks) pos/wks

30 Apr 77 **GONNA CAPTURE YOUR HEART** *Rocket ROKN 522* 18 8

BLUE (331 Top 500)
One of Britain's top global sellers this century: Duncan James, Anthony Costa, Lee Ryan and Simon Webbe. The London-based boy band, which was won countless awards including Best Pop Act at the 2003 Brits, saw first two albums go quadruple platinum in the UK (Singles: 100 weeks, Albums: 98 weeks) pos/wks

2 Jun 01 ● **ALL RISE** *Innocent SINCD 28* 4 13
8 Sep 01 ★ **TOO CLOSE** *Innocent SINCD 30* ■ 1 13
24 Nov 01 ★ **IF YOU COME BACK** *Innocent SINCD 32* ■ 1 13
30 Mar 02 ● **FLY BY II** *Innocent SINCD 33* 6 12
2 Nov 02 ● **ONE LOVE** *Innocent SINCD 41* 3 12
21 Dec 02 ★ **SORRY SEEMS TO BE THE HARDEST WORD (re-recording)** *Innocent SINDX 43* [1] ■ 1 17
29 Mar 03 ● **U MAKE ME WANNA** *Innocent SINCD 44* 4 10
1 Nov 03 ● **GUILTY** *Innocent SINCD 51* 2 9+
27 Dec 03 **SIGNED, SEALED, DELIVERED, I'M YOURS** *Innocent SINCD 54* [2] 11 1+
8 Dec 01 ★ **ALL RISE** *Innocent CDSIN 8* 1 63
16 Nov 02 ★ **ONE LOVE** *Innocent CDSIN 11* ■ 1 28
15 Nov 03 ★ **GUILTY** *Innocent CDSIN 13* ■ 1 7+

[1] Blue featuring Elton John [2] Blue featuring Stevie Wonder and Angie Stone

Babbity BLUE *UK, female vocalist (Singles: 2 weeks)* pos/wks

11 Feb 65 **DON'T MAKE ME (FALL IN LOVE WITH YOU)** *Decca F 12053* 48 2

Barry BLUE *UK, male vocalist – Barry Green (Singles: 48 weeks)* pos/wks

28 Jul 73 ● **DANCIN' (ON A SATURDAY NIGHT)** *Bell 1295* 2 15
3 Nov 73 ● **DO YOU WANNA DANCE?** *Bell 1336* 7 12
2 Mar 74 **SCHOOL LOVE** *Bell 1345* 11 9
3 Aug 74 **MISS HIT AND RUN** *Bell 1364* 26 7
26 Oct 74 **HOT SHOT** *Bell 1379* 23 5

See also CRY SISCO!

BLUE ADONIS featuring LIL' MISS MAX
Belgium, male production duo – Dirk de Boeck and Wim Perdaen with female vocalist (Singles: 3 weeks) pos/wks

17 Oct 98 **DISCO COP** *Serious SERR 002CD* 27 3

BLUE AEROPLANES *UK, male / female vocal / instrumental group (Singles: 3 weeks, Albums: 5 weeks)* pos/wks

17 Feb 90 **JACKET HANGS** *Ensign ENY 628* 72 1
26 May 90 **... AND STONES** *Ensign ENY 632* 63 2
24 Feb 90 **SWAGGER** *Ensign CHEN 13* 54 1
17 Aug 91 **BEATSONGS** *Ensign CHEN 21* 33 3
12 Mar 94 **LIFE MODEL** *Beggars Banquet BBQCD 143* 59 1

BLUE AMAZON
UK, male production duo / female vocalist (Singles: 2 weeks) pos/wks

17 May 97 **AND THEN THE RAIN FALLS** *Sony S2 BAS 301 CD* 53 1
1 Jul 00 **BREATHE** *Subversive SUB 61D* 73 1

BLUE BAMBOO
Belgium, male producer – Johan Gielen (Singles: 4 weeks) pos/wks

3 Dec 94 **ABC AND D ...** *Escapade CDJAPE 6* 23 4

See also AIRSCAPE; CUBIC 22; TRANSFORMER 2; BALEARIC BILL; Johan GIELEN presents ABNEA; SVENSON and GIELEN

BLUE BOY
UK, male producer – Alexis Blackmore (Singles: 16 weeks) pos/wks

1 Feb 97 ● **REMEMBER ME** *Pharm CDPHARM 1* 8 13
23 Aug 97 **SANDMAN** *Sidewalk CDSWALK 001* 25 3

BLUE CAPS – *See Gene VINCENT*

BLUE FEATHER
Holland, male vocal / instrumental group (Singles: 4 weeks) pos/wks

3 Jul 82 **LET'S FUNK TONIGHT** *Mercury MER 109* 50 4

BLUE FLAMES – *See Georgie FAME*

BLUE GRASS BOYS – *See Johnny DUNCAN and the BLUE GRASS BOYS*

BLUE HAZE
UK, male vocal / instrumental group (Singles: 6 weeks) pos/wks

18 Mar 72 **SMOKE GETS IN YOUR EYES** *A&M AMS 891* 32 6

BLUE JEANS – *See Bob B SOXX and the BLUE JEANS*

BLUE MELONS
UK, male / female vocal / instrumental group (Singles: 1 week) pos/wks

8 Jun 96 **DO WAH DIDDY DIDDY** *Fundamental FUNDCD 1* 70 1

BLUE MERCEDES
UK, male vocal / instrumental duo – Duncan Millar and David Titlow (Singles: 18 weeks) pos/wks

10 Oct 87 **I WANT TO BE YOUR PROPERTY** *MCA BONA 1* 23 11
13 Feb 88 **SEE WANT MUST HAVE** *MCA BONA 2* 57 2
23 Jul 88 **LOVE IS THE GUN** *MCA BONA 3* 46 5

BLUE MINK
UK / US, male vocal / instrumental group (Singles: 83 weeks) pos/wks

15 Nov 69 ● **MELTING POT** *Philips BF 1818* 3 15
28 Mar 70 ● **GOOD MORNING FREEDOM** *Philips BF 1838* 10 10
19 Sep 70 **OUR WORLD** *Philips 6006 042* 17 9
29 May 71 ● **BANNER MAN** *Regal Zonophone RZ 3034* 3 14
11 Nov 72 **STAY WITH ME (re)** *Regal Zonophone RZ 3064* 11 15
3 Mar 73 **BY THE DEVIL (I WAS TEMPTED)** *EMI 2007* 26 9
23 Jun 73 ● **RANDY** *EMI 2028* 9 11

See also DAVID and JONATHAN; PIPKINS

BLUE MURDER
UK, male vocal / instrumental group (Albums: 3 weeks) pos/wks

6 May 89 **BLUE MURDER** *Geffen WX 245* 45 3

BLUE NILE *UK, male vocal / instrumental group (Singles: 4 weeks, Albums: 10 weeks)* pos/wks

30 Sep 89 **THE DOWNTOWN LIGHTS** *Linn LKS 3* 67 1
29 Sep 90 **HEADLIGHTS ON THE PARADE** *Linn LKS 4* 72 1
19 Jan 91 **SATURDAY NIGHT** *Linn LKS 5* 50 2
19 May 84 **A WALK ACROSS THE ROOFTOPS** *Linn LKH 1* 80 2
21 Oct 89 **HATS** *Linn LKH 2* 12 4
22 Jun 96 **PEACE AT LAST** *Warner Bros. 9362458482* 13 4

BLUE ÖYSTER CULT *US, male vocal / instrumental group (Singles: 14 weeks, Albums: 40 weeks)* pos/wks

20 May 78 **(DON'T FEAR) THE REAPER** *CBS 6333* 16 14
3 Jul 76 **AGENTS OF FORTUNE** *CBS 81385* 26 10
4 Feb 78 **SPECTRES** *CBS 86050* 60 1
28 Oct 78 **SOME ENCHANTED EVENING** *CBS 86074* 18 4
18 Aug 79 **MIRRORS** *CBS 86087* 46 5
19 Jul 80 **CULTOSAURUS ERECTUS** *CBS 86120* 12 7
25 Jul 81 **FIRE OF UNKNOWN ORIGIN** *CBS 85137* 29 7
22 May 82 **EXTRATERRESTRIAL LIVE** *CBS 22203* 39 5
19 Nov 83 **THE REVOLUTION BY NIGHT** *CBS 25686* 95 1

BLUE PEARL *UK / US, male / female vocal / instrumental group (Singles: 29 weeks, Albums: 2 weeks)*

Date		Title	pos	wks
7 Jul 90	●	**NAKED IN THE RAIN** *Big Life BLR 23*	4	13
3 Nov 90		**LITTLE BROTHER** *Big Life BLR 32*	31	5
11 Jan 92		**(CAN YOU) FEEL THE PASSION** *Big Life BLR 67*	14	6
25 Jul 92		**MOTHER DAWN** *Big Life BLR 73*	50	2
27 Nov 93		**FIRE OF LOVE** *Logic 74321170292* [1]	71	1
4 Jul 98		**NAKED IN THE RAIN '98 (re-recording)** *Malarky MLKD 7*	22	2
1 Dec 90		**NAKED** *Big Life BLR LP4*	58	2

[1] Jungle High with Blue Pearl

BLUE RONDO A LA TURK *UK, male vocal / instrumental group (Singles: 9 weeks, Albums: 2 weeks)*

Date		Title	pos	wks
14 Nov 81		**ME AND MR SANCHEZ** *Virgin VS 463*	40	4
13 Mar 82		**KLACTOVEESEDSTEIN** *Diable Noir VS 476*	50	5
6 Nov 82		**CHEWING THE FAT** *Diable Noir V 2240*	80	2

BLUE ZOO
UK, male vocal / instrumental group (Singles: 17 weeks)

Date		Title	pos	wks
12 Jun 82		**I'M YOUR MAN** *Magnet MAG 224*	55	3
16 Oct 82		**CRY BOY CRY** *Magnet MAG 234*	13	10
28 May 83		**I JUST CAN'T (FORGIVE AND FORGET)** *Magnet MAG 241*	60	4

BLUEBELLS *UK, male vocal / instrumental group (Singles: 49 weeks, Albums: 15 weeks)*

Date		Title	pos	wks
12 Mar 83		**CATH / WILL SHE ALWAYS BE WAITING** *London LON 20*	62	2
9 Jul 83		**SUGAR BRIDGE (IT WILL STAND)** *London LON 27*	72	1
24 Mar 84		**I'M FALLING** *London LON 45*	11	12
23 Jun 84	●	**YOUNG AT HEART** *London LON 49*	8	12
1 Sep 84		**CATH (re-issue)** *London LON 54*	38	7
9 Feb 85		**ALL I AM (IS LOVING YOU)** *London LON 58*	58	3
27 Mar 93	★	**YOUNG AT HEART (re-issue)** *London LONCD 338*	1	12
11 Aug 84		**SISTERS** *London LONLP 1*	22	10
17 Apr 93		**THE SINGLES COLLECTION** *London 8284052*	27	5

BLUENOTES – See Harold MELVIN and the BLUENOTES

BLUES BAND *UK, male vocal / instrumental group (Singles: 2 weeks, Albums: 18 weeks)*

Date		Title	pos	wks
12 Jul 80		**BLUES BAND (EP)** *Arista BOOT 2*	68	2
8 Mar 80		**OFFICIAL BOOTLEG ALBUM** *Arista BBBP 101*	40	9
18 Oct 80		**READY** *Arista BB 2*	36	6
17 Oct 81		**ITCHY FEET** *Arista BB 3*	60	3

Tracks on Blues Band (EP): Maggie's Farm / Ain't it Tuff / Diddy Wah Diddy / Back Door Man

BLUES BROTHERS *US / Canada, male actors / vocal duo – John Belushi (d. 5 Mar 1982) and Dan Aykroyd (Singles: 8 weeks)*

Date		Title	pos	wks
7 Apr 90		**EVERYBODY NEEDS SOMEBODY TO LOVE** *East West A7591*	12	8

For the first two weeks, the flip side of 'Everybody Needs Somebody to Love' – 'Think' by Aretha Franklin – was listed

BLUETONES *UK, male vocal / instrumental group (Singles: 46 weeks, Albums: 50 weeks)*

Date		Title	pos	wks
17 Jun 95		**ARE YOU BLUE OR ARE YOU BLIND** *Superior Quality BLUE 001CD*	31	2
14 Oct 95		**BLUETONIC** *Superior Quality BLUE 002CD*	19	3
3 Feb 96	●	**SLIGHT RETURN** *Superior Quality BLUE 003CD*	2	8
11 May 96	●	**CUT SOME RUG / CASTLE ROCK (re)** *Superior Quality BLUE 005CD*	7	6
28 Sep 96	●	**MARBLEHEAD JOHNSON** *Superior Quality BLUE 006CD*	7	6
21 Feb 98	●	**SOLOMON BITES THE WORM** *Superior Quality BLUED 007*	10	3
9 May 98		**IF ...** *Superior Quality BLUED 009*	13	5
8 Aug 98		**SLEAZY BED TRACK** *Superior Quality BLUED 010*	35	2
4 Mar 00		**KEEP THE HOME FIRES BURNING** *Superior Quality BLUED 012*	13	3
20 May 00		**AUTOPHILIA** *Superior Quality BLUED 013*	18	3
6 Apr 02		**AFTER HOURS** *Superior Quality BLUED 016*	26	2
29 Mar 03		**FAST BOY / LIQUID LIPS** *Superior Quality BLUE 18CDS*	25	2
23 Aug 03		**NEVER GOING NOWHERE** *Superior Quality BLUE 020CDS*	40	1
24 Feb 96	★	**EXPECTING TO FLY** *Superior Quality BLUECD 004* ■	1	25
21 Mar 98	●	**RETURN TO THE LAST CHANCE SALOON** *Superior Quality BLUED 008*	10	16
27 May 00	●	**SCIENCE & NATURE** *Superior Quality BLUECD 014*	7	4
20 Apr 02		**THE SINGLES** *Superior Quality BLUECD 017*	14	4
24 May 03		**LUXEMBOURG** *Superior Quality BLUE019CD*	49	1

Colin BLUNSTONE *UK, male vocalist (Singles: 30 weeks)*

Date		Title	pos	wks
12 Feb 72		**SAY YOU DON'T MIND** *Epic EPC 7765*	15	9
11 Nov 72		**I DON'T BELIEVE IN MIRACLES** *Epic EPC 8434*	31	6
17 Feb 73		**HOW COULD WE DARE TO BE WRONG** *Epic EPC 1197*	45	2
14 Mar 81		**WHAT BECOMES OF THE BROKEN HEARTED** *Stiff BROKEN 1* [1]	13	10
29 May 82		**TRACKS OF MY TEARS** *PRT 7P 236*	60	2
15 Jan 83		**OLD AND WISE** *Arista ARIST 494* [2]	74	1

[1] Dave Stewart. Guest vocals: Colin Blunstone [2] Alan Parsons Project: Lead vocals by Colin Blunstone

See also ARGENT; Neil MacARTHUR; ZOMBIES

BLUR (89 Top 500)
Prime movers of Britpop: Damon Albarn (v/k), Graham Coxon (g), Alex James (b), Dave Rowntree (d). They won a record four Brit awards in 1995, and their first No.1 caused a media storm when it outpaced 'Roll with It' by Britpop rivals Oasis and was their best-selling single at 640,000 (Singles: 146 weeks, Albums: 307 weeks)

Date		Title	pos	wks
27 Oct 90		**SHE'S SO HIGH / I KNOW** *Food FOOD 26*	48	3
27 Apr 91	●	**THERE'S NO OTHER WAY** *Food FOOD 29*	8	8
10 Aug 91		**BANG** *Food FOOD 31*	24	4
11 Apr 92		**POPSCENE** *Food FOOD 37*	32	2
1 May 93		**FOR TOMORROW** *Food CDFOODS 40*	28	4
10 Jul 93		**CHEMICAL WORLD** *Food CDFOODS 45*	28	4
16 Oct 93		**SUNDAY SUNDAY** *Food CDFOOD 46*	26	3
19 Mar 94	●	**GIRLS AND BOYS** *Food CDFOODS 47*	5	7
11 Jun 94		**TO THE END** *Food CDFOODS 50*	16	5
3 Sep 94	●	**PARKLIFE** *Food CDFOOD 53*	10	7
19 Nov 94		**END OF A CENTURY** *Food CDFOOD 56*	19	3
26 Aug 95	★	**COUNTRY HOUSE (re)** *Food FOODS 63* ■	1	12
25 Nov 95	●	**THE UNIVERSAL** *Food CDFOODS 69*	5	9
24 Feb 96	●	**STEREOTYPES** *Food CDFOOD 73*	7	5
11 May 96	●	**CHARMLESS MAN** *Food CDFOOD 77*	5	6
1 Feb 97	★	**BEETLEBUM (re)** *Food CDFOODS 89* ■	1	7
19 Apr 97	●	**SONG 2** *Food CDFOODS 93*	2	5
28 Jun 97	●	**ON YOUR OWN** *Food CDFOOD 98*	5	5
27 Sep 97		**MOR** *Food CDFOOD 107*	15	3
6 Mar 99	●	**TENDER** *Food CDFOODS 117*	2	10
10 Jul 99		**COFFEE + TV** *Food CDFOODS 122*	11	7
27 Nov 99		**NO DISTANCE LEFT TO RUN (re)** *Food CDFOOD 123*	14	4
28 Oct 00	●	**MUSIC IS MY RADAR (re)** *Food / Parlophone CDFOODS 135*	10	9
26 Apr 03	●	**OUT OF TIME** *Parlophone CDR 6606*	5	9
19 Jul 03		**CRAZY BEAT** *Parlophone CDR 6610*	18	3
18 Oct 03		**GOOD SONG** *Parlophone CDR 6619*	22	2
7 Sep 91	●	**LEISURE** *Food FOODLP 6*	7	12
22 May 93		**MODERN LIFE IS RUBBISH** *Food FOODCD 9*	15	14
7 May 94	★	**PARKLIFE** *Food FOODCD 10* ■	1	106
23 Sep 95	★	**THE GREAT ESCAPE** *Food FOODCD 14* ■	1	47
22 Feb 97	★	**BLUR** *Food FOODCD 19* ■	1	65
27 Mar 99	★	**13** *Food FOODCD 29* ■	1	27
11 Nov 00	●	**THE BEST OF BLUR** *Food FOODCD 33*	3	28
17 May 03	★	**THINK TANK** *Parlophone 5829972* ■	1	8

Chart rules allow for a maximum of three formats; the 7-inch of 'Country House', already available on two CDs and cassette, was therefore listed separately

See also FAT LES; Graham COXON; GORILLAZ

BO SELECTA *UK, male rubber-faced comedian / vocalist – Avid Merrion (Leigh Francis) (Singles: 1 week)*

Date		Title	pos	wks
27 Dec 03	●	**PROPER CRIMBO** *BMG 82876581412*	4	1+

BOARDS OF CANADA *UK, male instrumental / production duo (Albums: 2 weeks)* pos/wks

2 Mar 02 **GEOGADDI** *Warp WARPCD 101* 21 2

BOB and EARL *US, male vocal duo – Bobby Relf and Earl Nelson (Singles: 13 weeks)* pos/wks

12 Mar 69 ● **HARLEM SHUFFLE** *Island WIP 6053* 7 13

BOB and MARCIA *Jamaica, male / female vocal duo – Bob Andy and Marcia Griffiths (Singles: 25 weeks)* pos/wks

14 Mar 70 ● **YOUNG, GIFTED AND BLACK** *Harry J HJ 6605* 5 12
5 Jun 71 **PIED PIPER** *Trojan TR 7818* 11 13

BOB THE BUILDER *UK, male silicone puppet building contractor – Neil Morrissey (Singles: 41 weeks, Albums: 12 weeks)* pos/wks

16 Dec 00 ★ **CAN WE FIX IT (2re)** *BBC Music WMSS 60372* ◆ 1 22
15 Sep 01 ★ **MAMBO NO.5** *BBC Music WMSS 60442* ■ 1 19
13 Oct 01 ● **THE ALBUM** *BBC Music WMSF 60472* 4 12

BOBBYSOCKS
Norway / Sweden, female vocal duo (Singles: 4 weeks) pos/wks

25 May 85 **LET IT SWING** *RCA PB 40127* 44 4

Su Su BOBIEN – *See MASS SYNDICATE featuring Su Su BOBIEN*

Andrea BOCELLI (423 Top 500) *Blind Italian operatic tenor who has sold more than 40 million albums worldwide, b. 22 Sep 1958, Lajatico. 'Romanza' sold 16 million copies worldwide; 'Sogno' topped the European chart and at times he had Top 3 places on the US classical chart (Singles: 24 weeks, Albums: 134 weeks)* pos/wks

24 May 97 ● **TIME TO SAY GOODBYE (CON TE PARTIRO)** *Coalition COLA 003CD* [1] 2 14
25 Sep 99 **CANTO DELLA TERRA (re)** *Polydor / Sugar 5613192* 24 9
18 Dec 99 **AVE MARIA** *Philips 4644852* 65 1
31 May 97 ● **ROMANZA** *Philips 4564562* 6 25
9 May 98 **ARIA – THE OPERA ALBUM** *Philips 4620332* 33 5
10 Apr 99 ● **SOGNO** *Polydor 5472212* 4 42
20 Nov 99 **SACRED ARIAS** *Philips 4626002* 20 12
23 Sep 00 **VERDI** *Philips 4646002* 17 10
27 Oct 01 ● **CIELI DI TOSCANA** *Polydor 5892452* 3 16
16 Nov 02 ● **SENTIMENTO** *Philips 4734102* 7 15
13 Feb 99 **VIAGGIO ITALIANO** *Philips 4621962* ....32 9+

[1] Sarah Brightman and Andrea Bocelli

'Canto Della Terra' was originally No.25 before re-entering and peaking one place higher in Jul 2000. 'Sentimento' features the London Symphony Orchestra and Lorin Maazel

See also Lorin MAAZEL

Karen BODDINGTON and Mark WILLIAMS
Australia / New Zealand, female / male vocal duo (Singles: 1 week) pos/wks

2 Sep 89 **HOME AND AWAY** *First Night SCORE 19* 73 1

BODINES *UK, male vocal / instrumental group (Albums: 1 week)* pos/wks

29 Aug 87 **PLAYED** *Pop BODL 2001* 94 1

BODY COUNT *US, male rap / instrumental group (Singles: 4 weeks, Albums: 2 weeks)* pos/wks

8 Oct 94 **BORN DEAD** *Rhyme Syndicate SYNDG 4* 28 2
17 Dec 94 **NECESSARY EVIL** *Virgin VSCDX 1529* 45 2
17 Sep 94 **BORN DEAD** *Rhyme Syndicate RSYND 2* 15 2

See also ICE-T

BODYSNATCHERS
UK, female vocal / instrumental group (Singles: 12 weeks) pos/wks

15 Mar 80 **LET'S DO ROCK STEADY** *2 Tone CHSTT 9* 22 9
19 Jul 80 **EASY LIFE** *2 Tone CHSTT 12* 50 3

Humphrey BOGART – *See Dooley WILSON*

Suzy BOGGUSS
US, female vocalist (Albums: 1 week) pos/wks

25 Sep 93 **SOMETHING UP MY SLEEVE** *Liberty CDEST 221* 69 1

Hamilton BOHANNON
US, male vocalist / instrumentalist – drums (Singles: 38 weeks) pos/wks

15 Feb 75 **SOUTH AFRICAN MAN** *Brunswick BR 16* 22 8
24 May 75 ● **DISCO STOMP** *Brunswick BR 19* 6 12
5 Jul 75 **FOOT STOMPIN' MUSIC** *Brunswick BR 21* 23 6
6 Sep 75 **HAPPY FEELING** *Brunswick BR 24* 49 3
26 Aug 78 **LET'S START THE DANCE** *Mercury 6167 700* 56 4
13 Feb 82 **LET'S START TO DANCE AGAIN** *London HL 10582* 49 5

BOILING POINT
US, male vocal / instrumental group (Singles: 6 weeks) pos/wks

27 May 78 **LET'S GET FUNKTIFIED** *Bang BANG 1312* 41 6

Marc BOLAN – *See T. REX*

CJ BOLLAND
Belgium, male producer (Singles: 10 weeks, Albums: 2 weeks) pos/wks

5 Oct 96 **SUGAR IS SWEETER** *Internal LIECD 35* 11 5
17 May 97 **THE PROPHET** *ffrr FCD 300* 19 3
3 Jul 99 **IT AIN'T GONNA BE ME** *Essential Recordings ESCD 5* 35 2
26 Oct 96 **THE ANALOGUE THEATRE** *Internal TRUCD 13* 43 2

See also RAVESIGNAL III

BOLSHOI
UK, male vocal / instrumental group (Albums: 1 week) pos/wks

3 Oct 87 **LINDY'S PARTY** *Beggars Banquet BEGA 86* 100 1

Michael BOLTON (154 Top 500)
Soulful rock balladeer / songwriter who initially recorded under his real name, Michael Bolotin (b. 26 Feb 1953, Connecticut, US), and fronted recording groups The Nomads and Blackjack (Singles: 113 weeks, Albums: 228 weeks) pos/wks

17 Feb 90 ● **HOW AM I SUPPOSED TO LIVE WITHOUT YOU** *CBS 655397 7* ▲ 3 10
28 Apr 90 ● **HOW CAN WE BE LOVERS** *CBS 655918 7* 10 10
21 Jul 90 **WHEN I'M BACK ON MY FEET AGAIN** *CBS 656077 7* 44 5
20 Apr 91 **LOVE IS A WONDERFUL THING** *Columbia 6567717* 23 8
27 Jul 91 **TIME LOVE AND TENDERNESS** *Columbia 6569897* 28 7
9 Nov 91 ● **WHEN A MAN LOVES A WOMAN** *Columbia 6574887* ▲ 8 9
8 Feb 92 **STEEL BARS** *Columbia 6577257* 17 6
9 May 92 **MISSING YOU NOW** *Columbia 6579917* [1] 28 4
31 Oct 92 **TO LOVE SOMEBODY** *Columbia 6584557* 16 6
26 Dec 92 **DRIFT AWAY** *Columbia 6588657* 18 5
13 Mar 93 **REACH OUT I'LL BE THERE** *Columbia 6588972* 37 4
13 Nov 93 **SAID I LOVED YOU BUT I LIED** *Columbia 6598762* 15 8
26 Feb 94 **SOUL OF MY SOUL** *Columbia 6601772* 32 3
14 May 94 **LEAN ON ME** *Columbia 6604132* 14 7
9 Sep 95 ● **CAN I TOUCH YOU ... THERE** *Columbia 6624385* 6 9
2 Dec 95 **A LOVE SO BEAUTIFUL** *Columbia 6627092* 27 5
16 Mar 96 **SOUL PROVIDER** *Columbia 6629812* 35 3
8 Nov 97 **THE BEST OF LOVE / GO THE DISTANCE** *Columbia 6652802* 14 4
17 Mar 90 ● **SOUL PROVIDER** *CBS 4653431* 4 72
11 Aug 90 **THE HUNGER** *CBS 4601631* 44 5
18 May 91 ● **TIME, LOVE AND TENDERNESS** *Columbia 4678121* ▲ 2 57
10 Oct 92 ● **TIMELESS – THE CLASSICS** *Columbia 4723022* ▲ 3 24
27 Nov 93 ● **THE ONE THING** *Columbia 4743552* 4 24
30 Sep 95 ● **GREATEST HITS 1985-1995** *Columbia 4810022* 2 30
22 Nov 97 **ALL THAT MATTERS** *Columbia 4885312* 20 7
2 May 98 **MY SECRET PASSION – THE ARIAS** *Sony Classical SK 63077* ..25 5
4 Dec 99 **TIMELESS – THE CLASSICS – VOL. 2** *Columbia 4960782* 50 2
6 Apr 02 **ONLY A WOMAN LIKE YOU** *Jive 9223522* 19 2

[1] Michael Bolton featuring Kenny G

Review of the Year

JANUARY 2003

Russian duo **t.A.T.u.** (Lena and Julia), who were controversially and statistically big news in 2003, spending four weeks at the top of the UK singles chart

Maurice Gibb of the **Bee Gees** dies while the group is charting with yet another Top 10 hit as composers, this time with 'Sacred Trust' by **One True Voice. Avril Lavigne** becomes the youngest solo female singer to top the UK album chart and **t.A.T.u.** become the first Russian act to score both a hit single and album in the UK. Fame Academy winner **David Sneddon's** debut disc 'Stop Living the Lie' enters at No.1, but with first-week sales only a 10th of Pop Idol winner **Will Young's** first release. The ground-breaking 'Mundian to Bach Ke' by **Panjabi MC** makes the Top 5. Across the Atlantic **David Gray's** show at Madison Square Garden grosses $500,000 and **Robbie Williams'** Escapology enters and peaks at No.43 on the US chart with first-week sales of just 21,000. The second series of American Idol and the first Canadian Idol are screened. At the American Music Awards, **Eminem** is the top winner with four trophies and his 'Lose Yourself' tops the US Hot 100 for a record (for a rap single) 11th week. **Norah Jones, Ashanti** and **Avril Lavigne** each receive five Grammy nominations and, after a 46-week climb, **Norah's** Come Away with Me finally tops the US chart. Top hip-hop producer and record company head Irv Gotti's office is raided because he was thought to have had ties with the Queens New York Supreme Team Drug Gang. Eight hundred million viewers around the world see **Shania Twain, No Doubt** and **Santana** perform, and The **Dixie Chicks** sing the national anthem at the Super Bowl. The US singles market appears to be in terminal decline as some releases in the Top 20 sales chart sell fewer than 1,000 copies. Country music is still as popular as ever, though, as the 50th anniversary of the death of the legendary **Hank Williams** is honoured with a show at the Grand Ole Opry house starring his son **Hank Williams Jr** and grandson **Hank Williams III.** In Spain every single, and six of the Top 10 albums, are by entrants in their version of Popstars. **Blue's** 'One Love' is a rare English-language entry in the Japanese Top 10 albums. Gone but never to be forgotten this month: **Doris Fisher,** composer of twice Top 20 hit 'You Always Hurt the One You Love' and chart-topper 'Whispering Grass', dies age 87 and 'Telephone Man' hitmaker **Meri Wilson** is killed in a car crash aged 53.

BOMB THE BASS *UK, male producer – Tim Simenon (Singles: 50 weeks, Albums: 16 weeks)*

Date		Title / Label	pos	wks
20 Feb 88	●	**BEAT DIS** *Mister-ron DOOD 1*	2	9
27 Aug 88	●	**MEGABLAST / DON'T MAKE ME WAIT** *Mister-ron DOOD 2* [1]	6	9
26 Nov 88	●	**SAY A LITTLE PRAYER** *Rhythm King DOOD 3* [2]	10	10
27 Jul 91	●	**WINTER IN JULY** *Rhythm King 6572757*	7	9
9 Nov 91		**THE AIR YOU BREATHE** *Rhythm King 6575387*	52	3
2 May 92		**KEEP GIVING ME LOVE** *Rhythm King 6579887*	62	2
1 Oct 94		**BUG POWDER DUST** *Stoned Heights BRCD 300* [3]	24	3
17 Dec 94		**DARKHEART** *Stoned Heights BRCD 305* [4]	35	3
1 Apr 95		**1 TO 1 RELIGION** *Stoned Heights BRCD 313* [5]	53	1
16 Sep 95		**SANDCASTLES** *Fourth & Broadway BRCD 324* [6]	54	1
22 Oct 88		**INTO THE DRAGON** *Rhythm King DOOD 1*	18	10
31 Aug 91		**UNKNOWN TERRITORY** *Rhythm King 4687740*	19	4
15 Apr 95		**CLEAR** *Fourth & Broadway BRCD 611*	22	2

[1] Bomb the Bass featuring Merlin and Antonia / Bomb the Bass featuring Lorraine and Lose [2] Bomb the Bass featuring Maureen [3] Bomb the Bass featuring Justin Warfield [4] Bomb the Bass featuring Spikey Tee [5] Bomb the Bass featuring Carlton [6] Bomb the Bass featuring Bernard Fowler

See also ANTONIA

BOMBALURINA featuring Timmy MALLETT *UK, male / female vocal group (Singles: 20 weeks, Albums: 5 weeks)*

Date		Title / Label	pos	wks
28 Jul 90	★	**ITSY BITSY TEENY WEENY YELLOW POLKA DOT BIKINI** *Carpet CRPT 1* [1]	1	13
24 Nov 90		**SEVEN LITTLE GIRLS SITTING IN THE BACKSEAT** *Carpet CRPT 2*	18	7
15 Dec 90		**HUGGIN' AN' A KISSIN'** *Polydor 8476481*	55	5

[1] Bombalurina

BOMBERS *Canada, male / female vocal / instrumental group (Singles: 10 weeks)*

Date		Title / Label	pos	wks
5 May 79		**(EVERYBODY) GET DANCIN'** *Flamingo FM 1*	37	7
18 Aug 79		**LET'S DANCE** *Flamingo FM 4*	58	3

BOMFUNK MC'S *Finland, male DJ / rap duo – Raymond Ebanks and DJ Gismo (Singles: 21 weeks, Albums: 2 weeks)*

Date		Title / Label	pos	wks
5 Aug 00	●	**FREESTYLER** *Dancepool DPS 2CD*	2	12
2 Dec 00		**UP ROCKING BEATS** *INCredible 6706132*	11	9
26 Aug 00		**IN STEREO** *EPIDROME 4943092*	33	2

BON *Germany, male vocal duo – Guy Gross and Claus Capek (Singles: 5 weeks)*

Date		Title / Label	pos	wks
3 Feb 01		**BOYS** *Epic 6707092*	15	5

BON JOVI (47 Top 500)

Globally popular New Jersey band: Jon Bon Jovi (v), Richie Sambora (g), David Bryan (k), Alec John Such (b), Tico Torres (d). The UK's biggest-selling album act of 1994. Estimated 75 million albums sold worldwide. Legendary fact: at one of their gigs a pig's head was thrown on stage. Best-selling single: 'Always' 560,500 (Singles: 232 weeks, Albums: 427 weeks)

Date		Title / Label	pos	wks
31 Aug 85		**HARDEST PART IS THE NIGHT** *Vertigo VER 22*	68	1
9 Aug 86		**YOU GIVE LOVE A BAD NAME** *Vertigo VER 26* ▲	14	10
25 Oct 86	●	**LIVIN' ON A PRAYER** *Vertigo VER 28* ▲	4	15
11 Apr 87		**WANTED DEAD OR ALIVE** *Vertigo JOV 1*	13	7
15 Aug 87		**NEVER SAY GOODBYE** *Vertigo JOV 2*	21	5
24 Sep 88		**BAD MEDICINE** *Vertigo JOV 3* ▲	17	7
10 Dec 88		**BORN TO BE MY BABY** *Vertigo JOV 4*	22	7
29 Apr 89		**I'LL BE THERE FOR YOU** *Vertigo JOV 5* ▲	18	7
26 Aug 89		**LAY YOUR HANDS ON ME** *Vertigo JOV 6*	18	6
9 Dec 89		**LIVING IN SIN** *Vertigo JOV 7*	35	6
24 Oct 92	●	**KEEP THE FAITH** *Jambco JOV 8*	5	6
23 Jan 93		**BED OF ROSES** *Jambco JOVCD 9*	13	6
15 May 93	●	**IN THESE ARMS** *Jambco JOVCD 10*	9	7
7 Aug 93		**I'LL SLEEP WHEN I'M DEAD** *Jambco JOVCD 11*	17	5
2 Oct 93		**I BELIEVE** *Jambco JOVCD 12*	11	6
26 Mar 94	●	**DRY COUNTY** *Jambco JOVCD 13*	9	6
24 Sep 94	●	**ALWAYS** *Jambco JOVCD 14*	2	18
17 Dec 94	●	**PLEASE COME HOME FOR CHRISTMAS (re)** *Jambco JOVCD 16*	7	10
25 Feb 95	●	**SOMEDAY I'LL BE SATURDAY NIGHT** *Jambco JOVDD 15*	7	7
10 Jun 95	●	**THIS AIN'T A LOVE SONG** *Mercury JOVCD 17*	6	9
30 Sep 95	●	**SOMETHING FOR THE PAIN** *Mercury JOVCD 18*	8	7
25 Nov 95	●	**LIE TO ME** *Mercury JOVCD 19*	10	8
9 Mar 96	●	**THESE DAYS** *Mercury JOVCD 20*	7	6
6 Jul 96		**HEY GOD** *Mercury JOVCD 21*	13	5
10 Apr 99		**REAL LIFE** *Reprise W 479CD*	21	5
3 Jun 00	●	**IT'S MY LIFE** *Mercury 5627682*	3	13
9 Sep 00	●	**SAY IT ISN'T SO (re)** *Mercury 5688972*	10	7
9 Dec 00		**THANK YOU FOR LOVING ME** *Mercury 5727302*	12	6
19 May 01	●	**ONE WILD NIGHT** *Mercury 5729502*	10	7
28 Sep 02	●	**EVERYDAY (re)** *Mercury 0639362*	5	6
21 Dec 02		**MISUNDERSTOOD** *Mercury 0638152*	21	5
24 May 03	●	**ALL ABOUT LOVIN' YOU (re)** *Mercury 9800242*	9	6
28 Apr 84		**BON JOVI** *Vertigo VERL 14*	71	3
11 May 85		**7800 FAHRENHEIT** *Vertigo VERL 24*	28	12
20 Sep 86	●	**SLIPPERY WHEN WET** *Vertigo VERH 38* ▲	6	123
1 Oct 88	★	**NEW JERSEY** *Vertigo VERH 62* ■ ▲	1	47
14 Nov 92	★	**KEEP THE FAITH** *Jambco 5141972* ■	1	70
22 Oct 94	★	**CROSSROAD – THE BEST OF BON JOVI** *Jambco 5229362* ■	1	68
1 Jul 95	★	**THESE DAYS** *Mercury 5282482* ■	1	50
10 Jun 00	★	**CRUSH** *Mercury 5425622* ■	1	29
26 May 01	●	**ONE WILD NIGHT – LIVE 1985-2001** *Mercury 5488652*	2	9
5 Oct 02	●	**BOUNCE** *Mercury 0633952*	2	9
15 Nov 03	●	**THIS LEFT FEELS RIGHT** *Mercury 9861391*	4	7+

See also Jon BON JOVI

Jon BON JOVI *US, male vocalist / instrumentalist – John Bongiovi Jr (Singles: 27 weeks, Albums: 41 weeks)*

Date		Title / Label	pos	wks
4 Aug 90		**BLAZE OF GLORY** *Vertigo JBJ 1* ▲	13	8
10 Nov 90		**MIRACLE** *Vertigo JBVJ 2*	29	5
14 Jun 97	●	**MIDNIGHT IN CHELSEA** *Mercury MERCD 488*	4	7
30 Aug 97	●	**QUEEN OF NEW ORLEANS** *Mercury MERCD 493*	10	4
15 Nov 97		**JANIE, DON'T TAKE YOUR LOVE TO TOWN** *Mercury 5749872*	13	3
25 Aug 90	●	**BLAZE OF GLORY / YOUNG GUNS II (FILM SOUNDTRACK)** *Vertigo 8464731*	2	23
28 Jun 97	●	**DESTINATION ANYWHERE** *Mercury 5360112*	2	18

See also BON JOVI

BOND *Australia / UK, female instrumental group (Albums: 21 weeks)*

Date		Title / Label	pos	wks
14 Oct 00		**BORN** *Decca 4670912*	16	18
16 Nov 02		**SHINE** *Decca 4734602*	26	3

Graham BOND *UK, male vocalist / instrumentalist – keyboards, d. 8 May 1974 (Albums: 2 weeks)*

Date		Title / Label	pos	wks
20 Jun 70		**SOLID BOND** *Warner Bros. WS 3001*	40	2

Ronnie BOND *UK, male vocalist (Singles: 5 weeks)*

Date		Title / Label	pos	wks
31 May 80		**IT'S WRITTEN ON YOUR BODY** *Mercury MER 13*	52	5

Gary 'U.S.' BONDS *US, male vocalist – Gary Anderson (Singles: 39 weeks, Albums: 8 weeks)*

Date		Title / Label	pos	wks
19 Jan 61		**NEW ORLEANS** *Top Rank JAR 527* [1]	16	11
20 Jul 61	●	**QUARTER TO THREE** *Top Rank JAR 575* [2] ▲	7	13
30 May 81		**THIS LITTLE GIRL** *EMI America EA 122*	43	6
22 Aug 81		**JOLE BLON** *EMI America EA 127*	51	3
31 Oct 81		**IT'S ONLY LOVE** *EMI America EA 128*	43	3
17 Jul 82		**SOUL DEEP** *EMI America EA 140*	59	3
22 Aug 81		**DEDICATION** *EMI America AML 3017*	43	3
10 Jul 82		**ON THE LINE** *EMI America AML 3022*	55	5

[1] U.S. Bonds [2] US Bonds

BONE *UK, male vocal / instrumental duo (Singles: 1 week)*

Date		Title / Label	pos	wks
2 Apr 94		**WINGS OF LOVE** *Deconstruction 74321176282*	55	1

BONE THUGS-N-HARMONY *US, male rap group (Singles: 26 weeks, Albums: 4 weeks)*

Date		Title / Label	pos	wks
4 Nov 95		**1ST OF THA MONTH** *Epic 6625172*	32	2
10 Aug 96	●	**THA CROSSROADS** *Epic 6635502* ▲	8	11

9 Nov 96	1ST OF THA MONTH (re-issue) *Epic 6638505*	15 4
15 Feb 97	DAYS OF OUR LIVEZ *East West A 3982CD*	37 2
26 Jul 97	LOOK INTO MY EYES *Epic 6647862*	16 3
24 May 03	HOME *Epic 6738302* [1]	19 4
31 Aug 96	E.1999 ETERNAL *Epic 4810382* ▲	39 3
9 Aug 97	THE ART OF WAR *Epic 4880802* ▲	42 1

[1] Bone Thugs-N-Harmony featuring Phil Collins

Elbow BONES and the RACKETEERS

US, male group leader and female backing group (Singles: 9 weeks) pos/wks

14 Jan 84	A NIGHT IN NEW YORK *EMI America EA 165*	33 9

BONEY M (174 Top 500)

Internationally successful West Indian vocal group: Bobby Farrell, Marcia Barrett, Liz Mitchell, Maisie Williams. This German-based quartet was assembled by producer Frank Farian (later behind controversial duo Milli Vanilli). Best-selling single: 'Rivers of Babylon' / 'Brown Girl in the Ring' 1,985,000 (Singles: 171 weeks, Albums: 143 weeks) pos/wks

18 Dec 76 ●	DADDY COOL *Atlantic K 10827*	6 13
12 Mar 77 ●	SUNNY *Atlantic K 10892*	3 10
25 Jun 77 ●	MA BAKER *Atlantic K 10965*	2 13
29 Oct 77 ●	BELFAST *Atlantic K 11020*	8 13
29 Apr 78 ★	RIVERS OF BABYLON / BROWN GIRL IN THE RING *Atlantic / Hansa K 11120* ◆	1 40
7 Oct 78 ●	RASPUTIN *Atlantic / Hansa K 11192*	2 10
2 Dec 78 ★	MARY'S BOY CHILD – OH MY LORD *Atlantic / Hansa K 11221* ◆	1 8
3 Mar 79 ●	PAINTER MAN *Atlantic / Hansa K 11255*	10 6
28 Apr 79 ●	HOORAY HOORAY, IT'S A HOLI-HOLIDAY *Atlantic / Hansa K 11279*	3 9
11 Aug 79	GOTTA GO HOME / EL LUTE *Atlantic / Hansa K 11351*	12 11
15 Dec 79	I'M BORN AGAIN *Atlantic / Hansa K 11410*	35 7
26 Apr 80	MY FRIEND JACK *Atlantic / Hansa K 11463*	57 5
14 Feb 81	CHILDREN OF PARADISE *Atlantic / Hansa K 11637*	66 2
21 Nov 81	WE KILL THE WORLD (DON'T KILL THE WORLD) *Atlantic / Hansa K 11689*	39 5
24 Dec 88	MEGAMIX / MARY'S BOY CHILD (re-mix) *Ariola 111947*	52 3
5 Dec 92 ●	BONEY M MEGAMIX *Arista 74321125127*	7 9
17 Apr 93	BROWN GIRL IN THE RING (re-mix) *Arista 74321137052*	38 3
8 May 99	MA BAKER (RE-MIX) – SOMEBODY SCREAMED *Logic 74321653872* [1]	22 2
29 Dec 01	DADDY COOL 2001 (re-mix) *BMG 74321913512*	47 2
23 Apr 77	TAKE THE HEAT OFF ME *Atlantic K 50314*	40 15
6 Aug 77	LOVE FOR SALE *Atlantic K 50385*	60 1
29 Jul 78 ★	NIGHT FLIGHT TO VENUS *Atlantic / Hansa K 50498*	1 65
29 Sep 79 ★	OCEANS OF FANTASY *Atlantic / Hansa K 50610* ■	1 18
12 Apr 80 ★	THE MAGIC OF BONEY M – 20 GOLDEN HITS *Atlantic / Hansa BMTV 1*	1 26
6 Sep 86	THE BEST OF 10 YEARS – 32 SUPERHITS *Stylus SMR 621*	35 5
27 Mar 93	THE GREATEST HITS *Telstar TCD 2656*	14 10
15 Dec 01	THE GREATEST HITS *BMG 74321896142*	66 3

[1] Boney M vs Horny United

'Brown Girl in the Ring' listed with 'Rivers of Babylon' only from 5 Aug 1978, peaking at No.2. 'El Lute' listed with 'Gotta Go Home' only from 29 Sep 1979. The 1988 and 1992 megamixes are different. The two 'The Greatest Hits' albums are different

BONFIRE

Germany, male vocal / instrumental group (Albums: 1 week) pos/wks

21 Oct 89	POINT BLANK *MSA ZL 74249*	74 1

BONIFACE

Seychelles, male vocalist – Bruce Boniface (Singles: 3 weeks) pos/wks

31 Aug 02	CHEEKY *Columbia 6729902*	25 3

Guest vocal by Lady Luck

Graham BONNET

UK, male vocalist (Singles: 15 weeks, Albums: 3 weeks) pos/wks

21 Mar 81 ●	NIGHT GAMES *Vertigo VER 1*	6 11
13 Jun 81	LIAR *Vertigo VER 2*	51 4
7 Nov 81	LINE UP *Mercury 6302151*	62 3

Graham BONNEY

UK, male vocalist – Graham Bradley (Singles: 8 weeks) pos/wks

24 Mar 66	SUPERGIRL *Columbia DB 7843*	19 8

BONNIE – *See DELANEY and BONNIE and FRIENDS*

BONNIE PRINCE BILLY

US, male vocalist / instrumentalist (Albums: 1 week) pos/wks

8 Feb 03	MASTER AND EVERYONE *Domino WIGCD121*	48 1

BONO

Ireland, male vocalist – Paul Hewson (Singles: 25 weeks) pos/wks

25 Jan 86	IN A LIFETIME *RCA PB 40535* [1]	20 5
10 Jun 89	IN A LIFETIME (re-issue) *RCA PB 42873* [1]	17 7
4 Dec 93 ●	I'VE GOT YOU UNDER MY SKIN *Island CID 578* [2]	4 9
9 Apr 94	IN THE NAME OF THE FATHER *Island CID 593* [3]	46 2
23 Oct 99	NEW DAY *Columbia 6682122* [4]	23 2

[1] Clannad featuring Bono [2] Frank Sinatra with Bono [3] Bono and Gavin Friday [4] Wyclef Jean featuring Bono

I've Got You Under My Skin was the listed B-side of 'Stay (Faraway, So Close)' by U2

See also U2

BONZO DOG DOO-DAH BAND *UK, male vocal / instrumental group (Singles: 14 weeks, Albums: 4 weeks)* pos/wks

6 Nov 68 ●	I'M THE URBAN SPACEMAN *Liberty LBF 15144*	5 14
18 Jan 69	DOUGHNUT IN GRANNY'S GREENHOUSE *Liberty LBS 83158*	40 1
30 Aug 69	TADPOLES *Liberty LBS 83257*	36 1
22 Jun 74	THE HISTORY OF THE BONZOS *United Artists UAD 60071*	41 2

Betty BOO *UK, female rapper – Alison Clarkson (Singles: 55 weeks, Albums: 25 weeks)* pos/wks

12 Aug 89 ●	HEY DJ – I CAN'T DANCE (TO THAT MUSIC YOU'RE PLAYING) / SKA TRAIN *Rhythm King LEFT 34* [1]	7 11
19 May 90 ●	DOIN' THE DO *Rhythm King LEFT 39*	7 12
11 Aug 90 ●	WHERE ARE YOU BABY? *Rhythm King LEFT 43*	3 10
1 Dec 90	24 HOURS *Rhythm King LEFT 45*	25 8
8 Aug 92	LET ME TAKE YOU THERE *WEA YZ 677*	12 8
3 Oct 92	I'M ON MY WAY *WEA YZ 693*	44 3
10 Apr 93	HANGOVER *WEA YZ 719CD*	50 3
22 Sep 90 ●	BOOMANIA *Rhythm King LEFTLP 12*	4 24
24 Oct 92	GRRR! IT'S BETTY BOO *WEA 4509909082*	62 1

[1] Beatmasters featuring Betty Boo

BOO RADLEYS *UK, male vocal / instrumental group (Singles: 27 weeks, Albums: 29 weeks)* pos/wks

20 Jun 92	DOES THIS HURT / BOO! FOREVER *Creation CRE 128*	67 1
23 Oct 93	WISH I WAS SKINNY *Creation CRESCD 169*	75 1
12 Feb 94	BARNEY (. . . & ME) *Creation CRESCD 178*	48 2
11 Jun 94	LAZARUS *Creation CRESCD 187*	50 2
11 Mar 95 ●	WAKE UP BOO! *Creation CRESCD 191*	9 8
13 May 95	FIND THE ANSWER WITHIN *Creation CRESCD 202*	37 3
29 Jul 95	IT'S LULU *Creation CRESCD 211*	25 2
7 Oct 95	FROM THE BENCH AT BELVIDERE *Creation CRESCD 214*	24 2
17 Aug 96	WHAT'S IN THE BOX (SEE WATCHA GOT) *Creation CRESCD 220*	25 2
19 Oct 96	C'MON KIDS *Creation CRESCD 236*	18 2
1 Feb 97	RIDE THE TIGER *Creation CRESCD 248X*	38 1
17 Oct 98	FREE HUEY *Creation CRESCD 299X*	54 1
4 Apr 92	EVERYTHING'S ALRIGHT FOREVER *Creation CRECD 120*	55 1
28 Aug 93	GIANT STEPS *Creation CRECD 149*	17 4
8 Apr 95 ★	WAKE UP! *Creation CRECD 179* ■	1 21
21 Sep 96	C'MON KIDS *Creation CRECD 194*	20 2
31 Oct 98	KINGSIZE *Creation CRECD 228*	62 1

BOO-YAA T.R.I.B.E.

US, male rap group (Singles: 6 weeks, Albums: 1 week) pos/wks

30 Jun 90	**PSYKO FUNK** *Fourth & Broadway BRW 179*	43	3
6 Nov 93	**ANOTHER BODY MURDERED** *Epic 6597942* [1]	26	3
14 Apr 90	NEW FUNKY NATION *Fourth & Broadway*	74	1

[1] Faith No More and Boo-Yaa T.R.I.B.E.

BOOGIE BOX HIGH

UK, male vocal / instrumental group – leader Andros Georgiou (Singles: 11 weeks) pos/wks

4 Jul 87 ●	**JIVE TALKIN'** *Hardback 7BOSS 4*	7	11

See also ALIEN VOICES featuring The THREE DEGREES; Andy G's STARSKY & HUTCH ALL STARS

BOOGIE DOWN PRODUCTIONS

US, male rap / production duo (Singles: 2 weeks, Albums: 9 weeks) pos/wks

4 Jun 88	**MY PHILOSOPHY / STOP THE VIOLENCE** *Jive JIVEX 170*	69	2
18 Jan 88	BY ALL MEANS NECESSARY *Jive HIP 63*	38	3
22 Jul 89	GHETTO MUSIC: THE BLUEPRINT OF HIP HOP *Jive HIP 80*	32	4
25 Aug 90	EDUTAINMENT *Jive HIP 100*	52	2

BOOKER T and the MG's

US, male instrumental group (Singles: 43 weeks, Albums: 5 weeks) pos/wks

11 Dec 68	**SOUL LIMBO** *Stax 102*	30	9
7 May 69 ●	**TIME IS TIGHT** *Stax 119*	4	18
30 Aug 69	**SOUL CLAP '69** *Stax 127*	35	4
15 Dec 79 ●	**GREEN ONIONS** *Atlantic K 10109*	7	12
25 Jul 64	GREEN ONIONS *London HAK 8182*	11	4
11 Jul 70	MCLEMORE AVENUE *Stax SXATS 1031*	70	1

BOOM!

UK, male / female vocal group (Singles: 5 weeks) pos/wks

27 Jan 01	**FALLING** *London LONCD 458*	11	5

Taka BOOM – *See Joey NEGRO; EYE TO EYE featuring Taka BOOM*

BOOM BOOM ROOM

UK, male vocal / instrumental group (Singles: 1 week) pos/wks

8 Mar 86	**HERE COMES THE MAN** *Fun After All FUN 101*	74	1

BOOMKAT

US, male / female vocal / instrumental / production duo – Kellin and Taryn Mann (Singles: 2 weeks) pos/wks

31 May 03	**THE WRECKONING** *Dreamworks 4504580*	37	2

BOOMTOWN RATS (295 Top 500)

New wave group named after a band in a Woody Guthrie novel. Fronted by charismatic Bob Geldof (b. 5 Oct 1954, Dublin), who was later knighted for organising Live Aid. The Mutt Lange-produced 'Rat Trap' was the first new wave No.1 (Singles: 123 weeks, Albums: 96 weeks) pos/wks

27 Aug 77	**LOOKING AFTER NO.1** *Ensign ENY 4*	11	9
19 Nov 77	**MARY OF THE 4TH FORM** *Ensign ENY 9*	15	9
15 Apr 78	**SHE'S SO MODERN** *Ensign ENY 13*	12	11
17 Jun 78 ●	**LIKE CLOCKWORK** *Ensign ENY 14*	6	13
14 Oct 78 ★	**RAT TRAP** *Ensign ENY 16*	1	15
21 Jul 79 ★	**I DON'T LIKE MONDAYS** *Ensign ENY 30*	1	12
17 Nov 79	**DIAMOND SMILES** *Ensign ENY 33*	13	10
26 Jan 80 ●	**SOMEONE'S LOOKING AT YOU** *Ensign ENY 34*	4	9
22 Nov 80 ●	**BANANA REPUBLIC** *Mercury BONGO 1*	3	11
31 Jan 81	**THE ELEPHANT'S GRAVEYARD (GUILTY)** *Mercury BONGO 2*	26	6
12 Dec 81	**NEVER IN A MILLION YEARS** *Mercury MER 87*	62	4
20 Mar 82	**HOUSE ON FIRE** *Mercury MER 91*	24	8
18 Feb 84	**TONIGHT** *Mercury MER 154*	73	1
19 May 84	**DRAG ME DOWN** *Mercury MER 163*	50	3
2 Jul 94	**I DON'T LIKE MONDAYS (re-issue)** *Vertigo VERCD 87*	38	2
17 Sep 77	BOOMTOWN RATS *Ensign ENVY 1*	18	11
8 Jul 78 ●	A TONIC FOR THE TROOPS *Ensign ENVY 3*	8	44
3 Nov 79 ●	THE FINE ART OF SURFACING *Ensign ENROX 11*	7	26
24 Jan 81 ●	MONDO BONGO *Mercury 6359 042*	6	7
3 Apr 82	V DEEP *Mercury 6359 082*	64	5
9 Jul 94 ●	LOUDMOUTH – THE BEST OF THE BOOMTOWN RATS AND BOB GELDOF *Vertigo 5222852* [1]	10	3

[1] Boomtown Rats and Bob Geldof

See also Bob GELDOF

Clint BOON EXPERIENCE

UK, male / female vocal / instrumental group (Singles: 3 weeks) pos/wks

6 Nov 99	**WHITE NO SUGAR** *Artful CDARTFUL 32*	61	1
5 Feb 00	**BIGGEST HORIZON** *Artful CDARTFUL 33*	70	1
5 Aug 00	**DO WHAT YOU DO (EARWORM SONG)** *Artful CDARTFUL 34*	63	1

Daniel BOONE

UK, male vocalist – Peter Lee Stirling (Singles: 25 weeks) pos/wks

14 Aug 71	**DADDY DON'T YOU WALK SO FAST** *Penny Farthing PEN 764*	17	15
1 Apr 72	**BEAUTIFUL SUNDAY (re)** *Penny Farthing PEN 781*	21	10

Debby BOONE

US, female vocalist (Singles: 2 weeks) pos/wks

24 Dec 77	**YOU LIGHT UP MY LIFE** *Warner Bros. / Curb K 17043* ▲	48	2

Pat BOONE (168 Top 500)

Major rival to Elvis in late 1950s, b. 1 Jun 1934, Florida. This clean-cut vocalist was voted the World's Outstanding Male Singer in the UK in 1957. He was seldom absent from the UK or US charts during the early rock 'n' roll years (Singles: 311 weeks, Albums: 12 weeks) pos/wks

18 Nov 55 ●	**AIN'T THAT A SHAME (re)** *London HLD 8172*	7	11
27 Apr 56 ★	**I'LL BE HOME (re)** *London HLD 8253*	1	24
27 Jul 56	**LONG TALL SALLY (re)** *London HLD 8291*	18	7
17 Aug 56	**I ALMOST LOST MY MIND** *London HLD 8303*	14	7
7 Dec 56 ●	**FRIENDLY PERSUASION (THEE I LOVE)** *London HLD 8346*	3	21
1 Feb 57 ●	**DON'T FORBID ME** *London HLD 8370*	2	16
26 Apr 57	**WHY BABY WHY** *London HLD 8404*	17	7
5 Jul 57 ●	**LOVE LETTERS IN THE SAND** *London HLD 8445* ▲	2	21
27 Sep 57 ●	**REMEMBER YOU'RE MINE / THERE'S A GOLDMINE IN THE SKY** *London HLD 8479*	5	18
6 Dec 57 ●	**APRIL LOVE** *London HLD 8512* ▲	7	23
13 Dec 57	**WHITE CHRISTMAS** *London HLD 8520*	29	1
4 Apr 58 ●	**A WONDERFUL TIME UP THERE** *London HLD 8574 (A)*	2	17
11 Apr 58 ●	**IT'S TOO SOON TO KNOW** *London HLD 8574 (B)*	7	12
27 Jun 58 ●	**SUGAR MOON** *London HLD 8640*	6	12
29 Aug 58	**IF DREAMS CAME TRUE** *London HLD 8675*	16	11
5 Dec 58	**GEE, BUT IT'S LONELY** *London HLD 8739*	30	1
16 Jan 59	**I'LL REMEMBER TONIGHT (2re)** *London HLD 8775*	18	9
10 Apr 59	**WITH THE WIND AND THE RAIN IN YOUR HAIR** *London HLD 8824*	21	3
22 May 59	**FOR A PENNY (re)** *London HLD 8855*	19	9
31 Jul 59	**'TWIXT TWELVE AND TWENTY (re)** *London HLD 8910*	18	7
23 Jun 60	**WALKING THE FLOOR OVER YOU (re)** *London HLD 9138*	39	8
6 Jul 61	**MOODY RIVER** *London HLD 9350* ▲	18	10
7 Dec 61 ●	**JOHNNY WILL** *London HLD 9461*	4	13
15 Feb 62	**I'LL SEE YOU IN MY DREAMS** *London HLD 9504*	27	9
24 May 62	**QUANDO, QUANDO, QUANDO** *London HLD 9543*	41	4
12 Jul 62 ●	**SPEEDY GONZALES** *London HLD 9573*	2	19
15 Nov 62	**THE MAIN ATTRACTION** *London HLD 9620*	12	11
22 Nov 58 ●	STARDUST *London HAD 2127*	10	1
28 May 60	HYMNS WE HAVE LOVED *London HAD 2228*	12	2
25 Jun 60	HYMNS WE LOVE *London HAD 2092*	14	1
24 Apr 76	PAT BOONE ORIGINALS *ABC ABSD 301*	16	8

'There's a Goldmine in the Sky' was listed only for the week of 27 Sep 1957. It peaked at No.23. 'A Wonderful Time Up There' and 'It's Too Soon to Know' were both on the same single release

BOOOM – *See Boris DLUGOSCH*

BOOT ROOM BOYZ – *See LIVERPOOL FC*

Duke BOOTEE – *See GRANDMASTER FLASH and the FURIOUS FIVE*

BOOTH and the BAD ANGEL *UK / US, male vocal / instrumental duo – Tim Booth and Angelo Badalamenti (Singles: 4 weeks, Albums: 2 weeks)*

Date		Title	pos	wks
22 Jun 96		I BELIEVE *Fontana BBCD 1*	25	3
11 Jul 98		FALL IN LOVE WITH ME *Mercury MERCD 503*	57	1
13 Jul 96		BOOTH AND THE BAD ANGEL *Fontana 5268522*	35	2

See also JAMES; Angelo BADALAMENTI

Ken BOOTHE *Jamaica, male vocalist (Singles: 22 weeks)*

Date		Title	pos	wks
21 Sep 74	★	EVERYTHING I OWN *Trojan TR 7920*	1	12
14 Dec 74		CRYING OVER YOU *Trojan TR 7944*	11	10

BOOTHILL FOOT-TAPPERS *UK, male / female vocal / instrumental group (Singles: 3 weeks)*

Date		Title	pos	wks
14 Jul 84		GET YOUR FEET OUT OF MY SHOES *Go! Discs TAP 1*	64	3

BOOTSY'S RUBBER BAND *US, male vocal / instrumental group (Singles: 3 weeks)*

Date		Title	pos	wks
8 Jul 78		BOOTZILLA *Warner Bros. K 17196*	43	3

BOOTZILLA ORCHESTRA – *See Malcolm McLAREN*

BOSS *US, male producer – David Morales (Singles: 1 week)*

Date		Title	pos	wks
27 Aug 94		CONGO *Cooltempo CDCOOL 296*	54	1

See also David MORALES; PULSE featuring Antoinette ROBERSON

BOSTON *US, male vocal / instrumental group (Singles: 13 weeks, Albums: 44 weeks)*

Date		Title	pos	wks
29 Jan 77		MORE THAN A FEELING *Epic EPC 4658*	22	8
7 Oct 78		DON'T LOOK BACK *Epic EPC 6653*	43	5
5 Feb 77		BOSTON *Epic EPC 81611*	11	20
9 Sep 78	●	DON'T LOOK BACK *Epic EPC 86057* ▲	9	10
4 Apr 81		BOSTON *Epic EPC 32038*	58	2
18 Oct 86		THIRD STAGE *MCA MCG 6017* ▲	37	11
25 Jun 94		WALK ON *MCA MCD 10973*	56	1

The two eponymous albums are different

Eve BOSWELL *Hungary, female vocalist – Eva Keleti, d. 13 Aug 1998 (Singles: 13 weeks)*

Date		Title	pos	wks
30 Dec 55	●	PICKIN' A-CHICKEN (2re) *Parlophone R 4082*	9	13

With Glen Somers and his Orchestra

Judy BOUCHER *St Vincent, female vocalist (Singles: 23 weeks, Albums: 1 week)*

Date		Title	pos	wks
4 Apr 87	●	CAN'T BE WITH YOU TONIGHT *Orbitone OR 721*	2	14
4 Jul 87		YOU CAUGHT MY EYE *Orbitone OR 722*	18	9
25 Apr 87		CAN'T BE WITH YOU TONIGHT *Orbitone OLP 024*	95	1

Peter BOUNCER – *See SHUT UP AND DANCE*

BOUNCING CZECKS *UK, male vocal / instrumental group (Singles: 1 week)*

Date		Title	pos	wks
29 Dec 84		I'M A LITTLE CHRISTMAS CRACKER *RCA 463*	72	1

BOUNTY KILLER *Jamaica, male rapper – Rodney Price (Singles: 1 week)*

Date		Title	pos	wks
27 Feb 99		IT'S A PARTY *Edel 0066135 BLA*	65	1

BOURGEOIS TAGG *US, male vocal / instrumental duo – Brent Bourgeois and Larry Tagg (Singles: 6 weeks)*

Date		Title	pos	wks
6 Feb 88		I DON'T MIND AT ALL *Island IS 353*	35	6

BOURGIE BOURGIE *UK, male vocal / instrumental group (Singles: 4 weeks)*

Date		Title	pos	wks
3 Mar 84		BREAKING POINT *MCA BOU 1*	48	4

Toby BOURKE with George MICHAEL *UK, male vocalists (Singles: 4 weeks)*

Date		Title	pos	wks
7 Jun 97	●	WALTZ AWAY DREAMING *Aegean AECD 01*	10	4

Aletia BOURNE – *See ANGELHEART*

BOW WOW WOW *UK / Burma, female / male vocal / instrumental group (Singles: 54 weeks, Albums: 38 weeks)*

Date		Title	pos	wks
26 Jul 80		C'30, C'60, C'90, GO *EMI 5088*	34	7
6 Dec 80		YOUR CASSETTE PET *EMI WOW 1*	58	6
28 Mar 81		W.O.R.K. (N.O. NAH NO NO MY DADDY DON'T) *EMI 5153*	62	3
15 Aug 81		PRINCE OF DARKNESS *RCA 100*	58	4
7 Nov 81		CHIHUAHUA *RCA 144*	51	4
30 Jan 82	●	GO WILD IN THE COUNTRY *RCA 175*	7	13
1 May 82		SEE JUNGLE (JUNGLE BOY) / TV SAVAGE *RCA 220*	45	3
5 Jun 82	●	I WANT CANDY *RCA 238*	9	8
31 Jul 82		LOUIS QUATORZE *RCA 263*	66	2
12 Mar 83		DO YOU WANNA HOLD ME? *RCA 314*	47	4
24 Oct 81		SEE JUNGLE! SEE JUNGLE! GO JOIN YOUR GANG YEAH! CITY ALL OVER GO APE CRAZY *RCA RCALP 00273000*	26	32
7 Aug 82		I WANT CANDY *EMI EMC 3416*	26	6

Your Cassette Pet listed as Louis Quatorze on 6 Dec 1980 only. Tracks on Your Cassette Pet (available only as a cassette) are: Louis Quatorze / Gold He Said / Umo-Sex-Al Apache / I Want My Baby on Mars / Sexy Eiffel Towers / Giant Sized Baby Thing / Fools Rush In / Radio G String. RCA 263 is disc version of track on EMI WOW 1 Cassette

BOWA featuring MALA *US, male / female vocal / instrumental duo (Singles: 1 week)*

Date		Title	pos	wks
7 Dec 91		DIFFERENT STORY *Dead Dead Good GOOD 8*	64	1

Dane BOWERS – *See TRUE STEPPERS*

David BOWIE (8 Top 500) *Chameleon-like singer / songwriter / entertainer b. David Jones, 8 Jan 1947, Brixton, London. Noted for his changes of character and fashion, he became Ziggy Stardust, Aladdin Sane and The Thin White Duke. His striking appearance was enhanced by an unfortunate school playground incident that changed the colour of one of his blue eyes to green after being stabbed by a compass. Voted most influential artist in an NME poll in 2000. Among his many accolades and awards, for both recording and songwriting, is the 1996 Brit Award for Outstanding Contribution to British Music. (He is the only act to reject induction into the Rock and Roll Hall of Fame.) No UK act can better the 10 albums he charted with simultaneously in the Top 100 in 1983, and no British male can match his eight No.1 albums. This often sampled performer has starred in movies, acted on Broadway, painted and recorded music with many of the world's leading acts. In 1999 he released the first virtual album and became the first major act to make a full album available for download, releasing the first enhanced CD single (1995) and being the first singer / songwriter to go to the stock market selling interest in his back catalogue, raising $55m in the process. Bowie has sold more than nine million UK singles (Singles: 452 weeks, Albums: 989 weeks)*

Date		Title	pos	wks
6 Sep 69	●	SPACE ODDITY (re) *Philips BF 1801*	5	14
24 Jun 72	●	STARMAN *RCA 2199*	10	11
16 Sep 72		JOHN, I'M ONLY DANCING *RCA 2263*	12	10
9 Dec 72	●	THE JEAN GENIE *RCA 2302*	2	13
14 Apr 73	●	DRIVE-IN SATURDAY SEATTLE – PHOENIX) *RCA 2352*	3	10
30 Jun 73	●	LIFE ON MARS? *RCA 2316*	3	13
15 Sep 73	●	THE LAUGHING GNOME *Deram DM 123*	6	12
20 Oct 73	●	SORROW *RCA 2424*	3	15
23 Feb 74	●	REBEL REBEL *RCA LPBO 5009*	5	7
20 Apr 74		ROCK 'N' ROLL SUICIDE *RCA LPBO 5021*	22	7
22 Jun 74		DIAMOND DOGS *RCA APBO 0293*	21	6
28 Sep 74	●	KNOCK ON WOOD *RCA 2466*	10	6
1 Mar 75		YOUNG AMERICANS *RCA 2523*	18	7
2 Aug 75		FAME *RCA 2579* ▲	17	8
11 Oct 75	★	SPACE ODDITY (re-issue) *RCA 2593*	1	10
29 Nov 75	●	GOLDEN YEARS *RCA 2640*	8	10
22 May 76		TVC 15 *RCA 2682*	33	4
19 Feb 77	●	SOUND AND VISION *RCA PB 0905*	3	11

15 Oct 77 HEROES *RCA PB 1121* 24 8
21 Jan 78 BEAUTY AND THE BEAST *RCA PB 1190* 39 3
2 Dec 78 BREAKING GLASS (EP) *RCA BOW 1* 54 7
5 May 79 ● BOYS KEEP SWINGING *RCA BOW 2* 7 10
21 Jul 79 D.J. *RCA BOW 3* 29 5
15 Dec 79 JOHN I'M ONLY DANCING (AGAIN) (1975) / JOHN I'M ONLY DANCING (1972) *RCA BOW 4* 12 8
1 Mar 80 ALABAMA SONG *RCA BOW 5* 23 5
16 Aug 80 ★ ASHES TO ASHES *RCA BOW 6* 1 10
1 Nov 80 ● FASHION *RCA BOW 7* 5 12
10 Jan 81 SCARY MONSTERS (AND SUPER CREEPS) *RCA BOW 8* 20 6
28 Mar 81 UP THE HILL BACKWARDS *RCA BOW 9* 32 6
14 Nov 81 ★ UNDER PRESSURE *EMI 5250* [1] 1 11
28 Nov 81 WILD IS THE WIND *RCA BOW 10* 24 10
6 Mar 82 BAAL (EP) *RCA BOW 11* 29 5
10 Apr 82 CAT PEOPLE (PUTTING OUT FIRE) *MCA 770* 26 6
27 Nov 82 ● PEACE ON EARTH – LITTLE DRUMMER BOY *RCA BOW 12* [2] 3 8
26 Mar 83 ★ LET'S DANCE *EMI America EA 152* ▲ 1 14
11 Jun 83 ● CHINA GIRL *EMI America EA 157* 2 8
24 Sep 83 ● MODERN LOVE *EMI America EA 158* 2 8
5 Nov 83 WHITE LIGHT, WHITE HEAT *RCA 372* 46 3
22 Sep 84 ● BLUE JEAN *EMI America EA 181* 6 8
8 Dec 84 TONIGHT *EMI America EA 187* 53 4
9 Feb 85 THIS IS NOT AMERICA (THE THEME FROM 'THE FALCON AND THE SNOWMAN') *EMI America EA 190* [3] 14 7
8 Jun 85 LOVING THE ALIEN (re) *EMI America EA 195* 19 7
7 Sep 85 ★ DANCING IN THE STREET *EMI America EA 204* [4] ■ 1 12
15 Mar 86 ● ABSOLUTE BEGINNERS *Virgin VS 838* 2 9
21 Jun 86 UNDERGROUND *EMI America EA 216* 21 6
8 Nov 86 WHEN THE WIND BLOWS *Virgin VS 906* 44 4
4 Apr 87 DAY-IN DAY-OUT *EMI America EA 230* 17 6
27 Jun 87 TIME WILL CRAWL *EMI America EA 237* 33 4
29 Aug 87 NEVER LET ME DOWN *EMI America EA 239* 34 6
7 Apr 90 FAME (re-mix) *EMI-USA FAME 90* 28 4
22 Aug 92 REAL COOL WORLD *Warner Bros. W 0127* 53 1
27 Mar 93 ● JUMP THEY SAY *Arista 74321139422* 9 6
12 Jun 93 BLACK TIE WHITE NOISE *Arista 74321148682* [5] 36 2
23 Oct 93 MIRACLE GOODNIGHT *Arista 74321162262* 40 2
4 Dec 93 BUDDHA OF SUBURBIA *Arista 74321177052* [6] 35 3
23 Sep 95 THE HEART'S FILTHY LESSON *RCA 74321307032* 35 2
2 Dec 95 STRANGERS WHEN WE MEET / THE MAN WHO SOLD THE WORLD (LIVE) *RCA 74321329402* 39 2
2 Mar 96 HALLO SPACEBOY *RCA 74321353842* 12 4
8 Feb 97 LITTLE WONDER *RCA 74321452072* 14 3
26 Apr 97 DEAD MAN WALKING *RCA 74321475852* 32 2
30 Aug 97 SEVEN YEARS IN TIBET *RCA 74321512542* 61 1
21 Feb 98 I CAN'T READ *Velvet ZYX 87578* 73 1
2 Oct 99 THURSDAY'S CHILD *Virgin VSCDT 1753* 16 3
18 Dec 99 UNDER PRESSURE (re-mix) *Parlophone CDQUEEN 28* [1] 14 7
5 Feb 00 SURVIVE *Virgin VSCDT 1767* 28 2
29 Jul 00 SEVEN *Virgin VSCDT 1776* 32 2
11 May 02 LOVING THE ALIEN (re-mix) *Positiva CDTIV 172* [7] 41 1
28 Sep 02 EVERYONE SAYS 'HI' *Columbia 6731342* 20 3
12 Jul 03 JUST FOR ONE DAY (HEROES) *Virgin DINST 263* [8] 73 1
1 Jul 72 ● THE RISE AND FALL OF ZIGGY STARDUST AND THE SPIDERS FROM MARS *RCA Victor SF 8287* 5 106
23 Sep 72 ● HUNKY DORY *RCA Victor SF 8244* 3 69
25 Nov 72 THE MAN WHO SOLD THE WORLD *RCA Victor LSP 4816* 26 22
25 Nov 72 SPACE ODDITY *RCA Victor LSP 4813* 17 37
5 May 73 ★ ALADDIN SANE *RCA Victor RS 1001* ■ 1 48
3 Nov 73 ★ PIN-UPS *RCA Victor RS 1003* ■ 1 21
8 Jun 74 ★ DIAMOND DOGS *RCA Victor APLI 0576* ■ 1 17
16 Nov 74 ● DAVID LIVE *RCA Victor APL 2 0771* 2 12
5 Apr 75 ● YOUNG AMERICANS *RCA Victor RS 1006* 2 12
7 Feb 76 ● STATION TO STATION *RCA Victor APLI 1327* 5 16
12 Jun 76 ● CHANGESONEBOWIE *RCA Victor RS 1055* 2 28
29 Jan 77 ● LOW *RCA Victor PL 12030* 2 18
29 Oct 77 ● HEROES *RCA Victor PL 12522* 3 18
14 Oct 78 ● STAGE *RCA Victor PL 02913* 5 10
9 Jun 79 ● LODGER *RCA Victor BOW LP 1* 4 17
27 Sep 80 ★ SCARY MONSTERS AND SUPER CREEPS *RCA Victor BOW LP 2* ■ 1 32
10 Jan 81 ● THE VERY BEST OF DAVID BOWIE *K-Tel NE 1111* 3 20
17 Jan 81 HUNKY DORY (re-issue) *RCA International INTS 5064* 32 51
31 Jan 81 THE RISE AND FALL OF ZIGGY STARDUST AND THE SPIDERS FROM MARS (re-issue) *RCA International INTS 5063* 33 62
28 Nov 81 CHANGESTWOBOWIE *RCA BOW LP 3* 24 17
6 Mar 82 ALADDIN SANE (re-issue) *RCA International INTS 5067* 49 24
14 Jan 83 RARE *RCA PL 45406* 34 11
23 Apr 83 ★ LET'S DANCE *EMI America AML 3029* ■ 1 56
30 Apr 83 PIN-UPS (re-issue) *RCA International INTS 5236* 57 15
30 Apr 83 THE MAN WHO SOLD THE WORLD (re-issue) *RCA International INTS 5237* 64 8
14 May 83 DIAMOND DOGS (re-issue) *RCA International INTS 5068* 60 14
11 Jun 83 LOW (re-issue) *RCA International INTS 5065* 75 8
11 Jun 83 HEROES (re-issue) *RCA International INTS 5066* 85 5
20 Aug 83 GOLDEN YEARS *RCA BOWLP 4* 33 5
5 Nov 83 ZIGGY STARDUST – THE MOTION PICTURE *RCA PL 84862* 17 6
28 Apr 84 FAME AND FASHION (BOWIE'S ALL TIME GREATEST HITS) *RCA PL 84919* 40 6
19 May 84 LOVE YOU TILL TUESDAY *Deram BOWIE 1* 53 4
6 Oct 84 ★ TONIGHT *EMI America DB 1* ■ 1 19
2 May 87 ● NEVER LET ME DOWN *EMI America AMLS 3117* 6 16
24 Mar 90 ★ CHANGESBOWIE *EMI DBTV 1* 1 29
14 Apr 90 HUNKY DORY (2nd re-issue) *EMI EMC 3572* 39 5
14 Apr 90 THE MAN WHO SOLD THE WORLD (2nd re-issue) *EMI EMC 3573* 64 1
14 Apr 90 SPACE ODDITY (re-issue) *EMI EMC 3571* 39 2
23 Jun 90 THE RISE AND FALL OF ZIGGY STARDUST AND THE SPIDERS FROM MARS (2nd re-issue) *EMI EMC 3577* 25 4
28 Jul 90 PIN-UPS (2nd re-issue) *EMI EMC 3580* 52 1
28 Jul 90 ALADDIN SANE (2nd re-issue) *EMI EMC 3579* 43 1
27 Oct 90 DIAMOND DOGS (2nd re-issue) *EMI EMC 3584* 67 3
4 May 91 STATION TO STATION (re-issue) *EMI EMD 1020* 54 1
4 May 91 YOUNG AMERICANS (re-issue) *EMI EMD 1021* 57 1
7 Sep 91 LOW (2nd re-issue) *EMI EMD 1027* 64 1
17 Apr 93 ★ BLACK TIE WHITE NOISE *Arista 74321136972* ■ 1 11
20 Nov 93 ● THE SINGLES COLLECTION *EMI CDEM 1512* 9 15
7 May 94 SANTA MONICA '72 *Trident GY 002* 74 1
7 Oct 95 ● OUTSIDE *RCA 74321310662* 8 4
15 Feb 97 ● EARTHLING *RCA 74321449442* 6 4
8 Nov 97 THE BEST OF DAVID BOWIE 1969 / 1974 *EMI 8218492* 13 17
2 May 98 THE BEST OF DAVID BOWIE 1974 / 1979 *EMI 4943002* 39 2
16 Oct 99 ● HOURS ... *Virgin CDV 2900* 5 5
7 Oct 00 ● BOWIE AT THE BEEB – THE BEST OF THE BBC RADIO SESSIONS 68-72 *EMI 5289582* 7 4
22 Jun 02 ● HEATHEN *Columbia 5082222* 5 18
20 Jul 02 THE RISE AND FALL OF ZIGGY STARDUST AND THE SPIDERS FROM MARS (3rd re-issue) *EMI 5398262* 36 2
16 Nov 02 BEST OF BOWIE *EMI 5398212* 11 23
27 Sep 03 ● REALITY *Columbia 5125552* 3 4

[1] Queen and David Bowie [2] David Bowie and Bing Crosby [3] David Bowie and the Pat Metheny Group [4] David Bowie and Mick Jagger [5] David Bowie featuring Al B Sure! [6] David Bowie featuring Lenny Kravitz [7] Scumfrog vs Bowie [8] David Guetta vs Bowie

The 1975 reissue of 1969's Space Oddity was part of a three-track single which also included Changes and Velvet Goldmine. Tracks on Breaking Glass (EP): Breaking Glass / Art Decade / Ziggy Stardust. All three versions of 'John I'm Only Dancing' are different. Tracks on Baal (EP): Baal's Hymn / Remembering Marie A / Ballad of the Adventurers / The Drowned Girl / Dirty Song

See also TIN MACHINE

BOWLING FOR SOUP *US, male vocal / instrumental group (Singles: 10 weeks, Albums: 4 weeks)*

pos/wks

17 Aug 02 ● GIRL ALL THE BAD GUYS WANT *Music for Nations CDKUT 194* 8 8
16 Nov 02 EMILY *Music for Nations CDKUT 198* 67 1
6 Sep 03 PUNK ROCK 101 *Music for Nations CDKUT 203* 43 1
7 Sep 02 DRUNK ENOUGH TO DANCE *Music for Nations CDMFN 282* 14 4

George BOWYER
UK, male vocalist (Singles: 2 weeks)

pos/wks

22 Aug 98 GUARDIANS OF THE LAND *Boys BYSCD 01* 33 2

BOX CAR RACER *US, male vocal / instrumental group (Singles: 1 week, Albums: 3 weeks)*

Date		Title / Label	pos	wks
6 Jul 02		**I FEEL SO** *MCA MCSTD 40290*	41	1
8 Jun 02		**BOX CAR RACER** *MCA 1129472*	27	3

BOX TOPS *US, male vocal / instrumental group (Singles: 33 weeks)*

Date		Title / Label	pos	wks
13 Sep 67	●	**THE LETTER** *Stateside SS 2044* ▲	5	12
20 Mar 68		**CRY LIKE A BABY** *Bell 1001*	15	12
23 Aug 69		**SOUL DEEP** *Bell 1068*	22	9

BOXCAR WILLIE *US, male vocalist – Lecil Martin, d. 12 Apr 1999 (Albums: 12 weeks)*

Date		Title / Label	pos	wks
31 May 80	●	**KING OF THE ROAD** *Warwick WW 5084*	5	12

BOY GEORGE *UK, male vocalist – George O'Dowd (Singles: 46 weeks, Albums: 15 weeks)*

Date		Title / Label	pos	wks
7 Mar 87	★	**EVERYTHING I OWN** *Virgin BOY 100*	1	9
6 Jun 87		**KEEP ME IN MIND** *Virgin BOY 101*	29	4
18 Jul 87		**SOLD** *Virgin BOY 102*	24	5
21 Nov 87		**TO BE REBORN** *Virgin BOY 103*	13	7
5 Mar 88		**LIVE MY LIFE** *Virgin BOY 105*	62	2
18 Jun 88		**NO CLAUSE 28** *Virgin BOY 106*	57	3
8 Oct 88		**DON'T CRY** *Virgin BOY 107*	60	2
4 Mar 89		**DON'T TAKE MY MIND ON A TRIP** *Virgin BOY 108*	68	2
19 Sep 92		**THE CRYING GAME** *Spaghetti CIAO 6*	22	4
12 Jun 93		**MORE THAN LIKELY** *Gee Street GESCD 49* [1]	40	3
1 Apr 95		**FUNTIME** *Virgin VSCDG 1538*	45	2
1 Jul 95		**IL ADORE** *Virgin VSCDX 1543*	50	2
21 Oct 95		**SAME THING IN REVERSE** *Virgin VSCDT 1561*	56	1
27 Jun 87		**SOLD** *Virgin V 2430*	29	6
13 Apr 91		**THE MARTYR MANTRAS** *More Protein CUMLP 1* [1]	60	1
2 Oct 93		**AT WORST ... THE BEST OF BOY GEORGE AND CULTURE CLUB** *Virgin VTCD 19* [2]	24	5
12 Mar 94		**THE DEVIL IN SISTER GEORGE** *Virgin VSCDG 1490*	26	2
3 Jun 95		**CHEAPNESS AND BEAUTY** *Virgin CDV 2780*	44	1

[1] PM Dawn featuring Boy George [1] Jesus Loves You [2] Boy George and Culture Club

See also CULTURE CLUB; JESUS LOVES YOU

BOY MEETS GIRL *US, male / female vocal duo – Shannon Rubicam and George Merrill (Singles: 13 weeks, Albums: 1 week)*

Date		Title / Label	pos	wks
3 Dec 88	●	**WAITING FOR A STAR TO FALL** *RCA PB 49519*	9	13
4 Feb 89		**REEL LIFE** *RCA PL 88414*	74	1

BOY WUNDA – *See* PROGRESS presents the BOY WUNDA

Max BOYCE *UK, male comedian / vocalist (Albums: 105 weeks)*

Date		Title / Label	pos	wks
5 Jul 75		**LIVE AT TREORCHY** *One Up OU 2033*	21	32
1 Nov 75	★	**WE ALL HAD DOCTORS' PAPERS** *EMI MB 101*	1	17
20 Nov 76	●	**THE INCREDIBLE PLAN** *EMI MB 102*	9	12
7 Jan 78		**THE ROAD AND THE MILES** *EMI MB 103*	50	3
11 Mar 78		**LIVE AT TREORCHY (re-issue)** *One Up OU 54043*	42	6
27 May 78	●	**I KNOW COS I WAS THERE** *EMI MAX 1001*	6	14
13 Oct 79		**NOT THAT I'M BIASED** *EMI MAX 1002*	27	13
15 Nov 80		**ME AND BILLY WILLIAMS** *EMI MAX 1003*	37	8

Jimmy BOYD *US, male vocalist (Singles: 22 weeks)*

Date		Title / Label	pos	wks
8 May 53	●	**TELL ME A STORY (re)** *Philips PB 126* [1]	5	16
27 Nov 53	●	**I SAW MOMMY KISSING SANTA CLAUS** *Columbia DB 3365* ▲	3	6

[1] Jimmy Boyd – Frankie Laine

Jacqueline BOYER *France, female vocalist (Singles: 2 weeks)*

Date		Title / Label	pos	wks
28 Apr 60		**TOM PILLIBI** *Columbia DB 4452*	33	2

BOYS *US, male vocal group (Singles: 5 weeks, Albums: 1 week)*

Date		Title / Label	pos	wks
12 Nov 88		**DIAL MY HEART** *Motown ZB 42245*	61	2
29 Sep 90		**CRAZY** *Motown ZB 44037*	57	3
1 Oct 77		**THE BOYS** *NEMS NEL 6001*	50	1

BOYSTEROUS *UK, male vocal group (Singles: 1 week)*

Date		Title / Label	pos	wks
22 Nov 03		**UP & DOWN** *Square Biz SBR 4*	53	1

BOYSTOWN GANG *US, male / female vocal group (Singles: 20 weeks)*

Date		Title / Label	pos	wks
22 Aug 81		**AIN'T NO MOUNTAIN HIGH ENOUGH – REMEMBER ME (MEDLEY)** *WEA DICK 1*	46	6
31 Jul 82	●	**CAN'T TAKE MY EYES OFF YOU** *ERC 101*	4	11
9 Oct 82		**SIGNED SEALED DELIVERED (I'M YOURS)** *ERC 102*	50	3

BOYZ – *See* HEAVY D and the BOYZ

BOYZ II MEN *US, male vocal quartet – brothers Nathan and Wanya Morris, Shawn Stockman, Michael McCary (Singles: 81 weeks, Albums: 46 weeks)*

Date		Title / Label	pos	wks
5 Sep 92	★	**END OF THE ROAD** *Motown TMG 1411* ▲	1	21
19 Dec 92		**MOTOWNPHILLY** *Motown TMG 1402*	23	6
27 Feb 93		**IN THE STILL OF THE NITE (I'LL REMEMBER)** *Motown TMGCD 1415*	27	4
3 Sep 94	●	**I'LL MAKE LOVE TO YOU (re)** *Motown TMGCD 1431* ▲	5	15
26 Nov 94		**ON BENDED KNEE** *Motown TMGCD 1433* ▲	20	3
22 Apr 95		**THANK YOU** *Motown TMGCD 1438*	26	3
8 Jul 95		**WATER RUNS DRY** *Motown TMGCD 1443*	24	3
9 Dec 95	●	**ONE SWEET DAY** *Columbia 6626035* [1] ▲	6	11
20 Jan 96		**HEY LOVER** *Def Jam DEFCD 14* [2]	17	4
20 Sep 97	●	**4 SEASONS OF LONELINESS** *Motown 8606992* ▲	10	6
6 Dec 97		**A SONG FOR MAMA** *Motown 8607372*	34	2
25 Jul 98		**CAN'T LET HER GO** *Motown 8607952*	23	3
31 Oct 92	●	**COOLEYHIGHHARMONY** *Motown 5300892*	7	18
24 Sep 94		**II** *Motown 5304312* ▲	17	5
4 Oct 97		**EVOLUTION** *Motown 5308222* ▲	12	5
23 Sep 00		**NATHAN MICHAEL SHAWN WANYA** *Universal 1592812*	54	1
16 Feb 02	●	**LEGACY – THE GREATEST HITS COLLECTION** *UMTV 0168882*	2	15
3 Aug 02		**FULL CIRCLE** *Arista 7822147412*	56	2

[1] Mariah Carey and Boyz II Men [2] LL Cool J featuring Boyz II Men

BOYZONE (107 Top 500)

Irish boy band vocal quintet who became international teen idols: Ronan Keating, Stephen Gately, Mikey Graham, Keith Duffy, Shane Lynch. They achieved the best ever start to a UK singles career with 16 consecutive Top 5 singles and sold more singles (6,435,711) than any other boy band. Best-selling single: 'No Matter What' 1,074,192 (Singles: 213 weeks, Albums: 203 weeks)

Date		Title / Label	pos	wks
10 Dec 94	●	**LOVE ME FOR A REASON** *Polydor 8512802*	2	13
29 Apr 95	●	**KEY TO MY LIFE** *Polydor PZCD 342*	3	8
12 Aug 95	●	**SO GOOD** *Polydor 5797732*	3	6
25 Nov 95	●	**FATHER AND SON** *Polydor 5775762*	2	16
9 Mar 96	●	**COMING HOME NOW** *Polydor 5775702*	4	9
19 Oct 96	★	**WORDS** *Polydor 5755372* ■	1	14
14 Dec 96	★	**A DIFFERENT BEAT (2re)** *Polydor 5732052* ■	1	15
22 Mar 97	●	**ISN'T IT A WONDER (re)** *Polydor 5735472*	2	14
2 Aug 97	●	**PICTURE OF YOU** *Polydor 5713112*	2	18
6 Dec 97	●	**BABY CAN I HOLD YOU / SHOOTING STAR** *Polydor 5691672*	2	14
2 May 98	★	**ALL THAT I NEED (re)** *Polydor 5698732* ■	1	14
15 Aug 98	★	**NO MATTER WHAT** *Polydor 5675672* ◆ ■	1	15
5 Dec 98	●	**I LOVE THE WAY YOU LOVE ME** *Polydor 5631992*	2	13
13 Mar 99	★	**WHEN THE GOING GETS TOUGH (re)** *Polydor 5699132* ■	1	16
22 May 99	★	**YOU NEEDED ME (re)** *Polydor 5639332* ■	1	15
4 Dec 99	●	**EVERY DAY I LOVE YOU** *Polydor 5615802*	3	13
2 Sep 95	★	**SAID AND DONE** *Polydor 5278012* ■	1	58
9 Nov 96	★	**A DIFFERENT BEAT** *Polydor 5337422* ■	1	24
6 Jun 98	★	**WHERE WE BELONG** *Polydor 5573982* ■	1	55
12 Jun 99	★	**... BY REQUEST** *Polydor 5475992* ■	1	57
29 Mar 03	●	**BALLADS – THE LOVE SONG COLLECTION** *Universal TV 0760742*	6	9

See also Ronan KEATING; Stephen GATELY; Mikey GRAHAM; KEITH 'N' SHANE

BRAD *US, male vocal / instrumental group (Singles: 1 week, Albums: 1 week)*

Date		Title / Label	pos	wks
26 Jun 93		**20TH CENTURY** *Epic 6592482*	64	1
15 May 93		**SHAME** *Epic 4735962*	72	1

Scott BRADLEY *UK, male vocalist (Singles: 1 week)*

Date		Title / Label	pos	wks
15 Oct 94		**ZOOM** *Hidden Agenda HIDDCD 1*	61	1

Paul BRADY *UK, male vocalist (Singles: 1 week, Albums: 1 week)*

Date		Title / Label	pos	wks
13 Jan 96		**THE WORLD IS WHAT YOU MAKE IT** *Mercury PBCD 5*	67	1
6 Apr 91		**TRICK OR TREAT** *Fontana 8484541*	62	1

Billy BRAGG (483 Top 500) *Renowned for his heartfelt political and personal lyrics, b. 20 Dec 1957, Barking, Essex. Bragg became a cult hero after a John Peel Radio 1 session in 1983. He has also diversified into political activism, broadcasting and numerous musical collaborations (Singles: 53 weeks, Albums: 89 weeks)*

Date		Title / Label	pos	wks
16 Mar 85		**BETWEEN THE WARS (EP)** *Go! Discs AGOEP 1*	15	6
28 Dec 85		**DAYS LIKE THESE** *Go! Discs GOD 8*	43	5
28 Jun 86		**LEVI STUBBS' TEARS** *Go! Discs GOD 12*	29	6
15 Nov 86		**GREETINGS TO THE NEW BRUNETTE** *Go! Discs GOD 15* [1]	58	2
14 May 88	★	**SHE'S LEAVING HOME** *Childline CHILD 1* [2]	1	11
10 Sep 88		**WAITING FOR THE GREAT LEAP FORWARDS** *Go! Discs GOD 23*	52	3
8 Jul 89		**WON'T TALK ABOUT IT** *Go.Beat GOD 33* [3]	29	6
6 Jul 91		**SEXUALITY** *Go! Discs GOD 56*	27	5
7 Sep 91		**YOU WOKE UP MY NEIGHBOURHOOD** *Go! Discs GOD 60*	54	2
29 Feb 92		**ACCIDENT WAITING TO HAPPEN (EP)** *Go! Discs GOD 67*	33	3
31 Aug 96		**UPFIELD** *Cooking Vinyl FRYCD 051*	46	1
17 May 97		**THE BOY DONE GOOD** *Cooking Vinyl FRYCD 064*	55	1
1 Jun 02		**TAKE DOWN THE UNION JACK** *Cooking Vinyl FRYCD 131* [4]	22	2
21 Jan 84		**LIFE'S A RIOT WITH SPY VS SPY** *Utility UTIL 1*	30	30
20 Oct 84		**BREWING UP WITH BILLY BRAGG** *Go! Discs AGOLP 4*	16	21
4 Oct 86	●	**TALKING WITH THE TAXMAN ABOUT POETRY** *Go! Discs AGOLP 6*	8	8
13 Jun 87		**BACK TO BASICS** *Go! Discs AGOLP 8*	37	4
1 Oct 88		**WORKERS PLAYTIME** *Go! Discs AGOLP 15*	17	4
12 May 90		**THE INTERNATIONALE** *Utility UTIL 11*	34	4
28 Sep 91	●	**DON'T TRY THIS AT HOME** *Go! Discs 8282791*	8	6
21 Sep 96		**WILLIAM BLOKE** *Cooking Vinyl COOKCD 100*	16	3
28 Jun 97		**BLOKE ON BLOKE** *Cooking Vinyl COOKCD 127*	72	1
11 Jul 98		**MERMAID AVENUE** *Elektra 7559622042* [1]	34	2
11 Sep 99		**REACHING TO THE CONVERTED** *Cooking Vinyl COOKCD 186*	41	2
10 Jun 00		**MERMAID AVENUE – VOL. 2** *Elektra 7559625222* [1]	61	1
16 Mar 02		**ENGLAND HALF ENGLISH** *Cooking Vinyl COOKCD 222* [2]	51	2
18 Oct 03		**MUST I PAINT YOU A PICTURE – THE ESSENTIAL** *Cooking Vinyl COOKCD266X*	49	1

[1] Billy Bragg with Johnny Marr and Kirsty MacColl [2] Billy Bragg with Cara Tivey [3] Norman Cook featuring Billy Bragg [4] Billy Bragg and the Blokes [1] Billy Bragg and Wilco [2] Billy Bragg and the Blokes

Tracks on Between the Wars (EP): Between the Wars / Which Side Are You On / World Turned Upside Down / It Says Here. Tracks on Accident Waiting to Happen (EP): Accident Waiting to Happen / Revolution / Sulk / The Warmest Room. 'She's Leaving Home' was listed with the flip side 'With a Little Help from My Friends' by Wet Wet Wet. 'Won't Talk About It' was listed with the flip side 'Blame It on the Bassline' by Norman Cook featuring MC Wildski

BRAIDS *US, female vocal duo – Zoe Ellis and Caitlin Cornwell (Singles: 3 weeks)*

Date		Title / Label	pos	wks
2 Nov 96		**BOHEMIAN RHAPSODY** *Atlantic A 5640CD*	21	3

BRAIN BASHERS
UK, male / female DJ / production duo (Singles: 1 week)

Date		Title / Label	pos	wks
1 Jul 00		**DO IT NOW** *Tidy Trax TIDY 137 CD*	64	1

BRAINBUG
Italy, male producer – Alberto Bertapelle (Singles: 7 weeks)

Date		Title / Label	pos	wks
3 May 97		**NIGHTMARE** *Positiva CDTIV 76*	11	5
22 Nov 97		**BENEDICTUS / NIGHTMARE** *Positiva CDTIV 86*	24	2

BRAINCHILD
Germany, male producer – Matthias Hoffmann (Singles: 2 weeks)

Date		Title / Label	pos	wks
30 Oct 99		**SYMMETRY C** *Multiply CDMULTY 55*	31	2

Wilfrid BRAMBELL and Harry H CORBETT
UK, male vocal TV comedy duo, Wilfrid Brambell d 18 Jan 1985, and Harry Corbett d. 21 Mar 1982 (Singles: 12 weeks, Albums: 34 weeks)

Date		Title / Label	pos	wks
28 Nov 63		**STEPTOE AND SON AT BUCKINGHAM PALACE (PARTS 1& 2)** *Pye 7N 15588*	25	12
23 Mar 63	●	**STEPTOE AND SON** *Pye NPL 18081*	4	28
11 Jan 64		**STEPTOE AND SON** *Pye GGL 0217*	14	5
14 Mar 64		**MORE JUNK** *Pye NPL 18090*	19	1

Bekka BRAMLETT – *See Joe COCKER*

BRAN VAN 3000 *Canada, male / female vocal / instrumental group (Singles: 15 weeks)*

Date		Title / Label	pos	wks
6 Jun 98		**DRINKING IN L.A.** *Capitol CDCL 802*	34	2
21 Aug 99	●	**DRINKING IN L.A. (re-issue)** *Capitol CDCL 811*	3	11
16 Jun 01		**ASTOUNDED** *Virgin VUSCD 194* [1]	40	2

[1] Bran Van 3000 featuring Curtis Mayfield

BRANCACCIO & AISHER *UK, male production duo – Luke Brancaccio and Bruce Aisher (Singles: 2 weeks)*

Date		Title / Label	pos	wks
16 Mar 02		**IT'S GONNA BE... (A LOVELY DAY)** *Credence CDCRED 017*	40	2

Michelle BRANCH
US, female vocalist (Singles: 18 weeks, Albums: 5 weeks)

Date		Title / Label	pos	wks
13 Apr 02		**EVERYWHERE** *Maverick W 577 CDX*	18	6
3 Aug 02		**ALL YOU WANTED** *Maverick W 585 CDX*	33	2
23 Nov 02		**THE GAME OF LOVE** *Arista 74321959442* [1]	16	8
12 Jul 03		**ARE YOU HAPPY NOW?** *Maverick W 613CD*	31	2
27 Apr 02		**THE SPIRIT ROOM** *Maverick 9362480972*	54	2
19 Jul 03		**HOTEL PAPER** *Maverick / Warner Bros MAV484262*	35	3

[1] Santana featuring Michelle Branch

BRAND NEW HEAVIES (393 Top 500)
Sophisticated funk / 'acid jazz' band, formed 1985 in London, UK. Remaining original members Simon Bartholomew (g), Andrew Levy (b) and Jan Kincaid (d, v) had vocal assistance on their hits from US females N'Dea Davenport (1991-95), Siedah Garrett (1997-98) and Carleen Anderson (1999-2000) (Singles: 68 weeks, Albums: 103 weeks)

Date		Title / Label	pos	wks
5 Oct 91		**NEVER STOP** *ffrr F 165*	43	3
15 Feb 92		**DREAM COME TRUE** *ffrr F 180*	24	4
18 Apr 92		**ULTIMATE TRUNK FUNK (EP)** *ffrr F 185*	19	6
1 Aug 92		**DON'T LET IT GO TO YOUR HEAD** *ffrr BNH 1*	24	4
19 Dec 92		**STAY THIS WAY** *ffrr BNH 2*	40	5
26 Mar 94		**DREAM ON DREAMER** *ffrr BNHCD 3*	15	4
11 Jun 94		**BACK TO LOVE** *ffrr BNHCD 4*	23	4
13 Aug 94		**MIDNIGHT AT THE OASIS** *ffrr BNHCD 5*	13	6
5 Nov 94		**SPEND SOME TIME** *ffrr BNHCD 6*	26	4
11 Mar 95		**CLOSE TO YOU** *ffrr BNHCD 7*	38	3
12 Apr 97		**SOMETIMES** *ffrr BNHCD 8*	11	5
28 Jun 97		**YOU ARE THE UNIVERSE** *ffrr GNHCD 9*	21	4
18 Oct 97	●	**YOU'VE GOT A FRIEND** *London BNHCD 10*	9	8
10 Jan 98		**SHELTER** *London BNHCD 11*	31	4
11 Sep 99		**SATURDAY NITE** *ffrr BNHCD12*	35	2
29 Jan 00		**APPARENTLY NOTHING** *ffrr BNHCD 13*	32	2
14 Mar 92		**BRAND NEW HEAVIES** *London 8283002*	25	16
5 Sep 92		**HEAVY RHYME EXPERIENCE: VOL.1** *Acid Jazz 8283352*	38	2
16 Apr 94	●	**BROTHER SISTER** *ffrr 8284902*	4	48
12 Nov 94		**ORIGINAL FLAVA** *Acid Jazz JAZIDCD 114*	64	1
3 May 97	●	**SHELTER** *ffrr 8288872*	5	33
25 Sep 99		**TRUNK FUNK – THE BEST OF THE BRAND NEW HEAVIES** *ffrr 3984291642*	13	3

The first 10 hits are credited 'featuring N'Dea Davenport' on either the sleeve or the label. She was replaced by Siedah Garrett from 1997 to 98 and Carleen Anderson from 1999. Tracks on Ultimate Trunk Funk (EP): Never Stop / Stay This Way / Mr Tanaka. BNH 2 is a re-mixed version of the track on the Ultimate Trunk Funk EP

BRAND X *UK, male vocal / instrumental group (Albums: 6 weeks)* pos/wks

21 May 77	**MOROCCAN ROLL** *Charisma CAS 1126*	37	5
11 Sep 82	**IS THERE ANYTHING ABOUT?** *CBS 85967*	93	1

Johnny BRANDON with the PHANTOMS
UK, male vocalist and instrumental group (Singles: 12 weeks) pos/wks

11 Mar 55 ●	**TOMORROW (re)** *Polygon P 1131* [1]	8	8
1 Jul 55	**DON'T WORRY** *Polygon P 1163*	18	4

[1] Johnny Brandon with the Phantoms and the Norman Warren Music

BRANDY *US, female vocalist / actress – Brandy Norwood (Singles: 83 weeks, Albums: 46 weeks)* pos/wks

10 Dec 94	**I WANNA BE DOWN** *Atlantic A7217CD*	44	3
3 Jun 95	**I WANNA BE DOWN (re-mix)** *Atlantic A 7186CD*	36	3
3 Feb 96	**SITTIN' UP IN MY ROOM** *Arista 74321344012*	30	4
6 Jun 98 ●	**THE BOY IS MINE** *Atlantic AT 0036CD* [1] ▲	2	20
10 Oct 98 ●	**TOP OF THE WORLD (re)** *Atlantic AT 0046CD* [2]	2	9
12 Dec 98	**HAVE YOU EVER?** *Atlantic AT 0058CD* ▲	13	8
19 Jun 99	**ALMOST DOESN'T COUNT** *Atlantic AT 0068CD1*	15	5
16 Jun 01 ●	**ANOTHER DAY IN PARADISE** *WEA WEA 327CD1* [3]	5	10
23 Feb 02 ●	**WHAT ABOUT US? (re)** *Atlantic AT 0125CD*	4	11
15 Jun 02	**FULL MOON (IMPORT)** *Atlantic 7567853092*	72	1
29 Jun 02	**FULL MOON** *Atlantic AT 130CD*	15	9
20 Jun 98	**NEVER S-A-Y NEVER** *Atlantic 7567830392*	19	31
9 Mar 02 ●	**FULL MOON** *Atlantic 7567931102*	9	15

[1] Brandy and Monica [2] Brandy featuring Mase [3] Brandy and Ray J

Laura BRANIGAN
US, female vocalist (Singles: 33 weeks, Albums: 18 weeks) pos/wks

18 Dec 82 ●	**GLORIA** *Atlantic K 11759*	6	13
7 Jul 84 ●	**SELF CONTROL** *Atlantic A 9676*	5	17
6 Oct 84	**THE LUCKY ONE** *Atlantic A 9636*	56	3
18 Aug 84	**SELF CONTROL** *Atlantic 780147*	16	14
24 Aug 85	**HOLD ME** *Atlantic 7812651*	64	4

BRASS CONSTRUCTION *US, male vocal / instrumental group (Singles: 35 weeks, Albums: 12 weeks)* pos/wks

3 Apr 76	**MOVIN'** *United Artists UP 36090*	23	6
5 Feb 77	**HA CHA CHA (FUNKTION)** *United Artists UP 36205*	37	5
26 Jan 80	**MUSIC MAKES YOU FEEL LIKE DANCING** *United Artists UP 615*	39	6
28 May 83	**WALKIN' THE LINE** *Capitol CL 292*	47	3
16 Jul 83	**WE CAN WORK IT OUT** *Capitol CL 299*	70	2
7 Jul 84	**PARTYLINE** *Capitol CL 335*	56	4
27 Oct 84	**INTERNATIONAL** *Capitol CL 341*	70	2
9 Nov 85	**GIVE AND TAKE** *Capitol CL 377*	62	3
28 May 88	**MOVIN' 1988 (re-mix)** *Syncopate SY 11*	24	4
20 Mar 76 ●	**BRASS CONSTRUCTION** *United Artists UAS 29923*	9	11
30 Jun 84	**RENEGADES** *Capitol EJ 24 0160*	94	1

BRASSTOOTH – *See BM DUBS present MR RUMBLE featuring BRASSTOOTH and KEE*

BRAT *UK, male vocalist – Roger Kitter (Singles: 8 weeks)* pos/wks

10 Jul 82	**CHALK DUST – THE UMPIRE STRIKES BACK** *Hansa SMASH 1*	19	8

BRAVADO
UK, male / female vocal / instrumental group (Singles: 3 weeks) pos/wks

18 Jun 94	**HARMONICA MAN** *Peach PEACHCD 5*	37	3

BRAVEHEARTS – *See QB FINEST featuring NAS & BRAVEHEARTS*

BRAVO ALL STARS *UK / US, male / female vocal / instrumental group (Singles: 2 weeks)* pos/wks

29 Aug 98	**LET THE MUSIC HEAL YOUR SOUL** *Edel 0039335 ERE*	36	2

Artists featured: Backstreet Boys, Aaron Carter, Scooter, 'N Sync, Caught in the Act, The Boyz, Blumchen, Gil, Squeezer, Mr President, Touche, R'N'G and the Moffatts

Alan BRAXE and Fred FALKE
France, male production duo (Singles: 3 weeks) pos/wks

25 Nov 00	**INTRO** *Vulture / Credence CDCRED 006*	35	3

Dhar BRAXTON *US, female vocalist (Singles: 8 weeks)* pos/wks

31 May 86	**JUMP BACK (SET ME FREE)** *Fourth & Broadway BRW 47*	32	8

Toni BRAXTON (290 Top 500) *Sultry, sexy soul / R&B vocalist, b. 7 Oct 1968, Maryland, US, who won Best New Artist Grammy in 1993, and was one of America's top-selling pop and R&B artists of the 1990s. Her biggest hits have been ballads from the pens of top writers Babyface, Diane Warren, R Kelly and Rodney Jerkins. Best-selling single: 'Un-Break My Heart' 770,000 (Singles: 86 weeks, Albums: 136 weeks)* pos/wks

18 Sep 93	**ANOTHER SAD LOVE SONG** *LaFace 74321163502*	51	2
15 Jan 94 ●	**BREATHE AGAIN** *LaFace 74321185442*	2	12
2 Apr 94	**ANOTHER SAD LOVE SONG (re-issue)** *LaFace 74321196682*	15	8
9 Jul 94	**YOU MEAN THE WORLD TO ME** *LaFace 74321214702*	30	5
3 Dec 94	**LOVE SHOULDA BROUGHT YOU HOME** *LaFace 74321249412*	33	3
13 Jul 96 ●	**YOU'RE MAKIN' ME HIGH** *LaFace 74321395402* ▲	7	11
2 Nov 96 ●	**UN-BREAK MY HEART** *LaFace 74321410632* ▲	2	19
24 May 97 ●	**I DON'T WANT TO** *LaFace 74321468612*	9	8
8 Nov 97	**HOW COULD AN ANGEL BREAK MY HEART** *LaFace 74321531982* [1]	22	4
29 Apr 00 ●	**HE WASN'T MAN ENOUGH** *LaFace 74321757852*	5	11
8 Mar 03	**HIT THE FREEWAY** *LaFace / Arista 82876506372* [2]	29	3
29 Jan 94 ●	**TONI BRAXTON** *LaFace 74321162682* ▲	4	33
29 Jun 96 ●	**SECRETS** *LaFace 73008260202*	10	81
6 May 00 ●	**THE HEAT** *LaFace 73008260692*	3	19
15 Nov 03	**ULTIMATE** *Arista 82876574852*	23	3

[1] Toni Braxton with Kenny G [2] Toni Braxton featuring Loon

BRAXTONS *US, female vocal group (Singles: 7 weeks)* pos/wks

1 Feb 97	**SO MANY WAYS** *Atlantic A 5469CD*	32	2
29 Mar 97	**THE BOSS** *Atlantic A 5441CD*	31	3
19 Jul 97	**SLOW FLOW** *Atlantic AT 0001CD*	26	2

BREAD (255 Top 500)
Internationally popular soft-rock group whose initial line-up was David Gates (v/g/k), James Griffin (g), Robb Royner (g) and Jim Gordon (d). Los Angeles formed quartet, wrote and originally recorded No.1 hits 'If' and 'Everything I Own' (Singles: 46 weeks, Albums: 198 weeks) pos/wks

1 Aug 70 ●	**MAKE IT WITH YOU** *Elektra 2101 010* ▲	5	14
15 Jan 72	**BABY I'M-A WANT YOU** *Elektra K 12033*	14	10
29 Apr 72	**EVERYTHING I OWN** *Elektra K 12041*	32	6
30 Sep 72	**THE GUITAR MAN** *Elektra K 12066*	16	9
25 Dec 76	**LOST WITHOUT YOUR LOVE** *Elektra K 12241*	27	7
26 Sep 70	**ON THE WATERS** *Elektra 2469005*	34	5
18 Mar 72 ●	**BABY I'M-A WANT YOU** *Elektra K 42100*	9	19
28 Oct 72 ●	**THE BEST OF BREAD** *Elektra K 42115*	7	100
27 Jul 74	**THE BEST OF BREAD VOLUME 2** *Elektra K 42161*	48	1
29 Jan 77	**LOST WITHOUT YOUR LOVE** *Elektra K 52044*	17	6
5 Nov 77 ★	**THE SOUND OF BREAD** *Elektra K 52062*	1	46
28 Nov 87	**THE VERY BEST OF BREAD** *Telstar STAR 2303*	84	2
5 Jul 97 ●	**ESSENTIALS** *Jive 9548354082* [1]	9	19

[1] David Gates and Bread

See also David GATES

BREAK MACHINE
US, male vocal group (Singles: 32 weeks, Albums: 16 weeks) pos/wks

4 Feb 84 ●	**STREET DANCE** *Record Shack SOHO 13*	3	14
12 May 84 ●	**BREAK DANCE PARTY (re)** *Record Shack SOHO 20*	9	10
11 Aug 84	**ARE YOU READY?** *Record Shack SOHO 24*	27	8
9 Jun 84	**BREAK MACHINE** *Record Shack SOHOLP 3*	17	16

BREAKBEAT ERA *UK, male / female instrumental / production trio (Singles: 5 weeks, Albums: 2 weeks)* pos/wks

18 Jul 98	**BREAKBEAT ERA** *XL Recordings XLS 95CD*	38	2
21 Aug 99	**ULTRA – OBSCENE** *XL Recordings XLS 107CD*	48	2

11 Mar 00 **BULLITPROOF** *XL Recordings XLS 115CD* 65 1
11 Sep 99 **ULTRA OBSCENE** *XL Recordings XLCD 130*.....31 2

BREAKFAST CLUB
US, male vocal / instrumental group (Singles: 3 weeks) pos/wks

27 Jun 87 **RIGHT ON TRACK** *MCA MCA 1146* 54 3

Julian BREAM
UK, male instrumentalist – guitar / lute (Albums: 2 weeks) pos/wks

27 Apr 96 **THE ULTIMATE GUITAR COLLECTION** *RCA Victor 74321337052* 66 2

BREATHE *UK, male vocal / instrumental group (Singles: 27 weeks, Albums: 5 weeks)* pos/wks

30 Jul 88 ● **HANDS TO HEAVEN** *Siren SRN 68* 4 12
22 Oct 88 **JONAH** *Siren SRN 95* 60 3
3 Dec 88 **HOW CAN I FALL?** *Siren SRN 102* 48 7
11 Mar 89 **DON'T TELL ME LIES** *Siren SRN 109* 45 5
8 Oct 88 **ALL THAT JAZZ** *Siren SRNLP 12*.....22 5

Freddy BRECK
Germany, male vocalist (Singles: 4 weeks) pos/wks

13 Apr 74 **SO IN LOVE WITH YOU** *Decca F 13481* 44 4

BRECKER BROTHERS *US, male vocal / instrumental duo – Randy and Michael Brecker (Singles: 5 weeks)* pos/wks

4 Nov 78 **EAST RIVER** *Arista ARIST 211* 34 5

BREEDERS *US / UK, female / male vocal / instrumental group (Singles: 7 weeks, Albums: 9 weeks)* pos/wks

18 Apr 92 **SAFARI (EP)** *4AD BAD 2003* 69 1
21 Aug 93 **CANNONBALL (EP)** *4AD BAD 3011CD* 40 3
6 Nov 93 **DIVINE HAMMER** *4AD BAD 3017CD* 59 1
23 Jul 94 **HEAD TO TOE (EP)** *4AD BADD 4012* 68 1
14 Sep 02 **SON OF THREE** *4AD BAD 2213CD* 72 1
9 Jun 90 **POD** *4AD CAD 0006* 22 3
11 Sep 93 ● **LAST SPLASH** *4AD CAD 3014CD*.....5 5
1 Jun 02 **TITLE TK** *4AD CAD 2205CD*.....51 1

Tracks on Safari (EP): Do You Love Me Now / Don't Call Home / Safari / So Sad About Us. Tracks on Cannonball (EP): Cannonball / Cro-Aloha / Lord of the Thighs / 900. Tracks on Head to Toe (EP): Head to Toe / Shocker in Gloom Town / Freed Pig

See also PIXIES; THROWING MUSES

BREEKOUT KREW *US, male vocal duo (Singles: 3 weeks)* pos/wks

24 Nov 84 **MATT'S MOOD** *London LON 59* 51 3

Ann BREEN *Ireland, female vocalist (Singles: 2 weeks)* pos/wks

19 Mar 83 **PAL OF MY CRADLE DAYS (re)** *Homespun HS 052* 69 2

Mark BREEZE – *See Darren STYLES & Mark BREEZE present INFEXTIOUS*

Jo BREEZER *UK, female vocalist (Singles: 2 weeks)* pos/wks

13 Oct 01 **VENUS AND MARS** *Columbia 6717612* 27 2

BRENDON
UK, male vocalist – Brendon Dunning (Singles: 9 weeks) pos/wks

19 Mar 77 **GIMME SOME** *Magnet MAG 80* 14 9

Maire BRENNAN
Ireland, female vocalist (Singles: 12 weeks, Albums: 2 weeks) pos/wks

16 May 92 **AGAINST THE WIND** *RCA PB 45399* 64 2
5 Jun 99 ● **SALTWATER** *Xtravaganza XTRAV 1CDS* [1] 6 10
13 Jun 92 **MAIRE** *RCA PD 75358* 53 2

[1] Chicane featuring Maire Brennan of Clannad

See also CLANNAD

Rose BRENNAN
Ireland, female vocalist (Singles: 9 weeks) pos/wks

7 Dec 61 **TALL DARK STRANGER** *Philips PB 1193* 31 9

Walter BRENNAN
US, male vocalist, d. 21 Sep 1974 (Singles: 3 weeks) pos/wks

28 Jun 62 **OLD RIVERS** *Liberty LIB 55436* 38 3

Tony BRENT *UK, male vocalist – Reginald Bretagne, d. 19 Jun 1993 (Singles: 52 weeks)* pos/wks

19 Dec 52 ● **WALKIN' TO MISSOURI (re)** *Columbia DB 3147* 7 7
2 Jan 53 ● **MAKE IT SOON (re)** *Columbia DB 3187* 9 7
23 Jan 53 **GOT YOU ON MY MIND** *Columbia DB 3226* 12 1
30 Nov 56 **CINDY, OH CINDY (re)** *Columbia DB 3844* 16 7
28 Jun 57 **DARK MOON** *Columbia DB 3950* 17 14
28 Feb 58 **THE CLOUDS WILL SOON ROLL BY (re)** *Columbia DB 4066* 20 5
5 Sep 58 **GIRL OF MY DREAMS** *Columbia DB 4177* 16 7
24 Jul 59 **WHY SHOULD I BE LONELY?** *Columbia DB 4304* 24 4

Bernard BRESSLAW *UK, male comedian / actor / vocalist, d. 11Jun 1993 (Singles: 11 weeks)* pos/wks

5 Sep 58 ● **MAD PASSIONATE LOVE** *HMV POP 522* 6 11

See also Michael MEDWIN, Bernard BRESSLAW, Alfie BASS and Leslie FYSON

Adrian BRETT
UK, male instrumentalist – flute (Albums: 11 weeks) pos/wks

10 Nov 79 **ECHOES OF GOLD** *Warwick WW 5062* 19 11

Paul BRETT *UK, male instrumentalist – guitar (Albums: 7 weeks)* pos/wks

19 Jul 80 **ROMANTIC GUITAR** *K-Tel ONE 1079* 24 7

Teresa BREWER
US, female vocalist – Theresa Breuer (Singles: 53 weeks) pos/wks

11 Feb 55 ● **LET ME GO LOVER** *Vogue/Coral Q 72043* [1] 9 10
13 Apr 56 ● **A TEAR FELL** *Vogue/Coral Q 72146* 2 15
13 Jul 56 ● **A SWEET OLD FASHIONED GIRL** *Vogue/Coral Q 72172* 3 15
10 May 57 **NORA MALONE** *Vogue/Coral Q 72224* 26 2
23 Jun 60 **HOW DO YOU KNOW IT'S LOVE** *Coral Q 72396* 21 11

[1] Teresa Brewer with The Lancers

BRIAN and MICHAEL *UK, male vocal duo – Kevin Parrott and Michael Coleman (Singles: 19 weeks)* pos/wks

25 Feb 78 ★ **MATCHSTALK MEN AND MATCHSTALK CATS AND DOGS (LOWRY'S SONG)** *Pye 7N 46035* 1 19

BRICK *US, male vocal / instrumental group (Singles: 4 weeks)* pos/wks

5 Feb 77 **DAZZ** *Bang 004* 36 4

Edie BRICKELL and the NEW BOHEMIANS *US, female / male vocal / instrumental group (Singles: 10 weeks, Albums: 19 weeks)* pos/wks

4 Feb 89 **WHAT I AM** *Geffen GEF 49* 31 7
27 May 89 **CIRCLE** *Geffen GEF 51* 74 1
1 Oct 94 **GOOD TIMES** *Geffen GFSTD 78* [1] 40 2
4 Feb 89 **SHOOTING RUBBERBANDS AT THE STARS** *Geffen WX 215* 25 17
10 Nov 90 **GHOST OF A DOG** *Geffen WX 386* 63 1
3 Sep 94 **PICTURE PERFECT MORNING** *Geffen GED 24715* [1] 59 1

[1] Edie Brickell [1] Edie Brickell

Alicia BRIDGES
US, female vocalist (Singles: 11 weeks) pos/wks

11 Nov 78 **I LOVE THE NIGHTLIFE (DISCO 'ROUND)** *Polydor 2066 936* 32 10
8 Oct 94 **I LOVE THE NIGHTLIFE (DISCO 'ROUND) (re-mix)** *Mother MUMCD 57* 61 1

Johnny BRIGGS – *See Amanda BARRIE and Johnny BRIGGS*

BRIGHOUSE AND RASTRICK BRASS BAND
UK, male brass band (Singles: 13 weeks, Albums: 11 weeks) pos/wks

12 Nov 77 ● THE FLORAL DANCE *Transatlantic BIG 548* 2 13
28 Jan 78 ● FLORAL DANCE *Logo 1001* 10 11

Bette BRIGHT
UK, female vocalist (Singles: 5 weeks) pos/wks

8 Mar 80 HELLO, I AM YOUR HEART *Korova KOW 3* 50 5

Sarah BRIGHTMAN
UK, female vocalist (Singles: 98 weeks, Albums: 31 weeks) pos/wks

11 Nov 78 ● I LOST MY HEART TO A STARSHIP TROOPER *Ariola / Hansa AHA 527* [1] 6 14
7 Apr 79 THE ADVENTURES OF THE LOVE CRUSADER *Ariola / Hansa AHA 538* [2] 53 5
30 Jul 83 HIM *Polydor POSP 625* [3] 55 4
23 Mar 85 ● PIE JESU *HMV WEBBER 1* [4] 3 8
11 Jan 86 ● THE PHANTOM OF THE OPERA *Polydor POSP 800* [5] 7 10
4 Oct 86 ● ALL I ASK OF YOU *Polydor POSP 802* [6] 3 16
10 Jan 87 ● WISHING YOU WERE SOMEHOW HERE AGAIN *Polydor POSP 803* 7 11
11 Jul 92 AMIGOS PARA SIEMPRE (FRIENDS FOR LIFE) *Really Useful RUR 10* [7] 11 11
24 May 97 ● TIME TO SAY GOODBYE (CON TE PARTIRO) *Coalition COLA 003CD* [8] 2 14
23 Aug 97 WHO WANTS TO LIVE FOREVER *Coalition COLA 014CD* 45 1
6 Dec 97 JUST SHOW ME HOW TO LOVE YOU *Coalition COLA 035CD* [9] 54 2
14 Feb 98 STARSHIP TROOPERS *Coalition COLA 040CD* 58 1
13 Feb 99 EDEN *Coalition COLA 065CD* 68 1
17 Jun 89 THE SONGS THAT GOT AWAY *Really Useful 839116 1* 48 2
8 Aug 92 AMIGOS PARA SIEMPRE (FREINDS FOR LIFE) *East West 4509902562* [1] 53 4
11 Nov 95 THE UNEXPECTED SONGS – SURRENDER *Really Useful 5277022* 45 2
14 Jun 97 ● TIMELESS *Coalition 630191812* 2 21
20 Jan 01 LA LUNA *East West 8573859152* 37 2

[1] Sarah Brightman and Hot Gossip [2] Sarah Brightman and the Starship Troopers [3] Sarah Brightman and the London Philharmonic [4] Sarah Brightman and Paul Miles-Kingston [5] Sarah Brightman and Steve Harley [6] Cliff Richard and Sarah Brightman [7] José Carreras and Sarah Brightman [8] Sarah Brightman and Andrea Bocelli [9] Sarah Brightman and the LSO featuring José Cura [1] José Carreras and Sarah Brightman

The listed flip side of 'Wishing You Were Somehow Here Again' was 'The Music of the Night' by Michael Crawford. COLA 040CD is a dance re-mix of AHA 527

See also Andrew LLOYD WEBBER

BRIGHTON AND HOVE ALBION FC
UK, male football team vocalists (Singles: 2 weeks) pos/wks

28 May 83 THE BOYS IN THE OLD BRIGHTON BLUE *Energy NRG 2* 65 2

BRILLIANT
UK, male / female vocal / instrumental group (Singles: 13 weeks, Albums: 1 week) pos/wks

19 Oct 85 IT'S A MAN'S MAN'S MAN'S WORLD *Food FOOD 5* 58 5
22 Mar 86 LOVE IS WAR *Food FOOD 6* 64 4
2 Aug 86 SOMEBODY *Food FOOD 7* 67 4
20 Sep 86 KISS THE LIPS OF LIFE *Food BRILL 1* 83 1

Danielle BRISEBOIS
US, female vocalist (Singles: 1 week) pos/wks

9 Sep 95 GIMME LITTLE SIGN *Epic 6610782* 75 1

Johnny BRISTOL
US, male vocalist (Singles: 16 weeks, Albums: 7 weeks) pos/wks

24 Aug 74 ● HANG ON IN THERE BABY *MGM 2006 443* 3 11
19 Jul 80 MY GUY – MY GIRL (MEDLEY) *Atlantic / Hansa K 11550* [1] 39 5
5 Oct 74 HANG ON IN THERE BABY *MGM 2315 303* 12 7

[1] Amii Stewart and Johnny Bristol

BRIT PACK *UK / Ireland, male vocal group (Singles: 2 weeks)* pos/wks

12 Feb 00 SET ME FREE *When! WENX 2000* 41 2

BRITISH SEA POWER *UK, male vocal / instrumental group (Singles: 3 weeks, Albums: 1 week)* pos/wks

12 Jul 03 CARRION / APOLOGIES TO INSECT LIFE *Rough Trade RTRADESCD 092* 36 1
1 Nov 03 REMEMBER ME *Rough Trade RTRADESCD 125* 30 2
14 Jun 03 THE DECLINE OF BRITISH SEA POWER *Rough Trade RTRADECD 090* 54 1

BRITS – *See VARIOUS ARTISTS (MONTAGES)*

Andrea BRITTON – *See OXYGEN featuring Andrea BRITTON*

BROCK LANDARS
UK, male vocal / production duo (Singles: 2 weeks) pos/wks

11 Jul 98 S.M.D.U. *Parlophone CDBLUE 001* 49 2

BRODSKY QUARTET – *See Elvis COSTELLO*

BROKEN ENGLISH
UK, male vocal / instrumental group (Singles: 13 weeks) pos/wks

30 May 87 COMIN' ON STRONG *EMI EM 5* 18 10
3 Oct 87 LOVE ON THE SIDE *EMI EM 55* 69 3

June BRONHILL and Thomas ROUND
Australia / UK, female / male vocal duo (Albums: 1 week) pos/wks

18 Jun 60 LILAC TIME *HMV CLP 1248* 17 1

BRONSKI BEAT (469 Top 500)
Electronic dance trio formed 1984 London, UK; Steve Bronski (k), Larry Steinbachek (k) and the plaintive falsetto of Jimmy Somerville (v), who left in 1985 for The Communards (replaced by John Foster). The first openly gay hit pop group split in 1989 (Singles: 78 weeks, Albums: 69 weeks) pos/wks

2 Jun 84 ● SMALLTOWN BOY *Forbidden Fruit BITE 1* 3 13
22 Sep 84 ● WHY? *Forbidden Fruit BITE 2* 6 10
1 Dec 84 IT AIN'T NECESSARILY SO *Forbidden Fruit BITE 3* 16 11
20 Apr 85 ● I FEEL LOVE (MEDLEY) *Forbidden Fruit BITE 4* [1] 3 12
30 Nov 85 ● HIT THAT PERFECT BEAT *Forbidden Fruit BITE 6* 3 14
29 Mar 86 COME ON, COME ON *Forbidden Fruit BITE 7* 20 7
1 Jul 89 CHA CHA HEELS *Arista 112331* [2] 32 7
2 Feb 91 SMALLTOWN BOY (re-mix) *London LON 287* [3] 32 4
20 Oct 84 ● THE AGE OF CONSENT *Forbidden Fruit BITLP 1* 4 53
21 Sep 85 HUNDREDS AND THOUSANDS *Forbidden Fruit BITLP 2* 24 6
10 May 86 TRUTHDARE DOUBLEDARE *Forbidden Fruit BITLP 3* 18 6
22 Sep 01 THE VERY BEST OF JIMMY SOMERVILLE BRONSKI BEAT AND THE COMMUNARDS *London 927412582* [1] 29 4

[1] Bronski Beat and Marc Almond [2] Eartha Kitt and Bronski Beat [3] Jimmy Somerville with Bronski Beat [1] Jimmy Somerville Bronski Beat and the Communards

Tracks on medley: I Feel Love / Love to Love You Baby / Johnny Remember Me

Jet BRONX and the FORBIDDEN *UK, male vocal / instrumental group – featuring TV presenter Loyd Grossman (Singles: 1 week)* pos/wks

17 Dec 77 AIN'T DOIN' NOTHIN' *Lightning LIG 50* 49 1

Michael BROOK – *See Nusrat Fateh Ali KHAN / Michael BROOK*

BROOK BROTHERS *UK, male vocal duo – Geoff and Ricky Brook (Singles: 35 weeks)* pos/wks

30 Mar 61 ● WARPAINT *Pye 7N 15333* 5 14
24 Aug 61 AIN'T GONNA WASH FOR A WEEK *Pye 7N 15369* 13 10
25 Jan 62 HE'S OLD ENOUGH TO KNOW BETTER *Pye 7N 15409* 37 1

Date		Title / Label	pos	wks
16 Aug 62		**WELCOME HOME BABY** *Pye 7N 15453*	**33**	6
21 Feb 63		**TROUBLE IS MY MIDDLE NAME** *Pye 7N 15498*	**38**	4

Bruno BROOKES – *See Liz KERSHAW and Bruno BROOKES*

BROOKLYN BOUNCE
Germany, male production duo and male / female vocal group (Singles: 1 week)

Date		Title / Label	pos	wks
30 May 98		**THE MUSIC'S GOT ME** *Club Tools 0064795 CLU*	**67**	1

BROOKLYN, BRONX and QUEENS – *See B B and Q BAND*

Elkie BROOKS (176 Top 500)
Husky-voiced female vocalist, professional at age 15, b. Elaine Bookbinder, 25 Feb 1945, Salford, UK. Blues, jazz then rock phases (in Vinegar Joe with Robert Palmer) followed by a solo career which featured an impressive 20-year run of 15 hit albums from 1977 (Singles: 91 weeks, Albums: 223 weeks)

Date		Title / Label	pos	wks
2 Apr 77	●	**PEARL'S A SINGER** *A&M AMS 7275*	**8**	9
20 Aug 77	●	**SUNSHINE AFTER THE RAIN** *A&M AMS 7306*	**10**	9
25 Feb 78		**LILAC WINE** *A&M AMS 7333*	**16**	7
3 Jun 78		**ONLY LOVE CAN BREAK YOUR HEART** *A&M AMS 7353*	**43**	5
11 Nov 78		**DON'T CRY OUT LOUD** *A&M AMS 7395*	**12**	11
5 May 79		**THE RUNAWAY** *A&M AMS 7428*	**50**	5
16 Jan 82		**FOOL IF YOU THINK IT'S OVER** *A&M AMS 8187*	**17**	10
1 May 82		**OUR LOVE** *A&M AMS 8214*	**43**	5
17 Jul 82		**NIGHTS IN WHITE SATIN** *A&M AMS 8235*	**33**	5
22 Jan 83		**GASOLINE ALLEY** *A&M AMS 8305*	**52**	5
22 Nov 86	●	**NO MORE THE FOOL** *Legend LM 4*	**5**	16
4 Apr 87		**BREAK THE CHAIN** *Legend LM 8*	**55**	3
11 Jul 87		**WE'VE GOT TONIGHT** *Legend LM 9*	**69**	1
18 Jun 77		TWO DAYS AWAY *A&M AMLH 68409*	**16**	20
13 May 78		SHOOTING STAR *A&M AMLH 64695*	**20**	13
13 Oct 79		LIVE AND LEARN *A&M AMLH 68509*	**34**	6
14 Nov 81	●	PEARLS *A&M ELK 1981*	**2**	79
13 Nov 82	●	PEARLS II *A&M ELK 1982*	**5**	25
14 Jul 84		MINUTES *A&M AML 68565*	**35**	7
8 Dec 84		SCREEN GEMS *EMI SCREEN 1*	**35**	11
6 Dec 86	●	NO MORE THE FOOL *Legend LMA 1*	**5**	23
27 Dec 86	●	THE VERY BEST OF ELKIE BROOKS *Telstar STAR 2284*	**10**	18
11 Jun 88		BOOKBINDER'S KID *Legend LMA 3*	**57**	3
18 Nov 89		INSPIRATIONS *Telstar STAR 2354*	**58**	3
13 Mar 93		ROUND MIDNIGHT *Castle Communications CTVCD 113*	**27**	4
16 Apr 94		NOTHIN' BUT THE BLUES *Castle Communications CTVCD 127*	**58**	2
13 Apr 96		AMAZING *Carlton Premiere 3036000282* [1]	**49**	2
15 Mar 97		THE VERY BEST OF ELKIE BROOKS *PolyGram TV 5407122*	**23**	7

[1] Elkie Brooks with the Royal Philharmonic Orchestra

The two 'The Very Best of Elkie Brooks' albums are different

Garth BROOKS
US, male vocalist (Singles: 15 weeks, Albums: 48 weeks)

Date		Title / Label	pos	wks
1 Feb 92		**SHAMELESS** *Capitol CL 646*	**71**	1
22 Jan 94		**THE RED STROKES / AIN'T GOING DOWN** *Liberty CDCLS 704*	**13**	5
16 Apr 94		**STANDING OUTSIDE THE FIRE** *Liberty CDCL 712*	**28**	4
18 Feb 95		**THE DANCE / FRIENDS IN LOW PLACES** *Capitol CDCL 735*	**36**	3
17 Feb 96		**SHE'S EVERY WOMAN** *Capitol CDCL 767*	**55**	1
13 Nov 99		**LOST IN YOU** *Capitol CDCL 814* [1]	**70**	1
15 Feb 92		ROPIN' THE WIND *Capitol CDESTU 2162* ▲	**41**	2
12 Feb 94	●	IN PIECES *Capitol CDEST 2212* ▲	**2**	11
24 Dec 94		THE HITS *Capitol CDP 8320812* ▲	**11**	21
2 Dec 95		FRESH HORSES *Capitol CDGB 1*	**22**	6
13 Dec 97		SEVENS *Capitol 8565992* ▲	**34**	7
28 Nov 98		DOUBLE LIVE *Capitol 4974242* ▲	**57**	1

[1] Garth Brooks as Chris Gaines

Harry BROOKS – *See STUDIO B / ROMEO and Harry BROOKS*

Mel BROOKS
US, male actor / rapper – Melvin Kaminsky (Singles: 10 weeks)

Date		Title / Label	pos	wks
18 Feb 84		**TO BE OR NOT TO BE (THE HITLER RAP)** *Island IS 158*	**12**	10

Meredith BROOKS
US, female vocal / instrumentalist (Singles: 13 weeks, Albums: 10 weeks)

Date		Title / Label	pos	wks
2 Aug 97	●	**BITCH** *Capital CDCL 790*	**6**	10
6 Dec 97		**I NEED** *Capital CDCLS 794*	**28**	2
7 Mar 98		**WHAT WOULD HAPPEN** *Capital CDCL 798*	**49**	1
23 Aug 97	●	BLURRING THE EDGES *Capitol CDEST 2298*	**5**	10

Norman BROOKS
Canada, male vocalist – Norman Arie (Singles: 1 week)

Date		Title / Label	pos	wks
12 Nov 54		**A SKY-BLUE SHIRT AND A RAINBOW TIE** *London L 1228*	**17**	1

Nigel BROOKS SINGERS
UK, male / female vocal choir (Albums: 17 weeks)

Date		Title / Label	pos	wks
29 Nov 75	●	SONGS OF JOY *K-Tel NE 706*	**5**	16
5 Jun 76		20 ALL TIME EUROVISION FAVOURITES *K-Tel NE 712*	**44**	1

BROS (448 Top 500)
Top teen appeal act; photogenic twins Matt Goss (v) and Luke Goss (d), b. 29 Sep 1968, London, UK, and Craig Logan (b) – who left in 1989. Sold out tours, broke sales records, created hysteria and won Brits Best Newcomer of 1988 award (Singles: 84 weeks, Albums: 69 weeks)

Date		Title / Label	pos	wks
5 Dec 87	●	**WHEN WILL I BE FAMOUS? (re)** *CBS ATOM 2*	**2**	15
19 Mar 88	●	**DROP THE BOY** *CBS ATOM 3*	**2**	10
18 Jun 88	★	**I OWE YOU NOTHING** *CBS ATOM 4*	**1**	11
17 Sep 88	●	**I QUIT** *CBS ATOM 5*	**4**	8
3 Dec 88	●	**CAT AMONG THE PIGEONS / SILENT NIGHT** *CBS ATOM 6*	**2**	8
29 Jul 89	●	**TOO MUCH** *CBS ATOM 7*	**2**	7
7 Oct 89	●	**CHOCOLATE BOX** *CBS ATOM 8*	**9**	6
16 Dec 89	●	**SISTER** *CBS ATOM 9*	**10**	6
10 Mar 90		**MADLY IN LOVE** *CBS ATOM 10*	**14**	4
13 Jul 91		**ARE YOU MINE?** *Columbia 6569707*	**12**	5
21 Sep 91		**TRY** *Columbia 6574047*	**27**	4
9 Apr 88	●	PUSH *CBS 460629 1*	**2**	54
28 Oct 89	●	THE TIME *CBS 465918 1*	**4**	13
12 Oct 91		CHANGING FACES *Columbia 4688171*	**18**	2

Act was duo for last six hits Act was a group for first album

BROTHER BEYOND
UK, male vocal / instrumental group (Singles: 58 weeks, Albums: 24 weeks)

Date		Title / Label	pos	wks
4 Apr 87		**HOW MANY TIMES** *EMI EMI 5591*	**62**	3
8 Aug 87		**CHAIN-GANG SMILE** *Parlophone R 6160*	**57**	3
23 Jan 88		**CAN YOU KEEP A SECRET?** *Parlophone R 6174*	**56**	4
30 Jul 88	●	**THE HARDER I TRY** *Parlophone R 6184*	**2**	14
5 Nov 88	●	**HE AIN'T NO COMPETITION** *Parlophone R 6193*	**6**	10
21 Jan 89		**BE MY TWIN** *Parlophone R 6195*	**14**	6
1 Apr 89		**CAN YOU KEEP A SECRET (re-mix)** *Parlophone R 6197*	**22**	5
28 Oct 89		**DRIVE ON** *Parlophone R 6233*	**39**	4
9 Dec 89		**WHEN WILL I SEE YOU AGAIN** *Parlophone R 6239*	**43**	5
10 Apr 90		**TRUST** *Parlophone R 6245*	**53**	2
19 Jan 91		**THE GIRL I USED TO KNOW** *Parlophone R 6265*	**48**	2
26 Nov 88	●	GET EVEN *Parlophone PCS 7327*	**9**	23
25 Nov 89		TRUST *Parlophone PCS 7337*	**60**	1

BROTHER BROWN featuring FRANK'EE
Denmark, male DJ / production duo and female vocalist (Singles: 5 weeks)

Date		Title / Label	pos	wks
2 Oct 99		**UNDER THE WATER** *ffrr FCD 367*	**18**	4
24 Nov 01		**STAR CATCHING GIRL** *Rulin / MOS RULIN 21CDS*	**51**	1

BROTHERHOOD
UK, male rap group (Singles: 1 week, Albums: 1 week)

Date		Title / Label	pos	wks
27 Jan 96		**ONE SHOT / NOTHING IN PARTICULAR** *Bite It BHOODD 3*	**55**	1
17 Feb 96		ELEMENTALZ *Bite It! BHOODCD 1*	**50**	1

BROTHERHOOD OF MAN
UK, male vocal quartet (Singles: 97 weeks, Albums: 40 weeks)

Date		Title / Label	pos	wks
14 Feb 70	●	**UNITED WE STAND** *Deram DM 284*	**10**	9
4 Jul 70		**WHERE ARE YOU GOING TO MY LOVE** *Deram DM 298*	**22**	10

13 Mar 76 ★	**SAVE YOUR KISSES FOR ME** *Pye 7N 45569* ◆	1	16
19 Jun 76	**MY SWEET ROSALIE** *Pye 7N 45602*	30	7
26 Feb 77 ●	**OH BOY (THE MOOD I'M IN)** *Pye 7N 45656*	8	12
9 Jul 77 ★	**ANGELO** *Pye 7N 45699*	1	12
14 Jan 78 ★	**FIGARO** *Pye 7N 46037*	1	11
27 May 78	**BEAUTIFUL LOVER** *Pye 7N 46071*	15	12
30 Sep 78	**MIDDLE OF THE NIGHT** *Pye 7N 46117*	41	6
3 Jul 82	**LIGHTNING FLASH** *EMI 5309*	67	2
24 Apr 76	LOVE AND KISSES FROM *Pye NSPL 18490*	20	8
12 Aug 78	B FOR BROTHERHOOD *Pye NSPL 18567*	18	9
7 Oct 78 ●	BROTHERHOOD OF MAN *K-Tel BML 7980*	6	15
29 Nov 80	SING 20 NUMBER ONE HITS *Warwick WW 5087*	14	8

BROTHERLOVE – *See PRATT and McCLAIN with BROTHERLOVE*

BROTHERS *UK, male vocal group (Singles: 9 weeks)*

		pos	wks
29 Jan 77 ●	**SING ME** *Bus Stop Bus 1054*	8	9

BROTHERS FOUR *US, male vocal group (Singles: 2 weeks)*

		pos	wks
23 Jun 60	**GREENFIELDS (re)** *Philips PB 1009*	40	2

BROTHERS GRIMM – *See JAZZ and the BROTHERS GRIMM*

BROTHERS IN RHYTHM *UK, male instrumental / production duo – Dave Seaman and Steve Anderson (Singles: 12 weeks)*

		pos	wks
16 Mar 91	**SUCH A GOOD FEELING** *Fourth & Broadway BRW 228*	64	2
14 Sep 91	**SUCH A GOOD FEELING (re-issue)** *Fourth & Broadway BRW 228 210*	14	8
30 Apr 94	**FOREVER AND A DAY** *Stress CDSTR 36* [1]	51	2

[1] Brothers in Rhythm present Charvoni

BROTHERS JOHNSON *US, male vocal / instrumental duo – George and Louis Johnson (Singles: 34 weeks, Albums: 22 weeks)*

		pos	wks
9 Jul 77	**STRAWBERRY LETTER 23** *A&M AMS 7297*	35	5
2 Sep 78	**AIN'T WE FUNKIN' NOW** *A&M AMS 7379*	43	6
4 Nov 78	**RIDE-O-ROCKET** *A&M AMS 7400*	50	4
23 Feb 80 ●	**STOMP** *A&M AMS 7509*	6	12
31 May 80	**LIGHT UP THE NIGHT** *A&M AMS 7526*	47	4
25 Jul 81	**THE REAL THING** *A&M AMS 8149*	50	3
19 Aug 78	BLAM!! *A&M AMLH 64714*	48	8
23 Feb 80	LIGHT UP THE NIGHT *A&M AMLK 63716*	22	12
18 Jul 81	WINNERS *A&M AMLK 63724*	42	2

BROTHERS LIKE OUTLAW featuring Alison EVELYN *UK, male / female vocal group (Singles: 1 week)*

		pos	wks
23 Jan 93	**GOOD VIBRATIONS** *Gee Street GESCD 44*	74	1

Edgar BROUGHTON BAND *UK, male vocal / instrumental group (Singles: 10 weeks, Albums: 6 weeks)*

		pos	wks
18 Apr 70	**OUT DEMONS OUT** *Harvest HAR 5015*	39	5
23 Jan 71	**APACHE DROPOUT (3re)** *Harvest HAR 5032*	33	5
20 Jun 70	SING BROTHER SING *Harvest SHVL 772*	18	4
5 Jun 71	THE EDGAR BROUGHTON BAND *Harvest SHVL 791*	28	2

Alison BROWN – *See BAR CODES featuring Alison BROWN*

Angie BROWN – *See BIZARRE INC; MOTIV 8*

Andrea BROWN – *See GOLDTRIX presents Andrea BROWN*

Bobby BROWN (339 Top 500)

Energetic swingbeat superstar, b. 5 Feb 1969, Massachusetts, who married Whitney Houston in 1992. He joined a re-formed New Edition in 1996, the vocal group in which he topped the chart with 'Candy Girl' as a 14-year-old (Singles: 131 weeks, Albums: 65 weeks)

		pos	wks
6 Aug 88	**DON'T BE CRUEL** *MCA MCA 1268*	42	7
17 Dec 88 ●	**MY PREROGATIVE** *MCA MCA 1299* ▲	6	17
25 Mar 89	**DON'T BE CRUEL (re-issue)** *MCA MCA 1310*	13	8
20 May 89 ●	**EVERY LITTLE STEP** *MCA MCA 1338*	6	9
15 Jul 89 ●	**ON OUR OWN (FROM GHOSTBUSTERS II)** *MCA MCA 1350*	4	9
23 Sep 89	**ROCK WIT'CHA** *MCA MCA 1367*	33	6
25 Nov 89	**RONI** *MCA MCA 1384*	21	7
9 Jun 90	**THE FREE STYLE MEGA-MIX** *MCA MCA 1421*	14	7
30 Jun 90	**SHE AIN'T WORTH IT** *London LON 265* [1] ▲	12	9
22 Aug 92	**HUMPIN' AROUND** *MCA MCS 1680*	19	6
17 Oct 92	**GOOD ENOUGH** *MCA MCS 1704*	41	4
19 Jun 93	**THAT'S THE WAY LOVE IS** *MCA MCSTD 1783*	56	2
22 Jan 94	**SOMETHING IN COMMON** *MCA MCSTD 1957* [2]	16	5
25 Jun 94 ●	**TWO CAN PLAY THAT GAME (re)** *MCA MCSTD 1973*	3	15
8 Jul 95 ●	**HUMPIN' AROUND (re-mix)** *MCA MCSTD 2073*	8	6
14 Oct 95	**MY PREROGATIVE (re-mix)** *MCA MCSTD 2094*	17	3
3 Feb 96	**EVERY LITTLE STEP (re-mix)** *MCA MCSTD 48004*	25	2
22 Nov 97	**FEELIN' INSIDE** *MCA MCSTD 48067*	40	1
21 Dec 02	**THUG LOVIN'** *Def Jam 0637872* [3]	15	8
28 Jan 89 ●	DON'T BE CRUEL *MCA MCF 3425* ▲	3	41
5 Aug 89	KING OF STAGE *MCA MCL 1886*	40	6
2 Dec 89	DANCE! ... YA KNOW IT! *MCA MCG 6074*	26	10
5 Sep 92	BOBBY *MCA MCAD 10695*	11	5
5 Aug 95	TWO CAN PLAY THAT GAME *MCA MCD 11334*	24	3

[1] Glenn Medeiros featuring Bobby Brown [2] Bobby Brown and Whitney Houston [3] Ja Rule featuring Bobby Brown

'Two Can Play That Game' reached its peak position of No.3 only on its re-entry in Apr 1995

Carl BROWN – *See DOUBLE TROUBLE*

Crazy World of Arthur BROWN *UK, male vocal / instrumental group (Singles: 14 weeks, Albums: 16 weeks)*

		pos	wks
26 Jun 68 ★	**FIRE** *Track 604 022*	1	14
6 Jul 68 ●	THE CRAZY WORLD OF ARTHUR BROWN *Track 612005*	2	16

Dennis BROWN *Jamaica, male vocalist – b. 1 Feb 1957, d.1 Jul 1999 (Singles: 18 weeks, Albums: 6 weeks)*

		pos	wks
3 Mar 79	**MONEY IN MY POCKET** *Lightning LV 5*	14	9
3 Jul 82	**LOVE HAS FOUND ITS WAY** *A&M AMS 8226*	47	6
11 Sep 82	**HALFWAY UP HALFWAY DOWN** *A&M AMS 8250*	56	3
26 Jun 82	LOVE HAS FOUND ITS WAY *A&M AMLH 64886*	72	6

Diana BROWN and Barrie K SHARPE *UK, female / male vocal duo (Singles: 11 weeks)*

		pos	wks
2 Jun 90	**THE MASTERPLAN** *ffrr F 133*	39	6
1 Sep 90	**SUN WORSHIPPERS (POSITIVE THINKING)** *ffrr F 144*	61	2
23 Mar 91	**LOVE OR NOTHING** *ffrr F 152*	71	1
27 Jun 92	**EATING ME ALIVE** *ffrr F 190*	53	2

Errol BROWN *UK, male vocalist (Singles: 13 weeks, Albums: 2 weeks)*

		pos	wks
4 Jul 87	**PERSONAL TOUCH** *WEA YZ 130*	25	8
28 Nov 87	**BODY ROCKIN'** *WEA YZ 162*	51	2
14 Feb 98	**IT STARTED WITH A KISS** *EMI CDHOT 101* [1]	18	3
9 Jun 01	STILL SEXY – THE ALBUM *Universal Music TV 138162*	44	2

[1] Hot Chocolate featuring Errol Brown

See also HOT CHOCOLATE

Foxy BROWN *US, female rapper – Inga Marchand (Singles: 25 weeks, Albums: 1 week)*

		pos	wks
21 Sep 96	**TOUCH ME TEASE ME** *Def Jam DEFCD 18* [1]	26	3
8 Mar 97	**GET ME HOME** *Def Jam DEFCD 32* [2]	11	5
10 May 97	**AIN'T NO PLAYA** *Northwestside 74321474842* [3]	31	2
21 Jun 97 ●	**I'LL BE** *Def Jam 5710432* [4]	9	5
11 Oct 97	**BIG BAD MAMMA** *Def Jam 5749792* [5]	12	3
25 Oct 97	**SUNSHINE** *Northwestside 74321528702* [6]	25	2
13 Mar 99	**HOT SPOT** *Def Jam 8708352*	31	2
8 Sep 01	**OH YEAH** *Der Jam 5887312*	27	3
6 Feb 99	CHYNA DOLL *Def Jam 5589332* ▲	51	1

[1] Case featuring Foxxy Brown [2] Foxy Brown featuring BLACKstreet [3] Jay-Z featuring Foxy Brown [4] Foxy Brown featuring Jay-Z [5] Foxy Brown featuring Dru Hill [6] Jay-Z featuring Babyface and Foxy Brown

Gloria D BROWN *US, female vocalist (Singles: 3 weeks)*

		pos	wks
8 Jun 85	THE MORE THEY KNOCK, THE MORE I LOVE YOU *10 TEN 52*	57	3

Horace BROWN

US, male vocalist (Singles: 7 weeks, Albums: 1 week)

		pos	wks
25 Feb 95	TASTE YOUR LOVE *Uptown MCSTD 2026*	58	1
18 May 96	ONE FOR THE MONEY *Motown 8605232*	12	4
12 Oct 96	THINGS WE DO FOR LOVE *Motown 8605712*	27	2
6 Jul 96	HORACE BROWN *Motown 5306942*	48	1

Ian BROWN *UK, male vocal / instrumentalist*

(Singles: 32 weeks, Albums: 35 weeks)

		pos	wks
24 Jan 98 ●	MY STAR *Polydor 5719872*	5	4
4 Apr 98	CORPSES *Polydor 5696552*	14	4
20 Jun 98	CAN'T SEE ME *Polydor 5440452*	21	3
20 Feb 99 ●	BE THERE *Mo Wax MW 108CD1* [1]	8	6
6 Nov 99	LOVE LIKE A FOUNTAIN *Polydor 5615162*	23	3
19 Feb 00 ●	DOLPHINS WERE MONKEYS *Polydor 5616372*	5	4
17 Jun 00	GOLDEN GAZE *Polydor 5618442*	29	2
29 Sep 01	F.E.A.R. *Polydor 5872842*	13	4
23 Feb 02	WHISPERS *Polydor 5705382*	33	2
14 Feb 98 ●	UNFINISHED MONKEY BUSINESS *Polydor 5395652*	4	24
20 Nov 99	GOLDEN GREATS *Polydor 5431412*	14	6
13 Oct 01 ●	MUSIC OF THE SPHERES *Polydor 5891262*	3	5

[1] Unkle featuring Ian Brown

See also STONE ROSES

James BROWN (426 Top 500)

'Soul Brother No.1', b. 3 May 1928, South Carolina, US. The most charted R&B performer of all time has influenced numerous musical styles since the mid-1950s. Only Elvis Presley has enjoyed more US pop chart entries (Singles: 104 weeks, Albums: 54 weeks)

		pos	wks
23 Sep 65	PAPA'S GOT A BRAND NEW BAG *London HL 9990* [1]	25	7
24 Feb 66	I GOT YOU *Pye International 7N 25350* [1]	29	6
16 Jun 66	IT'S A MAN'S MAN'S MAN'S WORLD *Pye International 7N 25371* [1]	13	9
10 Oct 70	GET UP I FEEL LIKE BEING A SEX MACHINE *Polydor 2001 071*	32	7
27 Nov 71	HEY AMERICA *Mojo 2093 006*	47	3
18 Sep 76	GET UP OFFA THAT THING *Polydor 2066 687*	22	6
29 Jan 77	BODY HEAT *Polydor 2066 763*	36	4
10 Jan 81	RAPP PAYBACK (WHERE IZ MOSES?) *RCA 28*	39	5
2 Jul 83	BRING IT ON . . . BRING IT ON *Sonet SON 2258*	45	4
1 Sep 84	UNITY (PART 1 – THE THIRD COMING) *Tommy Boy AFR 2* [2]	49	5
27 Apr 85	FROGGY MIX *Boiling Point FROG 1*	50	3
1 Jun 85	GET UP I FEEL LIKE BEING A SEX MACHINE (re) (re-issue) *Boiling Point POSP 751*	46	9
25 Jan 86 ●	LIVING IN AMERICA *Scotti Brothers A 6701*	5	10
18 Oct 86	GRAVITY *Scotti Brothers 650059 7*	65	2
30 Jan 88	SHE'S THE ONE *Urban URB 13*	45	3
23 Apr 88	THE PAYBACK MIX *Urban URB 17*	12	6
4 Jun 88	I'M REAL *Scotti Brothers JSB 1* [3]	31	4
23 Jul 88	I GOT YOU (I FEEL GOOD) (re-issue) *A&M AM 444*	52	3
16 Nov 91	GET UP (I FEEL LIKE BEING A) SEX MACHINE (2nd re-issue) *Polydor PO 185*	69	2
24 Oct 92	I GOT YOU (I FEEL GOOD) (re-mix) *FBI FBI 9* [4]	72	1
17 Apr 93	CAN'T GET ANY HARDER *Polydor PZCD 262*	59	2
17 Apr 99	FUNK ON AH ROLL *Inferno / Eagle EAGXA 073*	40	2
22 Apr 00	FUNK ON AH ROLL (re-mix) *Eagle EAGXS 127*	63	1
18 Oct 86	GRAVITY *Scotti Bros. SCT 57108*	85	3
25 Jun 88	I'M REAL *Scotti Bros. POLD 5230*	27	5
10 Oct 88	THE BEST OF JAMES BROWN – GODFATHER OF SOUL *K-Tel NE 1376*	17	21
16 Nov 91	SEX MACHINE – THE VERY BEST OF JAMES BROWN *Polydor 8458281*	19	22
11 May 02	THE GODFATHER – THE VERY BEST OF JAMES BROWN *UMTV 5898412*	30	3

[1] James Brown and the Famous Flames [2] Afrika Bambaataa and James Brown [3] James Brown featuring Full Force [4] James Brown vs Dakeyne

'Froggy Mix' is a medley of 12 James Brown songs. The listed flip side of 'I Got You (I Feel Good)' was 'Nowhere to Run' by Martha Reeves and the Vandellas

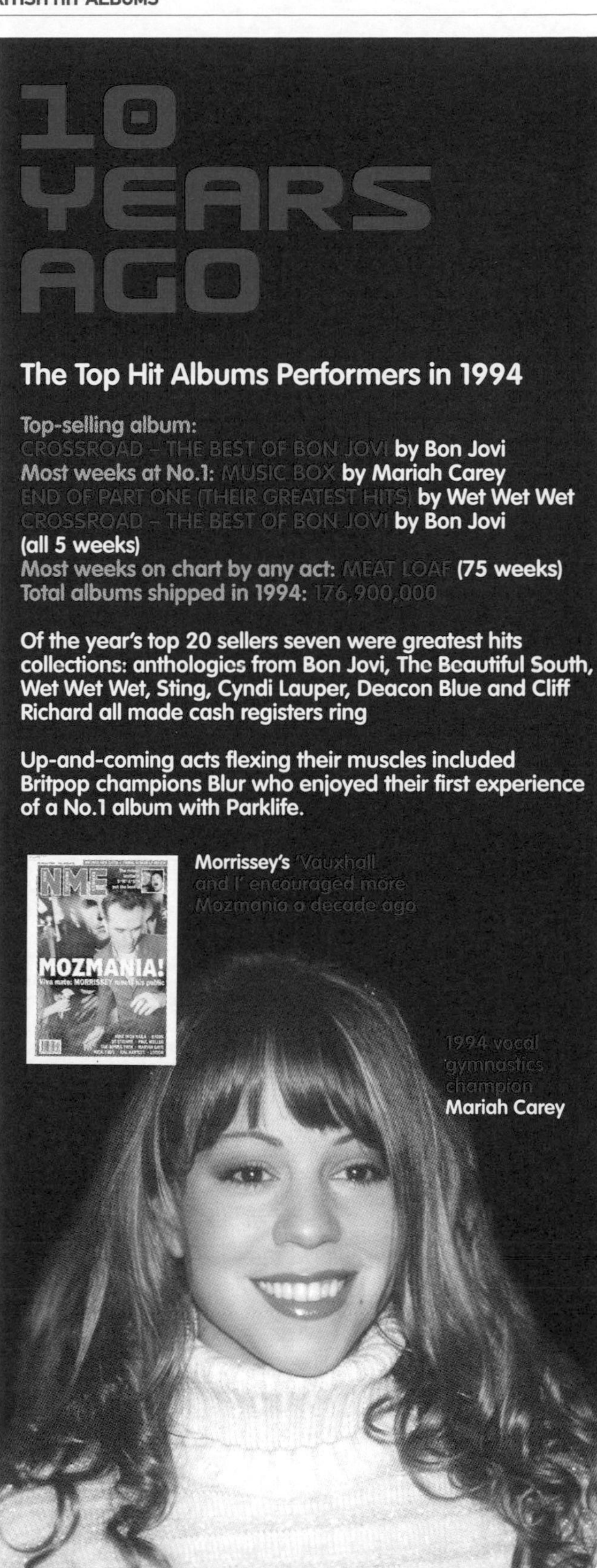

10 YEARS AGO
The Top Hit Albums Performers in 1994
Top-selling album:
CROSSROAD – THE BEST OF BON JOVI by Bon Jovi
Most weeks at No.1: MUSIC BOX by Mariah Carey
END OF PART ONE (THEIR GREATEST HITS) by Wet Wet Wet
CROSSROAD – THE BEST OF BON JOVI by Bon Jovi
(all 5 weeks)
Most weeks on chart by any act: MEAT LOAF (75 weeks)
Total albums shipped in 1994: 176,900,000
Of the year's top 20 sellers seven were greatest hits collections: anthologies from Bon Jovi, The Beautiful South, Wet Wet Wet, Sting, Cyndi Lauper, Deacon Blue and Cliff Richard all made cash registers ring
Up-and-coming acts flexing their muscles included Britpop champions Blur who enjoyed their first experience of a No.1 album with Parklife.
NME
MOZMANIA!
Morrissey's 'Vauxhall and I' encouraged more Mozmania a decade ago
1994 vocal gymnastics champion Mariah Carey

Jennifer BROWN
Sweden, female vocalist (Singles: 1 week)

Date		Title / Label	pos	wks
1 May 99		TUESDAY AFTERNOON *RCA 74321604092*	57	1

Joanne BROWN – *See Tony OSBORNE SOUND*

Jocelyn BROWN
US, female vocalist (Singles: 79 weeks)

Date		Title / Label	pos	wks
21 Apr 84		SOMEBODY ELSE'S GUY *Fourth & Broadway BRW 5*	13	9
22 Sep 84		I WISH YOU WOULD *Fourth & Broadway BRW 14*	51	3
15 Mar 86		LOVE'S GONNA GET YOU *Warner Bros. W 8889*	70	1
29 Jun 91	●	ALWAYS THERE *Talkin Loud TLK 10* [1]	6	9
14 Sep 91		SHE GOT SOUL *A&M AM 819* [2]	57	3
7 Dec 91	●	DON'T TALK JUST KISS *Tug SNOG 2* [3]	3	11
20 Mar 93		TAKE ME UP *A&M AMCD 210* [4]	61	1
11 Jun 94		NO MORE TEARS (ENOUGH IS ENOUGH) *Bell 74321209032* [5]	13	7
8 Oct 94		GIMME ALL YOUR LOVIN' *Bell 74321231322* [6]	22	3
13 Jul 96	●	KEEP ON JUMPIN' *Manifesto FESCD 11* [7]	8	6
10 May 97		IT'S ALRIGHT, I FEEL IT! *Talkin Loud TLCD 22* [8]	26	2
12 Jul 97	●	SOMETHING GOIN' ON *Manifesto FESCD 25* [7]	5	10
25 Oct 97		I AM THE BLACK GOLD OF THE SUN *Talkin Loud TLCD 26* [8]	31	2
22 Nov 97		HAPPINESS *Sony S3 KAMCD 2* [9]	45	1
2 May 98		FUN *INCredible INCRL 2CD*	33	2
29 Aug 98		AIN'T NO MOUNTAIN HIGH ENOUGH *INCredible INCRL 7CD*	35	2
27 Mar 99		I BELIEVE *Playola 0091705 PLA*	62	1
3 Jul 99		IT'S ALL GOOD *INCredible INCRL 14CD*	54	1
11 Mar 00		BELIEVE *Defected DFECT 14CD3* [10]	45	2
27 Jan 01		BELIEVE (re-mix) *Defected DFECT 26CDS* [10]	42	2
7 Sep 02		THAT'S HOW GOOD YOUR LOVE IS *Defected DFTD 057CDS* [11]	54	1

[1] Incognito featuring Jocelyn Brown [2] Jamestown featuring Jocelyn Brown [3] Right Said Fred. Guest vocals: Jocelyn Brown [4] Sonic Surfers featuring Jocelyn Brown [5] Kym Mazelle and Jocelyn Brown [6] Jocelyn Brown and Kym Mazelle [7] Todd Terry featuring Martha Wash and Jocelyn Brown [8] Nuyorican Soul featuring Jocelyn Brown [9] Kamasutra featuring Jocelyn Brown [10] Ministers De La Funk featuring Jocelyn Brown [11] Il Padrinos featuring Jocelyn Brown

See also Todd TERRY PROJECT

Joe BROWN and the BRUVVERS
UK, male vocalist / instrumentalist – guitar and male vocal instrumental group (Singles: 92 weeks, Albums: 47 weeks)

Date		Title / Label	pos	wks
17 Mar 60		THE DARKTOWN STRUTTERS' BALL *Decca F 11207*	34	6
26 Jan 61		SHINE *Pye 7N 15322* [1]	33	6
11 Jan 62		WHAT A CRAZY WORLD WE'RE LIVING IN *Piccadilly 7N 35024*	37	2
17 May 62	●	A PICTURE OF YOU *Piccadilly 7N 35047*	2	19
13 Sep 62		YOUR TENDER LOOK *Piccadilly 7N 35058*	31	6
15 Nov 62	●	IT ONLY TOOK A MINUTE (re) *Piccadilly 7N 35082*	6	14
7 Feb 63	●	THAT'S WHAT LOVE WILL DO *Piccadilly 7N 35106*	3	14
27 Jun 63		NATURE'S TIME FOR LOVE *Piccadilly 7N 35129*	26	6
26 Sep 63		SALLY ANN *Piccadilly 7N 35138*	28	9
29 Jun 67		WITH A LITTLE HELP FROM MY FRIENDS *Pye 7N 17339* [1]	32	4
14 Apr 73		HEY MAMA *Ammo AMO 101* [1]	33	6
1 Sep 62	●	A PICTURE OF YOU *Pye Golden Guinea GGL 0146*	3	39
25 May 63		JOE BROWN – LIVE *Piccadilly NPL 38006* [1]	14	8

[1] Joe Brown [1] Joe Brown

Karen BROWN – *See DJ's RULE*

Kathy BROWN *US, female vocalist (Singles: 9 weeks)*

Date		Title / Label	pos	wks
25 Nov 95		TURN ME OUT *Stress CDSTR 40*	44	2
20 Sep 97		TURN ME OUT (TURN TO SUGAR) (re-mix) *ffrr FCD* [1]	35	3
10 Apr 99		JOY *Azuli AZNYCDX 094*	63	1
5 May 01		LOVE IS NOT A GAME *Defected DFECT 31CDS* [2]	34	2
2 Jun 01		OVER YOU *Defected DFECT 28CDS* [3]	42	1

[1] Praxis featuring Kathy Brown [2] J Majik featuring Kathy Brown [3] Warren Clarke featuring Kathy Brown

Miquel BROWN *US, female vocalist (Singles: 7 weeks)*

Date		Title / Label	pos	wks
18 Feb 84		HE'S A SAINT, HE'S A SINNER *Record Shack SOHO 15*	68	4
24 Aug 85		CLOSE TO PERFECTION *Record Shack SOHO 48*	63	3

Palmer BROWN – *See BLAZE featuring Palmer BROWN*

Peter BROWN *US, male vocalist (Singles: 9 weeks)*

Date		Title / Label	pos	wks
11 Feb 78		DO YA WANNA GET FUNKY WITH ME *TK TKR 6009* [1]	43	4
17 Jun 78		DANCE WITH ME *TK TKR 6027*	57	5

[1] special background vocals: Betty Wright

Polly BROWN *UK, female vocalist (Singles: 5 weeks)*

Date		Title / Label	pos	wks
14 Sep 74		UP IN A PUFF OF SMOKE *GTO GT 2*	43	5

See also PICKETTYWITCH; SWEET DREAMS

Roy 'Chubby' BROWN *UK, male comedian – Royston Vasey (Singles: 22 weeks, Albums: 8 weeks)*

Date		Title / Label	pos	wks
13 May 95	●	LIVING NEXT DOOR TO ALICE (WHO THE F**K IS ALICE) (re) *N.O.W. CDWAG 245* [1]	3	19
21 Dec 96		ROCKIN' GOOD CHRISTMAS *PolyStar 5732612*	51	3
25 Nov 95		TAKE FAT AND PARTY *PolyStar 5297842*	29	7
7 Dec 96		FAT OUT OF HELL *PolyStar 5370602*	67	1

[1] Smokie featuring Roy 'Chubby' Brown

Sam BROWN
UK, female vocalist (Singles: 35 weeks, Albums: 30 weeks)

Date		Title / Label	pos	wks
11 Jun 88	●	STOP *A&M AM 440*	4	15
13 May 89		CAN I GET A WITNESS *A&M AM 509*	15	7
3 Mar 90		WITH A LITTLE LOVE *A&M AM 539*	44	4
5 May 90		KISSING GATE *A&M AM 549*	23	8
26 Aug 95		JUST GOOD FRIENDS *Dick Bros. DDICK 014CD1* [1]	63	1
11 Mar 89	●	STOP! *A&M AMA 5195*	4	18
14 Apr 90		APRIL MOON *A&M AMA 9014*	38	12

[1] Fish featuring Sam Brown

'Stop' reached its peak position of No.4 only on its re-entry in Feb 1989

Sharon BROWN *US, female vocalist (Singles: 11 weeks)*

Date		Title / Label	pos	wks
17 Apr 82		I SPECIALIZE IN LOVE *Virgin VS 494*	38	9
26 Feb 94		I SPECIALIZE IN LOVE (re-mix) *Deep Distraxion OILYCD 025*	62	2

Sleepy BROWN – *See OUTKAST*

BROWN SAUCE
UK, male / female vocal group (Singles: 12 weeks)

Date		Title / Label	pos	wks
12 Dec 81		I WANNA BE A WINNER *BBC RESL 101*	15	12

BROWN SUGAR – *See SEX CLUB featuring BROWN SUGAR*

Duncan BROWNE *UK, male vocalist (Singles: 8 weeks)*

Date		Title / Label	pos	wks
19 Aug 72		JOURNEY *RAK 135*	23	6
22 Dec 84		THEME FROM 'THE TRAVELLING MAN' *Towerbell TOW 64*	68	2

Jackson BROWNE *US, male vocalist / instrumentalist (Singles: 14 weeks, Albums: 38 weeks)*

Date		Title / Label	pos	wks
1 Jul 78		STAY *Asylum K 13128*	12	11
18 Oct 86		IN THE SHAPE OF A HEART *Elektra EKR 42*	66	2
25 Jun 94		EVERYWHERE I GO *Elektra EKR 184CD1*	67	1
4 Dec 76		THE PRETENDER *Asylum K 53048*	26	5
21 Jan 78		RUNNING ON EMPTY *Asylum K 53070*	28	7
12 Jul 80		HOLD OUT *Asylum K 52226* ▲	44	5
13 Aug 83		LAWYERS IN LOVE *Asylum 9602681*	37	7
8 Mar 86		LIVES IN THE BALANCE *Asylum EKT 31*	36	7
17 Jun 89		WORLD IN MOTION *Elektra EKT 50*	39	2
6 Nov 93		I'M ALIVE *Elektra 7559615242*	35	3
9 Mar 96		LOOKING EAST *Elektra 7559618672*	47	1
26 Oct 02		THE NAKED RIDE HOME *Elektra EA 7559627932*	53	1

Ronnie BROWNE – *See SCOTTISH RUGBY TEAM with Ronnie BROWNE*

Tom BROWNE

US, male instrumentalist – trumpet (Singles: 24 weeks) pos/wks

19 Jul 80	●	**FUNKIN' FOR JAMAICA (N.Y.)** *Arista ARIST 357*	10	11
25 Oct 80		**THIGHS HIGH (GRIP YOUR HIPS AND MOVE)** *Arista ARIST 367*	45	5
30 Jan 82		**FUNGI MAMA (BEBOPAFUNKADISCOLYPSO)** *Arista ARIST 450*	58	4
11 Jan 92		**FUNKIN' FOR JAMAICA (re-mix)** *Arista 114998*	45	4

BROWNS

US, male / female vocal group – Jim Ed, Maxine and Bonnie Brown (Singles: 13 weeks) pos/wks

18 Sep 59	●	**THE THREE BELLS** *RCA 1140* ▲	6	13

BROWNSTONE

US, female vocal group (Singles: 24 weeks, Albums: 16 weeks) pos/wks

1 Apr 95	●	**IF YOU LOVE ME** *MJJ 6614135*	8	12
15 Jul 95		**GRAPEVYNE** *MJJ 6620942*	16	4
23 Sep 95		**I CAN'T TELL YOU WHY** *MJJ 6623775*	27	2
17 May 97		**5 MILES TO EMPTY** *Epic 6640962*	12	4
27 Sep 97		**KISS AND TELL** *Epic 6649852*	21	2
29 Apr 95		**FROM THE BOTTOM UP** *MJJ 4773622*	18	13
31 May 97		**STILL CLIMBING** *MJJ Epic 4853882*	19	3

BROWNSVILLE STATION

US, male vocal / instrumental group (Singles: 6 weeks) pos/wks

2 Mar 74		**SMOKIN' IN THE BOYS' ROOM** *Philips 6073 834*	27	6

Dave BRUBECK QUARTET

US, male instrumental group (Singles: 30 weeks, Albums: 17 weeks) pos/wks

26Oct 61	●	**TAKE FIVE** *Fontana H 339*	6	15
8 Feb 62		**IT'S A RAGGY WALTZ** *Fontana H 352*	36	3
17 May 62		**UNSQUARE DANCE** *CBS AAG 102*	14	12
25 Jun 60		**TIME OUT** *Fontana TFL 5085*	11	1
7 Apr 62		**TIME FURTHER OUT** *Fontana TFL 5161* [1]	12	16

[1] Dave Brubeck

Tommy BRUCE and the BRUISERS

UK, male vocal / instrumental group (21 WEEKS) pos/wks

26 May 60	●	**AIN'T MISBEHAVIN'** *Columbia DB 4453*	3	16
8 Sep 60		**BROKEN DOLL** *Columbia DB 4498*	36	4
22 Feb 62		**BABETTE** *Columbia DB 4776* [1]	50	1

[1] Tommy Bruce

Jack BRUCE

UK male vocalist / instrumentalist – bass – John Asher (Albums: 9 weeks) pos/wks

27 Sep 69	●	**SONGS FOR A TAILOR** *Polydor 583058*	6	9

See also CREAM

Claudia BRÜCKEN

Germany, female vocalist (Singles: 2 weeks) pos/wks

11 Aug 90		**ABSOLUT(E)** *Island IS 471*	71	1
16 Feb 91		**KISS LIKE ETHER** *Island IS 479*	63	1

Bill BRUFORD – *See ANDERSON BRUFORD WAKEMAN HOWE; KING CRIMSON*

BRUISERS

UK, male instrumental group (Singles: 7 weeks) pos/wks

8 Aug 63		**BLUE GIRL (re)** *Parlophone R 5042*	31	7

Frank BRUNO

UK, male boxer / vocalist (Singles: 4 weeks) pos/wks

23 Dec 95		**EYE OF THE TIGER** *RCA 74321336282*	28	4

BRUNO and LIZ – *See Liz KERSHAW and Bruno BROOKES*

Tyrone BRUNSON

US, male instrumentalist – bass (Singles: 5 weeks) pos/wks

25 Dec 82		**THE SMURF** *Epic EPC A 3024*	52	5

Basil BRUSH featuring India BEAU

UK, male fox vocalist and female vocalist (Singles: 1 week) pos/wks

27 Dec 03		**BOOM BOOM / CHRISTMAS SLIDE** *Right RRBB 001*	44	1+

BRUVVERS – *See Joe BROWN and the BRUVVERS*

Dora BRYAN

UK, female actor / vocalist – Dora Broadbent (Singles: 6 weeks) pos/wks

5 Dec 63		**ALL I WANT FOR CHRISTMAS IS A BEATLE** *Fontana TF 427*	20	6

Kéllé BRYAN

UK, female vocalist (Singles: 4 weeks) pos/wks

2 Oct 99		**HIGHER THAN HEAVEN** *1st Avenue / Mercury MERCD 522*	14	4

See also ETERNAL

Anita BRYANT

US, female vocalist (Singles: 6 weeks) pos/wks

26 May 60		**PAPER ROSES (2re)** *London HLL 9144*	24	4
6 Oct 60		**MY LITTLE CORNER OF THE WORLD** *London HLL 9171*	48	2

Peabo BRYSON

US, male vocalist (Singles: 35 weeks) pos/wks

20 Aug 83	●	**TONIGHT I CELEBRATE MY LOVE** *Capitol CL 302* [1]	2	13
16 May 92	●	**BEAUTY AND THE BEAST** *Epic 6576607* [2]	9	7
17 Jul 93		**BY THE TIME THIS NIGHT IS OVER** *Arista 74321157142* [3]	56	3
11 Dec 93		**A WHOLE NEW WORLD (ALADDIN'S THEME)** *Columbia 6599002* [4] ▲	12	12

[1] Peabo Bryson and Roberta Flack [2] Celine Dion and Peabo Bryson [3] Kenny G with Peabo Bryson [4] Regina Belle and Peabo Bryson

See also Roberta FLACK

BUBBLEROCK – *See Jonathan KING*

Michael BUBLÉ

Canada, male vocalist (Albums: 11 weeks) pos/wks

18 Oct 03	●	**MICHAEL BUBLÉ** *Reprise 9362485352*	6	11+

Catherine BUCHANAN – *See JELLYBEAN*

Roy BUCHANAN

US, male instrumentalist – guitar, d. 14 Aug 1988 (Singles: 3 weeks) pos/wks

31 Mar 73		**SWEET DREAMS** *Polydor 2066 307*	40	3

BUCKETHEADS

US, male producer – Kenny Gonzalez (Singles: 16 weeks, Albums: 1 week) pos/wks

4 Mar 95	●	**THE BOMB! (THESE SOUNDS FALL INTO MY MIND)** *Positiva CDTIV 33*	5	13
20 Jan 96		**GOT MYSELF TOGETHER** *Positiva CDTIV 48*	12	3
27 Jan 96		**ALL IN THE MIND** *Positiva CDTIVA 1010*	74	1

Lindsey BUCKINGHAM

US, male vocalist (Singles: 7 weeks, Albums: 1 week) pos/wks

16 Jan 82		**TROUBLE** *Mercury MER 85*	31	7
8 Aug 92		**OUT OF THE CRADLE** *Mercury 5126582*	51	1

See also FLEETWOOD MAC

Jeff BUCKLEY

US, male vocalist / instrumentalist – guitar, d. 29 May 1997 (Singles: 3 weeks, Albums: 13 weeks) pos/wks

27 May 95		**LAST GOODBYE** *Columbia 6620422*	54	2
6 Jun 98		**EVERYBODY HERE WANTS YOU** *Columbia 6657912*	43	1
27 Aug 94		**GRACE** *Columbia 4759282*	50	7
23 May 98	●	**SKETCHES FOR MY SWEETHEART THE DRUNK** *Columbia 4886616*	7	4
20 May 00	●	**MYSTERY WHITE BOY – LIVE '95-'96** *Columbia 4979722*	8	2

BUCKS FIZZ 273 Top 500

Chart-topping mixed quartet: Cheryl Baker, Mike Nolan, Jay Aston (replaced by Shelley Preston in 1985) and Bobby G (Gubby). Formed for the 1981 Eurovision Song Contest, they were the last UK winners for 16 years (Singles: 150 weeks, Albums: 80 weeks) pos/wks

28 Mar 81 ★ MAKING YOUR MIND UP *RCA 56* 1 12
6 Jun 81 PIECE OF THE ACTION *RCA 88* 12 9
15 Aug 81 ONE OF THOSE NIGHTS *RCA 114* 20 10
28 Nov 81 ★ THE LAND OF MAKE BELIEVE *RCA 163* 1 16
27 Mar 82 ★ MY CAMERA NEVER LIES *RCA 202* 1 8
19 Jun 82 ● NOW THOSE DAYS ARE GONE *RCA 241* 8 9
27 Nov 82 ● IF YOU CAN'T STAND THE HEAT *RCA 300* 10 11
12 Mar 83 RUN FOR YOUR LIFE *RCA FIZ 1* 14 7
18 Jun 83 ● WHEN WE WERE YOUNG *RCA 342* 10 8
1 Oct 83 LONDON TOWN *RCA 363* 34 6
17 Dec 83 RULES OF THE GAME *RCA 380* 57 6
25 Aug 84 TALKING IN YOUR SLEEP *RCA FIZ 2* 15 9
27 Oct 84 GOLDEN DAYS *RCA FIZ 3* 42 4
29 Dec 84 I HEAR TALK *RCA FIZ 4* 34 8
22 Jun 85 YOU AND YOUR HEART SO BLUE *RCA PB 40233* 43 4
14 Sep 85 MAGICAL *RCA PB 40367* 57 3
7 Jun 86 ● NEW BEGINNING (MAMBA SEYRA) *Polydor POSP 794* 8 10
30 Aug 86 LOVE THE ONE YOU'RE WITH *Polydor POSP 813* 47 3
15 Nov 86 KEEP EACH OTHER WARM *Polydor POSP 835* 45 4
5 Nov 88 HEART OF STONE *RCA PB 42035* 50 3
8 Aug 81 BUCKS FIZZ *RCA RCALP 5050* 14 28
18 May 82 ● ARE YOU READY? *RCA RCALP 8000* 10 23
19 Mar 83 HAND CUT *RCA RCALP 6100* 17 13
3 Dec 83 GREATEST HITS *RCA RCA PL 70022* 25 13
24 Nov 84 I HEAR TALK *RCA PL 70397* 66 2
13 Dec 86 THE WRITING ON THE WALL *Polydor POHL 30* 89 1

BUCKSHOT LEFONQUE

US, male vocal / instrumental group (Singles: 1 week) pos/wks

6 Dec 97 ANOTHER DAY *Columbia 6653762* 65 1

Roy BUDD

UK, male instrumentalist – piano (Singles: 1 week, Albums: 1 week) pos/wks

10 Jul 99 GET CARTER *Cinephile CINX 1003* 68 1
19 Sep 98 GET CARTER (FILM SOUNDTRACK) *Cinephile CINCD 001* 68 1

Joe BUDDEN

US, male vocalist (Singles: 7 weeks, Albums: 1 week) pos/wks

19 Jul 03 PUMP IT UP *Def Jam / Mercury 9808879* 13 7
28 Jun 03 JOE BUDDEN *Def Jam / Mercury 9807936* 55 1

Harold BUDD / Liz FRASER / Robin GUTHRIE / Simon RAYMONDE

UK, male / female vocal / instrumental group (Albums: 2 weeks) pos/wks

22 Nov 86 THE MOON AND THE MELODIES *4AD CAD 611* 46 2

See also COCTEAU TWINS

BUDGIE *UK, male vocal / instrumental group (Singles: 2 weeks, Albums: 10 weeks)* pos/wks

3 Oct 81 KEEPING A RENDEZVOUS *RCA BUDGIE 3* 71 2
8 Jun 74 IN FOR THE KILL *MCA MCF 2546* 29 3
27 Sep 75 BANDOLIER *MCA MCF 2723* 36 4
31 Oct 81 NIGHT FLIGHT *RCA RCALP 6003* 68 2
23 Oct 82 DELIVER US FROM EVIL *RCA RCALP 6054* 62 1

BUFFALO G

Ireland, female vocal / rap duo – Olive Tucker and Naomi Lynch (Singles: 4 weeks) pos/wks

10 Jun 00 WE'RE REALLY SAYING SOMETHING (re) *Epic 6694182* 17 4

BUFFALO TOM *US, male vocal / instrumental group (Singles: 5 weeks, Albums: 5 weeks)* pos/wks

23 Oct 99 ● GOING UNDERGROUND: CARNATION *Ignition IGNSCD 16* 6 5
14 Mar 92 LET ME COME OVER *Situation Two SITU 36CD* 49 1
9 Oct 93 (BIG RED LETTER DAY) *Beggars Banquet BBQCD 142* 17 3
22 Jul 95 SLEEPY EYED *Beggars Banquet BBQCD 177* 31 1

B-side by: Liam Gallagher and Steve Cradock

BUG KANN and the PLASTIC JAM

UK, male / female vocal / instrumental group (Singles: 2 weeks) pos/wks

31 Aug 91 MADE IN TWO MINUTES *Optimum Dance BKPJ 1S* [1] 70 1
26 Feb 94 MADE IN 2 MINUTES (re-mix) *PWL International PWCD 286* 64 1

[1] Bug Kann and Plastic Jam featuring Patti Low and Doogie

BUGGLES *UK, male vocal / instrumental duo – Trevor Horn and Geoff Downes (Singles: 28 weeks, Albums: 6 weeks)* pos/wks

22 Sep 79 ★ VIDEO KILLED THE RADIO STAR *Island WIP 6524* 1 11
26 Jan 80 THE PLASTIC AGE *Island WIP 6540* 16 8
5 Apr 80 CLEAN, CLEAN *Island WIP 6584* 38 5
8 Nov 80 ELSTREE *Island WIP 6624* 55 4
16 Feb 80 THE AGE OF PLASTIC *Island ILPS 9585* 27 6

LTJ BUKEM *UK, male DJ / producer – Danny Williamson (Albums: 3 weeks)* pos/wks

8 Apr 00 JOURNEY INWARDS *Good Looking GLRAA 001* 40 3

James BULLER *UK, male vocalist (Singles: 1 week)* pos/wks

6 Mar 99 CAN'T SMILE WITHOUT YOU *BBC Music WMSS 60092* 51 1

Silvah BULLET – *See* Jonny L

BULLETPROOF

UK, male producer – Paul Chambers (Singles: 1 week) pos/wks

10 Mar 01 SAY YEAH / DANCE TO THE RHYTHM *Tidy Trax TIDY 148CD* 62 1

BUMP *UK, male instrumental / production duo – Marc Auerbach and Steve Travell (Singles: 5 weeks)* pos/wks

4 Jul 92 I'M RUSHING *Good Boy EDGE7 1* 40 4
11 Nov 95 I'M RUSHING (re-mix) *Deconstruction 74321320692* 45 1

BUMP & FLEX

UK, male / female vocal / production duo (Singles: 1 week) pos/wks

23 May 98 LONG TIME COMING *Heat Recordings HEATCD 014* 73 1

BUNKER KRU – *See* HARLEQUIN 4s / BUNKER KRU

BUNNYMEN – *See* ECHO and the BUNNYMEN

Emma BUNTON

UK, female vocalist (Singles: 56 weeks, Albums: 12 weeks) pos/wks

13 Nov 99 ● WHAT I AM *VC Recordings VCRD 53* [1] 2 12
14 Apr 01 ★ WHAT TOOK YOU SO LONG *Virgin VSCDT 1796* ■ 1 12
8 Sep 01 ● TAKE MY BREATH AWAY *Virgin VSCDT 1814* 5 9
22 Dec 01 WE'RE NOT GONNA SLEEP TONIGHT *Virgin VSCDT 1821* 20 5
7 Jun 03 ● FREE ME *19 / Universal 9807472* [2] 5 9
25 Oct 03 ● MAYBE *19 / Universal 9812785* [2] 6 9
28 Apr 01 ● A GIRL LIKE ME *Virgin CDV 2935* 4 12

[1] Tin Tin Out featuring Emma Bunton [2] Emma

See also SPICE GIRLS

Eric BURDON and WAR *UK, male vocalist and US, male vocal / instrumental group (Albums: 4 weeks)* pos/wks

3 Oct 70 ERIC BURDON DECLARES WAR *Polydor 2310041* 50 2
20 Feb 71 BLACKMAN'S BURDON *Liberty LDS 8400* 25 2

See also ANIMALS; WAR

Tim BURGESS

UK, male vocalist (Singles: 2 weeks, Albums: 1 week) pos/wks

6 Sep 03 I BELIEVE IN THE SPIRIT *PIAS Recordings PIASB 109CD* 44 1

15 Nov 03 **ONLY A BOY** *PIAS Recordings PIASB 119CD* 54 1
20 Sep 03 **I BELIEVE** *PIAS PIASB099CD* 38 1

See also CHARLATANS; ST ETIENNE

Geoffrey BURGON *UK, orchestra (Singles: 4 weeks)* pos/wks

26 Dec 81 **BRIDESHEAD THEME** *Chrysalis CHS 2562* 48 4

Keni BURKE *US, male vocalist (Singles: 4 weeks)* pos/wks

27 Jun 81 **LET SOMEBODY LOVE YOU** *RCA 93* 59 3
18 Apr 92 **RISIN' TO THE TOP** *RCA PB 49103* 70 1

Solomon BURKE – *See JUNKIE XL*

BURN *UK, male vocal / instrumental group (Singles: 2 weeks)* pos/wks

8 Jun 02 **THE SMILING FACE** *Hut / Virgin HUTCD 155* 72 1
29 Mar 03 **DRUNKEN FOOL** *Hut / Virgin HUTCD 166* 54 1

Jean-Jacques BURNEL
UK, male vocalist / instrumentalist – bass guitar (Albums: 6 weeks) pos/wks

21 Apr 79 **EUROMAN COMETH** *United Artists UAG 30214* 40 5
3 Dec 83 **FIRE AND WATER** *Epic EPC 25707* [1] 94 1

[1] Dave Greenfield and Jean-Jacques Burnel

See also Dave GREENFIELD; STRANGLERS

Hank C BURNETTE *Sweden, male multi-instrumentalist – Sven-Ake Hogberg (Singles: 8 weeks)* pos/wks

30 Oct 76 **SPINNING ROCK BOOGIE** *Sonet SON 2094* 21 8

Johnny BURNETTE
US, male vocalist, d. 1 Aug 1964 (Singles: 48 weeks) pos/wks

29 Sep 60 ● **DREAMIN'** *London HLG 9172* 5 16
12 Jan 61 ● **YOU'RE SIXTEEN** *London HLG 9254* 3 12
13 Apr 61 **LITTLE BOY SAD** *London HLG 9315* 12 12
10 Aug 61 **GIRLS** *London HLG 9388* 37 5
17 May 62 **CLOWN SHOES** *Liberty LIB 55416* 35 3

Rocky BURNETTE *US, male vocalist (Singles: 7 weeks)* pos/wks

17 Nov 79 **TIRED OF TOEIN' THE LINE** *EMI 2992* 58 7

Jerry BURNS *UK, female vocalist (Singles: 1 week)* pos/wks

25 Apr 92 **PALE RED** *Columbia 6579467* 64 1

Ray BURNS *UK, male vocalist (Singles: 19 weeks)* pos/wks

11 Feb 55 ● **MOBILE** *Columbia DB 3563* [1] 4 13
26 Aug 55 **THAT'S HOW A LOVE SONG WAS BORN** *Columbia DB 3640* [2] 14 6

[1] Ray Burns with Eric Jupp and His Orchestra [2] Ray Burns with the Coronets

BURRELLS – *See RESONANCE featuring The BURRELLS*

Malandra BURROWS *UK, female vocalist (Singles: 10 weeks)* pos/wks

1 Dec 90 **JUST THIS SIDE OF LOVE** *Yorkshire Television DALE 1* 11 8
18 Oct 97 **CARNIVAL IN HEAVEN** *Warner.esp WESP 001CD* 49 1
29 Aug 98 **DON'T LEAVE ME** *Warner.esp WESP 004CD* 54 1

Jenny BURTON *US, female vocalist (Singles: 2 weeks)* pos/wks

30 Mar 85 **BAD HABITS** *Atlantic A 9583* 68 2

BURUNDI STEIPHENSON BLACK
Burundi, drummers and chanters with orchestral additions by Mike Steiphenson of France (Singles: 14 weeks) pos/wks

13 Nov 71 **BURUNDI BLACK** *Barclay BAR 3* 31 14

BUS 75 – *See WHALE*

BUS STOP *UK, male production group (Singles: 19 weeks)* pos/wks

23 May 98 ● **KUNG FU FIGHTING** *All Around the World CDGLOBE 173* [1] 8 11
24 Oct 98 **YOU AIN'T SEEN NOTHIN' YET** *All Around the World CDGLOBE 187* [2] 22 4
10 Apr 99 **JUMP** *All Around the World CDGLOBE 186* 23 3
7 Sep 00 **GET IT ON** *All Around the World CDGLOBE225* [3] 59 1

[1] Bus Stop featuring Carl Douglas [2] Bus Stop featuring Randy Bachman [3] Bus Stop featuring T. Rex

See also FLIP & FILL

Lou BUSCH and his ORCHESTRA *US, orchestra and chorus – aka Joe 'Fingers' Carr, d. 19 Sep 1979 (Singles: 17 weeks)* pos/wks

27 Jan 56 ● **ZAMBESI** *Capitol CL 14504* 2 17

BUSH *UK, male vocal / instrumental group (Singles: 13 weeks, Albums: 18 weeks)* pos/wks

8 Jun 96 **MACHINEHEAD** *Interscope IND 95505* 48 2
1 Mar 97 ● **SWALLOWED** *Interscope IND 95528* 7 5
7 Jun 97 **GREEDY FLY** *Interscope IND 95536* 22 2
1 Nov 97 **BONE DRIVEN** *Interscope IND 95553* 49 1
4 Dec 99 **THE CHEMICALS BETWEEN US** *Trauma / Polydor 4972222* 46 1
18 Mar 00 **WARM MACHINE** *Trauma / Polydor 4972752* 45 1
3 Jun 00 **LETTING THE CABLES SLEEP** *Trauma / Polydor 4973352* 51 1
15 Jun 96 **SIXTEEN STONE** *Atlantic 6544925312* 42 3
1 Feb 97 ● **RAZORBLADE SUITCASE** *Interscope IND 90091* ▲ 4 12
6 Nov 99 **THE SCIENCE OF THINGS** *Trauma/Polydor 4904832* 28 2
10 Nov 01 **GOLDEN STATE** *Atlantic 7567834882* 53 1

Kate BUSH (91 Top 500)
Unmistakable singer / songwriter with operatic vocal ability, b. 30 Jul 1958, Kent. Discovered by Dave Gilmour of Pink Floyd. First British female to top the singles chart with a self-composed song and the first to have a UK No.1 album (Singles: 168 weeks, Albums: 281 weeks) pos/wks

11 Feb 78 ★ **WUTHERING HEIGHTS (re)** *EMI 2719* 1 13
10 Jun 78 ● **THE MAN WITH THE CHILD IN HIS EYES** *EMI 2806* 6 11
11 Nov 78 **HAMMER HORROR** *EMI 2887* 44 6
17 Mar 79 **WOW** *EMI 2911* 14 10
15 Sep 79 ● **ON STAGE (EP)** *EMI MIEP 2991* 10 9
26 Apr 80 **BREATHING** *EMI 5058* 16 7
5 Jul 80 ● **BABOOSHKA** *EMI 5085* 5 10
4 Oct 80 **ARMY DREAMERS** *EMI 5106* 16 9
6 Dec 80 **DECEMBER WILL BE MAGIC AGAIN** *EMI 5121* 29 7
11 Jul 81 **SAT IN YOUR LAP** *EMI 5201* 11 7
7 Aug 82 **THE DREAMING** *EMI 5296* 48 3
17 Aug 85 ● **RUNNING UP THAT HILL** *EMI KB 1* 3 11
26 Oct 85 **CLOUDBUSTING** *EMI KB 2* 20 6
1 Mar 86 **HOUNDS OF LOVE** *EMI KB 3* 18 5
10 May 86 **THE BIG SKY** *EMI KB 4* 37 3
1 Nov 86 ● **DON'T GIVE UP** *Virgin PGS 2* [1] 9 11
8 Nov 86 **EXPERIMENT IV** *EMI KB 5* 23 4
30 Sep 89 **THE SENSUAL WORLD** *EMI EM 102* 12 5
2 Dec 89 **THIS WOMAN'S WORK** *EMI EM 119* 25 5
10 Mar 90 **LOVE AND ANGER** *EMI EM 134* 38 3
7 Dec 91 **ROCKET MAN (I THINK IT'S GOING TO BE A LONG LONG TIME)** *Mercury TRIBO 2* 12 8
18 Sep 93 **RUBBERBAND GIRL** *EMI CDEM 280* 12 5
27 Nov 93 **MOMENTS OF PLEASURE** *EMI CDEM 297* 26 3
16 Apr 94 **THE RED SHOES** *EMI CDEMS 316* 21 3
30 Jul 94 **THE MAN I LOVE** *Mercury MERCD 408* [2] 27 2
19 Nov 94 **AND SO IS LOVE** *EMI CDEMS 355* 26 2
11 Mar 78 ● **THE KICK INSIDE** *EMI EMC 3223* 3 70
25 Nov 78 ● **LIONHEART** *EMI EMA 787* 6 36
20 Sep 80 ★ **NEVER FOR EVER** *EMI EMA 7964* ■ 1 23
25 Sep 82 ● **THE DREAMING** *EMI EMC 3419* 3 10
28 Sep 85 ★ **HOUNDS OF LOVE** *EMI KAB 1* ■ 1 52
22 Nov 86 ★ **THE WHOLE STORY** *EMI KBTV 1* 1 55
28 Oct 89 ● **THE SENSUAL WORLD** *EMI EMD 1010* 2 20
13 Nov 93 ● **THE RED SHOES** *EMI CDEMD 1047* 2 15

[1] Peter Gabriel and Kate Bush [2] Kate Bush and Larry Adler

Tracks on On Stage (EP): Them Heavy People / Don't Push Your Foot on the Heartbrake / James and the Cold Gun / L'Amour Looks Something Like You

BUSTED *UK, male vocal / instrumental group (Singles: 53 weeks, Albums: 60 weeks)* pos/wks

28 Sep 02 ● **WHAT I GO TO SCHOOL FOR** *Universal MCSTD 40294* 3 12
25 Jan 03 ● **YEAR 3000** *Universal MCSTD 40306* 2 15
3 May 03 ★ **YOU SAID NO** *Universal MCSTD 40318* ■ 1 10
23 Aug 03 ● **SLEEPING WITH THE LIGHT ON** *Universal MCSTD 40327* 3 10
22 Nov 03 ★ **CRASHED THE WEDDING** *Universal MCSTD 40345* ■ ....1 6+
12 Oct 02 ● **BUSTED** *Universal MCD 60084* ....2 55+
29 Nov 03 ● **A PRESENT FOR EVERYONE** *Universal MCD60090* ....2 5+

BUSTER *UK, male vocal / instrumental group (Singles: 1 week)* pos/wks

19 Jun 76 **SUNDAY** *RCA 2678* 49 1

Bernard BUTLER
UK, male vocal / instrumentalist (Singles: 9 weeks, Albums: 9 weeks) pos/wks

17 Jan 98 **STAY** *Creation CRESCD 281* 12 4
28 Mar 98 **NOT ALONE** *Creation CRESCD 289* 27 3
27 Jun 98 **A CHANGE OF HEART** *Creation CRESCD 297* 45 1
23 Oct 99 **YOU MUST GO ON** *Creation CRESCD 324* 44 1
18 Apr 98 **PEOPLE MOVE ON** *Creation CCRE 221* 11 8
6 Nov 99 **FRIENDS AND LOVERS** *Creation CRECD 248* 43 1

See also SUEDE; McALMONT and BUTLER

Jonathan BUTLER *South Africa, male vocalist / instrumentalist – guitar (Singles: 18 weeks, Albums: 14 weeks)* pos/wks

25 Jan 86 **IF YOU'RE READY (COME GO WITH ME)** *Jive JIVE 109* [1] 30 7
8 Aug 87 **LIES** *Jive JIVE 141* 18 11
12 Sep 87 **JONATHAN BUTLER** *Jive HIP 46* 12 11
4 Feb 89 **MORE THAN FRIENDS** *Jive HIP 70* 29 3

[1] Ruby Turner featuring Jonathan Butler

BUTTERSCOTCH
UK, male vocal group (Singles: 11 weeks) pos/wks

2 May 70 **DON'T YOU KNOW (SHE SAID HELLO)** *RCA 1937* 17 11

BUTTHOLE SURFERS *US, male vocal / instrumental group (Singles: 1 week, Albums: 2 weeks)* pos/wks

5 Oct 96 **PEPPER** *Capitol CDCL 778* 59 1
16 Mar 91 **PIOUHGD** *Rough Trade R 20812601* 68 1
3 Apr 93 **INDEPENDENT WORM SALOON** *Capitol CDEST 2192* 73 1

BUZZCOCKS *UK, male vocal / instrumental group (Singles: 53 weeks, Albums: 23 weeks)* pos/wks

18 Feb 78 **WHAT DO I GET?** *United Artists UP 36348* 37 3
13 May 78 **I DON'T MIND** *United Artists UP 36386* 55 2
15 Jul 78 **LOVE YOU MORE** *United Artists UP 36433* 34 6
23 Sep 78 **EVER FALLEN IN LOVE (WITH SOMEONE YOU SHOULDN'T'VE)** *United Artists UP 36455* 12 11
25 Nov 78 **PROMISES** *United Artists UP 36471* 20 10
10 Mar 79 **EVERYBODY'S HAPPY NOWADAYS** *United Artists UP 36499* ..29 6
21 Jul 79 **HARMONY IN MY HEAD** *United Artists UP 36541* 32 6
25 Aug 79 **SPIRAL SCRATCH (EP)** *New Hormones ORG 1* 31 6
6 Sep 80 **ARE EVERYTHING / WHY SHE'S A GIRL FROM THE CHAINSTORE** *United Artists BP 365* 61 3
25 Mar 78 **ANOTHER MUSIC IN A DIFFERENT KITCHEN** *United Artists UAG 30159* 15 11
7 Oct 78 **LOVE BITES** *United Artists UAG 30184* 13 9
6 Oct 79 **A DIFFERENT KIND OF TENSION** *United Artists UAG 30260* 26 3

Tracks on Spiral Scratch (EP): Breakdown / Time's Up / Boredom / Friends of Mine. Sleeve of EP (not the label) credits Buzzcocks with Howard Devoto. 'Why She's a Girl from the Chainstore' listed from 13 Sep 1980

BUZZY BUNCH – *See Celi BEE and the BUZZY BUNCH*

BY ALL MEANS
US, male vocal group (Singles: 2 weeks, Albums: 1 week) pos/wks

18 Jun 88 **I SURRENDER TO YOUR LOVE** *Fourth & Broadway BRW 102* ..65 2
16 Jul 88 **BY ALL MEANS** *Fourth & Broadway BRLP 520* 80 1

Max BYGRAVES (182 Top 500)
One of Britain's best-loved entertainers, b. 16 Oct, 1922, London. The comedian / singer / songwriter was the only British male in the first UK singles chart. He had five Top 20 'sing-a-long' hit albums in just 15 months of the 1970s (Singles: 131 weeks, Albums: 176 weeks) pos/wks

14 Nov 52 ● **COWPUNCHER'S CANTATA (3re)** *HMV B 10250* 6 8
14 May 54 ● **(THE GANG THAT SANG) HEART OF MY HEART** *HMV B 10654* ..7 8
10 Sep 54 ● **GILLY GILLY OSSENFEFFER KATZENELLEN BOGEN BY THE SEA (re)** *HMV B 10734* 7 8
21 Jan 55 **MISTER SANDMAN** *HMV B 10801* 16 1
18 Nov 55 ● **MEET ME ON THE CORNER** *HMV POP 116* 2 11
17 Feb 56 **THE BALLAD OF DAVY CROCKETT** *HMV POP 153* 20 1
25 May 56 **OUT OF TOWN** *HMV POP 164* 18 7
5 Apr 57 **HEART** *Decca F 10862* [1] 14 8
2 May 58 ● **YOU NEED HANDS / TULIPS FROM AMSTERDAM** *Decca F 11004* [2] 3 25
22 Aug 58 **LITTLE TRAIN / GOTTA HAVE RAIN** *Decca F 11046* 28 2
2 Jan 59 **(I LOVE TO PLAY) MY UKULELE** *Decca F 11077* 19 4
18 Dec 59 ● **JINGLE BELL ROCK** *Decca F 11176* 7 4
10 Mar 60 ● **FINGS AIN'T WOT THEY USED T'BE** *Decca F 11214* 5 15
28 Jul 60 **CONSIDER YOURSELF** *Decca F 11251* 50 1
1 Jun 61 **THE BELLS OF AVIGNON** *Decca F 11350* 36 5
19 Feb 69 **YOU'RE MY EVERYTHING (re)** *Pye 7N 17705* 34 4
6 Oct 73 **DECK OF CARDS** *Pye 7N 45276* 13 15
9 Dec 89 **WHITE CHRISTMAS** *Parkfield PMS 5012* 71 4
23 Sep 72 ● **SING ALONG WITH MAX** *Pye NSPL 18361* 4 44
2 Dec 72 **SING ALONG WITH MAX VOLUME 2** *Pye NSPL 18383* 11 23
5 May 73 ● **SINGALONGAMAX VOLUME 3** *Pye NSPL 18401* 5 30
29 Sep 73 ● **SINGALONGAMAX VOLUME 4** *Pye NSPL 18410* 7 12
15 Dec 73 **SINGALONGPARTY SONG** *Pye NSPL 18419* 15 6
12 Oct 74 **YOU MAKE ME FEEL LIKE SINGING A SONG** *Pye NSPL 18436* 39 3
7 Dec 74 **SINGALONGAXMAS** *Pye NSPL 18439* 21 6
13 Nov 76 ● **100 GOLDEN GREATS** *Ronco RTDX 2019* 3 21
28 Oct 78 **LINGALONGAMAX** *Ronco RPL 2033* 39 5
16 Dec 78 **THE SONG AND DANCE MEN** *Pye NSPL 18574* 67 1
19 Aug 89 ● **SINGALONGAWARYEARS** *Parkfield Music PMLP 5001* 5 19
25 Nov 89 **SINGALONGAWARYEARS VOLUME 2** *Parkfield Music PMLP 5006* 33 6

[1] Max Bygraves with Malcolm Lockyer and his Orchestra [2] Max Bygraves with the Clark Bros and both sides with Eric Rodgers and his Orchestra

Cowpuncher's Cantata is a medley with the following songs: Cry of the Wild Goose / Riders in the Sky / Mule Train / Jezebel. 'Tulips from Amsterdam' was listed with 'You Need Hands' from 9 May 1958

BYKER GROOOVE! *UK, female vocal group (Singles: 3 weeks)* pos/wks

24 Dec 94 **LOVE YOUR SEXY . . . !!** *Groove GROVD 01* 48 3

Charlie BYRD – *See Stan GETZ*

Debra BYRD – *See Barry MANILOW*

Donald BYRD *US, male instrumentalist – trumpet (Singles: 6 weeks, Albums: 3 weeks)* pos/wks

26 Sep 81 **LOVING YOU / LOVE HAS COME AROUND** *Elektra K 12559* 41 6
10 Oct 81 **LOVE BYRD** *Elektra K 52301* 70 3

Gary BYRD and the GB EXPERIENCE *US, male rapper and male / female vocal / instrumental group (Singles: 9 weeks)* pos/wks

23 Jul 83 ● **THE CROWN** *Motown TMGT 1312* 6 9

Features uncredited vocals by Stevie Wonder

BYRDS *US, male vocal / instrumental group (Singles: 52 weeks, Albums: 42 weeks)* pos/wks

17 Jun 65 ★ **MR TAMBOURINE MAN** *CBS 201765* ▲ 1 14
12 Aug 65 ● **ALL I REALLY WANT TO DO** *CBS 201796* 4 10
11 Nov 65 **TURN! TURN! TURN! (TO EVERYTHING THERE IS A SEASON** *CBS 202008* ▲ 26 8
5 May 66 **EIGHT MILES HIGH** *CBS 202067* 24 9
5 Jun 68 **YOU AIN'T GOING NOWHERE** *CBS 3411* 45 3

Date		Title / Label	pos	wks
13 Feb 71		**CHESTNUT MARE** *CBS 5322*	19	8
28 Aug 65	●	**MR TAMBOURINE MAN** *CBS BPG 62571*	7	12
9 Apr 66		**TURN TURN TURN** *CBS BPG 62652*	11	5
1 Oct 66		**5TH DIMENSION** *CBS BPG 62783*	27	2
22 Apr 67		**YOUNGER THAN YESTERDAY** *CBS SBPG 62988*	37	4
4 May 68		**THE NOTORIOUS BYRD BROTHERS** *CBS 63169*	12	11
24 May 69		**DR BYRDS AND MR HYDE** *CBS 63545*	15	1
14 Feb 70		**BALLAD OF EASY RIDER** *CBS 63795*	41	1
28 Nov 70		**UNTITLED** *CBS 66253*	11	4
14 Apr 73		**BYRDS** *Asylum SYLA 8754*	31	1
19 May 73		**HISTORY OF THE BYRDS** *CBS 68242*	47	1

David BYRNE

UK, male vocalist / instrumentalist (Albums: 18 weeks) pos/wks

Date		Title / Label	pos	wks
20 Apr 02	●	**LAZY** *Skint SKINT 74CD* [1]	2	13
21 Feb 81		**MY LIFE IN THE BUSH OF GHOSTS** *Polydor EGLP 48* [1]	29	8
21 Oct 89		**REI MOMO** *Warner Bros. WX 319*	52	2
14 Mar 92		**UH-OH** *Luaka Bop 7599267992*	26	5
4 Jun 94		**DAVID BYRNE** *Luaka Bop 9362455582*	44	2
19 May 01		**LOOK INTO THE EYEBALL** *Luaka Bop CDVUS 189*	58	1

[1] X-Press 2 featuring David Byrne [1] Brian Eno and David Byrne

See also TALKING HEADS; X-PRESS 2

Edward BYRNES and Connie STEVENS

US, male / female actors / vocal duo – Edward Brietenberger and Concetta Ingolia (Singles: 8 weeks) pos/wks

Date		Title / Label	pos	wks
5 May 60		**KOOKIE KOOKIE (LEND ME YOUR COMB)** *Warner Bros. WB 5*	27	8

BYSTANDERS

UK, male vocal / instrumental group (Singles: 1 week) pos/wks

Date		Title / Label	pos	wks
9 Feb 67		**98.6** *Piccadilly 7N 35363*	45	1

Andy C – *See SHIMON & Andy C*

Melanie C (418 Top 500)

Former Sporty Spice, (b. Melanie Chisholm, 12 Jan 1974, Liverpool, UK) has appeared on 11 No.1 hits – a total never bettered by any female artist. She is the only woman to top the UK chart solo and as part of a duo, quartet and quintet (Singles: 87 weeks, Albums: 72 weeks) pos/wks

Date		Title / Label	pos	wks
12 Dec 98	●	**WHEN YOU'RE GONE** *A&M 5828212* [1]	3	19
9 Oct 99	●	**GOIN' DOWN (re)** *Virgin VSCDT 1744*	4	6
4 Dec 99	●	**NORTHERN STAR** *Virgin VSCDT 1748*	4	11
1 Apr 00	★	**NEVER BE THE SAME AGAIN** *Virgin VSCDT 1762* [2] ■	1	16
19 Aug 00	★	**I TURN TO YOU** *Virgin VSCDT 1772* ■	1	12
9 Dec 00		**IF THAT WERE ME (re)** *Virgin VSCDT 1786*	18	10
8 Mar 03	●	**HERE IT COMES AGAIN (re)** *Virgin VSCDT 1842*	7	8
14 Jun 03		**ON THE HORIZON (re)** *Virgin VSCDT 1851*	14	3
22 Nov 03		**MELT / YEH YEH YEH** *Virgin VSCDX 1858*	27	2
30 Oct 99	●	**NORTHERN STAR** *Virgin CDVX 2893*	4	68
22 Mar 03	●	**REASON** *Virgin CDV2969*	5	4

[1] Bryan Adams featuring Melanie C [2] Melanie C / Lisa 'Left Eye' Lopes

See also SPICE GIRLS

Roy C

US, male vocalist – Roy C Hammond (Singles: 24 weeks) pos/wks

Date		Title / Label	pos	wks
21 Apr 66	●	**SHOTGUN WEDDING** *Island WI 273*	6	11
25 Nov 72	●	**SHOTGUN WEDDING (re-issue)** *UK 19*	8	13

C & C MUSIC FACTORY

US, male instrumental / production duo – Robert Clivilles and David Cole (d. 24 Jan 1995) featuring male / female vocalists / rappers. (Singles: 53 weeks, Albums: 14 weeks) pos/wks

Date		Title / Label	pos	wks
15 Dec 90	●	**GONNA MAKE YOU SWEAT (EVERYBODY DANCE NOW)** *CBS 6564540* [1] ▲	3	12
30 Mar 91		**HERE WE GO** *Columbia 6567557* [1]	20	7
6 Jul 91	●	**THINGS THAT MAKE YOU GO HMMM...** *Columbia 6566907* [1]	4	11
23 Nov 91		**JUST A TOUCH OF LOVE (EVERYDAY)** *Columbia 6575247* [2]	31	3
18 Jan 92		**PRIDE (IN THE NAME OF LOVE)** *Columbia 6577017* [3]	15	5
14 Mar 92		**A DEEPER LOVE** *Columbia 6578497* [3]	15	5
3 Oct 92		**KEEP IT COMIN' (DANCE TILL YOU CAN'T DANCE NO MORE)** *Columbia 6584307* [4]	34	3
27 Aug 94		**DO YOU WANNA GET FUNKY** *Columbia 6607622*	27	3
18 Feb 95		**I FOUND LOVE / TAKE A TOKE** *Columbia 6612112* [5]	26	2
11 Nov 95		**I'LL ALWAYS BE AROUND** *MCA MCSTD 40001*	42	2
9 Feb 91	●	**GONNA MAKE YOU SWEAT** *Columbia 4678141* [1]	8	13
28 Mar 92		**GREATEST REMIXES VOLUME 1** *Columbia 4694462* [2]	45	1

[1] C & C Music Factory (featuring Freedom Williams) [2] C & C Music Factory featuring Zelma Davis [3] Clivilles and Cole [4] C & C Music Factory featuring Q Unique and Deborah Cooper [5] C & C Music Factory / C & C Music Factory featuring Martha Wash [1] C&C Music Factory [2] Clivilles and Cole

C.C.S.

UK, male vocal / instrumental group (Singles: 55 weeks, Albums: 5 weeks) pos/wks

Date		Title / Label	pos	wks
31 Oct 70		**WHOLE LOTTA LOVE** *RAK 104*	13	13
27 Feb 71	●	**WALKIN'** *RAK 109*	7	16
4 Sep 71	●	**TAP TURNS ON THE WATER** *RAK 119*	5	13
4 Mar 72		**BROTHER** *RAK 126*	25	8
4 Aug 73		**THE BAND PLAYED THE BOOGIE** *RAK 154*	36	5
8 Apr 72		**CCS** *RAK SRAK 503*	23	5

CJ & CO

US, male vocal / instrumental group (Singles: 2 weeks) pos/wks

Date		Title / Label	pos	wks
30 Jul 77		**DEVIL'S GUN** *Atlantic K 10956*	43	2

CK & SUPREME TEAM

Holland / Belgium / US, production trio (Singles: 3 weeks) pos/wks

Date		Title / Label	pos	wks
11 Jan 03		**DREAMER** *Multiply CDMULTY 96*	23	3

CLS

US, male vocal / production duo (Singles: 1 week) pos/wks

Date		Title / Label	pos	wks
30 May 98		**CAN YOU FEEL IT** *Satellite 74321580162*	46	1

CM2 featuring Lisa LAW

UK, male production group and female vocalist (Singles: 1 week) pos/wks

Date		Title / Label	pos	wks
18 Jan 03		**FALL AT YOUR FEET** *Dance Pool 6732532*	66	1

C.O.D

US, male vocal / instrumental group (Singles: 2 weeks) pos/wks

Date		Title / Label	pos	wks
14 May 83		**IN THE BOTTLE** *Streetwave WAVE 2*	54	2

CRW

Italy, male producer – Mauro Picotto (Singles: 8 weeks) pos/wks

Date		Title / Label	pos	wks
26 Feb 00		**I FEEL LOVE** *VC Recordings VCRD 63*	15	4
25 Nov 00		**LOVIN'** *VC Recordings VCRD 77*	49	2

27 Apr 02 **LIKE A CAT** *BXR BXRC 0397* [1] 57 1
26 Oct 02 **PRECIOUS LIFE** *BXR BXRC 0395* [2] 57 1

[1] CRW featuring Veronika [2] CRW presents Veronika

See also Mauro PICOTTO

CZR featuring DELANO

US, male production group and US, male vocalist (Singles: 1 week) pos/wks

30 Sep 00 **I WANT YOU** *Credence CDCRED 002* 57 1

ÇA VA ÇA VA

UK, male vocal / instrumental group (Singles: 8 weeks) pos/wks

18 Sep 82 **WHERE'S ROMEO** *Regard RG 103* 49 5
19 Feb 83 **BROTHER BRIGHT** *Regard RG 105* 65 3

Montserrat CABALLÉ *Spain, female vocalist (Albums: 11 weeks)* pos/wks

22 Oct 88 **BARCELONA** *Polydor POLH 44* [1] 15 8
8 Aug 92 **FROM THE OFFICIAL BARCELONA GAMES CEREMONY** *RCA Red Seal 09026612042* [2] 41 3

[1] Freddie Mercury and Montserrat Caballé [2] Placido Domingo, José Carreras and Montserrat Caballé

CABANA

Brazil, male / female vocal / instrumental duo (Singles: 1 week) pos/wks

15 Jul 95 **BAILANDO CON LOBOS** *Hi-Life 5792512* 65 1

CABARET VOLTAIRE *UK, male vocal / instrumental group (Singles: 8 weeks, Albums: 11 weeks)* pos/wks

18 Jul 87 **DON'T ARGUE** *Parlophone R 6157* 69 2
4 Nov 89 **HYPNOTISED** *Parlophone R 6227* 66 2
12 May 90 **KEEP ON** *Parlophone R 6250* 55 2
18 Aug 90 **EASY LIFE** *Parlophone R 6261* 61 2
26 Jun 82 **2 X 45** *Rough Trade ROUGH 42* 98 1
13 Aug 83 **THE CRACKDOWN** *Some Bizzare CV 1* 31 5
10 Nov 84 **MICRO-PHONIES** *Some Bizzare CV 2* 69 1
3 Aug 85 **DRINKING GASOLINE** *Some Bizzare CVM 1* 71 2
26 Oct 85 **THE COVENANT THE SWORD AND THE ARM OF THE LORD** *Some Bizzare CV 3* 57 2

CABLE *UK, male vocal / instrumental group (Singles: 2 weeks)* pos/wks

14 Jun 97 **FREEZE THE ATLANTIC** *Infectious INFECT 38CD* 44 2

Albert CABRERA – *See David MORALES*

CACIQUE

UK, male / female vocal / instrumental group (Singles: 1 week) pos/wks

1 Jun 85 **DEVOTED TO YOU** *Diamond Duel DISC 1* 69 1

CACTUS WORLD NEWS *Ireland, male vocal / instrumental group (Singles: 7 weeks, Albums: 2 weeks)* pos/wks

8 Feb 86 **YEARS LATER** *MCA MCA 1024* 59 3
26 Apr 86 **WORLDS APART** *MCA MCA 1040* 58 3
20 Sep 86 **THE BRIDGE** *MCA MCA 1080* 74 1
24 May 86 **URBAN BEACHES** *MCA MCG 6005* 56 2

CADETS with Eileen REID *Ireland, male / female vocal / instrumental group (Singles: 1 week)* pos/wks

3 Jun 65 **JEALOUS HEART** *Pye 7N 15852* 42 1

Susan CADOGAN *Jamaica, female vocalist (Singles: 19 weeks)* pos/wks

5 Apr 75 ● **HURT SO GOOD** *Magnet MAG 23* 4 12
19 Jul 75 **LOVE ME BABY** *Magnet MAG 36* 22 7

CAESARS

Sweden, male vocal / instrumental group (Singles: 1 week) pos/wks

19 Apr 03 **JERK IT OUT** *Virgin DINSD 244* 60 1

Athena CAGE – *See Keith SWEAT*

Al CAIOLA *US, orchestra – Al Caiola – guitar (Singles: 6 weeks)* pos/wks

15 Jun 61 **THE MAGNIFICENT SEVEN** *HMV POP 889 / LONDON HLT 9294* 34 6

CAKE *US, male vocal / instrumental group (Singles: 7 weeks, Albums: 2 weeks)* pos/wks

22 Mar 97 **THE DISTANCE** *Capricorn 5742212* 22 3
31 May 97 **I WILL SURVIVE** *Capricorn 5744712* 29 2
1 May 99 **NEVER THERE** *Capricorn 8708112* 66 1
3 Nov 01 **SHORT SKIRT LONG JACKET** *Columbia 6720402* 63 1
5 Apr 97 **FASHION NUGGET** *Capricorn 5328672* 53 2

J.J. CALE

US, male vocalist / instrumentalist – guitar (Albums: 24 weeks) pos/wks

2 Oct 76 **TROUBADOUR** *Island ISA 5011* 53 1
25 Aug 79 **5** *Shelter ISA 5018* 40 6
21 Feb 81 **SHADES** *Shelter ISA 5021* 44 7
20 Mar 82 **GRASSHOPPER** *Shelter IFA 5022* 36 5
24 Sep 83 **#8** *Mercury MERL 22* 47 3
26 Sep 92 **NUMBER 10** *Silvertone ORECD 523* 58 2

John CALE – *See Lou REED; VELVET UNDERGROUND*

CALEXICO *US, male vocal / instrumental group (Albums: 2 weeks)* pos/wks

20 May 00 **HOT RAIL** *City Slang 201532* 57 1
22 Feb 03 **FEAST OF WIRE** *City Slang 5816932* 71 1

CALIBRE CUTS – *See VARIOUS ARTISTS (MONTAGES)*

CALIFORNIA SUNSHINE

Israel / Italy, male / female DJ / production group (Singles: 1 week) pos/wks

16 Aug 97 **SUMMER '89** *Perfecto PERF 143CD* 56 1

CALL *US, male vocal / instrumental group (Singles: 6 weeks)* pos/wks

30 Sep 89 **LET THE DAY BEGIN** *MCA MCA 1362* 42 6

Maria CALLAS *Greece, female vocalist – Cecilia Kalogeropoulou, d. 16 Sep 1978 (Albums: 19 weeks)* pos/wks

20 Jun 87 **THE MARIA CALLAS COLLECTION** *Stylus SMR 732* 50 7
24 Feb 96 **DIVA – THE ULTIMATE COLLECTION** *EMI CDEMTVD 113* 61 1
11 Nov 00 **POPULAR MUSIC FROM TV FILM AND OPERA** *EMI Classics CDC 5570502* 45 8
27 Oct 01 **THE BEST OF – ROMANTIC CALLAS – A COLLECTION OF ROMANTIC ARIAS AND DUETS** *EMI Classics CDC 5572112* ..32 3

Terry CALLIER *US, male vocalist (Singles: 4 weeks)* pos/wks

13 Dec 97 **BEST BIT (EP)** *Heavenly HVN 72CD* [1] 36 3
23 May 98 **LOVE THEME FROM SPARTACUS** *Talkin' Loud TLCD 32* 57 1

[1] Beth Orton featuring Terry Callier

Tracks on Best Bit (EP): Best Bit / Skimming Stone / Dolphins / Lean On Me

CALLING *US, male vocal / instrumental group (Singles: 15 weeks, Albums: 25 weeks)* pos/wks

29 Jun 02 **WHEREVER YOU WILL GO (import)** *RCA 74321912242* 64 1
6 Jul 02 ● **WHEREVER YOU WILL GO** *RCA 74321947652* 3 11
2 Nov 02 **ADRIENNE** *RCA 74321968352* 18 3
29 Jun 02 **CAMINO PALMERO** *RCA 74321916102* 12 25

Eddie CALVERT *UK, male instrumentalist (Singles: 80 weeks)* pos/wks

18 Dec 53 ★ **OH, MEIN PAPA** *Columbia DB 3337* 1 21
8 Apr 55 ★ **CHERRY PINK AND APPLE BLOSSOM WHITE** *Columbia DB 3581* 1 21
13 May 55 **STRANGER IN PARADISE** *Columbia DB 3594* 14 4
29 Jul 55 ● **JOHN AND JULIE** *Columbia DB 3624* 6 11
9 Mar 56 **ZAMBESI (re)** *Columbia DB 3747* 13 7

Date		Title / Label	pos	wks
7 Feb 58	●	**MANDY (LA PANSE)** *Columbia DB 3956*	9	14
20 Jun 58		**LITTLE SERENADE** *Columbia DB 4105*	28	2

Donnie CALVIN – *See ROCKER'S REVENGE featuring Donnie CALVIN*

CAMBRIDGE SINGERS – *See John RUTTER*

CAMEL

UK, male vocal / instrumental group (Albums: 47 weeks)

Date		Title / Label	pos	wks
24 May 75		**THE SNOW GOOSE** *Decca SKL 5207*	22	13
17 Apr 76		**MOON MADNESS** *Decca TXS 115*	15	6
17 Sep 77		**RAIN DANCES** *Decca TXS 124*	20	8
14 Oct 78		**BREATHLESS** *Decca TXS 132*	26	1
27 Oct 79		**I CAN SEE YOUR HOUSE FROM HERE** *Decca TXS 137*	45	3
31 Jan 81		**NUDE** *Decca SKL 5323*	34	7
15 May 82		**THE SINGLE FACTOR** *Decca SKL 5328*	57	5
21 Apr 84		**STATIONARY TRAVELLER** *Decca SKL 5334*	57	4

CAMEO

US, male vocal / instrumental group (Singles: 71 weeks, Albums: 47 weeks)

Date		Title / Label	pos	wks
31 Mar 84		**SHE'S STRANGE** *Club JAB 2*	37	8
13 Jul 85		**ATTACK ME WITH YOUR LOVE** *Club JAB 16*	65	2
14 Sep 85		**SINGLE LIFE** *Club JAB 21*	15	10
7 Dec 85		**SHE'S STRANGE (re-issue)** *Club JAB 25*	22	8
22 Mar 86		**A GOODBYE** *Club JAB 28*	65	2
30 Aug 86	●	**WORD UP** *Club JAB 38*	3	13
29 Nov 86		**CANDY** *Club JAB 43*	27	9
25 Apr 87		**BACK AND FORTH** *Club JAB 49*	11	9
17 Oct 87		**SHE'S MINE** *Club JAB 57*	35	4
29 Oct 88		**YOU MAKE ME WORK** *Club JAB 70*	74	1
28 Jul 01		**LOVERBOY (re)** *Virgin VUSCD 211* [1]	12	5
10 Aug 85		**SINGLE LIFE** *Club JABH 11*	66	12
18 Oct 86	●	**WORD UP** *Club JABH 19*	7	34
26 Nov 88		**MACHISMO** *Club 836002 1*	86	1

[1] Mariah featuring Cameo

Andy CAMERON

UK, male vocalist (Singles: 8 weeks)

Date		Title / Label	pos	wks
4 Mar 78	●	**ALLY'S TARTAN ARMY** *Klub 03*	6	8

CAMILLA – *See MOJOLATORS featuring CAMILLA*

Tony CAMILLO'S BAZUKA

US, male instrumental / vocal group (Singles: 5 weeks)

Date		Title / Label	pos	wks
31 May 75		**DYNOMITE (PART 1)** *A&M AMS 7168*	28	5

CAMISRA

UK, male DJ / producer – 'Tall Paul' Newman (Singles: 12 weeks)

Date		Title / Label	pos	wks
21 Feb 98	●	**LET ME SHOW YOU** *VC Recordings VCRD 31*	5	8
11 Jul 98		**FEEL THE BEAT** *VC Recordings VCRD 39*	32	2
22 May 99		**CLAP YOUR HANDS** *VC Recordings VCRD 49*	34	2

See also ESCRIMA; PARTIZAN; TALL PAUL; GRIFTERS

CAMOUFLAGE featuring MYSTI

UK, male / female vocal / instrumental group (Singles: 3 weeks)

Date		Title / Label	pos	wks
24 Sep 77		**BEE STING** *State STAT 58*	48	3

CAMP LO

US, male rap duo (Singles: 1 week)

Date		Title / Label	pos	wks
16 Aug 97		**LUCHINI AKA (THIS IS IT)** *ffrr FCD 305*	74	1

CAMPAG VELOCET

UK, male female vocal / instrumental group (Singles: 1 week)

Date		Title / Label	pos	wks
19 Feb 00		**VITO SATAN** *Pias Recordings PIASX 010CD*	75	1

Ali CAMPBELL

UK, male vocalist (Singles: 18 weeks, Albums: 11 weeks)

Date		Title / Label	pos	wks
20 May 95	●	**THAT LOOK IN YOUR EYE** *Kuff KUFFDG 1*	5	10
26 Aug 95		**LET YOUR YEAH BE YEAH** *Kuff KUFFD 2*	25	4
9 Dec 95		**SOMETHIN' STUPID** *Kuff KUFFDG 5* [1]	30	4
17 Jun 95	●	**BIG LOVE** *Kuff CDV 2783*	6	11

[1] Ali and Kibibi Campbell

See also Pato BANTON; UB40

Danny CAMPBELL and SASHA

UK, male vocalist and male DJ / producer (Singles: 1 week)

Date		Title / Label	pos	wks
31 Jul 93		**TOGETHER** *ffrr FCD 212*	57	1

See also SASHA

Don CAMPBELL – *See GENERAL SAINT*

Ellie CAMPBELL

UK, female vocalist (Singles: 5 weeks)

Date		Title / Label	pos	wks
3 Apr 99		**SWEET LIES** *Jive / Eastern Bloc 0519222*	42	1
14 Aug 99		**SO MANY WAYS** *Jive / Eastern Bloc 0519362*	26	3
9 Jun 01		**DON'T WANT YOU BACK** *Jive 9201302*	50	1

Ethna CAMPBELL

UK, female vocalist (Singles: 11 weeks)

Date		Title / Label	pos	wks
27 Dec 75		**THE OLD RUGGED CROSS** *Philips 6006 475*	33	11

Ian CAMPBELL FOLK GROUP

UK, male vocal / instrumental group (Singles: 5 weeks)

Date		Title / Label	pos	wks
11 Mar 65		**THE TIMES THEY ARE A-CHANGIN' (2re)** *Transatlantic SP 5*	42	5

Glen CAMPBELL (201 Top 500)

Top session guitarist and singer who became one of the biggest-selling country and easy listening artists of the 1960s, b. 22 Apr 1936, Arkansas, US. Other credits include part-time member of The Beach Boys and vocalist with The Crickets (Singles: 106 weeks, Albums: 185 weeks)

Date		Title / Label	pos	wks
29 Jan 69	●	**WICHITA LINEMAN** *Ember EMBS 261*	7	13
7 May 69		**GALVESTON** *Ember EMBS 263*	14	10
6 Dec 69	●	**ALL I HAVE TO DO IS DREAM** *Capitol CL 15619* [1]	3	14
7 Feb 70		**TRY A LITTLE KINDNESS** *Capitol CL 15622*	45	2
9 May 70	●	**HONEY COME BACK** *Capitol CL 15638*	4	19
26 Sep 70		**EVERYTHING A MAN COULD EVER NEED** *Capitol CL 15653*	32	5
21 Nov 70	●	**IT'S ONLY MAKE BELIEVE** *Capitol CL 15663*	4	14
27 Mar 71		**DREAM BABY (HOW LONG MUST I DREAM)** *Capitol CL 15674*	39	3
4 Oct 75	●	**RHINESTONE COWBOY** *Capitol CL 15824* ▲	4	12
26 Mar 77		**SOUTHERN NIGHTS** *Capitol CL 15907* ▲	28	6
30 Nov 02		**RHINESTONE COWBOY (GIDDY UP GIDDY UP)** *Serious SER 059CD* [2]	12	8
31 Jan 70		**GLEN CAMPBELL LIVE** *Capitol SB 21444*	16	14
28 Feb 70		**BOBBIE GENTRY AND GLEN CAMPBELL** *Capitol ST 2928* [1]	50	1
30 May 70		**TRY A LITTLE KINDNESS** *Capitol ESW 389*	37	10
12 Dec 70		**THE GLEN CAMPBELL ALBUM** *Capitol ST 22493*	16	5
27 Nov 71	●	**GLEN CAMPBELL'S GREATEST HITS** *Capitol ST 21885*	8	113
25 Oct 75		**RHINESTONE COWBOY** *Capitol ESW 11430*	38	9
20 Nov 76	★	**GLEN CAMPBELL'S TWENTY GOLDEN GREATS** *Capitol EMTV 2*	1	27
23 Apr 77		**SOUTHERN NIGHTS** *Capitol EST 11601*	51	1
22 Jul 89		**THE COMPLETE GLEN CAMPBELL** *Stylus SMR 979*	47	4
2 Oct 99		**MY HITS AND LOVE SONGS** *Capitol 5223002*	50	1

[1] Bobbie Gentry and Glen Campbell [2] Rikki and Daz featuring Glen Campbell
[1] Bobbie Gentry and Glen Campbell

Jo Ann CAMPBELL

US, female vocalist (Singles: 3 weeks)

Date		Title / Label	pos	wks
8 Jun 61		**MOTORCYCLE MICHAEL** *HMV POP 873*	41	3

Junior CAMPBELL

UK, male vocalist (Singles: 18 weeks)

Date		Title / Label	pos	wks
14 Oct 72	●	**HALLELUJAH FREEDOM** *Deram DM 364*	10	9
2 Jun 73		**SWEET ILLUSION** *Deram DM 387*	15	9

See also MARMALADE

Kibibi CAMPBELL – *See Ali CAMPBELL*

HAPPY 50TH BIRTHDAY ROCK 'N' ROLL

"What was the first rock 'n' roll record?" and "When and what was the first rock 'n' roll hit?" The first question is practically impossible to answer. Some might think it was Bill Haley's 'Rock Around the Clock' or Elvis's echo-drenched 'Heartbreak Hotel', but there were numerous acts and tracks with a rock 'n' roll sound, and often a rock 'n' roll lyric, before them. However, the second question is a little easier – or at least we are confident that we can pinpoint the period and the two records that could qualify for the title.

In October 1954, The Crew Cuts charted with their US No.1 'Sh-Boom'. It was a cover of an R&B smash written and recorded by New York vocal quintet The Chords, whose original recording was credited as "the record that launched a thousand doo-wop groups". Rock historians often deride The Crew Cuts' interpretation, but it certainly "rocked" more than other pop records of the time. And since it encouraged many pop performers to cut R&B songs, it hurried the rise of rock 'n' roll. The Crew Cuts did not consider themselves rock 'n' rollers; in fact, they had to be persuaded against their better judgement to record 'Sh-Boom', a song which owes something to the earlier hit '(Oh Baby Mine) I Get So Lonely' by The Four Knights and the old children's classic 'Gently Down the Stream'. The Crew Cuts, who were influenced by fellow Canadians The Four Lads, sang 'R&B-influenced barbershop harmony'. They were voted Top New Group in the US in 1954 and 'Sh-Boom' voted Top R&B Record of the Year in the prestigious jazz journal *Downbeat*. At the time they were considered cutting edge and attracted a large female fanbase. To paraphrase 'Sh-Boom', 'life was a dream' for the group, which had a long string of US hits with R&B covers. Sadly, The Chords, who "had nothing against the Crew Cuts", could not follow this gibberish gem and even a name change to the Sh-Booms did not help them.

There is no doubt that 'Shake, Rattle and Roll' by Bill Haley and the Comets, which charted in December 1954, was 100 per cent rock 'n' roll. Haley's first major US hit, the equally rocking 'Crazy Man Crazy', was overlooked here just like his previous 1954 release 'Rock Around the Clock'. Britain's teenagers instantly loved 'Shake, Rattle and Roll', though. The song was first recorded by Joe Turner in February 1954 and topped the US R&B chart in June, although, interestingly Joe says: "I was also singing a song of that title back in 1943." Haley and his Comets cleaned up the lyric and targeted their version at the pop market. Their aim was true. It launched Haley's very successful international career, introducing millions around the globe to rock 'n' roll. In Britain, it rocked the foundations of pop music when it shot into a Hit Parade crammed full of easy-on-the-ear songs and Christmas party piano medleys. When he was asked about the roots of rock, Haley always acknowledged his

The influential **Jesse Stone**, in the studio with the rather intimidated-looking trio **The Cookies**

debt to Turner: "Joe had a tremendous influence on my career, and on the birth of rock 'n' roll."

Before you make your choice about the first British rock 'n' roll hit, you might want to note that the original versions of both of these songs were produced and arranged by the same man, 'Shake, Rattle and Roll' composer Jesse Stone, who revealed, "I tried to design an R&B bass pattern that white kids could dance to."

Stone had an amazing life. As an infant at the turn of the century, he performed in his family's minstrel show. He worked with several early blues singers and first recorded in 1927. He led a jazz band in the 1930s and was a top R&B and jazz arranger (working with Jimmy Dorsey, Benny Goodman and Louis Jordan) in the 1940s. He wrote the first song Elvis ever sang on TV and was working with Buddy Holly at the time of the young star's premature death. The man who at one time was called the "New Cole Porter" died in 1999 at the age of 96. Perhaps Atlantic Records boss Ahmet Ertegun hit the nail on the head when he said, "Jesse Stone did more to develop the basic rock 'n' roll sound than anyone else." Maybe, then, the answer to "When was the first rock 'n' roll hit?" is simply "Fifty years ago in 1954 – back in the Stone Age".

Joe Turner, who claimed to have been singing a song titled 'Shake, Rattle and Roll' as far back as 1943

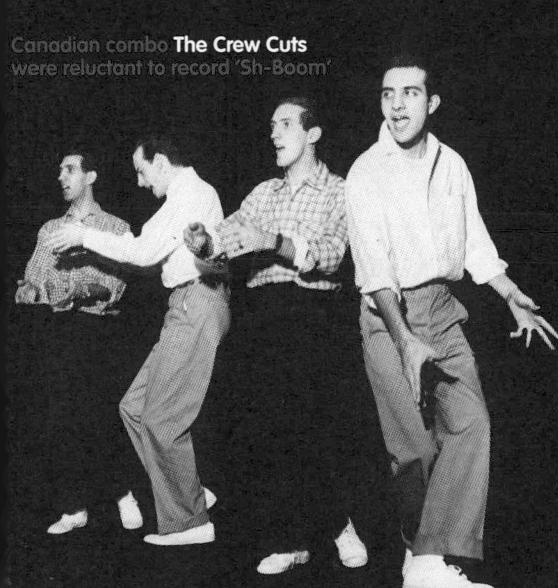

Canadian combo **The Crew Cuts** were reluctant to record 'Sh-Boom'

Naomi CAMPBELL *UK, female vocalist (Singles: 3 weeks)* pos/wks

24 Sep 94 **LOVE AND TEARS** *Epic 6608352* 40 3

Pat CAMPBELL *Ireland, male vocalist (Singles: 5 weeks)* pos/wks

15 Nov 69 **THE DEAL** *Major Minor MM 648* 31 5

Stan CAMPBELL *UK, male vocalist (Singles: 3 weeks)* pos/wks

6 Jun 87 **YEARS GO BY** *WEA YZ 127* 65 3

Tevin CAMPBELL *US, male vocalist (Singles: 2 weeks)* pos/wks

18 Apr 92 **TELL ME WHAT YOU WANT ME TO DO** *Qwest W 0102* 63 2

CAM'RON *US, male rapper – Cameron Giles (Singles: 27 weeks)* pos/wks

19 Sep 98 **HORSE AND CARRIAGE** *Epic 6662612* [1] 12 4
17 Aug 02 **OH BOY** *Roc-A-Fella 0639642* [2] 13 7
8 Feb 03 ● **HEY MA** *Roc-A-Fella 0637242* [2] 8 10
5 Apr 03 **BOY (I NEED YOU)** *Def Jam 0779282* [3] 17 6

[1] Cam'ron featuring Mase [2] Cam'ron featuring Juelz Santana [3] Mariah Carey featuring Cam'Ron

CAN *Germany, male vocal / instrumental group (Singles: 10 weeks)* pos/wks

28 Aug 76 **I WANT MORE** *Virgin VS 153* 26 10

CANDIDO *US, male multi-instrumentalist (Singles: 3 weeks)* pos/wks

18 Jul 81 **JINGO** *Excalibur EXC 102* 55 3

CANDLEWICK GREEN
UK, male vocal / instrumental group (Singles: 8 weeks) pos/wks

23 Feb 74 **WHO DO YOU THINK YOU ARE?** *Decca F 13480* 21 8

CANDY FLIP *UK, male vocal / instrumental duo – Rick Peel and Danny 'Dizzy' Deo (Singles: 14 weeks)* pos/wks

17 Mar 90 ● **STRAWBERRY FIELDS FOREVER** *Debut DEBT 3092* 3 10
14 Jul 90 **THIS CAN BE REAL** *Debut DEBT 3099* 60 4

CANDY GIRLS *UK, male / female instrumental / production duo – Rachel Auburn and Paul Masterson (Singles: 10 weeks)* pos/wks

30 Sep 95 **FEE FI FO FUM** *VC VCRD 1* [1] 23 4
24 Feb 96 **WHAM BAM** *VC VCRD 6* [1] 20 4
7 Dec 96 **I WANT CANDY** *Feverpitch CDFVR 1013* [2] 30 2

[1] Candy Girls featuring Sweet Pussy Pauline [2] Candy Girls featuring Valerie Malcolm

See also DOROTHY; SLEAZESISTERS; YOMANDA; HI-GATE; CLERGY; Paul MASTERSON presents SUSHI

CANDYLAND
UK, male vocal / instrumental group (Singles: 1 week) pos/wks

9 Mar 91 **FOUNTAIN O' YOUTH** *Non Fiction YES 4* 72 1

CANDYSKINS
UK, male vocal / instrumental group (Singles: 4 weeks) pos/wks

19 Oct 96 **MRS HOOVER** *Ultimate TOPP 051CD* 65 1
8 Feb 97 **MONDAY MORNING** *Ultimate TOPP 055CD* 34 2
3 May 97 **HANG MYSELF ON YOU** *Ultimate TOPP 059CD* 65 1

CANIBUS *US, male rapper – Germaine Williams (Singles: 3 weeks, Albums: 1 week)* pos/wks

27 Jun 98 **SECOND ROUND KO** *Universal UND 56198* 35 2
10 Oct 98 **HOW COME** *Interscope IND 95598* [1] 52 1
19 Sep 98 **CAN-I-BUS** *Universal UND 53222* 43 1

[1] Youssou N'Dour and Canibus

CANNED HEAT *US, male vocal / instrumental group (Singles: 41 weeks, Albums: 40 weeks)* pos/wks

24 Jul 68 ● **ON THE ROAD AGAIN** *Liberty LBS 15090* 8 15
1 Jan 69 **GOING UP THE COUNTRY** *Liberty LBF 15169* 19 10
17 Jan 70 ● **LET'S WORK TOGETHER** *Liberty LBF 15302* 2 15
11 Jul 70 **SUGAR BEE** *Liberty LBF 15350* 49 1
29 Jun 68 ● **BOOGIE WITH CANNED HEAT** *Liberty LBL 83103* 5 21
14 Feb 70 ● **CANNED HEAT COOKBOOK** *Liberty LBS 83303* 8 12
4 Jul 70 **CANNED HEAT '70 CONCERT** *Liberty LBS 83333* 15 3
10 Oct 70 **FUTURE BLUES** *Liberty LBS 83364* 27 4

Freddy CANNON *US, male vocalist – Freddy Picariello (Singles: 54 weeks, Albums: 11 weeks)* pos/wks

14 Aug 59 **TALLAHASSEE LASSIE** *Top Rank JAR 135* 17 8
1 Jan 60 ● **WAY DOWN YONDER IN NEW ORLEANS** *Top Rank JAR 247* 3 18
4 Mar 60 **CALIFORNIA HERE I COME** *Top Rank JAR 309* 25 3
17 Mar 60 **INDIANA** *Top Rank JAR309* 42 1
19 May 60 **THE URGE** *Top Rank JAR 369* 18 10
20 Apr 61 **MUSKRAT RAMBLE** *Top Rank JAR 548* 32 5
28 Jun 62 **PALISADES PARK** *Stateside SS 101* 20 9
27 Feb 60 ★ **THE EXPLOSIVE FREDDY CANNON** *Top Rank 25/108* 1 11

Blu CANTRELL
US, female vocalist (Singles: 33 weeks, Albums: 11 weeks) pos/wks

24 Nov 01 **HIT 'EM UP STYLE (OOPS!)** *Arista 74321891632* 12 9
19 Jul 03 **BREATHE (import)** *Arista 8786509842* [1] 59 3
9 Aug 03 ★ **BREATHE** *Arista 82876545722* [1] ■ 1 18
13 Dec 03 **MAKE ME WANNA SCREAM** *Arista 82876573382* 24 3+
9 Aug 03 **BITTERSWEET** *Arista 82876534042* 20 11

[1] Blu Cantrell Featuring Sean Paul

Jim CAPALDI
UK, male vocalist (Singles: 17 weeks) pos/wks

27 Jul 74 **IT'S ALL UP TO YOU** *Island WIP 6198* 27 6
25 Oct 75 ● **LOVE HURTS** *Island WIP 6246* 4 11

CAPERCAILLIE *UK / Ireland, male / female vocal / instrumental group (Singles: 3 weeks, Albums: 8 weeks)* pos/wks

23 May 92 **A PRINCE AMONG ISLANDS (EP)** *Survival ZB 45393* 39 2
17 Jun 95 **DARK ALAN (AILEIN DUINN)** *Survival SURCD 55* 65 1
25 Sep 93 **SECRET PEOPLE** *Arista 74321162742* 40 3
17 Sep 94 **CAPERCAILLIE** *Survival 74321229112* 61 1
4 Nov 95 **TO THE MOON** *Survival SURCD 019* 41 2
20 Sep 97 **BEAUTIFUL WASTELAND** *Survival SURCD 021* 55 2

Tracks on A Prince Among Islands (EP): Coisich a Ruin (Walk My Beloved) / Fagail Bhearnaraid (Leaving Bernaray) / The Lorn Theme / Gun Teann Mi Ris Na Ruinn Tha Seo (Remembrance)

CAPPADONNA
US, male rapper (Albums: 1 week) pos/wks

4 Apr 98 **THE PILLAGE** *Epic 4888502* 43 1

See also WU-TANG CLAN

CAPPELLA *Italy, male / female / production / vocal group (Singles: 68 weeks, Albums: 9 weeks)* pos/wks

9 Apr 88 **PUSH THE BEAT / BAUHAUS** *Fast Globe FGL 1* 60 2
6 May 89 **HELYOM HALIB** *Music Man MMPS 7004* 11 9
23 Sep 89 **HOUSE ENERGY REVENGE** *Music Man MMPS 7009* 73 1
27 Apr 91 **EVERYBODY** *ffrr F158* 66 1
18 Jan 92 **TAKE ME AWAY** *PWL Continental PWL 210* [1] 25 5
3 Apr 93 ● **U GOT 2 KNOW** *Internal Dance IDC 1* 6 11
14 Aug 93 **U GOT 2 KNOW (re-mix)** *Internal Dance IDCR 2* 43 3
23 Oct 93 ● **U GOT 2 LET THE MUSIC** *Internal Dance IDC 3* 2 12
19 Feb 94 ● **MOVE ON BABY** *Internal Dance IDC 4* 7 7
18 Jun 94 ● **U & ME** *Internal Dance IDCC 6* 10 7
15 Oct 94 **MOVE IT UP / BIG BEAT** *Internal Dance IDC 7* 16 6
16 Sep 95 **TELL ME THE WAY** *Systematic SYSCD 17* 17 3
6 Sep 97 **BE MY BABY** *Nukleuz PSNC 0072* 53 1
26 Mar 94 ● **U GOT 2 KNOW** *Internal Dance CAPPC 1* 10 9

[1] Cappella featuring Loleatta Holloway

See also 49ers

CAPRICCIO *UK, production duo (Singles: 2 weeks)* pos/wks

Date		Title / Label	pos	wks
27 Mar 99		EVERYBODY GET UP *Defected DEFECT 2CDS*	44	2

CAPRICE *US, female vocalist – Caprice Bourret (Singles: 5 weeks)* pos/wks

Date		Title / Label	pos	wks
4 Sep 99		OH YEAH *Virgin VSCDT 1745*	24	3
10 Mar 01		ONCE AROUND THE SUN *Virgin VSCDT 1750*	24	2

CAPRICORN *Belgium, male DJ (Singles: 1 week)* pos/wks

Date		Title / Label	pos	wks
29 Nov 97		20 HZ (NEW FREQUENCIES) *R&S RS 97126CD*	73	1

Tony CAPSTICK and the CARLTON MAIN / FRICKLEY COLLIERY BAND *UK, male vocalist and male instrumental group (Singles: 8 weeks)* pos/wks

Date		Title / Label	pos	wks
21 Mar 81	●	THE SHEFFIELD GRINDER / CAPSTICK COMES HOME *Dingles SID 27*	3	8

CAPTAIN BEAKY – See Keith MICHELL

CAPTAIN BEEFHEART and his MAGIC BAND *US, male vocal / instrumental group – Don Van Vliet (Albums: 8 weeks)* pos/wks

Date		Title / Label	pos	wks
6 Dec 69		TROUT MASK REPLICA *Straight STS 1053*	21	1
23 Jan 71		LICK MY DECALS OFF BABY *Straight STS 1063*	20	2
29 May 71		MIRROR MAN *Buddah 2365 002*	49	1
19 Feb 72		THE SPOTLIGHT KID *Reprise K 44162*	44	2
18 Sep 82		ICE CREAM FOR CROW *Virgin V 2337*	90	2

See also MAGIC BAND

CAPTAIN HOLLYWOOD PROJECT *US / Germany, male / female vocal / instrumental group (Singles: 31 weeks)* pos/wks

Date		Title / Label	pos	wks
22 Sep 90	●	I CAN'T STAND IT *BCM BCMR 395* [1]	7	10
24 Nov 90		ARE YOU DREAMING *BCM BCM 07504* [1]	17	10
27 Mar 93		ONLY WITH YOU *Pulse 8 CDLOSE 40*	67	1
6 Nov 93		MORE AND MORE *Pulse 8 CDLOSE 50*	23	5
5 Feb 94		IMPOSSIBLE *Pulse 8 CDLOSE 54*	29	3
11 Jun 94		ONLY WITH YOU (re-issue) *Pulse 8 CDLOSE 62*	61	1
1 Apr 95		FLYING HIGH *Pulse 8 CDLOSE 82*	58	1

[1] Twenty 4 Seven featuring Captain Hollywood

CAPTAIN SENSIBLE *UK, male vocalist – Ray Burns (Singles: 31 weeks, Albums: 3 weeks)* pos/wks

Date		Title / Label	pos	wks
26 Jun 82	★	HAPPY TALK *A&M CAP 1*	1	8
14 Aug 82		WOT! *A&M CAP 2*	26	7
24 Mar 84	●	GLAD IT'S ALL OVER / DAMNED ON 45 *A&M CAP 6*	6	10
28 Jul 84		THERE ARE MORE SNAKES THAN LADDERS *A&M CAP 7*	57	5
10 Dec 94		THE HOKEY COKEY *Have a Nice Day CDHOKEY 1*	71	1
11 Sep 82		WOMEN AND CAPTAIN FIRST *A&M AMLH 68548*	64	3

See also DAMNED

CAPTAIN and TENNILLE *US, male instrumentalist – keyboards and female vocalist, Daryl Dragon and Toni Tennille (Singles: 24 weeks, Albums: 6 weeks)* pos/wks

Date		Title / Label	pos	wks
2 Aug 75		LOVE WILL KEEP US TOGETHER *A&M AMS 7165* ▲	32	5
24 Jan 76		THE WAY I WANT TO TOUCH YOU *A&M AMS 7203*	28	6
4 Nov 78		YOU NEVER DONE IT LIKE THAT *A&M AMS 7384*	63	3
16 Feb 80	●	DO THAT TO ME ONE MORE TIME *Casablanca CAN 175* ▲	7	10
22 Mar 80		MAKE YOUR MOVE *Casablanca CAL 2060*	33	6

See also TENNILLE

Irene CARA *US, female actor / vocalist (Singles: 33 weeks)* pos/wks

Date		Title / Label	pos	wks
3 Jul 82	★	FAME *RSO 90*	1	16
4 Sep 82		OUT HERE ON MY OWN *RSO 66*	58	3
4 Jun 83	●	FLASHDANCE . . . WHAT A FEELING *Casablanca CAN 1016* ▲	2	14

CARAMBA *Sweden, male vocalist / multi-instrumentalist dog impersonator – Michael Tretow (Singles: 6 weeks)* pos/wks

Date		Title / Label	pos	wks
12 Nov 83		FEDORA (I'LL BE YOUR DAWG) *Billco BILL 101*	56	6

CARAVAN *UK, male vocal / instrumental group (Albums: 2 weeks)* pos/wks

Date		Title / Label	pos	wks
30 Aug 75		CUNNING STUNTS *Decca SKL 5210*	50	1
15 May 76		BLIND DOG AT ST DUNSTAN'S *BTM BTM 1007*	53	1

CARAVELLES *UK, female vocal duo – Lois Wilkinson and Andrea Simpson (Singles: 13 weeks)* pos/wks

Date		Title / Label	pos	wks
8 Aug 63	●	YOU DON'T HAVE TO BE A BABY TO CRY *Decca F 11697*	6	13

CARCASS *UK, male vocal / instrumental group (Albums: 2 weeks)* pos/wks

Date		Title / Label	pos	wks
6 Nov 93		HEARTWORK *Earache MOSH 097CD*	67	1
6 Jul 96		SWANSONG *Earache MOSH 160CD*	68	1

CARDIGANS *Sweden, female / male vocal / instrumental group (Singles: 67 weeks, Albums: 70 weeks)* pos/wks

Date		Title / Label	pos	wks
17 Jun 95		CARNIVAL (re) *Trampolene PZCD 345*	35	3
30 Sep 95		SICK AND TIRED *Stockholm 5773112*	34	3
17 Feb 96		RISE AND SHINE *Trampolene 5778252*	29	2
21 Sep 96		LOVEFOOL *Stockholm 5752952*	21	4
7 Dec 96		BEEN IT *Stockholm 5759672*	56	1
3 May 97	●	LOVEFOOL (re-issue) *Stockholm 5710502*	2	13
6 Sep 97		YOUR NEW CUCKOO *Stockholm 5716632*	35	2
17 Oct 98		MY FAVOURITE GAME *Stockholm 5679912*	14	18
6 Mar 99	●	ERASE / REWIND *Stockholm 5635332*	7	9
24 Jul 99		HANGING AROUND *Stockholm 5612682*	17	4
25 Sep 99	●	BURNING DOWN THE HOUSE *Gut CDGUT 26* [1]	7	7
22 Mar 03		FOR WHAT IT'S WORTH *Stockholm 0657232*	31	2
26 Jul 03		YOU'RE THE STORM *Stockholm 9809673*	74	1
8 Jul 95		LIFE *Stockholm 5235562*	51	9
12 Oct 96		FIRST BAND ON THE MOON *Stockholm 5331172*	18	10
31 Oct 98	●	GRAN TURISMO *Stockholm 5590812*	8	49
5 Apr 03		LONG GONE BEFORE MIDNIGHT *Stockholm / 0381092*	47	2

[1] Tom Jones and The Cardigans

See also A CAMP

CARE *UK, male vocal / instrumental duo (Singles: 4 weeks)* pos/wks

Date		Title / Label	pos	wks
12 Nov 83		FLAMING SWORD *Arista KBIRD 2*	48	4

Mariah CAREY (58 Top 500) *Record-shattering vocalist / songwriter, b. 27 Mar 1970, New York. Since her 1990 chart debut she has sold more than 120 million albums worldwide and has topped the US singles chart 15 times – only Elvis Presley has spent longer at the top. She had a brief, and much publicised, $20m per album deal with Virgin in 2001. Best-selling UK single: 'Without You' 559,200 (Singles: 282 weeks, Albums: 306 weeks)* pos/wks

Date		Title / Label	pos	wks
4 Aug 90	●	VISION OF LOVE *CBS 6559320* ▲	9	12
10 Nov 90		LOVE TAKES TIME *CBS 6563647* ▲	37	8
26 Jan 91		SOMEDAY *Columbia 6565837* ▲	38	5
1 Jun 91		THERE'S GOT TO BE A WAY *Columbia 6569317*	54	3
5 Oct 91		EMOTIONS *Columbia 6574037* ▲	17	9
11 Jan 92		CAN'T LET GO *Columbia 6576627*	20	7
18 Apr 92		MAKE IT HAPPEN *Columbia 6579417*	17	5
27 Jun 92	●	I'LL BE THERE *Columbia 6581377* ▲	2	9
21 Aug 93	●	DREAMLOVER *Columbia 6594445* ▲	9	10
6 Nov 93	●	HERO *Columbia 6598122* ▲	7	15
19 Feb 94	★	WITHOUT YOU *Columbia 6599192* ■	1	14
18 Jun 94	●	ANYTIME YOU NEED A FRIEND *Columbia 6603542*	8	10
17 Sep 94	●	ENDLESS LOVE (2re) *Epic 6608062* [1]	3	16
10 Dec 94	●	ALL I WANT FOR CHRISTMAS IS YOU *Columbia 6610702*	2	8
23 Sep 95	●	FANTASY *Columbia 6624952* ▲	4	11
9 Dec 95	●	ONE SWEET DAY *Columbia 6626035* [2] ▲	6	11
17 Feb 96	●	OPEN ARMS *Columbia 6629772*	4	6
22 Jun 96	●	ALWAYS BE MY BABY *Columbia 6633345* ▲	3	10
6 Sep 97	●	HONEY *Columbia 6650192* ▲	3	8
13 Dec 97		BUTTERFLY *Columbia 6653365*	22	6
13 Jun 98	●	MY ALL *Columbia 6660592* ▲	4	8
19 Dec 98	●	WHEN YOU BELIEVE (re) *Columbia 6667522* [3]	4	13
10 Apr 99		I STILL BELIEVE *Columbia 6670732*	16	7
6 Nov 99	●	HEARTBREAKER *Columbia 6683012* [4] ▲	5	13
11 Mar 00	●	THANK GOD I FOUND YOU (re) *Columbia 6690582* [5] ▲	10	10
30 Sep 00	★	AGAINST ALL ODDS (re) *Columbia 6698872* [6] ■	1	12
28 Jul 01		LOVERBOY (re) *Virgin VUSCD 211* [7]	12	5

29 Dec 01 **NEVER TOO FAR / DON'T STOP (FUNKIN' 4 JAMAICA)** *Virgin VUSCD 228* [8] 32 4
30 Nov 02 ● **THROUGH THE RAIN** *Mercury 0638072* 8 8
5 Apr 03 **BOY (I NEED YOU)** *Def Jam 0779282* [9] 17 6
7 Jun 03 ● **I KNOW WHAT YOU WANT** *J 82876528292* [10] 3 13
15 Sep 90 ● **MARIAH CAREY** *CBS 4668151* ▲ 6 40
26 Oct 91 ● **EMOTIONS** *Columbia 4688511* 4 40
18 Jul 92 ● **MTV UNPLUGGED EP** *Columbia 4718692* 3 10
11 Sep 93 ★ **MUSIC BOX** *Columbia 4742702* ■ ▲ 1 77
19 Nov 94 **MERRY CHRISTMAS** *Columbia 4773422* 32 7
7 Oct 95 ★ **DAYDREAM** *Columbia 4813672* ■ ▲ 1 46
20 Sep 97 ● **BUTTERFLY** *Columbia 4885372* ▲ 2 27
28 Nov 98 ● **#1'S** *Columbia 4926042* 10 32
13 Nov 99 ● **RAINBOW** *Columbia 4950652* 8 15
22 Sep 01 ● **GLITTER** *Virgin CDVUS 201* 10 3
15 Dec 01 **GREATEST HITS** *Columbia 5054612* 46 4
14 Dec 02 **CHARMBRACELET** *Island US / Mercury 0633842* 52 3
18 Oct 03 **THE REMIXES** *Columbia 5107542* 35 2

[1] Luther Vandross and Mariah Carey [2] Mariah Carey and Boyz II Men [3] Mariah Carey & Whitney Houston [4] Mariah Carey featuring Jay-Z [5] Mariah Carey featuring Joe and 98 Degrees [6] Mariah Carey featuring Westlife [7] Mariah featuring Cameo [8] Mariah Carey / Mariah Carey featuring Mystikal [9] Mariah Carey featuring Cam'Ron [10] Busta Rhymes and Mariah Carey featuring the Flipmode Squad

Although he is uncredited, 'I'll Be There' is a duet with Trey Lorenz

CARL – *See CLUBHOUSE*

Belinda CARLISLE (184 Top 500)

Lead vocalist of the first really successful all-girl rock group, The Go-Go's; b. 17 Aug 1958, Hollywood. She married the son of British-born film star James Mason in 1992 and her career fared even better in the UK than in her homeland. Joined a re-formed Go-Go's in 2001 (Singles: 145 weeks, Albums: 160 weeks) pos/wks

12 Dec 87 ★ **HEAVEN IS A PLACE ON EARTH** *Virgin VS 1036* ▲ 1 14
27 Feb 88 ● **I GET WEAK** *Virgin VS 1046* 10 9
7 May 88 ● **CIRCLE IN THE SAND** *Virgin VS 1074* 4 11
6 Aug 88 **MAD ABOUT YOU** *IRS IRM 118* 67 3
10 Sep 88 **WORLD WITHOUT YOU** *Virgin VS 1114* 34 6
10 Dec 88 **LOVE NEVER DIES . . .** *Virgin VS 1150* 54 5
7 Oct 89 ● **LEAVE A LIGHT ON** *Virgin VS 1210* 4 10
9 Dec 89 **LA LUNA** *Virgin VS 1230* 38 6
24 Feb 90 **RUNAWAY HORSES** *Virgin VS 1244* 40 5
26 May 90 **VISION OF YOU (re)** *Virgin VS 1264* 41 5
13 Oct 90 ● **(WE WANT) THE SAME THING** *Virgin VS 1319* 6 10
22 Dec 90 **SUMMER RAIN** *Virgin VS 1323* 23 10
28 Sep 91 **LIVE YOUR LIFE BE FREE** *Virgin VS 1370* 12 7
16 Nov 91 **DO YOU FEEL LIKE I FEEL** *Virgin VS 1383* 29 4
11 Jan 92 **HALF THE WORLD** *Virgin VS 1388* 35 4
29 Aug 92 **LITTLE BLACK BOOK** *Virgin VS 1428* 28 5
25 Sep 93 **BIGSCARYANIMAL** *Virgin VSCDT 1472* 12 6
27 Nov 93 **LAY DOWN YOUR ARMS** *Virgin VSCDG 1476* 27 6
13 Jul 96 ● **IN TOO DEEP** *Chrysalis CDCHS 5033* 6 7
21 Sep 96 ● **ALWAYS BREAKING MY HEART** *Chrysalis CDCHS 5037* 8 6
30 Nov 96 **LOVE IN THE KEY OF C** *Chrysalis CDCHS 5044* 20 3
1 Mar 97 **CALIFORNIA** *Chrysalis CDCHSS 5047* 31 2
27 Nov 99 **ALL GOD'S CHILDREN** *Virgin VSCDT 1756* 66 1
2 Jan 88 ● **HEAVEN ON EARTH** *Virgin V 2496* 4 54
4 Nov 89 ● **RUNAWAY HORSES** *Virgin V 2599* 4 39
26 Oct 91 ● **LIVE YOUR LIFE BE FREE** *Virgin V 2680* 7 16
19 Sep 92 ★ **THE BEST OF BELINDA VOLUME 1** *Virgin BELCD 1* 1 35
23 Oct 93 ● **REAL** *Virgin CDV 2725* 9 5
5 Oct 96 **A WOMAN & A MAN** *Chrysalis CDCHR 6115* 12 5
13 Nov 99 **A PLACE ON EARTH – THE GREATEST HITS** *Virgin CDV 2901* ..15 6

Bob CARLISLE *US, male vocalist (Singles: 2 weeks)* pos/wks

30 Aug 97 **BUTTERFLY KISSES** *Jive JIVECD 249* 56 2

Don CARLOS – *See SINGING DOGS*

Sara CARLSON – *See MANIC MCs featuring Sara CARLSON*

CARLTON

UK, male vocalist (Singles: 3 weeks) pos/wks

16 Feb 91 **LOVE AND PAIN** *Smith & Mighty SNM 4* 56 2
1 Apr 95 **1 TO 1 RELIGION** *Stoned Heights BRCD 313* [1] 53 1

[1] Bomb the Bass featuring Carlton

Carl CARLTON *US, male vocalist (Singles: 8 weeks)* pos/wks

18 Jul 81 **SHE'S A BAD MAMA JAMA (SHE'S BUILT, SHE'S STACKED)** *20th Century TC 2488* 34 8

Larry CARLTON – *See Mike POST*

Vanessa CARLTON

US, female vocalist (Singles: 14 weeks, Albums: 15 weeks) pos/wks

3 Aug 02 ● **A THOUSAND MILES** *A&M 4977542* 6 13
30 Nov 02 **ORDINARY DAY** *A&M 4978132* 53 1
15 Feb 03 **BIG YELLOW TAXI** *Geffen 4978302* [1] 16 9
27Jul 02 ● **BE NOT NOBODY** *A&M 4933672* 7 15

[1] Counting Crows featuring Vanessa Carlton

CARLTON MAIN / FRICKLEY COLLIERY BAND – *See Tony CAPSTICK and the CARLTON MAIN / FRICKLEY COLLIERY BAND*

CARMEL *UK, female / male vocal / instrumental group (Singles: 19 weeks, Albums: 11 weeks)* pos/wks

6 Aug 83 **BAD DAY** *London LON 29* 15 9
11 Feb 84 **MORE, MORE, MORE** *London LON 44* 23 7
14 Jun 86 **SALLY** *London LON 90* 60 3
1 Oct 83 **CARMEL** *Red Flame RFM 9* 94 2
24 Mar 84 **THE DRUM IS EVERYTHING** *London SH 8555* 19 8
27 Sep 86 **THE FALLING** *London LONLP 17* 88 1

Eric CARMEN

US, male vocalist (Singles: 7 weeks, Albums: 1 week) pos/wks

10 Apr 76 **ALL BY MYSELF** *Arista 42* 12 7
15 May 76 **ERIC CARMEN** *Arista ARTY 120* 58 1

Tracey CARMEN – *See RUTHLESS RAP ASSASSINS*

Jean CARN – *See Bobby M featuring Jean CARN*

Kim CARNEGIE

UK, female vocalist (Singles: 1 week) pos/wks

19 Jan 91 **JAZZ RAP** *Best ZB 44085* 73 1

Kim CARNES

US, female vocalist (Singles: 15 weeks, Albums: 16 weeks) pos/wks

9 May 81 ● **BETTE DAVIS EYES** *EMI America EA 121* ▲ 10 9
8 Aug 81 **DRAW OF THE CARDS** *EMI America EA 125* 49 4
9 Oct 82 **VOYEUR** *EMI America EA 143* 68 2
20 Jun 81 **MISTAKEN IDENTITY** *EMI America AML 3018* ▲ 26 16

CARNIVAL featuring RIP vs RED RAT *UK, male production duo and Jamaica, male vocalist (Singles: 1 week)* pos/wks

12 Sep 98 **ALL OF THE GIRLS (ALL AI-DI GIRL DEM)** *Pepper 0530072* 51 1

See also RIP PRODUCTIONS

Renato CAROSONE and his SEXTET *Italy, male vocalist (d. 27 Apr 2001) and instrumental backing group (Singles: 1 week)* pos/wks

4 Jul 58 **TORERO – CHA CHA CHA** *Parlophone R 4433* 25 1

Mary-Chapin CARPENTER *US, female vocalist / instrumentalist – guitar (Singles: 6 weeks, Albums: 9 weeks)* pos/wks

20 Nov 93 **HE THINKS HE'LL KEEP HER** *Columbia 6598632* 71 1
7 Jan 95 **ONE COOL REMOVE** *Columbia 6611342* [1] 40 3
3 Jun 95 **SHUT UP AND KISS ME** *Columbia 6613675* 35 2

29 Oct 94 STONES IN THE ROAD *Columbia CK 64327* 26 5
2 Nov 96 A PLACE IN THE WORLD *Columbia 4851822* 36 2
5 Jun 99 PARTY DOLL AND OTHER FAVOURITES *Columbia 4886592* 65 1
26 May 01 TIME*SEX*LOVE *Columbia 5023542* 57 1

[1] Shawn Colvin with Mary-Chapin Carpenter

CARPENTERS (30 Top 500)

All-time biggest-selling brother / sister duo: Karen Carpenter (v/d) (d. 4 Feb 1983), Richard Carpenter (k/v). This Connecticut couple was among the world's most popular pop / MOR acts of the 1970s before Karen's anorexia-related death (Singles: 173 weeks, Albums: 603 weeks) pos/wks

5 Sep 70 ● (THEY LONG TO BE) CLOSE TO YOU *A&M AMS 800* ▲ 6 18
9 Jan 71 WE'VE ONLY JUST BEGUN *A&M AMS 813* 28 7
18 Sep 71 SUPERSTAR / FOR ALL WE KNOW *A&M AMS 864* 18 13
1 Jan 72 MERRY CHRISTMAS DARLING *A&M AME 601* 45 1
23 Sep 72 ● I WON'T LAST A DAY WITHOUT YOU / GOODBYE TO LOVE *A&M AMS 7023* 9 16
7 Jul 73 ● YESTERDAY ONCE MORE *A&M AMS 7073* 2 17
20 Oct 73 ● TOP OF THE WORLD *A&M AMS 7086* ▲ 5 18
2 Mar 74 JAMBALAYA (ON THE BAYOU) / MR GUDER *A&M AMS 7098* 12 11
8 Jun 74 I WON'T LAST A DAY WITHOUT YOU (re-issue) *A&M AMS 7111* 32 5
18 Jan 75 ● PLEASE MR POSTMAN *A&M AMS 7141* ▲ 2 12
19 Apr 75 ● ONLY YESTERDAY *A&M AMS 7159* 7 10
30 Aug 75 SOLITAIRE *A&M AMS 7187* 32 5
20 Dec 75 SANTA CLAUS IS COMIN' TO TOWN *A&M AMS 7144* 37 4
27 Mar 76 THERE'S A KIND OF HUSH (ALL OVER THE WORLD) *A&M AMS 7219* 22 6
3 Jul 76 I NEED TO BE IN LOVE *A&M AMS 7238* 36 5
8 Oct 77 ● CALLING OCCUPANTS OF INTERPLANETARY CRAFT (THE RECOGNISED ANTHEM OF WORLD CONTACT DAY) *A&M AMS 7318* 9 9
11 Feb 78 SWEET, SWEET SMILE *A&M AMS 7327* 40 4
22 Oct 83 MAKE BELIEVE IT'S YOUR FIRST TIME *A&M AM 147* 60 3
8 Dec 90 MERRY CHRISTMAS DARLING / (THEY LONG TO BE) CLOSE TO YOU (re-issue) *A&M AM 716* 25 5
13 Feb 93 RAINY DAYS AND MONDAYS *A&M AMCD 0180* 63 2
24 Dec 94 TRYIN' TO GET THE FEELING AGAIN *A&M 5807612* 44 2
23 Jan 71 CLOSE TO YOU *A&M AMLS 998* 23 75
30 Oct 71 CARPENTERS *A&M AMLS 63502* 12 36
15 Apr 72 TICKET TO RIDE *A&M AMLS 64342* 20 3
23 Sep 72 A SONG FOR YOU *A&M AMLS 63511* 13 37
7 Jul 73 ● NOW & THEN *A&M AMLH 63519* 2 65
26 Jan 74 ★ THE SINGLES 1969-1973 *A&M AMLH 63601* ▲ 1 125
28 Jun 75 ★ HORIZON *A&M AMLK 64530* 1 27
23 Aug 75 TICKET TO RIDE (re-issue) *Hamlet AMLP 8001* 35 2
3 Jul 76 ● A KIND OF HUSH *A&M AMLK 64581* 3 15
8 Jan 77 LIVE AT THE PALLADIUM *A&M AMLS 68403* 28 3
8 Oct 77 PASSAGE *A&M AMLK 64703* 12 12
2 Dec 78 ● THE SINGLES 1974-1978 *A&M AMLT 19748* 2 27
27 Jun 81 MADE IN AMERICA *A&M AMLK 63723* 12 10
15 Oct 83 ● VOICE OF THE HEART *A&M AMLX 64954* 6 19
20 Oct 84 ● YESTERDAY ONCE MORE *EMI/A&M SING 1* 10 26
13 Jan 90 LOVELINES *A&M AMA 3931* 73 1
31 Mar 90 ★ ONLY YESTERDAY – THEIR GREATEST HITS *A&M AMA 1990* 1 82
15 Oct 94 INTERPRETATIONS *A&M 5402512* 29 10
22 Nov 97 LOVE SONGS *A&M 5408382* 47 8
9 Dec 00 GOLD – GREATEST HITS *A&M 4908652* 21 20

'I Won't Last a Day Without You' AMS 7023 listed by itself 23 Sep 1972 at No.49. 'Goodbye to Love', the other side, listed by itself from 30 Sep 1972, until the end of the record's chart run. 'Mr Guder' listed with 'Jambalaya' from 16 Mar 1974, until the end of the chart run

CARPET BOMBERS FOR PEACE *UK / US, male / female vocal / instrumental group (Singles: 1 week)* pos/wks

5 Apr 03 SALT IN THE WOUND *Jungle JUNG 066CD* 67 1

Dick CARR – *See Slim DUSTY*

Joe 'Fingers' CARR *US, male instrumentalist – piano – Lou Busch under a false name, d. 19 Sep 1979 (Singles: 5 weeks)* pos/wks

29 Jun 56 PORTUGUESE WASHERWOMAN *Capitol CL 14587* 20 5

See also Lou BUSCH and his Orchestra

Linda CARR *US, female vocalist (Singles: 12 weeks)* pos/wks

12 Jul 75 HIGHWIRE *Chelsea 2005 025* [1] 15 8
5 Jun 76 SOLD MY ROCK 'N' ROLL (GAVE IT FOR FUNKY SOUL) *Spark SRL 1139* [2] 36 4

[1] Linda Carr and the Love Squad [2] Linda and the Funky Boys

Lucy CARR *UK, female vocalist (Singles: 3 weeks)* pos/wks

25 Jan 01 MISSING YOU *Lickin LICKINCD 001* 28 2
9 Aug 03 THIS IS GOODBYE *Lickin LICKINCD 002* 41 1

Pearl CARR and Teddy JOHNSON

UK, female / male vocal duo (Singles: 19 weeks) pos/wks

20 Mar 59 SING LITTLE BIRDIE *Columbia DB 4275* 12 8
6 Apr 61 HOW WONDERFUL TO KNOW *Columbia DB 4603* [1] 23 11

[1] Teddy Johnson and Pearl Carr

Suzi CARR *US, female vocalist (Singles: 1 week)* pos/wks

8 Oct 94 ALL OVER ME *Cowboy RODEO 947CD* 45 1

Valerie CARR *US, female vocalist (Singles: 2 weeks)* pos/wks

4 Jul 58 WHEN THE BOYS TALK ABOUT THE GIRLS (re) *Columbia DB 4131* 29 2

Vikki CARR *US, female vocalist – Florencia Bisenta de Casillas Martinez Cardona (Singles: 26 weeks, Albums: 12 weeks)* pos/wks

1 Jun 67 ● IT MUST BE HIM (SEUL SUR SON ÉTOILE) *Liberty LIB 55917* 2 20
30 Aug 67 THERE I GO *Liberty LBF 15022* 50 1
12 Mar 69 WITH PEN IN HAND (2re) *Liberty LBF 15166* 39 5
22 Jul 67 WAY OF TODAY *Liberty SLBY 1331* 31 2
12 Aug 67 IT MUST BE HIM *Liberty LBS 83037* 12 10

Raffaella CARRA *Italy, female vocalist (Singles: 12 weeks)* pos/wks

15 Apr 78 ● DO IT, DO IT AGAIN *Epic EPC 6094* 9 12

Paul CARRACK

UK, male vocalist (Singles: 18 weeks, Albums: 8 weeks) pos/wks

16 May 87 WHEN YOU WALK IN THE ROOM *Chrysalis CHS 3109* 48 5
18 Mar 89 DON'T SHED A TEAR *Chrysalis CHS 3164* 60 3
6 Jan 96 EYES OF BLUE *IRS CDEIRS 192* 40 4
6 Apr 96 HOW LONG *IRS CDEIRS 193* 32 5
24 Aug 96 EYES OF BLUE (re-mix) *IRS CDEIRS 194* 45 1
3 Feb 96 BLUE VIEWS *I.R.S. EIRSCD 1075* 55 7
24 Jun 00 SATISFY MY SOUL *Carrack-UK PCARCD 1* 63 1

See also ACE; MIKE and the MECHANICS; SQUEEZE

CARRAPICHO – *See CHILLI featuring CARRAPICHO*

José CARRERAS (391 Top 500)

One of the world's foremost opera singers, b. 5 Dec 1946, Barcelona, Spain. The one-time prodigy is one of the world-acclaimed Three Tenors – the only chart-topping opera act – and his duet with Sarah Brightman headed the Australian chart (Singles: 19 weeks, Albums: 152 weeks) pos/wks

11 Jul 92 AMIGOS PARA SIEMPRE (FRIENDS FOR LIFE) *Really Useful RUR 10* [1] 11 11
30 Jul 94 LIBIAMO / LA DONNA E MOBILE *Teldec YZ 843CD* [2] 21 4
25 Jul 98 YOU'LL NEVER WALK ALONE *Decca 4607982* [3] 35 4
1 Oct 88 JOSÉ CARRERAS COLLECTION *Stylus SMR 860* 90 4
23 Dec 89 JOSÉ CARRERAS SINGS ANDREW LLOYD WEBBER *WEA WX 325* 42 6
1 Sep 90 ★ IN CONCERT *Decca 4304331* [1] 1 78
23 Feb 91 THE ESSENTIAL JOSÉ CARRERAS *Philips 4326921* 24 9

Date		Title / Label	pos	wks
6 Apr 91		**HOLLYWOOD GOLDEN CLASSICS** *East West WX 416*	47	3
8 Aug 92		**FROM THE BARCELONA GAMES CEREMONY** *RCA Red Seal 09026612042* [2]	41	3
8 Aug 92		**AMIGOS PARA SIEMPRE (FRIENDS FOR LIFE)** *East West 4509902562* [3]	53	4
16 Oct 93		**WITH A SONG IN MY HEART** *Teldec 4509923692*	73	1
25 Dec 93		**CHRISTMAS IN VIENNA** *Sony Classical SK 53358* [4]	71	2
10 Sep 94	★	**THE THREE TENORS IN CONCERT 1994** *Teldec 4509962002* [5]	1	26
3 Feb 96		**PASSION** *Erato 630125962*	21	8
29 Aug 98		**THE THREE TENORS IN PARIS 1998** *Decca 4605002* [1]	14	6
23 Dec 00		**THE THREE TENORS CHRISTMAS** *Sony Classical SK 89131* [6]	57	2

[1] José Carreras and Sarah Brightman [2] José Carreras featuring Placido Domingo and Luciano Pavarotti with Mehta [3] José Carreras, Placido Domingo and Luciano Pavarotti with Mehta [1] José Carreras, Placido Domingo and Luciano Pavarotti [2] Placido Domingo, José Carreras and Montserrat Caballé [3] José Carreras and Sarah Brightman [4] Placido Domingo, Diana Ross and José Carreras [5] José Carreras, Placido Domingo and Luciano Pavarotti conducted by Zubin Mehta [6] José Carreras Placido Domingo and Luciano Pavarotti featuring Zubin Mehta

Tia CARRERE

US, female actor / vocalist – Tia Carrere Samaha (Singles: 6 weeks) pos/wks

Date		Title / Label	pos	wks
30 May 92		**BALLROOM BLITZ** *Reprise W 0105*	26	6

Jim CARREY *Canada, male actor / vocalist (Singles: 3 weeks)* pos/wks

Date		Title / Label	pos	wks
21 Jan 95		**CUBAN PETE** *Columbia 6606625*	31	3

CARRIE

US / UK, male vocal / instrumental group (Singles: 2 weeks) pos/wks

Date		Title / Label	pos	wks
14 Mar 98		**MOLLY** *Island CID 687*	56	1
9 May 98		**CALIFORNIA SCREAMIN'** *Island CID 694*	55	1

Dina CARROLL (374 Top 500)

Brit award-winning Best Female Vocalist of 1994 b. 21 Aug 1968, Newmarket, UK. Soul / dance vocalist's 'So Close' was the biggest-selling debut album by a British female artist in the 1990s, and she was the only UK woman to have two simultaneous Top 10 singles that decade (in 1993) (Singles: 99 weeks, Albums: 80 weeks) pos/wks

Date		Title / Label	pos	wks
2 Feb 91	●	**IT'S TOO LATE** *Mercury ITM 3* [1]	8	14
15 Jun 91		**NAKED LOVE (JUST SAY YOU WANT ME)** *Mercury ITM 4* [2]	39	3
11 Jul 92		**AIN'T NO MAN** *A&M AM 0001*	16	8
10 Oct 92		**SPECIAL KIND OF LOVE** *A&M AM 0088*	16	5
5 Dec 92		**SO CLOSE** *A&M AM 0101*	20	8
27 Feb 93		**THIS TIME** *A&M AMCD 0184*	23	6
15 May 93		**EXPRESS** *A&M 580262-7*	12	6
16 Oct 93	●	**DON'T BE A STRANGER** *A&M 5803892*	3	13
11 Dec 93	●	**THE PERFECT YEAR** *A&M 5804812*	5	11
28 Sep 96	●	**ESCAPING** *Mercury / First Avenue DCCD 1*	3	8
21 Dec 96		**ONLY HUMAN** *Mercury / First Avenue DCCD 2*	33	4
24 Oct 98		**ONE, TWO, THREE** *Mercury / First Avenue MERCD 514*	16	4
24 Jul 99		**WITHOUT LOVE** *Manifesto / First Avenue FESCD 57*	13	7
16 Jun 01		**SOMEONE LIKE YOU** *Mercury / First Avenue 5689062*	38	2
30 Jan 93	●	**SO CLOSE** *A&M 5400342*	2	63
26 Oct 96	●	**ONLY HUMAN** *Mercury 5340962*	2	13
23 Jun 01		**THE VERY BEST OF DINA CARROLL** *Mercury 5489182*	15	4

[1] Quartz introducing Dina Carroll [2] Quartz and Dina Carroll

Ron CARROLL – *See SUPERFUNK; KLUSTER featuring Ron CARROLL*

Ronnie CARROLL

Ireland, male vocalist – Ronald Cleghorn (Singles: 50 weeks) pos/wks

Date		Title / Label	pos	wks
27 Jul 56		**WALK HAND IN HAND** *Philips PB 605*	13	8
29 Mar 57		**THE WISDOM OF A FOOL** *Philips PB 667*	20	2
31 Mar 60		**FOOTSTEPS** *Philips PB 1004*	36	3
22 Feb 62		**RING-A-DING GIRL** *Philips PB 1222*	46	3
2 Aug 62	●	**ROSES ARE RED** *Philips 326532 BF*	3	16
15 Nov 62		**IF ONLY TOMORROW** *Philips 326550 BF*	33	4
7 Mar 63	●	**SAY WONDERFUL THINGS** *Philips 326574 BF*	6	14

Jasper CARROTT *UK, male comedian / vocalist*

– Bob Davies (Singles: 15 weeks, Albums: 66 weeks) pos/wks

Date		Title / Label	pos	wks
16 Aug 75	●	**FUNKY MOPED / MAGIC ROUNDABOUT** *DJM DJS 388*	5	15
18 Oct 75	●	**RABBITS ON AND ON** *DJM DJLPS 462*	10	7
6 Nov 76		**CARROTT IN NOTTS** *DJM DJF 20482*	56	1
25 Nov 78		**THE BEST OF JASPER CARROTT** *DJM DJF 20549*	38	13
20 Oct 79		**THE UNRECORDED JASPER CARROTT** *DJM DJF 20560*	19	15
19 Sep 81		**BEAT THE CARROTT** *DJM DJF 20575*	13	16
25 Dec 82		**CARROTT'S LIB** *DJM DJF 20580*	80	3
19 Nov 83		**THE STUN (CARROTT TELLS ALL)** *DJF 20582*	57	8
7 Feb 87		**COSMIC CARROTT** *Portrait LAUGH 1*	66	3

CARS *US, male vocal / instrumental*

group (Singles: 51 weeks, Albums: 72 weeks) pos/wks

Date		Title / Label	pos	wks
11 Nov 78	●	**MY BEST FRIEND'S GIRL** *Elektra K 12301*	3	10
17 Feb 79		**JUST WHAT I NEEDED** *Elektra K 12312*	17	10
28 Jul 79		**LET'S GO** *Elektra K 12371*	51	4
5 Jun 82		**SINCE YOU'RE GONE** *Elektra K 13177*	37	4
29 Sep 84	●	**DRIVE (re)** *Elektra E 9706*	4	23
2 Dec 78		**CARS** *Elektra K 52088*	29	15
7 Jul 79		**CANDY-O** *Elektra K 52148*	30	6
6 Oct 84		**HEARTBEAT CITY** *Elektra 960296*	25	30
9 Nov 85		**THE CARS GREATEST HITS** *Elektra EKT 25*	27	19
5 Sep 87		**DOOR TO DOOR** *Elektra EKT 42*	72	2

'My Best Friend's Girl' was the first picture disc to make the singles chart. 'Drive', originally a No.5 hit, re-entered and peaked one place higher in Aug 1985

Alex CARTAÑA – *See LEE-CABRERA featuring Alex CARTAÑA*

Aaron CARTER

US, male vocalist (Singles: 33 weeks, Albums: 8 weeks) pos/wks

Date		Title / Label	pos	wks
29 Nov 97	●	**CRUSH ON YOU** *Ultra Pop 0099605 ULT*	9	8
7 Feb 98	●	**CRAZY LITTLE PARTY GIRL** *Ultra Pop 0099645 ULT*	7	6
28 Mar 98		**I'M GONNA MISS YOU FOREVER** *Ultra Pop 0099725 ULT*	24	5
4 Jul 98		**SURFIN' USA** *Ultra Pop 0099805 ULT*	18	5
16 Sep 00		**I WANT CANDY** *Jive 9250892*	31	3
28 Oct 00		**AARON'S PARTY (COME GET IT)** *Jive 9251272*	51	2
13 Apr 02		**LEAVE IT UP TO ME** *Jive 9253262*	22	4
28 Feb 98		**AARON CARTER** *Ultrapop 0099572 ULT*	12	8

Clarence CARTER *US, male vocalist (Singles: 13 weeks)* pos/wks

Date		Title / Label	pos	wks
10 Oct 70	●	**PATCHES** *Atlantic 2091 030*	2	13

Nick CARTER *US, male vocalist (Singles: 3 weeks)* pos/wks

Date		Title / Label	pos	wks
19 Oct 02		**HELP ME** *Jive 9254332*	17	3

See also BACKSTREET BOYS

CARTER – THE UNSTOPPABLE SEX MACHINE

UK, male vocal / instrumental duo – James 'Jim Bob' Morrison and Leslie 'Fruitbat' Carter (Singles: 46 weeks, Albums: 40 weeks) pos/wks

Date		Title / Label	pos	wks
26 Jan 91		**BLOODSPORT FOR ALL** *Rough Trade R 20112687*	48	2
22 Jun 91		**SHERIFF FATMAN** *Big Cat USM 1*	23	7
26 Oct 91		**AFTER THE WATERSHED** *Big Cat USM 2*	11	5
11 Jan 92		**RUBBISH** *Big Cat USM 3*	14	5
25 Apr 92	●	**THE ONLY LIVING BOY IN NEW CROSS** *Big Cat USM 4*	7	5
4 Jul 92		**DO RE ME SO FAR SO GOOD** *Chrysalis USM 5*	22	3
28 Nov 92		**THE IMPOSSIBLE DREAM** *Chrysalis USM 6*	21	3
4 Sep 93		**LEAN ON ME I WON'T FALL OVER** *Chrysalis CDUSM 7*	16	3
16 Oct 93		**LENNY AND TERENCE** *Chrysalis CDUSM 8*	40	2
12 Mar 94		**GLAM ROCK COPS** *Chrysalis CDUSMS 10*	24	3
19 Nov 94		**LET'S GET TATTOOS** *Chrysalis CDUSMS 30*	30	3
4 Feb 95		**THE YOUNG OFFENDER'S MUM** *Chrysalis CDUSMS 12*	34	3
30 Sep 95		**BORN ON THE 5TH OF NOVEMBER** *Chrysalis CDUSM 13*	35	2
2 Mar 91	●	**30 SOMETHING** *Rough Trade R2011 2702*	8	9
21 Sep 91		**101 DAMNATIONS** *Big Cat ABB 101*	29	6
1 Feb 92		**30 SOMETHING (re-issue)** *Chrysalis CHR 1897*	21	4
16 May 92	★	**1992 – THE LOVE ALBUM** *Chrysalis CCD 1946* ■	1	9
18 Sep 93	●	**POST HISTORIC MONSTERS** *Chrysalis CDCHR 7090*	5	4
26 Mar 94		**STARRY EYED AND BOLLOCK NAKED** *Chrysalis CDCHR 6069*	22	2
18 Feb 95	●	**WORRY BOMB** *Chrysalis CDCHRX 6096*	9	3

4 Oct 95 **STRAW DONKEY ... THE SINGLES** *Chrysalis CDCHR 6110* 37 2
5 Apr 97 **A WORLD WITHOUT DAVE** *Cooking Vinyl COOKCD 120* 73 1

:ARTER TWINS *Ireland, male vocal duo (Singles: 1 week)* pos/wks

8 Mar 97 **THE TWELFTH OF NEVER / TOO RIGHT TO BE** *RCA 74321453082* 61 1

Junior CARTIER *UK, male producer – Jon Carter (Singles: 1 week)* pos/wks

6 Nov 99 **WOMEN BEAT THEIR MEN** *Nucamp CAMPD 3X* 70 1

:ARTOONS *Denmark, male / female vocal / instrumental group (Singles: 30 weeks, Albums: 14 weeks)* pos/wks

3 Apr 99 ● **WITCH DOCTOR** *Flex / EMI CDTOONS 001* 2 13
9 Jun 99 ● **DOODAH! (re)** *Flex / EMI CDTOON 002* 7 12
4 Sep 99 **AISY WAISY** *Flex/ EMI CDTOONS 003* 16 5
7 Apr 99 **TOONAGE** *EMI 4966922* 17 14

;am CARTWRIGHT – *See VOLCANO*

:ARVELLS *UK, male vocalist / instrumentalist – Alan Carvell (Singles: 4 weeks)* pos/wks

6 Nov 77 **THE L.A. RUN** *Creole CR 143* 31 4

:ASCADES *US, male vocal group (Singles: 16 weeks)* pos/wks

8 Feb 63 ● **RHYTHM OF THE RAIN** *Warner Bros. WB 88* 5 16

:ASE *US, male rapper – Case Woodard (Singles: 15 weeks)* pos/wks

1 Sep 96 **TOUCH ME TEASE ME** *Def Jam DEFCD 18* [1] 26 3
0 Nov 01 **LIVIN' IT UP** *Def Jam 5888142* [2] 27 4
3 Aug 02 ● **LIVIN' IT UP (re-issue)** *Def Jam 0639782* [2] 5 8

[1] Case featuring Foxxy Brown [2] Ja Rule featuring Case

:d CASE
'K, male producer – Edward Makromallies (Singles: 5 weeks) pos/wks

1 Oct 00 **SOMETHING IN YOUR EYES** *Red Rose CDRROSE 003* 38 2
5 Sep 01 **WHO?** *Columbia 6718302* [1] 29 2
0 Jul 02 **GOOD TIMES** *Columbia 6727672* [2] 49 1

[1] Ed Case and Sweetie Irie [2] Ed Case featuring Skin

:rian and Brandon CASEY – *See NIVEA*

:atalie CASEY *UK, female actor / vocalist – youngest ever chart entrant at three years of age (Singles: 1 week)* pos/wks

7 Jan 84 **CHICK CHICK CHICKEN** *Polydor CHICK 1* 72 1

:ohnny CASH (160 Top 500)
Worldwide country music giant, b. 26 Feb, 1932, Arkansas, d. 12 Sep 2003. He scored 136 US country hits between 1956 and 2003. Elected to the Country Hall of Fame (1980) and R'n'R equivalent (1992) and enjoyed a renaissance late in his career, culminating in an MTV award for his version of Nine Inch Nails' 'Hurt' (Singles: 62 weeks, Albums: 272 weeks) pos/wks

3 Jun 65 **IT AIN'T ME BABE** *CBS 201760* 28 8
6 Sep 69 ● **A BOY NAMED SUE** *CBS 4460* 4 19
3 May 70 **WHAT IS TRUTH** *CBS 4934* 21 11
5 Apr 72 ● **A THING CALLED LOVE (re)** *CBS 7797* [1] 4 14
3 Jul 76 **ONE PIECE AT A TIME** *CBS 4287* [2] 32 7
0 May 03 **HURT / PERSONAL JESUS (re)** *American / Lost Highway 0779982* 39 3
3 Jul 66 **EVERYBODY LOVES A NUT** *CBS BPG 62717* 28 1
4 May 68 **FROM SEA TO SHINING SEA** *CBS 62972* 40 1
6 Jul 68 **OLD GOLDEN THROAT** *CBS 63316* 37 2
4 Aug 68 ● **JOHNNY CASH AT FOLSOM PRISON** *CBS 63308* 8 45
3 Aug 69 ● **JOHNNY CASH AT SAN QUENTIN** *CBS 63629* ▲ 2106
4 Oct 69 **GREATEST HITS VOLUME 1** *CBS 63062* 23 25
7 Mar 70 ● **HELLO I'M JOHNNY CASH** *CBS 63796* 6 16
5 Aug 70 ● **THE WORLD OF JOHNNY CASH** *CBS 66237* 5 25
2 Dec 70 **THE JOHNNY CASH SHOW** *CBS 64089* 18 6
8 Sep 71 **MAN IN BLACK** *CBS 64331* 18 7
13 Nov 71 **JOHNNY CASH** *Hallmark SHM 739* 43 2
20 May 72 ● **A THING CALLED LOVE** *CBS 64898* 8 11
14 Oct 72 **STAR PORTRAIT** *CBS 67201* 16 7
10 Jul 76 **ONE PIECE AT A TIME** *CBS 81416* 49 3
9 Oct 76 **THE BEST OF JOHNNY CASH** *CBS 10000* 48 2
2 Sep 78 **ITCHY FEET** *CBS 10009* 36 4
27 Aug 94 **THE MAN IN BLACK – THE DEFINITIVE COLLECTION** *Columbia MOODCD 35* 15 5
9 Mar 02 **MAN IN BLACK – THE VERY BEST OF JOHNNY CASH** *Columbia 5063452* 39 4

[1] Johnny Cash with the Evangel Temple Choir [2] Johnny Cash with the Tennessee Three

Pat CASH – *See John McENROE and Pat CASH with the FULL METAL RACKETS*

CA$HFLOW *US, male vocal / instrumental group (Singles: 8 weeks, Albums: 3 weeks)* pos/wks

24 May 86 **MINE ALL MINE / PARTY FREAK** *Club JAB 30* 15 8
28 Jun 86 **CASHFLOW** *Club JABH 17* 33 3

CASHMERE *US, male vocal / instrumental group (Singles: 11 weeks, Albums: 5 weeks)* pos/wks

19 Jan 85 **CAN I** *Fourth & Broadway BRW 19* 29 8
23 Mar 85 **WE NEED LOVE** *Fourth & Broadway BRW 22* 52 3
2 Mar 85 **CASHMERE** *Fourth & Broadway BRLP 503* 63 5

CASINO *UK, male vocal / production group (Singles: 2 weeks)* pos/wks

17 May 97 **SOUND OF EDEN** *Worx WORXCD 005* 52 1
10 Jul 99 **ONLY YOU** *Pow! CDPOW 006* 72 1

CASINOS *US, male vocal group (Singles: 7 weeks)* pos/wks

23 Feb 67 **THEN YOU CAN TELL ME GOODBYE** *President PT 123* 28 7

CASSANDRA – *See Rui DA SILVA featuring CASSANDRA*

David CASSIDY (293 Top 500)
Top teen idol of 1970s, b. 12 Apr 1950, New York. This photogenic singer / actor first found fame via the TV series The Partridge Family. His UK chart career took off as his US sales slowed down. Returned to Top 5 album chart in 2001 (Singles: 109 weeks, Albums: 110 weeks) pos/wks

8 Apr 72 ● **COULD IT BE FOREVER / CHERISH** *Bell 1224* 2 17
16 Sep 72 ★ **HOW CAN I BE SURE** *Bell 1258* 1 11
25 Nov 72 **ROCK ME BABY** *Bell 1268* 11 9
24 Mar 73 ● **I'M A CLOWN / SOME KIND OF A SUMMER** *Bell MABEL 4* 3 12
13 Oct 73 ★ **DAYDREAMER / THE PUPPY SONG** *Bell 1334* 1 15
11 May 74 ● **IF I DIDN'T CARE** *Bell 1350* 9 8
27 Jul 74 **PLEASE PLEASE ME** *Bell 1371* 16 6
5 Jul 75 **I WRITE THE SONGS / GET IT UP FOR LOVE** *RCA 2571* 11 8
25 Oct 75 **DARLIN'** *RCA 2622* 16 8
23 Feb 85 ● **THE LAST KISS** *Arista ARIST 589* 6 9
11 May 85 **ROMANCE (LET YOUR HEART GO)** *Arista ARIST 620* 54 6
20 May 72 ● **CHERISH** *Bell BELLS 210* 2 43
24 Feb 73 ● **ROCK ME BABY** *Bell BELLS 218* 2 20
24 Nov 73 ★ **DREAMS ARE NOTHIN' MORE THAN WISHES** *Bell BELLS 231* ..1 13
3 Aug 74 ● **CASSIDY LIVE** *Bell BELLS 243* 9 7
9 Aug 75 **THE HIGHER THEY CLIMB** *RCA Victor RS 1012* 22 5
8 Jun 85 **ROMANCE** *Arista 206 983* 20 6
13 Oct 01 ● **THEN AND NOW** *Universal Music TV 160822* 5 15
15 Nov 03 **A TOUCH OF BLUE** *Universal TV 9812859* 61 1

See also PARTRIDGE FAMILY

Eva CASSIDY (452 Top 500)
Unique singer / songwriter / instrumentalist – guitar, whose recording fame came after her death, b. 2 Feb 1963, Maryland, US, d. 2 Nov 1996. Worldwide success started when her fourth album, Songbird, was 'discovered' by the BBC. She is the only artist to score three posthumous No.1 albums in the UK (Singles: 10 weeks, Albums: 142 weeks) pos/wks

21 Apr 01 **OVER THE RAINBOW (3re)** *Blix Street / Hot HIT 16* 42 9
11 Oct 03 **YOU TAKE MY BREATH AWAY** *Blix Street / Hot HIT 27* 54 1

3 Jun 00 **TIME AFTER TIME** *Blix Street G 210073* 25 14
10 Feb 01 ★ **SONGBIRD** *Blix Street G 210045* 1 97
31 Aug 02 ★ **IMAGINE** *Blix Street / Hot G 210075* ■ 1 20
23 Aug 03 ★ **AMERICAN TUNE** *Blix Street / Hot G 210079* ■ 1 11

CASSIUS *France, DJ production duo – Philippe Zdar and Hubert Blanc-Francart (Singles: 13 weeks, Albums: 2 weeks)* pos/wks

23 Jan 99 ● **CASSIUS 1999** *Virgin DINSD 177* 7 7
15 May 99 **FEELING FOR YOU** *Virgin DINSD 181* 16 4
20 Nov 99 **LA MOUCHE** *Virgin DINSD 188* 53 1
5 Oct 02 **THE SOUND OF VIOLENCE** *Virgin DISND 241* 49 1
6 Feb 99 **1999** *Virgin CDVIR 76* 28 2

CAST 392 Top 500
The La's guitarist John Power (b. 14 Sep 1967, Liverpool) fronted this retro-sounding Merseyside Brit pop quartet, with Liam Tyson (g), Peter Wilkinson (b) and Keith O'Neill (d). Nominated for Best Newcomers at the 1995 Brit Awards (Singles: 55 weeks, Albums: 116 weeks) pos/wks

15 Jul 95 **FINETIME** *Polydor 5795072* 17 4
30 Sep 95 **ALRIGHT** *Polydor 5799272* 13 4
20 Jan 96 ● **SANDSTORM** *Polydor 5778732* 8 5
30 Mar 96 ● **WALKAWAY** *Polydor 5762852* 9 7
26 Oct 96 ● **FLYING** *Polydor 5754772* 4 5
5 Apr 97 ● **FREE ME (re)** *Polydor 5736512* 7 7
28 Jun 97 ● **GUIDING STAR** *Polydor 5711732* 9 6
13 Sep 97 ● **LIVE THE DREAM** *Polydor 5716852* 7 5
15 Nov 97 **I'M SO LONELY** *Polydor 5690592* 14 3
8 May 99 ● **BEAT MAMA** *Polydor 5635932* 9 5
7 Aug 99 **MAGIC HOUR** *Polydor 5612272* 28 3
28 Jul 01 **DESERT DROUGHT** *Polydor 5871752* 45 1
28 Oct 95 ● **ALL CHANGE** *Polydor 5293122* 7 67
26 Apr 97 ● **MOTHER NATURE CALLS** *Polydor 5375672* 3 42
29 May 99 ● **MAGIC HOUR** *Polydor 5471762* 6 7

CAST FROM CASUALTY
UK, male / female actors / vocal group (Singles: 6 weeks) pos/wks

14 Mar 98 ● **EVERLASTING LOVE** *Warner.esp WESP 003CD* 5 6

CAST OF THE NEW ROCKY HORROR SHOW
UK, male / female vocal group (Singles: 1 week) pos/wks

12 Dec 98 **THE TIMEWARP** *Damn It Janet DAMJAN 1CD* 57 1

Roy CASTLE *UK, male vocalist d. 2 Sep 1994 (Singles: 3 weeks)* pos/wks

22 Dec 60 **LITTLE WHITE BERRY** *Philips PB 1087* 40 3

CASUALS *UK, male vocal / instrumental group (Singles: 26 weeks)* pos/wks

14 Aug 68 ● **JESAMINE** *Decca F 22784* 2 18
4 Dec 68 **TOY** *Decca F 22852* 30 8

CAT *UK, male vocalist – Danny John-Jules (Singles: 4 weeks)* pos/wks

23 Oct 93 **TONGUE TIED** *EMI CDEM 286* 17 4

CATATONIA 381 Top 500 *Brit-nominated, chart-topping gregarious, Welsh indie-pop band formed Cardiff, 1991: Cerys Matthews (v: b. 11 Apr 1969, Swansea), Mark Roberts (g), Paul Jones (b), Owen Powell (g) and Aled Richards (d). Group split in 2001 and Matthews launched a solo career (Singles: 50 weeks, Albums: 125 weeks)* pos/wks

3 Feb 96 **SWEET CATATONIA** *Blanco Y Negro NEG 85CD* 61 1
4 May 96 **LOST CAT** *Blanco Y Negro NEG 88CD1* 41 1
7 Sep 96 **YOU'VE GOT A LOT TO ANSWER FOR** *Blanco Y Negro NEG 93CD1* 35 2
30 Nov 96 **BLEED** *Blanco Y Negro NEG 97CD1* 46 1
18 Oct 97 **I AM THE MOB** *Blanco Y Negro NEG 107CD* 40 2
31 Jan 98 ● **MULDER AND SCULLY** *Blanco Y Negro NEG 109CD* 3 10
2 May 98 ● **ROAD RAGE** *Blanco Y Negro NEG 112CD* 5 8
1 Aug 98 **STRANGE GLUE** *Blanco Y Negro NEG 113CD* 11 6
7 Nov 98 **GAME ON** *WEA NEG 114CD* 33 2
10 Apr 99 ● **DEAD FROM THE WAIST DOWN** *Blanco Y Negro NEG 115CD* 7 8
24 Jul 99 **LONDINIUM** *Blanco Y Negro NEG 117CD* 20 3
13 Nov 99 **KARAOKE QUEEN** *Blanco Y Negro NEG 119CD* 36 2
4 Aug 01 **STONE BY STONE (re)** *Blanco Y Negro NEG 134CD* 19 4
12 Oct 96 **WAY BEYOND BLUE** *Blanco Y Negro 630163052* 32 3
14 Feb 98 ★ **INTERNATIONAL VELVET** *Blanco Y Negro 3984208342* 1 93
24 Apr 99 ★ **EQUALLY CURSED AND BLESSED** *Blanco Y Negro 3984270942* ■ 1 23
18 Aug 01 ● **PAPER SCISSORS STONE** *Blanco Y Negro 8573888482* 6 4
14 Sep 02 **GREATEST HITS** *Blanco Y Negro 0927491942* 24 2

See also SPACE

CATCH *UK, male vocal / instrumental group (Singles: 1 week)* pos/wks

17 Nov 90 **FREE (C'MON)** *ffrr F 147* 70 1

CATCH *UK, male vocal / instrumental group (Singles: 6 week)* pos/wks

11 Oct 97 **BINGO** *Virgin VSCDT 1656* 23 4
21 Feb 98 **DIVE IN** *Virgin VSCDT 1665* 44 2

CATHERINE WHEEL *UK, male vocal / instrumental group (Singles: 12 weeks, Albums: 3 weeks)* pos/wks

23 Nov 91 **BLACK METALLIC (EP)** *Fontana CW 1* 68 1
8 Feb 92 **BALLOON** *Fontana CW 2* 59 1
18 Apr 92 **I WANT TO TOUCH YOU** *Fontana CW 3* 35 2
9 Jan 93 **30TH CENTURY MAN** *Fontana CWCD 4* 47 2
10 Jul 93 **CRANK** *Fontana CWCD 5* 66 1
16 Oct 93 **SHOW ME MARY** *Fontana CWCDA 6* 62 1
5 Aug 95 **WAYDOWN** *Fontana CWCD 7* 67 1
13 Dec 97 **DELICIOUS** *Chrysalis CDCHS 5071* 53 1
28 Feb 98 **MA SOLITUDA** *Chrysalis CDCHS 5077* 53 1
2 May 98 **BROKEN NOSE** *Chrysalis CDCHS 5086* 48 1
29 Feb 92 **FERMENT** *Fontana 5109032* 36 1
31 Jul 93 **CHROME** *Fontana 5180392* 58 1
16 May 98 **ADAM AND EVE** *Chrysalis 4930992* 53 1

Tracks on Black Metallic (EP): Black Metallic / Crawling Over Me / Let Me Down Again / Saccharine

CATHOLICS – *See Frank BLACK*

Lorraine CATO *UK, female vocalist (Singles: 3 weeks)* pos/wks

6 Feb 93 **HOW CAN YOU TELL ME IT'S OVER** *Columbia 6587662* 46 2
3 Aug 96 **I WAS MADE TO LOVE YOU** *MCA MCSTD 40055* 41 1

CATS *UK, male instrumental group (Singles: 2 weeks)* pos/wks

9 Apr 69 **SWAN LAKE (re)** *BAF 1* 48 2

CATS U.K. *UK, male instrumental group (Singles: 8 weeks)* pos/wks

6 Oct 79 **LUTON AIRPORT** *WEA K 18075* 22 8

Nick CAVE and the BAD SEEDS *Australia / Germany, male vocal / instrumental group (Singles: 13 weeks, Albums: 29 weeks)* pos/wks

11 Apr 92 **STRAIGHT TO YOU / JACK THE RIPPER** *Mute MUTE 140* 68 1
12 Dec 92 **WHAT A WONDERFUL WORLD** *Mute MUTE 151* [1] 72 1
9 Apr 94 **DO YOU LOVE ME** *Mute CDMUTE 160* 68 1
14 Oct 95 **WHERE THE WILD ROSES GROW** *Mute CDMUTE 185* [2] 11 4
9 Mar 96 **HENRY LEE** *Mute CDMUTE 189* [3] 36 1
22 Feb 97 **INTO MY ARMS** *Mute CDMUTE 192* 53 1
31 May 97 **(ARE YOU) THE ONE THAT I'VE BEEN...** *Mute CDMUTE 206* 67 1
31 Mar 01 **AS I SAT SADLY BY HER SIDE** *Mute CDMUTE 249* 42 1
2 Jun 01 **FIFTEEN FEET OF PURE WHITE SNOW** *Mute CDMUTE 262* 52 1
8 Mar 03 **BRING IT ON** *Mute CDMUTE 265* 58 1
2 Jun 84 **FROM HER TO ETERNITY** *Mute STUMM 17* 40 3
15 Jun 85 **THE FIRST BORN IS DEAD** *Mute STUMM 21* 53 1
30 Aug 86 **KICKING AGAINST THE PRICKS** *Mute STUMM 28* 89 1
1 Oct 88 **TENDER PREY** *Mute STUMM 52* 67 1
28 Apr 90 **THE GOOD SON** *Mute STUMM 76* 47 1
9 May 92 **HENRY'S DREAM** *Mute CDSTUMM 92* 29 2
18 Sep 93 **LIVE SEEDS** *Mute CDSTUMM 122* 67 1
30 Apr 94 **LET LOVE IN** *Mute LCDSTUMM 123* 12 2
17 Feb 96 ● **MURDER BALLADS** *Mute CDSTUMM 138* 8 5
15 Mar 97 **THE BOATMAN'S CALL** *Mute CDSTUMM 142* 22 3

23 May 98 **THE BEST OF NICK CAVE AND THE BAD SEEDS**
Mute LCDMUTEL 4 ....11 4
14 Apr 01 **NO MORE SHALL WE PART** *Mute CDSTUMM 164* 15 3
15 Feb 03 **NOCTURAMA** *Mute CDSTUMM207*....20 2

[1] Nick Cave and Shane MacGowan [2] Nick Cave and Kylie Minogue [3] Nick Cave and the Bad Seeds and PJ Harvey

See also BIRTHDAY PARTY

CAVE IN *US, male vocal / instrumental group (Singles: 1 week, Albums: 1 week)* pos/wks

31 May 03 **ANCHOR** *RCA 82876522982* 53 1
29 Mar 03 **ANTENNA** *RCA 82876507702* 67 1

CAVEMAN
UK, male rap group (Singles: 2 weeks, Albums: 2 weeks) pos/wks

9 Mar 91 **I'M READY** *Profile PROF 330* 65 2
3 Apr 91 **POSITIVE REACTION** *Profile FILER 406*....43 2

CECIL
UK, male vocal / instrumental group (Singles: 2 weeks) pos/wks

25 Oct 97 **HOSTAGE IN A FROCK** *Parlophone CDRS 6471* 68 1
28 Mar 98 **THE MOST TIRING DAY** *Parlophone CDR 6490* 69 1

CELEDA *US, female vocalist (Singles: 5 weeks)* pos/wks

5 Sep 98 **MUSIC IS THE ANSWER (DANCIN' AND PRANCIN)**
Twisted UK TWCD 10038 [1] 36 3
2 Jun 99 **BE YOURSELF** *Twisted UK TWCD 10049* 61 1
3 Oct 99 **MUSIC IS THE ANSWER (DANCIN' AND PRANCIN)**
Twisted UK TWCD 10052 [2] 50 1

[1] Danny Tenaglia and Celeda [2] Celeda with Danny Tenaglia

CELETIA *UK, female vocalist – Celetia Martin (Singles: 3 weeks)* pos/wks

1 Apr 98 **REWIND** *Big Life BLRD 142* 29 2
8 Aug 98 **RUNAWAY SKIES** *Big Life BLRD 144* 66 1

CELTIC CHORUS – *See LISBON LIONS featuring Martin O'NEILL & CELTIC CHORUS*

CELTIC SPIRIT *Ireland / UK, male vocal / instrumental group (Albums: 1 week)* pos/wks

1 Jan 98 **CELTIC DREAMS** *PolyGram TV 5399992* 62 1

CENOGINERZ
Holland, male producer – Michel Pollen (Singles: 1 week) pos/wks

2 Feb 02 **GIT DOWN** *Tripoli Trax TTRAX 081CD* 75 1

CENTORY
US, male rapper (Singles: 1 week) pos/wks

7 Dec 94 **POINT OF NO RETURN** *EMI CDEM 354* 67 1

CENTRAL LINE *UK, male vocal / instrumental group (Singles: 30 weeks, Albums: 5 weeks)* pos/wks

1 Jan 81 **(YOU KNOW) YOU CAN DO IT** *Mercury LINE 7*....67 3
5 Aug 81 **WALKING INTO SUNSHINE** *Mercury MER 78* 42 10
0 Jan 82 **DON'T TELL ME** *Mercury MER 90* 55 3
0 Nov 82 **YOU'VE SAID ENOUGH** *Mercury MER 117* 58 3
2 Jan 83 **NATURE BOY** *Mercury MER 131* 21 8
1 Jun 83 **SURPRISE SURPRISE** *Mercury MER 133* 48 3
3 Feb 82 **BREAKING POINT** *Mercury MERA 001* 64 5

CERRONE *France, male producer / multi-instrumentalist – Jean-Marc Cerrone (Singles: 21 weeks, Albums: 1 week)* pos/wks

5 Mar 77 **LOVE IN C MINOR** *Atlantic K 10895* 31 4
9 Jul 78 ● **SUPERNATURE** *Atlantic K 11089* 8 12
3 Jan 79 **JE SUIS MUSIC** *CBS 6918* 39 4
0 Aug 96 **SUPERNATURE (re-mix)** *Encore CDCOR 013* 66 1
0 Sep 78 **SUPERNATURE** *Atlantic K 50431*....60 1

A CERTAIN RATIO *UK, male vocal / instrumental group (Singles: 3 weeks, Albums: 3 weeks)* pos/wks

16 Jun 90 **WON'T STOP LOVING YOU** *A&M ACR 540* 55 3
30 Jan 82 **SEXTET** *Factory FACT 55*....53 3

Peter CETERA
US, male vocalist (Singles: 20 weeks, Albums: 4 weeks) pos/wks

2 Aug 86 ● **GLORY OF LOVE** *Full Moon W 8662* ▲ 3 13
21 Jun 97 ● **HARD TO SAY I'M SORRY** *La Face 74321481482* [1] 7 7
13 Sep 86 **SOLITUDE / SOLITAIRE** *Full Moon 9254741* 56 4

[1] Az Yet featuring Peter Cetera

See also CHICAGO

Frank CHACKSFIELD and his ORCHESTRA
UK, orchestra, leader d. 9 Jun 1995 (Singles: 41 weeks) pos/wks

3 Apr 53 ● **LITTLE RED MONKEY** *Parlophone R 3658* [1] 10 3
22 May 53 ● **TERRY'S THEME FROM 'LIMELIGHT'** *Decca F 10106* 2 24
12 Feb 54 ● **EBB TIDE** *Decca F 10122* 9 2
24 Feb 56 **IN OLD LISBON** *Decca F 10689* 15 4
18 May 56 **PORT-AU-PRINCE** *Decca F 10727* [2] 18 6
31 Aug 56 **DONKEY CART** *Decca F 10743* 26 2

[1] Frank Chacksfield's Tunesmiths, featuring Jack Jordan – clavioline
[2] Winifred Atwell and Frank Chacksfield

CHAIRMEN OF THE BOARD *US, male vocal / instrumental quartet – leader Norman (General) Johnson (Singles: 77 weeks)* pos/wks

22 Aug 70 ● **GIVE ME JUST A LITTLE MORE TIME** *Invictus INV 501* 3 13
14 Nov 70 ● **YOU'VE GOT ME DANGLING ON A STRING**
Invictus INV 504 ....5 13
20 Feb 71 **EVERYTHING'S TUESDAY** *Invictus INV 507* 12 9
15 May 71 **PAY TO THE PIPER** *Invictus INV 511* 34 7
4 Sep 71 **CHAIRMAN OF THE BOARD** *Invictus INV 516* 48 2
15 Jul 72 **WORKING ON A BUILDING OF LOVE** *Invictus INV 519* 20 8
7 Oct 72 **ELMO JAMES** *Invictus INV 524* 21 7
16 Dec 72 **I'M ON MY WAY TO A BETTER PLACE (re)**
Invictus INV 527 ....30 6
23 Jun 73 **FINDERS KEEPERS** *Invictus INV 530* 21 9
13 Sep 86 **LOVER BOY** *EMI EMI 5585* [1] 56 3

[1] Chairmen of the Board featuring General Johnson

CHAKACHAS *Belgium, male / female vocal / instrumental group (Singles: 8 weeks)* pos/wks

11 Jan 62 **TWIST TWIST** *RCA 1264* 48 1
27 May 72 **JUNGLE FEVER** *Polydor 2121 064* 29 7

George CHAKIRIS *US, male actor / vocalist (Singles: 1 week)* pos/wks

2 Jun 60 **HEART OF A TEENAGE GIRL** *Triumph RGM 1010* 49 1

CHAKKA BOOM BANG
Holland, male instrumental / production group (Singles: 1 week) pos/wks

20 Jan 96 **TOSSING AND TURNING** *Hooj Choons HOOJCD 39* 57 1

CHAKRA *UK, male production duo – Ricky Simmons and Steve Jones, and female vocalist (Singles: 5 weeks)* pos/wks

18 Jan 97 **I AM** *WEA WEA 091CD* 24 2
23 Aug 97 **HOME** *WEA WEA 116CD2* 46 1
23 Oct 99 **LOVE SHINES THROUGH** *WEA WEA 227CD* 67 1
26 Aug 00 **HOME (re-mix)** *WEA WEA 266CD* 47 1

See also ASCENSION; ESSENCE; LUSTRAL; SPACE BROTHERS; OXYGEN featuring Andrea BRITTON

CHALI 2NA – *See JURASSIC 5; DJ FORMAT featuring CHALI 2NA & AKIL*

Sue CHALONER
UK, female vocalist (Singles: 1 week) pos/wks

22 May 93 **MOVE ON UP** *Pulse 8 CDLOSE 41* 64 1

Richard CHAMBERLAIN
US, male actor / vocalist (Singles: 36 weeks, Albums: 8 weeks) pos/wks

7 Jun 62 **THEME FROM 'DR KILDARE' (THREE STARS WILL SHINE TONIGHT)** *MGM 1160* 12 10
1 Nov 62 **LOVE ME TENDER** *MGM 1173* 15 11
21 Feb 63 **HI-LILI, HI-LO** *MGM 1189* 20 9
18 Jul 63 **TRUE LOVE** *MGM 1205* 30 6
16 Mar 63 ● **RICHARD CHAMBERLAIN SINGS** *MGM C 923* 8 8

Bryan CHAMBERS – *See CLEPTOMANIACS featuring Bryan CHAMBERS*

CHAMELEON
UK, male vocal / instrumental group (Singles: 2 weeks) pos/wks

18 May 96 **THE WAY IT IS** *Stress CDSTR 65* 34 2

CHAMELEONS
UK, male vocal / instrumental group (Albums: 4 weeks) pos/wks

25 May 85 **WHAT DOES ANYTHING MEAN? BASICALLY** *Statik STAT LP 22* 60 2
20 Sep 86 **STRANGE TIMES** *Geffen 924 1191* 44 2

CHAMELEONS – *See LORI and The CHAMELEONS*

CHAMONIX – *See Kurtis MANTRONIK*

CHAMPAIGN *US, male / female vocal / instrumental group (Singles: 13 weeks, Albums: 4 weeks)* pos/wks

9 May 81 ● **HOW 'BOUT US** *CBS A 1046* 5 13
27 Jun 81 **HOW 'BOUT US** *CBS 84927* 38 4

CHAMPIONSHIP LEGEND – *See RAZE*

CHAMPS *US, male instrumental group (Singles: 10 weeks)* pos/wks

4 Apr 58 ● **TEQUILA** *London HLU 8580* ▲ 5 9
17 Mar 60 **TOO MUCH TEQUILA** *London HLH 9052* 49 1

CHAMPS BOYS *France, male instrumental group (Singles: 6 weeks)* pos/wks

19 Jun 76 **TUBULAR BELLS** *Philips 6006 519* 41 6

CHANCE – *See SUNKIDS featuring CHANCE*

Gene CHANDLER
US, male vocalist – Eugene Dixon (Singles: 29 weeks) pos/wks

5 Jun 68 **NOTHING CAN STOP ME** *Soul City SC 102* 41 4
3 Feb 79 **GET DOWN** *20th Century BTC 1040* 11 11
1 Sep 79 **WHEN YOU'RE NUMBER 1** *20th Century TC 2411* 43 5
28 Jun 80 **DOES SHE HAVE A FRIEND?** *20th Century TC 2451* 28 9

CHANELLE
US, female vocalist – Charlene Munford (Singles: 9 weeks) pos/wks

11 Mar 89 **ONE MAN** *Cooltempo COOL 183* 16 8
10 Dec 94 **ONE MAN (re-mix)** *Deep Distraxion OILYCD 031* 50 1

CHANGE *US, male / female vocal / instrumental group (Singles: 43 weeks, Albums: 23 weeks)* pos/wks

28 Jun 80 **A LOVER'S HOLIDAY / THE GLOW OF LOVE** *WEA K 79141* 14 8
6 Sep 80 **SEARCHING** *WEA K 79156* 11 10
2 Jun 84 **CHANGE OF HEART** *WEA YZ 7* 17 10
11 Aug 84 **YOU ARE MY MELODY** *WEA YZ 14* 48 4
16 Mar 85 **LET'S GO TOGETHER** *Cooltempo COOL 107* 37 7
25 May 85 **OH WHAT A FEELING** *Cooltempo COOL 109* 56 2
13 Jul 85 **MUTUAL ATTRACTION** *Cooltempo COOL 111* 60 2
19 May 84 **CHANGE OF HEART** *WEA WX 5* 34 17
27 Apr 85 **TURN ON THE RADIO** *Cooltempo CHR 1504* 39 6

See also Luther VANDROSS

CHANGING FACES *US, female vocal duo – Cassandra Lucas and Charisse Rose (Singles: 12 weeks)* pos/wks

24 Sep 94 **STROKE YOU UP** *Big Beat A 8251CD* 43 3
26 Jul 97 ● **G.H.E.T.T.O.U.T.** *Atlantic AT 0003CD* 10 5
1 Nov 97 **I GOT SOMEBODY ELSE** *Atlantic AT 0014CD* 42 1
4 Apr 98 **TIME AFTER TIME** *Atlantic AT 0027CD* [1] 35 2
1 Aug 98 **SAME TEMPO** *A&M 5826952* 53 1

[1] Changing Faces featuring Jay Z

Bruce CHANNEL *US, male vocalist (Singles: 28 weeks)* pos/wks

22 Mar 62 ● **HEY! BABY** *Mercury AMT 1171* ▲ 2 12
26 Jun 68 **KEEP ON** *Bell 1010* 12 16

CHANNEL X
Belgium, male / female vocal / instrumental group (Singles: 1 week) pos/wks

14 Dec 91 **GROOVE TO MOVE** *PWL Continental PWL 209* 67 1

CHANSON *US, male / female vocal group (Singles: 7 weeks)* pos/wks

13 Jan 79 **DON'T HOLD BACK** *Ariola ARO 140* 33 7

CHANTAL – *See MOONMAN*

CHANTAYS *US, male instrumental group (Singles: 14 weeks)* pos/wks

18 Apr 63 **PIPELINE** *London HLD 9696* 16 14

CHANTER SISTERS *UK, female vocal group (Singles: 5 weeks)* pos/wks

17 Jul 76 **SIDESHOW** *Polydor 2058 735* 43 5

CHAOS *UK, male vocal group (Singles: 2 weeks)* pos/wks

3 Oct 92 **FAREWELL MY SUMMER LOVE** *Arista 74321116397* 55 2

Harry CHAPIN
US, male vocalist d. 16 Jul 1981 (Singles: 5 weeks) pos/wks

11 May 74 **W.O.L.D.** *Elektra K 12133* 34 5

Michael CHAPMAN *UK, male vocalist (Albums: 1 week)* pos/wks

21 Mar 70 **FULLY QUALIFIED SURVIVOR** *Harvest SHVL 764* 45 1

Simone CHAPMAN – *See ILLEGAL MOTION featuring Simone CHAPMAN*

Tracy CHAPMAN (260 Top 500)
Modern folk vocalist / instrumentalist – guitar, whose socially conscious songs scored internationally, b. 20 Mar 1964, Ohio. Boosted by her appearance at Nelson Mandela's 70th birthday tribute show, her eponymous debut album sold more than 10 million copies and won the Grammy for Best New Act of 1988 (Singles: 15 weeks, Albums: 227 weeks) pos/wks

11 Jun 88 ● **FAST CAR** *Elektra EKR 73* 5 12
30 Sep 89 **CROSSROADS** *Elektra EKR 95* 61 3
21 May 88 ★ **TRACY CHAPMAN** *Elektra EKT 44* ▲ 1 188
14 Oct 89 ★ **CROSSROADS** *Elektra EKT 61* ■ 1 16
9 May 92 **MATTERS OF THE HEART** *Elektra 7559612152* 19 3
6 Oct 01 ● **COLLECTION** *Elektra 7559627002* 3 18
2 Nov 02 **LET IT RAIN** *Elektra 7559628362* 36 2

CHAPTERHOUSE *UK, male vocal / instrumental group (Singles: 3 weeks, Albums: 3 weeks)* pos/wks

30 Mar 91 **PEARL** *Dedicated STONE 003* 67 1
12 Oct 91 **MESMERISE** *Dedicated HOUSE 001* 60 2
11 May 91 **WHIRLPOOL** *Dedicated DEDLP 001* 23 3

CHAQUITO ORCHESTRA *UK, orchestra arranged and conducted by Johnny Gregory (Singles: 1 week, Albums: 2 weeks)* pos/wks

27 Oct 60 **NEVER ON SUNDAY** *Fontana H 265* [1] 50 1
24 Feb 68 **THIS IS CHAQUITO** *Fontana SFXL 50* [1] 36 1
4 Mar 72 **THRILLER THEMES** *Philips 6308 087* 48 1

[1] Chaquito and his Orchestra [1] Chaquito and Quedo Brass

See also QUEDO BRASS

CHARGE GBH *UK male vocal / instrumental group (Albums: 6 weeks)* pos/wks

14 Aug 82 CITY BABY ATTACKED BY RATS *Clay CLAYLP 4* 17 6

CHARLATANS (354 Top 500)

North country boys from Northwich, Cheshire, UK, who came to prominence as part of the 'Madchester' scene, Tim Burgess (v) b. 30 May 1968, Manchester, UK, and Rob Collins (k) b. 23 Feb 1963, d. 23 Jul 1996 (Singles: 77 weeks, Albums: 108 weeks) pos/wks

2 Jun 90 ● THE ONLY ONE I KNOW *Situation Two SIT 70T* 9 9
22 Sep 90 THEN *Situation Two SIT 74T* 12 5
9 Mar 91 OVER RISING *Situation Two SIT 76* 15 5
17 Aug 91 INDIAN ROPE *Dead Dead Good GOOD 1T* 57 1
9 Nov 91 ME. IN TIME *Situation Two SIT 84* 28 3
7 Mar 92 WEIRDO *Situation Two SIT 88* 19 4
18 Jul 92 TREMELO SONG (EP) *Situation Two SIT 97T* 44 2
5 Feb 94 CAN'T GET OUT OF BED *Beggars Banquet BBQ 27CD* 24 3
19 Mar 94 I NEVER WANT AN EASY LIFE IF ME AND HE WERE EVER TO GET THERE *Beggars Banquet BBQ 31CD* 38 1
2 Jul 94 JESUS HAIRDO *Beggars Banquet BBQ 32CD1* 48 2
7 Jan 95 CRASHIN' IN *Beggars Banquet BBQ 44CD* 31 2
27 May 95 JUST LOOKIN' / BULLET COMES *Beggars Banquet BBQ 55CD*32 3
26 Aug 95 JUST WHEN YOU'RE THINKIN' THINGS OVER *Beggars Banquet BBQ 60CD* 12 3
7 Sep 96 ● ONE TO ANOTHER *Beggars Banquet BBQ 301CD* 3 6
5 Apr 97 ● NORTH COUNTRY BOY (re) *Beggars Banquet BBQ 309CD* 4 6
21 Jun 97 ● HOW HIGH *Beggars Banquet BBQ 312CD* 6 5
1 Nov 97 TELLIN' STORIES *Beggars Banquet BBQ 318CD* 16 3
16 Oct 99 FOREVER *Universal MCSTD 40220* 12 3
18 Dec 99 MY BEAUTIFUL FRIEND *Universal MCSTD 40225* 31 3
27 May 00 IMPOSSIBLE *Universal MCSTD 40231* 15 3
8 Sep 01 LOVE IS THE KEY *Universal MCSTD 40262* 16 3
1 Dec 01 A MAN NEEDS TO BE TOLD *Universal MCSTD 40271* 31 2
20 Oct 90 ★ SOME FRIENDLY *Situation Two SITU 30* ■ 1 17
4 Apr 92 BETWEEN 10TH AND 11TH *Situation Two SITU 37CD* 21 4
2 Apr 94 ● UP TO OUR HIPS *Beggars Banquet BBQCD 147* 8 3
9 Sep 95 ★ THE CHARLATANS *Beggars Banquet BBQCD 174* ■ 1 13
3 May 97 ★ TELLIN' STORIES *Beggars Banquet BBQCD 190* ■ 1 28
7 Mar 98 ● MELTING POT *Beggars Banquet BBQCD 198* 4 25
30 Oct 99 ● US AND US ONLY *Universal MCD 60069* 2 10
22 Sep 01 ● WONDERLAND *Universal MCD 60076* 2 5
1 Jun 02 SONGS FROM THE OTHER SIDE *Beggars Banquet BEGL 2032CD* 55 1
3 Aug 02 LIVE IT LIKE YOU LOVE IT *Universal MCD 60080* 40 2

Tracks on Tremelo Song (EP): Tremelo Song / Happen to Die / Normality Swing

CHARLENE *US, female vocalist – Charlene Duncan (Singles: 12 weeks, Albums: 4 weeks)* pos/wks

15 May 82 ★ I'VE NEVER BEEN TO ME *Motown TMG 1260* 1 12
17 Jul 82 I'VE NEVER BEEN TO ME *Motown STML 12171* 43 4

Alex CHARLES – *See DJ INNOCENCE featuring Alex CHARLES*

Don CHARLES *UK, male vocalist (Singles: 5 weeks)* pos/wks

22 Feb 62 WALK WITH ME MY ANGEL *Decca F 11424* 39 5

Ray CHARLES (370 Top 500)

Rock era's first 'genius', b. Ray Charles Robinson, 23 Sep 1930, Georgia. This blind singer / songwriter / pianist and band leader had a US R&B chart career spanning seven decades. In 1994 he received a prestigious National Medal of Arts from US President Clinton (Singles: 130 weeks, Albums: 50 weeks) pos/wks

1 Dec 60 GEORGIA ON MY MIND (re) *HMV POP 792* ▲ 24 8
19 Oct 61 ● HIT THE ROAD JACK *HMV POP 935* ▲ 6 12
14 Jun 62 ★ I CAN'T STOP LOVING YOU *HMV POP 1034* ▲ 1 17
13 Sep 62 ● YOU DON'T KNOW ME *HMV POP 1064* 9 13
13 Dec 62 YOUR CHEATING HEART *HMV POP 1099* 13 8
28 Mar 63 DON'T SET ME FREE *HMV POP 1133* 37 3
16 May 63 ● TAKE THESE CHAINS FROM MY HEART *HMV POP 1161* 5 20
12 Sep 63 NO ONE *HMV POP 1202* 35 7
31 Oct 63 BUSTED *HMV POP 1221* 21 10
24 Sep 64 NO ONE TO CRY TO *HMV POP 1333* 38 3
21 Jan 65 MAKIN' WHOOPEE *HMV POP 1383* 42 4
10 Feb 66 CRYIN' TIME *HMV POP 1502* [1] 50 1
21 Apr 66 TOGETHER AGAIN *HMV POP 1519* 48 1
5 Jul 67 HERE WE GO AGAIN (re) *HMV POP 1595* 38 3
20 Dec 67 YESTERDAY *Stateside SS 2071* 44 4
31 Jul 68 ELEANOR RIGBY *Stateside SS 2120* 36 9
13 Jan 90 I'LL BE GOOD TO YOU *Qwest W 2697* [2] 21 7
28 Jul 62 ● MODERN SOUNDS IN COUNTRY AND WESTERN MUSIC *HMV CLP 1580* ▲ 6 16
23 Feb 63 MODERN SOUNDS IN COUNTRY AND WESTERN MUSIC VOLUME 2 *HMV CLP 1613* 15 5
20 Jul 63 GREATEST HITS *HMV CLP 1626* 16 5
5 Oct 68 GREATEST HITS VOLUME 2 *Stateside SSL 10241* 24 8
19 Jul 80 HEART TO HEART – 20 HOT HITS *London RAY TV 1* 29 5
24 Mar 90 THE COLLECTION *Arcade RCLP 101* 36 3
13 Mar 93 RAY CHARLES – THE LIVING LEGEND *Arcade ARC 94642* 48 3
25 Aug 01 THE DEFINITIVE RAY CHARLES *WSM 8122735562* 13 5

[1] With the Jack Halloran Singers and the Ray Charles Orchestra with the Raeletts
[2] Quincy Jones featuring Ray Charles and Chaka Khan

See also INXS

Suzette CHARLES *US, female vocalist (Singles: 2 weeks)* pos/wks

21 Aug 93 FREE TO LOVE AGAIN *RCA 74321158372* 58 2

Tina CHARLES *UK, female vocalist – Tina Hoskins (Singles: 63 weeks, Albums: 7 weeks)* pos/wks

7 Feb 76 ★ I LOVE TO LOVE (BUT MY BABY LOVES TO DANCE) *CBS 3937* 1 12
1 May 76 LOVE ME LIKE A LOVER *CBS 4237* 28 7
21 Aug 76 ● DANCE LITTLE LADY DANCE *CBS 4480* 6 13
4 Dec 76 ● DR LOVE *CBS 4779* 4 10
14 May 77 RENDEZVOUS *CBS 5174* 27 6
29 Oct 77 LOVE BUG – SWEETS FOR MY SWEET (MEDLEY) *CBS 5680* 26 4
11 Mar 78 I'LL GO WHERE YOUR MUSIC TAKES ME *CBS 6062* 27 8
30 Aug 86 I LOVE TO LOVE (re-mix) *DMC DECK 1* 67 3
3 Dec 77 HEART 'N' SOUL *CBS 82180* 35 7

See also 5000 VOLTS

CHARLES and EDDIE

US, male vocal duo – Charles Pettigrew (d. 6 Apr 2001) and Eddie Chacon (Singles: 30 weeks, Albums: 15 weeks) pos/wks

31 Oct 92 ★ WOULD I LIE TO YOU *Capitol CL 673* 1 17
20 Feb 93 N.Y.C. (CAN YOU BELIEVE THIS CITY) *Capitol CDCL 681* 33 5
22 May 93 HOUSE IS NOT A HOME *Capitol CDCLS 688* 29 4
13 May 95 24-7-365 *Capitol CDCLS 747* 38 4
12 Dec 92 DUOPHONIC *Capitol CDESTU 2186* 19 15

Dick CHARLESWORTH and his CITY GENTS *UK, male jazz band group – Dick Charlesworth – clarinet (Singles: 1 week)* pos/wks

4 May 61 BILLY BOY *Top Rank JAR 558* 43 1

CHARLISE – *See KID CREME*

CHARLOTTE *UK, female vocalist (Singles: 4 weeks)* pos/wks

12 Mar 94 QUEEN OF HEARTS *Big Life BLRD 106* 54 1
2 May 98 BE MINE *Parlophone Rhythm CDRHYTHM 10* 59 1
29 May 99 SKIN *Parlophone Rhythm Series CDRHYTHM 20* 56 1
4 Sep 99 SOMEDAY *Parlophone Rhythm Series CDRHYTHM 23* 74 1

CHARME *US, male / female vocal group (Singles: 2 weeks)* pos/wks

17 Nov 84 GEORGY PORGY *RCA 464* 68 2

CHARO and the SALSOUL ORCHESTRA

US, female vocalist and orchestra (Singles: 4 weeks) pos/wks

29 Apr 78 DANCE A LITTLE BIT CLOSER *Salsoul SSOL 101* 44 4

CHARVONI – *See BROTHERS IN RHYTHM*

CHAS and DAVE (402 Top 500)

Good-time 'rockney' music duo; Chas Hodges (k/v) b. 28 Dec 1943, and Dave Peacock (b/v), 24 May 1945. The lovable Londoners provide a mix of music hall, humorous 'knees-up' songs and early rock 'n' roll, which are ideal for pubs and parties (Singles: 66 weeks, Albums: 101 weeks)

Date	Title	pos	wks
11 Nov 78	**STRUMMIN' / I'M IN TROUBLE** *EMI 2874* [1]	52	3
26 May 79	**GERTCHA** *EMI 2947*	20	8
1 Sep 79	**THE SIDEBOARD SONG (GOT MY BEER IN THE SIDEBOARD HERE)** *EMI 2986*	55	3
29 Nov 80 ●	**RABBIT** *Rockney 9*	8	11
12 Dec 81	**STARS OVER 45** *Rockney KOR 12*	21	8
13 Mar 82 ●	**AIN'T NO PLEASING YOU** *Rockney KOR 14*	2	11
17 Jul 82	**MARGATE** *Rockney KOR 15*	46	4
19 Mar 83	**LONDON GIRLS** *Rockney KOR 17*	63	3
3 Dec 83	**MY MELANCHOLY BABY** *Rockney KOR 21*	51	6
3 May 86 ●	**SNOOKER LOOPY** *Rockney POT 147* [2]	6	9
5 Dec 81	**CHAS AND DAVE'S CHRISTMAS JAMBOREE BAG** *Warwick WW 5166 ?*	25	15
17 Apr 82	**MUSTN'T GRUMBLE** *Rockney 909*	35	11
8 Jan 83	**JOB LOT** *Rockney ROC 910*	59	15
15 Oct 83 ●	**CHAS AND DAVE'S KNEES UP – JAMBOREE BAG NO. 2** *Rockney / Towerbell ROC 911*	7	17
11 Aug 84	**WELL PLEASED** *Rockney ROC 912*	27	10
17 Nov 84	**CHAS AND DAVE'S GREATEST HITS** *Rockney ROC 913*	16	10
15 Dec 84	**CHAS AND DAVE'S CHRISTMAS JAMBOREE BAG (re-issue)** *Rockney ROCM 001*	87	1
9 Nov 85	**JAMBOREE BAG NUMBER 3** *Rockney ROC 914*	15	13
13 Dec 86	**CHAS AND DAVE'S CHRISTMAS CAROL ALBUM** *Telstar STAR 2293*	37	4
29 Apr 95 ●	**STREET PARTY** *Telstar TCD 2765*	3	5

[1] Chas and Dave with Rockney [2] Matchroom Mob with Chas and Dave

See also TOTTENHAM HOTSPUR FA CUP FINAL SQUAD

Tara CHASE – *See Sonny JONES featuring Tara CHASE*

CHEAP TRICK *US, male vocal / instrumental group (Singles: 14 weeks, Albums: 15 weeks)*

Date	Title	pos	wks
5 May 79	**I WANT YOU TO WANT ME** *Epic EPC 7258*	29	9
2 Feb 80	**WAY OF THE WORLD** *Epic EPC 8114*	73	2
31 Jul 82	**IF YOU WANT MY LOVE** *Epic EPC A 2406*	57	3
24 Feb 79	**CHEAP TRICK AT BUDOKAN** *Epic EPC 86083*	29	9
6 Oct 79	**DREAM POLICE** *Epic EPC 83522*	41	5
5 Jun 82	**ONE ON ONE** *Epic EPC 85740*	95	1

Oliver CHEATHAM *US, male vocalist (Singles: 22 weeks)*

Date	Title	pos	wks
2 Jul 83	**GET DOWN SATURDAY NIGHT** *MCA 828*	38	5
5 Apr 03 ★	**MAKE LUV** *Positiva CDTIV 187* [1] ■	1	15
6 Dec 03	**MUSIC & YOU** *Positiva CDTIV 197* [1]	38	2

[1] Room 5 featuring Oliver Cheatham

CHECK 1-2 – *See Craig McLACHLAN*

Chubby CHECKER *US, male vocalist – Ernest Evans (b. 3 Oct 1941) (Singles: 112 weeks, Albums: 7 weeks)*

Date	Title	pos	wks
22 Sep 60	**THE TWIST (2re)** *Columbia DB 4503* ▲	14	12
30 Mar 61	**PONY TIME** *Columbia DB 4591* ▲	27	6
17 Aug 61 ●	**LET'S TWIST AGAIN (3re)** *Columbia DB 4691*	2	34
5 Apr 62	**SLOW TWISTIN'** *Columbia DB 4808*	23	8
19 Apr 62	**TEACH ME TO TWIST** *Columbia DB 4802* [1]	45	1
9 Aug 62	**DANCIN' PARTY** *Columbia DB 4876*	19	13
1 Nov 62	**LIMBO ROCK** *Cameo Parkway P 849*	32	10
20 Dec 62	**JINGLE BELL ROCK** *Cameo Parkway C 205* [1]	40	3
31 Oct 63	**WHAT DO YA SAY** *Cameo Parkway P 806*	37	4
29 Nov 75 ●	**LET'S TWIST AGAIN / THE TWIST (re-issue)** *London HLU 10512*	5	10
18 Jun 88 ●	**THE TWIST (YO, TWIST)** *Urban URB 20* [2]	2	11
27 Jan 62	**TWIST WITH CHUBBY CHECKER** *Columbia 33SX 1315*	13	4
3 Mar 62	**FOR TWISTERS ONLY** *Columbia 33SX 1341*	17	3

[1] Chubby Checker and Bobby Rydell [2] Fat Boys and Chubby Checker

'The Twist' first charted in Sep 1960 peaking at No.49, then re-entered making No.44 a month later and No.14 in Jan 1962. 'Let's Twist Again' first charted in Aug 1961 peaking at No.37, then No.2 in Dec 1961, No.46 in Aug 1962 and No.49 a month later.

CHECKMATES – *See Emile FORD and the CHECKMATES*

CHECKMATES LTD

US, male vocal / instrumental group (Singles: 8 weeks)

Date	Title	pos	wks
15 Nov 69	**PROUD MARY** *A&M AMS 769*	30	8

Judy CHEEKS

US, female vocalist (Singles: 15 weeks)

Date	Title	pos	wks
13 Nov 93	**SO IN LOVE (THE REAL DEAL)** *Positiva CDTIV 6*	27	3
7 May 94	**REACH** *Positiva CDTIV 12*	17	4
4 Mar 95	**THIS TIME / RESPECT** *Positiva CDTIV 28*	23	2
17 Jun 95	**YOU'RE THE STORY OF MY LIFE / AS LONG AS YOU'RE GOOD TO ME** *Positiva CDTIV 34*	30	3
13 Jan 96	**REACH (re-mix)** *Positiva CDTIV 42*	22	3

CHEEKY GIRLS

Romania, female vocal duo – Monica and Gabriella Irimia (Singles: 33 weeks, Albums: 6 weeks)

Date	Title	pos	wks
14 Dec 02 ●	**CHEEKY SONG (TOUCH MY BUM)** *Multiply CDMULTY 97*	2	14
17 May 03 ●	**TAKE YOUR SHOES OFF** *Multiply CDMULTY 101*	3	10
16 Aug 03 ●	**HOORAY HOORAY (IT'S A CHEEKY HOLIDAY)** *Multiply CDMULTY 106*	3	7
20 Dec 03 ●	**HAVE A CHEEKY CHRISTMAS** *Multiply CDMULTY 110*	10	2+
23 Aug 03	**PARTYTIME** *Multiply MULTYCD 13*	14	6

CHEETAHS

UK, male vocal / instrumental group (Singles: 6 weeks)

Date	Title	pos	wks
1 Oct 64	**MECCA** *Philips BF 1362*	36	3
21 Jan 65	**SOLDIER BOY** *Philips BF 1383*	39	3

CHEF

US, male cartoon vocalist – Isaac Hayes (Singles: 13 weeks)

Date	Title	pos	wks
26 Dec 98 ★	**CHOCOLATE SALTY BALLS (PS I LOVE YOU)** *Columbia 6667985*	1	13

CHELSEA FC

UK, male football team vocalists (Singles: 22 weeks)

Date	Title	pos	wks
26 Feb 72 ●	**BLUE IS THE COLOUR** *Penny Farthing PEN 782*	5	12
14 May 94	**NO ONE CAN STOP US NOW** *RCA 74321210452*	23	3
17 May 97	**BLUE DAY** *WEA WEA 112CD* [1]	22	5
27 May 00	**BLUE TOMORROW** *Telstar TV CFCCD 2000*	22	2

[1] Suggs & Co featuring Chelsea Team

CHEMICAL BROTHERS (328 Top 500)

Internationally successful, Manchester-formed (1992), dance production duo Tom Rowlands and Ed Simons, originally named Dust Brothers (after their production heroes, who forced a name change). These Brit and Grammy winners are the first contemporary dance act to achieve three successive No. 1 albums (Singles: 68 weeks, Albums: 132 weeks)

Date	Title	pos	wks
17 Jun 95	**LEAVE HOME** *Junior Boy's Own CHEMSD 1*	17	4
9 Sep 95	**LIFE IS SWEET** *Junior Boy's Own CHEMSD 2*	25	3
27 Jan 96	**LOOPS OF FURY (EP)** *Junior Boy's Own CHEMSD 3*	13	1
12 Oct 96 ★	**SETTING SUN** *Junior Boy's Own CHEMSD 4* ■	1	7
5 Apr 97 ★	**BLOCK ROCKIN' BEATS (re)** *Virgin CHEMSD 5* ■	1	7
20 Sep 97	**ELEKTROBANK** *Virgin CHEMSD 6*	17	4
12 Jun 99 ●	**HEY BOY HEY GIRL** *Virgin CHEMSD 8*	3	10
14 Aug 99 ●	**LET FOREVER BE** *Virgin CHEMSD 9*	9	7
23 Oct 99	**OUT OF CONTROL** *Virgin CHEMSD 10*	21	4
22 Sep 01 ●	**IT BEGAN IN AFRIKA (re)** *Virgin CHEMSD 12*	8	6
26 Jan 02 ●	**STAR GUITAR (re)** *Virgin CHEMSD 14*	8	8
4 May 02	**COME WITH US / THE TEST** *Virgin CHEMSD 15*	14	3
27 Sep 03	**THE GOLDEN PATH** *Virgin CHEMSD 18* [1]	17	4
8 Jul 95 ●	**EXIT PLANET DUST** *Junior Boy's Own XDUSTCD 1*	9	41
19 Apr 97 ★	**DIG YOUR OWN HOLE** *Virgin XDUSTCD 2* ■	1	27
3 Jul 99 ★	**SURRENDER** *Virgin XDUSTCD 4* ■	1	47

9 Feb 02 ★	**COME WITH US** *Virgin XDUSTCD 5* ■	1	11
4 Oct 03 ●	**SINGLES 93-03** *Virgin XDUSTCDX 6*	9	6

[1] Chemical Brothers / Flaming Lips

Tracks on Loops of Fury (EP): Loops of Fury / (The Best Part of) Breaking Up / Get Upon It Like This / Chemical Beats. Uncredited vocal on 'Setting Sun' and 'Let Forever Be' by Noel Gallagher and on 'Out of Control' by Bernard Sumner

CHEQUERS

UK, male vocal / instrumental group (Singles: 10 weeks) pos/wks

18 Oct 75	**ROCK ON BROTHER** *Creole CR 111*	21	5
28 Feb 76	**HEY MISS PAYNE** *Creole CR 116*	32	5

CHER 70 Top 500

Perennially popular vocalist, b. Cherilyn LaPierre, 20 May 1946, California. She was half of the most successful husband / wife duo ever, Sonny and Cher, and had an equally stunning run of solo smashes. In 1990 at the age of 52, she became the oldest female solo singer to top the chart. Best-selling single: 'Believe' 1,672,108 (Singles: 229 weeks, Albums: 300 weeks) pos/wks

19 Aug 65 ●	**ALL I REALLY WANT TO DO** *Liberty LIB 66114*	9	10
31 Mar 66 ●	**BANG BANG (MY BABY SHOT ME DOWN)** *Liberty LIB 66160*	3	12
4 Aug 66	**I FEEL SOMETHING IN THE AIR** *Liberty LIB 12034*	43	2
22 Sep 66	**SUNNY** *Liberty LIB 12083*	32	5
6 Nov 71 ●	**GYPSYS, TRAMPS AND THIEVES** *MCA MU 1142* ▲	4	13
16 Feb 74	**DARK LADY (re)** *MCA 101* ▲	36	4
19 Dec 87 ●	**I FOUND SOMEONE** *Geffen GEF 31*	5	10
2 Apr 88	**WE ALL SLEEP ALONE** *Geffen GEF 35*	47	5
2 Sep 89 ●	**IF I COULD TURN BACK TIME** *Geffen GEF 59*	6	14
13 Jan 90	**JUST LIKE JESSE JAMES** *Geffen GEF 69*	11	11
7 Apr 90	**HEART OF STONE** *Geffen GEF 75*	43	5
11 Aug 90	**YOU WOULDN'T KNOW LOVE** *Geffen GEF 77*	55	3
13 Apr 91 ★	**THE SHOOP SHOOP SONG (IT'S IN HIS KISS)** *Epic 6566737*	1	15
13 Jul 91 ●	**LOVE AND UNDERSTANDING** *Geffen GFS 5*	10	8
12 Oct 91	**SAVE UP ALL YOUR TEARS** *Geffen GFS 11*	37	5
7 Dec 91	**LOVE HURTS** *Geffen GFS 16*	43	5
18 Apr 92	**COULD'VE BEEN YOU** *Geffen GFS 19*	31	4
14 Nov 92	**OH NO NOT MY BABY** *Geffen GFS 29*	33	4
16 Jan 93	**MANY RIVERS TO CROSS** *Geffen GFSTD 31*	37	3
6 Mar 93	**WHENEVER YOU'RE NEAR** *Geffen GFSTD 32*	72	1
15 Jan 94	**I GOT YOU BABE** *Geffen GFSTD 64* [1]	35	3
18 Mar 95 ★	**LOVE CAN BUILD A BRIDGE** *London COCD 1* [2]	1	8
28 Oct 95	**WALKING IN MEMPHIS** *WEA WEA 021CD1*	11	7
20 Jan 96 ●	**ONE BY ONE** *WEA WEA 032CD*	7	9
27 Apr 96	**NOT ENOUGH LOVE IN THE WORLD** *WEA WEA 052CD*	31	2
17 Aug 96	**THE SUN AIN'T GONNA SHINE ANYMORE** *WEA WEA 071CD*	26	3
31 Oct 98 ★	**BELIEVE (re)** *WEA WEA 175CD* ◆ ■ ▲	1	28
6 Mar 99 ●	**STRONG ENOUGH** *WEA WEA 201CD1*	5	10
19 Jun 99	**ALL OR NOTHING** *WEA WEA 212CD1*	12	7
6 Nov 99	**DOVE L'AMORE** *WEA WEA 230CD1*	21	3
17 Nov 01 ●	**THE MUSIC'S NO GOOD WITHOUT YOU** *WEA WEA 337CD*	8	10
2 Oct 65 ●	**ALL I REALLY WANT TO DO** *Liberty LBY 3058*	7	9
7 May 66	**SONNY SIDE OF CHER** *Liberty LBY 3072*	11	11
16 Jan 88	**CHER** *Geffen WX 132*	26	22
22 Jul 89 ●	**HEART OF STONE** *Geffen GEF 24239*	7	82
29 Jun 91 ★	**LOVE HURTS** *Geffen GEF 24427* ■	1	51
21 Nov 92 ★	**GREATEST HITS 1965-1992** *Geffen GED 24439* ■	1	33
18 Nov 95 ●	**IT'S A MAN'S WORLD** *WEA 0630126702*	10	18
7 Nov 98 ●	**BELIEVE** *WEA 3984253192*	7	44
20 Nov 99 ●	**THE GREATEST HITS** *WEA / Universal TV 8573804202*	7	24
1 Dec 01	**LIVING PROOF** *WEA 927424632*	46	2
6 Dec 03	**THE VERY BEST OF** *UMTV / WSM 5046685862*	35	4+

[1] Cher with Beavis and Butt-head
[2] Cher, Chrissie Hynde & Neneh Cherry with Eric Clapton

The catalogue number for 'Heart of Stone' changed from WX 262 during the album's chart run

See also SONNY and CHER; MEAT LOAF

CHERI *Canada, female vocal duo – Rosalind Hunt and Lyn Cullerier (Singles: 9 weeks)* pos/wks

19 Jun 82	**MURPHY'S LAW** *Polydor POSP 459*	13	9

CHEROKEES

UK, male vocal / instrumental group (Singles: 5 weeks) pos/wks

3 Sep 64	**SEVEN DAFFODILS** *Columbia DB 7341*	33	5

CHERRELLE *US, female vocalist – Cheryl Norton (Singles: 26 weeks, Albums: 9 weeks)* pos/wks

28 Dec 85 ●	**SATURDAY LOVE** *Tabu A 6829* [1]	6	11
1 Mar 86	**WILL YOU SATISFY?** *Tabu A 6927*	57	3
6 Feb 88	**NEVER KNEW LOVE LIKE THIS** *Tabu 6513827* [2]	26	7
6 May 89	**AFFAIR** *Tabu 654673 7*	67	2
24 Mar 90	**SATURDAY LOVE (re-mix)** *Tabu 6558007* [1]	55	2
2 Aug 97	**BABY COME TO ME** *One World OWECD 1* [2]	56	1
25 Jan 86	**HIGH PRIORITY** *Tabu TBU 26699*	17	9

[1] Cherrelle with Alexander O'Neal [2] Alexander O'Neal featuring Cherrelle

Don CHERRY *US, male vocalist d. 19 Oct 1995 (Singles: 11 weeks)* pos/wks

10 Feb 56 ●	**BAND OF GOLD** *Philips PB 549*	6	11

Eagle-Eye CHERRY

Sweden, male vocalist (Singles: 28 weeks, Albums: 32 weeks) pos/wks

4 Jul 98 ●	**SAVE TONIGHT** *Polydor 5695952*	6	13
14 Nov 98 ●	**FALLING IN LOVE AGAIN** *Polydor 5630252*	8	8
20 Mar 99	**PERMANENT TEARS** *Polydor 5636752*	43	1
29 Apr 00	**ARE YOU STILL HAVING FUN** *Polydor 5618032*	21	4
11 Nov 00	**LONG WAY AROUND** *Polydor 5677812* [1]	48	2
1 Aug 98 ●	**DESIRELESS** *Polydor 5372262*	3	29
20 May 00	**LIVING IN THE PRESENT FUTURE** *Polydor 5437442*	12	3

[1] Eagle-Eye Cherry featuring Neneh Cherry

Neneh CHERRY 467 Top 500

Sassy, strident rapper-singer, born Neneh Mariann Karlsson, 10 Mar 1964, Stockholm, Sweden, raised in New York and relocated to UK early 1980s. Stepdaughter of jazz trumpeter Don Cherry and sister of Eagle-Eye Cherry. Winner of 1990 Best New Female award in Rolling Stone and at the Brits (Singles: 98 weeks, Albums: 49 weeks) pos/wks

10 Dec 88 ●	**BUFFALO STANCE** *Circa YR 21*	3	13
20 May 89 ●	**MANCHILD** *Circa YR 30*	5	10
12 Aug 89	**KISSES ON THE WIND** *Circa YR 33*	20	6
23 Dec 89	**INNA CITY MAMMA** *Circa YR 42*	31	7
29 Sep 90	**I'VE GOT YOU UNDER MY SKIN** *Circa YR 53*	25	5
3 Oct 92	**MONEY LOVE** *Circa YR 83*	23	4
16 Jan 93	**BUDDY X** *Circa YRCD 98*	35	3
25 Jun 94 ●	**7 SECONDS (re)** *Columbia 6605082* [1]	3	25
18 Mar 95 ★	**LOVE CAN BUILD A BRIDGE** *London COCD 1* [2]	1	8
3 Aug 96 ●	**WOMAN** *Hut HUTCD 70*	9	7
14 Dec 96	**KOOTCHI** *Hut HUTDG 75*	38	2
22 Feb 97	**FEEL IT** *Hut HUTCD 79*	68	1
6 Nov 99	**BUDDY X 99** *4 Liberty LIBTCD 33* [3]	15	5
11 Nov 00	**LONG WAY AROUND** *Polydor 5677812* [4]	48	2
17 Jun 89 ●	**RAW LIKE SUSHI** *Circa CIRCA 8*	2	43
7 Nov 92	**HOMEBREW** *Circa CIRCD 25*	27	2
14 Sep 96	**MAN** *Hut CDHUT 38*	16	4

[1] Youssou N'Dour (featuring Neneh Cherry) [2] Cher, Chrissie Hynde and Neneh Cherry with Eric Clapton [3] Dreem Teem vs Neneh Cherry [4] Eagle-Eye Cherry featuring Neneh Cherry

See also RIP RIG AND PANIC

Cody CHESNUTT – *See ROOTS*

CHI-LITES *US, male vocal / instrumental group – leader Eugene Record (Singles: 89 weeks)* pos/wks

28 Aug 71	**(FOR GOD'S SAKE) GIVE MORE POWER TO THE PEOPLE** *MCA MU 1138*	32	6
15 Jan 72 ●	**HAVE YOU SEEN HER** *MCA MU 1146*	3	12
27 May 72	**OH GIRL** *MCA MU 1156* ▲	14	9
23 Mar 74 ●	**HOMELY GIRL** *Brunswick BR 9*	5	13
20 Jul 74	**I FOUND SUNSHINE** *Brunswick BR 12*	35	5
2 Nov 74 ●	**TOO GOOD TO BE FORGOTTEN** *Brunswick BR 13*	10	11

21 Jun 75 ●	**HAVE YOU SEEN HER / OH GIRL (re-issue)** *Brunswick BR 20*	5	9
13 Sep 75 ●	**IT'S TIME FOR LOVE** *Brunswick BR 25*	5	10
31 Jul 76 ●	**YOU DON'T HAVE TO GO** *Brunswick BR 34*	3	11
13 Aug 83	**CHANGING FOR YOU** *R & B RBS 215*	61	3

CHIC *US, male / female vocal / instrumental group – leaders Nile Rodgers and Bernard Edwards d. 18 Apr 1996 (Singles: 90 weeks, Albums: 47 weeks)*

		pos	wks
26 Nov 77 ●	**DANCE, DANCE, DANCE (YOWSAH, YOWSAH, YOWSAH)** *Atlantic K 11038*	6	12
1 Apr 78 ●	**EVERYBODY DANCE** *Atlantic K 11097*	9	11
18 Nov 78 ●	**LE FREAK** *Atlantic K 11209* ▲	7	16
24 Feb 79 ●	**I WANT YOUR LOVE** *Atlantic LV 16*	4	11
30 Jun 79 ●	**GOOD TIMES** *Atlantic K 11310* ▲	5	11
13 Oct 79	**MY FORBIDDEN LOVER** *Atlantic K 11385*	15	8
8 Dec 79	**MY FEET KEEP DANCING** *Atlantic K 11415*	21	9
12 Mar 83	**HANGIN'** *Atlantic A 9898*	64	1
19 Sep 87	**JACK LE FREAK** *Atlantic A 9198*	19	6
14 Jul 90	**MEGACHIC – CHIC MEDLEY** *East West A 7949*	58	2
15 Feb 92	**CHIC MYSTIQUE** *Warner Bros. W 0083*	48	3
3 Feb 79 ●	**C'EST CHIC** *Atlantic K 50565*	2	24
18 Aug 79	**RISQUE** *Atlantic K 50634*	29	12
15 Dec 79	**THE BEST OF CHIC** *Atlantic K 50686*	30	8
5 Dec 87	**FREAK OUT** *Telstar STAR 2319* [1]	72	3

[1] Chic and Sister Sledge

Megachic was a medley of Le Freak / Everybody Dance / Good Times / I Want Your Love

CHICAGO (306 Top 500)

Pioneering jazz-rock group included Peter Cetera (v / b) b. 13 Sep 1944. Group relocated from city of the same name to California, US, in 1967. Released longest numerical sequence of album titles (majority going platinum in the US) – the most recent being Chicago 26 (1999) (Singles: 81 weeks, Albums: 132 weeks)

		pos	wks
10 Jan 70 ●	**I'M A MAN** *CBS 4715* [1]	8	11
18 Jul 70 ●	**25 OR 6 TO 4** *CBS 5076*	7	13
9 Oct 76 ★	**IF YOU LEAVE ME NOW** *CBS 4603* ▲	1	16
5 Nov 77	**BABY, WHAT A BIG SURPRISE** *CBS 5672*	41	3
21 Aug 82 ●	**HARD TO SAY I'M SORRY** *Full Moon K 79301* ▲	4	15
27 Oct 84 ●	**HARD HABIT TO BREAK** *Full Moon W 9214*	8	13
26 Jan 85	**YOU'RE THE INSPIRATION** *Warner Bros. W 9126*	14	10
27 Sep 69 ●	**CHICAGO TRANSIT AUTHORITY** *CBS 66221* [1]	9	14
4 Apr 70 ●	**CHICAGO** *CBS 66233*	6	27
6 Mar 71 ●	**CHICAGO 3** *CBS 66260*	9	5
30 Sep 72	**CHICAGO 5** *CBS 69108* ▲	24	2
23 Oct 76	**CHICAGO X** *CBS 86010*	21	11
2 Oct 82	**CHICAGO 16** *Full Moon K 99235*	44	9
4 Dec 82	**LOVE SONGS** *TV TVA 6*	42	8
1 Dec 84	**CHICAGO 17** *Full Moon 925060*	24	20
25 Nov 89 ●	**THE HEART OF CHICAGO** *Reprise WX 328*	6	25
13 Feb 99	**THE HEART OF CHICAGO – 1967-1997** *Reprise 9362465542*	21	4
14 Sep 02	**THE CHICAGO STORY – THE COMPLETE GREATEST HITS** *Rhino 8122736302*	11	7

[1] Chicago Transit Authority [1] Chicago Transit Authority

CHICANE *UK, male producer / instrumentalist – Nick Bracegirdle (Singles: 52 weeks, Albums: 9 weeks)*

		pos	wks
21 Dec 96	**OFFSHORE** *Xtravaganza 0091005*	14	7
14 Jun 97	**SUNSTROKE** *Xtravaganza 0091125*	21	3
13 Sep 97	**OFFSHORE '97 (re-mix)** *Xtravaganza 0091255 EXT* [1]	17	4
20 Dec 97	**LOST YOU SOMEWHERE** *Xtravaganza 0091415*	35	3
10 Oct 98	**STRONG IN LOVE** *Xtravaganza 0091675EXT* [2]	32	2
5 Jun 99 ●	**SALTWATER** *Xtravaganza XTRAV 1CDS* [3]	6	10
18 Mar 00 ★	**DON'T GIVE UP** *Xtravaganza XTRAV 9CDS* [4] ■	1	14

TOP 10 ALBUMS BY WEEKS AT NO.1

South Pacific heads the list with more than two years' worth of chart-topping action. This Rodgers and Hammerstein film soundtrack also provided Captain Sensible with a No.1 song in 1982.

1. SOUTH PACIFIC – Soundtrack (115 weeks)
2. THE SOUND OF MUSIC – Soundtrack (70 weeks)
3. THE KING AND I – Soundtrack (47 weeks)
4. BRIDGE OVER TROUBLED WATER – Simon and Garfunkel (33 weeks)
5. PLEASE PLEASE ME – Beatles (30 weeks)
6. SGT. PEPPER'S LONELY HEARTS CLUB BAND – Beatles (27 weeks)
7. G.I. BLUES – Elvis Presley (22 weeks)
8. WITH THE BEATLES – Beatles (21 weeks)
9. A HARD DAY'S NIGHT – Beatles (21 weeks)
10. MY FAIR LADY (BROADWAY) – Original Cast (19 weeks)

Tie decided by total weeks on the entire chart

Composers **Richard Rodgers** and **Oscar Hammerstein II** occupy the top three slots in this list of chart-topping albums with real staying power

22 Jul 00 **NO ORDINARY MORNING / HALCYON** *Xtravaganza XTRAV 12CDS* 28 3
28 Oct 00 **AUTUMN TACTICS** *Xtravaganza XTRAV 17CDS* 44 2
8 Feb 03 **SALTWATER (re-mix)** *Xtravaganza XTRAV 35CDS* 43 2
8 Mar 03 **LOVE ON THE RUN** *WEA WEA 361CD* [5] 33 2
1 Nov 97 **FAR FROM THE MADDENING CROWDS** *Xtravaganza 0093172 EXT* 49 1
8 Apr 00 ● **BEHIND THE SUN** *Xtravaganza XTRAV 10CD* 10 8

[1] Chicane with Power Circle [2] Chicane featuring Mason [3] Chicane featuring Maire Brennan of Clannad [4] Chicane featuring Bryan Adams [5] Chicane featuring Peter Cunnah

Chicane are Disco Citizens under another name

CHICKEN SHACK *UK, male / female vocal / instrumental group – includes Christine Perfect / McVie (Singles: 19 weeks, Albums: 9 weeks)* pos/wks

7 May 69 **I'D RATHER GO BLIND** *Blue Horizon 57-3153* 14 13
6 Sep 69 **TEARS IN THE WIND** *Blue Horizon 57-3160* 29 6
22 Jul 68 **40 BLUE FINGERS FRESHLY PACKED** *Blue Horizon 763203* 12 8
15 Feb 69 ● **OK KEN?** *Blue Horizon 763209* 9 1

See also FLEETWOOD MAC; Christine McVIE

CHICKEN SHED *UK, youth theatre company (Singles: 6 weeks)* pos/wks

27 Dec 97 **I AM IN LOVE WITH THE WORLD** *Columbia 6654172* 15 6

CHICORY TIP
UK, male vocal / instrumental group (Singles: 34 weeks) pos/wks

29 Jan 72 ★ **SON OF MY FATHER** *CBS 7737* 1 13
20 May 72 **WHAT'S YOUR NAME** *CBS 8021* 13 8
31 Mar 73 **GOOD GRIEF CHRISTINA** *CBS 1258* 17 13

CHIEFTAINS *Ireland, male vocal / instrumental group (Singles: 4 weeks, Albums: 27 weeks)* pos/wks

18 Mar 95 **HAVE I TOLD YOU LATELY THAT I LOVE YOU** *RCA 74321271702* [1] 71 1
12 Jun 99 **I KNOW MY LOVE** *RCA Victor 74321670622* [2] 37 3
28 Mar 87 **JAMES GALWAY AND THE CHIEFTAINS IN IRELAND** *RCA Red Seal RL 85798* [1] 32 5
2 Jul 88 **IRISH HEARTBEAT** *Mercury MERH 124* [2] 18 7
4 Feb 95 **THE LONG BLACK VEIL** *RCA 74321251672* 17 9
6 Mar 99 **TEARS OF STONE** *RCA Victor 9026689682* 36 4
23 Mar 02 **THE WIDE WORLD OVER** *RCA Victor 9026639172* 37 2

[1] Chieftains with Van Morrison [2] Chieftains featuring The Corrs [1] James Galway and the Chieftains [2] Van Morrison and the Chieftains

CHIFFONS
US, female vocal group (Singles: 40 weeks) pos/wks

11 Apr 63 **HE'S SO FINE** *Stateside SS 172* ▲ 16 12
18 Jul 63 **ONE FINE DAY** *Stateside SS 202* 29 6
26 May 66 **SWEET TALKIN' GUY** *Stateside SS 512* 31 8
18 Mar 72 ● **SWEET TALKIN' GUY (re-issue)** *London HL 10271* 4 14

CHIKINKI
UK, male vocal / instrumental group (Singles: 1 week) pos/wks

29 Nov 03 **ASSASSINATOR 13** *Island CID 834* 72 1

CHILD
UK, male vocal / instrumental group (Singles: 22 weeks) pos/wks

29 Apr 78 **WHEN YOU WALK IN THE ROOM** *Ariola Hansa AHA 511* 38 5
22 Jul 78 ● **IT'S ONLY MAKE BELIEVE** *Ariola Hansa AHA 522* 10 12
28 Apr 79 **ONLY YOU (AND YOU ALONE)** *Ariola Hansa AHA 536* 33 5

Jane CHILD *Canada, female vocalist (Singles: 8 weeks)* pos/wks

12 May 90 **DON'T WANNA FALL IN LOVE** *Warner Bros. W 9817* 22 8

CHILDLINERS
UK / Australia, male / female vocal group (Singles: 6 weeks) pos/wks

16 Dec 95 ● **THE GIFT OF CHRISTMAS** *London LONCD 376* 9 6

CHILDREN FOR RWANDA
UK, male / female choir (Singles: 2 weeks) pos/wks

10 Sep 94 **LOVE CAN BUILD A BRIDGE** *East West YZ 849CD* 57 2

CHILDREN OF THE NIGHT
UK, male vocalist / producer (Singles: 2 weeks) pos/wks

26 Nov 88 **IT'S A TRIP (TUNE IN, TURN ON, DROP OUT)** *Jive JIVE 189* 52 2

CHILDREN OF THE REVOLUTION – *See KLF*

Toni CHILDS
US, female vocalist (Singles: 4 weeks, Albums: 1 week) pos/wks

25 Mar 89 **DON'T WALK AWAY** *A&M AM 462* 53 4
29 Apr 89 **UNION** *A&M AMA 5175* 73 1

CHILI HI FLY *Australia, male DJ / production duo – Simon Lewicki and Noel Burgess (Singles: 2 weeks)* pos/wks

18 Mar 00 **IS IT LOVE** *Ministry of Sound MOSCDS 141* 37 2

CHILL FAC-TORR
US, male vocal / instrumental group (Singles: 8 weeks) pos/wks

2 Apr 83 **TWIST (ROUND 'N' ROUND)** *Phillyworld PWS 109* 37 8

CHILLI featuring CARRAPICHO *US / Ghana / Brazil, male / female vocal / instrumental group (Singles: 1 week)* pos/wks

20 Sep 97 **TIC, TIC TAC** *Arista 74321511332* 59 1

CHIMES *UK, male / female vocal / instrumental group (Singles: 28 weeks, Albums: 19 weeks)* pos/wks

19 Aug 89 **1-2-3** *CBS 655166 7* 60 3
2 Dec 89 **HEAVEN (re)** *CBS 655432 7* 66 5
19 May 90 ● **I STILL HAVEN'T FOUND WHAT I'M LOOKING FOR** *CBS CHIM 1* 6 9
28 Jul 90 **TRUE LOVE** *CBS CHIM 2* 48 3
29 Sep 90 **HEAVEN (re-issue)** *CBS CHIM 3* 24 6
1 Dec 90 **LOVE COMES TO MIND** *CBS CHIM 4* 49 2
23 Jun 90 **THE CHIMES** *CBS 4664811* 17 19

CHIMIRA *South Africa, female vocalist (Singles: 1 week)* pos/wks

6 Dec 97 **SHOW ME HEAVEN** *Neoteric NRDCD 11* 70 1

CHINA BLACK *UK, male vocal / instrumental duo – Errol Reid and Simon Fung (Singles: 35 weeks, Albums: 4 weeks)* pos/wks

16 Jul 94 ● **SEARCHING (re)** *Wild Card CARDD 7* 4 20
29 Oct 94 **STARS** *Wild Card CARDD 9* 19 7
11 Feb 95 **ALMOST SEE YOU (SOMEWHERE)** *Wild Card CARDW 15* 31 2
3 Jun 95 **SWING LOW SWEET CHARIOT** *PolyGram TV SWLOW 2* [1] 15 6
11 Mar 95 **BORN** *Wild Card 5237552* 27 4

[1] Ladysmith Black Mambazo featuring China Black

CHINA CRISIS *UK, male vocal / instrumental group (Singles: 66 weeks, Albums: 68 weeks)* pos/wks

7 Aug 82 **AFRICAN AND WHITE** *Inevitable INEV 011* 45 5
22 Jan 83 **CHRISTIAN** *Virgin VS 562* 12 9
21 May 83 **TRAGEDY AND MYSTERY** *Virgin VS 587* 46 6
15 Oct 83 **WORKING WITH FIRE AND STEEL** *Virgin VS 620* 48 5
14 Jan 84 ● **WISHFUL THINKING** *Virgin VS 647* 9 8
10 Mar 84 **HANNA HANNA** *Virgin VS 665* 44 3
30 Mar 85 **BLACK MAN RAY** *Virgin VS 752* 14 9
1 Jun 85 **KING IN A CATHOLIC STYLE (WAKE UP)** *Virgin VS 765* 19 9
7 Sep 85 **YOU DID CUT ME** *Virgin VS 799* 54 3
8 Nov 86 **ARIZONA SKY** *Virgin VS 898* 47 4
24 Jan 87 **BEST KEPT SECRET** *Virgin VS 926* 36 5
20 Nov 82 **DIFFICULT SHAPES & PASSIVE RHYTHMS SOME PEOPLE THINK IT'S FUN TO ENTERTAIN** *Virgin V 2243* 21 18
12 Nov 83 **WORKING WITH FIRE AND STEEL – POSSIBLE POP SONGS VOLUME 2** *Virgin V 2286* 20 16

		pos/wks
11 May 85 ●	**FLAUNT THE IMPERFECTION** *Virgin V 2342*	**9** 22
6 Dec 86	**WHAT PRICE PARADISE** *Virgin V 2410*	**63** 6
13 May 89	**DIARY OF A HOLLOW HORSE** *Virgin V 2567*	**58** 2
15 Sep 90	**CHINA CRISIS COLLECTION** *Virgin V 2613*	**32** 4

CHINA DRUM *UK, male vocal / instrumental group (Singles: 4 weeks, Albums: 1 week)* pos/wks

2 Mar 96	**CAN'T STOP THESE THINGS** *Mantra MNT 8CD*	**65** 1
20 Apr 96	**LAST CHANCE** *Mantra MNT 10CD*	**60** 1
9 Aug 97	**FICTION OF LIFE** *Mantra MNT 21CD*	**65** 1
27 Sep 97	**SOMEWHERE ELSE** *Mantra MNT 022CD1*	**74** 1
11 May 96	**GOOSEFAIR** *Mantra MNTCD 1002*	**53** 1

Jonny CHINGAS
US, male instrumentalist (Singles: 6 weeks) pos/wks

19 Feb 83	**PHONE HOME** *CBS A 3121*	**43** 6

CHINGY *US, male rapper – Howard Bailey Jr (Singles: 5 weeks)* pos/wks

25 Oct 03	**RIGHT THURR** *Capitol CDCLS 849*	**17** 5

CHIPMUNKS *US, chipmunk vocal trio (Singles: 12 weeks)* pos/wks

24 Jul 59	**RAGTIME COWBOY JOE** *London HLU 8916* [1]	**11** 8
19 Dec 92	**ACHY BREAKY HEART** *Epic 6588837* [2]	**53** 3
14 Dec 96	**MACARENA** *Sony Wonder 6639981* [3]	**65** 1

[1] David Seville and the Chipmunks [2] Alvin and the Chipmunks featuring Billy Ray Cyrus [3] Los Del Chipmunks

The Chipmunk characters were created by David Seville, who died in 1972. His son resurrected the act in 1980

See also David SEVILLE

CHIPPENDALES
UK / US, male vocal group (Singles: 4 weeks) pos/wks

31 Oct 92	**GIVE ME YOUR BODY** *XSrhythm XSR 3*	**28** 4

George CHISHOLM – *See JOHNSTON BROTHERS*

CHOCOLATE PUMA *Holland, male production duo – DJ Dobri and DJ Zki (Rene ter Horst and Gaston Steenkist) (Singles: 9 weeks)* pos/wks

24 Mar 01 ●	**I WANNA BE U (re)** *Cream / Parlophone CREAM 13CD*	**6** 9

See also GOODMEN; JARK PRONGO; RHYTHMKILLAZ; TOMBA VIRA; RIVA featuring Dannii MINOGUE

CHOO CHOO PROJECT *US, male / female production / instrumental vocal duo – Harry Romero and Octahvia Lambert (Singles: 3 weeks)* pos/wks

15 Jan 00	**HAZIN' & PHAZIN'** *Defected DEFECT 10CDS*	**21** 3

See also José NUNEZ featuring OCTAHVIA; Harry 'Choo-Choo' ROMERO

CHOPS-EMC + EXTENSIVE
UK, male instrumental group and rapper (Singles: 1 week) pos/wks

8 Aug 92	**ME' ISRAELITES** *Faze 2 FAZE 6*	**60** 1

CHORDETTES
US, female vocal group (Singles: 25 weeks) pos/wks

17 Dec 54	**MR SANDMAN** *Columbia DB 3553* ▲	**11** 8
31 Aug 56 ●	**BORN TO BE WITH YOU** *London HLA 8302*	**8** 9
18 Apr 58 ●	**LOLLIPOP** *London HLD 8584*	**6** 8

CHORDS *UK, male vocal / instrumental group (Singles: 17 weeks, Albums: 3 weeks)* pos/wks

6 Oct 79	**NOW IT'S GONE** *Polydor 2059 141*	**63** 2
2 Feb 80	**MAYBE TOMORROW** *Polydor POSP 101*	**40** 5
26 Apr 80	**SOMETHING'S MISSING** *Polydor POSP 146*	**55** 3
12 Jul 80	**THE BRITISH WAY OF LIFE** *Polydor 2059 258*	**54** 3
18 Oct 80	**IN MY STREET** *Polydor POSP 185*	**50** 4
24 May 80	**SO FAR AWAY** *Polydor POLS 1019*	**30** 3

CHRIS and JAMES
UK, male instrumental / production duo (Singles: 3 weeks) pos/wks

17 Sep 94	**CALM DOWN (BASS KEEPS PUMPIN')** *Stress 12STR 38*	**74** 1
4 Nov 95	**FOX FORCE FIVE** *Stress CDSTR 61*	**71** 1
7 Nov 98	**CLUB FOR LIFE '98** *Stress CDSTR 85*	**66** 1

Neil CHRISTIAN
UK, male vocalist – Christopher Tidmarsh (Singles: 10 weeks) pos/wks

7 Apr 66	**THAT'S NICE** *Strike JH 301*	**14** 10

Roger CHRISTIAN *UK, male vocalist (Singles: 3 weeks)* pos/wks

30 Sep 89	**TAKE IT FROM ME** *Island IS 427*	**63** 3

CHRISTIANS (369 Top 500) *Soul / gospel-influenced UK pop group: vocalist brothers Russell, Roger (who went solo in 1986) and Garry Christian plus Henry Priestman (k/v). In1974, the brothers appeared on TV talent show Opportunity Knocks. Their self-titled debut album went double platinum (Singles: 84 weeks, Albums: 96 weeks)* pos/wks

31 Jan 87	**FORGOTTEN TOWN** *Island IS 291*	**22** 11
13 Jun 87	**HOOVERVILLE (AND THEY PROMISED US THE WORLD)** *Island IS 326*	**21** 10
26 Sep 87	**WHEN THE FINGERS POINT** *Island IS 335*	**34** 7
5 Dec 87	**IDEAL WORLD** *Island IS 347*	**14** 13
23 Apr 88	**BORN AGAIN** *Island IS 365*	**25** 7
15 Oct 88 ●	**HARVEST FOR THE WORLD** *Island IS 395*	**8** 7
20 May 89 ★	**FERRY 'CROSS THE MERSEY** *PWL PWL 41* [1] ■	**1** 7
23 Dec 89	**WORDS** *Island IS 450*	**18** 8
7 Apr 90	**I FOUND OUT** *Island IS 453*	**56** 2
15 Sep 90	**GREENBANK DRIVE** *Island IS 466*	**63** 2
5 Sep 92	**WHAT'S IN A WORD** *Island IS 536*	**33** 5
14 Nov 92	**FATHER** *Island IS 543*	**55** 2
6 Mar 93	**THE BOTTLE** *Island CID 549*	**39** 3
31 Oct 87 ●	**THE CHRISTIANS** *Island ILPS 9876*	**2** 68
27 Jan 90 ★	**COLOUR** *Island ILPS 9948* ■	**1** 17
10 Oct 92	**HAPPY IN HELL** *Island CID 9996*	**18** 3
20 Nov 93	**THE BEST OF THE CHRISTIANS** *Island CIDTV 6*	**22** 8

[1] Christians, Holly Johnson, Paul McCartney, Gerry Marsden and Stock Aitken Waterman

CHRISTIE *UK, male vocal / instrumental group (Singles: 37 weeks)* pos/wks

2 May 70 ★	**YELLOW RIVER** *CBS 4911*	**1** 22
10 Oct 70 ●	**SAN BERNADINO (re)** *CBS 5169*	**7** 14
25 Mar 72	**IRON HORSE** *CBS 7747*	**47** 1

David CHRISTIE *France, male vocalist (Singles: 12 weeks)* pos/wks

14 Aug 82 ●	**SADDLE UP** *KR KR 9*	**9** 12

John CHRISTIE *Australia, male vocalist (Singles: 6 weeks)* pos/wks

25 Dec 76	**HERE'S TO LOVE (AULD LANG SYNE)** *EMI 2554*	**24** 6

Lou CHRISTIE
US, male vocalist – Lugee Sacco (Singles: 35 weeks) pos/wks

24 Feb 66	**LIGHTNIN' STRIKES** *MGM 1297* ▲	**11** 8
28 Apr 66	**RHAPSODY IN THE RAIN** *MGM 1308*	**37** 2
13 Sep 69 ●	**I'M GONNA MAKE YOU MINE** *Buddah 201 057*	**2** 17
27 Dec 69	**SHE SOLD ME MAGIC** *Buddah 201 073*	**25** 8

Tony CHRISTIE *UK, male vocalist – Tony Fitzgerald (Singles: 54 weeks, Albums: 10 weeks)* pos/wks

9 Jan 71	**LAS VEGAS** *MCA MK 5058*	**21** 9
8 May 71 ●	**I DID WHAT I DID FOR MARIA** *MCA MK 5064*	**2** 17
20 Nov 71	**(IS THIS THE WAY TO) AMARILLO** *MCA MKS 5073*	**18** 13
10 Feb 73	**AVENUES AND ALLEYWAYS** *MCA MKS 5101*	**37** 4
17 Jan 76	**DRIVE SAFELY DARLIN'** *MCA 219*	**35** 4
23 Jan 99 ●	**WALK LIKE A PANTHER '98** *ffrr FCD 351* [1]	**10** 7
24 Jul 71	**I DID WHAT I DID FOR MARIA** *MCA MKPS 2016*	**37** 1
17 Feb 73	**WITH LOVING FEELING** *MCA MUPS 468*	**19** 2

31 May 75	**TONY CHRISTIE – LIVE** *MCA MCF 2703*	33	3
6 Nov 76	**BEST OF TONY CHRISTIE** *MCA MCF 2769*	28	4

[1] The All Seeing I featuring Tony Christie

Shawn CHRISTOPHER *US, female vocalist (Singles: 10 weeks)* pos/wks

4 May 91	**ANOTHER SLEEPLESS NIGHT** *Arista 114186*	50	4
21 Mar 92	**DON'T LOSE THE MAGIC** *Arista 115097*	30	5
2 Jul 94	**MAKE MY LOVE** *BTB BTBCD 502*	57	1

CHRON GEN
UK, male vocal / instrumental group (Albums: 3 weeks) pos/wks

3 Apr 82	**CHRONIC GENERATION** *Secret SEC 3*	53	3

CHUCKS *UK, male / female vocal group (Singles: 7 weeks)* pos/wks

24 Jan 63	**LOO-BE-LOO** *Decca F 11569*	22	7

CHUMBAWAMBA *UK, male / female vocal / instrumental group (Singles: 31 weeks, Albums: 10 weeks)* pos/wks

18 Sep 93	**ENOUGH IS ENOUGH** *One Little Indian 79 TP7CD* [1]	56	2
4 Dec 93	**TIMEBOMB** *One Little Indian 89 TP7CD*	59	1
23 Aug 97 ●	**TUBTHUMPING** *EMI CDEM 486*	2	20
31 Jan 98 ●	**AMNESIA** *EMI CDEM 498*	10	5
13 Jun 98	**TOP OF THE WORLD (OLE, OLE, OLE)** *EMI CDEM 511*	21	3
7 May 94	**ANARCHY** *One Little Indian TPLP 46CD*	29	2
4 Nov 95	**SWINGIN' WITH RAYMOND** *One Little Indian TPLP 66CDS*	70	1
13 Sep 97	**TUBTHUMPER** *EMI CDEMC 3773*	19	7

[1] Chumbawamba and Credit to the Nation

Chubby CHUNKS
UK, male instrumentalist / producer (Singles: 2 weeks) pos/wks

4 Jun 94	**TESTAMENT 4** *Cleveland City CLECD 13017* [1]	52	1
29 May 99	**I'M TELLIN YOU (re-mix)** *Cleveland City CLECD 13052* [2]	61	1

[1] Chubby Chunks Volume II [2] Chubby Chunks featuring Kim Ruffin

CHUPITO *Spain, male vocalist (Singles: 2 weeks)* pos/wks

23 Sep 95	**AMERICAN PIE** *Eternal WEA 018CD*	54	2

Charlotte CHURCH
UK, female vocalist (Singles: 14 weeks, Albums: 45 weeks) pos/wks

25 Dec 99	**JUST WAVE HELLO** *Sony Classical 6685312*	31	4
1 Feb 03 ●	**THE OPERA SONG (BRAVE NEW WORLD) (re)** *Direction 6734642* [1]	3	10
21 Nov 98 ●	**VOICE OF AN ANGEL** *Sony Classical SK 60957*	4	20
27 Nov 99 ●	**CHARLOTTE CHURCH** *Sony Classical SK 89003*	8	10
2 Dec 00	**DREAM A DREAM** *Sony Classical SK 89459*	30	6
3 Nov 01	**ENCHANTMENT** *Sony Classical SK 89710*	24	9

[1] Jurgen Vries featuirng CMC

Sir Winston CHURCHILL
UK, male statesman d. 24 Feb 1965 (Albums: 8 weeks) pos/wks

13 Feb 65 ●	**THE VOICE OF CHURCHILL** *Decca LXT 6200*	6	8

CHYNA – *See INCOGNITO*

CICA – *See PQM featuring CICA*

CICCONE YOUTH – *See SONIC YOUTH*

CICERO *UK, male vocalist – Dave Cicero (Singles: 12 weeks)* pos/wks

18 Jan 92	**LOVE IS EVERYWHERE** *Spaghetti CIAO 3*	19	8
18 Apr 92	**THAT LOVING FEELING** *Spaghetti CIAO 4*	46	3
1 Aug 92	**HEAVEN MUST HAVE SENT YOU BACK** *Spaghetti CIAO 5*	70	1

CINDERELLA *US, male vocal / instrumental group (Singles: 7 weeks, Albums: 8 weeks)* pos/wks

6 Aug 88	**GYPSY ROAD** *Vertigo VER 40*	54	2
4 Mar 89	**DON'T KNOW WHAT YOU GOT (TILL IT'S GONE)** *Vertigo VER 43*	54	2
17 Nov 90	**SHELTER ME** *Vertigo VER 51*	55	2
27 Apr 91	**HEARTBREAK STATION** *Vertigo VER 53*	63	1
23 Jul 88	**LONG COLD WINTER** *Vertigo VERH 59*	30	6
1 Dec 90	**HEARTBREAK STATION** *Vertigo 8480181*	36	2

CINDY and the SAFFRONS
UK, female vocal group (Singles: 3 weeks) pos/wks

15 Jan 83	**PAST, PRESENT AND FUTURE** *Stiletto STL 9*	56	3

CINEMATIC ORCHESTRA *UK, male orchestra (Albums: 2 weeks)* pos/wks

25 May 02	**EVERY DAY** *Ninja Tune ZENCD 59*	54	2

CINERAMA
UK, male / female vocal / instrumental duo (Singles: 1 week) pos/wks

18 Jul 98	**KERRY KERRY** *Cooking Vinyl FRYCD 072*	71	1

Gigliola CINQUETTI *Italy, female vocalist (Singles: 27 weeks)* pos/wks

23 Apr 64	**NON HO L'ETA PER AMARTI** *Decca F 21882*	17	17
4 May 74 ●	**GO (BEFORE YOU BREAK MY HEART)** *CBS 2294*	8	10

CIRCA featuring DESTRY
UK, male production group and US, male vocalist (Singles: 1 week) pos/wks

27 Nov 99	**SUN SHINING DOWN** *Inferno CDFERN 22*	70	1

CIRCUIT
UK, male / female vocal / instrumental group (Singles: 3 weeks) pos/wks

20 Jul 91	**SHELTER ME** *Cooltempo COOL 237*	44	2
1 Apr 95	**SHELTER ME (re-issue)** *Pukka CDPUKA 2*	50	1

CIRCULATION *UK, male production duo (Singles: 1 week)* pos/wks

1 Sep 01	**TURQUOISE** *Hooj Choons HOOJ 109*	64	1

CIRRUS *UK, male vocal group (Singles: 1 week)* pos/wks

30 Sep 78	**ROLLIN' ON** *Jet 123*	62	1

CITIZEN CANED
UK, male producer – Darren Tate (Singles: 2 weeks) pos/wks

7 Apr 01	**THE JOURNEY** *Serious SERR 029CD*	41	2

See also ANGELIC; Jurgen VRIES

CITY BEAT BAND – *See PRINCE CHARLES and the CITY BEAT BAND*

CITY BOY *UK, male vocal / instrumental group (Singles: 20 weeks)* pos/wks

8 Jul 78 ●	**5.7.0.5.** *Vertigo 6059 207*	8	12
28 Oct 78	**WHAT A NIGHT** *Vertigo 6059 211*	39	5
15 Sep 79	**THE DAY THE EARTH CAUGHT FIRE** *Vertigo 6059 238*	67	3

CITY GENTS – *See Dick CHARLESWORTH and his CITY GENTS*

CITY HIGH *US, male / female vocal / rap trio (Singles: 27 weeks)* pos/wks

6 Oct 01 ●	**WHAT WOULD YOU DO?** *Interscope / Polydor IND 97617*	3	17
16 Mar 02 ●	**CARAMEL** *Interscope / Polydor 4976742* [1]	9	10

[1] City High featuring Eve

CITY OF LONDON SINFONIA – *See John RUTTER*

CITY SPUD – *See NELLY*

CK – *See BADFELLAS featuring CK*

Gary CLAIL ON-U SOUND SYSTEM *UK, male vocal / instrumental group (Singles: 19 weeks, Albums: 2 weeks)* pos/wks

14 Jul 90	**BEEF** *RCA PB 43843* [1]	64	2

30 Mar 91 ● **HUMAN NATURE** *Perfecto PB 44401* 10 9
8 Jun 91 **ESCAPE** *Perfecto PB 44563* 44 3
14 Nov 92 **WHO PAYS THE PIPER** *Perfecto 74321117017* 31 3
22 May 93 **THESE THINGS ARE WORTH FIGHTING FOR** *Perfecto 74321147222* 45 2
4 May 91 **THE EMOTIONAL HOOLIGAN** *Perfecto PL 74965* 35 2

[1] Gary Clail On-U Sound System featuring Bim Sherman

See also PRIMAL SCREAM

CLAIRE – *See H & CLAIRE*

CLAIRE and FRIENDS *UK, female vocalist and young male / female friends (Singles: 11 weeks)* pos/wks

7 Jun 86 **IT'S 'ORRIBLE BEING IN LOVE (WHEN YOU'RE 8 1/2)** *BBC RESL 189* 13 11

CLANCY BROTHERS and Tommy MAKEM *Ireland, male vocal / instrumental group and male vocalist (Albums: 5 weeks)* pos/wks

16 Apr 66 **ISN'T IT GRAND BOYS** *CBS BPG 62674* 22 5

See also Tommy MAKEM

CLANNAD (362 Top 500) *Grammy-winning folk / new age / world music mainstays formed 1970, Co Donegal, Ireland, included Brennan siblings Maire (v/harp/k), Ciaran (g/k), Pol (k) and Ethne [Enya] (v/k) (1979-82). Gaelic-speaking group won a Bafta for Best Soundtrack in 1985 for 'Robin of Sherwood' (Singles: 29 weeks, Albums: 154 weeks)* pos/wks

6 Nov 82 ● **THEME FROM 'HARRY'S GAME'** *RCA 292* 5 10
2 Jul 83 **NEW GRANGE** *RCA 340* 65 1
12 May 84 **ROBIN (THE HOODED MAN)** *RCA HOOD 1* 42 5
25 Jan 86 **IN A LIFETIME** *RCA PB 40535* [1] 20 5
10 Jun 89 **IN A LIFETIME (re-issue)** *RCA PB 42873* [1] 17 7
10 Aug 91 **BOTH SIDES NOW** *MCA MCS 1546* [2] 74 1
2 Apr 83 **MAGICAL RING** *RCA RCALP 6072* 26 21
12 May 84 **LEGEND (MUSIC FROM ROBIN OF SHERWOOD)** *RCA PL 70188* 15 40
2 Jun 84 **MAGICAL RING (re-issue)** *RCA PL 70003* 91 1
26 Oct 85 **MACALLA** *RCA PL 70894* 33 24
7 Nov 87 **SIRIUS** *RCA PL 71513* 34 4
11 Feb 89 **ATLANTIC REALM** *BBC REB 727* 41 3
6 May 89 ● **PASTPRESENT** *RCA PL 74074* 5 26
20 Oct 90 **ANAM** *RCA PL 74762* 14 7
15 May 93 ● **BANBA** *RCA 74321139612* 5 11
6 Apr 96 **LORE** *RCA 74321300802* 14 7
31 May 97 **THE ULTIMATE COLLECTION** *RCA 74321486742* 46 4
11 Apr 98 **LANDMARKS** *RCA 74321560072* 34 2
18 Oct 03 **THE BEST OF – IN A LIFETIME** *RCA 82876564022* 23 4

[1] Clannad featuring Bono [2] Clannad and Paul Young

'Pastpresent' changed its catalogue number to 74321289812 during its chart run

Jimmy CLANTON *US, male vocalist (Singles: 1 week)* pos/wks

21 Jul 60 **ANOTHER SLEEPLESS NIGHT** *Top Rank JAR 382* 50 1

Eric CLAPTON (39 Top 500) *Rock / blues guitar player, b. Eric Clapp, 30 Mar 1945, Surrey. "Clapton is God" title bestowed on him by fans and media alike - also nicknamed 'Slowhand'. Prior to long and lucrative solo career he recorded with hitmakers The Yardbirds, Cream, Blind Faith and Derek and the Dominoes. Multi-Grammy-winning singer-guitarist and mega-grossing live performer (Singles: 150 weeks, Albums: 543 weeks)* pos/wks

20 Dec 69 **COMIN' HOME** *Atlantic 584 308* [1] 16 9
12 Aug 72 ● **LAYLA** *Polydor 2058 130* [2] 7 11
27 Jul 74 ● **I SHOT THE SHERIFF** *RSO 2090 132* ▲ 9 9
10 May 75 **SWING LOW SWEET CHARIOT** *RSO 2090 158* 19 9
16 Aug 75 **KNOCKIN' ON HEAVEN'S DOOR** *RSO 2090 166* 38 4
24 Dec 77 **LAY DOWN SALLY** *RSO 2090 264* 39 6
21 Oct 78 **PROMISES** *RSO 21* 37 7
6 Mar 82 ● **LAYLA (re-issue)** *RSO 87* [2] 4 10
5 Jun 82 **I SHOT THE SHERIFF (re-issue)** *RSO 88* 64 2
23 Apr 83 **THE SHAPE YOU'RE IN** *Duck W 9701* 75 1
16 Mar 85 **FOREVER MAN** *Warner Bros. W 9069* 51 4
4 Jan 86 **EDGE OF DARKNESS** *BBC RESL 178* [3] 65 3
17 Jan 87 **BEHIND THE MASK** *Duck W 8461* 15 11
20 Jun 87 **TEARING US APART** *Duck W 8299* [4] 56 3
27 Jan 90 **BAD LOVE** *Duck W 2644* 25 7
14 Apr 90 **NO ALIBIS** *Duck W 9981* 53 3
16 Nov 91 **WONDERFUL TONIGHT (LIVE)** *Duck W 0069* 30 7
8 Feb 92 ● **TEARS IN HEAVEN (re)** *Reprise W 0081* 5 12
1 Aug 92 **RUNAWAY TRAIN** *Rocket EJS 29* [5] 31 4
29 Aug 92 **IT'S PROBABLY ME** *A&M AM 883* [6] 30 5
3 Oct 92 **LAYLA (ACOUSTIC) (re-recording)** *Duck W 0134* 45 3
15 Oct 94 **MOTHERLESS CHILD** *Duck W 0271CD* 63 1
18 Mar 95 ★ **LOVE CAN BUILD A BRIDGE** *London COCD 1* [7] 1 8
20 Jul 96 **CHANGE THE WORLD** *Reprise W 0358CD* 18 5
4 Apr 98 **MY FATHER'S EYES** *Duck W 0443CD* 33 2
4 Jul 98 **CIRCUS** *Duck W 0447CD* 39 2
18 Nov 00 **FOREVER MAN (HOW MANY TIMES)** *ffrr FCD 386* [8] 26 2
30 Jul 66 ● **BLUES BREAKERS** *Decca LK 4804* [1] 6 17
5 Sep 70 **ERIC CLAPTON** *Polydor 2383021* 17 8
26 Aug 72 **HISTORY OF ERIC CLAPTON** *Polydor 2659 2478 027* 20 6
24 Mar 73 **IN CONCERT** *RSO 2659020* [2] 36 1
24 Aug 74 ● **461 OCEAN BOULEVARD** *RSO 2479 118* ▲ 3 19
12 Apr 75 **THERE'S ONE IN EVERY CROWD** *RSO 2479 132* 15 8
13 Sep 75 **E.C. WAS HERE** *RSO 2394 160* 14 6
11 Sep 76 ● **NO REASON TO CRY** *RSO 2479 179* 8 7
26 Nov 77 **SLOWHAND** *RSO 2479 201* 23 13
9 Dec 78 **BACKLESS** *RSO RSD 5001* 18 12
10 May 80 ● **JUST ONE NIGHT** *RSO RSDX 2* 3 12
7 Mar 81 **ANOTHER TICKET** *RSO RSD 5008* 18 8
24 Apr 82 **TIME PIECES – THE BEST OF ERIC CLAPTON** *RSO RSD 5010* 20 14
19 Feb 83 **MONEY & CIGARETTES** *Duck W 3773* 13 17
9 Jun 84 **BACKTRACKIN'** *Starblend ERIC 1* 29 16
23 Mar 85 ● **BEHIND THE SUN** *Duck 9251661* 8 14
6 Dec 86 ● **AUGUST** *Duck WX 71* 3 46
26 Sep 87 ● **THE CREAM OF ERIC CLAPTON** *Polydor ECTV 1* [3] 3 109
18 Nov 89 ● **JOURNEYMAN** *Duck WX 322* 2 32
26 Oct 91 **24 NIGHTS** *Duck WX 373* 17 7
12 Sep 92 ● **UNPLUGGED** *Duck 9362450242* ▲ 2 90
24 Sep 94 ★ **FROM THE CRADLE** *Duck 9362457352* ■ ▲ 1 18
21 Mar 98 ● **PILGRIM** *Duck 9362465772* 6 15
26 Jun 99 **BLUES** *Polydor 5471782* 52 2
30 Oct 99 ● **CLAPTON CHRONICLES – THE BEST OF ERIC CLAPTON** *Duck 9362475642* 6 21
24 Jun 00 **RIDING WITH THE KING** *Reprise 9362476122* [4] 15 15
15 Jul 00 **TIME PIECES – THE BEST OF ERIC CLAPTON (re-issue)** *Polydor 8000142* 73 2
17 Mar 01 ● **REPTILE** *Reprise 9362479662* 7 7
16 Nov 02 **LIVE ON TOUR 2001 – ONE MORE CAR ONE MORE RIDER** *Reprise 9362483972* 69 1

[1] Delaney and Bonnie and Friends featuring Eric Clapton [2] Derek and the Dominoes [3] Eric Clapton featuring Michael Kamen [4] Eric Clapton and Tina Turner [5] Elton John and Eric Clapton [6] Sting with Eric Clapton [7] Cher, Chrissie Hynde and Neneh Cherry with Eric Clapton [8] Beatchuggers featuring Eric Clapton
[1] John Mayall and Eric Clapton [2] Derek and the Dominos [3] Eric Clapton and Cream [4] B.B. King and Eric Clapton

From 9 Jul 93 'The Cream of Eric Clapton' was repackaged and was available as 'The Best of Eric Clapton'

See also DEREK and the DOMINOES; BLIND FAITH; CREAM

CLARISSA – *See DJ VISAGE featuring CLARISSA*

Dave CLARK FIVE (318 Top 500) *Beat Boom superstars from Tottenham, London: Dave Clark (d), Mike Smith (v/k), Lenny Davidson (g), Denis Payton (s), Rick Huxley (g). In the first years of the 'British Invasion', this foot-stomping quintet was second only to The Beatles in the US (Singles: 174 weeks, Albums: 31 weeks)* pos/wks

3 Oct 63 **DO YOU LOVE ME** *Columbia DB 7112* 30 6
21 Nov 63 ★ **GLAD ALL OVER** *Columbia DB 7154* 1 19
20 Feb 64 ● **BITS AND PIECES** *Columbia DB 7210* 2 11
28 May 64 ● **CAN'T YOU SEE THAT SHE'S MINE** *Columbia DB 7291* 10 11
13 Aug 64 **THINKING OF YOU BABY** *Columbia DB 7335* 26 4

22 Oct 64	ANYWAY YOU WANT IT *Columbia DB 7377*	25	5
14 Jan 65	EVERYBODY KNOWS *Columbia DB 7453*	37	4
11 Mar 65	REELIN' AND ROCKIN' *Columbia DB 7503*	24	8
27 May 65	COME HOME *Columbia DB 7580*	16	8
15 Jul 65 ●	CATCH US IF YOU CAN *Columbia DB 7625*	5	11
11 Nov 65	OVER AND OVER *Columbia DB 7744* ▲	45	4
19 May 66	LOOK BEFORE YOU LEAP *Columbia DB 7909*	50	1
16 Mar 67	YOU GOT WHAT IT TAKES *Columbia DB 8152*	28	8
1 Nov 67 ●	EVERYBODY KNOWS *Columbia DB 8286*	2	14
28 Feb 68	NO ONE CAN BREAK A HEART LIKE YOU *Columbia DB 8342*	28	7
18 Sep 68 ●	THE RED BALLOON *Columbia DB 8465*	7	11
27 Nov 68	LIVE IN THE SKY *Columbia DB 8505*	39	6
25 Oct 69	PUT A LITTLE LOVE IN YOUR HEART *Columbia DB 8624*	31	4
6 Dec 69 ●	GOOD OLD ROCK 'N' ROLL *Columbia DB 8638*	7	12
7 Mar 70 ●	EVERYBODY GET TOGETHER *Columbia DB 8660*	8	8
4 Jul 70	HERE COMES SUMMER *Columbia DB 8689*	44	3
7 Nov 70	MORE GOOD OLD ROCK 'N' ROLL *Columbia DB 8724*	34	6
1 May 93	GLAD ALL OVER (re-issue) *EMI CDEMCT 8*	37	3
18 Apr 64 ●	A SESSION WITH THE DAVE CLARK FIVE *Columbia 33SX 1598*	3	8
14 Aug 65 ●	CATCH US IF YOU CAN *Columbia 33SX 1756*	8	8
4 Mar 78 ●	25 THUMPING GREAT HITS *Polydor POLTV 7*	7	10
17 Apr 93	GLAD ALL OVER AGAIN *EMI CDEMTV 75*	28	5

'Everybody Knows' on DB 7453 and 'Everybody Knows' on DB 8286 are two different songs. The two Rock 'n' Roll titles are medleys as follows: Good Old Rock 'n' Roll / Sweet Little Sixteen / Long Tall Sally / Whole Lotta Shakin' Goin' On / Blue Suede Shoes / Lucille / Reelin' and Rockin' / Memphis Tennessee. More Good Old Rock 'n' Roll Music / Blueberry Hill / Good Golly Miss Molly / My Blue Heaven / Keep a Knockin' / Loving You / One Night / Lawdy Miss Clawdy

Dee CLARK

US, male vocalist d. 7 Dec 1990 (Singles: 9 weeks) pos/wks

2 Oct 59	JUST KEEP IT UP (AND SEE WHAT HAPPENS) *London HL 8915*	26	1
11 Oct 75	RIDE A WILD HORSE *Chelsea 2005 037*	16	8

Gary CLARK

UK, male vocalist (Singles: 8 weeks, Albums: 2 weeks) pos/wks

30 Jan 93	WE SAIL ON THE STORMY WATERS *Circa YRCDX 93*	34	4
3 Apr 93	FREEFLOATING *Circa YRCDX 94*	50	3
19 Jun 93	MAKE A FAMILY *Circa YRCDX 105*	70	1
8 May 93	TEN SHORT SONGS ABOUT LOVE *Circa CIRCD 23*	25	2

Loni CLARK

US, female vocalist (Singles: 6 weeks) pos/wks

5 Jun 93	RUSHING *A&M 5802862*	37	2
22 Jan 94	U *A&M 5804752*	28	3
17 Dec 94	LOVE'S GOT ME ON A TRIP SO HIGH *A&M 5808872*	59	1

Louis CLARK – *See ROYAL PHILHARMONIC ORCHESTRA*

Petula CLARK (197 Top 500)

Britain's most consistently successful female vocalist, b. 15 Nov 1932, Surrey. Before her 34-year chart span, she starred in movies and was voted Britain's Top TV Personality. First UK female to win a Grammy and to be named Top Female Vocalist of the Year in the US in 1966 (Singles: 247 weeks, Albums: 47 weeks) pos/wks

11 Jun 54 ●	THE LITTLE SHOEMAKER (re) *Polygon P 1117*	7	10
18 Feb 55	MAJORCA (re) *Polygon P 1146*	12	5
25 Nov 55 ●	SUDDENLY THERE'S A VALLEY *Pye Nixa N 15013*	7	10
26 Jul 57 ●	WITH ALL MY HEART *Pye Nixa N 15096*	4	18
15 Nov 57 ●	ALONE *Pye Nixa N 15112*	8	12
28 Feb 58	BABY LOVER *Pye Nixa N 15126*	12	7
26 Jan 61 ★	SAILOR *Pye 7N 15324*	1	15
13 Apr 61	SOMETHING MISSING *Pye 7N 15337*	44	1
13 Jul 61 ●	ROMEO *Pye 7N 15361*	3	15
16 Nov 61 ●	MY FRIEND THE SEA *Pye 7N 15389*	7	13
8 Feb 62	I'M COUNTING ON YOU *Pye 7N 15407*	41	2
28 Jun 62	YA YA TWIST (re) *Pye 7N 15448*	14	13
2 May 63	CASANOVA / CHARIOT *Pye 7N 15522*	39	7
12 Nov 64 ●	DOWNTOWN *Pye 7N 15722* ▲	2	15
11 Mar 65	I KNOW A PLACE *Pye 7N 15772*	17	8
12 Aug 65	YOU BETTER COME HOME *Pye 7N 15864*	44	3
14 Oct 65	ROUND EVERY CORNER *Pye 7N 15945*	43	3
4 Nov 65	YOU'RE THE ONE *Pye 7N 15991*	23	9
10 Feb 66 ●	MY LOVE *Pye 7N 17038* ▲	4	9
21 Apr 66	A SIGN OF THE TIMES *Pye 7N 17071*	49	1
30 Jun 66 ●	I COULDN'T LIVE WITHOUT YOUR LOVE *Pye 7N 17133*	6	11
2 Feb 67 ★	THIS IS MY SONG *Pye 7N 17258*	1	14
25 May 67	DON'T SLEEP IN THE SUBWAY *Pye 7N 17325*	12	11
13 Dec 67	THE OTHER MAN'S GRASS (IS ALWAYS GREENER) *Pye 7N 17416*	20	9
6 Mar 68	KISS ME GOODBYE *Pye 7N 17466*	50	1
30 Jan 71	THE SONG OF MY LIFE (re) *Pye 7N 45026*	32	12
15 Jan 72	I DON'T KNOW HOW TO LOVE HIM (re) *Pye 7N 45112*	47	2
19 Nov 88 ●	DOWNTOWN '88 (re-mix) *PRT PYS 19*	10	11
30 Jul 66	I COULDN'T LIVE WITHOUT YOUR LOVE *Pye NPL 18148*	11	10
4 Feb 67	HIT PARADE *Pye NPL 18159*	18	13
18 Feb 67	COLOUR MY WORLD *Pye NSPL 18171*	16	9
7 Oct 67	THESE ARE MY SONGS *Pye NSPL 18197*	38	3
6 Apr 68	THE OTHER MAN'S GRASS IS ALWAYS GREENER *Pye NSPL 18211*	37	1
5 Feb 77	20 ALL TIME GREATEST *K-Tel NE 945*	18	7
27 Apr 02	THE ULTIMATE COLLECTION *Sanctuary SANDD 111*	18	4

Roland CLARK – *See Armand VAN HELDEN; Azzido DA BASS*

Dave CLARKE

UK, male producer (Singles: 9 weeks, Albums: 2 weeks) pos/wks

30 Sep 95	RED THREE: THUNDER / STORM *Deconstruction 74321306992*	45	2
3 Feb 96	SOUTHSIDE *Bush 74321335382*	34	2
15 Jun 96	NO ONE'S DRIVING *Bush 74321380162*	37	2
8 Dec 01	THE COMPASS *Skint SKINT 73CD*	46	1
28 Dec 02	THE WOLF *Skint SKINT 78*	66	1
25 Oct 03	WAY OF LIFE *Skint SKINT 93CD*	59	1
17 Feb 96	ARCHIVE ONE *Bush / Deconstruction 74321320672*	36	2

Gilby CLARKE

US, male instrumentalist – guitar (Albums: 1 week) pos/wks

6 Aug 94	PAWNSHOP GUITARS *Virgin America CDVUS 76*	39	1

See also GUNS N' ROSES

John Cooper CLARKE

UK, male vocalist (Singles: 3 weeks, Albums: 9 weeks) pos/wks

10 Mar 79	GIMMIX! PLAY LOUD *Epic EPC 7009*	39	3
19 Apr 80	SNAP CRACKLE AND BOP *Epic EPC 84083*	26	7
5 Jun 82	ZIP STYLE METHOD *Epic EPC 85667*	97	2

Rick CLARKE *UK, male vocalist (Singles: 2 weeks)* pos/wks

30 Apr 88	I'LL SEE YOU ALONG THE WAY *WA WA 1*	63	2

Sharon D CLARKE – *See FPI PROJECT; SERIOUS ROPE*

Stanley CLARKE

US, male vocalist / instrumentalist – bass (Albums: 2 weeks) pos/wks

12 Jul 80	ROCKS PEBBLES AND SAND *Epic EPC 84342*	42	2

Warren CLARKE featuring Kathy BROWN

UK, male producer and US, female vocalist (Singles: 1 week) pos/wks

2 Jun 01	OVER YOU *Defected DFECT 28CDS*	42	1

Kelly CLARKSON

US, female vocalist (Singles: 13 weeks, Albums: 4 weeks) pos/wks

6 Sep 03 ●	MISS INDEPENDENT *S 82876553642*	6	10
29 Nov 03	LOW / THE TROUBLE WITH LOVE IS... *S 82876570702*	35	3
6 Sep 03	THANKFUL *S 82876540882* ▲	52	4

Julian CLARY – *See JOAN COLLINS FAN CLUB*

CLASH (244 Top 500)

Leading lights of the UK punk rock explosion: Joe Strummer (b. John Mellor, d. 23 Dec 2002) (v/g), Mick Jones (g/v), Paul Simonon (b), Topper Headon (d). Their third LP, 'London Calling' (first released 1979), was voted Best Album of the 1980s by Rolling Stone magazine. Inducted into the Rock and Roll Hall of Fame in 2003 (Singles: 135 weeks, Albums: 115 weeks)

Date		Title	pos	wks
2 Apr 77		**WHITE RIOT** *CBS 5058*	**38**	3
8 Oct 77		**COMPLETE CONTROL** *CBS 5664*	**28**	2
4 Mar 78		**CLASH CITY ROCKERS** *CBS 5834*	**35**	4
24 Jun 78		**(WHITE MAN) IN HAMMERSMITH PALAIS** *CBS 6383*	**32**	7
2 Dec 78		**TOMMY GUN** *CBS 6788*	**19**	10
3 Mar 79		**ENGLISH CIVIL WAR (JOHNNY COMES MARCHING HOME)** *CBS 7082*	**25**	6
19 May 79		**THE COST OF LIVING (EP)** *CBS 7324*	**22**	8
15 Dec 79		**LONDON CALLING** *CBS 8087*	**11**	10
9 Aug 80		**BANKROBBER** *CBS 8323*	**12**	10
6 Dec 80		**THE CALL UP** *CBS 9339*	**40**	6
24 Jan 81		**HITSVILLE UK** *CBS 9480*	**56**	4
25 Apr 81		**THE MAGNIFICENT SEVEN** *CBS 1133*	**34**	5
28 Nov 81		**THIS IS RADIO CLASH** *CBS A 1797*	**47**	6
1 May 82		**KNOW YOUR RIGHTS** *CBS A 2309*	**43**	3
26 Jun 82		**ROCK THE CASBAH** *CBS A 2429*	**30**	10
25 Sep 82		**SHOULD I STAY OR SHOULD I GO / STRAIGHT TO HELL** *CBS A 2646*	**17**	9
12 Oct 85		**THIS IS ENGLAND** *CBS A 6122*	**24**	5
12 Mar 88		**I FOUGHT THE LAW** *CBS CLASH 1*	**29**	5
7 May 88		**LONDON CALLING (re-issue)** *CBS CLASH 2*	**46**	3
21 Jul 90		**RETURN TO BRIXTON** *CBS 656072 7*	**57**	2
2 Mar 91	★	**SHOULD I STAY OR SHOULD I GO (re-issue)** *Columbia 6566677*	**1**	9
13 Apr 91		**ROCK THE CASBAH (re-issue)** *Columbia 6568147*	**15**	6
8 Jun 91		**LONDON CALLING (re-issue)** *Columbia 6569467*	**64**	2
30 Apr 77		CLASH *CBS 82000*	**12**	16
25 Nov 78	●	GIVE 'EM ENOUGH ROPE *CBS 82431*	**2**	14
22 Dec 79	●	LONDON CALLING *CBS CLASH 3*	**9**	21
20 Dec 80		SANDINISTA *CBS FSLN 1*	**19**	9
22 May 82	●	COMBAT ROCK *CBS FMLN 2*	**2**	23
16 Nov 85		CUT THE CRAP *CBS 26601*	**16**	3
2 Apr 88	●	THE STORY OF THE CLASH – VOLUME 1 *CBS 4602441*	**7**	21
16 Nov 91		THE SINGLES *Columbia 4689461*	**68**	2
16 Oct 99		FROM HERE TO ETERNITY *Columbia 4961832*	**13**	3
22 Mar 03		THE ESSENTIAL CLASH *Columbia 05109982*	**18**	3

Tracks on The Cost of Living (EP): I Fought the Law / Groovy Times / Gates of the West / Capital Radio. CBS CLASH 1 is a re-issue of a track from The Cost of Living (EP)

CLASS ACTION featuring Chris WILTSHIRE

US, female vocal group (Singles: 3 weeks)

Date	Title	pos	wks
7 May 83	**WEEKEND** *Jive JIVE 35*	**49**	3

CLASSICS IV

US, male vocal / instrumental group (Singles: 1 week)

Date	Title	pos	wks
28 Feb 68	**SPOOKY** *Liberty LBS 15051*	**46**	1

CLASSIX NOUVEAUX *UK, male vocal / instrumental group (Singles: 34 weeks, Albums: 6 weeks)*

Date	Title	pos	wks
28 Feb 81	**GUILTY** *Liberty BP 388*	**43**	7
16 May 81	**TOKYO** *Liberty BP 397*	**67**	3
8 Aug 81	**INSIDE OUTSIDE** *Liberty BP 403*	**45**	5
7 Nov 81	**NEVER AGAIN (THE DAYS TIME ERASED)** *Liberty BP 406*	**44**	4
13 Mar 82	**IS IT A DREAM** *Liberty BP 409*	**11**	9
29 May 82	**BECAUSE YOU'RE YOUNG** *Liberty BP 411*	**43**	4
30 Oct 82	**THE END ... OR THE BEGINNING** *Liberty BP 414*	**60**	2
30 May 81	NIGHT PEOPLE *Liberty LBG 30325*	**66**	2
24 Apr 82	LA VERITE *Liberty LBG 30346*	**44**	4

See also Sal SOLO

CLAWFINGER *Norway / Sweden, male vocal / instrumental group (Singles: 1 week)*

Date	Title	pos	wks
19 Mar 94	**WARFAIR** *East West YZ 804CD1*	**54**	1

Judy CLAY – *See William BELL*

Richard CLAYDERMAN (309 Top 500)

'The world's most successful pianist' according to Guinness World Records, b. Philippe Pagès (adopted great-grandmother's surname), 28 Dec 1953, Paris, France. He has sold in excess of 70 million albums and earned more than 250 gold and 70 platinum albums (Albums: 211 weeks)

Date		Title	pos	wks
13 Nov 82	●	RICHARD CLAYDERMAN *Decca SKL 5329*	**2**	64
8 Oct 83		THE MUSIC OF RICHARD CLAYDERMAN *Decca SKL 5333*	**21**	28
24 Nov 84		THE MUSIC OF LOVE *Decca SKL 5340*	**28**	21
1 Dec 84		CHRISTMAS *Decca SKL 5337*	**53**	5
23 Nov 85		THE CLASSIC TOUCH *Decca SKL 5343*	**17**	18
22 Nov 86		HOLLYWOOD AND BROADWAY *Decca SKL 5344*	**28**	9
28 Nov 87		SONGS OF LOVE *Decca SKL 5345*	**19**	13
3 Dec 88		A LITTLE NIGHT MUSIC *Decca Delphine 8281251*	**52**	5
25 Nov 89		THE LOVE SONGS OF ANDREW LLOYD WEBBER *Decca Delphine 8281751*	**18**	10
24 Nov 90		MY CLASSIC COLLECTION *Decca Delphine 8282281*	**29**	7
9 Nov 91		TOGETHER AT LAST *Delphine / Polydor 5115251* [1]	**14**	15
14 Nov 92		THE VERY BEST OF RICHARD CLAYDERMAN *Decca Delphine 8283362* [2]	**47**	5
19 Nov 94		IN HARMONY *Polydor 5238242* [1]	**28**	7
25 Nov 95		THE CARPENTERS COLLECTION *PolyGram TV 8286882*	**65**	2
20 Dec 97		THE BEST OF RICHARD CLAYDERMAN *Delphine DTVCD 700*	**73**	1
18 Sep 99		... WITH LOVE *Music Club MCTVCD 002*	**62**	1

[1] Richard Clayderman and James Last [2] Richard Clayderman with the Royal Philharmonic Orchestra

Adam CLAYTON and Larry MULLEN

Ireland, male instrumental duo (Singles: 12 weeks)

Date		Title	pos	wks
15 Jun 96	●	**THEME FROM 'MISSION: IMPOSSIBLE'** *Mother MUMCD 75*	**7**	12

See also U2

Merry CLAYTON

US, female vocalist (Singles: 1 week)

Date	Title	pos	wks
21 May 88	**YES** *RCA PB 49563*	**70**	1

CLAYTOWN TROUPE *UK, male vocal / instrumental group (Singles: 3 weeks, Albums: 1 week)*

Date	Title	pos	wks
16 Jun 90	**WAYS OF LOVE** *Island IS 464*	**57**	2
14 Mar 92	**WANTED IT ALL** *EMI USA MT 102*	**74**	1
21 Oct 89	THROUGH THE VEIL *Island ILPS 9933*	**72**	1

CLEA *UK, female vocal group (Singles: 3 weeks)*

Date	Title	pos	wks
4 Oct 03	**DOWNLOAD IT** *1967 CLEA 01CD*	**21**	3

Johnny CLEGG and SAVUKA *UK / South Africa, male vocal / instrumental group (Singles: 1 week)*

Date	Title	pos	wks
16 May 87	**SCATTERLINGS OF AFRICA** *EMI EMI 5605*	**75**	1

See also JULUKA

CLEOPATRA *UK, female vocal duo – Cleopatra, Zainam and Yonah Higgins (Singles: 44 weeks, Albums: 4 weeks)*

Date		Title	pos	wks
14 Feb 98	●	**CLEOPATRA'S THEME** *WEA WEA 133CD*	**3**	10
16 May 98	●	**LIFE AIN'T EASY** *WEA WEA 159CD1*	**4**	7
22 Aug 98	●	**I WANT YOU BACK** *WEA WEA 172CD1*	**4**	7
6 Mar 99		**A TOUCH OF LOVE** *WEA WEA 199CD1*	**24**	4
10 Apr 99	●	**THANK ABBA FOR THE MUSIC** *Epic ABCD 1* [1]	**4**	13
29 Jul 00		**COME AND GET ME** *WEA WEA 216CD1*	**29**	3
6 Jun 98		COMIN' ATCHA! *WEA 3984233562*	**20**	4

[1] Steps, Tina Cousins, Cleopatra, B*Witched, Billie

CLEPTOMANIACS featuring Bryan CHAMBERS

UK, male production group and vocalist (Singles: 3 weeks)

Date	Title	pos	wks
3 Feb 01	**ALL I DO** *Defected DFECT 27 CDS*	**23**	3

CLERGY *UK, male production duo – Paul Masterson and Judge Jules (Singles: 1 week)* pos/wks

20 Jul 02 **THE OBOE SONG** *ffrr DFCD 005* 50 1

See also CANDY GIRLS; DOROTHY; SLEAZESISTERS; YOMANDA; HI-GATE; Paul MASTERSON presents SUSHI

CLICK
US, male rap group (Singles: 1 week) pos/wks

29 Jun 96 **SCANDALOUS** *Jive JIVECD 393* 54 1

Jimmy CLIFF
Jamaica, male vocalist – James Chambers (Singles: 33 weeks) pos/wks

25 Oct 69 ● **WONDERFUL WORLD, BEAUTIFUL PEOPLE** *Trojan TR 690* 6 13
14 Feb 70 **VIETNAM (re)** *Trojan TR 7722* 46 3
8 Aug 70 ● **WILD WORLD** *Island WIP 6087* 8 12
19 Mar 94 **I CAN SEE CLEARLY NOW** *Columbia 6601982* 23 5

Buzz CLIFFORD *US, male vocalist (Singles: 13 weeks)* pos/wks

2 Mar 61 **BABY SITTIN' BOOGIE** *Fontana H 297* 17 13

Linda CLIFFORD *US, female vocalist (Singles: 13 weeks)* pos/wks

10 Jun 78 **IF MY FRIENDS COULD SEE ME NOW** *Curtom K 17163* 50 5
5 May 79 **BRIDGE OVER TROUBLED WATER** *RSO 30* 28 7
15 Sep 01 **RIDE THE STORM** *NRK Sound Division NRKCD 053* [1] 69 1

[1] Akabu featuring Linda Clifford

CLIMAX BLUES BAND *UK, male vocal / instrumental group (Singles: 9 weeks, Albums: 1 week)* pos/wks

9 Oct 76 ● **COULDN'T GET IT RIGHT** *BTM SBT 105* 10 9
13 Nov 76 **GOLD PLATED** *BTM 1009* 56 1

Simon CLIMIE *UK, male vocalist (Singles: 2 weeks)* pos/wks

19 Sep 92 **SOUL INSPIRATION** *Epic 6582837* 60 2

See also CLIMIE FISHER

CLIMIE FISHER *UK, male vocal / instrumental duo – Simon Climie and Rob Fisher d. 25 Aug 1999 (Singles: 44 weeks, Albums: 38 weeks)* pos/wks

5 Sep 87 **LOVE CHANGES (EVERYTHING)** *EMI EM 15* 67 2
12 Dec 87 ● **RISE TO THE OCCASION** *EMI EM 33* 10 11
12 Mar 88 ● **LOVE CHANGES (EVERYTHING) (re-mix)** *EMI EM 47* 2 12
21 May 88 **THIS IS ME** *EMI EM 58* 22 5
20 Aug 88 **I WON'T BLEED FOR YOU** *EMI EM 66* 35 4
24 Dec 88 **LOVE LIKE A RIVER** *EMI EM 81* 22 7
23 Sep 89 **FACTS OF LOVE** *EMI EM 103* 50 3
13 Feb 88 **EVERYTHING** *EMI EMC 3538* 14 36
21 Oct 89 **COMING IN FOR THE KILL** *EMI EMC 3565* 35 2

See also NAKED EYES

Patsy CLINE *US, female vocalist – Virginia Hensley d. 5 Mar 1963 (Singles: 17 weeks, Albums: 28 weeks)* pos/wks

26 Apr 62 **SHE'S GOT YOU** *Brunswick 05866* 43 1
29 Nov 62 **HEARTACHES** *Brunswick 05878* 31 5
8 Dec 90 **CRAZY** *MCA MCA 1465* 14 11
19 Jan 91 **DREAMING** *Platinum Music PLAT 303* 55 4
19 Jan 91 **SWEET DREAMS** *MCA MCG 6003* 18 10
5 Sep 92 **THE DEFINITIVE PATSY CLINE** *Arcade ARC 94992* 11 8
6 Jul 96 **THE VERY BEST OF PATSY CLINE** *MCA MCD 11483* 21 6

CLINIC *UK, male vocal / instrumental group (Singles: 3 weeks)* pos/wks

22 Apr 00 **THE RETURN OF EVIL BILL** *Domino RUG 093CD* 70 1
4 Nov 00 **THE SECOND LINE** *Domino RUG 116CD* 56 1
2 Mar 02 **WALKING WITH THEE** *Domino RUG 134CD* 65 1

George CLINTON *US, male vocalist (Singles: 10 weeks)* pos/wks

4 Dec 82 **LOOPZILLA** *Capitol CL 271* 57 5
26 Apr 86 **DO FRIES GO WITH THAT SHAKE** *Capitol CL 402* 57 2
27 Aug 94 **BOP GUN (ONE NATION)** *Fourth & Broadway BRCD 308* [1] 22 3

[1] Ice Cube featuring George Clinton

See also FUNKADELIC

CLIPSE *US, male rap duo – Gene and Terence Thornton (Singles: 5 weeks)* pos/wks

22 Feb 03 **WHEN THE LAST TIME** *Arista 82876502212* 41 2
24 May 03 **MA, I DON'T LOVE HER** *Arista 82876526482* [1] 38 3

[1] Clipse featuring Faith Evans

CLIVILLES & COLE – *See C & C MUSIC FACTORY*

CLOCK *UK, male production / vocal / instrumental duo (Singles: 70 weeks, Albums: 4 weeks)* pos/wks

30 Oct 93 **HOLDING ON** *Media MRLCD 007* 66 1
21 May 94 **THE RHYTHM** *Media MCSTD 1971* 28 2
10 Sep 94 **KEEP THE FIRES BURNING** *Media MCSTD 1998* 36 3
4 Mar 95 ● **AXEL F / KEEP PUSHIN'** *Media MCSTD 2041* 7 9
1 Jul 95 ● **WHOOMPH! (THERE IT IS)** *Media MCSTD 2059* 4 9
26 Aug 95 ● **EVERYBODY** *Media MCSTD 2077* 6 5
18 Nov 95 **IN THE HOUSE** *Media MCSTD 40005* 23 3
24 Feb 96 **HOLDING ON 4 U (re-mix)** *Media MCSTD 40019* 27 2
7 Sep 96 **OH WHAT A NIGHT** *Power Station MCSTD 40057* 13 10
22 Mar 97 ● **IT'S OVER** *Media MCSTD 40100* 10 5
18 Oct 97 **U SEXY THING** *Media MCSTD 40138* 11 9
17 Jan 98 **THAT'S THE WAY (I LIKE IT)** *Media MCSTD 40148* 11 4
11 Jul 98 **ROCK YOUR BODY** *Media MCSTD 40160* 30 3
28 Nov 98 **BLAME IT ON THE BOOGIE** *Media MCSTD 40191* 16 4
31 Jul 99 **SUNSHINE DAY** *Media MCSTD 40208* 58 1
23 Sep 95 **IT'S TIME ...** *Media MCD 11355* 27 2
5 Apr 97 **ABOUT TIME 2** *Media MCD 60032* 56 2

Rosemary CLOONEY *US, female vocalist (Singles: 81 weeks)* pos/wks

14 Nov 52 ● **HALF AS MUCH** *Columbia DB 3129* 3 9
5 Feb 54 ● **MAN (UH-HUH)** *Philips PB 220* 7 5
8 Oct 54 ★ **THIS OLE HOUSE** *Philips PB 336* ▲ 1 18
17 Dec 54 ★ **MAMBO ITALIANO** *Philips PB 382* [1] 1 16
20 May 55 ● **WHERE WILL THE DIMPLE BE?** *Philips PB 428* [1] 6 13
30 Sep 55 ● **HEY THERE** *Philips PB 494* ▲ 4 11
29 Mar 57 **MANGOS (re)** *Philips PB 671* 17 9

[1] Rosemary Clooney and the Mellomen

From 19 Feb 1954, other side of 'Man (Uh-Huh)', 'Woman (Uh-Huh)', by José Ferrer was also credited

CLOUD *UK, male instrumental group (Singles: 1 week)* pos/wks

31 Jan 81 **ALL NIGHT LONG / TAKE IT TO THE TOP** *UK Champagne FUNK 1* 72 1

CLOUDBURST – *See DISCO TEX presents CLOUDBURST*

CLOUT *South Africa, female vocal / instrumental group (Singles: 15 weeks)* pos/wks

17 Jun 78 ● **SUBSTITUTE** *Carrere EMI 2788* 2 15

CLUB NOUVEAU
US, male / female vocal / instrumental group (Singles: 12 weeks) pos/wks

21 Mar 87 ● **LEAN ON ME** *King Jay W 8430* ▲ 3 12

CLUB 69 *Austria / US, male producer / instrumentalist – Peter Rauhofer (Singles: 6 weeks)* pos/wks

5 Dec 92 **LET ME BE YOUR UNDERWEAR** *ffrr F 204* 33 5
14 Nov 98 **ALRIGHT** *Twisted UK TWCD 10039* [1] 70 1

[1] Club 69 featuring Suzanne Palmer

CLUBHOUSE
Italy, male vocal / instrumental group (Singles: 40 weeks) pos/wks

23 Jul 83 **DO IT AGAIN – BILLIE JEAN (MEDLEY)** *Island IS 132* 11 6

Date		Title / Label	Pos	Wks
3 Dec 83		**SUPERSTITION – GOOD TIMES (MEDLEY)** *Island IS 147*	59	3
1 Jul 89		**I'M A MAN – YEKE YEKE (MEDLEY)** *Music Man MMPS 7003*	69	3
20 Apr 91		**DEEP IN MY HEART (re)** *ffrr F 157*	55	4
4 Sep 93		**LIGHT MY FIRE (2re)** *PWL Continental PWCD 272* [1]	45	12
30 Apr 94	●	**LIGHT MY FIRE (re-mix)** *PWL Continental PWCD 288* [1]	7	8
23 Jul 94		**LIVING IN THE SUNSHINE** *PWL Continental PWCD 309* [1]	21	3
11 Mar 95		**NOWHERE LAND** *PWL International PWCD 318* [1]	56	1

[1] Clubhouse featuring Carl

CLUBZONE
UK / Germany, male vocal / instrumental group (Singles: 1 week) pos/wks

19 Nov 94		**HANDS UP** *Logic 74321236982*	50	1

CLUELESS
US, male / female vocal / production group (Singles: 1 week) pos/wks

5 Apr 97		**DON'T SPEAK** *ZYX ZYX 660738*	61	1

Jeremy CLYDE – *See Chad STUART and Jeremy CLYDE*

CLYDE VALLEY STOMPERS
UK, male instrumental group (Singles: 8 weeks) pos/wks

9 Aug 62		**PETER AND THE WOLF** *Parlophone R 4928*	25	8

CO-CO
UK, male / female vocal / instrumental group (Singles: 7 weeks) pos/wks

22 Apr 78		**BAD OLD DAYS** *Ariola Hansa AHA 513*	13	7

CO-OPERATION CHOIR – *See Peter E BENNETT with the CO-OPERATION CHOIR*

COAL CHAMBER
US, male vocal / instrumental group (Albums: 4 weeks) pos/wks

18 Sep 99		**CHAMBER MUSIC** *Roadrunner RR 86592*	21	2
18 May 02		**DARK DAYS** *Roadrunner RR 84842*	43	2

COAST TO COAST
UK, male vocal / instrumental group (Singles: 22 weeks) pos/wks

31 Jan 81	●	**(DO) THE HUCKLEBUCK** *Polydor POSP 214*	5	15
23 May 81		**LET'S JUMP THE BROOMSTICK** *Polydor POSP 249*	28	7

COAST 2 COAST featuring DISCOVERY
Ireland, male production duo and female vocalist (Singles: 1 week) pos/wks

16 Jun 01		**HOME** *Religion RLG 0126955*	44	1

COASTERS
US, male vocal group (Singles: 32 weeks) pos/wks

27 Sep 57		**SEARCHIN'** *London HLE 8450*	30	1
15 Aug 58		**YAKETY YAK** *London HLE 8665*	12	8
27 Mar 59	●	**CHARLIE BROWN** *London HLE 8819*	6	12
30 Oct 59		**POISON IVY** *London HLE 8938*	15	7
9 Apr 94		**SORRY BUT I'M GONNA HAVE TO PASS** *Rhino A 4519CD*	41	4

Odia COATES – *See Paul ANKA*

Luis COBOS
Spain, male orchestra conductor (Singles: 2 weeks, Albums: 1 week) pos/wks

16 Jun 90		**NESSUN DORMA FROM 'TURANDOT'** *Epic 656005 7* [1]	59	2
21 Apr 90		**OPERA EXTRAVAGANZA** *Epic MOOD 12*	72	1

[1] Luis Cobos featuring Placido Domingo

Eddie COCHRAN
US, male vocalist / instrumentalist d. 17 Apr 1960 (Singles: 90 weeks, Albums: 47 weeks) pos/wks

7 Nov 58		**SUMMERTIME BLUES** *London HLU 8702*	18	6
13 Mar 59	●	**C'MON EVERYBODY** *London HLU 8792*	6	13
16 Oct 59		**SOMETHIN' ELSE** *London HLU 8944*	22	3
22 Jan 60		**HALLELUJAH, I LOVE HER SO (re)** *London HLW 9022*	22	4
12 May 60	★	**THREE STEPS TO HEAVEN** *London HLG 9115*	1	15
6 Oct 60		**SWEETIE PIE** *London HLG 9196*	38	3
3 Nov 60		**LONELY** *London HLG 9196*	41	1
15 Jun 61		**WEEKEND** *London HLG 9362*	15	16
30 Nov 61		**JEANNIE, JEANNIE, JEANNIE** *London HLG 9460*	31	4
25 Apr 63		**MY WAY** *Liberty LIB 10088*	23	10
24 Apr 68		**SUMMERTIME BLUES (re-issue)** *Liberty LBF 15071*	34	8
13 Feb 88		**C'MON EVERYBODY (re-issue)** *Liberty EDDIE 501*	14	7
30 Jul 60		**SINGING TO MY BABY** *London HAU 2093*	19	1
1 Oct 60	●	**EDDIE COCHRAN MEMORIAL ALBUM** *London HAG 2267*	9	12
12 Jan 63		**CHERISHED MEMORIES** *Liberty LBY 1109*	15	3
20 Apr 63		**EDDIE COCHRAN MEMORIAL ALBUM (re-issue)** *Liberty LBY 1127*	11	18
19 Oct 63		**SINGING TO MY BABY (re-issue)** *Liberty LBY 1158*	20	1
9 May 70		**VERY BEST OF EDDIE COCHRAN** *Liberty LBS 83337*	34	3
18 Aug 79		**THE EDDIE COCHRAN SINGLES ALBUM** *United Artists UAK 30244*	39	6
16 Apr 88		**C'MON EVERYBODY** *Liberty ECR 1*	53	3

Brenda COCHRANE
Ireland, female vocalist (Albums: 14 weeks) pos/wks

14 Apr 90		**THE VOICE** *Polydor 8431411*	14	11
6 Apr 91		**IN DREAMS** *Polydor 8490341*	55	3

Tom COCHRANE
Canada, male vocalist (Singles: 2 weeks) pos/wks

27 Jun 92		**LIFE IS A HIGHWAY** *Capitol CL 660*	62	2

COCK ROBIN
US, male / female vocal / instrumental group (Singles: 12 weeks) pos/wks

31 May 86		**THE PROMISE YOU MADE** *CBS A 6764*	28	12

Joe COCKER
430 Top 500

Throaty, emotive pop / rock singer b. 20 May 1944, Sheffield, UK, whose first single was released in 1964. Remembered for a memorable performance at Woodstock, Cocker is still scoring Top 20 albums across Europe in the 21st century (Singles: 89 weeks, Albums: 68 weeks) pos/wks

22 May 68		**MARJORINE** *Regal-Zonophone RZ 3006*	48	1
2 Oct 68	★	**WITH A LITTLE HELP FROM MY FRIENDS** *Regal-Zonophone RZ 3013*	1	13
27 Sep 69	●	**DELTA LADY** *Regal-Zonophone RZ 3024*	10	11
4 Jul 70		**THE LETTER** *Regal-Zonophone RZ 3027*	39	6
26 Sep 81		**I'M SO GLAD I'M STANDING HERE TODAY** *MCA 741* [1]	61	3
15 Jan 83	●	**UP WHERE WE BELONG** *Island WIP 6830* [2] ▲	7	13
14 Nov 87		**UNCHAIN MY HEART** *Capitol CL 465*	46	4
13 Jan 90		**WHEN THE NIGHT COMES** *Capitol CL 535*	65	2
7 Mar 92		**(ALL I KNOW) FEELS LIKE FOREVER** *Capitol CL 645*	25	5
9 May 92		**NOW THAT THE MAGIC HAS GONE** *Capitol CL 657*	28	6
4 Jul 92		**UNCHAIN MY HEART (re-issue)** *Capitol CL 664*	17	6
21 Nov 92		**WHEN THE NIGHT COMES (re-issue)** *Capitol CL 674*	61	3
13 Aug 94		**THE SIMPLE THINGS** *Capitol CDCLS 722*	17	5
22 Oct 94		**TAKE ME HOME** *Capitol CDCLS 729* [3]	41	3
17 Dec 94		**LET THE HEALING BEGIN** *Capitol CDCLS 727*	32	5
23 Sep 95		**HAVE A LITTLE FAITH** *Capitol CDCLS 744*	67	2
12 Oct 96		**DON'T LET ME BE MISUNDERSTOOD** *Parlophone CDCLS 779*	53	1
26 Sep 70		**MAD DOGS AND ENGLISHMEN** *A&M AMLS 6002*	16	8
6 May 72		**JOE COCKER / WITH A LITTLE HELP FROM MY FRIENDS** *Double Back TOOFA 1/2*	29	4
30 Jun 84		**A CIVILISED MAN** *Capitol EJ 240139 1*	100	1
11 Apr 92		**NIGHT CALLS** *Capitol CDESTU 2167*	25	14
27 Jun 92	●	**THE LEGEND – THE ESSENTIAL COLLECTION** *PolyGram TV 5154112*	4	20
17 Sep 94	●	**HAVE A LITTLE FAITH** *Capitol CDEST 2233*	9	15
26 Oct 96		**ORGANIC** *Parlophone CDESTD 6*	49	1
20 Feb 99		**GREATEST HITS** *EMI 4977192*	24	2
23 Oct 99		**NO ORDINARY WORLD** *Parlophone 5230912*	63	1
15 Jun 02		**RESPECT YOURSELF** *Parlophone 5396432*	51	2

[1] Crusaders, featured vocalist Joe Cocker [2] Joe Cocker and Jennifer Warnes
[3] Joe Cocker featuring Bekka Bramlett

COCKEREL CHORUS
UK, male Tottenham Hotspur Football Club supporters vocal group (Singles: 12 weeks) pos/wks

24 Feb 73		**NICE ONE CYRIL** *Youngblood YB 1017*	14	12

COCKNEY REBEL – *See Steve HARLEY and COCKNEY REBEL*

COCKNEY REJECTS *UK, male vocal / instrumental group (Singles: 22 weeks, Albums: 17 weeks)*

Date		Title	pos	wks
1 Dec 79		**I'M NOT A FOOL** *EMI 5008*	65	2
16 Feb 80		**BADMAN** *EMI 5035*	65	3
26 Apr 80		**THE GREATEST COCKNEY RIP-OFF** *Zonophone Z 2*	21	7
17 May 80		**I'M FOREVER BLOWING BUBBLES** *Zonophone Z 4*	35	5
12 Jul 80		**WE CAN DO ANYTHING** *Zonophone Z 6*	65	2
25 Oct 80		**WE ARE THE FIRM** *Zonophone Z 10*	54	3
15 Mar 80		**GREATEST HITS VOLUME 1** *Zonophone ZONO 101*	22	11
25 Oct 80		**GREATEST HITS VOLUME 2** *Zonophone ZONO 102*	23	3
18 Apr 81		**GREATEST HITS VOLUME 3 (LIVE AND LOUD)** *Zonophone ZEM 101*	27	3

COCO *UK, female vocalist (Singles: 2 weeks)*

Date		Title	pos	wks
8 Nov 97		**I NEED A MIRACLE** *Positiva CDTIV 81*	39	2

See also FRAGMA

COCONUTS *US, female vocal group (Singles: 61 weeks)*

Date		Title	pos	wks
13 Jun 81		**ME NO POP I** *Ze WIP 6711* [1]	32	7
15 May 82	●	**I'M A WONDERFUL THING, BABY** *Ze WIP 6756* [2]	4	11
24 Jul 82	●	**STOOL PIGEON** *Ze WIP 6793* [2]	7	9
9 Oct 82	●	**ANNIE I'M NOT YOUR DADDY** *Ze WIP 6801* [2]	2	8
11 Dec 82		**DEAR ADDY** *Ze WIP 6840* [2]	29	7
11 Jun 83		**DID YOU HAVE TO LOVE ME LIKE YOU DID** *EMI America EA 156*	60	3
10 Sep 83		**THERE'S SOMETHING WRONG IN PARADISE** *Island IS 130* [2]	35	5
19 Nov 83		**THE LIFEBOAT PARTY** *Island IS 142* [2]	49	4
14 Apr 90		**THE SEX OF IT** *CBS 655698 7* [2]	29	5
10 Apr 93		**I'M A WONDERFUL THING BABY** *Island CID 551* [2]	60	2

[1] Kid Creole and the Coconuts present Coati Mundi [2] Kid Creole and the Coconuts

See also Kid CREOLE and the COCONUTS

COCTEAU TWINS *UK, male / female vocal / instrumental group (Singles: 25 weeks, Albums: 46 weeks)*

Date		Title	pos	wks
28 Apr 84		**PEARLY-DEWDROPS' DROPS** *4AD 405*	29	5
30 Mar 85		**AIKEA-GUINEA** *4AD AD 501*	41	3
23 Nov 85		**TINY DYNAMINE (EP)** *4AD BAD 510*	52	2
7 Dec 85		**ECHOES IN A SHALLOW BAY (EP)** *4AD BAD 511*	65	1
25 Oct 86		**LOVE'S EASY TEARS** *4AD AD 610*	53	1
8 Sep 90		**ICEBLINK LUCK** *4AD AD 0011*	38	3
2 Oct 93		**EVANGELINE** *Fontana CTCD 1*	34	2
18 Dec 93		**WINTER WONDERLAND / FROSTY THE SNOWMAN** *Fontana COCCD 1*	58	1
26 Feb 94		**BLUEBEARD** *Fontana CTCD 2*	33	2
7 Oct 95		**TWINLIGHTS (EP)** *Fontana CTCD 3*	59	1
4 Nov 95		**OTHERNESS (EP)** *Fontana CTCD 4*	59	1
30 Mar 96		**TISHBITE** *Fontana CTCD 5*	34	2
20 Jul 96		**VIOLAINE** *Fontana CTCD 6*	56	1
29 Oct 83		**HEAD OVER HEELS** *4AD CAD 313*	51	15
24 Nov 84		**TREASURE** *4AD CAD 412*	29	8
26 Apr 86	●	**VICTORIALAND** *4AD CAD 602*	10	7
1 Oct 88		**BLUE BELL KNOLL** *4AD CAD 807*	15	4
22 Sep 90	●	**HEAVEN OR LAS VEGAS** *4AD CAD 0012*	7	5
30 Oct 93		**FOUR-CALENDAR CAFÉ** *Fontana 5182592*	13	3
27 Apr 96		**MILK & KISSES** *Fontana 5145012*	17	3
28 Oct 00		**STARS AND TOPSOIL – A COLLECTION (1982-1990)** *4AD CAD 2K019CD*	63	1

Tracks on Tiny Dynamine (EP): Pink Orange Red / Ribbed and Veined / Plain Tiger / Sultitan Itan. Tracks on Echoes in a Shallow Bay (EP): Great Spangled Fritillary / Melonella / Pale Clouded White / Eggs and Their Shells. Tracks on Twinlights (EP): Golden-Vein / Half-Gifts / Pink Orange Red / Rilkean Heart. Tracks on Otherness (EP): Cherry Coloured Funk / Feet Like Fins / Seekers Who Are Lovers / Violaine

See also Harold BUDD / Liz FRASER / Robin GUTHRIE / Simon RAYMONDE

CODE RED *UK, male vocal group (Singles: 7 weeks)*

Date		Title	pos	wks
6 Jul 96		**I GAVE YOU EVERYTHING** *Polydor 5763992*	50	1
16 Nov 96		**THIS IS OUR SONG** *Polydor 5756332*	59	1
14 Jun 97		**CAN WE TALK...** *Polydor 5710992*	29	2
9 Aug 97		**IS THERE SOMEONE OUT THERE?** *Polydor 5714652*	34	2
4 Jul 98		**WHAT WOULD YOU DO IF...?** *Polydor 569932*	55	1

COFFEE *US, female vocal group (Singles: 13 weeks)*

Date		Title	pos	wks
27 Sep 80		**CASANOVA** *De-Lite MER 38*	13	10
6 Dec 80		**SLIP AND DIP / I WANNA BE WITH YOU** *De-Lite DE 1*	57	3

Alma COGAN *UK, female vocalist (Singles: 110 weeks)*

Date		Title	pos	wks
19 Mar 54	●	**BELL BOTTOM BLUES** *HMV B 10653*	4	9
27 Aug 54		**LITTLE THINGS MEAN A LOT (2re)** *HMV B 10717*	11	5
3 Dec 54	●	**I CAN'T TELL A WALTZ FROM A TANGO** *HMV B 10786*	6	11
27 May 55	★	**DREAMBOAT** *HMV B 10872*	1	16
23 Sep 55		**THE BANJO'S BACK IN TOWN** *HMV B 10917 (A)*	17	1
14 Oct 55		**GO ON BY** *HMV B 10917 (B)*	16	4
16 Dec 55		**TWENTY TINY FINGERS** *HMV POP 129(A)*	17	1
23 Dec 55	●	**NEVER DO A TANGO WITH AN ESKIMO** *HMV POP 129(B)*	6	5
30 Mar 56		**WILLIE CAN** *HMV POP 187* [1]	13	8
13 Jul 56		**THE BIRDS AND THE BEES** *HMV POP 223*	25	4
10 Aug 56		**WHY DO FOOLS FALL IN LOVE** *HMV POP 223*	22	3
2 Nov 56		**IN THE MIDDLE OF THE HOUSE (re)** *HMV POP 261*	20	4
18 Jan 57		**YOU, ME AND US** *HMV POP 284*	18	6
29 Mar 57		**WHATEVER LOLA WANTS (LOLA GETS)** *HMV POP 317*	26	2
31 Jan 58		**THE STORY OF MY LIFE** *HMV POP 433*	25	2
14 Feb 58		**SUGARTIME (re)** *HMV POP 450*	16	11
23 Jan 59		**LAST NIGHT ON THE BACK PORCH** *HMV POP 573*	27	2
18 Dec 59		**WE GOT LOVE** *HMV POP 670*	26	4
12 May 60		**DREAM TALK** *HMV POP 728*	48	1
11 Aug 60		**TRAIN OF LOVE** *HMV POP 760*	27	5
20 Apr 61		**COWBOY JIMMY JOE** *Columbia DB 4607*	37	6

[1] Alma Cogan with Desmond Lane – penny whistle

Shaye COGAN *US, female vocalist (Singles: 1 week)*

Date		Title	pos	wks
24 Mar 60		**MEAN TO ME** *MGM 1063*	40	1

Izhar COHEN and the ALPHA-BETA *Israel, male / female vocal group (Singles: 7 weeks)*

Date		Title	pos	wks
13 May 78		**A-BA-NI-BI** *Polydor 2001 781*	20	7

Leonard COHEN (443 Top 500)

Singer-songwriter and poet with a reputation for dark humour, b. 21 Sep 1934, Montreal, Canada. Jennifer Warnes devoted her 1987 set 'Famous Blue Raincoat' entirely to his compositions, and he inspired the 1991 multi-artist tribute compilation 'I'm Your Fan' (Albums: 154 weeks)

Date		Title	pos	wks
31 Aug 68		**SONGS OF LEONARD COHEN** *CBS 63241*	13	71
3 May 69	●	**SONGS FROM A ROOM** *CBS 63587*	2	26
24 Apr 71	●	**SONGS OF LOVE AND HATE** *CBS 69004*	4	18
28 Sep 74		**NEW SKIN FOR THE OLD CEREMONY** *CBS 69087*	24	3
10 Dec 77		**DEATH OF A LADIES' MAN** *CBS 86042*	35	5
16 Feb 85		**VARIOUS POSITIONS** *CBS 26222*	52	6
27 Feb 88		**I'M YOUR MAN** *CBS 460642 1*	48	13
6 Aug 88		**GREATEST HITS** *CBS 32644*	99	1
5 Dec 92		**THE FUTURE** *Columbia 4724982*	36	3
6 Aug 94		**COHEN LIVE** *Columbia 4771712*	35	4
20 Oct 01		**TEN NEW SONGS** *Columbia 5012022*	26	3
1 Feb 03		**THE ESSENTIAL** *Columbia 4979952*	70	1

Marc COHN *US, male vocalist (Singles: 15 weeks, Albums: 23 weeks)*

Date		Title	pos	wks
25 May 91		**WALKING IN MEMPHIS** *Atlantic A 7747*	66	4
10 Aug 91		**SILVER THUNDERBIRD** *Atlantic A 7657*	54	3
12 Oct 91		**WALKING IN MEMPHIS (re-issue)** *Atlantic A 7585*	22	5
29 May 93		**WALK THROUGH THE WORLD** *Atlantic A 7340CD*	37	3
29 Jun 91		**MARC COHN** *Atlantic 7567821781*	27	20
12 Jun 93		**THE RAINY SEASON** *Atlantic 7567824912*	24	3

COLA BOY *UK, male / female vocal / instrumental duo – Andrew Midgely and Janey Lee Grace (Singles: 7 weeks)*

Date		Title	pos	wks
6 Jul 91	●	**7 WAYS TO LOVE** *Arista 114526*	8	7

The 706 No.1 Albums

NO.1 ALBUMS OF THE 60S

Here is the complete chronological list of every UK chart-topping album from the 60s. All dates given are for an album's first week at No.1, not its first entry into the chart. The run at the top of the chart in weeks follows in brackets, followed by the US peak position of the album.

1960

12 Mar THE EXPLOSIVE FREDDY CANNON **Freddy Cannon** (1 week)
19 Mar SOUTH PACIFIC **Soundtrack** (19 weeks) US 1
30 Jul ELVIS IS BACK **Elvis Presley** (1 week) US 2
6 Aug SOUTH PACIFIC **Soundtrack** (5 weeks) US 1
10 Sep DOWN DRURY LANE TO MEMORY LANE **101 Strings** (5 weeks)
15 Oct SOUTH PACIFIC **Soundtrack** (13 weeks) US 1

1961

14 Jan G.I. BLUES **Elvis Presley** (7 weeks) US 1
4 Mar SOUTH PACIFIC **Soundtrack** (1 week) US 1
11 Mar G.I. BLUES **Elvis Presley** (3 weeks) US 1
1 Apr SOUTH PACIFIC **Soundtrack** (1 week) US 1
8 Apr G.I. BLUES **Elvis Presley** (12 weeks) US 1
1 Jul SOUTH PACIFIC **Soundtrack** (4 weeks) US 1
29Jul THE BLACK AND WHITE MINSTREL SHOW **George Mitchell Minstrels** (4 weeks)
26 Aug SOUTH PACIFIC **Soundtrack** (1 week) US 1
2 Sep THE BLACK AND WHITE MINSTREL SHOW **George Mitchell Minstrels** (1 week)
9 Sep SOUTH PACIFIC **Soundtrack** (1 week) US 1
16 Sep THE BLACK AND WHITE MINSTREL SHOW **George Mitchell Minstrels** (1 week)
23 Sep THE SHADOWS **Shadows** (4 weeks)
21 Oct THE BLACK AND WHITE MINSTREL SHOW **George Mitchell Minstrels** (1 week)
28 Oct THE SHADOWS **Shadows** (1 week)
4 Nov 21 TODAY **Cliff Richard** (1 week)
11 Nov ANOTHER BLACK AND WHITE MINSTREL SHOW **George Mitchell Minstrels** (8 weeks)

1962

6 Jan BLUE HAWAII **Elvis Presley** (1 week) US 1
13 Jan THE YOUNG ONES **Soundtrack Cliff Richard and the Shadows** (6 weeks)
24 Feb BLUE HAWAII **Elvis Presley** (17 weeks) US 1
23 Jun WEST SIDE STORY **Soundtrack** (5 weeks) US 1
28 Jul POT LUCK **Elvis Presley** (1 week) US 4
1 Sep WEST SIDE STORY **Soundtrack** (1 week) US 1
8 Sep POT LUCK **Elvis Presley** (1 week) US 4
15 Sep WEST SIDE STORY **Soundtrack** (1 week) US 1
22 Sep THE BEST OF BALL, BARBER AND BILK **Kenny Ball, Chris Barber and Acker Bilk** (1 week)
29 Sep WEST SIDE STORY **Soundtrack** (3 weeks) US 1
20 Oct THE BEST OF BALL, BARBER AND BILK **Kenny Ball, Chris Barber and Acker Bilk** (1 week)
27 Oct OUT OF THE SHADOWS **Shadows** (3 weeks)
17 Nov WEST SIDE STORY **Soundtrack** (1 week) US 1
24 Nov OUT OF THE SHADOWS **Shadows** (1 week)
1 Dec ON STAGE WITH GEORGE MITCHELL'S BLACK AND WHITE MINSTRELS **George Mitchell Minstrels** (2 weeks)
15 Dec WEST SIDE STORY **Soundtrack** (1 week) US 1
22 Dec OUT OF THE SHADOWS **Shadows** (1 week)
29 Dec THE BLACK AND WHITE MINSTREL SHOW **George Mitchell Minstrels** (2 weeks)

1963

12 Jan WEST SIDE STORY **Soundtrack** (1 week) US 1
19 Jan OUT OF THE SHADOWS **Shadows** (2 weeks)
2 Feb SUMMER HOLIDAY **Soundtrack Cliff Richard and the Shadows** (14 weeks)
11 May PLEASE PLEASE ME **Beatles** (30 weeks)
7 Dec WITH THE BEATLES **Beatles** (21 weeks)

1964

2 May ROLLING STONES **Rolling Stones** (12 weeks) US 11
25 Jul A HARD DAY'S NIGHT **Beatles** (21 weeks) US 1
19 Dec BEATLES FOR SALE **Beatles** (7 weeks)

1965

6 Feb ROLLING STONES NO.2 **Rolling Stones** (3 weeks) US 5
27 Feb BEATLES FOR SALE **Beatles** (1 week)
6 Mar ROLLING STONES NO.2 **Rolling Stones** (6 weeks) US 5
17 Apr THE FREEWHEELIN' BOB DYLAN **Bob Dylan** (1 week) US 22
24 Apr ROLLING STONES NO.2 **Rolling Stones** (1 week) US 5
1 May BEATLES FOR SALE **Beatles** (3 weeks)
22 May THE FREEWHEELIN' BOB DYLAN **Bob Dylan** (1 week) US 22
29 May BRINGING IT ALL BACK HOME **Bob Dylan** (1 week) US 6
5 Jun THE SOUND OF MUSIC **Soundtrack** (10 weeks) US 1
14 Aug HELP! **Beatles** (9 weeks) US 1
16 Oct THE SOUND OF MUSIC **Soundtrack** (10 weeks) US 1
25 Dec RUBBER SOUL **Beatles** (8 weeks) US 1

1966

19 Feb THE SOUND OF MUSIC **Soundtrack** (10 weeks) US 1
30 Apr AFTERMATH **Rolling Stones** (8 weeks) US 2
25 Jun THE SOUND OF MUSIC **Soundtrack** (7 weeks) US 1
13 Aug REVOLVER **Beatles** (7 weeks) US 1
1 Oct THE SOUND OF MUSIC **Soundtrack** (18 weeks) US 1

1967

4 Feb THE MONKEES **Monkees** (7 weeks) US 1
25 Mar THE SOUND OF MUSIC **Soundtrack** (7 weeks) US 1
13 May MORE OF THE MONKEES **Monkees** (1 week) US 1
20 May THE SOUND OF MUSIC **Soundtrack** (1 week) US 1
27 May MORE OF THE MONKEES **Monkees** (1 week) US 1
3 Jun THE SOUND OF MUSIC **Soundtrack** (1 week) US 1
10 Jun SGT. PEPPER'S LONELY HEARTS CLUB BAND **Beatles** (23 weeks) US 1
18 Nov THE SOUND OF MUSIC **Soundtrack** (1 week) US 1
25 Nov SGT. PEPPER'S LONELY HEARTS CLUB BAND **Beatles** (1 week) US 1
2 Dec THE SOUND OF MUSIC **Soundtrack** (3 weeks) US 1
23 Dec SGT. PEPPER'S LONELY HEARTS CLUB BAND **Beatles** (2 weeks) US 1

1967: MORE OF THE MONKEES Five weeks after the Monkees TV show premiered on BBC, Britain went Monkee crazy as the group made its UK album chart debut with chart-topper The Monkees, followed swiftly by a second No.1 three months later

1968

5 Jan VAL DOONICAN ROCKS BUT GENTLY Val Doonican (3 weeks)
27 Jan THE SOUND OF MUSIC Soundtrack (1 week) US 1
3 Feb SGT. PEPPER'S LONELY HEARTS CLUB BAND Beatles (1 week) US 1
0 Feb GREATEST HITS Four Tops (1 week) US 4
7 Feb GREATEST HITS Diana Ross and The Supremes (3 weeks) US 1
Mar JOHN WESLEY HARDING Bob Dylan (10 weeks) US 2
8 May SCOTT 2 Scott Walker (1 week)
25 May JOHN WESLEY HARDING Bob Dylan (3 weeks) US 2
5 Jun LOVE ANDY Andy Williams (1 week) US 8
22 Jun DOCK OF THE BAY Otis Redding (1 week) US 4
29 Jun OGDEN'S NUT GONE FLAKE Small Faces (6 weeks) US 159
0 Aug DELILAH Tom Jones (1 week)
7 Aug BOOKENDS Simon and Garfunkel (5 weeks) US 1
21 Sep DELILAH Tom Jones (1 week)
28 Sep BOOKENDS Simon and Garfunkel (2 weeks) US 1
2 Oct GREATEST HITS Hollies (6 week) US 11
23 Nov SOUND OF MUSIC Soundtrack (1 week) US 1
30 Nov GREATEST HITS Hollies (1 week) US 11
Dec THE BEATLES (WHITE ALBUM) Beatles (7 weeks) US 1

1969

25 Jan THE BEST OF THE SEEKERS Seekers (1 week)
Feb THE BEATLES (WHITE ALBUM) Beatles (1 week) US 1
Feb THE BEST OF THE SEEKERS Seekers (1 week)
5 Feb DIANA ROSS & THE SUPREMES JOIN THE TEMPTATIONS Diana Ross / Supremes / Temptations (4 weeks) US 2
5 Mar GOODBYE Cream (2 weeks) US 2
29 Mar THE BEST OF THE SEEKERS Seekers (2 weeks)
2 Apr GOODBYE Cream (1 week) US 2
9 Apr THE BEST OF THE SEEKERS Seekers (1 week)
26 Apr GOODBYE Cream (1 week) US 2
May THE BEST OF THE SEEKERS Seekers (1 week)
0 May ON THE THRESHOLD OF A DREAM Moody Blues (2 weeks) US 20
24 May NASHVILLE SKYLINE Bob Dylan (4 weeks) US 3
21 Jun HIS ORCHESTRA, HIS CHORUS, HIS SINGERS, HIS SOUND Ray Conniff (3 weeks)
2 Jul ACCORDING TO MY HEART Jim Reeves (4 weeks)
Aug STAND UP Jethro Tull (3 weeks) US 20
30 Aug FROM ELVIS IN MEMPHIS Elvis Presley (1 week) US 13
Sep STAND UP Jethro Tull (2 weeks) US 20
20 Sep BLIND FAITH Blind Faith (2 weeks) US 1
Oct ABBEY ROAD Beatles (11 weeks) US 1
20 Dec LET IT BLEED Rolling Stones (1 week) US 3
27 Dec ABBEY ROAD Beatles (6 weeks) US 1

COLD JAM featuring GRACE

US, male / female vocal / instrumental group (Singles: 2 weeks) pos/wks

28 Jul 90 **LAST NIGHT A DJ SAVED MY LIFE** *Big Wave BWR 39* 64 2

COLDCUT *UK, male production duo – Matt Black and Jonathan Moore (Singles: 39 weeks, Albums: 5 weeks)* pos/wks

20 Feb 88 ● **DOCTORIN' THE HOUSE** *Ahead of Our Time CCUT 27* [1] 6 9
10 Sep 88 **STOP THIS CRAZY THING** *Ahead of Our Time CCUT 4* [2] 21 7
25 Mar 89 **PEOPLE HOLD ON** *Ahead of Our Time CCUT 5* [3] 11 9
3 Jun 89 **MY TELEPHONE** *Ahead of Our Time CCUT 6* 52 2
16 Dec 89 **COLDCUT'S CHRISTMAS BREAK** *Ahead of Our Time CCUT 7* ..67 3
26 May 90 **FIND A WAY** *Ahead of Our Time CCUT 8* [4] 52 2
4 Sep 93 **DREAMER** *Arista 74321156642* 54 2
22 Jan 94 **AUTUMN LEAVES** *Arista 74321171052* 50 2
16 Aug 97 **MORE BEATS & PIECES** *Ninja Tune ZENCDS 58* 37 2
16 Jun 01 **REVOLUTION** *Ninja Tune ZENCDS 88* 67 1
29 Apr 89 **WHAT'S THAT NOISE** *Ahead of Our Time CCUTLP 1*.................20 4
20 Sep 97 **LET US PLAY!** *Ninja Tune ZENCD 30*...33 1

[1] Coldcut featuring Yazz and the Plastic Population [2] Coldcut featuring Junior Reid and the Ahead of Our Time Orchestra [3] Coldcut featuring Lisa Stansfield [4] Coldcut featuring Queen Latifah

COLDPLAY (280 Top 500) *Anthemic rock group with a social conscience. Chris Martin (v,k), Jonny Buckland (g), Guy Berryman (b) and Will Champion (d) formed while attending University College, London. The only act to have won both a Brit and a Grammy for each of their first two albums (Singles: 50 weeks, Albums: 177 weeks)* pos/wks

18 Mar 00 **SHIVER** *Parlophone CDR 6536* 35 3
8 Jul 00 ● **YELLOW** *Parlophone CDR 6538* 4 11
4 Nov 00 ● **TROUBLE** *Parlophone CDR 6549* 10 9
17 Aug 02 ● **IN MY PLACE** *Parlophone CDRS 6579* 2 10
23 Nov 02 ● **THE SCIENTIST** *Parlophone CDR 6588* 10 9
5 Apr 03 ● **CLOCKS** *Parlophone CDR 6594* 9 8
22 Jul 00 ★ **PARACHUTES** *Parlophone 5277832* ■ 1 111
7 Sep 02 ★ **A RUSH OF BLOOD TO THE HEAD** *Parlophone 5405042* ■ ......1 66+

Andy COLE *UK, male footballer / vocalist (Singles: 1 week)* pos/wks

18 Sep 99 **OUTSTANDING** *WEA WEA 224CD* 68 1

Cozy COLE

US, male instrumentalist – drums, d. 9 Jan 1981 (Singles: 1 week) pos/wks

5 Dec 58 **TOPSY (PARTS 1 AND 2)** *London HL 8750* 29 1

George COLE – *See Dennis WATERMAN*

Lloyd COLE (447 Top 500)

Introspective and inventive indie singer / songwriter / guitarist, b. 31 Jan 1961, Derbyshire, UK. Had most success with Glasgow-based band The Commotions before he relocated to the US in 1990. (Singles: 62 weeks, Albums: 92 weeks) pos/wks

26 May 84 **PERFECT SKIN (re)** *Polydor COLE 1* [1] 26 9
25 Aug 84 **FOREST FIRE** *Polydor COLE 2* [1] 41 6
17 Nov 84 **RATTLESNAKES** *Poldor COLE 3* [1] 65 2
14 Sep 85 **BRAND NEW FRIEND** *Polydor COLE 4* [1] 19 8
9 Nov 85 **LOST WEEKEND** *Polydor COLE 5* [1] 17 7
18 Jan 86 **CUT ME DOWN** *Polydor COLE 6* [1] 38 4
3 Oct 87 **MY BAG** *Polydor COLE 7* [1] 46 4
9 Jan 88 **JENNIFER SHE SAID** *Polydor COLE 8* [1] 31 5
23 Apr 88 **FROM THE HIP (EP)** *Polydor COLE 9* [1] 59 2
3 Feb 90 **NO BLUE SKIES** *Polydor COLE 11* 42 4
7 Apr 90 **DON'T LOOK BACK** *Polydor COLE 12* 59 3
31 Aug 91 **SHE'S A GIRL AND I'M A MAN** *Polydor COLE 14* 55 2
25 Sep 93 **SO YOU'D LIKE TO SAVE THE WORLD** *Fontana VIBE D1* 72 2
16 Sep 95 **LIKE LOVERS DO** *Fontana LCDD 1* 24 3
2 Dec 95 **SENTIMENTAL FOOL** *Fontana LCDD 2* 73 1
20 Oct 84 **RATTLESNAKES** *Polydor LCLP 1* [1] 13 30
30 Nov 85 ● **EASY PIECES** *Polydor LCLP 2* [1] 5 18
7 Nov 87 ● **MAINSTREAM** *Polydor LCLP 3* [1] 9 20
8 Apr 89 **19841989** *Polydor 837736 1* [1] 14 7
3 Mar 90 **LLOYD COLE** *Polydor 8419071* 11 6

28 Sep 91	DON'T GET WEIRD ON ME BABE *Polydor 5110931*	21	3
23 Oct 93	BAD VIBES *Fontana 5183182*	38	2
7 Oct 95	LOVE STORY *Fontana 5285292*	27	2
23 Jan 99	THE COLLECTION *Mercury 5381042*	24	4

[1] Lloyd Cole and the Commotions [1] Lloyd Cole and the Commotions

Tracks on From the Hip (EP): From the Hip / Please / Lonely Mile / Love Your Wife

MJ COLE *UK, male producer – Matt Coleman (Singles: 19 weeks, Albums: 4 weeks)*

		pos	wks
23 May 98	SINCERE *AM:PM 5826912*	38	2
6 May 00 ●	CRAZY LOVE *Talkin Loud TLCD 59*	10	7
12 Aug 00	SINCERE (re-mix) *Talkin Loud TLCD 60*	13	5
2 Dec 00	HOLD ON TO ME *Talkin Loud TLCD 62* [1]	35	2
29 Mar 03	WONDERING WHY *Talkin' Loud 0779522*	30	3
19 Aug 00	SINCERE *Talkin Loud 5425792*	14	4

[1] MJ Cole featuring Elizabeth Troy

Nat 'King' COLE (113 Top 500)

One of the 20th century's most distinctive song stylists, Nathaniel Adams Coles, b. 17 Mar 1917, Montgomery, Alabama, d. 15 Feb 1965. His 41-year chart span is proof that the highly regarded vocalist's recordings are timeless (Singles: 249 weeks, Albums: 150 weeks)

		pos	wks
14 Nov 52 ●	SOMEWHERE ALONG THE WAY *Capitol CL 13774*	3	7
19 Dec 52 ●	BECAUSE YOU'RE MINE (2re) *Capitol CL 13811*	6	4
2 Jan 53 ●	FAITH CAN MOVE MOUNTAINS (2re) *Capitol CL 13811*	10	4
24 Apr 53 ●	PRETEND *Capitol CL 13878*	2	18
14 Aug 53 ●	CAN'T I (2re) *Capitol CL 13937*	6	8
18 Sep 53 ●	MOTHER NATURE AND FATHER TIME *Capitol CL 13912*	7	7
16 Apr 54 ●	TENDERLY *Capitol CL 14061*	10	1
10 Sep 54 ●	SMILE *Capitol CL 14149*	2	14
8 Oct 54	MAKE HER MINE *Capitol CL 14149*	11	2
25 Feb 55 ●	A BLOSSOM FELL *Capitol CL 14235*	3	10
26 Aug 55	MY ONE SIN (re) *Capitol CL 14327*	17	2
27 Jan 56 ●	DREAMS CAN TELL A LIE *Capitol CL 14513*	10	9
11 May 56 ●	TOO YOUNG TO GO STEADY *Capitol CL 14573*	8	14
14 Sep 56	LOVE ME AS THOUGH THERE WERE NO TOMORROW (re) *Capitol CL 14621*	11	15
19 Apr 57 ●	WHEN I FALL IN LOVE *Capitol CL 14709*	2	20
5 Jul 57	WHEN ROCK AND ROLL CAME TO TRINIDAD *Capitol CL 14733*	28	1
18 Oct 57	MY PERSONAL POSSESSION *Capitol CL 14765* [1]	21	2
25 Oct 57	STARDUST *Capitol CL 14787*	24	2
29 May 59	YOU MADE ME LOVE YOU *Capitol CL 15017*	22	3
4 Sep 59	MIDNIGHT FLYER (re) *Capitol CL 15056*	23	4
12 Feb 60	TIME AND THE RIVER (2re) *Capitol CL 15111*	23	5
26 May 60 ●	THAT'S YOU *Capitol CL 15129*	10	8
10 Nov 60	JUST AS MUCH AS EVER *Capitol CL 15163*	18	10
2 Feb 61	THE WORLD IN MY ARMS *Capitol CL 15178*	36	10
16 Nov 61	LET TRUE LOVE BEGIN *Capitol CL 15224*	29	10
22 Mar 62	BRAZILIAN LOVE SONG (ANDORHINA PRETA) *Capitol CL 15241*	34	4
31 May 62	THE RIGHT THING TO SAY *Capitol CL 15250*	42	4
19 Jul 62	LET THERE BE LOVE *Capitol CL 15257* [2]	11	14
27 Sep 62 ●	RAMBLIN' ROSE *Capitol CL 15270*	5	14
20 Dec 62	DEAR LONELY HEARTS *Capitol CL 15280*	37	3
12 Dec 87 ●	WHEN I FALL IN LOVE (re-issue) *Capitol CL 15975*	4	7
22 Jun 91	UNFORGETTABLE *Elektra EKR 128* [3]	19	8
14 Dec 91	THE CHRISTMAS SONG *Capitol CL 641*	69	2
19 Mar 94	LET'S FACE THE MUSIC AND DANCE *EMI CDEM 312*	30	3
18 May 57 ★	LOVE IS THE THING *Capitol LCT 6129* ▲	1	14
19 Aug 61	STRING ALONG WITH NAT 'KING' COLE *Encore ENC 102*	12	9
20 Oct 62 ●	NAT 'KING' COLE SINGS AND THE GEORGE SHEARING QUINTET PLAYS *Capitol W 1675* [1]	8	7
27 Mar 65	UNFORGETTABLE NAT 'KING' COLE *Capitol W 20664*	11	8
7 Dec 68 ●	THE BEST OF NAT 'KING' COLE *Capitol ST 21139*	5	18
5 Dec 70	THE BEST OF NAT 'KING' COLE VOLUME 2 *Capitol ST 21687*	39	2
27 Nov 71	WHITE CHRISTMAS *MFP 5224* [2]	45	1
8 Apr 78 ★	20 GOLDEN GREATS *Capitol EMTV 9*	1	37
20 Nov 82 ●	GREATEST LOVE SONGS *Capitol EMTV 35*	7	26
26 Nov 88	CHRISTMAS WITH NAT 'KING' COLE *Stylus SMR 868*	25	9
23 Nov 91	UNFORGETTABLE NAT 'KING' COLE *EMI EMTV 61*	23	9
20 Nov 99	THE ULTIMATE COLLECTION *EMI 4995752*	26	7
15 Feb 03	LOVE SONGS *Capitol 05815132*	20	3

[1] Nat 'King' Cole and the Four Knights [2] Nat 'King' Cole with George Shearing [3] Natalie Cole and Nat 'King' Cole [1] Nat 'King' Cole and the George Shearing Quintet [2] Nat 'King' Cole and Dean Martin

The two 'Unforgettable Nat 'King' Cole' albums are different

Natalie COLE (451 Top 500)

Daughter of legendary Nat 'King' Cole who has a 20-year Grammy-winning span of her own, b. 6 Feb 1950, Los Angeles, US. 'Unforgettable' in 1991 was an electronically recorded duet with her late father. Nat and Natalie are the only dad and daughter who both have No.1 US albums (Singles: 87 weeks, Albums: 66 weeks)

		pos	wks
11 Oct 75	THIS WILL BE *Capitol CL 15834*	32	5
8 Aug 87	JUMP START *Manhattan MT 22*	44	8
26 Mar 88 ●	PINK CADILLAC *Manhattan MT 35*	5	12
25 Jun 88	EVERLASTING *Manhattan MT 46*	28	6
20 Aug 88	JUMP START (re-issue) *Manhattan MT 50*	36	5
26 Nov 88	I LIVE FOR YOUR LOVE *Manhattan MT 57*	23	14
15 Apr 89 ●	MISS YOU LIKE CRAZY *EMI-USA MT 63*	2	15
22 Jul 89	REST OF THE NIGHT *EMI-USA MT 69*	56	2
16 Dec 89	STARTING OVER AGAIN *EMI-USA MT 77*	56	4
21 Apr 90	WILD WOMEN DO *EMI-USA MT 81*	16	7
22 Jun 91	UNFORGETTABLE *Elektra EKR 128* [1]	19	8
16 May 92	THE VERY THOUGHT OF YOU *Elektra EKR 147*	71	1
17 Sep 83 ●	UNFORGETTABLE: A MUSICAL TRIBUTE TO NAT 'KING' COLE *CBS 10042* [1] ▲	5	16
7 May 88	EVERLASTING *Manhattan MTL 1012*	62	4
20 May 89 ●	GOOD TO BE BACK *EMI-USA MTL 1042*	10	12
27 Jul 91	UNFORGETTABLE – WITH LOVE *Elektra EKT 91*	11	29
26 Jun 93	TAKE A LOOK *Elektra 7559614962*	16	4
30 Nov 02	ASK A WOMAN WHO KNOWS *Verve 0654702*	63	1

[1] Natalie Cole and Nat 'King' Cole [1] Johnny Mathis and Natalie Cole

Paula COLE

US, female vocalist (Singles: 9 weeks, Albums: 1 week)

		pos	wks
28 Jun 97	WHERE HAVE ALL THE COWBOYS GONE? *Warner Bros. W 0406CD*	15	8
1 Aug 98	I DON'T WANT TO WAIT *Warner Bros. W 0422CD*	43	1
26 Jul 97	THIS FIRE *Warner Bros. 9362464242*	60	1

Naimee COLEMAN – *See AURORA*

COLETTE – *See SISTER BLISS*

John Ford COLEY – *See ENGLAND DAN and John Ford COLEY*

COLLAGE *US / Canada / Philippines, male vocal / instrumental group (Singles: 5 weeks)*

		pos	wks
21 Sep 85	ROMEO WHERE'S JULIET? *MCA MCA 1006*	46	5

COLLAPSED LUNG

UK, male vocal / instrumental group (Singles: 8 weeks)

		pos	wks
22 Jun 96	LONDON TONIGHT / EAT MY GOAL *Deceptive BLUFF 029CD*	31	3
30 May 98	EAT MY GOAL (re-issue) *Deceptive BLUFF 060CD*	18	5

Dave and Ansil COLLINS *Jamaica, male vocal / instrumental duo – Dave Barker and Ansil Collins (Singles: 27 weeks, Albums: 2 weeks)*

		pos	wks
27 Mar 71 ★	DOUBLE BARREL *Technique TE 901*	1	15
26 Jun 71 ●	MONKEY SPANNER *Technique TE 914* [1]	7	12
7 Aug 71	DOUBLE BARREL *Trojan TBL 162*	41	2

[1] Dave and Ansel Collins

Edwyn COLLINS *UK, male vocalist / instrumentalist (Singles: 25 weeks, Albums: 9 weeks)*

		pos	wks
11 Aug 84	PALE BLUE EYES *Swamplands SWP 1* [1]	72	2
12 Nov 94	EXPRESSLY (EP) *Setanta ZOP 001CD1*	42	3
17 Jun 95 ●	A GIRL LIKE YOU (re-issue) *Setanta ZOP 003CD*	4	14

2 Mar 96 **KEEP ON BURNING** *Setanta ZOP 004CD1* 45 2
2 Aug 97 **THE MAGIC PIPER (OF LOVE)** *Setanta SETCDA 041* 32 3
18 Oct 97 **ADIDAS WORLD** *Setanta SETCDB 045* 71 1
22 Jul 95 ● **GORGEOUS GEORGE** *Setanta AHOAON 058* 8 8
13 Sep 97 **I'M NOT FOLLOWING YOU** *Setanta SETCD 039* 55 1

1 Paul Quinn & Edwyn Collins

The only track on all formats of Expressly (EP) was 'A Girl Like You'

See also ORANGE JUICE

Felicia COLLINS – *See LUKK featuring Felicia COLLINS*

Jeff COLLINS *UK, male vocalist (Singles: 8 weeks)* pos/wks

18 Nov 72 **ONLY YOU** *Polydor 2058 287* 40 8

Joan COLLINS – *See Anthony NEWLEY Peter SELLERS Joan COLLINS*

Judy COLLINS

US, female vocalist (Singles: 86 weeks, Albums: 23 weeks) pos/wks

17 Jan 70 **BOTH SIDES NOW** *Elektra EKSN 45043* 14 11
5 Dec 70 ● **AMAZING GRACE (6re)** *Elektra 2101 020* 5 67
17 May 75 ● **SEND IN THE CLOWNS** *Elektra K 12177* 6 8
27 Feb 71 **WHALES AND NIGHTINGALES** *Elektra EKS 75010* 16 7
31 May 75 ● **JUDITH** *Elektra K 52019* 7 12
14 Dec 85 **AMAZING GRACE** *Telstar STAR 2265* 34 4

'Amazing Grace' re-entered in Jul, Sep, Nov, Dec 1971 and Apr, Sep, Dec 1972

Michelle COLLINS *UK, female actor / vocalist (Singles: 3 weeks)* pos/wks

27 Feb 99 **SUNBURN** *BBC Music WMSS 60082* 28 3

Phil COLLINS (19 Top 500)

Continually popular singer / songwriter / drummer / actor, b. 31 Jan, 1951, Chiswick, London. While at stage school he played the Artful Dodger in the West End production of 'Oliver!' and was an extra in the Beatles film 'A Hard Day's Night'. He first recorded with art rock band Flaming Youth before joining Genesis in 1970 (taking over lead vocals when Peter Gabriel left in 1975). He first recorded solo in 1981 and until 1996 combined a successful solo career with fronting the hit group. He was one of the world's top artists in the 1980s and 1990s, during which time he collected numerous singing and songwriting awards, had transatlantic album chart-toppers 'No Jacket Required' and '...But Seriously' (which sold in excess of 13 million globally) and scored seven US No.1 singles. Known for his charitable work, he was the only act to appear on stage in both London and Philadelphia in Live Aid, and played and sang on the Band Aid single. The multi-talented artist became a household name selling 80 million copies of his first six albums by the time he left stadium-fillers Genesis in 1996. Only members of The Beatles have appeared on more UK No.1 albums than this Songwriters' Hall of Fame member, who won an Oscar in 2000 for his music in Disney's 'Tarzan'. He is one of few British acts still selling well Stateside in the 21st century (Singles: 235 weeks, Albums: 803 weeks) pos/wks

17 Jan 81 ● **IN THE AIR TONIGHT** *Virgin VS102* 2 10
7 Mar 81 **I MISSED AGAIN** *Virgin VS 402* 14 8
30 May 81 **IF LEAVING ME IS EASY** *Virgin VS 423* 17 8
23 Oct 82 **THRU' THESE WALLS** *Virgin VS 524* 56 2
4 Dec 82 ★ **YOU CAN'T HURRY LOVE** *Virgin VS 531* 1 16
19 Mar 83 **DON'T LET HIM STEAL YOUR HEART AWAY** *Virgin VS 572* 45 5
7 Apr 84 ● **AGAINST ALL ODDS (TAKE A LOOK AT ME NOW)** *Virgin VS 674* ▲ 2 14
26 Jan 85 **SUSSUDIO** *Virgin VS 736* ▲ 12 9
9 Mar 85 ★ **EASY LOVER** *CBS A 4915* 1 ....1 12
13 Apr 85 ● **ONE MORE NIGHT** *Virgin VS 755* ▲ 4 9
27 Jul 85 **TAKE ME HOME** *Virgin VS 777* 19 9
23 Nov 85 ● **SEPARATE LIVES** *Virgin VS 818* 2 ▲ 4 13
18 Jun 88 ● **IN THE AIR TONIGHT (re-mix)** *Virgin VS 102* 4 9
3 Sep 88 ★ **A GROOVY KIND OF LOVE** *Virgin VS 1117* ▲ 1 13
26 Nov 88 ● **TWO HEARTS** *Virgin VS 1141* ▲ 6 11
4 Nov 89 ● **ANOTHER DAY IN PARADISE** *Virgin VS 1234* ▲ 2 11
27 Jan 90 ● **I WISH IT WOULD RAIN DOWN** *Virgin VS 1240* 7 9
28 Apr 90 **SOMETHING HAPPENED ON THE WAY TO HEAVEN** *Virgin VS 1251* 15 7
28 Jul 90 **THAT'S JUST THE WAY IT IS** *Virgin VS 1277* 26 5
6 Oct 90 **HANG IN LONG ENOUGH** *Virgin VS 1300* 34 3
8 Dec 90 **DO YOU REMEMBER (LIVE)** *Virgin VS 1305* 57 5
15 May 93 **HERO** *Atlantic A 7360* 3 ....56 3
30 Oct 93 ● **BOTH SIDES OF THE STORY (re)** *Virgin VSCDT 1500* 7 6
15 Jan 94 **EVERYDAY** *Virgin VSCDT 1505* 15 5
7 May 94 **WE WAIT AND WE WONDER** *Virgin VSCDT 1510* 45 2
5 Oct 96 ● **DANCE INTO THE LIGHT** *Face Value EW 066CD* 9 6
14 Dec 96 **IT'S IN YOUR EYES** *Face Value EW 076CD1* 30 4
12 Jul 97 **WEAR MY HAT** *Face Value EW 113CD* 43 2
7 Nov 98 **TRUE COLORS** *Virgin VSCDT 1715* 26 4
6 Nov 99 **YOU'LL BE IN MY HEART** *Edel / Walt Disney 0100735 DNY* 17 6
22 Sep 01 **IN THE AIR TONITE** *WEA WEA 331CD* 4 ....26 2
16 Nov 02 **CAN'T STOP LOVING YOU** *Face Value EW 254CD* 28 2
24 May 03 **HOME** *Epic 6738302* 5 ....19 4
29 Nov 03 **LOOK THROUGH MY EYES** *Walt Disney DISNEY 001* 61 1
21 Feb 81 ★ **FACE VALUE** *Virgin V 2185* ■ 1 274
13 Nov 82 ● **HELLO I MUST BE GOING** *Virgin V 2252* 2 163
2 Mar 85 ★ **NO JACKET REQUIRED** *Virgin V 2345* ■ ▲ 1 176
2 Dec 89 ★ **... BUT SERIOUSLY** *Virgin V 2620* ■ ▲ 1 72
17 Nov 90 ● **SERIOUS HITS ... LIVE!** *Virgin PCLP 1* 2 50
20 Nov 93 ★ **BOTH SIDES** *Virgin CDV 2800* ■ 1 21
2 Nov 96 ● **DANCE INTO THE LIGHT** *Face Value 630160002* 4 13
17 Oct 98 ★ **... HITS** *Virgin CDV 2870* ■ 1 27
23 Nov 02 **TESTIFY** *Face Value / East West 5046614842* 15 7

1 Philip Bailey (duet with Phil Collins) 2 Phil Collins and Marilyn Martin 3 David Crosby featuring Phil Collins 4 Lil' Kim featuring Phil Collins 5 Bone Thugs-N-Harmony featuring Phil Collins

See also GENESIS

Rodger COLLINS *US, male vocalist (Singles: 6 weeks)* pos/wks

3 Apr 76 **YOU SEXY SUGAR PLUM (BUT I LIKE IT)** *Fantasy FTC 132* 22 6

Willie COLLINS

US, male vocalist (Singles: 4 weeks, Albums: 1 week) pos/wks

28 Jun 86 **WHERE YOU GONNA BE TONIGHT?** *Capitol CL 410* 46 4
14 Jun 86 **WHERE YOU GONNA BE TONIGHT?** *Capitol EST 2012* 97 1

Willie COLON *US, male vocalist (Singles: 7 weeks)* pos/wks

28 Jun 86 **SET FIRE TO ME** *A&M AM 330* 41 7

COLOR ME BADD

US, male vocal group (Singles: 31 weeks, Albums: 22 weeks) pos/wks

18 May 91 ★ **I WANNA SEX YOU UP** *Giant W 0036* 1 14
3 Aug 91 ● **ALL 4 LOVE** *Giant W 0053* ▲ 5 10
12 Oct 91 **I ADORE MI AMOR** *Giant W 0067* ▲ 44 2
9 Nov 91 **I ADORE MI AMOR (re-issue)** *Giant W 0076* 59 2
22 Feb 92 **HEARTBREAKER** *Giant W 0078* 58 1
20 Nov 93 **TIME AND CHANCE** *Giant 74321168992* 62 1
16 Apr 94 **CHOOSE** *Giant 74321199432* 65 1
24 Aug 91 ● **CMB** *Giant WX 425* 3 22

COLORADO

UK, female vocal group (Singles: 3 weeks) pos/wks

21 Oct 78 **CALIFORNIA DREAMING** *Pinnacle PIN 67* 45 3

COLOSSEUM

UK, male vocal / instrumental group (Albums: 14 weeks) pos/wks

17 May 69 **COLOSSEUM** *Fontana S 5510* 15 1
22 Nov 69 **VALENTYNE SUITE** *Vertigo VO 1* 15 2
5 Dec 70 **DAUGHTER OF TIME** *Vertigo 6360 017* 23 5
26 Jun 71 **COLOSSEUM LIVE** *Bronze ICD 1* 17 6

COLOUR FIELD *UK, male vocal / instrumental group (Singles: 18 weeks, Albums: 8 weeks)* pos/wks

21 Jan 84 **THE COLOUR FIELD** *Chrysalis COLF 1* 43 4
28 Jul 84 **TAKE** *Chrysalis COLF 2* 70 1
26 Jan 85 **THINKING OF YOU** *Chrysalis COLF 3* 12 10

13 Apr 85 **CASTLES IN THE AIR** *Chrysalis COLF 4* 51 3
4 May 85 **VIRGINS AND PHILISTINES** *Chrysalis CHR 1480* 12 7
4 Apr 87 **DECEPTION** *Chrysalis CDL 1546* 95 1

COLOUR GIRL

UK, female vocalist – Rebecca Skingley (Singles: 5 weeks) pos/wks

11 Mar 00 **CAN'T GET USED TO LOSING YOU** *4 Liberty LIBT CD037* 31 3
9 Sep 00 **JOYRIDER (YOU'RE PLAYING WITH FIRE)** *4 Liberty LIBT CD039* 51 1
3 Feb 01 **MAS QUE NADA** *4 Liberty LIBTCD 040* [1] 57 1

[1] Colour Girl featuring PSG

COLOURBOX

UK, male vocal / instrumental group (Albums: 2 weeks) pos/wks

24 Aug 85 **COLOURBOX** *4AD CAD 508* 67 2

COLOURS featuring EMMANUEL & ESKA *UK, male instrumentalist / producer and female vocalist (Singles: 1 week)* pos/wks

27 Feb 99 **WHAT U DO** *Inferno CDFERN 12* 51 1

See also EN-CORE featuring Stephen EMMANUEL & ESKA; Nitin SAWHNEY

COLOURSOUND *UK, male production duo (Singles: 2 weeks)* pos/wks

28 Sep 02 **FLY WITH ME** *City Rockers ROCKERS 20CD* 49 2

Alice COLTRANE – *See SANTANA*

COLUMBO featuring OOE

UK, male production duo (Singles: 1 week) pos/wks

15 May 99 **ROCKABILLY BOB** *V2 / Milkgems VVR 5006903* 59 1

Shawn COLVIN

US, female vocalist (Singles: 12 weeks, Albums: 1 week) pos/wks

27 Nov 93 **I DON'T KNOW WHY** *Columbia 6598272* 62 1
12 Feb 94 **ROUND OF BLUES** *Columbia 6594282* 73 1
3 Sep 94 **EVERY LITTLE THING HE DOES IS MAGIC** *Columbia 6607742* 65 2
7 Jan 95 **ONE COOL REMOVE** *Columbia 6611342* [1] 40 3
12 Aug 95 **I DON'T KNOW WHY (re-issue)** *Columbia 6622725* 52 1
15 Mar 97 **GET OUT OF THIS HOUSE** *Columbia 6638522* 70 1
30 May 98 **SUNNY CAME HOME** *Columbia 6648022* 29 3
17 Sep 94 **COVER GIRL** *Columbia 4772402* 67 1

[1] Shawn Colvin with Mary-Chapin Carpenter

COMETS – *See Bill HALEY and His COMETS*

COMIC RELIEF

UK, charity ensemble of comedians (Albums: 8 weeks) pos/wks

10 May 86 ● **UTTERLY UTTERLY LIVE!** *WEA WX 51* 10 8

COMING OUT CREW

US, male / female vocal duo (Singles: 1 week) pos/wks

18 Mar 95 **FREE, GAY AND HAPPY** *Out on Vinyl CDOOV 002* 50 1

COMMANDER TOM

Germany, male producer – Tom Weyer (Singles: 1 week) pos/wks

23 Dec 00 **EYE BEE M** *Tripoli Trax TTRAX 069CD* 75 1

COMMENTATORS

UK, male impressionist – Rory Bremner (Singles: 7 weeks) pos/wks

22 Jun 85 **N-N-NINETEEN NOT OUT** *Oval 100* 13 7

COMMITMENTS (466 Top 500)

Irish band formed especially for Alan Parker's 1991 film of the same name. Led by vocalist Andrew Strong, with Angelina Ball, Maria Doyle, Bronagh Gallagher and Robert Arkins, their revivals of 1960s soul favourites became briefly, but hugely, popular (Singles: 1 week, Albums: 147 weeks) pos/wks

30 Nov 91 **MUSTANG SALLY** *MCA MCS 1598* 63 1
26 Oct 91 ● **THE COMMITMENTS (FILM SOUNDTRACK)** *MCA MCA 10286* 4 136
25 Apr 92 **THE COMMITMENTS VOLUME 2** *MCA MCAD 10506* 13 11

COMMODORES (237 Top 500)

Top-notch US R&B combo: Lionel Richie (v/k), William King (t), Thomas McClary (g), Milan Williams (var), Ronald LaPread (b), Walter Orange (d). They were among the 1970s' biggest-selling groups, but lost ground when songwriter Richie went solo in 1982 (Singles: 121 weeks, Albums: 135 weeks) pos/wks

24 Aug 74 **MACHINE GUN** *Tamla Motown TMG 902* 20 11
23 Nov 74 **THE ZOO (THE HUMAN ZOO)** *Tamla Motown TMG 924* 44 2
2 Jul 77 ● **EASY** *Motown TMG 1073* 9 10
8 Oct 77 **SWEET LOVE / BRICK HOUSE** *Motown TMG 1086* 32 6
11 Mar 78 **TOO HOT TA TROT / ZOOM** *Motown TMG 1096* 38 4
24 Jun 78 **FLYING HIGH** *Motown TMG 1111* 37 7
5 Aug 78 ★ **THREE TIMES A LADY** *Motown TMG 1113* ▲ 1 14
25 Nov 78 **JUST TO BE CLOSE TO YOU** *Motown TMG 1127* 62 4
25 Aug 79 ● **SAIL ON** *Motown TMG 1155* 8 10
3 Nov 79 ● **STILL** *Motown TMG 1166* ▲ 4 11
19 Jan 80 **WONDERLAND** *Motown TMG 1172* 40 4
1 Aug 81 **LADY (YOU BRING ME UP)** *Motown TMG 1238* 56 5
21 Nov 81 **OH NO** *Motown TMG 1245* 44 3
26 Jan 85 ● **NIGHTSHIFT** *Motown TMG 1371* 3 14
11 May 85 **ANIMAL INSTINCT** *Motown ZB 40097* 74 1
25 Oct 86 **GOIN' TO THE BANK** *Polydor POSPA 826* 43 4
13 Aug 88 **EASY (re-issue)** *Motown ZB 41793* 15 11
13 May 78 **LIVE!** *Motown TMSP 6007* 60 1
10 Jun 78 ● **NATURAL HIGH** *Motown STML 12087* 8 23
2 Dec 78 **GREATEST HITS** *Motown STML 12100* 19 16
18 Aug 79 **MIDNIGHT MAGIC** *Motown STMA 8032* 15 25
28 Jun 80 **HEROES** *Motown STMA 8034* 50 5
18 Jul 81 **IN THE POCKET** *Motown STML 12156* 69 5
14 Aug 82 ● **LOVE SONGS** *K-Tel NE 1171* 5 28
23 Feb 85 **NIGHTSHIFT** *Motown ZL 72343* 13 10
9 Nov 85 **THE VERY BEST OF THE COMMODORES** *Telstar STAR 2249* 25 13
6 May 95 **THE VERY BEST** *Motown 5305472* 26 3
22 Nov 03 ● **THE DEFINITIVE COLLECTION** *Universal TV 9861394* [1] 10 6+

[1] Lionel Richie / The Commodores

Group was US / UK for 1985 and 1986 hits Group was US only for first seven albums

COMMON *US, male rapper – Rasheed Lynn (Singles: 10 weeks)* pos/wks

8 Nov 97 **REMINDING ME (OF SEF)** *Relativity 6560762* [1] 59 1
14 Oct 00 **THE LIGHT / THE 6TH SENSE (SOMETHING U FEEL)** *MCA MCSTD 40237* 56 1
28 Apr 01 **GETO HEAVEN** *MCA MCSTD 40246* [2] 48 1
9 Feb 02 **DANCE FOR ME** *MCA MCSTD 40274* [3] 13 7

[1] Common featuring Chantay Savage [2] Common featuring Macy Gray [3] Mary J Blige featuring Common

COMMOTIONS – *See Lloyd COLE*

COMMUNARDS (442 Top 500)

Controversial, melodic pop duo consisted of Bronski Beat's Jimmy Somerville (v) b. 22 Jun 1961, Glasgow, Scotland, and Richard Coles (k), b. 23 Jun 1962, Northampton, UK. Their No.1 cover marked the song's third Top 20 reading within a decade (Singles: 76 weeks, Albums: 78 weeks) pos/wks

12 Oct 85 **YOU ARE MY WORLD** *London LON 77* 30 8
24 May 86 **DISENCHANTED** *London LON 89* 29 5
23 Aug 86 ★ **DON'T LEAVE ME THIS WAY** *London LON 103* [1] 1 14
29 Nov 86 ● **SO COLD THE NIGHT** *London LON 110* 8 10
21 Feb 87 **YOU ARE MY WORLD (87) (re-mix)** *London LON 123* 21 6
12 Sep 87 **TOMORROW** *London LON 143* 23 7
7 Nov 87 ● **NEVER CAN SAY GOODBYE** *London LON 158* 4 11
20 Feb 88 **FOR A FRIEND** *London LON 166* 28 7
11 Jun 88 **THERE'S MORE TO LOVE** *London LON 173* 20 8
2 Aug 86 ● **COMMUNARDS** *London LONLP 18* 7 45
17 Oct 87 ● **RED** *London LONLP 39* 4 29
22 Sep 01 **THE VERY BEST OF JIMMY SOMERVILLE, BRONSKI BEAT AND THE COMMUNARDS** *London 927412582* [1] 29 4

[1] Communards with Sarah Jane Morris [1] Jimmy Somerville, Bronski Beat and the Communards

Perry COMO (72 Top 500)

One of the 20th century's most enduring entertainers, b. 18 May 1912, Pennsylvania, d. 12 May 2001. This easy-on-the-ear relaxed balladeer launched his career in 1933, collected 150 US chart entries, hosted an Emmy-winning TV series, and continued to score hits past the age of 60 (Singles: 323 weeks, Albums: 202 weeks)

Date		Title	pos	wks
16 Jan 53	★	**DON'T LET THE STARS GET IN YOUR EYES** *HMV B 10400* [1] ▲	1	15
4 Jun 54	●	**WANTED (re)** *HMV B 10691* ▲	4	15
25 Jun 54	●	**IDLE GOSSIP** *HMV B 10667*	3	15
10 Dec 54		**PAPA LOVES MAMBO** *HMV B 10776*	16	1
30 Dec 55		**TINA MARIE** *HMV POP 103*	24	1
27 Apr 56		**JUKE BOX BABY** *HMV POP 191*	22	6
25 May 56	●	**HOT DIGGITY (DOG ZIGGITY BOOM)** *HMV POP 212*	4	13
21 Sep 56	●	**MORE (re)** *HMV POP 240*	10	12
28 Sep 56		**GLENDORA** *HMV POP 240*	18	6
7 Feb 58	★	**MAGIC MOMENTS** *RCA 1036*	1	17
7 Mar 58	●	**CATCH A FALLING STAR** *RCA 1036*	9	10
9 May 58	●	**KEWPIE DOLL** *RCA 1055*	9	7
30 May 58		**I MAY NEVER PASS THIS WAY AGAIN** *RCA 1062*	15	8
5 Sep 58		**MOON TALK** *RCA 1071*	17	11
7 Nov 58	●	**LOVE MAKES THE WORLD GO ROUND** *RCA 1086*	6	14
21 Nov 58		**MANDOLINS IN THE MOONLIGHT** *RCA 1086*	13	12
27 Feb 59	●	**TOMBOY** *RCA 1111*	10	12
10 Jul 59		**I KNOW** *RCA 1126* [2]	13	16
26 Feb 60	●	**DELAWARE** *RCA 1170*	3	14
10 May 62		**CATERINA (re)** *RCA 1283*	37	6
30 Jan 71	●	**IT'S IMPOSSIBLE** *RCA 2043*	4	23
15 May 71		**I THINK OF YOU** *RCA 2075*	14	11
21 Apr 73	●	**AND I LOVE YOU SO (re)** *RCA 2346*	3	35
25 Aug 73	●	**FOR THE GOOD TIMES** *RCA 2402*	7	27
8 Dec 73		**WALK RIGHT BACK** *RCA 2432*	33	10
25 May 74		**I WANT TO GIVE** *RCA LPBO 7518*	31	6
28 Jun 58	●	**WE GET LETTERS (VOL.2)** *RCA RD 27070*	4	7
8 Nov 58	●	**DEAR PERRY** *RCA RD 27078*	6	5
31 Jan 59	●	**COMO'S GOLDEN RECORDS** *RCA RD 27100*	4	5
10 Apr 71		**IT'S IMPOSSIBLE** *RCA Victor SF 8175*	13	13
7 Jul 73	★	**AND I LOVE YOU SO** *RCA Victor SF 8360*	1	109
24 Aug 74		**PERRY** *RCA Victor APLI 0585*	26	3
19 Apr 75		**MEMORIES ARE MADE OF HITS** *RCA Victor RS 1005*	14	16
25 Oct 75	★	**40 GREATEST HITS** *K-Tel NE 700*	1	34
3 Dec 83		**FOR THE GOOD TIMES** *Telstar STAR 2235*	41	6
17 Nov 01		**GOLD – GREATEST HITS** *RCA 74321865542*	55	2
4 Oct 03		**THE ESSENTIAL PERRY COMO** *Jive / RCA 82876560172*	54	2

[1] Perry Como with the Ramblers [2] with Mitchell Ayers' Orchestra and the Ray Charles Singers

LES COMPAGNONS DE LA CHANSON

France, male vocal group (Singles: 3 weeks)

Date		Title	pos	wks
9 Oct 59		**THE THREE BELLS (THE JIMMY BROWN SONG) (re)** *Columbia DB 4358*	21	3

COMPULSION

Ireland / Holland, male vocal / instrumental group (Albums: 1 week)

Date		Title	pos	wks
9 Apr 94		**COMFORTER** *One Little Indian TPLP 59CDL*	59	1

COMSAT ANGELS *UK, male vocal / instrumental group (Singles: 2 weeks, Albums: 9 weeks)*

Date		Title	pos	wks
21 Jan 84		**INDEPENDENCE DAY (re)** *Jive JIVE 54*	71	2
5 Sep 81		**SLEEP NO MORE** *Polydor POLS 1038*	51	5
18 Sep 82		**FICTION** *Polydor POLS 1075*	94	2
8 Oct 83		**LAND** *Jive HIP 8*	91	2

CON FUNK SHUN

US, male vocal / instrumental group (Singles: 2 weeks)

Date		Title	pos	wks
19 Jul 86		**BURNIN' LOVE** *Club JAB 32*	68	2

CONCEPT

US, male vocalist / instrumentalist – Eric Reed (Singles: 6 weeks)

Date		Title	pos	wks
14 Dec 85		**MR DJ** *Fourth & Broadway BRW 40*	27	6

CONDUCTOR & THE COWBOY *UK, male production duo – Lee Hallett and Adam Pracy (Singles: 2 weeks)*

Date		Title	pos	wks
20 May 00		**FEELING THIS WAY** *Serious SERR 016CD*	35	2

CONFEDERATES – *See Elvis COSTELLO*

CONGREGATION *UK, male / female choir (Singles: 14 weeks)*

Date		Title	pos	wks
27 Nov 71	●	**SOFTLY WHISPERING I LOVE YOU** *Columbia DB 8830*	4	14

CONGRESS

UK, male / female vocal / instrumental group (Singles: 4 weeks)

Date		Title	pos	wks
26 Oct 91		**40 MILES** *Inner Rhythm 7HEART 01*	26	4

CONJURE ONE

Canada, male producer – Rhys Fulber (Singles: 1 week)

Date		Title	pos	wks
15 Feb 03		**SLEEP / TEARS FROM THE MOON** *Nettwerk 331792*	42	1

Arthur CONLEY

US, male vocalist d. 17 Nov 2003 (Singles: 15 weeks)

Date		Title	pos	wks
27 Apr 67	●	**SWEET SOUL MUSIC** *Atlantic 584 083*	7	14
10 Apr 68		**FUNKY STREET** *Atlantic 583 175*	46	1

CONNELLS *US, male vocal / instrumental group (Singles: 11 weeks, Albums: 2 weeks)*

Date		Title	pos	wks
12 Aug 95		**74-75 (re)** *TVT LONCD 369*	14	11
9 Sep 95		**RING** *London 8286602*	36	2

Harry CONNICK Jr *US, male vocalist / instrumentalist – keyboards (Singles: 11 weeks, Albums: 67 weeks)*

Date		Title	pos	wks
25 May 91		**RECIPE FOR LOVE / IT HAD TO BE YOU** *Columbia 6568907*	32	6
3 Aug 91		**WE ARE IN LOVE** *Columbia 6572847*	62	2
23 Nov 91		**BLUE LIGHT RED LIGHT (SOMEONE'S THERE)** *Columbia 6575367*	54	3
22 Sep 90	●	**WE ARE IN LOVE** *CBS 4667361*	7	46
26 Oct 91		**BLUE LIGHT RED LIGHT** *Columbia 4690871*	16	11
30 Jan 93		**25** *Columbia 4728092*	35	2
12 Jun 93		**FOREVER FOR NOW** *Columbia 4738732*	32	5
27 Aug 94		**SHE** *Columbia 4768162*	21	3

Ray CONNIFF

US, male orchestra leader d. 12 Oct 2002 (Albums: 96 weeks)

Date		Title	pos	wks
28 May 60		**IT'S THE TALK OF THE TOWN** *Philips BBL 7354*	15	1
25 Jun 60		**S'AWFUL NICE** *Philips BBL 7281*	13	1
26 Nov 60	●	**HI-FI COMPANION ALBUM** *Philips BET 101*	3	44
20 May 61		**MEMORIES ARE MADE OF THIS** *Philips BBL 7439*	14	4
29 Dec 62		**S WONDERFUL 'S MARVELLOUS** *CBS DPG 66001*	18	3
29 Dec 62		**WE WISH YOU A MERRY CHRISTMAS** *CBS BPG 62092*	12	1
16 Apr 66		**HI-FI COMPANION ALBUM (re-issue)** *CBS DP 66011*	24	4
9 Sep 67		**SOMEWHERE MY LOVE** *CBS SBPG 62740*	34	3
21 Jun 69	★	**HIS ORCHESTRA HIS CHORUS HIS SINGERS HIS SOUND** *CBS SPR 27* ■	1	16
23 May 70		**BRIDGE OVER TROUBLED WATER** *CBS 64020*	30	14
12 Jun 71		**LOVE STORY** *CBS 64294*	34	1
19 Feb 72		**I'D LIKE TO TEACH THE WORLD TO SING** *CBS 64449*	17	4

Billy CONNOLLY

Scottish comedian b. 24 Nov 1942, Glasgow, who was formerly in folk group the Humblebums but went on to great acclaim as a TV personality and film actor (Singles: 31 weeks, Albums: 108 weeks)

Date		Title	pos	wks
1 Nov 75	★	**D.I.V.O.R.C.E.** *Polydor 2058 652*	1	10
17 Jul 76		**NO CHANCE (NO CHARGE)** *Polydor 2058 748*	24	5
25 Aug 79		**IN THE BROWNIES** *Polydor 2059 160*	38	7
9 Mar 85		**SUPER GRAN** *Stiff BUY 218*	32	9
20 Jul 74	●	**SOLO CONCERT** *Transatlantic TRA 279*	8	33
18 Jan 75	●	**COP YER WHACK OF THIS** *Polydor 2383 310*	10	29
20 Sep 75		**WORDS AND MUSIC** *Transatlantic TRA SAM 32*	34	10
6 Dec 75	●	**GET RIGHT INTAE HIM** *Polydor 2383 368*	6	14
11 Dec 76		**ATLANTIC BRIDGE** *Polydor 2383 419*	20	9

28 Jan 78 **RAW MEAT FOR THE BALCONY** *Polydor 2383 463* **57** 3
5 Dec 81 **THE PICK OF BILLY CONNOLLY** *Polydor POLTV 15* **23** 8
5 Dec 87 **BILLY AND ALBERT** *10 DIX 65* **81** 2

Sarah CONNOR featuring TQ

Germany, female vocalist and US, male rapper (Singles: 5 weeks) pos/wks

13 Oct 01 **LET'S GET BACK TO BED ... BOY** *Epic 67 18662* **16** 5

CONQUERING LION *UK, male vocal group (Singles: 1 week)* pos/wks

8 Oct 94 **CODE RED** *Mango CIDM 821* **53** 1

Leena CONQUEST and HIP HOP FINGER

US, female vocalist and male rapper (Singles: 1 week) pos/wks

18 Jun 94 **BOUNDARIES** *Natural Response 74321208522* **67** 1

Jess CONRAD

UK, male vocalist (Singles: 13 weeks) pos/wks

30 Jun 60 **CHERRY PIE** *Decca F 1123* **39** 1
26 Jan 61 **MYSTERY GIRL (re)** *Decca F 11315* **18** 10
11 Oct 62 **PRETTY JENNY** *Decca F 11511* **50** 2

CONSOLIDATED

US, male vocal / instrumental group (Albums: 1 week) pos/wks

30 Jul 94 **BUSINESS OF PUNISHMENT** *London 8285142* **53** 1

CONSORTIUM

UK, male vocal group (Singles: 9 weeks) pos/wks

12 Feb 69 **ALL THE LOVE IN THE WORLD** *Pye 7N 17635* **22** 9

Ann CONSUELO – *See SUBTERRANIA featuring Ann CONSUELO*

CONTOURS

US, male vocal group (Singles: 6 weeks) pos/wks

24 Jan 70 **JUST A LITTLE MISUNDERSTANDING**
Tamla Motown TMG 723 ....**31** 6

CONTRABAND *Germany / US, male / female vocal / instrumental group (Singles: 2 weeks)* pos/wks

20 Jul 91 **ALL THE WAY FROM MEMPHIS** *Impact American EM 195* **65** 2

CONTROL

UK, male / female vocal / instrumental group (Singles: 5 weeks) pos/wks

2 Nov 91 **DANCE WITH ME (I'M YOUR ECSTASY)**
All Around the World GLOBE 105 ....**17** 5

CONVERT *Belgium, male instrumental / production duo – Peter Ramson and Danny Van Wauwe (Singles: 7 weeks)* pos/wks

11 Jan 92 **NIGHTBIRD** *A&M AM 845* **39** 4
29 May 93 **ROCKIN' TO THE RHYTHM** *A&M 5802532* **42** 2
31 Jan 98 **NIGHTBIRD (re-issue)** *Wonderboy WBOYD 008* **45** 1

See also TRANSFORMER 2

Raz CONWAY – *See MORJAC featuring Raz CONWAY*

Russ CONWAY (250 Top 500)

Popular pianist and composer, b. Trevor Stanford, 2 Sep 1925, Bristol, d. 16 Nov 2000. Against the trends of the day this MOR piano player was the UK's top-selling artist in 1959 (Singles: 179 weeks, Albums: 69 weeks) pos/wks

29 Nov 57 **PARTY POPS** *Columbia DB 4031* **24** 5
29 Aug 58 **GOT A MATCH** *Columbia DB 4166* **30** 1
28 Nov 58 ● **MORE PARTY POPS** *Columbia DB 4204* **10** 7
23 Jan 59 **THE WORLD OUTSIDE (re)** *Columbia DB 4234* **24** 4
20 Feb 59 ★ **SIDE SADDLE** *Columbia DB 4256* **1** 30
15 May 59 ★ **ROULETTE** *Columbia DB 4298* **1** 19
21 Aug 59 ● **CHINA TEA** *Columbia DB 4337* **5** 13
13 Nov 59 ● **SNOW COACH** *Columbia DB 4368* **7** 9
20 Nov 59 ● **MORE AND MORE PARTY POPS** *Columbia DB 4373* **5** 8
4 Mar 60 **ROYAL EVENT** *Columbia DB 4418* **15** 8
21 Apr 60 **FINGS AIN'T WOT THEY USED T'BE** *Columbia DB 4422* **47** 1
19 May 60 **LUCKY FIVE** *Columbia DB 4457* **14** 9
29 Sep 60 **PASSING BREEZE** *Columbia DB 4508* **16** 10
24 Nov 60 **EVEN MORE PARTY POPS** *Columbia DB 4535* **27** 9
19 Jan 61 **PEPE** *Columbia DB 4564* **19** 9
25 May 61 **PABLO** *Columbia DB 4649* **45** 2
24 Aug 61 **SAY IT WITH FLOWERS** *Columbia DB 4665* [1] **23** 10
30 Nov 61 ● **TOY BALLOONS** *Columbia DB 4738* **7** 11
22 Feb 62 **LESSON ONE** *Columbia DB 4784* **21** 7
29 Nov 62 **ALWAYS YOU AND ME (re)** *Columbia DB 4934* **33** 7
22 Nov 58 ● **PACK UP YOUR TROUBLES** *Columbia 33SX 1120* **9** 5
2 May 59 ● **SONGS TO SING IN YOUR BATH** *Columbia 33SX 1149* **8** 10
19 Sep 59 ● **FAMILY FAVOURITES** *Columbia 33SX 1169* **3** 16
19 Dec 59 ● **TIME TO CELEBRATE** *Columbia 33SX 1197* **3** 7
26 Mar 60 ● **MY CONCERTO FOR YOU** *Columbia 33SX 1214* **5** 17
17 Dec 60 ● **PARTY TIME** *Columbia 33SX 1279* **7** 11
23 Apr 77 **RUSS CONWAY PRESENTS 24 PIANO GREATS**
Ronco RTL 2022 ....**25** 3

[1] Dorothy Squires and Russ Conway

'Always You and Me' featured Russ Conway talking as well as playing piano. Several of the discs were medleys as follows: Party Pops: When You're Smiling / I'm Looking over a Four-Leafed Clover / When You Wore a Tulip / Row Row Row / For Me and My Girl / Shine on Harvest Moon / By the Light of the Silvery Moon / Side By Side. More Party Pops: Music Music Music / If You Were the Only Girl in the World / Nobody's Sweetheart / Yes Sir That's My Baby / Some of these Days / Honeysuckle and the Bee / Hello Hello Who's Your Lady Friend / Shanty in Old Shanty Town. More and More Party Pops: Sheik of Araby / Who Were You With Last Night / Any Old Iron / Tiptoe Through the Tulips / If You Were the Only Girl in the World / When I Leave the World Behind. Even More Party Pops: Ain't She Sweet / I Can't Give You Anything But Love / Yes We Have No Bananas / I May Be Wrong / Happy Days And Lonely Nights / Glad Rag Doll

CONWAY BROTHERS *US, male vocal group (Singles: 10 weeks)* pos/wks

22 Jun 85 **TURN IT UP** *10 TEN 57* **11** 10

Ry COODER

US, male vocalist / instrumentalist – guitar (Albums: 49 weeks) pos/wks

11 Aug 79 **BOP TILL YOU DROP** *Warner Bros. K 56691* **36** 9
18 Oct 80 **BORDER LINE** *Warner Bros. K 56864* **35** 6
24 Apr 82 **THE SLIDE AREA** *Warner Bros. K 56976* **18** 12
14 Nov 87 **GET RHYTHM** *Warner Bros. WX 121* **75** 3
9 Apr 94 **TALKING TIMBUKTU** *World Circuit WCD 040* [1] **44** 3
5 Jul 97 **BUENA VISTA SOCIAL CLUB** *World Circuit WCD 050* **44** 15
8 Feb 03 **MAMBO SINUENDO** *Nonesuch 75597969612* [2] **40** 1

[1] Ali Farka Touri and Ry Cooder [2] Ry Cooder and Manuel Galbran

Martin COOK – *See Richard DENTON and Martin COOK*

Norman COOK

UK, male producer / multi-instrumentalist (Singles: 10 weeks) pos/wks

8 Jul 89 **WON'T TALK ABOUT IT / BLAME IT ON THE BASSLINE**
Go.Beat GOD 33 [1] **29** 6
21 Oct 89 **FOR SPACIOUS LIES** *Go.Beat GOD 37* [2] **48** 4

[1] Norman Cook featuring Billy Bragg / Norman Cook featuring MC Wildski
[2] Norman Cook featuring Lester

See also BEATS INTERNATIONAL; FATBOY SLIM; FREAKPOWER; HOUSEMARTINS; MIGHTY DUB KATZ; PIZZAMAN

Peter COOK and DUDLEY MOORE

UK, male comedy / vocal duo - Peter Cook, d. 9 Jan 1995 and Dudley Moore, d. 28 Mar 2002 (Singles: 15 weeks Albums: 34 weeks) pos/wks

17 Jun 65 **GOODBYE-EE** *Decca F 12158* **18** 10
15 Jul 65 **THE BALLAD OF SPOTTY MULDOON**
Decca F 12182 [1] **34** 5
21 May 66 **ONCE MORE WITH COOK** *Decca LK 4785* **25** 1
18 Sep 76 **DEREK AND CLIVE LIVE** *Island ILPS 9434* [1] **12** 25
24 Dec 77 **DEREK AND CLIVE COME AGAIN** *Virgin V 2094* [1] **18** 8

[1] Peter Cook [1] Derek and Clive

Brandon COOKE featuring Roxanne SHANTE

UK, male producer and US, female rapper (Singles: 3 weeks)

Date		Title / Label	pos	wks
29 Oct 88		**SHARP AS A KNIFE** *Club JAB 73*	**45**	3

Sam COOKE

US, male vocalist, d. 11 Dec 1964
(Singles: 82 weeks, Albums: 32 weeks)

Date		Title / Label	pos	wks
17 Jan 58		**YOU SEND ME** *London HLU 8506* ▲	**29**	1
14 Aug 59		**ONLY SIXTEEN** *HMV POP 642*	**23**	4
7 Jul 60		**WONDERFUL WORLD** *HMV POP 754*	**27**	8
29 Sep 60	●	**CHAIN GANG** *RCA 1202*	**9**	11
27 Jul 61	●	**CUPID** *RCA 1242*	**7**	14
8 Mar 62	●	**TWISTIN' THE NIGHT AWAY** *RCA 1277*	**6**	14
16 May 63		**ANOTHER SATURDAY NIGHT** *RCA 1341*	**23**	12
5 Sep 63		**FRANKIE AND JOHNNY** *RCA 1361*	**30**	6
22 Mar 86	●	**WONDERFUL WORLD (re-issue)** *RCA PB 49871*	**2**	11
10 May 86		**ANOTHER SATURDAY NIGHT (re-issue)** *RCA PB 49849*	**75**	1
26 Apr 86	●	**THE MAN AND HIS MUSIC** *RCA PL 87127*	**8**	27
25 Oct 03		**PORTRAIT OF A LEGEND 1951-1964** *Universal TV 9807446*	**30**	5

COOKIE CREW

UK, female rap duo – Susie Banfield and Debbie Pryce (Singles: 31 weeks, Albums: 4 weeks)

Date		Title / Label	pos	wks
9 Jan 88	●	**ROK DA HOUSE** *Rhythm King LEFT 11* [1]	**5**	11
7 Jan 89		**BORN THIS WAY (LET'S DANCE)** *ffrr FFR 19*	**23**	5
1 Apr 89		**GOT TO KEEP ON** *ffrr FFR 25*	**17**	9
15 Jul 89		**COME AND GET SOME** *ffrr F 110*	**42**	3
27 Jul 91		**SECRETS (OF SUCCESS)** *ffrr F159* [2]	**53**	3
6 May 89		**BORN THIS WAY!** *London 828134 1*	**24**	4

[1] Beatmasters featuring the Cookie Crew [2] Cookie Crew featuring Danny D

COOKIES *US, female vocal group (Singles: 1 week)*

Date		Title / Label	pos	wks
10 Jan 63		**CHAINS** *London HLU 9634*	**50**	1

COOL DOWN ZONE

UK, male / female vocal / instrumental group (Singles: 4 weeks)

Date		Title / Label	pos	wks
30 Jun 90		**HEAVEN KNOWS** *10 TEN 309*	**52**	4

COOL, the FAB, and the GROOVY present Quincy JONES

UK, male production duo, US, male group and US, male producer / instrumentalist (Singles: 1 week)

Date		Title / Label	pos	wks
1 Aug 98		**SOUL BOSSA NOVA** *Manifesto FESCD 48*	**47**	1

COOL JACK

Italy, male instrumental / production duo (Singles: 1 week)

Date		Title / Label	pos	wks
9 Nov 96		**JUS' COME** *AM:PM 5819892*	**44**	1

COOL NOTES

UK, male / female vocal / instrumental group (Singles: 28 weeks, Albums: 2 weeks)

Date		Title / Label	pos	wks
18 Aug 84		**YOU'RE NEVER TOO YOUNG** *Abstract Dance AD 1*	**42**	5
17 Nov 84		**I FORGOT** *Abstract Dance AD 2*	**63**	2
23 Mar 85		**SPEND THE NIGHT** *Abstract Dance AD 3*	**11**	9
13 Jul 85		**IN YOUR CAR** *Abstract Dance AD 4*	**13**	9
19 Oct 85		**HAVE A GOOD FOREVER** *Abstract Dance AD 5*	**73**	1
17 May 86		**INTO THE MOTION** *Abstract Dance AD 8*	**66**	2
9 Nov 85		**HAVE A GOOD FOREVER** *Abstract Dance ADLP 1*	**66**	2

Rita COOLIDGE

US, female vocalist (Singles: 24 weeks, Albums: 44 weeks)

Date		Title / Label	pos	wks
25 Jun 77	●	**WE'RE ALL ALONE** *A&M AMS 7295*	**6**	13
15 Oct 77		**(YOUR LOVE HAS LIFTED ME) HIGHER AND HIGHER (re)** *A&M AMS 7315*	**48**	2
4 Feb 78		**WORDS** *A&M AMS 7330*	**25**	8
25 Jun 83		**ALL TIME HIGH** *A&M AM 007*	**75**	1
6 Aug 77	●	**ANYTIME ANYWHERE** *A&M AMLH 64616*	**6**	28
6 May 78		**NATURAL ACT** *A&M AMLH 64690* [1]	**35**	4
8 Jul 78		**LOVE ME AGAIN** *A&M AMLH 64699*	**51**	1
14 Mar 81	●	**THE VERY BEST OF RITA COOLIDGE** *A&M AMLH 68520*	**6**	11

[1] Kris Kristofferson and Rita Coolidge

COOLIO *US, male rapper – Artis Ivey Jr*

(Singles: 62 weeks, Albums: 27 weeks)

Date		Title / Label	pos	wks
23 Jul 94		**FANTASTIC VOYAGE** *Tommy Boy TB 0617CD*	**41**	2
15 Oct 94		**I REMEMBER** *Tommy Boy TBXCD 635*	**73**	1
28 Oct 95	★	**GANGSTA'S PARADISE** *Tommy Boy MCSTD 2104* [1] ◆ ■ ▲	**1**	20
20 Jan 96	●	**TOO HOT** *Tommy Boy TBCD 718*	**9**	6
6 Apr 96		**1234 (SUMPIN' NEW)** *Tommy Boy TBCD 7721*	**13**	7
17 Aug 96		**IT'S ALL THE WAY LIVE (NOW)** *Tommy Boy TBCD 7731*	**34**	2
5 Apr 97	●	**HIT EM HIGH (THE MONSTARS' ANTHEM)** *Atlantic A 5449CD* [2]	**8**	6
7 Jun 97		**THE WINNER** *Atlantic A 5433CD*	**53**	1
19 Jul 97	●	**C U WHEN U GET THERE** *Tommy Boy TBCD 785* [3]	**3**	12
11 Oct 97		**OOH LA LA** *Tommy Boy TBCD 799*	**14**	5
29 Oct 94		**IT TAKES A THIEF** *Tommy Boy TBCD 1083*	**67**	1
18 Nov 95		**GANGSTA'S PARADISE** *Tommy Boy TBCD 1141*	**18**	24
13 Sep 97		**MY SOUL** *Tommy Boy TBCD 1180*	**28**	2

[1] Coolio featuring LV [2] B Real / Busta Rhymes / Coolio / LL Cool J / Method Man
[3] Coolio featuring 40 Thevz

COOLY'S HOT BOX – *See Roger SANCHEZ*

COOPER

Holland, male production trio (Singles: 2 weeks)

Date		Title / Label	pos	wks
11 Jan 03		**I BELIEVE IN LOVE** *Product PDT 05CDS*	**50**	2

Alice COOPER (262 Top 500)

The alter ego of shock-rock vocalist Vincent Furnier, b. 4 Feb 1948, Detroit, US. The transatlantic chart-topper's group was voted World's Top Band in 1972 in UK. Renowned for on-stage shock-horror theatrics (Singles: 104 weeks, Albums: 134 weeks)

Date		Title / Label	pos	wks
15 Jul 72	★	**SCHOOL'S OUT** *Warner Bros. K 16188*	**1**	12
7 Oct 72	●	**ELECTED** *Warner Bros. K 16214*	**4**	10
10 Feb 73	●	**HELLO HURRAY** *Warner Bros. K 16248*	**6**	12
21 Apr 73	●	**NO MORE MR NICE GUY** *Warner Bros. K 16262*	**10**	10
19 Jan 74		**TEENAGE LAMENT '74** *Warner Bros. K 16345*	**12**	7
21 May 77		**(NO MORE) LOVE AT YOUR CONVENIENCE** *Warner Bros. K 16935*	**44**	2
23 Dec 78		**HOW YOU GONNA SEE ME NOW** *Warner Bros. K 17270*	**61**	6
6 Mar 82		**SEVEN AND SEVEN IS (LIVE VERSION)** *Warner Bros. K 17924*	**62**	3
8 May 82		**FOR BRITAIN ONLY / UNDER MY WHEELS** *Warner Bros. K 17940*	**66**	2
18 Oct 86		**HE'S BACK (THE MAN BEHIND THE MASK)** *MCA MCA 1090*	**61**	2
9 Apr 88		**FREEDOM** *MCA MCA 1241*	**50**	3
29 Jul 89	●	**POISON** *Epic 655061 7*	**2**	11
7 Oct 89		**BED OF NAILS** *Epic ALICE 3*	**38**	5
2 Dec 89		**HOUSE OF FIRE** *Epic ALICE 4*	**65**	2
22 Jun 91		**HEY STOOPID** *Epic 6569837*	**21**	6
5 Oct 91		**LOVE'S A LOADED GUN** *Epic 6574387*	**38**	3
6 Jun 92		**FEED MY FRANKENSTEIN** *Epic 6580927*	**27**	3
28 May 94		**LOST IN AMERICA** *Epic 6603472*	**22**	3
23 Jul 94		**IT'S ME** *Epic 6605632*	**34**	2
5 Feb 72		**KILLER** *Warner Bros. K 56005*	**27**	18
22 Jul 72	●	**SCHOOL'S OUT** *Warner Bros. K 56007*	**4**	20
9 Sep 72		**LOVE IT TO DEATH** *Warner Bros. K 46177*	**28**	7
24 Mar 73	★	**BILLION DOLLAR BABIES** *Warner Bros. K 56013* ■ ▲	**1**	23
12 Jan 74		**MUSCLE OF LOVE** *Warner Bros. K 56018*	**34**	4
15 Mar 75		**WELCOME TO MY NIGHTMARE** *Anchor ANCL 2011*	**19**	8
24 Jul 76		**ALICE COOPER GOES TO HELL** *Warner Bros. K 56171*	**23**	7
28 May 77		**LACE AND WHISKY** *Warner Bros. K 56365*	**33**	3
23 Dec 78		**FROM THE INSIDE** *Warner Bros. K 56577*	**68**	3
17 May 80		**FLUSH THE FASHION** *Warner Bros. K 56805*	**56**	3
12 Sep 81		**SPECIAL FORCES** *Warner Bros. K 56927*	**96**	1
12 Nov 83		**DADA** *Warner Bros. 9239691*	**93**	1
1 Nov 86		**CONSTRICTOR** *MCA MCF 3341*	**41**	2
7 Nov 87		**RAISE YOUR FIST AND YELL** *MCA MCF 3392*	**48**	3
26 Aug 89	●	**TRASH** *Epic 465130 1*	**2**	12
13 Jul 91	●	**HEY STOOPID** *Epic 4684161*	**4**	7
18 Jun 94	●	**THE LAST TEMPTATION** *Epic 4765949*	**6**	6
24 Jun 00		**BRUTAL PLANET** *Eagle EAGCD 115*	**38**	1

10 Mar 01	**THE DEFINITIVE ALICE COOPER** *Rhino 8122735342*	**33** 5

For the first five hits, 'Alice Cooper' was the name of the entire group, not just of the lead vocalist Alice Cooper was US, male vocal / instrumental group for first five albums

Deborah COOPER – *See C & C MUSIC FACTORY*

Tommy COOPER
UK, male comedian / vocalist, d. 15 Apr 1984 (Singles: 3 weeks) pos/wks

29 Jun 61	**DON'T JUMP OFF THE ROOF DAD (re)** *Palette PG 9019*	**40** 3

COOPER TEMPLE CLAUSE
UK, male vocal / instrumental group (Singles: 10 weeks, Albums: 5 weeks) pos/wks

29 Sep 01	**LET'S KILL MUSIC** *Morning MORNING 9*	**41** 1
9 Feb 02	**FILM MAKER / BEEN TRAINING DOGS** *Morning MORNING 15*	**20** 3
18 May 02	**WHO NEEDS ENEMIES?** *Morning MORNING 23*	**22** 2
13 Sep 03	**PROMISES PROMISES** *Morning MORNING 30*	**19** 2
22 Nov 03	**BLIND PILOTS** *Morning MORNING 38*	**37** 2
23 Feb 02	**SEE THIS THROUGH AND LEAVE** *Morning MORNING 18*	**27** 3
20 Sep 03 ●	**KICK UP THE FIRE AND LET THE FLAMES BREAK LOOSE** *Morning MORNING36*	**5** 2

CO-ORDINATE – *See PESHAY*

Julian COPE
UK, male vocalist (Singles: 59 weeks, Albums: 35 weeks) pos/wks

19 Nov 83	**SUNSHINE PLAYROOM** *Mercury COPE 1*	**64** 1
31 Mar 84	**THE GREATNESS AND PERFECTION OF LOVE** *Mercury MER 155*	**52** 5
27 Sep 86	**WORLD SHUT YOUR MOUTH** *Island IS 290*	**19** 8
17 Jan 87	**TRAMPOLENE** *Island IS 305*	**31** 6
11 Apr 87	**EVE'S VOLCANO (COVERED IN SIN)** *Island IS 318*	**41** 5
24 Sep 88	**CHARLOTTE ANNE** *Island IS 380*	**35** 6
21 Jan 89	**5 O'CLOCK WORLD** *Island IS 399*	**42** 4
24 Jun 89	**CHINA DOLL** *Island IS 406*	**53** 2
9 Feb 91	**BEAUTIFUL LOVE** *Island IS 483*	**32** 6
20 Apr 91	**EAST EASY RIDER** *Island IS 492*	**51** 3
3 Aug 91	**HEAD** *Island IS 497*	**57** 2
8 Aug 92	**WORLD SHUT YOUR MOUTH (re-issue)** *Island IS 534*	**44** 3
17 Oct 92	**FEAR LOVES THIS PLACE** *Island IS 545*	**42** 2
12 Aug 95	**TRY TRY TRY** *Echo ECSCD 11*	**24** 3
27 Jul 96	**I COME FROM ANOTHER PLANET BABY** *Echo ECSCD 22*	**34** 2
5 Oct 96	**PLANETARY SIT-IN (EVERY GIRL HAS YOUR NAME)** *Echo ECSCD 25*	**34** 1
3 Mar 84	**WORLD SHUT YOUR MOUTH** *Mercury MERL 37*	**40** 4
24 Nov 84	**FRIED** *Mercury MERL 48*	**87** 1
14 Mar 87	**SAINT JULIAN** *Island ILPS 9861*	**11** 10
29 Oct 88	**MY NATION UNDERGROUND** *Island ILPS 9918*	**42** 2
16 Mar 91	**PEGGY SUICIDE** *Island ILPSD 9977*	**23** 7
15 Aug 92	**FLOORED GENIUS – THE BEST OF JULIAN COPE AND THE TEARDROP EXPLODES 1979-91** *Island CID 8000* [1]	**22** 3
31 Oct 92	**JEHOVAHKILL** *Island 5140522*	**20** 2
16 Jul 94	**AUTOGEDDON** *Echo ECHCD 1*	**16** 3
9 Sep 95	**JULIAN COPE PRESENTS 20 MOTHERS** *Echo ECHCD 5*	**20** 2
26 Oct 96	**INTERPRETER** *Echo ECHCD 12*	**39** 1

[1] Julian Cope and the Teardrop Explodes

See also TEARDROP EXPLODES

Imani COPPOLA
US, female vocalist / instrumentalist (Singles: 3 weeks) pos/wks

28 Feb 98	**LEGEND OF A COWGIRL** *Columbia 6656015*	**32** 3

See also BAHA MEN

The CORAL
UK, male vocal / instrumental group (Singles: 22 weeks, Albums: 43 weeks) pos/wks

27 Jul 02	**GOODBYE** *Deltasonic DLTCD 2005*	**21** 2
19 Oct 02	**DREAMING OF YOU** *Deltasonic DLTCD 2008*	**13** 5
15 Mar 03 ●	**DON'T THINK YOU'RE THE FIRST (re)** *Deltasonic DLTCDC 010*	**10** 4
26 Jul 03 ●	**PASS IT ON** *Deltasonic DLTCD 013*	**5** 7
18 Oct 03	**SECRET KISS** *Deltasonic DLTCD 015*	**25** 2
6 Dec 03	**BILL MCCAI** *Deltasonic DLTCD 017*	**23** 2
10 Aug 02 ●	**THE CORAL** *Deltasonic DLTCD 006*	**5** 34
9 Aug 03 ★	**MAGIC AND MEDICINE** *Deltasonic DLTCDPS014* ■	**1** 9

Harry H CORBETT – *See Wilfrid BRAMBELL and Harry H CORBETT*

Frank CORDELL and his ORCHESTRA
UK, orchestra, leader d. 6 Jul 1980 (Singles: 4 weeks) pos/wks

24 Aug 56	**SADIE'S SHAWL** *HMV POP 229*	**29** 2
16 Feb 61	**THE BLACK BEAR** *HMV POP 824*	**44** 2

Louise CORDET
UK, female vocalist – Louise Boisot (Singles: 13 weeks) pos/wks

5 Jul 62	**I'M JUST A BABY** *Decca F 11476*	**13** 13

CORDUROY
UK, male vocal / instrumental group (Albums: 1 week) pos/wks

8 Oct 94	**OUT OF HERE** *Acid Jazz JAZIDCD 107*	**73** 1

Chris CORNELL
US, male vocalist (Singles: 1 week, Albums: 1 week) pos/wks

23 Oct 99	**CAN'T CHANGE ME** *A&M 4971732*	**62** 1
2 Oct 99	**EUPHORIA MORNING** *A&M 4904222*	**31** 1

See also SOUNDGARDEN

Don CORNELL
US, male vocalist – Luigi Varlaro (Singles: 23 weeks) pos/wks

3 Sep 54 ★	**HOLD MY HAND** *Vogue Q 2013*	**1** 21
22 Apr 55	**STRANGER IN PARADISE** *Vogue Q 72073*	**19** 2

Lynn CORNELL
UK, female vocalist (Singles: 9 weeks) pos/wks

20 Oct 60	**NEVER ON SUNDAY** *Decca F 11277*	**30** 9

CORNERSHOP
UK, male vocal / instrumental duo (Singles: 18 weeks, Albums: 18 weeks) pos/wks

30 Aug 97	**BRIMFUL OF ASHA** *Wiiija WIJ 75CD*	**60** 1
28 Feb 98 ★	**BRIMFUL OF ASHA (re-mix)** *Wiiija WIJ 81CD* ■	**1** 12
16 May 98	**SLEEP ON THE LEFT SIDE** *Wiija WIJ 80CD*	**23** 3
16 Mar 02	**LESSONS LEARNED FROM ROCKY I TO ROCKY III** *Wiiija WIJ 129CD*	**37** 2
20 Sep 97	**WHEN I WAS BORN FOR THE 7TH TIME** *Wiiija WIJCD 1065*	**17** 15
13 Apr 02	**HANDCREAM FOR A GENERATION** *Wiiija WIJCD 1115*	**30** 3

Charlotte CORNWELL – *See Julie COVINGTON, Rula LENSKA, Charlotte CORNWELL and Sue JONES-DAVIES*

Hugh CORNWELL
UK, male vocalist / instrumentalist – guitar (Singles: 3 weeks, Albums: 1 week) pos/wks

24 Jan 87	**FACTS + FIGURES** *Virgin VS 922*	**61** 2
7 May 88	**ANOTHER KIND OF LOVE** *Virgin VS 945*	**71** 1
18 Jun 88	**WOLF** *Virgin V 2420*	**98** 1

See also STRANGLERS

CORO DE MUNJES DEL MONASTERIO BENEDICTINO DE SANTO DOMINGO DE SILOS
Spain, monastic choir (Albums: 28 weeks) pos/wks

5 Mar 94 ●	**CANTO GREGORIANO** *EMI Classics CMS 5652172*	**7** 25
17 Dec 94	**CANTO NOEL** *EMI Classics CDC 5552172*	**53** 3

See also MONKS CHORUS SILOS

CO-RO featuring TARLISA
Germany, male / female vocal / production group (Singles: 1 week) pos/wks

12 Dec 92	**BECAUSE THE NIGHT** *ZYX ZYX 68227*	**61** 1

CORONA *Brazil, male producer and female vocalist – Francesco Bontempi and Olga de Souza (Singles: 44 weeks, Albums: 7 weeks)* pos/wks

10 Sep 94 ● **THE RHYTHM OF THE NIGHT (re)** *WEA YZ 837CD1* 2 18
8 Apr 95 ● **BABY BABY** *Eternal YZ 919CD* 5 8
22 Jul 95 ● **TRY ME OUT** *Eternal YZ 955CD* 6 10
23 Dec 95 **I DON'T WANNA BE A STAR** *Eternal WEA 029CD* 22 6
22 Feb 97 **MEGAMIX** *Eternal WEA 092CD* 36 2
20 May 95 **THE RHYTHM OF THE NIGHT** *Eternal 0630103312* 18 7

CORONATION STREET CAST featuring Bill WADDINGTON
UK, male / female actors / vocal group (Singles: 3 weeks) pos/wks

16 Dec 95 **ALWAYS LOOK ON THE BRIGHT SIDE OF LIFE** *EMI Premier CDEMS 411* 35 3

The listed flip side of 'Always Look on the Bright Side of Life' was 'Something Stupid' by Amanda Barrie and Johnny Briggs

CORONETS *UK, male / female vocal group (Singles: 7 weeks)* pos/wks

26 Aug 55 **THAT'S HOW A LOVE SONG WAS BORN** *Columbia DB 3640* [1] 14 6
25 Nov 55 **TWENTY TINY FINGERS** *Columbia DB 3671* 20 1

[1] Ray Burns with the Coronets

CORRIES *UK, male vocal / instrumental duo – Ronnie Browne and Roy Williamson (Albums: 5 weeks)* pos/wks

9 May 70 **SCOTTISH LOVE SONGS** *Fontana 6309004* 46 4
16 Sep 72 **SOUND OF PIBROCH** *Columbia SCX 6511* 39 1

Briana CORRIGAN *UK, female vocalist (Singles: 2 weeks)* pos/wks

11 May 96 **LOVE ME NOW** *East West EW 041CD1* 48 2

See also BEAUTIFUL SOUTH

CORROSION OF CONFORMITY
US, male vocal / instrumental group (Albums: 1 week) pos/wks

14 Sep 96 **WISEBLOOD** *Columbia 4843282* 43 1

CORRS (97 Top 500) *Internationally successful Irish sisters and brother group: Andrea, Caroline, Sharon and Jim Corr. The quartet, which has sold more than five million albums in the UK, was voted Best International Group at 1999 Brits. 'Talk on Corners' was the top UK album in 1998 (Singles: 92 weeks, Albums: 347 weeks)* pos/wks

17 Feb 96 **RUNAWAY (re)** *Atlantic A 5727CD* 49 3
1 Feb 97 **LOVE TO LOVE YOU / RUNAWAY (re-issue)** *Atlantic A 5621CD* 62 1
25 Oct 97 **ONLY WHEN I SLEEP** *Atlantic AT 0015CD* 58 1
20 Dec 97 **I NEVER LOVED YOU ANYWAY** *Atlantic AT 0018CD* 43 2
28 Mar 98 **WHAT CAN I DO** *Atlantic AT 0029CD* 53 1
16 May 98 ● **DREAMS** *Atlantic AT 0032CD* 6 10
29 Aug 98 ● **WHAT CAN I DO (re-mix)** *Atlantic AT 0044CD* 3 11
28 Nov 98 ● **SO YOUNG** *Atlantic AT 0057CD1* 6 13
27 Feb 99 ● **RUNAWAY (re-mix)** *Atlantic AT 0062CD* 2 11
12 Jun 99 **I KNOW MY LOVE** *RCA Victor 74321670622* [1] 37 3
11 Dec 99 **RADIO** *Atlantic AT 0079CD* 18 9
15 Jul 00 ★ **BREATHLESS** *Atlantic AT 0084CD* ■ 1 13
11 Nov 00 **IRRESISTIBLE (re)** *Atlantic AT 0089CD* 20 7
28 Apr 01 **GIVE ME A REASON** *Atlantic AT 0097CD* 27 2
10 Nov 01 **WOULD YOU BE HAPPIER?** *Atlantic AT 0115CD* 14 5
2 Mar 96 ● **FORGIVEN NOT FORGOTTEN** *Atlantic 7567926122* 2 113
1 Nov 97 ★ **TALK ON CORNERS** *Atlantic 7567830512* 1 142
27 Nov 99 ● **UNPLUGGED** *Atlantic 7567809862* 7 26
29 Jul 00 ★ **IN BLUE** *Atlantic 7567833522* ■ 1 45
17 Nov 01 ● **THE BEST OF THE CORRS** *Atlantic 7567930732* 6 21

[1] Chieftains featuring The Corrs

CORRUPTED CRU featuring MC NEAT *UK, male rap / production duo – Scott Garcia and Michael Wood – and male rapper (Singles: 1 week)* pos/wks

2 Mar 02 **G.A.R.A.G.E.** *Red Rose CDRROSE 011* 59 1

See also Scott GARCIA featuring MC STYLES

Ferry CORSTEN *Holland, male producer (Singles: 3 weeks)* pos/wks

8 Jun 02 **PUNK** *Positiva CDTIV 173* 29 3

See also MOONMAN; SYSTEM F; VERACOCHA; GOURYELLA; STARPARTY; ALBION

CORTINA *UK, male producer – Ben Keen (Singles: 3 weeks)* pos/wks

24 Mar 01 **MUSIC IS MOVING** *Nukleuz NUKC 0159* 42 2
26 Jan 02 **ERECTION (TAKE IT TO THE TOP)** *Nukleuz NUKC 0352* [1] 48 1

[1] Cortina featuring BK and Madam Friction

See also BK

Vladimir COSMA *Hungary, orchestra (Singles: 1 week)* pos/wks

14 Jul 79 **DAVID'S SONG (MAIN THEME FROM 'KIDNAPPED')** *Decca FR 13841* 64 1

COSMIC BABY
Germany, male producer (Singles: 1 week, Albums: 1 week) pos/wks

26 Feb 94 **LOOPS OF INFINITY** *Logic 74321191432* 70 1
23 Apr 94 **THINKING ABOUT MYSELF** *Logic 74321196052* 60 1

COSMIC GATE *Germany, male production trio (Singles: 12 weeks)* pos/wks

4 Aug 01 ● **FIRE WIRE** *Data DATA 24 CDS* 9 7
11 May 02 **EXPLORATION OF SPACE** *Data DATA 30 CDS* 29 3
25 Jan 03 **THE WAVE / RAGING** *Nebula NEBCD 036* 48 2

COSMIC ROUGH RIDERS
UK, male vocal / instrumental group (Singles: 4 weeks) pos/wks

4 Aug 01 **REVOLUTION (IN THE SUMMERTIME)** *Poptones MC 5047SCD* 35 1
29 Sep 01 **THE PAIN INSIDE** *Poptones MC 5052SCD* 36 1
5 Jul 03 **BECAUSE YOU** *Measured MRCOSMIC 2SC* 34 1
20 Sep 03 **JUSTIFY THE RAIN** *Measured MRCOSMIC 3SCD* 39 1

COSMOS *UK, male producer / instrumentalist – Tom Middleton (Singles: 3 weeks)* pos/wks

18 Sep 99 **SUMMER IN SPACE** *Island Blue PFACD 3* 49 1
5 Oct 02 **TAKE ME WITH YOU** *Polydor 659952* 32 2

See also GLOBAL COMMUNICATION

Don COSTA
US, orchestra, leader d. 19 Jan 1983 (Singles: 10 weeks) pos/wks

13 Oct 60 **NEVER ON SUNDAY (re)** *London HLT 9195* 27 10

Nikka COSTA
US, female vocalist (Singles: 1 week) pos/wks

11 Aug 01 **LIKE A FEATHER** *Virgin VUSCD 199* 53 1

Elvis COSTELLO (112 Top 500) *ASCAP (US songwriter's body) Founders Award winner in 2003, b. Declan McManus, 25 Aug 1955, Liverpool, UK. He emerged during the punk explosion of 1976, but was soon accepted as a mainstream artist. Has clocked up 13 US Top 40 albums (Singles: 180 weeks, Albums: 224 weeks)* pos/wks

5 Nov 77 **WATCHING THE DETECTIVES** *Stiff BUY 20* 15 11
11 Mar 78 **(I DON'T WANT TO GO TO) CHELSEA** *Radar ADA 3* [1] 16 10
13 May 78 **PUMP IT UP** *Radar ADA 10* [1] 24 10
28 Oct 78 **RADIO RADIO** *Radar ADA 24* [1] 29 7
10 Feb 79 ● **OLIVER'S ARMY** *Radar ADA 31* [1] 2 12
12 May 79 **ACCIDENTS WILL HAPPEN** *Radar ADA 35* [1] 28 8
16 Feb 80 ● **I CAN'T STAND UP FOR FALLING DOWN** *F. Beat XX 1* [1] 4 8
12 Apr 80 **HIGH FIDELITY** *F. Beat XX 3* 30 5
7 Jun 80 **NEW AMSTERDAM** *F. Beat XX 5* 36 6
20 Dec 80 **CLUBLAND** *F. Beat XX 12* [1] 60 4
3 Oct 81 ● **A GOOD YEAR FOR THE ROSES** *F. Beat XX 17* 6 11
12 Dec 81 **SWEET DREAMS** *F. Beat XX 19* 42 8
10 Apr 82 **I'M YOUR TOY** *F. Beat XX 21* [2] 51 3
19 Jun 82 **YOU LITTLE FOOL** *F. Beat XX 26* 52 3
31 Jul 82 **MAN OUT OF TIME** *F. Beat XX 28* 58 2
25 Sep 82 **FROM HEAD TO TOE** *F. Beat XX 30* 43 4

Date		Title / Label	pos	wks
11 Dec 82		**PARTY PARTY** *A&M AMS 8267* [3]	48	6
11 Jun 83		**PILLS AND SOAP** *Imp IMP 001* [4]	16	4
9 Jul 83		**EVERYDAY I WRITE THE BOOK** *F. Beat XX 32*	28	8
17 Sep 83		**LET THEM ALL TALK** *F. Beat XX 33*	59	2
28 Apr 84		**PEACE IN OUR TIME** *Imposter TRUCE 1* [4]	48	3
16 Jun 84		**I WANNA BE LOVED / TURNING THE TOWN RED** *F. Beat XX 35*	25	6
25 Aug 84		**THE ONLY FLAME IN TOWN** *F. Beat XX 37*	71	2
4 May 85		**GREEN SHIRT (re)** *F. Beat ZB 40085*	68	2
1 Feb 86		**DON'T LET ME BE MISUNDERSTOOD** *F. Beat ZB 40555* [5]	33	4
30 Aug 86		**TOKYO STORM WARNING** *Imp IMP 007*	73	1
4 Mar 89		**VERONICA** *Warner Bros. W 7558*	31	6
20 May 89		**BABY PLAYS AROUND (EP)** *Warner Bros. W 2949*	65	1
4 May 91		**THE OTHER SIDE OF SUMMER** *Warner Bros. W 0025*	43	4
5 Mar 94		**SULKY GIRL** *Warner Bros. W 0234CD* [1]	22	3
30 Apr 94		**13 STEPS LEAD DOWN** *Warner Bros. W 0245CD* [1]	59	1
26 Nov 94		**LONDON'S BRILLIANT PARADE** *Warner Bros. W 0270CD1* [1]	48	2
11 May 96		**IT'S TIME** *Warner Bros. W 0348CD* [1]	58	1
1 May 99		**TOLEDO** *Mercury 8709652* [6]	72	1
31 Jul 99		**SHE (re)** *Mercury MERCD 521*	19	10
20 Apr 02		**TEAR OFF YOUR OWN HEAD (IT'S A DOLL REVOLUTION)** *Mercury 5828872*	58	1
6 Aug 77		**MY AIM IS TRUE** *Stiff SEEZ 3*	14	12
1 Apr 78	●	**THIS YEAR'S MODEL** *Radar RAD 3* [1]	4	14
20 Jan 79	●	**ARMED FORCES** *Radar RAD 14*	2	28
23 Feb 80	●	**GET HAPPY!!** *F-Beat XXLP 1*	2	14
31 Jan 81	●	**TRUST** *F-Beat XXLP 11* [1]	9	7
31 Oct 81	●	**ALMOST BLUE** *F-Beat XXLP 13*	7	18
10 Jul 82	●	**IMPERIAL BEDROOM** *F-Beat XXLP 17* [1]	6	12
6 Aug 83	●	**PUNCH THE CLOCK** *F-Beat XXLP 19* [1]	3	13
7 Jul 84	●	**GOODBYE CRUEL WORLD** *F-Beat ZL 70317* [1]	10	10
20 Apr 85	●	**THE BEST OF ELVIS COSTELLO – THE MAN** *Telstar STAR 2247* [1]	8	25
1 Mar 86		**KING OF AMERICA** *F-Beat ZL 70496* [2]	11	9
27 Sep 86		**BLOOD AND CHOCOLATE** *Imp XFIEND 80*	16	5
18 Feb 89	●	**SPIKE** *Warner Bros. WX 238*	5	16
28 Oct 89		**GIRLS GIRLS GIRLS** *Demon DFIEND 160* [1]	67	1
25 May 91	●	**MIGHTY LIKE A ROSE** *Warner Bros. WX 419*	5	6
30 Jan 93		**THE JULIET LETTERS** *Warner Bros. 9362451802* [3]	18	3
19 Mar 94	●	**BRUTAL YOUTH** *Warner Bros. 9362455352* [1]	2	5
12 Nov 94		**THE VERY BEST OF ELVIS COSTELLO AND THE ATTRACTIONS** *Demon DPAM 13* [1]	57	2
27 May 95		**KOJAK VARIETY** *Warner Bros. 9362459032*	21	2
12 Aug 95		**KING OF AMERICA (re-issue)** *Demon DPAM 11*	71	1
25 May 96		**ALL THIS USELESS BEAUTY** *Warner Bros. 9362461982*	28	3
10 Oct 98		**PAINTED FROM MEMORY** *Mercury 5380022* [4]	32	2
14 Aug 99	●	**THE VERY BEST OF ELVIS COSTELLO** *Universal Music TV 5464902*	4	10
31 Mar 01		**FOR THE STARS** *Deutsche Grammophon 4695302* [5]	67	1
27 Apr 02		**WHEN I WAS CRUEL** *Mercury 5868292*	17	4
27 Sep 03		**NORTH** *Deutsche Grammophon 9809165*	44	1

[1] Elvis Costello and the Attractions [2] Elvis Costello and the Attractions with the Royal Philharmonic Orchestra [3] Elvis Costello and the Attractions with the Royal Horn Guards [4] Imposter [5] The Costello Show featuring the Confederates [6] Elvis Costello / Burt Bacharach [1] Elvis Costello and the Attractions [2] Costello Show [3] Elvis Costello and the Brodsky Quartet [4] Elvis Costello with Burt Bacharach [5] Anne von Otter meets Elvis Costello

Tracks on Baby Plays Around (EP): Baby Plays Around / Poisoned Rose / Almost Blue / My Funny Valentine

See also BRODSKY QUARTET

COTTAGERS – *See Tony REES and The COTTAGERS*

Billy COTTON and His BAND *UK, male bandleader / vocalist, d. 25 Mar 1969, with band and chorus (Singles: 25 weeks)*

Date		Title / Label	pos	wks
1 May 53	●	**IN A GOLDEN COACH (THERE'S A HEART OF GOLD)** *Decca F 10058* [1]	3	10
18 Dec 53		**I SAW MOMMY KISSING SANTA CLAUS** *Decca F 10206* [2]	11	3
30 Apr 54	●	**FRIENDS AND NEIGHBOURS (re)** *Decca F 10299* [3]	3	12

[1] Billy Cotton and His Band, vocals by Doreen Stephens [2] Billy Cotton and His Band, vocals by the Mill Girls and the Bandits [3] Billy Cotton and His Band, vocals by the Bandits

Mike COTTON'S JAZZMEN *UK, male instrumental group – Mike Cotton – trumpet (Singles: 4 weeks)*

Date		Title / Label	pos	wks
20 Jun 63		**SWING THAT HAMMER** *Columbia DB 7029*	36	4

John COUGAR – *See John Cougar MELLENCAMP*

COUGARS *UK, male instrumental group (Singles: 8 weeks)*

Date		Title / Label	pos	wks
28 Feb 63		**SATURDAY NITE AT THE DUCK-POND** *Parlophone R 4989*	33	8

Phil COULTER *Ireland, male orchestra leader / instrumentalist – piano (Albums: 15 weeks)*

Date		Title / Label	pos	wks
13 Oct 84		**SEA OF TRANQUILITY** *K-Tel Ireland KLP 185*	46	14
18 May 85		**PHIL COULTER'S IRELAND** *K-Tel ONE 1296*	86	1

COUNCIL COLLECTIVE *UK / US, male / female vocal / instrumental group (Singles: 6 weeks)*

Date		Title / Label	pos	wks
22 Dec 84		**SOUL DEEP (PART 1)** *Polydor MINE 1*	24	6

COUNT INDIGO *UK, male vocalist (Singles: 1 week)*

Date		Title / Label	pos	wks
9 Mar 96		**MY UNKNOWN LOVE** *Cowboy RODEO 952CD*	59	1

COUNTING CROWS *US, male vocal / instrumental group (Singles: 23 weeks, Albums: 60 weeks)*

Date		Title / Label	pos	wks
30 Apr 94		**MR JONES** *Geffen GFSTD 69*	28	2
9 Jul 94		**ROUND HERE** *Geffen GFSTD 74*	70	1
15 Oct 94		**RAIN KING** *Geffen GFSTD 82*	49	3
19 Oct 96		**ANGELS OF THE SILENCES** *Geffen GFSTD 22182*	41	1
14 Dec 96		**A LONG DECEMBER (re)** *Geffen GFSTD 22190*	62	2
31 May 97		**DAYLIGHT FADING** *Geffen GFSTD 22247*	54	1
30 Oct 99		**HANGINAROUND** *Geffen 4971842*	46	1
29 Jun 02		**AMERICAN GIRLS** *Geffen 4977402*	33	2
15 Feb 03		**BIG YELLOW TAXI** *Geffen 4978302* [1]	16	9
21 Jun 03		**IF I COULD GIVE ALL MY LOVE** *Geffen GED 9806830*	50	1
12 Mar 94		**AUGUST AND EVERYTHING AFTER** *Geffen GED 24528*	16	38
26 Oct 96	●	**RECOVERING THE SATELLITES** *Geffen GED 24975* ▲	4	4
25 Jul 98		**ACROSS A WIRE – LIVE IN NEW YORK** *Geffen GED 25226*	27	4
13 Nov 99		**THIS DESERT LIFE** *Geffen 4904152*	19	3
20 Jul 02	●	**HARD CANDY** *Geffen 4933662*	9	11

[1] Counting Crows featuring Vanessa Carlton

COUNTRYMEN *UK, male vocal group (Singles: 2 weeks)*

Date		Title / Label	pos	wks
3 May 62		**I KNOW WHERE I'M GOING** *Piccadilly 7N 35029*	45	2

COURSE *Holland, male / female vocal / DJ / production group (Singles: 15 weeks)*

Date		Title / Label	pos	wks
19 Apr 97	●	**READY OR NOT** *The Brothers Organisation CDBRUV 2*	5	7
5 Jul 97	●	**AIN'T NOBODY** *The Brothers Organisation CDBRUV 3*	8	6
20 Dec 97		**BEST LOVE** *The Brothers Organisation CDBRUV 6*	51	2

Michael COURTNEY – *See LINCOLN CITY FC featuring Michael COURTNEY*

Tina COUSINS *UK, female vocalist (Singles: 42 weeks, Albums: 1 week)*

Date		Title / Label	pos	wks
15 Aug 98	●	**MYSTERIOUS TIMES** *Multiply CDMULTY 40* [1]	2	12
21 Nov 98		**PRAY** *Jive 0519162*	20	3
27 Mar 99		**KILLIN' TIME** *Jive / Eastern Bloc 0519232*	15	4
10 Apr 99	●	**THANK ABBA FOR THE MUSIC** *ABCD 1 Epic* [2]	4	13
10 Jul 99		**FOREVER** *Jive 0519332*	45	2
9 Oct 99		**ANGEL** *Ebul / Jive 0519432*	46	1

22 Apr 00 ● **JUST AROUND THE HILL** *Multiply CDMULTY 62* [1] 8 7
24 Jul 99 **KILLING TIME** *Jive/Eastern Bloc 519342* 50 1

[1] Sash! featuring Tina Cousins [2] Starring Steps, Tina Cousins, Cleopatra, B*Witched, Billie

Don COVAY *US, male vocalist (Singles: 6 weeks)* pos/wks

7 Sep 74 **IT'S BETTER TO HAVE (AND DON'T NEED)** *Mercury 6052 634* 29 6

Vincent COVELLO – *See BT*

COVENTRY CITY CUP FINAL SQUAD
UK, male football team vocalists (Singles: 2 weeks) pos/wks

23 May 87 **GO FOR IT!** *Sky Blue SKB 1* 61 2

COVER GIRLS *US, female vocal group (Singles: 4 weeks)* pos/wks

1 Aug 92 **WISHING ON A STAR** *Epic 6581437* 38 4

David COVERDALE
UK, male vocalist (Singles: 1 week, Albums: 2 weeks) pos/wks

7 Jun 97 **TOO MANY TEARS** *EMI CDEM 471* [1] 46 1
27 Feb 82 **NORTHWINDS** *Purple TTS 3513*....................78 1
7 Oct 00 **INTO THE LIGHT** *EMI 5281242* 75 1
21 Jun 97 **RESTLESS HEART** *EMI CDEMD 1104* [1] 34 2

[1] David Coverdale and Whitesnake [1] David Coverdale and Whitesnake

See also COVERDALE PAGE; DEEP PURPLE; WHITESNAKE

COVERDALE PAGE *UK, male vocal / instrumental duo – David Coverdale and Jimmy Page (Singles: 3 weeks, Albums: 8 weeks)* pos/wks

3 Jul 93 **TAKE ME FOR A LITTLE WHILE** *EMI CDEM 270* 29 2
23 Oct 93 **TAKE A LOOK AT YOURSELF** *EMI CDEM 279* 43 1
27 Mar 93 ● **COVERDALE PAGE** *EMI CDEMD 1041* 4 8

See also David COVERDALE; Jimmy PAGE

Julie COVINGTON *UK, female actor / vocalist (Singles: 29 weeks)* pos/wks

25 Dec 76 ★ **DON'T CRY FOR ME ARGENTINA (re)** *MCA 260* 1 18
3 Dec 77 **ONLY WOMEN BLEED** *Virgin VS 196* 12 11

See also Julie COVINGTON, Rula LENSKA, Charlotte CORNWELL and Sue JONES-DAVIES

Julie COVINGTON, Rula LENSKA, Charlotte CORNWELL and Sue JONES-DAVIES
UK, female actors / vocal group (Singles: 6 weeks) pos/wks

21 May 77 ● **OK?** *Polydor 2001 714* 10 6

See also Julie COVINGTON

Warren COVINGTON – *See Tommy DORSEY ORCHESTRA starring Warren COVINGTON*

COWBOY JUNKIES
Canada, male / female vocal / instrumental group (Albums: 7 weeks) pos/wks

24 Mar 90 **THE CAUTION HORSES** *RCA PL 90450* 33 4
15 Feb 92 **BLACK EYED MAN** *RCA PD 90620* 21 3

Patrick COWLEY – *See SYLVESTER*

Carl COX *UK, male producer (Singles: 19 weeks, Albums: 4 weeks)* pos/wks

28 Sep 91 **I WANT YOU (FOREVER)** *Perfecto PB 44885* [1] 23 7
8 Aug 92 **DOES IT FEEL GOOD TO YOU** *Perfecto PB 74321102877* [1] 35 3
6 Nov 93 **THE PLANET OF LOVE** *Perfecto 74321161772*....................44 2
9 Mar 96 **TWO PAINTINGS AND A DRUM (EP)** *Edel 0090715COX* 24 2
8 Jun 96 **SENSUAL SOPHIS-TI-CAT / THE PLAYER**
Ultimatum 0090875COX 25 2
12 Dec 98 **THE LATIN THEME** *Edel 0091685 COX* 52 1
22 May 99 **PHUTURE 2000** *Worldwide Ultimatum / Edel 0091715 COX* 40 2
15 Jun 96 **AT THE END OF THE CLICHÉ** *Ultimatum 0090752 COX*....................23 4

[1] DJ Carl Cox

Tracks on Two Paintings and a Drum (EP): Phoebus Apollo / Yum Yum / Siberian Snow Storm

Deborah COX *Canada, female vocalist (Singles: 8 weeks)* pos/wks

11 Nov 95 **SENTIMENTAL** *Arista 74321324962* 34 3
24 Feb 96 **WHO DO U LOVE** *Arista 74321337942* 31 3
31 Jul 99 **IT'S OVER NOW** *Arista 74321686942* 49 1
9 Oct 99 **NOBODY'S SUPPOSED TO BE HERE** *Arista 74321702102* 55 1

Michael COX *UK, male vocalist (Singles: 15 weeks)* pos/wks

9 Jun 60 ● **ANGELA JONES** *Triumph RGM 1011* 7 13
20 Oct 60 **ALONG CAME CAROLINE** *HMV POP 789* 41 2

Peter COX *UK, male vocalist (Singles: 6 weeks, Albums: 1 week)* pos/wks

2 Aug 97 **AIN'T GONNA CRY AGAIN** *Chrysalis CDCHS 5056* 37 2
15 Nov 97 **IF YOU WALK AWAY** *Chrysalis CDCHSS 5069* 24 2
20 Jun 98 **WHAT A FOOL BELIEVES** *Chrysalis CDCHS 5089* 39 2
29 Nov 97 **PETER COX** *Chrysalis CDCHR 6130*....................64 1

See also GO WEST

Graham COXON
UK, male vocalist / instrumentalist – guitar (Albums: 2 weeks) pos/wks

22 Aug 98 **THE SKY IS TOO HIGH** *Transcopic TRAN 005CD* 31 2

See also BLUR

CRACKER *US, male vocal / instrumental group (Singles: 9 weeks, Albums: 2 weeks)* pos/wks

28 May 94 **LOW (re)** *Virgin America VUSDG 80* 43 6
23 Jul 94 **GET OFF THIS** *Virgin America VUSCD 83* 41 3
25 Jun 94 **KEROSENE HAT** *Virgin America CDVUS 67*....................44 2

Sarah CRACKNELL
UK, female vocalist (Singles: 1 week) pos/wks

14 Sep 96 **ANYMORE** *Gut CDGUT 3* 39 1

See also SAINT ETIENNE

CRACKOUT
UK, male vocal / instrumental group (Singles: 2 weeks) pos/wks

22 Jun 02 **I AM THE ONE** *Hut / Virgin HUTCD 156* 72 1
9 Aug 03 **OUT OF OUR MINDS** *Hut / Virgin HUTCD 170* 63 1

CRADLE OF FILTH *UK, male vocal / instrumental group (Singles: 2 weeks, Albums: 4 weeks)* pos/wks

15 Mar 03 **BABALON A.D. (SO GLAD FOR THE MADNESS)**
Epic 6735549 ....35 2
16 May 98 **CRUELTY AND THE BEAST** *Music for Nations CDMFN 242* 48 1
11 Nov 00 **MIDIAN** *Music for Nations CDMFN 666*....................63 1
30 Jun 01 **BITTER SUITES TO SUCCUBI** *Snapper Music COF 001CD*..........63 1
22 Mar 03 **DAMNATION AND A DAY** *Epic 5109632*....................44 1

Steve CRADOCK – *See OCEAN COLOUR SCENE; BUFFALO TOM*

CRAIG
UK, male vocalist – Craig Phillips (Singles: 6 weeks) pos/wks

23 Dec 00 **AT THIS TIME OF YEAR (re)** *WEA WEA 321CD* 14 6

Robbie CRAIG – *See ARTFUL DODGER*

Floyd CRAMER
US, male instrumentalist – piano d. 31 Dec 1997 (Singles: 24 weeks) pos/wks

13 Apr 61 ★ **ON THE REBOUND** *RCA 1231* 1 14
20 Jul 61 **SAN ANTONIO ROSE** *RCA 1241* 36 8
23 Aug 62 **HOT PEPPER** *RCA 1301* 46 2

CRAMPS *US, male / female vocal / instrumental group (Singles: 4 weeks, Albums: 13 weeks)* pos/wks

9 Nov 85 **CAN YOUR PUSSY DO THE DOG?** *Big Beat NS 110* 68 1
10 Feb 90 **BIKINI GIRLS WITH MACHINE GUNS** *Enigma ENV 17* 35 3
25 Jun 83 **OFF THE BONE** *Illegal ILP 012*....................44 4

26 Nov 83	**SMELL OF FEMALE** *Big Beat NED 6*	**74** 2
1 Mar 86	**A DATE WITH ELVIS** *Big Beat WIKA 46*	**34** 6
24 Feb 90	**STAY SICK!** *Enigma ENVLP 1001*	**62** 1

CRANBERRIES (258 Top 500)

Irish rock quartet with a feverish international following, formed Co Limerick, 1991, fronted by Dolores O'Riordan (v). The group, which has sold more than 35 million albums worldwide, spent longer on the UK chart in 1995 (96 weeks) than any other act (Singles: 50 weeks, Albums: 193 weeks) pos/wks

27 Feb 93	**LINGER** *Island CID 556*	**74** 1
12 Feb 94	**LINGER (re-issue)** *Island CID 559*	**14** 11
7 May 94	**DREAMS** *Island CIDX 594*	**27** 5
1 Oct 94	**ZOMBIE** *Island CID 600*	**14** 6
3 Dec 94	**ODE TO MY FAMILY** *Island CIDX 601*	**26** 6
11 Mar 95	**I CAN'T BE WITH YOU** *Island CID 605*	**23** 5
12 Aug 95	**RIDICULOUS THOUGHTS** *Island CID 616*	**20** 3
20 Apr 96	**SALVATION** *Island CID 633*	**13** 5
13 Jul 96	**FREE TO DECIDE** *Island CID 637*	**33** 3
17 Apr 99	**PROMISES** *Island US / Mercury 5725912*	**13** 4
17 Jul 99	**ANIMAL INSTINCT** *Island US / Mercury 5621972*	**54** 1
13 Mar 93 ★	**EVERYBODY ELSE IS DOING IT SO WHY CAN'T WE?** *Island CID 8003*	**1** 86
15 Oct 94 ●	**NO NEED TO ARGUE** *Island CID 8029*	**2** 78
11 May 96 ●	**TO THE FAITHFUL DEPARTED** *Island CID 8048*	**2** 19
1 May 99 ●	**BURY THE HATCHET** *Island US/Mercury 5246442*	**7** 5
3 Nov 01	**WAKE UP AND SMELL THE COFFEE** *MCA 1127062*	**61** 1
28 Sep 02	**STARS – THE BEST OF 1992-2002** *Universal TV 0633862*	**20** 4

Les CRANE

US, male vocalist (Singles: 14 weeks) pos/wks

19 Feb 72 ●	**DESIDERATA** *Warner Bros. K 16119*	**7** 14

Whitfield CRANE – *See ICE-T; MOTÖRHEAD*

CRANES *UK, male / female vocal / instrumental group (Singles: 2 weeks, Albums: 2 weeks)* pos/wks

25 Sep 93	**JEWEL** *Dedicated CRANE 007CD*	**29** 1
3 Sep 94	**SHINING ROAD** *Dedicated CRANE 008CD1*	**57** 1
28 Sep 91	**WINGS OF JOY** *Dedicated DEDLP 003*	**52** 1
8 May 93	**FOREVER** *Dedicated DEDCD 009*	**40** 1

CRASH TEST DUMMIES

Canada, male / female vocal / instrumental group (Singles: 20 weeks, Albums: 23 weeks) pos/wks

23 Apr 94 ●	**MMM MMM MMM MMM** *RCA 74321201512*	**2** 11
16 Jul 94	**AFTERNOONS & COFFEESPOONS** *RCA 74321219622*	**23** 5
15 Apr 95	**THE BALLAD OF PETER PUMPKINHEAD** *RCA 74321276772* [1]	**30** 4
14 May 94 ●	**GOD SHUFFLED HIS FEET** *RCA 74321201522*	**2** 23

[1] Crash Test Dummies featuring Ellen Reid

CRASS *UK, male vocal / instrumental group (Albums: 2 weeks)* pos/wks

28 Aug 82	**CHRIST THE ALBUM** *Crass BOLLOX 2U2*	**26** 2

Beverley CRAVEN

UK, female vocalist / instrumentalist – keyboards (Singles: 33 weeks, Albums: 67 weeks) pos/wks

20 Apr 91 ●	**PROMISE ME** *Epic 6559437*	**3** 13
20 Jul 91	**HOLDING ON** *Epic 6565507*	**32** 7
5 Oct 91	**WOMAN TO WOMAN** *Epic 6574647*	**40** 5
7 Dec 91	**MEMORIES** *Epic 6576617*	**68** 2
25 Sep 93	**LOVE SCENES** *Epic 6595952*	**34** 4
20 Nov 93	**MOLLIE'S SONG** *Epic 6598132*	**61** 2
2 Mar 91 ●	**BEVERLEY CRAVEN** *Columbia 4670531*	**3** 52
9 Oct 93 ●	**LOVE SCENES** *Epic 4745172*	**4** 13
12 Jun 99	**MIXED EMOTIONS** *Epic 4941502*	**46** 2

Billy CRAWFORD *Philippines, male vocalist (Singles: 5 weeks)* pos/wks

10 Oct 98	**URGENTLY IN LOVE** *V2 VVR 5003063*	**48** 2
3 May 03	**YOU DIDN'T EXPECT THAT** *V2 VVR 5022083*	**35** 2
30 Aug 03	**TRACKIN'** *V2 VVR 5023103*	**32** 2

Jimmy CRAWFORD

UK, male vocalist – Ronald Lindsey (Singles: 11 weeks) pos/wks

8 Jun 61	**LOVE OR MONEY** *Columbia DB 4633*	**49** 1
16 Nov 61	**I LOVE HOW YOU LOVE ME** *Columbia DB 4717*	**18** 10

Michael CRAWFORD

UK, male actor / vocalist – Michael Dumble-Smith (Singles: 14 weeks, Albums: 73 weeks) pos/wks

10 Jan 87 ●	**THE MUSIC OF THE NIGHT** *Polydor POSP 803* [1]	**7** 11
15 Jan 94	**THE MUSIC OF THE NIGHT** *Columbia 6597382* [2]	**54** 3
28 Nov 87	**SONGS FROM THE STAGE AND SCREEN** *Telstar STAR 2308* [1]	**12** 13
2 Dec 89	**WITH LOVE** *Telstar STAR 2340*	**31** 7
9 Nov 91 ●	**MICHAEL CRAWFORD PERFORMS ANDREW LLOYD WEBBER** *Telstar STAR 2544*	**3** 36
13 Nov 93	**A TOUCH OF MUSIC IN THE NIGHT** *Telstar TCD 2676*	**12** 11
19 Nov 94	**THE LOVE SONGS ALBUM** *Telstar TCD 2748*	**64** 3
21 Nov 98	**ON EAGLE'S WINGS** *Atlantic 7567830762*	**65** 2
25 Dec 99	**THE MOST WONDERFUL TIME OF THE YEAR** *Telstar TV TTVCD 3111*	**69** 1

[1] Michael Crawford with the Royal Philharmonic Orchestra, conducted by David Caddick [2] Barbra Streisand (duet with Michael Crawford) [1] Michael Crawford with the London Symphony Orchestra

The flip side of POSP 803 – 'Wishing You Were Somehow Here Again' by Sarah Brightman – was also listed

Randy CRAWFORD (275 Top 500)

Soulful jazz-slanted song stylist, b. 18 Feb 1952, Georgia, US. Has surprisingly proved more successful in Europe than in her homeland, where she has yet to crack the pop Top 100. Winner of Brits Best Female Artist award in 1982 (Singles: 75 weeks, Albums: 155 weeks) pos/wks

21 Jun 80	**LAST NIGHT AT DANCELAND** *Warner Bros. K 17631*	**61** 2
30 Aug 80 ●	**ONE DAY I'LL FLY AWAY** *Warner Bros. K 17680*	**2** 11
30 May 81	**YOU MIGHT NEED SOMEBODY** *Warner Bros. K 17803*	**11** 13
8 Aug 81	**RAINY NIGHT IN GEORGIA** *Warner Bros. K 17840*	**18** 9
31 Oct 81	**SECRET COMBINATION** *Warner Bros. K 17872*	**48** 3
30 Jan 82	**IMAGINE (re)** *Warner Bros. K 17906*	**60** 2
5 Jun 82	**ONE HELLO** *Warner Bros. K 17948*	**48** 4
19 Feb 83	**HE REMINDS ME** *Warner Bros. K 17970*	**65** 2
8 Oct 83	**NIGHT LINE** *Warner Bros. W 9530*	**51** 4
29 Nov 86 ●	**ALMAZ** *Warner Bros. W 8583*	**4** 17
18 Jan 92	**DIAMANTE** *London LON 313* [1]	**44** 7
15 Nov 97	**GIVE ME THE NIGHT** *WEA WEA 142CD*	**60** 1
28 Jun 80 ●	**NOW WE MAY BEGIN** *Warner Bros. K 56791*	**10** 16
16 May 81 ●	**SECRET COMBINATION** *Warner Bros. K 56904*	**2** 60
12 Jun 82 ●	**WINDSONG** *Warner Bros. K 57011*	**7** 17
22 Oct 83	**NIGHTLINE** *Warner Bros. 9239761*	**37** 4
13 Oct 84 ●	**MISS RANDY CRAWFORD – THE GREATEST HITS** *K-Tel NE 1281*	**10** 17
28 Jun 86	**ABSTRACT EMOTIONS** *Warner Bros. WX 46*	**14** 10
10 Oct 87	**THE LOVE SONGS** *Telstar STAR 2299*	**27** 13
21 Oct 89	**RICH AND POOR** *Warner Bros. WX 308*	**63** 1
27 Mar 93 ●	**THE VERY BEST OF RANDY CRAWFORD** *Dino DINCD 58*	**8** 13
12 Feb 00	**LOVE SONGS – THE VERY BEST OF RANDY CRAWFORD** *Warner.ESP WMMCD 002*	**22** 4

[1] Zucchero with Randy Crawford

See also CRUSADERS

Robert CRAY BAND

US, male vocal / instrumental group (Singles: 5 weeks, Albums: 53 weeks) pos/wks

20 Jun 87	**RIGHT NEXT DOOR (BECAUSE OF ME)** *Mercury CRAY 3*	**50** 4
20 Apr 96	**BABY LEE** *Silvertone ORECD 81* [1]	**65** 1
12 Oct 85	**FALSE ACCUSATIONS** *Demon FIEND 43*	**68** 1
15 Nov 86	**STRONG PERSUADER** *Mercury MERH 97*	**34** 28
3 Sep 88	**DON'T BE AFRAID OF THE DARK** *Mercury MERH 129*	**13** 12

			pos	wks
22 Sep 90		**MIDNIGHT STROLL** *Mercury 8466521*	19	7
12 Sep 92		**I WAS WARNED** *Mercury 5127212*	29	3
16 Oct 93		**SHAME AND SIN** *Mercury 5185172*	48	1
20 May 95		**SOME RAINY MORNING** *Mercury 5269282* [1]	63	1

[1] John Lee Hooker with Robert Cray [1] Robert Cray

CRAZY ELEPHANT *US, male vocal group (Singles: 13 weeks)* pos/wks

			pos	wks
21 May 69		**GIMME GIMME GOOD LOVIN'** *Major Minor MM 609*	12	13

CRAZY HORSE – *See Neil YOUNG*

CRAZY TOWN *US, male vocal / rap / instrumental group (Singles: 19 weeks, Albums: 9 weeks)* pos/wks

			pos	wks
7 Apr 01	●	**BUTTERFLY** *Columbia 6710012* ▲	3	13
11 Aug 01		**REVOLVING DOOR** *Columbia 6714942*	23	5
30 Nov 02		**DROWNING** *Columbia 6733262*	50	1
21 Apr 01		**THE GIFT OF GAME** *Columbia 4952972*	15	9

CRAZYHEAD *UK, male vocal / instrumental group (Singles: 4 weeks)* pos/wks

			pos	wks
16 Jul 88		**TIME HAS TAKEN ITS TOLL ON YOU** *Food FOOD 12*	65	2
25 Feb 89		**HAVE LOVE, WILL TRAVEL (EP)** *Food SGE 2025*	68	2

Tracks on Have Love, Will Travel (EP): Have Love Will Travel / Out on a Limb (Live) / Baby Turpentine (Live) / Snake Eyes (Live)

CREAM (149 Top 500)

The first real 'supergroup' performed 1966-1968: Eric Clapton (g/v), Jack Bruce (b/v), Ginger Baker (d) Loud innovative blues-based trio, which introduced long solos to popular music, was the prototype for 1970s progressive rock bands. Inducted into Rock and Roll Hall of Fame in 1993 (Singles: 59 weeks, Albums: 290 weeks) pos/wks

			pos	wks
20 Oct 66		**WRAPPING PAPER** *Reaction 591 007*	34	6
15 Dec 66		**I FEEL FREE** *Reaction 591 011*	11	12
8 Jun 67		**STRANGE BREW** *Reaction 591 015*	17	9
5 Jun 68		**ANYONE FOR TENNIS (THE SAVAGE SEVEN THEME)** *Polydor 56 258*	40	3
9 Oct 68		**SUNSHINE OF YOUR LOVE** *Polydor 56 286*	25	7
15 Jan 69		**WHITE ROOM** *Polydor 56 300*	28	8
9 Apr 69		**BADGE** *Polydor 56 315*	18	10
28 Oct 72		**BADGE (re-issue)** *Polydor 2058 285*	42	4
24 Dec 66	●	**FRESH CREAM** *Reaction 593001*	6	16
18 Nov 67	●	**DISRAELI GEARS** *Reaction 594003*	5	42
17 Aug 68	●	**WHEELS OF FIRE (double)** *Polydor 583-031/2* ▲	3	26
17 Aug 68	●	**WHEELS OF FIRE (single)** *Polydor 583033*	7	13
8 Feb 69	●	**FRESH CREAM (re-issue)** *Reaction 594001*	7	2
15 Mar 69	★	**GOODBYE** *Polydor 583053* ■	1	28
8 Nov 69	●	**THE BEST OF CREAM** *Polydor 583060*	6	34
4 Jul 70	●	**LIVE CREAM** *Polydor 2383016*	4	15
24 Jun 72		**LIVE CREAM VOLUME 2** *Polydor 2383 119*	15	5
26 Sep 87	●	**THE CREAM OF ERIC CLAPTON** *Polydor ECTV* [1]	3	109

[1] Eric Clapton and Cream

From 9 Jul 93 'The Cream of Eric Clapton' was repackaged and was available as 'The Best of Eric Clapton'

See also Eric CLAPTON; Jack BRUCE

CREATION *UK, male vocal / instrumental group (Singles: 3 weeks)* pos/wks

			pos	wks
7 Jul 66		**MAKING TIME** *Planet PLF 116*	49	1
3 Nov 66		**PAINTER MAN** *Planet PLF 119*	36	2

CREATURES *UK, male / female vocal / instrumental group (Singles: 28 weeks, Albums: 9 weeks)* pos/wks

			pos	wks
3 Oct 81		**MAD EYED SCREAMER** *Polydor POSPD 354*	24	7
23 Apr 83		**MISS THE GIRL** *Wonderland SHE 1*	21	7
16 Jul 83		**RIGHT NOW** *Wonderland SHE 2*	14	10
14 Oct 89		**STANDING THERE** *Wonderland SHE 17*	53	2
27 Mar 99		**SAY** *Sioux SIOUX 6CD*	72	1
25 Oct 03		**GODZILLA** *Sioux SIOUX 14CD1*	53	1
28 May 83		**FEAST** *Wonderland SHELP 1*	17	9

See also SIOUXSIE and the BANSHEES

CREDIT TO THE NATION *UK, male rap group (Singles: 11 weeks, Albums: 3 weeks)* pos/wks

			pos	wks
22 May 93		**CALL IT WHAT YOU WANT** *One Little Indian 94 TP7CD*	57	3
18 Sep 93		**ENOUGH IS ENOUGH** *One Little Indian 79 TP7CD* [1]	56	2
12 Mar 94		**TEENAGE SENSATION** *One Little Indian 124 TP7CD*	24	3
14 May 94		**SOWING THE SEEDS OF HATRED** *One Little Indian 134 TP7CD*	72	1
22 Jul 95		**LIAR LIAR** *One Little Indian 144 TP7CD*	60	1
12 Sep 98		**TACKY LOVE SONG** *Chrysalis CDCHS 5097*	60	1
9 Apr 94		**TAKE DIS** *One Little Indian TPLP 44CDH*	20	3

[1] Chumbawamba and Credit to the Nation

CREED *US, male vocal / instrumental group (Singles: 13 weeks, Albums: 21 weeks)* pos/wks

			pos	wks
15 Jan 00		**HIGHER** *Epic 6683152*	47	1
20 Jan 01		**WITH ARMS WIDE OPEN** *Epic 6706952* ▲	13	5
29 Sep 01		**HIGHER (re-issue)** *Epic 6710642*	64	1
16 Mar 02		**MY SACRIFICE** *Epic 6723162*	18	5
3 Aug 02		**ONE LAST BREATH / BULLETS** *Epic 6728262*	47	1
3 Feb 01		**HUMAN CLAY** *Epic 4950276* ▲	29	4
1 Dec 01		**WEATHERED** *Epic 5049792* ▲	44	17

CREEDENCE CLEARWATER REVIVAL (419 Top 500)

Internationally successful combo which cleverly created original songs with 50s rock 'n' roll feel, fronted by John Fogerty b, 28 May 1945, California, US. Voted World's Top Group in UK Polls 1970/71 (beating The Beatles and The Rolling Stones) (Singles: 94 weeks, Albums: 65 weeks) pos/wks

			pos	wks
28 May 69	●	**PROUD MARY** *Liberty LBF 15223*	8	13
16 Aug 69	★	**BAD MOON RISING** *Liberty LBF 15230*	1	15
15 Nov 69		**GREEN RIVER** *Liberty LBF 15250*	19	11
14 Feb 70		**DOWN ON THE CORNER** *Liberty LBF 15283*	31	6
4 Apr 70	●	**TRAVELLIN' BAND (re)** *Liberty LBF 15310*	8	13
20 Jun 70	●	**UP AROUND THE BEND** *Liberty LBF 15354*	3	12
5 Sep 70		**LONG AS I CAN SEE THE LIGHT** *Liberty LBF 15384*	20	9
20 Mar 71		**HAVE YOU EVER SEEN THE RAIN** *Liberty LBF 15440*	36	6
24 Jul 71		**SWEET HITCH-HIKER** *United Artists UP 35261*	36	8
2 May 92		**BAD MOON RISING (re-issue)** *Epic 6580047*	71	1
24 Jan 70		**GREEN RIVER** *Liberty LBS 83273* ▲	20	6
28 Mar 70	●	**WILLY AND THE POOR BOYS** *Liberty LBS 83338*	10	24
2 May 70		**BAYOU COUNTRY** *Liberty LBS 83261*	62	1
12 Sep 70	★	**COSMO'S FACTORY** *Liberty LBS 83388* ■ ▲	1	15
23 Jan 71	●	**PENDULUM** *Liberty LBG 83400*	8	12
30 Jun 79		**GREATEST HITS** *Fantasy FT 558*	35	5
19 Oct 85		**THE CREEDENCE COLLECTION** *Impression IMDP 3*	68	2

See also John FOGARTY

CREME – *See GODLEY and CREME*

Kid CREOLE and the COCONUTS *US, male vocalist and female vocal group (Singles: 58 weeks, Albums: 54 weeks)* pos/wks

			pos	wks
13 Jun 81		**ME NO POP I** *Ze WIP 6711* [1]	32	7
15 May 82	●	**I'M A WONDERFUL THING, BABY** *Ze WIP 6756*	4	11
24 Jul 82	●	**STOOL PIGEON** *Ze WIP 6793*	7	9
9 Oct 82	●	**ANNIE I'M NOT YOUR DADDY** *Ze WIP 6801*	2	8
11 Dec 82		**DEAR ADDY** *Ze WIP 6840*	29	7
10 Sep 83		**THERE'S SOMETHING WRONG IN PARADISE** *Island IS 130*	35	5
19 Nov 83		**THE LIFEBOAT PARTY** *Island IS 142*	49	4
14 Apr 90		**THE SEX OF IT** *CBS 655698 7*	29	5
10 Apr 93		**I'M A WONDERFUL THING BABY (re-mix)** *Island CID 551*	60	2
22 May 82	●	**TROPICAL GANGSTERS** *Ze ILPS 7016*	3	40
26 Jun 82		**FRESH FRUIT IN FOREIGN PLACES** *Ze ILPS 7014*	99	1
17 Sep 83		**DOPPELGANGER** *Island ILPS 9743*	21	6
15 Sep 84		**CRE-OLE (THE BEST OF KID CREOLE AND THE COCONUTS)** *Island IMA 13*	21	7

[1] Kid Creole and the Coconuts present Coati Mundi

See also COCONUTS

CRESCENDO *UK / US, male / female vocal / instrumental duo – Serena and Steve Hitchcock (Singles: 5 weeks)* pos/wks

			pos	wks
23 Dec 95		**ARE YOU OUT THERE** *ffrr FCD 270*	20	5

CRESCENT

UK, male vocal / instrumental group (Singles: 3 weeks)

Date		Title / Label	pos	wks
18 May 02		**ON THE RUN** *Hut / Virgin HUTCD 153*	49	1
27 Jul 02		**TEST OF TIME** *Hut / Virgin HUTCD 157*	60	1
28 Sep 02		**SPINNIN' WHEELS** *Hut / Virgin HUTCD 160*	61	1

CRESTERS – *See Mike SAGAR and the CRESTERS*

CREW CUTS

Canada, male vocal group (Singles: 29 weeks)

Date		Title / Label	pos	wks
1 Oct 54		**SH-BOOM** *Mercury MB 3140* ▲	12	9
15 Apr 55	●	**EARTH ANGEL** *Mercury MB 3202*	4	20

Bernard CRIBBINS

UK, male actor / vocalist (Singles: 29 weeks)

Date		Title / Label	pos	wks
15 Feb 62	●	**HOLE IN THE GROUND** *Parlophone R 4869*	9	13
5 Jul 62	●	**RIGHT, SAID FRED** *Parlophone R 4923*	10	10
13 Dec 62		**GOSSIP CALYPSO** *Parlophone R 4961*	25	6

See also Howard BLAKE conducting the SINFONIA OF LONDON

CRICKETS (410 Top 500)

Band that originally featured Buddy Holly formed in Lubbock, Texas, US, best known members being Jerry Allison (d), Joe B Mauldin (b) and Sonny Curtis (g/v). Without Holly they recorded original versions of Top 10 hits 'I Fought the Law', 'Someone Someone', 'When You Ask About Love' and 'More Than I Can Say' (Singles: 97 weeks, Albums: 67 weeks)

Date		Title / Label	pos	wks
27 Sep 57	★	**THAT'LL BE THE DAY (re)** *Vogue Coral Q 72279* ▲	1	15
27 Dec 57	●	**OH BOY** *Coral Q 72298*	3	15
14 Mar 58	●	**MAYBE BABY** *Coral Q 72307*	4	10
25 Jul 58		**THINK IT OVER** *Coral Q 72329*	11	7
24 Apr 59		**LOVE'S MADE A FOOL OF YOU (re)** *Coral Q 72365*	26	2
15 Jan 60		**WHEN YOU ASK ABOUT LOVE** *Coral Q 72382*	27	1
12 May 60		**MORE THAN I CAN SAY** *Coral Q 72395*	42	1
26 May 60		**BABY MY HEART** *Coral Q 72395*	33	4
21 Jun 62	●	**DON'T EVER CHANGE** *Liberty LIB 55441*	5	13
24 Jan 63		**MY LITTLE GIRL** *Liberty LIB 10067*	17	9
6 Jun 63		**DON'T TRY TO CHANGE ME** *Liberty LIB 10092*	37	4
14 May 64		**YOU'VE GOT LOVE** *Coral Q 72472* [1]	40	6
2 Jul 64		**(THEY CALL HER) LA BAMBA** *Liberty LIB 55696*	21	10
19 Apr 58	●	**THE 'CHIRPING' CRICKETS** *Coral LVA 9081*	5	1
25 Mar 61		**IN STYLE WITH THE CRICKETS** *Coral LVA 9142*	13	7
27 Oct 62	●	**BOBBY VEE MEETS THE CRICKETS** *Liberty LBY 1086* [1]	2	27
11 Mar 78	★	**20 GOLDEN GREATS** *MCA EMTV 8* [2]	1	20
20 Feb 93	★	**WORDS OF LOVE** *PolyGram TV 5144872* [2]	1	9
28 Aug 99		**THE VERY BEST OF BUDDY HOLLY AND THE CRICKETS** *Universal Music TV 1120462* [2]	25	3

[1] Buddy Holly and The Crickets [1] Bobby Vee and the Crickets [2] Buddy Holly and the Crickets

Although not credited on the records, Buddy Holly was featured on the first four hits

See also Buddy HOLLY and the CRICKETS

CRIMINAL ELEMENT ORCHESTRA – *See Wally JUMP Jr and the CRIMINAL ELEMENT*

CRISPY AND COMPANY

US, male vocal / instrumental group (Singles: 11 weeks)

Date		Title / Label	pos	wks
16 Aug 75		**BRAZIL** *Creole CR 109*	26	5
27 Dec 75		**GET IT TOGETHER** *Creole CR 114* [1]	21	6

[1] Crispy & Co

CRITTERS

US, male vocal / instrumental group (Singles: 5 weeks)

Date		Title / Label	pos	wks
30 Jun 66		**YOUNGER GIRL** *London HL 10047*	38	5

Tony CROMBIE and His ROCKETS

UK, male vocal / instrumental group – Tony Crombie – drums, d. 18 Oct 1999 (Singles: 2 weeks)

Date		Title / Label	pos	wks
19 Oct 56		**TEACH YOU TO ROCK / SHORT'NIN' BREAD** *Columbia DB 3822*	25	2

CROOKLYN CLAN – *See FATMAN SCOOP featuring The CROOKLYN CLAN*

Bing CROSBY (487 Top 500)

The King of the Crooners. Bing released 2,500 tracks, 299 of which reached the US Top 20 (1931-1961) with estimated sales of more than 400 million, b. 3 May 1903, Washington, US, d.14 Oct 1977, Spain. 'White Christmas' (the most charted single in the US) unofficially could lay claim to being the world's best-seller with pre-chart figures having boosted sales well in excess of 30 million (Singles: 97 weeks, Albums: 45 weeks)

Date		Title / Label	pos	wks
14 Nov 52	●	**THE ISLE OF INNISFREE** *Brunswick 04900*	3	12
5 Dec 52	●	**ZING A LITTLE ZONG** *Brunswick 04981* [1]	10	2
19 Dec 52	●	**SILENT NIGHT, HOLY NIGHT** *Brunswick 03929*	8	2
19 Mar 54	●	**CHANGING PARTNERS (2re)** *Brunswick 05244*	9	3
7 Jan 55		**COUNT YOUR BLESSINGS INSTEAD OF SHEEP (re)** *Brunswick 05339*	11	3
29 Apr 55		**STRANGER IN PARADISE** *Brunswick 05410*	17	2
27 Apr 56		**IN A LITTLE SPANISH TOWN** *Brunswick 05543*	22	3
23 Nov 56	●	**TRUE LOVE** *Capitol CL 14645* [2]	4	27
24 May 57	●	**AROUND THE WORLD** *Brunswick 05674*	5	15
9 Aug 75		**THAT'S WHAT LIFE IS ALL ABOUT** *United Artists UP 35852*	41	4
3 Dec 77	●	**WHITE CHRISTMAS** *MCA 111* ▲	5	7
27 Nov 82	●	**PEACE ON EARTH – LITTLE DRUMMER BOY** *RCA BOW 12* [3]	3	8
17 Dec 83		**TRUE LOVE (re-issue)** *Capitol CL 315* [2]	70	3
21 Dec 85		**WHITE CHRISTMAS (re-issue)** *MCA BING 1*	69	2
19 Dec 98		**WHITE CHRISTMAS (2nd re-issue)** *MCA MCSRD 48105*	29	4
8 Oct 60	●	**JOIN BING AND SING ALONG** *Warner Bros. WM 4021*	7	11
21 Dec 74		**WHITE CHRISTMAS** *MCA MCF 2568*	45	3
20 Sep 75		**THAT'S WHAT LIFE IS ALL ABOUT** *United Artists UAG 2973*	28	6
5 Nov 77	●	**LIVE AT THE LONDON PALLADIUM** *K-Tel NE 951*	9	2
5 Nov 77		**THE BEST OF BING** *MCA MCF 2540*	41	7
17 Dec 77		**SEASONS** *Polydor 2442 151*	25	7
5 May 79		**SONGS OF A LIFETIME** *Philips 6641 923*	29	3
14 Dec 91		**CHRISTMAS WITH BING CROSBY** *Telstar STAR 2468*	66	3
23 Nov 96		**THE BEST OF BING CROSBY** *MCA MCD 11561*	59	3

[1] Bing Crosby and Jane Wyman [2] Bing Crosby and Grace Kelly [3] David Bowie and Bing Crosby

David CROSBY

US, male vocalist / instrumentalist (Singles: 3 weeks, Albums: 12 weeks)

Date		Title / Label	pos	wks
15 May 93		**HERO** *Atlantic A 7360* [1]	56	3
24 Apr 71		**IF ONLY I COULD REMEMBER MY NAME** *Atlantic 2401005*	12	7
13 May 72		**GRAHAM NASH AND DAVID CROSBY** *Atlantic K 50011* [1]	13	5

[1] David Crosby featuring Phil Collins [1] Graham Nash and David Crosby

See also CROSBY, STILLS, NASH and YOUNG; Phil COLLINS

CROSBY, STILLS, NASH and YOUNG

US / UK / Canada, male vocal / instrumental group (Singles: 12 weeks, Albums: 93 weeks)

Date		Title / Label	pos	wks
16 Aug 69		**MARRAKESH EXPRESS** *Atlantic 584 283* [1]	17	9
21 Jan 89		**AMERICAN DREAM** *Atlantic A 9003*	55	3
23 Aug 69		**CROSBY STILLS AND NASH** *Atlantic 588189* [1]	25	5
30 May 70	●	**DÉJÀ VU** *Atlantic 2401001* ▲	5	60
22 May 71	●	**FOUR-WAY STREET** *Atlantic 2956 004* ▲	5	12
21 May 74		**SO FAR** *Atlantic K 50023* ▲	25	6
9 Jul 77		**CSN** *Atlantic K 50369* [1]	23	9
6 Nov 99		**LOOKING FORWARD** *Reprise 9362474362*	54	1

[1] Crosby, Stills and Nash [1] Crosby, Stills and Nash

See also David CROSBY; Stephen STILLS; Graham NASH; Neil YOUNG

CROSS

UK / US, male vocal / instrumental group (Singles: 1 week, Albums: 2 weeks)

Date		Title / Label	pos	wks
17 Oct 87		**COWBOYS AND INDIANS** *Virgin VS 1007*	74	1
6 Feb 88		**SHOVE IT** *Virgin V 2477*	58	2

Review of the Year

FEBRUARY 2003

An average audience of 7.3 million watches the Brit awards but they don't see **Kelly** and **Sharon Osbourne** handing out trophies as planned; fears over terrorist activity prevent them from flying in for the event. Brit winners include **Will Young** with his breakthrough award, and **Ms Dynamite, Coldplay** and **Eminem** all bag two each. Other winners include **Liberty X, Sugababes, Blue, Pink, Red Hot Chili Peppers, Norah Jones** and **Tom Jones**, who is honoured with the special Contribution to British Music award. **Norah Jones** also comes away with five Grammy awards – the first time since **Christopher Cross** in 1980 that a single artist wins in all the major categories. The show, featuring a **Bee Gees** tribute by **'N Sync**, sees awards bestowed on **Coldplay, Santana, No Doubt, The Clash, Bruce Springsteen, Korn, Stevie Wonder, india.arie, Nelly and Johnny Cash**. **Etta James** receives a Lifetime Achievement Grammy. **Phil Spector** is arrested on suspicion of murdering movie actress **Lana Clarkson**. He hires Robert Shapiro from the O J Simpson team to defend him. The prestigious US R&B Foundations Pioneer Awards go to **Dionne Warwick, The Supremes, George Clinton, Dixie Cups, Johnny Nash and Clarence 'Frogman' Henry** among others. **Shakira's** 'Laundry Service' is certified a four-million seller in Europe and Erasure score a rare Top 20 best-selling single for a UK act in the US with 'Solsbury Hill'. The Mandela SOS concert takes place in South Africa. **Bono, Queen, Macy Gray, Coldplay, Dave Stewart, Nelly Furtado, Shaggy and Youssou N'Dour** all appear. **t.A.T.u.** become the first Russian act to top the chart and **Justin Timberlake's** 'Justified' finally hits No.1 in the UK album chart after a three-month residency,

Norah Jones, daughter of Ravi Shankar, struggles to keep her five Grammys under control

LL Cool J is even more patient. He has his first US No.1 with 'All I Have' 15 years and seven months after his chart debut, and '03 Bonnie & Clyde' gives **Jay-Z** his 21st hit in less than six years. The much talked-about Martin Bashir interview with **Michael Jackson** bags a 54 per cent TV audience in the UK and 23 per cent Stateside. **Kelly Rowland** becomes the first female to top the album chart as a solo artist and in a group. **2Pac** replaces **Elvis** as the artist with the most posthumous UK hit singles. **Massive Attack's** 100th Window enters the European Top 10 at No.1. It's a US sales record as **50 Cent's** major label album debut, Get Rich or Die Tryin', shifts 872,000 copies in its first four days – then 1.7 million in the first two weeks. Obituaries this month include balladeer **Malcolm Roberts**, the queen of skiffle **Nancy Whiskey** (born Anne Wilson) and **Howie Epstein** from Tom Petty's Heartbreakers.

Christopher CROSS *US, male vocalist – Christopher Geppert (Singles: 27 weeks, Albums: 93 weeks)* pos/wks

			pos	wks
19 Apr 80		**RIDE LIKE THE WIND** *Warner Bros. K 17582*	**69**	1
14 Feb 81		**SAILING** *Warner Bros. K 17695* ▲	**48**	6
17 Oct 81	●	**ARTHUR'S THEME (BEST THAT YOU CAN DO) (re)** *Warner Bros. K 17847* ▲	**7**	15
5 Feb 83		**ALL RIGHT** *Warner Bros. W 9843*	**51**	5
21 Feb 81		**CHRISTOPHER CROSS** *Warner Bros. K 56789*	**14**	77
19 Feb 83	●	**ANOTHER PAGE** *Warner Bros. W 3757*	**4**	16

It was not until 'Arthur's Theme' re-entered in Jan 1982 that it reached the peak position of No.7

CROW *Germany, male production duo – David Rzenno and David Nothroff (Singles: 1 week)* pos/wks

			pos	wks
19 May 01		**WHAT YA LOOKIN' AT** *Tidy Trax TIDY 153CD*	**60**	1

Sheryl CROW 232 Top 500

Multi-Grammy-winning pop singer / songwriter / instrumentalist – guitar, born 11 Feb 1962, Missouri, US. The one-time backing singer for Michael Jackson and George Harrison became the first US female soloist to score six UK hits off her debut LP (1993's Tuesday Night Music Club) (Singles: 89 weeks, Albums: 175 weeks) pos/wks

			pos	wks
18 Jun 94		**LEAVING LAS VEGAS** *A&M 5806472*	**66**	1
5 Nov 94	●	**ALL I WANNA DO** *A&M 5808452*	**4**	13
11 Feb 95		**STRONG ENOUGH** *A&M 5809212*	**33**	4
27 May 95		**CAN'T CRY ANYMORE** *A&M 5810552*	**33**	3
29 Jul 95		**RUN BABY RUN** *A&M 5811492*	**24**	4
11 Nov 95		**WHAT I CAN DO FOR YOU** *A&M 5812292*	**43**	1
21 Sep 96	●	**IF IT MAKES YOU HAPPY** *A&M 5819032*	**9**	6
30 Nov 96		**EVERYDAY IS A WINDING ROAD** *A&M 5820232*	**12**	6
29 Mar 97		**HARD TO MAKE A STAND** *A&M 5821492*	**22**	3
12 Jul 97	●	**A CHANGE WOULD DO YOU GOOD** *A&M 5822092*	**8**	5
18 Oct 97		**HOME** *A&M 0440312*	**25**	2
13 Dec 97		**TOMORROW NEVER DIES** *A&M 5824572*	**12**	9
12 Sep 98	●	**MY FAVORITE MISTAKE** *Polydor 5827632*	**9**	6
5 Dec 98		**THERE GOES THE NEIGHBORHOOD** *A&M 5828092*	**19**	7
6 Mar 99		**ANYTHING BUT DOWN** *A&M / Polydor 5828272*	**19**	4
11 Sep 99		**SWEET CHILD O' MINE** *Columbia 6678882*	**30**	3
13 Apr 02		**SOAK UP THE SUN** *A&M 4977042*	**16**	8
13 Jul 02		**STEVE MCQUEEN** *A&M 4977422*	**44**	1
1 Nov 03		**THE FIRST CUT IS THE DEEPEST** *A&M 9813556*	**37**	3
12 Feb 94	●	**TUESDAY NIGHT MUSIC CLUB** *A&M 5401262*	**8**	55
12 Oct 96	●	**SHERYL CROW** *A&M 5405902*	**5**	70
3 Oct 98	●	**THE GLOBE SESSIONS** *A&M 5409742*	**2**	32
20 Apr 02	●	**C'MON, C'MON** *A&M 4932622*	**2**	8
25 Oct 03	●	**THE VERY BEST OF SHERYL CROW** *A&M / Mercury 9861092*	**2**	10+

CROWD *International, male / female vocal / instrumental charity assembly (Singles: 11 weeks)* pos/wks

			pos	wks
1 Jun 85	★	**YOU'LL NEVER WALK ALONE** *Spartan BRAD 1*	**1**	11

CROWDED HOUSE 246 Top 500

Top Antipodean group evolved from Split Enz, and featured New Zealander Neil Finn (v/g/k). Formed 1986, they received Best International Group award at 1993 Brits, and played their last show (1996) to 100,000 people on the steps of the Sydney Opera House (Singles: 64 weeks, Albums: 186 weeks) pos/wks

			pos	wks
6 Jun 87		**DON'T DREAM IT'S OVER** *Capitol CL 438*	**27**	8
22 Jun 91		**CHOCOLATE CAKE** *Capitol CL 618*	**69**	2
2 Nov 91		**FALL AT YOUR FEET** *Capitol CL 626*	**17**	7
29 Feb 92	●	**WEATHER WITH YOU** *Capitol CL 643*	**7**	9
20 Jun 92		**FOUR SEASONS IN ONE DAY** *Capitol CL 655*	**26**	5
26 Sep 92		**IT'S ONLY NATURAL** *Capitol CL 661*	**24**	4
2 Oct 93		**DISTANT SUN** *Capitol CDCLS 697*	**19**	6
20 Nov 93		**NAILS IN MY FEET** *Capitol CDCLS 701*	**22**	4
19 Feb 94		**LOCKED OUT** *Capitol CDCLS 707*	**12**	4
11 Jun 94		**FINGERS OF LOVE** *Capitol CDCLS 715*	**25**	3
24 Sep 94		**PINEAPPLE HEAD** *Capitol CDCLS 723*	**27**	3
22 Jun 96		**INSTINCT** *Capitol CDCLS 774*	**12**	4
17 Aug 96		**NOT THE GIRL YOU THINK YOU ARE** *Capitol CDCLS 776*	**20**	3
9 Nov 96		**DON'T DREAM IT'S OVER (re-issue)** *Capitol CDCL 780*	**25**	2
13 Jul 91	●	**WOODFACE** *Capitol EST 2144*	**6**	86
23 Oct 93	●	**TOGETHER ALONE** *Capitol CDESTU 2215*	**4**	32
6 Jul 96	★	**RECURRING DREAM – THE VERY BEST OF CROWDED HOUSE** *Capitol CDEST 2283* ■	**1**	66
19 Feb 00		**AFTERGLOW** *Capitol 5237222*	**18**	2

See also FINN; Neil FINN; Tim FINN

CROWN HEIGHTS AFFAIR *US, male vocal / instrumental group (Singles: 34 weeks, Albums: 3 weeks)* pos/wks

			pos	wks
19 Aug 78		**GALAXY OF LOVE** *Mercury 6168 801*	**24**	10
11 Nov 78		**I'M GONNA LOVE YOU FOREVER** *Mercury 6168 803*	**47**	4
14 Apr 79		**DANCE LADY DANCE** *Mercury 6168 804*	**44**	4
3 May 80	●	**YOU GAVE ME LOVE** *De-Lite MER 9*	**10**	12
9 Aug 80		**YOU'VE BEEN GONE** *De-Lite MER 28*	**44**	4
23 Sep 78		**DREAM WORLD** *Philips 6372 754*	**40**	3

Julee CRUISE

US, female vocalist (Singles: 14 weeks, Albums: 30 weeks) pos/wks

			pos	wks
10 Nov 90	●	**FALLING** *Warner Bros. W 9544*	**7**	11
2 Mar 91		**ROCKIN' BACK INSIDE MY HEART** *Warner Bros. W 0004*	**66**	2
11 Sep 99		**IF I SURVIVE** *Distinctive DISNCD 55* [1]	**52**	1
17 Nov 90		**MUSIC FROM 'TWIN PEAKS'** *Warner Bros. 7599263161* [1]	**27**	25

[1] Hybrid featuring Julee Cruise [1] Angleo Badalamenti with Julee Cruise and Various Artists

CRUISERS – *See Dave BERRY*

CRUSADERS *US, male vocal / instrumental group – includes Wilton Felder (Singles: 16 weeks, Albums: 30 weeks)* pos/wks

			pos	wks
18 Aug 79	●	**STREET LIFE** *MCA 513*	**5**	11
26 Sep 81		**I'M SO GLAD I'M STANDING HERE TODAY** *MCA 741* [1]	**61**	3
7 Apr 84		**NIGHT LADIES** *MCA MCA 853*	**55**	2
21 Jul 79	●	**STREET LIFE** *MCA MCF 3008*	**10**	16
19 Jul 80		**RHAPSODY AND BLUE** *MCA MCG 4010*	**40**	5
12 Sep 81		**STANDING TALL** *MCA MCF 3122*	**47**	5
7 Apr 84		**GHETTO BLASTER** *MCA MCF 3176*	**46**	4

[1] Crusaders, featured vocalist Joe Cocker

Vocalist on 'Street Life' was Randy Crawford, though uncredited

CRUSH *UK, female vocal duo (Singles: 3 weeks)* pos/wks

			pos	wks
24 Feb 96		**JELLYHEAD** *Telstar CDSTAS 2809*	**50**	2
3 Aug 96		**LUV'D UP** *Telstar CDSTAS 2833*	**45**	1

Bobby CRUSH *UK, male instrumentalist – piano (Singles: 4 weeks, Albums: 12 weeks)* pos/wks

			pos	wks
4 Nov 72		**BORSALINO** *Philips 6006 248*	**37**	4
25 Nov 72		**BOBBY CRUSH** *Philips 6308 135*	**15**	7
18 Dec 82		**THE BOBBY CRUSH INCREDIBLE DOUBLE DECKER** *Warwick WW 5126/7*	**53**	5

CRY BEFORE DAWN

Ireland, male vocal / instrumental group (Singles: 2 weeks) pos/wks

			pos	wks
17 Jun 89		**WITNESS FOR THE WORLD** *Epic GONE 3*	**67**	2

CRY OF LOVE

US, male / female vocal / instrumental group (Singles: 1 week) pos/wks

			pos	wks
15 Jan 94		**BAD THING** *Columbia 6600462*	**60**	1

CRY SISCO! *UK, male producer – Barry Blue (Singles: 9 weeks)* pos/wks

			pos	wks
2 Sep 89		**AFRO DIZZI ACT (re)** *Escape AWOL 1*	**42**	9

See also Barry BLUE

CRYIN' SHAMES

UK, male vocal / instrumental group (Singles: 7 weeks) pos/wks

			pos	wks
31 Mar 66		**PLEASE STAY** *Decca F 12340*	**26**	7

CRYPT-KICKERS – *See Bobby 'Boris' PICKETT and the CRYPT-KICKERS*

CRYSTAL METHOD

US, male instrumental duo (Singles: 4 weeks)

Date	Title	pos	wks
11 Oct 97	**(CAN'T YOU) TRIP LIKE I DO** *Epic 6650862* [1]	39	2
7 Mar 98	**KEEP HOPE ALIVE** *Sony S2 CM 3CD*	71	1
8 Aug 98	**COMIN' BACK** *Sony S2 CM 4CD*	73	1

[1] Filter and The Crystal Method

CRYSTAL PALACE with the FAB FOUR

UK, male football team vocalists and UK, male vocal group (Singles: 2 weeks)

Date	Title	pos	wks
12 May 90	**GLAD ALL OVER / WHERE EAGLES FLY** *Parkfield PMS 5019*	50	2

CRYSTALS

US, female vocal group (Singles: 54 weeks)

Date	Title	pos	wks
22 Nov 62	**HE'S A REBEL** *London HLU 9611* ▲	19	13
20 Jun 63 ●	**DA DOO RON RON** *London HLU 9732*	5	16
19 Sep 63 ●	**THEN HE KISSED ME** *London HLU 9773*	2	14
5 Mar 64	**I WONDER** *London HLU 9852*	36	3
19 Oct 74	**DA DOO RON RON (re-issue)** *Warner Spector K 19010*	15	8

CSILLA

Hungary, female vocalist (Singles: 1 week)

Date	Title	pos	wks
13 Jul 96	**MAN IN THE MOON** *Worx WORXCD 001*	69	1

CUBAN BOYS

UK, male / female production group (Singles: 9 weeks)

Date	Title	pos	wks
25 Dec 99 ●	**COGNOSCENTI VS INTELLIGENTSIA (re)** *EMI CDCUBAN 001*	4	9

CUBIC 22

Belgium, male instrumental / production duo – Peter Ramson and Danny Van Wauwe (Singles: 7 weeks)

Date	Title	pos	wks
22 Jun 91	**NIGHT IN MOTION** *XL Recordings XLS 20*	15	7

See also AIRSCAPE; BLUE BAMBOO; TRANSFORMER 2; BALEARIC BILL; Johan GIELEN presents ABNEA; SVENSON and GIELEN

CUD

UK, male vocal / instrumental group (Singles: 16 weeks, Albums: 2 weeks)

Date	Title	pos	wks
19 Oct 91	**OH NO WON'T DO (EP)** *A&M AMB 829*	49	2
28 Mar 92	**THROUGH THE ROOF** *A&M AM 857*	44	2
30 May 92	**RICH AND STRANGE** *A&M AM 871*	24	3
15 Aug 92	**PURPLE LOVE BALLOON** *A&M AM 0024*	27	3
10 Oct 92	**ONCE AGAIN** *A&M AM 0081*	45	1
12 Feb 94	**NEUROTICA** *A&M 5805172*	37	2
2 Apr 94	**STICKS AND STONES** *A&M 5805472*	68	1
3 Sep 94	**ONE GIANT LOVE** *A&M 5807292*	52	2
11 Jul 92	**ASQUARIUS** *A&M 3953902*	30	1
23 Apr 94	**SHOWBIZ** *A&M 5402112*	46	1

Tracks on Oh No Won't Do (EP): Oh No Won't Do / Profession / Ariel / Price of Love

CUDDLES – *See Keith HARRIS and ORVILLE*

CUFFLINKS

US, male vocal group, leader – Ron Dante (Singles: 30 weeks)

Date	Title	pos	wks
29 Nov 69 ●	**TRACY** *MCA MU 1101*	4	16
14 Mar 70 ●	**WHEN JULIE COMES AROUND** *MCA MU 1112*	10	14

See also ARCHIES

Jamie CULLUM

UK, male vocalist / instrumentalist – piano (Albums: 9 weeks)

Date	Title	pos	wks
1 Nov 03 ●	**TWENTYSOMETHING** *UCJ 9865574*	5	9+

CULT (403 Top 500)

UK gothic rock stars who became US heavy rock heroes, previously recorded as Southern Death Cult and Death Cult. West Yorkshire band's constant members are Ian Astbury (v) and Billy Duffy (g). They relocated to the US in 1988 and topped the UK album chart with their hits collection in 1993 (Singles: 80 weeks, Albums: 86 weeks)

Date	Title	pos	wks
22 Dec 84	**RESURRECTION JOE** *Beggars Banquet BEG 122*	74	2
25 May 85	**SHE SELLS SANCTUARY (re)** *Beggars Banquet BEG 135*	15	19
5 Oct 85	**RAIN** *Beggars Banquet BEG 147*	17	8
30 Nov 85	**REVOLUTION** *Beggars Banquet BEG 152*	30	7
28 Feb 87	**LOVE REMOVAL MACHINE.** *Beggars Banquet BEG 182*	18	7
2 May 87	**LIL' DEVIL** *Beggars Banquet BEG 188*	11	7
22 Aug 87	**WILD FLOWER (DOUBLE SINGLE)** *Beggars Banquet BEG 195D*	24	2
29 Aug 87	**WILD FLOWER** *Beggars Banquet BEG 195*	30	4
1 Apr 89	**FIRE WOMAN** *Beggars Banquet BEG 228*	15	4
8 Jul 89	**EDIE (CIAO BABY)** *Beggars Banquet BEG 230*	32	5
18 Nov 89	**SUN KING / EDIE (CIAO BABY) (re-issue)** *Beggars Banquet BEG 235*	39	2
10 Mar 90	**SWEET SOUL SISTER** *Beggars Banquet BEG 241*	42	4
14 Sep 91	**WILD HEARTED SON** *Beggars Banquet BEG 255*	40	2
29 Feb 92	**HEART OF SOUL** *Beggars Banquet BEG 260*	51	1
30 Jan 93	**SHE SELLS SANCTUARY (re-mix)** *Beggars Banquet BEG 253CD*	15	4
8 Oct 94	**COMING DOWN** *Beggars Banquet BBQ 40CD*	50	1
7 Jan 95	**STAR** *Beggars Banquet BBQ 45CD*	65	1
18 Jun 83	**THE SOUTHERN DEATH CULT** *Beggars Banquet BEGA 46* [1]	43	3
8 Sep 84	**DREAMTIME** *Beggars Banquet BEGA 57*	21	8
26 Oct 85 ●	**LOVE** *Beggars Banquet BEGA 65*	4	22
18 Apr 87 ●	**ELECTRIC** *Beggars Banquet BEGA 80*	4	27
22 Apr 89 ●	**SONIC TEMPLE** *Beggars Banquet BEGA 98*	3	11
5 Oct 91 ●	**CEREMONY** *Beggars Banquet BEGA 122*	9	4
13 Feb 93 ★	**PURE CULT** *Beggars Banquet BEGACD 130* ■	1	8
22 Oct 94	**THE CULT** *Beggars Banquet BBQCD 164*	21	2
23 Jun 01	**BEYOND GOOD AND EVIL** *Atlantic 7567834402*	69	1

[1] Southern Death Cult

Tracks on double single: Wild Flower / Love Trooper / Outlaw (live) / Horse Nation (live)

CULT JAM – *See LISA LISA*

CULTURE

Jamaica, male vocal / instrumental group (Albums: 1 week)

Date	Title	pos	wks
1 Apr 78	**TWO SEVENS CLASH** *Lightning LIP 1*	60	1

Smiley CULTURE

UK, male vocalist – David Emanuel (Singles: 13 weeks)

Date	Title	pos	wks
15 Dec 84	**POLICE OFFICER** *Fashion FAD 7012*	12	10
6 Apr 85	**COCKNEY TRANSLATION** *Fashion FAD 7028*	71	1
13 Sep 86	**SCHOOLTIME CHRONICLE** *Polydor POSP 815*	59	2

CULTURE BEAT

UK / US / Germany, male / female vocal / instrumental group (Singles: 47 weeks, Albums: 10 weeks)

Date	Title	pos	wks
3 Feb 90	**CHERRY LIPS (DER ERDBEERMUND)** *Epic 6556337*	55	3
7 Aug 93 ★	**MR VAIN** *Epic 6594682*	1	15
6 Nov 93 ●	**GOT TO GET IT** *Epic 6597212*	4	11
15 Jan 94 ●	**ANYTHING** *Epic 6600252*	5	8
2 Apr 94	**WORLD IN YOUR HANDS** *Epic 6602292*	20	4
27 Jan 96	**INSIDE OUT** *Epic 6626562*	32	2
15 Jun 96	**CRYING IN THE RAIN** *Epic 6633582*	29	2
28 Sep 96	**TAKE ME AWAY** *Epic 6637552*	52	1
20 Sep 03	**MR VAIN RECALL (re-mix)** *East West EW 270CD*	51	1
25 Sep 93	**SERENITY** *Dance Pool 4741012*	13	10

CULTURE CLUB (210 Top 500)

Internationally successful London-based quartet, whose flamboyant lead singer, Boy George (b. George O'Dowd, 14 Jun 1961, Kent), attracted considerable media attention. In 1984, they won both Brit (Best Group) and Grammy awards (Best New Artist). Original members reunited for late 1990s tours. Best-selling single: 'Karma Chameleon' 1,405,000 (Singles: 119 weeks, Albums: 163 weeks)

Date	Title	pos	wks
18 Sep 82 ★	**DO YOU REALLY WANT TO HURT ME** *Virgin VS 518*	1	18
27 Nov 82 ●	**TIME (CLOCK OF THE HEART)** *Virgin VS 558*	3	12
9 Apr 83 ●	**CHURCH OF THE POISON MIND** *Virgin VS 571*	2	9
17 Sep 83 ★	**KARMA CHAMELEON** *Virgin VS 612* ◆ ▲	1	20
10 Dec 83 ●	**VICTIMS** *Virgin VS 641*	3	10
24 Mar 84 ●	**IT'S A MIRACLE** *Virgin VS 662*	4	9
6 Oct 84 ●	**THE WAR SONG** *Virgin VS 694*	2	8

1 Dec 84	THE MEDAL SONG (re) *Virgin VS 730*	32	5
15 Mar 86 ●	MOVE AWAY *Virgin VS 845*	7	7
31 May 86	GOD THANK YOU WOMAN *Virgin VS 861*	31	5
31 Oct 98 ●	I JUST WANNA BE LOVED *Virgin VSCDT 1710*	4	10
7 Aug 99	YOUR KISSES ARE CHARITY *Virgin VSCDT 1736*	25	4
27 Nov 99	COLD SHOULDER / STARMAN *Virgin VSCDT 1758*	43	2
16 Oct 82 ●	KISSING TO BE CLEVER *Virgin V 2232*	5	59
22 Oct 83 ★	COLOUR BY NUMBERS *Virgin V 2285* ■	1	56
3 Nov 84 ●	WAKING UP WITH THE HOUSE ON FIRE *Virgin V 2330*	2	13
12 Apr 86 ●	FROM LUXURY TO HEARTACHE *Virgin V 2380*	10	6
18 Apr 87 ●	THIS TIME *Virgin VTV 1*	8	10
2 Oct 93	AT WORST ... THE BEST OF BOY GEORGE AND CULTURE CLUB *Virgin VYCD 19* [1]	24	5
21 Nov 98	GREATEST MOMENTS *Virgin CDVX 2865*	15	13
4 Dec 99	DON'T MIND IF I DO *Virgin CDV 2887*	64	1

[1] Boy George and Culture Club

See also BOY GEORGE

Peter CUNNAH – *See D:REAM; CHICANE*

Larry CUNNINGHAM and the MIGHTY AVONS

Ireland, male vocal / instrumental group (Singles: 11 weeks)

		pos	wks
10 Dec 64	TRIBUTE TO JIM REEVES (re) *King KG 1016*	40	11

CUPID'S INSPIRATION

UK, male vocal / instrumental group (Singles: 19 weeks)

		pos	wks
19 Jun 68 ●	YESTERDAY HAS GONE *Nems 56 3500*	4	11
2 Oct 68	MY WORLD *Nems 56 3702*	33	8

José CURA – *See Sarah BRIGHTMAN*

Mike CURB CONGREGATION – *See Little Jimmy OSMOND*

CURE (146 Top 500)

Goth rock giants: Robert Smith (v/g), Lol Tolhurst (k), Simon Gallup (b), Porl Thompson (g), Boris Williams (d), who went from UK cult heroes to stadium-packing supergroup. Voted Best Group at 1991 Brit Awards (Singles: 145 weeks, Albums: 207 weeks)

		pos	wks
12 Apr 80	A FOREST *Fiction FICS 10*	31	8
4 Apr 81	PRIMARY *Fiction FICS 12*	43	6
17 Oct 81	CHARLOTTE SOMETIMES *Fiction FICS 14*	44	4
24 Jul 82	HANGING GARDEN *Fiction FICS 15*	34	4
27 Nov 82	LET'S GO TO BED (re) *Fiction FICS 17*	44	5
9 Jul 83	THE WALK *Fiction FICS 18*	12	8
29 Oct 83 ●	THE LOVE CATS *Fiction FICS 19*	7	11
7 Apr 84	THE CATERPILLAR *Fiction FICS 20*	14	7
27 Jul 85	IN BETWEEN DAYS *Fiction FICS 22*	15	10
21 Sep 85	CLOSE TO ME *Fiction FICS 23*	24	8
3 May 86	BOYS DON'T CRY *Fiction FICS 24*	22	6
18 Apr 87	WHY CAN'T I BE YOU? *Fiction FICS 25*	21	5
4 Jul 87	CATCH *Fiction FICS 26*	27	6
17 Oct 87	JUST LIKE HEAVEN *Fiction FICS 27*	29	5
20 Feb 88	HOT HOT HOT!!! *Fiction FICSX 28*	45	3
22 Apr 89 ●	LULLABY *Fiction FICS 29*	5	6
2 Sep 89	LOVESONG *Fiction FICS 30*	18	7
31 Mar 90	PICTURES OF YOU *Fiction FICS 34*	24	6
29 Sep 90	NEVER ENOUGH *Fiction FICS 35*	13	5
3 Nov 90	CLOSE TO ME (re-mix) *Fiction FICS 36*	13	5
28 Mar 92 ●	HIGH *Fiction FICS 39*	8	3
11 Apr 92	HIGH (re-mix) *Fiction FICSX 41*	44	1
23 May 92 ●	FRIDAY I'M IN LOVE *Fiction FICS 42*	6	7
17 Oct 92	A LETTER TO ELISE *Fiction FICS 46*	28	2
4 May 96	THE 13TH *Fiction 5764692*	15	2
29 Jun 96	MINT CAR *Fiction FISCD 52*	31	2
14 Dec 96	GONE *Fiction FICD 53*	60	1
29 Nov 97	WRONG NUMBER *Fiction FICD 54*	62	1
10 Nov 01	CUT HERE *Fiction 5873892*	54	1
2 Jun 79	THREE IMAGINARY BOYS *Fiction FIX 001*	44	3
3 May 80	17 SECONDS *Fiction FIX 004*	20	10
25 Apr 81	FAITH *Fiction FIX 6*	14	8
15 May 82 ●	PORNOGRAPHY *Fiction FIX D7*	8	9
3 Sep 83	BOYS DON'T CRY *Fiction SPELP 26*	71	7
24 Dec 83	JAPANESE WHISPERS *Fiction FIXM 8*	26	14
12 May 84 ●	THE TOP *Fiction FIXS 9*	10	10
3 Nov 84	CONCERT – THE CURE LIVE *Fiction FIXH 10*	26	4
7 Sep 85 ●	THE HEAD ON THE DOOR *Fiction FIXH 11*	7	13
31 May 86 ●	STANDING ON A BEACH – THE SINGLES *Fiction FIXH 12*	4	35
6 Jun 87 ●	KISS ME KISS ME KISS ME *Fiction FIXH 13*	6	15
13 May 89 ●	DISINTEGRATION *Fiction FIXH 14*	3	26
17 Nov 90 ●	MIXED UP *Fiction 8470991*	8	17
6 Apr 91 ●	ENTREAT *Fiction FIXH 17*	10	5
2 May 92 ★	WISH *Fiction FIXCD 20* ■	1	13
25 Sep 93	SHOW *Fiction FIXCD 25*	29	2
6 Nov 93	PARIS *Fiction FIXCD 26*	56	1
18 May 96 ●	WILD MOOD SWINGS *Fiction FIXCD 28*	9	6
15 Nov 97	GALORE – THE SINGLES 1987-1997 *Fiction FIXCD 30*	37	2
26 Feb 00	BLOODFLOWERS *Fiction FIXCD 31*	14	2
24 Nov 01	GREATEST HITS *Fiction 5894352*	33	5

The CD version of FIXH 12 was titled 'Staring at the Sea'

See also GLOVE

CURIOSITY KILLED THE CAT

UK, male vocal / instrumental group (Singles: 58 weeks, Albums: 27 weeks)

		pos	wks
13 Dec 86 ●	DOWN TO EARTH *Mercury CAT 2*	3	18
4 Apr 87	ORDINARY DAY *Mercury CAT 3*	11	7
20 Jun 87 ●	MISFIT *Mercury CAT 4*	7	9
19 Sep 87	FREE *Mercury CAT 5*	56	2
16 Sep 89	NAME AND NUMBER *Mercury CAT 6* [1]	14	9
25 Apr 92 ●	HANG ON IN THERE BABY *RCA PB 45377* [1]	3	10
29 Aug 92	I NEED YOUR LOVIN' *RCA 74321111377* [1]	47	2
30 Oct 93	GIMME THE SUNSHINE *RCA 74321168602* [1]	73	1
9 May 87 ★	KEEP YOUR DISTANCE *Mercury CATLP 1* ■	1	24
4 Oct 89	GETAHEAD *Mercury 842010 1*	29	3

[1] Curiosity

CURLS – *See Paul EVANS*

Mark CURRY – *See PUFF DADDY*

Chantal CURTIS

France, female vocalist (Singles: 3 weeks)

		pos	wks
14 Jul 79	GET ANOTHER LOVE *Pye 7P 5003*	51	3

TC CURTIS

Jamaica, male vocalist / instrumentalist (Singles: 4 weeks)

		pos	wks
23 Feb 85	YOU SHOULD HAVE KNOWN BETTER *Hot Melt VS 754*	50	4

CURVE

UK, male / female vocal / instrumental duo – Toni Halliday and Dean Garcia (Singles: 14 weeks, Albums: 6 weeks)

		pos	wks
16 Mar 91	THE BLINDFOLD (EP) *AnXious ANX 27*	68	1
25 May 91	COAST IS CLEAR *AnXious ANX 30*	34	3
9 Nov 91	CLIPPED *AnXious ANX 35*	36	2
7 Mar 92	FAIT ACCOMPLI *AnXious ANXT 36*	22	3
18 Jul 92	HORROR HEAD (EP) *AnXious ANXT 38*	31	2
4 Sep 93	BLACKERTHREETRACKER (EP) *AnXious ANXCD 42*	39	2
16 May 98	COMING UP ROSES *Universal UND 80489*	51	1
21 Mar 92	DOPPELGANGER *Anxious ANXCD 77*	11	3
19 Jun 93	RADIO SESSIONS *Anxious ANXCD 80*	72	1
25 Sep 93	CUCKOO *Anxious ANXCD 81*	23	2

Tracks on The Blindfold (EP): Ten Little Girls / I Speak Your Every Word / Blindfold / No Escape from Heaven. Tracks on Horror Head (EP): Horror Head / Falling Free / Mission from God / Today Is Not the Day. Only track available on all formats of Blackerthreetracker (EP): Missing Link

CURVED AIR

UK, male / female vocal / instrumental group (Singles: 12 weeks, Albums: 32 weeks)

		pos	wks
7 Aug 71 ●	BACK STREET LUV *Warner Bros. K 16092*	4	12
5 Dec 70 ●	AIR CONDITIONING *Warner Bros. WSX 3012*	8	21
9 Oct 71	CURVED AIR *Warner Bros. K 46092*	11	6
13 May 72	PHANTASMAGORIA *Reprise K 46158*	20	5

Malachi CUSH – *See MALACHI*

CUT 'N' MOVE *Denmark, male / female vocal / instrumental group (Singles: 4 weeks)* pos/wks

2 Oct 93	**GIVE IT UP** *EMI CDEM 273*	61	2
9 Sep 95	**I'M ALIVE** *EMI CDEM 375*	49	2

Frankie CUTLASS *US, male rapper (Singles: 1 week)* pos/wks

5 Apr 97	**THE CYPHER: PART 3** *Epic 6641445*	59	1

Adge CUTLER – *See WURZELS*

Jon CUTLER featuring E-MAN
US, male producer and male vocalist – Eric Clark (Singles: 2 weeks) pos/wks

19 Jan 02	**IT'S YOURS** *Direction 6720532*	38	2

CUTTING CREW *UK / Canada, male vocal / instrumental group (Singles: 37 weeks, Albums: 6 weeks)* pos/wks

16 Aug 86 ●	**(I JUST) DIED IN YOUR ARMS** *Siren SIREN 21* ▲	4	12
25 Oct 86	**I'VE BEEN IN LOVE BEFORE (re)** *Siren SIREN 29*	31	10
7 Mar 87	**ONE FOR THE MOCKINGBIRD** *Siren SIREN 40*	52	5
21 Nov 87	**I'VE BEEN IN LOVE BEFORE (re-mix)** *Siren SRN 29*	24	8
22 Jul 89	**(BETWEEN A) ROCK AND A HARD PLACE** *Siren SRN 108*	66	2
29 Nov 86	BROADCAST *Siren SIRENLP 7*	41	6

CYBERSONIK
US, male instrumentalist / producers (Singles: 1 week) pos/wks

10 Nov 90	**TECHNARCHY** *Champion CHAMP 264*	73	1

CYCLEFLY
Ireland, male vocal / instrumental group (Singles: 1 week) pos/wks

6 Apr 02	**NO STRESS** *Radioactive RAXTD 41*	68	1

CYGNUS X
Germany, male producer – A C Bousten (Singles: 5 weeks) pos/wks

11 Mar 00	**THE ORANGE THEME** *Hooj Choons HOOJ 88CD*	43	2
18 Aug 01	**SUPERSTRING** *Xtravaganza XTRAV 28CDS*	33	3

Johnny CYMBAL
Canada, male vocalist d. 16 Mar 1993 (Singles: 10 weeks) pos/wks

14 Mar 63	**MR BASS MAN** *London HLR 9682*	24	10

CYPRESS HILL
US, male rap group (Singles: 44 weeks, Albums: 67 weeks) pos/wks

31 Jul 93	**INSANE IN THE BRAIN** *Ruff House 6595332*	32	4
2 Oct 93	**WHEN THE SH.. GOES DOWN** *Ruff House 6596702*	19	4
11 Dec 93	**I AIN'T GOIN' OUT LIKE THAT** *Ruff House 6596902*	15	7
26 Feb 94	**INSANE IN THE BRAIN (re-issue)** *Ruff House 6601762*	21	4
7 May 94	**LICK A SHOT** *Ruff House 6603192*	20	3
7 Oct 95	**THROW YOUR SET IN THE AIR** *Ruff House 6623542*	15	3
17 Feb 96	**ILLUSIONS** *Columbia 6629052*	23	2
10 Oct 98	**TEQUILA SUNRISE** *Columbia 6664935*	23	2
10 Apr 99	**DR GREENTHUMB** *Columbia 6671202*	34	2
26 Jun 99	**INSANE IN THE BRAIN** *INCredible INCRL 17CD* [1]	19	3
29 Apr 00	**(RAP) SUPERSTAR / (ROCK) SUPERSTAR** *Columbia 6692642*	13	5
16 Sep 00	**HIGHLIFE / CAN'T GET THE BEST OF ME** *Columbia 6697892*	35	2
8 Dec 01	**LOWRIDER / TROUBLE (re)** *Columbia 6721662*	33	3
7 Aug 93	BLACK SUNDAY *Ruffhouse 4740752* ▲	13	49
11 Nov 95	CYPRESS HILL III (TEMPLES OF BOOM) *C olumbia 4781279*	11	5
24 Aug 96	UNRELEASED & REVAMPED (EP) *Columbia 4852302*	29	4
17 Oct 98	IV *Columbia 4916046*	25	3
6 May 00 ●	SKULL & BONES *Columbia 4951832*	6	5
15 Dec 01	STONED RAIDERS *Columbia 5041719*	71	1

[1] Jason Nevins vs Cypress Hill

Billy Ray CYRUS
US, male vocalist (Singles: 18 weeks, Albums: 10 weeks) pos/wks

25 Jul 92 ●	**ACHY BREAKY HEART** *Mercury MER 373*	3	10
10 Oct 92	**COULD'VE BEEN ME** *Mercury MER 378*	24	4
28 Nov 92	**THESE BOOTS ARE MADE FOR WALKIN'** *Mercury MER 384*	63	1
19 Dec 92	**ACHY BREAKY HEART** *Epic 6588837* [1]	53	3
29 Aug 92 ●	SOME GAVE ALL *Mercury 5106352* ▲	9	10

[1] Alvin and the Chipmunks featuring Billy Ray Cyrus

Holgar CZUKAY – *See David SYLVIAN*

Asher D
UK, male rapper (Singles: 2 weeks) pos/wks

4 Aug 01	**BABY, CAN I GET YOUR NUMBER** *East West EW 235CD* [1]	75	1
8 Jun 02	**BACK IN THE DAY / WHY ME** *Independiente ISOM 57MS*	43	1

[1] OBI Project featuring Harry, Asher D and DJ What?

See also SO SOLID CREW

Chuck D
US, male rapper – Carlton Ridenhour (Singles: 9 weeks) pos/wks

6 Jul 91	**BRING THE NOISE** *Island IS 490* [1]	14	5
26 Oct 96	**NO** *Mercury MERCD 476*	55	1
23 Jun 01	**ROCK DA FUNKY BEATS** *Xtrahard / Xtravaganza X2H3 CDS* [2]	19	3

[1] Anthrax featuring Chuck D [2] Public Domain featuring Chuck D

See also PUBLIC ENEMY

Crissy D – *See B15 PROJECT featuring Crissy D and Lady G*

Danny D – *See COOKIE CREW*

Juggy D – *See Rishi RICH PROJECT featuring Jay SEAN & JUGGY D*

Dimples D
US, female rapper – Crystal Smith (Singles: 10 weeks) pos/wks

17 Nov 90	**SUCKER DJ** *FBI FBI 11*	17	10

Longsy D
UK, male instrumentalist / producer (Singles: 7 weeks) pos/wks

4 Mar 89	**THIS IS SKA** *Big One VBIG 13*	56	7

Maxwell D
UK, male rapper – Maxwell Donaldson (Singles: 2 weeks)

Date	Title / Label	pos	wks
15 Sep 01	**SERIOUS** *4 Liberty LIBTCD 046*	38	2

Nikki D
US, female rapper – Nichelle Strong (Singles: 6 weeks)

Date	Title / Label	pos	wks
6 May 89	**MY LOVE IS SO RAW** *Def Jam 6548987* [1]	34	5
30 Mar 91	**DADDY'S LITTLE GIRL** *Def Jam 6567347*	75	1

[1] Alyson Williams featuring Nikki D

Vicky D
US, female vocalist (Singles: 6 weeks)

Date	Title / Label	pos	wks
13 Mar 82	**THIS BEAT IS MINE** *Virgin VS 486*	42	6

DB BOULEVARD
Italy, male production trio and female vocalist (Singles: 12 weeks)

Date	Title / Label	pos	wks
23 Feb 02 ●	**POINT OF VIEW** *Illustrious CDILL 002*	3	12

DBM
Germany, male / female vocal / instrumental group (Singles: 3 weeks)

Date	Title / Label	pos	wks
12 Nov 77	**DISCO BEATLEMANIA** *Atlantic K 11027*	45	3

D, B, M and T
UK, male vocal / instrumental group (Singles: 8 weeks)

Date	Title / Label	pos	wks
1 Aug 70	**MR PRESIDENT** *Fontana 6007 022*	33	8

See also Dave DEE, DOZY, BEAKY, MICK and TICH

D BO GENERAL – *See URBAN SHAKEDOWN*

D4
New Zealand, male vocal / instrumental group (Singles: 3 weeks)

Date	Title / Label	pos	wks
28 Sep 02	**GET LOOSE** *Infectious INFEC 117CDS*	64	1
7 Dec 02	**COME ON!** *Infectious INFEC 121CDS*	50	1
29 Mar 03	**LADIES MAN** *Infectious INFECT 122CDS*	41	1

D.H.S. *UK, male producer – Ben Stokes (Singles: 1 week)*

Date	Title / Label	pos	wks
9 Feb 02	**HOUSE OF GOD** *Club Tools 0135825 CLU*	72	1

D KAY & EPSILON featuring STAMINA MC
Austria / UK, production / vocal trio (Singles: 5 weeks)

Date	Title / Label	pos	wks
30 Aug 03	**BARCELONA** *Alphamagic / BC / BMG BCAU 001CD*	14	5

See also STAMINA MC; EPSILON

DMX *US, male rapper – Earl Simmons (Singles: 23 weeks, Albums: 11 weeks)*

Date	Title / Label	pos	wks
15 May 99	**SLIPPIN'** *Def Jam 8707552*	30	2
15 Dec 01	**WHO WE BE** *Def Jam 5888512*	34	4
3 May 03 ●	**X GON' GIVE IT TO YA** *Def Jam 0779042*	6	12
11 Oct 03	**WHERE THE HOOD AT?** *Def Jam 9811251*	16	5
3 Nov 01	**THE GREAT DEPRESSION** *Def Jam 5864502* ▲	20	3
27 Sep 03 ●	**GRAND CHAMP** *Def Jam / Mercury 9861021* ▲	6	8

D MOB *UK, male producer – Danny D (Singles: 48 weeks, Albums: 11 weeks)*

Date	Title / Label	pos	wks
15 Oct 88 ●	**WE CALL IT ACIEED** *ffrr FFR 13* [1]	3	12
3 Jun 89 ●	**IT IS TIME TO GET FUNKY** *ffrr F 107* [2]	9	10
21 Oct 89	**C'MON AND GET MY LOVE** *ffrr F 117* [3]	15	10
6 Jan 90 ●	**PUT YOUR HANDS TOGETHER** *ffrr F 124* [4]	7	8
7 Apr 90	**THAT'S THE WAY OF THE WORLD** *ffrr F 132* [3]	48	3
12 Feb 94	**WHY** *ffrr FCD 227* [3]	23	3
3 Sep 94	**ONE DAY** *ffrr FCDP 239*	41	2
11 Nov 89	**A LITTLE BIT OF THIS A LITTLE BIT OF THAT** *ffrr 8281591*	46	11

[1] D Mob featuring Gary Haisman [2] D Mob featuring LRS
[3] D Mob with Cathy Dennis [4] D Mob featuring Nuff Juice

DNA *UK, male production duo – Neal Slateford and Nick Bett (Singles: 29 weeks)*

Date	Title / Label	pos	wks
28 Jul 90 ●	**TOM'S DINER (re-mix)** *A&M AM 592* [1]	2	10
18 Aug 90	**LA SERENISSIMA** *Raw Bass RBASS 006*	34	8
3 Aug 91	**REBEL WOMAN** *DNA 7DNA 001* [2]	42	4
1 Feb 92	**CAN YOU HANDLE IT (re-recording)** *EMI EM 219* [3]	17	5
9 May 92	**BLUE LOVE (CALL MY NAME)** *EMI EM 226* [4]	66	2

[1] DNA featuring Suzanne Vega [2] DNA featuring Jazzi P [3] DNA featuring Sharon Redd [4] DNA featuring Joe Nye

D*NOTE
UK, male producer – Matt Winn (Singles: 3 weeks)

Date	Title / Label	pos	wks
12 Jul 97	**WAITING HOPEFULLY** *A&M 5822792*	46	1
15 Nov 97	**LOST AND FOUND** *VC VCRD 25*	59	1
27 Apr 02	**SHED MY SKIN** *Channel 4 Music C4M 00182*	73	1

D.O.P.
UK, male instrumental / production duo (Singles: 2 weeks)

Date	Title / Label	pos	wks
3 Feb 96	**STOP STARTING TO START STOPPING (EP)** *Hi-Life 5779472*	58	1
13 Jul 96	**GROOVY BEAT** *Hi-Life 5750652*	54	1

Tracks on Stop Starting to Stop Stopping (EP): Gusta / Dance to the House / Can You Feel It / How Do Y'All Feel

D.O.S.E. – *See Mark E SMITH*

D:REAM *UK, male vocal / instrumental / production duo (Singles: 74 weeks, Albums: 41 weeks)*

Date	Title / Label	pos	wks
4 Jul 92	**U R THE BEST THING** *FXU FXU 3*	72	1
30 Jan 93	**THINGS CAN ONLY GET BETTER** *Magnet MAG 1010CD*	24	5
24 Apr 93	**U R THE BEST THING (re-issue)** *Magnet MAG 1011CD*	19	8
31 Jul 93	**UNFORGIVEN** *Magnet MAG 1016CD*	29	3
2 Oct 93	**STAR / I LIKE IT** *Magnet MAG 1019CD*	26	4
8 Jan 94 ★	**THINGS CAN ONLY GET BETTER (re-issue)** *Magnet MAG 1020CD*	1	16
26 Mar 94 ●	**U R THE BEST THING (re-mix)** *Magnet MAG 1021CD*	4	10
18 Jun 94	**TAKE ME AWAY** *Magnet MAG 1025CD*	18	5
10 Sep 94	**BLAME IT ON ME** *Magnet MAG 1027CD*	25	5
8 Jul 95 ●	**SHOOT ME WITH YOUR LOVE** *Magnet MAG 1034CD*	7	7
9 Sep 95	**PARTY UP THE WORLD** *Magnet MAG 1037CD*	20	6
11 Nov 95	**THE POWER (OF ALL THE LOVE IN THE WORLD)** *Magnet MAG 1039CD*	40	1
3 May 97	**THINGS CAN ONLY GET BETTER (2nd re-issue)** *Magnet MAG 1050CD*	19	3
30 Oct 93 ●	**D:REAM ON VOLUME 1** *Magnet 4509933712*	5	37
30 Sep 95 ●	**WORLD** *Magnet 0630117962*	5	4

D:Ream was just Peter Cunnah from 1994

DSK *UK, male / female vocal / instrumental / production group (Singles: 4 weeks)*

Date	Title / Label	pos	wks
31 Aug 91	**WHAT WOULD WE DO / READ MY LIPS** *Boy's Own BOI 6*	46	3
22 Nov 97	**WHAT WOULD WE DO (re-mix)** *Fresh FRSHD 63*	55	1

DSM *US, male rap group (Singles: 4 weeks)*

Date	Title / Label	pos	wks
7 Dec 85	**WARRIOR GROOVE** *10 DAZZ 45-7*	68	4

DSP – *See Matt DAREY*

D-SHAKE
Holland, male producer – Adrianus De Mooy (Singles: 8 weeks)

Date	Title / Label	pos	wks
2 Jun 90	**YAAAH / TECHNO TRANCE** *Cooltempo COOL 213*	20	6
2 Feb 91	**MY HEART THE BEAT** *Cooltempo COOL 228*	42	2

D-SIDE
Ireland, male vocal group (Singles: 17 weeks)

Date	Title / Label	pos	wks
26 Apr 03 ●	**SPEECHLESS** *WEA WEA 366CD1*	9	8
26 Jul 03 ●	**INVISIBLE** *Blacklist / Edel / WEA WEA 369CD1*	7	6
13 Dec 03 ●	**REAL WORLD** *Blacklist / Edel 9814017*	9	3+

DT8 featuring Roxanne WILDE *UK, male producer – Darren Tate – and female vocalist (Singles: 3 weeks)* pos/wks

Date	Title / Label	pos	wks
3 May 03	DESTINATION *ffrr DFCD 007*	23	3

See also Jurgen VRIES

DTI *US, male vocal / instrumental group (Singles: 1 week)* pos/wks

Date	Title / Label	pos	wks
16 Apr 88	KEEP THIS FREQUENCY CLEAR *Premiere UK ERE 501*	73	1

D-TEK *UK, male instrumental / production group (Singles: 1 week)* pos/wks

Date	Title / Label	pos	wks
6 Nov 93	DROP THE ROCK (EP) *Positiva 12TIV 5*	70	1

Tracks on Drop the Rock (EP): Drop the Rock / Chunkafunk / Drop the Rock (re-mix) / Don't Breathe

D TRAIN *US, male vocal / instrumental duo – James Williams and Hubert Eaves III (Singles: 36 weeks, Albums: 4 weeks)* pos/wks

Date	Title / Label	pos	wks
6 Feb 82	YOU'RE THE ONE FOR ME *Epic EPC A 2016*	30	8
8 May 82	WALK ON BY *Epic EPC A 2298*	44	6
7 May 83	MUSIC PART 1 *Prelude A 3332*	23	7
16 Jul 83	KEEP GIVING ME LOVE *Prelude A 3497*	65	2
27 Jul 85	YOU'RE THE ONE FOR ME (re-mix) *Prelude ZB 40302*	15	11
12 Oct 85	MUSIC (re-mix) *Prelude ZB 40431*	62	2
8 May 82	D-TRAIN *Epic EPC 85683*	72	4

D12 *US, male rap group (Singles: 24 weeks, Albums: 17 weeks)* pos/wks

Date	Title / Label	pos	wks
17 Mar 01	● SH!T ON YOU *Interscope 4974962*	10	7
21 Jul 01	● PURPLE PILLS *Shady / Interscope 4975692*	2	12
17 Nov 01	FIGHT MUSIC *Shady / Interscope 4976522*	11	5
30 Jun 01	● DEVILS NIGHT *Shady / Interscope 4930792* ▲	2	17

Azzido DA BASS *Germany, male DJ / producer – Ingo Martens (Singles: 13 weeks)* pos/wks

Date	Title / Label	pos	wks
4 Mar 00	DOOMS NIGHT (re) *Club Tools 0067285 CLU*	46	3
21 Oct 00	● DOOMS NIGHT (re) (re-mix) *Club Tools 0120285 CLU*	8	9
23 Mar 02	SPEED (CAN YOU FEEL IT) *Club Tools 0135815 CLU* [1]	68	1

[1] Azzido Da Bass featuring Roland Clark

DA BRAT *US, female rapper (Singles: 3 weeks)* pos/wks

Date	Title / Label	pos	wks
22 Oct 94	FUNKDAFIED *Columbia 6609212*	65	1
29 Nov 97	SOCKIT2ME *East West E 3890CD* [1]	33	2

[1] Missy 'Misdemeanor' Elliott featuring Da Brat

DA CLICK *UK, male rap group / female vocalist (Singles: 8 weeks)* pos/wks

Date	Title / Label	pos	wks
16 Jan 99	GOOD RHYMES *ffrr FCD 353*	14	6
29 May 99	WE ARE DA CLICK *ffrr FCD 363*	38	2

DA FOOL *US, male DJ / producer – Mike Stewart (Singles: 2 weeks)* pos/wks

Date	Title / Label	pos	wks
16 Jan 99	NO GOOD *ffrr FCD 352*	38	2

Ricardo DA FORCE *UK, male rapper – Ricardo Lyte (Singles: 14 weeks)* pos/wks

Date	Title / Label	pos	wks
18 Mar 95	PUMP UP THE VOLUME *Stress CDSTR 49* [1]	51	2
16 Sep 95	● STAYIN' ALIVE *All Around the World CDGLOBE 131* [2]	2	11
31 Aug 96	WHY *ffrr FCD 280*	58	1

[1] Greed featuring Ricardo Da Force [2] N-Trance featuring Ricardo Da Force

See also N-TRANCE

DA HOOL *Germany, male instrumentalist / producer – Frank Tomiczek (Singles: 13 weeks)* pos/wks

Date	Title / Label	pos	wks
14 Feb 98	MEET HER AT THE LOVE PARADE *Manifesto FESCD 39*	15	4
22 Aug 98	BORA BORA *Manifesto FESCD 47*	35	3
28 Jul 01	MEET HER AT THE LOVE PARADE 2001 *Manifesto FESCD 85*	11	6

DA LENCH MOB *US, male rap group (Singles: 2 weeks)* pos/wks

Date	Title / Label	pos	wks
20 Mar 93	FREEDOM GOT AN A.K. *East West America A 8431CD*	51	2

DA MOB featuring JOCELYN BROWN *US, male / female vocal / instrumental group (Singles: 3 weeks)* pos/wks

Date	Title / Label	pos	wks
2 May 98	FUN *INCredible INCRL 2CD*	33	2
3 Jul 99	IT'S ALL GOOD *INCredible INCRL 14CD*	54	1

DA MUTTZ *UK, male production duo – Elliot Ireland and Alex Rizzo (Singles: 10 weeks)* pos/wks

Date	Title / Label	pos	wks
9 Dec 00	WASSUUP *Eternal WEA 319CD*	11	10

See also SHAFT

Rui DA SILVA featuring CASSANDRA *Portugal, male producer and UK, female vocalist – Cassandra Fox (Singles: 14 weeks)* pos/wks

Date	Title / Label	pos	wks
13 Jan 01	★ TOUCH ME *Kismet / Arista 74321823992* ■	1	14

DA SLAMMIN' PHROGZ *France, male production duo (Singles: 1 week)* pos/wks

Date	Title / Label	pos	wks
29 Apr 00	SOMETHING ABOUT THE MUSIC *WEA WEA 251CD*	53	1

DA TECHNO BOHEMIAN *Holland, male production trio (Singles: 1 week)* pos/wks

Date	Title / Label	pos	wks
25 Jan 97	BANGIN' BASS *Hi-Life 5731772*	63	1

Paul DA VINCI *UK, male vocalist – Paul Prewer (Singles: 8 weeks)* pos/wks

Date	Title / Label	pos	wks
20 Jul 74	YOUR BABY AIN'T YOUR BABY ANYMORE *Penny Farthing PEN 843*	20	8

See also RUBETTES

Terry DACTYL and the DINOSAURS *UK, male vocal / instrumental group (Singles: 16 weeks)* pos/wks

Date	Title / Label	pos	wks
15 Jul 72	● SEASIDE SHUFFLE *UK 5*	2	12
13 Jan 73	ON A SATURDAY NIGHT *UK 21*	45	4

Terry Dactyl is Jona Lewie

DADA *US, male vocal / instrumental group (Singles: 1 week)* pos/wks

Date	Title / Label	pos	wks
4 Dec 93	DOG *IRS CDEIRSS 185*	71	1

DADDY FREDDY – See Simon HARRIS

DADDY'S FAVOURITE *UK, male DJ / producer (Singles: 3 weeks)* pos/wks

Date	Title / Label	pos	wks
21 Nov 98	I FEEL GOOD THINGS FOR YOU *Go.Beat GONCD 12*	44	2
9 Oct 99	I FEEL GOOD THINGS FOR YOU (re-issue) *Go.Beat GOBCD 22*	50	1

DAFFY DUCK featuring the GROOVE GANG *Germany, male instrumental / production group (Singles: 3 weeks)* pos/wks

Date	Title / Label	pos	wks
6 Jul 91	PARTY ZONE *East West YZ 592*	58	3

DAFT PUNK *France, male instrumental / production duo – Thomas Bangalter and Guy Manuel de Homem-Christo (Singles: 35 weeks, Albums: 54 weeks)* pos/wks

Date	Title / Label	pos	wks
22 Feb 97	● DA FUNK / MUSIQUE *Soma / Virgin VSCDT 1625*	7	5
26 Apr 97	● AROUND THE WORLD *Virgin VSCDT 1633*	5	5
4 Oct 97	BURNIN' *Virgin VSCDT 1649*	30	2
28 Feb 98	REVOLUTION 909 *Virgin VSCDT 1682*	47	1
25 Nov 00	● ONE MORE TIME *Virgin VSCDT 1791*	2	12
23 Jun 01	DIGITAL LOVE *Virgin VSCDT 1810*	14	7
17 Nov 01	HARDER BETTER FASTER STRONGER *Virgin VSCDT 1822*	25	3
1 Feb 97	● HOMEWORK *Virgin CDV 2821*	8	17
24 Mar 01	● DISCOVERY *Virgin CDVX 2940*	2	37

Etienne DAHO – See SAINT ETIENNE

DAINTEES – See Martin STEPHENSON and the DAINTEES

DAISY CHAINSAW *UK, male / female vocal / instrumental group (Singles: 6 weeks, Albums: 1 week)* pos/wks

18 Jan 92	**LOVE YOUR MONEY** *Deva DEVA 001*	**26**	5
28 Mar 92	**PINK FLOWER / ROOM ELEVEN** *Deva 82 TP7*	**65**	1
10 Oct 92	**ELEVENTEEN** *Deva TPLP 100CD*	**62**	1

DAJAE – *See Junior SANCHEZ featuring DAJAE*

DAKEYNE – *See James BROWN; TINMAN*

DAKOTAS *UK, male instrumental group (Singles: 13 weeks)* pos/wks

11 Jul 63	**THE CRUEL SEA** *Parlophone R 5044*	**18**	13

See also Billy J KRAMER and the DAKOTAS

Jim DALE *UK, male vocalist – James Smith (Singles: 22 weeks)* pos/wks

11 Oct 57 ●	**BE MY GIRL** *Parlophone R 4343*	**2**	16
10 Jan 58	**JUST BORN (TO BE MY BABY)** *ParlophoneR 4376*	**27**	1
17 Jan 58	**CRAZY DREAM** *Parlophone R 4376*	**24**	2
7 Mar 58	**SUGARTIME** *Parlophone R 4402*	**25**	3

DALE and GRACE *US, male / female vocal duo (Singles: 2 weeks)* pos/wks

9 Jan 64	**I'M LEAVING IT UP TO YOU** *London HL 9807* ▲	**42**	2

DALE SISTERS *UK, female vocal trio – Julie, Hazel and Betty Dunderdale (Singles: 7 weeks)* pos/wks

17 Mar 60	**HEARTBEAT** *HMV POP 710* [1]	**33**	1
23 Nov 61	**MY SUNDAY BABY** *Ember S 140*	**36**	6

[1] England Sisters

DALEK I *UK male vocal / instrumental group (Albums: 2 weeks)* pos/wks

9 Aug 80	**COMPASS KUMPAS** *Backdoor OPEN 1*	**54**	2

DALI'S CAR *UK, male vocal / instrumental duo (Singles: 2 weeks, Albums: 1 week)* pos/wks

3 Nov 84	**THE JUDGEMENT IS THE MIRROR** *Paradox DOX 1*	**66**	2
1 Dec 84	**THE WAKING HOUR** *Paradox DOXLP 1*	**84**	1

DALLAS SUPERSTARS *Finland, male production duo – Heikki Liimatainen and Jaakko Slovaara (Singles: 1 week)* pos/wks

27 Sep 03	**HELIUM** *All Around the World CDGLOBE 289*	**64**	1

Roger DALTREY
UK, male vocalist (Singles: 46 weeks, Albums: 24 weeks) pos/wks

14 Apr 73 ●	**GIVING IT ALL AWAY** *Track 2094 110*	**5**	11
4 Aug 73	**I'M FREE** *Ode ODS 66302* [1]	**13**	10
14 May 77	**WRITTEN ON THE WIND** *Polydor 2121 319*	**46**	2
2 Aug 80	**FREE ME** *Polydor 2001 980*	**39**	6
11 Oct 80	**WITHOUT YOUR LOVE** *Polydor POSP 181*	**55**	4
3 Mar 84	**WALKING IN MY SLEEP** *WEA U 9686*	**56**	3
5 Oct 85	**AFTER THE FIRE** *10 TEN 69*	**50**	5
8 Mar 86	**UNDER A RAGING MOON** *10 TEN 81*	**43**	5
26 Jul 75	**RIDE A ROCK HORSE** *Polydor 2660 111*	**14**	10
4 Jun 77	**ONE OF THE BOYS** *Polydor 2442 146*	**45**	1
23 Aug 80	**MCVICAR (FILM SOUNDTRACK)** *Polydor POLD 5034*	**39**	11
2 Nov 85	**UNDER A RAGING MOON** *10 DIX 17*	**52**	2

[1] With London Symphony Orchestra and English Chamber Orchestra and English Chamber Choir – conducted by David Measham

See also The WHO

Glen DALY *UK, male vocalist (Albums: 2 weeks)* pos/wks

20 Nov 71	**GLASGOW NIGHT OUT** *Golden Guinea GGL 0479*	**28**	2

DAMAGE
UK, male vocal group (Singles: 59 weeks, Albums: 22 weeks) pos/wks

20 Jul 96	**ANYTHING** *Big Life BLRD 129*	**68**	1
12 Oct 96	**LOVE II LOVE** *Big Life BLRD 131*	**12**	6
14 Dec 96 ●	**FOREVER** *Big Life BLRD 132*	**6**	9
22 Mar 97 ●	**LOVE GUARANTEED (re)** *Big Life BLRDA 133*	**7**	7
17 May 97 ●	**WONDERFUL TONIGHT** *Big Life BLRDA 134*	**3**	8
9 Aug 97	**LOVE LADY** *Big Life BLRDB 137*	**33**	2
1 Jul 00 ●	**GHETTO ROMANCE** *Cooltempo CDCOOL 347*	**7**	7
28 Oct 00	**RUMOURS** *Cooltempo CDCOOLS 352*	**22**	4
31 Mar 01	**STILL BE LOVIN' YOU (re)** *Cooltempo CDCOOLS 355*	**11**	7
14 Jul 01	**SO WHAT IF I (re)** *Cooltempo CDCOOLS 357*	**12**	6
15 Dec 01	**AFTER THE LOVE HAS GONE** *Cooltempo CDCOOL 360*	**42**	2
19 Apr 97	**FOREVER** *Big Life BLRCD 31*	**13**	12
14 Apr 01	**SINCE YOU'VE BEEN GONE** *Cooltempo 5289592*	**16**	10

Carolina DAMAS – *See SUENO LATINO*

Bobby D'AMBROSIO featuring Michelle WEEKS
US, male DJ / producer and female vocalist (Singles: 3 weeks) pos/wks

2 Aug 97	**MOMENT OF MY LIFE** *Ministry of Sound MOSCDS 1*	**23**	3

DAMIAN *UK, male vocalist – Damian Davis (Singles: 26 weeks)* pos/wks

26 Dec 87	**THE TIME WARP 2** *Jive JIVE 160*	**51**	6
27 Aug 88	**THE TIME WARP 2 (re-issue)** *Jive JIVE 182*	**64**	3
19 Aug 89 ●	**THE TIME WARP (re-mix)** *Jive JIVE 209*	**7**	13
16 Dec 89	**WIG WAM BAM** *Jive JIVE 236*	**49**	4

'The Time Warp' is a re-mix of 'The Time Warp 2'

DAMNED
UK, male vocal / instrumental group – Dave Vanian, Brian James, Captain Sensible and Rat Scabies (Singles: 77 weeks, Albums: 54 weeks) pos/wks

5 May 79	**LOVE SONG** *Chiswick CHIS 112*	**20**	8
20 Oct 79	**SMASH IT UP** *Chiswick CHIS 116*	**35**	5
1 Dec 79	**I JUST CAN'T BE HAPPY TODAY** *Chiswick CHIS 120*	**46**	5
4 Oct 80	**HISTORY OF THE WORLD (PART 1)** *Chiswick CHIS 135*	**51**	4
28 Nov 81	**FRIDAY 13TH (EP)** *Stale One TRY 1*	**50**	4
10 Jul 82	**LOVELY MONEY** *Bronze BRO 149*	**42**	4
9 Jun 84	**THANKS FOR THE NIGHT** *Damned DAMNED 1*	**43**	4
30 Mar 85	**GRIMLY FIENDISH** *MCA GRIM 1*	**21**	7
22 Jun 85	**THE SHADOW OF LOVE (EDITION PREMIERE)** *MCA GRIM 2*	**25**	8
21 Sep 85	**IS IT A DREAM** *MCA GRIM 3*	**34**	4
8 Feb 86 ●	**ELOISE (re)** *MCA GRIM 4*	**3**	10
22 Nov 86	**ANYTHING** *MCA GRIM 5*	**32**	4
7 Feb 87	**GIGOLO** *MCA GRIM 6*	**29**	3
25 Apr 87	**ALONE AGAIN OR** *MCA GRIM 7*	**27**	6
28 Nov 87	**IN DULCE DECORUM** *MCA GRIM 8*	**72**	1
12 Mar 77	**DAMNED DAMNED DAMNED** *Stiff SEEZ 1*	**36**	10
17 Nov 79	**MACHINE GUN ETIQUETTE** *Chiswick CWK 3011*	**31**	5
29 Nov 80	**THE BLACK ALBUM** *Chiswick CWK 3015*	**29**	3
28 Nov 81	**THE BEST OF THE DAMNED** *Chiswick DAM 1*	**43**	12
23 Oct 82	**STRAWBERRIES** *Bronze BRON 542*	**15**	4
27 Jul 85	**PHANTASMAGORIA** *MCA MCF 3275*	**11**	17
13 Dec 86	**ANYTHING** *MCA MCG 6015*	**40**	2
12 Dec 87	**LIGHT AT THE END OF THE TUNNEL** *MCA MCSP 312*	**87**	1

Tracks on Friday 13th (EP): Disco Man / Limit Club / Billy Bad Breaks / Citadel

Kenny DAMON *US, male vocalist (Singles: 1 week)* pos/wks

19 May 66	**WHILE I LIVE** *Mercury MF 907*	**48**	1

Vic DAMONE *US, male vocalist – Vito Farinola (Singles: 22 weeks, Albums: 8 weeks)* pos/wks

6 Dec 57	**AN AFFAIR TO REMEMBER (OUR LOVE AFFAIR) (re)** *Philips PB 745*	**29**	2
9 May 58 ★	**ON THE STREET WHERE YOU LIVE** *Philips PB 819*	**1**	17
1 Aug 58	**THE ONLY MAN ON THE ISLAND** *Philips PB 837*	**24**	3
25 Apr 81	**NOW!** *RCA INTS 5080*	**28**	7
2 Apr 83	**VIC DAMONE SINGS THE GREAT SONGS** *CBS 32261*	**87**	1

Richie DAN
UK, male DJ / producer – Richard Gittens (Singles: 3 weeks) pos/wks

12 Aug 00	**CALL IT FATE** *Pure Silk CDPSR 1*	**34**	3

DANA *Ireland, female vocalist – Rosemary Brown (later Scallon) (Singles: 75 weeks, Albums: 2 weeks)* pos/wks

4 Apr 70 ★	**ALL KINDS OF EVERYTHING (re)** *Rex R 11054*	**1**	16
13 Feb 71	**WHO PUT THE LIGHTS OUT** *Rex R 11062*	**14**	11
25 Jan 75 ●	**PLEASE TELL HIM THAT I SAID HELLO** *GTO GT 6*	**8**	14
13 Dec 75 ●	**IT'S GONNA BE A COLD COLD CHRISTMAS** *GTO GT 45*	**4**	6
6 Mar 76	**NEVER GONNA FALL IN LOVE AGAIN** *GTO GT 55*	**31**	4
16 Oct 76	**FAIRYTALE** *GTO GT 66*	**13**	16
31 Mar 79	**SOMETHING'S COOKIN' IN THE KITCHEN** *GTO GT 243*	**44**	5
15 May 82	**I FEEL LOVE COMIN' ON** *Creole CR 32*	**66**	3
27 Dec 80	**EVERYTHING IS BEAUTIFUL** *Warwick WW 5099*	**43**	2

DANA – *See Mark PICCHIOTTI presents BASSTOY featuring DANA*

DANA INTERNATIONAL
Israel, transgender vocalist – Yaron Cohen (Singles: 4 weeks) pos/wks

27 Jun 98	**DIVA** *Dance Pool DANA 1CD*	**11**	4

DANCE CONSPIRACY
UK, male instrumental / production duo (Singles: 1 week) pos/wks

3 Oct 92	**DUB WAR** *XL Recordings XLT 34*	**72**	1

DANCE FLOOR VIRUS
Italy, male vocal / instrumental group (Singles: 2 weeks) pos/wks

21 Oct 95	**MESSAGE IN A BOTTLE** *Epic 6623742*	**49**	2

DANCE TO TIPPERARY
UK, male vocal / instrumental group (Singles: 2 weeks) pos/wks

24 May 03	**THE BHOYS ARE BACK IN TOWN** *Nede NRCD 2105*	**44**	2

DANCE 2 TRANCE *Germany, male instrumental / production duo – Rolf Ellmer and Dag Lerner (Singles: 8 weeks)* pos/wks

24 Apr 93	**P.OWER OF A.MERICAN N.ATIVES** *Logic 74321139582*	**25**	4
24 Jul 93	**TAKE A FREE FALL** *Logic 74321153602*	**36**	3
4 Feb 95	**WARRIOR** *Logic 74321257722*	**56**	1

See also JAM & SPOON featuring PLAVKA

Evan DANDO
US, male vocalist (Singles: 3 weeks, Albums: 1 week) pos/wks

24 Jun 95	**PERFECT DAY** *Virgin VSCDT 1552* [1]	**75**	1
31 May 03	**STOP MY HEAD** *Setanta SETCDA 127*	**38**	1
13 Dec 03	**IT LOOKS LIKE YOU** *Setanta SETCDA 130*	**68**	1
29 Mar 03	**BABY I'M BORED** *Setanta SETCD114*	**30**	1

[1] Kirsty MacColl and Evan Dando

See also LEMONHEADS

Suzanne DANDO
UK, female exercise instructor (Albums: 1 week) pos/wks

17 Mar 84	**SHAPE UP AND DANCE WITH SUZANNE DANDO** *Lifestyle LEG 21*	**87**	1

DANDY WARHOLS *US, male / female vocal / instrumental group (Singles: 30 weeks, Albums: 20 weeks)* pos/wks

28 Feb 98	**EVERY DAY SHOULD BE A HOLIDAY** *Capitol CDCL 797*	**29**	2
2 May 98	**NOT IF YOU WERE THE LAST JUNKIE ON EARTH** *Capitol CDCL 800*	**13**	4
8 Aug 98	**BOYS BETTER** *Capitol CDCLS 805*	**36**	2
10 Jun 00	**GET OFF** *Capitol CDCLS 821*	**38**	2
9 Sep 00	**BOHEMIAN LIKE YOU** *Capitol CDCL S823*	**42**	1
7 Jul 01	**GODLESS** *Capitol CDCL 829*	**66**	1
10 Nov 01 ●	**BOHEMIAN LIKE YOU (re-issue)** *Parlophone / Capitol CDCLX 823*	**5**	10
16 Mar 02	**GET OFF (re-issue)** *Parlophone / Capitol CDCL 835*	**34**	2
17 May 03	**WE USED TO BE FRIENDS** *Capitol CDCL 843*	**18**	3
9 Aug 03	**YOU WERE THE LAST HIGH** *Parlophone CDCL 845*	**34**	2
6 Dec 03	**PLAN A** *Parlophone CDCLS 851*	**66**	1
16 May 98	**COME DOWN** *Capitol 8365052*	**16**	8
24 Jun 00	**THIRTEEN TALES FROM URBAN BOHEMIA** *Capitol 8577872*	**32**	9
31 May 03	**WELCOME TO THE MONKEYHOUSE** *Parlophone 5901232*	**20**	3

DANDYS
UK, male vocal / instrumental group (Singles: 2 weeks) pos/wks

14 Mar 98	**YOU MAKE ME WANT TO SCREAM** *Artificial ATFCD 3*	**71**	1
30 May 98	**ENGLISH COUNTRY GARDEN** *Artificial ATFCD 4*	**57**	1

DANE *UK, male vocalist – Dane Bowers (Singles: 38 weeks)* pos/wks

29 Apr 00 ●	**BUGGIN** *Nulife 74321753342* [1]	**6**	8
26 Aug 00 ●	**OUT OF YOUR MIND (re)** *Nulife 74321782942* [2]	**2**	20
3 Mar 01 ●	**SHUT UP AND FORGET ABOUT IT** *Arista 74321835342*	**9**	5
7 Jul 01 ●	**ANOTHER LOVER** *Arista 74321863412*	**9**	5

[1] True Steppers featuring Dane Bowers [2] True Steppers and Dane Bowers featuring Victoria Beckham

See also ANOTHER LEVEL

D'ANGELO *US, male vocalist – Michael D'Angelo (Singles: 11 weeks, Albums: 5 weeks)* pos/wks

28 Oct 95	**BROWN SUGAR** *Cooltempo CDCOOL 307*	**24**	3
2 Mar 96	**CRUISIN'** *Cooltempo CDCOOL 316*	**31**	2
2 Mar 96	**COLD WORLD** *Geffen GFSTD 22114* [1]	**40**	2
15 Jun 96	**LADY** *Cooltempo CDCOOLS 323*	**21**	2
22 May 99	**BREAK UPS 2 MAKE UPS** *Def Jam 8709272* [2]	**33**	2
28 Oct 95	**BROWN SUGAR** *Cooltempo CTCD 46*	**57**	2
26 Feb 00	**VOODOO** *EMI 5250712* ▲	**21**	3

[1] Genius / GZA featuring D'Angelo [2] Method Man featuring D'Angelo

DANGER DANGER
US, male vocal / instrumental group (Singles: 5 weeks) pos/wks

8 Feb 92	**MONKEY BUSINESS** *Epic 6577517*	**42**	2
28 Mar 92	**I STILL THINK ABOUT YOU** *Epic 6578387*	**46**	2
13 Jun 92	**COMIN' HOME** *Epic 6581337*	**75**	1

DAN-I
UK, male vocalist – Selmore Lewinson (Singles: 9 weeks) pos/wks

10 Nov 79	**MONKEY CHOP** *Island WIP 6520*	**30**	9

Charlie DANIELS BAND *US, male vocal / instrumental group (Singles: 10 weeks, Albums: 1 week)* pos/wks

22 Sep 79	**THE DEVIL WENT DOWN TO GEORGIA** *Epic EPC 7737*	**14**	10
10 Nov 79	**MILLION MILE REFLECTIONS** *Epic EPC 83446*	**74**	1

Johnny DANKWORTH and His ORCHESTRA
UK, male orchestral group leader / instrumentalist – alto sax (Singles: 33 weeks) pos/wks

22 Jun 56 ●	**EXPERIMENTS WITH MICE** *Parlophone R 4185*	**7**	12
23 Feb 61 ●	**AFRICAN WALTZ** *Columbia DB 4590*	**9**	21

DANNII – *See Dannii MINOGUE*

DANNY and the JUNIORS
US, male vocal group (Singles: 19 weeks) pos/wks

17 Jan 58 ●	**AT THE HOP** *HMV POP 436* ▲	**3**	14
10 Jul 76	**AT THE HOP (re-issue)** *ABC 4123*	**39**	5

DANNY WILSON *UK, male vocal / instrumental group (Singles: 28 weeks, Albums: 11 weeks)* pos/wks

22 Aug 87 ●	**MARY'S PRAYER (re)** *Virgin VS 934*	**3**	18
17 Jun 89	**THE SECOND SUMMER OF LOVE** *Virgin VS 1186*	**23**	9
16 Sep 89	**NEVER GONNA BE THE SAME** *Virgin VS 1203*	**69**	1
30 Apr 88	**MEET DANNY WILSON** *Virgin V 2419*	**65**	5
29 Jul 89	**BEEBOP MOPTOP** *Virgin V 2594*	**24**	5
31 Aug 91	**SWEET DANNY WILSON** *Virgin V 2669*	**54**	1

It was not until 'Mary's Prayer' re-entered in Apr 1988 that it reached its peak position of No.3

DANSE SOCIETY *UK, male vocal / instrumental group (Singles: 5 weeks, Albums: 4 weeks)*

			pos	wks
27 Aug 83		WAKE UP *Society SOC 5*	61	3
5 Nov 83		HEAVEN IS WAITING *Society SOC 6*	60	2
11 Feb 84		HEAVEN IS WAITING *Society 205 972*	39	4

Steven DANTE *UK, male vocalist – Steven Dennis (Singles: 16 weeks, Albums: 1 week)*

			pos	wks
26 Sep 87		THE REAL THING *Chrysalis CHS 3167* [1]	13	10
9 Jul 88		I'M TOO SCARED *Cooltempo DANTE 1*	34	6
3 Sep 88		FIND OUT *Cooltempo CTLP 6*	87	1

[1] Jellybean featuring Steven Dante

Tonja DANTZLER *US, female vocalist (Singles: 1 week)*

			pos	wks
17 Dec 94		IN AND OUT OF MY LIFE *ffrr FCD 246*	66	1

DANY – *See DOUBLE DEE*

DANZIG *US, male vocal / instrumental group (Singles: 1 week)*

			pos	wks
14 May 94		MOTHER *American MOMDD 1*	62	1

DAPHNE *US, female vocalist (Singles: 1 week)*

			pos	wks
9 Dec 95		CHANGE *Stress CDSTR 54*	71	1

DAPHNE & CELESTE *US, female vocal duo – Daphne DeConcetto and Celeste Cruz (Singles: 28 weeks)*

			pos	wks
5 Feb 00	●	OOH STICK YOU! *Universal MCSTD 40209*	8	12
17 Jun 00		UGLY *Universal MCSTD 40232*	18	12
2 Sep 00		SCHOOL'S OUT *Universal MCSTD 40238*	12	4

Terence Trent D'ARBY (389 Top 500) *Unpredictable US pop / soul singer / songwriter, b. 15 Mar 1962, New York, US, whose success came after relocating to UK. Multi-million-selling, Grammy-winning debut album, 'Introducing the Hardline...', was a worldwide hit. Winner of 1988 Brit award for Best International Newcomer (Singles: 77 weeks, Albums: 96 weeks)*

			pos	wks
14 Mar 87	●	IF YOU LET ME STAY *CBS TRENT 1*	7	13
20 Jun 87	●	WISHING WELL *CBS TRENT 2* ▲	4	11
10 Oct 87		DANCE LITTLE SISTER (PART ONE) *CBS TRENT 3*	20	7
9 Jan 88	●	SIGN YOUR NAME *CBS TRENT 4*	2	10
20 Jan 90		TO KNOW SOMEONE DEEPLY IS TO KNOW SOMEONE SOFTLY *CBS TRENT 6*	55	3
17 Apr 93		DO YOU LOVE ME LIKE YOU SAY *Columbia 6590732*	14	6
19 Jun 93		DELICATE *Columbia 6593312* [1]	14	6
28 Aug 93		SHE KISSED ME *Columbia 6595922*	16	7
20 Nov 93		LET HER DOWN EASY *Columbia 6598642*	18	7
8 Apr 95		HOLDING ON TO YOU *Columbia 6614235*	20	6
5 Aug 95		VIBRATOR *Columbia 6622585*	57	1
25 Jul 87	★	INTRODUCING THE HARDLINE ACCORDING TO TERENCE TRENT D'ARBY *CBS 4509111* ■	1	67
4 Nov 89		NEITHER FISH NOR FLESH *CBS 4658091*	12	5
15 May 93	●	SYMPHONY OR DAMN *Columbia 4735612*	4	19
29 Apr 95		TERENCE TRENT D'ARBY'S VIBRATOR *Columbia 4785052*	11	5

[1] Terence Trent D'Arby featuring Des'ree

Richard DARBYSHIRE *UK, male vocalist (Singles: 7 weeks)*

			pos	wks
20 Aug 88		COMING BACK FOR MORE *Chrysalis JEL 4* [1]	41	3
24 Jul 93		THIS I SWEAR *Dome CDDOME 1003*	50	3
12 Feb 94		WHEN ONLY LOVE WILL DO *Dome CDDOME 1008*	54	1

[1] Jellybean featuring Richard Darbyshire

See also LIVING IN A BOX

DARE *UK, male vocal / instrumental group (Singles: 7 weeks, Albums: 1 week)*

			pos	wks
29 Apr 89		THE RAINDANCE *A&M AM 483*	62	2
29 Jul 89		ABANDON *A&M AM 519*	71	2
10 Aug 91		WE DON'T NEED A REASON *A&M AM 755*	52	2
5 Oct 91		REAL LOVE *A&M AM 824*	67	1
14 Sep 91		BLOOD FROM STONE *A&M 3953601*	48	1

DARE *Holland, female vocal trio (Singles: 1 week)*

			pos	wks
13 Sep 03		CHIHUAHUA *All Around the World CDGLOBE 311*	45	1

Matt DAREY *UK, male producer / instrumentalist (Singles: 17 weeks)*

			pos	wks
9 Oct 99		LIBERATION (TEMPTATION – FLY LIKE AN EAGLE) *Incentive CENT 1CDS* [1]	19	3
22 Apr 00		FROM RUSSIA WITH LOVE *Liquid Asset ASSET CD003* [2]	40	2
15 Jul 00		BEAUTIFUL *Incentive CENT 7CDS* [3]	21	4
20 Apr 02	●	BEAUTIFUL (re-mix) *Incentive CENT 38CDS* [4]	10	6
14 Dec 02		U SHINE ON *Incentive CENT 50CDS* [5]	34	2

[1] Matt Darey presents Mash Up [2] Matt Darey presents DSP [3] Matt Darey's Mash Up presents Marcella Woods [4] Matt Darey featuring Marcella Woods [5] Matt Darey and Marcella Woods

See also LOST TRIBE; MELT featuring Little Ms MARCIE; SUNBURST; MDM

Bobby DARIN (377 Top 500) *Singer / songwriter / actor and multi-instrumentalist who had pop, rock, R&B, country and MOR hits, b. Walden Robert Cassotto, 14 May 1936, New York, d. 20 Dec 1973. This Grammy winner was posthumously inducted into the Rock and Roll Hall of Fame in 1990 (Singles: 162 weeks, Albums: 15 weeks)*

			pos	wks
1 Aug 58		SPLISH SPLASH *London HLE 8666*	18	7
9 Jan 59		QUEEN OF THE HOP *London HLE 8737*	24	2
29 May 59	★	DREAM LOVER *London HLE 8867*	1	19
25 Sep 59	★	MACK THE KNIFE (2re) *London HLK 8939* ▲	1	18
29 Jan 60	●	LA MER (BEYOND THE SEA) (re) *London HLK 9034*	8	13
31 Mar 60	●	CLEMENTINE *London HLK 9086*	8	12
30 Jun 60		BILL BAILEY (re) *London HLK 9142*	34	2
16 Mar 61	●	LAZY RIVER *London HLK 9303*	2	13
6 Jul 61		NATURE BOY *London HLK 9375*	24	7
12 Oct 61	●	YOU MUST HAVE BEEN A BEAUTIFUL BABY *London HLK 9429*	10	11
26 Oct 61		THEME FROM 'COME SEPTEMBER' *London HLK 9407* [1]	50	1
21 Dec 61	●	MULTIPLICATION *London HLK 9474*	5	13
19 Jul 62	●	THINGS *London HLK 9575*	2	17
4 Oct 62		IF A MAN ANSWERS *Capitol CL 15272*	24	6
29 Nov 62		BABY FACE *London HLK 9624*	40	4
25 Jul 63		EIGHTEEN YELLOW ROSES *Capitol CL 15306*	37	4
13 Oct 66	●	IF I WERE A CARPENTER *Atlantic 584 051*	9	12
14 Apr 79		DREAM LOVER / MACK THE KNIFE (re-issue) *Lightning LIG 9017*	64	1
19 Mar 60	●	THIS IS DARIN *London HA 2235*	4	8
9 Apr 60		THAT'S ALL *London HAE 2172*	15	1
5 Oct 85		THE LEGEND OF BOBBY DARIN – HIS GREATEST HITS *Stylus SMR 8504*	39	6

[1] Bobby Darin Orchestra

DARIO G *UK, male DJ / production trio (Singles: 44 weeks, Albums: 4 weeks)*

			pos	wks
27 Sep 97	●	SUNCHYME *Eternal WEA 130CD*	2	18
20 Jun 98	●	CARNAVAL DE PARIS *Eternal WEA 162CD*	5	9
12 Sep 98		SUNMACHINE *Eternal WEA 173CD*	17	4
25 Mar 00		VOICES *Eternal WEA 256CD*	37	2
3 Feb 01	●	DREAM TO ME *Manifesto FESCD 79*	9	6
8 Jun 02		CARNAVAL 2002 (re-mix) *Eternal WEA 349CD*	34	3
25 Jan 03		HEAVEN IS CLOSER (FEELS LIKE HEAVEN) *Serious SER61CD*	39	2
11 Jul 98		SUNMACHINE *Eternal 3984233782*	26	4

DARIUS *UK, male vocalist – Darius Danesh (Singles: 43 weeks, Albums: 19 weeks)*

			pos	wks
10 Aug 02	★	COLOURBLIND *Mercury 639652* ■	1	16
7 Dec 02	●	RUSHES (re) *Mercury 0638042*	5	12
15 Mar 03	●	INCREDIBLE (WHAT I MEANT TO SAY) (re) *Mercury 0779772*	9	8
21 Jun 03		GIRL IN THE MOON (re) *Fontana 9808233*	21	3
14 Dec 02	●	DIVE IN *Mercury 0635922*	6	19

DARK MONKS *UK, male production duo (Singles: 1 week)* pos/wks

14 Sep 02 **INSANE** *Incentive CENT 45CDS* 62 1

DARK STAR
UK, male vocal / instrumental group (Singles: 6 weeks) pos/wks

26 Jun 99 **ABOUT 3AM** *Harvest CDEM 545* 50 1
15 Jan 00 **GRACEADELICA** *Harvest CDEMS 556* 25 3
13 May 00 **I AM THE SUN** *Harvest CDEMS 566* 31 2

DARKMAN *UK, male rapper – Brian Mitchell (Singles: 7 weeks)* pos/wks

14 May 94 **YABBA DABBA DOO** *Wild Card CARDD 6* 49 2
20 Aug 94 **WHO'S THE DARKMAN** *Wild Card CARDD 8* 46 2
3 Dec 94 **YABBA DABBA DOO (re-issue)** *Wild Card CARDD 11* 37 2
21 Oct 95 **BRAND NEW DAY** *Wild Card 5771892* 74 1

The DARKNESS *UK, male vocal / instrumental group (Singles: 19 weeks, Albums: 24 weeks)* pos/wks

8 Mar 03 **GET YOUR HANDS OFF MY WOMAN** *Must Destroy DUSTY 006CD* 43 2
28 Jun 03 **GROWING ON ME** *Must Destroy DUSTY 010CD* 11 5
4 Oct 03 ● **I BELIEVE IN A THING CALLED LOVE** *Must Destroy DARK 01CD* 2 11
27 Dec 03 ● **CHRISTMAS TIME (DON'T LET THE BELLS END)** *Must Destroy DARK 02CD* ....2 1+
19 Jul 03 ★ **PERMISSION TO LAND** *Must Destroy 5046674522* ....1 24+

DARLING BUDS *UK, male / female vocal / instrumental group (Singles: 20 weeks, Albums: 3 weeks)* pos/wks

8 Oct 88 **BURST** *Epic BLOND 1* 50 5
7 Jan 89 **HIT THE GROUND** *CBS BLOND 2* 27 5
25 Mar 89 **LET'S GO ROUND THERE** *CBS BLOND 3* 49 4
22 Jul 89 **YOU'VE GOT TO CHOOSE** *CBS BLOND 4* 45 3
2 Jun 90 **TINY MACHINE** *CBS BLOND 5* 60 2
12 Sep 92 **SURE THING** *Epic 6582157* 71 1
18 Feb 89 **POP SAID** *Epic 462894 1* 23 3

Guy DARRELL *UK, male vocalist (Singles: 13 weeks)* pos/wks

18 Aug 73 **I'VE BEEN HURT** *Santa Ponsa PNS 4* 12 13

James DARREN *US, male vocalist – James Ercolani (Singles: 25 weeks)* pos/wks

11 Aug 60 **BECAUSE THEY'RE YOUNG** *Pye International 7N 25059* 29 7
14 Dec 61 **GOODBYE CRUEL WORLD** *Pye International 7N 25116* 28 9
29 Mar 62 **HER ROYAL MAJESTY** *Pye International 7N 25125* 36 3
21 Jun 62 **CONSCIENCE** *Pye International 7N 25138* 30 6

DARTS (384 Top 500)
Britain's best-known doo-wop vocal group: line-up included Den Hegarty, Griff Fender, Rita Ray and Bob Fish. The popular London-based eight-piece band had three successive No.2 hits with revivals of early US rock 'n' roll and R&B songs (Singles: 117 weeks, Albums: 57 weeks) pos/wks

5 Nov 77 ● **DADDY COOL / THE GIRL CAN'T HELP IT** *Magnet MAG 100* 6 13
28 Jan 78 ● **COME BACK MY LOVE** *Magnet MAG 110* 2 12
6 May 78 ● **THE BOY FROM NEW YORK CITY** *Magnet MAG 116* 2 13
5 Aug 78 ● **IT'S RAINING** *Magnet MAG 126* 2 11
11 Nov 78 **DON'T LET IT FADE AWAY** *Magnet MAG 134* 18 11
10 Feb 79 ● **GET IT** *Magnet MAG 140* 10 9
21 Jul 79 ● **DUKE OF EARL** *Magnet MAG 147* 6 11
20 Oct 79 **CAN'T GET ENOUGH OF YOUR LOVE** *Magnet MAG 156* 43 6
1 Dec 79 **REET PETITE** *Magnet MAG 160* 51 7
31 May 80 **LET'S HANG ON** *Magnet MAG 174* 11 14
6 Sep 80 **PEACHES** *Magnet MAG 179* 66 3
29 Nov 80 **WHITE CHRISTMAS / SH-BOOM (LIFE COULD BE A DREAM)** *Magnet MAG 184* 48 7
3 Dec 77 ● **DARTS** *Magnet MAG 5020* 9 22
3 Jun 78 **EVERYONE PLAYS DARTS** *Magnet MAG 5022* 12 18
18 Nov 78 ● **AMAZING DARTS** *K-Tel / Magnet DLP 7981* 8 13
6 Oct 79 **DART ATTACK** *Magnet MAG 5030* 38 4

DARUDE *Finland, male producer – Ville Virtanen (Singles: 29 weeks)* pos/wks

24 Jun 00 ● **SANDSTORM** *Neo NEOCD 033* 3 15
25 Nov 00 ● **FEEL THE BEAT** *Neo NEOCD 045* 5 10
15 Sep 01 **OUT OF CONTROL (BACK FOR MORE)** *Neo NEOCD 067* 13 4

DAS EFX *US, male production / rap duo (Singles: 5 weeks)* pos/wks

7 Aug 93 **CHECK YO SELF** *Fourth & Broadway BRCD 283* [1] 36 4
25 Apr 98 **RAP SCHOLAR** *East West E 3853CD* [2] 42 1

[1] Ice Cube featuring Das EFX [2] Das EFX featuring Redman

DASHBOARD CONFESSIONAL
US, male vocalist – Chris Carrabba (Singles: 1 week) pos/wks

22 Nov 03 **HANDS DOWN** *Vagrant 9813790* 60 1

The DATSUNS *New Zealand, male vocal / instrumental group (Singles: 5 weeks, Albums: 3 weeks)* pos/wks

5 Oct 02 **IN LOVE** *V2 VVR 5020953* 25 2
22 Feb 03 **HARMONIC GENERATOR** *V2 VVR 5021223* 33 2
6 Sep 03 **MF FROM HELL** *V2 VVR 5021753* 55 1
19 Oct 02 **THE DATSUNS** *V2 VVR 1020962* 17 3

N'Dea DAVENPORT *US, female vocalist (Singles: 7 weeks)* pos/wks

11 Sep 93 **TRUST ME** *Cooltempo CDCOOL 278* [1] 34 2
20 Jun 98 **BRING IT ON** *Gee Street VVR5002033* 52 1
15 Dec 01 **YOU CAN'T CHANGE ME** *Defected DFECT 41CDS* [2] 25 4

[1] Guru featuring N'Dea Davenport [2] Roger Sanchez featuring Armand Van Helden and N'Dea Davenport

See also BRAND NEW HEAVIES; GURU

Anne-Marie DAVID *France, female vocalist (Singles: 9 weeks)* pos/wks

28 Apr 73 **WONDERFUL DREAM** *Epic EPC 1446* 13 9

Craig DAVID (329 Top 500)
Critically lauded singer / songwriter, b. 5 May 1981, Southampton, UK. At 18 years, 11 months and 10 days he was the youngest British male to write and sing a No.1. Won numerous awards for his songs, records and videos. Debut album 'Born to Do It' went gold in 24 countries with UK sales exceeding 1.5 million (Singles: 115 weeks, Albums: 85 weeks) pos/wks

11 Dec 99 ● **RE-REWIND THE CROWD SAY BO SELECTA** *Public Demand / Relentless RELENT 1CDS* [1] 2 17
15 Apr 00 ★ **FILL ME IN** *Wildstar CDWILD 28* ■ 1 14
15 Jul 00 ● **WOMAN TROUBLE** *Public Demand / ffrr FCD 380* [2] 6 10
5 Aug 00 ★ **7 DAYS (re)** *Wildstar CDWILD 30* ■ 1 15
2 Dec 00 ● **WALKING AWAY** *Wildstar CDWILD 35* 3 13
31 Mar 01 ● **RENDEZVOUS** *Wildstar CDWILD 36* 8 10
9 Nov 02 ● **WHAT'S YOUR FLAVA?** *Wildstar CDWILD 43* 8 10
1 Feb 03 ● **HIDDEN AGENDA** *Wildstar CDWILD 44* 10 6
10 May 03 ● **RISE & FALL** *Wildstar CDWILD 45* [3] 2 10
9 Aug 03 ● **SPANISH** *Wildstar CDWILD 49* 8 6
25 Oct 03 **WORLD FILLED WITH LOVE** *Wildstar CDWILD 51* 15 4
26 Aug 00 ★ **BORN TO DO IT** *Wildstar CDWILD 32* ■ 1 50
23 Nov 02 ● **SLICKER THAN YOUR AVERAGE** *Wildstar CDWILD 42* 4 35

[1] Artful Dodger featuring Craig David [2] Artful Dodger and Robbie Craig featuring Craig David [3] Craig David featuring Sting

FR DAVID *France, male vocalist – Robert Fitoussi (Singles: 13 weeks, Albums: 6 weeks)* pos/wks

2 Apr 83 ● **WORDS** *Carrere CAR 248* 2 12
18 Jun 83 **MUSIC** *Carrere CAR 282* 71 1
7 May 83 **WORDS** *Carrere CAL 145* 46 6

DAVID and JONATHAN *UK, male vocal duo – Roger Greenaway and Roger Cook (Singles: 22 weeks)* pos/wks

13 Jan 66 **MICHELLE** *Columbia DB 7800* 11 6
7 Jul 66 ● **LOVERS OF THE WORLD UNITE** *Columbia DB 7950* 7 16

See also BLUE MINK; PIPKINS

Jim DAVIDSON *UK, male vocalist (Singles: 4 weeks)*

		pos	wks
27 Dec 80	**WHITE CHRISTMAS / TOO RISKY** *Scratch SCR 001*	52	4

Paul DAVIDSON *Jamaica, male vocalist (Singles: 10 weeks)*

		pos	wks
27 Dec 75 ●	**MIDNIGHT RIDER** *Tropical ALO 56*	10	10

Dave DAVIES *UK, male vocalist (Singles: 17 weeks)*

		pos	wks
19 Jul 67 ●	**DEATH OF A CLOWN** *Pye 7N 17356*	3	10
6 Dec 67	**SUZANNAH'S STILL ALIVE** *Pye 7N 17429*	20	7

See also KINKS

Windsor DAVIES and Don ESTELLE *UK, male actors / vocal duo, Don Estelle, d. 2 Aug 2003 (Singles: 16 weeks, Albums: 8 weeks)*

		pos	wks
17 May 75 ★	**WHISPERING GRASS** *EMI 2290* [1]	1	12
25 Oct 75	**PAPER DOLL** *EMI 2361* [2]	41	4
10 Jan 76 ●	**SING LOFTY** *EMI EMC 3102* [1]	10	8

[1] Windsor Davies as BSM Williams and Don Estelle as Gunner Sugden (Lofty)
[2] Don Estelle and Windsor Davies [1] Don Estelle and Windsor Davies

Andrew DAVIS – *See BBC SYMPHONY ORCHESTRA SINGERS and CHORUS*

Billie DAVIS
UK, female vocalist – Carol Hedges (Singles: 33 weeks)

		pos	wks
30 Aug 62	**WILL I WHAT** *Parlophone R 4932* [1]	18	10
7 Feb 63 ●	**TELL HIM** *Decca F 11572*	10	12
30 May 63	**HE'S THE ONE** *Decca F 11658*	40	3
9 Oct 68	**I WANT YOU TO BE MY BABY** *Decca F 12823*	33	8

[1] Mike Sarne with Billie Davis

Billy DAVIS Jr – *See Marilyn McCOO and Billy DAVIS Jr*

Carl DAVIS and the ROYAL LIVERPOOL PHILHARMONIC ORCHESTRA
US, male conductor and orchestra (Albums: 4 weeks)

		pos	wks
19 Oct 91	**PAUL MCCARTNEY'S LIVERPOOL ORATORIO** *EMI Classics PAUL 1*	36	4

See also ROYAL LIVERPOOL PHILHARMONIC ORCHESTRA

Colin DAVIS – *See BBC SYMPHONY ORCHESTRA SINGERS and CHORUS*

Darlene DAVIS *US, female vocalist (Singles: 5 weeks)*

		pos	wks
7 Feb 87	**I FOUND LOVE** *Serious 7OUS 1*	55	5

John DAVIS and the MONSTER ORCHESTRA
US, male vocal / instrumental group (Singles: 2 weeks)

		pos	wks
10 Feb 79	**AIN'T THAT ENOUGH FOR YOU** *Miracle M 2*	70	2

Mac DAVIS *US, male vocalist (Singles: 22 weeks)*

		pos	wks
4 Nov 72	**BABY DON'T GET HOOKED ON ME** *CBS 8250* ▲	29	6
15 Nov 80	**IT'S HARD TO BE HUMBLE** *Casablanca CAN 210*	27	16

Miles DAVIS *US, male instrumentalist – trumpet, d. 28 Sep 1991 (Albums: 9 weeks)*

		pos	wks
11 Jul 70	**BITCHES BREW** *CBS 66236*	71	1
15 Jun 85	**YOU'RE UNDER ARREST** *CBS 26447*	88	1
18 Oct 86	**TUTU** *Warner Bros. 925490 1*	74	2
3 Jun 89	**AMANDLA** *Warner Bros. WX 250*	49	2
5 Oct 96	**THE VERY BEST OF MILES DAVIS** *Columbia SONYTV 17CD*	64	1
28 Apr 01	**KIND OF BLUE** *Columbia CK 64935*	63	2

Richie DAVIS – *See SHUT UP AND DANCE*

20 YEARS AGO

The Top Hit Albums Performers in 1984

Top-selling album: CAN'T SLOW DOWN by Lionel Richie
Longest run at No.1: LEGEND by Bob Marley and the Wailers (12 weeks)
Most weeks on chart by any act: DIRE STRAITS (116 weeks)
Total albums shipped in 1984: 100,200,000

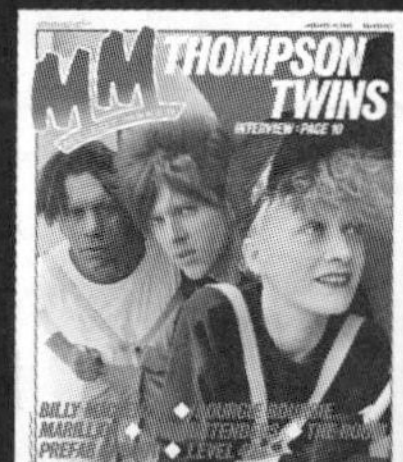

In addition to the above blockbusters, Billy Joel had the most albums on chart in a single week with six. The year was not a great one for female soloists. None reached the top of the album chart although two male/female acts, Thompson Twins and Eurythmics, did have No.1s.

Perhaps the biggest star of 1984 was 1984 itself. It was the first year to have three hit LPs named after it, with Van Halen, Rick Wakeman and Eurythmics all having albums titled *1984* in the record racks.

Keyboard wizard Rick Wakeman, one of three acts to name-check the year 1984 in an album title

Roy DAVIS Jr featuring Peven EVERETT
US, male producer, male vocalist (Singles: 4 weeks) pos/wks

1 Nov 97 **GABRIEL** *XL XLS 88CD* 22 4

Ruth DAVIS – *See Bo KIRKLAND and Ruth DAVIS*

Sammy DAVIS Jr *US, male vocalist, d. 16 May 1990 (Singles: 37 weeks, Albums: 1 week)* pos/wks

29 Jul 55 **SOMETHING'S GOTTA GIVE (re)** *Brunswick LAT 8296* 11 7
9 Sep 55 ● **LOVE ME OR LEAVE ME (re)** *Brunswick 05428* 8 8
30 Sep 55 **THAT OLD BLACK MAGIC** *Brunswick 05450* 16 1
7 Oct 55 **HEY THERE** *Brunswick 05469* 19 1
20 Apr 56 **IN A PERSIAN MARKET** *Brunswick 05518* 28 1
28 Dec 56 **ALL OF YOU** *Brunswick 05629* 28 1
16 Jun 60 **HAPPY TO MAKE YOUR ACQUAINTANCE** *Brunswick 05830* [1] 46 1
22 Mar 62 **WHAT KIND OF FOOL AM I? / GONNA BUILD A MOUNTAIN** *Reprise R 20048* 26 8
13 Dec 62 **ME AND MY SHADOW (re)** *Reprise R 20128* [2] 20 9
13 Apr 63 **SAMMY DAVIS JR AT THE COCONUT GROVE** *Reprise R 6063/2* 19 1

[1] Sammy Davis Jr and Carmen McRae [2] Frank Sinatra and Sammy Davis Jr

Skeeter DAVIS
US, female vocalist – Mary Penick (Singles: 13 weeks) pos/wks

14 Mar 63 **END OF THE WORLD** *RCA 1328* 18 13

TJ DAVIS *UK, female vocalist (Singles: 4 weeks)* pos/wks

27 Jul 96 **BRILLIANT FEELING** *Arista 74321380902* [1] 72 1
29 Dec 01 **WONDERFUL LIFE** *Melting Pot MPRCD 20* 42 3

[1] Full Monty Allstars featuring TJ Davis

Zelma DAVIS – *See C & C MUSIC FACTORY*

Spencer DAVIS GROUP *Big-selling Birmingham (UK) band: Spencer Davis (v/g), Peter York (d) and brothers Muff (b) and Steve Winwood (v/g/k). Both No.1s penned by reggae artist Jackie Edwards. Teenager Steve Winwood left 1967, and continued hit run with Blind Faith, Traffic and as a soloist (Singles: 71 weeks, Albums: 47 weeks)* pos/wks

5 Nov 64 **I CAN'T STAND IT** *Fontana TF 499* 47 3
25 Feb 65 **EVERY LITTLE BIT HURTS** *Fontana TF 530* 41 3
10 Jun 65 **STRONG LOVE (re)** *Fontana TF 571* 44 4
2 Dec 65 ★ **KEEP ON RUNNING** *Fontana TF 632* 1 14
24 Mar 66 ★ **SOMEBODY HELP ME** *Fontana TF 679* 1 10
1 Sep 66 **WHEN I COME HOME** *Fontana TF 739* 12 9
3 Nov 66 ● **GIMME SOME LOVING** *Fontana TF 762* 2 12
26 Jan 67 ● **I'M A MAN** *Fontana TF 785* 9 7
9 Aug 67 **TIME SELLER** *Fontana TF 854* 30 5
10 Jan 68 **MR SECOND CLASS** *United Artists UP 1203* 35 4
8 Jan 66 ● **THEIR 1ST LP** *Fontana TL 5242* 6 9
22 Jan 66 ● **THE 2ND LP** *Fontana TL 5295* 3 18
11 Sep 66 ● **AUTUMN '66** *Fontana TL 5359* 4 20

DAVIS PINCKNEY PROJECT – *See GO GO LORENZO and the DAVIS PINCKNEY PROJECT*

DAWN *US, male / female vocal trio – leader Tony Orlando, b. Michael Cassavitis (Singles: 109 weeks, Albums: 2 weeks)* pos/wks

16 Jan 71 ● **CANDIDA** *Bell 1118* 9 11
10 Apr 71 ★ **KNOCK THREE TIMES** *Bell 1146* ▲ 1 27
31 Jul 71 ● **WHAT ARE YOU DOING SUNDAY** *Bell 1169* [1] 3 12
10 Mar 73 ★ **TIE A YELLOW RIBBON ROUND THE OLE OAK TREE (re)** *Bell 1287* [1] ▲ 1 40
4 Aug 73 **SAY, HAS ANYBODY SEEN MY SWEET GYPSY ROSE** *Bell 1322* [1] 12 15
9 Mar 74 **WHO'S IN THE STRAWBERRY PATCH WITH SALLY** *Bell 1343* [2] 37 4
4 May 74 **GOLDEN RIBBONS** *Bell BELLS 236* 46 2

[1] Dawn featuring Tony Orlando [2] Tony Orlando and Dawn

Julie DAWN – *See Cyril STAPLETON and his ORCHESTRA*

Liz DAWN – *See Joe LONGTHORNE*

DAWN OF THE REPLICANTS *UK, male vocal / instrumental group (Singles: 2 weeks, Albums: 1 week)* pos/wks

7 Feb 98 **CANDLEFIRE** *East West EW 147CD1* 52 1
4 Apr 98 **HOGWASH FARM (THE DIESEL HANDS EP)** *East West EW 157CD* 65 1
28 Feb 98 **ONE HEAD, TWO ARMS, TWO LEGS** *East West 630196002* 62 1

Tracks on Hogwash Farm (The Diesel Hands EP): Hogwash Farm (re-built) / Night Train to Lichtenstein / The Duchess of Surin / Crow Valley

Dana DAWSON *US, female vocalist (Singles: 14 weeks)* pos/wks

15 Jul 95 ● **3 IS FAMILY** *EMI CDEM 378* 9 8
28 Oct 95 **GOT TO GIVE ME LOVE** *EMI CDEM 392* 27 2
4 May 96 **SHOW ME** *EMI CDEMS 423* 28 3
20 Jul 96 **HOW I WANNA BE LOVED** *EMI CDEMS 432* 42 1

Bobby DAY
US, male vocalist – Robert Byrd, d. 15 Jul 1990 (Singles: 2 weeks) pos/wks

7 Nov 58 **ROCKIN' ROBIN** *London HL 8726* 29 2

Darren DAY
UK, male vocalist (Singles: 7 weeks, Albums: 1 week) pos/wks

8 Oct 94 **YOUNG GIRL** *Bell 74321231082* 42 2
8 Jun 96 **SUMMER HOLIDAY MEDLEY** *RCA 74321384472* 17 4
9 May 98 **HOW CAN I BE SURE ?** *Eastcoast DDCD 001* 71 1
18 Apr 98 **DARREN DAY** *Eastcoast DAYCD 01* 62 1

Doris DAY (361 Top 500)
The Fifties' favourite singer / actress, b. Doris Kappelhoff, 3 Apr 1924, Cincinnati. The No.1 female movie star of that era also had numerous British hits (not to mention 25 US bestsellers) before the UK chart first started (Singles: 146 weeks, Albums: 37 weeks) pos/wks

14 Nov 52 ● **SUGARBUSH (re)** *Columbia DB 3123* [1] 8 8
21 Nov 52 ● **MY LOVE AND DEVOTION** *Columbia DB 3157* 10 2
3 Apr 53 **MA SAYS, PA SAYS** *Columbia DB3242* [2] 12 1
17 Apr 53 **FULL TIME JOB** *Columbia DB 3242* [2] 11 1
24 Jul 53 ● **LET'S WALK THAT-A-WAY** *Philips PB 157* [2] 4 14
2 Apr 54 ★ **SECRET LOVE** *Philips PB 230* ▲ 1 29
27 Aug 54 ● **THE BLACK HILLS OF DAKOTA** *Philips PB 287* 7 8
1 Oct 54 ● **IF I GIVE MY HEART TO YOU** *Philips PB 325* [3] 4 11
8 Apr 55 ● **READY, WILLING AND ABLE** *Philips PB 402* 7 9
9 Sep 55 **LOVE ME OR LEAVE ME** *Philips PB 479* 20 1
21 Oct 55 **I'LL NEVER STOP LOVING YOU (re)** *Philips PB 497* 17 3
29 Jun 56 ★ **WHATEVER WILL BE, WILL BE (QUE SERA, SERA)** *Philips PB 586* 1 22
13 Jun 58 **A VERY PRECIOUS LOVE** *Philips PB 799* 16 11
15 Aug 58 **EVERYBODY LOVES A LOVER (re)** *Philips PB 843* 25 4
12 Mar 64 ● **MOVE OVER DARLING** *CBS AAG 183* 8 16
18 Apr 87 **MOVE OVER DARLING (re-issue)** *CBS LEGS 1* 45 6
6 Jan 79 **20 GOLDEN GREATS** *Warwick PR 5053* 12 11
11 Nov 89 **A PORTRAIT OF DORIS DAY** *Stylus SMR 984* 32 9
6 Nov 93 **GREATEST HITS** *Telstar TCD 2659* 14 12
10 Dec 94 **THE LOVE ALBUM** *Vision VIS CD2* 64 3
20 Nov 99 **THE MAGIC OF THE MOVIES** *Columbia SONYTV 79CD* 63 1
20 Apr 02 **THE BEST OF DORIS DAY – 41 HOLLYWOOD GREATS** *Columbia 5079632* 73 1

[1] Doris Day and Frankie Laine [2] Doris Day and Johnnie Ray [3] Doris Day with The Mellomen

Inaya DAY
US, female vocalist – Inaya Davis (Singles: 3 weeks) pos/wks

22 May 99 **JUST CAN'T GET ENOUGH** *AM:PM CDAMPM 121* [1] 39 2
7 Oct 00 **FEEL IT** *Positiva CDTIV 141* 51 1

[1] Harry 'Choo Choo' Romero presents Inaya Day

See also Boris DLUGOSCH

Patti DAY *US, female vocalist (Singles: 1 week)* pos/wks

9 Dec 89 RIGHT BEFORE MY EYES *Debut DEBT 3080* 69 1

DAY ONE *UK, male vocal / instrumental duo (Singles: 1 week, Albums: 1 week)* pos/wks

13 Nov 99 I'M DOIN' FINE *Melankolic / Virgin SADD6* 68 1
25 Mar 00 ORDINARY MAN *Melankolic CDSAD 8* 70 1

DAYEENE *Sweden, female vocal duo (Singles: 1 week)* pos/wks

17 Jul 99 AND IT HURTS *Pukka CDPUKKA 20* 63 1

Taylor DAYNE *US, female vocalist – Leslie Wundermann (Singles: 54 weeks, Albums: 17 weeks)* pos/wks

23 Jan 88 ● TELL IT TO MY HEART *Arista 109616* 3 13
19 Mar 88 ● PROVE YOUR LOVE *Arista 109830* 8 10
11 Jun 88 I'LL ALWAYS LOVE YOU *Arista 111536* 41 7
18 Nov 89 WITH EVERY BEAT OF MY HEART *Arista 112760* 53 2
14 Apr 90 I'LL BE YOUR SHELTER *Arista 112996* 43 5
4 Aug 90 LOVE WILL LEAD YOU BACK *Arista 113277* ▲ 69 1
3 Jul 93 CAN'T GET ENOUGH OF YOUR LOVE *Arista 74321147852* 14 8
16 Apr 94 I'LL WAIT *Arista 74321203472* 29 3
4 Feb 95 ORIGINAL SIN (THEME FROM 'THE SHADOW') *Arista 74321223462* 63 1
18 Nov 95 SAY A PRAYER *Arista 74321324292* 58 1
13 Jan 96 TELL IT TO MY HEART (re-mix) *Arista 74321335962* 23 3
5 Mar 88 TELL IT TO MY HEART *Arista 208898* 24 17

DAYTON *US, male vocal group (Singles: 1 week)* pos/wks

10 Dec 83 THE SOUND OF MUSIC *Capitol CL 318* 75 1

DAZZ BAND
US, male vocal / instrumental group (Singles: 12 weeks) pos/wks

3 Nov 84 LET IT ALL BLOW *Motown TMG 1361* 12 12

Darryl D'BONNEAU – *See Barbara TUCKER; FONTANA featuring Darryl D'BONNEAU*

D'BORA *US, female vocalist – Deborah Walker (Singles: 4 weeks)* pos/wks

14 Sep 91 DREAM ABOUT YOU *Polydor PO 161* 75 1
1 Jul 95 GOING ROUND *Vibe MCSTD 2055* 40 2
30 Mar 96 GOOD LOVE REAL LOVE *Music Plant MCSTD 40023* 58 1

Nino DE ANGELO *Germany, male vocalist (Singles: 5 weeks)* pos/wks

21 Jul 84 GUARDIAN ANGEL *Carrere CAR 335* 57 5

DE BOS *Holland, male DJ / producer (Singles: 1 week)* pos/wks

25 Oct 97 ON THE RUN *Jive JIVECD 433* 51 1

Chris DE BURGH (145 Top 500)

Irish singing / songwriting son of a diplomat, b. Christopher Davidson, 15 Oct 1948, Argentina. The first act to enter the Swiss album chart at No.1. Despite his international album success, he will be best remembered for the No.1 he wrote for and about his wife. Daughter Rosanna was crowned Miss World in 2003 (Singles: 71 weeks, Albums: 281 weeks) pos/wks

23 Oct 82 DON'T PAY THE FERRYMAN *A&M AMS 8256* 48 5
12 May 84 HIGH ON EMOTION *A&M AM 190* 44 5
12 Jul 86 ★ THE LADY IN RED (re) *A&M AM 331* 1 15
20 Sep 86 FATAL HESITATION *A&M AM 346* 44 4
13 Dec 86 A SPACEMAN CAME TRAVELLING / THE BALLROOM OF ROMANCE *A&M AM 365* 40 5
12 Dec 87 THE SIMPLE TRUTH (A CHILD IS BORN) (re) *A&M AM 427* 55 3
29 Oct 88 ● MISSING YOU *A&M AM 474* 3 12
7 Jan 89 TENDER HANDS *A&M AM 486* 43 6
14 Oct 89 THIS WAITING HEART *A&M AM 528* 59 3
25 May 91 THE SIMPLE TRUTH (A CHILD IS BORN) (re-issue) *A&M RELF 1* 36 2
11 Apr 92 SEPARATE TABLES *A&M AM 863* 30 4
21 May 94 BLONDE HAIR BLUE JEANS *A&M 5805932* 51 1
9 Dec 95 THE SNOWS OF NEW YORK *A&M 5813132* 60 1
27 Sep 97 SO BEAUTIFUL *A&M 5823932* 29 4
18 Sep 99 WHEN I THINK OF YOU *A&M / Mercury 4971302* 59 1
12 Sep 81 BEST MOVES *A&M AMLH 68532* 65 4
9 Oct 82 THE GETAWAY *A&M AMLH 68549* 30 16
19 May 84 MAN ON THE LINE *A&M AMLX 65002* 11 24
29 Dec 84 ● THE VERY BEST OF CHRIS DE BURGH *Telstar STAR 2248* 6 70
24 Aug 85 SPANISH TRAIN AND OTHER STORIES *A&M AMLH 68343* 78 3
7 Jun 86 ● INTO THE LIGHT *A&M AM 5121* 2 59
4 Oct 86 CRUSADER *A&M AMLH 64746* 72 1
15 Oct 88 ★ FLYING COLOURS *A&M AMA 5224* ■ 1 30
4 Nov 89 ● FROM A SPARK TO A FLAME – THE VERY BEST OF CHRIS DE BURGH *A&M CDBLP 100* 4 29
22 Sep 90 HIGH ON EMOTION – LIVE FROM DUBLIN *A&M 3970861* 15 6
9 May 92 ● POWER OF TEN *A&M 3971882* 3 10
28 May 94 ● THIS WAY UP *A&M 5402332* 5 6
18 Nov 95 BEAUTIFUL DREAMS *A&M 5404322* 33 8
11 Oct 97 ● THE LOVE SONGS *A&M 5407942* 8 7
2 Oct 99 QUIET REVOLUTION *Mercury / A&M 4904462* 23 3
31 Mar 01 THE ULTIMATE COLLECTION – NOTES FROM PLANET EARTH *Mercury / A&M 4908992* 19 4
28 Sep 02 TIMING IS EVERYTHING *Mercury / A&M 4934292* 41 1

DE CASTRO SISTERS *Cuba, female vocal group (Singles: 1 week)* pos/wks

11 Feb 55 TEACH ME TONIGHT *London HL 8104* [1] 20 1

[1] De Castro Sisters with Skip Martin and his Orchestra

DE-CODE featuring Beverli SKEETE
UK, male / female vocal / instrumental group (Singles: 1 week) pos/wks

18 May 96 WONDERWALL / SOME MIGHT SAY *Neoteric NRCD 2* 69 1

Etienne DE CRECY
France, male DJ / producer (Singles: 3 weeks) pos/wks

28 Mar 98 PRIX CHOC REMIXES *Different DIF 007CD* 60 1
20 Jan 01 AM I WRONG *XL Recordings XLS 127 CD* 44 2

DE FUNK featuring F45
Italy / UK, male production / vocal group (Singles: 1 week) pos/wks

25 Sep 99 PLEASURE LOVE *INCredible INCS 3CD* 49 1

Lennie DE ICE *UK, male producer (Singles: 1 week)* pos/wks

17 Apr 99 WE ARE I. E. *Distinctive DISNCD 50* 61 1

DE LA SOUL (464 Top 500)

Brooklyn, New York vocal / production trio that replaced bitches and firearms with beads and flowers, Posdnous (Kelvin Mercer), Trugoy The Dove (David Joliceur) and Mase (Vincent Mason). 'Three Feet High and Rising' produced by Prince Paul spawned four hit singles, and was one of the most influential rap LPs of all time (Singles: 63 weeks, Albums: 86 weeks) pos/wks

8 Apr 89 ME MYSELF AND I *Big Life BLR 7* 22 8
8 Jul 89 SAY NO GO *Big Life BLR 10* 18 7
21 Oct 89 EYE KNOW *Big Life BLR 13* 14 7
23 Dec 89 ● THE MAGIC NUMBER / BUDDY *Big Life BLR 14* 7 8
24 Mar 90 MAMA GAVE BIRTH TO THE SOUL CHILDREN *Gee Street GEE 26* [1] 14 7
27 Apr 91 ● RING RING RING (HA HA HEY) *Big Life BLR 42* 10 7
3 Aug 91 A ROLLER SKATING JAM NAMED 'SATURDAYS' *Big Life BLR 55* 22 5
23 Nov 91 KEEPIN' THE FAITH *Big Life BLR 64* 50 2
18 Sep 93 BREAKADAWN *Big Life BLRD 103* 39 3
2 Apr 94 FALLIN' *Epic 6602622* [2] 59 1
29 Jun 96 STAKES IS HIGH *Tommy Boy TBCD 7730* 55 1
8 Mar 97 4 MORE *Tommy Boy TBCD 7779A* [3] 52 1
22 Jul 00 OOOH *Tommy Boy TBCD 2102* [4] 29 2
11 Nov 00 ALL GOOD *Tommy Boy TBCD 2154B* [5] 33 3
2 Mar 02 BABY PHAT *Tommy Boy TBCD 2359* 55 1
25 Mar 89 3 FEET HIGH AND RISING *Big Life DLSLP 1* 13 56
25 May 91 ● DE LA SOUL IS DEAD *Big Life BLRLP 8* 7 11
9 Oct 93 BUHLOONE MINDSTATE *Big Life BLRCD 25* 37 2

13 Jul 96 **STAKES IS HIGH** *Tommy Boy TBCD 1149* 42 1
9 Oct 99 **3 FEET HIGH AND RISING (RE-ISSUE)** *Tommy Boy TBCD 1019* 17 2
19 Aug 00 **ART OFFICIAL INTELLIGENCE: MOSAIC THUMP** *Tommy Boy TBCD 1348* 22 4
14 Jun 03 **THE BEST OF** *Rhino / Tommy Boy 8122736652* 17 10

[1] Queen Latifah + De La Soul [2] Teenage Fanclub and De La Soul [3] De La Soul featuring Zhané [4] De La Soul featuring Redman [5] De La Soul featuring Chaka Khan

'Buddy' listed only until 6 Jan 1990, peaking at No.8

See also JUNGLE BROTHERS

Donna DE LORY
US, female vocalist (Singles: 1 week) pos/wks

24 Jul 93 **JUST A DREAM** *MCA MCSTD 1750* 71 1

Vincent DE MOOR
Holland, male producer (Singles: 4 weeks) pos/wks

16 Aug 97 **FLOWTATION** *XL Recordings XLS 89CD* 54 1
7 Apr 01 **FLY AWAY** *VC Recordings VCRD 87* 30 3

See also VERACOCHA

DE NADA
UK, male / female production / vocal group (Singles: 7 weeks) pos/wks

25 Aug 01 **LOVE YOU ANYWAY** *Wildstar CDWILD 37* 15 4
9 Feb 02 **BRING IT ON TO MY LOVE** *Wildstar CDWILD 39* 24 3

DE NUIT *Italy, male production duo – Fabio Seveso and Francesco de Leo (Singles: 2 weeks)* pos/wks

23 Nov 02 **ALL THAT MATTERED (LOVE YOU DOWN)** *Credence CDCRED 029* 38 2

Lynsey DE PAUL *UK, female vocalist / instrumentalist – keyboards – Lynsey Rubin (Singles: 54 weeks)* pos/wks

19 Aug 72 ● **SUGAR ME** *MAM 81* 5 11
2 Dec 72 **GETTING A DRAG** *MAM 88* 18 8
27 Oct 73 **WON'T SOMEBODY DANCE WITH ME** *MAM 109* 14 7
8 Jun 74 **OOH I DO** *Warner Bros. K 16401* 25 6
2 Nov 74 ● **NO HONESTLY** *Jet 747* 7 11
22 Mar 75 **MY MAN AND ME** *Jet 750* 40 4
26 Mar 77 **ROCK BOTTOM** *Polydor 2058 859* [1] 19 7

[1] Lynsey De Paul and Mike Moran

Tullio DE PISCOPO
Italy, male vocalist (Singles: 4 weeks) pos/wks

28 Feb 87 **STOP BAJON . . . PRIMAVERA** *Greyhound GREY 9* 58 4

Manitas DE PLATA *France, male instrumentalist – guitar – Ricardo Baliardo (Albums: 1 week)* pos/wks

29 Jul 67 **FLAMENCO GUITAR** *Philips SBL 7786* 40 1

Rebecca DE RUVO
Sweden, female vocalist (Singles: 1 week) pos/wks

1 Oct 94 **I CAUGHT YOU OUT** *Arista 74321230782* 72 1

Teri DE SARIO *US, female vocalist (Singles: 5 weeks)* pos/wks

2 Sep 78 **AIN'T NOTHING GONNA KEEP ME FROM YOU** *Casablanca CAN 128* 52 5

Stephanie DE SYKES
UK, female vocalist – Stephanie Ryton (Singles: 17 weeks) pos/wks

20 Jul 74 ● **BORN WITH A SMILE ON MY FACE** *Bradley's BRAD 7409* [1] 2 10
19 Apr 75 **WE'LL FIND OUR DAY** *Bradley's BRAD 7509* 17 7

[1] Stephanie De Sykes with Rain

Tony DE VIT
UK, male DJ / producer, d. 2 Jul 1998 (Singles: 13 weeks) pos/wks

4 Mar 95 **BURNING UP** *Icon ICONCD 001* 25 3
12 Aug 95 **HOOKED** *Labello Dance LAD 18CD* [1] 28 2
9 Sep 95 **TO THE LIMIT** *X:Plode BANG 1CD* 44 2
30 May 96 **I'LL BE THERE** *Labello Dance LAD 25CD1* [1] 37 2
28 Oct 00 **DAWN** *Tidy Trax TIDY 140CD* 56 2
21 Dec 02 **I DON'T CARE** *Tidy Trax TIDY 181T* 65 1
12 Jul 03 **GIVE ME A REASON** *Tidy Trax TIDYTWO 123CD* [2] 53 1

[1] 99th Floor Elevators featuring Tony De Vit [2] Tony De Vit featuring Niki Mak

DEACON BLUE (163 Top 500) *Scottish sextet with fervent following, led by singer / songwriter Ricky Ross (v) and featuring his wife Lorraine McIntosh (v). Named after the Steely Dan song, they achieved five Top 5 albums, including the million-selling 'When the World Knows Your Name' (Singles: 112 weeks, Albums: 217 weeks)* pos/wks

23 Jan 88 **DIGNITY** *CBS DEAC 4* 31 8
9 Apr 88 **WHEN WILL YOU MAKE MY TELEPHONE RING** *CBS DEAC 5* ..34 7
16 Jul 88 **CHOCOLATE GIRL** *CBS DEAC 6* 43 7
15 Oct 88 ● **REAL GONE KID** *CBS DEAC 7* 8 13
4 Mar 89 **WAGES DAY** *CBS DEAC 8* 18 6
20 May 89 **FERGUS SINGS THE BLUES** *CBS DEAC 9* 14 6
16 Sep 89 **LOVE AND REGRET** *CBS DEAC 10* 28 5
6 Jan 90 **QUEEN OF THE NEW YEAR** *CBS DEAC 11* 21 5
25 Aug 90 ● **FOUR BACHARACH AND DAVID SONGS (EP)** *CBS DEAC 12* 2 9
25 May 91 **YOUR SWAYING ARMS** *Columbia 6568937* 23 4
27 Jul 91 ● **TWIST AND SHOUT** *Columbia 6573027* 10 9
12 Oct 91 **CLOSING TIME** *Columbia 6575027* 42 3
14 Dec 91 **COVER FROM THE SKY** *Columbia 6576737* 31 4
28 Nov 92 **YOUR TOWN** *Columbia 6587867* 14 8
13 Feb 93 **WILL WE BE LOVERS** *Columbia 6589732* 31 4
24 Apr 93 **ONLY TENDER LOVE** *Columbia 6591842* 22 4
17 Jul 93 **HANG YOUR HEAD** *Columbia 6594602* 21 3
2 Apr 94 **I WAS RIGHT AND YOU WERE WRONG** *Columbia 6602222* 32 3
28 May 94 **DIGNITY (re-issue)** *Columbia 6604485* 20 3
28 Apr 01 **EVERYTIME YOU SLEEP** *Papillon BTFLY 0011* 64 1
6 Jun 87 RAINTOWN *CBS 4505491* 14 77
15 Apr 89 ★ WHEN THE WORLD KNOWS YOUR NAME *CBS 4633211* ■ 1 54
22 Sep 90 ● OOH LAS VEGAS *CBS 4672421* 3 8
15 Jun 91 ● FELLOW HOODLUMS *Columbia 4685501* 2 27
13 Mar 93 ● WHATEVER YOU SAY SAY NOTHING *Columbia 4735272* 4 10
16 Apr 94 ★ OUR TOWN – THE GREATEST HITS *Columbia 4766422* 1 38
23 Oct 99 WALKING BACK HOME *Columbia 4963802* 39 2
12 May 01 HOMESICK *Papillon BTFLYCD 0014* 59 1

Tracks on Four Bacharach and David Songs (EP): I'll Never Fall in Love Again / The Look of Love / Message to Michael / Are You There (With Another Girl). 'Dignity' in 1994 was the original recording of the song first issued in 1987 when it failed to chart

DEAD CAN DANCE *Australia, male / female vocal / instrumental duo (Albums: 3 weeks)* pos/wks

25 Sep 93 INTO THE LABYRINTH *4AD CAD 3013CD* 47 1
29 Jun 96 SPIRITCHASER *4AD CAD 6008CD* 43 2

DEAD DRED
UK, male instrumental / production duo (Singles: 2 weeks) pos/wks

5 Nov 94 **DRED BASS** *Moving Shadow SHADOW 50CD* 60 2

DEAD END KIDS
UK, male vocal / instrumental group (Singles: 10 weeks) pos/wks

26 Mar 77 ● **HAVE I THE RIGHT** *CBS 4972* 6 10

DEAD KENNEDYS *US, male vocal / instrumental group (Singles: 9 weeks, Albums: 8 weeks)* pos/wks

1 Nov 80 **KILL THE POOR** *Cherry Red CHERRY 16* 49 3
30 May 81 **TOO DRUNK TO FUCK** *Cherry Red CHERRY 24* 36 6
13 Sep 80 FRESH FRUIT FOR ROTTING VEGETABLES *Cherry Red BRED 10* 33 6
4 Jul 87 GIVE ME CONVENIENCE *Alternative Tentacles VIRUS 5* 84 2

DEAD OR ALIVE *UK, male vocal / instrumental group (Singles: 73 weeks, Albums: 22 weeks)*

Date	Title / Label	pos	wks
24 Mar 84	**THAT'S THE WAY (I LIKE IT)** *Epic A 4271*	22	9
1 Dec 84 ★	**YOU SPIN ME ROUND (LIKE A RECORD)** *Epic A 4861*	1	23
20 Apr 85	**LOVER COME BACK TO ME** *Epic A 6086*	11	8
29 Jun 85	**IN TOO DEEP** *Epic A 6360*	14	8
21 Sep 85	**MY HEART GOES BANG (GET ME TO THE DOCTOR)** *Epic A 6571*	23	6
20 Sep 86	**BRAND NEW LOVER** *Epic A 650075 7*	31	4
10 Jan 87	**SOMETHING IN MY HOUSE** *Epic BURNS 1*	12	7
4 Apr 87	**HOOKED ON LOVE** *Epic BURNS 2*	69	2
3 Sep 88	**TURN ROUND AND COUNT 2 TEN** *Epic BURNS 4*	70	1
22 Jul 89	**COME HOME WITH ME BABY** *Epic BURNS 5*	62	2
17 May 03	**YOU SPIN ME ROUND (re-mix)** *Epic 6735782*	23	3
28 Apr 84	**SOPHISTICATED BOOM BOOM** *Epic EPC 25835*	29	3
25 May 85 ●	**YOUTHQUAKE** *Epic EPC 26420*	9	15
14 Feb 87	**MAD BAD AND DANGEROUS TO KNOW** *Epic 450 2571*	27	4

DEAD PREZ
US, male rap duo (Singles: 2 weeks)

Date	Title / Label	pos	wks
11 Mar 00	**HIP HOP** *Epic 6689862*	41	2

DEADLY SINS
UK / Italy, male vocal / instrumental duo (Singles: 2 weeks)

Date	Title / Label	pos	wks
30 Apr 94	**WE ARE GOING ON DOWN** *Ffrreedom TABCD 220*	45	2

DEAN – *See JAN and DEAN*

Hazell DEAN
UK, female vocalist (Singles: 71 weeks, Albums: 3 weeks)

Date	Title / Label	pos	wks
18 Feb 84	**EVERGREEN / JEALOUS LOVE** *Proto ENA 114*	63	3
21 Apr 84 ●	**SEARCHIN' (I GOTTA FIND A MAN)** *Proto ENA 109*	6	15
28 Jul 84 ●	**WHATEVER I DO (WHEREVER I GO)** *Proto ENA 119*	4	11
3 Nov 84	**BACK IN MY ARMS (ONCE AGAIN)** *Proto ENA 122*	41	4
2 Mar 85	**NO FOOL (FOR LOVE)** *Proto ENA 123*	41	5
12 Oct 85	**THEY SAY IT'S GONNA RAIN** *Parlophone R 6107*	58	4
2 Apr 88 ●	**WHO'S LEAVING WHO** *EMI EM 45*	4	11
25 Jun 88	**MAYBE (WE SHOULD CALL IT A DAY)** *EMI EM 62*	15	6
24 Sep 88	**TURN IT INTO LOVE** *EMI EM 71*	21	7
26 Aug 89	**LOVE PAINS** *Lisson DOLE 12*	48	4
23 Mar 91	**BETTER OFF WITHOUT YOU** *Lisson DOLE 19*	72	1
22 Oct 88	**ALWAYS** *EMI EMC 3546*	38	3

Jimmy DEAN
US, male vocalist – Seth Ward (Singles: 17 weeks)

Date	Title / Label	pos	wks
26 Oct 61 ●	**BIG BAD JOHN** *Philips PB 1187* ▲	2	13
8 Nov 62	**LITTLE BLACK BOOK** *CBS AAG 122*	33	4

Letitia DEAN and Paul MEDFORD
UK, female / male vocal / actor duo (Singles: 7 weeks)

Date	Title / Label	pos	wks
25 Oct 86	**SOMETHING OUTA NOTHING** *BBC RESL 203*	12	7

Sheryl DEANE – *See THRILLSEEKERS*

DEANNA – *See David MORALES*

DEAR JON
UK, female / male vocal / instrumental group (Singles: 1 week)

Date	Title / Label	pos	wks
22 Apr 95	**ONE GIFT OF LOVE** *MDMC DEVCS 2*	68	1

DEATH IN VEGAS *UK, male instrumental / production duo – Richard Fearless and Tim Holmes (Singles: 17 weeks, Albums: 16 weeks)*

Date	Title / Label	pos	wks
2 Aug 97	**DIRT** *Concrete HARD 27CD*	61	1
1 Nov 97	**ROCCO** *Concrete HARD 29CD*	51	1
12 Feb 00 ●	**AISHA** *Concrete HARD 43CD*	9	4
6 May 00	**DIRGE** *Concrete HARD 44CD*	24	2
21 Sep 02	**HANDS AROUND MY THROAT** *Concrete HARD 48CD*	36	1
28 Dec 02	**SCORPIO RISING (re)** *Concrete HARD 54CD1* [1]	14	8
29 Mar 97	**DEAD ELVIS** *Concrete HARD 22LPCD*	52	1
25 Sep 99	**THE CONTINO SESSIONS** *Concrete HARD 41CDU*	19	12
28 Sep 02	**SCORPIO RISING** *Concrete / BMG HARD 53CD2*	19	3

[1] Death in Vegas with Liam Gallagher. Uncredited vocal on 'Aisha' by Iggy Pop

DeBARGE
US, male / female vocal group (Singles: 17 weeks, Albums: 2 weeks)

Date	Title / Label	pos	wks
6 Apr 85 ●	**RHYTHM OF THE NIGHT** *Gordy TMG 1376*	4	14
21 Sep 85	**YOU WEAR IT WELL** *Gordy ZB 40345* [1]	54	3
25 May 85	**RHYTHM OF THE NIGHT** *Gordy ZL 72340*	94	2

[1] El DeBarge with DeBarge

See also Chico DeBARGE; El DeBARGE

Chico DeBARGE
US, male vocalist (Singles: 1 week)

Date	Title / Label	pos	wks
14 Mar 98	**IGGIN' ME** *Universal UND 56170*	50	1

See also DeBARGE

El DeBARGE
US, male vocalist (Singles: 3 weeks)

Date	Title / Label	pos	wks
28 Jun 86	**WHO'S JOHNNY ('SHORT CIRCUIT' THEME)** *Gordy ELD 1*	60	2
31 Mar 90	**SECRET GARDEN** *Qwest W 9992* [1]	67	1

[1] Quincy Jones featuring Al B Sure!, James Ingram, El DeBarge and Barry White

See also DeBARGE

Diana DECKER
US, female vocalist (Singles: 10 weeks)

Date	Title / Label	pos	wks
23 Oct 53 ●	**POPPA PICCOLINO (re)** *Columbia DB 3325*	2	10

DECLAN *UK, male vocalist – Declan Galbraith (Singles: 4 weeks, Albums: 3 weeks)*

Date	Title / Label	pos	wks
21 Dec 02	**TELL ME WHY** *EMI / Liberty CDDECS 004* [1]	29	4
5 Oct 02	**DECLAN** *EMI / Liberty 5416012*	44	3

[1] Declan featuring Young Voices Choir

DECOY AND ROY *Belgium, male production duo – Danny Van Wauwe and Roy Van Luffelen (Singles: 1 week)*

Date	Title / Label	pos	wks
1 Feb 03	**INNER LIFE** *Ministry of Sound / Data DATA 43CDS*	45	1

Dave DEE *UK, male vocalist (Singles: 4 weeks)*

Date	Title / Label	pos	wks
14 Mar 70	**MY WOMAN'S MAN** *Fontana TF 1074*	42	4

See also Dave DEE, DOZY, BEAKY, MICK and TICH

Jazzy DEE
US, male rapper / instrumentalist (Singles: 5 weeks)

Date	Title / Label	pos	wks
5 Mar 83	**GET ON UP** *Laurie LRS 101*	53	5

Joey DEE and the STARLITERS
US, male vocal / instrumental group (Singles: 8 weeks)

Date	Title / Label	pos	wks
8 Feb 62	**PEPPERMINT TWIST** *Columbia DB 4758* ▲	33	8

Kiki DEE *UK, female vocalist – Pauline Matthews (Singles: 79 weeks, Albums: 11 weeks)*

Date	Title / Label	pos	wks
10 Nov 73	**AMOUREUSE** *Rocket PIG 4*	13	13
7 Sep 74	**I'VE GOT THE MUSIC IN ME** *Rocket PIG 12* [1]	19	8
12 Apr 75	**(YOU DONT KNOW) HOW GLAD I AM** *Rocket PIG 16* [1]	33	4
3 Jul 76 ★	**DON'T GO BREAKING MY HEART** *Rocket ROKN 512* [2] ▲	1	14
11 Sep 76	**LOVING AND FREE / AMOUREUSE (re-issue)** *Rocket ROKN 515*	13	8
19 Feb 77	**FIRST THING IN THE MORNING** *Rocket ROKN 520*	32	5
11 Jun 77	**CHICAGO** *Rocket ROKN 526*	28	4
21 Feb 81	**STAR** *Ariola ARO 251*	13	10
23 May 81	**PERFECT TIMING** *Ariola ARO 257*	66	3
20 Nov 93 ●	**TRUE LOVE** *Rocket EJSCX 32* [2]	2	10
26 Mar 77	**KIKI DEE** *Rocket ROLA 3*	24	5

18 Jul 81	**PERFECT TIMING** *Ariola ARL 5050*	47 4
9 Apr 94	**THE VERY BEST OF KIKI DEE** *PolyGram TV 516728*	62 2

1 Kiki Dee Band 2 Elton John and Kiki Dee

On 18 Sep, 25 Sep and 2 Oct 1976, 'Loving and Free' was listed by itself. 'Chicago' was one side of a double-sided chart entry, the other being 'Bite Your Lip (Get Up and Dance)' by Elton John

Nancy DEE – *See BENELUX and Nancy DEE*

Suzanna DEE – *See SAINT featuring Suzanna DEE*

DEE DEE *Belgium, male production trio and female vocalist – Diana Trippaers (Singles: 9 weeks)* pos/wks

20 Jul 02	**FOREVER** *Incentive CENT 43CDS*	12 7
1 Mar 03	**THE ONE** *Incentive CENT 52CDS*	28 2

Trio includes Christophe Chantzis and Eric Vanspauwen (Ian Van Dahl)

Dave DEE, DOZY, BEAKY, MICK and TICH (431 Top 500)

Quirkily named UK quintet was very popular in late 1960s: Dave Dee (David Harman) (v), Dozy (Trevor Davies) (b), Beaky (John Dymond) (g), Mick (Michael Wilson) (d), Tich (Ian Amey) (g). Catchy productions and ultra-commercial songs (penned by managers Howard and Blaikley) ensured string of hits (Singles: 141 weeks, Albums: 15 weeks) pos/wks

23 Dec 65	**YOU MAKE IT MOVE** *Fontana TF 630*	26 8
3 Mar 66 ●	**HOLD TIGHT!** *Fontana TF 671*	4 17
9 Jun 66 ●	**HIDEAWAY** *Fontana TF 711*	10 11
15 Sep 66 ●	**BEND IT!** *Fontana TF 746*	2 12
8 Dec 66 ●	**SAVE ME** *Fontana TF 775*	3 10
9 Mar 67	**TOUCH ME, TOUCH ME** *Fontana TF 798*	13 9
18 May 67 ●	**OKAY!** *Fontana TF 830*	4 11
11 Oct 67 ●	**ZABADAK!** *Fontana TF 873*	3 14
14 Feb 68 ★	**THE LEGEND OF XANADU** *Fontana TF 903*	1 12
3 Jul 68 ●	**LAST NIGHT IN SOHO** *Fontana TF 953*	8 11
2 Oct 68	**THE WRECK OF THE 'ANTOINETTE'** *Fontana TF 971*	14 9
5 Mar 69	**DON JUAN** *Fontana TF 1000*	23 9
14 May 69	**SNAKE IN THE GRASS** *Fontana TF 1020*	23 8
2 Jul 66	**DAVE DEE DOZY BEAKY MICK AND TICH** *Fontana STL 5350*	11 10
7 Jan 67	**IF MUSIC BE THE FOOD OF LOVE ... PREPARE FOR INDIGESTION** *Fontana STL 5388*	27 5

DEEE-LITE *US / Russia / Japan, male / female vocal / instrumental group (Singles: 30 weeks, Albums: 19 weeks)* pos/wks

18 Aug 90 ●	**GROOVE IS IN THE HEART / WHAT IS LOVE** *Elektra EKR 114*	2 13
24 Nov 90	**POWER OF LOVE / DEEE-LITE THEME** *Elektra EKR 117*	25 7
23 Feb 91	**HOW DO YOU SAY . . . LOVE / GROOVE IS IN THE HEART (re-mix)** *Elektra EKR 118*	52 2
27 Apr 91	**GOOD BEAT** *Elektra EKR 122*	53 3
13 Jun 92	**RUNAWAY** *Elektra EKR 148*	45 3
30 Jul 94	**PICNIC IN THE SUMMERTIME** *Elektra EKR 186CD1*	43 2
8 Sep 90	**WORLD CLIQUE** *Elektra EKT 77*	14 18
4 Jul 92	**INFINITY WITHIN** *Elektra 7559613132*	37 1

'What Is Love' listed only from 25 Aug 1990

DEEJAY PUNK-ROC *US, male DJ / producer (Singles: 5 weeks, Albums: 1 week)* pos/wks

21 Mar 98	**DEAD HUSBAND** *Independiente ISOM 9MS*	71 1
9 May 98	**MY BEATBOX** *Independiente ISOM 12MS*	43 1
8 Aug 98	**FAR OUT** *Independiente ISOM 17MS*	43 2
20 Feb 99	**ROC-IN-IT** *Independiente ISOM 21MS* 1	59 1
30 May 98	**CHICKENEYE** *Independiente ISOM 5CD*	47 1

1 Deejay Punk-Roc vs Onyx

DEEJAY SVEN – *See MC MIKER 'G' and Deejay SVEN*

Carol DEENE *UK, female vocalist (Singles: 25 weeks)* pos/wks

26 Oct 61	**SAD MOVIES (MAKE ME CRY)** *HMV POP 922*	44 3
25 Jan 62	**NORMAN** *HMV POP 973*	24 8
5 Jul 62	**JOHNNY GET ANGRY** *HMV POP 1027*	32 4
23 Aug 62	**SOME PEOPLE** *HMV POP 1058*	25 10

Scotti DEEP

US, male producer / instrumentalist (Singles: 1 week) pos/wks

15 Mar 97	**BROOKLYN BEATS** *Xtravaganza 0090095*	67 1

DEEP BLUE

UK, male producer – Sean O'Keefe (Singles: 2 weeks) pos/wks

16 Apr 94	**HELICOPTER TUNE** *Moving Shadow SHADOW 41CD*	68 2

DEEP BLUE SOMETHING *US, male vocal / instrumental group (Singles: 17 weeks, Albums: 5 weeks)* pos/wks

6 Jul 96 ★	**BREAKFAST AT TIFFANY'S (re)** *Interscope IND 80032*	1 14
7 Dec 96	**JOSEY** *Interscope IND 95518*	27 3
5 Oct 96	**HOME** *Interscope IND 90002*	24 5

DEEP C

UK, male / female vocal / instrumental group (Singles: 3 weeks) pos/wks

19 Jan 91	**AFRICAN REIGN** *M & G MAGS 4*	75 1
8 Jun 91	**CHILL TO THE PANIC** *M & G MAGS 10*	73 2

DEEP COVER *UK, male production group (Singles: 1 week)* pos/wks

11 May 02	**SOUNDS OF EDEN (EVERYTIME I SEE THE GIRL)** *Attitude! 0158392*	63 1

Title on the label was incorrect. Should have read 'The Sound Of Eden'

See also TRU FAITH & DUB CONSPIRACY; SCOTT & LEON

DEEP CREED '94

US, male producer – Armand van Helden (Singles: 1 week) pos/wks

7 May 94	**CAN U FEEL IT** *Eastern Bloc BLOCCD 005*	59 1

DEEP DISH *Iran, male instrumental / production duo – Ali Shirazinia and Sharam Tayebi (Singles: 4 weeks, Albums: 2 weeks)* pos/wks

26 Oct 96	**STAY GOLD** *Deconstruction 74321418222*	41 1
1 Nov 97	**STRANDED** *Deconstruction 74321512232*	60 1
3 Oct 98	**THE FUTURE OF THE FUTURE (STAY GOLD)** *Deconstruction 74321616252* 1	31 2
18 Jul 98	**JUNK SCIENCE** *Deconstruction 74321580342*	37 2

1 Deep Dish with Everything but the Girl

DEEP FEELING

UK, male vocal / instrumental group (Singles: 5 weeks) pos/wks

25 Apr 70	**DO YOU LOVE ME** *Page One POF 165*	34 5

DEEP FOREST *France, male instrumental duo – Eric Mouquet and Michel Sanchez (Singles: 14 weeks, Albums: 17 weeks)* pos/wks

5 Feb 94 ●	**SWEET LULLABY** *Columbia 6599242*	10 6
21 May 94	**DEEP FOREST** *Columbia 6604115*	20 4
23 Jul 94	**SAVANNA DANCE** *Columbia 6606355*	28 2
24 Jun 95	**MARTA'S SONG** *Columbia 6621402*	26 2
26 Feb 94	**DEEP FOREST** *Columbia 4741782*	15 11
3 Jun 95	**BOHÈME** *Columbia 4786232*	12 5
31 Jan 98	**COMPARSA** *Columbia 4887252* 1	60 1

1 Deep Forest III

DEEP PURPLE (136 Top 500)

Long-running legendary heavy rock group. London band's ever-changing line-up ensured many spin-off groups, among them Rainbow (founded by ex-guitarist Ritchie Blackmore), Whitesnake (featuring ex-vocalist David Coverdale) and Gillan (started by ex-vocalist Ian Gillan) (Singles: 85 weeks, Albums: 278 weeks) pos/wks

15 Aug 70 ●	**BLACK NIGHT** *Harvest HAR 5020*	2 21
27 Feb 71 ●	**STRANGE KIND OF WOMAN** *Harvest HAR 5033*	8 12
13 Nov 71	**FIREBALL** *Harvest HAR 5045*	15 13
1 Apr 72	**NEVER BEFORE** *Purple PUR 102*	35 6
16 Apr 77	**SMOKE ON THE WATER** *Purple PUR 132*	21 7

15 Oct 77 **NEW LIVE AND RARE (EP)** *Purple PUR 135* 31 4
7 Oct 78 **NEW LIVE AND RARE II (EP)** *Purple PUR 137* 45 3
2 Aug 80 **BLACK NIGHT (re-issue)** *Harvest HAR 5210* 43 6
1 Nov 80 **NEW LIVE AND RARE III (EP)** *Harvest SHEP 101* 48 3
26 Jan 85 **PERFECT STRANGERS** *Polydor POSP 719* 48 3
15 Jun 85 **KNOCKING AT YOUR BACK DOOR / PERFECT STRANGERS** *Polydor POSP 749* 68 1
18 Jun 88 **HUSH** *Polydor PO 4* 62 2
20 Oct 90 **KING OF DREAMS** *RCA PB 49247* 70 1
2 Mar 91 **LOVE CONQUERS ALL** *RCA PB 49225* 57 2
24 Jun 95 **BLACK NIGHT (re-mix)** *EMI CDEM 382* 66 1
24 Jan 70 **CONCERTO FOR GROUP AND ORCHESTRA** *Harvest SHVL 767* 26 4
20 Jun 70 ● **DEEP PURPLE IN ROCK** *Harvest SHVL 777* 4 68
18 Sep 71 ★ **FIREBALL** *Harvest SHVL 793* 1 25
15 Apr 72 ★ **MACHINE HEAD** *Purple TPSA 7504* 1 24
6 Jan 73 **MADE IN JAPAN** *Purple TPSP 351* 16 14
17 Feb 73 ● **WHO DO WE THINK WE ARE** *Purple TPSA 7508* 4 11
2 Mar 74 ● **BURN** *Purple TPA 3505* 3 21
23 Nov 74 ● **STORM BRINGER** *Purple TPS 3508* 6 12
5 Jul 75 **24 CARAT PURPLE** *Purple TPSM 2002* 14 17
22 Nov 75 **COME TASTE THE BAND** *Purple TPSA 7515* 19 4
27 Nov 76 **DEEP PURPLE LIVE** *Purple TPSA 7517* 12 6
21 Apr 79 **THE MARK II PURPLE SINGLES** *Purple TPS 3514* 24 6
19 Jul 80 ★ **DEEPEST PURPLE** *Harvest EMTV 25* 1 15
13 Dec 80 **IN CONCERT** *Harvest SHDW 4121/4122* 30 8
4 Sep 82 **DEEP PURPLE LIVE IN LONDON** *Harvest SHSP 4124* 23 5
10 Nov 84 ● **PERFECT STRANGERS** *Polydor POLH 16* 5 15
29 Jun 85 **THE ANTHOLOGY** *Harvest PUR 1* 50 3
24 Jan 87 ● **THE HOUSE OF BLUE LIGHT** *Polydor POLH 32* 10 9
16 Jul 88 **NOBODY'S PERFECT** *Polydor PODV 10* 38 2
2 Nov 90 **SLAVES AND MASTERS** *RCA PL 90535* 45 2
7 Aug 93 **THE BATTLE RAGES ON ...** *RCA 74321154202* 21 3
17 Feb 96 **PURPENDICULAR** *RCA 74321338022* 58 1
31 Jan 98 **MADE IN JAPAN (RE-ISSUE)** *EMI 8578642* 73 1
24 Oct 98 **30: VERY BEST OF DEEP PURPLE** *EMI 4968072* 39 2

Tracks on New Live and Rare (EP): Black Night (Live) / Painted Horse / When a Blind Man Cries. New Live and Rare II (EP): Burn (Edited Version) / Coronarias Redig / Mistreated (Interpolating Rock Me Baby). New Live and Rare Volume 3 (EP): Smoke on the Water / Bird Has Flown / Grabsplatter

DEEP RIVER BOYS
US, male vocal group (Singles: 1 week) pos/wks

7 Dec 56 **THAT'S RIGHT** *HMV POP 263* 29 1

DEEPEST BLUE *Israel / UK, male production / vocal duo – Matti Schwartz and Joel Edwards (Singles: 8 weeks)* pos/wks

2 Aug 03 ● **DEEPEST BLUE** *Data / MoS DATA 55CDS* 7 8

Rick DEES and his CAST OF IDIOTS *US, male DJ / vocalist with male / female vocal / instrumental group (Singles: 9 weeks)* pos/wks

18 Sep 76 ● **DISCO DUCK (PART ONE)** *RSO 2090 204* ▲ 6 9

DEETAH *Chile, female vocalist (Singles: 10 weeks)* pos/wks

26 Sep 98 **RELAX** *ffrr FCDP 345* 11 8
1 May 99 **EL PARAISO RICO** *ffrr FCD 356* 39 2

DEF LEPPARD (183 Top 500)
Mainstream UK rock stalwarts who wooed US before their homeland: Joe Elliott (v), Phil Collen (g from 1983), Steve Clark (g) (d. 1991), Rick Savage (b), Rick Allen (d). In US they achieved the feat of two consecutive albums selling more than eight million (Singles: 116 weeks, Albums: 190 weeks) pos/wks

17 Nov 79 **WASTED** *Vertigo 6059 247* 61 3
23 Feb 80 **HELLO AMERICA** *Vertigo LEPP 1* 45 4
5 Feb 83 **PHOTOGRAPH** *Vertigo VER 5* 66 3
27 Aug 83 **ROCK OF AGES** *Vertigo VER 6* 41 4
1 Aug 87 ● **ANIMAL** *Bludgeon Riffola LEP 1* 6 9
19 Sep 87 **POUR SOME SUGAR ON ME** *Bludgeon Riffola LEP 2* 18 6
28 Nov 87 **HYSTERIA (re)** *Bludgeon Riffola LEP 3* 26 6
9 Apr 88 **ARMAGEDDON IT** *Bludgeon Riffola LEP 4* 20 5
16 Jul 88 **LOVE BITES** *Bludgeon Riffola LEP 5* ▲ 11 8
11 Feb 89 **ROCKET** *Bludgeon Riffola LEP 6* 15 7
28 Mar 92 ● **LET'S GET ROCKED** *Bludgeon Riffola DEF 7* 2 7
27 Jun 92 **MAKE LOVE LIKE A MAN** *Bludgeon Riffola LEP 7* 12 5
12 Sep 92 **HAVE YOU EVER NEEDED SOMEONE SO BAD** *Bludgeon Riffola LEP 8* 16 5
30 Jan 93 **HEAVEN IS** *Bludgeon Riffola LEPCD 9* 13 5
1 May 93 **TONIGHT** *Bludgeon Riffola LEPCD 10* 34 3
18 Sep 93 **TWO STEPS BEHIND** *Bludgeon Riffola LEPCD 12* 32 4
15 Jan 94 **ACTION** *Bludgeon Riffola LEPCD 13* 14 5
14 Oct 95 ● **WHEN LOVE AND HATE COLLIDE** *Bludgeon Riffola LEPCD 14* 2 10
4 May 96 **SLANG** *Bludgeon Riffola LEPCD 15* 17 5
13 Jul 96 **WORK IT OUT** *Bludgeon Riffola LEPCD 16* 22 3
28 Sep 96 **ALL I WANT IS EVERYTHING** *Bludgeon Riffola LEPCD 17* 38 2
30 Nov 96 **BREATHE A SIGH** *Bludgeon Riffola LEPCD 18* 43 1
24 Jul 99 **PROMISES** *Bludgeon Riffola 5621362* 41 1
9 Oct 99 **GOODBYE** *Bludgeon Riffola 5622892* 54 1
17 Aug 02 **NOW** *Bludgeon Riffola / Mercury 0639692* 23 2
26 Apr 03 **LONG LONG WAY TO GO** *Bludgeon Riffola 9800024* 40 2
22 Mar 80 **ON THROUGH THE NIGHT** *Vertigo 9102 040* 15 8
25 Jul 81 **HIGH 'N' DRY** *Vertigo 6359 045* 26 8
12 Mar 83 **PYROMANIA** *Vertigo VERS 2* 18 8
29 Aug 87 ★ **HYSTERIA** *Bludgeon Riffola HYSLP 1* ■ ▲ 1 101
11 Apr 92 ★ **ADRENALIZE** *Bludgeon Riffola 5109782* ■ ▲ 1 30
16 Oct 93 ● **RETRO ACTIVE** *Bludgeon Riffola 5183052* 6 5
4 Nov 95 ● **VAULT – GREATEST HITS 1980-1995** *Bludgeon Riffola 5286572* 3 14
25 May 96 ● **SLANG** *Bludgeon Riffola 5324932* 5 8
26 Jun 99 **EUPHORIA** *Bludgeon Riffola 5462442* 11 5
24 Aug 02 **X** *Bludgeon Riffola 0631202* 14 3

See also Mick RONSON with Joe ELLIOTT

DEFAULT
US, male vocal / instrumental group (Singles: 1 week) pos/wks

8 Feb 03 **WASTING MY TIME** *TVT / Island CID 809* 73 1

DEFINITION OF SOUND *UK, male rap duo – Donald weekes and Kevin Clark (Singles: 25 weeks, Albums: 3 weeks)* pos/wks

9 Mar 91 **WEAR YOUR LOVE LIKE HEAVEN** *Circa YR 61* 17 9
1 Jun 91 **NOW IS TOMORROW** *Circa YR 66* 46 4
8 Feb 92 **MOIRA JANE'S CAFE** *Circa YR 80* 34 4
19 Sep 92 **WHAT ARE YOU UNDER** *Circa YR 95* 68 1
14 Nov 92 **CAN I GET OVER** *Circa YR 97* 61 2
20 May 95 **BOOM BOOM** *Fontana DOSCD 1* 59 1
2 Dec 95 **PASS THE VIBES** *Fontana DOSCD 2* 23 3
24 Feb 96 **CHILD** *Fontana DOSCD 3* 48 1
29 Jun 91 **LOVE AND LIFE** *Circa CIRCA 14* 38 3

DEFTONES *US, male vocal / instrumental group (Singles: 9 weeks, Albums: 8 weeks)* pos/wks

21 Mar 98 **MY OWN SUMMER (SHOVE IT)** *Maverick W 0432CD* 29 2
11 Jul 98 **BE QUIET AND DRIVE (FAR AWAY)** *Maverick W 0445CD* 50 1
26 Aug 00 **CHANGE (IN THE HOUSE OF FLIES)** *Maverick W 531CD* 53 1
24 May 03 **MINERVA** *Maverick W 605CD* 15 3
4 Oct 03 **HEXAGRAM** *Maverick W 623CD* 68 2
8 Nov 97 **AROUND THE FUR** *Maverick 9362468102* 56 1
1 Jul 00 **WHITE PONY** *Maverick 9362477972* 13 2
24 Mar 01 **BACK TO SCHOOL (MINI MAGGIT)** *WEA 9362480822* 35 2
31 May 03 ● **THE DEFTONES** *Maverick 9362483912* 7 3

DEGREES OF MOTION featuring BITI
US, female vocal group (Singles: 21 weeks) pos/wks

25 Apr 92 **DO YOU WANT IT RIGHT NOW** *ffrr F 184* 31 5
18 Jul 92 **SHINE ON** *ffrr F 192* [1] 43 3
7 Nov 92 **SOUL FREEDOM – FREE YOUR SOUL** *ffrr FX 201* 64 1
19 Mar 94 ● **SHINE ON (re-mix)** *ffrr FCD 229* 8 8
25 Jun 94 **DO YOU WANT IT RIGHT NOW (re-mix)** *ffrr FCD 236* 26 4

[1] Degrees of Motion featuring Biti with Kit West

DEICIDE *US, male vocal / instrumental group (Albums: 1 week)* pos/wks

13 May 95 **ONCE UPON THE CROSS** *Roadrunner RR 89492* 66 1

DEJA *US, male / female vocal duo (Singles: 1 week)* pos/wks

29 Aug 87 **SERIOUS** *10 TEN 132* 75 1

DEJA VU *UK, male vocal / instrumental duo (Singles: 1 week)* pos/wks

5 Feb 94 **WHY WHY WHY** *Cowboy CDRODEO 941* 57 1

DEJURE *UK, male production duo – Ian Bland and Paul Fitzpatrick (Singles: 1 week)* pos/wks

23 Aug 03 **SANCTUARY** *Nebula NEBT 032* 62 1

See also DREAM FREQUENCY; RED

Desmond DEKKER and the ACES
Jamaica, male vocal / instrumental group – leader Desmond Dacres (Singles: 71 weeks, Albums: 4 weeks) pos/wks

12 Jul 67 **007 (SHANTY TOWN)** *Pyramid PYR 6004* 14 11
19 Mar 69 ★ **ISRAELITES** *Pyramid PYR 6058* 1 15
25 Jun 69 ● **IT MIEK** *Pyramid PYR 6068* 7 11
10 Jan 70 **PICKNEY GAL** *Pyramid PYR 6078* 42 3
22 Aug 70 ● **YOU CAN GET IT IF YOU REALLY WANT** *Trojan TR 7777* [1] 2 15
10 May 75 ● **ISRAELITES (re-recording)** *Cactus CT 57* [1] 10 9
30 Aug 75 **SING A LITTLE SONG** *Cactus CT 73* [1] 16 7
5 Jul 69 **THIS IS DESMOND DEKKER** *Trojan TTL 4* [1] 27 4

[1] Desmond Dekker [1] Desmond Dekker

DEL AMITRI (375 Top 500)
Stylish soft-rock band whose name is Greek for 'from the womb'. Core members Justin Currie (v,b) and Iain Harvie (g) formed the band in Glasgow, Scotland, 1983. 'Roll to Me' was one of the few UK records to reach the US Top 10 in the late 1990s (Singles: 71 weeks, Albums: 108 weeks) pos/wks

19 Aug 89 **KISS THIS THING GOODBYE** *A&M AM 515* 59 2
13 Jan 90 **NOTHING EVER HAPPENS** *A&M AM 536* 11 9
24 Mar 90 **KISS THIS THING GOODBYE (re-issue)** *A&M AM 551* 43 4
16 Jun 90 **MOVE AWAY JIMMY BLUE** *A&M AM 555* 36 6
3 Nov 90 **SPIT IN THE RAIN** *A&M AM 589* 21 6
9 May 92 **ALWAYS THE LAST TO KNOW** *A&M AM 870* 13 7
11 Jul 92 **BE MY DOWNFALL** *A&M AM 884* 30 4
12 Sep 92 **JUST LIKE A MAN** *A&M AM 0057* 25 4
23 Jan 93 **WHEN YOU WERE YOUNG** *A&M AMCD 0132* 20 3
18 Feb 95 **HERE AND NOW** *A&M 5809692* 21 4
29 Apr 95 **DRIVING WITH THE BRAKES ON** *A&M 5810072* 18 4
8 Jul 95 **ROLL TO ME** *A&M 5811312* 22 4
28 Oct 95 **TELL HER THIS** *A&M 5812172* 32 2
21 Jun 97 **NOT WHERE IT'S AT** *A&M 5822532* 21 3
6 Dec 97 **SOME OTHER SUCKER'S PARADE** *A&M 5824352* 46 1
13 Jun 98 **DON'T COME HOME TOO SOON** *A&M 5827052* 15 4
5 Sep 98 **CRY TO BE FOUND** *A&M MERCD 513* 40 2
13 Apr 02 **JUST BEFORE YOU LEAVE** *Mercury 4976972* 37 2
24 Feb 90 ● **WAKING HOURS** *A&M AMA 9006* 6 44
13 Jun 92 ● **CHANGE EVERYTHING** *A&M 3953852* 2 20
11 Mar 95 ● **TWISTED** *A&M 5403112* 3 25
12 Jul 97 ● **SOME OTHER SUCKER'S PARADE** *A&M 5407052* 6 5
19 Sep 98 ● **THE BEST OF DEL AMITRI – HATFUL OF RAIN** *Mercury / A&M 5409402* 5 11
20 Apr 02 **CAN YOU DO ME GOOD?** *Mercury / A&M 4932162* 30 3

DE'LACY *US, male / female vocal / instrumental group (Singles: 16 weeks, Albums: 1 week)* pos/wks

2 Sep 95 ● **HIDEAWAY** *Slip 'N' Slide 74321310472* 9 10
31 Aug 96 **THAT LOOK** *Slip 'N' Slide 74321398322* 19 4
14 Feb 98 **HIDEAWAY (re-mix)** *Slip 'N'Slide 74321561052* 21 2
1 Jul 95 **HIDEAWAY** *Slip 'n' Slide SLIP 023* 53 1

DELAGE *UK, female vocal group (Singles: 2 weeks)* pos/wks

15 Dec 90 **ROCK THE BOAT** *PWL / Polydor PO 113* 63 2

DELAKOTA *UK, male vocal / instrumental duo (Singles: 3 weeks, Albums: 1 week)* pos/wks

18 Jul 98 **THE ROCK** *Go.Beat GOBCD 10* 60 1
19 Sep 98 **C'MON CINCINNATI** *Go.Beat GOBCD 11* [1] 55 1
13 Feb 99 **555** *Go.Beat GOBCD 14* 42 1
3 Oct 98 **ONE LOVE** *Go! Beat 5578612* 58 1

[1] Delakota featuring Rose Smith

DELANEY and BONNIE and FRIENDS
US, male / female vocal duo – Delaney and Bonnie Bramlett, and instrumental group (Singles: 9 weeks, Albums: 3 weeks) pos/wks

20 Dec 69 **COMIN' HOME** *Atlantic 584 308* [1] 16 9
6 Jun 70 **ON TOUR** *Atlantic 2400013* 39 3

[1] Delaney and Bonnie and Friends featuring Eric Clapton

DELANO – *See CZR featuring DELANO*

The DELAYS
UK, male vocal / instrumental group (Singles: 1 week) pos/wks

2 Aug 03 **HEY GIRL** *Rough Trade RTRADESCD 102* 40 1

DELEGATION
UK, male vocal / instrumental group (Singles: 7 weeks) pos/wks

23 Apr 77 **WHERE IS THE LOVE (WE USED TO KNOW)** *State STAT 40* 22 6
20 Aug 77 **YOU'VE BEEN DOING ME WRONG** *State STAT 55* 49 1

DELERIUM *Canada, male production duo – Rhys Fulber and Bill Leeb (Singles: 24 weeks)* pos/wks

12 Jun 99 **SILENCE** *Nettwerk 398152* 73 1
5 Feb 00 **HEAVEN'S EARTH** *Nettwerk 331032* 44 1
14 Oct 00 ● **SILENCE (re-mix)** *Nettwerk 331072* [1] 3 16
7 Jul 01 **INNOCENTE (FALLING IN LOVE)** *Nettwerk 331172* [2] 32 3
24 Nov 01 **UNDERWATER** *Nettwerk 331422* [3] 33 2
12 Jul 03 **AFTER ALL** *Nettwerk 332012* [3] 46 1

[1] Delerium featuring Sarah McLachlan [2] Delerium featuring Leigh Nash
[3] Delerium featuring Rani [3] Delerium featuring Jael

Sarah McLachlan's vocals also featured, uncredited, on original hit version of 'Silence'

DELFONICS
US, male vocal group (Singles: 23 weeks) pos/wks

10 Apr 71 **DIDN'T I (BLOW YOUR MIND THIS TIME) (re)** *Bell 1099* 22 9
10 Jul 71 **LA-LA MEANS I LOVE YOU** *Bell 1165* 19 10
16 Oct 71 **READY OR NOT HERE I COME (CAN'T HIDE FROM LOVE)** *Bell 1175* 41 4

DELGADOS *UK, male / female vocal / instrumental group (Singles: 3 weeks, Albums: 3 weeks)* pos/wks

23 May 98 **PULL THE WIRES FROM THE WALL** *Chemikal CHEM 023CD* ..69 1
3 Jun 00 **AMERICAN TRILOGY** *Chemikal Underground CHEM 039CD* 61 1
1 Mar 03 **ALL YOU NEED IS HATE** *Mantra MNT 79CD* 72 1
20 Jun 98 **PELOTON** *Chemikal Underground CHEM 024CD* 56 1
29 Apr 00 **THE GREAT EASTERN** *Chemikal Underground CHEM 040CD* 72 1
26 Oct 02 **HATE** *Mantra/Beggars Banquet MNTCD 1031* 57 1

DELIRIOUS? *UK, male vocal / instrumental group (Singles: 17 weeks, Albums: 6 weeks)* pos/wks

1 Mar 97 **WHITE RIBBON DAY** *Furious? CDFURY 1* 41 2
17 May 97 **DEEPER** *Furious? CDFURY 2* 20 3
26 Jul 97 **PROMISE** *Furious? CDFURY 3* 20 2
15 Nov 97 **DEEPER (EP)** *Furious? CXFURY 4* 36 2
27 Mar 99 **SEE THE STAR** *Furious? CDFURY 5* 16 2
4 Mar 00 **IT'S OK** *Furious? CDFURY 6* 18 2
16 Jun 01 **WAITING FOR THE SUMMER** *Furious? CDFURY 7* 26 2
22 Dec 01 **I COULD SING OF YOUR LOVE FOREVER** *Furious? CDFURY 9* 40 2
28 Jun 97 **KING OF FOOLS** *Furious? FURYCD 1* 13 3
24 Apr 99 **MEZZAMORPHIS** *Furious? FURYCD 2* 25 2
18 Aug 01 **AUDIO LESSONOVER?** *Furious? FURYCD 4* 58 1

Tracks on Deeper (EP): Deeper / Summer of Love / Touch / Sanctify

'DELIVERANCE' SOUNDTRACK *US, male instrumental duo – Eric Weissberg on banjo and Steve Mandell on guitar (Singles: 7 weeks)* pos/wks

31 Mar 73 **DUELLING BANJOS** *Warner Bros. K 16223* **17** 7

DELLS *US, male vocal group (Singles: 9 weeks)* pos/wks

16 Jul 69 **I CAN SING A RAINBOW – LOVE IS BLUE (MEDLEY)** *Chess CRS 8099* **15** 9

DELORES – *See MONOBOY featuring DELORES*

DELRONS – *See REPARATA and The DELRONS*

DELSENA – *See Oris JAY presents DELSENA*

DELTA – *See David MORALES; Crystal WATERS*

DELUXE *US, female vocalist (Singles: 1 week)* pos/wks

18 Mar 89 **JUST A LITTLE MORE** *Unyque UNQ 5* **74** 1

Tim DELUXE
UK, male DJ / producer – Tim Liken (Singles: 9 weeks) pos/wks

20 Jul 02 **IT JUST WON'T DO** *Underwater H20 016CD* [1] **14** 7
4 Oct 03 **LESS TALK MORE ACTION** *Underwater H20 928CD* **45** 2

[1] Tim Deluxe featuring Sam Obernik

DEM 2 *UK, male production duo (Singles: 2 weeks)* pos/wks

24 Oct 98 **DESTINY** *Locked On LOX 101CD* **58** 2

DEMETREUS – *See Christian FALK featuring DEMETREUS*

DEMOLITION MAN – *See PRIZNA featuring DEMOLITION MAN*

DEMON *UK, male vocal / instrumental group (Albums: 5 weeks)* pos/wks

14 Aug 82 **THE UNEXPECTED GUEST** *Carrere CAL 139* **47** 3
2 Jul 83 **THE PLAGUE** *Clay CLAY LP 6* **73** 2

DEMON vs HEARTBREAKER
France, male production group (Singles: 1 week) pos/wks

19 May 01 **YOU ARE MY HIGH** *Source SOURCDSE 1032* **70** 1

D'EMPRESS – *See 187 LOCKDOWN*

Chaka DEMUS and PLIERS
Jamaica, male vocal duo (Singles: 55 weeks, Albums: 30 weeks) pos/wks

12 Jun 93 ● **TEASE ME** *Mango CIDM 806* **3** 15
18 Sep 93 ● **SHE DON'T LET NOBODY** *Mango CIDM 810* **4** 10
18 Dec 93 ★ **TWIST AND SHOUT (re)** *Mango CIDM 814* [1] **1** 14
12 Mar 94 **MURDER SHE WROTE** *Mango CIDM 812* **27** 4
18 Jun 94 **I WANNA BE YOUR MAN** *Mango CIDM 817* **19** 6
27 Aug 94 **GAL WINE** *Mango CIDM 818* **20** 4
31 Aug 96 **EVERY KINDA PEOPLE** *Island Jamaica IJCD 2005* **47** 1
30 Aug 97 **EVERY LITTLE THING SHE DOES IS MAGIC** *Virgin VSCDT 1654* **51** 1
10 Jul 93 ★ **TEASE ME** *Mango CIDM 1102* **1** 30

[1] Chaka Demus and Pliers featuring Jack Radics and Taxi Gang

Terry DENE
UK, male vocalist – Terry Williams (Singles: 20 weeks) pos/wks

7 Jun 57 **A WHITE SPORT COAT (re)** *Decca F 10895* **18** 7
19 Jul 57 **START MOVIN'** *Decca F 10914* **15** 8
16 May 58 **STAIRWAY OF LOVE** *Decca F 11016* **16** 5

DENISE and JOHNNY *UK, male / female vocal duo – Denise Van Outen and Johnny Vaughan (Singles: 12 weeks)* pos/wks

26 Dec 98 ● **ESPECIALLY FOR YOU (re)** *RCA 74321644722* **3** 12

See also THOSE 2 GIRLS; Andy WILLIAMS

Cathy DENNIS
UK, female vocalist (Singles: 68 weeks, Albums: 35 weeks) pos/wks

21 Oct 89 **C'MON AND GET MY LOVE** *ffrr F 117* [1] **15** 10
7 Apr 90 **THAT'S THE WAY OF THE WORLD** *ffrr F 132* [1] **48** 3
4 May 91 ● **TOUCH ME (ALL NIGHT LONG)** *Polydor CATH 3* **5** 10
20 Jul 91 **JUST ANOTHER DREAM** *Polydor CATH 2* **13** 7
5 Oct 91 **TOO MANY WALLS** *Polydor CATH 4* **17** 7
7 Dec 91 **EVERYBODY MOVE** *Polydor CATH 5* **25** 8
29 Aug 92 **YOU LIED TO ME** *Polydor CATH 6* **34** 4
21 Nov 92 **IRRESISTIBLE** *Polydor CATH 7* **24** 6
6 Feb 93 **FALLING** *Polydor CATHD 8* **32** 2
12 Feb 94 **WHY** *ffrr FCD 227* [1] **23** 3
10 Aug 96 **WEST END PAD** *Polydor 5752812* **25** 2
1 Mar 97 **WATERLOO SUNSET** *Polydor 5759612* **11** 5
21 Jun 97 **WHEN DREAMS TURN TO DUST** *Polydor 5711852* **43** 1
10 Aug 91 ● **MOVE TO THIS** *Polydor 8495031* **3** 31
23 Jan 93 ● **INTO THE SKYLINE** *Polydor 5139352* **8** 4

[1] D Mob with Cathy Dennis

Jackie DENNIS *UK, male vocalist (Singles: 10 weeks)* pos/wks

14 Mar 58 ● **LA DEE DAH** *Decca F 10992* **4** 9
27 Jun 58 **THE PURPLE PEOPLE EATER** *Decca F 11033* **29** 1

Stefan DENNIS *Australia, male vocalist (Singles: 8 weeks)* pos/wks

6 May 89 **DON'T IT MAKE YOU FEEL GOOD** *Sublime LIME 105* **16** 7
7 Oct 89 **THIS LOVE AFFAIR** *Sublime LIME 113* **67** 1

DENNISONS
UK, male vocal / instrumental group (Singles: 13 weeks) pos/wks

15 Aug 63 **BE MY GIRL** *Decca F 11691* **46** 6
7 May 64 **WALKING THE DOG** *Decca F 11880* **36** 7

Sandy DENNY
UK, female vocalist d. 21 Apr 1978 (Albums: 2 weeks) pos/wks

2 Oct 71 **THE NORTH STAR GRASSMAN AND THE RAVENS** *Island ILPS 9165* **31** 2

See also FAIRPORT CONVENTION

Richard DENTON and Martin COOK *UK, male orchestra leaders – instrumental duo, guitar and keyboards (Singles: 7 weeks)* pos/wks

15 Apr 78 **THEME FROM 'HONG KONG BEAT'** *BBC RESL 52* **25** 7

John DENVER (223 Top 500)
Unmistakable light tenor singer / songwriter / instrumentalist – guitar, with pop, country, folk and easy listening appeal: b. Henry John Deutschendorf, 31 Dec 1943, Roswell, New Mexico, d. 12 Oct 1997. One of America's top sellers in the 1970s amassed 19 platinum albums and four No.1 singles there (Singles: 22 weeks, Albums: 249 weeks) pos/wks

17 Aug 74 ★ **ANNIE'S SONG** *RCA APBO 0295* ▲ **1** 13
12 Dec 81 **PERHAPS LOVE** *CBS A 1905* [1] **46** 9
17 Mar 73 **ROCKY MOUNTAIN HIGH** *RCA SF 2308* **11** 15
2 Jun 73 **POEMS PRAYERS AND PROMISES** *RCA SF 8219* **19** 5
23 Jun 73 **RHYMES AND REASONS** *RCA Victor SF 8348* **21** 5
30 Mar 74 ● **THE BEST OF JOHN DENVER** *RCA Victor APLI 0374* **7** 69
7 Sep 74 ● **BACK HOME AGAIN** *RCA Victor APLI 0548* ▲ **3** 29
22 Mar 75 **AN EVENING WITH JOHN DENVER** *RCA Victor LSA 3211/12* **31** 4
11 Oct 75 **WIND SONG** *RCA Victor APLI 1183* ▲ **14** 21
15 May 76 ● **LIVE IN LONDON** *RCA Victor RS 1050* **2** 29
4 Sep 76 ● **SPIRIT** *RCA Victor APLI 1694* **9** 11
19 Mar 77 ● **BEST OF JOHN DENVER VOLUME 2** *RCA Victor PL 42120* **9** 9
11 Feb 78 **I WANT TO LIVE** *RCA PL 12561* **25** 5
21 Apr 79 **JOHN DENVER** *RCA Victor PL 13075* **68** 1
28 Nov 81 **PERHAPS LOVE** *CBS 73592* [1] **17** 21
22 Oct 83 **IT'S ABOUT TIME** *RCA RCALP 6087* **90** 2
1 Dec 84 **JOHN DENVER – THE COLLECTION** *Telstar STAR 2253* **20** 11
23 Aug 86 **ONE WORLD** *RCA PL 85811* **91** 3
22 Mar 97 **THE ROCKY MOUNTAIN COLLECTION** *RCA 7863668372* **19** 9

[1] Placido Domingo with John Denver [1] Placido Domingo and John Denver

Karl DENVER (446 Top 500)

Versatile Scottish singer with multi-octave vocal range, b. Angus McKenzie, 16 Dec 1934, Glasgow (d. 21 Dec 1998). This unique artist, whose yodel-laced style added colour and contrast to the charts, reached the Top 20 with his first five singles (Singles: 127 weeks, Albums: 27 weeks)

Date		Title	pos	wks
22 Jun 61	●	**MARCHETA** *Decca F 11360*	8	20
19 Oct 61	●	**MEXICALI ROSE** *Decca F 11395*	8	11
25 Jan 62	●	**WIMOWEH** *Decca F 11420*	4	17
22 Feb 62	●	**NEVER GOODBYE** *Decca F 11431*	9	18
7 Jun 62		**A LITTLE LOVE A LITTLE KISS** *Decca F 11470*	19	10
20 Sep 62		**BLUE WEEK-END** *Decca F 11505*	33	5
21 Mar 63		**CAN YOU FORGIVE ME** *Decca F 11608*	32	8
13 Jun 63		**INDIAN LOVE CALL** *Decca F 11674*	32	8
22 Aug 63		**STILL** *Decca F 11720*	13	15
5 Mar 64		**MY WORLD OF BLUE** *Decca F 11828*	29	6
4 Jun 64		**LOVE ME WITH ALL YOUR HEART** *Decca F 11905*	37	6
9 Jun 90		**LAZYITIS – ONE ARMED BOXER** *Factory FAC 2227* [1]	46	3
23 Dec 61	●	**WIMOWEH** *Ace of Clubs ACL 1098*	7	27

[1] Happy Mondays and Karl Denver

DENZIE – *See MONSTA BOY featuring DENZIE*

DEODATO

US, male multi-instrumentalist – Eumir Deodato (Singles: 9 weeks)

Date		Title	pos	wks
5 May 73	●	**ALSO SPRACH ZARATHUSTRA (2001)** *Creed Taylor CTI 4000*	7	9

DEPARTMENT S

UK, male vocal / instrumental group (Singles: 13 weeks)

Date		Title	pos	wks
4 Apr 81		**IS VIC THERE?** *RCA1003*	22	10
11 Jul 81		**GOING LEFT RIGHT** *Stiff BUY 118*	55	3

DEPECHE MODE (104 Top 500)

Consistently successful synth-led Essex band: Dave Gahan (v), Martin Gore (syn), Andy Fletcher (b, syn), Vince Clarke (syn, replaced 1982 by Alan Wilder). One of the world's best-selling groups, who reached the UK Top 10 with their first 13 albums (Singles: 240 weeks, Albums: 181 weeks)

Date		Title	pos	wks
4 Apr 81		**DREAMING OF ME** *Mute MUTE 013*	57	4
13 Jun 81		**NEW LIFE** *Mute MUTE 014*	11	15
19 Sep 81	●	**JUST CAN'T GET ENOUGH** *Mute MUTE 016*	8	10
13 Feb 82	●	**SEE YOU** *Mute MUTE 018*	6	10
8 May 82		**THE MEANING OF LOVE** *Mute MUTE 022*	12	8
28 Aug 82		**LEAVE IN SILENCE** *Mute BONG 1*	18	10
12 Feb 83		**GET THE BALANCE RIGHT** *Mute 7BONG 2*	13	8
23 Jul 83	●	**EVERYTHING COUNTS** *Mute 7BONG 3*	6	11
1 Oct 83		**LOVE IN ITSELF** *Mute 7BONG 4*	21	7
24 Mar 84	●	**PEOPLE ARE PEOPLE** *Mute 7BONG 5*	4	10
1 Sep 84	●	**MASTER AND SERVANT** *Mute 7BONG 6*	9	9
10 Nov 84		**SOMEBODY / BLASPHEMOUS RUMOURS** *Mute 7BONG 7*	16	6
11 May 85		**SHAKE THE DISEASE** *Mute BONG 8*	18	9
28 Sep 85		**IT'S CALLED A HEART** *Mute BONG 9*	18	4
22 Feb 86		**STRIPPED** *Mute BONG 10*	15	5
26 Apr 86		**A QUESTION OF LUST** *Mute BONG 11*	28	5
23 Aug 86		**A QUESTION OF TIME** *Mute BONG 12*	17	6
9 May 87		**STRANGELOVE** *Mute BONG 13*	16	5
5 Sep 87		**NEVER LET ME DOWN AGAIN** *Mute BONG 14*	22	4
9 Jan 88		**BEHIND THE WHEEL** *Mute BONG 15*	21	5
28 May 88		**LITTLE 15 (import)** *Mute LITTLE 15*	60	2
25 Feb 89		**EVERYTHING COUNTS** *Mute BONG 16*	22	7
9 Sep 89		**PERSONAL JESUS** *Mute BONG 17*	13	8
17 Feb 90	●	**ENJOY THE SILENCE** *Mute BONG 18*	6	9
19 May 90		**POLICY OF TRUTH** *Mute BONG 19*	16	6
29 Sep 90		**WORLD IN MY EYES** *Mute BONG 20*	17	6
27 Feb 93	●	**I FEEL YOU** *Mute CDBONG 21*	8	7
8 May 93		**WALKING IN MY SHOES** *Mute CDBONG 22*	14	4
25 Sep 93	●	**CONDEMNATION** *Mute CDBONG 23*	9	4
22 Jan 94	●	**IN YOUR ROOM** *Mute CDBONG 24*	8	4
15 Feb 97	●	**BARREL OF A GUN** *Mute CDBONG 25*	4	4
12 Apr 97	●	**IT'S NO GOOD** *Mute CDBONG 26*	5	5
28 Jun 97		**HOME** *Mute CDBONG 27*	23	4
1 Nov 97		**USELESS** *Mute CDBONG 28*	28	2
19 Sep 98		**ONLY WHEN I LOSE MYSELF** *Mute CDBONG 29*	17	3
5 May 01	●	**DREAM ON (re)** *Mute CDBONG 30*	6	5
11 Aug 01		**I FEEL LOVED** *Mute CDBONG 31*	12	6
17 Nov 01		**FREELOVE** *Mute CDBONG 32*	19	3
14 Nov 81	●	**SPEAK AND SPELL** *Mute STUMM 5*	10	33
9 Oct 82	●	**A BROKEN FRAME** *Mute STUMM 9*	8	11
3 Sep 83	●	**CONSTRUCTION TIME AGAIN** *Mute STUMM 13*	6	12
6 Sep 84	●	**SOME GREAT REWARD** *Mute STUMM 19*	5	12
26 Oct 85	●	**THE SINGLES 81-85** *Mute MUTEL 1*	6	22
29 Mar 86	●	**BLACK CELEBRATION** *Mute STUMM 26*	4	11
10 Oct 87	●	**MUSIC FOR THE MASSES** *Mute STUMM 47*	10	4
25 Mar 89	●	**101** *Mute STUMM 101*	5	8
31 Mar 90	●	**VIOLATOR** *Mute STUMM 64*	2	30
3 Apr 93	★	**SONGS OF FAITH AND DEVOTION** *Mute CDSTUMM 106* ■ ▲	1	16
26 Apr 97	★	**ULTRA** *Mute CDSTUMM 148* ■	1	11
10 Oct 98	●	**THE SINGLES 86-98** *Mute CDMUTEL 5*	5	6
7 Nov 98		**THE SINGLES 81-85 (re-issue)** *Mute LCDMUTEL 1*	57	1
26 May 01	●	**EXCITER** *Mute CDSTUMM 190*	9	4

'BONG 16' is a live version of 'BONG 3'

DEPTH CHARGE

UK, male producer – Jonathan Kane (Singles: 1 week)

Date		Title	pos	wks
29 Jul 95		**LEGEND OF THE GOLDEN SNAKE** *DC DC 01CD*	75	1

DER DRITTE RAUM

Germany, male producer – Andreas Kruger (Singles: 1 week)

Date		Title	pos	wks
4 Sep 99		**HALLE BOPP** *Additive 12AD 042*	75	1

DEREK and CLIVE – *See Peter COOK and Dudley MOORE*

DEREK and the DOMINOES – *See Eric CLAPTON*

Yves DERUYTER *Belgium, male DJ / producer (Singles: 3 weeks)*

Date		Title	pos	wks
14 Apr 01		**BACK TO EARTH** *UK Bonzai UKBONZAICD01*	63	1
19 Jan 02		**BACK TO EARTH (re-mix)** *UK Bonzai UKBONZAI 109CD*	56	2

DESERT *UK, male production duo (Singles: 1 week)*

Date		Title	pos	wks
20 Oct 01		**LETTIN' YA MIND GO** *Future Groove CDFGR 017*	74	1

DESERT EAGLE DISCS featuring Keisha WHITE

UK, male / female production / vocal group (Singles: 1 week)

Date		Title	pos	wks
1 Mar 03		**BIGGER BETTER DEAL** *Echo ECSCD 129*	67	1

DESERT SESSIONS *US / UK, male / female vocal / instrumental group (Singles: 2 weeks)*

Date		Title	pos	wks
15 Nov 03		**CRAWL HOME** *Island 9812964*	41	2

DESIDERIO *UK / Holland, male production duo / female vocalist (Singles: 1 week)*

Date		Title	pos	wks
3 Jun 00		**STARLIGHT** *Code Blue BLU 010CD*	57	1

Kevin DESIMONE – *See Barry MANILOW*

DESIRELESS

France, female vocalist (Singles: 19 weeks)

Date		Title	pos	wks
31 Oct 87		**VOYAGE VOYAGE** *CBS DESI 1*	53	6
14 May 88	●	**VOYAGE VOYAGE (re-mix)** *CBS DESI 2*	5	13

DESIYA featuring Melissa YIANNAKOU

UK, male / female vocal / instrumental duo (Singles: 1 week)

Date		Title	pos	wks
1 Feb 92		**COMIN' ON STRONG** *Black Market 12MKT 2*	74	1

DESKEE *UK, male instrumentalist (Singles: 3 weeks)*

Date		Title	pos	wks
3 Feb 90		**LET THERE BE HOUSE** *Big One VBIG 19*	52	2
8 Sep 90		**DANCE, DANCE** *Big One VBIG 22*	74	1

DES'REE *UK, female vocalist – Desiree Weekes (Singles: 73 weeks, Albums: 27 weeks)*

Date		Title / Label	pos	wks
31 Aug 91		FEEL SO HIGH *Dusted Sound 6573667*	51	5
11 Jan 92		FEEL SO HIGH (re-issue) *Dusted Sound 6576897*	13	7
21 Mar 92		MIND ADVENTURES *Dusted Sound 6578637*	43	3
27 Jun 92		WHY SHOULD I LOVE YOU *Dusted Sound 6580917*	44	3
19 Jun 93		DELICATE *Columbia 6593312* [1]	14	6
9 Apr 94		YOU GOTTA BE *Dusted Sound 6601342*	20	7
18 Jun 94		I AIN'T MOVIN' *Dusted Sound 6604672*	44	3
3 Sep 94		LITTLE CHILD *Dusted Sound 6604515*	69	1
11 Mar 95		YOU GOTTA BE (re-mix) *Dusted Sound 6613215*	14	8
20 Jun 98	●	LIFE *Sony S2 6659302*	8	15
7 Nov 98		WHAT'S YOUR SIGN? *Sony S2 6665162*	19	4
3 Apr 99	●	YOU GOTTA BE (2nd re-mix) *Dusted Sound / Sony S2 6668935*	10	8
16 Oct 99		AIN'T NO SUNSHINE *Universal Music TV 1564332* [2]	42	2
5 Apr 03		IT'S OKAY *Sony S2 6736492*	67	1
29 Feb 92		MIND ADVENTURES *Dusted Sound 4712632*	26	5
21 May 94		I AIN'T MOVIN' *Dusted Sound 4758432*	13	6
11 Jul 98		SUPERNATURAL *Sony S2 4897192*	16	16

[1] Terence Trent D'Arby featuring Des'ree [2] Ladysmith Black Mambazo featuring Des'ree with Kelly Rowland and Michelle Williams

DESTINY'S CHILD (249 Top 500) *Texas-based US female R&B quartet turned trio, fronted by co-writer and co-producer Beyoncé Knowles. Responsible for four US No.1s, They are the only US girl group to top the UK chart twice (Singles: 110 weeks, Albums: 138 weeks)*

Date		Title / Label	pos	wks
28 Mar 98	●	NO, NO, NO *Columbia 6656592* [1]	5	8
11 Jul 98		WITH ME *Columbia 6661472*	19	3
7 Nov 98		SHE'S GONE *Columbia 6664915* [2]	24	3
23 Jan 99		GET ON THE BUS *East West E 3780CD* [3]	15	5
24 Jul 99	●	BILLS, BILLS, BILLS *Columbia 6676902* ▲	6	9
30 Oct 99	●	BUG A BOO *Columbia 6681882*	9	7
8 Apr 00	●	SAY MY NAME *Columbia 6691882* ▲	3	11
29 Jul 00	●	JUMPIN' JUMPIN' *Columbia 6696292*	5	11
2 Dec 00	★	INDEPENDENT WOMEN PART 1 *Columbia 6705932* ■ ▲	1	15
28 Apr 01	★	SURVIVOR *Columbia 6711732* ■	1	13
4 Aug 01	●	BOOTYLICIOUS *Columbia 6717382* ▲	2	11
24 Nov 01	●	EMOTION *Columbia 6721112*	3	14
14 Mar 98		DESTINY'S CHILD *Columbia 4885352*	45	4
7 Aug 99	●	THE WRITING'S ON THE WALL *Columbia 4943942*	10	87
12 May 01	★	SURVIVOR *Columbia 5017832* ■ ▲	1	44
30 Mar 02		THIS IS THE REMIX *Columbia 5076272*	25	3

[1] Destiny's Child featuring Wyclef Jean [2] Matthew Marsden featuring Destiny's Child [3] Destiny's Child featuring Timbaland

See also BEYONCÉ; Kelly ROWLAND

DESTROYERS – *See George THOROGOOD and the DESTROYERS*

DESTRY – *See ZOO EXPERIENCE featuring DESTRY; CIRCA featuring DESTRY*

Marcella DETROIT *US, female vocalist – Marcella Levy (Singles: 16 weeks, Albums: 5 weeks)*

Date		Title / Label	pos	wks
12 Mar 94		I BELIEVE *London LONCD 347*	11	8
14 May 94		AIN'T NOTHING LIKE THE REAL THING *London LONCD 350* [1]	24	4
16 Jul 94		I'M NO ANGEL *London LOCDP 351*	33	4
9 Apr 94		JEWEL *London 8284912*	15	5

[1] Marcella Detroit and Elton John

See also SHAKESPEAR'S SISTER

DETROIT EMERALDS *US, male vocal group (Singles: 44 weeks)*

Date		Title / Label	pos	wks
10 Feb 73	●	FEEL THE NEED IN ME *Janus 6146 020*	4	15
5 May 73		YOU WANT IT YOU GOT IT *Westbound 6146 103*	12	9
11 Aug 73		I THINK OF YOU *Westbound 6146 104*	27	9
18 Jun 77		FEEL THE NEED (re-recording) *Atlantic K 10945*	12	11

DETROIT GRAND PU BAHS *US, male production / vocal group (Singles: 3 weeks)*

Date		Title / Label	pos	wks
8 Jul 00		SANDWICHES *Jive Electro 9230252*	29	3

DETROIT SPINNERS *US, male vocal quintet – included G C Cameron, Philippe Wynne (died on stage 1984) and John Edwards (Singles: 93 weeks, Albums: 3 weeks)*

Date		Title / Label	pos	wks
14 Nov 70		IT'S A SHAME *Tamla Motown TMG 755* [1]	20	11
21 Apr 73		COULD IT BE I'M FALLING IN LOVE *Atlantic K 10283*	11	11
29 Sep 73	●	GHETTO CHILD *Atlantic K 10359*	7	10
19 Oct 74		THEN CAME YOU *Atlantic K 10495* [2] ▲	29	6
11 Sep 76		THE RUBBERBAND MAN *Atlantic K 10807*	16	11
29 Jan 77		WAKE UP SUSAN *Atlantic K 10799*	29	6
7 May 77		COULD IT BE I'M FALLING IN LOVE (EP) *Atlantic K 10935*	32	3
23 Feb 80	★	WORKING MY WAY BACK TO YOU – FORGIVE ME GIRL – (MEDLEY) *Atlantic K 11432*	1	14
10 May 80		BODY LANGUAGE *Atlantic K 11392*	40	7
28 Jun 80	●	CUPID – I'VE LOVED YOU FOR A LONG TIME (MEDLEY) *Atlantic K 11498*	4	10
24 Jun 95		I'LL BE AROUND *Cooltempo CDCOOL 306* [3]	30	4
14 May 77		DETROIT SPINNERS' SMASH HITS *Atlantic K 50363*	37	3

[1] Motown Spinners [2] Dionne Warwicke and The Detroit Spinners [3] Rappin' 4-Tay featuring The Spinners

Tracks on Could It Be I'm Falling in Love (EP): Could It Be I'm Falling in Love / You're Throwing a Good Love Away / Games People Play / Lazy Susan

DETROIT WHEELS – *See Mitch RYDER and the DETROIT WHEELS*

DEUCE *UK, male / female vocal group (Singles: 23 weeks, Albums: 2 weeks)*

Date		Title / Label	pos	wks
21 Jan 95		CALL IT LOVE *London LONCD 355*	11	10
22 Apr 95	●	I NEED YOU *London LONCD 365*	10	5
19 Aug 95		ON THE BIBLE *London LONCD 368*	13	6
29 Jun 96		NO SURRENDER *Love This LUVTHISCD 10*	29	2
9 Sep 95		ON THE LOOSE! *London 8286642*	18	2

dEUS *Belgium, male vocal / instrumental group (Singles: 7 weeks, Albums: 1 week)*

Date		Title / Label	pos	wks
11 Feb 95		HOTEL LOUNGE (BE THE DEATH OF ME) *Island CID 603*	55	1
13 Jul 96		THEME FROM TURNPIKE (EP) *Island CID 630*	68	1
19 Oct 96		LITTLE ARITHMETICS *Island CID 643*	44	2
15 Mar 97		ROSES *Island CID 645*	56	1
24 Apr 99		INSTANT STREET *Island CID 742*	49	1
3 Jul 99		SISTER DEW *Island CID 750*	62	1
3 Apr 99		THE IDEAL CRASH *Island 5246432*	64	1

Tracks on Theme from Turnpike (EP): Theme from Turnpike / Worried About Satan / Overflow / My Little Contessa

David DEVANT & HIS SPIRIT WIFE *UK, male vocal / instrumental group (Singles: 2 weeks, Albums: 1 week)*

Date		Title / Label	pos	wks
5 Apr 97		GINGER *Rhythm King KIND 4CD*	54	1
21 Jun 97		THIS IS FOR REAL *Rhythm King KIND 5CD*	61	1
5 Jul 97		WORK, LOVELIFE, MISCELLANEOUS *Rhythm King KINDCD 1*	70	1

William DEVAUGHN *US, male vocalist (Singles: 10 weeks)*

Date		Title / Label	pos	wks
6 Jul 74		BE THANKFUL FOR WHAT YOU'VE GOT *Chelsea 2005 002*	31	5
20 Sep 80		BE THANKFUL FOR WHAT YOU'VE GOT (re-recording) *EMI 5101*	44	5

Sidney DEVINE *UK, male vocalist (Singles: 1 week, Albums: 11 weeks)*

Date		Title / Label	pos	wks
1 Apr 78		SCOTLAND FOREVER (EP) *Philips SCOT 1*	48	1
10 Apr 76		DOUBLE DEVINE *Philips 6625 019*	14	10
11 Dec 76		DEVINE TIME *Philips 6308 283*	49	1

Tracks on Scotland Forever (EP): Scotland Forever, Scots Wha' Hae, Flower of Scotland, Scottish Trilogy

DEVO *US, male vocal / instrumental group (Singles: 23 weeks, Albums: 22 weeks)*

Date		Title / Label	pos	wks
22 Apr 78		(I CAN'T ME GET NO) SATISFACTION *Stiff BOY 1*	41	8
13 May 78		JOCKO HOMO *Stiff DEV 1*	62	3

12 Aug 78	**BE STIFF** *Stiff BOY 2*	71	1
2 Sep 78	**COME BACK JONEE** *Virgin VS 223*	60	4
22 Nov 80	**WHIP IT** *Virgin VS 383*	51	7
16 Sep 78	**Q: ARE WE NOT MEN? A: NO WE ARE DEVO!** *Virgin V 2106*	12	7
23 Jun 79	**DUTY NOW FOR THE FUTURE** *Virgin V 2125*	49	6
24 May 80	**FREEDOM OF CHOICE** *Virgin V 2162*	47	5
5 Sep 81	**NEW TRADITIONALISTS** *Virgin V 2191*	50	4

DEVOTIONS – *See BELLE and the DEVOTIONS*

Howard DEVOTO

UK, male vocalist (Albums: 2 weeks) pos/wks

6 Aug 83	**JERKY VERSIONS OF THE DREAM** *Virgin V 2272*	57	2

See also BUZZCOCKS; MAGAZINE

DEXY'S MIDNIGHT RUNNERS (386 Top 500)

Maverick Birmingham, UK-based post-punk group which split up in 1987. Led throughout radical personnel and stylistic changes by Kevin Rowland (v/g), b 17 Aug 1953. Transatlantic No.1 'Come On Eileen' was the top selling UK single of 1982, selling 1,201,000 (Singles: 93 weeks, Albums: 80 weeks) pos/wks

19 Jan 80	**DANCE STANCE** *Oddball Productions R 6028*	40	6
22 Mar 80 ★	**GENO** *Late Night Feelings R 6033*	1	14
12 Jul 80 ●	**THERE THERE MY DEAR** *Late Night Feelings R 6038*	7	9
21 Mar 81	**PLAN B** *Parlophone R 6046*	58	2
11 Jul 81	**SHOW ME** *Mercury DEXYS 6*	16	9
20 Mar 82	**THE CELTIC SOUL BROTHERS** *Mercury DEXYS 8* [1]	45	4
3 Jul 82 ★	**COME ON EILEEN** *Mercury DEXYS 9* [1] ◆ ▲	1	17
2 Oct 82 ●	**JACKIE WILSON SAID (I'M IN HEAVEN WHEN YOU SMILE)** *Mercury DEXYS 10* [2]	5	7
4 Dec 82	**LET'S GET THIS STRAIGHT (FROM THE START) / OLD** *Mercury DEXYS 11* [2]	17	9
2 Apr 83	**THE CELTIC SOUL BROTHERS** *Mercury DEXYS 12* [2]	20	6
22 Nov 86	**BECAUSE OF YOU** *Mercury BRUSH 1*	13	10
26 Jul 80 ●	**SEARCHING FOR THE YOUNG SOUL REBELS** *Parlophone PCS 7213*	6	10
7 Aug 82 ●	**TOO-RYE-AY** *Mercury MERS 5*	2	46
26 Mar 83	**GENO** *EMI EMS 1007*	79	2
21 Sep 85	**DON'T STAND ME DOWN** *Mercury MERH 56*	22	6
8 Jun 91	**THE VERY BEST OF DEXY'S MIDNIGHT RUNNERS** *Mercury 8464601*	12	15
4 Oct 03	**LET'S MAKE THIS PRECIOUS – THE BEST OF DEXY'S MIDNIGHT RUNNERS** *EMI 5926802*	75	1

[1] Dexy's Midnight Runners with the Emerald Express
[2] Kevin Rowland and Dexy's Midnight Runners

DEXYS 12 is a different version from DEXYS 8

DHANY – *See KMC featuring DHANY*

DI – *See SHY FX; T-POWER*

Tony DI BART

UK, male vocalist (Singles: 19 weeks) pos/wks

9 Apr 94 ★	**THE REAL THING** *Cleveland City Blues CCBCD 15001*	1	12
20 Aug 94	**DO IT** *Cleveland City Blues CCBCD 15003*	21	4
20 May 95	**WHY DID YA** *Cleveland City Blues CCBCD 15004*	46	1
2 Mar 96	**TURN YOUR LOVE AROUND** *Cleveland City Blues CCBCD 15006*	66	1
17 Oct 98	**THE REAL THING (re-mix)** *Cleveland City CLECD 13050*	51	1

Jim DIAMOND

UK, male vocalist (Singles: 30 weeks, Albums: 5 weeks) pos/wks

3 Nov 84 ★	**I SHOULD HAVE KNOWN BETTER** *A&M AM 220*	1	13
2 Feb 85	**I SLEEP ALONE AT NIGHT** *A&M AM 229*	72	1
18 May 85	**REMEMBER I LOVE YOU** *A&M AM 247*	42	5
22 Feb 86 ●	**HI HO SILVER** *A&M AM 296*	5	11
22 May 93	**JIM DIAMOND** *PolyGram TV 8438472*	16	5

See also PhD

Neil DIAMOND (37 Top 500)

World-renowned singer / guitarist / songwriter, b. 24 Jan 1941, Brooklyn, US. First found international fame as writer of 'I'm a Believer' (Monkees), before going on to become one of the world's most popular live artists and biggest-selling album acts (20 platinum and 17 gold albums) (Singles: 121 weeks, Albums: 588 weeks) pos/wks

7 Nov 70 ●	**CRACKLIN' ROSIE** *Uni UN 529* ▲	3	17
20 Feb 71 ●	**SWEET CAROLINE** *Uni UN 531*	8	11
8 May 71 ●	**I AM . . . I SAID** *Uni UN 532*	4	12
13 May 72	**SONG SUNG BLUE** *Uni UN 538* ▲	14	13
14 Aug 76	**IF YOU KNOW WHAT I MEAN** *CBS 4398*	35	4
23 Oct 76	**BEAUTIFUL NOISE** *CBS 4601*	13	9
24 Dec 77	**DESIREE** *CBS 5869*	39	6
25 Nov 78 ●	**YOU DON'T BRING ME FLOWERS** *CBS 6803* [1] ▲	5	12
3 Mar 79	**FOREVER IN BLUE JEANS** *CBS 7047*	16	12
15 Nov 80	**LOVE ON THE ROCKS** *Capitol CL 16173*	17	12
14 Feb 81	**HELLO AGAIN** *Capitol CL 16176*	51	4
20 Nov 82	**HEARTLIGHT** *CBS A 2814*	47	7
21 Nov 92	**MORNING HAS BROKEN** *Columbia 6588267*	36	2
13 Mar 71	**GOLD** *Uni UNLS 116*	23	13
20 Mar 71	**TAP ROOT MANUSCRIPT** *Uni UNLS 117*	19	14
11 Dec 71	**STONES** *Uni UNLS 121*	18	14
5 Aug 72 ●	**MOODS** *Uni UNLS 128*	7	19
12 Jan 74	**HOT AUGUST NIGHT** *Uni ULD 1*	32	2
16 Feb 74	**JONATHAN LIVINGSTON SEAGULL** *CBS 69047*	35	1
9 Mar 74	**RAINBOW** *MCA MCF 2529*	39	5
29 Jul 74	**HIS 12 GREATEST HITS** *MCA MCF 2550*	13	78
9 Nov 74	**SERENADE** *CBS 69067*	11	14
10 Jul 76 ●	**BEAUTIFUL NOISE** *CBS 86004*	10	26
12 Mar 77 ●	**LOVE AT THE GREEK – RECORDED LIVE AT THE GREEK THEATRE** *CBS 95001*	3	32
6 Aug 77	**HOT AUGUST NIGHT (Re-issue)** *MCA MCSP 255*	60	1
17 Dec 77	**I'M GLAD YOU'RE HERE WITH ME TONIGHT** *CBS 86044*	16	12
25 Nov 78 ●	**20 GOLDEN GREATS** *MCA EMTV 14*	2	29
6 Jan 79	**YOU DON'T BRING ME FLOWERS** *CBS 86077*	15	23
19 Jan 80	**SEPTEMBER MORN** *CBS 86096*	14	11
22 Nov 80 ●	**THE JAZZ SINGER (FILM SOUNDTRACK)** *Capitol EAST12120*	3	110
28 Feb 81	**LOVE SONGS** *MCA MCF 3092*	43	6
5 Dec 81	**THE WAY TO THE SKY** *CBS 85343*	39	13
19 Jun 82	**12 GREATEST HITS VOLUME 2** *CBS 85844*	32	8
13 Nov 82	**HEARTLIGHT** *CBS 25073*	43	10
10 Dec 83	**THE VERY BEST OF NEIL DIAMOND** *K-Tel NE 1265*	33	11
28 Jul 84 ●	**PRIMITIVE** *CBS 86306*	7	10
24 May 86	**HEADED FOR THE FUTURE** *CBS 26952*	36	8
28 Nov 87	**HOT AUGUST NIGHT II** *CBS 460 4081*	74	4
25 Feb 89	**THE BEST YEARS OF OUR LIVES** *CBS 463201 1*	42	6
9 Nov 91	**LOVESCAPE** *Columbia 4688901*	36	13
4 Jul 92 ★	**THE GREATEST HITS 1966-1992** *Columbia 4715022*	1	30
28 Nov 92	**THE CHRISTMAS ALBUM** *Columbia 4724102*	50	6
9 Oct 93	**UP ON THE ROOF – SONGS FROM THE BRILL BUILDING** *Columbia 4743562*	28	10
17 Feb 96	**TENNESSEE MOON** *Columbia 4813782*	12	13
25 May 96	**THE BEST OF NEIL DIAMOND** *MCA MCD 11452*	68	1
31 Aug 96 ●	**THE ULTIMATE COLLECTION** *Sony TV / Universal MOODCD 45*	5	20
14 Nov 98	**THE MOVIE ALBUM – AS TIME GOES BY** *Columbia 4916552*	68	2
15 Sep 01	**THREE CHORD OPERA** *Columbia 5024932*	49	1
16 Mar 02	**THE ESSENTIAL** *Columbia 5010662*	11	12

[1] Barbra and Neil *(Barbra was Barbra Streisand)*

Gregg DIAMOND BIONIC BOOGIE

US, male / female vocal group, leader d. 14 Mar 1999 (Singles: 3 weeks) pos/wks

20 Jan 79	**CREAM (ALWAYS RISES TO THE TOP)** *Polydor POSP 18*	61	3

DIAMOND HEAD

UK, male vocal / instrumental group (Singles: 2 weeks, Albums: 9 weeks) pos/wks

11 Sep 82	**IN THE HEAT OF THE NIGHT** *MCA DHM 102*	67	2
23 Oct 82	**BORROWED TIME** *MCA DH 1001*	24	5
24 Sep 83	**CANTERBURY** *MCA DH 1002*	32	4

DIAMONDS

Canada / US, male vocal group (Singles: 17 weeks) pos/wks

31 May 57 ●	**LITTLE DARLIN'** *Mercury MT 148*	3	17

DIANA – *See Diana ROSS*

DICK and DEEDEE *US, male / female vocal duo – Dick St John (Richard Gosting, d. 27 Dec 2003) and Deedee Sperling (Singles: 3 weeks)*

Date	Title / Label	pos	wks
26 Oct 61	**THE MOUNTAIN'S HIGH** *London HLG 9408*	37	3

Charles DICKENS

UK, male vocalist – David Anthony (Singles: 8 weeks)

Date	Title / Label	pos	wks
1 Jul 65	**THAT'S THE WAY LOVE GOES** *Pye 7N 15887*	37	8

Gwen DICKEY

US, female vocalist (Singles: 13 weeks)

Date	Title / Label	pos	wks
27 Jan 90	**CAR WASH** *Swanyard SYR 7*	72	2
2 Jul 94	**AIN'T NOBODY (LOVES ME BETTER)** *X-clusive XCLU 010CD* [1]	21	4
14 Feb 98	**WISHING ON A STAR** *Northwestside 74321554632* [2]	13	4
31 Oct 98	**CAR WASH (re-recording)** *MCA MCSTD 48096* [3]	18	3

[1] KWS and Gwen Dickey
[2] Jay-Z featuring Gwen Dickey
[3] Rose Royce featuring Gwen Dickey

See also ROSE ROYCE

Neville DICKIE

UK, male instrumentalist – piano (Singles: 10 weeks)

Date	Title / Label	pos	wks
25 Oct 69	**ROBIN'S RETURN** *Major Minor MM 644*	33	10

DICKIES *US, male vocal / instrumental group (Singles: 28 weeks, Albums: 19 weeks)*

Date	Title / Label	pos	wks
16 Dec 78	**SILENT NIGHT** *A&M AMS 7403*	47	4
21 Apr 79 ●	**BANANA SPLITS (THE TRA LA LA SONG)** *A&M AMS 7431*	7	8
21 Jul 79	**PARANOID** *A&M AMS 7368*	45	6
15 Sep 79	**NIGHTS IN WHITE SATIN** *A&M AMS 7469*	39	5
16 Feb 80	**FAN MAIL** *A&M AMS 7504*	57	3
19 Jul 80	**GIGANTOR** *A&M AMS 7544*	72	2
17 Feb 79	**THE INCREDIBLE SHRINKING DICKIES** *A&M AMLE 64742*	18	17
24 Nov 79	**DAWN OF THE DICKIES** *A&M AMLE 68510*	60	2

Bruce DICKINSON

UK, male vocalist (Singles: 23 weeks, Albums: 15 weeks)

Date	Title / Label	pos	wks
28 Apr 90	**TATTOOED MILLIONAIRE** *EMI EM 138*	18	5
23 Jun 90	**ALL THE YOUNG DUDES** *EMI EM 142*	23	5
25 Aug 90	**DIVE! DIVE! DIVE!** *EMI EM 151*	45	2
4 Apr 92 ●	**(I WANT TO BE) ELECTED** *London LON 319* [1]	9	5
28 May 94	**TEARS OF THE DRAGON** *EMI CDEM 322*	28	2
8 Oct 94	**SHOOT ALL THE CLOWNS** *EMI CDEMS 341*	37	2
13 Apr 96	**BACK FROM THE EDGE** *Raw Power RAWX 1012*	68	1
3 May 97	**ACCIDENT OF BIRTH** *Raw Power RAWX 1042*	54	1
19 May 90	**TATTOOED MILLIONAIRE** *EMI EMC 3574*	14	9
18 Jun 94	**BALLS TO PICASSO** *EMI CDEMX 1057*	21	3
9 Mar 96	**SKUNKWORKS** *Raw Power RAWCD 106*	41	1
24 May 97	**ACCIDENT OF BIRTH** *Raw Power RAWCD 124*	53	1
26 Sep 98	**THE CHEMICAL WEDDING** *Air Raid AIRCD 1*	55	1

[1] Mr Bean and Smear Campaign featuring Bruce Dickinson

See also IRON MAIDEN

Barbara DICKSON (345 Top 500) *Noted folk-inflected pop singer, b. 27 Sep 1947, Dunfermline, Scotland. A familiar face on 1970s and 1980s TV who later received acclaim for theatrical forays (notably Willy Russell's 'Blood Brothers') and TV acting roles ('Band of Gold'). Awarded an OBE in 2002 (Singles: 49 weeks, Albums: 142 weeks)*

Date	Title / Label	pos	wks
17 Jan 76 ●	**ANSWER ME** *RSO 2090 174*	9	7
26 Feb 77	**ANOTHER SUITCASE IN ANOTHER HALL** *MCA 266*	18	7
19 Jan 80	**CARAVAN SONG** *Epic EPC 8103*	41	7
15 Mar 80	**JANUARY FEBRUARY** *Epic EPIC 8115*	11	10

TOP 10 COUNTRY HITS

Based on the UK chart performance of records that have entered the US country singles Top 40, here are the top 10 country records by weeks at No.1. The tie for position No.9 is decided by weeks at No.2.

Position - SONG - Act - (Weeks at No.1 / total weeks on the UK chart)

1. ROSE MARIE – Slim Whitman (11/19)
2. GIVE ME YOUR WORD – Tennessee Ernie Ford (7/24)
3. ALL I HAVE TO DO IS DREAM – Everly Brothers (7/21)
4. ALL SHOOK UP – Elvis Presley (7/21)
5. DISTANT DRUMS – Jim Reeves (5/25)
6. ARE YOU LONESOME TONIGHT? – Elvis Presley (4/15)
7. SIXTEEN TONS – Tennessee Ernie Ford (4/11)
8. WHOLE LOTTA WOMAN – Marvin Rainwater (3/15)
9. JAILHOUSE ROCK – Elvis Presley (3/14)
10. CRYING – Don McLean (3/14)

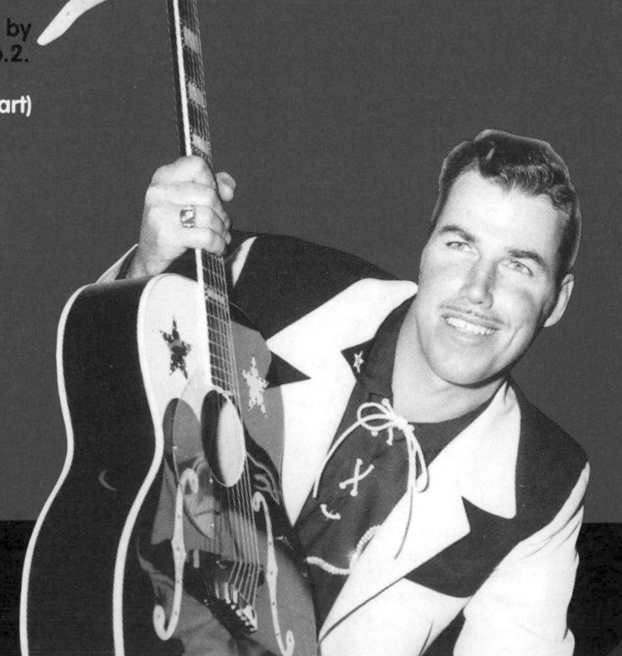

Slim Whitman sports his Lone Ranger outfit and contemplates his achievement in topping our chart with 'Rose Marie'

14 Jun 80 **IN THE NIGHT** *Epic EPC 8593* 48 2
5 Jan 85 ★ **I KNOW HIM SO WELL** *RCA CHESS 3* [1] 1 16
18 Jun 77 **MORNING COMES QUICKLY** *RSO 2394 188* 58 1
12 Apr 80 ● **THE BARBARA DICKSON ALBUM** *Epic EPC 84088* 7 12
16 May 81 **YOU KNOW IT'S ME** *Epic EPC 84551* 39 6
6 Feb 82 ● **ALL FOR A SONG** *Epic 10030* 3 37
24 Sep 83 **TELL ME IT'S NOT TRUE** *Legacy LLM 101* 100 1
23 Jun 84 **HEARTBEATS** *Epic EPC 25706* 21 8
12 Jan 85 ● **THE BARBARA DICKSON SONGBOOK** *K-Tel NE 1287* 5 19
23 Nov 85 **GOLD** *K-Tel ONE 1312* 11 18
15 Nov 86 **THE VERY BEST OF BARBARA DICKSON** *Telstar STAR 2276* 78 8
29 Nov 86 **THE RIGHT MOMENT** *K-Tel ONE 1335* 39 8
6 May 89 **COMING ALIVE AGAIN** *Telstar STAR 2349* 30 7
15 Aug 92 **DON'T THINK TWICE IT'S ALL RIGHT** *Columbia MOODCD 25* 32 5
28 Nov 92 **THE BEST OF ELAINE PAIGE AND BARBARA DICKSON** *Telstar TCD 2632* [1] 22 9
5 Mar 94 **PARCEL OF ROGUES** *Castle Communications CTVCD 126* 30 3

[1] Elaine Paige and Barbara Dickson [1] Elaine Paige and Barbara Dickson

'Tell Me It's Not True' is a mini-album featuring songs from the musical Blood Brothers

DICTATORS *US, male vocal / instrumental group (Singles: 2 weeks)* pos/wks

17 Sep 77 **SEARCH AND DESTROY (re)** *Asylum K 13091* 49 2

Bo DIDDLEY *US, male vocalist / instrumentalist, guitar – Ellas McDaniel (Singles: 10 weeks, Albums: 16 weeks)* pos/wks

10 Oct 63 **PRETTY THING** *Pye International 7N 25217* 34 6
18 Mar 65 **HEY GOOD LOOKIN'** *Chess CRS 8000* 39 4
5 Oct 63 **BO DIDDLEY** *Pye International NPL 28026* 11 8
9 Oct 63 **BO DIDDLEY IS A GUNSLINGER** *Pye NJL 33* 20 1
30 Nov 63 **BO DIDDLEY RIDES AGAIN** *Pye International NPL 28029* 19 1
15 Feb 64 **BO DIDDLEY'S BEACH PARTY** *Pye NPL 28032* 13 6

DIDDY *UK, male producer – Richard 'Diddy' Dearlove (Singles: 3 weeks)* pos/wks

19 Feb 94 **GIVE ME LOVE** *Positiva CDTIV 8* 52 1
12 Jul 97 **GIVE ME LOVE (re-mix)** *Feverpitch CDFVR 19* 23 2

See also BEDLAM

P DIDDY – *See PUFF DADDY*

DIDO (376 Top 500)

Record-breaking, multi-award-winning singer / songwriter, b. Florian Cloud de Bounevialle Armstrong, 25 Dec 1971, London. 'No Angel' (including the Eminem sampled 'Thank You') was the world's top selling album in 2001 (8.6 million) and is the UK's biggest selling debut album by a female artist (Singles: 49 weeks, Albums: 129 weeks) pos/wks

24 Apr 01 ● **HERE WITH ME** *Cheeky / Arista 74321832732* 4 12
2 Jun 01 ● **THANK YOU** *Cheeky / Arista 74321853042* 3 10
22 Sep 01 **HUNTER** *Cheeky / Arista 74321885452* 17 8
20 Apr 02 ● **ONE STEP TOO FAR** *Cheeky / Arista 74321926412* [1] 6 3
13 Sep 03 ● **WHITE FLAG** *Cheeky / Arista 82876546022* 2 13
13 Dec 03 ● **LIFE FOR RENT** *Cheeky / Arista 82876579462* ....8 3+
28 Oct 00 ★ **NO ANGEL** *Arista 743218832742* 1 117
11 Oct 03 ★ **LIFE FOR RENT** *Cheeky / Arista 82876545982* ■ ....1 12+

[1] Faithless featuring Dido

DIESEL PARK WEST *UK, male vocal / instrumental group (Singles: 15 weeks, Albums: 3 weeks)* pos/wks

4 Feb 89 **ALL THE MYTHS ON SUNDAY** *Food FOOD 17* 66 2
1 Apr 89 **LIKE PRINCES DO** *Food FOOD 19* 58 3
5 Aug 89 **WHEN THE HOODOO COMES** *Food FOOD 20* 62 2
18 Jan 92 **FALL TO LOVE** *Food FOOD 35* 48 3
21 Mar 92 **BOY ON TOP OF THE NEWS** *Food FOOD 36* 58 2
5 Sep 92 **GOD ONLY KNOWS** *Food FOOD 39* 57 3
11 Feb 89 **SHAKESPEARE ALABAMA** *Food FOODLP 2* 55 2
15 Feb 92 **DECENCY** *Food FOODCD 7* 57 1

DIFFERENT GEAR vs POLICE *UK / Italy, male production group and UK / US, male vocal / instrumental trio (Singles: 3 weeks)* pos/wks

5 Aug 00 **WHEN THE WORLD IS RUNNING DOWN** *Pagan PAGAN039CDS* 28 3

DIFFORD and TILBROOK *UK, male vocal / instrumental duo (Singles: 2 weeks, Albums: 3 weeks)* pos/wks

30 Jun 84 **LOVE'S CRASHING WAVES** *A&M AM 193* 57 2
14 Jul 84 **DIFFORD AND TILBROOK** *A&M AMLX 64985* 47 3

See also SQUEEZE

DIFF'RENT DARKNESS *UK, male vocal / instrumental group (Singles: 1 week)* pos/wks

27 Dec 03 **ORCHESTRAL MANOEUVRES IN THE DARKNESS** *Guided Missile GUIDE 49CD* ....66 1+

DIGABLE PLANETS *US, male / female vocal / instrumental group (Singles: 2 weeks)* pos/wks

13 Feb 93 **REBIRTH OF SLICK (COOL LIKE DAT)** *Pendulum EKR 159CD* ..67 2

Rah DIGGA – *See JAMELIA; OUTSIDAZ featuring Rah DIGGA and Melanie BLATT*

DIGITAL DREAM BABY *UK, male producer – Steven Teear (Singles: 4 weeks)* pos/wks

14 Dec 91 **WALKING IN THE AIR** *Columbia 6576067* 49 4

Hit is a dance re-mix of 'Walking in the Air' by vocalist Peter Auty

DIGITAL EXCITATION *Belgium, male producer – Frank de Wulf (Singles: 2 weeks)* pos/wks

29 Feb 92 **PURE PLEASURE** *R&S RSUK 10* 37 2

DIGITAL ORGASM *Belgium, male / female vocal / instrumental group (Singles: 14 weeks)* pos/wks

7 Dec 91 **RUNNING OUT OF TIME** *Dead Dead Good GOOD 009* 16 9
18 Apr 92 **STARTOUCHERS** *DDG International GOOD 13* 31 3
25 Jul 92 **MOOG ERUPTION** *DDG International GOOD 17* 62 2

DIGITAL UNDERGROUND *US, male rap group (Singles: 4 weeks, Albums: 2 weeks)* pos/wks

16 Mar 91 **SAME SONG** *Big Life BLR 40* 52 4
7 Apr 90 **SEX PACKETS** *BCM BCM 377LP* 59 1
30 Jun 90 **DOOWUTCHYALIKE / PACKET MAN** *BCM BCM 463X* 59 1

DILATED PEOPLES *US, male vocal / DJ / production group (Singles: 3 weeks, Albums: 1 week)* pos/wks

23 Feb 02 **WORST COMES TO WORST** *Capitol CDCL 834* 29 3
2 Mar 02 **EXPANSION TEAM** *Capitol 5314772* 55 1

DILEMMA *Italy, male instrumental / production group (Singles: 1 week)* pos/wks

6 Apr 96 **IN SPIRIT** *ffrr FCD 274* 42 1

Ricky DILLARD – *See Farley 'Jackmaster' FUNK*

DILLINJA *UK, male producer – Karl Francis (Singles: 8 weeks)* pos/wks

9 Nov 02 **TWIST 'EM OUT** *Renegade Hardware RH 40* 50 1
21 Dec 02 **LIVE OR DIE / SOUTH MANZ** *Valve VLV 007* 53 1
10 May 03 **THIS IS A WARNING / SUPER DJ** *Valve VLV 008* 47 1
28 Jun 03 **TWIST 'EM OUT (re-mix)** *Trouble on Vinyl TOV 56CD* [1] 35 3
27 Sep 03 **FAST CAR** *Valve VLV 011* 56 2

[1] Dilinja featuring Skibadee

Richard DIMBLEBY *UK, male broadcaster d. 22 Dec 1965 (Albums: 5 weeks)* pos/wks

4 Jun 66 **THE VOICE OF RICHARD DIMBLEBY** *MFP 1087* 14 5

DIMESTARS

UK, male / female vocal / instrumental group (Singles: 1 week)

Date		Title / Label	pos	wks
16 Jun 01		**MY SUPERSTAR** *Polydor 5870912*	72	1

D'INFLUENCE *UK, male / female vocal / instrumental group (Singles: 10 weeks, Albums: 1 week)*

Date		Title / Label	pos	wks
20 Jun 92		**GOOD LOVER** *East West A 8573* [1]	46	2
27 Mar 93		**GOOD LOVER (re-mix)** *East West America A 8439CD* [1]	61	1
24 Jun 95		**MIDNITE** *East West A 4418CD* [2]	58	1
16 Aug 97		**HYPNOTIZE** *Echo ECSCD 41*	33	2
11 Oct 97		**MAGIC** *Echo ECSCD 45*	45	1
5 Sep 98		**ROCK WITH YOU** *Echo ECSCD 56*	30	3
25 Oct 97		**LONDON** *Echo ECHCD 16*	56	1

[1] D-Influence [2] D*Influence

Paolo DINI – *See FPI PROJECT*

Mark DINNING

US, male vocalist, d. 22 Mar 1986 (Singles: 4 weeks)

Date		Title / Label	pos	wks
10 Mar 60		**TEEN ANGEL** *MGM 1053* ▲	37	4

DINOSAUR JR *US, male vocal / instrumental group (Singles: 13 weeks, Albums: 7 weeks)*

Date		Title / Label	pos	wks
2 Feb 91		**THE WAGON** *Blanco Y Negro NEG 48*	49	2
14 Nov 92		**GET ME** *Blanco Y Negro NEG 60*	44	1
30 Jan 93		**START CHOPPIN'** *Blanco Y Negro NEG 61CD*	20	3
12 Jun 93		**OUT THERE** *Blanco Y Negro NEG 63CD*	44	2
27 Aug 94		**FEEL THE PAIN** *Blanco Y Negro NEG 74CD*	25	3
11 Feb 95		**I DON'T THINK SO** *Blanco Y Negro NEG 77CD*	67	1
5 Apr 97		**TAKE A RUN AT THE SUN** *Blanco Y Negro NEG 103CD*	53	1
2 Mar 91		**GREEN MIND** *Blanco Y Negro BYN 24*	36	2
20 Feb 93	●	**WHERE YOU BEEN** *Blanco Y Negro 4509916272*	10	3
10 Sep 94		**WITHOUT A SOUND** *Blanco Y Negro 4509969332*	24	2

DINOSAURS – *See Terry DACTYL and the DINOSAURS*

DIO *UK / US, male vocal / instrumental group (Singles: 22 weeks, Albums: 48 weeks)*

Date		Title / Label	pos	wks
20 Aug 83		**HOLY DIVER** *Vertigo DIO 1*	72	2
29 Oct 83		**RAINBOW IN THE DARK** *Vertigo DIO 2*	46	3
11 Aug 84		**WE ROCK** *Vertigo DIO 3*	42	3
29 Sep 84		**MYSTERY** *Vertigo DIO 4*	34	4
10 Aug 85		**ROCK 'N' ROLL CHILDREN** *Vertigo DIO 5*	26	6
2 Nov 85		**HUNGRY FOR HEAVEN** *Vertigo DIO 6*	72	1
17 May 86		**HUNGRY FOR HEAVEN (re-issue)** *Vertigo DIO 7*	56	2
1 Aug 87		**I COULD HAVE BEEN A DREAMER** *Vertigo DIO 8*	69	1
11 Jun 83		**HOLY DIVER** *Vertigo VERS 5*	13	15
21 Jul 84	●	**THE LAST IN LINE** *Vertigo VERL 16*	4	14
7 Sep 85	●	**SACRED HEART** *Vertigo VERH 30*	4	6
5 Jul 86		**INTERMISSION** *Vertigo VERB 40*	22	5
22 Aug 87	●	**DREAM EVIL** *Vertigo VERH 46*	8	5
26 May 90		**LOCK UP THE WOLVES** *Vertigo 8460331*	28	3

DION

US, male vocalist – Dion DiMucci (Singles: 33 weeks)

Date		Title / Label	pos	wks
19 Jan 61		**LONELY TEENAGER** *Top Rank JAR 521*	47	1
2 Nov 61		**RUNAROUND SUE** *Top Rank JAR 586* ▲	11	9
15 Feb 62	●	**THE WANDERER** *HMV POP 971*	10	12
22 May 76		**THE WANDERER (re-issue)** *Philips 6146 700*	16	9
19 Aug 89		**KING OF THE NEW YORK STREETS** *Arista 112556*	74	2

DION and the BELMONTS

US, male vocal group (Singles: 2 weeks, Albums: 5 weeks)

Date		Title / Label	pos	wks
26 Jun 03		**A TEENAGER IN LOVE** *London HLU 8874*	28	2
12 Apr 80		**20 GOLDEN GREATS** *K-Tel NE 1057*	31	5

Celine DION (48 Top 500)

French-Canadian vocalist who won the 1988 Eurovision Song Contest (for Switzerland), b. 30 Mar 1968, Quebec. She has sold a reported 155 million albums worldwide and is the only female with two UK million-selling singles as a solo artist. Best-selling single: 'My Heart Will Go On' 1,312,551 (Singles: 250 weeks, Albums: 401 weeks)

Date		Title / Label	pos	wks
16 May 92	●	**BEAUTY AND THE BEAST** *Epic 6576607* [1]	9	7
4 Jul 92		**IF YOU ASKED ME TO (re)** *Epic 6581927*	57	5
14 Nov 92		**LOVE CAN MOVE MOUNTAINS** *Epic 6587787*	46	2
3 Apr 93		**WHERE DOES MY HEART BEAT NOW** *Epic 6563265*	72	1
29 Jan 94	●	**THE POWER OF LOVE** *Epic 6597992* ▲	4	10
23 Apr 94		**MISLED** *Epic 6602922*	40	3
22 Oct 94	★	**THINK TWICE** *Epic 6606422* ◆	1	31
20 May 95	●	**ONLY ONE ROAD** *Epic 6613535*	8	8
9 Sep 95	●	**TU M'AIMES ENCORE (TO LOVE ME AGAIN)** *Epic 6624255*	7	9
2 Dec 95		**MISLED (re-issue)** *Epic 6626495*	15	6
2 Mar 96	●	**FALLING INTO YOU** *Epic 6629795*	10	10
1 Jun 96	●	**BECAUSE YOU LOVED ME (THEME FROM 'UP CLOSE AND PERSONAL')** *Epic 6632382* ▲	5	16
5 Oct 96	●	**IT'S ALL COMING BACK TO ME NOW** *Epic 6637112*	3	14
21 Dec 96	●	**ALL BY MYSELF (re)** *Epic 6640622*	6	13
28 Jun 97		**CALL THE MAN** *Epic 6646922*	11	6
15 Nov 97	●	**TELL HIM** *Epic 6653052* [2]	3	15
20 Dec 97		**THE REASON** *Epic 6653812*	11	8
21 Feb 98	★	**MY HEART WILL GO ON** *Epic 6655472* ◆ ■ ▲	1	20
18 Jul 98	●	**IMMORTALITY** *Epic 6661682* [3]	5	12
28 Nov 98	●	**I'M YOUR ANGEL** *Epic 6666282* [4] ▲	3	13
10 Jul 99		**TREAT HER LIKE A LADY** *Epic 6675522*	29	3
11 Dec 99		**THAT'S THE WAY IT IS** *Epic 6684622*	12	11
8 Apr 00		**THE FIRST TIME EVER I SAW YOUR FACE (re)** *Epic 6691942*	19	7
23 Mar 02	●	**A NEW DAY HAS COME** *Epic 6725032*	7	10
31 Aug 02		**I'M ALIVE** *Epic 6730652*	17	6
7 Dec 02		**GOODBYE'S (THE SADDEST WORD)** *Epic 6733732*	38	2
20 Sep 03		**ONE HEART** *Columbia 6743482*	27	2
5 Mar 94	★	**THE COLOUR OF MY LOVE** *Epic 4747432*	1	109
16 Sep 95		**UNISON** *Epic 4672032*	55	3
7 Oct 95	●	**D'EUX** *Epic 4802862*	7	9
23 Mar 96	★	**FALLING INTO YOU** *Epic 4837928* ■ ▲	1	113
9 Nov 96		**LIVE A PARIS** *Epic 4866062*	53	1
15 Mar 97		**C'EST POUR VIVRE** *Nectar Masters NTRCD 076*	49	3
29 Nov 97	★	**LET'S TALK ABOUT LOVE** *Epic 4891592* ■ ▲	1	72
19 Sep 98		**S'IL SUFFISAIT D'AIMER** *Epic 4918592*	17	4
26 Sep 98		**CELINE DION** *Epic 4715089*	70	2
14 Nov 98		**THESE ARE SPECIAL TIMES** *Epic 4927302*	20	10
27 Nov 99	★	**ALL THE WAY ... A DECADE OF SONG** *Epic 4960942* ■ ▲	1	40
11 Nov 00		**THE COLLECTOR'S SERIES – VOLUME ONE** *Epic 5009952*	30	3
6 Apr 02	★	**A NEW DAY HAS COME** *Epic 5062262* ■ ▲	1	23
5 Apr 03	●	**ONE HEART** *Columbia 5108772*	4	9

[1] Celine Dion and Peabo Bryson [2] Barbra Streisand and Celine Dion [3] Celine Dion with special guests the Bee Gees [4] Celine Dion and R Kelly

Kathryn DION – *See 2 FUNKY 2 starring Kathryn DION*

DIONNE

Canada, female vocalist (Singles: 2 weeks)

Date		Title / Label	pos	wks
23 Sep 89		**COME GET MY LOVIN'** *Citybeat CBC 745*	69	2

Wasis DIOP featuring Lena FIAGBE

Senegal, male producer and UK, female singer (Singles: 2 weeks)

Date		Title / Label	pos	wks
10 Feb 96		**AFRICAN DREAM** *Mercury MERCD 453*	44	2

DIPPY – *See Keith HARRIS and ORVILLE*

DIRE STRAITS (14 Top 500)

Internationally acclaimed, album-orientated rock group fronted by Mark Knopfler (g/v) b. 12 Aug 1949, Glasgow. The London-based band was discovered after a demo tape was played on Charlie Gillett's Radio London show in 1977. Eponymous Knopfler-penned debut album (total cost just £12,500) was a transatlantic million-seller and, like their first single, 'Sultans of Swing', was even more successful in the US. By the early 1980s, they were global chart regulars, selling out shows across the US and Europe and attracting record-breaking crowds in Australasia. In 1983, they were voted Best British Group for the first time at the Brit Awards, and during that decade picked up countless other trophies. They released their most successful album, the Grammy and Brit winning 'Brothers in Arms', in 1985. 'It topped the chart in 22 countries (as did 'On Every Street') and sold more than nine million Stateside and nearly four million in the UK. The album included the US No.1 single 'Money for Nothing' (which featured co-writer Sting), the first video seen on MTV Europe. In 1991, the group started a record-shattering world tour, which was seen by more than seven million people in 25 countries and grossed about group £70m. In total Dire Straits sold in excess of 100 million albums around the globe (Singles: 119 weeks, Albums: 1,133 weeks) pos/wks

Date		Title	pos	wks
10 Mar 79	●	**SULTANS OF SWING** *Vertigo 6059 206*	8	11
28 Jul 79		**LADY WRITER** *Vertigo 6059 230*	51	6
17 Jan 81	●	**ROMEO AND JULIET** *Vertigo MOVIE 1*	8	11
4 Apr 81		**SKATEAWAY** *Vertigo MOVIE 2*	37	5
10 Oct 81		**TUNNEL OF LOVE** *Vertigo MUSIC 3*	54	3
4 Sep 82	●	**PRIVATE INVESTIGATIONS** *Vertigo DSTR 1*	2	8
22 Jan 83		**TWISTING BY THE POOL** *Vertigo DSTR 2*	14	7
18 Feb 84		**LOVE OVER GOLD (LIVE) / SOLID ROCK (LIVE)** *Vertigo DSTR 6*	50	3
20 Apr 85		**SO FAR AWAY** *Vertigo DSTR 9*	20	6
6 Jul 85	●	**MONEY FOR NOTHING** *Vertigo DSTR 10* ▲	4	16
26 Oct 85		**BROTHERS IN ARMS** *Vertigo DSTR 11*	16	13
11 Jan 86	●	**WALK OF LIFE** *Vertigo DSTR 12*	2	11
3 May 86		**YOUR LATEST TRICK** *Vertigo DSTR 13*	26	6
5 Nov 88		**SULTANS OF SWING (re-issue)** *Vertigo DSTR 15*	62	1
31 Aug 91		**CALLING ELVIS** *Vertigo DSTR 16*	21	4
2 Nov 91		**HEAVY FUEL** *Vertigo DSTR 17*	55	2
29 Feb 92		**ON EVERY STREET** *Vertigo DSTR 18*	42	2
27 Jun 92		**THE BUG** *Vertigo DSTR 19*	67	1
22 May 93		**ENCORES (EP)** *Vertigo DSCD 20*	31	3
22 Jul 78	●	**DIRE STRAITS** *Vertigo 9102 021*	5	132
23 Jun 79	●	**COMMUNIQUE** *Vertigo 9102 031*	5	32
25 Oct 80	●	**MAKING MOVIES** *Vertigo 6359 034*	4	251
2 Oct 82	★	**LOVE OVER GOLD** *Vertigo 6359 109* ■	1	200
24 Mar 84	●	**ALCHEMY – DIRE STRAITS LIVE** *Vertigo VERY 11*	3	163
25 May 85	★	**BROTHERS IN ARMS** *Vertigo VERH 25* ■ ▲	1	228
29 Oct 88	★	**MONEY FOR NOTHING** *Vertigo VERH 64* ■	1	64
21 Sep 91	★	**ON EVERY STREET** *Vertigo 5101601* ■	1	35
22 May 93	●	**ON THE NIGHT** *Vertigo 5147662*	4	7
8 Jul 95		**LIVE AT THE BBC** *Windsong WINDCD 072X*	71	1
31 Oct 98	●	**SULTANS OF SWING – THE VERY BEST OF DIRE STRAITS** *Vertigo 5586582*	6	20

Tracks on Encores (EP): Your Latest Trick / The Bug / Solid Rock / Local Hero (Wild Theme)

See also Mark KNOPFLER; David KNOPFLER; NOTTING HILLBILLIES

DIRECKT

UK, male instrumental / production duo – Mike 'E-Bloc' Kirwin and Danny 'Hibrid' Bennett (Singles: 2 weeks) pos/wks

Date		Title	pos	wks
13 Aug 94		**TWO FATT GUITARS (REVISITED)** *UFG UFG 7CD*	36	2

See also E-LUSTRIOUS

DIRECT DRIVE

UK, male / female vocal / instrumental group (Singles: 3 weeks) pos/wks

Date		Title	pos	wks
26 Jan 85		**ANYTHING?** *Polydor POSP 728*	67	2
4 May 85		**A.B.C. (FALLING IN LOVE'S NOT EASY)** *Boiling Point POSP 742*	75	1

DIRT DEVILS

UK / Finland, male production duo – Jon Grant and Paavo Siljamaki (Singles: 8 weeks) pos/wks

Date		Title	pos	wks
2 Feb 02		**THE DRILL** *NuLife / Arista 74321915262*	15	6
6 Dec 03		**MUSIC IS LIFE** *Nulife 82876571412*	53	2

DIRTY ROTTEN SCOUNDRELS – *See Lisa STANSFIELD*

DIRTY VEGAS

UK, male production trio (Singles: 11 weeks, Albums: 3 weeks) pos/wks

Date		Title	pos	wks
19 May 01		**DAYS GO BY** *Credence CDCRED 011*	27	4
3 Aug 02		**GHOSTS** *Credence CDCRED 028*	31	3
12 Oct 02		**DAYS GO BY (re-issue)** *Credence CDCRED 030*	16	4
17 Aug 02		**DIRTY VEGAS** *Credence 5399852*	40	3

DISCHARGE

UK, male vocal / instrumental group (Singles: 3 weeks, Albums: 5 weeks) pos/wks

Date		Title	pos	wks
24 Oct 81		**NEVER AGAIN** *Clay CLAY 6*	64	3
15 May 82		**HEAR NOTHING SEE NOTHING SAY NOTHING** *Clay CLAYLP 3*	40	5

DISCIPLES OF SOUL – *See LITTLE STEVEN*

DISCO ANTHEM

Holland, male producer – Lex van Coeverden (Singles: 2 weeks) pos/wks

Date		Title	pos	wks
18 Jun 94		**SCREAM** *Sweat MCSTD 1977*	47	2

DISCO CITIZENS

UK, male producer – Nick Bracegirdle (Singles: 5 weeks) pos/wks

Date		Title	pos	wks
22 Jul 95		**RIGHT HERE RIGHT NOW** *Deconstruction 74321293872*	40	2
12 Apr 97		**FOOTPRINT** *Xtravaganza 0091115*	34	2
4 Jul 98		**NAGASAKI BADGER** *Xtravaganza 0091595 EXT*	56	1

See also CHICANE

DISCO EVANGELISTS

UK, male instrumental / production group (Singles: 2 weeks) pos/wks

Date		Title	pos	wks
8 May 93		**DE NIRO** *Positiva CDTIV 2*	59	2

DISCO TEX & the SEX-O-LETTES

US, male vocalist / female vocal group (Singles: 22 weeks) pos/wks

Date		Title	pos	wks
23 Nov 74	●	**GET DANCING** *Chelsea 2005 013*	8	12
26 Apr 75	●	**I WANNA DANCE WIT CHOO (DOO DAT DANCE) – PART 1** *Chelsea 2005 024* [1]	6	10

[1] Disco Tex and the Sex-O-Lettes featuring Sir Monti Rock III

DISCO TEX presents CLOUDBURST

UK, male / female production / vocal group (Singles: 2 weeks) pos/wks

Date		Title	pos	wks
24 Mar 01		**I CAN CAST A SPELL** *Absolution CDABSOL 1*	35	2

See also FULL INTENTION; HUSTLERS CONVENTION featuring Dave LAUDAT and Ondrea DUVERNEY; SEX-O-SONIQUE

DISCOVERY – *See COAST 2 COAST featuring DISCOVERY*

DISPOSABLE HEROES OF HIPHOPRISY

US, male rap / instrumental duo – Michael Franti and Rono Tse (Singles: 7 weeks, Albums: 3 weeks) pos/wks

Date		Title	pos	wks
4 Apr 92		**TELEVISION THE DRUG OF THE NATION (re)** *Fourth & Broadway BRW 241*	44	6
30 May 92		**LANGUAGE OF VIOLENCE** *Fourth & Broadway 12BRW 248*	68	1
16 May 92		**HYPOCRISY IS THE GREATEST LUXURY** *Fourth & Broadway BRCD 584*	40	3

DISTANT SOUNDZ

UK, male production / vocal trio – Jack Berry, Mark Shrimpton and Rob Beaumont (Singles: 4 weeks) pos/wks

Date		Title	pos	wks
9 Mar 02		**TIME AFTER TIME** *W10 / Incentive CENT 36CDS*	20	4

Sacha DISTEL

France, male vocalist (Singles: 27 weeks, Albums: 14 weeks) pos/wks

Date		Title	pos	wks
10 Jan 70	●	**RAINDROPS KEEP FALLING ON MY HEAD (4re)** *Warner Bros. WB 7345*	10	27
2 May 70		**SACHA DISTEL** *Warner Bros. WS 3003*	21	14

The DISTILLERS

Australia / US, male / female vocal / instrumental group (Singles: 1 week, Albums: 1 week) pos/wks

Date		Title	pos	wks
15 Nov 03		**DRAIN THE BLOOD** *Sire W 628CD*	51	1
25 Oct 03		**CORAL FANG** *Sire 9362484202*	46	1

DISTORTED MINDS *UK, male production duo (Singles: 2 weeks)* pos/wks

29 Mar 03 **T-10 / THE TENTH PLANET** *Kaos KAOS 006* 43 2

DISTURBED *US, male vocal / instrumental group (Singles: 4 weeks, Albums: 1 week)* pos/wks

7 Apr 01 **VOICES** *Giant 74321848962* 52 1
28 Sep 02 **PRAYER** *Reprise W 591CD1* 31 2
14 Dec 02 **REMEMBER** *Reprise W 596CD1* 56 1
5 Oct 02 **BELIEVE** *Reprise 9362483582* 41 1

DIVA *Norway, female vocal duo (Singles: 2 weeks)* pos/wks

7 Oct 95 **THE SUN ALWAYS SHINES ON TV** *East West YZ 947CD* 53 1
20 Jul 96 **EVERYBODY (MOVE YOUR BODY)** *East West EW 035CD* 44 1

DIVA SURPRISE featuring Georgia JONES *US / Spain, male production duo – Walter Taieb and Giuseppe Nuzzo – and US, female vocalist (Singles: 2 weeks)* pos/wks

14 Nov 98 **ON THE TOP OF THE WORLD** *Positiva CDTIV 100* 29 2

See also ORIGINAL

DIVE *UK, male production duo – Sacha Collisson and Simon Greenaway (Singles: 1 week)* pos/wks

21 Feb 98 **BOOGIE** *WEA WEA 147CD1* 35 1

Hit featured vocalist Nasreen Shah
See also AURORA

DIVERSIONS *UK, male / female vocal / instrumental group (Singles: 3 weeks)* pos/wks

20 Sep 75 **FATTIE BUM BUM** *Gull GULS 18* 34 3

DIVINE *US, male vocalist – Harris Milstead, d. 7 Mar 1988 (Singles: 24 weeks)* pos/wks

15 Oct 83 **LOVE REACTION** *Design Communication DES 4* 65 2
14 Jul 84 **YOU THINK YOU'RE A MAN** *Proto ENA 118* 16 10
20 Oct 84 **I'M SO BEAUTIFUL** *Proto ENA 121* 52 2
27 Apr 85 **WALK LIKE A MAN** *Proto ENA 125* 23 7
20 Jul 85 **TWISTIN' THE NIGHT AWAY** *Proto ENA 127* 47 3

DIVINE *US, female vocal group (Singles: 1 week)* pos/wks

16 Oct 99 **LATELY** *Mushroom / Red Ant RA 002CDS* ▲ 52 1

DIVINE COMEDY *UK, male vocalist / instrumentalist – Neil Hannon (Singles: 38 weeks, Albums: 43 weeks)* pos/wks

29 Jun 96 **SOMETHING FOR THE WEEKEND** *Setanta SETCD 26* 14 5
24 Aug 96 **BECOMING MORE LIKE ALFIE** *Setanta SETCD 27* 27 2
16 Nov 96 **THE FROG PRINCESS** *Setanta SETCD 32* 15 2
22 Mar 97 **EVERYBODY KNOWS (EXCEPT YOU)** *Setanta SETCDA 038* 14 4
11 Apr 98 **SOMEDAY I'LL FIND YOU / I'VE BEEN TO A MARVELLOUS PARTY** *EMI CDTCB 001* [1] 28 3
26 Sep 98 **GENERATION SEX** *Setanta SETCDA 050* 19 3
28 Nov 98 **THE CERTAINTY OF CHANCE** *Setanta SETCDA 067* 49 1
6 Feb 99 ● **NATIONAL EXPRESS** *Setanta SETCDA 069* 8 7
21 Aug 99 **THE POP SINGER'S FEAR OF THE POLLEN COUNT** *Setanta SETCDA 070* 17 4
13 Nov 99 **GIN SOAKED BOY** *Setanta SETCDA 071* 38 2
10 Mar 01 **LOVE WHAT YOU DO** *Parlophone CDRS 6554* 26 2
26 May 01 **BAD AMBASSADOR** *Parlaphone CRDS 6558* 34 2
10 Nov 01 **PERFECT LOVESONG** *Parlophone CDR 6561* 42 1
11 May 96 **CASANOVA** *Setanta SETCD 25* 48 9
22 Feb 97 **A SHORT ALBUM ABOUT LOVE** *Setanta SETCD 036* 13 6
12 Sep 98 ● **FIN DE SIÈCLE** *Setanta SETCD 057* 9 14
11 Sep 99 ● **A SECRET HISTORY – THE BEST OF THE DIVINE COMEDY** *Setanta SETCD 100* 3 11
24 Mar 01 **REGENERATION** *Parlophone 5317612* 14 3

[1] Shola Ama and Craig Armstrong / Divine Comedy

DIVINE INSPIRATION *UK, male / female production / vocal group (Singles: 8 weeks)* pos/wks

18 Jan 03 ● **THE WAY (PUT YOUR HAND IN MY HAND)** *Data / MOS DATA 42CDS* 5 7
15 Nov 03 **WHAT WILL BE WILL BE (DESTINY)** *Heat Recordings HEATCD 036* 55 1

DIVINE WORKS *Germany, male producer – Claus Zundel (Albums: 2 weeks)* pos/wks

16 Aug 97 **DIVINE WORKS** *Virgin VTCD 119* 43 2

See also SACRED SPIRIT

DIVINYLS *Australia, male / female vocal / instrumental duo (Singles: 12 weeks, Albums: 1 week)* pos/wks

18 May 91 ● **I TOUCH MYSELF** *Virgin America VUS 36* 10 12
20 Jul 91 **DIVINYLS** *Virgin America VUSLP 30* 59 1

DIXIE CHICKS *US, female vocal / instrumental group (Singles: 7 weeks, Albums: 20 weeks)* pos/wks

3 Jul 99 **THERE'S YOUR TROUBLE** *Epic 6675162* 26 5
6 Nov 99 **READY TO RUN** *Epic 6682472* 53 1
19 Apr 03 **LANDSLIDE** *Columbia 6737392* 55 1
3 Jul 99 **WIDE OPEN SPACES** *Epic 4898422* 26 6
11 Sep 99 **FLY** *Epic 4951512* ▲ 38 2
22 Mar 03 **HOME** *Epic 5096032* ▲ 33 12

DIXIE CUPS *US, female vocal group (Singles: 16 weeks)* pos/wks

18 Jun 64 **CHAPEL OF LOVE** *Pye International 7N 25245* ▲ 22 8
13 May 65 **IKO IKO** *Red Bird RB 10024* 23 8

DIZZEE RASCAL *UK, male rapper – Dylan Mills (Singles: 14 weeks, Albums: 15 weeks)* pos/wks

7 Jun 03 **I LUV U** *XL Recordings XLS 165CD* 29 3
30 Aug 03 **FIX UP LOOK SHARP** *XL Recordings XLS 167CD* 17 5
22 Nov 03 **LUCKY STAR** *XL Recordings XLS 172CD* 23 4
6 Dec 03 **JUS' A RASCAL** *XL Recordings XLS 175CD* [1] 30 3
2 Aug 03 **BOY IN DA CORNER** *XL XLCD170* 23 15

[1] Basement Jaxx featuring Dizzee Rascal

DIZZY HEIGHTS *UK, male rapper (Singles: 4 weeks)* pos/wks

18 Dec 82 **CHRISTMAS RAPPING** *Polydor WRAP 1* 49 4

DJ ALIGATOR PROJECT *Denmark, male producer – Aliasghar Movasat (Singles: 11 weeks)* pos/wks

7 Sep 00 **THE WHISTLE SONG** *EMI CDBLOW 001* 57 1
19 Jan 02 ● **THE WHISTLE SONG (BLOW MY WHISTLE BITCH) (re-mix)** *All Around the World CDGLOBE 247* 5 10

DJ ARABESQUE – *See Mario PIU*

DJ BADMARSH and SHRI featuring UK APACHE *India / Yemen, male instrumental / production duo and UK, male rapper (Singles: 1 week)* pos/wks

28 Jul 01 **SIGNS** *Outcaste OUT 38CD1* 63 1

DJ BOBO *Switzerland, male DJ / producer – René Baumann (Singles: 7 weeks)* pos/wks

24 Sep 94 **EVERYBODY** *PWL Continental PWCD 312* 47 2
17 Jun 95 **LOVE IS ALL AROUND** *Avex UK AXEXCD 7* 49 2
25 Oct 03 **CHIHUAHUA** *Fuelin 82876559422* 36 3

DJ CHUCKY – *See XTM & DJ CHUCKY presents ANNIA*

DJ CHUS presents GROOVE FOUNDATION
Spain, male DJ / production duo (Singles: 1 week) pos/wks

2 Nov 02 **THAT FEELING** *Defected DFTD 055R* 65 1

DJ DADO *Italy, male producer – Roberto Gallo (Singles: 9 weeks)* pos/wks

6 Apr 96 ● **X-FILES** *ZYX ZYX 8065R8* 8 6
14 Mar 98 **COMING BACK** *ffrr TABCD 247* 63 1
11 Jul 98 **GIVE ME LOVE** *VC Recordings VCRD 37* [1] 59 1
8 May 99 **READY OR NOT** *Chemistry CDKEM 006* [2] 51 1

[1] DJ Dado vs Michelle weeks [2] DJ Dado and Simone Jay

DJ DAN presents NEEDLE DAMAGE
US, male DJ / production group (Singles: 1 week) pos/wks

5 May 01 **THAT ZIPPER TRACK** *Duty Free DF 026CD* 53 1

DJ DEE KLINE
UK, male DJ / producer – Nick Annand (Singles: 6 weeks) pos/wks

3 Jun 00 **I DON'T SMOKE** *East West EW 213CD* 11 6

DJ DISCIPLE
US, male DJ / producer (Singles: 1 week) pos/wks

12 Nov 94 **ON THE DANCEFLOOR** *Mother MUMCD 55* 67 1

DJ DUKE
Denmark, male producer – Ken Larson (Singles: 7 weeks) pos/wks

8 Jan 94 **BLOW YOUR WHISTLE** *ffrr FCD 228* 15 5
16 Jul 94 **TURN IT UP (SAY YEAH)** *ffrr FCD 235* 31 2

DJ E-Z ROCK – *See Rob BASE and DJ E-Z ROCK*

DJ EMPIRE presents Giorgio MORODER
Germany, male producer – Alexander Wilkie (Singles: 1 week) pos/wks

12 Feb 00 **THE CHASE (re-recording)** *LOGIC 731482* 46 1

DJ ERIC *UK, male production trio (Singles: 3 weeks)* pos/wks

13 Feb 99 **WE ARE LOVE** *Distinctive DISNCD 49* 37 2
10 Jun 00 **DESIRE** *Distinctive DISNCD 56* 67 1

DJ 'FAST' EDDIE
US, male producer (Singles: 15 weeks) pos/wks

11 Apr 87 **CAN U DANCE (re)** *Champion CHAMP 41* [1] 67 4
21 Jan 89 **HIP HOUSE / I CAN DANCE** *DJ International DJIN 5* 47 4
11 Mar 89 **YO YO GET FUNKY** *DJ International DJIN 7* 54 3
28 Oct 89 **GIT ON UP** *DJ International 655366 7* [2] 49 4

[1] Kenny 'Jammin' Jason and 'Fast' Eddie Smith
[2] DJ 'Fast' Eddie featuring Sundance

DJ FLAVOURS
UK, male producer – Neil Rumney (Singles: 4 weeks) pos/wks

11 Oct 97 **YOUR CARESS (ALL I NEED)** *All Around the World CDGLOBE 160* 19 4

DJ FORMAT featuring Chali 2NA & AKIL
UK, male DJ / producer and US, male rappers (Singles: 1 week) pos/wks

22 Mar 03 **WE KNOW SOMETHING YOU DON'T KNOW** *Genuine GEN 004CDX* 73 1

DJ FRESH *UK, male producer – Dan Stein (Singles: 1 week)* pos/wks

1 Nov 03 **DALICKS / TEMPLE OF DOOM** *Breakbeat Kaos BBK 001* 60 1

See also BAD COMPANY; FRESH BC

DJ GARRY
Belgium, male producer – Marino Stephano (Singles: 2 weeks) pos/wks

19 Jan 02 **DREAM UNIVERSE** *Xtravaganza XTRAV 32CDS* 36 2

DJ GERT
Belgium, male DJ / producer – Gert Rossenbacker (Singles: 1 week) pos/wks

26 May 01 **GIVE ME SOME MORE** *Mostika 23200253* 50 1

DJ GREGORY *France, male producer (Singles: 2 weeks)* pos/wks

9 Nov 02 **TROPICAL SOUNDCLASH** *Defected DFTD 061CD* 59 1
11 Oct 03 **ELLE / TROPICAL SOUNDCLASH (re-mix)** *Defected DFTD 077* 73 1

DJ HYPE *UK, male producer (Singles: 2 weeks, Albums: 1 week)* pos/wks

20 Mar 93 **SHOT IN THE DARK** *Suburban Base SUBBASE 20CD* 63 1
2 Jun 01 **CASINO ROYALE / DEAD A'S** *True Playaz TPRCD 004* [1] 58 1
30 Aug 97 **NEW FRONTIERS (EP)** *Parousia 74321501072* [1] 56 1

[1] DJ Zinc / DJ Hype [1] DJ Hype presents Ganja Kru

DJ INNOCENCE featuring Alex CHARLES
UK, male producer and male vocalist (Singles: 1 week) pos/wks

6 Apr 02 **SO BEAUTIFUL** *Echo ECSCD 119* 51 1

DJ JAZZY JEFF and FRESH PRINCE *US, male rap / DJ duo – Jeff Townes and Will Smith (Singles: 49 weeks, Albums: 15 weeks)* pos/wks

4 Oct 86 **GIRLS AIN'T NOTHING BUT TROUBLE** *Champion CHAMP 18* 21 8
3 Aug 91 ● **SUMMERTIME (re)** *Jive JIVECD 279* 8 12
9 Nov 91 **RING MY BELL** *Jive JIVECD 288* 53 2
11 Sep 93 ★ **BOOM! SHAKE THE ROOM** *Jive JIVECD 335* [1] 1 13
20 Nov 93 **I'M LOOKING FOR THE ONE (TO BE WITH ME)** *Jive JIVECD 345* [1] 24 4
19 Feb 94 **CAN'T WAIT TO BE WITH YOU** *Jive JIVECD 348* [1] 29 4
4 Jun 94 **TWINKLE TWINKLE (I'M NOT A STAR)** *Jive JIVECD 354* [1] 62 2
2 Dec 95 **BOOM! SHAKE THE ROOM (re-mix)** *Jive JIVECD 387* [1] 40 2
11 Jul 98 **LOVELY DAZE** *Jive 0518902* [2] 37 2
28 Feb 87 **ROCK THE HOUSE** *Champion CHAMP 1004* 97 1
21 May 88 **HE'S THE DJ I'M THE RAPPER** *Jive HIP 61* 68 2
14 Sep 91 **HOMEBASE** *Jive HIP 116* 69 1
11 Dec 93 **CODE RED** *Jive CHIP 140* [1] 50 6
16 May 98 **GREATEST HITS** *Jive 518482* [2] 20 5

[1] Jazzy Jeff and the Fresh Prince [2] DJ Jazzy Jeff and Fresh Prince
[1] Jazzy Jeff and the Fresh Prince [2] DJ Jazzy Jeff and Fresh Prince
'Summertime' re-entered and peaked at No.29 in Aug 1994
See also Will SMITH; JAZZY JEFF

DJ JEAN *Holland, DJ / producer – Jan Engelaar (Singles: 11 weeks)* pos/wks

11 Sep 99 ● **THE LAUNCH** *AM:PM CDAMPM 123* 2 11

DJ JURGEN presents Alice DEEJAY *Holland, male DJ / production group and female vocalist (Singles: 16 weeks)* pos/wks

31 Jul 99 ● **BETTER OFF ALONE** *Positiva CDTIV 113* 2 16

DJ KOOL
US, male rapper / DJ / producer – John Bowman (Singles: 7 weeks) pos/wks

22 Feb 97 ● **LET ME CLEAR MY THROAT** *American 74321452092* 8 7

DJ KRUSH *Japan, male producer (Singles: 2 weeks, Albums: 2 weeks)* pos/wks

16 Mar 96 **MEISO** *Mo Wax MW 042CD* 52 1
12 Oct 96 **ONLY THE STRONG SURVIVE** *Mo Wax MW 060CD* 71 1
3 Sep 94 **BAD BROTHERS** *Island IMCD 8024* [1] 58 1
11 Nov 95 **MEISO** *Mo Wax MW 039CD* 64 1

[1] Ronny Jordan meets DJ Krush

DJ LUCK & MC NEAT *UK, male DJ / producers – Joel Samuels and Michael Rose (Singles: 44 weeks)* pos/wks

25 Dec 99 ● **A LITTLE BIT OF LUCK** *Red Rose CORROSLE 1* 9 15
27 May 00 ● **MASTERBLASTER 2000** *Red Rose RROSE 002CD* [1] 5 8

7 Oct 00 ●	**AIN'T NO STOPPIN' US** *Red Rose CDRROSE 004* [2]	8 6
17 Mar 01	**PIANO LOCO** *Island CID 773*	12 8
8 Sep 01	**I'M ALL ABOUT YOU (re)** *Island CID 781* [3]	18 5
25 May 02	**IRIE** *Island CID 795* [4]	31 2

[1] DJ Luck and MC Neat featuring JJ [2] DJ Luck & MC Neat featuring JJ [3] DJ Luck and MC Neat featuring Ari Gold [4] Luck & Neat

DJ MANTA

Holland, male / female DJ / production trio (Singles: 1 week) pos/wks

9 Oct 99	**HOLDING ON** *AM:PM CDAMPM 125*	47 1

DJ MARKY & XRS *Brazil, male DJ / production duo – Marco da Silva and Nicassio de Oliveira (Singles: 8 weeks)* pos/wks

20 Jul 02	**LK 'CAROLINA CAROL BELA'** *V Recordings V 035* [1]	17 6
16 Nov 02	**LK (re-mix)** *V Recordings V 038*	45 2

[1] DJ Marky & XRS and Stamina MC

DJ MIKO *Italy, male producer – Quartobaro Manier (Singles: 10 weeks)* pos/wks

13 Aug 94 ●	**WHAT'S UP** *Systematic SYSCD 2*	6 10

DJ MILANO featuring SAMANTHA FOX

Italy, male DJ / producer and UK, female vocalist (Singles: 2 weeks) pos/wks

28 Mar 98	**SANTA MARIA** *All Around the World CDGLOBE 163*	31 2

[1] Hermes House Band and DJ Otzi

See also Samantha FOX

DJ MISJAH and DJ TIM *Holland, male instrumental / production duo – Misjah Van Der Heiden and Tim Hoogestegger (Singles: 4 weeks)* pos/wks

23 Mar 96	**ACCESS** *Ffrreedom TABCD 240*	16 3
27 May 00	**ACCESS (re-mix)** *Tripoli Trax TTRAXCD 063*	45 1

DJ MUGGS – *See TRICKY*

DJ NATION

UK, collection of UK DJs / producers (Singles: 2 weeks) pos/wks

9 Aug 03	**SUMMER EDITION** *Nukleuz 0542 FNUK*	59 2

DJ OTZI

Austria, male DJ / producer – Gerry Friedle (Singles: 48 weeks) pos/wks

18 Aug 01	**HEY BABY (import)** *EMI 8892462*	41 5
22 Sep 01 ★	**HEY BABY (UHH, AHH) (re)** *EMI CDOTZI 001* ■	1 24
1 Dec 01 ●	**DO WAH DIDDY** *EMI CDOTZI 002*	9 9
29 Dec 01	**X-MAS TIME** *EMI CDOTZI 003*	51 2
8 Jun 02 ●	**HEY BABY (THE UNOFFICIAL WORLD CUP REMIX) (re)** *EMI Austria / Liberty CDOTZI 004*	10 7
28 Dec 02	**LIVE IS LIFE** *EMI / Liberty CDLIVE 001* [1]	50 1

[1] Hermes House Band and DJ Otzi

DJ PIED PIPER and The MASTERS OF CEREMONIES

UK, male rap / production group (Singles: 14 weeks) pos/wks

2 Jun 01 ★	**DO YOU REALLY LIKE IT** *Relentless MOS RELMOS 1CDS* ■	1 14

DJ POWER

Italy, male producer – Steve Gambaroli (Singles: 2 weeks) pos/wks

7 Mar 92	**EVERYBODY PUMP** *Cooltempo COOL 252*	46 2

DJ PROFESSOR *Italy, male producer (Singles: 6 weeks)* pos/wks

10 Aug 91	**WE GOTTA DO IT** *Fourth & Broadway BRW 225* [1]	57 2
28 Mar 92	**ROCK ME STEADY** *PWL Continental PWL 219*	49 2
8 Oct 94	**ROCKIN' ME** *Citra CITRA 1CD* [2]	56 1
1 Mar 97	**WALKIN' ON UP** *Nukleuz MCSTD 40098* [3]	64 1

[1] DJ Professor featuring Francesco Zappala [2] Professor [3] DJ PROF-X-OR

DJ QUICKSILVER

Turkey / Belgium, male DJ / producer duo – Ohran Terzi and Tomasso De Donatis (Singles: 29 weeks, Albums: 3 weeks) pos/wks

5 Apr 97 ●	**BELLISSIMA** *Positiva CDTIV 72*	4 17
6 Sep 97 ●	**FREE** *Positiva CDTIVS 77*	7 7
21 Feb 98	**PLANET LOVE** *Positiva CDTIV 88*	12 5
7 Mar 98	**QUICKSILVER** *Positiva 4934942*	26 3

DJ QUIK – *See TONY TONI TONÉ*

DJ RAP *UK, female vocalist / DJ / producer – Charissa Saverio (Singles: 5 weeks)* pos/wks

4 Jul 98	**BAD GIRL** *Higher Ground HIGHS 8CD*	32 2
17 Oct 98	**GOOD TO BE ALIVE** *Higher Ground HIGHS 14CD*	36 2
3 Apr 99	**EVERYDAY GIRL** *Higher Ground HIGHS 19CD*	47 1

DJ ROLANDO AKA AZTEC MYSTIC

US, male DJ / producer – Rolando Rocha (Singles: 2 weeks) pos/wks

21 Oct 00	**JAGUAR** *430 West 430 WUKTCD1*	43 2

DJ SAKIN & FRIENDS

Germany, DJ / producer – Sakin Botzkurt (Singles: 18 weeks) pos/wks

20 Feb 99 ●	**PROTECT YOUR MIND (FOR THE LOVE OF A PRINCESS) (re)** *Positiva CDTIV 107*	4 11
5 Jun 99	**NOMANSLAND (DAVID'S SONG)** *Positiva CDTIV 112*	14 7

DJ SAMMY *Spain, male DJ / producer – Samuel Bouriah (Singles: 41 weeks, Albums: 9 weeks)* pos/wks

9 Nov 02 ★	**HEAVEN** *Data / MOS DATA 45CDS* [1] ■	1 19
8 Mar 03 ●	**THE BOYS OF SUMMER** *Data / MOS DATA 49CDS*	2 13
21 Jun 03 ●	**SUNLIGHT** *Data / MoS DATA 54CDS*	8 9
22 Mar 03	**HEAVEN** *Ministry of Sound DATACD 01*	14 9

[1] DJ Sammy and Yanou featuring Do

DJ SANDY vs HOUSETRAP *Germany, female DJ / producer – Sande De Sutter, and vocalist (Singles: 2 weeks)* pos/wks

1 Jul 00	**OVERDRIVE** *Positiva CDTIV 133*	32 2

DJ SCOT PROJECT

Germany, male DJ / producer (Singles: 2 weeks) pos/wks

27 Jul 96	**U (I GOT THE FEELING)** *Positiva CDTIV 55* [1]	66 1
14 Feb 98	**Y (HOW DEEP IS YOUR LOVE)** *Perfecto PERF 158CD1*	57 1

[1] Scot Project

DJ Doc SCOTT *UK, male producer (Singles: 2 weeks)* pos/wks

1 Feb 92	**NHS (EP)** *Absolute 2 ABS 001DJ*	64 2

Tracks on NHS (EP): Surgery / Night Nurse

DJ SCOTT featuring Lorna B *UK, male DJ – Scott Robertson, and female vocalist (Singles: 5 weeks)* pos/wks

28 Jan 95	**DO YOU WANNA PARTY** *Steppin' Out SPONCD 2*	36 3
1 Apr 95	**SWEET DREAMS** *Steppin' Out SPONCD 3*	37 2

DJ SEDUCTION

UK, male producer – John Kallum (Singles: 8 weeks) pos/wks

22 Feb 92	**HARDCORE HEAVEN / YOU AND ME** *Ffrreedom TAB 103*	26 5
11 Jul 92	**COME ON** *Ffrreedom TAB 111*	37 3

DJ SHADOW *US, male producer – Josh Davis (Singles: 11 weeks, Albums: 6 weeks)* pos/wks

25 Mar 95	**WHAT DOES YOUR SOUL LOOK LIKE** *Mo Wax MW 027CD*	59 1
14 Sep 96	**MIDNIGHT IN A PERFECT WORLD** *Mo Wax MW 057CD*	54 1
9 Nov 96	**STEM** *Mo Wax MW 058CD*	74 1
11 Oct 97	**HIGH NOON** *Mo Wax MW 063CD*	22 2
20 Dec 97	**CAMEL BOBSLED RACE** *Mo Wax MW 084CD*	62 1

24 Jan 98	**WHAT DOES YOUR SOUL LOOK LIKE (PART 1)** *Mo Wax MW 087*	54	1
1 Jun 02	**YOU CAN'T GO HOME AGAIN** *Mo Wax CID 797*	30	2
2 Nov 02	**SIX DAYS** *Island CID 807*	28	2
28 Sep 96	**ENDTRODUCING ...** *Mo Wax MW 059CD*	17	3
15 Jun 02 ●	**THE PRIVATE PRESS** *Island CID 8118*	8	3

DJ SHOG

Germany, male DJ / producer – Sven Greiner (Singles: 2 weeks) pos/wks

20 Jul 02	**THIS IS MY SOUND** *Nu Life 74321942272*	40	2

DJ SHORTY – *See Lenny FONTANA and DJ SHORTY*

DJ SKRIBBLE – *See MR REDS vs DJ SKRIBBLE*

DJ SNEAK featuring BEAR WHO? *Puerto Rico, male DJ / producer – Carlos Sosa and US, male DJ / producer (Singles: 3 weeks)* pos/wks

1 Feb 03	**FIX MY SINK** *Credence CDCREDS 033*	26	3

DJ SS *UK, male DJ / producer (Singles: 1 week)* pos/wks

20 Apr 02	**THE LIGHTER** *Formation FORM 12093*	63	1

DJ SUPREME

UK, male producer – Nick Destri (Singles: 11 weeks) pos/wks

5 Oct 96	**THA WILD STYLE** *Distinctive DISNCD 19*	39	2
3 May 97	**THA WILD STYLE (re-issue)** *Distinctive DISNCD 29*	24	2
6 Dec 97	**ENTER THE SCENE** *Distinctive DISNCD 40* [1]	49	1
21 Feb 98	**THA HORNS OF JERICHO** *All Around the World CDGLOBE 164*	29	2
16 Jan 99 ●	**UP TO THE WILDSTYLE** *All Around the World CDGLOBE 170* [2]	10	4

[1] DJ Supreme vs The Rhythm Masters [2] Porn Kings vs DJ Supreme

DJ TAUCHER

Germany, male DJ / producer – Ralf Armand Beck (Singles: 1 week) pos/wks

8 May 99	**CHILD OF THE UNIVERSE** *Additive 12AD 037*	74	1

DJ TIESTO

Holland, male producer – Tijs Verwest (Singles: 12 weeks) pos/wks

12 May 01	**FLIGHT 643** *Nebula NEBCD 016*	56	1
29 Sep 01	**URBAN TRAIN** *Nebula VCRD 95* [1]	22	3
13 Apr 02	**LETHAL INDUSTRY** *Nebula VCRD 103*	25	3
29 Jun 02	**643 (LOVE'S ON FIRE) (re-recording)** *Nebula VCRD 106* [2]	36	2
30 Nov 02	**OBSESSION** *Nebula NEBCD 029* [3]	56	1
11 Oct 03	**TRAFFIC** *Nebula NEBCD 052* [4]	48	2

[1] DJ Tiesto featuring Kirsty Hawshaw
[2] DJ Tiesto featuring Suzanne Palmer
[3] Tiesto and Junkie XL [4] Tiesto

See also GOURYELLA

DJ TIM – *See DJ MISJAH and DJ TIM*

DJ VISAGE featuring CLARISSA *Denmark / Germany, male DJ / producer and female vocalist (Singles: 1 week)* pos/wks

10 Jun 00	**THE RETURN (TIME TO SAY GOODBYE)** *One Step Music OSMCDS 13*	58	1

DJ WHAT? – *See OBI PROJECT featuring HARRY, ASHER D and DJ WHAT?*

DJ ZINC

UK, male DJ / producer – Benjamin Pettit (Singles: 6 weeks) pos/wks

18 Nov 00	**138 TREK** *Phaze One PHAZE CDX03*	27	3
2 Jun 01	**CASINO ROYALE / DEAD A'S** *True Playaz TPRCD 004* [1]	58	1
13 Apr 02	**REACHOUT** *True Playaz TPR 12039*	73	1
21 Sep 02	**FAIR FIGHT / AS WE DO** *Bingo Beats BING 008*	72	1

[1] DJ Zinc / DJ Hype

DJAIMIN *Switzerland, male producer (Singles: 2 weeks)* pos/wks

19 Sep 92	**GIVE YOU** *Cooltempo COOL 262*	45	2

DJD presents HYDRAULIC DOGS

UK, male production duo (Singles: 1 week) pos/wks

8 Jun 02	**SHAKE IT BABY** *Direction 6721812*	56	1

DJH featuring STEFY

Italy, male instrumental / production group (Singles: 14 weeks) pos/wks

16 Feb 91	**THINK ABOUT . . .** *RCA PB 44385*	22	6
13 Jul 91	**I LIKE IT** *RCA PB 44741*	16	7
19 Oct 91	**MOVE YOUR LOVE** *RCA PB 44965*	73	1

DJPC *Belgium, male producer (Singles: 5 weeks)* pos/wks

26 Oct 91	**INSSOMNIAK** *Hype 7PUM 005*	62	4
29 Feb 92	**INSSOMNIAK (re-issue)** *Hype PUMR 005*	64	1

DJ's RULE

Canada, male instrumental / production duo (Singles: 2 weeks) pos/wks

2 Mar 96	**GET INTO THE MUSIC** *Distinctive DISNCD 9*	72	1
5 Apr 97	**GET INTO THE MUSIC (re-mix)** *Distinctive DISNCDD27* [1]	65	1

[1] DJ's Rule featuring Karen Brown

DJUM DJUM – *See LEFTFIELD*

Boris DLUGOSCH *Germany, male producer (Singles: 8 weeks)* pos/wks

7 Dec 96	**KEEP PUSHIN'** *Manifesto FESCD 17* [1]	41	2
13 Sep 97	**HOLD YOUR HEAD UP HIGH** *Positiva CDTIV 79* [1]	23	2
16 Jun 01	**NEVER ENOUGH** *Positiva CDTIV 156* [2]	16	4

[1] Boris Dlugosch presents Booom! Vocals by Inaya Davis (aka Inaya Day) [2] Boris Dlugosch featuring Roisin Murphy

D'LUX

UK, male / female vocal / instrumental group (Singles: 1 week) pos/wks

22 Jun 96	**LOVE RESURRECTION** *Logic 74321371012*	58	1

DMAC

UK, male vocalist – Derek McDonald (Singles: 2 weeks) pos/wks

27 Jul 02	**THE WORLD SHE KNOWS** *Chrysalis CDCHS 5140*	33	2

D'MENACE *UK, male production duo – Sandy Rivera and John Alvarez (Singles: 3 weeks)* pos/wks

8 Aug 98	**DEEP MENACE (SPANK)** *Inferno CDFERN 8*	20	3

DO – *See DJ SAMMY*

Carl DOBKINS Jr *US, male vocalist (Singles: 1 week)* pos/wks

31 Mar 60	**LUCKY DEVIL** *Brunswick 05817*	44	1

Anita DOBSON

UK, female actor / vocalist (Singles: 13 weeks) pos/wks

9 Aug 86 ●	**ANYONE CAN FALL IN LOVE** *BBC RESL 191* [1]	4	9
18 Jul 87	**TALKING OF LOVE** *Parlophone R 6159*	43	4

[1] Anita Dobson featuring the Simon May Orchestra

DR ALBAN

Nigeria, male vocalist – Alban Nwapa (Singles: 28 weeks) pos/wks

5 Sep 92 ●	**IT'S MY LIFE** *Logic 115330*	2	12
14 Nov 92	**ONE LOVE** *Logic 74321108727*	45	2
10 Apr 93	**SING HALLELUJAH!** *Logic 74321136202*	16	8
26 Mar 94	**LOOK WHO'S TALKING** *Logic 74321195342*	55	3
13 Aug 94	**AWAY FROM HOME** *Logic 74321222682*	42	2
29 Apr 95	**SWEET DREAMS** *Logic 74321251552* [1]	59	1

[1] Swing featuring Dr Alban

DOCTOR and the MEDICS *UK, male / female vocal / instrumental group – lead vocal Clive Jackson (Singles: 25 weeks, Albums: 3 weeks)*

Date		Title	pos	wks
10 May 86	★	**SPIRIT IN THE SKY** *IRS IRM 113*	1	15
9 Aug 86		**BURN** *IRS IRM 119*	29	6
22 Nov 86		**WATERLOO** *IRS IRM 125* [1]	45	4
21 Jun 86		**LAUGHING AT THE PIECES** *MCA MIRG 1010*	25	3

[1] Doctor and the Medics featuring Roy Wood

DR DRE (444 Top 500)

Controversial rapper / producer and architect of West Coast gangsta rap, b. Andre Young, 18 Feb 1965, Los Angeles. Former member of NWA and founder of the Death Row label, whos acts include Snoop Dogg and Eminem (Singles: 76 weeks, Albums: 78 weeks)

Date		Title	pos	wks
22 Jan 94		**NUTHIN' BUT A 'G' THANG / LET ME RIDE** *Death Row A 8328CD*	31	3
3 Sep 94		**DRE DAY** *Death Row A 8292CD*	59	2
15 Apr 95		**NATURAL BORN KILLAZ** *Death Row A 8197CD* [1]	45	2
10 Jun 95		**KEEP THEIR HEADS RINGIN'** *Priority PTYCD 103*	25	4
13 Apr 96	●	**CALIFORNIA LOVE** *Death Row DRWCD 3* [2]	6	8
19 Oct 96	●	**NO DIGGITY** *Interscope IND 95003* [3] ▲	9	7
11 Jul 98		**ZOOM** *Interscope IND 95594* [4]	15	3
14 Aug 99	●	**GUILTY CONSCIENCE** *Interscope IND 4971282* [5]	5	8
25 Mar 00	●	**STILL D.R.E.** *Interscope 4972742* [6]	6	10
10 Jun 00	●	**FORGOT ABOUT DRE** *Interscope 4973412* [7]	7	9
3 Feb 01	●	**THE NEXT EPISODE** *Interscope 4974762* [6]	3	10
19 Jan 02	●	**BAD INTENTIONS** *Interscope 4973932* [8]	4	10
27 Nov 99	●	**2001** *Interscope 4904862*	4	76
9 Sep 00		**THE CHRONIC** *Interscope 7567922332*	52	2

[1] Dr Dre and Ice Cube [2] 2Pac featuring Dr Dre [3] BLACKstreet featuring Dr Dre [4] Dr Dre and LL Cool J [5] Eminem featuring Dr Dre [6] Dr Dre featuring Snoop Dogg [7] Dr Dre featuring Eminem [8] Dr. Dre featuring Knoc-Turn'al

DR FEELGOOD *UK, male vocal / instrumental group (Singles: 29 weeks, Albums: 33 weeks)*

Date		Title	pos	wks
11 Jun 77		**SNEAKIN' SUSPICION** *United Artists UP 36255*	47	3
24 Sep 77		**SHE'S A WIND UP** *United Artists UP 36304*	34	5
30 Sep 78		**DOWN AT THE DOCTORS** *United Artists UP 36444*	48	5
20 Jan 79	●	**MILK AND ALCOHOL** *United Artists UP 36468*	9	9
5 May 79		**AS LONG AS THE PRICE IS RIGHT** *United Artists YUP 36506*	40	6
8 Dec 79		**PUT HIM OUT OF YOUR MIND** *United Artists BP 306*	73	1
18 Oct 75		**MALPRACTICE** *United Artists UAS 29880*	17	6
2 Oct 76	★	**STUPIDITY** *United Artists UAS 29990*	1	9
4 Jun 77	●	**SNEAKIN' SUSPICION** *United Artists UAS 30075*	10	6
8 Oct 77		**BE SEEING YOU** *United Artists UAS 30123*	55	3
7 Oct 78		**PRIVATE PRACTICE** *United Artists UAG 30184*	41	5
2 Jun 79		**AS IT HAPPENS** *United Artists UAK 30239*	42	4

DR HOOK (233 Top 500)

Distinctive group fronted by vocalists Dennis Locorriere and Ray Sawyer; had eight years of regular UK / US hits. Early recordings often featured humorous anarchic Shel Silverstein songs, but this good-time New Jersey act had greater success with later gentler material (Singles: 104 weeks, Albums: 157 weeks)

Date		Title	pos	wks
24 Jun 72	●	**SYLVIA'S MOTHER** *CBS 7929* [1]	2	13
26 Jun 76	●	**A LITTLE BIT MORE** *Capitol CL 15871*	2	14
30 Oct 76	●	**IF NOT YOU** *Capitol CL 15885*	5	10
25 Mar 78		**MORE LIKE THE MOVIES** *Capitol CL 15967*	14	10
22 Sep 79	★	**WHEN YOU'RE IN LOVE WITH A BEAUTIFUL WOMAN** *Capitol CL 16039*	1	17
5 Jan 80	●	**BETTER LOVE NEXT TIME** *Capitol CL 16112*	8	8
29 Mar 80	●	**SEXY EYES** *Capitol CL 16127*	4	9
23 Aug 80		**YEARS FROM NOW** *Capitol CL 16154*	47	6
8 Nov 80		**SHARING THE NIGHT TOGETHER** *Capitol CL 16171*	43	4
22 Nov 80		**GIRLS CAN GET IT** *Mercury MER 51*	40	5
1 Feb 92		**WHEN YOU'RE IN LOVE WITH A BEAUTIFUL WOMAN (re-issue)** *Capitol EMCT 4*	44	4
6 Jun 92		**A LITTLE BIT MORE (re-issue)** *EMI EMCT 6*	47	4
25 Jun 76	●	**A LITTLE BIT MORE** *Capitol E-ST 23795*	5	42
29 Oct 77		**MAKING LOVE AND MUSIC** *Capitol EST 11632*	39	4
27 Oct 79		**PLEASURE AND PAIN** *Capitol EAST 11859*	47	6
17 Nov 79		**SOMETIMES YOU WIN** *Capitol EST 12018*	14	44
29 Nov 80		**RISING** *Mercury 6302 076*	44	5
6 Dec 80	●	**DR HOOK GREATEST HITS** *Capitol EST 26037*	2	28
14 Nov 81		**DR HOOK LIVE IN THE UK** *Capitol EST 26706*	90	1
13 Jun 92	●	**COMPLETELY HOOKED – THE BEST OF DR HOOK** *Capitol CDESTV 2*	3	19
13 Feb 99	●	**LOVE SONGS** *EMI 4979432*	8	8

[1] Dr Hook and the Medicine Show

DR JOHN *US, male vocalist / instrumentalist – piano – Malcolm Rebennack (Albums: 3 weeks)*

Date		Title	pos	wks
27 Jun 98		**ANUTHA ZONE** *Parlophone 4954902*	33	3

DR MOUTHQUAKE – *See E-ZEE POSSEE*

DR OCTAGON

US, male rapper / producer – Keith Thornton (Singles: 1 week)

Date		Title	pos	wks
7 Sep 96		**BLUE FLOWERS** *Mo Wax MW 055CD*	66	1

DOCTOR SPIN

UK, male instrumental / production duo (Singles: 8 weeks)

Date		Title	pos	wks
3 Oct 92	●	**TETRIS** *Carpet CRPT 4*	6	8

Ken DODD (226 Top 500)

Seasoned stand-up comedian-cum-balladeer, b. 8 Nov 1929, Liverpool. The tickling-stick-wielding troubadour was one of the most successful Merseyside acts in the mid-1960s, at times enjoying two Top 10 singles simultaneously. Biggest-selling single: 'Tears' 1,521,000 (Singles: 233 weeks, Albums: 36 weeks)

Date		Title	pos	wks
7 Jul 60	●	**LOVE IS LIKE A VIOLIN** *Decca F 11248*	8	18
15 Jun 61		**ONCE IN EVERY LIFETIME (2re)** *Decca F 11355*	28	18
1 Feb 62		**PIANISSIMO** *Decca F 11422*	21	15
29 Aug 63		**STILL** *Columbia DB 7094*	35	10
6 Feb 64		**EIGHT BY TEN** *Columbia DB 7191*	22	11
23 Jul 64		**HAPPINESS** *Columbia DB 7325*	31	13
26 Nov 64		**SO DEEP IS THE NIGHT** *Columbia DB 7398*	31	7
2 Sep 65	★	**TEARS** *Columbia DB 7659* ◆	1	24
18 Nov 65	●	**THE RIVER (LE COLLINE SONO IN FIORO)** *Columbia DB 7750*	3	14
12 May 66	●	**PROMISES** *Columbia DB 7914*	6	14
4 Aug 66		**MORE THAN LOVE** *Columbia DB 7976*	14	11
27 Oct 66		**IT'S LOVE** *Columbia DB 8031*	36	7
19 Jan 67		**LET ME CRY ON YOUR SHOULDER** *Columbia DB 8101*	11	10
30 Jul 69		**TEARS WON'T WASH AWAY THESE HEARTACHES** *Columbia DB 8600*	22	11
5 Dec 70		**BROKEN HEARTED (re)** *Columbia DB 8725*	15	10
10 Jul 71		**WHEN LOVE COMES ROUND AGAIN (L'ARCA DI NOE)** *Columbia DB 8796*	19	16
18 Nov 72		**JUST OUT OF REACH (OF MY TWO EMPTY ARMS)** *Columbia DB 8947*	29	11
29 Nov 75		**THINK OF ME (WHEREVER YOU ARE)** *EMI 2342*	21	8
26 Dec 81		**HOLD MY HAND** *Images IMGS 0002*	44	5
25 Dec 65	●	**TEARS OF HAPPINESS** *Columbia 33SX 1793*	6	12
23 Jul 66		**HITS FOR NOW AND ALWAYS** *Columbia SX 6060*	14	11
14 Jan 67		**FOR SOMEONE SPECIAL** *Columbia SCX 6224*	40	1
29 Nov 80	●	**20 GOLDEN GREATS OF KEN DODD** *Warwick WW 5098*	8	12

Rory DODD – *See Jim STEINMAN*

DODGY *UK, male vocal / instrumental group (Singles: 41 weeks, Albums: 54 weeks)*

Date		Title	pos	wks
8 May 93		**LOVEBIRDS** *A&M AMCD 0177*	65	2
3 Jul 93		**I NEED ANOTHER (EP)** *A&M 5803172*	67	2
6 Aug 94		**THE MELOD-EP** *Bostin 5806772*	53	1
1 Oct 94		**STAYING OUT FOR THE SUMMER** *Bostin 5807972*	38	2
7 Jan 95		**SO LET ME GO FAR** *Bostin 5809032*	30	3
11 Mar 95		**MAKING THE MOST OF** *Bostin 5809892* [1]	22	3
10 Jun 95		**STAYING OUT FOR THE SUMMER (re-mix)** *Bostin 5810952*	19	5
8 Jun 96		**IN A ROOM** *A&M 5816252*	12	6
10 Aug 96	●	**GOOD ENOUGH** *A&M 5818152*	4	8
16 Nov 96		**IF YOU'RE THINKING OF ME** *A&M 5819992*	11	4
15 Mar 97		**FOUND YOU** *A&M 5821332*	19	3
26 Sep 98		**EVERY SINGLE DAY** *A&M MERCD 512*	32	2
5 Jun 93		**THE DODGY ALBUM** *A&M 5400822*	75	1

5 Nov 94 **HOMEGROWN** *A&M 5402822* 28 14
29 Jun 96 ● **FREE PEACE SWEET** *A&M 5405732*..........7 38
17 Oct 98 **ACE A'S + KILLER B'S** *Mercury / A&M 5410182* 55 1

1 Dodgy with the Kick Horns

Tracks on I Need Another (EP): I Need Another / If I Fall / Hendre DDU. Tracks on The Melod-EP: Melodies Haunt You / The Snake / Don't Go / Summer Fayre

Tim DOG *US, male rapper (Singles: 3 weeks)* pos/wks

29 Oct 94 **BITCH WITH A PERM** *Dis-stress DISCD 1* 49 1
11 Feb 95 **MAKE WAY FOR THE INDIAN** *Island CID 586* 1 ....29 2

1 Apache Indian and Tim Dog

DOG EAT DOG *US, male vocal / instrumental group (Singles: 7 weeks, Albums: 2 weeks)* pos/wks

19 Aug 95 ● **NO FRONTS (re)** *Roadrunner RR 23312* 9 6
13 Jul 96 **ISMS** *Roadrunner RR 23083* 43 1
27 Jul 96 **PLAY GAMES** *Roadrunner RR 88762*..........40 2

It was not until the Apr 1996 re-entry that 'No Fronts' reached its peak position of No.9

Nate DOGG *US, male rapper – Nathan Hale (Singles: 45 weeks)* pos/wks

23 Jul 94 ● **REGULATE** *Death Row A 8290CD* 1 ....5 14
3 Feb 01 **OH NO** *Rawkus RWK 302* 2 ....24 4
25 Aug 01 **WHERE I WANNA BE (re)** *London LONCD 461* 3 ....14 7
29 Sep 01 **AREA CODES** *Def Jam 5887722* 4 ....25 3
1 Mar 03 **THE STREETS** *Def Jam 0779852* 5 ....48 2
12 Jul 03 ● **21 QUESTIONS** *Interscope 9807195* 6 ▲ 6 8
1 Nov 03 **OOH WEE** *Elektra E 7490CD* 7 ....15 7

1 Warren G and Nate Dogg 2 Mos Def and Nate Dogg featuring Pharoahe Monch 3 Shade Sheist featuring Nate Dogg and Kurupt 4 Ludacris featuring Nate Dogg 5 WC featuring Snoop Dogg and Nate Dogg 6 50 Cent featuring Nate Dogg 7 Mark Ronson featuring Ghostface Killah and Nate Dogg

DOGS D'AMOUR *UK, male vocal / instrumental group (Singles: 15 weeks, Albums: 12 weeks)* pos/wks

4 Feb 89 **HOW COME IT NEVER RAINS** *China CHINA 13* 44 3
5 Aug 89 **SATELLITE KID** *China CHINA 17*..........26 3
14 Oct 89 **TRAIL OF TEARS** *China CHINA 20* 47 3
23 Jun 90 **VICTIMS OF SUCCESS** *China CHINA 24* 36 3
15 Sep 90 **EMPTY WORLD** *China CHINA 27*..........61 2
19 Jun 93 **ALL OR NOTHING** *China WOKCD 2033*..........53 1
22 Oct 88 **IN THE DYNAMITE JET SALOON** *China WOL 8*..........97 1
25 Mar 89 **A GRAVEYARD OF EMPTY BOTTLES** *China 8390740* 16 4
30 Sep 89 **ERROL FLYNN** *China 8397001*..........22 3
6 Oct 90 **STRAIGHT** *China 8437961* 32 2
7 Sep 91 **DOG'S HITS AND THE BOOTLEG ALBUM** *China WOL 1020*..........58 1
15 May 93 **... MORE UNCHARTED HEIGHTS OF DISGRACE** *China WOLCD 1032* 30 1

Ken DOH *UK, male producer – Michael Devlin (Singles: 7 weeks)* pos/wks

30 Mar 96 ● **NAGASAKI (EP)** *ffrr FCD 272* 7 7

Tracks on Nagasaki (EP): Nagasaki (2 mixes) / I Need A Lover Tonight (2 mixes) / Kaki Traki

DOKKEN *US male vocal / instrumental group (Albums: 1 week)* pos/wks

21 Nov 87 **BACK FOR THE ATTACK** *Elektra EKT 43* 96 1

Joe DOLAN *Ireland, male vocalist (Singles: 40 weeks)* pos/wks

25 Jun 69 ● **MAKE ME AN ISLAND (re)** *Pye 7N 17738* 3 19
1 Nov 69 **TERESA** *Pye 7N 17833* 20 7
28 Feb 70 **YOU'RE SUCH A GOOD LOOKING WOMAN** *Pye 7N 17891* 17 13
17 Sep 77 **I NEED YOU** *Pye 7N 45702* 43 1

Thomas DOLBY *UK, male vocalist / multi-instrumentalist – Thomas Robertson (Singles: 51 weeks, Albums: 29 weeks)* pos/wks

3 Oct 81 **EUROPA AND THE PIRATE TWINS** *Parlophone R 6051* 48 3
14 Aug 82 **WINDPOWER** *Venice In Peril VIPS 103* 31 8
6 Nov 82 **SHE BLINDED ME WITH SCIENCE** *Venice In Peril VIPS 104* 49 4
16 Jul 83 **SHE BLINDED ME WITH SCIENCE (re-issue)** *Venice In Peril VIPS 105* 56 4
21 Jan 84 **HYPERACTIVE** *Parlophone Odeon R 6065* 17 9
31 Mar 84 **I SCARE MYSELF** *Parlophone Odeon R 6067*..........46 5
16 Apr 88 **AIRHEAD** *Manhattan MT 38* 53 3
9 May 92 **CLOSE BUT NO CIGAR** *Virgin VS 1410* 22 5
11 Jul 92 **I LOVE YOU GOODBYE** *Virgin VS 1417* 36 4
26 Sep 92 **SILK PYJAMAS** *Virgin VS 1430* 62 2
22 Jan 94 **HYPERACTIVE! (re-mix)** *Parlophone CDEMCTS 10*..........23 4
22 May 82 **THE GOLDEN AGE OF WIRELESS** *Venice in Peril VIP 1001* 65 10
18 Feb 84 **THE FLAT EARTH** *Parlophone Odeon PCS 2400341* 14 14
7 May 88 **ALIENS ATE MY BUICK** *Manhattan MTL 1020* 30 3
8 Aug 92 **ASTRONAUTS AND HERETICS** *Virgin CDV 2701* 35 2

Joe DOLCE MUSIC THEATRE *US, male vocalist (Singles: 10 weeks)* pos/wks

7 Feb 81 ★ **SHADDAP YOU FACE** *Epic EPC 9518* 1 10

DOLL *UK, male / female vocal / instrumental group (Singles: 8 weeks)* pos/wks

13 Jan 79 **DESIRE ME** *Beggars Banquet BEG 11* 28 8

DOLLAR (433 Top 500)

Photogenic teen-targeted UK vocal duo, who were originally one third of Guys and Dolls: David Van Day and Thereze Bazar. Their Top 10 hits came from writers as diverse as John Lennon, Paul McCartney, Trevor Horn, Erasure and themselves (Singles: 128 weeks, Albums: 28 weeks) pos/wks

11 Nov 78 **SHOOTING STAR** *Carrere EMI 2871* 14 12
19 May 79 **WHO WERE YOU WITH IN THE MOONLIGHT** *Carrere CAR 110* 14 12
18 Aug 79 ● **LOVE'S GOTTA HOLD ON ME** *Carrere CAR 122* 4 13
24 Nov 79 ● **I WANNA HOLD YOUR HAND** *Carrere CAR 131* 9 14
25 Oct 80 **TAKIN' A CHANCE ON YOU** *WEA K 18353* 62 3
15 Aug 81 **HAND HELD IN BLACK AND WHITE** *WEA BUCK 1* 19 12
14 Nov 81 ● **MIRROR MIRROR (MON AMOUR)** *WEA BUCK 2*..........4 17
20 Mar 82 **RING RING** *Carrere CAR 225*..........61 2
27 Mar 82 ● **GIVE ME BACK MY HEART** *WEA BUCK 3* 4 9
19 Jun 82 **VIDEOTHEQUE** *WEA BUCK 4* 17 10
18 Sep 82 **GIVE ME SOME KINDA MAGIC** *WEA BUCK 5* 34 6
16 Aug 86 **WE WALKED IN LOVE** *Arista DIME 1* 61 4
26 Dec 87 ● **O L'AMOUR** *London LON 146* 7 11
16 Jul 88 **IT'S NATURE'S WAY (NO PROBLEM)** *London LON 179* 58 3
15 Sep 79 **SHOOTING STARS** *Carrere CAL 111* 36 8
24 Apr 82 **THE VERY BEST OF DOLLAR** *Carrere CAL 3001* 31 9
30 Oct 82 **THE DOLLAR ALBUM** *WEA DTV 1*..........18 11

Placido DOMINGO (281 Top 500)

Perennially popular tenor b. 21 Jan 1941, Madrid, Spain. Brought an operatic quality to the pop charts, most successfully as one of The Three Tenors with a series of football World Cup tie-in concerts. Received an honorary knighthood in 2002 (Singles: 28 weeks, Albums: 199 weeks) pos/wks

12 Dec 81 **PERHAPS LOVE** *CBS A 1905* 1 ....46 9
27 May 89 **TILL I LOVED YOU** *CBS 654843 7* 2 ....24 9
16 Jun 90 **NESSUN DORMA FROM 'TURANDOT'** *Epic 656005 7* 3 ....59 2
30 Jul 94 **LIBIAMO / LA DONNA E MOBILE** *Teldec YZ 843CD* 4 ....21 4
25 Jul 98 **YOU'LL NEVER WALK ALONE** *Decca 4607982* 5 ....35 4
28 Nov 81 **PERHAPS LOVE** *CBS 73592* 1..........17 21
21 May 83 **MY LIFE FOR A SONG** *CBS 73683* 31 8
27 Dec 86 **PLACIDO DOMINGO COLLECTION** *Stylus SMR 625*..........30 14
23 Apr 88 **GREATEST LOVE SONGS** *CBS 44701*..........63 2
17 Jun 89 **GOYA ... A LIFE IN A SONG** *CBS 463294 1*..........36 4
17 Jun 89 **THE ESSENTIAL DOMINGO** *Deutsche Grammophon PDTV 1* ..20 8
1 Sep 90 ★ **IN CONCERT** *Decca 4304331* 2 ....1 78
24 Nov 90 **BE MY LOVE ... AN ALBUM OF LOVE** *EMI EMTV 54* 3..........14 12
7 Dec 91 **THE BROADWAY I LOVE** *East West 9031755901* 45 6
13 Jun 92 **DOMINGO: ARIAS AND SPANISH SONGS** *Deutsche Grammophon 4371122* 47 3
8 Aug 92 **FROM THE OFFICIAL BARCELONA GAMES CEREMONY** *RCA Red Seal 09026612042* 4 ....41 3
25 Dec 93 **CHRISTMAS IN VIENNA** *Sony Classical SK 53358* 5 ....71 2

Date		Title	Pos	Wks
10 Sep 94	★	**THE THREE TENORS IN CONCERT 1994** *Teldec 4509962002* [6]	1	26
10 Dec 94		**CHRISTMAS IN VIENNA II** *Sony Classical SK 64304* [7]	60	2
29 Aug 98		**THE THREE TENORS IN PARIS 1998** *Decca 4605002* [2]	14	6
28 Oct 00		**SONGS OF LOVE** *EMI CDC 5571042*	53	2
23 Dec 00		**THE THREE TENORS CHRISTMAS** *Sony Classical SK 89131* [8]	57	2

[1] Placido Domingo with John Denver [2] Placido Domingo and Jennifer Rush [3] Luis Cobos featuring Placido Domingo [4] José Carreras featuring Placido Domingo and Luciano Pavarotti with Mehta [5] José Carreras, Placido Domingo and Luciano Pavarotti with Mehta [1] Placido Domingo and John Denver [2] José Carreras, Placido Domingo and Luciano Pavarotti [3] Placido Domingo featuring The London Symphony Orchestra [4] Placido Domingo, José Carreras and Montserrat Caballé [5] Placido Domingo, Diana Ross and José Carreras [6] José Carreras, Placido Domingo and Luciano Pavarotti conducted by Zubin Mehta [7] Dionne Warwick and Placido Domingo [8] José Carreras, Placido Domingo and Luciano Pavarotti featuring Zubin Mehta

See also Andrew LLOYD WEBER

DOMINO

US, male rapper / vocalist – Shawn Ivy (Singles: 6 weeks) pos/wks

Date		Title	Pos	Wks
22 Jan 94		**GETTO JAM** *Chaos 6600402*	33	4
14 May 94		**SWEET POTATOE PIE** *Chaos 6603292*	42	2

Fats DOMINO

US, male vocalist / instrumentalist – piano (b. 26 Feb 1928) (Singles: 111 weeks, Albums: 1 week) pos/wks

Date		Title	Pos	Wks
27 Jul 56		**I'M IN LOVE AGAIN (re)** *London HLU 8280*	12	14
30 Nov 56	●	**BLUEBERRY HILL (re)** *London HLU 8330*	6	15
25 Jan 57		**AIN'T THAT A SHAME** *London HLU 8173*	23	2
1 Feb 57		**HONEY CHILE** *London HLU 8356*	29	1
29 Mar 57		**BLUE MONDAY (re)** *London HLP 8377*	23	2
19 Apr 57		**I'M WALKIN'** *London HLP 8407*	19	7
19 Jul 57		**VALLEY OF TEARS** *London HLP 8449*	25	1
28 Mar 58		**THE BIG BEAT** *London HLP 8575*	20	4
4 Jul 58		**SICK AND TIRED** *London HLP 8628*	26	1
22 May 59		**MARGIE** *London HLP 8865*	18	5
16 Oct 59		**I WANT TO WALK YOU HOME** *London HLP 8942*	14	5
18 Dec 59		**BE MY GUEST (re)** *London HLP 9005*	11	13
17 Mar 60		**COUNTRY BOY** *London HLP 9073*	19	11
21 Jul 60		**WALKING TO NEW ORLEANS** *London HLP 9163*	19	10
10 Nov 60		**THREE NIGHTS A WEEK** *London HLP 9198*	45	2
5 Jan 61		**MY GIRL JOSEPHINE** *London HLP 9244*	32	4
27 Jul 61		**IT KEEPS RAININ'** *London HLP 9374*	49	1
30 Nov 61		**WHAT A PARTY** *London HLP 9456*	43	1
29 Mar 62		**JAMBALAYA** *London HLP 9520*	41	1
31 Oct 63		**RED SAILS IN THE SUNSET** *HMV POP 1219*	34	6
24 Apr 76		**BLUEBERRY HILL (re-issue)** *United Artists UP 35797*	41	5
16 May 70		**VERY BEST OF FATS DOMINO** *Liberty LBS 83331*	56	1

DON PABLO'S ANIMALS

Italy, male production group (Singles: 10 weeks) pos/wks

Date		Title	Pos	Wks
19 May 90	●	**VENUS** *Rumour RUMA 18*	4	10

Siobhan DONAGHY

UK, female vocalist (Singles: 5 weeks) pos/wks

Date		Title	Pos	Wks
5 Jul 03		**OVERRATED (re)** *London LONCD 476*	19	4
27 Sep 03		**TWIST OF FATE** *London LONCD 481*	52	1

See also SUGABABES

DON-E

UK, male vocalist – Donald McLean (Singles: 8 weeks) pos/wks

Date		Title	Pos	Wks
9 May 92		**LOVE MAKES THE WORLD GO ROUND** *Fourth & Broadway BRW 242*	18	6
25 Jul 92		**PEACE IN THE WORLD** *Fourth & Broadway BRW 256*	41	1
28 Feb 98		**DELICIOUS** *Mushroom MUSH 20CD* [1]	52	1

[1] Deni Hines featuring Don-E

Lonnie DONEGAN (119 Top 500)

The 'King of Skiffle', b. 29 Apr 1931, Glasgow, Scotland, d. 3 Nov 2002. Britain's most successful and influential recording artist before The Beatles. Chalked up 28 successive Top 30 hits, and was the first UK male to score two US Top 10s. Album with Van Morrison and Chris Barber reached Top 20 in 2000 (Singles: 321 weeks, Albums: 68 weeks) pos/wks

Date		Title	Pos	Wks
6 Jan 56	●	**ROCK ISLAND LINE (2re)** *Decca F 10647* [1]	8	22
20 Apr 56	●	**LOST JOHN / STEWBALL (re)** *Pye Nixa N 15036* [1]	2	18
6 Jul 56		**SKIFFLE SESSION (EP)** *Pye Nixa NJE 1017* [1]	20	2
7 Sep 56	●	**BRING A LITTLE WATER, SYLVIE / DEAD OR ALIVE (re)** *Pye Nixa N 15071* [2]	7	13
21 Dec 56		**LONNIE DONEGAN SHOWCASE (LP)** *Pye Nixa NPT 19012* [2]	26	3
18 Jan 57	●	**DON'T YOU ROCK ME DADDY-O** *Pye Nixa N 15080* [2]	4	17
5 Apr 57	★	**CUMBERLAND GAP** *Pye Nixa N 15087* [2]	1	12
7 Jun 57	★	**GAMBLIN' MAN / PUTTIN' ON THE STYLE** *Pye Nixa N 15093* [2]	1	19
11 Oct 57	●	**MY DIXIE DARLING** *Pye Nixa N 15108* [2]	10	15
20 Dec 57		**JACK O' DIAMONDS** *Pye Nixa 7N 15116* [2]	14	7
11 Apr 58	●	**THE GRAND COOLIE DAM** *Pye Nixa 7N 15129* [2]	6	15
11 Jul 58		**SALLY DON'T YOU GRIEVE / BETTY, BETTY, BETTY** *Pye Nixa 7N 15148* [2]	11	7
26 Sep 58		**LONESOME TRAVELLER** *Pye Nixa 7N 15158* [2]	28	1
14 Nov 58		**LONNIE'S SKIFFLE PARTY** *Pye Nixa 7N 15165* [2]	23	5
21 Nov 58	●	**TOM DOOLEY** *Pye Nixa 7N 15172* [2]	3	14
6 Feb 59	●	**DOES YOUR CHEWING GUM LOSE ITS FLAVOUR (ON THE BEDPOST OVERNIGHT)** *Pye Nixa 7N 15181* [2]	3	12
8 May 59		**FORT WORTH JAIL** *Pye Nixa 7N 15198* [2]	14	5
26 Jun 59	●	**BATTLE OF NEW ORLEANS** *Pye 7N 15206* [2]	2	16
11 Sep 59		**SAL'S GOT A SUGAR LIP** *Pye 7N 15223* [2]	13	4
4 Dec 59		**SAN MIGUEL** *Pye 7N 15237* [2]	19	4
24 Mar 60	★	**MY OLD MAN'S A DUSTMAN** *Pye 7N 15256* [3]	1	13
26 May 60	●	**I WANNA GO HOME (THE WRECK OF THE 'JOHN B')** *Pye 7N 15267* [4]	5	17
25 Aug 60	●	**LORELEI** *Pye 7N 15275*	10	8
24 Nov 60		**LIVELY** *Pye 7N 15312* [3]	13	9
8 Dec 60		**VIRGIN MARY** *Pye 7N 15315*	27	5
11 May 61	●	**HAVE A DRINK ON ME** *Pye 7N 15354* [3]	8	15
31 Aug 61	●	**MICHAEL, ROW THE BOAT / LUMBERED** *Pye 7N 15371* [3]	6	11
18 Jan 62		**THE COMANCHEROS** *Pye 7N 15410*	14	10
5 Apr 62	●	**THE PARTY'S OVER** *Pye 7N 15424*	9	12
16 Aug 62		**PICK A BALE OF COTTON** *Pye 7N 15455* [3]	11	10
17 Nov 56	●	**LONNIE DONEGAN SHOWCASE** *Pye Nixa NPT 19012*	2	21
12 Jul 58	●	**LONNIE** *Pye Nixa NPT 19027*	3	13
1 Sep 62	●	**GOLDEN AGE OF DONEGAN** *Pye Golden Guinea GGL 0135*	3	23
9 Feb 63		**GOLDEN AGE OF DONEGAN VOLUME 2** *Pye Golden Guinea GGL 0170*	15	3
25 Feb 78		**PUTTING ON THE STYLE** *Chrysalis CHR 1158*	51	3
29 Jan 00		**THE SKIFFLE SESSIONS – LIVE IN BELFAST** *Venture CDVE 945* [1]	14	3
8 Mar 03		**PUTTIN' ON THE STYLE – THE GREATEST HITS** *Castle Music TVSAN002*	45	2

[1] Lonnie Donegan Skiffle Group [2] Lonnie Donegan and His Skiffle Group [3] Lonnie Donegan and His Group [4] Lonnie Donegan and Wally Stott's Orchestra [1] Van Morrison / Lonnie Donegan / Chris Barber

'Stewball' had one week on the chart by itself on 20 Apr 1956. 'Lost John', the other side, replaced it on 27 Apr 1956, but 'Stewball' was given co-billing with 'Lost John' for the weeks of 11, 18 and 25 May 1956, peaking only at No.7. 'Dead or Alive' was not listed with 'Bring a Little Water Sylvie' for the week 7 Sep 1956. 'Putting on the Style' was not listed with 'Gamblin' Man' for the weeks of 7 and 14 Jun 1956. Tracks on Skiffle Session (EP): Railroad Bill / Stockalee / Ballad of Jesse James / Ol' Riley. Tracks on Lonnie Donegan Showcase (LP): Wabash Cannonball / How Long / How Long Blues / Nobody's Child / I Shall Not Be Moved / I'm Alabammy Bound / I'm a Rambling Man / Wreck of the Old '97 / Frankie and Johnny

Tanya DONELLY

US, female vocalist / instrumentalist (Singles: 2 weeks, Albums: 1 week) pos/wks

Date		Title	Pos	Wks
30 Aug 97		**PRETTY DEEP** *4AD BAD 7007CD*	55	1
6 Dec 97		**THE BRIGHT LIGHT** *4AD BAD 7012CD*	64	1
20 Sep 97		**LOVESONGS FOR UNDERDOGS** *4AD CAD 7008CD*	36	1

See also BELLY

UK NO.1 ALBUM DEBUTS

A chronological list of all the acts that have the best chart debuts imaginable – straight in at No.1 with their first album entry on the UK chart

BAY CITY ROLLERS 12/10/74 ROLLIN'
SEX PISTOLS 12/11/77
NEVER MIND THE BOLLOCKS HERE'S THE SEX PISTOLS
PRETENDERS 19/01/80 PRETENDERS
PHIL COLLINS 21/02/81 FACE VALUE
ABC 03/07/82 THE LEXICON OF LOVE
BONNIE TYLER 16/04/83
FASTER THAN THE SPEED OF NIGHT
WHAM! 09/07/83 FANTASTIC
HOWARD JONES 17/03/84 HUMAN'S LIB
FRANKIE GOES TO HOLLYWOOD 10/11/84
WELCOME TO THE PLEASURE DOME
CURIOSITY KILLED THE CAT 09/05/87 KEEP YOUR DISTANCE
SWING OUT SISTER 23/05/87 IT'S BETTER TO TRAVEL
TERENCE TRENT D'ARBY 25/07/87
INTRODUCING THE HARDLINE ACCORDING TO
GEORGE MICHAEL 14/11/87 FAITH
RICK ASTLEY 28/11/87 WHENEVER YOU NEED SOMEBODY
JOHNNY HATES JAZZ 23/01/88 TURN BACK THE CLOCK
MORRISSEY 26/03/88 VIVA HATE
HOLLY JOHNSON 06/05/89 BLAST
CHARLATANS 20/10/90 SOME FRIENDLY
FARM 16/03/91 SPARTACUS
SEAL 01/06/91 SEAL
ANNIE LENNOX 18/04/92 DIVA
MICHAEL BALL 30/05/92 MICHAEL BALL
EAST 17 27/02/93 WALTHAMSTOW
SUEDE 10/04/93 SUEDE
JAMIROQUAI 26/06/93 EMERGENCY ON PLANET EARTH
OASIS 10/09/94 DEFINITELY MAYBE
ELASTICA 25/03/95 ELASTICA
BLACK GRAPE 19/08/95
IT'S GREAT WHEN YOU'RE STRAIGHT ... YEAH
BOYZONE 02/09/95 SAID AND DONE
ROBSON GREEN AND JEROME FLYNN 25/11/95
ROBSON & JEROME
BLUETONES 24/02/96 EXPECTING TO FLY
ASH 18/05/96 1977
KULA SHAKER 28/09/96 K
PETER ANDRE 12/10/96 NATURAL
SPICE GIRLS 16/11/96 SPICE
MANSUN 01/03/97 ATTACK OF THE GREY LANTERN
GARY BARLOW 07/06/97 OPEN ROAD
WU-TANG CLAN 14/06/97 WU-TANG FOREVER
HANSON 21/06/97 MIDDLE OF NOWHERE
EMBRACE 20/06/98 THE GOOD WILL OUT
FIVE 04/07/98 FIVE
RICHARD ASHCROFT 08/07/00 ALONE WITH EVERBODY
COLDPLAY 22/07/00 PARACHUTES
RONAN KEATING 12/08/00 RONAN
CRAIG DAVID 26/08/00 BORN TO DO IT
HEAR'SAY 07/04/01 POPSTARS
STAIND 01/09/01 BREAK THE CYCLE
WILL YOUNG 19/10/02 FROM NOW ON
KELLY ROWLAND 15/02/03 SIMPLY DEEP
BEYONCÉ 05/07/03 DANGEROUSLY IN LOVE

Bonnie Tyler, the first woman to bag a UK album chart-topper with her first hit album straight in at No.1

DONNAS *US, female vocal / instrumental group (Singles: 3 weeks)* pos/wks

12 Apr 03	**TAKE IT OFF** *Atlantic AT 0148CD*	38	2
5 Jul 03	**WHO INVENTED YOU?** *Atlantic AT 0156CD*	61	1

Ral DONNER *US, male vocalist, d. 6 Apr 1984 (Singles: 10 weeks)* pos/wks

21 Sep 61	**YOU DON'T KNOW WHAT YOU'VE GOT (UNTIL YOU LOSE IT)** *Parlophone R 4820*	25	10

DONOVAN 390 Top 500

Acclaimed Celtic singer / songwriter, b. Donovan Leitch, 10 May 1946, Glasgow. Initially dubbed British version of Bob Dylan, he enjoyed massive fame on both sides of the Atlantic in the 'flower power' years of the late 1960s (Singles: 100 weeks, Albums: 73 weeks) pos/wks

25 Mar 65 ●	**CATCH THE WIND** *Pye 7N 15801*	4	13
3 Jun 65 ●	**COLOURS** *Pye 7N 15866*	4	12
11 Nov 65	**TURQUOISE** *Pye 7N 15984*	30	6
8 Dec 66 ●	**SUNSHINE SUPERMAN** *Pye 7N 17241* ▲	2	11
9 Feb 67 ●	**MELLOW YELLOW** *Pye 7N 17267*	8	8
25 Oct 67 ●	**THERE IS A MOUNTAIN** *Pye 7N 17403*	8	11
21 Feb 68 ●	**JENNIFER JUNIPER** *Pye 7N 17457*	5	11
29 May 68 ●	**HURDY GURDY MAN** *Pye 7N 17537*	4	10
4 Dec 68	**ATLANTIS** *Pye 7N 17660*	23	8
9 Jul 69	**GOO GOO BARABAJAGAL (LOVE IS HOT)** *Pye 7N 17778* [1]	12	9
1 Dec 90	**JENNIFER JUNIPER** *Fontana SYP 1*	68	1
5 Jun 65 ●	**WHAT'S BIN DID AND WHAT'S BIN HID** *Pye NPL 18117*	3	16
6 Nov 65	**FAIRY TALE** *Pye NPL 18128*	20	2
8 Jul 67	**SUNSHINE SUPERMAN** *Pye NPL 18181*	25	7
14 Oct 67 ●	**UNIVERSAL SOLDIER** *Marble Arch MAL 718*	5	18
11 May 68	**A GIFT FROM A FLOWER TO A GARDEN** *Pye NSPL 20000*	13	14
12 Sep 70	**OPEN ROAD** *Dawn DNLS 3009*	30	4
24 Mar 73	**COSMIC WHEELS** *Epic EPC 65450*	15	12

[1] Donovan with the Jeff Beck Group

Jason DONOVAN 266 Top 500

The top teen idol of the late 1980s, b. 1 Jun 1968, Melbourne. The Australian actor turned singer had an impressive array of UK hits after leaving TV soap 'Neighbours'. His debut LP, 'Ten Good Reasons', was the UK's top-selling album of 1989 (Singles: 137 weeks, Albums: 99 weeks) pos/wks

10 Sep 88 ●	**NOTHING CAN DIVIDE US** *PWL PWL 17*	5	12
10 Dec 88 ★	**ESPECIALLY FOR YOU** *PWL PWL 24* [1]	1	14
4 Mar 89 ★	**TOO MANY BROKEN HEARTS** *PWL PWL 32*	1	13
10 Jun 89 ★	**SEALED WITH A KISS** *PWL PWL 39* ■	1	10
9 Sep 89 ●	**EVERY DAY (I LOVE YOU MORE)** *PWL PWL 43*	2	9
9 Dec 89 ●	**WHEN YOU COME BACK TO ME** *PWL PWL 46*	2	11
7 Apr 90 ●	**HANG ON TO YOUR LOVE** *PWL PWL 51*	8	7
30 Jun 90	**ANOTHER NIGHT** *PWL PWL 58*	18	5
1 Sep 90 ●	**RHYTHM OF THE RAIN** *PWL PWL 60*	9	6
27 Oct 90	**I'M DOING FINE** *PWL PWL 69*	22	6
18 May 91	**RSVP** *PWL PWL 80*	17	5
22 Jun 91 ★	**ANY DREAM WILL DO** *Really Useful RUR 7*	1	12
24 Aug 91 ●	**HAPPY TOGETHER** *PWL PWL 203*	10	6
7 Dec 91	**JOSEPH MEGA REMIX (re-mix)** *Really Useful RUR 9* [2]	13	8
18 Jul 92	**MISSION OF LOVE** *Polydor PO 222*	26	4
28 Nov 92	**AS TIME GOES BY** *Polydor PO 245*	26	6
7 Aug 93	**ALL AROUND THE WORLD** *Polydor PZCD 278*	41	3
13 May 89 ★	**TEN GOOD REASONS** *PWL HF 7*	1	54
9 Jun 90 ●	**BETWEEN THE LINES** *PWL HF 14*	2	26
28 Sep 91 ●	**GREATEST HITS** *PWL HF 20*	9	17
11 Sep 93	**ALL AROUND THE WORLD** *Polydor 8477452*	27	2

[1] Kylie Minogue and Jason Donovan [2] Jason Donovan and Original London Cast featuring Linzi Hately, David Easter and Johnny Amobi

See also Stage Cast Recordings – JOSEPH and the AMAZING TECHNICOLOUR DREAMCOAT

DOOBIE BROTHERS *US, male vocal / instrumental group (Singles: 45 weeks, Albums: 30 weeks)* pos/wks

9 Mar 74	**LISTEN TO THE MUSIC** *Warner Bros. K 16208*	29	7
7 Jun 75	**TAKE ME IN YOUR ARMS (ROCK ME A LITTLE WHILE)** *Warner Bros. K 16559*	29	5
17 Feb 79	**WHAT A FOOL BELIEVES (re)** *Warner Bros. K 17314* ▲	31	11
14 Jul 79	**MINUTE BY MINUTE** *Warner Bros. K 17411*	47	4
24 Jan 87	**WHAT A FOOL BELIEVES (re-issue)** *Warner Bros. W 8451* [1]	57	3
29 Jul 89	**THE DOCTOR** *Capitol CL 536*	73	2
27 Nov 93 ●	**LONG TRAIN RUNNIN'** *Warner Bros. W 0217CD*	7	10
14 May 94	**LISTEN TO THE MUSIC (re-mix)** *Warner Bros. W 0228CD*	37	3
30 Mar 74	**WHAT WERE ONCE VICES ARE NOW HABITS** *Warner Bros. K 56206*	19	10
17 May 75	**STAMPEDE** *Warner Bros. K 56094*	14	11
10 Apr 76	**TAKIN' IT TO THE STREETS** *Warner Bros. K 56196*	42	2
19 Sep 77	**LIVING ON THE FAULT LINE** *Warner Bros. K 56383*	25	5
11 Oct 80	**ONE STEP CLOSER** *Warner Bros. K 56824*	53	2

[1] Doobie Brothers featuring Michael McDonald

See also Michael McDONALD

DOOGIE – *See BUG KANN and the PLASTIC JAM*

DOOLALLY *UK, male production duo – Stephen Mende and Daniel Langsmen (Singles: 16 weeks)* pos/wks

14 Nov 98	**STRAIGHT FROM THE HEART (re)** *Locked On LOX 104CD*	20	10
7 Aug 99 ●	**STRAIGHT FROM THE HEART (re-issue)** *Chocolate Boy / Locked On LOX 112CD*	9	6

See also SHANKS & BIGFOOT

DOOLEYS *UK, male vocal / instrumental group (Singles: 83 weeks, Albums: 27 weeks)* pos/wks

13 Aug 77	**THINK I'M GONNA FALL IN LOVE WITH YOU** *GTO GT 95*	13	10
12 Nov 77 ●	**LOVE OF MY LIFE** *GTO GT 110*	9	11
13 May 78	**DON'T TAKE IT LYIN' DOWN** *GTO GT 220*	60	3
2 Sep 78	**A ROSE HAS TO DIE** *GTO GT 229*	11	11
10 Feb 79	**HONEY I'M LOST** *GTO GT 242*	24	9
16 Jun 79 ●	**WANTED** *GTO GT 249*	3	14
22 Sep 79 ●	**THE CHOSEN FEW** *GTO GT 258*	7	11
8 Mar 80	**LOVE PATROL** *GTO GT 260*	29	7
6 Sep 80	**BODY LANGUAGE** *GTO GT 276*	46	4
10 Oct 81	**AND I WISH** *GTO GT 300*	52	3
30 Jun 79 ●	**THE BEST OF THE DOOLEYS** *GTO GTTV 038*	6	21
3 Nov 79	**THE CHOSEN FEW** *GTO GTLP 040*	56	4
25 Oct 80	**FULL HOUSE** *GTO GTTV 050*	54	2

Val DOONICAN 177 Top 500

Popular balladeer and TV host, b. 3 Feb 1928, Waterford, Ireland. This relaxed crooner, who was known for his rocking chair and multicoloured jumpers, had five successive Top 10 albums in the Swinging Sixties (Singles: 143 weeks, Albums: 170 weeks) pos/wks

15 Oct 64 ●	**WALK TALL** *Decca F 11982*	3	21
21 Jan 65 ●	**THE SPECIAL YEARS (re)** *Decca F 12049*	7	13
8 Apr 65	**I'M GONNA GET THERE SOMEHOW** *Decca F 12118*	25	5
17 Mar 66 ●	**ELUSIVE BUTTERFLY** *Decca F 12358*	5	12
3 Nov 66 ●	**WHAT WOULD I BE** *Decca F 12505*	2	17
23 Feb 67	**MEMORIES ARE MADE OF THIS** *Decca F 12566*	11	12
25 May 67	**TWO STREETS** *Decca F 12608*	39	4
18 Oct 67 ●	**IF THE WHOLE WORLD STOPPED LOVIN'** *Pye 7N 17396*	3	19
21 Feb 68	**YOU'RE THE ONLY ONE** *Pye 7N 17465*	37	4
12 Jun 68	**NOW** *Pye 7N 17534*	43	2
23 Oct 68	**IF I KNEW THEN WHAT I KNOW NOW** *Pye 7N 17616*	14	13
23 Apr 69	**RING OF BRIGHT WATER** *Pye 7N 17713*	48	1
4 Dec 71	**MORNING** *Philips 6006 177*	12	13
10 Mar 73	**HEAVEN IS MY WOMAN'S LOVE (re)** *Philips 6028 031*	34	7
12 Dec 64 ●	**THE LUCKY 13 SHADES OF VAL DOONICAN** *Decca LK 4648*	2	27
3 Dec 66 ●	**GENTLE SHADES OF VAL DOONICAN** *Decca LK 4831*	5	52
2 Dec 67 ★	**VAL DOONICAN ROCKS BUT GENTLY** *Pye NSPL 18204*	1	23
30 Nov 68 ●	**VAL** *Pye NSPL 18236*	6	11
14 Jun 69 ●	**THE WORLD OF VAL DOONICAN** *Decca SPA 3*	2	31
13 Dec 69	**SOUNDS GENTLE** *Pye NSPL 18321*	22	9
19 Dec 70	**THE MAGIC OF VAL DOONICAN** *Philips 6642 003*	34	3
27 Nov 71	**THIS IS VAL DOONICAN** *Philips 6382 017*	40	1
22 Feb 75	**I LOVE COUNTRY MUSIC** *Philips 9299261*	37	2
21 May 77	**SOME OF MY BEST FRIENDS ARE SONGS** *Philips 6641 607*	29	5
24 Mar 90	**SONGS FROM MY SKETCH BOOK** *Parkfield PMLP 5014*	33	6

DOOP *Holland, male instrumental duo – Ferry Ridderhof and Peter Garnefski (Singles: 12 weeks)* pos/wks

12 Mar 94 ★ **DOOP** *Citybeat CBE 774CD* 1 12

DOORS 498 Top 500

Controversial, uncompromising rock band. Formed 1965 in Los Angeles, 'Lizard King' Jim Morrison (v) d. 1971, Ray Manzarek (k), Robby Krieger (g) and John Densmore (d) were 1993 Rock and Roll Hall of Fame inductees but did not score a UK Top 10 single until 1991 and album until 2000 (Singles: 42 weeks, Albums: 99 weeks) pos/wks

16 Aug 67 **LIGHT MY FIRE** *Elektra EKSN 45014* ▲ 49 1
28 Aug 68 **HELLO, I LOVE YOU** *Elektra EKSN 45037* ▲ 15 12
16 Oct 71 **RIDERS ON THE STORM (re)** *Elektra K 12021* 22 11
20 Mar 76 **RIDERS ON THE STORM (re-issue)** *Elektra K 12203* 33 5
3 Feb 79 **HELLO I LOVE YOU (re-issue)** *Elektra K 12215* 71 2
27 Apr 91 **BREAK ON THROUGH** *Elektra EKR 121* 64 2
1 Jun 91 ● **LIGHT MY FIRE (re-issue)** *Elektra EKR 125* 7 8
10 Aug 91 **RIDERS ON THE STORM (2nd re-issue)** *Elektra EKR 131* 68 1
28 Sep 68 WAITING FOR THE SUN *Elektra EKS7 4024* ▲ 16 10
11 Apr 70 MORRISON HOTEL *Elektra EKS 75007* 12 8
26 Sep 70 ABSOLUTELY LIVE *Elektra 2665 002* 69 1
31 Jul 71 L.A. WOMAN *Elektra K 42090* 28 4
1 Apr 72 WEIRD SCENES INSIDE THE GOLD MINE *Elektra K 62009* 50 1
29 Oct 83 ALIVE SHE CRIED *Elektra 9602691* 36 5
4 Jul 87 LIVE AT THE HOLLYWOOD BOWL *Elektra EKT 40* 51 3
6 Apr 91 THE DOORS (FILM SOUNDTRACK) *Elektra EKT 85* 11 17
20 Apr 91 THE BEST OF THE DOORS *Elektra EKT 21* 17 18
20 Apr 91 THE DOORS *Elektra K 42012* 43 13
1 Jun 91 IN CONCERT *Elektra EKT 88* 24 5
21 Mar 98 THE BEST OF THE DOORS (re-issue) *Elektra K 9603452* 37 8
23 Sep 00 ● THE BEST OF THE DOORS (2nd re-issue) *Elektra 7559624682* 9 6

DOPE SMUGGLAZ
UK, male DJ / production trio (Singles: 5 weeks) pos/wks

5 Dec 98 **THE WORD** *Mushroom PERFCDS 1* 62 1
7 Aug 99 **DOUBLE DOUBLE DUTCH** *Perfecto PERF2CDS* 15 4

Charlie DORE *UK, female vocalist (Singles: 2 weeks)* pos/wks

17 Nov 79 **PILOT OF THE AIRWAVES** *Island WIP 6526* 66 2

Andrea DORIA
Italy, male producer / instrumentalist (Singles: 1 week) pos/wks

26 Apr 03 **BUCCI BAG** *Southern Fried ECB 38CDS* 57 1

DOROTHY *UK, male producer / instrumentalist – Paul Masterson (Singles: 5 weeks)* pos/wks

9 Dec 95 **WHAT'S THAT TUNE (DOO DOO DOO DOO DOO-DOO-DOO-DOO-DOO-DOO)** *RCA 74321330912* 31 5

See also CANDY GIRLS; SLEAZESISTERS; YOMANDA; HI-GATE; CLERGY; Paul MASTERSON presents SUSHI

Lee DORSEY *US, male vocalist, d. 1 Dec 1986 (Singles: 36 weeks, Albums: 3 weeks)* pos/wks

3 Feb 66 **GET OUT OF MY LIFE, WOMAN** *Stateside SS 485* 22 7
5 May 66 **CONFUSION** *Stateside SS 506* 38 6
11 Aug 66 ● **WORKING IN THE COALMINE** *Stateside SS 528* 8 11
27 Oct 66 ● **HOLY COW** *Stateside SS 552* 6 12
17 Dec 66 NEW LEE DORSEY *Stateside SSL 10192* 34 3

Marc DORSEY *US, male vocalist (Singles: 1 week)* pos/wks

19 Jun 99 **IF YOU REALLY WANNA KNOW** *Jive 0522592* 58 1

Tommy DORSEY ORCHESTRA starring Warren COVINGTON
US, orchestra with Warren Covington, male instrumentalist – trombone, leader Tommy Dorsey d. 26 Nov 1956 (Singles: 19 weeks) pos/wks

17 Oct 58 ● **TEA FOR TWO CHA CHA** *Brunswick 05757* 3 19

DOUBLE *Switzerland, male vocal / instrumental duo – Kurt Maloo and Felix Haug (Singles: 10 weeks, Albums: 4 weeks)* pos/wks

25 Jan 86 ● **THE CAPTAIN OF HER HEART** *Polydor POSP 779* 8 9
5 Dec 87 **DEVIL'S BALL** *Polydor POSP 888* 71 1
8 Mar 86 BLUE *Polydor POLD 5187* 69 4

DOUBLE DEE
Italy, male producer – Davide Domenella (Singles: 5 weeks) pos/wks

1 Dec 90 **FOUND LOVE** *Epic 6563766* [1] 63 2
25 Nov 95 **FOUND LOVE (re-mix)** *Sony S3 DANUCD 1* [1] 33 2
27 Sep 03 **SHINING** *Positiva CDTIV 194* 58 1

[1] Double Dee featuring Dany

DOUBLE 99 *UK, male instrumental / production duo – Tim Liken and Omar Adimora (Singles: 9 weeks)* pos/wks

31 May 97 **RIPGROOVE** *Satellite 74321485132* 31 3
1 Nov 97 **RIPGROOVE (re-mix)** *Satellite 74321529322* 14 6

See also RIP PRODUCTIONS

007 – *See RED RAW featuring 007*

DOUBLE SIX
UK, male vocal / instrumental group (Singles: 2 weeks) pos/wks

19 Sep 98 **REAL GOOD** *Multiply CDMULTY 39* 66 1
12 Jun 99 **BREAKDOWN** *Multiply CDMULTY 50* 59 1

DOUBLE TROUBLE *UK, male instrumental / production duo – Leigh Guest and Michael Menson (Singles: 35 weeks, Albums: 1 week)* pos/wks

27 May 89 **JUST KEEP ROCKIN'** *Desire WANT 9* [1] 11 12
7 Oct 89 ● **STREET TUFF** *Desire WANT 18* [2] 3 14
12 May 90 **TALK BACK** *Desire WANT 27* [3] 71 1
30 Jun 90 **LOVE DON'T LIVE HERE ANYMORE** *Desire WANT 32* [4] 21 6
15 Jun 91 **RUB-A-DUB** *Desire WANT 41* 66 2
4 Aug 90 AS ONE *Desire LULP 6* 73 1

[1] Double Trouble and the Rebel MC [2] Rebel MC and Double Trouble [3] With vocals by Janette Sewell [4] Double Trouble featuring Janette Sewell and Carl Brown

See Stevie Ray VAUGHAN and DOUBLE TROUBLE

DOUBLE TROUBLE – *See also AIRHEADZ*

DOUBLE YOU?
Italy, male vocalist – Willie Morales (Singles: 3 weeks) pos/wks

2 May 92 **PLEASE DON'T GO** *ZYX ZYX 67487* 41 3

Rob DOUGAN *Australia, male vocalist / instrumentalist / producer (Singles: 4 weeks)* pos/wks

4 Apr 98 **FURIOUS ANGELS** *Cheeky CHEKCD 025* 62 1
6 Jul 02 **CLUBBED TO DEATH** *Cheeky / Arista 74321941702* 24 3

See also OUR TRIBE / ONE TRIBE; SPHINX

Carl DOUGLAS *Jamaica, male vocalist (Singles: 39 weeks)* pos/wks

17 Aug 74 ★ **KUNG FU FIGHTING** *Pye 7N 45377* ▲ 1 13
30 Nov 74 **DANCE THE KUNG FU** *Pye 7N 45418* 35 5
3 Dec 77 **RUN BACK** *Pye 7N 46018* 25 10
23 May 98 ● **KUNG FU FIGHTING** *All Around the World CDGLOBE 173* [1] 8 11

[1] Bus Stop featuring Carl Douglas

Second listing for Kung Fu Fighting was not a re-mix of the original but Douglas's 1974 hit vocal sampled and used in a new recording by Bus Stop

Carol DOUGLAS *US, female vocalist (Singles: 4 weeks)* pos/wks

22 Jul 78 **NIGHT FEVER** *Gull GULS 61* 66 4

Craig DOUGLAS *UK, male vocalist – Terence Perkins (b. 13 Aug 1941) (Singles: 113 weeks, Albums: 2 weeks)* pos/wks

12 Jun 59 **A TEENAGER IN LOVE** *Top Rank JAR 133* 13 11

7 Aug 59 ★ **ONLY SIXTEEN** *Top Rank JAR 159* **1** 15
22 Jan 60 ● **PRETTY BLUE EYES** *Top Rank JAR 268* **4** 15
28 Apr 60 ● **THE HEART OF A TEENAGE GIRL** *Top Rank JAR 340* **10** 9
11 Aug 60 **OH! WHAT A DAY** *Top Rank JAR 406* **43** 1
20 Apr 61 ● **A HUNDRED POUNDS OF CLAY** *Top Rank JAR 556* **9** 9
29 Jun 61 ● **TIME** *Top Rank JAR 569* **9** 14
22 Mar 62 ● **WHEN MY LITTLE GIRL IS SMILING** *Top Rank JAR 610* **9** 13
28 Jun 62 ● **OUR FAVOURITE MELODIES** *Columbia DB 4854* **9** 10
18 Oct 62 **OH, LONESOME ME** *Decca F 11523* **15** 12
28 Feb 63 **TOWN CRIER** *Decca F 11575* **36** 4
6 Aug 60 **CRAIG DOUGLAS** *Top Rank BUY 049* **17** 2

DOVE *Ireland, male / female vocal group (Singles: 2 weeks)* pos/wks

11 Sep 99 **DON'T DREAM** *ZTT 135CD* **37** 2

DOVES *UK, male vocal / instrumental group (Singles: 15 weeks, Albums: 40 weeks)* pos/wks

14 Aug 99 **HERE IT COMES** *Casino CHIP 003CD* **73** 1
1 Apr 00 **THE CEDAR ROOM** *Heavenly HVN 95CD* **33** 2
10 Jun 00 **CATCH THE SUN** *Heavenly HVN 96CD* **32** 2
11 Nov 00 **THE MAN WHO TOLD EVERYTHING** *Heavenly HVN 98CD* **32** 2
27 Apr 02 ● **THERE GOES THE FEAR** *Heavenly HVN 111CD* **3** 3
3 Aug 02 **POUNDING** *Heavenly HVN 116CD* **21** 3
26 Oct 02 **CAUGHT BY THE RIVER** *Heavenly HVN 126CDS* **29** 2
15 Apr 00 **LOST SOULS** *Heavenly HVNLP 26CD* **16** 16
11 May 02 ★ **THE LAST BROADCAST** *Heavenly HVNLP 35CD* ■ **1** 23
11 Oct 03 **LOST SIDES** *Heavenly HVNLP 46CDX* **50** 1

DOWLANDS *UK, male vocal group (Singles: 7 weeks)* pos/wks

9 Jan 64 **ALL MY LOVING** *Oriole CB 1897* **33** 7

DOWN *US, male vocal / instrumental group (Albums: 1 week)* pos/wks

30 Sep 95 **NOLA** *Atlantic 7559618302* **68** 1

Robert DOWNEY Jr *US, male actor / vocalist (Singles: 1 week)* pos/wks

30 Jan 93 **SMILE** *Epic 6589052* **68** 1

Don DOWNING *US, male vocalist (Singles: 10 weeks)* pos/wks

10 Nov 73 **LONELY DAYS, LONELY NIGHTS** *People PEO 102* **32** 10

Will DOWNING
US, male vocalist (Singles: 35 weeks, Albums: 28 weeks) pos/wks

2 Apr 88 **A LOVE SUPREME** *Fourth & Broadway BRW 90* **14** 10
25 Jun 88 **IN MY DREAMS** *Fourth & Broadway BRW 104* **34** 6
1 Oct 88 **FREE** *Fourth & Broadway BRW 112* **58** 5
21 Jan 89 **WHERE IS THE LOVE** *Fourth & Broadway BRW 122* [1] **19** 7
28 Oct 89 **TEST OF TIME** *Fourth & Broadway BRW 146* **67** 2
24 Feb 90 **COME TOGETHER AS ONE** *Fourth & Broadway BRW 159* **48** 4
18 Sep 93 **THERE'S NO LIVING WITHOUT YOU** *Fourth & Broadway BRCD 278* **67** 1
26 Mar 88 **WILL DOWNING** *Fourth & Broadway BRLP 518* **20** 23
18 Nov 89 **COME TOGETHER AS ONE** *Fourth & Broadway BRLP 538* **36** 2
6 Apr 91 **A DREAM FULFILLED** *Fourth & Broadway BRLP 565* **43** 3

[1] Mica Paris and Will Downing

Jason DOWNS featuring MILK *US, male vocalist and US, male rapper (Singles: 6 weeks, Albums: 1 week)* pos/wks

12 May 01 **WHITE BOY WITH A FEATHER** *Pepper 9230412* **19** 5
14 Jul 01 **CATS IN THE CRADLE** *Pepper 9230442* **65** 1
28 Jul 01 **WHITE BOY WITH A FEATHER** *Pepper 9230452* **64** 1

DOWNSIDE ABBEY – *See MONKS and CHOIRBOYS of DOWNSIDE ABBEY*

Lamont DOZIER – *See HOLLAND-DOZIER featuring Lamont DOZIER*

Charlie DRAKE *UK, male comedian / vocalist – Charles Sprigall (Singles: 37 weeks)* pos/wks

8 Aug 58 ● **SPLISH SPLASH** *Parlophone R 4461* **7** 11
24 Oct 58 **VOLARE** *Parlophone R 4478* **28** 2
27 Oct 60 **MR CUSTER** *Parlophone R 4701* **12** 12
5 Oct 61 **MY BOOMERANG WON'T COME BACK** *Parlophone R 4824* **14** 11
1 Jan 72 **PUCKWUDGIE** *Columbia DB 8829* **47** 1

DRAMATIS
UK, male vocal / instrumental group (Singles: 8 weeks) pos/wks

5 Dec 81 **LOVE NEEDS NO DISGUISE** *Beggars Banquet BEG 68* [1] **33** 7
13 Nov 82 **I CAN SEE HER NOW** *Rocket XPRES 83* **57** 1

[1] Gary Numan and Dramatis

Rusty DRAPER *US, male vocalist – Farrell H Draper, b. 25 Jan 1923, d. 28 Mar 2003 (Singles: 4 weeks)* pos/wks

11 Aug 60 **MULE SKINNER BLUES** *Mercury AMT 1101* **39** 4

DREAD ZEPPELIN *US, male vocal / instrumental group (Singles: 3 weeks, Albums: 2 weeks)* pos/wks

1 Dec 90 **YOUR TIME IS GONNA COME** *IRS DREAD 1* **59** 1
13 Jul 91 **STAIRWAY TO HEAVEN** *IRS DREAD 2* **62** 2
11 Aug 90 **UN-LED-ED** *IRS EIRSA 1042* **71** 2

DREADZONE
UK, male instrumental group (Singles: 15 weeks, Albums: 5 weeks) pos/wks

6 May 95 **ZION YOUTH** *Virgin VSCDG 1537* **49** 2
29 Jul 95 **CAPTAIN DREAD** *Virgin VSCDG 1541* **49** 2
23 Sep 95 **MAXIMUM (EP)** *Virgin VSCDT 1555* **56** 2
6 Jan 96 **LITTLE BRITAIN** *Virgin VSCDG 1565* **20** 6
30 Mar 96 **LIFE LOVE AND UNITY** *Virgin VSCDT 1583* **56** 1
10 May 97 **EARTH ANGEL** *Virgin VSCDT 1593* **51** 1
26 Jul 97 **MOVING ON** *Virgin VSCDT 1635* **58** 1
10 Jun 95 **SECOND LIGHT** *Virgin CDV 2778* **37** 4
9 Aug 97 **BIOLOGICAL RADIO** *Virgin CDV 2808* **45** 1

Tracks on Maximum (EP): Maximum / Fight the Power 95 / One Way

DREAM *US, female vocal group (Singles: 7 weeks)* pos/wks

17 Mar 01 **HE LOVES U NOT** *Puff Daddy / Arista 74321823542* **17** 7

DREAM ACADEMY *UK, male / female vocal / instrumental group (Singles: 10 weeks, Albums: 2 weeks)* pos/wks

30 Mar 85 **LIFE IN A NORTHERN TOWN** *Blanco Y Negro NEG 10* **15** 8
14 Sep 85 **THE LOVE PARADE** *Blanco Y Negro NEG 16* **68** 2
12 Oct 85 **THE DREAM ACADEMY** *Blanco Y Negro BYN 6* **58** 2

DREAM FREQUENCY
UK, male producer – Ian Bland (Singles: 12 weeks) pos/wks

12 Jan 91 **LOVE PEACE AND HARMONY** *Citybeat CBE 756* **71** 2
25 Jan 92 **FEEL SO REAL** *Citybeat CBE 763* [1] **23** 5
25 Apr 92 **TAKE ME** *Citybeat CBE 768* **39** 3
21 May 94 **GOOD TIMES / THE DREAM** *Citybeat CBE 773CD* **67** 1
10 Sep 94 **YOU MAKE ME FEEL MIGHTY REAL** *Citybeat CBE 775CD* **65** 1

[1] Dream Frequency featuring Debbie Sharp

See also RED; BEAT RENEGADES

DREAM THEATER
US, male vocal / instrumental group (Albums: 1 week) pos/wks

15 Oct 94 **AWAKE** *East West 7567901262* **65** 1

DREAM WARRIORS
Canada, male rap group (Singles: 19 weeks, Albums: 7 weeks) pos/wks

14 Jul 90 **WASH YOUR FACE IN MY SINK** *Fourth & Broadway BRW 183* **16** 8
24 Nov 90 **MY DEFINITION OF A BOOMBASTIC JAZZ STYLE** *Fourth & Broadway BRW 197* **13** 8
2 Mar 91 **LUDI** *Fourth & Broadway BRW 206* **39** 3
16 Feb 91 **AND NOW THE LEGACY BEGINS** *Fourth & Broadway BRLP 560* **18** 7

DREAMCATCHER
UK, male / female production / vocal trio (Singles: 4 weeks) pos/wks

12 Jan 02 **I DON'T WANNA LOSE MY WAY** *Positiva CDTIVS 157* **14** 4

DREAMERS – *See FREDDIE and the DREAMERS*

DREAMHOUSE
UK, male vocal / instrumental group (Singles: 2 weeks) pos/wks

3 Jun 95 **STAY** *Chase CDPALACE 1* **62** 2

DREAMKEEPER *UK, female vocal duo (Albums: 1 week)* pos/wks

9 Aug 97 **SPIRIT OF RELAXATION** *Flute SPIRICD 1* **71** 1

DREAMWEAVERS
US, male / female vocal group (Singles: 18 weeks) pos/wks

10 Feb 56 ★ **IT'S ALMOST TOMORROW** *Brunswick 05515* **1** 18

DREEM TEEM *UK, male DJ / production trio (Singles: 14 weeks)* pos/wks

13 Dec 97 **THE THEME** *4 Liberty 74321542032* **34** 4
6 Nov 99 **BUDDY X 99** *4 Liberty LIBTCD 33* [1] **15** 5
15 Dec 01 **IT AIN'T ENOUGH** *ffrr / Public Demand FCD 401* [2] **20** 5

[1] Dreem Teem vs Neneh Cherry [2] Dreem Teem vs Artful Dodger featuring MZ May and MC Alistair

DRELLS – *See Archie BELL and the DRELLS*

Eddie DRENNON and B.B.S. UNLIMITED
US, male vocal / instrumental group (Singles: 6 weeks) pos/wks

28 Feb 76 **LET'S DO THE LATIN HUSTLE**
Pye International 7N 25702 ....**20** 6

Alan DREW *UK, male vocalist (Singles: 2 weeks)* pos/wks

26 Sep 63 **ALWAYS THE LONELY ONE** *Columbia DB 7090* **48** 2

DRIFTERS 207 Top 500
Ever-changing, ever-popular US group, founded in 1953 by Clyde McPhatter (d. 1972) and still active today, with erstwhile members including Ben E King, Johnny Moore (d. 1998) and Rudy Lewis (d. 1964). Inducted into Rock and Roll Hall of Fame in 1988 (Singles: 176 weeks, Albums: 109 weeks) pos/wks

8 Jan 60 **DANCE WITH ME** (re) *London HLE 8988* **17** 5
3 Nov 60 ● **SAVE THE LAST DANCE FOR ME** *London HLK 9201* ▲ **2** 18
16 Mar 61 **I COUNT THE TEARS** *London HLK 9287* **28** 6
5 Apr 62 **WHEN MY LITTLE GIRL IS SMILING** *London HLK 9522* **31** 3
10 Oct 63 **I'LL TAKE YOU HOME** *London HLK 9785* **37** 5
24 Sep 64 **UNDER THE BOARDWALK** *Atlantic AT 4001* **45** 4
8 Apr 65 **AT THE CLUB** *Atlantic AT 4019* **35** 7
29 Apr 65 **COME ON OVER TO MY PLACE** *Atlantic AT 4023* **40** 5
2 Feb 67 **BABY WHAT I MEAN** *Atlantic 584 065* **49** 1
25 Mar 72 ● **AT THE CLUB / SATURDAY NIGHT AT THE MOVIES** (re)
(re-issue) *Atlantic K 10148* **3** 20
26 Aug 72 ● **COME ON OVER TO MY PLACE (re-issue)** *Atlantic K 10216* **9** 11
4 Aug 73 ● **LIKE SISTER AND BROTHER** *Bell 1313* **7** 12
15 Jun 74 ● **KISSIN' IN THE BACK ROW OF THE MOVIES** *Bell 1358* **2** 13
12 Oct 74 ● **DOWN ON THE BEACH TONIGHT** *Bell 1381* **7** 9
8 Feb 75 **LOVE GAMES** *Bell 1396* **33** 6
6 Sep 75 ● **THERE GOES MY FIRST LOVE** *Bell 1433* **3** 12
29 Nov 75 ● **CAN I TAKE YOU HOME LITTLE GIRL** *Bell 1462* **10** 10
13 Mar 76 **HELLO HAPPINESS** *Bell 1469* **12** 8
11 Sep 76 **EVERY NITE'S A SATURDAY NIGHT WITH YOU** *Bell 1491* **29** 7
18 Dec 76 ● **YOU'RE MORE THAN A NUMBER IN MY LITTLE RED BOOK**
Arista 78 ....**5** 12
14 Apr 79 **SAVE THE LAST DANCE FOR ME / WHEN MY LITTLE GIRL IS SMILING (re-issue)** *Lightning LIG 9014* **69** 2
18 May 68 **GOLDEN HITS** *Atlantic 588103* **27** 7
10 Jun 72 **GOLDEN HITS (RE-ISSUE)** *Atlantic K 40018* **26** 8
8 Nov 75 ● **24 ORIGINAL HITS** *Atlantic K 60106* **2** 34
13 Dec 75 **LOVE GAMES** *Bell BELLS 246* **51** 1
18 Oct 86 **THE VERY BEST OF THE DRIFTERS** *Telstar STAR 2280* **24** 15
14 Mar 87 **STAND BY ME (THE ULTIMATE COLLECTION)**
Atlantic WX 90 [1] **14** 8
20 Oct 90 **THE VERY BEST OF BEN E. KING & THE DRIFTERS**
Telstar STAR 2373 [1] **15** 16
7 Nov 98 **THE VERY BEST OF BEN E. KING & THE DRIFTERS**
Warner.ESP/Global TV RADCD 108 [1] **41** 3
17 May 03 ● **THE DEFINITIVE** *Atlantic WSMCD137* **8** 17

[1] Ben E. King & the Drifters

'Saturday Night at the Movies' received chart credit with 'At the Club' only after the re-issue's return to the chart on 8 Apr 1972 The two albums entitled 'The Very Best Of Ben E. King & The Drifters' are different

DRIFTERS – *See SHADOWS*

DRIFTWOOD *Holland, male production trio (Singles: 2 weeks)* pos/wks

1 Feb 03 **FREELOADER** *Positiva CDTIV 185* **32** 2

Julie DRISCOLL, Brian AUGER and the TRINITY *UK, female vocalist / male instrumental group (Singles: 16 weeks, Albums: 13 weeks)* pos/wks

17 Apr 68 ● **THIS WHEEL'S ON FIRE** *Marmalade 598 006* **5** 16
8 Jun 68 **OPEN** *Marmalade 608002* **12** 13

DRIVER 67 *UK, male vocalist – Paul Phillips (Singles: 12 weeks)* pos/wks

23 Dec 78 ● **CAR 67** *Logo GO 336* **7** 12

DRIZABONE *UK / US, male / female vocal / instrumental group (Singles: 18 weeks, Albums: 1 week)* pos/wks

22 Jun 91 **REAL LOVE** *Fourth & Broadway BRW 223* [1] **16** 8
26 Oct 91 **CATCH THE FIRE** *Fourth & Broadway BRW 232* [1] **54** 2
23 Apr 94 **PRESSURE** *Fourth & Broadway BRCD 264* **33** 2
15 Oct 94 **BRIGHTEST STAR** *Fourth & Broadway BRCD 293* **45** 2
4 Mar 95 **REAL LOVE (re-recording)** *Fourth & Broadway BRCD 311* **24** 4
19 Nov 94 **CONSPIRACY** *Fourth & Broadway BRCD 593* **72** 1

[1] Driza Bone

Frank D'RONE *US, male vocalist (Singles: 6 weeks)* pos/wks

22 Dec 60 **STRAWBERRY BLONDE (THE BAND ROCKED ON)**
Mercury AMT 1123 ....**24** 6

DROWNING POOL *US, male vocal / instrumental group (Singles: 3 weeks, Albums: 1 week)* pos/wks

27 Apr 02 **BODIES** *Epic 6723172* **34** 2
10 Aug 02 **TEAR AWAY** *Epic 6729832* **65** 1
16 Feb 02 **SINNER** *Epic 5040912* **70** 1

DRU HILL
US, male vocal group (Singles: 42 weeks, Albums: 7 weeks) pos/wks

15 Feb 97 **TELL ME** *Fourth & Broadway BRCD 342* **30** 3
10 May 97 **IN MY BED** *Fourth & Broadway BRCD 353* **16** 3
11 Oct 97 **BIG BAD MAMMA** *Def Jam 5749792* [1] **12** 3
6 Dec 97 **5 STEPS** *Island Black Music CID 675* **22** 3
24 Oct 98 ● **HOW DEEP IS YOUR LOVE** (re) *Island Black Music CID 725* [2] ..**9** 8
6 Feb 99 ● **THESE ARE THE TIMES** *Island Black Music CID 733* **4** 6
10 Jul 99 ● **WILD WILD WEST** *Columbia 6675962* [3] ▲ **2** 16
7 Nov 98 **ENTER THE DRU** *Island Black Music 5245422* **42** 7

[1] Foxy Brown featuring Dru Hill [2] Dru Hill featuring Redman [3] Will Smith featuring Dru Hill - additional vocals Kool Moe Dee

See also SISQO

DRUGSTORE *UK / US / Brazil, male / female vocal / instrumental group (Singles: 5 weeks, Albums: 3 weeks)* pos/wks

10 Jun 95 **FADER** *Honey HONCD 7* **72** 1
2 May 98 **EL PRESIDENT** *Roadrunner RR 22369* **20** 3
4 Jul 98 **SOBER** *Roadrunner RR22303* **68** 1
8 Apr 95 **DRUGSTORE** *Honey 8286170* **31** 2
16 May 98 **WHITE MAGIC FOR LOVERS** *Roadrunner RR 87112* **45** 1

Additional vocals on 'El President' by Thom Yorke

DRUM CLUB *UK, male instrumental / production duo (Singles: 1 week, Albums: 1 week)* pos/wks

6 Nov 93 **SOUND SYSTEM** *Butterfly BFLD 10* **62** 1
20 Aug 94 **DRUMS ARE DANGEROUS** *Butterfly BFLCD 10* **53** 1

DRUM THEATRE
UK, male vocal / instrumental group (Singles: 8 weeks) pos/wks

15 Feb 86 **LIVING IN THE PAST** *Epic A 6798* **67** 2
17 Jan 87 **ELDORADO** *Epic EMU 1* **44** 6

DRUMSOUND & Simon 'BASSLINE' SMITH *UK, male production duo – Andy Wright and Simon Smith (Singles: 1 week)* pos/wks

26 Jul 03 **JUNGLIST** *Technique TECH 021* **67** 1

DRUNKENMUNKY
Holland, male production group (Singles: 2 weeks) pos/wks

4 Oct 03 **E** *All Around the World CDGLOBE 285* **41** 2

DRUPI *Italy, male vocalist – Giampiero Anelli (Singles: 12 weeks)* pos/wks

1 Dec 73 **VADO VIA** *A&M AMS 7083* **17** 12

DTOX
UK, male / female vocal / instrumental group (Singles: 1 week) pos/wks

21 Nov 92 **SHATTERED GLASS** *Vitality VITal 1* **75** 1

John DU CANN *UK, male vocalist (Singles: 6 weeks)* pos/wks

22 Sep 79 **DON'T BE A DUMMY** *Vertigo 6059 241* **33** 6

John DU PREZ – *See MODERN ROMANCE*

DUB CONSPIRACY – *See TRU FAITH & DUB CONSPIRACY*

DUB PISTOLS
UK, male vocal / instrumental / production group (Singles: 2 weeks) pos/wks

10 Oct 98 **CYCLONE** *CONCRETE HARD 36CD* **63** 1
18 Oct 03 **PROBLEM IS** *Distinctive DISNCD 107* [1] **66** 1

[1] Dub Pistols featuring Terry Hall

DUB WAR *UK, male vocal / instrumental group (Singles: 5 weeks)* pos/wks

3 Jun 95 **STRIKE IT** *Earache MOSH 138CD* **70** 1
27 Jan 96 **ENEMY MAKER** *Earache MOSH 147CD* **41** 2
24 Aug 96 **CRY DIGNITY** *Earache MOSH 163CDD* **59** 1
29 Mar 97 **MILLION DOLLAR LOVE** *Earache MOSH 170CD1* **73** 1

DUBLINERS *Ireland, male vocal / instrumental group (Singles: 45 weeks, Albums: 91 weeks)* pos/wks

30 Mar 67 ● **SEVEN DRUNKEN NIGHTS** *Major Minor MM 506* **7** 17
30 Aug 67 **BLACK VELVET BAND** *Major Minor MM 530* **15** 15
20 Dec 67 **MAIDS, WHEN YOU'RE YOUNG NEVER WED AN OLD MAN** *Major Minor MM 551* **43** 3
28 Mar 87 ● **THE IRISH ROVER** *Stiff BUY 258* [1] **8** 8
16 Jun 90 **JACK'S HEROES / WHISKEY IN THE JAR** *Pogue Mahone YZ 500* [1] **63** 2
13 May 67 ● **A DROP OF THE HARD STUFF** *Major Minor MMLP 3* **5** 41
9 Sep 67 **BEST OF THE DUBLINERS** *Transatlantic TRA 158* **25** 11
7 Oct 67 ● **MORE OF THE HARD STUFF** *Major Minor MMLP 5* **8** 23
2 Mar 68 **DRINKIN' AND COURTIN'** *Major Minor SMLP 14* **31** 3
25 Apr 87 **THE DUBLINERS 25 YEARS CELEBRATION** *Stylus SMR 731* **43** 10
22 Mar 03 **SPIRIT OF THE IRISH** *Sanctuary TVSAN003* **19** 3

[1] Pogues and the Dubliners

DUBSTAR *UK, female / male vocal / instrumental group (Singles: 26 weeks, Albums: 20 weeks)* pos/wks

8 Jul 95 **STARS** *Food CDFOOD 61* **40** 3
30 Sep 95 **ANYWHERE** *Food CDFOOD 67* **37** 3
6 Jan 96 **NOT SO MANIC NOW** *Food CDFOOD 71* **18** 5
30 Mar 96 **STARS (re-issue)** *Food CDFOODS 75* **15** 6
3 Aug 96 **ELEVATOR SONG** *Food CDFOOD 80* **25** 2
19 Jul 97 **NO MORE TALK** *Food CDFOOD 96* **20** 3
20 Sep 97 **CATHEDRAL PARK** *Food CDFOOD 104* **41** 1
7 Feb 98 **I WILL BE YOUR GIRLFRIEND** *Food CDFOODS 108* **28** 2
27 May 00 **I (FRIDAY NIGHT)** *Food CDFOODS 128* **37** 1
21 Oct 95 **DISGRACEFUL** *Food FOODCDX 13* **30** 18
4 Oct 97 **GOODBYE** *Food FOODCD 23* **18** 2

Ricardo 'Rikrok' DUCENT – *See SHAGGY*

Hilary DUFF
US, female vocalist (Singles: 7 weeks, Albums: 1 week) pos/wks

1 Nov 03 ● **SO YESTERDAY** *Hollywood HOL 003CD1* **9** 7
15 Nov 03 **METAMORPHOSIS** *Hollywood 5046692682* ▲ **69** 1

Mary DUFF – *See Daniel O'DONNELL*

DUFFO *Australia, male vocalist (Singles: 2 weeks)* pos/wks

24 Mar 79 **GIVE ME BACK ME BRAIN** *Beggars Banquet BEG 15* **60** 2

Stephen 'Tin Tin' DUFFY
UK, male vocalist (Singles: 24 weeks, Albums: 7 weeks) pos/wks

9 Jul 83 **HOLD IT** *Curve X 9763* [1] **55** 4
2 Mar 85 ● **KISS ME** *10 TIN 2* **4** 11
18 May 85 **ICING ON THE CAKE** *10 TIN 3* **14** 9
20 Apr 85 **THE UPS AND DOWNS** *10 DIX 5* **35** 7

[1] Tin Tin

DUKE *UK, male vocalist (Singles: 6 weeks)* pos/wks

25 May 96 **SO IN LOVE WITH YOU** *Encore CDCOR 009* **66** 1
26 Oct 96 **SO IN LOVE WITH YOU (re-issue)** *Pukka CDPUKKA 11* **22** 4
11 Nov 00 **SO IN LOVE WITH YOU (re-mix)** *48k / Perfecto SPECT 08CDS* **65** 1

George DUKE *US, male vocalist / instrumentalist – keyboards (Singles: 6 weeks, Albums: 4 weeks)* pos/wks

12 Jul 80 **BRAZILIAN LOVE AFFAIR** *Epic EPC 8751* **36** 6
26 Jul 80 **BRAZILIAN LOVE AFFAIR** *Epic EPC 84311* **33** 4

DUKES
UK, male vocal duo (Singles: 13 weeks) pos/wks

17 Oct 81 **MYSTERY GIRL** *WEA K 18867* **47** 7
1 May 82 **THANK YOU FOR THE PARTY** *WEA K 19136* **53** 6

DUKES – *See Steve EARLE*

Candy DULFER *Holland, female instrumentalist – saxophone (Singles: 14 weeks, Albums: 11 weeks)* pos/wks

24 Feb 90 ● **LILY WAS HERE** *RCA ZB 43045* [1] **6** 12
4 Aug 90 **SAXUALITY** *RCA PB 43769* **60** 2
18 Aug 90 **SAXUALITY** *RCA PL 74661* **27** 9
13 Mar 93 **SAX-A-GO-GO** *Ariola 4321111812* **56** 2

[1] David A Stewart featuring Candy Dulfer

DUM DUMS *UK, male vocal / instrumental group (Singles: 15 weeks, Albums: 2 weeks)* pos/wks

11 Mar 00 **EVERYTHING** *Good Behavior CDGOOD 1* **21** 5
8 Jul 00 **CAN'T GET YOU OUT OF MY THOUGHTS** *Good Behaviour GD GOOD 2* **18** 5
23 Sep 00 **YOU DO SOMETHING TO ME** *Good Behaviour CD GOLD 3* **27** 3
17 Feb 01 **ARMY OF TWO** *Good Behaviour CDGOOD 5* **27** 2
30 Sep 00 **IT GOES WITHOUT SAYING** *Good Behaviour CDGOOD 4* **27** 2

Thuli DUMAKUDE *South Africa, female vocalist (Singles: 1 week)* pos/wks

2 Jan 88 **THE FUNERAL (SEPTEMBER 25, 1977)** *MCA MCA 1228* **75** 1

The listed flip side of 'The Funeral' was 'Cry Freedom' by George Fenton and Jonas Gwangwa

John DUMMER and Helen APRIL

UK, male / female vocal duo (Singles: 3 weeks) pos/wks

Date		Title / Label	pos	wks
28 Aug 82		**BLUE SKIES** *Speed SPEED 8*	54	3

DUMONDE

Germany, male / female production / vocal group (Singles: 3 weeks) pos/wks

Date		Title / Label	pos	wks
27 Jan 01		**TOMORROW** *Variation VART 6*	60	1
19 May 01		**NEVER LOOK BACK** *Manifesto FESCD 83*	36	2

DUNBLANE

UK, male / female vocal / instrumental group (Singles: 15 weeks) pos/wks

Date		Title / Label	pos	wks
21 Dec 96	★	**KNOCKIN' ON HEAVEN'S DOOR / THROW THESE GUNS AWAY** *BMG 74321442182* ■	1	15

DUNCAN – *See PJ & DUNCAN*

Johnny DUNCAN and the BLUE GRASS BOYS

US, male vocalist (d. 15 Jul 2000) and UK, instrumental group (Singles: 20 weeks) pos/wks

Date		Title / Label	pos	wks
26 Jul 57	●	**LAST TRAIN TO SAN FERNANDO** *Columbia DB 3959*	2	17
25 Oct 57		**BLUE, BLUE HEARTACHES** *Columbia DB 3996*	27	1
29 Nov 57		**FOOTPRINTS IN THE SNOW (re)** *Columbia DB 4029*	27	2

David DUNDAS

UK, male vocalist (Singles: 14 weeks) pos/wks

Date		Title / Label	pos	wks
24 Jul 76	●	**JEANS ON** *Air CHS 2094*	3	9
9 Apr 77		**ANOTHER FUNNY HONEYMOON** *Air CHS 2136*	29	5

Errol DUNKLEY

Jamaica, male vocalist (Singles: 14 weeks) pos/wks

Date		Title / Label	pos	wks
22 Sep 79		**O.K. FRED** *Scope SC 6*	11	11
2 Feb 80		**SIT DOWN AND CRY** *Scope SC 11*	52	3

Clive DUNN

UK, male actor / vocalist (Singles: 28 weeks) pos/wks

Date		Title / Label	pos	wks
28 Nov 70	★	**GRANDAD (re)** *Columbia DB 8726*	1	28

Simon DUPREE and the BIG SOUND

UK, male vocal / instrumental group (Singles: 16 weeks, Albums: 1 week) pos/wks

Date		Title / Label	pos	wks
22 Nov 67	●	**KITES** *Parlophone R 5646*	9	13
3 Apr 68		**FOR WHOM THE BELL TOLLS** *Parlophone R 5670*	43	3
16 Aug 67		**WITHOUT RESERVATIONS** *Parlophone PCS 7029*	39	1

DURAN DURAN (54 Top 500)

New Romantics turned teen idols: Simon Le Bon (v), Nick Rhodes (k), John Taylor (b), Andy Taylor (g), Roger Taylor (d). The Birmingham band's successive Top 10 hits included 'A View to a Kill', the best-selling James Bond theme ever in the UK and the US. The three Taylors were unrelated (Singles: 222 weeks, Albums: 401 weeks) pos/wks

Date		Title / Label	pos	wks
21 Feb 81		**PLANET EARTH** *EMI 5137*	12	11
9 May 81		**CARELESS MEMORIES** *EMI 5168*	37	7
25 Jul 81	●	**GIRLS ON FILM** *EMI 5206*	5	11
28 Nov 81		**MY OWN WAY** *EMI 5254*	14	11
15 May 82	●	**HUNGRY LIKE THE WOLF** *EMI 5295*	5	12
21 Aug 82	●	**SAVE A PRAYER** *EMI 5327*	2	9
13 Nov 82	●	**RIO** *EMI 5346*	9	11
26 Mar 83	★	**IS THERE SOMETHING I SHOULD KNOW?** *EMI 5371* ■	1	9
29 Oct 83	●	**UNION OF THE SNAKE (re)** *EMI 5429*	3	11
4 Feb 84	●	**NEW MOON ON MONDAY** *EMI DURAN 1*	9	7
28 Apr 84	★	**THE REFLEX** *EMI DURAN 2* ▲	1	14
3 Nov 84	●	**THE WILD BOYS** *Parlophone DURAN 3*	2	14
18 May 85	●	**A VIEW TO A KILL** *Parlophone DURAN 007* ▲	2	16
1 Nov 86	●	**NOTORIOUS (re)** *EMI DDN 45*	7	7
21 Feb 87		**SKIN TRADE** *EMI TRADE 1*	22	6
25 Apr 87		**MEET EL PRESIDENTE** *EMI TOUR 1*	24	5
1 Oct 88		**I DON'T WANT YOUR LOVE** *EMI YOUR 1*	14	5
7 Jan 89	●	**ALL SHE WANTS IS** *EMI DD 11*	9	5
22 Apr 89		**DO YOU BELIEVE IN SHAME?** *EMI DD 12*	30	4
16 Dec 89		**BURNING THE GROUND** *EMI DD 13*	31	5
4 Aug 90		**VIOLENCE OF SUMMER (LOVE'S TAKING OVER)** *Parlophone DD 14*	20	4
17 Nov 90		**SERIOUS** *Parlophone DD 15*	48	3
30 Jan 93	●	**ORDINARY WORLD** *Parlophone CDDDS 16*	6	9
10 Apr 93		**COME UNDONE** *Parlophone CDDDS 17*	13	8
4 Sep 93		**TOO MUCH INFORMATION** *Parlophone CDDDS 18*	35	3
25 Mar 95		**PERFECT DAY** *Parlophone CDDDS 20*	28	4
17 Jun 95		**WHITE LINES (DON'T DO IT)** *Parlophone CDDD 19* [1]	17	5
24 May 97		**OUT OF MY MIND** *Virgin VSCDT 1639*	21	2
30 Jan 99		**ELECTRIC BARBARELLA** *EMI CDELEC 2000*	23	3
10 Jun 00		**SOMEONE ELSE NOT ME** *Hollywood / Edel 0108845 HWR*	53	1
27 Jun 81	●	**DURAN DURAN** *EMI EMC 3372*	3	118
22 May 82	●	**RIO** *EMI EMC 3411*	2	109
3 Dec 83	★	**SEVEN AND THE RAGGED TIGER** *EMI DD 1* ■	1	47
24 Nov 84	●	**ARENA** *Parlophone DD 2*	6	31
6 Dec 86		**NOTORIOUS** *EMI DDN 331*	16	16
29 Oct 88		**BIG THING** *EMI DDB 33*	15	5
25 Nov 89	●	**DECADE** *EMI DDX 10*	5	16
1 Sep 90	●	**LIBERTY** *Parlophone PCSD 112*	8	4
27 Feb 93	●	**DURAN DURAN (THE WEDDING ALBUM)** *Parlophone CDDB 34*	4	23
8 Apr 95		**THANK YOU** *Parlophone CDDDB 36*	12	3
21 Nov 98		**GREATEST** *EMI 4962392*	15	27
27 Mar 99		**STRANGE BEHAVIOUR** *EMI 4939722*	70	1
1 Jul 00		**POP TRASH** *Hollywood 0107512 HWR*	53	1

[1] Duran Duran featuring Melle Mel and Grandmaster Flash and the Furious Five

Group was UK / US from 1989 and were billed as Duranduran on EMI DDB 33

See also ARCADIA; POWER STATION

Jimmy DURANTE

US, male vocalist / comedian, d. 29 Jan 1980 (Singles: 1 week) pos/wks

Date		Title / Label	pos	wks
14 Dec 96		**MAKE SOMEONE HAPPY** *Warner Bros. W 0385CD*	69	1

Deanna DURBIN

Canada, female vocalist (Albums: 4 weeks) pos/wks

Date		Title / Label	pos	wks
30 Jan 82		**THE BEST OF DEANNA DURBIN** *MCA International MCL 1634*	84	4

Judith DURHAM

Australia, female vocalist (Singles: 5 weeks, Albums: 16 weeks) pos/wks

Date		Title / Label	pos	wks
15 Jun 67		**THE OLIVE TREE** *Columbia DB 8207*	33	5
23 Apr 94	●	**A CARNIVAL OF HITS** *EMI CDEMTV 83* [1]	7	14
30 Mar 96		**MONA LISAS** *EMI Premier CDJDTV 1*	46	2

[1] Judith Durham and the Seekers

See also SEEKERS

Ian DURY and the BLOCKHEADS (373 Top 500)

Art college lecturer turned witty vocalist / songwriter, b. 12 May 1942, Billericay, Essex; d. 27 Mar 2000. Ex-Kilburn and the High Roads member (1970-76) played final show at the prestigious London Palladium. A 2001 tribute album included Paul McCartney and Robbie Williams (Singles: 56 weeks, Albums: 123 weeks) pos/wks

Date		Title / Label	pos	wks
29 Apr 78	●	**WHAT A WASTE!** *Stiff BUY 27*	9	12
9 Dec 78	★	**HIT ME WITH YOUR RHYTHM STICK** *Stiff BUY 38* [1]	1	15
4 Aug 79	●	**REASONS TO BE CHEERFUL (PT. 3)** *Stiff BUY 50*	3	8
30 Aug 80		**I WANT TO BE STRAIGHT** *Stiff BUY 90*	22	7
15 Nov 80		**SUPERMAN'S BIG SISTER** *Stiff BUY 100*	51	3
25 May 85		**HIT ME WITH YOUR RHYTHM STICK (re-mix)** *Stiff BUY 214*	55	4
26 Oct 85		**PROFOUNDLY IN LOVE WITH PANDORA** *EMI EMI 5534* [2]	45	5
27 Jul 91		**HIT ME WITH YOUR RHYTHM STICK '91** *Flying FLYR 1*	73	1
11 Mar 00		**DRIP FED FRED** *Virgin VSCDT 1768* [3]	55	1
22 Oct 77	●	**NEW BOOTS AND PANTIES!!** *Stiff SEEZ 4* [1]	5	90
2 Jun 79	●	**DO IT YOURSELF** *Stiff SEEZ 14*	2	18
6 Dec 80		**LAUGHTER** *Stiff SEEZ 30*	48	4
10 Oct 81		**LORD UPMINSTER** *Polydor POLD 5042*	53	4
4 Feb 84		**4000 WEEKS HOLIDAY** *Polydor POLD 5112* [2]	54	2
11 Jul 98		**MR LOVE PANTS** *Ronnie Harris DUR 1*	57	2
9 Oct 99		**REASONS TO BE CHEERFUL – THE VERY BEST OF IAN DURY AND THE BLOCKHEADS** *EMI 5228882*	40	2
30 Mar 02		**TEN MORE TURNIPS FROM THE TIP** *Ronnie Harris DUR 2*	60	1

[1] Ian and the Blockheads [2] Ian Dury [3] Madness featuring Ian Dury
[1] Ian Dury [2] Ian Dury and the Music Students

See also HATFIELD and THE NORTH

DUST BROTHERS

US, male production duo (Singles: 1 week) pos/wks

11 Dec 99	**THIS IS YOUR LIFE** *Restless 74321713962*	**60**	1

DUST JUNKYS *UK, male vocal / instrumental /group (Singles: 5 weeks, Albums: 2 weeks)* pos/wks

15 Nov 97	**(NONSTOPOPERATION)** *Polydor 5719732*	**47**	2
28 Feb 98	**WHAT TIME IS IT?** *Polydor 5694912*	**39**	2
16 May 98	**NOTHIN' PERSONAL** *Polydor 5699092*	**62**	1
21 Mar 98	**DONE AND DUSTED** *Polydor 5570432*	**35**	2

DUSTED *UK, male production / instrumental duo – Roland Armstrong and Mark Bates (Singles: 2 weeks)* pos/wks

20 Jan 01	**ALWAYS REMEMBER TO RESPECT AND HONOUR YOUR MOTHER PART ONE** *Go! Beat / Polydor GOBCD 36*	**31**	2

Vocal by 12-year-old choirboy Alan Young

See also FAITHLESS; OUR TRIBE / ONE TRIBE; ROLLO; SPHINX

Slim DUSTY *Australia, male vocalist – David Kirkpatrick D. 19 Sep 2003 (Singles: 15 weeks)* pos/wks

30 Jan 59 ●	**A PUB WITH NO BEER** *Columbia DB 4212* [1]	**3**	15

[1] Slim Dusty with Dick Carr and his Bushlanders

DUTCH FORCE

Holland, male producer – Benno De Goeij (Singles: 2 weeks) pos/wks

6 May 00	**DEADLINE** *Inferno CDFERN 27*	**35**	2

Ondrea DUVERN – *See HUSTLERS CONVENTION featuring Dave LAUDAT and Ondrea DUVERNEY*

DWEEB

UK, male / female vocal / instrumental trio (Singles: 2 weeks) pos/wks

22 Feb 97	**SCOOBY DOO** *Blanco Y Negro NEG 100CD*	**63**	1
7 Jun 97	**OH YEAH, BABY** *Blanco Y Negro NEG 102CD1*	**70**	1

Sarah DWYER – *See LANGE*

Bob DYLAN (32 Top 500)

The most influential folk / rock vocalist / guitarist ever, b. Robert Zimmerman, 24 May 1941, Minnesota, US. The legendary performer, who led the 1960s folk music movement, redefined the term and, indeed, image of the singer / songwriter. He was still adding to his impressive tally of Top 5 UK and US albums in 2002 (Singles: 137 weeks, Albums: 614 weeks) pos/wks

25 Mar 65 ●	**TIMES THEY ARE A-CHANGIN'** *CBS 201751*	**9**	11
29 Apr 65 ●	**SUBTERRANEAN HOMESICK BLUES** *CBS 201753*	**9**	9
17 Jun 65	**MAGGIE'S FARM** *CBS 201781*	**22**	8
19 Aug 65 ●	**LIKE A ROLLING STONE** *CBS 201811*	**4**	12
28 Oct 65 ●	**POSITIVELY 4TH STREET** *CBS 201824*	**8**	12
27 Jan 66	**CAN YOU PLEASE CRAWL OUT YOUR WINDOW** *CBS 201900*	**17**	5
14 Apr 66	**ONE OF US MUST KNOW (SOONER OR LATER)** *CBS 202053*	**33**	5
12 May 66 ●	**RAINY DAY WOMEN NOS. 12 & 35** *CBS 202307*	**7**	8
21 Jul 66	**I WANT YOU** *CBS 202258*	**16**	9
14 May 69	**I THREW IT ALL AWAY** *CBS 4219*	**30**	6
13 Sep 69 ●	**LAY LADY LAY** *CBS 4434*	**5**	12
10 Jul 71	**WATCHING THE RIVER FLOW** *CBS 7329*	**24**	9
6 Oct 73	**KNOCKIN' ON HEAVEN'S DOOR** *CBS 1762*	**14**	9
7 Feb 76	**HURRICANE** *CBS 3878*	**43**	4
29 Jul 78	**BABY STOP CRYING** *CBS 6499*	**13**	11
28 Oct 78	**IS YOUR LOVE IN VAIN** *CBS 6718*	**56**	3
20 May 95	**DIGNITY** *Columbia 6620762*	**33**	2
11 Jul 98	**LOVE SICK** *Columbia 6659972*	**64**	1
14 Oct 00	**THINGS HAVE CHANGED** *Columbia 6693792*	**58**	1
23 May 64 ★	**THE FREEWHEELIN' BOB DYLAN** *CBS BPG 62193*	**1**	49
11 Jul 64 ●	**THE TIMES THEY ARE A-CHANGIN'** *CBS BPG 62251*	**4**	20
21 Nov 64 ●	**ANOTHER SIDE OF BOB DYLAN** *CBS BPG 62429*	**8**	19
8 May 65	**BOB DYLAN** *CBS BPG 62022*	**13**	6
15 May 65 ★	**BRINGING IT ALL BACK HOME** *CBS BPG 62515*	**1**	29
9 Oct 65 ●	**HIGHWAY 61 REVISITED** *CBS BPG 62572*	**4**	15
20 Aug 66 ●	**BLONDE ON BLONDE** *CBS DDP 66012*	**3**	15
14 Jan 67 ●	**GREATEST HITS** *CBS SBPG 62847*	**6**	82
2 Mar 68 ★	**JOHN WESLEY HARDING** *CBS SBPG 63252*	**1**	29
17 May 69 ★	**NASHVILLE SKYLINE** *CBS 63601*	**1**	42
11 Jul 70 ★	**SELF PORTRAIT** *CBS 66250* ■	**1**	15
28 Nov 70 ★	**NEW MORNING** *CBS 69001* ■	**1**	11
25 Dec 71	**MORE BOB DYLAN GREATEST HITS** *CBS 67238/9*	**12**	15
29 Sep 73	**PAT GARRETT & BILLY THE KID (FILM SOUNDTRACK)** *CBS 69042*	**29**	11
23 Feb 74 ●	**PLANET WAVES** *Island ILPS 9261* ▲	**7**	8
13 Jul 74 ●	**BEFORE THE FLOOD** *Asylum IDBD 1*	**8**	7
15 Feb 75 ●	**BLOOD ON THE TRACKS** *CBS 69097* ▲	**4**	16
26 Jul 75 ●	**THE BASEMENT TAPES** *CBS 88147*	**8**	10
31 Jan 76 ●	**DESIRE** *CBS 86003* ▲	**3**	35
9 Oct 76 ●	**HARD RAIN** *CBS 86016*	**3**	7
1 Jul 78 ●	**STREET LEGAL** *CBS 86067*	**2**	20
26 May 79 ●	**BOB DYLAN AT BUDOKAN** *CBS 96004*	**4**	19
8 Sep 79 ●	**SLOW TRAIN COMING** *CBS 86095*	**2**	13
28 Jun 80 ●	**SAVED** *CBS 86113*	**3**	8
29 Aug 81 ●	**SHOT OF LOVE** *CBS 85178*	**6**	8
12 Nov 83 ●	**INFIDELS** *CBS 25539*	**9**	12
15 Dec 84	**REAL LIVE** *CBS 26334*	**54**	2
22 Jun 85	**EMPIRE BURLESQUE** *CBS 86313*	**11**	6
2 Aug 86	**KNOCKED OUT LOADED** *CBS 86326*	**35**	5
23 Apr 88	**GREATEST HITS VOLUME 3** *CBS 460907 1*	**47**	3
25 Jun 88	**DOWN IN THE GROOVE** *CBS 460267 1*	**32**	3
18 Feb 89	**DYLAN AND THE DEAD** *CBS 463381 1* [1]	**38**	3
14 Oct 89 ●	**OH MERCY** *CBS 465800 1*	**6**	7
22 Sep 90	**UNDER THE RED SKY** *CBS 4671881*	**13**	3
13 Apr 91	**THE BOOTLEG SERIES VOLUMES 1-3** *Columbia 4680861*	**32**	5
14 Nov 92	**GOOD AS I BEEN TO YOU** *Columbia 4727102*	**18**	3
20 Nov 93	**WORLD GONE WRONG** *Columbia 474 8572*	**35**	2
29 Apr 95 ●	**UNPLUGGED** *Columbia 4783742*	**10**	5
14 Jun 97 ●	**THE BEST OF BOB DYLAN** *Columbia SONYTV 28CD*	**6**	18
11 Oct 97 ●	**TIME OUT OF MIND** *Columbia 4869362*	**10**	6
24 Oct 98	**LIVE AT THE ROYAL ALBERT HALL** *Legacy 4914852*	**19**	2
20 May 00	**THE BEST OF BOB DYLAN – VOLUME 2** *Columbia 4983612*	**22**	2
2 Jun 01 ●	**THE ESSENTIAL BOB DYLAN** *Columbia STVCD 116*	**9**	12
22 Sep 01 ●	**LOVE AND THEFT** *Columbia 5043642*	**3**	5
7 Dec 02	**LIVE 1975 – THE ROLLING THUNDER REVUE** *Columbia 5101403*	**69**	1

[1] Bob Dylan and the Grateful Dead

See also TRAVELING WILBURYS

DYNAMITE MC & ORIGIN UNKNOWN

UK, male rapper – Dominic Smith, and production duo (Singles: 1 week) pos/wks

20 Sep 03	**HOTNESS** *Ram RAMM 45*	**66**	1

DYNAMIX II featuring TOO TOUGH TEE

US, male vocal / instrumental group and rapper (Singles: 4 weeks) pos/wks

8 Aug 87	**JUST GIVE THE DJ A BREAK** *Cooltempo COOL 151*	**50**	4

DYNASTY

US, male / female vocal / instrumental group (Singles: 20 weeks) pos/wks

13 Oct 79	**I DON'T WANT TO BE A FREAK (BUT I CAN'T HELP MYSELF)** *Solar FB 1694*	**20**	13
9 Aug 80	**I'VE JUST BEGUN TO LOVE YOU** *Solar SO 10*	**51**	4
21 May 83	**DOES THAT RING A BELL** *Solar E 9911*	**53**	3

Ronnie DYSON

US, male vocalist, d. 10 Nov 1990 (Singles: 6 weeks) pos/wks

4 Dec 71	**WHEN YOU GET RIGHT DOWN TO IT** *CBS 7449*	**34**	6

Katherine E
US, female vocalist (Singles: 7 weeks) pos/wks

6 Apr 91	**I'M ALRIGHT** *Dead Dead Good GOOD 2*	41	5
18 Jan 92	**THEN I FEEL GOOD** *PWL Continental PWL 13*	56	2

Lizz E – *See FRESH 4 featuring Lizz E*

Sheila E
US, female vocalist / instrumentalist – percussion – Sheila Escovedo (Singles: 9 weeks) pos/wks

23 Feb 85	**THE BELLE OF ST MARK** *Warner Bros. W 9180*	18	9

E-LUSTRIOUS
UK, male instrumental / production duo – Mike Kirwin and Danny Bennett (Singles: 2 weeks) pos/wks

15 Feb 92	**DANCE NO MORE** *MOS MOS 001T* [1]	58	1
2 Jul 94	**IN YOUR DANCE** *UFG UFG 6CD*	69	1

[1] E-Lustrious featuring Deborah French

See also DIRECKT

E-MALE
UK, male vocal / instrumental group (Singles: 1 week) pos/wks

31 Jan 98	**WE ARE E-MALE** *East West EW 137CD*	44	1

E-MAN – *See Jon CUTLER featuring E-MAN*

EMF
UK, male vocal / instrumental group (Singles: 50 weeks, Albums: 22 weeks) pos/wks

3 Nov 90	● **UNBELIEVABLE** *Parlophone R 6273* ▲	3	13
2 Feb 91	● **I BELIEVE** *Parlophone R 6279*	6	7
27 Apr 91	**CHILDREN** *Parlophone R 6288*	19	5
31 Aug 91	**LIES** *Parlophone R 6295*	28	3
2 May 92	**UNEXPLAINED (EP)** *Parlophone SGE 2026*	18	4
19 Sep 92	**THEY'RE HERE** *Parlophone R 6321*	29	3
21 Nov 92	**IT'S YOU** *Parlophone R 6327*	23	3
25 Feb 95	**PERFECT DAY** *Parlophone CDRS 6401*	27	3
8 Jul 95	● **I'M A BELIEVER** *Parlophone CDR 6412* [1]	3	8
28 Oct 95	**AFRO KING** *Parlophone CDRS 6416*	51	1
18 May 91	● **SCHUBERT DIP** *Parlophone PCS 7353*	3	19
10 Oct 92	**STIGMA** *Parlophone CDPCSD 122*	19	2
18 Mar 95	**CHA CHA CHA** *Parlophone CDPCSD 165*	30	1

[1] EMF and Reeves and Mortimer

Tracks on Unexplained (EP): Getting Through / Far From Me / The Same / Search and Destroy

E-MOTION
UK, male vocal / instrumental duo – Alan Angus and Justin Oliver (Singles: 7 weeks) pos/wks

3 Feb 96	**THE NAUGHTY NORTH AND THE SEXY SOUTH** *Soundproof MCSTD 40017*	20	3
17 Aug 96	**I STAND ALONE** *Soundproof MCSTD 40061*	60	1
26 Oct 96	**THE NAUGHTY NORTH AND THE SEXY SOUTH (re-mix)** *Soundproof MCSTD 40076*	17	3

EPMD
US, male rap / DJ duo (Singles: 1 week, Albums: 1 week) pos/wks

15 Aug 98	**STRICTLY BUSINESS** *Parlophone CDR 6502* [1]	43	1
16 Feb 91	**BUSINESS AS USUAL** *Def Jam 4676971*	69	1

[1] Kurtis Mantronik vs EPMD

E-ROTIC
Germany / US, male / female vocal / instrumental group (Singles: 2 weeks) pos/wks

3 Jun 95	**MAX DON'T HAVE SEX WITH YOUR EX** *Stip CDSTIP 2*	45	2

E-SMOOVE featuring Latanza WATERS
US, male producer – Eric Miller and and US, female vocalist (Singles: 1 week) pos/wks

15 Aug 98	**DEJA VU** *AM:PM 5827671*	63	1

See also THICK D; PRAISE CATS

E STREET BAND – *See Bruce SPRINGSTEEN*

E-TRAX
Germany, male production duo (Singles: 1 week) pos/wks

9 Jun 01	**LET'S ROCK** *Tidy Trax TIDY 155CD*	60	1

E-TYPE
Sweden, male vocalist (Singles: 2 weeks) pos/wks

23 Sep 95	**THIS IS THE WAY** *Ffrreedom TABCD 237*	53	1
24 Jun 00	**CAMPIONE 2000** *Polydor 1580822*	58	1

E.U. – *See SALT-N-PEPA*

EYC
US, male vocal group (Singles: 36 weeks, Albums: 5 weeks) pos/wks

11 Dec 93	**FEELIN' ALRIGHT** *MCA MCSTD 1952*	16	8
5 Mar 94	**THE WAY YOU WORK IT** *MCA MCSTD 1963*	14	7
14 May 94	**NUMBER ONE** *MCA MCSTD 1976*	27	5
30 Jul 94	**BLACK BOOK** *MCA MCSTD 1987*	13	6
10 Dec 94	**ONE MORE CHANCE** *MCA MCSTD 2025*	25	6
23 Sep 95	**OOH-AH-AA (I FEEL IT)** *Gasoline Alley MCSTD 2096*	33	2
2 Dec 95	**IN THE BEGINNING** *Gasoline Alley MCSTD 2107*	41	2
16 Apr 94	**EXPRESS YOURSELF CLEARLY** *MCA MCD 11061*	14	5

E-Z ROLLERS
UK, male / female vocal / instrumental group (Singles: 4 weeks) pos/wks

24 Apr 99	**WALK THIS LAND** *Moving Shadow 130CD1*	18	3
8 Feb 03	**BACK TO LOVE** *Moving Shadow 159CD*	61	1

E-ZEE POSSEE
UK, male / female vocal / instrumental group (Singles: 16 weeks) pos/wks

26 Aug 89	**EVERYTHING STARTS WITH AN 'E' (re)** *More Protein PROT 1*	15	9
20 Jan 90	**LOVE ON LOVE** *More Protein PROT 3* [1]	59	3
30 Jun 90	**THE SUN MACHINE** *More Protein PROT 4*	62	3
21 Sep 91	**BREATHING IS E-ZEE** *More Protein PROT 12* [2]	72	1

[1] E-Zee Possee With Dr Mouthquake [2] E-Zee Possee featuring Tara Newley

'Everything Starts with an 'E' did not reach its peak position until it re-entered in Mar 1990

EAGLES
(79 Top 500) *Legendary west coast rock group, which includes Glenn Frey (v/g), Don Henley (v/d) and Joe Walsh (v/g), all successful solo artists in their own right. America's biggest-selling album group disbanded in 1982, but reunited recently for very successful tours. No album in the US has outsold 'Their Greatest Hits 1971-1975' (27 million) (Singles: 52 weeks, Albums: 437 weeks)* pos/wks

9 Aug 75	**ONE OF THESE NIGHTS** *Asylum AYM 543* ▲	23	7
1 Nov 75	**LYIN' EYES** *Asylum AYM 548*	23	7

Date		Title / Label	Pos	Wks
6 Mar 76		**TAKE IT TO THE LIMIT** *Asylum K 13029*	12	7
15 Jan 77		**NEW KID IN TOWN** *Asylum K 13069* ▲	20	7
16 Apr 77	●	**HOTEL CALIFORNIA** *Asylum K 13079* ▲	8	10
16 Dec 78		**PLEASE COME HOME FOR CHRISTMAS** *Asylum K 13145*	30	5
13 Oct 79		**HEARTACHE TONIGHT** *Asylum K 12394* ▲	40	5
1 Dec 79		**THE LONG RUN** *Elektra K 12404*	66	2
13 Jul 96		**LOVE WILL KEEP US ALIVE** *Geffen GFSTD 21980*	52	1
25 Oct 03		**HOLE IN THE WORLD** *Eagles 8122745472*	69	1
27 Apr 74		**ON THE BORDER** *Asylum SYL 9016*	28	9
12 Jul 75	●	**ONE OF THESE NIGHTS** *Asylum SYLA 8759* ▲	8	41
12 Jul 75		**DESPERADO** *Asylum SYLL 9011*	39	9
6 Mar 76	●	**THEIR GREATEST HITS 1971-1975** *Asylum K 53017* ▲	2	77
25 Dec 76	●	**HOTEL CALIFORNIA** *Asylum K 53051* ▲	2	70
13 Oct 79	●	**THE LONG RUN** *Asylum K 52181* ▲	4	16
22 Nov 80		**LIVE** *Asylum K 62032*	24	13
18 May 85	●	**THE BEST OF EAGLES** *Asylum EKT 5*	8	74
23 Jul 94	●	**THE VERY BEST OF THE EAGLES** *Elektra 9548323752*	4	55
19 Nov 94		**HELL FREEZES OVER** *Geffen GED 24725* ▲	18	21
9 Jun 01	●	**THE VERY BEST OF THE EAGLES** *Elektra 7559626802*	3	48
1 Nov 03		**THE COMPLETE GREATEST HITS** *WSM 8122737312*	27	4

Robert EARL *UK, male vocalist – Brian Budge (Singles: 27 weeks)* pos/wks

Date		Title / Label	Pos	Wks
25 Apr 58		**I MAY NEVER PASS THIS WAY AGAIN** *Philips PB 805*	14	13
24 Oct 58		**MORE THAN EVER (COME PRIMA) (re)** *Philips PB 867*	26	4
13 Feb 59		**THE WONDERFUL SECRET OF LOVE** *Philips PB 891*	17	10

Charles EARLAND *US, male instrumentalist – keyboards, d. 11 Dec 1999 (Singles: 5 weeks)* pos/wks

Date		Title / Label	Pos	Wks
19 Aug 78		**LET THE MUSIC PLAY** *Mercury 6167 703*	46	5

Steve EARLE *US, male vocalist / instrumentalist – guitar (Singles: 7 weeks, Albums: 21 weeks)* pos/wks

Date		Title / Label	Pos	Wks
15 Oct 88		**COPPERHEAD ROAD** *MCA MCA 1280*	45	6
31 Dec 88		**JOHNNY COME LATELY** *MCA MCA 1301*	75	1
4 Jul 87		**EXIT 0** *MCA MCF 3379*	77	2
19 Nov 88		**COPPERHEAD ROAD** *MCA MCF 3426*	42	8
7 Jul 90		**THE HARD WAY** *MCA MCG 6095* [1]	22	4
19 Oct 91		**SHUT UP AND DIE LIKE AN AVIATOR** *MCA MCA 10315* [1]	62	1
23 Mar 96		**I FEEL ALRIGHT** *Transatlantic TRACD 227*	44	3
18 Oct 97		**EL COROZON** *Warner Bros. 9362467892*	59	1
6 Mar 99		**THE MOUNTAIN** *Grapevine GRACD 252* [2]	51	1
17 Jun 00		**TRANSCENDENTAL BLUES** *Epic 4980749*	32	1

[1] Steve Earle and the Dukes [2] Steve Earle and the Del McCoury Band

See also Del McCOURY BAND

EARLY MUSIC CONSORT directed by David MUNROW *UK, male / female instrumental group (Singles: 1 week)* pos/wks

Date		Title / Label	Pos	Wks
3 Apr 71		**HENRY VIII SUITE (EP)** *BBC RESL 1*	49	1

Tracks on Henry VIII Suite (EP): Fanfare, Passomezo du Roy, Gaillarde d'Éscosse / Pavane, Mille Ducats / Larocque Gaillarde / Allemande / Wedding March, La Mourisque / If Love Now Reigned / Ronde, Pourquoi

EARTH WIND AND FIRE (195 Top 500)

Colourful, mystical, Los Angeles-based group noted for flamboyant stage performances. Formed by Maurice White (d/v) and included Philip Bailey (v), Ronnie Laws (s/fl) and Verdine White (b). Few R&B acts outsold them in the late 1970s, when they achieved eight successive US Top 10 albums (Singles: 128 weeks, Albums: 167 weeks) pos/wks

Date		Title / Label	Pos	Wks
12 Feb 77		**SATURDAY NITE** *CBS 4835*	17	9
11 Feb 78		**FANTASY** *CBS 6056*	14	10
13 May 78		**JUPITER** *CBS 6267*	41	5
29 Jul 78		**MAGIC MIND (re)** *CBS 6490*	54	5
7 Oct 78		**GOT TO GET YOU INTO MY LIFE** *CBS 6553*	33	7
9 Dec 78	●	**SEPTEMBER** *CBS 6922*	3	13
12 May 79	●	**BOOGIE WONDERLAND** *CBS 7292* [1]	4	13
28 Jul 79	●	**AFTER THE LOVE HAS GONE** *CBS 7721*	4	10
6 Oct 79		**STAR** *CBS 7902*	16	8
15 Dec 79		**CAN'T LET GO** *CBS 8077*	46	7
8 Mar 80		**IN THE STONE** *CBS 8252*	53	3
11 Oct 80		**LET ME TALK** *CBS 8982*	29	5
20 Dec 80		**BACK ON THE ROAD** *CBS 9377*	63	4
7 Nov 81	●	**LET'S GROOVE** *CBS A 1679*	3	13
6 Feb 82		**I'VE HAD ENOUGH** *CBS A 1959*	29	6
5 Feb 83		**FALL IN LOVE WITH ME** *CBS A 2927*	47	4
7 Nov 87		**SYSTEM OF SURVIVAL** *CBS EWF 1*	54	3
31 Jul 99		**SEPTEMBER (re-mix)** *INCredible INCR 24CD*	25	3
21 Jan 78		**ALL 'N' ALL** *CBS 86051*	13	23
16 Dec 78	●	**THE BEST OF EARTH WIND AND FIRE VOLUME 1** *CBS 83284*	6	42
23 Jun 79	●	**I AM** *CBS 86084*	5	41
1 Nov 80	●	**FACES** *CBS 88498*	10	6
14 Nov 81		**RAISE!** *CBS 85272*	14	22
19 Feb 83		**POWERLIGHT** *CBS 25120*	22	7
10 May 86	●	**THE COLLECTION** *K-Tel NE 1322*	5	13
28 Nov 92		**THE VERY BEST OF EARTH WIND AND FIRE** *Telstar TCD 2631*	40	6
28 Sep 96		**BOOGIE WONDERLAND – THE VERY BEST OF EARTH WIND AND FIRE** *Telstar TCD 2879*	29	4
7 Aug 99		**THE ULTIMATE COLLECTION** *Columbia SONYTV 66CD*	34	3

[1] Earth Wind and Fire with The Emotions

EARTHLING *UK, male vocal / instrumental duo (Singles: 2 weeks, Albums: 1 week)* pos/wks

Date		Title / Label	Pos	Wks
14 Oct 95		**ECHO ON MY MIND PART II** *Cooltempo CDCOOL 312*	61	1
1 Jun 96		**BLOOD MUSIC (EP)** *Cooltempo CDCOOL 319*	69	1
3 Jun 95		**RADAR** *Cooltempo CTCD 44*	66	1

Tracks on Blood Music (EP): First Transmission / Because the Night / Soup or No Soup / Infinite M

EAST 57th STREET featuring Donna ALLEN *UK, male production trio and US, female vocalist (Singles: 3 weeks)* pos/wks

Date		Title / Label	Pos	Wks
11 Oct 97		**SATURDAY** *AM:PM 5823752*	29	3

EAST OF EDEN *UK, male instrumental group (Singles: 12 weeks, Albums: 2 weeks)* pos/wks

Date		Title / Label	Pos	Wks
17 Apr 71	●	**JIG-A-JIG** *Deram DM 297*	7	12
14 Mar 70		**SNAFU** *Deram SML 1050*	29	2

EAST 17 (221 Top 500)

London-based singing, rapping and dancing lads with international teen appeal: Tony Mortimer (v/k), Brian Harvey (v), John Hendy (v), Terry Coldwell (v). Bad press and personal problems resulted in main songwriter Mortimer quitting, and a name change to E-17 for their short-lived 1998 comeback. Biggest-selling single: 'Stay Another Day' 910,000 (Singles: 170 weeks, Albums: 102 weeks) pos/wks

Date		Title / Label	Pos	Wks
29 Aug 92	●	**HOUSE OF LOVE** *London LON 325*	10	9
14 Nov 92		**GOLD (re)** *London LON 331*	28	8
30 Jan 93	●	**DEEP** *London LOCDP 334*	5	10
10 Apr 93		**SLOW IT DOWN** *London LONCD 339*	13	7
26 Jun 93		**WEST END GIRLS** *London LONCD 344*	11	7
4 Dec 93	●	**IT'S ALRIGHT** *London LONCD 345*	3	14
14 May 94	●	**AROUND THE WORLD** *London LONCD 349*	3	13
1 Oct 94	●	**STEAM** *London LONCD 353*	7	8
3 Dec 94	★	**STAY ANOTHER DAY (re)** *London LONCD 354*	1	16
25 Mar 95	●	**LET IT RAIN** *London LONCD 363*	10	7
17 Jun 95		**HOLD MY BODY TIGHT** *London LONCD 367*	12	7
4 Nov 95	●	**THUNDER** *London LONCD 373*	4	14
10 Feb 96	●	**DO U STILL** *London LONCD 379*	7	7
10 Aug 96		**SOMEONE TO LOVE** *London LONCD 385*	16	8
2 Nov 96	●	**IF YOU EVER** *London LONCD 388* [1]	2	15
18 Jan 97	●	**HEY CHILD** *London LONCD 390* [2]	3	5
14 Nov 98	●	**EACH TIME** *Telstar CDSTAS 3017* [3]	2	10
13 Mar 99		**BETCHA CAN'T WAIT** *Telstar CDSTAS 3031* [3]	12	5
27 Feb 93	★	**WALTHAMSTOW** *London 8283732* ■	1	33
29 Oct 94	●	**STEAM** *London 8285422*	3	36
25 Nov 95	●	**UP ALL NIGHT** *London 8286992*	7	15
16 Nov 96	●	**AROUND THE WORLD – HIT SINGLES – THE JOURNEY SO FAR** *London 8288522* [1]	3	16
28 Nov 98		**RESURRECTION** *Telstar TCD 3015* [2]	43	2

[1] East 17 featuring Gabrielle [2] East Seventeen [3] E-17

[1] East Seventeen [2] E-17

'Walthamstow' changed its catalogue number to 8284262 during its chart run

EAST SIDE BEAT

Italy, male vocal / instrumental duo – Carl Fanini and Francesco Petrocchi (Singles: 18 weeks) pos/wks

Date		Title / Label	pos	wks
30 Nov 91	●	**RIDE LIKE THE WIND** *ffrr F 176*	3	11
19 Dec 92		**ALIVE AND KICKING** *ffrr F 206*	26	6
29 May 93		**YOU'RE MY EVERYTHING** *ffrr FCD 207*	65	1

EASTERHOUSE

UK, male vocal / instrumental group (Albums: 1 week) pos/wks

Date		Title / Label	pos	wks
28 Jun 86		**CONTENDERS** *Rough Trade ROUGH 94*	91	1

EASTERN LANE

UK, male vocal / instrumental group (Singles: 1 week) pos/wks

Date		Title / Label	pos	wks
15 Nov 03		**FEED YOUR ADDICTION** *Rough Trade RTRADECD 132*	72	1

Sheena EASTON (494 Top 500)

Scotland's most successful act Stateside, b. Sheena Orr, 27 Apr 1959, Glasgow. This vocalist was first seen in TV documentary 'The Big Time'. Reached the big time on both sides of the Atlantic and won the Grammy for Best New Artist of 1981 (Singles: 104 weeks, Albums: 37 weeks) pos/wks

Date		Title / Label	pos	wks
5 Apr 80	●	**MODERN GIRL (re)** *EMI 5042*	8	15
19 Jul 80	●	**9 TO 5** *EMI 5066* ▲	3	15
25 Oct 80		**ONE MAN WOMAN** *EMI 5114*	14	6
14 Feb 81		**TAKE MY TIME** *EMI 5135*	44	5
2 May 81		**WHEN HE SHINES** *EMI 5166*	12	8
27 Jun 81	●	**FOR YOUR EYES ONLY** *EMI 5195*	8	13
12 Sep 81		**JUST ANOTHER BROKEN HEART** *EMI 5232*	33	8
5 Dec 81		**YOU COULD HAVE BEEN WITH ME** *EMI 5252*	54	3
31 Jul 82		**MACHINERY** *EMI 5326*	38	5
12 Feb 83		**WE'VE GOT TONIGHT** *Liberty UP 658* [1]	28	7
21 Jan 89		**THE LOVER IN ME** *MCA MCA 1289*	15	8
18 Mar 89		**DAYS LIKE THIS** *MCA MCA 1325*	43	3
15 Jul 89		**101** *MCA MCA 1348*	54	2
18 Nov 89		**THE ARMS OF ORION** *Warner Bros. W 2757* [2]	27	5
9 Dec 00		**GIVING UP GIVING IN** *Universal MCSTD 40244*	54	1
31 Jan 81		**TAKE MY TIME** *EMI EMC 3354*	17	19
3 Oct 81		**YOU COULD HAVE BEEN WITH ME** *EMI EMC 3378*	33	6
25 Sep 82		**MADNESS MONEY AND MUSIC** *EMI EMC 3414*	44	4
15 Oct 83		**BEST KEPT SECRET** *EMI EMC 1077951*	99	1
4 Mar 89		**THE LOVER IN ME** *MCA MCG 6036*	30	7

[1] Kenny Rogers and Sheena Easton [2] Prince with Sheena Easton

'Modern Girl' reached its peak position only on re-entry in Aug 1980

See also PRINCE

EASTSIDE CONNECTION

US, disco aggregation (Singles: 3 weeks) pos/wks

Date		Title / Label	pos	wks
8 Apr 78		**YOU'RE SO RIGHT FOR ME** *Creole CR 149*	44	3

Clint EASTWOOD *US, male actor / vocalist (Singles: 2 weeks)* pos/wks

Date		Title / Label	pos	wks
7 Feb 70		**I TALK TO THE TREES** *Paramount PARA 3004*	18	2

This is the flip of 'Wand'rin Star' by Lee Marvin and was listed with Marvin's A-side for two weeks only

Clint EASTWOOD and GENERAL SAINT

UK, male vocal duo (Singles: 8 weeks, Albums: 3 weeks) pos/wks

Date		Title / Label	pos	wks
29 Sep 84		**LAST PLANE (ONE WAY TICKET)** *MCA MCA 910*	51	3
2 Apr 94		**OH CAROL!** *Copasetic COPCD 0009*	54	5
6 Feb 82		**TWO BAD DJ** *Greensleeves GREL 24*	99	2
28 May 83		**STOP THAT TRAIN** *Greensleeves GREL 53*	98	1

EASY RIDERS – *See Frankie LAINE*

EASYBEATS *Australia / Holland / UK, male vocal / instrumental group (Singles: 24 weeks)* pos/wks

Date		Title / Label	pos	wks
27 Oct 66	●	**FRIDAY ON MY MIND** *United Artists UP 1157*	6	15
10 Apr 68		**HELLO, HOW ARE YOU** *United Artists UP 2209*	20	9

EASYWORLD

UK, male vocal / instrumental trio (Singles: 4 weeks) pos/wks

Date		Title / Label	pos	wks
1 Jun 02		**BLEACH** *Jive 9253552*	67	1
21 Sep 02		**YOU & ME** *Jive 9254092*	57	1
8 Feb 03		**JUNKIES** *Jive 9254522*	40	1
18 Oct 03		**2ND AMENDMENT** *Jive 82876554692*	42	1

EAT

UK / US, male / female vocal / instrumental group (Singles: 1 week) pos/wks

Date		Title / Label	pos	wks
12 Jun 93		**BLEED ME WHITE** *Fiction FICCD 48*	73	1

EAT STATIC *UK, male production duo – Marv Pepler and Joie Hinton (Singles: 3 weeks, Albums: 5 weeks)* pos/wks

Date		Title / Label	pos	wks
22 Feb 97		**HYBRID** *Planet Dog BARK 024CD*	41	1
27 Sep 97		**INTERCEPTOR** *Planet Dog BARK 030CD*	44	1
27 Jun 98		**CONTACT...** *Planet Dog BARK 033CD*	67	1
15 May 93		**ABDUCTION** *Planet Dog BARKCD 1*	62	1
25 Jun 94		**IMPLANT** *Planet Dog BARKCD 005*	13	3
25 Oct 97		**SCIENCE OF THE GODS** *Planet Dog BARKCD 029*	60	1

Cleveland EATON

US, male instrumentalist – keyboards (Singles: 6 weeks) pos/wks

Date		Title / Label	pos	wks
23 Sep 78		**BAMA BOOGIE WOOGIE** *Gull GULS 63*	35	6

EAV

Austria, male vocal / instrumental group (Singles: 4 weeks) pos/wks

Date		Title / Label	pos	wks
27 Sep 86		**BA-BA-BANKROBBERY (ENGLISH VERSION)** *Columbia DB 9139*	63	4

EAZY-E *US, male rapper – Eric Wright, d. 26 Mar 1995 (Singles: 3 weeks, Albums: 1 week)* pos/wks

Date		Title / Label	pos	wks
6 Jan 96		**JUST TAH LET YOU KNOW** *Epic 6628162*	30	3
10 Feb 96		**STR8 OFF THA STREETZ OF MUTHAPHUKKIN COMPTON** *Ruthless 4835762*	66	1

See also NWA

ECHO and the BUNNYMEN (353 Top 500)

Cult alternative rock group originally from Liverpool, UK, who named themselves after their drum machine. Ian McCulloch (v), b. 5 May 1959, front man of this moody and atmospheric group, went solo in 1988. Original line-up regrouped in 1997 (Singles: 86 weeks, Albums: 100 weeks) pos/wks

Date		Title / Label	pos	wks
17 May 80		**RESCUE** *Korova KOW 1*	62	1
18 Apr 81		**SHINE SO HARD (EP)** *Korova ECHO 1*	37	4
18 Jul 81		**A PROMISE** *Korova KOW 15*	49	4
29 May 82		**THE BACK OF LOVE** *Korova KOW 24*	19	7
22 Jan 83	●	**THE CUTTER** *Korova KOW 26*	8	8
16 Jul 83		**NEVER STOP** *Korova KOW 28*	15	7
28 Jan 84	●	**THE KILLING MOON** *Korova KOW 32*	9	6
21 Apr 84		**SILVER** *Korova KOW 34*	30	5
14 Jul 84		**SEVEN SEAS** *Korova KOW 35*	16	7
19 Oct 85		**BRING ON THE DANCING HORSES** *Korova KOW 43*	21	7
13 Jun 87		**THE GAME** *WEA YZ 134*	28	4
1 Aug 87		**LIPS LIKE SUGAR** *WEA YZ 144*	36	4
20 Feb 88		**PEOPLE ARE STRANGE** *WEA YZ 175*	29	5
2 Mar 91		**PEOPLE ARE STRANGE (re-issue)** *East West YZ 567*	34	4
28 Jun 97	●	**NOTHING LASTS FOREVER** *London LOCDP 396*	8	6
13 Sep 97		**I WANT TO BE THERE WHEN YOU COME** *London LONCD 399*	30	2
8 Nov 97		**DON'T LET IT GET YOU DOWN** *London LOCDP 406*	50	1
27 Mar 99		**RUST** *London LONCD 424*	22	3
5 May 01		**IT'S ALRIGHT** *Cooking Vinyl FRYCD 104*	41	1
26 Jul 80		**CROCODILES** *Korova KODE 1*	17	6
6 Jun 81	●	**HEAVEN UP HERE** *Korova KODE 3*	10	16
12 Feb 83	●	**PORCUPINE** *Korova KODE 6*	2	17
12 May 84	●	**OCEAN RAIN** *Korova KODE 8*	4	26
23 Nov 85	●	**SONGS TO LEARN & SING** *Korova KODE 13*	6	15
18 Jul 87	●	**ECHO AND THE BUNNYMEN** *WEA WX 108*	4	9
21 Jun 97		**BALLYHOO – THE BEST OF ECHO AND THE BUNNYMEN** *Korova 630191032*	59	1
26 Jul 97	●	**EVERGREEN** *London 8289052*	8	7

		pos	wks
17 Apr 99	**WHAT ARE YOU GOING TO DO WITH YOUR LIFE?** *London 5560802*	21	2
26 May 01	**FLOWERS** *Cooking Vinyl COOKCD 208*	56	1

Tracks on 'Shine So Hard' (EP): Crocodiles, All That Jazz, Zimbo, Over the Wall

ECHOBASS

UK, male producer – Simon Woodgate (Singles: 1 week)

		pos	wks
14 Jul 01	**YOU ARE THE WEAKEST LINK** *House of Bush CDANNE 001*	53	1

ECHOBEATZ *UK, male DJ / production duo – Dave De Braie and Paul Moody (Singles: 5 weeks)*

		pos	wks
25 Jul 98 ●	**MAS QUE NADA** *Eternal WEA 176CD*	10	5

ECHOBELLY *UK / Sweden, male / female vocal / instrumental group (Singles: 16 weeks, Albums: 28 weeks)*

		pos	wks
2 Apr 94	**INSOMNIAC** *Fauve FAUV 1CD*	47	1
2 Jul 94	**I CAN'T IMAGINE THE WORLD WITHOUT ME** *Fauve FAUV 2CD*	39	2
5 Nov 94	**CLOSE...BUT** *Fauve FAUV 4CD*	59	1
2 Sep 95	**GREAT THINGS** *Fauve FAUV 5CD*	13	3
4 Nov 95	**KING OF THE KERB** *Fauve FAUV 7CD*	25	3
2 Mar 96	**DARK THERAPY** *Fauve FAUV 8CD*	20	3
23 Aug 97	**THE WORLD IS FLAT** *Epic 6648152*	31	2
8 Nov 97	**HERE COMES THE BIG RUSH** *Epic 6652452*	56	1
3 Sep 94 ●	**EVERYONE'S GOT ONE** *Fauve FAUV 3CD*	8	3
30 Sep 95 ●	**ON** *Fauve FAUV 6CD*	4	24
22 Nov 97	**LUSTRA** *Epic 4889672*	47	1

See also LITHIUM and Sonya MADAN

Billy ECKSTINE

US, male vocalist, d. 8 Mar 1993 (Singles: 48 weeks)

		pos	wks
12 Nov 54 ●	**NO ONE BUT YOU** *MGM 763*	3	17
27 Sep 57	**PASSING STRANGERS** *Mercury MT 164* [1]	22	2
13 Feb 59 ●	**GIGI** *Mercury AMT 1018*	8	14
12 Mar 69	**PASSING STRANGERS (re-issue)** *Mercury MF 1082* [1]	20	15

[1] Billy Eckstine and Sarah Vaughan

ECLIPSE *Italy, male producer / instrumentalist – Gianni Bini (Singles: 4 weeks)*

		pos	wks
14 Aug 99	**MAKES ME LOVE YOU** *Azuli AZNYCDX 100*	25	4

See also BINI & MARTINI; HOUSE OF GLASS; GOODFELLAS featuring Lisa MILLETT

Silvio ECOMO

Holland, male producer (Singles: 1 week)

		pos	wks
15 Jul 00	**STANDING** *Hooj Choons HOOJ 098CD*	70	1

EDDIE and the HOT RODS *UK, male vocal / instrumental group (Singles: 26 weeks, Albums: 9 weeks)*

		pos	wks
11 Sep 76	**LIVE AT THE MARQUEE (EP)** *Island IEP 2*	43	5
13 Nov 76	**TEENAGE DEPRESSION** *Island WIP 6354*	35	4
23 Apr 77	**I MIGHT BE LYING** *Island WIP 6388*	44	3
13 Aug 77 ●	**DO ANYTHING YOU WANNA DO** *Island WIP 6401* [1]	9	10
21 Jan 78	**QUIT THIS TOWN** *Island WIP 6411*	36	4
18 Dec 76	**TEENAGE DEPRESSION** *Island ILPS 9457*	43	1
3 Dec 77	**LIFE ON THE LINE** *Island ILPS 9509*	27	3
24 Mar 79	**THRILLER** *Island ILPS 9563*	50	1
24 Jul 82	**WILD DOGS** *Arista SPART 1196* [1]	75	4

[1] Rods [1] Rods

Tracks on Live at the Marquee (EP): 96 Tears / Get out of Denver / Medley: Gloria / Satisfaction

EDDY

UK, female vocalist (Singles: 2 weeks)

		pos	wks
9 Jul 94	**SOMEDAY** *Positiva CDTIV 14*	49	2

Duane EDDY (202 Top 500)

Twangy guitar legend, b. 26 Apr 1938, New York. Early rock's No.1 solo instrumentalist assembled a long string of UK and US hit singles and was one of the first rock acts to score on the album charts (Singles: 202 weeks, Albums: 88 weeks)

		pos	wks
5 Sep 58	**REBEL-ROUSER** *London HL 8669* [1]	19	10
2 Jan 59	**CANNONBALL** *London HL 8764* [2]	22	4
19 Jun 59 ●	**PETER GUNN (re)** *London HLW 8879*	6	11
24 Jul 59	**YEP!** *London HLW B8879*	17	5
4 Sep 59	**FORTY MILES OF BAD ROAD** *London HLW 8929*	11	9
18 Dec 59	**SOME KIND-A EARTHQUAKE** *London HLW 9007*	12	5
19 Feb 60	**BONNIE CAME BACK** *London HLW 9050*	12	11
28 Apr 60 ●	**SHAZAM!** *London HLW 9104*	4	13
21 Jul 60 ●	**BECAUSE THEY'RE YOUNG** *London HLW 9162*	2	18
10 Nov 60	**KOMMOTION** *London HLW 9225*	13	10
12 Jan 61 ●	**PEPE** *London HLW 9257*	2	14
20 Apr 61 ●	**THEME FROM DIXIE** *London HLW 9324*	7	10
22 Jun 61	**RING OF FIRE** *London HLW 9370*	17	10
14 Sep 61	**DRIVIN' HOME** *London HLW 9406*	30	4
5 Oct 61	**CARAVAN** *Parlophone R 4826*	42	3
24 May 62	**DEEP IN THE HEART OF TEXAS** *RCA 1288*	19	8
23 Aug 62 ●	**BALLAD OF PALADIN** *RCA 1300* [3]	10	10
8 Nov 62 ●	**(DANCE WITH THE) GUITAR MAN** *RCA 1316* [4]	4	16
14 Feb 63	**BOSS GUITAR** *RCA 1329* [4]	27	8
30 May 63	**LONELY BOY LONELY GUITAR** *RCA 1344* [4]	35	4
29 Aug 63	**YOUR BABY'S GONE SURFIN'** *RCA 1357* [4]	49	1
8 Mar 75 ●	**PLAY ME LIKE YOU PLAY YOUR GUITAR** *GTO GT 11* [4]	9	9
22 Mar 86 ●	**PETER GUNN (re-recording)** *China WOK 6* [5]	8	9
6 Jun 59 ●	**HAVE 'TWANGY' GUITAR WILL TRAVEL** *London HAW 2160*	6	3
31 Oct 59 ●	**SPECIALLY FOR YOU** *London HAW 2191*	6	8
19 Mar 60 ●	**THE TWANG'S THE THANG** *London HAW 2236*	2	25
26 Nov 60	**SONGS OF OUR HERITAGE** *London HAW 2285*	13	5
1 Apr 61 ●	**A MILLION DOLLARS' WORTH OF TWANG** *London HAW 2325*	5	19
9 Jun 62	**A MILLION DOLLARS' WORTH OF TWANG VOLUME 2** *London HAW 2435*	18	1
21 Jul 62 ●	**TWISTIN' AND TWANGIN'** *RCA RD 27264*	8	12
8 Dec 62	**TWANGY GUITAR – SILKY STRINGS** *RCA RD 7510*	13	11
16 Mar 63	**DANCE WITH THE GUITAR MAN** *RCA RD 7545*	14	4

[1] Duane Eddy and His Twangy Guitar [2] Duane Eddy His Twangy Guitar & The Rebels [3] Duane Eddy – Orchestra conducted by Bob Thompson [4] Duane Eddy and The Rebelettes [5] Art of Noise featuring Duane Eddy

EDDY and the SOUL BAND

US, male / female vocal / instrumental group (Singles: 7 weeks)

		pos	wks
23 Feb 85	**THE THEME FROM 'SHAFT'** *Club JAB 11*	13	7

Randy EDELMAN

US, male vocalist / instrumentalist – piano (Singles: 18 weeks)

		pos	wks
6 Mar 76	**CONCRETE AND CLAY** *20th Century BTC 2261*	11	7
18 Sep 76	**UPTOWN, UPTEMPO WOMAN** *20th Century BTC 2225*	25	7
15 Jan 77	**YOU** *20th Century BTC 2253*	49	2
17 Jul 82	**NOBODY MADE ME** *Rocket XPRES 81*	60	2

EDELWEISS *Austria, male / female vocal / instrumental group (Singles: 10 weeks)*

		pos	wks
29 Apr 89 ●	**BRING ME EDELWEISS** *WEA YZ 353*	5	10

EDEN *UK / Australia, male / female vocal / instrumental group (Singles: 2 weeks)*

		pos	wks
6 Mar 93	**DO U FEEL 4 ME** *Logic 74321135422*	51	2

Lyn EDEN – *See SMOKIN BEATS featuring Lyn EDEN*

EDISON LIGHTHOUSE *UK, male vocal / instrumental group – lead vocal Tony Burrows (Singles: 13 weeks)*

		pos	wks
24 Jan 70 ★	**LOVE GROWS (WHERE MY ROSEMARY GOES)** *Bell 1091*	1	12
30 Jan 71	**IT'S UP TO YOU PETULA** *Bell 1136*	49	1

EDMONTON SYMPHONY ORCHESTRA – *See PROCOL HARUM*

Dave EDMUNDS *UK, male vocalist / instrumentalist – guitar (Singles: 93 weeks, Albums: 21 weeks)* pos/wks

21 Nov 70 ★ **I HEAR YOU KNOCKING** *MAM 1* [1] ... **1** 14
20 Jan 73 ● **BABY I LOVE YOU** *Rockfield ROC 1* ... **8** 13
9 Jun 73 ● **BORN TO BE WITH YOU** *Rockfield ROC 2* ... **5** 12
2 Jul 77 **I KNEW THE BRIDE** *Swansong SSK 19411* ... **26** 8
30 Jun 79 ● **GIRLS TALK** *Swansong SSK 19418* ... **4** 11
22 Sep 79 **QUEEN OF HEARTS** *Swansong SSK 19419* ... **11** 9
24 Nov 79 **CRAWLING FROM THE WRECKAGE** *Swansong SSK 19420* ... **59** 4
9 Feb 80 **SINGING THE BLUES** *Swansong SSK 19422* ... **28** 8
28 Mar 81 **ALMOST SATURDAY NIGHT** *Swansong SSK 19424* ... **58** 3
20 Jun 81 **THE RACE IS ON** *Swansong SSK 19425* [2] ... **34** 6
26 Mar 83 **SLIPPING AWAY** *Arista ARIST 522* ... **60** 4
7 Apr 90 **KING OF LOVE** *Capitol CL 568* ... **68** 1
23 Jun 79 **REPEAT WHEN NECESSARY** *Swansong SSK 59409* ... **39** 12
18 Apr 81 **TWANGIN'** *Swansong SSK 59411* ... **37** 4
3 Apr 82 **D.E. 7TH** *Arista SPART 1184* ... **60** 3
30 Apr 83 **INFORMATION** *Arista 205 348* ... **92** 2

[1] Dave Edmunds' Rockpile [2] Dave Edmunds and the Stray Cats

See also ROCKPILE

Alton EDWARDS *Zimbabwe, male vocalist (Singles: 9 weeks)* pos/wks

9 Jan 82 **I JUST WANNA (SPEND SOME TIME WITH YOU)** *Streetwave STRA 1897* ... **20** 9

Dennis EDWARDS *US, male vocalist (Singles: 10 weeks, Albums: 1 week)* pos/wks

24 Mar 84 **DON'T LOOK ANY FURTHER (re)** *Gordy TMG 1334* [1] ... **45** 10
14 Apr 84 **DON'T LOOK ANY FURTHER** *Gordy ZL 72148* ... **91** 1

[1] Dennis Edwards featuring Siedah Garrett

The re-entry peaked at No.55 in Jun 1987

Rupie EDWARDS *Jamaica, male vocalist (Singles: 16 weeks)* pos/wks

23 Nov 74 ● **IRE FEELINGS (SKANGA)** *Cactus CT 38* ... **9** 10
8 Feb 75 **LEGO SKANGA** *Cactus CT 51* ... **32** 6

Todd EDWARDS *US, male DJ / producer (Albums: 1 week)* pos/wks

24 Aug 96 **SAVED MY LIFE** *ffrr FX 279* ... **69** 1

Tommy EDWARDS *US, male vocalist, d. 23 Oct 1969 (Singles: 18 weeks)* pos/wks

3 Oct 58 ★ **IT'S ALL IN THE GAME** *MGM 989* ▲ ... **1** 17
7 Aug 59 **MY MELANCHOLY BABY** *MGM 1020* ... **29** 1

EEK-A-MOUSE *Jamaica – male vocalist (Albums: 3 weeks)* pos/wks

14 Aug 82 **SKIDIP** *Greensleeves GREL 41* ... **61** 3

EELS *US, male vocal / instrumental group (Singles: 23 weeks, Albums: 40 weeks)* pos/wks

15 Feb 97 ● **NOVOCAINE FOR THE SOUL** *Dreamworks DRMCD 22174* ... **10** 5
17 May 97 ● **SUSAN'S HOUSE** *Dreamworks DRMCD 22238* ... **9** 5
13 Sep 97 **YOUR LUCKY DAY IN HELL** *Dreamworks DRMCD 22277* ... **35** 2
26 Sep 98 **LAST STOP: THIS TOWN** *Dreamworks DRMCD 22346* ... **23** 3
12 Dec 98 **CANCER FOR THE CURE** *Dreamworks DRMCD 22373* ... **60** 1
26 Feb 00 **MR E'S BEAUTIFUL BLUES** *Dreamworks DRMCD 4509762* ... **11** 4
24 Jun 00 **FLYSWATTER** *Dreamworks DRMCD 4509462* ... **55** 1
22 Sep 01 **SOULJACKER PART 1** *Dreamworks DRMCD 4508922* ... **30** 2
8 Feb 97 ● **BEAUTIFUL FREAK** *Dreamworks DRMD 50001* ... **5** 27
3 Oct 98 **ELECTRO-SHOCK BLUES** *Dreamworks DRD 50052* ... **12** 4
11 Mar 00 ● **DAISIES OF THE GALAXY** *Dreamworks 4502182* ... **8** 5
6 Oct 01 **SOULJACKER** *Dreamworks 4503462* ... **12** 2
14 Jun 03 **SHOOTENANNY** *Dreamworks 4504588* ... **35** 2

EFUA *UK, female vocalist (Singles: 5 weeks)* pos/wks

3 Jul 93 **SOMEWHERE** *Virgin VSCDT 1463* ... **42** 5

EGG *UK, male vocal / instrumental group (Singles: 1 week)* pos/wks

30 Jan 99 **GETTING AWAY WITH IT** *Indochina ID 079CD* ... **58** 1

EGGS ON LEGS *UK, male vocalist (Singles: 1 week)* pos/wks

23 Sep 95 **COCK A DOODLE DO IT** *Avex UK AVEXCD 18* ... **42** 1

EGYPTIAN EMPIRE *UK, male producer – Tim Taylor (Singles: 2 weeks)* pos/wks

24 Oct 92 **THE HORN TRACK** *Ffrreedom TAB 115* ... **61** 2

EIFFEL 65 *Italy, male vocal trio (Singles: 36 weeks, Albums: 4 weeks)* pos/wks

21 Aug 99 **BLUE (DA BA DEE) (import)** *Logic 74321688212* ... **39** 5
25 Sep 99 ★ **BLUE (DA BA DEE)** *Eternal WEA 226CD1* ◆ ■ ... **1** 21
19 Feb 00 ● **MOVE YOUR BODY** *Eternal WEA 255CD1* ... **3** 10
4 Mar 00 **EUROPOP** *Eternal 8573814552* ... **12** 4

18 WHEELER *UK, male vocal / instrumental group (Singles: 1 week)* pos/wks

15 Mar 97 **STAY** *Creation CRESCD 249* ... **59** 1

EIGHTH WONDER *UK, male / female vocal / instrumental group (Singles: 25 weeks, Albums: 4 weeks)* pos/wks

2 Nov 85 **STAY WITH ME** *CBS A 6594* ... **65** 2
20 Feb 88 ● **I'M NOT SCARED** *CBS SCARE 1* ... **7** 13
25 Jun 88 **CROSS MY HEART** *CBS 651552 7* ... **13** 8
1 Oct 88 **BABY BABY** *CBS BABE 1* ... **65** 2
23 Jul 88 **FEARLESS** *CBS 460628 1* ... **47** 4

EIGHTIES MATCHBOX B-LINE DISASTER *UK, male vocal / instrumental group (Singles: 5 weeks)* pos/wks

28 Sep 02 **CELEBRATE YOUR MOTHER** *No Death / Island MCSTD 40296* **66** 1
18 Jan 03 **PSYCHOSIS SAFARI** *No Death / Island MCSTD 40308* ... **26** 2
24 May 03 **CHICKEN** *No Death / Island MCSCD 40317* ... **30** 2

801 *UK, male vocal / instrumental group (Albums: 2 weeks)* pos/wks

20 Nov 76 **801 LIVE** *Island ILPS 9444* ... **52** 2

808 STATE *UK, DJ / production / instrumental group (Singles: 70 weeks, Albums: 20 weeks)* pos/wks

18 Nov 89 ● **PACIFIC** *ZTT ZANG 1* ... **10** 9
31 Mar 90 **THE EXTENDED PLEASURE OF DANCE (EP)** *ZTT ZANG 2T* ... **56** 1
2 Jun 90 ● **THE ONLY RHYME THAT BITES** *ZTT ZANG 3* [1] ... **10** 10
15 Sep 90 **TUNES SPLITS THE ATOM** *ZTT ZANG 6* [1] ... **18** 7
10 Nov 90 ● **CUBIK / OLYMPIC** *ZTT ZANG 5* ... **10** 10
16 Feb 91 ● **IN YER FACE** *ZTT ZANG 14* ... **9** 6
27 Apr 91 **OOOPS** *ZTT ZANG 19* [2] ... **42** 3
17 Aug 91 **LIFT / OPEN YOUR MIND** *ZTT ZANG 20* ... **38** 4
29 Aug 92 **TIME BOMB / NIMBUS** *ZTT ZANG 33* ... **59** 1
12 Dec 92 **ONE IN TEN (re-mix)** *ZTT ZANG 39* [3] ... **17** 8
30 Jan 93 **PLAN 9** *ZTT ZANG 38CD* ... **50** 2
26 Jun 93 **10 X 10** *ZTT ZANG 42CD* ... **67** 1
13 Aug 94 **BOMBADIN** *ZTT ZANG 54CD* ... **67** 1
29 Jun 96 **BOND** *ZTT ZANG 80CD* ... **57** 1
8 Feb 97 **LOPEZ** *ZTT ZANG 87CD* ... **20** 2
16 May 98 **PACIFIC / CUBIK (re-mix)** *ZTT ZTT 98CD1* ... **21** 3
6 Mar 99 **THE ONLY RHYME THAT BITES (re-mix)** *ZTT ZTT 125CD* [1] ... **53** 1
16 Dec 89 **NINETY** *ZTT ZTT 2* ... **57** 5
16 Mar 91 ● **EX:EL** *ZTT ZTT 6* ... **4** 10
13 Feb 93 **GORGEOUS** *ZTT 4509911002* ... **17** 3
30 May 98 **808:88:98** *ZTT ZTT 100CD* ... **40** 2

[1] MC Tunes versus 808 State [2] 808 State featuring Bjork [3] 808 State vs UB40

Tracks on The Extended Pleasure of Dance (EP): Cobra Bora / Ancodia / Cubik. 'Cubik' is a re-issue of one of the tracks from The Extended Pleasure of Dance (EP). 'Lopez' features the uncredited vocals of James Dean Bradfield, lead singer of the Manic Street Preachers

COMPILATION ALBUM CHART-TOPPERS

This chronological list contains every No.1 compilation album since these albums were removed from the main chart to form their own Top 20 in January 1989. The albums marked with an * indicate that the chart-topper had more than one stay at the top

CHART ENTRY DATE / **ALBUM TITLE** / LABEL / **WEEKS ON CHART**

14 Jan 1989 **NOW THAT'S WHAT I CALL MUSIC! 13** EMI/Virgin/Polygram **1**
21 Jan 1989 **THE PREMIERE COLLECTION** Really Useful/Polydor **3***
4 Feb 1989 **THE MARQUEE – 30 LEGENDARY YEARS** Polydor **4**
4 Mar 1989 **THE AWARDS** Telstar/BPI **1**
18 Mar 1989 **DEEP HEAT** Telstar **1**
25 Mar 1989 **UNFORGETTABLE 2** EMI **1**
1 Mar 1989 **NOW THAT'S WHAT I CALL MUSIC! 14** EMI/Virgin/Polygram **7**
20 May 1989 **NITE FLITE 2** CBS **2**
3 May 1989 **HITS 10** CBS/WEA/BMG **6**
15 May 1989 **NOW DANCE '89** EMI/Virgin **6**
26 May 1989 **NOW THAT'S WHAT I CALL MUSIC! 15** EMI/Virgin/Polygram **5**
30 Sep 1989 **DEEP HEAT 4 – PLAY WITH FIRE** Telstar **5**
4 Sep 1989 **SMASH HITS PARTY '89** Dover **3**
25 Sep 1989 **THE 80'S ALBUM OF THE DECADE** EMI **1**
2 Sep 1989 **NOW THAT'S WHAT I CALL MUSIC! 16** EMI/Virgin/Polygram **6**
20 Jan 1990 **PURE SOFT METAL** Stylus **5***
3 Feb 1990 **DEEP HEAT 5 – FEED THE FEVER** Telstar **2**
10 Mar 1990 **NOW DANCE 901** EMI/Virgin/Polygram **4**
7 Apr 1990 **DEEP HEAT 6 – THE SIXTH SENSE** Telstar **2**
21 Apr 1990 **JUST THE TWO OF US** CBS **2**
5 May 1990 **NOW THAT'S WHAT I CALL MUSIC! 17** EMI/Virgin **5**
9 Jun 1990 **CLASSIC EXPERIENCE 11** EMI **4**
7 Jul 1990 **DEEP HEAT 7 – SEVENTH HEAVEN** Telstar **1**
14 Jul 1990 **SMASH HITS – RAVE!** Dover **2**
28 Jul 1990 **NOW DANCE 902** EMI/Virgin **3**
18 Aug 1990 **KNEBWORTH THE ALBUM** Polydor **2**
1 Sep 1990 **MEGABASS** Telstar **4**
29 Sep 1990 **SLAMMIN'** A&M **1**
6 Oct 1990 **THAT LOVING FEELING VOL. 3** Dino **3**
27 Oct 1990 **MISSING YOU – AN ALBUM OF LOVE** EMI **3**
17 Nov 1990 **NOW DANCE 903** EMI/Virgin **2**
1 Dec 1990 **NOW THAT'S WHAT I CALL MUSIC! 18** EMI/Virgin **6**
19 Jan 1990 **DIRTY DANCING (OST)** RCA **2**
2 Feb 1991 **DEEP HEAT 9 NINTH LIFE** Telstar **2**
16 Feb 1991 **THE LOST BOYS** Atlantic **1**
23 Feb 1991 **AWESOME!!** EMI **3**
16 Mar 1991 **UNCHAINED MELODIES** Telstar **3**
6 Apr 1991 **NOW THAT'S WHAT I CALL MUSIC! 19** EMI/Virgin/Polygram **5**
11 May 1991 **THINKING OF YOU...** Columbia **2**
25 May 1991 **SMASH HITS MASSIVE!** Dover **2**
8 May 1991 **THE ESSENTIAL MOZART** Decca **2***
15 Jun 1991 **THE RHYTHM DIVINE** Dino **1**
29 Jun 1991 **WINGS OF LOVE** A&M **5**
3 Aug 1991 **THIN ICE 2 – THE FIRST SHIVER** Telstar **1**
10 Aug 1991 **PURPLE RAINBOWS** Polydor **1**
17 Aug 1991 **THE HITS ALBUM** Sony/BMG **2**
31 Aug 1991 **THE SOUND OF THE SUBURBS** Columbia **3**
21 Sep 1991 **GROOVY GHETTO** Arcade **2**
5 Oct 1991 **NOW DANCE 91** EMI/Virgin/Polygram **3**
26 Oct 1991 **2 ROOMS – ELTON JOHN** Mercury **1**
2 Nov 1991 **HARDCORE ECSTASY** Dino **4**
30 Nov 1991 **NOW THAT'S WHAT I CALL MUSIC! 20** EMI/Virgin/Polygram **7**
18 Jan 1992 **ESSENTIAL HARDCORE** Dino **1**
25 Jan 1992 **THE ULTIMATE RAVE** EMI/Virgin/Polygram **4**
22 Feb 1992 **THE AWARDS 1992** Polygram **2**
7 Mar 1992 **ULTIMATE HARDCORE** Telstar **2**
21 Mar 1992 **SOUL EMOTION** Polygram **3**
11 Apr 1992 **ALL WOMAN** Quality TV **2**
25 Apr 1992 **NOW THAT'S WHAT I CALL MUSIC! 21** EMI/Virgin/Polygram **5**
30 May 1992 **THE RAVE GENER8TOR** Cookie Jar **2**
13 Jun 1992 **EARTHRISE – THE RAINFOREST ALBUM** Elf **1**
20 Jun 1992 **MODERN LOVE** Polygram **1**
27 Jun 1992 **HEARTBEAT** Columbia **4**
25 Jul 1992 **KT3 – KAOS THEORY 3** Telstar **2**
8 Aug 1992 **NOW THAT'S WHAT I CALL MUSIC! 22** EMI/Virgin **8**
3 Oct 1992 **SIXTIES BEAT** Dino **1**
10 Oct 1992 **ALL WOMAN 2** Quality TV **1**
17 Oct 1992 **ENERGY RUSH** Dino **2**
31 Oct 1992 **THE ULTIMATE...** Columbia **1**
7 Nov 1992 **THE BEST OF DANCE 92** Telstar **2***
14 Nov 1992 **THE ULTIMATE COUNTRY COLLECTION** Columbia **1**

28 Nov 1992 **NOW THAT'S WHAT I CALL MUSIC! 23** EMI/Virgin **5**
2 Jan 1993 **THE BODYGUARD (OST)** Arista **11****
27 Feb 1993 **HITS 93 VOL 1** Telstar **3**
3 Apr 1993 **BLUES BROTHER SOUL SISTER** Dino **1**
10 Apr 1993 **ENERGY RUSH PRESENTS DANCE HITS 93** Dino **3**
8 May 1993 **NOW THAT'S WHAT I CALL MUSIC! 24** EMI/Virgin/Polygram **6**
19 Jun 1993 **ORIGINALS** Columbia **1**
26 Jun 1993 **NOW DANCE 93** EMI/Virgin/Polygram **2**
10 Jul 1993 **100 PERCENT DANCE** Telstar **1**
17 Jul 1993 **BEST DANCE ALBUM...EVER!** Virgin **4**
14 Aug 1993 **NOW THAT'S WHAT I CALL MUSIC! 25** EMI/Virgin/Polygram **5**
18 Sep 1993 **DANCE ADRENALIN** Telstar **2**
2 Oct 1993 **100% DANCE VOL 2** Telstar **4***
16 Oct 1993 **NOW! 1993** EMI/Virgin/Polygram **1**
6 Nov 1993 **NOW DANCE – THE BEST OF '93** EMI/Virgin/Polygram **1**
13 Nov 1993 **BEST OF DANCE '93** Telstar **2**
27 Nov 1993 **NOW THAT'S WHAT I CALL MUSIC! 26** EMI/Virgin/Polygram **8**
22 Jan 1994 **THE SOUND OF KISS 100FM** Polygram TV **1**
29 Jan 1994 **NOW DANCE 94 VOLUME 1** EMI/Virgin/Polygram **2**
12 Feb 1994 **SWEET SOUL HARMONIES** Virgin **1**
19 Feb 1994 **DANCE HITS 94 – VOL 1** Telstar **3**
12 Mar 1994 **SOUL DEVOTION** Polygram **4**
9 Apr 1994 **NOW THAT'S WHAT I CALL MUSIC! 27** EMI/Virgin/Polygram **4**
7 May 1994 **DANCE ZONE LEVEL ONE** Polygram TV **4**
4 Jun 1994 **ENERGY RUSH – XTERMIN8** Dino **1**
11 Jun 1994 **DANCE HITS '94 VOLUME 2** Telstar **1**
18 Jun 1994 **PURE MOODS** Virgin **3**
9 Jul 1994 **NOW DANCE – SUMMER 94** EMI/Virgin **1**
16 Jul 1994 **DANCE ZONE – LEVEL TWO** Polygram TV **2**
30 Jul 1994 **IT'S THE ULTIMATE DANCE ALBUM** Telstar **2**
13 Aug 1994 **NOW THAT'S WHAT I CALL MUSIC! 28** EMI/Virgin/Polygram **5**
17 Sep 1903 **THE BEST ROCK ALBUM IN THE WORLD … EVER!** Virgin **4***
8 Oct 1994 **DANCE LEVEL – LEVEL 3** Polygram **1**
15 Oct 1994 **NOW THAT'S WHAT I CALL MUSIC! 1994** EMI/Virgin/Polygram **4**
19 Nov 1994 **THE LOVE ALBUM** Virgin **1**
26 Nov 1994 **NOW THAT'S WHAT I CALL MUSIC! 29** EMI/Virgin/Polygram **9**
28 Jan 1995 **THE BEST OF HEARTBEAT** Columbia **1**
4 Feb 1995 **THE BEST PUNK ALBUM IN THE WORLD … EVER!** Virgin **1**
11 Feb 1995 **DANCE MANIA 95 – VOLUME 1** Pure Music **2**
25 Feb 1995 **ON A DANCE TIP** Global Television **3**
18 Mar 1995 **SMASH HITS 95 – VOLUME 1** Telstar **1**
25 Mar 1995 **DANCE ZONE LEVEL 4** Polygram **2**
8 Apr 1995 **DANCE MANIA 95 – VOLUME 2** Pure Music **2**
22 Mar 1995 **NOW THAT'S WHAT I CALL MUSIC! 30** EMI/Virgin/Polygram **4**
20 May 1995 **ON A DANCE TIP 2** Global Television **3**
10 Jun 1995 **TOP OF THE POPS 1** Columbia **2**
24 Jun 1995 **DANCE ZONE – LEVEL FIVE** Polygram TV **3**
15 Jul 1995 **DANCE MANIA 95 – VOLUME 3** Pure Music **3**
5 Aug 1995 **THE BEST SUMMER … EVER!** Virgin **1**
12 Aug 1995 **NOW THAT'S WHAT I CALL MUSIC! 31** EMI/Virgin/Polygram **4**
9 Sep 1995 **DANCE ZONE – LEVEL SIX** Polygram TV **1**
16 Sep 1995 **HELP – WAR CHILD** Go! Discs **2**
30 Sep 1995 **HEARTBEAT – FOREVER YOURS** Columbia **6**
11 Nov 1995 **THE GREASTEST PARTY ALBUM UNDER THE SUN!** EMI TV **1**
18 Nov 1995 **PURE SWING IV** Dino **1**
25 Nov 1995 **NOW THAT'S WHAT I CALL MUSIC! 32** EMI/Virgin/Polygram **6**
6 Jan 1996 **HITS 96** Global TV/Warner TV **4**
3 Feb 1996 **SISTERS OF SWING** Polygram TV **1**
10 Feb 1996 **THE BEST … ALBUM IN THE WORLD … EVER! 2** Virgin **2**
24 Feb 1996 **THE NO. 1 LOVE ALBUM** Polygram TV **1**
2 Mar 1996 **IN THE MIX 96** Virgin **4**
30 Mar 1996 **NOW THAT'S WHAT I CALL MUSIC! 33** EMI/Virgin/Polygram **5**
4 May 1996 **DANCE ZONE – LEVEL SEVEN** Polygram TV **1**
11 May 1996 **BOYZ OF SWING** Polygram TV **1**
18 May 1996 **NEW HITS 96** Warner.ESP/Global TV//Sony **9**
20 Jul 1996 **BIG MIX 96** EMI TV/Warner.ESP **4**
17 Aug 1996 **THE BEST DANCE ALBUM IN THE WORLD … EVER! 6** Virgin **1**
24 Aug 1996 **NOW THAT'S WHAT I CALL MUSIC! 34** EMI/Virgin/Polygram **7**
12 Oct 1996 **IN THE MIX 96 – 3** Virgin **1**
19 Oct 1996 **KISS IN IBIZA '96** Polygram TV **4**
16 Nov 1996 **HUGE HITS 1996** Warner ESP/Global TV **2**
30 Nov 1996 **NOW THAT'S WHAT I CALL MUSIC! 35** EMI/Virgin/Polygram **7**
18Jan 1997 **THE ANNUAL II – PETE TONG and BOY GEORGE** Ministry of Sound **5***
15 Feb 1997 **IN THE MIX 97** Virgin **1**
1 Mar 1997 **CLUB MIX 97 – 2** Polygram TV **2**
15 Mar 1997 **THE SOUL ALBUM** Virgin **1**
22 Mar 1997 **THE BEST … ALBUM IN THE WORLD … EVER! 5** Virgin/EMI TV **1**
29 Mar 1997 **DANCE NATION 3 – PETE TONG & JUDGE JULES** Ministry of Sound **1**

COMPILATION ALBUM CHART-TOPPERS CONTINUED

5 Apr 1997 **NOW THAT'S WHAT I CALL MUSIC! 36** EMI/Virgin/Polygram **3**
26 Apr 1997 **NEW HITS 1997** Warner.ESP/Global TV **4**
24 May 1997 **BIG MIX 97** Warner/Virgin/EMI **2**
7 Jun 1997 **SMASH HITS – SUMER 97** Virgin/EMI **1**
14 Jun 1997 **THE BEST CLUB ANTHEMS … EVER!** Virgin/EMI **4**
12 Jul 1997 **THE BEST DISCO ALBUM IN THE WORLD … EVER!** Virgin/EMI **2**
26 Jul 1997 **NOW THAT'S WHAT I CALL MUSIC! 37** EMI/Virgin/Polygram **4**
23 Aug 1997 **FRESH HITS 1997** Warner.ESP/Global TV **3**
13 Sep 1997 **IBIZA UNCOVERED** Virgin/EMI **4***
4 Oct 1997 **KISS IN IBIZA 97** Polygram TV **1**
18 Oct 1997 **BIG MIX 97 – VOLUME 2** Virgin/EMI/Warner.ESP **1**
25 Oct 1997 **THE BEST … ANTHEMS … EVER!** Virgin/EMI **1**
1 Nov 1997 **NOW DANCE 97** Virgin/EMI **1**
8 Nov 1997 **HUGE HITS 1997** Warner.ESP/Global//Sony **1**
15 Nov 1997 **THE ANNUAL III – PETE TONG & BOY GEORGE** Ministry of Sound **2**
29 Nov 1997 **NOW THAT'S WHAT I CALL MUSIC! 38** EMI/Virgin/Polygram **4***
13 Dec 1997 **DIANA PRINCESS OF WALES – TRIBUTE** Diana Memorial Fund **4**
24 Jan 1998 **THE EIGHTIES MIX** Global TV/Polygram **2**
7 Feb 1998 **ULTIMATE CLUB MIX** Polygram TV **1**
14 Feb 1998 **IN THE MIX 98** Virgin/EMI **2***
21 Feb 1998 **LOVE** Polygram **1**
7 Mar 1998 **FANTASTIC '80'S!** Columbia **1**
14 Mar 98 **THE FULL MONTY** RCA Victor **3**
4 Apr 1998 **NEW HITS 98** Warner.Esp/Global TV/Sony **2**
18 Apr 1998 **NOW THAT'S WHAT I CALL MUSIC! 39** EMI/Virgin/Polygram **8**
13 Jun 1998 **THE BOX HITS 98 – VOLUME 2** Telstar **3**
4 Jul 1998 **FRESH HITS 98** Warner.ESP/Global/Sony **6**
15 Aug 1998 **NOW THAT'S WHAT I CALL MUSIC! 40** EMI/Virgin/Polygram **4**
12 Sep 1998 **THE IBIZA ANNUAL** Ministry of Sound **1**
19 Sep 1998 **BIG HITS 98** Warner.ESP/Global//Sony **5**
24 Oct 1998 **IN THE MIX IBIZA** Virgin/EMI **1**
31 Nov 1998 **THE BEST CHART HITS ALBUM IN THE WORLD … EVER!** Virgin/EMI **1**
7 Nov 1998 **HUGE HITS 1998** Warner.ESP/Global TV/Sony **2***
14 Nov 1998 **THE ANNUAL IV –– JUDGE JULES AND BOY GEORGE** Ministry of Sound **2**
5 Dec 1998 **NOW THAT'S WHAT I CALL MUSIC! 41** EMI/Virgin/Polygram **7**
23 Jan 1999 **THE BEST CLUB ANTHEMS 99 … EVER!** Virgin/EMI **1**
30 Jan 1999 **CLUBBER'S GUIDE TO … NINETY NINE** Ministry of Sound **2**
13 Jan 1999 **EUPHORIA** Telstar TV **2***
20 Feb 1999 **LOVE SONGS** Polygram TV/Warner **1**
6 Mar 1999 **KISS HOUSE NATION** Polygram TV **2**
20 Mar 1999 **ESPECIALLY FOR YOU** Columbia/Sony TV **1**
27 Mar 1999 **DANCE NATION SIX – TALL PAUL/B BLOCK** Ministry of Sound **1**
3 Apr 1999 **NEW HITS 99** Warner.ESP/Global/Sony **1**
10 Apr 1999 **NOW THAT'S WHAT I CALL MUSIC! 42** EMI/Virgin/Universal **7**
29 May 1999 **TRANCE NATION** Ministry of Sound **3**
19 Jun 1999 **CLUBBERS GUIDE TO IBIZA – SUMMER '99** Ministry Of Sound **2**
3 Jul 1999 **FRESH HITS 99** Warner.ESP/Global **3**
24 Jul 1999 **THE BEST DANCE ALBUM IN THE WORLD … EVER! 9** Virgin/EMI **1**
31 Jul 1999 **NOW THAT'S WHAT I CALL MUSIC! 43** EMI/Virgin/Universal **4**
28 Aug 1999 **BIZA ANNUAL 99** Ministry of Sound **1**
4 Sep 1999 **BIG HITS 99** Warner.ESP/Global TV **2**
18 Sep 1999 **KISS IBIZA 99** Universal TV **3**
9 Oct 1999 **TOP OF THE POPS 99 VOL. 2** Universal TV **1**
16 Oct 1999 **TRANCE NATION 2** Ministry of Sound **1**
23 Oct 1999 **LAND OF MY FATHERS** Universal TV **1**
30 Oct 1999 **NOW DANCE 2000** Virgin/EMI **1**
6 Nov 1999 **HUGE HITS 99** Warner.ESP/Global TV//Sony **4**
4 Dec 1999 **NOW! 44** EMI/Virgin/Universal **8**
29 Jan 2000 **CLUBBER'S GUIDE TO … 2000** Ministry of Sound **2**
12 Feb 2000 **AGIA NAPA – FANTASY ISLAND** Telstar **1**
19 Feb 2000 **THE LOVE SONGS ALBUM** Warner/Universal TV/Global TV **1**
26 Feb 2000 **REWIND – THE SOUND OF UK GARAGE** Ministry of Sound **1**
5 Mar 2000 **THE BEACH (OST)** London **3**
25 Mar 2000 **NEW HITS 2000** Warner.ESP/Global TV/Sony TV **2**
8 Apr 2000 **NEW WOMAN 2000** Virgin **1**
15 Apr 2000 **DANCE NATION – TALL PAUL/BRANDON BLOCK** Ministry of Sound **1**
22 Apr 2000 **GIRLS 2K** Virgin **1**
29 Apr 2000 **NOW! 45** EMI/Virgin/Universal **6**
10 Jun 2000 **CLUBBER'S GUIDE TO IBIZA – SUMMER 2000** Ministry of Sound **1**
17 Jun 2000 **TOP OF THE POPS 2000 – VOL 2** Universal Music TV **1**
24 Jun 2000 **CLUB MIX IBIZA 2000** Universal Music TV **3**

15 Jul 2000 **FRESH HITS – VOL 1** Warner.ESP/Global TV/Sony TV **2**
29 Jul 2000 **KISS CLUBLIFE SUMMER 2000** Universal Music TV **1**
5 Aug 2000 **NOW! 46** EMI/Virgin/Universal **4**
2 Sep 2000 **THE IBIZA ANNUAL – SUMMER 2000** Ministry of Sound **3**
23 Sep 2000 **KISS IBIZA 2000** Universal Music TV **2**
7 Oct 2000 **TRANCE NATION 4** Ministry of Sound **3**
28 Oct 2000 **CLUBMIX 2000 – VOL 2** Universal Music TV **1**
4 Nov 2000 **NOW DANCE 2001** Virgin **1**
11 Nov 2000 **THE ANNUAL 2000 – JUDGE JULES/TALL PAUL** Ministry of Sound **2**
25 Nov 2000 **CREAM ANTHEMS 2001** Virgin **1**
2 Dec 2000 **NOW! 47** EMI/Virgin/Universal **7**
20 Jan 2001 **CLUBBERS GUIDE TO 2001** Ministry of Sound **2**
3 Feb 2001 **BREAKDOWN - VERY BEST OF EUPHORIC DANCE** BMG Commercial/Telstar **2**
17 Feb 2001 **THE CHILLOUT SESSION** Ministry of Sound **7**
31 Mar 2001 **NEW WOMAN 2001** Virgin **1**
7 Apr 2001 **THE ANNUAL – SPRING 2001** Ministry of Sound **2**
21 Apr 2001 **NOW! 48** EMI/Virgin/Universal **3**
12 May 2001 **BRIDGET JONES'S DIARY (OST)** Mercury **6**
23 Jun 2001 **CAPITOL GOLD LEGENDS** Virgin/EMI **7**
11 Aug 2001 **NOW! 49** EMI/Virgin/Universal **6**
22 Sep 2001 **THE CLASSIC CHILLOUT ALBUM** Columbia **2***
29 Sep 2001 **HITS 50** BMG/Sony/Telstar/WSM **2**
20 Oc 2001 **PEPSI CHART 2002** Virgin/EMI **2**
3 Nov 2001 **NOW DANCE 2002** Virgin/EMI **2**
17 Nov 2001 **THE ANNUAL 2002** Ministry of Sound **2**
1 Dec 2001 **NOW! 50** EMI/Virgin/Universal **7**
19 Jan 2002 **CLUBBERS GUIDE TO 2002** Ministry of Sound **3**
9 Feb 2002 **THE BEST CLUB ANTHEMS 2002** Virgin/EMI **1**
16 Feb 2002 **CLUB MIX 2002** Universal TV **1**
23 Feb 2002 **LOVE SO STRONG** WSM **1**
2 Mar 2002 **SCHOOLDISCO.COM – SPRING TERM** Columbia **2**
16 Mar 2002 **NEW WOMAN 2002** Virgin TV **1**
23 Mar 2002 **SUPERCHARGED** Universal TV **2**
6 Apr 2002 **NOW! 51** EMI/Virgin **3***
20 Apr 2002 **POP IDOL –THE BIG BAND ALBUM** S/RCA **4**
25 May 2002 **KISSTORY – DANCE CLASSICS** Universal TV **1**
1 Jun 2002 **THE BEST SUMMER ALBUM 2002** Sony TV/WSM **1**
8 Jun 2002 **CLUBBERS GUIDE TO IBIZA 2002** Ministry of Sound **1**
15 Jun 2002 **SMASH! HITS – SUMMER 2002** EMI/Virgin/Universal **1**
22 Jun 2002 **CAPITOL GOLD ROCK LEGENDS** EMI Virgin **1**
29 Jun 2002 **THE VERY BEST OF MTV UNPLUGGED** WSM/Universal TV **1**
6 Jul 2002 **CLUBLAND – THE RIDE OF YOUR LIFE** Universal TV **4**
3 Aug 2002 **NOW! 52** EMI/Virgin/Universal TV **5**
7 Sep 2002 **THE VERY BEST OF PURE R&B – THE SUMMER COLLECTION** BMG/Telstar TV **1**
14 Sep 2002 **SMASH! HITS – LET'S PARTY** EMI Virgin/Universal TV **5**
19 Oct 2002 **NEW WOMAN – THE AUTUMN COLLECTION** EMI Virgin **1**
26 Oct 2002 **NOW DANCE 2003** EMI Virgin **1**
2 Nov 2002 **HITS 54** BMG/Sony/Telstar/WSM **2**
16 Nov 2002 **THE ANNUAL 2003** Ministry of Sound **1**
23 Nov 2002 **CLUBLAND II – THE RIDE OF YOUR LIFE** All Around the World/Universal TV **1**
30 Nov 2002 **NOW THAT'S WHAT I CALL MUSIC! 53** EMI/Virgin/Universal TV **7**
18 Jan 2003 **CLUBBERS GUIDE 2003** Ministry of Sound **1**
25 Jan 2003 **8 MILE (OST)** Interscope **3**
15 Feb 2003 **LOVE – ETERNAL LOVESONGS** Universal TV **2**
1 Mar 2003 **CLUB MIX 2003** Universal TV 1
8 Mar 2003 **THE VERY BEST OF MTV UNPLUGGED 2** Universal TV/WSM **2**
22 Mar 2003 **THE VERY BEST OF COLD FEET (TV SOUNDTRACK)** Universal TV **3**
12 Apr 2003 **HITS 53** BMG/Sony/Telstar/WSM **2**
26 Apr 2003 **NOW THAT'S WHAT I CALL MUSIC! 54** EMI/Virgin/Universal TV **7**
14 June 2003 **POWER BALLADS** EMI Virgin **3**
5 Jul 2003 **CLUBLANDS III – THE SOUND OF THE SUMMER** All Around the World/Universal TV **3**
26 Jul 2003 **HITS 56** BMG/Sony/Telstar/WSM **1**
2 Aug 2003 **NOW! 55** EMI/Virgin/Universal TV **5**
6 Sep 2003 **KISS PRESENT R&B COLLABORATIONS** Sony TV/Universal TV **3**
27 Sept 2003 **CLUBMIX SUMMER 2003** All Around the World/Universal TV **2**
11 Oct 2003 **NOW DECADES** EMI/Virgin/Universal TV **3**
1 Nov 2003 **GREASEMANIA (TV SOUNDTRACK)** Polydor/s **1**
8 Nov 2003 **NOW DANCE 2004** EMI Virgin **1**
15 Nov 2003 **WESTWOOD – PLATINUM EDITION 2003** Def Jam **1**
22 Nov 2003 **CLUBLAND 4** All Around the World/Universal TV **1**
29 Nov 2003 **NOW THAT'S WHAT I CALL MUSIC! 56** EMI/Virgin/Universal TV **1**

88.3 – *See Lisa MAY*

Ludovico EINAUDI *Italy, male vocalist (Albums: 4 weeks)* pos/wks

13 Sep 03 **ECHOES – THE COLLECTION** *BMG 82876550892* **40** 4

EINSTEIN *UK, male rapper (Singles: 6 weeks)* pos/wks

18 Nov 89 **ANOTHER MONSTERJAM** *ffrr F 116* [1] **65** 1
15 Dec 90 **TURN IT UP** *Swanyard SYD 9* [2] **42** 4
24 Aug 96 **THE POWER 96** *Arista 74321398672* [3] **42** 1

[1] Simon Harris featuring Einstein [2] Technotronic featuring Melissa and Einstein [3] Snap featuring Einstein

See also AMBASSADORS OF FUNK featuring MC MARIO

EL COCO *US, male vocal / instrumental group (Singles: 4 weeks)* pos/wks

14 Jan 78 **COCOMOTION** *Pye International 7N 25761* **31** 4

EL MARIACHI
US, male producer – Roger Sanchez (Singles: 2 weeks) pos/wks

9 Nov 96 **CUBA** *ffrr FCD 286* **38** 2

See also FUNK JUNKEEZ; Roger SANCHEZ

ELASTICA *UK, female / male vocal / instrumental group (Singles: 12 weeks, Albums: 27 weeks)* pos/wks

12 Feb 94 **LINE UP** *Deceptive BLUFF 004CD* **20** 3
22 Oct 94 **CONNECTION** *Deceptive BLUFF 010CD* **17** 4
25 Feb 95 **WAKING UP** *Deceptive BLUFF 011CD* **13** 4
24 Jun 00 **MAD DOG** *Deceptive BLUFF 077CD* **44** 1
25 Mar 95 ★ **ELASTICA** *Deceptive BLUFF 014CD* ■ **1** 25
15 Apr 00 **THE MENACE** *Deceptive BLUFF 075CD*....................**24** 2

ELATE
UK, male / female vocal / instrumental trio (Singles: 2 weeks) pos/wks

26 Jul 97 **SOMEBODY LIKE YOU** *VC VCRD 22* **38** 2

Donnie ELBERT
US, male vocalist, d. 26 Jan 1989 (Singles: 29 weeks) pos/wks

8 Jan 72 ● **WHERE DID OUR LOVE GO?** *London HL 10352* **8** 10
26 Feb 72 **I CAN'T HELP MYSELF** *Avco 6105 009* **11** 10
29 Apr 72 **A LITTLE PIECE OF LEATHER** *London HL 10370* **27** 9

ELBOW *UK, male vocal / instrumental group (Singles: 10 weeks, Albums: 9 weeks)* pos/wks

5 May 01 **RED** *V2 VVR 5016153* **36** 1
21 Jul 01 **POWDER BLUE** *V2 VVR 5016163* **41** 1
20 Oct 01 **NEWBORN** *V2 VVR 5016173* **42** 1
16 Feb 02 **ASLEEP IN THE BACK / COMING SECOND** *V2 VVR 5018703* **19** 3
16 Aug 03 **FALLEN ANGEL** *V2 VVR 5021803* **19** 3
8 Nov 03 **FUGITIVE MOTEL** *V2 VVR 5021823* **44** 1
19 May 01 **ASLEEP IN THE BACK** *V2 VVR 1015882* **14** 5
30 Aug 03 ● **CAST OF THOUSANDS** *V2 VVR1021812*....................**7** 4

ELECTRA *UK, male vocal / instrumental group (Singles: 7 weeks)* pos/wks

6 Aug 88 **JIBARO** *ffrr FFR 9* **54** 3
30 Dec 89 **IT'S YOUR DESTINY / AUTUMN LOVE** *London F 121* **51** 4

ELECTRAFIXION *UK, male vocal / instrumental group (Singles: 6 weeks, Albums: 2 weeks)* pos/wks

19 Nov 94 **ZEPHYR** *WEA YZ 865CD* **47** 2
9 Sep 95 **LOWDOWN** *WEA YZ 977CD* **54** 2
4 Nov 95 **NEVER** *Spacejunk WEA 022CD* **58** 1
16 Mar 96 **SISTER PAIN** *Spacejunk WEA 037CD1* **27** 1
7 Oct 95 **BURNED** *Spacejunk 0630112482*....................**38** 2

ELECTRASY *UK, male vocal / instrumental group (Singles: 7 weeks, Albums: 1 week)* pos/wks

13 Jun 98 **LOST IN SPACE** *MCA MCSTD 40171* **60** 1
5 Sep 98 **MORNING AFTERGLOW** *MCA MCSTD 40184* **19** 4
28 Nov 98 **BEST FRIEND'S GIRL** *MCA MCSXD 40195* **41** 2
26 Sep 98 **BEAUTIFUL INSANE** *MCA MCD 60051*....................**48** 1

ELECTRIBE 101 *UK / Germany, male / female vocal / instrumental group (Singles: 15 weeks, Albums: 3 weeks)* pos/wks

28 Oct 89 **TELL ME WHEN THE FEVER ENDED** *Mercury MER 310* **32** 5
24 Feb 90 **TALKING WITH MYSELF** *Mercury MER 316* **23** 5
22 Sep 90 **YOU'RE WALKING** *Mercury MER 328* **50** 3
10 Oct 98 **TALKING WITH MYSELF (re-mix)** *Manifesto FESDD 49* **39** 2
20 Oct 90 **ELECTRIBAL MEMORIES** *Mercury 8429651* **26** 3

ELECTRIC BOYS
Sweden, male vocal / instrumental group (Albums: 1 week) pos/wks

6 Jun 92 **GROOVUS MAXIMUS** *Vertigo 5122552* **61** 1

ELECTRIC LIGHT ORCHESTRA *49* **Top 500**
Ground-breaking and innovative UK group, fronted by multi-talented Jeff Lynne (v/g) from Birmingham and originally included Roy Wood (The Move). Their unique sound, which featured an orchestral string section, helped them to achieve numerous transatlantic hits (Singles: 255 weeks, Albums: 393 weeks) pos/wks

29 Jul 72 ● **10538 OVERTURE** *Harvest HAR 5053* **9** 8
27 Jan 73 ● **ROLL OVER BEETHOVEN** *Harvest HAR 5063* **6** 10
6 Oct 73 **SHOWDOWN** *Harvest HAR 5077* **12** 10
9 Mar 74 **MA-MA-MA-BELLE** *Warner Bros. K 16349* **22** 8
10 Jan 76 ● **EVIL WOMAN** *Jet 764* **10** 8
3 Jul 76 **STRANGE MAGIC** *Jet 779* **38** 3
13 Nov 76 ● **LIVIN' THING** *Jet UP 36184* **4** 12
19 Feb 77 ● **ROCKARIA!** *Jet UP 36209* **9** 9
21 May 77 ● **TELEPHONE LINE** *Jet UP 36254* **8** 10
29 Oct 77 **TURN TO STONE** *Jet UP 36313* **18** 12
28 Jan 78 ● **MR BLUE SKY** *Jet UP 36342* **6** 11
10 Jun 78 ● **WILD WEST HERO** *Jet JET 109* **6** 14
7 Oct 78 ● **SWEET TALKIN' WOMAN** *Jet 121* **6** 9
9 Dec 78 **THE ELO EP** *Jet ELO 1* **34** 8
19 May 79 ● **SHINE A LITTLE LOVE** *Jet 144* **6** 10
21 Jul 79 ● **THE DIARY OF HORACE WIMP** *Jet 150* **8** 9
1 Sep 79 ● **DON'T BRING ME DOWN** *Jet 153* **3** 9
17 Nov 79 ● **CONFUSION / LAST TRAIN TO LONDON** *Jet 166* **8** 10
24 May 80 **I'M ALIVE** *Jet 179* **20** 9
21 Jun 80 ★ **XANADU** *Jet 185* [1] **1** 11
2 Aug 80 **ALL OVER THE WORLD** *Jet 195* **11** 8
22 Nov 80 **DON'T WALK AWAY** *Jet 7004* **21** 10
1 Aug 81 ● **HOLD ON TIGHT** *Jet 7011* [2] **4** 12
24 Oct 81 **TWILIGHT** *Jet 7015* **30** 7
9 Jan 82 **TICKET TO THE MOON / HERE IS THE NEWS** *Jet 7018* [3] **24** 8
18 Jun 83 **ROCK 'N' ROLL IS KING** *Jet A 3500* **13** 9
3 Sep 83 **SECRET MESSAGES** *Jet A 3720* **48** 3
1 Mar 86 **CALLING AMERICA** *Epic A 6844* **28** 7
11 May 91 **HONEST MEN PART TWO** *Telstar ELO 100* [4] **60** 1
12 Aug 72 **ELECTRIC LIGHT ORCHESTRA** *Harvest SHVL 797*....................**32** 4
31 Mar 73 **ELECTRIC LIGHT ORCHESTRA II** *Harvest SHVL 806* **35** 1
11 Dec 76 ● **A NEW WORLD RECORD** *United Artists UAG 30017*....................**6** 100
12 Nov 77 ● **OUT OF THE BLUE** *United Artists UAR 100*....................**4** 108
6 Jan 79 **THREE LIGHT YEARS** *Jet JET BX 1* **38** 9
16 Jun 79 ★ **DISCOVERY** *Jet JET LX 500* ■ **1** 46
1 Dec 79 ● **ELO'S GREATEST HITS** *Jet JET LX 525*....................**7** 18
8 Aug 81 ★ **TIME** *Jet JETLP 236*....................**1** 32
2 Jul 83 ● **SECRET MESSAGES** *Jet JET LX 527* **4** 15
15 Mar 86 ● **BALANCE OF POWER** *Epic EPC 26467* **9** 12
16 Dec 89 **THE GREATEST HITS** *Telstar STAR 2370* **23** 21
1 Jun 91 **ELECTRIC LIGHT ORCHESTRA PART II** *Telstar STAR 2503* [1] **34** 4
2 Jul 94 ● **THE VERY BEST OF THE ELECTRIC LIGHT ORCHESTRA** *Dino DINCD 90*....................**4** 11
8 Nov 97 **LIGHT YEARS – THE VERY BEST OF ELECTRIC LIGHT ORCHESTRA** *Epic 4890392*....................**60** 4
23 Jun 01 **ZOOM** *Epic 5025002*....................**34** 2
3 Nov 01 **THE ULTIMATE COLLECTION** *Columbia STVCD 126* **18** 6

[1] Olivia Newton-John and Electric Light Orchestra [2] ELO [3] ELO ('Here Is the News' only) [4] Electric Light Orchestra Part 2 [1] ELO Part 2

'Here Is the News' listed from 16 Jan 1982. Tracks on The ELO EP: Can't Get It Out of My Head / Strange Magic / Ma-Ma-Ma-Belle / Evil Woman 'A New World Record' changed label number to JET LP 200 and 'Out of the Blue' changed to JET DP 400 during their chart runs. 'The Greatest Hits' was also issued under the title 'The Very Best of Electric Light Orchestra' with the same track listings and catalogue number

ELECTRIC PRUNES
US, male vocal / instrumental group (Singles: 5 weeks) pos/wks

9 Feb 67 **I HAD TOO MUCH TO DREAM (LAST NIGHT)** *Reprise RS 20532* 49 1
11 May 67 **GET ME TO THE WORLD ON TIME** *Reprise RS 20564* 42 4

ELECTRIC SIX *US, male vocal / instrumental group (Singles: 22 weeks, Albums: 10 weeks)* pos/wks

18 Jan 03 ● **DANGER! HIGH VOLTAGE** *XL Recordings XLS 151CD* 2 11
14 Jun 03 ● **GAY BAR** *XL Recordings XLS 158CD* 5 10
25 Oct 03 **DANCE COMMANDER** *XL Recordings XLS 170CD* 40 1
12 Jul 03 ● **FIRE** *XL XLCD169* 7 10

ELECTRIC SOFT PARADE *UK, male vocal / instrumental group (Singles: 5 weeks, Albums: 3 weeks)* pos/wks

4 Aug 01 **EMPTY AT THE END / SUMATRAN** *DB DB 006CD7* [1] 65 1
10 Nov 01 **THERE'S A SILENCE** *DB DB 007CD7* 52 1
16 Mar 02 **SILENT TO THE DARK II** *DB DB 008CD7* 23 2
1 Jun 02 **EMPTY AT THE END / THIS GIVEN LINE** *DB DB 009CD7* 39 1
16 Feb 02 **HOLES IN THE WALL** *DB DB 002CDLP* 35 2
25 Oct 03 **THE AMERICAN ADVENTURE** *BMG 82876563692* 45 1

[1] Soft Parade

The 2002 version of 'Empty at the End' is a re-recording

ELECTRIC SUN – *See Uli Jon ROTH and ELECTRIC SUN*

ELECTRIC WIND ENSEMBLE
UK, male instrumental group (Albums: 9 weeks) pos/wks

18 Feb 84 **HAUNTING MELODIES** *Nouveau Music NML 1007* 28 9

ELECTRIQUE BOUTIQUE
UK / France, male production group (Singles: 2 weeks) pos/wks

26 Aug 00 **REVELATION** *Data DATA 14CDS* 37 2

ELECTRONIC *UK, male vocal / instrumental group (Singles: 36 weeks, Albums: 24 weeks)* pos/wks

16 Dec 89 **GETTING AWAY WITH IT** *Factory FAC 2577* 12 9
27 Apr 91 ● **GET THE MESSAGE** *Factory FAC 2877* 8 7
21 Sep 91 **FEEL EVERY BEAT** *Factory FAC 3287* 39 4
4 Jul 92 ● **DISAPPOINTED** *Parlophone R 6311* 6 5
6 Jul 96 **FORBIDDEN CITY** *Parlophone CDR 6436* 14 4
28 Sep 96 **FOR YOU** *Parlophone CDR 6445* 16 2
15 Feb 97 **SECOND NATURE** *Parlophone CDR 6455* 35 2
24 Apr 99 **VIVID** *Parlopbone CDR 6514* 17 3
8 Jun 91 ● **ELECTRONIC** *Factory FACT 290* 2 16
20 Jul 96 ● **RAISE THE PRESSURE** *Parlophone CDPCS 7382* 8 5
8 May 99 ● **TWISTED TENDERNESS** *Parlophone 5201462* 9 3

ELECTRONICAS
Holland, male instrumental group (Singles: 8 weeks) pos/wks

19 Sep 81 **ORIGINAL BIRD DANCE** *Polydor POSP 360* 22 8

ELECTROSET
UK, male instrumental / production group (Singles: 4 weeks) pos/wks

21 Nov 92 **HOW DOES IT FEEL** *ffrr F 203* 27 3
15 Jul 95 **SENSATION** *Ffrreedom TABCD 231* 69 1

ELEGANTS *US, male vocal group (Singles: 2 weeks)* pos/wks

26 Sep 58 **LITTLE STAR** *HMV POP 520* ▲ 25 2

ELEMENT FOUR *UK, male production duo – Paul Oakenfold and Andy Gray (Singles: 11 weeks)* pos/wks

9 Sep 00 ● **BIG BROTHER UK TV THEME (re)** *Channel 4 Music C4M 00072* 4 11

ELEPHANT MAN
Jamaica, male vocalist – O'Neil Bryan (Singles: 3 weeks) pos/wks

22 Nov 03 **PON DE RIVER, PON DE BANK** *Atlantic AT 0168CD* 29 3

ELEVATION
UK, male instrumental / production duo (Singles: 1 week) pos/wks

23 May 92 **CAN U FEEL IT** *Nova Mute 12NOMU 3* 62 1

ELEVATOR SUITE
UK, male production / instrumental trio (Singles: 1 week) pos/wks

12 Aug 00 **BACK AROUND** *Infectious INFECT 85CDS* 71 1

ELEVATORMAN
UK, male instrumental / production group (Singles: 4 weeks) pos/wks

14 Jan 95 **FUNK AND DRIVE** *Wired WIRED 211* 37 3
1 Jul 95 **FIRED UP** *Wired WIRED 216* 44 1

Danny ELFMAN
US, male orchestra leader (Albums: 6 weeks) pos/wks

12 Aug 89 **BATMAN** *Warner Bros. WX 287* 45 6

ELGINS
US, male / female vocal group (Singles: 20 weeks) pos/wks

1 May 71 ● **HEAVEN MUST HAVE SENT YOU** *Tamla Motown TMG 771* 3 13
9 Oct 71 **PUT YOURSELF IN MY PLACE** *Tamla Motown TMG 787* 28 7

ELIAS and his ZIG-ZAG JIVE FLUTES
South Africa, male instrumental group (Singles: 14 weeks) pos/wks

25 Apr 58 ● **TOM HARK** *Columbia DB 4109* 2 14

Yvonne ELLIMAN
US, female vocalist (Singles: 44 weeks) pos/wks

29 Jan 72 **I DON'T KNOW HOW TO LOVE HIM** *MCA MMKS 5077* 47 1
6 Nov 76 ● **LOVE ME** *RSO 2090 205* 6 13
7 May 77 **HELLO STRANGER** *RSO 2090 236* 26 5
13 Aug 77 **I CAN'T GET YOU OUT OF MY MIND** *RSO 2090 251* 17 13
6 May 78 ● **IF I CAN'T HAVE YOU** *RSO 2090 266* ▲ 4 12

'I Don't Know How to Love Him' was one of four tracks on a maxi-single, two of which were credited during the disc's one week on the chart. The other track credited was 'Superstar' by Murray Head

Duke ELLINGTON *US, male band leader / instrumentalist – piano, d. 24 May 1974 (Singles: 4 weeks, Albums: 2 weeks)* pos/wks

5 Mar 54 ● **SKIN DEEP** *Philips PB 243* [1] 7 4
8 Apr 61 **NUT CRACKER SUITE** *Philips BBL 7418* 11 2

[1] Duke Ellington and his Orchestra with Louis Bellson (drums)

Lance ELLINGTON
UK, male vocalist (Singles: 1 week) pos/wks

21 Aug 93 **LONELY (HAVE WE LOST OUR LOVE)** *RCA 74321158332* 57 1

Ray ELLINGTON *UK, male vocal / instrumental group, leader d. 27 Feb 1985 (Singles: 4 weeks)* pos/wks

15 Nov 62 **THE MADISON (re)** *Ember S 102* 36 4

Bern ELLIOTT and the FENMEN
UK, male vocal / instrumental group (Singles: 22 weeks) pos/wks

21 Nov 63 **MONEY** *Decca F 11770* 14 13
19 Mar 64 **NEW ORLEANS** *Decca F 11852* 24 9

Joe ELLIOTT – *See Mick RONSON with Joe ELLIOTT*

Missy 'Misdemeanor' ELLIOTT

453 Top 500 *Leading female rapper / songwriter / producer / arranger and record label (Gold Mind) boss, b. Melissa Elliott, Virginia, 1 Jul 1972. Award-winning hip hop / R&B legend, who first surfaced in group Sista in 1992, has recorded with numerous artists and charted with 14 of them (Singles: 99 weeks, Albums: 53 weeks)*

Date	Title	pos	wks
30 Aug 97	**THE RAIN (SUPA DUPA FLY)** *East West E 3919 CD*	16	3
29 Nov 97	**SOCKIT2ME** *East West E 3890CD* [1]	33	2
25 Apr 98	**BEEP ME 911** *East West E 3859CD*	14	3
22 Aug 98	**MAKE IT HOT** *East West E 3821 CD* [2]	22	4
22 Aug 98	**HIT 'EM WIT DA HEE** *East West E3824 CD1* [3]	25	3
26 Sep 98 ★	**I WANT YOU BACK** *Virgin VSCDT 1716* [4] ■	1	9
21 Nov 98	**5 MINUTES** *Elektra E 3803CD* [5]	72	1
13 Mar 99	**HERE WE COME** *Virgin DINSD 179* [6]	43	1
25 Sep 99	**ALL N MY GRILL** *Elektra E 3742 CD* [7]	20	4
22 Jan 00	**HOT BOYZ** *Elektra E 7002CD* [8]	18	3
28 Apr 01 ●	**GET UR FREAK ON** *East West / Elektra E 7206CD*	4	11
18 Aug 01 ●	**ONE MINUTE MAN** *Elektra E 7245CD* [9]	10	8
13 Oct 01	**SUPERFREAKON** *East West / Elektra 7559672550*	72	1
22 Dec 01	**SON OF A GUN (I BETCHA THINK THIS SONG IS ABOUT YOU) (re)** *Virgin VUSCD 232* [10]	13	9
6 Apr 02 ●	**4 MY PEOPLE** *Goldmind / Elektra E 7286CD*	5	13
16 Nov 02 ●	**WORK IT** *Goldmind / Elektra E7344CD* [11]	6	9
22 Mar 03 ●	**GOSSIP FOLKS** *Elektra E 7380CD* [12]	9	9
22 Nov 03 ●	**PASS THAT DUTCH** *East West E 7509CD*	10	6+
10 Jul 99	**DA REAL WORLD** *Elektra 7559624362*	42	2
26 May 01 ●	**MISS E ... SO ADDICTIVE** *Elektra 7559626392*	10	26
23 Nov 02	**UNDER CONSTRUCTION** *Elektra 7559628132*	23	22
6 Dec 03	**THIS IS NOT A TEST** *Elektra 7559629052*	49	3

[1] Missy 'Misdemeanor' Elliott featuring Da Brat [2] Nicole featuring Missy 'Misdemeanor' Elliott and Mocha [3] Missy 'Misdemeanor' Elliott featuring Lil' Kim [4] Melanie B featuring Missy 'Misdemeanor' Elliott [5] Lil' Mo featuring Missy 'Misdemeanor' Elliott [6] Timbaland / Missy Elliott and Magoo [7] Missy 'Misdemeanor' Elliott featuring MC Solaar [8] Missy 'Misdemeanor' Elliott featuring Nas, Eve and Q Tip [9] Missy 'Misdemeanor' Elliott featuring Ludacris [10] Janet with Carly Simon featuring Missy Elliott [11] Missy Elliott [12] Missy Elliott featuring Ludacris

Greg ELLIS – *See Reva RICE and Greg ELLIS*

Joey B ELLIS

US, male rapper (Singles: 10 weeks)

Date	Title	pos	wks
16 Feb 91	**GO FOR IT (HEART AND FIRE)** *Capitol CL 601* [1]	20	8
18 May 91	**THOUGHT U WERE THE ONE FOR ME** *Capitol CL 614*	58	2

[1] Rocky V featuring Joey B Ellis and Tynetta Hare

Shirley ELLIS

US, female vocalist (Singles: 17 weeks)

Date	Title	pos	wks
6 May 65 ●	**THE CLAPPING SONG** *London HLR 9961*	6	13
8 Jul 78	**THE CLAPPING SONG (EP)** *MCA MCEP 1*	59	4

Tracks on The Clapping Song (EP): The Clapping Song / Ever See a Diver Kiss His Wife While the Bubbles Bounce Above the Water / The Name Game / The Nitty Gritty. 'The Clapping Song' itself qualifies as a re-issue

ELLIS, BEGGS and HOWARD

UK, male vocal / instrumental group (Singles: 8 weeks)

Date	Title	pos	wks
2 Jul 88	**BIG BUBBLES, NO TROUBLES (re)** *RCA PB 42089*	41	8

Peak position reached on its re-entry in Mar 89

Sophie ELLIS-BEXTOR

UK, female vocalist (Singles: 81 weeks, Albums: 46 weeks)

Date	Title	pos	wks
26 Aug 00 ★	**GROOVEJET (IF THIS AIN'T LOVE)** *Positiva CDTIV 137* ■ [1]	1	24
25 Aug 01 ●	**TAKE ME HOME (A GIRL LIKE ME)** *Polydor 5872312*	2	12
15 Dec 01 ●	**MURDER ON THE DANCEFLOOR** *Polydor 5704942*	2	16
22 Jun 02 ●	**GET OVER YOU / MOVE THIS MOUNTAIN** *Polydor 5708332*	3	13
16 Nov 02	**MUSIC GETS THE BEST OF ME** *Polydor 0659222*	14	10
25 Oct 03 ●	**MIXED UP WORLD** *Polydor 9812108*	7	6
15 Sep 01 ●	**READ MY LIPS** *Polydor 5891742*	2	44
8 Nov 03	**SHOOT FROM THE HIP** *Polydor 9865834*	19	2

[1] Spiller, lead vocals by Sophie Ellis-Bextor

See also THEAUDIENCE; SPILLER

Jennifer ELLISON

UK, female vocalist (Singles: 10 weeks)

Date	Title	pos	wks
28 Aug 03 ●	**BABY I DON'T CARE** *East West EW 268CD1*	6	10

Ben ELTON

UK, male comedian (Albums: 2 weeks)

Date	Title	pos	wks
14 Nov 87	**MOTORMOUTH** *Mercury BENLP 1*	86	2

ELWOOD

US, male rapper / vocalist – Elwood Strickland (Singles: 1 week)

Date	Title	pos	wks
26 Aug 00	**SUNDOWN** *Palm Pictures PPCD 70342*	72	1

EMBRACE

UK, male vocal / instrumental group (Singles: 38 weeks, Albums: 39 weeks)

Date	Title	pos	wks
17 May 97	**FIREWORKS EP** *Hut HUTCD 84*	34	2
19 Jul 97	**ONE BIG FAMILY EP** *Hut HUTCD 86*	21	3
8 Nov 97 ●	**ALL YOU GOOD GOOD PEOPLE (EP)** *Hut HUTCD 90*	8	4
6 Jun 98 ●	**COME BACK TO WHAT YOU KNOW** *Hut HUTCD 93*	6	8
29 Aug 98 ●	**MY WEAKNESS IS NONE OF YOUR BUSINESS** *Hut HUTCD 103*	9	4
13 Nov 99	**HOOLIGAN** *Hut HUTCD 123*	18	3
25 Mar 00	**YOU'RE NOT ALONE** *Hut / Virgin HUTCD 126*	14	3
10 Jun 00	**SAVE ME (re)** *Hut / Virgin HUTCD 133*	29	3
19 Aug 00	**I WOULDN'T WANNA HAPPEN TO YOU** *Hut / Virgin HUTCD 137*	23	2
1 Sep 01	**WONDER (re)** *Hut / Virgin HUTCD 142*	14	4
17 Nov 01	**MAKE IT LAST** *Hut / Virgin HUTCD 144*	35	2
20 Jun 98 ★	**THE GOOD WILL OUT** *Hut CDHUT 46* ■	1	21
8 Apr 00 ●	**DRAWN FROM MEMORY** *Hut CDHUT 60*	8	13
15 Sep 01 ●	**IF YOU'VE NEVER BEEN** *Hut CDHUT 68*	9	3
6 Apr 02	**FIREWORKS (SINGLES 1997-2002)** *Hut CDHUT 74*	36	2

Tracks on Fireworks (EP): The Last Gas / Now You're Nobody / Blind / Fireworks. Tracks on One Big Family (EP): One Big Family / Dry Kids / You've Only Got to Stop to Get Better / Butter Wouldn't Melt. Tracks on All You Good Good People (EP): All You Good Good People / You Don't Amount to Anything – This Time / The Way I Do / Free Ride

EMERSON – *See SASHA*

Keith EMERSON

UK, male instrumentalist – keyboards (Singles: 5 weeks)

Date	Title	pos	wks
10 Apr 76	**HONKY TONK TRAIN BLUES** *Manticore K 13513*	21	5

See also EMERSON, LAKE and PALMER; EMERSON, LAKE and POWELL

EMERSON, LAKE and PALMER

465 Top 500 *Pioneering armour-plated progressive rock supertrio, Keith Emerson, ex-Nice (k), Greg Lake, ex-King Crimson, (v,b,g) and Carl Palmer, ex-Atomic Rooster and Crazy World of Arthur Brown (d). Their classical-orientated rock helped change the face of 1970s music (Singles: 13 weeks, Albums: 135 weeks)*

Date	Title	pos	wks
4 Jun 77 ●	**FANFARE FOR THE COMMON MAN** *Atlantic K 10946*	2	13
5 Dec 70 ●	**EMERSON, LAKE AND PALMER** *Island ILPS 9132*	4	28
19 Jun 71 ★	**TARKUS** *Island ILPS 9155*	1	17
4 Dec 71 ●	**PICTURES AT AN EXHIBITION** *Island HELP 1*	3	5
8 Jul 72 ●	**TRILOGY** *Island ILPS 9186*	2	29
22 Dec 73 ●	**BRAIN SALAD SURGERY** *Manticore K 53501*	2	17
24 Aug 74 ●	**WELCOME BACK MY FRIENDS TO THE SHOW THAT NEVER ENDS – LADIES AND GENTLEMEN: EMERSON, LAKE AND PALMER** *Manticore K 63500*	5	5
9 Apr 77 ●	**WORKS** *Atlantic K 80009*	9	25
10 Dec 77	**WORKS VOLUME 2** *Atlantic K 50422*	20	5
9 Dec 78	**LOVE BEACH** *Atlantic K50552*	48	4

See also ASIA; Keith EMERSON; Greg LAKE

EMERSON, LAKE and POWELL

UK, male vocal / instrumental group (Albums: 5 weeks)

Date	Title	pos	wks
14 Jun 86	**EMERSON, LAKE AND POWELL** *Polydor POLD 5191*	35	5

See also EMERSON LAKE and PALMER; Greg LAKE; Cozy POWELL; Keith EMERSON

Dick EMERY

UK, male actor / vocalist, d. 2 Jan 1983 (Singles: 8 weeks) pos/wks

26 Feb 69	**IF YOU LOVE HER** *Pye 7N 17644*	32	4
13 Jan 73	**YOU ARE AWFUL** *Pye 7N 45202*	43	4

EMILIA

Sweden, female vocalist – Emilia Rydberg (Singles: 14 weeks) pos/wks

12 Dec 98 ●	**BIG BIG WORLD** *Universal UMD 87190*	5	13
1 May 99	**GOOD SIGN** *Universal UMD 87206*	54	1

EMINEM (114 Top 500)

Controversy-courting, chainsaw-wielding, multi-award-winning rap superstar, whose real name is Marshall Mathers (aka Slim Shady) b. 17 Oct 1974, Detroit. The 2003 Brit and Oscar winner is the most successful rap artist in UK chart history (Singles: 140 weeks, Albums: 257 weeks) pos/wks

10 Apr 99 ●	**MY NAME IS (re)** *Interscope IND 95638*	2	12
14 Aug 99 ●	**GUILTY CONSCIENCE** *Interscope IND 4971282* [1]	5	8
10 Jun 00 ●	**FORGOT ABOUT DRE** *Interscope 4973412* [2]	7	9
8 Jul 00 ★	**THE REAL SLIM SHADY** *Interscope 4973792* ■	1	15
14 Oct 00 ●	**THE WAY I AM** *Interscope 4974252*	8	9
16 Dec 00 ★	**STAN (re)** *Interscope IND 97470* ■	1	17
1 Sep 01	**SCARY MOVIES** *Mole UK MOLE UK 045* [3]	63	1
1 Jun 02 ★	**WITHOUT ME** *Interscope 4977282* ■	1	16
28 Sep 02 ●	**CLEANIN' OUT MY CLOSET (2re)** *Interscope 4973942*	4	13
14 Dec 02 ★	**LOSE YOURSELF** *Interscope 4978282* ■ ▲	1	21
15 Mar 03 ●	**SING FOR THE MOMENT** *Interscope 4978612*	6	10
19 Jul 03 ●	**BUSINESS** *Interscope 9809382*	6	9
24 Apr 99 ●	**THE SLIM SHADY LP** *Interscope IND 90321*	10	114
3 Jun 00 ★	**THE MARSHALL MATHERS LP** *Interscope 4906292* ▲	1	74
8 Jun 02 ★	**THE EMINEM SHOW** *Interscope 4932902* ■ ▲	1	69

[1] Eminem featuring Dr. Dre
[2] Dr Dre featuring Eminem
[3] Bad meets Evil featuring Eminem & Royce Da 5'9"

'Stan' features uncredited vocal by Dido

EMMA

UK, female vocalist – Emma Booth (Singles: 6 weeks) pos/wks

28 Apr 90	**GIVE A LITTLE LOVE BACK TO THE WORLD** *Big Wave BWR 33*	33	6

EMMANUEL & ESKA – *See COLOURS featuring EMMANUEL & ESKA; EN-CORE featuring Stephen EMMANUEL & ESKA*

EMMIE

UK, female vocalist – Emma Morton-Smith (Singles: 9 weeks) pos/wks

23 Jan 99 ●	**MORE THAN THIS** *Indirect / Manifesto FESCD 52*	5	8
16 Feb 02	**I WON'T LET YOU DOWN** *Decode / Telstar CDSTAS 3210* [1]	53	1

[1] W.I.P. featuring Emmie

See also INDIEN

EMOTIONS

US, female vocal group (Singles: 28 weeks) pos/wks

10 Sep 77 ●	**BEST OF MY LOVE** *CBS 5555* ▲	4	10
24 Dec 77	**I DON'T WANNA LOSE YOUR LOVE** *CBS 5819*	40	5
12 May 79 ●	**BOOGIE WONDERLAND** *CBS 7292* [1]	4	13

[1] Earth Wind and Fire with The Emotions

Alec EMPIRE

Germany, male producer (Singles: 1 week, Albums: 1 week) pos/wks

13 Apr 02	**ADDICTED TO YOU** *Digital Hardcore DHRMCD 38*	64	1
4 May 02	**INTELLIGENCE & SACRIFICE** *Digital Hardcore DHRCD 29*	71	1

EMPIRION

UK, male instrumental / production group (Singles: 2 weeks) pos/wks

6 Jul 96	**NARCOTIC INFLUENCE** *XL XLS 72CD*	64	1
21 Jun 97	**BETA** *XL XLS 77CD*	75	1

EN VOGUE

US, female vocal group (Singles: 83 weeks, Albums: 52 weeks) pos/wks

5 May 90 ●	**HOLD ON** *East West America 7908*	5	11
21 Jul 90	**LIES** *East West America 7893*	44	4
4 Apr 92 ●	**MY LOVIN' (re)** *East West America A 8578*	4	12
15 Aug 92	**GIVING HIM SOMETHING HE CAN FEEL** *East West America A 8524*	44	3
7 Nov 92	**FREE YOUR MIND / GIVING HIM SOMETHING HE CAN FEEL (re-issue)** *East West America A 8468*	16	8
16 Jan 93	**GIVE IT UP TURN IT LOOSE** *East West America A 8445CD*	22	4
10 Apr 93	**LOVE DON'T LOVE YOU** *East West America A 8424CD*	64	1
9 Oct 93	**RUNAWAY LOVE** *East West America A 8359CD*	36	3
19 Mar 94 ●	**WHATTA MAN** *ffrr FCD 222* [1]	7	10
11 Jan 97 ●	**DON'T LET GO (LOVE)** *East West A 3976CD*	5	16
14 Jun 97	**WHATEVER** *East West E 3642CD*	14	5
6 Sep 97	**TOO GONE, TOO LONG** *East West E 3908CD*	20	3
28 Nov 98	**HOLD ON (re-mix)** *East West E 3796 CD*	53	1
1 Jul 00	**RIDDLE** *Elektra E 7053CD*	33	2
2 Jun 90	**BORN TO SING** *Atlantic 7567820841*	23	13
23 May 92 ●	**FUNKY DIVAS** *East West America 7567921212*	4	29
28 Jun 97 ●	**EV3** *East West 7559620972*	9	8
31 Oct 98	**BEST OF EN VOGUE** *East West 7559623222*	39	2

[1] Salt-N-Pepa with En Vogue

EN-CORE featuring Stephen EMMANUEL & ESKA

UK, male producer – Stephen Boreland and female vocalist – Eska Mtungwazi (Singles: 2 weeks) pos/wks

9 Sep 00	**COOCHY COO** *VC Recordings VCRD 72*	32	2

ENCORE

France, female vocalist – Sabine Ohmes (Singles: 4 weeks) pos/wks

14 Feb 98	**LE DISC JOCKEY** *Sum CDSUM 2*	12	4

ENERGISE

UK, male vocal / instrumental group (Singles: 1 week) pos/wks

16 Feb 91	**REPORT TO THE DANCEFLOOR** *Network NWKT 16*	69	1

ENERGY 52 *Germany, male DJ / producer – Paul Schmitz-Moormann (Singles: 11 weeks)* pos/wks

8 Mar 97	**CAFÉ DEL MAR** *Hooj Choons HOOJCD 51*	51	1
25 Jul 98	**CAFÉ DEL MAR (re-mix)** *Hooj Choons HOOJ 64CD*	12	6
12 Oct 02	**CAFÉ DEL MAR (2nd re-mix)** *Lost Language LOST 019CD*	24	4

ENERGY ORCHARD *Ireland, male vocal / instrumental group (Singles: 6 weeks, Albums: 2 weeks)* pos/wks

27 Jan 90	**BELFAST** *MCA MCA 1392*	52	4
7 Apr 90	**SAILORTOWN** *MCA MCA 1402*	73	2
12 May 90	**ENERGY ORCHARD** *MCA MCG 6083*	53	2

Harry ENFIELD

UK, male comedian / vocalist (Singles: 7 weeks) pos/wks

7 May 88 ●	**LOADSAMONEY (DOIN' UP THE HOUSE)** *Mercury DOSH 1*	4	7

ENGLAND BOYS

UK, male vocal group (Singles: 3 weeks) pos/wks

8 Jun 02	**GO ENGLAND** *Phonogram 5829592*	26	3

ENGLAND DAN and John Ford COLEY *US, male vocal duo – Dan Seals and John Ford Coley (Singles: 12 weeks)* pos/wks

25 Sep 76	**I'D REALLY LOVE TO SEE YOU TONIGHT** *Atlantic K 10810*	26	7
23 Jun 79	**LOVE IS THE ANSWER** *Big Tree K 11296*	45	5

ENGLAND RUGBY WORLD CUP SQUAD – *See UNION featuring the ENGLAND WORLD CUP SQUAD*

ENGLAND SISTERS – *See DALE SISTERS*

ENGLAND SUPPORTERS' BAND

UK, male instrumental group (Singles: 4 weeks) pos/wks

Date		Title / Label	Pos	Wks
27 Jun 98		**THE GREAT ESCAPE** *V2 VVR 5002163*	46	2
24 Jun 00		**THE GREAT ESCAPE 2000 (re-recording)** *V2 VVR 5014293*	26	2

ENGLAND UNITED

UK, male / female vocal / instrumental group (Singles: 11 weeks) pos/wks

Date		Title / Label	Pos	Wks
13 Jun 98	●	**(HOW DOES IT FEEL TO BE) ON TOP OF THE WORLD (re)** *London LONCD 414*	9	11

ENGLAND WORLD CUP SQUAD

UK, male football team vocalists (Singles: 48 weeks, Albums: 18 weeks) pos/wks

Date		Title / Label	Pos	Wks
18 Apr 70	★	**BACK HOME (re)** *Pye 7N 17920*	1	17
10 Apr 82	●	**THIS TIME (WE'LL GET IT RIGHT) / ENGLAND, WE'LL FLY THE FLAG** *England ER 1*	2	13
19 Apr 86		**WE'VE GOT THE WHOLE WORLD AT OUR FEET / WHEN WE ARE FAR FROM HOME** *Columbia DB 9128*	66	2
21 May 88		**ALL THE WAY** *MCA GOAL 1* [1]	64	2
2 Jun 90	★	**WORLD IN MOTION . . .** *Factory / MCA FAC 2937* [2]	1	12
15 Jun 02		**WORLD IN MOTION (re-issue)** *London / MCA NUDOCD 12* [2]	43	2
16 May 70	●	**THE WORLD BEATERS SING THE WORLD BEATERS** *Pye NSPL 18337* [1]	4	8
15 May 82		**THIS TIME** *K-Tel NE 1169* [1]	37	10

[1] England Football Team and the 'sound' of Stock, Aitken and Waterman
[2] Englandneworder (comprised New Order plus Keith Allen with England footballer / rapper John Barnes and the rest of the England World Cup squad
[1] England Football World Cup Squad

ENGLAND'S BARMY ARMY

UK, 5,000 male / female vocal cricket supporters (Singles: 1 week) pos/wks

Date		Title / Label	Pos	Wks
12 Jun 99		**COME ON ENGLAND!** *Wildstar CDWILD 20*	45	1

ENGLISH CHAMBER ORCHESTRA – *See Kiri TE KANAWA; John WILLIAMS; Andrew LLOYD WEBBER; Nigel KENNEDY; John BARRY*

Kim ENGLISH

US, female vocalist (Singles: 7 weeks) pos/wks

Date		Title / Label	Pos	Wks
23 Jul 94		**NITE LIFE** *Hi-Life PZCD 323*	35	2
4 Mar 95		**TIME FOR LOVE** *Hi-Life HICD 8*	48	1
9 Sep 95		**I KNOW A PLACE** *Hi-Life 5798072*	52	1
30 Nov 96		**NITE LIFE (re-mix)** *Hi-Life 5755332*	35	2
26 Apr 97		**SUPERNATURAL** *Hi-Life 5736972*	50	1

Scott ENGLISH

US, male vocalist (Singles: 10 weeks) pos/wks

Date		Title / Label	Pos	Wks
9 Oct 71		**BRANDY** *Horse HOSS 7*	12	10

ENIAC – *See Tom NOVY*

ENIGMA

UK, male / female vocal / instrumental group (Singles: 15 weeks, Albums: 3 weeks) pos/wks

Date		Title / Label	Pos	Wks
23 May 81		**AIN'T NO STOPPING** *Creole CR 9*	11	8
8 Aug 81		**I LOVE MUSIC** *Creole CR 14*	25	7
5 Sep 81		AIN'T NO STOPPIN' *Creole CRX 1*	80	3

ENIGMA (350 Top 500)

New-age, ambient and dance fusion sculpted by Michael Cretu, b. 18 May 1957, Bucharest, Romania (aided by German wife Sandra Lauer and producer Frank Peterson). Title of Gregorian chant-sampling international debut hit 'Sadeness' – referring to Marquis de Sade – was shortened for UK release (Singles: 45 weeks, Albums: 142 weeks) pos/wks

Date		Title / Label	Pos	Wks
15 Dec 90	★	**SADNESS PART 1** *Virgin International DINS 101*	1	12
30 Mar 91		**MEA CULPA PART II** *Virgin International DINS 104*	55	3
10 Aug 91		**PRINCIPLES OF LUST** *Virgin International DINS 110*	59	2
11 Jan 92		**THE RIVERS OF BELIEF** *Virgin International DINS 112*	68	2
29 Jan 94	●	**RETURN TO INNOCENCE** *Virgin International DINSD 123*	3	14
14 May 94		**THE EYES OF TRUTH** *Virgin International DINSD 126*	21	4
20 Aug 94		**AGE OF LONELINESS** *Virgin International DINSD 135*	21	5
25 Jan 97		**BEYOND THE INVISIBLE** *Virgin International DINSD 155*	26	2
19 Apr 97		**T.N.T. FOR THE BRAIN** *Virgin International DINSD 161*	60	1
22 Dec 90	★	**MCMXC a.D. – THE LIMITED EDITION** *Virgin International VIR 11*	1	83
19 Feb 94	★	**THE CROSS OF CHANGES** *Virgin International CDVIR 20* [1] ■	1	35
7 Dec 96		**LE ROI EST MORT VIVE LE ROI!** *Virgin CDVIR 60*	12	12
29 Jan 00	●	**THE SCREEN BEHIND THE MIRROR** *Virgin CDVIR 100*	7	6
17 Nov 01		**LOVE SENSUALITY DEVOTION – THE GREATEST HITS** *Virgin CDVIR 150*	29	4
20 Sep 03		**VOYAGEUR** *Virgin CDVIRX 211*	46	2

[1] Enigma 2

Brian ENO

UK, male instrumentalist – keyboards (Albums: 16 weeks) pos/wks

Date		Title / Label	Pos	Wks
9 Mar 74		**HERE COME THE WARM JETS** *Island ILPS 9268*	26	2
21 Oct 78		**MUSIC FOR FILMS** *Polydor 2310 623*	55	1
21 Feb 81		**MY LIFE IN THE BUSH OF GHOSTS** *Polydor EGLP 48* [1]	29	8
8 May 82		**AMBIENT 4 ON LAND** *EG EGED 20*	93	1
12 Sep 92		**NERVE NET** *Opal 9362450332*	70	1
24 Sep 94		**WAH WAH** *Fontana 5228272* [2]	11	2
14 Oct 95		**SPINNER** *All Saints ASCD 023* [3]	71	1

[1] Brian Eno and David Byrne
[2] James and Brian Eno
[3] Brian Eno and Jah Wobble

See also ROXY MUSIC

ENTOMBED

Sweden, male vocal / instrumental band (Albums: 1 week) pos/wks

Date		Title / Label	Pos	Wks
15 Mar 97		**TO RIDE SHOOT STRAIGHT AND SPEAK THE TRUTH** *Threeman Recordings CDMFN 216*	75	1

ENUFF Z'NUFF

US, male vocal / instrumental group (Albums: 1 week) pos/wks

Date		Title / Label	Pos	Wks
13 Apr 91		**STRENGTH** *Atco 7567916381*	56	1

ENYA (156 Top 500)

The world's top selling new age artist, b. Eithne Ni Brennan, 17 May 1961, Co Donegal, Ireland. Multi-award winning ex-Clannad member (1980-82), whose sales top 60 million, was the world's biggest-selling female artist in 2001 (15 million albums) (Singles: 65 weeks, Albums: 274 weeks) pos/wks

Date		Title / Label	Pos	Wks
15 Oct 88	★	**ORINOCO FLOW** *WEA YZ 312*	1	13
24 Dec 88		**EVENING FALLS . . .** *WEA YZ 356*	20	4
10 Jun 89		**STORMS IN AFRICA (PART II)** *WEA YZ 368*	41	4
19 Oct 91		**CARIBBEAN BLUE** *WEA YZ 604*	13	7
7 Dec 91		**HOW CAN I KEEP FROM SINGING?** *WEA YZ 365*	32	5
1 Aug 92	●	**BOOK OF DAYS** *WEA YZ 640*	10	6
14 Nov 92		**THE CELTS** *WEA YZ 705*	29	4
18 Nov 95	●	**ANYWHERE IS** *WEA WEA 023CD*	7	12
7 Dec 96		**ON MY WAY HOME** *WEA WEA 047CD*	26	2
13 Dec 97		**ONLY IF...** *WEA WEA 143CD*	43	2
25 Nov 00		**ONLY TIME** *WEA WEA 316CD*	32	3
31 Mar 01		**WILD CHILD** *WEA WEA 324CD*	72	1
2 Feb 02		**MAY IT BE** *WEA W 578CD*	50	2
6 Jun 87		**ENYA** *BBC REB 605*	69	4
15 Oct 88	●	**WATERMARK** *WEA WX 199*	5	92
16 Nov 91	★	**SHEPHERD MOONS** *WEA WX 431* ■	1	90
28 Nov 92	●	**THE CELTS** *WEA 4509911672*	10	19
2 Dec 95	●	**THE MEMORY OF TREES** *WEA 0630128792*	5	24
15 Nov 97	●	**PAINT THE SKY WITH STARS – THE BEST OF ENYA** *WEA 3984208952*	4	28
2 Dec 00	●	**A DAY WITHOUT RAIN** *WEA 8573859862*	6	17

'The Celts' is a repackaged and re-issued version of 'Enya'

EON

UK, male producer – Ian Bela (Singles: 1 week) pos/wks

Date		Title / Label	Pos	Wks
17 Aug 91		**FEAR: THE MINDKILLER** *Vinyl Solution STORM 33*	63	1

EPSILON – *See D KAY & EPSILON featuring STAMINA MC*

EQUALS *UK, male vocal / instrumental group (Singles: 69 weeks, Albums: 10 weeks)*

Date		Title	pos	wks
21 Feb 68		**I GET SO EXCITED** *President PT 180*	44	4
1 May 68	★	**BABY COME BACK (re)** *President PT 135*	1	18
21 Aug 68		**LAUREL AND HARDY** *President PT 200*	35	5
27 Nov 68		**SOFTLY SOFTLY** *President PT 222*	48	3
2 Apr 69		**MICHAEL AND THE SLIPPER TREE** *President PT 240*	24	7
30 Jul 69	●	**VIVA BOBBY JOE** *President PT 260*	6	14
27 Dec 69		**RUB A DUB DUB** *President PT 275*	34	7
19 Dec 70	●	**BLACK SKIN BLUE EYED BOYS** *President PT 325*	9	11
18 Nov 67	●	**UNEQUALLED EQUALS** *President PTL 1006*	10	9
9 Mar 68		**EQUALS EXPLOSION** *President PTLS 1015*	32	1

See also Eddy GRANT

ERASURE (68 Top 500)

Award-winning UK duo formed by Vince Clarke (k) and Andy Bell (v). After hits with Depeche Mode, Yazoo and The Assembly, this act was Clarke's greatest success, scoring 16 Top 10 singles and having five albums enter at No.1 (Singles: 212 weeks, Albums: 323 weeks)

Date		Title	pos	wks
5 Oct 85		**WHO NEEDS LOVE LIKE THAT** *Mute MUTE 40*	55	2
25 Oct 86	●	**SOMETIMES** *Mute MUTE 51*	2	17
28 Feb 87		**IT DOESN'T HAVE TO BE** *Mute MUTE 56*	12	9
30 May 87	●	**VICTIM OF LOVE** *Mute MUTE 61*	7	9
3 Oct 87	●	**THE CIRCUS** *Mute MUTE 66*	6	10
5 Mar 88	●	**SHIP OF FOOLS** *Mute MUTE 74*	6	8
11 Jun 88		**CHAINS OF LOVE** *Mute MUTE 83*	11	7
1 Oct 88	●	**A LITTLE RESPECT** *Mute MUTE 85*	4	10
10 Dec 88	●	**CRACKERS INTERNATIONAL (EP)** *Mute MUTE 93*	2	13
30 Sep 89	●	**DRAMA!** *Mute MUTE 89*	4	8
9 Dec 89		**YOU SURROUND ME** *Mute MUTE 99*	15	9
10 Mar 90	●	**BLUE SAVANNAH** *Mute MUTE 109*	3	10
2 Jun 90		**STAR** *Mute MUTE 111*	11	7
29 Jun 91	●	**CHORUS** *Mute MUTE 125*	3	9
21 Sep 91	●	**LOVE TO HATE YOU** *Mute MUTE 131*	4	9
7 Dec 91		**AM I RIGHT? (EP)** *Mute MUTE 134*	15	6
11 Jan 92		**AM I RIGHT (EP) (re-mix)** *Mute L12MUTE 134*	22	3
28 Mar 92	●	**BREATH OF LIFE** *Mute MUTE 142*	8	6
13 Jun 92	★	**ABBA-ESQUE (EP)** *Mute MUTE 144* ■	1	12
7 Nov 92	●	**WHO NEEDS LOVE (LIKE THAT) (re-mix)** *Mute MUTE 150*	10	4
23 Apr 94	●	**ALWAYS** *Mute CDMUTE 152*	4	9
30 Jul 94	●	**RUN TO THE SUN** *Mute CDMUTE 153*	6	5
3 Dec 94		**I LOVE SATURDAY** *Mute CDMUTE 166*	20	6
23 Sep 95		**STAY WITH ME** *Mute CDMUTE 174*	15	4
9 Dec 95		**FINGERS AND THUMBS (COLD SUMMER'S DAY)** *Mute CDMUTE 178*	20	3
18 Jan 97		**IN MY ARMS** *Mute CDMUTE 190*	13	4
8 Mar 97		**DON'T SAY YOUR LOVE IS KILLING ME** *Mute CDMUTE 195*	23	2
21 Oct 00		**FREEDOM** *Mute CDMUTE 244*	27	2
18 Jan 03	●	**SOLSBURY HILL** *Mute CDMUTE 275*	10	3
19 Apr 03		**MAKE ME SMILE (COME UP AND SEE ME)** *Mute CDMUTE 292*	14	3
25 Oct 03		**OH L'AMOUR** *Mute CDMUTE 312*	13	3
14 Jun 86		**WONDERLAND** *Mute STUMM 25*	71	7
11 Apr 87	●	**THE CIRCUS** *Mute STUMM 35*	6	107
30 Apr 88	★	**THE INNOCENTS** *Mute STUMM 55* ■	1	78
28 Oct 89	★	**WILD!** *Mute STUMM 75* ■	1	48
26 Oct 91	★	**CHORUS** *Mute STUMM 95* ■	1	25
28 Nov 92	★	**POP! – THE FIRST 20 HITS** *Mute CDMUTEL 2* ■	1	26
28 May 94	★	**I SAY I SAY I SAY** *Mute LCDSTUMM 115* ■	1	15
4 Nov 95		**ERASURE** *Mute CDSTUMM 145*	14	5
12 Apr 97	●	**COWBOY** *Mute CDSTUMM 155*	10	4
4 Nov 00		**LOVEBOAT** *Mute CDSTUMM 175*	45	1
8 Feb 03		**OTHER PEOPLE'S SONGS** *Mute CDSTUMM215*	17	2
1 Nov 03		**HITS! THE VERY BEST OF ERASURE** *Mute LCDMUTEL10*	15	5

Tracks on Crackers International (EP): Stop / The Hardest Part / Knocking on Your Door / She Won't Be Home. Tracks on Am I Right (EP): Am I Right / Carry On Clangers / Let It Flow / Waiting for Sex. Tracks on Am I Right (Re-mix EP): Am I Right / Chorus / Love to Hate You / Perfect Stranger. Tracks on Abba-esque (EP): Lay All Your Love on Me / SOS / Take a Chance on Me / Voulez-Vous. 'Take a Chance on Me' credits MC Kinky

See also ASSEMBLY; KINKY

ERIC and the GOOD GOOD FEELING

UK, male / female vocal / instrumental group (Singles: 1 week)

Date	Title	pos	wks
3 Jun 89	**GOOD GOOD FEELING** *Equinox EQN 1*	73	1

ERIK *UK, female vocalist (Singles: 5 weeks)*

Date	Title	pos	wks
10 Apr 93	**LOOKS LIKE I'M IN LOVE AGAIN** *PWL Sanctuary PWCD 252* [1]	46	2
29 Jan 94	**GOT TO BE REAL** *PWL International PWCD 278*	42	2
1 Oct 94	**WE GOT THE LOVE** *PWL International PWCD 305*	55	1

[1] Key West featuring Erik

ERIN – *See BBG; SHUT UP AND DANCE*

ERIRE – *See SCIENCE DEPARTMENT featuring ERIRE*

EROTIC DRUM BAND

Canada, male / female vocal / instrumental group (Singles: 3 weeks)

Date	Title	pos	wks
9 Jun 79	**LOVE DISCO STYLE** *Scope SC 1*	47	3

ERUPTION *Jamaica, male / female vocal / instrumental group (Singles: 21 weeks)*

Date		Title	pos	wks
18 Feb 78	●	**I CAN'T STAND THE RAIN** *Atlantic K 11068* [1]	5	11
21 Apr 79	●	**ONE WAY TICKET** *Atlantic / Hansa K 11266*	9	10

[1] Eruption featuring Precious Wilson

Michelle ESCOFFERY – *See ARTFUL DODGER*

Shaun ESCOFFERY *UK, male vocalist (Singles: 2 weeks)*

Date	Title	pos	wks
10 Mar 01	**SPACE RIDER** *Oyster Music OYSCD 4*	52	1
20 Jul 02	**DAYS LIKE THIS** *Oyster Music OYSCDS 8*	53	1

ESCORTS *UK, male vocal / instrumental group (Singles: 2 weeks)*

Date	Title	pos	wks
2 Jul 64	**THE ONE TO CRY** *Fontana TF 474*	49	2

ESCRIMA *UK, male producer – Paul Newman (Singles: 4 weeks)*

Date	Title	pos	wks
11 Feb 95	**TRAIN OF THOUGHT** *Ffrreedom TABCD 225*	36	2
7 Oct 95	**DEEPER** *Hooj Choons TABCD 236*	27	2

See also CAMISRA; PARTIZAN; TALL PAUL; GRIFTERS

ESKA – *See COLOURS featuring EMMANUEL & ESKA; EN-CORE featuring Stephen EMMANUEL & ESKA; Nitin SAWHNEY*

ESKIMOS & EGYPT

UK, male vocal / instrumental group (Singles: 4 weeks)

Date	Title	pos	wks
13 Feb 93	**FALL FROM GRACE** *One Little Indian EEF 96CD*	51	2
29 May 93	**UK-USA** *One Little Indian 99 TP7CD*	52	2

ESPIRITU *UK / France, male / female vocal / instrumental duo – Vanessa Quinones and Chris Chaplin (Singles: 10 weeks)*

Date	Title	pos	wks
6 Mar 93	**CONQUISTADOR** *Heavenly HVN 28CD*	47	2
7 Aug 93	**LOS AMERICANOS** *Heavenly HVN 33CD*	45	2
20 Aug 94	**BONITA MANANA** *Columbia 6606925*	50	1
25 Mar 95	**ALWAYS SOMETHING THERE TO REMIND ME** *WEA YZ 911CD* [1]	14	5

[1] Tin Tin Out featuring Espiritu

ESSENCE *UK, male production group – Ricky Simmonds and Stephen Jones, and female vocalist (Singles: 2 weeks)*

Date	Title	pos	wks
21 Mar 98	**THE PROMISE** *Innocent SINCD 1*	27	2

See also ASCENSION; CHAKRA; LUSTRAL; SPACE BROTHERS; OXYGEN featuring Andrea BRITTON

ESSEX *US, male / female vocal group (Singles: 5 weeks)*

Date	Title	pos	wks
8 Aug 63	**EASIER SAID THAN DONE** *Columbia DB 7077* ▲	41	5

David ESSEX (127 Top 500) *Actor / teeny-bop star turned popular entertainer, b. David Cook, 23 Jul 1947, London. This singer / songwriter was voted No.1 British Male Vocalist (1974) and was a teen idol for more than a decade. Starred in the stage show 'Godspell' and graduated successfully to films (Singles: 199 weeks, Albums: 178 weeks)*

Date		Title / Label	pos	wks
18 Aug 73	●	ROCK ON *CBS 1693*	3	11
10 Nov 73	●	LAMPLIGHT *CBS 1902*	7	15
11 May 74		AMERICA *CBS 2176*	32	5
12 Oct 74	★	GONNA MAKE YOU A STAR *CBS 2492*	1	17
14 Dec 74	●	STARDUST *CBS 2828*	7	10
5 Jul 75	●	ROLLING STONE *CBS 3425*	5	7
13 Sep 75	★	HOLD ME CLOSE *CBS 3572*	1	10
6 Dec 75		IF I COULD *CBS 3776*	13	8
20 Mar 76		CITY LIGHTS *CBS 4050*	24	4
16 Oct 76		COMING HOME *CBS 4486*	24	6
17 Sep 77		COOL OUT TONIGHT *CBS 5495*	23	6
11 Mar 78		STAY WITH ME BABY *CBS 6063*	45	5
19 Aug 78	●	OH WHAT A CIRCUS *Mercury 6007 185*	3	11
21 Oct 78		BRAVE NEW WORLD *CBS 6705*	55	3
3 Mar 79		IMPERIAL WIZARD *Mercury 6007 202*	32	8
5 Apr 80	●	SILVER DREAM MACHINE (PART 1) *Mercury BIKE 1*	4	11
14 Jun 80		HOT LOVE *Mercury HOT 11*	57	4
26 Jun 82		ME AND MY GIRL (NIGHT-CLUBBING) *Mercury MER 107*	13	10
11 Dec 82	●	A WINTER'S TALE *Mercury MER 127*	2	10
4 Jun 83		THE SMILE *Mercury ESSEX 1*	52	4
27 Aug 83	●	TAHITI (FROM 'MUTINY ON THE BOUNTY') *Mercury BOUNT 1*	8	11
26 Nov 83		YOU'RE IN MY HEART (re) *Mercury ESSEX 2*	59	6
23 Feb 85		FALLING ANGELS RIDING *Mercury ESSEX 5*	29	7
18 Apr 87		MYFANWY *Arista RIS 11*	41	7
26 Nov 94		TRUE LOVE WAYS *PolyGram TV TLWCD 2* [1]	38	3
24 Nov 73	●	ROCK ON *CBS 65823*	7	22
19 Oct 74	●	DAVID ESSEX *CBS 69088*	2	24
27 Sep 75	●	ALL THE FUN OF THE FAIR *CBS 69160*	3	20
5 Jun 76		ON TOUR *CBS 95000*	51	1
30 Oct 76		OUT ON THE STREET *CBS 86017*	31	9
8 Oct 77		GOLD AND IVORY *CBS 86038*	29	4
6 Jan 79		THE DAVID ESSEX ALBUM *CBS 10011*	29	7
31 Mar 79		IMPERIAL WIZARD *Mercury 9109 616*	12	9
12 Jun 80		HOT LOVE *Mercury 6359 017*	75	1
19 Jun 82		STAGE-STRUCK *Mercury MERS 4*	31	15
27 Nov 82		THE VERY BEST OF DAVID ESSEX *TV TVA 4*	37	11
15 Oct 83		MUTINY *Mercury MERH 30*	39	4
17 Dec 83		THE WHISPER *Mercury MERH 34*	67	6
6 Dec 86		CENTRE STAGE *K-Tel ONE 1333*	82	4
19 Oct 91		HIS GREATEST HITS *Mercury 5103081*	13	13
10 Apr 93	●	COVER SHOT *PolyGram TV 5145632*	3	8
22 Oct 94		BACK TO BACK *PolyGram TV 5237902*	33	2
9 Dec 95		MISSING YOU *PolyGram TV 5295822*	26	9
17 May 97		A NIGHT AT THE MOVIES *PolyGram TV 5376082*	14	5
13 Jun 98		GREATEST HITS *PolyGram TV 5584842*	31	4

[1] David Essex and Catherine Zeta Jones

'Mutiny' is a studio recording of a musical that was not staged until 1985. Both this album and the eventual stage production starred David Essex and Frank Finlay

Gloria ESTEFAN (101 Top 500) *Latin music's leading lady, b. Gloria Fajardo, 1 Sep 1957, Cuba. Successes in the dance and MOR fields have pushed her total world sales to a reported 70 million, with two of the vocalist's albums passing the one-million sales mark in the UK (Singles: 182 weeks, Albums: 247 weeks)*

Date		Title / Label	pos	wks
16 Jul 88	●	ANYTHING FOR YOU *Epic 651673 7* [1] ▲	10	16
22 Oct 88	●	1-2-3 (re) *Epic 652958 7* [1]	9	10
17 Dec 88		RHYTHM IS GONNA GET YOU *Epic 654514 7* [1]	16	9
11 Feb 89	●	CAN'T STAY AWAY FROM YOU *Epic 651444 7* [1]	7	12
15 Jul 89	●	DON'T WANNA LOSE YOU *Epic 655054 0* ▲	6	10
16 Sep 89		OYE MI CANTO (HEAR MY VOICE) *Epic 655287 7*	16	8
25 Nov 89		GET ON YOUR FEET *Epic 655450 7*	23	7
3 Mar 90		HERE WE ARE *Epic 6554737*	23	6
26 May 90		CUTS BOTH WAYS *Epic 655982 7*	49	5
26 Jan 91		COMING OUT OF THE DARK *Epic 6565747* ▲	25	5
6 Apr 91		SEAL OUR FATE *Epic 6567737*	24	7
8 Jun 91		REMEMBER ME WITH LOVE *Epic 6569687*	22	6
21 Sep 91		LIVE FOR LOVING YOU *Epic 6573827*	33	5
24 Oct 92		ALWAYS TOMORROW *Epic 6583977*	24	4
12 Dec 92	●	MIAMI HIT MIX / CHRISTMAS THROUGH YOUR EYES *Epic 6588377*	8	9
13 Feb 93		I SEE YOUR SMILE *Epic 6589612*	48	2
3 Apr 93		GO AWAY *Epic 6590952*	13	6
3 Jul 93		MI TIERRA *Epic 6593512*	36	3
14 Aug 93		IF WE WERE LOVERS / CON LOS ANOS QUE ME QUEDAN *Epic 6595702*	40	3
18 Dec 93		MONTUNO *Epic 6599972*	55	2
15 Oct 94		TURN THE BEAT AROUND *Epic 6606822*	21	6
3 Dec 94		HOLD ME, THRILL ME, KISS ME (re) *Epic 6610802*	11	11
18 Feb 95		EVERLASTING LOVE *Epic 6611595*	19	5
25 May 96		REACH (re) *Epic 6632642*	15	8
24 Aug 96		YOU'LL BE MINE (PARTY TIME) *Epic 6636505*	18	3
14 Dec 96		I'M NOT GIVING YOU UP *Epic 6640222*	28	3
6 Jun 98		HEAVEN'S WHAT I FEEL *Epic 6660042*	17	4
10 Oct 98		OYE *Epic 6664645*	33	2
16 Jan 99		DON'T LET THIS MOMENT END *Epic 6667472*	28	2
8 Jan 00		MUSIC OF MY HEART *Epic 6685272* [2]	34	3
19 Nov 88	★	ANYTHING FOR YOU *Epic 4631251* [1]	1	54
5 Aug 89	★	CUTS BOTH WAYS *Epic 4651451* ■	1	64
16 Feb 91	●	INTO THE LIGHT *Epic 4677821*	2	36
14 Nov 92	●	GREATEST HITS *Epic 4723322*	2	47
10 Jul 93		MI TIERRA *Epic 4737992*	11	11
29 Oct 94	●	HOLD ME THRILL ME KISS ME *Epic 4774162*	5	19
21 Oct 95		ABRIENDO PUERTAS *Epic 4809922*	70	1
15 Jun 96		DESTINY *Epic 4839322*	12	9
13 Jun 98		GLORIA! *Epic 4898502*	16	4
27 May 00		ALMA CARIBENA – CARIBBEAN SOUL *Epic 4976172*	44	1
24 Feb 01		GREATEST HITS VOL. II *Epic 5016372*	60	1

[1] Gloria Estefan and Miami Sound Machine [2] 'N Sync / Gloria Estefan [1] Gloria Estefan and Miami Sound Machine

'Christmas Through Your Eyes' was listed only from 19 Dec 1992

See also MIAMI SOUND MACHINE

EST'ELLE – *See BLAK TWANG*

Don ESTELLE and Windsor DAVIES
UK, male vocal duo, Don Estelle d. 2 Aug 2003 (Albums: 8 weeks)

Date		Title / Label	pos	wks
10 Jan 76	●	SING LOFTY *EMI EMC 3102*	10	8

Don ESTELLE – *See Windsor DAVIES and Don ESTELLE*

ESTHERO – *See Ian POOLEY*

Deon ESTUS
US, male vocalist / instrumentalist – bass (Singles: 7 weeks)

Date		Title / Label	pos	wks
25 Jan 86		MY GUY – MY GIRL (MEDLEY) *Sedition EDIT 3310* [1]	63	3
29 Apr 89		HEAVEN HELP ME *Mika MIKA 2*	41	4

[1] Amii Stewart and Deon Estus

ETA *Denmark, male instrumental group (Singles: 5 weeks)*

Date		Title / Label	pos	wks
28 Jun 97		CASUAL SUB (BURNING SPEAR) *East West EW 110CD*	28	3
31 Jan 98		CASUAL SUB (BURNING SPEAR) (re-mix) *East West Dance EW 145CD*	28	2

ETERNAL (193 Top 500) *London-based vocal group with across-the-board appeal: sisters Easther and Vernett Bennett, Kelle Bryan, Louise Nurding. First all-female act to shift more than one million copies of an album in the UK. Louise left for a successful solo career in 1995 followed by Kelle four years later. Best-selling single 'I Wanna Be the Only One' 600,000 (Singles: 134 weeks, Albums: 163 weeks)*

Date		Title / Label	pos	wks
2 Oct 93	●	STAY *EMI CDEM 283*	4	9
15 Jan 94	●	SAVE OUR LOVE *EMI CDEM 296*	8	7
30 Apr 94	●	JUST A STEP FROM HEAVEN *EMI CDEM 311*	8	10
20 Aug 94		SO GOOD *EMI CDEMS 339*	13	7
5 Nov 94	●	OH BABY I . . . *EMI CDEM 353*	4	13
24 Dec 94		CRAZY *EMI CDEMX 364*	15	7

			pos	wks
21 Oct 95	●	POWER OF A WOMAN *EMI CDEM 396*	5	8
9 Dec 95	●	I AM BLESSED *EMI CDEMS 408*	7	12
9 Mar 96	●	GOOD THING *EMI CDEM 419*	8	6
17 Aug 96	●	SOMEDAY *EMI CDEMS 439*	4	9
7 Dec 96	●	SECRETS *EMI CDEM 459*	9	7
8 Mar 97	●	DON'T YOU LOVE ME *EMI CDEMS 465*	3	7
31 May 97	★	I WANNA BE THE ONLY ONE *EMI CDEM 472* [1] ■	1	15
11 Oct 97	●	ANGEL OF MINE *EMI CDEM 493*	4	13
30 Oct 99		WHAT 'CHA GONNA DO *EMI CDEM 552*	16	4
11 Dec 93	●	ALWAYS & FOREVER *EMI CDEMD 1053*	2	76
11 Nov 95	●	POWER OF A WOMAN *EMI CDEMD 1090*	6	31
29 Mar 97	●	BEFORE THE RAIN *EMI CDEMD 1103*	3	29
1 Nov 97	●	GREATEST HITS *EMI 8217982*	2	27

[1] Eternal featuring BeBe Winans

ETHER *UK, male vocal / instrumental group (Singles: 1 week)* pos/wks

			pos	wks
28 Mar 98		WATCHING YOU *Parlophone CDR 6491*	74	1

Melissa ETHERIDGE *US, female vocalist (Albums: 2 weeks)* pos/wks

			pos	wks
30 Sep 89		BRAVE AND CRAZY *Island ILPS 9939*	63	1
9 May 92		NEVER ENOUGH *Island CID 9990*	56	1

ETHICS *Holland, male producer – Patrick Prinz (Singles: 5 weeks)* pos/wks

			pos	wks
25 Nov 95		TO THE BEAT OF THE DRUM (LA LUNA) *VC VCRD 5*	13	5

See also ARTEMESIA; MOVIN' MELODIES; SUBLIMINAL CUTS

ETHIOPIANS
Jamaica, male vocal / instrumental group (Singles: 6 weeks) pos/wks

			pos	wks
13 Sep 67		TRAIN TO SKAVILLE *Rio RIO 130*	40	6

Tony ETORIA *UK, male vocalist (Singles: 8 weeks)* pos/wks

			pos	wks
4 Jun 77		I CAN PROVE IT *GTO GT 89*	21	8

Nellie ETTISON – *See ARTIFICIAL FUNK featuring Nellie ETTISON*

EUROGROOVE *UK, male / female vocal group (Singles: 7 weeks)* pos/wks

			pos	wks
20 May 95		MOVE YOUR BODY *Avex UK AVEXCD 4*	29	2
5 Aug 95		DIVE TO PARADISE *Avex UK AVEXCD 10*	31	2
21 Oct 95		IT'S ON YOU (SCAN ME) *Avex UK AVEXCD 17*	25	2
3 Feb 96		MOVE YOUR BODY (re-mix) *Avex UK AVEXCD 22*	44	1

EUROPE *Sweden, male vocal / instrumental group – lead vocal Joey Tempest (Singles: 50 weeks, Albums: 43 weeks)* pos/wks

			pos	wks
1 Nov 86	★	THE FINAL COUNTDOWN *Epic A 7127*	1	15
31 Jan 87		ROCK THE NIGHT *Epic EUR 1*	12	9
18 Apr 87		CARRIE *Epic EUR 2*	22	8
20 Aug 88		SUPERSTITIOUS *Epic EUR 3*	34	5
1 Feb 92		I'LL CRY FOR YOU *Epic 6576977*	28	5
21 Mar 92		HALFWAY TO HEAVEN *Epic 6578517*	42	4
25 Dec 99		THE FINAL COUNTDOWN 2000 (re-recording) *Epic 6685042*	36	4
22 Nov 86	●	THE FINAL COUNTDOWN *Epic EPC 26808*	9	37
17 Sep 88		OUT OF THIS WORLD *Epic 4624491*	12	5
19 Oct 91		PRISONERS IN PARADISE *Epic 4687551*	61	1

EUROPEANS
UK, male vocal / instrumental group (Albums: 1 week) pos/wks

			pos	wks
11 Feb 84		LIVE *A&M SCOT 1*	100	1

EURYTHMICS (42 Top 500)
Innovative and internationally popular duo formed by Brit award-winning Scottish vocalist Annie Lennox and multi-instrumentalist / songwriter / producer Dave Stewart, formerly known as The Tourists. The most charted male / female duo in the UK, whose greatest hits album sold more than two million copies in the UK and in Europe (Singles: 208 weeks, Albums: 476 weeks) pos/wks

			pos	wks
4 Jul 81		NEVER GONNA CRY AGAIN *RCA 68*	63	3
20 Nov 82	●	LOVE IS A STRANGER (re) *RCA DA 1*	6	13
12 Feb 83	●	SWEET DREAMS (ARE MADE OF THIS) *RCA DA 2* ▲	2	14
9 Jul 83	●	WHO'S THAT GIRL? *RCA DA 3*	3	10
5 Nov 83	●	RIGHT BY YOUR SIDE *RCA DA 4*	10	11
21 Jan 84	●	HERE COMES THE RAIN AGAIN *RCA DA 5*	8	8
3 Nov 84	●	SEXCRIME (NINETEEN EIGHTY FOUR) *Virgin VS 728*	4	13
19 Jan 85		JULIA *Virgin VS 734*	44	4
20 Apr 85		WOULD I LIE TO YOU? *RCA PB 40101*	17	8
6 Jul 85	★	THERE MUST BE AN ANGEL (PLAYING WITH MY HEART) *RCA PB 40247*	1	13
2 Nov 85	●	SISTERS ARE DOIN' IT FOR THEMSELVES *RCA PB 40339* [1]	9	11
11 Jan 86		IT'S ALRIGHT (BABY'S COMING BACK) *RCA PB 40375*	12	8
14 Jun 86		WHEN TOMORROW COMES *RCA DA 7*	30	6
6 Sep 86	●	THORN IN MY SIDE *RCA DA 8*	5	11
29 Nov 86		THE MIRACLE OF LOVE *RCA DA 9*	23	9
28 Feb 87		MISSIONARY MAN *RCA DA 10*	31	4
24 Oct 87		BEETHOVEN (I LOVE TO LISTEN TO) *RCA DA 11*	25	5
26 Dec 87		SHAME *RCA DA 14*	41	6
9 Apr 88		I NEED A MAN *RCA DA 15*	26	5
11 Jun 88		YOU HAVE PLACED A CHILL IN MY HEART *RCA DA 16*	16	8
26 Aug 89		REVIVAL *RCA DA 17*	26	6
4 Nov 89		DON'T ASK ME WHY *RCA DA 19*	25	6
3 Feb 90		THE KING AND QUEEN OF AMERICA *RCA DA 20*	29	5
12 May 90		ANGEL *RCA DA 21*	23	6
9 Mar 91		LOVE IS A STRANGER (re-issue) *RCA PB 44265*	46	3
16 Nov 91		SWEET DREAMS (ARE MADE OF THIS) '91 *RCA PB 45031*	48	2
16 Oct 99		I SAVED THE WORLD TODAY *RCA 74321695632*	11	6
5 Feb 00		17 AGAIN *RCA 74321726262*	27	4
12 Feb 83	●	SWEET DREAMS (ARE MADE OF THIS) *RCA RCALP 6063*	3	60
26 Nov 83	★	TOUCH *RCA PL 70109*	1	48
9 Jun 84		TOUCH DANCE *RCA PG 70354*	31	5
24 Nov 84		1984 (FOR THE LOVE OF BIG BROTHER) *Virgin V 1984*	23	17
11 May 85	●	BE YOURSELF TONIGHT *RCA PL 70711*	3	80
12 Jul 86	●	REVENGE *RCA PL 71050*	3	52
21 Nov 87	●	SAVAGE *RCA PL 71555*	7	33
23 Sep 89	★	WE TOO ARE ONE *RCA PL 74251* ■	1	32
30 Mar 91	★	GREATEST HITS *RCA PL 74856* ■	1	122
27 Nov 93		EURYTHMICS LIVE 1983-1989 *RCA 74321171452*	22	7
30 Oct 99	●	PEACE *RCA 74321695622*	4	20

[1] Eurythmics and Aretha Franklin

'Love Is a Stranger' reached its peak position when it re-entered in Apr 1983

EUSEBE
UK, male / female vocal group (Singles: 3 weeks) pos/wks

			pos	wks
26 Aug 95		SUMMERTIME HEALING *Mama's Yard CDMAMA 4*	32	3

EVANESCENCE *US, male / female, vocal / instrumental group (Singles: 25 weeks, Albums: 34 weeks)* pos/wks

			pos	wks
31 May 03		BRING ME TO LIFE (import) *Epic 8734881* [1]	60	2
14 Jun 03	★	BRING ME TO LIFE *Epic 6739762* ■ [1]	1	17
4 Oct 03	●	GOING UNDER *Epic / Wind Up 6743522*	8	6
10 May 03	★	FALLEN *Epic 5108792*	1	34+

[1] Evanescence featuring Paul McCoy

EVANGEL TEMPLE CHOIR – *See Johnny CASH*

Faith EVANS
US, female vocalist (Singles: 43 weeks, Albums: 1 week) pos/wks

			pos	wks
14 Oct 95		YOU USED TO LOVE ME *Puff Daddy 74321299812*	42	2
23 Nov 96		STRESSED OUT *Jive JIVECD 404* [1]	33	2
28 Jun 97	★	I'LL BE MISSING YOU *Puff Daddy 74321499102* [2] ◆ ■ ▲	1	21
14 Nov 98		LOVE LIKE THIS *Puff Daddy 74321625592*	24	4
1 May 99		ALL NIGHT LONG *Puff Daddy / Arista 74321665692* [3]	23	3
1 May 99		GEORGY PORGY *Warner Bros. W478CD2* [4]	28	3
30 Dec 00		HEARTBREAK HOTEL *Arista 74321820572* [5]	25	5
24 May 03		MA, I DON'T LOVE HER *Arista 82876526482* [6]	38	3
7 Nov 98		KEEP THE FAITH *Arista 74321614672*	69	1

[1] A Tribe Called Quest featuring Faith Evans and Raphael Saadiq [2] Puff Daddy and Faith Evans featuring 112 [3] Faith Evans featuring Puff Daddy [4] Eric Benet featuring Faith Evans [5] Whitney Houston featuring Faith Evans and Kelly Price [6] Clipse featuring Faith Evans

Maureen EVANS

UK, female vocalist (Singles: 37 weeks) pos/wks

22 Jan 60	**THE BIG HURT** *Oriole CB 1533*	**26**	2
17 Mar 60	**LOVE KISSES AND HEARTACHES** *Oriole CB 1540*	**44**	1
2 Jun 60	**PAPER ROSES** *Oriole CB 1550*	**40**	5
29 Nov 62 ●	**LIKE I DO** *Oriole CB 1760*	**3**	18
27 Feb 64	**I LOVE HOW YOU LOVE ME** *Oriole CB 1906*	**34**	11

Paul EVANS

US, male vocalist (Singles: 14 weeks) pos/wks

27 Nov 59	**SEVEN LITTLE GIRLS SITTING IN THE BACK SEAT** *London HLL 8968* [1]	**25**	1
31 Mar 60	**MIDNITE SPECIAL** *London HLL 9045*	**41**	1
16 Dec 78 ●	**HELLO, THIS IS JOANNIE (THE TELEPHONE ANSWERING MACHINE SONG)** *Spring 2066 932*	**6**	12

[1] Paul Evans and The Curls

EVASIONS *UK, male / female vocal / rap / instrumental group (Singles: 8 weeks)* pos/wks

13 Jun 81	**WIKKA WRAP** *Groove GP 107*	**20**	8

E.V.E. *UK / US, female vocal group (Singles: 5 weeks)* pos/wks

1 Oct 94	**GROOVE OF LOVE** *Gasoline Alley MCSTD 2007*	**30**	3
28 Jan 95	**GOOD LIFE** *Gasoline Alley MCSTD 2038*	**39**	2

EVE *US, female rapper – Eve Jeffers (Singles: 49 weeks, Albums: 13 weeks)* pos/wks

22 Jan 00	**HOT BOYZ** *Elektra E 7002CD* [1]	**18**	3
19 May 01 ●	**WHO'S THAT GIRL** *Interscope 4975572*	**6**	8
25 Aug 01 ●	**LET ME BLOW YA MIND** *Interscope / Polydor 4975932* [2]	**4**	12
9 Mar 02	**BROTHA PART II** *J 74321922142* [3]	**37**	2
16 Mar 02 ●	**CARAMEL** *Interscope / Polydor 4976742* [4]	**9**	10
5 Oct 02 ●	**GANGSTA LOVIN'** *Ruff Ryders / Interscope 4978042* [5]	**6**	8
12 Apr 03	**SATISFACTION** *Ruff Ryders / Interscope 4978262*	**20**	4
6 Dec 03	**NOT TODAY** *Geffen MCSTD 40349* [6]	**40**	2
11 Aug 01	**SCORPION** *Interscope 4930212*	**22**	8
7 Sep 02	**EVE-OLUTION** *Interscope/Polydor 4934722*	**47**	5

[1] Missy 'Misdemeanor' Elliott featuring Nas, Eve and Q Tip
[2] Eve featuring Gwen Stefani [3] Angie Stone featuring Alicia Keys and Eve
[4] City High featuring Eve [5] Eve featuring Alicia Keys
[6] Mary J Blige featuring Eve

Jessica EVE – *See WHO DA FUNK*

Alison EVELYN – *See BROTHERS LIKE OUTLAW featuring Alison EVELYN*

EVERCLEAR *US, male vocal / instrumental group (Singles: 7 weeks, Albums: 3 weeks)* pos/wks

1 Jun 96	**HEARTSPARK DOLLARSIGN** *Capitol CDCLS 773*	**48**	2
31 Aug 96	**SANTA MONICA (WATCH THE WORLD DIE)** *Capitol CDCL 775*	**40**	2
9 May 98	**EVERYTHING TO EVERYONE** *Capitol CDCL 799*	**41**	1
14 Oct 00	**WONDERFUL** *Capital CDCLS 824*	**36**	2
14 Mar 98	**SO MUCH FOR THE AFTERGLOW** *Capitol 8365032*	**63**	1
19 Aug 00	**SONGS FROM AN AMERICAN MOVIE – VOL. ONE – LEARNING HOW TO SMILE** *Capitol 5278642*	**51**	1
28 Apr 01	**SONGS FROM AN AMERICAN MOVIE – VOL. TWO – GOOD TIME FOR A BAD ATTITUDE** *Capitol 5304192*	**69**	1

Betty EVERETT

US, female vocalist, d. 18 Aug 2001 (Singles: 14 weeks) pos/wks

14 Jan 65	**GETTING MIGHTY CROWDED** *Fontana TF 520*	**29**	7
30 Oct 68	**IT'S IN HIS KISS (THE SHOOP SHOOP SONG)** *President PT 215*	**34**	7

Kenny EVERETT

UK, male DJ / vocalist, d. 4 Apr 1995 (Singles: 12 weeks) pos/wks

12 Nov 77	**CAPTAIN KREMMEN (RETRIBUTION)** *DJM DJS 10810* [1]	**32**	4
26 Mar 83 ●	**SNOT RAP** *RCA KEN 1*	**9**	8

[1] Kenny Everett and Mike Vickers

Peven EVERETT – *See Roy DAVIS Jr featuring Peven EVERETT*

EVERLAST

US, male vocalist – Erik Schrody (Singles: 5 weeks, Albums: 1 week) pos/wks

27 Feb 99	**WHAT IT'S LIKE** *Tommy Boy TBCD 7470*	**34**	2
3 Jul 99	**ENDS** *Tommy Boy TBCD 346*	**47**	1
20 Jan 01	**BLACK JESUS** *Tommy Boy TBCD 2180*	**37**	2
13 Mar 99	**WHITEY FORD SINGS THE BLUES** *Tommy Boy TBCD 1236*	**65**	1

See also HOUSE OF PAIN

Phil EVERLY

US, male vocalist (Singles: 24 weeks, Albums: 1 week) pos/wks

6 Nov 82	**LOUISE** *Capitol CL 266*	**47**	6
19 Feb 83 ●	**SHE MEANS NOTHING TO ME** *Capitol CL 276* [1]	**9**	9
10 Dec 94	**ALL I HAVE TO DO IS DREAM (re)** *EMI CDEMS 359* [2]	**14**	9
7 May 83	**PHIL EVERLY** *Capitol EST 27670*	**61**	1

[1] Phil Everly and Cliff Richard [2] Cliff Richard and Phil Everly

'All I Have to Do Is Dream' was listed with its flip side 'Miss You Nights' by Cliff Richard

See also EVERLY BROTHERS

EVERLY BROTHERS (83 Top 500)

Rock 'n' roll's foremost vocal duo: Don b. 1 Feb 1937 and Phil Everly b. 19 Jan 1939. The Kentucky-based brothers' distinctive harmony sound has influenced scores of later groups including The Beatles. The duo, voted World's Top Group by NME readers in 1958, was supported by The Rolling Stones on 1963 UK tour. They achieved a long string of transatlantic hits, many of which were self-composed. They were the first duo / group inducted into the Rock and Roll Hall of Fame, and were awarded a Lifetime Grammy in 1997. In 2001 they were elected into the Country Music Hall of Fame and their home state erected statues in their honour. Total UK single sales were 4,827,957 (Singles: 344 weeks, Albums: 130 weeks) pos/wks

12 Jul 57 ●	**BYE BYE LOVE** *London HLA 8440*	**6**	16
8 Nov 57 ●	**WAKE UP LITTLE SUSIE** *London HLA 8498* ▲	**2**	13
23 May 58 ★	**ALL I HAVE TO DO IS DREAM / CLAUDETTE** *London HLA 8618* ▲	**1**	21
12 Sep 58 ●	**BIRD DOG** *London HLA 8685* ▲	**2**	16
23 Jan 59 ●	**PROBLEMS** *London HLA 8781*	**6**	12
22 May 59	**TAKE A MESSAGE TO MARY (2re)** *London HLA 8863*	**20**	10
29 May 59	**POOR JENNY** *London B-HLA 8863*	**14**	11
11 Sep 59 ●	**('TIL) I KISSED YOU** *London HLA 8934*	**2**	15
12 Feb 60	**LET IT BE ME (re)** *London HLA 9039*	**13**	10
14 Apr 60 ★	**CATHY'S CLOWN** *Warner Bros. WB 1* ▲	**1**	18
14 Jul 60 ●	**WHEN WILL I BE LOVED** *London HLA 9157*	**4**	16
22 Sep 60 ●	**LUCILLE / SO SAD (TO WATCH GOOD LOVE GO BAD)** *Warner Bros. WB 19*	**4**	15
15 Dec 60	**LIKE STRANGERS** *London HLA 9250*	**11**	10
9 Feb 61 ★	**WALK RIGHT BACK / EBONY EYES** *Warner Bros. WB 33*	**1**	16
15 Jun 61 ★	**TEMPTATION** *Warner Bros. WB 42*	**1**	15
5 Oct 61	**MUSKRAT / DON'T BLAME ME** *Warner Bros. WB 50*	**20**	6
18 Jan 62 ●	**CRYING IN THE RAIN** *Warner Bros. WB 56*	**6**	15
17 May 62	**HOW CAN I MEET HER** *Warner Bros. WB 67*	**12**	10
25 Oct 62	**NO ONE CAN MAKE MY SUNSHINE SMILE** *Warner Bros. WB 79*	**11**	11
21 Mar 63	**SO IT WILL ALWAYS BE** *Warner Bros. WB 94*	**23**	11
13 Jun 63	**IT'S BEEN NICE (GOODNIGHT)** *Warner Bros. WB 99*	**26**	5
17 Oct 63	**THE GIRL SANG THE BLUES** *Warner Bros. WB 109*	**25**	9
16 Jul 64	**THE FERRIS WHEEL** *Warner Bros. WB 135*	**22**	10
3 Dec 64	**GONE, GONE, GONE (re)** *Warner Bros. WB 146*	**36**	6
6 May 65	**THAT'LL BE THE DAY** *Warner Bros. WB 158*	**30**	4
20 May 65 ●	**THE PRICE OF LOVE** *Warner Bros. WB 161*	**2**	14
26 Aug 65	**I'LL NEVER GET OVER YOU** *Warner Bros. WB 5639*	**35**	5
21 Oct 65	**LOVE IS STRANGE** *Warner Bros. WB 5649*	**11**	9

Date		Title / Label	pos	wks
8 May 68		**IT'S MY TIME** *Warner Bros. WB 7192*	39	6
22 Sep 84		**ON THE WINGS OF A NIGHTINGALE** *Mercury MER 170*	41	9
2 Jul 60	●	**IT'S EVERLY TIME** *Warner Bros. WM 4006*	2	23
15 Oct 60	●	**FABULOUS STYLE OF THE EVERLY BROTHERS** *London HAA 2266*	4	11
4 Mar 61	●	**A DATE WITH THE EVERLY BROTHERS** *Warner Bros. WM 4028*	3	14
21 Jul 62		**INSTANT PARTY** *Warner Bros. WM 4061*	20	1
12 Sep 70	●	**ORIGINAL GREATEST HITS** *CBS 66255*	7	16
8 Jun 74		**THE VERY BEST OF THE EVERLY BROTHERS** *Warner Bros. K 46008*	43	1
29 Nov 75	●	**WALK RIGHT BACK WITH THE EVERLYS** *Warner Bros. K 56118*	10	10
9 Apr 77		**LIVING LEGENDS** *Warwick WW 5027*	12	10
18 Dec 82		**LOVE HURTS** *K-Tel NE 1197*	22	22
7 Jan 84		**EVERLY BROTHERS REUNION CONCERT** *Impression IMDP 1*	47	6
3 Nov 84		**THE EVERLY BROTHERS** *Mercury MERH 44*	36	4
29 May 93		**THE GOLDEN YEARS OF THE EVERLY BROTHERS – THEIR 24 GREATEST HITS** *Warner Bros. 9548319922*	26	5
1 Jun 02	●	**THE DEFINITIVE EVERLY BROTHERS** *WSM 927473042*	10	7

'All I Have to Do Is Dream' was listed without Claudette for its first week on the chart but, from 30 May 1958, both sides charted for 20 more weeks.

See also Phil EVERLY

EVERTON FOOTBALL CLUB

UK, male football team vocalists (Singles: 8 weeks) pos/wks

Date		Title / Label	pos	wks
11 May 85		**HERE WE GO** *Columbia DB 9106* [1]	14	5
20 May 95		**ALL TOGETHER NOW** *MDMC DEVCS 3*	24	3

[1] Everton 1985

EVERYTHING BUT THE GIRL (279 Top 500)

Introspective pop duo formed 1982, Hull, UK: Tracey Thorn (v) b. 26 Sep 1962, Ben Watt (k) b. 6 Dec 1962. Gained greatest popularity after mid-90s conversion to low-key dance music. Remix of 'Missing' was the first single to spend an uninterrupted year on the US chart. Best-selling single 'Missing' 870,000 (Singles: 96 weeks, Albums: 132 weeks) pos/wks

Date		Title / Label	pos	wks
12 May 84		**EACH AND EVERY ONE** *Blanco Y Negro NEG 1*	28	7
21 Jul 84		**MINE** *Blanco Y Negro NEG 3*	58	2
6 Oct 84		**NATIVE LAND** *Blanco Y Negro NEG 6*	73	2
2 Aug 86		**COME ON HOME** *Blanco Y Negro NEG 21*	44	7
11 Oct 86		**DON'T LEAVE ME BEHIND** *Blanco Y Negro NEG 23*	72	2
13 Feb 88		**THESE EARLY DAYS** *Blanco Y Negro NEG 30*	75	1
9 Jul 88	●	**I DON'T WANT TO TALK ABOUT IT** *Blanco Y Negro NEG 34*	3	9
27 Jan 90		**DRIVING** *Blanco Y Negro NEG 40*	54	2
22 Feb 92		**COVERS (EP)** *Blanco Y Negro NEG 54*	13	6
24 Apr 93		**THE ONLY LIVING BOY IN NEW YORK (EP)** *Blanco Y Negro NEG 62CD*	42	5
19 Jun 93		**I DIDN'T KNOW I WAS LOOKING FOR LOVE (EP)** *Blanco Y Negro NEG 64CD*	72	1
4 Jun 94		**ROLLERCOASTER (EP)** *Blanco Y Negro NEG 69CD*	65	1
20 Aug 94		**MISSING** *Blanco Y Negro NEG 71CD1*	69	1
28 Oct 95	●	**MISSING (re-mix)** *Blanco Y Negro NEG 84CD*	3	22
20 Apr 96	●	**WALKING WOUNDED** *Virgin VSCDT 1577*	6	6
29 Jun 96	●	**WRONG** *Virgin VSCDT 1589*	8	7
5 Oct 96		**SINGLE** *Virgin VSCDT 1600*	20	3
7 Dec 96		**DRIVING (re-mix)** *Blanco Y Negro NEG 99CD1*	36	2
1 Mar 97		**BEFORE TODAY** *Virgin VSCDT 1624*	25	2
3 Oct 98		**THE FUTURE OF THE FUTURE (STAY GOLD)** *Deconstruction 74321616252* [1]	31	2
25 Sep 99		**FIVE FATHOMS** *Virgin VSCDT 1742*	27	3
4 Mar 00		**TEMPERAMENTAL** *Virgin VSCDT 1761*	72	1
27 Jan 01		**TRACEY IN MY ROOM** *VC Recordings VCRD 78* [2]	34	2
16 Jun 84		**EDEN** *Blanco Y Negro BYN 2*	14	22
27 Apr 85	●	**LOVE NOT MONEY** *Blanco Y Negro BYN 3*	10	9
6 Sep 86		**BABY THE STARS SHINE BRIGHT** *Blanco Y Negro BYN 9*	22	9
12 Mar 88		**IDLEWILD** *Blanco Y Negro BYN 14*	13	9
6 Aug 88		**IDLEWILD (re-issue)** *Blanco Y Negro BYN 16*	21	6
17 Feb 90	●	**THE LANGUAGE OF LIFE** *Blanco Y Negro BYN 21*	10	6
5 Oct 91		**WORLDWIDE** *Blanco Y Negro BYN 25*	29	5
22 May 93	●	**HOME MOVIES – THE BEST OF EVERYTHING BUT THE GIRL** *Blanco Y Negro 4509923192*	5	8
25 Jun 94		**AMPLIFIED HEART** *Blanco Y Negro 4509964822*	20	15
18 May 96	●	**WALKING WOUNDED** *Virgin CDV 2803*	4	27
9 Nov 96		**THE BEST OF EVERYTHING BUT THE GIRL** *Blanco Y Negro 630166372*	23	12
9 Oct 99		**TEMPERAMENTAL** *Virgin CDV 2892*	16	3
2 Nov 02		**LIKE THE DESERTS MISS THE RAIN** *Virgin CDV 2966*	58	1

[1] Deep Dish with Everything but the Girl [2] EBTG vs Soul Vision

Tracks on Covers (EP): Love Is Strange / Tougher Than the Rest / Time After Time / Alison. Tracks on The Only Living Boy in New York (EP): The Only Living Boy in New York / Birds / Gabriel / Horses in the Room. Tracks on I Didn't Know I Was Looking for Love (EP): I Didn't Know I Was Looking for Love / My Head Is My Only House Unless It Rains / Political Science / A Piece of My Mind. Tracks on Rollercoaster (EP): Rollercoaster / Straight Back to You / Lights of Te Touan / I Didn't Know I Was Looking for Love (demo)

E'VOKE *UK, female vocal duo*

– Marlaine Gordon and Kerry Potter (Singles: 9 weeks) pos/wks

Date		Title / Label	pos	wks
25 Nov 95		**RUNAWAY** *Ffrreedom TABCD 238*	30	3
24 Aug 96		**ARMS OF LOREN** *Manifesto FESCD 10*	25	3
2 Feb 02		**ARMS OF LOREN (re-mix)** *Inferno CDFERN 001*	31	3

EVOLUTION

UK, male / female vocal / instrumental group (Singles: 12 weeks) pos/wks

Date		Title / Label	pos	wks
20 Mar 93		**LOVE THING** *Deconstruction 74321134272*	32	2
3 Jul 93		**EVERYBODY DANCE** *Deconstruction 74321152012*	19	5
8 Jan 94		**EVOLUTIONDANCE PART ONE (EP)** *Deconstruction 74321171912*	52	3
4 Nov 95		**LOOK UP TO THE LIGHT** *Deconstruction 74321318042*	55	1
19 Oct 96		**YOUR LOVE IS CALLING** *Deconstruction 74321422872*	60	1

Tracks on Evolutiondance Part One (EP): Escape 2 Alcatraz (remix) / Everybody / Don't Stop the Rain

EX PISTOLS

UK, male vocal / instrumental group (Singles: 2 weeks) pos/wks

Date		Title / Label	pos	wks
2 Feb 85		**LAND OF HOPE AND GLORY** *Virginia PISTOL 76*	69	2

EXCITERS

US, male / female vocal group (Singles: 7 weeks) pos/wks

Date		Title / Label	pos	wks
21 Feb 63		**TELL HIM** *United Artists UP 1011*	46	1
4 Oct 75		**REACHING FOR THE BEST** *20th Century BTC 1005*	31	6

EXETER BRAMDEAN BOYS' CHOIR

UK, male choir (Singles: 3 weeks) pos/wks

Date		Title / Label	pos	wks
18 Dec 93		**REMEMBERING CHRISTMAS** *Golden Sounds DSCC 1*	46	3

EXILE

US, male vocal / instrumental group (Singles: 18 weeks) pos/wks

Date		Title / Label	pos	wks
19 Aug 78	●	**KISS YOU ALL OVER** *RAK 279* ▲	6	12
12 May 79		**HOW COULD THIS GO WRONG** *RAK 293*	67	2
12 Sep 81		**HEART AND SOUL** *RAK 333*	54	4

EXODUS

US, male vocal / instrumental group (Albums: 1 week) pos/wks

Date		Title / Label	pos	wks
11 Feb 89		**FABULOUS DISASTER** *Music For Nations MFN 90*	67	1

EXOTERIX

UK, male producer – Duncan Millar (Singles: 2 weeks) pos/wks

Date		Title / Label	pos	wks
24 Apr 93		**VOID** *Positiva CDTIV 1*	58	1
5 Feb 94		**SATISFY MY LOVE** *Union UCRCD 26*	62	1

EXOTICA featuring Itsy FOSTER *UK / Italy, male / female vocal / instrumental group (Singles: 1 week)* pos/wks

Date		Title / Label	pos	wks
16 Sep 95		**THE SUMMER IS MAGIC** *Polydor 5798392*	68	1

EXPLOITED *UK, male vocal / instrumental group (Singles: 13 weeks, Albums: 26 weeks)* pos/wks

		pos	wks
18 Apr 81	**DOGS OF WAR** *Secret SHH 110*	63	4
17 Oct 81	**DEAD CITIES** *Secret SHH 120*	31	5
5 Dec 81	**DON'T LET 'EM GRIND YOU DOWN** *Superville EXP 1003* [1]	70	1
8 May 82	**ATTACK** *Secret SHH 130*	50	3
16 May 81	**PUNK'S NOT DEAD** *Secret SEC 1*	20	11
14 Nov 81	**EXPLOITED LIVE** *Superville EXPLP 2001*	52	3
19 Jun 82	**TROOPS OF TOMORROW** *Secret SEC 8*	17	12

[1] Exploited and Anti-Pasti

EXPOSE
US, female vocal group (Singles: 1 week) pos/wks

		pos	wks
28 Aug 93	**I'LL NEVER GET OVER YOU (GETTING OVER ME)** *Arista 74321158962*	75	1

EXPRESS OF SOUND
Italy, male instrumental / production group (Singles: 1 week) pos/wks

		pos	wks
2 Nov 96	**REAL VIBRATION (WANT LOVE)** *Positiva CDTIV 66*	45	1

EXPRESSOS
UK, male / female vocal / instrumental group (Singles: 5 weeks) pos/wks

		pos	wks
21 Jun 80	**HEY GIRL** *WEA K 18246*	60	3
14 Mar 81	**TANGO IN MONO** *WEA K 18431*	70	2

EXTENSIVE – *See CHOPS-EMC + EXTENSIVE*

EXTREME *US, male vocal / instrumental group (Singles: 46 weeks, Albums: 75 weeks)* pos/wks

		pos	wks
8 Jun 91	**GET THE FUNK OUT** *A&M AM 737*	19	7
27 Jul 91 ●	**MORE THAN WORDS** *A&M AM 792* ▲	2	11
12 Oct 91	**DECADENCE DANCE** *A&M AM 773*	36	3
23 Nov 91	**HOLE HEARTED** *A&M AM 839*	12	7
2 May 92	**SONG FOR LOVE** *A&M AM 698*	12	6
5 Sep 92	**REST IN PEACE** *A&M AM 0055*	13	5
14 Nov 92	**STOP THE WORLD** *A&M AM 0096*	22	2
6 Feb 93	**TRAGIC COMIC** *A&M AMCD 0156*	15	4
11 Mar 95	**HIP TODAY** *A&M 5809932*	44	1
1 Jun 91	**EXTREME II PORNOGRAFFITTI** *A&M 3953131*	12	61
26 Sep 92 ●	**III SIDES TO EVERY STORY** *A&M 5400062*	2	11
11 Feb 95 ●	**WAITING FOR THE PUNCHLINE** *A&M 5403052*	10	3

EYE TO EYE featuring Taka BOOM
UK, male producer – Stuart Crichton, and US, female vocalist (Singles: 2 weeks) pos/wks

		pos	wks
9 Jun 01	**JUST CAN'T GET ENOUGH (NO NO NO NO)** *Xtravaganza XTRAV 25CD*	36	2

See also MUKKAA; UMBOZA

EYES CREAM
Italy, male producer – Agostino Carollo (Singles: 1 week) pos/wks

		pos	wks
16 Oct 99	**FLY AWAY (BYE BYE)** *Accolade CDAC 001*	53	1

TOP 10 ALBUMS BY WEEKS ON CHART

These are the long stayers that have a claim to being the most popular and certainly the most enduring albums of all time. Surprisingly, Bat Out of Hell, Dark Side of the Moon and Simon and Garfunkel's Greatest Hits did not manage one single week at No.1 during a total of 21 years' worth of chart action.

1. RUMOURS – **Fleetwood Mac** (477 weeks)
2. BAT OUT OF HELL – **Meat Loaf** (474 weeks)
3. GREATEST HITS – **Queen** (450 weeks)
4. THE SOUND OF MUSIC – **Original Film Soundtrack** (381 weeks)
5. DARK SIDE OF THE MOON – **Pink Floyd** (364 weeks)
6. LEGEND – **Bob Marley and the Wailers** (330 weeks)
7. GOLD – GREATEST HITS – **Abba** (328 weeks)
8. SOUTH PACIFIC – **Original Film Soundtrack** (313 weeks)
9. BRIDGE OVER TROUBLED WATER – **Simon and Garfunkel** (307 weeks)
10. SIMON AND GARFUNKEL'S GREATEST HITS – **Simon and Garfunkel** (283 weeks)

In front of the penetrating gaze of drummer **Mick Fleetwood**, a photographer captures the full Mac clan with their gold discs awarded for the enduring success of 'Rumours'

Adam F *UK, male producer – Adam Fenton (Singles: 22 weeks, Albums: 3 weeks)*

Date	Title	pos	wks
27 Sep 97	**CIRCLES** *Positiva CDFJ 002*	20	3
7 Mar 98	**MUSIC IN MY MIND** *Positiva CDFJ 003*	27	3
15 Sep 01	**SMASH SUMTHIN'** *Def Jam 5886932* [1]	11	7
1 Dec 01	**STAND CLEAR** *Chrysalis CDEM 597* [2]	43	1
6 Apr 02	**WHERE'S MY...?** *EMI CDEMS 598* [3]	37	2
27 Apr 02	**METROSOUND** *Kaos KAOS 001P* [4]	54	1
8 Jun 02	**STAND CLEAR (re-mix)** *Kaos KAOSCD 002* [2]	50	1
31 Aug 02	**SMASH SUMTHIN' (re-mix)** *Kaos KAOSCD 003* [5]	47	2
14 Dec 02	**DIRTY HARRY'S REVENGE** *Kaos KAOS 004* [6]	50	2
15 Nov 97	COLOURS *Positiva 8217252*	47	1
22 Sep 01	KAOS – THE ANTI-ACOUSTIC WARFARE *Chrysalis 5342502*	44	2

[1] Redman featuring Adam F [2] Adam F featuring M.O.P. [3] Adam F featuring Lil' Mo [4] Adam F and J Majik [5] Adam F featuring Redman [6] Adam F featuring Beenie Man

F A B *UK, male producers (Singles: 11 weeks Albums: 3 weeks)*

Date	Title	pos	wks
7 Jul 90 ●	**THUNDERBIRDS ARE GO** *Brothers Organisation FAB 1* [1]	5	8
20 Oct 90	**THE PRISONER** *Brothers Organisation FAB 6* [2]	56	2
1 Dec 90	**THE STINGRAY MEGAMIX** *Brothers Organisation FAB 2* [3]	66	1
10 Nov 90	POWER THEMES 90 *Telstar STAR 2430*	53	3

[1] F A B featuring MC Parker [2] F A B featuring MC Number 6 [3] F A B featuring Aqua Marina

FBI – *See REDHEAD KINGPIN and The FBI*

FC KAHUNA *UK, male production duo (Singles: 3 weeks)*

Date	Title	pos	wks
6 Apr 02	**GLITTERBALL** *City Rockers ROCKERS 11CD*	64	1
20 Jul 02	**MACHINE SAYS YES** *City Rockers ROCKERS 18CD*	58	1
22 Mar 03	**HAYLING** *Skint SKINT 84CD*	49	1

F45 – *See DE FUNK featuring F45*

FFWD *UK / Germany, male instrumental group (Albums: 1 week)*

Date	Title	pos	wks
13 Aug 94	FFWD *Inter INTA 001CD*	48	1

FKW *UK, male vocal / instrumental group (Singles: 8 weeks)*

Date	Title	pos	wks
2 Oct 93	**NEVER GONNA (GIVE YOU UP)** *PWL International PWCD 273*	48	2
11 Dec 93	**SEIZE THE DAY** *PWL International PWCD 279*	45	2
5 Mar 94	**JINGO** *PWL International PWCD 283*	30	3
4 Jun 94	**THIS IS THE WAY** *PWL International PWCD 307*	63	1

FLB – *See FAT LARRY'S BAND*

F.L.O. – *See Rahni HARRIS and F.L.O.*

FM *UK, male vocal / instrumental group (Singles: 11 weeks, Albums: 3 weeks)*

Date	Title	pos	wks
31 Jan 87	**FROZEN HEART** *Portrait DIDGE 1*	64	2
20 Jun 87	**LET LOVE BE THE LEADER** *Portrait MERV 1*	71	2
5 Aug 89	**BAD LUCK** *Epic 655031 7*	54	4
7 Oct 89	**SOMEDAY (YOU'LL COME RUNNING)** *CBS DINK 1*	64	2
10 Feb 90	**EVERYTIME I THINK OF YOU** *Epic DINK 2*	73	1
20 Sep 86	INDISCREET *Portrait PRT 26827*	76	1
14 Oct 89	TOUGH IT OUT *Epic 465589 1*	34	2

FPI PROJECT *Italy, male instrumental / production group (Singles: 17 weeks)*

Date	Title	pos	wks
9 Dec 89 ●	**GOING BACK TO MY ROOTS / RICH IN PARADISE** *Rumour RUMAT 9*	9	12
9 Mar 91	**EVERYBODY (ALL OVER THE WORLD)** *Rumour RUMA 29*	65	3
7 Aug 93	**COME ON (AND DO IT)** *Synthetic SYNTH 006CD*	59	1
13 Mar 99	**EVERYBODY (ALL OVER THE WORLD) (re-mix)** *99 North CDNTH 14*	67	1

'Going Back to My Roots' was a vocal track available in two formats and featured either Paolo Dini or Sharon Dee Clarke

FYC – *See FINE YOUNG CANNIBALS*

FAB! *Ireland, female vocal group (Singles: 1 week)*

Date	Title	pos	wks
1 Aug 98	**TURN AROUND** *Break Records BRCX 107*	59	1

FAB FOR featuring Robert OWENS *Germany / Italy, male production duo and US, male vocalist (Singles: 1 week)*

Date	Title	pos	wks
15 Feb 03	**LAST NIGHT A DJ BLEW MY MIND** *Illustrious CDILL 013*	34	1

Shelley FABARES *US, female vocalist / actor (Singles: 4 weeks)*

Date	Title	pos	wks
26 Apr 62	**JOHNNY ANGEL** *Pye International 7N 25132* ▲	41	4

FABIAN *US, male vocalist (Singles: 1 week)*

Date	Title	pos	wks
10 Mar 60	**HOUND DOG MAN** *HMV POP 695*	46	1

Lara FABIAN *Belgium, female vocalist (Singles: 1 week)*

Date	Title	pos	wks
28 Oct 00	**I WILL LOVE AGAIN** *Columbia 6694062*	63	1

FABOLOUS *US, male rapper – John Jackson (Singles: 11 weeks, Albums: 10 weeks)*

Date	Title	pos	wks
16 Aug 03	**CAN'T LET YOU GO** *Elektra E 7408CD* [1]	14	5
1 Nov 03	**INTO YOU** *Elektra E 7470CD* [2]	18	6
2 Aug 03	STREET DREAMS *East West 7559627912*	51	10

[1] Fabolous featuring Mike Shorey and Lil' Mo [2] Fabolous featuring Tamia

FABULOUS BAKER BOYS *UK, male DJ / production trio (Singles: 2 weeks)*

Date	Title	pos	wks
15 Nov 97	**OH BOY** *Multiply CDMULTY 28*	34	2

FACE – *See David MORALES*

FACES *UK, male vocal / instrumental group (Singles: 46 weeks, Albums: 61 weeks)*

Date	Title	pos	wks
18 Dec 71 ●	**STAY WITH ME** *Warner Bros. K 16136*	6	14
17 Feb 73 ●	**CINDY INCIDENTALLY** *Warner Bros. K 16247*	2	9
8 Dec 73 ●	**POOL HALL RICHARD / I WISH IT WOULD RAIN** *Warner Bros. K 16341*	8	11
7 Dec 74	**YOU CAN MAKE ME DANCE SING OR ANYTHING (EVEN TAKE THE DOG FOR A WALK, MEND A FUSE, FOLD AWAY THE IRONING BOARD, OR ANY OTHER DOMESTIC SHORT COMINGS)** *Warner Bros. K 16494* [1]	12	9
4 Jun 77	**THE FACES (EP)** *Riva 8*	41	3

4 Apr 70 **FIRST STEP** *Warner Bros. WS 3000* 45 1
8 May 71 **LONG PLAYER** *Warner Bros. W 3011* 31 7
25 Dec 71 ● **A NOD'S AS GOOD AS A WINK ... TO A BLIND HORSE** *Warner Bros. K 56006* 2 22
21 Apr 73 ★ **OOH-LA-LA** *Warner Bros. K 56011* 1 13
26 Jan 74 ● **OVERTURE AND BEGINNERS** *Mercury 9100 001* [1] 3 7
21 May 77 **THE BEST OF THE FACES** *Riva RVLP 3* 24 6
7 Nov 92 **THE BEST OF ROD STEWART AND THE FACES 1971-1975** *Mercury 5141802* [1] 58 1
1 Nov 03 **CHANGING FACES – THE VERY BEST OF ROD STEWART AND THE FACES** *Universal TV 9812604* [1] 13 4

[1] Faces / Rod Stewart [1] Rod Stewart and the Faces

Tracks on The Faces (EP): Memphis / You Can Make Me Dance Sing or Anything / Stay with Me / Cindy Incidentally

See also Rod STEWART

FACTORY OF UNLIMITED RHYTHM

Jamaica, male / female vocal / instrumental group (Singles: 1 week) pos/wks

1 Jun 96 **THE SWEETEST SURRENDER** *Kuff KUFFD 6* 59 1

Donald FAGEN

US, male vocalist (Singles: 2 weeks, Albums: 25 weeks) pos/wks

3 Jul 93 **TOMORROW'S GIRLS** *Reprise W 0180CDX* 46 2
20 Oct 82 **THE NIGHTFLY** *Warner Bros. 923696* 44 16
5 Jun 93 ● **KAMAKIRIAD** *Reprise 9362452302* 3 9

See also STEELY DAN

Joe FAGIN

UK, male vocalist (Singles: 20 weeks) pos/wks

7 Jan 84 ● **THAT'S LIVIN' ALRIGHT** *Towerbell TOW 46* 3 11
5 Apr 86 **BACK WITH THE BOYS AGAIN / GET IT RIGHT** *Towerbell TOW 84* 53 9

Jad FAIR – *See TEENAGE FANCLUB*

Yvonne FAIR

US, female vocalist, d. 6 Mar 1994 (Singles: 11 weeks) pos/wks

24 Jan 76 ● **IT SHOULD HAVE BEEN ME** *Tamla Motown TMG 1013* 5 11

FAIR WEATHER *UK, male vocal / instrumental group – leader Andy Fairweather-Low (Singles: 12 weeks)*

pos/wks

18 Jul 70 ● **NATURAL SINNER** *RCA 1977* 6 12

See also AMEN CORNER

FAIRGROUND ATTRACTION

UK, female / male vocal / instrumental group – lead vocal Eddi Reader (Singles: 27 weeks, Albums: 54 weeks) pos/wks

16 Apr 88 ★ **PERFECT** *RCA PB 41845* 1 13
30 Jul 88 ● **FIND MY LOVE** *RCA PB 42079* 7 10
19 Nov 88 **A SMILE IN A WHISPER** *RCA PB 42249* 75 1
28 Jan 89 **CLARE** *RCA PB 42607* 49 3
28 May 88 ● **THE FIRST OF A MILLION KISSES** *RCA PL 71696* 2 52
30 Jun 90 **AY FOND KISS** *RCA PL 74596* 55 2

Group was male only on last album

See also Eddi READER

FAIRPORT CONVENTION *UK, male / female vocal / instrumental (Singles: 9 weeks, Albums: 41 weeks)*

pos/wks

23 Jul 69 **SI TU DOIS PARTIR (re)** *Island WIP 6064* 21 9
2 Aug 69 **UNHALFBRICKING** *Island ILPS 9102* 12 8
17 Jan 70 **LIEGE AND LIEF** *Island ILPS 9115* 17 15
18 Jul 70 **FULL HOUSE** *Island ILPS 9130* 13 11
3 Jul 71 ● **ANGEL DELIGHT** *Island ILPS 9162* 8 5
12 Jul 75 **RISING FOR THE MOON** *Island ILPS 9313* 52 1
28 Jan 89 **RED AND GOLD** *New Routes RUE 002* 74 1

Andy FAIRWEATHER-LOW

UK, male vocalist (Singles: 18 weeks) pos/wks

21 Sep 74 ● **REGGAE TUNE** *A&M AMS 7129* 10 8
6 Dec 75 ● **WIDE EYED AND LEGLESS** *A&M AMS 7202* 6 10

See also AMEN CORNER; FAIR WEATHER

Adam FAITH (192 Top 500)

Teen-idol vocalist turned top actor then financial wizard, b. Terence Nelhams, 23 Jun 1940, London, d. 8 Mar 2003. One of the most charted acts of the 1960s; became the first UK artist to lodge initial seven hits in the Top 5. Also one of the first UK acts to record original songs regularly (Singles: 252 weeks, Albums: 46 weeks) pos/wks

20 Nov 59 ★ **WHAT DO YOU WANT?** *Parlophone R 4591* 1 19
22 Jan 60 ★ **POOR ME** *Parlophone R 4623* 1 18
14 Apr 60 ● **SOMEONE ELSE'S BABY** *Parlophone R 4643* 2 13
30 Jun 60 ● **JOHNNY COMES MARCHING HOME / MADE YOU** *Parlophone R 4665* [1] 5 13
15 Sep 60 ● **HOW ABOUT THAT!** *Parlophone R 4689* [1] 4 14
17 Nov 60 ● **LONELY PUP (IN A CHRISTMAS SHOP)** *Parlophone R 4708* 4 11
9 Feb 61 ● **WHO AM I! / THIS IS IT!** *Parlophone R 4735* 5 14
27 Apr 61 **EASY GOING ME** *Parlophone R 4766* 12 10
20 Jul 61 **DON'T YOU KNOW IT** *Parlophone R 4807* 12 10
26 Oct 61 ● **THE TIME HAS COME** *Parlophone R 4837* 4 14
18 Jan 62 **LONESOME** *Parlophone R 4864* [1] 12 9
3 May 62 ● **AS YOU LIKE IT** *Parlophone R 4896* [1] 5 15
30 Aug 62 ● **DON'T THAT BEAT ALL** *Parlophone R 4930* [2] 8 11
13 Dec 62 **BABY TAKE A BOW** *Parlophone R 4964* 22 6
31 Jan 63 **WHAT NOW** *Parlophone R 4990* [2] 31 5
11 Jul 63 **WALKIN' TALL** *Parlophone R 5039* 23 6
19 Sep 63 ● **THE FIRST TIME** *Parlophone R 5061* [3] 5 13
12 Dec 63 **WE ARE IN LOVE** *Parlophone R 5091* [3] 11 12
12 Mar 64 **IF HE TELLS YOU** *Parlophone R 5109* [3] 25 9
28 May 64 **I LOVE BEING IN LOVE WITH YOU** *Parlophone R 5138* [3] 33 6
26 Nov 64 **A MESSAGE TO MARTHA (KENTUCKY BLUEBIRD)** *Parlophone R 5201* 12 11
11 Feb 65 **STOP FEELING SORRY FOR YOURSELF** *Parlophone R 5235* 23 6
17 Jun 65 **SOMEONE'S TAKEN MARIA AWAY** *Parlophone R 5289* 34 5
20 Oct 66 **CHERYL'S GOIN' HOME** *Parlophone R 5516* 46 2
19 Nov 60 ● **ADAM** *Parlophone PMC 1128* 6 36
11 Feb 61 **BEAT GIRL (FILM SOUNDTRACK)** *Columbia 33SX 1225* 11 3
24 Mar 62 **ADAM FAITH** *Parlophone PMC 1162* 20 1
25 Sep 65 **FAITH ALIVE** *Parlophone PMC 1249* 19 1
19 Dec 81 **20 GOLDEN GREATS** *Warwick WW 5113* 61 3
27 Nov 93 **MIDNIGHT POSTCARDS** *PolyGram TV 8213982* 43 2

[1] With John Barry and His Orchestra [2] Adam Faith with Johnny Keating and His Orchestra [3] Adam Faith and The Roulettes

Horace FAITH

Jamaica, male vocalist – Horace Smith (Singles: 10 weeks) pos/wks

12 Sep 70 **BLACK PEARL** *Trojan TR 7790* 13 10

Percy FAITH

Canada, orchestra, leader d. 9 Feb 1976 (Singles: 31 weeks) pos/wks

4 Mar 60 ● **THE THEME FROM 'A SUMMER PLACE'** *Philips PB 989* ▲ 2 31

FAITH BROTHERS *UK, male vocal / instrumental group (Singles: 6 weeks, Albums: 1 week)*

pos/wks

13 Apr 85 **THE COUNTRY OF THE BLIND** *Siren SIREN 2* 63 3
6 Jul 85 **A STRANGER ON HOME GROUND** *Siren SIREN 4* 69 3
9 Nov 85 **EVENTIDE** *Siren SIRENLP 1* 66 1

FAITH, HOPE AND CHARITY

US, male / female vocal group (Singles: 4 weeks) pos/wks

31 Jan 76 **JUST ONE LOOK** *RCA 2632* 38 4

FAITH, HOPE AND CHARITY

UK, female vocal group (Singles: 3 weeks) pos/wks

23 Jun 90 **BATTLE OF THE SEXES** *WEA YZ 480* 53 3

FAITH NO MORE

US, male vocal instrumental group (Singles: 65 weeks, Albums: 74 weeks)

Date		Title / Label	pos	wks
6 Feb 88		**WE CARE A LOT** *Slash LASH 17*	53	3
10 Feb 90		**EPIC** *Slash LASH 21*	37	4
14 Apr 90		**FROM OUT OF NOWHERE** *Slash LASH 24*	23	6
14 Jul 90		**FALLING TO PIECES** *Slash LASH 25*	41	3
8 Sep 90		**EPIC (re-issue)** *Slash LASH 26*	25	5
6 Jun 92	●	**MIDLIFE CRISIS** *Slash LASH 37*	10	5
15 Aug 92		**A SMALL VICTORY** *Slash LASH 39*	29	5
12 Sep 92		**A SMALL VICTORY (re-mix)** *Slash LASHX 40*	55	1
21 Nov 92		**EVERYTHING'S RUINED** *Slash LASH 43*	28	3
16 Jan 93	●	**I'M EASY / BE AGGRESSIVE (re)** *Slash LACDP 44*	3	8
6 Nov 93		**ANOTHER BODY MURDERED** *Epic 6597942* [1]	26	3
11 Mar 95		**DIGGING THE GRAVE** *Slash LASCD 51*	16	4
27 May 95		**RICOCHET** *Slash LASCD 53*	27	2
29 Jul 95		**EVIDENCE** *Slash LASCD 54*	32	3
31 May 97		**ASHES TO ASHES** *Slash LASCD 61*	15	3
16 Aug 97		**LAST CUP OF SORROW** *Slash LASCD 62*	51	1
13 Dec 97		**THIS TOWN AIN'T BIG ENOUGH FOR BOTH OF US** *Roadrunner RR 22513* [2]	40	2
17 Jan 98		**ASHES TO ASHES (re-issue)** *Slash LACDP 63*	29	3
7 Nov 98		**I STARTED A JOKE** *Slash LASCD 65*	49	1
17 Feb 90		**THE REAL THING** *Slash 8281541*	30	35
16 Feb 91		**LIVE AT THE BRIXTON ACADEMY** *Slash 8282381*	20	4
20 Jun 92	●	**ANGEL DUST** *Slash 8283212*	2	25
25 Mar 95	●	**KING FOR A DAY FOOL FOR A LIFETIME** *Slash 8285602*	5	6
21 Jun 97	●	**ALBUM OF THE YEAR** *Slash 8289012*	7	3
21 Nov 98		**WHO CARES A LOT? – THE GREATEST HITS** *Slash 5560572*	37	1

[1] Faith No More and Boo-Yaa T.R.I.B.E. [2] Sparks vs Faith No More

Marianne FAITHFULL

UK, female vocalist (Singles: 59 weeks, Albums: 19 weeks)

Date		Title / Label	pos	wks
13 Aug 64	●	**AS TEARS GO BY** *Decca F 11923*	9	13
18 Feb 65	●	**COME AND STAY WITH ME** *Decca F 12075*	4	13
6 May 65	●	**THIS LITTLE BIRD** *Decca F 12162*	6	11
22 Jul 65	●	**SUMMER NIGHTS** *Decca F 12193*	10	10
4 Nov 65		**YESTERDAY** *Decca F 12268*	36	4
9 Mar 67		**IS THIS WHAT I GET FOR LOVING YOU?** *Decca F 22524*	43	2
24 Nov 79		**THE BALLAD OF LUCY JORDAN** *Island WIP 6491*	48	6
5 Jun 65		**COME MY WAY** *Decca LK 4688*	12	7
5 Jun 65		**MARIANNE FAITHFULL** *Decca LK 4689*	15	2
24 Nov 79		**BROKEN ENGLISH** *Island M1*	57	3
17 Oct 81		**DANGEROUS ACQUAINTANCES** *Island ILPS 9648*	45	4
26 Mar 83		**A CHILD'S ADVENTURE** *Island ILPS 9734*	99	1
8 Aug 87		**STRANGE WEATHER** *Island ILPS 9874*	78	2

FAITHLESS

UK, male / female vocal / instrumental group (Singles: 72 weeks, Albums: 43 weeks)

Date		Title / Label	pos	wks
5 Aug 95		**SALVA MEA (SAVE ME)** *Cheeky CHEKCD 008*	30	2
9 Dec 95		**INSOMNIA** *Cheeky CHEKCD 010*	27	2
23 Mar 96		**DON'T LEAVE** *Cheeky CHEKCD 012*	34	2
26 Oct 96	●	**INSOMNIA (re-issue)** *Cheeky CHEKCD 017*	3	13
21 Dec 96	●	**SALVA MEA (re-mix)** *Cheeky CHEKCD 018*	9	7
26 Apr 97	●	**REVERENCE** *Cheeky CHEKCD 019*	10	3
15 Nov 97		**DON'T LEAVE (re-mix)** *Cheeky CHEKXCD 024*	21	2
5 Sep 98	●	**GOD IS A DJ** *Cheeky CHEKCD 028*	6	8
5 Dec 98		**TAKE THE LONG WAY HOME** *Cheeky CHEKCD 031*	15	6
1 May 99		**BRING MY FAMILY BACK** *Cheeky CHEKCD 035*	14	5
16 Jun 01	●	**WE COME 1** *Cheeky 74321850842*	3	10
29 Sep 01		**MUHAMMAD ALI** *Cheeky 74321886442*	29	4
29 Dec 01		**TARANTULA** *Cheeky 74321903592*	29	5
20 Apr 02	●	**ONE STEP TOO FAR** *Cheeky / Arista 74321926412* [1]	6	3
23 Nov 96		**REVERENCE** *Cheeky CHEKCD 500*	26	14
3 Oct 98	●	**SUNDAY 8PM** *Cheeky CHEKCD 503*	10	7
30 Jun 01	●	**OUTROSPECTIVE** *Cheeky 74321850832*	4	22

[1] Faithless featuring Dido

See also OUR TRIBE / ONE TRIBE; ROLLO; SPHINX; DUSTED

FALCO

Austria, male vocalist – Johann Holzel, d. 6 Feb 1998 (Singles: 26 weeks, Albums: 15 weeks)

Date		Title / Label	pos	wks
22 Mar 86	★	**ROCK ME AMADEUS** *A&M AM 278* ▲	1	15
31 May 86	●	**VIENNA CALLING** *A&M AM 318*	10	8
2 Aug 86		**JEANNY** *A&M AM 333*	68	1
27 Sep 86		**THE SOUND OF MUSIK** *WEA U 8591*	61	2
26 Apr 86		**FALCO 3** *A&M AMA 5105*	32	15

Christian FALK featuring DEMETREUS

Sweden, male producer and male vocalist (Singles: 3 weeks)

Date		Title / Label	pos	wks
26 Aug 00		**MAKE IT RIGHT** *London LONCD 452*	22	3

Fred FALKE – *See Alan BRAXE and Fred FALKE*

FALL

UK, male / female vocal / instrumental group – leader Mark E Smith (Singles: 26 weeks, Albums: 32 weeks)

Date		Title / Label	pos	wks
13 Sep 86		**MR PHARMACIST** *Beggars Banquet BEG 168*	75	1
20 Dec 86		**HEY! LUCIANI** *Beggars Banquet BEG 176*	59	1
9 May 87		**THERE'S A GHOST IN MY HOUSE** *Beggars Banquet BEG 187*	30	4
31 Oct 87		**HIT THE NORTH** *Beggars Banquet BEG 200*	57	5
30 Jan 88		**VICTORIA** *Beggars Banquet BEG 206*	35	3
26 Nov 88		**BIG NEW PRINZ / JERUSALEM (DOUBLE SINGLE)** *Beggars Banquet FALL 2/3*	59	2
27 Jan 90		**TELEPHONE THING** *Cog Sinister SIN 4*	58	1
8 Sep 90		**WHITE LIGHTNING** *Cog Sinister SIN 6*	56	2
14 Mar 92		**FREE RANGE** *Cog Sinister SINS 8*	40	1
17 Apr 93		**WHY ARE PEOPLE GRUDGEFUL** *Permanent CDSPERM 9*	43	1
25 Dec 93		**BEHIND THE COUNTER** *Permanent CDSPERM 13*	75	1
30 Apr 94		**15 WAYS** *Permanent CDSPERM 14*	65	1
17 Feb 96		**THE CHISELERS** *Jet JETSCD 500*	60	1
21 Feb 98		**MASQUERADE** *Artful CDARTFUL 1*	69	1
14 Dec 02		**THE FALL VS 2003** *Action TAKE 020CD*	64	1
20 Mar 82		**HEX ENDUCTION HOUR** *Kamera KAM 005*	71	3
20 Oct 84		**THE WONDERFUL AND FRIGHTENING WORLD OF ...** *Beggars Banquet BEGA 58*	62	2
5 Oct 85		**THE NATION'S SAVING GRACE** *Beggars Banquet BEGA 67*	54	2
11 Oct 86		**BEND SINISTER** *Beggars Banquet BEGA 75*	36	3
12 Mar 88		**THE FRENZ EXPERIMENT** *Beggars Banquet BEGA 91*	19	4
12 Nov 88		**I AM KURIOUS ORANJ** *Beggars Banquet BEGA 96*	54	2
8 Jul 89		**SEMINAL LIVE** *Beggars Banquet BBL 102*	40	2
3 Mar 90		**EXTRICATE** *Cog Sinister 8422041*	31	3
15 Sep 90		**458489 B-SIDES** *Beggars Banquet BEGA 111*	44	2
4 May 91		**SHIFT WORK** *Cog Sinister 8485941*	17	2
28 Mar 92		**CODE: SELFISH** *Cog Sinister 5121622*	21	1
8 May 93	●	**INFOTAINMENT SCAN** *Permanent PERMCD 12*	9	3
14 May 94		**MIDDLE CLASS REVOLT** *Permanent PERMCD 16*	48	1
11 Mar 95		**CEREBRAL CAUSTIC** *Permanent PERMCD 30*	67	1
22 Jun 96		**THE LIGHT USER SYNDROME** *Jet JETCD 1012*	54	1

Tracks on 'Big New Prinz / Jerusalem' double single: Big New Prinz / Wrong Place Right Time Number Two / Jerusalem / Acid Priest 2088. Tracks on 'The Fall vs 2003': Susan vs Youthclub (& remix) / Janey vs Johnny

See also Mark E SMITH

FALLACY

UK, male producer - Daniel Fahey (Singles: 4 weeks)

Date		Title / Label	pos	wks
22 Jun 02		**THE GROUNDBREAKER** *Wordplay WORDCD 036* [1]	47	2
24 May 03		**BIG N BASHY** *Virgin VSCDT 1847* [2]	45	2

[1] Fallacy and Fusion [2] Fallacy featuring Tubby T

Harold FALTERMEYER

Germany, male instrumentalist – keyboards (Singles: 23 weeks)

Date		Title / Label	pos	wks
23 Mar 85	●	**AXEL F (re)** *MCA MCA 949*	2	22
24 Aug 85		**FLETCH THEME** *MCA MCA 991*	74	1

'Axel F' reached its peak position in Jun 1985

Agnetha FALTSKOG

Sweden, female vocalist (Singles: 12 weeks, Albums: 17 weeks)

Date		Title / Label	pos	wks
28 May 83		**THE HEAT IS ON** *Epic A 3436*	35	6
13 Aug 83		**WRAP YOUR ARMS AROUND ME** *Epic A 3622*	44	5
22 Oct 83		**CAN'T SHAKE LOOSE** *Epic A 3812*	63	1

			pos	wks
11 Jun 83		**WRAP YOUR ARMS AROUND ME** *Epic EPC 25505*	18	13
4 May 85		**EYES OF A WOMAN** *Epic EPC 26446*	38	3
12 Mar 88		**I STAND ALONE** *WEA WX 150*	72	1

See also ABBA

Georgie FAME (351 Top 500)

Critically acclaimed R&B / jazz vocalist / keyboard player, b. Clive Powell, 26 Jun 1943, Lancashire, UK. The one-time rock 'n' roll tour musician, who had a string of Sixties hits, is still a popular performer, often working with contemporaries such as Van Morrison and Bill Wyman (Singles: 115 weeks, Albums: 72 weeks)

			pos	wks
17 Dec 64	★	**YEH, YEH** *Columbia DB 7428* [1]	1	12
4 Mar 65		**IN THE MEANTIME** *Columbia DB 7494* [1]	22	8
29 Jul 65		**LIKE WE USED TO BE** *Columbia DB 7633* [1]	33	7
28 Oct 65		**SOMETHING** *Columbia DB 7727* [1]	23	7
23 Jun 66	★	**GET AWAY** *Columbia DB 7946* [1]	1	11
22 Sep 66		**SUNNY** *Columbia DB 8015*	13	8
22 Dec 66		**SITTING IN THE PARK** *Columbia DB 8096* [1]	12	10
23 Mar 67		**BECAUSE I LOVE YOU** *CBS 202587*	15	8
13 Sep 67		**TRY MY WORLD** *CBS 2945*	37	5
13 Dec 67	★	**THE BALLAD OF BONNIE AND CLYDE** *CBS 3124*	1	13
9 Jul 69		**PEACEFUL** *CBS 4295*	16	9
13 Dec 69		**SEVENTH SON** *CBS 4659*	25	7
10 Apr 71		**ROSETTA** *CBS 7108* [2]	11	10
17 Oct 64		FAME AT LAST *Columbia 33SX 1638*	15	8
14 May 66	●	SWEET THINGS *Columbia SX 6043*	6	22
15 Oct 66	●	SOUND VENTURE *Columbia SX 6076*	9	9
11 Mar 67		HALL OF FAME *Columbia SX 6120*	12	18
1 Jul 67		TWO FACES OF FAME *CBS SBPG 63018*	22	15

[1] Georgie Fame and the Blue Flames [2] Fame and Price Together

FAMILY *UK, male vocal / instrumental group (Singles: 44 weeks, Albums: 41 weeks)*

			pos	wks
1 Nov 69		**NO MULE'S FOOL** *Reprise RS 27001*	29	7
22 Aug 70		**STRANGE BAND** *Reprise RS 27009*	11	12
17 Jul 71	●	**IN MY OWN TIME** *Reprise K 14090*	4	13
23 Sep 72		**BURLESQUE** *Reprise K 14196*	13	12
10 Aug 68		MUSIC IN THE DOLLS HOUSE *Reprise RLP 6312*	35	3
22 Mar 69	●	FAMILY ENTERTAINMENT *Reprise RSLP 6340*	6	3
7 Feb 70	●	A SONG FOR ME *Reprise RSLP 9001*	4	13
28 Nov 70	●	ANYWAY *Reprise RSX 9005*	7	7
20 Nov 71		FEARLESS *Reprise K 54003*	14	2
30 Sep 72		BANDSTAND *Reprise K 54006*	15	10
29 Sep 73		IT'S ONLY A MOVIE *Raft RA 58501*	30	3

FAMILY CAT *UK, male vocal / instrumental group (Singles: 4 weeks, Albums: 1 week)*

			pos	wks
28 Aug 93		**AIRPLANE GARDENS / ATMOSPHERIC ROAD** *Dedicated FCUK 003CD*	69	1
21 May 94		**WONDERFUL EXCUSE** *Dedicated 74321208432*	48	1
30 Jul 94		**GOLDENBOOK** *Dedicated 74321220072*	42	2
4 Jul 92		FURTHEST FROM THE SUN *Dedicated DEDCD 007*	55	1

FAMILY COOKIN' – *See LIMMIE and the FAMILY COOKIN'*

FAMILY DOGG *UK, male / female vocal group (Singles: 14 weeks)*

			pos	wks
28 May 69	●	**A WAY OF LIFE** *Bell 1055*	6	14

FAMILY FOUNDATION

UK, male / female vocal / instrumental group (Singles: 4 weeks)

			pos	wks
13 Jun 92		**XPRESS YOURSELF** *380 PEW 1*	42	4

FAMILY STAND *US, male / female vocal / instrumental group (Singles: 13 weeks, Albums: 3 weeks)*

			pos	wks
31 Mar 90	●	**GHETTO HEAVEN** *East West A 7997*	10	11
17 Jan 98		**GHETTO HEAVEN (re-mix)** *Perfecto PERF 156CD1*	30	2
19 May 90		CHAIN *Atlantic WX 349*	52	3

FAMILY STONE – *See SLY and the FAMILY STONE*

FAMOUS FLAMES – *See James BROWN*

FANTASTIC FOUR

US, male vocal group (Singles: 4 weeks)

			pos	wks
24 Feb 79		**B.Y.O.F. (BRING YOUR OWN FUNK)** *Atlantic LV 14*	62	4

FANTASTICS *US, male vocal group (Singles: 12 weeks)*

			pos	wks
27 Mar 71	●	**SOMETHING OLD, SOMETHING NEW** *Bell 1141*	9	12

FANTASY UFO

UK, male instrumental group (Singles: 6 weeks)

			pos	wks
29 Sep 90		**FANTASY** *XL XLT 15*	56	3
10 Aug 91		**MIND BODY SOUL** *Strictly Underground YZ 591* [1]	50	3

[1] Fantasy UFO featuring Jay Groove

FAR CORPORATION *UK / US / Germany / Switzerland, male vocal / instrumental group (Singles: 11 weeks)*

			pos	wks
26 Oct 85	●	**STAIRWAY TO HEAVEN** *Arista ARIST 639*	8	11

Don FARDON

UK, male vocalist – Donald Maughn (Singles: 22 weeks)

			pos	wks
18 Apr 70		**BELFAST BOY** *Young Blood YB 1010*	32	5
10 Oct 70	●	**INDIAN RESERVATION** *Young Blood YB 1015*	3	17

FARGETTA

Italy / UK, male producer – Mario Fargetta (Singles: 3 weeks)

			pos	wks
[illegible]		[illegible] [1]	[illegible]	[illegible]
10 Aug 96		**THE MUSIC IS MOVING** *Arista 74321381572*	74	1

[1] Fargetta and Anne-Marie Smith

See also TAMPERER featuring MAYA

Chris FARLOWE *UK, male vocalist – John Deighton (Singles: 36 weeks, Albums: 3 weeks)*

			pos	wks
27 Jan 66		**THINK (re)** *Immediate IM 023*	37	3
23 Jun 66	★	**OUT OF TIME** *Immediate IM 035* [1]	1	13
27 Oct 66		**RIDE ON BABY** *Immediate IM 038*	31	7
16 Feb 67		**MY WAY OF GIVING IN** *Immediate IM 041*	48	1
29 Jun 67		**MOANIN'** *Immediate IM 056*	46	2
13 Dec 67		**HANDBAGS AND GLADRAGS** *Immediate IM 065*	33	6
27 Sep 75		**OUT OF TIME (re-issue)** *Immediate IMS 101*	44	4
2 Apr 66		14 THINGS TO THINK ABOUT *Immediate IMLP 005*	19	1
10 Dec 66		THE ART OF CHRIS FARLOWE *Immediate IMLP 006*	37	2

[1] Chris Farlowe and The Thunderbirds

FARM *UK, male vocal / instrumental group (Singles: 54 weeks, Albums: 17 weeks)*

			pos	wks
5 May 90		**STEPPING STONE / FAMILY OF MAN** *Produce MILK 101*	58	4
1 Sep 90	●	**GROOVY TRAIN** *Produce MILK 102*	6	10
8 Dec 90	●	**ALL TOGETHER NOW** *Produce MILK 103*	4	12
13 Apr 91		**SINFUL! (SCARY JIGGIN' WITH DR LOVE)** *Siren SRN 138* [1]	28	5
4 May 91		**DON'T LET ME DOWN** *Produce MILK 104*	36	3
24 Aug 91		**MIND** *Produce MILK 105*	31	4
14 Dec 91		**LOVE SEE NO COLOUR** *Produce MILK 106*	58	4
4 Jul 92		**RISING SUN** *End Product 6581737*	48	3
17 Oct 92		**DON'T YOU WANT ME** *End Product 6584687*	18	5
2 Jan 93		**LOVE SEE NO COLOUR (re-mix)** *End Product 6588682*	35	4
16 Mar 91	★	SPARTACUS *Produce MILKLP 1* ■	1	17

[1] Pete Wylie with The Farm

FARMERS BOYS *UK, male vocal / instrumental group (Singles: 17 weeks, Albums: 1 week)*

			pos	wks
9 Apr 83		**MUCK IT OUT!** *EMI 5380*	48	6
30 Jul 83		**FOR YOU** *EMI 5401*	66	3
4 Aug 84		**IN THE COUNTRY** *EMI FAB 2*	44	5
3 Nov 84		**PHEW WOW** *EMI FAB 3*	59	3
29 Oct 83		GET OUT AND WALK *EMI EMC 1077991*	49	1

John FARNHAM
Australia, male vocalist (Singles: 17 weeks, Albums: 9 weeks) pos/wks

25 Apr 87 ● **YOU'RE THE VOICE** *Wheatley PB 41093* 6 17
11 Jul 87 WHISPERING JACK *RCA PL 71224* 35 9

FARRAR – *See MARVIN WELCH and FARRAR; WELCH*

Joanne FARRELL *US, female vocalist (Singles: 2 weeks)* pos/wks

24 Jun 95 **ALL I WANNA DO** *Big Beat A 8194CD* 40 2

Joe FARRELL *US, male instrumentalist – saxophone, d. 10 Jan 1986 (Singles: 4 weeks)* pos/wks

16 Dec 78 **NIGHT DANCING** *Warner Bros. LV 2* 57 4

Dionne FARRIS *US, female vocalist (Singles: 6 weeks)* pos/wks

18 Mar 95 **I KNOW (re)** *Columbia 6613542* 41 5
7 Jun 97 **HOPELESS** *Columbia 6645165* 42 1

Gene FARRIS *US, male producer (Singles: 1 week)* pos/wks

20 Dec 03 **WELCOME TO CHICAGO** *Defected DFTD 081* 74 1

Gene FARROW with the GF BAND
UK, male vocal / instrumental group (Singles: 8 weeks) pos/wks

1 Apr 78 **MOVE YOUR BODY (re)** *Magnet MAG 109* 33 6
5 Aug 78 **DON'T STOP NOW (re)** *Magnet MAG 125* 71 2

FASCINATIONS *US, female vocal group (Singles: 6 weeks)* pos/wks

3 Jul 71 **GIRLS ARE OUT TO GET YOU** *Mojo 2092 004* 32 6

FASHION *UK, male vocal / instrumental group (Singles: 12 weeks, Albums: 17 weeks)* pos/wks

3 Apr 82 **STREETPLAYER (MECHANIK)** *Arista ARIST 456* 46 5
21 Aug 82 **LOVE SHADOW** *Arista ARIST 483* 51 5
18 Feb 84 **EYE TALK** *Epic A 4106* 69 2
3 Jul 82 ● FABRIQUE *Arista SPART 1185* 10 16
16 Jun 84 TWILIGHT OF IDOLS *De Stijl EPC 25909* 69 1

Susan FASSBENDER *UK, female vocalist (Singles: 8 weeks)* pos/wks

17 Jan 81 **TWILIGHT CAFE** *CBS 9468* 21 8

FAST FOOD ROCKERS
UK, male / female vocal group (Singles: 22 weeks) pos/wks

28 Jun 03 ● **FAST FOOD SONG** *Better the Devil BTD 1CD* 2 14
18 Oct 03 ● **SAY CHEESE (SMILE PLEASE)** *Better the Devil BTD 5CD* 10 7
27 Dec 03 **I LOVE CHRISTMAS** *Better the Devil BTD 6CDX* 25 1+

FASTBALL *US, male vocal / instrumental trio (Singles: 5 weeks)* pos/wks

3 Oct 98 **THE WAY** *Polydor 5699472* 21 5

FASTER PUSSYCAT
US, male vocal / instrumental group (Albums: 3 weeks) pos/wks

16 Sep 89 WAKE ME WHEN IT'S OVER *Elektra EKT 64* 35 2
22 Aug 92 WHIPPED! *Elektra 7559611242* 58 1

FASTWAY *UK, male vocal / instrumental group (Singles: 1 week, Albums: 2 weeks)* pos/wks

2 Apr 83 **EASY LIVIN'** *CBS A 3196* 74 1
30 Apr 83 FASTWAY *CBS 25359* 43 2

FAT BOYS
US, male rap group (Singles: 29 weeks, Albums: 5 weeks) pos/wks

4 May 85 **JAIL HOUSE RAP** *Sutra U 9123* 63 2
22 Aug 87 ● **WIPEOUT** *Urban URB 5* [1] 2 12
18 Jun 88 ● **THE TWIST (YO, TWIST)** *Urban URB 20* [2] 2 11
5 Nov 88 **LOUIE LOUIE** *Urban URB 26* 46 4
3 Oct 87 CRUSHIN' *Urban URBLP 3* 49 4
30 Jul 88 COMING BACK HARD AGAIN *Urban URBLP 13* 98 1

[1] Fat Boys and the Beach Boys [2] Fat Boys and Chubby Checker

FAT JOE *US, male rapper (Singles: 17 weeks, Albums: 10 weeks)* pos/wks

1 Apr 00 **FEELIN' SO GOOD** *Columbia 6691972* [1] 15 6
30 Mar 02 **WE THUGGIN'** *Atlantic AT 0124CD* 48 1
25 May 02 ● **WHAT'S LUV?** *Atlantic AT 0128CD* [2] 4 8
14 Dec 02 **CRUSH TONIGHT** *Atlantic AT 0142CD* [3] 42 2
27 Apr 02 JEALOUS ONES STILL ENVY (J.O.S.E.) *Atlantic 7567834722* 19 10

[1] Jennifer Lopez featuring Big Pun and Fat Joe [2] Fat Joe featuring Ashanti
[3] Fat Joe featuring Ginuwine

Sleeve, not label, of 'We Thuggin'' has credit 'featuring R. Kelly'

FAT LADY SINGS *Ireland, male vocal / instrumental group (Singles: 2 weeks, Albums: 1 week)* pos/wks

17 Jul 93 **DRUNKARD LOGIC** *East West YZ 756CD* 56 2
18 May 91 TWIST *East West WX 418* 50 1

FAT LARRY'S BAND *US, male vocal / instrumental group (Singles: 26 weeks, Albums: 4 weeks)* pos/wks

2 Jul 77 **CENTER CITY** *Atlantic K 10951* 31 5
10 Mar 79 **BOOGIE TOWN** *Fantasy FTC 168* [1] 46 4
18 Aug 79 **LOOKING FOR LOVE TONIGHT** *Fantasy FTC 179* [2] 46 6
18 Sep 82 ● **ZOOM** *Virgin VS 546* 2 11
9 Oct 82 BREAKIN' OUT *Virgin V 2229* 58 4

[1] FLB [2] Fat Larry's Band (FLB)

FAT LES *UK, male / female vocal group – includes Alex James (Singles: 22 weeks)* pos/wks

20 Jun 98 ● **VINDALOO** *Telstar CDSTAS 2982* 2 12
19 Dec 98 **NAUGHTY CHRISTMAS (GOBLIN IN THE OFFICE)** *Turtleneck NECKCD 001* 21 5
17 Jun 00 ● **JERUSALEM (re)** *Parlophone CDR 6540* [1] 10 5

[1] Fat Les 2000

See also BLUR; ME ME ME

FATBACK BAND *US, male vocal / instrumental group (Singles: 67 weeks, Albums: 7 weeks)* pos/wks

6 Sep 75 **YUM, YUM (GIMME SOME)** *Polydor 2066 590* 40 6
6 Dec 75 **(ARE YOU READY) DO THE BUS STOP** *Polydor 2066 637* 18 10
21 Feb 76 ● **(DO THE) SPANISH HUSTLE** *Polydor 2066 656* 10 7
29 May 76 **PARTY TIME** *Polydor 2066 682* 41 4
14 Aug 76 **NIGHT FEVER** *Spring 2066 706* 38 4
12 Mar 77 **DOUBLE DUTCH** *Spring 2066 777* 31 4
9 Aug 80 **BACKSTROKIN'** *Spring POSP 149* [1] 41 9
23 Jun 84 ● **I FOUND LOVIN' (re)** *Master Mix CHE 8401* 7 16
4 May 85 **GIRLS ON MY MIND** *Atlantic / Cotillion FBACK 1* [1] 69 2
6 Sep 86 **I FOUND LOVIN' (re-issue)** *Important TAN 10* 55 5
6 Mar 76 RAISING HELL *Polydor 2391 203* 19 6
4 Jul 87 FATBACK LIVE *Start STL 12* 80 1

[1] Fatback

FATBOY SLIM (355 Top 500) *Multi-aliased, superstar DJ / producer Norman Cook (b. Quentin Cook, 31 Jul 1963, Bromley, Kent, UK) finally achieved a solo No.1 in this guise, having already topped the chart with Housemartins and Beats International. Married TV / radio presenter Zoe Ball in 1999 (Singles: 73 weeks, Albums: 111 weeks)* pos/wks

3 May 97 **GOING OUT OF MY HEAD** *Skint SKINT 19CD* 57 1
1 Nov 97 **EVERYBODY NEEDS A 303** *Skint SKINT 31CD* 34 2
20 Jun 98 ● **THE ROCKAFELLER SKANK** *Skint SKINT 35CD* 6 10
17 Oct 98 ● **GANGSTER TRIPPIN'** *Skint SKINT 39CD* 3 8
16 Jan 99 ★ **PRAISE YOU** *Skint SKINT 42CD* ■ 1 12
1 May 99 ● **RIGHT HERE RIGHT NOW** *Skint SKINT 46CD* 2 10
1 May 99 **BADDER BADDER SCHWING** *Eye Q EYEUK 040CD* [1] 34 2
28 Oct 00 ● **SUNSET (BIRD OF PREY) (re)** *Skint SKINT 58CD* 9 13
20 Jan 01 **DEMONS** *Skint SKINT 60CD* [2] 16 5

5 May 01	●	**STAR 69** *Skint SKINT 64CD*	10	7
15 Sep 01		**YA MAMA / SONG FOR SHELTER** *Skint SKINT 71CD*	30	2
26 Jan 02		**RETOX** *Skint SKINT FAT 18*	73	1
28 Sep 96		**BETTER LIVING THROUGH CHEMISTRY** *Skint BRASSIC 2CD*	69	3
31 Oct 98	★	**YOU'VE COME A LONG WAY BABY** *Skint BRASSIC 11CD*	1	86
18 Nov 00	●	**HALFWAY BETWEEN THE GUTTER AND THE STARS** *Skint BRASSIC 20CD*	8	22

[1] Freddy Fresh featuring Fatboy Slim [2] Fatboy Slim featuring Macy Gray

See also BEATS INTERNATIONAL; Norman COOK; FREAKPOWER; HOUSEMARTINS; MIGHTY DUB KATZ; PIZZAMAN; URBAN ALL STARS

FATHER ABRAHAM – *See SMURFS*

FATHER ABRAPHART and the SMURPS – *See Jonathan KING*

FATHER KILCOYNE – *See POPE JOHN PAUL II*

FATIMA MANSIONS *Ireland, male vocal / instrumental group (Singles: 11 weeks, Albums: 1 week)*

			pos	wks
23 May 92		**EVIL MAN** *Radioactive SKX 56*	59	1
1 Aug 92		**1000 %** *Radioactive SKX 59*	61	3
19 Sep 92	●	**(EVERYTHING I DO) I DO IT FOR YOU** *Columbia 6583827*	7	6
6 Aug 94		**THE LOYALISER** *Kitchenware SKCD 67*	58	1
6 Jun 92		**VALHALLA AVENUE** *Radioactive KWCD 18*	52	1

'(Everything I Do) I Do It for You' was listed with 'Theme from M.A.S.H. (Suicide Is Painless)' by Manic Street Preachers

FATMAN SCOOP featuring The CROOKLYN CLAN *US, male DJ / rapper – Isaac Freeman III (Singles: 9 weeks)*

			pos	wks
1 Nov 03	★	**BE FAITHFUL** *Def Jam 9812716* ■	1	9+

FEAR FACTORY *US, male vocal / instrumental group (Singles: 1 week, Albums: 6 weeks)*

			pos	wks
9 Oct 99		**CARS** *Roadrunner RR 21893*	57	1
1 Jul 95		**DEMANUFACTURE** *Roadrunner RR 89565*	27	1
14 Jun 97		**REMANUFACTURE – CLONING TECHNOLOGY** *Roadrunner RR 88342*	22	1
8 Aug 98		**OBSOLETE** *Roadrunner RR 87522*	20	2
5 May 01		**DIGIMORTAL** *Roadrunner RR 85612*	24	2

Phil FEARON *UK, male vocalist (Singles: 63 weeks, Albums: 9 weeks)*

			pos	wks
23 Apr 83	●	**DANCING TIGHT** *Ensign ENY 501* [1]	4	11
30 Jul 83		**WAIT UNTIL TONIGHT (MY LOVE)** *Ensign ENY 503* [1]	20	8
22 Oct 83		**FANTASY REAL** *Ensign ENY 507* [2]	41	6
10 Mar 84	●	**WHAT DO I DO** *Ensign ENY 510* [2]	5	10
14 Jul 84	●	**EVERYBODY'S LAUGHING** *Ensign ENY 514* [2]	10	10
15 Jun 85		**YOU DON'T NEED A REASON** *Ensign ENY 517* [2]	42	4
27 Jul 85		**THIS KIND OF LOVE** *Ensign ENY 521* [3]	70	3
2 Aug 86	●	**I CAN PROVE IT** *Ensign PF 1*	8	9
15 Nov 86		**AIN'T NOTHING BUT A HOUSEPARTY** *Ensign PF 2*	60	2
25 Aug 84	●	**PHIL FEARON AND GALAXY** *Ensign ENCL 2* [1]	8	8
14 Sep 85		**THIS KIND OF LOVE** *Ensign ENCL 4* [1]	98	1

[1] Galaxy featuring Phil Fearon [2] Phil Fearon and Galaxy [3] Phil Fearon and Galaxy featuring Dee Galdes [1] Phil Fearon and Galaxy

FEEDER *UK, male vocal / instrumental group (Singles: 56 weeks, Albums: 43 weeks)*

			pos	wks
8 Mar 97		**TANGERINE** *Echo ECSCD 32*	60	1
10 May 97		**CEMENT** *Echo ECSCX 36*	53	1
23 Aug 97		**CRASH** *Echo ECSCD 42*	48	1
18 Oct 97		**HIGH** *Echo ECSCD 44*	24	2
28 Feb 98		**SUFFOCATE** *Echo ECSCX 52*	37	1
3 Apr 99		**DAY IN DAY OUT** *Echo ECSCD 75*	31	2
12 Jun 99		**INSOMNIA** *Echo ECSCD 77*	22	3
21 Aug 99		**YESTERDAY WENT TOO SOON** *Echo ECSCD 79*	20	3
20 Nov 99		**PAPERFACES** *Echo ECSCD 85*	41	2
20 Jan 01	●	**BUCK ROGERS** *Echo ECSCD 106*	5	6
14 Apr 01		**SEVEN DAYS IN THE SUN (re)** *Echo ECSCD 107*	14	6
14 Jul 01		**TURN** *Echo ECSCD 116*	27	2
22 Dec 01		**JUST A DAY (EP)** *Echo ECSCD 121*	12	7
12 Oct 02		**COME BACK AROUND (re)** *Echo ECSCD 130*	14	5
25 Jan 03	●	**JUST THE WAY I'M FEELING** *Echo ECSCD 133*	10	8
17 May 03		**FORGET ABOUT TOMORROW** *Echo ECSCD 135*	12	4
4 Oct 03		**FIND THE COLOUR** *Echo ECSCD 145*	24	2
31 May 97		**POLYTHENE** *Echo ECHCD 15*	65	1
11 Sep 99	●	**YESTERDAY WENT TOO SOON** *Echo ECHCD 28*	8	3
5 May 01	●	**ECHO PARK** *Echo ECHCD 34*	5	9
2 Nov 02	●	**COMFORT IN SOUND** *Echo ECHCD 43*	6	30

Tracks on 'Just a Day' (EP): CD1 features 'Just a Day', 'Can't Stand Losing You', 'Piece By Piece' (last track is video only). CD 2 features 'Just a Day' (Full version), 'Emily', Slowburn', Just a Day (video)

Wilton FELDER *US, male instrumentalist – tenor sax (Singles: 7 weeks, Albums: 3 weeks)*

			pos	wks
1 Nov 80		**INHERIT THE WIND** *MCA 646*	39	5
16 Feb 85		**(NO MATTER HOW HIGH I GET) I'LL STILL BE LOOKIN' UP TO YOU** *MCA MCA 919* [1]	63	2
23 Feb 85		**SECRETS** *MCA MCF 3237*	77	3

[1] Wilton Felder featuring Bobby Womack and introducing Alltrinna Grayson

Bobby Womack uncredited vocalist on 'Inherit the Wind'

See also CRUSADERS

FELICIA – *See B.M.R. featuring FELICIA*

José FELICIANO *Puerto Rico, male vocalist / instrumentalist – guitar (Singles: 23 weeks, Albums: 40 weeks)*

			pos	wks
18 Sep 68	●	**LIGHT MY FIRE** *RCA 1715*	6	16
18 Oct 69		**AND THE SUN WILL SHINE** *RCA 1871*	25	7
2 Nov 68	●	**FELICIANO** *RCA Victor SF 7946*	6	36
29 Nov 69		**JOSE FELICIANO** *RCA Victor SF 8044*	29	2
14 Feb 70		**10 TO 23** *RCA SF 7946*	38	1
22 Aug 70		**FIREWORKS** *RCA SF 8124*	65	1

FELIX *UK, male producer – Francis Wright (Singles: 29 weeks, Albums: 4 weeks)*

			pos	wks
8 Aug 92	●	**DON'T YOU WANT ME** *Deconstruction 74321110507*	6	11
24 Oct 92		**IT WILL MAKE ME CRAZY** *Deconstruction 74321118137*	11	6
22 May 93		**STARS** *Deconstruction 74321147102*	29	3
12 Aug 95	●	**DON'T YOU WANT ME (re-mix)** *Deconstruction 74321293972*	10	5
19 Oct 96		**DON'T YOU WANT ME (2nd re-mix)** *Deconstruction 74321418142*	17	4
10 Apr 93		**#1** *Deconstruction 74321137002*	26	4

Gil FELIX – *See INFRARED vs Gil FELIX*

Julie FELIX *US, female vocalist / instrumentalist – guitar (Singles: 19 weeks, Albums: 4 weeks)*

			pos	wks
18 Apr 70		**IF I COULD (EL CONDOR PASA)** *RAK 101*	19	11
17 Oct 70		**HEAVEN IS HERE** *RAK 105*	22	8
11 Sep 66		**CHANGES** *Fontana TL 5368*	27	4

FELIX DA HOUSECAT *US, male producer – Felix Stallings Jr (Singles: 5 weeks)*

			pos	wks
6 Sep 97		**DIRTY MOTHA** *Manifesto FESCD 29*	66	1
14 Jul 01		**SILVER SCREEN SHOWER SCENE** *City Rockers ROCKERS 1CD*	55	1
2 Mar 02		**WHAT DOES IT FEEL LIKE?** *City Rockers ROCKERS 8CD*	66	1
5 Oct 02		**SILVER SCREEN SHOWER SCENE (re-mix)** *City Rockers ROCKERS 19CD*	39	2

FELLY – *See TECHNOTRONIC*

FELON *UK, female vocalist – Simone Locker (Singles: 2 weeks)*

			pos	wks
23 Mar 02		**GET OUT** *Serious SERR 032CD*	31	2

FE-M@IL *UK, female vocal group (Singles: 2 weeks)* pos/wks

5 Aug 00	**FLEE FLY FLO** *Jive 9250592*	46	2

FEMME FATALE
US, male / female vocal / instrumental group (Singles: 2 weeks) pos/wks

11 Feb 89	**FALLING IN AND OUT OF LOVE** *MCA MCA 1309*	69	2

FENDERMEN *US, male vocal / instrumental duo – Phil Humphrey and Jim Sundquist – guitars (Singles: 9 weeks)* pos/wks

18 Aug 60	**MULE SKINNER BLUES (2re)** *Top Rank JAR 395*	32	9

FENIX TX
US, male vocal / instrumental group (Singles: 1 week) pos/wks

11 May 02	**THREESOME** *MCA MCSTD 40279*	66	1

FENMEN – *See Bern ELLIOTT and the FENMEN*

George FENTON and Jonas GWANGWA *UK / South Africa, male instrumental / production duo (Singles: 1 week)* pos/wks

2 Jan 88	**CRY FREEDOM** *MCA MCA 1228*	75	1

The listed flip side of 'Cry Freedom' was 'The Funeral' by Thuli Dumakude

Peter FENTON *UK, male vocalist (Singles: 3 weeks)* pos/wks

10 Nov 66	**MARBLE BREAKS IRON BENDS** *Fontana TF 748*	46	3

Shane FENTON and the FENTONES
UK, male instrumental group (Singles: 32 weeks) pos/wks

26 Oct 61	**I'M A MOODY GUY** *Parlophone R 4827*	22	8
1 Feb 62	**WALK AWAY** *Parlophone R 4866*	38	5
5 Apr 62	**IT'S ALL OVER NOW** *Parlophone R 4883*	29	7
19 Apr 62	**THE MEXICAN** *Parlophone R 4899* [1]	41	3
12 Jul 62	**CINDY'S BIRTHDAY** *Parlophone R 4921*	19	8
27 Sep 62	**THE BREEZE AND I** *Parlophone R 4937* [1]	48	1

[1] The Fentones

FERGIE
Ireland, male DJ / producer – Robert Ferguson (Singles: 5 weeks) pos/wks

9 Sep 00	**DECEPTION** *Duty Free DF 020CD*	47	1
25 Nov 00	**HOOVERS & HORNS** *Nukleuz NUKC 0185* [1]	57	2
10 Aug 02	**THE BASS EP** *Duty Free / Decode DFTELCX 004*	47	2

[1] Fergie & BK

Tracks on The Bass EP: Mixes of 'Bass Generator' / 'Bass Has Got Me On'

Sheila FERGUSON *US, female vocalist (Singles: 1 week)* pos/wks

5 Feb 94	**WHEN WILL I SEE YOU AGAIN** *XSrhythm CDSTAS 2711*	60	1

See also THREE DEGREES

FERKO STRING BAND
US, male instrumental group (Singles: 2 weeks) pos/wks

12 Aug 55	**ALABAMA JUBILEE** *London HL 8140*	20	2

Luisa FERNANDEZ *Spain, female vocalist (Singles: 8 weeks)* pos/wks

11 Nov 78	**LAY LOVE ON YOU** *Warner Bros. K 17061*	31	8

Pamela FERNANDEZ
US, female vocalist (Singles: 3 weeks) pos/wks

17 Sep 94	**KICKIN' IN THE BEAT** *Ore AG 5CD*	43	2
3 Jun 95	**LET'S START OVER / KICKIN' IN THE BEAT (re-mix)** *Ore AG 9CD*	59	1

FERRANTE and TEICHER *US, male instrumental duo – Arthur Ferrante and Louis Teicher – piano (Singles: 18 weeks)* pos/wks

18 Aug 60	**THEME FROM 'THE APARTMENT'** *London HLT 9164*	44	1
9 Mar 61 ●	**EXODUS (THEME FROM 'EXODUS')** *London HLT 9298 and HMV POP 881*	6	17

Exodus (Theme from 'Exodus') available first on London, then on HMV when the US label, United Artists, changed its UK outlet

Ibrahim FERRER
Cuba, male vocalist / instrumentalist – piano (Albums: 3 weeks) pos/wks

5 Jun 99	**BUENA VISTA SOCIAL CLUB PRESENTS IBRAHIM FERRER** *World Circuit WCD 055*	42	3

José FERRER *US, male actor / vocalist – José Vincente Ferrer y Centron, d. 26 Jan 1992 (Singles: 3 weeks)* pos/wks

19 Feb 54 ●	**WOMAN (UH-HUH)** *Philips PB220*	7	3

'Woman (Uh-Huh)' coupled with 'Man (Uh-Huh)' by Rosemary Clooney

Tony FERRINO
UK, male vocalist – comedian Steve Coogan (Singles: 2 weeks) pos/wks

23 Nov 96	**HELP YOURSELF / BIGAMY AT CHRISTMAS** *RCA 74321430302*	42	2

Bryan FERRY 88 Top 500
Stylish and sauve UK vocalist / songwriter, b. 26 Sep 1945, Tyne and Wear. This sophisticated singer split his time between solo career and fronting the visually stimulating and innovative Roxy Music. Both acts continue to have album success in the new millennium (Singles: 133 weeks, Albums: 325 weeks) pos/wks

29 Sep 73 ●	**A HARD RAIN'S A-GONNA FALL** *Island WIP 6170*	10	9
25 May 74	**THE 'IN' CROWD** *Island WIP 6196*	13	6
31 Aug 74	**SMOKE GETS IN YOUR EYES** *Island WIP 6205*	17	8
5 Jul 75	**YOU GO TO MY HEAD** *Island WIP 6234*	33	3
12 Jun 76 ●	**LET'S STICK TOGETHER (LET'S WORK TOGETHER)** *Island WIP 6307*	4	10
7 Aug 76 ●	**EXTENDED PLAY (EP)** *Island IEP 1*	7	9
5 Feb 77 ●	**THIS IS TOMORROW** *Polydor 2001 704*	9	9
14 May 77	**TOKYO JOE** *Polydor 2001 711*	15	7
13 May 78	**WHAT GOES ON** *Polydor POSP 3*	67	2
5 Aug 78	**SIGN OF THE TIMES** *Polydor 2001 798*	37	8
11 May 85 ●	**SLAVE TO LOVE** *EG FERRY 1*	10	9
31 Aug 85	**DON'T STOP THE DANCE** *EG FERRY 2*	21	7
7 Dec 85	**WINDSWEPT** *EG FERRY 3*	46	3
29 Mar 86	**IS YOUR LOVE STRONG ENOUGH?** *EG FERRY 4*	22	7
10 Oct 87	**THE RIGHT STUFF** *Virgin VS 940*	37	6
13 Feb 88	**KISS AND TELL** *Virgin VS 1034*	41	5
29 Oct 88	**LET'S STICK TOGETHER (re-mix)** *EG EGO 44*	12	7
11 Feb 89	**THE PRICE OF LOVE (re-mix)** *EG EGO 46*	49	3
22 Apr 89	**HE'LL HAVE TO GO** *EG EGO 48*	63	1
6 Mar 93	**I PUT A SPELL ON YOU** *Virgin VSCDG 1400*	18	5
29 May 93	**WILL YOU LOVE ME TOMORROW** *Virgin VSCDG 1455*	23	5
4 Sep 93	**GIRL OF MY BEST FRIEND** *Virgin VSCDG 1488*	57	2
29 Oct 94	**YOUR PAINTED SMILE** *Virgin VSCDG 1508*	52	1
11 Feb 95	**MAMOUNA** *Virgin VSCDG 1528*	57	1
3 Nov 73 ●	**THESE FOOLISH THINGS** *Island ILPS 9249*	5	42
20 Jul 74 ●	**ANOTHER TIME ANOTHER PLACE** *Island ILPS 9284*	4	25
2 Oct 76	**LET'S STICK TOGETHER** *Island ILPSX 1*	19	5
5 Mar 77 ●	**IN YOUR MIND** *Polydor 2302 055*	5	17
30 Sep 78	**THE BRIDE STRIPPED BARE** *Polydor POLD 5003*	13	5
15 Jun 85 ★	**BOYS AND GIRLS** *EG EGLP 62* ■	1	44
26 Apr 86 ★	**STREET LIFE – 20 GREAT HITS** *EG EGTV 1* [1] ■	1	77
14 Nov 87 ●	**BÊTE NOIRE** *Virgin V 2474*	9	16
19 Nov 88 ●	**THE ULTIMATE COLLECTION** *EG EGTV 2* [1]	6	35
3 Apr 93 ●	**TAXI** *Virgin CDV 2700*	2	14
17 Sep 94	**MAMOUNA** *Virgin CDV 2751*	11	4
4 Nov 95	**MORE THAN THIS – THE BEST OF BRYAN FERRY AND ROXY MUSIC** *Virgin CDV 2791* [1]	15	15
6 Nov 99	**AS TIME GOES BY** *Virgin CDVIR 89*	16	10
22 Jul 00	**SLAVE TO LOVE** *Virgin CDV 2921*	11	11
11 May 02 ●	**FRANTIC** *Virgin CDVIR 167*	6	5

[1] Bryan Ferry and Roxy Music

Tracks on Extended Play (EP): Price of Love / Shame Shame Shame / Heart on My Sleeve / It's Only Love

FERRY AID
International, male / female charity ensemble (Singles: 7 weeks) pos/wks

4 Apr 87 ★ **LET IT BE** *The Sun AID 1* ■ 1 7

FEVER featuring Tippa IRIE
UK, male production / instrumental group with male vocalist (Singles: 1 week) pos/wks

8 Jul 95 **STAYING ALIVE 95** *Telstar CDSTAS 2776* 48 1

Lena FIAGBE
UK, female vocalist (Singles: 13 weeks) pos/wks

24 Jul 93 **YOU COME FROM EARTH** *Mother MUMCD 42* [1] 69 1
23 Oct 93 **GOTTA GET IT RIGHT** *Mother MUMCD 44* 20 5
16 Apr 94 **WHAT'S IT LIKE TO BE BEAUTIFUL** *Mother MUMCD 49* 52 3
25 Jun 94 **VISIONS** *Mother MUMCD 53* 48 2
10 Feb 96 **AFRICAN DREAM** *Mercury MERCD 453* [2] 44 2

[1] Lena [2] Wasis Diop featuring Lena Fiagbe

Karel FIALKA
UK, male vocalist / multi-instrumentalist (Singles: 12 weeks) pos/wks

17 May 80 **THE EYES HAVE IT** *Blueprint BLU 2005* 52 4
5 Sep 87 ● **HEY MATTHEW** *IRS IRM 140* 9 8

FIAT LUX
UK, male vocal / instrumental group (Singles: 4 weeks) pos/wks

28 Jan 84 **SECRETS** *Polydor FIAT 2* 65 3
17 Mar 84 **BLUE EMOTION** *Polydor FIAT 3* 59 1

FICTION FACTORY
UK, male vocal / instrumental group (Singles: 11 weeks) pos/wks

14 Jan 84 ● **(FEELS LIKE) HEAVEN** *CBS A 3996* 6 9
17 Mar 84 **GHOST OF LOVE** *CBS A 3819* 64 2

FIDDLER'S DRAM
UK, male / female vocal / instrumental group (Singles: 9 weeks) pos/wks

15 Dec 79 ● **DAYTRIP TO BANGOR (DIDN'T WE HAVE A LOVELY TIME)** *Dingle's SID 211* 3 9

FIDELFATTI featuring RONNETTE
Italy, male producer and female vocalist (Singles: 1 week) pos/wks

27 Jan 90 **JUST WANNA TOUCH ME** *Urban URB 46* 65 1

Brad FIEDEL
Germany, male arranger (Albums: 7 weeks) pos/wks

31 Aug 91 **TERMINATOR 2 (FILM SOUNDTRACK)** *Vareses Sarabande VS 5335* 26 7

Billy FIELD
Australia, male vocalist (Singles: 3 weeks) pos/wks

12 Jun 82 **YOU WEREN'T IN LOVE WITH ME** *CBS A 2344* 67 3

Ernie FIELDS and his ORCHESTRA
US, orchestra – leader d. 11 May 1997 (Singles: 8 weeks) pos/wks

25 Dec 59 **IN THE MOOD** *London HL 8985* 13 8

Gracie FIELDS
UK, female vocalist – Grace Stansfield, d. 27 Sep 1979 (Singles: 15 weeks, Albums: 3 weeks) pos/wks

31 May 57 ● **AROUND THE WORLD (re)** *Columbia DB 3953* 8 9
6 Nov 59 **LITTLE DONKEY (re)** *Columbia DB 4360* 20 6
20 Dec 75 **THE GOLDEN YEARS** *Warwick WW 5007* 48 3

Richard 'Dimples' FIELDS
US, male vocalist, d. 15 Jan 2000 (Singles: 4 weeks) pos/wks

20 Feb 82 **I'VE GOT TO LEARN TO SAY NO** *Epic EPC A 1918* 56 4

FIELDS OF THE NEPHILIM
UK, male vocal / instrumental group (Singles: 10 weeks, Albums: 9 weeks) pos/wks

24 Oct 87 **BLUE WATER** *Situation Two SIT 48* 75 1
4 Jun 88 **MOONCHILD** *Situation Two SIT 52* 28 3
27 May 89 **PSYCHONAUT** *Situation Two ST 57* 35 3
4 Aug 90 **FOR HER LIGHT** *Beggars Banquet BEG 244T* 54 1
24 Nov 90 **SUMERLAND (DREAMED)** *Beggars Banquet BEG 250* 37 1
28 Sep 02 **FROM THE FIRE** *Jungle JUNG 65CD* 62 1
30 May 87 **DAWNRAZOR** *Situation 2 SITU 18* 62 2
17 Sep 88 **THE NEPHILIM** *Situation 2 SITU 22* 14 3
6 Oct 90 **ELIZIUM** *Beggars Banquet BEGA 115* 22 2
6 Apr 91 **EARTH INFERNO** *Beggars Banquet BEGA 120* 39 2

FIERCE
UK, female vocal group (Singles: 23 weeks, Albums: 2 weeks) pos/wks

9 Jan 99 **RIGHT HERE RIGHT NOW** *Wildstar CDWILD 13* 25 5
15 May 99 **DAYZ LIKE THAT** *Wildstar CDWILD 19* 11 5
14 Aug 99 **SO LONG** *Wildstar CDWILD 27* 15 5
12 Feb 00 ● **SWEET LOVE 2K** *Wildstar CDWILD 34* 3 8
28 Aug 99 **RIGHT HERE RIGHT NOW** *Wildstar CDWILD 14* 27 2

5TH DIMENSION
US, male / female vocal group (Singles: 21 weeks) pos/wks

16 Apr 69 **AQUARIUS / LET THE SUNSHINE IN (MEDLEY)** *Liberty LBF 15193* ▲ 11 12
17 Jan 70 **WEDDING BELL BLUES** *Liberty LBF 15288* ▲ 16 9

50 CENT
US, male rapper – Curtis Jackson (Singles: 41 weeks, Albums: 43 weeks) pos/wks

22 Feb 03 ● **IN DA CLUB** *Interscope 4978742* ▲ 3 24
12 Jul 03 ● **21 QUESTIONS** *Interscope 9807195* [1] ▲ 6 8
18 Oct 03 **P.I.M.P. (import)** *Interscope 9811812CD* 74 1
25 Oct 03 ● **P.I.M.P.** *Interscope 9812333* 5 8
1 Mar 03 ● **GET RICH OR DIE TRYIN'** *Interscope ISC4935442* ▲ ..... 2 43+

[1] 50 Cent featuring Nate Dogg

5050
UK, male production duo – Jason Powell and Andy Lysandrou (Singles: 2 weeks) pos/wks

13 Oct 01 **WHO'S COMING ROUND** *Obsessive FIFTYCD 01* 54 1
23 Mar 02 **BAD BOYS HOLLER BOO** *Logic 74321910202* 73 1

50 GRIND featuring POKEMON ALLSTARS
UK, male vocal / instrumental group and Pokemon popsters (Singles: 1 week) pos/wks

22 Dec 01 **GOTTA CATCH 'EM ALL** *Recognition CDREC 21* 57 1

52ND STREET
UK, male / female vocal / instrumental group (Singles: 13 weeks, Albums: 1 week) pos/wks

2 Nov 85 **TELL ME (HOW IT FEELS)** *10 TEN 74* 54 5
11 Jan 86 **YOU'RE MY LAST CHANCE** *10 TEN 89* 49 4
8 Mar 86 **I CAN'T LET YOU GO** *10 TEN 114* 57 4
19 Apr 86 **CHILDREN OF THE NIGHT** *10 DIX 25* 71 1

53RD & 3RD – *See Jonathan KING*

56K featuring BEJAY
UK, male / female production / vocal group (Singles: 1 week) pos/wks

19 Apr 03 **SAVE A PRAYER** *Kontor 0146495* 46 1

FILTER
US, male vocal / instrumental duo – Richard Patrick and Brian Liesgang (Singles: 5 weeks, Albums: 2 weeks) pos/wks

11 Oct 97 **(CAN'T YOU) TRIP LIKE I DO** *Epic 6650862* [1] 39 2
18 Mar 00 **TAKE A PICTURE** *Reprise W 515CD* 25 3
4 Sep 99 **TITLE OF RECORD** *Reprise 9362473882* 75 1
10 Aug 02 **THE AMALGAMUT** *Reprise 9362479632* 68 1

[1] Filter and The Crystal Method

FINAL CUT – *See TRUE FAITH and Bridgette GRACE with FINAL CUT*

FINCH
US, male vocal / instrumental group (Singles: 2 weeks) pos/wks

5 Apr 03 **LETTERS TO YOU** *Drive-Thru / MCA MCSTD 40310* 39 2

FINE YOUNG CANNIBALS (349 Top 500)

Politically aware pop / soul trio from Birmingham, UK: Roland Gift (v), ex-Beat members Andy Cox (g) and David Steele (b). Unmistakable vocalist Gift also acted in films, most notably 1989's Scandal. FYC, who were among 1989's biggest selling acts worldwide, won (and returned) two Brit awards in 1990 (Singles: 81 weeks, Albums: 107 weeks)

Date		Title / Label	pos	wks
8 Jun 85	●	**JOHNNY COME HOME** *London LON 68*	8	13
9 Nov 85		**BLUE** *London LON 79*	41	6
11 Jan 86	●	**SUSPICIOUS MINDS** *London LON 82*	8	9
12 Apr 86		**FUNNY HOW LOVE IS** *London LON 88*	58	4
21 Mar 87	●	**EVER FALLEN IN LOVE** *London LON 121*	9	10
7 Jan 89	●	**SHE DRIVES ME CRAZY** *London LON 199* ▲	5	11
15 Apr 89	●	**GOOD THING** *London LON 218* ▲	7	8
19 Aug 89		**DON'T LOOK BACK** *London LON 220*	34	4
18 Nov 89		**I'M NOT THE MAN I USED TO BE** *London LON 244*	20	8
24 Feb 90		**I'M NOT SATISFIED** *London LON 252*	46	3
16 Nov 96		**THE FLAME** *ffrr LONCD 389*	17	3
11 Jan 97		**SHE DRIVES ME CRAZY (re-mix)** *ffrr LONCD 391*	36	2
21 Dec 85		FINE YOUNG CANNIBALS *London LONLP 16*	11	27
18 Feb 89	★	THE RAW AND THE COOKED *London 8280691* ■	1	66
15 Dec 90		THE RAW AND THE REMIX *London 8282211* [1]	61	1
23 Nov 96	●	THE FINEST *ffrr 8288542*	10	13

[1] FYC

'The Raw and The Remix' is a remix album of 'The Raw and the Cooked'

See also TWO MEN, A DRUM MACHINE AND A TRUMPET

FINITRIBE

UK, male instrumental / production group (Singles: 2 weeks)

Date		Title / Label	pos	wks
11 Jul 92		**FOREVERGREEN** *One Little Indian 74 TP12F*	51	1
19 Nov 94		**BRAND NEW** *ffrr FCD 247*	69	1

FINK BROTHERS

UK, male vocal / instrumental duo (Singles: 4 weeks)

Date		Title / Label	pos	wks
9 Feb 85		**MUTANTS IN MEGA CITY ONE** *Zarjazz JAZZ 2*	50	4

Frank FINLAY – *See David ESSEX*

FINN

New Zealand, male vocal / instrumental duo – Neil and Tim Finn (Singles: 5 weeks, Albums: 3 weeks)

Date		Title / Label	pos	wks
14 Oct 95		**SUFFER NEVER** *Parlophone CDRS 6417*	29	3
9 Dec 95		**ANGEL'S HEAP** *Parlophone CDRS 6421*	41	2
28 Oct 95		FINN *Parlophone CDFINN 1*	15	3

See also CROWDED HOUSE; Neil FINN; Tim FINN

Micky FINN – *See URBAN SHAKEDOWN*

Neil FINN

New Zealand, male vocalist / instrumentalist (Singles: 6 weeks, Albums: 15 weeks)

Date		Title / Label	pos	wks
13 Jun 98		**SHE WILL HAVE HER WAY** *Parlophone CDR 6495*	26	2
17 Oct 98		**SINNER** *Parlophone CDR 6505*	39	1
7 Apr 01		**WHEREVER YOU ARE** *Parlophone CDRS 6557*	32	2
22 Sep 01		**HOLE IN THE ICE** *Parlophone CDRS 6563*	43	1
27 Jun 98	●	TRY WHISTLING THIS *Parlophone 4951392*	5	11
21 Apr 01		ONE NIL *Parlophone 5320392*	14	4

See also CROWDED HOUSE; FINN

Tim FINN

New Zealand, male vocalist (Singles: 6 weeks, Albums: 2 weeks)

Date		Title / Label	pos	wks
26 Jun 93		**PERSUASION** *Capitol 6592482*	43	3
18 Sep 93		**HIT THE GROUND RUNNING** *Capitol CDCLS 694*	50	3
10 Jul 93		BEFORE AND AFTER *Capitol CDEST 2202*	29	2

See also CROWDED HOUSE; FINN

Johnnie FIORI – *See BARKIN BROTHERS featuring Johnnie FIORI*

Elisa FIORILLO

US, female vocalist (Singles: 14 weeks)

Date		Title / Label	pos	wks
28 Nov 87	●	**WHO FOUND WHO** *Chrysalis CHS JEL 1* [1]	10	10
13 Feb 88		**HOW CAN I FORGET YOU** *Chrysalis ELISA 1*	50	4

[1] Jellybean featuring Elisa Fiorillo

FIRE INC – *See Jim STEINMAN*

FIRE ISLAND

UK, male instrumental / production group (Singles: 7 weeks)

Date		Title / Label	pos	wks
8 Aug 92		**IN YOUR BONES / FIRE ISLAND** *Boy's Own BOIX 11*	66	1
12 Mar 94		**THERE BUT FOR THE GRACE OF GOD** *Junior Boy's Own JBO 18CD* [1]	32	3
4 Mar 95		**IF YOU SHOULD NEED A FRIEND** *Junior Boy's Own JBO 26CDS* [2]	51	1
11 Apr 98		**SHOUT TO THE TOP** *JBO JNR 5001573* [3]	23	2

[1] Fire Island featuring Love Nelson [2] Fire Island featuring Mark Anthoni
[3] Fire Island featuring Loleatta Holloway

See also HELLER & FARLEY PROJECT; Pete HELLER; STYLUS TROUBLE

FIREBALLS

US, male vocal / instrumental group (Singles: 17 weeks)

Date		Title / Label	pos	wks
27 Jul 61		**QUITE A PARTY** *Pye International 7N 25092*	29	9
14 Nov 63		**SUGAR SHACK (re)** *London HLD 9789* [1] ▲	45	8

[1] Jimmy Gilmer and The Fireballs

FIREHOUSE

US, male vocal / instrumental group (Singles: 2 weeks)

Date		Title / Label	pos	wks
13 Jul 91		**DON'T TREAT ME BAD** *Epic 6567807*	71	1
19 Dec 92		**WHEN I LOOK INTO YOUR EYES** *Epic 6588347*	65	1

FIRM

UK, male vocal / instrumental group (Singles: 21 weeks, Albums: 8 weeks)

Date		Title / Label	pos	wks
17 Jul 82		**ARTHUR DALEY ('E'S ALRIGHT)** *Bark HID 1*	14	9
6 Jun 87	★	**STAR TREKKIN'** *Bark TREK 1*	1	12
2 Mar 85		THE FIRM *Atlantic 7812391*	15	5
5 Apr 86		MEAN BUSINESS *Atlantic WX 35*	46	3

FIRM featuring Dawn ROBINSON

US, male rap group, and US, female vocalist (Singles: 3 weeks)

Date		Title / Label	pos	wks
29 Nov 97		**FIRM BIZ** *Columbia 6651612*	18	3

FIRST CHOICE

US, female vocal group (Singles: 21 weeks)

Date		Title / Label	pos	wks
19 May 73		**ARMED AND EXTREMELY DANGEROUS** *Bell 1297*	16	10
4 Aug 73	●	**SMARTY PANTS** *Bell 1324*	9	11

FIRST CIRCLE

US, male vocal / instrumental group (Albums: 2 weeks)

Date		Title / Label	pos	wks
2 May 87		BOYS' NIGHT OUT *EMI America AML 3118*	70	2

FIRST CLASS

UK, male vocal group (Singles: 10 weeks)

Date		Title / Label	pos	wks
15 Jun 74		**BEACH BABY** *UK 66*	13	10

FIRST EDITION – *See Kenny ROGERS*

FIRST LIGHT

UK, male vocal / instrumental duo (Singles: 5 weeks)

Date		Title / Label	pos	wks
21 May 83		**EXPLAIN THE REASONS** *London LON 26*	65	3
28 Jan 84		**WISH YOU WERE HERE** *London LON 43*	71	2

FIRSTBORN

Ireland, male producer – Oisin Lunny (Singles: 1 week)

Date		Title / Label	pos	wks
19 Jun 99		**THE MOOD CLUB** *Independiente ISOM 28MS*	69	1

The 706 No.1 Albums

NO.1 ALBUMS OF THE 70S

Here is the complete chronological list of every UK chart-topping album from the 70s. All dates given are for an album's first week at No.1, not its first entry into the chart. The run at the top of the chart in weeks follows in brackets, followed by the US peak position of the album.

1970

7 Feb **LED ZEPPELIN II Led Zeppelin** (1 week) US 1
14 Feb **BRITISH MOTOWN CHARTBUSTERS VOL.3 Various** (1 week)
21 Feb **BRIDGE OVER TROUBLED WATER Simon and Garfunkel** (13 weeks) US 1
23 May **LET IT BE Beatles** (3 weeks) US 1
13 Jun **BRIDGE OVER TROUBLED WATER Simon and Garfunkel** (4 weeks) US 1
11 Jul **SELF PORTRAIT Bob Dylan** (1 week) US 4
18 Jul **BRIDGE OVER TROUBLED WATER Simon and Garfunkel** (5 weeks) US 1
22 Aug **A QUESTION OF BALANCE Moody Blues** (3 weeks) US 3
12 Sep **COSMO'S FACTORY Creedence Clearwater Revival** (1 week) US 1
19 Sep **GET YOUR YA-YA'S OUT! Rolling Stones** (2 weeks) US 6
3 Oct **BRIDGE OVER TROUBLED WATER Simon and Garfunkel** (1 week) US 1
10 Oct **PARANOID Black Sabbath** (1 week) US 12
17 Oct **BRIDGE OVER TROUBLED WATER Simon and Garfunkel** (1 week) US 1
24 Oct **ATOMIC HEART MOTHER Pink Floyd** (1 week) US 55
31 Oct **MOTOWN CHARTBUSTERS VOL.4 Various** (1 week)
7 Nov **LED ZEPPELIN III Led Zeppelin** (3 weeks) US 1
28 Nov **NEW MORNING Bob Dylan** (1 week) US 7
5 Dec **GREATEST HITS Andy Williams** (1 week) US 42
12 Dec **LED ZEPPELIN III Led Zeppelin** (1 week) US 1
19 Dec **GREATEST HITS Andy Williams** (4 weeks) US 42

1971

16 Jan **BRIDGE OVER TROUBLED WATER Simon and Garfunkel** (3 weeks) US 1
6 Feb **ALL THINGS MUST PASS George Harrison** (6 weeks)
3 Apr **HOME LOVING MAN Andy Williams** (2 weeks)
17 Apr **MOTOWN CHARTBUSTERS VOL.5 Various** (3 weeks)
8 May **STICKY FINGERS Rolling Stones** (4 weeks) US 1
5 Jun **RAM Paul McCartney** (2 weeks) US 2
19 Jun **STICKY FINGERS Rolling Stones** (1 week) US 1
26 Jun **TARKUS Emerson Lake and Palmer** (1 week) US 9
3 Jul **BRIDGE OVER TROUBLED WATER Simon and Garfunkel** (5 weeks) US 1
7 Aug **HOT HITS 6 Various** (1 week)
14 Aug **EVERY GOOD BOY DESERVES FAVOUR Moody Blues** (1 week) US 2
21 Aug **TOP OF THE POPS VOL.18 Various** (3 weeks)
11 Sep **BRIDGE OVER TROUBLED WATER Simon and Garfunkel** (1 week) US 1
18 Sep **WHO'S NEXT Who** (1 week) US 4
25 Sep **FIREBALL Deep Purple** (1 week) US 32
2 Oct **EVERY PICTURE TELLS A STORY Rod Stewart** (4 weeks) US 1
30 Oct **IMAGINE John Lennon / Plastic Ono Band** (2 weeks) US 1
13 Nov **EVERY PICTURE TELLS A STORY Rod Stewart** (2 weeks) US 1
27 Nov **TOP OF THE POPS VOL. 20 Various** (1 week)
4 Dec **FOUR SYMBOLS Led Zeppelin** (2 weeks) US 2
18 Dec **ELECTRIC WARRIOR T. Rex** (6 weeks) US 32

1972

29 Jan **CONCERT FOR BANGLADESH Various** (1 week) US 2
5 Feb **ELECTRIC WARRIOR T. Rex** (6 weeks) US 32
19 Feb **NEIL REID Neil Reid** (3 weeks)
11 Mar **HARVEST Neil Young** (1 week) US 1
18 Mar **PAUL SIMON Paul Simon** (1 week) US 4
25 Mar **FOG ON THE TYNE Lindisfarne** (4 weeks)
22 Apr **MACHINE HEAD Deep Purple** (2 weeks) US 7
6 May **PROPHETS, SEERS AND SAGES AND THE ANGELS OF THE AGES / MY PEOPLE WERE FAIR AND HAD SKY IN THEIR HAIR BUT NOW THEY'RE CONTENT TO WEAR STARS ON THEIR BROWS T. Rex** (1 week)
13 May **MACHINE HEAD Deep Purple** (1 week)
20 May **BOLAN BOOGIE T. Rex** (3 weeks)
10 Jun **EXILE ON MAIN STREET Rolling Stones** (1 week) US 1
17 Jun **20 DYNAMIC HITS Various** (8 weeks)
12 Aug **20 FANTASTIC HITS Various** (5 weeks)
16 Sep **NEVER A DULL MOMENT Rod Stewart** (2 weeks) US 2
30 Sep **20 FANTASTIC HITS Various** (1 week)
7 Oct **20 ALL TIME HITS OF THE FIFTIES Various** (8 weeks)
2 Dec **25 ROCKIN' AND ROLLIN' GREATS Various** (3 weeks)
23 Dec **20 ALL TIME HITS OF THE FIFTIES Various** (3 weeks)

1973

13 Jan **SLAYED? Slade** (1 week) US 69
20 Jan **BACK TO FRONT Gilbert O'Sullivan** (1 week) US 48
27 Jan **SLAYED? Slade** (2 weeks) US 69
10 Feb **DON'T SHOOT ME I'M ONLY THE PIANO PLAYER Elton John** (6 weeks) US 1
24 Mar **BILLION DOLLAR BABIES Alice Cooper** (1 week) US 1
31 Mar **FLASHBACK GREAT HITS OF THE SIXTIES Various** (2 weeks)
14 Apr **HOUSES OF THE HOLY Led Zeppelin** (2 weeks) US 1
28 Apr **OOH-LA-LA Faces** (1 week) US 21
5 May **ALADDIN SANE David Bowie** (5 weeks) US 17
9 Jun **PURE GOLD Various** (3 weeks)
30 Jun **THAT'LL BE THE DAY Various** (3 weeks)
18 Aug **WE CAN MAKE IT Peters and Lee** (2 weeks)
1 Sep **SING IT AGAIN ROD Rod Stewart** (3 weeks) US 31
22 Sep **GOAT'S HEAD SOUP Rolling Stones** (2 weeks) US 1
6 Oct **SLADEST Slade** (3 weeks) US 129
27 Oct **HELLO Status Quo** (1 week)
3 Nov **PIN UPS David Bowie** (5 weeks) US 23
8 Dec **STRANDED Roxy Music** (1 week) US 186
15 Dec **DREAMS ARE NOTHIN' MORE THAN WISHES David Cassidy** (1 week)
22 Dec **GOODBYE YELLOW BRICK ROAD Elton John** (2 weeks) US 1

1974

5 Jan **TALES FROM TOPOGRAPHIC OCEANS Yes** (2 weeks) US 6
19 Jan **SLADEST Slade** (1 week) US 129
26 Jan **AND I LOVE YOU SO Perry Como** (1 week) US 34
2 Feb **THE SINGLES 1969-73 Carpenters** (4 weeks) US 1
2 Mar **OLD, NEW, BORROWED AND BLUE Slade** (1 week)
9 Mar **THE SINGLES 1969-73 Carpenters** (11 weeks) US 1
25 May **JOURNEY TO THE CENTRE OF THE EARTH Rick Wakeman** (1 week) US 3

1973: SLADEST Slade's second No.1 album of this year, a success amplified by the release of their 'Merry Xmas Everybody' single in December

1979: PARALLEL LINES Blondie's hit single-packed No.1 went on to amass worldwide sales approaching 20 million

1 Jun THE SINGLES 1969-73 Carpenters (1 week) US 1
8 Jun DIAMOND DOGS David Bowie (4 weeks) US 5
6 Jul THE SINGLES 1969-73 Carpenters (1 week) US 1
13 Jul CARIBOU Elton John (2 weeks) US 1
27 Jul BAND ON THE RUN Wings (7 weeks) US 1
14 Sep HERGEST RIDGE Mike Oldfield (3 weeks) US 87
5 Oct TUBULAR BELLS Mike Oldfield (1 week) US 3
12 Oct ROLLIN' Bay City Rollers (1 week)
19 Oct SMILER Rod Stewart (1 week) US 13
26 Oct ROLLIN' Bay City Rollers (1 week)
2 Nov SMILER Rod Stewart (1 week) US 13
9 Nov ROLLIN' Bay City Rollers (2 weeks)
23 Nov ELTON JOHN'S GREATEST HITS Elton John (11 weeks) US 1

1975

8 Feb HIS GREATEST HITS Engelbert Humperdinck (3 weeks) US 103
1 Mar ON THE LEVEL Status Quo (2 weeks)
15 Mar PHYSICAL GRAFFITI Led Zeppelin (1 week) US 1
22 Mar 20 GREATEST HITS Tom Jones (4 weeks)
19 Apr THE BEST OF THE STYLISTICS Stylistics (2 weeks) US 41
3 May ONCE UPON A STAR Bay City Rollers (3 weeks)
24 May THE BEST OF THE STYLISTICS Stylistics (5 weeks) US 41
28 Jun VENUS AND MARS Wings (1 week) US 1
5 Jul HORIZON Carpenters (2 weeks) US 13
19 Jul VENUS AND MARS Wings (1 week) US 1
26 Jul HORIZON Carpenters (3 weeks) US 13
16 Aug THE BEST OF THE STYLISTICS Stylistics (2 weeks) US 41
30 Aug ATLANTIC CROSSING Rod Stewart (5 weeks) US 9
4 Oct WISH YOU WERE HERE Pink Floyd (1 week) US 1
11 Oct ATLANTIC CROSSING Rod Stewart (2 weeks) US 9
25 Oct 40 GOLDEN GREATS Jim Reeves (3 weeks)
15 Nov WE ALL HAD DOCTORS' PAPERS Max Boyce (1 week)
22 Nov 40 GREATEST HITS Perry Como (5 weeks)
27 Dec A NIGHT AT THE OPERA Queen (2 weeks) US 4

1976

10 Jan 40 GREATEST HITS Perry Como (1 week)
17 Jan A NIGHT AT THE OPERA Queen (2 weeks) US 4
31 Jan THE BEST OF ROY ORBISON Roy Orbison (1 week)
7 Feb THE VERY BEST OF SLIM WHITMAN Slim Whitman (6 weeks)
20 Mar BLUE FOR YOU Status Quo (3 weeks)
10 Apr ROCK FOLLIES TV Soundtrack (2 weeks)
24 Apr PRESENCE Led Zeppelin (1 week) US 1
1 May ROCK FOLLIES TV Soundtrack (1 week)
8 May GREATEST HITS Abba (9 weeks) US 48
10 Jul A NIGHT ON THE TOWN Rod Stewart (2 weeks) US 2
24 Jul 20 GOLDEN GREATS Beach Boys (10 weeks)
2 Oct BEST OF THE STYLISTICS VOL.2 Stylistics (1 week)
9 Oct STUPIDITY Dr Feelgood (1 week)
16 Oct GREATEST HITS Abba (2 weeks) US 48
30 Oct SOUL MOTION Various (2 weeks)
13 Nov THE SONG REMAINS THE SAME Led Zeppelin (1 week) US 2
20 Nov 22 GOLDEN GUITAR GREATS Bert Weedon (1 week)
27 Nov 20 GOLDEN GREATS Glen Campbell (6 weeks)

1977

8 Jan A DAY AT THE RACES Queen (1 week) US 5
15 Jan ARRIVAL Abba (1 week) US 20
22 Jan RED RIVER VALLEY Slim Whitman (4 weeks)
19 Feb 20 GOLDEN GREATS Shadows (6 weeks)
2 Apr PORTRAIT OF SINATRA Frank Sinatra (2 weeks)
16 Apr ARRIVAL Abba (9 weeks) US 20
18 Jun LIVE AT THE HOLLYWOOD BOWL Beatles (1 week) US 2
25 Jun THE MUPPET SHOW Muppets (1 week)
2 Jul A STAR IS BORN (Soundtrack) Barbra Streisand (2 weeks) US 1
16 Jul THE JOHNNY MATHIS COLLECTION Johnny Mathis (4 weeks)
13 Aug GOING FOR THE ONE Yes (2 weeks) US 8
27 Aug 20 ALL TIME GREATS Connie Francis (2 weeks)
10 Sep 40 GREATEST HITS Elvis Presley (1 week)
17 Sep 20 GOLDEN GREATS Diana Ross and the Supremes (7 weeks)
5 Nov 40 GOLDEN GREATS Cliff Richard (1 week)
12 Nov NEVER MIND THE BOLLOCKS HERE'S THE SEX PISTOLS Sex Pistols (2 weeks) US 106
26 Nov THE SOUND OF BREAD Bread (2 weeks)
10 Dec DISCO FEVER Various (6 weeks)

1978

21 Jan THE SOUND OF BREAD Bread (1 week)
28 Jan RUMOURS Fleetwood Mac (1 week) US 1
4 Feb THE ALBUM Abba (7 weeks) US 14
25 Mar 20 GOLDEN GREATS Buddy Holly and the Crickets (3 weeks) US 55
15 Apr 20 GOLDEN GREATS Nat 'King' Cole (3 weeks)
6 May SATURDAY NIGHT FEVER Soundtrack (18 weeks) US 1
9 Sep NIGHT FLIGHT TO VENUS Boney M (4 weeks) US 134
7 Oct GREASE Soundtrack (13 weeks) US 1

1979

6 Jan GREATEST HITS Showaddywaddy (2 weeks)
20 Jan DON'T WALK – BOOGIE Various (3 weeks)
10 Feb ACTION REPLAY Various (1 week)
17 Feb PARALLEL LINES Blondie (4 weeks) US 6
17 Mar SPIRITS HAVING FLOWN Bee Gees (2 weeks) US 1
31 Mar GREATEST HITS VOL.2 Barbra Streisand (4 weeks) US 1
28 Apr THE VERY BEST OF LEO SAYER Leo Sayer (3 weeks)
19 May VOULEZ-VOUS Abba (4 weeks) US 19
16 Jun DISCOVERY Electric Light Orchestra (5 weeks) US 5
21 Jul REPLICAS Tubeway Army (1 week) US 124
28 Jul THE BEST DISCO ALBUM IN THE WORLD Various (6 weeks)
8 Sep IN THROUGH THE OUT DOOR Led Zeppelin (2 weeks) US 1
22 Sep THE PLEASURE PRINCIPLE Gary Numan (1 week) US 16
29 Sep OCEANS OF FANTASY Boney M (1 week)
6 Oct THE PLEASURE PRINCIPLE Gary Numan (1 week) US 16
13 Oct EAT TO THE BEAT Blondie (1 week) US 17
REGGATTA DE BLANC Police (4 weeks) US 25
Note: Two charts published this week due to a change in chart collation
10 Nov TUSK Fleetwood Mac (1 week) US 4
17 Nov GREATEST HITS VOL.2 Abba (3 weeks) US 46
8 Dec GREATEST HITS Rod Stewart (5 weeks) US 22

FISCHER-Z *UK, male vocal / instrumental group (Singles: 7 weeks, Albums: 1 week)* pos/wks

26 May 79 **THE WORKER** *United Artists UP 36509* 53 5
3 May 80 **SO LONG** *United Artists BP 342* 72 2
23 Jun 79 **WORD SALAD** *United Artists UAG 30232* 66 1

FISCHERSPOONER *US, male vocal / instrumental duo – Warren Fischer and Casey Spooner (Singles: 3 weeks)* pos/wks

20 Jul 02 **EMERGE** *Ministry of Sound FSMOS 1CDS* 25 3

FISH *UK, male vocalist – Derek Dick (Singles: 20 weeks, Albums: 17 weeks)* pos/wks

18 Oct 86 **SHORT CUT TO SOMEWHERE** *Charisma CB 426* [1] 75 1
28 Oct 89 **STATE OF MIND** *EMI EM 109* 32 3
6 Jan 90 **BIG WEDGE** *EMI EM 125* 25 4
17 Mar 90 **A GENTLEMAN'S EXCUSE ME** *EMI EM 135* 30 3
28 Sep 91 **INTERNAL EXILE** *Polydor FISHY 1* 37 2
11 Jan 92 **CREDO** *Polydor FISHY 2* 38 2
4 Jul 92 **SOMETHING IN THE AIR** *Polydor FISHY 3* 51 2
16 Apr 94 **LADY LET IT LIE** *Dick Bros. DDICK 3CD1* 46 1
1 Oct 94 **FORTUNES OF WAR** *Dick Bros. DDICK 008CD1* 67 1
26 Aug 95 **JUST GOOD FRIENDS** *Dick Bros. DDICK 014CD1* [2] 63 1
10 Feb 90 ● **VIGIL IN A WILDERNESS OF MIRRORS** *EMI EMD 1015* 5 6
9 Nov 91 **INTERNAL EXILE** *Polydor 5110491* 21 3
30 Jan 93 **SONGS FROM THE MIRROR** *Polydor 5174992* 46 2
11 Jun 94 **SUITS** *Dick Bros. DDICK 004CD* 18 2
16 Sep 95 **YANG** *Dick Bros. DDICK 012CD* 52 1
16 Sep 95 **YIN** *Dick Bros. DDICK 011CD* 58 1
31 May 97 **SUNSETS ON EMPIRE** *Dick Bros. DDICK 25CD* 42 1
1 May 99 **RAINGODS WITH ZIPPOS** *Roadrunner RR 86772* 57 1

[1] Fish and Tony Banks [2] Fish featuring Sam Brown

See also Tony BANKS; MARILLION

FISHBONE *US, male vocal / instrumental group (Singles: 3 weeks, Albums: 1 week)* pos/wks

1 Aug 92 **EVERYDAY SUNSHINE / FIGHT THE YOUTH** *Columbia 6581937* 60 2
28 Aug 93 **SWIM** *Columbia 6596252* 54 1
13 Jul 91 **THE REALITY OF MY SURROUNDINGS** *Columbia 4676151* 75 1

Cevin FISHER
US, male DJ / producer (Singles: 9 weeks) pos/wks

3 Oct 98 **THE FREAKS COME OUT** *Ministry of Sound MOSCDS 127* [1] 34 2
20 Feb 99 **(YOU GOT ME) BURNING UP** *Wonderboy WBOYD 013* [2] 14 4
7 Aug 99 **MUSIC SAVED MY LIFE** *Sm:)e Communications SM 90982* 67 1
20 Jan 01 **IT'S A GOOD LIFE** *Wonderboy WBOYD 022* [3] 54 1
24 Feb 01 **LOVE YOU SOME MORE** *Subversive SUB 68D* [4] 60 1

[1] Cevin Fisher's Big Break [2] Cevin Fisher / Loleatta Holloway [3] Cevin Fisher featuring Ramona Kelly [4] Cevin Fisher featuring Shelia Smith

Eddie FISHER
US, male vocalist (Singles: 105 weeks) pos/wks

2 Jan 53 ★ **OUTSIDE OF HEAVEN (re)** *HMV B 10362* 1 17
23 Jan 53 ● **EVERYTHING I HAVE IS YOURS (re)** *HMV B 10398* 8 5
1 May 53 ● **DOWNHEARTED** *HMV B 10450* 3 15
22 May 53 ★ **I'M WALKING BEHIND YOU** *HMV B 10489* [1] ▲ 1 18
6 Nov 53 ● **WISH YOU WERE HERE** *HMV B 10564* 8 9
22 Jan 54 ● **OH MY PAPA (O MEIN PAPA) (3re)** *HMV B 10614* ▲ 9 4
29 Oct 54 **I NEED YOU NOW (2re)** *HMV B 10755* ▲ 13 10
18 Mar 55 ● **(I'M ALWAYS HEARING) WEDDING BELLS** *HMV B 10839* 5 11
23 Nov 56 ● **CINDY, OH CINDY** *HMV POP 273* 5 16

[1] Eddie Fisher with Sally Sweetland (soprano)

Mark FISHER featuring Dotty GREEN *UK, male instrumentalist – keyboards and female vocalist (Singles: 2 weeks)* pos/wks

29 Jun 85 **LOVE SITUATION** *Total Control TOCO 3* 59 2

Toni FISHER *US, female vocalist, d. 12 Feb 1999 (Singles: 1 week)* pos/wks

12 Feb 60 **THE BIG HURT** *Top Rank JAR 261* 30 1

FITS OF GLOOM *UK / Italy, male vocal duo (Singles: 4 weeks)* pos/wks

4 Jun 94 **HEAVEN** *Media MCSTD 1981* 47 2
5 Nov 94 **THE POWER OF LOVE** *Media MCSTD 2016* [1] 49 2

[1] Fits of Gloom featuring Lizzy Mack

Ella FITZGERALD *US, female vocalist, d. 15 June 1996 (Singles: 29 weeks, Albums: 57 weeks)* pos/wks

23 May 58 **THE SWINGIN' SHEPHERD BLUES** *HMV POP 486* 15 5
16 Oct 59 **BUT NOT FOR ME (re)** *HMV POP 657* 25 3
21 Apr 60 **MACK THE KNIFE** *HMV POP 736* 19 9
6 Oct 60 **HOW HIGH THE MOON** *HMV POP 782* 46 1
22 Nov 62 **DESAFINADO (re)** *Verve VS 502* 38 6
30 Apr 64 **CAN'T BUY ME LOVE** *Verve VS 519* 34 5
19 Jul 58 ● **ELLA FITZGERALD SINGS THE IRVING BERLIN SONG BOOK** *HMV CLP 1183* 5 1
11 Jun 60 **ELLA SINGS GERSHWIN** *Brunswick LA 8648* 13 3
18 Jun 60 **ELLA AT THE OPERA HOUSE** *Columbia 3SX 10126* 16 1
23 Jul 60 **ELLA SINGS GERSHWIN VOLUME 5** *HMV CLP 1353* 18 2
10 May 80 **THE INCOMPARABLE ELLA** *Polydor POLTV 9* 40 7
27 Feb 88 **A PORTRAIT OF ELLA FITZGERALD** *Stylus SMR 847* 42 10
19 Nov 94 **ESSENTIAL ELLA** *PolyGram TV 5239902* 35 14
23 Mar 96 **FOREVER ELLA** *Verve / PolyGram TV 5293872* 19 6
15 Feb 03 **GOLD** *Verve 654842* 15 13

Scott FITZGERALD
UK, male vocalist – William McPhail (Singles: 12 weeks) pos/wks

14 Jan 78 ● **IF I HAD WORDS** *Pepper UP 36333* [1] 3 10
7 May 88 **GO** *PRT PYS 10* 52 2

[1] Scott Fitzgerald and Yvonne Keeley with the St Thomas More School Choir

FIVE 276 Top 500
Superior all-boy vocal group: 'Abs' Breen, 'J' Brown, Sean Conlon, Rich Neville, Scott Robinson. Eponymous debut album sold more than four million worldwide. The only UK act to reach the Top 10 with every one of their first 11 releases split in 2001 (Singles: 133 weeks, Albums: 96 weeks) pos/wks

13 Dec 97 ● **SLAM DUNK (DA FUNK)** *RCA 74321537352* 10 9
14 Mar 98 ● **WHEN THE LIGHTS GO OUT** *RCA 74321562312* 4 9
20 Jun 98 ● **GOT THE FEELIN'** *RCA 74321584892* 3 13
12 Sep 98 ● **EVERYBODY GET UP** *RCA 74321613752* 2 12
28 Nov 98 ● **UNTIL THE TIME IS THROUGH** *RCA 74321632602* 2 12
31 Jul 99 ● **IF YA GETTIN' DOWN** *RCA 74321689692* 2 12
6 Nov 99 ★ **KEEP ON MOVIN'** *RCA 74321709862* ■ 1 17
18 Mar 00 ● **DON'T WANNA LET YOU GO** *RCA 74321745292* 9 12
29 Jul 00 ★ **WE WILL ROCK YOU (re)** *RCA 74321774022* [1] ■ 1 13
25 Aug 01 ★ **LET'S DANCE** *RCA 74321875962* ■ 1 12
3 Nov 01 ● **CLOSER TO ME (re)** *RCA 74321900742* 4 12
4 Jul 98 ★ **FIVE** *RCA 74321589762* ■ 1 36
20 Nov 99 ● **INVINCIBLE** *RCA 74321713922* 4 39
8 Sep 01 ● **KINGSIZE** *RCA 74321875972* 3 11
1 Dec 01 ● **GREATEST HITS** *RCA 74321913432* 9 10

[1] Five and Queen

See also ABS

FIVE FOR FIGHTING
US, male vocalist / instrumentalist – John Ondrasik (Singles: 1 week) pos/wks

1 Jun 02 **SUPERMAN (IT'S NOT EASY)** *Columbia 6727202* 48 1

FIVE PENNY PIECE
UK, male / female vocal / instrumental group (Albums: 6 weeks) pos/wks

24 Mar 73 **MAKING TRACKS** *Columbia SCX 6536* 37 1
3 Jul 76 ● **KING COTTON** *EMI EMC 3129* 9 5

FIVE SMITH BROTHERS *UK, male vocal group (Singles: 1 week)* pos/wks

22 Jul 55 **I'M IN FAVOUR OF FRIENDSHIP** *Decca F 10527* 20 1

FIVE STAR (199 Top 500) *Britain's best known black family act: Deniece, Doris, Stedman, Lorraine and Delroy Pearson. The Essex-based group became the youngest act to top the LP chart with the UK million-seller 'Silk and Steel'. In 1987 they were voted Top British Group in Smash Hits and at Brit Awards. They relocated to the US and had some R&B chart success (Singles: 140 weeks, Albums: 153 weeks)*

Date		Title	pos	wks
4 May 85		**ALL FALL DOWN** *Tent PB 40039*	**15**	12
20 Jul 85		**LET ME BE THE ONE** *Tent PB 40193*	**18**	9
14 Sep 85		**LOVE TAKE OVER** *Tent PB 40353*	**25**	9
16 Nov 85		**RSVP** *Tent PB 40445*	**45**	5
11 Jan 86	●	**SYSTEM ADDICT** *Tent PB 40515*	**3**	11
12 Apr 86	●	**CAN'T WAIT ANOTHER MINUTE** *Tent PB 40697*	**7**	10
26 Jul 86	●	**FIND THE TIME** *Tent PB 40799*	**7**	10
13 Sep 86	●	**RAIN OR SHINE** *Tent PB 40901*	**2**	11
22 Nov 86		**IF I SAY YES** *Tent PB 40981*	**15**	9
7 Feb 87	●	**STAY OUT OF MY LIFE** *Tent PB 41131*	**9**	8
18 Apr 87	●	**THE SLIGHTEST TOUCH** *Tent PB 41265*	**4**	9
22 Aug 87		**WHENEVER YOU'RE READY** *Tent PB 41477*	**11**	6
10 Oct 87		**STRONG AS STEEL** *Tent PB 41565*	**16**	7
5 Dec 87		**SOMEWHERE SOMEBODY** *Tent PB 41661*	**23**	6
4 Jun 88		**ANOTHER WEEKEND** *Tent PB 42081*	**18**	4
6 Aug 88		**ROCK MY WORLD** *Tent PB 42145*	**28**	4
17 Sep 88		**THERE'S A BRAND NEW WORLD** *Tent PB 42235*	**61**	2
19 Nov 88		**LET ME BE YOURS** *Tent PB 42343*	**51**	3
8 Apr 89		**WITH EVERY HEARTBEAT** *Tent PB 42693*	**49**	2
10 Mar 90		**TREAT ME LIKE A LADY** *Tent FIVE 1*	**54**	2
7 Jul 90		**HOT LOVE** *Tent FIVE 2*	**68**	1
3 Aug 85		LUXURY OF LIFE *Tent PL 70735*	12	70
30 Aug 86	★	SILK AND STEEL *Tent PL 71100*	1	58
26 Sep 87	●	BETWEEN THE LINES *Tent PL 71505*	7	17
27 Aug 88		ROCK THE WORLD *Tent PL 71747*	17	5
21 Oct 89		GREATEST HITS *Tent PL 74080*	53	3

FIVE THIRTY *UK, male vocal / instrumental group (Singles: 4 weeks, Albums: 1 week)*

Date		Title	pos	wks
4 Aug 90		**ABSTAIN** *East West YZ 530*	**75**	1
25 May 91		**13TH DISCIPLE** *East West YZ 577*	**67**	1
3 Aug 91		**SUPERNOVA** *East West YZ 594*	**75**	1
2 Nov 91		**YOU (EP)** *East West YZ 624*	**72**	1
31 Aug 91		BED *East West WX 530*	57	1

Tracks on You (EP): You / Cuddly Drug / Slow Train into the Ocean

5000 VOLTS *UK, male / female vocal / instrumental group (Singles: 18 weeks)*

Date		Title	pos	wks
6 Sep 75	●	**I'M ON FIRE** *Philips 6006 464*	**4**	9
24 Jul 76	●	**DOCTOR KISS-KISS** *Philips 6006 533*	**8**	9

Vocals (uncredited) on 'I'm on Fire' by Tina Charles

FIXATE *UK, male vocal group (Singles: 1 week)*

Date		Title	pos	wks
14 Jul 01		**24/7** *Epark EPKFIX CD1*	**42**	1

FIXX *UK, male vocal / instrumental group (Singles: 8 weeks, Albums: 7 weeks)*

Date		Title	pos	wks
24 Apr 82		**STAND OR FALL** *MCA FIXX 2*	**54**	4
17 Jul 82		**RED SKIES** *MCA FIXX 3*	**57**	4
22 May 82		SHUTTERED ROOM *MCA FX 1001*	54	6
21 May 83		REACH THE BEACH *MCA FX 1002*	91	1

Roberta FLACK
US, female vocalist (Singles: 79 weeks, Albums: 45 weeks)

Date		Title	pos	wks
27 May 72		**THE FIRST TIME EVER I SAW YOUR FACE** *Atlantic K 10161* ▲	**14**	14
5 Aug 72		**WHERE IS THE LOVE** *Atlantic K 10202* [1]	**29**	7
17 Feb 73	●	**KILLING ME SOFTLY WITH HIS SONG** *Atlantic K 10282* ▲	**6**	14
24 Aug 74		**FEEL LIKE MAKIN' LOVE** *Atlantic K 10467* ▲	**34**	7
6 May 78		**THE CLOSER I GET TO YOU** *Atlantic K 11099* [2]	**42**	4
17 May 80	●	**BACK TOGETHER AGAIN** *Atlantic K 11481* [1]	**3**	11
30 Aug 80		**DON'T MAKE ME WAIT TOO LONG** *Atlantic K 11555*	**44**	7
20 Aug 83	●	**TONIGHT I CELEBRATE MY LOVE** *Capitol CL 302* [3]	**2**	13
29 Jul 89		**UH-UH OOH-OOH LOOK OUT (HERE IT COMES)** *Atlantic A 8941*	**72**	2
15 Jul 72		FIRST TAKE *Atlantic K 40040* ▲	47	2
13 Oct 73		KILLING ME SOFTLY *Atlantic K 50021*	40	2
7 Jun 80		ROBERTA FLACK AND DONNY HATHAWAY *Atlantic K 50696* [1]	31	7
17 Sep 83		BORN TO LOVE *Capitol EST 7122841* [2]	15	10
31 Mar 84		ROBERTA FLACK'S GREATEST HITS *K-Tel NE 1269*	35	14
19 Feb 94	●	SOFTLY WITH THESE SONGS – THE BEST OF ROBERTA FLACK *Atlantic 7567824982*	7	10

[1] Roberta Flack and Donny Hathaway [2] Roberta Flack with Donny Hathaway [3] Peabo Bryson and Roberta Flack [1] Roberta Flack and Donny Hathaway [2] Peabo Bryson and Roberta Flack

FLAJ – *See GETO BOYS featuring FLAJ*

The FLAMING LIPS *US, male vocal / instrumental group (Singles: 15 weeks, Albums: 17 weeks)*

Date		Title	pos	wks
9 Mar 96		**THIS HERE GIRAFFE** *Warner Bros. W 0335CD*	**72**	1
26 Jun 99		**RACE FOR THE PRIZE** *Warner Bros. W 494CD1*	**39**	2
20 Nov 99		**WAITIN' FOR A SUPERMAN** *Warner Bros. W 505CD1*	**73**	1
31 Aug 02		**DO YOU REALIZE??** *Warner Bros. WEA W 586CD*	**32**	2
25 Jan 03		**YOSHIMI BATTLES THE PINK ROBOTS PT. 1** *Warner Bros. W 597CD1*	**18**	3
5 Jun 03		**FIGHT TEST** *Warner Bros. W611 CD1*	**28**	2
27 Sep 03		**THE GOLDEN PATH** *Virgin CHEMSD 18* [1]	**17**	4
29 May 99		THE SOFT BULLETIN *Warner Bros. 9362473932*	39	2
27 Jul 02		YOSHIMI BATTLES THE PINK ROBOTS *Warner Bros. 9362481412*	13	15

[1] Chemical Brothers / Flaming Lips

FLAMINGOS
US, male vocal group (Singles: 5 weeks)

Date		Title	pos	wks
4 Jun 69		**THE BOOGALOO PARTY** *Philips BF 1786*	**26**	5

Michael FLANDERS
UK, male vocalist, d. 14 Apr 1975 (Singles: 3 weeks)

Date		Title	pos	wks
27 Feb 59		**THE LITTLE DRUMMER BOY (re)** *Parlophone R 4528*	**20**	3

With the Michael Sammes Singers

FLASH and the PAN *Australia, male vocal / instrumental group (Singles: 15 weeks, Albums: 2 weeks)*

Date		Title	pos	wks
23 Sep 78		**AND THE BAND PLAYED ON (DOWN AMONG THE DEAD MEN)** *Ensign ENY 15*	**54**	4
21 May 83	●	**WAITING FOR A TRAIN** *Easybeat EASY 1*	**7**	11
16 Jul 83		PAN-ORAMA *Easy Beat EASLP 100*	69	2

Lester FLATT and Earl SCRUGGS
US, male instrumental duo – banjo (Singles: 6 weeks)

Date		Title	pos	wks
15 Nov 67		**FOGGY MOUNTAIN BREAKDOWN** *CBS 3038 and Mercury MF 1007*	**39**	6

The versions on the two labels were not the same cuts; CBS had a 1965 recording, Mercury a 1949 recording. The chart did not differentiate and listed both together

Fogwell FLAX and the ANKLEBITERS from FREEHOLD JUNIOR SCHOOL
UK, male vocalist and school choir (Singles: 2 weeks)

Date		Title	pos	wks
26 Dec 81		**ONE NINE FOR SANTA** *EMI 5255*	**68**	2

FLEE-REKKERS
UK, male instrumental group (Singles: 13 weeks)

Date		Title	pos	wks
19 May 60		**GREEN JEANS** *Triumph RGM 1008*	**23**	13

FLEETWOOD MAC (18 Top 500)
Record-breaking, Anglo-American, soft-rock superstars, who started as a British blues band. Members included Mick Fleetwood (d), John McVie (b), Peter Green (g), Christine McVie (k/v), Lindsey Buckingham (g/v), Stevie Nicks (v). They made their live debut at 1967 Windsor Jazz and Blues Festival

and by 1969 were one of Britain's most popular bands, thanks partly to Green's hypnotic composition 'Albatross' (which returned to the Top 3 in 1973). Green left shortly before McVie's future wife, Christine (voted Top British Female Singer in 1969 MM poll), joined from Chicken Shack. Group's Stateside breakthrough came with chart-topping second eponymous album, with featured two new members: American singer / songwriters Buckingham and Nicks. Grammy Hall of Fame album 'Rumours' topped the US chart for 31 weeks. It has sold 19 million in America and is 10 times platinum in the UK, where it has spent longer on the chart than any album. Group members concentrated on solo projects in the 1980s, reconvening in 1987 for the hit-packed 'Tango in the Night'. They split again in 1990, reunited briefly for President Clinton's inaugural concert in 1993 and in 1997, Fleetwood, Buckingham, Nicks and the McVie's live recording 'The Dance' topped the US chart. In 1998 they received the Outstanding Contribution to British Music Award at the Brits and were inducted into the Rock and Roll Hall of Fame (Singles: 223 weeks, Albums: 879 weeks) pos/wks

10 Apr 68 **BLACK MAGIC WOMAN** *Blue Horizon 57 3138* 37 7
17 Jul 68 **NEED YOUR LOVE SO BAD** *Blue Horizon 57 3139* 31 13
4 Dec 68 ★ **ALBATROSS** *Blue Horizon 57 3145* 1 20
16 Apr 69 ● **MAN OF THE WORLD** *Immediate IM 080* 2 14
23 Jul 69 **NEED YOUR LOVE SO BAD (re) (re-issue)** *Blue Horizon 57 3157* 32 9
4 Oct 69 ● **OH WELL** *Reprise RS 27000* 2 16
23 May 70 ● **THE GREEN MANALISHI (WITH THE TWO-PRONG CROWN)** *Reprise RS 27007* 10 12
12 May 73 ● **ALBATROSS (re-issue)** *CBS 8306* 2 15
13 Nov 76 **SAY YOU LOVE ME** *Reprise K 14447* 40 4
19 Feb 77 **GO YOUR OWN WAY** *Warner Bros. K 16872* 38 4
30 Apr 77 **DON'T STOP** *Warner Bros. K 16930* 32 5
9 Jul 77 **DREAMS** *Warner Bros. K 16969* ▲ 24 9
22 Oct 77 **YOU MAKE LOVING FUN** *Warner Bros. K 17013* 45 2
11 Mar 78 **RHIANNON** *Reprise K 14430* 46 3
6 Oct 79 ● **TUSK** *Warner Bros. K 17468* 6 10
22 Dec 79 **SARA** *Warner Bros. K 17533* 37 8
25 Sep 82 **GYPSY** *Warner Bros. K 17997* 46 3
18 Dec 82 ● **OH DIANE** *Warner Bros. FLEET 1* 9 15
4 Apr 87 ● **BIG LOVE** *Warner Bros. W 8398* 9 12
11 Jul 87 **SEVEN WONDERS** *Warner Bros. W 8317* 56 4
26 Sep 87 ● **LITTLE LIES** *Warner Bros. W 8291* 5 12
26 Dec 87 **FAMILY MAN** *Warner Bros. W 8114* 54 5
2 Apr 88 ● **EVERYWHERE** *Warner Bros. W 8143* 4 10
18 Jun 88 **ISN'T IT MIDNIGHT** *Warner Bros. W 7860* 60 2
17 Dec 88 **AS LONG AS YOU FOLLOW** *Warner Bros. W 7644* 66 3
5 May 90 **SAVE ME** *Warner Bros. W 9866* 53 3
25 Aug 90 **IN THE BACK OF MY MIND** *Warner Bros. W 9739* 58 3
2 Mar 68 ● **FLEETWOOD MAC** *Blue Horizon BPG 763200* 4 37
7 Sep 68 ● **MR WONDERFUL** *Blue Horizon 763205* 10 11
30 Aug 69 **THE PIOUS BIRD OF GOOD OMEN** *Blue Horizon 763215* 18 4
4 Oct 69 ● **THEN PLAY ON** *Reprise RSLP 9000* 6 11
10 Oct 70 **KILN HOUSE** *Reprise RSLP 9004* 39 2
19 Feb 72 **GREATEST HITS** *CBS 69011* 36 13
6 Nov 76 **FLEETWOOD MAC** *Reprise K 54043* ▲ 23 19
26 Feb 77 ★ **RUMOURS** *Warner Bros. K 56344* ▲ 1 477
27 Oct 79 ★ **TUSK** *Warner Bros. K 66088* 1 26
13 Dec 80 **FLEETWOOD MAC LIVE** *Warner Bros. K 66097* 31 9
10 Jul 82 ● **MIRAGE** *Warner Bros. K 56592* ▲ 5 39
25 Apr 87 ★ **TANGO IN THE NIGHT** *Warner Bros. WX 65* 1 115
3 Dec 88 ● **GREATEST HITS** *Warner Bros. WX 221* 3 53
21 Apr 90 ★ **BEHIND THE MASK** *Warner Bros. WX 335* ■ 1 21
23 Sep 95 **LIVE AT THE BBC** *Essential EDFCD 297* 48 2
21 Oct 95 **TIME** *Warner Bros. 9362459202* 47 1
6 Sep 97 **THE DANCE** *Reprise 9362467022* ▲ 15 10
26 Oct 02 ● **THE VERY BEST OF FLEETWOOD MAC** *WSM 8122736352* ....7 21+
10 May 03 ● **SAY YOU WILL** *WEA WB48467* 6 8

Group was UK and male only pre-1976 and for 'Live at the BBC' album. All the above albums are different although some are identically titled. 'Greatest Hits' in 1972 changed its catalogue number to 4607041 during its chart run

See also CHICKEN SHACK; Peter GREEN; Christine PERFECT

FLEETWOODS *US, male / female vocal trio (Singles: 8 weeks)* pos/wks

24 Apr 59 ● **COME SOFTLY TO ME** *London HLU 8841* ▲ 6 8

John 'OO' FLEMING *UK, male DJ / producer (Singles: 3 weeks)* pos/wks

25 Dec 99 **LOST IN EMOTION** *React CDREACT 170* 74 1
12 Aug 00 **FREE** *React CDREACT 186* 61 1
2 Feb 02 **BELFAST TRANCE** *Nebula BELFCD 001* [1] 74 1

[1] John 'OO' Fleming vs Simple Minds

FLESH & BONES

Belgium, male / female production / vocal trio (Singles: 1 week) pos/wks

10 Aug 02 **I LOVE YOU** *Multiply CDMULTY 86* 70 1

FLICKMAN *Italy, male production duo – Andreas Mazzali and Giuliano Orlandi (Singles: 6 weeks)* pos/wks

4 Mar 00 **THE SOUND OF BAMBOO** *Inferno CDFERN 25* 11 5
28 Apr 01 **HEY! PARADISE** *Inferno CDFERN 37* 69 1

KC FLIGHTT *US, male rapper (Singles: 5 weeks)* pos/wks

1 Apr 89 **PLANET E** *RCA PT 49404* 48 4
12 May 01 **VOICES** *Hooj Choons HOOJ 106CD* [1] 59 1

[1] KC Flightt vs Funky Junction

Dread FLIMSTONE and the MODERN TONE AGE FAMILY

US, male vocal / instrumental group (Singles: 1 week) pos/wks

30 Nov 91 **FROM THE GHETTO** *Urban URB 87* 66 1

Berni FLINT

UK, male vocalist (Singles: 11 weeks, Albums: 6 weeks) pos/wks

19 Mar 77 ● **I DON'T WANT TO PUT A HOLD ON YOU** *EMI 2599* 3 10
23 Jul 77 **SOUTHERN COMFORT** *EMI 2621* 48 1
2 Jul 77 **I DON'T WANT TO PUT A HOLD ON YOU** *EMI EMC 3184* 37 6

FLINTLOCK

UK, male vocal / instrumental group (Singles: 5 weeks) pos/wks

29 May 76 **DAWN** *Pinnacle P 8419* 30 5

FLIP & FILL *UK, male production duo – Graham Turner and Mark Hall (Singles: 34 weeks, Albums: 7 weeks)* pos/wks

24 Mar 01 **TRUE LOVE NEVER DIES** *All Around the World CDGLOBE 240* [1] 34 3
2 Feb 02 ● **TRUE LOVE NEVER DIES (re-mix)** *All Around the World CDGLOBE 248* [1] 7 10
27 Jul 02 ● **SHOOTING STAR** *All Around the World CDGLOBE 258* 3 10
18 Jan 03 **I WANNA DANCE WITH SOMEBODY (re)** *All Around the World CDGLOBE 275* 13 7
22 Mar 03 **SHAKE YA SHIMMY** *All Around the World CDGLOBE 213* [2] ..28 2
28 Jun 03 **FIELD OF DREAMS** *All Around the World CDGLOBE 273* [3] ..28 2
19 Jul 03 **FLOOR FILLAS** *UMTV / AATW 0392192* 29 7

[1] Flip and Fill featuring Kelly Llorenna [2] Porn Kings vs Flip and Fill featuring 740 Boyz [3] Flip and Fill featuring Jo James

'Shooting Star' features uncredited vocal by Karen Parry

See also BUS STOP

FLIPMODE SQUAD

US, male / female production / rap group (Singles: 14 weeks) pos/wks

31 Oct 98 **CHA CHA CHA** *Elektra E 3810CD* 54 1
7 Jun 03 ● **I KNOW WHAT YOU WANT** *J 82876528292* [1] 3 13

[1] Busta Rhymes and Mariah Carey featuring the Flipmode Squad

FLOATERS

US, male vocal group (Singles: 11 weeks, Albums: 8 weeks) pos/wks

23 Jul 77 ★ **FLOAT ON** *ABC 4187* 1 11
20 Aug 77 **FLOATERS** *ABC ABCL 5229* 17 8

FLOCK *UK male vocal / instrumental group (Albums: 2 weeks)* pos/wks

2 May 70 **FLOCK** *CBS 63733* 59 2

A FLOCK OF SEAGULLS *UK, male vocal / instrumental group (Singles: 46 weeks, Albums: 59 weeks)*

Date	Title	pos	wks
27 Mar 82	**I RAN** *Jive JIVE 14*	**43**	6
12 Jun 82	**SPACE AGE LOVE SONG** *Jive JIVE 17*	**34**	6
6 Nov 82 ●	**WISHING (IF I HAD A PHOTOGRAPH OF YOU)** *Jive JIVE 25*	**10**	12
23 Apr 83	**NIGHTMARES** *Jive JIVE 33*	**53**	3
25 Jun 83	**TRANSFER AFFECTION** *Jive JIVE 41*	**38**	5
14 Jul 84	**THE MORE YOU LIVE, THE MORE YOU LOVE** *Jive JIVE 62*	**26**	11
19 Oct 85	**WHO'S THAT GIRL (SHE'S GOT IT)** *Jive JIVE 106*	**66**	3
17 Apr 82	A FLOCK OF SEAGULLS *Jive HOP 201*	**32**	44
7 May 83	LISTEN *Jive HIP 4*	**16**	10
1 Sep 84	THE STORY OF A YOUNG HEART *Jive HIP 14*	**30**	5

FLOETRY *UK, female vocal duo (Singles: 1 week)*

Date	Title	pos	wks
26 Apr 03	**FLOETIC** *Dreamworks 4507752*	**73**	1

FLOORPLAY
UK, male instrumental / production duo (Singles: 1 week)

Date	Title	pos	wks
27 Jan 96	**AUTOMATIC** *Perfecto PERF 115CD*	**50**	1

FLOWERED UP *UK, male vocal / instrumental group (Singles: 17 weeks, Albums: 3 weeks)*

Date	Title	pos	wks
28 Jul 90	**IT'S ON** *Heavenly HVN 3*	**54**	4
24 Nov 90	**PHOBIA** *Heavenly HVN 7*	**75**	1
11 May 91	**TAKE IT** *London FUP 1*	**34**	4
17 Aug 91	**IT'S ON / EGG RUSH (re-recording)** *London FUP 2*	**38**	3
2 May 92	**WEEKENDER** *Heavenly HVN 16*	**20**	5
7 Sep 91	A LIFE WITH BRIAN *London 8282441*	**23**	3

FLOWERPOT MEN *UK, male vocal group (Singles: 12 weeks)*

Date	Title	pos	wks
23 Aug 67 ●	**LET'S GO TO SAN FRANCISCO** *Deram DM 142*	**4**	12

Mike FLOWERS POPS
UK, male / female vocal / instrumental group (Singles: 14 weeks)

Date	Title	pos	wks
30 Dec 95 ●	**WONDERWALL (re)** *London LONCD 378*	**2**	9
8 Jun 96	**LIGHT MY FIRE / PLEASE RELEASE ME** *London LONCD 384*	**39**	2
28 Dec 96	**DON'T CRY FOR ME ARGENTINA** *Love This LUVTHIS 16*	**30**	3

Eddie FLOYD
US, male vocalist (Singles: 29 weeks, Albums: 5 weeks)

Date	Title	pos	wks
2 Feb 67	**KNOCK ON WOOD (re)** *Atlantic 584 041*	**19**	18
16 Mar 67	**RAISE YOUR HAND** *Stax 601 001*	**42**	3
9 Aug 67	**THINGS GET BETTER** *Stax 601 016*	**31**	8
29 Apr 67	KNOCK ON WOOD *Stax 589006*	**36**	5

FLUFFY
UK, female vocal / instrumental group (Singles: 2 weeks)

Date	Title	pos	wks
17 Feb 96	**HUSBAND** *Parkway PARK 006CD*	**58**	1
5 Oct 96	**NOTHING** *Virgin VSCDT 1614*	**52**	1

FLUKE *UK, male instrumental / production group (Singles: 20 weeks, Albums: 3 weeks)*

Date	Title	pos	wks
20 Mar 93	**SLID** *Circa YRCD 103*	**59**	1
19 Jun 93	**ELECTRIC GUITAR** *Circa YRCD 104*	**58**	2
11 Sep 93	**GROOVY FEELING** *Circa YRCD 106*	**45**	3
23 Apr 94	**BUBBLE** *Circa YRCD 110*	**37**	2
29 Jul 95	**BULLET** *Circa YRCD 121*	**23**	3
16 Dec 95	**TOSH** *Circa YRCD 122*	**32**	3
16 Nov 96	**ATOM BOMB** *Circa YRCD 125*	**20**	3
31 May 97	**ABSURD** *Virgin YRCD 126*	**25**	2
27 Sep 97	**SQUIRT** *Circa YRCD 127*	**46**	1
23 Oct 93	SIX WHEELS ON MY WAGON *Circa CIRCDX 27*	**41**	1
19 Aug 95	OTO *Circa CIRCD 31*	**44**	1
11 Oct 97	RISOTTO *Virgin CIRCD 33*	**45**	1

See also LUCKY MONKEYS

FLUSH – *See SLADE*

FLYING LIZARDS *UK, male / female vocal / instrumental group (Singles: 16 weeks, Albums: 3 weeks)*

Date	Title	pos	wks
4 Aug 79 ●	**MONEY** *Virgin VS 276*	**5**	10
9 Feb 80	**TV** *Virgin VS 325*	**43**	6
16 Feb 80	FLYING LIZARDS *Virgin V 2150*	**60**	3

FLYING PICKETS
UK, male vocal group (Singles: 20 weeks, Albums: 22 weeks)

Date	Title	pos	wks
26 Nov 83 ★	**ONLY YOU** *10 TEN 14*	**1**	11
21 Apr 84 ●	**WHEN YOU'RE YOUNG AND IN LOVE** *10 TEN 20*	**7**	8
8 Dec 84	**WHO'S THAT GIRL** *10 GIRL 1*	**71**	1
17 Dec 83	LIVE AT THE ALBANY EMPIRE *AVM AVMLP 0001*	**48**	11
9 Jun 84	LOST BOYS *10 DIX 4*	**11**	11

Jerome FLYNN – *See ROBSON & JEROME*

FLYTRONIX – *See PESHAY*

FOCUS *Holland, male instrumental group (Singles: 21 weeks, Albums: 65 weeks)*

Date	Title	pos	wks
20 Jan 73	**HOCUS POCUS** *Polydor 2001 211*	**20**	10
27 Jan 73 ●	**SYLVIA** *Polydor 2001 422*	**4**	11
11 Nov 72 ●	MOVING WAVES *Polydor 2931 002*	**2**	34
2 Dec 72 ●	FOCUS 3 *Polydor 2383 016*	**6**	15
20 Oct 73	FOCUS AT THE RAINBOW *Polydor 2442 118*	**23**	5
25 May 74	HAMBURGER CONCERTO *Polydor 2442 124*	**20**	5
9 Aug 75	FOCUS *Polydor 2384 070*	**23**	6

FOG
US, male DJ / producer – Ralph Falcon (Singles: 4 weeks)

Date	Title	pos	wks
19 Feb 94	**BEEN A LONG TIME** *Columbia 6601212*	**44**	2
6 Jun 98	**BEEN A LONG TIME (re-mix)** *Pukka CDPUKKA 16*	**27**	2

See also FUNKY GREEN DOGS

Dan FOGELBERG
US, male vocalist (Singles: 4 weeks, Albums: 3 weeks)

Date	Title	pos	wks
15 Mar 80	**LONGER** *Epic EPC 8230*	**59**	4
29 Mar 80	PHOENIX *Epic EPC 83317*	**42**	3

John FOGERTY
US, male vocalist / instrumentalist – guitar (Albums: 11 weeks)

Date	Title	pos	wks
16 Feb 85	CENTERFIELD *Warner Bros. 9252031* ▲	**48**	11

See also CREEDENCE CLEARWATER REVIVAL

Ben FOLDS FIVE *US, male vocal / instrumental group (Singles: 12 weeks, Albums: 7 weeks)*

Date	Title	pos	wks
14 Sep 96	**UNDERGROUND** *Caroline CDCAR 008*	**37**	2
1 Mar 97	**BATTLE OF WHO COULD CARE LESS** *Epic 6642302*	**26**	3
7 Jun 97	**KATE** *Epic 6645365*	**39**	2
18 Apr 98	**BRICK** *Epic 6656612*	**26**	3
24 Apr 99	**ARMY** *Epic 6672182*	**28**	2
29 Sep 01	**ROCKIN' THE SUBURBS** *Epic 6718492* [1]	**53**	1
15 Mar 97	WHATEVER AND EVER AMEN *Epic 4866982*	**30**	3
24 Jan 98	NAKED BABY PHOTOS *Caroline CAR 7554*	**65**	1
8 May 99	THE UNAUTHORIZED BIOGRAPHY OF REINHOLD MESSNER *Epic 4933122*	**22**	2
6 Oct 01	ROCKIN' THE SUBURBS *Epic 5040632* [1]	**73**	1

[1] Ben Folds [1] Ben Folds

Ellen FOLEY
US, female vocalist (Albums: 3 weeks)

Date	Title	pos	wks
17 Nov 79	NIGHT OUT *Epic EPC 83718*	**68**	1
4 Apr 81	SPIRIT OF ST LOUIS *Epic EPC 84809*	**57**	2

FOLK IMPLOSION
US, male vocal / instrumental duo (Singles: 1 week)

Date	Title	pos	wks
15 Jun 96	**NATURAL ONE** *London LONCD 382*	**45**	1

Jane FONDA

US, female actor / exercise instructor (Albums: 51 weeks) pos/wks

29 Jan 83 ● JANE FONDA'S WORKOUT RECORD *CBS 88581* 7 47
22 Sep 84 JANE FONDA'S WORKOUT RECORD: NEW AND IMPROVED *CBS 88640* 60 4

Claudia FONTAINE – *See BEATMASTERS*

FONTANA featuring Darryl D'BONNEAU

US, male producer and male vocalist (Singles: 1 week) pos/wks

24 Mar 01 POW POW POW *Strictly Rhythm SRUKCD 01* 62 1

Lenny FONTANA and DJ SHORTY

US, male production duo – Lenny Fontana and Dominik Huebler (Singles: 2 weeks) pos/wks

4 Mar 00 CHOCOLATE SENSATION *ffrr FCD 375* 39 2

Wayne FONTANA

UK, male vocalist – Glyn Ellis (Singles: 76 weeks, Albums: 1 week) pos/wks

11 Jul 63 HELLO JOSEPHINE *Fontana TF 404* [1] 46 2
28 May 64 STOP LOOK AND LISTEN *Fontana TF 451* [1] 37 4
8 Oct 64 ● UM, UM, UM, UM, UM, UM *Fontana TF 497* [1] 5 15
4 Feb 65 ● GAME OF LOVE *Fontana TF 535* [1] ▲ 2 11
17 Jun 65 JUST A LITTLE BIT TOO LATE *Fontana TF 579* [1] 20 7
30 Sep 65 SHE NEEDS LOVE *Fontana TF 611* [1] 32 6
9 Dec 65 IT WAS EASIER TO HURT HER *Fontana TF 642* 36 6
21 Apr 66 COME ON HOME *Fontana TF 684* 16 12
25 Aug 66 GOODBYE BLUEBIRD *Fontana TF 737* 49 1
8 Dec 66 PAMELA, PAMELA *Fontana TF 770* 11 12
20 Feb 65 WAYNE FONTANA AND THE MINDBENDERS *Fontana TL 5230* [1] 18 1

[1] Wayne Fontana and the Mindbenders
[1] Wayne Fontana and the Mindbenders

See also MINDBENDERS

FOO FIGHTERS

US, male vocal / instrumental group (Singles: 50 weeks, Albums: 86 weeks) pos/wks

1 Jul 95 ● THIS IS A CALL *Roswell CDCL 753* 5 4
16 Sep 95 I'LL STICK AROUND *Roswell CDCL 757* 18 3
2 Dec 95 FOR ALL THE COWS *Roswell CDCL 762* 28 2
6 Apr 96 BIG ME *Roswell CDCL 768* 19 3
10 May 97 MONKEY WRENCH *Roswell CDCLS 788* 12 4
30 Aug 97 EVERLONG *Roswell CDCL 792* 18 3
31 Jan 98 MY HERO *Roswell CDCL 796* 21 2
29 Aug 98 WALKING AFTER YOU: BEACON LIGHT *Elektra E 4100CD* [1] 20 3
30 Oct 99 LEARN TO FLY *RCA 74321706622* 21 3
30 Sep 00 BREAKOUT *RCA 74321790102* 29 3
16 Dec 00 NEXT YEAR *RCA 74321809262* 42 2
18 Jan 03 TIMES LIKE THESE *RCA 74321989552* 12 5
19 Oct 02 ● ALL MY LIFE *RCA 74321973152* 5 9
18 Jan 03 TIMES LIKE THESE *RCA 74321989552* 12 5
5 Jul 03 LOW *RCA 82876522562* 21 2
4 Oct 03 HAVE IT ALL *RCA 82876563702* 37 2
8 Jul 95 ● FOO FIGHTERS *Roswell CDSET 2266* 3 17
24 May 97 ● THE COLOUR AND THE SHAPE *Roswell CDEST 2295* 3 12
13 Nov 99 ● THERE IS NOTHING LEFT TO LOSE *RCA 74321716992* 10 16
2 Nov 02 ★ ONE BY ONE *RCA 74321973482* ■ 1 41

[1] Foo Fighters: Ween

FOOL BOONA

UK, male DJ / producer – Colin Tevendale (Singles: 1 week) pos/wks

10 Apr 99 POPPED!! *Virgin / VC Recordings / Uber Disko VCRD 46* 52 1

FOOL'S GARDEN

Germany, male vocal / instrumental group (Singles: 4 weeks) pos/wks

25 May 96 LEMON TREE *Encore CDCOR 014* 61 1
3 Aug 96 LEMON TREE (re-issue) *Encore CDCOR 018* 26 3

FOR REAL

US, female vocal group (Singles: 2 weeks) pos/wks

1 Jul 95 YOU DON'T KNOW NOTHIN' *A&M 5811232* 54 1
12 Jul 97 LIKE I DO *Rowdy 74321486582* 45 1

Steve FORBERT

US, male vocalist (Albums: 3 weeks) pos/wks

9 Jun 79 ALIVE ON ARRIVAL *Epic EPC 83308* 56 1
24 Nov 79 JACK RABBIT SLIM *Epic EPC 83879* 54 2

Bill FORBES

UK, male vocalist (Singles: 1 week) pos/wks

15 Jan 60 TOO YOUNG *Columbia DB 4386* 29 1

David FORBES

UK, male producer (Singles: 1 week) pos/wks

25 Aug 01 QUESTIONS (MUST BE ASKED) *Serious SERR 031CD* 57 1

FORBIDDEN – *See Jet BRONX and the FORBIDDEN*

FORCE & STYLES featuring Kelly LLORENNA

UK, male DJ duo and female vocalist (Singles: 1 week) pos/wks

25 Jul 98 HEART OF GOLD *Diverse VERSE 2CD* 55 1

FORCE MD'S

US, male vocal group (Singles: 9 weeks) pos/wks

12 Apr 86 TENDER LOVE *Tommy Boy IS 269* 23 9

Clinton FORD

UK, male vocalist – Ian Stopford Harrison (Singles: 25 weeks, Albums: 4 weeks) pos/wks

23 Oct 59 OLD SHEP *Oriole CB 1500* 27 1
17 Aug 61 TOO MANY BEAUTIFUL GIRLS *Oriole CB 1623* 48 1
8 Mar 62 FANLIGHT FANNY *Oriole CB 1706* 22 10
5 Jan 67 RUN TO THE DOOR *Piccadilly 7N 35361* 25 13
26 May 62 CLINTON FORD *Oriole PS 40021* 16 4

Emile FORD and the CHECKMATES

UK, male vocal / instrumental group – Emile Sweatman (Singles: 89 weeks) pos/wks

30 Oct 59 ★ WHAT DO YOU WANT TO MAKE THOSE EYES AT ME FOR? *Pye 7N 15225* 1 26
5 Feb 60 ● ON A SLOW BOAT TO CHINA *Pye 7N 15245* 3 15
26 May 60 YOU'LL NEVER KNOW WHAT YOU'RE MISSING ('TIL YOU TRY) *Pye 7N 15268* 12 9
1 Sep 60 THEM THERE EYES *Pye 7N 15282* [1] 18 16
8 Dec 60 ● COUNTING TEARDROPS *Pye 7N 15314* 4 12
2 Mar 61 WHAT AM I GONNA DO *Pye 7N 15331* 33 6
18 May 61 HALF OF MY HEART (re) *Piccadilly 7N 35003* [2] 42 4
8 Mar 62 I WONDER WHO'S KISSING HER NOW *Piccadilly 7N 35033* [2] 43 1

[1] Emile Ford: The Babs Knight Group and Johnny Keating Music [2] Emile Ford

Lita FORD

UK, female vocalist (Singles: 7 weeks, Albums: 4 weeks) pos/wks

17 Dec 88 KISS ME DEADLY *RCA PB 49575* 75 1
20 May 89 CLOSE MY EYES FOREVER *Dreamland PB 49409* [1] 47 3
11 Jan 92 SHOT OF POISON *RCA PB 49145* 63 3
26 May 84 DANCIN' ON THE EDGE *Vertigo VERL 13* 96 1
23 Jun 90 STILETTO *RCA PL 82090* 66 1
25 Jan 92 DANGEROUS CURVES *RCA PD 90592* 51 2

[1] Lita Ford duet with Ozzy Osbourne

Martyn FORD ORCHESTRA

UK, orchestra (Singles: 3 weeks) pos/wks

14 May 77 LET YOUR BODY GO DOWNTOWN *Mountain TOP 26* 38 3

Mary FORD – *See Les PAUL and Mary FORD*

Penny FORD

US, female vocalist (Singles: 7 weeks) pos/wks

4 May 85 DANGEROUS *Total Experience FB 49975* [1] 43 5
29 May 93 DAYDREAMING *Columbia 6590592* 43 2

[1] Pennye Ford

See also SNAP!

Tennessee Ernie FORD

US, male vocalist, d. 17 Oct 1991 (Singles: 42 weeks)

			pos	wks
21 Jan 55	★	**GIVE ME YOUR WORD** *Capitol CL 14005*	1	24
6 Jan 56	★	**SIXTEEN TONS** *Capitol CL 14500* ▲	1	11
13 Jan 56	●	**THE BALLAD OF DAVY CROCKETT** *Capitol CL 14506*	3	7

Julia FORDHAM

UK, female vocalist (Singles: 32 weeks, Albums: 36 weeks)

			pos	wks
2 Jul 88		**HAPPY EVER AFTER** *Circa YR 15*	27	9
25 Feb 89		**WHERE DOES THE TIME GO?** *Circa YR 23*	41	5
31 Aug 91		**I THOUGHT IT WAS YOU** *Circa YR 69*	64	2
18 Jan 92		**LOVE MOVES (IN MYSTERIOUS WAYS)** *Circa YR 73*	19	9
30 May 92		**I THOUGHT IT WAS YOU (re-mix)** *Circa YR 90*	45	3
30 Apr 94		**DIFFERENT TIME DIFFERENT PLACE** *Circa YRCD 111*	41	3
23 Jul 94		**I CAN'T HELP MYSELF** *Circa YRCD 116*	62	1
18 Jun 88		JULIA FORDHAM *Circa CIRCA 4*	20	22
21 Oct 89		PORCELAIN *Circa CIRCA 10*	13	5
2 Nov 91		SWEPT *Circa CIRCA 18*	33	6
21 May 94		FALLING FORWARD *Circa CIRCD 28*	21	3

FOREIGNER (320 Top 500)

Melodic Anglo-American rock group which amassed six US Top 10 albums. Featured Londoner Mick Jones (g) and New York native Lou Gramm (v). 'Waiting for a Girl Like You' stayed at No.2 in the US for a record-breaking 10 weeks (Singles: 78 weeks, Albums: 126 weeks)

			pos	wks
6 May 78		**FEELS LIKE THE FIRST TIME** *Atlantic K 11086*	39	6
15 Jul 78		**COLD AS ICE** *Atlantic K 10986*	24	10
28 Oct 78		**HOT BLOODED** *Atlantic K 11167*	42	3
24 Feb 79		**BLUE MORNING, BLUE DAY** *Atlantic K 11236*	45	4
29 Aug 81		**URGENT** *Atlantic K 11665*	54	4
10 Oct 81		**JUKE BOX HERO** *Atlantic K 11678*	48	4
12 Dec 81	●	**WAITING FOR A GIRL LIKE YOU** *Atlantic K 11696*	8	13
8 May 82		**URGENT (re-issue)** *Atlantic K 11728*	45	5
8 Dec 84	★	**I WANT TO KNOW WHAT LOVE IS** *Atlantic A 9596* ▲	1	16
6 Apr 85		**THAT WAS YESTERDAY** *Atlantic A 9571*	28	6
22 Jun 85		**COLD AS ICE (re-mix)** *Atlantic A 9539*	64	2
19 Dec 87		**SAY YOU WILL** *Atlantic A 9169*	71	4
22 Oct 94		**WHITE LIE** *Arista 74321232862*	58	1
26 Aug 78		DOUBLE VISION *Atlantic K 50476*	32	5
25 Jul 81	●	4 *Atlantic K 50796* ▲	5	62
18 Dec 82		RECORDS *Atlantic A 0999*	58	11
22 Dec 84	★	AGENT PROVOCATEUR *Atlantic 7819991*	1	32
19 Dec 87		INSIDE INFORMATION *Atlantic WX 143*	64	7
6 Jul 91		UNUSUAL HEAT *Atlantic WX 424*	56	1
2 May 92		THE VERY BEST OF FOREIGNER *Atlantic 7567805112*	19	7
12 Nov 94		MR MOONLIGHT *Arista 74321232852*	59	1

FORMATIONS *US, male vocal group (Singles: 11 weeks)*

			pos	wks
31 Jul 71		**AT THE TOP OF THE STAIRS (re)** *Mojo 2027 001*	28	11

George FORMBY *UK, male vocalist / instrumentalist – ukulele – George Hoy Booth, d. 6 Mar 1961 (Singles: 3 weeks)*

			pos	wks
21 Jul 60		**HAPPY GO LUCKY ME / BANJO BOY** *Pye 7N 15269*	40	3

See also 2 IN A TENT

FORREST

US, male vocalist – Forrest M Thomas Jr (Singles: 20 weeks)

			pos	wks
26 Feb 83	●	**ROCK THE BOAT** *CBS A 3163*	4	10
14 May 83		**FEEL THE NEED IN ME** *CBS A 3411*	17	8
17 Sep 83		**ONE LOVER (DON'T STOP THE SHOW)** *CBS A 3734*	67	2

Sharon FORRESTER *Jamaica, female vocalist (Singles: 1 week)*

			pos	wks
11 Feb 95		**LOVE INSIDE** *ffrr FCD 253*	50	1

Lance FORTUNE

UK, male vocalist – Chris Morris (Singles: 18 weeks)

			pos	wks
19 Feb 60	●	**BE MINE** *Pye 7N 15240*	4	13
5 May 60		**THIS LOVE I HAVE FOR YOU** *Pye 7N 15260*	26	5

FORTUNES

UK, male vocal / instrumental group (Singles: 65 weeks)

			pos	wks
8 Jul 65	●	**YOU'VE GOT YOUR TROUBLES** *Decca F 12173*	2	14
7 Oct 65	●	**HERE IT COMES AGAIN** *Decca F 12243*	4	14
3 Feb 66		**THIS GOLDEN RING** *Decca F 12321*	15	9
11 Sep 71	●	**FREEDOM COME, FREEDOM GO** *Capitol CL 15693*	6	17
29 Jan 72	●	**STORM IN A TEACUP** *Capitol CL 15707*	7	11

45 KING (DJ MARK THE 45 KING)

US, male producer – Mark James (Singles: 6 weeks)

			pos	wks
28 Oct 89		**THE KING IS HERE/THE 900 NUMBER (re)** *Dance Trax DRX 9*	60	6

49ERS *Italy, male producer – Gianfranco Bortolotti (Singles: 27 weeks, Albums: 5 weeks)*

			pos	wks
16 Dec 89	●	**TOUCH ME** *Fourth & Broadway BRW 157*	3	13
17 Mar 90		**DON'T YOU LOVE ME** *Fourth & Broadway BRW 167*	12	6
9 Jun 90		**GIRL TO GIRL** *Fourth & Broadway BRW 174*	31	3
6 Jun 92		**GOT TO BE FREE** *Fourth & Broadway BRW 255*	46	2
29 Aug 92		**THE MESSAGE** *Fourth & Broadway BRW 257*	68	1
18 Mar 95		**ROCKIN' MY BODY** *Media MCSTD 2021* [1]	31	2
10 Mar 90		THE 49ERS *Fourth & Broadway BRLP 547*	51	5

[1] 49ers featuring Ann-Marie Smith

See also CAPPELLA

Itsy FOSTER – *See EXOTICA featuring Itsy FOSTER*

Lawrence FOSTER – *See LONDON SYMPHONY ORCHESTRA*

Penny FOSTER – *See STAGECOACH featuring Penny FOSTER*

FOSTER and ALLEN (247 Top 500)

Ever-popular Irish duo formed 1975; Mike Foster (accordion/v), Tony Allen (g/v). The folk-based performers have sold a reported 20 million albums globally, and are the only act to have at least one hit album per year between 1983 and 1999 (Singles: 47 weeks, Albums: 203 weeks)

			pos	wks
27 Feb 82		**A BUNCH OF THYME** *Ritz RITZ 5*	18	11
30 Oct 82		**OLD FLAMES** *Ritz RITZ 028*	51	8
19 Feb 83		**MAGGIE** *Ritz RITZ 025*	27	9
29 Oct 83		**I WILL LOVE YOU ALL MY LIFE** *Ritz RITZ 056*	49	6
30 Jun 84		**JUST FOR OLD TIME'S SAKE** *Ritz RITZ 066*	47	6
29 Mar 86		**AFTER ALL THESE YEARS** *Ritz RITZ 106*	43	7
14 May 83		MAGGIE *Ritz RITZLP 0012*	72	6
5 Nov 83		I WILL LOVE YOU ALL OF MY LIFE *Ritz RITZLP 0015*	71	6
17 Nov 84		THE VERY BEST OF FOSTER AND ALLEN *Ritz RITZ LPTV 1*	18	18
29 Mar 86		AFTER ALL THESE YEARS *Ritz RITZLP 0032*	82	8
25 Oct 86		REMINISCING *Stylus SMR 623*	11	15
27 Jun 87		LOVE SONGS – THE VERY BEST OF FOSTER AND ALLEN VOLUME 2 *Ritz RITZLP 0036*	92	1
10 Oct 87		REFLECTIONS *Stylus SMR 739*	16	16
30 Apr 88		REMEMBER YOU'RE MINE *Stylus SMR 853*	16	15
28 Oct 89		THE MAGIC OF FOSTER AND ALLEN – THEIR GREATEST HITS *Stylus SMR 989*	29	12
9 Dec 89		FOSTER AND ALLEN'S CHRISTMAS COLLECTION *Stylus SMR 995*	40	4
10 Nov 90		SOUVENIRS *Telstar STAR 2457*	15	12
8 Dec 90		THE CHRISTMAS COLLECTION *Telstar STAR 2459*	44	4
2 Nov 91		MEMORIES *Telstar STAR 2527*	18	11
31 Oct 92		HEART STRINGS *Telstar TCD 2608*	37	10
23 Oct 93		BY REQUEST *Telstar TCD 2670*	14	12
5 Nov 94		SONGS WE LOVE TO SING *Telstar TCD 2741*	41	9
4 Nov 95		100 GOLDEN GREATS *Telstar TCD 2791*	30	12
2 Nov 96		SOMETHING SPECIAL – 100 GOLDEN LOVE SONGS *Telstar TCD 2846*	46	10
26 Apr 97		SHADES OF GREEN *Telstar TCD 2899*	55	2
15 Nov 97		BEST FRIENDS *Telstar TV TTVCD 2935*	36	8
12 Dec 98		GREATEST HITS *Telstar TV TTVCD 3000*	52	4
25 Dec 99		ONE DAY AT A TIME *Telstar TV TTVCD 3090*	61	1
15 Nov 03		BY SPECIAL REQUEST – THE VERY BEST OF FOSTER AND ALLEN *DMG TV DMGTV003*	30	7+

FOTHERINGAY

UK, male / female vocal / instrumental group (Albums: 6 weeks) pos/wks

11 Jul 70 **FOTHERINGAY** *Island ILPS 9125* 18 6

FOUNDATION featuring Natalie ROSSI

Holland, male producers and UK, female vocalist (Singles: 2 weeks) pos/wks

12 Jul 03 **ALL OUT OF LOVE** *Fuelin 82876513292* 40 2

FOUNDATIONS *Trinidad / Jamaica / Dominica / UK / Sri Lanka, male vocal / instrumental group (Singles: 57 weeks)* pos/wks

27 Sep 67 ★ **BABY NOW THAT I'VE FOUND YOU** *Pye 7N 17366* 1 16
24 Jan 68 **BACK ON MY FEET AGAIN** *Pye 7N 17417* 18 10
1 May 68 **ANY OLD TIME (YOU'RE LONELY AND SAD) (re)** *Pye 7N 17503* 48 2
20 Nov 68 ● **BUILD ME UP BUTTERCUP** *Pye 7N 17636* 2 15
12 Mar 69 ● **IN THE BAD BAD OLD DAYS (BEFORE YOU LOVED ME)** *Pye 7N 17702* 8 10
13 Sep 69 **BORN TO LIVE, BORN TO DIE** *Pye 7N 17809* 46 3
12 Dec 98 **BUILD ME UP BUTTERCUP (re-issue)** *Castle NEEX 1001* 71 1

FOUNTAINS OF WAYNE *US, male vocal / instrumental group (Singles: 7 weeks, Albums: 1 week)* pos/wks

22 Mar 97 **RADIATION VIBE** *Atlantic 7567956262* 32 2
10 May 97 **SINK TO THE BOTTOM** *Atlantic A 5612CD* 42 1
26 Jul 97 **SURVIVAL CAR** *Atlantic AT 0004CD* 53 1
27 Dec 97 **I WANT AN ALIEN FOR CHRISTMAS** *Atlantic AT 0020CD* 36 2
20 Mar 99 **DENISE** *Atlantic AT 0053CD* 57 1
7 Jun 97 **FOUNTAINS OF WAYNE** *Atlantic 7567927252* 67 1

FOUR ACES *US, male vocal group (Singles: 40 weeks)* pos/wks

30 Jul 54 ● **THREE COINS IN THE FOUNTAIN (re)** *Brunswick 05308* [1] 5 6
7 Jan 55 ● **MISTER SANDMAN** *Brunswick 05355* [1] 9 5
20 May 55 ● **STRANGER IN PARADISE** *Brunswick 05418* 6 6
18 Nov 55 ● **LOVE IS A MANY SPLENDORED THING** *Brunswick 05480* [1] ▲ 2 13
19 Oct 56 **A WOMAN IN LOVE** *Brunswick 05589* [1] 19 3
4 Jan 57 **FRIENDLY PERSUASION (THEE I LOVE)** *Brunswick 05623* [1] 29 1
23 Jan 59 **THE WORLD OUTSIDE** *Brunswick 05773* 18 6

[1] Four Aces featuring Al Alberts

FOUR BUCKETEERS

UK, male / female vocal group (Singles: 6 weeks) pos/wks

3 May 80 **THE BUCKET OF WATER SONG** *CBS 8393* 26 6

FOUR ESQUIRES *US, male vocal group (Singles: 2 weeks)* pos/wks

31 Jan 58 **LOVE ME FOREVER** *London HLO 8533* 23 2

4 HERO *UK, male instrumental / production group (Singles: 6 weeks, Albums: 7 weeks)* pos/wks

24 Nov 90 **MR KIRK'S NIGHTMARE** *Reinforced RIVET 1203* 73 2
9 May 92 **COOKIN' UP YAH BRAIN** *Reinforced RIVET 1216* 59 2
15 Aug 98 **STAR CHASERS** *Talkin' Loud TLCD 36* 41 1
3 Nov 01 **LES FLEUR** *Talkin' Loud TLCD 66* 53 1
25 Jul 98 **TWO PAGES** *Talkin Loud 5584622* 38 6
10 Nov 01 **CREATING PATTERNS** *Talkin Loud 5860572* 65 1

'Mr Kirk's Nightmare' was titled 'Combat Dancing (EP)' in its first week on chart

4-SKINS

UK, male vocal instrumental group (Albums: 4 weeks) pos/wks

17 Apr 82 **THE GOOD THE BAD AND THE 4-SKINS** *Secret SEC 4* 80 4

400 BLOWS

UK, male vocal / instrumental duo (Singles: 4 weeks) pos/wks

29 Jun 85 **MOVIN'** *Illuminated ILL 61* 54 4

FOUR JAYS – *See Billy FURY*

FOUR KESTRELS – *See Billy FURY*

FOUR KNIGHTS *US, male vocal group (Singles: 11 weeks)* pos/wks

4 Jun 54 ● **(OH BABY MINE) I GET SO LONELY (re)** *Capitol CL 14076* 5 11

FOUR LADS *Canada, male vocal group (Singles: 23 weeks)* pos/wks

19 Dec 52 ● **FAITH CAN MOVE MOUNTAINS (re)** *Columbia DB 3154* [1] 7 3
22 Oct 54 ● **RAIN, RAIN, RAIN** *Philips PB 311* [2] 8 16
28 Apr 60 **STANDING ON THE CORNER** *Philips PB 1000* 34 4

[1] Johnnie Ray and The Four Lads [2] Frankie Laine and The Four Lads

4 NON BLONDES *US, female / male vocal / instrumental group (Singles: 19 weeks, Albums: 18 weeks)* pos/wks

19 Jun 93 ● **WHAT'S UP** *Interscope A 8412CD* 2 17
16 Oct 93 **SPACEMAN** *Interscope A 8349CD* 53 2
17 Jul 93 ● **BIGGER BETTER FASTER MORE!** *Interscope 7567921122* 4 18

4 OF US *Ireland, male vocal / instrumental group (Singles: 6 weeks, Albums: 1 week)* pos/wks

27 Feb 93 **SHE HITS ME** *Columbia 6589192* 35 4
1 May 93 **I MISS YOU** *Columbia 6591722* 62 2
20 Mar 93 **MAN ALIVE** *Columbia 4723262* 64 1

FOUR PENNIES *UK, male vocal / instrumental group – lead vocal Lionel Morton (Singles: 56 weeks, Albums: 5 weeks)* pos/wks

16 Jan 64 **DO YOU WANT ME TO (re)** *Philips BF 1296* 47 2
2 Apr 64 ★ **JULIET** *Philips BF 1322* 1 15
16 Jul 64 **I FOUND OUT THE HARD WAY** *Philips BF 1349* 14 11
29 Oct 64 **BLACK GIRL** *Philips BF 1366* 20 12
7 Oct 65 **UNTIL IT'S TIME FOR YOU TO GO** *Philips BF 1435* 19 11
17 Feb 66 **TROUBLE IS MY MIDDLE NAME** *Philips BF 1469* 32 5
7 Nov 64 **TWO SIDES OF FOUR PENNIES** *Philips BL 7642* 13 5

FOUR PREPS *US, male vocal group (Singles: 23 weeks)* pos/wks

13 Jun 58 ● **BIG MAN** *Capitol CL 14873* 2 14
26 May 60 **GOT A GIRL (re)** *Capitol CL 15128* 28 7
2 Nov 61 **MORE MONEY FOR YOU AND ME (MEDLEY)** *Capitol CL 15217* 39 2

Tracks on medley: Mr Blue / Alley Oop / Smoke Gets in Your Eyes / In This Whole Wide World / A Worried Man / Tom Dooley / A Teenager in Love. All songs feature new lyrics

FOUR SEASONS *296* **Top 500**

No.1 US group of the early 1960s: Frankie Valli (v), Bob Gaudio (k/v), Nick Massi (b/v) (died 2000), Tommy DeVito (g/v). Falsetto-voiced Valli's quartet, the first group to score three US No.1s in succession, has a chart span there of almost 40 years (Singles: 151 weeks, Albums: 68 weeks) pos/wks

4 Oct 62 ● **SHERRY** *Stateside SS 122* ▲ 8 16
17 Jan 63 **BIG GIRLS DON'T CRY** *Stateside SS 145* ▲ 13 10
28 Mar 63 **WALK LIKE A MAN** *Stateside SS 169* ▲ 12 12
27 Jun 63 **AIN'T THAT A SHAME** *Stateside SS 194* 38 3
27 Aug 64 ● **RAG DOLL** *Philips BF 1347* [1] ▲ 2 13
18 Nov 65 ● **LET'S HANG ON** *Philips BF 1439* [1] 4 16
31 Mar 66 **WORKIN' MY WAY BACK TO YOU** *Philips BF 1474* [2] 50 3
2 Jun 66 **OPUS 17 (DON'T YOU WORRY 'BOUT ME)** *Philips BF 1493* [2] 20 9
29 Sep 66 **I'VE GOT YOU UNDER MY SKIN** *Philips BF 1511* [2] 12 11
12 Jan 67 **TELL IT TO THE RAIN** *Philips BF 1538* [2] 37 5
19 Apr 75 ● **THE NIGHT** *Mowest MW 3024* [3] 7 9
20 Sep 75 ● **WHO LOVES YOU** *Warner Bros. / Curb K 16602* 6 9
31 Jan 76 ★ **DECEMBER, 1963, (OH, WHAT A NIGHT)** *Warner Bros. / Curb K 16688* ▲ 1 10
24 Apr 76 ● **SILVER STAR** *Warner Bros. / Curb K 16742* 3 9
27 Nov 76 **WE CAN WORK IT OUT** *Warner Bros. / Curb K 16845* 34 4
18 Jun 77 **RHAPSODY** *Warner Bros. / Curb K 16932* 37 3
20 Aug 77 **DOWN THE HALL** *Warner Bros. / Curb K 16982* 34 5
29 Oct 88 **DECEMBER, 1963 (OH, WHAT A NIGHT) (re-mix)** *BR 45277* [3] 49 4
6 Jul 63 **SHERRY** *Stateside SL 10033* 20 1
10 Apr 71 **EDIZIONE D'ORO** *Philips 6640002* 11 7
20 Nov 71 **THE BIG ONES** *Philips 6336208* 37 1
6 Mar 76 **THE FOUR SEASONS STORY** *Private Stock DAPS 1001* 20 8
6 Mar 76 **WHO LOVES YOU** *Warner Bros. K 56179* 12 17

20 Nov 76 ● **GREATEST HITS** *K-Tel NE 942*..............................4 6
21 May 88 **THE COLLECTION** *Telstar STAR 2320* [1]..............................38 9
7 Mar 92 ● **THE VERY BEST OF FRANKIE VALLI AND THE FOUR SEASONS** *PolyGram TV 5131192* [1]..............................7 15
13 Oct 01 **THE DEFINITIVE FRANKIE VALLI AND THE FOUR SEASONS** *WSM 8122735552* [1]..............................26 4

[1] Four Seasons with the sound of Frankie Valli [2] Four Seasons with Frankie Valli [3] Frankie Valli and the Four Seasons [1] Frankie Valli and the Four Seasons

4 STRINGS

Holland, male / female production / vocal duo (Singles: 13 weeks) pos/wks

23 Dec 00 **DAY TIME** *AM:PM 139*..............................48 3
11 May 02 **(TAKE ME AWAY) INTO THE NIGHT (re)** *Nebula / Virgin VCRD 107* 15 7
14 Sep 02 **DIVING** *Nebula VCRD 108*..............................38 2
13 Sep 03 **LET IT RAIN** *Nebula NEBCD 049*..............................49 1

See also MADELYNE

FOUR TET

UK, male DJ / producer – Keiran Hebden (Albums: 1 week) pos/wks

17 May 03 **ROUNDS** *Domino WIDCD126*..............................60 1

4 THE CAUSE *US, male / female vocal group (Singles: 9 weeks)* pos/wks

10 Oct 98 **STAND BY ME** *RCA 74321622442*..............................12 9

FOUR TOPS (62 Top 500)

Unmistakable R&B vocal group from Detroit: Levi Stubbs, Renaldo Benson, Lawrence Payton (d. 1997), Abdul Fakir. The legendary Motown act performed together for a record 44 years (until Payton's death) and were inducted into the Rock and Roll Hall of Fame in 1990 (Singles: 318 weeks, Albums: 256 weeks) pos/wks

1 Jul 65 **I CAN'T HELP MYSELF** *Tamla Motown TMG 515* ▲..............................23 9
2 Sep 65 **IT'S THE SAME OLD SONG** *Tamla Motown TMG 528*..............................34 8
21 Jul 66 **LOVING YOU IS SWEETER THAN EVER** *Tamla Motown TMG 568*..............................21 12
13 Oct 66 ★ **REACH OUT I'LL BE THERE** *Tamla Motown TMG 579* ▲..............................1 16
12 Jan 67 ● **STANDING IN THE SHADOWS OF LOVE** *Tamla Motown TMG 589*..............................6 8
30 Mar 67 ● **BERNADETTE** *Tamla Motown TMG 601*..............................8 10
15 Jun 67 **SEVEN ROOMS OF GLOOM** *Tamla Motown TMG 612*..............................12 9
11 Oct 67 **YOU KEEP RUNNING AWAY** *Tamla Motown TMG 623*..............................26 7
13 Dec 67 ● **WALK AWAY RENEE** *Tamla Motown TMG 634*..............................3 11
13 Mar 68 ● **IF I WERE A CARPENTER** *Tamla Motown TMG 647*..............................7 11
21 Aug 68 **YESTERDAY'S DREAMS** *Tamla Motown TMG 665*..............................23 15
13 Nov 68 **I'M IN A DIFFERENT WORLD** *Tamla Motown TMG 675*..............................27 13
28 May 69 **WHAT IS A MAN** *Tamla Motown TMG 698*..............................16 11
27 Sep 69 **DO WHAT YOU GOTTA DO** *Tamla Motown TMG 710*..............................11 11
21 Mar 70 ● **I CAN'T HELP MYSELF (re-issue)** *Tamla Motown TMG 732*..............................10 11
30 May 70 ● **IT'S ALL IN THE GAME (re)** *Tamla Motown TMG 736*..............................5 16
3 Oct 70 ● **STILL WATER (LOVE) (re)** *Tamla Motown TMG 752*..............................10 12
1 May 71 **JUST SEVEN NUMBERS (CAN STRAIGHTEN OUT MY LIFE)** *Tamla Motown TMG 770*..............................36 5
26 Jun 71 **RIVER DEEP MOUNTAIN HIGH** *Tamla Motown TMG 777* [1]..............................11 10
25 Sep 71 ● **SIMPLE GAME** *Tamla Motown TMG 785*..............................3 11
20 Nov 71 **YOU GOTTA HAVE LOVE IN YOUR HEART** *Tamla Motown TMG 793* [1]..............................25 10
11 Mar 72 **BERNADETTE (re-issue)** *Tamla Motown TMG 803*..............................23 7
5 Aug 72 **WALK WITH ME TALK WITH ME DARLING** *Tamla Motown TMG 823*..............................32 6
18 Nov 72 **KEEPER OF THE CASTLE** *Probe PRO 575*..............................18 9
10 Nov 73 **SWEET UNDERSTANDING LOVE** *Probe PRO 604*..............................29 10
17 Oct 81 ● **WHEN SHE WAS MY GIRL** *Casablanca CAN 1005*..............................3 10
19 Dec 81 **DON'T WALK AWAY** *Casablanca CAN 1006*..............................16 11
6 Mar 82 **TONIGHT I'M GONNA LOVE YOU ALL OVER** *Casablanca CAN 1008*..............................43 4
26 Jun 82 **BACK TO SCHOOL AGAIN** *RSO 89*..............................62 2
23 Jul 88 **REACH OUT I'LL BE THERE (re-mix)** *Motown ZB 41943*..............................11 9
17 Sep 88 **INDESTRUCTIBLE** *Arista 111717* [2]..............................55 4
3 Dec 88 ● **LOCO IN ACAPULCO** *Arista 111850*..............................7 13
25 Feb 89 **INDESTRUCTIBLE** *Arista 112074* [2]..............................30 7
19 Nov 66 ● **FOUR TOPS ON TOP** *Tamla Motown TML 11037*..............................9 23
11 Feb 67 ● **FOUR TOPS LIVE!** *Tamla Motown STML 11041*..............................4 72
25 Nov 67 ● **REACH OUT** *Tamla Motown STML 11056*..............................4 34
20 Jan 68 ★ **GREATEST HITS** *Tamla Motown STML 11061*..............................1 67
8 Feb 69 **YESTERDAY'S DREAMS** *Tamla Motown STML 11087*..............................37 1
27 Jun 70 **STILL WATERS RUN DEEP** *Tamla Motown STML 11149*..............................29 8
29 May 71 ● **MAGNIFICENT SEVEN** *Tamla Motown STML 11179* [1]..............................6 11
27 Nov 71 **FOUR TOPS' GREATEST HITS VOLUME 2** *Tamla Motown STML 11195*..............................25 10
10 Nov 73 **THE FOUR TOPS STORY 1964-72** *Tamla Motown TMSP 11241/2*..............................35 5
13 Feb 82 **THE BEST OF THE FOUR TOPS** *K-Tel NE 1160*..............................13 13
8 Dec 90 **THEIR GREATEST HITS** *Telstar STAR 2437*..............................47 6
19 Sep 92 **THE SINGLES COLLECTION** *PolyGram TV 5157102*..............................11 5
30 Mar 02 **AT THEIR VERY BEST – TEMPTATIONS / FOUR TOPS** *Universal TV 5830142*..............................18 1

[1] Supremes and The Four Tops [2] Four Tops featuring Smokey Robinson
[1] Supremes and Four Tops

The original US recording of 'Indestructible' was not issued until after the chart run of the UK-only mix 2002 'At Their Very Best' album appeared only in the UK Compilation Chart and not in the standard Top 75

4TUNE 500

UK, male / female production group (Singles: 1 week) pos/wks

16 Aug 03 **DANCING IN THE DARK** *Black Gold BLGD 04C501*..............................75 1

4 VINI featuring Elisabeth TROY *UK, male vocal / production group and female vocalist (Singles: 1 week)* pos/wks

18 May 02 **FOREVER YOUNG** *Botchit & Scarper BOS 2CD033*..............................75 1

4CLUBBERS

Germany, male production group (Singles: 1 week) pos/wks

14 Sep 02 **CHILDREN** *Code Blue BLU 026CD*..............................45 1

See also FUTURE BREEZE

4MANDU

UK, male vocal group (Singles: 6 weeks) pos/wks

29 Jul 95 **THIS IS IT** *Final Vinyl 74321291222*..............................45 3
17 Feb 96 **DO IT FOR LOVE** *Arista 74321343902*..............................45 2
15 Jun 96 **BABY DON'T GO** *Arista 74321375914*..............................47 1

FOURMOST

UK, male vocal / instrumental group (Singles: 64 weeks) pos/wks

12 Sep 63 ● **HELLO LITTLE GIRL** *Parlophone R 5056*..............................9 17
26 Dec 63 **I'M IN LOVE** *Parlophone R 5078*..............................17 12
23 Apr 64 ● **A LITTLE LOVING** *Parlophone R 5128*..............................6 13
13 Aug 64 **HOW CAN I TELL HER** *Parlophone R 5157*..............................33 4
26 Nov 64 **BABY I NEED YOUR LOVIN'** *Parlophone R 5194*..............................24 12
9 Dec 65 **GIRLS, GIRLS, GIRLS** *Parlophone R 5379*..............................33 6

14-18 *UK, male vocalist – Pete Waterman (Singles: 4 weeks)* pos/wks

1 Nov 75 **GOODBYE-EE** *Magnet MAG 48*..............................33 4

See also STOCK AITKEN WATERMAN

40 THEVZ – *See COOLIO*

Bernard FOWLER – *See BOMB THE BASS*

FOX *UK / US, male / female vocal / instrumental group (Singles: 29 weeks, Albums: 8 weeks)* pos/wks

15 Feb 75 ● **ONLY YOU CAN** *GTO GT 8*..............................3 11
10 May 75 **IMAGINE ME IMAGINE YOU** *GTO GT 21*..............................15 8
10 Apr 76 ● **S-S-S-SINGLE BED** *GTO GT 57*..............................4 10
17 May 75 ● **FOX** *GTO GTLP 001*..............................7 8

Noosha FOX *UK, female vocalist (Singles: 6 weeks)* pos/wks

12 Nov 77 **GEORGINA BAILEY** *GTO GT 106*..............................31 6

See also FOX

Samantha FOX
UK, female vocalist (Singles: 73 weeks, Albums: 18 weeks)

Date		Title / Label	pos	wks
22 Mar 86	●	**TOUCH ME (I WANT YOUR BODY)** *Jive FOXY 1*	3	10
28 Jun 86	●	**DO YA DO YA (WANNA PLEASE ME)** *Jive FOXY 2*	10	7
6 Sep 86		**HOLD ON TIGHT** *Jive FOXY 3*	26	5
13 Dec 86		**I'M ALL YOU NEED** *Jive FOXY 4*	41	6
30 May 87	●	**NOTHING'S GONNA STOP ME NOW** *Jive FOXY 5*	8	9
25 Jul 87		**I SURRENDER (TO THE SPIRIT OF THE NIGHT)** *Jive FOXY 6*	25	7
17 Oct 87		**I PROMISE YOU (GET READY)** *Jive FOXY 7*	58	3
19 Dec 87		**TRUE DEVOTION** *Jive FOXY 8*	62	3
21 May 88		**NAUGHTY GIRLS (NEED LOVE TOO)** *Jive FOXY 9*	31	5
19 Nov 88		**LOVE HOUSE** *Jive FOXY 10*	32	6
28 Jan 89		**I ONLY WANNA BE WITH YOU** *Jive FOXY 11*	16	8
17 Jun 89		**I WANNA HAVE SOME FUN** *Jive FOXY 12*	63	2
28 Mar 98		**SANTA MARIA** *All Around the World CDGLOBE 163* [1]	31	2
26 Jul 86		**TOUCH ME** *Jive HIP 39*	17	10
1 Aug 87		**SAMANTHA FOX** *Jive HIP 48*	22	6
18 Feb 89		**I WANNA HAVE SOME FUN** *Jive HIP 72*	46	2

[1] DJ Milano featuring Samantha Fox

See also SOX

Bruce FOXTON *UK, male vocalist / instrumentalist – bass (Singles: 9 weeks, Albums: 4 weeks)*

Date		Title / Label	pos	wks
30 Jul 83		**FREAK** *Arista BFOX 1*	23	5
29 Oct 83		**THIS IS THE WAY** *Arista BFOX 2*	56	3
21 Apr 84		**IT MAKES ME WONDER** *Arista BFOX 3*	74	1
12 May 84		**TOUCH SENSITIVE** *Arista 206 251*	68	4

See also JAM

Inez FOXX
US, female vocalist (Singles: 8 weeks)

Date		Title / Label	pos	wks
23 Jul 64		**HURT BY LOVE** *Sue WI 323*	40	3
19 Feb 69		**MOCKINGBIRD (re)** *United Artists UP 2269* [1]	33	5

[1] Inez and Charlie Foxx

John FOXX *UK, male vocalist – Dennis Leigh (Singles: 31 weeks, Albums: 17 weeks)*

Date		Title / Label	pos	wks
26 Jan 80		**UNDERPASS** *Virgin VS 318*	31	8
29 Mar 80		**NO-ONE DRIVING (DOUBLE SINGLE)** *Virgin VS 338*	32	4
19 Jul 80		**BURNING CAR** *Virgin VS 360*	35	7
8 Nov 80		**MILES AWAY** *Virgin VS 382*	51	3
29 Aug 81		**EUROPE (AFTER THE RAIN)** *Virgin VS 393*	40	5
2 Jul 83		**ENDLESSLY** *Virgin VS 543*	66	3
17 Sep 83		**YOUR DRESS** *Virgin VS 615*	61	1
2 Feb 80		**METAMATIC** *Metalbeat V 2146*	18	7
3 Oct 81		**THE GARDEN** *Virgin V 2194*	24	6
8 Oct 83		**THE GOLDEN SECTION** *Virgin V 2233*	27	3
5 Oct 85		**IN MYSTERIOUS WAYS** *Virgin V 2355*	85	1

Tracks on double single: No One Driving / Glimmer / This City / Mr No

FRAGGLES *UK / US, puppets from TV series (Singles: 8 weeks, Albums: 4 weeks)*

Date		Title / Label	pos	wks
18 Feb 84		**'FRAGGLE ROCK' THEME** *RCA 389*	33	8
21 Apr 84		**FRAGGLE ROCK** *RCA PL 70221*	38	4

FRAGMA *Germany / Spain, male / female production / vocal group (Singles: 45 weeks, Albums: 12 weeks)*

Date		Title / Label	pos	wks
25 Sep 99		**TOCA ME** *Positiva CDTIV 120*	11	6
22 Apr 00	★	**TOCA'S MIRACLE (re-mix)** *Positiva CDTIV 128* [1] ■	1	17
13 Jan 01	●	**EVERYTIME YOU NEED ME** *Positiva CDTIV 147* [2]	3	11
19 May 01	●	**YOU ARE ALIVE** *Positiva CDTIVS 153*	4	9
8 Dec 01		**SAY THAT YOU'RE HERE** *Illustrious CDILLS 001*	25	2
27 Jan 01		**TOCA** *Positiva 8506770*	19	12

[1] Fragma, vocals by Co Co [2] Fragma featuring Maria Rubia

Roddy FRAME *UK, male vocalist / instrumentalist (Singles: 2 weeks, Albums: 1 week)*

Date		Title / Label	pos	wks
19 Sep 98		**REASON FOR LIVING** *Independiente ISOM 18MS*	45	2
3 Oct 98		**THE NORTH STAR** *Independiente ISOM 7CD*	55	1

See also AZTEC CAMERA

Peter FRAMPTON
UK, male vocalist (Singles: 24 weeks, Albums: 49 weeks)

Date		Title / Label	pos	wks
1 May 76	●	**SHOW ME THE WAY** *A&M AMS 7218*	10	12
11 Sep 76		**BABY I LOVE YOUR WAY** *A&M AMS 7246*	43	5
6 Nov 76		**DO YOU FEEL LIKE WE DO** *A&M AMS 7260*	39	4
23 Jul 77		**I'M IN YOU** *A&M AMS 7298*	41	3
22 May 76	●	**FRAMPTON COMES ALIVE!** *A&M AMLM 63703* ▲	6	39
18 Jun 77		**I'M IN YOU** *A&M AMLK 64039*	19	10

See also HERD; HUMBLE PIE

Connie FRANCIS (217 Top 500) *The original Italian-American queen of pop, b. Concetta Franconero, 12 Dec 1938, New Jersey. The most successful international female vocalist of the 1950s and 1960s, the first female teenager to register a UK No.1 single and the first female solo artist to top the UK album chart (Singles: 244 weeks, Albums: 31 weeks)*

Date		Title / Label	pos	wks
4 Apr 58	★	**WHO'S SORRY NOW** *MGM 975*	1	25
27 Jun 58		**I'M SORRY I MADE YOU CRY** *MGM 982*	11	10
22 Aug 58	★	**CAROLINA MOON / STUPID CUPID** *MGM 985*	1	19
31 Oct 58		**I'LL GET BY** *MGM 993*	19	6
21 Nov 58		**FALLIN'** *MGM 993*	20	5
26 Dec 58		**YOU ALWAYS HURT THE ONE YOU LOVE** *MGM 998*	13	7
13 Feb 59	●	**MY HAPPINESS (re)** *MGM 1001*	4	15
3 Jul 59	●	**LIPSTICK ON YOUR COLLAR** *MGM 1018*	3	16
11 Sep 59		**PLENTY GOOD LOVIN'** *MGM 1036*	18	6
4 Dec 59		**AMONG MY SOUVENIRS** *MGM 1046*	11	10
17 Mar 60		**VALENTINO** *MGM 1060*	27	8
19 May 60	●	**MAMA / ROBOT MAN** *MGM 1076*	2	19
18 Aug 60	●	**EVERYBODY'S SOMEBODY'S FOOL** *MGM 1086* ▲	5	13
3 Nov 60	●	**MY HEART HAS A MIND OF ITS OWN** *MGM 1100* ▲	3	15
12 Jan 61		**MANY TEARS AGO** *MGM 1111*	12	9
16 Mar 61	●	**WHERE THE BOYS ARE / BABY ROO** *MGM 1121*	5	14
15 Jun 61		**BREAKIN' IN A BRAND NEW BROKEN HEART** *MGM 1136*	12	11
14 Sep 61	●	**TOGETHER** *MGM 1138*	6	11
14 Dec 61		**BABY'S FIRST CHRISTMAS** *MGM 1145*	30	4
26 Apr 62		**DON'T BREAK THE HEART THAT LOVES YOU** *MGM 1157* ▲	39	3
2 Aug 62	●	**VACATION** *MGM 1165*	10	9
20 Dec 62		**I'M GONNA BE WARM THIS WINTER** *MGM 1185*	48	1
10 Jun 65		**MY CHILD** *MGM 1271*	26	6
20 Jan 66		**JEALOUS HEART** *MGM 1293*	44	2
26 Mar 60		**ROCK 'N' ROLL MILLION SELLERS** *MGM C 804*	12	1
11 Feb 61		**CONNIE'S GREATEST HITS** *MGM C 831*	16	3
18 Jun 77	★	**20 ALL TIME GREATS** *Polydor 2391 290*	1	22
24 Apr 93		**THE SINGLES COLLECTION** *PolyGram TV 5191312*	12	5

Baby Roo listed with 'Where the Boys Are' for first eight weeks only

Jill FRANCIS *UK, female vocalist (Singles: 1 week)*

Date		Title / Label	pos	wks
3 Jul 93		**MAKE LOVE TO ME** *Glady Wax GW 003CD*	70	1

Claude FRANÇOIS
France, male vocalist, d. 11 Mar 1978 (Singles: 4 weeks)

Date		Title / Label	pos	wks
10 Jan 76		**TEARS ON THE TELEPHONE** *Bradley's BRAD 7528*	35	4

Female vocal: Kathy Barnet

Joe FRANK – *See HAMILTON, Joe FRANK and REYNOLDS*

FRANK AND WALTERS *Ireland, male vocal / instrumental group (Singles: 13 weeks, Albums: 1 week)*

Date		Title / Label	pos	wks
21 Mar 92		**HAPPY BUSMAN** *Setanta HOO 2*	49	2
12 Sep 92		**THIS IS NOT A SONG** *Setanta HOO 3*	46	3
9 Jan 93		**AFTER ALL** *Setanta HOOCD 4*	11	5
17 Apr 93		**FASHION CRISIS HITS NEW YORK** *Setanta HOOCD 5*	42	3
7 Nov 92		**TRAINS BOATS AND PLANES** *Setanta 8283692*	36	1

Review of the Year

MARCH 2003

Lisa Marie Presley who was born on 1 Feb 1969, the same month in which Dad entered the UK singles chart with 'Guitar Man'

US singles sales are lower than at any time since the early 1950s. Ashanti has her first three hit singles simultaneously in the US Top 10 – a feat last achieved by The Beatles in 1964. As Celine Dion signs a $10m deal with Daimler/Chrysler motors, Sony claims her world album sales are now in excess of 155 million. Norah Jones's 'Come Away with Me' is No.1 in both the UK and European album charts with British sales of more than one million. It makes Norah, who completes a whole year at the top of the US jazz chart, only the fourth act to top the UK and US album chart simultaneously with a debut release. The Monkees, Blind Faith and Men at Work had all done it before. Charlotte Church and Josh Groban duet at the closing ceremony of the Winter Olympics. 'Babalon AD (So Glad for the Madness)' by Cradle of Filth becomes the first DVD-only single to enter the UK Top 40. Brenda Lee's autobiography, Little Miss Dynamite – The Life And Times of…, is published. Gareth Gates scores his fourth No.1 in less than 12 months, equalling the feat of Elvis, Madonna and Frank Ifield. Oasis score their 15th consecutive Top 5 single with Liam's 'Songbird'. Australia's most successful folk group The Seekers start their farewell tour and 60-year-old Paul McCartney, enjoying his 60th hit album, plays his first European dates in 10 years as his Back in the World tour gets under way. Smokey Robinson receives one of America's highest honours, the National Medal of Arts, from President Bush at the White House. Lisa Marie Presley's first chart album enters higher Stateside (No.5) than her dad's debut had (No.11). The Dixie Chicks break a record set by the Backstreet Boys when they sell more than $49m worth of tickets (867,000) in one weekend. On a similar theme, Bruce Springsteen overtakes the one-venue ticket record set by The Rolling Stones, when 550,000 tickets (gross $37.8m) are purchased for 10 shows at the Giants Stadium in his home state of New Jersey. New inductees into the Rock and Roll Hall of Fame include AC/DC, The Police, The Clash, The Righteous Brothers and Floyd Cramer. Bob Geldof receives a Lifetime Achievement trophy from the Irish Music Awards. Cat Stevens records his first new pop track in 25 years: the peace song 'Angel of War'. Reborn in the USA premieres on British TV; the eventual winner will be Spandau Ballet's Tony Hadley. Gareth Gates and The Kumars' revival of 'Spirit in the Sky' shifts more than 273,000 copies in its first week and accounts for one third of that week's total sales. Teen sensation Utada Hikaru is named Japan's domestic act of the year with sales of 6.4 million albums. The Japanese also appreciate Avril Lavigne, who, with sales of just below 900,000, is the top English-speaking artist. Chicago walks off with the Best Film Oscar – the first musical to do so since Oliver! back in 1968. Eminem's 'Lose Yourself' is voted Best Original Song; he is the only nominee who does not bother to attend the ceremony. The Top DVDs are now regularly outselling the top CDs in America and Fleetwood Mac's 'Peacekeeper' becomes the first download-only single to make the US Hot 100 chart. Saddest news from the month … Leading 1960s teen idol Adam Faith dies (age 62), as does R&B hitmaker Brandi Wells, Hank Ballard – the inventor of the Twist, Ian Samwell, who penned friend Cliff Richard's first hits including 'Move It', Rusty Draper and acclaimed singer/songwriter Alice Martineau age 31.

Brenda Lee's new biography is the not uncommon but fascinating tale of a poor girl raised in the red-clay backwoods of Georgia and who became a Vegas headliner at age 12 and gets to tour with The Beatles, record with Jimmy Page, sing for the Queen, write with Michael McDonald and became the only female inducted into the Rock and Roll and Country Music Halls of fame

FRANKE *UK, male vocalist – Franke Pharoah (Singles: 3 weeks)* pos/wks

Date		Title	pos	wks
7 Nov 92		**UNDERSTAND THIS GROOVE** *China WOK 2028*	60	2
21 May 94		**LOVE COME HOME** *Triangle BLUESCD 001* [1]	73	1

[1] Our Tribe with Franke Pharoah and Kristine W

FRANK'EE – *See BROTHER BROWN featuring FRANK'EE*

FRANKIE GOES TO HOLLYWOOD 259 Top 500

Fiercely marketed, controversial and regularly re-mixed Merseyside-based quintet fronted by Holly Johnson (b. 19 Feb 1960, Sudan). First act since Gerry and the Pacemakers to hit No.1 with initial three releases. During July 1984, 'Two Tribes' and 'Relax' held top two places in the chart. Total UK single sales were 5,008,067. Best-selling single: 'Relax' 1,910,000 (Singles: 147 weeks, Albums: 95 weeks) pos/wks

Date		Title	pos	wks
26 Nov 83	★	**RELAX (re)** *ZTT ZTAS 1* ◆	1	52
16 Jun 84	★	**TWO TRIBES (re)** *ZTT ZTAS 3* ◆ ■	1	21
1 Dec 84	★	**THE POWER OF LOVE (re)** *ZTT ZTAS 5*	1	12
30 Mar 85	●	**WELCOME TO THE PLEASURE DOME** *ZTT ZTAS 7*	2	11
6 Sep 86	●	**RAGE HARD** *ZTT ZTAS 22*	4	7
22 Nov 86		**WARRIORS (OF THE WASTELAND)** *ZTT ZTAS 25*	19	8
7 Mar 87		**WATCHING THE WILDLIFE** *ZTT ZTAS 26*	28	6
2 Oct 93	●	**RELAX (re-issue)** *ZTT FGTH 1CD*	5	7
20 Nov 93		**WELCOME TO THE PLEASURE DOME (re-mix)** *ZTT FGTH 2CD*	18	3
18 Dec 93	●	**THE POWER OF LOVE (re-issue)** *ZTT FGTH 3CD*	10	7
26 Feb 94		**TWO TRIBES (re-mix)** *ZTT FGTH 4CD*	16	3
1 Jul 00	●	**THE POWER OF LOVE (re-mix)** *ZTT ZTT 150CD*	6	6
9 Sep 00		**TWO TRIBES (re-mix)** *ZTT ZTT 154CD*	17	3
18 Nov 00		**WELCOME TO THE PLEASURE DOME (re-mix)** *ZTT 166CD*	45	1
10 Nov 84	★	**WELCOME TO THE PLEASUREDOME** *ZTT ZTTIQ 1* ■	1	66
1 Nov 86	●	**LIVERPOOL** *ZTT ZTTIQ 8*	5	13
30 Oct 93	●	**BANG! – THE GREATEST HITS OF FRANKIE GOES TO HOLLYWOOD** *ZTT 4509939122*	4	15
7 Oct 00		**MAXIMUM JOY** *ZTT ZTT 165CD*	54	1

Aretha FRANKLIN 229 Top 500

The 'Queen of Soul Music', b. 25 Mar 1942, Tennessee, US. With six decades of recording behind her, this legendary gospel-influenced vocalist has won countless awards and amassed more R&B hits than any other female in her homeland (Singles: 182 weeks, Albums: 85 weeks) pos/wks

Date		Title	pos	wks
8 Jun 67	●	**RESPECT** *Atlantic 584 115* ▲	10	14
23 Aug 67		**BABY I LOVE YOU** *Atlantic 584 127*	39	4
20 Dec 67		**CHAIN OF FOOLS / SATISFACTION (re)** *Atlantic 584 157*	37	7
13 Mar 68		**SINCE YOU'VE BEEN GONE (SWEET SWEET BABY)** *Atlantic 584 172*	47	1
22 May 68		**THINK** *Atlantic 584 186*	26	9
7 Aug 68	●	**I SAY A LITTLE PRAYER** *Atlantic 584 206*	4	14
22 Aug 70		**DON'T PLAY THAT SONG** *Atlantic 2091 027*	13	11
2 Oct 71		**SPANISH HARLEM** *Atlantic 2091 138*	14	9
8 Sep 73		**ANGEL** *Atlantic K 10346*	37	5
16 Feb 74		**UNTIL YOU COME BACK TO ME (THAT'S WHAT I'M GONNA DO)** *Atlantic K 10399*	26	8
6 Dec 80		**WHAT A FOOL BELIEVES** *Arista ARIST 377*	46	7
19 Sep 81		**LOVE ALL THE HURT AWAY** *Arista ARIST 428* [1]	49	3
4 Sep 82		**JUMP TO IT** *Arista ARIST 479*	42	5
23 Jul 83		**GET IT RIGHT** *Arista ARIST 537*	74	2
13 Jul 85		**FREEWAY OF LOVE (re)** *Arista ARIST 624*	51	6
2 Nov 85	●	**SISTERS ARE DOIN' IT FOR THEMSELVES** *RCA PB 40339* [2]	9	11
23 Nov 85		**WHO'S ZOOMIN' WHO** *Arista ARIST 633*	11	14
22 Feb 86		**ANOTHER NIGHT** *Arista ARIST 657*	54	6
25 Oct 86		**JUMPIN' JACK FLASH** *Arista ARIST 678*	58	3
31 Jan 87	★	**I KNEW YOU WERE WAITING (FOR ME)** *Epic DUET 1* [3] ▲	1	9
14 Mar 87		**JIMMY LEE** *Arista RIS 6*	46	4
6 May 89		**THROUGH THE STORM** *Arista 112185* [4]	41	3
9 Sep 89		**IT ISN'T, IT WASN'T, IT AIN'T NEVER GONNA BE** *Arista 112545* [5]	29	5
7 Apr 90		**THINK** *East West A 7951*	31	2
27 Jul 91		**EVERYDAY PEOPLE** *Arista 114420*	69	1
12 Feb 94	●	**A DEEPER LOVE** *Arista 74321187022*	5	7
25 Jun 94		**WILLING TO FORGIVE** *Arista 74321213342*	17	7
9 May 98		**A ROSE IS STILL A ROSE** *Arista 74321569742*	22	4
26 Sep 98		**HERE WE GO AGAIN** *Arista 74321612742*	68	1
12 Aug 67		**I NEVER LOVED A MAN** *Atlantic 587006*	36	2
13 Apr 68		**LADY SOUL** *Atlantic 588099*	25	18
14 Sep 68	●	**ARETHA NOW** *Atlantic 588114*	6	11
18 Jan 86		**WHO'S ZOOMIN' WHO?** *Arista 2072 02*	49	12
24 May 86		**THE FIRST LADY OF SOUL** *Stylus SMR 8506*	89	1
8 Nov 86		**ARETHA** *Arista 208 020*	51	13
3 Jun 89		**THROUGH THE STORM** *Arista 209842*	46	1
19 Mar 94		**GREATEST HITS 1980-1994** *Arista 74321162022*	27	3
29 Oct 94		**QUEEN OF SOUL – THE VERY BEST OF ARETHA FRANKLIN** *Atlantic 8122713962*	20	5
21 Nov 98		**GREATEST HITS** *Global Television RADCD 110*	38	10
15 Jun 02		**RESPECT – THE VERY BEST OF ARETHA FRANKLIN** *BMG TV/WSM 927470542*	15	9

[1] Aretha Franklin and George Benson [2] Eurythmics and Aretha Franklin [3] Aretha Franklin and George Michael [4] Aretha Franklin and Elton John [5] Aretha Franklin and Whitney Houston

'Think' is a re-recording. It was the flip side of 'Everybody Needs Somebody to Love' by Blues Brothers and was listed for the first two weeks of that record's run

Erma FRANKLIN

US, female vocalist d. 7 Sep 2002 (Singles: 10 weeks) pos/wks

Date		Title	pos	wks
10 Oct 92	●	**(TAKE A LITTLE) PIECE OF MY HEART** *Epic 6583847*	9	10

Rodney FRANKLIN *US, male instrumentalist – piano (Singles: 9 weeks, Albums: 2 weeks)* pos/wks

Date		Title	pos	wks
19 Apr 80	●	**THE GROOVE** *CBS 8529*	7	9
24 May 80		**YOU'LL NEVER KNOW** *CBS 83812*	64	2

Chevelle FRANKLYN / BEENIE MAN

Jamaica, female / male vocalists (Singles: 1 week) pos/wks

Date		Title	pos	wks
20 Sep 97		**DANCEHALL QUEEN** *Island Jamaica IJCD 2018*	70	1

FRANTIC FIVE – *See Don LANG*

FRANTIQUE

US, female vocal group (Singles: 12 weeks) pos/wks

Date		Title	pos	wks
11 Aug 79	●	**STRUT YOUR FUNKY STUFF** *Philadelphia Int. PIR 7728*	10	12

FRANZ FERDINAND

UK, male vocal / instrumental group (Singles: 1 week) pos/wks

Date		Title	pos	wks
20 Sep 03		**DARTS OF PLEASURE** *Domino RUG 164CD*	44	1

Elizabeth FRASER – *See COCTEAU TWINS; FUTURE SOUND OF LONDON; Ian McCULLOCH; MASSIVE ATTACK*

Wendy FRASER – *See Patrick SWAYZE featuring Wendy FRASER*

FRASH *UK, male vocal / instrumental group (Singles: 1 week)* pos/wks

Date		Title	pos	wks
18 Feb 95		**HERE I GO AGAIN** *PWL International FLIPCD 1*	69	1

LIZ FRAZER – *See Harold BUDD / Liz FRAZER / Robin GUTHRIE / Susan RAYMONDE*

FRAZIER CHORUS *UK, male / female vocal / instrumental group (Singles: 14 weeks, Albums: 2 weeks)* pos/wks

Date		Title	pos	wks
4 Feb 89		**DREAM KITCHEN** *Virgin VS 1145*	57	3
15 Apr 89		**TYPICAL!** *Virgin VS 1174*	53	2
15 Jul 89		**SLOPPY HEART** *Virgin VS 1192*	73	1
9 Jun 90		**CLOUD 8** *Virgin VS 1252*	52	3
25 Aug 90		**NOTHING** *Virgin VS 1284*	51	3
16 Feb 91		**WALKING ON AIR** *Virgin VS 1330*	60	2
20 May 89		**SUE** *Virgin V 2578*	56	1
16 Mar 91		**RAY** *Virgin VFC 2654*	66	1

FREAK OF NATURE

US / Denmark, male vocal / instrumental group (Albums: 1 week) pos/wks

Date		Title	pos	wks
1 Oct 94		**GATHERING OF FREAKS** *Music for Nations CDMFN 169*	66	1

FREAKY REALISTIC *UK / Japan, male / female vocal / instrumental group (Singles: 3 weeks)* pos/wks

Date		Title	pos	wks
3 Apr 93		**KOOCHIE RYDER** *Frealism FRECD 2*	52	2
3 Jul 93		**LEONARD NIMOY** *Frealism FRECD 3*	71	1

FREAKPOWER *UK / Canada, male vocal / instrumental group (Singles: 20 weeks, Albums: 5 weeks)* pos/wks

Date		Title	pos	wks
16 Oct 93		**TURN ON TUNE IN COP OUT** *Fourth & Broadway BRCD 284* [1]	29	5
26 Feb 94		**RUSH** *Fourth & Broadway BRCD 291*	62	2
18 Mar 95	●	**TURN ON TUNE IN COP OUT (re-issue)** *Fourth & Broadway BRCD 317*	3	9
8 Jun 96		**NEW DIRECTION** *Fourth & Broadway BRCD 331*	60	1
9 May 98		**NO WAY** *Deconstruction 74321578572*	29	3
15 Apr 95		**DRIVE-THRU BOOTY** *Fourth & Broadway BRCDX 606* [1]	11	5

[1] Freak Power [1] Freak Power

See also BEATS INTERNATIONAL; Norman COOK; FATBOY SLIM; HOUSEMARTINS; MIGHTY DUB KATZ; PIZZAMAN

FREAKYMAN *Holland, male producer – Andre Van Den Bosch (Singles: 1 week)* pos/wks

Date		Title	pos	wks
27 Sep 97		**DISCOBUG '97** *Xtravaganza 0091285 EXT*	68	1

Stan FREBERG *US, male vocalist / comedian (Singles: 5 weeks)* pos/wks

Date		Title	pos	wks
19 Nov 54		**SH-BOOM** *Capitol CL 14187* [1]	15	2
27 Jul 56		**ROCK ISLAND LINE / HEARTBREAK HOTEL (re)** *Capitol CL 14608* [2]	24	2
12 May 60		**THE OLD PAYOLA ROLL BLUES** *Capitol CL 15122* [3]	40	1

[1] Stan Freberg with the Toads [2] Stan Freberg and his Sniffle Group [3] Stan Freberg with Jesse White

FRED & ROXY *UK, female vocal duo – Phaedra and Roxanna Aslami (Singles: 2 weeks)* pos/wks

Date		Title	pos	wks
5 Feb 00		**SOMETHING FOR THE WEEKEND** *Echo ECSCD 81*	36	2

John FRED and the PLAYBOY BAND *US, male vocal / instrumental group (Singles: 12 weeks)* pos/wks

Date		Title	pos	wks
3 Jan 68	●	**JUDY IN DISGUISE (WITH GLASSES)** *Pye International 7N 25442* ▲	3	12

FREDDIE and the DREAMERS *UK, male vocal / instrumental group – leader – Freddie Garrity (Singles: 85 weeks, Albums: 26 weeks)* pos/wks

Date		Title	pos	wks
9 May 63	●	**IF YOU GOTTA MAKE A FOOL OF SOMEBODY** *Columbia DB 7032*	3	14
8 Aug 63	●	**I'M TELLING YOU NOW** *Columbia DB 7086* ▲	2	11
7 Nov 63	●	**YOU WERE MADE FOR ME** *Columbia DB 7147*	3	15
20 Feb 64		**OVER YOU** *Columbia DB 7214*	13	11
14 May 64		**I LOVE YOU BABY** *Columbia DB 7286*	16	8
16 Jul 64		**JUST FOR YOU** *Columbia DB 7322*	41	3
5 Nov 64	●	**I UNDERSTAND** *Columbia DB 7381*	5	15
22 Apr 65		**A LITTLE YOU** *Columbia DB 7526*	26	5
4 Nov 65		**THOU SHALT NOT STEAL** *Columbia DB 7720*	44	3
9 Nov 63	●	**FREDDIE AND THE DREAMERS** *Columbia 33SX 1577*	5	26

Dee FREDRIX *UK, female vocalist (Singles: 5 weeks)* pos/wks

Date		Title	pos	wks
27 Feb 93		**AND SO I WILL WAIT FOR YOU** *East West YZ 725CD*	56	4
3 Jul 93		**DIRTY MONEY** *East West YZ 750CD*	74	1

FREE *UK, male vocal / instrumental group (Singles: 75 weeks, Albums: 63 weeks)* pos/wks

Date		Title	pos	wks
6 Jun 70	●	**ALL RIGHT NOW (re)** *Island WIP 6082*	2	25
1 May 71	●	**MY BROTHER JAKE** *Island WIP 6100*	4	11
27 May 72		**LITTLE BIT OF LOVE** *Island WIP 6129*	13	10
13 Jan 73	●	**WISHING WELL** *Island WIP 6146*	7	10
18 Feb 78		**FREE (EP) (re)** *Island IEP 6*	11	10
9 Feb 91	●	**ALL RIGHT NOW (re-mix)** *Island IS 486*	8	9
11 Jul 70	●	**FIRE AND WATER** *Island ILPS 9120*	2	18
23 Jan 71		**HIGHWAY** *Island ILPS 9138*	41	2
26 Jun 71	●	**FREE LIVE!** *Island ILPS 9160*	4	12
17 Jun 72	●	**FREE AT LAST** *Island ILPS 9192*	9	9
3 Feb 73	●	**HEARTBREAKER** *Island ILPS 9217*	9	7
16 Mar 74	●	**THE FREE STORY** *Island ISLD 4*	2	6
2 Mar 91	●	**THE BEST OF FREE – ALL RIGHT NOW** *Island ILPTV 2*	9	9

'All Right Now' re-entry peaked at No.15 in Jul 1973 and the 'Free' (EP) re-entered in Oct 1982 peaking at No.57. Tracks on the 'Free' (EP): All Right Now (long version) / My Brother Jake (re-issue) / Wishing Well (re-issue)

See also BAD COMPANY

FREE – *See Wyclef JEAN; Pras MICHEL; QUEEN; QUEEN LATIFAH*

FREE ASSOCIATION *UK, male / female vocal / instrumental group (Singles: 2 weeks)* pos/wks

Date		Title	pos	wks
12 Apr 03		**EVERYBODY KNOWS** *Ramp RAMP 001CDS*	74	1
13 Sep 03		**SUGARMAN** *13 Amp 9809471*	53	1

FREE SPIRIT *UK, male / female vocal duo (Singles: 1 week)* pos/wks

Date		Title	pos	wks
13 May 95		**NO MORE RAINY DAYS** *Columbia 6612822*	68	1

FREE THE SPIRIT *UK, male instrumental duo – Nick Magnus and Ron Edwards (Albums: 42 weeks)* pos/wks

Date		Title	pos	wks
4 Feb 95	●	**PAN PIPE MOODS** *PolyGram TV 5271972*	2	26
4 Nov 95		**PAN PIPE MOODS TWO** *PolyGram TV 5293952*	18	11
25 May 96		**PAN PIPE MOODS IN PARADISE** *PolyGram TV 5319612*	26	5

FREEEZ *UK, male vocal / instrumental group (Singles: 48 weeks, Albums: 18 weeks)* pos/wks

Date		Title	pos	wks
7 Jun 80		**KEEP IN TOUCH** *Calibre CAB 103*	49	3
7 Feb 81	●	**SOUTHERN FREEEZ** *Beggars Banquet BEG 51* [1]	8	11
18 Apr 81		**FLYING HIGH** *Beggars Banquet BEG 55*	35	5
18 Jun 83	●	**I.O.U.** *Beggars Banquet BEG 96*	2	15
1 Oct 83		**POP GOES MY LOVE** *Beggars Banquet BEG 98*	26	6
17 Jan 87		**I.O.U. (re-mix)** *Citybeat CBE 709* [2]	23	6
30 May 87		**SOUTHERN FREEEZ (re-mix)** *Total Control TOCO 14* [1]	63	2
7 Feb 81		**SOUTHERN FREEEZ** *Beggars Banquet BEGA 22*	17	15
22 Oct 83		**GONNA GET YOU** *Beggars Banquet BEGA 48*	46	3

[1] Freeez featuring Ingrid Mansfield Allman [2] Freeez featuring John Rocca

FREEFALL featuring Jan JOHNSTON *UK / Australia, male DJ / production duo – Alan Bremner and Anthony Pappalardo, and female vocalist (Singles: 5 weeks)* pos/wks

Date		Title	pos	wks
28 Nov 98		**SKYDIVE** *Stress CDSTR 89*	75	1
22 Jul 00		**SKYDIVE (re-mix)** *Renaissance Recordings RENCDS 002*	43	2
8 Sep 01		**SKYDIVE (I FEEL WONDERFUL) (2nd re-mix)** *Incentive CENT 22CDS*	35	2

FREEFALL featuring PSYCHOTROPIC *UK / US, male instrumental / production group (Singles: 1 week)* pos/wks

Date		Title	pos	wks
27 Jul 91		**FEEL SURREAL** *ffrr FX 160*	63	1

FREEHOLD JUNIOR SCHOOL – *See Fogwell FLAX and the ANKLEBITERS from FREEHOLD JUNIOR SCHOOL*

FREELAND *UK / Chile, male / female production / vocal / instrumental group (Singles: 2 weeks)* pos/wks

Date		Title	pos	wks
13 Sep 03		**WE WANT YOUR SOUL** *Maximise Profit FREECDS 01*	35	2

Claire FREELAND *UK, female vocalist (Singles: 1 week)* pos/wks

Date		Title	pos	wks
10 Jul 01		**FREE** *Statuesque CDSTATU 1*	44	1

FREESTYLERS *UK, male instrumental / vocal group (Singles: 5 weeks, Albums: 3 weeks)* pos/wks

Date		Title	pos	wks
7 Feb 98		**B-BOY STANCE** *Freskanova FND 7* [1]	23	3
14 Nov 98		**WARNING** *Freskanova FND 14* [2]	68	1

24 Jul 99 **HERE WE GO** *Freskanova FND 19* 45 1
15 Aug 98 **WE ROCK HARD** *Freskanova FNTCD 4* 33 3

1 Freestylers featuring Tenor Fly 2 Freestylers featuring Navigator

FREHLEY'S COMET
US, male vocal / instrumental group (Albums: 1 week) pos/wks

18 Jun 88 **SECOND SIGHTING** *Atlantic 781862 1* 79 1

See also KISS

FREIHEIT
Germany, male vocal / instrumental group (Singles: 9 weeks) pos/wks

17 Dec 88 **KEEPING THE DREAM ALIVE** *CBS 652989 7* 14 9

Deborah FRENCH – *See E-LUSTRIOUS*

Nicki FRENCH *UK, female vocalist (Singles: 18 weeks)* pos/wks

15 Oct 94 ● **TOTAL ECLIPSE OF THE HEART (re)** *Bags of Fun BAGSCD 1* 5 13
22 Apr 95 **FOR ALL WE KNOW** *Bags of Fun BAGSCD 4* 42 2
15 Jul 95 **DID YOU EVER REALLY LOVE ME** *Love This LUVTHISCD 2* 55 1
27 May 00 **DON'T PLAY THAT SONG AGAIN** *RCA 74321764572* 34 2

'Total Eclipse of the Heart' peaked at No.5 on re-entry in Jan 1995

FRENCH AFFAIR
France, male production duo / female vocalist (Singles: 3 weeks) pos/wks

16 Sep 00 **MY HEART GOES BOOM** *Arista 74321780562* 44 3

Freddy FRESH
US, male producer – Frederick Schmid (Singles: 3 weeks) pos/wks

1 May 99 **BADDER BADDER SCHWING** *Eye Q EYEUK 040CD* 1 ....34 2
31 Jul 99 **WHAT IT IS** *Eye Q EYEUK 043CD* 63 1

1 Freddy Fresh featuring Fatboy Slim

FRESH BC
UK, male production group (Singles: 1 week) pos/wks

25 Oct 03 **SIGNAL / BIG LOVE** *Ram RAMM 46* 58 1

See also BAD COMPANY; DJ FRESH

Doug E FRESH and the GET FRESH CREW
US, male rap / DJ group (Singles: 11 weeks) pos/wks

9 Nov 85 ● **THE SHOW** *Cooltempo COOL 116* 7 11

FRESH 4 featuring Lizz E *UK, male DJ / production group and female vocalist (Singles: 9 weeks)* pos/wks

7 Oct 89 ● **WISHING ON A STAR** *10 TEN 287* 10 9

FRESH PRINCE – *See DJ JAZZY JEFF and The FRESH PRINCE*

FRESHIES *UK, male vocal / instrumental group (Singles: 3 weeks)* pos/wks

14 Feb 81 **I'M IN LOVE WITH THE GIRL ON A CERTAIN MANCHESTER MEGASTORE CHECKOUT DESK** *MCA 670* 54 3

Matt FRETTON *UK, male vocalist (Singles: 5 weeks)* pos/wks

11 Jun 83 **IT'S SO HIGH** *Chrysalis MATT 1* 50 5

FREUR *UK, male vocal / instrumental group (Singles: 4 weeks)* pos/wks

23 Apr 83 **DOOT DOOT** *CBS A 3141* 59 4

Glenn FREY
US, male vocalist (Singles: 20 weeks, Albums: 9 weeks) pos/wks

2 Mar 85 **THE HEAT IS ON** *MCA MCA 941* 12 12
22 Jun 85 **SMUGGLER'S BLUES** *BBC RESL 170* 22 8
6 Jul 85 **THE ALLNIGHTER** *MCA MCF 3277* 31 9

See also EAGLES

FRIDA *Norway, female vocalist – Anni-Frid Lyngstad (Singles: 12 weeks, Albums: 8 weeks)* pos/wks

21 Aug 82 **I KNOW THERE'S SOMETHING GOING ON** *Epic EPC A2603* 43 7
17 Dec 83 **TIME** *Epic A 3983* 1 ....45 5
18 Sep 82 **SOMETHING'S GOING ON** *Epic EPC 85966* 18 7
20 Oct 84 **SHINE** *Epic EPC 26178* 67 1

1 Frida and B A Robertson

See also ABBA

Gavin FRIDAY – *See BONO*

Ralph FRIDGE
Germany, male producer – Ralf Fritsch (Singles: 4 weeks) pos/wks

24 Apr 99 **PARADISE** *Additive 12AD 036* 68 1
8 Apr 00 **ANGEL** *Incentive CENT 6CDS* 20 3

Dean FRIEDMAN
US, male vocalist / instrumentalist – keyboards (Singles: 22 weeks, Albums: 14 weeks) pos/wks

3 Jun 78 **WOMAN OF MINE** *Lifesong LS 401* 52 5
23 Sep 78 ● **LUCKY STARS** *Lifesong LS 402* 3 10
18 Nov 78 **LYDIA** *Lifesong LS 403* 31 7
21 Oct 78 **WELL WELL SAID THE ROCKING CHAIR** *Lifesong LSLP 6019* 21 14

'Lucky Stars' features uncredited vocals by Denise Marsa

FRIENDS AGAIN
UK, male vocal / instrumental group (Singles: 3 weeks) pos/wks

4 Aug 84 **THE FRIENDS AGAIN EP** *Mercury FA 1* 59 3

Tracks on The Friends Again EP: Lullaby on Board / Wand You Wave / Thank You for Being an Angel

FRIENDS OF MATTHEW
UK, male / female vocal / instrumental group (Singles: 1 week) pos/wks

10 Jul 99 **OUT THERE** *Serious SERR 007CD* 61 1

FRIGID VINEGAR
UK, male rap / production duo (Singles: 1 week) pos/wks

21 Aug 99 **DOGMONAUT 2000 (IS THERE ANYONE OUT THERE?)** *Gut CDGUT 27* 53 1

FRIJID PINK
US, male vocal / instrumental group (Singles: 16 weeks) pos/wks

28 Mar 70 ● **THE HOUSE OF THE RISING SUN** *Deram DMR 288* 4 16

Robert FRIPP *UK, male instrumentalist (Albums: 3 weeks)* pos/wks

12 May 79 **EXPOSURE** *Polydor EGLP 101* 71 1
17 Jul 93 **THE FIRST DAY** *Virgin CDVX 2712* 1 ....21 2

1 David Sylvian and Robert Fripp

See also KING CRIMSON

Jane FROMAN
US, female vocalist, d. 22 Apr 1980 (Singles: 4 weeks) pos/wks

17 Jun 55 **I WONDER** *Capitol CL 14254* 14 4

FRONT 242 *Belgium / US, male vocal / instrumental group (Singles: 1 week, Albums: 3 weeks)* pos/wks

1 May 93 **RELIGION** *RRE RRE 106CD* 46 1
2 Feb 91 **TYRANNY FOR YOU** *RRE RRE 011* 49 1
22 May 93 **06:21:03: 11 UP EVIL** *RRE RRE 021CD* 44 1
4 Sep 93 **05:22:09: 12 OFF** *RRE RRE 022CD* 46 1

FROU FROU
UK, male / female production / vocal duo (Singles: 1 week) pos/wks

6 Jul 02 **BREATHE IN** *Island CID 799* 44 1

Christian FRY

UK, male vocalist (Singles: 3 weeks) pos/wks

14 Nov 98 **YOU GOT ME** *Mushroom MUSH 33CDS* 45 2
3 Apr 99 **WON'T YOU SAY** *Mushroom MUSH 46CDS* 48 1

FUGAZI *US, male vocal / instrumental group (Singles: 1 week, Albums: 7 weeks)* pos/wks

20 Oct 01 **FURNITURE** *Dischord DIS 129CD* 61 1
21 Sep 91 **STEADY DIET OF NOTHING** *Dischord DISCHORD 60* 63 1
19 Jun 93 **IN ON THE KILLTAKER** *Dischord DIS 70CD* 24 2
13 May 95 **RED MEDICINE** *Dischord DIS 90CD* 18 2
25 Apr 98 **END HITS** *Dischord DIS 110CD* 47 1
20 Oct 01 **THE ARGUMENT** *Dischord DIS 130CD* 63 1

FUGEES

US / Haiti, male / female vocal / rap / production trio – Lauryn Hill, Wyclef Jean, Pras Michel (Singles: 65 weeks, Albums: 72 weeks) pos/wks

6 Apr 96 **FU-GEE-LA** *Columbia 6630662* 21 5
8 Jun 96 ★ **KILLING ME SOFTLY** *Columbia 6633435* ◆ ■ 1 20
14 Sep 96 ★ **READY OR NOT** *Columbia 6637215* 1 12
30 Nov 96 ● **NO WOMAN, NO CRY** *Columbia 6639925* 2 9
15 Mar 97 ● **RUMBLE IN THE JUNGLE** *Mercury 5740692* 3 8
28 Jun 97 **WE TRYING TO STAY ALIVE** *Columbia 6646815* [1] 13 5
6 Sep 97 **THE SWEETEST THING** *Columbia 6649785* [2] 18 4
27 Sep 97 **GUANTANAMERA** *Columbia 6650852* [1] 25 2
30 Mar 96 ● **THE SCORE** *Columbia 4835492* ▲ 3 70
7 Dec 96 **BOOTLEG VERSIONS** *Columbia 4868242* 55 2

[1] Wyclef Jean and The Refugee Allstars [2] Refugee Camp Allstars featuring Lauryn Hill

FULL CIRCLE

US, male vocal group (Singles: 5 weeks) pos/wks

7 Mar 87 **WORKIN' UP A SWEAT** *EMI America EA 229* 41 5

FULL FORCE

US, male vocal / instrumental group (Singles: 37 weeks) pos/wks

4 May 85 **I WONDER IF I TAKE YOU HOME (re)** *CBS A 6057* [1] 12 17
21 Dec 85 ● **ALICE I WANT YOU JUST FOR ME** *CBS A 6640* 9 11
21 May 88 **NAUGHTY GIRLS (NEED LOVE TOO)** *Jive FOXY 9* 31 5
4 Jun 88 **I'M REAL** *Scotti Brothers JSB 1* [2] 31 4

[1] Lisa Lisa and Cult Jam with Full Force [2] James Brown featuring Full Force

FULL INTENTION

UK, male instrumental / production group (Singles: 8 weeks) pos/wks

6 Apr 96 **AMERICA (I LOVE AMERICA)** *Stress CDSTR 56* 32 2
10 Aug 96 **UPTOWN DOWNTOWN** *Stress CDSTR 67* 61 1
26 Jul 97 **SHAKE YOUR BODY (DOWN TO THE GROUND)** *Sugar Daddy CDSTR 82* 34 2
22 Nov 97 **AMERICA (I LOVE AMERICA) (re-mix)** *Sugar Daddy CDSTRX 56* 56 1
6 Jun 98 **YOU ARE SOMEBODY** *Sugar Daddy CDSD 001* 75 1
1 Sep 01 **I'LL BE WAITING** *Rulin RULIN 17CDS* [1] 44 1

[1] Full Intention presents Shena

See also HUSTLERS CONVENTION featuring Dave LAUDAT and Ondrea DUVERNEY; SEX-O-SONIQUE; SHENA; DISCO TEX presents CLOUDBURST

FULL METAL RACKETS – *See John McENROE and Pat CASH with the FULL METAL RACKETS*

FULL MONTY ALLSTARS featuring TJ DAVIS

UK, male vocal / instrumental group with UK, female vocalist (Singles: 1 week) pos/wks

27 Jul 96 **BRILLIANT FEELING** *Arista 74321380902* 72 1

Bobby FULLER FOUR *US, male vocal / instrumental group, leader d. 18 Jul 1966 (Singles: 4 weeks)* pos/wks

14 Apr 66 **I FOUGHT THE LAW** *London HL 10030* 33 4

FUN BOY THREE *UK, male vocal / instrumental trio – leader Terry Hall (Singles: 70 weeks, Albums: 40 weeks)* pos/wks

7 Nov 81 **THE LUNATICS (HAVE TAKEN OVER THE ASYLUM)** *Chrysalis CHS 2563* 20 12
13 Feb 82 ● **IT AIN'T WHAT YOU DO IT'S THE WAY THAT YOU DO IT** *Chrysalis CHS 2570* [1] 4 10
10 Apr 82 ● **REALLY SAYING SOMETHING** *Deram NANA 1* [2] 5 10
8 May 82 **THE TELEPHONE ALWAYS RINGS** *Chrysalis CHS 2609* 17 9
31 Jul 82 **SUMMERTIME** *Chrysalis CHS 2629* 18 8
15 Jan 83 **THE MORE I SEE (THE LESS I BELIEVE)** *Chrysalis CHS 2664* 68 1
5 Feb 83 ● **TUNNEL OF LOVE** *Chrysalis CHS 2678* 10 10
30 Apr 83 ● **OUR LIPS ARE SEALED** *Chrysalis FUNB 1* 7 10
20 Mar 82 ● **THE FUNBOY THREE** *Chrysalis CHR 1383* 7 20
19 Feb 83 **WAITING** *Chrysalis CHR 1417* 14 20

[1] Fun Boy Three and Bananarama [2] Bananarama with Fun Boy Three

See also COLOUR FIELD; SPECIALS; VEGAS

FUN DA MENTAL

UK, male rap group (Albums: 1 week) pos/wks

25 Jun 94 **SEIZE THE TIME** *Nation NATCD 33* 74 1

FUN LOVIN' CRIMINALS (456 Top 500)

Hip-hop and funk-blending trio formed New York City 1993: Huey Morgan (v/g), Brian 'Fast' Leiser (b/k) and Steve Borgovini (d). The act, whose catalogue includes the Pulp Fiction sampling 'Scooby Snacks' and Barry White tribute 'Love Unlimited', is more popular in UK than in the US (Singles: 32 weeks, Albums: 120 weeks) pos/wks

8 Jun 96 **THE GRAVE AND THE CONSTANT** *Chrysalis CDCHS 5031* 72 1
17 Aug 96 **SCOOBY SNACKS** *Chrysalis CDCHS 5034* 22 3
16 Nov 96 **THE FUN LOVIN' CRIMINAL** *Chrysalis CDCHS 5040* 26 3
29 Mar 97 **KING OF NEW YORK** *Chrysalis CDCHS 5049* 28 3
5 Jul 97 **I'M NOT IN LOVE / SCOOBY SNACKS** *Chrysalis CDCHS 5060* 12 5
15 Aug 98 **LOVE UNLIMITED** *Chrysalis CDCHS 5096* 18 4
17 Oct 98 **BIG NIGHT OUT** *Chrysalis CDCHSS 5101* 29 2
8 May 99 **KOREAN BODEGA** *Chrysalis CDCHS 5108* 15 3
17 Feb 01 ● **LOCO** *Chrysalis CDCHSS 5121* 5 6
1 Sep 01 **BUMP / RUN DADDY RUN** *Chrysalis CDCHSS 5128* 50 1
13 Sep 03 **TOO HOT** *Sanctuary SANXD 205* 61 1
13 Jul 96 ● **COME FIND YOURSELF** *Chrysalis CDCHR 6113* 7 71
5 Sep 98 ● **100% COLOMBIAN** *Chrysalis 4970562* 3 26
11 Dec 99 **MIMOSA** *Chrysalis 5234592* 37 9
10 Mar 01 ● **LOCO** *Chrysalis 5314712* 5 6
3 Aug 02 **BAG OF HITS – 15 INTERGLOBAL CHARTSTOPPERS** *Chrysalis 5399542* 11 6
20 Sep 03 **WELCOME TO POPPY'S** *Sanctuary SANCD187* 20 2

FUNERAL FOR A FRIEND *UK, male vocal / instrumental group (Singles: 5 weeks, Albums: 3 weeks)* pos/wks

9 Aug 03 **JUNEAU** *Infectious EW 269CD1* 19 3
18 Oct 03 **SHE DROVE ME TO DAYTIME TELEVISION** *Infectious / East West EW 274CD1* 20 2
25 Oct 03 **CASUALLY DRESSED AND DEEP IN CONVERSATION** *Infectious 2564609472* 12 3

Farley 'Jackmaster' FUNK

US, male producer – Farley Williams (Singles: 16 weeks) pos/wks

23 Aug 86 ● **LOVE CAN'T TURN AROUND** *DJ International LON 105* 10 12
11 Feb 89 **AS ALWAYS** *Champion CHAMP 90* [1] 49 2
14 Dec 96 **LOVE CAN'T TURN AROUND** *4 Liberty LIBTCD 27* [2] 40 2

[1] Farley 'Jackmaster' Funk presents Ricky Dillard [2] Farley 'Jackmaster' Funk with Darryl Pandy

'Love Can't Turn Around' in 1996 is a re-recording

FUNK D'VOID

Sweden, male producer – Lars Sandberg (Singles: 1 week) pos/wks

20 Oct 01 **DIABLA** *Soma SOMA 112* 70 1

FUNK JUNKEEZ

US, male DJ / producer – Roger Sanchez (Singles: 1 week) pos/wks

Date	Title	pos	wks
21 Feb 98	**GOT FUNK** *Evocative EVOKE 1CDS*	57	1

See also EL MARIACHI; Roger SANCHEZ

FUNK MASTERS

UK, male / female vocal / instrumental group (Singles: 12 weeks) pos/wks

Date	Title	pos	wks
18 Jun 83 ●	**IT'S OVER** *Master Funk Records 7MP 004*	8	12

Features Gonzales on horns and uncredited vocals by Juliet Roberts

FUNKADELIC

US, male vocal / instrumental group – leader George Clinton (Singles: 13 weeks, Albums: 5 weeks) pos/wks

Date	Title	pos	wks
9 Dec 78 ●	**ONE NATION UNDER A GROOVE (PART 1)** *Warner Bros. K 17246*	9	12
21 Aug 99	**MOTHERSHIP RECONNECTION** *Virgin DINSD 185* [1]	55	1
23 Dec 78	**ONE NATION UNDER A GROOVE** *Warner Bros. K 56539*	56	5

[1] Scott Grooves featuring Parliament / Funkadelic

FUNKAPOLITAN

UK, male vocal / instrumental group (Singles: 7 weeks) pos/wks

Date	Title	pos	wks
22 Aug 81	**AS TIME GOES BY** *London LON 001*	41	7

FUNKDOOBIEST

US, male rap group (Singles: 6 weeks, Albums: 1 week) pos/wks

Date	Title	pos	wks
11 Dec 93	**WOPBABALUBOP** *Immortal 6597112*	37	4
5 Mar 94	**BOW WOW WOW** *Immortal 6594052*	34	2
15 Jul 95	**BROTHAS DOOBIE** *Epic 4783812*	62	1

FUNKSTAR DE LUXE

Denmark, male producer / instrumentalist – Matt Ottesen (Singles: 18 weeks) pos/wks

Date	Title	pos	wks
25 Sep 99 ●	**SUN IS SHINING** *Club Tools / Edel 0066895 CLU* [1]	3	10
22 Jan 00	**RAINBOW COUNTRY** *Club Tools 0067225CLU* [1]	11	6
13 May 00	**WALKIN IN THE NAME** *Club Tools 0067375 CLU* [2]	42	1
25 Nov 00	**PULL UP TO THE BUMPER** *Club Tools 0120375 CLU* [3]	60	1

[1] Bob Marley vs Funkstar De Luxe [2] Funkstar De Luxe vs Terry Maxx [3] Grace Jones vs Funkstar De Luxe

FUNKY BOYS – *See Linda CARR*

FUNKY BUNCH – *See MARKY MARK and the FUNKY BUNCH*

FUNKY CHOAD featuring Nick SKITZ

Australia / Italy, male production duo and Australia, male vocalist (Singles: 1 week) pos/wks

Date	Title	pos	wks
29 Aug 98	**THE ULTIMATE** *ffrr FCD 341*	51	1

FUNKY GREEN DOGS

US, male / female vocal / production group (Singles: 6 weeks) pos/wks

Date	Title	pos	wks
12 Apr 97	**FIRED UP!** *Twisted UK TWCD 10016*	17	3
28 Jun 97	**THE WAY** *Twisted UK TWCD 10026*	43	1
20 Jun 98	**UNTIL THE DAY** *Twisted UK TWCD 10034*	75	1
27 Feb 99	**BODY** *Twisted UK TWCD 110041*	46	1

See also FOG

FUNKY JUNCTION – *See KC FLIGHTT*

FUNKY POETS

US, male vocal group (Singles: 1 week) pos/wks

Date	Title	pos	wks
7 May 94	**BORN IN THE GHETTO** *Epic 6603522*	72	1

FUNKY WORM

UK, male / female vocal / instrumental group (Singles: 14 weeks) pos/wks

Date	Title	pos	wks
30 Jul 88	**HUSTLE! (TO THE MUSIC . . .)** *Fon FON 15*	13	8
26 Nov 88	**THE SPELL!** *Fon FON 16*	61	3
20 May 89	**U + ME = LOVE** *Fon FON 19*	46	3

FUREYS with Davey ARTHUR

Ireland, male vocal duo – Finbar and Eddie Fury, and UK, male vocalist (Singles: 14 weeks, Albums: 38 weeks) pos/wks

Date	Title	pos	wks
10 Oct 81	**WHEN YOU WERE SWEET SIXTEEN** *Ritz RITZ 003*	14	11
3 Apr 82	**I WILL LOVE YOU (EV'RY TIME WHEN WE ARE GONE)** *Ritz RITZ 012* [1]	54	3
8 May 82	**WHEN YOU WERE SWEET SIXTEEN** *Ritz RITZLP 0004*	99	1
10 Nov 84	**GOLDEN DAYS** *K-Tel ONE 1283*	17	19
26 Oct 85	**AT THE END OF THE DAY** *K-Tel ONE 1310*	35	11
21 Nov 87	**FUREYS FINEST** *Telstar HSTAR 2311*	65	7

[1] The Fureys

FURIOUS FIVE – *See GRANDMASTER FLASH and the FURIOUS FIVE*

FURNITURE

UK, male / female vocal / instrumental group (Singles: 10 weeks) pos/wks

Date	Title	pos	wks
14 Jun 86	**BRILLIANT MIND** *Stiff BUY 251*	21	10

Nelly FURTADO

Canada, female vocalist (Singles: 34 weeks, Albums: 48 weeks) pos/wks

Date	Title	pos	wks
10 Mar 01 ●	**I'M LIKE A BIRD** *Dreamworks 4509192*	5	16
1 Sep 01 ●	**TURN OFF THE LIGHT** *Dreamworks DRMDM 50891*	4	10
19 Jan 02	**...ON THE RADIO (REMEMBER THE DAYS)** *Dreamworks DRMDM 50856*	18	6
20 Dec 03	**POWERLESS (SAY WHAT YOU WANT)** *Dreamworks 4504645*	13	2+
24 Mar 01 ●	**WHOA NELLY!** *Dreamworks 4502852*	3	47
6 Dec 03	**FOLKLORE** *Dreamworks / Polydor 4505089*	62	1

Billy FURY (162 Top 500)

Early British rock 'n' roll star, b. Ronald Wycherley, 17 Apr 1940, Liverpool, d. 28 Jan 1983. First talent-spotted and 'Christened' Billy Fury by impresario Larry Parnes at a gig in Liverpool where he is remembered by a statue unveiled in his hometown in 2003. He appeared in the 1965 film 'I've Gotta Horse' and in 1982 starred in 'That'll Be the Day'. Fury has equalled The Beatles' record of 24 hits in the 1960s, and spent his 281 weeks on chart without ever bagging a chart-topping single or album (Singles: 281 weeks, Albums: 51 weeks) pos/wks

Date	Title	pos	wks
27 Feb 59	**MAYBE TOMORROW (re)** *Decca F 11102*	18	9
26 Jun 59	**MARGO** *Decca F 11128*	28	1
10 Mar 60 ●	**COLETTE** *Decca F 11200*	9	10
26 May 60	**THAT'S LOVE** *Decca F 11237* [1]	19	11
22 Sep 60	**WONDROUS PLACE** *Decca F 11267*	25	9
19 Jan 61	**A THOUSAND STARS** *Decca F 11311*	14	10
27 Apr 61	**DON'T WORRY** *Decca F 11334* [2]	40	2
11 May 61 ●	**HALFWAY TO PARADISE** *Decca F 11349*	3	23
7 Sep 61 ●	**JEALOUSY** *Decca F 11384*	2	12
14 Dec 61 ●	**I'D NEVER FIND ANOTHER YOU** *Decca F 11409*	5	15
15 Mar 62	**LETTER FULL OF TEARS** *Decca F 11437*	32	6
3 May 62 ●	**LAST NIGHT WAS MADE FOR LOVE** *Decca F 11458*	4	16
19 Jul 62 ●	**ONCE UPON A DREAM** *Decca F 11485*	7	13
25 Oct 62	**BECAUSE OF LOVE** *Decca F 11508*	18	14
14 Feb 63 ●	**LIKE I'VE NEVER BEEN GONE** *Decca F11582*	3	15
16 May 63 ●	**WHEN WILL YOU SAY I LOVE YOU** *Decca F 11655*	3	12
25 Jul 63 ●	**IN SUMMER** *Decca F 11701*	5	11
3 Oct 63	**SOMEBODY ELSE'S GIRL** *Decca F 11744*	18	7
2 Jan 64	**DO YOU REALLY LOVE ME TOO? (FOOLS ERRAND)** *Decca F 11792*	13	10
30 Apr 64	**I WILL** *Decca F 11888*	14	12
23 Jul 64 ●	**IT'S ONLY MAKE BELIEVE** *Decca F 11939*	10	10
14 Jan 65	**I'M LOST WITHOUT YOU** *Decca F 12048*	16	10
22 Jul 65 ●	**IN THOUGHTS OF YOU** *Decca F 12178*	9	11
16 Sep 65	**RUN TO MY LOVIN' ARMS** *Decca F 12230*	25	7
10 Feb 66	**I'LL NEVER QUITE GET OVER YOU** *Decca F 12325*	35	5
4 Aug 66	**GIVE ME YOUR WORD** *Decca F 12459*	27	7
4 Sep 82	**LOVE OR MONEY** *Polydor POSP 488*	57	5
13 Nov 82	**DEVIL OR ANGEL** *Polydor POSP 528*	58	4
4 Jun 83	**FORGET HIM** *Polydor POSP 558*	59	4
4 Jun 60	**THE SOUND OF FURY** *Decca LF 1329*	18	2
23 Sep 61 ●	**HALFWAY TO PARADISE** *Ace Of Clubs ACL 1083*	5	9
11 May 63 ●	**BILLY** *Decca LK 4533*	6	21

26 Oct 63	**WE WANT BILLY** *Decca LK 4548*	14 2
19 Feb 83	**THE BILLY FURY HIT PARADE** *Decca TAB 37*	44 15
26 Mar 83	**THE ONE AND ONLY BILLY FURY** *Polydor POLD 5069*	54 2

1 Billy Fury with The Four Jays 2 Billy Fury with The Four Kestrels

FUSE *Canada male instrumentalist – keyboards – Richie Hawtin (Albums: 1 week)*

		pos/wks
19 Jun 93	**DIMENSION INTRUSION** *Warp WARPCD 12*	63 1

See also PLASTIK MAN

FUSED *Sweden, male instrumental / production duo and female vocalist (Singles: 1 week)*

		pos/wks
20 Mar 99	**THIS PARTY SUCKS!** *Columbia 6669302*	64 1

FUTURE BREEZE *Germany, male production duo – Markus Boehme and Martin Hensing (Singles: 11 weeks)*

		pos/wks
6 Sep 97	**WHY DON'T YOU DANCE WITH ME** *AM:PM 5823312*	50 1
20 Jan 01	**SMILE** *Nebula NEBCD 014*	67 1
13 Apr 02	**TEMPLE OF DREAMS** *Ministry of Sound / DATA 31 CDS*	21 6
28 Dec 02	**OCEAN OF ETERNITY** *Ministry of Sound / DATA 44 CDS*	46 3

See also 4CLUBBERS

FUTURE FORCE *UK / US, male / female vocal / instrumental duo (Singles: 1 week)*

		pos/wks
17 Aug 96	**WHAT YOU WANT** *AM:PM 5816592*	47 1

FUTURE SOUND OF LONDON *UK, male instrumental / production duo – Brian Dougans and Gary Cobain (Singles: 25 weeks, Albums: 10 weeks)*

		pos/wks
23 May 92	**PAPUA NEW GUINEA** *Jumpin' & Pumpin' TOT 17*	22 6
6 Nov 93	**CASCADE** *Virgin VSCDT 1478*	27 3
30 Jul 94	**EXPANDER** *Jumpin' & Pumpin' CDSTOT 37*	72 1
13 Aug 94	**LIFEFORMS** *Virgin VSCDT 1484* 1	14 3
27 May 95	**FAR-OUT SON OF LUNG AND THE RAMBLINGS OF A MADMAN** *Virgin VSCDT 1540*	22 3
26 Oct 96	**MY KINGDOM** *Virgin VSCDT 1605*	13 3
12 Apr 97	**WE HAVE EXPLOSIVE** *Virgin VSCDX 1616*	12 3
29 Sep 01	**PAPUA NEW GUINEA 2001 (re-mix)** *Jumpin' & Pumpin' CDSTOT 44*	28 3
18 Jul 92	**ACCELERATOR** *Jumpin' & Pumpin' CDTOT 2*	75 1
4 Jun 94 ●	**LIFEFORMS** *Virgin CDV 2722*	6 5
17 Dec 94	**ISDN** *Virgin CDV 2755*	62 1
17 Jun 95	**ISDN (REMIX)** *Virgin CDVX 2755*	44 1
9 Nov 96	**DEAD CITIES** *Virgin CDVX 2814*	26 2

1 F.S.O.L. vocals by Elizabeth Fraser

See also HUMANOID; AMORPHOUS ANDROGYNOUS

The FUTUREHEADS *UK, male vocal / instrumental group (Singles: 1 week)*

		pos/wks
9 Aug 03	**FIRST DAY** *Fantastic Plastic FPS 036*	58 1

FUTURESHOCK *UK, male production duo and male vocalist (Singles: 3 weeks)*

		pos/wks
15 Mar 03	**ON MY MIND** *Junior / Parlophone CDR 6595* 1	51 1
16 Aug 03	**PRIDE'S PARANOIA** *Junior / Parlophone CDR 6616*	60 1
1 Nov 03	**LATE AT NIGHT** *Parlophone CDR 6617*	73 1

1 Futureshock featuring Ben Onono

FUZZBOX – *See WE'VE GOT A FUZZBOX AND WE'RE GONNA USE IT*

Leslie FYSON – *See Michael MEDWIN, Bernard BRESSLAW, Alfie BASS and Leslie FYSON*

Ali G and SHAGGY *UK, male comedian / rapper – Sacha Baron Cohen and Jamaica, male vocalist – Orville Burrell (Singles: 14 weeks)*

		pos/wks
23 Mar 02 ●	**ME JULIE** *Island CID 793*	2 14

Bobby G *UK, male vocalist (Singles: 12 weeks)*

		pos/wks
1 Dec 84	**BIG DEAL (2re)** *BBC RESL 151*	46 12

See also BUCKS FIZZ

Dennis G – *See WIDEBOYS featuring Dennis G*

Gina G *Australia, female vocalist – Gina Gardiner (Singles: 51 weeks, Albums: 4 weeks)*

		pos/wks
6 Apr 96 ★	**OOH AAH ... JUST A LITTLE BIT (2re)** *Eternal WEA 041CD*	1 25
9 Nov 96 ●	**I BELONG TO YOU** *Eternal WEA 081CD*	6 11
22 Mar 97 ●	**FRESH!** *Eternal WEA 095CD*	6 7
7 Jun 97	**TI AMO** *Eternal WEA 107CD1*	11 5
6 Sep 97	**GIMME SOME LOVE** *Eternal WEA 101CD1*	25 2
15 Nov 97	**EVERY TIME I FALL** *Eternal WEA 134CD*	52 1
5 Apr 97	**FRESH!** *Eternal 630178402*	12 4

Hurricane G – *See PUFF DADDY*

Kenny G *US, male instrumentalist – saxophone – Kenny Gorelick (Singles: 26 weeks, Albums: 58 weeks)*

		pos/wks
21 Apr 84	**HI! HOW YA DOIN'?** *Arista ARIST 561*	70 3
30 Aug 86	**WHAT DOES IT TAKE (TO WIN YOUR LOVE)** *Arista ARIST 672*	64 2
4 Jul 87	**SONGBIRD** *Arista RIS 18*	22 7
9 May 92	**MISSING YOU NOW** *Columbia 6579917* 1	28 4
24 Apr 93	**FOREVER IN LOVE** *Arista 74321145552*	47 3
17 Jul 93	**BY THE TIME THIS NIGHT IS OVER** *Arista 74321157142* 2	56 3
8 Nov 97	**HOW COULD AN ANGEL BREAK MY HEART** *LaFace 74321531982* 3	22 4
17 Mar 84	**G FORCE** *Arista 206 168*	56 5
8 Aug 87	**DUOTONES** *Arista 207 792*	28 5
14 Apr 90	**MONTAGE** *Arista 210621*	32 7
15 May 93 ●	**BREATHLESS** *Arista 07822186462*	4 27
19 Oct 96	**THE MOMENT** *Arista 7822189352*	19 9
13 Dec 97	**GREATEST HITS** *Arista 7822189912*	38 5

1 Michael Bolton featuring Kenny G 2 Kenny G with Peabo Bryson 3 Toni Braxton with Kenny G

Warren G *US, male rapper – Warren Griffin (Singles: 60 weeks, Albums: 10 weeks)* pos/wks

23 Jul 94 ● **REGULATE** *Death Row A 8290CD* [1] 5 14
12 Nov 94 **THIS DJ (re)** *RAL RALCD 1* 12 7
25 Mar 95 **DO YOU SEE** *RAL RALCD 3* 29 2
23 Nov 96 ● **WHAT'S LOVE GOT TO DO WITH IT** *Interscope IND 97008* [2] 2 12
22 Feb 97 ● **I SHOT THE SHERIFF** *Mercury DEFCD 31* 2 8
31 May 97 **SMOKIN' ME OUT** *Def Jam 5744432* [3] 14 5
10 Jan 98 **PRINCE IGOR** *Def Jam 5749652* [4] 15 7
24 Jan 98 **ALL NIGHT ALL RIGHT** *Mushroom MUSH 21CD* [5] 16 4
16 Mar 02 **LOOKIN' AT YOU** *Universal MCSTD 40275* [6] 60 1
6 Aug 94 **REGULATE ... G FUNK ERA** *RAL 5233352* 25 6
8 Mar 97 **TAKE A LOOK OVER YOUR SHOULDER (REALITY)** *Def Jam 5334842* 20 4

[1] Warren G and Nate Dogg [2] Warren G featuring Adina Howard [3] Warren G featuring Ron Isley [4] Warren G featuring Sissel [5] Peter Andre featuring Warren G [6] Warren G featuring Toi

Andy G's STARSKY & HUTCH ALL STARS *UK, male producer (Singles: 1 week)* pos/wks

3 Oct 98 **STARSKY & HUTCH – THE THEME** *Virgin VSCDT 1708* 51 1

GBH *UK, male vocal / instrumental group (Singles: 5 weeks)* pos/wks

6 Feb 82 **NO SURVIVORS** *Clay CLAY 8* 63 2
20 Nov 82 **GIVE ME FIRE** *Clay CLAY 16* 69 3

G-CLEFS *US, male vocal group (Singles: 12 weeks)* pos/wks

30 Nov 61 **I UNDERSTAND** *London HLU 9433* 17 12

G CLUB presents BANDA SONORA *UK, male producer – Gerald Elms (Singles: 1 week)* pos/wks

19 Oct 02 **PRESSURE COOKER** *Defected DFTD 060CDS* 46 1

G NATION featuring ROSIE *UK, male production duo – Jake Moses and Mark Smith – and UK, female vocalist (Singles: 1 week)* pos/wks

9 Aug 97 **FEEL THE NEED** *Cooltempo CDCOOL 327* 58 1

G.O.S.H. *UK, male / female charity ensemble (Singles: 11 weeks)* pos/wks

28 Nov 87 **THE WISHING WELL** *MBS GOSH 1* 22 11

G.Q. *US, male vocal / instrumental group (Singles: 6 weeks)* pos/wks

10 Mar 79 **DISCO NIGHTS – (ROCK FREAK)** *Arista ARIST 245* 42 6

GSP *UK, male instrumental / production duo – Ian Gallivan and Justin Stride (Singles: 3 weeks)* pos/wks

3 Oct 92 **THE BANANA SONG** *Yoyo YOYO 1* 37 3

GTO *UK, male / female instrumental / production duo – Lee Newman and Michael Wells (Singles: 7 weeks)* pos/wks

4 Aug 90 **PURE** *Cooltempo COOL 218* 57 3
7 Sep 91 **LISTEN TO THE RHYTHM FLOW / BULLFROG** *React REACT 7001* 72 2
2 May 92 **ELEVATION** *React REACT 4* 59 2

See also TECHNOHEAD; TRICKY DISCO

GTR *UK, male vocal / instrumental group (Albums: 4 weeks)* pos/wks

19 Jul 86 **GTR** *Arista 207 716* 41 4

See also Steve HACKETT; Steve HOWE

G TOM MAC – *See LOST BROTHERS featuring G TOM MAC*

G-UNIT *US, male rap trio – leader – 50 Cent (Singles: 1 week, Albums: 5 weeks)* pos/wks

27 Dec 03 **STUNT 101** *Interscope 9815335* ....29 1+
29 Nov 03 **BEG FOR MERCY** *Interscope / Polydor 9861498* ....13 5+

Eric GABLE *US, male vocalist (Singles: 1 week)* pos/wks

19 Mar 94 **PROCESS OF ELIMINATION** *Epic 6602282* 63 1

Peter GABRIEL (164 Top 500)

Award-winning singer / songwriter, b. 13 Feb 1950, Surrey, UK. Fronted Genesis until 1975, when replaced by Phil Collins. He broke through internationally with 'Sledgehammer', which also made him a video innovator. He is the driving force behind the Womad festival and is a tireless Amnesty International supporter (Singles: 114 weeks, Albums: 215 weeks) pos/wks

9 Apr 77 **SOLSBURY HILL** *Charisma CB 301* 13 9
9 Feb 80 ● **GAMES WITHOUT FRONTIERS** *Charisma CB 354* 4 11
10 May 80 **NO SELF CONTROL** *Charisma CB 360* 33 6
23 Aug 80 **BIKO** *Charisma CB 370* 38 3
25 Sep 82 **SHOCK THE MONKEY** *Charisma SHOCK 1* 58 5
9 Jul 83 **I DON'T REMEMBER** *Charisma GAB 1* 62 3
2 Jun 84 **WALK THROUGH THE FIRE** *Virgin VS 689* 69 3
26 Apr 86 ● **SLEDGEHAMMER** *Virgin PGS 1* ▲ 4 16
1 Nov 86 ● **DON'T GIVE UP** *Virgin PGS 2* [1] 9 11
28 Mar 87 **BIG TIME** *Charisma PGS 3* 13 7
11 Jul 87 **RED RAIN** *Charisma PGS 4* 46 3
21 Nov 87 **BIKO (LIVE)** *Charisma PGS 6* 49 6
3 Jun 89 **SHAKIN' THE TREE** *Virgin VS 1167* [2] 61 3
22 Dec 90 **SOLSBURY HILL / SHAKING THE TREE (re-issue)** *Virgin VS 1322* [3] 57 4
19 Sep 92 **DIGGING IN THE DIRT** *Realworld PGS 7* 24 4
16 Jan 93 ● **STEAM** *Realworld PGSDG 8* 10 7
3 Apr 93 **BLOOD OF EDEN** *Realworld PGSDG 9* 43 4
25 Sep 93 **KISS THAT FROG** *Realworld PGSDG 10* 46 3
25 Jun 94 **LOVETOWN** *Epic 6604802* 49 2
3 Sep 94 **SW LIVE (EP)** *Realworld PGSCD 11* 39 2
11 Jan 03 **MORE THAN THIS** *Realworld PGSCD 14* 47 2
12 Mar 77 ● **PETER GABRIEL** *Charisma CDS 4006* 7 19
17 Jun 78 ● **PETER GABRIEL** *Charisma CDS 4013* 10 8
7 Jun 80 ★ **PETER GABRIEL** *Charisma CDS 4019* 1 18
18 Sep 82 ● **PETER GABRIEL** *Charisma PG 4* 6 16
18 Jun 83 ● **PETER GABRIEL PLAYS LIVE** *Charisma PGDL 1* 8 9
30 Apr 85 **BIRDY (FILM SOUNDTRACK)** *Charisma CAS 1167* 51 3
31 May 86 ★ **SO** *Virgin PG 5* ■ 1 76
17 Jun 89 **PASSION** *Virgin RWLP 1* 29 5
1 Dec 90 **SHAKING THE TREE – 16 GOLDEN GREATS** *Virgin PGTV 6* 11 18
10 Oct 92 ● **US** *Realworld PGCD 7* 2 29
10 Sep 94 ● **SECRET WORLD LIVE** *Realworld PGDCD 8* 10 4
24 Jun 00 **OVO** *Realworld PGCD 9* 24 2
5 Oct 02 **UP** *Realworld PGCD 11* 11 4
15 Nov 03 **HIT** *Realworld 5952372* 29 4

[1] Peter Gabriel and Kate Bush [2] Youssou N'Dour and Peter Gabriel [3] Peter Gabriel / Youssou N'Dour and Peter Gabriel

Tracks available on all formats of SW Live (EP): Red Rain / San Jacinto. First four albums are different

GABRIELLE (180 Top 500)

Eyepatch-wearing soul / pop vocalist, born Louisa Gabrielle Bobb, 16 May 1970, London, UK. Broke record for highest chart debut when 'Dreams' entered at No.2. Voted Best British Newcomer at 1994 Brit Awards and Best British Female Vocalist in 1997. Best-selling single: 'Dreams' 513,200 (Singles: 144 weeks, Albums: 165 weeks) pos/wks

19 Jun 93 ★ **DREAMS** *Go.Beat GODCD 99* 1 15
2 Oct 93 ● **GOING NOWHERE** *Go.Beat GODCD 106* 9 7
11 Dec 93 **I WISH** *Go.Beat GODCD 108* 26 5
26 Feb 94 **BECAUSE OF YOU** *Go.Beat GODCD 109* 24 5
24 Feb 96 ● **GIVE ME A LITTLE MORE TIME** *Go.Beat GODCD 139* 5 18
22 Jun 96 **FORGET ABOUT THE WORLD** *Go.Beat GODCD 146* 23 5
5 Oct 96 **IF YOU REALLY CARED** *Go.Beat GODCD 153* 15 5
2 Nov 96 ● **IF YOU EVER** *London LONCD 388* [1] 2 15
1 Feb 97 ● **WALK ON BY** *Go.Beat GODCD 159* 7 8
9 Oct 99 ● **SUNSHINE** *Go.Beat GOBCD 23* 9 8
5 Feb 00 ★ **RISE** *Go.Beat / Polydor GOBCD 25* ■ 1 15
17 Jun 00 ● **WHEN A WOMAN** *Go.Beat / Polydor GOBCD 27* 6 8
4 Nov 00 **SHOULD I STAY** *Go.Beat / Polydor GOBCD 32* 13 7
21 Apr 01 ● **OUT OF REACH** *Go.Beat / Polydor GOLCD 39* 4 16

3 Nov 01 ● **DON'T NEED THE SUN TO SHINE (TO MAKE ME SMILE)** *Go.Beat / Polydor GOBCD 47* 9 7
30 Oct 93 ● **FIND YOUR WAY** *Go! Beat 8284412*....9 22
8 Jun 96 **GABRIELLE** *Go! Beat 8287242*....11 30
30 Oct 99 ★ **RISE** *Go! Beat 5477682*....1 87
24 Nov 01 ● **DREAMS CAN COME TRUE – GREATEST HITS VOL. 1** *Go! Beat 5893742*....2 26

[1] East 17 featuring Gabrielle

Yvonne GAGE *US, female vocalist (Singles: 4 weeks)* pos/wks

16 Jun 84 **DOIN' IT IN A HAUNTED HOUSE** *Epic A 4519*....45 4

Danni'elle GAHA *Australia, female vocalist (Singles: 7 weeks)* pos/wks

1 Aug 92 **STUCK IN THE MIDDLE** *Epic 6581247*....68 2
27 Feb 93 **DO IT FOR LOVE** *Epic 6584612*....52 2
12 Jun 93 **SECRET LOVE** *Epic 6592212*....41 3

Dave GAHAN
UK, male vocalist (Singles: 6 weeks, Albums: 2 weeks) pos/wks

7 Jun 03 **DIRTY STICKY FLOORS** *Mute CDMUTE 294*....18 2
30 Aug 03 **I NEED YOU** *Mute CDMUTE 301*....27 2
8 Nov 03 **BOTTLE LIVING** *Mute CDMUTE 310*....36 2
14 Jun 03 **PAPER MONSTERS** *Mute CDSTUMM216*....36 2

See also DEPECHE MODE

Billy and Sarah GAINES
US, male / female vocal duo (Singles: 1 week) pos/wks

14 Jun 97 **I FOUND SOMEONE** *Expansion CDEXP 27*....48 1

Rosie GAINES *US, female vocalist (Singles: 15 weeks)* pos/wks

11 Nov 95 **I WANT U** *Motown 8604852*....70 1
31 May 97 ● **CLOSER THAN CLOSE** *Big Bang CDBBANG 1*....4 12
29 Nov 97 **I SURRENDER** *Big Bang CDBBANG 2*....39 2

Serge GAINSBOURG – See Jane BIRKIN and Serge GAINSBOURG

GALA *Italy, female vocalist – Gala Rizzatto (Singles: 24 weeks)* pos/wks

19 Jul 97 ● **FREED FROM DESIRE** *Big Life BLRD 135*....2 14
6 Dec 97 **LET A BOY CRY** *Big Life BLRD 140*....11 8
22 Aug 98 **COME INTO MY LIFE** *Big Life BLRD 147*....38 2

GALAXY – See Phil FEARON

Manuel GABAN – See Ry COODER

Dee GALDES – See Phil FEARON; BABY D

Eve GALLAGHER *UK, female vocalist (Singles: 8 weeks)* pos/wks

1 Dec 90 **LOVE COME DOWN (re)** *More Protein PROT 6*....61 4
15 Apr 95 **YOU CAN HAVE IT ALL** *Cleveland City CLECD 13023*....43 2
28 Oct 95 **LOVE COME DOWN (re-recording)** *Cleveland City CLECD 13028*....57 1
6 Jul 96 **HEARTBREAK** *React CDREACT 78* [1]....44 1

[1] Mrs Wood featuring Eve Gallagher

Liam GALLAGHER – See OASIS; DEATH IN VEGAS; BUFFALO TOM

Rory GALLAGHER *Ireland, male vocalist / instrumentalist – guitar, d. 14 Jun 1995 (Albums: 43 weeks)* pos/wks

29 May 71 **RORY GALLAGHER** *Polydor 2383044*....32 2
4 Dec 71 **DEUCE** *Polydor 2383076*....39 1
20 May 72 ● **LIVE! IN EUROPE** *Polydor 2383 112*....9 15
24 Feb 73 **BLUE PRINT** *Polydor 2383 189*....12 7
17 Nov 73 **TATTOO** *Polydor 2383 230*....32 3
27 Jul 74 **IRISH TOUR '74** *Polydor 2659 031*....36 2
30 Oct 76 **CALLING CARD** *Chrysalis CHR 1124*....32 1
22 Sep 79 **TOP PRIORITY** *Chrysalis CHR 1235*....56 4
8 Nov 80 **STAGE STRUCK** *Chrysalis CHR 1280*....40 3
8 May 82 **JINX** *Chrysalis CHR 1359*....68 5

See also TASTE

GALLAGHER and LYLE *UK, male vocal / instrumental duo – Benny Gallagher and Graham Lyle (Singles: 27 weeks, Albums: 44 weeks)* pos/wks

28 Feb 76 ● **I WANNA STAY WITH YOU** *A&M AMS 7211*....6 9
22 May 76 ● **HEART ON MY SLEEVE** *A&M AMS 7227*....6 10
11 Sep 76 **BREAKAWAY** *A&M AMS 7245*....35 4
29 Jan 77 **EVERY LITTLE TEARDROP** *A&M AMS 7274*....32 4
28 Feb 76 ● **BREAKAWAY** *A&M AMLH 68348*....6 35
29 Jan 77 **LOVE ON THE AIRWAYS** *A&M AMLH 64620*....19 9

Patsy GALLANT *Canada, female vocalist (Singles: 9 weeks)* pos/wks

10 Sep 77 ● **FROM NEW YORK TO L.A.** *EMI 2620*....6 9

GALLEON *France, male production duo (Singles: 2 weeks)* pos/wks

20 Apr 02 **SO I BEGIN** *Epic 6724102*....36 2

Luke GALLIANA *UK, male vocalist (Singles: 1 week)* pos/wks

12 May 01 **TO DIE FOR** *Jive 9201272*....42 1

GALLIANO *UK, male / female vocal / instrumental group (Singles: 14 weeks, Albums: 15 weeks)* pos/wks

30 May 92 **SKUNK FUNK** *Talkin Loud TLK 23*....41 2
1 Aug 92 **PRINCE OF PEACE** *Talkin Loud TLK 24*....47 3
10 Oct 92 **JUS' REACH (RECYCLED)** *Talkin Loud TLK 29*....66 2
28 May 94 **LONG TIME GONE** *Talkin Loud TLKCD 48*....15 3
30 Jul 94 **TWYFORD DOWN** *Talkin Loud TLKCD 49*....37 2
27 Jul 96 **EASE YOUR MIND** *Talkin Loud TLCD 10*....45 2
20 Jun 92 **A JOYFUL NOISE UNTO THE CREATOR** *Talkin Loud 8480802*....28 3
11 Jun 94 ● **THE PLOT THICKENS** *Talkin Loud 5224522*....7 12

GALLON DRUNK
UK, male vocal / instrumental group (Albums: 1 week) pos/wks

13 Mar 93 **FROM THE HEART OF TOWN** *Clawfist HUNKACDL 005*....67 1

James GALWAY *UK, male instrumentalist – flute (Singles: 13 weeks, Albums: 100 weeks)* pos/wks

27 May 78 ● **ANNIE'S SONG** *RCA Red Seal RB 5085* [1]....3 13
27 May 78 **THE MAGIC FLUTE OF JAMES GALWAY** *RCA Red Seal LRLI 5131*....43 6
1 Jul 78 **THE MAN WITH THE GOLDEN FLUTE** *RCA Red Seal LRLI 5127*....52 3
9 Sep 78 ● **JAMES GALWAY PLAYS SONGS FOR ANNIE** *RCA Red Seal RL 25163*....7 40
15 Dec 79 **SONGS OF THE SEASHORE** *Solar RL 25253*....39 6
31 May 80 **SOMETIMES WHEN WE TOUCH** *RCA PL 25296* [1]....15 14
18 Dec 82 **THE JAMES GALWAY COLLECTION** *Telstar STAR 2224*....41 8
8 Dec 84 **IN THE PINK** *RCA Red Seal RL 85315* [2]....62 6
28 Mar 87 **JAMES GALWAY AND THE CHIEFTAINS IN IRELAND** *RCA Red Seal RL 85798* [3]....32 5
17 Apr 93 **THE ESSENTIAL FLUTE OF JAMES GALWAY** *RCA Victor 74321133852*....30 5
18 Feb 95 **I WILL ALWAYS LOVE YOU** *RCA Victor 74321262212*....59 2
20 Jul 96 **CLASSICAL MEDITATIONS** *RCA Victor 74321377312*....45 5

[1] James Galway, flute, National Philharmonic Orchestra; Charles Gerhart, conductor [1] Cleo Laine and James Galway [2] James Galway and Henry Mancini with the National Philharmonic Orchestra [3] James Galway and the Chieftains

GAMBAFREAKS *Italy, male production duo (Singles: 2 weeks)* pos/wks

12 Sep 98 **INSTANT REPLAY** *Evocative EVOKE 7CDS* [1]....57 1
13 May 00 **DOWN DOWN DOWN** *Azuli AZNYCDX 116*....57 1

[1] Gambafreaks featuring Paco Rivaz

GANG OF FOUR *UK, male vocal / instrumental group (Singles: 5 weeks, Albums: 9 weeks)* pos/wks

16 Jun 79 **AT HOME HE'S A TOURIST** *EMI 2956*....58 3

22 May 82	**I LOVE A MAN IN UNIFORM** *EMI 5299*	65 2
13 Oct 79	ENTERTAINMENT *EMI EMC 3313*	45 3
21 Mar 81	SOLID GOLD *EMI EMC 3364*	52 2
29 May 82	SONGS OF THE FREE *EMI EMC 3412*	61 4

GANG STARR *US, male rap duo – Christopher Martin and Keith Elam (Singles: 8 weeks, Albums: 10 weeks)* pos/wks

13 Oct 90	**JAZZ THING** *CBS 356377 7*	66 2
23 Feb 91	**TAKE A REST** *Cooltempo COOL 230*	63 1
25 May 91	**LOVESICK** *Cooltempo COOL 234*	50 3
13 Jun 92	**2 DEEP** *Cooltempo COOL 256*	67 2
26 Jan 91	STEP IN THE ARENA *Cooltempo ZCTLP 21*	36 3
12 Mar 94	HARD TO EARN *Cooltempo CTCD 38*	29 3
11 Apr 98	MOMENT OF TRUTH *Cooltempo 8590322*	43 1
7 Aug 99	FULL CLIP: A DECADE OF GANG STARR *Cooltempo 5211892*	47 2
5 Jul 03	THE OWNERZ *Virgin CDVUS235*	74 1

See also GURU

GANJA KRU – *See DJ HYPE presents GANJA KRU*

GANT *UK, production duo – Julian Jonah and Danny Harrison (Singles: 1 week)* pos/wks

27 Dec 97	**SOUND BWOY BURIAL / ALL NIGHT LONG** *Positiva CDTIV 85*	67 1

GAP BAND *US, male vocal / instrumental group – Charlie, Ronnie and Robert Wilson (Singles: 82 weeks, Albums: 3 weeks)* pos/wks

12 Jul 80 ●	**OOPS UP SIDE YOUR HEAD** *Mercury MER 22*	6 14
27 Sep 80	**PARTY LIGHTS** *Mercury MER 37*	30 8
27 Dec 80	**BURN RUBBER ON ME (WHY YOU WANNA HURT ME)** *Mercury MER 52*	22 11
11 Apr 81	**HUMPIN'** *Mercury MER 63*	36 6
27 Jun 81	**YEARNING FOR YOUR LOVE** *Mercury MER 73*	47 4
5 Jun 82	**EARLY IN THE MORNING** *Mercury MER 97*	55 3
19 Feb 83	**OUTSTANDING** *Total Experience TE 001*	68 2
31 Mar 84	**SOMEDAY** *Total Experience TE 5*	17 8
23 Jun 84	**JAMMIN' IN AMERICA** *Total Experience TE 6*	64 2
13 Dec 86 ●	**BIG FUN** *Total Experience FB 49779*	4 12
14 Mar 87	**HOW MUSIC CAME ABOUT (BOP B DA B DA DA)** *Total Experience FB 49755*	61 2
11 Jul 87	**OOPS UPSIDE YOUR HEAD (re-mix)** *Club JAB 54*	20 8
18 Feb 89	**I'M GONNA GIT YOU SUCKA** *Arista 112016*	63 2
7 Feb 87	GAP BAND 8 *Total Experience FL 89992*	47 3

GARBAGE (268 Top 500) *Missing link between techno and grunge, formed Madison, Wisconsin, 1993; includes Shirley Manson (b. Edinburgh, Scotland, v/g) and Butch Vig (d), who produced Nirvana and Smashing Pumpkins. 'Shut Your Mouth' was the first Top 20 single to spend only one week in the Top 75 (Singles: 66 weeks, Albums: 169 weeks)* pos/wks

19 Aug 95	**SUBHUMAN** *Mushroom D 1138*	50 1
30 Sep 95	**ONLY HAPPY WHEN IT RAINS** *Mushroom D 1199*	29 3
2 Dec 95	**QUEER** *Mushroom D 1237*	13 4
23 Mar 96 ●	**STUPID GIRL** *Mushroom D 1271*	4 7
23 Nov 96 ●	**MILK (re)** *Mushroom D 1494* [1]	10 8
9 May 98 ●	**PUSH IT** *Mushroom MUSH 28CDS*	9 5
18 Jul 98 ●	**I THINK I'M PARANOID** *Mushroom MUSH 35CDS*	9 5
17 Oct 98	**SPECIAL** *Mushroom MUSH 39CDS*	15 4
6 Feb 99 ●	**WHEN I GROW UP** *Mushroom MUSH 43CDS*	9 7
5 Jun 99	**YOU LOOK SO FINE** *Mushroom MUSH 49CDS*	19 4
27 Nov 99	**THE WORLD IS NOT ENOUGH** *Radioactive RAXTD 40*	11 9
6 Oct 01	**ANDROGYNY** *Mushroom MUSH 94CDS*	24 2
2 Feb 02	**CHERRY LIPS (GO BABY GO!)** *Mushroom MUSH 98CDS*	22 4
20 Apr 02	**BREAKING UP THE GIRL** *Mushroom MUSH 101CDS*	27 2
5 Oct 02	**SHUT YOUR MOUTH** *Mushroom MUSH 106CDS*	20 1
14 Oct 95 ●	GARBAGE *Mushroom D 31450*	6 100
23 May 98 ★	VERSION 2.0 *Mushroom MUSH 29CD* ■	1 65
13 Oct 01 ●	BEAUTIFUL GARBAGE *Mushroom MUSH 95CD*	6 4

[1] Garbage featuring Tricky

Jan GARBAREK *Norway, male instrumentalist – saxophone (Albums: 1 week)* pos/wks

4 May 96	VISIBLE WORLD *ECM 5290862*	69 1

Adam GARCIA *Australia, male vocalist (Singles: 5 weeks)* pos/wks

16 May 98	**NIGHT FEVER** *Polydor 5697972*	15 5

Scott GARCIA featuring MC STYLES *UK, male producer and UK, male rapper – Scott Garcia and Daryl Turner (Singles: 3 weeks)* pos/wks

1 Nov 97	**A LONDON THING** *Connected CDCONNECT 1*	29 3

See also CORRUPTED CRU featuring MC NEAT

Boris GARDINER *Jamaica, male vocalist / instrumentalist (Singles: 38 weeks)* pos/wks

17 Jan 70	**ELIZABETHAN REGGAE (re)** *Duke DU 39*	14 14
26 Jul 86 ★	**I WANT TO WAKE UP WITH YOU** *Revue REV 733*	1 15
4 Oct 86	**YOU'RE EVERYTHING TO ME** *Revue REV 735*	11 8
27 Dec 86	**THE MEANING OF CHRISTMAS** *Revue REV 740*	69 1

The first copies of 'Elizabethan Reggae', an instrumental, were printed with the label incorrectly crediting Byron Lee as the performer. The charts for the first entry, and the first four weeks of the re-entry, all reprinted this error. All charts and discs printed after 28 Feb 1970 gave Boris Gardiner the credit he deserved

Paul GARDINER *UK, male instrumentalist – bass (Singles: 4 weeks)* pos/wks

25 Jul 81	**STORMTROOPER IN DRAG** *Beggars Banquet BEG 61*	49 4

Uncredited vocalist is Gary Numan

Art GARFUNKEL *US, male vocalist (Singles: 37 weeks, Albums: 64 weeks)* pos/wks

13 Sep 75 ★	**I ONLY HAVE EYES FOR YOU** *CBS 3575*	1 11
3 Mar 79 ★	**BRIGHT EYES** *CBS 6947* ◆	1 19
7 Jul 79	**SINCE I DON'T HAVE YOU** *CBS 7371*	38 7
13 Oct 73	ANGEL CLARE *CBS 69021*	14 7
1 Nov 75 ●	BREAKAWAY *CBS 86002*	7 10
18 Mar 78	WATER MARK *CBS 86054*	25 5
21 Apr 79 ●	FATE FOR BREAKFAST *CBS 86082*	2 20
19 Sep 81	SCISSORS CUT *CBS 85259*	51 3
17 Nov 84	THE ART GARFUNKEL ALBUM *CBS 10046*	12 13
14 Dec 96	THE VERY BEST OF ART GARFUNKEL – ACROSS AMERICA *Virgin VTCD 113*	35 6

See also SIMON and GARFUNKEL

Judy GARLAND *US, female vocalist – Frances Gumm, d. 22 Jan 1969 (Singles: 2 weeks, Albums: 3 weeks)* pos/wks

10 Jun 55	**THE MAN THAT GOT AWAY** *Philips PB 366*	18 2
3 Mar 62	JUDY AT CARNEGIE HALL *Capitol W 1569* ▲	13 3

Jessica GARLICK *UK, female vocalist (Singles: 6 weeks)* pos/wks

25 May 02	**COME BACK** *Columbia 6725662*	13 6

Errol GARNER *US, male instrumentalist – piano, d. 2 Jan 1977 (Albums: 1 week)* pos/wks

14 Jul 62	CLOSE UP IN SWING *Philips BBL 7579*	20 1

Laurent GARNIER *France, male DJ / producer (Singles: 4 weeks)* pos/wks

15 Feb 97	**CRISPY BACON** *F Communications F 055CD*	60 1
22 Apr 00	**MAN WITH THE RED FACE** *F Communications F 119CD*	65 1
11 Nov 00	**GREED / THE MAN WITH THE RED FACE (re-issue)** *F Communications F 127CDUK*	36 2

Lee GARRETT *US, male vocalist (Singles: 7 weeks)* pos/wks

29 May 76	**YOU'RE MY EVERYTHING** *Chrysalis CHS 2087*	15 7

Leif GARRETT *US, male vocalist (Singles: 14 weeks)* pos/wks

20 Jan 79 ●	**I WAS MADE FOR DANCIN'** *Scotti Brothers K 11202*	4 10
21 Apr 79	**FEEL THE NEED** *Scotti Brothers K 11274*	38 4

Lesley GARRETT

UK, female vocalist (Singles: 10 weeks, Albums: 44 weeks) pos/wks

Date		Title / Label	pos	wks
6 Nov 93		**AVE MARIA** *Internal Affairs KGBD 012* [1]	16	10
12 Feb 94		**THE ALBUM** *Telstar TCD 2709*	25	7
18 Nov 95		**SOPRANO IN RED** *Silva Classics SILKTVCD 1*	59	8
19 Oct 96		**SOPRANO IN HOLLYWOOD** *Silva Classics SILKTVCD 2*	53	4
18 Oct 97		**THE SOPRANO'S GREATEST HITS** *Silva Classics SILKTVCD 3*	53	2
22 Nov 97		**A SOPRANO INSPIRED** *Conifer Classics 75605513292*	48	7
14 Nov 98		**LESLEY GARRETT** *BBC / BMG Conifer 75605513382*	34	8
27 May 00		**I WILL WAIT FOR YOU** *BBC / BMG Conifer 75605513542*	28	7
24 Nov 01		**TRAVELLING LIGHT** *EMI Classics CDC 5572512*	75	1

[1] Lesley Garrett and Amanda Thompson

Siedah GARRETT – *See BRAND NEW HEAVIES; Dennis EDWARDS; Michael JACKSON*

David GARRICK

UK, male vocalist – Philip Core (Singles: 16 weeks) pos/wks

Date		Title / Label	pos	wks
9 Jun 66		**LADY JANE** *Piccadilly 7N 35317*	28	7
22 Sep 66		**DEAR MRS APPLEBEE** *Piccadilly 7N 35335*	22	9

GARY'S GANG

US, male vocal / instrumental group (Singles: 18 weeks) pos/wks

Date		Title / Label	pos	wks
24 Feb 79	●	**KEEP ON DANCIN'** *CBS 7109*	8	10
2 Jun 79		**LET'S LOVEDANCE TONIGHT** *CBS 7328*	49	4
6 Nov 82		**KNOCK ME OUT** *Arista ARIST 499*	45	4

Barbara GASKIN – *See Dave STEWART*

GAT DECOR

UK, male instrumental / production group (Singles: 10 weeks) pos/wks

Date		Title / Label	pos	wks
16 May 92		**PASSION** *Effective EFFS 1*	29	4
9 Mar 96	●	**PASSION (re-mix)** *Way Of Life WAYDA 1*	6	6

See also PHUNKY PHANTOM; REST ASSURED

Stephen GATELY

Ireland, male vocalist (Singles: 19 weeks, Albums: 4 weeks) pos/wks

Date		Title / Label	pos	wks
10 Jun 00	●	**NEW BEGINNING / BRIGHT EYES** *A&M / Polydor 5618192*	3	11
14 Oct 00		**I BELIEVE** *Polydor 5877472*	11	4
12 May 01		**STAY** *A&M / Mercury 5870672*	13	4
1 Jul 00	●	**NEW BEGINNING** *A&M 5439102*	9	4

See also BOYZONE

David GATES

US, male vocalist (Singles: 2 weeks, Albums: 11 weeks) pos/wks

Date		Title / Label	pos	wks
22 Jul 78		**TOOK THE LAST TRAIN** *Elektra K 12307*	50	2
31 May 75		**NEVER LET HER GO** *Elektra K 52012*	32	1
29 Jul 78		**GOODBYE GIRL** *Elektra K 52091*	28	3
12 Oct 02		**THE DAVID GATES SONGBOOK – A LIFETIME OF MUSIC** *Jive 0927491402*	11	7

See also BREAD

Gareth GATES

UK, male vocalist (Singles: 104 weeks, Albums: 21 weeks) pos/wks

Date		Title / Label	pos	wks
30 Mar 02	★	**UNCHAINED MELODY (2re)** *S 74321930882* ◆ ■	1	30
20 Jul 02	★	**ANYONE OF US (STUPID MISTAKE)** *S 74321950602* ■	1	15
5 Oct 02	★	**THE LONG AND WINDING ROAD / SUSPICIOUS MINDS** *S 74321965972* [1] ■	1	18
21 Dec 02	●	**WHAT MY HEART WANTS TO SAY (re)** *S 743211985592*	5	13
22 Mar 03	★	**SPIRIT IN THE SKY** *S 82876511202* [2] ■	1	15
20 Sep 03	●	**SUNSHINE (re)** *S 82876560032*	3	10
13 Dec 03	●	**SAY IT ISN'T SO** *S 82876583412*	4	3+
9 Nov 02	●	**WHAT MY HEART WANTS TO SAY** *S 74321975172*	2	17
4 Oct 03		**GO YOUR OWN WAY** *S 82876557452*	11	4

[1] Will Young and Gareth Gates / Gareth Gates
[2] Gareth Gates featuring The Kumars

GAY DAD

UK, male / female vocal / instrumental group (Singles: 10 weeks, Albums: 4 weeks) pos/wks

Date		Title / Label	pos	wks
30 Jan 99	●	**TO EARTH WITH LOVE** *London LONCD 413*	10	4
5 Jun 99		**JOY!** *London LONCD 428*	22	3
14 Aug 99		**OH JIM** *London LONCD 437*	47	1
31 Mar 01		**NOW ALWAYS AND FOREVER** *B Unique BUN 004CD*	41	1
22 Sep 01		**TRANSMISSION** *B Unique BUN 009CD*	58	1
19 Jun 99		**LEISURE NOISE** *London 5561032*	14	4

GAY GORDON and the MINCE PIES

UK, male / female vocal / instrumental group (Singles: 5 weeks) pos/wks

Date		Title / Label	pos	wks
6 Dec 86		**THE ESSENTIAL WALLY PARTY MEDLEY** *Lifestyle XY 2*	60	5

GAYE BYKERS ON ACID

UK, male vocal / instrumental group (Singles: 2 weeks, Albums: 1 week) pos/wks

Date		Title / Label	pos	wks
31 Oct 87		**GIT DOWN (SHAKE YOUR THANG)** *Purple Fluid VS 1008*	54	2
14 Nov 87		**DRILL YOUR OWN HOLE** *Virgin V 2478*	95	1

Marvin GAYE

117 Top 500 *One of soul's most innovative and successful singer / songwriters, b. 2 Apr 1939, Washington DC, d. 1 Apr 1984. He went from doo-wop group member and session drummer to superstar. Posthumously awarded a Lifetime Achievement Grammy Award in 1996 (Singles: 202 weeks, Albums: 189 weeks)* pos/wks

Date		Title / Label	pos	wks
30 Jul 64		**ONCE UPON A TIME** *Stateside SS 316* [1]	50	1
10 Dec 64		**HOW SWEET IT IS** *Stateside SS 360*	49	1
29 Sep 66		**LITTLE DARLIN' (I NEED YOU)** *Tamla Motown TMG 574*	50	1
26 Jan 67		**IT TAKES TWO** *Tamla Motown TMG 590* [2]	16	11
17 Jan 68		**IF I COULD BUILD MY WHOLE WORLD AROUND YOU** *Tamla Motown TMG 635* [3]	41	7
12 Jun 68		**AIN'T NOTHIN' LIKE THE REAL THING** *Tamla Motown TMG 655* [3]	34	7
2 Oct 68		**YOU'RE ALL I NEED TO GET BY** *Tamla Motown TMG 668* [3]	19	19
22 Jan 69		**YOU AIN'T LIVIN' TILL YOU'RE LOVIN'** *Tamla Motown TMG 681* [3]	21	8
12 Feb 69	★	**I HEARD IT THROUGH THE GRAPEVINE** *Tamla Motown TMG 686* ▲	1	15
4 Jun 69		**GOOD LOVIN' AIN'T EASY TO COME BY (re)** *Tamla Motown TMG 697* [3]	26	8
23 Jul 69	●	**TOO BUSY THINKING 'BOUT MY BABY** *Tamla Motown TMG 705*	5	16
15 Nov 69	●	**ONION SONG** *Tamla Motown TMG 715* [3]	9	12
9 May 70	●	**ABRAHAM, MARTIN AND JOHN** *Tamla Motown TMG 734*	9	14
11 Dec 71		**SAVE THE CHILDREN** *Tamla Motown TMG 796*	41	6
22 Sep 73		**LET'S GET IT ON** *Tamla Motown TMG 868* ▲	31	7
23 Mar 74	●	**YOU ARE EVERYTHING** *Tamla Motown TMG 890* [4]	5	12
20 Jul 74		**STOP LOOK LISTEN (TO YOUR HEART)** *Tamla Motown TMG 906* [4]	25	8
7 May 77	●	**GOT TO GIVE IT UP (PT.1)** *Motown TMG 1069* ▲	7	10
24 Feb 79		**POPS, WE LOVE YOU** *Motown TMG 1136* [5]	66	5
30 Oct 82	●	**(SEXUAL) HEALING** *CBS A 2855*	4	14
8 Jan 83		**MY LOVE IS WAITING** *CBS A 3048*	34	5
18 May 85		**SANCTIFIED LADY** *CBS A 4894*	51	4
26 Apr 86	●	**I HEARD IT THROUGH THE GRAPEVINE (re-issue)** *Tamla Motown ZB 40701*	8	8
14 May 94		**LUCKY LUCKY ME** *Motown TMGCD 1426*	67	1
6 Oct 01		**MUSIC** *Polydor 4976222* [6]	36	2
16 Mar 68		**GREATEST HITS** *Tamla Motown STML 11065*	40	1
22 Aug 70		**GREATEST HITS** *Tamla Motown STML 11153* [1]	60	4
19 Jan 71	●	**DIANA AND MARVIN** *Tamla Motown STMA 8015* [2]	6	43
10 Nov 73		**LET'S GET IT ON** *Tamla Motown STMA 8013*	39	1
15 May 76		**I WANT YOU** *Tamla Motown STML 12025*	22	5
30 Oct 76		**THE BEST OF MARVIN GAYE** *Tamla Motown STML 12042*	56	1
28 Feb 81		**IN OUR LIFETIME** *Motown STML 12149*	48	4
29 Aug 81		**DIANA AND MARVIN (re-issue)** *Motown STMS 5001* [2]	78	2
20 Nov 82	●	**MIDNIGHT LOVE** *CBS 85977*	10	16
12 Nov 83		**GREATEST HITS** *Telstar STAR 2234*	13	61
15 Jun 85		**DREAM OF A LIFETIME** *CBS 26239*	46	4
12 Nov 88		**LOVE SONGS** *Telstar STAR 2331* [3]	69	9
2 Nov 90		**LOVE SONGS** *Telstar STAR 2427*	39	5
9 Apr 94	●	**THE VERY BEST OF MARVIN GAYE** *Motown 5302922*	3	18
24 Jul 99		**WHAT'S GOING ON** *Motown 5308832*	56	4

		pos	wks
19 Feb 00 ●	**THE LOVE SONGS** *UMTV/Motown 5454702*	8	7
1 Sep 01	**THE VERY BEST OF MARVIN GAYE** *Motown 143672*	15	4

[1] Marvin Gaye and Mary Wells [2] Marvin Gaye and Kim Weston [3] Marvin Gaye and Tammi Terrell [4] Diana Ross and Marvin Gaye [5] Diana Ross, Marvin Gaye, Smokey Robinson and Stevie Wonder [6] Erick Sermon featuring Marvin Gaye [1] Marvin Gaye and Tammi Terrell [2] Diana Ross and Marvin Gaye [3] Marvin Gaye and Smokey Robinson

The two 'Greatest Hits' and 'The Very Best of Marvin Gaye' albums are different

Crystal GAYLE *US, female vocalist – Brenda Gail Webb (Singles: 28 weeks, Albums: 25 weeks)*

		pos	wks
12 Nov 77 ●	**DON'T IT MAKE MY BROWN EYES BLUE** *United Artists UP 36307*	5	14
26 Aug 78	**TALKING IN YOUR SLEEP** *United Artists UP 36422*	11	14
21 Jan 78	**WE MUST BELIEVE IN MAGIC** *United Artists UAG 30108*	15	7
23 Sep 78	**WHEN I DREAM** *United Artists UAG 30169*	25	8
22 Mar 80 ●	**THE CRYSTAL GAYLE SINGLES ALBUM** *United Artists UAG 30287*	7	10

Michelle GAYLE *UK, female vocalist (Singles: 52 weeks, Albums: 13 weeks)*

		pos	wks
7 Aug 93	**LOOKING UP** *RCA 74321154532*	11	6
24 Sep 94 ●	**SWEETNESS** *RCA 74321230192*	4	16
17 Dec 94	**I'LL FIND YOU** *RCA 74321247762*	26	7
27 May 95	**FREEDOM** *RCA 74321284692*	16	6
26 Aug 95	**HAPPY JUST TO BE WITH YOU** *RCA 74321302692*	11	7
8 Feb 97 ●	**DO YOU KNOW** *RCA 74321419282*	6	6
26 Apr 97	**SENSATIONAL** *RCA 74321419302*	14	4
22 Oct 94	**MICHELLE GAYLE** *RCA 74321234122*	30	10
10 May 97	**SENSATIONAL** *RCA 74321419322*	17	3

Roy GAYLE – *See MIRAGE*

GAYLE & GILLIAN *Australia, female vocal duo (Singles: 2 weeks)*

		pos	wks
3 Jul 93	**MAD IF YA DON'T** *Mushroom CDMUSH 1*	75	1
19 Mar 94	**WANNA BE YOUR LOVER** *Mushroom D 11598*	62	1

Gloria GAYNOR *US, female vocalist (Singles: 73 weeks, Albums: 17 weeks)*

		pos	wks
7 Dec 74 ●	**NEVER CAN SAY GOODBYE** *MGM 2006 463*	2	13
8 Mar 75	**REACH OUT, I'LL BE THERE** *MGM 2006 499*	14	8
9 Aug 75	**ALL I NEED IS YOUR SWEET LOVIN'** *MGM 2006 531*	44	3
17 Jan 76	**HOW HIGH THE MOON** *MGM 2006 558*	33	4
3 Feb 79 ★	**I WILL SURVIVE** *Polydor 2095 017* ▲	1	15
6 Oct 79	**LET ME KNOW (I HAVE A RIGHT)** *Polydor STEP 5*	32	7
24 Dec 83	**I AM WHAT I AM (FROM 'LA CAGE AUX FOLLES')** *Chrysalis CHS 2765*	13	12
26 Jun 93 ●	**I WILL SURVIVE (re-mix)** *Polydor PZCD 270*	5	10
3 Jun 00	**LAST NIGHT** *Logic 74321738082*	67	1
8 Mar 75	**NEVER CAN SAY GOODBYE** *MGM 2315 321*	32	8
24 Mar 79	**LOVE TRACKS** *Polydor 2391 385*	31	7
16 Aug 86	**THE POWER OF GLORIA GAYNOR** *Stylus SMR 618*	81	2

GAZ *US, male vocal / instrumental group (Singles: 4 weeks)*

		pos	wks
24 Feb 79	**SING SING** *Salsoul SSOL 116*	60	4

GAZZA *UK, male footballer / vocalist – Paul Gascoigne (Singles: 14 weeks)*

		pos	wks
10 Nov 90 ●	**FOG ON THE TYNE (REVISITED)** *Best ZB 44083* [1]	2	9
22 Dec 90	**GEORDIE BOYS (GAZZA RAP)** *Best ZB 44229*	31	5

[1] Gazza and Lindisfarne

Nigel GEE *UK, male producer (Singles: 1 week)*

		pos	wks
27 Jan 01	**HOOTIN'** *Neo NEOCD 040*	57	1

J GEILS BAND *US, male vocal / instrumental group (Singles: 20 weeks, Albums: 15 weeks)*

		pos	wks
9 Jun 79	**ONE LAST KISS** *EMI America AM 507*	74	1
13 Feb 82 ●	**CENTERFOLD** *EMI America EA 135* ▲	3	9
10 Apr 82	**FREEZE-FRAME** *EMI America EA 134*	27	7
26 Jun 82	**ANGEL IN BLUE** *EMI America EA 138*	55	3
27 Feb 82	**FREEZE-FRAME** *EMI America AML 3020* ▲	12	15

Bob GELDOF *Ireland, male vocalist (Singles: 15 weeks, Albums: 10 weeks)*

		pos	wks
1 Nov 86	**THIS IS THE WORLD CALLING** *Mercury BOB 101*	25	5
21 Feb 87	**LOVE LIKE A ROCKET** *Mercury BOB 102*	61	3
23 Jun 90	**THE GREAT SONG OF INDIFFERENCE** *Mercury BOB 104*	15	6
7 May 94	**CRAZY** *Vertigo VERCX 85*	65	1
6 Dec 86	**DEEP IN THE HEART OF NOWHERE** *Mercury BOBLP 1*	79	1
4 Aug 90	**THE VEGETARIANS OF LOVE** *Mercury 8462501*	21	6
9 Jul 94 ●	**LOUDMOUTH – THE BEST OF THE BOOMTOWN RATS AND BOB GELDOF** *Vertigo 5222832* [1]	10	3

[1] Boomtown Rats and Bob Geldof

See also BOOMTOWN RATS

GEM – *See OUR TRIBE / ONE TRIBE*

GEMINI *UK, male vocal duo – Michael and David Smallwood (Singles: 7 weeks)*

		pos	wks
30 Sep 95	**EVEN THOUGH YOU BROKE MY HEART** *EMI CDEMS 391*	40	3
10 Feb 96	**STEAL YOUR LOVE AWAY** *EMI CDEMS 407*	37	2
29 Jun 96	**COULD IT BE FOREVER** *EMI CDEMS 426*	38	2

GEMS FOR JEM *UK, male instrumental / production duo – Steve McCutcheon and Darren Pearce (Singles: 2 weeks)*

		pos	wks
6 May 95	**LIFTING ME HIGHER** *Box 21 CDSBOKS 3*	28	2

GENE *UK, male vocal / instrumental group (Singles: 22 weeks, Albums: 14 weeks)*

		pos	wks
13 Aug 94	**BE MY LIGHT BE MY GUIDE** *Costermonger COST 002CD*	54	1
12 Nov 94	**SLEEP WELL TONIGHT** *Costermonger COST 003CD*	36	2
4 Mar 95	**HAUNTED BY YOU** *Costermonger COST 004CD*	32	2
22 Jul 95	**OLYMPIAN** *Costermonger COST 005CD*	18	2
13 Jan 96	**FOR THE DEAD** *Costermonger COST 006CD*	14	3
2 Nov 96	**FIGHTING FIT** *Costermonger COST 009CD*	22	2
1 Feb 97	**WE COULD BE KINGS** *Polydor COSCD 10*	17	2
10 May 97	**WHERE ARE THEY NOW?** *Polydor COSCD 11*	22	2
9 Aug 97	**SPEAK TO ME SOMEONE** *Polydor COSCD 12*	30	2
27 Feb 99	**AS GOOD AS IT GETS** *Polydor COSCD 14*	23	2
24 Apr 99	**FILL HER UP** *Polydor COSCD 15*	36	2
1 Apr 95 ●	**OLYMPIAN** *Costermonger 5274462*	8	6
3 Feb 96	**TO SEE THE LIGHTS** *Costermonger GENE 002CD*	11	3
1 Mar 97 ●	**DRAWN TO THE DEEP END** *Polydor GENEC 3*	8	3
13 Mar 99	**REVELATIONS** *Polydor GENEC 4*	25	2

GENE AND JIM ARE INTO SHAKES *UK, male vocal / instrumental duo (Singles: 2 weeks)*

		pos	wks
19 Mar 88	**SHAKE! (HOW ABOUT A SAMPLING, GENE?)** *Rough Trade RT 216*	68	2

GENE LOVES JEZEBEL *UK, male vocal / instrumental group (Singles: 7 weeks, Albums: 5 weeks)*

		pos	wks
29 Mar 86	**SWEETEST THING** *Beggars Banquet BEG 156*	75	1
14 Jun 86	**HEARTACHE** *Beggars Banquet BEG 161*	71	2
5 Sep 87	**THE MOTION OF LOVE** *Beggars Banquet BEG 192*	56	3
5 Dec 87	**GORGEOUS** *Beggars Banquet BEG 202*	68	1
19 Jul 87	**DISCOVER** *Beggars Banquet BEGA 73*	32	4
24 Oct 87	**HOUSE OF DOLLS** *Beggars Banquet BEGA 87*	81	1

GENERAL DEGREE – *See Richie STEPHENS*

GENERAL LEVY *UK, male vocalist – Paul Levy (Singles: 13 weeks)*

		pos	wks
4 Sep 93	**MONKEY MAN** *ffrr FCD 214*	75	1
18 Jun 94	**INCREDIBLE** *Renk RENK 42 CD* [1]	39	3
10 Sep 94 ●	**INCREDIBLE (re-mix)** *Renk CD RENK 44* [1]	8	9

[1] M-Beat featuring General Levy

GENERAL PUBLIC

UK, male vocal / instrumental group (Singles: 4 weeks)

Date		Title	pos	wks
10 Mar 84		**GENERAL PUBLIC** *Virgin VS 659*	60	3
2 Jul 94		**I'LL TAKE YOU THERE** *Epic 6605532*	73	1

See also BEAT

GENERAL SAINT

UK, male vocalist (Singles: 9 weeks, Albums: 5 weeks)

Date		Title	pos	wks
29 Sep 84		**LAST PLANE (ONE WAY TICKET)** *MCA MCA 910* [1]	51	3
2 Apr 94		**OH CAROL!** *Copasetic COPCD 0009* [1]	54	5
6 Aug 94		**SAVE THE LAST DANCE FOR ME** *Copasetic COPCD 12* [2]	75	1
6 Feb 82		**TWO BAD DJ** *Greensleeves GREL 24* [1]	99	2
28 May 83		**STOP THAT TRAIN** *Greensleeves GREL 53* [1]	98	1

[1] Clint Eastwood and General Saint [2] General Saint featuring Don Campbell

[1] Clint Eastwood and General Saint

GENERATION X *UK, male vocal / instrumental group (Singles: 31 weeks, Albums: 9 weeks)*

Date		Title	pos	wks
17 Sep 77		**YOUR GENERATION** *Chrysalis CHS 2165*	36	4
11 Mar 78		**READY STEADY GO** *Chrysalis CHS 2207*	47	3
20 Jan 79		**KING ROCKER** *Chrysalis CHS 2261*	11	9
7 Apr 79		**VALLEY OF THE DOLLS** *Chrysalis CHS 2310*	23	7
30 Jun 79		**FRIDAY'S ANGELS** *Chrysalis CHS 2330*	62	2
18 Oct 80		**DANCING WITH MYSELF** *Chrysalis CHS 2444* [1]	62	2
24 Jan 81		**DANCING WITH MYSELF (EP)** *Chrysalis CHS 2488* [1]	60	4
8 Apr 78		**GENERATION X** *Chrysalis CHR 1169*	29	4
17 Feb 79		**VALLEY OF THE DOLLS** *Chrysalis CHR 1193*	51	5

[1] Gen X

Tracks on Dancing with Myself (EP): Dancing with Myself / Untouchables / Rock On / King Rocker

See also Billy IDOL

GENERATOR

Holland, male producer – Robert Smit (Singles: 1 week)

Date		Title	pos	wks
23 Oct 99		**WHERE ARE YOU NOW?** *Tidy Trax TIDY 130CD*	60	1

GENESIS

44 Top 500 *Perennially popular UK group. Stalwart members are Tony Banks (k) and Mike Rutherford (g); others included Peter Gabriel (v), Phil Collins (v/d), Steve Hackett (g). These progressive 1970s rockers became a major act in the 1980s and had 10 consecutive Top 3 albums (Singles: 187 weeks, Albums: 491 weeks)*

Date		Title	pos	wks
6 Apr 74		**I KNOW WHAT I LIKE (IN YOUR WARDROBE)** *Charisma CB 224*	21	7
26 Feb 77		**YOUR OWN SPECIAL WAY** *Charisma CB 300*	43	3
28 May 77		**SPOT THE PIGEON (EP)** *Charisma GEN 001*	14	7
11 Mar 78	●	**FOLLOW YOU FOLLOW ME** *Charisma CB 309*	7	13
8 Jul 78		**MANY TOO MANY** *Charisma CB 315*	43	5
15 Mar 80	●	**TURN IT ON AGAIN** *Charisma CB 356*	8	10
17 May 80		**DUCHESS** *Charisma CB 363*	46	5
13 Sep 80		**MISUNDERSTANDING** *Charisma CB 369*	42	5
22 Aug 81	●	**ABACAB** *Charisma CB 388*	9	8
31 Oct 81		**KEEP IT DARK** *Charisma CB 391*	33	4
13 Mar 82		**MAN ON THE CORNER** *Charisma CB 393*	41	5
22 May 82	●	**3 X 3 (EP)** *Charisma GEN 1*	10	8
3 Sep 83	●	**MAMA** *Virgin / Charisma MAMA 1*	4	10
12 Nov 83		**THAT'S ALL** *Charisma / Virgin TATA 1*	16	11
11 Feb 84		**ILLEGAL ALIEN (re)** *Charisma / Virgin AL 1*	46	4
31 May 86		**INVISIBLE TOUCH** *Virgin GENS 1* ▲	15	8
30 Aug 86		**IN TOO DEEP** *Virgin GENS 2*	19	9
22 Nov 86		**LAND OF CONFUSION** *Virgin GENS 3*	14	12
14 Mar 87		**TONIGHT TONIGHT TONIGHT** *Virgin GENS 4*	18	6
20 Jun 87		**THROWING IT ALL AWAY** *Virgin GENS 5*	22	8
2 Nov 91	●	**NO SON OF MINE (re)** *Virgin GENS 6*	6	7
11 Jan 92	●	**I CAN'T DANCE** *Virgin GENS 7*	7	9
18 Apr 92		**HOLD ON MY HEART** *Virgin GENS 8*	16	5
25 Jul 92		**JESUS HE KNOWS ME** *Virgin GENS 9*	20	7
21 Nov 92	●	**INVISIBLE TOUCH (LIVE)** *Virgin GENS 10*	7	4
20 Feb 93		**TELL ME WHY** *Virgin GENDG 11*	40	3
27 Sep 97		**CONGO** *Virgin GENSD 12*	29	2
13 Dec 97		**SHIPWRECKED** *Virgin GENDX14*	54	1
7 Mar 98		**NOT ABOUT US** *Virgin GENSD 15*	66	1
14 Oct 72		**FOXTROT** *Charisma CAS 1058*	12	7
11 Aug 73	●	**GENESIS LIVE** *Charisma CLASS 1*	9	10
20 Oct 73	●	**SELLING ENGLAND BY THE POUND** *Charisma CAS 1074*	3	21
11 May 74		**NURSERY CRYME** *Charisma CAS 1052*	39	1
7 Dec 74	●	**THE LAMB LIES DOWN ON BROADWAY** *Charisma CGS 101*	10	6
28 Feb 76	●	**A TRICK OF THE TAIL** *Charisma CDS 4001*	3	39
15 Jan 77	●	**WIND AND WUTHERING** *Charisma CDS 4005*	7	22
29 Oct 77	●	**SECONDS OUT** *Charisma GE 2001*	4	17
15 Apr 78	●	**AND THEN THERE WERE THREE** *Charisma CDS 4010*	3	32
5 Apr 80	★	**DUKE** *Charisma CBR 101* ■	1	30
26 Sep 81	★	**ABACAB** *Charisma CBR 102* ■	1	27
12 Jun 82	●	**THREE SIDES LIVE** *Charisma GE 2002*	2	19
15 Oct 83	★	**GENESIS** *Charisma GENLP 1* ■	1	51
31 Mar 84		**NURSERY CRYME (re-issue)** *Charisma CHC 22*	68	1
21 Apr 84		**TRESPASS** *Charisma CHC 12*	98	1
21 Jun 86	★	**INVISIBLE TOUCH** *Charisma GENLP 2* ■	1	96
23 Nov 91	★	**WE CAN'T DANCE** *Virgin GENLP 3* ■	1	61
28 Nov 92	●	**LIVE – THE WAY WE WALK VOLUME ONE: THE SHORTS** *Virgin GENCD 4*	3	18
23 Jan 93	★	**LIVE – THE WAY WE WALK VOLUME TWO: THE LONGS** *Virgin GENCD 5* ■	1	9
13 Sep 97	●	**CALLING ALL STATIONS** *Virgin GENCD 6*	2	7
4 Jul 98		**ARCHIVE 1967-75** *Virgin CDBOX 6*	35	1
6 Nov 99	●	**TURN IT ON AGAIN – THE HITS** *Virgin GENCDX 8*	4	15

Tracks on Spot the Pigeon (EP): Match of the Day / Pigeons / Inside and Out. Tracks on 3 x 3 (EP): Paperlate / You Might Recall / Me and Virgil

See also Tony BANKS; Phil COLLINS; Peter GABRIEL; Steve HACKETT; MIKE and the MECHANICS

Lee A GENESIS – *See Bob SINCLAR*

GENEVA *UK, male vocal / instrumental group (Singles: 9 weeks, Albums: 2 weeks)*

Date		Title	pos	wks
26 Oct 96		**NO ONE SPEAKS** *Nude NUD 22CD*	32	2
8 Feb 97		**INTO THE BLUE** *Nude NUD 25CD*	26	2
31 May 97		**TRANQUILIZER** *Nude NUD 28 CD1*	24	2
16 Aug 97		**BEST REGRETS** *Nude NUD 31CD1*	38	1
27 Nov 99		**DOLLARS IN THE HEAVENS** *Nude NUD 46CD1*	59	1
11 Mar 00		**IF YOU HAVE TO GO** *Nude NUD 49CD1*	69	1
21 Jun 97		**FURTHER** *Nude NUDE 7CD*	20	2

GENEVIEVE *UK, female vocalist – Susan Hunt (Singles: 1 week)*

Date		Title	pos	wks
5 May 66		**ONCE** *CBS 202061*	43	1

GENIUS CRU *UK, male production group (Singles: 7 weeks)*

Date		Title	pos	wks
3 Feb 01		**BOOM SELECTION** *Incentive CENT 17CDS*	12	5
27 Oct 01		**COURSE BRUV** *Incentive CENT 28CDS*	39	2

GENIUS / GZA – *See GZA / GENIUS*

Jackie GENOVA

UK, female exercise instructor (Albums: 2 weeks)

Date		Title	pos	wks
21 May 83		**WORK THAT BODY** *Island ILPS 9732*	74	2

Bobbie GENTRY *US, female vocalist – Roberta Streeter (Singles: 48 weeks, Albums: 2 weeks)*

Date		Title	pos	wks
13 Sep 67		**ODE TO BILLIE JOE** *Capitol CL 15511* ▲	13	11
30 Aug 69	★	**I'LL NEVER FALL IN LOVE AGAIN** *Capitol CL 15606*	1	19
6 Dec 69	●	**ALL I HAVE TO DO IS DREAM** *Capitol CL 15619* [1]	3	14
21 Feb 70		**RAINDROPS KEEP FALLING ON MY HEAD** *Capitol CL 15626*	40	4
25 Oct 69		**TOUCH 'EM WITH LOVE** *Capitol EST 155*	21	1
28 Feb 70		**BOBBIE GENTRY AND GLEN CAMPBELL** *Capitol ST 2928* [1]	50	1

[1] Bobbie Gentry and Glen Campbell [1] Bobbie Gentry and Glen Campbell

GEORDIE *UK, male vocal / instrumental group (Singles: 35 weeks)*

Date		Title	pos	wks
2 Dec 72		**DON'T DO THAT** *Regal Zonophone RZ 3067*	32	7
17 Mar 73	●	**ALL BECAUSE OF YOU** *EMI 2008*	6	13
16 Jun 73		**CAN YOU DO IT** *EMI 2031*	13	9
25 Aug 73		**ELECTRIC LADY** *EMI 2048*	32	6

Lowell GEORGE *US male vocalist / instrumentalist – guitar, d. 29 Jun 1979 (Albums: 1 week)* pos/wks

21 Apr 79 THANKS BUT I'LL EAT IT HERE *Warner Bros. K 56487* 71 1

See also LITTLE FEAT

Robin GEORGE
UK, male vocalist (Singles: 2 weeks, Albums: 3 weeks) pos/wks

27 Apr 85 HEARTLINE *Bronze BRO 191* 68 2
2 Mar 85 DANGEROUS MUSIC *Bronze BRON 554* 65 3

Sophia GEORGE
Jamaica, female vocalist (Singles: 11 weeks) pos/wks

7 Dec 85 ● GIRLIE GIRLIE *Winner WIN 01* 7 11

GEORGIA SATELLITES *US, male vocal / instrumental group (Singles: 8 weeks, Albums: 9 weeks)* pos/wks

7 Feb 87 KEEP YOUR HANDS TO YOURSELF *Elektra EKR 50* 69 1
16 May 87 BATTLESHIP CHAINS *Elektra EKR 58* 44 4
21 Jan 89 HIPPY HIPPY SHAKE *Elektra EKR 86* 63 3
7 Feb 87 GEORGIA SATELLITES *Elektra 980 4961* 52 7
2 Jul 88 OPEN ALL NIGHT *Elektra EKT 47* 39 2

GEORGIE PORGIE
US, male producer (Singles: 3 weeks) pos/wks

12 Aug 95 EVERYBODY MUST PARTY *Vibe MCSTD 2068* 61 1
4 May 96 TAKE ME HIGHER *Music Plant MCSTD 40031* 61 1
26 Aug 00 LIFE GOES ON *Neo NEOCD 039* 54 1

GEORGIO *US, male vocalist (Singles: 3 weeks)* pos/wks

20 Feb 88 LOVER'S LANE *Motown ZB 41611* 54 3

Danyel GÉRARD *France, male vocalist (Singles: 12 weeks)* pos/wks

18 Sep 71 BUTTERFLY *CBS 7454* 11 12

GERIDEAU *US, male vocalist (Singles: 2 weeks)* pos/wks

27 Aug 94 BRING IT ALL BACK 2 LUV *Fruittree FTREE 10CD* [1] 65 1
4 Jul 98 MASQUERADE *Inferno CDFERN7* 63 1

[1] Project featuring Gerideau

Lisa GERRARD – *See Hans ZIMMER*

GERRY and the PACEMAKERS (480 Top 500)
Record-breaking Merseybeat band: Gerry Marsden (v/g), Les Chadwick (b), Les McGuire (p), Freddie Marsden (d). Second Liverpool group to chart (after The Beatles), but first to reach No.1 and first act ever to top UK chart with their initial three singles (Singles: 114 weeks, Albums: 29 weeks) pos/wks

14 Mar 63 ★ HOW DO YOU DO IT? *Columbia DB 4987* 1 18
30 May 63 ★ I LIKE IT *Columbia DB 7041* 1 15
10 Oct 63 ★ YOU'LL NEVER WALK ALONE *Columbia DB 7126* 1 19
16 Jan 64 ● I'M THE ONE *Columbia DB 7189* 2 15
16 Apr 64 ● DON'T LET THE SUN CATCH YOU CRYING *Columbia DB 7268* ..6 11
3 Sep 64 IT'S GONNA BE ALL RIGHT *Columbia DB 7353* ..24 7
17 Dec 64 ● FERRY 'CROSS THE MERSEY *Columbia DB 7437* 8 13
25 Mar 65 I'LL BE THERE *Columbia DB 7504* 15 9
18 Nov 65 WALK HAND IN HAND *Columbia DB 7738* 29 7
26 Oct 63 ● HOW DO YOU LIKE IT? *Columbia 33SX 1546* 2 28
6 Feb 65 FERRY CROSS THE MERSEY *Columbia 33SX 1676* 19 1

GET FRESH CREW – *See Doug E FRESH and the GET FRESH CREW*

GET READY *UK, male vocal group (Singles: 1 week)* pos/wks

3 Jun 95 WILD WILD WEST *Mega GACXCD 2698* 65 1

GETO BOYS featuring FLAJ
US, male rap group (Singles: 1 week) pos/wks

11 May 96 THE WORLD IS A GHETTO *Virgin America VUSCD 104* 49 1

Stan GETZ *US, male instrumentalist – tenor sax – Stanley Gayetzsky, d. 6 Jun 1991 (Singles: 29 weeks, Albums: 7 weeks)* pos/wks

8 Nov 62 DESAFINADO *HMV POP 1061* [1] 11 13
23 Jul 64 THE GIRL FROM IPANEMA (GAROTA DE IPANEMA) *Verve VS 520* [2] 29 10
25 Aug 84 THE GIRL FROM IPANEMA (re-issue) *Verve IPA 1* [3] 55 6
23 Feb 63 JAZZ SAMBA *Verve SULP 9013* [1] 15 7

[1] Stan Getz and Charlie Byrd [2] Stan Getz and Joao Gilberto [3] Astrud Gilberto
[1] Stan Getz and Charlie Byrd

The re-issue of 'The Girl from Ipanema' was credited only to Astrud Gilberto, the vocalist, even though it was exactly the same recording as the original hit

Angela GHEORGIU – *See Roberto ALAGNA / Angela GHEORGIU*

Amanda GHOST *UK, female vocalist (Singles: 1 week)* pos/wks

8 Apr 00 IDOL *Warner Brothers W 518CD* 63 1

GHOST DANCE
UK, male vocal / instrumental group (Singles: 2 weeks) pos/wks

17 Jun 89 DOWN TO THE WIRE *Chrysalis CHS 3376* 66 2

GHOSTFACE KILLAH *US, male rapper – Dennis Coles (Singles: 20 weeks, Albums: 2 weeks)* pos/wks

12 Jul 97 ALL THAT I GOT IS YOU *Epic 6646842* 11 4
23 Jan 99 ● I WANT YOU FOR MYSELF *Northwestside 74321643632* [1] 2 8
4 Nov 00 MISS FAT BOOTY – PART II *Rawkus RWK 282CD* [2] 64 1
1 Nov 03 OOH WEE *Elektra E 7490CD* [3] 15 7
9 Nov 96 IRONMAN *Epic 4853892* 38 2

[1] Another Level / Ghostface Killah [2] Mos Def featuring Ghostface Killah [3] Mark Ronson featuring Ghostface Killah and Nate Dogg

See also WU-TANG CLAN

Andy GIBB *UK, male vocalist, d. 10 Mar 1988 (Singles: 30 weeks, Albums: 9 weeks)* pos/wks

25 Jun 77 I JUST WANNA BE YOUR EVERYTHING *RSO 2090 237* ▲ 26 7
13 May 78 SHADOW DANCING *RSO 001* ▲ 42 6
12 Aug 78 ● AN EVERLASTING LOVE *RSO 015* 10 10
27 Jan 79 (OUR LOVE) DON'T THROW IT ALL AWAY *RSO 26* 32 7
19 Aug 78 SHADOW DANCING *RSO RSS 0001* 15 9

Barry GIBB *UK, male vocalist (Albums: 2 weeks)* pos/wks

20 Oct 84 NOW VOYAGER *Polydor POLH 14* 85 2

See also BEE GEES; Barbra STREISAND

Robin GIBB
UK, male vocalist (Singles: 25 weeks, Albums: 1 week) pos/wks

9 Jul 69 ● SAVED BY THE BELL (re) *Polydor 56-337* 2 17
7 Feb 70 AUGUST OCTOBER *Polydor 56-371* 45 3
11 Feb 84 ANOTHER LONELY NIGHT IN NEW YORK *Polydor POSP 668* ..71 1
1 Feb 03 PLEASE *SPV Recordings SPV 05571463* 23 4
15 Feb 03 MAGNET *SPV Recordings SPV08571472* 43 1

See also BEE GEES

Beth GIBBONS & RUSTIN' MAN
UK, female vocalist and male producer / instrumentalist – Paul Webb (Singles: 1 week, Albums: 2 weeks) pos/wks

15 Mar 03 TOM THE MODEL *Go! Beat GOBCD 55* 70 1
9 Nov 02 OUT OF SEASON *Go! Beat 665742* 28 2

See also PORTISHEAD; TALK TALK

Steve GIBBONS BAND *UK, male vocal / instrumental group (Singles: 14 weeks, Albums: 3 weeks)* pos/wks

6 Aug 77 TULANE *Polydor 2058 889* 12 10
13 May 78 EDDY VORTEX *Polydor 2059 017* 56 4
22 Oct 77 CAUGHT IN THE ACT *Polydor 2478 112* 22 3

2003 UK FACTS AND STATS

UK album sales were up 6.8 per cent in 2003 with total sales of 159.3 million – a staggering figure when you consider that the majority of the world suffered decreased sales.

Although sales of singles were down 29.2 per cent in 2003 (with total sales of 30.9 million), indications are that within a relatively short period of time paid downloads could more than make up for the shortfall. In America this is already the case, with paid downloads easily outselling physical singles for the last six months of 2003. Back in the UK, it may be not so much a question of will paid downloads work but which downloading system will be the most used. This could mean that we see a major change in the make-up of the Top 75, with popular old tracks making the charts alongside current releases – as they do on the American download chart. Apple was bullish about its download performance and announced 25 million paid downloads since business opened Stateside in April. However, it's still far too early to write off the CD single. In 2003 record companies came up with several ideas to save the single, including price cuts and reduction in content.

Biggest-selling singles act of 2003
BLACK EYED PEAS 848,000

Biggest-selling albums act of 2003
DIDO 2,369,000

Biggest-selling DVD of 2003
WHAT WE DID LAST SUMMER by ROBBIE WILLIAMS 263,178

Most popular ring tone of 2003
IN DA CLUB by 50 CENT

Most played record on radio in 2003
MAKE LUV by ROOM 5 FEATURING OLIVER CHEATHAM 57,186 plays

The pace of the singles chart continued to slow down in 2003. There were just 23 No.1s, almost half as many as were in 2000, and the average single was spending longer on the chart – two facts which may bode well for the future. However, the UK still has the world's fastest moving chart. Other good signs for the record industry in 2003 include the increased sales of music DVDs (up 79.9 per cent) and ring tones ('In Da Club' being the most popular track on both sides of the Atlantic), and the fact that it was a record summer for live acts in the UK and that US tour grosses passed the $2bn mark for the first time. Pop Idol-type TV shows still supplied many of the world's biggest-selling acts in a year in which British artists increased their share of sales both inside and outside the UK.

Finally, The Rolling Stones proved once again that they were still the biggest live draw when they grossed $299,520,225 for their Licks world tour, the most profitable of the year and second only to an all-time record set by their very own Voodoo Lounge extravaganza in 1994-96.

TOP 10 SINGLES OF 2003

1. **WHERE IS THE LOVE? Black Eyed Peas** 625,198
2. **SPIRIT IN THE SKY Gareth Gates featuring The Kumars** 552,598
3. **IGNITION REMIX R Kelly** 478,369
4. **MAD WORLD Michael Andrews featuring Gary Jules** 394,627
5. **LEAVE RIGHT NOW Will Young** 381,088
6. **ALL THE THINGS SHE SAID t.A.T.u.** 337,829
7. **CHANGES Ozzy and Kelly Osbourne** 333,869
8. **BREATHE Blu Cantrell featuring Sean Paul** 330,032
9. **MAKE LUV Room 5 featuring Oliver Cheatham** 316,750
10. **CHRISTMAS TIME (DON'T LET THE BELLS END) The Darkness** 313,530

TOP 10 ALBUMS OF 2003

1. **LIFE FOR RENT Dido** 2,168,302
2. **JUSTIFIED Justin Timberlake** 1,404,272
3. **STRIPPED Christina Aguilera** 1,264,059
4. **GOTTA GET THRU THIS Daniel Bedingfield** 1,112,143
5. **COME AWAY WITH ME Norah Jones** 1,071,671
6. **PERMISSION TO LAND The Darkness** 1,027,803
7. **A RUSH OF BLOOD TO THE HEAD Coldplay** 985,587
8. **NUMBER ONES Michael Jackson** 960,848
9. **BUSTED Busted** 907,331
10. **IN TIME – THE BEST OF 1988-2003 R.E.M.** 907,282

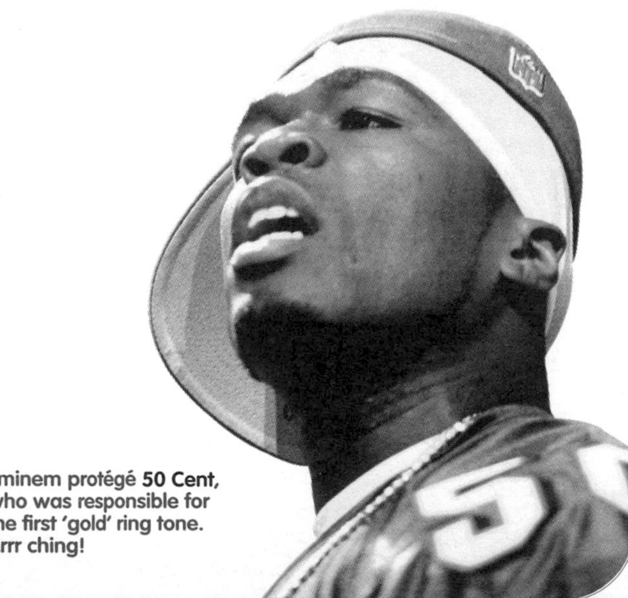

Eminem protégé 50 Cent, who was responsible for the first 'gold' ring tone. Krrr ching!

Georgia GIBBS
US, female vocalist – Freda Gibbons (Singles: 2 weeks) pos/wks

22 Apr 55 **TWEEDLE DEE** *Mercury MB 3196* 20 1
13 Jul 56 **KISS ME ANOTHER** *Mercury MT 110* 25 1

Debbie GIBSON *US female vocalist / producer (Singles: 70 weeks, Albums: 52 weeks)* pos/wks

26 Sep 87 **ONLY IN MY DREAMS (re)** *Atlantic A 9322* 11 12
23 Jan 88 ● **SHAKE YOUR LOVE** *Atlantic A 9187* 7 8
7 May 88 **OUT OF THE BLUE** *Atlantic A 9091* 19 7
9 Jul 88 ● **FOOLISH BEAT** *Atlantic A 9059* ▲ 9 9
15 Oct 88 **STAYING TOGETHER** *Atlantic A 9020* 53 2
28 Jan 89 **LOST IN YOUR EYES** *Atlantic A 8970* ▲ 34 7
29 Apr 89 **ELECTRIC YOUTH** *Atlantic A 8919* 14 8
19 Aug 89 **WE COULD BE TOGETHER** *Atlantic A 8896* 22 8
9 Mar 91 **ANYTHING IS POSSIBLE** *Atlantic A 7735* 51 2
3 Apr 93 **SHOCK YOUR MAMA** *Atlantic A 7386CD* 74 1
24 Jul 93 **YOU'RE THE ONE THAT I WANT** *Epic 6595222* [1] 13 6
30 Jan 88 **OUT OF THE BLUE** *Atlantic WX 139*....................26 35
11 Feb 89 ● **ELECTRIC YOUTH** *Atlantic WX 231* ▲ 8 16
30 Mar 91 **ANYTHING IS POSSIBLE** *Atlantic WX 399*....................69 1

[1] Craig McLachlan and Debbie Gibson

'Only in My Dreams' made its peak position on re-entry in Mar 1988

Don GIBSON *US, male vocalist / instrumentalist – guitar d. 17 Nov 2003 (Singles: 16 weeks, Albums: 10 weeks)* pos/wks

31 Aug 61 **SEA OF HEARTBREAK** *RCA 1243* 14 13
1 Feb 62 **LONESOME NUMBER ONE** *RCA 1272* 47 3
22 Mar 80 **COUNTRY NUMBER ONE** *Warwick WW 5079*....................13 10

Wayne GIBSON *UK, male vocalist (Singles: 13 weeks)* pos/wks

3 Sep 64 **KELLY** *Pye 7N 15680* 48 2
23 Nov 74 **UNDER MY THUMB** *Pye Disco Demand DDS 2001* 17 11

GIBSON BROTHERS *Martinique, male vocal / instrumental group (Singles: 54 weeks, Albums: 3 weeks)* pos/wks

10 Mar 79 **CUBA** *Island WIP 6483* 41 9
21 Jul 79 ● **OOH! WHAT A LIFE** *Island WIP 6503* 10 12
17 Nov 79 ● **QUE SERA MI VIDA (IF YOU SHOULD GO)** *Island WIP 6525* 5 11
23 Feb 80 **CUBA / BETTER DO IT SALSA (re-issue)** *Island WIP 6561* 12 9
12 Jul 80 **MARIANA** *Island WIP 6617* 11 10
9 Jul 83 **MY HEART'S BEATING WILD (TIC TAC TIC TAC)** *Stiff BUY 184* ..56 3
30 Aug 80 **ON THE RIVIERA** *Island ILPS 9620* 50 3

GIDEA PARK
UK, male vocal group – includes Adrian Baker (Singles: 19 weeks) pos/wks

4 Jul 81 **BEACH BOY GOLD** *Sonet SON 2162* 11 13
12 Sep 81 **SEASONS OF GOLD** *Polo POLO 14* 28 6

Johan GIELEN presents ABNEA
Belgium, male producer (Singles: 1 week) pos/wks

18 Aug 01 **VELVET MOODS** *Data DATA 17T* 74 1

See also AIRSCAPE; BLUE BAMBOO; BALEARIC BILL; SVENSON and GIELEN

GIFTED *UK, male instrumentalist (Singles: 1 week)* pos/wks

23 Aug 97 **DO I** *Perfecto PERF 140CD* 60 1

GIGOLO AUNTS
US, male vocal / instrumental group (Singles: 4 weeks) pos/wks

23 Apr 94 **MRS WASHINGTON** *Fire BLAZE 68CD* 74 1
13 May 95 **WHERE I FIND MY HEAVEN** *Fire BLAZE 87CD* 29 3

Astrud GILBERTO – *See Stan GETZ*

Bebel GILBERTO *Brazil, female vocalist (Albums: 5 weeks)* pos/wks

31 Aug 02 **TANTO TEMPO** *East West 0927474072* 49 5

Joao GILBERTO – *See Stan GETZ*

Jane GILCHRIST – *See Denise LEIGH*

Donna GILES
US, female vocalist (Singles: 4 weeks) pos/wks

13 Aug 94 **AND I'M TELLING YOU I'M NOT GOING** *Ore AG 4CD* 43 2
10 Feb 96 **AND I'M TELLING YOU I'M NOT GOING (re-issue)** *Ore AGR 4CD* 27 2

Johnny GILL
US, male vocalist (Singles: 12 weeks, Albums: 3 weeks) pos/wks

23 Feb 91 **WRAP MY BODY TIGHT** *Motown ZB 44271* 57 2
28 Nov 92 **SLOW AND SEXY** *Epic 6587727* [1] 17 7
17 Jul 93 **THE FLOOR** *Motown TMGCD 1416* 53 1
29 Jan 94 **A CUTE SWEET LOVE ADDICTION** *Motown TMGCD 1420* 46 2
19 Jun 93 **PROVOCATIVE** *Motown 5302062* 41 3

[1] Shabba Ranks featuring Johnny Gill

See also NEW EDITION

Vince GILL – *See Amy GRANT; Barbra STREISAND*

GILLAN *UK, male vocal / instrumental group (Singles: 46 weeks, Albums: 53 weeks)* pos/wks

14 Jun 80 **SLEEPING ON THE JOB** *Virgin VS 355* 55 3
4 Oct 80 **TROUBLE** *Virgin VS 377* 14 6
14 Feb 81 **MUTUALLY ASSURED DESTRUCTION** *Virgin VSK 103* 32 5
21 Mar 81 **NEW ORLEANS** *Virgin VS 406* 17 10
20 Jun 81 **NO LAUGHING IN HEAVEN** *Virgin VS 425* 31 6
10 Oct 81 **NIGHTMARE** *Virgin VS 441* 36 6
23 Jan 82 **RESTLESS** *Virgin VS 465* 25 7
4 Sep 82 **LIVING FOR THE CITY** *Virgin VS 519* 50 3
17 Jul 76 **CHILD IN TIME** *Polydor 2490 136* [1]....................55 1
20 Oct 79 **MR UNIVERSE** *Acrobat ACRO 3* 11 6
16 Aug 80 ● **GLORY ROAD** *Virgin V 2171* 3 12
25 Apr 81 ● **FUTURE SHOCK** *Virgin VK 2196*....................2 13
7 Nov 81 **DOUBLE TROUBLE** *Virgin VGD 3506*....................12 15
2 Oct 82 **MAGIC** *Virgin V 2238* 17 6

[1] Ian Gillan Band

See also Ian GILLAN

Ian GILLAN *UK, male vocalist (Albums: 1 week)* pos/wks

28 Jul 90 **NAKED THUNDER** *Teldec 9031718991* 63 1

See also DEEP PURPLE; BLACK SABBATH; GILLAN

GILLETTE – *See 20 FINGERS*

Stuart GILLIES *UK, male vocalist (Singles: 10 weeks)* pos/wks

31 Mar 73 **AMANDA** *Philips 6006 293* 13 10

Jimmy GILMER – *See FIREBALLS*

Thea GILMORE
UK, female vocalist (Singles: 2 weeks, Albums: 1 week) pos/wks

16 Aug 03 **JULIET (KEEP THAT IN MIND)** *Hungry Dog YRGNUHS 1* 35 1
8 Nov 03 **MAINSTREAM** *Hungry Dog YRGNUH 53* 50 1
23 Aug 03 **AVALANCHE** *Hungry Dog YRGNUHA 1*....................63 1

David GILMOUR
UK, male vocalist / instrumentalist – guitar (Albums: 18 weeks) pos/wks

10 Jun 78 **DAVID GILMOUR** *Harvest SHVL 817* 17 9
17 Mar 84 **ABOUT FACE** *Harvest SHSP 2400791* 21 9

See also PINK FLOYD

James GILREATH *US, male vocalist (Singles: 10 weeks)* pos/wks

2 May 63 **LITTLE BAND OF GOLD** *Pye International 7N 25190* 29 10

Jim GILSTRAP *US, male vocalist (Singles: 11 weeks)*

				pos/wks	
5 Mar 75	●	**SWING YOUR DADDY**	*Chelsea 2005 021*	4	11

Gordon GILTRAP *UK, male instrumentalist – guitar (Singles: 10 weeks, Albums: 7 weeks)*

				pos/wks	
4 Jan 78		**HEARTSONG**	*Electric WOT 19*	21	7
28 Apr 79		**FEAR OF THE DARK**	*Electric WOT 29* [1]	58	3
8 Feb 78		**PERILOUS JOURNEY**	*Electric TRIX 4*	29	7

[1] Gordon Giltrap Band

GIN BLOSSOMS *US, male vocal / instrumental group (Singles: 12 weeks, Albums: 6 weeks)*

				pos/wks	
5 Feb 94		**HEY JEALOUSY**	*Fontana GINCD 3*	24	5
6 Apr 94		**FOUND OUT ABOUT YOU**	*Fontana GINCD 4*	40	3
0 Feb 96		**TIL I HEAR IT FROM YOU**	*A&M 5812272*	39	2
27 Apr 96		**FOLLOW YOU DOWN**	*A&M 5815512*	30	2
26 Feb 94		**NEW MISERABLE EXPERIENCE**	*Fontana 3954032*	53	4
24 Feb 96		**CONGRATULATIONS I'M SORRY**	*A&M 5404702*	42	2

GINGERBREADS – *See GOLDIE and the GINGERBREADS*

GINUWINE *US, male rapper – Elgin Lumpkin (Singles: 27 weeks, Albums: 2 weeks)*

				pos/wks	
25 Jan 97		**PONY**	*Epic 6641282*	16	6
24 May 97		**TELL ME DO U WANNA**	*Epic 6645272*	16	3
6 Sep 97	●	**WHEN DOVES CRY**	*Epic 6649245*	10	5
4 Mar 98		**HOLLER**	*Epic 6653372*	13	4
3 Mar 99	●	**WHAT'S SO DIFFERENT?**	*Epic 6670522*	10	4
4 Dec 02		**CRUSH TONIGHT**	*Atlantic AT 0142CD* [1]	42	2
7 Jun 03		**HELL YEAH**	*Epic 6739242*	27	3
28 Mar 98		**GINUWINE ... THE BACHELOR**	*Epic 4853912*	74	1
27 Mar 99		**100% GINUWINE**	*Epic 4919922*	42	1

[1] Fat Joe featuring Ginuwine

GIPSY KINGS *France, male vocal / instrumental group (Singles: 2 weeks, Albums: 65 weeks)*

				pos/wks	
3 Sep 94		**HITS MEDLEY**	*Columbia 6606022*	53	2
5 Apr 89		**GIPSY KINGS**	*Telstar STAR 2355*	16	29
25 Nov 89		**MOSAÏQUE**	*Telstar STAR 2398*	27	13
3 Jul 91		**ESTE MUNDO**	*Columbia 4686481*	19	7
6 Aug 94		**GREATEST HITS**	*Columbia 4772422*	11	11
24 Jul 99		**VOLARE – THE VERY BEST OF THE GIPSY KINGS**	*Columbia SONYTV 69CD*	20	5

Martine GIRAULT *UK, female vocalist (Singles: 7 weeks)*

				pos/wks	
29 Aug 92		**REVIVAL**	*ffrr FX 195*	53	2
30 Jan 93		**REVIVAL (re-issue)**	*ffrr FCD 205*	37	3
28 Oct 95		**BEEN THINKING ABOUT YOU**	*RCA 74321316142*	63	1
1 Feb 97		**REVIVAL (re-mix)**	*RCA 74321432162*	61	1

GIRESSE *UK, male DJ / production duo (Singles: 1 week)*

				pos/wks	
4 Apr 01		**MON AMI**	*Inferno CDFERN 36*	61	1

GIRL *UK, male vocal / instrumental group (Singles: 3 weeks, Albums: 6 weeks)*

				pos/wks	
2 Apr 80		**HOLLYWOOD TEASE**	*Jet 176*	50	3
9 Feb 80		**SHEER GREED**	*Jet JETLP 224*	33	5
3 Jan 82		**WASTED YOUTH**	*Jet JETLP 238*	92	1

GIRL NEXT DOOR – *See M&S presents GIRL NEXT DOOR*

GIRL THING *UK / Holland, female vocal group (Singles: 13 weeks)*

				pos/wks	
1 Jul 00	●	**LAST ONE STANDING (re)**	*RCA 74321762412*	8	10
8 Nov 00		**GIRLS ON TOP**	*RCA 74321801162*	25	3

GIRLFRIEND *Australia, female vocal group (Singles: 6 weeks)*

				pos/wks	
0 Jan 93		**TAKE IT FROM ME**	*Arista 74321114252*	47	4
5 May 93		**GIRL'S LIFE**	*Arista 74321138452*	68	2

GIRLS ALOUD
UK, female vocal group (Singles: 49 weeks, Albums: 16 weeks)

				pos/wks	
28 Dec 02	★	**SOUND OF THE UNDERGROUND**	*Polydor 0658272* ■	1	21
24 May 03	●	**NO GOOD ADVICE**	*Polydor 9800051*	2	14
30 Aug 03	●	**LIFE GOT COLD**	*Polydor 9810656*	3	9
29 Nov 03	●	**JUMP**	*Polydor 9814103*	2	5+
7 Jun 03	●	**SOUNDS OF THE UNDERGROUND**	*Polydor 9865315*	2	16+

GIRLS AT OUR BEST
UK, male / female vocal / instrumental group (Albums: 3 weeks)

				pos/wks	
7 Nov 81		**PLEASURE**	*Happy Birthday RVLP 1*	60	3

GIRLS @ PLAY *UK, female vocal group (Singles: 7 weeks)*

				pos/wks	
24 Feb 01		**AIRHEAD**	*GSM GSMCDR 1*	18	5
13 Oct 01		**RESPECTABLE**	*Redbus RBMCD101*	29	2

GIRLSCHOOL *UK, female vocal / instrumental group (Singles: 25 weeks, Albums: 23 weeks)*

				pos/wks	
2 Aug 80		**RACE WITH THE DEVIL**	*Bronze BRO 100*	49	6
21 Feb 81	●	**ST VALENTINE'S DAY MASSACRE (EP)**	*Bronze BRO 116* [1]	5	8
11 Apr 81		**HIT AND RUN**	*Bronze BRO 118*	32	6
11 Jul 81		**C'MON LET'S GO**	*Bronze BRO 126*	42	3
3 Apr 82		**WILDLIFE (EP)**	*Bronze BRO 144*	58	2
5 Jul 80		**DEMOLITION**	*Bronze BRON 525*	28	10
25 Apr 81	●	**HIT 'N' RUN**	*Bronze BRON 534*	5	6
12 Jun 82		**SCREAMING BLUE MURDER**	*Bronze BRON 541*	27	6
12 Nov 83		**PLAY DIRTY**	*Bronze BRON 548*	66	1

[1] Motörhead and Girlschool (also known as Headgirl)

Tracks on St Valentine's Day Massacre (EP): Please Don't Touch / Emergency / Bomber. Tracks on Wildlife (EP): Don't Call It Love / Wildlife / Don't Stop

Junior GISCOMBE – *See JUNIOR*

GITTA *Denmark / Italy, male / female vocal / instrumental group (Singles: 1 week)*

				pos/wks	
19 Aug 00		**NO MORE TURNING BACK**	*Pepper 9230302*	54	1

GLADIATORS
UK, male / female vocal group (Singles: 1 week)

				pos/wks	
30 Nov 96		**THE BOYS ARE BACK IN TOWN**	*RCA 74321417002*	70	1

GLADIATORS – *See NERO and the GLADIATORS*

GLAM
Italy, male instrumental / production group (Singles: 2 weeks)

				pos/wks	
1 May 93		**HELL'S PARTY**	*Six6 SIXCD 001*	42	2

GLAM METAL DETECTIVES
UK, male / female vocal group (Singles: 2 weeks)

				pos/wks	
11 Mar 95		**EVERYBODY UP!**	*ZTT ZANG 62CD*	29	2

GLAMMA KID *UK, male vocalist / rapper – Lyael Constable (Singles: 25 weeks, Albums: 1 week)*

				pos/wks	
21 Nov 98		**FASHION '98**	*WEA WEA 179CD*	49	1
17 Apr 99	●	**TABOO**	*WEA WEA 203CD* [1]	10	8
27 Nov 99	●	**WHY**	*WEA WEA 229 CD1*	10	10
2 Sep 00		**BILLS 2 PAY (re)**	*WEA WEA 268CD*	17	6
16 Sep 00		**KIDOLOGY**	*WEA 3984298572*	66	1

[1] Glamma Kid featuring Shola Ama

GLASS TIGER
Canada, male vocal / instrumental group (Singles: 18 weeks)

				pos/wks	
18 Oct 86		**DON'T FORGET ME (WHEN I'M GONE)**	*Manhattan MT 13*	29	9
31 Jan 87		**SOMEDAY**	*Manhattan MT 17*	66	2
26 Oct 91		**MY TOWN**	*EMI EM 212*	33	7

'My Town' features the uncredited vocals of Rod Stewart

Mayson GLEN ORCHESTRA – *See Paul HENRY and the Mayson GLEN ORCHESTRA*

GLENN and CHRIS

UK, male footballers / vocal duo – Glenn Hoddle and Chris Waddle (Singles: 8 weeks)

Date		Title / Label	pos	wks
18 Apr 87		**DIAMOND LIGHTS** *Record Shack KICK 1*	12	8

Gary GLITTER (224 Top 500)

Glitter rock giant, b. Paul Gadd, 8 May 1940, Oxfordshire, UK. Started recording in 1960 (as Paul Raven), and was the first act to put his first 11 hits into the Top 10. This singer / songwriter remained a popular live performer until he was jailed in 1999. Biggest-selling single: 'I Love You Love Me Love' 1,140,000 (Singles: 170 weeks, Albums: 100 weeks)

Date		Title / Label	pos	wks
10 Jun 72	●	**ROCK AND ROLL (PARTS 1 & 2)** *Bell 1216*	2	15
23 Sep 72	●	**I DIDN'T KNOW I LOVED YOU (TILL I SAW YOU ROCK 'N' ROLL)** *Bell 1259*	4	11
20 Jan 73	●	**DO YOU WANNA TOUCH ME? (OH YEAH)** *Bell 1280*	2	11
7 Apr 73	●	**HELLO! HELLO! I'M BACK AGAIN** *Bell 1299*	2	14
21 Jul 73	★	**I'M THE LEADER OF THE GANG (I AM!)** *Bell 1321*	1	12
17 Nov 73	★	**I LOVE YOU LOVE ME LOVE** *Bell 1337* ◆ ■	1	14
30 Mar 74	●	**REMEMBER ME THIS WAY** *Bell 1349*	3	8
15 Jun 74	★	**ALWAYS YOURS** *Bell 1359*	1	9
23 Nov 74	●	**OH YES! YOU'RE BEAUTIFUL** *Bell 1391*	2	10
3 May 75	●	**LOVE LIKE YOU AND ME** *Bell 1423*	10	6
21 Jun 75	●	**DOING ALRIGHT WITH THE BOYS** *Bell 1429*	6	7
8 Nov 75		**PAPA OOM MOW MOW** *Bell 1451*	38	5
13 Mar 76		**YOU BELONG TO ME** *Bell 1473*	40	5
22 Jan 77		**IT TAKES ALL NIGHT LONG** *Arista 85*	25	6
16 Jul 77		**A LITTLE BOOGIE WOOGIE IN THE BACK OF MY MIND** *Arista 112*	31	5
20 Sep 80		**GARY GLITTER (EP)** *GTO GT 282*	57	3
10 Oct 81		**AND THEN SHE KISSED ME** *Bell BELL 1497*	39	5
5 Dec 81		**ALL THAT GLITTERS** *Bell BELL 1498*	48	5
23 Jun 84		**DANCE ME UP** *Arista ARIST 570*	25	5
1 Dec 84	●	**ANOTHER ROCK AND ROLL CHRISTMAS** *Arista ARIST 592*	7	7
10 Oct 92		**AND THE LEADER ROCKS ON (MEGAMIX / MEDLEY)** *EMI EM 252*	58	2
21 Nov 92		**THROUGH THE YEARS** *EMI EM 256*	49	3
16 Dec 95		**HELLO HELLO I'M BACK AGAIN (AGAIN!)** *Carlton Sounds 3036000192*	50	2
21 Oct 72	●	**GLITTER** *Bell BELLS 216*	8	40
16 Jun 73	●	**TOUCH ME** *Bell BELLS 222*	2	33
29 Jun 74	●	**REMEMBER ME THIS WAY** *Bell BELLS 237*	5	14
27 Mar 76		**GARY GLITTER'S GREATEST HITS** *Bell BELLS 262*	33	5
14 Nov 92		**MANY HAPPY RETURNS – THE HITS** *EMI CDEMTV 68*	35	8

'Rock and Roll Part 1' not listed with 'Part 2' for weeks of 10 and 17 Jun 1972. Tracks on Gary Glitter (EP): I'm the Leader of the Gang (I Am) / Rock and Roll (Part 2) / Hello Hello I'm Back Again / Do You Wanna Touch Me? (Oh Yeah). All were re-issues. 'Hello Hello I'm Back Again (Again!)' in 1995 is a re-recording. All That Glitters was a medley of re-recordings: I'm the Leader of the Gang (I Am) / Do You Wanna Touch Me (Oh Yeah) / Doing Alright with the Boys / I Didn't Know I Loved You (Till I Saw You Rock'n' Roll) / Rock and Roll (Part 2). And the Leader Rocks On was a medley of I'm the Leader of the Gang (I Am) / Come On, Come In, Get On / Rock On / I Didn't Know I Loved You (Till I Saw You Rock 'N' Roll) / Do You Wanna Touch Me (Oh Yeah) / Hello! I'm Back Again

GLITTER BAND *UK, male vocal / instrumental group (Singles: 60 weeks, Albums: 17 weeks)*

Date		Title / Label	pos	wks
23 Mar 74	●	**ANGEL FACE** *Bell 1348*	4	10
3 Aug 74	●	**JUST FOR YOU** *Bell 1368*	10	8
19 Oct 74	●	**LET'S GET TOGETHER AGAIN** *Bell 1383*	8	8
18 Jan 75	●	**GOODBYE MY LOVE** *Bell 1395*	2	9
12 Apr 75	●	**THE TEARS I CRIED** *Bell 1416*	8	8
9 Aug 75		**LOVE IN THE SUN** *Bell 1437*	15	8
28 Feb 76	●	**PEOPLE LIKE YOU AND PEOPLE LIKE ME** *Bell 1471*	5	9
14 Sep 74		**HEY** *Bell BELLS 241*	13	12
3 May 75		**ROCK 'N' ROLL DUDES** *Bell BELLS 253*	17	4
19 Jun 76		**GREATEST HITS** *Bell BELLS 264*	52	1

See also Gary GLITTER

GLOBAL COMMUNICATION

UK, male instrumental / production duo (Singles: 1 week)

Date		Title / Label	pos	wks
11 Jan 97		**THE WAY / THE DEEP** *Dedicated GLOBA 002CD*	51	1

See also COSMOS

GLOVE *UK, male vocal / instrumental group (Singles: 3 weeks, Albums: 3 weeks)*

Date		Title / Label	pos	wks
20 Aug 83		**LIKE AN ANIMAL** *Wonderland SHE 3*	52	3
17 Sep 83		**BLUE SUNSHINE** *Wonderland SHELP 2*	35	3

See also CURE; SIOUXSIE and the BANSHEES

Dana GLOVER

US, female vocalist (Singles: 1 week, Albums: 2 weeks)

Date		Title / Label	pos	wks
10 May 03		**THINKING OVER** *Dreamworks 4507762*	38	1
17 May 03		**TESTIMONY** *Dreamworks / Polydor 04504522*	43	2

GLOWORM *UK / US, male vocal / instrumental group (Singles: 17 weeks)*

Date		Title / Label	pos	wks
6 Feb 93		**I LIFT MY CUP** *Pulse 8 CDLOSE 37*	20	4
14 May 94	●	**CARRY ME HOME** *Go.Beat GODCD 112*	9	11
6 Aug 94		**I LIFT MY CUP (re-issue)** *Pulse 8 CDLOSE 67*	46	2

GO GO LORENZO and the DAVIS PINCKNEY PROJECT

US, male vocal / instrumental group (Singles: 8 weeks)

Date		Title / Label	pos	wks
6 Dec 86		**YOU CAN DANCE IF YOU WANT TO** *Boiling Point POSP 836*	46	8

GO-GO's *US, female vocal / instrumental group (Singles: 10 weeks, Albums: 4 weeks)*

Date		Title / Label	pos	wks
15 May 82		**OUR LIPS ARE SEALED** *IRS GDN 102*	47	6
26 Jan 91		**COOL JERK** *IRS AM 712*	60	1
18 Feb 95		**THE WHOLE WORLD LOST ITS HEAD** *IRS CDEIRS 190*	29	3
21 Aug 82		**VACATION** *IRS SP 70031*	75	3
18 Mar 95		**RETURN TO THE VALLEY OF THE GO-GO'S** *IRS EIRSCD 1071*	52	1

See also Belinda CARLISLE; Jane WIEDLIN

GO WEST (323 Top 500)

Songwriting duo specialising in radio-friendly white soul sounds; Peter Cox (v) and Richard Drummie (g/k/v). Best Newcomers at the 1986 Brit awards had US Top 10 hit with 'King of Wishful Thinking', from the soundtrack of Pretty Woman (Singles: 85 weeks, Albums: 119 weeks)

Date		Title / Label	pos	wks
23 Feb 85	●	**WE CLOSE OUR EYES** *Chrysalis CHS 2850*	5	14
11 May 85		**CALL ME** *Chrysalis GOW 1*	12	10
3 Aug 85		**GOODBYE GIRL** *Chrysalis GOW 2*	25	7
23 Nov 85		**DON'T LOOK DOWN – THE SEQUEL** *Chrysalis GOW 3*	13	10
29 Nov 86		**TRUE COLOURS** *Chrysalis GOW 4*	48	7
9 May 87		**I WANT TO HEAR IT FROM YOU** *Chrysalis GOW 5*	43	3
12 Sep 87		**THE KING IS DEAD** *Chrysalis GOW 6*	67	2
28 Jul 90		**THE KING OF WISHFUL THINKING** *Chrysalis GOW 8*	18	10
17 Oct 92		**FAITHFUL** *Chrysalis GOW 9*	13	6
16 Jan 93		**WHAT YOU WON'T DO FOR LOVE** *Chrysalis CDGOWS 10*	15	5
27 Mar 93		**STILL IN LOVE** *Chrysalis CDGOWS 11*	43	3
2 Oct 93		**TRACKS OF MY TEARS** *Chrysalis CDGOWS 12*	16	5
4 Dec 93		**WE CLOSE OUR EYES (re-mix)** *Chrysalis CDGOWS 13*	40	3
13 Apr 85	●	**GO WEST / BANGS AND CRASHES** *Chrysalis CHR 1495*	8	83
6 Jun 87		**DANCING ON THE COUCH** *Chrysalis CDL 1550*	19	5
14 Nov 92		**INDIAN SUMMER** *Chrysalis CDCHR 1964*	13	16
16 Oct 93	●	**ACES AND KINGS – THE BEST OF GO WEST** *Chrysalis CDCHR 6050*	5	15

'Bangs and Crashes' is an album of remixed versions of Go West tracks and some new material. From 31 May 1986 both records were available together as a double album

GO-BETWEENS *Australia, male / female vocal / instrumental group (Albums: 2 weeks)*

Date		Title / Label	pos	wks
13 Jun 87		**TALLULAH** *Beggars Banquet BEGA 81*	91	1
10 Sep 88		**16 LOVERS LANE** *Beggars Banquet BEGA 95*	81	1

GOATS *US, male rap group (Singles: 2 weeks, Albums: 1 week)*

Date		Title / Label	pos	wks
29 May 93		AAAH D YAAA / TYPICAL AMERICAN *Ruff House 6593032*	53	2
27 Aug 94		NO GOATS NO GLORY *Columbia 4769372*	58	1

'Typical American' listed only from 5 Jun 1993, peaking at No.65

GOD MACHINE *US, male vocal / instrumental group (Singles: 2 weeks, Albums: 1 week)*

Date		Title / Label	pos	wks
30 Jan 93		HOME *Fiction FICCD 47*	65	2
20 Feb 93		SCENES FROM THE SECOND STOREY *Fiction 5171562*	55	1

GODFATHERS
UK, male vocal / instrumental group (Albums: 3 weeks)

Date		Title / Label	pos	wks
13 Feb 88		BIRTH SCHOOL WORK DEATH *Epic 460263 1*	80	2
20 May 89		MORE SONGS ABOUT LOVE AND HATE *Epic 463394 1*	49	1

GODIEGO
Japan / US, male vocal / instrumental group (Singles: 11 weeks)

Date		Title / Label	pos	wks
15 Oct 77		THE WATER MARGIN *BBC RESL 50*	37	4
16 Feb 80		GANDHARA *BBC RESL 66*	56	7

'The Water Margin' is the English version of the song, which shared chart credit with the Japanese language version by Pete Mac Jr

GODLEY and CREME *UK, male vocal / instrumental duo – Kevin Godley and Lol Creme (Singles: 36 weeks, Albums: 34 weeks)*

Date		Title / Label	pos	wks
12 Sep 81	●	UNDER YOUR THUMB *Polydor POSP 322*	3	11
21 Nov 81	●	WEDDING BELLS *Polydor POSP 369*	7	11
30 Mar 85		CRY (re) *Polydor POSP 732*	19	14
19 Nov 77		CONSEQUENCES *Mercury CONS 017*	52	1
9 Sep 78		L *Mercury 9109 611*	47	2
17 Oct 81		ISMISM *Polydor POLD 5043*	29	13
29 Aug 87	●	CHANGING FACES – THE VERY BEST OF 10cc AND GODLEY AND CREME *ProTV TGCLP 1* [1]	4	18

[1] 10cc and Godley and Creme

See also 10cc; HOTLEGS

GOD'S PROPERTY
US, male / female gospel choir (Singles: 1 week)

Date		Title / Label	pos	wks
22 Nov 97		STOMP *B-rite Music IND 95559*	60	1

GODSPEED YOU BLACK EMPEROR!
Canada, male vocal / instrumental group (Albums: 1 week)

Date		Title / Label	pos	wks
21 Oct 00		LIFT YOUR SKINNY FISTS LIKE ANTENNAS TO HEAVEN *Kranky KRANK 043*	66	1

Alex GOLD featuring Philip OAKEY
UK, male producer and male vocalist (Singles: 1 week)

Date		Title / Label	pos	wks
26 Apr 03		L.A. TODAY *Xtravaganza XTRAV 37CDS*	68	1

See also HUMAN LEAGUE

Andrew GOLD *US, male vocalist / instrumentalist – piano (Singles: 36 weeks, Albums: 7 weeks)*

Date		Title / Label	pos	wks
2 Apr 77		LONELY BOY *Asylum K 13076*	11	9
25 Mar 78	●	NEVER LET HER SLIP AWAY *Asylum K 13112*	5	13
24 Jun 78		HOW CAN THIS BE LOVE *Asylum K 13126*	19	10
14 Oct 78		THANK YOU FOR BEING A FRIEND *Asylum K 13135*	42	4
15 Apr 78		ALL THIS AND HEAVEN TOO *Asylum K 53072*	31	7

See also WAX

Ari GOLD – *See DJ LUCK & MC NEAT*

Brian and Tony GOLD – *See RED DRAGON with Brian and Tony GOLD; SHAGGY*

GOLD BLADE
UK, male vocal / instrumental group (Singles: 1 week)

Date		Title / Label	pos	wks
22 Mar 97		STRICTLY HARDCORE *Ultimate TOPP 056CD*	64	1

GOLDBUG
UK, male / female vocal / instrumental group (Singles: 5 weeks)

Date		Title / Label	pos	wks
27 Jan 96	●	WHOLE LOTTA LOVE *Acid Jazz JAZID 125CD*	3	5

GOLDEN BOY with MISS KITTIN *Germany, male producer and France, female vocalist (Singles: 1 week)*

Date		Title / Label	pos	wks
7 Sep 02		RIPPIN KITTEN *Illustrious CDILL 007*	67	1

GOLDEN EARRING *Holland, male vocal / instrumental group (Singles: 16 weeks, Albums: 4 weeks)*

Date		Title / Label	pos	wks
8 Dec 73	●	RADAR LOVE *Track 2094 116*	7	13
8 Oct 77		RADAR LOVE *Polydor 2121 335*	44	3
2 Feb 74		MOONTAN *Track 2406 112*	24	4

The 8 Oct 1977 version of Radar Love credits Golden Earring 'Live'

GOLDEN GIRLS *UK, male producer / instrumentalist – Mike Hazell (Singles: 3 weeks)*

Date		Title / Label	pos	wks
3 Oct 98		KINETIC *Distinctive DISNCD 46*	38	2
4 Dec 99		KINETIC (re-mix) *Distinctive DISNCD 59*	56	1

GOLDENSCAN *UK, male DJ / production duo (Singles: 1 week)*

Date		Title / Label	pos	wks
11 Nov 00		SUNRISE *VC Recordings VCRD 79*	52	1

GOLDFINGER
US, male vocal / instrumental group (Singles: 1 week)

Date		Title / Label	pos	wks
22 Jun 02		OPEN YOUR EYES *Jive 9270052*	75	1

GOLDFRAPP *UK, male / female vocal / instrumental group (Singles: 10 weeks, Albums: 11 weeks)*

Date		Title / Label	pos	wks
23 Jun 01		UTOPIA *Mute CDMUTE 264*	62	1
17 Nov 01		PILOTS *Mute CDMUTE 267*	68	1
26 Apr 03		TRAIN *Mute CDMUTE 291*	23	3
2 Aug 03		STRICT MACHINE *Mute CDMUTE 295*	25	3
15 Nov 03		TWIST *Mute CDMUTE 311*	31	2
25 Aug 01		FELT MOUNTAIN *Mute CDSTUMM 188*	57	5
10 May 03		BLACK CHERRY *Mute CDSTUMM196*	19	6

GOLDIE *UK, male vocal / instrumental group (Singles: 11 weeks)*

Date		Title / Label	pos	wks
27 May 78	●	MAKING UP AGAIN *Bronze BRO 50*	7	11

GOLDIE *UK, male producer – Clifford Price (Singles: 16 weeks, Albums: 16 weeks)*

Date		Title / Label	pos	wks
3 Dec 94		INNER CITY LIFE *ffrr FCD 251* [1]	49	2
9 Sep 95		ANGEL *ffrr FCD 266*	41	3
11 Nov 95		INNER CITY LIFE (re-mix) *ffrr FCD 267*	39	2
1 Nov 97		DIGITAL *ffrr FCD 316* [2]	13	3
24 Jan 98		TEMPERTEMPER *ffrr FCD 325* [2]	13	4
18 Apr 98		BELIEVE *ffrr FCD 332*	36	2
19 Aug 95	●	TIMELESS *ffrr 8286142*	7	12
14 Feb 98		SATURNZ RETURN *ffrr 8289902*	15	4

[1] Goldie presents Metalheadz [2] Goldie featuring KRS One

GOLDIE and the GINGERBREADS
US, female vocal / instrumental group (Singles: 5 weeks)

Date		Title / Label	pos	wks
25 Feb 65		CAN'T YOU HEAR MY HEART BEAT? *Decca F 12070*	25	5

GOLDRUSH
UK, male vocal / instrumental group (Singles: 2 weeks)

Date		Title / Label	pos	wks
22 Jun 02		SAME PICTURE *Virgin VSCDT 1833*	64	1
7 Sep 02		WIDE OPEN SKY *Virgin VSCDT 1834*	70	1

Bobby GOLDSBORO *US, male vocalist (Singles: 47 weeks)*

Date		Title / Label	pos	wks
17 Apr 68	●	HONEY *United Artists UP2215* ▲	2	15
4 Aug 73	●	SUMMER (THE FIRST TIME) *United Artists UP35558*	9	10
3 Aug 74		HELLO, SUMMERTIME *United Artists UP35705*	14	10
29 Mar 75	●	HONEY (re-issue) *United Artists UP35633*	2	12

Glen GOLDSMITH
UK, male vocalist (Singles: 24 weeks, Albums: 9 weeks) pos/wks

7 Nov 87	**I WON'T CRY** *Reproduction PB 41493*	34	7
12 Mar 88	**DREAMING** *Reproduction PB 41711*	12	11
11 Jun 88	**WHAT YOU SEE IS WHAT YOU GET** *Reproduction PB 42075*	33	5
3 Sep 88	**SAVE A LITTLE BIT** *Reproduction PB 42147*	73	1
23 Jul 88	WHAT YOU SEE IS WHAT YOU GET *RCA PL 71750*	14	9

GOLDTRIX presents Andrea BROWN
UK, male production / instrumental duo and US, female vocalist (Singles: 9 weeks) pos/wks

19 Jan 02 ●	**IT'S LOVE (TRIPPIN') (re)** *AM:PM / Serious / Evolve CDAMPM 152*	6	9

GOMEZ
UK, male vocal / instrumental group (Singles: 16 weeks, Albums: 99 weeks) pos/wks

11 Apr 98	**78 STONE WOBBLE** *Hut HUTCD 95*	44	1
13 Jun 98	**GET MYSELF ARRESTED** *Hut HUTCD 97*	45	1
12 Sep 98	**WHIPPIN' PICCADILLY** *Hut HUTCD 105*	35	3
10 Jul 99	**BRING IT ON** *Hut HUTCD 112*	21	3
11 Sep 99	**RHYTHM & BLUES ALIBI** *Hut HUTCD 114*	18	3
27 Nov 99	**WE HAVEN'T TURNED AROUND** *Hut HUTCD 117*	38	2
16 Mar 02	**SHOT SHOT** *Hut / Virgin HUTCD 149*	28	2
15 Jun 02	**SOUND OF SOUNDS / PING ONE DOWN** *Hut / Virgin HUTCD 154*	48	1
25 Apr 98	BRING IT ON *Hut CDHUTX 49*	11	60
25 Sep 99 ●	LIQUID SKIN *Hut CDHUT 54*	2	28
7 Oct 00 ●	ABANDONED SHOPPING TROLLEY HOTLINE *Hut CDHUTX 64*	10	4
30 Mar 02 ●	IN OUR GUN *Hut CDHUT 72*	8	7

Leroy GOMEZ – *See SANTA ESMERALDA and Leroy GOMEZ*

GOMPIE
Holland, male vocal / instrumental group (Singles: 12 weeks) pos/wks

20 May 95	**ALICE (WHO THE X IS ALICE) (LIVING NEXT DOOR TO ALICE) (re)** *Habana HABSCD 5*	17	12

GONZALES – *See FUNK MASTERS*

GONZALEZ
UK / US, male vocal / instrumental group (Singles: 11 weeks) pos/wks

31 Mar 79	**HAVEN'T STOPPED DANCING YET** *Sidewalk SID 102*	15	11

GOO GOO DOLLS
US, male vocal / instrumental trio (Singles: 4 weeks, Albums: 2 weeks) pos/wks

1 Aug 98	**IRIS** *Reprise W 0449CD*	50	1
27 Mar 99	**SLIDE** *Edel / Hollywood / Third Rail 0102035 HWR*	43	1
17 Jul 99	**IRIS (re-issue)** *Hollywood 0102485 HWR*	26	2
31 Jul 99	DIZZY UP THE GIRL *Hollywood 0102042 HWR*	47	1
4 May 02	GUTTERFLOWER *Warner Bros. 9362483112*	56	1

GOOD CHARLOTTE
US, male vocal / instrumental group (Singles: 25 weeks, Albums: 38 weeks) pos/wks

15 Feb 03 ●	**LIFESTYLES OF THE RICH AND FAMOUS** *Epic 6735562*	8	10
17 May 03 ●	**GIRLS AND BOYS** *Epic 6738772*	6	9
30 Aug 03 ●	**THE ANTHEM** *Epic 6742555*	10	4
20 Dec 03	**THE YOUNG AND THE HOPELESS / HOLD ON** *Epic 6745432*	34	2+
25 Jan 03	THE YOUNG AND THE HOPELESS *Epic 5094889*	15	38

GOOD GIRLS
US, female vocal group (Singles: 1 week) pos/wks

24 Jul 93	**JUST CALL ME** *Motown TMGCD 1417*	75	1

GOODBYE MR MACKENZIE
UK, male / female vocal / instrumental group – includes Shirley Manson (Singles: 13 weeks, Albums: 4 weeks) pos/wks

20 Aug 88	**GOODBYE MR MACKENZIE** *Capitol CL 501*	62	2
11 Mar 89	**THE RATTLER** *Capitol CL 522*	37	6
29 Jul 89	**GOODWILL CITY / I'M SICK OF YOU** *Capitol CL 538*	49	2
21 Apr 90	**LOVE CHILD** *Parlophone R 6247*	52	2
23 Jun 90	**BLACKER THAN BLACK** *Parlophone R 6257*	61	1
22 Apr 89	GOOD DEEDS AND DIRTY RAGS *Capitol EST 2089*	26	3
16 Mar 91	HAMMER AND TONGS *Radioactive RAR 10227*	61	1

Roger GOODE featuring Tasha BAXTER
South Africa, male DJ / producer and female vocalist (Singles: 2 weeks) pos/wks

13 Apr 02	**IN THE BEGINNING** *ffrr DFCD 004*	33	2

GOODFELLAS featuring Lisa MILLETT
Italy, male production duo – Paolo Martini and Gianni Bini – and UK, female vocalist (Singles: 2 weeks) pos/wks

21 Jul 01	**SOUL HEAVEN** *Direction 6713852*	27	2

See also ECLIPSE; BINI & MARTINI; HOUSE OF GLASS

GOODFELLAZ
US, male vocal trio (Singles: 2 weeks) pos/wks

10 May 97	**SUGAR HONEY ICE TEA** *Wild Card 5736132*	25	2

GOODIES
UK, male comedy / vocal group (Singles: 38 weeks, Albums: 11 weeks) pos/wks

7 Dec 74 ●	**THE INBETWEENIES / FATHER CHRISTMAS DO NOT TOUCH ME** *Bradley's BRAD 7421*	7	9
15 Mar 75 ●	**FUNKY GIBBON / SICK-MAN BLUES** *Bradley's BRAD 7504*	4	10
21 Jun 75	**BLACK PUDDING BERTHA (THE QUEEN OF NORTHERN SOUL)** *Bradley's BRAD 7517*	19	7
27 Sep 75	**NAPPY LOVE / WILD THING** *Bradley's BRAD 7524*	21	6
13 Dec 75	**MAKE A DAFT NOISE FOR CHRISTMAS** *Bradley's BRAD 7533*	20	6
8 Nov 75	THE NEW GOODIES LP *Bradley's BRADL 1010*	25	11

Cuba GOODING
US, male vocalist (Singles: 2 weeks) pos/wks

19 Nov 83	**HAPPINESS IS JUST AROUND THE BEND** *London LON 41*	72	2

Benny GOODMAN
US male instrumentalist – clarinet, d. 13 Jun 1986 (Albums: 1 week) pos/wks

3 Apr 71	BENNY GOODMAN TODAY *Decca DDS 3*	49	1

GOODMEN
Holland, male instrumental / production duo – Rene Terhorst and Gaston Steenkist (Singles: 19 weeks) pos/wks

7 Aug 93 ●	**GIVE IT UP (re)** *Fresh Fruit TABCD 118*	5	19

See also JARK PRONGO; RHYTHMKILLAZ; CHOCOLATE PUMA; TOMBA VIRA; RIVA featuring Dannii MINOGUE

Delta GOODREM
Australia, female vocalist (Singles: 36 weeks, Albums: 25 weeks) pos/wks

22 Mar 03 ●	**BORN TO TRY** *Epic 6736342*	3	13
28 Jun 03 ●	**LOST WITHOUT YOU** *Epic 6739555*	4	11
4 Oct 03 ●	**INNOCENT EYES** *Epic 6743152*	9	9
13 Dec 03	**NOT ME, NOT I** *Epic 6745372*	18	3+
12 Jul 03 ●	INNOCENT EYES *Epic 5109512*	2	25+

Ron GOODWIN and His ORCHESTRA
UK, orchestra leader, d. 8 Jan 2003 (Singles: 24 weeks, Albums: 1 week) pos/wks

15 May 53 ●	**TERRY'S THEME FROM 'LIMELIGHT'** *Parlophone R 3686*	3	23
28 Oct 55	**BLUE STAR (THE MEDIC THEME)** *Parlophone R 4074*	20	1
2 May 70	LEGEND OF THE GLASS MOUNTAIN *Studio Two TWO 220* [1]	49	1

[1] Ron Goodwin

See also Eamonn ANDREWS

GOODY GOODY
US, female vocal duo (Singles: 5 weeks) pos/wks

2 Dec 78	**#1 DEE JAY** *Atlantic LV 3*	55	5

GOOMBAY DANCE BAND
Germany / Montserrat, male / female vocal / instrumental group (Singles: 16 weeks, Albums: 9 weeks) pos/wks

27 Feb 82 ★	**SEVEN TEARS** *Epic EPC A 1242*	1	12
15 May 82	**SUN OF JAMAICA** *Epic EPC A 2345*	50	4
10 Apr 82	SEVEN TEARS *Epic EPC 85702*	16	9

GOONS *UK, male comedy / vocal group (Singles: 30 weeks, Albums: 31 weeks)*

Date		Title	pos	wks
29 Jun 56	●	**I'M WALKING BACKWARDS FOR CHRISTMAS / BLUEBOTTLE BLUES** *Decca F 10756*	4	10
14 Sep 56	●	**BLOODNOK'S ROCK 'N' ROLL CALL / THE YING TONG SONG** *Decca F 10780*	3	10
21 Jul 73	●	**YING TONG SONG (re-issue)** *Decca F 13414*	9	10
28 Nov 59	●	**BEST OF THE GOON SHOWS** *Parlophone PMC 1108*	8	14
17 Dec 60		**BEST OF THE GOON SHOWS VOLUME 2** *Parlophone PMC 1129*	12	6
4 Nov 72	●	**LAST GOON SHOW OF ALL** *BBC Radio Enterprise REB 142*	8	11

'Bluebottle Blues' listed only from 13 Jul 1956. It peaked at No.5

See also Peter SELLERS; Harry SECOMBE; Spike MILLIGAN

Lonnie GORDON *US, female vocalist (Singles: 23 weeks)*

Date		Title	pos	wks
24 Jun 89		**(I'VE GOT YOUR) PLEASURE CONTROL** *ffrr F 106* [1]	60	3
27 Jan 90	●	**HAPPENIN' ALL OVER AGAIN** *Supreme SUPE 159*	4	10
11 Aug 90		**BEYOND YOUR WILDEST DREAMS** *Supreme SUPE 167*	48	2
17 Nov 90		**IF I HAVE TO STAND ALONE** *Supreme SUPE 181*	68	1
4 May 91		**GONNA CATCH YOU** *Supreme SUPE 185*	32	5
7 Oct 95		**LOVE EVICTION** *X:Plode BANG 2CD* [2]	32	2

[1] Simon Harris featuring Lonnie Gordon [2] Quartz Lock featuring Lonnie Gordon

Lesley GORE *US, female vocalist – Born Lesley Goldstein, 2 May 1946 (Singles: 20 weeks)*

Date		Title	pos	wks
20 Jun 63	●	**IT'S MY PARTY** *Mercury AMT 1205* ▲	9	12
24 Sep 64		**MAYBE I KNOW** *Mercury MF 829*	20	8

Martin L GORE *UK, male vocalist (Singles: 1 week, Albums: 1 week)*

Date		Title	pos	wks
26 Apr 03		**STARDUST** *Mute CDMUTE 296*	44	1
24 Jun 89		**COUNTERFEIT EP** *Mute STUMM 67*	51	1

See also DEPECHE MODE

GORILLAZ *UK / US, animated male vocal / instrumental / production group (Singles: 39 weeks, Albums: 53 weeks)*

Date		Title	pos	wks
17 Mar 01	●	**CLINT EASTWOOD** *Parlophone CDR 6552*	4	17
7 Jul 01	●	**19/2000** *Parlophone CDR 6559*	6	10
3 Nov 01		**ROCK THE HOUSE** *Parlophone CDRS 6565*	18	8
9 Mar 02		**TOMORROW COMES TODAY (re)** *Parlophone CDR 6573*	33	3
3 Aug 02		**LIL' DUB CHEFIN'** *Parlophone CDR 6584* [1]	73	1
7 Apr 01	●	**GORILLAZ** *Parlophone 5311380*	3	52
23 Mar 02		**G SIDES** *Parlophone 536942*	65	1

[1] Space Monkeyz vs Gorillaz

GORKY'S ZYGOTIC MYNCI *UK, male / female vocal / instrumental group (Singles: 8 weeks, Albums: 2 weeks)*

Date		Title	pos	wks
9 Nov 96		**PATIO SONG** *Fontana GZMCD 1*	41	1
29 Mar 97		**DIAMOND DEW** *Fontana GZMCD 2*	42	1
21 Jun 97		**YOUNG GIRLS & HAPPY ENDINGS / DARK NIGHT** *Fontana GZMCD 3*	49	1
6 Jun 98		**SWEET JOHNNY** *Fontana GZMCD 4*	60	1
29 Aug 98		**LET'S GET TOGETHER (IN OUR MINDS)** *Fontana GZMCD 5*	43	1
2 Oct 99		**SPANISH DANCE TROUPE** *Mantra / Beggars Banquet MNT 47CD*	47	1
4 Mar 00		**POODLE ROCKIN'** *Mantra / Beggars Banquet MNT 52CD*	52	1
15 Sep 01		**STOOD ON GOLD** *Mantra / Beggars Banquet MNT 64CD*	65	1
19 Apr 97		**BARAFUNDLE** *Fontana 5347692*	46	1
12 Sep 98		**GORKY 5** *Fontana 5588222*	67	1

Eydie GORME *US, female vocalist (Singles: 33 weeks)*

Date		Title	pos	wks
24 Jan 58		**LOVE ME FOREVER** *HMV POP 432*	21	5
21 Jun 62	●	**YES MY DARLING DAUGHTER** *CBS AAG 105*	10	9
31 Jan 63		**BLAME IT ON THE BOSSA NOVA** *CBS AAG 131*	32	6
22 Aug 63	●	**I WANT TO STAY HERE** *CBS AAG 163* [1]	3	13

[1] Steve and Eydie

See also Steve LAWRENCE

Luke GOSS and the BAND OF THIEVES *UK, male vocal / instrumental group (Singles: 3 weeks)*

Date		Title	pos	wks
12 Jun 93		**SWEETER THAN THE MIDNIGHT RAIN** *Sabre CDSAB 1*	52	2
21 Aug 93		**GIVE ME ONE MORE CHANCE** *Sabre CDSAB 2*	68	1

See also BROS

Matt GOSS *UK, male vocalist (Singles: 7 weeks)*

Date		Title	pos	wks
26 Aug 95		**THE KEY** *Atlas 5811532*	40	2
27 Apr 96		**IF YOU WERE HERE TONIGHT** *Atlas 5762932*	23	3
15 Nov 03		**I'M COMING WITH YA** *Concept CDCON 49*	22	2

See also BROS

Irv GOTTI *US, male producer / rapper (Singles: 10 weeks, Albums: 3 weeks)*

Date		Title	pos	wks
12 Oct 02	●	**DOWN 4 U (2re)** *Murder Inc 0639002* [1]	4	10
20 Jul 02		**IRV GOTTI PRESENTS THE INC** *Murder Inc / Mercury 630332* [1]	68	3

[1] Irv Gotti presents Ja Rule, Ashanti, Charli Baltimore and Vita [1] Irv Gotti presents the Inc

Nigel GOULDING – *See Abigail MEAD and Nigel GOULDING*

Graham GOULDMAN *UK, male vocalist (Singles: 4 weeks)*

Date		Title	pos	wks
23 Jun 79		**SUNBURN** *Mercury SUNNY 1*	52	4

See also 10 CC; WAX

GOURYELLA *Holland, male production duo – Tijs Verwest and Ferry Corsten (Singles: 11 weeks)*

Date		Title	pos	wks
10 Jul 99		**GOURYELLA** *Code Blue BLU 001CD*	15	7
4 Dec 99		**WALHALLA** *Code Blue BLU 006CD*	27	2
23 Dec 00		**TENSHI** *Code Blue BLUE 017CD*	45	2

See also MOONMAN; SYSTEM F; VERACOCHA; STARPARTY; ALBION; Ferry CORSTEN

GRACE *UK, female vocalist – Dominique Atkins (Singles: 24 weeks)*

Date		Title	pos	wks
8 Apr 95	●	**NOT OVER YET** *Perfecto PERF 104CD*	6	8
23 Sep 95		**I WANT TO LIVE** *Perfecto PERF 109CD*	30	2
24 Feb 96		**SKIN ON SKIN** *Perfecto PERF 116CD*	21	3
1 Jun 96		**DOWN TO EARTH** *Perfecto PERF 120CD*	20	2
28 Sep 96		**IF I COULD FLY** *Perfecto PERF 127CD*	29	2
3 May 97		**HAND IN HAND** *Perfecto PERF 129CD*	38	1
26 Jul 97		**DOWN TO EARTH (re-mix)** *Perfecto PERF 142CD1*	29	2
14 Aug 99		**NOT OVER YET 99** *Code Blue BLU 004CD1* [1]	16	4

[1] Planet Perfecto featuring Grace

Bridgette GRACE – *See TRUE FAITH and Bridgette GRACE with FINAL CUT*

GRACE BROTHERS *UK, male instrumental duo (Singles: 1 week)*

Date		Title	pos	wks
20 Apr 96		**ARE YOU BEING SERVED** *EMI Premier PRESCD 1*	51	1

Charlie GRACIE *US, male vocalist / instrumentalist – guitar – Charlie Graci (Singles: 41 weeks)*

Date		Title	pos	wks
19 Apr 57		**BUTTERFLY** *Parlophone R 4290*	12	8
14 Jun 57	●	**FABULOUS** *Parlophone R 4313*	8	16
23 Aug 57	●	**I LOVE YOU SO MUCH IT HURTS / WANDERIN' EYES (2re)** *London HLU 8467*	6	16
10 Jan 58		**COOL BABY** *London HLU 8521*	26	1

'I Love You So Much It Hurts' and 'Wanderin' Eyes' were listed together for two weeks, then listed separately for a further two and 12 weeks respectively

GRAFITI *UK, male producer – Mike Skinner (Singles: 2 weeks)*

Date		Title	pos	wks
30 Aug 03		**WHAT IS THE PROBLEM?** *679 Recordings 679L 021CD*	37	2

See also the STREETS

Eve GRAHAM – *See NEW SEEKERS*

Jaki GRAHAM

UK, female vocalist (Singles: 75 weeks, Albums: 10 weeks) pos/wks

23 Mar 85 ●	**COULD IT BE I'M FALLING IN LOVE** *Chrysalis GRAN 6* [1]	5	11
29 Jun 85 ●	**ROUND AND ROUND** *EMI JAKI 4*	9	11
31 Aug 85	**HEAVEN KNOWS** *EMI JAKI 5*	59	3
16 Nov 85	**MATED** *EMI JAKI 6* [1]	20	10
3 May 86 ●	**SET ME FREE** *EMI JAKI 7*	7	12
9 Aug 86	**BREAKING AWAY** *EMI JAKI 8*	16	8
15 Nov 86	**STEP RIGHT UP** *EMI JAKI 9*	15	12
9 Jul 88	**NO MORE TEARS** *EMI JAKI 12*	60	2
24 Jun 89	**FROM NOW ON** *EMI JAKI 15*	73	2
16 Jul 94	**AIN'T NOBODY** *Pulse 8 CDLOSE 64*	44	2
4 Feb 95	**YOU CAN COUNT ON ME** *Avex UK AVEXCD 1*	62	1
8 Jul 95	**ABSOLUTE E-SENSUAL** *Avex UK AVEXCD 5*	69	1
14 Sep 85	HEAVEN KNOWS *EMI JK 1*	48	5
20 Sep 86	BREAKING AWAY *EMI EMC 3514*	25	5

[1] David Grant and Jaki Graham

Larry GRAHAM

US, male vocalist / instrumentalist – bass (Singles: 4 weeks) pos/wks

3 Jul 82	**SOONER OR LATER** *Warner Bros. K 17925*	54	4

See also SLY and the FAMILY STONE

Mikey GRAHAM *Ireland, male vocalist (Singles: 6 weeks)* pos/wks

10 Jun 00	**YOU'RE MY ANGEL** *Public PR 001CDS*	13	5
14 Apr 01	**YOU COULD BE MY EVERYTHING** *Public PR 003CDS*	62	1

See also BOYZONE

Ron GRAINER ORCHESTRA

UK, orchestra, leader d. 21 Feb 1981 (Singles: 7 weeks) pos/wks

9 Dec 78	**A TOUCH OF VELVET – A STING OF BRASS** *Casino Classics CC 5*	60	7

GRAM'MA FUNK – *See GROOVE ARMADA; ILLICIT featuring GRAM'MA FUNK*

GRAND FUNK RAILROAD *US, male vocal / instrumental group (Singles: 1 week, Albums: 1 week)* pos/wks

6 Feb 71	**INSIDE LOOKING OUT** *Capitol CL 15668*	40	1
13 Feb 71	GRAND FUNK LIVE *Capital E-STDW 1/2*	29	1

GRAND PLAZ

UK, male instrumental / production group (Singles: 4 weeks) pos/wks

8 Sep 90	**WOW WOW – NA NA** *Urban URB 60*	41	4

GRAND PRIX *UK, male vocal / instrumental group (Singles: 1 week, Albums: 2 weeks)* pos/wks

27 Feb 82	**KEEP ON BELIEVING** *RCA 162*	75	1
18 Jun 83	SAMURAI *Chrysalis CHR 1430*	65	2

GRAND PUBA *US, male rapper – Maxwell Dixon (Singles: 6 weeks)* pos/wks

13 Jan 96	**WHY YOU TREAT ME SO BAD** *Virgin VSCDT 1566* [1]	11	5
30 Mar 96	**WILL YOU BE MY BABY** *GHQ 74321339092* [2]	53	1

[1] Shaggy featuring Grand Puba [2] Infiniti featuring Grand Puba

GRAND THEFT AUDIO

UK, male vocal / instrumental group (Singles: 1 week) pos/wks

24 Mar 01	**WE LUV U** *Sci-Fi SCIFI 1CD*	70	1

GRANDAD ROBERTS AND HIS SON ELVIS

UK, male vocal duo (Singles: 1 week) pos/wks

20 Jun 98	**MEAT PIE SAUSAGE ROLL** *WEA WEA 160CD*	67	1

GRANDADDY *US, male vocal / instrumental group (Singles: 6 weeks, Albums: 6 weeks)* pos/wks

2 Sep 00	**HEWLETT'S DAUGHTER** *V2 VVR 5014333*	71	1
10 Feb 01	**THE CRYSTAL LAKE** *V2 VVR 5015153*	38	2
14 Jun 03	**NOW IT'S ON** *V VVR 25022243*	23	2
6 Sep 03	**EL CAMINOS IN THE WEST** *V2 VVR 5023663*	48	1
20 May 00	THE SOPHTWARE SLUMP *V2 VVR 1012252*	36	4
21 Jun 03	SUMDAY *V2 VVR1022232*	22	2

GRANDMASTER FLASH and the FURIOUS FIVE

US, male vocal / rapper / producer / DJ group (Singles: 92 weeks, Albums: 20 weeks) pos/wks

28 Aug 82 ●	**THE MESSAGE** *Sugarhill SHL 117*	8	9
22 Jan 83	**MESSAGE II (SURVIVAL)** *Sugarhill SH 119* [1]	74	2
19 Nov 83 ●	**WHITE LINES (DON'T DON'T DO IT) (3re)** *Sugarhill SH 130* [2]	7	43
30 Jun 84	**BEAT STREET BREAKDOWN** *Atlantic A 9659* [3]	42	7
22 Sep 84	**WE DON'T WORK FOR FREE** *Sugarhill SH 136* [3]	45	4
15 Dec 84 ●	**STEP OFF (PART 1)** *Sugarhill SH 139* [3]	8	12
16 Feb 85	**SIGN OF THE TIMES** *Elektra E 9677* [4]	72	1
16 Mar 85	**PUMP ME UP** *Sugarhill SH 141* [3]	45	6
8 Jan 94	**WHITE LINES (DON'T DO IT) (re-mix)** *WGAF WGAFCD 103* [2]	59	3
17 Jun 95	**WHITE LINES (DON'T DO IT)** *Parlophone CDDD 19* [5]	17	5
23 Oct 82	THE MESSAGE *Sugar Hill SHLP 1007*	77	3
23 Jun 84	GREATEST MESSAGES *Sugar Hill SHLP 5552*	41	16
23 Feb 85	THEY SAID IT COULDN'T BE DONE *Elektra 9603891*	95	1

[1] Melle Mel and Duke Bootee [2] Grandmaster and Melle Mel [3] Grandmaster Melle Mel and the Furious Five [4] Grandmaster Flash [5] Duran Duran featuring Melle Mel and Grandmaster Flash and the Furious Five

1983's original *'White Lines (Don't, Don't Do It) re-entered in 1984 (twice) and 1985*

GRANDMASTER MELLE MEL

US, male rapper – Melvin Glover (Albums: 5 weeks) pos/wks

20 Oct 84	WORK PARTY *Sugar Hill SHLP 5553*	45	5

GRANDMIXER D.ST.

US, male DJ / producer – Derek Howells (Singles: 3 weeks) pos/wks

24 Dec 83	**CRAZY CUTS (re)** *Island IS 146*	71	3

GRANGE HILL CAST *UK, male / female vocal charity assembly / TV show cast (Singles: 6 weeks)* pos/wks

19 Apr 86 ●	**JUST SAY NO** *BBC RESL 183*	5	6

Gerri GRANGER *US, female vocalist (Singles: 3 weeks)* pos/wks

30 Sep 78	**I GO TO PIECES (EVERYTIME)** *Casino Classics CC3*	50	3

Amy GRANT

US, female vocalist (Singles: 39 weeks, Albums: 15 weeks) pos/wks

11 May 91 ●	**BABY BABY** *A&M AM 727* ▲	2	13
3 Aug 91	**EVERY HEARTBEAT** *A&M AM 783*	25	7
2 Nov 91	**THAT'S WHAT LOVE IS FOR** *A&M AM 666*	60	3
15 Feb 92	**GOOD FOR ME** *A&M AM 810*	60	1
13 Aug 94	**LUCKY ONE** *A&M 5807322*	60	1
22 Oct 94	**SAY YOU'LL BE MINE** *A&M 5808292*	41	2
24 Jun 95	**BIG YELLOW TAXI** *A&M 5809972*	20	10
14 Oct 95	**HOUSE OF LOVE** *A&M 5812332* [1]	46	2
22 Jun 91	HEART IN MOTION *A&M 3953211*	25	15

[1] Amy Grant with Vince Gill

Andrea GRANT *UK, female vocalist (Singles: 1 week)* pos/wks

14 Nov 98	**REPUTATIONS (JUST BE GOOD TO ME)** *WEA WEA 192CD*	75	1

Boysie GRANT – *See Ezz RECO and The LAUNCHERS with Boysie GRANT*

David GRANT

UK, male vocalist (Singles: 59 weeks, Albums: 7 weeks) pos/wks

30 Apr 83	**STOP AND GO** *Chrysalis GRAN 1*	19	9
16 Jul 83 ●	**WATCHING YOU WATCHING ME** *Chrysalis GRAN 2*	10	13
8 Oct 83	**LOVE WILL FIND A WAY** *Chrysalis GRAN 3*	24	6
26 Nov 83	**ROCK THE MIDNIGHT** *Chrysalis GRAN 4*	46	4
23 Mar 85 ●	**COULD IT BE I'M FALLING IN LOVE** *Chrysalis GRAN 6* [1]	5	11
16 Nov 85	**MATED** *EMI JAKI 6* [1]	20	10

Date		Title	pos	wks
1 Aug 87		**CHANGE** *Polydor POSP 871*	**55**	4
12 May 90		**KEEP IT TOGETHER** *Fourth & Broadway BRW 169*	**56**	2
5 Nov 83		**DAVID GRANT** *Chrysalis CHR 1448*	**32**	6
18 May 85		**HOPES AND DREAMS** *Chrysalis CHR 1483*	**96**	1

[1] David Grant and Jaki Graham

See also LINX

Eddy GRANT (397 Top 500)

Former lead guitarist and songwriter for UK group The Equals, b. 5 Mar 1948, Plaisance, Guyana. Left group 1972, went into production and formed own label, Ice. Remix of transatlantic No.2 'Electric Avenue' returned him to the heights in 2001 (Singles: 107 weeks, Albums: 62 weeks)

Date		Title	pos	wks
2 Jun 79		**LIVING ON THE FRONT LINE** *Ensign ENY 26*	**11**	11
15 Nov 80	●	**DO YOU FEEL MY LOVE?** *Ensign ENY 45*	**8**	11
4 Apr 81		**CAN'T GET ENOUGH OF YOU** *Ensign ENY 207*	**13**	10
25 Jul 81		**I LOVE YOU, YES I LOVE YOU** *Ensign ENY 216*	**37**	6
16 Oct 82	★	**I DON'T WANNA DANCE** *Ice ICE 56*	**1**	15
15 Jan 83	●	**ELECTRIC AVENUE** *Ice ICE 57*	**2**	9
19 Mar 83		**LIVING ON THE FRONT LINE / DO YOU FEEL MY LOVE (re-issue)** *Mercury MER 135*	**47**	4
23 Apr 83		**WAR PARTY** *Ice ICE 58*	**42**	4
29 Oct 83		**TILL I CAN'T TAKE LOVE NO MORE** *Ice ICE 60*	**42**	7
19 May 84		**ROMANCING THE STONE** *Ice ICE 61*	**52**	3
23 Jan 88	●	**GIMME HOPE JO'ANNA** *Ice ICE 78701*	**7**	12
27 May 89		**WALKING ON SUNSHINE** *Blue Wave R 6217*	**63**	2
9 Jun 01	●	**ELECTRIC AVENUE (re) (re-mix)** *Ice / East West EW 232CD*	**5**	12
24 Nov 01		**WALKING ON SUNSHINE (re-mix)** *Ice / East West EW 242CD*	**57**	1
30 May 81		**CAN'T GET ENOUGH** *Ice ICELP 21*	**39**	6
27 Nov 82	●	**KILLER ON THE RAMPAGE** *Ice ICELP 3023*	**7**	23
17 Nov 84		**ALL THE HITS** *K-Tel NE 1284*	**23**	10
1 Jul 89		**WALKING ON SUNSHINE (THE BEST OF EDDY GRANT)** *Parlophone PCSD 108*	**20**	8
19 May 01	●	**THE GREATEST HITS** *East West 8573885972*	**3**	15

Gogi GRANT

US, female vocalist – Audrey Arinsberg (Singles: 11 weeks)

Date		Title	pos	wks
29 Jun 56	●	**THE WAYWARD WIND** *London HLB 8282* ▲	**9**	11

Julie GRANT

UK, female vocalist – Vivienne Foreman (Singles: 17 weeks)

Date		Title	pos	wks
3 Jan 63		**UP ON THE ROOF** *Pye 7N 15483*	**33**	3
28 Mar 63		**COUNT ON ME** *Pye 7N 15508*	**24**	9
24 Sep 64		**COME TO ME** *Pye 7N 15684*	**31**	5

Rudy GRANT *Guyana, male vocalist (Singles: 3 weeks)*

Date		Title	pos	wks
14 Feb 81		**LATELY** *Ensign ENY 202*	**58**	3

GRANT LEE BUFFALO

US, male vocal / instrumental group (Albums: 5 weeks)

Date		Title	pos	wks
10 Jul 93		**FUZZY** *Slash 8283892*	**74**	1
1 Oct 94		**MIGHTY JOE MOON** *Slash 8285412*	**24**	2
15 Jun 96		**COPPEROPOLIS** *Slash 8287602*	**34**	2

GRAPEFRUIT

UK, male vocal / instrumental group (Singles: 19 weeks)

Date		Title	pos	wks
14 Feb 68		**DEAR DELILAH** *RCA 1656*	**21**	9
14 Aug 68		**C'MON MARIANNE** *RCA 1716*	**31**	10

GRASS-SHOW

Sweden, male vocal / instrumental group (Singles: 2 weeks)

Date		Title	pos	wks
22 Mar 97		**1962** *Food CDFOOD 90*	**53**	1
23 Aug 97		**OUT OF THE VOID** *Food CDFOOD 103*	**75**	1

GRATEFUL DEAD

US, male vocal / instrumental group (Albums: 14 weeks)

Date		Title	pos	wks
19 Sep 70		**WORKINGMAN'S DEAD** *Warner Bros. WS 1869*	**69**	2
20 Feb 71		**AMERICAN BEAUTY** *Warner Bros. WS 1893*	**27**	2
3 Aug 74		**GRATEFUL DEAD FROM THE MARS HOTEL** *Atlantic K 59302*	**47**	1
1 Nov 75		**BLUES FOR ALLAH** *United Artists UAS 29895*	**45**	1
4 Sep 76		**STEAL YOUR FACE** *United Artists UAS 60131/2*	**42**	1
20 Aug 77		**TERRAPIN STATION** *Arista SPARTY 1016*	**30**	1
19 Sep 87		**IN THE DARK** *Arista 208 564*	**57**	3
18 Feb 89		**DYLAN AND THE DEAD** *CBS 4633811* [1]	**38**	3

[1] Bob Dylan and the Grateful Dead

GRAVEDIGGAZ

US, male rap group (Singles: 6 weeks, Albums: 1 week)

Date		Title	pos	wks
11 Mar 95		**SIX FEET DEEP (EP)** *Gee Street GESCD 62*	**64**	1
5 Aug 95		**THE HELL (EP)** *Fourth & Broadway BRCD 326* [1]	**12**	3
24 Jan 98		**THE NIGHT THE EARTH CRIED** *Gee Street GEE 5001013*	**44**	1
25 Apr 98		**UNEXPLAINED** *Gee Street GEE 5001623*	**48**	1
4 Oct 97		**THE PICK THE SICKLE AND THE SHOVEL** *Gee Street GEE 1000562*	**24**	1

[1] Tricky vs The Gravediggaz

Tracks on Six Feet Deep (EP): Bang Your Head / Mommy / Suicide. Tracks on The Hell (EP): Hell Is Round the Corner / Hell Is Round the Corner (remix) / Psychosis / Tonite Is a Special Nite

See also RZA; WU-TANG CLAN

David GRAY (265 Top 500) *Acoustic singer / songwriter sensation*

b. Manchester, 13 Jun 1968. The Ivor Novello award-winning, modern-day troubadour took 66 weeks to top the UK album chart with his two-million-selling 'White Ladder'. One of the few UK acts to score Stateside in the 21st century (Singles: 40 weeks, Albums: 197 weeks)

Date		Title	pos	wks
4 Dec 99		**PLEASE FORGIVE ME** *IHT IHTCDS 003*	**72**	1
1 Jul 00	●	**BABYLON** *IHT / East West EW 215CD1*	**5**	12
28 Oct 00		**PLEASE FORGIVE ME (re-issue)** *IHT / East West EW 219CD*	**18**	6
17 Mar 01		**THIS YEAR'S LOVE** *IHT / East West EW 228CD1*	**20**	5
28 Jul 01		**SAIL AWAY** *IHT / East West EW 234CD*	**26**	6
29 Dec 01		**SAY HELLO WAVE GOODBYE** *IHT / East West EW 244CD*	**26**	4
21 Dec 02		**THE OTHER SIDE** *IHT / East West EW 259CD*	**35**	3
19 Apr 03		**BE MINE** *IHT / East West EW 264CD*	**23**	3
13 May 00	★	**WHITE LADDER** *East West 8573829832*	**1**	143
12 Aug 00	●	**LOST SONGS 95-98** *IHT IHTCD 002*	**7**	11
14 Jul 01		**THE EP'S 92-94** *Hut CDHUT 67*	**68**	1
9 Nov 02	★	**A NEW DAY AT MIDNIGHT** *East West 5046616582* ■	**1**	42

See also ORBITAL

David GRAY and Tommy TYCHO

UK, male vocalist and Australia, orchestra leader (Albums: 6 weeks)

Date		Title	pos	wks
16 Oct 76		**ARMCHAIR MELODIES** *K-Tel NE 927*	**21**	6

See also Tommy TYCHO

Dobie GRAY

US, male vocalist – Lawrence Brown (Singles: 11 weeks)

Date		Title	pos	wks
25 Feb 65		**THE 'IN' CROWD** *London HL 9953*	**25**	7
27 Sep 75		**OUT ON THE FLOOR** *Black Magic BM 107*	**42**	4

Dorian GRAY *UK, male vocalist (Singles: 7 weeks)*

Date		Title	pos	wks
27 Mar 68		**I'VE GOT YOU ON MY MIND** *Parlophone R 5667*	**36**	7

Les GRAY *UK, male vocalist (Singles: 5 weeks)*

Date		Title	pos	wks
26 Feb 77		**A GROOVY KIND OF LOVE** *Warner Bros. K 16883*	**32**	5

See also MUD

Macy GRAY *US, female vocalist – Natalie McIntyre (Singles: 52 weeks, Albums: 80 weeks)*

Date		Title	pos	wks
3 Jul 99		**DO SOMETHING** *Epic 6675932*	**51**	1
9 Oct 99	●	**I TRY** *Epic 6681832*	**6**	22
25 Mar 00		**STILL (re)** *Epic 6689822*	**18**	9
5 Aug 00		**WHY DIDN'T YOU CALL ME (re)** *Epic 6696682*	**38**	3
20 Jan 01		**DEMONS** *Skint SKINT 60CD* [1]	**16**	5
28 Apr 01		**GETO HEAVEN** *MCA MCSTD 40246* [2]	**48**	1
12 May 01		**REQUEST LINE** *Interscope 4970532* [3]	**31**	3

		pos	wks
15 Sep 01	**SWEET BABY** *Epic 6718822* [4]	**23**	4
8 Dec 01	**SEXUAL REVOLUTION** *Epic 6721462*	**45**	1
3 May 03	**WHEN I SEE YOU** *Epic 6738402*	**26**	3
17 Jul 99 ●	**ON HOW LIFE IS** *Epic 4944232*	3	67
29 Sep 01 ★	**THE ID** *Epic 5040892* ■	1	8
10 May 03	**THE TROUBLE WITH BEING MYSELF** *Epic 5108102*	17	5

[1] Fatboy Slim featuring Macy Gray [2] Common featuring Macy Gray [3] Black Eyed Peas featuring Macy Gray [4] Macy Gray featuring Erykah Badu

Barry GRAY ORCHESTRA *UK, orchestra (Singles: 8 weeks)*

		pos	wks
11 Jul 81	**THUNDERBIRDS** *PRT 7P 216*	**61**	2
14 Jun 86	**JOE 90 (THEME) / CAPTAIN SCARLET THEME** *PRT 7PX 354* [1]	**53**	6

[1] Barry Gray Orchestra with Peter Beckett – keyboards

Alltrinna GRAYSON – *See Wilton FELDER*

GREASE – *See TRICKY*

GREAT WHITE *US, male vocal / instrumental group (Singles: 5 weeks, Albums: 1 week)*

		pos	wks
24 Feb 90	**HOUSE OF BROKEN LOVE** *Capitol CL 562*	**44**	2
16 Feb 91	**CONGO SQUARE** *Capitol CL 605*	**62**	1
7 Sep 91	**CALL IT ROCK 'N' ROLL** *Capitol CL 625*	**67**	2
9 Mar 91	**HOOKED** *Capitol EST 2138*	43	1

Martin GRECH *UK, male vocalist (Singles: 1 week, Albums: 2 weeks)*

		pos	wks
12 Oct 02	**OPEN HEART ZOO** *DTOX / Island CID 811*	**68**	1
3 Aug 02	**OPEN HEART ZOO** *Island CID 8119*	54	2

Buddy GRECO *US, male vocalist – Armando Greco (Singles: 8 weeks)*

		pos	wks
7 Jul 60	**THE LADY IS A TRAMP** *Fontana H 255*	**26**	8

GREED featuring Ricardo DA FORCE *UK, male instrumental duo and UK, male rapper (Singles: 2 weeks)*

		pos	wks
18 Mar 95	**PUMP UP THE VOLUME** *Stress CDSTR 49*	**51**	2

GREEDIES *Ireland / UK / US, male vocal / instrumental group (Singles: 5 weeks)*

		pos	wks
15 Dec 79	**A MERRY JINGLE** *Vertigo GREED 1*	**28**	5

Al GREEN *US, male vocalist (Singles: 68 weeks, Albums: 31 weeks)*

		pos	wks
9 Oct 71 ●	**TIRED OF BEING ALONE** *London HLU 10337*	**4**	13
8 Jan 72 ●	**LET'S STAY TOGETHER** *London HLU 10348* ▲	**7**	12
20 May 72	**LOOK WHAT YOU DONE FOR ME** *London HLU 10369*	**44**	4
19 Aug 72	**I'M STILL IN LOVE WITH YOU** *London HLU 10382*	**35**	5
16 Nov 74	**SHA-LA-LA (MAKE ME HAPPY)** *London HLU 10470*	**20**	11
15 Mar 75	**L.O.V.E. (LOVE)** *London HLU 10482*	**24**	8
3 Dec 88	**PUT A LITTLE LOVE IN YOUR HEART** *A&M AM 484* [1]	**28**	8
21 Oct 89	**THE MESSAGE IS LOVE** *Breakout USA 668* [2]	**38**	5
2 Oct 93	**LOVE IS A BEAUTIFUL THING** *Arista 74321162692*	**56**	2
26 Apr 75	**AL GREEN'S GREATEST HITS** *London SHU 8481*	18	16
1 Oct 88	**HI LIFE – THE BEST OF AL GREEN** *K-Tel NE 1420*	34	7
24 Oct 92	**AL** *Beechwood AGREECD 1*	41	2
16 Feb 02	**L-O-V-E: THE ESSENTIAL AL GREEN** *Hi ALTV 2002*	18	6

[1] Annie Lennox and Al Green [2] Arthur Baker and the Backbeat Disciples featuring Al Green

Dotty GREEN – *See Mark FISHER featuring Dotty GREEN*

Jesse GREEN *Jamaica, male vocalist (Singles: 26 weeks)*

		pos	wks
7 Aug 76	**NICE AND SLOW** *EMI 2492*	**17**	12
18 Dec 76	**FLIP** *EMI 2564*	**26**	8
11 Jun 77	**COME WITH ME** *EMI 2615*	**29**	6

Peter GREEN *UK male vocalist / instrumentalist – guitar – Peter Greenbaum (Albums: 19 weeks)*

		pos	wks
9 Jul 79	**IN THE SKIES** *Creole PULS 101*	32	13
24 May 80	**LITTLE DREAMER** *PUK PULS 102*	34	4
24 May 97	**SPLINTER GROUP** *Artisan SARCD 101*	71	1
30 May 98	**THE ROBERT JOHNSON SONGBOOK** *Artisan SARCD 002* [1]	57	1

[1] Peter Green with Nigel Watson and the Splinter Group

See also FLEETWOOD MAC;

Robson GREEN *UK, male vocalist (Albums: 4 weeks)*

		pos	wks
14 Dec 02	**MOMENT IN TIME** *T2 TCD3300*	49	4

See also ROBSON & JEROME

GREEN DAY (496 Top 500)

Superior US punk pop trio, formed California 1989: Billie Joe Armstrong (v/g), Mike Dirnt (d) and Tre Cool (Frank Wright III). Grammy winners were Top Modern Rock act in US in 1995 and 'Dookie' earned US diamond album (10 million sales) (Singles: 43 weeks, Albums: 98 weeks)

		pos	wks
20 Aug 94	**BASKET CASE** *Reprise W 0257CD*	**55**	2
29 Oct 94	**WELCOME TO PARADISE** *Reprise W 0269CDX*	**20**	3
28 Jan 95 ●	**BASKET CASE (re-issue)** *Reprise W 0279CD*	**7**	6
18 Mar 95	**LONGVIEW** *Reprise W 0278CD*	**30**	3
20 May 95	**WHEN I COME AROUND** *Reprise W 0294CD*	**27**	3
7 Oct 95	**GEEK STINK BREATH** *Reprise W 0320CD*	**16**	3
6 Jan 96	**STUCK WITH ME** *Reprise W 0327CD*	**24**	3
6 Jul 96	**BRAIN STEW / JADED** *Reprise W 0339CD*	**28**	2
11 Oct 97	**HITCHIN' A RIDE** *Reprise W 0424CD*	**25**	2
31 Jan 98	**TIME OF YOUR LIFE (GOOD RIDDANCE)** *Reprise W 0430CD1*	**11**	5
9 May 98	**REDUNDANT** *Reprise W 0438CD1*	**27**	2
30 Sep 00	**MINORITY** *Reprise W 532CD*	**18**	3
23 Dec 00	**WARNING** *Reprise W 548CD1*	**27**	4
10 Nov 01	**WAITING** *Reprise W 570CD*	**34**	2
5 Nov 94	**DOOKIE** *Reprise 9362457952*	13	55
21 Oct 95 ●	**INSOMNIAC** *Reprise 936240462*	8	5
25 Oct 97	**NIMROD** *Reprise 9362467942*	11	11
14 Oct 00 ●	**WARNING** *Reprise 9362480302*	4	14
24 Nov 01	**INTERNATIONAL SUPERHITS!** *Reprise 9362481452*	15	10
13 Jul 02	**SHENANIGANS** *Reprise 9362482082*	32	3

GREEN JELLY *US, male vocal / instrumental group (Singles: 15 weeks, Albums: 10 weeks)*

		pos	wks
5 Jun 93 ●	**THREE LITTLE PIGS** *Zoo 74321151422*	**5**	8
14 Aug 93	**ANARCHY IN THE UK** *Zoo 74321159052*	**27**	3
25 Dec 93	**I'M THE LEADER OF THE GANG** *Arista 74321174892* [1]	**25**	4
3 Jul 93	**CEREAL KILLER SOUNDTRACK** *Zoo 72445110382*	18	10

[1] Hulk Hogan with Green Jelly

GREEN ON RED *US, male vocal / instrumental group (Albums: 1 week)*

		pos	wks
26 Oct 85	**NO FREE LUNCH** *Mercury MERM 78*	99	1

GREEN VELVET *US, male DJ / producer – Curtis Jones (Singles: 2 weeks)*

		pos	wks
25 May 02	**LA LA LAND** *Credence CDCRED 025*	**29**	2

Gavin GREENAWAY – *See Hans ZIMMER*

Norman GREENBAUM *US, male vocalist (Singles: 20 weeks)*

		pos	wks
21 Mar 70 ★	**SPIRIT IN THE SKY** *Reprise RS 20885*	**1**	20

Lorne GREENE *Canada, male actor / vocalist, d. 11 Sep 1987 (Singles: 8 weeks)*

		pos	wks
17 Dec 64	**RINGO** *RCA 1428* ▲	**22**	8

Dave GREENFIELD – *See Jean-Jacques BURNEL*

GREENSLADE
UK, male vocal / instrumental group (Albums: 3 weeks) pos/wks

14 Sep 74 SPYGLASS GUEST *Warner Bros. K 56055* 34 3

Lee GREENWOOD *US, male vocalist (Singles: 6 weeks)* pos/wks

19 May 84 THE WIND BENEATH MY WINGS *MCA 877* 49 6

Christina GREGG *UK, female exercise instructor (Albums: 1 week)* pos/wks

27 May 78 MUSIC 'N' MOTION *Warwick WW 5041* 51 1

Iain GREGORY *UK, male vocalist (Singles: 2 weeks)* pos/wks

4 Jan 62 CAN'T YOU HEAR THE BEAT OF A BROKEN HEART *Pye 7N 15397* 39 2

Johnny GREGORY – *See CHAQUITO and his ORCHESTRA; Russ HAMILTON*

Band of the GRENADIER GUARDS – *See ST JOHN'S COLLEGE SCHOOL CHOIR and the Band of the GRENADIER GUARDS*

GREYHOUND
Jamaica, male vocal / instrumental group (Singles: 33 weeks) pos/wks

26 Jun 71 ● BLACK AND WHITE *Trojan TR 7820* 6 13
8 Jan 72 MOON RIVER *Trojan TR 7848* 12 11
25 Mar 72 I AM WHAT I AM *Trojan TR 7853* 20 9

GRID
UK, male instrumental / production duo – Richard Norris and Dave Ball (Singles: 47 weeks, Albums: 4 weeks) pos/wks

7 Jul 90 FLOATATION *East West YZ 475* 60 2
29 Sep 90 A BEAT CALLED LOVE *East West YZ 498* 64 4
25 Jul 92 FIGURE OF 8 *Virgin VSTG 1421* 50 3
3 Oct 92 HEARTBEAT *Virgin VST 1427* 72 2
13 Mar 93 CRYSTAL CLEAR *Virgin VSCDT 1442* 27 4
30 Oct 93 TEXAS COWBOYS *Deconstruction 74321167762* 21 3
4 Jun 94 ● SWAMP THING *Deconstruction 74321205842* 3 17
17 Sep 94 ROLLERCOASTER *Deconstruction 74321230772* 19 4
3 Dec 94 TEXAS COWBOYS (re-issue) *Deconstruction 74321244032* 17 6
23 Sep 95 DIABLO *Deconstruction 74321308402* 32 2
1 Oct 94 EVOLVER *Deconstruction 74321227182* 14 3
14 Oct 95 MUSIC FOR DANCING *Deconstruction 74321276702* 67 1

Zaine GRIFF *New Zealand, male vocalist (Singles: 6 weeks)* pos/wks

16 Feb 80 TONIGHT *Automatic K 17547* 54 3
31 May 80 ASHES AND DIAMONDS *Automatic K 17610* 68 3

Billy GRIFFIN *US, male vocalist (Singles: 12 weeks)* pos/wks

8 Jan 83 HOLD ME TIGHTER IN THE RAIN *CBS A 2935* 17 9
14 Jan 84 SERIOUS *CBS A 4053* 64 3

See also MIRACLES

Clive GRIFFIN *UK, male vocalist (Singles: 5 weeks)* pos/wks

24 Jun 89 HEAD ABOVE WATER *Mercury STEP 4* 60 2
11 May 91 I'LL BE WAITING *Mercury STEP 6* 56 3

Nanci GRIFFITH *US, female vocalist (Albums: 27 weeks)* pos/wks

28 Mar 88 LITTLE LOVE AFFAIRS *MCA MCF 3413* 78 1
23 Sep 89 STORMS *MCA MCG 6066* 38 3
28 Sep 91 LATE NIGHT GRANDE HOTEL *MCA MCA 10306* 40 5
20 Mar 93 OTHER VOICES / OTHER ROOMS *MCA MCD 10796* 18 6
13 Nov 93 THE BEST OF NANCI GRIFFITH *MCA MCD 10966* 27 4
1 Oct 94 FLYER *MCA MCD 11155* 20 4
5 Apr 97 BLUE ROSES FROM THE MOONS *Elektra 7559620152* 64 3
11 Aug 01 CLOCK WITHOUT HANDS *Elektra 7559626602* 61 1

Roni GRIFFITH *US, female vocalist (Singles: 4 weeks)* pos/wks

30 Jun 84 (THE BEST PART OF) BREAKING UP *Making Waves SURF 101* 63 4

TOP 20 FEMALE ALBUM ARTISTS

Top 20 is compiled using total weeks on the UK albums chart for all female solo artists

1. **MADONNA** – 1,026 weeks (15 hit albums)
2. **DIANA ROSS** – 589 weeks (44 hit albums)
3. **TINA TURNER** – 521 weeks (8 hit albums)
4. **BARBRA STREISAND** – 467 weeks (24 hit albums)
5. **CELINE DION** – 401 weeks (14 hit albums)
6. **WHITNEY HOUSTON** – 377 weeks (7 hit albums)
7. **CHER** – 320 weeks (13 hit albums)
8. **MARIAH CAREY** – 306 weeks (13 hit albums)
9. **SHIRLEY BASSEY** – 294 weeks (36 hit albums)
10. **KATE BUSH** – 281 weeks (8 hit albums)
11. **KYLIE MINOGUE** – 279 weeks (13 hit albums)
12. **ENYA** – 274 weeks (7 hit albums)
13. **JANET JACKSON** – 268 weeks (7 hit albums)
14. **GLORIA ESTEFAN** – 247 weeks (11 hit albums)
15. **TRACY CHAPMAN** – 227 weeks (5 hit albums)
16. **ELKIE BROOKS** – 223 weeks (15 hit albums)
17. **SADE** – 213 weeks (7 hit albums)
18. **SHANIA TWAIN** – 210 weeks (4 hit albums)
19. **ALANIS MORISSETTE** – 208 weeks (4 hit albums)
20. **NANA MOUSKOURI** – 205 weeks (11 hit albums)

Shirley Bassey and Kate Bush, the UK's top two female album artists

GRIFTERS *UK, male production duo – Paul Newman and Brandon Block (Singles: 1 week)* pos/wks

20 Feb 99	**FLASH** *Duty Free DF 004CD*	63	1

See also CAMISRA; ESCRIMA; PARTIZAN; TALL PAUL

GRIM NORTHERN SOCIAL *UK, male vocal / instrumental group (Singles: 1 week)* pos/wks

6 Sep 03	**URBAN PRESSURE** *One Little Indian 353 TP7CD*	60	1

GRIMETHORPE COLLIERY BAND *UK, male brass band (Albums: 4 weeks)* pos/wks

6 Jun 98	**BRASSED OFF (FILM SOUNDTRACK)** *RCA Victor 9026687572*	36	4

See also Peter SKELLERN

Josh GROBAN *US, male vocalist (Albums: 8 weeks)* pos/wks

15 Feb 03	**JOSH GROBAN** *Reprise 9362481542*	28	8

Jay GROOVE – See FANTASY UFO

GROOVE ARMADA *UK, male production / instrumental duo – Andy Cato and Tom Findlay (Singles: 27 weeks, Albums: 30 weeks)* pos/wks

8 May 99	**IF EVERYBODY LOOKED THE SAME** *Pepper 0530292*	25	2
7 Aug 99	**AT THE RIVER** *Pepper 0530062*	19	5
27 Nov 99	**I SEE YOU BABY (re)** *Pepper 9230002* [1]	17	6
25 Aug 01	**SUPERSTYLIN' (re)** *Pepper 9230472*	12	7
17 Nov 01	**MY FRIEND** *Pepper 9230532*	36	2
2 Nov 02	**PURPLE HAZE** *Pepper 9230642*	36	2
17 May 03	**EASY** *Pepper 9230712*	31	2
6 Sep 03	**BUT I FEEL GOOD** *Pepper 82876551792*	50	1
5 Jun 99	**VERTIGO** *Pepper 530332*	23	19
6 May 00	**THE REMIXES** *Pepper 9230102*	68	1
22 Sep 01 ●	**GOODBYE COUNTRY (HELLO NIGHTCLUB)** *Pepper 9230492*	5	8
16 Nov 02	**LOVEBOX** *Pepper 9230662*	41	2

[1] Groove Armada featuring Gram'ma Funk

See also WEEKEND PLAYERS

GROOVE CONNEKTION 2 *UK, male producer / instrumentalist (Singles: 1 week)* pos/wks

11 Apr 98	**CLUB LONELY** *XL Recordings XLT 94CD*	54	1

GROOVE CORPORATION *UK / Italy, male / female vocal / instrumental group (Singles: 1 week)* pos/wks

16 Apr 94	**RAIN** *Six6 SIXCD 109*	71	1

GROOVE FOUNDATION – See DJ CHUS presents GROOVE FOUNDATION

GROOVE GANG – See DAFFY DUCK featuring the GROOVE GANG

GROOVE GENERATION featuring Leo SAYER *UK, male production group (Singles: 3 weeks)* pos/wks

8 Aug 98	**YOU MAKE ME FEEL LIKE DANCING** *Brothers Org. CDBRUV 8*	32	3

GROOVE THEORY *US, male / female production vocal duo – Bryce Wilson and Amel Larrieux (Singles: 3 weeks)* pos/wks

18 Nov 95	**TELL ME** *Epic 6623882*	31	3

See also MANTRONIX

GROOVERIDER *UK, male DJ / producer – Ray Bingham (Singles: 3 weeks, Albums: 1 week)* pos/wks

26 Sep 98	**RAINBOWS OF COLOUR** *Higher Ground HIGHS 13CD*	40	2
19 Jun 99	**WHERE'S JACK THE RIPPER** *Higher Ground HIGHS 20CD*	61	1
10 Oct 98	**MYSTERIES OF FUNK** *Higher Ground HIGH 6CD*	50	1

Scott GROOVES *US, male DJ / producer (Singles: 3 weeks)* pos/wks

16 May 98	**EXPANSIONS** *Soma Recordings SOMA 65CDS* [1]	68	1
28 Nov 98	**MOTHERSHIP RECONNECTION** *Soma Recordings SOMA 71CDS*	55	1
21 Aug 99	**MOTHERSHIP RECONNECTION** *Virgin DINSD 185* [2]	55	1

[1] Scott Grooves featuring Roy Ayers [2] Scott Grooves featuring Parliament / Funkadelic

Henry GROSS *US, male vocalist (Singles: 4 weeks)* pos/wks

28 Aug 76	**SHANNON** *Life Song ELS 45002*	32	4

GROUND LEVEL *Australia, male instrumental / production group (Singles: 2 weeks)* pos/wks

30 Jan 93	**DREAMS OF HEAVEN** *Faze 2 CDFAZE 14*	54	2

GROUNDHOGS *UK, male vocal / instrumental group (Albums: 51 weeks)* pos/wks

6 Jun 70 ●	**THANK CHRIST FOR THE BOMB** *Liberty LBS 83295*	9	13
27 Mar 71 ●	**SPLIT** *Liberty LBG 83401*	5	28
18 Mar 72 ●	**WHO WILL SAVE THE WORLD** *United Artists UAG 29237*	8	9
13 Jul 74	**SOLID** *WWA WWA 004*	31	1

GROUP THERAPY *US, male rap group (Singles: 1 week)* pos/wks

30 Nov 96	**EAST COAST / WEST COAST KILLAS** *Interscope IND 95516*	51	1

Boring Bob GROVER – See PIRANHAS

Sir Charles GROVES – See ROYAL PHILHARMONIC ORCHESTRA

GUESS WHO *Canada, male vocal / instrumental group (Singles: 14 weeks)* pos/wks

16 Feb 67	**HIS GIRL** *King KG 1044*	45	1
9 May 70	**AMERICAN WOMAN (re)** *RCA 1943* ▲	19	13

David GUETTA featuring Chris WILLIS *France, male producer and US, male vocalist (Singles: 2 weeks)* pos/wks

31 Aug 02	**LOVE, DON'T LET ME GO** *Virgin DINSD 243* [1]	46	1
12 Jul 03	**JUST FOR ONE DAY (HEROES)** *Virgin DINST 263* [2]	73	1

[1] David Guetta featuring Chris Willis [2] David Guetta vs Bowie

GUILDFORD CATHEDRAL CHOIR *UK, choir (Albums: 4 weeks)* pos/wks

10 Dec 66	**CHRISTMAS CAROLS FROM GUILDFORD CATHEDRAL** *MFP 1104*	23	4

Record credits Barry Rose as conductor

GUITAR CORPORATION *UK, male instrumental group (Albums: 5 weeks)* pos/wks

15 Feb 92	**IMAGES** *Quality Television QTVCD 002*	41	5

GUN *UK, male vocal / instrumental trio (Singles: 11 weeks)* pos/wks

20 Nov 68 ●	**RACE WITH THE DEVIL** *CBS 3734*	8	11

GUN *UK, male vocal / instrumental group (Singles: 46 weeks, Albums: 23 weeks)* pos/wks

1 Jul 89	**BETTER DAYS** *A&M AM 505*	33	9
16 Sep 89	**MONEY (EVERYBODY LOVES HER)** *A&M AM 520*	73	2
11 Nov 89	**INSIDE OUT** *A&M AM 531*	57	2
10 Feb 90	**TAKING ON THE WORLD** *A&M AM 541*	50	3
14 Jul 90	**SHAME ON YOU** *A&M AM 573*	33	4
14 Mar 92	**STEAL YOUR FIRE** *A&M AM 851*	24	4
2 May 92	**HIGHER GROUND** *A&M AM 869*	48	2
4 Jul 92	**WELCOME TO THE REAL WORLD** *A&M AM 885*	43	2
9 Jul 94 ●	**WORD UP** *A&M 5806672*	8	7
24 Sep 94	**DON'T SAY IT'S OVER** *A&M 5807572*	19	3
25 Feb 95	**THE ONLY ONE** *A&M 5809552*	29	3
15 Apr 95	**SOMETHING WORTHWHILE** *A&M 5810452*	39	2

26 Apr 97 **CRAZY YOU** *A&M 5821932* [1] 21 2
12 Jul 97 **MY SWEET JANE** *A&M 5822792* [1] 51 1
22 Jul 89 **TAKING ON THE WORLD** *A&M AMA 7007*....44 10
18 Apr 92 **GALLUS** *A&M 3953832* 14 4
13 Aug 94 ● **SWAGGER** *A&M 5402542* 5 7
24 May 97 **0141 632 6326** *A&M 5407232*....32 2

[1] G.U.N.

GUNS N' ROSES (81 Top 500)

Often controversial Los Angeles-based band. Best known line-up included Axl Rose (b. William Bailey) (v), Slash (b. Saul Hudson) (g), Izzy Stradlin (b. Jeffrey Isbell) (g). The only act to hold the top two album spots in both the UK and the US on the week of releasing both records: Use Your Illusion I and II in 1991 (Singles: 107 weeks, Albums: 379 weeks) pos/wks

3 Oct 87 **WELCOME TO THE JUNGLE** *Geffen GEF 30* 67 2
20 Aug 88 **SWEET CHILD O' MINE** *Geffen GEF 43* ▲ 24 8
29 Oct 88 **WELCOME TO THE JUNGLE / NIGHTRAIN (re-issue)** *Geffen GEF 47* 24 5
18 Mar 89 ● **PARADISE CITY** *Geffen GEF 50* 6 9
3 Jun 89 ● **SWEET CHILD O' MINE (re-issue)** *Geffen GEF 55* 6 9
1 Jul 89 ● **PATIENCE** *Geffen GEF 56* 10 7
2 Sep 89 **NIGHTRAIN (re-issue)** *Geffen GEF 60* 17 5
13 Jul 91 ● **YOU COULD BE MINE** *Geffen GFS 6* 3 10
21 Sep 91 ● **DON'T CRY** *Geffen GFS 9* 8 4
21 Dec 91 ● **LIVE AND LET DIE** *Geffen GFS 17* 5 7
7 Mar 92 ● **NOVEMBER RAIN** *Geffen GFS 18* 4 5
23 May 92 ● **KNOCKIN' ON HEAVEN'S DOOR** *Geffen GFS 21* 2 9
21 Nov 92 ● **YESTERDAYS / NOVEMBER RAIN (re-issue)** *Geffen GFS 27* 8 9
29 May 93 **THE CIVIL WAR (EP)** *Geffen GFSTD 43* 11 3
20 Nov 93 ● **AIN'T IT FUN** *Geffen GFSTD 62* 9 3
4 Jun 94 ● **SINCE I DON'T HAVE YOU** *Geffen GFSTD 70* 10 6
14 Jan 95 ● **SYMPATHY FOR THE DEVIL** *Geffen GFSTD 86* 9 6
1 Aug 87 ● **APPETITE FOR DESTRUCTION** *Geffen WX 125* ▲ 5 158
17 Dec 88 **G N' R LIES** *Geffen WX 218* 22 41
28 Sep 91 ● **USE YOUR ILLUSION I** *Geffen GEF 24415*....2 84
28 Sep 91 ★ **USE YOUR ILLUSION II** *Geffen GEF 24420* ■ ▲ 1 84
4 Dec 93 ● **THE SPAGHETTI INCIDENT?** *Geffen GED 24617*....2 10
11 Dec 99 **LIVE – ERA '87-'93** *Geffen 4905142* 45 2

The re-issue of 'November Rain' was listed only from 28 Nov 1992. Tracks on The Civil War (EP): Civil War / Garden of Eden / Dead Horse / Interview

See also Duff MCKAGAN; SLASH'S SNAKEPIT; GILBY CLARKE

GUNSHOT

UK, male rap group (Albums: 1 week) pos/wks

19 Jun 93 **PATRIOT GAMES** *Vinyl Solution STEAM 43CD* 60 1

David GUNSON

UK, male after-dinner speaker (Albums: 2 weeks) pos/wks

25 Dec 82 **WHAT GOES UP MIGHT COME DOWN** *Big Ben BB 0012* 92 2

Peter GUNZ – See LORD TARIQ and Peter GUNZ

GURU

US, male rapper / producer – Keith Elam (Singles: 12 weeks, Albums: 12 weeks) pos/wks

11 Sep 93 **TRUST ME** *Cooltempo CDCOOL 278* [1] 34 2
13 Nov 93 **NO TIME TO PLAY** *Cooltempo CDCOOL 282* [2] 25 3
19 Aug 95 **WATCH WHAT YOU SAY** *Cooltempo CDCOOL 308* [3] 28 3
18 Nov 95 **FEEL THE MUSIC** *Cooltempo CDCOOLS 313* 34 2
13 Jul 96 **LIVIN' IN THIS WORLD / LIFESAVER** *Cooltempo CDCOOL 320* 61 1
16 Dec 00 **KEEP YOUR WORRIES** *Virgin VUSCD 177* [4] 57 1
29 May 93 **JAZZMATAZZ** *Cooltempo CTCD 34*....58 2
15 Jul 95 **JAZZMATAZZ VOLUME II – THE NEW REALITY** *Cooltempo CTCD 47*....12 9
14 Oct 00 **STREETSOUL** *Virgin CDVUS 178* [1] 74 1

[1] Guru featuring N'Dea Davenport [2] Guru featuring Dee C Lee [3] Guru featuring Chaka Khan [4] Guru's Jazzmatazz featuring Angie Stone [1] Guru's Jazzmatazz

See also GANG STARR

GURU JOSH

UK, male producer – Paul Walden (Singles: 14 weeks, Albums: 2 weeks) pos/wks

24 Feb 90 ● **INFINITY** *Deconstruction PB 43475* 5 10
16 Jun 90 **WHOSE LAW (IS IT ANYWAY)?** *Deconstruction PB 43647* 26 4
14 Jul 90 **INFINITY** *Deconstruction PL 74701* 41 2

Adrian GURVITZ

UK, male vocalist (Singles: 16 weeks) pos/wks

30 Jan 82 ● **CLASSIC** *RAK 339* 8 13
12 Jun 82 **YOUR DREAM** *RAK 343* 61 3

G.U.S. (Footwear) BAND and the MORRISTOWN ORPHEUS CHOIR

UK, male / female groups (Albums: 1 week) pos/wks

3 Oct 70 **LAND OF HOPE AND GLORY** *Columbia SCX 6406* 54 1

See also MORRISTOWN ORPHEUS CHOIR

GUSGUS

Iceland, male / female vocal / instrumental group (Singles: 5 weeks) pos/wks

21 Feb 98 **POLYESTERDAY** *4AD BAD 8002CD* 55 1
13 Mar 99 **LADYSHAVE** *4AD BAD 9001CD* 64 1
24 Apr 99 **STARLOVERS** *4AD BADD 9004CD*....62 1
8 Feb 03 **DAVID** *Underwater H20 022CD* 52 1
28Jun 03 **CALL OF THE WILD** *Underwater H20 032CD* 75 1

GUSTO

US, male producer – Edward Green (Singles: 8 weeks) pos/wks

2 Mar 96 ● **DISCO'S REVENGE** *Manifesto FESCD 6* 9 5
7 Sep 96 **LET'S ALL CHANT** *Manifesto FESCD 13* 21 3

Arlo GUTHRIE

US, male vocalist (Albums: 1 week) pos/wks

7 Mar 70 **ALICE'S RESTAURANT** *Reprise RSLP 6267* 44 1

Gwen GUTHRIE

US, female vocalist, d. 3 Feb 1999 (Singles: 25 weeks, Albums: 14 weeks) pos/wks

19 Jul 86 ● **AIN'T NOTHIN' GOIN' ON BUT THE RENT** *Boiling Point POSP 807* 5 12
11 Oct 86 **(THEY LONG TO BE) CLOSE TO YOU** *Boiling Point POSP 822* ..25 7
14 Feb 87 **GOOD TO GO LOVER / OUTSIDE IN THE RAIN** *Boiling Point POSP 841* 37 4
4 Sep 93 **AIN'T NOTHIN' GOIN' ON BUT THE RENT (re-mix)** *Polydor PZCD 276* 42 2
23 Aug 86 **GOOD TO GO LOVER** *Boiling Point POLD 5201*....42 14

Robin GUTHRIE – See Harold BUDD / Liz FRASER / Robin GUTHRIE / Simon RAYMONDE

GUY

US, male vocal group - includes Aaron Hall and Teddy Riley (Singles: 4 weeks, Albums: 1 week) pos/wks

4 May 91 **HER** *MCA MCS 1575* 58 4
5 Feb 00 **III** *MCA 1121702* 55 1

Buddy GUY

US, male vocalist / instrumentalist – guitar (Albums: 9 weeks) pos/wks

22 Jun 91 **DAMN RIGHT I'VE GOT THE BLUES** *Silvertone ORELP 516* 43 5
13 Mar 93 **FEELS LIKE RAIN** *Silvertone ORECD 525* 36 4

A GUY CALLED GERALD

UK, male producer – Gerald Simpson (Singles: 23 weeks, Albums: 2 weeks) pos/wks

8 Apr 89 **VOODOO RAY (re)** *Rham! RS 804* 12 18
16 Dec 89 **FX / EYES OF SORROW** *Subscape AGCG 1* 52 5
14 Apr 90 **AUTOMANIKK** *Subscape 4664821* 68 1
1 Apr 95 **BLACK SECRET TECHNOLOGY** *Juice Box JBCD 25*....64 1

GUYS 'N' DOLLS

UK, male / female vocal group (Singles: 33 weeks, Albums: 1 week) pos/wks

1 Mar 75 ● **THERE'S A WHOLE LOT OF LOVING** *Magnet MAG 20* [1] 2 11
17 May 75 **HERE I GO AGAIN** *Magnet MAG 30* 33 5
21 Feb 76 ● **YOU DON'T HAVE TO SAY YOU LOVE ME** *Magnet MAG 50* 5 8

6 Nov 76	**STONEY GROUND** *Magnet MAG 76*	**38** 4
13 May 78	**ONLY LOVING DOES IT** *Magnet MAG 115*	**42** 5
31 May 75	**GUYS 'N' DOLLS** *Magnet MAG 5005*	**43** 1

1 Guys & Dolls

GUYVER *UK, male producer – Guy Mearns (Singles: 1 week)* pos/wks

29 Mar 03	**TRAPPED / DIFFERENCES** *Tidy Two TIDYTWO 118*	**72** 1

Jonas GWANGWA – *See George FENTON and Jonas GWANGWA*

GWENT CHORALE – *See Bryn YEMM*

GYPSYMEN
US, male producer – Todd Terry (Singles: 2 weeks) pos/wks

11 Aug 01	**BABARABATIRI** *Sound Design SDES 09CDS*	**32** 2

See also Todd TERRY PROJECT

GYRES *UK, male vocal / instrumental group (Singles: 2 weeks)* pos/wks

13 Apr 96	**POP COP** *Sugar SUGA 9CD*	**71** 1
6 Jul 96	**ARE YOU READY** *Sugar SUGA 11CD*	**71** 1

GZA / GENIUS
US, male rapper – Gary Crice (Singles: 2 weeks, Albums: 2 weeks) pos/wks

2 Mar 96	**COLD WORLD** *Geffen GFSTD 22114* 1	**40** 2
2 Dec 95	**LIQUID SWORDS** *Geffen GED 24813*	**73** 1
10 Jul 99	**BENEATH THE SURFACE** *MCA MCD 11969*	**64** 1

1 Genius / GZA featuring D'Angelo

See also WU-TANG CLAN

H & CLAIRE *UK, male / female vocal duo – Ian Watkins and Claire Richards (Singles: 25 weeks, Albums: 1 week)* pos/wks

18 May 02 ●	**DJ** *WEA WEA 347CD*	**3** 11
24 Aug 02 ●	**HALF A HEART (re)** *WEA WEA 359CDX*	**8** 6
16 Nov 02 ●	**ALL OUT OF LOVE (re)** *WEA WEA 360CD*	**10** 8
30 Nov 02	**ANOTHER YOU ANOTHER ME** *WEA 0927494622*	**58** 1

See also STEPS

HHC *UK, male DJ / production duo (Singles: 1 week)* pos/wks

19 Apr 97	**WE'RE NOT ALONE** *Perfecto PERF 138CD*	**44** 1

H 20 *UK, male vocal / instrumental group (Singles: 16 weeks)* pos/wks

21 May 83	**DREAM TO SLEEP** *RCA 330*	**17** 10
13 Aug 83	**JUST OUTSIDE OF HEAVEN** *RCA 349*	**38** 6

H20 *US / Switzerland, male / female vocal / instrumental group (Singles: 4 weeks)* pos/wks

14 Sep 96	**NOBODY'S BUSINESS** *AM:PM 5818832* 1	**19** 3
30 Aug 97	**SATISFIED (TAKE ME HIGHER)** *AM:PM 5823252*	**66** 1

1 H20 featuring Billie

HWA featuring SONIC THE HEDGEHOG
UK, male producer – Jeremy Healy (Singles: 6 weeks) pos/wks

5 Dec 92	**SUPERSONIC** *Internal Affairs KGB 008*	**33** 6

See also Jeremy HEALY and AMOS; HAYSI FANTAYZEE

HABIT
UK, male vocal / instrumental group (Singles: 2 weeks) pos/wks

30 Apr 88	**LUCY** *Virgin VS 1063*	**56** 2

Steve HACKETT *UK, male vocalist / instrumentalist – guitar (Singles: 2 weeks, Albums: 38 weeks)* pos/wks

2 Apr 83	**CELL 151** *Charisma CELL 1*	**66** 2
1 Nov 75	**VOYAGE OF THE ACOLYTE** *Charisma CAS 1111*	**26** 4
6 May 78	**PLEASE DON'T TOUCH** *Charisma CDS 4012*	**38** 5
26 May 79	**SPECTRAL MORNINGS** *Charisma CDS 4017*	**22** 11
21 Jun 80 ●	**DEFECTOR** *Charisma CDS 4018*	**9** 7
29 Aug 81	**CURED** *Charisma CDS 4021*	**15** 5
30 Apr 83	**HIGHLY STRUNG** *Charisma HACK 1*	**16** 3
19 Nov 83	**BAY OF KINGS** *Lamborghini LMGLP 3000*	**70** 1
22 Sep 84	**TILL WE HAVE FACES** *Lamborghini LMGLP 4000*	**54** 2

See also GENESIS; GTR

HADDAWAY *Trinidad and Tobago, male vocalist – Nester Haddaway (Singles: 52 weeks, Albums: 16 weeks)* pos/wks

5 Jun 93 ●	**WHAT IS LOVE** *Logic 74321148502*	**2** 15
25 Sep 93 ●	**LIFE** *Logic 74321164212*	**6** 9
18 Dec 93 ●	**I MISS YOU** *Logic 74321181522*	**9** 14
2 Apr 94 ●	**ROCK MY HEART** *Logic 74321194122*	**9** 9
24 Jun 95	**FLY AWAY** *Logic 74321286942*	**20** 3
23 Sep 95	**CATCH A FIRE** *Logic 74321306652*	**39** 2
23 Oct 93 ●	**HADDAWAY – THE ALBUM** *Logic 74321169222*	**9** 16

Tony HADLEY
UK, male vocalist (Singles: 9 weeks, Albums: 6 weeks) pos/wks

7 Mar 92	**LOST IN YOUR LOVE** *EMI EM 222*	**42** 4
29 Aug 92	**FOR YOUR BLUE EYES ONLY** *EMI EM 234*	**67** 2
16 Jan 93	**THE GAME OF LOVE** *EMI CDEM 254*	**72** 1
10 May 97	**DANCE WITH ME** *VC VCRD 17* 1	**35** 2
20 Sep 97	**TONY HADLEY** *PolyGram TV 5393012*	**45** 3
10 May 03	**TRUE BALLADS** *Universal TV 382882*	**31** 3

1 Tin Tin Out featuring Tony Hadley

See also SPANDAU BALLET

Sammy HAGAR *US, male vocalist / instrumentalist – guitar (Singles: 15 weeks, Albums: 19 weeks)* pos/wks

15 Dec 79	**THIS PLANET'S ON FIRE (BURN IN HELL) / SPACE STATION NO.5** *Capitol CL 16114*	**52** 5
16 Feb 80	**I'VE DONE EVERYTHING FOR YOU** *Capitol CL 16120*	**36** 5
24 May 80	**HEARTBEAT / LOVE OR MONEY** *Capitol RED 1*	**67** 2
16 Jan 82	**PIECE OF MY HEART (re)** *Geffen GEFA 1884*	**67** 3
29 Sep 79	**STREET MACHINE** *Capitol EST 11983*	**38** 4
22 Mar 80	**LOUD AND CLEAR** *Capitol EST 25330*	**12** 8
7 Jun 80	**DANGER ZONE** *Capitol EST 12069*	**25** 3
13 Feb 82	**STANDING HAMPTON** *Geffen GEF 85456*	**84** 2
4 Jul 87	**SAMMY HAGAR** *Geffen WX 114*	**86** 2

See also MONTROSE; VAN HALEN; HAGAR SHCON AARONSON SHRIEVE

HAGAR SCHON AARONSON SHRIEVE
US, male vocal / instrumental group (Albums: 1 week) pos/wks

Date	Title	pos	wks
19 May 84	**THROUGH THE FIRE** *Geffen GEF 25893*	92	1

See also Sammy HAGAR

Paul HAIG *UK, male vocalist (Singles: 3 weeks, Albums: 2 weeks)* pos/wks

Date	Title	pos	wks
28 May 83	**HEAVEN SENT** *Island IS 111*	74	3
22 Oct 83	**RHYTHM OF LIFE** *Crepuscule ILPS 9742*	82	2

HAIRCUT 100 *UK, male vocal / instrumental group – includes Nick Heyward (Singles: 47 weeks, Albums: 34 weeks)* pos/wks

Date	Title	pos	wks
24 Oct 81 ●	**FAVOURITE SHIRTS (BOY MEETS GIRL)** *Arista CLIP 1*	4	14
30 Jan 82 ●	**LOVE PLUS ONE** *Arista CLIP 2*	3	12
10 Apr 82 ●	**FANTASTIC DAY** *Arista CLIP 3*	9	9
21 Aug 82 ●	**NOBODY'S FOOL** *Arista CLIP 4*	9	7
6 Aug 83	**PRIME TIME** *Polydor HC 1*	46	5
6 Mar 82 ●	**PELICAN WEST** *Arista HCC 100*	2	34

Curtis HAIRSTON *US, male vocalist, b. 10 Oct 1961, d. 18 Jan 1996 (Singles: 16 weeks)* pos/wks

Date	Title	pos	wks
15 Oct 83	**I WANT YOU (ALL TONIGHT)** *RCA 368*	44	5
27 Apr 85	**I WANT YOUR LOVIN' (JUST A LITTLE BIT)** *London LON 66*	13	7
6 Dec 86	**CHILLIN' OUT** *Atlantic A 9335*	57	4

Gary HAISMAN – *See D MOB*

HAL featuring Gillian ANDERSON
UK, male production trio and US, female vocalist (Singles: 3 weeks) pos/wks

Date	Title	pos	wks
24 May 97	**EXTREMIS** *Virgin VSCDT 1636*	23	3

HALE and PACE and the STONKERS *UK, male comedy duo – Gareth Hale and Norman Pace, and backing group (Singles: 7 weeks)* pos/wks

Date	Title	pos	wks
9 Mar 91 ★	**THE STONK** *London LON 296*	1	7

Bill HALEY and His COMETS (274 Top 500) *Original 'King of Rock 'n' Roll', b. 6 Jul 1925, Detroit, d. 9 Feb 1981. The kiss-curl hairstyled frontman introduced rock to the world via a string of 1950s smashes, including 'Rock Around the Clock', the only record to return to the Top 20 on five occasions, selling 1,392,000 (Singles: 199 weeks, Albums: 31 weeks)* pos/wks

Date	Title	pos	wks
17 Dec 54 ●	**SHAKE, RATTLE AND ROLL** *Brunswick 05338*	4	14
7 Jan 55 ★	**ROCK AROUND THE CLOCK (5re)** *Brunswick 05317* ◆ ▲	1	36
15 Apr 55	**MAMBO ROCK** *Brunswick 05405*	14	2
30 Dec 55 ●	**ROCK-A-BEATIN' BOOGIE** *Brunswick 05509*	4	9
9 Mar 56 ●	**SEE YOU LATER, ALLIGATOR (re)** *Brunswick 05530*	7	21
25 May 56 ●	**THE SAINTS ROCK 'N ROLL** *Brunswick 05565*	5	24
17 Aug 56 ●	**ROCKIN' THROUGH THE RYE (re)** *Brunswick 05582*	3	23
14 Sep 56	**RAZZLE DAZZLE** *Brunswick 05453*	13	8
9 Nov 56 ●	**RIP IT UP** *Brunswick 05615*	4	18
9 Nov 56	**ROCK 'N' ROLL STAGE SHOW (LP)** *Brunswick LAT 8139*	30	1
23 Nov 56	**RUDY'S ROCK (re)** *Brunswick 05616*	26	5
1 Feb 57	**ROCK THE JOINT** *London HLF 8371*	20	4
8 Feb 57 ●	**DON'T KNOCK THE ROCK** *Brunswick 05640*	7	8
3 Apr 68	**ROCK AROUND THE CLOCK (re-issue)** *MCA MU 1013*	20	11
16 Mar 74	**ROCK AROUND THE CLOCK (2nd re-issue)** *MCA 128*	12	10
25 Apr 81	**HALEY'S GOLDEN MEDLEY** *MCA 694*	50	5
4 Aug 56 ●	**ROCK AROUND THE CLOCK** *Brunswick LAT 8117*	2	17
20 Oct 56 ★	**ROCK 'N' ROLL STAGE SHOW** *Brunswick LAT 8139*	1	8
16 Feb 57 ●	**ROCK THE JOINT** *London HAF 2037*	5	1
18 May 68	**ROCK AROUND THE CLOCK** *Ace Of Hearts AH 13*	34	5

'Rock Around the Clock' peaked at No.15 on its first visit to the chart, then re-entered peaking at No.1 in Oct 1955, No.5 in Sep 1956, No.24 in Dec 1956, No.25 in Jan 1957 and No.22 later that same month. Tracks on Rock 'n' Roll Stage Show (LP): Calling All Comets / Rockin' Through the Rye / A Rockin' Little Tune / Hide and Seek / Hey There Now / Goofin' Around / Hook Line and Sinker / Rudy's Rock / Choo Choo Ch'Boogie / Blue Comets Rock / Hot Dog Buddy Buddy / Tonight's the Night. Occasionally, some of the 'Rock Around the Clock' labels billed the song as '(We're Gonna) Rock Around the Clock'. Haley's Golden Medley comprised: Rock Around The Clock / Rock-a-Beatin=Boogie / Shake, Rattle and Roll / Choo Choo Ch'Boogie / See You Later Alligator

HALF MAN HALF BISCUIT
UK, male vocal / instrumental group (Albums: 14 weeks) pos/wks

Date	Title	pos	wks
8 Feb 86	**BACK IN THE D.H.S.S.** *Probe Plus PROBE 4*	60	9
21 Feb 87	**BACK AGAIN IN THE D.H.S.S.** *Probe Plus PROBE 8*	59	5

Aaron HALL *US, male vocalist (Singles: 3 weeks)* pos/wks

Date	Title	pos	wks
13 Jun 92	**DON'T BE AFRAID** *MCA MCS 1632*	56	2
23 Oct 93	**GET A LITTLE FREAKY WITH ME** *MCA MCSTD 1936*	66	1

See also GUY

Audrey HALL *Jamaica, female vocalist (Singles: 20 weeks)* pos/wks

Date	Title	pos	wks
25 Jan 86	**ONE DANCE WON'T DO** *Germain DG7-1985*	20	11
5 Jul 86	**SMILE** *Germain DG 15*	14	9

Daryl HALL
US, male vocalist (Singles: 26 weeks, Albums: 9 weeks) pos/wks

Date	Title	pos	wks
2 Aug 86	**DREAMTIME** *RCA HALL 1*	28	8
25 Sep 93	**I'M IN A PHILLY MOOD (re)** *Epic 6595555*	52	4
8 Jan 94	**STOP LOVING ME STOP LOVING YOU** *Epic 6599982*	30	6
14 May 94	**HELP ME FIND A WAY TO YOUR HEART** *Epic 6604102*	70	1
2 Jul 94	**GLORYLAND** *Mercury MERCD 404* [1]	36	4
10 Jun 95	**WHEREVER WOULD I BE** *Columbia 6620592* [2]	44	3
23 Aug 86	**THREE HEARTS IN THE HAPPY ENDING MACHINE** *RCA PL 87196*	26	5
23 Oct 93	**SOUL ALONE** *Epic 4732912*	55	4

[1] Daryl Hall and the Sounds of Blackness [2] Dusty Springfield and Daryl Hall

See also Daryl HALL and John OATES

Daryl HALL and John OATES (264 Top 500)
Soul-influenced US duo: Daryl Hall (v), b. 11 Oct 1948, Philadelphia and John Oates (g) b. 7 Apr 1949, New York. Met at university in 1967, eventually becoming the most successful duo in US singles chart history, with 16 Top 10s and six No.1s (Singles: 84 weeks, Albums: 154 weeks) pos/wks

Date	Title	pos	wks
16 Oct 76	**SHE'S GONE** *Atlantic K 10828*	42	4
14 Jun 80	**RUNNING FROM PARADISE** *RCA RUN 1*	41	6
20 Sep 80	**YOU'VE LOST THAT LOVIN' FEELIN'** *RCA 1*	55	3
15 Nov 80	**KISS ON MY LIST** *RCA 15* ▲	33	8
23 Jan 82 ●	**I CAN'T GO FOR THAT (NO CAN DO)** *RCA 172* ▲	8	10
10 Apr 82	**PRIVATE EYES** *RCA 134* ▲	32	7
30 Oct 82 ●	**MANEATER** *RCA 290* ▲	6	11
22 Jan 83	**ONE ON ONE** *RCA 305*	63	3
30 Apr 83	**FAMILY MAN** *RCA 323*	15	7
12 Nov 83	**SAY IT ISN'T SO** *RCA 375*	69	3
10 Mar 84	**ADULT EDUCATION** *RCA 396*	63	2
20 Oct 84	**OUT OF TOUCH** *RCA 449* ▲	48	5
9 Feb 85	**METHOD OF MODERN LOVE** *RCA 472*	21	8
22 Jun 85	**OUT OF TOUCH (re-mix)** *RCA PB 49967*	62	3
21 Sep 85	**A NIGHT AT THE APOLLO LIVE!** *RCA PB 49935* [1]	58	2
29 Sep 90	**SO CLOSE** *Arista 113600* [2]	69	1
26 Jan 91	**EVERYWHERE I LOOK** *Arista 113980*	74	1
3 Jul 76	**HALL AND OATES** *RCA Victor APL1 1144*	56	1
18 Sep 76	**BIGGER THAN BOTH OF US** *RCA Victor APL1 1467*	25	7
15 Oct 77	**BEAUTY ON A BACK STREET** *RCA PL 12300*	40	2
6 Feb 82 ●	**PRIVATE EYES** *RCA RCALP 6001*	8	21
23 Oct 82	**H2O** *RCA RCALP 6056*	24	35
29 Oct 83	**ROCK 'N' SOUL PART 1** *RCA PL 84858*	16	45
27 Oct 84	**BIG BAM BOOM** *RCA PL 85309*	28	13
28 Sep 85	**HALL & OATES LIVE AT THE APOLLO WITH DAVID RUFFIN AND EDDIE KENDRICK** *RCA PL 87035*	32	5
18 Jun 88	**OOH YEAH!** *RCA 208895*	52	3
27 Oct 90	**CHANGE OF SEASON** *Arista 210548*	44	2
19 Oct 91 ●	**THE BEST OF DARYL HALL AND JOHN OATES – LOOKING BACK** *Arista PL 90388*	9	16
6 Oct 01	**THE ESSENTIAL COLLECTION** *RCA 74321886972*	26	2
12 Apr 03	**DO IT FOR LOVE** *Sanctuary SANCD166*	37	2

[1] Daryl Hall and John Oates featuring David Ruffin and Eddie Kendrick [2] Hall and Oates

'A Night at the Apollo Live!' is a medley of 'The Way You Do the Things You Do' and 'My Girl'

Lynden David Hall *UK, male vocalist / instrumentalist (Singles: 12 weeks, Albums: 4 weeks)* pos/wks

		pos	wks
25 Oct 97	**SEXY CINDERELLA** *Cooltempo CDCOOL 328*	45	2
14 Mar 98	**DO I QUALIFY?** *Cooltempo CDCOOLS 331*	26	2
4 Jul 98	**CRESCENT MOON** *Cooltempo CDCOOL 333*	45	1
31 Oct 98	**SEXY CINDERELLA (re-issue)** *Cooltempo CDCOOLS 340*	17	3
11 Mar 00	**FORGIVE ME** *Cooltempo CDCOOLS 346*	30	2
27 May 00	**SLEEPING WITH VICTOR** *Cooltempo CDCOOL 348*	49	1
23 Sep 00	**LET'S DO IT AGAIN** *Cooltempo CDCOOL 351*	69	1
14 Nov 98	**MEDICINE 4 MY PAIN** *Cooltempo 4959952*	43	2
10 Jun 00	**THE OTHER SIDE** *Cooltempo 5261492*	36	2

Pam HALL *Jamaica, female vocalist (Singles: 4 weeks)* pos/wks

		pos	wks
16 Aug 86	**DEAR BOOPSIE** *Bluemountain BM 027*	54	4

Terry HALL *UK, male vocalist (Singles: 7 weeks, Albums: 1 week)* pos/wks

		pos	wks
11 Nov 89	**MISSING** *Chrysalis CHS 3381*	75	1
27 Aug 94	**FOREVER J** *AnXious ANX 1024CDX*	67	1
12 Nov 94	**SENSE** *AnXious ANX 1027CD*	54	2
28 Oct 95	**RAINBOWS (EP)** *AnXious ANX 1033CD1*	62	1
14 Jun 97	**BALLAD OF A LANDLORD** *Southsea Bubble CDBUBBLE 1*	50	1
18 Oct 03	**PROBLEM IS** *Distinctive DISNCD 107* [1]	66	1
18 Oct 97	**LAUGH** *Southsea Bubble Co CDBUBBLE 3*	50	1

[1] Dub Pistols featuring Terry Hall

The sleeve, not the label, of 'Missing' credits Terry, Blair and Anouchka. Tracks on Rainbows (EP) CD1: Chasing a Rainbow / Mistakes / See No Evil (live) / Ghost Town (live) and CD2: Chasing a Rainbow / Our Lips are Sealed (live) / Thinking of You (live) / Ghost Town (live)

See also FUN BOY THREE; SPECIALS; VEGAS

Toni HALLIDAY – *See LEFTFIELD; Paul VAN DYK*

Geri HALLIWELL 458 Top 500

Headline-grabbing former Ginger Spice (b. 6 Aug 1972, Watford, UK) sang on seven Spice Girls chart-toppers before achieving more solo No.1s than any other UK female. She is the only person to score as many as four consecutive No.1s both as a solo artist and as part of group (Singles: 93 weeks, Albums: 58 weeks) pos/wks

		pos	wks
22 May 99 ●	**LOOK AT ME (re)** *EMI CDEM 542*	2	14
28 Aug 99 ★	**MI CHICO LATINO** *EMI CDEM 548* ■	1	13
13 Nov 99 ★	**LIFT ME UP (re)** *EMI CDEM 554* ■	1	17
25 Mar 00 ★	**BAG IT UP (re)** *EMI CDEMS 560* ■	1	13
12 May 01 ★	**IT'S RAINING MEN** *EMI CDEMS 584* ■	1	15
11 Aug 01 ●	**SCREAM IF YOU WANNA GO FASTER (re)** *EMI CDEMS 595*	8	11
8 Dec 01 ●	**CALLING** *EMI CDEMS 606*	7	10
19 Jun 99 ●	**SCHIZOPHONIC** *EMI 5210092*	4	43
26 May 01 ●	**SCREAM IF YOU WANNA GO FASTER** *EMI 5333692*	5	15

See also SPICE GIRLS

HALO *UK, male vocal / instrumental group (Singles: 3 weeks)* pos/wks

		pos	wks
16 Feb 02	**COLD LIGHT OF DAY** *S2 6723072*	49	1
1 Jun 02	**SANCTIMONIOUS** *S2 6725962*	44	1
7 Sep 02	**NEVER ENDING** *S2 6730125*	56	1

HALO JAMES *UK, male vocal / instrumental group (Singles: 24 weeks, Albums: 4 weeks)* pos/wks

		pos	wks
7 Oct 89	**WANTED** *Epic HALO 1*	45	5
23 Dec 89 ●	**COULD HAVE TOLD YOU SO** *Epic HALO 2*	6	12
17 Mar 90	**BABY** *Epic HALO 3*	43	4
19 May 90	**MAGIC HOUR** *Epic HALO 4*	59	3
14 Apr 90	**WITNESS** *Epic 466761*	18	4

HAMBURG STUDENTS' CHOIR
Germany, male vocal group (Albums: 6 weeks) pos/wks

		pos	wks
17 Dec 60	**HARK THE HERALD ANGELS SING** *Pye GGL 0023*	11	6

Ashley HAMILTON *US, male vocalist (Singles: 4 weeks)* pos/wks

		pos	wks
14 Jun 03	**WIMMIN' (re)** *Columbia 673902*	27	4

George HAMILTON IV
US, male vocalist (Singles: 13 weeks, Albums: 11 weeks) pos/wks

		pos	wks
7 Mar 58	**WHY DON'T THEY UNDERSTAND** *HMV POP 429*	22	9
18 Jul 58	**I KNOW WHERE I'M GOIN' (re)** *HMV POP 505*	23	4
10 Apr 71	**CANADIAN PACIFIC** *RCA SF 8062*	45	1
10 Feb 79	**REFLECTIONS** *Lotus WH 5008*	25	9
13 Nov 82	**SONGS FOR A WINTER'S NIGHT** *Ronco RTL 2082*	94	1

Lynne HAMILTON *UK, female vocalist (Singles: 11 weeks)* pos/wks

		pos	wks
29 Apr 89 ●	**ON THE INSIDE (THEME FROM 'PRISONER: CELL BLOCK H')** *A1 A1 311*	3	11

Russ HAMILTON
UK, male vocalist – Ronald Hulme (Singles: 26 weeks) pos/wks

		pos	wks
24 May 57 ●	**WE WILL MAKE LOVE** *Oriole CB 1359*	2	20
27 Sep 57	**WEDDING RING** *Oriole CB 1388* [1]	20	6

[1] Russ Hamilton with Johnny Gregory and His Orchestra with The Tonettes

HAMILTON, Joe FRANK and REYNOLDS
US, male vocal group (Singles: 6 weeks) pos/wks

		pos	wks
13 Sep 75	**FALLIN' IN LOVE** *Pye International 7N 25690* ▲	33	6

Marvin HAMLISCH
US, male instrumentalist – piano (Singles: 13 weeks) pos/wks

		pos	wks
30 Mar 74	**THE ENTERTAINER** *MCA 121*	25	13

HAMMER – *See MC HAMMER*

Jan HAMMER *Czech Republic, male instrumentalist – keyboards (Singles: 26 weeks, Albums: 12 weeks)* pos/wks

		pos	wks
12 Oct 85 ●	**MIAMI VICE THEME** *MCA MCA 1000* ▲	5	8
19 Sep 87 ●	**CROCKETT'S THEME** *MCA MCA 1193*	2	12
1 Jun 91	**CROCKETT'S THEME (re-issue) / CHANCER** *MCA MCS 1541*	47	6
14 Nov 87	**ESCAPE FROM TV** *MCA MCF 3407*	34	12

Albert HAMMOND *Gibraltar, male vocalist (Singles: 11 weeks)* pos/wks

		pos	wks
30 Jun 73	**FREE ELECTRIC BAND** *Mums 1494*	19	11

See also FAMILY DOGG

Beres HAMMOND – *See Maxi PRIEST*

HAMPENBERG *Denmark, male / female vocal / instrumental / production group (Singles: 2 weeks)* pos/wks

		pos	wks
21 Sep 02	**DUCKTOY** *Serious SERR 49CD*	30	2

Herbie HANCOCK *US, male vocalist / instrumentalist – keyboards (Singles: 41 weeks, Albums: 24 weeks)* pos/wks

		pos	wks
26 Aug 78	**I THOUGHT IT WAS YOU** *CBS 6530*	15	9
3 Feb 79	**YOU BET YOUR LOVE** *CBS 7010*	18	10
30 Jul 83 ●	**ROCKIT** *CBS A 3577*	8	12
8 Oct 83	**AUTODRIVE** *CBS A 3802*	33	4
21 Jan 84	**FUTURE SHOCK** *CBS A 4075*	54	3
4 Aug 84	**HARDROCK** *CBS A 4616*	65	3
9 Sep 78	**SUNLIGHT** *CBS 82240*	27	6
24 Feb 79	**FEETS DON'T FAIL ME NOW** *CBS 83491*	28	8
27 Aug 83	**FUTURE SHOCK** *CBS 25540*	27	10

Tony HANCOCK
UK, male comedian d. 25 Jun 1968 (Albums: 51 weeks) pos/wks

		pos	wks
9 Apr 60 ●	**THIS IS HANCOCK** *Pye NPL 10845*	2	22
12 Nov 60	**PIECES OF HANCOCK** *Pye NPL 18054*	17	2
3 Mar 62	**HANCOCK** *Pye NPL 18068*	12	23
14 Sep 63	**THIS IS HANCOCK (re-issue)** *Pye Golden Guinea GGL 0206*	16	4

HANDBAGGERS
UK, male / female vocal / instrumental group (Singles: 1 week) pos/wks

		pos	wks
15 Jun 96	**U FOUND OUT** *Tidy Trax TIDY 104CD*	55	1

Vernon HANDLEY – *See Nigel KENNEDY*

HANDLEY FAMILY
UK, male / female vocal group (Singles: 7 weeks)

Date		Title	pos	wks
7 Apr 73		**WAM BAM** *GL 100*	30	7

HANI *US, male DJ / producer (Singles: 1 week)*

Date		Title	pos	wks
11 Mar 00		**BABY WANTS TO RIDE** *Neo NEO CD025*	70	1

Jayn HANNA *UK, female vocalist (Singles: 2 weeks)*

Date		Title	pos	wks
13 Apr 96		**LOVELIGHT (RIDE ON A LOVE TRAIN)** *VC VCRD 10*	42	1
1 Feb 97		**LOST WITHOUT YOU** *VC VCRD 16*	44	1

HANNAH
UK, female vocalist – Hannah Waddingham (Singles: 2 weeks)

Date		Title	pos	wks
21 Oct 00		**OUR KIND OF LOVE** *Telstar CDSTAS 3149*	41	2

HANNAH – *See MAN WITH NO NAME*

HANNAH and her SISTERS – *See Hannah JONES*

Bo HANNSON
Sweden, multi-instrumentalist (Albums: 7 weeks)

Date		Title	pos	wks
18 Nov 72		**LORD OF THE RINGS** *Charisma CAS 1059*	32	7

HANOI ROCKS *Finland / UK, male vocal / instrumental group (Singles: 2 weeks, Albums: 4 weeks)*

Date		Title	pos	wks
7 Jul 84		**UP AROUND THE BEND** *CBS A 4513*	61	2
11 Jun 83		**BACK TO MYSTERY CITY** *Lick LICLP 1*	87	1
20 Oct 84		**TWO STEPS FROM THE MOVE** *CBS 26066*	28	3

HANSON *US, male vocal / instrumental group (Singles: 47 weeks, Albums: 31 weeks)*

Date		Title	pos	wks
7 Jun 97	★	**MMMBOP** *Mercury 5745012* ■ ▲	1	13
13 Sep 97	●	**WHERE'S THE LOVE** *Mercury 5749032*	4	9
22 Nov 97	●	**I WILL COME TO YOU** *Mercury 5680672*	5	9
28 Mar 98		**WEIRD** *Mercury 5685412*	19	5
4 Jul 98		**THINKING OF YOU (re)** *Mercury 5688132*	23	7
29 Apr 00		**IF ONLY** *Mercury 5627502*	15	4
21 Jun 97	★	**MIDDLE OF NOWHERE** *Mercury 5346152* ■	1	29
13 Jun 98		**3 CAR GARAGE – INDIE RECORDINGS 95-96** *Mercury 5583992*	39	1
13 May 00		**THIS TIME AROUND** *Mercury 5427212*	33	1

John HANSON
UK, male vocalist (Albums: 12 weeks)

Date		Title	pos	wks
23 Apr 60		**THE STUDENT PRINCE** *Pye NPL 18046*	17	1
2 Sep 61	●	**THE STUDENT PRINCE / THE VAGABOND KING** *Pye GGL 0086*	9	7
10 Dec 77		**JOHN HANSON SINGS 20 SHOWTIME GREATS** *K-Tel NE 1002*	16	4

HAPPENINGS
US, male vocal group (Singles: 14 weeks)

Date		Title	pos	wks
18 May 67		**I GOT RHYTHM** *Stateside SS 2013*	28	9
16 Aug 67		**MY MAMMY** *Pye International 7N 25501 and BT Puppy BTS 45530*	34	5

Pye gave the US BT Puppy label its own identification halfway through the success of 'My Mammy'

HAPPY CLAPPERS *UK, male / female vocal / instrumental group (Singles: 19 weeks)*

Date		Title	pos	wks
3 Jun 95		**I BELIEVE** *Shindig SHIN 4CD*	21	3
26 Aug 95		**HOLD ON** *Shindig SHIN 7CD*	27	2
18 Nov 95	●	**I BELIEVE (re-issue)** *Shindig SHIN 9CD*	7	8
15 Jun 96		**CAN'T HELP IT** *Coliseum TOGA 004CD*	18	3
21 Dec 96		**NEVER AGAIN** *Coliseum TOGA 012CD*	49	1
22 Nov 97		**I BELIEVE (re-mix)** *Coalition COLA 027CD*	28	2

HAPPY MONDAYS *UK, male vocal / instrumental group (Singles: 53 weeks, Albums: 58 weeks)*

Date		Title	pos	wks
30 Sep 89		**WFL** *Factory FAC 2327*	68	2
25 Nov 89		**MADCHESTER RAVE ON (EP)** *Factory FAC 2427*	19	14
7 Apr 90	●	**STEP ON** *Factory FAC 2727*	5	11
9 Jun 90		**LAZYITIS – ONE ARMED BOXER** *Factory FAC 2227* [1]	46	3
20 Oct 90	●	**KINKY AFRO** *Factory FAC 3027*	5	7
9 Mar 91		**LOOSE FIT** *Factory FAC 3127*	17	7
30 Nov 91		**JUDGE FUDGE** *Factory FAC 3327*	24	3
19 Sep 92		**STINKIN THINKIN** *Factory FAC 3627*	31	3
21 Nov 92		**SUNSHINE AND LOVE** *Factory FAC 3727*	62	1
22 May 99		**THE BOYS ARE BACK IN TOWN** *London LONCD 432*	24	2
27 Jan 90		**BUMMED** *Factory FACT 220*	59	14
17 Nov 90	●	**PILLS 'N' THRILLS AND BELLYACHES** *Factory FACT 320*	4	30
12 Oct 91		**LIVE** *Factory FACT 322*	21	3
10 Oct 92		**... YES PLEASE!** *Factory FACD 420*	14	3
18 Nov 95		**LOADS – THE BEST OF THE HAPPY MONDAYS** *Factory Once 5203432*	41	2
5 Jun 99		**GREATEST HITS** *London 5561052*	11	4
6 Jul 02		**PILLS 'N' THRILLS AND BELLYACHES (re-issue)** *London 3984282512*	47	2

[1] Happy Mondays and Karl Denver

Tracks on Madchester Rave On (EP): Hallelujah / Holy Ghost / Clap Your Hands / Rave On

See also BLACK GRAPE

HAR MAR SUPERSTAR
US, male vocalist – Sean Tillman (Singles: 1 week)

Date		Title	pos	wks
5 Jul 03		**EZ PASS** *B Unique BUN 054CDS*	59	1

Ed HARCOURT
UK, male vocalist (Singles: 2 weeks, Albums: 1 week)

Date		Title	pos	wks
2 Feb 02		**APPLE OF MY EYE** *Heavenly HVN 107CDS*	61	1
15 Feb 03		**ALL OF YOUR DAYS WILL BE BLESSED** *Heavenly HVN 127CDS*	35	1
1 Mar 03		**FROM EVERY SPHERE** *Heavenly HVNLP39CD*	39	1

Paul HARDCASTLE
UK, male producer (Singles: 66 weeks, Albums: 5 weeks)

Date		Title	pos	wks
7 Apr 84		**YOU'RE THE ONE FOR ME – DAYBREAK – AM** *Total Control TOCO 1*	41	4
28 Jul 84		**GUILTY** *Total Control TOCO 2*	55	3
22 Sep 84		**RAIN FOREST** *Bluebird BR 8*	41	5
17 Nov 84		**EAT YOUR HEART OUT** *Cooltempo COOL 102*	59	4
4 May 85	★	**19** *Chrysalis CHS 2860*	1	16
15 Jun 85		**RAIN FOREST (re-issue)** *Bluebird / 10 BR 15*	53	4
9 Nov 85		**JUST FOR MONEY** *Chrysalis CASH 1*	19	5
1 Feb 86	●	**DON'T WASTE MY TIME** *Chrysalis PAUL 1* [1]	8	11
21 Jun 86		**FOOLIN' YOURSELF** *Chrysalis PAUL 2*	51	3
11 Oct 86		**THE WIZARD** *Chrysalis PAUL 3*	15	6
9 Apr 88		**WALK IN THE NIGHT** *Chrysalis PAUL 4*	54	3
4 Jun 88		**40 YEARS** *Chrysalis PAUL 5*	53	2
30 Nov 85		**PAUL HARDCASTLE** *Chrysalis CHR 1517*	53	5

[1] Paul Hardcastle featuring Carol Kenyon

'Just for Money' features the voices of Laurence Olivier, Bob Hoskins, Ed O'Ross and Alan Talbot, who are credited on the sleeve only

See also SILENT UNDERDOG

HARDCORE RHYTHM TEAM
UK, male vocal / production group (Singles: 1 week)

Date		Title	pos	wks
14 Mar 92		**HARDCORE – THE FINAL CONFLICT** *Furious FRUT 001*	69	1

Duane HARDEN – *See POWERHOUSE; Armand VAN HELDEN*

HARDFLOOR *Germany, male instrumental / production group (Singles: 6 weeks, Albums: 1 week)*

Date		Title	pos	wks
26 Dec 92		**HARDTRANCE ACPERIENCE** *Harthouse UK HARTUK 1*	56	4
10 Apr 93		**TRANCESCRIPT** *Harthouse UK HARTUK 5CD*	72	1
25 Oct 97		**ACPERIENCE (re-mix)** *Eye-q EYEUK 018CD1*	60	1
29 Jun 96		**HOME RUN** *Harthouse HHCD 019*	68	1

Ronan HARDIMAN *Ireland, male composer (Albums: 8 weeks)* pos/wks

Date	Title	pos	wks
2 Nov 96	MICHAEL FLATLEY'S LORD OF THE DANCE *PolyGram TV 5337572*	37	8

Tim HARDIN *US, male vocalist, d. 29 Dec 1980 (Singles: 1 week)* pos/wks

Date	Title	pos	wks
5 Jan 67	HANG ON TO A DREAM *Verve VS 1504*	50	1

Carolyn HARDING – *See PROSPECT PARK / Carolyn HARDING*

Mike HARDING
UK, male vocalist / comedian (Singles: 8 weeks, Albums: 24 weeks) pos/wks

Date	Title	pos	wks
2 Aug 75	ROCHDALE COWBOY *Rubber ADUB 3*	22	8
30 Aug 75	MRS 'ARDIN'S KID *Rubber RUB 011*	24	6
10 Jul 76	ONE MAN SHOW *Philips 6625 022*	19	10
11 Jun 77	OLD FOUR EYES IS BACK *Philips 6308 290*	31	6
24 Jun 78	CAPTAIN PARALYTIC AND THE BROWN ALE COWBOY *Philips 6641 798*	60	2

Françoise HARDY *France, female vocalist (Singles: 27 weeks)* pos/wks

Date	Title	pos	wks
25 Jun 64	TOUS LES GARÇONS ET LES FILLES *Pye 7N 15653*	36	7
31 Dec 64	ET MÊME *Pye 7N 15740*	31	5
25 Mar 65	ALL OVER THE WORLD *Pye 7N 15802*	16	15

Tynetta HARE – *See Joey B ELLIS*

Niki HARIS – *See SNAP!*

Morten HARKET *Norway, male vocalist (Singles: 1 week)* pos/wks

Date	Title	pos	wks
19 Aug 95	A KIND OF CHRISTMAS CARD *Warner Bros. W 0304CD*	53	1

See also A-HA

HARLEM COMMUNITY CHOIR – *See John LENNON*

HARLEQUIN 4s / BUNKER KRU *US, male / female vocal / instrumental group with UK, male production duo (Singles: 4 weeks)* pos/wks

Date	Title	pos	wks
19 Mar 88	SET IT OFF *Champion CHAMP 64*	55	4

Steve HARLEY and COCKNEY REBEL *UK, male vocal / instrumental group – leader Steve Nice (Singles: 69 weeks, Albums: 52 weeks)* pos/wks

Date	Title	pos	wks
11 May 74 ●	JUDY TEEN *EMI 2128* [1]	5	11
10 Aug 74 ●	MR SOFT *EMI 2191* [1]	8	9
8 Feb 75 ★	MAKE ME SMILE (COME UP AND SEE ME) *EMI 2263*	1	9
7 Jun 75	MR RAFFLES (MAN, IT WAS MEAN) *EMI 2299*	13	6
31 Jul 76 ●	HERE COMES THE SUN *EMI 2505* [2]	10	7
6 Nov 76	(I BELIEVE) LOVE'S A PRIMA DONNA *EMI 2539* [2]	41	4
20 Oct 79	FREEDOM'S PRISONER *EMI 2994* [2]	58	3
13 Aug 83	BALLERINA (PRIMA DONNA) *Stiletto STL 14* [2]	51	5
11 Jan 86 ●	THE PHANTOM OF THE OPERA *Polydor POSP 800* [3]	7	10
25 Apr 92	MAKE ME SMILE (COME UP AND SEE ME) (re-issue) *EMI EMCT 5* [2]	46	2
30 Dec 95	MAKE ME SMILE (COME UP AND SEE ME) (2nd re-issue) *EMI CDHARLEY 1*	33	3
22 Jun 74 ●	THE PSYCHOMODO *EMI EMC 3033* [1]	8	20
22 Mar 75 ●	THE BEST YEARS OF OUR LIVES *EMI EMC 3068*	4	19
14 Feb 76	TIMELESS FLIGHT *EMI EMA 775*	18	6
27 Nov 76	LOVE'S A PRIMA DONNA *EMI EMC 3156*	28	3
30 Jul 77	FACE TO FACE – A LIVE RECORDING *EMI EMSP 320*	40	4

[1] Cockney Rebel [2] Steve Harley [3] Sarah Brightman and Steve Harley
[1] Cockney Rebel

HARLEY QUINNE *UK, male vocal group (Singles: 8 weeks)* pos/wks

Date	Title	pos	wks
14 Oct 72	NEW ORLEANS *Bell 1255*	19	8

HARMONIUM *UK, male production / instrumental duo - Stewart and Bradley Palmer (Albums: 4 weeks)* pos/wks

Date	Title	pos	wks
21 Mar 98	SPIRIT OF TRANQUILITY *Global Television RADCD 79*	25	4

See also BLOWING FREE; HYPNOSIS; IN TUNE; JAMES BOYS; RAINDANCE; SCHOOL OF EXCELLENCE

HARMONIX
UK, male producer – Hamish Brown (Singles: 2 weeks) pos/wks

Date	Title	pos	wks
30 Mar 96	LANDSLIDE *Deconstruction 74321330762*	28	2

HARMONY GRASS
UK, male vocal / instrumental group (Singles: 7 weeks) pos/wks

Date	Title	pos	wks
29 Jan 69	MOVE IN A LITTLE CLOSER BABY *RCA 1772*	24	7

Ben HARPER *US, male vocalist / instrumentalist (Singles: 1 week)* pos/wks

Date	Title	pos	wks
4 Apr 98	FADED *Virgin VUSCD 134*	54	1

Charlie HARPER *UK, male vocalist (Singles: 1 week)* pos/wks

Date	Title	pos	wks
19 Jul 80	BARMY LONDON ARMY *Gem GEMS 35*	68	1

Roy HARPER
UK, male vocalist / instrumentalist – guitar (Albums: 9 weeks) pos/wks

Date	Title	pos	wks
9 Mar 74	VALENTINE *Harvest SHSP 4027*	27	1
21 Jun 75	H.Q. *Harvest SHSP 4046*	31	2
12 Mar 77	BULLINAMINGVASE *Harvest SHSP 4060*	25	2
16 Mar 85	WHATEVER HAPPENED TO JUGULA? *Beggars Banquet BEGA 60* [1]	44	4

[1] Roy Harper and Jimmy Page

HARPERS BIZARRE *US, male vocal group (Singles: 13 weeks)* pos/wks

Date	Title	pos	wks
30 Mar 67	59TH STREET BRIDGE SONG (FEELIN' GROOVY) *Warner Bros. WB 5890*	34	7
4 Oct 67	ANYTHING GOES *Warner Bros. WB 7063*	33	6

HARPO *Sweden, male vocalist – Jan Svensson (Singles: 6 weeks)* pos/wks

Date	Title	pos	wks
17 Apr 76	MOVIE STAR *DJM DJS 400*	24	6

T HARRINGTON – *See Rahni HARRIS and F.L.O.*

Anita HARRIS
UK, female vocalist (Singles: 50 weeks, Albums: 5 weeks) pos/wks

Date	Title	pos	wks
29 Jun 67 ●	JUST LOVING YOU *CBS 2724*	6	30
11 Oct 67	THE PLAYGROUND *CBS 2991*	46	3
24 Jan 68	ANNIVERSARY WALTZ *CBS 3211*	21	9
14 Aug 68	DREAM A LITTLE DREAM OF ME *CBS 3637*	33	8
27 Jan 68	JUST LOVING YOU *CBS SBPG 63182*	29	5

Emmylou HARRIS *US, female vocalist / instrumentalist – guitar (Singles: 6 weeks, Albums: 37 weeks)* pos/wks

Date	Title	pos	wks
6 Mar 76	HERE, THERE & EVERYWHERE *Reprise K 14415*	30	6
14 Feb 76	ELITE HOTEL *Reprise K 54060*	17	11
29 Jan 77	LUXURY LINER *Warner Bros. K 56344*	17	6
4 Feb 78	QUARTER MOON IN A TEN CENT TOWN *Warner Bros. K 56433*	40	5
29 Mar 80	HER BEST SONGS *K-Tel NE 1058*	36	3
14 Feb 81	EVANGELINE *Warner Bros. K 56880*	53	4
14 Mar 87	TRIO *Warner Bros. 9254911* [1]	60	4
7 Oct 95	WRECKING BALL *Grapevine GRACD 102*	46	1
29 Aug 98	SPYBOY *Grapevine GRACD 241*	57	1
30 Sep 00	RED DIRT GIRL *Grapevine GRACD 103*	45	1
4 Oct 03	STUMBLE INTO GRACE *Nonesuch 7559798052*	52	1

[1] Dolly Parton / Emmylou Harris / Linda Ronstadt

Jet HARRIS *UK, male instrumentalist – bass (Singles: 18 weeks)* pos/wks

Date	Title	pos	wks
24 May 62	BESAME MUCHO *Decca F 11466*	22	7
16 Aug 62	MAIN TITLE THEME (FROM 'THE MAN WITH THE GOLDEN ARM') *Decca F 11488*	12	11

See also Jet HARRIS and Tony MEEHAN; The SHADOWS

Jet HARRIS and Tony MEEHAN
UK, male instrumental duo – bass and drums (Singles: 39 weeks) pos/wks

Date	Title	pos	wks
10 Jan 63 ★	DIAMONDS *Decca F 11563*	1	13

			pos	wks
25 Apr 63	●	**SCARLETT O'HARA** *Decca F 11644*	2	13
5 Sep 63	●	**APPLEJACK** *Decca F 11710*	4	13

See also Jet HARRIS; Tony MEEHAN; The SHADOWS

Keith HARRIS and ORVILLE

UK, male ventriloquist vocalist with duck (Singles: 20 weeks, Albums: 1 week)

			pos	wks
18 Dec 82	●	**ORVILLE'S SONG** *BBC RESL 124*	4	11
24 Dec 83		**COME TO MY PARTY** *BBC RESL 138* [1]	44	4
14 Dec 85		**WHITE CHRISTMAS** *Columbia DB 9121*	40	5
4 Jun 83		**AT THE END OF THE RAINBOW** *BBC REH 465* [1]	92	1

[1] Keith Harris and Orville with Dippy [1] Keith Harris, Orville and Cuddles

Major HARRIS

US, male vocalist (Singles: 9 weeks)

			pos	wks
9 Aug 75		**LOVE WON'T LET ME WAIT** *Atlantic K 10585*	37	7
5 Nov 83		**ALL MY LIFE** *London LON 37*	61	2

Max HARRIS

UK, orchestra (Singles: 10 weeks)

			pos	wks
1 Dec 60		**GURNEY SLADE** *Fontana H 282*	11	10

Rahni HARRIS and F.L.O.

US, male instrumental group (Singles: 7 weeks)

			pos	wks
16 Dec 78		**SIX MILLION STEPS (WEST RUNS SOUTH)** *Mercury 6007 198*	43	7

Hit has credit 'vocals by T Harrington and O Rasbury'

Richard HARRIS

Ireland, male actor / vocalist, d. 25 Oct 2002 (Singles: 18 weeks)

			pos	wks
26 Jun 68	●	**MACARTHUR PARK** *RCA 1699*	4	12
8 Jul 72		**MACARTHUR PARK (re-issue)** *Probe GFF 101*	38	6

Rochelle HARRIS – *See ANGELHEART*

Rolf HARRIS

Australia, male vocalist (Singles: 77 weeks, Albums: 1 week)

			pos	wks
21 Jul 60	●	**TIE ME KANGAROO DOWN SPORT** *Columbia DB 4483* [1]	9	13
25 Oct 62	●	**SUN ARISE** *Columbia DB 4888*	3	16
28 Feb 63		**JOHNNY DAY** *Columbia DB 4979*	44	2
16 Apr 69		**BLUER THAN BLUE** *Columbia DB 8553*	30	8
22 Nov 69	★	**TWO LITTLE BOYS (re)** *Columbia DB 8630*	1	25
13 Feb 93	●	**STAIRWAY TO HEAVEN** *Vertigo VERCD 73*	7	6
1 Jun 96		**BOHEMIAN RHAPSODY** *Living Beat LBECD 41*	50	1
25 Oct 97		**SUN ARISE (re-recording)** *EMI CDROO 001*	26	3
14 Oct 00		**FINE DAY** *Tommy Boy TBCD 2155*	24	3
1 Nov 97		**CAN YOU TELL WHAT IT IS YET?** *EMI 8218802*	70	1

[1] Rolf Harris with his wobble board and The Rhythm Spinners

Ronnie HARRIS

UK, male vocalist (Singles: 3 weeks)

			pos	wks
24 Sep 54		**THE STORY OF TINA** *Columbia DB 3499*	12	3

Sam HARRIS

US, male vocalist (Singles: 2 weeks)

			pos	wks
9 Feb 85		**HEARTS ON FIRE / OVER THE RAINBOW** *Motown TMG 1370*	67	2

Simon HARRIS

UK, male / DJ producer (Singles: 17 weeks)

			pos	wks
19 Mar 88		**BASS (HOW LOW CAN YOU GO)** *ffrr FFR 4*	12	6
29 Oct 88		**HERE COMES THAT SOUND** *ffrr FFR 12*	38	4
24 Jun 89		**(I'VE GOT YOUR) PLEASURE CONTROL** *ffrr F 106* [1]	60	3
18 Nov 89		**ANOTHER MONSTERJAM** *ffrr F 116* [2]	65	1
10 Mar 90		**RAGGA HOUSE (ALL NIGHT LONG)** *Living Beat 7SMASH 9* [3]	56	3

[1] Simon Harris featuring Lonnie Gordon [2] Simon Harris featuring Einstein [3] Simon Harris featuring Daddy Freddy

See also AMBASSADORS OF FUNK featuring MC MARIO

George HARRISON

(378 Top 500) *Former Beatles guitarist, much inspired by Eastern musicians, born 25 Feb 1943, Liverpool, UK, died 29 Nov 2001. First ex-Beatle to score a solo UK No.1 single and only soloist to top the chart twice with the same single. Although not credited as a George Harrison album, the triple disc Concert for Bangladesh was instigated and performed by him and star guests such as Ravi Shankar, Bob Dylan, Eric Clapton and Ringo Starr (Singles: 94 weeks, Albums: 82 weeks)*

			pos	wks
23 Jan 71	★	**MY SWEET LORD** *Apple R 5884* ▲	1	17
14 Aug 71	●	**BANGLA-DESH** *Apple R 5912*	10	9
2 Jun 73	●	**GIVE ME LOVE (GIVE ME PEACE ON EARTH)** *Apple R 5988* ▲	8	10
21 Dec 74		**DING DONG** *Apple R 6002*	38	5
11 Oct 75		**YOU** *Apple R 6007*	38	5
10 Mar 79		**BLOW AWAY** *Dark Horse K 17327*	51	5
23 May 81		**ALL THOSE YEARS AGO** *Dark Horse K 17807*	13	7
24 Oct 87	●	**GOT MY MIND SET ON YOU** *Dark Horse W 8178* ▲	2	14
6 Feb 88		**WHEN WE WAS FAB** *Dark Horse W 8131*	25	7
25 Jun 88		**THIS IS LOVE** *Dark Horse W 7913*	55	3
26 Jan 02	★	**MY SWEET LORD (re-issue)** *Parlophone CDR 6571*	1	10
24 May 03		**ANY ROAD** *Parlophone CDRS 6601*	37	2
26 Dec 70	★	**ALL THINGS MUST PASS** *Apple STCH 639* ▲	1	24
7 Jul 73	●	**LIVING IN THE MATERIAL WORLD** *Apple PAS 10006* ▲	2	12
18 Oct 75		**EXTRA TEXTURE (READ ALL ABOUT IT)** *Apple PAS 10009*	16	4
18 Dec 76		**THIRTY THREE AND A THIRD** *Dark Horse K 56319*	35	4
17 Mar 79		**GEORGE HARRISON** *Dark Horse K 56562*	39	5
13 Jun 81		**SOMEWHERE IN ENGLAND** *Dark Horse K 56870*	13	4
14 Nov 87	●	**CLOUD NINE** *Dark Horse WX 123*	10	23
3 Feb 01		**ALL THINGS MUST PASS (re-issue)** *Parlophone 5304742*	68	2
30 Nov 02		**BRAINWASHED** *Parlophone 5803450*	29	4

See also BEATLES; TRAVELING WILBURYS

Jane HARRISON

UK, female operatic vocalist (Albums: 1 week)

			pos	wks
4 Feb 89		**NEW DAY** *Stylus SMR 869*	70	1

Noel HARRISON

UK, male vocalist (Singles: 14 weeks)

			pos	wks
26 Feb 69	●	**THE WINDMILLS OF YOUR MIND** *Reprise RS 20758*	8	14

HARRY

UK, female vocalist – Victoria Harrison (Singles: 2 weeks)

			pos	wks
2 Nov 02		**SO REAL** *Dirty Word DWRCD 003*	53	1
19 Apr 03		**UNDER THE COVERS (EP)** *Dirty Word DWRCD 005*	43	1

Tracks on Under the Covers (EP): 'Imagination' / 'Push It (Real Good)' / She's in Parties

HARRY – *See OBI PROJECT featuring HARRY, ASHER D and DJ WHAT?*

Deborah HARRY

US, female vocalist (Singles: 52 weeks, Albums: 53 weeks)

			pos	wks
1 Aug 81		**BACKFIRED** *Chrysalis CHS 2526* [1]	32	6
15 Nov 86	●	**FRENCH KISSIN' IN THE USA** *Chrysalis CHS 3066* [1]	8	10
28 Feb 87		**FREE TO FALL** *Chrysalis CHS 3093* [1]	46	4
9 May 87		**IN LOVE WITH LOVE** *Chrysalis CHS 3128* [1]	45	5
7 Oct 89		**I WANT THAT MAN** *Chrysalis CHS 3369*	13	10
2 Dec 89		**BRITE SIDE** *Chrysalis CHS 3452*	59	4
31 Mar 90		**SWEET AND LOW** *Chrysalis CHS 3491*	57	3
5 Jan 91		**WELL DID YOU EVAH!** *Chrysalis CHS 3646* [2]	42	4
3 Jul 93		**I CAN SEE CLEARLY NOW** *Chrysalis CDCHSS 4900*	23	4
18 Sep 93		**STRIKE ME PINK** *Chrysalis CDCHSS 5000*	46	2
8 Aug 81	●	**KOO KOO** *Chrysalis CHR 1347* [1]	6	7
29 Nov 86		**ROCKBIRD** *Chrysalis CHR 1540* [1]	31	11
17 Dec 88		**ONCE MORE INTO THE BLEACH** *Chrysalis CJB 2* [2]	50	4
28 Oct 89		**DEF DUMB AND BLONDE** *Chrysalis CHR 1650*	12	7
16 Mar 91	●	**THE COMPLETE PICTURE – THE VERY BEST OF DEBORAH HARRY AND BLONDIE** *Chrysalis CHR 1817* [2]	3	22
31 Jul 93		**DEBRAVATION** *Chrysalis CDCHR 6033*	24	2

[1] Debbie Harry [2] Deborah Harry and Iggy Pop [1] Debbie Harry [2] Deborah Harry and Blondie

See also BLONDIE

HARRY J ALL STARS
Jamaica, male instrumental group (Singles: 25 weeks) pos/wks

25 Oct 69 ● **LIQUIDATOR** *Trojan TR 675* 9 20
29 Mar 80 **LIQUIDATOR (re-issue)** *Trojan TRO 9063* 42 5

Re-issue of 'Liquidator' coupled with re-issue of 'Long Shot Kick De Bucket' by The Pioneers

Keef HARTLEY BAND
UK, male vocal / instrumental group (Albums: 3 weeks) pos/wks

5 Sep 70 **THE TIME IS NEAR** *Deram SML 1071* 41 3

Richard HARTLEY / Michael REED ORCHESTRA *UK, male instrumentalist – synthesizer, orchestra (Singles: 10 weeks)* pos/wks

25 Feb 84 ● **THE MUSIC OF TORVILL AND DEAN (EP)** *Safari SKATE 1* 9 10

Tracks on EP: Bolero / Capriccio Espagnole Opus 34 (Nos. 4 and 5) by Richard Hartley; Barnum on Ice / Discoskate by the Michael Reed Orchestra

Dan HARTMAN *US, male vocalist (Singles: 34 weeks)* pos/wks

21 Oct 78 ● **INSTANT REPLAY** *Blue Sky SKY 6706* 8 15
13 Jan 79 **THIS IS IT** *Blue Sky SKY 6999* 17 8
18 May 85 **SECOND NATURE** *MCA MCA 957* 66 2
24 Aug 85 **I CAN DREAM ABOUT YOU** *MCA MCA 988* 12 8
1 Apr 95 **KEEP THE FIRE BURNIN'** *Columbia 6611552* [1] 49 1

[1] Dan Hartman starring Loleatta Holloway

HARVEY *UK, male rapper – Michael Harvey (Singles: 2 weeks)* pos/wks

7 Sep 02 **GET UP AND MOVE** *Go! Beat GOBCD 52* 24 2

Alex HARVEY – *See SENSATIONAL ALEX HARVEY BAND*

Brian HARVEY *UK, male vocalist (Singles: 5 weeks)* pos/wks

28 Apr 01 **STRAIGHT UP NO BENDS** *Edel 0126605 ERE* 26 2
27 Oct 01 **LOVING YOU (OLE OLE OLE)** *Blacklist 0132325 ERE* [1] 20 3

[1] Brian Harvey and the Refugee Crew

See also EAST 17; TRUE STEPPERS

Richard HARVEY and FRIENDS
UK, male instrumental group (Albums: 1 week) pos/wks

6 May 89 **EVENING FALLS** *Telstar STAR 2350* 72 1

Lee HARVEY – *See N*E*R*D*

PJ HARVEY *UK, female vocalist – Polly Jean Harvey (Singles: 22 weeks, Albums: 33 weeks)* pos/wks

29 Feb 92 **SHEELA-NA-GIG** *Too Pure PURE 008* 69 1
1 May 93 **50 FT QUEENIE** *Island CID 538* 27 2
17 Jul 93 **MAN-SIZE** *Island CID 569* 42 2
18 Feb 95 **DOWN BY THE WATER** *Island CID 607* 38 2
22 Jul 95 **C'MON BILLY** *Island CID 614* 29 2
28 Oct 95 **SEND HIS LOVE TO ME** *Island CID 610* 34 2
9 Mar 96 **HENRY LEE** *Mute CDMUTE 189* [1] 36 1
23 Nov 96 **THAT WAS MY VEIL** *Island CID 648* [2] 75 1
26 Sep 98 **A PERFECT DAY ELISE** *Island CID 718* 25 2
23 Jan 99 **THE WIND** *Island CID 730* 29 2
25 Nov 00 **GOOD FORTUNE** *Island CID 769* 41 2
10 Mar 01 **A PLACE CALLED HOME** *Island CID 771* 43 2
20 Oct 01 **THIS IS LOVE** *Island CID 785* 41 1
11 Apr 92 **DRY** *Too Pure PURECD 10* 11 5
8 May 93 ● **RID OF ME** *Island CID 8002* 3 4
30 Oct 93 **4-TRACK DEMOS** *Island IMCD 170* 19 2
11 Mar 95 **TO BRING YOU MY LOVE** *Island CID 8035* 12 6
5 Oct 96 **DANCE HALL AT LOUSE POINT** *Island CID 8051* [1] 46 1
10 Oct 98 **IS THIS DESIRE?** *Island CID 8076* 17 2
4 Nov 00 **STORIES FROM THE CITY STORIES FROM THE SEA** *Island CID 8099* 23 13

[1] Nick Cave and the Bad Seeds and PJ Harvey [2] John Parish + Polly Jean Harvey
[1] John Parish + Polly Jean Harvey

Until 1995 PJ Harvey was the name of the entire group, not just the lead singer

Steve HARVEY
UK, male vocalist (Singles: 6 weeks) pos/wks

28 May 83 **SOMETHING SPECIAL** *London LON 25* 46 4
29 Oct 83 **TONIGHT** *London LON 36* 63 2

HARVEY DANGER
US, male vocal / instrumental group (Singles: 1 week) pos/wks

1 Aug 98 **FLAGPOLE SITTA** *Slash LASCD 64* 57 1

Gordon HASKELL
UK, male vocalist (Singles: 6 weeks, Albums: 11 weeks) pos/wks

29 Dec 01 ● **HOW WONDERFUL YOU ARE** *Flying Sparks TDBCDS 04* 2 6
19 Jan 02 ● **HARRY'S BAR** *East West 927439762* 2 10
26 Oct 02 **SHADOWS ON THE WALL** *Flying Sparks TDBCD 068* 44 1

David HASSELHOFF
US, male vocalist / actor (Singles: 2 weeks) pos/wks

13 Nov 93 **IF I COULD ONLY SAY GOODBYE** *Arista 74321172262* 35 2

Tony HATCH *UK, orchestra (Singles: 1 week)* pos/wks

4 Oct 62 **OUT OF THIS WORLD** *Pye 7N 15460* 50 1

Juliana HATFIELD *US, female vocalist / instrumentalist – guitar (Singles: 2 weeks, Albums: 3 weeks)* pos/wks

11 Sep 93 **MY SISTER** *Mammoth YZ 767CD* [1] 71 1
18 Mar 95 **UNIVERSAL HEART-BEAT** *East West YZ 916CD* 65 1
14 Aug 93 **BECOME WHAT YOU ARE** *Mammoth 4509935292* [1] 44 2
8 Apr 95 **ONLY EVERYTHING** *East West 4509998862* 59 1

[1] Juliana Hatfield Three [1] Juliana Hatfield Three

HATFIELD AND THE NORTH
UK, male / female vocal / instrumental group (Albums: 1 week) pos/wks

29 Mar 75 **ROTTERS CLUB** *Virgin V 2030* 43 1

See also Ian DURY

Donny HATHAWAY – *See Roberta FLACK*

Lalah HATHAWAY *US, female vocalist (Singles: 10 weeks)* pos/wks

1 Sep 90 **HEAVEN KNOWS** *Virgin America VUS 28* 66 2
2 Feb 91 **BABY DON'T CRY** *Virgin America VUS 35* 54 3
27 Jul 91 **FAMILY AFFAIR** *Ten TEN 369* [1] 37 5

[1] BEF featuring Lalah Hathaway

HATIRAS featuring SLARTA JOHN *Canada, male producer – George Hatiris and UK, male rapper – Mark James (Singles: 5 weeks)* pos/wks

27 Jan 01 **SPACED INVADER** *Defected DFECT 25CDS* 14 5

HAVANA
UK, male instrumental / production group (Singles: 1 week) pos/wks

6 Mar 93 **ETHNIC PRAYER** *Limbo LIMBO 007CD* 71 1

HAVEN *UK, male vocal / instrumental group (Singles: 6 weeks, Albums: 3 weeks)* pos/wks

22 Sep 01 **LET IT LIVE** *Radiate RDT 3* 72 1
2 Feb 02 **SAY SOMETHING** *Radiate RDT 4* 24 3
4 May 02 **TIL THE END** *Radiate RDT 6* 28 2
16 Feb 02 **BETWEEN THE SENSES** *Radiate RDTCD 1* 26 3

Nic HAVERSON *UK, male vocalist (Singles: 3 weeks)* pos/wks

30 Jan 93 **HEAD OVER HEELS** *Telstar CDHOH 1* 48 3

Chesney HAWKES
UK, male vocalist (Singles: 26 weeks, Albums: 8 weeks) pos/wks

23 Feb 91 ★ **THE ONE AND ONLY** *Chrysalis CHS 3627* 1 16

22 Jun 91	**I'M A MAN NOT A BOY** *Chrysalis CHS 3708*	**27** 5
28 Sep 91	**SECRETS OF THE HEART** *Chrysalis CHS 3681*	**57** 3
29 May 93	**WHAT'S WRONG WITH THIS PICTURE** *Chrysalis CDCHS 3969*	**63** 1
12 Jan 02	**STAY AWAY BABY JANE** *Arc DSART 13*	**74** 1
13 Apr 91	BUDDY'S SONG (FILM SOUNDTRACK) *Chrysalis CHR 1812*	18 8

Screamin' Jay HAWKINS

US, male vocalist, d. 12 Feb 2000 (Singles: 3 weeks) pos/wks

3 Apr 93	**HEART ATTACK AND VINE** *Columbia 6591092*	**42** 3

Sophie B HAWKINS

US, female vocalist (Singles: 37 weeks, Albums: 6 weeks) pos/wks

4 Jul 92	**DAMN I WISH I WAS YOUR LOVER** *Columbia 6581077*	**14** 9
12 Sep 92	**CALIFORNIA HERE I COME** *Columbia 6583177*	**53** 3
6 Feb 93	**I WANT YOU** *Columbia 6587772*	**49** 2
13 Aug 94	**RIGHT BESIDE YOU** *Columbia 6606915*	**13** 12
26 Nov 94	**DON'T DON'T TELL ME NO** *Columbia 6610152*	**36** 5
11 Mar 95	**AS I LAY ME DOWN** *Columbia 6612125*	**24** 6
1 Aug 92	TONGUES AND TAILS *Columbia 4688232*	46 2
3 Sep 94	WHALER *Columbia 4765122*	46 4

Ted HAWKINS

US, male vocalist / instrumentalist – guitar, d. 1 Jan 1995 (Albums: 1 week) pos/wks

18 Apr 87	HAPPY HOUR *Windows on the World WOLP 2*	82 1

Edwin HAWKINS SINGERS

US, male / female vocal group (Singles: 13 weeks) pos/wks

21 May 69	● **OH HAPPY DAY (re)** *Buddah 201 048*	**2** 13

Kirsty HAWKSHAW

UK, female vocalist (Singles: 7 weeks) pos/wks

24 Jun 00	**DREAMING** *Headspace HEDSCD 002* [1]	**38** 2
29 Sep 01	**URBAN TRAIN** *Nebula VCRD 95* [2]	**22** 3
21 Sep 02	**STEALTH** *Distinctive Breaks DISNCD 90* [3]	**67** 1
23 Nov 02	**FINE DAY** *Mainline CDMAIN 002*	**62** 1

[1] BT featuring Kirsty Hawkshaw [2] DJ Tiesto featuring Kirsty Hawshaw [3] Way Out West featuring Kirsty Hawkshaw

See also OPUS III

HAWKWIND

UK, male vocal / instrumental group (Singles: 28 weeks, Albums: 101 weeks) pos/wks

1 Jul 72	● **SILVER MACHINE (2re)** *United Artists UP 35381*	**3** 22
11 Aug 73	**URBAN GUERRILLA** *United Artists UP 35566*	**39** 3
19 Jul 80	**SHOT DOWN IN THE NIGHT** *Bronze BRO 98*	**59** 3
6 Nov 71	IN SEARCH OF SPACE *United Artists UAS 29202*	18 19
23 Dec 72	DOREMI FASOL LATIDO *United Artists UAS 29364*	14 5
2 Jun 73	● SPACE RITUAL ALIVE *United Artists UAD 60037/8*	9 5
21 Sep 74	HALL OF THE MOUNTAIN GRILL *United Artists UAG 29672*	16 5
31 May 75	WARRIOR ON THE EDGE OF TIME *United Artists UAG 29766*	13 7
24 Apr 76	ROAD HAWKS *United Artists UAK 29919*	34 4
18 Sep 76	ASTONISHING SOUNDS AMAZING MUSIC *Charisma CDS 4004*	33 5
9 Jul 77	QUARK STRANGENESS AND CHARM *Charisma CDS 4008*	30 6
21 Oct 78	25 YEARS ON *Charisma CD 4014* [1]	48 3
30 Jun 79	PXR 5 *Charisma CDS4016*	59 5
9 Aug 80	LIVE 1979 *Bronze BRON 527*	15 7
8 Nov 80	LEVITATION *Bronze BRON 530*	21 4
24 Oct 81	SONIC ATTACK *RCA RCALP 5004*	19 5
22 May 82	CHURCH OF HAWKWIND *RCA RCALP 9004*	26 6
23 Oct 82	CHOOSE YOUR MASQUES *RCA RCALP 6055*	29 5
5 Nov 83	ZONES *Flicknife SHARP 014*	57 2
25 Feb 84	HAWKWIND *Liberty SLS 1972921*	75 1
16 Nov 85	CHRONICLE OF THE BLACK SWORD *Flicknife SHARP 033*	65 2
14 May 88	THE XENON CODEX *GWR GWLP 26*	79 2
6 Oct 90	SPACE BANDITS *GWR GWLP 103*	70 1
23 May 92	ELECTRIC TEPEE *Essential ESSCD 181*	53 1
6 Nov 93	IT IS THE BUSINESS OF THE FUTURE TO BE DANGEROUS *Essential ESCDCD 196*	75 1

[1] Hawklords

'Silver Machine' re-entries were in 1978 and 1983

Bill HAYES

US, male vocalist (Singles: 9 weeks) pos/wks

6 Jan 56	● **THE BALLAD OF DAVY CROCKETT** *London HLA 8220* [1] ▲	**2** 9

[1] Bill Hayes with Archie Bleyer's Orchestra

Darren HAYES

Australia, male vocalist (Singles: 30 weeks, Albums: 28 weeks) pos/wks

30 Mar 02	● **INSATIABLE** *Columbia 6723995*	**8** 14
20 Jul 02	**STRANGE RELATIONSHIP** *Columbia 6728685*	**15** 8
16 Nov 02	**I MISS YOU (re)** *Columbia 6733312*	**20** 5
1 Feb 03	**CRUSH (1980 ME)** *Columbia 6734902*	**19** 3
13 Apr 02	● SPIN *Columbia 5053192*	2 28

See also SAVAGE GARDEN

Gemma HAYES

Ireland, female vocalist (Singles: 2 weeks, Albums: 1 week) pos/wks

25 May 02	**HANGING AROUND** *Source SOURCD 046*	**62** 1
10 Aug 02	**LET A GOOD THING GO** *Source SOURCD 051*	**54** 1
8 Jun 02	NIGHT ON MY SIDE *Source CDSOUR 049*	52 1

Isaac HAYES

US, male vocalist / multi-instrumentalist (Singles: 35 weeks, Albums: 14 weeks) pos/wks

4 Dec 71	● **THEME FROM 'SHAFT'** *Stax 2025 069* ▲	**4** 12
3 Apr 76	● **DISCO CONNECTION** *ABC 4100* [1]	**10** 9
26 Dec 98	★ **CHOCOLATE SALTY BALLS (PS I LOVE YOU)** *Columbia 6667985* [2]	**1** 13
30 Sep 00	**THEME FROM SHAFT (re-recording)** *LaFace / Arista 74321792582*	**53** 1
18 Dec 71	SHAFT *Polydor 2659 007* ▲	17 13
12 Feb 72	BLACK MOSES *Stax 2628 004*	38 1

[1] Isaac Hayes Movement [2] Chef

HAYSI FANTAYZEE

UK, male / female production / vocal duo – Jeremy Healy and Kate Garner (Singles: 25 weeks, Albums: 5 weeks) pos/wks

24 Jul 82	**JOHN WAYNE IS BIG LEGGY** *Regard RG 100*	**11** 10
13 Nov 82	**HOLY JOE** *Regard RG 104*	**51** 3
22 Jan 83	**SHINY SHINY** *Regard RG 106*	**16** 10
25 Jun 83	**SISTER FRICTION** *Regard RG 108*	**62** 2
26 Feb 83	BATTLE HYMNS FOR CHILDREN SINGING *Regard RGLP 6000*	53 5

Justin HAYWARD

UK, male vocalist (Singles: 20 weeks, Albums: 35 weeks) pos/wks

25 Oct 75	● **BLUE GUITAR** *Threshold TH 21* [1]	**8** 7
8 Jul 78	● **FOREVER AUTUMN** *CBS 6368* [2]	**5** 13
29 Mar 75	● BLUE JAYS *Threshold THS 12* [1]	4 18
5 Mar 77	SONGWRITER *Deram SDL 15*	28 5
19 Jul 80	NIGHT FLIGHT *Decca TXS 138*	41 4
19 Oct 85	MOVING MOUNTAINS *Towerbell TOWLP 15*	78 1
28 Oct 89	CLASSIC BLUE *Trax MODEM 1040* [2]	47 7

[1] Justin Hayward and John Lodge [2] From Jeff Wayne's 'War of the Worlds' featuring Justin Hayward [1] Justin Hayward and John Lodge [2] Justin Hayward Mike Batt and the London Philharmonic Orchestra

See also MOODY BLUES

Leon HAYWOOD

US, male vocalist (Singles: 11 weeks) pos/wks

15 Mar 80	**DON'T PUSH IT DON'T FORCE IT** *20th Century Fox TC 2443*	**12** 11

HAYWOODE

UK, female vocalist – Sharon Haywoode (Singles: 31 weeks) pos/wks

17 Sep 83	**A TIME LIKE THIS** *CBS A 3651*	**48** 7
29 Sep 84	**I CAN'T LET YOU GO** *CBS A 4664*	**63** 4
13 Apr 85	**ROSES** *CBS A 6069*	**65** 3
5 Oct 85	**GETTING CLOSER** *CBS A 6582*	**67** 2
21 Jun 86	**ROSES (re-issue)** *CBS A 7224*	**11** 11
13 Sep 86	**I CAN'T LET YOU GO (re-issue)** *CBS 650076 7*	**50** 4

2003 NO.1 SINGLES

Something old (Oliver Cheatham), something new (David Sneddon), something borrowed (Westlife), but nothing by Blue …

DATE / **SINGLE** / **ACT** / WEEKS AT NO.1

4 Jan SOUND OF THE UNDERGROUND – **Girls Aloud** 3 (total including 2003 = 4)
25 Jan STOP LIVING THE LIE – **David Sneddon** 2
8 Feb ALL THE THINGS SHE SAID – **t.A.T.u.** 4
8 Mar BEAUTIFUL – **Christina Aguilera** 2
22 Mar SPIRIT IN THE SKY – **Gareth Gates featuring the Kumars** 2
5 Apr MAKE LUV – **Room 5 featuring Oliver Cheatham** 4
3 May YOU SAID NO – **Busted** 1
10 May LONELINESS – **Tomcraft** 1
17 May IGNITION – **R Kelly** 4
14 Jun BRING ME TO LIFE – **Evanescence** 4
12 Jul CRAZY IN LOVE – **Beyoncé** 3
2 Aug NEVER GONNA LEAVE YOUR SIDE – **Daniel Bedingfield** 1
9 Aug BREATHE – **Blu Cantrell featuring Sean Paul** 4
6 Sep ARE YOU READY FOR LOVE? – **Elton John** 1
13 Sep WHERE IS THE LOVE? – **Black Eyed Peas** 6
25 Oct HOLE IN THE HEAD – **Sugababes** 1
1 Nov BE FAITHFUL – **Fatman Scoop featuring the Crooklyn Clan** 2
15 Nov SLOW – **Kylie Minogue** 1
22 Nov CRASHED THE WEDDING – **Busted** 1
29 Nov MANDY – **Westlife** 1
6 Dec LEAVE RIGHT NOW – **Will Young** 2
20 Dec CHANGES – **Ozzy and Kelly Osbourne** 1
27 Dec MAD WORLD – **Michael Andrews featuring Gary Jules** 1 (total into 2004 = 3)

Black Eyed Peas, who managed the longest stay at No.1 this century with six weeks at the top. The beatboxing trio, which first charted in 1998, was joined by new member, female vocalist Fergie, a 40-piece orchestra and buddy Justin Timberlake on its autumn chart-topper

The unstoppable Busted are primed for world domination following their two 2003 chart-toppers. A Monkees-style Christmas TV special, a forthcoming cameo in 'Scooby Doo 2', and an invitation to contribute a song to the new 'Thunderbirds' movie plus more quality catchy hits will follow this year

Ofra HAZA
Israel, female vocalist, d. 23 Feb 2000 (Singles: 12 weeks) pos/wks

		pos	wks
30 Apr 88	**IM NIN'ALU** *WEA YZ 190*	15	8
17 Jun 95	**MY LOVE IS FOR REAL** *Virgin America VUSCD 91* [1]	28	3
3 Apr 99	**BABYLON** *Warner Esp. WESP 006CD1* [2]	65	1

[1] Paula Abdul featuring Ofra Haza [2] Black Dog featuring Ofra Haza

HAZE – *See Sandy RIVERA*

HAZIZA *Sweden, male production duo (Singles: 1 week)* pos/wks

		pos	wks
28 Apr 01	**ONE MORE** *Tidy Trax TIDY 152T*	75	1

Lee HAZLEWOOD – *See Nancy SINATRA*

HAZZARDS *US, female vocal duo – Sydney Maresca and Anne Harris (Singles: 1 week)* pos/wks

		pos	wks
22 Nov 03	**GAY BOYFRIEND** *Better The Devil BTD 3CD*	67	1

Murray HEAD *UK, male vocalist (Singles: 15 weeks)* pos/wks

		pos	wks
29 Jan 72	**SUPERSTAR** *MCA MMKS 5077*	47	1
10 Nov 84	**ONE NIGHT IN BANGKOK (re)** *RCA CHESS 1*	12	14

'Superstar' was one of four tracks on a maxi single, two of which were credited during the disc's one week on the chart. The other track credited was 'I Don't Know How to Love Him' by Yvonne Elliman

Roy HEAD *US, male vocalist (Singles: 5 weeks)* pos/wks

		pos	wks
4 Nov 65	**TREAT HER RIGHT** *Vocalion V-P 9248*	30	5

HEADBANGERS
UK, male vocal / instrumental group (Singles: 3 weeks) pos/wks

		pos	wks
10 Oct 81	**STATUS ROCK** *Magnet MAG 206*	60	3

HEADBOYS
UK, male vocal / instrumental group (Singles: 8 weeks) pos/wks

		pos	wks
22 Sep 79	**THE SHAPE OF THINGS TO COME** *RSO 40*	45	8

HEADGIRL – *See GIRLSCHOOL; MOTÖRHEAD*

Max HEADROOM – *See ART OF NOISE*

HEADS
UK, male instrumental group (Singles: 4 weeks) pos/wks

		pos	wks
21 Jun 86	**AZTEC LIGHTNING (THEME FROM BBC WORLD CUP GRANDSTAND)** *BBC RESL 184*	45	4

HEADS with Shaun RYDER
US / UK, male / female vocal / instrumental group (Singles: 1 week) pos/wks

		pos	wks
9 Nov 96	**DON'T TAKE MY KINDNESS FOR WEAKNESS** *Radioactive MCSTD 48024*	60	1

Heads are Talking Heads minus lead singer David Byrne

See also TALKING HEADS

HEADSWIM *UK, male vocal / instrumental group (Singles: 5 weeks, Albums: 2 weeks)* pos/wks

		pos	wks
25 Feb 95	**CRAWL** *Epic 6612252*	64	1
14 Feb 98	**TOURNIQUET** *Epic 6650442*	30	3
16 May 98	**BETTER MADE** *Epic 6658402*	42	1
30 May 98	**DESPITE YOURSELF** *Epic 4877262*	24	2

Jeff HEALEY BAND
Canada, male vocal / instrumental group (Albums: 16 weeks) pos/wks

		pos	wks
14 Jan 89	**SEE THE LIGHT** *Arista 209441*	58	7
9 Jun 90	**HELL TO PAY** *Arista 210815*	18	6
28 Nov 92	**FEEL THIS** *Arista 74321120872*	72	1
18 Mar 95	**COVER TO COVER** *Arista 74321238882*	50	2

Jeremy HEALY and AMOS *UK, male production / vocal duo – Jeremy Healy and Amos Pizzey (Singles: 7 weeks)* pos/wks

		pos	wks
12 Oct 96	**STAMP!** *Positiva CDTIV 65*	11	5
31 May 97	**ARGENTINA** *Positiva CDTIV 74*	30	2

See also HWA featuring SONIC THE HEDGEHOG

Imogen HEAP – *See URBAN SPECIES*

HEAR 'N' AID *International, male / female vocal / instrumental charity assembly (Singles: 6 weeks)* pos/wks

		pos	wks
19 Apr 86	**STARS** *Vertigo HEAR 1*	26	6

HEAR'SAY *UK, male / female vocal group (Singles: 60 weeks, Albums: 32 weeks)* pos/wks

		pos	wks
24 Mar 01	★ **PURE AND SIMPLE** *Polydor 5870069* ◆ ■	1	25
7 Jul 01	★ **THE WAY TO YOUR LOVE (re)** *Polydor 5871482* ■	1	17
8 Dec 01	● **EVERYBODY** *Polydor 5705122*	4	11
24 Aug 02	● **LOVIN' IS EASY (re)** *Polydor 5708542*	6	7
7 Apr 01	★ **POPSTARS** *Polydor 5498212* ■	1	27
15 Dec 01	**EVERYBODY** *Polydor 5895412*	24	5

See also Myleene KLASS; Kym MARSH

HEART 297 Top 500
Giants of Stateside AOR, who first tasted success in Canada and are regarded as key players on the Seattle music scene. Fronted by Californian-born Wilson sisters Ann (v/g/f) b. 19 Jun 1951 and Nancy (g/v) b. 16 Mar 1954. UK chart career began a full decade after US debut (Singles: 76 weeks, Albums: 143 weeks) pos/wks

		pos	wks
29 Mar 86	**THESE DREAMS** *Capitol CL 394* ▲	62	4
13 Jun 87	● **ALONE** *Capitol CL 448* ▲	3	16
19 Sep 87	**WHO WILL YOU RUN TO** *Capitol CL 457*	30	7
12 Dec 87	**THERE'S THE GIRL** *Capitol CL 473*	34	7
5 Mar 88	● **NEVER / THESE DREAMS (re-issue)** *Capitol CL 482*	8	9
14 May 88	**WHAT ABOUT LOVE** *Capitol CL 487*	14	6
22 Oct 88	**NOTHIN' AT ALL** *Capitol CL 507*	38	3
24 Mar 90	● **ALL I WANNA DO IS MAKE LOVE TO YOU** *Capitol CL 569*	8	13
28 Jul 90	**I DIDN'T WANT TO NEED YOU** *Capitol CL 580*	47	3
17 Nov 90	**STRANDED** *Capitol CL 595*	60	2
14 Sep 91	**YOU'RE THE VOICE** *Capitol CLS 624*	56	2
20 Nov 93	**WILL YOU BE THERE (IN THE MORNING)** *Capitol CDCLS 700*	19	4
22 Jan 77	**DREAMBOAT ANNIE** *Arista ARTY 139*	36	8
23 Jul 77	**LITTLE QUEEN** *Portrait PRT 82075*	34	4
19 Jun 82	**PRIVATE AUDITION** *Epic EPC 85792*	77	2
26 Oct 85	**HEART** *Capitol EJ 2403721* ▲	19	43
6 Jun 87	● **BAD ANIMALS** *Capitol ESTU 2032*	7	56
14 Apr 90	● **BRIGADE** *Capitol ESTU 2121*	3	20
28 Sep 91	**ROCK THE HOUSE 'LIVE'** *Capitol ESTU 2154*	45	2
11 Dec 93	**DESIRE WALKS ON** *Capitol CDEST 2216*	32	2
19 Apr 97	**THESE DREAMS – GREATEST HITS** *Capitol CDEMC 3765*	33	6

'Heart' changed label number during its chart run to Capitol LOVE 1

HEARTBEAT
UK, male / female vocal / instrumental group (Singles: 5 weeks) pos/wks

		pos	wks
24 Oct 87	**TEARS FROM HEAVEN** *Priority P 17*	32	4
23 Apr 88	**THE WINNER** *Priority P 19*	70	1

HEARTBEAT COUNTRY
UK, male vocalist – Bill Maynard (Singles: 1 week) pos/wks

		pos	wks
31 Dec 94	**HEARTBEAT** *MMM MMM 01CD*	75	1

HEARTBREAKER – *See DEMON vs HEARTBREAKER*

HEARTBREAKERS
US, male vocal / instrumental group (Albums: 1 week) pos/wks

		pos	wks
5 Nov 77	**L.A.M.F.** *Track 2409 218*	55	1

HEARTBREAKERS – *See Tom PETTY and the HEARTBREAKERS*

HEARTISTS
Italy, male DJ / production trio (Singles: 5 weeks) pos/wks

			pos	wks
9 Aug 97		**BELO HORIZONTI** *VC VCRD 23*	42	3
31 Jan 98		**BELO HORIZONTI (re-mix)** *VC VCRD 28*	40	2

HEARTLESS CREW
UK, male DJ / production trio (Singles: 3 weeks, Albums: 2 weeks) pos/wks

			pos	wks
25 May 02		**THE HEARTLESS THEME AKA 'THE SUPERGLUE RIDDIM'** *East West HEART 02CD*	21	3
28 Jun 03		**WHY (LOOKING BACK)** *East West HEART 03CD*	50	1
18 May 02	●	**HEARTLESS CREW PRESENTS CRISP BISCUIT VOL.1** *East West 927460172*	10	2

Ted HEATH and his MUSIC
UK, orchestra, leader d. 18 Nov 1969 (Singles: 56 weeks, Albums: 5 weeks) pos/wks

			pos	wks
16 Jan 53		**VANESSA** *Decca F 9983*	11	1
3 Jul 53	●	**HOT TODDY** *Decca F 10093*	6	11
23 Oct 53	●	**DRAGNET (4re)** *Decca F 10176*	9	5
12 Feb 54	●	**SKIN DEEP** *Decca F 10246*	9	3
6 Jul 56		**THE FAITHFUL HUSSAR** *Decca F 10746*	18	9
14 Mar 58	●	**SWINGIN' SHEPHERD BLUES** *Decca F 11000*	3	14
11 Apr 58		**TEQUILA** *Decca F 11003*	21	6
4 Jul 58		**TOM HARK** *Decca F 11025*	24	2
5 Oct 61		**SUCU SUCU (re)** *Decca F 11392*	36	5
21 Apr 62		**BIG BAND PERCUSSION** *Decca PFM 24004*	17	5

HEATWAVE
UK / US, male vocal / instrumental group (Singles: 80 weeks, Albums: 27 weeks) pos/wks

			pos	wks
22 Jan 77	●	**BOOGIE NIGHTS** *GTO GT 77*	2	14
7 May 77		**TOO HOT TO HANDLE / SLIP YOUR DISC TO THIS** *GTO GT 91*	15	11
14 Jan 78		**THE GROOVE LINE** *GTO GT 115*	12	8
3 Jun 78		**MIND BLOWING DECISIONS** *GTO GT 226*	12	11
4 Nov 78	●	**ALWAYS AND FOREVER / MIND BLOWING DECISIONS (re-mix)** *GTO GT 236*	9	14
26 May 79		**RAZZLE DAZZLE** *GTO GT 248*	43	5
17 Jan 81		**GANGSTERS OF THE GROOVE** *GTO GT 285*	19	8
21 Mar 81		**JITTERBUGGIN'** *GTO GT 290*	34	7
1 Sep 90		**MIND BLOWING DECISIONS (re-recording)** *Brothers Organisation HW 1*	65	2
11 Jun 77		**TOO HOT TO HANDLE** *GTO GTLP 013*	46	2
6 May 78		**CENTRAL HEATING** *GTO GTLP 027*	26	15
14 Feb 81		**CANDLES** *GTO GTLP 047*	29	9
23 Feb 91		**GANGSTERS OF THE GROOVE – 90'S MIX** *Telstar STAR 2434*	56	1

HEAVEN 17 (302 Top 500)
Politically astute electronic pop trio from Sheffield, UK: Martyn Ware (k), Ian Craig Marsh (k) (both previously in Human League) and Glenn Gregory (v). Named after a fictional band in cult film A Clockwork Orange, they reunited and played their first ever gigs in 1997 (Singles: 87 weeks, Albums: 128 weeks) pos/wks

			pos	wks
21 Mar 81		**(WE DON'T NEED THIS) FASCIST GROOVE THANG** *Virgin VS 400*	45	5
5 Sep 81		**PLAY TO WIN** *Virgin VS 433*	46	7
14 Nov 81		**PENTHOUSE AND PAVEMENT** *Virgin VS 455*	57	3
30 Oct 82		**LET ME GO** *Virgin VS 532*	41	6
16 Apr 83	●	**TEMPTATION** *Virgin VS 570*	2	13
25 Jun 83	●	**COME LIVE WITH ME** *Virgin VS 607*	5	11
10 Sep 83		**CRUSHED BY THE WHEELS OF INDUSTRY** *Virgin VS 628*	17	7
1 Sep 84		**SUNSET NOW** *Virgin VS 708*	24	6
27 Oct 84		**THIS IS MINE** *Virgin VS 722*	23	7
19 Jan 85		**. . . (AND THAT'S NO LIE)** *Virgin VS 740*	52	5
17 Jan 87		**TROUBLE** *Virgin VS 920*	51	3
21 Nov 92	●	**TEMPTATION (re-mix)** *Virgin VS 1446*	4	11
27 Feb 93		**(WE DON'T NEED THIS) FASCIST GROOVE THANG (re-mix)** *Virgin VSCDT 1451*	40	2
10 Apr 93		**PENTHOUSE AND PAVEMENT (re-mix)** *Virgin VSCDT 1457*	54	1
26 Sep 81		**PENTHOUSE AND PAVEMENT** *Virgin V 2208*	14	76
7 May 83	●	**THE LUXURY GAP** *Virgin V 2253*	4	36
6 Oct 84		**HOW MEN ARE** *B.E.F. V 2326*	12	11
12 Jul 86		**ENDLESS** *Virgin TCVB/CDV 2383*	70	2
29 Nov 86		**PLEASURE ONE** *Virgin V 2400*	78	1
20 Mar 93		**HIGHER AND HIGHER – THE BEST OF HEAVEN 17** *Virgin CDV 2717*	31	2

Carol Kenyon is the uncredited vocalist on 'Temptation'. 'Fascist Groove Thang' in 1993 is a re-recording

HEAVENS CRY
Holland, male production duo (Singles: 2 weeks) pos/wks

			pos	wks
6 Oct 01		**TILL TEARS DO US PART (re)** *Tidy Trax 158 CD*	68	2

HEAVY D and the BOYZ
Jamaica / US, male rap / vocal duo (Singles: 28 weeks, Albums: 3 weeks) pos/wks

			pos	wks
6 Dec 86		**MR BIG STUFF** *MCA MCA 1106*	61	8
15 Jul 89		**WE GOT OUR OWN THANG** *MCA MCA 23942*	69	2
6 Jul 91	●	**NOW THAT WE FOUND LOVE** *MCA MCS 1550*	2	12
28 Sep 91		**IS IT GOOD TO YOU** *MCA MCS 1564*	46	3
8 Oct 94		**THIS IS YOUR NIGHT** *MCA MCSTD 2010*	30	3
10 Aug 91		**PEACEFUL JOURNEY** *MCA MCA 10289*	40	3

HEAVY PETTIN'
UK, male vocal / instrumental group (Singles: 2 weeks, Albums: 4 weeks) pos/wks

			pos	wks
17 Mar 84		**LOVE TIMES LOVE** *Polydor HEP 3*	69	2
29 Oct 83		**LETTIN' LOOSE** *Polydor HEPLP 1*	55	2
13 Jul 85		**ROCK AIN'T DEAD** *Polydor HEPLP 2*	81	2

HEAVY STEREO
UK, male vocal / instrumental group (Singles: 4 weeks) pos/wks

			pos	wks
22 Jul 95		**SLEEP FREAK** *Creation CRESCD 203*	46	1
28 Oct 95		**SMILER** *Creation CRESCD 213*	46	1
10 Feb 96		**CHINESE BURN** *Creation CRESCD 218*	45	1
24 Aug 96		**MOUSE IN A HOLE** *Creation CRESCD 230*	53	1

HEAVY WEATHER
US, male vocalist – Peter Lee (Singles: 1 week) pos/wks

			pos	wks
29 Jun 96		**LOVE CAN'T TURN AROUND** *Pukka CDPUKKA 6*	56	1

Bobby HEBB
US, male vocalist (Singles: 15 weeks) pos/wks

			pos	wks
8 Sep 66		**SUNNY** *Philips BF 1503*	12	9
19 Aug 72		**LOVE LOVE LOVE** *Philips 6051 023*	32	6

HED BOYS
UK, male instrumental / production duo – Dave Lee and Andrew Livingstone (Singles: 6 weeks) pos/wks

			pos	wks
6 Aug 94		**GIRLS + BOYS** *Deconstruction 74321223322*	21	4
4 Nov 95		**GIRLS + BOYS (re-mix)** *Deconstruction 74321322032*	36	2

See also Li KWAN; RAVEN MAIZE; Joey NEGRO; Z FACTOR; JAKATTA; AKABU featuring Linda CLIFFORD; PHASE II; IL PADRINOS featuring Jocelyn BROWN

(HED) PLANET EARTH
US, male rap / vocal / instrumental group (Albums: 1 week) pos/wks

			pos	wks
2 Sep 00		**BROKE** *Music For Nations CDMFN 262*	73	1

HEDGEHOPPERS ANONYMOUS
UK, male vocal / instrumental group (Singles: 12 weeks) pos/wks

			pos	wks
30 Sep 65	●	**IT'S GOOD NEWS WEEK** *Decca F 12241*	5	12

HEFNER
UK, male vocal / instrumental group (Singles: 3 weeks) pos/wks

			pos	wks
26 Aug 00		**GOOD FRUIT** *Too Pure PURE 108CDS*	50	1
14 Oct 00		**THE GREEDY UGLY PEOPLE** *Too Pure PURE 111CDS*	64	1
8 Sep 01		**ALAN BEAN** *Too Pure PURE 118CDS*	58	1

Neal HEFTI
US, male orchestra (Singles: 4 weeks) pos/wks

			pos	wks
9 Apr 88		**BATMAN THEME** *RCA PB 49571*	55	4

Den HEGARTY
UK, male vocalist (Singles: 2 weeks) pos/wks

			pos	wks
31 Mar 79		**VOODOO VOODOO** *Magnet MAG 143*	73	2

See also DARTS

Anita HEGERLAND – *See Mike OLDFIELD*

HEINZ *UK, male vocalist – Heinz Burt, d. 7 Apr 2000 (Singles: 35 weeks)* pos/wks

8 Aug 63 ● **JUST LIKE EDDIE** *Decca F 11693* 5 15
28 Nov 63 **COUNTRY BOY** *Decca F 11768* 26 9
27 Feb 64 **YOU WERE THERE** *Decca F 11831* 26 8
15 Oct 64 **QUESTIONS I CAN'T ANSWER** *Columbia DB 7374* 39 2
18 Mar 65 **DIGGIN' MY POTATOES** *Columbia DB 7482* [1] 49 1

[1] Heinz and the Wild Boys

See also TORNADOS

HELICOPTER *UK, male instrumental / production duo – Dylan Barnes and Rob Davy (Singles: 4 weeks)* pos/wks

27 Aug 94 **ON YA WAY** *Helicopter TIG 007CD* 32 2
22 Jun 96 **ON YA WAY (re-mix)** *Systematic SYSCD 27* 37 2

See also MUTINY UK

HELIOCENTRIC WORLD
UK, male / female vocal / instrumental group (Singles: 2 weeks) pos/wks

14 Jan 95 **WHERE'S YOUR LOVE BEEN** *Talkin Loud TLKCD 51* 71 2

HELIOTROPIC featuring Verna V *UK, male production duo – Nick Hale and Gez Dewar – with female vocalist (Singles: 2 weeks)* pos/wks

16 Oct 99 **ALIVE** *Multiply CDMULTY 52* 33 2

HELL IS FOR HEROES *UK, male vocal / instrumental group (Singles: 7 weeks, Albums: 2 weeks)* pos/wks

9 Feb 02 **YOU DROVE ME TO IT** *Wishakismo CDWISH 003* 63 1
17 Aug 02 **I CAN CLIMB MOUNTAINS** *Chrysalis CDCHS 5143* 41 2
2 Nov 02 **NIGHT VISION** *Chrysalis CDCHSS 5147* 38 1
1 Feb 03 **YOU DROVE ME TO IT (re-issue)** *EMI CDCHSS 5149* 28 2
17 May 05 **RETREAT** *EMI CDEMS 619* 39 1
15 Feb 03 THE NEON HANDSHAKE *EMI 5409232* 16 2

See also SYMPOSIUM

Pete HELLER *UK, male DJ / producer (Singles: 7 weeks)* pos/wks

15 May 99 **BIG LOVE** *Essential Recordings ESCD 4* 12 7

HELLER & FARLEY PROJECT *UK, male instrumental / production duo – Pete Heller and Terry Farley (Singles: 7 weeks)* pos/wks

24 Feb 96 **ULTRA FLAVA** *AM:PM 5814372* 22 3
28 Dec 96 **ULTRA FLAVA (re-mix)** *AM:PM 5820552* 32 4

See also FIRE ISLAND; Pete HELLER; STYLUS TROUBLE

HELLO
UK, male vocal / instrumental group (Singles: 21 weeks) pos/wks

9 Nov 74 ● **TELL HIM** *Bell 1377* 6 12
18 Oct 75 ● **NEW YORK GROOVE** *Bell 1438* 9 9

HELLOWEEN *US, male vocal / instrumental group (Singles: 7 weeks, Albums: 9 weeks)* pos/wks

27 Aug 88 **DR STEIN** *Noise International 7HELLO 1* 57 3
12 Nov 88 **I WANT OUT** *Noise International 7HELLO 2* 69 2
2 Mar 91 **KIDS OF THE CENTURY** *EMI EM 178* 56 2
17 Sep 88 KEEPER OF THE SEVEN KEYS PART 2 *Noise International NUK 117* 24 5
15 Apr 89 LIVE IN THE UK *EMI EMC 3558* 26 2
23 Mar 91 PINK BUBBLES GO APE *EMI EMC 3588* 41 2

HELMET *US, male vocal / instrumental group (Albums: 1 week)* pos/wks

2 Jul 94 BETTY *Interscope 6544924042* 38 1

Bobby HELMS *US, male vocalist, d. 19 Jul 1997 (Singles: 7 weeks)* pos/wks

29 Nov 57 **MY SPECIAL ANGEL** *Brunswick 05721* [1] 22 3
21 Feb 58 **NO OTHER BABY** *Brunswick 05730* 30 1
1 Aug 58 **JACQUELINE** *Brunswick 05748* [1] 20 3

[1] Bobby Helms with the Anita Kerr Singers

Jimmy HELMS *US, male vocalist (Singles: 10 weeks)* pos/wks

24 Feb 73 ● **GONNA MAKE YOU AN OFFER YOU CAN'T REFUSE** *Cube BUG 27* 8 10

See also LONDONBEAT

HELTAH SKELTAH and ORIGINOO GUNN CLAPPAZ as the FABULOUS FIVE
US, male rap / vocal / production group (Singles: 1 week) pos/wks

1 Jun 96 **BLAH** *Priority PTYCD 117* 60 1

HEMSTOCK – *See Paul VAN DYK*

Ainslie HENDERSON *UK, male vocalist (Singles: 7 weeks)* pos/wks

8 Mar 03 ● **KEEP ME A SECRET (re)** *Mercury 0779812* 5 7

Eddie HENDERSON
US, male instrumentalist – trumpet (Singles: 6 weeks) pos/wks

28 Oct 78 **PRANCE ON** *Capitol CL 16015* 44 6

Joe 'Mr Piano' HENDERSON
UK, male instrumentalist – piano, d. 4 May 1980 (Singles: 23 weeks) pos/wks

3 Jun 55 **SING IT WITH JOE** *Polygon P 1167* 14 4
2 Sep 55 **SING IT AGAIN WITH JOE** *Polygon P 1184* 18 3
25 Jul 58 **TRUDIE (re)** *Pye Nixa N 15147* 14 14
23 Oct 59 **TREBLE CHANCE** *Pye 7N 15224* 28 1
24 Mar 60 **OOH! LA! LA!** *Pye 7N 15257* 44 1

First two hits are medleys as follows: Sing It with Joe: Margie / I'm Nobody's Sweetheart / Somebody Stole My Gal / Moonlight Bay / By the Light of the Silvery Moon / Cuddle Up a Little Closer. Sing It Again with Joe: Put Your Arms Around Me Honey / Ain't She Sweet / When You're Smiling / Shine on Harvest Moon / My Blue Heaven / Show Me the Way to Go Home

Wayne HENDERSON – *See Roy AYERS*

Billy HENDRIX
Germany, male producer – Sharam Khososi (Singles: 2 weeks) pos/wks

12 Sep 98 **THE BODY SHINE (EP)** *Hooj Choons HOOJ 65CD* 55 2

Tracks on The Body Shine (EP): The Body Shine / Funky Shine / Colour Systems Inc's Amber Dub / Timewriter re-mix

See also THREE 'N ONE

Jimi HENDRIX EXPERIENCE (132 Top 500)
Guitar ace and hugely influential 20th-century icon, b. Johnny Allen Hendrix, 27 Nov 1942, Seattle, US, renamed James Marshall Hendrix, d. 18 Sep 1970, London. After being 'discovered' and then managed by Animals' bassist Chas Chandler, the left-handed guitarist and vocalist formed The Jimi Hendrix Experience, featuring Mitch Mitchell (d) and Noel Redding (b, d. 11 May 2003). His timeless appeal consistently generates annual global sales of about three million albums (Singles: 88 weeks, Albums: 282 weeks) pos/wks

29 Dec 66 ● **HEY JOE** *Polydor 56 139* 6 11
23 Mar 67 ● **PURPLE HAZE** *Track 604 001* 3 14
11 May 67 ● **THE WIND CRIES MARY** *Track 604 004* 6 11
30 Aug 67 **BURNING OF THE MIDNIGHT LAMP** *Track 604 007* 18 9
23 Oct 68 ● **ALL ALONG THE WATCHTOWER** *Track 604 025* 5 11
16 Apr 69 **CROSSTOWN TRAFFIC** *Track 604 029* 37 3
7 Nov 70 ★ **VOODOO CHILE** *Track 2095 001* 1 13
30 Oct 71 **GYPSY EYES / REMEMBER** *Track 2094 010* 35 5
12 Feb 72 **JOHNNY B GOODE** *Polydor 2001 277* [1] 35 5
21 Apr 90 **CROSSTOWN TRAFFIC (re-issue)** *Polydor PO 71* [1] 61 3
20 Oct 90 **ALL ALONG THE WATCHTOWER (EP)** *Polydor PO 100* [1] 52 3
27 May 67 ● ARE YOU EXPERIENCED *Track 612001* [1] 2 33
16 Dec 67 ● AXIS: BOLD AS LOVE *Track 613003* [1] 5 16
27 Apr 68 ● SMASH HITS *Track 613004* [1] 4 25

		pos	wks
18 May 68	**GET THAT FEELING** *London HA 8349* [2]	39	2
16 Nov 68 ●	**ELECTRIC LADYLAND** *Track 613008/9* [1] ▲	6	12
4 Jul 70 ●	**BAND OF GYPSIES** *Track 2406001*	6	22
3 Apr 71 ●	**CRY OF LOVE** *Track 2408101*	2	14
28 Aug 71 ●	**EXPERIENCE** *Ember NR 5057*	9	6
20 Nov 71	**JIMI HENDRIX AT THE ISLE OF WIGHT** *Track 2302 016*	17	2
4 Dec 71	**RAINBOW BRIDGE** *Reprise K 44159*	16	8
5 Feb 72 ●	**HENDRIX IN THE WEST** *Polydor 2302 018*	7	14
11 Nov 72	**WAR HEROES** *Polydor 2302 020*	23	3
21 Jul 73	**SOUNDTRACK RECORDINGS FROM THE FILM 'JIMI HENDRIX'** *Warner Bros. K 64017*	37	1
29 Mar 75	**JIMI HENDRIX** *Polydor 2343 080*	35	4
30 Aug 75	**CRASH LANDING** *Polydor 2310 398*	35	3
29 Nov 75	**MIDNIGHT LIGHTNING** *Polydor 2310 415*	46	1
14 Aug 82	**THE JIMI HENDRIX CONCERTS** *CBS 88592*	16	11
19 Feb 83	**THE SINGLES ALBUM** *Polydor PODV 6*	77	4
11 Mar 89	**RADIO ONE** *Castle Collectors CCSLP 212*	30	6
3 Nov 90 ●	**CORNERSTONES 1967-1970** *Polydor 8472311*	5	16
14 Nov 92	**THE ULTIMATE EXPERIENCE** *PolyGram TV 5172352*	25	26
30 Apr 94 ●	**BLUES** *Polydor 5210372*	10	3
13 Aug 94	**WOODSTOCK** *Polydor 5233842*	32	3
10 May 97	**FIRST RAYS OF THE NEW RISING SUN** *MCA MCD 11599*	37	2
2 Aug 97	**ELECTRIC LADYLAND (re-issue)** *MCA MCD 11600*	47	1
13 Sep 97 ●	**EXPERIENCE HENDRIX – THE BEST OF JIMI HENDRIX** *Telstar TV TTVCD 2930*	10	29
13 Jun 98	**BBC SESSIONS** *MCA MCD 11742* [1]	42	2
20 Jul 02 ●	**VOODOO CHILD – THE JIMI HENDRIX COLLECTION** *UMTV 1703222*	10	13

[1] Jimi Hendrix [1] Jimi Hendrix Experience [2] Jimi Hendrix and Curtis Knight

Tracks on All Along the Watchtower (EP): All Along the Watchtower / Voodoo Chile / Hey Joe (re-issues)

Nona HENDRYX

US, female vocalist (Singles: 2 weeks)

		pos	wks
16 May 87	**WHY SHOULD I CRY** *EMI America EA 234*	60	2

See also LaBELLE

Don HENLEY *US, male vocalist / instrumentalist – drums (Singles: 30 weeks, Albums: 30 weeks)*

		pos	wks
12 Feb 83	**DIRTY LAUNDRY** *Asylum E 9894*	59	3
9 Feb 85	**THE BOYS OF SUMMER** *Geffen A 4945*	12	10
29 Jul 89	**THE END OF THE INNOCENCE** *Geffen GEF 57*	48	5
3 Oct 92	**SOMETIMES LOVE JUST AIN'T ENOUGH** *MCA MCS 1692* [1]	22	6
18 Jul 98	**BOYS OF SUMMER (re-issue)** *Geffen GFSTD 22350*	12	6
9 Mar 85	**BUILDING THE PERFECT BEAST** *Geffen GEF 25939*	14	11
8 Jul 89	**THE END OF THE INNOCENCE** *Geffen WX 253*	17	16
3 Jun 00	**INSIDE JOB** *Warner Bros. 9362470832*	25	3

[1] Patty Smyth with Don Henley

See also EAGLES

Cassius HENRY *UK, male vocalist (Singles: 2 weeks)*

		pos	wks
30 Mar 02	**BROKE** *Blacklist 0130265 ERE*	31	2

Clarence 'Frogman' HENRY

US, male vocalist / instrumentalist – keyboards (Singles: 35 weeks)

		pos	wks
4 May 61 ●	**BUT I DO** *Pye International 7N 25078*	3	19
13 Jul 61 ●	**YOU ALWAYS HURT THE ONE YOU LOVE** *Pye International 7N 25089*	6	12
21 Sep 61	**LONELY STREET / WHY CAN'T YOU** *Pye International 7N 25108*	42	2
17 Jul 93	**(I DON'T KNOW WHY) BUT I DO (re-issue)** *MCA MCSTD 1797*	65	2

Kevin HENRY – *See* LA MIX

Paul HENRY and the Mayson GLEN ORCHESTRA

UK, male vocalist / orchestra (Singles: 2 weeks)

		pos	wks
14 Jan 78	**BENNY'S THEME** *Pye 7N 46027*	39	2

Pauline HENRY

UK, female vocalist (Singles: 21 weeks, Albums: 1 week)

		pos	wks
18 Sep 93	**TOO MANY PEOPLE** *Sony S2 6595942*	38	2
6 Nov 93	**FEEL LIKE MAKING LOVE** *Sony S2 6597972*	12	7
29 Jan 94	**CAN'T TAKE YOUR LOVE** *Sony S2 6599902*	30	3
21 May 94	**WATCH THE MIRACLE START** *Sony S2 6602772*	54	1
30 Sep 95	**SUGAR FREE** *Sony S2 6624362*	57	2
23 Dec 95	**LOVE HANGOVER** *Sony S2 6626132*	37	3
24 Feb 96	**NEVER KNEW LOVE LIKE THIS** *Sony S2 6629382* [1]	40	2
1 Jun 96	**HAPPY** *Sony S2 6630692*	46	1
19 Feb 94	**PAULINE** *Sony S2 4747442*	45	1

[1] Pauline Henry featuring Wayne Marshall

See also CHIMES

Pierre HENRY

France, male instrumentalist (Singles: 1 week)

		pos	wks
4 Oct 97	**PSYCHE ROCK** *Hi-Life 4620312*	58	1

HEPBURN *UK, female vocal / instrumental group (Singles: 15 weeks, Albums: 2 weeks)*

		pos	wks
29 May 99 ●	**I QUIT** *Columbia 6674012*	8	7
28 Aug 99	**BUGS** *Columbia 6677382*	14	5
19 Feb 00	**DEEP DEEP DOWN** *Columbia 6683382*	16	3
11 Sep 99	**HEPBURN** *Columbia 4948352*	28	2

Band and Chorus of HER MAJESTY'S GUARDS DIVISION

UK, military band (Albums: 4 weeks)

		pos	wks
22 Nov 75	**30 SMASH HITS OF THE WAR YEARS** *Warwick WW 5006*	38	4

HERBALISER *UK, male DJ / production duo – Jake Wherry and Ollie 'Teeba' Trattles (Albums: 1 week)*

		pos	wks
30 Mar 02	**SOMETHING WICKED THIS WAY COMES** *Ninja Tune ZENCD 64*	71	1

HERD *UK, male vocal / instrumental group – includes Peter Frampton (Singles: 35 weeks, Albums: 1 week)*

		pos	wks
13 Sep 67 ●	**FROM THE UNDERWORLD** *Fontana TF 856*	6	13
20 Dec 67	**PARADISE LOST** *Fontana TF 887*	15	9
10 Apr 68 ●	**I DON'T WANT OUR LOVING TO DIE** *Fontana TF 925*	5	13
24 Feb 68	**PARADISE LOST** *Fontana STL 5458*	38	1

See also Peter FRAMPTON

HERMAN'S HERMITS (289 Top 500)

Manchester quintet fronted by teenage vocalist Peter Noone, b. 5 Nov 1947, whose US popularity in the mid-1960s rivalled The Beatles. This band sold more than 40 million records and at times had three singles simultaneously in the US Top 20 (Singles: 211 weeks, Albums: 11 weeks)

		pos	wks
20 Aug 64 ★	**I'M INTO SOMETHING GOOD** *Columbia DB 7338*	1	15
19 Nov 64	**SHOW ME GIRL** *Columbia DB 7408*	19	9
18 Feb 65 ●	**SILHOUETTES** *Columbia DB 7475*	3	12
29 Apr 65 ●	**WONDERFUL WORLD** *Columbia DB 7546*	7	9
2 Sep 65	**JUST A LITTLE BIT BETTER** *Columbia DB 7670*	15	9
23 Dec 65 ●	**A MUST TO AVOID** *Columbia DB 7791*	6	11
24 Mar 66	**YOU WON'T BE LEAVING** *Columbia DB 7861*	20	7
23 Jun 66	**THIS DOOR SWINGS BOTH WAYS** *Columbia DB 7947*	18	7
6 Oct 66 ●	**NO MILK TODAY** *Columbia DB 8012*	7	11
1 Dec 66	**EAST WEST** *Columbia DB 8076*	37	7
9 Feb 67 ●	**THERE'S A KIND OF HUSH** *Columbia DB 8123*	7	11
17 Jan 68	**I CAN TAKE OR LEAVE YOUR LOVING** *Columbia DB 8327*	11	9
1 May 68	**SLEEPY JOE** *Columbia DB 8404*	12	10
17 Jul 68 ●	**SUNSHINE GIRL** *Columbia DB 8446*	8	14
18 Dec 68 ●	**SOMETHING'S HAPPENING** *Columbia DB 8504*	6	15
23 Apr 69 ●	**MY SENTIMENTAL FRIEND** *Columbia DB 8563*	2	12
8 Nov 69	**HERE COMES THE STAR** *Columbia DB 8626*	33	9
7 Feb 70 ●	**YEARS MAY COME, YEARS MAY GO (re)** *Columbia DB 8656*	7	12
23 May 70	**BET YER LIFE I DO** *RAK 102*	22	10
14 Nov 70	**LADY BARBARA** *RAK 106* [1]	13	12
18 Sep 65	**HERMAN'S HERMITS** *Columbia 33SX 1727*	16	2

25 Sep 71	THE MOST OF HERMAN'S HERMITS *MFP 5216*	14 5
8 Oct 77	GREATEST HITS *K-Tel NE 1001*	37 4

[1] Peter Noone and Herman's Hermits

See also Peter NOONE

HERMES HOUSE BAND *Holland, male / female vocal / instrumental group (Singles: 14 weeks)* pos/wks

15 Dec 01 ●	**COUNTRY ROADS** *EMI / Liberty CDHHB 001*	7 12
13 Apr 02	**QUE SERA SERA** *EMI / Liberty CDHHB 002*	53 1
28 Dec 02	**LIVE IS LIFE** *EMI / Liberty CDLIVE 001* [1]	50 1

[1] Hermes House Band and DJ Otzi

HERNANDEZ *UK, male vocalist (Singles: 3 weeks)* pos/wks

15 Apr 89	**ALL MY LOVE** *Epic HER 1*	58 3

Patrick HERNANDEZ *Guadeloupe, male vocalist (Singles: 14 weeks)* pos/wks

16 Jun 79 ●	**BORN TO BE ALIVE** *Gem GEM 4*	10 14

HERREYS *Sweden, male vocal group (Singles: 3 weeks)* pos/wks

26 May 84	**DIGGI LOO-DIGGI LEY** *Panther PAN 5*	46 3

Kristin HERSH *US, female vocalist (Singles: 3 weeks, Albums: 5 weeks)* pos/wks

22 Jan 94	**YOUR GHOST** *4AD BAD 4001CD*	45 2
16 Apr 94	**STRINGS** *4AD BAD 4006CD*	60 1
5 Feb 94 ●	HIPS AND MAKERS *4AD CAD 4002CD*	7 4
14 Feb 98	STRANGE ANGELS *4AD CAD 8003CD*	64 1

See also THROWING MUSES

Nick HEYWARD *UK, male vocalist (Singles: 65 weeks, Albums: 13 weeks)* pos/wks

19 Mar 83	**WHISTLE DOWN THE WIND** *Arista HEY 1*	13 8
4 Jun 83	**TAKE THAT SITUATION** *Arista HEY 2*	11 10
24 Sep 83	**BLUE HAT FOR A BLUE DAY** *Arista HEY 3*	14 8
3 Dec 83	**ON A SUNDAY** *Arista HEY 4*	52 5
2 Jun 84	**LOVE ALL DAY** *Arista HEY 5*	31 6
3 Nov 84	**WARNING SIGN (re)** *Arista HEY 6*	25 9
8 Jun 85	**LAURA** *Arista HEY 8*	45 4
10 May 86	**OVER THE WEEKEND** *Arista HEY 9*	43 5
10 Sep 88	**YOU'RE MY WORLD** *Warner Bros. W 7758*	67 2
21 Aug 93	**KITE** *Epic 6594882*	44 2
16 Oct 93	**HE DOESN'T LOVE YOU LIKE I DO** *Epic 6597282*	58 2
30 Sep 95	**THE WORLD** *Epic 6623845*	47 2
13 Jan 96	**ROLLERBLADE** *Epic 6627912*	37 2
29 Oct 83 ●	NORTH OF A MIRACLE *Arista NORTH 1*	10 13

See also HAIRCUT 100

HI-FIVE *US, male vocal group (Singles: 8 weeks)* pos/wks

1 Jun 91	**I LIKE THE WAY (THE KISSING GAME)** *Jive JIVE 271* ▲	43 6
24 Oct 92	**SHE'S PLAYING HARD TO GET** *Jive JIVE 316*	55 2

HI-GATE *UK, male production duo – Julius (Judge Jules) O'Riordan and Paul Masterson (Singles: 14 weeks)* pos/wks

29 Jan 00 ●	**PITCHIN' (IN EVERY DIRECTION)** *Incentice CENT 3CD*	6 6
26 Aug 00	**I CAN HEAR VOICES / CANED AND UNABLE** *Incentive CENT 9 CDS*	12 5
7 Apr 01	**GONNA WORK IT OUT** *Incentive CENT 20CDS*	25 3

See also CANDY GIRLS; DOROTHY; SLEAZESISTERS; YOMANDA; CLERGY; Paul MASTERSON presents SUSHI

HI GLOSS *US, disco aggregation (Singles: 13 weeks)* pos/wks

8 Aug 81	**YOU'LL NEVER KNOW** *Epic EPC A 1387*	12 13

HI JACK *US, male vocal group (Albums: 1 week)* pos/wks

19 Oct 91	THE HORNS OF JERICHO *Warner Bros. 7599263861*	54 1

HI-LUX *UK, male instrumental / production duo (Singles: 3 weeks)* pos/wks

18 Feb 95	**FEEL IT** *Cheeky CHEKCD 006*	41 2
2 Sep 95	**NEVER FELT THIS WAY / FEEL IT (re-issue)** *Champion CHAMPCD 319*	58 1

HI POWER *Germany, male rap group (Singles: 1 week)* pos/wks

1 Sep 90	**CULT OF SNAP / SIMBA GROOVE** *Rumour RUMAT 24*	73 1

HI-TEK featuring JONELL *US, male producer – Tony Cottrell (Singles: 1 week)* pos/wks

20 Oct 01	**ROUND & ROUND** *Rawkus RWK 3432*	73 1

HI-TEK 3 featuring YA KID K *Belgium, male / female vocal / instrumental group (Singles: 10 weeks)* pos/wks

3 Feb 90	**SPIN THAT WHEEL** *Brothers Organisation BORG 1*	69 3
29 Sep 90	**SPIN THAT WHEEL (TURTLES GET REAL) (re-issue)** *Brothers Organisation BORG 16*	15 7

See also TECHNOTRONIC

HI TENSION *UK, male vocal / instrumental group (Singles: 23 weeks, Albums: 4 weeks)* pos/wks

6 May 78	**HI TENSION** *Island WIP 6422*	13 12
12 Aug 78 ●	**BRITISH HUSTLE / PEACE ON EARTH** *Island WIP 6446*	8 11
6 Jan 79	HI TENSION *Island ILPS 9564*	74 4

'Peace on Earth' credited with 'British Hustle' from 2 Sep 1978 to end of record's chart run

John HIATT *US, male vocalist (Albums: 3 weeks)* pos/wks

7 Jul 90	STOLEN MOMENTS *A&M 3953101*	72 1
11 Sep 93	PERFECTLY GOOD GUITAR *A&M 5401302*	67 1
11 Nov 95	WALK ON *Capitol CDP 8334162*	74 1

Al HIBBLER *US, male vocalist, d. 24 Apr 2001 (Singles: 17 weeks)* pos/wks

13 May 55 ●	**UNCHAINED MELODY** *Brunswick 05420*	2 17

Hinda HICKS *UK, female vocalist (Singles: 15 weeks, Albums: 4 weeks)* pos/wks

7 Mar 98	**IF YOU WANT ME** *Island CID 689*	25 3
16 May 98	**YOU THINK YOU OWN ME** *Island CID 700*	19 4
15 Aug 98	**I WANNA BE YOUR LADY** *Island CID 709*	14 5
24 Oct 98	**TRULY** *Island CID 721*	31 2
14 Oct 00	**MY REMEDY** *Island CID 765*	61 1
29 Aug 98	HINDA *Island CID 8068*	20 4

HIDDEN CAMERAS *Canada, male vocal collective (Singles: 1 week)* pos/wks

14 Jun 03	**A MIRACLE** *Rough Trade RTRADESC 105*	70 1

Bertie HIGGINS *US, male vocalist (Singles: 4 weeks)* pos/wks

5 Jun 82	**KEY LARGO** *Epic EPC A 2168*	60 4

HIGH *UK, male vocal group (Singles: 11 weeks, Albums: 2 weeks)* pos/wks

25 Aug 90	**UP AND DOWN** *London LON 272*	53 4
27 Oct 90	**TAKE YOUR TIME** *London LON 280*	56 2
12 Jan 91	**BOX SET GO** *London LONG 286*	28 3
6 Apr 91	**MORE . . .** *London LON 297*	67 2
17 Nov 90	SOMEWHERE SOON *London 8282241*	59 2

HIGH CONTRAST *UK, male producer – Lincoln Barrett (Singles: 2 weeks)* pos/wks

1 Jun 02	**GLOBAL LOVE** *Hospital NHS 44CD*	68 1
9 Aug 03	**BASEMENT TRACK** *Hospital NHS 60*	65 1

HIGH FIDELITY *UK, male vocal / instrumental group (Singles: 1 week)* pos/wks

25 Jul 98	**LUV DUP** *Plastique FAKE 03CDS*	70 1

HIGH LLAMAS
UK, male vocal / instrumental group (Albums: 1 week)

		pos	wks
6 Apr 96	**HAWAII** *Alpaca Park CDWOOL 2*	62	1

HIGH NUMBERS
UK, male vocal / instrumental group (Singles: 4 weeks)

		pos	wks
5 Apr 80	**I'M THE FACE** *Back Door DOOR 4*	49	4

The High Numbers were an early version of The Who

HIGH SOCIETY
UK, male vocal / instrumental group (Singles: 4 weeks)

		pos	wks
15 Nov 80	**I NEVER GO OUT IN THE RAIN** *Eagle ERS 002*	53	4

HIGHLY LIKELY
UK, male vocal / instrumental group (Singles: 4 weeks)

		pos	wks
21 Apr 73	**WHATEVER HAPPENED TO YOU ('LIKELY LADS' THEME)** *BBC RESL 10*	35	4

HIGHWAYMEN
US, male vocal group (Singles: 18 weeks)

		pos	wks
7 Sep 61 ★	**MICHAEL** *HMV POP 910* ▲	1	14
7 Dec 61	**THE GYPSY ROVER (re)** *HMV POP 948*	41	4

HIJACK
UK, male rap group (Singles: 3 weeks)

		pos	wks
6 Jan 90	**THE BADMAN IS ROBBIN'** *Rhyme Syndicate 655517 7*	56	3

Benny HILL
UK, male comedian / vocalist, d. 20 Apr 1992 (Singles: 43 weeks, Albums: 8 weeks)

		pos	wks
16 Feb 61	**GATHER IN THE MUSHROOMS** *Pye 7N 15327*	12	8
1 Jun 61	**TRANSISTOR RADIO** *Pye 7N 15359*	24	6
16 May 63	**HARVEST OF LOVE** *Pye 7N 15520*	20	8
13 Nov 71 ★	**ERNIE (THE FASTEST MILKMAN IN THE WEST)** *Columbia DB 8833*	1	17
30 May 92	**ERNIE (THE FASTEST MILKMAN IN THE WEST) (re-issue)** *EMI ERN 1*	29	4
11 Dec 71 ●	**WORDS AND MUSIC** *Columbia SCX 6479*	9	8

Chris HILL
UK, male vocalist / DJ / producer (Singles: 14 weeks)

		pos	wks
6 Dec 75 ●	**RENTA SANTA** *Philips 6006 491*	10	7
4 Dec 76 ●	**BIONIC SANTA** *Philips 6006 551*	10	7

Dan HILL
Canada, male vocalist (Singles: 13 weeks)

		pos	wks
18 Feb 78	**SOMETIMES WHEN WE TOUCH (re)** *20th Century BTC 2355*	13	13

Faith HILL
US, female vocalist (Singles: 34 weeks, Albums: 29 weeks)

		pos	wks
14 Nov 98	**THIS KISS** *Warner Brothers W463CD*	13	11
17 Apr 99	**LET ME LET GO** *Warner Bros. W473CD*	72	1
20 May 00	**BREATHE** *WEA WEA 520CD*	33	2
21 Apr 01	**THE WAY YOU LOVE ME** *Warner Brothers W51CD*	15	5
30 Jun 01 ●	**THERE YOU'LL BE** *Warner Brothers W 563CD*	3	11
13 Oct 01	**BREATHE (re-mix)** *Warner Brothers W 572CD*	36	2
26 Oct 02	**CRY** *Warner Brothers W 593CD*	25	2
3 Jun 00	**BREATHE** *Warner Bros. 9362473732* ▲	19	16
27 Oct 01 ●	**THERE YOU'LL BE** *Warner Bros. 9362482402*	6	11
9 Nov 02	**CRY** *Warner Bros. 9362483682* ▲	29	2

Lauryn HILL
US, female vocalist (Singles: 35 weeks, Albums: 74 weeks)

		pos	wks
6 Sep 97	**THE SWEETEST THING** *Columbia 6649785* [1]	18	4
27 Dec 97	**ALL MY TIME** *World Entertainment OWECD 2*	57	1
3 Oct 98 ●	**DOO WOP (THAT THING)** *Ruffhouse 6665152* ▲	3	7
27 Feb 99 ●	**EX-FACTOR (re)** *Columbia / Ruffhouse 6669452*	4	10
10 Jul 99	**EVERYTHING IS EVERYTHING** *Columbia / Ruffhouse 6675742*	19	6
11 Dec 99	**TURN YOUR LIGHTS DOWN LOW** *Columbia 6684362* [2]	15	7
10 Oct 98 ●	**THE MISEDUCATION OF LAURYN HILL** *Columbia 4898432* ▲	2	72
18 May 02	**MTV UNPLUGGED 2.0** *Columbia 5080032*	40	2

[1] Refugee Camp Allstars featuring Lauryn Hill [2] Bob Marley featuring Lauryn Hill

See also FUGEES

Lonnie HILL
US, male vocalist (Singles: 4 weeks)

		pos	wks
22 Mar 86	**GALVESTON BAY** *10 TEN 111*	51	4

Roni HILL
US, female vocalist (Singles: 4 weeks)

		pos	wks
7 May 77	**YOU KEEP ME HANGIN' ON – STOP IN THE NAME OF LOVE (MEDLEY)** *Creole CR 138*	36	4

Vince HILL
UK, male vocalist (Singles: 91 weeks, Albums: 10 weeks)

		pos	wks
7 Jun 62	**THE RIVER'S RUN DRY (re)** *Piccadilly 7N 35043*	41	2
6 Jan 66	**TAKE ME TO YOUR HEART AGAIN** *Columbia DB 7781*	13	11
17 Mar 66	**HEARTACHES** *Columbia DB 7852*	28	5
2 Jun 66	**MERCI CHERI** *Columbia DB 7924*	36	6
9 Feb 67 ●	**EDELWEISS** *Columbia DB 8127*	2	17
11 May 67	**ROSES OF PICARDY** *Columbia DB 8185*	13	11
27 Sep 67	**LOVE LETTERS IN THE SAND** *Columbia DB 8268*	23	9
26 Jun 68	**THE IMPORTANCE OF YOUR LOVE** *Columbia DB 8414*	32	12
12 Feb 69	**DOESN'T ANYBODY KNOW MY NAME?** *Columbia DB 8515*	50	1
25 Oct 69	**LITTLE BLUE BIRD** *Columbia DB 8616*	42	1
25 Sep 71	**LOOK AROUND (AND YOU'LL FIND ME THERE)** *Columbia DB 8804*	12	16
20 May 67	**EDELWEISS** *Columbia SCX 6141*	23	9
29 Apr 78	**THAT LOVING FEELING** *K-Tel NE 1017*	51	1

Steve HILLAGE
UK, male vocalist / instrumentalist – guitar (Albums: 41 weeks)

		pos	wks
3 May 75	**FISH RISING** *Virgin V 2031*	33	3
16 Oct 76 ●	**L** *Virgin V 2066*	10	12
22 Oct 77	**MOTIVATION RADIO** *Virgin V 2777*	28	5
29 Apr 78	**GREEN VIRGIN** *Virgin 2098*	30	8
17 Feb 79	**LIVE HERALD** *Virgin VGD 3502*	54	5
5 May 79	**RAINBOW DOME MUSIC** *Virgin VR 1*	52	5
27 Oct 79	**OPEN** *Virgin V 2135*	71	1
5 Mar 83	**FOR TO NEXT** *Virgin V 2244*	48	2

HILLMAN MINX
UK / France, male / female vocal / instrumental group (Singles: 1 week)

		pos	wks
5 Sep 98	**I'VE HAD ENOUGH** *Mercury MERCD 509*	72	1

HILLTOPPERS
US, male vocal group (Singles: 30 weeks)

		pos	wks
27 Jan 56 ●	**ONLY YOU (AND YOU ALONE) (re)** *London HLD 8221*	3	23
14 Sep 56	**TRYIN'** *London HLD 8298*	30	1
5 Apr 57	**MARIANNE (re)** *London HLD 8381*	20	6

Ronnie HILTON
UK, male vocalist – Adrian Hill (b. 26 Jan 1926, d. 21 Feb 2001) (Singles: 136 weeks)

		pos	wks
26 Nov 54 ●	**I STILL BELIEVE** *HMV B 10785*	3	14
10 Dec 54	**VENI VIDI VICI** *HMV B 10785*	12	8
11 Mar 55 ●	**A BLOSSOM FELL** *HMV B 10808*	10	5
26 Aug 55	**STARS SHINE IN YOUR EYES** *HMV B 10901*	13	7
11 Nov 55	**THE YELLOW ROSE OF TEXAS** *HMV B 10924*	15	2
10 Feb 56	**YOUNG AND FOOLISH (2re)** *HMV POP 154*	17	3
20 Apr 56 ★	**NO OTHER LOVE** *HMV POP 198*	1	14
29 Jun 56 ●	**WHO ARE WE** *HMV POP 221*	6	12
21 Sep 56	**A WOMAN IN LOVE** *HMV POP 248*	30	1
9 Nov 56	**TWO DIFFERENT WORLDS** *HMV POP 274*	13	13
24 May 57 ●	**AROUND THE WORLD** *HMV POP 338*	4	18
2 Aug 57	**WONDERFUL! WONDERFUL!** *HMV POP 364*	27	2
21 Feb 58	**MAGIC MOMENTS** *HMV POP 446*	22	2
18 Apr 58	**I MAY NEVER PASS THIS WAY AGAIN (2re)** *HMV POP 468* [1]	27	3
9 Jan 59	**THE WORLD OUTSIDE** *HMV POP 559* [1]	18	6
21 Aug 59	**THE WONDER OF YOU** *HMV POP 638*	22	3

21 May 64 **DON'T LET THE RAIN COME DOWN** *HMV POP 1291* **21** 10
11 Feb 65 **A WINDMILL IN OLD AMSTERDAM** *HMV POP 1378* **23** 13

[1] Ronnie Hilton with the Michael Sammes Singers

HIM *Finland, male vocal / instrumental group (Singles: 2 weeks, Albums: 1 week)* pos/wks

17 May 03 **BURIED ALIVE BY LOVE** *RCA 82876523162* **30** 2
26 Apr 03 **LOVE METAL** *RCA 82876505012*....................**55** 1

HINDSIGHT
UK, male vocal / instrumental group (Singles: 3 weeks) pos/wks

5 Sep 87 **LOWDOWN** *Circa YR 5* **62** 3

Deni HINES *Australia, female vocalist (Singles: 6 weeks)* pos/wks

14 Jun 97 **IT'S ALRIGHT** *Mushroom D 1593* **35** 2
20 Sep 97 **I LIKE THE WAY** *Mushroom MUSH 7CDX* **37** 2
28 Feb 98 **DELICIOUS** *Mushroom MUSH 20CD* [1] **52** 1
23 May 98 **JOY** *Mushroom MUSH 30CDS* **47** 1

[1] Deni Hines featuring Don-E

Gregory HINES – *See Luther VANDROSS*

HIPSWAY *UK, male vocal / instrumental group (Singles: 21 weeks, Albums: 23 weeks)* pos/wks

13 Jul 85 **THE BROKEN YEARS** *Mercury MER 193* **72** 3
14 Sep 85 **ASK THE LORD** *Mercury MER 195* **72** 1
22 Feb 86 **THE HONEYTHIEF** *Mercury MER 212* **17** 9
10 May 86 **ASK THE LORD (re-recording)** *Mercury LORD 1* **50** 5
20 Sep 86 **LONG WHITE CAR** *Mercury MER 230* **55** 2
1 Apr 89 **YOUR LOVE** *Mercury MER 279* **66** 1
19 Apr 86 **HIPSWAY** *Mercury MERH 85* **42** 23

David HIRSCHFELDER
Australia, male composer (Albums: 9 weeks) pos/wks

8 Feb 97 **SHINE (FILM SOUNDTRACK)** *Philips 4547102* **46** 9

The HISS
US, male vocal / instrumental group (Singles: 3 weeks) pos/wks

1 Mar 03 **TRIUMPH** *Loog / Polydor 0657782* **53** 1
9 Aug 03 **CLEVER KICKS** *Polydor 9809465*....................**49** 1
15 Nov 03 **BACK ON THE RADIO** *Polydor 9813415* **65** 1

HISTORY featuring Q-TEE
UK, male production duo and female rapper (Singles: 5 weeks) pos/wks

21 Apr 90 **AFRIKA** *SBK SBK 7008* **42** 5

Carol HITCHCOCK
Australia, female vocalist (Singles: 5 weeks) pos/wks

30 May 87 **GET READY** *A&M AM 391* **56** 5

HITHOUSE *Holland, male producer – Peter Slaghuis d. 5 Sep 1991 (Singles: 13 weeks)* pos/wks

5 Nov 88 **JACK TO THE SOUND OF THE UNDERGROUND** *Supreme SUPE 137* **14** 12
19 Aug 89 **MOVE YOUR FEET TO THE RHYTHM OF THE BEAT** *Supreme SUPE 149* **69** 1

HITMAN HOWIE TEE – *See REAL ROXANNE*

The HIVES *Sweden, male vocal / instrumental group (Singles: 5 weeks, Albums: 30 weeks)* pos/wks

23 Feb 02 **HATE TO SAY I TOLD YOU SO** *Burning Heart BHR 1059* **23** 3
18 May 02 **MAIN OFFENDER** *Poptones MC 5076SCD* **24** 2
12 Jan 02 ● **YOUR NEW FAVOURITE BAND** *Poptones MC 5055CD*....................**7** 30

Helen HOBSON – *See Cliff RICHARD*

Edmund HOCKRIDGE *Canada, male vocalist (Singles: 18 weeks)* pos/wks

17 Feb 56 ● **YOUNG AND FOOLISH (2re)** *Nixa N 15039* **10** 9
11 May 56 **NO OTHER LOVE (2re)** *Nixa N 15048* **24** 4
31 Aug 56 **BY THE FOUNTAINS OF ROME** *Pye Nixa N 15063* **17** 5

Eddie HODGES *US, male vocalist (Singles: 10 weeks)* pos/wks

28 Sep 61 **I'M GONNA KNOCK ON YOUR DOOR** *London HLA 9369* **37** 6
9 Aug 62 **(GIRLS GIRLS GIRLS) MADE TO LOVE** *London HLA 9576* **37** 4

Roger HODGSON
UK, male vocalist / instrumentalist (Albums: 4 weeks) pos/wks

20 Oct 84 **IN THE EYE OF THE STORM** *A&M AMA 5004* **70** 4

See also SUPERTRAMP

Mani HOFFMAN – *See SUPERMEN LOVERS featuring Mani Hoffman*

Gerard HOFFNUNG
UK, male comedian, d. 28 Sep 1959 (Albums: 20 weeks) pos/wks

3 Sep 60 ● **AT THE OXFORD UNION** *Decca LF 1330* **4** 20

Susanna HOFFS
US, female vocalist (Singles: 8 weeks, Albums: 2 weeks) pos/wks

2 Mar 91 **MY SIDE OF THE BED** *Columbia 6565547*....................**44** 4
11 May 91 **UNCONDITIONAL LOVE** *Columbia 6567827*....................**65** 2
19 Oct 96 **ALL I WANT** *London LONCD 387* **32** 2
6 Apr 91 **WHEN YOU'RE A BOY** *Columbia 4672021* **56** 2

See also BANGLES

Hulk HOGAN with GREEN JELLY
US, male wrestler / vocalist – Terry Bollea – and US, male vocal / instrumental group (Singles: 4 weeks) pos/wks

25 Dec 93 **I'M THE LEADER OF THE GANG** *Arista 74321174892* **25** 4

See also GREEN JELLY

HOGGBOY *UK, male vocal / instrumental group (Singles: 1 week)* pos/wks

27 Apr 02 **SHOULDN'T LET THE SIDE DOWN** *Sobriety SOB4 CDA* **74** 1

Christopher HOGWOOD – *See 007; ACADEMY OF ST MARTIN IN THE FIELDS; ACADEMY OF ANCIENT MUSIC conducted by Christopher HOGWOOD*

Demi HOLBORN *UK, female vocalist (Singles: 2 weeks)* pos/wks

27 Jul 02 **I'D LIKE TO TEACH THE WORLD TO SING** *Universal Classics & Jazz 0190982* **27** 2

HOLDEN & THOMPSON *UK, male producer and female vocalist – James Holden and Julie Thompson (Singles: 1 week)* pos/wks

17 May 03 **NOTHING** *Loaded LOAD 98CD* **51** 1

HOLE *US, female / male vocal / instrumental group (Singles: 15 weeks, Albums: 10 weeks)* pos/wks

17 Apr 93 **BEAUTIFUL SON** *City Slang EFA 0491603* **54** 1
9 Apr 94 **MISS WORLD** *City Slang EFA 049362* **64** 1
15 Apr 95 **DOLL PARTS** *Geffen GFSTD 91* **16** 3
29 Jul 95 **VIOLET** *Geffen GFSTD 94* **17** 2
12 Sep 98 **CELEBRITY SKIN** *Geffen GFSTD 22345* **19** 4
30 Jan 99 **MALIBU** *Geffen GFSTD 22369* **22** 2
10 Jul 99 **AWFUL** *Geffen INTDE 97098* **42** 2
12 Oct 91 **PRETTY ON THE INSIDE** *City Slang E 04071*....................**59** 1
23 Apr 94 **LIVE THROUGH THIS** *City Slang EFA 049352* **13** 5
19 Sep 98 **CELEBRITY SKIN** *Geffen GED 25164* **11** 4

HOLE IN ONE
Holland, male DJ / producer – Marcel Hol (Singles: 2 weeks) pos/wks

15 Feb 97 **LIFE'S TOO SHORT** *Manifesto FESCD 21* **36** 2

Billie HOLIDAY
US, female vocalist, d. 17 Jul 1959 (Albums: 11 weeks)

Date		Title / Label	pos	wks
16 Nov 85		THE LEGEND OF BILLIE HOLIDAY *MCA BHTV 1*	60	10
6 Sep 97		LADY DAY – THE VERY BEST OF BILLIE HOLIDAY *Sony TV / Universal MOODCD 52*	63	1

Jools HOLLAND and his RHYTHM & BLUES ORCHESTRA
UK, male vocal / instrumentalist – piano (Singles: 3 weeks, Albums: 57 weeks)

Date		Title / Label	pos	wks
24 Feb 01		I'M IN THE MOOD FOR LOVE *Warner Esp WSMS 001CD* [1]	29	3
5 May 90		WORLD OF HIS OWN *IRS EIRSA 1018* [1]	71	1
26 Oct 96		SEX & JAZZ & ROCK & ROLL *Coliseum HF 51CD*	38	2
25 Oct 97		LIFT THE LID *Coalition 3984205252*	50	1
1 Dec 01	●	SMALL WORLD BIG BAND *WSM 927426562* [2]	8	37
30 Nov 02		SMALL WORLD BIG BAND VOLUME TWO – MORE FRIENDS *WSM 0927494192*	17	11
29 Nov 03		SMALL WORLD BIG BAND FRIENDS 3 – JACK O THE GREEN *Radar RADAR001CD*	39	5+

[1] Jools Holland and Jamiroquai [1] Jools Holland [2] Jools Holland and his Rhythm & Blues Orchestra and Friends

See also SQUEEZE

HOLLAND-DOZIER featuring Lamont DOZIER
US, male vocal duo (Singles: 5 weeks)

Date		Title / Label	pos	wks
28 Oct 72		WHY CAN'T WE BE LOVERS *Invictus INV 525*	29	5

Jennifer HOLLIDAY *US, female vocalist (Singles: 6 weeks)*

Date		Title / Label	pos	wks
4 Sep 82		AND I'M TELLING YOU I'M NOT GOING *Geffen GEF A 2644*	32	6

Michael HOLLIDAY *UK, male vocalist – Norman Milne, d. 29 Oct 1963 (Singles: 66 weeks)*

Date		Title / Label	pos	wks
30 Mar 56		NOTHIN' TO DO (re) *Columbia DB 3746*	20	3
15 Jun 56		HOT DIGGITY (DOG ZIGGITY BOOM) / THE GAL WITH THE YALLER SHOES (2re) *Columbia DB 3783*	13	11
5 Oct 56		TEN THOUSAND MILES *Columbia DB 3813*	24	3
17 Jan 58	★	THE STORY OF MY LIFE *Columbia DB 4058*	1	15
14 Mar 58		IN LOVE *Columbia DB 4087*	26	3
16 May 58	●	STAIRWAY OF LOVE *Columbia DB 4121*	3	13
11 Jul 58		I'LL ALWAYS BE IN LOVE WITH YOU *Columbia DB 4155*	27	1
1 Jan 60	★	STARRY EYED *Columbia DB 4378* [1]	1	13
14 Apr 60		SKYLARK *Columbia DB 4437*	39	3
1 Sep 60		LITTLE BOY LOST *Columbia DB 4475*	50	1

[1] Michael Holliday with the Michael Sammes Singers

When 'Hot Diggity (Dog Ziggity Boom) / Gal With the Yaller Shoes' re-entered the chart on 3 Aug 1956, 'Hot Diggity (Dog Ziggity Boom)' was listed by itself on 3 Aug and 10 Aug. Both sides were listed on 17 Aug – 'Gal with the Yaller Shoes' peaking at No.25

HOLLIES (85 Top 500) *Distinctive, influential and well-respected Manchester group with UK single sales totaling 4,597,450: Allan Clarke (v), Graham Nash (g), Tony Hicks (g), Eric Haydock (b), Bobby Elliott (d). They were among the most regular chart visitors of the 1960s, and their No.1s span 23 years (Singles: 318 weeks, Albums: 154 weeks)*

Date		Title / Label	pos	wks
30 May 63		(AIN'T THAT) JUST LIKE ME *Parlophone R 5030*	25	10
29 Aug 63		SEARCHIN' *Parlophone R 5052*	12	14
21 Nov 63	●	STAY *Parlophone R 5077*	8	16
27 Feb 64	●	JUST ONE LOOK *Parlophone R 5104*	2	13
21 May 64	●	HERE I GO AGAIN *Parlophone R 5137*	4	12
17 Sep 64	●	WE'RE THROUGH *Parlophone R 5178*	7	11
28 Jan 65	●	YES I WILL *Parlophone R 5232*	9	13
27 May 65	★	I'M ALIVE *Parlophone R 5287*	1	14
2 Sep 65	●	LOOK THROUGH ANY WINDOW *Parlophone R 5322*	4	11
9 Dec 65		IF I NEEDED SOMEONE *Parlophone R 5392*	20	9
24 Feb 66	●	I CAN'T LET GO *Parlophone R 5409*	2	10
23 Jun 66	●	BUS STOP *Parlophone R 5469*	5	9
13 Oct 66	●	STOP STOP STOP *Parlophone R 5508*	2	12
16 Feb 67	●	ON A CAROUSEL *Parlophone R 5562*	4	11
1 Jun 67	●	CARRIE-ANNE *Parlophone R 5602*	3	11
27 Sep 67		KING MIDAS IN REVERSE *Parlophone R 5637*	18	8
27 Mar 68	●	JENNIFER ECCLES *Parlophone R 5680*	7	11
2 Oct 68		LISTEN TO ME *Parlophone R 5733*	11	11
5 Mar 69	●	SORRY SUZANNE *Parlophone R 5765*	3	12
4 Oct 69	●	HE AIN'T HEAVY, HE'S MY BROTHER *Parlophone R 5806*	3	15
18 Apr 70	●	I CAN'T TELL THE BOTTOM FROM THE TOP *Parlophone R 5837*	7	10
3 Oct 70		GASOLINE ALLEY BRED *Parlophone R 5862*	14	7
22 May 71		HEY WILLY *Parlophone R 5905*	22	7
26 Feb 72		THE BABY *Polydor 2058 199*	26	6
2 Sep 72		LONG COOL WOMAN IN A BLACK DRESS *Parlophone R 5939*	32	8
13 Oct 73		THE DAY THAT CURLY BILLY SHOT DOWN CRAZY SAM MCGHEE *Polydor 2058 403*	24	6
9 Feb 74	●	THE AIR THAT I BREATHE *Polydor 2058 435*	2	13
14 Jun 80		SOLDIER'S SONG *Polydor 2059 246*	58	3
29 Aug 81		HOLLIEDAZE (A MEDLEY) *EMI 5229*	28	7
3 Sep 88	★	HE AIN'T HEAVY, HE'S MY BROTHER (re-issue) *EMI EM 74*	1	11
3 Dec 88		THE AIR THAT I BREATHE (re-issue) *EMI EM 80*	60	5
20 Mar 93		THE WOMAN I LOVE *EMI CDEM 264*	42	2
15 Feb 64	●	STAY WITH THE HOLLIES *Parlophone PMC 1220*	2	25
2 Oct 65	●	HOLLIES *Parlophone PMC 1261*	8	14
16 Jul 66		WOULD YOU BELIEVE? *Parlophone PMC 7008*	16	8
17 Dec 66		FOR CERTAIN BECAUSE *Parlophone PCS 17011*	12	7
17 Jun 67		EVOLUTION *Parlophone PCS 7022*	13	10
17 Aug 68	★	THE HOLLIES' GREATEST HITS *Parlophone PCS 7057*	1	27
17 May 69	●	HOLLIES SIGN DYLAN *Parlophone PCS 7078*	3	7
28 Nov 70		CONFESSIONS OF THE MIND *Parlophone PCS 7117*	30	5
16 Mar 74		HOLLIES *Polydor 2383 262*	38	3
19 Mar 77	●	HOLLIES LIVE HITS *Polydor 2383 428*	4	12
22 Jul 78	●	20 GOLDEN GREATS *EMI EMTV 11*	2	20
1 Oct 88		ALL THE HITS AND MORE *EMI EM 1301*	51	5
3 Apr 93		THE AIR THAT I BREATHE – THE BEST OF THE HOLLIES *EMI CDEMTV 74*	15	7
5 Apr 03		GREATEST HITS *EMI 5820122*	21	4

The 1972 hit 'The Baby' featured Swedish lead vocalist Mikael Rickfors. Holliedaze (A Medley) comprised: Just One Look / Here I Go Again / I'm Alive / I Can't Let Go / Long Cool Woman in a Black Dress / Bus Stop / Carrie-Anne The two 'Hollies' albums are different

See also Graham NASH

Mark HOLLIS *UK, male vocal / instrumentalist (Albums: 1 week)*

Date		Title / Label	pos	wks
14 Feb 98		MARK HOLLIS *Polydor 5376882*	53	1

See also TALK TALK

Laurie HOLLOWAY – *See SOUTH BANK ORCHESTRA*

Loleatta HOLLOWAY *US, female vocalist (Singles: 21 weeks)*

Date		Title / Label	pos	wks
31 Aug 91		GOOD VIBRATIONS *Interscope A 8764* [1] ▲	14	7
18 Jan 92		TAKE ME AWAY *PWL Continental PWL 210* [2]	25	5
26 Mar 94		STAND UP *Six6 SIXCD 111*	68	1
1 Apr 95		KEEP THE FIRE BURNIN' *Columbia 6611552* [3]	49	1
11 Apr 98		SHOUT TO THE TOP *JBO JNR 5001573* [4]	23	2
20 Feb 99		(YOU GOT ME) BURNING UP *Wonderboy WBOYD 013* [5]	14	4
25 Nov 00		DREAMIN' *Defected DFECT 22CDS*	59	1

[1] Marky Mark and the Funky Bunch featuring Loleatta Holloway [2] Cappella featuring Loleatta Holloway [3] Dan Hartman starring Loleatta Holloway [4] Fire Island featuring Loleatta Holloway [5] Cevin Fisher / Loleatta Holloway

HOLLOWAY & CO
UK, male producer – Nicky Holloway (Singles: 1 week)

Date		Title / Label	pos	wks
21 Aug 99		I'LL DO ANYTHING – TO MAKE YOU MINE *INCredible INCS 2CD*	58	1

Buddy HOLLY (71 Top 500) *Highly respected and exceptionally influential singer / songwriter, b. Charles Hardin Holley, 7 Sep 1936, Texas, US, d. 3 Feb 1959 (aka 'the day the music died'). Despite a relatively brief career, his records and songs are still frequently heard around the globe (Singles: 190 weeks, Albums: 339 weeks)*

Date		Title / Label	pos	wks
6 Dec 57	●	PEGGY SUE *Coral Q 72293*	6	17
14 Mar 58		LISTEN TO ME *Coral Q 72288*	16	2

			pos	wks
20 Jun 58	●	**RAVE ON** *Coral Q 72325*	5	14
29 Aug 58		**EARLY IN THE MORNING** *Coral Q 72333*	17	4
16 Jan 59		**HEARTBEAT** *Coral Q 72346*	30	1
27 Feb 59	★	**IT DOESN'T MATTER ANYMORE** *Coral Q 72360*	1	21
31 Jul 59		**MIDNIGHT SHIFT** *Brunswick 05800*	26	3
11 Sep 59		**PEGGY SUE GOT MARRIED** *Coral Q 72376*	13	10
28 Apr 60		**HEARTBEAT (re-issue)** *Coral Q 72392*	30	3
26 May 60		**TRUE LOVE WAYS** *Coral Q 72397*	25	7
20 Oct 60		**LEARNING THE GAME** *Coral Q 72411*	36	3
26 Jan 61		**WHAT TO DO** *Coral Q 72419*	34	6
6 Jul 61		**BABY I DON'T CARE / VALLEY OF TEARS** *Coral Q 72432*	12	14
15 Mar 62		**LISTEN TO ME (re-issue)** *Coral Q 72449*	48	1
13 Sep 62		**REMINISCING** *Coral Q 72455*	17	11
14 Mar 63	●	**BROWN-EYED HANDSOME MAN** *Coral Q 72459*	3	17
6 Jun 63	●	**BO DIDDLEY** *Coral Q 72463*	4	12
5 Sep 63	●	**WISHING** *Coral Q 72466*	10	11
19 Dec 63		**WHAT TO DO (re-recording)** *Coral Q 72469*	27	8
14 May 64		**YOU'VE GOT LOVE** *Coral Q 72472* [1]	40	6
10 Sep 64		**LOVE'S MADE A FOOL OF YOU** *Coral Q 72475*	39	6
3 Apr 68		**PEGGY SUE / RAVE ON (re-issue)** *MCA MU 1012*	32	9
10 Dec 88		**TRUE LOVE WAYS (re-issue)** *MCA MCA 1302*	65	4
2 May 59	●	**THE BUDDY HOLLY STORY** *Coral LVA 9105*	2	156
15 Oct 60	●	**THE BUDDY HOLLY STORY VOLUME 2** *Coral LVA 9127*	7	14
21 Oct 61	●	**THAT'LL BE THE DAY** *Ace Of Hearts AH 3*	5	14
6 Apr 63	●	**REMINISCING** *Coral LVA 9212*	2	31
13 Jun 64	●	**BUDDY HOLLY SHOWCASE** *Coral LVA 9222*	3	16
26 Jun 65		**HOLLY IN THE HILLS** *Coral LVA 9227*	13	6
15 Jul 67	●	**BUDDY HOLLY'S GREATEST HITS** *Ace of Hearts AH 148*	9	40
12 Apr 69		**GIANT** *MCA MUPS 371*	13	1
21 Aug 71		**BUDDY HOLLY'S GREATEST HITS (re-issue)** *Coral CP 8*	32	6
12 Jul 75		**BUDDY HOLLY'S GREATEST HITS (2nd re-issue)** *Coral CDLM 8007*	42	3
11 Mar 78	★	**20 GOLDEN GREATS** *MCA EMTV 8* [1]	1	20
8 Sep 84		**BUDDY HOLLY'S GREATEST HITS (3rd re-issue)** *MCA MCL 1618*	100	1
18 Feb 89	●	**TRUE LOVE WAYS** *Telstar STAR 2339*	8	11
20 Feb 93	★	**WORDS OF LOVE** *PolyGram TV 5144872* [1] ■	1	9
7 Dec 96		**THE VERY BEST OF BUDDY HOLLY** *Dino DINCD 133*	24	8
28 Aug 99		**THE VERY BEST OF BUDDY HOLLY AND THE CRICKETS** *Universal Music TV 1120462* [1]	25	3

[1] Buddy Holly and The Crickets [1] Buddy Holly and the Crickets

Buddy Holly's version of 'Love's Made a Fool of You' is not the same version as the Crickets' hit of 1959, on which Holly did not appear. 'Valley of Tears' was not listed together with 'Baby I Don't Care' until 13 Jul 1961

See also CRICKETS

HOLLY and the IVYS

UK, male / female vocal / instrumental group (Singles: 4 weeks)

			pos	wks
19 Dec 81		**CHRISTMAS ON 45** *Decca SANTA 1*	40	4

HOLLYWOOD ARGYLES

US, male vocal group (Singles: 10 weeks)

			pos	wks
21 Jul 60		**ALLEY-OOP** *London HLU 9146* ▲	24	10

HOLLYWOOD BEYOND *UK, male group (Singles: 14 weeks)*

			pos	wks
12 Jul 86	●	**WHAT'S THE COLOUR OF MONEY?** *WEA YZ 76*	7	10
20 Sep 86		**NO MORE TEARS** *WEA YZ 81*	47	4

Eddie HOLMAN *US, male vocalist (Singles: 13 weeks)*

			pos	wks
19 Oct 74	●	**(HEY THERE) LONELY GIRL** *ABC 4012*	4	13

Dave HOLMES *UK, male producer (Singles: 1 week)*

			pos	wks
26 May 01		**DEVOTION** *Tidy Trax TIDY 154CD*	66	1

David HOLMES

UK, male producer (Singles: 8 weeks, Albums: 5 weeks)

			pos	wks
6 Apr 96		**GONE** *Go! Discs GODCD 140*	75	1
23 Aug 97		**GRITTY SHAKER** *Go.Beat GOBCD 2*	53	1
10 Jan 98		**DON'T DIE JUST YET** *Go.Beat GOLCD 6*	33	3
4 Apr 98		**MY MATE PAUL** *Go.Beat GOBCD 8*	39	2
19 Aug 00		**69 POLICE** *Go.Beat / Polydor GOBCD 30*	53	1
22 Jul 95		**THIS FILM'S CRAP LET'S SLASH THE SEATS** *Go! Discs 8286312*	51	1
13 Sep 97		**LET'S GET KILLED** *Go! Beat 5391002*	34	2
24 Jun 00		**BOW DOWN TO THE EXIT SIGN** *Go! Beat 5438662*	22	2

Rupert HOLMES *US, male vocalist (Singles: 14 weeks)*

			pos	wks
12 Jan 80		**ESCAPE (THE PINA COLADA SONG)** *Infinity INF 120* ▲	23	7
22 Mar 80		**HIM** *MCA 565*	31	7

John HOLT

Jamaica, male vocalist (Singles: 14 weeks, Albums: 2 weeks)

			pos	wks
14 Dec 74	●	**HELP ME MAKE IT THROUGH THE NIGHT** *Trojan TR 7909*	6	14
1 Feb 75		**A THOUSAND VOLTS OF HOLT** *Trojan TRLS 75*	42	2

Nichola HOLT *UK, female vocalist (Singles: 1 week)*

			pos	wks
21 Oct 00		**THE GAME** *RCA 74321798992*	72	1

HOME *UK, male vocal / instrumental group (Albums: 1 week)*

			pos	wks
11 Nov 72		**DREAMER** *CBS 67522*	41	1

A HOMEBOY, a HIPPIE and a FUNKI DREDD

UK, male vocal / instrumental group (Singles: 9 weeks)

			pos	wks
13 Oct 90		**TOTAL CONFUSION** *Tam Tam 7TTT 031*	56	3
29 Dec 90		**FREEDOM** *Tam Tam 7TTT 039*	68	4
8 Jan 94		**HERE WE GO AGAIN** *Polydor PZCD 302*	57	2

HONDY

Italy, male / female production / vocal group (Singles: 2 weeks)

			pos	wks
12 Apr 97		**HONDY (NO ACCESS)** *Manifesto FESCD 20*	26	2

HONEYBUS

UK, male vocal / instrumental group (Singles: 12 weeks)

			pos	wks
20 Mar 68	●	**I CAN'T LET MAGGIE GO** *Deram DM 182*	8	12

HONEYCOMBS *UK, male / female vocal / instrumental group – lead vocal Dennis D'Ell (Dalziel) (Singles: 39 weeks)*

			pos	wks
23 Jul 64	★	**HAVE I THE RIGHT** *Pye 7N 15664*	1	15
22 Oct 64		**IS IT BECAUSE** *Pye 7N 15705*	38	6
29 Apr 65		**SOMETHING BETTER BEGINNING** *Pye 7N 15827*	39	4
5 Aug 65		**THAT'S THE WAY** *Pye 7N 15890*	12	14

HONEYCRACK *UK, male vocal / instrumental group (Singles: 9 weeks, Albums: 1 week)*

			pos	wks
4 Nov 95		**SITTING AT HOME** *Epic 6625382*	42	2
24 Feb 96		**GO AWAY** *Epic 6628642*	41	2
11 May 96		**KING OF MISERY** *Epic 6631472*	32	2
20 Jul 96		**SITTING AT HOME (re-issue)** *Epic 6635032*	32	2
16 Nov 96		**ANYWAY** *EG EGO 52A*	67	1
1 Jun 96		**PROZAIC** *Epic 4842302*	34	1

HONEYDRIPPERS *UK / US, male vocal / instrumental group (Singles: 3 weeks, Albums: 10 weeks)*

			pos	wks
2 Feb 85		**SEA OF LOVE** *Es Paranza YZ 33*	56	3
1 Dec 84		**THE HONEYDRIPPERS VOLUME ONE** *Es Paranza 790220*	56	10

See also Robert PLANT

HONEYZ *UK / France, female vocal trio (Singles: 57 weeks, Albums: 22 weeks)*

			pos	wks
5 Sep 98	●	**FINALLY FOUND** *1st Avenue / Mercury HNZCD 1*	4	12
19 Dec 98	●	**END OF THE LINE (re)** *1st Avenue / Mercury HNZCD 2*	5	14
24 Apr 99	●	**LOVE OF A LIFETIME** *1st Avenue / Mercury HNZCD 3*	9	9
23 Oct 99	●	**NEVER LET YOU DOWN** *1st Avenue / Mercury HNZCD 4*	7	6
11 Mar 00	●	**WON'T TAKE IT LYING DOWN (re)** *1st Avenue / Mercury HNZCD 5*	7	8

			pos	wks
28 Oct 00		**NOT EVEN GONNA TRIP (2re)** *1st Avenue / Mercury HNZCD 7*	24	5
18 Aug 01		**I DON'T KNOW** *1st Avenue / Mercury HNZCD 8*	28	3
5 Dec 98		**WONDER NO.8** *Mercury 5588142*	33	22

See also ANOTHERSIDE

HONKY *UK, male vocal / instrumental group (Singles: 5 weeks)*

			pos	wks
28 May 77		**JOIN THE PARTY** *Creole CR 137*	28	5

HONKY *UK, male vocal / instrumental group (Singles: 5 weeks)*

			pos	wks
30 Oct 93		**THE HONKY DOODLE DAY EP** *ZTT ZANG 45CD*	61	1
19 Feb 94		**THE WHISTLER** *ZTT ZANG 48CD*	41	2
20 Apr 96		**HIP HOP DON'T YA DROP** *Higher Ground HIGHS 1CD*	70	1
10 Aug 96		**WHAT'S GOIN DOWN** *Higher Ground HIGHS 2CD*	49	1

Tracks on The Honky Doodle Day EP: KKK (Boom Boom Tra La La La) / Honky Doodle Dub / Chains

HOOBASTANK
US, male vocal / instrumental group (Singles: 2 weeks)

			pos	wks
13 Apr 02		**CRAWLING IN THE DARK** *Mercury 5828622*	47	2

Peter HOOK – *See HYBRID featuring Peter HOOK; MONACO: NEW ORDER; JOY DIVISION*

Frank HOOKER and POSITIVE PEOPLE
US, male / female vocal / instrumental group (Singles: 4 weeks)

			pos	wks
5 Jul 80		**THIS FEELIN'** *DJM DJS 10947*	48	4

John Lee HOOKER *US, male vocalist / instrumentalist – guitar, d. 21 Jun 2001 (Singles: 23 weeks, Albums: 31 weeks)*

			pos	wks
11 Jun 64		**DIMPLES** *Stateside SS 297*	23	10
24 Oct 92		**BOOM BOOM** *Pointblank POB 3*	16	5
16 Jan 93		**BOOGIE AT RUSSIAN HILL** *Pointblank POBDX 4*	53	2
15 May 93		**GLORIA** *Exile VANCD 11* [1]	31	3
11 Feb 95		**CHILL OUT (THINGS GONNA CHANGE)** *Pointblank POBD 10*	45	2
20 Apr 96		**BABY LEE** *Silvertone ORECD 81* [2]	65	1
4 Feb 67		**HOUSE OF THE BLUES** *Marble Arch MAL 663*	34	2
11 Nov 89		**THE HEALER** *Silvertone ORELP 508*	63	8
21 Sep 91	●	**MR LUCKY** *Silvertone ORELP 519*	3	10
7 Nov 92		**BOOM BOOM** *Pointblank VPBCD 12*	15	4
4 Mar 95		**CHILL OUT** *Pointblank VPBCD 22*	23	5
22 Mar 97		**DON'T LOOK BACK** *Pointblank VPBCD 39*	63	2

[1] Van Morrison and John Lee Hooker [2] John Lee Hooker with Robert Cray

HOOTERS
US, male vocal / instrumental group (Singles: 9 weeks)

			pos	wks
21 Nov 87		**SATELLITE** *CBS 651168 7*	22	9

HOOTIE & THE BLOWFISH *US, male vocal / instrumental group (Singles: 6 weeks, Albums: 30 weeks)*

			pos	wks
25 Feb 95		**HOLD MY HAND** *Atlantic A 7230CD*	50	3
27 May 95		**LET HER CRY** *Atlantic A 7188CD*	75	1
4 May 96		**OLD MAN AND ME (WHEN I GET TO HEAVEN)** *Atlantic A 5513CD*	57	1
7 Nov 98		**I WILL WAIT** *Atlantic AT 0048CD*	57	1
18 Mar 95		**CRACKED REAR VIEW** *Atlantic 7826132* ▲	12	11
4 May 96	●	**FAIRWEATHER JOHNSON** *Atlantic 7567828862* ▲	9	16
26 Sep 98		**MUSICAL CHAIRS** *Atlantic 7567831362*	15	3

HOPE A.D.
UK, male producer – David Hope (Singles: 1 week)

			pos	wks
4 Jun 94		**TREE FROG** *Sun-Up SUN 003CD*	73	1

See also MIND OF KANE

HOPE OF THE STATES
UK, male vocal / instrumental group (Singles: 2 weeks)

			pos	wks
11 Oct 03		**ENEMIES / FRIENDS** *Sony Music 6742572*	25	2

Mary HOPKIN *UK, female vocalist / instrumentalist – guitar (Singles: 74 weeks, Albums: 9 weeks)*

			pos	wks
4 Sep 68	★	**THOSE WERE THE DAYS** *Apple 2*	1	21
2 Apr 69	●	**GOODBYE** *Apple 10*	2	14
31 Jan 70	●	**TEMMA HARBOUR** *Apple 22*	6	11
28 Mar 70	●	**KNOCK KNOCK WHO'S THERE** *Apple 26*	2	14
31 Oct 70		**THINK ABOUT YOUR CHILDREN (re)** *Apple 30*	19	9
31 Jul 71		**LET MY NAME BE SORROW** *Apple 34*	46	1
20 Mar 76		**IF YOU LOVE ME (I WON'T CARE)** *Good Earth GD 2*	32	4
1 Mar 69	●	**POSTCARD** *Apple SAPCOR 5*	3	9

See also OASIS

Anthony HOPKINS *UK, male actor / vocalist (Singles: 1 week)*

			pos	wks
27 Dec 86		**DISTANT STAR** *Juice AA 5*	75	1

Nick HORNBY – *See PRETENDERS*

James HORNER
US, male composer / conductor (Albums: 82 weeks)

			pos	wks
31 Jan 98	★	**TITANIC (FILM SOUNDTRACK)** *Sony Classical SK 63213* [1]	1	55
12 Sep 98	●	**BACK TO TITANIC** *Sony Classical SK 60691*	10	18
23 Sep 95		**BRAVEHEART (FILM SOUNDTRACK)** *Decca 4482952* [2]	27	9

[1] James Horner - vocals by Sissel [2] London Symphony Orchestra conductor James Horner

Bruce HORNSBY and the RANGE *US, male vocal / instrumental group (Singles: 15 weeks, Albums: 54 weeks)*

			pos	wks
2 Aug 86		**THE WAY IT IS** *RCA PB 49805* ▲	15	10
25 Apr 87		**MANDOLIN RAIN** *RCA PB 49769*	70	1
28 May 88		**THE VALLEY ROAD** *RCA PB 49561*	44	4
13 Sep 86		**THE WAY IT IS** *RCA PL 89901*	16	26
14 May 88		**SCENES FROM THE SOUTHSIDE** *RCA PL 86686*	18	18
30 Jun 90		**A NIGHT ON THE TOWN** *RCA PL 82041*	23	7
8 May 93		**HARBOR LIGHTS** *RCA 07863661142*	32	3

HORNY UNITED – *See BONEY M*

Jane HORROCKS *UK, female actor / vocalist (Albums: 1 week)*

			pos	wks
21 Oct 00		**THE FURTHER ADVENTURES OF LITTLE VOICE** *Liberty 5287542*	63	1

HORSE *UK, female / male vocal / instrumental group (Singles: 10 weeks, Albums: 4 weeks)*

			pos	wks
24 Nov 90		**CAREFUL** *Capitol CL 587*	52	3
21 Aug 93		**SHAKE THIS MOUNTAIN** *Oxygen GASPD 7*	52	2
23 Oct 93		**GOD'S HOME MOVIE** *Oxygen GASXD 10*	56	1
15 Jan 94		**CELEBRATE** *Oxygen GASPD 11*	49	2
5 Apr 97		**CAREFUL (re-mix)** *Stress CDSTRX 79*	44	2
23 Jun 90		**THE SAME SKY** *Echo Chamber EST 2123*	44	2
13 Nov 93		**GOD'S HOME MOVIE** *Oxygen MCD 10935*	42	2

HORSLIPS
Ireland, male vocal / instrumental group (Albums: 3 weeks)

			pos	wks
30 Apr 77		**THE BOOK OF INVASIONS – A CELTIC SYMPHONY** *DJM DJF 20498*	39	3

Johnny HORTON
US, male vocalist, d. 5 Nov 1960 (Singles: 15 weeks)

			pos	wks
26 Jun 59		**THE BATTLE OF NEW ORLEANS** *Philips PB 932* ▲	16	4
19 Jan 61		**NORTH TO ALASKA** *Philips PB 1062*	23	11

HOT ACTION COP
US, male vocal / instrumental group (Singles: 1 week)

			pos	wks
14 Jun 03		**FEVER FOR THE FLAVA** *Lava AT 0152CD*	41	1

HOT BLOOD *France, male instrumental group (Singles: 5 weeks)*

			pos	wks
9 Oct 76		**SOUL DRACULA** *Creole CR 132*	32	5

Review of the Year

APRIL 2003

Billy Fury's statue is unveiled in his native Liverpool 20 years after his death, a ceremony attended by Fury's wife and brother at the Museum of Liverpool Life

S Club announce on stage to their fans on Easter Monday that they are calling it a day. **Gareth Gates's** 'Anyone of Us (Stupid Mistake)' flies high across Europe, making it the most successful single outside the UK by a reality TV pop star. **Pink Floyd's** epic Dark Side of the Moon returns to the top of the US catalogue album chart in its 1,352nd chart week. (That's 26 years.) Despite not showing on the US Hot 100, **Sophie Ellis-Bextor's** 'Murder on the Dancefloor' makes the American dance Top 10 and appears in the US sales Top 40 alongside **Daniel Bedingfield's** 'If You're Not the One', which makes No.2. Comments which **The Dixie Chicks** make in the UK about President Bush result in their US country No.1 single 'Travelin' Soldier' dropping from No.3 to outside the Top 60. While we're in the country, **LeAnn Rimes's** 'How Do I Live' spends a record 300th week on the US country sales chart – bringing her total chart weeks (with just nine singles) to 747. A record 11 of the Top 12 places on the Japanese singles chart are taken by the same act: the duo B/Z (pronounced Beez), who are **Tak Matsumoto and Koshi Inabi. The Yardbirds** make a comeback, releasing their new album and tour in the US for the first time since 1968. The five-DVD set, **The Beatles Anthology**, breaks DVD music sales records but is swiftly pushed down to third spot in the video chart by **Gareth Gates** and **Will Young** releases. **Tom Jones** revival of 'Black Betty' makes the Italian Top 10. US groups **The White Stripes** and **Linkin Park** debut at No.1 on the UK album chart with Elephant and Meteora, with respective first week sales of 194,000 and 93,000. A seven-foot high statue of **Billy Fury** is unveiled in the courtyard of the Museum of Liverpool Life and fellow Scouser **Paul McCartney** buys the publishing rights to the songs of rock 'n' roll pioneer **Carl Perkins**. **Ronan Keating** and his longtime manager, **Louis Walsh**, go their separate ways.

Soul superstar **Luther Vandross** suffers a very bad stroke. Twenty years after his only previous hit, 55-year-old **Oliver Cheatham** tops the UK singles chart in the company of Room 5. In a single week, 14 of the top 15 singles on the Spanish chart are by artists featured in Operación Triunfo (their Popstars meets Fame Academy show). An announcement reveals that the UK now has more music TV stations (23) than any other country. Apple launches its download operation and one million tracks are downloaded in the first seven days (with five million in the first eight weeks). Sad losses this month include **Edwin Starr**, famed for his anti-war classic 'War' who dies during the invasion of Iraq age 61. **Cholly Atkins** (Charles Atkinson), choreographer of the first boy band, **Frankie Lymon and the Teenagers**, **The Temptations, The Miracles, O'Jays, Tavares, Gladys Knight and the Pips** and **The Shirelles**, right through to **New Kids on the Block**, dies age 89. Also departing planet pop are **Felice Bryant** who, with husband **Boudleaux**, won 58 songwriting awards and penned many of the **Everly Brothers'** biggest hits. **Little Eva**, the loco-motion girl, dies age 59, as does the high priestess of soul **Nina Simone.**

Apple launches its download operation and one million tracks are downloaded in the first seven days

HOT BUTTER *US, production duo – Bill and Steve Jerome featuring Stan Free (Singles: 19 weeks)* pos/wks

22 Jul 72 ● **POPCORN (re)** *Pye International 7N 25583* **5** 19

HOT CHOCOLATE 98 Top 500

London-based band who were chart regulars throughout the 1970s and 1980s. Group founders were West Indian-born Errol Brown (v) and Tony Wilson (b/v). The act had at least one hit every year between 1970 and 1984 and 'You Sexy Thing' made the Top 10 in three decades: 70s, 80s and 90s (Singles: 283 weeks, Albums: 153 weeks) pos/wks

15 Aug 70 ● **LOVE IS LIFE** *RAK 103* **6** 12
6 Mar 71 **YOU COULD HAVE BEEN A LADY** *RAK 110* **22** 9
28 Aug 71 ● **I BELIEVE (IN LOVE)** *RAK 118* **8** 11
28 Oct 72 **YOU'LL ALWAYS BE A FRIEND** *RAK 139* **23** 8
14 Apr 73 ● **BROTHER LOUIE** *RAK 149* **7** 10
18 Aug 73 **RUMOURS** *RAK 157* **44** 3
16 Mar 74 ● **EMMA** *RAK 168* **3** 10
30 Nov 74 **CHERI BABE** *RAK 188* **31** 9
24 May 75 **DISCO QUEEN** *RAK 202* **11** 7
9 Aug 75 ● **A CHILD'S PRAYER** *RAK 212* **7** 10
8 Nov 75 ● **YOU SEXY THING** *RAK 221* **2** 12
20 Mar 76 **DON'T STOP IT NOW** *RAK 230* **11** 8
26 Jun 76 **MAN TO MAN** *RAK 238* **14** 8
21 Aug 76 **HEAVEN IS IN THE BACK SEAT OF MY CADILLAC** *RAK 240* **25** 8
18 Jun 77 ★ **SO YOU WIN AGAIN** *RAK 259* **1** 11
26 Nov 77 ● **PUT YOUR LOVE IN ME** *RAK 266* **10** 9
4 Mar 78 **EVERY 1'S A WINNER** *RAK 270* **12** 11
2 Dec 78 **I'LL PUT YOU TOGETHER AGAIN (FROM DEAR ANYONE)** *RAK 286* **13** 11
19 May 79 **MINDLESS BOOGIE** *RAK 292* **46** 5
28 Jul 79 **GOING THROUGH THE MOTIONS** *RAK 296* **53** 4
3 May 80 ● **NO DOUBT ABOUT IT** *RAK 310* **2** 11
19 Jul 80 **ARE YOU GETTING ENOUGH OF WHAT MAKES YOU HAPPY** *RAK 318* **17** 7
13 Dec 80 **LOVE ME TO SLEEP** *RAK 324* **50** 5
30 May 81 **YOU'LL NEVER BE SO WRONG** *RAK 331* **52** 4
17 Apr 82 ● **GIRL CRAZY** *RAK 341* **7** 11
10 Jul 82 ● **IT STARTED WITH A KISS** *RAK 344* **5** 12
25 Sep 82 **CHANCES** *RAK 350* **32** 5
7 May 83 ● **WHAT KINDA BOY YOU LOOKING FOR (GIRL)** *RAK 357* **10** 9
17 Sep 83 **TEARS ON THE TELEPHONE** *RAK 363* **37** 5
4 Feb 84 **I GAVE YOU MY HEART (DIDN'T I)** *RAK 369* **13** 10
17 Jan 87 ● **YOU SEXY THING (re-mix)** *EMI 5592* **10** 10
4 Apr 87 **EVERY 1'S A WINNER (re-mix)** *EMI 5607* **69** 2
6 Mar 93 **IT STARTED WITH A KISS (re-issue)** *EMI CDEMCTS 7* **31** 5
22 Nov 97 ● **YOU SEXY THING (re-issue)** *EMI CDHOT 100* **6** 8
14 Feb 98 **IT STARTED WITH A KISS (2nd re-issue)** *EMI CDHOT 101* [1] **18** 3
15 Nov 75 **HOT CHOCOLATE** *RAK SRAK 516* **34** 7
7 Aug 76 **MAN TO MAN** *RAK SRAK 522* **32** 7
20 Nov 76 ● **GREATEST HITS** *RAK SRAK 524* **6** 35
8 Apr 78 **EVERY 1'S A WINNER** *RAK SRAK 531* **30** 8
15 Dec 79 ● **20 HOTTEST HITS** *RAK EMTV 22* **3** 19
25 Sep 82 **MYSTERY** *RAK SRAK 549* **24** 7
21 Feb 87 ★ **THE VERY BEST OF HOT CHOCOLATE** *RAK EMTV 42* **1** 28
20 Mar 93 ★ **THEIR GREATEST HITS** *EMI CDEMTV 73* **1** 42

[1] Hot Chocolate featuring Errol Brown

HOT GOSSIP – *See Sarah BRIGHTMAN*

HOT HOT HEAT *Canada, male vocal / instrumental group (Singles: 4 weeks, Albums: 2 weeks)* pos/wks

5 Apr 03 **BANDAGES** *B Unique BUN 045CDS* **25** 3
9 Aug 03 **NO, NOT NOW** *Sub Pop W 615CD* **38** 1
12 Apr 03 **MAKE UP THE BREAKDOWN** *WEA 5046646202* **35** 2

HOT HOUSE

UK, male / female vocal / instrumental group (Singles: 3 weeks) pos/wks

14 Feb 87 **DON'T COME TO STAY** *Deconstruction CHEZ 1* **74** 1
24 Sep 88 **DON'T COME TO STAY (re-issue)** *Deconstruction PB 42233* **70** 2

HOT 'N' JUICY – *See MOUSSE T*

HOT RODS – *See EDDIE and the HOT RODS*

HOT STREAK

US, male vocal / instrumental group (Singles: 8 weeks) pos/wks

10 Sep 83 **BODY WORK** *Polydor POSP 642* **19** 8

HOTHOUSE FLOWERS *Ireland, male vocal / instrumental group (Singles: 36 weeks, Albums: 51 weeks)* pos/wks

14 May 88 **DON'T GO** *London LON 174* **11** 8
23 Jul 88 **I'M SORRY** *London LON 187* **53** 3
12 May 90 **GIVE IT UP** *London LON 258* **30** 5
28 Jul 90 **I CAN SEE CLEARLY NOW** *London LON 269* **23** 7
20 Oct 90 **MOVIES** *London LON 276* **68** 2
13 Feb 93 **EMOTIONAL TIME** *London LONCD 335* **38** 4
8 May 93 **ONE TONGUE** *London LOCDP 340* **45** 3
19 Jun 93 **ISN'T IT AMAZING** *London LOCDP 343* **46** 2
27 Nov 93 **THIS IS IT (YOUR SOUL)** *London LONCD 346* **67** 1
16 May 98 **YOU CAN LOVE ME NOW** *London LONCD 410* **65** 1
18 Jun 88 ● **PEOPLE** *London LONLP 58* **2** 19
16 Jun 90 ● **HOME** *London 8281971* **5** 21
20 Mar 93 ● **SONGS FROM THE RAIN** *London 8283502* **7** 11

HOTLEGS

UK, male vocal / instrumental group (Singles: 14 weeks) pos/wks

4 Jul 70 ● **NEANDERTHAL MAN** *Fontana 6007 019* **2** 14

See also 10cc, GODLEY and CREME

HOTSHOTS *UK, male vocal group (Singles: 15 weeks)* pos/wks

2 Jun 73 ● **SNOOPY VS THE RED BARON** *Mooncrest MOON 5* **4** 15

Steven HOUGHTON

UK, male actor / vocalist (Singles: 22 weeks, Albums: 7 weeks) pos/wks

29 Nov 97 ● **WIND BENEATH MY WINGS** *RCA 74321529272* **3** 15
7 Mar 98 **TRULY (re)** *RCA 74321558552* **23** 7
29 Nov 97 **STEVEN HOUGHTON** *RCA 74321542592* **21** 7

HOUSE – *See A HOUSE*

HOUSE ENGINEERS

UK, male vocal / instrumental duo (Singles: 2 weeks) pos/wks

5 Dec 87 **GHOST HOUSE** *Syncopate SY 8* **69** 2

HOUSE OF GLASS

Italy, male production duo – Gianni Bini and Paolo Martini (Singles: 1 week) pos/wks

14 Apr 01 **DISCO DOWN** *Azuli AZNY 138* **72** 1

See also ECLIPSE; BINI & MARTINI; GOODFELLAS featuring Lisa MILLETT

HOUSE OF LOVE *UK, male vocal / instrumental group (Singles: 21 weeks, Albums: 14 weeks)* pos/wks

22 Apr 89 **NEVER** *Fontana HOL 1* **41** 2
18 Nov 89 **I DON'T KNOW WHY I LOVE YOU** *Fontana HOL 2* **41** 3
3 Feb 90 **SHINE ON** *Fontana HOL 3* **20** 4
7 Apr 90 **BEATLES AND THE STONES** *Fontana HOL 4* **36** 4
26 Oct 91 **THE GIRL WITH THE LONELIEST EYES** *Fontana HOL 5* **58** 1
2 May 92 **FEEL** *Fontana HOL 6* **45** 3
27 Jun 92 **YOU DON'T UNDERSTAND** *Fontana HOL 7* **46** 3
5 Dec 92 **CRUSH ME** *Fontana HOL 810* **67** 1
10 Mar 90 ● **THE HOUSE OF LOVE** *Fontana 8422931* **8** 10
10 Nov 90 **THE HOUSE OF LOVE** *Fontana 8469781* **49** 1
18 Jul 92 **BABE RAINBOW** *Fontana 5125492* **34** 2
3 Jul 93 **AUDIENCE WITH THE MIND** *Fontana 5148802* **38** 1

Identically titled albums are different

HOUSE OF PAIN

US, male rap group (Singles: 24 weeks, Albums: 7 weeks) pos/wks

10 Oct 92 **JUMP AROUND** *Ruffness XLS 32* **32** 4

22 May 93 ● JUMP AROUND / TOP O' THE MORNING TO YA (re-issue) *Ruffness XL 43CD* 8 7
23 Oct 93 SHAMROCKS AND SHENANIGANS / WHO'S THE MAN *Ruffness XLS 46CD* 23 4
16 Jul 94 ON POINT *Ruffness XLS 52CD* 19 3
12 Nov 94 IT AIN'T A CRIME *Ruffness XLS 55CD1* 37 2
1 Jul 95 OVER THERE (I DON'T CARE) *Ruffness XLS 61CD1* 20 3
5 Oct 96 FED UP *Tommy Boy TBCD 7744* 68 1
21 Nov 92 HOUSE OF PAIN *XL XLCD 111* 73 1
30 Jul 94 ● SAME AS IT EVER WAS *XL XLCD 115* 8 6

HOUSE OF VIRGINISM

Sweden, male vocal / instrumental group (Singles: 6 weeks) pos/wks

20 Nov 93 I'LL BE THERE FOR YOU (DOYA DODODO DOYA) *ffrr FCD 221* 29 3
30 Jul 94 REACHIN *ffrr FCD 238* 35 2
17 Feb 96 EXCLUSIVE *Logic 74321324102* [1] 67 1

[1] Apollo presents House of Virginism

HOUSE OF ZEKKARIYAS – *See WOMACK and WOMACK*

HOUSE TRAFFIC *Italy / UK, male / female vocal / production group (Singles: 3 weeks)* pos/wks

4 Oct 97 EVERY DAY OF MY LIFE *Logic 74321249442* 24 3

HOUSEMARTINS *UK, male vocal / instrumental group fronted by Norman Cook (b) and Paul Heaton (v) (Singles: 60 weeks, Albums: 71 weeks)* pos/wks

8 Mar 86 SHEEP (re) *Go! Discs GOD 9* 54 4
7 Jun 86 ● HAPPY HOUR *Go! Discs GOD 11* 3 13
4 Oct 86 THINK FOR A MINUTE *Go! Discs GOD 13* 18 8
6 Dec 86 ★ CARAVAN OF LOVE *Go! Discs GOD 16* 1 11
23 May 87 FIVE GET OVER EXCITED *Go! Discs GOD 18* 11 6
5 Sep 87 ME AND THE FARMER *Go! Discs GOD 19* 15 5
21 Nov 87 BUILD *Go! Discs GOD 21* 15 8
23 Apr 88 THERE IS ALWAYS SOMETHING THERE TO REMIND ME *Go! Discs GOD 22* 35 4
10 May 03 CHANGE THE WORLD *Free 2 Air 0146685F2A* [1] 51 1
5 Jul 86 ● LONDON 0 HULL 4 *Go! Discs AGOLP 7* 3 41
27 Dec 86 THE HOUSEMARTINS' CHRISTMAS SINGLES BOX *Go! Discs GOD 816* 84 1
3 Oct 87 ● THE PEOPLE WHO GRINNED THEMSELVES TO DEATH *Go! Discs AGOLP 9* 9 18
21 May 88 ● NOW THAT'S WHAT I CALL QUITE GOOD! *Go! Discs AGOLP 11* 8 11

[1] Dino Lenny vs the Housemartins

See also YES; GTR; ASIA; ANDERSON BRUFORD WAKEMAN HOWE

See also Norman COOK; BEAUTIFUL SOUTH; BISCUIT BOY

HOUSEMASTER BOYZ and the RUDE BOY OF HOUSE

US, male vocal / instrumental group (Singles: 14 weeks) pos/wks

9 May 87 ● HOUSE NATION (re) *Magnetic Dance MAGD 1* 8 14

HOUSETRAP – *See DJ SANDY vs HOUSETRAP*

Thelma HOUSTON *US, female vocalist (Singles: 22 weeks)* pos/wks

5 Feb 77 DON'T LEAVE ME THIS WAY *Motown TMG 1060* ▲ 13 8
27 Jun 81 IF YOU FEEL IT *RCA 77* 48 4
1 Dec 84 YOU USED TO HOLD ME SO TIGHT *MCA MCA 932* 49 8
21 Jan 95 DON'T LEAVE ME THIS WAY (re-recording) *Dynamo DYND 001* 35 2

Whitney HOUSTON (40 Top 500)

Multi-award-winning, record-shattering vocalist b. 9 Aug 1963, New Jersey, US. She has scored a record seven successive No.1s in the US. In 2001and with sales exceeding 140 million behind her, she signed a record-breaking $100m recording deal. Best-selling single: 'I Will Always Love You' 1,355,055 (Singles: 315 weeks, Albums: 377 weeks) pos/wks

16 Nov 85 ★ SAVING ALL MY LOVE FOR YOU *Arista ARIST 640* ▲ 1 16
25 Jan 86 ● HOW WILL I KNOW *Arista ARIST 656* ▲ 5 12
25 Jan 86 HOLD ME *Asylum EKR 32* [1] 44 5
12 Apr 86 ● GREATEST LOVE OF ALL *Arista ARIST 658* ▲ 8 11
23 May 87 ★ I WANNA DANCE WITH SOMEBODY (WHO LOVES ME) *Arista RIS 1* ▲ 1 16
22 Aug 87 DIDN'T WE ALMOST HAVE IT ALL *Arista RIS 31* ▲ 14 8
14 Nov 87 ● SO EMOTIONAL *Arista RIS 43* ▲ 5 11
12 Mar 88 WHERE DO BROKEN HEARTS GO *Arista 109793* ▲ 14 8
28 May 88 ● LOVE WILL SAVE THE DAY *Arista 111516* 10 7
24 Sep 88 ★ ONE MOMENT IN TIME *Arista 111613* 1 12
9 Sep 89 IT ISN'T, IT WASN'T, IT AIN'T NEVER GONNA BE *Arista 112545* [2] 29 5
20 Oct 90 ● I'M YOUR BABY TONIGHT (re) *Arista 113594* ▲ 5 10
22 Dec 90 ALL THE MAN THAT I NEED *Arista 114000* ▲ 13 10
6 Jul 91 MY NAME IS NOT SUSAN *Arista 114510* 29 5
28 Sep 91 I BELONG TO YOU *Arista 114727* 54 2
14 Nov 92 ★ I WILL ALWAYS LOVE YOU (re) *Arista 74321120657* ◆ ▲ 1 29
20 Feb 93 ● I'M EVERY WOMAN *Arista 74321131502* 4 11
24 Apr 93 ● I HAVE NOTHING *Arista 74321146142* 3 10
31 Jul 93 RUN TO YOU *Arista 74321153332* 15 6
6 Nov 93 QUEEN OF THE NIGHT *Arista 74321169302* 14 5
22 Jan 94 SOMETHING IN COMMON *MCA MCSTD 1957* [3] 16 5
18 Nov 95 EXHALE (SHOOP SHOOP) *Arista 74321332472* ▲ 11 9
24 Feb 96 COUNT ON ME *Arista 74321345842* [4] 12 6
21 Dec 96 STEP BY STEP *Arista 74321449332* 13 13
29 Mar 97 I BELIEVE IN YOU AND ME *Arista 74321468602* 16 5
19 Dec 98 ● WHEN YOU BELIEVE (re) *Columbia 6667522* [5] 4 13
6 Mar 99 ● IT'S NOT RIGHT (BUT IT'S OK) *Arista 74321652402* 3 15
3 Jul 99 ● MY LOVE IS YOUR LOVE *Arista 74321672862* 2 12
11 Dec 99 I LEARNED FROM THE BEST *Arista 74321723992* 19 11
17 Jun 00 ● IF I TOLD YOU THAT (re) *Arista 74321766282* [6] 9 11
14 Oct 00 ● COULD I HAVE THIS KISS FOREVER *Arista 74321795992* [7] 7 8
30 Dec 00 HEARTBREAK HOTEL *Arista 74321820572* [8] 25 5
9 Nov 02 WHATCHULOOKINAT *Arista 74321973062* 13 3
14 Dec 85 ● WHITNEY HOUSTON *Arista 206978* ▲ 2 119
13 Jun 87 ★ WHITNEY *Arista 208141* ■ ▲ 1 101
17 Nov 90 ● I'M YOUR BABY TONIGHT *Arista 211039* 4 29
4 Jan 97 THE PREACHER'S WIFE (FILM SOUNDTRACK) *Arista 74321441252* 35 7
28 Nov 98 ● MY LOVE IS YOUR LOVE *Arista 7822190372* 4 68
27 May 00 ★ THE GREATEST HITS *Arista 74321757392* ■ 1 50
16 Feb 02 LOVE WHITNEY *Arista 74321910272* 22 3

[1] Teddy Pendergrass with Whitney Houston [2] Aretha Franklin and Whitney Houston [3] Bobby Brown and Whitney Houston [4] Whitney Houston and CeCe Winans [5] Mariah Carey & Whitney Houston [6] Whitney Houston / George Michael [7] Whitney Houston and Enrique Iglesias [8] Whitney Houston featuring Faith Evans and Kelly Price

'I Will Always Love You' re-entered peaking at No.25 in Dec 1993

Adina HOWARD *US, female vocalist (Singles: 16 weeks)* pos/wks

4 Mar 95 FREAK LIKE ME (re) *East West A 4473CD* 33 4
23 Nov 96 ● WHAT'S LOVE GOT TO DO WITH IT *Interscope IND 97008* [1] 2 12

[1] Warren G featuring Adina Howard

Billy HOWARD *UK, male comedian / vocalist (Singles: 12 weeks)* pos/wks

13 Dec 75 ● KING OF THE COPS *Penny Farthing PEN 892* 6 12

Miki HOWARD *US, female vocalist (Singles: 2 weeks)* pos/wks

26 May 90 UNTIL YOU COME BACK (THAT'S WHAT I'M GONNA DO) *East West 7935* 67 2

Nick HOWARD *Australia, male vocalist (Singles: 1 week)* pos/wks

21 Jan 95 EVERYBODY NEEDS SOMEBODY *Bell 74321220942* 64 1

Robert HOWARD – *See Kym MAZELLE; BLOW MONKEYS*

Steve HOWE

UK, male vocal / instrumentalist – guitar (Albums: 6 weeks) pos/wks

15 Nov 75 BEGINNINGS *Atlantic K 50151* 22 4
24 Nov 79 THE STEVE HOWE ALBUM *Atlantic K 50621* 68 2

See also YES; GTR; ASIA; ANDERSON BRUFORD WAKEMAN HOWE

HOWLIN' WOLF *US, male vocalist – Chester Burnette, d. 10 Jan 1976 (Singles: 5 weeks)* pos/wks

4 Jun 64 **SMOKESTACK LIGHTNIN'** *Pye International 7N 25244* 42 5

HUDDERSFIELD CHORAL SOCIETY
UK, choir (Albums: 14 weeks) pos/wks

15 Mar 86 ● **THE HYMNS ALBUM** *EMI EMTV 40* 8 10
13 Dec 86 **THE CAROLS ALBUM** *EMI EMTV 43* 29 4

Al HUDSON *US, male vocalist (Singles: 20 weeks)* pos/wks

9 Sep 78 **DANCE, GET DOWN (FEEL THE GROOVE) / HOW DO YOU DO** *ABC 4229* 57 4
15 Sep 79 **YOU CAN DO IT** *MCA 511* [1] 15 10
8 Dec 79 **MUSIC** *MCA 542* [2] 56 6

[1] Al Hudson and the Partners [2] One Way featuring Al Hudson

Lavine HUDSON *UK, female vocalist (Singles: 3 weeks)* pos/wks

21 May 88 **INTERVENTION** *Virgin VS 1067* 57 3

HUDSON-FORD *UK, male vocal / instrumental duo – Richard Hudson and John Ford (Singles: 20 weeks)* pos/wks

18 Aug 73 ● **PICK UP THE PIECES** *A&M AMS 7078* 8 9
16 Feb 74 **BURN BABY BURN** *A&M AMS 7096* 15 9
29 Jun 74 **FLOATING IN THE WIND** *A&M AMS 7116* 35 2

See also MONKS

HUE AND CRY *UK, male vocal / instrumental duo – Pat and Greg Kane (Singles: 59 weeks, Albums: 74 weeks)* pos/wks

13 Jun 87 ● **LABOUR OF LOVE** *Circa YR 4* 6 16
19 Sep 87 **STRENGTH TO STRENGTH** *Circa YR 6* 46 5
30 Jan 88 **I REFUSE** *Circa YR 8* 47 3
22 Oct 88 **ORDINARY ANGEL** *Circa YR 18* 42 6
28 Jan 89 **LOOKING FOR LINDA** *Circa YR 24* 15 9
6 May 89 **VIOLENTLY (EP)** *Circa YR 29* 21 6
30 Sep 89 **SWEET INVISIBILITY** *Circa YR 37* 55 3
25 May 91 **MY SALT HEART** *Circa YR 64* 47 3
3 Aug 91 **LONG TERM LOVERS OF PAIN (EP)** *Circa YR 71* 48 3
11 Jul 92 **PROFOUNDLY YOURS** *Fidelity FIDEL 1* 74 1
13 Mar 93 **LABOUR OF LOVE (re-mix)** *Circa HUESCD 1* 25 4
7 Nov 87 **SEDUCED AND ABANDONED** *Circa CIRCA 2* 22 11
10 Dec 88 ● **REMOTE / THE BITTER SUITE** *Circa CIRCA 6* 10 48
29 Jun 91 ● **STARS CRASH DOWN** *Circa CIRCA 15* 10 9
29 Aug 92 **TRUTH AND LOVE** *Fidelity FIDELCD 1* 33 2
10 Apr 93 **LABOURS OF LOVE – THE BEST OF HUE AND CRY** *Circa HACCD 1* 27 4

Tracks on Violently (EP): Violently / The Man with the Child In His Eyes / Calamity John. Tracks on Long Term Lovers of Pain (EP): Long Term Lovers of Pain / Heart of Saturday Night / Remembrance and Gold / Stars Crash Down 'Remote' re-entered the chart on 16 Dec 89 when it was made available with the free album 'The Bitter Suite'

HUES CORPORATION
US, male / female vocal group (Singles: 16 weeks) pos/wks

27 Jul 74 ● **ROCK THE BOAT** *RCA APBO 0232* ▲ 6 10
19 Oct 74 **ROCKIN' SOUL** *RCA PB 10066* 24 6

HUFF & HERB *UK, male DJ / production duo – Ben Langmaid and Jeff Patterson (Singles: 4 weeks)* pos/wks

6 Dec 97 **FEELING GOOD** *Planet 3 GXY 2018CD* 31 3
7 Nov 98 **FEELING GOOD '98 (re-mix)** *Planet 3 GXY 2020CD* 69 1

See also HUFF & PUFF

HUFF & PUFF *UK, male instrumental / production duo – Ben Langmaid and Roland Armstrong (Singles: 4 weeks)* pos/wks

2 Nov 96 **HELP ME MAKE IT** *Skyway SKYWCD 4* 31 2
21 Jun 97 **HELP ME MAKE IT (re-mix)** *Skyway SKYWCD 8* 37 2

See also FAITHLESS; HUFF & HERB; OUR TRIBE / ONE TRIBE; ROLLO; DUSTED

David HUGHES *UK, male vocalist – Geoffrey Paddison, d. 19 Oct 1972 (Singles: 1 week)* pos/wks

21 Sep 56 **BY THE FOUNTAINS OF ROME** *Philips PB 606* 27 1

HUGO and LUIGI *US, orchestra and chorus, leaders – Hugo Peretti and Luigi Creatore (Singles: 2 weeks)* pos/wks

24 Jul 59 **LA PLUME DE MA TANTE** *RCA 1127* 29 2

Alan HULL *UK, male vocalist, d. 17 Nov 1995 (Albums: 3 weeks)* pos/wks

28 Jul 73 **PIPEDREAM** *Charisma CAS 1069* 29 3

See also LINDISFARNE

HUMAN LEAGUE (105 Top 500)
Early-1980s UK pop sensation. Fronted by Phil Oakey (b. 2 Oct 1955, Sheffield) (v/syn) and joined in 1980 by vocalists Joanne Catherall and Susanne Sulley. The group, which also topped the US chart, won Best Newcomers at the 1982 Brit Awards. Best-selling single: 'Don't You Want Me' 1,430,000 (Singles: 156 weeks, Albums: 263 weeks) pos/wks

3 May 80 **HOLIDAY 80 (DOUBLE SINGLE) (re)** *Virgin SV 105* 46 10
21 Jun 80 **EMPIRE STATE HUMAN** *Virgin VS 351* 62 2
28 Feb 81 **BOYS AND GIRLS** *Virgin VS 395* 48 4
2 May 81 **THE SOUND OF THE CROWD** *Virgin VS 416* 12 10
8 Aug 81 ● **LOVE ACTION (I BELIEVE IN LOVE)** *Virgin VS 435* 3 13
10 Oct 81 ● **OPEN YOUR HEART** *Virgin VS 453* 6 9
5 Dec 81 ★ **DON'T YOU WANT ME** *Virgin VS 466* ◆ ▲ 1 13
9 Jan 82 ● **BEING BOILED** *EMI FAST 4* 6 9
20 Nov 82 ● **MIRROR MAN** *Virgin VS 522* 2 10
23 Apr 83 ● **(KEEP FEELING) FASCINATION** *Virgin VS 569* 2 9
5 May 84 **THE LEBANON (re)** *Virgin VS 672* 11 7
30 Jun 84 **LIFE ON YOUR OWN** *Virgin VS 688* 16 6
17 Nov 84 **LOUISE** *Virgin VS 723* 13 10
23 Aug 86 ● **HUMAN** *Virgin VS 880* ▲ 8 8
22 Nov 86 **I NEED YOUR LOVING** *Virgin VS 900* 72 1
15 Oct 88 **LOVE IS ALL THAT MATTERS** *Virgin VS 1025* 41 5
18 Aug 90 **HEART LIKE A WHEEL** *Virgin VS 1262* 29 5
7 Jan 95 ● **TELL ME WHEN** *East West YZ 882CD1* 6 9
18 Mar 95 **ONE MAN IN MY HEART** *East West YZ 904CD1* 13 8
17 Jun 95 **FILLING UP WITH HEAVEN** *East West YZ 944CD1* 36 2
28 Oct 95 **DON'T YOU WANT ME (re-mix)** *Virgin VSCDT 1557* 16 3
20 Jan 96 **STAY WITH ME TONIGHT** *East West EW 020CD* 40 2
11 Aug 01 **ALL I EVER WANTED** *Papillon BTFLYS 0012* 47 1
31 May 80 **TRAVELOGUE** *Virgin V 2160* 16 42
22 Aug 81 **REPRODUCTION** *Virgin V 2133* 34 23
24 Oct 81 ★ **DARE** *Virgin V 2192* 1 72
17 Jul 82 ● **LOVE AND DANCING** *Virgin OVED 6* [1] 3 52
19 May 84 ● **HYSTERIA** *Virgin V 2315* 3 18
20 Sep 86 ● **CRASH** *Virgin V 2391* 7 6
12 Nov 88 ● **GREATEST HITS** *Virgin HLTV 1* 3 24
22 Sep 90 **ROMANTIC?** *Virgin V 2624* 24 2
4 Feb 95 ● **OCTOPUS** *East West 4509987502* 6 12
11 Nov 95 **GREATEST HITS** *Virgin CDV 2792* 28 8
18 Aug 01 **SECRETS** *Papillon BTFLYCD 0019* 44 1
27 Sep 03 **THE VERY BEST OF THE HUMAN LEAGUE** *Virgin HLCDX2* 24 3

[1] League Unlimited Orchestra

'Holiday 80 (Double Single)' reached its peak position only on re-entry in 1982. Tracks on double single: Being Boiled / Marianne / Rock and Roll – Nightclubbing / Dancevision *Both Greatest Hits albums are different*

HUMAN MOVEMENT featuring Sophie MOLETA *UK, male production duo and Australia, female vocalist (Singles: 1 week)* pos/wks

3 Feb 01 **LOVE HAS COME AGAIN** *Renaissance Recordings RENCDS 005* 53 1

HUMAN NATURE
Australia, male vocal group (Singles: 7 weeks) pos/wks

10 May 97 **WISHES** *Epic 6644485* 44 1
30 Aug 97 **WHISPER YOUR NAME** *Epic 6649465* 53 1
10 Mar 01 **HE DON'T LOVE YOU** *Epic 6708922* 18 4
30 Jun 01 **WHEN WE WERE YOUNG** *Epic 6713792* 43 1

HUMAN RESOURCE

Holland, male instrumental / production group (Singles: 14 weeks) pos/wks

14 Sep 91	**DOMINATOR** *R&S RSUK 4*	36	7
21 Dec 91	**THE COMPLETE DOMINATOR (re-mix)** *R&S RSUK 4X*	18	7

HUMANOID

UK, male producer – Brian Dougans (Singles: 14 weeks) pos/wks

26 Nov 88	**STAKKER HUMANOID** *Westside WSR 12*	17	8
22 Apr 89	**SLAM** *Westside WSR 14*	54	2
8 Aug 92	**STAKKER HUMANOID (re-issue)** *Jumpin' + Pumpin' TOT 27*	40	3
3 Mar 01	**STAKKER HUMANOID (re-mix)** *Jumpin' + Pumpin' CDSTOT 43*	65	1

See also FUTURE SOUND OF LONDON

HUMATE

Germany, male production trio (Singles: 4 weeks) pos/wks

30 Jan 99	**LOVE STIMULATION** *Deviant DVNT 22CDS*	18	4

HUMBLE PIE *UK, male vocal / instrumental group – includes Peter Frampton (Singles: 10 weeks, Albums: 10 weeks)* pos/wks

23 Aug 69 ●	**NATURAL BORN BUGIE** *Immediate IM 082*	4	10
6 Sep 69	**AS SAFE AS YESTERDAY IS** *Immediate IMSP 025*	32	1
22 Jan 72	**ROCKING AT THE FILLMORE** *A&M AMLH 63506*	32	2
15 Apr 72	**SMOKIN'** *A&M AMLS 64342*	28	5
7 Apr 73	**EAT IT** *A&M AMLS 6004*	34	2

See also Peter FRAMPTON

Engelbert HUMPERDINCK (77 Top 500)

Internationally popular cabaret entertainer and easy-on-the-ear vocalist, b. Arnold Dorsey, 2 May 1936, Madras, India. After a slow career start, an unlikely name change helped him to become one of the biggest-earning performers of the 1960s. This Vegas veteran was the UK's biggest-selling artist of 1967 and has reportedly amassed a personal fortune of £100m. Best-selling single: 'Release Me' 1,365,000 (Singles: 239 weeks, Albums: 255 weeks) pos/wks

26 Jan 67 ★	**RELEASE ME** *Decca F 12541* ◆	1	56
25 May 67 ●	**THERE GOES MY EVERYTHING** *Decca F 12610*	2	29
23 Aug 67 ★	**THE LAST WALTZ** *Decca F 12655* ◆	1	27
10 Jan 68 ●	**AM I THAT EASY TO FORGET** *Decca F 12722*	3	13
24 Apr 68 ●	**A MAN WITHOUT LOVE** *Decca F 12770*	2	15
25 Sep 68 ●	**LES BICYCLETTES DE BELSIZE** *Decca F 12834*	5	15
5 Feb 69 ●	**THE WAY IT USED TO BE** *Decca F 12879*	3	14
9 Aug 69	**I'M A BETTER MAN (FOR HAVING LOVED YOU)** *Decca F 12957*	15	13
15 Nov 69 ●	**WINTER WORLD OF LOVE** *Decca F 12980*	7	13
30 May 70	**MY MARIE** *Decca F 13032*	31	7
12 Sep 70	**SWEETHEART (re)** *Decca F 13068*	22	7
11 Sep 71	**ANOTHER TIME, ANOTHER PLACE** *Decca F 13212*	13	12
4 Mar 72	**TOO BEAUTIFUL TO LAST** *Decca F 13281*	14	10
20 Oct 73	**LOVE IS ALL (re)** *Decca F 13443*	44	4
30 Jan 99	**QUANDO QUANDO QUANDO** *The Hit Label HLC 15*	40	3
6 May 00	**HOW TO WIN YOUR LOVE** *Universal TV 8822682*	59	1
20 May 67 ●	**RELEASE ME** *Decca SKL 4868*	6	58
25 Nov 67 ●	**THE LAST WALTZ** *Decca SKL 4901*	3	33
3 Aug 68 ●	**A MAN WITHOUT LOVE** *Decca SKL 4939*	3	45
1 Mar 69 ●	**ENGELBERT** *Decca SKL 4985*	3	8
6 Dec 69 ●	**ENGELBERT HUMPERDINCK** *Decca SKL 5030*	5	23
11 Jul 70	**WE MADE IT HAPPEN** *Decca SKL 5054*	17	11
18 Sep 71	**ANOTHER TIME ANOTHER PLACE** *Decca SKL 5097*	48	1
26 Feb 72	**LIVE AT THE RIVIERA LAS VEGAS** *Decca TXS 105*	45	1
21 Dec 74 ★	**ENGELBERT HUMPERDINCK – HIS GREATEST HITS** *Decca SKL 5198*	1	34
4 May 85	**GETTING SENTIMENTAL** *Telstar STAR 2254*	35	10
4 Apr 87	**THE ENGELBERT HUMPERDINCK COLLECTION** *Telstar STAR 2294*	35	9
10 Jun 95	**LOVE UNCHAINED** *EMI CDEMTV 94*	16	6
8 Apr 00 ●	**AT HIS VERY BEST** *Universal Music TV 8449742*	5	14
20 Oct 01	**I WANT TO WAKE UP WITH YOU** *Universal Music TV 149462*	42	2

HUNDRED REASONS *UK, male vocal / instrumental group (Singles: 12 weeks, Albums: 7 weeks)* pos/wks

18 Aug 01	**EP TWO** *Columbia 6713922*	47	1
15 Dec 01	**EP THREE** *Columbia 6720782*	37	2
9 Mar 02	**IF I COULD** *Columbia 6724402*	19	3
18 May 02	**SILVER** *Columbia 6726642*	15	3
28 Sep 02	**FALTER** *Columbia 6731452*	38	1
15 Nov 03	**THE GREAT TEST** *Columbia 6743762*	29	2
1 Jun 02 ●	**IDEAS ABOVE OUR STATION** *Columbia 5081482*	6	7

Tracks on EP Two: Remmus / Soapbox / Shine. Tracks on EP Three: I'll Find You / Sunny / Slow Motion

Peter HUNNIGALE – See ARSENAL FC

Geraldine HUNT *Canada, female vocalist (Singles: 5 weeks)* pos/wks

25 Oct 80	**CAN'T FAKE THE FEELING** *Champagne FIZZ 501*	44	5

Lisa HUNT – See LOVESTATION

Marsha HUNT *US, female vocalist (Singles: 3 weeks)* pos/wks

21 May 69	**WALK ON GILDED SPLINTERS** *Track 604 030*	46	2
2 May 70	**KEEP THE CUSTOMER SATISFIED** *Track 604 037*	41	1

Tommy HUNT *US, male vocalist (Singles: 17 weeks)* pos/wks

11 Oct 75	**CRACKIN' UP** *Spark SRL 1132*	39	5
21 Aug 76	**LOVING ON THE LOSING SIDE** *Spark SRL 1146*	28	9
4 Dec 76	**ONE FINE MORNING** *Spark SRL 1148*	44	3

HUNTER featuring Ruby TURNER *UK, male gladiator / vocalist and UK, female vocalist (Singles: 1 week)* pos/wks

9 Dec 95	**SHAKABOOM!** *Telstar HUNTCD 1*	64	1

Alfonzo HUNTER

US, male rap / instrumentalist (Singles: 2 weeks) pos/wks

22 Feb 97	**JUST THE WAY** *Cooltempo CDCOOL 326*	38	2

Ian HUNTER

UK, male vocalist (Singles: 10 weeks, Albums: 26 weeks) pos/wks

3 May 75	**ONCE BITTEN TWICE SHY** *CBS 3194*	14	10
12 Apr 75	**IAN HUNTER** *CBS 80710*	21	15
29 May 76	**ALL AMERICAN ALIEN BOY** *CBS 81310*	29	4
5 May 79	**YOU'RE NEVER ALONE WITH A SCHIZOPHRENIC** *Chrysalis CHR 1214*	49	3
26 Apr 80	**WELCOME TO THE CLUB** *Chrysalis CJT 6*	61	2
29 Aug 81	**SHORT BACK 'N' SIDES** *Chrysalis CHR 1326*	79	2

See also MOTT THE HOOPLE

Tab HUNTER

US, male actor / vocalist – Andrew Arthur Kelm (Singles: 30 weeks) pos/wks

8 Feb 57 ★	**YOUNG LOVE** *London HLD 8380* ▲	1	18
12 Apr 57 ●	**NINETY-NINE WAYS (re)** *London HLD 8410*	5	12

Terry HUNTER *US, male DJ / producer (Singles: 1 week)* pos/wks

26 Jul 97	**HARVEST FOR THE WORLD** *Delirious DELICD 4*	48	1

Steve 'Silk' HURLEY *US, male producer (Singles: 9 weeks)* pos/wks

10 Jan 87 ★	**JACK YOUR BODY** *DJ International LON 117*	1	9

See also VOICES OF LIFE; JM SILK

HURLEY & TODD *UK / South Africa, male production duo – Ross Hurley and Drew Todd (Singles: 2 weeks)* pos/wks

29 Apr 00	**SUNSTORM** *Multiply CDMULTY 58*	38	2

HURRAH! *UK, male vocal / instrumental group (Albums: 1 week)* pos/wks

28 Feb 87	**TELL GOD I'M HERE** *Kitchenware 208 201*	71	1

HURRICANE – See PUFF DADDY

HURRICANE #1 *UK, male vocal / instrumental group (Singles: 17 weeks, Albums: 3 weeks)*

		pos/wks
10 May 97	**STEP INTO MY WORLD** *Creation CRESCD 253*	29 2
5 Jul 97	**JUST ANOTHER ILLUSION** *Creation CRESCD 264*	35 2
6 Sep 97	**CHAIN REACTION** *Creation CRESCD 271*	30 2
1 Nov 97	**STEP INTO MY WORLD (re-mix)** *Creation CRESCD 276*	19 3
21 Feb 98	**ONLY THE STRONGEST WILL SURVIVE** *Creation CRERSCD 285*	19 6
24 Oct 98	**RISING SIGN** *Creation CRESCD 303*	47 1
3 Apr 99	**THE GREATEST HIGH** *Creation CRESCD 309*	43 1
27 Sep 97	HURRICANE #1 *Creation CRECD 206*	11 2
1 May 99	ONLY THE STRONG WILL SURVIVE *Creation CRECD 237*	55 1

HURRICANES – See JOHNNY and the HURRICANES

Phil HURTT *US, male vocalist (Singles: 5 weeks)*

		pos/wks
11 Nov 78	**GIVING IT BACK** *Fantasy FTC 161*	36 5

HUSAN – See BHANGRA KNIGHTS vs HUSAN

HÜSKER DÜ *US, male vocal / instrumental group (Albums: 1 week)*

		pos/wks
14 Feb 87	WAREHOUSE: SONGS AND STORIES *Warner Bros. 925 5441*	72 1

See also Bob MOULD; SUGAR

HUSTLERS CONVENTION featuring Dave LAUDAT and Ondrea DUVERNEY *UK, male production duo with male vocalist and US, female vocalist (Singles: 1 week)*

		pos/wks
20 May 95	**DANCE TO THE MUSIC** *Stress CDSTR 53*	71 1

See also FULL INTENTION; SEX-O-SONIQUE; DISCO TEX presents CLOUDBURST

Willie HUTCH *US, male vocalist (Singles: 8 weeks)*

		pos/wks
4 Dec 82	**IN AND OUT** *Motown TMG 1285*	51 7
6 Jul 85	**KEEP ON JAMMIN'** *Motown ZB 40173*	73 1

June HUTTON *US, female vocalist, d. 2 May 1973 (Singles: 7 weeks)*

		pos/wks
7 Aug 53 ●	**SAY YOU'RE MINE AGAIN (re)** *Capitol CL 13918*	6 7

HYBRID *UK, male production trio (Singles: 5 weeks, Albums: 1 week)*

		pos/wks
10 Jul 99	**FINISHED SYMPHONY** *Distinctive DISNCD 52*	58 1
11 Sep 99	**IF I SURVIVE** *Distinctive DISNCD 55* [1]	52 1
3 Jun 00	**KID 2000** *Virgin / EMI VTS CD2* [2]	32 2
20 Sep 03	**TRUE TO FORM** *Distinctive DISNCD 111* [3]	59 1
25 Sep 99	WIDE ANGLE *Distinctive DISNCD 54*	45 1

[1] Hybrid featuring Julee Cruise [2] Hybrid featuring Chrissie Hynde [3] Hybrid featuring Peter Hook

HYDRAULIC DOGS – See DJD presents HYDRAULIC DOGS

Brian HYLAND *US, male vocalist (Singles: 72 weeks)*

		pos/wks
7 Jul 60 ●	**ITSY BITSY TEENIE WEENIE YELLOW POLKADOT BIKINI** *London HLR 9161* ▲	8 13
20 Oct 60	**FOUR LITTLE HEELS** *London HLR 9203*	29 6
10 May 62 ●	**GINNY COME LATELY** *HMV POP 1013*	5 15
2 Aug 62 ●	**SEALED WITH A KISS** *HMV POP 1051*	3 15
8 Nov 62	**WARMED OVER KISSES** *HMV POP 1079*	28 6
27 Mar 71	**GYPSY WOMAN (re)** *Uni UN 530*	42 6
28 Jun 75 ●	**SEALED WITH A KISS (re-issue)** *ABC 4059*	7 11

Sheila HYLTON *Jamaica, female vocalist (Singles: 12 weeks)*

		pos/wks
15 Sep 79	**BREAKFAST IN BED** *United Artists BP 304*	57 5
17 Jan 81	**THE BED'S TOO BIG WITHOUT YOU** *Island WIP 6671*	35 7

Phyllis HYMAN *US, female vocalist, d. 30 Jun 1995 (Singles: 9 weeks, Albums: 1 week)*

		pos/wks
16 Feb 80	**YOU KNOW HOW TO LOVE ME** *Arista ARIST 323*	47 6
12 Sep 81	**YOU SURE LOOK GOOD TO ME** *Arista ARIST 424*	56 3
20 Sep 86	LIVING ALL ALONE *Philadelphia International PHIL 4001*	97 1

Dick HYMAN TRIO *US, male instrumental trio – Dick Hyman, keyboards (Singles: 10 weeks)*

		pos/wks
16 Mar 56 ●	**THEME FROM 'THE THREEPENNY OPERA'** *MGM 890*	9 10

Chrissie HYNDE *US, female vocalist / instrumentalist (Singles: 38 weeks)*

		pos/wks
3 Aug 85 ★	**I GOT YOU BABE** *DEP International DEP20* [1]	1 13
18 Jun 88 ●	**BREAKFAST IN BED** *DEP International DEP29* [1]	6 11
12 Oct 91	**SPIRITUAL HIGH (STATE OF INDEPENDENCE)** *Arista 114528* [2]	66 2
23 Jan 93	**SPIRITUAL HIGH (STATE OF INDEPENDENCE) (re-mix)** *Arista 74321 127712* [2]	47 2
18 Mar 95 ★	**LOVE CAN BUILD A BRIDGE** *London CO CD1* [3]	1 8
3 Jun 00	**KID 2000** *Virgin / EMI VTS CD2* [4]	32 2

[1] UB40 featuring Chrissie Hynde [2] Moodswings featuring Chrissie Hynde [3] Cher, Chrissie Hynde and Neneh Cherry with Eric Clapton [4] Hybrid featuring Chrissie Hynde

See also PRETENDERS

HYPER GO GO *UK, male instrumental / production duo – Jamie Diplock and Alex Bell (Singles: 15 weeks)*

		pos/wks
22 Aug 92	**HIGH** *Deconstruction 74321110497*	30 5
31 Jul 93	**NEVER LET GO** *Positiva CDTIV 3*	45 3
5 Feb 94	**RAISE** *Positiva CDTIV 9*	36 2
26 Nov 94	**IT'S ALRIGHT** *Positiva CDTIV 20*	49 1
6 Apr 96	**DO WATCHA DO** *Avex UK AVEXCD 24* [1]	54 1
12 Oct 96	**HIGH (re-mix)** *Distinctive DISNCD 24*	32 2
12 Apr 97	**DO WATCHA DO (re-mix)** *Distinctive DISNCD 28* [1]	60 1

[1] Hyper Go Go and Adeva

HYPERLOGIC *UK, male instrumental / production trio (Singles: 3 weeks)*

		pos/wks
29 Jul 95	**ONLY ME** *Systematic SYSCD 15*	35 2
9 May 98	**ONLY ME (re-mix)** *Tidy Trax TIDY 113CD1*	48 1

HYPERSTATE *UK, male / female vocal / instrumental duo (Singles: 1 week)*

		pos/wks
6 Feb 93	**TIME AFTER TIME** *M & G MAGCD 34*	71 1

HYPNOSIS *UK, male production / instrumental duo - Stewart and Bradley Palmer (Albums: 16 weeks)*

		pos/wks
17 Aug 96	VOICES OF TRANQUILITY *Dino DINCD 123*	16 12
15 Mar 97	VOICES OF TRANQUILITY – VOLUME 2 *Dino DINCD 135*	32 4

See also BLOWING FREE; HARMONIUM; IN TUNE; JAMES BOYS; RAINDANCE; SCHOOL OF EXCELLENCE

HYPNOTIST *UK, male producer – Caspar Pound (Singles: 5 weeks)*

		pos/wks
28 Sep 91	**THE HOUSE IS MINE** *Rising High RSN 4*	65 2
21 Dec 91	**THE HARDCORE EP** *Rising High RSN 13*	68 3

Tracks on The Hardcore EP: Hardcore U Know the Score / The Ride / Night of the Livin' E Heads / God of the Universe

HYSTERIC EGO *UK, male producer – Rob White (Singles: 8 weeks)*

		pos/wks
31 Aug 96	**WANT LOVE** *WEA WEA 070CD*	28 4
21 Jun 97	**MINISTRY OF LOVE** *WEA WEA 094CD*	39 2
28 Feb 98	**WANT LOVE – THE REMIXES** *WEA WEA 150CD*	46 1
13 Feb 99	**TIME TO GET BACK** *WEA WEA 198CD*	50 1

HYSTERICS
UK, male vocal / instrumental group (Singles: 5 weeks)

Date	Title / Label	pos	wks
12 Dec 81	**JINGLE BELLS LAUGHING ALL THE WAY** *Record Delivery KA 5*	44	5

HYSTERIX
UK, male / female vocal / instrumental group (Singles: 4 weeks)

Date	Title / Label	pos	wks
7 May 94	**MUST BE THE MUSIC** *Deconstruction 74321207362*	40	3
18 Feb 95	**EVERYTHING** *Deconstruction 74321236882*	65	1

I AM KLOOT
UK, male vocal / instrumental group (Singles: 2 weeks, Albums: 1 week)

Date	Title / Label	pos	wks
14 Jun 03	**LIFE IN A DAY** *Echo ECSCD 140*	43	1
20 Sep 03	**3 FEET TALL** *Echo ECDCD 143*	46	1
27 Sep 03	I AM KLOOT *Echo ECHCD46*	68	1

I KAMANCHI
UK, male production duo – Krust and Die (Singles: 1 week)

Date	Title / Label	pos	wks
14 Jun 03	**NEVER CAN TELL / SOUL BEAT CALLING** *Full Cycle FCY 052*	69	1

I-LEVEL
UK, male vocal / instrumental group (Singles: 9 weeks, Albums: 4 weeks)

Date	Title / Label	pos	wks
16 Apr 83	**MINEFIELD** *Virgin VS 563*	52	6
18 Jun 83	**TEACHER** *Virgin VS 595*	56	3
9 Jul 83	I-LEVEL *Virgin V 2270*	50	4

I MONSTER
UK, male production / vocal duo – Dean Honer and Jarrod Gosling (Singles: 6 weeks)

Date	Title / Label	pos	wks
16 Jun 01	**DAYDREAM IN BLUE** *Instant Karma KARMA 7 CD*	20	6

IQ
UK, male vocal / instrumental group (Albums: 1 week)

Date	Title / Label	pos	wks
22 Jun 85	THE WAKE *Sahara SAH 136*	72	1

Janis IAN
US, female vocalist (Singles: 10 weeks)

Date	Title / Label	pos	wks
17 Nov 79	**FLY TOO HIGH** *CBS 7936*	44	7
28 Jun 80	**THE OTHER SIDE OF THE SUN** *CBS 8611*	44	3

IAN VAN DAHL
Belgium, male / female production / vocal group – leader – AnneMie Coenen (Singles: 46 weeks, Albums: 7 weeks)

Date	Title / Label	pos	wks
21 Jul 01 ●	**CASTLES IN THE SKY** *Nulife 74321867142*	3	16
22 Dec 01 ●	**WILL I** *Nulife 74321903402*	5	13
1 Jun 02 ●	**REASON** *Nulife 74321938722*	8	8
12 Oct 02	**TRY** *Nulife 74321967942*	15	5
1 Nov 03	**I CAN'T LET YOU GO** *Nulife 82876570712*	20	4
8 Jun 02 ●	ACE *NuLife 74321934812*	7	7

ICE CUBE
US, male rapper – O'Shea Jackson (Singles: 23 weeks, Albums: 11 weeks)

Date	Title / Label	pos	wks
27 Mar 93	**IT WAS A GOOD DAY** *Fourth & Broadway BRCD 270*	27	4
7 Aug 93	**CHECK YO SELF** *Fourth & Broadway BRCD 283* [1]	36	4
11 Sep 93	**WICKED** *Fourth & Broadway BRCD 282*	62	1
18 Dec 93	**REALLY DOE** *Fourth & Broadway BRCD 302*	66	1
26 Mar 94	**YOU KNOW HOW WE DO IT (re)** *Fourth & Broadway BRCD 303*	41	5
27 Aug 94	**BOP GUN (ONE NATION)** *Fourth & Broadway BRCD 308* [2]	22	3
11 Mar 95	**HAND OF THE DEAD BODY** *Virgin America VUSCD 88* [3]	41	2
15 Apr 95	**NATURAL BORN KILLAZ** *Death Row A 8197CD* [4]	45	2
22 Mar 97	**THE WORLD IS MINE** *Jive JIVECD 419*	60	1
28 Jul 90	AMERIKKKA'S MOST WANTED *Fourth & Broadway BRLP 551*	48	5
9 Mar 91	KILL AT WILL *Fourth & Broadway BRLM 572*	66	3
5 Dec 92	THE PREDATOR *Fourth & Broadway BRCD 592* ▲	73	1
18 Dec 93	LETHAL INJECTION *Fourth & Broadway BRCD 609*	52	1
1 Apr 00	WAR & PEACE – VOL. II (THE PEACE DISC) *Priority CDPTY 183*	56	1

[1] Ice Cube featuring Das EFX [2] Ice Cube featuring George Clinton [3] Scarface featuring Ice Cube [4] Dr Dre and Ice Cube

ICE MC
UK, male rapper – Ian Campbell (Singles: 5 weeks)

Date	Title / Label	pos	wks
6 Aug 94	**THINK ABOUT THE WAY (BOM DIGI DIGI BOM...)** *WEA YZ 829CD*	42	2
8 Apr 95	**IT'S A RAINY DAY** *Eternal YZ 902CD*	73	1
14 Sep 96	**BOM DIGI BOM (THINK ABOUT THE WAY) (re-issue)** *Eternal WEA 073CD*	38	2

ICE-T
US, male rapper – Tracy Morrow (Singles: 29 weeks, Albums: 15 weeks)

Date	Title / Label	pos	wks
18 Mar 89	**HIGH ROLLERS** *Sire W 7574*	63	2
17 Feb 90	**YOU PLAYED YOURSELF** *Sire W 9994*	64	2
29 Sep 90	**SUPERFLY 1990** *Capitol CL 586* [1]	48	3
8 May 93	**I AIN'T NEW TA THIS** *Rhyme Syndicate SYNDD 1*	62	2
18 Dec 93	**THAT'S HOW I'M LIVIN'** *Rhyme Syndicate SYNDD 2*	21	6
9 Apr 94	**GOTTA LOTTA LOVE** *Rhyme Syndicate SYNDD 3*	24	4
10 Dec 94	**BORN TO RAISE HELL** *Fox 74321230152* [2]	47	2
1 Jun 96	**I MUST STAND** *Rhyme Syndicate SYNDD 5*	23	3
7 Dec 96	**THE LANE** *Rhyme Syndicate SYNDD 6*	18	5
21 Oct 89	THE ICEBERG / FREEDOM OF SPEECH *Warner Bros. WX 316*	42	2
25 May 91	OG – ORIGINAL GANGSTER *Sire WX 412*	38	4
3 Apr 93	HOME INVASION *Rhyme Syndicate RSYND 1*	15	7
8 Jun 96	VI: RETURN OF THE REAL *Virgin RSYND 3*	26	2

[1] Curtis Mayfield and Ice-T [2] Motörhead / Ice-T / Whitfield Crane

ICEBERG SLIMM
UK, male rapper – Duane Dyer (Singles: 2 weeks)

Date	Title / Label	pos	wks
7 Oct 00	**NURSERY RHYMES** *Polydor 5877632*	37	2

ICEHOUSE
Australia, male vocal / instrumental group (Singles: 28 weeks, Albums: 7 weeks)

Date	Title / Label	pos	wks
5 Feb 83	**HEY LITTLE GIRL** *Chrysalis CHS 2670*	17	10
23 Apr 83	**STREET CAFE** *Chrysalis COOL 1*	62	4
3 May 86	**NO PROMISES** *Chrysalis CHS 2978*	72	1
29 Aug 87	**CRAZY (re)** *Chrysalis CHS 3156*	38	9
14 May 88	**ELECTRIC BLUE** *Chrysalis CHS 3239*	53	4
5 Mar 83	LOVE IN MOTION *Chrysalis CHR 1390*	64	6
2 Apr 88	MAN OF COLOURS *Chrysalis CHR 1592*	93	1

ICICLE WORKS
UK, male vocal / instrumental group – lead vocal Ian McNabb (Singles: 28 weeks, Albums: 19 weeks)

Date	Title / Label	pos	wks
24 Dec 83	**LOVE IS A WONDERFUL COLOUR** *Beggars Banquet BEG 99*	15	8
10 Mar 84	**BIRDS FLY (WHISPER TO A SCREAM) / IN THE CAULDRON OF LOVE** *Beggars Banquet BEG 108*	53	4
26 Jul 86	**UNDERSTANDING JANE** *Beggars Banquet BEG 160*	52	3

4 Oct 86	**WHO DO YOU WANT FOR YOUR LOVE?** *Beggars Banquet BEG 172*	**54**	4
14 Feb 87	**EVANGELINE** *Beggars Banquet BEG 181*	**53**	4
30 Apr 88	**LITTLE GIRL LOST** *Beggars Banquet BEG 215*	**59**	4
17 Mar 90	**MOTORCYCLE RIDER** *Epic WORKS 100*	**73**	1
31 Mar 84	**THE ICICLE WORKS** *Beggars Banquet BEGA 50*	**24**	6
28 Sep 85	**THE SMALL PRICE OF A BICYCLE** *Beggars Banquet BEGA 61*	**55**	3
1 Mar 86	**SEVEN SINGLES DEEP** *Beggars Banquet BEGA 71*	**52**	2
21 Mar 87	**IF YOU WANT TO DEFEAT YOUR ENEMY SING HIS SONG** *Beggars Banquet BEGA 78*	**28**	4
14 May 88	**BLIND** *Beggars Banquet IWA 2*	**40**	3
5 Sep 92	**THE BEST OF THE ICICLE WORKS** *Beggars Banquet BEGA 124CD*	**60**	1

ICON *UK, male / female vocal / instrumental duo (Singles: 1 week)* pos/wks

15 Jun 96	**TAINTED LOVE** *Eternal WEA 057CD*	**51**	1

IDEAL *UK, male producer – Jon Da Silva (Singles: 2 weeks)* pos/wks

6 Aug 94	**HOT** *Cleveland City CLECD 13019*	**49**	2

IDEAL U.S. featuring LIL' MO

US, male vocal group and female vocalist (Singles: 3 weeks) pos/wks

23 Sep 00	**WHATEVER** *Virgin VUSCD172*	**31**	3

IDES OF MARCH

US, male vocal / instrumental group (Singles: 9 weeks) pos/wks

6 Jun 70	**VEHICLE** *Warner Bros. WB 7378*	**31**	9

Eric IDLE featuring Richard WILSON

UK, male actors / vocalists (Singles: 3 weeks) pos/wks

17 Dec 94	**ONE FOOT IN THE GRAVE** *Victa CDVICTA 1*	**50**	3

See also MONTY PYTHON

IDLEWILD *UK, male vocal / instrumental group (Singles: 30 weeks, Albums: 13 weeks)* pos/wks

9 May 98	**A FILM FOR THE FUTURE** *Food CDFOOD 111*	**53**	1
25 Jul 98	**EVERYONE SAYS YOU'RE SO FRAGILE** *Food CDFOOD 113*	**47**	1
24 Oct 98	**I'M A MESSAGE** *Food CDFOOD 114*	**41**	1
13 Feb 99	**WHEN I ARGUE I SEE SHAPES** *Food CDFOOD 116*	**19**	2
2 Oct 99	**LITTLE DISCOURAGE** *Food CDFOOD 124*	**24**	2
8 Apr 00	**ACTUALLY IT'S DARKNESS** *Food CDFOOD127*	**23**	3
24 Jun 00	**THESE WOODEN IDEAS** *Food CDFOOD 132*	**32**	3
28 Oct 00	**ROSEABILITY** *Food CDFOODS 134*	**38**	2
4 May 02 ●	**YOU HELD THE WORLD IN YOUR ARMS** *Parlophone CDRS 6575*	**9**	4
13 Jul 02	**AMERICAN ENGLISH** *Parlophone CDRS 6582*	**15**	7
2 Nov 02	**LIVE IN A HIDING PLACE** *Parlophone CDRS 6587*	**26**	2
22 Feb 03	**A MODERN WAY OF LETTING GO** *Parlophone CDR 6598*	**28**	2
7 Nov 98	**HOPE IS IMPORTANT** *Food FOODCD 28*	**53**	1
22 Apr 00	**100 BROKEN WINDOWS** *Food FOODCD 32*	**15**	4
27 Jul 02 ●	**THE REMOTE PART** *Parlophone 5402430*	**3**	8

Billy IDOL (316 Top 500)

Snarling rock 'n' roll rebel of the 1980s. Former vocalist of punk hitmakers Generation X, b. William Broad, 30 Nov 1955, Middlesex, UK. He had his greatest success in the US, where four singles reached the Top 10 and 'Mony Mony' reached No.1 (Singles: 106 weeks, Albums: 100 weeks) pos/wks

11 Sep 82	**HOT IN THE CITY** *Chrysalis CHS 2625*	**58**	4
24 Mar 84	**REBEL YELL** *Chrysalis IDOL 2*	**62**	2
30 Jun 84	**EYES WITHOUT A FACE** *Chrysalis IDOL 3*	**18**	11
29 Sep 84	**FLESH FOR FANTASY** *Chrysalis IDOL 4*	**54**	3
13 Jul 85 ●	**WHITE WEDDING** *Chrysalis IDOL 5*	**6**	15
14 Sep 85 ●	**REBEL YELL (re-issue)** *Chrysalis IDOL 6*	**6**	12
4 Oct 86	**TO BE A LOVER** *Chrysalis IDOL 8*	**22**	8
7 Mar 87	**DON'T NEED A GUN** *Chrysalis IDOL 9*	**26**	5
13 Jun 87	**SWEET SIXTEEN** *Chrysalis IDOL 10*	**17**	9
3 Oct 87 ●	**MONY MONY** *Chrysalis IDOL 11* ▲	**7**	10
16 Jan 88	**HOT IN THE CITY (re-mix)** *Chrysalis IDOL 12*	**13**	9
13 Aug 88	**CATCH MY FALL** *Chrysalis IDOL 13*	**63**	3
28 Apr 90	**CRADLE OF LOVE** *Chrysalis IDOL 14*	**34**	4
11 Aug 90	**L.A. WOMAN** *Chrysalis IDOL 15*	**70**	2
22 Dec 90	**PRODIGAL BLUES** *Chrysalis IDOL 16*	**47**	4
26 Jun 93	**SHOCK TO THE SYSTEM** *Chrysalis CDCHS 3994*	**30**	3
10 Sep 94	**SPEED** *Fox 74321223472*	**47**	2
8 Jun 85 ●	**VITAL IDOL** *Chrysalis CUX 1502*	**7**	34
28 Sep 85	**REBEL YELL** *Chrysalis CHR 1450*	**36**	11
1 Nov 86 ●	**WHIPLASH SMILE** *Chrysalis CDL 1514*	**8**	20
2 Jul 88 ●	**IDOL SONGS: 11 OF THE BEST** *Chrysalis BILTVD 1*	**2**	25
12 May 90	**CHARMED LIFE** *Chrysalis CHR 1735*	**15**	8
10 Jul 93	**CYBERPUNK** *Chrysalis CDCHR 6000*	**20**	2

The IDOLS *UK, male / female vocal group (Singles: 1 week)* pos/wks

27 Dec 03 ●	**HAPPY XMAS (WAR IS OVER)** *S 82876583822*	**5**	1+

Frank IFIELD (251 Top 500)

Early 60s superstar, b. 30 Nov 1937, Coventry, UK, and raised in Australia. This pop vocalist / yodeller had four No.1s in 12 months with revivals of US standards. Unlike many of his early 1960s UK contemporaries, his records also did well internationally. Best-selling single: 'I Remember You' 1,096,000 (Singles: 163 weeks, Albums: 83 weeks) pos/wks

19 Feb 60	**LUCKY DEVIL (re)** *Columbia DB 4399*	**22**	8
29 Sep 60	**GOTTA GET A DATE** *Columbia DB 4496*	**49**	1
5 Jul 62 ★	**I REMEMBER YOU** *Columbia DB 4856* ◆	**1**	28
25 Oct 62 ★	**LOVESICK BLUES** *Columbia DB 4913*	**1**	17
24 Jan 63 ★	**THE WAYWARD WIND** *Columbia DB 4960*	**1**	13
11 Apr 63 ●	**NOBODY'S DARLIN' BUT MINE** *Columbia DB 7007*	**4**	16
27 Jun 63 ★	**CONFESSIN' (THAT I LOVE YOU)** *Columbia DB 7062*	**1**	16
17 Oct 63	**MULE TRAIN** *Columbia DB 7131*	**22**	6
9 Jan 64 ●	**DON'T BLAME ME** *Columbia DB 7184*	**8**	13
23 Apr 64	**ANGRY AT THE BIG OAK TREE** *Columbia DB 7263*	**25**	8
23 Jul 64	**I SHOULD CARE** *Columbia DB 7319*	**33**	3
1 Oct 64	**SUMMER IS OVER** *Columbia DB 7355*	**25**	6
19 Aug 65	**PARADISE** *Columbia DB 7655*	**26**	9
23 Jun 66	**NO ONE WILL EVER KNOW** *Columbia DB 7940*	**25**	4
8 Dec 66	**CALL HER YOUR SWEETHEART** *Columbia DB 8078*	**24**	11
7 Dec 91	**SHE TAUGHT ME HOW TO YODEL** *EMI 7YODEL 1* [1]	**40**	4
16 Feb 63 ●	**I'LL REMEMBER YOU** *Columbia 33SX 1467*	**3**	36
21 Sep 63 ●	**BORN FREE** *Columbia 33SX 1462*	**3**	32
28 Mar 64 ●	**BLUE SKIES** *Columbia 55SX 1588*	**10**	12
19 Dec 64 ●	**GREATEST HITS** *Columbia 33SX 1633*	**9**	3

[1] Frank Ifield featuring the Backroom Boys

Enrique IGLESIAS (440 Top 500)

Multi-award-winning Latin superstar; b. 8 May 1975, Madrid, Spain – son of Julio Iglesias. Together they're the only father and son who both topped the UK singles chart. In the last three years of the 20th century, he sold 13 million albums and earned 132 platinum discs around the globe (Singles: 79 weeks, Albums: 75 weeks) pos/wks

11 Sep 99 ●	**BAILAMOS** *Interscope IND 97131* ▲	**4**	9
18 Dec 99	**RHYTHM DIVINE** *Interscope 4972242*	**45**	2
14 Oct 00 ●	**COULD I HAVE THIS KISS FOREVER** *Arista 74321795992* [1]	**7**	8
2 Feb 02 ★	**HERO** *Interscope IND 97671* [2] ■	**1**	19
27 Apr 02	**ESCAPE (import)** *Interscope 4976922* [2]	**71**	2
25 May 02 ●	**ESCAPE** *Interscope 4977062* [2]	**3**	14
7 Sep 02	**LOVE TO SEE YOU CRY** *Interscope IND 97760*	**12**	7
7 Dec 02	**MAYBE** *Interscope 4978222* [2]	**12**	9
26 Apr 03	**TO LOVE A WOMAN** *Mercury 0779082* [3]	**19**	4
29 Nov 03	**ADDICTED** *Interscope 9814327*	**11**	5+
26 Jan 02 ★	**ESCAPE** *Interscope 4931822*	**1**	71
6 Dec 03	**SEVEN** *Interscope / Polydor 9861477*	**13**	4+

[1] Whitney Houston and Enrique Iglesias [2] Enrique [3] Lionel Richie featuring Enrique Iglesias

Julio IGLESIAS (245 Top 500)

Spain's most successful vocalist of all time with reported worldwide sales of more than 225 million albums; b. 23 Sep 1943, Madrid. Suave singer was still adding to his hits and awards in the late 1990s, and his son Enrique is currently one of the world's top-selling artists (Singles: 75 weeks, Albums: 175 weeks) pos/wks

24 Oct 81 ★	**BEGIN THE BEGUINE (VOLVER A EMPEZAR)** *CBS A 1612*	**1**	14

6 Mar 82 ● **QUIEREME MUCHO (YOURS)** *CBS A 1939* 3 9
9 Oct 82 **AMOR** *CBS A 2801* 32 7
9 Apr 83 **HEY!** *CBS JULIO 1* 31 7
7 Apr 84 **TO ALL THE GIRLS I'VE LOVED BEFORE** *CBS A 4252* [1] 17 10
7 Jul 84 **ALL OF YOU** *CBS A 4522* [2] 43 8
6 Aug 88 ● **MY LOVE** *CBS JULIO 2* [3] 5 11
4 Jun 94 **CRAZY (re)** *Columbia 6603695* 43 5
26 Nov 94 **FRAGILE (re)** *Columbia 6610192* 53 4
7 Nov 81 **DE NINA A MUJER** *CBS 85063* 43 5
28 Nov 81 ● **BEGIN THE BEGUINE** *CBS 85462* 5 28
16 Oct 82 **AMOR** *CBS 25103* 14 14
2 Jul 83 ● **JULIO** *CBS 10038* 5 17
1 Sep 84 **1100 BEL AIR PLACE** *CBS 86308* 14 14
19 Oct 85 **LIBRA** *CBS 26623* 61 4
3 Sep 88 **NON STOP** *CBS 460990 1* 33 14
1 Dec 90 **STARRY NIGHT** *CBS 4672841* 27 20
28 May 94 ● **CRAZY** *Columbia 4747382* 6 37
12 Aug 95 ● **LA CARRETERA** *Columbia 4807042* 6 6
30 Nov 96 **TANGO** *Columbia 4866752* 56 3
7 Nov 98 **MY LIFE – THE GREATEST HITS** *Columbia 4910902* 18 9
22 Jul 00 **NOCHE DE CUATRO LUNAS** *Columbia 4974222* 32 3
19 Jul 03 **LOVE SONGS** *Columbia 5126042* 64 1

[1] Julio Iglesias and Willie Nelson [2] Julio Iglesias and Diana Ross [3] Julio Iglesias featuring Stevie Wonder

IGNORANTS *UK, male vocal duo (Singles: 3 weeks)* pos/wks

25 Dec 93 **PHAT GIRLS** *Spaghetti CIOCD 8* 59 3

IIO *US, male / female production / vocal duo – Marcus Moser and Nadia Li (Singles: 15 weeks)* pos/wks

10 Nov 01 ● **RAPTURE** *Made / Data / MoS DATA 27CDS* 2 12
14 Jun 03 **AT THE END** *Free 2 Air 0148065F2A* 20 3

IKARA COLT
UK, male / female vocal / instrumental group (Singles: 1 week) pos/wks

2 Mar 02 **RUDD** *Fantastic Plastic FPS 029* 72 1

IL PADRINOS featuring Jocelyn BROWN
UK, male production duo – Dave Lee and Danny Rampling with US, female vocalist (Singles: 1 week) pos/wks

7 Sep 02 **THAT'S HOW GOOD YOUR LOVE IS** *Defected DFTD 057CDS* 54 1

See also HED BOYS; Li KWAN; RAVEN MAIZE; Joey NEGRO; Z FACTOR; JAKATTA; AKABU featuring Linda CLIFFORD; PHASE II

ILLEGAL MOTION featuring Simone CHAPMAN
UK, male / female vocal / instrumental duo (Singles: 1 week) pos/wks

9 Oct 93 **SATURDAY LOVE** *Arista 74321163032* 67 1

ILLICIT featuring GRAM'MA FUNK
UK, male production duo with US, female vocalist (Singles: 1 week) pos/wks

2 Sep 00 **CHEEKY ARMADA** *Yola YOLACDX 01* 72 1

ILS *UK, male producer (Singles: 1 week)* pos/wks

23 Feb 02 **NEXT LEVEL** *Marine Parade MAPA 012* 75 1

IMAANI *UK, female vocalist – Imaani Saleem (aka Melanie Crosdale) (Singles: 7 weeks)* pos/wks

9 May 98 **WHERE ARE YOU** *EMI CDEM 510* 15 7

IMAGINATION (282 Top 500)
Distinctive London-based trio, which created a unique blend of soul and dance music: Leee John (v), Ashley Ingram (v/k), Errol Kennedy (d). One of the most original British acts of the early 1980s, they were fronted by a charismatic and flamboyant lead singer (Singles: 105 weeks, Albums: 122 weeks) pos/wks

16 May 81 ● **BODY TALK** *R & B RBS 201* 4 18
5 Sep 81 **IN AND OUT OF LOVE** *R & B RBS 202* 16 9
14 Nov 81 **FLASHBACK** *R & B RBS 206* 16 13
6 Mar 82 ● **JUST AN ILLUSION** *R & B RBS 208* 2 11
26 Jun 82 ● **MUSIC AND LIGHTS** *R & B RBS 210* 5 9
25 Sep 82 **IN THE HEAT OF THE NIGHT** *R & B RBS 211* 22 8
11 Dec 82 **CHANGES** *R & B RBS 213* 31 8
4 Jun 83 **LOOKING AT MIDNIGHT** *R & B RBS 214* 29 7
5 Nov 83 **NEW DIMENSIONS** *R & B RBS 216* 56 3
26 May 84 **STATE OF LOVE** *R & B RBS 218* 67 2
24 Nov 84 **THANK YOU MY LOVE** *R & B RBS 219* 22 15
16 Jan 88 **INSTINCTUAL** *RCA PB 41697* 62 2
24 Oct 81 **BODY TALK** *R & B RBLP 1001* 20 53
11 Sep 82 ● **IN THE HEAT OF THE NIGHT** *R & B RBLP 1002* 7 29
14 May 83 ● **NIGHT DUBBING** *R & B RBDUB 1* 9 20
12 Nov 83 **SCANDALOUS** *R & B RBLP 1004* 25 8
12 Aug 89 ● **IMAGINATION – ALL THE HITS** *Stylus SMR 985* 4 12

IMAJIN *US, male vocal group (Singles: 7 weeks)* pos/wks

27 Jun 98 **SHORTY (YOU KEEP PLAYING WITH MY MIND)** *Jive 0521212* [1] 22 3
20 Feb 99 **NO DOUBT** *Jive 0521772* 42 2
24 Apr 99 **BOUNCE, ROCK, SKATE, ROLL** *Jive 0522142* 45 1
12 Feb 00 **FLAVA** *Jive 9250012* 64 1

[1] Imajin featuring Keith Murray

Natalie IMBRUGLIA (436 Top 500)
Australian actor turned sultry pop singer b. 4 Feb 1975, Sydney. 'Neighbours' star (1991-94) won six Arias (Australian music awards) in 1998, and two Brits in 1999. Although only a No.2 hit, the Grammy-nominated 'Torn' is among the UK's all-time Top 100 best-sellers (Singles: 53 weeks, Albums: 102 weeks) pos/wks

8 Nov 97 ● **TORN** *RCA 74321527982* 2 17
14 Mar 98 ● **BIG MISTAKE** *RCA 74321566782* 2 10
6 Jun 98 **WISHING I WAS THERE** *RCA 74321585062* 19 5
17 Oct 98 ● **SMOKE** *RCA 74321621942* 5 7
10 Nov 01 **THAT DAY (re)** *RCA 74321896792* 11 5
23 Mar 02 ● **WRONG IMPRESSION** *RCA 74321928352* 10 7
3 Aug 02 **BEAUTY ON THE FIRE** *RCA 74321947022* 26 2
6 Dec 97 ● **LEFT OF THE MIDDLE** *RCA 74321544412* 5 87
17 Nov 01 **WHITE LILIES ISLAND** *RCA 74321891212* 15 15

IMMACULATE FOOLS *UK, male vocal / instrumental group (Singles: 4 weeks, Albums: 4 weeks)* pos/wks

26 Jan 85 **IMMACULATE FOOLS** *A&M AM 227* 51 4
11 May 85 **HEARTS OF FORTUNE** *A&M AMA 5030* 65 4

IMMATURE featuring SMOOTH
US, male vocal group and US, female vocalist (Singles: 2 weeks) pos/wks

16 Mar 96 **WE GOT IT** *MCA MCSTD 48009* 26 2

IMPALAS
US, male vocal group (Singles: 1 week) pos/wks

21 Aug 59 **SORRY (I RAN ALL THE WAY HOME)** *MGM 1015* 28 1

IMPEDANCE
UK, male producer – Daniel Haydon (Singles: 4 weeks) pos/wks

11 Nov 89 **TAINTED LOVE** *Jumpin' & Pumpin' TOT 4* 54 4

IMPERIAL DRAG
UK, male vocal / instrumental group (Singles: 1 week) pos/wks

12 Oct 96 **BOY OR A GIRL** *Columbia 6632992* 54 1

IMPERIAL TEEN
US, male / female vocal / instrumental group (Singles: 1 week) pos/wks

7 Sep 96 **YOU'RE ONE** *Slash LASCD 57* 69 1

See also FAITH NO MORE

IMPERIALS *US, male vocal group (Singles: 9 weeks)* pos/wks

24 Dec 77 **WHO'S GONNA LOVE ME** *Power Exchange PX 266* 17 9

IMPERIALS QUARTET – *See Elvis PRESLEY*

IMPOSTER – *See Elvis COSTELLO*

IMPRESSIONS *US, male vocal group (Singles: 10 weeks)* pos/wks

		pos	wks
22 Nov 75	**FIRST IMPRESSIONS** *Curtom K 16638*	16	10

IN CROWD
UK, male vocal / instrumental group (Singles: 1 week) pos/wks

		pos	wks
20 May 65	**THAT'S HOW STRONG MY LOVE IS** *Parlophone R 5276*	48	1

IN TUA NUA
Ireland, male / female vocal / instrumental group (Singles: 2 weeks) pos/wks

		pos	wks
14 May 88	**ALL I WANTED** *Virgin VS 1072*	69	2

IN TUNE *UK, male instrumental / production duo – Bradley and Stewart Palmer (Albums: 3 weeks)* pos/wks

		pos	wks
17 Jun 95	**ACOUSTIC MOODS** *Global Television RADCD 13*	21	3

See also BLOWING FREE; HYPNOSIS; IN TUNE; JAMES BOYS; RAINDANCE; SCHOOL OF EXCELLENCE

INAURA *UK, male vocal / instrumental group (Singles: 1 week)* pos/wks

		pos	wks
18 May 96	**COMA AROMA** *EMI CDEM 421*	57	1

INCANTATION *UK, male instrumental group (Singles: 12 weeks, Albums: 52 weeks)* pos/wks

		pos	wks
4 Dec 82	**CACHARPAYA (ANDES PUMPSA DAESI)** *Beggars Banquet BEG 84*	12	12
11 Dec 82 ●	**CACHARPAYA (PANPIPES OF THE ANDES)** *Beggars Banquet BEGA 39*	9	26
17 Dec 83	**DANCE OF THE FLAMES** *Beggars Banquet BEGA 49*	61	7
28 Dec 85	**BEST OF INCANTATION – MUSIC FROM THE ANDES** *West Five CODA 19*	28	19

INCOGNITO *UK, male / female vocal / instrumental group (Singles: 38 weeks, Albums: 19 weeks)* pos/wks

		pos	wks
15 Nov 80	**PARISIENNE GIRL** *Ensign ENY 44*	73	2
29 Jun 91 ●	**ALWAYS THERE** *Talkin Loud TLK 10* [1]	6	9
14 Sep 91	**CRAZY FOR YOU** *Talkin Loud TLK 14* [2]	59	2
6 Jun 92	**DON'T YOU WORRY 'BOUT A THING** *Talkin Loud TLK 21*	19	6
15 Aug 92	**CHANGE** *Talkin Loud TLK 26*	52	2
21 Aug 93	**STILL A FRIEND OF MINE** *Talkin Loud TLKCD 42*	47	2
20 Nov 93	**GIVIN' IT UP** *Talkin Loud TLKCD 44*	43	2
12 Mar 94	**PIECES OF A DREAM** *Talkin Loud TLKCD 46*	35	2
27 May 95	**EVERYDAY** *Talkin Loud TLKCD 55*	23	3
5 Aug 95	**I HEAR YOUR NAME** *Talkin Loud TLKCD 56*	42	3
11 May 96	**JUMP TO MY LOVE / ALWAYS THERE (re-recording)** *Talkin Loud TLCD 7*	29	3
26 Oct 96	**OUT OF THE STORM** *Talkin Loud TLCD 14*	57	1
10 Apr 99	**NIGHTS OVER EGYPT** *Talkin Loud TLCD 40*	56	1
18 Apr 81	**JAZZ FUNK** *Ensign ENVY 504*	28	8
27 Jul 91	**INSIDE LIFE** *Talkin Loud 8485461*	44	2
4 Jul 92	**TRIBES VIBES AND SCRIBES** *Talkin Loud 5123632*	41	2
6 Nov 93	**POSITIVITY** *Talkin Loud 5182602*	55	2
17 Jun 95	**100 DEGREES AND RISING** *Talkin Loud 5280002*	11	4
1 Jun 96	**REMIXED** *Talkin Loud 5323092*	56	1

[1] Incognito featuring Jocelyn Brown [2] Incognito featuring Chyna

INCREDIBLE STRING BAND
UK, male / female vocal / instrumental group (Albums: 37 weeks) pos/wks

		pos	wks
21 Oct 67	**5000 SPIRITS OR THE LAYERS OF THE ONION** *Elektra EUKS 257*	25	5
6 Apr 68 ●	**HANGMAN'S BEAUTIFUL DAUGHTER** *Elektra EVKS7 258*	5	21
20 Jul 68	**THE INCREDIBLE STRING BAND** *Elektra EKL 254*	34	3
24 Jan 70	**CHANGING HORSES** *Elektra EKS 74057*	30	1
9 May 70	**I LOOKED UP** *Elektra 2469002*	30	4
31 Oct 70	**U** *Elektra 2665001*	34	2
30 Oct 71	**LIQUID ACROBAT AS REGARDS THE AIR** *Island ILPS 9172*	46	1

INCUBUS *US, male vocal / instrumental group (Singles: 8 weeks, Albums: 4 weeks)* pos/wks

		pos	wks
20 May 00	**PARDON ME** *Epic 6693462*	61	1
23 Jun 01	**DRIVE** *Epic 6713782*	40	2
2 Feb 02	**WISH YOU WERE HERE** *Epic 6722552*	27	3
14 Sep 02	**ARE YOU IN?** *Epic 6728482*	34	2
3 Nov 01	**MORNING VIEW** *Epic 5040612*	15	4

INDEEP *US, male / female vocal / rap group (Singles: 11 weeks)* pos/wks

		pos	wks
22 Jan 83	**LAST NIGHT A DJ SAVED MY LIFE** *Sound of New York SNY 1*	13	9
14 May 83	**WHEN BOYS TALK** *Sound of New York SNY 3*	67	2

INDIA *US, female vocalist – Linda Caballero (Singles: 15 weeks)* pos/wks

		pos	wks
26 Feb 94	**LOVE AND HAPPINESS (YEMAYA Y OCHUN)** *Cooltempo CDCOOL 287* [1]	50	2
5 Aug 95	**I CAN'T GET NO SLEEP** *A&M 5811412* [2]	44	2
16 Mar 96	**OYE COMO VA** *Media MCSTD 40013* [3]	36	2
8 Feb 97	**RUNAWAY** *Talkin Loud TLCD20* [4]	24	4
19 Jul 97	**OYE COMO VA (re-issue)** *Nukleuz MCSTD 40120* [3]	56	1
31 Jul 99	**TO BE IN LOVE** *Defected DEFECT 5CDS* [5]	23	3
6 Jul 02	**BACKFIRED** *SuSu CDSUSU 4* [6]	62	1

[1] River Ocean featuring India [2] Masters at Work presents India [3] Tito Puente Jr and the Latin Rhythm featuring Tito Puente, India and Cali Aleman [4] Nuyorican Soul featuring India [5] MAW presents India [6] Masters at Work featuring India

INDIAN VIBES
UK, male vocal / instrumental group (Singles: 2 weeks) pos/wks

		pos	wks
24 Sep 94	**MATHAR** *Virgin International DINSD 136*	68	1
2 May 98	**MATHAR (re-mix)** *VC Recordings VCRD 32*	52	1

INDIEN *UK, male / female production / vocal duo – Mark Hadfield and Emma Morton-Smith (Singles: 1 week)* pos/wks

		pos	wks
9 Aug 03	**SHOW ME LOVE** *Concept CDCON 40*	69	1

See also EMMIE

INDIGO GIRLS *US, female vocal / instrumental duo – Amy Ray and Emily Saliers (Albums: 3 weeks)* pos/wks

		pos	wks
11 Jun 94	**SWAMP OPHELIA** *Epic 4759312*	66	1
15 Jul 95	**4.5** *Epic 4804392*	43	2

INDO *US, female vocal duo (Singles: 3 weeks)* pos/wks

		pos	wks
18 Apr 98	**R U SLEEPING** *Satellite 74321568212*	31	3

INDUSTRY STANDARD *UK, male DJ / production duo – Clayton Mitchell and Dave Dellar (Singles: 3 weeks)* pos/wks

		pos	wks
10 Jan 98	**VOLUME 1 (WHAT YOU WANT WHAT YOU NEED)** *Satellite 74321543742*	34	3

INFA RIOT *UK, male vocal / instrumental group (Albums: 4 weeks)* pos/wks

		pos	wks
7 Aug 82	**STILL OUT OF ORDER** *Secret SEC 7*	42	4

INFEXTIOUS – *See Darren STYLES & Mark BREEZE present INFEXTIOUS*

INFINITI – *See GRAND PUBA*

INFRARED vs Gil FELIX *UK / Switzerland, production duo and Brazil, male vocalist / guitarist. (Singles: 1 week)* pos/wks

		pos	wks
4 Oct 03	**CAPOEIRA** *Infrared INFRA 24CD*	67	1

INGRAM *US, male vocal / instrumental group (Singles: 2 weeks)* pos/wks

		pos	wks
11 Jun 83	**SMOOTHIN' GROOVIN'** *Streetwave WAVE 3*	56	2

James INGRAM
US, male vocalist (Singles: 42 weeks, Albums: 19 weeks) pos/wks

		pos	wks
12 Feb 83	**BABY COME TO ME** *Qwest K 15005* [1] ▲	11	10
18 Feb 84	**YAH MO B THERE (2re)** *Qwest 9394* [2]	12	16

11 Jul 87 ● SOMEWHERE OUT THERE *MCA MCA 1132* [3] 8 13
31 Mar 90 SECRET GARDEN *Qwest W 9992* [4] 67 1
16 Apr 94 THE DAY I FALL IN LOVE *Columbia 6600282* [5] 64 2
31 Mar 84 IT'S YOUR NIGHT *Qwest 9239701*....25 17
30 Aug 86 NEVER FELT SO GOOD *Qwest WX 44* 72 2

[1] Patti Austin and James Ingram [2] James Ingram with Michael McDonald [3] Linda Ronstadt and James Ingram [4] Quincy Jones featuring Al B Sure!, James Ingram, El DeBarge and Barry White [5] Dolly Parton and James Ingram

INK SPOTS
US, male vocal group (Singles: 4 weeks) pos/wks

29 Apr 55 ● MELODY OF LOVE *Parlophone R 3977* 10 4

John INMAN *UK, male actor / vocalist (Singles: 6 weeks)* pos/wks

25 Oct 75 ARE YOU BEING SERVED SIR? *DJM DJS 602* 39 6

INMATES
UK, male vocal / instrumental group (Singles: 9 weeks) pos/wks

8 Dec 79 THE WALK *Radar ADA 47* 36 9

INME *UK, male vocal / instrumental group (Singles: 5 weeks, Albums: 2 weeks)* pos/wks

27 Jul 02 UNDERDOSE *Music for Nations CDKUT 195* 66 1
28 Sep 02 FIREFLY *Music for Nations CDKUT 197* 43 1
18 Jan 03 CRUSHED LIKE FRUIT *Music for Nations CDKUT 200* 25 2
26 Apr 03 NEPTUNE *Music for Nations CDKUT 201* 46 1
8 Feb 03 OVERGROWN EDEN *Music for Nations CDMFNX275* 15 2

INNER CIRCLE *Jamaica, male vocal / instrumental group (Singles: 35 weeks, Albums: 2 weeks)* pos/wks

24 Feb 79 EVERYTHING IS GREAT *Island WIP 6472* 37 8
12 May 79 STOP BREAKING MY HEART *Island WIP 6488* 50 3
31 Oct 92 ● SWEAT (A LA LA LA LA LONG) (re) *Magnet 9031776802* 3 19
31 Jul 93 BAD BOYS *Magnet MAG 1017CD* 52 3
10 Sep 94 GAMES PEOPLE PLAY *Magnet MAG 1026CD* 67 2
29 May 93 BAD TO THE BONE *Magnet 9031776772*....44 2

'Sweat (A La La La La Long)' made peak position on re-entry in May 1993

INNER CITY *US, male vocal / production group (Singles: 81 weeks, Albums: 39 weeks)* pos/wks

3 Sep 88 ● BIG FUN *10 TEN 240* [1] 8 14
10 Dec 88 ● GOOD LIFE *10 TEN 249*....4 12
22 Apr 89 ● AIN'T NOBODY BETTER *10 TEN 252* 10 7
29 Jul 89 DO YOU LOVE WHAT YOU FEEL *10 TEN 273* 16 7
18 Nov 89 WATCHA GONNA DO WITH MY LOVIN' *10 TEN 290* 12 9
13 Oct 90 THAT MAN (HE'S ALL MINE) *10 TEN 334*....42 4
23 Feb 91 TILL WE MEET AGAIN *Ten TEN 337* 47 2
7 Dec 91 LET IT REIGN *Ten TEN 392* 51 2
4 Apr 92 HALLELUJAH '92 *Ten TEN 398* 22 4
13 Jun 92 PENNIES FROM HEAVEN *Ten TEN 405* 24 4
12 Sep 92 PRAISE *Ten TENX 408* 59 2
27 Feb 93 TILL WE MEET AGAIN (re-mix) *Ten TENCD 414* 55 1
14 Aug 93 BACK TOGETHER AGAIN *Six6 SIXCD 104* 49 1
5 Feb 94 DO YA *Six6 SIXCD 107* 44 2
9 Jul 94 SHARE MY LIFE *Six6 SIXCD 114* 62 1
10 Feb 96 YOUR LOVE *Six6 SIXCD 127*....28 2
5 Oct 96 DO ME RIGHT *Six6 SIXXCD 2*....47 1
6 Feb 99 ● GOOD LIFE (BUENA VIDA) (re-recording) *Pias Recordings PIASX 002CD* 10 6
20 May 89 ● PARADISE *10 DIX 81*....3 30
10 Feb 90 PARADISE REMIXED *10 XID 81* 17 6
11 Jul 92 PRAISE *Ten 4718862*....52 1
15 May 93 TESTAMENT 93 *Ten CDOVD 438* 33 2

[1] Inner City featuring Kevin Saunderson

INNER SANCTUM
Canada, male producer – Steve Bolton (Singles: 1 week) pos/wks

23 May 98 HOW SOON IS NOW *Malarky MLKD 6* 75 1

INNERZONE ORCHESTRA
US, male producer – Carl Craig (Singles: 1 week) pos/wks

28 Sep 96 BUG IN THE BASSBIN *Mo Wax MW 049CD* 68 1

INNOCENCE *UK, male / female vocal / instrumental group (Singles: 33 weeks, Albums: 20 weeks)* pos/wks

3 Mar 90 NATURAL THING *Cooltempo COOL 201* 16 7
21 Jul 90 SILENT VOICE *Cooltempo COOL 212* 37 5
13 Oct 90 LET'S PUSH IT *Cooltempo COOL 220* 25 6
8 Dec 90 A MATTER OF FACT *Cooltempo COOL 223* 37 7
30 Mar 91 REMEMBER THE DAY *Cooltempo COOL 226* 56 2
20 Jun 92 I'LL BE THERE *Cooltempo COOL 255* 26 3
3 Oct 92 ONE LOVE IN MY LIFETIME *Cooltempo COOL 263* 40 2
21 Nov 92 BUILD *Cooltempo COOL 267* 72 1
10 Nov 90 BELIEF *Cooltempo CTLP 20*....24 19
31 Oct 92 BUILD *Cooltempo CTCD 26*....66 1

INSANE CLOWN POSSE
US, male rap duo (Singles: 2 weeks) pos/wks

17 Jan 98 HALLS OF ILLUSION *Island CID 685* 56 1
6 Jun 98 HOKUS POKUS *Island CIDX 705* 53 1

INSPIRAL CARPETS
UK, male vocal / instrumental group (Singles: 51 weeks, Albums: 36 weeks) pos/wks

18 Nov 89 MOVE *Cow DUNG 6*....49 2
17 Mar 90 THIS IS HOW IT FEELS *Cow DUNG 7* 14 8
30 Jun 90 SHE COMES IN THE FALL *Cow DUNG 10* 27 6
17 Nov 90 ISLAND HEAD (EP) *Cow DUNG 11* 21 4
30 Mar 91 CARAVAN *Cow DUNG 13* 30 5
22 Jun 91 PLEASE BE CRUEL *Cow DUNG 15* 50 2
29 Feb 92 DRAGGING ME DOWN *Cow DUNG 16* 12 5
30 May 92 TWO WORLDS COLLIDE *Cow DUNG 17* 32 2
19 Sep 92 GENERATIONS *Cow DUNG 18T*....28 3
14 Nov 92 BITCHES BREW *Cow DUNG 20T* 36 2
5 Jun 93 HOW IT SHOULD BE *Cow DUNG 22CD* 49 1
22 Jan 94 SATURN 5 *Cow DUNG 23CD* 20 4
5 Mar 94 I WANT YOU *Cow DUNG 24CD* [1]....18 3
7 May 94 UNIFORM *Cow DUNG 26CD* 51 1
16 Sep 95 JOE *Cow DUNG 27CD* 37 2
26 Jul 03 COME BACK TOMORROW *Mute DUNG 31CD* 43 1
5 May 90 ● LIFE *Cow DUNG 8*....2 21
4 May 91 ● THE BEAST INSIDE *Cow DUNG 14*....5 6
17 Oct 92 REVENGE OF THE GOLDFISH *Cow DUNG 19*....17 3
19 Mar 94 ● DEVIL HOPPING *Cow LDUNG 25CD* 10 3
30 Sep 95 THE SINGLES *Cow CDMOOTEL 3*....17 3

[1] Inspiral Carpets featuring Mark E Smith

Tracks on Island Head (EP): Biggest Mountain / Gold Top / Weakness / I'll Keep It In Mind

INSPIRATIONAL CHOIR
US, male / female choir (Singles: 11 weeks, Albums: 4 weeks) pos/wks

22 Dec 84 ABIDE WITH ME *Epic A 4997* 44 5
14 Dec 85 ABIDE WITH ME (re-issue) *Portrait A 4997* 36 6
18 Jan 86 SWEET INSPIRATION *Portrait PRT 10048*....59 4

Label credits the Royal Choral Society

INSPIRATIONS *UK, male instrumentalist – keyboards – Neil Palmer (Albums: 35 weeks)* pos/wks

29 Apr 95 ● PAN PIPE INSPIRATIONS *Pure Music PMCD 7011* 10 10
23 Sep 95 ● PAN PIPE DREAMS *Pure Music PMCD 7016* 10 8
11 Nov 95 PURE EMOTIONS *Pure Music PMCD 7023* 37 4
6 Apr 96 PAN PIPE IMAGES *Telstar TCD 2819* 23 6
12 Oct 96 THE VERY BEST OF THE PAN PIPES *Telstar TCD 2845* 37 7

INSTANT FUNK
US, male vocal / instrumental group (Singles: 5 weeks) pos/wks

20 Jan 79 GOT MY MIND MADE UP *Salsoul SSOL 114*....46 5

INTASTELLA

UK, male / female vocal / instrumental group (Singles: 6 weeks) pos/wks

25 May 91	**DREAM SOME PARADISE** *MCA MCS 1520*	69	1
24 Aug 91	**PEOPLE** *MCA MCS 1559*	74	2
16 Nov 91	**CENTURY** *MCA MCS 1585*	70	2
23 Sep 95	**THE NIGHT** *Planet 3 GXY 2005CD*	60	1

INTELLIGENT HOODLUM *US, male rapper (Singles: 3 weeks)* pos/wks

6 Oct 90	**BACK TO REALITY** *A&M AM 598*	55	3

INTENSO PROJECT

UK, male production / vocal group (Singles: 4 weeks) pos/wks

17 Aug 02	**LUV DA SUNSHINE** *Inferno CDFERN 47*	22	2
26 Jul 03	**YOUR MUSIC** *Concept CDCON 43* [1]	32	2

[1] Intenso Project featuring Laura Jaye

INTERACTIVE

Germany, male instrumental / production group (Singles: 6 weeks) pos/wks

13 Apr 96	**FOREVER YOUNG** *Ffrreedom TABCD 235*	28	4
8 Mar 03	**FOREVER YOUNG (re-mix)** *All Around the World CDGLOBE 253*	37	2

INTERPOL *US, male vocal / instrumental group (Singles: 3 weeks)* pos/wks

23 Nov 02	**OBSTACLE 1** *Matador OLE 5702*	72	1
26 Apr 03	**SAY HELLO TO THE ANGELS / NYC** *Matador OLE 5822*	65	1
27 Sep 03	**OBSTACLE 1 (re-mix)** *Matador OLE 5942*	41	1

INTI ILLIMANI-GUAMARY *Chile, male vocal / instrumental group – pan pipes (Albums: 7 weeks)* pos/wks

17 Dec 83	**THE FLIGHT OF THE CONDOR – ORIGINAL TV SOUNDTRACK** *BBC REB 440*	62	7

INTRUDERS *US, male vocal group (Singles: 21 weeks)* pos/wks

13 Apr 74	**I'LL ALWAYS LOVE MY MAMA** *Philadelphia International PIR 2159*	32	7
6 Jul 74	**WIN, PLACE OR SHOW (SHE'S A WINNER)** *Philadelphia International PIR 2212*	14	9
22 Dec 84	**WHO DO YOU LOVE?** *Streetwave KHAN 34*	65	5

INVADERS OF THE HEART – *See Jah WOBBLE'S INVADERS of the HEART*

INVISIBLE GIRLS – *See Pauline MURRAY and the INVISIBLE GIRLS*

INVISIBLE MAN

UK, male producer – Graham Mew (Singles: 1 week) pos/wks

17 Apr 99	**GIVE A LITTLE LOVE** *Serious SERR 006CD*	48	1

INXS (130 Top 500)

Stadium-packing rock sextet led by Australian Michael Hutchence (b. 22 Jan 1960, Sydney; d. 22 Nov 1997). Both Hutchence and group won Brit awards in 1991, and the video for their US chart-topper 'Need You Tonight' won five MTV awards in 1988 (Singles: 132 weeks, Albums: 240 weeks) pos/wks

19 Apr 86		**WHAT YOU NEED** *Mercury INXS 5*	51	6
28 Jun 86		**LISTEN LIKE THIEVES** *Mercury INXS 6*	46	7
30 Aug 86		**KISS THE DIRT (FALLING DOWN THE MOUNTAIN)** *Mercury INXS 7*	54	3
24 Oct 87		**NEED YOU TONIGHT** *Mercury INXS 8* ▲	58	3
9 Jan 88		**NEW SENSATION** *Mercury INXS 9*	25	6
12 Mar 88		**DEVIL INSIDE** *Mercury INXS 10*	47	5
25 Jun 88		**NEVER TEAR US APART** *Mecury INXS 11*	24	7
12 Nov 88	●	**NEED YOU TONIGHT (re-issue)** *Mercury INXS 12*	2	11
8 Apr 89		**MYSTIFY** *Mercury INXS 13*	14	7
15 Sep 90		**SUICIDE BLONDE** *Mercury INXS 14*	11	6
8 Dec 90		**DISAPPEAR** *Mercury INXS 15*	21	8
26 Jan 91		**GOOD TIMES** *Atlantic A 7751* [1]	18	8
30 Mar 91		**BY MY SIDE** *Mercury INXS 16*	42	4
13 Jul 91		**BITTER TEARS** *Mercury INXS 17*	30	3
2 Nov 91		**SHINING STAR (EP)** *Mercury INXS 18*	27	3
18 Jul 92		**HEAVEN SENT** *Mercury INXS 19*	31	3
5 Sep 92		**BABY DON'T CRY** *Mercury INXS 20*	20	5
14 Nov 92		**TASTE IT** *Mercury INXS 23*	21	4
13 Feb 93		**BEAUTIFUL GIRL** *Mercury INXCD 24*	23	5
23 Oct 93		**THE GIFT** *Mercury INXCD 25*	11	4
11 Dec 93		**PLEASE (YOU GOT THAT . . .)** *Mercury INXCD 26*	50	3
22 Oct 94		**THE STRANGEST PARTY (THESE ARE THE TIMES)** *Mercury INXCD 27*	15	5
22 Mar 97		**ELEGANTLY WASTED** *Mercury INXCD 28*	20	4
7 Jun 97		**EVERYTHING** *Mercury INXDD 29*	71	1
18 Aug 01		**PRECIOUS HEART (re)** *Duty Free / Decode DFTELCD 001* [2]	14	5
3 Nov 01		**I'M SO CRAZY (re)** *Credence CDCRED 016* [3]	19	6
8 Feb 86		**LISTEN LIKE THIEVES** *Mercury MERH 82*	48	15
28 Nov 87	●	**KICK** *Mercury MERH 114*	9	103
6 Oct 90	●	**X** *Mercury 8466681*	2	44
16 Nov 91	●	**LIVE BABY LIVE** *Mercury 5105801*	8	9
15 Aug 92	★	**WELCOME TO WHEREVER YOU ARE** *Mercury 5125072* ■	1	33
13 Nov 93	●	**FULL MOON DIRTY HEARTS** *Mercury 5186372*	3	8
12 Nov 94	●	**THE GREATEST HITS** *Mercury 5262302*	3	22
19 Apr 97		**ELEGANTLY WASTED** *Mercury 5346132*	16	3
26 Oct 02		**DEFINITIVE INXS** *Mercury 0633562*	15	3

[1] Jimmy Barnes and INXS [2] Tall Paul vs Inxs [3] Par-T-One vs Inxs

Tracks on Shining Star (EP): Shining Star / Send a Message (Live) / Faith in Each Other (Live) / Bitter Tears (Live). Although uncredited, 'Please (You Got That...)' is a duet with Ray Charles

See also MAX Q

Tony IOMMI – *See BLACK SABBATH*

Sweetie IRIE – *See ASWAD; SCRITTI POLITTI; Ed CASE*

Tippa IRIE *UK, male vocalist – Anthony Henry (Singles: 14 weeks)* pos/wks

22 Mar 86	**HELLO DARLING** *Greensleeves / UK Bubblers TIPPA 4*	22	7
19 Jul 86	**HEARTBEAT** *Greensleeves / UK Bubblers TIPPA 5*	59	3
15 May 93	**SHOUTING FOR THE GUNNERS** *London LONCD 342* [1]	34	3
8 Jul 95	**STAYING ALIVE 95** *Telstar CDSTAS 2776* [2]	48	1

[1] Arsenal FA Cup Squad featuring Tippa Irie and Peter Hunnigale [2] Fever featuring Tippa Irie

IRON MAIDEN (128 Top 500)

Legendary London-based group named after a medieval torture device. Lead vocalists have included Paul Di'Anno and Blaze Bayley, but it was with front man Bruce Dickinson that they enjoyed a period as one of the world's top metal bands. Their post-Christmas chart-topper 'Bring Your Daughter to the Slaughter' is the lowest first week sale for a No.1 with 29,918 copies (Singles: 168 weeks, Albums: 208 weeks) pos/wks

23 Feb 80		**RUNNING FREE** *EMI 5032*	34	5
7 Jun 80		**SANCTUARY** *EMI 5065*	29	5
8 Nov 80		**WOMEN IN UNIFORM** *EMI 5105*	35	4
14 Mar 81		**TWILIGHT ZONE / WRATH CHILD** *EMI 5145*	31	5
27 Jun 81		**PURGATORY** *EMI 5184*	52	3
26 Sep 81		**MAIDEN JAPAN (EP)** *EMI 5219*	43	4
20 Feb 82	●	**RUN TO THE HILLS** *EMI 5263*	7	10
15 May 82		**THE NUMBER OF THE BEAST** *EMI 5287*	18	8
23 Apr 83		**FLIGHT OF ICARUS** *EMI 5378*	11	6
2 Jul 83		**THE TROOPER** *EMI 5397*	12	7
18 Aug 84		**2 MINUTES TO MIDNIGHT** *EMI 5849*	11	6
3 Nov 84		**ACES HIGH** *EMI 5502*	20	5
5 Oct 85		**RUNNING FREE (LIVE)** *EMI 5532*	19	5
14 Dec 85		**RUN TO THE HILLS (LIVE)** *EMI 5542*	26	6
6 Sep 86		**WASTED YEARS** *EMI 5583*	18	4
22 Nov 86		**STRANGER IN A STRANGE LAND (re)** *EMI 5589*	22	6
26 Mar 88	●	**CAN I PLAY WITH MADNESS** *EMI EM 49*	3	6
13 Aug 88	●	**THE EVIL THAT MEN DO** *EMI EM 64*	5	6
19 Nov 88	●	**THE CLAIRVOYANT** *EMI EM 79*	6	8
18 Nov 89	●	**INFINITE DREAMS (re)** *EMI EM 117*	6	6
22 Sep 90	●	**HOLY SMOKE** *EMI EM 153*	3	4
5 Jan 91	★	**BRING YOUR DAUGHTER . . . TO THE SLAUGHTER** *EMI EMPD 171* ■	1	5
25 Apr 92	●	**BE QUICK OR BE DEAD** *EMI EM 229*	2	4
11 Jul 92		**FROM HERE TO ETERNITY** *EMI EMS 240*	21	4

			pos	wks
13 Mar 93	●	**FEAR OF THE DARK (LIVE)** *EMI CDEMS 263*	8	3
16 Oct 93	●	**HALLOWED BE THY NAME (LIVE)** *EMI CDEM 288*	9	3
7 Oct 95	●	**MAN ON THE EDGE** *EMI CDEMS 398*	10	3
21 Sep 96		**VIRUS** *EMI CDEM 443*	16	3
21 Mar 98		**THE ANGEL AND THE GAMBLER** *EMI CDEM 507*	18	3
20 May 00	●	**THE WICKER MAN** *EMI CDEMS 568*	9	4
4 Nov 00		**OUT OF THE SILENT PLANET** *EMI CDEM 576*	20	3
23 Mar 02	●	**RUN TO THE HILLS (re-recording)** *EMI CDEM 612*	9	4
13 Sep 03	●	**WILDEST DREAMS** *EMI CDEM 627*	6	6
6 Dec 03		**RAINMAKER** *EMI CDEM 633*	13	4+
26 Apr 80	●	**IRON MAIDEN** *EMI EMC 3330*	4	15
28 Feb 81		**KILLERS** *EMI EMC 3357*	12	8
10 Apr 82	★	**THE NUMBER OF THE BEAST** *EMI EMC 3400* ■	1	31
28 May 83	●	**PIECE OF MIND** *EMI EMA 800*	3	18
15 Sep 84	●	**POWERSLAVE** *EMI POWER 1*	2	13
15 Jun 85		**IRON MAIDEN (re-issue)** *Fame FA 4131211*	71	2
26 Oct 85	●	**LIVE AFTER DEATH** *EMI RIP 1*	2	14
11 Oct 86	●	**SOMEWHERE IN TIME** *EMI EMC 3512*	3	12
20 Jun 87		**THE NUMBER OF THE BEAST (re-issue)** *Fame FA 3178*	98	1
23 Apr 88	★	**SEVENTH SON OF A SEVENTH SON** *EMI EMD 1006* ■	1	18
24 Feb 90	●	**RUNNING FREE / SANCTUARY** *EMI IRN 1*	10	4
3 Mar 90	●	**WOMEN IN UNIFORM / TWILIGHT ZONE** *EMI IRN 2*	10	3
10 Mar 90	●	**PURGATORY / MAIDEN JAPAN** *EMI IRN 3*	5	3
17 Mar 90	●	**RUN TO THE HILLS / THE NUMBER OF THE BEAST** *EMI IRN 4*	3	2
24 Mar 90	●	**FLIGHT OF ICARUS / THE TROOPER** *EMI IRN 5*	7	2
31 Mar 90		**2 MINUTES TO MIDNIGHT / ACES HIGH** *EMI IRN 6*	11	2
7 Apr 90	●	**RUNNING FREE (LIVE) / RUN TO THE HILLS (LIVE)** *EMI IRN 7*	9	2
14 Apr 90	●	**WASTED YEARS / STRANGER IN A STRANGE LAND** *EMI IRN 8*	9	2
21 Apr 90	●	**CAN I PLAY WITH MADNESS / THE EVIL THAT MEN DO** *EMI IRN 9*	10	3
28 Apr 90		**THE CLAIRVOYANT / INFINITE DREAMS (LIVE)** *EMI IRN 10*	11	2
13 Oct 90	●	**NO PRAYER FOR THE DYING** *EMI EMD 1017*	2	14
23 May 92	★	**FEAR OF THE DARK** *EMI CDEMD 1032* ■	1	5
3 Apr 93	●	**A REAL LIVE ONE** *EMI CDEMD 1042*	3	4
30 Oct 93		**A REAL DEAD ONE** *EMI CDEMD 1048*	12	3
20 Nov 93		**LIVE AT DONNINGTON** *EMI CDDON 1*	23	1
14 Oct 95	●	**THE X FACTOR** *EMI CDEMD 1087*	8	4
5 Oct 96		**BEST OF THE BEAST** *EMI CDEMD 1097*	16	5
4 Apr 98		**VIRTUAL XI** *EMI 4939152*	16	2
10 Jun 00	●	**BRAVE NEW WORLD** *EMI 5266052*	7	4
6 Apr 02		**ROCK IN RIO** *EMI 5386430*	15	3
16 Nov 02		**EDWARD THE GREAT – THE GREATEST HITS** *EMI 05431032*	57	1
20 Sep 03	●	**DANCE OF DEATH** *EMI 5923402*	2	5

'Run to the Hills' (re-recording) is a live version Entries from Feb to Apr 1990 are double 12-inch singles made ineligible for the singles chart by their retail price

IRONHORSE

Canada, male vocal / instrumental group (Singles: 3 weeks)

			pos	wks
5 May 79		**SWEET LUI-LOUISE** *Scotti Brothers K 11271*	60	3

See also Randy BACHMAN

Big Dee IRWIN

US, male vocalist – Difosco Erwin, d. 27 Aug 1995 (Singles: 17 weeks)

			pos	wks
21 Nov 63	●	**SWINGING ON A STAR** *Colpix PX 11010*	7	17

Single was a vocal duet by Big Dee Irwin and Little Eva (uncredited)

Gregory ISAACS

Jamaica, male vocalist (Albums: 6 weeks)

			pos	wks
12 Sep 81		**MORE GREGORY** *Charisma PREX 9*	93	1
4 Sep 82		**NIGHT NURSE** *Island ILPS 9721*	32	5

Chris ISAAK

US, male vocalist (Singles: 22 weeks, Albums: 38 weeks)

			pos	wks
24 Nov 90	●	**WICKED GAME** *London LON 279*	10	10
2 Feb 91		**BLUE HOTEL** *Reprise W 0005*	17	7
3 Apr 93		**CAN'T DO A THING (TO STOP ME)** *Reprise W 0161CD*	36	3
10 Jul 93		**SAN FRANCISCO DAYS** *Reprise W 0182CD*	62	1
2 Oct 99		**BABY DID A BAD BAD THING** *Reprise W 503CD*	44	1
26 Jan 91	●	**WICKED GAME** *Reprise WX 406*	3	30
24 Apr 93		**SAN FRANCISCO DAYS** *Reprise 9362451162*	12	5
3 Jun 95		**FOREVER BLUE** *Reprise 9362458452*	27	3

ISHA-D

UK, male / female vocal / instrumental duo – Phil Coxon and Beverley Reppion (Singles: 4 weeks)

			pos	wks
22 Jul 95		**STAY (TONIGHT)** *Cleveland City Blues CCBCD 15005*	28	3
5 Jul 97		**STAY (re-issue)** *Satellite 74321498212*	58	1

Ronald ISLEY – *See Warren G; ISLEY BROTHERS; R KELLY; Rod STEWART*

ISLEY BROTHERS

US, male vocal / instrumental group – Ronald, O'Kelly (d. 1986) and Rudolph Isley (Singles: 108 weeks, Albums: 24 weeks)

			pos	wks
25 Jul 63		**TWIST AND SHOUT** *Stateside SS 112*	42	1
28 Apr 66	●	**THIS OLD HEART OF MINE (IS WEAK FOR YOU) (re)** *Tamla Motown TMG 555*	3	17
1 Sep 66		**I GUESS I'LL ALWAYS LOVE YOU** *Tamla Motown TMG 572*	45	2
15 Jan 69		**I GUESS I'LL ALWAYS LOVE YOU (re-issue)** *Tamla Motown TMG 683*	11	9
16 Apr 69	●	**BEHIND A PAINTED SMILE** *Tamla Motown TMG 693*	5	12
25 Jun 69		**IT'S YOUR THING** *Major Minor MM 621*	30	5
30 Aug 69		**PUT YOURSELF IN MY PLACE** *Tamla Motown TMG 708*	13	11
22 Sep 73		**THAT LADY** *Epic EPC 1704*	14	9
19 Jan 74		**HIGHWAYS OF MY LIFE** *Epic EPC 1980*	25	8
25 May 74		**SUMMER BREEZE** *Epic EPC 2244*	16	8
10 Jul 76	●	**HARVEST FOR THE WORLD** *Epic EPC 4369*	10	8
13 May 78		**TAKE ME TO THE NEXT PHASE** *Epic EPC 6292*	50	4
3 Nov 79		**IT'S A DISCO NIGHT (ROCK DON'T STOP)** *Epic EPC 7911*	14	11
16 Jul 83		**BETWEEN THE SHEETS** *Epic A 3513*	52	3
14 Dec 68		**THIS OLD HEART OF MINE** *Tamla Motown STML 11034*	23	6
14 Aug 76		**HARVEST FOR THE WORLD** *Epic EPC 81268*	50	5
14 May 77		**GO FOR YOUR GUNS** *Epic EPC 86027*	46	2
24 Jun 78		**SHOWDOWN** *Epic EPC 86039*	50	1
5 Mar 88		**GREATEST HITS** *Telstar STAR 2306*	41	10

'This Old Heart of Mine (Is Weak for You)' originally peaked at No.47 before making No.3 in Nov 1968

ISLEY JASPER ISLEY

US, male vocal / instrumental group (Singles: 5 weeks)

			pos	wks
23 Nov 85		**CARAVAN OF LOVE** *Epic A 6612*	52	5

ISOTONIK

UK, male producer – Chris Paul (Singles: 9 weeks)

			pos	wks
11 Jan 92		**DIFFERENT STROKES** *Ffrreedom TAB 101*	12	5
2 May 92		**EVERYWHERE I GO / LET'S GET DOWN** *Ffrreedom TAB 108*	25	4

'Let's Get Down' listed only from 9 May 1992

See also Chris PAUL

IT BITES

UK, male vocal / instrumental group (Singles: 21 weeks, Albums: 12 weeks)

			pos	wks
12 Jul 86	●	**CALLING ALL THE HEROES** *Virgin VS 872*	6	12
18 Oct 86		**WHOLE NEW WORLD** *Virgin VS 896*	54	3
23 May 87		**THE OLD MAN AND THE ANGEL** *Virgin VS 941*	72	1
13 May 89		**STILL TOO YOUNG TO REMEMBER** *Virgin VS 1184*	66	3
24 Feb 90		**STILL TOO YOUNG TO REMEMBER (re-issue)** *Virgin VS 1238*	60	2
6 Sep 86		**THE BIG LAD IN THE WINDMILL** *Virgin V 2378*	35	5
2 Apr 88		**ONCE AROUND THE WORLD** *Virgin V 2456*	43	3
24 Jun 89		**EAT ME IN ST LOUIS** *Virgin V 2591*	40	3
31 Aug 91		**THANK YOU AND GOODNIGHT** *Virgin VGD 24233*	59	1

IT'S A BEAUTIFUL DAY

US, male / female vocal / instrumental group (Albums: 3 weeks)

			pos	wks
23 May 70		**IT'S A BEAUTIFUL DAY** *CBS 63722*	58	1
18 Jul 70		**MARRYING MAIDEN** *CBS 66236*	45	2

IT'S IMMATERIAL

UK, male vocal / instrumental group (Singles: 10 weeks, Albums: 3 weeks)

			pos	wks
12 Apr 86		**DRIVING AWAY FROM HOME (JIM'S TUNE)** *Siren SIREN 15*	18	7
2 Aug 86		**ED'S FUNKY DINER (FRIDAY NIGHT, SATURDAY MORNING)** *Siren SIREN 24*	65	3
27 Sep 86		**LIFE'S HARD AND THEN YOU DIE** *Siren SIRENLP 4*	62	3

ITTY BITTY BOOZY WOOZY *Holland, male instrumental / production duo – Addy Van Der Zwan and Koen Groeneveld (Singles: 2 weeks)* pos/wks

25 Nov 95	**TEMPO FIESTA (PARTY TIME)** *Systematic SYSCD 23*	**34**	2

See also KLUBBHEADS

Burl IVES *US, male vocalist, d. 14 Apr 1995 (Singles: 25 weeks)* pos/wks

25 Jan 62 ●	**A LITTLE BITTY TEAR** *Brunswick 05863*	**9**	15
17 May 62	**FUNNY WAY OF LAUGHIN'** *Brunswick 05868*	**29**	10

IVY LEAGUE *UK, male vocal group (Singles: 31 weeks)* pos/wks

4 Feb 65 ●	**FUNNY HOW LOVE CAN BE** *Piccadilly 7N 35222*	**8**	9
6 May 65	**THAT'S WHY I'M CRYING** *Piccadilly 7N 35228*	**22**	8
24 Jun 65 ●	**TOSSING AND TURNING** *Piccadilly 7N 35251*	**3**	13
14 Jul 66	**WILLOW TREE** *Piccadilly 7N 35326*	**50**	1

IZIT
UK, male / female vocal / instrumental group (Singles: 3 weeks) pos/wks

2 Dec 89	**STORIES** *ffrr F 122*	**52**	3

Ray J
US, male vocalist – Willie Ray Norwood Jr (Singles: 12 weeks) pos/wks

17 Oct 98	**THAT'S WHY I LIE** *Atlantic AT 0049CD*	**71**	1
16 Jun 01 ●	**ANOTHER DAY IN PARADISE** *WEA WEA 327CD1* [1]	**5**	10
11 Aug 01	**WAIT A MINUTE** *Atlantic AT 0106CD* [2]	**54**	1

[1] Brandy and Ray J [2] Ray J featuring Lil' Kim

J.A.L.N. BAND
UK / Jamaica, male vocal / instrumental group (Singles: 17 weeks) pos/wks

11 Sep 76	**DISCO MUSIC / I LIKE IT** *Magnet MAG 73*	**21**	9
27 Aug 77	**I GOT TO SING** *Magnet MAG 97*	**40**	4
1 Jul 78	**GET UP (AND LET YOURSELF GO)** *Magnet MAG 118*	**53**	4

JB's ALL STARS
UK, male / female vocal / instrumental group (Singles: 4 weeks) pos/wks

11 Feb 84	**BACKFIELD IN MOTION** *RCA Victor RCA 384*	**48**	4

JC *UK, male producer (Singles: 1 week)* pos/wks

7 Feb 98	**SO HOT** *East West EW 146CD*	**74**	1

JC001 *UK, male rapper (Singles: 4 weeks)* pos/wks

24 Apr 93	**NEVER AGAIN** *AnXious ANX 1012CD*	**67**	2
26 Jun 93	**CUPID** *AnXious ANX 1014CD*	**56**	2

JD – *See SNOOP DOGG*

JD aka 'DREADY'
UK, male vocalist – Karl Jairzhino Daniel (Singles: 1 week) pos/wks

2 Aug 03	**SIGNAL** *Independiente SSB 2MS*	**64**	1

JDS *Italy / UK, male DJ / production duo – Julian Napolitano and Darren Pearce (Singles: 3 weeks)* pos/wks

27 Sep 97	**NINE WAYS** *ffrr FCD 310*	**61**	1
23 May 98	**LONDON TOWN** *Jive 0530042*	**49**	1
3 Mar 01	**NINE WAYS (re-mix)** *ffrr FCD 391*	**47**	1

JFK *UK, male producer (Singles: 3 weeks)* pos/wks

15 Sep 01	**GOOD GOD** *Y2K Y2K 025CD*	**71**	1
26 Jan 02	**WHIPLASH** *Y2K Y2K 027CD*	**47**	1
4 May 02	**THE SOUND OF BLUE** *Y2K Y2K 030CD*	**55**	1

JJ *UK, male / female vocal / instumental duo (Singles: 3 weeks)* pos/wks

9 Feb 91	**IF THIS IS LOVE** *Columbia 6566097*	**55**	3

JJ – *See DJ LUCK & MC NEAT*

JJ72 *Ireland, male / female vocal / instrumental group (Singles: 13 weeks, Albums: 22 weeks)* pos/wks

3 Jun 00	**LONG WAY SOUTH** *Lakota LAK 0015CD*	**68**	1
26 Aug 00	**OXYGEN** *Lakota LAK 0016CD*	**23**	3
4 Nov 00	**OCTOBER SWIMMER** *Lakota LAK 0018CD*	**29**	3
10 Feb 01	**SNOW** *Lakota LAK 0019CD*	**21**	3
12 Oct 02	**FORMULAE** *Lakota / Columbia 6731592*	**28**	2
22 Feb 03	**ALWAYS AND FOREVER** *Columbia 6734322*	**43**	1
9 Sep 00	JJ72 *Lakota LAKCD 0017*	**16**	20
26 Oct 02	I TO SKY *Lakota 5095292*	**20**	2

JKD BAND
UK, male vocal / instrumental group (Singles: 4 weeks) pos/wks

1 Jul 78	**DRAGON POWER** *Satril SAT 132*	**58**	4

JMD – *See TYREE*

JM SILK
US, male vocal / instrumental duo (Singles: 6 weeks) pos/wks

25 Oct 86	**I CAN'T TURN AROUND** *RCA PB 49793*	**62**	3
7 Mar 87	**LET THE MUSIC TAKE CONTROL** *RCA PB 49767*	**47**	3

J PAC
UK, male vocal / instrumental duo (Singles: 2 weeks) pos/wks

22 Jul 95	**ROCK 'N' ROLL (DOLE)** *East West YZ 953CD*	**51**	2

JT and the BIG FAMILY
Italy, male / female vocal / instrumental group (Singles: 8 weeks) pos/wks

3 Mar 90 ●	**MOMENTS IN SOUL** *Champion CHAMP 237*	**7**	8

JT PLAYAZ *UK, male production trio (Singles: 4 weeks)* pos/wks

5 Apr 97	**JUST PLAYIN'** *Pukka CDJTP 1*	**30**	3
2 May 98	**LET'S GET DOWN** *MCA MCSTD 40161*	**64**	1

JTQ
UK, male instrumental group (Singles: 6 weeks, Albums: 5 weeks) pos/wks

3 Apr 93	**LOVE THE LIFE** *Big Life BLRD 93* [1]	**34**	3
3 Jul 93	**SEE A BRIGHTER DAY** *Big Life BLRDA 97* [1]	**49**	2
25 Feb 95	**LOVE WILL KEEP US TOGETHER** *Acid Jazz JAZID 112CD* [2]	**63**	1
1 May 93	SUPERNATURAL FEELING *Big Life BLRCD 21* [1]	**36**	3
29 Oct 94	EXTENDED PLAY *Acid Jazz JAZID 110CD*	**70**	1
11 Mar 95	IN THE HAND OF THE INEVITABLE *Acid Jazz JAZID CD115*	**63**	1

[1] JTQ with Noel McKoy [2] JTQ featuring Alison Limerick [1] JTQ with Noel McKoy [2] James Taylor Quartet

JX *UK, male producer – Jake Williams (Singles: 33 weeks)* pos/wks

Date		Title / Label	pos	wks
2 Apr 94		**SON OF A GUN** *Internal Dance IDC 5*	13	6
1 Apr 95		**YOU BELONG TO ME** *Ffrreedom TABCD 227*	17	5
19 Aug 95	●	**SON OF A GUN (re-mix)** *Ffrreedom TABCD 233*	6	6
18 May 96	●	**THERE'S NOTHING I WON'T DO** *Ffrreedom TABCD 241*	4	13
8 Mar 97		**CLOSE TO YOUR HEART** *Ffrreedom TABCD 245*	18	3

JXL – *See JUNKIE XL*

JA RULE (421 Top 500) *Mobo winner Jeffrey Atkins (hence JA), b. New York, 29 Feb 1976. One of this millennium's most regular transatlantic chart entrants, and one of just five acts to replace themselves at the top of the US chart (Singles: 94 weeks, Albums: 65 weeks)* pos/wks

Date		Title / Label	pos	wks
13 Mar 99		**CAN I GET A...** *Def Jam 5668472* [1]	24	3
3 Mar 01		**BETWEEN YOU AND ME** *Def Jam 5727402* [2]	26	3
10 Nov 01		**LIVIN' IT UP** *Def Jam 5888142* [3]	27	4
10 Nov 01	●	**I'M REAL** *Epic 6720322* [4] ▲	4	15
2 Feb 02	●	**ALWAYS ON TIME** *Def Jam 5889462* [5] ▲	6	13
23 Mar 02	●	**AIN'T IT FUNNY** *Epic 6724922* [6] ▲	4	13
3 Aug 02	●	**LIVIN' IT UP (re-issue)** *Def Jam 0639782* [3]	5	8
24 Aug 02		**RAINY DAYZ** *MCA MCSTD 40288* [7]	17	5
12 Oct 02	●	**DOWN 4 U (2re)** *Murder Inc 0639002* [8]	4	10
21 Dec 02		**THUG LOVIN'** *Def Jam 0637872* [9]	15	8
29 Mar 03		**MESMERIZE** *Murder Inc / Mercury 0779582* [5]	12	8
6 Dec 03	●	**CLAP BACK / REIGNS** *Def Jam / Mercury 9814618*	9	4+
27 Oct 01	●	**PAIN IS LOVE** *Def Jam 5864372* ▲	3	50
30 Nov 02		**THE LAST TEMPTATION** *Def Jam / Mercury 0635432*	14	13
15 Nov 03		**BLOOD IN MY EYE** *Def Jam / Mercury 9861329*	51	2

[1] Jay-Z featuring Amil & Ja Rule [2] Ja Rule featuring Christina Milian [3] Ja Rule featuring Case [4] Jennifer Lopez featuring Ja Rule [5] Ja Rule featuring Ashanti [6] Jennifer Lopez featuring Ja Rule & Caddillac Tah [7] Mary J Blige featuring Ja Rule [8] Irv Gotti presents Ja Rule, Ashanti, Charli Baltimore and Vita [9] Ja Rule featuring Bobby Brown

JACK 'N' CHILL
UK, male instrumental group (Singles: 21 weeks) pos/wks

Date		Title / Label	pos	wks
6 Jun 87	●	**THE JACK THAT HOUSE BUILT (re)** *Oval / 10 / Virgin TEN 174*	6	16
9 Jul 88		**BEATIN' THE HEAT** *10 TEN 234*	42	5

'The Jack That House Built' reached its peak position only on re-entry in Jan 1988

Terry JACKS *Canada, male vocalist (Singles: 21 weeks)* pos/wks

Date		Title / Label	pos	wks
23 Mar 74	★	**SEASONS IN THE SUN** *Bell 1344* ▲	1	12
29 Jun 74	●	**IF YOU GO AWAY** *Bell 1362*	8	9

See also POPPY FAMILY

Chad JACKSON
UK, male DJ / producer – Mark Chadwick (Singles: 10 weeks) pos/wks

Date		Title / Label	pos	wks
2 Jun 90	●	**HEAR THE DRUMMER (GET WICKED)** *Big Wave BWR 36*	3	10

Dee D JACKSON
UK, female vocalist – Deirdre Cozier (Singles: 14 weeks) pos/wks

Date		Title / Label	pos	wks
22 Apr 78	●	**AUTOMATIC LOVER** *Mercury 6007 171*	4	9
2 Sep 78		**METEOR MAN** *Mercury 6007 182*	48	5

Freddie JACKSON
US, male vocalist (Singles: 31 weeks, Albums: 48 weeks) pos/wks

Date		Title / Label	pos	wks
23 Nov 85		**YOU ARE MY LADY** *Capitol CL 379*	49	4
22 Feb 86		**ROCK ME TONIGHT (FOR OLD TIME'S SAKE)** *Capitol CL 358*	18	9
11 Oct 86		**TASTY LOVE** *Capitol CL 428*	73	1
7 Feb 87		**HAVE YOU EVER LOVED SOMEBODY** *Capitol CL 437*	33	6
9 Jul 88		**NICE 'N' SLOW** *Capitol CL 502*	56	2
15 Oct 88		**CRAZY (FOR ME)** *Capitol CL 510*	41	3
5 Sep 92		**ME AND MRS JONES** *Capitol CL 668*	32	5
15 Jan 94		**MAKE LOVE EASY** *RCA 74321179162*	70	1
18 May 85		**ROCK ME TONIGHT** *Capitol EJ 24403161*	27	22
8 Nov 86		**JUST LIKE THE FIRST TIME** *Capitol EST 2023*	30	15
30 Jul 88		**DON'T LET LOVE SLIP AWAY** *Capitol EST 2067*	24	9
17 Nov 90		**DO ME AGAIN** *Capitol EST 2134E*	48	2

Gisele JACKSON *US, female vocalist (Singles: 1 week)* pos/wks

Date		Title / Label	pos	wks
30 Aug 97		**LOVE COMMANDMENTS** *Manifesto FESCD 28*	54	1

Janet JACKSON (64 Top 500) *Multi-award-winning, record-breaking vocalist / performer, b. 16 May 1966, Indiana, US. Although not an overnight sensation, the youngest of the talented Jackson family has amassed a staggering collection of gold albums and singles. Best-selling single 'Together Again' 741,000 (Singles: 288 weeks, Albums: 268 weeks)* pos/wks

Date		Title / Label	pos	wks
22 Mar 86	●	**WHAT HAVE YOU DONE FOR ME LATELY** *A&M AM 308*	3	14
31 May 86		**NASTY** *A&M AM 316*	19	9
9 Aug 86	●	**WHEN I THINK OF YOU** *A&M AM 337* ▲	10	10
1 Nov 86		**CONTROL** *A&M AM 359*	42	5
21 Mar 87	●	**LET'S WAIT AWHILE** *Breakout USA 601*	3	10
13 Jun 87		**PLEASURE PRINCIPLE** *Breakout USA 604*	24	5
14 Nov 87		**FUNNY HOW TIME FLIES (WHEN YOU'RE HAVING FUN)** *A&M Breakout USA 613*	59	2
2 Sep 89		**MISS YOU MUCH** *Breakout USA 663* ▲	22	7
4 Nov 89		**RHYTHM NATION** *Breakout USA 673*	23	5
27 Jan 90		**COME BACK TO ME** *Breakout USA 681*	20	7
31 Mar 90		**ESCAPADE** *Breakout USA 684* ▲	17	7
7 Jul 90		**ALRIGHT** *A&M USA 693*	20	5
8 Sep 90		**BLACK CAT** *A&M AM 587* ▲	15	6
27 Oct 90		**LOVE WILL NEVER DO (WITHOUT YOU)** *A&M AM 700* ▲	34	4
15 Aug 92	●	**THE BEST THINGS IN LIFE ARE FREE** *Perspective PERSS 7400* [1]	2	13
8 May 93	●	**THAT'S THE WAY LOVE GOES** *Virgin VSCDG 1460* ▲	2	10
31 Jul 93		**IF** *Virgin VSCDT 1474*	14	7
20 Nov 93	●	**AGAIN** *Virgin VSCDG 1481* ▲	6	11
12 Mar 94		**BECAUSE OF LOVE** *Virgin VSCDG 1488*	19	4
18 Jun 94		**ANY TIME ANY PLACE** *Virgin VSCDT 1501*	13	5
26 Nov 94		**YOU WANT THIS** *Virgin VSCDT 1519*	14	3
18 Mar 95	●	**WHOOPS NOW / WHAT'LL I DO** *Virgin VSCDT 1533*	9	8
10 Jun 95	●	**SCREAM (re)** *Epic 6620222* [2]	3	13
24 Jun 95		**SCREAM (re-mix)** *Epic 6621277* [2]	43	2
23 Sep 95	●	**RUNAWAY** *A&M 5811972*	6	7
16 Dec 95	●	**THE BEST THINGS IN LIFE ARE FREE (re-mix)** *A&M 5813092* [3]	7	7
6 Apr 96		**TWENTY FOREPLAY** *A&M 5815112*	22	4
4 Oct 97	●	**GOT 'TIL IT'S GONE** *Virgin VSCDG 1666* [4]	6	9
13 Dec 97	●	**TOGETHER AGAIN** *Virgin VSCDG 1670* [5] ▲	4	19
4 Apr 98	●	**I GET LONELY** *Virgin VSCDT 1683* [6]	5	7
27 Jun 98		**GO DEEP** *Virgin VSCDT 1680* [5]	13	5
19 Dec 98		**EVERY TIME** *Virgin VSCDT 1720* [5]	46	1
17 Apr 99		**GIRLFRIEND / BOYFRIEND** *Interscope IND 95640* [7]	11	7
1 May 99	●	**WHAT'S IT GONNA BE?!** *Elektra E3762CD1* [8]	6	7
19 Aug 00	●	**DOESN'T REALLY MATTER** *Def Soul 5629152* ▲	5	11
21 Apr 01	●	**ALL FOR YOU** *Virgin VSCDT 1801* ▲ [5]	3	11
11 Aug 01		**SOMEONE TO CALL MY LOVER** *Virgin VSCDT 1813* [5]	11	5
22 Dec 01		**SON OF A GUN (I BETCHA THINK THIS SONG IS ABOUT YOU) (re)** *Virgin VUSCD 232* [9]	13	9
28 Sep 02	●	**FEEL IT BOY (re)** *Virgin VUSCD 258* [10]	9	7
5 Apr 86	●	**CONTROL** *A&M AMA 5016* ▲	8	72
14 Nov 87		**CONTROL – THE REMIXES** *Breakout MIXLP 1*	20	14
30 Sep 89	●	**JANET JACKSON'S RHYTHM NATION 1814** *A&M AMA 3920* ▲	4	43
29 May 93	★	**JANET / JANET. REMIXED** *Virgin CDV 2720* ■ ▲	1	57
14 Oct 95	●	**DESIGN OF A DECADE 1986-1996** *A&M 5404222*	2	21
18 Oct 97	●	**THE VELVET ROPE** *Virgin CDV 2860* [1] ▲	6	43
5 May 01	●	**ALL FOR YOU** *Virgin CDV 2950* [1] ▲	2	18

[1] Luther Vandross and Janet Jackson with special guests BBD and Ralph Tresvant [2] Michael Jackson and Janet Jackson [3] Luther Vandross and Janet Jackson [4] Janet featuring Q-Tip and Joni Mitchell [5] Janet [6] Janet featuring BLACKstreet [7] BLACKstreet with Janet [8] Busta Rhymes featuring Janet [9] Janet with Carly Simon featuring Missy Elliott [10] Beenie Man featuring Janet [1] Janet

From 25 Mar 95 'Janet' was listed with the remix album 'Janet Remixed'

See also Herb ALPERT and the TIJUANA BRASS

Jermaine JACKSON
US, male vocalist (Singles: 43 weeks, Albums: 12 weeks) pos/wks

Date		Title / Label	pos	wks
10 May 80	●	**LET'S GET SERIOUS** *Motown TMG 1183*	8	11
26 Jul 80		**BURNIN' HOT** *Motown TMG 1194*	32	6

Date		Title / Label	Pos	Wks
30 May 81		**YOU LIKE ME DON'T YOU** *Motown TMG 1222*	41	5
12 May 84		**SWEETEST SWEETEST** *Arista JJK 1*	52	4
27 Oct 84		**WHEN THE RAIN BEGINS TO FALL** *Arista ARIST 584* [1]	68	2
16 Feb 85	●	**DO WHAT YOU DO** *Arista ARIST 609*	6	13
21 Oct 89		**DON'T TAKE IT PERSONAL** *Arista 112634*	69	2
31 May 80		**LET'S GET SERIOUS** *Motown STML 12127*	22	6
12 May 84		**DYNAMITE** *Arista 206 317*	57	6

[1] Jermaine Jackson and Pia Zadora

'Let's Get Serious' features uncredited vocals of Stevie Wonder

See also JACKSONS

Joe JACKSON (438 Top 500)

Many faceted singer / songwriter and pianist, b. 11 Aug 1955, Staffordshire. Unique and critically acclaimed recording artist whose five Grammy nominations ran from 1979 to 2001 (when Symphony No.1 became his first winner). His original 1980s band reunited in 2003 (Singles: 49 weeks, Albums: 106 weeks) pos/wks

Date		Title / Label	Pos	Wks
4 Aug 79		**IS SHE REALLY GOING OUT WITH HIM?** *A&M AMS 7459*	13	9
12 Jan 80	●	**IT'S DIFFERENT FOR GIRLS** *A&M AMS 7493*	5	9
4 Jul 81		**JUMPIN' JIVE** *A&M AMS 8145* [1]	43	5
8 Jan 83	●	**STEPPIN' OUT** *A&M AMS 8262*	6	8
12 Mar 83		**BREAKING US IN TWO** *A&M AM 101*	59	4
28 Apr 84		**HAPPY ENDING** *A&M AM 186*	58	3
7 Jul 84		**BE MY NUMBER TWO** *A&M AM 200*	70	2
7 Jun 86		**LEFT OF CENTER** *A&M AM 320* [2]	32	9
17 Mar 79		**LOOK SHARP** *A&M AMLH 64743*	40	11
13 Oct 79		**I'M THE MAN** *A&M AMLH 64794*	12	16
18 Oct 80		**BEAT CRAZY** *A&M AMLH 64837*	42	3
4 Jul 81		**JUMPIN' LIVE** *A&M AMLH 68530* [1]	14	14
3 Jul 82	●	**NIGHT AND DAY** *A&M AMLH 64906*	3	27
7 Apr 84		**BODY AND SOUL** *A&M AMLX 65000*	14	14
5 Apr 86		**BIG WORLD** *A&M JWA 3*	41	5
7 May 88		**LIVE 1980-86** *A&M AMA 6706*	66	2
29 Apr 89		**BLAZE OF GLORY** *A&M AMA 5249*	36	3
15 Sep 90	●	**STEPPING OUT – THE VERY BEST OF JOE JACKSON** *A&M 3970521*	7	9
11 May 91		**LAUGHTER AND LUST** *Virgin America VUSLP 34*	41	2

[1] Joe Jackson's Jumpin' Jive [2] Suzanne Vega featuring Joe Jackson [1] Joe Jackson's Jumpin' Jive

Michael JACKSON (9 Top 500)

The self-proclaimed 'King of Pop' b. 29 Aug 1958, Indiana, US, is arguably the best-known living musical entertainer. The youngest vocalist (age 11, fronting the Jackson Five) to top the US singles chart, he was also the first artist to enter that chart at No.1 (with 'You Are Not Alone'). In 1991 he became the first US act to enter the UK chart at No.1 since Elvis Presley in 1960 (whose daughter, Lisa Marie, he married in 1994). This outstanding, innovative singer / songwriter and performer has broken countless other records for his singles, albums, videos and tours. 'Thriller' is the world's biggest-selling record with global sales estimates varying between 47 and 51.2 million, including 26 million in the US alone. It topped the US album chart for an unprecedented 37 weeks and had a record 12 Grammy nominations. Also on the album front, 'History' sold more copies in its first week than any previous double album. 'Dangerous' sold a staggering 10 million worldwide in its first month and 'Invincible' returned him to the top in 2001. Both 'Thriller' and 'Bad' have sold more than three million copies in the UK. Jackson, whose private life and physical appearance have attracted much media attention, was the first entertainer to earn more than $100m in a year, and the first to receive an award for selling at least 100 million albums outside of the US. Of his 11 million plus UK single sales, 'Earth Song' was the best-seller with 1,038,821 copies sold (Singles: 512 weeks, Albums: 913 weeks) pos/wks

Date		Title / Label	Pos	Wks
12 Feb 72	●	**GOT TO BE THERE** *Tamla Motown TMG 797*	5	11
20 May 72	●	**ROCKIN' ROBIN** *Tamla Motown TMG 816*	3	14
19 Aug 72	●	**AIN'T NO SUNSHINE** *Tamla Motown TMG 826*	8	11
25 Nov 72	●	**BEN** *Tamla Motown TMG 834* ▲	7	14
18 Nov 78		**EASE ON DOWN THE ROAD** *MCA 396* [1]	45	4
15 Sep 79	●	**DON'T STOP 'TIL YOU GET ENOUGH** *Epic EPC 7763* ▲	3	12
24 Nov 79	●	**OFF THE WALL** *Epic EPC 8045*	7	10
9 Feb 80	●	**ROCK WITH YOU** *Epic EPC 8206* ▲	7	9
3 May 80	●	**SHE'S OUT OF MY LIFE** *Epic EPC 8384*	3	9
26 Jul 80		**GIRLFRIEND** *Epic EPC 8782*	41	5
23 May 81	★	**ONE DAY IN YOUR LIFE** *Motown TMG 976*	1	14
1 Aug 81		**WE'RE ALMOST THERE** *Motown TMG 977*	46	4
6 Nov 82	●	**THE GIRL IS MINE (re)** *Epic EPC A 2729* [2]	8	10
29 Jan 83	★	**BILLIE JEAN** *Epic EPC A 3084* ▲	1	15
9 Apr 83	●	**BEAT IT** *Epic EPC A 3258* ▲	3	12
11 Jun 83	●	**WANNA BE STARTIN' SOMETHIN'** *Epic A 3427*	8	9
23 Jul 83		**HAPPY (LOVE THEME FROM 'LADY SINGS THE BLUES')** *Tamla Motown TMG 986*	52	3
15 Oct 83	●	**SAY SAY SAY** *Parlophone R 6062* [3] ▲	2	15
19 Nov 83	●	**THRILLER** *Epic A 3643*	10	18
31 Mar 84		**P.Y.T. (PRETTY YOUNG THING)** *Epic A 4136*	11	8
2 Jun 84	●	**FAREWELL MY SUMMER LOVE** *Motown TMG 1342*	7	12
11 Aug 84		**GIRL YOU'RE SO TOGETHER** *Motown TMG 1355*	33	8
8 Aug 87	★	**I JUST CAN'T STOP LOVING YOU** *Epic 650202 7* ▲	1	9
26 Sep 87	●	**BAD** *Epic 651155 7* ▲	3	11
5 Dec 87	●	**THE WAY YOU MAKE ME FEEL** *Epic 651275 7* ▲	3	10
20 Feb 88		**MAN IN THE MIRROR** *Epic 651388 7* ▲	21	5
16 Apr 88	●	**I WANT YOU BACK** *Motown ZB 41919* [4]	8	9
28 May 88		**GET IT** *Motown ZB 41883* [5]	37	4
16 Jul 88	●	**DIRTY DIANA** *Epic 651546 7* ▲	4	8
10 Sep 88		**ANOTHER PART OF ME** *Epic 652844 7*	15	6
26 Nov 88	●	**SMOOTH CRIMINAL** *Epic 653026 7*	8	10
25 Feb 89	●	**LEAVE ME ALONE** *Epic 654672 7*	2	9
15 Jul 89		**LIBERIAN GIRL** *Epic 654947 0*	13	6
23 Nov 91	★	**BLACK OR WHITE** *Epic 6575987* ■ ▲	1	10
18 Jan 92		**BLACK OR WHITE (re-mix)** *Epic 6577316*	14	4
15 Feb 92	●	**REMEMBER THE TIME / COME TOGETHER** *Epic 6577747*	3	8
2 May 92	●	**IN THE CLOSET** *Epic 6580187*	8	6
25 Jul 92	●	**WHO IS IT** *Epic 6581797*	10	7
12 Sep 92		**JAM** *Epic 6583607*	13	5
5 Dec 92	●	**HEAL THE WORLD** *Epic 6584887*	2	15
27 Feb 93	●	**GIVE IN TO ME** *Epic 6590692*	2	9
10 Jul 93	●	**WILL YOU BE THERE** *Epic 6592222*	9	8
18 Dec 93		**GONE TOO SOON** *Epic 6599762*	33	5
10 Jun 95	●	**SCREAM (re)** *Epic 6620222* [6]	3	13
24 Jun 95		**SCREAM (re-mix)** *Epic 6621277* [6]	43	2
2 Sep 95	★	**YOU ARE NOT ALONE** *Epic 6623102* ▲	1	15
9 Dec 95	★	**EARTH SONG** *Epic 6626955* ◆ ■	1	17
20 Apr 96	●	**THEY DON'T CARE ABOUT US (2re)** *Epic 6629502*	4	14
24 Aug 96	●	**WHY** *Epic 6629502* [7]	2	9
16 Nov 96	●	**STRANGER IN MOSCOW (re)** *Epic 6637872*	4	11
3 May 97	★	**BLOOD ON THE DANCEFLOOR** *Epic 6644625* ■	1	9
19 Jul 97	●	**HISTORY / GHOSTS** *Epic 6647962*	5	8
20 Oct 01	●	**YOU ROCK MY WORLD** *Epic 6720292*	2	15
22 Dec 01		**CRY** *Epic 6721822*	25	4
6 Dec 03	●	**ONE MORE CHANCE** *Epic 6744802*	5	4+
3 Jun 72		**GOT TO BE THERE** *Tamla Motown STML 11205*	37	5
13 Jan 73		**BEN** *Tamla Motown STML 11220*	17	7
29 Sep 79	●	**OFF THE WALL** *Epic EPC 84368*	5	186
4 Jul 81		**THE BEST OF MICHAEL JACKSON** *Motown STMR 9009*	11	18
18 Jul 81		**ONE DAY IN YOUR LIFE** *Motown STML 12158*	29	8
11 Dec 82	★	**THRILLER** *Epic EPC 85930* ▲	1	190
12 Feb 83		**E.T. – THE EXTRA TERRESTRIAL** *MCA 7000*	82	2
9 Jul 83	★	**18 GREATEST HITS** *Telstar STAR 2232* [1]	1	58
3 Dec 83		**MICHAEL JACKSON 9 SINGLE PACK** *Epic MJ 1*	66	3
9 Jun 84	●	**FAREWELL MY SUMMER LOVE** *Motown ZL 72227*	9	14
15 Nov 86		**DIANA ROSS, MICHAEL JACKSON, GLADYS KNIGHT, STEVIE WONDER. THEIR VERY BEST BACK TO BACK** *PRIORITY TV PTVR 2* [2]	21	10
12 Sep 87	★	**BAD** *Epic EPC 4502901* ■ ▲	1	122
31 Oct 87		**LOVE SONGS** *Telstar STAR 2298* [3]	12	24
26 Dec 87		**THE MICHAEL JACKSON MIX** *Stylus SMR 745*	27	25
30 Jul 88		**SOUVENIR SINGLES PACK** *Epic MJ 5*	91	1
30 Nov 91	★	**DANGEROUS** *Epic 4658021* ■ ▲	1	96
29 Feb 92		**MOTOWN'S GREATEST HITS** *Motown 5300142*	53	2
15 Aug 92		**TOUR SOUVENIR PACK** *Epic MJ 4*	32	3
24 Jun 95	★	**HISTORY – PAST PRESENT AND FUTURE BOOK 1** *Epic 4747092* ■ ▲	1	78
24 May 97	★	**BLOOD ON THE DANCE FLOOR – HISTORY IN THE MIX** *Epic 4875002* ■	1	16
19 Jul 97	●	**THE BEST OF MICHAEL JACKSON AND THE JACKSON 5IVE – THE MOTOWN YEARS** *PolyGram TV 5308042* [4]	5	12
10 Nov 01	★	**INVINCIBLE** *Epic 4951742* ■ ▲	1	12

24 Nov 01 **GREATEST HITS – HISTORY VOLUME 1** *Epic 5018692*..........15 16
29 Nov 03 ★ **NUMBER ONES** *Epic 5138002* ■ ....1 5+

[1] Diana Ross and Michael Jackson [2] Michael Jackson and Paul McCartney [3] Paul McCartney and Michael Jackson [4] Michael Jackson with the Jackson Five [5] Stevie Wonder and Michael Jackson [6] Michael Jackson and Janet Jackson [7] 3T featuring Michael Jackson [1] Michael Jackson plus the Jackson Five [2] Diana Ross / Michael Jackson / Gladys Knight / Stevie Wonder [3] Diana Ross and Michael Jackson [4] Michael Jackson and the Jackson Five

The sleeve of 'I Just Can't Stop Loving You' credits Siedah Garrett but the label does not. 'Come Together' was listed only from 7 Mar 1992. It peaked at No.10. Chart rules allow for a maximum of three formats; the additional three formats of 'Scream' – which each included re-mixed versions – were therefore listed separately (see 24 Jun 1995) 'Off the Wall' changed its catalogue number to 4500861 during its chart run. From 14 Jan 89 when multi-artist albums were excluded from the main chart 'Love Songs' was listed in the compilation albums chart

See also JACKSONS; VARIOUS ARTISTS

Mick JACKSON *UK, male vocalist (Singles: 16 weeks)* pos/wks

30 Sep 78 **BLAME IT ON THE BOOGIE** *Atlantic K 11102*..........15 8
3 Feb 79 **WEEKEND** *Atlantic K 11224*..........38 8

Millie JACKSON
US, female vocalist (Singles: 8 weeks, Albums: 7 weeks) pos/wks

18 Nov 72 **MY MAN, A SWEET MAN** *Mojo 2093 022*..........50 1
10 Mar 84 **I FEEL LIKE WALKIN' IN THE RAIN** *Sire W 9348*..........55 2
15 Jun 85 **ACT OF WAR** *Rocket EJS 8* [1]..........32 5
18 Feb 84 **E.S.P.** *Sire 250382*..........59 5
6 Apr 85 **LIVE AND UNCENSORED** *Important TADLP 001*..........81 2

[1] Elton John and Millie Jackson

Stonewall JACKSON *US, male vocalist (Singles: 2 weeks)* pos/wks

17 Jul 59 **WATERLOO** *Philips PB 941*..........24 2

Tony JACKSON – *See Q; SWEET DREAMS*

Tony JACKSON and the VIBRATIONS *UK, male vocal / instrumental group – leader d. 18 Aug 2003 (Singles: 3 weeks)* pos/wks

8 Oct 64 **BYE BYE BABY** *Pye 7N 15685*..........38 3

See also SEARCHERS

Wanda JACKSON *US, female vocalist (Singles: 11 weeks)* pos/wks

1 Sep 60 **LET'S HAVE A PARTY** *Capitol CL 15147*..........32 8
26 Jan 61 **MEAN MEAN MAN (re)** *Capitol CL 15176*..........40 3

JACKSON SISTERS *US, female vocal group (Singles: 2 weeks)* pos/wks

20 Jun 87 **I BELIEVE IN MIRACLES** *Urban URB 4*..........72 2

JACKSONS (121 Top 500) *One of the world's biggest-selling and most popular groups: brothers Jackie, Tito, Jermaine, Marlon and solo superstar Michael Jackson, with Randy joining in 1977. The Indiana quintet topped the US chart with their first four hits, and have reportedly sold more than 100 million records (Singles: 235 weeks, Albums: 152 weeks)* pos/wks

31 Jan 70 ● **I WANT YOU BACK** *Tamla Motown TMG 724* [1] ▲..........2 13
16 May 70 ● **ABC** *Tamla Motown TMG 738* [1] ▲..........8 11
1 Aug 70 ● **THE LOVE YOU SAVE** *Tamla Motown TMG 746* [1] ▲..........7 9
21 Nov 70 ● **I'LL BE THERE** *Tamla Motown TMG 758* [1] ▲..........4 16
10 Apr 71 **MAMA'S PEARL** *Tamla Motown TMG 769* [1]..........25 7
17 Jul 71 **NEVER CAN SAY GOODBYE** *Tamla Motown TMG 778* [1]..........33 7
11 Nov 72 ● **LOOKIN' THROUGH THE WINDOWS** *Tamla Motown TMG 833* [1]..........9 11
23 Dec 72 **SANTA CLAUS IS COMING TO TOWN** *Tamla Motown TMG 837* [1]..........43 3
17 Feb 73 ● **DOCTOR MY EYES** *Tamla Motown TMG 842* [1]..........9 10
9 Jun 73 **HALLELUJAH DAY** *Tamla Motown TMG 856* [1]..........20 9
8 Sep 73 **SKYWRITER** *Tamla Motown TMG 865* [1]..........25 8
9 Apr 77 **ENJOY YOURSELF** *Epic EPC 5063*..........42 4
4 Jun 77 ★ **SHOW YOU THE WAY TO GO** *Epic EPC 5266*..........1 10
13 Aug 77 **DREAMER** *Epic EPC 5458*..........22 9
5 Nov 77 **GOIN' PLACES** *Epic EPC 5732*..........26 7
11 Feb 78 **EVEN THOUGH YOU'VE GONE** *Epic EPC 5919*..........31 4
23 Sep 78 ● **BLAME IT ON THE BOOGIE** *Epic EPC 6683*..........8 12
3 Feb 79 **DESTINY** *Epic EPC 6983*..........39 6
24 Mar 79 ● **SHAKE YOUR BODY (DOWN TO THE GROUND)** *Epic EPC 7181*..4 12
25 Oct 80 **LOVELY ONE** *Epic EPC 9302*..........29 6
13 Dec 80 **HEARTBREAK HOTEL** *Epic EPC 9391*..........44 6
28 Feb 81 ● **CAN YOU FEEL IT** *Epic EPC 9554*..........6 15
4 Jul 81 ● **WALK RIGHT NOW** *Epic EPC A 1294*..........7 11
7 Jul 84 **STATE OF SHOCK** *Epic A 4431* [2]..........14 8
8 Sep 84 **TORTURE** *Epic A 4675*..........26 6
16 Apr 88 ● **I WANT YOU BACK (re-mix)** *Motown ZB 41913* [3]..........8 9
13 May 89 **NOTHIN' (THAT COMPARES 2 U)** *Epic 654808 7*..........33 6
21 Mar 70 **DIANA ROSS PRESENTS THE JACKSON FIVE** *Tamla Motown STML 11142* [1]..........16 4
15 Aug 70 **ABC** *Tamla Motown STML 11153* [1]..........22 6
7 Oct 72 **GREATEST HITS** *Tamla Motown STML 11212* [1]..........26 14
18 Nov 72 **LOOKIN' THROUGH THE WINDOWS** *Tamla Motown STML 11214* [1]..........16 8
16 Jul 77 **THE JACKSONS** *Epic EPC 86009*..........54 1
3 Dec 77 **GOIN' PLACES** *Epic EPC 86035*..........45 1
5 May 79 **DESTINY** *Epic EPC 83200*..........33 7
11 Oct 80 **TRIUMPH** *Epic EPC 86112*..........13 16
12 Dec 81 **LIVE** *Epic EPC 88562*..........53 9
9 Jul 83 ★ **18 GREATEST HITS** *Telstar STAR 2232* [2]..........1 58
21 Jul 84 ● **VICTORY** *Epic EPC 86303*..........3 13
1 Jul 89 **2300 JACKSON ST** *Epic 463352 1*..........39 3
19 Jul 97 ● **THE BEST OF MICHAEL JACKSON AND THE JACKSON 5IVE – THE MOTOWN YEARS** *PolyGram TV 5308042* [3]..........5 12

[1] Jackson Five [2] Jacksons, lead vocals Mick Jagger and Michael Jackson [3] Michael Jackson with the Jackson Five [1] Jackson Five [2] Michael Jackson plus the Jackson Five [3] Michael Jackson and the Jackson 5ive

See also Michael JACKSON; Jermaine JACKSON

JACKY – *See Jackie LEE*

JACQUELINE – *See MACK VIBE featuring JACQUELINE*

JADA – *See SKIP RAIDERS featuring JADA*

JADE *US, female vocal group (Singles: 28 weeks, Albums: 3 weeks)* pos/wks

20 Mar 93 ● **DON'T WALK AWAY** *Giant W 0160CD*..........7 8
3 Jul 93 **I WANNA LOVE YOU** *Giant 74321151662*..........13 7
18 Sep 93 **ONE WOMAN** *Giant 74321165122*..........22 5
5 Feb 94 **ALL THRU THE NITE** *Giant 74321187552* [1]..........32 3
11 Feb 95 **EVERY DAY OF THE WEEK** *Giant 74321260242*..........19 5
29 May 93 **JADE TO THE MAX** *Giant 74321148002*..........43 3

[1] P.O.V. featuring Jade

JADE 4 U – *See Praga KHAN*

JAEL – *See DELERIUM*

JAGGED EDGE
UK, male vocal / instrumental group (Singles: 2 weeks) pos/wks

15 Sep 90 **YOU DON'T LOVE ME** *Polydor PO 97*..........66 2

JAGGED EDGE featuring NELLY
US, male vocal group and male rapper (Singles: 3 weeks) pos/wks

27 Oct 01 **WHERE THE PARTY AT?** *Columbia 6719012*..........25 3

See also NELLY; NIVEA

Mick JAGGER
UK, male vocalist (Singles: 43 weeks, Albums: 24 weeks) pos/wks

14 Nov 70 **MEMO FROM TURNER** *Decca F 13067*..........32 5
7 Jul 84 **STATE OF SHOCK** *Epic A 4431* [1]..........14 8
16 Feb 85 **JUST ANOTHER NIGHT** *CBS A 4722*..........32 6
7 Sep 85 ★ **DANCING IN THE STREET** *EMI America EA 204* [2] ■..........1 12
12 Sep 87 **LET'S WORK** *CBS 651028 7*..........31 7

Date		Title	Pos	Wks
6 Feb 93		**SWEET THING** *Atlantic A 7410CD*	24	4
23 Mar 02		**VISIONS OF PARADISE** *Virgin VUSCD 240*	43	1
16 Mar 85	●	**SHE'S THE BOSS** *CBS 86310*	6	11
26 Sep 87		**PRIMITIVE COOL** *CBS 460 1231*	26	5
20 Feb 93		**WANDERING SPIRIT** *Atlantic 7567824362*	12	4
1 Dec 01		**GODDESS IN THE DOORWAY** *Virgin CDVUS 214*	44	4

[1] Jacksons, lead vocals Mick Jagger and Michael Jackson [2] David Bowie and Mick Jagger

See also ROLLING STONES

JAGS *UK, male vocal / instrumental group (Singles: 11 weeks)*

Date		Title	pos	wks
8 Sep 79		**BACK OF MY HAND** *Island WIP 6501*	17	10
2 Feb 80		**WOMAN'S WORLD** *Island WIP 6531*	75	1

JAHEIM *US, male rapper – Jaheim Hoagland (Singles: 10 weeks, Albums: 1 week)*

Date		Title	pos	wks
24 Mar 01		**COULD IT BE** *Warner Bros. W 551CD*	33	3
11 Aug 01		**JUST IN CASE** *Warner Bros. W 564CD*	34	2
29 Jun 02		**JUST IN CASE (re-mix)** *Warner Bros. WEA W 581CD*	38	3
8 Mar 03		**FABULOUS** *Warner Bros. WEA W 598CD*	41	2
7 Apr 01		**GHETTO LOVE** *Warner Bros. 9362474522*	50	1

JAHMALI – *See BLAK TWANG*

JAIMESON
UK, male producer – Jamie Williams (Singles: 18 weeks)

Date		Title	pos	wks
25 Jan 03	●	**TRUE** *V2 / JDid JAD 5021363* [1]	4	10
23 Aug 03	●	**COMPLETE** *V2 / JDid JAD 5021713*	4	8

[1] Jaimeson featuring Angel Blu

JAKATTA
UK, male producer – Dave Lee (Singles: 30 weeks, Albums: 4 weeks)

Date		Title	pos	wks
24 Feb 01	●	**AMERICAN DREAM (re)** *Rulin RULIN 15CDS*	3	14
11 Aug 01		**AMERICAN DREAM (re-mix)** *Rulin RULIN 20CDS*	63	1
16 Feb 02	●	**SO LONELY** *Rulin RULIN 25CDS*	8	5
12 Oct 02	●	**MY VISION** *Rulin RULIN 26CDS* [1]	6	8
1 Jan 03		**ONE FINE DAY** *MoS / RULIN 29CDS*	39	2
26 Oct 02		**VISIONS** *Rulin RULINCD 01*	12	4

[1] Jakatta featuring Seal

See also HED BOYS; Li KWAN; RAVEN MAIZE; Joey NEGRO; SEAL; Z FACTOR; AKABU featuring Linda CLIFFORD; PHASE II; IL PADRINOS featuring Jocelyn BROWN

JAM 110 Top 500 *Influential and extremely popular punk-based mod trio from Surrey: Paul Weller (v/g), Bruce Foxton (b), Rick Buckler (d). They hold the record for the most simultaneous Top 75 singles with 13 (all reactivated by their 1982 dissolution). Mass waves of re-entries dominated the charts on 26 Apr 1980 and 22 Jan 1983. Total single sales were 5,094,055 (Singles: 206 weeks, Albums: 199 weeks)*

Date		Title	pos	wks
7 May 77		**IN THE CITY (2re)** *Polydor 2058 866*	40	14
23 Jul 77		**ALL AROUND THE WORLD (2re)** *Polydor 2058 903*	13	15
5 Nov 77		**THE MODERN WORLD (2re)** *Polydor 2058 945*	36	11
11 Mar 78		**NEWS OF THE WORLD (2re)** *Polydor 2058 995*	27	12
26 Aug 78		**DAVID WATTS / 'A' BOMB IN WARDOUR STREET (2re)** *Polydor 2059 054*	25	15
21 Oct 78		**DOWN IN THE TUBE STATION AT MIDNIGHT (re)** *Polydor POSP 8*	15	13
17 Mar 79		**STRANGE TOWN (2re)** *Polydor POSP 34*	15	18
25 Aug 79		**WHEN YOU'RE YOUNG (re)** *Polydor POSP 69*	17	11
3 Nov 79	●	**THE ETON RIFLES (re)** *Polydor POSP 83*	3	15
22 Mar 80	★	**GOING UNDERGROUND / DREAMS OF CHILDREN (re)** *Polydor POSP 113* ■	1	15
23 Aug 80	★	**START (re)** *Polydor 2059 266*	1	10
7 Feb 81		**THAT'S ENTERTAINMENT (import)** *Metronome 0030 364*	21	7
6 Jun 81	●	**FUNERAL PYRE** *Polydor POSP 257*	4	6
24 Oct 81	●	**ABSOLUTE BEGINNERS** *Polydor POSP 350*	4	6
13 Feb 82	★	**TOWN CALLED MALICE / PRECIOUS (re)** *Polydor POSP 400* ■	1	9
3 Jul 82	●	**JUST WHO IS THE FIVE O'CLOCK HERO** *Polydor 2059 504*	8	5
18 Sep 82	●	**THE BITTEREST PILL (I EVER HAD TO SWALLOW)** *Polydor POSP 505*	2	7
4 Dec 82	★	**BEAT SURRENDER** *Polydor POSP 540* ■	1	9
29 Jan 83		**THAT'S ENTERTAINMENT** *Polydor POSP 482*	60	3
29 Jun 91		**THAT'S ENTERTAINMENT (re-issue)** *Polydor PO 155*	57	2
11 Oct 97		**THE BITTEREST PILL (I EVER HAD TO SWALLOW) (re-issue)** *Polydor 5715992*	30	2
11 May 02		**IN THE CITY (re-issue)** *Polydor 5876117*	36	1
28 May 77		**IN THE CITY** *Polydor 2383 447*	20	18
26 Nov 77		**THIS IS THE MODERN WORLD** *Polydor 2383 475*	22	5
11 Nov 78	●	**ALL MOD CONS** *Polydor POLD 5008*	6	17
24 Nov 79	●	**SETTING SONS** *Polydor POLD 5028*	4	19
6 Dec 80	●	**SOUND AFFECTS** *Polydor POLD 5035*	2	19
20 Mar 82	★	**THE GIFT** *Polydor POLD 5055* ■	1	24
18 Dec 82	●	**DIG THE NEW BREED** *Polydor POLD 5075*	2	15
27 Aug 83		**IN THE CITY (re-issue)** *Polydor SPELP 27*	100	1
22 Oct 83	●	**SNAP!** *Polydor SNAP 1*	2	30
13 Jul 91	●	**GREATEST HITS** *Polydor 8495541*	2	21
18 Apr 92		**EXTRAS** *Polydor 5131772*	15	4
6 Nov 93		**LIVE JAM** *Polydor 5196672*	28	2
27 Jul 96		**THE JAM COLLECTION** *Polydor 5314932*	58	1
7 Jun 97	●	**DIRECTION REACTION CREATION** *Polydor 5371432*	8	4
25 Oct 97	●	**THE VERY BEST OF THE JAM** *Polydor / PolyGram TV 5374232*	9	10
18 May 02	●	**THE SOUND OF THE JAM** *Polydor 5897812*	3	7
15 Jun 02		**THE JAM AT THE BBC** *Polydor 5896902*	33	2

See also Bruce FOXTON; Paul WELLER

JAM & SPOON featuring PLAVKA
Germany, male production duo – Rolf Ellmer and Markus Loeffel and female vocalist (Singles: 26 weeks, Albums: 1 week)

Date		Title	pos	wks
2 May 92		**TALES FROM A DANCEOGRAPHIC OCEAN (EP)** *R&S RSUK 14* [1]	49	1
6 Jun 92		**THE COMPLETE STELLA (re-mix)** *R&S RSUK 14X* [1]	66	2
26 Feb 94		**RIGHT IN THE NIGHT (FALL IN LOVE WITH MUSIC)** *Epic 6600822*	31	4
24 Sep 94		**FIND ME (ODYSSEY TO ANYOONA)** *Epic 6608082*	37	3
10 Jun 95	●	**RIGHT IN THE NIGHT (FALL IN LOVE WITH MUSIC) (re-issue)** *Epic 6620182*	10	8
16 Sep 95		**FIND ME (ODYSSEY TO ANYOONA) (re-issue)** *Epic 6623242*	22	3
25 Nov 95		**ANGEL (LADADI O-HEYO)** *Epic 6626382*	26	2
30 Aug 97		**KALEIDOSCOPE SKIES** *Epic 6647614*	48	1
2 Mar 02		**BE ANGELED** *Nulife / Arista 74321878992* [2]	31	2
19 Feb 94		**TRIPOMATIC FAIRYTALES 2001** *Epic 4749282* [1]	71	1

[1] Jam and Spoon [2] Jam & Spoon featuring Rea [1] Jam and Spoon

Tracks on Tales From a Danceographic Ocean (EP): Stella / Keep on Movin' / My First Fantastic FF. 'The Complete Stella' is a re-mix of a track from the EP

See also DANCE 2 TRANCE; STORM; TOKYO GHETTO PUSSY

JAM MACHINE
Italy / US, male vocal / instrumental group (Singles: 1 week)

Date		Title	pos	wks
23 Dec 89		**EVERYDAY** *Deconstruction PB 43299*	68	1

JAM ON THE MUTHA
UK, male vocal / instrumental group (Singles: 2 weeks)

Date		Title	pos	wks
11 Aug 90		**HOTEL CALIFORNIA** *M & G MAGS 3*	62	2

JAM TRONIK *Germany, male / female vocal / instrumental group (Singles: 7 weeks)*

Date		Title	pos	wks
24 Mar 90		**ANOTHER DAY IN PARADISE** *Debut DEBT 3093*	19	7

JAMAICA UNITED
Jamaica, male vocal ensemble (Singles: 1 week)

Date		Title	pos	wks
4 Jul 98		**RISE UP** *Columbia 6660522*	54	1

JAMELIA *UK, female vocalist – Jamelia Davis (Singles: 34 weeks, Albums: 4 weeks)*

Date		Title	pos	wks
31 Jul 99		**I DO** *Parlophone Rhythm Series CDRHYTHM 21*	36	2
4 Mar 00	●	**MONEY** *Parlophone Rhythm Series CDRYTHM 27* [1]	5	9
24 Jun 00		**CALL ME** *Parlophone Rhythm Series CDRHYTHM 28*	11	5
21 Oct 00		**BOY NEXT DOOR** *Parlophone Rhythm Series CDRHYTHM 29*	42	2

21 Jun 03	BOUT *Parlophone CDRS 6597* [2]	37	2
27 Sep 03 ●	SUPERSTAR *Parlophone CDR 6615*	3	14+
8 Jul 00	DRAMA *Parlophone Rhythm 5272272*	39	2
11 Oct 03	THANK YOU *Parlophone 5837772*	65	2

[1] Jamelia featuring Beenie Man [2] Jamelia featuring Rah Digga

JAMES (254 Top 500)

Anthemic indie pop band formed in 1982 in Manchester, UK, by mainstays Tim Booth (v) and Larry Gott (g). After several hitless years, critically acclaimed releases and record company changes, they became one of the most consistently successful acts of the 1990s (Singles: 89 weeks, Albums: 155 weeks)

		pos	wks
12 May 90	HOW WAS IT FOR YOU? *Fontana JIM 5*	32	3
7 Jul 90	COME HOME *Fontana JIM 6*	32	4
8 Dec 90	LOSE CONTROL *Fontana JIM 7*	38	5
30 Mar 91 ●	SIT DOWN *Fontana JIM 8*	2	10
30 Nov 91 ●	SOUND *Fontana JIM 9*	9	7
1 Feb 92	BORN OF FRUSTRATION *Fontana JIM 10*	13	6
4 Apr 92	RING THE BELLS *Fontana JIM 11*	37	2
18 Jul 92	SEVEN (EP) *Fontana JIM 12*	46	2
11 Sep 93	SOMETIMES *Fontana JIMCD 13*	18	4
13 Nov 93	LAID *Fontana JIMCD 14*	25	4
2 Apr 94	JAM J / SAY SOMETHING *Fontana JIMCD 15*	24	4
22 Feb 97 ●	SHE'S A STAR *Fontana JIMCD 16*	9	5
3 May 97	TOMORROW *Fontana JIMCD 17*	12	3
5 Jul 97	WALTZING ALONG *Fontana JIMCD 18*	23	4
21 Mar 98	DESTINY CALLING *Fontana JIMCD 19*	17	4
6 Jun 98	RUNAGROUND *Fontana JIMCD 20*	29	2
21 Nov 98 ●	SIT DOWN (re-mix) *Fontana JIMCD 21*	7	7
31 Jul 99	I KNOW WHAT I'M HERE FOR *Mercury JIMCD22*	22	5
16 Oct 99	JUST LIKE FRED ASTAIRE *Mercury JIMCD 23*	17	3
25 Dec 99	WE'RE GOING TO MISS YOU *Mercury JIMCD 24*	48	2
7 Jul 01	GETTING AWAY WITH IT (ALL MESSED UP) *Mercury JIMCD 25*	22	3
2 Aug 86	STUTTER *Blanco Y Negro JIMLP 1*	68	2
8 Oct 88	STRIP MINE *Sire JIMLP 2*	90	1
16 Jun 90 ●	GOLD MOTHER *Fontana 8485951*	2	34
29 Feb 92 ●	SEVEN *Fontana 5109322*	2	14
9 Oct 93 ●	LAID *Fontana 5149432*	3	16
24 Sep 94	WAH WAH *Fontana 5228272* [1]	11	2
8 Mar 97 ●	WHIPLASH *Fontana 5343542*	9	19
4 Apr 98 ★	THE BEST OF JAMES *Fontana 5368982* ■	1	53
23 Oct 99 ●	MILLIONAIRES *Mercury 5467892*	2	11
14 Jul 01	PLEASED TO MEET YOU *Mercury 5861462*	11	3

[1] James and Brian Eno

Tracks on Seven (EP): Seven / Goalie's Ball / William Burroughs / Still Alive. 'Say Something' listed with 'Jam J' only for first two weeks of record's run

David JAMES

UK, male DJ / producer (Singles: 1 week)

		pos	wks
11 Aug 01	ALWAYS A PERMANENT STATE *Hooj Choons HOOJ 108CD*	60	1

Dick JAMES

UK, male vocalist – Isaac Vapnic, d. 1 Feb 1986 (Singles: 13 weeks)

		pos	wks
20 Jan 56	ROBIN HOOD / THE BALLAD OF DAVY CROCKETT (re) *Parlophone R 4117*	14	9
11 Jan 57	GARDEN OF EDEN *Parlophone R 4255*	18	4

'Robin Hood' is with Stephen James and his Chums. 'The Ballad of Davy Crockett' listed only from 18 May 1956

Etta JAMES

US, female vocalist – Jamesetta Hawkins (Singles: 7 weeks)

		pos	wks
10 Feb 96 ●	I JUST WANT TO MAKE LOVE TO YOU *MCA MCSTD 48003*	5	7

Freddie JAMES

Canada, male vocalist (Singles: 3 weeks)

		pos	wks
24 Nov 79	GET UP AND BOOGIE *Warner Bros. K 17478*	54	3

Holly JAMES – *See Jason NEVINS*

Jo JAMES – *See FLIP and FILL*

Joni JAMES

US, female vocalist – Joan Babbo (Singles: 2 weeks)

		pos	wks
6 Mar 53	WHY DON'T YOU BELIEVE ME? *MGM 582* ▲	11	1
30 Jan 59	THERE MUST BE A WAY *MGM 1002*	24	1

Rick JAMES

US, male vocalist (Singles: 30 weeks, Albums: 2 weeks)

		pos	wks
8 Jul 78	YOU AND I *Motown TMG 1110*	46	7
7 Jul 79	I'M A SUCKER FOR YOUR LOVE *Motown TMG 1146* [1]	43	8
6 Sep 80	BIG TIME *Motown TMG 1198*	41	6
4 Jul 81	GIVE IT TO ME BABY *Motown TMG 1229*	47	3
12 Jun 82	STANDING ON THE TOP (PART 1) *Motown TMG 1263* [2]	53	3
3 Jul 82	DANCE WIT' ME *Motown TMG 1266*	53	3
24 Jul 82	THROWIN' DOWN *Motown STML 12167*	93	2

[1] Teena Marie, co-lead vocals Rick James [2] Temptations featuring Rick James

Sonny JAMES

US, male vocalist – James Loden (Singles: 8 weeks)

		pos	wks
30 Nov 56	THE CAT CAME BACK *Capitol CL 14635*	30	1
8 Feb 57	YOUNG LOVE *Capitol CL 14683*	11	7

Wendy JAMES

UK, female vocalist (Singles: 4 weeks, Albums: 1 week)

		pos	wks
20 Feb 93	THE NAMELESS ONE *MCA MCSTD 1732*	34	3
17 Apr 93	LONDON'S BRILLIANT *MCA MCSTD 1763*	62	1
20 Mar 93	NOW AIN'T THE TIME FOR YOUR TEARS *MCA MCD 10800*	43	1

See also TRANSVISION VAMP

Jimmy JAMES and the VAGABONDS

UK, male vocal / instrumental group (Singles: 25 weeks)

		pos	wks
11 Sep 68	RED RED WINE *Pye 7N 17579*	36	8
24 Apr 76	I'LL GO WHERE YOUR MUSIC TAKES ME *Pye 7N 45585*	23	8
17 Jul 76 ●	NOW IS THE TIME *Pye 7N 45606*	5	9

Tommy JAMES and the SHONDELLS

US, male vocal / instrumental group (Singles: 25 weeks)

		pos	wks
21 Jul 66	HANKY PANKY *Roulette RK 7000* ▲	38	7
5 Jun 68 ★	MONY MONY *Major Minor MM 567*	1	18

JAMES BOYS

UK, male vocal duo – Bradley and Stewart Palmer (Singles: 6 weeks)

		pos	wks
19 May 73	OVER AND OVER *Penny Farthing PEN 806*	39	6

JAMESON and VIPER

UK, male production / rap duo (Singles: 1 week)

		pos	wks
14 Sep 02	SELECTA (URBAN HEROES) *Universal Soundproof SPR 1CD*	51	1

See also REFLEX featuring MC VIPER

JAMESTOWN featuring Jocelyn BROWN

US, male instrumentalist / producer – Kent Brainerd and US, female vocalist (Singles: 1 week)

		pos	wks
27 Mar 99	I BELIEVE *Playola 0091705 PLA*	62	1

See also Jocelyn BROWN

JAMIROQUAI (140 Top 500)

One of world's biggest-selling acts of the late 1990s features headdress-wearing vocalist Jay Kay, b. 30 Dec 1969, Manchester, UK. Group, whose videos have also earned numerous accolades, sold seven million copies of 1996 album 'Travelling Without Moving' and 1999 album 'Synkronized' topped many European charts (Singles: 141 weeks, Albums: 215 weeks)

		pos	wks
31 Oct 92	WHEN YOU GONNA LEARN (re) *Acid Jazz JAZID 46*	52	3
13 Mar 93 ●	TOO YOUNG TO DIE *Sony S2 6590112*	10	7
5 Jun 93	BLOW YOUR MIND *Sony S2 6592972*	12	6
14 Aug 93	EMERGENCY ON PLANET EARTH *Sony S2 6595782*	32	3
25 Sep 93	WHEN YOU GONNA LEARN (re-issue) *Sony S2 6596952*	28	3
8 Oct 94	SPACE COWBOY *Sony S2 6608512*	17	5
19 Nov 94	HALF THE MAN *Sony S2 6610032*	15	8
1 Jul 95 ●	STILLNESS IN TIME *Sony S2 6620255*	9	5

1 Jun 96	DO U KNOW WHERE YOU'RE COMING FROM *Renk CDRENK 63* [1]	12 5
31 Aug 96 ●	VIRTUAL INSANITY *Sony S2 6636132*	3 11
7 Dec 96 ●	COSMIC GIRL *Sony S2 6638292*	6 10
10 May 97 ●	ALRIGHT *Sony S2 6643252*	6 5
13 Dec 97	HIGH TIMES *Sony S2 6653702*	20 6
25 Jul 98 ★	DEEPER UNDERGROUND *Sony S2 6662182* ■	1 11
5 Jun 99 ●	CANNED HEAT *Sony S2 6673022*	4 10
25 Sep 99	SUPERSONIC *Sony S2 6678392*	22 4
11 Dec 99	KING FOR A DAY *Sony S2 6679732*	20 7
24 Feb 01	I'M IN THE MOOD FOR LOVE *Warner Esp WSMS 001CD* [2]	29 3
25 Aug 01 ●	LITTLE L *Sony S2 6717182*	5 11
1 Dec 01	YOU GIVE ME SOMETHING *Sony S2 6720072*	16 9
9 Mar 02	LOVE FOOLOSOPHY (re) *Sony S2 6723252*	14 6
20 Jul 02	CORNER OF THE EARTH *Sony S2 6727882*	31 3
26 Jun 93 ★	EMERGENCY ON PLANET EARTH *Sony S2 4740692* ■	1 32
29 Oct 94 ●	THE RETURN OF THE SPACE COWBOY *Sony S2 4778132*	2 29
21 Sep 96 ●	TRAVELLING WITHOUT MOVING *Sony S2 4839999*	2 74
26 Jun 99 ★	SYNKRONIZED *Sony S2 4945172* ■	1 29
15 Sep 01 ★	A FUNK ODYSSEY *Sony S2 5040692* ■	1 51

[1] M-Beat featuring Jamiroquai [2] Jools Holland and Jamiroquai

JAMMERS *US, male vocal / instrumental group (Singles: 2 weeks)* pos/wks

29 Jan 83	BE MINE TONIGHT *Salsoul Sal 101*	65 2

JamX & DeLEON *Germany, male production duo – Jürgen Mutschall and Dominik DeLeon (Singles: 2 weeks)* pos/wks

7 Sep 02	CAN U DIG IT? *Serious SERR 052CD*	40 2

JAN and DEAN *US, male vocal duo – Jan Berry and Dean Torrence (Singles: 18 weeks, Albums: 2 weeks)* pos/wks

24 Aug 61	HEART AND SOUL *London HLH 9395*	24 8
15 Aug 63	SURF CITY *Liberty LIB 55580* ▲	26 10
12 Jul 80	THE JAN AND DEAN STORY *K-Tel NE 1084*	67 2

JAN and KJELD *Denmark, male vocal duo – Jan and Kjeld Wennick (Singles: 4 weeks)* pos/wks

21 Jul 60	BANJO BOY *Ember S 101*	36 4

JANE'S ADDICTION *US, male vocal / instrumental group (Singles: 10 weeks, Albums: 5 weeks)* pos/wks

23 Mar 91	BEEN CAUGHT STEALING *Warner Bros. W 0011*	34 3
1 Jun 91	CLASSIC GIRL *Warner Bros. W 0031*	60 1
26 Jul 03	JUST BECAUSE *Capitol CDCL 847*	14 4
8 Nov 03	TRUE NATURE *Parlophone CDCL 850*	41 2
8 Sep 90	RITUAL DE LO HABITUAL *Warner Bros. WX 306*	37 2
2 Aug 03	STRAYS *Parlophone 5921972*	14 3

Horst JANKOWSKI, His Orchestra and Chorus *Germany, male instrumentalist – piano (Singles: 18 weeks)* pos/wks

29 Jul 65 ●	A WALK IN THE BLACK FOREST *Mercury MF 861*	3 18

Samantha JANUS *UK, female vocalist (Singles: 3 weeks)* pos/wks

11 May 91	A MESSAGE TO YOUR HEART *Hollywood HWD 104*	30 3

Philip JAP *UK, male vocalist (Singles: 8 weeks)* pos/wks

31 Jul 82	SAVE US *A&M AMS 8217*	53 4
25 Sep 82	TOTAL ERASURE *A&M JAP 1*	41 4

JAPAN (300 Top 500) *Rock quintet which subsequently became New Romantic figureheads fronted by David Sylvian (v), b. David Batt, 23 Feb 1958, London, UK, who later recorded critically acclaimed solo work. Group folded in 1982, but full line-up briefly reconvened as Rain Tree Crow in 1991 (Singles: 81 weeks, Albums: 135 weeks)* pos/wks

18 Oct 80	GENTLEMEN TAKE POLAROIDS *Virgin VS 379*	60 2
9 May 81	THE ART OF PARTIES *Virgin VS 409*	48 5
19 Sep 81	QUIET LIFE *Hansa HANSA 6*	19 9
7 Nov 81	VISIONS OF CHINA *Virgin VS 436*	32 12
23 Jan 82	EUROPEAN SON *Hansa HANSA 10*	31 6
20 Mar 82 ●	GHOSTS *Virgin VS 472*	5 8
22 May 82	CANTONESE BOY *Virgin VS 502*	24 6
3 Jul 82 ●	I SECOND THAT EMOTION *Hansa HANSA 12*	9 11
9 Oct 82	LIFE IN TOKYO *Hansa HANSA 17*	28 6
20 Nov 82	NIGHT PORTER *Virgin VS 554*	29 9
12 Mar 83	ALL TOMORROW'S PARTIES *Hansa HANSA 18*	38 4
21 May 83	CANTON (LIVE) *Virgin VS 581*	42 3
9 Feb 80	QUIET LIFE *Ariola Hansa AHAL 8011*	53 8
15 Nov 80	GENTLEMEN TAKE POLAROIDS *Virgin V 2180*	45 10
26 Sep 81	ASSEMBLAGE *Hansa HANLP 1*	26 46
28 Nov 81	TIN DRUM *Virgin V 2209*	12 50
18 Jun 83 ●	OIL ON CANVAS *Virgin VD 2513*	5 14
8 Dec 84	EXORCISING GHOSTS *Virgin VGD 3510*	45 7

See also RAIN TREE CROW; David SYLVIAN

JARK PRONGO *Holland, male production duo – Rene Ter Horst and Gaston Steenkist (Singles: 1 week)* pos/wks

3 Apr 99	MOVIN' THRU YOUR SYSTEM *Hooj Choons HOOJ 72CD*	58 1

See also GOODMEN; RHYTHMKILLAZ; CHOCOLATE PUMA; TOMBA VIRA; RIVA featuring Dannii MINOGUE

Jeff JARRATT and Don REEDMAN *UK, male producers (Albums: 8 weeks)* pos/wks

22 Nov 80	MASTERWORKS *K-Tel ONE 1093*	39 8

See also Pierre BELMONDE

Jean-Michel JARRE (216 Top 500) *Distinctive synthesizer wizard b. 24 Aug 1948, Lyon, France (son of composer / conductor Maurice), has sold more than 55 million albums worldwide. His spectacular, futuristic, live sound-and-light extravaganzas have frequently broken attendance records (Singles: 40 weeks, Albums: 236 weeks)* pos/wks

27 Aug 77 ●	OXYGENE PART IV *Polydor 2001 721*	4 9
20 Jan 79	EQUINOXE PART 5 *Polydor POSP 20*	45 5
23 Aug 86	FOURTH RENDEZ-VOUS *Polydor POSP 788*	65 4
5 Nov 88	REVOLUTIONS *Polydor PO 25*	52 2
7 Jan 89	LONDON KID *Polydor PO 32* [1]	52 3
7 Oct 89	OXYGENE PART IV (re-mix) *Polydor PO 55*	65 2
26 Jun 93	CHRONOLOGIE PART 4 *Polydor POCS 274*	55 2
30 Oct 93	CHRONOLOGIE PART 4 (re-mix) *Polydor POCS 274*	56 1
22 Mar 97	OXYGENE 8 *Epic 6643232*	17 3
5 Jul 97	OXYGENE 10 *Epic 6647152*	21 2
11 Jul 98	RENDEZ-VOUS '98 *Epic 6661102* [2]	12 6
26 Feb 00	C'EST LA VIE *Epic 6689302* [3]	40 1
20 Aug 77 ●	OXYGENE *Polydor 2310 555*	2 24
16 Dec 78	EQUINOXE *Polydor POLD 5007*	11 26
6 Jun 81 ●	MAGNETIC FIELDS *Polydor POLS 1033*	6 17
15 May 82 ●	THE CONCERTS IN CHINA *Polydor PODV 3*	6 17
12 Nov 83	THE ESSENTIAL JEAN-MICHEL JARRE *Polystar PROLP 3*	14 29
24 Nov 84	ZOOLOOK *Polydor POLH 15*	47 14
12 Apr 86 ●	RENDEZ-VOUS *Polydor POLH 27*	9 38
18 Jul 87	EN CONCERT HOUSTON / LYON *Polydor POLH 36*	18 15
8 Oct 88 ●	REVOLUTIONS *Polydor POLH 45*	2 13
14 Oct 89	JARRE LIVE *Polydor 841258 1*	16 4
23 Jun 90	WAITING FOR COUSTEAU *Dreyfus 8436141*	14 10
26 Oct 91	IMAGES – THE BEST OF JEAN-MICHEL JARRE *Dreyfus 5113061*	14 12
5 Jun 93	CHRONOLOGIE *Polydor 5193732*	11 8
28 May 94	CHRONOLOGIE PART 6 *Polydor 5195792*	60 1
1 Mar 97	OXYGENE 7-13 *Epic 4869849*	11 5
23 May 98	ODYSSEY THROUGH O2 *Epic 4897646*	50 2
12 Feb 00	METAMORPHOSES *Epic 4960222*	37 1

[1] Jean-Michel Jarre featuring Hank Marvin [2] Jean-Michel Jarre and Apollo 440 [3] Jean-Michel Jarre featuring Natacha Atlas

Al JARREAU *US, male vocalist (Singles: 30 weeks, Albums: 37 weeks)* pos/wks

26 Sep 81	WE'RE IN THIS LOVE TOGETHER *Warner Bros. K 17849*	55 4
14 May 83	MORNIN' *WEA U9929*	28 6
16 Jul 83	TROUBLE IN PARADISE *WEA Int. U9871*	36 5

24 Sep 83 **BOOGIE DOWN** *WEA U9814* ... 63 3
16 Nov 85 **DAY BY DAY** *Polydor POSP 770* [1] ... 53 3
5 Apr 86 **THE MUSIC OF GOODBYE (LOVE THEME FROM 'OUT OF AFRICA')** *MCA MCA 1038* [2] ... 75 1
7 Mar 87 ● **'MOONLIGHTING' THEME** *WEA U8407* ... 8 8
5 Sep 81 **BREAKING AWAY** *Warner Bros. K 56917* ... 60 8
30 Apr 83 **JARREAU** *WEA International U 0070* ... 39 18
17 Nov 84 **HIGH CRIME** *WEA 250807* ... 81 1
13 Sep 86 **L IS FOR LOVER** *WEA International 253 0801* ... 45 10

[1] Shakatak featuring Al Jarreau [2] Melissa Manchester and Al Jarreau

Kenny 'Jammin' JASON and DJ 'Fast' Eddie SMITH

US, male DJ / production duo (Singles: 4 weeks) pos/wks

11 Apr 87 **CAN U DANCE (re)** *Champion CHAMP 41* ... 67 4

JAVELLS featuring Nosmo KING

UK, male vocalist – Stephen Gold (Singles: 8 weeks) pos/wks

9 Nov 74 **GOODBYE NOTHING TO SAY** *Pye Disco Demand DDS 2003* ... 26 8

See also TRUTH

JAVINE *UK, female vocalist – Javine Hylton (Singles: 14 weeks)* pos/wks

19 Jul 03 ● **REAL THINGS** *Innocent SINCD 46* ... 4 9
22 Nov 03 **SURRENDER (YOUR LOVE)** *Innocent SINCD 52* ... 15 5

Peter JAY and the JAYWALKERS *UK, male instrumental group – Peter Jay – drums (Singles: 11 weeks)* pos/wks

8 Nov 62 **CAN CAN '62** *Decca F 11531* ... 31 11

Oris JAY presents DELSENA

Holland, male producer – Peran van Dijk and UK, female vocalist (Singles: 2 weeks) pos/wks

23 Mar 02 **TRIPPIN'** *Gusto CDGUS 3* ... 42 2

Simone JAY – *See DJ DADO*

JAYDEE

Holland, male DJ / producer – Robin Albers (Singles: 3 weeks) pos/wks

20 Sep 97 **PLASTIC DREAMS** *R&S RS 97117CD* ... 18 3

Laura JAYE – *See INTENSO PROJECT*

Ollie JAYE – *See JON THE DENTIST vs Ollie JAYE*

JAYHAWKS

US, male / female vocal / instrumental group (Singles: 1 week, Albums: 4 weeks) pos/wks

15 Jul 95 **BAD TIME** *American 74321291632* ... 70 1
25 Feb 95 **TOMORROW THE GREEN GRASS** *American 74321236802* ... 41 1
3 May 97 **SOUND OF LIES** *American Recordings 74321464062* ... 61 1
20 May 00 **SMILE** *Columbia 4979712* ... 60 1
19 Apr 03 **RAINY DAY MUSIC** *American 0771362* ... 70 1

JAY-Z *US, male rapper – Shawn Carter (Singles: 121 weeks, Albums: 16 weeks)* pos/wks

1 Mar 97 **CAN'T KNOCK THE HUSTLE** *Northwestside 74321447192* [1] 30 2
10 May 97 **AIN'T NO PLAYA** *Northwestside 74321474842* [2] ... 31 2
21 Jun 97 ● **I'LL BE** *Def Jam 75710432* [3] ... 9 5
23 Aug 97 **WHO YOU WIT** *Qwest W 0411CD* ... 65 1
25 Oct 97 **SUNSHINE** *Northwestside 74321528702* [4] ... 25 2
14 Feb 98 **WISHING ON A STAR** *Northwestside 74321554632* [5] ... 13 4
27 Jun 98 **THE CITY IS MINE** *Northwestside 74321588012* [6] ... 38 2
12 Dec 98 ● **HARD KNOCK LIFE (GHETTO ANTHEM)** *Northwestside 74321635332* ... 2 11
13 Mar 99 **CAN I GET A...** *Def Jam 5668472* [7] ... 24 3
10 Apr 99 **BE ALONE NO MORE** *Northwestside 74321658472* [8] ... 11 9
19 Jun 99 **LOBSTER & SCRIMP** *Virgin DINSD 186* [9] ... 48 1
6 Nov 99 ● **HEARTBREAKER** *Columbia 6683012* [10] ▲ ... 5 13
4 Dec 99 **WHAT YOU THINK OF THAT** *Def Jam 8708292* ... 58 1
26 Feb 00 **ANYTHING** *Def Jam 5626502* ... 18 4
24 Jun 00 **BIG PIMPIN'** *Def Jam 5627742* ... 29 3
16 Dec 00 **I JUST WANNA LOVE U (GIVE IT 2 ME)** *Def Jam 5727462* ... 17 8
23 Jun 01 **FIESTA** *Jive 9252142* [11] ... 23 3
27 Oct 01 **IZZO (H.O.V.A.)** *Roc-a-Fella / Def Jam 5888152* ... 21 4
19 Jan 02 **GIRLS, GIRLS, GIRLS (re)** *Roc-a-Fella / Def Jam 5889062* ... 11 7
25 May 02 **HONEY** *Jive 9253662* [12] ... 35 2
1 Feb 03 ● **'03 BONNIE & CLYDE** *Roc-a-Fella 0770102* [13] ... 2 12
26 Apr 03 **EXCUSE ME MISS** *Roc-a-Fella 0779122* ... 17 7
5 Jul 03 **JOGI / BEWARE OF THE BOYS** *Showbiz / Dharma DHARMA ICDS* [14] ... 25 3
16 Aug 03 **FRONTIN'** *Arista 8267655332* [15] ... 6 10
20 Dec 03 **CHANGE CLOTHES** *Roc-a-Fella 9815225* ... 35 2+
29 Sep 01 **THE BLUEPRINT** *Roc-a-Fella 5863962* ... 30 4
30 Mar 02 **CHAPTER ONE** *Roc-a-Fella 74321920462* ... 65 1
30 Mar 02 **THE BEST OF BOTH WORLDS** *Jive 9223512* [1] ... 37 2
30 Nov 02 **THE BLUEPRINT 2 – THE GIFT & THE CURSE** *Def Jam / Mercury 0633812* ▲ ... 23 7
29 Nov 03 **THE BLACK ALBUM** *Roc-a-fella / Mercury 9861121* ▲ ... 40 2

[1] Jay-Z featuring Mary J Blige [2] Jay-Z featuring Foxy Brown [3] Foxy Brown featuring Jay-Z [4] Jay-Z featuring Babyface and Foxy Brown [5] Jay-Z featuring Gwen Dickey [6] Jay-Z featuring BLACKstreet [7] Jay-Z featuring Amil & Ja Rule [8] Another Level featuring Jay-Z [9] Timbaland featuring Jay-Z [10] Mariah Carey featuring Jay-Z [11] R Kelly featuring Jay-Z [12] R Kelly & Jay-Z [13] Jay-Z featuring Beyonce Knowles [14] Panjabi MC / Panjabi MC featuring Jay-Z [15] Pharrell Williams featuring Jay-Z [1] R. Kelly and Jay-Z

JAZZ and the BROTHERS GRIMM

UK, male vocal / instrumental group (Singles: 2 weeks) pos/wks

9 Jul 88 **(LET'S ALL GO BACK) DISCO NIGHTS** *Ensign ENY 616* ... 57 2

JAZZY JEFF – *See DJ JAZZY JEFF and The FRESH PRINCE*

JAZZY JEFF & The FRESH PRINCE – *See DJ JAZZY JEFF and The FRESH PRINCE*

JAZZY M

UK, male DJ / producer – Michael Connelly (Singles: 2 weeks) pos/wks

21 Oct 00 **JAZZIN' THE WAY YOU KNOW** *Perfecto PERF 08CDS* ... 47 2

Norma JEAN – *See Romina JOHNSON*

Wyclef JEAN *US, male rapper / vocalist / producer (Singles: 75 weeks, Albums: 23 weeks)* pos/wks

28 Jun 97 **WE TRYING TO STAY ALIVE** *Columbia 6646815* [1] ... 13 5
27 Sep 97 **GUANTANAMERA** *Columbia 6650852* [1] ... 25 2
28 Mar 98 ● **NO, NO, NO** *Columbia 6656592* [2] ... 5 8
16 May 98 ● **GONE TILL NOVEMBER** *Columbia 6658712* ... 3 9
14 Nov 98 ● **ANOTHER ONE BITES THE DUST** *Dreamworks DRMCD 22364* [3] ... 5 6
23 Oct 99 **NEW DAY** *Columbia 6682122* [4] ... 23 2
16 Sep 00 ● **IT DOESN'T MATTER** *Columbia 6697782* [5] ... 3 8
16 Dec 00 ● **911** *Columbia 6706122* [6] ... 9 10
21 Jul 01 ● **PERFECT GENTLEMEN** *Columbia 6710522* ... 4 14
8 Dec 01 **WISH YOU WERE HERE (re)** *Columbia 6721562* ... 28 5
6 Jul 02 **TWO WRONGS** *Columbia 6728902* [7] ... 14 6
5 Jul 97 **THE CARNIVAL** *Columbia 4874422* [1] ... 40 6
2 Sep 00 ● **THE ECLEFTIC – 2 SIDES II A BOOK** *Columbia 4979792* ... 5 15
20 Jul 02 **MASQUERADE** *Columbia 5078542* ... 30 2

[1] Wyclef Jean and The Refugee Allstars [2] Destiny's Child featuring Wyclef Jean [3] Queen with Wyclef Jean featuring Pras and Free [4] Wyclef Jean featuring Bono [5] Wyclef Jean featuring The Rock and Melky Sedeck [6] Wyclef Jean featuring Mary J Blige [7] Wyclef Jean featuring Claudette Ortiz [1] Wyclef Jean and the Refugee Allstars

See also FUGEES

THE JEEVAS

UK, male vocal / instrumental group (Singles: 1 week) pos/wks

22 Mar 03 **ONCE UPON A TIME IN AMERICA** *Cowboy Music COWCDA 005* ... 61 1

JEFFERSON *UK, male vocalist – Geoff Turton (Singles: 8 weeks)*

		pos	wks
9 Apr 69	COLOUR OF MY LOVE *Pye 7N 17706*	22	8

JEFFERSON AIRPLANE *US / UK, female / male vocal / instrumental group (Singles: 41 weeks. Albums: 34 weeks)*

		pos	wks
26Jan 80	JANE *Grunt FB 1750* [1]	21	9
16 Nov 85	WE BUILT THIS CITY *RCA PB 49929* [2] ▲	12	12
8 Feb 86	SARA *RCA FB 49893* [2] ▲	66	3
11 Apr 87 ★	NOTHING'S GONNA STOP US NOW *Grunt FB 49757* [2] ▲	1	17
28 Jun 69	BLESS ITS POINTED LITTLE HEAD *RCA SF 8019*	38	1
7 Mar 70	VOLUNTEERS *RCA SF 8076*	34	7
13 Feb 71	BLOWS AGAINST THE EMPIRE *RCA SF 8163* [1]	12	6
2 Oct 71	BARK *Grunt FTR 1001*	42	1
2 Sep 72	LONG JOHN SILVER *Grunt FTR 1007*	30	1
31 Jul 76	SPITFIRE *Grunt RFL 1557* [2]	30	2
9 Feb 80	FREEDOM AT POINT ZERO *Grunt FL 13452* [2]	22	11
18 Jul 87	NO PROTECTION *Grunt FL 86413* [3]	26	5

[1] Jefferson Starship [2] Starship
[1] Paul Kantner and Jefferson Airplane [2] Jefferson Starship [3] Starship

See also Grace SLICK; Paul KANTNER

JEFFERSON STARSHIP – *See JEFFERSON AIRPLANE*

Garland JEFFREYS *US, male vocalist (Singles: 1 week)*

		pos	wks
8 Feb 92	HAIL HAIL ROCK 'N' ROLL *RCA PB 49171*	72	1

JELLYBEAN *US, male producer – John Benitez (Singles: 47 weeks, Albums: 35 weeks)*

		pos	wks
1 Feb 86	SIDEWALK TALK *EMI America EA 210* [1]	47	4
26 Sep 87	THE REAL THING *Chrysalis CHS 3167* [2]	13	10
28 Nov 87 ●	WHO FOUND WHO *Chrysalis CHS JEL 1* [3]	10	10
12 Dec 87	JINGO *Chrysalis JEL 2*	12	10
12 Mar 88	JUST A MIRAGE *Chrysalis JEL 3* [4]	13	10
20 Aug 88	COMING BACK FOR MORE *Chrysalis JEL 4* [5]	41	3
31 Oct 87	JUST VISITING THIS PLANET *Chrysalis CHR 1569*	15	28
3 Sep 88	ROCKS THE HOUSE! *Chrysalis CJB 1*	16	7

[1] Jellybean featuring Catherine Buchanan [2] Jellybean featuring Steven Dante [3] Jellybean featuring Elisa Fiorillo [4] Jellybean featuring Adele Bertei [5] Jellybean featuring Richard Darbyshire

JELLYFISH *US, male vocal / instrumental group (Singles: 20 weeks, Albums: 2 weeks)*

		pos	wks
26 Jan 91	THE KING IS HALF UNDRESSED *Charisma CUSS 1*	39	6
27 Apr 91	BABY'S COMING BACK *Charisma CUSS 2*	51	4
3 Aug 91	THE SCARY-GO-ROUND EP *Charisma CUSS 3*	49	3
26 Oct 91	I WANNA STAY HOME *Charisma CUSS 4*	59	2
1 May 93	THE GHOST AT NUMBER ONE *Charisma CUSDG 10*	43	3
17 Jul 93	NEW MISTAKE *Charisma CUSDG 11*	55	2
22 May 93	SPILT MILK *Charisma CDCUS 20*	21	2

Tracks on The Scary-Go-Round EP: Now She Knows She's Wrong / Bedspring Kiss / She Still Loves Him (Live) / Baby's Coming Back (Live)

JEMINI *UK, male / female vocal duo – Jemma Abbey and Chris Crosby (Singles: 3 weeks)*

		pos	wks
7 Jun 03	CRY BABY *Integral INTEG 001CD*	15	3

Karl JENKINS – *See ADIEMUS*

JERU THE DAMAJA *US, male rapper (Singles: 1 week)*

		pos	wks
7 Dec 96	YA PLAYIN YASELF *ffrr FCD 289*	67	1

JESSICA *Sweden, female vocalist (Singles: 1 week)*

		pos	wks
20 Mar 99	HOW WILL I KNOW (WHO YOU ARE) *Jive 0522412*	47	1

JESSY *Belgium, female vocalist – Jessy de Smet (Singles: 3 weeks)*

		pos	wks
12 Apr 03	LOOK AT ME NOW *Data / Ministry of Sound DATA 46CDS*	29	3

JESUS AND MARY CHAIN *UK, male vocal / instrumental group (Singles: 59 weeks, Albums: 40 weeks)*

		pos	wks
2 Mar 85	NEVER UNDERSTAND *Blanco Y Negro NEG 8*	47	4
8 Jun 85	YOU TRIP ME UP *Blanco Y Negro NEG 13*	55	3
12 Oct 85	JUST LIKE HONEY *Blanco Y Negro NEG 17*	45	3
26 Jul 86	SOME CANDY TALKING *Blanco Y Negro NEG 19*	13	5
2 May 87 ●	APRIL SKIES *Blanco Y Negro NEG 24*	8	6
15 Aug 87	HAPPY WHEN IT RAINS *Blanco Y Negro NEG 25*	25	5
7 Nov 87	DARKLANDS *Blanco Y Negro NEG 29*	33	4
9 Apr 88	SIDEWALKING *Blanco Y Negro NEG 32*	30	3
23 Sep 89	BLUES FROM A GUN *Blanco Y Negro NEG 41*	32	2
18 Nov 89	HEAD ON *Blanco Y Negro NEG 42*	57	2
8 Sep 90	ROLLERCOASTER (EP) *Blanco Y Negro NEG 45*	46	2
15 Feb 92 ●	REVERENCE *Blanco Y Negro NEG 55*	10	4
14 Mar 92	FAR GONE AND OUT *Blanco Y Negro NEG 56*	23	3
4 Jul 92	ALMOST GOLD *Blanco Y Negro NEG 57*	41	2
10 Jul 93	SOUND OF SPEED (EP) *Blanco Y Negro NEG 66CD*	30	2
30 Jul 94	SOMETIMES ALWAYS *Blanco Y Negro NEG 70CD*	22	3
22 Oct 94	COME ON *Blanco Y Negro NEG 73CD1*	52	2
17 Jun 95	I HATE ROCK 'N' ROLL *Blanco Y Negro NEG 81CD*	61	1
18 Apr 98	CRACKING UP *Creation CRESCD 292*	35	2
30 May 98	ILOVEROCKNROLL *Creation CRESCD 296*	38	1
30 Nov 85	PSYCHOCANDY *Blanco Y Negro BYN 7*	31	10
12 Sep 87 ●	DARKLANDS *Blanco Y Negro BYN 11*	5	7
30 Apr 88 ●	BARBED WIRE KISSES *Blanco Y Negro BYN 15*	9	7
21 Oct 89	AUTOMATIC *Blanco Y Negro BYN 20*	11	4
4 Apr 92	HONEY'S DEAD *Blanco Y Negro 9031765542*	14	5
24 Jul 93	THE SOUND OF SPEED *Blanco Y Negro 4509931052*	15	3
27 Aug 94	STONED AND DETHRONED *Blanco Y Negro 4509967172*	13	3
13 Jun 98	MUNKI *Creation CRECD 232*	47	1

Tracks on Rollercoaster (EP): Rollercoaster / Silverblade / Lowlife / Tower of Song. Tracks on Sound of Speed (EP): Snakedriver / Something I Can't Have / Write Record Release Blues / Little Red Rooster

JESUS JONES *UK, male vocal / instrumental group (Singles: 52 weeks, Albums: 31 weeks)*

		pos	wks
25 Feb 89	INFO-FREAKO *Food FOOD 18*	42	3
8 Jul 89	NEVER ENOUGH *Food FOOD 21*	42	3
23 Sep 89	BRING IT ON DOWN *Food FOOD 22*	46	3
7 Apr 90	REAL REAL REAL *Food FOOD 24*	19	8
6 Oct 90	RIGHT HERE RIGHT NOW *Food FOOD 25*	31	4
12 Jan 91 ●	INTERNATIONAL BRIGHT YOUNG THING *Food FOOD 27*	7	7
2 Mar 91	WHO? WHERE? WHY? *Food FOOD 28*	21	7
20 Jul 91	RIGHT HERE RIGHT NOW (re-issue) *Food FOOD 30*	31	4
9 Jan 93 ●	THE DEVIL YOU KNOW *Food CDPERV 1*	10	5
10 Apr 93	THE RIGHT DECISION *Food CDPERV 2*	36	3
10 Jul 93	ZEROES & ONES *Food CDFOODS 44*	30	3
14 Jun 97	THE NEXT BIG THING *Food CDFOOD 95*	49	1
16 Aug 97	CHEMICAL #1 *Food CDFOOD 102*	71	1
14 Oct 89	LIQUIDIZER *Food FOODLP 3*	32	3
9 Feb 91 ★	DOUBT *Food FOODLP 5* ■	1	24
6 Feb 93 ●	PERVERSE *Food FOODCD 8*	6	4

JESUS LIZARD *US, male vocal / instrumental group (Singles: 2 weeks, Albums: 1 week)*

		pos	wks
6 Mar 93	PUSS *Touch And Go TG 83CD*	12	2
10 Sep 94	DOWN *Touch And Go TG 131CD*	64	1

The listed flip side of 'Puss' was 'Oh, the Guilt' by Nirvana

JESUS LOVES YOU *UK, male vocalist – Boy George (Singles: 18 weeks, Albums: 1 week)*

		pos	wks
11 Nov 89	AFTER THE LOVE *More Protein PROT 2*	68	1
23 Feb 91	BOW DOWN MISTER *More Protein PROT 8*	27	8
8 Jun 91	GENERATIONS OF LOVE *More Protein PROT 10*	35	8
12 Dec 92	SWEET TOXIC LOVE *Virgin VS 1449*	65	1
13 Apr 91	THE MARTYR MANTRAS *More Protein CUMLP 1*	60	1

See also BOY GEORGE; CULTURE CLUB

JET *Australia, male vocal / instrumental group (Singles: 4 weeks, Albums: 4 weeks)* pos/wks

6 Sep 03	**ARE YOU GONNA BE MY GIRL?** *Elektra E 7456CD1*	23	2
15 Nov 03	**ROLLOVER DJ** *Elektra E 748CCD1*	34	2
27 Sep 03	GET BORN *Elektra 7559628922*	17	4

JETHRO TULL 186 Top 500 *Unique folk / rock outfit, fronted by the unmistakable, eccentrically dressed Ian Anderson (fl/v), who ranked among the world's top album sellers of the progressive rock era. Surprisingly, they picked up the first ever Grammy for hard rock / heavy metal in 1989 (Singles: 68 weeks, Albums: 236 weeks)* pos/wks

1 Jan 69	**LOVE STORY** *Island WIP 6048*	29	8
14 May 69 ●	**LIVING IN THE PAST** *Island WIP 6056*	3	14
1 Nov 69 ●	**SWEET DREAM** *Chrysalis WIP 6070*	7	11
24 Jan 70 ●	**TEACHER / THE WITCH'S PROMISE** *Chrysalis WIP 6077*	4	9
18 Sep 71	**LIFE IS A LONG SONG / UP THE POOL** *Chrysalis WIP 6106*	11	8
11 Dec 76	**RING OUT SOLSTICE BELLS (EP)** *Chrysalis CXP 2*	28	6
15 Sep 84	**LAP OF LUXURY** *Chrysalis TULL 1*	70	2
16 Jan 88	**SAID SHE WAS A DANCER** *Chrysalis TULL 4*	55	4
21 Mar 92	**ROCKS ON THE ROAD** *Chrysalis TULLX 7*	47	3
22 May 93	**LIVING IN THE (SLIGHTLY MORE RECENT) PAST** *Chrysalis CDCHSS 3970*	32	3
2 Nov 68 ●	THIS WAY *Island ILPS 9085*	10	22
9 Aug 69 ★	STAND UP *Island ILPS 9103* ■	1	29
9 May 70 ●	BENEFIT *Island ILPS 9123*	3	13
3 Apr 71 ●	AQUALUNG *Island ILPS 9145*	4	21
18 Mar 72 ●	THICK AS A BRICK *Chrysalis CHR 1003* ▲	5	14
15 Jul 72 ●	LIVING IN THE PAST *Chrysalis CJT 1*	8	11
28 Jul 73	A PASSION PLAY *Chrysalis CHR 1040* ▲	13	8
2 Nov 74	WAR CHILD *Chrysalis CHR 1067*	14	4
27 Sep 75	MINSTREL IN THE GALLERY *Chrysalis CHR 1082*	20	6
31 Jan 76	M.U. THE BEST OF JETHRO TULL *Chrysalis CHR 1078*	44	5
15 May 76	TOO OLD TO ROCK 'N' ROLL: TOO YOUNG TO DIE *Chrysalis CHR 1111*	25	10
19 Feb 77	SONGS FROM THE WOOD *Chrysalis CHR 1132*	13	12
29 Apr 78	HEAVY HORSES *Chrysalis CHR 1175*	20	10
14 Oct 78	LIVE BURSTING OUT *Chrysalis CJT 4*	17	8
6 Oct 79	STORM WATCH *Chrysalis CDL 1238*	27	4
6 Sep 80	A *Chrysalis CDL 1301*	25	5
17 Apr 82	BROADSWORD AND THE BEAST *Chrysalis CDL 1380*	27	19
15 Sep 84	UNDER WRAPS *Chrysalis CDL 1461*	18	5
2 Nov 85	ORIGINAL MASTERS *Chrysalis JTTV 1*	63	3
19 Sep 87	CREST OF A KNAVE *Chrysalis CDL 1590*	19	10
9 Jul 88	20 YEARS OF JETHRO TULL *Chrysalis TBOX 1*	78	1
2 Sep 89	ROCK ISLAND *Chrysalis CHR 1708*	18	6
14 Sep 91	CATFISH RISING *Chrysalis CHR 1886*	27	3
26 Sep 92	A LITTLE LIGHT MUSIC *Chrysalis CCD 1954*	34	2
16 Sep 95	ROOTS TO BRANCHES *Chrysalis CDCHR 6109*	20	3
29 Jun 96	AQUALUNG *Chrysalis CD25 AQUA1*	53	1
4 Sep 99	J-TULL DOT COM *Papillon BTFLYCD 0001*	44	1

Tracks on Ring Out Solstice Bells (EP): Ring Out Solstice Bells / March the Mad Scientist / The Christmas Song / Pan Dance. 'Living in the (Slightly More Recent) Past' is a live version of the original

JETS *UK, male vocal / instrumental group (Singles: 38 weeks, Albums: 6 weeks)* pos/wks

22 Aug 81	**SUGAR DOLL** *EMI 5211*	55	3
31 Oct 81	**YES TONIGHT JOSEPHINE** *EMI 5247*	25	11
6 Feb 82	**LOVE MAKES THE WORLD GO ROUND** *EMI 5262*	21	9
24 Apr 82	**THE HONEYDRIPPER** *EMI 5289*	58	3
9 Oct 82	**SOMEBODY TO LOVE** *EMI 5342*	56	3
6 Aug 83	**BLUE SKIES** *EMI 5405*	53	3
17 Dec 83	**ROCKIN' AROUND THE CHRISTMAS TREE** *PRT 7P 297*	62	4
13 Oct 84	**PARTY DOLL** *PRT JETS 2*	72	2
10 Apr 82	100 PERCENT COTTON *EMI EMC 3399*	30	6

JETS *US, male / female vocal / instrumental group (Singles: 19 weeks, Albums: 4 weeks)* pos/wks

31 Jan 87 ●	**CRUSH ON YOU** *MCA MCA 1048*	5	13
25 Apr 87	**CURIOSITY** *MCA MCA 1119*	41	4
28 May 88	**ROCKET 2 U** *MCA MCA 1226*	69	2
11 Apr 87	CRUSH ON YOU *MCA MCF 3312*	57	4

Joan JETT and the BLACKHEARTS *US, female vocalist with male vocal / instrumental group (Singles: 21 weeks, Albums: 7 weeks)* pos/wks

24 Apr 82 ●	**I LOVE ROCK 'N' ROLL** *Epic EPC A 2152* ▲	4	10
10 Jul 82	**CRIMSON AND CLOVER** *Epic EPC A 2485*	60	3
20 Aug 88	**I HATE MYSELF FOR LOVING YOU** *London LON 195*	46	6
31 Mar 90	**DIRTY DEEDS** *Chrysalis CHS 3518* [1]	69	1
19 Feb 94	**I LOVE ROCK & ROLL (re-issue)** *Reprise W 0232CD*	75	1
8 May 82	I LOVE ROCK 'N' ROLL *Epic EPC 85686*	25	7

[1] Joan Jett

JEWEL *US, female vocalist – Jewel Kilcher (Singles: 9 weeks, Albums: 4 weeks)* pos/wks

14 Jun 97	**WHO WILL SAVE YOUR SOUL** *Atlantic A 8514CD*	52	1
9 Aug 97	**YOU WERE MEANT FOR ME (re)** *Atlantic A 5463CD*	32	3
21 Nov 98	**HANDS** *Atlantic AT 0055CD*	41	2
26 Jun 99	**DOWN SO LONG** *Atlantic AT 0069CD*	38	2
30 Aug 03	**INTUITION** *Atlantic W 619CD*	52	1
28 Nov 98	SPIRIT *Atlantic 7567829502*	54	1
9 Mar 02	THIS WAY *Atlantic 7567835192*	34	3

JEZ & CHOOPIE *UK / Israel, male DJ / production duo – Jeremy Ansell and David Geyra (Singles: 2 weeks)* pos/wks

21 Mar 98	**YIM** *Multiply CDMULTY 31*	36	2

JHELISA *US, female vocalist (Singles: 1 week)* pos/wks

1 Jul 95	**FRIENDLY PRESSURE** *Dorado DOR 040CD*	75	1

JICKS – *See Stephen MALKMUS*

JIGSAW *UK, male vocal / instrumental group (Singles: 16 weeks)* pos/wks

1 Nov 75 ●	**SKY HIGH** *Splash CPI 1*	9	11
6 Aug 77	**IF I HAVE TO GO AWAY** *Splash CP 11*	36	5

JILTED JOHN *UK, male vocalist – Graham Fellows (Singles: 12 weeks)* pos/wks

12 Aug 78 ●	**JILTED JOHN** *EMI International INT 567*	4	12

JIMMY EAT WORLD *US, male vocal / instrumental group (Singles: 6 weeks, Albums: 4 weeks)* pos/wks

17 Nov 01	**SALT SWEAT SUGAR** *Dreamworks 4508782*	60	1
9 Feb 02	**THE MIDDLE** *Dreamworks 4508482*	26	3
15 Jun 02	**SWEETNESS** *Dreamworks 4508342*	38	2
9 Feb 02	JIMMY EAT WORLD *Dreamworks 4503482*	62	4

JIMMY THE HOOVER *UK, male / female vocal / instrumental group (Singles: 8 weeks)* pos/wks

25 Jun 83	**TANTALISE (WO WO EE YEH YEH)** *Innervision A 3406*	18	8

JINGLE BELLES *US / UK, female vocal group (Singles: 4 weeks)* pos/wks

17 Dec 83	**CHRISTMAS SPECTRE** *Passion PASH 14*	37	4

JINNY *Italy, female vocalist – Janine Brown (Singles: 16 weeks)* pos/wks

29 Jun 91	**KEEP WARM** *Virgin VS 1356*	68	3
22 May 93	**FEEL THE RHYTHM** *Logic 401633001022*	74	1
15 Jul 95	**KEEP WARM (re-mix)** *Multiply CDMULTY 5*	11	8
16 Dec 95	**WANNA BE WITH YOU** *Multiply CDMULTY 8*	30	4

JIVE BUNNY and the MASTERMIXERS *UK, male DJ / production duo – Andy Pickles and Les Hemstock (Singles: 68 weeks, Albums: 29 weeks)* pos/wks

15 Jul 89 ★	**SWING THE MOOD** *Music Factory Dance MFD 001*	1	19
14 Oct 89 ★	**THAT'S WHAT I LIKE** *Music Factory Dance MFD 002*	1	12
16 Dec 89 ★	**LET'S PARTY** *Music Factory Dance MFD 003* ■	1	6
17 Mar 90 ●	**THAT SOUNDS GOOD TO ME** *Music Factory Dance MFD 004*	4	6

25 Aug 90 ● **CAN CAN YOU PARTY** *Music Factory Dance MFD 007* 8 6
17 Nov 90 **LET'S SWING AGAIN** *Music Factory Dance MFD 009* 19 5
22 Dec 90 **THE CRAZY PARTY MIXES** *Music Factory Dance MFD 010* 13 5
23 Mar 91 **OVER TO YOU JOHN (HERE WE GO AGAIN)** *Music Factory Dance MFD 012* 28 5
20 Jul 91 **HOT SUMMER SALSA** *Music Factory Dance MFD 013* 43 2
23 Nov 91 **ROCK 'N' ROLL DANCE PARTY** *Music Factory Dance MFD 015* 48 2
9 Dec 89 ● **JIVE BUNNY – THE ALBUM** *Telstar STAR 2390* 2 22
8 Dec 90 **IT'S PARTY TIME** *Telstar STAR 2449* 23 7

See also Liz KERSHAW and Bruno BROOKES

JO JO GUNNE

US, male vocal / instrumental group (Singles: 12 weeks) pos/wks

25 Mar 72 ● **RUN RUN RUN** *Asylum AYM 501* 6 12

JOAN COLLINS FAN CLUB

UK, male comedian / vocalist – Julian Clary (Singles: 3 weeks) pos/wks

18 Jun 88 **LEADER OF THE PACK** *10 TEN 227* 60 3

John Paul JOANS *UK, male vocalist (Singles: 7 weeks)* pos/wks

19 Dec 70 **THE MAN FROM NAZARETH (re)** *RAK 107* 25 7

JOBABE – *See REAL & RICHARDSON featuring JOBABE*

JOBOXERS *UK, male vocal / instrumental group (Singles: 33 weeks, Albums: 5 weeks)* pos/wks

19 Feb 83 ● **BOXERBEAT** *RCA BOX 1* 3 15
21 May 83 ● **JUST GOT LUCKY** *RCA BOXX 2* 7 9
13 Aug 83 **JOHNNY FRIENDLY** *RCA BOXX 3* 31 8
12 Nov 83 **JEALOUS LOVE** *RCA BOXX 4* 72 1
24 Sep 83 **LIKE GANGBUSTERS** *RCA BOXXLP 1* 18 5

JOCASTA *UK, male vocal / instrumental group (Singles: 2 weeks)* pos/wks

15 Feb 97 **GO** *Epic 6641415* 50 1
3 May 97 **CHANGE ME** *Epic 6643902* 60 1

JOCKMASTER B.A. – *See MAD JOCKS featuring JOCKMASTER B.A.*

JOCKO *US, male DJ / rapper – Jocko Henderson, d. 15 Jul 2000 (Singles: 3 weeks)* pos/wks

23 Feb 80 **RHYTHM TALK** *Philadelphia International PIR 8222* 56 3

JODE featuring YO-HANS

UK, male / female vocal duo (Singles: 2 weeks) pos/wks

19 Dec 98 **WALK...(THE DOG) LIKE AN EGYPTIAN** *Logic 74321640332* 48 2

JODECI

US, male vocal group (Singles: 19 weeks, Albums: 8 weeks) pos/wks

16 Jan 93 **CHERISH** *Uptown MCSTD 1726* 56 2
11 Dec 93 **CRY FOR YOU** *Uptown MCSTD 1951* 56 1
16 Jul 94 **FEENIN'** *Uptown MCSTD 1984* 18 3
28 Jan 95 **CRY FOR YOU (re-issue)** *Uptown MCSTD 2039* 20 3
24 Jun 95 **FREEK 'N YOU** *Uptown MCSTD 2072* 17 5
9 Dec 95 **LOVE U 4 LIFE** *Uptown MCSTD 2105* 23 3
25 May 96 **GET ON UP** *MCA MCSTD 48010* 20 2
29 Jul 95 ● **THE SHOW THE AFTER PARTY THE HOTEL** *Uptown MCD 11258* 4 8

See also K-Ci & JoJo

JODIE *Australia, female vocalist (Singles: 1 week)* pos/wks

25 Feb 95 **ANYTHING YOU WANT** *Mercury MERCD 423* 47 1

JOE *US, male vocalist – Joseph Thomas (Singles: 45 weeks, Albums: 9 weeks)* pos/wks

22 Jan 94 **I'M IN LUV** *Mercury JOECD 1* 22 4
25 Jun 94 **THE ONE FOR ME** *Mercury JOECD 2* 34 2
22 Oct 94 **ALL OR NOTHING** *Mercury JOECD 3* 56 1
27 Apr 96 **ALL THE THINGS (YOUR MAN WON'T DO)** *Island CID 634* 34 3
14 Jun 97 **DON'T WANNA BE A PLAYER** *Jive JIVECD 410* 16 3
27 Sep 97 **THE LOVE SCENE** *Jive JIVECD 430* 22 2
10 Jan 98 **GOOD GIRLS** *Jive JIVECD 442* 29 3
22 Aug 98 **NO ONE ELSE COMES CLOSE** *Jive 0521682* 41 2
31 Oct 98 **ALL THAT I AM** *Jive 0518532* 52 1
11 Mar 00 ● **THANK GOD I FOUND YOU (re)** *Columbia 6690582* [1] ▲ 10 10
15 Jul 00 **TREAT HER LIKE A LADY** *Jive 9250772* 60 1
17 Feb 01 ● **STUTTER** *Jive 9251632* [2] ▲ 7 8
5 May 01 **I WANNA KNOW** *Jive 9252102* 37 2
16 Feb 02 **LET'S STAY HOME TONIGHT** *Jive 9253222* 29 2
14 Sep 02 **WHAT IF A WOMAN** *Jive 9253962* 53 1
12 Feb 94 **EVERYTHING** *Vertigo 5188072* 53 1
9 Aug 97 **ALL THAT I AM** *Jive CHIP 183* 26 4
29 Apr 00 **MY NAME IS JOE** *Jive 9220352* 46 4

[1] Mariah Carey featuring Joe and 98 Degrees [2] Joe featuring Mystikal

JOE PUBLIC *US, male rap group (Singles: 5 weeks)* pos/wks

11 Jul 92 **LIVE AND LEARN** *Columbia 6575267* 43 4
28 Nov 92 **I'VE BEEN WATCHIN'** *Columbia 6587657* 75 1

Billy JOEL (76 Top 500) *Platinum-plated singer / songwriter / pianist, b. 9 May 1949, Long Island, US. This relatively youthful Grammy Living Legend Award recipient was the first artist to have five albums pass the seven-million mark Stateside. Best-selling single: 'Uptown Girl' 974,000 (Singles: 146 weeks, Albums: 349 weeks)* pos/wks

11 Feb 78 **JUST THE WAY YOU ARE** *CBS 5872* 19 9
24 Jun 78 **MOVIN' OUT (ANTHONY'S SONG)** *CBS 6412* 35 6
2 Dec 78 **MY LIFE** *CBS 6821* 12 15
28 Apr 79 **UNTIL THE NIGHT** *CBS 7242* 50 3
12 Apr 80 **ALL FOR LEYNA** *CBS 8325* 40 4
9 Aug 80 **IT'S STILL ROCK AND ROLL TO ME** *CBS 8753* ▲ 14 11
15 Oct 83 ★ **UPTOWN GIRL** *CBS A 3775* 1 17
10 Dec 83 ● **TELL HER ABOUT IT** *CBS A 3655* ▲ 4 10
18 Feb 84 ● **AN INNOCENT MAN** *CBS A 4142* 8 10
28 Apr 84 **THE LONGEST TIME** *CBS A 4280* 25 8
23 Jun 84 **LEAVE A TENDER MOMENT ALONE / GOODNIGHT SAIGON** *CBS A 4521* 29 7
22 Feb 86 **SHE'S ALWAYS A WOMAN / JUST THE WAY YOU ARE (re-issue)** *CBS A 6862* 53 1
20 Sep 86 **A MATTER OF TRUST** *CBS 650057 7* 52 4
30 Sep 89 ● **WE DIDN'T START THE FIRE** *CBS JOEL 1* ▲ 7 10
16 Dec 89 **LENINGRAD** *CBS JOEL 3* 53 4
10 Mar 90 **I GO TO EXTREMES** *CBS JOEL 2* 70 2
29 Aug 92 **ALL SHOOK UP** *Columbia 6583437* 27 4
31 Jul 93 ● **THE RIVER OF DREAMS** *Columbia 6595432* 3 14
23 Oct 93 **ALL ABOUT SOUL** *Columbia 6597362* 32 4
26 Feb 94 **NO MAN'S LAND** *Columbia 6599202* 50 3
25 Mar 78 **THE STRANGER** *CBS 82311* 25 40
25 Nov 78 ● **52ND STREET** *CBS 83181* ▲ 10 43
22 Mar 80 ● **GLASS HOUSES** *CBS 86108* ▲ 9 24
10 Oct 81 **SONGS IN THE ATTIC** *CBS 85273* 57 3
2 Oct 82 **THE NYLON CURTAIN** *CBS 85959* 27 8
10 Sep 83 ● **AN INNOCENT MAN** *CBS 25554* 2 95
4 Feb 84 **COLD SPRING HARBOUR** *CBS 32400* 95 1
23 Jun 84 **PIANO MAN** *CBS 32002* 98 1
20 Jul 85 ● **GREATEST HITS – VOLUME I & VOLUME II** *CBS 88666* 7 39
16 Aug 86 **THE BRIDGE** *CBS 86323* 38 10
28 Nov 87 **KOHYEPT – LIVE IN LENINGRAD** *CBS 460 4071* 92 1
4 Nov 89 ● **STORM FRONT** *CBS 4656581* ▲ 5 25
14 Aug 93 ● **RIVER OF DREAMS** *Columbia 4738722* ▲ 3 26
1 Nov 97 **GREATEST HITS – VOLUME III** *Columbia 4882362* 23 4
13 Jun 98 **GREATEST HITS – VOLUMES I II & III** *Columbia 4912742* 33 4
27 May 00 **2000 YEARS – THE MILLENNIUM CONCERT** *Columbia 4979812* 68 1
31 Mar 01 ● **THE ULTIMATE COLLECTION** *Columbia SONYTV 98CD* 4 24

'Goodnight Saigon' listed only from 30 Jun 1984

JOHANN *Germany, male producer – Johann Bley (Singles: 1 week)* pos/wks

16 Mar 96 **NEW KICKS** *Perfecto PERF 118CD* 54 1

Angela JOHN – *See José PADILLA featuring Angela JOHN*

Elton JOHN (6 | Top 500) *Flamboyant singer / songwriter / pianist, b. Reginald Dwight, 25 Mar 1947, Pinner, Middlesex, UK. Almost as famous for his outrageous wardrobe as his music, Elton was the biggest-selling pop act of the 1970s, and has sold more albums in the UK and US than any British male singer, with total worldwide sales exceeding 150 million. He is the only British act to enter the US singles chart at No.1 and also recorded the first two albums to enter the US chart at No.1. He holds the record for headlining appearances at New York's Madison Square Garden. Elton, twice chairman of Watford Football Club, is the only act to chart every year from 1971 to 1999 in the UK and US. His Greatest Hits album has sold more than 16 million in the US and he has topped the US adult contemporary chart a record 16 times. 'Candle in the Wind 1997' (which he performed at the funeral of Diana, Princess of Wales) topped the chart in almost every country. In the UK it sold nearly five million in six weeks and in the US had record advance orders of 8.7 million (and total sales in excess of 11 million). It also spent a staggering three years in the Canadian Top 20, which included 45 weeks at No.1. It is the world's best-selling single, with sales of 33 million (4,864,611 in the UK). Elton's UK singles sales now amount to more than 13 million. His lyric-writing partners have included, most influentially, Bernie Taupin and, more recently, Sir Tim Rice. He became Sir Elton John in 1998 (Singles: 623 Weeks, Albums: 970 weeks)* pos/wks

23 Jan 71 ● **YOUR SONG** *DJM DJS 233* ... 7 12
22 Apr 72 ● **ROCKET MAN (I THINK IT'S GOING TO BE A LONG LONG TIME)** *DJM DJX 501* ... 2 13
9 Sep 72 **HONKY CAT** *DJM DJS 269* ... 31 6
4 Nov 72 ● **CROCODILE ROCK** *DJM DJS 271* ▲ ... 5 14
20 Jan 73 ● **DANIEL** *DJM DJS 275* ... 4 10
7 Jul 73 ● **SATURDAY NIGHT'S ALRIGHT FOR FIGHTING** *DJM DJX 502* ... 7 9
29 Sep 73 ● **GOODBYE YELLOW BRICK ROAD** *DJM DJS 285* ... 6 16
8 Dec 73 **STEP INTO CHRISTMAS** *DJM DJS 290* ... 24 7
2 Mar 74 **CANDLE IN THE WIND** *DJM DJS 297* ... 11 9
1 Jun 74 **DON'T LET THE SUN GO DOWN ON ME** *DJM DJS 302* ... 16 8
14 Sep 74 **THE BITCH IS BACK** *DJM DJS 322* ... 15 7
23 Nov 74 ● **LUCY IN THE SKY WITH DIAMONDS** *DJM DJS 340* ▲ ... 10 10
8 Mar 75 **PHILADELPHIA FREEDOM** *DJM DJS 354* [1] ▲ ... 12 9
28 Jun 75 **SOMEONE SAVED MY LIFE TONIGHT** *DJM DJS 385* ... 22 5
4 Oct 75 **ISLAND GIRL** *DJM DJS 610* ▲ ... 14 8
20 Mar 76 ● **PINBALL WIZARD** *DJM DJS 652* ... 7 7
3 Jul 76 ★ **DON'T GO BREAKING MY HEART** *Rocket ROKN 512* [2] ▲ ... 1 14
25 Sep 76 **BENNIE AND THE JETS** *DJM DJS 10705* ▲ ... 37 5
13 Nov 76 **SORRY SEEMS TO BE THE HARDEST WORD** *Rocket ROKN 517* ... 11 10
26 Feb 77 **CRAZY WATER** *Rocket ROKN 521* ... 27 6
11 Jun 77 **BITE YOUR LIP (GET UP AND DANCE)** *Rocket ROKN 526* ... 28 4
15 Apr 78 **EGO** *Rocket ROKN 538* ... 34 6
21 Oct 78 **PART TIME LOVE** *Rocket XPRES 1* ... 15 13
16 Dec 78 ● **SONG FOR GUY** *Rocket XPRES 5* ... 4 10
12 May 79 **ARE YOU READY FOR LOVE** *Rocket XPRES 13* ... 42 6
24 May 80 **LITTLE JEANNIE** *Rocket XPRES 32* ... 33 7
23 Aug 80 **SARTORIAL ELOQUENCE** *Rocket XPRES 41* ... 44 5
21 Mar 81 **I SAW HER STANDING THERE** *DJM DJS 10965* [3] ... 40 4
23 May 81 **NOBODY WINS** *Rocket XPRES 54* ... 42 5
27 Mar 82 ● **BLUE EYES** *Rocket XPRES 71* ... 8 10
12 Jun 82 **EMPTY GARDEN** *Rocket XPRES 77* ... 51 4
30 Apr 83 ● **I GUESS THAT'S WHY THEY CALL IT THE BLUES** *Rocket XPRES 91* ... 5 15
30 Jul 83 ● **I'M STILL STANDING** *Rocket EJS 1* ... 4 11
15 Oct 83 **KISS THE BRIDE** *Rocket EJS 2* ... 20 7
10 Dec 83 **COLD AS CHRISTMAS (IN THE MIDDLE OF THE YEAR)** *Rocket EJS 3* ... 33 6
26 May 84 ● **SAD SONGS (SAY SO MUCH)** *Rocket PH 7* ... 7 12
11 Aug 84 ● **PASSENGERS** *Rocket EJS 5* ... 5 11
20 Oct 84 **WHO WEARS THESE SHOES** *Rocket EJS 6* ... 50 3
2 Mar 85 **BREAKING HEARTS (AIN'T WHAT IT USED TO BE)** *Rocket EJS 7* ... 59 3
15 Jun 85 **ACT OF WAR** *Rocket EJS 8* [4] ... 32 5
12 Oct 85 ● **NIKITA** *Rocket EJS 9* ... 3 13
9 Nov 85 **THAT'S WHAT FRIENDS ARE FOR** *Arista ARIST 638* [5] ▲ ... 16 9
7 Dec 85 **WRAP HER UP** *Rocket EJS 10* ... 12 10
1 Mar 86 **CRY TO HEAVEN** *Rocket EJS 11* ... 47 4
4 Oct 86 **HEARTACHE ALL OVER THE WORLD** *Rocket EJS 12* ... 45 4
29 Nov 86 **SLOW RIVERS** *Rocket EJS 13* [6] ... 44 8
20 Jun 87 **FLAMES OF PARADISE** *CBS 6508657* [7] ... 59 3
16 Jan 88 ● **CANDLE IN THE WIND** *Rocket EJS 15* ... 5 11
4 Jun 88 **I DON'T WANNA GO ON WITH YOU LIKE THAT** *Rocket EJS 16* 30 8
3 Sep 88 **TOWN OF PLENTY** *Rocket EJS 17* ... 74 1
6 May 89 **THROUGH THE STORM** *Arista 112185* [8] ... 41 3
26 Aug 89 **HEALING HANDS** *Rocket EJS 19* ... 45 5
4 Nov 89 **SACRIFICE** *Rocket EJS 20* ... 55 3
9 Jun 90 ★ **SACRIFICE / HEALING HANDS (re-issue)** *Rocket EJS 22* ... 1 15
18 Aug 90 **CLUB AT THE END OF THE STREET / WHISPERS** *Rocket EJS 23* ... 47 3
20 Oct 90 **YOU GOTTA LOVE SOMEONE** *Rocket EJS 24* ... 33 4
15 Dec 90 **EASIER TO WALK AWAY (re)** *Rocket EJS 25* ... 63 2
7 Dec 91 ★ **DON'T LET THE SUN GO DOWN ON ME** *Epic 6576467* [9] ■ ▲ ... 1 10
6 Jun 92 ● **THE ONE** *Rocket EJS 28* ... 10 8
1 Aug 92 **RUNAWAY TRAIN** *Rocket EJS 29* [10] ... 31 4
7 Nov 92 **THE LAST SONG** *Rocket EJS 30* ... 21 4
22 May 93 **SIMPLE LIFE** *Rocket EJSCD 31* ... 44 2
20 Nov 93 ● **TRUE LOVE** *Rocket EJSCX 32* [2] ... 2 10
26 Feb 94 ● **DON'T GO BREAKING MY HEART (re-recording)** *Rocket EJRCD 33* [11] ... 7 7
14 May 94 **AIN'T NOTHING LIKE THE REAL THING** *London LONCD 350* [12] ... 24 4
9 Jul 94 **CAN YOU FEEL THE LOVE TONIGHT** *Mercury EJCD 34* ... 14 9
8 Oct 94 **CIRCLE OF LIFE** *Rocket EJSCD 35* ... 11 12
4 Mar 95 **BELIEVE** *Rocket EJSCD 36* ... 15 7
20 May 95 **MADE IN ENGLAND** *Rocket EJSCD 37* ... 18 5
3 Feb 96 **PLEASE** *Rocket EJSCD 40* ... 33 3
14 Dec 96 ● **LIVE LIKE HORSES** *Rocket LLHDD 1* [13] ... 9 6
20 Sep 97 ★ **CANDLE IN THE WIND 1997 / SOMETHING ABOUT THE WAY YOU LOOK TONIGHT** *Rocket PTCD 1* ◆ ■ ▲ ... 1 24
14 Feb 98 **RECOVER YOUR SOUL** *Rocket EJSCD 42* ... 16 3
13 Jun 98 **IF THE RIVER CAN BEND** *Rocket EJSDD 43* ... 32 2
6 Mar 99 ● **WRITTEN IN THE STARS (re)** *Mercury EJSCD 45* [14] ... 10 8
6 Oct 01 ● **I WANT LOVE** *Rocket / Mercury 5887062* ... 9 10
26 Jan 02 **THIS TRAIN DON'T STOP THERE ANYMORE** *Rocket / Mercury 588962* ... 24 4
13 Apr 02 **ORIGINAL SIN** *Rocket / Mercury 5889992* ... 39 2
27 Jul 02 ● **YOUR SONG (re)** *Mercury 639972* [15] ... 4 10
21 Dec 02 ★ **SORRY SEEMS TO BE THE HARDEST WORD (re-recording)** *Innocent SINDX 43* [16] ■ ... 1 17
19 Jul 03 **ARE YOU READY FOR LOVE (12" re-mix)** *Southern Fried ECB 50LOVE* ... 66 1
6 Sep 03 ★ **ARE YOU READY FOR LOVE (re-mix)** *Southern Fried ECB 50CDS* ... 1 13

23 May 70 ● **ELTON JOHN** *DJM DJLPS 406* ... 5 22
16 Jan 71 ● **TUMBLEWEED CONNECTION** *DJM DJLPS 410* ... 2 20
1 May 71 **THE ELTON JOHN LIVE ALBUM 17-11-70** *DJM DJLPS 414* ... 20 2
20 May 72 **MADMAN ACROSS THE WATER** *DJM DJLPH 420* ... 41 2
3 Jun 72 ● **HONKY CHATEAU** *DJM DJLPH 423* ▲ ... 2 23
10 Feb 73 ★ **DON'T SHOOT ME I'M ONLY THE PIANO PLAYER** *DJM DJLPH 427* ■ ▲ ... 1 42
3 Nov 73 ★ **GOODBYE YELLOW BRICK ROAD** *DJM DJLPO 1001* ▲ ... 1 84
13 Jul 74 ★ **CARIBOU** *DJM DJLPH 439* ■ ▲ ... 1 18
23 Nov 74 ★ **ELTON JOHN'S GREATEST HITS** *DJM DJLPH 442* ■ ▲ ... 1 84
7 Jun 75 ● **CAPTAIN FANTASTIC AND THE BROWN DIRT COWBOY** *DJM DJLPX 1* ▲ ... 2 24
8 Nov 75 ● **ROCK OF THE WESTIES** *DJM DJLPH 464* ▲ ... 5 12
15 May 76 ● **HERE AND THERE** *DJM DJLPH 473* ... 6 9
6 Nov 76 ● **BLUE MOVES** *Rocket ROSP 1* ... 3 15
15 Oct 77 ● **ELTON JOHN'S GREATEST HITS VOLUME 2** *DJM DJH 20520* ... 6 24
4 Nov 78 ● **A SINGLE MAN** *Rocket TRAIN 1* ... 8 26
20 Oct 79 **VICTIM OF LOVE** *Rocket HISPD 125* ... 41 3
8 Mar 80 **LADY SAMANTHA** *DJM 22085* ... 56 2
31 May 80 **21 AT 33** *Rocket HISPD 126* ... 12 13
25 Oct 80 **THE VERY BEST OF ELTON JOHN** *K-Tel NE 1094* ... 24 13
30 May 81 **THE FOX** *Rocket TRAIN 16* ... 12 12
17 Apr 82 **JUMP UP** *Rocket HISPD 127* ... 13 12
6 Nov 82 **LOVE SONGS** *TV TVA 3* ... 39 13
11 Jun 83 ● **TOO LOW FOR ZERO** *Rocket HISPD 24* ... 7 73
30 Jun 84 ● **BREAKING HEARTS** *Rocket HISPD 25* ... 2 23
16 Nov 85 ● **ICE ON FIRE** *Rocket HISPD 26* ... 3 23

15 Nov 86 **LEATHER JACKETS** *Rocket EJLP 1* 24 9
12 Sep 87 **LIVE IN AUSTRALIA** *Rocket EJBXL 1* [1] 43 7
16 Jul 88 **REG STRIKES BACK** *Rocket EJLP 3* 18 6
23 Sep 89 ★ **SLEEPING WITH THE PAST** *Rocket 8388391* 1 42
10 Nov 90 ★ **THE VERY BEST OF ELTON JOHN** *Rocket 8469471* ■ 1 97
27 Jun 92 ● **THE ONE** *Rocket 5123602* 2 18
4 Dec 93 ● **DUETS** *Rocket 5184782* 5 18
1 Apr 95 ● **MADE IN ENGLAND** *Rocket 5261852* 3 14
18 Nov 95 ● **LOVE SONGS** *Rocket 5287882* 4 48
11 Oct 97 ● **THE BIG PICTURE** *Rocket 5362662* 3 23
3 Apr 99 **ELTON JOHN AND TIM RICE'S AIDA** *Mercury 5246512* [2] 29 2
25 Nov 00 ● **ONE NIGHT ONLY – THE GREATEST HITS** *Mercury 5483342* 7 13
13 Oct 01 ● **SONGS FROM THE WEST COAST** *Mercury 5863302* 2 34
20 Oct 01 **GOODBYE YELLOW BRICK ROAD (re-issue)** *Rocket 5281592* 41 4
23 Nov 02 ● **THE GREATEST HITS 1970 – 2002** *Mercury 634992* ....3 41+

[1] Elton John Band [2] Elton John and Kiki Dee [3] Elton John Band featuring John Lennon and the Muscle Shoals Horns [4] Elton John and Millie Jackson [5] Dionne Warwick and Friends featuring Elton John, Stevie Wonder and Gladys Knight [6] Elton John and Cliff Richard [7] Jennifer Rush and Elton John [8] Aretha Franklin and Elton John [9] George Michael and Elton John [10] Elton John and Eric Clapton [11] Elton John with RuPaul [12] Marcella Detroit and Elton John [13] Elton John and Luciano Pavarotti [14] Elton John and LeAnn Rimes [15] Elton John & Alessandro Safina [16] Blue featuring Elton John [1] Elton John and the Melbourne Symphony Orchestra [2] Elton John and Friends

'Bite Your Lip (Get Up and Dance)' was one side of a double-sided chart entry, the other being 'Chicago' by Kiki Dee. 'Wrap Her Up' features George Michael as uncredited co-vocalist. 'Candle in the Wind' 1988 was a live recording 'Live in Australia' reappeared in 1988 as EJLP 2; EJB XL 1 was the original 'de luxe' version. The two 'The Very Best of Elton John' albums are different

See also MELBOURNE SYMPHONY ORCHESTRA

Robert JOHN

US, male vocalist – Robert John Pedrick (Singles: 13 weeks) pos/wks

17 Jul 68 **IF YOU DON'T WANT MY LOVE** *CBS 3436* 42 5
20 Oct 79 **SAD EYES** *EMI American EA 101* ▲ 31 8

JOHNNA *US, female vocalist (Singles: 3 weeks)* pos/wks

10 Feb 96 **DO WHAT YOU FEEL** *PWL International PWL 323CD* 43 2
11 May 96 **IN MY DREAMS** *PWL International PWL 325CD* 66 1

JOHNNY and CHARLEY *Spain, male vocal duo (Singles: 1 week)* pos/wks

14 Oct 65 **LA YENKA** *Pye International 7N 25326* 49 1

JOHNNY and the HURRICANES

US, male instrumental quintet (Singles: 88 weeks, Albums: 5 weeks) pos/wks

9 Oct 59 ● **RED RIVER ROCK** *London HL 8948* 3 16
25 Dec 59 **REVEILLE ROCK** *London HL 9017* 14 5
17 Mar 60 ● **BEATNIK FLY** *London HLI 9072* 8 19
16 Jun 60 ● **DOWN YONDER** *London HLX 9134* 8 11
29 Sep 60 ● **ROCKING GOOSE** *London HLX 9190* 3 20
2 Mar 61 **JA-DA** *London HLX 9289* 14 9
6 Jul 61 **OLD SMOKIE / HIGH VOLTAGE** *London HLX 9378* 24 8
3 Dec 60 **STORMSVILLE** *London HAI 2269* 18 1
1 Apr 61 **BIG SOUND OF JOHNNY AND THE HURRICANES** *London HAK 2322* 14 4

JOHNNY CORPORATE

US, male production duo (Singles: 2 weeks) pos/wks

28 Oct 00 **SUNDAY SHOUTIN'** *Defected DFECT 21CDS* 45 2

JOHNNY HATES JAZZ *UK, male vocal / instrumental group (Singles: 45 weeks, Albums: 39 weeks)* pos/wks

11 Apr 87 ● **SHATTERED DREAMS** *Virgin VS 948* 5 14
29 Aug 87 **I DON'T WANT TO BE A HERO** *Virgin VS 1000* 11 10
21 Nov 87 **TURN BACK THE CLOCK** *Virgin VS 1017* 12 11
27 Feb 88 **HEART OF GOLD** *Virgin VS 1045* 19 7
9 Jul 88 **DON'T SAY IT'S LOVE** *Virgin VS 1081* 48 3
23 Jan 88 ★ **TURN BACK THE CLOCK** *Virgin V 2475* ■ 1 39

JOHNSON

UK, male / female vocal / instrumental duo (Singles: 1 week) pos/wks

27 Mar 99 **SAY YOU LOVE ME** *Higher Ground HIGHS 18CD* 56 1

Andreas JOHNSON

Sweden, male vocalist (Singles: 12 weeks, Albums: 2 weeks) pos/wks

5 Feb 00 ● **GLORIOUS** *WEA WEA 254CD* 4 11
27 May 00 **THE GAMES WE PLAY** *WEA WEA 264* 41 1
19 Feb 00 **LIEBLING** *WEA 3984269142* 46 2

Bryan JOHNSON

UK, male vocalist, d. 18 Oct 1995 (Singles: 11 weeks) pos/wks

10 Mar 60 **LOOKING HIGH, HIGH, HIGH** *Decca F 11213* 20 11

Carey JOHNSON

Australia, male vocalist (Singles: 8 weeks) pos/wks

25 Apr 87 **REAL FASHION REGGAE STYLE** *Oval TEN 170* 19 8

Denise JOHNSON

UK, female vocalist (Singles: 4 weeks) pos/wks

24 Aug 91 **DON'T FIGHT IT FEEL IT** *Creation CRE 110* [1] 41 2
14 May 94 **RAYS OF THE RISING SUN** *Magnet MAG 1022CD* 45 2

[1] Primal Scream featuring Denise Johnson

Don JOHNSON

US, male actor / vocalist (Singles: 12 weeks) pos/wks

18 Oct 86 **HEARTBEAT** *Epic 650064 7* 46 5
5 Nov 88 **TILL I LOVED YOU (LOVE THEME FROM 'GOYA')** *CBS BARB 2* [1] 16 7

[1] Barbra Streisand and Don Johnson

General JOHNSON – *See CHAIRMEN OF THE BOARD*

Holly JOHNSON

UK, male vocalist (Singles: 38 weeks, Albums: 17 weeks) pos/wks

14 Jan 89 ● **LOVE TRAIN** *MCA MCA 1306* 4 11
1 Apr 89 ● **AMERICANOS** *MCA MCA 1323* 4 11
20 May 89 ★ **FERRY 'CROSS THE MERSEY** *PWL PWL 41* [1] ■ 1 7
24 Jun 89 **ATOMIC CITY** *MCA MCA 1342* 18 4
30 Sep 89 **HEAVEN'S HERE** *MCA MCA 1365* 62 2
1 Dec 90 **WHERE HAS LOVE GONE?** *MCA MCA 1460* 73 1
25 Dec 99 **THE POWER OF LOVE** *Pleasure Dome PLDCD 1005* 56 2
6 May 89 ★ **BLAST** *MCA MCG 6042* ■ 1 17

[1] Christians, Holly Johnson, Paul McCartney, Gerry Marsden and Stock Aitken Waterman

See also FRANKIE GOES TO HOLLYWOOD

Howard JOHNSON

US, male vocalist (Singles: 6 weeks) pos/wks

4 Sep 82 **KEEPIN' LOVE NEW / SO FINE** *A&M USA 1221* 45 6

'Keepin' Love New' listed 4 Sep 1982 only

Johnny JOHNSON and the BANDWAGON

US, male vocal group (Singles: 50 weeks) pos/wks

16 Oct 68 ● **BREAKIN' DOWN THE WALLS OF HEARTACHE** *Direction 58-3670* [1] 4 15
5 Feb 69 **YOU** *Direction 58-3923* 34 4
28 May 69 **LET'S HANG ON** *Direction 58-4180* 36 6
25 Jul 70 ● **SWEET INSPIRATION (re)** *Bell 1111* 10 13
28 Nov 70 ● **(BLAME IT) ON THE PONY EXPRESS** *Bell 1128* 7 12

[1] Bandwagon

Kevin JOHNSON *Australia, male vocalist (Singles: 6 weeks)* pos/wks

11 Jan 75 **ROCK 'N ROLL (I GAVE YOU THE BEST YEARS OF MY LIFE)** *UK UKR 84* 23 6

Laurie JOHNSON ORCHESTRA

UK, orchestra (Singles: 14 weeks) pos/wks

Date		Title	pos	wks
28 Sep 61	●	SUCU SUCU *Pye 7N 15383*	9	12
17 May 97		THEME FROM 'THE PROFESSIONALS' *Virgin VSCDT 1643* [1]	36	2

[1] Laurie Johnson's London Big Band

Linton Kwesi JOHNSON *Jamaica, male poet (Albums: 8 weeks)* pos/wks

Date		Title	pos	wks
30 Jun 79		FORCE OF VICTORY *Island ILPS 9566*	66	1
31 Oct 80		BASS CULTURE *Island ILPS 9605*	46	5
10 Mar 84		MAKING HISTORY *Island ILPS 9770*	73	2

LJ JOHNSON *US, male vocalist (Singles: 6 weeks)* pos/wks

Date		Title	pos	wks
7 Feb 76		YOUR MAGIC PUT A SPELL ON ME *Philips 6006 492*	27	6

Lou JOHNSON *US, male vocalist (Singles: 2 weeks)* pos/wks

Date		Title	pos	wks
26 Nov 64		A MESSAGE TO MARTHA (KENTUCKY BLUEBIRD) *London HL 9929*	36	2

Marv JOHNSON

US, male vocalist, d. 16 May 1993 (Singles: 40 weeks) pos/wks

Date		Title	pos	wks
12 Feb 60	●	YOU GOT WHAT IT TAKES *London HLT 9013*	7	17
5 May 60		I LOVE THE WAY YOU LOVE *London HLT 9109*	35	3
11 Aug 60		AIN'T GONNA BE THAT WAY *London HLT 9165*	50	1
22 Jan 69	●	I'LL PICK A ROSE FOR MY ROSE *Tamla Motown TMG 680*	10	11
25 Oct 69		I MISS YOU BABY *Tamla Motown TMG 713*	25	8

Orlando JOHNSON – *See SECCHI featuring Orlando JOHNSON*

Paul JOHNSON

UK, male vocalist (Singles: 7 weeks, Albums: 3 weeks) pos/wks

Date		Title	pos	wks
21 Feb 87		WHEN LOVE COMES CALLING *CBS PJOHN 1*	52	5
25 Feb 89		NO MORE TOMORROWS *CBS PJOHN 7*	67	2
4 Jul 87		PAUL JOHNSON *CBS 450640 1*	63	2
16 Sep 89		PERSONAL *CBS 463284 1*	70	1

Paul JOHNSON

US, male producer / instrumentalist (Singles: 8 weeks) pos/wks

Date		Title	pos	wks
25 Sep 99	●	GET GET DOWN *Defected DEFECT 7CDS*	5	8

Puff JOHNSON *US, female vocalist (Singles: 6 weeks)* pos/wks

Date		Title	pos	wks
18 Jan 97		OVER AND OVER *Columbia 6640345*	20	4
12 Apr 97		FOREVER MORE *Work 644075*	29	2

Romina JOHNSON *UK, female vocalist (Singles: 13 weeks)* pos/wks

Date		Title	pos	wks
4 Mar 00	●	MOVIN TOO FAST (re) *Locked On XL LOX 117CD* [1]	2	12
17 Jun 00		MY FORBIDDEN LOVER *51 Lexington CDLEX 1* [2]	59	1

[1] Artful Dodger and Romina Johnson [2] Romina Johnson featuring Luci Martin and Norma Jean

Syleena JOHNSON *US, female vocalist (Singles: 2 weeks)* pos/wks

Date		Title	pos	wks
26 Oct 02		TONIGHT I'M GONNA LET GO *Jive 9254252*	38	2

Sleeve credits Syleena Johnson featuring Busta Rhymes, Rampage, Sham & Spliff Star (of Flipmode Squad)

Teddy JOHNSON – *See Pearl CARR and Teddy JOHNSON*

JOHNSTON BROTHERS *UK, male vocal group – leader Johnny Johnston (Johnny Reine) (Singles: 33 weeks)* pos/wks

Date		Title	pos	wks
3 Apr 53	●	OH, HAPPY DAY *Decca F 10071*	4	8
5 Nov 54		WAIT FOR ME, DARLING *Decca F 10362* [1]	18	1
21 Jan 55		HAPPY DAYS AND LONELY NIGHTS *Decca F 10389*	14	2
7 Oct 55	★	HERNANDO'S HIDEAWAY *Decca F 10608*	1	13
30 Dec 55	●	JOIN IN AND SING AGAIN *Decca F 10636* [2]	9	1
13 Apr 56		NO OTHER LOVE *Decca F 10721*	22	1
30 Nov 56		IN THE MIDDLE OF THE HOUSE *Decca F 10781*	27	1
7 Dec 56		JOIN IN AND SING NO.3 (re) *Decca F 10814*	24	2
8 Feb 57		GIVE HER MY LOVE *Decca F 10828*	27	1
19 Apr 57		HEART *Decca F 10860*	23	3

[1] Joan Regan with The Johnston Brothers [2] Johnson Brothers and The George Chisholm Sour-Note Six

The following two hits were medleys: Join In and Sing Again: Sheik of Araby / Yes Sir That's My Baby / California Here I Come / Some of These Days / Charleston / Margie. Join In and Sing (No.3): Coal Black Morning / When You're Smiling / Alexander's Ragtime Band / Sweet Sue Just You / When You Wore a Tulip / If You Were the Only Girl in the World

Bruce JOHNSTON

US, male instrumentalist – keyboards (Singles: 4 weeks) pos/wks

Date		Title	pos	wks
27 Aug 77		PIPELINE *CBS 5514*	33	4

See also BEACH BOYS

James A JOHNSTON *US, male producer (Albums: 17 weeks)* pos/wks

Date		Title	pos	wks
13 Nov 99		WORLD WRESTLING FEDERATION – THE MUSIC – VOLUME 4 *Koch International 333612*	44	9
10 Mar 01		WORLD WRESTLING FEDERATION – THE MUSIC – VOLUME 5 *Koch KOCCD 8830*	11	8

Jan JOHNSTON *UK, female vocalist (Singles: 12 weeks)* pos/wks

Date		Title	pos	wks
8 Feb 97		TAKE ME BY THE HAND *AM:PM 5821012* [1]	28	2
28 Nov 98		SKYDIVE *Stress CDSTR 89* [2]	75	1
12 Feb 00		LOVE WILL COME *Xtravaganza XTRAV6CDS* [2]	31	2
22 Jul 00		SKYDIVE (re-mix) *Renaissance Recordings RENCDS 002* [3]	43	2
21 Apr 01		FLESH *Perfecto PERF 05CDS*	36	2
28 Jul 01		SILENT WORDS *Perfecto PERF 16CDS*	57	1
8 Sep 01		SKYDIVE (I FEEL WONDERFUL) (2nd re-mix) *Incentive CENT 22CDS* [3]	35	2

[1] Submerge featuring Jan Johnston [2] Tomski featuring Jan Johnston [3] Freefall featuring Jan Johnston

Sabrina JOHNSTON *US, female vocalist (Singles: 19 weeks)* pos/wks

Date		Title	pos	wks
7 Sep 91	●	PEACE *East West YZ 616*	8	10
7 Dec 91		FRIENDSHIP *East West YZ 637*	58	4
11 Jul 92		I WANNA SING *East West YZ 661*	46	2
3 Oct 92		PEACE (re-mix) *Epic 6584377*	35	2
13 Aug 94		SATISFY MY LOVE *Champion CHAMPCD 311*	62	1

The listed flipside of 'Peace' (re-mix) was 'Gypsy Woman' (re-mix) by Crystal Waters

Brian JOHNSTONE

UK, male broadcaster, d. 5 Jan 1994 (Albums: 3 weeks) pos/wks

Date		Title	pos	wks
5 Mar 94		AN EVENING WITH JOHNNERS *Listen For Pleasure LFP 7742*	46	3

James JOLIS – *See Barry MANILOW*

JOLLY BROTHERS

Jamaica, male vocal / instrumental group (Singles: 7 weeks) pos/wks

Date		Title	pos	wks
28 Jul 79		CONSCIOUS MAN *United Artists UP 36415*	46	7

JOLLY ROGER *UK, male instrumentalist / producer – Eddie Richards (Singles: 12 weeks)* pos/wks

Date		Title	pos	wks
10 Sep 88		ACID MAN *10 TEN 236*	23	12

Al JOLSON

US, male vocalist – Asa Yoelson d. 23 Oct 1950 (Albums: 11 weeks) pos/wks

Date		Title	pos	wks
14 Mar 81		20 GOLDEN GREATS *MCA MCTV 4*	18	7
17 Dec 83		THE AL JOLSON COLLECTION *Ronco RON LP 5*	67	4

JOMALSKI – *See WILDCHILD*

JOMANDA *US, female vocal group (Singles: 10 weeks)* pos/wks

Date		Title	pos	wks
22 Apr 89		MAKE MY BODY ROCK *RCA PB 42749*	44	3
29 Jun 91		GOT A LOVE FOR YOU *Giant W 0040*	43	4

Date	Title / Label	pos	wks
11 Sep 93	**I LIKE IT** *Big Beat A 8377CD*	**67**	1
13 Nov 93	**NEVER** *Big Beat A 8347CD*	**40**	2

JON and VANGELIS

UK, male vocalist and Greece, male multi-instrumentalist – Jon Anderson and Evangelos Papathanassiou (Singles: 28 weeks, Albums: 53 weeks) pos/wks

Date	Title / Label	pos	wks
5 Jan 80 ●	**I HEAR YOU NOW** *Polydor POSP 96*	**8**	11
12 Dec 81 ●	**I'LL FIND MY WAY HOME** *Polydor JV 1*	**6**	13
30 Jul 83	**HE IS SAILING** *Polydor JV 4*	**61**	2
18 Aug 84	**STATE OF INDEPENDENCE** *Polydor JV 5*	**67**	2
26 Jan 80 ●	**SHORT STORIES** *Polydor POLD 5030*	**4**	11
11 Jul 81	**THE FRIENDS OF MR CAIRO** *Polydor POLD 5039*	**17**	8
23 Jan 82 ●	**THE FRIENDS OF MR CAIRO (re-issue)** *Polydor POLD 5053*	**6**	15
2 Jul 83	**PRIVATE COLLECTION** *Polydor POLH 4*	**22**	10
11 Aug 84	**THE BEST OF JON AND VANGELIS** *Polydor POLH 6*	**42**	9

See also Jon ANDERSON; VANGELIS

JON OF THE PLEASED WIMMIN

UK, male DJ / producer – Jonathan Cooper (Singles: 5 weeks) pos/wks

Date	Title / Label	pos	wks
18 Feb 95	**PASSION** *Perfecto YZ 884CD*	**27**	3
6 Apr 96	**GIVE ME STRENGTH** *Perfecto PERF 119CD*	**30**	2

JON THE DENTIST vs Ollie JAYE

UK, male DJs / producers (Singles: 2 weeks) pos/wks

Date	Title / Label	pos	wks
24 Jul 99	**IMAGINATION** *Tidy Trax TIDY 126CD*	**72**	1
10 Jun 00	**FEEL SO GOOD** *Tidy Trax TIDY 135CD*	**72**	1

JONAH

Holland, male production group (Singles: 4 weeks) pos/wks

Date	Title / Label	pos	wks
22 Jul 00	**SSSST (LISTEN)** *VC Recordings VCRD 69*	**25**	4

JONELL – *See HI-TEK featuring JONELL*

Aled JONES 367 Top 500

Angelic choirboy turned broadcaster. Welsh boy soprano b. 29 Dec 1970, Llandegfan, Anglesey, who matured into a baritone has performed in classical, traditional, religious and pop styles. In July 1985, he became the youngest soloist to feature on simultaneous Top 10 albums (Singles: 24 weeks, Albums: 157 weeks) pos/wks

Date	Title / Label	pos	wks
20 Jul 85	**MEMORY: THEME FROM THE MUSICAL 'CATS'** *BBC RESL 175*	**42**	4
30 Nov 85 ●	**WALKING IN THE AIR** *HMV ALED 1*	**5**	11
14 Dec 85	**PICTURES IN THE DARK** *Virgin VS 836* [1]	**50**	6
20 Dec 86	**A WINTER STORY** *HMV ALED 2*	**51**	3
27 Apr 85 ●	**VOICES FROM THE HOLY LAND** *BBC REC 564* [1]	**6**	43
29 Jun 85 ●	**ALL THROUGH THE NIGHT** *BBC REH 569* [1]	**2**	44
23 Nov 85	**ALED JONES WITH THE BBC WELSH CHORUS** *10 / BBC AJ 1* [1]	**11**	10
22 Feb 86	**WHERE E'ER YOU WALK** *10 DIX 21*	**36**	6
12 Jul 86	**PIE JESU** *10 AJ 2*	**25**	16
29 Nov 86	**AN ALBUM OF HYMNS** *Telstar STAR 2272*	**18**	11
14 Mar 87	**ALED (MUSIC FROM THE TV SERIES)** *10 AJ 3*	**52**	6
5 Dec 87	**THE BEST OF ALED JONES** *10 AJ 5*	**59**	5
26 Oct 02	**ALED** *UCJ 0644792*	**27**	9
11 Oct 03	**HIGHER** *UCJ 9865579*	**21**	7

[1] Mike Oldfield featuring Aled Jones, Anita Hegerland and Barry Palmer [1] Aled Jones with the BBC Welsh Chorus

Barbara JONES

Jamaica, female vocalist – Barbara Nation (Singles: 7 weeks) pos/wks

Date	Title / Label	pos	wks
31 Jan 81	**JUST WHEN I NEEDED YOU MOST** *Sonet SON 2221*	**31**	7

Catherine Zeta JONES

UK, female actor / vocalist (Singles: 9 weeks) pos/wks

Date	Title / Label	pos	wks
19 Sep 92	**FOR ALL TIME** *Columbia 6583547*	**36**	5
26 Nov 94	**TRUE LOVE WAYS** *PolyGram TV TLWCD 2* [1]	**38**	3
1 Apr 95	**IN THE ARMS OF LOVE** *Wow! WOWCD 7101*	**72**	1

[1] David Essex and Catherine Zeta Jones

Donell JONES

US, male vocalist (Singles: 20 weeks, Albums: 5 weeks) pos/wks

Date	Title / Label	pos	wks
15 Feb 97	**KNOCKS ME OFF MY FEET** *LaFace 74321458502*	**58**	1
22 Jan 00 ●	**U KNOW WHAT'S UP** *LaFace 74321722752*	**2**	11
20 May 00	**SHORTY (GOT HER EYES ON ME)** *Laface 74321748902*	**19**	3
2 Dec 00	**TRUE STEP TONIGHT** *Nulife 74321811312* [1]	**25**	3
24 Aug 02	**YOU KNOW THAT I LOVE YOU** *Arista 74321956962*	**41**	2
29 Jan 00	**WHERE I WANNA BE** *LaFace 73008260602*	**47**	3
22 Jun 02	**LIFE GOES ON** *Arista 74321941552*	**62**	2

[1] True Steppers featuring Brian Harvey and Donell Jones

Georgia JONES – *See DIVA SURPRISE featuring Georgia JONES; PLUX featuring Georgia JONES*

Glenn JONES *US, male vocalist (Albums: 1 week)* pos/wks

Date	Title / Label	pos	wks
31 Oct 87	**GLENN JONES** *Jive HIP 51*	**62**	1

Grace JONES *Jamaica, female vocalist – Grace Mendoza (Singles: 46 weeks, Albums: 80 weeks)* pos/wks

Date	Title / Label	pos	wks
26 Jul 80	**PRIVATE LIFE** *Island WIP 6629*	**17**	8
20 Jun 81	**PULL UP TO THE BUMPER** *Island WIP 6696*	**53**	4
30 Oct 82	**THE APPLE STRETCHING / NIPPLE TO THE BOTTLE** *Island WIP 6779*	**50**	4
9 Apr 83	**MY JAMAICAN GUY** *Island IS 103*	**56**	3
12 Oct 85	**SLAVE TO THE RHYTHM** *ZTT IS 206*	**12**	8
18 Jan 86	**PULL UP TO THE BUMPER / LA VIE EN ROSE (re-issue)** *Island IS 240*	**12**	9
1 Mar 86	**LOVE IS THE DRUG** *Island IS 266*	**35**	4
15 Nov 86	**I'M NOT PERFECT (BUT I'M PERFECT FOR YOU)** *Manhattan MT 15*	**56**	3
7 May 94	**SLAVE TO THE RHYTHM (re-mix)** *Zance ZANG 50CD1*	**28**	2
25 Nov 00	**PULL UP TO THE BUMPER** *Club Tools 0120375 CLU* [1]	**60**	1
30 Aug 80	**WARM LEATHERETTE** *Island ILPS 9592*	**45**	2
23 May 81	**NIGHTCLUBBING** *Island ILPS 9624*	**35**	16
20 Nov 82	**LIVING MY LIFE** *Island ILPS 9722*	**15**	22
9 Nov 85	**SLAVE TO THE RHYTHM** *ZTT GRACE 1*	**12**	8
14 Dec 85 ●	**ISLAND LIFE** *Island GJ 1*	**4**	30
29 Nov 86	**INSIDE STORY** *Manhattan MTL 1007*	**61**	2

[1] Grace Jones vs Funkstar De Luxe

'La Vie en Rose' was listed only from 1 Feb 1986

Hannah JONES *US, female vocalist (Singles: 9 weeks)* pos/wks

Date	Title / Label	pos	wks
14 Sep 91	**BRIDGE OVER TROUBLED WATER** *Dance Pool 6565467*	**21**	8
30 Jan 93	**KEEP IT ON** *TMRC CDTMRC 7*	**67**	1

Howard JONES 284 Top 500

Accomplished singer / songwriter, b. 23 Feb 1955, Southampton, UK, who was a regular chart visitor in the mid-1980s with his brand of synth-based pop. Jones, who was equally popular in the US, appeared at Live Aid (Singles: 103 weeks, Albums: 122 weeks) pos/wks

Date	Title / Label	pos	wks
17 Sep 83 ●	**NEW SONG (re)** *WEA HOW 1*	**3**	15
26 Nov 83 ●	**WHAT IS LOVE** *WEA HOW 2*	**2**	15
18 Feb 84	**HIDE AND SEEK** *WEA HOW 3*	**12**	9
26 May 84 ●	**PEARL IN THE SHELL** *WEA HOW 4*	**7**	10
11 Aug 84 ●	**LIKE TO GET TO KNOW YOU WELL** *WEA HOW 5*	**4**	12
9 Feb 85 ●	**THINGS CAN ONLY GET BETTER** *WEA HOW 6*	**6**	8
20 Apr 85 ●	**LOOK MAMA** *WEA HOW 7*	**10**	6
29 Jun 85	**LIFE IN ONE DAY** *WEA HOW 8*	**14**	7
15 Mar 86	**NO ONE IS TO BLAME** *WEA HOW 9*	**16**	7
4 Oct 86	**ALL I WANT** *WEA HOW 10*	**35**	4
29 Nov 86	**YOU KNOW I LOVE YOU...DON'T YOU?** *WEA HOW 11*	**43**	3
21 Mar 87	**LITTLE BIT OF SNOW** *WEA HOW 12*	**70**	1
4 Mar 89	**EVERLASTING LOVE** *WEA HOW 13*	**62**	3
11 Apr 92	**LIFT ME UP** *East West HOW 15*	**52**	3
17 Mar 84 ★	**HUMAN'S LIB** *WEA WX 1* ■	**1**	57
8 Dec 84	**THE 12" ALBUM** *WEA WX 14*	**15**	33
23 Mar 85 ●	**DREAM INTO ACTION** *WEA WX 15*	**2**	25
25 Oct 86 ●	**ONE TO ONE** *WEA WX 68*	**10**	4
1 Apr 89	**CROSS THAT LINE** *WEA WX 225*	**64**	1
5 Jun 93	**THE BEST OF HOWARD JONES** *East West 4509927012*	**36**	2

Jack JONES *US, male vocalist (Albums: 70 weeks)* pos/wks

29 Apr 72	●	**A SONG FOR YOU** *RCA Victor SF 8228*	9 6
3 Jun 72	●	**BREAD WINNERS** *RCA Victor SF 8280*	7 36
7 Apr 73	●	**TOGETHER** *RCA Victor SF 8342*	8 10
23 Feb 74	●	**HARBOUR** *RCA Victor APLI 0408*	10 5
19 Feb 77		**THE FULL LIFE** *RCA Victor PL 12067*	41 5
21 May 77	●	**ALL TO YOURSELF** *RCA TVL 2*	10 8

Janie JONES
UK, female vocalist – Marion Mitchell (Singles: 3 weeks) pos/wks

27 Jan 66		**WITCHES BREW** *HMV POP 1495*	46 3

Jimmy JONES *US, male vocalist (Singles: 47 weeks)* pos/wks

17 Mar 60	●	**HANDY MAN (re)** *MGM 1051*	3 24
16 Jun 60	★	**GOOD TIMIN'** *MGM 1078*	1 15
8 Sep 60		**I JUST GO FOR YOU** *MGM 1091*	35 4
17 Nov 60		**READY FOR LOVE** *MGM 1103*	46 1
30 Mar 61		**I TOLD YOU SO** *MGM 1123*	33 3

Juggy JONES
US, male multi-instrumentalist – Henry Murray (Singles: 4 weeks) pos/wks

7 Feb 76		**INSIDE AMERICA** *Contempo CS 2080*	39 4

Kelly JONES – *See MANCHILD*

Lavinia JONES *South Africa, female vocalist (Singles: 2 weeks)* pos/wks

18 Feb 95		**SING IT TO YOU (DEE-DOOB-DEE-DOO)** *Virgin International DINDG 142*	45 2

Mick JONES – *See AZTEC CAMERA; CLASH*

Norah JONES *US, female vocalist / instrumentalist – keyboards (Singles: 3 weeks, Albums: 86 weeks)* pos/wks

25 May 02		**DON'T KNOW WHY** *Parlophone CDCL 836*	59 1
17 Aug 02		**FEELIN' THE SAME WAY** *Parlophone CDCL 838*	72 1
13 Sep 03		**DON'T KNOW WHY (re-issue) / I'LL BE YOUR BABY TONIGHT** *Parlophone CDCL 848*	67 1
11 May 02	★	**COME AWAY WITH ME** *Parlophone 5386092* ▲	1 86+

Oran 'Juice' JONES *US, male vocalist (Singles: 14 weeks)* pos/wks

15 Nov 86	●	**THE RAIN** *Def Jam A 7303*	4 14

Paul JONES *UK, male vocalist – Paul Pond (Singles: 34 weeks)* pos/wks

6 Oct 66	●	**HIGH TIME** *HMV POP 1554*	4 15
19 Jan 67	●	**I'VE BEEN A BAD, BAD BOY** *HMV POP 1576*	5 9
23 Aug 67		**THINKIN' AIN'T FOR ME (re)** *HMV POP 1602*	32 8
5 Feb 69		**AQUARIUS** *Columbia DB 8514*	45 2

See also BLUES BAND; MANFRED MANN

Quincy JONES *US, male producer / instrumentalist – keyboards (Singles: 42 weeks, Albums: 41 weeks)* pos/wks

29 Jul 78		**STUFF LIKE THAT** *A&M AMS 7367*	34 9
11 Apr 81		**AI NO CORRIDA (I-NO-KO-REE-DA)** *A&M AMS 8109* [1]	14 10
20 Jun 81		**RAZZAMATAZZ** *A&M AMS 8140*	11 9
5 Sep 81		**BETCHA' WOULDN'T HURT ME** *A&M AMS 8157*	52 3
13 Jan 90		**I'LL BE GOOD TO YOU** *Qwest W 2697* [2]	21 7
31 Mar 90		**SECRET GARDEN** *Qwest W 9992* [3]	67 1
14 Sep 96		**STOMP** *Qwest W 0372CD* [4]	28 2
1 Aug 98		**SOUL BOSSA NOVA** *Manifesto FESCD 48* [5]	47 1
18 Apr 81		**THE DUDE** *A&M AMLK 63721*	19 25
20 Mar 82		**THE BEST** *A&M AMLH 68542*	41 4
20 Jan 90		**BACK ON THE BLOCK** *Qwest WX 313*	26 12

[1] Quincy Jones featuring Dune [2] Quincy Jones featuring Ray Charles and Chaka Khan [3] Quincy Jones featuring Al B Sure!, James Ingram, El DeBarge and Barry White [4] Quincy Jones featuring Melle Mel, Coolio, Yo-Yo, Shaquille O'Neal, The Luniz [5] Cool, the Fab and the Groovy present Quincy Jones

Uncredited vocals on 'Stuff Like That' were by Ashford and Simpson and Chaka Khan, and on 'Razzamatazz' and 'Betcha' Wouldn't Hurt Me' by Patti Austin

Rickie Lee JONES *US, female vocalist / instrumentalist – guitar (Singles: 9 weeks, Albums: 39 weeks)* pos/wks

23 Jun 79		**CHUCK E'S IN LOVE** *Warner Bros. K 17390*	18 9
16 Jun 79		**RICKIE LEE JONES** *Warner Bros. K 56628*	18 19
8 Aug 81		**PIRATES** *Warner Bros. K 56816*	37 11
2 Jul 83		**GIRL AT HER VOLCANO** *Warner Bros. 9238051*	51 3
13 Oct 84		**THE MAGAZINE** *Warner Bros. 925117*	40 4
7 Oct 89		**FLYING COWBOYS** *Geffen WX 309*	50 2

Shirley JONES – *See PARTRIDGE FAMILY*

Sonny JONES featuring Tara CHASE *Germany, male vocalist and Canada, female rapper (Singles: 2 weeks)* pos/wks

7 Oct 00		**FOLLOW YOU FOLLOW ME** *Logic 74321772892*	42 2

Tammy JONES
UK, female vocalist (Singles: 10 weeks, Albums: 5 weeks) pos/wks

26 Apr 75	●	**LET ME TRY AGAIN** *Epic EPC 3211*	5 10
12 Jul 75		**LET ME TRY AGAIN** *Epic EPC 80853*	38 5

Tom JONES 24 Top 500
Unmistakable entertainer who has been an international headliner for five decades, b Thomas Woodward, 7 Jun, 1940, South Wales (re-named after the popular 1963 film). Despite failure of his first two Joe Meek-produced singles, the Welsh wonder became one of world's most popular singers, with hits in the pop, country, R&B and easy listening fields. The Vegas veteran, who hosted his own very successful late-1960s TV series, has had hits on 10 labels. This 60-something sex symbol, who was the top British solo singer of the 1960s on both sides of Atlantic, had his best-selling album in 1999 with 'Reload' and received an Outstanding Contribution to British Music Brit Award in 2003. Best-selling single: 'Green, Green Grass of Home' 1,205,000 (Singles: 394 weeks, Albums: 509 weeks) pos/wks

11 Feb 65	★	**IT'S NOT UNUSUAL** *Decca F 12062*	1 14
6 May 65		**ONCE UPON A TIME** *Decca F 12121*	32 4
8 Jul 65		**WITH THESE HANDS** *Decca F 12191*	13 11
12 Aug 65		**WHAT'S NEW PUSSYCAT?** *Decca F 12203*	11 10
13 Jan 66		**THUNDERBALL** *Decca F 12292*	35 4
19 May 66		**ONCE THERE WAS A TIME / NOT RESPONSIBLE** *Decca F 12390*	18 9
18 Aug 66		**THIS AND THAT** *Decca F 12461*	44 3
10 Nov 66	★	**GREEN, GREEN GRASS OF HOME** *Decca F 22511* ◆	1 22
16 Feb 67	●	**DETROIT CITY** *Decca F 22555*	8 10
13 Apr 67	●	**FUNNY FAMILIAR FORGOTTEN FEELINGS** *Decca F 12599*	7 15
26 Jul 67	●	**I'LL NEVER FALL IN LOVE AGAIN** *Decca F 12639*	2 25
22 Nov 67	●	**I'M COMING HOME** *Decca F 12693*	2 16
28 Feb 68	●	**DELILAH** *Decca F 12747*	2 17
17 Jul 68	●	**HELP YOURSELF** *Decca F 12812*	5 26
27 Nov 68		**A MINUTE OF YOUR TIME** *Decca F 12854*	14 15
14 May 69	●	**LOVE ME TONIGHT** *Decca F 12924*	9 12
13 Dec 69	●	**WITHOUT LOVE (re)** *Decca F 12990*	10 12
18 Apr 70	●	**DAUGHTER OF DARKNESS** *Decca F 13013*	5 15
15 Aug 70		**I (WHO HAVE NOTHING) (re)** *Decca F 13061*	16 11
16 Jan 71		**SHE'S A LADY (re)** *Decca F 13113*	13 10
5 Jun 71		**PUPPET MAN (re)** *Decca F 13183*	49 2
23 Oct 71	●	**TILL** *Decca F 13236*	2 15
1 Apr 72	●	**THE YOUNG NEW MEXICAN PUPPETEER** *Decca F 13298*	6 12
14 Apr 73		**LETTER TO LUCILLE** *Decca F 13393*	31 8
7 Sep 74		**SOMETHING 'BOUT YOU BABY I LIKE** *Decca F 13550*	36 5
16 Apr 77		**SAY YOU'LL STAY UNTIL TOMORROW** *EMI 2583*	40 3
18 Apr 87	●	**A BOY FROM NOWHERE** *Epic OLE 1*	2 12
30 May 87		**IT'S NOT UNUSUAL (re-issue)** *Decca F 103*	17 8
2 Jan 88		**I WAS BORN TO BE ME** *Epic OLE 4*	61 1
29 Oct 88	●	**KISS** *China CHINA 11* [1]	5 7
29 Apr 89		**MOVE CLOSER** *Jive JIVE 203*	49 3
26 Jan 91		**COULDN'T SAY GOODBYE** *Dover ROJ 10*	51 2
16 Mar 91		**CARRYING A TORCH** *Dover ROJ 12*	57 2
4 Jul 92		**DELILAH (re-issue)** *The Hit Label TOM 10*	68 2
6 Feb 93		**ALL YOU NEED IS LOVE** *Childline CHILDCD 93*	19 4
5 Nov 94		**IF I ONLY KNEW** *ZTT ZANG 59CD*	11 9
25 Sep 99	●	**BURNING DOWN THE HOUSE** *Gut CDGUT 26* [2]	7 7
18 Dec 99		**BABY, IT'S COLD OUTSIDE** *Gut CDGUT 29* [3]	17 7

18 Mar 00 ● **MAMA TOLD ME NOT TO COME** *Gut CDGUT 031* [4] 4 7
20 May 00 ● **SEX BOMB** *Gut CDGUT 33* [5] 3 10
18 Nov 00 **YOU NEED LOVE LIKE I DO** *GUT CDGUT 36* [6] 24 3
9 Nov 02 **TOM JONES INTERNATIONAL** *V2 VVR5021083* 31 2
8 Mar 03 **BLACK BETTY / I WHO HAVE NOTHING** *V2 VVR 5021763* 50 2
5 Jun 65 **ALONG CAME JONES** *Decca LK 6693* 11 5
8 Oct 66 **FROM THE HEART** *Decca LK 4814* 23 8
8 Apr 67 ● **GREEN GREEN GRASS OF HOME** *Decca SKL 4855* 3 49
24 Jun 67 ● **LIVE AT THE TALK OF THE TOWN** *Decca SKL 4874* 6 90
30 Dec 67 ● **13 SMASH HITS** *Decca SKL 4909* 5 49
27 Jul 68 ★ **DELILAH** *Decca SKL 4946* 1 29
21 Dec 68 ● **HELP YOURSELF** *Decca SKL 4982* 4 9
28 Jun 69 ● **THIS IS TOM JONES** *Decca SKL 5007* 2 20
15 Nov 69 ● **TOM JONES LIVE IN LAS VEGAS** *Decca SKL 5032* 2 45
25 Apr 70 ● **TOM** *Decca SKL 5045* 4 18
14 Nov 70 ● **I WHO HAVE NOTHING** *Decca SKL 5072* 10 10
29 May 71 ● **SHE'S A LADY** *Decca SKL 5089* 9 7
27 Nov 71 **LIVE AT CAESAR'S PALACE** *Decca DKL 1/1 1/2* 27 5
24 Jun 72 **CLOSE UP** *Decca SKL 5132* 17 4
23 Jun 73 **THE BODY AND SOUL OF TOM JONES** *Decca SKL 5162* 31 1
5 Jan 74 **GREATEST HITS** *Decca SKL 5176* 15 13
22 Mar 75 ★ **20 GREATEST HITS** *Decca TJD 1/1 1/2* ■ 1 21
7 Oct 78 **I'M COMING HOME** *Lotus WH 5001* 12 9
16 May 87 **THE GREATEST HITS** *Telstar STAR 2296* 16 12
13 May 89 **AT THIS MOMENT** *Jive TOMTV 1* 34 3
8 Jul 89 **AFTER DARK** *Stylus SMR 978* 46 4
6 Apr 91 **CARRYING A TORCH** *Dover ADD 20* 44 4
27 Jun 92 ● **THE COMPLETE TOM JONES** *The Hit Label 8442862* 8 6
26 Nov 94 **THE LEAD AND HOW TO SWING IT** *ZTT 6544924982* 55 1
14 Nov 98 **THE ULTIMATE HITS COLLECTION** *PolyGram TV 8449012* 26 6
9 Oct 99 ★ **RELOAD** *Gut GUTCD 009* ■ 1 65
16 Nov 02 **MR. JONES** *V2 VVR 1021072* 36 2
1 Mar 03 ● **GREATEST HITS** *Universal TV 8828632* 2 14

[1] Art of Noise featuring Tom Jones [2] Tom Jones and The Cardigans [3] Tom Jones and Cerys Matthews [4] Tom Jones and Stereophonics [5] Tom Jones and Mousse T [6] Tom Jones and Heather Small

'I Who Have Nothing' (08 Mar 2003) is a re-recording

Sue JONES-DAVIES – *See Julie COVINGTON, Rula LENSKA, Charlotte CORNWELL and Sue JONES-DAVIES*

JONESTOWN *US, male vocal duo (Singles: 1 week)* pos/wks

13 Jun 98 **SWEET THANG** *Universal UMD 70376* 49 1

Janis JOPLIN
US, female vocalist d. 4 Oct 1970 (Albums: 14 weeks) pos/wks

13 Mar 71 **PEARL** *CBS 64188* ▲ 20 4
22 Jul 72 **JANIS JOPLIN IN CONCERT** *CBS 67241* 30 6
29 Aug 98 **THE ULTIMATE COLLECTION** *Columbia SONYTV 52CD* 26 4

Alison JORDAN *UK, female vocalist (Singles: 4 weeks)* pos/wks

9 May 92 **BOY FROM NEW YORK CITY** *Arista 74321100427* 23 4

Dick JORDAN *UK, male vocalist (Singles: 4 weeks)* pos/wks

17 Mar 60 **HALLELUJAH, I LOVE HER SO** *Oriole CB 1534* 47 1
9 Jun 60 **LITTLE CHRISTINE** *Oriole CB 1548* 39 3

Jack JORDAN – *See Frank CHACKSFIELD and his ORCHESTRA*

Montell JORDAN
US, male vocalist (Singles: 21 weeks, Albums: 3 weeks) pos/wks

13 May 95 **THIS IS HOW WE DO IT** *Def Jam DEFCD 07* ▲ 11 8
2 Sep 95 **SOMETHIN' 4 DA HONEYZ** *Def Jam DEFCD 10* 15 4
19 Oct 96 **I LIKE** *Def Jam DEFCD 19* [1] 24 3
23 May 98 **LET'S RIDE** *Def Jam 5686912* [2] 25 2
8 Apr 00 **GET IT ON TONITE** *Def Soul 5627222* 15 4
24 Jun 95 **THIS IS HOW WE DO IT** *RAL 5271792* 53 2
14 Sep 96 **MORE ...** *Def Jam 5331912* 66 1

[1] Montell Jordan featuring Slick Rick [2] Montell Jordan featuring Master P and Silkk the Shocker

Ronny JORDAN *UK, male instrumentalist – guitar – Ronnie Simpson (Singles: 7 weeks, Albums: 7 weeks)* pos/wks

1 Feb 92 **SO WHAT!** *Antilles ANN 14* 32 4
25 Sep 93 **UNDER YOUR SPELL** *Island CID 565* 72 1
15 Jan 94 **TINSEL TOWN** *Island CID 566* 64 1
28 May 94 **COME WITH ME** *Island CID 584* 63 1
7 Mar 92 **THE ANTIDOTE** *Island CID 9988* 52 4
9 Oct 93 **THE QUIET REVOLUTION** *Island CID 8009* 49 2
3 Sep 94 **BAD BROTHERS** *Island IMCD 8024* [1] 58 1

[1] Ronny Jordan meets DJ Krush

JORDANAIRES – *See Elvis PRESLEY*

JORIO *US, male producer – Fred Jorio (Singles: 1 week)* pos/wks

24 Feb 01 **REMEMBER ME** *Wonderboy WBOYD 021* 54 1

David JOSEPH *UK, male vocalist (Singles: 21 weeks)* pos/wks

26 Feb 83 **YOU CAN'T HIDE (YOUR LOVE FROM ME)** *Island IS 101* 13 9
28 May 83 **LET'S LIVE IT UP (NITE PEOPLE)** *Island IS 116* 26 5
18 Feb 84 **JOYS OF LIFE** *Island IS 153* 61 2
31 May 86 **EXPANSIONS '86 (EXPAND YOUR MIND)** *Fourth & Broadway BRW 48* [1] 58 5

[1] Chris Paul featuring David Joseph

See also HI TENSION

Dawn JOSEPH – *See LOGO featuring Dawn JOSEPH*

Mark JOSEPH
UK, male vocalist – Mark Joseph Muzsnyai (Singles: 2 weeks) pos/wks

1 Mar 03 **GET THROUGH** *Mark Joseph MJR 003* 38 1
30 Aug 03 **FLY** *14 th Floor MJM 010* 28 1

Martyn JOSEPH *UK, male vocalist (Singles: 10 weeks)* pos/wks

20 Jun 92 **DOLPHINS MAKE ME CRY** *Epic 6581347* 34 4
12 Sep 92 **WORKING MOTHER** *Epic 6582937* 65 1
9 Jan 93 **PLEASE SIR** *Epic 6588552* 45 3
3 Jun 95 **TALK ABOUT IT IN THE MORNING** *Epic 6613342* 43 2

JOURNEY *US, male vocal / instrumental group (Singles: 9 weeks, Albums: 30 weeks)* pos/wks

27 Feb 82 **DON'T STOP BELIEVIN'** *CBS A 1728* 62 4
11 Sep 82 **WHO'S CRYING NOW** *CBS A 2725* 46 5
20 Mar 82 **ESCAPE** *CBS 85138* ▲ 32 16
19 Feb 83 ● **FRONTIERS** *CBS 25261* 6 8
6 Aug 83 **EVOLUTION** *CBS 32342* 100 1
24 May 86 **RAISED ON RADIO** *CBS 26902* 22 5

Ruth JOY
UK, female vocalist – Ann Saunderson (Singles: 4 weeks) pos/wks

26 Aug 89 **DON'T PUSH IT** *MCA RJOY 1* 66 2
22 Feb 92 **FEEL** *MCA MCS 1574* 67 1
14 Nov 92 **WALKING ON SUNSHINE** *Network NWK 55* [1] 71 1

[1] Krush featuring Ruth Joy

JOY DIVISION *UK, male vocal / instrumental group (Singles: 24 weeks, Albums: 33 weeks)* pos/wks

28 Jun 80 **LOVE WILL TEAR US APART (re)** *Factory FAC 23* 13 16
18 Jun 88 **ATMOSPHERE** *Factory FAC 2137* 34 5
17 Jun 95 **LOVE WILL TEAR US APART (re-mix)** *London YOJCD 1* 19 3
26 Jul 80 ● **CLOSER** *Factory FACT 25* 6 8
30 Aug 80 **UNKNOWN PLEASURES** *Factory FACT 10* 71 1
17 Oct 81 ● **STILL** *Factory FACT 40* 5 12
23 Jul 88 ● **1977-1980 SUBSTANCE** *Factory FAC 250* 7 8
1 Jul 95 **PERMANENT** *London 8286242* 16 3
7 Feb 98 **HEART AND SOUL** *London 8289682* 70 1

'Love Will Tear Us Apart' re-entered and peaked at No.19 in Oct 1983

See also HI TENSION

JOY STRINGS

UK, male / female vocal / instrumental group (Singles: 11 weeks) pos/wks

Date	Title / Label	pos	wks
27 Feb 64	**IT'S AN OPEN SECRET** *Regal-Zonophone RZ 501*	32	7
17 Dec 64	**A STARRY NIGHT** *Regal-Zonophone RZ 504*	34	4

JOYRIDER *UK, male vocal / instrumental group (Singles: 4 weeks)* pos/wks

Date	Title / Label	pos	wks
27 Jul 96	**RUSH HOUR** *Paradox PDOXD 012*	22	3
28 Sep 96	**ALL GONE AWAY** *A&M 5819552*	54	1

JU JU HOUNDS – *See Izzy STRADLIN*

JUDAS PRIEST *UK, male vocal / instrumental group (Singles: 51 weeks, Albums: 78 weeks)* pos/wks

Date	Title / Label	pos	wks
20 Jan 79	**TAKE ON THE WORLD** *CBS 6915*	14	10
12 May 79	**EVENING STAR** *CBS 7312*	53	4
29 Mar 80	**LIVING AFTER MIDNIGHT** *CBS 8379*	12	7
7 Jun 80	**BREAKING THE LAW** *CBS 8644*	12	6
23 Aug 80	**UNITED** *CBS 8897*	26	8
21 Feb 81	**DON'T GO** *CBS 9520*	51	3
25 Apr 81	**HOT ROCKIN'** *CBS A 1153*	60	3
21 Aug 82	**YOU'VE GOT ANOTHER THING COMIN'** *CBS A 2611*	66	2
21 Jan 84	**FREEWHEEL BURNIN'** *CBS A 4054*	42	3
23 Apr 88	**JOHNNY B GOODE** *Atlantic A 9114*	64	2
15 Sep 90	**PAINKILLER** *CBS 656273 7*	74	1
23 Mar 91	**A TOUCH OF EVIL** *Columbia 6565897*	58	1
24 Apr 93	**NIGHT CRAWLER** *Columbia 6590972*	63	1
14 May 77	**SIN AFTER SIN** *CBS 82008*	23	6
25 Feb 78	**STAINED GLASS** *CBS 82430*	27	5
11 Nov 78	**KILLING MACHINE** *CBS 83135*	32	9
6 Oct 79 ●	**UNLEASHED IN THE EAST** *CBS 83852*	10	8
19 Apr 80 ●	**BRITISH STEEL** *CBS 84160*	4	17
7 Mar 81	**POINT OF ENTRY** *CBS 84834*	14	5
17 Jul 82	**SCREAMING FOR VENGEANCE** *CBS 85941*	11	9
28 Jan 84	**DEFENDERS OF THE FAITH** *CBS 25713*	19	5
19 Apr 86	**TURBO** *CBS 26641*	33	4
13 Jun 87	**PRIEST LIVE** *CBS 450 6391*	47	2
28 May 88	**RAM IT DOWN** *CBS 461108 1*	24	5
22 Sep 90	**PAINKILLER** *CBS 4672901*	26	2
8 May 93	**METAL WORKS 73-93** *Columbia 4730502*	37	1

JUDGE DREAD *UK, male vocalist – Alex Hughes, d. 13 Mar 1998 (Singles: 95 weeks, Albums: 14 weeks)* pos/wks

Date	Title / Label	pos	wks
26 Aug 72	**BIG SIX** *Big Shot BI 608*	11	27
9 Dec 72 ●	**BIG SEVEN** *Big Shot BI 613*	8	18
21 Apr 73	**BIG EIGHT** *Big Shot BI 619*	14	10
5 Jul 75 ●	**JE T'AIME (MOI NON PLUS)** *Cactus CT 65*	9	9
27 Sep 75	**BIG TEN** *Cactus CT 77*	14	7
6 Dec 75	**CHRISTMAS IN DREADLAND / COME OUTSIDE** *Cactus CT 80*	14	7
8 May 76	**THE WINKLE MAN** *Cactus CT 90*	35	4
28 Aug 76	**Y VIVA SUSPENDERS** *Cactus CT 99*	27	4
2 Apr 77	**5TH ANNIVERSARY (EP)** *Cactus CT 98*	31	4
14 Jan 78	**UP WITH THE COCK / BIG PUNK** *Cactus CT 110*	49	1
16 Dec 78	**HOKEY COKEY / JINGLE BELLS** *EMI 2881*	59	4
6 Dec 75	**BEDTIME STORIES** *Cactus CTLP 113*	26	12
7 Mar 81	**40 BIG ONES** *Creole BIG 1*	51	2

Tracks on 5th Anniversary (EP): Jamaica Jerk (Off) / Bring Back the Skins / End of the World / Big Everything. 'Y Viva Suspenders' was listed, additionally, with 'Confessions of a Bouncer' in its second week on the chart

JUICE *Denmark, female vocal trio (Singles: 3 weeks)* pos/wks

Date	Title / Label	pos	wks
18 Apr 98	**BEST DAYS** *Chrysalis CDCHS 5081*	28	2
22 Aug 98	**I'LL COME RUNNIN'** *Chrysalis CDCHS 5090*	48	1

JUICY *US, male / female vocal duo (Singles: 5 weeks)* pos/wks

Date	Title / Label	pos	wks
22 Feb 86	**SUGAR FREE** *Epic A 6917*	45	5

JUICY LUCY *UK, male vocal / instrumental group (Singles: 17 weeks, Albums: 5 weeks)* pos/wks

Date	Title / Label	pos	wks
7 Mar 70	**WHO DO YOU LOVE** *Vertigo V 1*	14	12
10 Oct 70	**PRETTY WOMAN (re)** *Vertigo 6059 015*	44	5
18 Apr 70	**JUICY LUCY** *Vertigo VO 2*	41	4
21 Nov 70	**LIE BACK AND ENJOY IT** *Vertigo 6360 014*	53	1

Gary JULES – *See Michael ANDREWS featuring Gary JULES*

Thomas JULES-STOCK

UK, male vocalist (Singles: 1 week) pos/wks

Date	Title / Label	pos	wks
15 Aug 98	**DIDN'T I TELL YOU TRUE** *Mercury MERCD 501*	59	1

JULIA and COMPANY

US, male / female vocal group (Singles: 10 weeks) pos/wks

Date	Title / Label	pos	wks
3 Mar 84	**BREAKIN' DOWN (SUGAR SAMBA)** *London LON 46*	15	8
23 Feb 85	**I'M SO HAPPY** *Next Plateau LON 61*	56	2

JULUKA *UK / South Africa, male / female vocal / instrumental group (Singles: 4 weeks, Albums: 3 weeks)* pos/wks

Date	Title / Label	pos	wks
12 Feb 83	**SCATTERLINGS OF AFRICA** *Safari ZULU 1*	44	4
23 Jul 83	**SCATTERLINGS** *Safari SHAKA 1*	50	3

See also Johnny CLEGG and SAVUKA

JUMP *UK, male instrumental group (Singles: 1 week)* pos/wks

Date	Title / Label	pos	wks
1 Mar 97	**FUNKATARIUM** *Heat Recordings HEATCD 005*	56	1

Wally JUMP Jr and the CRIMINAL ELEMENT

US, male producer – Arthur Baker (Singles: 19 weeks) pos/wks

Date	Title / Label	pos	wks
28 Feb 87	**TURN ME LOOSE** *London LON 126*	60	2
5 Sep 87	**PUT THE NEEDLE TO THE RECORD** *Cooltempo COOL 150* [1]	63	3
12 Dec 87	**TIGHTEN UP – I JUST CAN'T STOP DANCIN'** *Breakout USA 621*	24	7
19 Mar 88	**PRIVATE PARTY** *Breakout USA 624*	57	3
6 Oct 90	**EVERYBODY (RAP)** *Deconstruction PB 44701* [2]	30	4

[1] Criminal Element Orchestra [2] Criminal Element Orchestra and Wendell Williams

JUMPING JACKS – *See Danny PEPPERMINT and the JUMPING JACKS*

Rosemary JUNE

US, female vocalist (Singles: 9 weeks) pos/wks

Date	Title / Label	pos	wks
23 Jan 59	**(I'LL BE WITH YOU) IN APPLE BLOSSOM TIME** *Pye International 7N 25005*	14	9

JUNGLE BOOK

US, male / female vocal group (Singles: 8 weeks) pos/wks

Date	Title / Label	pos	wks
8 May 93	**THE JUNGLE BOOK GROOVE** *Hollywood HWCD 128*	14	8

JUNGLE BROTHERS *US, male rap duo – Nathaniel Hall and Michael Small (Singles: 35 weeks, Albums: 3 weeks)* pos/wks

Date	Title / Label	pos	wks
22 Oct 88	**I'LL HOUSE YOU** *Gee Street GEE 003* [1]	22	5
18 Mar 89	**BLACK IS BLACK / STRAIGHT OUT OF THE JUNGLE** *Gee Street GEE 15*	72	1
31 Mar 90	**WHAT 'U' WAITIN' '4'** *Eternal W 9865*	35	5
21 Jul 90	**DOIN' OUR OWN DANG** *Eternal W 9754*	33	6
19 Jul 97	**BRAIN** *Gee Street GEE 5000388*	52	1
29 Nov 97	**JUNGLE BROTHER (re)** *Gee Street GEE 5000493*	18	5
11 Jul 98	**I'LL HOUSE YOU '98 (re-mix)** *Gee Street FCD 338*	26	5
28 Nov 98	**BECAUSE I GOT IT LIKE THAT** *Gee Street GEE 5003593*	32	2
10 Jul 99	**V.I.P.** *Gee Street / V2 GEE 5007953*	33	3
6 Nov 99	**GET DOWN** *Gee Street / V2 GEE 5010153*	52	1
25 Mar 00	**FREAKIN' YOU** *Gee Street GEE 5008808*	70	1
3 Feb 90	**DONE BY THE FORCES OF NATURE** *Eternal WX 332*	41	3

[1] Richie Rich meets The Jungle Brothers

'Doin' Our Own Dang' features the uncredited De La Soul and Monie Love. 'Jungle Brother' reached its peak position on re-entering the chart in May 1998

JUNGLE HIGH with BLUE PEARL

UK / Germany, male production / instrumental duo and UK / US, male / female vocal / instrumental group (Singles: 1 week) pos/wks

Date	Title / Label	pos	wks
27 Nov 93	**FIRE OF LOVE** *Logic 74321170292*	71	1

See also BLUE PEARL

JUNIOR *UK, male vocalist – Norman Giscombe (Singles: 57 weeks, Albums: 14 weeks)* pos/wks

			pos	wks
24 Apr 82	●	**MAMA USED TO SAY** *Mercury MER 98*	7	13
10 Jul 82		**TOO LATE** *Mercury MER 112*	20	9
25 Sep 82		**LET ME KNOW / I CAN'T HELP IT** *Mercury MER 116*	53	3
23 Apr 83		**COMMUNICATION BREAKDOWN** *Mercury MER 134*	57	3
8 Sep 84		**SOMEBODY** *London LON 50*	64	2
9 Feb 85		**DO YOU REALLY (WANT MY LOVE)** *London LON 60*	47	4
30 Nov 85		**OH LOUISE** *London LON 75*	74	3
4 Apr 87	●	**ANOTHER STEP (CLOSER TO YOU)** *MCA KIM 5* [1]	6	11
25 Aug 90		**STEP OFF** *MCA MCA 1432* [2]	63	3
15 Aug 92		**THEN CAME YOU** *MCA MCS 1676* [2]	32	5
31 Oct 92		**ALL OVER THE WORLD** *MCA MCS 1691* [2]	74	1
5 Jun 82		**JI** *Mercury MERS 3*	28	14

[1] Kim Wilde and Junior [2] Junior Giscombe

JUNIOR JACK
Italy, male producer – Vito Lucente (Singles: 10 weeks) pos/wks

			pos	wks
16 Dec 00		**MY FEELING** *Defected DFECT 24CDS*	31	4
2 Mar 02		**THRILL ME** *VC Recordings VCRD 102*	29	3
27 Sep 03		**E SAMBA** *Defected DFTD0 76CDS*	34	3

JUNIOR M.A.F.I.A.
US, male / female rap ensemble (Singles: 2 weeks) pos/wks

			pos	wks
3 Feb 96		**I NEED YOU TONIGHT** *Big Beat A 8130CD* [1]	66	1
19 Oct 96		**GETTIN' MONEY** *Big Beat A 5674CD*	63	1

[1] Junior M.A.F.I.A. featuring Aaliyah

JUNIOR SENIOR
Denmark, male vocal / instrumental duo – Jesper Mortensen and Jeppe Laursen (Singles: 20 weeks, Albums: 3 weeks) pos/wks

			pos	wks
8 Mar 03	●	**MOVE YOUR FEET** *Mercury 0198192*	3	17
9 Aug 03		**RHYTHM BANDITS** *Mercury 9810210*	22	3
22 Mar 03		**D-D-DON'T DON'T STOP THE BEAT** *Mercury FROG0262CD*	29	3

JUNIORS – *See DANNY and the JUNIORS*

JUNKIE XL
Holland, male producer – Tom Holkenborg (Singles: 15 weeks) pos/wks

			pos	wks
22 Jul 00		**ZEROTONINE** *Manifesto FESCD71*	63	1
22 Jun 02	★	**A LITTLE LESS CONVERSATION** *RCA 74321943572* [1] ■	1	12
30 Nov 02		**OBSESSION** *Nebula NEBCD 029* [2]	56	1
7 Jun 03		**CATCH UP TO MY STEP** *Roadrunner RR 20209* [3]	63	1

[1] Elvis vs JXL [2] Tiesto and Junkie XL [3] Junkie XL featuring Solomon Burke

JUNO REACTOR
UK / Germany, male production duo (Singles: 1 week) pos/wks

			pos	wks
8 Feb 97		**JUNGLE HIGH** *Perfecto PERF 133CD*	45	1

JURASSIC 5
US, male rap group (Singles: 4 weeks, Albums: 6 weeks) pos/wks

			pos	wks
25 Jul 98		**JAYOU** *Pan PAN 018CD*	56	1
24 Oct 98		**CONCRETE SCHOOLYARD** *Pan PAN 020CD*	35	3
13 Jun 98		**JURASSIC 5** *Pan PAN 015CD*	70	1
1 Jul 00		**QUALITY CONTROL** *Interscope 4907102*	23	3
19 Oct 02		**POWER IN NUMBERS** *Interscope 4934372*	46	2

Christopher JUST *Austria, male producer (Singles: 2 weeks)* pos/wks

			pos	wks
13 Dec 97		**I'M A DISCO DANCER** *Slut Trax SLUT 001CD*	72	1
6 Feb 99		**I'M A DISCO DANCER (re-mix)** *XL Recordings XLS 105CD*	69	1

JUST 4 JOKES featuring MC RB
UK, male production duo and male rapper (Singles: 1 week) pos/wks

			pos	wks
28 Sep 02		**JUMP UP** *Serious SERR 050CD*	67	1

JUST LUIS
Spain, male vocalist – Luis Sierra Pizarro (Singles: 3 weeks) pos/wks

			pos	wks
14 Oct 95		**AMERICAN PIE (re)** *Pro-Activ CDPTV 1*	31	3

Jimmy JUSTICE
UK, male vocalist – James Little (Singles: 35 weeks) pos/wks

			pos	wks
29 Mar 62	●	**WHEN MY LITTLE GIRL IS SMILING** *Pye 7N 15421*	9	13
14 Jun 62	●	**AIN'T THAT FUNNY** *Pye 7N 15443*	8	11
23 Aug 62		**SPANISH HARLEM** *Pye 7N 15457*	20	11

JUSTIFIED ANCIENTS OF MU MU *UK, male vocal / production duo – Bill Drummond and Jimmy Cauty (Singles: 6 weeks)* pos/wks

			pos	wks
9 Nov 91	●	**IT'S GRIM UP NORTH (re)** *KLF Communications JAMS 028*	10	6

See also KLF; TIMELORDS; 2K

JUSTIN *UK, male vocalist – Justin Osuji (Singles: 13 weeks)* pos/wks

			pos	wks
22 Aug 98		**THIS BOY** *Virgin STCDT 1*	34	2
16 Jan 99		**OVER YOU** *Virgin STCDT 2*	11	4
17 Jul 99		**IT'S ALL ABOUT YOU** *Innocent STCDT 3*	34	3
22 Jan 00		**LET IT BE ME** *Innocent STCDTX 4*	15	4

Bill JUSTIS
US, male instrumentalist – alto sax, d. 15 Jul 1982 (Singles: 8 weeks) pos/wks

			pos	wks
10 Jan 58		**RAUNCHY (re)** *London HLS 8517*	11	8

Patrick JUVET *Switzerland, male vocalist (Singles: 19 weeks)* pos/wks

			pos	wks
2 Sep 78		**GOT A FEELING** *Casablanca CAN 127*	34	7
4 Nov 78		**I LOVE AMERICA** *Casablanca CAN 132*	12	12

BRITISH HIT SINGLES & ALBUMS

K

BRITISH HIT SINGLES AND ALBUMS

Frank K featuring Wiston OFFICE
Italy / US, male vocal / instrumental duo (Singles: 1 week) pos/wks

			pos	wks
26 Jan 91		**EVERYBODY LET'S SOMEBODY LOVE** *Urban URB 66*	61	1

Leila K
Sweden, female rapper – Leila El Khalifi (Singles: 22 weeks) pos/wks

			pos	wks
25 Nov 89	●	**GOT TO GET** *Arista 112696* [1]	8	14
17 Mar 90		**ROK THE NATION** *Arista 112971* [1]	41	3
23 Jan 93		**OPEN SESAME** *Polydor PQCD 1*	23	4
3 Jul 93		**ÇA PLANE POUR MOI** *Polydor PQCD 3*	69	1

[1] Rob 'n' Raz featuring Leila K

KC & THE SUNSHINE BAND *US, male vocal / instrumental group – leader – Harry Wayne Casey (Singles: 104 weeks)* pos/wks

			pos	wks
17 Aug 74	●	**QUEEN OF CLUBS** *Jayboy BOY 88*	7	12
23 Nov 74		**SOUND YOUR FUNKY HORN** *Jayboy BOY 83*	17	9

29 Mar 75 **GET DOWN TONIGHT** *Jayboy BOY 93* ▲ 21 9
2 Aug 75 ● **THAT'S THE WAY (I LIKE IT)** *Jayboy BOY 99* ▲ 4 10
22 Nov 75 **I'M SO CRAZY ('BOUT YOU)** *Jayboy BOY 101* 34 3
17 Jul 76 **(SHAKE, SHAKE, SHAKE) SHAKE YOUR BOOTY** *Jayboy BOY 110* ▲ 22 8
11 Dec 76 **KEEP IT COMIN' LOVE** *Jayboy BOY 112* 31 8
30 Apr 77 **I'M YOUR BOOGIE MAN** *TK XB 2167* ▲ 41 4
6 May 78 **BOOGIE SHOES** *TK TKR 6025* 34 5
22 Jul 78 **IT'S THE SAME OLD SONG** *TK TKR 6037* 47 5
8 Dec 79 ● **PLEASE DON'T GO** *TK TKR 7558* ▲ 3 12
16 Jul 83 ★ **GIVE IT UP** *Epic EPC A 3017* 1 14
24 Sep 83 **(YOU SAID) YOU'D GIMME SOME MORE** *Epic A 2760* 41 3
11 May 91 **THAT'S THE WAY I LIKE IT (re-mix)** *Music Factory Dance M7FAC 2* 59 2
30Aug 75 **KC AND THE SUNSHINE BAND** *Jayboy JSL 9* 26 7
1 Mar 80 ● **GREATEST HITS** *TK TKR 83385* 10 6
27 Aug 83 **ALL IN A NIGHT'S WORK** *Epic EPC 85847* 46 4

K-CI & JOJO *US, male vocal duo – Cedric and Joel Hailey (Singles: 29 weeks, Albums: 3 weeks)* pos/wks

27 Jul 96 **HOW DO YOU WANT IT** *Death Row DRWCD 4* [1] ▲ 17 4
23 Aug 97 **YOU BRING ME UP** *MCA MCSTD 48057* 21 2
18 Apr 98 ● **ALL MY LIFE** *MCA MCSTD 48076* ▲ 8 11
19 Sep 98 **DON'T RUSH (TAKE LOVE SLOWLY)** *MCA MCSTD 48090* 16 3
2 Oct 99 **TELL ME IT'S REAL** *MCA MCSTD 40211* 40 2
23 Sep 00 **TELL ME IT'S REAL (re-mix)** *AM:PM CDAMPM 135* 16 5
12 May 01 **CRAZY** *MCA MCSTD 40253* 35 2
28 Jun 97 **LOVE ALWAYS** *MCA MCD 11613* 51 2
3 Jul 99 **IT'S REAL** *MCA MCD 11975* 56 1

[1] 2Pac featuring K-Ci and JoJo

See also JODECI

K CREATIVE
UK, male vocal / instrumental group (Singles: 2 weeks) pos/wks

7 Mar 92 **THREE TIMES A MAYBE** *Talkin Loud TLK 17* 58 2

The listed flipside of 'Three Times a Maybe' was 'Feed the Feeling' by Perception

Ernie K-DOE
US, male vocalist – Ernest Kador, d. 5 Jul 2001 (Singles: 7 weeks) pos/wks

11 May 61 **MOTHER-IN-LAW** *London HLU 9330* ▲ 29 7

K-GEE *UK, male producer – Karl Gordon (Singles: 3 weeks)* pos/wks

4 Nov 00 **I DON'T REALLY CARE** *Instant Karma KARMA 3CD* 22 3

K.I.D.
Antilles, male / female vocal / instrumental group (Singles: 4 weeks) pos/wks

28 Feb 81 **DON'T STOP** *EMI 5143* 49 4

K-KLASS *UK, male / female vocal / instrumental group (Singles: 31 weeks, Albums: 1 week)* pos/wks

4 May 91 **RHYTHM IS A MYSTERY** *Deconstruction CREED 11* [1] 61 2
9 Nov 91 ● **RHYTHM IS A MYSTERY (re-issue)** *Deconstruction R 6302* [2] ..3 10
25 Apr 92 **SO RIGHT** *Deconstruction R 6309* 20 5
7 Nov 92 **DON'T STOP** *Deconstruction R 6325* 32 3
27 Nov 93 **LET ME SHOW YOU** *Deconstruction CDR 6367* 13 7
28 May 94 **WHAT YOU'RE MISSING** *Deconstruction CDRS 6380* 24 3
1 Aug 98 **BURNIN'** *Parlophone CDK 2001* 45 1
4 Jun 94 **UNIVERSAL** *Deconstruction CDPCSDX 149* 73 1

[1] K-Klass featuring Bobbie Depasois [2] K-Klass with vocals by Bobbie Depasois

KLF *UK, male vocal / instrumental duo – Bill Drummond and Jimmy Cauty (Singles: 51 weeks, Albums: 46 weeks)* pos/wks

11 Aug 90 ● **WHAT TIME IS LOVE? (LIVE AT TRANCENTRAL)** *KLF Communications KLF 004* [1] 5 12
19 Jan 91 ★ **3 AM ETERNAL** *KLF Communications KLF 005* [1] 1 11
4 May 91 ● **LAST TRAIN TO TRANCENTRAL** *KLF Communications KLF 008* 2 9
7 Dec 91 ● **JUSTIFIED AND ANCIENT** *KLF Communications KLF 099* [2] ..2 12
7 Mar 92 ● **AMERICA: WHAT TIME IS LOVE? (re-mix)** *KLF Communications KLFUSA 004* 4 7
16 Mar 91 ● **THE WHITE ROOM** *KLF Communications JAMSLP 6* 3 46

[1] KLF featuring the Children of the Revolution [2] KLF guest vocals: Tammy Wynette

See also JUSTIFIED ANCIENTS OF MU MU; TIMELORDS; 2K

KMC featuring DHANY
Italy, male production duo, and female vocalist (Singles: 2 weeks) pos/wks

25 May 02 **I FEEL SO FINE** *Incentive CENT 39CDS* 33 2

KP & ENVYI *US, female vocal / rap duo – Kia Philips and Susan Hedgepath (Singles: 4 weeks)* pos/wks

13 Jun 98 **SWING MY WAY** *East West E 3849 CD* 14 4

KRS ONE *US, male rapper – Lawrence Parker (Singles: 8 weeks, Albums: 1 week)* pos/wks

18 May 96 **RAPPAZ R N DAINJA** *Jive JIVECD 396* 47 1
8 Feb 97 **WORD PERFECT** *Jive JIVECD 418* 70 1
26 Apr 97 **STEP INTO A WORLD (RAPTURE'S DELIGHT)** *Jive JIVECD 411* 24 2
20 Sep 97 **HEARTBEAT / A FRIEND** *Jive JIVECD 431* 66 1
1 Nov 97 **DIGITAL** *ffrr FCD 316* [1] 13 3
31 May 97 **I GOT NEXT** *Jive CHIP 179* 58 1

[1] Goldie featuring KRS One

K7
US, male vocal / rap group (Singles: 22 weeks, Albums: 3 weeks) pos/wks

11 Dec 93 ● **COME BABY COME** *Big Life BLRD 105* 3 16
2 Apr 94 **HI DE HO** *Big Life BLRD 108* [1] 17 5
25 Jun 94 **ZUNGA ZENG** *Big Life BLRD 111* [1] 63 1
5 Feb 94 **SWING BATTA SWING** *Big Life BLRCD 27* 27 3

[1] K7 and the Swing Kids

K3M
Italy, male / female vocal / instrumental duo (Singles: 1 week) pos/wks

21 Mar 92 **LISTEN TO THE RHYTHM** *PWL Continental PWL 214* 71 1

K2 FAMILY
UK, male production / rap / vocal group (Singles: 3 weeks) pos/wks

27 Oct 01 **BOUNCING FLOW** *Relentless RELENT 22CD* 27 3

K-WARREN featuring LEE-O *UK, male producer – Kevin Warren Williams and UK, male vocalist – Leo Ihenacho (Singles: 2 weeks)* pos/wks

5 May 01 **COMING HOME** *Go! Beat GOBCD 41* 32 2

KWS *UK, male vocal / instrumental group (Singles: 36 weeks)* pos/wks

25 Apr 92 ★ **PLEASE DON'T GO / GAME BOY** *Network NWK 46* 1 16
22 Aug 92 ● **ROCK YOUR BABY** *Network NWK 54* 8 7
12 Dec 92 **HOLD BACK THE NIGHT** *Network NWK 65* [1] 30 5
5 Jun 93 **CAN'T GET ENOUGH OF YOUR LOVE** *Network NWKCD 72* 71 1
9 Apr 94 **IT SEEMS TO HANG ON** *X-clusive XCLU 006CD* 58 1
2 Jul 94 **AIN'T NOBODY (LOVES ME BETTER)** *X-clusive XCLU 010CD* [2] 21 4
19 Nov 94 **THE MORE I GET THE MORE I WANT** *X-clusive XCLU 011CD* [3] 35 2

[1] KWS features guest vocal from The Trammps [2] KWS and Gwen Dickey [3] KWS featuring Teddy Pendergrass

'Game Boy' was listed only from 9 May 1992

KYO – *See BEDROCK*

KACI *US, female vocalist – Kaci Battaglia (Singles: 23 weeks, Albums: 2 weeks)* pos/wks

10 Mar 01 **PARADISE** *Curb / London CUBC 61* 11 9
28 Jul 01 **TU AMOR** *Curb / London CUBC 71* 24 3

2 Feb 02 ●	**I THINK I LOVE YOU** *Curb / London CUBC 076*	**10** 10
9 Aug 03	**I'M NOT ANYBODY'S GIRL** *Curb / London CUBC 091*	**55** 1
16 Feb 02	PARADISE *Curb/London 927402192*	**47** 2

Joshua KADISON

US, male vocalist (Singles: 19 weeks, Albums: 4 weeks) pos/wks

26 Feb 94	**JESSIE (re)** *SBK CDSBK 43*	**48** 5
12 Nov 94	**BEAUTIFUL IN MY EYES** *SBK CDSBK 50*	**65** 1
29 Apr 95	**JESSIE (re-issue)** *SBK CDSBK 53*	**15** 10
12 Aug 95	**BEAUTIFUL IN MY EYES (re-issue)** *SBK CDSBK 55*	**37** 3
27 May 95	PAINTED DESERT SERENADE *SBK SBKCD 22*	**45** 4

KADOC

UK / Spain, male vocal / instrumental group (Singles: 11 weeks) pos/wks

6 Apr 96	**THE NIGHTTRAIN** *Positiva CDTIV 26*	**14** 8
17 Aug 96	**YOU GOT TO BE THERE** *Positiva CDTIV 58*	**45** 1
23 Aug 97	**ROCK THE BELLS** *Manifesto FESCD 30*	**34** 2

Bert KAEMPFERT and His Orchestra *Germany, orchestra, leader d. 21 Jun 1980 (Singles: 10 weeks, Albums: 104 weeks)* pos/wks

23 Dec 65	**BYE BYE BLUES** *Polydor BM 56 504*	**24** 10
5 Mar 66 ●	BYE BYE BLUES *Polydor BM 84086*	**4** 22
16 Apr 66	BEST OF BERT KAEMPFERT *Polydor 84012*	**27** 1
28 May 66	SWINGING SAFARI *Polydor LPHM 46384*	**20** 15
30 Jul 66	STRANGERS IN THE NIGHT *Polydor LPHM 84053*	**13** 26
4 Feb 67	RELAXING SOUND OF BERT KAEMPFERT *Polydor 583501*	**33** 3
18 Feb 67	BERT KAEMPFERT – BEST SELLER *Polydor 583551*	**25** 18
29 Apr 67	HOLD ME *Polydor 184072*	**36** 5
26 Aug 67	KAEMPFERT SPECIAL *Polydor 236207*	**24** 5
19 Jun 71	ORANGE COLOURED SKY *Polydor 2310091*	**49** 1
5 Jul 80	SOUNDS SENSATIONAL *Polydor POLTB 10*	**17** 8

KAJAGOOGOO *UK, male vocal / instrumental group – lead vocal Limahl (Singles: 50 weeks, Albums: 23 weeks)* pos/wks

22 Jan 83 ★	**TOO SHY** *EMI 5359*	**1** 13
2 Apr 83 ●	**OOH TO BE AH** *EMI 5383*	**7** 8
4 Jun 83	**HANG ON NOW** *EMI 5394*	**13** 7
17 Sep 83 ●	**BIG APPLE** *EMI 5423*	**8** 8
3 Mar 84	**THE LION'S MOUTH** *EMI 5449*	**25** 7
5 May 84	**TURN YOUR BACK ON ME** *EMI 5646*	**47** 4
21 Sep 85	**SHOULDN'T DO THAT** *Parlophone R 6106* [1]	**63** 3
30 Apr 83 ●	WHITE FEATHERS *EMI EMC 3433*	**5** 20
26 May 84	ISLANDS *EMI KAJA 1*	**35** 3

[1] Kaja

KALEEF *UK, male rap / vocal group (Singles: 12 weeks)* pos/wks

30 Mar 96	**WALK LIKE A CHAMPION** *Payday KACD 5* [1]	**23** 3
7 Dec 96	**GOLDEN BROWN** *Unity UNITY 010CD*	**22** 4
14 Jun 97	**TRIALS OF LIFE** *Unity UNITY 012CD*	**75** 1
11 Oct 97	**I LIKE THE WAY (THE KISSING GAME)** *Unity UNITY 015CD1*	**58** 1
24 Jan 98	**SANDS OF TIME** *Unity UNITY 016CD*	**26** 3

[1] Kaliphz featuring Prince Naseem

Preeya KALIDAS *UK, female vocalist (Singles: 2 weeks)* pos/wks

13 Jul 02	**SHAKALAKA BABY** *Sony Classical 6726322*	**38** 2

KALIN TWINS

US, male vocal duo – Herb and Hal Kalin (Singles: 18 weeks) pos/wks

18 Jul 58 ★	**WHEN** *Brunswick 05751*	**1** 18

KALLAGHAN – *See N'n'G featuring KALLAGHAN*

Kitty KALLEN *US, female vocalist (Singles: 23 weeks)* pos/wks

2 Jul 54 ★	**LITTLE THINGS MEAN A LOT** *Brunswick 05287* ▲	**1** 23

Gunter KALLMAN CHOIR

Germany, male / female vocal group (Singles: 3 weeks) pos/wks

24 Dec 64	**ELISABETH SERENADE** *Polydor NH 24678*	**39** 3

KAMASUTRA featuring Jocelyn BROWN *Italy, male DJ / production duo and US, female vocalist (Singles: 1 week)* pos/wks

22 Nov 97	**HAPPINESS** *Sony S2 KAMCD 2*	**45** 1

See also Jocelyn BROWN

Nick KAMEN

UK, male vocalist (Singles: 33 weeks, Albums: 7 weeks) pos/wks

8 Nov 86 ●	**EACH TIME YOU BREAK MY HEART** *WEA YZ 90*	**5** 12
28 Feb 87	**LOVING YOU IS SWEETER THAN EVER** *WEA YZ 106*	**16** 9
16 May 87	**NOBODY ELSE** *WEA YZ 122*	**47** 3
28 May 88	**TELL ME** *WEA YZ 184*	**40** 5
28 Apr 90	**I PROMISED MYSELF** *WEA YZ 454*	**50** 4
18 Apr 87	NICK KAMEN *WEA WX 84*	**34** 7

Ini KAMOZE *Jamaica, male vocalist (Singles: 15 weeks)* pos/wks

7 Jan 95 ●	**HERE COMES THE HOTSTEPPER** *Columbia 6610472* ▲	**4** 15

KANDI *US, female vocalist – Kandi Burruss (Singles: 10 weeks)* pos/wks

11 Nov 00 ●	**DON'T THINK I'M NOT** *Columbia 6705102*	**9** 10

KANDIDATE

UK, male vocal / instrumental group (Singles: 28 weeks) pos/wks

19 Aug 78	**DON'T WANNA SAY GOODNIGHT** *RAK 280*	**47** 6
17 Mar 79	**I DON'T WANNA LOSE YOU** *RAK 289*	**11** 12
4 Aug 79	**GIRLS GIRLS GIRLS** *RAK 295*	**34** 7
22 Mar 80	**LET ME ROCK YOU** *RAK 306*	**58** 3

Eden KANE *India, male vocalist (Singles: 73 weeks)* pos/wks

1 Jun 61 ★	**WELL I ASK YOU** *Decca F 11353*	**1** 21
14 Sep 61 ●	**GET LOST** *Decca F 11381*	**10** 11
18 Jan 62 ●	**FORGET ME NOT** *Decca F 11418*	**3** 14
10 May 62 ●	**I DON'T KNOW WHY** *Decca F 11460*	**7** 13
30 Jan 64 ●	**BOYS CRY** *Fontana TF 438*	**8** 14

KANE GANG *UK, male vocal / instrumental group (Singles: 37 weeks, Albums: 12 weeks)* pos/wks

19 May 84	**SMALLTOWN CREED** *Kitchenware SK 11*	**60** 2
7 Jul 84	**CLOSEST THING TO HEAVEN** *Kitchenware SK 15*	**12** 11
10 Nov 84	**RESPECT YOURSELF (re)** *Kitchenware SK 16*	**21** 11
9 Mar 85	**GUN LAW** *Kitchenware SK 20*	**53** 4
27 Jun 87	**MOTORTOWN** *Kitchenware SK 30*	**45** 5
16 Apr 88	**DON'T LOOK ANY FURTHER** *Kitchenware SK 33*	**52** 4
23 Feb 85	THE BAD AND LOWDOWN WORLD OF THE KANE GANG *Kitchenware KWLP 2*	**21** 8
8 Aug 87	MIRACLE *Kitchenware KWLP 7*	**41** 4

KANSAS *US, male vocal / instrumental group (Singles: 7 weeks)* pos/wks

1 Jul 78	**CARRY ON WAYWARD SON** *Kirshner KIR 4932*	**51** 7

Mory KANTE *Guinea, male vocalist (Singles: 14 weeks)* pos/wks

23 Jul 88	**YEKE YEKE** *London LON 171*	**29** 9
11 Mar 95	**YEKE YEKE (re-issue)** *Ffrreedom TABCD 226*	**25** 3
30 Nov 96	**YEKE YEKE (re-mix)** *ffrr FCD 288*	**28** 2

Paul KANTNER and JEFFERSON AIRPLANE

US, male vocalist / instrumentalist (Albums: 6 weeks) pos/wks

13 Feb 71	BLOWS AGAINST THE EMPIRE *RCA SF 8163*	**12** 6

See also JEFFERSON AIRPLANE

KAOMA *France, male / female vocal / instrumental group (Singles: 20 weeks)* pos/wks

21 Oct 89 ●	**LAMBADA** *CBS 655011 7*	**4** 18
27 Jan 90	**DANCANDO LAMBADA** *CBS 655235 7*	**62** 2

KAOTIC CHEMISTRY

UK, male instrumental / production group (Singles: 1 week) pos/wks

31 Oct 92	**LSD (EP)** *Moving Shadow SHADOW 20*	**68** 1

Tracks on LSD (EP): Space Cakes / LSD / Illegal Substances / Drumtrip II

FASTEST SELLING ALBUMS

Based on the fastest time to sell one million copies of an album from release date

Remarkably, the fastest this century is 1 by The Beatles with the one-million mark reached in just 26 days. The all-time record-breakers are as follows:

All-time record
One million in 17 days:
BE HERE NOW
Oasis 1997

All-time male solo record
One million in 29 days:
SWING WHEN YOU'RE WINNING
Robbie Williams 2001

All-time female solo record
One million in 50 days:
LIFE FOR RENT
Dido 2003

All-time duo record
One million in 26 days:
ROBSON & JEROME
Robson & Jerome 1996

Dido, whose follow-up to 'No Angel', 'Life for Rent', sold one million copies in 50 days, shifting 102,500 on day one and 400,351 in the first week on its way to the record

KARAJA *Germany, female vocalist (Singles: 1 week)* pos/wks

19 Oct 02 **SHE MOVES (LA LA LA)** *Ministry of Sound / Substance SUBS 14CDS* 42 1

KARIN – *See UNIQUE 3*

KARIYA *US, female vocalist (Singles: 9 weeks)* pos/wks

8 Jul 89 **LET ME LOVE YOU FOR TONIGHT (re)** *Sleeping Bag SBUK 4* ..44 9

Mick KARN *UK, male instrumentalist – bass – Anthony Michaelides (Singles: 6 weeks, Albums: 4 weeks)* pos/wks

9 Jul 83 **AFTER A FASHION** *Musicfest FEST 1* [1] 39 4
17 Jan 87 **BUOY** *Virgin VS 910* [2] 63 2
20 Nov 82 **TITLES** *Virgin V 2249* 74 3
28 Feb 87 **DREAMS OF REASON PRODUCE MONSTERS** *Virgin V 2389* 89 1

[1] Midge Ure and Mick Karn [2] Mick Karn featuring David Sylvian

See also JAPAN

KARTOON KREW *US, rap / instrumental group (Singles: 6 weeks)* pos/wks

7 Dec 85 **INSPECTOR GADGET** *Champion CHAMP 6* 58 6

KASENETZ-KATZ SINGING ORCHESTRAL CIRCUS *US, male vocal / instrumental group (Singles: 15 weeks)* pos/wks

20 Nov 68 **QUICK JOEY SMALL (RUN JOEY RUN)** *Buddah 201 022* 19 15

KATCHA *UK, male DJ / producer (Singles: 1 week)* pos/wks

21 Aug 99 **TOUCHED BY GOD** *Hooj Choons HOOJ 77CD* 57 1

KATOI *Thailand, female DJ / producer (Singles: 1 week)* pos/wks

29 Mar 03 **TOUCH YOU** *Arista Dance 74321964492* 70 1

KATRINA and the WAVES *US / UK, female / male vocal / instrumental group (Singles: 34 weeks, Albums: 7 weeks)* pos/wks

4 May 85 ● **WALKING ON SUNSHINE** *Capitol CL 354* 8 12
5 Jul 86 **SUN STREET** *Capitol CL 407* 22 9
8 Jun 96 **WALKING ON SUNSHINE (re-issue)** *EMI Premier PRESCD 2* 53 1
10 May 97 ● **LOVE SHINE A LIGHT** *Eternal WEA 106CD1* 3 12
8 Jun 85 **KATRINA AND THE WAVES** *Capitol KTW 1* 28 6
10 May 86 **WAVES** *Capitol EST 2010* 70 1

KAVANA *UK, male vocalist – Anthony Kavanagh (Singles: 26 weeks, Albums: 2 weeks)* pos/wks

11 May 96 **CRAZY CHANCE** *Nemesis NMSD 1* 35 3
24 Aug 96 **WHERE ARE YOU** *Nemesis NMSD 2* 26 2
11 Jan 97 ● **I CAN MAKE YOU FEEL GOOD** *Nemesis NMSDX 3* 8 5
19 Apr 97 ● **MFEO** *Nemesis NMSD 4* 8 4
13 Sep 97 **CRAZY CHANCE 97 (re-recording)** *Nemesis NMSD 5* 16 3
29 Aug 98 **SPECIAL KIND OF SOMETHING** *Virgin VSCDT 1704* 13 4
12 Dec 98 **FUNKY LOVE (re)** *Virgin VSCDT 1711* 32 3
20 Mar 99 **WILL YOU WAIT FOR ME** *Virgin VSCDT 1726* 29 2
10 May 97 **KAVANA** *Nemesis CDNMS 1* 29 2

Niamh KAVANAGH *Ireland, female vocalist (Singles: 5 weeks)* pos/wks

12 Jun 93 **IN YOUR EYES** *Arista 74321154152* 24 5

KAWALA *UK, male vocal / instrumental / production group (Singles: 1 week)* pos/wks

26 Feb 00 **HUMANISTIC** *Pepper 9230022* 68 1

Janet KAY *UK, female vocalist – Janet Bogle (Singles: 24 weeks)* pos/wks

9 Jun 79 ● **SILLY GAMES** *Scope SC 2* 2 14
11 Aug 90 **SILLY GAMES** *Arista 113452* [1] 22 7
11 Aug 90 **SILLY GAMES (re-mix)** *Music Factory Dance MFD 006* 62 3

[1] Lindy Layton featuring Janet Kay

Danny KAYE *US, male actor / vocalist – David Kaminsky, d. 3 Mar 1987 (Singles: 10 weeks)* pos/wks

27 Feb 53 ● **WONDERFUL COPENHAGEN** *Brunswick 05023* 5 10

With Gordon Jenkins and his Orchestra and Chorus

KAYE SISTERS *UK, female vocal group (Singles: 45 weeks)* pos/wks

25 May 56 **IVORY TOWER** *HMV POP 209* [1] 20 5
1 Nov 57 ● **GOT-TA HAVE SOMETHING IN THE BANK, FRANK** *Philips PB 751* [2] 8 11
3 Jan 58 **SHAKE ME I RATTLE / ALONE** *Philips PB 752* 27 1
1 May 59 ● **COME SOFTLY TO ME** *Philips PB 913* [2] 9 9
7 Jul 60 ● **PAPER ROSES** *Philips PB 1024* 7 19

[1] Three Kayes [2] Frankie Vaughan and The Kaye Sisters

KAYESTONE *UK, male DJ / production duo (Singles: 1 week)* pos/wks

29 Jul 00 **ATMOSPHERE** *Distinctive DISNCD 62* 55 1

KÉ *US, male vocalist (Singles:1 Week)* pos/wks

13 Apr 96 **STRANGE WORLD** *Venture 74321349412* 73 1

Johnny KEATING *UK, orchestra (Singles: 14 weeks)* pos/wks

1 Mar 62 ● **THEME FROM 'Z CARS' (JOHNNY TODD)** *Piccadilly 7N 35032* 8 14

Ronan KEATING (307 Top 500)

Record-setting Irish vocalist, b. 3 Mar 1977, Dublin, who is still adding to his unprecedented chart start of 25 Top 10 singles (23 of them making the Top 5) including those as a member of Boyzone. In addition six of his eight albums (including two solo) entered at No.1. He formerly co-managed Westlife. Best-selling single: 'When You Say Nothing at All' 528,600 (Singles: 109 weeks, Albums: 102 weeks) pos/wks

7 Aug 99 ★ **WHEN YOU SAY NOTHING AT ALL (2re)** *Polydor 5612902* ■ 1 17
22 Jul 00 ★ **LIFE IS A ROLLERCOASTER** *Polydor 5619362* ■ 1 14
2 Dec 00 ● **THE WAY YOU MAKE ME FEEL (re)** *Polydor 5878852* 6 12
28 Apr 01 ● **LOVIN' EACH DAY** *Polydor 5876872* 2 14
18 May 02 ★ **IF TOMORROW NEVER COMES** *Polydor 5707182* ■ 1 15
21 Sep 02 ● **I LOVE IT WHEN WE DO (2re)** *Polydor 5709032* 5 10
7 Dec 02 ● **WE'VE GOT TONIGHT** *Polydor 0658612* [1] 4 13
10 May 03 ● **THE LONG GOODBYE** *Polydor 0657372* 3 10
22 Nov 03 ● **LOST FOR WORDS** *Polydor 9813304* 9 4
12 Aug 00 ★ **RONAN** *Polydor 5491032* ■ 1 56
1 Jun 02 ★ **DESTINATION** *Polydor 5897892* ■ 1 41
29 Nov 03 **TURN IT ON** *Polydor 9865882* ....21 5+

[1] Ronan Keating featuring Lulu

KEE – *See BM DUBS present MR RUMBLE featuring BRASSTOOTH and KEE*

Kevin KEEGAN *UK, male footballer / vocalist (Singles: 6 weeks)* pos/wks

9 Jun 79 **HEAD OVER HEELS IN LOVE** *EMI 2965* 31 6

KEEL *US, male vocal / instrumental group (Albums: 2 weeks)* pos/wks

17 May 86 **THE FINAL FRONTIER** *Vertigo VERH 33* 83 2

Howard KEEL *US, male vocalist – Harold Leek (Albums: 36 weeks)* pos/wks

14 Apr 84 ● **AND I LOVE YOU SO** *Warwick WW 5137* 6 19
9 Nov 85 **REMINISCING – THE HOWARD KEEL COLLECTION** *Telstar STAR 2259* 20 12
28 Mar 88 **JUST FOR YOU** *Telstar STAR 2318* 51 5

Yvonne KEELEY – *See Scott FITZGERALD*

Nelson KEENE *UK, male vocalist – Malcolm Holland (Singles: 5 weeks)* pos/wks

25 Aug 60 **IMAGE OF A GIRL (re)** *HMV POP 771* 37 5

KEITH *US, male vocalist – James Keefer (Singles: 8 weeks)* pos/wks

Date		Title	Pos	Wks
26 Jan 67		**98.6** *Mercury MF 955*	24	7
16 Mar 67		**TELL ME TO MY FACE** *Mercury MF 968*	50	1

KEITH 'N' SHANE *Ireland, male vocal duo – Keith Duffy and Shane Lynch (Singles: 3 weeks)* pos/wks

Date		Title	Pos	Wks
23 Dec 00		**GIRL YOU KNOW IT'S TRUE** *Polydor 5879462*	36	3

See also BOYZONE

KELIS *US, female vocalist – Kelis Rogers (Singles: 38 weeks, Albums: 13 weeks)* pos/wks

Date		Title	Pos	Wks
26 Feb 00		**CAUGHT OUT THERE (import)** *Virgin 8965102CD*	52	1
4 Mar 00	●	**CAUGHT OUT THERE (re)** *Virgin VUSCD 158*	4	12
17 Jun 00		**GOOD STUFF** *Virgin VUSCD 164*	19	5
8 Jul 00		**GOT YOUR MONEY** *Elektra E 7077CD* [1]	11	8
21 Oct 00		**GET ALONG WITH YOU** *Virgin VUSCD 174*	51	1
3 Nov 01		**YOUNG FRESH N' NEW** *Virgin VUSCD 212*	32	2
5 Oct 02		**HELP ME** *Perfecto PERF 42CDS* [2]	65	1
23 Aug 03	●	**FINEST DREAMS** *Virgin RXCD 2* [3]	8	5
23 Aug 03		**LET'S GET ILL** *Bad Boy / Universal / Island MCSTD 40331* [4]	25	3
11 Mar 00		**KALEIDOSCOPE** *Virgin CDVUS 167*	43	13

[1] Ol' Dirty Bastard featuring Kelis [2] Timo Maas featuring Kelis [3] Richard X featuring Kelis [4] P Diddy featuring Kelis

Jerry KELLER *US, male vocalist (Singles: 14 weeks)* pos/wks

Date		Title	Pos	Wks
28 Aug 59	★	**HERE COMES SUMMER** *London HLR 8890*	1	14

Frank KELLY *Ireland, male actor / vocalist – Francis O'Kelly (Singles: 5 weeks)* pos/wks

Date		Title	Pos	Wks
24 Dec 83		**CHRISTMAS COUNTDOWN (re)** *Ritz RITZ 062*	26	5

Re-entry peaked at No.54 in Dec 1984

Frankie KELLY *US, male vocalist / instrumentalist (Singles: 2 weeks)* pos/wks

Date		Title	Pos	Wks
2 Nov 85		**AIN'T THAT THE TRUTH** *10 TEN 87*	65	2

Grace KELLY – *See* Bing CROSBY

Keith KELLY *UK, male vocalist – Michael Pailthorpe (Singles: 5 weeks)* pos/wks

Date		Title	Pos	Wks
5 May 60		**TEASE ME (MUST YOU ALWAYS) (re)** *Parlophone R 4640*	27	4
18 Aug 60		**LISTEN LITTLE GIRL** *Parlophone R 4676*	47	1

R KELLY (171 Top 500)

Phenomenally successful R&B vocalist, b. Robert Kelly, 8 Jan 1971, Chicago, US, whose writing and production skills are constantly in demand by other top artists. Amazingly, 1998 album 'R' yielded seven Top 20 hits but never reached the Top 20 itself. Best-selling single: 'I Believe I Can Fly' 673,000 (Singles: 196 weeks, Albums: 121 weeks) pos/wks

Date		Title	Pos	Wks
9 May 92		**SHE'S GOT THAT VIBE** *Jive JIVET 292* [1]	57	2
20 Nov 93		**SEX ME** *Jive JIVECD 346* [1]	75	1
14 May 94		**YOUR BODY'S CALLIN'** *Jive JIVECD 353*	19	4
3 Sep 94		**SUMMER BUNNIES** *Jive JIVECD 358*	23	3
22 Oct 94	●	**SHE'S GOT THAT VIBE (re-issue)** *Jive JIVECD 364*	3	13
21 Jan 95	●	**BUMP 'N' GRIND** *Jive JIVECD 368* ▲	8	9
6 May 95		**THE 4 PLAY EPS** *Jive JIVECD 376*	23	3
11 Nov 95		**YOU REMIND ME OF SOMETHING** *Jive JIVECD 388*	24	3
2 Mar 96		**DOWN LOW (NOBODY HAS TO KNOW)** *Jive JIVECD 392* [2]	23	3
22 Jun 96		**THANK GOD IT'S FRIDAY** *Jive JIVECD 395*	14	4
29 Mar 97	★	**I BELIEVE I CAN FLY** *Jive JIVECD 415*	1	17
19 Jul 97	●	**GOTHAM CITY** *Jive JIVECD 428*	9	8
18 Jul 98	●	**BE CAREFUL (re)** *Jive 0521452* [3]	7	7
26 Sep 98		**HALF ON A BABY** *Jive 0521802*	16	4
14 Nov 98		**HOME ALONE** *Jive 0522392* [4]	17	5
28 Nov 98	●	**I'M YOUR ANGEL** *Epic 6666282* [5] ▲	3	13
31 Jul 99		**DID YOU EVER THINK** *Jive 0523612*	20	5
16 Oct 99	●	**IF I COULD TURN BACK THE HANDS OF TIME (import) (re)** *Jive 0523182*	2	21
19 Feb 00		**SATISFY YOU (import) (re)** *Bad Boy / Arista 792832* [6]	73	2
11 Mar 00	●	**SATISFY YOU** *Bad Boy / Arista 74321745592* [6]	8	8
22 Apr 00		**ONLY THE LOOT CAN MAKE ME HAPPY / WHEN A WOMAN'S FED UP / I CAN'T SLEEP BABY (IF I)** *Jive 9250282*	24	3
21 Oct 00		**I WISH** *Jive 9251262*	12	6
31 Mar 01		**THE STORM IS OVER NOW** *Jive 9251782*	18	6
23 Jun 01		**FIESTA** *Jive 9252142* [7]	23	3
2 Mar 02	●	**THE WORLD'S GREATEST** *Jive 9253242*	4	12
25 May 02		**HONEY** *Jive 9253662* [8]	35	2
17 May 03	★	**IGNITION** *Jive 9254972* ■	1	20
23 Aug 03	●	**SNAKE** *Jive 82876547232* [9]	10	5
15 Nov 03		**STEP IN THE NAME / THOIA THONG** *Jive 82876573912*	14	4
29 Feb 92		**BORN INTO THE 90'S** *Jive CHIP 123* [1]	67	1
27 Nov 93		**12 PLAY** *Jive CHIP 144*	20	44
25 Nov 95		**R KELLY** *Jive CHIP 166* ▲	18	10
21 Nov 98		**R** *Jive 517932*	27	26
18 Nov 00		**TP-2.COM** *Jive 9220262* ▲	21	3
30 Mar 02		**THE BEST OF BOTH WORLDS** *Jive 9223512* [2]	37	2
1 Mar 03	●	**CHOCOLATE FACTORY** *Jive 9225082* ▲	10	22
4 Oct 03	●	**THE R IN R & B – GREATEST HITS – VOL.1** *Jive 82876561792*	4	13+

[1] R Kelly and Public Announcement [2] R Kelly featuring Ronald Isley [3] Sparkle featuring R Kelly [4] R Kelly featuring Keith Murray [5] Celine Dion and R Kelly [6] Puff Daddy featuring R Kelly [7] R Kelly featuring Jay-Z [8] R Kelly & Jay-Z [9] R Kelly featuring Big Tigger [1] R Kelly and Public Announcement [2] R Kelly and Jay-Z

The 4 Play EP was available on two CDs, each featuring 'Your Body's Callin'' and three further tracks

Ramona KELLY – *See* Cevin FISHER

Roberta KELLY *US, female vocalist (Singles: 3 weeks)* pos/wks

Date		Title	Pos	Wks
21 Jan 78		**ZODIACS (re)** *Oasis/Hansa 3*	44	3

KELLY FAMILY *Ireland, male / female vocal / instrumental group (Singles: 1 week)* pos/wks

Date		Title	Pos	Wks
21 Oct 95		**AN ANGEL** *EMI CDEM 390*	69	1

Tricia Lee KELSHALL – *See* WAY OUT WEST

Johnny KEMP *Barbados, male vocalist (Singles: 1 week)* pos/wks

Date		Title	Pos	Wks
27 Aug 88		**JUST GOT PAID** *CBS 651470 7*	68	1

Tara KEMP *US, female vocalist (Singles: 2 weeks)* pos/wks

Date		Title	Pos	Wks
20 Apr 91		**HOLD YOU TIGHT** *Giant W 0020*	69	2

Felicity KENDAL *UK, female actor / exercise instructor (Albums: 47 weeks)* pos/wks

Date		Title	Pos	Wks
19 Jun 82		**SHAPE UP AND DANCE (VOLUME 1)** *Lifestyle LEG 1*	29	47

Eddie KENDRICK – *See* Daryl HALL and John OATES

Graham KENDRICK *UK, male vocalist (Singles: 4 weeks)* pos/wks

Date		Title	Pos	Wks
9 Sep 89		**LET THE FLAME BURN BRIGHTER** *Power P 30*	55	4

Eddie KENDRICKS *US, male vocalist, d. 5 Oct 1992 (Singles: 20 weeks)* pos/wks

Date		Title	Pos	Wks
3 Nov 73		**KEEP ON TRUCKIN'** *Tamla Motown TMG 873* ▲	18	14
16 Mar 74		**BOOGIE DOWN** *Tamla Motown TMG 888*	39	4
21 Sep 85		**A NIGHT AT THE APOLLO LIVE!** *RCA PB 49935* [1]	58	2

[1] Daryl Hall and John Oates featuring David Ruffin and Eddie Kendrick

A Night at the Apollo Live! is a medley of 'The Way You Do the Things You Do' and 'My Girl'. Kendricks dropped the 's' from his name for last hit

See also TEMPTATIONS

KENICKIE *UK, female / male vocal / instrumental group (Singles: 13 weeks, Albums: 5 weeks)*

Date	Title	pos	wks
14 Sep 96	**PUNKA** *Emidisc CDDISC 001*	43	2
16 Nov 96	**MILLIONAIRE SWEEPER** *Emidisc CDDISC 002*	60	1
11 Jan 97	**IN YOUR CAR** *Emidisc CDDISC 005*	24	3
3 May 97	**NIGHTLIFE** *Emidisc CDDISC 006*	27	2
5 Jul 97	**PUNKA (re-issue)** *Emidisc CDDISC 007*	38	2
6 Jun 98	**I WOULD FIX YOU** *EMI CDEM 513*	36	2
22 Aug 98	**STAY IN THE SUN** *EMI CDEMS 520*	43	1
24 May 97 ●	**AT THE CLUB** *Emidisc ADISCCD 002*	9	3
12 Sep 98	**GET IN** *EMI 4958512*	32	2

Jane KENNAWAY and STRANGE BEHAVIOUR
UK, female vocalist with male instrumental group (Singles: 3 weeks)

Date	Title	pos	wks
24 Jan 81	**I.O.U.** *Deram DM 436*	65	3

Brian KENNEDY
Ireland, male vocalist (Singles: 8 weeks, Albums: 4 weeks)

Date	Title	pos	wks
22 Jun 96	**A BETTER MAN** *RCA 74321382642*	28	3
21 Sep 96	**LIFE, LOVE AND HAPPINESS** *RCA 74321409921*	27	3
5 Apr 97	**PUT THE MESSAGE IN THE BOX** *RCA 74321462272*	37	2
31 Mar 90	**THE GREAT WAR OF WORDS** *RCA PL 74475*	64	1
19 Oct 96	**A BETTER MAN** *RCA 74321409132*	19	3

Kevin KENNEDY *UK, male actor / vocalist (Singles: 1 week)*

Date	Title	pos	wks
24 Jun 00	**BULLDOG NATION** *D2m 74321759742*	70	1

Nigel KENNEDY
UK, male instrumentalist – violin (Albums: 124 weeks)

Date	Title	pos	wks
1 Mar 86	**ELGAR: VIOLIN CONCERTO** *EMI EMX 4120581* [1]	97	1
7 Oct 89 ●	**VIVALDI: THE FOUR SEASONS** *EMI NIGE 2* [2]	3	81
5 May 90	**MENDELSSOHN / BRUCH / SCHUBERT** *HMV 7496631* [3]	28	15
6 Apr 91	**BRAHMS: VIOLIN CONCERTO** *EMI NIGE 3*	16	12
22 Feb 92	**JUST LISTEN ...** *EMI Classics CDNIGE 4*	56	1
21 Nov 92	**BEETHOVEN: VIOLIN CONCERTO** *EMI Classics CDC 7545742* [4]	40	6
29 Jun 96	**KAFKA** *EMI CDEMD 1095*	67	1
6 Nov 99	**CLASSIC KENNEDY** *EMI Classics CDC 5568902* [2]	51	6
2 Nov 02	**NIGEL KENNEDY'S GREATEST HITS** *EMI Classics 5574112*	71	1

[1] Nigel Kennedy with the London Philharmonic Orchestra conducted by Vernon Handley [2] Nigel Kennedy with the English Chamber Orchestra [3] Nigel Kennedy with Jeffrey Tate and the English Chamber Orchestra [4] Nigel Kennedy with Klaus Tennstedt and the North German Radio Symphony Orchestra

KENNY *Ireland, male vocalist – Tony Kenny (Singles: 16 weeks)*

Date	Title	pos	wks
3 Mar 73	**HEART OF STONE** *RAK 144*	11	13
30 Jun 73	**GIVE IT TO ME NOW** *RAK 153*	38	3

KENNY *UK, male vocal / instrumental group (Singles: 39 weeks, Albums: 1 week)*

Date	Title	pos	wks
7 Dec 74 ●	**THE BUMP** *RAK 186*	3	15
8 Mar 75 ●	**FANCY PANTS** *RAK 196*	4	9
7 Jun 75	**BABY I LOVE YOU, OK!** *RAK 207*	12	7
16 Aug 75 ●	**JULIE ANNE** *RAK 214*	10	8
17 Jan 76	**THE SOUND OF SUPER K** *RAK SRAK 518*	56	1

Although uncredited, all lead and background vocals on 'The Bump' were performed by Barry Palmer

Gerard KENNY
US, male vocalist (Singles: 21 weeks, Albums: 4 weeks)

Date	Title	pos	wks
9 Dec 78	**NEW YORK, NEW YORK** *RCA PB 5117*	43	8
21 Jun 80	**FANTASY (re)** *RCA PB 5256*	34	6
18 Feb 84	**THE OTHER WOMAN, THE OTHER MAN** *Impression IMS 3*	69	4
4 May 85	**NO MAN'S LAND** *WEA YZ 38*	56	3
21 Jul 79	**MADE IT THROUGH THE RAIN** *RCA Victor PL 25218*	19	4

KENT *Sweden, male vocal / instrumental group (Singles: 1 week)*

Date	Title	pos	wks
13 Mar 99	**747** *RCA 74321645912*	61	1

Klark KENT *US, male vocalist / multi-instrumentalist – Stewart Copeland (Singles: 4 weeks)*

Date	Title	pos	wks
26 Aug 78	**DON'T CARE** *A&M AMS 7376*	48	4

See also POLICE

Carol KENYON – *See Paul HARDCASTLE; HEAVEN 17; RAPINATION*

KERBDOG *Ireland, male vocal / instrumental group (Singles: 5 weeks, Albums: 1 week)*

Date	Title	pos	wks
12 Mar 94	**DRY RISER** *Vertigo VERCC 83*	60	1
6 Aug 94	**DUMMY CRUSHER** *Vertigo VERCD 86*	37	2
12 Oct 96	**SALLY** *Fontana KERCD 2*	69	1
29 Mar 97	**MEXICAN WAVE** *Fontana KERCD 3*	49	1
12 Apr 97	**ON THE TURN** *Fontana 5329992*	64	1

Dick KERR – *See Slim DUSTY*

Anita KERR SINGERS – *See Bobby HELMS*

KERRI and MICK
Australia, female / male vocal duo (Singles: 3 weeks)

Date	Title	pos	wks
28 Apr 84	**'SONS AND DAUGHTERS' THEME** *A1 A1 286*	68	3

KERRI-ANN
Ireland, female vocalist (Singles: 1 week)

Date	Title	pos	wks
8 Aug 98	**DO YOU LOVE ME BOY?** *Raglan Road 5671012*	58	1

KERRI B – *See SYSTEM presents KERRI B*

Liz KERSHAW and Bruno BROOKES
UK, male / female DJ / vocal duo (Singles: 3 weeks)

Date	Title	pos	wks
2 Dec 89	**IT TAKES TWO BABY** *Spartan CIN 101* [1]	53	2
1 Dec 90	**LET'S DANCE** *Jive BRUNO 1* [2]	54	1

[1] Liz Kershaw, Bruno Brookes, Jive Bunny and Londonbeat [2] Bruno and Liz and the Radio 1 DJ Posse

Nik KERSHAW *348 Top 500*
One time jazz-funk guitarist whose melodic pop repertoire made him a mid-1980s teen idol, b. 1 Mar 1958, Bristol, UK. His 50 weeks on the singles chart in 1984 beat all other soloists. He appeared at Live Aid, and penned hits for Let Loose, The Hollies and a No.1 for Chesney Hawkes (Singles: 89 weeks, Albums: 100 weeks)

Date	Title	pos	wks
19 Nov 83	**I WON'T LET THE SUN GO DOWN ON ME** *MCA MCA 816*	47	5
28 Jan 84 ●	**WOULDN'T IT BE GOOD** *MCA NIK 2*	4	14
14 Apr 84	**DANCING GIRLS** *MCA NIK 3*	13	9
16 Jun 84 ●	**I WON'T LET THE SUN GO DOWN ON ME (re-issue)** *MCA NIK 4*	2	13
15 Sep 84	**HUMAN RACING** *MCA NIK 5*	19	7
17 Nov 84 ●	**THE RIDDLE** *MCA NIK 6*	3	11
16 Mar 85 ●	**WIDE BOY** *MCA NIK 7*	9	8
3 Aug 85 ●	**DON QUIXOTE** *MCA NIK 8*	10	7
30 Nov 85	**WHEN A HEART BEATS** *MCA NIK 9*	27	7
11 Oct 86	**NOBODY KNOWS** *MCA NIK 10*	44	3
13 Dec 86	**RADIO MUSICOLA** *MCA NIK 11*	43	2
4 Feb 89	**ONE STEP AHEAD** *MCA NIK 12*	55	1
27 Feb 99	**SOMEBODY LOVES YOU** *Eagle EAGXA 023*	70	1
7 Aug 99	**SOMETIMES** *Wall of Sound WALLD 054* [1]	56	1
10 Mar 84 ●	**HUMAN RACING** *MCA MCF 3197*	5	61
1 Dec 84 ●	**THE RIDDLE** *MCA MCF 3245*	8	36
8 Nov 86	**RADIO MUSICOLA** *MCA MCG 6016*	47	3

[1] Les Rythmes Digitales featuring Nik Kershaw

KEVIN and PERRY – *See PRECOCIOUS BRATS featuring KEVIN and PERRY*

KEVIN THE GERBIL
UK, male gerbil vocalist (Singles: 6 weeks)

Date	Title	pos	wks
4 Aug 84	**SUMMER HOLIDAY** *Magnet RAT 3*	50	6

KEY WEST featuring ERIK *UK, male producer – Richard Hewson and female vocalist (Singles: 2 weeks)*

Date		Title / Label	pos	wks
10 Apr 03		**LOOKS LIKE I'M IN LOVE AGAIN** *PWL Sanctuary PWCD 252*	46	2

See also RAH BAND

KEYNOTES – *See Dave KING*

Alicia KEYS *US, female vocalist / instrumentalist – keyboards (Singles: 38 weeks, Albums: 82 weeks)*

Date		Title / Label	pos	wks
10 Nov 01	●	**FALLIN'** *J 74321903692* ▲	3	10
9 Mar 02		**BROTHA PART II** *J 74321922142* [1]	37	2
30 Mar 02		**A WOMAN'S WORTH** *J 74321928692*	18	8
20 Jul 02		**HOW COME YOU DON'T CALL ME** *J 74321943122*	26	3
5 Oct 02	●	**GANGSTA LOVIN'** *Ruff Ryders / Interscope 4978042* [2]	6	8
7 Dec 02		**GIRLFRIEND** *J 74321974972*	24	5
20 Dec 03		**YOU DON'T KNOW MY NAME** *J 82876581612*	19	2+
22 Sep 01	●	**SONGS IN A MINOR** *J 80813200022* ▲	6	79
13 Dec 03		**THE DIARY OF ALICIA KEYS** *J 82876586202* ▲	13	3+

[1] Angie Stone featuring Alicia Keys and Eve [2] Eve featuring Alicia Keys

Chaka KHAN (484 Top 500) *Powerful and influential soul diva b. Yvette Stevens, 23 Mar 1953, Illinois, US. Fronted funk troupe Rufus for six years and went solo in 1978. Prince-penned 'I Feel for You' was the first UK No.1 to feature rap elements (courtesy of Grandmaster Melle Mel) (Singles: 97 weeks, Albums: 45 weeks)*

Date		Title / Label	pos	wks
2 Dec 78		**I'M EVERY WOMAN** *Warner Bros. K 17269*	11	13
31 Mar 84	●	**AIN'T NOBODY** *Warner Bros. RCK 1* [1]	8	12
20 Oct 84	★	**I FEEL FOR YOU** *Warner Bros. W 9209*	1	16
19 Jan 85		**THIS IS MY NIGHT** *Warner Bros. W 9097*	14	6
20 Apr 85		**EYE TO EYE** *Warner Bros. W 9009*	16	7
12 Jul 86		**LOVE OF A LIFETIME** *Warner Bros. W 8671*	52	4
21 Jan 89		**IT'S MY PARTY** *Warner Bros. W 7678*	71	2
6 May 89	●	**I'M EVERY WOMAN (re-mix)** *Warner Bros. W 2963*	8	8
8 Jul 89	●	**AIN'T NOBODY (re-mix)** *Warner Bros. W 2880* [1]	6	9
7 Oct 89		**I FEEL FOR YOU (re-mix)** *Warner Bros. W 2764*	45	2
13 Jan 90		**I'LL BE GOOD TO YOU** *Qwest W 2697* [2]	21	7
28 Mar 92		**LOVE YOU ALL MY LIFETIME** *Warner Bros. W 0087*	49	3
17 Jul 93		**DON'T LOOK AT ME THAT WAY** *Warner Bros. W 0192CD*	73	1
19 Aug 95		**WATCH WHAT YOU SAY** *Cooltempo CDCOOL 308* [3]	28	3
1 Mar 97		**NEVER MISS THE WATER** *Reprise W 1393CD* [4]	59	1
11 Nov 00		**ALL GOOD** *Tommy Boy TBCD 2154B* [5]	33	3
21 Apr 84		**STOMPIN' AT THE SAVOY** *Warner Bros. 923679* [1]	64	5
20 Oct 84		**I FEEL FOR YOU** *Warner Bros. 925 162*	15	22
9 Aug 86		**DESTINY** *Warner Bros. WX 45*	77	2
3 Jun 89		**LIFE IS A DANCE – THE REMIX PROJECT** *Warner Bros. WX 268*	14	15
4 Sep 99		**BEST OF CHAKA KHAN – I'M EVERY WOMAN** *Warner.ESP 9362475072*	62	1

[1] Rufus and Chaka Khan [2] Quincy Jones featuring Ray Charles and Chaka Khan [3] Guru featuring Chaka Khan [4] Chaka Khan featuring Me'Shell Ndegeocello [5] De La Soul featuring Chaka Khan [1] Rufus and Chaka Khan

See also Quincy JONES

Nusrat Fateh Ali KHAN / Michael BROOK *Pakistan, male vocalist and Canada, male producer / instrumentalist (Albums: 1 week)*

Date		Title / Label	pos	wks
6 Apr 96		**NIGHT SONG** *Realworld CDRW 50*	65	1

Praga KHAN *Belgium, male producer – Maurice Engelen (Singles: 9 weeks)*

Date		Title / Label	pos	wks
4 Apr 92		**FREE YOUR BODY / INJECTED WITH A POISON** *Profile PROFT 347* [1]	16	6
11 Jul 92		**RAVE ALERT** *Profile PROF 369*	39	2
24 Nov 01		**INJECTED WITH A POISON (re-mix)** *Nukleuz NUKC 0238*	52	1

[1] Praga Khan featuring Jade 4 U

Aram KHATCHATURIAN / VIENNA PHILHARMONIC ORCHESTRA *Russia, male conductor and Austria, orchestra (Albums: 15 weeks)*

Date		Title / Label	pos	wks
22 Jan 72		**SPARTACUS** *Decca SXL 6000*	16	15

Mary KIANI *UK, female vocalist (Singles: 15 weeks)*

Date		Title / Label	pos	wks
12 Aug 95		**WHEN I CALL YOUR NAME** *Mercury MERCD 440*	18	4
23 Dec 95		**I GIVE IT ALL TO YOU / I IMAGINE** *Mercury MERCD 449*	35	4
27 Apr 96		**LET THE MUSIC PLAY** *Mercury MERCD 456*	19	3
18 Jan 97		**100%** *Mercury MERCD 469*	23	3
21 Jun 97		**WITH OR WITHOUT YOU** *Mercury MERCD 487*	46	1

KICK HORNS – *See DODGY*

KICK SQUAD *UK / Germany, male vocal / instrumental group (Singles: 2 weeks)*

Date		Title / Label	pos	wks
10 Nov 90		**SOUND CLASH (CHAMPION SOUND)** *Kickin KICK 2*	59	2

KICKING BACK with TAXMAN *UK, male / female vocal / instrumental duo with male rapper (Singles: 8 weeks)*

Date		Title / Label	pos	wks
17 Mar 90		**DEVOTION** *10 TEN 297*	47	4
7 Jul 90		**EVERYTHING** *10 TEN 307*	54	4

KICKS LIKE A MULE *UK, male instrumental / production duo – Nick Halkes and Richard Russell (Singles: 6 weeks)*

Date		Title / Label	pos	wks
1 Feb 92	●	**THE BOUNCER** *Tribal Bass TRIBE 3S*	7	6

KID CREME *Belgium, male producer – Nicolas Skaravilli (Singles: 3 weeks)*

Date		Title / Label	pos	wks
22 Mar 03		**DOWN AND UNDER (TOGETHER)** *Ink NIBNE 13CD* [1]	55	1
10 May 03		**HYPNOTISING** *Positiva CDTIV 189* [2]	31	2

[1] Kid Creme featuring MC Shurakano [2] Kid Creme featuring Charlise

KID 'N' PLAY *US, male rap duo (Singles: 7 weeks)*

Date		Title / Label	pos	wks
18 Jul 87		**LAST NIGHT** *Cooltempo COOL 148*	71	1
26 Mar 88		**DO THIS MY WAY** *Cooltempo COOL 164*	48	3
17 Sep 88		**GITTIN' FUNKY** *Cooltempo COOL 168*	55	3

KID ROCK *US, male vocalist / rapper – Robert Ritchie (Singles: 8 weeks, Albums: 1 week)*

Date		Title / Label	pos	wks
23 Oct 99		**COWBOY** *Atlantic AT 0076CD*	36	2
9 Sep 00		**AMERICAN BAD ASS** *Atlantic AT 0085CD*	25	4
12 May 01		**BAWITDABA** *Atlantic AT 0098CD*	41	2
10 Jun 00		**THE HISTORY OF ROCK** *Atlantic 7567833142*	73	1

KID UNKNOWN *UK, male producer – Paul Fitzpatrick (Singles: 1 week)*

Date		Title / Label	pos	wks
2 May 92		**NIGHTMARE** *Warp WAP 20CD*	64	1

Carol KIDD featuring Terry WAITE *UK, female / male vocal duo (Singles: 3 weeks)*

Date		Title / Label	pos	wks
17 Oct 92		**WHEN I DREAM** *The Hit Label HLS 1*	58	3

Johnny KIDD and the PIRATES *UK, male vocal / instrumental group, leader d. 7 Oct 1966 (Singles: 62 weeks)*

Date		Title / Label	pos	wks
12 Jun 59		**PLEASE DON'T TOUCH (re)** *HMV POP 615* [1]	25	5
12 Feb 60		**YOU GOT WHAT IT TAKES** *HMV POP 698*	25	3
16 Jun 60	★	**SHAKIN' ALL OVER** *HMV POP 753*	1	19
6 Oct 60		**RESTLESS** *HMV POP 790*	22	7
13 Apr 61		**LINDA LU** *HMV POP 853*	47	1
10 Jan 63		**A SHOT OF RHYTHM AND BLUES** *HMV POP 1088*	48	1
25 Jul 63	●	**I'LL NEVER GET OVER YOU** *HMV POP 1173*	4	15
28 Nov 63		**HUNGRY FOR LOVE** *HMV POP 1228*	20	10
30 Apr 64		**ALWAYS AND EVER** *HMV POP 1269*	46	1

[1] Johnny Kidd

Nicole KIDMAN *Australia, female actor / vocalist (Singles: 17 weeks)*

Date		Title / Label	pos	wks
6 Oct 01		**COME WHAT MAY** *Interscope / Polydor 4976302* [1]	27	5
22 Dec 01	★	**SOMETHIN' STUPID** *Chrysalis CDCHS 5132* [2] ■	1	12

[1] Nicole Kidman & Ewan McGregor [2] Robbie Williams and Nicole Kidman

KIDS FROM 'FAME' 449 Top 500

TV's original 'Fame' academy students along with singing dance teacher Debbie Allen. These US actors / singers (backed by session musicians), who spent 12 weeks at No.1 with their debut album, oddly failed to crack the Top 40 in their homeland (Singles: 36 weeks, Albums: 117 weeks) pos/wks

			pos	wks
14 Aug 82	●	**HI-FIDELITY** *RCA 254* [1]	5	10
2 Oct 82	●	**STARMAKER** *RCA 280*	3	10
11 Dec 82		**MANNEQUIN** *RCA 299* [2]	50	6
9 Apr 83		**FRIDAY NIGHT (LIVE VERSION)** *RCA 320*	13	10
24 Jul 82	★	**THE KIDS FROM 'FAME'** *BBC REP 447*	1	45
16 Oct 82	●	**THE KIDS FROM 'FAME' AGAIN** *RCA RCALP 6057*	2	21
26 Feb 83	●	**THE KIDS FROM 'FAME' LIVE** *BBC KIDLP 003*	8	28
14 May 83		**THE KIDS FROM 'FAME' SONGS** *BBC KIDLP 004*	14	16
20 Aug 83		**THE KIDS FROM 'FAME' SING FOR YOU** *BBC KIDLP 005*	28	7

[1] Kids from Fame featuring Valerie Landsberg [2] Kids from Fame featuring Gene Anthony Ray

Greg KIHN BAND

US, male vocal / instrumental group (Singles: 2 weeks) pos/wks

			pos	wks
23 Apr 83		**JEOPARDY** *Beserkley E 9847*	63	2

KILLAH PRIEST *US, male rapper (Singles: 1 week)* pos/wks

			pos	wks
7 Feb 98		**ONE STEP** *Geffen GFSTD 22318*	45	1

KILLER MIKE *US, male rappers – Michael Render (Singles: 9 weeks)* pos/wks

			pos	wks
6 Apr 02		**THE WHOLE WORLD** *Laface 74321917592* [1]	19	5
27 Jul 02		**LAND OF A MILLION DRUMS** *Atlantic AT 0134CD* [2]	46	1
10 May 03		**A.D.I.D.A.S.** *Columbia 6738652* [3]	22	3

[1] Outkast featuring Killer Mike [2] Outkast featuring Killer Mike and Sleepy Brown [3] Killer Mike featuring Big Boi

KILLING JOKE *UK, male vocal / instrumental group (Singles: 50 weeks, Albums: 35 weeks)* pos/wks

			pos	wks
23 May 81		**FOLLOW THE LEADERS** *Malicious Damage EGMDS 101*	55	5
20 Mar 82		**EMPIRE SONG** *Malicious Damage EGO 4*	43	4
30 Oct 82		**BIRDS OF A FEATHER** *EG EGO 10*	64	2
25 Jun 83		**LET'S ALL (GO TO THE FIRE DANCES)** *EG EGO 11*	51	3
15 Oct 83		**ME OR YOU?** *EG EGO 14*	57	1
7 Apr 84		**EIGHTIES** *EG EGO 16*	60	5
21 Jul 84		**A NEW DAY** *EG EGO 17*	56	2
2 Feb 85		**LOVE LIKE BLOOD** *EG EGO 20*	16	9
30 Mar 85		**KINGS AND QUEENS** *EG EGO 21*	58	3
16 Aug 86		**ADORATIONS** *EG EGO 27*	42	6
18 Oct 86		**SANITY** *EG EGO 30*	70	1
7 May 94		**MILLENNIUM** *Butterfly BFLD 12*	34	2
16 Jul 94		**THE PANDEMONIUM SINGLE** *Butterfly BFLD 17*	28	3
4 Feb 95		**JANA** *Butterfly BFLDA 21*	54	1
23 Mar 96		**DEMOCRACY** *Butterfly BFLDA 33*	39	1
26 Jul 03		**LOOSE CANNON** *Zuma ZUMAD 004*	25	2
25 Oct 80		**KILLING JOKE** *Polydor EGMD 545*	39	4
20 Jun 81		**WHAT'S THIS FOR** *Malicious Damage EGMD 550*	42	4
8 May 82		**REVELATIONS** *Malicious Damage EGMD 3*	12	6
27 Nov 82		**'HA' – KILLING JOKE LIVE** *EG EGMDT 4*	66	2
23 Jul 83		**FIRE DANCES** *EG EGMD 5*	29	3
9 Mar 85		**NIGHT TIME** *EG EGLP 61*	11	9
22 Nov 86		**BRIGHTER THAN A THOUSAND SUNS** *EG EGLP 66*	54	1
9 Jul 88		**OUTSIDE THE GATE** *EG EGLP 73*	92	1
6 Aug 94		**PANDEMONIUM** *Butterfly BFLCD 9*	16	3
13 Apr 96		**DEMOCRACY** *Butterfly BFLCD 17*	71	1
9 Aug 03		**KILLING JOKE** *Zuma ZUMACD002*	43	1

KILLS *UK, male / female, vocal / instrumental group (Singles: 1 week, Albums: 1 week)* pos/wks

			pos	wks
26 Apr 03		**FRIED MY LITTLE BRAINS** *Domino RUG 154CD*	55	1
22 Mar 03		**KEEP ON YOUR MEAN SIDE** *Domino WIGCD124*	47	1

Andy KIM

Canada, male vocalist – Andrew Joachim (Singles: 12 weeks) pos/wks

			pos	wks
24 Aug 74	●	**ROCK ME GENTLY** *Capitol CL 15787* ▲	2	12

KIMERA with the LONDON SYMPHONY ORCHESTRA

Korea, female vocalist and UK, orchestra (Albums: 4 weeks) pos/wks

			pos	wks
26 Oct 85		**HITS ON OPERA** *Stylus SMR 8505*	38	4

See also LONDON SYMPHONY ORCHESTRA

KINANE *Ireland, female vocalist (Singles: 4 weeks)* pos/wks

			pos	wks
18 May 96		**ALL THE LOVER I NEED** *Coliseum TOGA 003CD* [1]	59	1
21 Sep 96		**THE WOMAN IN ME** *Coliseum TOGA 007CD* [1]	73	1
16 May 98		**HEAVEN** *Coalition COLA 047CD*	49	1
22 Aug 98		**SO FINE** *Coalition COLA 055CD1*	63	1

[1] Bianca Kinane

KINESIS

UK, male vocal / instrumental group (Singles: 3 weeks) pos/wks

			pos	wks
22 Mar 03		**...AND THEY OBEY** *Independiente ISOM 68MS*	63	1
28 Jun 03		**FOREVER REELING** *Independiente ISOM 74MS*	65	1
27 Sep 03		**ONE WAY MIRROR** *Independiente ISOM 77MS*	71	1

KING *UK / Ireland, male vocal / instrumental group, leader – Paul King (Singles: 44 weeks, Albums: 32 weeks)* pos/wks

			pos	wks
12 Jan 85	●	**LOVE AND PRIDE** *CBS A 4988*	2	14
23 Mar 85		**WON'T YOU HOLD MY HAND NOW** *CBS A 6094*	24	8
17 Aug 85	●	**ALONE WITHOUT YOU** *CBS A 6308*	8	9
19 Oct 85		**THE TASTE OF YOUR TEARS** *CBS A 6618*	11	9
11 Jan 86		**TORTURE** *CBS A 6761*	23	4
9 Feb 85	●	**STEPS IN TIME** *CBS 26095*	6	21
23 Nov 85		**BITTER SWEET** *CBS 86320*	16	11

Albert KING – *See Gary MOORE*

B B KING *US, male vocalist / instrumentalist – guitar – Riley King (Singles: 10 weeks, Albums: 24 weeks)* pos/wks

			pos	wks
15 Apr 89	●	**WHEN LOVE COMES TO TOWN** *Island IS 411* [1]	6	7
18 Jul 92		**SINCE I MET YOU BABY** *Virgin VS 1423* [2]	59	3
25 Aug 79		**TAKE IT HOME** *MCA MCF 3010*	60	5
1 May 99		**HIS DEFINITIVE GREATEST HITS** *Universal Music TV 5473402*	24	4
24 Jun 00		**RIDING WITH THE KING** *Reprise 9362476122* [1]	15	15

[1] U2 with B B King [2] Gary Moore and B B King [1] B B King and Eric Clapton

Ben E KING *US, male vocalist – Benjamin Nelson (Singles: 35 weeks, Albums: 30 weeks)* pos/wks

			pos	wks
2 Feb 61		**FIRST TASTE OF LOVE** *London HLK 9258*	27	11
22 Jun 61		**STAND BY ME (re)** *London HLK 9358*	27	7
5 Oct 61		**AMOR, AMOR** *London HLK 9416*	38	4
14 Feb 87	★	**STAND BY ME (re-issue)** *Atlantic A 9361*	1	11
4 Jul 87		**SAVE THE LAST DANCE FOR ME** *Manhattan MT 25*	69	2
1 Jul 67		**SPANISH HARLEM** *Atlantic 590001*	30	3
14 Mar 87		**STAND BY ME (THE ULTIMATE COLLECTION)** *Atlantic WX 90* [1]	14	8
20 Oct 90		**THE VERY BEST OF BEN E KING & THE DRIFTERS** *Telstar STAR 2373* [1]	15	16
7 Nov 98		**THE VERY BEST OF BEN E KING & THE DRIFTERS** *Warner.ESP / Global TV RADCD 108* [1]	41	3

[1] Ben E King & the Drifters

Both 'Very Best of...' albums are different

See also DRIFTERS

Carole KING *US, female vocalist / instrumentalist – piano – Carole Klein (Singles: 29 weeks, Albums: 108 weeks)* pos/wks

			pos	wks
20 Sep 62	●	**IT MIGHT AS WELL RAIN UNTIL SEPTEMBER** *London HLU 9591*	3	13
7 Aug 71	●	**IT'S TOO LATE** *A&M AMS 849* ▲	6	12
28 Oct 72		**IT MIGHT AS WELL RAIN UNTIL SEPTEMBER (re-issue)** *London HL 10391*	43	4
24 Jul 71	●	**TAPESTRY** *A&M AMLS 2025* ▲	4	90
15 Jan 72		**MUSIC** *A&M AMLH 67013* ▲	18	10
2 Dec 72		**RHYMES AND REASONS** *Ode 77016*	40	2

7 Feb 98	TAPESTRY (re-issue) *Epic CD 32110*	24	3
30 Sep 00	NATURAL WOMAN – THE VERY BEST OF CAROLE KING *Columbia SONYTV 93CD*	31	3

Dave KING
UK, male vocalist, d. 17 Apr 2002 (Singles: 29 weeks) pos/wks

17 Feb 56 ●	MEMORIES ARE MADE OF THIS *Decca F 10684* [1]	5	15
13 Apr 56	YOU CAN'T BE TRUE TO TWO *Decca F 10720* [1]	11	9
21 Dec 56	CHRISTMAS AND YOU *Decca F 10791*	23	2
24 Jan 58	THE STORY OF MY LIFE *Decca F 10973*	20	3

[1] Dave King featuring The Keynotes

Denis KING – *See KING BROTHERS; STUTZ BEARCATS and The Denis KING ORCHESTRA*

Diana KING
Jamaica, female vocalist (Singles: 22 weeks, Albums: 2 weeks) pos/wks

8 Jul 95 ●	SHY GUY *Columbia 6621682*	2	13
28 Oct 95	AIN'T NOBODY *Columbia 6625495*	13	5
1 Nov 97	I SAY A LITTLE PRAYER *Columbia 6651472*	17	4
12 Aug 95	TOUGHER THAN LOVE *Columbia 4777562*	50	2

Evelyn 'Champagne' KING
US, female vocalist (Singles: 76 weeks, Albums: 9 weeks) pos/wks

13 May 78	SHAME *RCA PC 1122*	39	23
3 Feb 79	I DON'T KNOW IF IT'S RIGHT *RCA PB 1386*	67	2
27 Jun 81	I'M IN LOVE *RCA 95* [1]	27	11
26 Sep 81	IF YOU WANT MY LOVIN' *RCA 131* [1]	43	6
28 Aug 82 ●	LOVE COME DOWN *RCA 249* [1]	7	13
20 Nov 82	BACK TO LOVE *RCA 287* [1]	40	4
19 Feb 83	GET LOOSE *RCA 315* [1]	45	5
9 Nov 85	YOUR PERSONAL TOUCH *RCA PB 49915*	37	5
29 Mar 86	HIGH HORSE *RCA PB 49891*	55	3
23 Jul 88	HOLD ON TO WHAT YOU'VE GOT *Manhattan MT 49*	47	3
10 Oct 92	SHAME (re-mix) *Network NWKTEN 56* [2]	74	1
11 Sep 82	GET LOOSE *RCA RCALP 3093*	35	9

[1] Evelyn King [2] Altern 8 vs Evelyn King

Jonathan KING
UK, male vocalist (Singles: 128 weeks) pos/wks

29 Jul 65 ●	EVERYONE'S GONE TO THE MOON *Decca F 12187*	4	11
10 Jan 70	LET IT ALL HANG OUT *Decca F 12988*	26	7
16 Jan 71	IT'S THE SAME OLD SONG *B & C CB 139* [1]	19	9
3 Apr 71	SUGAR SUGAR *RCA 2064* [2]	12	14
29 May 71	LAZY BONES *Decca F 13177*	23	8
20 Nov 71	HOOKED ON A FEELING *Decca F 13241*	23	10
5 Feb 72	FLIRT! *Decca F 13276*	22	9
14 Oct 72 ●	LOOP DI LOVE *UK 7* [3]	4	13
26 Jan 74	(I CAN'T GET NO) SATISFACTION *UK 53* [4]	29	5
6 Sep 75 ●	UNA PALOMA BLANCA (WHITE DOVE) *UK 105*	5	11
20 Sep 75	CHICK-A-BOOM (DON'T YA JES LOVE IT) *UK 2012 002* [5]	36	4
7 Feb 76	IN THE MOOD *UK 121* [6]	46	3
26 Jun 76 ●	IT ONLY TAKES A MINUTE *UK 135* [7]	9	9
7 Oct 78	ONE FOR YOU, ONE FOR ME *GTO GT 237*	29	6
16 Dec 78	LICK A SMURP FOR CHRISTMAS (ALL FALL DOWN) *Petrol GAS 1 / Magnet MAG 139* [8]	58	4
16 Jun 79	YOU'RE THE GREATEST LOVER *UK International INT 586*	67	2
3 Nov 79	GLORIA *Ariola ARO 198*	65	3

[1] Weathermen [2] Sakkarin [3] Shag [4] Bubblerock [5] 53rd and 3rd featuring the Sound of Shag [6] Sound 9418 [7] One Hundred Ton and a Feather [8] Father Abraphart and the Smurps

Mark KING
UK, male vocalist / instrumentalist – bass (Albums: 2 weeks) pos/wks

21 Jul 84	INFLUENCES *Polydor MKLP 1*	77	2

See also LEVEL 42

Nosmo KING – *See JAVELLS featuring Nosmo KING*

Paul KING
UK, male vocalist (Singles: 3 weeks) pos/wks

2 May 87	I KNOW *CBS PKING 1*	59	3

See also KING

Solomon KING
US, male vocalist (Singles: 28 weeks, Albums: 1 week) pos/wks

3 Jan 68 ●	SHE WEARS MY RING *Columbia DB 8325*	3	18
1 May 68	WHEN WE WERE YOUNG *Columbia DB 8402*	21	10
22 Jun 68	SHE WEARS MY RING *Columbia SCX 6250*	40	1

Tony KING – *See Kylie MINOGUE*

KING ADORA
UK, male vocal / instrumental group (Singles: 6 weeks, Albums: 1 week) pos/wks

4 Nov 00	SMOULDER *Superior Quality / A&M RQSD 010CD*	62	1
3 Mar 01	SUFFOCATE *Superior Quality / A&M RQS 11DD*	39	2
26 May 01	BIONIC *Superior Quality / A&M RQS 012CD*	30	2
31 May 03	BORN TO LOSE / KAMIKAZE *MHR MHRCD 001*	68	1
2 Jun 01	VIBRATE YOU *Superior Quality RQS 13CD*	30	1

KING BEE
UK, male rapper (Singles: 6 weeks) pos/wks

26 Jan 91	MUST BEE THE MUSIC *Columbia 6565827* [1]	44	4
23 Mar 91	BACK BY DOPE DEMAND *First Bass 7RUFF 6X*	61	2

[1] King Bee featuring Michele

KING BROTHERS
UK, male vocal / instrumental group (Singles: 74 weeks) pos/wks

31 May 57 ●	A WHITE SPORT COAT (AND A PINK CARNATION) *Parlophone R 4310*	6	14
9 Aug 57	IN THE MIDDLE OF AN ISLAND *Parlophone R 4338*	19	13
6 Dec 57	WAKE UP LITTLE SUSIE *Parlophone R 4367*	22	3
31 Jan 58	PUT A LIGHT IN THE WINDOW (2re) *Parlophone R 4389*	25	4
14 Apr 60 ●	STANDING ON THE CORNER *Parlophone R 4639*	4	11
28 Jul 60	MAIS OUI *Parlophone R 4672*	16	10
12 Jan 61	DOLL HOUSE *Parlophone R 4715*	21	8
2 Mar 61	76 TROMBONES *Parlophone R 4737*	19	11

KING CRIMSON
UK / US, male vocal / instrumental group (Albums: 55 weeks) pos/wks

1 Nov 69 ●	IN THE COURT OF THE CRIMSON KING *Island ILPS 9111*	5	18
30 May 70 ●	IN THE WAKE OF POSEIDON *Island ILPS 9127*	4	13
16 Jan 71	LIZARD *Island ILPS 9141*	29	2
8 Jan 72	ISLANDS *Island ILPS 9175*	30	1
7 Apr 73	LARKS' TONGUES IN ASPIC *Island ILPS 9230*	20	4
13 Apr 74	STARLESS AND BIBLE BLACK *Island ILPS 9275*	28	2
26 Oct 74	RED *Island ILPS 9308*	45	1
10 Oct 81	DISCIPLINE *EG EGLP 49*	41	4
26 Jun 82	BEAT *EG EGLP 51*	39	5
31 Mar 84	THREE OF A PERFECT PAIR *EG EGLP 55*	30	4
15 Apr 95	THRAK *Virgin KCCDY 1*	58	1

See also Greg LAKE; Bill BRUFORD; Robert FRIPP

KING KURT
UK, male vocal / instrumental group (Singles: 16 weeks, Albums: 5 weeks) pos/wks

15 Oct 83	DESTINATION ZULULAND *Stiff BUY 189*	36	6
28 Apr 84	MACK THE KNIFE *Stiff BUY 199*	55	4
4 Aug 84	BANANA BANANA *Stiff BUY 206*	54	4
15 Nov 86	AMERICA *Polydor KURT 1*	73	1
2 May 87	THE LAND OF RING DANG DO *Polydor KURT 2*	67	1
10 Dec 83	OOH WALLAH WALLAH *Stiff SEEZ 52*	99	1
8 Mar 86	BIG COCK *Stiff SEEZ 62*	50	4

KING SUN-D'MOET
US, male rap / DJ duo (Singles: 3 weeks) pos/wks

11 Jul 87	HEY LOVE *Flame MELT 5*	66	3

KING TRIGGER
UK, male / female vocal / instrumental group (Singles: 4 weeks) pos/wks

14 Aug 82	THE RIVER *Chrysalis CHS 2623*	57	4

KINGDOM COME
US, male vocal / instrumental group (Singles: 2 weeks, Albums: 10 weeks)

Date		Title	pos	wks
16 Apr 88		**GET IT ON** *Polydor KCS 1*	75	1
6 May 89		**DO YOU LIKE IT** *Polydor KCS 3*	73	1
28 Mar 88		**KINGDOM COME** *Polydor KCLP 1*	43	6
13 May 89		**IN YOUR FACE** *Polydor 839192 1*	25	4

KINGMAKER
UK, male vocal / instrumental group (Singles: 22 weeks, Albums: 10 weeks)

Date		Title	pos	wks
18 Jan 92		**IDIOTS AT THE WHEEL (EP)** *Scorch SCORCH 3*	30	3
23 May 92		**EAT YOURSELF WHOLE** *Scorch SCORCHG 5*	15	3
31 Oct 92		**ARMCHAIR ANARCHIST** *Scorch SCORCHG 6*	47	2
8 May 93		**10 YEARS ASLEEP** *Scorch CDSCORCHS 8*	15	4
19 Jun 93		**QUEEN JANE** *Scorch CDSCORS 9*	29	4
30 Oct 93		**SATURDAY'S NOT WHAT IT USED TO BE** *Scorch CDSCORCH 10*	63	1
15 Apr 95		**YOU AND I WILL NEVER SEE THINGS EYE TO EYE** *Scorch CDSCORCHS 11*	33	3
3 Jun 95		**IN THE BEST POSSIBLE TASTE (PART 2)** *Scorch CDSCORCHS 12*	41	2
19 Oct 91		**EAT YOURSELF WHOLE** *Scorch CHR 1878*	29	3
29 May 93		**SLEEPWALKING** *Scorch CDCHR 6014*	15	7

Tracks on Idiots at the Wheel (EP): Really Scrape the Sky / Revelation / Every Teenage Suicide / Strip Away

Choir of KING'S COLLEGE, CAMBRIDGE
UK, male / female choir (Albums: 3 weeks)

Date		Title	pos	wks
11 Dec 71		**THE WORLD OF CHRISTMAS** *Argo SPAA 104*	38	3

KING'S X
US male vocal / instrumental group (Albums: 4 weeks)

Date		Title	pos	wks
1 Jul 89		**GRETCHEN GOES TO NEBRASKA** *Atlantic WX 279*	52	1
10 Nov 90		**FAITH HOPE LOVE** *Megaforce 756821451*	70	1
28 Mar 92		**KING'S X** *Atlantic 7567805062*	46	1
12 Feb 94		**DOGMAN** *Atlantic 7567825582*	49	1

KINGS OF CONVENIENCE
Norway, male vocal / instrumental duo (Singles: 2 weeks, Albums: 1 week)

Date		Title	pos	wks
21 Apr 01		**TOXIC GIRL** *Source SOURCDSE 1025*	44	1
14 Jul 01		**FAILURE** *Source SOURCD 036*	63	1
10 Feb 01		**QUIET IS THE NEW LOUD** *Source SOURCD 019*	72	1

KINGS OF LEON
US, male vocal / instrumental group (Singles: 9 weeks, Albums: 19 weeks)

Date		Title	pos	wks
8 Mar 03		**HOLY ROLLER NOVOCAINE** *Hand Me Down / HMD 21*	53	1
14 Jun 03		**WHAT I SAW** *Hand Me Down HMD 23*	22	3
23 Aug 03		**MOLLY'S CHAMBERS** *Hand Me Down HMD 29*	23	3
1 Nov 03		**WASTED TIME** *Hand Me Down HMD 32*	51	2
19 Jul 03	●	**YOUTH AND YOUNG MANHOOD** *Hand Me Down HMD27*	3	19

KINGS OF SWING ORCHESTRA
Australia, orchestra (Singles: 5 weeks, Albums: 11 weeks)

Date		Title	pos	wks
1 May 82		**SWITCHED ON SWING** *Philips SWING 1*	48	5
29 May 82		**SWITCHED ON SWING** *K-Tel ONE 1166*	28	11

KINGS OF TOMORROW
US, male production / instrumental duo – Sandy Rivera and Jason Sealee (Singles: 7 weeks)

Date		Title	pos	wks
14 Apr 01		**FINALLY** *Distance DI 2029* [1]	54	1
29 Sep 01		**FINALLY (re-mix)** *Defected DFECT 37CDS* [1]	24	3
13 Apr 02		**YOUNG HEARTS** *Defected DFECT 46CDS*	45	2
25 Oct 03		**DREAMS / THROUGH** *Defected DFTD 079*	74	1

[1] Kings of Tomorrow featuring Julie McKnight

See also Sandy RIVERA; LAYO & BUSHWACKA!

KINGSMEN
US, male vocal / instrumental group (Singles: 7 weeks)

Date		Title	pos	wks
30 Jan 64		**LOUIE LOUIE** *Pye International 7N 25231*	26	7

KINGSTON TRIO
US, male vocal / instrumental group (Singles: 15 weeks)

Date		Title	pos	wks
21 Nov 58	●	**TOM DOOLEY** *Capitol CL 14951* ▲	5	14
4 Dec 59		**SAN MIGUEL** *Capitol CL 15073*	29	1

KINKS
141 Top 500 *Well-respected and innovative London band, who had few equals in the 1960s: Ray Davies (v/g), Dave Davies (g), Pete Quaife (b), Mick Avory (d). Ray Davies, regarded as one of rock's premier songwriters, remains active 40 years after the group's first hit (Singles: 215 weeks, Albums: 139 weeks)*

Date		Title	pos	wks
13 Aug 64	★	**YOU REALLY GOT ME** *Pye 7N 15673*	1	12
29 Oct 64	●	**ALL DAY AND ALL OF THE NIGHT** *Pye 7N 15714*	2	14
21 Jan 65	★	**TIRED OF WAITING FOR YOU** *Pye 7N 15759*	1	10
25 Mar 65		**EVERYBODY'S GONNA BE HAPPY** *Pye 7N 15813*	17	8
27 May 65	●	**SET ME FREE** *Pye 7N 15854*	9	11
5 Aug 65	●	**SEE MY FRIEND** *Pye 7N 15919*	10	9
2 Dec 65	●	**TILL THE END OF THE DAY** *Pye 7N 15981*	8	12
3 Mar 66	●	**DEDICATED FOLLOWER OF FASHION** *Pye 7N 17064*	4	11
9 Jun 66	★	**SUNNY AFTERNOON** *Pye 7N 17125*	1	13
24 Nov 66	●	**DEAD END STREET** *Pye 7N 17222*	5	11
11 May 67	●	**WATERLOO SUNSET** *Pye 7N 17321*	2	11
18 Oct 67	●	**AUTUMN ALMANAC** *Pye 7N 17400*	3	11
17 Apr 68		**WONDERBOY** *Pye 7N 17468*	36	5
17 Jul 68		**DAYS** *Pye 7N 17573*	12	10
16 Apr 69		**PLASTIC MAN** *Pye 7N 17724*	31	4
10 Jan 70		**VICTORIA** *Pye 7N 17865*	33	4
4 Jul 70	●	**LOLA** *Pye 7N 17961*	2	14
12 Dec 70	●	**APEMAN** *Pye 7N 45016*	5	14
27 May 72		**SUPERSONIC ROCKET SHIP** *RCA 2211*	16	8
27 Jun 81		**BETTER THINGS** *Arista ARIST 415*	46	5
6 Aug 83		**COME DANCING** *Arista ARIST 502*	12	9
15 Oct 83		**DON'T FORGET TO DANCE** *Arista ARIST 524*	58	3
15 Oct 83		**YOU REALLY GOT ME (re-issue)** *PRT KD1*	47	4
18 Jan 97		**THE DAYS EP** *When! WENX 1016*	35	2
17 Oct 64	●	**KINKS** *Pye NPL 18096*	3	25
13 Mar 65	●	**KINDA KINKS** *Pye NPL 18112*	3	15
4 Dec 65	●	**KINKS KONTROVERSY** *Pye NPL 18131*	9	12
11 Sep 66	●	**WELL RESPECTED KINKS** *Marble Arch MAL 612*	5	31
5 Nov 66		**FACE TO FACE** *Pye NPL 18149*	12	11
14 Oct 67		**SOMETHING ELSE** *Pye NSPL 18193*	35	2
2 Dec 67	●	**SUNNY AFTERNOON** *Marble Arch MAL 716*	9	11
23 Oct 71		**GOLDEN HOUR OF THE KINKS** *Golden Hour GH 501*	21	4
14 Oct 78		**20 GOLDEN GREATS** *Ronco RPL 2031*	19	6
5 Nov 83		**KINKS GREATEST HITS – DEAD END STREET** *PRT KINK 1*	96	1
16 Sep 89		**THE ULTIMATE COLLECTION** *Castle Communications CTVLP 001*	35	7
18 Sep 93		**THE DEFINITIVE COLLECTION** *PolyGram TV 5164652*	18	7
12 Apr 97		**THE VERY BEST OF THE KINKS** *PolyGram TV 5375542*	42	3
8 Jun 02		**THE ULTIMATE COLLECTION** *Sanctuary SANDD 109*	32	4

Tracks on The Days EP: Days / You Really Got Me / Dead End Street / Lola

'The Ultimate Collection' in 2002 is an expanded version of the 1989 release

KINKY
UK, female rapper (Singles: 1 week)

Date		Title	pos	wks
24 Aug 96		**EVERYBODY** *Feverpitch CDFVR 1009*	71	1

See also ERASURE

KINKY MACHINE
UK, male vocal / instrumental group (Singles: 4 weeks)

Date		Title	pos	wks
6 Mar 93		**SUPERNATURAL GIVER** *Lemon LEMON 006CD*	70	1
29 May 93		**SHOCKAHOLIC** *Oxygen GASPD 5*	70	1
14 Aug 93		**GOING OUT WITH GOD** *Oxygen GASPD 9*	74	1
2 Jul 94		**10 SECOND BIONIC MAN** *Oxygen GASPD 14*	66	1

Fern KINNEY
US, female vocalist – Fern Kinney-Lewis (Singles: 11 weeks)

Date		Title	pos	wks
16 Feb 80	★	**TOGETHER WE ARE BEAUTIFUL** *WEA K 79111*	1	11

KINSHASA BAND – *See Johnny WAKELIN*

KIOKI *Japan, male vocalist (Singles: 1 week)* pos/wks

17 Aug 02 **DO & DON'T FOR LOVE** *V2 VVR 5020803* 66 1

KIRA *Belgium, female vocalist (Singles: 5 weeks)* pos/wks

1 Mar 03 ● **I'LL BE YOUR ANGEL** *Nulife 74321970362* 9 5

Kathy KIRBY
UK, female vocalist (Singles: 54 weeks, Albums: 8 weeks) pos/wks

15 Aug 63 **DANCE ON** *Decca F 11682* 11 13
7 Nov 63 ● **SECRET LOVE** *Decca F 11759* 4 18
20 Feb 64 ● **LET ME GO LOVER!** *Decca F 11832* 10 11
7 May 64 **YOU'RE THE ONE** *Decca F 11892* 17 9
4 Mar 65 **I BELONG** *Decca F 12087* 36 3
4 Jan 64 16 HITS FROM STARS AND GARTERS *Decca LK 5475* 11 8

Bo KIRKLAND and Ruth DAVIS
US, male / female vocal duo (Singles: 9 weeks) pos/wks

4 Jun 77 **YOU'RE GONNA GET NEXT TO ME** *EMI International INT 532* 12 9

Dominic KIRWAN *Ireland, male vocalist (Albums: 1 week)* pos/wks

1 Nov 97 THE MUSIC'S BACK *Ritz RITZCD 0084* 54 1

KISS *US / Israel, male vocal / instrumental group (Singles: 57 weeks, Albums: 71 weeks)* pos/wks

30 Jun 79 **I WAS MADE FOR LOVIN' YOU** *Casablanca CAN 152* 50 7
20 Feb 82 **A WORLD WITHOUT HEROES** *Casablanca KISS 002* 55 3
30 Apr 83 **CREATURES OF THE NIGHT** *Casablanca KISS 4* 34 4
29 Oct 83 **LICK IT UP** *Vertigo KISS 5* 31 5
8 Sep 84 **HEAVEN'S ON FIRE** *Vertigo VER 12* 43 3
9 Nov 85 **TEARS ARE FALLING** *Vertigo KISS 6* 57 2
3 Oct 87 ● **CRAZY CRAZY NIGHTS** *Vertigo KISS 7* 4 9
5 Dec 87 **REASON TO LIVE** *Vertigo KISS 8* 33 7
10 Sep 88 **TURN ON THE NIGHT** *Vertigo KISS 9* 41 3
18 Nov 89 **HIDE YOUR HEART** *Vertigo KISS 10* 59 2
31 Mar 90 **FOREVER** *Vertigo KISS 11* 65 2
11 Jan 92 ● **GOD GAVE ROCK AND ROLL TO YOU II** *Interscope A 8696* 4 8
9 May 92 **UNHOLY** *Mercury KISS 12* 26 2
29 May 76 DESTROYER *Casablanca CBSP 4008* 22 5
25 Jun 76 ALIVE! *Casablanca CBSP 401* 49 2
17 Dec 77 ALIVE *Casablanca CALD 5004* 60 1
7 Jul 79 DYNASTY *Casablanca CALH 2051* 50 6
28 Jun 80 UNMASKED *Mercury 6302 032* 48 3
5 Dec 81 THE ELDER *Casablanca 6302 163* 51 3
26 Jun 82 KILLERS *Casablanca CANL 1* 42 6
6 Nov 82 CREATURES OF THE NIGHT *Casablanca CANL 4* 22 4
8 Oct 83 ● LICK IT UP *Vertigo VERL 9* 7 7
6 Oct 84 ANIMALIZE *Vertigo VERL 18* 11 4
5 Oct 85 ASYLUM *Vertigo VERH 32* 12 3
7 Nov 87 ● CRAZY NIGHTS *Vertigo VERH 49* 4 14
10 Dec 88 SMASHES THRASHES AND HITS *Vertigo 836759 1* 62 2
4 Nov 89 HOT IN THE SHADE *Fontana 838913 1* 35 2
23 May 92 ● REVENGE *Mercury 8480372* 10 3
29 May 93 ALIVE III *Mercury 5148272* 24 2
23 Mar 96 MTV UNPLUGGED *Mercury 5289502* 74 1
12 Jul 97 GREATEST HITS *PolyGram TV 5361592* 58 2
3 Oct 98 PSYCHO-CIRCUS *Mercury 5589922* 47 1

See also Vinnie VINCENT

KISS AMC *UK, female rap duo (Singles: 5 weeks)* pos/wks

1 Jul 89 **A BIT OF U2 (re)** *Syncopate SY 29* 58 4
3 Feb 90 **MY DOCS** *Syncopate XAMC 1* 66 1

Before its re-entry in Aug '89, due to copyright problems, 'A Bit of U2' was credited simply as 'A Bit Of…'

KISSING THE PINK *UK, male / female vocal / instrumental group (Singles: 14 weeks, Albums: 5 weeks)* pos/wks

5 Mar 83 **LAST FILM** *Magnet KTP 3* 19 14
4 Jun 83 NAKED *Magnet KTPL 1001* 54 5

Mac and Katie KISSOON
Trinidad / UK, male / female vocal duo (Singles: 33 weeks) pos/wks

19 Jun 71 **CHIRPY CHIRPY CHEEP CHEEP** *Young Blood YB 1026* 41 1
18 Jan 75 ● **SUGAR CANDY KISSES** *Polydor 2058 531* 3 10
3 May 75 ● **DON'T DO IT BABY** *State STAT 4* 9 8
30 Aug 75 **LIKE A BUTTERFLY** *State STAT 9* 18 9
15 May 76 **THE TWO OF US** *State STAT 21* 46 5

Kevin KITCHEN
UK, male vocalist (Singles: 3 weeks) pos/wks

20 Apr 85 **PUT MY ARMS AROUND YOU** *China WOK 1* 64 3

KITCHENS OF DISTINCTION
UK, male vocal / instrumental group (Albums: 2 weeks) pos/wks

30 Mar 91 STRANGE FREE WORLD *One Little Indian TPLP 19* 45 1
15 Aug 92 THE DEATH OF COOL *One Little Indian TPLP 39CD* 72 1

Joy KITIKONTI
Italy, male producer – Massimo Chiticonti (Singles: 2 weeks) pos/wks

17 Nov 01 **JOYENERGIZER** *BXR BXRC 0347* 57 2

Eartha KITT *US, female vocalist (Singles: 34 weeks, Albums: 1 week)* pos/wks

1 Apr 55 ● **UNDER THE BRIDGES OF PARIS (re)** *HMV B 10647* 7 10
3 Dec 83 **WHERE IS MY MAN** *Record Shack SOHO 11* 36 11
7 Jul 84 **I LOVE MEN** *Record Shack SOHO 21* 50 3
12 Apr 86 **THIS IS MY LIFE** *Record Shack SOHO 61* 73 1
1 Jul 89 **CHA CHA HEELS** *Arista 112331* [1] 32 7
5 Mar 94 **IF I LOVE YA THEN I NEED YA IF I NEED YA THEN I WANT YOU AROUND** *RCA 74321190342* 43 2
11 Feb 61 REVISITED *London HA 2296* 17 1

[1] Eartha Kitt and Bronski Beat

KITTIE *Canada, female vocal / instrumental group (Singles: 2 weeks)* pos/wks

25 Mar 00 **BRACKISH** *Epic 6691292* 46 1
22 Jul 00 **CHARLOTTE** *Epic 6696222* 60 1

Myleene KLASS *UK, female vocalist / instrumentalist – keyboards (Albums: 3 weeks)* pos/wks

1 Nov 03 MOVING ON *UCJ 9865632* 32 3

See also HEAR'SAY

KLAXONS
Belgium, male vocal / instrumental group (Singles: 6 weeks) pos/wks

10 Dec 83 **THE CLAP CLAP SOUND** *PRT 7P 290* 45 6

KLEA *UK, male / female production / vocal / rap trio (Singles: 1 week)* pos/wks

7 Sep 02 **TIC TOC** *Incentive CENT 41CDS* 61 1

KLEEER *US, male / female vocal / instrumental group (Singles: 10 weeks, Albums: 1 week)* pos/wks

17 Mar 79 **KEEEP YOUR BODY WORKIN'** *Atlantic LV 21* 51 6
14 Mar 81 **GET TOUGH** *Atlantic 11560* 49 4
6 Jul 85 SEEEKRET *Atlantic 7812541* 96 1

DD KLEIN – *See ALIVE featuring DD KLEIN*

KLESHAY *UK, female vocal trio (Singles: 5 weeks)* pos/wks

19 Sep 98 **REASONS** *Epic KLE 1CD* 33 2
20 Feb 99 **RUSH** *Epic KLE 2CD* 19 3

KLUBBHEADS
Holland, male instrumental / production group (Singles: 10 weeks) pos/wks

11 May 96 ● **KLUBBHOPPING** *AM:PM 5815572* 10 6
16 Aug 97 **DISCOHOPPING** *AM:PM 5823032* 35 2
15 Aug 98 **KICKIN' HARD** *Wonderboy WBOYD 011* 36 2

See also ITTY BITTY BOOZY WOOZY

Review of the Year

MAY 2003

A newcomer to the Top 40 this month and the pages of this book is **Mark Joseph**. Nothing unusual about that, you might think. However, his remarkable chart debut is achieved from a single on his self-funded label, which was available only in Virgin record shops. **Busted** are the first act in chart history to have their first three singles enter the chart at No.3, No.2 and No.1 respectively. During this month rock officially overtakes pop in album sales and **Madonna** performs for 600 fans at HMV in Oxford Circus. **Jemini** become the first UK entry to score nul point in the Eurovision Song Contest in Latvia which was won by Turkey's Sertab. **Justin Timberlake's** Justified passes the million sales mark in the UK (not bad for a singer whose group, **'N Sync**, never had a Top 10 album). **Coldplay** headline at the Hollywood Bowl and pick up an Ivor Novello Song Award as do **David Gray**, **Cathy Dennis**, **Bryan Ferry**, **UB40** and **Brian Wilson**. Seventy-year-old **Yoko Ono** hits the Top 40 with a remix of her only solo hit 'Walking on Thin Ice', and a record 61,000 copies of **Paul McCartney's** Back in the World DVD are sold in the first week in the US. S Club Juniors rename themselves **S Club 8**. **Erasure's** update of 'Make Me Smile (Come Up and See Me)' is one of an impressive four UK singles in the US Top 40 sales chart. **Ruben Studdard** wins American Idol 2 with **Clay Aiken** the runner-up. **Etta James** receives a star on the Hollywood Walk of Fame as do Holland, Dozier and Holland, whose compositions, it is announced, have been played more than 100 million times on US radio. **t.A.T.u.'s** album 200km/h in the Wrong Lane heads the Japanese chart which also contains a rare UK visitor, **Sarah Brightman**, with 'Harem'. The Bacharach and David musical The Look of Love opens on Broadway. 'In Da Club' by **50 Cent** becomes the first "gold" ring tone with 500,000 paid downloads putting the rapper within the elite few who have three simultaneous entries in the US Top 10. He also has a record nine different tracks on the US R&B/hip-hop chart and bags the top two US R&B album slots. Forty-four years after their US chart debut with 'Shout', **The Isley Brothers** enter the US album chart at No.1 with Body Kiss. **Elvis Costello** receives the prestigious ASCAP Founders Award. **Ronan Keating** completes a record-breaking 24 UK Top 10 entries in a row, with his composition 'The Long Goodbye'. **Marilyn Manson's** album The Golden Age of Grotesque is a chart-topper in numerous countries including the US, where it makes a spectacular record-breaking drop of 20 places from its peak. She might be more interested in gardening these days but **Kim Wilde** bounces back with a big German hit 'Anyplace, Anytime, Anywhere', with another 80s female favourite Nena. More comebacks … 71-year-old **Johnny Cash** returns to the UK singles chart after 27 years away with 'Hurt'/'Personal Jesus' and remixes of two previous chart-toppers by Dead or Alive and Snap! simultaneously enter the Top 75. The pop world loses some legendary figures this month. They number record producer and record label boss **Mickie Most**, **Johnny Cash's** wife **June Carter Cash**, **Jimi Hendrix Experience** drummer **Noel Redding** (who dies age 57) and Glitter band main man **Gerry Shephard**, aged just 51.

2003 UK Eurovision entrants Jemini, pictured at London's Latvian Embassy, which hosted a Eurovision-style launch of the 16th edition of British Hit Singles. The duo failed spectacularly to follow in the footstep of other invited guests including past winners Bucks Fizz, Brotherhood of Man and Katrina of Katrina and the waves

22 year old do-it-yourself pop star Mark Joseph

Earl KLUGH – *See George BENSON*

KLUSTER featuring Ron CARROLL
France, male DJ / production duo (Singles: 1 week) pos/wks

28 Apr 01 MY LOVE *Scorpio Music 1928112* 73 1

KNACK *US, male vocal / instrumental group (Singles: 12 weeks, Albums: 2 weeks)* pos/wks

30 Jun 79 ● MY SHARONA *Capitol CL 16087* ▲ 6 10
13 Oct 79 GOOD GIRLS DON'T *Capitol CL 16097* 66 2
4 Aug 79 GET THE KNACK *Capitol EST 11948* ▲ 65 2

KNACK – *See MOUNT RUSHMORE presents THE KNACK*

Beverley KNIGHT *UK, female vocalist – Beverley Smith (Singles: 40 weeks, Albums: 38 weeks)* pos/wks

8 Apr 95 FLAVOUR OF THE OLD SCHOOL *Dome CDDOME 101* 50 2
2 Sep 95 DOWN FOR THE ONE *Dome CDDOME 102* 55 1
21 Oct 95 FLAVOUR OF THE OLD SCHOOL (re-mix) *Dome CDDOME 105* 33 2
23 Mar 96 MOVING ON UP (ON THE RIGHT SIDE) *Dome CDDOME 107* 42 1
30 May 98 MADE IT BACK *Parlophone Rhythm CDRHYTHM 11* [1] 21 3
22 Aug 98 REWIND (FIND A WAY) *Parlophone Rhythm CDRHYTHS 13* 40 2
10 Apr 99 MADE IT BACK (re-mix) *Parlophone Rhythm CDRHYTHM 18* 19 5
17 Jul 99 GREATEST DAY *Parlophone Rhythm CDRHYTHS 22* 14 5
4 Dec 99 SISTA SISTA *Parlophone Rhythm CDRHYTHM 26* 31 2
17 Nov 01 GET UP *Parlophone CDRS 6564* 17 4
9 Mar 02 ● SHOULDA WOULDA COULDA *Parlophone CDRS 6570* 10 9
6 Jul 02 GOLD *Parlophone CDRS 6580* 27 4
5 Sep 98 PRODIGAL SISTA *Parlophone Rhythm 4962962* 42 14
23 Mar 02 ● WHO I AM *Parlophone 5360320* 7 24

[1] Beverley Knight featuring Redman

Curtis KNIGHT – *See Jimi HENDRIX EXPERIENCE*

Frederick KNIGHT *US, male vocalist (Singles: 10 weeks)* pos/wks

10 Jun 72 I'VE BEEN LONELY SO LONG *Stax 2025 098* 22 10

Gladys KNIGHT and the PIPS (188 Top 500) *One of soul music's foremost female singers for almost 40 years; b. 28 May 1944, Georgia, US. The celebrated vocalist (who first appeared on US TV aged eight) and her family quartet The Pips (they split in 1989) were inducted into the Rock and Roll Hall of Fame in 1996 (Singles: 187 weeks, Albums: 117 weeks)* pos/wks

8 Jun 67 TAKE ME IN YOUR ARMS AND LOVE ME *Tamla Motown TMG 604* 13 15
27 Dec 67 I HEARD IT THROUGH THE GRAPEVINE *Tamla Motown TMG 629* 47 1
17 Jun 72 JUST WALK IN MY SHOES *Tamla Motown TMG 813* 35 8
25 Nov 72 HELP ME MAKE IT THROUGH THE NIGHT *Tamla Motown TMG 830* 11 17
3 Mar 73 THE LOOK OF LOVE *Tamla Motown TMG 844* 21 9
26 May 73 NEITHER ONE OF US (WANTS TO BE THE FIRST TO SAY GOODBYE) *Tamla Motown TMG 855* 31 7
5 Apr 75 ● THE WAY WE WERE – TRY TO REMEMBER *Buddah BDS 428* 4 15
2 Aug 75 ● BEST THING THAT EVER HAPPENED TO ME *Buddah BDS 432* 7 10
15 Nov 75 PART TIME LOVE *Buddah BDS 438* 30 5
8 May 76 ● MIDNIGHT TRAIN TO GEORGIA *Buddah BDS 444* ▲ 10 9
21 Aug 76 MAKE YOURS A HAPPY HOME *Buddah BDS 447* 35 4
6 Nov 76 SO SAD THE SONG *Buddah BDS 448* 20 9
15 Jan 77 NOBODY BUT YOU *Buddah BDS 451* 34 2
28 May 77 ● BABY DON'T CHANGE YOUR MIND *Buddah BDS 458* 4 12
24 Sep 77 HOME IS WHERE THE HEART IS *Buddah BDS 460* 35 4
8 Apr 78 THE ONE AND ONLY (re) *Buddah BDS 470* 32 5
24 Jun 78 COME BACK AND FINISH WHAT YOU STARTED *Buddah BDS 473* 15 13
30 Sep 78 IT'S A BETTER THAN GOOD TIME *Buddah BDS 478* 59 4
30 Aug 80 TASTE OF BITTER LOVE *CBS 8890* 35 6
8 Nov 80 BOURGIE, BOURGIE *CBS 9081* 32 6
26 Dec 81 WHEN A CHILD IS BORN *CBS S 1758* [1] 74 2
9 Nov 85 THAT'S WHAT FRIENDS ARE FOR *Arista ARIST 638* [2] ▲ 16 9
16 Jan 88 LOVE OVERBOARD *MCA MCA 1223* 42 4
10 Jun 89 ● LICENCE TO KILL *MCA MCA 1339* [3] 6 11
31 May 75 I FEEL A SONG *Buddah BDLP 4030* 20 15
28 Feb 76 ● THE BEST OF GLADYS KNIGHT & THE PIPS *Buddah BDLH 5013* 6 43
16 Jul 77 STILL TOGETHER *Buddah BDLH 5014* 42 3
12 Nov 77 ● 30 GREATEST *K-Tel NE 1004* 3 22
4 Oct 80 A TOUCH OF LOVE *K-Tel NE 1090* 16 6
4 Feb 84 THE COLLECTION – 20 GREATEST HITS *Starblend NITE 1* 43 5
15 Nov 86 DIANA ROSS, MICHAEL JACKSON, GLADYS KNIGHT, STEVIE WONDER. THEIR VERY BEST BACK TO BACK *Priority TV PTVR 2* [1] 21 10
27 Feb 88 ALL OUR LOVE *MCA MCF 3409* 80 1
28 Oct 89 THE SINGLES ALBUM *PolyGram GKTV 1* 13 10
29 Mar 97 THE SINGLES ALBUM (re-issue) *PolyGram TV 8420032* 69 2

[1] Johnny Mathis and Gladys Knight [2] Dionne Warwick and Friends featuring Elton John, Stevie Wonder and Gladys Knight [3] Gladys Knight [1] Diana Ross / Michael Jackson / Gladys Knight / Stevie Wonder

Jordan KNIGHT *US, male vocalist (Singles: 9 weeks)* pos/wks

16 Oct 99 ● GIVE IT TO YOU (re) *Interscope 4971672* 5 9

See also NEW KIDS ON THE BLOCK

Robert KNIGHT *US, male vocalist (Singles: 26 weeks)* pos/wks

17 Jan 68 EVERLASTING LOVE *Monument MON 1008* 40 2
24 Nov 73 ● LOVE ON A MOUNTAIN TOP *Monument MNT 1875* 10 16
9 Mar 74 EVERLASTING LOVE (re-issue) *Monument MNT 2106* 19 8

KNIGHTSBRIDGE STRINGS
UK, male orchestra (Albums: 1 week) pos/wks

25 Jun 60 STRING SWAY *Top Rank BUY 017* 20 1

KNOC-TURN'AL – *See DR DRE*

David KNOPFLER
UK, male vocalist / instrumentalist – guitar (Albums: 1 week) pos/wks

19 Nov 83 RELEASE *Peach River DAVID 1* 82 1

See also DIRE STRAITS

Mark KNOPFLER *UK, male vocalist / instrumentalist – guitar (Singles: 7 weeks, Albums: 60 weeks)* pos/wks

12 Mar 83 GOING HOME (THEME OF 'LOCAL HERO') *Vertigo DSTR 4* 56 3
16 Mar 96 DARLING PRETTY *Vertigo VERCD 88* 33 2
25 May 96 CANNIBALS *Vertigo VERCD 89* 42 2
16 Apr 83 LOCAL HERO (FILM SOUNDTRACK) *Vertigo VERL 4* 14 11
20 Oct 84 CAL (FILM SOUNDTRACK) *Vertigo VERH 17* 65 3
24 Nov 90 NECK AND NECK *CBS 4674351* [1] 41 11
6 Apr 96 ● GOLDEN HEART *Vertigo 5147322* 9 17
7 Oct 00 ● SAILING TO PHILADELPHIA *Mercury 5429812* 4 13
12 Oct 02 ● THE RAGPICKER'S DREAM *Mercury 0632932* 7 5

[1] Chet Atkins and Mark Knopfler

See also DIRE STRAITS

KNOWLEDGE *Italy, male production duo (Singles: 1 week)* pos/wks

8 Nov 97 AS (UNTIL THE DAY) *ffrr FCD 312* 70 1

Buddy KNOX *US, male vocalist, d. 14 Feb 1999 (Singles: 5 weeks)* pos/wks

10 May 57 PARTY DOLL *Columbia DB 3914* ▲ 29 3
16 Aug 62 SHE'S GONE *Liberty LIB 55473* 45 2

Frankie KNUCKLES
US, male producer (Singles: 19 weeks, Albums: 2 weeks) pos/wks

17 Jun 89 TEARS *ffrr F 108* [1] 50 3
21 Oct 89 YOUR LOVE *Trax TRAXT 3* 59 4
27 Jul 91 THE WHISTLE SONG *Virgin America VUS 47* 17 5
23 Nov 91 IT'S HARD SOMETIMES *Virgin America VUS 52* 67 1
6 Jun 92 RAIN FALLS *Virgin America VUST 60* [2] 48 2

27 May 95 **TOO MANY FISH** *Virgin America VUSCD 89* [3] **34** 2
18 Nov 95 **WHADDA U WANT (FROM ME)** *Virgin America VUSCD 98* [3] **36** 2
17 Aug 91 **BEYOND THE MIX** *Virgin America VUSLP 6* **59** 2

[1] Frankie Knuckles presents Satoshi Tomiie [2] Frankie Knuckles featuring Lisa Michaelis [3] Frankie Knuckles featuring Adeva

Moe KOFFMAN QUARTETTE *Canada, male instrumental group, Moe Koffman – flute, d. 28 Mar 2001 (Singles: 2 weeks)* pos/wks

28 Mar 58 **SWINGIN' SHEPHERD BLUES** *London HLJ 8549* **23** 2

Mike KOGLIN *Germany, male producer (Singles: 4 weeks)* pos/wks

28 Nov 98 **THE SILENCE** *Multiply CDMULTY 44* **20** 2
29 May 99 **ON MY WAY** *Multiply CDMULTY 51* [1] **28** 2

[1] Mike Koglin featuring Beatrice

KOKOMO
US, male instrumentalist – piano – Jimmy Wisner (Singles: 7 weeks) pos/wks

13 Apr 61 **ASIA MINOR** *London HLU 9305* **35** 7

KOKOMO
UK, male / female vocal / instrumental group (Singles: 3 weeks) pos/wks

29 May 82 **A LITTLE BIT FURTHER AWAY** *CBS A 2064* **45** 3

KON KAN *Canada, male vocal / instrumental duo – Barry Harris and Kevin Wynne (Singles: 13 weeks)* pos/wks

4 Mar 89 ● **I BEG YOUR PARDON** *Atlantic A 8969* **5** 13

John KONGOS *South Africa, male vocalist / multi-instrumentalist (Singles: 25 weeks, Albums: 2 weeks)* pos/wks

22 May 71 ● **HE'S GONNA STEP ON YOU AGAIN** *Fly BUG 8* **4** 14
20 Nov 71 ● **TOKOLOSHE MAN** *Fly BUG 14* **4** 11
15 Jan 72 **KONGOS** *Fly HIFLY 7* **29** 2

KONKRETE *UK, female production duo (Singles: 1 week)* pos/wks

22 Sep 01 **LAW UNTO MYSELF** *Perfecto PERF 23CDS* **60** 1

KONTAKT *UK, male production duo – Scott Attrill and Jim Sullivan (Singles: 4 weeks)* pos/wks

20 Sep 03 **SHOW ME A SIGN** *Nulife 82876557432* **19** 4

KOOL and the GANG (169 Top 500)
One of the most consistently successful R&B acts, hailing from New Jersey and including Robert 'Kool' Bell (b) and James 'JT' Taylor (v). The band spent 10 years as top US R&B stars before starting an impressive run of international hits (Singles: 208 weeks, Albums: 115 weeks) pos/wks

27 Oct 79 ● **LADIES NIGHT** *Mercury KOOL 7* **9** 12
19 Jan 80 **TOO HOT** *Mercury KOOL 8* **23** 8
12 Jul 80 **HANGIN' OUT** *De-Lite KOOL 9* **52** 4
1 Nov 80 ● **CELEBRATION** *De-Lite KOOL 10* ▲ **7** 13
21 Feb 81 **JONES VS JONES / SUMMER MADNESS** *De-Lite KOOL 11* **17** 11
30 May 81 **TAKE IT TO THE TOP** *De-Lite DE 2* **15** 9
31 Oct 81 **STEPPIN' OUT** *De-Lite DE 4* **12** 13
19 Dec 81 ● **GET DOWN ON IT** *De-Lite DE 5* **3** 12
6 Mar 82 **TAKE MY HEART (YOU CAN HAVE IT IF YOU WANT IT)** *De-Lite DE 6* **29** 7
7 Aug 82 **BIG FUN** *De-Lite DE 7* **14** 8
16 Oct 82 ● **OOH LA LA LA (LET'S GO DANCIN')** *De-Lite DE 9* **6** 9
4 Dec 82 **HI DE HI, HI DE HO** *De-Lite DE 14* **29** 8
10 Dec 83 **STRAIGHT AHEAD** *De-Lite DE 15* **15** 10
11 Feb 84 ● **JOANNA / TONIGHT** *De-Lite DE 16* **2** 11
14 Apr 84 ● **(WHEN YOU SAY YOU LOVE SOMEBODY) IN THE HEART** *De-Lite DE 17* **7** 8
24 Nov 84 **FRESH** *De-Lite DE 18* **11** 12
9 Feb 85 **MISLED** *De-Lite DE 19* **28** 5
11 May 85 ● **CHERISH** *De-Lite DE 20* **4** 22
2 Nov 85 **EMERGENCY** *De-Lite DE 21* **50** 3
22 Nov 86 **VICTORY (re)** *Club JAB 44* **30** 12
21 Mar 87 **STONE LOVE** *Club JAB 47* **45** 4
31 Dec 88 **CELEBRATION (re-mix)** *Club JAB 78* **56** 5
6 Jul 91 **GET DOWN ON IT (re-mix)** *Mercury MER 346* **69** 1
27 Dec 03 ● **LADIES NIGHT** *Innocent SINCD 53* [1] .... **8** 1+
21 Nov 81 ● **SOMETHING SPECIAL** *De-Lite DSR 001* **10** 20
2 Oct 82 **AS ONE** *De-Lite DSR 3* **49** 10
7 May 83 ● **TWICE AS KOOL** *De-Lite PROLP 2* **4** 23
14 Jan 84 **IN THE HEART** *De-Lite DSR 4* **18** 23
15 Dec 84 **EMERGENCY** *De-Lite DSR 6* **47** 25
12 Nov 88 **THE SINGLES COLLECTION** *De-Lite KGTV 1* **28** 13
27 Oct 90 **KOOL LOVE** *Telstar STAR 2435* **50** 1

[1] Atomic Kitten featuring Kool and the Gang

'Jones vs Jones' and 'Summer Madness' were labelled as A and B sides with 'Funky Stuff' and 'Hollywood Swinging' as the C and D sides of a two-disc release

KOOL ROCK STEADY – *See TYREE*

KOON + STEPHENSON – *See WESTBAM*

KORGIS *UK, male vocal / instrumental duo (Singles: 27 weeks, Albums: 4 weeks)* pos/wks

23 Jun 79 **IF I HAD YOU** *Rialto TREB 103* **13** 12
24 May 80 ● **EVERYBODY'S GOT TO LEARN SOMETIME** *Rialto TREB 115* **5** 12
30 Aug 80 **IF IT'S ALRIGHT WITH YOU BABY** *Rialto TREB 118* **56** 3
26 Jul 80 **DUMB WAITERS** *Rialto TENOR 104* **40** 4

KORN *US, male vocal / instrumental group (Singles: 25 weeks, Albums: 17 weeks)* pos/wks

19 Oct 96 **NO PLACE TO HIDE** *Epic 6638452* **26** 2
15 Feb 97 **A.D.I.D.A.S.** *Epic 6642042* **22** 2
7 Jun 97 **GOOD GOD** *Epic 6646585* **25** 2
22 Aug 98 **GOT THE LIFE** *Epic 6663912* **23** 2
8 May 99 **FREAK ON A LEASH** *Epic 6672522* **24** 2
12 Feb 00 **FALLING AWAY FROM ME** *Epic 6688692* **24** 2
3 Jun 00 **MAKE ME BAD** *Epic 6694332* **25** 2
1 Jun 02 **HERE TO STAY** *Epic 6727425* **12** 5
21 Sep 02 **THOUGHTLESS** *Epic 6731572* **37** 2
23 Aug 03 **DID MY TIME** *Epic 6741422* **15** 4
26 Oct 96 **LIFE IS PEACHY** *Epic 4853692* **32** 2
29 Aug 98 ● **FOLLOW THE LEADER** *Epic 4912212* ▲ **5** 4
27 Nov 99 **ISSUES** *Epic 4963592* ▲ **37** 1
22 Jun 02 ● **UNTOUCHABLES** *Epic 5017700* **4** 9
6 Dec 03 **TAKE A LOOK IN THE MIRROR** *Epic 05133253* **53** 1

KOSHEEN *UK, male / female production / vocal trio (Singles: 31 weeks, Albums: 29 weeks)* pos/wks

17 Jun 00 **EMPTY SKIES / HIDE U** *Moksha Recordings MOKSHA 05CD* ..**73** 1
14 Apr 01 **(SLIP & SLIDE) SUICIDE** *Moksha Recordings MOKSHA 07CD* **50** 2
1 Sep 01 ● **HIDE U (re) (re-mix)** *Arista 74321879412* **6** 7
22 Dec 01 **CATCH** *Moksha / Arista 74321913722* **15** 8
4 May 02 **HUNGRY** *Moksha / Arista 74321934382* **13** 4
31 Aug 02 **HARDER** *Moksha / Arista 74321954452* **53** 1
9 Aug 03 ● **ALL IN MY HEAD (re)** *Moksha / Arista 82876527242* **7** 7
1 Nov 03 **WASTING MY TIME** *Moksha / Arista 82876570022* **49** 1
29 Sep 01 ● **RESIST** *Arista 74321880812* **8** 23
23 Aug 03 ● **KOKOPELLI** *Moksha / Arista 82876527232* **7** 6

KOWDEAN – *See OXIDE & NEUTRINO*

KRAFTWERK (463 Top 500) *German electronic robot 'n' roll pioneers: Ralf Hutter (k/v), Florian Schneider (prc/v), Karl Bartos (prc), Wolfgang Flur (prc). First German act to top the UK singles chart, they influenced disco and synth pop movements and helped to lay the foundation stones for hip hop (Singles: 76 weeks, Albums: 73 weeks)* pos/wks

10 May 75 **AUTOBAHN** *Vertigo 6147 012* **11** 9
28 Oct 78 **NEON LIGHTS** *Capitol CL 15998* **53** 3
9 May 81 **POCKET CALCULATOR** *EMI 5175* **39** 6
11 Jul 81 ★ **COMPUTER LOVE / THE MODEL (re)** *EMI 5207* **1** 21
20 Feb 82 **SHOWROOM DUMMIES** *EMI 5272* **25** 5
6 Aug 83 **TOUR DE FRANCE (re)** *EMI 5413* **22** 19
1 Jun 91 **THE ROBOTS** *EMI EM 192* **20** 4

2 Nov 91	RADIOACTIVITY (re-mix) *EMI EM 201*	43	2
23 Oct 99	TOUR DE FRANCE (re-issue) *EMI 8874210*	61	1
18 Mar 00	EXPO 2000 *EMI CDEM 562*	27	2
19 Jul 03	TOUR DE FRANCE 2003 (re-mix) *EMI CDEM 626*	20	4
17 May 75 ●	AUTOBAHN *Vertigo 6360 620*	4	18
20 May 78 ●	THE MAN-MACHINE *Capitol EST 11728*	9	13
23 May 81	COMPUTER WORLD *EMI EMC 3370*	15	22
6 Feb 82	TRANS-EUROPE EXPRESS *Capitol EST 11603*	49	7
22 Jun 85	AUTOBAHN (re-issue) *Parlophone AUTO 1*	61	3
15 Nov 86	ELECTRIC CAFÉ *EMI EMD 1001*	58	2
22 Jun 91	THE MIX *EMI EM 1408*	15	6
16 Aug 03	TOUR DE FRANCE SOUNDTRACKS *EMI 5917082*	21	2

'Computer Love / The Model' did not make No.1 until re-entry in Dec 1981. 'Tour de France' also peaked at No.24 after re-entry in Aug 84.

Diana KRALL
US, female vocalist instrumentalist – piano (Albums: 14 weeks) pos/wks

12 Jun 99	WHEN I LOOK IN YOUR EYES *Verve 503042*	72	1
29 Sep 01	THE LOOK OF LOVE *Verve 5498462*	23	7
23 Nov 02	LIVE IN PARIS *Verve 0653692*	30	6

Billy J KRAMER and the DAKOTAS
UK, male vocal / instrumental group (Singles: 71 weeks, Albums: 17 weeks) pos/wks

2 May 63 ●	DO YOU WANT TO KNOW A SECRET? *Parlophone R 5023*	2	15
1 Aug 63 ★	BAD TO ME *Parlophone R 5049*	1	14
7 Nov 63 ●	I'LL KEEP YOU SATISFIED *Parlophone R 5073*	4	13
27 Feb 64 ★	LITTLE CHILDREN *Parlophone R 5105*	1	13
23 Jul 64 ●	FROM A WINDOW *Parlophone R 5156*	10	8
20 May 65	TRAINS AND BOATS AND PLANES *Parlophone R 5285*	12	8
16 Nov 63	LISTEN TO BILLY J KRAMER *Parlophone PMC 1209*	11	17

KRANKIES
UK, male / female vocal duo (Singles: 6 weeks) pos/wks

7 Feb 81	FAN'DABI'DOZI (re) *Monarch MON 21*	46	6

Alison KRAUSS and UNION STATION
US, female vocal instrumentalist – fiddle and instrumental group (Albums: 1 week) pos/wks

25 Aug 01	NEW FAVORITE *Rounder RRCD 0495*	72	1

Lenny KRAVITZ (364 Top 500)
Grammy and Brit-winning, genre-defying vocalist and multi-instrumentalist, who has worked with Madonna, Mick Jagger, David Bowie and Stevie Wonder, b. 26 May 1964, New York City. His Greatest Hits album reached the Top 10 in 25 countries and sold more than seven million globally (Singles: 69 weeks, Albums: 113 weeks) pos/wks

2 Jun 90	MR CABDRIVER *Virgin America VUS 20*	58	2
4 Aug 90	LET LOVE RULE *Virgin America VUS 26*	39	4
30 Mar 91	ALWAYS ON THE RUN *Virgin America VUS 34*	41	3
15 Jun 91	IT AIN'T OVER TIL IT'S OVER *Virgin America VUS 43*	11	8
14 Sep 91	STAND BY MY WOMAN *Virgin America VUS 45*	55	3
20 Feb 93 ●	ARE YOU GONNA GO MY WAY *Virgin America VUSDG 65*	4	11
22 May 93	BELIEVE *Virgin America VUSCD 72*	30	5
28 Aug 93	HEAVEN HELP *Virgin America VUSDG 73*	20	7
4 Dec 93	IS THERE ANY LOVE IN YOUR HEART *Virgin America VUSDG 76*	52	2
4 Dec 93	BUDDHA OF SUBURBIA *Arista 74321177052* [1]	35	3
9 Sep 95	ROCK AND ROLL IS DEAD *Virgin America VUSCD 93*	22	3
23 Dec 95	CIRCUS *Virgin America VUSCD 96*	54	2
2 Mar 96	CAN'T GET YOU OFF MY MIND *Virgin America VUSCD 100*	54	2
16 May 98	IF YOU CAN'T SAY NO *Virgin VUSCD 130*	48	2
10 Oct 98	I BELONG TO YOU *Virgin VUSCD 138*	75	1
20 Feb 99 ★	FLY AWAY *Virgin VUSCD 141* ■	1	10
6 Apr 02	STILLNESS OF HEART *Virgin VUSCD 236*	44	1
26 May 90	LET LOVE RULE *Virgin America VUSLP 10*	56	4
13 Apr 91 ●	MAMA SAID *Virgin America VUSLP 31*	8	27
13 Mar 93 ★	ARE YOU GONNA GO MY WAY *Virgin America CDVUS 60* ■	1	47
23 Sep 95 ●	CIRCUS *Virgin America CDVUS 86*	5	4
23 May 98	5 *Virgin CDVUS 140*	18	13
4 Nov 00	GREATEST HITS *Virgin CDVUSX 183*	12	17
10 Nov 01	LENNY *Virgin CDVUS 213*	55	1

[1] David Bowie featuring Lenny Kravitz

KRAZE
US, male / female vocal / instrumental group (Singles: 6 weeks) pos/wks

22 Oct 88	THE PARTY *MCA MCA 1288*	29	5
17 Jun 89	LET'S PLAY HOUSE *MCA MCA 1337*	71	1

KREUZ
UK, male vocal group (Singles: 1 week, Albums: 2 weeks) pos/wks

8 Jul 95	PARTY ALL NIGHT *Diesel DES 004C*	75	1
18 Mar 95	KREUZ KONTROL *Diesel DESCD 01*	48	2

Chantal KREVIAZUK
Canada, female vocalist (Singles: 1 week) pos/wks

6 Mar 99	LEAVING ON A JET PLANE *Epic 6666272*	59	1

KREW-KATS
UK, male instrumental group (Singles: 10 weeks) pos/wks

9 Mar 61	TRAMBONE (re) *HMV POP 840*	33	10

KRIS KROSS
US, male rap duo – Chris Kelly and Chris Smith (Singles: 22 weeks, Albums: 8 weeks) pos/wks

30 May 92 ●	JUMP *Ruff House 6578547* ▲	2	8
25 Jul 92	WARM IT UP *Ruff House 6582187*	16	6
17 Oct 92	I MISSED THE BUS *Ruff House 6583927*	57	1
19 Dec 92	IT'S A SHAME *Ruff House 6588587*	31	5
11 Sep 93	ALRIGHT *Ruff House 6595652*	47	2
27 Jun 92	TOTALLY KROSSED OUT *Columbia 4714342* ▲	31	8

Marty KRISTIAN – *See NEW SEEKERS*

Kris KRISTOFFERSON – *See Rita COOLIDGE*

Chad KROEGER featuring Josey SCOTT
Canada / US, male vocal / instrumental duo (Singles: 14 weeks) pos/wks

22 Jun 02 ●	HERO *Roadrunner RR 20463*	4	14

See also NICKLEBACK; SALIVA

KROKUS
Switzerland / Malta, male vocal / instrumental group (Singles: 2 weeks, Albums: 11 weeks) pos/wks

16 May 81	INDUSTRIAL STRENGTH (EP) *Ariola ARO 258*	62	2
21 Feb 81	HARDWARE *Ariola ARL 5064*	44	4
20 Feb 82	ONE VICE AT A TIME *Arista SPART 1189*	28	5
16 Apr 83	HEADHUNTER *Arista 205 255*	74	2

Tracks on Industrial Strength (EP): Bedside Radio / Easy Rocker / Celebration / Bye Bye Baby

KRUSH
UK, male / female vocal / instrumental group (Singles: 16 weeks) pos/wks

5 Dec 87 ●	HOUSE ARREST *Club JAB 63*	3	15
14 Nov 92	WALKING ON SUNSHINE *Network NWK 55* [1]	71	1

[1] Krush featuring Ruth Joy

KRUSH PERSPECTIVE
US, female vocal group (Singles: 2 weeks) pos/wks

16 Jan 93	LET'S GET TOGETHER (SO GROOVY NOW) *Perspective PERD 7416*	61	2

KRUST
UK, male producer / instrumentalist – Keith Thompson (Singles: 2 weeks) pos/wks

23 Oct 99	CODED LANGUAGE *Talkin Loud TLCD 51* [1]	66	1
26 Jan 02	SNAPPED IT *Full Cycle FCY 034*	58	1

[1] Krust featuring Saul Williams

KULA SHAKER
UK, male vocal / instrumental group (Singles: 48 weeks, Albums: 54 weeks) pos/wks

4 May 96	GRATEFUL WHEN YOU'RE DEAD – JERRY WAS THERE *Columbia KULACD 2*	35	3
6 Jul 96 ●	TATTVA *Columbia KULACD 3*	4	8
7 Sep 96 ●	HEY DUDE *Columbia KULACD 4*	2	7
23 Nov 96 ●	GOVINDA *Columbia KULACD 5*	7	8

Date		Title / Label	pos	wks
8 Mar 97	●	**HUSH (re)** *Columbia KULACD 6*	2	9
2 May 98	●	**SOUND OF DRUMS** *Columbia KULA 21CD*	3	6
6 Mar 99		**MYSTICAL MACHINE GUN** *Columbia KULA 22CD*	14	3
15 May 99		**SHOWER YOUR LOVE** *Columbia KULA 23CD*	14	4
28 Sep 96	★	K *Columbia SHAKER 1CDK* ■	1	44
20 Mar 99	●	PEASANTS PIGS & ASTRONAUTS *Columbia SHAKER 2CD*	9	10

KULAY *Philippines, male / female vocal group (Singles: 1 week)* pos/wks

12 Sep 98		**DELICIOUS** *INCredible INCRL 4CD*	73	1

KUMARA *Holland, male production duo (Singles: 1 week)* pos/wks

7 Sep 00		**SNAP YOUR FINGAZ** *Y2K Y2K 018CD*	70	1

KUMARS – *See Gareth GATES*

Charlie KUNZ *US, male instrumentalist – piano, d. 16 Mar 1958 (Singles: 4 weeks, Albums: 11 weeks)* pos/wks

17 Dec 54		**PIANO MEDLEY NO.114 (re)** *Decca F 10419*	16	4
14 Jun 69	●	THE WORLD OF CHARLIE KUNZ *Decca SPA 15*	9	11

Medley titles: There Must Be a Reason / Hold My Hand / If I Give My Heart to You / Little Things Mean a Lot / Make Her Mine / My Son My Son

KURSAAL FLYERS
UK, male vocal / instrumental group (Singles: 10 weeks) pos/wks

20 Nov 76		**LITTLE DOES SHE KNOW** *CBS 4689*	14	10

KURUPT *US, male rapper (Singles: 10 weeks)* pos/wks

25 Aug 01		**WHERE I WANNA BE (re)** *London LONCD461* [1]	14	7
13 Oct 01		**IT'S OVER** *Pias Recordings PIASB 024CD*	21	3

[1] Shade Sheist featuring Nate Dogg and Kurupt

KUT KLOSE *US, female vocal group (Singles: 1 week)* pos/wks

29 Apr 95		**I LIKE** *Elektra EKR 200CD*	72	1

Li KWAN *UK, male producer – Dave Lee (Singles: 2 weeks)* pos/wks

17 Dec 94		**I NEED A MAN** *Deconstruction 74321252192*	51	2

See also HED BOYS; RAVEN MAIZE; Joey NEGRO; Z FACTOR; JAKATTA; AKABU featuring Linda CLIFFORD; PHASE II; IL PADRINOS featuring Jocelyn BROWN

KY-MANI – *See PM DAWN*

Jonny L *UK, male vocalist / instrumentalist / producer (Singles: 2 weeks)* pos/wks

28 Aug 93		**OOH I LIKE IT** *XL Recordings XLS 44CD*	73	1
31 Oct 98		**20 DEGREES** *XL Recordings XLS 103CD* [1]	66	1

[1] Jonny L featuring Silvah Bullet

LA GANZ *US, male vocal / instrumental group (Singles: 1 week)* pos/wks

9 Nov 96		**LIKE A PLAYA** *Jive JIVECD 405*	75	1

L.A. GUNS *US, male / female vocal / instrumental group (Singles: 4 weeks, Albums: 4 weeks)* pos/wks

30 Nov 91		**SOME LIE 4 LOVE** *Mercury MER 358*	61	1
21 Dec 91		**THE BALLAD OF JAYNE** *Mercury MER 361*	53	3
5 Mar 88		L.A. GUNS *Vertigo VERH 55*	73	1
30 Sep 89		COCKED AND LOADED *Vertigo 8385921*	45	2
13 Jul 91		HOLLYWOOD VAMPIRES *Mercury 8496041*	44	1

LA MIX
UK, male / female production / vocal duo – Les Adams and Emma Frielich (Singles: 25 weeks) pos/wks

10 Oct 87		**DON'T STOP (JAMMIN')** *Breakout USA 615*	47	4
21 May 88	●	**CHECK THIS OUT** *Breakout USA 629*	6	7
8 Jul 89		**GET LOOSE** *Breakout USA 659* [1]	25	6
16 Sep 89		**LOVE TOGETHER** *Breakout USA 662* [2]	66	2
15 Sep 90		**COMING BACK FOR MORE** *A&M AM 579*	50	3
19 Jan 91		**MYSTERIES OF LOVE** *A&M AM 707*	46	2
23 Mar 91		**WE SHOULDN'T HOLD HANDS IN THE DARK** *A&M AM 755*	69	1

[1] LA Mix featuring Jazzi P [2] LA Mix featuring Kevin Henry

LCD *UK, male production group (Singles: 9 weeks)* pos/wks

27 Jun 98		**ZORBA'S DANCE** *Virgin VSCDT 1693*	20	5
9 Oct 99		**ZORBA'S DANCE (re-issue)** *Virgin VSCDT 1757*	22	4

LFO *UK, male instrumental / production group (Singles: 15 weeks, Albums: 3 weeks)* pos/wks

14 Jul 90		**LFO** *Warp WAP 5*	12	10
6 Jul 91		**WE ARE BACK / NURTURE** *Warp 7WAP 14*	47	3
1 Feb 92		**WHAT IS HOUSE (EP)** *Warp WAP 17*	62	2
3 Aug 91		FREQUENCIES *Warp WARPLP 3*	42	2
10 Feb 96		ADVANCE *Warp WARPCD 39*	44	1

Tracks on What Is House (EP): Tan Ta Ra / Mashed Potato / What Is House / Syndrome

LL COOL J (478 Top 500)
With a moniker abbreviated from Ladies Love Cool James, this whizz kid was born James Todd Smith, 18 Jun 1968, New York, US. The first solo rap act to score a UK Top 10 hit with 'I Need Love', which was also the first successful rap 'ballad', he has amassed a record eight US No.1 rap hits (Singles: 101 weeks, Albums: 43 weeks) pos/wks

4 Jul 87		**I'M BAD** *Def Jam 650856 7*	71	1
12 Sep 87	●	**I NEED LOVE** *Def Jam 651101 7*	8	10
21 Nov 87		**GO CUT CREATOR GO** *Def Jam LLCJ 1*	66	2
13 Feb 88		**GOING BACK TO CALI / JACK THE RIPPER** *Def Jam LLCJ 2*	37	4
10 Jun 89		**I'M THAT TYPE OF GUY** *Def Jam LLCJ 3*	43	5
1 Dec 90		**AROUND THE WAY GIRL / MAMA SAID KNOCK YOU OUT** *Def Jam 6564470*	41	4
9 Mar 91		**AROUND THE WAY GIRL (re-mix)** *Columbia 6564470*	36	4
10 Apr 93		**HOW I'M COMIN'** *Def Jam 6591692*	37	2
20 Jan 96		**HEY LOVER** *Def Jam DEFCD 14* [1]	17	4
1 Jun 96		**DOIN' IT** *Def Jam DEFCD 15* [2]	15	3
5 Oct 96	●	**LOUNGIN'** *Def Jam DEFCD 30*	7	8
8 Feb 97	★	**AIN'T NOBODY** *Geffen GFSTD 22195* ■	1	9
5 Apr 97	●	**HIT EM HIGH (THE MONSTARS' ANTHEM)** *Atlantic A 5449CD* [3]	8	6
1 Nov 97	●	**PHENOMENON** *Def Jam 5681172*	9	5
28 Mar 98	●	**FATHER** *Def Jam 5685292*	10	5
11 Jul 98		**ZOOM** *Interscope IND 95594* [4]	15	3
5 Dec 98		**INCREDIBLE** *Jive 0522102* [5]	52	1
26 Oct 02	●	**LUV U BETTER** *Def Jam 0638722*	7	7
22 Feb 03		**PARADISE** *Def Jam 0637032* [6]	18	5
22 Mar 03	●	**ALL I HAVE** *Epic 6736782* [7] ▲	2	13
15 Feb 86		RADIO *Def Jam DEF 26745*	71	1
13 Jun 87		BIGGER AND DEFFER *Def Jam 450 5151*	54	19
8 Jul 89		WALKING WITH A PANTHER *Def Jam 465112 1*	43	3
13 Oct 90		MAMA SAID KNOCK YOU OUT *Def Jam 4673151*	49	2

17 Apr 93	**14 SHOTS TO THE DOME** *Def Jam 4736782*	74 1
16 Nov 96	**ALL WORLD** *Def Jam 5341252*	23 8
25 Oct 97	**PHENOMENON** *Def Jam 5391862*	37 4
23 Sep 00	**G.O.A.T. FEATURING JAMES T SMITH – THE GREATEST OF ALL TIME** *Def Jam 5429972* ▲	29 2
2 Nov 02	**10** *Def Jam 0632192*	26 3

[1] LL Cool J featuring Boyz II Men [2] LL Cool J, guest vocals by LeShaun [3] B Real / Busta Rhymes / Coolio / LL Cool J / Method Man [4] Dr Dre and LL Cool J [5] Keith Murray featuring LL Cool J [6] LL Cool J featuring Amerie [7] Jennifer Lopez featuring LL Cool J

'Jack the Ripper' listed only from 20 Feb 1988

LNR *US, male vocal / instrumental duo (Singles: 2 weeks)*

		pos/wks
3 Jun 89	**WORK IT TO THE BONE** *Kool Kat KOOL 501*	64 2

LRS – *See D MOB*

LSG *Germany, male DJ / producer – Oliver Lieb (Singles: 1 week)*

		pos/wks
10 May 97	**NETHERWORLD** *Hooj Choons HOOJCD 52*	63 1

L7 *US, female vocal / instrumental group (Singles: 18 weeks, Albums: 8 weeks)*

		pos/wks
4 Apr 92	**PRETEND WE'RE DEAD** *Slash LASH 34*	21 7
30 May 92	**EVERGLADE** *Slash LASH 36*	27 3
12 Sep 92	**MONSTER** *Slash LASH 38*	33 3
28 Nov 92	**PRETEND WE'RE DEAD (re-issue)** *Slash LASH 42*	50 3
9 Jul 94	**ANDRES** *Slash LASCD 48*	34 2
2 May 92	**BRICKS ARE HEAVY** *Slash 8283072*	24 6
23 Jul 94	**HUNGRY FOR STINK** *Slash 8285312*	26 2

L.T.D. *US, male vocal / instrumental group (Singles: 3 weeks)*

		pos/wks
9 Sep 78	**HOLDING ON (WHEN LOVE IS GONE)** *A&M AMS 7378*	70 3

LV *US, male vocalist – Larry Sanders (Singles: 25 weeks)*

		pos/wks
28 Oct 95 ★	**GANGSTA'S PARADISE** *Tommy Boy MCSTD 2104* [1] ◆ ■ ▲	1 20
23 Dec 95	**THROW YOUR HANDS UP / GANGSTA'S PARADISE** *Tommy Boy TBCD 699*	24 4
4 May 96	**I AM LV** *Tommy Boy TBCD 7724*	64 1

[1] Coolio featuring LV

The version of 'Gangsta's Paradise' coupled with 'Throw Your Hands Up' is a re-recorded version without Coolio's vocals

LWS *Italy, male instrumental group (Singles: 1 week)*

		pos/wks
29 Oct 94	**GOSP** *Transworld TRANNY 4CD*	65 1

LA BELLE EPOQUE *France, female vocal duo (Singles: 14 weeks)*

		pos/wks
27 Aug 77 ●	**BLACK IS BLACK (re)** *Harvest HAR 5133*	2 14

LA BOUCHE *US, male / female rap / vocal duo – Lane McCray and Melanie Thornton (Singles: 12 weeks)*

		pos/wks
24 Sep 94	**SWEET DREAMS** *Bell 74321223912*	63 1
15 Jul 95	**BE MY LOVER** *Arista 74321265402*	27 4
30 Sep 95	**FALLING IN LOVE** *Arista 74321305102*	43 2
2 Mar 96	**BE MY LOVER (re-mix)** *Arista 74321339822*	25 4
7 Sep 96	**SWEET DREAMS (re-issue)** *Arista 74321398542*	44 1

Sam LA MORE *Australia, male producer – Sam Littlemore (Singles: 1 week)*

		pos/wks
5 Apr 03	**TAKIN' HOLD** *Underwater H20 023X*	70 1

LA NA NEE NEE NOO NOO – *See BANANARAMA*

LA FLEUR *Holland, male / female vocal / instrumental group (Singles: 4 weeks)*

		pos/wks
30 Jul 83	**BOOGIE NIGHTS** *Proto ENA 111*	51 4

Danny LA RUE *UK, male vocalist – Daniel Carroll (Singles: 9 weeks)*

		pos/wks
18 Dec 68	**ON MOTHER KELLY'S DOORSTEP** *Page One POF 108*	33 9

LA TREC – *See SASH!*

LaBELLE *US, female vocal group – lead vocal Patti LaBelle (Singles: 9 weeks)*

		pos/wks
22 Mar 75	**LADY MARMALADE (VOULEZ-VOUS COUCHER AVEC MOI CE SOIR?)** *Epic EPC 2852* ▲	17 9

Patti LaBELLE *US, female vocalist – Patricia Holt (Singles: 21 weeks, Albums: 17 weeks)*

		pos/wks
3 May 86 ●	**ON MY OWN** *MCA MCA 1045* [1] ▲	2 13
2 Aug 86	**OH, PEOPLE** *MCA MCA 1075*	26 6
3 Sep 94	**THE RIGHT KINDA LOVER** *MCA MCSTD 1995*	50 2
24 May 86	**WINNER IN YOU** *MCA MCF 3319* ▲	30 17

[1] Patti LaBelle and Michael McDonald

See also LaBELLE

Tiff LACEY – *See REDD SQUARE featuring Tiff LACEY*

LADIES CHOICE *UK, male vocal / instrumental group (Singles: 4 weeks)*

		pos/wks
25 Jan 86	**FUNKY SENSATION** *Sure Delight SD 01*	41 4

LADIES FIRST *UK, female vocal trio (Singles: 7 weeks)*

		pos/wks
24 Nov 01	**MESSIN'** *Polydor 5873422*	30 2
13 Apr 02	**I CAN'T WAIT** *Polydor 5706912*	19 5

LADY G – *See B-15 PROJECT featuring Crissy D and LADY G*

LADY J – *See RAZE*

LADY OF RAGE *US, female rapper (Singles: 1 week)*

		pos/wks
8 Oct 94	**AFRO PUFFS** *Interscope A 8288CD*	72 1

LADY SAW *Jamaica, female vocalist – Marion Hall (Singles: 3 weeks)*

		pos/wks
16 Dec 00	**BUMP N GRIND (I AM FEELING HOT TONIGHT)** *Telstar CDSTAS 3129* [1]	59 1
20 Oct 01	**SINCE I MET YOU LADY / SPARKLE OF MY EYES** *DEP International DEPD 55* [2]	40 2

[1] M Dubs featuring Lady Saw [2] UB40 featuring Lady Saw

LADYSMITH BLACK MAMBAZO *South Africa, male vocal group (Singles: 26 weeks, Albums: 69 weeks)*

		pos/wks
3 Jun 95	**SWING LOW SWEET CHARIOT** *PolyGram TV SWLOW 2* [1]	15 6
3 Jun 95	**WORLD IN UNION '95** *PolyGram TV RUGBY 2* [2]	47 5
15 Nov 97	**INKANYEZI NEZAZI (THE STAR AND THE WISEMAN)** *A&M 5823892*	33 3
11 Jul 98	**THE STAR AND THE WISEMAN (re-issue)** *AM:PM 5825692*	63 1
16 Oct 99	**AIN'T NO SUNSHINE** *Universal Music TV 1564332* [3]	42 2
18 Dec 99	**I SHALL BE THERE** *Glow Worm / Epic 6683332* [4]	13 9
11 Apr 87	**SHAKA ZULU** *Warner Bros. WX 94*	34 11
22 Nov 97	**HEAVENLY** *A&M 5407902*	53 16
3 Oct 98 ●	**THE BEST OF LADYSMITH BLACK MAMBAZO – THE STAR AND THE WISEMAN** *PolyGram TV 5652982*	2 34
16 Oct 99	**IN HARMONY** *Universal Music TV 1537392*	15 5
12 May 01	**THE ULTIMATE COLLECTION** *Universal Music TV 5566822*	37 3

[1] Ladysmith Black Mambazo featuring China Black [2] Ladysmith Black Mambazo featuring PJ Powers [3] Ladysmith Black Mambazo featuring Des'ree [4] B*Witched featuring Ladysmith Black Mambazo

'The Best of Ladysmith Black Mambazo – The Star and the Wiseman' changed label to Universal Music TV from 13 Mar 99

LADYTRON
UK / Bulgaria, male / female vocal production group (Singles: 3 weeks)

Date		Title	pos	wks
7 Dec 02		**SEVENTEEN** *Telstar / Invicta Hi-Fi CDSTAS 3284*	68	1
22 Mar 03		**BLUE JEANS** *Invicta Hi-Fi / Telstar CDSTAS 3311*	43	1
12 Jul 03		**EVIL** *Invicta Hi-Fi / Telstar CDSTAS 3331*	44	1

LAGUNA *Italy, male DJ / production duo – Cristiano Spiller and Tommy Vee (Singles: 2 weeks)*

Date		Title	pos	wks
1 Nov 97		**SPILLER FROM RIO (DO IT EASY)** *Positiva CDTIV 83*	40	2

See also SPILLER

LAID BACK
Denmark, male vocal / instrumental duo (Singles: 4 weeks)

Date		Title	pos	wks
5 May 90		**BAKERMAN** *Arista 112356*	44	4

LAIN – *See WOOKIE*

Cleo LAINE *UK, female vocalist – Clementina Campbell (Singles: 14 weeks, Albums: 37 weeks)*

Date		Title	pos	wks
29 Dec 60		**LET'S SLIP AWAY** *Fontana H 269*	42	1
14 Sep 61	●	**YOU'LL ANSWER TO ME** *Fontana H 326*	5	13
7 Jan 78		BEST OF FRIENDS *RCA RS 1094* [1]	18	22
2 Dec 78		CLEO *Arcade ADEP 37*	68	1
31 May 80		SOMETIMES WHEN WE TOUCH *RCA PL 25296* [2]	15	14

[1] Cleo Laine and John Williams [2] Cleo Laine and James Galway

Frankie LAINE 178 Top 500
Powerful-voiced No.1 hitmaker of the pre-rock years, b. Frank Lovecchio, 30 Mar 1913, Chicago, US. He spent an unequalled 27 weeks at the top of the UK chart in 1953, including a record 18 by 'I Believe'. At one time he had three singles in the Top 5 (Singles: 282 weeks, Albums: 29 weeks)

Date		Title	pos	wks
14 Nov 52	●	**HIGH NOON (DO NOT FORSAKE ME)** *Columbia DB 3113*	7	7
14 Nov 52	●	**SUGARBUSH (re)** *Columbia DB 3123* [1]	8	8
20 Mar 53		**THE GIRL IN THE WOOD** *Columbia DB 2907*	11	1
3 Apr 53	★	**I BELIEVE** *Philips PB 117*	1	36
8 May 53	●	**TELL ME A STORY (re)** *Philips PB 126* [2]	5	16
4 Sep 53	●	**WHERE THE WINDS BLOW** *Philips PB 167*	2	12
16 Oct 53	★	**HEY JOE!** *Philips PB 172*	1	8
30 Oct 53	★	**ANSWER ME** *Philips PB 196*	1	17
8 Jan 54	●	**BLOWING WILD** *Philips PB 207*	2	12
26 Mar 54	●	**GRANADA (re)** *Philips PB 242*	9	2
16 Apr 54	●	**THE KID'S LAST FIGHT** *Philips PB 258*	3	10
13 Aug 54	●	**MY FRIEND** *Philips PB 316*	3	15
8 Oct 54	●	**THERE MUST BE A REASON** *Philips PB 306*	9	9
22 Oct 54	●	**RAIN, RAIN, RAIN** *Philips PB 311* [3]	8	16
11 Mar 55		**IN THE BEGINNING** *Philips PB 404*	20	1
24 Jun 55	●	**COOL WATER** *Philips PB 465* [4]	2	22
15 Jul 55	●	**STRANGE LADY IN TOWN** *Philips PB 478*	6	13
11 Nov 55		**HUMMING BIRD** *Philips PB 498*	16	1
25 Nov 55	●	**HAWK-EYE** *Philips PB 519*	7	8
20 Jan 56	●	**SIXTEEN TONS** *Philips PB 539* [4]	10	3
4 May 56		**HELL HATH NO FURY** *Philips PB 585*	28	1
7 Sep 56	★	**A WOMAN IN LOVE** *Philips PB 617*	1	21
28 Dec 56		**MOONLIGHT GAMBLER (re)** *Philips PB 638*	13	13
26 Apr 57		**LOVE IS A GOLDEN RING** *Philips PB 676* [5]	19	5
4 Oct 57		**GOOD EVENING FRIENDS / UP ABOVE MY HEAD, I HEAR MUSIC IN THE AIR** *Philips PB 708* [6]	25	4
13 Nov 59	●	**RAWHIDE (re)** *Philips PB 965*	6	20
11 May 61		**GUNSLINGER** *Philips PB 1135*	50	1
24 Jun 61	●	HELL BENT FOR LEATHER *Philips BBL 7468*	7	23
24 Sep 77	●	THE VERY BEST OF FRANKIE LAINE *Warwick PR 5032*	7	6

[1] Doris Day and Frankie Laine [2] Jimmy Boyd - Frankie Laine [3] Frankie Laine and The Four Lads [4] Frankie Laine with The Mellomen [5] Frankie Laine and The Easy Riders [6] Frankie Laine and Johnnie Ray

Greg LAKE
UK, male vocalist (Singles: 12 weeks, Albums: 3 weeks)

Date		Title	pos	wks
6 Dec 75	●	**I BELIEVE IN FATHER CHRISTMAS (2re)** *Manticore K 13511*	2	12
17 Oct 81		GREG LAKE *Chrysalis CHR 1357*	62	3

Re-entries occurred in Dec '82 and Dec '83

See also EMERSON, LAKE and PALMER; EMERSON LAKE and POWELL; KING CRIMSON

LAMB *UK, male / female vocal / production duo – Andy Barlow and Louise Rhodes (Singles: 4 weeks, Albums: 2 weeks)*

Date		Title	pos	wks
29 Mar 97		**GORECKI** *Fontana LAMCD 4*	30	2
3 Apr 99		**B LINE** *Fontana LAMCD 5*	52	1
22 May 99		**ALL IN YOUR HANDS** *Fontana LAMCD 6*	71	1
29 May 99		FEAR OF FOURS *Fontana 5588212*	37	1
20 Oct 01		WHAT SOUND *Mercury 5865382*	54	1

Annabel LAMB
UK, female vocalist (Singles: 7 weeks, Albums: 1 week)

Date		Title	pos	wks
27 Aug 83		**RIDERS ON THE STORM** *A&M AM 131*	27	7
28 Apr 84		THE FLAME *A&M AMLX 68564*	84	1

LAMBCHOP *US, male / female vocal / instrumental group (Singles: 1 week, Albums: 3 weeks)*

Date		Title	pos	wks
20 May 00		**UP WITH PEOPLE** *City Slang 201592*	66	1
19 Feb 00		NIXON *City Slang 201522*	60	1
2 Mar 02		IS A WOMAN *City Slang 201902*	38	2

LAMBRETTAS *UK, male vocal / instrumental group (Singles: 24 weeks, Albums: 8 weeks)*

Date		Title	pos	wks
1 Mar 80	●	**POISON IVY** *Rocket XPRESS 25*	7	12
24 May 80		**D-A-A-ANCE** *Rocket XPRESS 33*	12	8
23 Aug 80		**ANOTHER DAY (ANOTHER GIRL)** *Rocket XPRESS 36*	49	4
5 Jul 80		BEAT BOYS IN THE JET AGE *Rocket TRAIN 10*	28	8

LAMPIES
UK, male / female / canine cartoon vocal group (Singles: 3 weeks)

Date		Title	pos	wks
22 Dec 01		**LIGHT UP THE WORLD FOR CHRISTMAS** *Bluecrest LAMPCD 001*	48	3

LANCASTRIANS
UK, male vocal / instrumental group (Singles: 2 weeks)

Date		Title	pos	wks
24 Dec 64		**WE'LL SING IN THE SUNSHINE** *Pye 7N 15732*	44	2

Major LANCE *US, male vocalist d. 3 Sep 1994 (Singles: 2 weeks)*

Date		Title	pos	wks
13 Feb 64		**UM, UM, UM, UM, UM, UM** *Columbia DB 7205*	40	2

LANCERS – *See Teresa BREWER*

Valerie LANDSBERG – *See KIDS FROM 'FAME'*

Charlie LANDSBOROUGH
UK, male vocalist / instrumentalist – guitar (Albums: 19 weeks)

Date		Title	pos	wks
12 Oct 96		WITH YOU IN MIND *Ritz RITZCD 0078*	49	6
8 Nov 97		FURTHER DOWN THE ROAD *Ritz RITZCD 0085*	42	3
10 Oct 98		THE VERY BEST OF CHARLIE LANDSBOROUGH *Ritz RZCD 0087*	41	2
2 Oct 99		STILL CAN'T SAY GOODBYE *Ritz RZCD 0092*	39	2
16 Aug 03		SMILE *Telstar Premiere TPECD5516*	37	6

LANDSCAPE *UK, male vocal / instrumental group (Singles: 20 weeks, Albums: 12 weeks)*

Date		Title	pos	wks
28 Feb 81	●	**EINSTEIN A GO-GO** *RCA 22*	5	13
23 May 81		**NORMAN BATES** *RCA 60*	40	7
21 Mar 81		FROM THE TEAROOMS OF MARS TO THE HELLHOLES OF URANUS *RCA RCALP 5003*	13	12

Desmond LANE – *See Alma COGAN; Cyril STAPLETON and his ORCHESTRA*

Ronnie LANE *UK, male vocalist d. 4 Jun 1997 (Singles: 12 weeks, Albums: 4 weeks)*

Date		Title	pos	wks
12 Jan 74		**HOW COME?** *GM GMS 011* [1]	11	8

15 Jun 74 **THE POACHER** *GM GMS 024* 36 4
17 Aug 74 **ANYMORE FOR ANYMORE** . . *GM GML 1013* [1] 48 1
15 Oct 77 **ROUGH MIX** *Polydor 2442147* [2] 44 3

[1] Ronnie Lane accompanied by the band Slim Chance [1] Ronnie Lane with the band Slim Chance [2] Pete Townshend and Ronnie Lane

See also SMALL FACES

Emma LANFORD – *See MOUSSE T*

Don LANG *UK, male vocalist / instrumentalist – trombone – Gordon Langhorn d. 3 Aug 1992 (Singles: 18 weeks)* pos/wks

4 Nov 55 **CLOUDBURST (2re)** *HMV POP 115* 16 4
5 Jul 57 **SCHOOL DAY (RING! RING! GOES THE BELL)** *HMV POP 350* [1] 26 2
23 May 58 ● **WITCH DOCTOR** *HMV POP 488* [1] 5 11
10 Mar 60 **SINK THE BISMARCK** *HMV POP 714* 43 1

[1] Don Lang and his Frantic Five

kd lang *Canada, female vocalist – Katherine Dawn Lang (Singles: 25 weeks, Albums: 71 weeks)* pos/wks

16 May 92 **CONSTANT CRAVING** *Sire W 0100* 52 4
22 Aug 92 **CRYING** *Virgin America VUS 63* [1] 13 6
27 Feb 93 **CONSTANT CRAVING (re-issue)** *Sire W 0157CD* 15 8
1 May 93 **THE MIND OF LOVE (WHERE IS YOUR HEAD, KATHRYN?)** *Sire W 0170CD1* 72 1
26 Jun 93 **MISS CHATELAINE** *Sire W 0181CDX* 68 2
11 Dec 93 **JUST KEEP ME MOVING** *Sire W 0227CD* 59 1
30 Sep 95 **IF I WERE YOU** *Sire W 0319CD* 53 1
18 May 96 **YOU'RE OK** *Warner Bros. W 0332CD* 44 2
28 Mar 92 ● **INGENUE** *Sire 7599268402* 3 52
13 Nov 93 **EVEN COWGIRLS GET THE BLUES** *Sire 9362454332* 36 2
14 Oct 95 ● **ALL YOU CAN EAT** *Warner Bros. 9362460342* 7 5
12 Jul 97 **DRAG** *Warner Bros. 9362466232* 19 3
15 Jul 00 **INVINCIBLE SUMMER** *Warner Bros. 9362476052* 17 6
5 Jul 03 **A WONDERFUL WORLD** *Columbia 5098702* [1] 33 3

[1] Roy Orbison (duet with kd lang) [1] Tony Bennett & kd lang

Thomas LANG
UK, male vocalist (Singles: 3 weeks, Albums: 1 week) pos/wks

30 Jan 88 **THE HAPPY MAN** *Epic VOW 4* 67 3
20 Feb 88 **SCALLYWAG JAZ** *Epic 450996 1* 92 1

LANGE
UK, male producer – Stuart Langelaan (Singles: 8 weeks) pos/wks

19 Jun 99 **I BELIEVE** *Additive 12 AD039* [1] 68 1
19 Jan 02 ● **DRIFTING AWAY** *VC Recordings VCRD 101* [2] 9 6
22 Feb 03 **DON'T THINK IT (FEEL IT)** *Nebula NEBCD 037* [3] 59 1

[1] Lange featuring Sarah Dwyer [2] Lange featuring Skye [3] Lange featuring Leah

LANTERNS
UK, male / female vocal / instrumental trio (Singles: 1 week) pos/wks

6 Feb 99 **HIGHRISE TOWN** *Columbia 6665712* 50 1

Mario LANZA *US, male vocalist – Alfredo Cocozza d. 7 Oct 1959 (Singles: 32 weeks, Albums: 64 weeks)* pos/wks

14 Nov 52 ● **BECAUSE YOU'RE MINE** *HMV DA 2017* 3 24
4 Feb 55 **DRINKING SONG** *HMV DA 2065* 13 1
18 Feb 55 **I'LL WALK WITH GOD (re)** *HMV DA 2062* 18 2
22 Apr 55 **SERENADE (re)** *HMV DA 2065* 15 3
14 Sep 56 **SERENADE (re)** *HMV DA 2085* 25 2
11 Aug 56 ● **SONGS FROM 'THE STUDENT PRINCE' AND OTHER FAMOUS MELODIES** *HMV ALP 1186* ▲ 5 1
6 Dec 58 ● **THE STUDENT PRINCE / THE GREAT CARUSO** *RCA RB 16113* ..4 21
23 Jul 60 ● **THE GREAT CARUSO: MARIO LANZA SINGS CARUSO FAVOURITES** *RCA RB 16112* 3 15
9 Jan 71 **HIS GREATEST HITS VOLUME 1** *RCA LSB 4000* 39 1
5 Sep 81 **THE LEGEND OF MARIO LANZA** *K-Tel NE 1110* 29 11
14 Nov 87 **A PORTRAIT OF MARIO LANZA** *Stylus SMR 741* 49 8
12 Mar 94 **MARIO LANZA – THE ULTIMATE COLLECTION** *RCA Victor 74321185742* 13 7

DA 2065 and DA 2085 are two different songs Both sides of RB 16113 are film soundtrack recordings

LAPTOP *US, male vocalist / instrumentalist – Jesse Hartman (Singles: 1 week)* pos/wks

12 Jun 99 **NOTHING TO DECLARE** *Island CID 744* 74 1

LARD *UK, male vocal / instrumental group (Albums: 1 week)* pos/wks

6 Oct 90 **THE LAST TEMPTATION OF REID** *Alternative Tentacles VIRUS 84* 69 1

Julius LAROSA *US, male vocalist (Singles: 9 weeks)* pos/wks

4 Jul 58 **TORERO** *RCA 1063* 15 9

LA's *UK, male vocal / instrumental group (Singles: 20 weeks, Albums: 20 weeks)* pos/wks

14 Jan 89 **THERE SHE GOES** *Go! Discs GOLASEP 2* 59 4
15 Sep 90 **TIMELESS MELODY** *Go! Discs GOLAS 4* 57 2
3 Nov 90 **THERE SHE GOES (re-issue)** *Go! Discs GOLAS 5* 13 9
16 Feb 91 **FEELIN'** *Go! Discs GOLAS 6* 43 3
10 May 97 **FEVER PITCH THE EP** *Blanco Y Negro NEG 104CD* [1] 65 1
2 Oct 99 **THERE SHE GOES (2nd re-issue)** *Polydor 5614032* 65 1
13 Oct 90 **THE LA'S** *Go! Discs 8282021* 30 20

[1] Pretenders, La's, Orlando, Neil MacColl, Nick Hornby

Tracks on Fever Pitch the EP: Goin' Back – Pretenders / There She Goes – La's / How Can We Hang on to a Dream – Orlando / Football – Neil MacColl, Boo Hewerdine and Nick Hornby

LAS KETCHUP *Spain, female vocal trio (Singles: 26 weeks)* pos/wks

2 Sep 02 **THE KETCHUP SONG (ASEREJE) (import)** *Columbia 6729602CD* 49 4
19 Oct 02 ★ **THE KETCHUP SONG (ASEREJE)** *Columbia 6731932* ■ 1 22

Denise LASALLE
US, female vocalist – Denise Craig (Singles: 13 weeks) pos/wks

15 Jun 85 ● **MY TOOT TOOT** *Epic A 6334* 6 13

LASGO *Belgium, male / female production / vocal / instrumental trio (Singles: 30 weeks, Albums: 3 weeks)* pos/wks

9 Mar 02 ● **SOMETHING** *Positiva CDTIV 169* 4 15
24 Aug 02 ● **ALONE** *Positiva CDTIVS 176* 7 8
30 Nov 02 **PRAY** *Positiva CDTIVS 182* 17 7
7 Sep 02 **SOME THINGS** *Positiva 5419362* 30 3

Lisa LASHES *UK, female DJ / producer (Singles: 3 weeks)* pos/wks

8 Jul 00 **UNBELIEVABLE** *Tidy Trax TIDY 138CD* 63 1
25 Oct 03 **WHAT CAN YOU DO 4 ME?** *Tidy Trax TIDY 194CD* 52 2

James LAST 90 Top 500
The most charted big band formed in 1964 and fronted by German producer / arranger/ conductor and composer b. Hans Last 17 Apr 1929. Known for his non-stop dance party records he has sold in excess of 50 million albums around the globe (Singles: 4 weeks, Albums: 446 weeks) pos/wks

3 May 80 **THE SEDUCTION (LOVE THEME)** *Polydor PD 2071* [1] 48 4
15 Apr 67 ● **THIS IS JAMES LAST** *Polydor 104678* [1] 6 48
22 Jul 67 **HAMMOND A-GO-GO** *Polydor 249043* 27 10
26 Aug 67 **LOVE THIS IS MY SONG** *Polydor 583553* 32 2
26 Aug 67 **NON-STOP DANCING** *Polydor 236203* 35 1
22 Jun 68 **JAMES LAST GOES POP** *Polydor 249160* 32 3
8 Feb 69 **DANCING '68 VOLUME 1** *Polydor 249216* 40 1
31 May 69 **TRUMPET A-GO-GO** *Polydor 249239* 13 1
9 Aug 69 **NON-STOP DANCING '69** *Polydor 249294* 26 1
24 Jan 70 **NON-STOP DANCING '69/2** *Polydor 249354* 27 3
23 May 70 **NON-STOP EVERGREENS** *Polydor 249370* 26 1
11 Jul 70 **NON-STOP DANCING '70** *Polydor 237104* 44 1
11 Jul 70 **CLASSICS UP TO DATE** *Polydor 249371* 67 1

Date		Title	Label	Pos	Wks
24 Oct 70		VERY BEST OF JAMES LAST	*Polydor 2371054*	45	4
8 May 71		NON-STOP DANCING '71	*Polydor 2371111*	21	4
26 Jun 71		SUMMER HAPPENING	*Polydor 2371133*	38	1
18 Sep 71		BEACH PARTY 2	*Polydor 2371211*	47	1
2 Oct 71		YESTERDAY'S MEMORIES	*Contour 2870117*	17	14
16 Oct 71		NON-STOP DANCING 12	*Polydor 2371141*	30	3
19 Feb 72		NON-STOP DANCING 13	*Polydor 2371189*	32	2
4 Mar 72		POLKA PARTY	*Polydor 2371190*	22	3
29 Apr 72		JAMES LAST IN CONCERT	*Polydor 2371191*	13	6
24 Jun 72		VOODOO PARTY	*Polydor 2371235*	45	1
16 Sep 72		CLASSICS UP TO DATE VOLUME 2	*Polydor 184061*	49	1
30 Sep 72		LOVE MUST BE THE REASON	*Polydor 2371281*	32	2
27 Jan 73		THE MUSIC OF JAMES LAST	*Polydor 2683010*	19	12
24 Feb 73		NON-STOP DANCING VOLUME 14	*Polydor 2371319*	27	3
24 Feb 73		JAMES LAST IN RUSSIA	*Polydor 2371293*	12	9
28 Jul 73		OLE	*Polydor 2371384*	24	5
1 Sep 73		NON-STOP DANCING VOLUME 15	*Polydor 2371376*	34	2
20 Apr 74		NON-STOP DANCING VOLUME 16	*Polydor 2371444*	43	2
29 Jun 74		IN CONCERT VOLUME 2	*Polydor 2371320*	49	1
23 Nov 74		GOLDEN MEMORIES	*Polydor 2371472*	39	2
26 Jul 75	●	TEN YEARS NON-STOP JUBILEE	*Polydor 2660111*	5	16
2 Aug 75		VIOLINS IN LOVE	*K-Tel I*	60	1
22 Nov 75	●	MAKE THE PARTY LAST	*Polydor 2371612*	3	19
8 May 76		CLASSICS UP TO DATE VOLUME 3	*Polydor 2371538*	54	1
6 May 78		EAST TO WEST	*Polydor 2630092*	49	4
14 Apr 79	●	LAST THE WHOLE NIGHT LONG	*Polydor PTD 001*	2	45
23 Aug 80		THE BEST FROM 150 GOLD RECORDS	*Polydor 2681 211*	56	3
1 Nov 80		CLASSICS FOR DREAMING	*Polydor POLTV 11*	12	18
14 Feb 81		ROSES FROM THE SOUTH	*Polydor 2372 051*	41	5
21 Nov 81		HANSIMANIA	*Polydor POLTV 14*	18	13
28 Nov 81		LAST FOREVER	*Polydor 2630 135*	88	2
5 Mar 83		BLUEBIRD	*Polydor POLD 5072*	57	3
30 Apr 83		NON-STOP DANCING '83 – PARTY POWER	*Polydor POLD 5094*	56	2
30 Apr 83		THE BEST OF MY GOLD RECORDS	*Polydor PODV 7*	42	5
3 Dec 83		THE GREATEST SONGS OF THE BEATLES	*Polydor POLD 5119*	52	8
24 Mar 84		THE ROSE OF TRALEE AND OTHER IRISH FAVOURITES	*Polydor POLD 5131*	21	11
13 Oct 84		PARADISE	*Polydor POLD 5163*	74	2
8 Dec 84		JAMES LAST IN SCOTLAND	*Polydor POLD 5166*	68	9
14 Sep 85		LEAVE THE BEST TO LAST	*Polydor PROLP 7*	11	27
18 Apr 87		BY REQUEST	*Polydor POLH 34*	22	11
26 Nov 88		DANCE DANCE DANCE	*Polydor JLTV 1*	38	8
14 Apr 90		CLASSICS BY MOONLIGHT	*Polydor 8432181*	12	12
15 Jun 91	●	POP SYMPHONIES	*Polydor 8494291*	10	11
9 Nov 91		TOGETHER AT LAST	*Delphine/Polydor 5115251* [2]	14	15
12 Sep 92		VIVA ESPAÑA	*PolyGram TV 5172202*	23	5
20 Nov 93		JAMES LAST PLAYS ANDREW LLOYD WEBBER	*Polydor 5199102*	12	10
19 Nov 94		IN HARMONY	*Polydor 5238242* [2]	28	7
18 Nov 95		THE VERY BEST OF JAMES LAST & HIS ORCHESTRA	*Polydor 5295562*	36	7
28 Mar 98		POP SYMPHONIES 2	*Polydor 5396242* [3]	32	3
24 Apr 99		COUNTRY ROADS	*Polydor/Universal TV 5474022*	18	5
3 Nov 01		JAMES LAST AND HIS ORCHESTRA PLAYS ABBA	*Polydor 5891982* [3]	29	4
6 Sep 03		THE CLASSICAL COLLECTION	*UCJ 9810457*	44	3

[1] James Last Band [1] James Last Band [2] Richard Clayderman and James Last [3] James Last and his Orchestra

LAST RHYTHM

Italy, male instrumental / production group (Singles: 1 week) pos/wks

Date		Title	Label	Pos	Wks
14 Sep 96		LAST RHYTHM	*Stress CDSTR 76*	62	1

LATE SHOW

UK, male vocal / instrumental group (Singles: 6 weeks) pos/wks

Date		Title	Label	Pos	Wks
3 Mar 79		BRISTOL STOMP	*Decca F 13822*	40	6

LATIN QUARTER *UK, male / female vocal / instrumental group (Singles: 10 weeks, Albums: 3 weeks)*

pos/wks

Date		Title	Label	Pos	Wks
18 Jan 86		RADIO AFRICA	*Rockin' Horse RH 102*	19	9
18 Apr 87		NOMZAMO (ONE PEOPLE ONE CAUSE)	*Rockin' Horse RH 113*	73	1
1 Mar 86		MODERN TIMES	*Rockin' Horse RHLP 1*	91	2
6 Jun 87		MICK AND CAROLINE	*Rockin' Horse 208 142*	96	1

LATIN RHYTHM – *See Tito PUENTE Jr and The LATIN RHYTHM featuring Tito PUENTE, INDIA and Cali ALEMAN*

LATIN THING *Canada / Spain, male / female vocal / instrumental group (Singles: 1 week)*

pos/wks

Date		Title	Label	Pos	Wks
13 Jul 96		LATIN THING	*Faze 2 CDFAZE 33*	41	1

Gino LATINO *Italy, male producer – Lorenzo Cherubini (Singles: 7 weeks)*

pos/wks

Date		Title	Label	Pos	Wks
20 Jan 90		WELCOME	*ffrr F 126*	17	7

LATINO RAVE – *See VARIOUS ARTISTS (MONTAGES)*

LATOUR *US, male vocalist / producer – William LaTour (Singles: 7 weeks)*

pos/wks

Date		Title	Label	Pos	Wks
8 Jun 91		PEOPLE ARE STILL HAVING SEX	*Polydor PO 147*	15	7

Stacy LATTISAW *US, female vocalist (Singles: 14 weeks)*

pos/wks

Date		Title	Label	Pos	Wks
14 Jun 80	●	JUMP TO THE BEAT	*Atlantic / Cotillion K 11496*	3	11
30 Aug 80		DYNAMITE	*Atlantic K 11554*	51	3

Dave LAUDAT – *See HUSTLERS CONVENTION featuring Dave LAUDAT and Ondrea DUVERNEY*

LAUNCHERS – *See Ezz RECO and The LAUNCHERS with Boysie GRANT*

Cyndi LAUPER (341 Top 500) *Flamboyant and versatile singer / songwriter, b. 20 Jun 1953, New York, US. Her debut album, 'She's So Unusual' (1983), spawned four Top 5 US singles, and she won a Grammy for Best New Artist of 1984 (easily outpacing her major female rival, Madonna) (Singles: 103 weeks, Albums: 92 weeks)*

pos/wks

Date		Title	Label	Pos	Wks
14 Jan 84	●	GIRLS JUST WANT TO HAVE FUN	*Portrait A 3943*	2	12
24 Mar 84	●	TIME AFTER TIME (re)	*Portrait A 4290* ▲	3	17
1 Sep 84		SHE BOP	*Portrait A 4620*	46	5
17 Nov 84		ALL THROUGH THE NIGHT	*Portrait A 4849*	64	2
20 Sep 86		TRUE COLOURS	*Portrait 650026 7* ▲	12	11
27 Dec 86		CHANGE OF HEART (re)	*Portrait CYNDI 1*	67	2
28 Mar 87		WHAT'S GOING ON	*Portrait CYN 1*	57	3
20 May 89	●	I DROVE ALL NIGHT	*Epic CYN 4*	7	12
5 Aug 89		MY FIRST NIGHT WITHOUT YOU	*Epic CYN 5*	53	4
30 Dec 89		HEADING WEST	*Epic CYN 6*	68	1
6 Jun 92		THE WORLD IS STONE	*Epic 6579707*	15	7
13 Nov 93		THAT'S WHAT I THINK	*Epic 6598782*	31	4
8 Jan 94		WHO LET IN THE RAIN	*Epic 6590392*	32	4
17 Sep 94	●	HEY NOW (GIRLS JUST WANT TO HAVE FUN)	*Epic 6608072*	4	13
11 Feb 95		I'M GONNA BE STRONG	*Epic 6611962*	37	2
26 Aug 95		COME ON HOME	*Epic 6614255*	39	2
1 Feb 97		YOU DON'T KNOW	*Epic 6641845*	27	2
18 Feb 84		SHE'S SO UNUSUAL	*Portrait PRT 25792*	16	32
11 Oct 86		TRUE COLORS	*Portrait PRT 26948*	25	12
1 Jul 89	●	A NIGHT TO REMEMBER	*Epic 462499 1*	9	12
27 Nov 93		HAT FULL OF STARS	*Epic 4730542*	56	1
3 Sep 94	●	TWELVE DEADLY CYNS ... AND THEN SOME	*Epic 4773632*	2	34
22 Feb 97		SISTERS OF AVALON	*Epic 4853702*	59	1

'Hey Now (Girls Just Want to Have Fun)' is a re-recording of her first hit

LAUREL and HARDY *UK / US, male comedians / actors / vocal duo – Stan Laurel d. 23 Feb 1965, Oliver Hardy d. 7 Aug 1957, with US, male vocal group (Singles: 10 weeks, Albums: 4 weeks)*

pos/wks

Date		Title	Label	Pos	Wks
22 Nov 75	●	THE TRAIL OF THE LONESOME PINE	*United Artists UP 36026* [1]	2	10
6 Dec 75		THE GOLDEN AGE OF HOLLYWOOD COMEDY	*United Artists UAG 29676*	55	4

[1] Laurel and Hardy with the Avalon Boys featuring Chill Wills

LAUREL and HARDY
UK, male vocal / instrumental reggae duo (Singles: 2 weeks pos/wks

2 Apr 83 **CLUNK CLINK** *CBS A 3213* 65 2

LAURNEA
US, female vocalist – Laurnea Wilkinson (Singles: 2 weeks) pos/wks

12 Jul 97 **DAYS OF YOUTH** *Epic 6646932* 36 2

Lauren LAVERNE – *See KENICKIE; MINT ROYALE*

Avril LAVIGNE
Canada, female vocalist (Singles: 36 weeks, Albums: 55 weeks) pos/wks

7 Sep 02 **COMPLICATED (import) (re)** *RCA 74321955782* 64 2
5 Oct 02 ● **COMPLICATED** *Arista 74321965962* 3 9
28 Dec 02 ● **SK8ER BOI** *Arista 74321979782* 8 9
12 Apr 03 ● **I'M WITH YOU** *Arista 82876506712* 7 10
19 Jul 03 **LOSING GRIP (re)** *Arista 82876534542* 22 6
14 Sep 02 ★ **LET GO** *Arista 74321949312* 1 55

LAW
UK / US, male vocal / instrumental duo (Albums: 1 week) pos/wks

6 Apr 91 **THE LAW** *Atlantic 7567821951* 61 1

Joanna LAW *UK, female vocalist (Singles: 8 weeks)* pos/wks

7 Jul 90 **FIRST TIME EVER** *Citybeat CBE 752* 67 3
14 Sep 96 **THE GIFT** *Deconstruction 74321401912* [1] 15 5

[1] Way Out West featuring Miss Joanna Law

Law's contribution to 'The Gift' is a sample from 'First Time Ever'

Lisa LAW – *See CM2 featuring Lisa LAW*

Steve LAWLER *UK, male DJ / producer (Singles: 1 week)* pos/wks

11 Nov 00 **RISE 'IN** *Bedrock BEDRCDS 008* 50 1

Belle LAWRENCE *UK, female vocalist (Singles: 1 week)* pos/wks

30 Mar 02 **EVERGREEN** *Euphoric CDUPH 024* 73 1

Billy LAWRENCE – *See RAMPAGE featuring Billy LAWRENCE*

Joey LAWRENCE
US, male vocalist (Singles: 15 weeks, Albums: 3 weeks) pos/wks

26 Jun 93 **NOTHIN' MY LOVE CAN'T FIX** *EMI CDEM 271* 13 7
28 Aug 93 **I CAN'T HELP MYSELF** *EMI CDEM 277* 27 4
30 Oct 93 **STAY FOREVER** *EMI CDEM 289* 41 3
19 Sep 98 **NEVER GONNA CHANGE MY MIND** *Curb CUBC 34* 49 1
31 Jul 93 **JOEY LAWRENCE** *EMI CDEMC 3657* 39 3

Lee LAWRENCE
UK, male vocalist – Leon Siroto d. Feb 1961 (Singles: 10 weeks) pos/wks

20 Nov 53 ● **CRYING IN THE CHAPEL (re)** *Decca F 10177* 7 6
2 Dec 55 **SUDDENLY THERE'S A VALLEY (re)** *Columbia DB 3681* 14 4

With Ray Martin and his Orchestra

Sophie LAWRENCE
UK, female vocalist (Singles: 7 weeks) pos/wks

3 Aug 91 **LOVE'S UNKIND** *IQ ZB 44821* 21 7

Steve LAWRENCE
US, male vocalist – Sidney Leibowitz (Singles: 27 weeks) pos/wks

21 Apr 60 ● **FOOTSTEPS** *HMV POP 726* 4 13
18 Aug 60 **GIRLS, GIRLS, GIRLS** *London HLT 9166* 49 1
22 Aug 63 ● **I WANT TO STAY HERE** *CBS AAG 163* [1] 3 13

[1] Steve and Eydie

See also Eydie GORME

Syd LAWRENCE
UK, orchestra – leader d. 5 May 1998 (Albums: 9 weeks) pos/wks

8 Aug 70 **MORE MILLER AND OTHER BIG BAND MAGIC** *Philips 6642 001* 14 4
25 Dec 71 **MUSIC OF GLENN MILLER IN SUPER STEREO** *Philips 6641017* 43 2
25 Dec 71 **SYD LAWRENCE WITH THE GLENN MILLER SOUND** *Fontana SFL 13178* 31 2
26 Feb 72 **SOMETHING OLD SOMETHING NEW** *Philips 6308 090* 34 1

Ronnie LAWS
US, male vocalist / instrumentalist – saxophone (Albums: 1 week) pos/wks

17 Oct 81 **SOLID GROUND** *Liberty LBG 30336* 100 1

LAYO & BUSHWACKA! *UK, male DJ / production duo – Layo Paskin and Matthew Benjamin (Singles: 12 weeks, Albums: 1 week)* pos/wks

22 Jun 02 **LOVE STORY** *XL Recordings XLS 144CD* 30 2
25 Jan 03 ● **LOVE STORY (VS FINALLY)** *XL Recordings XLS 154CD* 8 7
16 Aug 03 **IT'S UP TO YOU (SHINING THROUGH)** *XL Recordings XLS 163CD* 25 3
13 Jul 02 **NIGHT WORKS** *XL Recordings XLCD 154* 61 1

The 2003 entry of 'Love Story' is so called because it combines the original track with the vocal from 'Finally' by Kings of Tomorrow featuring Julie McKnight

Lindy LAYTON *UK, female vocalist (Singles: 28 weeks)* pos/wks

10 Feb 90 ★ **DUB BE GOOD TO ME** *Go. Beat GOD 39* [1] 1 13
11 Aug 90 **SILLY GAMES** *Arista 113452* [2] 22 7
26 Jan 91 **ECHO MY HEART** *Arista 113845* 42 2
31 Aug 91 **WITHOUT YOU (ONE AND ONE)** *Arista 114636* 71 2
24 Apr 93 **WE GOT THE LOVE** *PWL International PWCD 250* 38 3
30 Oct 93 **SHOW ME** *PWL International PWCD 275* 47 1

[1] Beats International featuring Lindy Layton [2] Lindy Layton featuring Janet Kay

Peter LAZONBY *UK, male DJ / producer (Singles: 1 week)* pos/wks

10 Jun 00 **SACRED CYCLES** *Hooj Choons HOOJ 93CD* 49 1

Doug LAZY
US, male rapper – Gene Finley (Singles: 9 weeks, Albums: 1 week) pos/wks

15 Jul 89 **LET IT ROLL** *Atlantic A 8866* [1] 27 5
4 Nov 89 **LET THE RHYTHM PUMP** *Atlantic A 8784* 45 3
26 May 90 **LET THE RHYTHM PUMP (re-mix)** *East West A 7919* 63 1
10 Mar 90 **DOUG LAZY GETTIN' CRAZY** *Atlantic 7567820661* 65 1

[1] Raze presents Doug Lazy

Keith LE BLANC – *See Malcolm X*

LE CLICK *Sweden / US, male / female vocal duo – Kayo Shekoni and Robert Haynes (Singles: 2 weeks)* pos/wks

30 Aug 97 **CALL ME** *Logic 74321509672* 38 2

Kele LE ROC *UK, female vocalist – Kelly Biggs (Singles: 17 weeks, Albums: 2 weeks)* pos/wks

31 Oct 98 ● **LITTLE BIT OF LOVIN'** *1st Avenue / Wild Card / Polydor 5672812* 8 7
27 Mar 99 ● **MY LOVE** *1st Avenue / Wild Card / Polydor 5636112* 8 7
30 Sep 00 **THINKING OF YOU** *Telstar CDSTAS 3136* [1] 70 1
7 Jun 03 **FEELIN' U** *London FCD 409* [2] 34 2
10 Apr 99 **EVERYBODY'S SOMEBODY** *Wild Card 5596662* 44 2

[1] Curtis Lynch Jr featuring Kele Le Roc and Red Rat [2] Shy FX and T-Power featuring Kele Le Roc

LEAGUE UNLIMITED ORCHESTRA – *See HUMAN LEAGUE*

LEAH – *See LANGE*

Vicky LEANDROS *Greece, female vocalist (Singles: 29 weeks)* pos/wks

8 Apr 72 ● **COME WHAT MAY** *Philips 6000 049* 2 16

Date	Title / Label	pos	wks
23 Dec 72	**THE LOVE IN YOUR EYES (2re)** *Philips 6000 081*	40	8
7 Jul 73	**WHEN BOUZOUKIS PLAYED (re)** *Philips 6000 111*	44	5

Denis LEARY *US, male comedian / vocalist (Singles: 2 weeks)*

Date	Title / Label	pos	wks
13 Jan 96	**ASSHOLE** *A&M 5813352*	58	2

LEAVES *Iceland, male vocal / instrumental group (Singles: 1 week, Albums: 1 week)*

Date	Title / Label	pos	wks
18 May 02	**RACE** *B Unique BUN 020CDS*	66	1
31 Aug 02	BREATHE *B Unique 0927487392*	71	1

LED ZEPPELIN (74 Top 500) *Hard rock's most successful album act: Robert Plant (v), Jimmy Page (g), John Paul Jones (b/k), John Bonham (d) d. 1980. Innovative, pioneering quartet has sold more than 100 million albums in the US alone, where it scored seven No.1s from 1969-2003 (Singles: 2 weeks, Albums: 495 weeks)*

Date	Title / Label	pos	wks
13 Sep 97	**WHOLE LOTTA LOVE** *Atlantic AT00 13CD*	21	2
12 Apr 69 ●	LED ZEPPELIN *Atlantic 588171*	6	71
8 Nov 69 ★	LED ZEPPELIN II *Atlantic 588198* ▲	1	136
7 Nov 70 ★	LED ZEPPELIN 3 *Atlantic 2401002* ■ ▲	1	40
27 Nov 71 ★	FOUR SYMBOLS (LED ZEPPELIN 4) *Atlantic K 2401012*	1	69
14 Apr 73 ★	HOUSES OF THE HOLY *Atlantic K 50014* ■ ▲	1	13
15 Mar 75 ★	PHYSICAL GRAFFITI *Swan Song SSK 89400* ■ ▲	1	27
24 Apr 76 ★	PRESENCE *Swan Song SSK 59402* ■ ▲	1	14
6 Nov 76 ★	THE SONG REMAINS THE SAME *Swan Song SSK 89402*	1	15
8 Sep 79 ★	IN THROUGH THE OUT DOOR *Swan Song SSK 59410* ■ ▲	1	16
4 Dec 82 ●	CODA *Swan Song A 0051*	4	7
27 Oct 90 ●	REMASTERS *Atlantic ZEP 1*	10	45
10 Nov 90	LED ZEPPELIN *Atlantic 7567821441*	48	2
9 Oct 93	LED ZEPPELIN BOXED SET II *Atlantic 7567824772*	56	1
29 Nov 97	BBC SESSIONS *Atlantic 7567830612*	23	7
1 Apr 00	LATTER DAYS – THE BEST OF LED ZEPPELIN VOLUME TWO *Atlantic 7567832782*	40	1
1 Apr 00	EARLY DAYS – THE BEST OF LED ZEPPELIN VOLUME ONE *Atlantic 7567832682*	55	1
8 Mar 03	VERY BEST OF – EARLY DAYS & LATTER DAYS *Atlantic 7567836195*	11	23
7 Jun 03 ●	HOW THE WEST WAS WON *Atlantic 7567835872* ▲	5	7

Led Zeppelin 2' changed label / number to Atlantic K 40037 and 'Four Symbols' changed to Atlantic K 50008 during their runs. The fourth Led Zeppelin album appeared in the chart under various guises: 'The Fourth Led Zeppelin Album' 'Runes', 'The New Led Zeppelin Album', 'Led Zeppelin 4' and 'Four Symbols'. The two albums titled Led Zeppelin are different. (The 1990 entry was a boxed set of old and previously unreleased material.)

See also Robert PLANT; COVERDALE / PAGE

Angel LEE *UK, female vocalist – Angelique Beckford (Singles: 1 week)*

Date	Title / Label	pos	wks
3 Jun 00	**WHAT'S YOUR NAME?** *WEA WEA 258CD*	39	1

Ann LEE *UK, female vocalist – Annerley Gordon (Singles: 21 weeks)*

Date	Title / Label	pos	wks
11 Sep 99	**2 TIMES (import)** *ZYX ZYX 90188*	57	2
16 Oct 99 ●	**2 TIMES** *Systematic SYSCD 31*	2	16
4 Mar 00	**VOICES** *Systematic SYSCD 32*	27	3

Brenda LEE (219 Top 500) *Biggest-selling teenage female vocalist of the early rock years; b. Brenda Tarpley, 11 Dec 1944, Georgia, US. 'Little Miss Dynamite', who first recorded aged 11, had back-to-back UK / US hits in the early 1960s. She was inducted into the Country Music Hall of Fame in 1997 (Singles: 210 weeks, Albums: 64 weeks)*

Date	Title / Label	pos	wks
17 Mar 60 ●	**SWEET NUTHIN'S (re)** *Brunswick 05819*	4	19
30 Jun 60	**I'M SORRY** *Brunswick 05833* ▲	12	16
20 Oct 60	**I WANT TO BE WANTED** *Brunswick 05839* ▲	31	6
19 Jan 61	**LET'S JUMP THE BROOMSTICK** *Brunswick 05823*	12	15
6 Apr 61	**EMOTIONS** *Brunswick 05847*	45	1
20 Jul 61	**DUM DUM** *Brunswick 05854*	22	8
16 Nov 61	**FOOL NUMBER ONE** *Brunswick 05860*	38	3
8 Feb 62	**BREAK IT TO ME GENTLY** *Brunswick 05864*	46	2
5 Apr 62 ●	**SPEAK TO ME PRETTY** *Brunswick 05867*	3	12
21 Jun 62 ●	**HERE COMES THAT FEELING** *Brunswick 05871*	5	12
13 Sep 62	**IT STARTED ALL OVER AGAIN** *Brunswick 05876*	15	11
29 Nov 62 ●	**ROCKIN' AROUND THE CHRISTMAS TREE** *Brunswick 05880*	6	7
17 Jan 63 ●	**ALL ALONE AM I** *Brunswick 05882*	7	17
28 Mar 63 ●	**LOSING YOU** *Brunswick 05886*	10	16
18 Jul 63	**I WONDER** *Brunswick 05891*	14	9
31 Oct 63	**SWEET IMPOSSIBLE YOU** *Brunswick 05896*	28	6
9 Jan 64 ●	**AS USUAL** *Brunswick 05899*	5	15
9 Apr 64	**THINK** *Brunswick 05903*	26	8
10 Sep 64	**IS IT TRUE** *Brunswick 05915*	17	8
10 Dec 64	**CHRISTMAS WILL BE JUST ANOTHER LONELY DAY** *Brunswick 05921*	25	5
4 Feb 65	**THANKS A LOT** *Brunswick 05927*	41	2
29 Jul 65	**TOO MANY RIVERS** *Brunswick 05936*	22	12
24 Nov 62	ALL THE WAY *Brunswick LAT 8383*	20	2
16 Feb 63	BRENDA – THAT'S ALL *Brunswick LAT 8516*	13	9
13 Apr 63 ●	ALL ALONE AM I *Brunswick LAT 8530*	8	20
16 Jul 66	BYE BYE BLUES *Brunswick LAT 8649*	21	2
1 Nov 80	LITTLE MISS DYNAMITE *Warwick WW 5083*	15	11
7 Jan 84	25TH ANNIVERSARY *MCA MCLD 609*	65	4
30 Mar 85	THE VERY BEST OF BRENDA LEE *MCA LETV 1*	16	9
15 Oct 94	THE VERY BEST OF BRENDA LEE ... WITH LOVE *Telstar TCD 2738*	20	7

Byron LEE – *See Boris GARDINER*

Curtis LEE *US, male vocalist (Singles: 2 weeks)*

Date	Title / Label	pos	wks
31 Aug 61	**PRETTY LITTLE ANGEL EYES (re)** *London HLX 9397*	47	2

Dave LEE – *See HED BOYS; Li KWAN; RAVEN MAIZE; Joey NEGRO; Z FACTOR; JAKATTA; AKABU featuring Linda CLIFFORD; IL PADRINOS featuring Jocelyn BROWN*

Dee C LEE *UK, female vocalist – Diane Sealey (Singles: 20 weeks)*

Date	Title / Label	pos	wks
9 Nov 85 ●	**SEE THE DAY** *CBS A 6570*	3	12
8 Mar 86	**COME HELL OR WATERS HIGH** *CBS A 6869*	46	5
13 Nov 93	**NO TIME TO PLAY** *Cooltempo CDCOOL 282* [1]	25	3

[1] Guru featuring Dee C Lee

See also STYLE COUNCIL

Garry LEE and SHOWDOWN *Canada, male vocal / instrumental group (Singles: 3 weeks)*

Date	Title / Label	pos	wks
31 Jul 93	**THE RODEO SONG** *Party Dish VCD 101*	44	3

Jackie LEE *UK, female vocalist – Jackie Hopkins (Singles: 31 weeks)*

Date	Title / Label	pos	wks
10 Apr 68 ●	**WHITE HORSES** *Philips BF 1647* [1]	10	14
2 Jan 71	**RUPERT** *Pye 7N 45003*	14	17

[1] Jacky

Jacknife LEE – *See RUN-DMC*

Leapy LEE *UK, male vocalist – Lee Graham (Singles: 28 weeks)*

Date	Title / Label	pos	wks
21 Aug 68 ●	**LITTLE ARROWS** *MCA MU 1028*	2	21
20 Dec 69	**GOOD MORNING (re)** *MCA MK 5021*	29	7

Murphy LEE – *See NELLY*

Peggy LEE *US, female vocalist – Norma Jean Egstrom d. 22 Jan 2002 (Singles: 29 weeks, Albums: 23 weeks)*

Date	Title / Label	pos	wks
24 May 57 ●	**MR WONDERFUL** *Brunswick 05671*	5	13
15 Aug 58 ●	**FEVER** *Capitol CL 14902*	5	11
23 Mar 61	**TILL THERE WAS YOU (re)** *Capitol CL 15184*	30	4
22 Aug 92	**FEVER (re-issue)** *Capitol PEG 1*	75	1
4 Jun 60 ●	LATIN A LA LEE *Capitol T 1290*	8	15
11 Jun 60	BEAUTY AND THE BEAT *Capitol T 1219* [1]	16	6
20 May 61	BEST OF PEGGY LEE VOLUME 2 *Brunswick LAT 8355*	18	1
21 Oct 61	BLACK COFFEE *Ace of Hearts AH 5*	20	1

[1] Peggy Lee and George Shearing

Toney LEE *US, male vocalist (Singles: 4 weeks)* pos/wks

Date		Title / Label	pos	wks
29 Jan 83		**REACH UP** *TMT TMT 2*	64	4

Tracey LEE *US, male vocalist (Singles: 1 week)* pos/wks

Date		Title / Label	pos	wks
19 Jul 97		**THE THEME** *Universal UND 56133*	51	1

LEE-CABRERA *US, male production duo (Singles: 9 weeks)* pos/wks

Date		Title / Label	pos	wks
12 Apr 03		**SHAKE IT (NO TE MUEVAS TANTO)** *Credence 12CDRED 035*	58	1
6 Sep 03		**SHAKE IT (MOVE A LITTLE CLOSER)** *Credence CDCRED 039* [1]	16	6
15 Nov 03		**SPECIAL 2003** *Credence CDCRED 040*	45	2

[1] Lee-Cabrera featuring Alex Cartaña

LEEDS UNITED FC
UK, male football team vocalists (Singles: 13 weeks) pos/wks

Date		Title / Label	pos	wks
29 Apr 72	●	**LEEDS UNITED** *Chapter One SCH 168*	10	10
25 Apr 92		**LEEDS, LEEDS, LEEDS (re)** *Q Music LUFC 2*	54	3

Carol LEEMING – *See STAXX featuring Carol LEEMING*

Raymond LEFÈVRE
France, orchestra (Singles: 2 weeks, Albums: 9 weeks) pos/wks

Date		Title / Label	pos	wks
15 May 68		**SOUL COAXING** *Major Minor MM 559*	46	2
7 Oct 67	●	**RAYMOND LEFÈVRE** *Major Minor MMLP 4*	10	7
17 Feb 68		**RAYMOND LEFÈVRE VOLUME 2** *Major Minor SMLP 13*	37	2

LEFTFIELD *UK, male instrumental / production duo – Neil Barnes and Paul Daley (Singles: 23 weeks, Albums: 113 weeks)* pos/wks

Date		Title / Label	pos	wks
12 Dec 92		**SONG OF LIFE** *Hard Hands HAND 002T*	59	1
13 Nov 93		**OPEN UP** *Hard Hands HAND 009CD* [1]	13	5
25 Mar 95		**ORIGINAL** *Hard Hands HAND 18CD* [2]	18	3
5 Aug 95		**THE AFRO-LEFT EP** *Hard Hands HAND 23CD* [3]	22	3
20 Jan 96		**RELEASE THE PRESSURE** *Hard Hands HAND 29CD*	13	3
18 Sep 99	●	**AFRIKA SHOX** *Hard Hands HAND 057CD1* [4]	7	5
11 Dec 99		**DUSTED (re)** *Hard Hands HAND 058CD1* [5]	28	3
11 Feb 95	●	**LEFTISM** *Hard Hands HANDCD 2*	3	93
2 Oct 99	★	**RHYTHM AND STEALTH** *Higher Ground / Hard Hands HANDCD 4* ■	1	20

[1] Leftfield Lydon [2] Leftfield Halliday [3] Leftfield featuring Djum Djum
[4] Leftfield / Bambaataa [5] Leftfield / Roots Manuva

Tracks on The Afro-Left EP: Afro-Left / Afro Ride / Afro Central / Afro Sol

LEGEND B *Germany, male production duo (Singles: 1 week)* pos/wks

Date		Title / Label	pos	wks
22 Feb 97		**LOST IN LOVE** *Perfecto PERF 132CD*	45	1

Tom LEHRER *US, male comedian / vocalist (Albums: 26 weeks)* pos/wks

Date		Title / Label	pos	wks
8 Nov 58	●	**SONGS BY TOM LEHRER** *Decca LF 1311*	7	19
25 Jun 60	●	**AN EVENING WASTED WITH TOM LEHRER** *Decca LK 4332*	7	7

Jody LEI *South Africa, female vocalist (Singles: 2 weeks)* pos/wks

Date		Title / Label	pos	wks
22 Feb 03		**SHOWDOWN** *Independiente ISOM 66MS*	34	2

Denise LEIGH and Jane GILCHRIST
UK, female vocalists (Albums: 2 weeks) pos/wks

Date		Title / Label	pos	wks
8 Nov 03		**OPERATUNITY WINNERS** *EMI Classics 05575942*	60	2+

LEILANI
UK, female vocalist – Leilani Sen (Singles: 7 weeks) pos/wks

Date		Title / Label	pos	wks
6 Feb 99		**MADNESS THING** *ZTT ZTT 124CD*	19	4
12 Jun 99		**DO YOU WANT ME?** *ZTT ZTT 134CD*	40	2
3 Jun 00		**FLYING ELVIS** *ZTT ZTT 145CD*	73	1

Paul LEKAKIS *US, male vocalist (Singles: 4 weeks)* pos/wks

Date		Title / Label	pos	wks
30 May 87		**BOOM BOOM (LET'S GO BACK TO MY ROOM)** *Champion CHAMP 43*	60	4

LEMAR *UK, male vocalist – Lemar Obika (Singles: 16 weeks, Albums: 4 weeks)* pos/wks

Date		Title / Label	pos	wks
30 Aug 03	●	**DANCE (WITH U)** *Sony Music 6741325*	2	11
29 Nov 03	●	**50/50 / LULLABY** *Sony Music 6744182*	5	5+
6 Dec 03		**DEDICATED** *Sony Music 5137912*	17	4+

LEMON JELLY *UK, male production duo – Fred Deakin and Nick Franglan (Singles: 5 weeks, Albums: 6 weeks)* pos/wks

Date		Title / Label	pos	wks
19 Oct 02		**SPACE WALK** *Impotent Fury / XL Recordings IFXLS 150CD*	36	2
1 Feb 03		**NICE WEATHER FOR DUCKS** *Impotent Fury / XL Recordings IFXLS 156CD*	16	3
2 Nov 02		**LOST HORIZONS** *Impotent Fury / XL IFXLCD 160*	20	6

LEMON PIPERS
US, male vocal / instrumental group (Singles: 16 weeks) pos/wks

Date		Title / Label	pos	wks
7 Feb 68	●	**GREEN TAMBOURINE** *Pye International 7N 25444* ▲	7	11
1 May 68		**RICE IS NICE** *Pye International 7N 25454*	41	5

LEMON TREES
UK, male vocal / instrumental group (Singles: 9 weeks) pos/wks

Date		Title / Label	pos	wks
26 Sep 92		**LOVE IS IN YOUR EYES** *Oxygen GASP 1*	75	1
7 Nov 92		**THE WAY I FEEL** *Oxygen GASP 2*	62	2
13 Feb 93		**LET IT LOOSE** *Oxygen GASPD 3*	55	2
17 Apr 93		**CHILD OF LOVE** *Oxygen GASPD 4*	55	3
3 Jul 93		**I CAN'T FACE THE WORLD** *Oxygen GASPD 6*	52	1

LEMONESCENT *UK, female vocal group (Singles: 4 weeks)* pos/wks

Date		Title / Label	pos	wks
29 Jun 02		**BEAUTIFUL** *Supertone SUPTCD 1*	70	1
9 Nov 02		**SWING MY HIPS (SEX DANCE)** *Supertone SUPTCD 2*	48	1
5 Apr 03		**HELP ME MAMA** *Supertone SUPTCD 4*	36	1
21 Jun 03		**CINDERELLA** *Supertone SUPTCD 8*	31	1

LEMONHEADS *US / Australia, male vocal / instrumental group – lead vocal Evan Dando (Singles: 26 weeks, Albums: 32 weeks)* pos/wks

Date		Title / Label	pos	wks
17 Oct 92		**IT'S A SHAME ABOUT RAY** *Atlantic A 7423*	70	1
5 Dec 92		**MRS ROBINSON / BEIN' AROUND** *Atlantic A 7401*	19	9
6 Feb 93		**CONFETTI / MY DRUG BUDDY** *Atlantic A 7430CD*	44	2
10 Apr 93		**IT'S A SHAME ABOUT RAY (re-issue)** *Atlantic A 5764CD*	31	3
16 Oct 93		**INTO YOUR ARMS** *Atlantic A 7302CD*	14	4
27 Nov 93		**IT'S ABOUT TIME** *Atlantic A 7296CD*	57	2
14 May 94		**BIG GAY HEART** *Atlantic A 7259CD*	55	2
28 Sep 96		**IF I COULD TALK I'D TELL YOU** *Atlantic A 5561CD*	39	2
14 Dec 96		**IT'S ALL TRUE** *Atlantic A 5635CD*	61	1
1 Aug 92		**IT'S A SHAME ABOUT RAY** *Atlantic 7567824602*	33	16
23 Oct 93	●	**COME ON FEEL THE LEMONHEADS** *Atlantic 7567825372*	5	14
12 Oct 96		**CAR BUTTON CLOTH** *Atlantic 7567927262*	28	2

Group was male / female for first album and all singles up to and including 'It's a Shame About Ray (re-issue)' except A 7401

LEN *Canada, male / female DJ / vocal group (Singles: 15 weeks)* pos/wks

Date		Title / Label	pos	wks
18 Dec 99	●	**STEAL MY SUNSHINE** *Columbia 6685062*	8	13
10 Jun 00		**CRYPTIK SOULS CREW** *Columbia 6693832*	28	2

LENA – *See Lena FIAGBE*

John LENNON (67 Top 500)
One of the 20th century's greatest musical talents, b. 9 Oct 1940, Liverpool, d. 8 Dec 1980. World-famous singer / songwriter who, together with Paul McCartney, fronted The Beatles and penned their hits. Three of his singles topped the UK chart in the two months after his murder in New York. He was recently included in the BBC's Top 10 Great Britons of all time. Best-selling single: 'Imagine' 1,486,581 (Singles: 199 weeks, Albums: 337 weeks) pos/wks

Date		Title / Label	pos	wks
9 Jul 69	●	**GIVE PEACE A CHANCE (re)** *Apple 13* [1]	2	18
1 Nov 69		**COLD TURKEY** *Apple APPLES 1001* [1]	14	8
21 Feb 70	●	**INSTANT KARMA** *Apple APPLES 1003* [2]	5	9
20 Mar 71	●	**POWER TO THE PEOPLE** *Apple R 5892* [3]	7	9
9 Dec 72	●	**HAPPY XMAS (WAR IS OVER) (4re)** *Apple R 5970* [4]	2	26
24 Nov 73		**MIND GAMES** *Apple R 5994*	26	9

		pos	wks
19 Oct 74	**WHATEVER GETS YOU THRU' THE NIGHT** *Apple R 5998* [5] ▲	36	4
8 Feb 75	**#9 DREAM** *Apple R 6003*	23	8
3 May 75	**STAND BY ME** *Apple R 6005*	30	7
1 Nov 75 ★	**IMAGINE (re)** *Apple R 6009* ◆	1	24
8 Nov 80 ★	**(JUST LIKE) STARTING OVER** *Geffen K 79186* ▲	1	15
24 Jan 81 ★	**WOMAN** *Geffen K 79195*	1	11
21 Mar 81	**I SAW HER STANDING THERE** *DJM DJS 10965* [6]	40	4
4 Apr 81	**WATCHING THE WHEELS** *Geffen K 79207*	30	6
20 Nov 82	**LOVE** *Parlophone R 6059*	41	7
21 Jan 84 ●	**NOBODY TOLD ME** *Ono Music / Polydor POSP 700*	6	6
17 Mar 84	**BORROWED TIME** *Polydor POSP 701*	32	6
30 Nov 85	**JEALOUS GUY** *Parlophone R 6117*	65	2
10 Dec 88	**IMAGINE / JEALOUS GUY / HAPPY XMAS (WAR IS OVER) (re-issue)** *Parlophone R 6199*	45	5
25 Dec 99 ●	**IMAGINE (re) (re-issue)** *Parlophone CDR 6534*	3	13
20 Dec 03	**HAPPY XMAS (WAR IS OVER) (re-issue)** *Parlophone CDR 6627* [7]	33	2+
16 Jan 71 ●	**JOHN LENNON / PLASTIC ONO BAND** *Apple PCS 7124* [1]	8	11
30 Oct 71 ★	**IMAGINE** *Apple PAS 10004* [2] ■ ▲	1	101
14 Oct 72	**SOMETIME IN NEW YORK CITY** *Apple PCSP 716* [3]	11	6
8 Dec 73	**MIND GAMES** *Apple PCS 7165*	13	12
19 Oct 74 ●	**WALLS AND BRIDGES** *Apple PCTC 253* ▲	6	10
8 Mar 75 ●	**ROCK 'N' ROLL** *Apple PCS 7169*	6	28
8 Nov 75 ●	**SHAVED FISH** *Apple PCS 7173*	8	29
22 Nov 80 ★	**DOUBLE FANTASY** *Geffen K 99131* [4] ▲	1	36
20 Nov 82 ★	**THE JOHN LENNON COLLECTION** *Parlophone EMTV 37*	1	43
4 Feb 84 ●	**MILK AND HONEY** *Polydor POLH 5* [4]	3	13
8 Mar 86	**LIVE IN NEW YORK CITY** *Parlophone PCS 7031*	55	3
22 Oct 88	**IMAGINE (FILM SOUNDTRACK)** *Parlophone PCSP 722*	64	6
8 Nov 97 ●	**LENNON LEGEND – THE VERY BEST OF JOHN LENNON** *Parlophone 8219542*	4	37
14 Nov 98	**ANTHOLOGY** *Capitol 8306142*	62	1
26 Feb 00	**IMAGINE (re-issue)** *Parlophone 5248582*	51	1

[1] Plastic Ono Band [2] Lennon, Ono and the Plastic Ono Band [3] John Lennon / Plastic Ono Band [4] John and Yoko and the Plastic Ono Band with the Harlem Community Choir [5] John Lennon with the Plastic Ono Nuclear Band [6] Elton John Band featuring John Lennon and the Muscle Shoals Horns [7] John and Yoko and the Plastic Ono Band

'Give Peace a Chance' re-entry made No.33 in Jan 1981. 'Happy Xmas (War Is Over)' peaked at No.4 in Dec 1972, No.48 in Jan 1975, and No.2 in Dec 1980, and the re-entry made No.28 in Dec 1981 and peaked at No.56 in Dec 1982. 'Imagine' peaked at No.6 in 1975, and topped the chart on re-entry in Dec 1980

[1] John Lennon and the Plastic Ono Band [2] John Lennon and the Plastic Ono Band with the Flux Fiddlers [3] John and Yoko Lennon with the Plastic Ono Band and Elephant's Memor [4] John Lennon and Yoko Ono

'Imagine' changed its label credit to Parlophone PAS 10004 between its initial chart run and later runs. 'Imagine – Music from the Motion Picture' includes Beatle's tracks

See also BEATLES

Julian LENNON

UK, male vocalist (Singles: 47 weeks, Albums: 20 weeks)

		pos	wks
6 Oct 84 ●	**TOO LATE FOR GOODBYES** *Charisma JL 1*	6	11
15 Dec 84	**VALOTTE** *Charisma JL 2*	55	6
9 Mar 85	**SAY YOU'RE WRONG** *Charisma JL 3*	75	1
7 Dec 85	**BECAUSE** *EMI 5538*	40	7
11 Mar 89	**NOW YOU'RE IN HEAVEN** *Virgin VS 1154*	59	3
24 Aug 91 ●	**SALTWATER** *Virgin VS 1361*	6	13
30 Nov 91	**HELP YOURSELF** *Virgin VS 1379*	53	2
25 Apr 92	**GET A LIFE** *Virgin VS 1398*	56	3
23 May 98	**DAY AFTER DAY** *Music from Another JULIAN 4CD*	66	1
3 Nov 84	**VALOTTE** *Charisma JLLP 1*	20	15
5 Apr 86	**THE SECRET VALUE OF DAYDREAMING** *Charisma CAS 1171*	93	1
5 Oct 91	**HELP YOURSELF** *Virgin V 2668*	42	4

Annie LENNOX (308 Top 500)

Innovative, ground-breaking singer / songwriter who has remained consistently successful around the globe: b. 25 Dec, 1954, Aberdeen, Scotland. Former focal point of Tourists and Eurythmics has won more Brit awards than any other female performer and won an Oscar for best song in 2004 for 'Into the West' from The Lord of the Rings: The Return of the King (Singles: 68 weeks, Albums: 143 weeks)

		pos	wks
3 Dec 88	**PUT A LITTLE LOVE IN YOUR HEART** *A&M AM 484* [1]	28	8
28 Mar 92 ●	**WHY** *RCA PB 45317*	5	8
6 Jun 92	**PRECIOUS** *RCA 74321100257*	23	5
22 Aug 92 ●	**WALKING ON BROKEN GLASS** *RCA 74321107227*	8	8
31 Oct 92	**COLD** *RCA 74321116902*	26	4
13 Feb 93 ●	**LITTLE BIRD / LOVE SONG FOR A VAMPIRE** *RCA 74321133832*	3	12
18 Feb 95 ●	**NO MORE 'I LOVE YOU'S** *RCA 74321257162*	2	12
10 Jun 95	**A WHITER SHADE OF PALE** *RCA 74321284822*	16	6
30 Sep 95	**WAITING IN VAIN** *RCA 74321316132*	31	3
9 Dec 95	**SOMETHING SO RIGHT** *RCA 74321332392* [2]	44	2
18 Apr 92 ★	**DIVA** *RCA PD 75326* ■	1	80
18 Mar 95 ★	**MEDUSA** *RCA 74321257172* ■	1	49
21 Jun 03 ●	**BARE** *RCA 82876524052*	3	14

[1] Annie Lennox and Al Green [2] Annie Lennox featuring Paul Simon

See also EURYTHMICS; TOURISTS

Dino LENNY *Italy, male producer (Singles: 2 weeks)*

		pos	wks
4 May 02	**I FEEL STEREO** *Incentive CENT 40CDS*	60	1
10 May 03	**CHANGE THE WORLD** *Free 2 Air 0146685F2A* [1]	51	1

[1] Dino Lenny vs the Housemartins

Rula LENSKA – *See Julie COVINGTON, Rula LENSKA, Charlotte CORNWELL and Sue JONES-DAVIES*

Phillip LEO *UK, male vocalist (Singles: 3 weeks)*

		pos	wks
23 Jul 94	**SECOND CHANCE** *EMI CDEM 327*	57	2
25 Mar 95	**THINKING ABOUT YOUR LOVE** *EMI CDEM 358*	64	1

Deke LEONARD

UK, male vocalist / instrumentalist – guitar (Albums: 1 week)

		pos	wks
13 Apr 74	**KAMIKAZE** *United Artists UAG 29544*	50	1

See also MAN

Paul LEONI

UK, male instrumentalist – pan flute (Albums: 19 weeks)

		pos	wks
24 Sep 83	**FLIGHTS OF FANCY** *Nouveau Music NML 1002*	17	19

LES RYTHMES DIGITALES *UK, male DJ / producer – Jacques Lu Cont (Stuart Price) (Singles: 3 weeks, Albums: 1 week)*

		pos	wks
25 Apr 98	**MUSIC MAKES YOU LOSE CONTROL** *Wall of Sound WALLD 037*	69	1
7 Aug 99	**SOMETIMES** *Wall of Sound WALLD 054* [1]	56	1
30 Oct 99	**JACQUES YOUR BODY (MAKE ME SWEAT)** *Wall of Sound WALLD 060*	60	1
5 Jun 99	**DARKDANCER** *Wall Of Sound WALLCD 021*	53	1

[1] Les Rythmes Digitales featuring Nik Kershaw

LeSHAUN – *See LL COOL J*

LESS THAN JAKE *US, male vocal / instrumental group (Singles: 3 weeks, Albums: 2 weeks)*

		pos	wks
5 Aug 00	**ALL MY BEST FRIENDS ARE METALHEADS** *Golf CDSHOLE 027*	51	1
8 Sep 01	**GAINESVILLE ROCK CITY** *Golf CDSHOLE 48*	57	1
24 May 03	**SHE'S GONNA BREAK SOON** *Sire W 606CD*	39	1
31 May 03	**ANTHEM** *Sire 9362484852*	37	2

LESTER – *See Norman COOK*

Ketty LESTER

US, female vocalist – Revoyda Frierson (Singles: 16 weeks)

		pos	wks
19 Apr 62 ●	**LOVE LETTERS** *London HLN 9527*	4	12
19 Jul 62	**BUT NOT FOR ME** *London HLN 9574*	45	4

LET LOOSE *UK, male vocal / instrumental group (Singles: 62 weeks, Albums: 15 weeks)*

		pos	wks
24 Apr 93	**CRAZY FOR YOU** *Vertigo VERCD 74*	44	3

Date		Title / Label	Pos	Wks
9 Apr 94		**SEVENTEEN** *Mercury MERCD 400*	44	2
25 Jun 94	●	**CRAZY FOR YOU (re) (re-issue)** *Mercury MERCD 402*	2	24
22 Oct 94		**SEVENTEEN (re) (re-mix)** *Mercury MERCD 406*	11	9
28 Jan 95		**ONE NIGHT STAND** *Mercury MERCD 419*	12	6
29 Apr 95	●	**BEST IN ME** *Mercury MERCD 428*	8	5
4 Nov 95		**EVERYBODY SAY EVERYBODY DO (re)** *Mercury MERCD 446*	29	4
22 Jun 96	●	**MAKE IT WITH YOU** *Mercury MERCD 464*	7	6
7 Sep 96		**TAKE IT EASY** *Mercury MERCD 472*	25	2
16 Nov 96		**DARLING BE HOME SOON** *Mercury MERCD 475*	65	1
19 Nov 94		LET LOOSE *Mercury 5260182*	20	14
5 Oct 96		ROLLERCOASTER *Mercury 5329552*	42	1

Gerald LETHAN – *See WALL OF SOUND featuring Gerald LETHAN*

LETTERMEN *US, male vocal group (Singles: 3 weeks)* pos/wks

Date		Title / Label	Pos	Wks
23 Nov 61		**THE WAY YOU LOOK TONIGHT** *Capitol CL 15222*	36	3

LEVEL 42 (111 Top 500) *Critically acclaimed Isle of Wight / Hong Kong / London band: Mark King (v/b), Boon Gould (g), Mike Lindup (k/v), Phil Gould (d). Boasting a world-class bass player in King, they went from Brit-funk cult heroes to international stardom (Singles: 177 weeks, Albums: 228 weeks)* pos/wks

Date		Title / Label	Pos	Wks
30 Aug 80		**LOVE MEETING LOVE** *Polydor POSP 170*	61	4
18 Apr 81		**LOVE GAMES** *Polydor POSP 234*	38	6
8 Aug 81		**TURN IT ON** *Polydor POSP 286*	57	6
14 Nov 81		**STARCHILD** *Polydor POSP 343*	47	4
8 May 82		**ARE YOU HEARING (WHAT I HEAR)?** *Polydor POSP 396*	49	5
2 Oct 82		**WEAVE YOUR SPELL** *Polydor POSP 500*	43	4
15 Jan 83		**THE CHINESE WAY** *Polydor POSP 538*	24	8
16 Apr 83		**OUT OF SIGHT, OUT OF MIND** *Polydor POSP 570*	41	4
30 Jul 83	●	**THE SUN GOES DOWN (LIVING IT UP)** *Polydor POSP 622*	10	12
22 Oct 83		**MICRO KID** *Polydor POSP 643*	37	5
1 Sep 84		**HOT WATER** *Polydor POSP 697*	18	9
3 Nov 84		**THE CHANT HAS BEGUN** *Polydor POSP 710*	41	5
21 Sep 85	●	**SOMETHING ABOUT YOU** *Polydor POSP 759*	6	17
7 Dec 85		**LEAVING ME NOW** *Polydor POSP 776*	15	11
26 Apr 86	●	**LESSONS IN LOVE** *Polydor POSP 790*	3	13
14 Feb 87	●	**RUNNING IN THE FAMILY** *Polydor POSP 842*	6	10
25 Apr 87	●	**TO BE WITH YOU AGAIN** *Polydor POSP 855*	10	7
12 Sep 87	●	**IT'S OVER** *Polydor POSP 900*	10	8
12 Dec 87		**CHILDREN SAY** *Polydor POSP 911*	22	6
3 Sep 88		**HEAVEN IN MY HANDS** *Polydor PO 14*	12	5
29 Oct 88		**TAKE A LOOK** *Polydor PO 24*	32	4
21 Jan 89		**TRACIE** *Polydor PO 34*	25	5
28 Oct 89		**TAKE CARE OF YOURSELF** *Polydor PO 58*	39	3
17 Aug 91		**GUARANTEED** *RCA PB 44745*	17	4
19 Oct 91		**OVERTIME** *RCA PB 44997*	62	2
18 Apr 92		**MY FATHER'S SHOES** *RCA PB 45271*	55	1
26 Feb 94		**FOREVER NOW** *RCA 74321190272*	19	4
30 Apr 94		**ALL OVER YOU** *RCA 74321205662*	26	2
6 Aug 94		**LOVE IN A PEACEFUL WORLD** *RCA 74321220332*	31	3
29 Aug 81		LEVEL 42 *Polydor POLS 1036*	20	18
10 Apr 82		THE EARLY TAPES JULY-AUGUST 1980 *Polydor POLS 1064*	46	6
18 Sep 82		THE PURSUIT OF ACCIDENTS *Polydor POLD 5067*	17	16
3 Sep 83	●	STANDING IN THE LIGHT *Polydor POLD 5110*	9	13
13 Oct 84		TRUE COLOURS *Polydor POLH 10*	14	8
6 Jul 85		A PHYSICAL PRESENCE *Polydor POLH 23*	28	5
26 Oct 85	●	WORLD MACHINE *Polydor POLH 25*	3	72
28 Mar 87	●	RUNNING IN THE FAMILY *Polydor POLH 42*	2	54
1 Oct 88	●	STARING AT THE SUN *Polydor POLH 50*	2	11
18 Nov 89	●	LEVEL BEST *Polydor LEVTV 1*	5	15
14 Sep 91	●	GUARANTEED *RCA PL 75005*	3	5
26 Mar 94	●	FOREVER NOW *RCA 74321189962*	8	3
7 Nov 98		THE VERY BEST OF LEVEL 42 *Polydor 5593732*	41	2

See also Mark KING

LEVELLERS (499 Top 500)

Folk punk band with an anti-authoritarian reputation, formed Brighton 1988 and fronted by Mark Chadwick. Despite some negative music press, they have built a large and loyal following. Oddly, none of their 19 hit singles reached the Top 10 (Singles: 59 weeks, Albums: 81 weeks) pos/wks

Date		Title / Label	Pos	Wks
21 Sep 91		**ONE WAY** *China WOK 2008*	51	2
7 Dec 91		**FAR FROM HOME** *China WOK 2010*	71	1
23 May 92		**15 YEARS (EP)** *China WOKX 2020*	11	5
10 Jul 93		**BELARUSE** *China WOKCD 2034*	12	5
30 Oct 93		**THIS GARDEN** *China WOKCD 2039*	12	4
14 May 94		**JULIE (EP)** *China WOKCD 2042*	17	3
12 Aug 95		**HOPE ST** *China WOKCD 2059*	12	5
14 Oct 95		**FANTASY** *China WOKCD 2067*	16	3
23 Dec 95		**JUST THE ONE** *China WOKCD 2076* [1]	12	8
20 Jul 96		**EXODUS – LIVE** *China WOKCD 2082*	24	2
9 Aug 97		**WHAT A BEAUTIFUL DAY** *China WOKCD 2088*	13	5
18 Oct 97		**CELEBRATE** *China WOKCD 2089*	28	2
20 Dec 97		**DOG TRAIN** *China WOKCD 2090*	24	5
14 Mar 98		**TOO REAL** *China WOKCD 2091*	46	1
24 Oct 98		**BOZOS** *China WOKCD 2096*	44	2
6 Feb 99		**ONE WAY (re-recording)** *China WOKCD 2102*	33	2
9 Sep 00		**HAPPY BIRTHDAY REVOLUTION** *China EW218CD*	57	1
21 Sep 02		**COME ON** *Eagle / Hag EHAGXS 001*	44	1
18 Jan 03		**WILD AS ANGELS EP** *Eagle / Hag EHAGXS 003*	34	2
19 Oct 91		LEVELLING THE LAND *China WOL 1022*	14	30
4 Sep 93	●	LEVELLERS *China WOLCD 1034*	2	14
9 Sep 95	★	ZEITGEIST *China WOLCD 1064*	1	14
31 Aug 96		BEST LIVE – HEADLIGHTS WHITE LINES BLACK TAR RIVERS *China WOLCDX 1074*	13	4
6 Sep 97	●	MOUTH TO MOUTH *China WOLCD 1084*	5	6
7 Nov 98		ONE WAY OF LIFE – BEST OF THE LEVELLERS *China / Jive 521732*	15	11
16 Sep 00		HELLO PIG *China 8573843392*	28	2

[1] Levellers, special guest Joe Strummer

Tracks on 15 Years (EP): 15 Years / Dance Before the Storm / The River Flow (Live) / Plastic Jeezus. Tracks on Julie (EP): Julie / English Civil War / Lowlands of Holland / 100 Years of Solitude

LEVERT

US, male vocal group (Singles: 10 weeks, Albums: 1 week) pos/wks

Date		Title / Label	Pos	Wks
22 Aug 87	●	**CASANOVA** *Atlantic A 9217*	9	10
29 Aug 87		THE BIG THROWDOWN *Atlantic 7817731*	86	1

LEVERT SWEAT GILL *US, male vocal group (Singles: 7 weeks)* pos/wks

Date		Title / Label	Pos	Wks
14 Mar 98		**MY BODY** *East West E 3857CD*	21	3
6 Jun 98		**CURIOUS** *East West E 3842CD*	23	2
12 Sep 98		**DOOR #1** *East West E 3817CD*	45	2

See also Keith SWEAT; Johnny GILL

Hank LEVINE *US, orchestra (Singles: 4 weeks)* pos/wks

Date		Title / Label	Pos	Wks
21 Dec 61		**IMAGE** *HMV POP 947*	45	4

LEVITATION

UK, male vocal / instrumental group (Albums: 1 week) pos/wks

Date		Title / Label	Pos	Wks
16 May 92		NEED FOR NOT *Rough Trade R 2862*	45	1

LEVITICUS *UK, male producer (Singles: 1 week)* pos/wks

Date		Title / Label	Pos	Wks
25 Mar 95		**BURIAL** *ffrr FCD 255*	66	1

Barrington LEVY *Jamaica, male vocalist (Singles: 13 weeks)* pos/wks

Date		Title / Label	Pos	Wks
2 Feb 85		**HERE I COME** *London LON 62*	41	4
15 Jun 91		**TRIBAL BASE** *Desire WANT 44* [1]	20	6
24 Sep 94		**WORK** *MCA MCSTD 2003*	65	1
13 Oct 01		**HERE I COME (SING DJ)** *Nulife / Arista 74321895622* [2]	37	2

[1] Rebel MC featuring Tenor Fly and Barrington Levy [2] Talisman P featuring Barrington Levy

Here I Come (Sing DJ) is a re-recording of Here I Come

Jona LEWIE *UK, male vocalist – John Lewis (Singles: 20 weeks)* pos/wks

Date		Title / Label	Pos	Wks
10 May 80		**YOU'LL ALWAYS FIND ME IN THE KITCHEN AT PARTIES** *Stiff BUY 73*	16	9
29 Nov 80	●	**STOP THE CAVALRY** *Stiff BUY 104*	3	11

On some copies first title was simply 'Kitchen at Parties'

See also Terry DACTYL and the DINOSAURS

TV AND RADIO COMPILATION ALBUMS

A chronological list of all the TV-and radio-related compilation albums giving, among others, Alan Titchmarsh, the Daleks, the Fonz, and the Royal Family their 15 minutes of fame in chart history

CHART ENTRY DATE / ALBUM TITLE / LABEL / PEAK POSITION / WEEKS ON CHART

13 Dec 1958 JACK GOOD'S OH BOY! Parlophone 9 14
4 Mar 1961 HUCKLEBERRY HOUND Pye 10 12
2 Mar 1963 THAT WAS THE WEEK THAT WAS Parlophone 11 9
14 Sep 1963 THE BEST OF RADIO LUXEMBOURG Pye Golden Guinea 14 2
8 Feb 1964 READY STEADY GO! Decca 20 1
28 Mar 1964 STARS FROM STARS AND GARTERS Pye 17 2
7 Aug 1971 THE WORLD OF YOUR 100 BEST TUNES Decca 10 22
9 Oct 1971 THE WORLD OF YOUR 100 BEST TUNES VOLUME 2 Decca 9 13
4 Nov 1972 THE BBC 1922-1972 (TV AND RADIO EXTRACTS) BBC 16 7
8 Dec 1973 MUSIC FOR A ROYAL WEDDING BBC 7 6
4 Jan 1975 BBC TV'S BEST OF TOP OF THE POPS Super Beeb 21 5
27 Sep 1975 THE WORLD OF YOUR 100 BEST TUNES VOLUME 10 Decca 41 4
6 Dec 1975 SUPERSONIC Stallion 21 6
13 Dec 1975 THE TOP 25 FROM YOUR 100 BEST TUNES Decca 21 5
10 Apr 1976 ROCK FOLLIES Island 1 15
29 May 1976 HAMILTON'S HOT SHOTS Warwick 15 5
5 Jun 1976 EUROVISION FAVOURITES K-Tel 44 1
22 Oct 1977 10 YEARS OF HITS – RADIO ONE Super Beeb 39 3
11 Mar 1978 FONZIE'S FAVOURITES Warner Bros. 8 16
8 Apr 1978 PENNIES FROM HEAVEN World Records 10 17
1 Jul 1978 MORE PENNIES FROM HEAVEN World Records 31 4
9 Dec 1978 STARS ON SUNDAY BY REQUEST Curzon Sounds 65 3
15 Dec 1979 FAWLTY TOWERS BBC 25 10
7 Feb 1981 FAWLTY TOWERS VOLUME 2 (TV ORIGINAL CAST) BBC 26 7
14 Feb 1981 THE HITCH-HIKER'S GUIDE TO THE GALAXY VOLUME 2 Original 47 4
1 Aug 1981 THE MUSIC OF COSMOS RCA 43 10
1 Aug 1981 ROYAL ROMANCE Windsor 84 1
8 Aug 1981 THE OFFICIAL BBC ALBUM OF THE ROYAL WEDDING BBC 1 11
21 Nov 1981 BRIDESHEAD REVISITED Chrysalis 50 12
19 Dec 1981 WE ARE MOST AMUSED (THE BEST OF BRITISH COMEDY) Ronco/Charisma 30 9
23 Oct 1982 ON THE AIR – 60 YEARS OF BBC THEME MUSIC BBC 85 3
26 Nov 1983 REILLY ACE OF THEMES Red Bus 54 6
4 Feb 1984 ORIGINAL MUSIC FROM AUF WIEDERSEHEN, PET Towerbell 21 6
18 Feb 1984 THE TUBE K-Tel 30 6
18 May 1985 VICTORY IN EUROPE – BROADCASTS FROM BBC CORRESPONDENTS BBC 61 1
28 Sep 1985 THE TV HITS ALBUM Towerbell 26 13
26 Oct 1985 MUSIC FROM THE TELEVISION SERIES 'MIAMI VICE' BBC/MCA 11 9
16 Nov 1985 THE EASTENDERS SING-A-LONG ALBUM BBC 33 10
23 Nov 1985 TELLY HITS – 16 TOP TV THEMES Stylus 34 6
15 Feb 1986 JONATHAN KING'S ENTERTAINMENT USA Stylus 6 11
12 Apr 1986 THE TV HITS ALBUM TWO – 16 ORIGINAL HIT TV THEMES Towerbell 19 7
5 Jul 1986 TELLY HITS 2 – 16 TOP TV THEMES Stylus 68 2
26 Jul 1986 MUSIC FROM THE TELEVISION SERIES 'MIAMI VICE' (re-issue) MCA 94 1

TV and radio comedy genius Peter Cook was a key contributor and writer to the BBC's That Was the Week That Was (see 1963). Cook, whose other chart listings wit[h] Dudley Moore and Derek and Clive are recorded elsewhere in this book, is picture[d] with another great British comedian who was even more successful in the music stakes, Beatle John Lennon

9 Aug 1986 ROYAL WEDDING BBC **55 1**
18 Oct 1986 THE VERY BEST OF ENTERTAINMENT USA VOLUME 2 Priority **44 4**
11 Nov 1986 SIMON BATES – OUR TUNE Polydor **58 5**
26 Dec 1986 MUSIC FROM THE BBC TV SERIES 'THE SINGING DETECTIVE' BBC **10 24**
27 Jun 1987 THE ROCK 'N' ROLL YEARS 1964-67 BBC **71 2**
27 Jun 1987 THE ROCK 'N' ROLL YEARS 1968-71 BBC **77 1**
27 Jun 1987 THE ROCK 'N' ROLL YEARS 1956-59 BBC **80 2**
27 Jun 1987 THE ROCK 'N' ROLL YEARS 1960-63 BBC **84 1**
3 Oct 1987 MOONLIGHTING – THE TV SOUNDTRACK ALBUM MCA **50 6**
17 Oct 1987 MIAMI VICE 2 MCA **71 4**
28 Nov 1987 THE CHART SHOW – DANCE HITS 1987 Chrysalis **39 6**
26 Mar 1988 THE CHART SHOW – ROCK THE NATION Dover **16 8**
1 Oct 1988 MOONLIGHTING 2 WEA **5 9**
1 Oct 1988 MIAMI VICE III MCA **95 1**
8 Oct 1988 ONES ON 1 BBC **10 7**
24 Dec 1988 THE BEIDERBECKE COLLECTION Dormouse **89 2**

The new compilations Top 20 chart is used from this point in 1988 except where an album's peak position is listed as higher than 20, indicating that it is taken from the main official albums chart

14 Jan 1989 THE BEIDERBECKE COLLECTION Dormouse **14 5**
20 May 1989 THE CHART SHOW – ROCK THE NATION 2 Dover **8 4**
3 Jun 1989 THE CHART SHOW – DANCE MASTERS Dover **4 7**
17 Jun 1989 RAY MOORE – A PERSONAL CHOICE BBC **7 4**
23 Sep 1989 TV TUNES K-Tel **17 3**
17 Feb 1990 PENNIES FROM HEAVEN BBC **8 13**
16 Feb 1991 BRITS 1991 – THE MAGIC OF BRITISH MUSIC Telstar **7 6**
21 Sep 1991 THE OLD GREY WHISTLE TEST – BEST OF THE TEST Windsong International **13 3**
22 Feb 1992 THE AWARDS 1992 PolyGram TV **1 9**
27 Jun 1992 HEARTBEAT Columbia **1 4**
18 Jul 1992 DOCTOR WHO – THE EVIL OF THE DALEKS BBC **72 1**
25 Jul 1992 32 ONES ON ONE – RADIO 1'S 25TH BIRTHDAY Connoisseur Collection **8 10**
17 Oct 1992 BEST OF CAPITAL GOLD – 24 CARAT CLASSIC HITS The Hit Label **20 1**
31 Oct 1992 SMASHIE AND NICEY PRESENT LET'S ROCK! EMI **8 4**
28 Nov 1992 GLADIATORS PolyGram TV **11 10**
30 Jan 1993 THE BEST OF THE CLASSICAL BITS Philips/PolyGram TV **7 10**
13 Feb 1993 HEAD OVER HEELS Telstar **3 9**
20 Feb 1993 THE AWARDS 1993 PolyGram TV **3 7**
13 Mar 1993 LIPSTICK ON YOUR COLLAR – 28 ORIGINAL HITS OF THE 50S PolyGram TV **2 13**
17 Apr 1993 THE CHART SHOW – THE ULTIMATE ROCK ALBUM The Hit Label **4 11**
12 Jun 1993 CLASSIC COMMERCIALS Decca **8 6**
12 Jun 1993 THE PIG ATTRACTION FEATURING PINKY AND PERKY Telstar **19 2**
3 Jul 1993 ROADSHOW HITS – 21 YEARS OF RADIO 1 FM ROADSHOW Connoisseur Collection **18 2**
7 Aug 1993 THE BIG BREAKFAST ALBUM Arcade **8 5**
14 Aug 1993 DOCTOR WHO – THE POWER OF THE DALEKS BBC **71 1**
18 Sep 1993 DOCTOR WHO – THE PARADISE OF DEATH BBC **48 1**
2 Oct 1993 THE CHART SHOW – ULTIMATE ROCK 2 The Hit Label 13 **10 3**
23 Oct 1993 TALES FROM THE CITY PolyGram TV **17 2**
20 Nov 1993 RETURN OF THE GLADIATORS PolyGram TV **20 1**
22 Jan 1994 THE SOUND OF KISS 100FM PolyGram TV **1 4**
4 Jun 1994 TOP GEAR Epic **3 13**
16 Jul 1994 THE CHART SHOW – THE ULTIMATE BLUES ALBUM The Hit Label **13 3**

TV AND RADIO COMPILATION ALBUMS CONTINUED

22 Oct 1994 **DR HILARY JONES' CLASSIC RELAXATION** PolyGram TV **13 2**
28 Jan 1995 **THE BEST OF HEARTBEAT** Columbia **1 6**
20 May 1995 **THE CHART SHOW PRESENTS CHART MACHINE** PolyGram TV **18 2**
27 May 1995 **TOP GEAR 2** Columbia **4 6**
10 Jun 1995 **TOP OF THE POPS 1** Columbia **1 6**
24 Jun 1995 **TOP GEAR CLASSICS – TURBO CLASSICS** Deutsche Grammophon **17 1**
5 Aug 1995 **THE CHART SHOW DANCE ALBUM** PolyGram TV **6 3**
30 Sep 1995 **HEARTBEAT – FOREVER YOURS** Columbia **1 17**
18 Nov 1995 **THE CORONATION STREET ALBUM EMI** Premier **20 1**
2 Dec 1995 **TOP OF THE POPS 2** Columbia **14 7**
9 Mar 1996 **TOP GEAR 3** Columbia **11 4**
20 Apr 1996 **HALL OF FAME** Classic FM **13 4**
17 Aug 1996 **EVENING SESSION – PRIORITY TUNES** Virgin **11 4**
17 Aug 1996 **INDEPENDENCE DAY UK** Speaking Volumes **66 2**
9 Nov 1996 **TOP GEAR – ON THE ROAD AGAIN** EMI TV **12 3**
2 Aug 1997 **AFTER THE BREAK** Columbia **17 1**
13 Sep 1997 **IBIZA UNCOVERED** Virgin/EMI **1 10**
27 Sep 1997 **DIANA, PRINCESS OF WALES 1961-1997 – FUNERAL SERVICE** BBC Worldwide Classics **3 5**
8 Nov 1997 **READY STEADY GO! – NUMBER ONE SIXTIES ALBUM** PolyGram TV **10 2**
21 Mar 1998 **READY STEADY GO! – SIXTIES MOTOWN SOUND** PolyGram TV **5 5**
16 May 1998 **A SONG FOR EUROTRASH** EMI **19 1**
30 May 1998 **DAVE PEARCE PRESENTS DANCE ANTHEMS** PolyGram TV **4 7**
22 Aug 1998 **IBIZA UNCOVERED 2** Virgin/EMI **2 9**
22 Aug 1998 **ROCK THE DANCEFLOOR** All Around the World **9 2**
26 Sep 1998 **TOP GEAR ANTHEMS** Virgin/EMI **6 6**
3 Oct 1998 **STARSKY & HUTCH PRESENTS 70sFUNKSOULJAZZDISCO** Virgin/EMI **13 2**
17 Oct 1998 **DAVE PEARCE PRESENTS DANCE ANTHEMS VOLUME 2** PolyGram TV **5 3**
17 Oct 1998 **THE HEART OF THE 80S & 90S** Universal **9 3**
5 Dec 1998 **CHEF AID – THE SOUTH PARK ALBUM** Columbia **2 14**
5 Dec 1998 **CHRIS TARRANT PRESENTS ULTIMATE PARTY MEGAMIX** Telstar TV **17 1**
3 Apr 1999 **ROCK THE DANCEFLOOR 2** All Around the World **7 1**
3 Apr 1999 **LIVE & KICKING – VIEWERS CHOICE PART 1** Virgin/EMI **12 3**
10 Apr 1999 **CLUBZONE – DANCING IN THE CITY** Warner.ESP/Radio City/3 Beat **20 1**
17 Apr 1999 **QUEER AS FOLK – THE WHOLE THING. SORTED** Almighty **2 9**
12 Jun 1999 **SONGS FROM DAWSON'S CREEK** Columbia **3 11**
10 Jul 1999 **CHRIS TARRANT'S ULTIMATE SUMMER PARTY** Telstar TV **15 2**
24 Jul 1999 **DAVE PEARCE PRESENTS 40 CLASSIC DANCE ANTHEMS** Universal Music TV **5 6**
28 Aug 1999 **MTV IBIZA 99** Columbia **10 3**
2 Oct 1999 **IBIZA UNCOVERED – THE RETURN** Virgin/EMI **2 7**
16 Oct 1999 **RELAX ...** Classic FM **11 7**
23 Oct 1999 **DAVE PEARCE PRESENTS 40 CLASSIC DANCE ANTHEMS 2** Universal Music TV **7 3**
23 Oct 1999 **SEX, CHIPS & ROCK 'N' ROLL** Virgin/EMI **12 1**
20 Nov 1999 **ABBAMANIA** Polydor/Universal Music TV **2 14**
20 Nov 1999 **BUFFY THE VAMPIRE SLAYER – THE ALBUM** Columbia **7 2**
27 Nov 1999 **MUSIC OF THE MILLENNIUM** Universal/Virgin/EMI **2 16**
18 Dec 1999 **RADIO 2 – SONGS OF THE CENTURY** Global TV **9 8**
12 Feb 2000 **AGIA NAPA – FANTASY ISLAND – THE BEST UPFRONT & CLASSIC UK GARAGE** Telstar TV **1 6**
26 Feb 2000 **QUEER AS FOLK 2 – SAME MEN. NEW TRACKS** Channel 4 Music **5 5**

11 Mar 2000 **THE GRIMLEYS – ORIGINAL TV SOUNDTRACK** Global Television **17 1**
8 Apr 2000 **SWITCHED ON – THE COOL SOUND OF TV ADVERTISING** Telstar TV **9 4**
22 Apr 2000 **POKEMON – 2 B A MASTER** Koch **20 1**
29 Apr 2000 **TREVOR NELSON'S RHYTHM NATION** INCredible **9 4**
29 Apr 2000 **TV 2000** Columbia **16 2**
6 May 2000 **HALL OF FAME 2000** Classic FM **10 8**
20 May 2000 **ALAN TITCHMARSH – IN A COUNTRY GARDEN** Sony Classical **20 1**
22 Jul 2000 **HAPPY & GLORIOUS** Decca **20 1**
26 Aug 2000 **BIG BROTHER – THE ORIGINAL SOUNDTRACK** Bazal/Channel 4 Music **17 3**
30 Sep 2000 **YOUNG GUNS GO FOR IT – HEROES OF THE 80'S** Virgin/EMI **10 4**
7 Oct 2000 **PEPSI CHART 2001** Virgin/EMI **2 8**
14 Oct 2000 **CD:UK – 40 WICKED HITS – YOU KNOW WHERE IT'S AT!** Universal/BMG/Sony Music TV **7 4**
14 Oct 2000 **BBC RADIO 2 COUNTRY HITS** BMG TV/Telstar TV **20 1**
28 Oct 2000 **SONGS FROM DAWSON'S CREEK – VOLUME 2** Columbia **5 3**
4 Nov 2000 **CLASSIC FM – RELAX MORE** Classic FM **7 8**
11 Nov 2000 **STEVE WRIGHT'S SUNDAY LOVE SONGS** BBC Music/Universal Music TV **6 19**
18 Nov 2000 **JAMIE OLIVER'S COOKIN' – MUSIC TO COOK BY** Columbia **14 1**
2 Dec 2000 **MUSIC OF THE MILLENNIUM 2** Universal/EMI/Virgin **6 10**
23 Dec 2000 **CONTENDERS FOR THE RECORD OF THE YEAR 2000 BMG** Commercial/Telstar **13 3**
30 Dec 2000 **MOTOWN MANIA** Universal Music TV/BMG **9 2**
30 Dec 2000 **MORE COLD FEET** BMG TV Projects **18 1**
20 Jan 2001 **THE GREATEST NO.1 SINGLES** Virgin/EMI/Universal Music TV **2 12**
3 Feb 2001 **THE LICK – PRESENTED BY TREVOR NELSON** Universal Music TV/Def Soul **3 7**
3 Feb 2001 **CD:UK – MORE WICKED HITS** Universal/BMG/Sony Music TV **9 3**
3 Mar 2001 **THE NEW PEPSI CHART ALBUM** Virgin/EMI **2 7**
31 Mar 2001 **AYIA NAPA – RETURN TO FANTASY ISLAND** BMG/Telstar TV **18 2**
14 Apr 2001 **THE SOUND OF CLASSIC FM** Classic FM **16 3**
26 May 2001 **TRIGGER HAPPY TV – SOUNDTRACK TO SERIES 2** Channel 4 Music **15 2**
23 Jun 2001 **CAPITAL GOLD LEGENDS** Virgin/EMI **1 20**
30 Jun 2001 **ROCK THE DANCEFLOOR 5** All Around the World **19 1**
7 Jul 2001 **95.8 CAPITAL FM'S PARTY IN THE PARK FOR THE PRINCE'S TRUST** Universal Music TV **2 5**
1 Sep 2001 **PURE FLAVA – MIXED BY STEVE 'SMOOTH' SUTHERLAND** WSM/Universal Music TV **10 4**
20 Oct 2001 **PEPSI CHART 2002** Virgin/EMI **1 7**
27 Oct 2001 **CLASSIC FM – TIME TO RELAX** Classic FM **9 6**
17 Nov 2001 **CAPITAL GOLD LEGENDS II** Virgin/EMI **2 7**
17 Nov 2001 **ALL TOGETHER NOW – CHILDREN'S FAVOURITE TV THEMES** Universal Music TV **11 5**
24 Nov 2001 **STEVE WRIGHT'S SUNDAY LOVE SONGS – VOLUME 2** BBC/Universal Music TV **12 3**
8 Dec 2001 **COLD FEET** Universal Music TV **13 8**
20 Apr 2002 **POP IDOL – THE BIG BAND ALBUM** S **1 10**
6 Jul 2002 **PARTY AT THE PALACE** Universal TV/Virgin **6 3**
21 Dec 2002 **FAME ACADEMY** Mercury **2 7**
15 Mar 2003 **THE VERY BEST OF COLD FEET** Universal **1 10**
6 Sep 2003 **FAME ACADEMY – BEE GEES SPECIAL** Polydor **17 1**
11 Oct 2003 **FAME ACADEMY – THE FINALISTS** Polydor **2 6**
1 Nov 2003 **BUFFY THE VAMPIRE SLAYER** Virgin/EMI **12 2**
1 Nov 2003 **GREASEMANIA** * Polydor/S **1 3**
8 Nov 2003 **CAPITAL GOLD – LOVE LEGENDS** Virgin/EMI **5 1**

CJ LEWIS *UK, male vocalist (Singles: 32 weeks, Albums: 2 weeks)* pos/wks

23 Apr 94 ● **SWEETS FOR MY SWEET** *Black Market BMITD 017* 3 13
23 Jul 94 ● **EVERYTHING IS ALRIGHT (UPTIGHT)** *Black Market BMITD 019* 10 7
8 Oct 94 **BEST OF MY LOVE** *Black Market BMITD 021* 13 6
17 Dec 94 **DOLLARS** *Black Market BMITD 023* 34 4
9 Sep 95 **R TO THE A** *Black Market BMITD 030* 34 2
3 Sep 94 **DOLLARS** *Black Market MCD 11131* 44 2

Danny J LEWIS *UK, male producer (Singles: 2 weeks)* pos/wks

20 Jun 98 **SPEND THE NIGHT** *Locked On LOX 98CD* 29 2

Darlene LEWIS *US, female vocalist (Singles: 4 weeks)* pos/wks

16 Apr 94 **LET THE MUSIC (LIFT YOU UP)** *KMS / Eastern Bloc KMSCD 10* 16 4

All formats of 'Let the Music Lift You Up' featured versions by Loveland featuring Rachel McFarlane and also by Darlene Lewis

Dee LEWIS *UK, female vocalist (Singles: 5 weeks)* pos/wks

18 Jun 88 **BEST OF MY LOVE** *Mercury DEE 3* 47 5

Donna LEWIS
UK, female vocalist (Singles: 16 weeks, Albums: 1 week) pos/wks

7 Sep 96 ● **I LOVE YOU ALWAYS FOREVER** *Atlantic A 5495CD* 5 14
8 Feb 97 **WITHOUT LOVE** *Atlantic A 5468CD* 39 2
12 Oct 96 **NOW IN A MINUTE** *Atlantic 7567827622* 52 1

Gary LEWIS and the PLAYBOYS *US, male vocal / instrumental group, leader – Gary Levitch (Singles: 7 weeks)* pos/wks

8 Feb 75 **MY HEART'S SYMPHONY** *United Artists UP 35780* 36 7

Huey LEWIS and the NEWS 417 Top 500
One of the most popular 1980s US acts, formed in San Francisco in 1980. Leader b. Hugh Cregg III, 5 Jul 1950, New York. The Grammy and Brit-winning band took 'The Power of Love' into the Top 20 twice within six months (Singles: 66 weeks, Albums: 94 weeks) pos/wks

27 Oct 84 **IF THIS IS IT** *Chrysalis CHS 2803* 39 6
31 Aug 85 **THE POWER OF LOVE** *Chrysalis HUEY 1* ▲ 11 10
23 Nov 85 **HEART AND SOUL (EP)** *Chrysalis HUEY 2* 61 4
8 Feb 86 ● **THE POWER OF LOVE / DO YOU BELIEVE IN LOVE (re-issue)** *Chrysalis HUEY 3* 9 12
10 May 86 **THE HEART OF ROCK AND ROLL** *Chrysalis HUEY 4* 49 3
23 Aug 86 **STUCK WITH YOU** *Chrysalis HUEY 5* ▲ 12 12
6 Dec 86 **HIP TO BE SQUARE** *Chrysalis HUEY 6* 41 8
21 Mar 87 **SIMPLE AS THAT** *Chrysalis HUEY 7* 47 5
16 Jul 88 **PERFECT WORLD** *Chrysalis HUEY 10* 48 6
14 Sep 85 **SPORTS** *Chrysalis CHR 1412* ▲ 23 24
20 Sep 86 ● **FORE!** *Chrysalis CDL 1534* ▲ 8 52
6 Aug 88 **SMALL WORLD** *Chrysalis CDL 1622* 12 8
18 May 91 **HARD AT PLAY** *Chrysalis CHR 1847* 39 2
21 Nov 92 **THE HEART OF ROCK & ROLL – THE BEST OF HUEY LEWIS AND THE NEWS** *Chrysalis CDCHR 1934* 23 8

Tracks on Heart and Soul (EP): Heart and Soul / Hope You Love Me Like You Say You Do / Heart of Rock and Roll / Buzz Buzz Buzz. 'Do You Believe in Love' listed only from 15 Feb 1986

Jerry LEWIS
US, male actor / vocalist – Joseph Levitch (Singles: 8 weeks) pos/wks

8 Feb 57 **ROCK-A-BYE YOUR BABY WITH A DIXIE MELODY (re)** *Brunswick 05636* 12 8

Jerry Lee LEWIS *US, male vocalist / instrumentalist – piano (Singles: 68 weeks, Albums: 6 weeks)* pos/wks

27 Sep 57 ● **WHOLE LOTTA SHAKIN' GOIN' ON (re)** *London HLS 8457* 8 11
20 Dec 57 ★ **GREAT BALLS OF FIRE** *London HLS 8529* 1 12
11 Apr 58 ● **BREATHLESS** *London HLS 8592* 8 7
23 Jan 59 **HIGH SCHOOL CONFIDENTIAL** *London HLS 8780* 12 6
1 May 59 **LOVIN' UP A STORM** *London HLS 8840* 28 1
9 Jun 60 **BABY, BABY, BYE BYE** *London HLS 9131* 47 1
4 May 61 ● **WHAT'D I SAY (re)** *London HLS 9335* 10 14
6 Sep 62 **SWEET LITTLE SIXTEEN** *London HLS 9584* 38 5
14 Mar 63 **GOOD GOLLY MISS MOLLY** *London HLS 9688* 31 6
6 May 72 **CHANTILLY LACE** *Mercury 6052 141* 33 5
2 Jun 62 **JERRY LEE LEWIS VOLUME 2** *London HA 2440* 14 6

Linda LEWIS
UK, female vocalist (Singles: 31 weeks, Albums: 4 weeks) pos/wks

2 Jun 73 **ROCK-A-DOODLE-DOO** *Raft RA 18502* 15 11
12 Jul 75 ● **IT'S IN HIS KISS** *Arista 17* 6 8
17 Apr 76 **BABY I'M YOURS** *Arista 43* 33 6
2 Jun 79 **I'D BE SURPRISINGLY GOOD FOR YOU** *Ariola ARO 166* 40 5
19 Aug 00 **REACH OUT** *Skint SKINT 54CD* [1] 61 1
9 Aug 75 **NOT A LITTLE GIRL ANYMORE** *Arista ARTY 109* 40 4

[1] Midfield General featuring Linda Lewis

Linda Gail LEWIS – *See Van MORRISON*

Ramsey LEWIS *US, male instrumentalist – piano (Singles: 8 weeks, Albums: 4 weeks)* pos/wks

15 Apr 72 **WADE IN THE WATER** *Chess 6145 004* 31 8
21 May 66 **HANG ON RAMSEY** *Chess CRL 4520* [1] 20 4

[1] Ramsey Lewis Trio

Shirley LEWIS – *See Arthur BAKER*

John LEYTON *UK, male vocalist / actor (Singles: 70 weeks)* pos/wks

3 Aug 61 ★ **JOHNNY REMEMBER ME** *Top Rank JAR 577* 1 15
5 Oct 61 ● **WILD WIND** *Top Rank JAR 585* 2 10
28 Dec 61 **SON THIS IS SHE** *HMV POP 956* 15 10
15 Mar 62 **LONE RIDER** *HMV POP 992* 40 5
3 May 62 **LONELY CITY** *HMV POP 1014* 14 11
23 Aug 62 **DOWN THE RIVER NILE** *HMV POP 1054* 42 3
21 Feb 63 **CUPBOARD LOVE** *HMV POP 1122* 22 12
18 Jul 63 **I'LL CUT YOUR TAIL OFF (re)** *HMV POP 1175* 36 3
20 Feb 64 **MAKE LOVE TO ME** *HMV POP 1264* [1] 49 1

[1] John Leyton and the LeRoys

LEYTON BUZZARDS
UK, male vocal / instrumental group (Singles: 5 weeks) pos/wks

3 Mar 79 **SATURDAY NIGHT (BENEATH THE PLASTIC PALM TREES)** *Chrysalis CHS 2288* 53 5

LIBERACE *US, male instrumentalist – piano (Wladziu Valentino Liberace) d. 4 Feb 1987 (Singles: 2 weeks)* pos/wks

17 Jun 55 **UNCHAINED MELODY** *Philips PB 430* 20 1
19 Oct 56 **I DON'T CARE (AS LONG AS YOU CARE FOR ME)** *Columbia DB 3834* 28 1

'I Don't Care' featured Liberace as vocalist too

LIBERATION *UK, male instrumental / production duo – William Linch and David Cooper (Singles: 3 weeks)* pos/wks

24 Oct 92 **LIBERATION** *ZYX ZYX 68657* 28 3

LIBERTINES *UK, male vocal / instrumental group (Singles: 10 weeks, Albums: 3 weeks)* pos/wks

15 Jun 02 **WHAT A WASTER** *Rough Trade RTRADESCD 054* 37 2
12 Oct 02 **UP THE BRACKET** *Rough Trade RTRADESCD 064* 29 2
25 Jan 03 **TIME FOR HEROES** *Rough Trade RTRADESCD 074* 20 2
30 Aug 03 **DON'T LOOK BACK INTO THE SUN** *Rough Trade TRADESCD199* 11 4
2 Nov 02 **UP THE BRACKET** *Rough Trade RTRADECD 065* 35 3

LIBERTY X *UK, male / female vocal group (Singles: 71 weeks, Albums: 60 weeks)* pos/wks

6 Oct 01 ● **THINKING IT OVER** *V2 VVR 5017773* [1] 5 8
15 Dec 01 **DOIN' IT** *V2 VVR 5017793* [1] 14 6

25 May 02 ★ **JUST A LITTLE** *V2 VVR 5018963* ■ 1 16
21 Sep 02 ● **GOT TO HAVE YOUR LOVE** *V2 VVR 5020503* 2 12
14 Dec 02 ● **HOLDING ON FOR YOU** *V2 VVR 5020763* 5 11
29 Mar 03 ● **BEING NOBODY** *Virgin RXCD 1* [2] 3 11
1 Nov 03 ● **JUMPIN' (re)** *V2 VVR 5023543* 6 7
8 Jun 02 ● **THINKING IT OVER** *V2 VVR 1017782* 3 56
15 Nov 03 **BEING SOMEBODY** *V2 VVR1023562* 12 4

[1] Liberty [2] Richard X vs Liberty X

LIBIDO
Norway, male vocal / instrumental group (Singles: 1 week) pos/wks

31 Jan 98 **OVERTHROWN** *Fire BLAZE 119CD* 53 1

LIBRA presents TAYLOR
US, male / female production / vocal trio (Singles: 3 weeks) pos/wks

26 Oct 96 **ANOMALY – CALLING YOUR NAME** *Platipus PLATCD 24* 71 1
18 Mar 00 **ANOMALY – CALLING YOUR NAME (re-mix)** *Platipus PLATCD 56* 43 2

LICK THE TINS
UK, male / female vocal / instrumental group (Singles: 8 weeks) pos/wks

29 Mar 86 **CAN'T HELP FALLING IN LOVE** *Sedition EDIT 3308* 42 8

Oliver LIEB presents SMOKED
Germany, male producer (Singles: 1 week) pos/wks

30 Sep 00 **METROPOLIS** *Duty Free DF 019CD* 72 1

See also LSG

Ben LIEBRAND
Holland, male DJ / producer (Singles: 2 weeks) pos/wks

9 Jun 90 **PULS(T)AR** *Epic LIEB 1* 68 2

LIEUTENANT PIGEON
UK, male / female instrumental group (Singles: 29 weeks) pos/wks

16 Sep 72 ★ **MOULDY OLD DOUGH** *Decca F 13278* 1 19
16 Dec 72 **DESPERATE DAN** *Decca F 13365* 17 10

LIFEHOUSE
US, male vocal / instrumental group (Singles: 4 weeks) pos/wks

8 Sep 01 **HANGING BY A MOMENT** *Dreamworks / Polydor 4975612* 25 4

LIFFORD – *See ARTFUL DODGER*

LIGHT OF THE WORLD *UK, male vocal / instrumental group (Singles: 25 weeks, Albums: 1 week)* pos/wks

14 Apr 79 **SWINGIN'** *Ensign ENY 22* 45 5
14 Jul 79 **MIDNIGHT GROOVIN'** *Ensign ENY 29* 72 1
18 Oct 80 **LONDON TOWN** *Ensign ENY 43* 41 5
17 Jan 81 **I SHOT THE SHERIFF** *Ensign ENY 46* 40 5
28 Mar 81 **I'M SO HAPPY / TIME** *Ensign MER 64* 35 6
21 Nov 81 **RIDE THE LOVE TRAIN** *EMI 5242* 49 3
24 Jan 81 **ROUND TRIP** *Ensign ENVY 14* 73 1

LIGHTER SHADE OF BROWN
US, male vocal duo (Singles: 3 weeks) pos/wks

9 Jul 94 **HEY DJ** *Mercury MERCD 401* 33 3

Gordon LIGHTFOOT *Canada, male vocalist / instrumentalist – guitar (Singles: 26 weeks, Albums: 2 weeks)* pos/wks

19 Jun 71 **IF YOU COULD READ MY MIND** *Reprise RS 20974* 30 9
3 Aug 74 **SUNDOWN** *Reprise K 14327* ▲ 33 7
15 Jan 77 **THE WRECK OF THE EDMUND FITZGERALD** *Reprise K 14451* 40 4
16 Sep 78 **DAYLIGHT KATY** *Warner Bros. K 17214* 41 6
20 May 72 **DON QUIXOTE** *Reprise K 44166* 44 1
17 Aug 74 **SUNDOWN** *Reprise K 54020* ▲ 45 1

Terry LIGHTFOOT'S NEW ORLEANS JAZZMEN *UK, vocalist / instrumentalist – clarinet – and male band (Singles: 17 weeks)* pos/wks

7 Sep 61 **TRUE LOVE** *Columbia DB 4696* 33 4
23 Nov 61 **KING KONG** *Columbia SCD 2165* 29 12
3 May 62 **TAVERN IN THE TOWN** *Columbia DB 4822* 49 1

LIGHTFORCE *Germany, male production duo (Singles: 1 week)* pos/wks

28 Oct 00 **JOIN ME** *Slinky Music SLINKY 004CD* 53 1

LIGHTHOUSE FAMILY 147 Top 500 *Smooth, easy-on-the-ear pop / soul duo formed in Newcastle-upon-Tyne, UK; Nigerian-born Tunde Baiyewu (v) and Londoner Paul Tucker (k). After a slow start, their debut album 'Ocean Drive' (1995) sold 1.6 million in the UK and made a name for them in the rest of Europe (Singles: 89 weeks, Albums: 263 weeks)* pos/wks

27 May 95 **LIFTED** *Wild Card CARDW 17* 61 2
14 Oct 95 **OCEAN DRIVE** *Wild Card 5797072* 34 3
10 Feb 96 ● **LIFTED (re-issue)** *Wild Card 5779432* 4 10
1 Jun 96 **OCEAN DRIVE (re-issue)** *Wild Card 5766192* 11 8
21 Sep 96 **GOODBYE HEARTBREAK** *Wild Card 5753492* 14 6
21 Dec 96 **LOVING EVERY MINUTE** *Wild Card 5731012* 20 7
11 Oct 97 ● **RAINCLOUD** *Wild Card 5717932* 6 7
10 Jan 98 ● **HIGH** *Polydor 5691492* 4 14
27 Jun 98 ● **LOST IN SPACE** *Polydor 5670592* 6 8
10 Oct 98 **QUESTION OF FAITH** *Wild Card 5673932* 21 5
9 Jan 99 **POSTCARD FROM HEAVEN** *Wild Card 5633952* 24 6
24 Nov 01 ● **(I WISH I KNEW HOW IT WOULD FEEL TO BE) FREE – ONE** *Wild Card / Polydor 5873812* 6 9
9 Mar 02 **RUN** *Wild Card / Polydor 5705702* 30 3
6 Jul 02 **HAPPY** *Wild Card / Polydor 5707902* 51 1
18 Nov 95 ● **OCEAN DRIVE** *Wild Card 5237872* 3 154
1 Nov 97 ● **POSTCARDS FROM HEAVEN** *Wild Card 5395162* 2 73
1 Dec 01 ● **WHATEVER GETS YOU THROUGH THE DAY** *Wild Card 5894122* 7 18
30 Nov 02 **GREATEST HITS** *Wild Card/Polydor 0654482* 23 6
19 Apr 03 ● **THE VERY BEST OF** *Wild Card/Polydor 0761662* 9 12

LIGHTNING SEEDS 253 Top 500
Conceived as a 'perfect pop' studio project by producer and group veteran Ian Broudie (v/g) 4 Aug 1958, Liverpool, UK. England's most popular footballing anthem, 'Three Lions', became the first song to top the charts twice with different lyrics (Singles: 104 weeks, Albums: 140 weeks) pos/wks

22 Jul 89 **PURE** *Ghetto GTG 4* 16 8
14 Mar 92 **THE LIFE OF RILEY** *Virgin VS 1402* 28 6
30 May 92 **SENSE** *Virgin VS 1414* 31 5
20 Aug 94 **LUCKY YOU** *Epic 6606282* 43 2
14 Jan 95 **CHANGE** *Epic 6609865* 13 6
15 Apr 95 **MARVELLOUS** *Epic 6614265* 24 5
22 Jul 95 **PERFECT** *Epic 6621792* 18 5
21 Oct 95 **LUCKY YOU (re-issue)** *Epic 6625182* 15 6
9 Mar 96 **READY OR NOT** *Epic 6629672* 20 4
1 Jun 96 ★ **THREE LIONS (THE OFFICIAL SONG OF THE ENGLAND FOOTBALL TEAM)** *Epic 6632732* [1] ■ 1 15
2 Nov 96 **WHAT IF... (re)** *Epic 6638635* 14 4
18 Jan 97 **SUGAR COATED ICEBERG** *Epic 6640432* 12 4
26 Apr 97 ● **YOU SHOWED ME** *Epic 6643282* 8 5
13 Dec 97 **WHAT YOU SAY** *Epic 6653572* 41 5
20 Jun 98 ★ **THREE LIONS '98** *Epic 6660982* [1] ■ 1 13
27 Nov 99 **LIFE'S TOO SHORT (re)** *Epic 6681502* 27 4
18 Mar 00 **SWEETEST SOUL SENSATIONS** *Epic 6689422* 67 1
15 Jun 02 **THREE LIONS '98 (re) (re-issue)** *Epic 6728152* [2] 16 6
10 Feb 90 **CLOUDCUCKOOLAND** *Ghetto GHETT 3* 50 2
18 Apr 92 **SENSE** *Virgin CDV 2690* 53 1
17 Sep 94 **JOLLIFICATION** *Epic 4772379* 12 58
18 May 96 **PURE LIGHTNING SEEDS** *Virgin CDV 2805* 27 9
23 Nov 96 **DIZZY HEIGHTS** *Epic 4866402* 11 26
22 Nov 97 ● **LIKE YOU DO ... BEST OF THE LIGHTNING SEEDS** *Epic 4890342* 5 42
4 Dec 99 **TILT** *Epic 4962632* 46 2

[1] Baddiel and Skinner and the Lightning Seeds [2] Baddiel, Skinner and the Lightning Seeds

LIL BOW WOW

US, male rapper – Rashad Moss (Singles: 9 weeks) pos/wks

14 Apr 01 ● **BOW WOW (THAT'S MY NAME)** *So So Def / Columbia 6709832* 6 9

LIL' DEVIOUS *UK, male production duo – Mark Baker and Gary Little (Singles: 1 week)* pos/wks

15 Sep 01 **COME HOME** *Rulin RULIN 16CDS* 55 1

See also PERCY FILTH

LIL' KIM *US, female vocalist – Kimberly Jones (Singles: 56 weeks, Albums: 1 week)* pos/wks

26 Apr 97 **NO TIME** *Atlantic A 5594CD* [1] 45 1
5 Jul 97 **CRUSH ON YOU (re)** *Atlantic AT 0002CD* 23 5
16 Aug 97 **NOT TONIGHT** *Atlantic AT 0007CD* 11 5
22 Aug 98 **HIT 'EM WIT DA HEE** *East West E3824 CD1* [2] 25 3
5 Feb 00 **NOTORIOUS B.I.G.** *Puff Daddy / Arista 74321737312* [3] 16 5
2 Sep 00 **NO MATTER WHAT THEY SAY** *Atlantic 7567846972* 35 2
30 Jun 01 ★ **LADY MARMALADE** *Interscope / Polydor 4975612* [4] ■ ▲ 1 16
11 Aug 01 **WAIT A MINUTE** *Atlantic AT 0106CD* [5] 54 1
22 Sep 01 **IN THE AIR TONITE** *WEA WEA 331CD* [6] 26 2
10 May 03 **THE JUMP OFF** *Atlantic AT 0151CD* [7] 16 7
20 Sep 03 ● **CAN'T HOLD US DOWN** *RCA 87876556332* [8] 6 9
8 Jul 00 **THE NOTORIOUS K.I.M.** *Atlantic 7567928402* 67 1

[1] Lil' Kim featuring Puff Daddy [2] Missy 'Misdemeanor' Elliott featuring Lil' Kim [3] Notorious B.I.G. featuring Puff Daddy and Lil' Kim [4] Christina Aguilera, Lil' Kim, Mya and Pink [5] Ray J featuring Lil' Kim [6] Lil' Kim featuring Phil Collins [7] Lil' Kim featuring Mr Cheeks [8] Christina Aguilera featuring Lil' Kim

'Crush on You' peaked at No.23 when it re-entered in Oct '97

LIL' LOUIS *US, male producer – Marvin Burns (Singles: 21 weeks, Albums: 5 weeks)* pos/wks

29 Jul 89 ● **FRENCH KISS** *ffrr FX 115* 2 11
13 Jan 90 **I CALLED U** *ffrr F 123* 16 6
26 Sep 92 **SAVED MY LIFE** *ffrr FX 197* [1] 74 1
12 Aug 00 **HOW'S YOUR EVENING SO FAR** *ffrr FCD 384* [2] 23 3
26 Aug 89 **FRENCH KISSES** *ffrr 828170 1* 35 5

[1] Lil' Louis and the World [2] Josh Wink and Lil' Louis

See also BLACK MAGIC

LIL' MISS MAX – See BLUE ADONIS featuring LIL' MISS MAX

LIL' MO *US, female vocalist – Cynthia Long (Singles: 12 weeks)* pos/wks

21 Nov 98 **5 MINUTES** *Elektra E 3803CD* [1] 72 1
23 Sep 00 **WHATEVER** *Virgin VUSCD 172* [2] 31 3
6 Apr 02 **WHERE'S MY...?** *EMI CDEMS 598* [3] 37 2
15 Feb 03 **IF I COULD GO!** *Elektra E 7331CD* [4] 61 1
16 Aug 03 **CAN'T LET YOU GO** *Elektra E 7408CD* [5] 14 5

[1] Lil' Mo featuring Missy 'Misdemeanor' Elliott [2] Ideal U.S. featuring Lil' Mo [3] Adam F featuring Lil' Mo [4] Angie Martinez featuring Lil' Mo and Sacario [5] Fabolous featuring Mike Shorey and Lil' Mo

LIL MO' YIN YANG *US, male instrumental / production duo – Erick 'More' Morillo and 'Lil' Louis Vega (Singles: 2 weeks)* pos/wks

9 Mar 96 **REACH** *Multiply CDMULTY 9* 28 2

See also Erick 'More' MORILLO presents RAW; PIANOHEADZ; REEL 2 REAL featuring The MAD STUNTMAN

LIL' ROMEO *US, male rapper (Singles: 1 week)* pos/wks

22 Sep 01 **MY BABY** *Priority PTYCD 136* 67 1

L'IL T – See MANIJAMA featuring MUKUPA & L'IL T

LILY – See MAXIMA featuring LILY

LILYS *US, male vocal / instrumental group (Singles: 4 weeks)* pos/wks

21 Feb 98 **A NANNY IN MANHATTAN** *Che CHE 77CD* 16 4

LIMA – See Tom NOVY

LIMAHL *UK, male vocalist – Chris Hamill (Singles: 25 weeks, Albums: 3 weeks)* pos/wks

5 Nov 83 **ONLY FOR LOVE (re)** *EMI LML 1* 16 8
2 Jun 84 **TOO MUCH TROUBLE** *EMI LML 2* 64 3
13 Oct 84 ● **NEVER ENDING STORY** *EMI LML 3* 4 14
1 Dec 84 **DON'T SUPPOSE** *EMI PLML 1* 63 3

See also KAJAGOOGOO

Alison LIMERICK

UK, female vocalist (Singles: 41 weeks, Albums: 2 weeks) pos/wks

30 Mar 91 **WHERE LOVE LIVES** *Arista 144208* 27 8
12 Oct 91 **COME BACK (FOR REAL LOVE)** *Arista 114530* 53 2
21 Dec 91 **MAGIC'S BACK (THEME FROM 'THE GHOSTS OF OXFORD STREET')** *RCA PB 45223* [1] 42 4
29 Feb 92 **MAKE IT ON MY OWN** *Arista 114996* 16 6
18 Jul 92 **GETTIN' IT RIGHT** *Arista 74321102867* 57 2
28 Nov 92 **HEAR MY CALL** *Arista 115337* 73 1
8 Jan 94 **TIME OF OUR LIVES** *Arista 74321180332* 36 4
19 Mar 94 **LOVE COME DOWN** *Arista 74321191952* 36 2
25 Feb 95 **LOVE WILL KEEP US TOGETHER** *Acid Jazz JAZID 112CD* [2] 63 1
6 Jul 96 ● **WHERE LOVE LIVES (re-mix)** *Arista 74321381592* 9 6
14 Sep 96 **MAKE IT ON MY OWN (re-mix)** *Arista 74321407812* 30 2
23 Aug 97 **PUT YOUR FAITH IN ME** *MBA XES 9001* 42 1
15 Mar 03 **WHERE LOVE LIVES (re-mix)** *Arista Dance 74321981442* 44 2
4 Apr 92 **AND STILL I RISE** *Arista 262365* 53 2

[1] Malcolm McLaren featuring Alison Limerick [2] JTQ featuring Alison Limerick

LIMIT *Holland, male vocal / instrumental duo – Bernard Oates and Rob van Schaik (Singles: 8 weeks)* pos/wks

5 Jan 85 **SAY YEAH** *Portrait A 4808* 17 8

LIMMIE and the FAMILY COOKIN'

US, male / female vocal group (Singles: 28 weeks) pos/wks

21 Jul 73 ● **YOU CAN DO MAGIC** *Avco 6105 019* 3 13
20 Oct 73 **DREAMBOAT** *Avco 6105 025* 31 5
6 Apr 74 ● **A WALKIN' MIRACLE** *Avco 6105 027* 6 10

LIMP BIZKIT (434 Top 500)

Masters of the metal, punk and hip hop mixing 'rapcore' genre, formed 1995, Florida, include Fred Durst (v) and Wes Borland (g), who was replaced in 2003 by Mike Smith (ex-Snot). Award-winning quintet has sold 30 million albums worldwide (Singles: 60 weeks, Albums: 95 weeks) pos/wks

15 Jul 00 ● **TAKE A LOOK AROUND (THEME FROM 'MI:2')** *Interscope 4973682* 3 13
11 Nov 00 **MY GENERATION (re)** *Interscope IND 97448* 15 8
27 Jan 01 ★ **ROLLIN'** *Interscope IND 97474* ■ 1 13
23 Jun 01 ● **MY WAY** *Interscope 4975732* 6 10
10 Nov 01 **BOILER** *Interscope 4976362* 18 5
27 Sep 03 ● **EAT YOU ALIVE** *Interscope 9811757* 10 7
6 Dec 03 **BEHIND BLUE EYES** *Interscope 9814744* 18 4+
3 Jul 99 ● **SIGNIFICANT OTHER** *Interscope IND 90335* ▲ 10 37
9 Sep 00 **THREE DOLLAR BILL Y'ALL$** *Interscope IND 90124* 50 5
28 Oct 00 ★ **CHOCOLATE STARFISH AND THE HOT DOG FLAVORED WATER** *Interscope 4907932* ▲ 1 48
4 Oct 03 ● **RESULTS MAY VARY** *Interscope 9860971* 7 5

LINA *US, female vocalist (Singles: 1 week)* pos/wks

3 Mar 01 **PLAYA NO MO'** *Atlantic AT 0094CD* 46 1

LINCOLN CITY FC featuring Michael COURTNEY

UK, male football team and male vocalist (Singles: 1 week) pos/wks

4 May 02 **CHIRPY CHIRPY CHEEP CHEEP / JAGGED END** *Nap Music SLCPD 0001* 64 1

Bob LIND *US, male vocalist (Singles: 10 weeks)* pos/wks

10 Mar 66 ● **ELUSIVE BUTTERFLY** *Fontana TF 670* 5 9
26 May 66 **REMEMBER THE RAIN** *Fontana TF 702* 46 1

LINDA and the FUNKY BOYS – *See Linda CARR*

LINDISFARNE 388 Top 500

Perennial folk-rock hybrid, who blended wistful sensitivity, social sentiments and boozy revelry, formed 1969 Newcastle-upon-Tyne; included Alan Hull (d.1996, v/g/p) and Ray Jackson (g). 'Fog on the Tyne' was the top-selling album by a UK act in 1971 (Singles: 55 weeks, Albums: 118 weeks) pos/wks

Date		Title / Label	pos	wks
26 Feb 72	●	**MEET ME ON THE CORNER** *Charisma CB 173*	5	11
13 May 72	●	**LADY ELEANOR** *Charisma CB 153*	3	11
23 Sep 72		**ALL FALL DOWN** *Charisma CB 191*	34	5
3 Jun 78	●	**RUN FOR HOME** *Mercury 6007 177*	10	15
7 Oct 78		**JUKE BOX GYPSY** *Mercury 6007 187*	56	4
10 Nov 90	●	**FOG ON THE TYNE (REVISITED)** *Best ZB 44083* [1]	2	9
30 Oct 71	★	**FOG ON THE TYNE** *Charisma CAS 1050*	1	56
15 Jan 72	●	**NICELY OUT OF TUNE** *Charisma CAS 1025*	8	30
30 Sep 72	●	**DINGLY DELL** *Charisma CAS 1057*	5	10
11 Aug 73		**LINDISFARNE LIVE** *Charisma CLASS 2*	25	6
18 Oct 75		**FINEST HOUR** *Charisma CAS 1108*	55	1
24 Jun 78		**BACK AND FOURTH** *Mercury 9109 609*	22	11
9 Dec 78		**MAGIC IN THE AIR** *Mercury 6641 877*	71	1
23 Oct 82		**SLEEPLESS NIGHTS** *LMP GET 1*	59	3

[1] Gazza and Lindisfarne

See also Alan HULL

LINDSAY *UK, female vocalist (Singles: 4 weeks)* pos/wks

Date		Title / Label	pos	wks
12 May 01		**NO DREAM IMPOSSIBLE** *Universal TV 1589562*	32	4

LINER *UK, male vocal / instrumental group (Singles: 6 weeks)* pos/wks

Date		Title / Label	pos	wks
10 Mar 79		**KEEP REACHING OUT FOR LOVE** *Atlantic K 11235*	49	3
26 May 79		**YOU AND ME** *Atlantic K 11285*	44	3

Andy LING *UK, male producer (Singles: 1 week)* pos/wks

Date		Title / Label	pos	wks
13 May 00		**FIXATION** *Hooj Choons HOOJ 094CD*	55	1

Laurie LINGO and the DIPSTICKS *UK, male DJ / vocal duo – Dave Lee Travis and Paul Burnett (Singles: 7 weeks)* pos/wks

Date		Title / Label	pos	wks
17 Apr 76	●	**CONVOY GB** *State STAT 23*	4	7

LINK *US, male rapper (Singles: 1 week)* pos/wks

Date		Title / Label	pos	wks
7 Nov 98		**WHATCHA GONE DO?** *Relativity 6666055*	48	1

LINKIN PARK 380 Top 500

Pioneering alternative metal / rap-rock sextet formed Los Angeles. Members include Chester Bennington (v), Mike Shinoda (rap/v) and Joseph Hahn (DJ). Grammy-winning 'Hybrid Theory' was top-selling US album of 2001 with 4.8 million (world total more than 17 million) (Singles: 55 weeks, Albums: 121 weeks) pos/wks

Date		Title / Label	pos	wks
27 Jan 01		**ONE STEP CLOSER** *Warner Brothers W 550CD*	24	4
21 Apr 01		**CRAWLING** *Warner Brothers W 556CD*	16	8
30 Jun 01		**PAPERCUT** *Warner Brothers W 562CD*	14	6
20 Oct 01	●	**IN THE END** *Warner Brothers W 569CD*	8	9
3 Aug 02	●	**H! VLTG3 / PTS.OF.ATHRTY** *Warner Brothers W 588CD*	9	6
29 Mar 03	●	**SOMEWHERE I BELONG** *Warner Brothers W 602CD*	10	8
21 Jun 03		**FAINT** *Warner Brothers W 610CD1*	15	8
20 Sep 03		**NUMB** *Warner Brothers W 622CD1*	14	6
20 Jan 01	●	**(HYBRID THEORY)** *Warner Bros. 9362477552*	4	77
10 Aug 02	●	**REANIMATION** *Warner Bros. 9362483542*	3	8
29 Mar 03	★	**METEORA** *Warner Bros. 9362484612* ■ ▲	1	33
6 Dec 03		**LIVE IN TEXAS** *Warner Bros. WB485632*	47	3

'Reanimation' is a remix album of songs from 'Hybrid Theory'

See also X-ECUTIONERS featuring Mike SHINODA and Mr HAHN of LINKIN PARK

LINOLEUM *UK, male / female vocal / instrumental group (Singles: 1 week)* pos/wks

Date		Title / Label	pos	wks
12 Jul 97		**MARQUIS** *Lino Vinyl LINO 004CD1*	73	1

LINUS LOVES featuring Sam OBERNIK *UK, male producer – Linus O'Brien and female vocalist (Singles: 3 weeks)* pos/wks

Date		Title / Label	pos	wks
22 Nov 03		**STAND BACK** *Data / MoS DATA 62CD*	31	3

LINX *UK, male vocal / instrumental duo – David Grant and Peter 'Sketch' Martin (Singles: 45 weeks, Albums: 23 weeks)* pos/wks

Date		Title / Label	pos	wks
20 Sep 80		**YOU'RE LYING** *Chrysalis CHS 2461*	15	10
7 Mar 81	●	**INTUITION** *Chrysalis CHS 2500*	7	11
13 Jun 81		**THROW AWAY THE KEY** *Chrysalis CHS 2519*	21	9
5 Sep 81		**SO THIS IS ROMANCE** *Chrysalis CHS 2546*	15	9
21 Nov 81		**CAN'T HELP MYSELF** *Chrysalis CHS 2565*	55	3
10 Jul 82		**PLAYTHING** *Chrysalis CHS 2621*	48	3
28 Mar 81	●	**INTUITION** *Chrysalis CHR 1332*	8	19
31 Oct 81		**GO AHEAD** *Chrysalis CHR 1358*	35	4

LIONROCK *UK, male producer – Justin Robertson (Singles: 14 weeks, Albums: 3 weeks)* pos/wks

Date		Title / Label	pos	wks
5 Dec 92		**LIONROCK** *Deconstruction 74321124381*	63	1
8 May 93		**PACKET OF PEACE** *Deconstruction 74321144372*	32	3
23 Oct 93		**CARNIVAL** *Deconstruction 74321164862*	34	2
27 Aug 94		**TRIPWIRE** *Deconstruction 74321204702*	44	1
6 Apr 96		**STRAIGHT AT YER HEAD** *Deconstruction 74321342972*	33	2
27 Jul 96		**FIRE UP THE SHOESAW** *Deconstruction 74321382652*	43	1
14 Mar 98		**RUDE BOY ROCK** *Concrete HARD 31CD*	20	3
30 May 98		**SCATTER & SWING** *Concrete HARD 35CD*	54	1
20 Apr 96		**AN INSTINCT FOR DETECTION** *Deconstruction 74321342812*	30	2
28 Mar 98		**CITY DELIRIOUS** *Concrete HARD 32LPCD*	73	1

LIPPS INC *US, male / female vocal / instrumental group (Singles: 13 weeks)* pos/wks

Date		Title / Label	pos	wks
17 May 80	●	**FUNKYTOWN** *Casablanca CAN 194* ▲	2	13

LIQUID *UK, male producer – Eamon Downes (Singles: 20 weeks)* pos/wks

Date		Title / Label	pos	wks
21 Mar 92		**SWEET HARMONY** *XL Recordings XLS 28*	15	6
5 Sep 92		**THE FUTURE MUSIC (EP)** *XL Recordings XLT 33*	59	2
20 Mar 93		**TIME TO GET UP** *XL Recordings XLS 40CD*	46	2
8 Jul 95		**SWEET HARMONY (re-mix) / ONE LOVE FAMILY** *XL Recordings XLS 65CD*	14	6
21 Oct 95		**CLOSER** *XL Recordings XLS 66CD*	47	2
25 Jul 98		**STRONG** *Higher Ground HIGHS 7CD*	59	1
21 Oct 00		**ORLANDO DAWN** *Xtravaganza XTRAV 16CDS*	53	1

Tracks on The Future Music (EP): Liquid Is Liquid / Music / House (Is a Feeling) / The Year 3000. On the first two hits act also included Shane Heneghan

LIQUID CHILD *Germany, male production duo – Tobias Menguser and Jürgen Herbarth (Singles: 2 weeks)* pos/wks

Date		Title / Label	pos	wks
23 Oct 99		**DIVING FACES** *Essential Recordings ESCD 9*	25	2

LIQUID GOLD *UK, male / female vocal / instrumental group (Singles: 46 weeks, Albums: 3 weeks)* pos/wks

Date		Title / Label	pos	wks
2 Dec 78		**ANYWAY YOU DO IT** *Creole CR 159*	41	7
23 Feb 80	●	**DANCE YOURSELF DIZZY** *Polo POLO 1*	2	14
31 May 80	●	**SUBSTITUTE** *Polo POLO 4*	8	9
1 Nov 80		**THE NIGHT THE WINE AND THE ROSES** *POLO 6*	32	7
28 Mar 81		**DON'T PANIC** *Polo POLO 8*	42	5
21 Aug 82		**WHERE DID WE GO WRONG** *Polo POLO 23*	56	4
16 Aug 80		**LIQUID GOLD** *Polo POLP 101*	34	3

LIQUID OXYGEN *US, male producer (Singles: 2 weeks)* pos/wks

Date		Title / Label	pos	wks
28 Apr 90		**THE PLANET DANCE (MOVE YA BODY)** *Champion CHAMP 242*	56	2

LIQUID PEOPLE *UK, male production duo (Singles: 2 weeks)* pos/wks

Date		Title / Label	pos	wks
20 Jul 02		**MONSTER** *Defected DFECT 49* [1]	67	1
21 Jun 03		**IT'S MY LIFE** *Nebula NEBCD 045* [2]	64	1

[1] Liquid People vs Simple Minds [2] Liquid People vs Talk Talk

LIQUID STATE featuring Marcella WOODS *UK, male production duo with female vocalist (Singles: 1 week)* pos/wks

Date		Title / Label	pos	wks
30 Mar 02		**FALLING** *Perfecto PERF 29CDS*	60	1

LISA LISA

US, female vocalist – Lisa Velez (Singles: 32 weeks)

Date	Title	pos	wks
4 May 85	**I WONDER IF I TAKE YOU HOME (re)** *CBS A 6057* [1]	12	17
31 Oct 87	**LOST IN EMOTION** *CBS 651036 7* [2] ▲	58	4
13 Jul 91	**LET THE BEAT HIT 'EM** *Columbia 6572867* [2]	17	6
24 Aug 91	**LET THE BEAT HIT 'EM PART 2** *Columbia 6573747* [2]	49	2
26 Mar 94	**SKIP TO MY LU** *Chrysalis CDCHS 5006*	34	3
21 Sep 85	**LISA LISA AND CULT JAM WITH FULL FORCE** *CBS 26593* [1]	96	1

[1] Lisa Lisa and Cult Jam with Full Force [2] Lisa Lisa and Cult Jam [1] Lisa Lisa and Cult Jam with Full Force

LISA MARIE – *See Malcolm McLAREN*

LISA MARIE EXPERIENCE

UK, male instrumental / production duo – Dean Marriot and Neil Hynde (Singles: 15 weeks)

Date	Title	pos	wks
27 Apr 96	● **KEEP ON JUMPIN' (re)** *ffrr FCD 271*	7	13
10 Aug 96	**DO THAT TO ME** *Positiva CDTIV 57*	33	2

LISBON LIONS featuring Martin O'NEILL & CELTIC CHORUS

UK, male football supporters vocal group (Singles: 4 weeks)

Date	Title	pos	wks
11 May 02	**THE BEST DAY OF OUR LIVES** *Concept CDCON 32*	17	4

LIT

US, male vocal / instrumental group (Singles: 7 weeks, Albums: 1 week)

Date	Title	pos	wks
26 Jun 99	**MY OWN WORST ENEMY** *RCA 74321669992*	16	4
25 Sep 99	**ZIP – LOCK** *RCA 74321701852*	60	1
19 Aug 00	**OVER MY HEAD** *Capitol 8889532*	37	2
10 Jul 99	**A PLACE IN THE SUN** *RCA 7863677752*	52	1

LITHIUM and Sonya MADAN

US, male producer – Victor Imbres and UK, female vocalist (Singles: 2 weeks)

Date	Title	pos	wks
1 Mar 97	**RIDE A ROCKET** *ffrr FCD 293*	40	2

See also ECHOBELLY

De Etta LITTLE and Nelson PIGFORD

US, female / male vocal duo (Singles: 5 weeks)

Date	Title	pos	wks
13 Aug 77	**YOU TAKE MY HEART AWAY** *United Artists UP 36257*	35	5

LITTLE ANGELS

UK, male vocal / instrumental group (Singles: 41 weeks, Albums: 15 weeks)

Date	Title	pos	wks
4 Mar 89	**BIG BAD EP** *Polydor LTLEP 2*	74	1
24 Feb 90	**KICKING UP DUST** *Polydor LTL 5*	46	4
12 May 90	**RADICAL YOUR LOVER** *Polydor LTL 6* [1]	34	4
4 Aug 90	**SHE'S A LITTLE ANGEL** *Polydor LTL 7*	21	3
2 Feb 91	**BONEYARD** *Polydor LTL 8*	33	4
30 Mar 91	**PRODUCT OF THE WORKING CLASS** *Polydor LTL 9*	40	2
1 Jun 91	**YOUNG GODS** *Polydor LTL 10*	34	2
20 Jul 91	**I AIN'T GONNA CRY** *Polydor LTL 11*	26	3
7 Nov 92	**TOO MUCH TOO YOUNG** *Polydor LTL 12*	22	3
9 Jan 93	**WOMANKIND** *Polydor LTLCD 13*	12	5
24 Apr 93	**SOAPBOX** *Polydor LTLCD 14*	33	4
25 Sep 93	**SAIL AWAY** *Polydor LTLCD 15*	45	3
9 Apr 94	**TEN MILES HIGH** *Polydor LTLCD 16*	18	3
2 Mar 91	**YOUNG GODS** *Polydor 8478461*	17	6
6 Feb 93	★ **JAM** *Polydor 5176422* ■	1	5
23 Apr 94	**LITTLE OF THE PAST** *Polydor 5219362*	20	2
2 Jul 94	**TOO POSH TO MOSH TOO GOOD TO LAST!** *Essential ESSCD 213*	18	2

[1] Little Angels featuring the Big Bad Horns

Tracks on Big Bad EP: She's a Little Angel / Don't Waste My Time / Better Than the Rest / Sex in Cars

LITTLE ANTHONY and the IMPERIALS

US, male vocal group (Singles: 4 weeks)

Date	Title	pos	wks
31 Jul 76	**BETTER USE YOUR HEAD** *United Artists UP 36141*	42	4

LITTLE BENNY and the MASTERS

US, male rapper / instrumentalist – trumpet – and male instrumental group (Singles: 7 weeks)

Date	Title	pos	wks
2 Feb 85	**WHO COMES TO BOOGIE** *Bluebird 10 BR 13*	33	7

LITTLE CAESAR

UK, male vocalist (Singles: 3 weeks)

Date	Title	pos	wks
9 Jun 90	**THE WHOLE OF THE MOON** *A1 EAU 1*	68	3

LITTLE EVA

US, female vocalist – Eva Boyd d. 10 Apr 2003 (Singles: 45 weeks)

Date	Title	pos	wks
6 Sep 62	● **THE LOCO-MOTION (re)** *London HL 9581* ▲	2	28
3 Jan 63	**KEEP YOUR HANDS OFF MY BABY** *London HLU 9633*	30	5
7 Mar 63	**LET'S TURKEY TROT** *London HLU 9687*	13	12

'Loco-motion' re-entry peaked at No.11 in Jul 1972

See also Big Dee IRWIN

LITTLE FEAT

US, male vocal / instrumental group (Albums: 19 weeks)

Date	Title	pos	wks
6 Dec 75	**THE LAST RECORD ALBUM** *Warner Bros. K 56156*	36	3
21 May 77	● **TIME LOVES A HERO** *Warner Bros. K 56349*	8	11
11 Mar 78	**WAITING FOR COLUMBUS** *Warner Bros. K 66075*	43	1
1 Dec 79	**DOWN ON THE FARM** *Warner Bros. K 56667*	46	3
8 Aug 81	**HOY-HOY!** *Warner Bros. K 666100*	76	1

See also Lowell GEORGE

LITTLE LOUIE – *See Louie VEGA*

LITTLE MS MARCIE – *See MELT featuring LITTLE Ms MARCIE*

LITTLE RICHARD

US, male vocalist / instrumentalist – piano, Richard Penniman (Singles: 116 weeks)

Date	Title	pos	wks
14 Dec 56	**RIP IT UP** *London HLO 8336*	30	1
8 Feb 57	● **LONG TALL SALLY** *London HLO 8366*	3	16
22 Feb 57	**TUTTI FRUTTI** *London HLO 8366*	29	1
8 Mar 57	**SHE'S GOT IT (re)** *London HLO 8382*	15	9
15 Mar 57	● **THE GIRL CAN'T HELP IT** *London HLO 8382*	9	11
28 Jun 57	● **LUCILLE** *London HLO 8446*	10	9
13 Sep 57	**JENNY JENNY** *London HLO 8470*	11	5
29 Nov 57	**KEEP A KNOCKIN'** *London HLO 8509*	21	7
28 Feb 58	● **GOOD GOLLY MISS MOLLY** *London HLU 8560*	8	9
11 Jul 58	**OOH! MY SOUL (re)** *London HLO 8647*	22	4
2 Jan 59	● **BABY FACE** *London HLU 8770*	2	15
3 Apr 59	**BY THE LIGHT OF THE SILVERY MOON** *London HLU 8831*	17	5
5 Jun 59	**KANSAS CITY** *London HLU 8868*	26	5
11 Oct 62	**HE GOT WHAT HE WANTED (BUT HE LOST WHAT HE HAD)** *Mercury AMT 1189*	38	4
4 Jun 64	**BAMA LAMA BAMA LOO** *London HL 9896*	20	7
2 Jul 77	**GOOD GOLLY MISS MOLLY / RIP IT UP** *Creole CR 140*	37	4
14 Jun 86	**GREAT GOSH A'MIGHTY! (IT'S A MATTER OF TIME)** *MCA MCA 1049*	62	2
25 Oct 86	**OPERATOR** *WEA YZ 89*	67	2

The 1977 versions of 'Good Golly Miss Molly' and 'Rip It Up' on Creole are re-recordings

LITTLE STEVEN

US, male vocalist / instrumentalist – guitar (Singles: 3 weeks, Albums: 4 weeks)

Date	Title	pos	wks
23 May 87	**BITTER FRUIT** *Manhattan MT 21*	66	3
6 Nov 82	**MEN WITHOUT WOMEN** *EMI America 3027* [1]	73	2
6 Jun 87	**FREEDOM NO COMPROMISE** *Manhattan MTL 1010*	52	2

[1] Little Steven and the Disciples of Soul

LITTLE T – *See REBEL MC*

LITTLE TONY and his BROTHERS

Italy, male vocal group, leader – Anthony Ciacci (Singles: 3 weeks)

Date	Title	pos	wks
15 Jan 60	**TOO GOOD** *Decca F 11190*	19	3

LITTLE TREES

Denmark, female vocal group (Singles: 7 weeks)

Date	Title	pos	wks
1 Sep 01	**HELP! I'M A FISH** *RCA 74321874652*	11	7

LITTLE VILLAGE

UK / US, male vocal / instrumental group (Albums: 4 weeks) pos/wks

29 Feb 92 **LITTLE VILLAGE** *Reprise 7599267132* 23 4

LIVE

US, male vocal / instrumental group (Singles: 13 weeks, Albums: 9 weeks) pos/wks

18 Feb 95 **I ALONE** *Radioactive RAXTD 13* 48 4
1 Jul 95 **SELLING THE DRAMA** *Radioactive RAXTD 17* 30 2
7 Oct 95 **ALL OVER YOU** *Radioactive RAXTD 20* 48 1
13 Jan 96 **LIGHTNING CRASHES** *Radioactive RAXTD 23* 33 2
15 Mar 97 **LAKINI'S JUICE** *Radioactive RAD 49023* 29 2
12 Jul 97 **FREAKS** *Radioactive RAXTD 29* 60 1
5 Feb 00 **THE DOLPHIN'S CRY** *Radioactive RAXTD 39* 62 1
15 Jul 95 **THROWING COPPER** *Radioactive RAD 10997* ▲ 37 6
29 Mar 97 **SECRET SAMADHI** *Radioactive RAD 11590* ▲ 31 2
16 Oct 99 **THE DISTANCE TO HERE** *Radioactive RAD 11966* 56 1

LIVE ELEMENT

US, male production duo – Greg Bahary and Chris Malinchak (Singles: 2 weeks) pos/wks

26 Jan 02 **BE FREE** *Strictly Rhythm SRUKCD 11* 26 2

LIVE REPORT

UK, male vocal / instrumental group (Singles: 1 week) pos/wks

20 May 89 **WHY DO I ALWAYS GET IT WRONG** *Brouhaha CUE 7* 73 1

LIVERPOOL EXPRESS

UK, male vocal / instrumental group (Singles: 26 weeks) pos/wks

26 Jun 76 **YOU ARE MY LOVE** *Warner Bros. K 16743* 11 9
16 Oct 76 **HOLD TIGHT** *Warner Bros. K 16799* 46 2
18 Dec 76 **EVERY MAN MUST HAVE A DREAM** *Warner Bros. K 16854* 17 11
4 Jun 77 **DREAMIN'** *Warner Bros. K 16933* 40 4

LIVERPOOL FC

UK, male football team vocalists (Singles: 21 weeks) pos/wks

28 May 77 **WE CAN DO IT (EP)** *State STAT 50* 15 4
23 Apr 83 **LIVERPOOL (WE'RE NEVER GONNA...) / LIVERPOOL (ANTHEM)** *Mean MEAN 102* 54 4
17 May 86 **SITTING ON THE TOP OF THE WORLD** *Columbia DB 9116* 50 2
14 May 88 ● **ANFIELD RAP (RED MACHINE IN FULL EFFECT)** *Virgin LFC 1* 3 6
18 May 96 ● **PASS AND MOVE (IT'S THE LIVERPOOL GROOVE)** *Telstar LFCCD 96* [1] 4 5

[1] Liverpool FC and the Boot Room Boyz

Tracks on We Can Do It (EP): We Can Do It / Liverpool Lou / We Shall Not Be Moved / You'll Never Walk Alone

LIVIN' JOY

US / Italy, male / female vocal / instrumental group – leader Paolo Visnadi (Singles: 44 weeks, Albums: 2 weeks) pos/wks

3 Sep 94 **DREAMER** *Undiscovered MCSTD 1993* 18 6
13 May 95 ★ **DREAMER (re-mix)** *Undiscovered MCSTD 2056* ■ 1 11
15 Jun 96 ● **DON'T STOP MOVIN'** *Undiscovered MCSTD 40041* 5 14
2 Nov 96 ● **FOLLOW THE RULES** *Undiscovered MCSTD 40081* 9 5
5 Apr 97 **WHERE CAN I FIND LOVE** *Undiscovered MCSTD 40108* 12 4
23 Aug 97 **DEEP IN YOU** *Universal MCSTD 40136* 17 4
16 Nov 96 **DON'T STOP MOVIN'** *Undiscovered MCD 60023* 41 2

See also ALEX PARTY

LIVING COLOUR

US, male vocal / instrumental group (Singles: 22 weeks, Albums: 22 weeks) pos/wks

27 Oct 90 **TYPE** *Epic LCL 7* 75 1
2 Feb 91 **LOVE REARS ITS UGLY HEAD** *Epic 6565937* 12 11
1 Jun 91 **SOLACE OF YOU** *Epic 6569087* 33 5
26 Oct 91 **CULT OF PERSONALITY** *Epic 6575357* 67 2
20 Feb 93 **LEAVE IT ALONE** *Epic 6589762* 34 2
17 Apr 93 **AUSLANDER** *Epic 6591732* 53 1
15 Sep 90 **TIME'S UP** *Epic 4669201* 20 19
6 Mar 93 **STAIN** *Epic 4728562* 19 3

LIVING IN A BOX

UK, male vocal / instrumental group – including Richard Derbyshire (Singles: 62 weeks, Albums: 35 weeks) pos/wks

4 Apr 87 ● **LIVING IN A BOX** *Chrysalis LIB 1* 5 13
13 Jun 87 **SCALES OF JUSTICE** *Chrysalis LIB 2* 30 6
26 Sep 87 **SO THE STORY GOES** *Chrysalis LIB 3* [1] 34 8
30 Jan 88 **LOVE IS THE ART** *Chrysalis LIB 4* 45 4
18 Feb 89 ● **BLOW THE HOUSE DOWN** *Chrysalis LIB 5* 10 9
10 Jun 89 **GATECRASHING** *Chrysalis LIB 6* 36 6
23 Sep 89 ● **ROOM IN YOUR HEART** *Chrysalis LIB 7* 5 13
30 Dec 89 **DIFFERENT AIR (re)** *Chrysalis LIB 8* 57 3
9 May 87 **LIVING IN A BOX** *Chrysalis CDL 1547* 25 19
8 Jul 89 **GATECRASHING** *Chrysalis CDL 1676* 21 16

[1] Living in a Box featuring Bobby Womack

Dandy LIVINGSTONE

Jamaica, male vocalist – Robert Livingstone Thompson (Singles: 19 weeks) pos/wks

2 Sep 72 **SUZANNE BEWARE OF THE DEVIL** *Horse HOSS 16* 14 11
13 Jan 73 **BIG CITY / THINK ABOUT THAT** *Horse HOSS 25* 26 8

LLAMA FARMERS

UK, male / female vocal / instrumental group (Singles: 2 weeks) pos/wks

6 Feb 99 **BIG WHEELS** *Beggars Banquet BBQ 333CD* 67 1
15 May 99 **GET THE KEYS AND GO** *Beggars Banquet BBQ 335CD* 74 1

Kelly LLORENNA

UK, female vocalist (Singles: 32 weeks, Albums: 2 weeks) pos/wks

7 May 94 **SET YOU FREE** *All Around the World CDGLOBE 124* [1] 39 4
24 Feb 96 **BRIGHTER DAY** *Pukka CDPUKKA 5* 43 2
25 Jul 98 **HEART OF GOLD** *Diverse VERSE 2CD* [2] 55 1
24 Mar 01 **TRUE LOVE NEVER DIES** *All Around the World CDGLOBE 240* [3] 34 3
2 Feb 02 ● **TRUE LOVE NEVER DIES (re-mix)** *All Around the World CDGLOBE 248* [3] 7 10
6 Jul 02 ● **TELL IT TO MY HEART** *All Around the World CDGLOBE 256* 9 8
30 Nov 02 **HEART OF GOLD** *All Around the World CDGLOBE 271* 19 4
7 Dec 02 **ALL CLUBBED UP – THE BEST OF KELLY LLORENNA** *Universal TV 0666082* 62 2

[1] N-Trance featuring Kelly Llorenna [2] Force and Styles featuring Kelly Llorenna
[3] Flip and Fill featuring Kelly Llorenna

See also N-TRANCE

Andrew LLOYD WEBBER

UK, male composer / producer (Albums: 37 weeks) pos/wks

11 Feb 78 ● **VARIATIONS** *MCA MCF 2824* 2 19
23 Mar 85 ● **REQUIEM** *HMV ALW 1* 4 18

'Variations' features cellist Julian Lloyd Webber. 'Requiem' credits Placido Domingo, Sarah Brightman, Paul Miles-Kingston, Winchester Cathedral Choir and the English Chamber Orchestra conducted by Lorin Maazel

See also ENGLISH CHAMBER ORCHESTRA; Lorin MAAZEL; WINCHESTER CATHEDRAL CHOIR

Julian LLOYD WEBBER

UK, male instrumentalist – cello (Albums: 19 weeks) pos/wks

14 Sep 85 **PIECES** *Polydor PROLP 6* 59 5
21 Feb 87 **ELGAR CELLO CONCERTO** *Philips 416 3541* 94 1
27 Oct 90 **LLOYD WEBBER PLAYS LLOYD WEBBER** *Philips 4322911* 15 13

First two albums credit the London Symphony Orchestra and the third credits the Royal Philharmonic Orchestra.

See also LONDON SYMPHONY ORCHESTRA; ROYAL PHILHARMONIC ORCHESTRA; Andrew LLOYD WEBBER

Don LLOYDIE – *See SOUNDMAN and Don LLOYDIE with Elisabeth TROY*

LO FIDELITY ALLSTARS

UK, male vocal / instrumental group (Singles: 5 weeks, Albums: 4 weeks) pos/wks

11 Oct 97 **DISCO MACHINE GUN** *Skint SKINT 30CD* 50 1
2 May 98 **VISION INCISION** *Skint SKINT 33CD* 30 2

28 Nov 98 **BATTLEFLAG** *Skint SKINT 38CD* [1] 36 2
6 Jun 98 **HOW TO OPERATE WITH A BLOWN MIND** *Skint BRASSIC 8CD* 15 4

[1] Lo Fidelity Allstars featuring Pigeonhed

LOBO *US, male vocalist – Kent LaVoie (Singles: 25 weeks)* pos/wks

19 Jun 71 ● **ME AND YOU AND A DOG NAMED BOO** *Philips 6073 801* 4 14
8 Jun 74 ● **I'D LOVE YOU TO WANT ME** *UK 68* 5 11

LOBO
Holland, male vocalist – Imrich Lobo (Singles: 11 weeks) pos/wks

25 Jul 81 ● **THE CARIBBEAN DISCO SHOW** *Polydor POSP 302* 8 11

LOCK 'N' LOAD *Holland, male DJ / production duo – Francis Rooijen and Nilz Pijpers (Singles: 13 weeks)* pos/wks

15 Apr 00 ● **BLOW YA MIND (re)** *Pepper 9230162* 6 11
3 Mar 01 **HOUSE SOME MORE** *Pepper 9230422* 45 2

Josef LOCKE *Ireland, male vocalist – Joseph McLaughlin, d. 15 Oct 1999 (Albums: 20 weeks)* pos/wks

28 Jun 69 **THE WORLD OF JOSEF LOCKE TODAY** *Decca SPA 21* 29 1
21 Mar 92 ● **HEAR MY SONG (THE BEST OF JOSEF LOCKE)** *EMI CDGO 2034* 7 17
27 Jun 92 **TAKE A PAIR OF SPARKLING EYES** *EMI CDGO 2038* 41 2

Hank LOCKLIN *US, male vocalist (Singles: 41 weeks)* pos/wks

11 Aug 60 ● **PLEASE HELP ME, I'M FALLING** *RCA 1188* 9 19
15 Feb 62 **FROM HERE TO THERE TO YOU** *RCA 1273* 44 3
15 Nov 62 **WE'RE GONNA GO FISHIN'** *RCA 1305* 18 11
5 May 66 **I FEEL A CRY COMING ON** *RCA 1510* 29 8

LOCKSMITH
US, male vocal / instrumental group (Singles: 6 weeks) pos/wks

23 Aug 80 **UNLOCK THE FUNK** *Arista ARIST 364* 42 6

LOCOMOTIVE
UK, male vocal / instrumental group (Singles: 8 weeks) pos/wks

16 Oct 68 **RUDI'S IN LOVE** *Parlophone R 5718* 25 8

John LODGE
UK, male vocalist / instrumentalist – guitar (Albums: 20 weeks) pos/wks

29 Mar 75 ● **BLUE JAYS** *Threshold THS 12* [1] 4 18
19 Feb 77 **NATURAL AVENUE** *Decca TXS 120* 38 2

[1] Justin Hayward and John Lodge

See also MOODY BLUES

LODGER
UK, male / female vocal / instrumental group (Singles: 2 weeks) pos/wks

2 May 98 **I'M LEAVING** *Island CID 693* 40 2

Lisa LOEB and NINE STORIES *US, female / male vocal / instrumental group (Singles: 17 weeks, Albums: 2 weeks)* pos/wks

3 Sep 94 ● **STAY (I MISSED YOU)** *RCA 74321212522* ▲ 6 15
16 Sep 95 **DO YOU SLEEP?** *Geffen GFSTD 96* 45 2
7 Oct 95 **TAILS** *Geffen GED 24734*.....39 2

Nils LOFGREN *US, male vocalist / instrumentalist – guitar (Singles: 3 weeks, Albums: 30 weeks)* pos/wks

8 Jun 85 **SECRETS IN THE STREET** *Towerbell TOW 68* 53 3
17 Apr 76 ● **CRY TOUGH** *A&M AMLH 64573* 8 11
26 Mar 77 **I CAME TO DANCE** *A&M AMLH 64628*.....30 4
5 Nov 77 **NIGHT AFTER NIGHT** *A&M AMLH 68439*.....38 2
26 Sep 81 **NIGHT FADES AWAY** *Backstreet MCF 3121* 50 3
1 May 82 **A RHYTHM ROMANCE** *A&M AMLH 68543*.....100 1
6 Jul 85 **FLIP** *Towerbell TOWLP 11* 36 7
5 Apr 86 **CODE OF THE ROAD** *Towerbell TOWDLP 17* 86 1
27 Apr 91 **SILVER LINING** *Essential ESSLP 145* 61 1

Johnny LOGAN *Ireland, male vocalist – Sean Sherrard (Singles: 24 weeks, Albums: 1 week)* pos/wks

3 May 80 ★ **WHAT'S ANOTHER YEAR** *Epic EPC 8572* 1 8
23 May 87 ● **HOLD ME NOW** *Epic LOG 1* 2 11
22 Aug 87 **I'M NOT IN LOVE** *Epic LOG 2* 51 5
22 Aug 87 **HOLD ME NOW** *CBS 451 0731* 83 1

Kenny LOGGINS
US, male vocalist / instrumentalist (Singles: 21 weeks) pos/wks

28 Apr 84 ● **FOOTLOOSE** *CBS A 4101* ▲ 6 10
1 Nov 86 **DANGER ZONE** *CBS A 7188* 45 11

LOGO featuring Dawn JOSEPH
UK, male production duo and female vocalist (Singles: 1 week) pos/wks

8 Dec 01 **DON'T PANIC** *Manifesto FESCD 89* 42 1

LOLA *US, female vocalist (Singles: 1 week)* pos/wks

28 Mar 87 **WAX THE VAN** *Syncopate SY 1* 65 1

LOLLY *UK, female vocalist – Anna Klumby (Singles: 44 weeks, Albums: 12 weeks)* pos/wks

10 Jul 99 ● **VIVA LA RADIO** *Polydor 5639492* 6 9
18 Sep 99 ● **MICKEY** *Polydor 5613682* 4 10
4 Dec 99 ● **BIG BOYS DON'T CRY / ROCKIN' ROBIN** *Polydor 5615552* 10 9
6 May 00 **PER SEMPRE AMORE (FOREVER IN LOVE) (re)** *Polydor 5617882* 11 10
9 Sep 00 **GIRLS JUST WANNA HAVE FUN** *Polydor 5619762* 14 6
2 Oct 99 **MY FIRST ALBUM** *Polydor 5479622*.....21 12

Alain LOMBARD – *See Mady MESPLE and Danielle MILLET with the PARIS OPÉRA-COMIQUE ORCHESTRA conducted by Alain LOMBARD*

Julie LONDON
US, female vocalist – Julie Peck d. 18 Oct 2000 (Singles: 3 weeks) pos/wks

5 Apr 57 **CRY ME A RIVER** *London HLU 8240* 22 3

Laurie LONDON
UK, male vocalist (Singles: 12 weeks) pos/wks

8 Nov 57 **HE'S GOT THE WHOLE WORLD IN HIS HANDS** *Parlophone R 4359* 12 12

With Geoff Love his Orchestra and Chorus

LONDON BOYS *UK, male vocal duo – Edem Ephraim and Dennis Fuller, both d. 21 Sep 1996 (Singles: 46 weeks, Albums: 29 weeks)* pos/wks

10 Dec 88 ● **REQUIEM (re)** *WEA YZ 345* 4 21
1 Jul 89 ● **LONDON NIGHTS** *WEA YZ 393* 2 9
16 Sep 89 **HARLEM DESIRE** *WEA YZ 415* 17 7
2 Dec 89 **MY LOVE** *WEA YZ 433* 46 6
16 Jun 90 **CHAPEL OF LOVE** *East West YZ 458* 75 1
19 Jan 91 **FREEDOM** *East West YZ 554* 54 2
29 Jul 89 ● **THE TWELVE COMMANDMENTS OF DANCE** *WEA WX 278*.....2 29

'Reqium' peaked at No.4 after re-entering in April 1989

LONDON COMMUNITY GOSPEL CHOIR – *See Sal SOLO*

LONDON PHILHARMONIC CHOIR
UK, male / female choir (Albums: 20 weeks) pos/wks

3 Dec 60 ● **THE MESSIAH** *Pye Golden Guinea GGL 0062* [1] 10 7
13 Nov 76 ● **SOUND OF GLORY** *Arcade ADEP 25* [2] 10 10
13 Apr 91 **PRAISE – 18 CHORAL MASTERPIECES** *Pop & Arts PATLP 301* [3] 54 3

[1] London Philharmonic Choir with the London Orchestra conducted by Peter Susskind [2] London Philharmonic Choir with the National Philharmonic Orchestra conducted by John Aldiss [3] London Philharmonic Choir with the National Philharmonic Orchestra

See also John ALDISS; Walter SUSSKIND; ADIEMUS

LONDON PHILHARMONIC ORCHESTRA *(Albums: 22 weeks)* pos/wks

23 Apr 60	**RAVEL'S BOLERO** *London HAV 2189*	15	4
8 Apr 61	**VICTORY AT SEA** *Pye GGL 0073*	12	1
21 May 83 ●	**DRESSED FOR THE OCCASION** *EMI EMC 3432* [1]	7	17

[1] Cliff Richard and the London Philharmonic Orchestra

See also Nigel KENNEDY; Ennio MORRICONE; Justin HAYWARD; Cliff RICHARD

LONDON STRING CHORALE
UK, orchestra / choir (Singles: 13 weeks) pos/wks

15 Dec 73	**GALLOPING HOME (re)** *Polydor 2058 280*	31	13

LONDON SYMPHONY ORCHESTRA 278 Top 500
Formed in 1904, one of the chart's largest acts. Principal conductors have included André Previn and Sir Colin Davis. Famous for global tours and soundtrack recordings, they achieved greatest chart success with symphonic arrangements of rock classics (Singles: 7 weeks, Albums: 221 weeks) pos/wks

6 Jan 79	**THEME FROM 'SUPERMAN' (MAIN TITLE)** *Warner Bros. K 17292*	32	5
6 Dec 97	**JUST SHOW ME HOW TO LOVE YOU** *Coaltion COLA 035CD* [1]	54	2
18 Mar 72	**TOP TV THEMES** *Studio Two STWO 372*	13	7
16 Dec 72 ●	**THE STRAUSS FAMILY** *Polydor 2659 014* [1]	2	21
5 Jul 75	**MUSIC FROM 'EDWARD VII'** *Polydor 2659 041*	52	1
18 Dec 76	**THE SNOW GOOSE** *RCA RS 1088* [2]	49	1
21 Jan 78	**STAR WARS (FILM SOUNDTRACK)** *20th Century BTD 541*	21	12
8 Jul 78 ●	**CLASSIC ROCK** *K-Tel ONE 1009*	3	39
10 Feb 79	**CLASSIC ROCK – THE SECOND MOVEMENT** *K-Tel NE 1039*	26	8
5 Jan 80	**RHAPSODY IN BLACK** *K-Tel ONE 1063*	34	5
1 Aug 81 ●	**CLASSIC ROCK – ROCK CLASSICS** *K-Tel ONE 1123*	5	23
27 Nov 82	**THE BEST OF CLASSIC ROCK** *K-Tel ONE 1080*	35	11
27 Aug 83	**CLASSIC ROCK – ROCK SYMPHONIES** *K-Tel ONE 1243*	40	9
26 Oct 85	**HITS ON OPERA** *Stylus SMR 8505* [3]	38	4
16 Nov 85	**THE POWER OF CLASSIC ROCK** *Portrait PRT 10049*	13	15
14 Nov 87	**CLASSIC ROCK COUNTDOWN** *CBS MOOD 3*	32	16
18 Nov 89	**CLASSIC ROCK – THE LIVING YEARS** *CBS MOOD 9*	51	6
18 Jan 92	**WIND OF CHANGE – CLASSIC ROCK** *Columbia MOODCD 19* [4]	24	8
19 Nov 94	**THE WORKS OF RICE AND LLOYD WEBBER** *Vision VISCD 4*	55	2
23 Sep 95	**BRAVEHEART (FILM SOUNDTRACK)** *Decca 4482952* [5]	27	9
25 Oct 97	**PAUL MCCARTNEY'S STANDING STONE** *EMI Classics CDC 5564842* [6]	34	2
15 May 99 ●	**STAR WARS – THE PHANTOM MENACE (FILM SOUNDTRACK)** *Sony Classical SK 61816*	8	17
11 May 02	**STAR WARS EPISODE II – ATTACK OF THE CLONES (FILM SOUNDTRACK)** *Sony Classical SK 89932*	15	5

[1] Sarah Brightman and the LSO featuring José Cura [1] London Symphony Orchestra conducted by Cyril Ornadel [2] Spike Milligan with London Symphony Orchestra [3] Kimera featuring the London Symphony Orchestra [4] London Symphony Orchestra and the Royal Choral Society [5] London Symphony Orchestra conductor James Horner [6] London Symphony Orchestra conducted by Lawrence Foster

Orchestra conducted by John Williams for singles 'Star Wars – The Phantom Menace' and 'Star Wars Episode II – Attack of the Clones' are conducted by John Williams

See also Andrea BOCELLI

LONDON WELSH MALE VOICE CHOIR
UK, male choir (Albums: 10 weeks) pos/wks

5 Sep 81	**SONGS OF THE VALLEYS** *K-Tel NE 1117*	61	10

LONDONBEAT *UK / US, male vocal group – includes Jimmy Helms (Singles: 47 weeks, Albums: 6 weeks)* pos/wks

26 Nov 88	**9 AM (THE COMFORT ZONE)** *AnXious ANX 008*	19	10
18 Feb 89	**FAILING IN LOVE AGAIN** *AnXious ANX 007*	60	2
2 Dec 89	**IT TAKES TWO BABY** *Spartan CIN 101* [1]	53	2
1 Sep 90 ●	**I'VE BEEN THINKING ABOUT YOU** *AnXious ANX 14* ▲	2	13
24 Nov 90	**A BETTER LOVE** *AnXious ANX 21*	52	5
2 Mar 91	**NO WOMAN NO CRY** *AnXious ANX 25*	64	2
20 Jul 91	**A BETTER LOVE (re-issue)** *AnXious ANX 32*	23	6
27 Jun 92	**YOU BRING ON THE SUN** *AnXious ANX 37*	32	4
24 Oct 92	**THAT'S HOW I FEEL ABOUT YOU** *AnXious ANX 40*	69	1
8 Apr 95	**I'M JUST YOUR PUPPET ON A . . . (STRING)** *AnXious 74321270982*	55	1
20 May 95	**COME BACK** *AnXious 74321226682*	69	1
13 Oct 90	**IN THE BLOOD** *AnXious ZL 74810*	34	6

[1] Liz Kershaw, Bruno Brookes, Jive Bunny and Londonbeat

See also Jimmy HELMS

LONE JUSTICE *US, female / male vocal / instrumental group (Singles: 4 weeks, Albums: 5 weeks)* pos/wks

7 Mar 87	**I FOUND LOVE** *Geffen GEF 18*	45	4
6 Jul 85	**LONE JUSTICE** *Geffen GEF 26288*	49	2
8 Nov 86	**SHELTER** *Geffen WX 73*	84	3

LONE STAR
UK, male vocal / instrumental group (Albums: 7 weeks) pos/wks

2 Oct 76	**LONE STAR** *Epic EPC 81545*	47	1
17 Sep 77	**FIRING ON ALL SIX** *CBS 82213*	36	6

LONESTAR
US, male vocal / instrumental group (Singles: 24 weeks) pos/wks

15 Apr 00	**AMAZED** *BMG / Grapevine 74321742582* ▲	21	22
7 Sep 00	**SMILE** *BMG / Grapevine 74321786132*	55	2

Shorty LONG
US, male vocalist – Frederick Long d. 29 Jun 1969 (Singles: 7 weeks) pos/wks

17 Jul 68	**HERE COMES THE JUDGE** *Tamla Motown TMG 663*	30	7

LONG AND THE SHORT
UK, male vocal / instrumental group (Singles: 8 weeks) pos/wks

10 Sep 64	**THE LETTER** *Decca F 11964*	35	5
24 Dec 64	**CHOC ICE** *Decca F 12043*	40	3

LONG RYDERS *US, male vocal / instrumental group (Singles: 4 weeks, Albums: 1 week)* pos/wks

5 Oct 85	**LOOKING FOR LEWIS AND CLARKE** *Island IS 237*	59	4
16 Nov 85	**STATE OF OUR UNION** *Island ILPS 9802*	66	1

LONGPIGS *UK, male vocal / instrumental group (Singles: 17 weeks, Albums: 10 weeks)* pos/wks

22 Jul 95	**SHE SAID** *Mother MUMCD 66*	67	1
28 Oct 95	**JESUS CHRIST** *Mother MUMCD 68*	61	1
17 Feb 96	**FAR** *Mother MUMCD 71*	37	2
13 Apr 96	**ON AND ON** *Mother MUMCD 74*	16	3
22 Jun 96	**SHE SAID (re-issue)** *Mother MUMCD 77*	16	4
5 Oct 96	**LOST MYSELF** *Mother MUMCD 82*	22	3
9 Oct 99	**BLUE SKIES** *Mother MUMCD 113*	21	2
18 Dec 99	**THE FRANK SONATA** *Mother MUMCD 114*	57	1
11 May 96	**THE SUN IS OFTEN OUT** *Mother MUMCD 9602*	26	9
23 Oct 99	**MOBILE HOME** *Mother MUMCD 9901*	33	1

Joe LONGTHORNE
UK, male vocalist (Singles: 6 weeks, Albums: 32 weeks) pos/wks

30 Apr 94	**YOUNG GIRL** *EMI CDEM 310*	61	2
10 Dec 94	**PASSING STRANGERS** *EMI CDEM 362* [1]	34	4
3 Dec 88	**THE JOE LONGTHORNE SONGBOOK** *Telstar STAR 2353*	16	12
29 Jul 89	**ESPECIALLY FOR YOU** *Telstar STAR 2365*	22	10
9 Dec 89	**THE JOE LONGTHORNE CHRISTMAS ALBUM** *Telstar STAR 2385*	44	4
13 Nov 93	**I WISH YOU LOVE** *EMI CDEMC 3662*	47	4
8 Oct 94	**LIVE AT THE ROYAL ALBERT HALL** *Premier CDDPR 126*	57	2

[1] Joe Longthorne and Liz Dawn

LONGVIEW *UK, male vocal / instrumental group (Singles: 5 weeks, Albums: 2 weeks)* pos/wks

26 Oct 02	**WHEN YOU SLEEP** *4:45 Recordings LVIEW 02CD*	74	1
8 Feb 03	**NOWHERE** *4:45 Recordings LVIEW 03CD*	72	1
19 Jul 03	**FURTHER** *14th Floor 14 FLR 01CD1*	27	2

11 Oct 03 **CAN'T EXPLAIN** *14th Floor 14FLR 02CD1* 51 1
2 Aug 03 **MERCURY** *14th Floor 5046668862* 45 2

LONYO
UK, male vocalist / producer – Lonyo Engele (Singles: 9 weeks) pos/wks

8 Jul 00 ● **SUMMER OF LOVE** *Riverhorse RIVH CD3* [1] 8 7
7 Apr 01 **GARAGE GIRLS** *Riverhorse RIVHCD 12* [2] 39 2

[1] Lonyo – Comme Ci Comme Ça [2] Lonyo featuring MC Onyx Stone

LOOK *UK, male vocal / instrumental group (Singles: 15 weeks)* pos/wks

20 Dec 80 ● **I AM THE BEAT** *MCA 647* 6 12
29 Aug 81 **FEEDING TIME** *MCA 736* 50 3

LOON – *See PUFF DADDY; Toni BRAXTON*

LOOP *UK, male vocal / instrumental group (Albums: 2 weeks)* pos/wks

4 Feb 89 **FADE OUT** *Chapter 22 CHAPLP 34* 51 1
3 Feb 90 **A GILDED ETERNITY** *Situation Two SITU 27* 39 1

LOOP DA LOOP
UK, male producer – Nick Dresti (Singles: 4 weeks) pos/wks

7 Jun 97 **GO WITH THE FLOW** *Manifesto FESCD 24* 47 1
20 Feb 99 **HAZEL** *Manifesto FESCD 53* 20 3

LOOSE ENDS *UK, male / female vocal / instrumental trio (Singles: 76 weeks, Albums: 41 weeks)* pos/wks

25 Feb 84 **TELL ME WHAT YOU WANT** *Virgin VS 658* 74 1
28 Apr 84 **EMERGENCY (DIAL 999)** *Virgin VS 677* 41 6
21 Jul 84 **CHOOSE ME (RESCUE ME)** *Virgin VS 697* 59 3
23 Feb 85 **HANGIN' ON A STRING (CONTEMPLATING)** *Virgin VS 748* 13 13
11 May 85 **MAGIC TOUCH** *Virgin VS 761* 16 7
27 Jul 85 **GOLDEN YEARS** *Virgin VS 795* 59 4
14 Jun 86 **STAY A LITTLE WHILE, CHILD** *Virgin VS 819* 52 5
20 Sep 86 **SLOW DOWN** *Virgin VS 884* 27 7
29 Nov 86 **NIGHTS OF PLEASURE** *Virgin VS 919* 42 7
4 Jun 88 **MR BACHELOR** *Virgin VS 1080* 50 4
25 Aug 90 **DON'T BE A FOOL** *10 TEN 312* 13 9
17 Nov 90 **LOVE'S GOT ME** *10 TEN 330* 40 4
20 Jun 92 **HANGIN' ON A STRING (re-mix)** *Ten TEN 406* 25 5
5 Sep 92 **MAGIC TOUCH (re-mix)** *Ten TEN 409* 75 1
21 Apr 84 **A LITTLE SPICE** *Virgin V 2301* 46 9
20 Apr 85 **SO WHERE ARE YOU?** *Virgin V 2340* 13 13
18 Oct 86 **ZAGORA** *Virgin V 2384* 15 8
2 Jul 88 **THE REAL CHUCKEEBOO** *Virgin V 2528* 52 4
22 Sep 90 **LOOK HOW LONG** *Ten DIX 94* 19 5
19 Sep 92 **TIGHTEN UP VOLUME 1** *Ten DIXCD 112* 40 2

Lisa 'Left Eye' LOPES
US, female rapper, d. 25 Apr 2002 (Singles: 20 weeks) pos/wks

1 Apr 00 ★ **NEVER BE THE SAME AGAIN (re)** *Virgin VSCDT 1762* [1] ■ 1 16
27 Oct 01 **THE BLOCK PARTY** *La Face / Arista 74321895912* 16 4

[1] Melanie C / Lisa 'Left Eye' Lopes

See also TLC

Jennifer LOPEZ (220 Top 500) *Globally successful, photogenic singer / actress, J.Lo, b. 24 Jul 1970, Bronx, New York, starred in such movies as 'The Wedding Planner', 'The Cell' and 'Selena' (life story of an earlier Latin superstar) (Singles: 136 weeks, Albums: 137 weeks)* pos/wks

3 Jul 99 ● **IF YOU HAD MY LOVE** *Columbia 6675772* ▲ 4 13
13 Nov 99 ● **WAITING FOR TONIGHT** *Columbia 6683072* 5 12
1 Apr 00 **FEELIN' SO GOOD** *Columbia 6691972* [1] 15 6
20 Jan 01 ★ **LOVE DON'T COST A THING (re)** *Epic 6707282* ■ 1 11
12 May 01 ● **PLAY (re)** *Epic 6712272* 3 12
18 Aug 01 ● **AIN'T IT FUNNY (re)** *Epic 6717592* 3 9
10 Nov 01 ● **I'M REAL** *Epic 6720322* [2] ▲ 4 15
23 Mar 02 ● **AIN'T IT FUNNY** *Epic 6724922* [3] ▲ 4 13
13 Jul 02 ● **I'M GONNA BE ALRIGHT** *Epic 6728442* [4] 3 10
30 Nov 02 ● **JENNY FROM THE BLOCK** *Epic 6733572* 3 13
22 Mar 03 ● **ALL I HAVE** *Epic 6736782* [5] ▲ 2 13
21 Jun 03 **I'M GLAD** *Epic 6740152* 11 9
17 Jul 99 **ON THE 6** *Columbia 4949302* 14 30
3 Feb 01 ● **J.LO** *Epic 5005502* ▲ 2 48
30 Mar 02 ● **J TO THA L-O! – THE REMIXES** *Epic 5060242* ▲ 4 27
7 Dec 02 **THIS IS ME... THEN** *Epic 5101282* 14 32

[1] Jennifer Lopez featuring Big Pun and Fat Joe [2] Jennifer Lopez featuring Ja Rule [3] Jennifer Lopez featuring Ja Rule & Caddillac Tah [4] Jennifer Lopez featuring Nas [5] Jennifer Lopez featuring LL Cool J

Trini LOPEZ
US, male vocalist (Singles: 37 weeks, Albums: 42 weeks) pos/wks

12 Sep 63 ● **IF I HAD A HAMMER** *Reprise R 20198* 4 17
12 Dec 63 **KANSAS CITY** *Reprise R 20236* 35 5
12 May 66 **I'M COMING HOME CINDY** *Reprise R 20455* 28 5
6 Apr 67 **GONNA GET ALONG WITHOUT YA NOW** *Reprise R 20547* 41 5
19 Dec 81 **TRINI TRAX** *RCA 154* 59 5
26 Oct 63 ● **TRINI LOPEZ AT P.J.'S** *Reprise R 6093* 7 25
25 Mar 67 ● **TRINI LOPEZ IN LONDON** *Reprise RSLP 6238* 6 17

LO-PRO – *See X-PRESS 2*

Jeff LORBER
US, male vocalist / instrumentalist – keyboards (Albums: 2 weeks) pos/wks

18 May 85 **STEP BY STEP** *Club JABH 9* 97 2

L'ORCHESTRE ELECTRONIQUE
UK, male synthesized orchestra (Albums: 1 week) pos/wks

29 Oct 83 **SOUND WAVES** *Nouveau Musique NML 1005* 75 1

LORD ROCKINGHAM'S XI *UK, male / female instrumental group – leader Harry Robinson (Singles: 21 weeks)* pos/wks

24 Oct 58 ★ **HOOTS MON** *Decca F 11059* [1] 1 17
6 Feb 59 **WEE TOM** *Decca F 11104* [1] 16 3
25 Sep 93 **HOOTS MON (re-issue)** *Decca 8820982* 60 1

[1] Jack Good presents Lord Rockingham's XI

LORD TANAMO
Trinidad and Tobago, male vocalist (Singles: 2 weeks) pos/wks

1 Dec 90 **I'M IN THE MOOD FOR LOVE** *Mooncrest MOON 1009* 58 2

LORD TARIQ and Peter GUNZ *US, male vocal / rap duo – Sean Hamilton and Peter Panky (Singles: 3 weeks)* pos/wks

2 May 98 **DEJA VU (UPTOWN BABY)** *Columbia 6658722* 21 3

Erin LORDAN – *See ASCENSION; BBG; SHUT UP AND DANCE*

Jerry LORDAN
UK, male vocalist d. 24 Jul 1995 (Singles: 16 weeks) pos/wks

8 Jan 60 **I'LL STAY SINGLE (re)** *Parlophone R 4588* 26 3
26 Feb 60 **WHO COULD BE BLUER (re)** *Parlophone R 4627* 16 11
2 Jun 60 **SING LIKE AN ANGEL** *Parlophone R 4653* 36 2

Traci LORDS *US, female vocalist (Singles: 1 week)* pos/wks

7 Oct 95 **FALLEN ANGEL** *Radioactive RAXTD 18* 72 1

LORDS OF THE UNDERGROUND
US, male rap group (Albums: 1 week) pos/wks

12 Nov 94 **KEEPERS OF THE FUNK** *Pendulum CDCHR 6088* 68 1

Sophia LOREN – *See Peter SELLERS*

Trey LORENZ
US, male vocalist – Lloyd Lorenz Smith (Singles: 5 weeks) pos/wks

21 Nov 92 **SOMEONE TO HOLD** *Epic 6587857* 65 2
30 Jan 93 **PHOTOGRAPH OF MARY** *Epic 6589542* 38 3

See also Mariah CAREY

LORI and the CHAMELEONS
UK, female / male vocal / instrumental group (Singles: 1 week)

Date		Title / Label	pos	wks
8 Dec 79		**TOUCH** *Sire SIR 4025*	**70**	1

LORRAINE – *See BOMB THE BASS*

LOS BRAVOS *Spain / Germany, male vocal / instrumental group (Singles: 24 weeks, Albums: 1 week)*

Date		Title / Label	pos	wks
30 Jun 66	●	**BLACK IS BLACK** *Decca F 22419*	**2**	13
8 Sep 66		**I DON'T CARE** *Decca F 22484*	**16**	11
8 Oct 64		BLACK IS BLACK *Decca LK 4822*	**29**	1

LOS DEL CHIPMUNKS – *See CHIPMUNKS*

LOS DEL MAR featuring Wil VELOZ
Cuba / Canada, male vocal / instrumental group (Singles: 7 weeks)

Date		Title / Label	pos	wks
8 Jun 96		**MACARENA (re)** *Pulse 8 CDLOSE 101*	**43**	7

LOS DEL RIO *Spain, male vocal / instrumental duo – Antonio Monge and Rafael Perdigones (Singles: 19 weeks)*

Date		Title / Label	pos	wks
1 Jun 96	●	**MACARENA (re)** *RCA 74321345372* ▲	**2**	19

LOS INDIOS TABAJARAS *Brazil, male instrumental guitar duo – Natalicio and Antenor Lima (Singles: 17 weeks)*

Date		Title / Label	pos	wks
31 Oct 63	●	**MARIA ELENA** *RCA 1365*	**5**	17

LOS LOBOS *US, male vocal / instrumental group – lead vocal David Hildago (Singles: 24 weeks, Albums: 9 weeks)*

Date		Title / Label	pos	wks
6 Apr 85		**DON'T WORRY BABY / WILL THE WOLF SURVIVE** *London LASH 4*	**57**	4
18 Jul 87	★	**LA BAMBA** *Slash LASH 13* ▲	**1**	11
26 Sep 87		**COME ON LET'S GO** *Slash LASH 14*	**18**	9
6 Apr 85		HOW WILL THE WOLF SURVIVE? *Slash SLMP 3*	**77**	6
7 Feb 87		BY THE LIGHT OF THE MOON *Slash SLAP 13*	**77**	3

LOS NINOS *UK, male instrumental group (Albums: 1 week)*

Date		Title / Label	pos	wks
22 Jul 95		FRAGILE – MYSTICAL SOUNDS OF THE PANPIPE *Pearls DPWKF 4253*	**74**	1

LOS POP TOPS
Spain, male vocal group (Singles: 6 weeks)

Date		Title / Label	pos	wks
9 Oct 71		**MAMY BLUE** *A&M AMS 859*	**35**	6

LOS UMBRELLOS
Denmark, male / female vocal trio (Singles: 2 weeks)

Date		Title / Label	pos	wks
3 Oct 98		**NO TENGO DINERO** *Virgin VUSCD 139*	**33**	2

Joe LOSS and his ORCHESTRA *UK, orchestra, leader d. 6 Jun 1990 (Singles: 52 weeks, Albums: 10 weeks)*

Date		Title / Label	pos	wks
29 Jun 61		**WHEELS CHA CHA** *HMV POP 880*	**21**	21
19 Oct 61		**SUCU SUCU** *HMV POP 937*	**48**	1
29 Mar 62		**THE MAIGRET THEME** *HMV POP 995*	**20**	10
1 Nov 62		**MUST BE MADISON** *HMV POP 1075*	**20**	13
5 Nov 64		**MARCH OF THE MODS (2re)** *HMV POP 1351*	**31**	7
30 Oct 71		ALL-TIME PARTY HITS *MFP 5227*	**24**	10

See also George MITCHELL MINSTRELS

LOST
UK, male / instrumental / production duo (Singles: 1 week)

Date		Title / Label	pos	wks
22 Jun 91		**TECHNO FUNK** *Perfecto PT 44560*	**75**	1

LOST BOYZ
US, male rap group (Singles: 2 weeks, Albums: 1 week)

Date		Title / Label	pos	wks
2 Nov 96		**MUSIC MAKES ME HIGH** *Universal MCSTD 48015*	**42**	1
12 Jul 97		**LOVE, PEACE & NAPPINESS** *Universal UND 56131*	**57**	1
6 Jul 96		LEGAL DRUG MONEY *Universal UND 53010*	**64**	1

LOST BROTHERS featuring G Tom MAC
UK, male production group and male vocalist (Singles: 2 weeks)

Date		Title / Label	pos	wks
20 Dec 03		**CRY LITTLE SISTER (I NEED U NOW)** *Incentive CENT 60CDS*	**21**	2+

LOST IT.COM
UK, male vocal / production duo (Singles: 1 week)

Date		Title / Label	pos	wks
7 Apr 01		**ANIMAL** *Perfecto PERF 13CDS*	**70**	1

LOST TRIBE *UK, male production duo – Matt Darey and Red Jerry (Singles: 4 weeks)*

Date		Title / Label	pos	wks
11 Sep 99		**GAMEMASTER** *Hooj Choons HOOJ 81CD*	**24**	3
6 Dec 03		**GAMEMASTER (re-mix)** *Liquid Asset ASSETCD 12015*	**61**	1

See also Matt DAREY; MELT featuring Little Ms MARCIE; SUNBURST; MDM

LOST WITNESS
UK, male production duo and female vocalist (Singles: 13 weeks)

Date		Title / Label	pos	wks
29 May 99		**HAPPINESS HAPPENING** *Ministry of Sound MOSCDS 129*	**18**	4
18 Sep 99		**RED SUN RISING** *Ministry of Sound MOSCDS 133*	**22**	3
16 Dec 00		**7 COLOURS** *Data DATA 15CDS*	**28**	3
18 May 02		**DID I DREAM (SONG TO THE SIREN)** *Ministry of Sound / Data DATA 28CDS*	**28**	3

LOSTPROPHETS *UK, male vocal / instrumental group (Singles: 8 weeks, Albums: 8 weeks)*

Date		Title / Label	pos	wks
8 Dec 01		**SHINOBI VS DRAGON NINJA** *Visible Noise TORMENT 16*	**41**	2
23 Mar 02		**THE FAKE SOUND OF PROGRESS** *Visible Noise TORMENT 19*	**21**	3
15 Nov 03		**BURN BURN** *Visible Noise TORMENT 29CD*	**17**	3
2 Mar 02		THE FAKE SOUND OF PROGRESS *Visible Noise TORMENT 10CD*	**44**	8

LOTUS EATERS *UK, male vocal / instrumental duo – Peter Coyle and Jerry Kelley (Singles: 16 weeks, Albums: 1 week)*

Date		Title / Label	pos	wks
2 Jul 83		**FIRST PICTURE OF YOU** *Sylvan SYL 1*	**15**	12
8 Oct 83		**YOU DON'T NEED SOMEONE NEW** *Sylvan SYL 2*	**53**	4
16 Jun 84		NO SENSE OF SIN *Sylvan 206 263*	**96**	1

Bonnie LOU
US, female vocalist – Bonnie Lou Kath (Singles: 10 weeks)

Date		Title / Label	pos	wks
5 Feb 54	●	**TENNESSEE WIG WALK** *Parlophone R 3730*	**4**	10

Lippy LOU *UK, female rapper (Singles: 2 weeks)*

Date		Title / Label	pos	wks
22 Apr 95		**LIBERATION** *More Protein PROCD 105*	**57**	2

Louchie LOU and Michie ONE *UK, female rap duo – Louise Gold and Michelle Charles (Singles: 36 weeks)*

Date		Title / Label	pos	wks
29 May 93	●	**SHOUT** *ffrr FCD 211*	**7**	8
14 Aug 93		**SOMEBODY ELSE'S GUY** *ffrr FCD 216*	**54**	2
26 Aug 95		**GET DOWN ON IT** *China WOKCD 2054*	**58**	1
13 Apr 96	●	**CECILIA (2re)** *WEA WEA 042CD1* [1]	**4**	19
15 Jun 96		**GOOD SWEET LOVIN'** *Indochina ID 050CD*	**34**	2
21 Sep 96		**NO MORE ALCOHOL** *WEA WEA 065CD1* [1]	**24**	4

[1] Suggs featuring Louchie Lou and Michie One

LOUD
UK, male vocal / instrumental group (Singles: 2 weeks)

Date		Title / Label	pos	wks
28 Mar 92		**EASY** *China WOK 2016*	**67**	2

John D LOUDERMILK *US, male vocalist (Singles: 10 weeks)*

Date		Title / Label	pos	wks
4 Jan 62		**THE LANGUAGE OF LOVE** *RCA 1269*	**13**	10

James LOUGHRAN – *See BBC SYMPHONY ORCHESTRA SINGERS and CHORUS*

Louie LOUIE *US, male vocalist (Singles: 5 weeks)*

Date		Title / Label	pos	wks
19 Dec 92		**THE THOUGHT OF IT** *Hardback YZ 724*	**34**	5

LOUISE 488 Top 500 *First British female to have a string of Top 20s as both a group member (she exited Eternal in July 1995) and as a solo singer, b. Louise Nurding, 4 Nov 1974, south London. The vocalist, who has sung on 18 Top 20 entries, is married to footballer Jamie Redknapp (Singles: 83 weeks, Albums: 59 weeks)*

Date		Title / Label	pos	wks
7 Oct 95	●	**LIGHT OF MY LIFE** *EMI CDEMS 397*	8	8
16 Mar 96		**IN WALKED LOVE** *EMI CDEMS 413*	17	6
8 Jun 96	●	**NAKED** *EMI CDEM 431*	5	8
31 Aug 96	●	**UNDIVIDED LOVE** *EMI CDEM 441*	5	6
30 Nov 96	●	**ONE KISS FROM HEAVEN** *EMI CDEM 454*	9	7
4 Oct 97	●	**ARMS AROUND THE WORLD** *EMI CDEM 490*	4	7
29 Nov 97	●	**LET'S GO ROUND AGAIN** *EMI CDEM 500*	10	9
4 Apr 98		**ALL THAT MATTERS (re)** *1st Avenue CDEM 506*	11	6
29 Jul 00	●	**2 FACED** *1st Avenue / EMI CDEMS 570*	3	8
11 Nov 00		**BEAUTIFUL INSIDE** *1st Avenue / EMI CDEMS 575*	13	4
8 Sep 01	●	**STUCK IN THE MIDDLE WITH YOU** *1st Avenue / EMI CDEM 600*	4	9
27 Sep 03	●	**PANDORA'S KISS / DON'T GIVE UP** *Positive POSCDS 001*	5	5
6 Jul 96	●	**NAKED** *EMI CDEMC 3748*	7	31
18 Oct 97	●	**WOMAN IN ME** *EMI 8219032*	5	19
12 Aug 00		**ELBOW BEACH** *EMI 5276142*	12	4
22 Sep 01	●	**CHANGING FACES – THE BEST OF LOUISE** *EMI 5349672*	9	5

See also ETERNAL

Jacques LOUSSIER
France, male instrumentalist – piano (Albums: 3 weeks)

Date		Title / Label	pos	wks
30 Mar 85		**THE BEST OF PLAY BACH** *Start STL 1*	58	3

LOVE *US, male vocal / instrumental group (Albums: 9 weeks)*

Date		Title / Label	pos	wks
24 Feb 68		**FOREVER CHANGES** *Elektra EKS7 4013*	24	7
16 May 70		**OUT HERE** *Harvest Show 3/4*	29	2

Darlene LOVE
US, female vocalist – Darlene Wright (Singles: 5 weeks)

Date		Title / Label	pos	wks
19 Dec 92		**ALL ALONE ON CHRISTMAS (re)** *Arista 74321124767*	31	5

Re-entry made No.72 in Jan 1994

See also CRYSTALS

Geoff LOVE
UK, male orchestra leader, d. 8 Jul 1991 (Albums: 28 weeks)

Date		Title / Label	pos	wks
7 Aug 71		**BIG WAR MOVIE THEMES** *MFP 5171*	11	20
21 Aug 71		**BIG WESTERN MOVIE THEMES** *MFP 5204*	38	3
30 Oct 71		**BIG LOVE MOVIE THEMES** *MFP 5221*	28	5

See also Laurie LONDON; MANUEL and The MUSIC OF THE MOUNTAINS

Helen LOVE
UK, male / female vocal / instrumental group (Singles: 2 weeks)

Date		Title / Label	pos	wks
20 Sep 97		**DOES YOUR HEART GO BOOM** *Che CHE 72CD*	71	1
19 Sep 98		**LONG LIVE THE UK MUSIC SCENE** *Che CHE 82CD*	65	1

Monie LOVE *UK, female rapper – Simone Johnson (Singles: 51 weeks, Albums: 3 weeks)*

Date		Title / Label	pos	wks
4 Feb 89		**I CAN DO THIS** *Cooltempo COOL 177*	37	4
24 Jun 89		**GRANDPA'S PARTY** *Cooltempo COOL 184*	16	9
14 Jul 90		**MONIE IN THE MIDDLE** *Cooltempo COOL 210*	46	3
22 Sep 90		**IT'S A SHAME (MY SISTER)** *Cooltempo COOL 219* [1]	12	8
1 Dec 90		**DOWN TO EARTH** *Cooltempo COOL 222*	31	6
6 Apr 91		**RING MY BELL** *Cooltempo COOL 224* [2]	20	5
25 Jul 92		**FULL TERM LOVE** *Cooltempo COOL 258*	34	4
13 Mar 93		**BORN 2 B.R.E.E.D.** *Cooltempo CDCOOL 269*	18	5
12 Jun 93		**IN A WORD OR 2 / THE POWER** *Cooltempo CDCOOL 273*	33	3
21 Aug 93		**NEVER GIVE UP** *Cooltempo CDCOOL 276*	41	2
22 Apr 00		**SLICE OF DA PIE** *Relentless RELENT 2CDS*	29	2
20 Oct 90		**DOWN TO EARTH** *Cooltempo CTLP 14*	30	3

[1] Monie Love featuring True Image [2] Monie Love vs Adeva

Vikki LOVE – *See JUNGLE BROTHERS; NUANCE featuring Vikki LOVE*

LOVE AFFAIR *UK, male vocal / instrumental group – lead vocal Steve Ellis (Singles: 56 weeks)*

Date		Title / Label	pos	wks
3 Jan 68	★	**EVERLASTING LOVE** *CBS 3125*	1	12
17 Apr 68	●	**RAINBOW VALLEY** *CBS 3366*	5	13
11 Sep 68	●	**A DAY WITHOUT LOVE** *CBS 3674*	6	12
19 Feb 69		**ONE ROAD** *CBS 3994*	16	9
16 Jul 69	●	**BRINGING ON BACK THE GOOD TIMES** *CBS 4300*	9	10

LOVE AND MONEY *UK, male vocal / instrumental group (Singles: 23 weeks, Albums: 2 weeks)*

Date		Title / Label	pos	wks
24 May 86		**CANDYBAR EXPRESS** *Mercury MONEY 1*	56	4
25 Apr 87		**LOVE AND MONEY** *Mercury MONEY 4*	68	4
17 Sep 88		**HALLELUIAH MAN** *Fontana MONEY 5*	63	4
14 Jan 89		**STRANGE KIND OF LOVE** *Fontana MONEY 6*	45	5
25 Mar 89		**JOCELYN SQUARE** *Fontana MONEY 7*	51	4
16 Nov 91		**WINTER** *Fontana MONEY 9*	52	2
29 Oct 88		**STRANGE KIND OF LOVE** *Fontana SFLP 7*	71	1
3 Aug 91		**DOGS IN THE TRAFFIC** *Fontana 8489931*	41	1

LOVE BITE
Italy, male / female production / vocal group (Singles: 1 week)

Date		Title / Label	pos	wks
7 Oct 00		**TAKE YOUR TIME** *AM:PM CDAMPM134*	56	1

LOVE CITY GROOVE *UK, male / female vocal / rap / instrumental group (Singles: 11 weeks)*

Date		Title / Label	pos	wks
8 Apr 95	●	**LOVE CITY GROOVE** *Planet 3 GXY 2003CD*	7	11

LOVE CONNECTION *Italy / Germany, male / female vocal / production group (Singles: 1 week)*

Date		Title / Label	pos	wks
2 Dec 00		**THE BOMB** *Multiply CDMULTY 63*	53	1

LOVE DECADE
UK, male / female vocal / instrumental group (Singles: 14 weeks)

Date		Title / Label	pos	wks
6 Jul 91		**DREAM ON (IS THIS A DREAM)** *All Around the World GLOBE 100*	52	2
23 Nov 91		**SO REAL** *All Around the World GLOBE 106*	14	7
11 Apr 92		**I FEEL YOU** *All Around the World GLOBE 107*	34	3
6 Feb 93		**WHEN THE MORNING COMES** *All Around the World CDGLOBE 114*	69	1
17 Feb 96		**IS THIS A DREAM** *All Around the World CDGLOBE 132*	39	1

'Is This a Dream' in 1996 is a re-recording

LOVE DECREE
UK, male vocal / instrumental group (Singles: 4 weeks)

Date		Title / Label	pos	wks
16 Sep 89		**SOMETHING SO REAL (CHINHEADS THEME)** *Ariola 112642*	61	4

LOVE / HATE *US, male vocal / instrumental group (Singles: 4 weeks, Albums: 5 weeks)*

Date		Title / Label	pos	wks
30 Nov 91		**EVIL TWIN** *Columbia 6575967*	59	1
4 Apr 92		**WASTED IN AMERICA** *Columbia 6578897*	38	3
7 Mar 92		**WASTED IN AMERICA** *Columbia 4694532*	20	4
24 Jul 93		**LET'S RUMBLE** *RCA 74321153112*	24	1

LOVE INC *Jamaica / Canada, male / female production / vocal duo – Simone Denny and Chris Sheppard (Singles: 20 weeks)*

Date		Title / Label	pos	wks
28 Dec 02	●	**YOU'RE A SUPERSTAR** *Nulife / Arista 74321973842*	7	13
31 May 03	●	**BROKEN BONES** *Nulife / Arista 82876523172*	8	7

LOVE INCORPORATED featuring MC NOISE
UK, male vocal / production duo (Singles: 3 weeks)

Date		Title / Label	pos	wks
9 Feb 91		**LOVE IS THE MESSAGE** *Love EVOL 1*	59	3

LOVE NELSON – *See FIRE ISLAND*

LOVE REACTION – *See ZODIAC MINDWARP and the LOVE REACTION*

LOVE SCULPTURE *UK, instrumental group (Singles: 14 weeks)* pos/wks

27 Nov 68 ● **SABRE DANCE** *Parlophone R 5744* 5 14

See also Dave EDMUNDS

LOVE SQUAD – *See Linda CARR*

A LOVE SUPREME
UK, male vocal / instrumental group (Singles: 2 weeks) pos/wks

17 Apr 99 **NIALL QUINN'S DISCO PANTS** *A Love Supreme / Cherry Red CDVINNIE 3* 59 2

[LOVE] TATTOO
Australia, male producer – Stephen Allkins (Singles: 1 week) pos/wks

6 Oct 01 **DROP SOME DRUMS** *Positiva CDTIV 162* 58 1

LOVE TO INFINITY
UK, male / female vocal / instrumental group (Singles: 4 weeks) pos/wks

24 Jun 95 **KEEP LOVE TOGETHER** *Mushroom D 00467* 38 2
18 Nov 95 **SOMEDAY** *Mushroom D 1143* 75 1
3 Aug 96 **PRAY FOR LOVE** *Mushroom D 1213* 69 1

LOVE TRIBE *US, male / female vocal / instrumental duo – Tanya Walters and Dewey Bullock (Singles: 3 weeks)* pos/wks

29 Jun 96 **STAND UP** *AM:PM 5816272* 23 3

LOVE UNLIMITED *US, female vocal group (Singles: 19 weeks)* pos/wks

17 Jun 72 **WALKIN' IN THE RAIN WITH THE ONE I LOVE** *Uni UN 539* 14 10
25 Jan 75 **IT MAY BE WINTER OUTSIDE (BUT IN MY HEART IT'S SPRING)** *20th Century BTC 2149* 11 9

LOVE UNLIMITED ORCHESTRA
US, orchestra (Singles: 10 weeks) pos/wks

2 Feb 74 ● **LOVE'S THEME** *Pye International 7N 25635* ▲ 10 10

LOVEBUG
UK, male / female production / vocal trio (Singles: 2 weeks) pos/wks

18 Oct 03 **WHO'S THE DADDY** *Sony Music 6742702* 35 2

LOVEBUG STARSKI
US, male rapper – Kevin Smith (Singles: 9 weeks) pos/wks

31 May 86 **AMITYVILLE (THE HOUSE ON THE HILL)** *Epic A 7182* 12 9

LOVEDEEJAY AKEMI – *See YOSH presents LOVEDEEJAY AKEMI*

LOVEHAPPY
US / UK, male / female vocal / instrumental group (Singles: 3 weeks) pos/wks

18 Feb 95 **MESSAGE OF LOVE** *MCA MCSTD 2040* 37 2
20 Jul 96 **MESSAGE OF LOVE (re-mix)** *MCA MCSTD 40052* 70 1

Bill LOVELADY *UK, male vocalist (Singles: 10 weeks)* pos/wks

18 Aug 79 **REGGAE FOR IT NOW** *Charisma CB 337* 12 10

LOVELAND featuring the voice of Rachel McFARLANE
UK, male / female vocal / instrumental group (Singles: 15 weeks) pos/wks

16 Apr 94 **LET THE MUSIC (LIFT YOU UP)** *KMS / Eastern Bloc KMSCD 10* 16 4
5 Nov 94 **(KEEP ON) SHINING / HOPE (NEVER GIVE UP)** *Eastern Bloc BLOCCD 016* 37 2
14 Jan 95 **I NEED SOMEBODY** *Eastern Bloc BLOCCD 019* 21 3
10 Jun 95 **DON'T MAKE ME WAIT** *Eastern Bloc BLOC 20CD* 22 3
2 Sep 95 **THE WONDER OF LOVE** *Eastern Bloc BLOC 22CD* 53 1
11 Nov 95 **I NEED SOMEBODY (re-mix)** *Eastern Bloc BLOC 23CD* 38 2

All formats of 'Let the Music (Lift You Up)' featured versions by Loveland featuring Rachel McFarlane and also by Darlene Lewis

LOVER SPEAKS
UK, male vocal / instrumental duo (Singles: 5 weeks) pos/wks

16 Aug 86 **NO MORE 'I LOVE YOU'S'** *A&M AM 326* 58 5

Michael LOVESMITH *US, male vocalist (Singles: 1 week)* pos/wks

5 Oct 85 **AIN'T NOTHIN' LIKE IT** *Motown ZB 40369* 75 1

LOVESTATION
UK, male / female vocal / instrumental group (Singles: 21 weeks) pos/wks

13 Mar 93 **SHINE ON ME** *RCA 743211337912* [1] 71 1
13 Nov 93 **BEST OF MY LOVE** *Fresh FRSHD 1* 73 1
18 Mar 95 **LOVE COME RESCUE ME** *Fresh FRSHD 22* 42 2
1 Aug 98 **TEARDROPS** *Fresh FRSHD 65* 14 6
5 Dec 98 **SENSUALITY** *Fresh FRSHD 71* 16 7
5 Feb 00 **TEARDROPS (re-mix)** *Fresh FRSHD 79* 24 4

[1] Lovestation featuring Lisa Hunt

Lyle LOVETT *US, male vocalist (Albums: 2 weeks)* pos/wks

8 Oct 94 **I LOVE EVERYBODY** *MCA MCD 10808* 54 1
29 Jun 96 **THE ROAD TO ENSENADA** *MCA MCD 11409* 62 1

Lene LOVICH *US, female vocalist – Lili Marlene Premilovich (Singles: 38 weeks, Albums: 17 weeks)* pos/wks

17 Feb 79 ● **LUCKY NUMBER** *Stiff BUY 42* 3 11
12 May 79 **SAY WHEN** *Stiff BUY 46* 19 10
20 Oct 79 **BIRD SONG** *Stiff BUY 53* 39 7
29 Mar 80 **WHAT WILL I DO WITHOUT YOU** *Stiff BUY 69* 58 3
14 Mar 81 **NEW TOY** *Stiff BUY 97* 53 5
27 Nov 82 **IT'S YOU ONLY YOU (MEIN SCHMERZ)** *Stiff BUY 164* 68 2
17 Mar 79 **STATELESS** *Stiff SEEZ 7* 35 11
2 Feb 80 **FLEX** *Stiff SEEZ 19* 19 6

LOVIN' SPOONFUL *US / Canada, male vocal / instrumental group (Singles: 33 weeks, Albums: 11 weeks)* pos/wks

14 Apr 66 ● **DAYDREAM** *Pye International 7N 25361* 2 13
14 Jul 66 ● **SUMMER IN THE CITY** *Kama Sutra KAS 200* ▲ 8 11
5 Jan 67 **NASHVILLE CATS** *Kama Sutra KAS 204* 26 7
9 Mar 67 **DARLING BE HOME SOON** *Kama Sutra KAS 207* 44 2
7 May 66 ● **DAYDREAM** *Pye NPL 28078* 8 11

LOVINDEER *Jamaica, male vocalist (Singles: 3 weeks)* pos/wks

27 Sep 86 **MAN SHORTAGE** *TSOJ TS 1* 69 3

Gary LOW *Italy, male vocalist (Singles: 3 weeks)* pos/wks

8 Oct 83 **I WANT YOU** *Savoir Faire FAIS 004* 52 3

Patti LOW – *See BUG KANN and the PLASTIC JAM*

Jim LOWE *US, male vocalist (Singles: 9 weeks)* pos/wks

26 Oct 56 ● **THE GREEN DOOR** *London HLD 8317* [1] 8 9

[1] Jim Lowe and the High Fives

Nick LOWE
UK, male vocalist (Singles: 27 weeks, Albums: 17 weeks) pos/wks

11 Mar 78 ● **I LOVE THE SOUND OF BREAKING GLASS** *Radar ADA 1* 7 8
9 Jun 79 **CRACKING UP** *Radar ADA 34* 34 5
25 Aug 79 **CRUEL TO BE KIND** *Radar ADA 43* 12 11
26 May 84 **HALF A BOY AND HALF A MAN** *F. Beat XX 34* 53 3
11 Mar 78 **THE JESUS OF COOL** *Radar RAD 1* 22 9
23 Jun 79 **LABOUR OF LUST** *Radar RAD 21* 43 6
20 Feb 82 **NICK THE KNIFE** *F-Beat XXLP 14* 99 2

See also ROCKPILE

LOWGOLD *UK, male vocal / instrumental group (Singles: 4 weeks, Albums: 2 weeks)* pos/wks

30 Sep 00 **BEAUTY DIES YOUNG** *Nude NUD 52CD* 67 1
10 Feb 01 **MERCURY** *Nude NUD 53CD* 48 1
12 May 01 **COUNTERFEIT** *Nude NUD 55CD* 52 1

8 Sep 01	BEAUTY DIES YOUNG (re-mix) *Nude NUD 59CD*	40	1
24 Feb 01	JUST BACKWARD OF SQUARE *Nude NUDE 17CD*	33	2

LOWRELL *US, male vocalist – Lowrell Simon (Singles: 9 weeks)*

		pos	wks
24 Nov 79	MELLOW MELLOW RIGHT ON *AVI AVIS 108*	37	9

LUCAS
Denmark, male vocalist – Lucas Secon (Singles: 4 weeks)

		pos	wks
6 Aug 94	LUCAS WITH THE LID OFF *WEA YZ 832CD*	37	4

Carrie LUCAS *US, female vocalist (Singles: 6 weeks)*

		pos	wks
16 Jun 79	DANCE WITH YOU *Solar FB 1482*	40	6

Tammy LUCAS – *See Teddy RILEY*

LUCIANA *UK, female vocalist (Singles: 5 weeks)*

		pos	wks
23 Apr 94	GET IT UP FOR LOVE *Chrysalis CDCHS 5008*	55	2
6 Aug 94	IF YOU WANT *Chrysalis CDCHS 5009*	47	2
5 Nov 94	WHAT GOES AROUND / ONE MORE RIVER *Chrysalis CDCHS 5015*	67	1

LUCID
UK, male / female vocal / instrumental group (Singles: 15 weeks)

		pos	wks
8 Aug 98 ●	I CAN'T HELP MYSELF *ffrr FCD 339*	7	8
27 Feb 99	CRAZY *ffrr / Delirious / Indirect FCD 355*	14	5
16 Oct 99	STAY WITH ME TILL DAWN *ffrr FCD 368*	25	2

LUCKY MONKEYS
UK, male instrumental group (Singles: 1 week)

		pos	wks
9 Nov 96	BJANGO *Hi-Life 5757132*	50	1

See also FLUKE

LUCY PEARL *US, male / female vocal / rap / instrumental / production trio (Singles: 7 weeks)*

		pos	wks
29 Jul 00	DANCE TONIGHT *Virgin VSCDT 1775*	36	2
25 Nov 00	DON'T MESS WITH MY MAN *Virgin VSCDT 1778*	20	4
28 Jul 01	WITHOUT YOU *Virgin VSCDT 1805*	51	1

LUDACRIS *US, male rapper – Christopher Bridges (Singles: 42 weeks, Albums: 6 weeks)*

		pos	wks
9 Jun 01	WHAT'S YOUR FANTASY *Def Jam 5729842*	19	5
18 Aug 01 ●	ONE MINUTE MAN *Elektra E 7245CD* [1]	10	8
29 Sep 01	AREA CODES *Def Jam 5887722* [2]	25	3
22 Jun 02	ROLLOUT (MY BUSINESS) *Def Jam 5829632*	20	7
5 Oct 02	SATURDAY (OOOH OOOH) *Def Jam 0639142*	31	2
9 Nov 02	WHY DON'T WE FALL IN LOVE *Columbia 6732212* [3]	40	2
22 Mar 03 ●	GOSSIP FOLKS *Elektra E 7380CD* [4]	9	9
22 Nov 03	STAND UP *Def Jam / Mercury 9814001* [5]	14	6+
29 Jun 02	WORD OF MOUF *Def Jam 5864462*	57	2
18 Oct 03	CHICKEN 'N' BEER *Def Jam / Mercury 9861137* ▲	44	4

[1] Missy 'Misdemeanor' Elliott featuring Ludacris [2] Ludacris featuring Nate Dogg [3] Amerie featuring Ludacris [4] Missy Elliott featuring Ludacris [5] Ludacris featuring Shawnna

Baz LUHRMANN *Australia, male producer (Singles: 16 weeks)*

		pos	wks
12 Jun 99 ★	EVERYBODY'S FREE (TO WEAR SUNSCREEN) – THE SUNSCREEN SONG (CLASS OF '99) *EMI CDBAZ 001* ■	1	16

Uncredited vocals by actor Lee Perry

Robin LUKE *US, male vocalist (Singles: 6 weeks)*

		pos	wks
17 Oct 58	SUSIE DARLIN' (2re) *London HLD 8676*	23	6

LUKK featuring Felicia COLLINS
US, male / female vocal / instrumental group (Singles: 1 week)

		pos	wks
28 Sep 85	ON THE ONE *Important TAN 6*	72	1

LULU (315 Top 500) *One of Scotland's best-known female vocalists, b. Marie Lawrie, 3 Nov 1948, Strathclyde. She scored her first hit aged 15, had a US chart-topper ('To Sir with Love') aged 18, won the Eurovision Song Contest aged 20, and finally reached No.1 aged 44 (Singles: 188 weeks, Albums: 18 weeks)*

		pos	wks
14 May 64 ●	SHOUT *Decca F 11884* [1]	7	13
12 Nov 64	HERE COMES THE NIGHT *Decca F 12017*	50	1
17 Jun 65 ●	LEAVE A LITTLE LOVE *Decca F 12169*	8	11
2 Sep 65	TRY TO UNDERSTAND *Decca F 12214*	25	8
13 Apr 67 ●	THE BOAT THAT I ROW *Columbia DB 8169*	6	11
29 Jun 67	LET'S PRETEND *Columbia DB 8221*	11	11
8 Nov 67	LOVE LOVES TO LOVE LOVE *Columbia DB 8295*	32	6
28 Feb 68 ●	ME, THE PEACEFUL HEART *Columbia DB 8358*	9	9
5 Jun 68	BOY *Columbia DB 8425*	15	7
6 Nov 68 ●	I'M A TIGER *Columbia DB 8500*	9	13
12 Mar 69 ●	BOOM BANG-A-BANG *Columbia DB 8550*	2	13
22 Nov 69	OH ME OH MY (I'M A FOOL FOR YOU BABY) *Atco 226008*	47	2
26 Jan 74 ●	THE MAN WHO SOLD THE WORLD *Polydor 2001 490*	3	9
19 Apr 75	TAKE YOUR MAMA FOR A RIDE *Chelsea 2005 022*	37	4
12 Dec 81	I COULD NEVER MISS YOU (MORE THAN I DO) (re) *Alfa ALFA 1700*	62	5
19 Jul 86 ●	SHOUT *Jive LULU1 / Decca SHOUT 1*	8	11
30 Jan 93	INDEPENDENCE *Dome CDDOME 1001*	11	5
3 Apr 93	I'M BACK FOR MORE *Dome CDDOME 1002* [2]	27	5
4 Sep 93	LET ME WAKE UP IN YOUR ARMS *Dome CDDOME 1005*	51	2
9 Oct 93 ★	RELIGHT MY FIRE *RCA 74321167722* [3] ■	1	14
27 Nov 93	HOW 'BOUT US *Dome CDDOME 1007*	46	3
27 Aug 94	GOODBYE BABY AND AMEN *Dome CDDOME 1011*	40	2
26 Nov 94	EVERY WOMAN KNOWS *Dome CDDOME 1013*	44	2
29 May 99	HURT ME SO BAD *Rocket / Mercury 5726132*	42	2
8 Jan 00	BETTER GET READY *Mercury 5625852*	59	1
18 Mar 00	WHERE THE POOR BOYS DANCE *Mercury 1568452*	24	5
7 Dec 02 ●	WE'VE GOT TONIGHT *Polydor 0658612* [4]	4	13
25 Sep 71	THE MOST OF LULU *MFP 5215*	15	6
6 Mar 93	INDEPENDENCE *Dome DOMECD 1*	67	1
1 Jun 02 ●	TOGETHER *Mercury 630212*	4	9
22 Nov 03	THE GREATEST HITS *Mercury / Universal TV 9865879*	35	2

[1] Lulu and The Luvvers [2] Lulu and Bobby Womack [3] Take That featuring Lulu [4] Ronan Keating featuring Lulu

The newly recorded 'Shout' entered the chart on 19 Jul 1986, and the next week the original Decca version by Lulu and The Luvvers also charted. For all subsequent weeks Gallup amalgamated both versions under one entry and we have added an extra week on chart for the 'double week' to take account of this

Bob LUMAN *US, male vocalist d. 27 Dec 1978 (Singles: 21 weeks, Albums: 1 week)*

		pos	wks
8 Sep 60 ●	LET'S THINK ABOUT LIVING *Warner Bros. WB 18*	6	18
15 Dec 60	WHY, WHY, BYE, BYE *Warner Bros. WB 28*	46	1
4 May 61	THE GREAT SNOWMAN *Warner Bros. WB 37*	49	2
14 Jan 61	LET'S THINK ABOUT LIVING *Warner Bros. WM 4025*	18	1

LUMIDEE *US, female vocalist (Singles: 14 weeks, Albums: 3 weeks)*

		pos	wks
9 Aug 03 ●	NEVER LEAVE YOU – UH OOH, UH OOOH! *Universal MCSTD 40328*	2	13
29 Nov 03	CRASHIN' A PARTY *Universal MCSTD 40341* [1]	55	1
16 Aug 03	ALMOST FAMOUS *Universal 9860622*	70	3

[1] Lumidee featuring N.O.R.E.

LUNIZ *US, male rap duo – Jerrold 'Yukmouth' Ellis Jr and Garrick 'Knumbskull' Husbands (Singles: 18 weeks, Albums: 3 weeks)*

		pos	wks
17 Feb 96 ●	I GOT 5 ON IT *Virgin America VUSCD 101*	3	13
11 May 96	PLAYA HATA *Virgin America VUSCD 103*	20	3
31 Oct 98	I GOT 5 ON IT (re-mix) *Virgin VCRD 41*	28	2
16 Mar 96	OPERATION STACKOLA *Virgin VUSMC 94*	41	3

LUPINE HOWL
UK, male vocal / instrumental group (Singles: 1 week)

		pos	wks
22 Jan 00	VAPORIZER *Vinyl Hiss VHISSCD 001*	68	1

TOP 10 INSTRUMENTALS

The top 10 instrumental hit singles based on weeks on chart, not surprisingly, show Somerset-born clarinettist Acker Bilk in the top spot. Despite the fact that Eddie Calvert's instrumental 'Oh, Mein Papa' was at No.1 for a record-breaking nine weeks, it just fails to make the cut here with 21 chart weeks in total. Shadows chart-toppers 'Apache' and 'Wonderful Land' also fail by a whisker, bubbling under on 21 and 19 weeks respectively. Ties in this list are determined by each single's peak chart position.

1. STRANGER ON THE SHORE – Mr Acker Bilk with the Leon Young String Chorale (55 weeks on chart)
2. ALBATROSS – Fleetwood Mac (35 weeks on chart)
3. SIDE SADDLE – Russ Conway (30 weeks on chart)
4. THE THEME FROM 'A SUMMER PLACE' – Percy Faith and His Orchestra (31 weeks on chart)
5. TELSTAR – Tornados (25 weeks on chart)
6. AMAZING GRACE – Royal Scots Dragoon Guards (27 weeks on chart)
7. THE GOOD, THE BAD AND THE UGLY – Hugo Montenegro His Orchestra and Chorus (25 weeks on chart)
8. TERRY'S THEME FROM 'LIMELIGHT' – Frank Chacksfield and His Orchestra (24 weeks on chart)
9. PETITE FLEUR – Chris Barber's Jazz Band (24 weeks on chart)
10. THE SONG FROM 'THE MOULIN ROUGE' – Mantovani and his Orchestra (23 weeks on chart)

Acker Bilk, attracting a bevy of beauties to the swimming baths, is determined to search for the very best acoustics in which to perform his laid-back classic 'Stranger on the Shore'

LURKERS *UK, male vocal / instrumental group (Singles: 11 weeks, Albums: 1 week)*

		pos/wks	
3 Jun 78	**AIN'T GOT A CLUE** *Beggars Banquet BEG 6*	**45**	3
5 Aug 78	**I DON'T NEED TO TELL HER** *Beggars Banquet BEG 9*	**49**	4
3 Feb 79	**JUST THIRTEEN** *Beggars Banquet BEG 14*	**66**	2
9 Jun 79	**OUT IN THE DARK / CYANIDE** *Beggars Banquet BEG 19*	**72**	1
17 Nov 79	**NEW GUITAR IN TOWN** *Beggars Banquet BEG 28*	**72**	1
1 Jul 78	FULHAM FALLOUT *Beggars Banquet BEGA 2*	57	1

LUSCIOUS JACKSON *US, female vocal / instrumental group (Singles: 5 weeks, Albums: 1 week)*

		pos/wks	
18 Mar 95	**DEEP SHAG / CITYSONG** *Capitol CDCL 739*	**69**	1
21 Oct 95	**HERE** *Capitol CDCL 758*	**59**	1
12 Apr 97	**NAKED EYE** *Capitol CDCL 786*	**25**	2
3 Jul 99	**LADYFINGERS** *Grand Royal / Parlophone CDCL 813*	**43**	1
26 Apr 97	FEVER IN FEVER OUT *Capitol CDEST 2290*	55	1

LUSH *UK, female / male vocal / instrumental group (Singles: 19 weeks, Albums: 10 weeks)*

		pos/wks	
10 Mar 90	**MAD LOVE (EP)** *4AD BAD 003*	**55**	1
27 Oct 90	**SWEETNESS AND LIGHT** *4AD BAD 0013*	**47**	2
19 Oct 91	**NOTHING NATURAL** *4AD AD 1016*	**43**	2
11 Jan 92	**FOR LOVE (EP)** *4AD BAD 2001*	**35**	2
11 Jun 94	**HYPOCRITE** *4AD BAD 4008CD*	**52**	2
11 Jun 94	**DESIRE LINES** *4AD BAD 4010CD*	**60**	1
20 Jan 96	**SINGLE GIRL** *4AD BAD 6001CD*	**21**	3
9 Mar 96	**LADYKILLERS** *4AD BAD 6002CD*	**22**	3
27 Jul 96	**500 (SHAKE BABY SHAKE)** *4AD BAD 6009CD*	**21**	3
8 Feb 92 ●	SPOOKY *4AD CAD 2002CD*	7	3
25 Jun 94	SPLIT *4AD CAD 4011CD*	19	2
30 Mar 96 ●	LOVELIFE *4AD CAD 6004CD*	8	5

Tracks on Mad Love (EP): De-Luxe / Leaves Me Cold / Downer / Thoughtforms. Tracks on For Love (EP): For Love / Starlust / Outdoor Miner / Astronaut

LUSTRAL *UK, male DJ / production duo – Ricky Simmons and Steve Jones (Singles: 3 weeks)*

		pos/wks	
18 Oct 97	**EVERYTIME** *Hooj Choons HOOJCD 55*	**60**	1
4 Dec 99	**EVERYTIME (re-mix)** *Hooj Choons HOOJ 83CD*	**30**	2

See also ASCENSION; CHAKRA; SPACE BROTHERS; OXYGEN featuring Andrea BRITTON

LUVVERS – *See LULU*

LUZON *US, male producer – Stacy Burket (Singles: 1 week)*

		pos/wks	
14 Jul 01	**THE BAGUIO TRACK** *Renaissance RENCDS 006*	**67**	1

Annabella LWIN *Burma, female vocalist (Singles: 1 week)*

		pos/wks	
28 Jan 95	**DO WHAT YOU DO** *Sony S2 6611235*	**61**	1

John LYDON *UK, male vocalist (Singles: 6 weeks)*

		pos/wks	
13 Nov 93	**OPEN UP** *Hard Hands HAND 009CD* [1]	**13**	5
2 Aug 97	**SUN** *Virgin VUSCD 122*	**42**	1

[1] Leftfield Lydon

See also PUBLIC IMAGE LTD; SEX PISTOLS

Frankie LYMON and the TEENAGERS *US, male vocal group, leader d. 28 Feb 1968 (Singles: 38 weeks)*

		pos/wks	
29 Jun 56 ★	**WHY DO FOOLS FALL IN LOVE** *Columbia DB 3772* [1]	**1**	16
29 Mar 57	**I'M NOT A JUVENILE DELINQUENT** *Columbia 33 DB 3878*	**12**	7
12 Apr 57 ●	**BABY, BABY** *Columbia DB 3878*	**4**	12
20 Sep 57	**GOODY GOODY** *Columbia DB 3983*	**24**	3

[1] Teenagers featuring Frankie Lymon

Des LYNAM featuring WIMBLEDON CHORAL SOCIETY *UK, male vocalist / TV presenter with choir (Singles: 3 weeks)*

		pos/wks	
12 Dec 98	**IF – READ TO FAURÉ'S 'PAVANE'** *BBC Worldwide WMSS 60062*	**45**	3

Curtis LYNCH Jr featuring Kele LE ROC and RED RAT
UK, male producer with female vocalist and Jamaica, male vocalist (Singles: 1 week)

			pos	wks
30 Sep 00		THINKING OF YOU *Telstar CDSTAS3136*	70	1

See also Kele LE ROC

Kenny LYNCH *UK, male vocalist (Singles: 59 weeks)*

			pos	wks
30 Jun 60		MOUNTAIN OF LOVE *HMV POP 751*	33	3
13 Sep 62		PUFF (re) *HMV POP 1057*	33	6
6 Dec 62	●	UP ON THE ROOF *HMV POP 1090*	10	12
20 Jun 63	●	YOU CAN NEVER STOP ME LOVING YOU *HMV POP 1165*	10	14
16 Apr 64		STAND BY ME *HMV POP 1280*	39	7
27 Aug 64		WHAT AM I TO YOU (re) *HMV POP 1321*	37	6
17 Jun 65		I'LL STAY BY YOU *HMV POP 1430*	29	7
20 Aug 83		HALF THE DAY'S GONE AND WE HAVEN'T EARNED A PENNY *Satril SAT 510*	50	4

Liam LYNCH *US, male vocalist (Singles: 9 weeks)*

			pos	wks
7 Dec 02	●	UNITED STATES OF WHATEVER *Global Warming WARMCD 17*	10	9

Cheryl LYNN *US, female vocalist (Singles: 2 weeks)*

			pos	wks
8 Sep 84		ENCORE *Streetwave KHAN 23*	68	2

Patti LYNN *UK, female vocalist (Singles: 5 weeks)*

			pos	wks
10 May 62		JOHNNY ANGEL *Fontana H 391*	37	5

Tami LYNN *US, female vocalist (Singles: 20 weeks)*

			pos	wks
22 May 71	●	I'M GONNA RUN AWAY FROM YOU *Mojo 2092 001*	4	14
3 May 75		I'M GONNA RUN AWAY FROM YOU (re-issue) *Contempo Raries CS 9026*	36	6

Vera LYNN *UK, female vocalist – Vera Welch (Singles: 46 weeks, Albums: 15 weeks)*

			pos	wks
14 Nov 52	●	AUF WIEDERSEH'N SWEETHEART *Decca F 9927* ▲	10	1
14 Nov 52	●	FORGET-ME-NOT (re) *Decca F 9985*	5	6
14 Nov 52	●	THE HOMING WALTZ *Decca F 9959*	9	3
5 Jun 53		THE WINDSOR WALTZ *Decca F 10092*	11	1
15 Oct 54	★	MY SON, MY SON *Decca F 10372* [1]	1	14
8 Jun 56		WHO ARE WE *Decca F 10715*	30	1
26 Oct 56		A HOUSE WITH LOVE IN IT *Decca F 10799*	17	13
15 Mar 57		THE FAITHFUL HUSSAR (DON'T CRY MY LOVE) *Decca F 10846*	29	2
21 Jun 57		TRAVELLIN' HOME *Decca F 10903*	20	5
21 Nov 81		20 FAMILY FAVOURITES *EMI EMTV 28*	25	12
9 Sep 89		WE'LL MEET AGAIN *Telstar STAR 2369*	44	3

[1] Vera Lynn with Frank Weir, his saxophone, his Orchestra and Chorus

Jeff LYNNE *UK, male vocalist (Singles: 4 weeks, Albums: 4 weeks)*

			pos	wks
30 Jun 90		EVERY LITTLE THING *Reprise W 9799*	59	4
4 Aug 90		ARMCHAIR THEATRE *Reprise WX 347*	24	4

See also ELECTRIC LIGHT ORCHESTRA; TRAVELING WILBURYS

Shelby LYNNE *US, female vocalist (Singles: 1 week)*

			pos	wks
29 Apr 00		LEAVIN' *Mercury 5627372*	73	1

Philip LYNOTT *Ireland, male vocalist / instrumentalist d. 4 Jan 1986 (Singles: 36 weeks, Albums: 16 weeks)*

			pos	wks
5 Apr 80		DEAR MISS LONELY HEARTS *Vertigo SOLO 1*	32	6
21 Jun 80		KING'S CALL *Vertigo SOLO 2*	35	6
21 Mar 81		YELLOW PEARL (re) *Vertigo SOLO 3*	14	12
18 May 85	●	OUT IN THE FIELDS *10 TEN 49* [1]	5	10
24 Jan 87		KING'S CALL (re-mix) *Vertigo LYN 1*	68	2
26 Apr 80		SOLO IN SOHO *Vertigo 9102 038*	28	6
14 Nov 87		SOLDIER OF FORTUNE – THE BEST OF PHIL LYNOTT AND THIN LIZZY *Telstar STAR 2300* [1]	55	10

[1] Gary Moore and Phil Lynott [1] Phil Lynott and Thin Lizzy

'Yellow Pearl' made its peak position on re-entry in Dec 1981

See also THIN LIZZY; Gary MOORE

LYNYRD SKYNYRD *US, male vocal / instrumental group (Singles: 21 weeks, Albums: 19 weeks)*

			pos	wks
11 Sep 76		SWEET HOME ALABAMA / DOUBLE TROUBLE (2re) *MCA 251*	21	21
3 May 75		NUTHIN' FANCY *MCA MCF 2700*	43	1
28 Feb 76		GIMME BACK MY BULLETS *MCA MCF 2744*	34	5
6 Nov 76		ONE MORE FOR THE ROAD *MCA MCPS 279*	17	4
12 Nov 77		STREET SURVIVORS *MCA MCG 3525*	13	4
4 Nov 78		SKYNYRD'S FIRST AND LAST *MCA MCG 3529*	50	1
9 Feb 80		GOLD AND PLATINUM *MCA MCSP 308*	49	4

Sweet Home Alabama / Double Trouble was the chart listing for what was also alternatively listed as the Freebird EP for the two re-entries which peaked at No.43 in Dec 1979 and No.21 in 1982. 1976 chart peak was No.31

Barbara LYON *US, female vocalist d. 10 Jul 1985 (Singles: 12 weeks)*

			pos	wks
24 Jun 55		STOWAWAY *Columbia DB 3619*	12	8
21 Dec 56		LETTER TO A SOLDIER *Columbia DB 3865*	27	4

LYTE FUNKIE ONES *US, male vocal / rap group (Singles: 20 weeks, Albums: 1 week)*

			pos	wks
22 May 99		CAN'T HAVE YOU *Logic 74321649152*	54	1
18 Sep 99		SUMMER GIRLS *Logic 74321701152*	16	7
5 Feb 00	●	GIRL ON TV *Logic 74321717582*	6	9
27 Apr 02		EVERY OTHER TIME *Logic 74321925502*	24	3
26 Feb 00		LYTE FUNKIE ONES *Logic 74321706832*	62	1

Humphrey LYTTELTON BAND *UK, male jazz band – Humphrey Lyttelton – trumpet (Singles: 6 weeks)*

			pos	wks
13 Jul 56		BAD PENNY BLUES *Parlophone R 4184*	19	6

Kevin LYTTLE *St. Vincent, male vocalist (Singles: 10 weeks)*

			pos	wks
25 Oct 03	●	TURN ME ON *Atlantic AT 0167CD*	2	10+

M *UK, male vocalist / multi-instrumentalist – Robin Scott (Singles: 39 weeks)*

			pos	wks
7 Apr 79	●	POP MUZIK *MCA 413* ▲	2	14
8 Dec 79		MOONLIGHT AND MUZAK *MCA 541*	33	9
15 Mar 80		THAT'S THE WAY THE MONEY GOES *MCA 570*	45	5
22 Nov 80		OFFICIAL SECRETS *MCA 650*	64	2
10 Jun 89		POP MUZIK (re-mix) *Freestyle FRS 1*	15	9

Bobby M featuring Jean CARN
US, male / female vocal / instrumental duo (Singles: 3 weeks) pos/wks

29 Jan 83 **LET'S STAY TOGETHER** *Gordy TMG 1288* 53 3

M and O BAND *UK, male vocal / instrumental duo – Muff Murfin and Colin Owen (Singles: 6 weeks)* pos/wks

28 Feb 76 **LET'S DO THE LATIN HUSTLE** *Creole CR 120* 16 6

M&S presents GIRL NEXT DOOR
UK, male production duo and female vocalist (Singles: 13 weeks) pos/wks

7 Apr 01 ● **SALSOUL NUGGET (IF U WANNA)** *ffrr FCD 393* 6 13

MBD – *See SO SOLID CREW*

M-BEAT *UK, male producer – Marlon Hart (Singles: 24 weeks)* pos/wks

18 Jun 94 **INCREDIBLE** *Renk RENK 42CD* [1] 39 3
10 Sep 94 ● **INCREDIBLE (re-mix)** *Renk CDRENK 44* [1] 8 9
17 Dec 94 **SWEET LOVE** *Renk CDRENK 49* [2] 18 7
1 Jun 96 **DO U KNOW WHERE YOU'RE COMING FROM** *Renk CDRENK 63* [3] 12 5

[1] M-Beat featuring General Levy [2] M-Beat featuring Nazlyn [3] M-Beat featuring Jamiroquai

M-D-EMM *UK, male producer – Mark Ryder (Singles: 3 weeks)* pos/wks

22 Feb 92 **GET DOWN** *Strictly Underground 7STUR 13* 55 2
30 May 92 **MOVE YOUR FEET** *Strictly Underground STUR 15* 67 1

See also Mark RYDER

MDM *UK, male producer – Matt Darey (Singles: 1 week)* pos/wks

27 Oct 01 **MASH IT UP** *Nulife / Arista 74321870472* 66 1

See also LOST TRIBE; Matt DAREY; MELT featuring Little Ms MARCIE; SUNBURST

M DUBS featuring LADY SAW
UK / Jamaica, male producer / female vocalist (Singles: 1 week) pos/wks

16 Dec 00 **BUMP N GRIND (I AM FEELING HOT TONIGHT)** *Telstar CDSTAS 3129* 59 1

MFSB *US, orchestra (Singles: 18 weeks)* pos/wks

27 Apr 74 **TSOP (THE SOUND OF PHILADELPHIA)** *Philadelphia International PIR 2289* [1] ▲ 22 9
26 Jul 75 **SEXY** *Philadelphia International PIR 3381* 37 5
31 Jan 81 **MYSTERIES OF THE WORLD** *Sound of Philadelphia PIR 9501* 41 4

[1] MFSB featuring the Three Degrees

M FACTOR *UK, male DJ / production duo – Danny Harrison and Julian Jonah (Singles: 4 weeks)* pos/wks

6 Jul 02 **MOTHER** *Serious SERR 042CD* 18 3
26 Jul 03 **COME TOGETHER** *Credence CDCRED 037* 46 1

MG's – *See BOOKER T and the MG's*

MK *US, male producer – Mark Kinchen (Singles: 3 weeks)* pos/wks

4 Feb 95 **ALWAYS** *Activ CDTV 3* [1] 69 1
27 May 95 **BURNING '95** *Activ CDTVR 6* 44 2

[1] MK featuring Alana

Alana appears on both hits, although she is credited only on the first

M + M *Canada, male / female vocal duo (Singles: 4 weeks)* pos/wks

28 Jul 84 **BLACK STATIONS WHITE STATIONS** *RCA 426* 46 4

M + M are Martha and a Muffin

See also MARTHA and the MUFFINS

MN8 *UK / Trinidad, male vocal group (Singles: 38 weeks, Albums: 4 weeks)* pos/wks

4 Feb 95 ● **I'VE GOT A LITTLE SOMETHING FOR YOU** *Columbia 6608802* 2 13
29 Apr 95 ● **IF YOU ONLY LET ME IN** *Columbia 6613252* 6 7
15 Jul 95 ● **HAPPY** *Columbia 6622192* 8 7
4 Nov 95 **BABY IT'S YOU (re)** *Columbia 6624522* 22 3
24 Feb 96 **PATHWAY TO THE MOON** *Columbia 6629212* 25 2
31 Aug 96 **TUFF ACT TO FOLLOW** *Columbia 6635345* 15 3
26 Oct 96 **DREAMING** *Columbia 6638302* 21 3
27 May 95 **TO THE NEXT LEVEL** *Columbia 4802802* 13 4

MNO
Belgium, male instrumental / production group (Singles: 2 weeks) pos/wks

28 Sep 91 **GOD OF ABRAHAM** *A&M AM 820* 66 2

M.O.P. *US, male rap duo – Jamal Grinnage and Eric Murry (Singles: 20 weeks, Albums: 3 weeks)* pos/wks

12 May 01 ● **COLD AS ICE** *Epic 6711762* 4 10
18 Aug 01 ● **ANTE UP (re)** *Epic 6717882* [1] 7 8
1 Dec 01 **STAND CLEAR** *Chrysalis CDEM 597* [2] 43 1
8 Jun 02 **STAND CLEAR (re-mix)** *Kaos KAOSCD 002* [2] 50 1
25 Aug 01 **WARRIORZ** *Epic 4982779* 40 3

[1] M.O.P. featuring Busta Rhymes [2] Adam F featuring M.O.P.

M1 *UK, male producer (Singles: 1 week)* pos/wks

22 Feb 03 **HEAVEN SENT** *Inferno CDFERN 51* 72 1

M PEOPLE (109 Top 500) *Clubland favourites turned pop soul sophisticates: Heather Small (v), backed by Paul Heard and Mike Pickering (both k / prog). In 1994 this Manchester act was voted Best British Dance Act at the Brits and won the 1993 Mercury Music Prize for their LP 'Elegant Slumming' (Singles: 137 weeks, Albums: 278 weeks)* pos/wks

26 Oct 91 **HOW CAN I LOVE YOU MORE?** *Deconstruction PB 44855* 29 9
7 Mar 92 **COLOUR MY LIFE** *Deconstruction PB 45241* 35 4
18 Apr 92 **SOMEDAY** *Deconstruction PB 45369* [1] 38 3
10 Oct 92 **EXCITED** *Deconstruction 74321116337* 29 5
6 Feb 93 ● **HOW CAN I LOVE YOU MORE? (re-mix)** *Deconstruction 74321130232* 8 8
26 Jun 93 ● **ONE NIGHT IN HEAVEN** *Deconstruction 74321151852* 6 11
25 Sep 93 ● **MOVING ON UP** *Deconstruction 74321166162* 2 11
4 Dec 93 ● **DON'T LOOK ANY FURTHER** *Deconstruction 74321177112* 9 10
12 Mar 94 ● **RENAISSANCE** *Deconstruction 74321194132* 5 7
17 Sep 94 **ELEGANTLY AMERICAN: ONE NIGHT IN HEAVEN / MOVING ON UP (EP) (re-mix)** *Deconstruction 74321231882* ..31 2
19 Nov 94 ● **SIGHT FOR SORE EYES** *Deconstruction 74321245472* 6 9
4 Feb 95 ● **OPEN YOUR HEART** *Deconstruction 74321261532* 9 7
24 Jun 95 ● **SEARCH FOR THE HERO** *Deconstruction 74321287962* 9 7
14 Oct 95 **LOVE RENDEZVOUS** *Deconstruction 74321319282* 32 4
25 Nov 95 **ITCHYCOO PARK** *Deconstruction 74321330732* 11 8
4 Oct 97 ● **JUST FOR YOU** *BMG 74321523002* 8 7
6 Dec 97 **FANTASY ISLAND (re)** *BMG 74321542932* 33 9
28 Mar 98 ● **ANGEL STREET** *M People 74321564182* 8 6
7 Nov 98 **TESTIFY** *M People 74321621742* 12 6
13 Feb 99 **DREAMING** *M People 74321645352* 13 4
6 Mar 93 **NORTHERN SOUL** *Deconstruction 74321117772* 53 2
16 Oct 93 ● **ELEGANT SLUMMING** *Deconstruction 74321166782* 2 87
26 Nov 94 ● **BIZARRE FRUIT / BIZARRE FRUIT II** *Deconstruction 74321240812* 3 115
16 Sep 95 **NORTHERN SOUL (re-issue)** *RCA PD 75157* 26 3
25 Oct 97 ● **FRESCO** *M People 74321524902* 2 40
14 Nov 98 ● **THE BEST OF M PEOPLE** *M People 74321613872* 2 31

[1] M People with Heather Small

From 9 Dec 95 'Bizarre Fruit' was listed with the remix album 'Bizarre Fruit II'

M3 *UK, male / female production / vocal trio (Singles: 2 weeks)* pos/wks

30 Oct 99 **BAILAMOS** *Inferno CDFERN 21* 40 2

M2M *Norway, female vocal / instrumental duo – Marit Larsen and Marion Raven (Singles: 6 weeks)* pos/wks

1 Apr 00 **DON'T SAY YOU LOVE ME** *Atlantic AT 0081CD* 16 6

MSG – *See Michael SCHENKER GROUP*

MXM *Italy, male / female vocal / instrumental group (Singles: 1 week)* pos/wks

2 Jun 90 **NOTHING COMPARES 2 U** *London LON 267* 68 1

Timo MAAS *Germany, male DJ / producer (Singles: 10 weeks, Albums: 3 weeks)* pos/wks

1 Apr 00 **DER SCHIEBER** *48k / Perfecto SPECT 07CDS* 50 1
30 Sep 00 **UBIK** *Perfecto PERF 10CDS* [1] 33 2
23 Feb 02 **TO GET DOWN** *Perfecto PERF 30CDS* 14 4
11 May 02 **SHIFTER** *Perfecto PERF 31CDS* [2] 38 2
5 Oct 02 **HELP ME** *Perfecto PERF 42CDS* [3] 65 1
16 Mar 02 LOUD *Perfecto PERFALB 08CD* 41 3

[1] Timo Mass featuring Martin Bettinghaus [2] Timo Maas featuring MC Chickaboo [3] Timo Maas featuring Kelis

Lorin MAAZEL – *See Andrea BOCELLI; Andrew LLOYD WEBBER*

Pete MAC Jr *US, male vocalist (Singles: 4 weeks)* pos/wks

15 Oct 77 **THE WATER MARGIN** *BBC RESL 50* 37 4

This is the Japanese version of the song which shared chart credit with the English-language version by Godiego

See also GODIEGO

Scott MAC – *See SIGNUM*

MAC BAND featuring the McCAMPBELL BROTHERS *US, male vocal group (Singles: 17 weeks, Albums: 3 weeks)* pos/wks

18 Jun 88 ● **ROSES ARE RED** *MCA MCA 1264* 8 13
10 Sep 88 **STALEMATE** *MCA MCA 1271* 40 4
20 Aug 88 THE MAC BAND *MCA MCC 6032* 61 3

'Stalemate' credits the McCampbell Brothers on the sleeve only, not on the label

Keith MAC PROJECT *UK, male / female vocal / instrumental group (Singles: 1 week)* pos/wks

25 Jun 94 **DE DAH DAH (SPICE OF LIFE)** *Public Demand PPDCD 3* 66 1

Lara McALLEN – *See ANGEL CITY featuring Lara McALLEN*

David McALMONT *UK, male vocalist (Singles: 5 weeks)* pos/wks

27 Apr 96 **HYMN** *Blanco Y Negro NEG 87CD* [1] 65 1
9 Aug 97 **LOOK AT YOURSELF** *Hut HUTCD 87* 40 2
22 Nov 97 **DIAMONDS ARE FOREVER** *East West EW 141CD* [2] 39 2

[1] Ultramarine featuring David McAlmont [2] David McAlmont / David Arnold

See also McALMONT and BUTLER

McALMONT & BUTLER *UK, male vocal / instrumental duo – David McAlmont and Bernard Butler (Singles: 17 weeks, Albums: 10 weeks)* pos/wks

27 May 95 ● **YES** *Hut HUTCD 53* 8 8
4 Nov 95 **YOU DO** *Hut HUTCD 57* 17 4
10 Aug 02 **FALLING** *Chrysalis CDCHS 5141* 23 3
9 Nov 02 **BRING IT BACK** *Chrysalis CDCHSS 5145* 36 2
9 Dec 95 THE SOUND OF McALMONT AND BUTLER *Hut CDHUT 32* 33 8
24 Aug 02 BRING IT BACK *Chrysalis 5399772* 18 2

See also Bernard BUTLER; David McALMONT

Neil MacARTHUR *UK, male vocalist – Colin Blunstone (Singles: 5 weeks)* pos/wks

5 Feb 69 **SHE'S NOT THERE** *Deram DM 225* 34 5

David MacBETH *UK, male vocalist (Singles: 4 weeks)* pos/wks

30 Oct 59 **MR BLUE** *Pye 7N 15231* 18 4

Nicko McBRAIN *UK, male vocalist / instrumentalist – drums (Singles: 1 week)* pos/wks

13 Jul 91 **RHYTHM OF THE BEAST** *EMI NICK 01* 72 1

See also IRON MAIDEN

Frankie McBRIDE *Ireland, male vocalist (Singles: 15 weeks, Albums: 3 weeks)* pos/wks

9 Aug 67 **FIVE LITTLE FINGERS** *Emerald MD 1081* 19 15
17 Feb 68 FRANKIE McBRIDE *Emerald SLD 28* 29 3

MACC LADS *UK, male vocal / instrumental group (Albums: 1 week)* pos/wks

7 Oct 89 FROM BEER TO ETERNITY *Hectic House HHLP 12* 72 1

Dan McCAFFERTY *UK, male vocalist (Singles: 3 weeks)* pos/wks

13 Sep 75 **OUT OF TIME** *Mountain TOP 1* 41 3

CW McCALL *US, male vocalist – William Fries (Singles: 10 weeks)* pos/wks

14 Feb 76 ● **CONVOY** *MGM 2006 560* ▲ 2 10

Noel McCALLA – *See BIGFELLA featuring Noel McCALLA*

David McCALLUM *UK, male actor / vocalist (Singles: 4 weeks)* pos/wks

14 Apr 66 **COMMUNICATION** *Capitol CL 15439* 32 4

McCAMPBELL BROTHERS – *See MAC BAND featuring the McCAMPBELL BROTHERS*

Linda McCARTNEY *US, female vocalist – Linda Eastman, d. 17 Apr 1998 (Singles: 7 weeks, Albums: 24 weeks)* pos/wks

28 Aug 71 **BACK SEAT OF MY CAR** *Apple R 5914* [1] 39 5
21 Nov 98 **WIDE PRAIRIE** *Parlophone CDR 6510* 74 1
6 Feb 99 **THE LIGHT COMES FROM WITHIN** *Parlophone CDR 6513* 56 1
5 Jun 71 ★ RAM *Apple PAS 10003* [1] ■ 1 24

[1] Paul and Linda McCartney [1] Paul and Linda McCartney

See also Paul McCARTNEY; WINGS

Paul McCARTNEY (20 Top 500)

Pop's most successful singer / songwriter and the richest man in British music, b. 18 Jun, 1942, Liverpool. His composition 'Yesterday' is the world's most recorded song and has had more than seven million plays on US radio alone. This entertainer, known for his charitable work, has broken attendance records around the world; his 50-date 2002 US tour grossed a record $100m and a 1999 internet show attracted at least 50 million hits. Winner of a record number of Ivor Novello Awards, he was awarded the only Rhodium record (from Guinness) to honour outstanding sales and received Lifetime Achievement Grammy (1990) and knighthood (1997). He has reportedly amassed a personal fortune of £500m. Sir Paul is the only artist to have No.1s as a solo artist, part of a duo, trio, quartet, quintet and charity group. Mull of Kintyre / Girls' School' at 2,050,000 is his best-seller (Singles: 410 weeks, Albums: 570 weeks) pos/wks

27 Feb 71 ● **ANOTHER DAY** *Apple R 5889* 2 12
28 Aug 71 **BACK SEAT OF MY CAR** *Apple R 5914* [1] 39 5
26 Feb 72 **GIVE IRELAND BACK TO THE IRISH** *Apple R 5936* [2] 16 8
27 May 72 ● **MARY HAD A LITTLE LAMB** *Apple R 5949* [2] 9 11
9 Dec 72 ● **HI, HI, HI / C MOON** *Apple R 5973* [2] 5 13
7 Apr 73 ● **MY LOVE** *Apple R 5985* [3] ▲ 9 11
9 Jun 73 ● **LIVE AND LET DIE (re)** *Apple R 5987* [2] 9 14
3 Nov 73 **HELEN WHEELS** *Apple R 5993* [3] 12 12
2 Mar 74 ● **JET** *Apple R 5996* [3] 7 9
6 Jul 74 ● **BAND ON THE RUN** *Apple R 5997* [3] ▲ 3 11
9 Nov 74 **JUNIOR'S FARM** *Apple R 5999* [3] 16 10
31 May 75 ● **LISTEN TO WHAT THE MAN SAID** *Capitol R 6006* [2] ▲ 6 8
18 Oct 75 **LETTING GO** *Capitol R 6008* [2] 41 3
15 May 76 ● **SILLY LOVE SONGS** *Parlophone R 6014* [2] ▲ 2 11
7 Aug 76 ● **LET 'EM IN** *Parlophone R 6015* [2] 2 10
19 Feb 77 **MAYBE I'M AMAZED** *Parlophone R 6017* [2] 28 5
19 Nov 77 ★ **MULL OF KINTYRE / GIRLS' SCHOOL** *Capitol R 6018* [2] ◆ 1 17
1 Apr 78 ● **WITH A LITTLE LUCK** *Parlophone R 6019* [2] ▲ 5 9
1 Jul 78 **I'VE HAD ENOUGH** *Parlophone R 6020* [2] 42 7
9 Sep 78 **LONDON TOWN** *Parlophone R 6021* [2] 60 4
7 Apr 79 ● **GOODNIGHT TONIGHT** *Parlophone R 6023* [2] 5 10
16 Jun 79 **OLD SIAM SIR** *Parlophone R 6026* [2] 35 6
1 Sep 79 **GETTING CLOSER / BABY'S REQUEST** *Parlophone R 6027* [2] ..60 3

1 Dec 79 ● WONDERFUL CHRISTMASTIME *Parlophone R 6029* 6 8
19 Apr 80 ● COMING UP *Parlophone R 6035* ▲ 2 9
21 Jun 80 ● WATERFALLS *Parlophone R 6037* 9 8
10 Apr 82 ★ EBONY AND IVORY *Parlophone 6054* [4] ▲ 1 10
3 Jul 82 TAKE IT AWAY *Parlophone R 6056* 15 10
9 Oct 82 TUG OF WAR *Parlophone R 6057* 53 3
6 Nov 82 ● THE GIRL IS MINE (re) *Epic EPC A 2729* [5] 8 10
15 Oct 83 ● SAY SAY SAY *Parlophone R 6062* [6] ▲ 2 15
17 Dec 83 ★ PIPES OF PEACE *Parlophone R 6064* 1 12
6 Oct 84 ● NO MORE LONELY NIGHTS (BALLAD) *Parlophone R 6080* 2 15
24 Nov 84 ● WE ALL STAND TOGETHER (re) *Parlophone R 6086* [7] 3 18
30 Nov 85 SPIES LIKE US *Parlophone R 6118* 13 10
26 Jul 86 PRESS *Parlophone R 6133* 25 8
13 Dec 86 ONLY LOVE REMAINS *Parlophone R 6148* 34 5
28 Nov 87 ● ONCE UPON A LONG AGO *Parlophone R 6170* 10 7
20 May 89 MY BRAVE FACE *Parlophone R 6213* 18 5
20 May 89 ★ FERRY 'CROSS THE MERSEY *PWL PWL 41* [8] ■ 1 7
29 Jul 89 THIS ONE *Parlophone R 6223* 18 6
25 Nov 89 FIGURE OF EIGHT *Parlophone R 6235* 42 3
17 Feb 90 PUT IT THERE *Parlophone R 6246* 32 2
20 Oct 90 BIRTHDAY *Parlophone R 6271* 29 3
8 Dec 90 ALL MY TRIALS *Parlophone CDR 6278* 35 5
9 Jan 93 HOPE OF DELIVERANCE *Parlophone CDR 6330* 18 6
6 Mar 93 C'MON PEOPLE *Parlophone CDRS 6338* 41 3
10 May 97 YOUNG BOY *Parlophone CDRS 6462* 19 3
19 Jul 97 THE WORLD TONIGHT *Parlophone CDR 6472* 23 2
27 Dec 97 BEAUTIFUL NIGHT *Parlophone CDR 6489* 25 4
6 Nov 99 NO OTHER BABY / BROWN EYED HANDSOME MAN *Parlophone CDR 6527* 42 2
10 Nov 01 FROM A LOVER TO A FRIEND *Parlophone CDR 6567* 45 2
2 May 70 ● McCARTNEY *Apple PCS 7102* ▲ 2 32
5 Jun 71 ★ RAM *Apple PAS 10003* [1] ■ 1 24
18 Dec 71 WILD LIFE *Apple PCS 7142* [2] 11 9
19 May 73 ● RED ROSE SPEEDWAY *Apple PCTC 251* [3] ▲ 5 16
15 Dec 73 ★ BAND ON THE RUN *Apple PAS 10007* [3] ▲ 1 124
21 Jun 75 ★ VENUS AND MARS *Apple PCTC 254* [2] ▲ 1 29
17 Apr 76 ● WINGS AT THE SPEED OF SOUND *Apple PAS 10010* [2] ▲ 2 35
15 Jan 77 ● WINGS OVER AMERICA *Parlophone PAS 720* [2] ▲ 8 22
15 Apr 78 ● LONDON TOWN *Parlophone PAS 10012* [2] 4 23
16 Dec 78 ● WINGS GREATEST HITS *Parlophone PCTC 256* [2] 5 32
23 Jun 79 ● BACK TO THE EGG *Parlophone PCTC 257* [2] 6 15
31 May 80 ★ McCARTNEY II *Parlophone PCTC 258* ■ 1 18
7 Mar 81 THE McCARTNEY INTERVIEW *EMI CHAT 1* 34 4
8 May 82 ★ TUG OF WAR *Parlophone PCTC 259* ■ ▲ 1 27
12 Nov 83 ● PIPES OF PEACE *Parlophone PCTC 1652301* 4 23
3 Nov 84 ★ GIVE MY REGARDS TO BROAD STREET *Parlophone PCTC 2* ■ 1 21
13 Sep 86 ● PRESS TO PLAY *Parlophone PCSD 103* 8 6
14 Nov 87 ● ALL THE BEST! *Parlophone PMTV 1* 2 21
17 Jun 89 ★ FLOWERS IN THE DIRT *Parlophone PCSD 106* 1 20
17 Nov 90 TRIPPING THE LIVE FANTASTIC *Parlophone PCST 7346* 17 11
1 Jun 91 ● UNPLUGGED – THE OFFICIAL BOOTLEG *Parlophone PCSD 116* 7 3
12 Oct 91 CHOBA B CCCP (THE RUSSIAN ALBUM) *Parlophone CDPCSD 117* 63 1
13 Feb 93 ● OFF THE GROUND *Parlophone CDPCSD 125* 5 4
20 Nov 93 PAUL IS LIVE *Parlophone PDPCSD 147* 34 2
17 May 97 ● FLAMING PIE *Parlophone CDPCSD 171* 2 15
27 Mar 99 BAND ON THE RUN (re-issue) *Parlophone 4991762* [3] 69 1
16 Oct 99 RUN DEVIL RUN *Parlophone 5223512* 12 11
19 May 01 ● WINGSPAN – HITS AND HISTORY *P arlophone 5328502* 5 7
24 Nov 01 DRIVING RAIN *Parlophone 5355102* 46 1
29 Mar 03 ● BACK IN THE WORLD *Parlophone 5830052* 5 13

[1] Paul and Linda McCartney [2] Wings [3] Paul McCartney and Wings [4] Paul McCartney with Stevie Wonder [5] Michael Jackson and Paul McCartney [6] Paul McCartney and Michael Jackson [7] Paul McCartney and the Frog Chorus [8] Christians, Holly Johnson, Paul McCartney, Gerry Marsden and Stock Aitken Waterman [1] Paul and Linda McCartney [2] Wings [3] Paul McCartney and Wings

R 6027 credits no label at all, although the number is a Parlophone one

See also BEATLES; WINGS

Kirsty MacCOLL *UK, female vocalist, d. 18 Dec 2000 (Singles: 65 weeks, Albums: 58 weeks)* pos/wks

13 Jun 81 THERE'S A GUY WORKS DOWN THE CHIPSHOP SWEARS HE'S ELVIS *Polydor POSP 250* 14 9
19 Jan 85 ● A NEW ENGLAND *Stiff BUY 216* 7 10
15 Nov 86 GREETINGS TO THE NEW BRUNETTE *Go! Discs GOD 15* [1] 58 2
5 Dec 87 ● FAIRYTALE OF NEW YORK *Pogue Mahone NY 7* [2] 2 9
8 Apr 89 FREE WORLD *Virgin KMA 1* 43 6
1 Jul 89 DAYS *Virgin KMA 2* 12 9
25 May 91 WALKING DOWN MADISON *Virgin VS 1348* 23 7
17 Aug 91 MY AFFAIR *Virgin VS 1354* 56 2
14 Dec 91 FAIRYTALE OF NEW YORK (re-issue) *PM YZ 628* [2] 36 5
4 Mar 95 CAROLINE *Virgin VSCDX 1517* 58 2
24 Jun 95 PERFECT DAY *Virgin VSCDT 1552* [3] 75 1
29 Jul 95 DAYS (re-issue) *Virgin VSCDT 1558* 42 3
20 May 89 KITE *Virgin KMLP 1* 34 12
6 Jul 91 ELECTRIC LANDLADY *Virgin V 2663* 17 8
12 Mar 94 TITANIC DAYS *ZTT 4509947112* 46 2
18 Mar 95 ● GALORE – THE BEST OF KIRSTY MacCOLL *Virgin CDV 2763* 6 27
1 Apr 00 TROPICAL BRAINSTORM *V2 VVR 1009872* 39 9

[1] Billy Bragg with Johnny Marr and Kirsty MacColl [2] Pogues featuring Kirsty MacColl [3] Kirsty MacColl and Evan Dando

Neil MacCOLL – *See LA's; PRETENDERS*

Marilyn McCOO and Billy DAVIS Jr *US, female / male vocal duo (Singles: 9 weeks)* pos/wks

19 Mar 77 ● YOU DON'T HAVE TO BE A STAR (TO BE IN MY SHOW) *ABC 4147* ▲ 7 9

Del McCOURY BAND – *See Steve EARLE*

Paul McCOY BAND – *See EVANESCENCE*

Van McCOY *US, orchestra, leader d. 6 Jul 1979 (Singles: 36 weeks, Albums: 11 weeks)* pos/wks

31 May 75 ● THE HUSTLE *Avco 6105 038* [1] ▲ 3 12
1 Nov 75 CHANGE WITH THE TIMES *Avco 6105 042* 36 4
12 Feb 77 SOUL CHA CHA *H & L 6105 065* 34 6
9 Apr 77 ● THE SHUFFLE *H & L 6105 076* 4 14
5 Jul 75 DISCO BABY *Avco 9109 004* [1] 32 11

[1] Van McCoy with the Soul City Symphony [1] Van McCoy with the Soul City Symphony

McCOYS *US, male vocal / instrumental group (Singles: 18 weeks)* pos/wks

2 Sep 65 ● HANG ON SLOOPY *Immediate IM 001* ▲ 5 14
16 Dec 65 FEVER *Immediate IM 021* 44 4

George McCRAE *US, male vocalist (Singles: 62 weeks, Albums: 29 weeks)* pos/wks

29 Jun 74 ★ ROCK YOUR BABY *Jayboy BOY 85* ▲ 1 14
5 Oct 74 ● I CAN'T LEAVE YOU ALONE *Jayboy BOY 90* 9 9
14 Dec 74 YOU CAN HAVE IT ALL *Jayboy BOY 92* 23 9
22 Mar 75 SING A HAPPY SONG *Jayboy BOY 95* 38 4
19 Jul 75 ● IT'S BEEN SO LONG *Jayboy BOY 100* 4 11
18 Oct 75 I AIN'T LYIN' *Jayboy BOY 105* 12 7
24 Jan 76 HONEY I *Jayboy BOY 107* 33 4
25 Feb 84 ONE STEP CLOSER (TO LOVE) *President PT 522* 57 4
3 Aug 74 ROCK YOUR BABY *Jayboy JSL 3* 13 28
13 Sep 75 GEORGE McCRAE *Jayboy JSL 10* 54 1

Gwen McCRAE *US, female vocalist (Singles: 5 weeks)* pos/wks

30 Apr 88 ALL THIS LOVE THAT I'M GIVING *Flame MELT 7* 63 2
13 Feb 93 ALL THIS LOVE I'M GIVING *KTDA CDKTDA 2* [1] 36 3

[1] Music and Mystery featuring Gwen McCrae

McCRARYS *US, male / female vocal group (Singles: 4 weeks)* pos/wks

31 Jul 82 LOVE ON A SUMMER NIGHT *Capitol CL 251* 52 4

Mindy McCREADY *US, female vocalist (Singles: 3 weeks)* pos/wks

1 Aug 98 OH ROMEO *BNA 74321597242* 41 3

Ian McCULLOCH

UK, male vocalist (Singles: 15 weeks, Albums: 4 weeks) pos/wks

15 Dec 84 **SEPTEMBER SONG** *Korova KOW 40* **51** 5
2 Sep 89 **PROUD TO FALL** *WEA YZ 417* **51** 4
12 May 90 **CANDLELAND (THE SECOND COMING)** *East West YZ 452* [1] **75** 1
22 Feb 92 **LOVER LOVER LOVER** *East West YZ 643* **47** 4
26 Apr 03 **SLIDING** *Cooking Vinyl FRYCD 146* **61** 1
7 Oct 89 **CANDLELAND** *WEA WX 303* **18** 3
21 Mar 92 **MYSTERIO** *East West 9031762642* **46** 1

[1] Ian McCulloch featuring Elizabeth Fraser

See also ECHO and the BUNNYMEN

Martine McCUTCHEON

UK, female actor / vocalist (Singles: 65 weeks, Albums: 36 weeks) pos/wks

18 Nov 95 **ARE YOU MAN ENOUGH** *Avex UK AVEX CD 14* [1] **62** 1
17 Apr 99 ★ **PERFECT MOMENT (re)** *Innocent SINCD 7* ■ **1** 20
11 Sep 99 ● **I'VE GOT YOU** *Innocent SINCD 12* **6** 10
4 Dec 99 ● **TALKING IN YOUR SLEEP / LOVE ME** *Innocent SINCD 14* **6** 16
4 Nov 00 ● **I'M OVER YOU** *Innocent SINCD 20* **2** 10
3 Feb 01 ● **ON THE RADIO** *Innocent SINCD 21* **7** 8
18 Sep 99 ● **YOU ME & US** *Innocent CDSIN 4* **2** 20
25 Nov 00 **WISHING** *Innocent CDSIN 7* **25** 14
14 Dec 02 **MUSICALITY** *EMI / Liberty 5805492* **55** 2

[1] Uno Clio featuring Martine McCutcheon

Gene McDANIELS *US, male vocalist (Singles: 2 weeks)* pos/wks

16 Nov 61 **TOWER OF STRENGTH (re)** *London HLG 9448* **49** 2

Julie McDERMOTT – *See AWESOME 3; THIRD DIMENSION featuring Julie McDERMOTT*

Charles McDEVITT SKIFFLE GROUP featuring Nancy WHISKEY

UK, male / female vocal / instrumental group, Nancy Whiskey d. 1 Feb 2003 (Singles: 20 weeks) pos/wks

12 Apr 57 ● **FREIGHT TRAIN (re)** *Oriole CB 1352* **5** 18
14 Jun 57 **GREENBACK DOLLAR (re)** *Oriole CB 1371* **28** 2

Jane McDONALD

UK, female vocalist (Singles: 7 weeks, Albums: 39 weeks) pos/wks

26 Dec 98 ● **CRUISE INTO CHRISTMAS MEDLEY** *Focus Music Int CDFM 2* .. **10** 7
25 Jul 98 ★ **JANE McDONALD** *Focus Music International FMCD 1* ■ **1** 27
17 Jun 00 ● **INSPIRATION** *Universal Music TV 1578612* **6** 9
27 Oct 01 **LOVE AT THE MOVIES** *Universal Music TV 149472* **24** 3

Michael McDONALD *US, male vocalist / instrumentalist (Singles: 49 weeks, Albums: 49 weeks)* pos/wks

18 Feb 84 **YAH MO B THERE (2re)** *Qwest W 9394* [1] **12** 16
3 May 86 ● **ON MY OWN** *MCA MCA 1045* [2] ▲ **2** 13
26 Jul 86 **I KEEP FORGETTIN'** *Warner Bros K 17992* **43** 6
6 Sep 86 **SWEET FREEDOM** *MCA MCA 1073* **12** 10
24 Jan 87 **WHAT A FOOL BELIEVES (re-issue)** *Warner Bros. W 8451* [3] **57** 3
5 Oct 02 **SWEET FREEDOM** *Serious SERR 55CD* [4] **54** 1
22 Nov 86 ● **SWEET FREEDOM: BEST OF MICHAEL McDONALD** *Warner Bros. WX 67* **6** 35
26 May 90 **TAKE IT TO HEART** *Reprise WX 285* **35** 4
17 Mar 01 **THE VERY BEST OF MICHAEL McDONALD** *Rhino 8122735302* .. **21** 6
17 May 03 **MOTOWN** *Universal TV 9800233* **29** 4

[1] James Ingram with Michael McDonald [2] Patti LaBelle and Michael McDonald [3] Doobie Brothers featuring Michael McDonald [4] Safri Duo featuring Michael McDonald

'Yah Mo B There' first chart listing in Feb 1984 peaked at No.44 and the first re-entry in Apr 1984 peaked at No.69. The 1985 second re-entry was a re-mix of the original hit with the same catalogue number. The 2002 release of 'Sweet Freedom' features re-recorded vocals

See also DOOBIE BROTHERS

Carrie McDOWELL *US, female vocalist (Singles: 3 weeks)* pos/wks

26 Sep 87 **UH UH NO NO CASUAL SEX** *Motown ZV 41501* **68** 3

John McENROE and Pat CASH with the FULL METAL RACKETS

US / Australia, male vocal / instrumental duo with UK, backing group (Singles: 1 week) pos/wks

13 Jul 91 **ROCK 'N' ROLL** *Music for Nations KUT 141* **66** 1

Reba McENTIRE *US, female vocalist (Singles: 1 week)* pos/wks

19 Jun 99 **DOES HE LOVE YOU** *MCA Nashville MCSTD 55569* **62** 1

MACEO & THE MACKS

US, male vocal / instrumental group (Singles: 5 weeks) pos/wks

16 May 87 **CROSS THE TRACK (WE BETTER GO BACK)** *Urban URBX1* **54** 5

McFADDEN and WHITEHEAD *US, male vocal duo – Gene McFadden and John Whitehead (Singles: 10 weeks)* pos/wks

19 May 79 ● **AIN'T NO STOPPIN' US NOW** *Philadelphia International PIR 7365* **5** 10

Rachel McFARLANE *UK, female vocalist (Singles: 17 weeks)* pos/wks

1 Aug 98 **LOVER** *Multiply CDMULTY 37* **38** 2
16Apr 94 **LET THE MUSIC (LIFT YOU UP)** *KMS / Eastern Bloc KMSCD 10* [1] **16** 4
5 Nov 94 **(KEEP ON) SHINING / HOPE (NEVER GIVE UP)** *Eastern Bloc BLOCCD 016* [1] **37** 2
14 Jan 95 **I NEED SOMEBODY** *Eastern Bloc BLOCCD 019* [1] **21** 3
10 Jun 95 **DON'T MAKE ME WAIT** *Eastern Bloc BLOC 20CD* [1] **22** 3
2 Sep 95 **THE WONDER OF LOVE** *Eastern Bloc BLOC 22CD* [1] **53** 1
11 Nov 95 **I NEED SOMEBODY (re-mix)** *Eastern Bloc BLOC 23CD* [1] **38** 2

[1] Loveland featuring the voice of Rachel McFarlane

Bobby McFERRIN

US, male vocalist (Singles: 15 weeks, Albums: 1 week) pos/wks

24 Sep 88 ● **DON'T WORRY BE HAPPY** *Manhattan MT 56* ▲ **2** 11
17 Dec 88 **THINKIN' ABOUT YOUR BODY** *Manhattan BLUE 6* **46** 4
29 Oct 88 **SIMPLE PLEASURES** *Manhattan MTL 1018* **92** 1

McGANNS *UK, male actors / vocal trio (Singles: 4 weeks)* pos/wks

14 Nov 98 **JUST MY IMAGINATION** *Coalition COLA 062CD* **59** 1
6 Feb 99 **A HEARTBEAT AWAY** *Coalition COLA 069CD* **42** 3

Kate and Anna McGARRIGLE

Canada, female vocal duo (Albums: 4 weeks) pos/wks

26 Feb 77 **DANCER WITH BRUISED KNEES** *Warner Bros. K 56356* **35** 4

Mike McGEAR

UK, male vocalist – Michael McCartney (Singles: 4 weeks) pos/wks

5 Oct 74 **LEAVE IT** *Warner Bros. K 16446* **36** 4

See also SCAFFOLD

Maureen McGOVERN *US, female vocalist (Singles: 8 weeks)* pos/wks

5 Jun 76 **THE CONTINENTAL** *20th Century BTC 2222* **16** 8

Shane MacGOWAN

UK, male vocalist (Singles: 9 weeks, Albums: 3 weeks) pos/wks

12 Dec 92 **WHAT A WONDERFUL WORLD** *Mute MUTE 151* [1] **72** 1
3 Sep 94 **THE CHURCH OF THE HOLY SPOOK** *ZTT ZANG 57CD* [2] **74** 1
15 Oct 94 **THAT WOMAN'S GOT ME DRINKING** *ZTT ZANG 56CD* [2] **34** 3
29 Apr 95 **HAUNTED** *ZTT ZANG 65CD* [3] **30** 2
20 Apr 96 **MY WAY** *ZTT ZANG 79CD* **29** 2
29 Oct 94 **THE SNAKE** *ZTT 4509981042* [1] **37** 2
8 Nov 97 **THE CROCK OF GOLD** *ZTT MACG 002CD* [1] **59** 1

[1] Nick Cave and Shane MacGowan [2] Shane MacGowan and the Popes [3] Shane MacGowan and Sinead O'Connor [1] Shane MacGowan and the Popes

See also POGUES

Ewan McGREGOR – *See PF PROJECT featuring Ewan McGREGOR; Nicole KIDMAN*

Freddie McGREGOR *Jamaica, male vocalist (Singles: 16 weeks)* pos/wks

27 Jun 87 ● JUST DON'T WANT TO BE LONELY *Germain DG 24* 9 11
19 Sep 87 THAT GIRL (GROOVY SITUATION) *Polydor POSP 884* 47 5

Mary MacGREGOR
US, female vocalist (Singles: 10 weeks, Albums: 1 week) pos/wks

19 Feb 77 ● TORN BETWEEN TWO LOVERS *Ariola America AA 111* ▲ 4 10
23 Apr 77 TORN BETWEEN TWO LOVERS *Ariola America AAS 1504* 59 1

McGUINNESS FLINT *UK, male vocal / instrumental group (Singles: 26 weeks, Albums: 2 weeks)* pos/wks

21 Nov 70 ● WHEN I'M DEAD AND GONE *Capitol CL 15662* 2 14
1 May 71 ● MALT AND BARLEY BLUES *Capitol CL 15682* 5 12
23 Jan 71 ● McGUINNESS FLINT *Capitol EAST 22625* 9 2

Barry McGUIRE *US, male vocalist (Singles: 13 weeks)* pos/wks

9 Sep 65 ● EVE OF DESTRUCTION *RCA 1469* ▲ 3 13

McGUIRE SISTERS *US, female vocal group (Singles: 24 weeks)* pos/wks

1 Apr 55 NO MORE *Vogue Coral Q 72050* 20 1
15 Jul 55 SINCERELY *Vogue Coral Q 72050* ▲ 14 4
1 Jun 56 DELILAH JONES *Vogue Coral Q 72161* 24 2
14 Feb 58 SUGARTIME *Coral Q 72305* 14 6
1 May 59 MAY YOU ALWAYS (re) *Coral Q 72356* 15 11

MACHEL *Trinidad, male vocalist (Singles: 2 weeks)* pos/wks

14 Sep 96 COME DIG IT *London LONCD 386* 56 2

MACHINE HEAD *UK, male vocal / instrumental group (Singles: 4 weeks, Albums: 9 weeks)* pos/wks

27 May 95 OLD *Roadrunner RR 23403* 43 2
6 Dec 97 TAKE MY SCARS *Roadrunner RR 22573* 73 1
18 Dec 99 FROM THIS DAY *Roadrunner RR 21383* 74 1
20 Aug 94 BURN MY EYES *Roadrunner RR 90169* 25 3
5 Apr 97 THE MORE THINGS CHANGE ... *Roadrunner RR 88602* 16 3
21 Aug 99 THE BURNING RED *Roadrunner RR 86512* 13 2
13 Oct 01 SUPERCHARGER *Roadrunner 12085002* 34 1

Billy MACK *UK, male actor / vocalist – Bill Nighy (Singles: 1 week)* pos/wks

27 Dec 03 CHRISTMAS IS ALL AROUND *Island CID 841* 26 1+

Craig MACK *US, male rapper (Singles: 5 weeks)* pos/wks

12 Nov 94 FLAVA IN YA EAR *Bad Boy 74321242582* 57 2
1 Apr 95 GET DOWN *Puff Daddy 74321263402* 54 1
7 Jun 97 SPIRIT *Perspective 5822312* [1] 35 2

[1] Sound of Blackness featuring Craig Mack

Lizzy MACK *UK, female vocalist (Singles: 3 weeks)* pos/wks

5 Nov 94 THE POWER OF LOVE *Media MCSTD 2016* [1] 49 2
4 Nov 95 DON'T GO *Power Station MCSTD 40004* 52 1

[1] Fits of Gloom featuring Lizzy Mack

Lonnie MACK
US, male instrumentalist – guitar (Singles: 3 weeks) pos/wks

14 Apr 79 MEMPHIS *Lightning LIG 9011* 47 3

'Memphis' was coupled with 'Let's Dance' by Chris Montez as a double A-side

MACK VIBE featuring JACQUELINE
US, male / female vocal / instrumental duo (Singles: 1 week) pos/wks

4 Feb 95 I CAN'T LET YOU GO *MCA MCSTD 20020* 53 1

Duff McKAGAN
US, male vocalist / instrumentalist – bass (Albums: 2 weeks) pos/wks

9 Oct 93 BELIEVE IN ME *Geffen GED 24605* 27 2

See also Guns N' Roses

McKAY *US, female vocalist – Stephanie McKay (Singles: 1 week)* pos/wks

23 Aug 03 TAKE ME OVER *Go! Beat GOBCD 57* 65 1

Maria McKEE
US, female vocalist (Singles: 23 weeks, Albums: 6 weeks) pos/wks

15 Sep 90 ★ SHOW ME HEAVEN *Epic 656303 7* 1 14
26 Jan 91 BREATHE *Geffen GFS 1* 59 1
1 Aug 92 SWEETEST CHILD *Geffen GFS 23* 45 4
22 May 93 I'M GONNA SOOTHE YOU *Geffen GFSTD 39* 35 3
18 Sep 93 I CAN'T MAKE IT ALONE *Geffen GFSTD 53* 74 1
24 Jun 89 MARIA McKEE *Geffen WX 270* 49 3
12 Jun 93 YOU GOTTA SIN TO GET SAVED *Geffen GED 24508* 26 3

Kenneth McKELLAR
UK, male vocalist (Singles: 4 weeks, Albums: 10 weeks) pos/wks

10 Mar 66 A MAN WITHOUT LOVE *Decca F 12341* 30 4
28 Jun 69 THE WORLD OF KENNETH McKELLAR *Decca SPA 11* 27 7
31 Jan 70 ECCO DI NAPOLI *Decca SKL 5018* 45 3

Terence McKENNA – *See SHAMEN*

Billy MacKENZIE
UK, male vocalist – b. 27 Mar 1957, d. 22 Jan 1997 (Albums: 1 week) pos/wks

18 Oct 97 BEYOND THE SUN *Nude NUDE 8CD* 64 1

See also ASSOCIATES

Gisele MacKENZIE *Canada, female vocalist – Gisele LaFleche, d. 5 Sep 2003 (Singles: 6 weeks)* pos/wks

17 Jul 53 ● SEVEN LONELY DAYS (2re) *Capitol CL 13920* 6 6

Scott McKENZIE
US, male vocalist – Philip Blondheim (Singles: 18 weeks) pos/wks

12 Jul 67 ★ SAN FRANCISCO (BE SURE TO WEAR SOME FLOWERS IN YOUR HAIR) *CBS 2816* 1 17
1 Nov 67 LIKE AN OLD TIME MOVIE *CBS 3009* [1] 50 1

[1] The Voice of Scott McKenzie

Ken MACKINTOSH his SAXOPHONE and his ORCHESTRA
UK, orchestra (Singles: 9 weeks) pos/wks

15 Jan 54 ● THE CREEP (re) *HMV BD 1295* 10 2
7 Feb 58 RAUNCHY *HMV POP 426* 19 6
10 Mar 60 NO HIDING PLACE *HMV POP 713* 45 1

Brian McKNIGHT *US, male vocalist (Singles: 4 weeks)* pos/wks

6 Jun 98 ANYTIME *Motown 8607752* 48 2
3 Oct 98 YOU SHOULD BE MINE *Motown 8608412* 36 2

Julie McKNIGHT *US, female vocalist (Singles: 6 weeks)* pos/wks

14 Apr 01 FINALLY *Distance DI 2029* [1] 54 1
29 Sep 01 FINALLY (re-mix) *Defected DFECT 37CDS* [1] 24 3
15 Jun 02 HOME *Defected DFECT 51 CDS* 61 1
23 Nov 02 DIAMOND LIFE *Distance DI 2409* [2] 52 1

[1] Kings of Tomorrow featuring Julie McKnight [2] Louie Vega and Jay 'Sinister' Sealee starring Julie McKnight

See also LAYO & BUSHWACKA!

Vivienne McKONE *UK, female vocalist (Singles: 5 weeks)* pos/wks

25 Jul 92 SING (OOH-EE-OOH) *ffrr F 183* 47 4
31 Oct 92 BEWARE *ffrr F 202* 69 1

McKOY *UK, male / female vocal group (Singles: 2 weeks)* pos/wks

6 Mar 93 FIGHT *Rightrack CDTUM 1* 54 2

Noel McKOY – *See JTQ; McKOY*

Craig McLACHLAN *Australia, male actor / vocalist (Singles: 40 weeks, Albums: 11 weeks)*

			pos	wks
16 Jun 90	●	**MONA** *Epic 655784 7* [1]	2	11
4 Aug 90		**AMANDA** *Epic 656170 7* [1]	19	6
10 Nov 90		**I ALMOST FELT LIKE CRYING** *Epic 656310 7* [1]	50	3
23 May 92		**ONE REASON WHY** *Epic 6580677*	29	6
14 Nov 92		**ON MY OWN** *Epic 6584677*	59	2
24 Jul 93		**YOU'RE THE ONE THAT I WANT** *Epic 6595222* [2]	13	6
25 Dec 93		**GREASE** *Epic 6600242*	44	4
8 Jul 95		**EVERYDAY** *MDMC DEVCS 6* [3]	65	2
21 Jul 90	●	**CRAIG McLACHLAN AND CHECK 1-2** *Epic 4663471* [1]	10	11

[1] Craig McLachlan and Check 1-2 [2] Craig McLachlan and Debbie Gibson [3] Craig McLachlan and the Culprits [1] Craig McLachlan and Check 1-2

Sarah McLACHLAN *Canada, female vocalist / instrumentalist – guitar (Singles: 24 weeks, Albums: 2 weeks)*

			pos	wks
3 Oct 98		**ADIA** *Arista 74321613902*	18	5
14 Oct 00	●	**SILENCE (re-mix)** *Nettwerk 331072* [1]	3	16
2 Feb 02		**ANGEL (re-mix)** *Nettwerk 331482*	36	3
17 Oct 98		**SURFACING** *Arista 189702*	47	2

[1] Delerium featuring Sarah McLachlan

See also DELERIUM

Tommy McLAIN *US, male vocalist (Singles: 1 week)*

			pos	wks
8 Sep 66		**SWEET DREAMS** *London HL 10065*	49	1

Malcolm McLAREN *UK, male vocalist (Singles: 65 weeks, Albums: 41 weeks)*

			pos	wks
4 Dec 82	●	**BUFFALO GALS** *Charisma MALC 1* [1]	9	12
26 Feb 83		**SOWETO** *Charisma MALC 2* [2]	32	5
2 Jul 83	●	**DOUBLE DUTCH** *Charisma MALC 3*	3	13
17 Dec 83		**DUCK FOR THE OYSTER** *Charisma MALC 4*	54	5
1 Sep 84		**MADAM BUTTERFLY (UN BEL DI VEDREMO)** *Charisma MALC 5*	13	9
27 May 89		**WALTZ DARLING** *Epic WALTZ 2* [3]	31	8
19 Aug 89		**SOMETHING'S JUMPIN' IN YOUR SHIRT** *Epic WALTZ 3* [4]	29	7
25 Nov 89		**HOUSE OF THE BLUE DANUBE** *Epic WALTZ 4* [3]	73	1
21 Dec 91		**MAGIC'S BACK (THEME FROM 'THE GHOSTS OF OXFORD STREET')** *RCA PB 45223* [5]	42	4
3 Oct 98		**BUFFALO GALS STAMPEDE (re-mix)** *Virgin VSCDT 1717* [6]	65	1
4 Jun 83		**DUCK ROCK** *Charisma MMLP 1*	18	17
26 May 84		**WOULD YA LIKE MORE SCRATCHIN'** *Charisma CLAM 1* [1]	44	4
29 Dec 84		**FANS** *Charisma MMDL 2*	47	8
15 Jul 89		**WALTZ DARLING** *Epic 460736 1* [2]	30	11
20 Aug 94		**PARIS** *No! NOCD 101*	44	1

[1] Malcolm McLaren and the World's Famous Supreme Team [2] Malcolm McLaren and the McLarenettes [3] Malcolm McLaren and the Bootzilla Orchestra [4] Malcolm McLaren and the Bootzilla Orchestra featuring Lisa Marie [5] Malcolm McLaren featuring Alison Limerick [6] Malcolm McLaren and the World's Famous Supreme Team plus Rakim and Roger Sanchez [1] Malcolm McLaren and the World's Famous Supreme Team [2] Malcolm McLaren and the Bootzilla Orchestra

Mahavishnu John McLAUGHLIN – *See SANTANA; MAHAVISHNU ORCHESTRA*

Bitty McLEAN *UK, male vocalist (Singles: 50 weeks, Albums: 11 weeks)*

			pos	wks
31 Jul 93	●	**IT KEEP RAININ' (TEARS FROM MY EYES)** *Brilliant CDBRIL 1*	2	15
30 Oct 93		**PASS IT ON** *Brilliant CDBRIL 2*	35	3
15 Jan 94	●	**HERE I STAND** *Brilliant CDBRIL 3*	10	6
9 Apr 94	●	**DEDICATED TO THE ONE I LOVE** *Brilliant CDBRIL 4*	6	10
6 Aug 94		**WHAT GOES AROUND** *Brilliant CDBRIL 5*	36	3
8 Apr 95		**OVER THE RIVER** *Brilliant CDBRIL 9*	27	4
17 Jun 95		**WE'VE ONLY JUST BEGUN** *Brilliant CDBRIL 10*	23	5
30 Sep 95		**NOTHING CAN CHANGE THIS LOVE** *Brilliant CDBRIL 11*	55	2
27 Jan 96		**NATURAL HIGH** *Brilliant CDBRIL 12*	63	1
5 Oct 96		**SHE'S ALRIGHT** *Kuff KUFFD 9*	53	1
19 Feb 94		**JUST TO LET YOU KNOW** *Brilliant BRILCD 1*	19	11

Don McLEAN (414 Top 500) *Celebrated singer / songwriter / instrumentalist – guitar, b. 2 Oct, 1945, New York, US. The 8.5 minute 'American Pie', which was America's top single of 1972, is regarded as one of the all-time great rock era records. No.1 song 'Killing Me Softly' was written about him (Singles: 68 weeks, Albums: 92 weeks)*

			pos	wks
22 Jan 72	●	**AMERICAN PIE** *United Artists UP 35325* ▲	2	16
13 May 72	★	**VINCENT** *United Artists UP 35359*	1	15
14 Apr 73		**EVERYDAY** *United Artists UP 35519*	38	5
10 May 80	★	**CRYING** *EMI 5051*	1	14
17 Apr 82		**CASTLES IN THE AIR** *EMI 5258*	47	8
5 Oct 91		**AMERICAN PIE (re-issue)** *Liberty EMCT 3*	12	10
11 Mar 72	●	**AMERICAN PIE** *United Artists UAS 29285* ▲	3	54
17 Jun 72		**TAPESTRY** *United Artists UAS 29350*	16	12
24 Nov 73		**PLAYIN' FAVOURITES** *United Artists UAG 29528*	42	2
14 Jun 80		**CHAIN LIGHTNING** *EMI International INS 3025*	19	9
27 Sep 80	●	**THE VERY BEST OF DON McLEAN** *United Artists UAG 30314*	4	12
15 Apr 00		**AMERICAN PIE – THE GREATEST HITS** *Capitol 5258472*	30	3

Jackie McLEAN *US, male instrumentalist – alto sax (Singles: 4 weeks)*

			pos	wks
7 Jul 79		**DOCTOR JACKYLL AND MISTER FUNK** *RCA PB 1575*	53	4

Phil McLEAN *US, male vocalist (Singles: 4 weeks)*

			pos	wks
18 Jan 62		**SMALL SAD SAM** *Top Rank JAR 597*	34	4

Andy McNAB *UK, male soldier (Albums: 2 weeks)*

			pos	wks
21 May 94		**BRAVO TWO ZERO** *PolyGram TV 5222002*	45	2

Ian McNABB *UK, male vocalist (Singles: 6 weeks, Albums: 5 weeks)*

			pos	wks
23 Jan 93		**IF LOVE WAS LIKE GUITARS** *This Way Up WAY 233*	67	1
2 Jul 94		**YOU MUST BE PREPARED TO DREAM** *This Way Up WAY 3199* [1]	54	1
17 Sep 94		**GO INTO THE LIGHT** *This Way Up WAY 3699*	66	2
27 Apr 96		**DON'T PUT YOUR SPELL ON ME** *This Way Up WAY 5033*	72	1
6 Jul 96		**MERSEYBEAST** *This Way Up WAY 5266*	74	1
30 Jan 93		**TRUTH AND BEAUTY** *This Way Up 5143782*	51	1
16 Jul 94		**HEAD LIKE A ROCK** *This Way Up 5222982*	29	2
18 May 96		**MERSEYBEAST** *This Way Up 5242152*	30	2

[1] Ian McNabb featuring Ralph Molina and Billy Talbot

See also ICICLE WORKS

Lutricia McNEAL *US, female vocalist (Singles: 43 weeks, Albums: 16 weeks)*

			pos	wks
29 Nov 97	●	**AIN'T THAT JUST THE WAY** *Wildstar CXSTAS 2907*	6	18
23 May 98	●	**STRANDED** *Wildstar CXSTAS 2973*	3	12
26 Sep 98	●	**SOMEONE LOVES YOU HONEY** *Wildstar CDWILD 9*	9	7
19 Dec 98		**THE GREATEST LOVE YOU'LL NEVER KNOW** *Wildstar CDWILD 11*	17	6
25 Jul 98		**LUTRICIA McNEAL** *Wildstar CDWILD 5*	16	16

Patrick MacNEE and Honor BLACKMAN *UK, male / female actors / vocal duo (Singles: 7 weeks)*

			pos	wks
1 Dec 90	●	**KINKY BOOTS** *Deram KINKY 1*	5	7

Rita MacNEIL *Canada, female vocalist (Singles: 10 weeks, Albums: 4 weeks)*

			pos	wks
6 Oct 90		**WORKING MAN** *Polydor PO 98*	11	10
24 Nov 90		**REASON TO BELIEVE** *Polydor 8471061*	32	4

Clyde McPHATTER *US, male vocalist d. 13 Jun 1972 (Singles: 1 week)*

			pos	wks
24 Aug 56		**TREASURE OF LOVE** *London HLE 8293*	27	1

See also DRIFTERS

Carmen McRAE – *See Sammy DAVIS Jr*

Tom McRAE *UK, male vocalist (Singles: 1 week, Albums: 2 weeks)* pos/wks

24 May 03 KARAOKE SOUL *DB DB 016CD* 48 1
15 Feb 03 JUST LIKE BLOOD *DB DB006CDLP* 26 2

Ian McSHANE *UK, male actor / vocalist (Albums: 7 weeks)* pos/wks

21 Nov 92 FROM BOTH SIDES NOW *PolyGram TV 5176192* 40 7

Ralph McTELL *UK, male vocalist / instrumentalist – guitar – Ralph May (Singles: 18 weeks, Albums: 17 weeks)* pos/wks

7 Dec 74 ● STREETS OF LONDON *Reprise K 14380* 2 12
20 Dec 75 DREAMS OF YOU *Warner Bros. K 16648* 36 6
18 Nov 72 NOT TILL TOMORROW *Reprise K 44210* 36 1
2 Mar 74 EASY *Reprise K 54013* 31 4
15 Feb 75 STREETS *Warner Bros. K 56105* 13 12

Christine McVIE *UK, female vocalist (Albums: 4 weeks)* pos/wks

11 Feb 84 CHRISTINE MCVIE *Warner Bros. 92 5059* 58 4

See also CHICKEN SHACK; FLEETWOOD MAC

David McWILLIAMS
UK, male vocalist d. 9 Jan 2002 (Albums: 9 weeks) pos/wks

10 Jun 67 DAVID McWILLIAMS SINGS *Major Minor MMLP 2* 38 2
4 Nov 67 DAVID McWILLIAMS VOLUME 2 *Major Minor MMLP 10* 23 6
9 Mar 68 DAVID McWILLIAMS VOLUME 3 *Major Minor MMLP 11* 39 1

MAD COBRA featuring Richie STEPHENS
Jamaica / UK, male vocal duo (Singles: 2 weeks) pos/wks

15 May 93 LEGACY *Columbia 6592852* 64 2

MAD DONNA *UK, female vocalist (Singles: 4 weeks)* pos/wks

4 May 02 THE WHEELS ON THE BUS *Star Harbour / All Around the World DISCO 0202R* 17 4

MAD JOCKS featuring JOCKMASTER B.A.
UK, male vocal / instrumental group (Singles: 9 weeks) pos/wks

19 Dec 87 JOCK MIX 1 *Debut DEBT 3037* 46 5
18 Dec 93 PARTY FOUR (EP) *SMP CDSSKM 24* 57 4

Tracks on Party Four (EP): No Lager / Here We Go Again / Jock Party Mix / Jock Jak Mix

MAD MOSES
US, male DJ / producer – 'Mad' Mitch Moses (Singles: 1 week) pos/wks

16 Aug 97 PANTHER PARTY *Hi-Life 5744932* 50 1

MAD SEASON
UK, male vocal / instrumental group (Albums: 1 week) pos/wks

25 Mar 95 ABOVE *Columbia 4785072* 41 1

MAD STUNTMAN – *See REEL 2 REAL featuring The MAD STUNTMAN*

MADAM FRICTION – *See CORTINA*

Sonya MADAN – *See LITHIUM and Sonya MADAN*

MADASUN *UK, female vocal group (Singles: 13 weeks)* pos/wks

11 Mar 00 DON'T YOU WORRY *V2 VVR 5011523* 14 6
27 May 00 WALKING ON WATER *V2 VVR 5012418* 14 4
2 Sep 00 FEEL GOOD *V2 VVR 5012983* 29 3

Danny MADDEN *US, male vocalist (Singles: 2 weeks)* pos/wks

14 Jul 90 THE FACTS OF LIFE *Eternal YZ 473* 72 2

MADDER ROSE *US, male / female vocal / instrumental group (Singles: 2 weeks, Albums: 2 weeks)* pos/wks

26 Mar 94 PANIC ON *Atlantic A 8301CD* 65 1
16 Jul 94 CAR SONG *Seed A 7256CD* 68 1
9 Apr 94 PANIC ON *Atlantic 7567825812* 52 2

MADDOG – *See STRETCH 'N' VERN present MADDOG*

MADE IN LONDON
UK / Norway, female vocal group (Singles: 6 weeks) pos/wks

13 May 00 DIRTY WATER *RCA 74321746192* 15 5
9 Sep 00 SHUT YOUR MOUTH *RCA 74321772602* 74 1

MADELYNE
Holland, male producer – Carlo Resoort (Singles: 1 week) pos/wks

7 Sep 02 BEAUTIFUL CHILD (A DEEPER LOVE) *Xtravaganza XTRAV 36CDS* 63 1

See also 4 STRINGS

MADEMOISELLE
France, male production / instrumental duo (Singles: 1 week) pos/wks

8 Sep 01 DO YOU LOVE ME *RCA 74321878952* 56 1

MAD'HOUSE *France / Holland, male / female production / vocal group (Singles: 14 weeks, Albums: 1 week)* pos/wks

17 Aug 02 ● LIKE A PRAYER *Serious SERR 046CD* 3 11
9 Nov 02 HOLIDAY *Serious SER 058CD* 24 3
31 Aug 02 ABSOLUTELY MAD *Serious / Mercury SERRCD 001* 57 1

MADISON AVENUE
Australia, male producer – Andy Van Dorsselaer – and female vocalist – Cheyne Coates (Singles: 25 weeks, Albums: 1 week) pos/wks

13 Nov 99 DON'T CALL ME BABY (2re) *VC Recordings VCRD 56* 30 6
20 May 00 ★ DON'T CALL ME BABY (re-issue) *VC Recordings VCRD 64* ■ 1 12
21 Oct 00 ● WHO THE HELL ARE YOU *VC Recordings VCRD 70* 10 5
27 Jan 01 EVERYTHING YOU NEED *VC Recordings VCRD 82* 33 2
4 Nov 00 THE POLYESTER EMBASSY *VC Recordings CDVCR 7* 74 1

MADNESS 43 Top 500
London-based band whose ska-rooted 'nutty' sound earned them a huge haul of hits. This good-time septet fronted by Graham 'Suggs' McPherson (b. 13 Jan 1961) spent more weeks on the chart in the 1980s than any other group (Singles: 268 weeks, Albums: 414 weeks) pos/wks

1 Sep 79 THE PRINCE *2 Tone TT 3* 16 11
10 Nov 79 ● ONE STEP BEYOND... *Stiff BUY 56* 7 14
5 Jan 80 ● MY GIRL *Stiff BUY 62* 3 10
5 Apr 80 ● WORK REST AND PLAY (EP) *Stiff BUY 71* 6 8
13 Sep 80 ● BAGGY TROUSERS *Stiff BUY 84* 3 20
22 Nov 80 ● EMBARRASSMENT *Stiff BUY 102* 4 12
24 Jan 81 ● THE RETURN OF THE LOS PALMAS SEVEN *Stiff BUY 108* 7 11
25 Apr 81 ● GREY DAY *Stiff BUY 112* 4 10
26 Sep 81 ● SHUT UP *Stiff BUY 126* 7 9
5 Dec 81 ● IT MUST BE LOVE *Stiff BUY 134* 4 12
20 Feb 82 CARDIAC ARREST *Stiff BUY 140* 14 10
22 May 82 ★ HOUSE OF FUN *Stiff BUY 146* 1 9
24 Jul 82 ● DRIVING IN MY CAR *Stiff BUY 153* 4 8
27 Nov 82 ● OUR HOUSE *Stiff BUY 163* 5 13
19 Feb 83 ● TOMORROW'S (JUST ANOTHER DAY) / MADNESS (IS ALL IN THE MIND) *Stiff BUY 169* 8 9
20 Aug 83 ● WINGS OF A DOVE *Stiff BUY 181* 2 10
5 Nov 83 ● THE SUN AND THE RAIN *Stiff BUY 192* 5 10
11 Feb 84 MICHAEL CAINE *Stiff BUY 196* 11 8
2 Jun 84 ONE BETTER DAY *Stiff BUY 201* 17 7
31 Aug 85 YESTERDAY'S MEN *Zarjazz JAZZ 5* 18 7
26 Oct 85 UNCLE SAM *Zarjazz JAZZ 7* 21 11
1 Feb 86 SWEETEST GIRL *Zarjazz JAZZ 8* 35 6
8 Nov 86 (WAITING FOR) THE GHOST TRAIN (re) *Zarjazz JAZZ 9* 18 8
19 Mar 88 I PRONOUNCE YOU *Virgin VS 1054* 1 44 4
15 Feb 92 ● IT MUST BE LOVE (re-issue) *Virgin VS 1405* 6 9
25 Apr 92 HOUSE OF FUN (re-issue) *Virgin VS 1413* 40 3
8 Aug 92 MY GIRL (re-issue) *Virgin VS 1425* 27 4
28 Nov 92 THE HARDER THEY COME *Go! Discs GOD 93* 44 3
27 Feb 93 NIGHT BOAT TO CAIRO *Virgin VSCDT 1447* 56 2

31 Jul 99	●	**LOVESTRUCK** *Virgin VSCDT 1737*	10	7
6 Nov 99		**JOHNNY THE HORSE** *Virgin VSCDT 1740*	44	2
11 Mar 00		**DRIP FED FRED** *Virgin VSCDT 1768* [2]	55	1
3 Nov 79	●	**ONE STEP BEYOND ...** *Stiff SEEZ 17*	2	78
4 Oct 80	●	**ABSOLUTELY** *Stiff SEEZ 29*	2	46
10 Oct 81	●	**MADNESS 7** *Stiff SEEZ 39*	5	29
1 May 82	★	**COMPLETE MADNESS** *Stiff HIT-TV 1*	1	88
13 Nov 82	●	**MADNESS PRESENTS THE RISE AND FALL** *Stiff SEEZ 46*	10	22
3 Mar 84	●	**KEEP MOVING** *Stiff SEEZ 53*	6	19
12 Oct 85		**MAD NOT MAD** *Zarjazz JZLP 1*	16	9
6 Dec 86		**UTTER MADNESS** *Zarjazz JZLP 2*	29	8
7 May 88		**THE MADNESS** *Virgin V 2507*	65	1
7 Mar 92	★	**DIVINE MADNESS** *Virgin CDV 2692*	1	96
14 Nov 92		**MADSTOCK** *Go! Discs 8283672*	22	9
13 Jun 98		**THE HEAVY HEAVY HITS** *Virgin CDV 2862*	19	5
13 Nov 99		**WONDERFUL** *Virgin CDV 2889*	17	2
2 Nov 02		**OUR HOUSE – THE ORIGINAL SONGS** *Virgin CDV 2965*	45	2

[1] The Madness [2] Madness featuring Ian Dury

Tracks on Work Rest and Play (EP): Night Boat to Cairo / Deceives the Eye / The Young and the Old / Don't Quote Me on That. 'Night Boat to Cairo' in 1993 is a re-issue of a track from the Work Rest and Play EP

See also SUGGS

MADONNA (5 Top 500)

The most successful female chart act of all time in the UK and US, with world sales in excess of 145 million records with almost 15 million UK singles, b. Madonna Ciccone, 16 Aug 1958, Michigan. Continually ground-breaking and trend-setting, this often controversial artist has amassed an unequalled 35 consecutive UK Top 10 singles (includes two re-entries, a remix and a re-issue) and an unbeatable tally of Top 5 entries. She has also had more UK No.1 singles and albums than any other female soloist, and at one time held the top two slots on the singles chart (1985). Her accumulated UK Top 10 entries are more than The Beatles and Rolling Stones combined, and her album 'The Immaculate Collection' has sold more than 3.6 million copies in the UK alone. In the US, the multi-award-winning singer holds the female record for 27 consecutive Top 20 entries and 16 successive Top 5s plus a dozen No.1s – 10 of which she wrote. Madonna has produced more No.1s than any female, played to packed stadiums around the globe and starred in several successful films. Her 2000 album 'Music' topped the chart in 26 countries and shipped five million albums. She was again voted Best International Female Singer at the 2001 Brits and grossed £40m for the 28 US dates of her Drowned World Tour – the highest figure for a female performer in that year. She is also the most performed artist on the TV show 'Stars in Their Eyes', with eight impressions in the first 14 series (Singles: 611 weeks, Albums: 1026 weeks)

			pos	wks
14 Jan 84	●	**HOLIDAY (re)** *Sire W 9405*	2	21
17 Mar 84		**LUCKY STAR** *Sire W 9522*	14	9
2 Jun 84	●	**BORDERLINE (re)** *Sire W 9260*	2	13
17 Nov 84	●	**LIKE A VIRGIN** *Sire W 9210* ▲	3	18
2 Mar 85	●	**MATERIAL GIRL** *Sire W 9083*	3	10
8 Jun 85	●	**CRAZY FOR YOU** *Geffen A 6323* ▲	2	15
27 Jul 85	★	**INTO THE GROOVE** *Sire W 8934*	1	14
21 Sep 85	●	**ANGEL** *Sire W 8881*	5	9
12 Oct 85	●	**GAMBLER (re)** *Geffen A 6585*	4	12
7 Dec 85	●	**DRESS YOU UP** *Sire W 8848*	5	11
26 Apr 86	●	**LIVE TO TELL** *Sire W 8717* ▲	2	12
28 Jun 86	★	**PAPA DON'T PREACH** *Sire W 8636* ▲	1	14
4 Oct 86	★	**TRUE BLUE** *Sire W 8550*	1	15
13 Dec 86	●	**OPEN YOUR HEART** *Sire W 8480* ▲	4	9
4 Apr 87	★	**LA ISLA BONITA** *Sire W 8378*	1	11
18 Jul 87	★	**WHO'S THAT GIRL** *Sire W 8341* ▲	1	10
19 Sep 87	●	**CAUSING A COMMOTION** *Sire W 8224*	4	9
12 Dec 87	●	**THE LOOK OF LOVE** *Sire W 8115*	9	7
18 Mar 89	★	**LIKE A PRAYER** *Sire W 7539* ▲	1	12
3 Jun 89	●	**EXPRESS YOURSELF** *Sire W 2948*	5	10
16 Sep 89	●	**CHERISH** *Sire W 2883*	3	8
16 Dec 89	●	**DEAR JESSIE** *Sire W 2668*	5	9
7 Apr 90	★	**VOGUE** *Sire W 9851* ▲	1	14
21 Jul 90	●	**HANKY PANKY** *Sire W 9789*	2	9
8 Dec 90	●	**JUSTIFY MY LOVE** *Sire W 9000* ▲	2	10
2 Mar 91	●	**CRAZY FOR YOU (re-mix)** *Sire W 0008*	2	8
13 Apr 91	●	**RESCUE ME** *Sire W 0024*	3	8
8 Jun 91	●	**HOLIDAY (re-issue)** *Sire W 0037*	5	7
25 Jul 92	●	**THIS USED TO BE MY PLAYGROUND** *Sire W 0122* ▲	3	9
17 Oct 92	●	**EROTICA (re)** *Maverick W 0138*	3	9
12 Dec 92	●	**DEEPER AND DEEPER** *Maverick W 0146*	6	9
6 Mar 93	●	**BAD GIRL** *Maverick W 0154CD*	10	7
3 Apr 93	●	**FEVER** *Maverick W 0168CD*	6	6
31 Jul 93	●	**RAIN** *Maverick W 0190CD*	7	8
2 Apr 94	●	**I'LL REMEMBER** *Maverick W 0240CD*	7	8
8 Oct 94	●	**SECRET** *Maverick W 0268CD*	5	9
17 Dec 94		**TAKE A BOW** *Maverick W 0278CD* ▲	16	9
25 Feb 95	●	**BEDTIME STORY (re)** *Maverick W 0285CD*	4	9
26 Aug 95	●	**HUMAN NATURE** *Maverick W 0300CD*	8	5
4 Nov 95	●	**YOU'LL SEE** *Maverick W 0324CD*	5	13
6 Jan 96		**OH FATHER** *Maverick W 0326CD*	16	6
23 Mar 96		**ONE MORE CHANCE** *Maverick W 0337CD*	11	4
2 Nov 96	●	**YOU MUST LOVE ME (2re)** *Warner Bros. W 0378CD*	10	6
28 Dec 96	●	**DON'T CRY FOR ME ARGENTINA** *Warner Bros. W 0384CD*	3	12
29 Mar 97	●	**ANOTHER SUITCASE IN ANOTHER HALL** *Warner Bros. W 0388CD*	7	5
7 Mar 98	★	**FROZEN** *Maverick W 0433CD* ■	1	13
9 May 98	●	**RAY OF LIGHT (re)** *Maverick W 0444CD*	2	10
5 Sep 98	●	**DROWNED WORLD (SUBSTITUTE FOR LOVE)** *Maverick W 0453CD1*	10	5
5 Dec 98	●	**THE POWER OF GOODBYE / LITTLE STAR** *Maverick W 459CD*	6	9
13 Mar 99	●	**NOTHING REALLY MATTERS (re)** *Maverick W 471CD*	7	9
19 Jun 99	●	**BEAUTIFUL STRANGER** *Maverick W 495CD*	2	16
11 Mar 00	★	**AMERICAN PIE (re)** *Maverick W 519CD* ■	1	14
2 Sep 00	★	**MUSIC** *Maverick W 537CD1* ■ ▲	1	23
9 Dec 00	●	**DON'T TELL ME** *Maverick W 547CD1*	4	10
28 Apr 01	●	**WHAT IT FEELS LIKE FOR A GIRL (re)** *Maverick W 533CD*	7	11
9 Nov 02	●	**DIE ANOTHER DAY** *Warner W 595CD*	3	16
19 Apr 03		**AMERICAN LIFE (import)** *Maverick 166582*	57	1
26 Apr 03	●	**AMERICAN LIFE** *Maverick W 603CD1*	2	11
19 Jul 03	●	**HOLLYWOOD** *Maverick W 614CD1*	2	7
22 Nov 03	●	**ME AGAINST THE MUSIC** *Jive 82876576432* [1]	2	6+
20 Dec 03		**LOVE PROFUSION** *Maverick W 634CD1*	11	2+
11 Feb 84	●	**MADONNA / THE FIRST ALBUM** *Sire 923867*	6	123
24 Nov 84	★	**LIKE A VIRGIN** *Sire 925157* ▲	1	152
12 Jul 86	★	**TRUE BLUE** *Sire WX 54* ■ ▲	1	85
28 Nov 87	●	**YOU CAN DANCE** *Sire WX 76*	5	16
1 Apr 89	★	**LIKE A PRAYER** *Sire WX 239* ■ ▲	1	70
2 Jun 90	●	**I'M BREATHLESS** *Sire WX 351*	2	20
24 Nov 90	★	**THE IMMACULATE COLLECTION** *Sire WX 370* ■	1	207
24 Oct 92	●	**EROTICA** *Maverick 9362450312*	2	38
5 Nov 94	●	**BEDTIME STORIES** *Maverick 9362457672*	2	27
18 Nov 95	●	**SOMETHING TO REMEMBER** *Maverick 9362461002*	3	29
9 Nov 96	★	**EVITA (FILM SOUNDTRACK)** *Warner Bros. 9362464322*	1	36
14 Mar 98	★	**RAY OF LIGHT** *Maverick 9362468472* ■	1	116
30 Sep 00	★	**MUSIC** *Maverick 9362478652* ■ ▲	1	64
24 Nov 01	●	**GHV2: GREATEST HITS VOLUME 2** *Maverick 9362480002*	2	24
3 May 03	★	**AMERICAN LIFE** *Maverick / Warner Bros 9362484542* ■ ▲	1	19

[1] Britney Spears featuring Madonna

Re-entries: 'Holiday' originally peaked at No.6 in 1984 making No.2 only on re-entry in Aug 1985. 'Borderline' peaked at No.56 on its first chart visit before making No.2 on re-entry in Jan 1986

From 22 Aug 85 'Madonna' was repacked as 'The First Album' Sire WX 22. 'Like a Virgin' changed label number to Sire WX 20 during its chart run

Lisa MAFFIA

UK, female vocalist (Singles: 23 weeks, Albums: 1 week)

			pos	wks
30 Dec 00	●	**NO GOOD 4 ME** *East West OXIDE 02CD* [1]	6	8
3 May 03	●	**ALL OVER** *Independiente ISOM 69MS*	2	11
9 Aug 03		**IN LOVE** *Independiente ISOM 75MS*	13	4
23 Aug 03		**FIRST LADY** *Independiente ISOM 39CD*	44	1

[1] Oxide & Neutrino featuring Megaman, Romeo and Lisa Maffia

See also SO SOLID CREW

MAGAZINE

UK, male vocal / instrumental group, lead vocal – Howard Devoto (Singles: 7 weeks, Albums: 24 weeks)

			pos	wks
11 Feb 78		**SHOT BY BOTH SIDES** *Virgin VS 200*	41	4
26 Jul 80		**SWEET HEART CONTRACT** *Virgin VS 368*	54	3

		pos	wks
24 Jun 78	**REAL LIFE** *Virgin V 2100*	29	8
14 Apr 79	**SECONDHAND DAYLIGHT** *Virgin V 2121*	38	8
10 May 80	**CORRECT USE OF SOAP** *Virgin V 2156*	28	4
13 Dec 80	**PLAY** *Virgin V 2184*	69	1
27 Jun 81	**MAGIC MURDER AND THE WEATHER** *Virgin V 2200*	39	3

See also Howard DEVOTO

MAGIC AFFAIR *US / Germany, male / female vocal / instrumental group (Singles: 8 weeks)*

		pos	wks
4 Jun 94	**OMEN III** *EMI CDEM 317*	17	4
27 Aug 94	**GIVE ME ALL YOUR LOVE** *EMI CDEM 340*	30	2
5 Nov 94	**IN THE MIDDLE OF THE NIGHT** *EMI CDEM 349*	38	2

MAGIC BAND – *See CAPTAIN BEEFHEART and his MAGIC BAND*

MAGIC LADY *US, female vocal duo (Singles: 3 weeks)*

		pos	wks
14 May 88	**BETCHA CAN'T LOSE (WITH MY LOVE)** *Motown ZB 42003*	58	3

MAGIC LANTERNS *UK, male vocal / instrumental group (Singles: 3 weeks)*

		pos	wks
7 Jul 66	**EXCUSE ME BABY (2re)** *CBS 202094*	44	3

MAGIK J – *See Ian POOLEY*

MAGNA CARTA *UK, male vocal / instrumental group (Albums: 2 weeks)*

		pos	wks
8 Aug 70	**SEASONS** *Vertigo 6360 003*	55	2

MAGNUM *UK, male vocal / instrumental group (Singles: 26 weeks, Albums: 47 weeks)*

		pos	wks
22 Mar 80	**MAGNUM (DOUBLE SINGLE)** *Jet 175*	47	6
12 Jul 86	**LONELY NIGHT** *Polydor POSP 798*	70	2
19 Mar 88	**DAYS OF NO TRUST** *Polydor POSP 910*	32	4
7 May 88	**START TALKING LOVE** *Polydor POSP 920*	22	4
2 Jul 88	**IT MUST HAVE BEEN LOVE** *Polydor POSP 930*	33	4
23 Jun 90	**ROCKIN' CHAIR** *Polydor PO 88*	27	4
25 Aug 90	**HEARTBROKE AND BUSTED** *Polydor PO 94*	49	2
16 Sep 78	**KINGDOM OF MADNESS** *Jet JETLP 210*	58	1
19 Apr 80	**MARAUDER** *Jet JETLP 230*	34	5
6 Mar 82	**CHASE THE DRAGON** *Jet JETLP 235*	17	7
21 May 83	**THE ELEVENTH HOUR** *Jet JETLP 240*	38	4
25 May 85	**ON A STORYTELLER'S NIGHT** *FM WKFM LP 34*	24	7
4 Oct 86	**VIGILANTE** *Polydor POLD 5198*	24	5
9 Apr 88 ●	**WINGS OF HEAVEN** *Polydor POLD 5221*	5	9
21 Jul 90 ●	**GOODNIGHT L.A.** *Polydor 8435681*	9	5
14 Sep 91	**THE SPIRIT** *Polydor 5111691*	50	1
24 Oct 92	**SLEEPWALKING** *Music For Nations CDMFN 143*	27	2
18 Jun 94	**ROCK ART** *EMI CDEMD 1066*	57	1

Tracks on double single: Invasion / Kingdom of Madness / All of My Life / Great Adventure

MAGOO *UK, male vocal / instrumental group (Singles: 1 week)*

		pos	wks
4 Apr 98	**BLACK SABBATH / SWEET LEAF** *Fierce Panda NING 47CD* [1]	60	1

[1] Magoo : Mogwai

MAGOO – *See Missy 'Misdemeanor' ELLIOTT; TIMBALAND*

Sean MAGUIRE *UK, male vocalist / actor (Singles: 34 weeks, Albums: 3 weeks)*

		pos	wks
20 Aug 94	**SOMEONE TO LOVE** *Parlophone CDR 6390*	14	7
5 Nov 94	**TAKE THIS TIME (re)** *Parlophone CDR 6395*	27	5
25 Mar 95	**SUDDENLY** *Parlophone CDR 6403*	18	5
24 Jun 95	**NOW I'VE FOUND YOU** *Parlophone CDLEEPYS 1*	22	3
18 Nov 95	**YOU TO ME ARE EVERYTHING** *Parlophone CDR 6420*	16	3
25 May 96	**GOOD DAY** *Parlophone CDR 6432*	12	4
3 Aug 96	**DON'T PULL YOUR LOVE** *Parlophone CDR 6440*	14	4
29 Mar 97	**TODAY'S THE DAY** *Parlophone CDR 6459*	27	3
26 Nov 94	**SEAN MAGUIRE** *Parlophone CDPCSDX 164*	75	1
15 Jun 96	**SPIRIT** *Parlophone CDPCSD 169*	43	2

MAHAVISHNU ORCHESTRA *UK / US, male instrumental group (Albums: 14 weeks)*

		pos	wks
31 Mar 73	**BIRDS OF FIRE** *CBS 65321*	20	5
28 Jul 73 ●	**LOVE DEVOTION SURRENDER** *CBS 69037* [1]	7	9

[1] Carlos Santana and Mahavishnu John McLaughlin

Siobhan MAHER – *See OCEANIC*

MAHLATHINI and the MAHOTELLA QUEENS – *See ART OF NOISE*

MAI TAI *Guyana, female vocal group (Singles: 30 weeks, Albums: 1 week)*

		pos	wks
25 May 85 ●	**HISTORY** *Virgin VS 773*	8	13
3 Aug 85 ●	**BODY AND SOUL** *Virgin VS 801*	9	13
15 Feb 86	**FEMALE INTUITION** *Virgin VS 844*	54	4
6 Jul 85	**HISTORY** *Virgin V 2359*	91	1

MAIN INGREDIENT *US, male vocal group – includes Cuba Gooding (Singles: 7 weeks)*

		pos	wks
29 Jun 74	**JUST DON'T WANT TO BE LONELY** *RCA APBO 0205*	27	7

MAISONETTES *UK, male / female vocal group (Singles: 12 weeks)*

		pos	wks
11 Dec 82 ●	**HEARTACHE AVENUE** *Ready Steady Go! RSG 1*	7	12

MAJESTICS *UK, male / female vocal group (Albums: 4 weeks)*

		pos	wks
4 Apr 87	**TUTTI FRUTTI** *BBC REN 629*	64	4

J MAJIK *UK, male producer – Jamie Spratling (Singles: 3 weeks)*

		pos	wks
5 May 01	**LOVE IS NOT A GAME** *Defected DFECT 31CDS* [1]	34	2
27 Apr 02	**METROSOUND** *Kaos KAOS 001P* [2]	54	1

[1] J Majik featuring Kathy Brown [2] Adam F and J Majik

Niki MAK – *See Tony DE VIT*

MAKADOPOULOS and his GREEK SERENADERS *Greece, male vocal / instrumental group (Singles: 14 weeks)*

		pos	wks
20 Oct 60	**NEVER ON SUNDAY** *Palette PG 9005*	36	14

MAKAVELI – *See 2PAC*

Tommy MAKEM – *See CLANCY BROTHERS and Tommy MAKEM*

Jack E MAKOSSA *Kenya, male producer (Singles: 5 weeks)*

		pos	wks
12 Sep 87	**THE OPERA HOUSE** *Champion CHAMP 50*	48	5

MALA – *See BOWA featuring MALA*

MALACHI *UK, male vocalist – Malachi Cush (Singles: 1 week, Albums: 4 weeks)*

		pos	wks
19 Apr 03	**JUST SAY YOU LOVE ME** *Mercury / Universal TV 0779072*	49	1
5 Apr 03	**MALACHI** *Mercury / Universal TV 0772802*	17	4

MALAIKA *US, female vocalist (Singles: 1 week)*

		pos	wks
31 Jul 93	**GOTTA KNOW (YOUR NAME)** *A&M 5802732*	68	1

Carl MALCOLM *Jamaica, male vocalist (Singles: 8 weeks)*

		pos	wks
13 Sep 75 ●	**FATTIE BUM BUM** *UK 108*	8	8

Valerie MALCOLM – *See CANDY GIRLS*

Stephen MALKMUS *US, male vocalist (Singles: 1 week, Albums: 2 weeks)*

		pos	wks
28 Apr 01	**DISCRETION GROVE** *Domino RUG 123CD*	60	1
24 Feb 01	**STEPHEN MALKMUS** *Domino Recordings WIGCD 90*	49	1
29 Mar 03	**PIG LIB** *Domino Recordings WIGCD122X* [1]	63	1

[1] Stephen Malkmus & The Jicks

The 706 No.1 Albums

NO.1 ALBUMS OF THE 80S

Here is the complete chronological list of every UK chart-topping album from the 80s. All dates given are for an album's first week at No.1, not its first entry into the chart. The run at the top of the chart in weeks follows in brackets, followed by the US peak position of the album.

1980
12 Jan GREATEST HITS VOL.2 **Abba** (1 week) US 46
19 Jan PRETENDERS **Pretenders** (4 weeks) US 9
16 Feb THE LAST DANCE **Various** (2 weeks)
1 Mar STRING OF HITS **Shadows** (3 weeks)
22 Mar TEARS AND LAUGHTER **Johnny Mathis** (2 weeks)
5 Apr DUKE **Genesis** (2 weeks) US 11
19 Apr GREATEST HITS **Rose Royce** (2 weeks)
3 May SKY 2 **Sky** (2 weeks)
17 May THE MAGIC OF BONEY M **Boney M** (2 weeks)
31 May McCARTNEY II **Paul McCartney** (2 weeks) US 3
14 Jun PETER GABRIEL **Peter Gabriel** (2 weeks) US 22
28 Jun FLESH AND BLOOD **Roxy Music** (1 week) US 35
5 Jul EMOTIONAL RESCUE **Rolling Stones** (2 weeks) US 1
19 Jul THE GAME **Queen** (2 weeks) US 1
2 Aug DEEPEST PURPLE **Deep Purple** (1 week) US 148
9 Aug BACK IN BLACK **AC/DC** (2 weeks) US 4
23 Aug FLESH AND BLOOD **Roxy Music** (3 weeks) US 35
13 Sep TELEKON **Gary Numan** (1 week) US 64
20 Sep NEVER FOR EVER **Kate Bush** (1 week)
27 Sep SCARY MONSTERS AND SUPER CREEPS **David Bowie** (2 weeks) US 12
11 Oct ZENYATTA MONDATTA **Police** (4 weeks) US 5
8 Nov GUILTY **Barbra Streisand** (2 weeks) US 1
22 Nov SUPER TROUPER **Abba** (9 weeks) US 17

1981
24 Jan KINGS OF THE WILD FRONTIER **Adam and the Ants** (2 weeks) US 44
7 Feb DOUBLE FANTASY **John Lennon** (2 weeks) US 1
21 Feb FACE VALUE **Phil Collins** (3 weeks) US 7
14 Mar KINGS OF THE WILD FRONTIER **Adam and the Ants** (10 weeks) US 44
23 May STARS ON 45 **Starsound** (5 weeks) US 9
27 Jun NO SLEEP TIL HAMMERSMITH **Motörhead** (1 week)
4 Jul DISCO DAZE AND DISCO NITES **Various** (1 week)
11 Jul LOVE SONGS **Cliff Richard** (1 week)
15 Aug THE OFFICIAL BBC ALBUM OF THE ROYAL WEDDING (2 weeks)
29 Aug TIME **Electric Light Orchestra** (2 weeks) US 16
12 Sep DEAD RINGER **Meat Loaf** (2 weeks) US 45
26 Sep ABACAB **Genesis** (2 weeks) US 7
10 Oct GHOST IN THE MACHINE **Police** (3 weeks) US 2
31 Oct DARE **Human League** (1 week) US 3
7 Nov SHAKY **Shakin' Stevens** (1 week)
14 Nov GREATEST HITS **Queen** (4 weeks) US 14
12 Dec CHART HITS '81 **Various** (1 week)
19 Dec THE VISITORS **Abba** (3 weeks) US 29

1982
9 Jan DARE **Human League** (3 weeks) US 3
30 Jan LOVE SONGS **Barbra Streisand** (7 weeks)
20 Mar THE GIFT **Jam** (1 week) US 82
27 Mar LOVE SONGS **Barbra Streisand** (2 weeks)
10 Apr THE NUMBER OF THE BEAST **Iron Maiden** (2 weeks) US 33
24 Apr 1982 **Status Quo** (1 week)
1 May BARRY LIVE IN BRITAIN **Barry Manilow** (1 week)
8 May TUG OF WAR **Paul McCartney** (2 weeks) US 1
12 Jun COMPLETE MADNESS **Madness** (2 weeks)
22 Jun AVALON **Roxy Music** (2 weeks) US 53
3 Jul THE LEXICON OF LOVE **ABC** (3 weeks) US 24
24 Jul FAME **Soundtrack** (1 week) US 7 and THE LEXICON OF LOVE **ABC** (1 week) US 24
31 Jul FAME **Soundtrack** (1 week) US 7
7 Aug KIDS FROM FAME **Kids from Fame** (8 weeks) US 146
2 Oct LOVE OVER GOLD **Dire Straits** (4 weeks) US 19
30 Oct KIDS FROM FAME **Kids from Fame** (4 weeks) US 146
27 Nov THE SINGLES – THE FIRST TEN YEARS **Abba** (1 week) US 62
4 Dec THE JOHN LENNON COLLECTION **John Lennon** (6 weeks) US 33

1983
15 Jan RAIDERS OF THE POP CHARTS **Various** (2 weeks)
29 Jan BUSINESS AS USUAL **Men at Work** (5 weeks) US 1
5 Mar THRILLER **Michael Jackson** (1 week) US 1
12 Mar WAR **U2** (1 week) US 12
19 Mar THRILLER **Michael Jackson** (1 week) US 1
26 Mar THE HURTING **Tears for Fears** (1 week) US 73
2 Apr THE FINAL CUT **Pink Floyd** (2 weeks) US 6
16 Apr FASTER THAN THE SPEED OF NIGHT **Bonnie Tyler** (1 week) US 4
23 Apr LET'S DANCE **David Bowie** (3 weeks) US 4
14 May TRUE **Spandau Ballet** (1 week) US 19
21 May THRILLER **Michael Jackson** (5 weeks) US 1
25 Jun SYNCHRONICITY **Police** (2 weeks) US 1
9 Jul FANTASTIC! **Wham!** (2 weeks) US 83
23 Jul YOU AND ME BOTH **Yazoo** (2 weeks) US 69
6 Aug THE VERY BEST OF THE BEACH BOYS **Beach Boys** (2 weeks)
20 Aug 18 GREATEST HITS **Michael Jackson plus the Jackson Five** (3 weeks)
10 Sep THE VERY BEST OF THE BEACH BOYS **Beach Boys** (1 week)
17 Sep NO PARLEZ **Paul Young** (1 week) US 79
24 Sep LABOUR OF LOVE **UB40** (1 week) US 14
1 Oct NO PARLEZ **Paul Young** (2 weeks) US 79
15 Oct GENESIS **Genesis** (1 week) US 9
22 Oct COLOUR BY NUMBERS **Culture Club** (3 weeks) US 2
12 Nov CAN'T SLOW DOWN **Lionel Richie** (1 week) US 1
19 Nov COLOUR BY NUMBERS **Culture Club** (2 weeks) US 2
3 Dec SEVEN AND THE RAGGED TIGER **Duran Duran** (1 week) US 8
10 Dec NO PARLEZ **Paul Young** (1 week) US 79
17 Dec NOW THAT'S WHAT I CALL MUSIC! **Various** (4 weeks)

1984
14 Jan NO PARLEZ **Paul Young** (1 week) US 79
21 Jan NOW THAT'S WHAT I CALL MUSIC! **Various** (1 week)
28 Jan THRILLER **Michael Jackson** (1 week) US 1
4 Feb TOUCH **Eurythmics** (2 weeks) US 7
18 Feb SPARKLE IN THE RAIN **Simple Minds** (1 week) US 64
25 Feb INTO THE GAP **Thompson Twins** (3 weeks) US 10
17 Mar HUMAN'S LIB **Howard Jones** (2 weeks) US 59

1983: SEVEN AND THE RAGGED TIGER In the midst of a world tour, Duran Duran hit the top spot for one week with this Alex Sadkin, Ian Little and Duran Duran produced album

1986: SO This Peter Gabriel chart-topper features guest appearances from Kate Bush, P P Arnold, Laurie Anderson, Nile Rodgers, Jim Kerr and Stewart Copeland

31 Mar CAN'T SLOW DOWN **Lionel Richie** (2 weeks) US 1
14 Apr NOW THAT'S WHAT I CALL MUSIC! 2 **Various** (5 weeks)
19 May LEGEND **Bob Marley and the Wailers** (12 weeks) US 54
11 Aug NOW THAT'S WHAT I CALL MUSIC! 3 **Various** (8 weeks)
6 Oct TONIGHT **David Bowie** (1 week) US 11
13 Oct THE UNFORGETTABLE FIRE **U2** (2 weeks) US 12
27 Oct STEEL TOWN **Big Country** (1 week) US 70
3 Nov GIVE MY REGARDS TO BROAD STREET **Paul McCartney** (1 week) US 21
10 Nov WELCOME TO THE PLEASURE DOME **Frankie Goes to Hollywood** (1 week) US 33
17 Nov MAKE IT BIG **Wham!** (2 weeks) US 1
1 Dec THE HITS ALBUM / THE HITS TAPE **Various** (7 weeks)

1985

19 Jan ALF **Alison Moyet** (1 week) US 45
26 Jan AGENT PROVOCATEUR **Foreigner** (3 weeks) US 4
16 Feb BORN IN THE USA **Bruce Springsteen** (1 week) US 1
23 Feb MEAT IS MURDER **Smiths** (1 week) US 110
2 Mar NO JACKET REQUIRED **Phil Collins** (5 weeks) US 1
6 Apr THE SECRET OF ASSOCIATION **Paul Young** (1 week) US 19
13 Apr HITS 2 **Various** (6 weeks)
25 May BROTHERS IN ARMS **Dire Straits** (2 weeks) US 1
8 Jun OUR FAVOURITE SHOP **Style Council** (1 week)
15 Jun BOYS AND GIRLS **Bryan Ferry** (2 weeks) US 63
29 Jun MISPLACED CHILDHOOD **Marillion** (1 week) US 47
6 Jul BORN IN THE USA **Bruce Springsteen** (4 weeks) US 1
3 Aug BROTHERS IN ARMS **Dire Straits** (2 weeks) US 1
17 Aug NOW THAT'S WHAT I CALL MUSIC! 5 **Various** (5 weeks)
21 Sep LIKE A VIRGIN **Madonna** (1 week) US 1
28 Sep HOUNDS OF LOVE **Kate Bush** (1 week) US 30
26 Oct THE LOVE SONGS **George Benson** (1 week)
2 Nov ONCE UPON A TIME **Simple Minds** (1 week) US 10
9 Nov THE LOVE SONGS **George Benson** (1 week)
16 Nov PROMISE **Sade** (2 weeks) US 1
30 Nov THE GREATEST HITS OF 1985 **Various** (1 week)
7 Dec NOW THAT'S WHAT I CALL MUSIC! 6 **Various** (2 weeks)
21 Dec NOW! – THE CHRISTMAS ALBUM **Various** (2 weeks)

1986

4 Jan NOW THAT'S WHAT I CALL MUSIC! 6 **Various** (2 weeks)
18 Jan BROTHERS IN ARMS **Dire Straits** (10 weeks) US 1
29 Mar HITS 4 **Various** (4 weeks)
26 Apr STREET LIFE – 20 GREAT HITS **Bryan Ferry / Roxy Music** (5 weeks) US 100
31 May SO **Peter Gabriel** (2 weeks) US 2
14 Jun A KIND OF MAGIC **Queen** (1 week) US 46
21 Jun INVISIBLE TOUCH **Genesis** (3 weeks) US 3
12 Jul TRUE BLUE **Madonna** (6 weeks) US 1
23 Aug NOW THAT'S WHAT I CALL MUSIC! 7 **Various** (5 weeks)
27 Sep SILK AND STEEL **Five Star** (1 week) US 80
4 Oct GRACELAND **Paul Simon** (5 weeks) US 3
8 Nov EVERY BREATH YOU TAKE – THE SINGLES **Police** (2 weeks) US 7
22 Nov HITS 5 **Various** (2 weeks)
6 Dec NOW THAT'S WHAT I CALL MUSIC! 8 **Various** (6 weeks)

1987

17 Jan THE WHOLE STORY **Kate Bush** (2 weeks) US 76
31 Jan GRACELAND **Paul Simon** (3 weeks) US 3
21 Feb PHANTOM OF THE OPERA **Original London Cast** (3 weeks) US 33
14 Mar THE VERY BEST OF HOT CHOCOLATE **Hot Chocolate** (1 week)
21 Mar THE JOSHUA TREE **U2** (2 weeks) US 1
4 Apr NOW THAT'S WHAT I CALL MUSIC! 9 **Various** (5 weeks)
9 May KEEP YOUR DISTANCE **Curiosity Killed the Cat** (2 weeks) US 55
23 May IT'S BETTER TO TRAVEL **Swing Out Sister** (2 weeks) US 40
6 Jun LIVE IN THE CITY OF LIGHT **Simple Minds** (1 week) US 96
13 Jun WHITNEY **Whitney Houston** (6 weeks) US 1
25 Jul INTRODUCING THE HARDLINE ACCORDING TO TERENCE TRENT D'ARBY **Terence Trent D'Arby** (1 week) US 4
1 Aug HITS 6 **Various** (4 weeks)
29 Aug HYSTERIA **Def Leppard** (1 week) US 1
5 Sep HITS 6 **Various** (1 week)
12 Sep BAD **Michael Jackson** (5 weeks) US 1
17 Oct TUNNEL OF LOVE **Bruce Springsteen** (1 week) US 1
24 Oct NOTHING LIKE THE SUN **Sting** (1 week) US 9
31 Oct TANGO IN THE NIGHT **Fleetwood Mac** (2 weeks) US 7
14 Nov FAITH **George Michael** (1 week) US 1
21 Nov BRIDGE OF SPIES **T'Pau** (1 week)
28 Nov WHENEVER YOU NEED SOMEBODY **Rick Astley** (1 week) US 10
5 Dec NOW THAT'S WHAT I CALL MUSIC! 10 **Various** (6 weeks)

1988

16 Jan POPPED IN SOULED OUT **Wet Wet Wet** (1 week) US 123
23 Jan TURN BACK THE CLOCK **Johnny Hates Jazz** (1 week) US 56
30 Jan INTRODUCING THE HARDLINE ACCORDING TO TERENCE TRENT D'ARBY **Terence Trent D'Arby** (8 weeks) US 4
26 Mar VIVA HATE **Morrissey** (1 week) US 48
2 Apr NOW THAT'S WHAT I CALL MUSIC! 11 **Various** (3 weeks)
23 Apr SEVENTH SON OF A SEVENTH SON **Iron Maiden** (1 week) US 12
30 Apr THE INNOCENTS **Erasure** (1 week) US 49
7 May TANGO IN THE NIGHT **Fleetwood Mac** (2 weeks) US 7
21 May LOVESEXY **Prince** (1 week) US 11
28 May TANGO IN THE NIGHT **Fleetwood Mac** (1 week) US 7
4 Jun NITE FLITE **Various** (4 weeks)
2 Jul TRACY CHAPMAN **Tracy Chapman** (3 weeks) US 1
23 Jul NOW THAT'S WHAT I CALL MUSIC! 12 **Various** (5 weeks)
27 Aug KYLIE **Kylie Minogue** (4 weeks) US 53
24 Sep HOT CITY NIGHTS **Various** (1 week)
1 Oct NEW JERSEY **Bon Jovi** (2 weeks) US 1
15 Oct FLYING COLOURS **Chris de Burgh** (1 week)
22 Oct RATTLE AND HUM **U2** (1 week) US 1
29 Oct MONEY FOR NOTHING **Dire Straits** (3 weeks) US 62
19 Nov KYLIE **Kylie Minogue** (2 weeks) US 53
3 Dec NOW THAT'S WHAT I CALL MUSIC! 13 **Various** (3 weeks)
24 Dec PRIVATE COLLECTION **Cliff Richard** (2 weeks)

NO.1 ALBUMS OF THE 80S CONTINUED

1989

7 Jan NOW THAT'S WHAT I CALL MUSIC! 13 Various (1 week)

(From 14 January 1989, compilation albums were excluded from the main chart)

14 Jan THE INNOCENTS Erasure (1 week) US 49
21 Jan THE LEGENDARY ROY ORBISON Roy Orbison (3 weeks)
11 Feb TECHNIQUE New Order (1 week) US 32
18 Feb THE RAW AND THE COOKED Fine Young Cannibals (1 week) US 1
25 Feb A NEW FLAME Simply Red (4 weeks) US 22
25 Mar ANYTHING FOR YOU Gloria Estefan and Miami Sound Machine (1 week)
1 Apr LIKE A PRAYER Madonna (2 weeks) US 1
15 Apr WHEN THE WORLD KNOWS YOUR NAME Deacon Blue (2 weeks)
29 Apr A NEW FLAME Simply Red (1 week) US 22
6 May BLAST Holly Johnson (1 week)
13 May STREET FIGHTING YEARS Simple Minds (1 week) US 70
20 May TEN GOOD REASONS Jason Donovan (2 weeks)
3 Jun THE MIRACLE Queen (1 week) US 24
10 Jun TEN GOOD REASONS Jason Donovan (2 weeks)
24 Jun FLOWERS IN THE DIRT Paul McCartney (1 week) US 21
1 Jul BATMAN (SOUNDTRACK) Prince (1 week) US 1
8 Jul VELVETEEN Transvision Vamp (1 week)
15 Jul CLUB CLASSICS VOLUME ONE Soul II Soul (1 week) US 14
22 Jul A NEW FLAME Simply Red (2 weeks) US 22
5 Aug CUTS BOTH WAYS Gloria Estefan (6 weeks) US 8
16 Sep ASPECTS OF LOVE Original Cast (1 week)
23 Sep WE TOO ARE ONE Eurythmics (1 week) US 34
30 Sep FOREIGN AFFAIR Tina Turner (1 week) US 31
7 Oct THE SEEDS OF LOVE Tears for Fears (1 week) US 8
14 Oct CROSSROADS Tracy Chapman (1 week) US 9
21 Oct ENJOY YOURSELF Kylie Minogue (1 week)
28 Oct WILD! Erasure (2 weeks) US 57
11 Nov THE ROAD TO HELL Chris Rea (3 weeks) US 107
2 Dec ...BUT SERIOUSLY Phil Collins (8 weeks) US 1

1989: CLUB CLASSICS VOLUME ONE Jazzie B and Nellee Hooper produced this debut album from Soul II Soul which features the sublime 'Keep On Movin''

Timmy MALLETT – *See BOMBALURINA featuring Timmy MALLETT*

Yngwie J MALMSTEEN

Sweden, male instrumentalist – guitar (Albums: 11 weeks) pos/wks

		pos	wks
21 May 88	ODYSSEY *Polydor POLD 5224*	27	7
4 Nov 89	TRIAL BY FIRE – LIVE IN LENINGRAD *Polydor 839726 1*	65	1
28 Apr 90	ECLIPSE *Polydor 8434611*	43	2
29 Feb 92	FIRE AND ICE *Elektra 7559611372*	57	1

Raul MALO *US, male vocalist (Singles: 1 week)* pos/wks

		pos	wks
18 May 02	I SAID I LOVE YOU *Gravity 74321923082*	57	1

See also MAVERICKS

MAMA CASS

US, female vocalist – Ellen Cohen, d. 29 Jul 1974 (Singles: 27 weeks) pos/wks

		pos	wks
14 Aug 68	DREAM A LITTLE DREAM OF ME *RCA 1726*	11	12
16 Aug 69 ●	IT'S GETTING BETTER *Stateside SS 8021*	8	15

See also MAMAS and the PAPAS

MAMA'S BOYS

Ireland, male vocal / instrumental group (Albums: 4 weeks) pos/wks

		pos	wks
6 Apr 85	POWER AND PASSION *Jive HIP 24*	55	4

MAMAS and the PAPAS (485 Top 500)

Folk / rock harmony quartet who helped to make California the focal point of mid-60s music; singer/songwriter John Phillips (d. 2001) and wife Michelle, Canadian Dennis Doherty and (Mama) Cass Elliott (d. 1974). Quartet split 1968 with Cass becoming solo hitmaker and Michelle an actress (Singles: 71 weeks, Albums: 71 weeks) pos/wks

		pos	wks
28 Apr 66	CALIFORNIA DREAMIN' *RCA 1503*	23	9
12 May 66 ●	MONDAY MONDAY *RCA 1516* ▲	3	13
28 Jul 66	I SAW HER AGAIN *RCA 1533*	11	11
9 Feb 67	WORDS OF LOVE *RCA 1564*	47	3
6 Apr 67 ●	DEDICATED TO THE ONE I LOVE *RCA 1576*	2	17
26 Jul 67 ●	CREEQUE ALLEY *RCA 1613*	9	11
2 Aug 97 ●	CALIFORNIA DREAMIN' (re-issue) *MCA MCSTD 48058*	9	7
25 Jun 66 ●	THE MAMAS AND PAPAS *RCA Victor RD 7803*	3	18
28 Jan 67	CASS JOHN MICHELLE DENNY *RCA Victor SF 7639*	24	6
24 Jun 67 ●	MAMAS AND PAPAS DELIVER *RCA Victor SF 7880*	4	22
26 Apr 69 ●	HITS OF GOLD *Stateside S 5007*	7	2
18 Jun 77 ●	THE BEST OF THE MAMAS AND PAPAS *Arcade ADEP 30*	6	13
28 Jan 95	CALIFORNIA DREAMIN' – THE VERY BEST OF THE MAMAS AND THE PAPAS *PolyGram TV 5239732*	14	6
6 Sep 97	CALIFORNIA DREAMIN' – GREATEST HITS OF THE MAMAS AND THE PAPAS *Telstar TV TTVCD 2931*	30	4

See also MAMA CASS

MAMBAS – *See Marc ALMOND*

Cheb MAMI – *See STING*

MAN *UK, male vocal / instrumental group (Albums: 11 weeks)* pos/wks

		pos	wks
20 Oct 73	BACK INTO THE FUTURE *United Artists UAD 60053/4*	23	3
25 May 74	RHINOS WINOS AND LUNATICS *United Artists UAG 29631*	24	4
11 Oct 75	MAXIMUM DARKNESS *United Artists UAG 29872*	25	2
17 Apr 76	WELSH CONNECTION *MCA MCF 2753*	40	2

A MAN CALLED ADAM

UK, male / female vocal / instrumental group (Singles: 4 weeks) pos/wks

		pos	wks
29 Sep 90	BAREFOOT IN THE HEAD (re) *Big Life BLR 28*	60	4

MAN TO MAN

US, male vocal / instrumental duo (Singles: 19 weeks) pos/wks

		pos	wks
13 Sep 86 ●	MALE STRIPPER (2re) *Bolts BOLTS 4* [1]	4	16
4 Jul 87	I NEED A MAN / ENERGY'S EUROBEAT *Bolts BOLTS 5*	43	3

[1] Man 2 Man meet Man Parrish

'Male Stripper' reached its peak position on its second re-entry in Feb 1987

MAN WITH NO NAME

UK, male producer – Martin Freeland (Singles: 6 weeks) pos/wks

30 Sep 95 **FLOOR-ESSENCE** *Perfecto PERF 108CD* 68 1
20 Jan 96 **PAINT A PICTURE** *Perfecto PERF 114CD* [1] 42 2
12 Oct 96 **TELEPORT / SUGAR RUSH** *Perfecto PERF 126CD* 55 1
2 May 98 **VAVOOM!** *Perfecto PERF 159CD1* 43 1
18 Jul 98 **THE FIRST DAY (HORIZON)** *Perfecto PERF 164CD* 72 1

[1] Man with No Name featuring Hannah

MANASSAS – *See Stephen STILLS*

Melissa MANCHESTER – *See Al JARREAU*

MANCHESTER BOYS CHOIR *UK, male choir (Albums: 2 weeks)* pos/wks

21 Dec 85 **THE NEW SOUND OF CHRISTMAS** *K-Tel ONE 1314* 80 2

MANCHESTER UNITED FOOTBALL CLUB

UK, male football team vocalists (Singles: 56 weeks) pos/wks

8 May 76 **MANCHESTER UNITED** *Decca F 13633* 50 1
21 May 83 **GLORY GLORY MAN UNITED** *EMI 5390* 13 5
18 May 85 ● **WE ALL FOLLOW MAN UNITED** *Columbia DB 9107* 10 5
19 Jun 93 **UNITED (WE LOVE YOU)** *Living Beat LBECD 026* [1] 37 2
30 Apr 94 ★ **COME ON YOU REDS** *PolyGram TV MANU 2* 1 15
13 May 95 ● **WE'RE GONNA DO IT AGAIN** *PolyGram TV MANU 952* [2] 6 6
4 May 96 ● **MOVE MOVE MOVE (THE RED TRIBE) (re)** *Music Collection MANUCD 1* [3] 6 15
29 May 99 **LIFT IT HIGH (ALL ABOUT BELIEF) (re)** *Music Collection MANUCD 4* [4] 11 7

[1] Manchester United and the Champions [2] Manchester United Football Squad featuring Stryker [3] 1996 Manchester United FA Cup Squad [4] 1999 Manchester United Squad

MANCHILD *UK, male production duo – Max Odell and Brett Parker (Singles: 2 weeks)* pos/wks

16 Sep 00 **THE CLICHES ARE TRUE** *One Little Indian 176 TP7CD* [1] 60 1
25 Aug 01 **NOTHING WITHOUT ME** *One Little Indian 183 TP7CD* 40 1

[1] Manchild featuring Kelly Jones

Henry MANCINI & His ORCHESTRA *US, orchestra / chorus, leader d. 14 Jun 1994 (Singles: 23 weeks, Albums: 23 weeks)* pos/wks

7 Dec 61 **MOON RIVER (re)** *RCA 1256* 44 3
24 Sep 64 ● **HOW SOON** *RCA 1414* 10 12
25 Mar 72 **THEME FROM 'CADE'S COUNTY'** *RCA 2182* 42 1
11 Feb 84 **MAIN THEME FROM 'THE THORN BIRDS'** *Warner Bros. 9677* 23 7
16 Oct 76 **HENRY MANCINI** *Arcade ADEP 24* 26 8
30 Jun 84 **MAMMA** *Decca 411959* [1] 96 1
8 Dec 84 **IN THE PINK** *RCA Red Seal RL 85315* [2] 62 6
13 Dec 86 **THE HOLLYWOOD MUSICALS** *CBS 4502581* [3] 46 8

[1] Luciano Pavarotti with the Henry Mancini Orchestra [2] James Galway and Henry Mancini and the National Philharmonic Orchestra [3] Johnny Mathis and Henry Mancini

Steve MANDELL – *See 'DELIVERANCE' SOUNDTRACK*

MANFRED MANN (170 Top 500)

One of the most regular chart entrants of the 1960s: Manfred Mann (k), Mike Vickers (g), Tom McGuinness (b), Mike Hugg (d), Paul Jones (v) – Jones was replaced by Mike D'Abo in 1966. They were the first group from the south of England to top the US charts during 1964's so-called 'British Invasion' (Singles: 217 weeks, Albums: 100 weeks) pos/wks

23 Jan 64 ● **5-4-3-2-1** *HMV POP 1252* 5 13
16 Apr 64 **HUBBLE BUBBLE (TOIL AND TROUBLE)** *HMV POP 1282* 11 8
16 Jul 64 ★ **DO WAH DIDDY DIDDY** *HMV POP 1320* ▲ 1 14
15 Oct 64 ● **SHA LA LA** *HMV POP 1346* 3 12
14 Jan 65 ● **COME TOMORROW** *HMV POP 1381* 4 9
15 Apr 65 **OH NO, NOT MY BABY** *HMV POP 1413* 11 10
16 Sep 65 ● **IF YOU GOTTA GO, GO NOW** *HMV POP 1466* 2 12
21 Apr 66 ★ **PRETTY FLAMINGO** *HMV POP 1523* 1 12
7 Jul 66 **YOU GAVE ME SOMEBODY TO LOVE** *HMV POP 1541* 36 4
4 Aug 66 ● **JUST LIKE A WOMAN** *Fontana TF 730* 10 10
27 Oct 66 ● **SEMI-DETACHED SUBURBAN MR JAMES** *Fontana TF 757* 2 12
30 Mar 67 ● **HA! HA! SAID THE CLOWN** *Fontana TF 812* 4 11
25 May 67 **SWEET PEA** *Fontana TF 828* 36 4
24 Jan 68 ★ **MIGHTY QUINN** *Fontana TF 897* 1 11
12 Jun 68 ● **MY NAME IS JACK** *Fontana TF 943* 8 11
18 Dec 68 ● **FOX ON THE RUN** *Fontana TF 985* 5 12
30 Apr 69 ● **RAGAMUFFIN MAN** *Fontana TF 1013* 8 11
8 Sep 73 ● **JOYBRINGER** *Vertigo 6059 083* [1] 9 10
28 Aug 76 ● **BLINDED BY THE LIGHT** *Bronze BRO 29* [1] ▲ 6 10
20 May 78 ● **DAVY'S ON THE ROAD AGAIN** *Bronze BRO 52* [1] 6 12
17 Mar 79 **YOU ANGEL YOU** *Bronze BRO 68* [1] 54 5
7 Jul 79 **DON'T KILL IT CAROL** *Bronze BRO 77* [1] 45 4
19 Sep 64 ● **FIVE FACES OF MANFRED MANN** *HMV CLP 1731* 3 24
23 Oct 65 ● **MANN MADE** *HMV CLP 1911* 7 11
17 Sep 66 **MANN MADE HITS** *HMV CLP 3559* 11 17
29 Oct 66 **AS IS** *Fontana TL 5377* 22 4
21 Jan 67 **SOUL OF MANN** *HMV CSD 3594* 40 1
17 Jun 78 **WATCH** *Bronze BRON 507* [1] 33 6
24 Mar 79 **ANGEL STATION** *Bronze BRON 516* [1] 30 8
15 Sep 79 ● **SEMI-DETACHED SUBURBAN** *EMI EMTV 19* 9 14
26 Feb 83 **SOMEWHERE IN AFRIKA** *Bronze BRON 543* [1] 87 1
18 Sep 86 ● **THE ROARING SILENCE** *Bronze ILPS 9357* [1] 10 9
23 Jan 93 **AGES OF MANN** *PolyGram TV 5143622* 23 4
10 Sep 94 **THE VERY BEST OF MANFRED MANN'S EARTH BAND** *Arcade ARC 3100162* [1] 69 1

[1] Manfred Mann's Earth Band [1] Manfred Mann's Earth Band

MANHATTAN TRANSFER (429 Top 500)

Multi-faceted four-part harmony vocal group formed New York, US, 1969, whose recordings include songs from the 1930s to the 80s. Their nostalgic sound earned them 10 Grammy awards, although, oddly, their No.1 single did not chart in the US (Singles: 72 weeks, Albums: 85 weeks) pos/wks

7 Feb 76 **TUXEDO JUNCTION** *Atlantic K 10670* 24 6
5 Feb 77 ★ **CHANSON D'AMOUR** *Atlantic K 10886* 1 13
28 May 77 **DON'T LET GO** *Atlantic K 10930* 32 6
18 Feb 78 **WALK IN LOVE (re)** *Atlantic K 11075* 12 12
20 May 78 **ON A LITTLE STREET IN SINGAPORE** *Atlantic K 11136* 20 9
16 Sep 78 **WHERE DID OUR LOVE GO / JE VOULAIS (TE DIRE QUE JE T'ATTENDS)** *Atlantic K 11182* 40 4
23 Dec 78 **WHO, WHAT, WHEN, WHERE, WHY** *Atlantic K 11233* 49 6
17 May 80 **TWILIGHT ZONE – TWILIGHT TONE (MEDLEY)** *Atlantic K 11476* 25 8
21 Jan 84 **SPICE OF LIFE** *Atlantic A 9728* 19 8
12 Mar 77 **COMING OUT** *Atlantic K 50291* 12 20
19 Mar 77 **MANHATTAN TRANSFER** *Atlantic K 50138* 49 7
25 Feb 78 ● **PASTICHE** *Atlantic K 50444* 10 34
11 Nov 78 ● **LIVE** *Atlantic K 50540* 4 17
17 Nov 79 **EXTENSIONS** *Atlantic K 50674* 63 3
18 Feb 84 **BODIES AND SOULS** *Atlantic 780104* 53 4

MANHATTANS

US, male vocal group (Singles: 31 weeks, Albums: 3 weeks) pos/wks

19 Jun 76 ● **KISS AND SAY GOODBYE** *CBS 4317* ▲ 4 11
2 Oct 76 ● **HURT** *CBS 4562* 4 11
23 Apr 77 **IT'S YOU** *CBS 5093* 43 3
26 Jul 80 **SHINING STAR** *CBS 8624* 45 4
6 Aug 83 **CRAZY** *CBS A 3578* 63 2
14 Aug 76 **MANHATTANS** *CBS 81513* 37 3

M.A.N.I.C.

UK, male vocal / production duo (Singles: 1 week) pos/wks

18 Apr 92 **I'M COMIN' HARDCORE** *Union City UCRT 2* 60 1

MANIC MCs featuring Sara CARLSON

UK, male production duo and female vocalist (Singles: 5 weeks) pos/wks

12 Aug 89 **MENTAL** *RCA PB 43037* 30 5

MANIC STREET PREACHERS (142 Top 500)

Best-selling Welsh act of the 1990s; James Dean Bradfield (v/g), Nicky Wire (b), Sean Moore (d) and Richey Edwards (v/g – missing since 1995 and officially declared dead in 2002). Won trophies for the Best British Group and Best Album at the 1997 and 1999 Brit Awards (Singles: 150 weeks, Albums: 203 weeks)

Date		Title	pos	wks
25 May 91		YOU LOVE US *Heavenly HVN 10*	62	2
10 Aug 91		STAY BEAUTIFUL *Columbia 6573377*	40	3
9 Nov 91		LOVE'S SWEET EXILE / REPEAT *Columbia 6575827*	26	3
1 Feb 92		YOU LOVE US (re-issue) *Columbia 6577247*	16	4
28 Mar 92		SLASH 'N' BURN *Columbia 6578737*	20	4
13 Jun 92		MOTORCYCLE EMPTINESS *Columbia 6580837*	17	6
19 Sep 92	●	THEME FROM M.A.S.H. (SUICIDE IS PAINLESS) *Columbia 6583827*	7	6
21 Nov 92		LITTLE BABY NOTHING *Columbia 6587967*	29	3
12 Jun 93		FROM DESPAIR TO WHERE *Columbia 6593372*	25	4
31 Jul 93		LA TRISTESSE DURERA (SCREAM TO A SIGH) *Columbia 6594772*	22	5
2 Oct 93		ROSES IN THE HOSPITAL *Columbia 6597272*	15	3
12 Feb 94		LIFE BECOMING A LANDSLIDE *Columbia 6600702*	36	2
11 Jun 94		FASTER / PCP *Epic 6604472*	16	3
13 Aug 94		REVOL *Epic 6606862*	22	3
15 Oct 94		SHE IS SUFFERING *Epic 6608952*	25	3
27 Apr 96	●	A DESIGN FOR LIFE (re) *Epic 6630705*	2	11
3 Aug 96	●	EVERYTHING MUST GO *Epic 6634685*	5	6
12 Oct 96	●	KEVIN CARTER *Epic 6637752*	9	4
14 Dec 96	●	AUSTRALIA *Epic 6640442*	7	7
13 Sep 97		MOTORCYCLE EMPTINESS (re-issue) *Epic MANIC 5CD*	41	2
13 Sep 97		YOU LOVE US (2nd re-issue) *Epic MANIC 3CD*	49	1
13 Sep 97		LITTLE BABY NOTHING (re-issue) *Epic MANIC 6CD*	50	1
13 Sep 97		STAY BEAUTIFUL (re-issue) *Epic MANIC 1CD*	52	1
13 Sep 97		SLASH 'N' BURN (re-issue) *Epic MANIC 4CD*	54	1
13 Sep 97		LOVE'S SWEET EXILE (re-issue) *Epic MANIC 2CD*	55	1
5 Sep 98	★	IF YOU TOLERATE THIS YOUR CHILDREN WILL BE NEXT (re) *Epic 6663452* ■	1	11
12 Dec 98		THE EVERLASTING *Epic 6666862*	11	8
20 Mar 99	●	YOU STOLE THE SUN FROM MY HEART *Epic 6669532*	5	8
17 Jul 99		TSUNAMI *Epic 6674112*	11	5
22 Jan 00	★	THE MASSES AGAINST THE CLASSES (re) *Epic 6685302* ■	1	7
10 Mar 01	●	FOUND THAT SOUL (re) *Epic 6708332*	9	4
10 Mar 01	●	SO WHY SO SAD *Epic 6708322*	8	7
16 Jun 01		OCEAN SPRAY *Epic 6712532*	15	4
22 Sep 01		LET ROBESON SING *Epic 6717732*	19	2
26 Oct 02	●	THERE BY THE GRACE OF GOD (re) *Epic 6731662*	6	5
22 Feb 92		GENERATION TERRORISTS *Columbia 4710602*	13	17
3 Jul 93	●	GOLD AGAINST THE SOUL *Columbia 4640642*	8	11
10 Sep 94	●	THE HOLY BIBLE *Epic 4774219*	6	4
1 Jun 96	●	EVERYTHING MUST GO *Epic 4839302*	2	82
26 Sep 98	★	THIS IS MY TRUTH TELL ME YOURS *Epic 4917039* ■	1	60
31 Mar 01	●	KNOW YOUR ENEMY *Epic 5018802*	2	14
9 Nov 02	●	FOREVER DELAYED – THE GREATEST HITS *Epic 5095519*	4	12
26 Jul 03		LIPSTICK TRACES – A SECRET HISTORY OF *Sony Music 5123862*	11	3

The listed flipside of 'Theme From M.A.S.H. (Suicide Is Painless)' was '(Everything I Do) I Do It for You' by Fatima Mansions

MANIJAMA featuring MUKUPA & L'IL T

UK, male / female production / vocal group (Singles: 1 week)

Date	Title	pos	wks
8 Feb 03	NO NO NO *Defected DFTD 058CDS*	66	1

Barry MANILOW (82 Top 500)

Middle-of-the-road superstar, b. Barry Pincus, 17 Jun 1946, Brooklyn, US. This crowd-pulling singer / songwriter / pianist with a vast and loyal following on both sides of the Atlantic has sold in excess of 50 million albums (Singles: 136 weeks, Albums: 343 weeks)

Date		Title	pos	wks
22 Feb 75		MANDY *Arista 1* ▲	11	9
6 May 78		CAN'T SMILE WITHOUT YOU *Arista 176*	43	7
29 Jul 78		SOMEWHERE IN THE NIGHT / COPACABANA (AT THE COPA) *Arista 196*	42	10
23 Dec 78		COULD IT BE MAGIC *Arista ARIST 229*	25	10
8 Nov 80		LONELY TOGETHER *Arista ARIST 373*	21	13
7 Feb 81		I MADE IT THROUGH THE RAIN *Arista ARIST 384*	37	6
11 Apr 81		BERMUDA TRIANGLE *Arista ARIST 406*	15	9
26 Sep 81		LET'S HANG ON *Arista ARIST 429*	12	11
12 Dec 81		THE OLD SONGS *Arista ARIST 443*	48	8
20 Feb 82		IF I SHOULD LOVE AGAIN *Arista ARIST 453*	66	2
17 Apr 82		STAY *Arista ARIST 464* [1]	23	8
16 Oct 82	●	I WANNA DO IT WITH YOU *Arista ARIST 495*	8	8
4 Dec 82		I'M GONNA SIT RIGHT DOWN AND WRITE MYSELF A LETTER *Arista ARIST 503*	36	7
25 Jun 83		SOME KIND OF FRIEND *Arista ARIST 516*	48	2
27 Aug 83		YOU'RE LOOKING HOT TONIGHT *Arista ARIST 542*	47	6
10 Dec 83		READ 'EM AND WEEP *Arista ARIST 551*	17	7
8 Apr 89		PLEASE DON'T BE SCARED *Arista 112186*	35	5
10 Apr 93		COPACABANA (AT THE COPA) (re-mix) *Arista 74321136912*	22	4
20 Nov 93		COULD IT BE MAGIC 1993 *Arista 74321174882*	36	3
6 Aug 94		LET ME BE YOUR WINGS *EMI CDEM 336* [2]	73	1
23 Sep 78		EVEN NOW *Arista SPART 1047*	12	28
3 Mar 79	●	MANILOW MAGIC – THE BEST OF BARRY MANILOW *Arista ARTV 2*	3	151
20 Oct 79		ONE VOICE *Arista SPART 1106*	18	7
29 Nov 80	●	BARRY *Arista DLART 2*	5	34
25 Apr 81		GIFT SET *Arista BOX 1*	62	1
3 Oct 81	●	IF I SHOULD LOVE AGAIN *Arista BMAN 1*	5	26
1 May 82	★	BARRY LIVE IN BRITAIN *Arista ARTV 4* ■	1	23
27 Nov 82	●	I WANNA DO IT WITH YOU *Arista BMAN 2*	7	9
8 Oct 83	●	A TOUCH MORE MAGIC *Arista BMAN 3*	10	12
1 Dec 84		2:00 AM PARADISE CAFÉ *Arista 206 496*	28	6
16 Nov 85		MANILOW *RCA PL 87044*	40	6
20 Feb 88		SWING STREET *Arista 208860*	81	1
20 May 89		SONGS TO MAKE THE WHOLE WORLD SING *Arista 209927*	20	4
17 Mar 90		LIVE ON BROADWAY *Arista 303785*	19	3
30 Jun 90		THE SONGS 1975-1990 *Arista 303868*	13	7
2 Nov 91		SHOWSTOPPERS *Arista 212091*	53	3
3 Apr 93		HIDDEN TREASURES *Arista 74321135682*	36	7
27 Nov 93		GREATEST HITS – THE PLATINUM COLLECTION *Arista 74321175452*	37	6
5 Nov 94		SINGIN' WITH THE BIG BANDS *Arista 07822187712*	54	2
30 Nov 96		SUMMER OF '78 *Arista 7822188092*	66	2
21 Nov 98		MANILOW SINGS SINATRA *Arista 7822190332*	72	2
25 May 02		HERE AT THE MAYFLOWER *Columbia 5077342*	18	3

[1] Barry Manilow featuring Kevin Desimone and James Jolis [2] Barry Manilow and Debra Byrd

ARIST 464 was available as both a live and studio recording

MANIX

UK, male / female vocal / instrumental group (Singles: 6 weeks)

Date	Title	pos	wks
23 Nov 91	MANIC MINDS *Reinforced RIVET 1209*	63	2
7 Mar 92	OBLIVION (HEAD IN THE CLOUDS) (EP) *Reinforced RIVET 1212*	43	3
8 Aug 92	RAINBOW PEOPLE *Reinforced RIVET 1221*	57	1

Tracks on Oblivion (Head in the Clouds) (EP): Oblivion (Head in the Clouds) / Never Been to Belgium (Gotta Rush) / I Can't Stand It / You Held My Hand

MANKEY *UK, male producer – Andy Manston (Singles: 1 week)*

Date	Title	pos	wks
16 Nov 96	BELIEVE IN ME *Frisky DISKY 3*	74	1

MANKIND

UK, male instrumental group (Singles: 12 weeks)

Date	Title	pos	wks
25 Nov 78	DR WHO *Pinnacle PIN 71*	25	12

Aimee MANN

US, female vocalist (Singles: 9 weeks, Albums: 3 weeks)

Date	Title	pos	wks
31 Oct 87	TIME STAND STILL *Vertigo RUSH 13* [1]	42	3
28 Aug 93	I SHOULD'VE KNOWN *Imago 72787250437*	55	2
20 Nov 93	STUPID THING *Imago 72787250527*	47	2
5 Mar 94	I SHOULD'VE KNOWN (re-issue) *Imago 72787250602*	45	2
18 Sep 93	WHATEVER *Imago 72787210172*	39	1
11 Nov 95	I'M WITH STUPID *Geffen GED 24951*	51	1
14 Sep 02	LOST IN SPACE *V2 VVR 1020882*	72	1

[1] Rush with Aimee Mann

Roberto MANN
UK, male orchestra leader (Albums: 9 weeks) pos/wks

9 Dec 67 GREAT WALTZES *Deram SML 1010* 19 9

Shelley MANN
US, male instrumentalist – drums, d. 29 Sep 1984 (Albums: 1 week) pos/wks

18 Jun 60 MY FAIR LADY *Vogue LAC 12100* 20 1

Johnny MANN SINGERS
US, male / female vocal group (Singles: 13 weeks) pos/wks

12 Jul 67 ● UP-UP AND AWAY *Liberty LIB 55972* 6 13

MANOWAR
US, male vocal / instrumental group (Albums: 3 weeks) pos/wks

18 Feb 84 HAIL TO ENGLAND *Music For Nations MFN 19* 83 2
6 Oct 84 SIGN OF THE HAMMER *10 DIX 10* 73 1

MANSUN *UK, male vocal / instrumental group (Singles: 44 weeks, Albums: 27 weeks)* pos/wks

6 Apr 96 ONE (EP) *Parlophone CDR 6430* 37 2
15 Jun 96 TWO (EP) *Parlophone CDR 6437* 32 2
21 Sep 96 THREE (EP) *Parlophone CDR 6447* 19 3
17 Dec 96 WIDE OPEN SPACE *Parlophone CDR 6453* 15 4
15 Feb 97 ● SHE MAKES MY NOSE BLEED *Parlophone CDR 6453* 9 5
10 May 97 TAXLOSS *Parlophone CDRS 6465* 15 3
18 Oct 97 ● CLOSED FOR BUSINESS *Parlophone CDRS6482* 10 3
11 Jul 98 ● LEGACY (EP) *Parlophone CDRS 6497* 7 4
5 Sep 98 BEING A GIRL (PART ONE) (EP) *Parlophone CDR 6503* 13 3
7 Nov 98 NEGATIVE *Parlophone CDR 6508* 27 2
13 Feb 99 SIX *Parlophone CDR 6511* 16 3
12 Aug 00 ● I CAN ONLY DISAPPOINT U *Parlophone CDR 6544* 8 6
18 Nov 00 ELECTRIC MAN *Parlophone CDR 6550* 23 2
10 Feb 01 FOOL *Parlophone CDRS 6553* 28 2
1 Mar 97 ★ ATTACK OF THE GREY LANTERN *Parlophone CDPCS 7387* ■ ..1 19
19 Sep 98 ● SIX *Parlophone 4967232* 6 4
26 Aug 00 LITTLE KIX *Parlophone 5277822* 12 4

Tracks on One (EP): Egg Shaped Fred / Ski Jump Nose / Lemonade Secret Drinker / Thief. Tracks on Two (EP): Take It Easy Chicken / Drastic Sturgeon / The Greatest Pain / Moronica. Tracks on Three (EP): Stripper Vicar / An Open Letter to the Lyrical Trainspotter / No One Knows Us / Things Keep Falling Off Buildings. Tracks on Legacy (EP): CD#1 Legacy (Extended version) / Can't Afford to Die / Spasm of Identity / Check Under the Bed. CD#2 Legacy / Wide Open Space (The Perfecto Remix) / GSOH / Face in the Crowd. Tracks on Being a Girl (Part One) (EP): Being a Girl / I Care / Been Here Before / Hideout / Railings

MANTOVANI (340 Top 500) *Britain's most successful album act before The Beatles, leader b. Annunzio Paulo Mantovani, 15 Nov 1905, Venice, Italy, d. 29 Mar 1980. UK orchestra was the first act to sell a million stereo albums, and had six albums simultaneously in the US Top 30 in 1959 (Singles: 52 weeks, Albums: 143 weeks)* pos/wks

19 Dec 52 ● WHITE CHRISTMAS *Decca F 10017* 6 3
29 May 53 ★ THE SONG FROM THE MOULIN ROUGE (2re) *Decca F 10094* 1 23
23 Oct 53 ● SWEDISH RHAPSODY (re) *Decca F 10168* 2 18
11 Feb 55 LONELY BALLERINA (re) *Decca F 10395* 16 4
31 May 57 AROUND THE WORLD *Decca F 10888* 20 4
21 Feb 59 ● CONTINENTAL ENCORES *Decca LK 4298* 4 12
18 Feb 61 CONCERT SPECTACULAR *Decca LK 4377* 16 2
16 Apr 66 ● MANTOVANI MAGIC *Decca LK 7949* 3 15
15 Oct 66 MR MUSIC – MANTOVANI *Decca LK 4809* 24 3
14 Jan 67 ● MANTOVANI'S GOLDEN HITS *Decca SKL 4818* 10 35
30 Sep 67 HOLLYWOOD *Decca SKL 4887* 37 1
14 Jun 69 ● THE WORLD OF MANTOVANI *Decca SPA 1* 6 31
4 Oct 69 ● THE WORLD OF MANTOVANI VOLUME 2 *Decca SPA 36* 4 19
16 May 70 MANTOVANI TODAY *Decca SKL 5003* 16 8
26 Feb 72 TO LOVERS EVERYWHERE *Decca SKL 5112* 44 1
3 Nov 79 ● 20 GOLDEN GREATS *Warwick WW 5067* 9 13
16 Mar 85 MANTOVANI MAGIC *Telstar STAR 2237* [1] 52 3

[1] Mantovani Orchestra conducted by Roland Shaw

See also David WHITFIELD; Roland SHAW

Kurtis MANTRONIK *US, male vocalist / instrumentalist / producer – Kurtis Khaleel (Singles: 6 weeks)* pos/wks

15 Aug 98 STRICTLY BUSINESS *Parlophone CDR 6502* [1] 43 1
9 Nov 02 77 STRINGS *Southern Fried ECB 35* [2] 71 1
28 Jun 03 HOW DID YOU KNOW *Southern Fried ECB 43CDS* [2] 16 4

[1] Kurtis Mantronik vs EPMD [2] Kurtis Mantronik presents Chamonix

MANTRONIX *US / Jamaica, male production / rap duo – Curtis Kahleel, MC Tee (Toure Embden) replaced Bryce Wilson (1989) (Singles: 48 weeks, Albums: 17 weeks)* pos/wks

22 Feb 86 LADIES *10 TEN 116* 55 4
17 May 86 BASSLINE *10 TEN 118* 34 6
7 Feb 87 WHO IS IT? *10 TEN 137* 40 6
4 Jul 87 SCREAM (PRIMAL SCREAM) *10 TEN 169* 46 4
30 Jan 88 SING A SONG (BREAK IT DOWN) *10 TEN 206* 61 2
12 Mar 88 SIMPLE SIMON (YOU GOTTA REGARD) *10 TEN 217* 72 2
6 Jan 90 ● GOT TO HAVE YOUR LOVE *Capitol CL 559* [1] 4 11
12 May 90 ● TAKE YOUR TIME *Capitol CL 573* [1] 10 7
2 Mar 91 DON'T GO MESSIN' WITH MY HEART *Capitol CL 608* 22 5
22 Jun 91 STEP TO ME (DO ME) *Capitol CL 613* 59 1
29 Mar 86 THE ALBUM *10 DIX 37* 45 3
13 Dec 86 MUSICAL MADNESS *10 DIX 50* 66 3
2 Apr 88 IN FULL EFFECT *10 DIX 74* 39 3
17 Feb 90 THIS SHOULD MOVE YA *Capitol EST 2117* 18 6
30 Mar 91 THE INCREDIBLE SOUND MACHINE *Capitol EST 2139* 36 2

[1] Mantronix featuring Wondress

MANUEL and The MUSIC OF THE MOUNTAINS
UK, orchestra, leader – Geoff Love d. 8 Jul 1991 (Singles: 31 weeks, Albums: 38 weeks) pos/wks

28 Aug 59 THE HONEYMOON SONG (2re) *Columbia DB 4323* 22 9
13 Oct 60 NEVER ON SUNDAY *Columbia DB 4515* 29 10
13 Oct 66 SOMEWHERE MY LOVE *Columbia DB 7969* 42 2
31 Jan 76 ● RODRIGO'S GUITAR CONCERTO DE ARANJUEZ (THEME FROM 2ND MOVEMENT) *EMI 2383* 3 10
10 Sep 60 MUSIC OF THE MOUNTAINS *Columbia 33SX 1212* 17 1
7 Aug 71 THIS IS MANUEL *Studio Two STWO 5* 18 19
31 Jan 76 ● CARNIVAL *Studio Two TWO 337* 3 18

See also MUSIC OF THE MOUNTAINS; Geoff LOVE

Roots MANUVA *UK, male rapper – Rodney Hylton Smith (Singles: 6 weeks, Albums: 4 weeks)* pos/wks

11 Dec 99 DUSTED (re) *Hard Hands HAND 058CD1* [1] 28 3
4 Aug 01 WITNESS (1 HOPE) *Big Dada BDCDS 022* 45 2
20 Oct 01 DREAMY DAYS *Big Dada BDCDS 033* 53 1
25 Aug 01 RUN COME SAVE ME *Big Dada BDCD 032* 33 3
20 Jul 02 DUB COME SAVE ME *Big Dada BDCD 040* 75 1

[1] Leftfield / Roots Manuva

Phil MANZANERA *UK, male vocalist / instrumentalist – guitar – Philip Targett-Adams (Albums: 1 week)* pos/wks

24 May 75 DIAMOND HEAD *Island ILPS 9315* 40 1

See also ROXY MUSIC

MARATHON
Germany / UK, male vocal / instrumental group (Singles: 3 weeks) pos/wks

25 Jan 92 MOVIN' *Ten TEN 395* 36 3

MARAUDERS
UK, male vocal / instrumental group (Singles: 4 weeks) pos/wks

8 Aug 63 THAT'S WHAT I WANT (re) *Decca F 11695* 43 4

MARBLES *UK, male vocal duo – Graham Bonnet and Trevor Gordon (Singles: 18 weeks)* pos/wks

25 Sep 68 ● ONLY ONE WOMAN *Polydor 56 272* 5 12
26 Mar 69 THE WALLS FELL DOWN *Polydor 56 310* 28 6

See also Graham BONNET

MARC and the MAMBAS – *See Marc ALMOND*

MARC et CLAUDE *Germany, male DJ / production duo – Marc Romboy and Klaus Derichs (Singles: 15 weeks)* pos/wks

21 Nov 98	**LA** *Positiva CDTIV 104*	28	3
22 Jul 00	**I NEED YOUR LOVIN' (LIKE THE SUNSHINE)** *Positiva CDTIV 136*	12	7
6 Apr 02	**TREMBLE** *Positiva CDTIVS 170*	29	3
19 Apr 03	**LOVING YOU '03** *Positive CDTIV 190*	37	2

MARCELS
US, male vocal group – lead vocal Cornelius Harp (Singles: 17 weeks) pos/wks

13 Apr 61 ★	**BLUE MOON** *Pye International 7N 25073* ▲	1	13
8 Jun 61	**SUMMERTIME** *Pye International 7N 25083*	46	4

Little Peggy MARCH
US, female vocalist – Margaret Battavio (Singles: 7 weeks) pos/wks

12 Sep 63	**HELLO HEARTACHE, GOODBYE LOVE** *RCA 1362*	29	7

MARCO POLO
Italy, male instrumental / production duo (Singles: 1 week) pos/wks

8 Apr 95	**A PRAYER TO THE MUSIC** *Hi-Life HICD 7*	65	1

MARCY PLAYGROUND *US, male vocal / instrumental trio (Singles: 3 weeks, Albums: 1 week)* pos/wks

18 Apr 98	**SEX AND CANDY** *EMI CDEM 508*	29	3
9 May 98	**MARCY PLAYGROUND** *EMI 8535692*	61	1

MARDI GRAS
UK, male vocal / instrumental group (Singles: 9 weeks) pos/wks

5 Aug 72	**TOO BUSY THINKING ABOUT MY BABY** *Bell 1226*	19	9

MARIA – *See Maria NAYLER*

Kelly MARIE
UK, female vocalist – Jacqueline McKinnon (Singles: 36 weeks) pos/wks

2 Aug 80 ★	**FEELS LIKE I'M IN LOVE** *Calibre PLUS 1*	1	16
18 Oct 80	**LOVING JUST FOR FUN** *Calibre PLUS 4*	21	7
7 Feb 81	**HOT LOVE** *Calibre PLUS 5*	22	10
30 May 81	**LOVE TRIAL** *Calibre PLUS 7*	51	3

Rose MARIE
Ireland, female vocalist (Singles: 5 weeks, Albums: 35 weeks) pos/wks

19 Nov 83	**WHEN I LEAVE THE WORLD BEHIND (2re)** *A1 284*	63	5
13 Apr 85	**ROSE MARIE SINGS JUST FOR YOU** *A1 RMTV 1*	30	13
24 May 86	**SO LUCKY** *A1-Spartan RMLP 2*	62	3
14 Nov 87	**SENTIMENTALLY YOURS** *Telstar STAR 2302*	22	11
19 Nov 88	**TOGETHER AGAIN** *Telstar STAR 2333*	52	7
23 Mar 96	**MEMORIES OF HOME** *Telstar TCD 2788*	51	1

Teena MARIE
US, female vocalist – Mary Brockert (Singles: 28 weeks) pos/wks

7 Jul 79	**I'M A SUCKER FOR YOUR LOVE** *Motown TMG 1146* [1]	43	8
31 May 80 ●	**BEHIND THE GROOVE** *Motown TMG 1185*	6	10
11 Oct 80	**I NEED YOUR LOVIN'** *Motown TMG 1203*	28	6
26 Mar 88	**OOO LA LA LA** *Epic 651423 7*	74	2
10 Nov 90	**SINCE DAY ONE** *Epic 656429 7*	69	2

[1] Teena Marie, co-lead vocals Rick James

MARILLION 228 Top 500
Progressive rock group formed in Buckinghamshire and originally named after Tolkien's novel Silmarillion. They reached their peak of popularity in the 80s, when fronted by Scottish vocalist / songwriter Fish (b. Derek Dick, 25 Apr 1958). When Fish left in 1989 the band continued to make regular visits to the charts with Steve Hogarth in the role of vocalist / songwriter (Singles: 103 weeks, Albums: 165 weeks) pos/wks

20 Nov 82	**MARKET SQUARE HEROES (re)** *EMI 5351*	53	8
12 Feb 83	**HE KNOWS YOU KNOW** *EMI 5362*	35	4
18 Jun 83	**GARDEN PARTY** *EMI 5393*	16	5
11 Feb 84	**PUNCH AND JUDY** *EMI MARIL 1*	29	4
12 May 84	**ASSASSING** *EMI MARIL 2*	22	5
18 May 85 ●	**KAYLEIGH** *EMI MARIL 3*	2	14
7 Sep 85 ●	**LAVENDER** *EMI MARIL 4*	5	9
30 Nov 85	**HEART OF LOTHIAN** *EMI MARIL 5*	29	6
23 May 87 ●	**INCOMMUNICADO** *EMI MARIL 6*	6	5
25 Jul 87	**SUGAR MICE** *EMI MARIL 7*	22	5
7 Nov 87	**WARM WET CIRCLES** *EMI MARIL 8*	22	4
26 Nov 88	**FREAKS (LIVE)** *EMI MARIL 9*	24	3
9 Sep 89	**HOOKS IN YOU** *Capitol MARIL 10*	30	3
9 Dec 89	**UNINVITED GUEST** *EMI MARIL 11*	53	2
14 Apr 90	**EASTER** *EMI MARIL 12*	34	2
8 Jun 91	**COVER MY EYES (PAIN AND HEAVEN)** *EMI MARIL 13*	34	4
3 Aug 91	**NO ONE CAN** *EMI MARIL 14*	33	4
5 Oct 91	**DRY LAND** *EMI MARIL 15*	34	2
23 May 92	**SYMPATHY** *EMI MARIL 16*	17	3
1 Aug 92	**NO ONE CAN (re-issue)** *EMI MARIL 17*	26	4
26 Mar 94	**THE HOLLOW MAN** *EMI CDEMS 307*	30	2
7 May 94	**ALONE AGAIN IN THE LAP OF LUXURY** *EMI CDEMS 318*	53	3
10 Jun 95	**BEAUTIFUL** *EMI CDMARILS 18*	29	2
26 Mar 83 ●	**SCRIPT FOR A JESTER'S TEAR** *EMI EMC 3429*	7	31
24 Mar 84 ●	**FUGAZI** *EMI EMC 2400851*	5	20
17 Nov 84 ●	**REAL TO REEL** *EMI JEST 1*	8	22
29 Jun 85 ★	**MISPLACED CHILDHOOD** *EMI MRL 2* ■	1	41
4 Jul 87 ●	**CLUTCHING AT STRAWS** *EMI EMD 1002*	2	15
23 Jul 88	**B SIDES THEMSELVES** *EMI EMS 1295*	64	6
10 Dec 88	**THE THIEVING MAGPIE** *EMI MARIL 1*	25	6
7 Oct 89 ●	**SEASON'S END** *EMI EMD 1011 22*	7	4
6 Jul 91 ●	**HOLIDAYS IN EDEN** *EMI EMD 1022*	7	7
20 Jun 92	**A SINGLES COLLECTION 1982-1992** *EMI CDEMD 1033*	27	2
19 Feb 94 ●	**BRAVE** *EMI CDEMC 1054*	10	4
8 Jul 95	**AFRAID OF SUNLIGHT** *EMI CDEMD 1079*	16	2
6 Apr 96	**MADE AGAIN** *EMI CDEMD 1094*	37	1
3 May 97	**THIS STRANGE ENGINE** *Raw Power RAWCD 121*	27	2
3 Oct 98	**RADIATION** *Raw Power RAWCD 126*	35	1
30 Oct 99	**MARILLION.COM** *Intact/Raw Power RAWCD 144*	53	1

See also FISH

MARILYN
UK, male vocalist – Peter Robinson (Singles: 26 weeks) pos/wks

5 Nov 83 ●	**CALLING YOUR NAME** *Mercury MAZ 1*	4	12
11 Feb 84	**CRY AND BE FREE** *Mercury MAZ 2*	31	6
21 Apr 84	**YOU DON'T LOVE ME** *Mercury MAZ 3*	40	7
13 Apr 85	**BABY U LEFT ME (IN THE COLD)** *Mercury MAZ 4*	70	1

MARILYN MANSON *US, male vocal / instrumental group (Singles: 37 weeks, Albums: 15 weeks)* pos/wks

7 Jun 97	**THE BEAUTIFUL PEOPLE** *Nothing 95541*	18	3
20 Sep 97	**TOURNIQUET** *Nothing 95552*	28	2
21 Nov 98	**THE DOPE SHOW** *Nothing 95610*	12	3
26 Jun 99	**ROCK IS DEAD** *Maverick W 486CD*	23	2
18 Nov 00	**DISPOSABLE TEENS** *Nothing 4974372*	12	3
3 Mar 01	**THE FIGHT SONG** *Nothing / Interscope 4974902*	24	3
15 Sep 01	**THE NOBODIES** *Nothing IND97604*	34	2
30 Mar 02 ●	**TAINTED LOVE** *Maverick / Warner Bros. W 579CD*	5	11
14 Jun 03	**MOBSCENE** *Interscope / Polydor 9807726*	13	6
13 Sep 03	**THIS IS THE NEW S**T** *Interscope / Polydor 9810793*	29	2
26 Oct 96	**ANTICHRIST SUPERSTAR** *Interscope IND 90086*	73	1
26 Sep 98 ●	**MECHANICAL ANIMALS** *Interscope IND 90273* ▲	8	4
27 Nov 99	**THE LAST TOUR ON EARTH** *Interscope 4905242*	61	1
25 Nov 00	**HOLY WOOD** *Nothing 4908292*	23	2
24 May 03 ●	**THE GOLDEN AGE OF GROTESQUE** *Interscope / Polydor 9800093* ▲	4	7

Marino MARINI and his QUARTET
Italy, male vocalist and instrumental group (Singles: 23 weeks) pos/wks

3 Oct 58	**VOLARE (NEL BLU DIPINTO DI BLU)** *Durium DC 16632*	13	7
10 Oct 58 ●	**COME PRIMA** *Durium DC 16632*	2	14
20 Mar 59	**CIAO CIAO BAMBINA (PIOVE) (re)** *Durium DC 16636*	24	2

Review of the Year

JUNE 2003

S Club's last single, the aptly titled 'Say Goodbye', follows all of their previous 10 releases into the Top 5. Mike Stock scores his 58th Top 10 with 'Fast Food Song' by the nattily named Fast Food Rockers. Ashanti scores her seventh straight Top 20 entry in 16 months with 'Rock wit U (Awww Baby)'. Led Zeppelin lead the US album chart and Music Video chart with the 1970s-recorded How the West Was Won. It is their seventh US No.1 and is the first three-CD (or more) set to top the US chart for five years. For the first time in the century two UK albums are simultaneously in the US Top 5: Bare by Annie Lennox and Radiohead's Hail to the Thief. Metallica's St Anger heads the charts in 13 countries (including Japan) and Shirley Bassey clocks up a record 36th album hit for a UK female artist with Thank You for the Years. American Idol 2 runner-up Clay Aiken's debut single, 'This Is the Night', sells 393,000 copies in the first week Stateside – a figure not bettered since Elton John's record-shattering 'Candle in the Wind 1997'. He is also the first artist ever to make his US chart debut at No.1. Little Richard is inducted into the Songwriters' Hall of Fame. At the half-way point in 2003 singles sales are down a massive 36 per cent and albums up 12 per cent compared with last year.

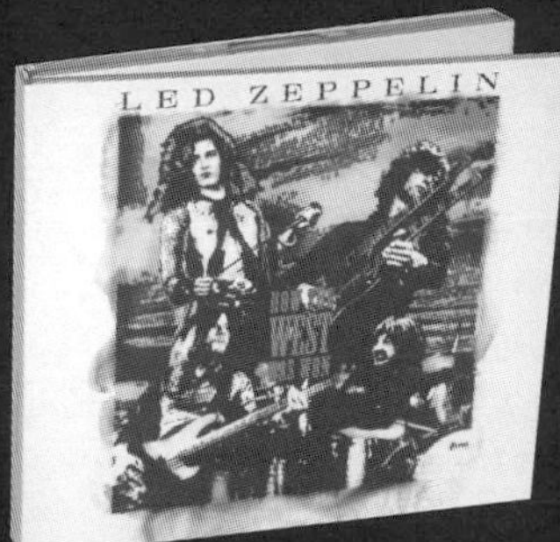

Led Zeppelin's seventh US No.1 album

Metallica: big in Japan in June and No.1 in 12 other territories

MARIO *US, male vocalist – Mario Barrett (Singles: 6 weeks)*

Date		Title	pos	wks
12 Apr 03		**JUST A FRIEND** *J 82876508082*	18	4
12 Jul 03		**C'MON** *J 82876528282*	28	2

MARION *UK, male vocal / instrumental group (Singles: 9 weeks, Albums: 2 weeks)*

Date		Title	pos	wks
25 Feb 95		**SLEEP** *London LONCD 360*	53	1
13 May 95		**TOYS FOR BOYS** *London LONCD 366*	57	1
21 Oct 95		**LET'S ALL GO TOGETHER** *London LONCD 371*	37	2
3 Feb 96		**TIME** *London LONCD 377*	29	2
30 Mar 96		**SLEEP (re-mix)** *London LONCD 381*	17	2
7 Mar 98		**MIYAKO HIDEAWAY** *London LONCD 403*	45	1
17 Feb 96	●	**THIS WORLD AND BODY** *London 8286952*	10	2

MARK 'OH
Germany, male producer – Marko Albrecht (Singles: 3 weeks)

Date		Title	pos	wks
6 May 95		**TEARS DON'T LIE** *Systematic SYSCD 9*	24	3

Pigmeat MARKHAM
US, male vocalist / comedian, d. 13 Dec 1981 (Singles: 8 weeks)

Date		Title	pos	wks
17 Jul 68		**HERE COMES THE JUDGE** *Chess CRS 8077*	19	8

Biz MARKIE *US, male rapper (Singles: 2 weeks)*

Date		Title	pos	wks
26 May 90		**JUST A FRIEND** *Cold Chillin' W 9823*	55	2

Yannis MARKOPOULOS
Greece, orchestra (Singles: 8 weeks, Albums: 8 weeks)

Date		Title	pos	wks
17 Dec 77		**WHO PAYS THE FERRYMAN?** *BBC RESL 51*	11	8
26 Aug 78		**WHO PAYS THE FERRYMAN** *BBC REB 315*	22	8

Guy MARKS
US, male vocalist – Mario Scarpo d. 28 Nov 1987 (Singles: 8 weeks)

Date		Title	pos	wks
13 May 78		**LOVING YOU HAS MADE ME BANANAS** *ABC 4211*	25	8

MARKSMEN – *See Houston WELLS and the MARKSMEN*

MARKY MARK and the FUNKY BUNCH *US, male / female vocal / rap / instrumental group (Singles: 14 weeks, Albums: 1 week)*

Date		Title	pos	wks
31 Aug 91		**GOOD VIBRATIONS** *Interscope A 8764* [1] ▲	14	7
2 Nov 91		**WILDSIDE** *Interscope A 8674*	42	3
12 Dec 92		**YOU GOTTA BELIEVE** *Interscope A 8480*	54	4
5 Oct 91		**MUSIC FOR THE PEOPLE** *Interscope 7567917371*	61	1

[1] Marky Mark and the Funky Bunch featuring Loleatta Holloway

Bob MARLEY and the WAILERS (38 Top 500)
Legendary, globally successful Jamaican group, fronted by Bob Marley, nicknamed 'Tuff Gong', b. 6 Apr 1945, Jamaica, d. 11 May 1981, Miami, (v/g). Varying line-up included Peter Tosh b. 19 Oct 1944, Jamaica, d. 11 Sep 1987, Jamaica, (v/g), Bunny Wailer (v/prc). Their compilation 'Legend' is the biggest-selling reggae album in the UK and the US with combined sales of more than 12 million (Singles: 167 weeks, Albums: 536 weeks)

Date		Title	pos	wks
27 Sep 75	●	**NO WOMAN NO CRY (re)** *Island WIP 6244*	8	18
25 Jun 77		**EXODUS** *Island WIP 6390*	14	9
10 Sep 77		**WAITING IN VAIN** *Island WIP 6402*	27	6
10 Dec 77	●	**JAMMING / PUNKY REGGAE PARTY** *Island WIP 6410*	9	12
25 Feb 78	●	**IS THIS LOVE** *Island WIP 6420*	9	9
10 Jun 78		**SATISFY MY SOUL** *Island WIP 6440*	21	10
20 Oct 79		**SO MUCH TROUBLE IN THE WORLD** *Island WIP 6510*	56	4
21 Jun 80	●	**COULD YOU BE LOVED** *Island WIP 6610*	5	12
13 Sep 80		**THREE LITTLE BIRDS** *Island WIP 6641*	17	9
7 May 83	●	**BUFFALO SOLDIER** *Island/Tuff Gong IS 108*	4	12
21 Apr 84	●	**ONE LOVE – PEOPLE GET READY** *Island IS 169*	5	11
23 Jun 84		**WAITING IN VAIN (re-issue)** *Island IS 180*	31	7
8 Dec 84		**COULD YOU BE LOVED (re-issue)** *Island IS 210*	71	2
18 May 91		**ONE LOVE – PEOPLE GET READY (re-issue)** *Tuff Gong TGX 1*	42	3
19 Sep 92	●	**IRON LION ZION** *Tuff Gong TGX 2*	5	9
28 Nov 92		**WHY SHOULD I / EXODUS (re)** *Tuff Gong TGX 3*	42	4
20 May 95		**KEEP ON MOVING** *Tuff Gong TGXCD 4*	17	4
8 Jun 96		**WHAT GOES AROUND COMES AROUND** *Anansi ANACS 002*	42	1
25 Sep 99	●	**SUN IS SHINING** *Club Tools / Edel 0066895 CLU* [1]	3	10
11 Dec 99		**TURN YOUR LIGHTS DOWN LOW** *Columbia 6684362* [2]	15	7
22 Jan 00		**RAINBOW COUNTRY** *Club Tools 0067225CLU* [1]	11	6
24 Jun 00		**JAMMIN'** *Tuff Gong TGXCD 9* [3]	42	2
4 Oct 75		**NATTY DREAD** *Island ILPS 9281*	43	5
20 Dec 75		**LIVE!** *Island ILPS 9376*	38	11
8 May 76		**RASTAMAN VIBRATION** *Island ILPS 9383*	15	13
11 Jun 77	●	**EXODUS** *Island ILPS 9498*	8	56
1 Apr 78	●	**KAYA** *Island ILPS 9517*	4	24
16 Dec 78		**BABYLON BY BUS** *Island ISLD 11*	40	11
13 Oct 79		**SURVIVAL** *Island ILPS 9542*	20	6
28 Jun 80	●	**UPRISING** *Island ILPS 9596*	6	17
28 May 83	●	**CONFRONTATION** *Island ILPS 9760*	5	19
19 May 84	★	**LEGEND – THE BEST OF BOB MARLEY AND THE WAILERS** *Tuff Gong BMWX 1* ■	1	330
28 Jul 86		**REBEL MUSIC** *Island ILPS 9843*	54	3
3 Oct 92	●	**SONGS OF FREEDOM** *Tuff Gong TGCBX 1* [1]	10	5
3 Jun 95	●	**NATURAL MYSTIC** *Tuff Gong BMWCD 2*	5	8
4 Sep 99		**THE SUN IS SHINING** *Club Tools CLU 66730* [2]	40	3
2 Jun 01	●	**ONE LOVE – THE VERY BEST OF BOB MARLEY AND THE WAILERS** *Tuff Gong BMWCD 3*	5	16
7 Jul 01		**LIVELY UP YOURSELF** *Music Collection 12691* [1]	75	1
10 Nov 01		**ONE LOVE – THE VERY BEST OF BOB MARLEY AND THE WAILERS** *Tuff Gong 5865512*	24	8

[1] Bob Marley vs Funkstar De Luxe [2] Bob Marley featuring Lauryn Hill [3] Bob Marley featuring MC Lyte [1] Bob Marley [2] Bob Marley vs Funkstar De Luxe

'No Woman No Cry' on first chart visit made No.22 before making its peak position on re-entry in Jun 1981. 'Exodus' on Tuff Gong TGX 3 listed with 'Why Should I' only from 5 Dec 1992, and is a different version from the Island hit. It peaked at No.53 The second 'One Love – The Very Best of Bob Marley and the Wailers' album is a repackaged version of the 2 Jun 01 album and includes a bonus CD of rare tracks; 'The Sun Is Shining' is an import single that was too long to be eligible for the singles chart; 'Live' returned to the chart in 1981 under the title 'Live at the Lyceum'

Ziggy MARLEY and the MELODY MAKERS *Jamaica, male / female vocal / instrumental group (Singles: 11 weeks)*

Date		Title	pos	wks
11 Jun 88		**TOMORROW PEOPLE** *Virgin VS 1049*	22	10
23 Sep 89		**LOOK WHO'S DANCING** *Virgin America VUS 5*	65	1

Lene MARLIN *Norway, female vocalist – Lene Marlin Pederson (Singles: 20 weeks, Albums: 34 weeks)*

Date		Title	pos	wks
11 Mar 00	●	**SITTING DOWN HERE** *Virgin DINSD 183*	5	11
16 Sep 00		**UNFORGIVABLE SINNER** *Virgin DINSD 202*	13	6
13 Jan 01		**WHERE I'M HEADED** *Virgin DINSD 196*	31	2
4 Oct 03		**YOU WEREN'T THERE** *Virgin DINSD 262*	59	1
25 Mar 00		**PLAYING MY GAME** *Virgin CDVIR 83*	18	34

MARLO *UK, male vocal / instrumental group (Singles: 1 week)*

Date		Title	pos	wks
24 Jul 99		**HOW DO I KNOW?** *Polydor 5611362*	56	1

MARMALADE *UK, male vocal / instrumental group – includes Junior Campbell (Singles: 130 weeks)*

Date		Title	pos	wks
22 May 68	●	**LOVIN' THINGS** *CBS 3412*	6	13
23 Oct 68		**WAIT FOR ME MARIANNE** *CBS 3708*	30	5
4 Dec 68	★	**OB-LA-DI, OB-LA-DA** *CBS 3892*	1	20
11 Jun 69	●	**BABY MAKE IT SOON** *CBS 4287*	9	13
20 Dec 69	●	**REFLECTIONS OF MY LIFE** *Decca F 12982*	3	12
18 Jul 70	●	**RAINBOW** *Decca F 13035*	3	14
27 Mar 71		**MY LITTLE ONE** *Decca F 13135*	15	11
4 Sep 71	●	**COUSIN NORMAN** *Decca F 13214*	6	11
27 Nov 71		**BACK ON THE ROAD (re)** *Decca F 13251*	35	8
1 Apr 72	●	**RADANCER** *Decca F 13297*	6	12
21 Feb 76	●	**FALLING APART AT THE SEAMS** *Target TGT 105*	9	11

MARMION *Spain / Holland, male instrumental / production duo (Singles: 2 weeks)*

Date		Title	pos	wks
18 May 96		**SCHONEBERG** *Hooj Choons HOOJCD 43*	53	1
14 Feb 98		**SCHONEBERG (re-mix)** *ffrr FCD 324*	56	1

Johnny MARR – *See Billy BRAGG; ELECTRONIC; Kirsty MacCOLL; SMITHS*

MARRADONA
UK, male DJ / production group (Singles: 5 weeks) pos/wks

26 Feb 94 OUT OF MY HEAD *Peach PWCD 282* 38 3
26 Jul 97 OUT OF MY HEAD 97 (re-mix) *Soopa SPCD 1* 39 2

Neville MARRINER and the ACADEMY OF ST MARTIN IN THE FIELDS
UK, male conductor and chamber orchestra (Albums: 6 weeks) pos/wks

6 Apr 85 AMADEUS (FILM SOUNDTRACK) *London LONDP 6* 64 6

M/A/R/R/S
UK, male instrumental / production group (Singles: 14 weeks) pos/wks

5 Sep 87 ★ PUMP UP THE VOLUME / ANITINA (THE FIRST TIME I SEE SHE DANCE) *4AD AD 70* 1 14

MARS VOLTA
US, male vocal / instruemtal group (Singles: 2 weeks, Albums: 6 weeks) pos/wks

11 Oct 03 INERTIATIC ESP *Universal MCSTD 40332* 42 2
5 Jul 03 DE-LOUSED IN THE COMATORIUM *Universal 9860460* 43 1

Bernie MARSDEN
UK, male vocalist / instrumentalist – guitar (Albums: 2 weeks) pos/wks

5 Sep 81 LOOK AT ME NOW *Parlophone PCF 7217* 71 2

See also WHITESNAKE

Gerry MARSDEN – *See CHRISTIANS, Holly JOHNSON, Paul McCARTNEY, Gerry MARSDEN and STOCK AITKEN WATERMAN; GERRY and the PACEMAKERS*

Matthew MARSDEN
UK, male actor / vocalist (Singles: 10 weeks) pos/wks

11 Jul 98 THE HEART'S LONE DESIRE *Columbia 6661152* 13 7
7 Nov 98 SHE'S GONE *Columbia 6664915* [1] 24 3

[1] Matthew Marsden featuring Destiny's Child

Kym MARSH
UK, female vocalist (Singles: 21 weeks, Albums: 3 weeks) pos/wks

19 Apr 03 ● CRY *Island MCSTD 40314* 2 12
19 Jul 03 ● COME ON OVER *Universal MCSTD 40323* 10 7
8 Nov 03 SENTIMENTAL *Universal MCSTD 40340* 35 2
2 Aug 03 ● STANDING TALL *Universal 9800035* 9 3

See also HEAR'SAY

Stevie MARSH *UK, female vocalist (Singles: 4 weeks)* pos/wks

4 Dec 59 IF YOU WERE THE ONLY BOY IN THE WORLD (re) *Decca F 11181* 24 4

MARSHA – *See SHAGGY*

Amanda MARSHALL *Canada, female vocalist (Albums: 2 weeks)* pos/wks

3 Aug 96 AMANDA MARSHALL *Epic 4837912* 47 2

Joy MARSHALL *UK, female vocalist (Singles: 2 weeks)* pos/wks

23 Jun 66 THE MORE I SEE YOU *Decca F 12422* 34 2

Keith MARSHALL *UK, male vocalist (Singles: 10 weeks)* pos/wks

4 Apr 81 ONLY CRYING *Arrival PIK 2* 12 10

Louise Clare MARSHALL – *See SILICONE SOUL featuring Louise Clare MARSHALL*

Wayne MARSHALL *UK, male vocalist (Singles: 7 weeks)* pos/wks

1 Oct 94 OOH AAH (G-SPOT) *Soultown SOULCDS 322* 29 3
3 Jun 95 SPIRIT *Soultown SOULCDS 00352* 58 1
24 Feb 96 NEVER KNEW LOVE LIKE THIS *Sony S2 6629382* [1] 40 2
7 Dec 96 G SPOT (re-mix) *MBA INTER 9006* 50 1

[1] Pauline Henry featuring Wayne Marshall

MARSHALL HAIN *UK, male / female vocal / instrumental duo – Julian Marshall and Kit Hain (Singles: 19 weeks)* pos/wks

3 Jun 78 ● DANCING IN THE CITY *Harvest HAR 5157* 3 15
14 Oct 78 COMING HOME *Harvest HAR 5168* 39 4

MARTAY featuring ZZ TOP *UK, female rapper – Melone McKenzy and US, male vocal / instrumental trio (Singles: 2 weeks)* pos/wks

16 Oct 99 GIMME ALL YOUR LOVIN' 2000 *Riverhorse RIVHCD 2* 28 2

Lena MARTELL *UK, female vocalist – Helen Thomson (Singles: 18 weeks, Albums: 71 weeks)* pos/wks

29 Sep 79 ★ ONE DAY AT A TIME *Pye 7N 46021* 1 18
25 May 74 THAT WONDERFUL SOUND OF LENA MARTELL *Pye SPL 18427* 35 2
8 Jan 77 THE BEST OF LENA MARTELL *Pye NSPL 18506* 13 16
27 May 78 THE LENA MARTELL COLLECTION *Ronco RTL 2028* 12 19
20 Oct 79 ● LENA'S MUSIC ALBUM *Pye N 123* 5 18
19 Apr 80 ● BY REQUEST *Ronco RTL 2046* 9 9
29 Nov 80 BEAUTIFUL SUNDAY *Ronco RTL 2052* 23 7

MARTHA and the MUFFINS *Canada, female / male vocal / instrumental group (Singles: 10 weeks, Albums: 6 weeks)* pos/wks

1 Mar 80 ● ECHO BEACH *Dindisc DIN 9* 10 10
15 Mar 80 METRO MUSIC *DinDisc DID 1* 34 6

See also M + M

MARTHA and the VANDELLAS – *See Martha REEVES and The VANDELLAS*

MARTIKA *US, female vocalist – Marta Marrera (Singles: 57 weeks, Albums: 52 weeks)* pos/wks

29 Jul 89 ● TOY SOLDIERS *CBS 655049 7* ▲ 5 11
14 Oct 89 ● I FEEL THE EARTH MOVE *CBS 655294 7* 7 14
13 Jan 90 MORE THAN YOU KNOW *CBS 655526 7* 15 7
17 Mar 90 WATER *CBS 655731 7* 59 3
17 Aug 91 ● LOVE . . . THY WILL BE DONE *Columbia 6573137* 9 9
30 Nov 91 MARTIKA'S KITCHEN *Columbia 6575687* 17 10
22 Feb 92 COLOURED KISSES *Columbia 6577097* 41 3
16 Sep 89 MARTIKA *CBS 463355 1* 11 37
7 Sep 91 MARTIKA'S KITCHEN *Columbia 4671891* 15 15

Juan MARTIN and the ROYAL PHILHARMONIC ORCHESTRA *Spain, male instrumentalist – guitar and UK, orchestra (Singles: 57 weeks, Albums: 9 weeks)* pos/wks

28 Jan 84 ● LOVE THEME FROM 'THE THORN BIRDS' *WEA X 9518* 10 7
11 Feb 84 SERENADE *K-Tel NE 1267* 21 9

See also ROYAL PHILHARMONIC ORCHESTRA

Billie Ray MARTIN *Germany, female vocalist – Birgit Dieckmann (Singles: 20 weeks, Albums: 2 weeks)* pos/wks

19 Nov 94 YOUR LOVING ARMS *Magnet MAG 1028CD* 38 3
20 May 95 ● YOUR LOVING ARMS (re-mix) *Magnet MAG 1031CD* 6 10
2 Sep 95 RUNNING AROUND TOWN *Magnet MAG 1035CD* 29 2
6 Jan 96 IMITATION OF LIFE *Magnet MAG 1040CD* 29 3
6 Apr 96 SPACE OASIS *Magnet MAG 1042CD* 66 1
21 Aug 99 HONEY *React CDREACT 129* 54 1
3 Feb 96 DEADLINE FOR MY MEMORIES *Magnet 630121802* 46 2

Dean MARTIN (288 Top 500)
Acclaimed vocalist / entertainer / film actor and cabaret performer, b. Dino Crocetti, 7 Jun 1917, Ohio, d. 25 Dec 1995. He first found fame partnering Jerry Lewis (1946-56), and had a long and successful solo career. He was a member of Frank Sinatra's 'Rat Pack' and had an impressive 46-year chart span (Singles: 163 weeks, Albums: 59 weeks) pos/wks

18 Sep 53 ● KISS (re) *Capitol CL 13893* 5 8
22 Jan 54 ● THAT'S AMORE *Capitol CL 14008* 2 11
1 Oct 54 ● SWAY *Capitol CL 14138* 6 7
22 Oct 54 HOW DO YOU SPEAK TO AN ANGEL (re) *Capitol CL 14150* 15 6
28 Jan 55 ● THE NAUGHTY LADY OF SHADY LANE *Capitol CL 14226* 5 10

4 Feb 55 MAMBO ITALIANO *Capitol CL 14227* ... 14 2
25 Feb 55 ● LET ME GO, LOVER *Capitol CL 14226* ... 3 9
1 Apr 55 ● UNDER THE BRIDGES OF PARIS *Capitol CL 14255* ... 6 8
10 Feb 56 ★ MEMORIES ARE MADE OF THIS *Capitol CL 14523* ▲ ... 1 16
2 Mar 56 YOUNG AND FOOLISH *Capitol CL 14519* ... 20 1
27 Apr 56 INNAMORATA *Capitol CL 14507* ... 21 3
22 Mar 57 THE MAN WHO PLAYS THE MANDOLINO *Capitol CL 14690* ... 21 2
13 Jun 58 ● RETURN TO ME *Capitol CL 14844* ... 2 22
29 Aug 58 ● VOLARE (NEL BLU DIPINTO DI BLU) *Capitol CL 14910* ... 2 14
27 Aug 64 EVERYBODY LOVES SOMEBODY *Reprise R 20281* ▲ ... 11 13
12 Nov 64 THE DOOR IS STILL OPEN TO MY HEART *Reprise R 20307* ... 42 4
5 Feb 69 ● GENTLE ON MY MIND (re) *Reprise RS 23343* ... 2 24
22 Jun 96 THAT'S AMORE (re-issue) *EMI Premier PRESCD 3* ... 43 2
21 Aug 99 SWAY (re-issue) *Capitol CDSWAY 001* ... 66 1
13 May 61 THIS TIME I'M SWINGIN'! *Capitol T 1442* ... 18 1
25 Feb 67 AT EASE WITH DEAN *Reprise RSLP 6322* ... 35 1
4 Nov 67 WELCOME TO MY WORLD *Philips DBL 001* ... 39 1
12 Oct 68 DEAN MARTIN'S GREATEST HITS VOLUME 1 *Reprise RSLP 6301* ... 40 1
22 Feb 69 ● GENTLE ON MY MIND *Reprise RSLP 6330* ... 9 8
22 Feb 69 ● THE BEST OF DEAN MARTIN *Capitol ST 21194* ... 9 1
27 Nov 71 WHITE CHRISTMAS *MFP 524* [1] ... 45 1
13 Nov 76 ● 20 ORIGINAL DEAN MARTIN HITS *Reprise K 54066* ... 7 11
5 Jun 99 ● THE VERY BEST OF DEAN MARTIN – THE CAPITOL & REPRISE YEARS *EMI 4967212* ... 5 29
26 Aug 00 THE VERY BEST OF DEAN MARTIN VOLUME 2 – THE CAPITOL & REPRISE YEARS *Capitol 5277712* ... 40 2
16 Feb 02 LOVE SONGS *Capitol 5377482* ... 24 3

[1] Nat 'King' Cole and Dean Martin

George MARTIN *UK, male producer (Albums: 13 weeks)* pos/wks

4 Apr 98 ● IN MY LIFE *Echo ECHCD 20* ... 5 13

See also BEATLES

Juan MARTIN – *See ROYAL PHILHARMONIC ORCHESTRA*

Linda MARTIN

Ireland, female vocalist (Singles: 2 weeks) pos/wks

30 May 92 WHY ME *Columbia 6581317* ... 59 2

Luci MARTIN – *See Romina JOHNSON*

Marilyn MARTIN – *See Phil COLLINS*

Ray MARTIN and his CHORUS and ORCHESTRA

UK, orchestra, leader d. 7 Feb 1988 (Singles: 11 weeks) pos/wks

14 Nov 52 ● BLUE TANGO (re) *Columbia DB 3051* ... 8 4
4 Dec 53 ● SWEDISH RHAPSODY (re) *Columbia DB 3346* ... 4 4
15 Jun 56 THE CAROUSEL WALTZ (re) *Columbia DB 3771* ... 24 3

See also Lee LAWRENCE

Ricky MARTIN 458 Top 500

Ex-boy band singer and soap star b. Enrique Martin Morales, 24 Dec 1971, Puerto Rico. The performer who put the Latin into platinum sold 15 million of his eponymous album, recorded the world's biggest-selling football single ('The Cup of Life') and has the world's biggest-selling Spanish language album ('Vuelve'). Biggest-selling UK single 'Livin' La Vida Loca' 775,700 (Singles: 75 weeks, Albums: 75 weeks) pos/wks

20 Sep 97 ● (UN, DOS, TRES) MARIA *Columbia 6649595* ... 6 6
11 Jul 98 THE CUP OF LIFE *Columbia 6661502* ... 29 3
17 Jul 99 ★ LIVIN' LA VIDA LOCA *Columbia 6676402* ■ ▲ ... 1 17
20 Nov 99 SHAKE YOUR BON-BON *Columbia 6683412* ... 12 9
29 Apr 00 ● PRIVATE EMOTION *Columbia 6692692* [1] ... 9 9
4 Nov 00 ● SHE BANGS *Columbia 6705422* ... 3 15
10 Mar 01 ● NOBODY WANTS TO BE LONELY *Columbia 6709462* [2] ... 4 12
28 Jul 01 LOADED *Columbia 6714642* ... 19 4
12 Jun 99 ● RICKY MARTIN *Columbia 4944060* ▲ ... 2 48
18 Nov 00 SOUND LOADED *Columbia 4977692* ... 14 21
1 Dec 01 THE BEST OF RICKY MARTIN *Columbia 5050192* ... 42 6

[1] Ricky Martin featuring Meja [2] Ricky Martin and Christina Aguilera

Tony MARTIN

US, male vocalist – Alvin Morris Jr (Singles: 28 weeks) pos/wks

22 Apr 55 ● STRANGER IN PARADISE *HMV B 10849* ... 6 13
13 Jul 56 ● WALK HAND IN HAND *HMV POP 222* ... 2 15

Both with Hugo Winterhalter's Orchestra and Chorus

Vince MARTIN – *See TARRIERS*

Wink MARTINDALE *US, male vocalist (Singles: 41 weeks)* pos/wks

4 Dec 59 ● DECK OF CARDS (3re) *London HLD 8962* ... 5 29
20 Oct 73 DECK OF CARDS (re-issue) *Dot DOT 109* ... 22 12

'Deck of Cards' on the London label made No.18 in 1959 re-entering at No.28 in Jan 1960, again at No.45 in Mar 1960 before making No.5 with the third re-entry in Apr 1963

Alice MARTINEAU

UK, female vocalist, d. 6 Mar 2003 (Singles: 1 week) pos/wks

23 Nov 02 IF I FALL *Epic 6732332* ... 45 1

Angie MARTINEZ featuring Lil' MO & SACARIO

US, female vocal / rap trio (Singles: 1 week) pos/wks

15 Feb 03 IF I COULD GO! *Elektra E 7331CD* ... 61 1

Al MARTINO *US, male vocalist – Alfred Cini (Singles: 87 weeks)* pos/wks

14 Nov 52 ★ HERE IN MY HEART *Capitol CL 13779* ▲ ... 1 18
21 Nov 52 ● TAKE MY HEART *Capitol CL 13769* ... 9 1
30 Jan 53 ● NOW *Capitol CL 13835* ... 3 12
10 Jul 53 ● RACHEL (re) *Capitol CL 13879* ... 10 5
4 Jun 54 ● WANTED (2re) *Capitol CL 14128* ... 4 16
1 Oct 54 ● THE STORY OF TINA *Capitol CL 14163* ... 10 8
23 Sep 55 THE MAN FROM LARAMIE (re) *Capitol CL 14343* ... 19 3
31 Mar 60 SUMMERTIME *Top Rank JAR 312* ... 49 1
29 Aug 63 I LOVE YOU BECAUSE *Capitol CL 15300* ... 48 1
22 Aug 70 ● SPANISH EYES (re) *Capitol CL 15430* ... 5 22

'Spanish Eyes' peaked only at No.49 in 1970 before re-entering in Jul 1973 to make No.5

John MARTYN *UK, male vocalist / instrumentalist – guitar (Singles: 2 weeks, Albums: 30 weeks)* pos/wks

24 Mar 01 DELIVER ME *Multiply CDMULTY 72* [1] ... 31 2
4 Feb 78 ONE WORLD *Island ILPS 9492* ... 54 1
1 Nov 80 GRACE AND DANGER *Island ILPS 9560* ... 54 2
26 Sep 81 GLORIOUS FOOL *Geffen K 99178* ... 25 7
4 Sep 82 WELL KEPT SECRET *WEA K 99255* ... 20 7
17 Nov 84 SAPPHIRE *Island ILPS 9779* ... 57 2
8 Mar 86 PIECE BY PIECE *Island ILPS 9807* ... 28 4
10 Oct 92 COULDN'T LOVE YOU MORE *Permanent PERMCD 9* ... 65 2
10 Aug 96 AND *Go! Discs 8287982* ... 32 3
4 Apr 98 THE CHURCH WITH ONE BELL *Independiente ISOM 3CD* ... 51 1
3 Jun 00 GLASGOW WALKER *Independiente ISOM 15CD* ... 66 1

[1] Sister Bliss featuring John Martyn

MARVELETTES *US, female vocal group (Singles: 10 weeks)* pos/wks

15 Jun 67 WHEN YOU'RE YOUNG AND IN LOVE *Tamla Motown TMG 609* ... 13 10

MARVIN and TAMARA *UK, male / female vocal duo – Marvin Simmonds and Tamara Nicole (Singles: 9 weeks)* pos/wks

7 Aug 99 GROOVE MACHINE *Epic 6675582* ... 11 5
25 Dec 99 NORTH, SOUTH, EAST, WEST *Epic 6684902* ... 38 4

Hank MARVIN *UK, male vocalist / instrumentalist – guitar – Brian Rankin (Singles: 36 weeks, Albums: 72 weeks)* pos/wks

13 Sep 69 ● THROW DOWN A LINE *Columbia DB 8615* [1] ... 7 9
21 Feb 70 THE JOY OF LIVING *Columbia DB 8657* [1] ... 25 8
6 Mar 82 DON'T TALK *Polydor POSP 420* ... 49 4
22 Mar 86 ★ LIVING DOLL *WEA YZ 65* [2] ... 1 11

7 Jan 89	**LONDON KID** *Polydor PO 32* [3]	52 3
17 Oct 92	**WE ARE THE CHAMPIONS** *PolyGram TV PO 229* [4]	66 1
22 Nov 69	**HANK MARVIN** *Columbia SCX 6352*	14 2
20 Mar 82	**WORDS AND MUSIC** *Polydor POLD 5054*	66 3
31 Oct 92	**INTO THE LIGHT** *Polydor 5171482*	18 10
20 Nov 93	**HEARTBEAT** *PolyGram TV 52132222*	17 9
22 Oct 94	**THE BEST OF HANK MARVIN AND THE SHADOWS** *PolyGram TV 5238212* [1]	19 11
18 Nov 95	**HANK PLAYS CLIFF** *PolyGram TV 5294262*	33 7
23 Nov 96	**HANK PLAYS HOLLY** *PolyGram TV 5337132*	34 7
5 Apr 97	**HANK PLAYS LIVE** *PolyGram TV 5374282*	71 1
22 Nov 97	**PLAY ANDREW LLOYD WEBBER AND TIM RICE** *PolyGram TV 5394792* [1]	41 6
14 Nov 98	**VERY BEST OF HANK MARVIN AND THE SHADOWS – THE FIRST 40 YEARS** *PolyGram TV 5592112* [1]	56 5
15 Apr 00	**MARVIN AT THE MOVIES** *Universal Music TV 1570572*	17 5
20 Apr 02 ●	**GUITAR PLAYER** *UMTV 171242*	10 6

[1] Cliff and Hank [2] Cliff Richard and The Young Ones featuring Hank B Marvin [3] Jean-Michel Jarre featuring Hank Marvin [4] Hank Marvin featuring Brian May [1] Hank Marvin and the Shadows

See also SHADOWS; MARVIN, WELCH and FARRAR

Lee MARVIN

US, male actor / vocalist – d. 28 Aug 1987 (Singles: 23 weeks) pos/wks

7 Feb 70 ★	**WAND'RIN' STAR (2re)** *Paramount PARA 3004*	1 23

'I Talk to the Trees' by Clint Eastwood, the flip side of 'Wand'rin' Star', was listed with 'Wand'rin' Star' for 7 Feb and 14 Feb 1970 only

MARVIN THE PARANOID ANDROID

UK, male robot (Singles: 4 weeks) pos/wks

16 May 81	**MARVIN** *Polydor POSP 261*	53 4

MARVIN, WELCH and FARRAR

UK, male vocal / instrumental group (Albums: 4 weeks) pos/wks

3 Apr 71	**MARVIN, WELCH AND FARRAR** *Regal Zonophone SRZA 8502*	30 4

See also Hank MARVIN; SHADOWS

Richard MARX

US, male vocalist (Singles: 75 weeks, Albums: 42 weeks) pos/wks

27 Feb 88	**SHOULD'VE KNOWN BETTER** *Manhattan MT 32*	50 5
14 May 88	**ENDLESS SUMMER NIGHTS** *Manhattan MT 39*	50 3
17 Jun 89	**SATISFIED** *EMI-USA MT 64* ▲	52 4
2 Sep 89 ●	**RIGHT HERE WAITING** *EMI-USA MT 72* ▲	2 10
11 Nov 89	**ANGELIA** *EMI-USA MT 74*	45 4
24 Mar 90	**TOO LATE TO SAY GOODBYE** *EMI-USA MT 80*	38 3
7 Jul 90	**CHILDREN OF THE NIGHT** *EMI-USA MT 84*	54 2
1 Sep 90	**ENDLESS SUMMER NIGHTS / HOLD ON TO THE NIGHTS (re-issue)** *EMI-USA MT 89* ▲	60 2
19 Oct 91	**KEEP COMING BACK** *Capitol CL 634*	55 2
9 May 92 ●	**HAZARD** *Capitol CL 654*	3 15
29 Aug 92	**TAKE THIS HEART** *Capitol CL 667*	13 6
28 Nov 92	**CHAINS AROUND MY HEART** *Capitol CL 676*	29 6
29 Jan 94	**NOW AND FOREVER** *Capitol CDCLS 703*	13 6
30 Apr 94	**SILENT SCREAM** *Capitol CDCLS 714*	32 4
13 Aug 94	**THE WAY SHE LOVES ME** *Capitol CDCL 721*	38 3
9 Apr 88	**RICHARD MARX** *Manhattan MTL 1017*	68 2
20 May 89 ●	**REPEAT OFFENDER** *EMI-USA MTL 1043* ▲	8 12
16 Nov 91 ●	**RUSH STREET** *Capitol ESTU 2158*	7 20
19 Feb 94	**PAID VACATION** *Capitol CDESTU 2208*	11 5
21 Feb 98	**GREATEST HITS** *Capitol 8219142*	34 3

MARXMAN

UK / Ireland, rap / instrumental group (Singles: 5 weeks, Albums: 1 week) pos/wks

6 Mar 93	**ALL ABOUT EVE** *Talkin Loud TLKCD 35*	28 4
1 May 93	**SHIP AHOY** *Talkin Loud TLKCD 39*	64 1
3 Apr 93	**33 REVOLUTIONS PER MINUTE** *Talkin Loud 5145382*	69 1

Sinead O'Connor provides uncredited vocals on 'Ship Ahoy'

MARY JANE GIRLS

US, female vocal group (Singles: 15 weeks, Albums: 9 weeks) pos/wks

21 May 83	**CANDY MAN** *Motown TMG 1301*	60 4
25 Jun 83	**ALL NIGHT LONG** *Gordy TMG 1309*	13 9
8 Oct 83	**BOYS** *Gordy TMG 1315*	74 1
18 Feb 95	**ALL NIGHT LONG (re-mix)** *Motown TMGCD 1436*	51 1
28 May 83	**MARY JANE GIRLS** *Gordy STML 12189*	51 9

MARY MARY

US, female vocal duo – Erica and Tina Atkins (Singles: 14 weeks) pos/wks

10 Jun 00 ●	**SHACKLES (PRAISE YOU)** *Columbia 6694202*	5 12
18 Nov 00	**I SINGS** *Columbia 6699742*	32 2

Carolyne MAS

US, female vocalist (Singles: 2 weeks) pos/wks

2 Feb 80	**QUOTE GOODBYE QUOTE** *Mercury 6167 873*	71 2

MASAI

UK, female vocal duo – Sharon Amos and Anna Crane (Singles: 1 week) pos/wks

1 Mar 03	**DO THAT THING** *Concept CDCON 36*	42 1

MA$E

US, male rapper – Mason Betha (Singles: 53 weeks, Albums: 9 weeks) pos/wks

29 Mar 97	**CAN'T NOBODY HOLD ME DOWN** *Arista 74321464552* [1] ▲	19 4
9 Aug 97 ●	**MO MONEY MO PROBLEMS** *Puff Daddy 74321492492* [2] ▲	6 10
27 Dec 97 ●	**FEEL SO GOOD** *Puff Daddy 74321526442*	10 8
18 Apr 98	**WHAT YOU WANT** *Puff Daddy74321578772* [3]	15 5
19 Sep 98	**HORSE AND CARRIAGE** *Epic 6662612* [4]	12 4
10 Oct 98 ●	**TOP OF THE WORLD (re)** *Atlantic AT 0046CD* [5]	2 9
12 Dec 98 ●	**TAKE ME THERE** *Interscope IND 95620* [6]	7 9
10 Jul 99	**GET READY** *Puff Daddy / Arista 74321682602* [7]	32 4
24 Jan 98	**HARLEM WORLD** *Puff Daddy 78612730172* ▲	53 7
24 Jul 99	**DOUBLE UP** *Puff Daddy 74321674332*	47 2

[1] Puff Daddy featuring Mase [2] Notorious B.I.G. featuring Puff Daddy and Mase [3] Mase featuring Total [4] Cam'ron featuring Mase [5] Brandy featuring Mase [6] BLACKstreet and Mya featuring Mase and Blinky Blink [7] Mase featuring BLACKstreet

MASH

US, male vocal / instrumental group (Singles: 12 weeks) pos/wks

10 May 80 ★	**THEME FROM M*A*S*H (SUICIDE IS PAINLESS)** *CBS 8536*	1 12

MASH!

UK / US, male / female vocal group (Singles: 3 weeks) pos/wks

21 May 94	**U DON'T HAVE TO SAY U LOVE ME** *React CDREACT 37*	37 2
4 Feb 95	**LET'S SPEND THE NIGHT TOGETHER** *Playa CDXPLAYA 2*	66 1

MASH UP – *See Matt DAREY*

MASON – *See CHICANE*

Barbara MASON

US, female vocalist (Singles: 5 weeks) pos/wks

21 Jan 84	**ANOTHER MAN** *Streetwave KHAN 3*	45 5

Glen MASON

UK, male vocalist – Tommy Lennon (Singles: 7 weeks) pos/wks

28 Sep 56	**GLENDORA** *Parlophone R 4203*	28 2
16 Nov 56	**THE GREEN DOOR** *Parlophone R 4244*	24 5

John MASON

UK, male instrumentalist (Albums: 1 week) pos/wks

27 Dec 75	**STRINGS OF SCOTLAND** *Philips 6382 108*	50 1

Mary MASON

UK, female vocalist (Singles: 6 weeks) pos/wks

8 Oct 77	**ANGEL OF THE MORNING – ANY WAY THAT YOU WANT ME (MEDLEY)** *Epic EPC 5552*	27 6

MASQUERADE

UK, male / female vocal group (Singles: 10 weeks) pos/wks

11 Jan 86	**ONE NATION** *Streetwave KHAN 59*	54 6
5 Jul 86	**(SOLUTION TO) THE PROBLEM (re)** *Streetwave KHAN 67*	64 4

MASS ORDER *US, male vocal / instrumental duo – Eugene Hanes and Marc Valentine (Singles: 5 weeks)*

Date	Title	pos	wks
14 Mar 92	**LIFT EVERY VOICE (TAKE ME AWAY)** *Columbia 6577487*	35	3
23 May 92	**LET'S GET HAPPY** *Columbia 6580737*	45	2

MASS PRODUCTION *US, male vocal / instrumental group (Singles: 7 weeks)*

Date	Title	pos	wks
12 Mar 77	**WELCOME TO OUR WORLD (OF MERRY MUSIC)** *Atlantic K 10898*	44	3
17 May 80	**SHANTE** *Atlantic K 11475*	59	4

MASS SYNDICATE featuring Su Su BOBIEN *US, male producer and US, female vocalist (Singles: 1 week)*

Date	Title	pos	wks
24 Oct 98	**YOU DON'T KNOW** *ffrr FCD 347*	71	1

MASSED WELSH CHOIRS *UK, male voice choir (Albums: 7 weeks)*

Date	Title	pos	wks
9 Aug 69 ●	**CYMANSA GANN** *BBC REC 53 M*	5	7

Zeitia MASSIAH *UK, female vocalist (Singles: 2 weeks)*

Date	Title	pos	wks
12 Mar 94	**I SPECIALIZE IN LOVE** *Union City UCRCD 27*	74	1
24 Sep 94	**THIS IS THE PLACE** *Virgin VSCDT 1511*	62	1

MASSIEL *Spain, female vocalist (Singles: 4 weeks)*

Date	Title	pos	wks
24 Apr 68	**LA LA LA** *Philips BF 1667*	35	4

MASSIVE ATTACK (231 Top 500)

Trip hop titans who emerged from Bristol's legendary Wild Bunch: mainstays Robert '3-D' Del Naja (v), Grant 'Daddy-G' Marshall (v) and Andrew 'Mushroom' Vowles (k). Brit-nominated band entered the European chart at No.1 in 2003 with '100th Window' (which featured Del Naja only) (Singles: 44 weeks, Albums: 222 weeks)

Date	Title	pos	wks
23 Feb 91	**UNFINISHED SYMPATHY** *Wild Bunch WBRS 2* [1]	13	9
8 Jun 91	**SAFE FROM HARM** *Wild Bunch WBRS 3*	25	6
22 Feb 92	**MASSIVE ATTACK (EP)** *Wild Bunch WBRS 4*	27	4
29 Oct 94	**SLY** *Wild Bunch WBRDX 5*	24	4
21 Jan 95	**PROTECTION** *Wild Bunch WBRX 6* [2]	14	4
1 Apr 95	**KARMACOMA** *Wild Bunch WBRX 7*	28	4
19 Jul 97	**RISINGSON** *Circa WBRX 8*	11	3
9 May 98 ●	**TEARDROP** *Virgin WBRX 9*	10	6
25 Jul 98	**ANGEL** *Virgin WBRX 10*	30	2
8 Mar 03	**SPECIAL CASES** *Virgin VSCDT 1839*	15	2
20 Apr 91	**BLUE LINES** *Wild Bunch WBRLP 1*	13	84
8 Oct 94 ●	**PROTECTION / NO PROTECTION** *Wild Bunch WBRCD 2*	4	78
2 May 98 ★	**MEZZANINE** *Virgin WBRCD 4* ■	1	54
22 Feb 03 ★	**100TH WINDOW** *Virgin CDV2967* ■	1	6

[1] Massive [2] Massive Attack featuring Tracey Thorn

Vocals on first three releases by Shara Nelson. Tracks on Massive Attack (EP): Hymn of the Big Wheel / Home of the Whale / Be Thankful / Any Love. Teardrop features an uncredited vocal by Elizabeth Fraser from Cocteau Twins From 4 Mar 95 'Protection' was listed with the remix album 'No Protection'

See also Shara NELSON; NICOLETTE

MASSIVO featuring TRACY *UK, male / female vocal / instrumental group (Singles: 11 weeks)*

Date	Title	pos	wks
26 May 90	**LOVING YOU** *Debut DEBT 3097*	25	11

MASTER P – *See Montell JORDAN*

MASTER SINGERS *UK, male vocal group (Singles: 8 weeks)*

Date	Title	pos	wks
14 Apr 66	**HIGHWAY CODE** *Parlophone R 5428*	25	6
17 Nov 66	**WEATHER FORECAST (re)** *Parlophone R 5523*	45	2

MASTERMIXERS – *See JIVE BUNNY and the MASTERMIXERS*

Sammy MASTERS *US, male vocalist – Samuel Lawmaster (Singles: 5 weeks)*

Date	Title	pos	wks
9 Jun 60	**ROCKIN' RED WING** *Warner Bros. WB 10*	36	5

MASTERS AT WORK *US, male production / instrumental duo – 'Lil' Louis Vega and Kenny 'Dope' Gonzales (Singles: 6 weeks)*

Date	Title	pos	wks
5 Aug 95	**I CAN'T GET NO SLEEP** *A&M 5811412* [1]	44	2
31 Jul 99	**TO BE IN LOVE** *Defected DEFECT 5CDS* [2]	23	3
6 Jul 02	**BACKFIRED** *SuSu CDSUSU 4* [3]	62	1

[1] Masters at Work presents India [2] MAW presents India [3] Masters at Work featuring India

See also NUYORICAN SOUL

MASTERS of CEREMONIES – *See DJ PIED PIPER and The MASTERS OF CEREMONIES*

Paul MASTERSON presents SUSHI *UK, male producer (Singles: 2 weeks)*

Date	Title	pos	wks
2 Nov 02	**THE EARTHSHAKER** *Nulife 74321970372*	35	2

See also CANDY GIRLS; DOROTHY; SLEAZESISTERS; YOMANDA; HI-GATE; CLERGY

MATCH *UK, male vocal / instrumental group (Singles: 3 weeks)*

Date	Title	pos	wks
16 Jun 79	**BOOGIE MAN** *Flamingo FM 2*	48	3

MATCHBOX *UK, male vocal / instrumental group (Singles: 66 weeks, Albums: 14 weeks)*

Date	Title	pos	wks
3 Nov 79	**ROCKABILLY REBEL** *Magnet MAG 155*	18	12
19 Jan 80	**BUZZ BUZZ A DIDDLE IT** *Magnet MAG 157*	22	8
10 May 80	**MIDNITE DYNAMOS** *Magnet MAG 169*	14	12
27 Sep 80 ●	**WHEN YOU ASK ABOUT LOVE** *Magnet MAG 191*	4	12
29 Nov 80	**OVER THE RAINBOW – YOU BELONG TO ME (MEDLEY)** *Magnet MAG 192*	15	11
4 Apr 81	**BABES IN THE WOOD** *Magnet MAG 193*	46	6
1 Aug 81	**LOVE'S MADE A FOOL OF YOU** *Magnet MAG 194*	63	3
29 May 82	**ONE MORE SATURDAY NIGHT** *Magnet MAG 223*	63	2
2 Feb 80	**MATCHBOX** *Magnet MAG 5031*	44	5
11 Oct 80	**MIDNITE DYNAMOS** *Magnet MAG 5036*	23	9

MATCHBOX TWENTY *US, male vocal / instrumental group (Singles: 5 weeks, Albums: 5 weeks)*

Date	Title	pos	wks
11 Apr 98	**PUSH** *Atlantic AT 0021CD* [1]	38	2
4 Jul 98	**3 AM** *Atlantic AT 0034CD* [1]	64	1
17 Feb 01	**IF YOU'RE GONE** *Atlantic AT 0090CD*	50	1
22 Feb 03	**DISEASE** *Atlantic AT 0145CD*	50	1
25 Apr 98	**YOURSELF OR SOMEONE LIKE YOU** *Atlantic 7567927212* [1]	50	1
3 Jun 00	**MAD SEASON BY MATCHBOX TWENTY** *Atlantic 7567833392*	31	2
8 Mar 03	**MORE THAN YOU THINK YOU ARE** *Atlantic 7567931702*	31	2

[1] Matchbox 20

MATCHROOM MOB – *See CHAS and DAVE*

Mireille MATHIEU *France, female vocalist (Singles: 7 weeks, Albums: 1 week)*

Date	Title	pos	wks
13 Dec 67	**LA DERNIÈRE VALSE** *Columbia DB 8323*	26	7
2 Mar 68	**MIREILLE MATHIEU** *Columbia SCX 6210*	39	1

Johnny MATHIS (135 Top 500)

Legendary MOR vocal superstar, b. 30 Sep 1935, San Francisco, US. Frank Sinatra and Elvis Presley are the only males with more hit albums in the US, where his greatest hits album charted for almost 10 years – a record for a solo performer (Singles: 138 weeks, Albums: 228 weeks)

Date	Title	pos	wks
23 May 58	**TEACHER, TEACHER** *Fontana H 130*	27	5
26 Sep 58 ●	**A CERTAIN SMILE** *Fontana H 142*	4	16
19 Dec 58	**WINTER WONDERLAND** *Fontana H 165*	17	3
7 Aug 59 ●	**SOMEONE** *Fontana H 199*	6	15
27 Nov 59	**THE BEST OF EVERYTHING** *Fontana H 218*	30	1
29 Jan 60	**MISTY (re)** *Fontana H 219*	12	12
24 Mar 60	**YOU ARE BEAUTIFUL (re)** *Fontana H 234*	38	9
28 Jul 60	**STARBRIGHT** *Fontana H 254*	47	2
6 Oct 60 ●	**MY LOVE FOR YOU** *Fontana H 267*	9	18
4 Apr 63	**WHAT WILL MARY SAY** *CBS AAG 135*	49	1

25 Jan 75 ●	I'M STONE IN LOVE WITH YOU *CBS 2653*	10	12
13 Nov 76 ★	WHEN A CHILD IS BORN (SOLEADO) *CBS 4599*	1	12
25 Mar 78 ●	TOO MUCH, TOO LITTLE, TOO LATE *CBS 6164* [1] ▲	3	14
29 Jul 78	YOU'RE ALL I NEED TO GET BY *CBS 6483* [1]	45	6
11 Aug 79	GONE, GONE, GONE *CBS 7730*	15	10
26 Dec 81	WHEN A CHILD IS BORN *CBS S 1758* [2]	74	2
8 Nov 58 ●	WARM *Fontana TBA TFL 5015*	6	2
24 Jan 59 ●	SWING SOFTLY *Fontana TBA TFL 5039*	10	1
13 Feb 60 ●	RIDE ON A RAINBOW *Fontana TFL 5061*	10	2
10 Dec 60 ●	RHYTHMS AND BALLADS OF BROADWAY *Fontana SET 101*	6	10
17 Jun 61	I'LL BUY YOU A STAR *Fontana TFL 5143*	18	1
16 May 70	RAINDROPS KEEP FALLING ON MY HEAD *CBS 63587*	23	10
3 Apr 71	LOVE STORY *CBS 64334*	27	5
9 Sep 72	FIRST TIME EVER I SAW YOUR FACE *CBS 64930*	40	3
16 Dec 72	MAKE IT EASY ON YOURSELF *CBS 65161*	49	1
8 Mar 75	I'M COMING HOME *CBS 65690*	18	11
5 Apr 75	THE HEART OF A WOMAN *CBS 80533*	39	2
26 Jul 75	WHEN WILL I SEE YOU AGAIN *CBS 80738*	13	10
3 Jul 76	I ONLY HAVE EYES FOR YOU *CBS 81329*	14	12
19 Feb 77	GREATEST HITS VOLUME IV *CBS 86022*	31	5
18 Jun 77 ★	THE JOHNNY MATHIS COLLECTION *CBS 10003*	1	40
17 Dec 77	SWEET SURRENDER *CBS 86036*	55	1
29 Apr 78 ●	YOU LIGHT UP MY LIFE *CBS 86055*	3	19
26 Aug 78	THAT'S WHAT FRIENDS ARE FOR *CBS 86068* [1]	16	11
7 Apr 79	THE BEST DAYS OF MY LIFE *CBS 86080*	38	5
3 Nov 79	MATHIS MAGIC *CBS 86103*	59	4
8 Mar 80 ★	TEARS AND LAUGHTER *CBS 10019*	1	15
12 Jul 80	ALL FOR YOU *CBS 86115*	20	8
19 Sep 81 ●	CELEBRATION *CBS 10028*	9	16
15 May 82	FRIENDS IN LOVE *CBS 85652*	34	7
17 Sep 83 ●	UNFORGETTABLE: A MUSICAL TRIBUTE TO NAT 'KING' COLE *CBS 10042* [2]	5	16
15 Sep 84	A SPECIAL PART OF ME *CBS 25475*	45	3
13 Dec 86	THE HOLLYWOOD MUSICALS *CBS 4502581* [3]	46	8

[1] Johnny Mathis and Deniece Williams [2] Johnny Mathis and Gladys Knight
[1] Johnny Mathis and Deniece Williams [2] Johnny Mathis and Natalie Cole
[3] Johnny Mathis and Henry Mancini

Ivan MATIAS *US, male vocalist (Singles: 1 week)*

		pos	wks
6 Apr 96	SO GOOD (TO COME HOME TO) / I'VE HAD ENOUGH *Arista 74321345072*	69	1

MATT BIANCO *UK, male vocal / instrumental duo (Singles: 65 weeks, Albums: 67 weeks)*

		pos	wks
11 Feb 84	GET OUT OF YOUR LAZY BED *WEA BIANCO 1*	15	8
14 Apr 84	SNEAKING OUT THE BACK DOOR / MATT'S MOOD *WEA YZ 3*	44	7
10 Nov 84	HALF A MINUTE *WEA YZ 26*	23	10
2 Mar 85	MORE THAN I CAN BEAR *WEA YZ 34*	50	7
5 Oct 85	YEH YEH *WEA YZ 46*	13	10
1 Mar 86	JUST CAN'T STAND IT *WEA YZ 62*	66	2
14 Jun 86	DANCING IN THE STREET *WEA YZ 72*	64	3
4 Jun 88	DON'T BLAME IT ON THAT GIRL / WAP-BAM-BOOGIE *WEA YZ 188*	11	13
27 Aug 88	GOOD TIMES *WEA YZ 302*	55	3
4 Feb 89	NERVOUS / WAP-BAM-BOOGIE (re-mix) *WEA YZ 328*	59	2
8 Sep 84	WHOSE SIDE ARE YOU ON *WEA WX 7*	35	39
22 Mar 86	MATT BIANCO *WEA WX 35*	26	13
9 Jul 88	INDIGO *WEA WX 181*	23	13
2 Nov 90	THE BEST OF MATT BIANCO *East West WX 376*	49	2

'Matt's Mood' credited only from 5 May 1984. Act was a UK / Poland, male / female vocal / instrumental group before 1986

Kathy MATTEA *US, female vocalist (Albums: 2 weeks)*

		pos	wks
15 Apr 95	READY FOR THE STORM (FAVOURITE CUTS) *Mercury 5280062*	61	1
8 Feb 97	LOVE TRAVELS *Mercury 5328992*	65	1

Al MATTHEWS *US, male vocalist (Singles: 8 weeks)*

		pos	wks
23 Aug 75	FOOL *CBS 3429*	16	8

Dave MATTHEWS BAND *US, male vocal / instrumental group (Singles: 2 weeks)*

		pos	wks
1 Dec 01	THE SPACE BETWEEN *RCA 74321883192*	35	2

Cerys MATTHEWS *UK, female vocalist (Singles: 8 weeks, Albums: 5 weeks)*

		pos	wks
18 Dec 99	BABY, IT'S COLD OUTSIDE *Gut CDGUT 29* [1]	17	7
2 Aug 03	CAUGHT IN THE MIDDLE *Blano Y Negro NEG 147CD1*	47	1
31 May 03	COCKAHOOP *Blanco Y Negro 2564603062*	30	5

[1] Tom Jones and Cerys Matthews

See also CATATONIA; Tom JONES

John MATTHEWS – *See UNDERCOVER*

MATTHEWS' SOUTHERN COMFORT *UK, male vocal / instrumental group – lead vocalist Ian Matthews (Singles: 18 weeks, Albums: 4 weeks)*

		pos	wks
26 Sep 70 ★	WOODSTOCK *Uni UNS 526*	1	18
25 Jul 70	SECOND SPRING *Uni UNLS 112*	52	4

MATUMBI *UK, male vocal / instrumental group (Singles: 7 weeks)*

		pos	wks
29 Sep 79	POINT OF VIEW (SQUEEZE A LITTLE LOVIN) *Matumbi RIC 101*	35	7

Susan MAUGHAN *UK, female vocalist (Singles: 25 weeks)*

		pos	wks
11 Oct 62 ●	BOBBY'S GIRL *Philips 326544 BF*	3	19
14 Feb 63	HAND A HANDKERCHIEF TO HELEN *Philips 326562 BF*	41	3
9 May 63	SHE'S NEW TO YOU *Philips 326586 BF*	45	3

MAUREEN *UK, female vocalist – Maureen Walsh (Singles: 22 weeks)*

		pos	wks
26 Nov 88 ●	SAY A LITTLE PRAYER *Rhythm King DOOD 3* [1]	10	10
16 Jun 90	THINKING OF YOU *Urban URB 55* [2]	11	9
12 Jan 91	WHERE HAS ALL THE LOVE GONE *Urban URB 65*	51	3

[1] Bomb the Bass featuring Maureen [2] Maureen Walsh

Some copies of 'Thinking of You' were credited simply to Maureen

Paul MAURIAT and his ORCHESTRA *France, orchestra (Singles: 14 weeks)*

		pos	wks
21 Feb 68	LOVE IS BLUE (L'AMOUR EST BLEU) *Philips BF 1637* ▲	12	14

MAVERICKS *US, male vocal / instrumental group – leader Raul Malo (Singles: 23 weeks, Albums: 60 weeks)*

		pos	wks
2 May 98 ●	DANCE THE NIGHT AWAY *MCA Nashville MCSTD 48081*	4	18
26 Sep 98	I'VE GOT THIS FEELING *MCA Nashville MCSTD 48095*	27	4
5 Jun 99	SOMEONE SHOULD TELL HER *MCA Nashville MCSTD 55567*	45	1
11 May 96	MUSIC FOR ALL OCCASIONS *MCA MCD 11344*	56	1
14 Mar 98 ●	TRAMPOLINE *MCA Nashville UMD 80456*	10	48
4 Dec 99	THE BEST OF THE MAVERICKS *Mercury / Universal TV 1701202*	40	9
4 Oct 03	MAVERICKS *Sanctuary SANCD 192*	65	2

MAW – *See MASTERS AT WORK*

MAX LINEN *UK, male production duo (Singles: 1 week)*

		pos	wks
17 Nov 01	THE SOULSHAKER *Global Cuts GC 73CD*	55	1

MAX Q *Australia, male vocal / instrumental duo (Singles: 3 weeks, Albums: 1 week)*

		pos	wks
17 Feb 90	SOMETIMES *Mercury MXQ 2*	53	3
4 Nov 89	MAX Q *Mercury 838942 1*	69	1

See also INXS

MAX WEBSTER *Canada, male vocal / instrumental group (Singles: 3 weeks)*

		pos	wks
19 May 79	PARADISE SKIES *Capitol CL 16079*	43	3

MAXEE *US, female vocalist (Singles: 1 week)* pos/wks

17 Mar 01 **WHEN I LOOK INTO YOUR EYES** *Mercury 5628702* 55 1

MAXIM
UK, male producer / vocalist – Keith Palmer (Singles: 3 weeks) pos/wks

10 Jun 00 **CARMEN QUEASY** *XL Recordings XLS 119CD* 33 2
23 Sep 00 **SCHEMING** *XL Recordings XLS 121CD* 53 1

Sleeve of 'Carmen Queasy' credits 'vocal by Skin' (from Skunk Anansie)

See also PRODIGY

MAXIMA featuring LILY *UK / Spain, male / female vocal / instrumental duo (Singles: 2 weeks)* pos/wks

14 Aug 93 **IBIZA** *Yo! Yo! CDLILY 1* 55 2

MAXTREME *Holland, male production group (Singles: 1 week)* pos/wks

9 Mar 02 **MY HOUSE IS YOUR HOUSE** *Y2K Y2K 028CD* 66 1

MAXWELL *US, male vocalist – Maxwell Menard (Singles: 10 weeks, Albums: 20 weeks)* pos/wks

11 May 96 **...TIL THE COPS COME KNOCKIN'** *Columbia 6631792* 63 1
24 Aug 96 **ASCENSION NO ONE'S GONNA LOVE YOU SO DON'T EVER WONDER** *Columbia 6636265* 39 3
1 Mar 97 **SUMTHIN' SUMTHIN' THE MANTRA** *Columbia 6638642* 27 3
24 May 97 **ASCENSION DON'T EVER WONDER (re-issue)** *Columbia 6645952* 28 3
13 Apr 96 **URBAN HANG SUITE** *Columbia 4836992* 39 10
26 Jul 97 **MTV UNPLUGGED (EP)** *Columbia 4882922* 45 2
4 Jul 98 **EMBRYA** *Columbia 4894202* 11 6
22 Sep 01 **NOW** *Columbia 4974542* ▲ 46 2

MAXX *UK / Sweden / Germany, male / female vocal / instrumental group (Singles: 24 weeks, Albums: 1 week)* pos/wks

21 May 94 ● **GET-A-WAY** *Pulse 8 CDLOSE 59* 4 12
6 Aug 94 ● **NO MORE (I CAN'T STAND IT)** *Pulse 8 CDLOSE 66* 8 8
29 Oct 94 **YOU CAN GET IT** *Pulse 8 CDLOSE 75* 21 3
22 Jul 95 **I CAN MAKE YOU FEEL LIKE** *Pulse 8 CDLOSE 88* 56 1
23 Jul 94 **TO THE MAXXIMUM** *Pulse 8 PULSE 15CD* 66 1

Terry MAXX – *See FUNKSTAR DE LUXE*

Billy MAY and his Orchestra *US, orchestra (Singles: 10 weeks)* pos/wks

27 Apr 56 ● **MAIN TITLE THEME FROM 'MAN WITH THE GOLDEN ARM'** *Capitol CL 14551* 9 10

Brian MAY *UK, male vocalist / instrumentalist – guitar (Singles: 33 weeks, Albums: 23 weeks)* pos/wks

5 Nov 83 **STAR FLEET** *EMI 5436* [1] 65 3
7 Dec 91 ● **DRIVEN BY YOU** *Parlophone R 6304* 6 9
5 Sep 92 ● **TOO MUCH LOVE WILL KILL YOU** *Parlophone R 6320* 5 9
17 Oct 92 **WE ARE THE CHAMPIONS** *PolyGram TV PO 229* [2] 66 1
21 Nov 92 **BACK TO THE LIGHT** *Parlophone R 6329* 19 4
19 Jun 93 **RESURRECTION** *Parlophone CDRS 6351* [3] 23 3
18 Dec 93 **LAST HORIZON** *Parlophone CDR 6371* 51 2
6 Jun 98 **THE BUSINESS** *Parlophone CDR 6498* 51 1
12 Sep 98 **WHY DON'T WE TRY AGAIN** *Parlophone CDR 6504* 44 1
12 Nov 83 **STAR FLEET PROJECT** *EMI SFLT 1078061* [1] 35 4
10 Oct 92 ● **BACK TO THE LIGHT** *Parlophone CDPCSD 123* 6 14
19 Feb 94 **LIVE AT THE BRIXTON ACADEMY** *Parlophone CDPCSD 150* [2] 20 3
13 Jun 98 **ANOTHER WORLD** *Parlophone 4949732* 23 2

[1] Brian May and Friends [2] Hank Marvin featuring Brian May [3] Brian May with Cozy Powell [1] Brian May and Friends [2] Brian May Band

See also QUEEN

Lisa MAY *UK, female vocalist (Singles: 2 weeks)* pos/wks

15 Jul 95 **WISHING ON A STAR** *Urban Gorilla UG 3CD* [1] 61 1
14 Sep 96 **THE CURSE OF VOODOO RAY** *Fontana VOOCD 1* 64 1

[1] 88.3 featuring Lisa MAY

Mary MAY *UK, female vocalist (Singles: 1 week)* pos/wks

27 Feb 64 **ANYONE WHO HAD A HEART** *Fontana TF 440* 49 1

Shernette MAY *UK, female vocalist (Singles: 1 week)* pos/wks

6 Jun 98 **ALL THE MAN THAT I NEED** *Virgin VSCDT 1691* 50 1

Simon MAY
UK, male vocalist / conductor (Singles: 21 weeks) pos/wks

9 Oct 76 ● **THE SUMMER OF MY LIFE** *Pye 7N 45627* 7 8
21 May 77 **WE'LL GATHER LILACS – ALL MY LOVING (MEDLEY) (re)** *Pye 7N 45688* 49 2
26 Oct 85 **HOWARD'S WAY** *BBC RESL 174* [1] 21 11
27 Sep 86 **SIMON'S WAY** *BBC REB 594* [1] 59 7

[1] Simon May Orchestra [1] Simon May Orchestra

See also Anita DOBSON; Marti WEBB

MAYA – *See TAMPERER featuring MAYA*

John MAYALL
UK, male vocalist / instrumentalist – guitar (Albums: 115 weeks) pos/wks

30 Jul 66 ● **BLUES BREAKERS** *Decca LK 4804* [1] 6 17
4 Mar 67 ● **A HARD ROAD** *Decca SKL 4853* 10 19
23 Sep 67 ● **CRUSADE** *Decca SKL 4890* 8 14
25 Nov 67 **THE BLUES ALONE** *Ace Of Clubs SCL 1243* 24 5
16 Mar 68 **DIARY OF A BAND VOLUME 1** *Decca SKL 4918* 27 9
16 Mar 68 **DIARY OF A BAND VOLUME 2** *Decca SKL 4919* 28 5
20 Jul 68 ● **BARE WIRES** *Decca SKL 4945* 3 17
18 Jan 69 **BLUES FROM LAUREL CANYON** *Decca SKL 4972* 33 3
23 Aug 69 **LOOKING BACK** *Decca SKL 5010* 14 7
15 Nov 69 **THE TURNING POINT** *Polydor 583571* 11 7
11 Apr 70 ● **EMPTY ROOMS** *Polydor 583580* 9 8
12 Dec 70 **U.S.A. UNION** *Polydor 2425020* 50 1
26 Jun 71 **BACK TO THE ROOTS** *Polydor 2657005* 31 2
17 Apr 93 **WAKE UP CALL** *Silvertone ORECD 527* 61 1

[1] John Mayall and Eric Clapton

John MAYER *US, male vocalist (Singles: 1 week, Albums: 1 week)* pos/wks

23 Aug 03 **NO SUCH THING** *Columbia 6732322* 42 1
25 Oct 03 **HEAVIER THINGS** *Columbia 5134722* ▲ 74 1

Curtis MAYFIELD *US, male vocalist / instrumentalist – guitar, d. 26 Dec 1999 (Singles: 20 weeks, Albums: 5 weeks)* pos/wks

31 Jul 71 **MOVE ON UP** *Buddah 2011 080* 12 10
2 Dec 78 **NO GOODBYES** *Atlantic LV 1* 65 3
30 May 87 **(CELEBRATE) THE DAY AFTER YOU** *RCA MONK 6* [1] 52 2
29 Sep 90 **SUPERFLY 1990** *Capitol CL 586* [2] 48 3
16 Jun 01 **ASTOUNDED** *Virgin VUSCD 194* [3] 40 2
20 Mar 71 **CURTIS** *Buddah 2318 015* 30 1
31 Mar 73 **SUPERFLY** *Buddah 2318 065* ▲ 26 2
15 Feb 97 **NEW WORLD ORDER** *Warner Bros. 9362463482* 44 2

[1] Blow Monkeys with Curtis Mayfield [2] Curtis Mayfield and Ice-T [3] Bran Van 3000 featuring Curtis Mayfield

MAYTALS
Jamaica, male vocal / instrumental group (Singles: 4 weeks) pos/wks

25 Apr 70 **MONKEY MAN (re)** *Trojan TR 7711* 47 4

MAYTE *US, female vocalist (Singles: 1 week)* pos/wks

18 Nov 95 **IF EYE LOVE U 2 NIGHT** *NPG 0061635* 67 1

MAZE featuring Frankie BEVERLY *US, male vocal / instrumental group (Singles: 14 weeks, Albums: 25 weeks)* pos/wks

20 Jul 85 **TOO MANY GAMES** *Capitol CL 363* 36 7
23 Aug 86 **I WANNA BE WITH YOU** *Capitol CL 421* 55 3
27 May 89 **JOY AND PAIN** *Capitol CL 531* [1] 57 4
7 May 83 **WE ARE ONE** *Capitol EST 12262* 38 6
9 Mar 85 **CAN'T STOP THE LOVE** *Capitol MAZE 1* 41 12

		pos	wks
27 Sep 86	**LIVE IN LOS ANGELES** *Capitol ESTSP 24*	70	2
16 Sep 89	**SILKY SOUL** *Warner Bros. WX 301*	43	5

[1] Maze

Kym MAZELLE

US, female vocalist – Kimberley Grigsby (Singles: 66 weeks)

		pos	wks
12 Nov 88	**USELESS (I DON'T NEED YOU NOW)** *Syncopate SY 18*	53	3
14 Jan 89 ●	**WAIT** *RCA PB 42595* [1]	7	10
25 Mar 89	**GOT TO GET YOU BACK** *Syncopate SY 25*	29	4
7 Oct 89	**LOVE STRAIN** *Syncopate SY 30*	52	3
20 Jan 90	**WAS THAT ALL IT WAS** *Syncopate SY 32*	33	6
26 May 90	**USELESS (I DON'T NEED YOU NOW) (re-mix)** *Syncopate SY 36*	48	2
24 Nov 90	**MISSING YOU** *Ten TEN 345* [2]	22	7
25 May 91	**NO ONE CAN LOVE YOU MORE THAN ME** *Parlophone R 6287*	62	2
26 Dec 92	**LOVE ME THE RIGHT WAY** *Arista 74321128097* [3]	22	10
11 Jun 94	**NO MORE TEARS (ENOUGH IS ENOUGH)** *Bell 74321209032* [4]	13	7
8 Oct 94	**GIMME ALL YOUR LOVIN'** *Bell 74321231322* [5]	22	3
23 Dec 95	**SEARCHING FOR THE GOLDEN EYE** *Eternal WEA 027CD* [6]	40	3
28 Sep 96	**LOVE ME THE RIGHT WAY (re-mix)** *Logic 74321404442* [3]	55	1
16 Aug 97	**YOUNG HEARTS RUN FREE** *EMI CDEM 488*	20	4
19 Feb 00	**TRULY** *Island Blue PFACD 4* [7]	55	1

[1] Robert Howard and Kym Mazelle [2] Soul II Soul featuring Kym Mazelle [3] Rapination and Kym Mazelle [4] Kym Mazelle and Jocelyn Brown [5] Jocelyn Brown and Kym Mazelle [6] Motiv 8 and Kym Mazelle [7] Peshay featuring Kym Mazelle

MAZZY STAR *US, male / female vocal / instrumental group (Singles: 3 weeks, Albums: 2 weeks)*

		pos	wks
27 Aug 94	**FADE INTO YOU** *Capitol CDCL 720*	48	1
2 Nov 96	**FLOWERS IN DECEMBER** *Capitol CDCL 781*	40	2
9 Oct 93	**SO TONIGHT THAT I MIGHT SEE** *Capitol CDEST 2206*	68	1
16 Nov 96	**AMONG MY SWAN** *Capitol CDEST 2288*	57	1

MC ALISTAIR – *See DREEM TEEM*

MC CHICKABOO – *See Timo MAAS*

MC DUKE *UK, male rapper (Singles: 1 week)*

		pos	wks
11 Mar 89	**I'M RIFFIN (ENGLISH RASTA)** *Music of Life 7NOTE 25*	75	1

MC ERIC – *See TECHNOTRONIC*

MC FIXX IT – *See ANTICAPPELLA*

MC HAMMER *US, male rapper – Stanley Burrell (Singles: 68 weeks, Albums: 67 weeks)*

		pos	wks
9 Jun 90 ●	**U CAN'T TOUCH THIS** *Capitol CL 578*	3	16
6 Oct 90 ●	**HAVE YOU SEEN HER** *Capitol CL 590*	8	7
8 Dec 90 ●	**PRAY** *Capitol CL 599*	8	10
23 Feb 91	**HERE COMES THE HAMMER** *Capitol CL 610*	15	5
1 Jun 91	**YO!! SWEETNESS** *Capitol CL 616*	16	5
20 Jul 91	**(HAMMER HAMMER) THEY PUT ME IN THE MIX** *Capitol CL 607*	20	4
26 Oct 91	**2 LEGIT 2 QUIT** *Capitol CL 636* [1]	60	2
21 Dec 91 ●	**ADDAMS GROOVE** *Capitol CL 642* [1]	4	9
21 Mar 92	**DO NOT PASS ME BY** *Capitol CL 650* [1]	14	6
12 Mar 94	**IT'S ALL GOOD** *RCA 74321188612* [1]	52	2
13 Aug 94	**DON'T STOP** *RCA 74321220012* [1]	72	1
3 Jun 95	**STRAIGHT TO MY FEET** *Priority PTYCD 102* [2]	57	1
28 Jul 90 ●	**PLEASE HAMMER DON'T HURT 'EM** *Capitol EST 2120* ▲	8	59
6 Apr 91	**LET'S GET IT STARTED** *Capitol EST 2140*	46	2
2 Nov 91	**TOO LEGIT TO QUIT** *Capitol ESTP 26* [1]	41	6

[1] Hammer [2] Hammer featuring Deion Saunders [1] Hammer

MC IMAGE – *See Jhay PALMER featuring MC IMAGE*

MC KIE – *See TEEBONE featuring MC KIE and MC SPARKS*

MC LETHAL *UK, male producer (Singles: 1 week)*

		pos	wks
14 Nov 92	**THE RAVE DIGGER** *Network NWKT 60*	66	1

MC LYTE *US, female rapper – Lana Moorer (Singles: 16 weeks)*

		pos	wks
15 Jan 94	**RUFFNECK** *Atlantic A 8336CD*	67	1
29 Jun 96	**KEEP ON KEEPIN' ON** *East West A 4287CD* [1]	39	2
18 Jan 97	**COLD ROCK A PARTY** *East West A 3975CD*	15	4
19 Apr 97	**KEEP ON KEEPIN' ON (re-issue)** *East West A 3950CD1* [1]	27	2
5 Sep 98	**I CAN'T MAKE A MISTAKE** *Elektra E 3813CD*	46	1
19 Dec 98	**IT'S ALL YOURS** *East West E 3789CD* [2]	36	4
24 Jun 00	**JAMMIN'** *Tuff Gong TGXCD 9* [3]	42	2

[1] MC Lyte featuring Xscape [2] MC Lyte featuring Gina Thompson [3] Bob Marley featuring MC Lyte

MC MALIBU – *See ROUND SOUND presents ONYX STONE & MC MALIBU*

MC MARIO – *See AMBASSADORS OF FUNK featuring MC MARIO*

MC MIKEE FREEDOM – *See NOMAD*

MC MIKER 'G' and Deejay SVEN *Holland, male vocal / instrumental rap duo – Lucien Witteveen and Sven Van Veen (Singles: 7 weeks)*

		pos	wks
6 Sep 86 ●	**HOLIDAY RAP** *Debut DEBT 3008*	6	7

MC NEAT – *See DJ LUCK & MC NEAT; CORRUPTED CRU featuring MC NEAT*

MC NOISE – *See LOVE INCORPORATED featuring MC NOISE*

MC NUMBER 6 – *See FAB*

MC ONYX STONE – *See LONYO*

MC PARKER – *See FAB*

MC RB – *See SUNSHIP featuring MCRB; JUST 4 JOKES featuring MC RB*

MC SAR – *See REAL McCOY*

MC SHURAKANO – *See KID CREME*

MC SKAT KAT and the STRAY MOB

US, male cartoon feline rap / vocal group (Singles: 2 weeks)

		pos	wks
9 Nov 91	**SKAT STRUT** *Virgin America VUS 51*	64	2

MC SOLAAR – *See Missy 'Misdemeanor' ELLIOTT; URBAN SPECIES*

MC SPARKS – *See TEEBONE featuring MC KIE and MC SPARKS*

MC SPY-D + FRIENDS

UK, male / female vocal / instrumental group (Singles: 2 weeks)

		pos	wks
11 Mar 95	**THE AMAZING SPIDER-MAN** *Parlophone CDR 6404*	37	2

MC STYLES – *See Scott GARCIA featuring MC STYLES*

MC TUNES *UK, male rapper – Nicholas Lockett (Singles: 19 weeks, Albums: 3 weeks)*

		pos	wks
2 Jun 90 ●	**THE ONLY RHYME THAT BITES** *ZTT ZANG 3* [1]	10	10
15 Sep 90	**TUNES SPLITS THE ATOM** *ZTT ZANG 6* [1]	18	7
1 Dec 90	**PRIMARY RHYMING** *ZTT ZANG 10*	67	1
6 Mar 99	**THE ONLY RHYME THAT BITES (re-mix)** *ZTT ZTT 125CD* [1]	53	1
13 Oct 90	**THE NORTH AT ITS HEIGHTS** *ZTT ZTT 3*	26	3

[1] MC Tunes versus 808 State

MC VIPER – *See REFLEX featuring MC VIPER*

MC WILDSKI *UK, male rapper (Singles: 10 weeks)*

		pos	wks
8 Jul 89	**BLAME IT ON THE BASSLINE** *Go.Beat GOD 33* [1]	29	6
3 Mar 90	**WARRIOR** *Arista 112956*	49	4

[1] Norman Cook featuring MC Wildski

'Blame It on the Bassline' was listed with 'Won't Talk About It' by Norman Cook featuring Billy Bragg

ME AND YOU featuring WE THE PEOPLE BAND *Jamaica / UK, male / female vocal / instrumental group (Singles: 9 weeks)* pos/wks

28 Jul 79	**YOU NEVER KNOW WHAT YOU'VE GOT** *Laser LAS 8*	31	9

ME ME ME *UK, male vocal / instrumental group (Singles: 4 weeks)* pos/wks

17 Aug 96	**HANGING AROUND** *Indolent DUFF 005CD*	19	4

See also FAT LES

Abigail MEAD and Nigel GOULDING *UK / US, female / male producers – Vivian Kubrick and Nigel Goulding (Singles: 10 weeks)* pos/wks

26 Sep 87 ●	**FULL METAL JACKET (I WANNA BE YOUR DRILL INSTRUCTOR)** *Warner Bros. W 8187*	2	10

Vaughn MEADER *US, male comedian (Albums: 8 weeks)* pos/wks

29 Dec 62	**THE FIRST FAMILY** *London HAA 8048* ▲	12	8

MEAT BEAT MANIFESTO *UK, male production duo (Singles: 1 week)* pos/wks

20 Feb 93	**MINDSTREAM** *Play It Again Sam BIAS 232CD*	55	1

MEAT LOAF (23 Top 500)

Larger-than-life vocalist / actor, b. Marvin Lee Aday, 27 Sep 1948, Dallas, US. His collaborations with producer / songwriter Jim Steinman resulted in some of rock's finest recordings. His album 'Bat Out of Hell' sold more than 25 million copies and spent almost 10 years in total in the UK chart. Best-selling single 'I'd Do Anything for Love (But I Won't Do That)' 761,200 (Singles: 152 weeks, Albums: 784 weeks) pos/wks

20 May 78	**YOU TOOK THE WORDS RIGHT OUT OF MY MOUTH** *Epic EPC 5980*	33	8
19 Aug 78	**TWO OUT OF THREE AIN'T BAD** *Epic EPC 6281*	32	8
10 Feb 79	**BAT OUT OF HELL** *Epic EPC 7018*	15	7
26 Sep 81	**I'M GONNA LOVE HER FOR BOTH OF US** *Epic EPCA 1580*	62	3
28 Nov 81 ●	**DEAD RINGER FOR LOVE** *Epic EPCA 1697*	5	17
28 May 83	**IF YOU REALLY WANT TO** *Epic A 3357*	59	2
24 Sep 83	**MIDNIGHT AT THE LOST AND FOUND** *Epic A 3748*	17	8
14 Jan 84	**RAZOR'S EDGE** *Epic A 4080*	41	3
6 Oct 84	**MODERN GIRL** *Arista ARIST 585*	17	9
22 Dec 84	**NOWHERE FAST** *Arista ARIST 600*	67	4
23 Mar 85	**PIECE OF THE ACTION** *Arista ARIST 603*	47	5
30 Aug 86	**ROCK 'N' ROLL MERCENARIES** *Arista ARIST 666* [1]	31	6
22 Jun 91	**DEAD RINGER FOR LOVE (re-issue)** *Epic 6569827*	53	2
27 Jun 92	**TWO OUT OF THREE AIN'T BAD (re-issue)** *Epic 6574917*	69	1
9 Oct 93 ★	**I'D DO ANYTHING FOR LOVE (BUT I WON'T DO THAT)** *Virgin VSCDT 1443* ▲	1	19
18 Dec 93 ●	**BAT OUT OF HELL (re-issue)** *Epic 6600062*	8	9
19 Feb 94	**ROCK AND ROLL DREAMS COME THROUGH** *Virgin VSCDT 1479*	11	7
7 May 94	**OBJECTS IN THE REAR VIEW MIRROR MAY APPEAR CLOSER THAN THEY ARE** *Virgin VSCDT 1492*	26	4
28 Oct 95 ●	**I'D LIE FOR YOU (AND THAT'S THE TRUTH)** *Virgin VSCDT 1563*	2	11
27 Jan 96 ●	**NOT A DRY EYE IN THE HOUSE** *Virgin VSCDT 1567*	7	6
27 Apr 96	**RUNNIN' FOR THE RED LIGHT (I GOTTA LIFE)** *Virgin VSCDX 1582*	21	3
17 Apr 99	**IS NOTHING SACRED** *Virgin VSCDT 1734* [2]	15	4
26 Apr 03	**COULDN'T HAVE SAID IT BETTER** *Mercury 0656842*	31	2
6 Dec 03	**MAN OF STEEL** *Mercury 9815114*	21	4+
11 Mar 78 ●	**BAT OUT OF HELL** *Cleveland International EPC 82419*	9	474
12 Sep 81 ★	**DEAD RINGER** *Epic EPC 83645* ■	1	46
7 May 83 ●	**MIDNIGHT AT THE LOST AND FOUND** *Epic EPC 25243*	7	23
10 Nov 84 ●	**BAD ATTITUDE** *Arista 206 619*	8	16
26 Jan 85 ●	**HITS OUT OF HELL** *Epic EPC 26156*	2	80
11 Oct 86	**BLIND BEFORE I STOP** *Arista 207 741*	28	6
7 Nov 87	**LIVE AT WEMBLEY** *RCA 208599*	60	2
18 Sep 93 ★	**BAT OUT OF HELL II – BACK INTO HELL** *Virgin CDV 2710* ■ ▲	1	59
22 Oct 94	**ALIVE IN HELL** *Pure Music PMCD 7002*	33	4
11 Nov 95 ●	**WELCOME TO THE NEIGHBOURHOOD** *Virgin CDV 2799*	3	27
14 Nov 98	**THE VERY BEST OF MEAT LOAF** *Virgin / Sony TV CDV 2868*	14	33+
3 May 02 ●	**COULDN'T HAVE SAID IT BETTER** *Mercury 0761192*	4	14

[1] Meat Loaf featuring John Parr [2] Meat Loaf featuring Patti Russo

'Dead Ringer for Love' features Cher as uncredited co-vocalist. 'I'd Do Anything for Love (But I Won't Do That) features uncredited vocals by Lorraine Crosby (aka Mrs Loud) 'Hits Out of Hell' changed catalogue number to 4504471 during its chart run

MECHANICS – *See MIKE and the MECHANICS*

MECO *US, orchestra – leader Meco Monardo (Singles: 9 weeks)* pos/wks

1 Oct 77 ●	**STAR WARS THEME – CANTINA BAND** *RCA XB 1028* ▲	7	9

Glenn MEDEIROS *US, male vocalist (Singles: 26 weeks, Albums: 2 weeks)* pos/wks

18 Jun 88 ★	**NOTHING'S GONNA CHANGE MY LOVE FOR YOU** *London LON 184*	1	13
3 Sep 88	**LONG AND LASTING LOVE (ONCE IN A LIFETIME)** *London LON 202*	42	4
30 Jun 90	**SHE AIN'T WORTH IT** *London LON 265* [1] ▲	12	9
8 Oct 88	**NOT ME** *London LONLP 68*	63	2

[1] Glenn Medeiros featuring Bobby Brown

Paul MEDFORD – *See Letitia DEAN and Paul MEDFORD*

MEDIAEVAL BAEBES *UK, female vocal group (Albums: 7 weeks)* pos/wks

29 Nov 97	**SALVA NOS** *Venture CDVE 935*	62	6
31 Oct 98	**WORLDES BLYSSE** *Venture CDVE 941*	73	1

MEDICINE HEAD *UK, male vocal / instrumental duo – John Fiddler and Peter Hope Evans (Singles: 37 weeks)* pos/wks

26 Jun 71	**(AND THE) PICTURES IN THE SKY** *Dandelion DAN 7003*	22	8
5 May 73 ●	**ONE AND ONE IS ONE** *Polydor 2001 432*	3	13
4 Aug 73	**RISING SUN** *Polydor 2058 389*	11	9
9 Feb 74	**SLIP AND SLIDE** *Polydor 2058 436*	22	7

MEDICINE SHOW – *See DR HOOK*

MEDICS – *See DOCTOR and the MEDICS*

Bill MEDLEY *US, male vocalist (Singles: 29 weeks)* pos/wks

31 Oct 87 ●	**(I'VE HAD) THE TIME OF MY LIFE (re)** *RCA PB 49625* [1] ▲	6	23
27 Aug 88	**HE AIN'T HEAVY, HE'S MY BROTHER** *Scotti Brothers PO 10*	25	6

[1] Bill Medley and Jennifer Warnes

'(I've Had) The Time of My Life' re-entered in Dec 1990 peaking at No.8

See also RIGHTEOUS BROTHERS

MEDWAY *US, male producer – Jesse Skeens (Singles: 2 weeks)* pos/wks

29 Apr 00	**FAT BASTARD (EP)** *Hooj Choons HOOJ 92CD*	69	1
10 Mar 01	**RELEASE** *Hooj Choons HOOJ 105*	67	1

Tracks on Fat Bastard (EP): Release / Flanker / Faith

Michael MEDWIN, Bernard BRESSLAW, Alfie BASS and Leslie FYSON *UK, male actors / vocalists (Singles: 9 weeks)* pos/wks

30 May 58 ●	**THE SIGNATURE TUNE OF 'THE ARMY GAME'** *HMV POP 490*	5	9

See also Bernard BRESSLAW

MEECHIE *US, female vocalist (Singles: 1 week)* pos/wks

2 Sep 95	**YOU BRING ME JOY** *Vibe MCSTD 2069*	74	1

Tony MEEHAN *UK, male instrumental group – Tony Meehan – drums (Singles: 4 weeks)* pos/wks

16 Jan 64	**SONG OF MEXICO** *Decca F 11801*	39	4

See also Jet HARRIS and Tony MEEHAN; SHADOWS

MEEKER *UK, female vocal / production duo (Singles: 1 week)* pos/wks

			pos	wks
26 Feb 00		**SAVE ME** *Underwater H20 009 CD*	60	1

MEGA CITY FOUR *UK, male vocal / instrumental group (Singles: 7 weeks, Albums: 3 weeks)* pos/wks

			pos	wks
19 Oct 91		**WORDS THAT SAY** *Big Life MEGA 2*	66	1
8 Feb 92		**STOP (EP)** *Big Life MEGA 3*	36	2
16 May 92		**SHIVERING SAND** *Big Life MEGA 4*	35	2
1 May 93		**IRON SKY** *Big Life MEGAD 5*	48	1
17 Jul 93		**WALLFLOWER** *Big Life MEGAD 6*	69	1
17 Jun 89		TRANZOPHOBIA *Decoy DYL 3*	67	1
7 Mar 92		SEBASTOPOL ROAD *Big Life MEGCD 1*	41	1
22 May 93		MAGIC BULLETS *Big Life MEGCD 3*	57	1

Tracks on Stop (EP): Stop / Desert Song / Back to Zero / Overlap

MEGABASS – *See VARIOUS ARTISTS (MONTAGES)*

MEGADETH *US, male vocal / instrumental group (Singles: 32 weeks, Albums: 26 weeks)* pos/wks

			pos	wks
19 Dec 87		**WAKE UP DEAD** *Capitol CL 476*	65	2
27 Feb 88		**ANARCHY IN THE UK** *Capitol CL 480*	45	3
21 May 88		**MARY JANE** *Capitol CL 489*	46	2
13 Jan 90		**NO MORE MR NICE GUY** *SBK SBK 4*	13	6
29 Sep 90		**HOLY WARS . . . THE PUNISHMENT DUE** *Capitol CLP 588*	24	3
16 Mar 91		**HANGAR 18** *Capitol CLS 604*	26	4
27 Jun 92		**SYMPHONY OF DESTRUCTION** *Capitol CLS 662*	15	3
24 Oct 92		**SKIN O' MY TEETH** *Capitol CLP 669*	13	3
29 May 93		**SWEATING BULLETS** *Capitol CDCL 682*	26	3
7 Jan 95		**TRAIN OF CONSEQUENCES** *Capitol CDCL 730*	22	3
26 Mar 88		SO FAR SO GOOD ... SO WHAT! *Capitol EST 2053*	18	5
6 Oct 90	●	RUST IN PEACE *Capitol EST 2132*	8	4
18 Jul 92	●	COUNTDOWN TO EXTINCTION *Capitol CDESTU 2175*	5	8
5 Nov 94	●	YOUTHANASIA / HIDDEN TREASURE *Capitol CDEST 2244*	6	5
19 Jul 97		CRYPTIC WRITINGS *Capitol CDEST 2297*	38	1
18 Sep 99		RISK *Capitol 4991340*	29	2
26 May 01		THE WORLD NEEDS A HERO *Metal Is MISCD 006*	45	1

From 25 Mar 95 'Youthanasia' was listed with a bonus album 'Hidden Treasure'

MEGAMAN – *See OXIDE & NEUTRINO*

MEHTA – *See José CARRERAS*

Dieter MEIER – *See X-PRESS 2; YELLO*

MEJA *Sweden, female vocalist – Meja Beckman (Singles: 14 weeks)* pos/wks

			pos	wks
24 Oct 98		**ALL 'BOUT THE MONEY** *Columbia 6665662*	12	5
29 Apr 00	●	**PRIVATE EMOTION** *Columbia 6692692* [1]	9	9

[1] Ricky Martin featuring Meja

MEKKA *UK, male producer – Jake Williams (Singles: 1 week)* pos/wks

			pos	wks
24 Mar 01		**DIAMOND BACK** *Perfecto PERF 12CDS*	67	1

MEKON featuring Roxanne SHANTE *UK, male producer – John Gosling and US, female rapper (Singles: 1 week)* pos/wks

			pos	wks
23 Sep 00		**WHAT'S GOING ON** *Wall of Sound WALD 064*	43	1

Melle MEL – *See GRANDMASTER FLASH and the FURIOUS FIVE; GRANDMASTER MELLE MEL*

MEL and KIM *UK, female vocal duo – Mel Appleby, d.18 Jan 1990, and Kim Appleby (Singles: 51 weeks, Albums: 25 weeks)* pos/wks

			pos	wks
20 Sep 86	●	**SHOWING OUT (GET FRESH AT THE WEEKEND)** *Supreme SUPE 107*	3	19
7 Mar 87	★	**RESPECTABLE** *Supreme SUPE 111*	1	15
11 Jul 87	●	**F.L.M.** *Supreme SUPE 113*	7	10
27 Feb 88	●	**THAT'S THE WAY IT IS** *Supreme SUPE 117*	10	7
25 Apr 87	●	F.L.M. *Supreme SU 2*	3	25

See also Kim APPLEBY

MEL and KIM – *See Mel SMITH; Kim WILDE*

George MELACHRINO ORCHESTRA *UK, orchestra, leader d. 18 Jun 1965 (Singles: 9 weeks)* pos/wks

			pos	wks
12 Oct 56		**AUTUMN CONCERTO** *HMV B 10958*	18	9

MELANIE *US, female vocalist / instrumentalist – guitar – Melanie Safka (Singles: 35 weeks, Albums: 66 weeks)* pos/wks

			pos	wks
26 Sep 70	●	**RUBY TUESDAY (re)** *Buddah 2011 038*	9	15
16 Jan 71		**WHAT HAVE THEY DONE TO MY SONG MA** *Buddah 2011038*	39	1
1 Jan 72	●	**BRAND NEW KEY** *Buddah 2011 105* ▲	4	12
16 Feb 74		**WILL YOU LOVE ME TOMORROW** *Neighbourhood NBH 9*	37	5
24 Sep 83		**EVERY BREATH OF THE WAY** *Neighbourhood HOOD NB1*	70	2
19 Sep 70	●	CANDLES IN THE RAIN *Buddah 2318009*	5	31
16 Jan 71		LEFTOVER WINE *Buddah 2318011*	22	4
29 May 71	●	THE GOOD BOOK *Buddah 2322 001*	9	9
8 Jan 72		GATHER ME *Buddah 2322 002*	14	14
1 Apr 72		GARDEN IN THE CITY *Buddah 2318 054*	19	6
7 Oct 72		THE FOUR SIDES OF MELANIE *Buddah 2659 013*	23	2

MELBOURNE SYMPHONY ORCHESTRA – *See Elton JOHN*

MELKY SEDECK *US, male / female vocal / instrumental duo – Melky and Sedeck Jean (Singles: 9 weeks)* pos/wks

			pos	wks
8 May 99		**RAW** *MCA MCSTD 48107*	50	1
16 Sep 00	●	**IT DOESN'T MATTER** *Columbia 6697782* [1]	3	8

[1] Wyclef Jean featuring The Rock and Melky Sedeck

John Cougar MELLENCAMP *US, male vocalist / instrumentalist – guitar (Singles: 18 weeks, Albums: 31 weeks)* pos/wks

			pos	wks
23 Oct 82		**JACK AND DIANE** *Riva RIVA 37* [1] ▲	25	8
1 Feb 86		**SMALL TOWN** *Riva JCM 5*	53	4
10 May 86		**R.O.C.K. IN THE USA** *Riva JCM 6*	67	3
3 Sep 94		**WILD NIGHT** *Mercury MERCD 409* [2]	34	3
6 Nov 82		AMERICAN FOOL *Riva RVLP 16* [1] ▲	37	6
3 Mar 84		UH-HUH *Riva RIVL 1*	92	1
3 Oct 87		THE LONESOME JUBILEE *Mercury MERH 109*	31	12
27 May 89		BIG DADDY *Mercury MERH 838220 1*	25	4
19 Oct 91		WHENEVER WE WANTED *Mercury 5101511*	39	2
18 Sep 93		HUMAN WHEELS *Mercury 5180882*	37	2
17 Jan 98		THE BEST THAT I COULD DO *PolyGram TV 5367382* [2]	25	4

[1] John Cougar [2] John Mellencamp featuring Me'Shell Ndegeocello [1] John Cougar [2] John Mellencamp

MELLOMEN – *See Rosemary CLOONEY; Doris DAY; Frankie LAINE*

Will MELLOR *UK, male actor / vocalist (Singles: 9 weeks)* pos/wks

			pos	wks
28 Feb 98	●	**WHEN I NEED YOU** *Unity UNITY 017RCD*	5	6
27 Jun 98		**NO MATTER WHAT I DO** *Jive 0540012*	23	3

MELLOW TRAX *Germany, male producer – Christian Schwarnweber (Singles: 2 weeks)* pos/wks

			pos	wks
14 Oct 00		**OUTTA SPACE** *Substance SUBS 3CDS*	41	2

MELODIANS *Jamaica, male vocal / instrumental group (Singles: 1 week)* pos/wks

			pos	wks
10 Jan 70		**SWEET SENSATION** *Trojan TR 695*	41	1

MELODY MAKERS – *See Ziggy MARLEY and the MELODY MAKERS*

MELT featuring LITTLE MS MARCIE *UK, male producer – Matt Darey – and female vocalist (Singles: 1 week)* pos/wks

			pos	wks
8 Apr 00		**HARD HOUSE MUSIC** *WEA WEA 257CD*	59	1

See also LOST TRIBE; Matt DAREY; SUNBURST; MDM

MELTDOWN *UK / US, male instrumental / production duo (Singles: 1 week)* pos/wks

			pos	wks
27 Apr 96		**MY LIFE IS IN YOUR HANDS** *Sony S3 DANU 7CD*	44	1

STAGE MUSICALS

A complete chronological listing of all the charting stage recordings, including the music from Broadway, the West End, opera and military parades. The majority of these albums appear in the main official charts. Those that appear only in the compilation charts are marked *

CHART ENTRY DATE / **ALBUM TITLE** / LABEL / **PEAK POSITION / WEEKS ON CHART**

4 Aug 1956 **SALAD DAYS (LONDON) –** Oriole **5 1**
10 May 1958 **MY FAIR LADY (BROADWAY)** Philips **2 129**
24 Jan 1959 **WEST SIDE STORY (BROADWAY)** Philips **3 27**
26 Mar 1960 **FINGS AIN'T WOT THEY USED TO BE (LONDON)** Decca **5 11**
26 Mar 1960 **AT THE DROP OF A HAT (LONDON)** Parlophone **9 1**
2 Apr 1960 **FLOWER DRUM SONG (BROADWAY)** Philips **2 27**
7 May 1960 **FOLLOW THAT GIRL (LONDON)** HMV **5 9**
21 May 1960 **MOST HAPPY FELLA (BROADWAY)** Philips **6 13**
21 May 1960 **MAKE ME AN OFFER (LONDON)** HMV **18 1**
28 May 1960 **FLOWER DRUM SONG (LONDON)** HMV **10 3**
25 Jun 1960 **SHOWBOAT (STUDIO RECORDING)** HMV **12 1**
9 Jul 1960 **MOST HAPPY FELLA (LONDON)** HMV **19 1**
30 Jul 1960 **WEST SIDE STORY (BROADWAY)** Philips **14 1**
10 Sep 1960 **OLIVER! (LONDON)** Decca **4 91**
11 Mar 1961 **KING KONG (SOUTH AFRICA)** Decca **12 8**
6 May 1961 **MUSIC MAN (LONDON)** JMH **8 13**
24 Jun 1961 **THE SOUND OF MUSIC (BROADWAY)** Philips **4 19**
22 Jul 1961 **BEYOND THE FRINGE (LONDON)** Parlophone **13 17**
22 Jul 1961 **BYE BYE BIRDIE (LONDON)** Philips **17 3**
29 Jul 1961 **THE SOUND OF MUSIC (LONDON)** HMV **4 68**
9 Sep 1961 **STOP THE WORLD – I WANT TO GET OFF (LONDON)** Decca **8 14**
14 Jul 1962 **BLITZ (LONDON)** HMV **7 21**
18 May 1963 **HALF A SIXPENCE (LONDON)** Decca **20 2**
3 Aug 1963 **PICKWICK (LONDON)** Philips **12 10**
4 Jan 1964 **MY FAIR LADY (BROADWAY)** CBS **19 1**
22 Feb 1964 **AT THE DROP OF ANOTHER HAT (LONDON)** Parlophone **12 11**
3 Oct 1964 **CAMELOT (BROADWAY)** CBS **10 12**
16 Jan 1965 **CAMELOT (LONDON)** HMV **19 1**
11 Mar 1967 **FIDDLER ON THE ROOF (LONDON)** CBS **4 50**
28 Dec 1968 **HAIR (LONDON)** Polydor **3 94**
30 Aug 1969 **THE WORLD OF OLIVER (LONDON) (re-issue)** Decca **23 4**
6 Sep 1969 **HAIR (BROADWAY)** RCA **29 3**
12 Sep 1970 **EDINBURGH MILITARY TATTOO 1970** Waverley **34 4**
18 Sep 1971 **EDINBURGH MILITARY TATTOO 1971** Waverley **44 1**
8 Jan 1972 **JESUS CHRIST SUPERSTAR (STUDIO RECORDING)** MCA **6 20**
19 Feb 1972 **GODSPELL (LONDON)** Bell **25 17**
22 Jan 1977 **EVITA (STUDIO RECORDING)** MCA **4 35**
17 Jun 1978 **WHITE MANSIONS (STUDIO RECORDING)** A & M **51 3**
18 Nov 1978 **EVITA (LONDON)** MCA **24 18**
1 Aug 1981 **CATS (LONDON)** Polydor **6 26**
6 Nov 1982 **MACK AND MABEL (BROADWAY)** MCA **38 7**

FIDDLER ON THE ROOF Can any one song in stage musical history be more associated with one person than 'If I Were a Rich Man' and Topol? Other stand-out tracks from this 1967 original cast recording include 'Matchmaker, Matchmaker' and 'Sunrise, Sunset'

LES MISÉRABLES This 1985 release of Victor Hugo's novel turned musical featured the original London cast

4 Aug 1984 STARLIGHT EXPRESS (LONDON) Starlight/Polydor 21 9
8 Sep 1984 SONG AND DANCE RCA 46 4
10 Nov 1984 CHESS (STUDIO RECORDING) RCA 10 16
12 Jan 1985 BREAKDANCE 2 – ELECTRIC BOOGALOO Polydor 34 20
18 May 1985 WEST SIDE STORY (STUDIO RECORDING) Deutsche Grammophon 11 32
2 Nov 1985 CHESS PIECES (STUDIO RECORDING) Telstar 87 3
9 Nov 1985 OVATION – THE BEST OF ANDREW LLOYD WEBBER K-Tel 34 12
7 Dec 1985 PERFORMANCE – THE VERY BEST OF TIM RICE AND ANDREW LLOYD WEBBER Telstar 33 7
15 Feb 1986 LES MISÉRABLES (LONDON) First Night 72 4
10 May 1986 WEST SIDE STORY – HIGHLIGHTS (STUDIO RECORDING) Deutsche Grammophon 72 6
17 May 1986 DAVE CLARK'S 'TIME' (STUDIO RECORDING) EMI 21 6
11 Oct 1986 SOUTH PACIFIC (STUDIO RECORDING) CBS 5 24
21 Feb 1987 THE PHANTOM OF THE OPERA (LONDON) Really Useful 1 141
27 Jun 1987 MATADOR (STUDIO RECORDING) Epic 26 5
21 Nov 1987 MY FAIR LADY (STUDIO RECORDING) Decca 41 12
12 Nov 1988 ANDREW LLOYD WEBBER – THE PREMIERE COLLECTION Polydor 3 9
14 Jan 1989 ANDREW LLOYD WEBBER – THE PREMIERE COLLECTION * Polydor 1 55
16 Sep 1989 ASPECTS OF LOVE (LONDON) Polydor 1 29
10 Feb 1990 MILESTONES – 20 ROCK OPERAS * Telstar 6 11
24 Feb 1990 MISS SAIGON (LONDON) Geffen 4 11
19 May 1990 A NIGHT AT THE OPERA * Telstar 2 12
1 Dec 1990 THE BEST FROM THE MGM MUSICALS * EMI 12 4
29 Jun 1991 FIVE GUYS NAMED MOE (LONDON) First Night 59 1
31 Aug 1991 JOSEPH AND THE AMAZING TECHNICOLOR DREAMCOAT Really Useful 1 38
16 Nov 1991 ESSENTIAL OPERA * Decca 2 28
11 Jul 1992 THE ULTIMATE OPERA COLLECTION * Erato 14 5
10 Oct 1992 THE KING AND I (STUDIO RECORDING) Philips 57 2
28 Nov 1992 THE PREMIERE COLLECTION ENCORE – ANDREW LLOYD WEBBER * Really Useful 2 11
5 Dec 1992 TAKE 2: OPERA FAVOURITES/ORCHESTRAL CLASSICS * Masterworks 18 3
10 Apr 1993 LEONARD BERNSTEIN'S 'WEST SIDE STORY' (STUDIO RECORDING) IMG 33 5
10 Apr 1993 THE NEW STARLIGHT EXPRESS (LONDON) Really Useful 42 2
11 Sep 1993 SUNSET BOULEVARD (LONDON) Really Useful 11 4
2 Oct 1993 GREASE (LONDON) Epic 20 3
6 Nov 1993 ESSENTIAL OPERA 2 * Decca 17 2
19 Mar 1994 I KNOW THEM SO WELL – TIM RICE * PolyGram TV 2 7
5 Nov 1994 THE VERY BEST OF ANDREW LLOYD WEBBER * Really Useful 3 13
1 Apr 1995 OLIVER! (1994 LONDON CAST) First Night 36 3
11 May 1996 LES MISÉRABLES – 10TH ANNIVERSARY CONCERT First Night 32 7
16 Nov 1996 MARTIN GUERRE (LONDON) First Night 58 1
14 Dec 1996 HEATHCLIFF LIVE (THE SHOW) (LONDON) EMI 41 1
27 Jun 1998 CHICAGO – THE MUSICAL (LONDON) RCA Victor 61 1
22 Aug 1998 SATURDAY NIGHT FEVER (LONDON) Polydor 17 6
31 Oct 1998 SONGS FROM ANDREW LLOYD WEBBER AND JIM STEINMAN'S WHISTLE DOWN THE WIND * Really Useful/Polydor 3 4
13 Nov 1999 MAMMA MIA! (LONDON) Polydor 56 2
4 Aug 2001 MY FAIR LADY (2001 LONDON CAST RECORDING) First Night 73 1
17 Nov 2001 THE OPERA ALBUM 2002 * Virgin/EMI 7 6
8 Dec 2001 ANDREW LLOYD WEBBER – GOLD * Really Useful/Polydor 5 4
29 Jun 2002 A R RAHMAN'S BOMBAY DREAMS (LONDON) Sony Classical 61 1

Katie MELUA *Georgia, female vocalist / instrumentalist – guitar (Singles: 3 weeks, Albums: 7 weeks)* pos/wks

13 Dec 03 ● **THE CLOSEST THING TO CRAZY** *Dramatico DRAMCDS 003* ....10 3+
15 Nov 03 **CALL OFF THE SEARCH** *Dramatico DRAMCD0002* ....37 7+

Harold MELVIN and The BLUENOTES
US, male vocal group, leader d. 24 Mar 1997 (Singles: 52 weeks) pos/wks

13 Jan 73 ● **IF YOU DON'T KNOW ME BY NOW** *CBS 8496* 9 9
12 Jan 74 **THE LOVE I LOST (PART 1)** *Philadelphia International PIR 1879* 21 8
13 Apr 74 **SATISFACTION GUARANTEED (OR TAKE YOUR LOVE BACK)** *Philadelphia International PIR 2187* 32 6
31 May 75 **GET OUT (AND LET ME CRY)** *Route RT 06* [1] 35 5
28 Feb 76 **WAKE UP EVERYBODY (PART 1)** *Philadelphia International PIR 3866* 23 7
22 Jan 77 ● **DON'T LEAVE ME THIS WAY** *Philadelphia International PIR 4909* [2] 5 10
2 Apr 77 **REACHING FOR THE WORLD** *ABC 4161* [1] 48 1
28 Apr 84 **DON'T GIVE ME UP** *London LON 47* [1] 59 4
4 Aug 84 **TODAY'S YOUR LUCKY DAY** *London LON 52* [3] 66 2

[1] Harold Melvin and the Blue Notes [2] Harold Melvin and the Bluenotes featuring Theodore Pendergrass [3] Harold Melvin and the Blue Notes featuring Nikko

MEMBERS *UK, male vocal / instrumental group (Singles: 14 weeks, Albums: 5 weeks)* pos/wks

3 Feb 79 **THE SOUND OF THE SUBURBS** *Virgin VS 242* 12 9
7 Apr 79 **OFFSHORE BANKING BUSINESS** *Virgin VS 248* 31 5
28 Apr 79 **AT THE CHELSEA NIGHTCLUB** *Virgin V 2120* 45 5

MEMBERS OF MAYDAY *Germany, male production duo – Klaus Jankuhn and Maximilian Lenz (Singles: 4 weeks)* pos/wks

23 Jun 01 **10 IN 01** *Deviant DVNT 42CDS* 31 3
13 Apr 02 **SONIC EMPIRE** *Low Spirit DVNT 49CDS* 59 1

MEMPHIS BLEEK featuring JAY-Z
US, male rappers (Singles: 1 week) pos/wks

4 Dec 99 **WHAT YOU THINK OF THAT** *Def Jam 8708292* 58 1

See also JAY-Z

MEN AT WORK *Australia / UK, male vocal / instrumental group – lead vocal Colin James Hay (Singles: 39 weeks, Albums: 71 weeks)* pos/wks

30 Oct 82 **WHO CAN IT BE NOW?** *Epic EPC A 2392* ▲ 45 5
8 Jan 83 ★ **DOWN UNDER** *Epic EPC A 1980* ▲ 1 12
9 Apr 83 **OVERKILL** *Epic EPC A 3220* 21 10
2 Jul 83 **IT'S A MISTAKE** *Epic EPC A 3475* 33 6
10 Sep 83 **DR HECKYLL AND MR JIVE** *Epic EPC A 3668* 31 6
15 Jan 83 ★ **BUSINESS AS USUAL** *Epic EPC 85669* ▲ 1 44
30 Apr 83 ● **CARGO** *Epic EPC 25372* 8 27

MEN OF VIZION
US, male vocal group (Singles: 2 weeks) pos/wks

27 Mar 99 **DO YOU FEEL ME? (...FREAK YOU)** *MJJ / Epic 6670912* 36 2

MEN THEY COULDN'T HANG *UK, male vocal / instrumental group (Singles: 4 weeks, Albums: 9 weeks)* pos/wks

2 Apr 88 **THE COLOURS** *Magnet SELL 6* 61 4
27 Jul 85 **NIGHT OF A THOUSAND CANDLES** *Imp FIEND 50* 91 2
8 Nov 86 **HOW GREEN IS THE VALLEY** *MCA MCF 3337* 68 2
23 Apr 88 **WAITING FOR BONAPARTE** *Magnet MAGL 5075* 41 2
6 May 89 **SILVER TOWN** *Silvertone ORELP 503* 39 2
1 Sep 90 **THE DOMINO CLUB** *Silvertone ORELP 512* 53 1

MEN WITHOUT HATS *Canada, male vocal / instrumental group (Singles: 11 weeks, Albums: 1 week)* pos/wks

8 Oct 83 ● **THE SAFETY DANCE** *Statik TAK 1* 6 11
12 Nov 83 **RHYTHM OF YOUTH** *Statik STATLP 10* 96 1

Sergio MENDES *Brazil, male conductor (Singles: 5 weeks)* pos/wks

9 Jul 83 **NEVER GONNA LET YOU GO** *A&M AM 118* 45 5

Uncredited vocals by Joe Pizzulo and Leza Miller

Andrea MENDEZ *UK, female vocalist (Singles: 1 week)* pos/wks

3 Aug 96 **BRING ME LOVE** *AM:PM 5817872* 44 1

MENSWEAR *UK, male vocal / instrumental group (Singles: 18 weeks, Albums: 6 weeks)* pos/wks

15 Apr 95 **I'LL MANAGE SOMEHOW** *Laurel LAUCD 4* 49 1
1 Jul 95 **DAYDREAMER** *Laurel LAUCD 5* 14 4
30 Sep 95 **STARDUST** *Laurel LAUCD 6* 16 3
16 Dec 95 **SLEEPING IN** *Laurel LAUCD 7* 24 3
23 Mar 96 ● **BEING BRAVE** *Laurel LAUCD 8* 10 4
7 Sep 96 **WE LOVE YOU** *Laurel LAUCD 11* 22 3
21 Oct 95 **NUISANCE** *Laurel 8286792* 11 6

MENTAL AS ANYTHING
Australia, male vocal / instrumental group (Singles: 13 weeks) pos/wks

7 Feb 87 ● **LIVE IT UP** *Epic ANY 1* 3 13

Natalie MERCHANT *US, female vocalist (Albums: 3 weeks)* pos/wks

1 Jul 95 **TIGERLILY** *Elektra 7559617452* 39 2
13 Jun 98 **OPHELIA** *Elektra 7559621962* 52 1

See also 10,000 MANIACS

Freddie MERCURY 477 Top 500
Gregarious, versatile lead singer of Queen, b. Faroukh Bulsara, 5 Sep 1946, Zanzibar, Africa, d. 24 Nov 1991. UK-based performer was one of rock music's all-time great showmen, whose music has raised millions of pounds for Aids charities (Singles: 79 weeks, Albums: 65 weeks) pos/wks

22 Sep 84 ● **LOVE KILLS** *CBS A 4735* 10 8
20 Apr 85 **I WAS BORN TO LOVE YOU** *CBS A 6019* 11 10
13 Jul 85 **MADE IN HEAVEN** *CBS A 6413* 57 4
21 Sep 85 **LIVING ON MY OWN** *CBS A 6555* 50 3
24 May 86 **TIME** *EMI EMI 5559* 32 5
7 Mar 87 ● **THE GREAT PRETENDER** *Parlophone R 6151* 4 9
7 Nov 87 ● **BARCELONA** *Polydor POSP 887* [1] 8 9
8 Aug 92 ● **BARCELONA (re-issue)** *Polydor PO 221* [1] 2 8
12 Dec 92 ● **IN MY DEFENCE** *Parlophone R 6331* 8 7
6 Feb 93 **THE GREAT PRETENDER (re-issue)** *Parlophone CDR 6336* 29 3
31 Jul 93 ★ **LIVING ON MY OWN (re-mix)** *Parlophone CDR 6355* 1 13
11 May 85 ● **MR BAD GUY** *CBS 86312* 6 23
22 Oct 88 **BARCELONA** *Polydor POLH 44* [1] 15 8
28 Nov 92 ● **THE FREDDIE MERCURY ALBUM** *Parlophone CDPCSD 124* 4 25
4 Nov 00 **SOLO – THE VERY BEST OF FREDDIE MERCURY** *Parlophone 5280472* 13 9

[1] Freddie Mercury and Montserrat Caballé [1] Freddie Mercury and Montserrat Caballé

See also QUEEN

MERCURY REV *US, male vocal / instrumental group (Singles: 12 weeks, Albums: 17 weeks)* pos/wks

14 Nov 98 **GODDESS ON A HIWAY** *V2 VVR 5003323* 51 1
6 Feb 99 **DELTA SUN BOTTLENECK STOMP** *V2 VVR 5005413* 26 2
22 May 99 **OPUS 40** *V2 VVR 5006963* 31 2
28 Aug 99 **GODDESS ON A HIWAY (re-issue)** *V2 VVR 5008493* 26 2
6 Oct 01 **NITE AND FOG** *V2 VVR 5017723* 47 1
26 Jan 02 **THE DARK IS RISING** *V2 VVR 5018713* 16 3
27 Jul 02 **LITTLE RHYMES** *V2 VVR 5019783* 51 1
12 Jun 93 **BOCES** *Beggars Banquet BBQCD 140* 43 1
17 Oct 98 **DESERTER'S SONGS** *V2 VVR 1002772* 27 12
8 Sep 01 **ALL IS DREAM** *V2 VVR 1017528* 11 4

MERCY MERCY
UK, male vocal / instrumental group (Singles: 2 weeks) pos/wks

21 Sep 85 **WHAT ARE WE GONNA DO ABOUT IT?** *Ensign ENY 522* 59 2

MERLE and ROY

UK, female / male vocal / instrumental duo (Albums: 5 weeks) pos/wks

Date		Title / Label	pos	wks
26 Sep 87		**REQUESTS** *Mynod Mawr RMBR 8713*	**74**	5

MERLIN – *See BEATMASTERS; BOMB THE BASS*

MERO *UK, male vocal duo – Tommy Clark and Derek McDonald (Singles: 2 weeks)* pos/wks

Date		Title / Label	pos	wks
25 Mar 00		**IT MUST BE LOVE** *RCA 74321664772*	**33**	2

Tony MERRICK *UK, male vocalist (Singles: 1 week)* pos/wks

Date		Title / Label	pos	wks
2 Jun 66		**LADY JANE** *Columbia DB 7913*	**49**	1

MERSEYBEATS *UK, male vocal / instrumental group (Singles: 64 weeks, Albums: 9 weeks)* pos/wks

Date		Title / Label	pos	wks
12 Sep 63		**IT'S LOVE THAT REALLY COUNTS** *Fontana TF 412*	**24**	12
16 Jan 64	●	**I THINK OF YOU** *Fontana TF 431*	**5**	17
16 Apr 64		**DON'T TURN AROUND** *Fontana TF 459*	**13**	11
9 Jul 64		**WISHIN' AND HOPIN'** *Fontana TF 482*	**13**	10
5 Nov 64		**LAST NIGHT** *Fontana TF 504*	**40**	3
14 Oct 65		**I LOVE YOU, YES I DO** *Fontana TF 607*	**22**	8
20 Jan 66		**I STAND ACCUSED** *Fontana TF 645*	**38**	3
20 Jun 64		**THE MERSEYBEATS** *Fontana TL 5210*	**12**	9

MERSEYS *UK, male vocal duo (Singles: 13 weeks)* pos/wks

Date		Title / Label	pos	wks
28 Apr 66	●	**SORROW** *Fontana TF 694*	**4**	13

MERTON PARKAS

UK, male vocal / instrumental group (Singles: 6 weeks) pos/wks

Date		Title / Label	pos	wks
4 Aug 79		**YOU NEED WHEELS** *Beggars Banquet BEG 22*	**40**	6

MERZ *UK, male vocalist / instrumentalist – Conrad Lambert (Singles: 2 weeks)* pos/wks

Date		Title / Label	pos	wks
17 Jul 99		**MANY WEATHERS APART** *Epic 6674972*	**48**	1
16 Oct 99		**LOVELY DAUGHTER** *Epic 6679132*	**60**	1

MESCALEROS – *See Joe STRUMMER*

Mady MESPLE and Danielle MILLET with the PARIS OPÉRA-COMIQUE ORCHESTRA conducted by Alain LOMBARD

France, female vocal duo and orchestra (Singles: 4 weeks) pos/wks

Date		Title / Label	pos	wks
6 Apr 85		**FLOWER DUET (FROM 'LAKMÉ')** *EMI 5481*	**47**	4

MESSIAH

UK, male instrumental / production group (Singles: 13 weeks) pos/wks

Date		Title / Label	pos	wks
20 Jun 92		**TEMPLE OF DREAMS** *Kickin KICK 12S*	**20**	5
26 Sep 92		**I FEEL LOVE** *Kickin KICK 22S* [1]	**19**	5
27 Nov 93		**THUNDERDOME** *WEA YZ 790CD1*	**29**	3

[1] Messiah featuring Precious Wilson

METAL GURUS

UK, male vocal / instrumental group (Singles: 2 weeks) pos/wks

Date		Title / Label	pos	wks
8 Dec 90		**MERRY XMAS EVERYBODY** *Mercury GURU 1*	**55**	2

METALHEADZ – *See GOLDIE*

METALLICA 330 Top 500

Perennially popular hard rock group formed in 1981 in Los Angeles by Denmark-born Lars Ulrich (d) and fronted by James Hetfield (v/g). Festival favourites and multi-award winners have sold more than 60 million albums in the US alone and their latest album topped the chart in 13 countries (Singles: 70 weeks, Albums: 129 weeks) pos/wks

Date		Title / Label	pos	wks
22 Aug 87		**THE $5.98 EP – GARAGE DAYS RE-REVISITED** *Vertigo METAL 112*	**27**	4
3 Sep 88		**HARVESTER OF SORROW** *Vertigo METAL 212*	**20**	3
22 Apr 89		**ONE** *Vertigo METAL 5*	**13**	7
10 Aug 91	●	**ENTER SANDMAN** *Vertigo METAL 7*	**5**	4
9 Nov 91		**THE UNFORGIVEN** *Vertigo METAL 8*	**15**	4
2 May 92	●	**NOTHING ELSE MATTERS** *Vertigo METAL 10*	**6**	6
31 Oct 92		**WHEREVER I MAY ROAM** *Vertigo METAL 9*	**25**	4
20 Feb 93		**SAD BUT TRUE** *Vertigo METCD 11*	**20**	3
1 Jun 96	●	**UNTIL IT SLEEPS** *Vertigo METCD 12*	**5**	4
28 Sep 96		**HERO OF THE DAY** *Vertigo METCD 13*	**17**	4
7 Dec 96		**MAMA SAID** *Vertigo METCD 14*	**19**	2
22 Nov 97		**THE MEMORY REMAINS** *Vertigo METCD 15*	**13**	3
7 Mar 98		**THE UNFORGIVEN II** *Vertigo METDD 17*	**15**	4
4 Jul 98		**FUEL** *Vertigo METCD 16*	**31**	2
27 Feb 99		**WHISKEY IN THE JAR** *Vertigo METCD 19*	**29**	2
12 Aug 00		**I DISAPPEAR** *Hollywood 0113875 HWR*	**35**	3
5 Jul 03	●	**ST ANGER** *Vertigo 9865412*	**9**	8
4 Oct 03		**FRANTIC** *Vertigo 9811513*	**16**	3
11 Aug 84		**RIDE THE LIGHTNING** *Music For Nations MFN 27*	**87**	2
15 Mar 86		**MASTER OF PUPPETS** *Music For Nations MFN 60*	**41**	4
17 Sep 88	●	**... AND JUSTICE FOR ALL** *Vertigo VERH 61*	**4**	6
19 May 90		**THE GOOD THE BAD AND THE LIVE** *Vertigo 8754871*	**56**	1
24 Aug 91	★	**METALLICA** *Vertigo 5100221* ■ ▲	**1**	72
11 Dec 93		**LIVE SHIT – BINGE AND PURGE** *Vertigo 5187250*	**54**	1
15 Jun 96	★	**LOAD** *Vertigo 5326182* ■ ▲	**1**	18
5 Oct 96		**HERO OF THE DAY** *Vertigo METCY 13*	**47**	1
29 Nov 97	●	**RELOAD** *Vertigo 5364092* ▲	**4**	9
5 Dec 98		**GARAGE INC.** *Vertigo 5383512*	**29**	2
4 Dec 99		**S&M** *Vertigo 5467972*	**33**	2
14 Jun 03	●	**ST ANGER** *Vertigo 9865338* ▲	**3**	11

Tracks on The $5.98 EP: Garage Days Re-Revisited : Helpless / Crash Course in Brain Surgery / The Small Hours / Last Caress / Green Hell 'Live Shit – Binge and Purge' is a boxed set containing two CDs three video cassettes and a book

METEOR SEVEN

Germany, male producer – Jans Ebert (Singles: 1 week) pos/wks

Date		Title / Label	pos	wks
18 May 02		**UNIVERSAL MUSIC** *Bulletproof PROOF 16CD*	**71**	1

METEORS *UK, male vocal / instrumental group (Singles: 2 weeks, Albums: 3 weeks)* pos/wks

Date		Title / Label	pos	wks
26 Feb 83		**JOHNNY REMEMBER ME** *ID EYE 1*	**66**	2
26 Feb 83		**WRECKIN' CREW** *I.D. NOSE 1*	**53**	3

Pat METHENY GROUP – *See David BOWIE*

METHOD MAN *US, male rapper – Clifford Smith (Singles: 19 weeks, Albums: 4 weeks)* pos/wks

Date		Title / Label	pos	wks
29 Apr 95		**RELEASE YO' SELF** *Def Jam DEFCD 6*	**46**	1
29 Jul 95	●	**I'LL BE THERE FOR YOU - YOU'RE ALL I NEED TO GET BY** *Def Jam DEFCD 11* [1]	**10**	5
5 Apr 97	●	**HIT EM HIGH (THE MONSTARS' ANTHEM)** *Atlantic A 5449CD* [2]	**8**	6
22 May 99		**BREAK UPS 2 MAKE UPS** *Def Jam 8709272* [3]	**33**	2
27 Sep 03		**LOVE @ 1ST SIGHT** *MCA MCSTD 40338* [4]	**18**	5
28 Nov 98		**TICAL 2000: JUDGEMENT DAY** *Def Jam 5589202*	**49**	1
9 Oct 99		**BLACKOUT!** *Def Jam 5466092* [1]	**45**	3

[1] Method Man featuring Mary J Blige [2] B Real / Busta Rhymes / Coolio / LL Cool J / Method Man [3] Method Man featuring D'Angelo [4] Mary J Blige featuring Method Man [1] Method Man and Redman

See also WU-TANG CLAN

MEW

Denmark, male vocal / instrumental group (Singles: 3 weeks) pos/wks

Date		Title / Label	pos	wks
5 Mar 03		**COMFORTING SOUNDS** *Epic 6736432*	**48**	1
28 Jun 03		**AM I WRY? NO** *Epic 6739395*	**47**	1
27 Dec 03		**SHE CAME HOME FOR CHRISTMAS** *Epic 6744942*	**55**	1+

MEZZOFORTE *Iceland, male instrumental group (Singles: 10 weeks, Albums: 10 weeks)* pos/wks

Date		Title / Label	pos	wks
5 Mar 83		**GARDEN PARTY** *Steinar STE 705*	**17**	9
11 Jun 83		**ROCKALL** *Steinar STE 710*	**75**	1
5 Mar 83		**SURPRISE SURPRISE** *Steinar STELP 02*	**23**	9
2 Jul 83		**CATCHING UP WITH MEZZOFORTE** *Steinar STELP 03*	**95**	1

MIAMI SOUND MACHINE *Cuba, male / female vocal / instrumental group (Singles: 72 weeks)*

Date		Title / Label	pos	wks
11 Aug 84	●	**DR BEAT** *Epic A 4614*	6	14
17 May 86		**BAD BOY** *Epic A 6537*	16	11
16 Jul 88	●	**ANYTHING FOR YOU** *Epic 651673 7* [1] ▲	10	16
22 Oct 88	●	**1-2-3 (re)** *Epic 652958 7* [1]	9	10
17 Dec 88		**RHYTHM IS GONNA GET YOU** *Epic 654514 7* [1]	16	9
11 Feb 89	●	**CAN'T STAY AWAY FROM YOU** *Epic 651 444 7* [1]	7	12

[1] Gloria Estefan and Miami Sound Machine

See also Gloria ESTEFAN

George MICHAEL (61 Top 500)

Previously half of internationally celebrated duo Wham!, b. Georgios Panayiotou, 25 Jun 1963, London, UK. This multi-talented, award-winning singer / songwriter / producer / arranger and instrumentalist has successfully made the difficult transition from teeny-bopper hero to world-renowned solo star. Best-selling single: 'Careless Whisper' 1,365,995 (Singles: 264 weeks, Albums: 313 weeks)

Date		Title / Label	pos	wks
4 Aug 84	★	**CARELESS WHISPER** *Epic A 4603* ◆ ▲	1	17
5 Apr 86	★	**A DIFFERENT CORNER** *Epic A 7033*	1	10
31 Jan 87	★	**I KNEW YOU WERE WAITING (FOR ME)** *Epic DUET 2* [1] ▲	1	9
13 Jun 87	●	**I WANT YOUR SEX** *Epic LUST 1*	3	10
24 Oct 87	●	**FAITH** *Epic EMU 3* ▲	2	12
9 Jan 88		**FATHER FIGURE** *Epic EMU 4* ▲	11	6
23 Apr 88	●	**ONE MORE TRY** *Epic EMU 5* ▲	8	7
16 Jul 88		**MONKEY** *Epic EMU 6* ▲	13	6
3 Dec 88		**KISSING A FOOL** *Epic EMU 7*	18	6
25 Aug 90	●	**PRAYING FOR TIME** *Epic GEO 1* ▲	6	7
27 Oct 90		**WAITING FOR THAT DAY** *Epic GEO 2*	23	5
15 Dec 90		**FREEDOM!** *Epic GEO 3*	28	6
16 Feb 91		**HEAL THE PAIN** *Epic 6566477*	31	4
30 Mar 91		**COWBOYS AND ANGELS** *Epic 6567747*	45	3
7 Dec 91	★	**DON'T LET THE SUN GO DOWN ON ME** *Epic 6576467* [2] ■ ▲	1	10
13 Jun 92	●	**TOO FUNKY** *Epic 6580587*	4	9
1 May 93	★	**FIVE LIVE (EP) (re)** *Parlophone CDRS 6340* [3] ■	1	12
20 Jan 96	★	**JESUS TO A CHILD (2re)** *Virgin VSCDG 1571* ■	1	13
4 May 96	★	**FASTLOVE** *Virgin VSCDG 1579* ■	1	14
31 Aug 96	●	**SPINNING THE WHEEL** *Virgin VSCDG 1595*	2	12
1 Feb 97	●	**OLDER / I CAN'T MAKE YOU LOVE ME (re)** *Virgin VSCDG 1626*	3	9
10 May 97	●	**STAR PEOPLE '97 (re)** *Virgin VSCDG 1641*	2	13
7 Jun 97	●	**WALTZ AWAY DREAMING** *Aegean AECD 01* [4]	10	4
20 Sep 97	●	**YOU HAVE BEEN LOVED / THE STRANGEST THING '97** *Virgin VSCDG 1663*	2	8
31 Oct 98	●	**OUTSIDE (re)** *Epic 6665625*	2	16
13 Mar 99	●	**AS** *Epic 6670122* [5]	4	10
17 Jun 00	●	**IF I TOLD YOU THAT (re)** *Arista 74321766282* [6]	9	11
30 Mar 02	●	**FREEEK!** *Polydor 5706812*	7	10
10 Aug 02		**SHOOT THE DOG (re)** *Polydor 5709242*	12	5
14 Nov 87	★	**FAITH** *Epic 4600001* ■ ▲	1	77
15 Sep 90	★	**LISTEN WITHOUT PREJUDICE VOLUME 1** *Epic 4672951* ■	1	57
25 May 96	★	**OLDER** *Virgin CDV 2802* ■	1	99
21 Nov 98	★	**LADIES & GENTLEMEN – THE BEST OF GEORGE MICHAEL** *Epic 4917052* ■	1	63
18 Dec 99	●	**SONGS FROM THE LAST CENTURY** *Virgin CDVX 2920*	2	17

[1] Aretha Franklin and George Michael [2] George Michael and Elton John [3] George Michael and Queen with Lisa Stansfield [4] Toby Bourke with George Michael [5] George Michael and Mary J Blige [6] Whitney Houston / George Michael

Tracks on Five Live (EP): Somebody to Love / These Are the Days of Our Lives / Calling You / Papa Was a Rolling Stone – Killer (medley). The first track on the EP features Queen, the second Queen and Lisa Stansfield

See also Elton JOHN; Lisa MOORISH

MICHAELA *UK, female vocalist (Singles: 6 weeks)*

Date		Title / Label	pos	wks
2 Sep 89		**H-A-P-P-Y RADIO** *London H 1*	62	4
28 Apr 90		**TAKE GOOD CARE OF MY HEART** *London WAC 90*	66	2

Lisa MICHAELIS – *See Frankie KNUCKLES*

Pras MICHEL *US, male rapper / producer – Prakazrel Michael (Singles: 36 weeks, Albums: 3 weeks)*

Date		Title / Label	pos	wks
27 Jun 98	●	**GHETTO SUPASTAR (THAT IS WHAT YOU ARE)** *Interscope IND 95593* [1]	2	17
7 Nov 98	●	**BLUE ANGELS** *Ruffhouse 6666215* [2]	6	10
14 Nov 98	●	**ANOTHER ONE BITES THE DUST** *Dreamworks DRMCD 22364* [3]	5	6
1 Sep 01		**MISS CALIFORNIA** *Elektra E 7192CD* [4]	25	3
14 Nov 98		**GHETTO SUPASTAR** *Columbia 4914892*	44	3

[1] Pras Michel featuring Ol' Dirty Bastard introducing Mya [2] Pras [3] Queen with Wyclef Jean featuring Pras and Free [4] Dante Thomas featuring Pras

See also FUGEES

MICHELE – *See KING BEE*

Keith MICHELL *Australia, male actor / vocalist (Singles: 25 weeks, Albums: 12 weeks)*

Date		Title / Label	pos	wks
27 Mar 71		**I'LL GIVE YOU THE EARTH (TOUS LES BATEAUX, TOUS LES OISEAUX) (re)** *Spark SRL 1046*	30	11
26 Jan 80	●	**CAPTAIN BEAKY / WILFRED THE WEASEL** *Polydor POSP 106*	5	10
29 Mar 80		**THE TRIAL OF HISSING SID** *Polydor HISS 1* [1]	53	4
9 Feb 80		**CAPTAIN BEAKY AND HIS BAND** *Polydor 238 3462*	28	12

[1] Keith Michell, Captain Beaky and his Band

MICHELLE *Trinidad, female vocalist (Singles: 1 week)*

Date		Title / Label	pos	wks
8 Jun 96		**STANDING HERE ALL ALONE** *Positiva CDTIV 54*	69	1

Yvette MICHELLE *US, female vocalist – Michele Bryant (Singles: 3 weeks)*

Date		Title / Label	pos	wks
5 Apr 97		**I'M NOT FEELING YOU** *Loud 74321465222*	36	3

Lloyd MICHELS – *See MISTURA featuring Lloyd MICHELS*

MICK and PAT – *See PAT and MICK*

MICROBE *UK, male vocalist – Ian Doody (Singles: 7 weeks)*

Date		Title / Label	pos	wks
14 May 69		**GROOVY BABY** *CBS 4158*	29	7

MICRODISNEY *Ireland, male vocal / instrumental group (Singles: 3 weeks)*

Date		Title / Label	pos	wks
21 Feb 87		**TOWN TO TOWN** *Virgin VS 927*	55	3

MIDDLE OF THE ROAD *UK, male / female vocal / instrumental group (Singles: 76 weeks)*

Date		Title / Label	pos	wks
5 Jun 71	★	**CHIRPY CHIRPY CHEEP CHEEP** *RCA 2047*	1	34
4 Sep 71	●	**TWEEDLE DEE, TWEEDLE DUM** *RCA 2110*	2	17
11 Dec 71	●	**SOLEY SOLEY** *RCA 2151*	5	12
25 Mar 72		**SACRAMENTO (A WONDERFUL TOWN) (re)** *RCA 2184*	23	7
29 Jul 72		**SAMSON AND DELILAH** *RCA 2237*	26	6

MIDDLESBROUGH FC featuring Bob MORTIMER and Chris REA *UK, male football team / vocal group (Singles: 1 week)*

Date		Title / Label	pos	wks
24 May 97		**LET'S DANCE** *Magnet EW 112CD*	44	1

See also Chris REA

MIDFIELD GENERAL featuring Linda LEWIS *UK, male producer – Damian Harris, and UK, female vocalist (Singles: 1 week)*

Date		Title / Label	pos	wks
19 Aug 00		**REACH OUT** *Skint / SKINT 54CD*	61	1

See also Linda LEWIS

MIDGET *UK, male vocal / instrumental group (Singles: 2 weeks)*

Date		Title / Label	pos	wks
31 Jan 98		**ALL FALL DOWN** *Radarscope TINYCDS 6X*	57	1
18 Apr 98		**INVISIBLE BALLOON** *Radarscope TINYCDS 7*	66	1

MIDI XPRESS

UK, male vocal / instrumental duo (Singles: 1 week) pos/wks

11 May 96 CHASE *Labello Dance LAD 26CD* 73 1

Bette MIDLER

US, female vocalist (Singles: 27 weeks, Albums: 40 weeks) pos/wks

17 Jun 89 ● WIND BENEATH MY WINGS *Atlantic A 8972* ▲ 5 12
13 Oct 90 ● FROM A DISTANCE (re) *Atlantic A 7820* 6 14
5 Dec 98 MY ONE TRUE FRIEND *Warner Brothers W 460CD* 58 1
15 Jul 89 BEACHES (FILM SOUNDTRACK) *Atlantic 7819931* 21 9
13 Jul 91 ● SOME PEOPLE'S LIVES *Atlantic 7567821291* 5 11
15 Feb 92 FOR THE BOYS (FILM SOUNDTRACK) *Atlantic 7567823292* 75 1
30 Oct 93 ● EXPERIENCE THE DIVINE – GREATEST HITS *Atlantic 7567824972* 3 15
25 Nov 95 BETTE OF ROSES *Atlantic 7567828232* 55 4

'From a Distance' peaked at No.6 in Jun 1991

MIDNIGHT COWBOY SOUNDTRACK

US, orchestra (Singles: 4 weeks) pos/wks

8 Nov 80 MIDNIGHT COWBOY *United Artists UP 634* 47 4

MIDNIGHT OIL *Australia, male vocal / instrumental group (Singles: 32 weeks, Albums: 21 weeks)* pos/wks

23 Apr 88 BEDS ARE BURNING *Sprint OIL 1* 48 5
2 Jul 88 THE DEAD HEART *Sprint OIL 2* 68 2
25 Mar 89 ● BEDS ARE BURNING (re-issue) *Sprint OIL 3* 6 13
1 Jul 89 THE DEAD HEART (re-issue) *Sprint OIL 4* 62 4
10 Feb 90 BLUE SKY MINE *CBS OIL 5* 66 2
17 Apr 93 TRUGANINI *Columbia 6590492* 29 4
3 Jul 93 MY COUNTRY *Columbia 6593702* 66 1
6 Nov 93 IN THE VALLEY *Columbia 6598492* 60 1
25 Jun 88 DIESEL AND DUST *CBS 4600051* 19 16
10 Mar 90 BLUE SKY MINING *CBS 4656531* 28 3
1 May 93 EARTH AND SUN AND MOON *Columbia 4736052* 27 2

MIDNIGHT STAR *US, male / female vocal / instrumental group (Singles: 26 weeks, Albums: 6 weeks)* pos/wks

23 Feb 85 OPERATOR *Solar MCA 942* 66 2
28 Jun 86 HEADLINES *Solar MCA 1065* 16 8
4 Oct 86 ● MIDAS TOUCH *Solar MCA 1096* 8 10
7 Feb 87 ENGINE NO.9 *Solar MCA 1117* 64 3
2 May 87 WET MY WHISTLE *Solar MCA 1127* 60 3
2 Feb 85 PLANETARY INVASION *Solar MCF 3251* 85 2
5 Jul 86 HEADLINES *Solar MCF 3322* 42 4

MIDNITE BAND – *See Tony RALLO and the MIDNITE BAND*

MIGHTY AVENGERS

UK, male vocal / instrumental group (Singles: 2 weeks) pos/wks

26 Nov 64 SO MUCH IN LOVE *Decca F 11962* 46 2

MIGHTY AVONS – *See Larry CUNNINGHAM and the MIGHTY AVONS*

MIGHTY DUB KATZ

UK, male producer – Norman Cook (Singles: 6 weeks) pos/wks

7 Dec 96 JUST ANOTHER GROOVE *ffrr FCD 287* 43 1
2 Aug 97 MAGIC CARPET RIDE *ffrr FCD 306* 24 4
7 Dec 02 LET THE DRUMS SPEAK *Southern Fried ECB 31X* 73 1

See also BEATS INTERNATIONAL; Norman COOK; FATBOY SLIM; FREAKPOWER; HOUSEMARTINS; PIZZAMAN

MIGHTY LEMON DROPS *UK, male vocal / instrumental group (Singles: 6 weeks, Albums: 5 weeks)* pos/wks

13 Sep 86 THE OTHER SIDE OF YOU *Blue Guitar AZUR 1* 67 1
18 Apr 87 OUT OF HAND *Blue Guitar AZUR 4* 66 3
23 Jan 88 INSIDE OUT *Blue Guitar AZUR 6* 74 2
4 Oct 86 HAPPY HEAD *Blue Guitar AZLP 1* 58 2
27 Feb 88 THE WORLD WITHOUT END *Blue Guitar AZLP 4* 34 3

MIGHTY MIGHTY BOSSTONES *US, male vocal / instrumental group (Singles: 6 weeks, Albums: 2 weeks)* pos/wks

25 Apr 98 THE IMPRESSION THAT I GET *Mercury 5748432* 12 5
27 Jun 98 THE RASCAL KING *Mercury 5661092* 63 1
16 May 98 LET'S FACE IT *Mercury 5344722* 40 2

MIGHTY MORPH'N POWER RANGERS *US, male / female vocal group (Singles: 13 weeks, Albums: 3 weeks)* pos/wks

17 Dec 94 ● POWER RANGERS (3re) *RCA 74321253022* 3 13
24 Dec 94 POWER RANGERS – THE ALBUM *RCA 74321252982* 50 3

MIGHTY WAH! *UK, male vocal / instrumental group – leader Pete Wylie (Albums: 11 weeks)* pos/wks

18 Jul 81 NAH-POO = THE ART OF BLUFF *Eternal CLASSIC 1* [1] 33 5
4 Aug 84 A WORD TO THE WISE GUY *Beggars Banquet BEGA 54* 28 6

[1] Wah!

See also WAH!

MIGIL FIVE *UK, male vocal / instrumental group (Singles: 20 weeks)* pos/wks

19 Mar 64 ● MOCKINGBIRD HILL *Pye 7N 15597* 10 13
4 Jun 64 NEAR YOU *Pye 7N 15645* 31 7

MIG29 *Italy, male instrumental / production group (Singles: 2 weeks)* pos/wks

22 Feb 92 MIG29 *Champion CHAMP 292* 62 2

MIKAELA – *See SUPERCAR*

MIKE *UK, male producer – Mark Jolley (Singles: 2 weeks)* pos/wks

19 Nov 94 TWANGLING THREE FINGERS IN A BOX *Pukka CDMIKE 100* 40 2

MIKE and the MECHANICS (404 Top 500)

Adult-orientated, radio-friendly pop act formed by Genesis guitarist Mike Rutherford b. 2 Oct 1950, Surrey. Vocalists included former Ace front man Paul Carrack and ex-Sad Café singer Paul Young (d. 2000). 'The Living Years' has been heard more than two million times on US radio (Singles: 67 weeks, Albums: 99 weeks) pos/wks

15 Feb 86 SILENT RUNNING (ON DANGEROUS GROUND) *WEA U 8908* 21 9
31 May 86 ALL I NEED IS A MIRACLE *WEA U 8765* 53 4
14 Jan 89 ● THE LIVING YEARS *WEA U 7717* ▲ 2 11
16 Mar 91 WORD OF MOUTH *Virgin VS 1345* 13 10
15 Jun 91 A TIME AND PLACE *Virgin VS 1351* 58 3
8 Feb 92 EVERYBODY GETS A SECOND CHANCE *Virgin VS 1396* 56 4
25 Feb 95 OVER MY SHOULDER *Virgin VSCDT 1526* 12 9
17 Jun 95 A BEGGAR ON A BEACH OF GOLD *Virgin VSCDT 1535* 33 5
2 Sep 95 ANOTHER CUP OF COFFEE *Virgin VSCDT 1554* 51 4
17 Feb 96 ALL I NEED IS A MIRACLE (re-mix) *Virgin VSCDT 1576* 27 4
1 Jun 96 SILENT RUNNING (re-issue) *Virgin VSCDT 1585* 61 1
5 Jun 99 NOW THAT YOU'VE GONE *Virgin VSCDT 1732* 35 2
28 Aug 99 WHENEVER I STOP *Virgin VSCDT 1743* 73 1
15 Mar 86 MIKE AND THE MECHANICS *WEA WX 49* 78 3
26 Nov 88 ● THE LIVING YEARS *WEA WX 203* 2 19
27 Apr 91 WORD OF MOUTH *Virgin V 2662* 11 7
18 Mar 95 ● BEGGAR ON A BEACH OF GOLD *Virgin CDV 2772* 9 33
2 Mar 96 THE LIVING YEARS (re-issue) *Atlantic K 2560042* 67 2
16 Mar 96 ● HITS *Virgin CDV 2797* 3 31
12 Jun 99 MIKE AND THE MECHANICS *Virgin CDV 2885* 14 4

The two 'Mike and the Mechanics' albums are different

See also Mike RUTHERFORD

MIKI and GRIFF *UK, female / male vocal duo – Barbara Salisbury d. 20 Apr 1989, and Emyr Griffith d. 24 Sep 1995 (Singles: 25 weeks)* pos/wks

2 Oct 59 HOLD BACK TOMORROW *Pye 7N 15213* [1] 26 2
13 Oct 60 ROCKIN' ALONE *Pye 7N 15296* [2] 44 3
1 Feb 62 A LITTLE BITTY TEAR *Pye 7N 15412* 16 13
22 Aug 63 I WANT TO STAY HERE *Pye 7N 15555* 23 7

[1] Lonnie Donegan presents Miki and Griff with the Lonnie Donegan Group
[2] Miki and Griff with the Lonnie Donegan Group

Buddy MILES – *See SANTANA*

John MILES *UK, male vocalist / instrumentalist (Singles: 30 weeks, Albums: 25 weeks)* pos/wks

18 Oct 75		**HIGHFLY** *Decca F 13595*	**17** 6
20 Mar 76	●	**MUSIC** *Decca F 13627*	**3** 9
16 Oct 76		**REMEMBER YESTERDAY** *Decca F 13667*	**32** 5
18 Jun 77	●	**SLOW DOWN** *Decca F 13709*	**10** 10
27 Mar 76	●	**REBEL** *Decca SKL 5231*	**9** 10
26 Feb 77		**STRANGER IN THE CITY** *Decca TXS 118*	**37** 3
1 Apr 78		**ZARAGON** *Decca TXS 126*	**43** 5
21 Apr 79		**MORE MILES PER HOUR** *Decca TXS 135*	**46** 5
29 Aug 81		**MILES HIGH** *EMI EMC 3374*	**96** 2

Robert MILES *Italy, male instrumentalist – keyboards – Roberto Concina (Singles: 49 weeks, Albums: 51 weeks)* pos/wks

24 Feb 96	●	**CHILDREN** *Deconstruction 74321348322*	**2** 18
8 Jun 96	●	**FABLE (2re)** *Deconstruction 74321382622*	**7** 9
16 Nov 96	●	**ONE & ONE** *Deconstruction 74321427692* [1]	**3** 17
29 Nov 97		**FREEDOM** *Deconstruction 74321536952* [2]	**15** 4
28 Jul 01		**PATHS** *Salt SALT 002CD* [3]	**74** 1
22 Jun 96	●	**DREAMLAND** *Deconstruction 74321391262*	**7** 48
6 Dec 97		**23AM** *Deconstruction 74321541132*	**42** 3

[1] Robert Miles featuring Maria Nayler [2] Robert Miles featuring Kathy Sledge [3] Robert Miles featuring Nina Miranda

June MILES-KINGSTON – *See Jimmy SOMERVILLE*

Paul MILES-KINGSTON – *See Sarah BRIGHTMAN*

Christina MILIAN *US, female vocalist (Singles: 30 weeks, Albums: 11 weeks)* pos/wks

3 Mar 01		**BETWEEN YOU AND ME** *Def Jam 5727402* [1]	**26** 3
26 Jan 02	●	**AM TO PM** *Def Soul 5889332*	**3** 11
29 Jun 02	●	**WHEN YOU LOOK AT ME** *Def Soul 5829802*	**3** 10
9 Nov 02	●	**IT'S ALL GRAVY** *Relentless RELENT 32CD* [2]	**9** 6
2 Feb 02		**CHRISTINA MILIAN** *Def Soul 5867392*	**23** 11

[1] Ja Rule featuring Christina Milian [2] Romeo featuring Christina Milian

MILK – *See Jason DOWNS featuring MILK*

MILK AND HONEY featuring Gali ATARI *Israel, male / female vocal / instrumental group (Singles: 8 weeks)* pos/wks

14 Apr 79	●	**HALLELUJAH** *Polydor 2001 870*	**5** 8

MILK & SUGAR *Germany, male production duo – Michael Kronenberger and Steffan Harning (Singles: 7 weeks)* pos/wks

12 Jan 02		**LOVE IS IN THE AIR** *Positiva CDTIV 166* [1]	**25** 3
11 Oct 03		**LET THE SUNSHINE IN** *Data / MoS DATA 64CDS* [2]	**18** 4

[1] Milk and Sugar vs John Paul Young [2] Milk and Sugar featuring Lizzy Pattinson

MILK INC *Belgium, male / female production / vocal duo – Regi Penxten and An Vervoort (Singles: 21 weeks, Albums: 1 week)* pos/wks

28 Feb 98		**GOOD ENOUGH (LA VACHE)** *Malarky MLKD 5* [1]	**23** 3
25 May 02	●	**IN MY EYES** *All Around the World CDGLOBE 252*	**9** 8
21 Sep 02	●	**WALK ON WATER** *Positiva CDTIV 179*	**10** 6
11 Jan 03		**LAND OF THE LIVING** *Positiva CDTIVS 184*	**18** 4
5 Oct 02		**MILK INC** *Positiva 5419532*	**47** 1

[1] Milk Incorporated

MILKY *Italy, male production duo and Egypt, female vocalist (Singles: 7 weeks)* pos/wks

31 Aug 02	●	**JUST THE WAY YOU ARE** *Multiply CDMULTY 87*	**8** 6
7 Dec 02		**IN MY MIND** *Multiply CDMULTY 92*	**48** 1

MILL GIRLS – *See Billy COTTON and His BAND*

MILLA *US, female vocalist (Singles: 1 week)* pos/wks

18 Jun 94		**GENTLEMAN WHO FELL** *SBK CDSBK 49*	**65** 1

Dominic MILLER *Argentina, male instrumentalist (Albums: 3 weeks)* pos/wks

14 Jun 03		**SHAPES** *BBC Music WMSF60702*	**38** 3

Frankie MILLER *UK, male vocalist (Singles: 32 weeks, Albums: 1 week)* pos/wks

4 Jun 77		**BE GOOD TO YOURSELF** *Chrysalis CHS 2147*	**27** 6
14 Oct 78	●	**DARLIN'** *Chrysalis CHS 2255*	**6** 15
20 Jan 79		**WHEN I'M AWAY FROM YOU** *Chrysalis CHS 2276*	**42** 5
21 Mar 92		**CALEDONIA** *MCS MCS 2001*	**45** 6
14 Apr 79		**FALLING IN LOVE** *Chrysalis CHR 1220*	**54** 1

Gary MILLER *UK, male vocalist – Neville Williams d. 15 Jun 1968 (Singles: 35 weeks)* pos/wks

21 Oct 55		**THE YELLOW ROSE OF TEXAS** *Nixa N 15004*	**13** 5
13 Jan 56	●	**ROBIN HOOD** *Nixa N 15020*	**10** 6
11 Jan 57		**GARDEN OF EDEN (re)** *Pye Nixa N 15070*	**14** 7
19 Jul 57		**WONDERFUL, WONDERFUL** *Pye Nixa N 15094*	**29** 1
17 Jan 58		**THE STORY OF MY LIFE** *Pye Nixa N 15120*	**14** 6
21 Dec 61		**THERE GOES THAT SONG AGAIN / THE NIGHT IS YOUNG (AND YOU'RE SO BEAUTIFUL) (re)** *Pye 7N 15404*	**29** 10

'The Night Is Young' listed with 'There Goes That Song Again' only for weeks 21 and 28 Dec 1961 and 4 Jan 1962. It peaked at No.32

Glenn MILLER *US, orchestra leader, Glenn Miller – trombone, d. 15 Dec 1944 (Singles: 9 weeks, Albums: 82 weeks)* pos/wks

12 Mar 54		**MOONLIGHT SERENADE** *HMV BD 5942*	**12** 1
24 Jan 76		**MOONLIGHT SERENADE / LITTLE BROWN JUG / IN THE MOOD** *RCA 2644* ▲	**13** 8
28 Jan 61	●	**GLENN MILLER PLAYS SELECTIONS FROM 'THE GLENN MILLER STORY' AND OTHER HITS** *RCA 27068 0023*	**10** 18
5 Jul 69	●	**THE BEST OF GLENN MILLER** *RCA International 1002*	**5** 14
6 Sep 69		**NEARNESS OF YOU** *RCA International INTS 1019*	**30** 2
25 Apr 70		**A MEMORIAL 1944-1969** *RCA GM 1*	**18** 17
25 Dec 71		**THE REAL GLENN MILLER AND HIS ORCHESTRA PLAY THE ORIGINAL MUSIC OF THE FILM 'THE GLENN MILLER STORY' AND OTHER HITS** *RCA International NTS 1157*	**28** 2
14 Feb 76		**A LEGENDARY PERFORMER** *RCA Victor DPM 2065*	**41** 5
14 Feb 76		**A LEGENDARY PERFORMER VOLUME 2** *RCA Victor CPL 11349*	**53** 2
9 Apr 77	●	**THE UNFORGETTABLE GLENN MILLER** *RCA Victor TVL 1*	**4** 8
20 Mar 93		**THE ULTIMATE GLENN MILLER** *Bluebird 74321131372*	**11** 6
25 Feb 95		**THE LOST RECORDINGS** *Happy Days CDHD 4012*	**22** 6
18 Oct 03		**IN THE MOOD – THE DEFINITIVE GLENN MILLER** *BMG 82876560302*	**43** 2

US No.1 symbol refers only to 'In the Mood' which hit the top spot in 1939 'The Real Glenn Miller and His Orchestra Play ...' is a re-titled re-issue of the first album

Jody MILLER *US, female vocalist (Singles: 1 week)* pos/wks

21 Oct 65		**HOME OF THE BRAVE** *Capitol CL 15415*	**49** 1

Leza MILLER – *See Sergio MENDES*

Mitch MILLER his Orchestra and Chorus *US, orchestra and chorus (Singles: 13 weeks)* pos/wks

7 Oct 55	●	**THE YELLOW ROSE OF TEXAS** *Philips PB 505* ▲	**2** 13

Ned MILLER *US, male vocalist (Singles: 22 weeks)* pos/wks

14 Feb 63	●	**FROM A JACK TO A KING** *London HL 9658*	**2** 21
18 Feb 65		**DO WHAT YOU DO DO WELL** *London HL 9937*	**48** 1

Roger MILLER *US, male vocalist / instrumentalist – guitar, d. 25 Oct 1992 (Singles: 42 weeks)* pos/wks

18 Mar 65	★	**KING OF THE ROAD** *Philips BF 1397*	**1** 15
3 Jun 65		**ENGINE ENGINE NO.9** *Philips BF 1416*	**33** 5
21 Oct 65		**KANSAS CITY STAR** *Philips BF 1437*	**48** 1

Date		Title / Label	pos	wks
16 Dec 65		**ENGLAND SWINGS (re)** *Philips BF 1456*	13	8
27 Mar 68		**LITTLE GREEN APPLES (2re)** *Mercury MF 1021*	19	13

Steve MILLER BAND *US, male vocal / instrumental group (Singles: 36 weeks, Albums: 51 weeks)*

Date		Title / Label	pos	wks
23 Oct 76		**ROCK 'N ME** *Mercury 6078 804* ▲	11	9
19 Jun 82	●	**ABRACADABRA** *Mercury STEVE 3* ▲	2	11
4 Sep 82		**KEEPS ME WONDERING WHY** *Mercury STEVE 4*	52	3
11 Aug 90	★	**THE JOKER** *Capitol CL 583* ▲	1	13
12 Jun 76		FLY LIKE AN EAGLE *Mercury 9286 177*	11	17
4 Jun 77		BOOK OF DREAMS *Mercury 9286 456*	12	12
19 Jun 82	●	ABRACADABRA *Mercury 6302 204*	10	16
7 May 83		STEVE MILLER BAND LIVE! *Mercury MERL 18*	79	2
6 Oct 90		THE BEST OF 1968-1973 *Capitol EST 2133*	34	3
10 Oct 98		GREATEST HITS *PolyGram TV 5592402*	58	1

Suzi MILLER and the JOHNSTON BROTHERS *UK, female vocalist – Renee Lester and male vocal group (Singles: 2 weeks)*

Date		Title / Label	pos	wks
21 Jan 55		**HAPPY DAYS AND LONELY NIGHTS** *Decca F 10389*	14	2

Lisa MILLETT – *See BABY BUMPS; SHEER BRONZE featuring Lisa MILLETT; A.T.F.C. presents ONEPHATDEEVA; GOODFELLAS featuring Lisa MILLETT*

MILLI VANILLI *France / Germany, male duo – Rob Pilatus (d. 2 Apr 1998) and Fabrice Morvan (Singles: 50 weeks, Albums: 25 weeks)*

Date		Title / Label	pos	wks
1 Oct 88	●	**GIRL YOU KNOW IT'S TRUE** *Cooltempo COOL 170*	3	13
17 Dec 88		**BABY DON'T FORGET MY NUMBER** *Cooltempo COOL 178* ▲	16	11
22 Jul 89		**BLAME IT ON THE RAIN (re)** *Cooltempo COOL 180* ▲	52	10
30 Sep 89	●	**GIRL I'M GONNA MISS YOU** *Cooltempo COOL 191* ▲	2	15
10 Mar 90		**ALL OR NOTHING** *Cooltempo COOL 199*	74	1
21 Jan 89	●	ALL OR NOTHING / 2X2 *Cooltempo CTLP 11*	6	25

'All or Nothing' was repackaged and available with a free re-mix album 2X2 from 16 Oct 89 onwards

MILLICAN and NESBIT *UK, male vocal duo – Alan Millican and Tim Nesbit (Singles: 14 weeks, Albums: 24 weeks)*

Date		Title / Label	pos	wks
1 Dec 73		**VAYA CON DIOS (MAY GOD BE WITH YOU)** *Pye 7N 45310*	20	11
18 May 74		**FOR OLD TIME'S SAKE** *Pye 7N 45357*	38	3
23 Mar 74	●	MILLICAN AND NESBIT *Pye NSPL 18428*	3	21
4 Jan 75		EVERYBODY KNOWS MILLICAN AND NESBIT *Pye NSPL 18446*	23	3

MILLIE *Jamaica, female vocalist – Millie Small (Singles: 33 weeks)*

Date		Title / Label	pos	wks
12 Mar 64	●	**MY BOY LOLLIPOP** *Fontana TF 449*	2	18
25 Jun 64		**SWEET WILLIAM** *Fontana TF 479*	30	9
11 Nov 65		**BLOODSHOT EYES** *Fontana TF 617*	48	1
25 Jul 87		**MY BOY LOLLIPOP (re-issue)** *Island WIP 6574*	46	5

Spike MILLIGAN *UK, male comedian / vocalist d. 27 Feb 2002 (Albums: 5 weeks)*

Date		Title / Label	pos	wks
25 Nov 61		MILLIGAN PRESERVED *Parlophone PMC 1152*	11	4
18 Dec 76		THE SNOW GOOSE *RCA RS 1088* [1]	49	1

[1] Spike Milligan with the London Symphony Orchestra

See also Harry SECOMBE, Peter SELLERS and Spike MILLIGAN; GOONS; LONDON SYMPHONY ORCHESTRA

MILLION DAN *UK, male rapper (Singles: 1 week)*

Date		Title / Label	pos	wks
27 Sep 03		**DOGZ N SLEDGEZ** *Gut CDGUT 52*	66	1

MILLIONAIRE HIPPIES *UK, male producer – Danny Rampling (Singles: 4 weeks)*

Date		Title / Label	pos	wks
18 Dec 93		**I AM THE MUSIC HEAR ME!** *Deconstruction 74321175432*	52	3
10 Sep 94		**C'MON** *Deconstruction 74321229372*	59	1

Garry MILLS *UK, male vocalist (Singles: 31 weeks)*

Date		Title / Label	pos	wks
7 Jul 60	●	**LOOK FOR A STAR** *Top Rank JAR 336*	7	14
20 Oct 60		**TOP TEEN BABY** *Top Rank JAR 500*	24	12
22 Jun 61		**I'LL STEP DOWN** *Decca F 11358*	39	5

Hayley MILLS *UK, female actor / vocalist (Singles: 11 weeks)*

Date		Title / Label	pos	wks
19 Oct 61		**LET'S GET TOGETHER** *Decca F 21396*	17	11

Stephanie MILLS *US, female vocalist (Singles: 33 weeks)*

Date		Title / Label	pos	wks
18 Oct 80	●	**NEVER KNEW LOVE LIKE THIS BEFORE** *20th Century TC 2460*	4	14
23 May 81		**TWO HEARTS** *20th Century TC 2492* [1]	49	5
15 Sep 84		**THE MEDICINE SONG** *Club JAB 8*	29	9
5 Sep 87		**(YOU'RE PUTTIN') A RUSH ON ME** *MCA MCA 1187*	62	2
1 May 93		**NEVER DO YOU WRONG** *MCA MCSTD 1767*	57	2
10 Jul 93		**ALL DAY ALL NIGHT** *MCA MCSTD 1778*	68	1

[1] Stephanie Mills featuring Teddy Pendergrass

Warren MILLS *Zambia, male vocalist (Singles: 1 week)*

Date		Title / Label	pos	wks
28 Sep 85		**SUNSHINE** *Jive JIVE 99*	74	1

MILLS BROTHERS *US, male vocal group (Singles: 1 week)*

Date		Title / Label	pos	wks
9 Jan 53	●	**THE GLOW WORM** *Brunswick 05007*	10	1

MILLTOWN BROTHERS *UK, male vocal / instrumental group (Singles: 16 weeks, Albums: 5 weeks)*

Date		Title / Label	pos	wks
2 Feb 91		**WHICH WAY SHOULD I JUMP?** *A&M AM 711*	38	5
13 Apr 91		**HERE I STAND** *A&M AM 758*	41	4
6 Jul 91		**APPLE GREEN** *A&M AM 787*	43	4
22 May 93		**TURN OFF** *A&M 5802692*	55	1
17 Jul 93		**IT'S ALL OVER NOW BABY BLUE** *A&M 5803332*	48	2
23 Mar 91		SLINKY *A&M 3953461*	27	5

CB MILTON *Holland, male vocalist (Singles: 5 weeks)*

Date		Title / Label	pos	wks
21 May 94		**IT'S A LOVING THING** *Logic 74321208062*	49	2
25 Mar 95		**IT'S A LOVING THING (re-mix)** *Logic 74321267212*	34	2
19 Aug 95		**HOLD ON** *Logic 74321292112*	62	1

Garnet MIMMS and TRUCKIN' CO *US, male vocalist and male instrumental group (Singles: 1 week)*

Date		Title / Label	pos	wks
25 Jun 77		**WHAT IT IS** *Arista 109*	44	1

MIND OF KANE *UK, male producer – David Hope (Singles: 1 week)*

Date		Title / Label	pos	wks
27 Jul 91		**STABBED IN THE BACK** *Deja Vu DJV 007*	64	1

See also HOPE A.D.

MINDBENDERS *UK, male vocal / instrumental group (Singles: 79 weeks, Albums: 5 weeks)*

Date		Title / Label	pos	wks
11 Jul 63		**HELLO JOSEPHINE** *Fontana TF 404* [1]	46	2
28 May 64		**STOP LOOK AND LISTEN** *Fontana TF 451* [1]	37	4
8 Oct 64	●	**UM, UM, UM, UM, UM, UM** *Fontana TF 497* [1]	5	15
4 Feb 65	●	**GAME OF LOVE** *Fontana TF 535* [1] ▲	2	11
17 Jun 65		**JUST A LITTLE BIT TOO LATE** *Fontana TF 579* [1]	20	7
30 Sep 65		**SHE NEEDS LOVE** *Fontana TF 611* [1]	32	6
13 Jan 66	●	**A GROOVY KIND OF LOVE** *Fontana TF 644*	2	14
5 May 66		**CAN'T LIVE WITH YOU CAN'T LIVE WITHOUT YOU** *Fontana TF 697*	28	7
25 Aug 66		**ASHES TO ASHES** *Fontana TF 731*	14	9
20 Sep 67		**THE LETTER** *Fontana TF 869*	42	4
20 Feb 65		WAYNE FONTANA AND THE MINDBENDERS *Fontana TL 5230*	18	1
25 Jun 66		THE MINDBENDERS *Fontana TL 5324*	28	4

[1] Wayne Fontana and the Mindbenders

See also Wayne FONTANA

MINDFUNK *US, male vocal / instrumental group (Albums: 1 week)*

Date		Title / Label	pos	wks
15 May 93		DROPPED *Megaforce CDZAZ 3*	60	1

MINDS OF MEN *UK, male / female vocal / instrumental group (Singles: 1 week)*

Date		Title / Label	pos	wks
22 Jun 96		**BRAND NEW DAY** *Perfecto PERF 121CD*	41	1

Sal MINEO

US, male vocalist / actor d. 12 Feb 1976 (Singles: 11 weeks) pos/wks

Date		Title	pos	wks
12 Jul 57		**START MOVIN' (IN MY DIRECTION)** *Philips PB 707*	16	11

Marcello MINERBI *Italy, orchestra (Singles: 16 weeks)* pos/wks

Date		Title	pos	wks
22 Jul 65	●	**ZORBA'S DANCE** *Durium DRS 54001*	6	16

MINIMAL FUNK 2 *Italy, male production duo (Singles: 2 weeks)* pos/wks

Date		Title	pos	wks
18 Jul 98		**THE GROOVY THANG** *Cleveland City CLECD 13046*	65	1
18 May 02		**DEFINITION OF HOUSE** *Junior BRG 033* [1]	63	1

[1] Minimal Funk

MINIMALISTIX *Belgium, male production duo – Andy Vandierendonck and Peter Bellaert (Singles: 7 weeks)* pos/wks

Date		Title	pos	wks
16 Mar 02		**CLOSE COVER** *Data DATA 32CDS*	12	5
19 Jul 03		**MAGIC FLY** *Data / MoS DATA 48CDS*	36	2

MINIPOPS

UK, male / female vocal group (Singles: 2 weeks, Albums: 12 weeks) pos/wks

Date		Title	pos	wks
26 Dec 87		**SONGS FOR CHRISTMAS '87 (EP)** *Bright BULB 9*	39	2
26 Dec 81		**MINIPOPS** *K-Tel NE 1102*	63	7
19 Feb 83		**WE'RE THE MINIPOPS** *K-Tel ONE 1187*	54	5

Tracks on Songs for Christmas '87 (EP): Thanks for Giving Us Christmas / The Man in Red / Christmas Time Around the World / Shine On

MINISTERS DE LA FUNK

US, male production trio (Singles: 4 weeks) pos/wks

Date		Title	pos	wks
11 Mar 00		**BELIEVE** *Defected DFECT 14CDS*	45	2
27 Jan 01		**BELIEVE (re-mix)** *Defected DFECT 26CDS* [1]	42	2

[1] Ministers De La Funk featuring Jocelyn Brown

MINISTRY *US, male vocal / instrumental group (Singles: 3 weeks, Albums: 6 weeks)* pos/wks

Date		Title	pos	wks
8 Aug 92		**NWO** *Sire W 0125TE*	49	1
6 Jan 96		**THE FALL** *Warner Bros. W 0328CD*	53	2
25 Jul 92		**PSALM 69** *Sire 7599267272*	33	5
10 Feb 96		**FILTH PIG** *Warner Bros. 9362458382*	43	1

See also REVOLTING COCKS

MINK DeVILLE

US, male vocal / instrumental group (Singles: 9 weeks) pos/wks

Date		Title	pos	wks
6 Aug 77		**SPANISH STROLL** *Capitol CLX 103*	20	9

MINKY *UK, male producer – Gary Dedman (Singles: 1 week)* pos/wks

Date		Title	pos	wks
30 Oct 99		**THE WEEKEND HAS LANDED** *Offbeat OFFCD 1001*	70	1

Liza MINNELLI

US, female vocalist (Singles: 15 weeks, Albums: 27 weeks) pos/wks

Date		Title	pos	wks
12 Aug 89	●	**LOSING MY MIND** *Epic ZEE 1*	6	7
7 Oct 89		**DON'T DROP BOMBS** *Epic ZEE 2*	46	3
25 Nov 89		**SO SORRY I SAID** *Epic ZEE 3*	62	2
3 Mar 90		**LOVE PAINS** *Epic ZEE 4*	41	3
7 Apr 73	●	**LIZA WITH A 'Z'** *CBS 65212*	9	15
16 Jun 73		**THE SINGER** *CBS 65555*	45	1
21 Oct 89	●	**RESULTS** *Epic 465511 1*	6	10
6 Jul 96		**GENTLY** *Angel CDQ 8354702*	58	1

Dannii MINOGUE (486 Top 500)

Australia, singer / actor, b. 20 Oct 1971, who like older sister Kylie had a chart comeback in 2001. The Minogues have had more singles success than any other sisters (Singles: 113 weeks, Albums: 29 weeks) pos/wks

Date		Title	pos	wks
30 Mar 91	●	**LOVE AND KISSES** *MCA MCS 1529*	8	8
18 May 91		**SUCCESS** *MCA MCS 1538*	11	7
27 Jul 91	●	**JUMP TO THE BEAT** *MCA MCS 1556*	8	6
19 Oct 91		**BABY LOVE** *MCA MCS 1580*	14	6
14 Dec 91		**I DON'T WANNA TAKE THIS PAIN** *MCA MCS 1600*	40	5
1 Aug 92		**SHOW YOU THE WAY TO GO** *MCA MCS 1671*	30	3
12 Dec 92		**LOVE'S ON EVERY CORNER** *MCA MCSR 1723*	44	4
17 Jul 93	●	**THIS IS IT** *MCA MCSTD 1790*	10	8
2 Oct 93		**THIS IS THE WAY** *MCA MCSTD 1935*	27	3
11 Jun 94		**GET INTO YOU** *Mushroom D 11751*	36	2
23 Aug 97	●	**ALL I WANNA DO** *Eternal WEA 119CD* [1]	4	8
1 Nov 97		**EVERYTHING I WANTED** *Eternal WEA 137CD* [1]	15	4
28 Mar 98		**DISREMEMBRANCE** *Eternal WEA 153CD* [1]	21	3
1 Dec 01	●	**WHO DO YOU LOVE NOW (STRINGER)** *ffrr DFCD 002* [2]	3	15
16 Nov 02	●	**PUT THE NEEDLE ON IT** *London LONCD 470*	7	11
15 Mar 03	●	**I BEGIN TO WONDER** *London LONCD 473*	2	11
21 Jun 03	●	**DON'T WANNA LOSE THIS FEELING (re)** *London LONCD 478*	5	9
15 Jun 91	●	**LOVE AND KISSES** *MCA MCA 10340*	8	20
16 Oct 93		**GET INTO YOU** *MCA MCD 10909*	52	1
20 Sep 97		**GIRL** *Eternal 3984205482* [1]	57	1
29 Mar 03	●	**NEON NIGHTS** *London 2564600032*	8	7

[1] Dannii [2] Riva featuring Dannii Minogue [1] Dannii

Kylie MINOGUE (56 Top 500)

Aussie teen soap star turned sex siren, b. 28 May 1968, Melbourne, Australia. She has had the best ever chart start for a female soloist with 13 successive Top 10 entries and has the longest span of UK No.1 singles of any female solo artist – 15 years and nine months. Best-selling single: 'Can't Get You Out of My Head' 1,037,235 (Singles: 333 weeks, Albums: 279 weeks) pos/wks

Date		Title	pos	wks
23 Jan 88	★	**I SHOULD BE SO LUCKY** *PWL PWL 8*	1	16
14 May 88	●	**GOT TO BE CERTAIN** *PWL PWL 12*	2	12
6 Aug 88	●	**THE LOCO-MOTION** *PWL PWL 14*	2	11
22 Oct 88	●	**JE NE SAIS PAS POURQUOI** *PWL PWL 21*	2	13
10 Dec 88	★	**ESPECIALLY FOR YOU** *PWL PWL 24* [1]	1	14
6 May 89	★	**HAND ON YOUR HEART** *PWL PWL 35*	1	11
5 Aug 89	●	**WOULDN'T CHANGE A THING** *PWL PWL 42*	2	9
4 Nov 89	●	**NEVER TOO LATE** *PWL PWL 45*	4	10
20 Jan 90	★	**TEARS ON MY PILLOW** *PWL PWL 47*	1	8
12 May 90	●	**BETTER THE DEVIL YOU KNOW** *PWL PWL 56*	2	10
3 Nov 90	●	**STEP BACK IN TIME** *PWL PWL 64*	4	8
2 Feb 91	●	**WHAT DO I HAVE TO DO** *PWL PWL 72*	6	8
1 Jun 91	●	**SHOCKED** *PWL PWL 81* [2]	6	7
7 Sep 91		**WORD IS OUT** *PWL PWL 204*	16	5
2 Nov 91	●	**IF YOU WERE WITH ME NOW** *PWL PWL 208* [3]	4	7
30 Nov 91		**KEEP ON PUMPIN' IT** *PWL PWL 207* [4]	49	1
25 Jan 92	●	**GIVE ME JUST A LITTLE MORE TIME** *PWL PWL 212*	2	8
25 Apr 92		**FINER FEELINGS** *PWL International PWL 227*	11	6
22 Aug 92		**WHAT KIND OF FOOL (HEARD ALL THAT BEFORE)** *PWL International PWL 241*	14	5
28 Nov 92		**CELEBRATION** *PWL International PWL 257*	20	7
10 Sep 94	●	**CONFIDE IN ME** *Deconstruction 74321227482*	2	9
26 Nov 94		**PUT YOURSELF IN MY PLACE** *Deconstruction 74321246572*	11	9
22 Jul 95		**WHERE IS THE FEELING** *Deconstruction 74321293612*	16	3
14 Oct 95		**WHERE THE WILD ROSES GROW** *Mute CDMUTE 185* [5]	11	4
20 Sep 97		**SOME KIND OF BLISS** *Deconstruction 74321517252*	22	5
6 Dec 97		**DID IT AGAIN** *Deconstruction 74321535702*	14	6
21 Mar 98		**BREATHE** *Deconstruction 74321570132*	14	4
31 Oct 98		**GBI** *Arthrob ART 021CD* [6]	63	1
1 Jul 00	★	**SPINNING AROUND** *Parlophone CDRS 6542* ■	1	11
23 Sep 00	●	**ON A NIGHT LIKE THIS (re)** *Parlophone CDRS 6546*	2	8
21 Oct 00	●	**KIDS (2re)** *Chrysalis CDCHS 5119* [7]	2	19
23 Dec 00	●	**PLEASE STAY** *Parlophone CDRS 6551*	10	7
29 Sep 01	★	**CAN'T GET YOU OUT OF MY HEAD** *Parlophone CDRS 6562* ◆ ■	1	25
2 Mar 02	●	**IN YOUR EYES** *Parlophone CDRS 6569*	3	17
22 Jun 02	●	**LOVE AT FIRST SIGHT** *Parlophone CDRS 6577*	2	12
23 Nov 02	●	**COME INTO MY WORLD** *Parlophone CDR 6590*	8	10
15 Nov 03	★	**SLOW** *Parlophone CDR 6625* ■	1	7+
16 Jul 88	★	**KYLIE** *PWL HF 3*	1	67
21 Oct 89	★	**ENJOY YOURSELF** *PWL HF 9* ■	1	33
24 Nov 90	●	**RHYTHM OF LOVE** *PWL HF 18*	9	22
26 Oct 91		**LET'S GET TO IT** *PWL HF 21*	15	12
5 Sep 92	★	**GREATEST HITS** *PWL International HFCD 25* ■	1	10
1 Oct 94	●	**KYLIE MINOGUE** *Deconstruction 74321227492*	4	15
4 Apr 98	●	**KYLIE MINOGUE** *Deconstruction 74321517272*	10	4
15 Aug 98		**MIXES** *Deconstruction 74321587152*	63	1
7 Oct 00	●	**LIGHT YEARS** *Parlophone 5284002*	2	28
28 Oct 00		**HITS PLUS** *Deconstruction 74321785342*	41	1

13 Oct 01 ★ **FEVER** *Parlophone 5358042* ■ 1 70
30 Nov 02 **GREATEST HITS 87-92** *PWL 9224682* 20 11
29 Nov 03 ● **BODY LANGUAGE** *Parlophone 5957582* ....6 5+

[1] Kylie Minogue and Jason Donovan [2] Kylie Minogue / rap by Jazzie P [3] Kylie Minogue and Keith Washington [4] Visionmasters with Tony King and Kylie Minogue [5] Nick Cave and Kylie Minogue [6] Towa Tei featuring Kylie Minogue [7] Robbie Williams / Kylie Minogue

Both eponymously titled albums are different; The 2002 'Greatest Hits' has a slightly different tracklisting to the 1992 album and includes an additional CD of remixes

Morris MINOR and the MAJORS
UK, male vocal / rap group (Singles: 11 weeks) pos/wks

19 Dec 87 ● **STUTTER RAP (NO SLEEP 'TIL BEDTIME)** *10 TEN 203* 4 11

Sugar MINOTT *Jamaica, male vocalist (Singles: 16 weeks)* pos/wks

28 Mar 81 ● **GOOD THING GOING (WE'VE GOT A GOOD THING GOING)** *RCA 58* 4 12
17 Oct 81 **NEVER MY LOVE** *RCA 138* 52 4

MINT CONDITION *US, male vocal group (Singles: 3 weeks)* pos/wks

21 Jun 97 **WHAT KIND OF MAN WOULD I BE** *Wild Card 5710492* 38 2
4 Oct 97 **LET ME BE THE ONE** *Wild Card 5717132* 63 1

MINT JULEPS *UK, female vocal group (Singles: 7 weeks)* pos/wks

22 Mar 86 **ONLY LOVE CAN BREAK YOUR HEART** *Stiff BUY 241* 62 2
30 May 87 **EVERY KINDA PEOPLE** *Stiff BUY 257* 58 5

MINT ROYALE *UK, male production duo – Neil Claxton and Chris Baker (Singles: 10 weeks)* pos/wks

5 Feb 00 **DON'T FALTER** *Faith & Hope FHCD 014* [1] 15 4
6 May 00 **TAKE IT EASY** *Faith & Hope FHCD 016* 66 1
7 Sep 02 **SEXIEST MAN IN JAMAICA** *Faith & Hope FHCD 025* 20 3
8 Feb 03 **BLUE SONG** *Faith & Hope FHCD 030* 35 2

[1] Mint Royale featuring Lauren Laverne

MINTY
Australia, female vocalist – Angela Kelly (Singles: 1 week) pos/wks

23 Jan 99 **I WANNA BE FREE** *Virgin VSCDT 1728* 67 1

MINUTEMAN
UK, male vocal / instrumental group (Singles: 3 weeks) pos/wks

20 Jul 02 **BIG BOY** *Ignition IGNSCD 225* 69 1
21 Sep 02 **5000 MINUTES OF PAIN** *Ignition IGNSCD 27* 75 1
15 Feb 03 **BIG BOY / MOTHER FIXATION** *Ignition IGNSCD 28* 45 1

MIRACLES – *See Smokey ROBINSON and the MIRACLES*

MIRAGE *UK, male vocal / instrumental group (Singles: 35 weeks, Albums: 33 weeks)* pos/wks

14 Jan 84 **GIVE ME THE NIGHT (MEDLEY)** *Passion PASH 15* [1] 49 4
9 May 87 ● **JACK MIX II / III** *Debut DEBT 3022* 4 11
25 Jul 87 **SERIOUS MIX** *Debut DEBT 3028* 42 4
7 Nov 87 ● **JACK MIX IV** *Debut DEBT 3035* 8 10
27 Feb 88 **JACK MIX VII** *Debut DEBT 3042* 50 3
2 Jul 88 **PUSH THE BEAT** *Debut DEBT 3050* 67 2
11 Nov 89 **LATINO HOUSE** *Debut DEBT 3085* 70 1
26 Dec 87 ● **THE BEST OF MIRAGE – JACK MIX '88** *Stylus SMR 746* 7 15
25 Jun 88 ● **JACK MIX IN FULL EFFECT** *Stylus SMR 856* 7 12
7 Jan 89 **ROYAL MIX '89** *Stylus SMR 871* 34 6

[1] Mirage featuring Roy Gayle

'Jack Mix III' listed with 'Jack Mix II' only from 6 Jun 1987

MIRAGE *UK, male instrumental trio (Albums: 3 weeks)* pos/wks

23 Sep 95 **CLASSIC GUITAR MOODS** *PolyGram TV 5290562* 25 3

Nina MIRANDA – *See Robert MILES*

Danny MIRROR
Holland, male vocalist – Eddy Ouwens (Singles: 9 weeks) pos/wks

17 Sep 77 ● **I REMEMBER ELVIS PRESLEY (THE KING IS DEAD)** *Sonet SON 2121* 4 9

MIRRORBALL *UK, male production duo – Jamie White and Jamie Ford – and female vocalist (Singles: 5 weeks)* pos/wks

13 Feb 99 **GIVEN UP** *Multiply CDMULTY 46* 12 4
24 Jun 00 **BURNIN'** *Multiply CDMULTY 56* 47 1

See also PF PROJECT featuring Ewan McGREGOR; TZANT

MIRWAIS
France, male producer – Mirwais Ahmadzais (Singles: 3 weeks) pos/wks

20 May 00 **DISCO SCIENCE** *Epic 6693102* 68 1
23 Dec 00 **NAIVE SONG** *Epic 6706922* 50 2

MISHKA
Bermuda, male vocalist – Alexander Mishka Frith (Singles: 2 weeks) pos/wks

15 May 99 **GIVE YOU ALL THE LOVE** *Creation CRESCD 311* 34 2

MISS BEHAVIN'
UK, female DJ / producer – Nichola Potterton (Singles: 1 week) pos/wks

18 Jan 03 **SUCH A GOOD FEELIN'** *Tidy Two TIDYTWO 115CD* 62 1

MISS JANE *UK, female vocalist (Singles: 1 week)* pos/wks

30 Oct 99 **IT'S A FINE DAY** *G1 Recordings G 1001CD* 62 1

MISS KITTIN – *See GOLDEN BOY with MISS KITTIN*

MISS SHIVA *Germany, female DJ / producer – Khadra Bungardt (Singles: 2 weeks)* pos/wks

10 Nov 01 **DREAMS** *VC Recordings VCRD 99* 30 2

MISS X *UK, female vocalist – Joyce Blair (Singles: 6 weeks)* pos/wks

1 Aug 63 **CHRISTINE** *Ember S 175* 37 6

MS DYNAMITE *UK, female rapper / vocalist – Niomi McLean Daley (Singles: 58 weeks, Albums: 42 weeks)* pos/wks

23 Jun 01 **BOOO!** *ffrr / Public Demand / Social Circles FCD 399* [1] 12 6
1 Jun 02 ● **IT TAKES MORE** *Polydor 5707982* 7 10
7 Sep 02 ● **DY-NA-MI-TEE** *Polydor 5709782* 5 10
14 Dec 02 **PUT HIM OUT** *Polydor 0658942* 19 6
22 Jun 02 ● **A LITTLE DEEPER** *Polydor 5899552* 10 42

[1] Sticky featuring Ms Dynamite

MISSION *UK, male vocal / instrumental group (Singles: 58 weeks, Albums: 48 weeks)* pos/wks

14 Jun 86 **SERPENTS KISS** *Chapter 22 CHAP 6* 70 3
26 Jul 86 **GARDEN OF DELIGHT / LIKE A HURRICANE** *Chapter 22 CHAP 7* 49 4
18 Oct 86 **STAY WITH ME** *Mercury MYTH 1* 30 4
17 Jan 87 **WASTELAND** *Mercury MYTH 2* 11 6
14 Mar 87 **SEVERINA** *Mercury MYTH 3* 25 5
13 Feb 88 **TOWER OF STRENGTH** *Mercury MYTH 4* 12 7
23 Apr 88 **BEYOND THE PALE** *Mercury MYTH 6* 32 4
13 Jan 90 **BUTTERFLY ON A WHEEL** *Mercury MYTH 8* 12 4
10 Mar 90 **DELIVERANCE** *Mercury MYTH 9* 27 4
2 Jun 90 **INTO THE BLUE** *Mercury MYTH 10* 32 3
17 Nov 90 **HANDS ACROSS THE OCEAN** *Mercury MYTH 11* 28 2
25 Apr 92 **NEVER AGAIN** *Mercury MYTH 12* 34 3
20 Jun 92 **LIKE A CHILD AGAIN** *Mercury MYTH 13* 30 2
17 Oct 92 **SHADES OF GREEN** *Vertigo MYTH 14* 49 2
8 Jan 94 **TOWER OF STRENGTH (re-mix)** *Vertigo MYTCD 15* 33 3
26 Mar 94 **AFTERGLOW** *Vertigo MYTCD 16* 53 1
4 Feb 95 **SWOON** *Neverland HOOKCD 002* 73 1
22 Nov 86 **GOD'S OWN MEDICINE** *Mercury MERH 102* 14 20
4 Jul 87 **THE FIRST CHAPTER** *Mercury MISH 1* 35 4

12 Mar 88 ● **CHILDREN** *Mercury MISH 2* **2** 9
17 Feb 90 ● **CARVED IN SAND** *Mercury 8422511* **7** 8
2 Nov 90 **GRAINS OF SAND** *Mercury 8469371* **28** 2
4 Jul 92 **MASQUE** *Vertigo 5121212* **23** 2
19 Feb 94 **SUM AND SUBSTANCE** *Vertigo 5184472* **49** 1
25 Feb 95 **NEVERLAND** *Neverland SMEECD 001* **58** 1
15 Jun 96 **BLUE** *Equator SMEECD 002* **73** 1

MISSJONES *US, female vocalist (Singles: 1 week)* pos/wks

10 Oct 98 **2 WAY STREET** *Motown 8608572* **49** 1

MISTA E

UK, male producer – Damon Rochefort (Singles: 5 weeks) pos/wks

10 Dec 88 **DON'T BELIEVE THE HYPE** *Urban URB 28* **41** 5

See also NOMAD

MIS-TEEQ

UK, female vocal group (Singles: 69 weeks, Albums: 52 weeks) pos/wks

20 Jan 01 ● **WHY** *Inferno / Telstar CDFERN 35* **8** 7
23 Jun 01 ● **ALL I WANT** *Inferno / Telstar CDSTAS 3184* **2** 11
27 Oct 01 ● **ONE NIGHT STAND** *Inferno / Telstar CDSTAS 3208* **5** 12
2 Mar 02 ● **B WITH ME** *Inferno / Telstar CDSTAS 3243* **5** 8
29 Jun 02 ● **ROLL ON / THIS IS HOW WE DO IT** *Inferno / Telstar CDSTAS 3255* **7** 7
29 Mar 03 ● **SCANDALOUS** *Telstar CDSTAS 3319* **2** 11
12 Jul 03 ● **CAN'T GET IT BACK** *Telstar CDSTAS 3337* **8** 9
29 Nov 03 **STYLE** *Telstar CDSTAS 3369* **13** 4
10 Nov 01 ● **LICKIN' ON BOTH SIDES** *Inferno/Telstar TCD 3212* **3** 31
12 Apr 03 ● **EYE CANDY** *Telstar TCD3304* **6** 21

MR and MRS SMITH

UK, male / female instrumental / production group (Singles: 1 week) pos/wks

12 Oct 96 **GOTTA GET LOOSE** *Hooj Choons HOOJCD 46* **70** 1

MR BEAN and SMEAR CAMPAIGN featuring Bruce DICKINSON *UK, male comedian – Rowan Atkinson – and male vocalist (Singles: 5 weeks)* pos/wks

4 Apr 92 ● **(I WANT TO BE) ELECTED** *London LON 319* **9** 5

MR BIG

UK, male vocal / instrumental group (Singles: 14 weeks) pos/wks

12 Feb 77 ● **ROMEO** *EMI 2567* **4** 10
21 May 77 **FEEL LIKE CALLING HOME** *EMI 2610* **35** 4

MR BIG *US, male vocal / instrumental group (Singles: 17 weeks, Albums: 14 weeks)* pos/wks

7 Mar 92 ● **TO BE WITH YOU** *Atlantic A 7514* ▲ **3** 11
23 May 92 **JUST TAKE MY HEART** *Atlantic A 7490* **26** 4
8 Aug 92 **GREEN TINTED SIXTIES MIND** *Atlantic A 7468* **72** 1
20 Nov 93 **WILD WORLD** *Atlantic A 7310CD* **59** 1
22Jul 89 **MR. BIG** *Atlantic 781990 1* **60** 1
13 Apr 91 **LEAN INTO IT** *Atlantic 7567822091* **28** 12
2 Oct 93 **BUMP AHEAD** *Atlantic 7567824952* **61** 1

MR BLOBBY

UK, male pink and yellow spotted blob vocalist (Singles: 16 weeks) pos/wks

4 Dec 93 ★ **MR BLOBBY** *Destiny Music CDDMUS 104* **1** 12
16 Dec 95 **CHRISTMAS IN BLOBBYLAND** *Destiny DMUSCD 108* **36** 4

MR BLOE *UK, male instrumental group (Singles: 18 weeks)* pos/wks

9 May 70 ● **GROOVIN' WITH MR BLOE** *DJM DJS 216* **2** 18

MR BUNGLE

US, male vocal / instrumental group (Albums: 1 week) pos/wks

21 Sep 91 **MR BUNGLE** *London 8282671* **57** 1

Mr CHEEKS – *See LIL' KIM*

MR FINGERS

US, male producer – Larry Heard (Singles: 5 weeks) pos/wks

17 Mar 90 **WHAT ABOUT THIS LOVE** *ffrr F 131* **74** 1
7 Mar 92 **CLOSER** *MCA MCS 1601* **50** 3
23 May 92 **ON MY WAY** *MCA MCS 1630* **71** 1

MR FOOD

UK, male vocalist (Singles: 3 weeks) pos/wks

9 Jun 90 **. . . AND THAT'S BEFORE ME TEA!** *Tangible TGB 005* **62** 3

Mr HAHN – *See LINKIN PARK; X-ECUTIONERS featuring Mike SHINODA and Mr HAHN of LINKIN PARK*

MR HANKEY

US, male Christmas excrement vocalist (Singles: 6 weeks) pos/wks

25 Dec 99 ● **MR HANKEY THE CHRISTMAS POO** *Columbia 6685582* **4** 6

MR JACK

Belgium, male producer – Lucente Vito (Singles: 2 weeks) pos/wks

25 Jan 97 **WIGGLY WORLD** *Extravaganza 0090965* **32** 2

MR LEE

US, male producer – Leroy Haggard (Singles: 6 weeks) pos/wks

6 Aug 88 **PUMP UP LONDON** *Breakout USA 639* **64** 2
11 Nov 89 **GET BUSY (re)** *Jive JIVE 231* **41** 4

MR MISTER *US, male vocal / instrumental group (Singles: 22 weeks, Albums: 24 weeks)* pos/wks

21 Dec 85 ● **BROKEN WINGS** *RCA PB 49945* ▲ **4** 13
1 Mar 86 **KYRIE** *RCA PB 49927* ▲ **11** 9
15 Feb 86 ● **WELCOME TO THE REAL WORLD** *RCA PL 89647* ▲ **6** 24

MR OIZO

France, male producer – Quentin Dupieux (Singles: 15 weeks) pos/wks

3 Apr 99 ★ **FLAT BEAT (re)** *F Communications / Pias Recordings F 104CDUK* ■ **1** 15

MR PINK presents The PROGRAM

UK, male producer – Leiam Sullivan (Singles: 4 weeks) pos/wks

19 Jan 02 **LOVE AND AFFECTION** *Manifesto FESCD 90* **22** 4

MR PRESIDENT

Germany, male / female vocal group (Singles: 13 weeks) pos/wks

14 Jun 97 ● **COCO JAMBOO** *WEA WEA 110CD* **8** 11
20 Sep 97 **I GIVE YOU MY HEART** *WEA WEA 126CD* **52** 1
25 Apr 98 **JOJO ACTION** *WEA WEA 156CD* **73** 1

MR REDS vs. DJ SKRIBBLE *UK, male producers – Reduan Nabbach and Scott Ialachi (Singles: 5 weeks)* pos/wks

24 May 03 **EVERYBODY COME ON (CAN U FEEL IT)** *ffrr FCD 410* **13** 6

MR ROY

UK, male instrumental / production group (Singles: 6 weeks) pos/wks

7 May 94 **SOMETHING ABOUT YOU** *Fresh FRSHD 11* **74** 1
21 Jan 95 **SAVED** *Fresh FRSHD 21* **24** 4
16 Dec 95 **SOMETHING ABOUT U (CAN'T BE BEAT) (re-mix)** *Fresh FRSHCD 33* **49** 1

MR SCRUFF *UK, male DJ / producer – Andy Carthy (Singles: 1 week, Albums: 2 weeks)* pos/wks

14 Dec 02 **SWEETSMOKE** *Ninja Tune ZENCDS 12124* **75** 1
21 Sep 02 **TROUSER JAZZ** *Ninja Tune ZENCD 65* **29** 2

MR RUMBLE – *See BM DUBS present MR RUMBLE featuring BRASSTOOTH and KEE*

MR SHABZ – *See SO SOLID CREW*

MR SMASH & FRIENDS featuring The ENGLAND SUPPORTER'S BAND *UK, male vocal football supporters group (Singles: 1 week)* pos/wks

8 Jun 02 WE'RE COMING OVER *RGR RGRCD 2* 67 1

See also MADNESS

MR V *UK, male producer – Rob Villiers (Singles: 2 weeks)* pos/wks

6 Aug 94 GIVE ME LIFE *Cheeky CHEKCD 005* 40 2

MR VEGAS *Jamaica, male vocalist – Clifford Smith (Singles:7 weeks)* pos/wks

22 Aug 98 HEADS HIGH *Greensleeves GRECD 650* 71 1
13 Nov 99 HEADS HIGH (re-issue) *Greensleeves GRECD 785* 16 6

MRS MILLS *UK, female instrumentalist – piano – Gladys Mills d. 1978 (Singles: 6 weeks, Albums: 13 weeks)* pos/wks

14 Dec 61 MRS MILLS MEDLEY *Parlophone R 4856* 18 5
31 Dec 64 MRS MILLS PARTY MEDLEY *Parlophone R 5214* 50 1
10Dec 66 COME TO MY PARTY *Parlophone PMC 7010* 17 7
28 Dec 68 MRS. MILLS' PARTY PIECES *Parlophone PCS 7066* 32 3
13 Dec 69 LET'S HAVE ANOTHER PARTY *Parlophone PCS 7035* 23 2
6 Nov 71 I'M MIGHTY GLAD *MFP 5225* 49 1

Mrs Mills' Medley: I Want to Be Happy / Sheik of Araby / Baby Face / Somebody Stole My Gal / Ma (He's Making Eyes At Me) / Swanee / Ain't She Sweet / California Here I Come. Mrs Mills Party Medley: You Made Me Love You (I Didn't Want To Do It) / Shine on Harvest Moon / I Don't Want to Set the World on Fire / Around the World / Ramona / Charmaine

MRS WOOD *UK, female producer – Jane Wood (Singles: 6 weeks)* pos/wks

16 Sep 95 JOANNA *React CDREACT 066* 40 2
6 Jul 96 HEARTBREAK *React CDREACT 78* [1] 44 1
4 Oct 97 JOANNA (re-mix) *React CDREACT 107* 34 2
15 Aug 98 1234 *React CDREACT 121* 54 1

[1] Mrs Wood featuring Eve Gallagher

MISTURA featuring Lloyd MICHELS *US, male instrumental group, Lloyd Michels – trumpet (Singles: 10 weeks)* pos/wks

15 May 76 THE FLASHER *Route RT 30* 23 10

Des MITCHELL
UK / Belgium, male DJ / production trio (Singles: 5 weeks) pos/wks

29 Jan 00 ● (WELCOME) TO THE DANCE *Code Blue BLUE 0087CD1* 5 5

Guy MITCHELL (407 Top 500) *Extremely popular pre-rock vocalist, b. Al Cernik, 27 Feb 1927, Detroit, US, d. 1 Jul 1999. He appeared on the first and last charts of the 1950s, and was one of most consistently successful singers and performers of that decade (Singles: 165 weeks)* pos/wks

14 Nov 52 ● FEET UP! *Columbia DB 3151* 2 10
13 Feb 53 ★ SHE WEARS RED FEATHERS (re) *Columbia DB 3238* 1 16
24 Apr 53 ● PRETTY LITTLE BLACK-EYED SUSIE *Columbia DB 3255* 2 11
28 Aug 53 ★ LOOK AT THAT GIRL *Philips PB 162* 1 14
6 Nov 53 ● CHICKA BOOM (re) *Philips PB 178* 4 15
18 Dec 53 ● CLOUD LUCKY SEVEN *Philips PB 210A* 2 16
19 Feb 54 ● THE CUFF OF MY SHIRT (2re) *Philips PB 225* 9 3
26 Feb 54 SIPPIN' SODA *Philips PB 210B* 11 1
30 Apr 54 ● A DIME AND A DOLLAR (re) *Philips PB 248* 8 5
7 Dec 56 ★ SINGING THE BLUES *Philips PB 650* ▲ 1 22
15 Feb 57 ● KNEE DEEP IN THE BLUES *Philips PB 669* 3 12
26 Apr 57 ★ ROCK-A-BILLY *Philips PB 685* 1 14
26 Jul 57 IN THE MIDDLE OF A DARK, DARK NIGHT / SWEET STUFF (re) *Philips PB 712* 25 4
11 Oct 57 CALL ROSIE ON THE PHONE *Philips PB 743* 17 6
27 Nov 59 ● HEARTACHES BY THE NUMBER (re) *Philips PB 964* ▲ 5 16

Joni MITCHELL (490 Top 500) *Canada's first lady of bohemian folk rock, b. Roberta Anderson, 7 Nov 1943, Fort Macleod, Alberta. The highly respected and influential singer / songwriter and guitarist, whose compositions also included No.1 hit 'Woodstock', has four decades of album hits (and five in the US) (Singles: 24 weeks, Albums: 118 weeks)* pos/wks

13 Jun 70 BIG YELLOW TAXI *Reprise RS 20906* 11 15
4 Oct 97 ● GOT 'TIL IT'S GONE *Virgin VSCDG 1666* [1] 6 9
6 Jun 70 ● LADIES OF THE CANYON *Reprise RSLP 6376* 8 25
24 Jul 71 ● BLUE *Reprise K 44128* 3 18
16 Mar 74 COURT AND SPARK *Asylum SYLA 8756* 14 11
1 Feb 75 MILES OF AISLES *Asylum SYSP 902* 34 4
27 Dec 75 THE HISSING OF SUMMER LAWNS *Asylum SYLA 8763* 14 10
11 Dec 76 HEJIRA *Asylum K 53053* 11 5
21 Jan 78 DON JUAN'S RECKLESS DAUGHTER *Asylum K 63003* 20 7
14 Jul 79 MINGUS *Asylum K 53091* 24 7
4 Oct 80 SHADOWS AND LIGHT *Elektra K 62030* 63 3
4 Dec 82 WILD THINGS RUN FAST *Geffen GEF 25102* 32 8
30 Nov 85 DOG EAT DOG *Geffen GEF 26455* 57 3
2 Apr 88 CHALK MARK IN A RAIN STORM *Geffen WX 141* 26 7
9 Mar 91 NIGHT RIDE HOME *Geffen GEF 24302* 25 5
5 Nov 94 TURBULENT INDIGO *Reprise 9362457862* 53 2
10 Oct 98 TAMING THE TIGER *Reprise 9362464512* 57 1
11 Mar 00 BOTH SIDES NOW *Reprise 9362476202* 50 2

[1] Janet featuring Q-Tip and Joni Mitchell

VSCDG 1666 uses samples from RS 20906

George MITCHELL MINSTRELS (200 Top 500)
Last and biggest selling British minstrel band, leader b. 27 Feb 1917, Falkirk, Scotland, d. 27 Aug 2002. Although definitely non-PC now, this ensemble, which featured Tony Mercer and Dai Francis, had an extremely popular TV series and amassed record-breaking sales (Albums: 292 weeks) pos/wks

26 Nov 60 ★ THE BLACK AND WHITE MINSTREL SHOW *HMV CLP 1399* 1 142
21 Oct 61 ★ ANOTHER BLACK AND WHITE MINSTREL SHOW *HMV CLP 1460* 1 64
20 Oct 62 ★ ON STAGE WITH THE GEORGE MITCHELL MINSTRELS *HMV CLP 1599* 1 26
2 Nov 63 ● ON TOUR WITH THE GEORGE MITCHELL MINSTRELS *HMV CLP 1667* 6 18
12 Dec 64 ● SPOTLIGHT ON THE GEORGE MITCHELL MINSTRELS *HMV CLP 1803* 6 7
4 Dec 65 ● MAGIC OF THE MINSTRELS *HMV CLP 1917* 9 7
26 Nov 66 HERE COME THE MINSTRELS *HMV CLP 3579* 11 11
16 Dec 67 SHOWTIME *HMV CSD 3642* 26 2
14 Dec 68 SING THE IRVING BERLIN SONGBOOK *Columbia SCX 6267* 33 1
19 Dec 70 THE MAGIC OF CHRISTMAS *Columbia SCX 6431* 32 4
19 Nov 77 ● 30 GOLDEN GREATS *EMI EMTV 7* [1] 10 10

[1] George Mitchell Minstrels with the Joe Loss Orchestra

Willie MITCHELL
US, male instrumentalist – guitar (Singles: 3 weeks) pos/wks

24 Apr 68 SOUL SERENADE *London HLU 10186* 43 1
11 Dec 76 THE CHAMPION *London HL 10545* 47 2

MIX FACTORY
UK, male / female vocal / instrumental group (Singles: 2 weeks) pos/wks

30 Jan 93 TAKE ME AWAY (PARADISE) *All Around the World CDGLOBE 120* 51 2

MIXMASTER
Italy, male producer – Daniele Davoli (Singles: 10 weeks) pos/wks

4 Nov 89 ● GRAND PIANO *BCM BCM 344* 9 10

See also BLACK BOX

MIXTURES
Australia, male vocal / instrumental group (Singles: 21 weeks) pos/wks

16 Jan 71 ● THE PUSHBIKE SONG *Polydor 2058 083* 2 21

Hank MIZELL
US, male vocalist d. Dec 1992 (Singles: 13 weeks) pos/wks

20 Mar 76 ● JUNGLE ROCK *Charly CS 1005* 3 13

MOBB DEEP *US, male rap group (Albums: 1 week)* pos/wks

23 Nov 96 HELL ON EARTH *Loud 74321425582* 67 1

MOBILES

UK, male / female vocal / instrumental group (Singles: 14 weeks) pos/wks

9 Jan 82 ● **DROWNING IN BERLIN** *Rialto RIA 3* 9 10
27 Mar 82 **AMOUR AMOUR** *Rialto RIA 5* 45 4

MOBO ALLSTARS *UK / US, male / female vocal / instrumental group (Singles: 3 weeks)* pos/wks

26 Dec 98 **AIN'T NO STOPPING US NOW** *PolyGram TV 5632302* 47 3

Artists featured include: Another Level, Shola Ama, Kéllé Bryan, Celetia, Cleopatra, Damage, Des'ree, D'Influence, E17, Michelle Gayle, Glamma Kid, Lynden David Hall, Hinda Hicks, Honeyz, Kle'Shay, Kele Le Roc, Beverley Knight, Tony Momrelle, Nine Yards, Mica Paris, Karen Ramirez, Connor Reeves, Roachford, 7th Son, Byron Stingily, Truce, Soundproof, Ultimate Kaos

MOBY (332 Top 500) *Genre-bending, maverick producer / vocalist b. Richard Hall, 11 Sep 1965, New York, US. Descendant of 'Moby Dick' author, Herman Melville. The Brit and Grammy-nominated 'Play' was the UK's biggest-selling independent album of 2000 and went platinum in more than 20 countries (Singles: 70 weeks, Albums: 128 weeks)* pos/wks

27 Jul 91 ● **GO (re)** *Outer Rhythm FOOT 15* 10 10
3 Jul 93 **I FEEL IT** *Equinox AXISCD 001* 38 3
11 Sep 93 **MOVE** *Mute CDMUTE 158* 21 5
28 May 94 **HYMN** *Mute CDMUTE 161* 31 2
29 Oct 94 **FEELING SO REAL** *Mute CDMUTE 173* 30 2
25 Feb 95 **EVERY TIME YOU TOUCH ME** *Mute CDMUTE 176* 28 3
1 Jul 95 **INTO THE BLUE** *Mute CDMUTE 179A* 34 2
7 Sep 96 **THAT'S WHEN I REACH FOR MY REVOLVER** *Mute CDMUTE 184* 50 1
15 Nov 97 ● **JAMES BOND THEME (re)** *Mute CDMUTE 210* 8 8
5 Sep 98 **HONEY** *Mute CDMUTE 218* 33 2
8 May 99 **RUN ON** *Mute CDMUTE 221* 33 2
24 Jul 99 **BODYROCK** *Mute CDMUTE 225* 38 2
23 Oct 99 **WHY DOES MY HEART FEEL SO BAD?** *Mute CDMUTE 230* 16 4
18 Mar 00 **NATURAL BLUES** *Mute CDMUTE 251* 11 6
24 Jun 00 ● **PORCELAIN** *Mute CDMUTE 252* 5 6
28 Oct 00 **WHY DOES MY HEART FEEL SO BAD? (re-issue)** *Mute CDMUTE 255* 17 5
11 May 02 **WE ARE ALL MADE OF STARS** *Mute CDMUTE 268* 11 4
31 Aug 02 **EXTREME WAYS** *Mute CDMUTE 270* 39 1
16 Nov 02 **IN THIS WORLD** *Mute CDMUTE 276* 35 2
25 Mar 95 **EVERYTHING IS WRONG / MIXED & REMIXED** *Mute LCDSTUMM 130* 21 7
5 Oct 96 **ANIMAL RIGHTS** *Mute LCDSTUMM 150* 38 1
29 May 99 ★ **PLAY** *Mute CDSTUMM 172* 1 81
1 Jul 00 **I LIKE TO SCORE** *Mute CDSTUMM 168* 54 2
4 Nov 00 **PLAY / THE B SIDES** *Mute LCDSTUMM 172* 24 3
25 May 02 ★ **18** *Mute CDSTUMM 202* ■ 1 34

MOCA – *See David MORALES*

MOCHA – *See Missy 'Misdemeanor' ELLIOTT; Nicole RAY*

MOCK TURTLES *UK, male / female vocal / instrumental group (Singles: 18 weeks, Albums: 4 weeks)* pos/wks

9 Mar 91 **CAN YOU DIG IT?** *Siren SRN 136* 18 11
29 Jun 91 **AND THEN SHE SMILES** *Siren SRN 139* 44 4
15 Mar 03 **CAN YOU DIG IT? (re-mix)** *Virgin CDMOCK 001* 19 3
25 May 91 **TURTLE SOUP** *Imaginary ILLUSION 012* 54 1
27 Jul 91 **TWO SIDES** *Siren SRNLP31* 33 3

MODERN EON

UK, male vocal / instrumental group (Albums: 1 week) pos/wks

13 Jun 81 **FICTION TALES** *DinDisc DID 11* 65 1

MODERN LOVERS – *See Jonathan RICHMAN and the MODERN LOVERS*

MODERN ROMANCE *UK, male vocal / instrumental group (Singles: 77 weeks, Albums: 13 weeks)* pos/wks

15 Aug 81 **EVERYBODY SALSA** *WEA K 18815* 12 10
7 Nov 81 ● **AY AY AY AY MOOSEY** *WEA K 18883* 10 12
30 Jan 82 **QUEEN OF THE RAPPING SCENE (NOTHING EVER GOES THE WAY YOU PLAN)** *WEA K 18928* 37 8
14 Aug 82 **CHERRY PINK AND APPLE BLOSSOM WHITE** *WEA K 19245* [1] 15 8
13 Nov 82 ● **BEST YEARS OF OUR LIVES** *WEA ROM 1* 4 13
26 Feb 83 ● **HIGH LIFE** *WEA ROM 2* 8 8
7 May 83 **DON'T STOP THAT CRAZY RHYTHM** *WEA ROM 3* 14 6
6 Aug 83 ● **WALKING IN THE RAIN** *WEA X 9733* 7 12
16 Apr 83 **TRICK OF THE LIGHT** *WEA X 0127* 53 7
3 Dec 83 **PARTY TONIGHT** *Ronco RON LP 3* 45 6

[1] Modern Romance featuring John du Prez

MODERN TALKING *Germany, male vocal / instrumental duo – Thomas Anders and Dieter Bohlen (Singles: 22 weeks, Albums: 3 weeks)* pos/wks

15 Jun 85 **YOU'RE MY HEART, YOU'RE MY SOUL (re)** *Magnet MAG 277* ..56 7
12 Oct 85 **YOU CAN WIN IF YOU WANT** *Magnet MAG 282* 70 2
16 Aug 86 ● **BROTHER LOUIE** *RCA PB 40875* 4 10
4 Oct 86 **ATLANTIS IS CALLING (S.O.S. FOR LOVE)** *RCA PB 40969* 55 3
11 Oct 86 **READY FOR ROMANCE** *RCA PL 71133* 76 3

MODETTES

UK, female vocal / instrumental group (Singles: 6 weeks) pos/wks

12 Jul 80 **PAINT IT BLACK** *Deram DET-R 1* 42 5
18 Jul 81 **TONIGHT** *Deram DET 3* 68 1

MODJO *France, male production / vocal duo – Yann Destangol and Romain Tranchart (Singles: 29 weeks)* pos/wks

16 Sep 00 ★ **LADY (HEAR ME TONIGHT)** *Polydor 5877582* ■ 1 20
14 Apr 01 **CHILLIN'** *Polydor 5870092* 12 8
6 Oct 01 **WHAT I MEAN** *Polydor 5873462* 59 1

Domenico MODUGNO

Italy, male vocalist d. 6 Aug 1994 (Singles: 13 weeks) pos/wks

5 Sep 58 ● **VOLARE (NEL BLU DIPINTO DI BLU)** *Oriole ICB 5000* ▲ 10 12
27 Mar 59 **CIAO CIAO BAMBINA (PIOVE)** *Oriole CB 1489* 29 1

MOFFATTS *Canada, male vocal / instrumental group (Singles: 6 weeks, Albums: 1 week)* pos/wks

20 Feb 99 **CRAZY** *Chrysalis CDEM 533* 16 3
26 Jun 99 **UNTIL YOU LOVED ME** *Chrysalis CDEM 541* 36 2
23 Oct 99 **MISERY** *EMI CDEM 551* 47 1
6 Mar 99 **CHAPTER 1: A NEW BEGINNING** *Chrysalis 4992072* 62 1

MOGUAI *Germany, male producer – Andre Tegeler (Singles: 1 week)* pos/wks

8 Feb 03 **U KNOW Y** *Hope HOPECDS 038* 62 1

MOGWAI

UK, male instrumental group (Singles: 3 weeks, Albums: 7 weeks) pos/wks

4 Apr 98 **SWEET LEAF / BLACK SABBATH** *Fierce Panda NING 47CD* [1] 60 1
11 Apr 98 **FEAR SATAN (re-mix)** *Eye-Q EYEUK 032CD* 57 1
11 Jul 98 **NO EDUCATION NO FUTURE (F**K THE CURFEW)** *Chemikal CHEM 026CD* 68 1
8 Nov 97 **YOUNG TEAM** *Chemikal Underground CHEM 018CD* 75 1
10 Apr 99 **COME ON DIE YOUNG** *Chemikal Underground CHEM 033CD* ..29 2
12 May 01 **ROCK ACTION** *Southpaw PAWCD 1* 23 2
21 Jun 03 **HAPPY SONGS FOR HAPPY PEOPLE** *PIAS PIASX035CD* 47 2

[1] Mogwai: Magoo

MOHAWKS *UK, male vocal / instrumental group – leader Alan Hawkshaw (Singles: 2 weeks)* pos/wks

24 Jan 87 **THE CHAMP** *Pama PM 1* 58 2

Frank'o MOIRAGHI featuring AMNESIA *Italy, male / female vocal / instrumental duo (Singles: 4 weeks)* pos/wks

1 Jun 96 **FEEL MY BODY** *Multiply CDMULTY 10* 39 2
26 Oct 96 **FEEL MY BODY (re-mix)** *Multiply CDMULTY 15* 40 2

MOIST *Canada, male vocal / instrumental group (Singles: 10 weeks, Albums: 3 weeks)* pos/wks

12 Nov 94 **PUSH** *Chrysalis CDCHS 5016* 35 3

MOST HIT ALBUMS

Our Top 20 acts chart, defined by most hit albums (not including re-issues), is dominated by male artists and split almost equally between US and British performers. Ties are separated by chart positions of the albums in question.

1. ELVIS PRESLEY 106 hit albums
2. JAMES LAST 64
3. FRANK SINATRA 62
4. CLIFF RICHARD 56
5. DIANA ROSS 52
6. BOB DYLAN 45
7. ROLLING STONES 43
8. SHADOWS 43
9. DAVID BOWIE 39
10. ELTON JOHN 39
11. SHIRLEY BASSEY 36
12. NEIL DIAMOND 35
13. NEIL YOUNG 34
14. STATUS QUO 33
15. BEATLES 32
16. ROD STEWART 32
17. IRON MAIDEN 30
18. BEACH BOYS 30
19. VAN MORRISON 30
20. PAUL McCARTNEY 29

The two Neils, Diamond and Young, side by side in this chart with 69 hit albums between them

25 Feb 95 **SILVER** *Chrysalis CDCHS 5019* **50** 2
29 Apr 95 **FREAKY BE BEAUTIFUL** *Chrysalis CDCHS 5022* **47** 2
19 Aug 95 **PUSH (re-issue)** *Chrysalis CDCHS 5024* **20** 3
26 Aug 95 **SILVER** *Chrysalis CDCHR 6080* **49** 3

MOJO *UK, male instrumental group (Singles: 3 weeks)* pos/wks

22 Aug 81 **DANCE ON** *Creole CR 17* **70** 3

MOJOLATORS featuring CAMILLA
US, male production duo and female vocalist (Singles: 1 week) pos/wks

6 Oct 01 **DRIFTING** *Multiply CDMULTY 81* **52** 1

MOJOS *UK, male vocal / instrumental group (Singles: 26 weeks)* pos/wks

26 Mar 64 ● **EVERYTHING'S ALRIGHT** *Decca F 11853* **9** 11
11 Jun 64 **WHY NOT TONIGHT** *Decca F 11918* **25** 10
10 Sep 64 **SEVEN DAFFODILS** *Decca F 11959* **30** 5

MOKENSTEF *US, female vocal group (Singles: 1 week)* pos/wks

23 Sep 95 **HE'S MINE** *Def Jam DEFCD 13* **70** 1

MOLELLA featuring the OUTHERE BROTHERS *Italy, male producer and US, male rap / vocal duo (Singles: 10 weeks)* pos/wks

16 Dec 95 ● **IF YOU WANNA PARTY** *Eternal WEA 030CD* **9** 10

Sophie MOLETA – *See HUMAN MOVEMENT featuring Sophie MOLETA*

Ralph MOLINA – *See Ian McNABB*

Brian MOLKO – *See ALPINESTARS featuring Brian MOLKO*

Sam MOLLISON – *See SASHA*

MOLLY HALF HEAD
UK, male vocal / instrumental group (Singles: 1 week) pos/wks

3 Jun 95 **SHINE** *Columbia 6620732* **73** 1

MOLLY HATCHET
US, male vocal / instrumental group (Albums: 1 week) pos/wks

25 Jan 86 **DOUBLE TROUBLE – LIVE** *Epic EPC 88670* **94** 1

MOLOKO *Ireland / UK, male / female vocal / instrumental duo – Roisin Murphy and Mark Brydon (Singles: 39 weeks, Albums: 30 weeks)* pos/wks

24 Feb 96 **DOMINOID** *Echo ECSCD 016* **65** 1
25 May 96 **FUN FOR ME** *Echo ECSCD 20* **36** 2
20 Jun 98 **THE FLIPSIDE** *Echo ECSCD 54* **53** 1
27 Mar 99 **SING IT BACK** *Echo ECSCD 71* **45** 2
4 Sep 99 ● **SING IT BACK (re-mix)** *Echo ECSCD 82* **4** 9
1 Apr 00 ● **THE TIME IS NOW** *Echo ECSCD 88* **2** 10
5 Aug 00 **PURE PLEASURE SEEKER** *Echo ECSCD 99* **21** 5
1 Mar 03 **FAMILIAR FEELING** *Echo ECSCD 131* **10** 4
25 Nov 00 **INDIGO** *Echo ECSCD 104* **51** 1
5 Jul 03 **FOREVER MORE** *Echo ECSCD 136* **17** 4
5 Sep 98 **I AM NOT A DOCTOR** *Echo ECHCD 21* **64** 1
22 Apr 00 ● **THINGS TO MAKE AND DO** *Echo ECHCD 31* **3** 26
15 Mar 03 **STATUES** *Echo ECHCD44* **18** 3

See also PSYCHEDELIC WALTONS

MOMBASSA *UK, male production duo (Singles: 1 week)* pos/wks

8 Mar 97 **CRY FREEDOM** *Soundproof SPCD 021* **63** 1

MOMENTS *US, male vocal group (Singles: 32 weeks)* pos/wks

8 Mar 75 ● **GIRLS** *All Platinum 6146 302* [1] **3** 10
19 Jul 75 ● **DOLLY MY LOVE** *All Platinum 6146 306* **10** 9

Date		Title / Label	pos	wks
25 Oct 75		**LOOK AT ME (I'M IN LOVE)** *All Platinum 6146 309*	42	4
22 Jan 77	●	**JACK IN THE BOX** *All Platinum 6146 318*	7	9

[1] Moments and Whatnauts

Tony MOMRELLE *UK, male vocalist (Singles: 1 week)*

Date		Title / Label	pos	wks
15 Aug 98		**LET ME SHOW YOU** *Art & Soul ART 1CDS*	67	1

MONACO *UK, male vocal / instrumental duo – Peter Hook and David Potts (Singles: 11 weeks, Albums: 3 weeks)*

Date		Title / Label	pos	wks
15 Mar 97		**WHAT DO YOU WANT FROM ME?** *Polydor 5731912*	11	6
31 May 97		**SWEET LIPS** *Polydor 5710552*	18	4
20 Sep 97		**SHINE (SOMEONE WHO NEEDS ME)** *Polydor 5714182*	55	1
21 Jun 97		MUSIC FOR PLEASURE *Polydor 5372422*	11	3

See also *NEW ORDER; JOY DIVISION*

Pharoahe MONCH

US, male rapper – Troy Jamerson (Singles: 11 weeks)

Date		Title / Label	pos	wks
19 Feb 00		**SIMON SAYS** *Rawkus RWK 205CD*	24	2
19 Aug 00		**LIGHT** *Rawkus RWK 259CD*	72	1
3 Feb 01		**OH NO** *Rawkus RWK 302* [1]	24	4
1 Dec 01		**GOT YOU** *Priority PTYCD 145*	27	3
14 Sep 02		**THE LIFE** *MCA MCSTD 402292* [2]	50	1

[1] Mos Def and Nate Dogg featuring Pharoahe Monch [2] Styles and Pharoahe Monch

Jay MONDI and the LIVING BASS

US, male / female vocal / instrumental group (Singles: 3 weeks)

Date		Title / Label	pos	wks
24 Mar 90		**ALL NIGHT LONG** *10 TEN 304*	63	3

MONDO KANE

UK, male vocal / instrumental group (Singles: 3 weeks)

Date		Title / Label	pos	wks
16 Aug 86		**NEW YORK AFTERNOON** *Lisson DOLE 2*	70	3

MONE *US, female vocalist (Singles: 2 weeks)*

Date		Title / Label	pos	wks
12 Aug 95		**WE CAN MAKE IT** *A&M 5811592*	64	1
16 Mar 96		**MOVIN'** *AM:PM 5814392*	48	1

Zoot MONEY and the BIG ROLL BAND

UK, male vocal / instrumental group, leader – George Bruno Money (Singles: 8 weeks, Albums: 3 weeks)

Date		Title / Label	pos	wks
18 Aug 66		**BIG TIME OPERATOR** *Columbia DB 7975*	25	8
15 Oct 66		ZOOT *Columbia SX 6075*	23	3

MONEY MARK *US, male vocal / instrumentalist / producer – Mark Ramos-Nishita (Singles: 3 weeks, Albums: 6 weeks)*

Date		Title / Label	pos	wks
28 Feb 98		**HAND IN YOUR HEAD** *Mo Wax MW 066CD*	40	2
6 Jun 98		**MAYBE I'M DEAD** *Mo Wax MW 089CD1*	45	1
9 Sep 95		MARK'S KEYBOARD REPAIR *Mo Wax MW 034CD*	35	2
16 May 98		PUSH THE BUTTON *Mo Wax MW 090CD*	17	4

MONICA *US, female vocalist – Monica Arnold (Singles: 37 weeks, Albums: 10 weeks)*

Date		Title / Label	pos	wks
29 Jul 95		**DON'T TAKE IT PERSONAL (JUST ONE OF DEM DAYS)** *Arista 74321301452*	32	3
17 Feb 96		**LIKE THIS AND LIKE THAT** *Rowdy 74321344222*	33	2
8 Jun 96		**BEFORE YOU WALK OUT OF MY LIFE** *Rowdy 74321374042*	22	3
24 May 97		**FOR YOU I WILL** *Atlantic A 5437CD*	27	2
6 Jun 98	●	**THE BOY IS MINE** *Atlantic AT 0036 CD* [1] ▲	2	20
17 Oct 98	●	**THE FIRST NIGHT** *Rowdy 74321619342* ▲	6	6
4 Sep 99		**ANGEL OF MINE** *Arista 74321692892* ▲	55	1
25 Jul 98		THE BOY IS MINE *Arista 7822190112*	52	10

[1] Brandy and Monica

MONIFAH *US, female vocalist – Monifah Carter (Singles: 2 weeks)*

Date		Title / Label	pos	wks
30 Jan 99		**TOUCH IT** *Universal UND 56218*	29	2

TS MONK

US, male / female vocal / instrumental group (Singles: 6 weeks)

Date		Title / Label	pos	wks
7 Mar 81		**BON BON VIE** *Mirage K 11653*	63	2
25 Apr 81		**CANDIDATE FOR LOVE** *Mirage K 11648*	58	4

MONKEES (294 Top 500)

The world's top act of 1967: Davy Jones (v/g), Mike Nesmith (v/g), Peter Tork (v/k), Mickey Dolenz (v/d). This Anglo-American quartet was hand-picked for a Beatles-style TV series, which helped to rocket them, albeit briefly, to the very top (Singles: 101 weeks, Albums: 118 weeks)

Date		Title / Label	pos	wks
5 Jan 67	★	**I'M A BELIEVER** *RCA 1560* ▲	1	17
26 Jan 67		**LAST TRAIN TO CLARKSVILLE** *RCA 1547* ▲	23	7
6 Apr 67	●	**A LITTLE BIT ME, A LITTLE BIT YOU** *RCA 1580*	3	12
22 Jun 67	●	**ALTERNATE TITLE** *RCA 1604*	2	12
16 Aug 67		**PLEASANT VALLEY SUNDAY** *RC 1620*	11	8
15 Nov 67	●	**DAYDREAM BELIEVER** *RCA 1645* ▲	5	17
27 Mar 68		**VALLERI** *RCA 1673*	12	8
26 Jun 68		**DW WASHBURN** *RCA 1706*	17	6
26 Mar 69		**TEAR DROP CITY** *RCA 1802*	46	1
25 Jun 69		**SOMEDAY MAN** *RCA 1824*	47	1
15 Mar 80		**THE MONKEES EP** *Arista ARIST 326*	33	9
18 Oct 86		**THAT WAS THEN, THIS IS NOW** *Arista ARIST 673*	68	1
1 Apr 89		**THE MONKEES EP** *Arista 112157*	62	2
28 Jan 67	★	THE MONKEES *RCA Victor SF 7844* ▲	1	36
15 Apr 67	★	MORE OF THE MONKEES *RCA Victor SF 7868* ▲	1	25
8 Jul 67	●	HEADQUARTERS *RCA Victor SF 7886* ▲	2	19
13 Jan 68	●	PISCES AQUARIUS CAPRICORN & JONES LTD. *RCA Victor SF 7912* ▲	5	11
28 Nov 81		THE MONKEES *Arista DARTY 12*	99	1
15 Apr 89		HEY HEY IT'S THE MONKEES – GREATEST HITS *K-Tel NE 1432*	12	9
22 Mar 97		HERE THEY COME ... THE GREATEST HITS OF THE MONKEES *Warner.ESP/Telstar 9548352182*	15	10
10 Mar 01		THE DEFINITIVE MONKEES *WSM 8573866922*	15	7

Tracks on Arista 326 EP: I'm a Believer / Daydream Believer / Last Train to Clarksville / A Little Bit Me a Little Bit You. Tracks on Arista 112157 EP: Daydream Believer / Monkees Theme / Last Train to Clarksville The two albums titled 'The Monkees' are different

MONKEY MAFIA

UK, male vocal / instrumental / DJ / production group (Singles: 3 weeks, Albums: 1 week)

Date		Title / Label	pos	wks
10 Aug 96		**WORK MI BODY** *Heavenly HVN 53CD* [1]	75	1
7 Jun 97		**15 STEPS (EP)** *Heavenly HVN 67CD*	67	1
2 May 98		**LONG AS I CAN SEE THE LIGHT** *Heavenly HVN 84CD*	51	1
16 May 98		SHOOT THE BOSS *Heavenly HVNLP 21CD*	69	1

[1] Monkey Mafia featuring Patra

Tracks on 15 Steps (EP): Lion in the Hall / Krash the Decks: Slaughter the Vinyl / Metro Love / Beats in the Hall

MONKS

UK, male vocal / instrumental duo – Richard Hudson and John Ford (Singles: 9 weeks)

Date		Title / Label	pos	wks
21 Apr 79		**NICE LEGS SHAME ABOUT HER FACE** *Carrere CAR 104*	19	9

The Monks were Hudson-Ford under a different name

MONKS AND CHOIRBOYS OF DOWNSIDE ABBEY

UK, male monastic choir (Albums: 6 weeks)

Date		Title / Label	pos	wks
2 Nov 96		THE ABBEY *Virgin VTCD 99*	54	5
3 Jan 98		GREGORIAN MOODS *Virgin/EMI VTCD 171*	59	1

MONKS CHORUS SILOS – See *CORO DE MUNJES DEL MONASTERIO BENEDICTINO DE SANTO DOMINGO DE SILOS*

MONKS OF AMPLEFORTH ABBEY

UK, monastic choir (Albums: 2 weeks)

Date		Title / Label	pos	wks
17 Jun 95		VISION OF PEACE *Classic FM CFMCD 1783*	73	2

MONO *UK, male / female vocal / instrumental duo (Singles: 1 week, Albums: 1 week)* pos/wks

2 May 98	LIFE IN MONO *Echo ECSCD 64*	60 1
8 Aug 98	FORMICA BLUES *Echo ECHCD 17*	71 1

MONOBOY featuring DELORES *Ireland, male producer – Ian Masterson and female vocalist (Singles: 1 week)* pos/wks

7 Jul 01	THE MUSIC IN YOU *Perfecto PERF 18CDS*	50 1

MONOCHROME SET
UK, male vocal / instrumental group (Albums: 4 weeks) pos/wks

3 May 80	STRANGE BOUTIQUE *DinDisc DID 4*	62 4

Tony MONOPOLY *Australia, male vocalist (Albums: 4 weeks)* pos/wks

12 Jun 76	TONY MONOPOLY *BUK BULP 2000*	25 4

Matt MONRO 489 Top 500
Superior British balladeer and former bus driver, b. Terence Parsons, 1 Dec 1930, London, d. 7 Feb 1985. This Sinatra-styled vocalist, who was renamed by hitmaker Winifred Atwell, had few MOR equals in the 1960s. In 1961, Billboard magazine named him Top International Act and Most Promising Male Singer (Singles: 127 weeks, Albums: 15 weeks) pos/wks

15 Dec 60 ●	PORTRAIT OF MY LOVE *Parlophone R 4714*	3 16
9 Mar 61 ●	MY KIND OF GIRL *Parlophone R 4755*	5 12
18 May 61	WHY NOT NOW / CAN THIS BE LOVE *Parlophone R 4775*	24 9
28 Sep 61	GONNA BUILD A MOUNTAIN *Parlophone R 4819*	44 3
8 Feb 62 ●	SOFTLY AS I LEAVE YOU *Parlophone R 4868*	10 18
14 Jun 62	WHEN LOVE COMES ALONG *Parlophone R 4911*	46 3
8 Nov 62	MY LOVE AND DEVOTION *Parlophone R 4954*	29 5
14 Nov 63	FROM RUSSIA WITH LOVE *Parlophone R 5068*	20 13
17 Sep 64 ●	WALK AWAY *Parlophone R 5171*	4 20
24 Dec 64	FOR MAMA *Parlophone R 5215*	23 4
25 Mar 65	WITHOUT YOU *Parlophone R 5251*	37 4
21 Oct 65 ●	YESTERDAY *Parlophone R 5348*	8 12
24 Nov 73	AND YOU SMILED *EMI 2091*	28 8
7 Aug 65	I HAVE DREAMED *Parlophone PMC 1250*	20 1
17 Sep 66	THIS IS THE LIFE *Capitol T 2540*	25 2
26 Aug 67	INVITATION TO THE MOVIES *Capitol ST 2730*	30 1
15 Mar 80 ●	HEARTBREAKERS *EMI EMTV 23*	5 11

Gerry MONROE *UK, male vocalist (Singles: 57 weeks)* pos/wks

23 May 70 ●	SALLY *Chapter One CH 122*	4 20
19 Sep 70	CRY *Chapter One CH 128*	38 5
14 Nov 70 ●	MY PRAYER *Chapter One CH 132*	9 12
17 Apr 71	IT'S A SIN TO TELL A LIE *Chapter One CH 144*	13 12
21 Aug 71	LITTLE DROPS OF SILVER *Chapter One CH 152*	37 6
12 Feb 72	GIRL OF MY DREAMS *Chapter One CH 159*	43 2

Hollis P MONROE *Canada, male producer (Singles: 1 week)* pos/wks

24 Apr 99	I'M LONELY *City Beat CBE 778CD*	51 1

MONSOON
UK, male / female vocal / instrumental group (Singles: 12 weeks) pos/wks

3 Apr 82	EVER SO LONELY *Mobile Suit Corp CORP 2*	12 9
5 Jun 82	SHAKTI (THE MEANING OF WITHIN) *Mobile Suit Corp CORP 4*	41 3

MONSTA BOY featuring DENZIE
UK, male production / vocal instrumental duo (Singles: 3 weeks) pos/wks

7 Oct 00	SORRY (I DIDN'T KNOW) *Locked On LOX 125CD*	25 3

MONSTER MAGNET *US, male vocal / instrumental group (Singles: 6 weeks, Albums: 2 weeks)* pos/wks

29 May 93	TWIN EARTH *A&M 5802812*	67 1
18 Mar 95	NEGASONIC TEENAGE WARHEAD *A&M 5809812*	49 1
6 May 95	DOPES TO INFINITY *A&M 5810332*	58 1
23 Jan 99	POWERTRIP *A&M 5828232*	39 2
6 Mar 99	SPACE LORD *A&M 5632752*	45 1
1 Apr 95	DOPES TO INFINITY *A&M 5403152*	51 1
13 Jun 98	POWERTRIP *A&M 5409082*	65 1

MONTAGE
UK, female vocal trio (Singles: 1 week) pos/wks

15 Feb 97	THERE AIN'T NOTHIN' LIKE THE LOVE *Wildcard 5733172*	64 1

MONTANA SEXTET
US, male instrumental group (Singles: 1 week) pos/wks

15 Jan 83	HEAVY VIBES *Virgin VS 560*	59 1

MONTANO vs THE TRUMPET MAN
UK, male production / instrumental duo (Singles: 1 week) pos/wks

18 Sep 99	ITZA TRUMPET THING *Serious SERR 010CD*	46 1

Hugo MONTENEGRO His Orchestra and Chorus
US, orchestra, leader d. 6 Feb 1981 (Singles: 26 weeks) pos/wks

11 Sep 68 ★	THE GOOD, THE BAD AND THE UGLY (re) *RCA 1727*	1 25
8 Jan 69	HANG 'EM HIGH *RCA 1771*	50 1

Chris MONTEZ
US, male vocalist – Ezekiel Montanez (Singles: 61 weeks) pos/wks

4 Oct 62 ●	LET'S DANCE *London HLU 9596*	2 18
17 Jan 63 ●	SOME KINDA FUN *London HLU 9650*	10 9
30 Jun 66 ●	THE MORE I SEE YOU *Pye International 7N 25369*	3 13
22 Sep 66	THERE WILL NEVER BE ANOTHER YOU *Pye International 7N 25381*	37 4
14 Oct 72 ●	LET'S DANCE (re-issue) *London HLU 10205*	9 14
14 Apr 79	LET'S DANCE (2nd re-issue) *Lightning LIG 9011*	47 3

The second re-issue of 'Let's Dance' on Lightning was coupled with 'Memphis' by Lonnie Mack as a double A-side

MONTROSE *US, male vocal / instrumental group (Singles: 2 weeks, Albums: 1 week)* pos/wks

28 Jun 80	SPACE STATION NUMBER 5 / GOOD ROCKIN' TONIGHT *Warner Brothers WB HM 9*	71 2
15 Jun 74	MONTROSE *Warner Bros. K 46276*	43 1

MONTROSE AVENUE
UK, male vocal / instrumental group (Singles: 4 weeks) pos/wks

28 Mar 98	WHERE DO I STAND? *Columbia 6656072*	38 2
20 Jun 98	SHINE *Columbia 6660012*	58 1
17 Oct 98	START AGAIN *Columbia 6664255*	59 1

MONTY PYTHON'S FLYING CIRCUS
UK, male vocal / comedy group (Singles: 9 weeks, Albums: 33 weeks) pos/wks

5 Oct 91 ●	ALWAYS LOOK ON THE BRIGHT SIDE OF LIFE *Virgin PYTH 1* [1]	3 9
30 Oct 71	ANOTHER MONTY PYTHON RECORD *Charisma CAS 1049*	26 3
27 Jan 73	MONTY PYTHON'S PREVIOUS ALBUM *Charisma CAS 1063*	39 3
23 Feb 74	MATCHING TIE & HANDKERCHIEF *Charisma CAS 1080*	49 2
27 Jul 74	LIVE AT DRURY LANE *Charisma CLASS 4*	19 8
9 Aug 75	THE ALBUM OF THE SOUNDTRACK OF THE TRAILER OF THE FILM OF MONTY PYTHON AND THE HOLY GRAIL *Charisma CAS 1003*	45 4
24 Nov 79	LIFE OF BRIAN *Warner Bros. K 56751*	63 3
18 Oct 80	MONTY PYTHON'S CONTRACTUAL OBLIGATION ALBUM *Charisma CAS 1152*	13 8
16 Nov 91	MONTY PYTHON SINGS *Virgin MONT 1*	62 2

[1] Monty Python

See also Eric IDLE

MONYAKA
US / Jamaica, male vocal / instrumental group (Singles: 8 weeks) pos/wks

10 Sep 83	GO DEH YAKA (GO TO THE TOP) *Polydor POSP 641*	14 8

MOOD

UK, male vocal / instrumental group (Singles: 10 weeks) pos/wks

6 Feb 82	**DON'T STOP** *RCA 171*	59	4
22 May 82	**PARIS IS ONE DAY AWAY** *RCA 211*	42	5
30 Oct 82	**PASSION IN DARK ROOMS** *RCA 276*	74	1

MOODSWINGS / CHRISSIE HYNDE *UK, male production group and US, female vocalist (Singles: 4 weeks)* pos/wks

12 Oct 91	**SPIRITUAL HIGH (STATE OF INDEPENDENCE)** *Arista 114528*	66	2
23 Jan 93	**SPIRITUAL HIGH (STATE OF INDEPENDENCE) (re-mix)** *Arista 74321127712*	47	2

See also PRETENDERS

MOODY BLUES (92 Top 500)

Long-lived and internationally popular cosmic rock quintet from Birmingham, UK. Line-up has included Denny Laine (v/g), Ray Thomas (fl/v), Mike Pinder, (k/v), Graeme Edge (d), Justin Hayward (v/g) and John Lodge (b/v). This album-orientated act has sold more than 50 million records worldwide (Singles: 114 weeks, Albums: 335 weeks) pos/wks

10 Dec 64 ★	**GO NOW** *Decca F 12022*	1	14
4 Mar 65	**I DON'T WANT TO GO ON WITHOUT YOU** *Decca F 12095*	33	9
10 Jun 65	**FROM THE BOTTOM OF MY HEART** *Decca F 12166*	22	9
18 Nov 65	**EVERYDAY** *Decca F 12266*	44	2
27 Dec 67 ●	**NIGHTS IN WHITE SATIN (2re)** *Deram DM 161*	9	34
7 Aug 68	**VOICES IN THE SKY** *Deram DM 196*	27	10
4 Dec 68	**RIDE MY SEE-SAW** *Deram DM 213*	42	1
2 May 70 ●	**QUESTION** *Threshold TH 4*	2	12
6 May 72	**ISN'T LIFE STRANGE** *Threshold TH 9*	13	10
10 Feb 73	**I'M JUST A SINGER (IN A ROCK & ROLL BAND)** *Threshold TH 13*	36	4
20 Aug 83	**BLUE WORLD** *Threshold TH 30*	35	5
25 Jun 88	**I KNOW YOU'RE OUT THERE SOMEWHERE** *Polydor POSP 921*	52	4
27 Jan 68	**DAYS OF FUTURE PASSED** *Deram SML 707*	27	16
3 Aug 68 ●	**IN SEARCH OF THE LOST CHORD** *Deram SML 711*	5	32
3 May 69 ★	**ON THE THRESHOLD OF A DREAM** *Deram SML 1035*	1	73
6 Dec 69 ●	**TO OUR CHILDREN'S CHILDREN'S CHILDREN** *Threshold THS 1*	2	44
15 Aug 70 ★	**A QUESTION OF BALANCE** *Threshold THS 3*	1	19
7 Aug 71 ★	**EVERY GOOD BOY DESERVES FAVOUR** *Threshold THS 5*	1	21
2 Dec 72 ●	**SEVENTH SOJOURN** *Threshold THS 7* ▲	5	18
16 Nov 74	**THIS IS THE MOODY BLUES** *Threshold MB 1/2*	14	18
24 Jun 78 ●	**OCTAVE** *Decca TXS 129*	6	18
10 Nov 79	**OUT OF THIS WORLD** *K-Tel NE 1051*	15	10
23 May 81 ●	**LONG DISTANCE VOYAGER** *Threshold TXS 139* ▲	7	19
10 Sep 83	**THE PRESENT** *Threshold TXS 140*	15	8
10 May 86	**THE OTHER SIDE OF LIFE** *Threshold POLD 5190*	24	6
25 Jun 88	**SUR LA MER** *Polydor POLH 43*	21	5
20 Jan 90	**GREATEST HITS** *Threshold 8406591*	71	1
13 Jul 91	**KEYS OF THE KINGDOM** *Threshold 8494331*	54	2
5 Oct 96	**THE VERY BEST OF THE MOODY BLUES** *PolyGram TV 5358002*	13	15
22 Apr 00	**THE VERY BEST OF THE MOODY BLUES (re-issue) / STRANGE TIMES** *Universal Music TV 5414242*	19	6
11 May 02	**THE VERY BEST OF THE MOODY BLUES** *UMTV 5833442*	27	4

'Nights in White Satin' reached No.19 on its original chart visit then peaked at No.9 in Dec 1972, climbing to No.14 on its re-entry in Nov 1979

The Very Best of in 2002 is an expanded version of the 1996 album

Michael MOOG

US, male producer – Shivaun Gaines (Singles: 3 weeks) pos/wks

11 Dec 99	**THAT SOUND** *ffrr FCD 374*	32	2
25 Aug 01	**YOU BELONG TO ME** *Strictly Rhythm SRUKECD 04*	62	1

MOOGWAI

Switzerland / Holland, production duo (Singles: 2 weeks) pos/wks

6 May 00	**VIOLA** *Platipus PLATCD 71*	55	1
26 May 01	**THE LABYRINTH** *Platipus PLATCD 83*	68	1

MOONMAN

Holland, male DJ / producer – Ferry Corsten (Singles: 4 weeks) pos/wks

9 Aug 97	**DON'T BE AFRAID** *Heat Recordings HEATCD 009*	60	1
27 Nov 99	**DON'T BE AFRAID '99 (re-mix)** *Heat Recordings HEATCD 022*	41	2
7 Oct 00	**GALAXIA** *Heat Recordings HEATCD 025* [1]	50	1

[1] Moonman featuring Chantal

See also SYSTEM F; VERACOCHA; GOURYELLA; STARPARTY; ALBION; Ferry CORSTEN

MOONTREKKERS *UK, male instrumental group (Singles: 1 week)* pos/wks

2 Nov 61	**NIGHT OF THE VAMPIRE** *Parlophone R 4814*	50	1

MOONY *Italy, female vocalist – Monica Bragato (Singles: 9 weeks)* pos/wks

15 Jun 02 ●	**DOVE (I'LL BE LOVING YOU)** *Positiva / Cream CDMNY 1*	9	8
1 Mar 03	**ACROBATS (LOOKING FOR BALANCE)** *WEA WEA 363CD*	64	1

Ian MOOR *UK, male vocalist (Albums: 2 weeks)* pos/wks

7 Oct 00	**NATURALLY** *BMG TV Projects 74321783862*	38	2

Chanté MOORE *US, female vocalist (Singles: 11 weeks)* pos/wks

20 Mar 93	**LOVE'S TAKEN OVER** *MCA MCSTD 1744*	54	3
4 Mar 95	**FREE / SAIL ON** *MCA MCSTD 2042*	69	1
7 Apr 01	**STRAIGHT UP (re)** *MCA MCSTD 40250*	11	7

Christy MOORE *Ireland, male vocalist (Albums: 8 weeks)* pos/wks

4 May 91	**SMOKE AND STRONG WHISKEY** *Newberry CM 21*	49	3
21 Sep 91	**THE CHRISTY MOORE COLLECTION** *East West WX 434*	69	1
6 Nov 93	**KING PUCK** *Equator ATLASCD 003*	66	2
14 Sep 96	**GRAFFITI TONGUE** *Grapevine GRACD 215*	35	2

Dorothy MOORE *US, female vocalist (Singles: 24 weeks)* pos/wks

19 Jun 76 ●	**MISTY BLUE** *Contempo CS 2087*	5	12
16 Oct 76	**FUNNY HOW TIME SLIPS AWAY** *Contempo CS 2092*	38	3
15 Oct 77	**I BELIEVE YOU** *Epic EPC 5573*	20	9

Dudley MOORE *UK, male comedian / vocalist / instrumentalist – piano (Albums: 24 weeks)* pos/wks

4 Dec 65	**THE OTHER SIDE OF DUDLEY MOORE** *Decca LK 4732*	11	9
11 Jun 66	**GENUINE DUD** *Decca LK 4788*	13	10
26 Jan 91	**ORCHESTRA!** *Decca 4308361* [1]	38	5

[1] Sir George Solti and Dudley Moore

See also Peter COOK and Dudley MOORE

Gary MOORE (314 Top 500)

Noted blues guitarist, b. 4 Apr 1952, Belfast. Played in early 1970s Irish band Skid Row (with Phil Lynott) as well as Thin Lizzy and Colosseum II before successfully launching his solo career (Singles: 103 weeks, Albums: 104 weeks) pos/wks

21 Apr 79 ●	**PARISIENNE WALKWAYS** *MCA 419*	8	11
21 Jan 84	**HOLD ON TO LOVE** *10 TEN 13*	65	3
11 Aug 84	**EMPTY ROOMS** *10 TEN 25*	51	5
18 May 85 ●	**OUT IN THE FIELDS** *10 TEN 49* [1]	5	10
27 Jul 85	**EMPTY ROOMS (re-issue)** *10 TEN 58*	23	8
20 Dec 86	**OVER THE HILLS AND FAR AWAY** *10 TEN 134*	20	8
28 Feb 87	**WILD FRONTIER** *10 TEN 159*	35	5
9 May 87	**FRIDAY ON MY MIND** *10 TEN 164*	26	6
29 Aug 87	**THE LONER** *10 TEN 178*	53	5
5 Dec 87	**TAKE A LITTLE TIME (DOUBLE SINGLE)** *10 TEN 190*	75	1
14 Jan 89	**AFTER THE WAR** *Virgin GMS 1*	37	4
18 Mar 89	**READY FOR LOVE** *Virgin GMS 2*	56	2
24 Mar 90	**OH PRETTY WOMAN** *Virgin VS 1233* [2]	48	3
12 May 90	**STILL GOT THE BLUES (FOR YOU)** *Virgin VS 1267*	31	7
18 Aug 90	**WALKING BY MYSELF** *Virgin VS 1281*	48	5
15 Dec 90	**TOO TIRED** *Virgin VS 1306*	71	1
22 Feb 92	**COLD DAY IN HELL** *Virgin VS 1393*	24	5
9 May 92	**STORY OF THE BLUES** *Virgin VS 1412*	40	4
18 Jul 92	**SINCE I MET YOU BABY** *Virgin VS 1423* [3]	59	3
24 Oct 92	**SEPARATE WAYS** *Virgin VS 1437*	59	1
8 May 93	**PARISIENNE WALKWAYS (re-recording)** *Virgin VSCDX 1456*	32	4

		pos	wks
17 Jun 95	NEED YOUR LOVE SO BAD *Virgin VSCDG 1546*	48	2
3 Feb 79	BACK ON THE STREETS *MCA MCF 2853*	70	1
16 Oct 82	CORRIDORS OF POWER *Virgin V 2245*	30	6
18 Feb 84	VICTIMS OF THE FUTURE *10 DIX 2*	12	7
13 Oct 84	WE WANT MOORE! *10 GMDL 1*	32	3
14 Sep 85	RUN FOR COVER *10 DIX 16*	12	8
12 Jul 86	ROCKIN' EVERY NIGHT *10 XID 1*	99	1
14 Mar 87 ●	WILD FRONTIER *10 DIX 56*	8	14
11 Feb 89	AFTER THE WAR *Virgin V 2575*	23	5
7 Apr 90	STILL GOT THE BLUES *Virgin V 2612*	13	26
21 Mar 92 ●	AFTER HOURS *Virgin CDV 2684*	4	13
22 May 93 ●	BLUES ALIVE *Virgin CDVX 2716*	8	5
26 Nov 94	BALLADS AND BLUES 1982-1994 *Virgin CDV 2768*	33	6
10 Jun 95	BLUES FOR GREENEY *Virgin CDV 2784*	14	5
7 Jun 97	DARK DAYS IN PARADISE *Virgin CDV 2826*	43	2
31 Oct 98	OUT IN THE FIELDS – THE VERY BEST OF GARY MOORE *Virgin CDVX 2871*	54	1
24 Mar 01	BACK TO THE BLUES *Sanctuary SANCD 072*	53	1

1 Gary Moore and Phil Lynott 2 Gary Moore featuring Albert King 3 Gary Moore and B.B. King

'Parisienne Walkways' features uncredited vocals by Phil Lynott. Tracks on double single: Take a Little Time / Out in the Fields / All Messed Up / Thunder Rising

See also BBM

Jackie MOORE *US, female vocalist (Singles: 5 weeks)*

		pos	wks
15 Sep 79	THIS TIME BABY *CBS 7722*	49	5

Lynsey MOORE – *See RAMSEY and FEN featuring Lynsey MOORE*

Mandy MOORE
US, female vocalist (Singles: 18 weeks, Albums: 1 week)

		pos	wks
6 May 00 ●	CANDY *Epic 6693452*	6	13
19 Aug 00	I WANNA BE WITH YOU *Epic 6695922*	21	5
20 May 00	I WANNA BE WITH YOU *Epic 4982769*	52	1

Mark MOORE – *See S EXPRESS*

Melba MOORE
US, female vocalist – Melba Hill (Singles: 29 weeks)

		pos	wks
15 May 76 ●	THIS IS IT *Buddah BDS 443*	9	8
26 May 79	PICK ME UP, I'LL DANCE *Epic EPC 7234*	48	5
9 Oct 82	LOVE'S COMIN' AT YA *EMI America EA 146*	15	8
15 Jan 83	MIND UP TONIGHT *Capitol CL 272*	22	6
5 Mar 83	UNDERLOVE *Capitol CL 281*	60	2

Ray MOORE
UK, male DJ / vocalist d. Jan 1989 (Singles: 9 weeks)

		pos	wks
29 Nov 86	O' MY FATHER HAD A RABBIT *Play PLAY 213*	24	7
5 Dec 87	BOG EYED JOG *Play PLAY 224*	61	2

Sam MOORE and Lou REED
US, male vocal duo (Singles: 10 weeks)

		pos	wks
17 Jan 87	SOUL MAN *A&M AM 364*	30	10

See also SAM and DAVE; Lou REED

Tina MOORE
US, female vocalist (Singles: 18 weeks)

		pos	wks
30 Aug 97 ●	NEVER GONNA LET YOU GO *Delirious 74321511052*	7	15
25 Apr 98	NOBODY BETTER *RCA 74321571612*	20	3

Lisa MOORISH
UK, female vocalist – Lisa Morrish (Singles: 11 weeks)

		pos	wks
7 Jan 95	JUST THE WAY IT IS *Go.Beat GODCD 123*	42	3
19 Aug 95	I'M YOUR MAN *Go.Beat GODCD 128*	24	3
3 Feb 96	MR FRIDAY NIGHT *Go.Beat GODCD 137*	24	3
18 May 96	LOVE FOR LIFE *Go.Beat GODCD 145*	37	2

'I'm Your Man' features the uncredited vocals of George Michael

Angel MORAES *US, male producer (Singles: 2 weeks)*

		pos	wks
16 Nov 96	HEAVEN KNOWS – DEEP DEEP DOWN *ffrr FCD 282*	72	1
17 May 97	I LIKE IT *AM:PM 5871792*	70	1

David MORALES *US, male DJ / producer (Singles: 21 weeks)*

		pos	wks
10 Jul 93	GIMME LUV (EENIE MEENIE MINY MO) *Mercury MERCD 390*	37	3
20 Nov 93	THE PROGRAM *Mercury MERCD 396*	66	1
24 Aug 96	IN DE GHETTO *Manifesto FESCD 12* 1	35	2
15 Aug 98 ●	NEEDIN' U *Manifesto FESCD 46* 2	8	8
24 Jun 00	HIGHER *Azuli AZNYCDX 120* 3	41	2
20 Jan 01	NEEDIN' U II *Manifesto FESCD 78* 4	11	5

1 David Morales and the Bad Yard Club featuring Crystal Waters and Delta 2 David Morales presents The Face 3 David Morales and Albert Cabrera present Moca featuring Deanna 4 David Morales presents The Face featuring Juliet Roberts

'Needin' U II' is a remix of the 1998 hit with additional vocals

See also BOSS; PULSE featuring Antoinette ROBERSON

Mike MORAN – *See Lynsey DE PAUL*

Patrick MORAZ
Switzerland, male instrumentalist – keyboards (Albums: 8 weeks)

		pos	wks
10 Apr 76	PATRICK MORAZ *Charisma CDS 4002*	28	7
23 Jul 77	OUT IN THE SUN *Charisma CDS 4007*	44	1

MORCHEEBA *UK, male / female vocal / instrumental group (Singles: 14 weeks, Albums: 108 weeks)*

		pos	wks
13 Jul 96	TAPE LOOP *Indochina ID 045CD*	42	1
5 Oct 96	TRIGGER HIPPIE *Indochina ID 052CD*	40	2
15 Feb 97	THE MUSIC THAT WE HEAR (MOOG ISLAND) *Indochina ID 054CD*	47	1
11 Oct 97	SHOULDER HOLSTER *Indochina ID 064CD*	53	1
11 Apr 98	BLINDFOLD *Indochina ID 070CD*	56	1
20 Jun 98	LET ME SEE *Indochina ID 076CD*	46	1
29 Aug 98	PART OF THE PROCESS *China WOKCD 2097*	38	2
5 Aug 00	ROME WASN'T BUILT IN A DAY *East West EW 214CD*	34	3
31 Mar 01	WORLD LOOKING IN *East West EW 225CD*	48	1
6 Jul 02	OTHERWISE *East West EW 247CD*	64	1
12 Apr 97	WHO CAN YOU TRUST? *Indochina ZEN 009CD*	57	3
28 Mar 98	BIG CALM *Indochina ZEN 017CD*	18	71
22 Jul 00 ●	FRAGMENTS OF FREEDOM *East West 8573836022*	6	14
13 Jul 02 ●	CHARANGO *East West 927469632*	7	8
12 Jul 03 ●	PARTS OF THE PROCESS *East West 5046658702*	6	12

MORDRED *UK, male vocal / instrumental group (Albums: 1 week)*

		pos	wks
16 Feb 91	IN THIS LIFE *Noise International NO 1591*	70	1

MORE *UK, male vocal / instrumental group (Singles: 2 weeks)*

		pos	wks
14 Mar 81	WE ARE THE BAND *Atlantic K 11561*	59	2

MORE FIRE CREW
UK, vocal / rap / production group (Singles: 10 weeks)

		pos	wks
25 Jan 03	BACK THEN *Go Beat GOBCD 54*	45	2
16 Mar 02 ●	OI! *Go Beat GOBCD 48* 1	8	8

1 Platinum 45 featuring More Fire Crew

MOREL
US, male vocalist / producer – Richard Morel (Singles: 1 week)

		pos	wks
12 Aug 00	TRUE (THE FAGGOT IS YOU) *Hooj Choons HOOJ 097CD*	64	1

George MOREL featuring Heather WILDMAN
US, male / female vocal / instrumental duo (Singles: 2 weeks)

		pos	wks
26 Oct 96	LET'S GROOVE *Positiva CDTIV 62*	42	2

MORGAN *UK, male vocal / instrumental duo (Singles: 1 week)*

		pos	wks
27 Nov 99	MISS PARKER *Source CDSOUR 002*	74	1

Debelah MORGAN *US, female vocalist (Singles: 9 weeks)* pos/wks

24 Feb 01 ● DANCE WITH ME *Atlantic AT 0087CD* 10 9

Derrick MORGAN *Jamaica, male vocalist (Singles: 1 week)* pos/wks

17 Jan 70 MOON HOP *Crab 32* 49 1

Jamie J MORGAN *US, male vocalist (Singles: 6 weeks)* pos/wks

10 Feb 90 WALK ON THE WILD SIDE *Tabu 655596 7* 27 6

Jane MORGAN

US, female vocalist – Jane Currier (Singles: 22 weeks) pos/wks

5 Dec 58 ★ THE DAY THE RAINS CAME *London HLR 8751* 1 16
22 May 59 IF ONLY I COULD LIVE MY LIFE AGAIN *London HLR 8810* 27 1
21 Jul 60 ROMANTICA *London HLR 9120* 39 5

Meli'sa MORGAN *US, female vocalist (Singles: 7 weeks)* pos/wks

9 Aug 86 FOOL'S PARADISE *Capitol CL 415* 41 5
25 Jun 88 GOOD LOVE *Capitol CL 483* 59 2

Ray MORGAN *UK, male vocalist (Singles: 6 weeks)* pos/wks

25 Jul 70 THE LONG AND WINDING ROAD *B & C CB 128* 32 6

Erick 'More' MORILLO presents RAW *US, male DJ / producer / instrumentalist and female vocalist (Singles: 1 week)* pos/wks

4 Feb 95 HIGHER (FEEL IT) *A&M 5809412* 74 1

See also LIL MO' YIN YANG; PIANOHEADZ; REAL TO REEL

Alanis MORISSETTE (234 Top 500)

Internationally successful, frank and rebellious, Canadian singer / songwriter / instrumentalist – guitar, b. 1 Jun 1974, Ottawa. The child prodigy's Brit and Grammy-winning, 30-million selling 'Jagged Little Pill' became the first album by a female to top the US and UK charts simultaneously (Singles: 53 weeks, Albums: 208 weeks) pos/wks

5 Aug 95 YOU OUGHTA KNOW *Maverick W 0307CD* 22 7
28 Oct 95 HAND IN MY POCKET *Maverick W 0312CD* 26 3
24 Feb 96 YOU LEARN *Maverick W 0334CD* 24 4
20 Apr 96 IRONIC *Maverick W 0343CD* 11 9
3 Aug 96 ● HEAD OVER FEET *Maverick W 0355CD* 7 7
7 Dec 96 ALL I REALLY WANT *Maverick W 0382CD* 59 1
31 Oct 98 ● THANK U *Maverick W 0458CD* 5 10
13 Mar 99 JOINING YOU *Maverick W 472CD1* 28 2
31 Jul 99 SO PURE *Maverick W 492CD1* 38 2
2 Mar 02 HANDS CLEAN *Maverick W 574CD* 12 7
17 Aug 02 PRECIOUS ILLUSIONS *Maverick W 582CD* 53 1
26 Aug 95 ★ JAGGED LITTLE PILL *Maverick 9362459012* ▲ 1 172
14 Nov 98 ● SUPPOSED FORMER INFATUATION JUNKIE *Maverick 9362470942* ▲ 3 21
4 Dec 99 MTV UNPLUGGED *Maverick 9362475892* 56 5
16 Mar 02 ● UNDER RUG SWEPT *Maverick 9362482722* ▲ 2 10

MORJAC featuring Raz CONWAY

Denmark, male production duo and male vocalist (Singles: 2 weeks) pos/wks

11 Oct 03 STARS *Credence CDCRED 036* 38 2

Giorgio MORODER

Italy, male instrumentalist – synthesizer (Singles: 36 weeks) pos/wks

24 Sep 77 FROM HERE TO ETERNITY *Oasis 1* [1] 16 10
17 Mar 79 CHASE *Casablanca CAN 144* 48 6
22 Sep 84 ● TOGETHER IN ELECTRIC DREAMS *Virgin VS 713* [2] 3 13
29 Jun 85 GOOD-BYE BAD TIMES *Virgin VS 772* [3] 44 5
11 Jul 98 CARRY ON *Almighty CDALMY 120* [4] 65 1
12 Feb 00 THE CHASE (re-recording) *Logic 74321732112* [5] 46 1

[1] Giorgio [2] Giorgio Moroder and Phil Oakey [3] Philip Oakey and Giorgio Moroder [4] Donna Summer and Giorgio Moroder [5] DJ Empire presents Giorgio Moroder

Joseph MOROVITZ – *See SOUTH BANK ORCHESTRA*

Ennio MORRICONE

Italy, orchestra (Singles: 12 weeks, Albums: 16 weeks) pos/wks

11 Apr 81 ● CHI MAI (THEME FROM THE TV SERIES 'THE LIFE AND TIMES OF DAVID LLOYD GEORGE') *BBC RESL 92* 2 12
2 May 81 THIS IS ENNIO MORRICONE *EMI THIS 33* 23 5
9 May 81 CHI MAI *BBC REH 414* 29 6
7 Mar 87 THE MISSION (FILM SOUNDTRACK) *Virgin V 2402* [1] 73 4
30 Sep 00 THE VERY BEST OF ENNIO MORRICONE *Virgin CDV 2929* 48 1

[1] Ennio Morricone and the London Philharmonic Orchestra

See also London Philharmonic Orchestra

Sarah Jane MORRIS – *See COMMUNARDS*

Diana MORRISON – *See Michael BALL*

Dorothy Combs MORRISON – *See Edwin HAWKINS SINGERS*

Mark MORRISON

UK, male vocalist (Singles: 68 weeks, Albums: 39 weeks) pos/wks

22 Apr 95 CRAZY *WEA YZ 907CD* 19 4
16 Sep 95 LET'S GET DOWN *WEA WEA 001CD* 39 2
16 Mar 96 ★ RETURN OF THE MACK (re) *WEA WEA 040CD* 1 24
27 Jul 96 ● CRAZY (re) (re-mix) *WEA WEA 054CD1* 6 9
19 Oct 96 ● TRIPPIN' *WEA WEA 079CD1* 8 6
21 Dec 96 ● HORNY *WEA WEA 090CD1* 5 9
15 Mar 97 ● MOAN & GROAN *WEA WEA 096CD1* 7 6
20 Sep 97 WHO'S THE MACK! *WEA WEA 128CD1* 13 5
4 Sep 99 BEST FRIEND *WEA WEA 221CD1* [1] 23 3
4 May 96 ● RETURN OF THE MACK *WEA 630145862* 4 38
27 Sep 97 ONLY GOD CAN JUDGE ME *WEA 630195392* 50 1

[1] Mark Morrison and Conner Reeves

Van MORRISON (194 Top 500)

Critically acclaimed singer / songwriter has amassed many international hits over five decades, b. 31 Aug 1945, Belfast, UK. Received Outstanding Contribution Brit award (1994) and OBE (1996), and 'Brown Eyed Girl' achieved more than five million radio plays Stateside (Singles: 21 weeks, Albums: 276 weeks) pos/wks

20 Oct 79 BRIGHT SIDE OF THE ROAD *Mercury 6001 121* 63 3
1 Jul 89 HAVE I TOLD YOU LATELY *Polydor VANS 1* 74 1
9 Dec 89 WHENEVER GOD SHINES HIS LIGHT *Polydor VANS 2* [1] 20 6
15 May 93 GLORIA *Exile VANCD 11* [2] 31 3
18 Mar 95 HAVE I TOLD YOU LATELY THAT I LOVE YOU *RCA 74321271702* [3] 71 1
10 Jun 95 DAYS LIKE THIS *Exile VANCD 12* 65 1
2 Dec 95 NO RELIGION *Exile 5775792* 54 1
1 Mar 97 THE HEALING GAME *Exile 5733912* 46 1
6 Mar 99 PRECIOUS TIME *Pointblank / Virgin POBD 14* 36 2
22 May 99 BACK ON TOP *Exile / Pointblank / Virgin POBD 15* 69 1
18 May 02 HEY MR DJ *Polydor / Exile 5705962* 58 1
18 Apr 70 MOONDANCE *Warner Bros. WS 1835* 32 2
13 Feb 71 VAN MORRISON, HIS BAND AND STREET CHOIR *Warner Bros. WS 1884* 18 6
11 Aug 73 HARD NOSE THE HIGHWAY *Warner Bros. K 46242* 22 3
16 Nov 74 VEEDON FLEECE *Warner Bros. K 56068* 41 1
7 May 77 A PERIOD OF TRANSITION *Warner Bros. K 56322* 23 5
21 Oct 78 WAVELENGTH *Warner Bros. K 56526* 27 6
8 Sep 79 INTO THE MUSIC *Vertigo 9120 852* 21 9
20 Sep 80 THE COMMON ONE *Mercury 6302 021* 53 3
27 Feb 82 BEAUTIFUL VISION *Mercury 6302 122* 31 14
26 Mar 83 INARTICULATE SPEECH OF THE HEART *Mercury MERL 16* 14 8
3 Mar 84 LIVE AT THE GRAND OPERA HOUSE BELFAST *Mercury MERL 36* 47 4
9 Feb 85 A SENSE OF WONDER *Mercury MERH 54* 25 5
2 Aug 86 NO GURU NO METHOD NO TEACHER *Mercury MERH 94* 27 5
19 Sep 87 POETIC CHAMPIONS COMPOSE *Mercury MERH 110* 26 6
2 Jul 88 IRISH HEARTBEAT *Mercury MERH 124* [1] 18 7
10 Jun 89 AVALON SUNSET *Polydor 839262 1* 13 14
7 Apr 90 ● THE BEST OF VAN MORRISON *Polydor 8419701* 4 87
20 Oct 90 ● ENLIGHTENMENT *Polydor 8471001* 5 14
21 Sep 91 ● HYMNS TO THE SILENCE *Polydor 8490261* 5 6
27 Feb 93 THE BEST OF VAN MORRISON VOLUME 2 *Polydor 5177602* 31 3

12 Jun 93 ● **TOO LONG IN EXILE** *Exile 5192192* 4 9
30 Apr 94 ● **A NIGHT IN SAN FRANCISCO** *Polydor 5212902* 8 5
24 Jun 95 ● **DAYS LIKE THIS** *Exile 5273072* 5 15
15 Mar 97 ● **THE HEALING GAME** *Exile 5371012* 10 7
27 Jun 98 **THE PHILOSOPHER'S STONE** *Exile 5317892* 20 3
20 Mar 99 **BACK ON TOP** *Pointblank VPBCD 50* 11 16
29 Jan 00 **THE SKIFFLE SESSIONS – LIVE IN BELFAST** *Venture CDVE 945* [2] 14 3
7 Oct 00 **YOU WIN AGAIN** *Pointblank VPBCD 54* [3] 34 2
25 May 02 ● **DOWN THE ROAD** *Exile 5891772* 6 6
1 Nov 03 **WHAT'S WRONG WITH THIS PICTURE?** *Blue Note 5901672* 43 2

[1] Van Morrison with Cliff Richard [2] Van Morrison and John Lee Hooker [3] Chieftains with Van Morrison [1] Van Morrison and the Chieftains [2] Van Morrison / Lonnie Donegan / Chris Barber [3] Van Morrison and Linda Gail Lewis

'Have I Told You Lately That I Love You' is a re-recording of his second hit

See also THEM

MORRISSEY *UK, male vocalist – Stephen Morrissey (Singles: 74 weeks, Albums: 51 weeks)* pos/wks

27 Feb 88 ● **SUEDEHEAD** *HMV POP 1618* 5 6
11 Jun 88 ● **EVERYDAY IS LIKE SUNDAY** *HMV POP 1619* 9 6
11 Feb 89 ● **LAST OF THE FAMOUS INTERNATIONAL PLAYBOYS** *HMV POP 1620* 6 5
29 Apr 89 ● **INTERESTING DRUG** *HMV POP 1621* 9 4
25 Nov 89 **OUIJA BOARD OUIJA BOARD** *HMV POP 1622* 18 4
5 May 90 **NOVEMBER SPAWNED A MONSTER** *HMV POP 1623* 12 4
20 Oct 90 **PICCADILLY PALARE** *HMV POP 1624* 18 2
23 Feb 91 **OUR FRANK** *HMV POP 1625* 26 3
13 Apr 91 **SING YOUR LIFE** *HMV POP 1626* 33 2
27 Jul 91 **PREGNANT FOR THE LAST TIME** *HMV POP 1627* 25 4
12 Oct 91 **MY LOVE LIFE** *HMV POP 1628* 29 2
9 May 92 **WE HATE IT WHEN OUR FRIENDS BECOME SUCCESSFUL** *HMV POP 1629* 17 3
18 Jul 92 **YOU'RE THE ONE FOR ME, FATTY** *HMV POP 1630* 19 3
19 Dec 92 **CERTAIN PEOPLE I KNOW** *HMV POP 1631* 35 4
12 Mar 94 ● **THE MORE YOU IGNORE ME THE CLOSER I GET** *Parlophone CDR 6372* 8 3
11 Jun 94 **HOLD ON TO YOUR FRIENDS** *Parlophone CDR 6383* 47 2
20 Aug 94 **INTERLUDE** *Parlophone CDR 6365* [1] 25 2
28 Jan 95 **BOXERS** *Parlophone CDR 6400* 23 3
2 Sep 95 **DAGENHAM DAVE** *RCA Victor 74321299802* 26 2
9 Dec 95 **THE BOY RACER** *RCA Victor 74321332952* 36 2
23 Dec 95 **SUNNY** *Parlophone CDR 6243* 42 2
2 Aug 97 **ALMA MATTERS** *Island CID 667* 16 3
18 Oct 97 **ROY'S KEEN** *Island CID 671* 42 1
10 Jan 98 **SATAN REJECTED MY SOUL** *Island CID 686* 39 2
26 Mar 88 ★ **VIVA HATE** *HMV CSD 3787* ■ 1 20
27 Oct 90 ● **BONA DRAG** *HMV CLP 3788* 9 4
16 Mar 91 ● **KILL UNCLE** *HMV CSD 3789* 8 4
8 Aug 92 ● **YOUR ARSENAL** *HMV CDCSD 3790* 4 5
22 May 93 **BEETHOVEN WAS DEAF** *HMV CDCSD 3791* 13 2
26 Mar 94 ★ **VAUXHALL AND I** *Parlophone CDPCSD 148* ■ 1 5
18 Feb 95 **WORLD OF MORRISSEY** *Parlophone CDPCSD 163* 15 2
9 Sep 95 ● **SOUTHPAW GRAMMAR** *RCA Victor 74321299532* 4 3
23 Aug 97 ● **MALADJUSTED** *Island CID 8059* 8 3
20 Sep 97 **THE BEST OF MORRISSEY – SUEDEHEAD** *EMI CDEMC 3771* 26 3

[1] Morrissey and Siouxsie

See also SMITHS

MORRISSEY MULLEN *UK, male vocal / instrumental duo (Albums: 11 weeks)* pos/wks

18 Jul 81 **BADNESS** *Beggars Banquet BEGA 27* 43 5
3 Apr 82 **LIFE ON THE WIRE** *Beggars Banquet BEGA 33* 47 5
23 Apr 83 **IT'S ABOUT TIME** *Beggars Banquet BEGA 44* 95 1

MORRISTON ORPHEUS MALE VOICE CHOIR – *See ALARM*

MORRISTOWN ORPHEUS CHOIR – *See G.U.S. (FOOTWEAR) BAND and the MORRISTOWN ORPHEUS CHOIR*

Buddy MORROW *US, orchestra – Muni Zudecoff (Singles: 1 week)* pos/wks

20 Mar 53 **NIGHT TRAIN** *HMV B 10347* 12 1

Bob MORTIMER – *See MIDDLESBROUGH FC featuring Bob MORTIMER and Chris REA; EMF*

MOS DEF *US, male rapper – Dante Smith (Singles: 6 weeks)* pos/wks

24 Jun 00 **UMI SAYS** *Rawkus RWK 232CD* 60 1
4 Nov 00 **MISS FAT BOOTY – PART II** *Rawkus RWK 282CD* [1] 64 1
3 Feb 01 **OH NO** *Rawkus RWK 302* [2] 24 4

[1] Mos Def featuring Ghostface Killah [2] Mos Def and Nate Dogg featuring Pharoahe Monch

Kate MOSS – *See PRIMAL SCREAM*

Mickie MOST *UK, male vocalist, d. 30 May 2003 (Singles: 1 week)* pos/wks

25 Jul 63 **MR PORTER** *Decca F 11664* 45 1

MOTELS *US / UK, male / female vocal / instrumental group (Singles: 7 weeks)* pos/wks

11 Oct 80 **WHOSE PROBLEM?** *Capitol CL 16162* 42 4
10 Jan 81 **DAYS ARE O.K.** *Capitol CL 16149* 41 3

Wendy MOTEN *US, female vocalist (Singles: 13 weeks, Albums: 2 weeks)* pos/wks

5 Feb 94 ● **COME IN OUT OF THE RAIN** *EMI-USA CDMT 105* 8 9
14 May 94 **SO CLOSE TO LOVE** *EMI-USA CDMTS 106* 35 4
19 Mar 94 **WENDY MOTEN** *EMI CDMTL 1073* 42 2

MOTHER *UK, male instrumental / production duo – Jools Brettle and Lee Fisher (Singles: 4 weeks)* pos/wks

12 Jun 93 **ALL FUNKED UP** *Bosting BYSNCD 101* 34 2
1 Oct 94 **GET BACK** *Six6 SIXT 119* 73 1
31 Aug 96 **ALL FUNKED UP (re-mix)** *Six6 SIXXCD 1* 66 1

MOTHER EARTH *UK, male vocal / instrumental group (Albums: 2 weeks)* pos/wks

5 Mar 94 **THE PEOPLE TREE** *Acid Jazz JAZIDCD 083* 45 2

MOTHERS OF INVENTION *US, male vocal / instrumental group (Albums: 12 weeks)* pos/wks

29 Jun 68 **WE'RE ONLY IN IT FOR THE MONEY** *Verve SVLP 9199* 32 5
28 Mar 70 **BURNT WEENY SANDWICH** *Reprise RSLP 6370* 17 3
3 Oct 70 **WEASELS RIPPED MY FLESH** *Reprise RSLP 2028* 28 4

See also Frank ZAPPA

MOTHER'S PRIDE *UK, male DJ / production duo (Singles: 2 weeks)* pos/wks

21 Mar 98 **FLORIBUNDA** *Heat Recordings HEATCD 013* 42 1
6 Nov 99 **LEARNING TO FLY** *Devolution DEVR 001CDS* 54 1

MOTIV 8 *UK, male producer – Steve Rodway (Singles: 10 weeks)* pos/wks

17 Jul 93 **ROCKIN' FOR MYSELF** *Nuff Respect NUFF 002CD* [1] 67 1
7 May 94 **ROCKIN' FOR MYSELF (re-mix)** *WEA YZ 814CD* 18 4
21 Oct 95 **BREAK THE CHAIN** *Eternal WEA 010CD* 31 2
23 Dec 95 **SEARCHING FOR THE GOLDEN EYE** *Eternal WEA 027CD* [2] 40 3

[1] Motiv 8 featuring Angie Brown [2] Motiv 8 and Kym Mazelle

MOTIVATION *Holland, male producer – Francis Louwers (Singles: 1 week)* pos/wks

17 Nov 01 **PARA MI** *Definitive CDDEF 1* 71 1

MOTIVO – *See SNAP!*

MÖTLEY CRÜE *US, male vocal / instrumental group (Singles: 28 weeks, Albums: 26 weeks)*

		pos/wks	
24 Aug 85	**SMOKIN' IN THE BOYS ROOM** *Elektra EKR 16*	71	2
8 Feb 86	**HOME SWEET HOME / SMOKIN' IN THE BOYS ROOM (re-issue)** *Elektra EKR 33*	51	3
1 Aug 87	**GIRLS, GIRLS, GIRLS** *Elektra EKR 59*	26	6
16 Jan 88	**YOU'RE ALL I NEED / WILD SIDE** *Elektra EKR 65*	23	4
4 Nov 89	**DR FEELGOOD** *Elektra EKR 97*	50	3
12 May 90	**WITHOUT YOU** *Elektra EKR 109*	39	3
7 Sep 91	**PRIMAL SCREAM** *Elektra EKR 133*	32	2
11 Jan 92	**HOME SWEET HOME (re-mix)** *Elektra EKR 136*	37	2
5 Mar 94	**HOOLIGAN'S HOLIDAY** *Elektra EKR 180CDX*	36	2
19 Jul 97	**AFRAID** *Elektra E 3936 CD1*	58	1
13 Jul 85	**THEATRE OF PAIN** *Elektra EKT 8*	36	3
30 May 87	**GIRLS GIRLS GIRLS** *Elektra EKT 39*	14	11
16 Sep 89 ●	**DR FEELGOOD** *Elektra EKT 59* ▲	4	7
19 Oct 91	**DECADE OF DECADENCE '81-'91** *Elektra EKT 95*	20	3
26 Mar 94	**MÖTLEY CRÜE** *Elektra 7559615342*	17	2

'Wild Side' listed with 'You're All I Need' only from 30 Jan 1988. It peaked at No.26

See also Vince NEIL

MOTÖRHEAD (357 Top 500) *Unashamedly loud mainstays of UK heavy rock formed in 1975 after Lemmy (v/b) (b. Ian Kilmister 24 Dec 1945, Stoke-on-Trent, UK) left Hawkwind. Much admired in punk circles, they helped to pave the way for 1980s heavy metal bands such as Metallica (Singles: 81 weeks, Albums: 103 weeks)*

		pos/wks	
16 Sep 78	**LOUIE LOUIE (re)** *Bronze BRO 60*	68	2
10 Mar 79	**OVERKILL (re)** *Bronze BRO 67*	39	7
30 Jun 79	**NO CLASS** *Bronze BRO 78*	61	4
1 Dec 79	**BOMBER** *Bronze BRO 85*	34	7
3 May 80 ●	**THE GOLDEN YEARS (EP)** *Bronze BRO 92*	8	7
1 Nov 80	**ACE OF SPADES** *Bronze BRO 106*	15	12
22 Nov 80	**BEER DRINKERS AND HELL RAISERS** *Big Beat SWT 61*	43	4
21 Feb 81 ●	**ST VALENTINE'S DAY MASSACRE (EP)** *Bronze BRO 116* [1]	5	8
11 Jul 81 ●	**MOTÖRHEAD (LIVE)** *Bronze BRO 124*	6	7
3 Apr 82	**IRON FIST** *Bronze BRO 146*	29	5
21 May 83	**I GOT MINE** *Bronze BRO 165*	46	2
30 Jul 83	**SHINE** *Bronze BRO 167*	59	2
1 Sep 84	**KILLED BY DEATH** *Bronze BRO 185*	51	2
5 Jul 86	**DEAF FOREVER** *GWR GWR 2*	67	1
5 Jan 91	**THE ONE TO SING THE BLUES** *Epic 6565787*	45	3
14 Nov 92	**'92 TOUR (EP)** *Epic 6588096*	63	1
11 Sep 93	**ACE OF SPADES (re-issue)** *WGAF CDWGAF 101*	23	5
10 Dec 94	**BORN TO RAISE HELL** *Fox 74321230152* [2]	47	2
24 Sep 77	**MOTÖRHEAD** *Chiswick WIK 2*	43	5
24 Mar 79	**OVERKILL** *Bronze BRON 515*	24	11
27 Oct 79	**BOMBER** *Bronze BRON 523*	12	13
8 Dec 79	**ON PAROLE** *United Artists LBR 1004*	65	2
8 Nov 80 ●	**ACE OF SPADES** *Bronze BRON 531*	4	16
27 Jun 81 ★	**NO SLEEP 'TIL HAMMERSMITH** *Bronze BRON 535* ■	1	21
17 Apr 82 ●	**IRON FIST** *Bronze BRNA 539*	6	9
26 Feb 83	**WHAT'S WORDS WORTH** *Big Beat NED 2*	71	2
4 Jun 83	**ANOTHER PERFECT DAY** *Bronze BRON 546*	20	4
15 Sep 84	**NO REMORSE** *Bronze PROTV MOTOR 1*	14	6
9 Aug 86	**ORGASMATRON** *GWR GWLP 1*	21	4
5 Sep 87	**ROCK 'N' ROLL** *GWR GWLP 14*	34	3
15 Oct 88	**NO SLEEP AT ALL** *GWR GWR 31*	79	1
2 Feb 91	**1916** *Epic 4674811*	24	4
8 Aug 92	**MARCH OR DIE** *Epic 4717232*	60	1
9 Sep 00	**THE BEST OF MOTÖRHEAD** *Metal Is MISDD 002*	52	1

[1] Motörhead and Girlschool (also known as Headgirl) [2] Motörhead / Ice-T / Whitfield Crane

Tracks on The Golden Years (EP): Dead Men Tell No Tales / Too Late Too Late / Leaving Here / Stone Dead Forever. Tracks on St Valentine's Day Massacre (EP): Please Don't Touch / Emergency / Bomber. Tracks on '92 Tour (EP): Hellraiser / You Better Run / Going to Brazil / Ramones

MOTORS *UK, male vocal / instrumental group (Singles: 29 weeks, Albums: 6 weeks)*

		pos/wks	
24 Sep 77	**DANCING THE NIGHT AWAY** *Virgin VS 186*	42	4
10 Jun 78 ●	**AIRPORT** *Virgin VS 219*	4	13
19 Aug 78	**FORGET ABOUT YOU** *Virgin VS 222*	13	9
12 Apr 80	**LOVE AND LONELINESS** *Virgin VS 263*	58	3
15 Oct 77	**THE MOTORS** *Virgin V 2089*	46	5
3 Jun 78	**APPROVED BY THE MOTORS** *Virgin V 2101*	60	1

MOTOWN SPINNERS – *See DETROIT SPINNERS*

MOTT THE HOOPLE *UK, male vocal / instrumental group – leader Ian Hunter (Singles: 55 weeks, Albums: 32 weeks)*

		pos/wks	
12 Aug 72 ●	**ALL THE YOUNG DUDES** *CBS 8271*	3	11
16 Jun 73	**HONALOOCHIE BOOGIE** *CBS 1530*	12	9
8 Sep 73 ●	**ALL THE WAY FROM MEMPHIS** *CBS 1764*	10	8
24 Nov 73 ●	**ROLL AWAY THE STONE** *CBS 1895*	8	12
30 Mar 74	**THE GOLDEN AGE OF ROCK 'N' ROLL** *CBS 2177*	16	7
22 Jun 74	**FOXY, FOXY** *CBS 2439*	33	5
2 Nov 74	**SATURDAY GIG** *CBS 2754*	41	3
2 May 70	**MOTT THE HOOPLE** *Island ILPS 9108*	66	1
17 Oct 70	**MAD SHADOWS** *Island ILPS 9119*	48	2
17 Apr 71	**WILD LIFE** *Island ILPS 9144*	44	2
23 Sep 72	**ALL THE YOUNG DUDES** *CBS 65184*	21	4
11 Aug 73 ●	**MOTT** *CBS 69038*	7	15
13 Apr 74	**THE HOOPLE** *CBS 69062*	11	5
23 Nov 74	**LIVE** *CBS 69093*	32	2
4 Oct 75	**DRIVE ON** *CBS 69154*	45	1

Bob MOULD *US, male vocalist / instumentalist (Albums: 2 weeks)*

		pos/wks	
11 May 96	**BOB MOULD** *Creation CRECD 188*	52	1
5 Sep 98	**THE LAST DOG AND PONY SHOW** *Creation CRECD 215*	58	1

See also HÜSKER DÜ; SUGAR

MOUNT RUSHMORE presents THE KNACK
UK, male production duo with female vocalist (Singles: 1 week)

		pos/wks	
3 Apr 99	**YOU BETTER** *Universal MCSTD 40192*	53	1

MOUNTAIN
US / Canada, male vocal / instrumental group (Albums: 4 weeks)

		pos/wks	
5 Jun 71	**NANTUCKET SLEIGHRIDE** *Island ILPS 9148*	43	1
8 Jul 72	**THE ROAD GOES EVER ON** *Island ILPS 9199*	21	3

Nana MOUSKOURI (299 Top 500) *Greece's No.1 musical export, b. 15 Oct 1934, Athens. Distinctive, bespectacled, folk-based singer / guitarist, who collected the first of her numerous worldwide gold and platinum records in 1961, became a Member of the European Parliament in 1994 (Singles: 11 weeks, Albums: 205 weeks)*

		pos/wks	
11 Jan 86 ●	**ONLY LOVE** *Philips PH 38*	2	11
7 Jun 69 ●	**OVER AND OVER** *Fontana S 5511*	10	97
4 Apr 70 ●	**THE EXQUISITE NANA MOUSKOURI** *Fontana STL 5536*	10	25
10 Oct 70	**RECITAL '70** *Fontana 6312 003*	68	1
3 Apr 71	**TURN ON THE SUN** *Fontana 6312 008*	16	15
29 Jul 72	**BRITISH CONCERT** *Fontana 6651 003*	29	11
28 Apr 73	**SONGS FROM HER TV SERIES** *Fontana 6312 036*	29	11
28 Sep 74	**SPOTLIGHT ON NANA MOUSKOURI** *Fontana 6641 197*	38	6
10 Jul 76 ●	**PASSPORT** *Philips 9101 061*	3	16
22 Feb 86	**ALONE** *Philips PHH 3*	19	10
8 Oct 88	**THE MAGIC OF NANA MOUSKOURI** *Philips NMTV 1*	44	8
3 Mar 01	**AT HER VERY BEST** *Philips 5485492*	39	5

MOUSSE T
Germany, male producer – Mustafa Gundogdu (Singles: 28 weeks)

		pos/wks	
6 Jun 98 ●	**HORNY** *AM:PM 5826712* [1]	2	17
20 May 00 ●	**SEX BOMB** *Gut CDGUT 33* [2]	3	10
10 Aug 02	**FIRE** *Serious SERR 44CD* [3]	58	1

[1] Mousse T vs Hot 'N' Juicy [2] Tom Jones and Mousse T [3] Mousse T featuring Emma Lanford

MOUTH and MACNEAL
Holland, male / female vocal duo (Singles: 10 weeks)

		pos/wks	
4 May 74 ●	**I SEE A STAR** *Decca F 13504*	8	10

MOVE *UK, male vocal / instrumental group – included Carl Wayne and Roy Wood (Singles: 110 weeks, Albums: 9 weeks)* pos/wks

Date		Title / Label	pos	wks
5 Jan 67	●	**NIGHT OF FEAR** *Deram DM 109*	2	10
6 Apr 67	●	**I CAN HEAR THE GRASS GROW** *Deram DM 117*	5	10
6 Sep 67	●	**FLOWERS IN THE RAIN** *Regal Zonophone RZ3001*	2	13
7 Feb 68	●	**FIRE BRIGADE** *Regal Zonophone RZ3005*	3	11
25 Dec 68	★	**BLACKBERRY WAY** *Regal Zonophone RZ3015*	1	12
23 Jul 69		**CURLY** *Regal Zonophone RZ3021*	12	12
25 Apr 70	●	**BRONTOSAURUS** *Regal Zonophone RZ3026*	7	10
3 Jul 71		**TONIGHT** *Harvest HAR 5038*	11	10
23 Oct 71		**CHINATOWN** *Harvest HAR 5043*	23	8
13 May 72	●	**CALIFORNIA MAN** *Harvest HAR 5050*	7	14
13 Apr 68		MOVE *Regal Zonophone SLPZ 1002*	15	9

MOVEMENT
US, male vocal / instrumental group (Singles: 2 weeks) pos/wks

Date		Title / Label	pos	wks
24 Oct 92		**JUMP!** *Arista 74321116677*	57	2

MOVEMENT 98 featuring Carroll THOMPSON
UK, male / female vocal / instrumental group (Singles: 8 weeks) pos/wks

Date		Title / Label	pos	wks
19 May 90		**JOY AND HEARTBREAK** *Circa YR 45*	27	5
15 Sep 90		**SUNRISE** *Circa YR 51*	58	3

MOVIN' MELODIES
Holland, male producer – Patrick Prinz (Singles: 3 weeks) pos/wks

Date		Title / Label	pos	wks
22 Oct 94		**LA LUNA** *Effective EFFS 017CD* [1]	64	1
29 Jun 96		**INDICA** *Hooj Choons HOOJCD 44*	62	1
26 Jul 97		**ROLLERBLADE** *Movin' Melodies 5822352*	71	1

[1] Movin' Melodies Production

See also ARTEMESIA; ETHICS; SUBLIMINAL CUTS

Alison MOYET (190 Top 500)
After five Top 20 hits with Yazoo, the distinctive, bluesy-voiced vocalist (b. 18 Jun 1961, Essex, UK), nicknamed Alf, enjoyed a string of solo successes. Her biggest hits included revivals of songs made popular by Billie Holiday and Ketty Lester (Singles: 107 weeks, Albums: 194 weeks) pos/wks

Date		Title / Label	pos	wks
23 Jun 84	●	**LOVE RESURRECTION** *CBS A 4497*	10	11
13 Oct 84	●	**ALL CRIED OUT** *CBS A 4757*	8	11
1 Dec 84		**INVISIBLE** *CBS A 4930*	21	10
16 Mar 85	●	**THAT OLE DEVIL CALLED LOVE** *CBS A 6044*	2	10
29 Nov 86	●	**IS THIS LOVE?** *CBS MOYET 1*	3	16
7 Mar 87	●	**WEAK IN THE PRESENCE OF BEAUTY** *CBS MOYET 2*	6	10
30 May 87		**ORDINARY GIRL** *CBS MOYET 3*	43	4
28 Nov 87	●	**LOVE LETTERS** *CBS MOYET 5*	4	10
6 Apr 91		**IT WON'T BE LONG** *Columbia 6567577*	50	4
1 Jun 91		**WISHING YOU WERE HERE** *Columbia 6569397*	72	1
12 Oct 91		**THIS HOUSE** *Columbia 6575157*	40	5
16 Oct 93		**FALLING** *Columbia 6595962*	42	3
12 Mar 94		**WHISPERING YOUR NAME** *Columbia 6601622*	18	7
28 May 94		**GETTING INTO SOMETHING** *Columbia 6603565*	51	2
22 Oct 94		**ODE TO BOY** *Columbia 6607952*	59	1
26 Aug 95		**SOLID WOOD** *Columbia 6623265*	44	2
17 Nov 84	★	ALF *CBS 26229*	1	84
18 Apr 87	●	RAINDANCING *CBS 450 1521*	2	52
4 May 91		HOODOO *Columbia 4682721*	11	6
2 Apr 94		ESSEX *Columbia 4759552*	24	4
3 Jun 95	★	SINGLES *Columbia 4806632* ■	1	35
22 Sep 01		THE ESSENTIAL ALISON MOYET *Columbia STVCD 123*	16	4
31 Aug 02		HOMETIME *Sanctuary SANCD 128*	18	9

See also YAZOO

MOZAIC *UK, female vocal group (Singles: 7 weeks)* pos/wks

Date		Title / Label	pos	wks
5 Aug 95		**SING IT (THE HALLELUJAH SONG)** *Perfecto PERF 106CD*	14	4
10 Aug 96		**RAYS OF THE RISING SUN** *Perfecto PERF 123CD*	32	2
30 Nov 96		**MOVING UP MOVING ON** *Perfecto PERF 131CD*	62	1

MTUME *US, male / female vocal / instrumental group (Singles: 12 weeks, Albums: 1 week)* pos/wks

Date		Title / Label	pos	wks
14 May 83		**JUICY FRUIT** *Epic A 3424*	34	9
22 Sep 84		**PRIME TIME** *Epic A 4720*	57	3
6 Oct 84		YOU ME AND HE *Epic EPC 26077*	85	1

MUD (333 Top 500)
Rock 'n' roll-influenced Seventies stars: Les Gray (v), Rob Davis (g/v), Ray Stiles (b/v), Dave Mount (d/v). After joining RAK Records and teaming with writers / producers Nicky Chinn and Mike Chapman, this good-time British band had a noteworthy run of hits, including three No.1s. Davis is now one of the UK's most successful songwriters, writing No.1 hits for Kylie Minogue and Spiller (Singles: 139 weeks, Albums: 58 weeks) pos/wks

Date		Title / Label	pos	wks
10 Mar 73		**CRAZY** *RAK 146*	12	12
23 Jun 73		**HYPNOSIS** *RAK 152*	16	13
27 Oct 73	●	**DYNA-MITE** *RAK 159*	4	12
19 Jan 74	★	**TIGER FEET** *RAK 166*	1	11
13 Apr 74	●	**THE CAT CREPT IN** *RAK 170*	2	9
27 Jul 74	●	**ROCKET** *RAK 178*	6	9
30 Nov 74	★	**LONELY THIS CHRISTMAS (re)** *RAK 187*	1	13
15 Feb 75	●	**THE SECRETS THAT YOU KEEP** *RAK 194*	3	9
26 Apr 75	★	**OH BOY** *RAK 201*	1	9
21 Jun 75	●	**MOONSHINE SALLY** *RAK 208*	10	7
2 Aug 75		**ONE NIGHT** *RAK 213*	32	4
4 Oct 75	●	**L'L'LUCY** *Private Stock PVT 41*	10	6
29 Nov 75	●	**SHOW ME YOU'RE A WOMAN** *Private Stock PVT 45*	8	8
15 May 76		**SHAKE IT DOWN** *Private Stock PVT 65*	12	8
27 Nov 76	●	**LEAN ON ME** *Private Stock PVT 85*	7	9
28 Sep 74	●	MUD ROCK *RAK SRAK 508*	8	35
26 Jul 75	●	MUD ROCK VOLUME 2 *RAK SRAK 513*	6	12
1 Nov 75		MUD'S GREATEST HITS *RAK SRAK 6755*	25	6
27 Dec 75		USE YOUR IMAGINATION *Private Stock PVLP 1003*	33	5

'Lonely This Christmas' re-entered peaking at No.61 in Dec 1985

See also Les GRAY

MUDHONEY *US, male vocal / instrumental group (Singles: 2 weeks, Albums: 5 weeks)* pos/wks

Date		Title / Label	pos	wks
17 Aug 91		**LET IT SLIDE** *Subpop SP 15154*	60	1
24 Oct 92		**SUCK YOU DRY** *Reprise W 0137*	65	1
31 Aug 91		EVERY GOOD BOY DESERVES FUDGE *Subpop SP 18160*	34	2
17 Oct 92		PIECE OF CAKE *Reprise 9362450902*	39	2
8 Apr 95		MY BROTHER THE COW *Reprise 9362458402*	70	1

MUDLARKS *UK, male / female vocal group (Singles: 19 weeks)* pos/wks

Date		Title / Label	pos	wks
2 May 58	●	**LOLLIPOP** *Columbia DB 4099*	2	9
6 Jun 58	●	**BOOK OF LOVE** *Columbia DB 4133*	8	9
27 Feb 59		**THE LOVE GAME** *Columbia DB 4250*	30	1

MUFFINS – *See MARTHA and the MUFFINS*

Idris MUHAMMAD
US, male instrumentalist – drums (Singles: 3 weeks) pos/wks

Date		Title / Label	pos	wks
17 Sep 77		**COULD HEAVEN EVER BE LIKE THIS** *Kudu 935*	42	3

Vocal by Frank Floyd

MUKKAA *UK, male instrumental / production duo – Stuart Crichton and Billy Kiltie (Singles: 1 week)* pos/wks

Date		Title / Label	pos	wks
27 Feb 93		**BURUCHACCA** *Limbo LIMBO 008*	74	1

See also UMBOZA; EYE TO EYE featuring Taka BOOM

MUKUPA – *See MANIJAMA featuring MUKUPA & L'IL T*

Maria MULDAUR
US, female vocalist – Maria D'Amato (Singles: 8 weeks) pos/wks

Date		Title / Label	pos	wks
29 Jun 74		**MIDNIGHT AT THE OASIS** *Reprise K 14331*	21	8

MULL HISTORICAL SOCIETY *UK, male vocal / instrumental group – leader Colin MacIntyre (Singles: 6 weeks, Albums: 4 weeks)* pos/wks

Date		Title / Label	pos	wks
21 Jul 01		**ANIMAL CANNABUS** *Rough Trade RTRADESCD 021*	53	1
9 Feb 02		**WATCHING XANADU** *Blanco Y Negro NEG 138CD*	36	2
1 Mar 03		**THE FINAL ARREARS** *Blanco Y Negro NEG 144CD*	32	2
14 Jun 03		**AM I WRONG** *Blanco Y Negro NEG 146CD*	51	1

		pos/wks
27 Oct 01	LOSS *Blanco Y Negro 927413072*	43 1
15 Mar 03	US *Blanco Y Negro 09276499562*	19 3

Arthur MULLARD – *See Hylda BAKER and Arthur MULLARD*

Larry MULLEN – *See Adam CLAYTON and Larry MULLEN; U2*

Gerry MULLIGAN and Ben WEBSTER

US, male instrumental duo – baritone and tenor sax, Gerry Mulligan d. 20 Jan 1996, Ben Webster d. 20 Sep 1973 (Albums: 1 week)

		pos/wks
24 Sep 60	GERRY MULLIGAN MEETS BEN WEBSTER *HMV CLP 1373*	15 1

Shawn MULLINS

US, male vocalist (Singles: 11 weeks, Albums: 1 week)

		pos/wks
6 Mar 99 ●	LULLABY *Columbia 6669592*	9 10
2 Oct 99	WHAT IS LIFE *Columbia 6678212*	62 1
20 Mar 99	SOUL'S CORE *Columbia 4930372*	60 1

MULU

UK, male / female vocal / instrumental duo (Singles: 1 week)

		pos/wks
2 Aug 97	PUSSYCAT *Dedicated MULU 003CD1*	50 1

Omero MUMBA

Ireland, male vocalist (Singles: 2 weeks)

		pos/wks
20 Jul 02	LIL' BIG MAN *Polydor 5708852*	42 2

Samantha MUMBA

Ireland, female vocalist (Singles: 69 weeks, Albums: 16 weeks)

		pos/wks
8 Jul 00 ●	GOTTA TELL YOU *Wild Card / Polydor 5618832*	2 12
28 Oct 00 ●	BODY II BODY *Wild Card / Polydor 5877742*	5 12
3 Mar 01 ●	ALWAYS COME BACK TO YOUR LOVE *Wild Card / Polydor 5879252*	3 15
22 Sep 01 ●	BABY COME ON OVER *Wild Card / Polydor 5872352*	5 10
22 Dec 01 ●	LATELY *Wild Card / Polydor 5705232*	6 12
26 Oct 02 ●	I'M RIGHT HERE (re) *Wild Card / Polydor 0659372*	5 8
11 Nov 00 ●	GOTTA TELL YOU *Wild Card 5492262*	9 16

Coati MUNDI – *See Kid CREOLE and the COCONUTS*

MUNDY *Ireland, male vocalist (Singles: 2 weeks)*

		pos/wks
3 Aug 96	TO YOU I BESTOW *Epic MUNDY 1CD*	60 1
5 Oct 96	LIFE'S A CINCH *Epic MUNDY 2CD*	75 1

MUNGO JERRY *UK, male vocal / instrumental group – leader Ray Dorset (Singles: 88 weeks, Albums: 14 weeks)*

		pos/wks
6 Jun 70 ★	IN THE SUMMERTIME *Dawn DNX 2502*	1 20
6 Feb 71 ★	BABY JUMP (re) *Dawn DNX 2505*	1 13
29 May 71 ●	LADY ROSE *Dawn DNX 2510*	5 12
18 Sep 71	YOU DON'T HAVE TO BE IN THE ARMY TO FIGHT IN THE WAR *Dawn DNX 2513*	13 8
22 Apr 72	OPEN UP *Dawn DNX 2514*	21 8
7 Jul 73 ●	ALRIGHT, ALRIGHT, ALRIGHT *Dawn DNS 1037*	3 12
10 Nov 73	WILD LOVE *Dawn DNS 1051*	32 5
6 Apr 74	LONG LEGGED WOMAN DRESSED IN BLACK *Dawn DNS 1061*	13 9
29 May 99	SUPPORT THE TOON – IT'S YOUR DUTY (EP) *Saraja TOONCD 001* [1]	57 1
8 Aug 70	MUNGO JERRY *Dawn DNLS 3008*	13 6
10 Apr 71	ELECTRONICALLY TESTED *Dawn DNLS 3020*	14 8

[1] Mungo Jerry and Toon Travellers

Tracks on Support the Toon – It's Your Duty (EP): Blaydon Races / Going to Wembley / Bottle of Beer

MUNICH MACHINE

Germany, male instrumental group (Singles: 8 weeks)

		pos/wks
10 Dec 77	GET ON THE FUNK TRAIN *Oasis OASIS 2*	41 4
4 Nov 78	A WHITER SHADE OF PALE *Oasis OASIS 5* [1]	42 4

[1] Munich Machine introducing Chris Bennett

MUNROS featuring David METHREN

UK, male pipe band (Albums: 3 weeks)

		pos/wks
27 Jun 98	THE LONE PIPER *Virgin VTCD185*	46 3

David MUNROW – *See EARLY MUSIC CONSORT directed by David MUNROW*

MUPPETS

US, male / female vocal / instrumental puppet ensemble – leader Kermit the Frog (Singles: 15 weeks, Albums: 45 weeks)

		pos/wks
28 May 77 ●	HALFWAY DOWN THE STAIRS *Pye 7N 45698*	7 8
17 Dec 77	THE MUPPET SHOW MUSIC HALL EP *Pye 7NX 8004*	19 7
11 Jun 77 ★	THE MUPPET SHOW *Pye NSPH 19*	1 35
25 Feb 78	THE MUPPET SHOW VOLUME 2 *Pye NSPH 21*	16 10

'Halfway Down the Stairs' is sung by Jerry Nelson as Kermit the Frog's nephew, Robin. Tracks on The Muppet Show Music Hall EP: Don't Dilly Dally on the Way / Waiting at the Church / The Boy in the Gallery / Wotcher (Knocked 'Em in the Old Kent Road)

MURDERDOLLS *US, male vocal / instrumental group (Singles: 4 weeks, Albums: 1 week)*

		pos/wks
16 Nov 02	DEAD IN HOLLYWOOD *Roadrunner RR 20223*	54 1
26 Jul 03	WHITE WEDDING *Roadrunner RR 20155*	24 3
31 Aug 02	BEYOND THE VALLEY OF THE MURDERDOLLS *Roadrunner RR 84262*	40 1

Lydia MURDOCK

US, female vocalist (Singles: 9 weeks)

		pos/wks
24 Sep 83	SUPERSTAR *Korova KOW 30*	14 9

Shirley MURDOCK

US, female vocalist (Singles: 2 weeks)

		pos/wks
12 Apr 86	TRUTH OR DARE *Elektra EKR 36*	60 2

Eddie MURPHY – *See Shabba RANKS*

Noel MURPHY *Ireland, male vocalist (Singles: 4 weeks)*

		pos/wks
27 Jun 87	MURPHY AND THE BRICKS *Murphy's STACK 1*	57 4

Peter MURPHY *UK, male vocalist (Albums: 1 week)*

		pos/wks
26 Jul 86	SHOULD THE WORLD FAIL TO FALL APART *Beggars Banquet BEGA 69*	82 1

See also BAUHAUS

Roisin MURPHY – *See MOLOKO; PSYCHEDELIC WALTONS*

Walter MURPHY and the BIG APPLE BAND

US, orchestra (Singles: 9 weeks)

		pos/wks
10 Jul 76	A FIFTH OF BEETHOVEN *Private Stock PVT 59* ▲	28 9

Anne MURRAY

Canada, female vocalist (Singles: 40 weeks, Albums: 10 weeks)

		pos/wks
24 Oct 70	SNOWBIRD *Capitol CL 15654*	23 17
21 Oct 72	DESTINY *Capitol CL 15734*	41 4
9 Dec 78	YOU NEEDED ME *Capitol CL 16011* ▲	22 14
21 Apr 79	I JUST FALL IN LOVE AGAIN *Capitol CL 16069*	58 2
19 Apr 80	DAYDREAM BELIEVER *Capitol CL 16123*	61 3
3 Oct 81	THE VERY BEST OF ANNE MURRAY *Capitol EMTV 31*	14 10

Keith MURRAY *US, male rapper (Singles: 10 weeks)*

		pos/wks
2 Nov 96	THE RHYME *Jive JIVECD 407*	59 1
27 Jun 98	SHORTY (YOU KEEP PLAYING WITH MY MIND) *Jive 0521212* [1]	22 3
14 Nov 98	HOME ALONE *Jive 0522392* [2]	17 5
5 Dec 98	INCREDIBLE *Jive 0522102* [3]	52 1

[1] Imajin featuring Keith Murray [2] R Kelly featuring Keith Murray [3] Keith Murray featuring LL Cool J

Pauline MURRAY and the INVISIBLE GIRLS
UK, female vocalist with male (really) vocal / instrumental group (Singles: 2 weeks, Albums: 4 weeks) pos/wks

2 Aug 80 **DREAM SEQUENCE (ONE)** *Illusive IVE 1* 67 2
11 Oct 80 **PAULINE MURRAY AND THE INVISIBLE GIRLS** *Elusive 2394 227* 25 4

Ruby MURRAY
UK, female vocalist (b. 29 Mar 1935, d. 17 Dec 1996) (Singles: 114 weeks) pos/wks

3 Dec 54 ● **HEARTBEAT** *Columbia DB 3542* 3 16
28 Jan 55 ★ **SOFTLY, SOFTLY (re)** *Columbia DB 3558* 1 23
4 Feb 55 ● **HAPPY DAYS AND LONELY NIGHTS** *ColumbiaDB 3577* 6 8
4 Mar 55 ● **LET ME GO LOVER** *Columbia DB 3577* 5 7
18 Mar 55 ● **IF ANYONE FINDS THIS, I LOVE YOU** *Columbia DB 3580* [1] 4 11
1 Jul 55 ● **EVERMORE** *Columbia DB 3617* 3 17
14 Oct 55 ● **I'LL COME WHEN YOU CALL** *Columbia DB 3643* 6 7
31 Aug 56 **YOU ARE MY FIRST LOVE (re)** *Columbia DB 3770* 16 5
12 Dec 58 **REAL LOVE** *Columbia DB 4192* 18 6
5 Jun 59 ● **GOODBYE JIMMY, GOODBYE (re)** *Columbia DB 4305* 10 14

[1] Ruby Murray with Anne Warren

Junior MURVIN
Jamaica, male vocalist – Mervin Smith (Singles: 9 weeks) pos/wks

3 May 80 **POLICE AND THIEVES** *Island WIP 6539* 23 9

MUSE
UK, male vocal / instrumental group (Singles: 41 weeks, Albums: 55 weeks) pos/wks

26 Jun 99 **UNO** *Mushroom / Taste Media MUSH 50CDS* 73 1
18 Sep 99 **CAVE** *Mushroom / Taste Media MUSH 58CDS* 52 1
4 Dec 99 **MUSCLE MUSEUM** *Mushroom / Taste Media MUSH 66CDS* 43 2
4 Mar 00 **SUNBURN** *Mushroom / Taste Media MUSH 68CDS* 22 2
17 Jun 00 **UNINTENDED** *Mushroom / Taste Media MUSH 72CDS* 20 4
21 Oct 00 **MUSCLE MUSEUM (re-issue)** *Mushroom / Taste Media MUSH 84CDS* 25 3
24 Mar 01 **PLUG IN BABY** *Mushroom / Taste Media MUSH 89CDS* 11 5
16 Jun 01 **NEW BORN** *Mushroom / Taste Media MUSH 92CDS* 12 4
1 Sep 01 **BLISS** *Mushroom / Taste Media MUSH 96CDS* 22 2
1 Dec 01 **HYPER MUSIC / FEELING GOOD** *Mushroom MUSH 97CDS* 24 3
29 Jun 02 **DEAD STAR / IN YOUR WORLD** *Mushroom MUSH 104CDS* 13 3
20 Sep 03 ● **TIME IS RUNNING OUT** *East West EW 272CD* 8 8
13 Dec 03 **HYSTERIA** *East West EW 278CD* ....17 3+
16 Oct 99 **SHOWBIZ** *Mushroom MUSH 59CD* 29 16
30 Jun 01 ● **ORIGIN OF SYMMETRY** *Mushroom MUSH 93CD* 3 24
13 Jul 02 ● **HULLABALOO** *Mushroom MUSH 105CD* 10 4
4 Oct 03 ★ **ABSOLUTION** *East West 5046685872* ■ ....1 11+

MUSIC
UK, male vocal / instrumental group (Singles: 8 weeks, Albums: 5 weeks) pos/wks

31 Aug 02 **TAKE THE LONG ROAD AND WALK IT** *Hut / Virgin HUTCD 158* ..14 3
30 Nov 02 **GETAWAY** *Hut / Virgin HUTCD162* 26 2
1 Mar 03 **THE TRUTH IS NO WORDS** *Hut / Virgin VSCDT 1845* 18 3
14 Sep 02 ● **THE MUSIC** *Hut / Virgin CDHUTX 76* 4 5

MUSIC and MYSTERY featuring Gwen McCRAE
UK, male production group and US, female vocalist (Singles: 3 weeks) pos/wks

13 Feb 93 **ALL THIS LOVE I'M GIVING** *KTDA CDKTDA 2* 36 3

MUSIC OF THE MOUNTAINS – *See MANUEL and The MUSIC OF THE MOUNTAINS*

MUSIC RELIEF '94
UK, male / female vocal / instrumental group (Singles: 1 week) pos/wks

5 Nov 94 **WHAT'S GOING ON** *Jive RWANDACD 1* 70 1

MUSIC STUDENTS – *See Ian DURY and the BLOCKHEADS*

MUSICAL YOUTH
UK, male vocal / instrumental group – lead vocal Dennis Seaton (Singles: 55 weeks, Albums: 22 weeks) pos/wks

25 Sep 82 ★ **PASS THE DUTCHIE (re)** *MCA YOU 1* 1 13
20 Nov 82 **YOUTH OF TODAY** *MCA YOU 2* 13 9
12 Feb 83 ● **NEVER GONNA GIVE YOU UP** *MCA YOU 3* 6 10
16 Apr 83 **HEARTBREAKER** *MCA YOU 4* 44 3
9 Jul 83 **TELL ME WHY** *MCA YOU 5* 33 6
22 Oct 83 **007** *MCA YOU 6* 26 6
14 Jan 84 **SIXTEEN** *MCA YOU 7* 23 8
4 Dec 82 **THE YOUTH OF TODAY** *MCA YOULP 1* 24 22

See also Donna SUMMER

MUSIQ – *See ROOTS*

MUSIQUE
US, female vocal group (Singles: 12 weeks) pos/wks

18 Nov 78 **IN THE BUSH** *CBS 6791* 16 12

MUSIQUE vs U2
UK, male production duo – Nick Hanson and Moussa Clarke – and Ireland, male vocal / instrumental group (Singles: 5 weeks) pos/wks

2 Jun 01 **NEW YEAR'S DUB (re)** *Serious SERR 030CD* 15 5

See also PF PROJECT featuring Ewan McGREGOR

MUSTAFAS – *See STAIFFI and his MUSTAFAS*

MUTINY UK
UK, male production duo – Dylan Barnes and Rob Davy (Singles: 3 weeks) pos/wks

19 May 01 **SECRETS** *Sunflower VCRD 86* 47 1
25 Aug 01 **VIRUS** *VC Recordings VCRD 91* 42 2

Vocals on 'Secrets' by Lorraine Cato

See also HELICOPTER

MUTTON BIRDS
New Zealand, male vocal / instrumental group (Albums: 1 week) pos/wks

12 Jul 97 **ENVY OF ANGELS** *Virgin CDVIR 55* 64 1

MY BLOODY VALENTINE
UK, male / female vocal / instrumental group (Singles: 5 weeks, Albums: 2 weeks) pos/wks

5 May 90 **SOON** *Creation CRE 073* 41 3
16 Feb 91 **TO HERE KNOWS WHEN** *Creation CRE 085* 29 2
23 Nov 91 **LOVELESS** *Creation CRELP 060* 24 2

MY LIFE STORY
UK, male / female vocal / instrumental group (Singles: 12 weeks, Albums: 1 week) pos/wks

17 Aug 96 **12 REASONS WHY I LOVE HER** *Parlophone CDR 6442* 32 2
9 Nov 96 **SPARKLE** *Parlophone CDR 6450* 34 2
1 Mar 97 **THE KING OF KISSINGDOM** *Parlophone CDRS 6457* 35 1
17 May 97 **STRUMPET** *Parlophone CDR 6464* 27 2
23 Aug 97 **DUCHESS** *Parlophone CDR 6474* 39 1
19 Jun 99 **IT'S A GIRL THING** *IT ITR 001* 37 2
30 Oct 99 **EMPIRE LINE** *IT ITR 003* 58 1
19 Feb 00 **WALK / DON'T WALK** *IT ITR 007* 48 1
22 Mar 97 **THE GOLDEN MILE** *Parlophone CDPCS 7386* 36 1

MY MORNING JACKET
US, male vocal / instrumental group (Albums: 1 week) pos/wks

20 Sep 03 **IT STILL MOVES** *RCA 82876559252* 62 1

MY VITRIOL
UK, male / female vocal / instrumental group (Singles: 7 weeks, Albums: 2 weeks) pos/wks

22 Jul 00 **CEMENTED SHOES** *Infectious INFECT 89CDS* 65 1
11 Nov 00 **PIECES** *Infectious INFECT 94CDS* 56 1
24 Feb 01 **ALWAYS: YOUR WAY** *Infectious INFECT 95CDS* 31 2
19 May 01 **GROUNDED** *Infectious INFECT 97CD* 29 2
27 Jul 02 **MOODSWINGS / THE GENTLE ART OF CHOKING** *Infectious INFECT 107CDSX* 39 1
17 Mar 01 **FINELINES** *Infectious INFECT 96CD* 24 2

SPORTING COMPILATIONS

This list comprises all the sports-related compilation albums not attributed to a single act in the main A-Z listing of the book.

CHART ENTRY DATE / ALBUM TITLE / LABEL / PEAK POSITION / WEEKS ON CHART

3 Aug 85 THE MAGIC OF TORVILL AND DEAN Stylus 35 9
5 Dec 87 SPECIAL OLYMPICS – A VERY SPECIAL CHRISTMAS A&M 19 6
29 Feb 92 GOLD: 18 EPIC SPORTING ANTHEMS Telstar 15 3
15 Aug 92 BARCELONA GOLD Warner Bros. 15 2
5 Mar 94 FACE THE MUSIC – TORVILL AND DEAN PolyGram TV 8 3
10 Jun 95 WORLD IN UNION – ANTHEMS PolyGram TV 8 4
1 Jun 96 THE BEAUTIFUL GAME – UEFA EURO '96 RCA 10 6
29 Jun 96 THE BEST FOOTIE ANTHEMS IN THE WORLD…EVER! Virgin 5 5
27 Jun 98 ALL NEW – THE BEST FOOTIE ANTHEMS IN THE WORLD…EVER! Virgin EMI 6 3
27 Jun 98 ALLEZ! OLA! OLEZ! Columbia 8 3
16 Oct 99 LAND OF MY FATHERS OFFICIAL 1999 RUGBY WORLD CUP ALBUM Decca / Universal Music TV 1 6
15 Apr 00 WORLD WRESTLING FEDERATION AGGRESSION Priority 13 8
17 Jun 00 THE BEST FOOTIE ANTHEMS…EVER! Virgin EMI 4 3
24 Jun 00 UEFA EURO 2000 – THE OFFICIAL ALBUM Universal Music TV 15 1
20 Apr 02 WWF FORECABLE ENTRY Columbia 13 2
8 Jun 02 JUMPERS 4 GOALPOSTS WSM 4 4
11 Oct 03 WORLD IN UNION 2003 Decca 10 4

'World in Union 2003' is the latest addition to the list of rugby compilation albums, featuring Bryn Terfel, Shirley Bassey, Russell Watson, Aled Jones, Tom Jones, Max Boyce, Kiri Te Kanawa, The Three Tenors, Kenneth McKellar and many more

MYA *US, female vocalist – Mya Harrison (Singles: 66 weeks)* pos/wks

27 Jun 98 ● GHETTO SUPASTAR (THAT IS WHAT YOU ARE) *Interscope IND 95593* [1] 2 17
12 Dec 98 ● TAKE ME THERE *Interscope IND 95620* [2] 7 9
10 Feb 01 ● CASE OF THE EX *Interscope 4974772* 3 11
24 Mar 01 GIRLS DEM SUGAR *Virgin VUSCD 173* [3] 13 5
9 Jun 01 FREE *Interscope 4975002* 11 6
30 Jun 01 ★ LADY MARMALADE *Interscope / Polydor 4975612* [4] ■ ▲ 1 16
20 Sep 03 MY LOVE IS LIKE... WO *Interscope / Polydor 9810305* 33 2

[1] Pras Michel featuring Ol' Dirty Bastard introducing Mya [2] BLACKstreet and Mya featuring Mase and Blinky Blink [3] Beenie Man featuring Mya [4] Christina Aguilera, Lil' Kim, Mya and Pink

Tim MYCROFT – *See SOUNDS NICE featuring Tim MYCROFT*

Alicia MYERS *US, female vocalist (Singles: 3 weeks)* pos/wks

1 Sep 84 YOU GET THE BEST FROM ME (SAY, SAY, SAY) *MCA MCA 914* 58 3

Billie MYERS
UK, female vocalist (Singles: 12 weeks, Albums: 9 weeks) pos/wks

11 Apr 98 ● KISS THE RAIN *Universal UND 56182* 4 9
25 Jul 98 TELL ME *Universal UND 56201* 28 3
2 May 98 GROWING PAINS *Universal UND 53100* 19 9

Richard MYHILL *UK, male vocalist (Singles: 9 weeks)* pos/wks

1 Apr 78 IT TAKES TWO TO TANGO *Mercury 6007 167* 17 9

Alannah MYLES
Canada, female vocalist (Singles: 17 weeks, Albums: 21 weeks) pos/wks

17 Mar 90 ● BLACK VELVET *East West A 8742* ▲ 2 15
16 Jun 90 LOVE IS *East West A 8918* 61 2
28 Apr 90 ● ALANNAH MYLES *Atlantic 7819561* 3 21

Marie MYRIAM *France, female vocalist (Singles: 4 weeks)* pos/wks

28 May 77 L'OISEAU ET L'ENFANT *Polydor 2056 634* 42 4

MYRON
US male vocalist (Singles: 1 week) pos/wks

22 Nov 97 WE CAN GET DOWN *Island Black Music CID 677* 74 1

MYSTERIANS – *See ? (QUESTION MARK) and the MYSTERIANS*

MYSTERY
Holland, male production duo (Singles: 2 weeks) pos/wks

6 Oct 01 MYSTERY *Inferno CDFERN 42* 56 1
10 Aug 02 ALL I EVER WANTED (DEVOTION) *Xtravaganza XTRAV 33CDS* 57 1

MYSTI – *See CAMOUFLAGE featuring MYSTI*

MYSTIC MERLIN
US, male vocal / instrumental group (Singles: 9 weeks) pos/wks

26 Apr 80 JUST CAN'T GIVE YOU UP *Capitol CL 16133* 20 9

MYSTIC 3
UK / Italy, male production group – aka Blockster (Singles: 1 week) pos/wks

24 Jun 00 SOMETHING'S GOIN' ON *Rulin RULIN 2CDS* 63 1

MYSTICA *Israel, male production trio (Singles: 2 weeks)* pos/wks

24 Jan 98 EVER REST *Perfecto PERF 152CD* 62 1
9 May 98 AFRICAN HORIZON *Perfecto PERF 161CD* 59 1

MYSTIKAL
US, male rapper – Michael Tyler (Singles: 23 weeks) pos/wks

9 Dec 00 SHAKE YA ASS *Jive 9251552* 30 5
17 Feb 01 ● STUTTER *Jive 9251632* [1] ▲ 7 8
29 Dec 01 NEVER TOO FAR / DON'T STOP (FUNKIN' 4 JAMAICA) *Virgin VUSCD 228* [2] 32 4
3 Mar 01 DANGER (BEEN SO LONG) *Jive 9251722* [3] 28 3
23 Feb 02 BOUNCIN' BACK (BUMPIN' ME AGAINST THE WALL) *Jive 9253272* 45 1

			pos	wks
10 May 03		**DON'T MESS WITH MY MAN (re-mix)** *Jive 9254822* [4]	33	2

[1] Joe featuring Mystikal [2] Mariah Carey / Mariah Carey featuring Mystikal [3] Mystikal featuring Nivea [4] Nivea featuring Brian and Brandon Casey of Jagged Edge and Mystikal

MYTOWN *Ireland, male vocal group (Singles: 2 weeks)* pos/wks

			pos	wks
13 Mar 99		**PARTY ALL NIGHT** *Universal UND 56231*	22	2

MZ MAY – *See DREEM TEEM*

N-JOI
UK, male instrumental / production group (Singles: 28 weeks) pos/wks

			pos	wks
27 Oct 90		**ANTHEM** *Deconstruction PB 44041*	45	5
2 Mar 91		**ADRENALIN (EP)** *Deconstruction PT 44344*	23	5
6 Apr 91	●	**ANTHEM (re-issue)** *Deconstruction PB 44445*	8	8
22 Feb 92		**LIVE IN MANCHESTER (PARTS 1 + 2)** *Deconstruction PT 45252*	12	5
24 Jul 93		**THE DRUMSTRUCK EP** *Deconstruction 74321154832*	33	3
17 Dec 94		**PAPILLON** *Deconstruction 74321252132*	70	1
8 Jul 95		**BAD THINGS** *Deconstruction 74321277292*	57	1

Tracks on Adrenalin (EP): Adrenalin / The Kraken / Rhythm Zone / Phoenix. Tracks on The Drumstruck EP: The Void / Boom Bass / Drumstruck

NKOTB – *See NEW KIDS ON THE BLOCK*

N'n'G featuring KALLAGHAN
UK, male / female production / vocal group (Singles: 6 weeks) pos/wks

			pos	wks
1 Apr 00		**RIGHT BEFORE MY EYES** *Urban Heat UHTCD 003*	12	6

N.O.R.E.
US, male rapper – Victor Santiago (Singles: 8 weeks, Albums: 1 week) pos/wks

			pos	wks
21 Sep 02		**NOTHIN'** *Def Jam 639262*	11	7
29 Nov 03		**CRASHIN' A PARTY** *Def Jam MCSTD 40341* [1]	55	1
25 Jul 98		**N.O.R.E.** *Penalty Recordings PENCD 3077* [1]	72	1

[1] Lumidee featuring N.O.R.E. [1] Noreaga

NPG – *See NEW POWER GENERATION*

NRG *UK, male DJ / production duo (Singles: 2 weeks)* pos/wks

			pos	wks
29 Mar 97		**NEVER LOST HIS HARDCORE** *Top Banana TOPCD 04*	71	1
12 Dec 98		**NEVER LOST HIS HARDCORE (re-mix)** *Top Banana TOPCD 010*	61	1

'N SYNC
US, male vocal group (Singles: 79 weeks, Albums: 32 weeks) pos/wks

			pos	wks
13 Sep 97		**TEARIN' UP MY HEART** *Arista 74321505152*	40	2
22 Nov 97		**I WANT YOU BACK** *Arista 74321541122*	62	1
27 Feb 99	●	**I WANT YOU BACK (re) (re-issue)** *Transcontinental / Northwestside 74321646972*	5	10
26 Jun 99	●	**TEARIN' UP MY HEART (re) (re-issue)** *Northwestside / Arista 74321675832*	9	10
8 Jan 00		**MUSIC OF MY HEART** *Epic 6685272* [1]	34	3
11 Mar 00	●	**BYE BYE BYE** *Jive 9250202*	3	8
22 Jul 00		**I'LL NEVER STOP** *Jive 9250762*	13	6
16 Sep 00	●	**IT'S GONNA BE ME** *Jive 9251082* ▲	9	8
2 Dec 00		**THIS I PROMISE YOU** *Jive 9251302*	21	7
21 Jul 01	●	**POP** *Jive 9252422*	9	8
8 Dec 01		**GONE (re)** *Jive 9252772*	24	4
27 Apr 02	●	**GIRLFRIEND** *Jive 9253312* [2]	2	12
17 Jul 99		**'N SYNC** *Northwestside 74321681902*	30	2
1 Apr 00		**NO STRINGS ATTACHED** *Jive 9220272* ▲	14	22
4 Aug 01		**CELEBRITY** *Jive 9222032* ▲	12	8

[1] 'N Sync / Gloria Estefan [2] 'N Sync featuring Nelly

See also Justin TIMBERLAKE

NT GANG
Germany, male vocal / instrumental group (Singles: 1 week) pos/wks

			pos	wks
2 Apr 88		**WAM BAM** *Cooltempo COOL 163*	71	1

N-TRANCE *UK, male production duo – Dale Longworth and Kevin O'Toole (Singles: 83 weeks)* pos/wks

			pos	wks
7 May 94		**SET YOU FREE** *All Around the World CDGLOBE 124* [1]	39	4
22 Oct 94		**TURN UP THE POWER** *All Around the World CDGLOBE 125*	23	3
14 Jan 95	●	**SET YOU FREE (re-mix)** *All Around the World CDGLOBE 126*	2	15
16 Sep 95	●	**STAYIN' ALIVE** *All Around the World CDGLOBE 131* [2]	2	11
24 Feb 96		**ELECTRONIC PLEASURE** *All Around the World CDGLOBE 135*	11	4
5 Apr 97		**D.I.S.C.O.** *All Around the World CDGLOBE 153*	11	6
23 Aug 97		**THE MIND OF THE MACHINE** *All Around the World CDGLOBE 159*	15	4
1 Nov 97	●	**DA YA THINK I'M SEXY** *All Around the World CDGLOBE 150* [3]	7	10
12 Sep 98		**PARADISE CITY** *All Around the World CDGLOBE 140*	28	3
19 Dec 98		**TEARS IN THE RAIN** *All Around the World CDGLOBE 185*	53	1
20 May 00		**SHAKE YA BODY** *All Around the World CDGLOBE 204*	37	1
22 Sep 01	●	**SET YOU FREE (2nd re-mix)** *All Around the World CDGLOBE 242*	4	11
14 Sep 02	●	**FOREVER (re)** *All Around the World CDGLOBE 257*	6	8
19 Jul 03		**DESTINY** *All Around the World CDGLOBE 282*	37	2

[1] N-Trance featuring Kelly Llorenna [2] N-Trance featuring Ricardo Da Force [3] N-Trance featuring Rod Stewart

Although she is vocalist on all versions of 'Set You Free', Kelly Llorenna is given label credit only on the first entry. Similarly, Ricardo da Force appears on several tracks but receives label credit only for 'Stayin' Alive'

N-TYCE
UK, female vocal group (Singles: 15 weeks, Albums: 1 week) pos/wks

			pos	wks
5 Jul 97		**HEY DJ! (PLAY THAT SONG)** *Telstar CDSTAS 2885*	20	2
13 Sep 97		**WE COME TO PARTY** *Telstar CDSTAS 2915*	12	4
28 Feb 98		**TELEFUNKIN'** *Telstar CDSTAS 2944*	16	5
6 Jun 98		**BOOM BOOM** *Telstar CDSTAS 2971*	18	4
20 Jun 98		**ALL DAY EVERY DAY** *Telstar TCD 2945*	44	1

N.W.A. *US, male rap group (Singles: 15 weeks, Albums: 11 weeks)* pos/wks

			pos	wks
9 Sep 89		**EXPRESS YOURSELF (re)** *Fourth & Broadway BRW 144*	26	9
1 Sep 90		**GANGSTA, GANGSTA** *Fourth & Broadway BRW 191*	70	1
10 Nov 90		**100 MILES AND RUNNIN'** *Fourth & Broadway BRW 200*	38	3

23 Nov 91	**ALWAYZ INTO SOMETHIN'** *Fourth & Broadway BRW 238* 60	2
30 Sep 89	**STRAIGHT OUTTA COMPTON** *Fourth & Broadway BRLP 534*....41	6
15 Jun 91	**EFIL4ZAGGIN** *Fourth & Broadway BRLP 562* ▲ 25	2
31 Aug 96	**GREATEST HITS** *Priority CDPTY 126* 56	1
5 Jul 03	**STRAIGHT OUTTA COMPTON (re-issue)** *Priority 5379362* 35	4

'Express Yourself' made No.50 on its first visit and peaked at No.26 on re-entry in May 1990

NYCC *Germany, male rap trio (Singles: 6 weeks)* pos/wks

30 May 98	**FIGHT FOR YOUR RIGHT (TO PARTY)** *Control 0042645 CON* 14	5
19 Sep 98	**CAN YOU FEEL IT (ROCK DA HOUSE)** *Control 0042785 CON* 68	1

NADA SURF
US, male vocal / instrumental group (Singles: 1 week) pos/wks

24 May 03	**INSIDE OF LOVE** *Heavenly HVN 133CD* 73	1

Jimmy NAIL (422 Top 500) *Singer / songwriter, b. James Michael Aloysius Bradford, 1954, Newcastle, UK, whose R&B mixed with a Geordie take on country provided a flip side to his acting career which included key characters in both 'Auf Wiedersehen, Pet' and 'Spender'. His longest stay on the charts was courtesy of another TV series, 'Crocodile Shoes', in which he combined acting and singing (Singles: 73 weeks, Albums: 85 weeks)* pos/wks

27 Apr 85 ●	**LOVE DON'T LIVE HERE ANYMORE** *Virgin VS 764* 3	11
11 Jul 92 ★	**AIN'T NO DOUBT** *East West YZ 686* 1	12
3 Oct 92	**LAURA** *East West YZ 702* 58	2
26 Nov 94 ●	**CROCODILE SHOES (2re)** *East West YZ 867CD* 4	20
11 Feb 95	**COWBOY DREAMS** *East West YZ 878CD*......................................13	7
6 May 95	**CALLING OUT YOUR NAME** *East West YZ 935CD* 65	1
28 Oct 95	**BIG RIVER** *East West EW 008CD* 18	5
23 Dec 95	**LOVE** *East West EW 018CD* 33	4
3 Feb 96	**BIG RIVER (re-mix)** *East West EW 024CD* 72	2
16 Nov 96	**COUNTRY BOY** *East West EW 070CD* 25	8
21 Nov 98	**THE FLAME STILL BURNS** *London LONCD 420* [1] 47	1
8 Aug 92 ●	**GROWING UP IN PUBLIC** *East West 4509901442*..............................2	12
3 Dec 94 ●	**CROCODILE SHOES** *East West 4509985562* 2	31
18 Nov 95 ●	**BIG RIVER** *East West 0630128232* 8	15
30 Nov 96 ●	**CROCODILE SHOES II** *East West 630169352*.................................10	13
18 Oct 97 ●	**THE NAIL FILE – THE BEST OF JIMMY NAIL** *East West 3984207392* 8	14

[1] Jimmy Nail with Strange Fruit

NAILBOMB
Brazil / UK, male vocal / instrumental duo (Albums: 1 week) pos/wks

2 Apr 94	**POINT BLANK** *Roadrunner RR 90552* 62	1

NAKATOMI
UK, male / female production group (Singles: 4 weeks) pos/wks

7 Feb 98	**CHILDREN OF THE NIGHT** *Peach PCHCD 006* 47	2
26 Oct 02	**CHILDREN OF THE NIGHT (re-mix)** *Jive 9254212* 31	2

NAKED EYES *UK, male vocal / instrumental duo – Pete Byrne and Rob Fisher d. 25 Aug 1999 (Singles: 3 weeks)* pos/wks

23 Jul 83	**ALWAYS SOMETHING THERE TO REMIND ME** *RCA 348* 59	3

See also CLIMIE FISHER

NALIN I.N.C. *Germany, male production duo (Singles: 1 week)* pos/wks

28 Mar 98	**PLANET VIOLET** *Logic 74321565702* 51	1

See also NALIN & KANE

NALIN & KANE *Germany, male DJ / production duo – Andy Nalin and Harry Cane (Singles: 6 weeks)* pos/wks

1 Nov 97	**BEACHBALL** *ffrr FCD 318* 48	1
3 Oct 98	**BEACHBALL (re-mix)** *LONDON FCD349* 17	5

See also NALIN I.N.C.

NANA – *See ARCHITECHS*

NAPALM DEATH
UK, male vocal / instrumental band (Albums: 3 weeks) pos/wks

15 Sep 90	**HARMONY OF CORRUPTION** *Earache MOSH 19* 67	1
30 May 92	**UTOPIA BANISHED** *Earache MOSH 53CD* 58	1
3 Feb 96	**DIATRIBES** *Earache MOSH 141CDD* 73	1

NAPOLEON XIV
US, male vocalist – Jerry Samuels (Singles: 10 weeks) pos/wks

4 Aug 66 ●	**THEY'RE COMING TO TAKE ME AWAY, HA-HAAA!** *Warner Bros. WB 5831* 4	10

NARADA – *See Narada Michael WALDEN*

NARCOTIC THRUST *UK, male / female production duo and female vocalist (Singles: 3 weeks)* pos/wks

10 Aug 02	**SAFE FROM HARM** *ffrr FCD 406* 24	3

Michelle NARINE – *See BIG BASS vs Michelle NARINE*

NAS *US, male rapper – Nasir Jones (Singles: 55 weeks, Albums: 16 weeks)* pos/wks

28 May 94	**IT AIN'T HARD TO TELL** *Columbia 6604702* 64	1
17 Aug 96	**IF I RULED THE WORLD** *Columbia 6634022* 12	7
25 Jan 97	**STREET DREAMS** *Columbia 6641302* 12	4
14 Jun 97	**HEAD OVER HEELS** *Epic 6645942* [1] 18	3
29 May 99	**HATE ME NOW** *Columbia 6672562* [2] 14	6
15 Jan 00	**NASTRADAMUS** *Columbia 6685572* 24	3
22 Jan 00	**HOT BOYZ** *Elektra E 7002CD* [3] 18	3
21 Apr 01	**OOCHIE WALLY** *Columbia 67010852* [4] 30	3
2 Feb 02	**GOT UR SELF A ... (re)** *Columbia 6723022* 30	5
13 Jul 02 ●	**I'M GONNA BE ALRIGHT** *Epic 6728442* [5] 3	10
25 Jan 03	**MADE YOU LOOK** *Columbia 6734792* 27	3
5 Apr 03	**I CAN** *Columbia 6737382* 19	7
13 Jul 96	**IT WAS WRITTEN** *Columbia 4841962* ▲...38	6
17 Apr 99	**I AM ...** *Columbia 4894192* ▲ 31	4
25 Jan 03	**GOD'S SON** *Columbia 5098115*...57	6

[1] Allure featuring NAS [2] Nas featuring Puff Daddy [3] Missy 'Misdemeanor' Elliott featuring Nas, Eve and Q Tip [4] QB Finest featuring Nas & Bravehearts [5] Jennifer Lopez featuring Nas

Graham NASH *UK, male vocalist (Albums: 13 weeks)* pos/wks

26 Jun 71	**SONGS FOR BEGINNERS** *Atlantic 2401011* 13	8
13 May 72	**GRAHAM NASH AND DAVID CROSBY** *Atlantic K 50011* [1] 13	5

[1] Graham Nash and David Crosby

See also CROSBY, STILLS, NASH & YOUNG; HOLLIES

Johnny NASH
US, male vocalist, (Singles: 106 weeks, Albums: 17 weeks) pos/wks

7 Aug 68 ●	**HOLD ME TIGHT** *Regal Zonophone RZ 3010* 5	16
8 Jan 69 ●	**YOU GOT SOUL** *Major Minor MM 586* 6	12
2 Apr 69 ●	**CUPID (re)** *Major Minor MM 603* 6	12
1 Apr 72	**STIR IT UP** *CBS 7800* 13	12
24 Jun 72 ●	**I CAN SEE CLEARLY NOW** *CBS 8113* ▲ 5	15
7 Oct 72 ●	**THERE ARE MORE QUESTIONS THAN ANSWERS** *CBS 8351* 9	9
14 Jun 75 ★	**TEARS ON MY PILLOW** *CBS 3220* 1	11
11 Oct 75	**LET'S BE FRIENDS** *CBS 3597* 42	3
12 Jun 76	**(WHAT A) WONDERFUL WORLD** *Epic EPC 4294* 25	7
9 Nov 85	**ROCK ME BABY** *2000 AD FED 19* 47	4
15 Apr 89	**I CAN SEE CLEARLY NOW (re-mix)** *Epic JN 1* 54	5
5 Aug 72	**I CAN SEE CLEARLY NOW** *CBS 64860*...39	6
10 Dec 77	**JOHNNY NASH COLLECTION** *Epic EPC 10008*...................................18	11

Leigh NASH – *See DELERIUM*

NASH THE SLASH
Canada, male vocalist / instrumentalist – violin (Albums: 1 week) pos/wks

21 Feb 81	**CHILDREN OF THE NIGHT** *DinDisc DID 9* 61	1

NASHVILLE TEENS
UK, male vocal / instrumental group (Singles: 36 weeks) pos/wks

9 Jul 64 ● **TOBACCO ROAD** *Decca F 11930* 6 13
22 Oct 64 ● **GOOGLE EYE** *Decca F 12000* 10 10
4 Mar 65 **FIND MY WAY BACK HOME** *Decca F 12089* 34 6
20 May 65 **THIS LITTLE BIRD** *Decca F 12143* 38 4
3 Feb 66 **THE HARD WAY (re)** *Decca F 12316* 45 3

NATASHA *UK, female vocalist – Natasha England (Singles: 16 weeks, Albums: 3 weeks)* pos/wks

5 Jun 82 ● **IKO IKO** *Towerbell TOW 22* 10 11
4 Sep 82 **THE BOOM BOOM ROOM** *Towerbell TOW 25* 44 5
9 Oct 82 **CAPTURED** *Towerbell TOWLP 2* 53 3

Ultra NATÉ *US, female vocalist – Ultra Naté Wyche (Singles: 39 weeks, Albums: 4 weeks)* pos/wks

9 Dec 89 **IT'S OVER NOW** *Eternal YZ 440* 62 3
23 Feb 91 **IS IT LOVE?** *Eternal YZ 509* [1] 71 1
29 Jan 94 **SHOW ME** *Warner Bros. W 0219CD* 62 1
14 Jun 97 ● **FREE** *AM:PM 5822432* 4 17
24 Jan 98 **FREE (re-mix)** *AM:PM 5825012* 33 2
18 Apr 98 ● **FOUND A CURE** *AM:PM 5826452* 6 7
25 Jul 98 **NEW KIND OF MEDICINE** *AM:PM 5827492* 14 5
22 Jul 00 **DESIRE** *AM:PM CDAMPM133* 40 2
9 Jun 01 **GET IT UP (THE FEELING)** *AM:PM CDAMPM 140* 51 1
9 May 98 **SITUATION: CRITICAL** *AM:PM 5408242* 17 4

[1] Basement Boys present Ultra Naté

NATIONAL BRASS BAND
UK, orchestra (Albums: 10 weeks) pos/wks

10 May 80 **GOLDEN MELODIES** *K-Tel ONE 1075* 15 10

NATIONAL PHILHARMONIC ORCHESTRA – *See James GALWAY*

NATIVE
UK, male production duo (Singles: 2 weeks) pos/wks

10 Feb 01 **FEEL THE DRUMS** *Slinky Music SLINKY 009 CD* 46 2

NATURAL
US, male vocal group (Singles: 2 weeks) pos/wks

10 Aug 02 **PUT YOUR ARMS AROUND ME** *Ariola 74321947892* 32 2

NATURAL BORN CHILLERS *UK, male production duo – Arif Salih and Lee Parker (Singles: 3 weeks)* pos/wks

1 Nov 97 **ROCK THE FUNKY BEAT** *East West EW 138CD1* 30 3

NATURAL BORN GROOVES *Belgium, male DJ / production duo – Burn Boon and Jaco van Rijsvijck (Singles: 3 weeks)* pos/wks

2 Nov 96 **FORERUNNER** *XL XLS 76CD* 64 1
19 Apr 97 **GROOVEBIRD** *Positiva CDTIV 75* 21 2

NATURAL LIFE
UK, male / female vocal / instrumental group (Singles: 3 weeks) pos/wks

7 Mar 92 **NATURAL LIFE** *Tribe NLIFE 3* 47 3

NATURAL SELECTION
US, male vocal / instrumental duo (Singles: 2 weeks) pos/wks

9 Nov 91 **DO ANYTHING** *East West A 8724* 69 2

NATURALS
UK, male vocal / instrumental group (Singles: 9 weeks) pos/wks

20 Aug 64 **I SHOULD HAVE KNOWN BETTER** *Parlophone R 5165* 24 9

David NAUGHTON
US, male actor / vocalist (Singles: 6 weeks) pos/wks

25 Aug 79 **MAKIN' IT** *RSO 32* 44 6

NAUGHTY BY NATURE
US, male rap group (Singles: 18 weeks, Albums: 5 weeks) pos/wks

9 Nov 91 **O.P.P.** *Big Life BLR 62* 73 1
20 Jun 92 **O.P.P. (re-issue)** *Big Life BLR 74* 35 3
30 Jan 93 **HIP HOP HOORAY** *Big Life BLRD 89* 22 3
19 Jun 93 **IT'S ON** *Big Life BLRD 99* 48 2
27 Nov 93 **HIP HOP HOORAY (re-mix)** *Big Life BLRDA 104* 20 4
29 Apr 95 **FEEL ME FLOW** *Big Life BLRD 115* 23 3
11 Sep 99 **JAMBOREE** *Arista 74321692882* [1] 51 1
19 Oct 02 **FEELS GOOD (DON'T WORRY BOUT A THING)** *Island CID 806* [2] 44 1
6 Mar 93 **19 NAUGHTY III** *Big Life BLRCD 23* 40 2
27 May 95 **POVERTY'S PARADISE** *Big Life BLRCD 28* 20 3

[1] Naughty By Nature featuring Zhané [2] Naughty By Nature featuring 3LW

NAVIGATOR – *See FREESTYLERS*

Maria NAYLER *UK, female vocalist (Singles: 26 weeks)* pos/wks

9 Mar 96 **BE AS ONE** *Deconstruction 74321342962* [1] 17 4
16 Nov 96 ● **ONE & ONE** *Deconstruction 74321427692* [2] 3 17
7 Mar 98 **NAKED AND SACRED** *Deconstruction 74321534242* 32 3
5 Sep 98 **WILL YOU BE WITH ME / LOVE IS THE GOD** *Deconstruction 74321591772* 65 1
27 May 00 **ANGRY SKIES** *Deconstruction 74321759492* 42 1

[1] Sasha and Maria [2] Robert Miles featuring Maria Nayler

NAZARETH *UK, male vocal / instrumental group (Singles: 75 weeks, Albums: 51 weeks)* pos/wks

5 May 73 ● **BROKEN DOWN ANGEL** *Mooncrest MOON 1* 9 11
21 Jul 73 ● **BAD BAD BOY** *Mooncrest MOON 9* 10 9
13 Oct 73 **THIS FLIGHT TONIGHT** *Mooncrest MOON 14* 11 13
23 Mar 74 **SHANGHAI'D IN SHANGHAI** *Mooncrest MOON 22* 41 4
14 Jun 75 **MY WHITE BICYCLE** *Mooncrest MOON 47* 14 8
15 Nov 75 **HOLY ROLLER** *Mountain TOP 3* 36 4
24 Sep 77 **HOT TRACKS (EP)** *Mountain NAZ 1* 15 11
18 Feb 78 **GONE DEAD TRAIN** *Mountain NAZ 002* 49 2
13 May 78 **PLACE IN YOUR HEART (re)** *Mountain TOP 37* 70 2
27 Jan 79 **MAY THE SUNSHINE** *Mountain NAZ 003* 22 8
28 Jul 79 **STAR** *Mountain TOP 45* 54 3
26 May 73 **RAZAMANAZ** *Mooncrest CREST 1* 11 25
24 Nov 73 ● **LOUD 'N' PROUD** *Mooncrest CREST 4* 10 7
18 May 74 **RAMPANT** *Mooncrest CREST 15* 13 3
13 Dec 75 **GREATEST HITS** *Mountain TOPS 108* 54 1
3 Feb 79 **NO MEAN CITY** *Mountain TOPS 123* 34 9
28 Feb 81 **THE FOOL CIRCLE** *NEMS NEL 6019* 60 3
3 Oct 81 **NAZARETH LIVE** *NEMS NELD 102* 78 3

Tracks on Hot Tracks (EP): Love Hurts / This Flight Tonight / Broken Down Angel / Hair of the Dog

NAZLYN – *See M-BEAT*

Me'Shell NDEGEOCELLO
US, female vocalist / instrumentalist – bass (Singles: 5 weeks) pos/wks

12 Feb 94 **IF THAT'S YOUR BOYFRIEND (HE WASN'T LAST NIGHT)** *Maverick W 0223CD1* 74 1
3 Sep 94 **WILD NIGHT** *Mercury MERCD 409* [1] 34 3
1 Mar 97 **NEVER MISS THE WATER** *Reprise W 0393CD* [2] 59 1

[1] John Mellencamp featuring Me'Shell Ndegeocello [2] Chaka Khan featuring Me'Shell Ndegeocello

Youssou N'DOUR *Senegal, male vocalist (Singles: 35 weeks)* pos/wks

3 Jun 89 **SHAKIN' THE TREE** *Virgin VS 1167* [1] 61 3
22 Dec 90 **SHAKIN' THE TREE (re-issue)** *Virgin VS 1322* [1] 57 4
25 Jun 94 ● **7 SECONDS (re)** *Columbia 6605082* [2] 3 25
14 Jan 95 **UNDECIDED** *Columbia 6609712* 53 2
10 Oct 98 **HOW COME** *Interscope IND 95598* [3] 52 1

[1] Youssou N'Dour and Peter Gabriel [2] Youssou N'Dour (featuring Neneh Cherry) [3] Youssou N'Dour and Canibus

The re-issue of 'Shaking the Tree' was listed with its flip side, 'Solsbury Hill' by Peter Gabriel

NEARLY GOD *UK, male / female vocal / instrumental group – includes Tricky (Singles: 2 weeks, Albums: 4 weeks)* pos/wks

20 Apr 96	**POEMS** *Durban Poison DPCD 3*	28	2
4 May 96 ●	**NEARLY GOD** *Durban Poison DPCD 1001*	10	4

Dr Martin NEARY – See WESTMINSTER ABBEY CHOIR

Terry NEASON *UK, female vocalist (Singles: 1 week)* pos/wks

25 Jun 94	**LIFEBOAT** *WEA YZ 830*	72	1

NEBULA II
UK, male instrumental / production group (Singles: 3 weeks) pos/wks

1 Feb 92	**SEANCE / ATHEAMA** *Reinforced RIVET 1211*	55	2
16 May 92	**FLATLINERS** *J4M 12NEBULA 2*	54	1

NED'S ATOMIC DUSTBIN *UK, male vocal / instrumental group (Singles: 24 weeks, Albums: 8 weeks)* pos/wks

14 Jul 90	**KILL YOUR TELEVISION** *Chapter 22 CHAP 48*	53	2
27 Oct 90	**UNTIL YOU FIND OUT** *Chapter 22 CHAP 52*	51	2
9 Mar 91	**HAPPY** *Columbia 6566807*	16	4
21 Sep 91	**TRUST** *Furtive 6574627*	21	4
10 Oct 92	**NOT SLEEPING AROUND** *Furtive 6583866*	19	3
5 Dec 92	**INTACT** *Furtive 6588166*	36	6
25 Mar 95	**ALL I ASK OF MYSELF IS THAT I HOLD TOGETHER** *Furtive 6613565*	33	2
15 Jul 95	**STUCK** *Furtive 6620562*	64	1
9 Feb 91	**BITE (import)** *Rough Trade Germany RTD 14011831*	72	1
13 Apr 91 ●	**GOD FODDER** *Furtive 4681121*	4	5
31 Oct 92	**ARE YOU NORMAL?** *Furtive 4726332*	13	2

Raja NEE *US, female vocalist (Singles: 2 weeks)* pos/wks

4 Mar 95	**TURN IT UP** *Perspective 5874872*	42	2

NEEDLE DAMAGE – See DJ DAN presents NEEDLE DAMAGE

Joey NEGRO *UK, male producer – Dave Lee (Singles: 15 weeks)* pos/wks

16 Nov 91	**DO WHAT YOU FEEL** *Ten TEN 391* [1]	36	3
21 Dec 91	**REACHIN' (re-mix)** *Republic LIC 160* [1]	70	1
18 Jul 92	**ENTER YOUR FANTASY (EP)** *Ten TEN 397*	35	3
25 Sep 93	**WHAT HAPPENED TO THE MUSIC** *Virgin VSCD 1466*	51	2
19 Feb 00 ●	**MUST BE THE MUSIC** *Incentive CENT 4CDS* [2]	8	5
16 Sep 00	**SATURDAY** *Yola YOLA CDX03* [2]	41	1

[1] Joey Negro presents Phase II [2] Joey Negro featuring Taka Boom

Tracks on Enter Your Fantasy (EP): Love Fantasy / Get Up / Enter Your Mind / Everybody

See also HED BOYS; Li KWAN; RAVEN MAIZE; Z FACTOR; JAKATTA; AKABU featuring Linda CLIFFORD; PHASE II; IL PADRINOS featuring Jocelyn BROWN

neil *UK, male actor / vocalist – Nigel Planer (Singles: 10 weeks)* pos/wks

14 Jul 84 ●	**HOLE IN MY SHOE** *WEA YZ 10*	2	10

Vince NEIL *US, male vocalist (Singles: 1 week, Albums: 1 week)* pos/wks

3 Oct 92	**YOU'RE INVITED (BUT YOUR FRIEND CAN'T COME)** *Hollywood HWD 123*	63	1
8 May 93	**EXPOSED** *Warner Bros. 9362452602*	44	1

See also MÖTLEY CRÜE

NEJA *Italy, female vocalist (Singles: 1 week)* pos/wks

26 Sep 98	**RESTLESS (I KNOW YOU KNOW)** *Panorama CDPAN 1*	47	1

NEK *Italy, male vocalist (Singles: 1 week)* pos/wks

29 Aug 98	**LAURA** *Coalition COLA 054CD*	59	1

NELLY (395 Top 500) *Southern rap superstar, b. Cornell Haynes 2 Nov 1974, Travis, Texas. Leader of the St. Louis rap pack, the St. Lunatics, was the first act since The Beatles to have initial two US No.1 hits replace each other at the top (Singles: 101 weeks, Albums: 69 weeks)* pos/wks

11 Nov 00 ●	**(HOT S**T) COUNTRY GRAMMAR** *Universal MCSTD 40242*	7	9
24 Feb 01	**E.I** *Universal MCSTD 40249*	11	5
19 May 01 ●	**RIDE WIT ME** *Universal MCSTD 40252* [1]	3	12
15 Sep 01	**BATTER UP** *Universal MCSTD 40261* [2]	28	3
27 Oct 01	**WHERE THE PARTY AT?** *Columbia MCSTD 6719012* [3]	25	3
27 Apr 02 ●	**GIRLFRIEND** *Jive 9253312* [4]	2	12
29 Jun 02 ●	**HOT IN HERRE** *Universal MCSTD 40289* ▲	4	15
26 Oct 02 ★	**DILEMMA** *Universal MCSTD 40299* [5] ■ ▲	1	21
15 Mar 03 ●	**WORK IT** *Universal MCSCD 40312* [6]	7	11
20 Sep 03 ●	**SHAKE YA TAILFEATHER** *Bad Boy MCSTD 40337* [7] ▲	10	7
13 Dec 03	**IZ U** *Universal MCSTD 40346*	36	3+
3 Feb 01	**COUNTRY GRAMMAR** *Universal 1577432* ▲	14	31
13 Jul 02 ●	**NELLYVILLE** *Universal 186902* ▲	2	38

[1] Nelly featuring City Spud [2] Nelly and St Lunatics [3] Jagged Edge featuring Nelly [4] 'N Sync featuring Nelly [5] Nelly featuring Kelly Rowland [6] Nelly featuring Justin Timberlake [7] Nelly, P Diddy and Murphy Lee

NELSON *US, male vocal duo (Singles: 3 weeks)* pos/wks

27 Oct 90	**(CAN'T LIVE WITHOUT YOUR) LOVE AND AFFECTION** *DGC GEF 82* ▲	54	3

Bill NELSON *UK, male vocalist / instrumentalist – guitar and synthesizer (Singles: 12 weeks, Albums: 21 weeks)* pos/wks

24 Feb 79	**FURNITURE MUSIC** *Harvest HAR 5176* [1]	59	3
5 May 79	**REVOLT INTO STYLE** *Harvest HAR 5183* [1]	69	2
5 Jul 80	**DO YOU DREAM IN COLOUR?** *Cocteau COQ 1*	52	4
13 Jun 81	**YOUTH OF NATION ON FIRE** *Mercury WILL 2*	73	3
24 Feb 79	**SOUND ON SOUND** *Harvest SHSP 4095* [1]	33	5
23 May 81 ●	**QUIT DREAMING AND GET ON THE BEAM** *Mercury 6359 055*	7	6
3 Jul 82	**THE LOVE THAT WHIRLS (DIARY OF A THINKING HEART)** *Mercury WHIRL 3*	28	4
14 May 83	**CHIMERA** *Mercury MERB 19*	30	5
3 May 86	**GETTING THE HOLY GHOST ACROSS** *Portrait PRT 26602*	91	1

[1] Bill Nelson's Red Noise [1] Bill Nelson's Red Noise

See also BE BOP DELUXE; RED NOISE

Phyllis NELSON
US, female vocalist (Singles: 24 weeks, Albums: 10 weeks) pos/wks

23 Feb 85 ★	**MOVE CLOSER** *Carrere CAR 337*	1	21
21 May 94	**MOVE CLOSER (re-issue)** *EMI CDEMCT 9*	34	3
20 Apr 85	**MOVE CLOSER** *Carrere CAL 203*	29	10

Ricky NELSON (461 Top 500) *TV star turned teen idol and later singer / songwriter b. 8 May 1940, New Jersey, d. 31 Dec 1985. He was virtually raised on a US radio / TV family show. In the 1950s, he enjoyed sales on a par with Elvis Presley and Pat Boone. Both his father and his two sons also topped the US chart (1935 and 1990) (Singles: 150 weeks)* pos/wks

21 Feb 58	**STOOD UP (re)** *London HLP 8542*	27	2
22 Aug 58 ●	**POOR LITTLE FOOL (re)** *London HLP 8670* ▲	4	14
7 Nov 58 ●	**SOMEDAY** *London HLP 8732*	9	13
21 Nov 58	**I GOT A FEELING** *London HLP 8732*	27	1
17 Apr 59 ●	**IT'S LATE** *London HLP 8817*	3	20
15 May 59	**NEVER BE ANYONE ELSE BUT YOU (re)** *London HLP 8817*	14	10
4 Sep 59	**SWEETER THAN YOU** *London HLP 8927*	19	3
11 Sep 59	**JUST A LITTLE TOO MUCH** *London HLP 8927*	11	8
15 Jan 60	**I WANNA BE LOVED** *London HLP 9021*	30	1
7 Jul 60	**YOUNG EMOTIONS** *London HLP 9121*	48	1
1 Jun 61 ●	**HELLO MARY LOU / TRAVELLIN' MAN** *London HLP 9347* ▲	2	18
16 Nov 61	**EVERLOVIN'** *London HLP 9440* [1]	23	5
29 Mar 62	**YOUNG WORLD** *London HLP 9524*	19	13
30 Aug 62	**TEENAGE IDOL** *London HLP 9583* [1]	39	4
17 Jan 63	**IT'S UP TO YOU** *London HLP 9648* [1]	22	9
17 Oct 63	**FOOLS RUSH IN** *Brunswick 05895* [1]	12	9
30 Jan 64	**FOR YOU** *Brunswick 05900* [1]	14	10
21 Oct 72	**GARDEN PARTY** *MCA MU 1165* [1]	41	4
24 Aug 91	**HELLO MARY LOU (GOODBYE HEART) (re-issue)** *Liberty EMCT 2*	45	5

[1] Rick Nelson

Sandy NELSON
US, male instrumentalist – drums (Singles: 42 weeks) pos/wks

6 Nov 59 ● **TEEN BEAT (re)** *Top Rank JAR 197* 9 12
14 Dec 61 ● **LET THERE BE DRUMS** *London HLP 9466* 3 16
22 Mar 62 **DRUMS ARE MY BEAT** *London HLP 9521* 30 6
7 Jun 62 **DRUMMIN' UP A STORM** *London HLP 9558* 39 8

Shara NELSON
UK, female vocalist (Singles: 23 weeks, Albums: 11 weeks) pos/wks

24 Jul 93 **DOWN THAT ROAD** *Cooltempo CDCOOL 275* 19 6
18 Sep 93 **ONE GOODBYE IN TEN** *Cooltempo CDCOOL 279* 21 5
12 Feb 94 **UPTIGHT** *Cooltempo CDCOOL 286* 19 5
4 Jun 94 **NOBODY** *Cooltempo CDCOOL 290* 49 1
10 Sep 94 **INSIDE OUT / DOWN THAT ROAD (re-mix)** *Cooltempo CDCOOLX 295* 34 3
16 Sep 95 **ROUGH WITH THE SMOOTH** *Cooltempo CDCOOL 311* 30 2
5 Dec 98 **SENSE OF DANGER** *Pagan PAGAN 024CDS* [1] 61 1
2 Oct 93 **WHAT SILENCE KNOWS** *Cooltempo CTCD 35* 22 9
7 Oct 95 **FRIENDLY FIRE** *Cooltempo CTCD 48* 44 2

[1] Presence featuring Shara Nelson

See also MASSIVE ATTACK

Shelley NELSON – *See TIN TIN OUT*

Willie NELSON *US, male vocalist / instrumentalist / instrumentalist – guitar (Singles: 13 weeks)* pos/wks

31 Jul 82 **ALWAYS ON MY MIND** *CBS A 2511* 49 3
7 Apr 84 **TO ALL THE GIRLS I'VE LOVED BEFORE** *CBS A 4252* [1] 17 10

[1] Julio Iglesias and Willie Nelson

NENA *Germany, female / male vocal / instrumental group – lead vocal Gabriele (Nena) Kerner (Singles: 14 weeks, Albums: 5 weeks)* pos/wks

4 Feb 84 ★ **99 RED BALLOONS** *Epic A 4074* 1 12
5 May 84 **JUST A DREAM** *Epic H 3249* 70 2
24 Mar 84 **NENA** *Epic EPC 25925* 31 5

NEPTUNES *US, male production / vocal / rap duo – Pharrell Williams and Chad Hugo, Albums: 8 weeks)* pos/wks

30 Aug 03 ● **THE NEPTUNES PRESENT ... CLONES** *Arista 82876533852* ▲ ..2 8

'The Neptunes Present ... Clones' appeared on the Compilations Chart only

*See also Pharrell WILLIAMS; N*E*R*D*

N*E*R*D *US, male vocal / production / instrumental trio (Singles: 10 weeks, Albums: 14 weeks)* pos/wks

9 Jun 01 **LAPDANCE** *Virgin VUSCD 196* [1] 33 2
10 Aug 02 **ROCK STAR** *Virgin VUSCD 253* 15 4
29 Mar 03 **PROVIDER / LAPDANCE (re-mix)** *Virgin VUSCD 262* [2] 20 4
17 Aug 02 **IN SEARCH OF ...** *Virgin CDVUSX 216* 41 14

[1] N*E*R*D featuring Lee Harvey and Vita [2] N*E*R*D / N*E*R*D featuring Lee Harvey and Vita

See also Pharrell WILLIAMS; NEPTUNES

NERIO'S DUBWORK – *See Darryl PANDY*

Frances NERO
US, female vocalist (Singles: 9 weeks) pos/wks

13 Apr 91 **FOOTSTEPS FOLLOWING ME** *Debut DEBT 3109* 17 9

NERO and the GLADIATORS
UK, male instrumental group (Singles: 6 weeks) pos/wks

23 Mar 61 **ENTRY OF THE GLADIATORS (re)** *Decca F 11329* 37 5
27 Jul 61 **IN THE HALL OF THE MOUNTAIN KING** *Decca F 11367* 48 1

Ann NESBY *US, female vocalist (Singles: 3 weeks)* pos/wks

21 Dec 96 **WITNESS (EP)** *AM:PM 5875612* 42 2
17 May 97 **HOLD ON (EP)** *AM:PM 5822332* 75 1

Tracks on Witness (EP): Can I Get a Witness / (mix) / In the Spirit / I'm Still Wearing Your Name. Tracks on Hold On (EP): Hold On (Mousse T's Uplifting Garage Edit) / Hold On (Mousse T's Hard Soul Remix) / Hold On (Klub Head Mix) / This weekend (Laidback Mix)

Michael NESMITH
US, male vocalist / instrumentalist – guitar (Singles: 6 weeks) pos/wks

26 Mar 77 **RIO** *Island WIP 6373* 28 6

See also MONKEES

NETWORK
UK, male vocal / instrumental group (Singles: 4 weeks) pos/wks

12 Dec 92 **BROKEN WINGS** *Chrysalis CHS 3923* 46 4

NEVADA
UK, male / female vocal / instrumental group (Singles: 1 week) pos/wks

8 Jan 83 **IN THE BLEAK MID WINTER** *Polydor POSP 203* 71 1

NEVADA – *See STEREOPOL featuring NEVADA*

NEVE – *See Y-TRAXX*

Robbie NEVIL
US, male vocalist (Singles: 24 weeks, Albums: 1 week) pos/wks

20 Dec 86 ● **C'EST LA VIE** *Manhattan MT 14* 3 11
2 May 87 **DOMINOES** *Manhattan MT 19* 26 6
11 Jul 87 **WOT'S IT TO YA** *Manhattan MT 24* 43 7
13 Jun 87 **C'EST LA VIE** *Manhattan MTL 1006* 93 1

Aaron NEVILLE – *See NEVILLE BROTHERS; Linda RONSTADT*

NEVILLE BROTHERS *US, male vocal / instrumental group (Singles: 7 weeks, Albums: 3 weeks)* pos/wks

25 Nov 89 **WITH GOD ON OUR SIDE** *A&M AM 545* 47 6
7 Jul 90 **BIRD ON A WIRE** *A&M AM 568* 72 1
18 Aug 90 **BROTHER'S KEEPER** *A&M 3953121* 35 3

Jason NEVINS
US, male DJ / producer (Singles: 29 weeks) pos/wks

21 Feb 98 **IT'S LIKE THAT (German import)** *Columbia 6652932* [1] 63 3
14 Mar 98 **IT'S LIKE THAT (US import)** *Columbia 6652932* [1] 65 1
21 Mar 98 ★ **IT'S LIKE THAT** *Sm:)e Communications SM 90652* [1] ◆ ■ 1 16
18 Apr 98 **IT'S TRICKY (import)** *Epidrome EPD 6656982* [1] 74 1
26 Jun 99 **INSANE IN THE BRAIN** *INCredible INCRL 17CD* [2] 19 3
16 Aug 03 ● **I'M IN HEAVEN** *Free 2 Air / Incentive 0148665F2A* [3] 9 5

[1] Run-DMC vs Jason Nevins [2] Jason Nevins vs Cypress Hill [3] Jason Nevins featuring UKNY / Holly James

NEW ATLANTIC *UK, male instrumental / production duo – Richard Lloyd and Cameron Saunders (Singles: 15 weeks)* pos/wks

29 Feb 92 **I KNOW** *3 Beat 3BT 1* 12 7
3 Oct 92 **INTO THE FUTURE** *3 Beat 3BT 2* [1] 70 1
13 Feb 93 **TAKE OFF SOME TIME** *3 Beat 3BTCD 14* 64 1
26 Nov 94 **THE SUNSHINE AFTER THE RAIN** *Ffrreedom TABCD 223* [2] 26 6

[1] New Atlantic featuring Linda Wright [2] New Atlantic / U4EA featuring Berri

'The Sunshine After the Rain' was re-issued in 1995, credited simply to the vocalist Berri

See also BERRI

NEW BOHEMIANS – *See Edie BRICKELL and the NEW BOHEMIANS*

Choir of NEW COLLEGE, OXFORD / Edward HIGGINBOTTOM
UK, choir / conductor (Albums: 7 weeks) pos/wks

12 Oct 96 **AGNUS DEI** *Erato 630146342* 49 5
18 Apr 98 **AGNUS DEI II** *Erato 3984216592* 57 2

NEW EDITION
US, male vocal / rap group – Bobby Brown, Johnny Gill, and Ralph Tresvant (Singles: 36 weeks, Albums: 3 weeks)

Date		Title	pos	wks
16 Apr 83	★	**CANDY GIRL** *London LON 21*	1	13
13 Aug 83		**POPCORN LOVE** *London LON 31*	43	5
23 Feb 85		**MR TELEPHONE MAN** *MCA MCA 938*	19	9
15 Apr 89		**CRUCIAL** *MCA MCA 23934*	70	1
10 Aug 96		**HIT ME OFF** *MCA MCSTD 48014*	20	4
7 Jun 97		**SOMETHING ABOUT YOU** *MCA MCSTD 48032*	16	4
14 Sep 96		**HOME AGAIN** *MCA MCD 11480* ▲	22	3

See also BELL BIV DEVOE

NEW FAST AUTOMATIC DAFFODILS
UK, male vocal / instrumental group (Albums: 2 weeks)

Date		Title	pos	wks
17 Nov 90		**PIGEON HOLE** *Play It Again Sam BIAS 185*	49	1
24 Oct 92		**BODY EXIT MIND** *Play It Again Sam BIAS 205CD*	57	1

NEW FOUND GLORY
US, male / female vocal group (Singles: 5 weeks, Albums: 8 weeks)

Date		Title	pos	wks
16 Jun 01		**HIT OR MISS (WAITED TOO LONG)** *MCA 1558232*	58	1
3 Aug 02		**MY FRIENDS OVER YOU** *MCA MCSTD 40286*	30	3
19 Oct 02		**HEAD ON COLLISION** *MCA MCSTD 40298*	64	1
29 Jun 02	●	**STICKS AND STONES** *MCA 1129452*	10	8

A NEW GENERATION
UK, male vocal / instrumental group (Singles: 5 weeks)

Date		Title	pos	wks
26 Jun 68		**SMOKEY BLUES AWAY** *Spark SRL 1007*	38	5

NEW KIDS ON THE BLOCK (336 Top 500)
Highest-earning boy band of all time: Jordan and Jon Knight, Donnie Wahlberg, Danny Wood, Joey McIntyre. Formed Boston, US, by producer / manager Maurice Starr as pop version of his act New Edition. In 1990, they grossed a reported $861m and became the first group to score eight UK Top 10 entries in a year (Singles: 90 weeks, Albums: 106 weeks)

Date		Title	pos	wks
16 Sep 89		**HANGIN' TOUGH** *CBS BLOCK 1*	52	4
11 Nov 89	★	**YOU GOT IT (THE RIGHT STUFF)** *CBS BLOCK 2*	1	13
6 Jan 90	★	**HANGIN' TOUGH (re-issue)** *CBS BLOCK 3* ▲	1	9
17 Mar 90	●	**I'LL BE LOVING YOU (FOREVER)** *CBS BLOCK 4* ▲	5	8
12 May 90	●	**COVER GIRL** *CBS BLOCK 5*	4	8
16 Jun 90	●	**STEP BY STEP** *CBS BLOCK 6* ▲	2	7
4 Aug 90	●	**TONIGHT** *CBS BLOCK 7*	3	10
13 Oct 90	●	**LET'S TRY AGAIN / DIDN'T I BLOW YOUR MIND** *CBS BLOCK 8*	8	5
8 Dec 90	●	**THIS ONE'S FOR THE CHILDREN** *CBS BLOCK 9*	9	7
9 Feb 91		**GAMES** *CBS 6566267*	14	4
18 May 91		**CALL IT WHAT YOU WANT** *Columbia 6567857*	12	5
14 Dec 91	●	**IF YOU GO AWAY** *Columbia 6576667*	9	5
19 Feb 94		**DIRTY DAWG** *Columbia 6600362* [1]	27	3
26 Mar 94		**NEVER LET YOU GO** *Columbia 6602072* [1]	42	2
9 Dec 89	●	**HANGIN' TOUGH** *CBS 4608741* ▲	2	41
30 Jun 90	★	**STEP BY STEP** *CBS 4666861* ■ ▲	1	31
2 Nov 90	●	**NEW KIDS ON THE BLOCK** *CBS 4675041*	6	13
15 Dec 90		**MERRY MERRY CHRISTMAS** *CBS 4659071*	13	5
2 Mar 91		**NO MORE GAMES – THE REMIX ALBUM** *Columbia 4674941*	15	11
21 Dec 91		**H.I.T.S.** *Columbia 4694381*	50	4
12 Mar 94		**FACE THE MUSIC** *Columbia 4743592* [1]	36	1

[1] NKOTB [1] NKOTB

NEW MODEL ARMY
UK, male vocal / instrumental group (Singles: 33 weeks, Albums: 21 weeks)

Date		Title	pos	wks
27 Apr 85		**NO REST** *EMI NMA 1*	28	5
3 Aug 85		**BETTER THAN THEM / NO SENSE** *EMI NMA 2*	49	2
30 Nov 85		**BRAVE NEW WORLD** *EMI NMA 3*	57	1
8 Nov 86		**51ST STATE** *EMI NMA 4*	71	2
28 Feb 87		**POISON STREET** *EMI NMA 5*	64	1
26 Sep 87		**WHITE COATS (EP)** *EMI NMA 6*	50	3
21 Jan 89		**STUPID QUESTIONS** *EMI NMA 7*	31	3
11 Mar 89		**VAGABONDS** *EMI NMA 8*	37	3
10 Jun 89		**GREEN AND GREY** *EMI NMA 9*	37	3
8 Sep 90		**GET ME OUT** *EMI NMA 10*	34	3
3 Nov 90		**PURITY** *EMI NMA 11*	61	2
8 Jun 91		**SPACE** *EMI NMA 12*	39	2
20 Feb 93		**HERE COMES THE WAR** *Epic 6589352*	25	2
24 Jul 93		**LIVING IN THE ROSE (THE BALLADS EP)** *Epic 6592492*	51	1
12 May 84		**VENGEANCE** *Abstract ABT 008*	73	5
25 May 85		**NO REST FOR THE WICKED** *EMI NMAL 1*	22	3
11 Oct 86		**THE GHOST OF CAIN** *EMI EMC 3516*	45	3
18 Feb 89		**THUNDER AND CONSOLATION** *EMI EMC 3552*	20	3
6 Oct 90		**IMPURITY** *EMI EMC 3581*	23	2
22 Jun 91		**RAW MELODY MEN** *EMI EMC 3595*	43	2
10 Apr 93		**THE LOVE OF HOPELESS CAUSES** *Epic 4735622*	22	2
25 Apr 98		**STRANGE BROTHERHOOD** *Eagle EAGCD 021*	72	1

Better Than Them / No Sense are the lead tracks from The Acoustic EP which included the following tracks: Better Than Them / No Sense / Adrenalin / Trust. Tracks on White Coats (EP): White Coats / The Charge / Chinese Whispers / My Country. Tracks on Living in the Rose (The Ballads EP): Living in the Rose / Drummy B / Marry the Sea / Sleepwalking

NEW MUSIK
UK, male vocal / instrumental group (Singles: 27 weeks, Albums: 11 weeks)

Date		Title	pos	wks
6 Oct 79		**STRAIGHT LINES** *GTO GT 255*	53	5
19 Jan 80		**LIVING BY NUMBERS** *GTO GT 261*	13	8
26 Apr 80		**THIS WORLD OF WATER** *GTO GT 268*	31	7
12 Jul 80		**SANCTUARY** *GTO GT 275*	31	7
17 May 80		**FROM A TO B** *GTO GTLP 041*	35	9
14 Mar 81		**ANYWHERE** *GTO GTLP 044*	68	2

NEW ORDER (155 Top 500)
Innovative Mancunian group featuring three former members of critically acclaimed Joy Division: Bernard Sumner (v/g), Peter Hook (b), Stephen Morris (d), and augmented by Gillian Gilbert (k). 'Blue Monday' remains the UK's biggest-selling 12-inch single of all time and is their best-selling single (all formats totalling 1,001,400) (Singles: 191 weeks, Albums: 149 weeks)

Date		Title	pos	wks
14 Mar 81		**CEREMONY** *Factory FAC 33*	34	5
3 Oct 81		**PROCESSION / EVERYTHING'S GONE GREEN** *Factory FAC 53*	38	5
22 May 82		**TEMPTATION** *Factory FAC 63*	29	7
19 Mar 83	●	**BLUE MONDAY (2re)** *Factory FAC 73* ◆	9	38
3 Sep 83		**CONFUSION** *Factory FAC 93*	12	7
28 Apr 84		**THIEVES LIKE US** *Factory FAC 103*	18	5
25 May 85		**THE PERFECT KISS** *Factory FAC 123*	46	4
9 Nov 85		**SUB-CULTURE** *Factory FAC 133*	63	4
29 Mar 86		**SHELLSHOCK** *Factory FAC 143*	28	5
27 Sep 86		**STATE OF THE NATION** *Factory FAC 153*	30	3
27 Sep 86		**THE PEEL SESSIONS (1ST JUNE 1982) (EP)** *Strange Fruit SFPS 001*	54	1
15 Nov 86		**BIZARRE LOVE TRIANGLE** *Factory FAC 163*	56	2
1 Aug 87	●	**TRUE FAITH** *Factory FAC 183/7*	4	10
19 Dec 87		**TOUCHED BY THE HAND OF GOD** *Factory FAC 1937*	20	7
7 May 88	●	**BLUE MONDAY (re-mix)** *Factory FAC 737*	3	11
10 Dec 88		**FINE TIME** *Factory FAC 2237*	11	8
11 Mar 89		**ROUND AND ROUND** *Factory FAC 2637*	21	7
9 Sep 89		**RUN 2** *Factory FAC 273*	49	2
2 Jun 90	★	**WORLD IN MOTION . . .** *Factory / MCA FAC 2937* [1]	1	12
17 Apr 93	●	**REGRET** *Centredate Co. NUOCD 1*	4	7
3 Jul 93		**RUINED IN A DAY** *Centredate Co. NUOCD 2*	22	4
4 Sep 93		**WORLD (THE PRICE OF LOVE)** *Centredate Co. NUOCD 3*	13	5
18 Dec 93		**SPOOKY** *Centredate Co. NUOCD 4*	22	4
19 Nov 94	●	**TRUE FAITH (re-mix)** *Centredate Co. NUOCD 5*	9	8
21 Jan 95		**NINETEEN63** *London NUOCD 6*	21	4
5 Aug 95		**BLUE MONDAY (2nd re-mix)** *London NUOCD 7*	17	4
25 Aug 01	●	**CRYSTAL** *London NUOCD 8*	8	4
1 Dec 01		**60 MILES AN HOUR** *London NUOCD 9*	29	2
27 Apr 02		**HERE TO STAY** *London NUOCD 11*	15	3
15 Jun 02		**WORLD IN MOTION (re-issue)** *London / MCA NUDOCD 12* [1]	43	2
30 Nov 02		**CONFUSION (re-mix)** *Whacked WACKT 002CD* [2]	64	1
28 Nov 81		**MOVEMENT** *Factory FACT 50*	30	10
14 May 83	●	**POWER CORRUPTION AND LIES** *Factory FACT 75*	4	29
25 May 85	●	**LOW-LIFE** *Factory FACT 100*	7	10
11 Oct 86	●	**BROTHERHOOD** *Factory FACT 150*	9	5
29 Aug 87	●	**SUBSTANCE 1987** *Factory FACT 200*	3	37
11 Feb 89	★	**TECHNIQUE** *Factory FACT 275* ■	1	14
22 Feb 92		**BBC RADIO 1 LIVE IN CONCERT** *Windsong International WINCD 011*	33	2
15 May 93	★	**REPUBLIC** *London 8284132* ■	1	19

17 Jul 93 **SUBSTANCE 1987 (re-issue)** *London 5200082* 32 2
3 Dec 94 ● **? (THE BEST OF NEW ORDER) / ? (THE REST OF NEW ORDER)** *Centredate Co. 8285802* 4 17
8 Sep 01 ● **GET READY** *London 8573896212* 6 4

[1] Englandneworder [2] Arthur Baker vs New Order

Group was male only on first hit. 'Blue Monday''s first visit to the chart peaked at No.12 with the first re-entry making No.9 in Oct 1983 and the second peaking at No.52 in Jan 1984. 'Blue Monday' in 1988 is a re-mixed version of the original 1983 hit which was made available on seven-inch for the first time, hence the slight difference in catalogue number. Sales for the re-mix and the original were combined from 7 May 1988 onwards when calculating its chart position. Tracks on The Peel Sessions (1st June 1982) (EP): Turn the Heater On / We All Stand / Too Late / 5-8-6. Englandneworder comprised New Order plus Keith Allen with England footballer / rapper John Barnes and the rest of the England World Cup squad From 2 Sep 95 '? (The Best Of)' was listed with the remix album '? (The Rest Of)'

See also ELECTRONIC; JOY DIVISION; MONACO; The OTHER TWO

NEW ORLEANS JAZZMEN – *See Terry LIGHTFOOT'S NEW ORLEANS JAZZMEN*

NEW POWER GENERATION *US, male / female vocal / instrumental group (Singles: 64 weeks, Albums: 3 weeks)* pos/wks

31 Aug 91 ● **GETT OFF** *Paisley Park W 0056* [1] 4 8
21 Sep 91 **CREAM** *Paisley Park W 0061* [1] ▲ 15 7
7 Dec 91 **DIAMONDS AND PEARLS** *Paisley Park W 0075* [1] 25 6
28 Mar 92 **MONEY DON'T MATTER 2 NIGHT** *Paisley Park W 0091* [1] 19 5
27 Jun 92 **THUNDER** *Paisley Park W 0113* [1] 28 3
18 Jul 92 ● **SEXY MF / STROLLIN'** *Paisley Park W 0123* [1] 4 7
10 Oct 92 ● **MY NAME IS PRINCE** *Paisley Park W 0132* [1] 7 5
14 Nov 92 **MY NAME IS PRINCE (re-mix)** *Paisley Park W 0142T* [1] 51 1
5 Dec 92 **7** *Paisley Park W 0147* [1] 27 6
13 Mar 93 **THE MORNING PAPERS** *Paisley Park W 0162CD* [1] 52 3
1 Apr 95 **GET WILD** *NPG 0061045* [2] 19 4
19 Aug 95 **THE GOOD LIFE (re)** *NPG 0061515* 15 8
21 Nov 98 **COME ON** *RCA 74321634722* 65 1
8 Apr 95 **EXODUS** *NPG 0061032* 11 3

[1] Prince and the New Power Generation [2] NPG

'The Good Life' peaked at No.29 on its first visit before re-entering at the peak position in Jul 1997

See also PRINCE

NEW RADICALS *US, male vocalist – Gregg Alexander (Singles: 18 weeks, Albums: 14 weeks)* pos/wks

3 Apr 99 ● **YOU GET WHAT YOU GIVE** *MCA MCSTD 48111* 5 17
25 Sep 99 **SOMEDAY WE'LL KNOW** *MCA MCSTD 40217* 48 1
17 Apr 99 ● **MAYBE YOU'VE BEEN BRAINWASHED TOO** *MCA MCD 11858* ..10 14

NEW SEEKERS (343 Top 500)

UK / Australia, male / female vocal / instrumental group – Keith Potger Eve Graham, Lyn Paul, Peter Doyle, Paul Layton and Marty Kristian. Hits included a Coca-Cola advertisement and a Eurovision entry. The group sold more than 25 million records worldwide and equalled the eight Top 20 entries by The Seekers. Biggest-selling single 'I'd Like to Teach the World to Sing' (Singles: 143 weeks, Albums: 49 weeks) pos/wks

17 Oct 70 **WHAT HAVE THEY DONE TO MY SONG MA (re)** *Philips 6006 027* 44 2
10 Jul 71 ● **NEVER ENDING SONG OF LOVE** *Philips 6006 125* 2 19
18 Dec 71 ★ **I'D LIKE TO TEACH THE WORLD TO SING (IN PERFECT HARMONY)** *Polydor 2058 184* 1 21
4 Mar 72 ● **BEG, STEAL OR BORROW** *Polydor 2058 201* 2 13
10 Jun 72 ● **CIRCLES** *Polydor 2058 242* 4 16
2 Dec 72 **COME SOFTLY TO ME** *Polydor 2058 315* [1] 20 11
24 Feb 73 **PINBALL WIZARD – SEE ME, FEEL ME (MEDLEY)** *Polydor 2058 338* 16 8
7 Apr 73 **NEVERTHELESS (I'M IN LOVE WITH YOU)** *Polydor 2068 340* [2] 34 5
16 Jun 73 **GOODBYE IS JUST ANOTHER WORD** *Polydor 2058 368* 36 5
24 Nov 73 ★ **YOU WON'T FIND ANOTHER FOOL LIKE ME** *Polydor 2058 421* [3] 1 16
9 Mar 74 ● **I GET A LITTLE SENTIMENTAL OVER YOU** *Polydor 2058 439* [3] 5 9
14 Aug 76 **IT'S SO NICE (TO HAVE YOU HOME)** *CBS 4391* 44 4
29 Jan 77 **I WANNA GO BACK** *CBS 4786* 25 4
15 Jul 78 **ANTHEM (ONE DAY IN EVERY WEEK)** *CBS 6413* 21 10
5 Feb 72 **NEW COLOURS** *Polydor 2383 066* 40 4
1 Apr 72 ● **WE'D LIKE TO TEACH THE WORLD TO SING** *Polydor 2883 103* ..2 25
12 Aug 72 **NEVER ENDING SONG OF LOVE** *Polydor 2383 126* 35 4
14 Oct 72 **CIRCLES** *Polydor 2442 102* 23 5
21 Apr 73 **NOW** *Polydor 2383 195* 47 2
30 Mar 74 **TOGETHER** *Polydor 2383 264* 12 9

[1] New Seekers featuring Marty Kristian [2] Eve Graham and the New Seekers [3] New Seekers featuring Lyn Paul

NEW TONE AGE FAMILY – *See Dread FLIMSTONE and the MODERN TONE AGE FAMILY*

NEW VAUDEVILLE BAND *UK, male vocal / instrumental group (Singles: 43 weeks)* pos/wks

8 Sep 66 ● **WINCHESTER CATHEDRAL** *Fontana TF 741* ▲ 4 19
26 Jan 67 ● **PEEK-A-BOO** *Fontana TF 784* [1] 7 11
11 May 67 **FINCHLEY CENTRAL** *Fontana TF 824* 11 9
2 Aug 67 **GREEN STREET GREEN** *Fontana TF 853* 37 4

[1] New Vaudeville Band featuring Tristram

NEW VISION *US, male vocal / instrumental duo – Samuel Morales and Albert Cabrera (Singles: 2 weeks)* pos/wks

29 Jan 00 **(JUST) YOU AND ME** *AM:PM CDAMPM 128* 23 2

See also LEE-CABRERA; David MORALES

NEW WORLD *Australia, male vocal / instrumental group (Singles: 53 weeks)* pos/wks

27 Feb 71 **ROSE GARDEN** *RAK 111* 15 11
3 Jul 71 ● **TOM-TOM TURNAROUND** *RAK 117* 6 15
4 Dec 71 **KARA, KARA** *RAK 123* 17 13
13 May 72 ● **SISTER JANE** *RAK 130* 9 13
12 May 73 **ROOFTOP SINGING** *RAK 148* 50 1

NEW WORLD THEATRE ORCHESTRA *UK, orchestra (Albums: 1 week)* pos/wks

24 Dec 60 **LET'S DANCE TO THE HITS OF THE 30'S AND 40'S** *Pye Golden Guinea GGL 0026* 20 1

NEW YORK CITY *US, male vocal group (Singles: 11 weeks)* pos/wks

21 Jul 73 **I'M DOIN' FINE NOW** *RCA 2351* 20 11

NEW YORK SKYY *US, male / female vocal / instrumental group (Singles: 2 weeks, Albums: 2 weeks)* pos/wks

16 Jan 82 **LET'S CELEBRATE (re)** *Epic EPC A 1898* 67 2
21 Jun 86 **FROM THE LEFT SIDE** *Capitol EST 2014* [1] 85 1

[1] Skyy

NEWBEATS *US, male vocal group (Singles: 22 weeks)* pos/wks

10 Sep 64 **BREAD AND BUTTER** *Hickory 1269* 15 9
23 Oct 71 ● **RUN, BABY, RUN** *London HLE 10341* 10 13

Booker NEWBERRY III *US, male vocalist (Singles: 11 weeks)* pos/wks

28 May 83 ● **LOVE TOWN** *Polydor POSP 613* 6 8
8 Oct 83 **TEDDY BEAR** *Polydor POSP 637* 44 3

Mickey NEWBURY *US, male vocalist / instrumentalist – guitar – Milton Newbury, d. 29 Sep 2002 (Singles: 5 weeks)* pos/wks

1 Jul 72 **AMERICAN TRILOGY** *Elektra K 12047* 42 5

NEWCLEUS *US, male rap / instrumental group (Singles: 6 weeks, Albums: 2 weeks)* pos/wks

3 Sep 83 **JAM ON REVENGE (THE WIKKI WIKKI SONG)** *Beckett BKS 8* ..44 6
25 Aug 84 **JAM ON REVENGE** *Sunnyview SVLP 6600* 84 2

Bob NEWHART *US, male comedian (Albums: 37 weeks)* pos/wks

Date		Title	pos	wks
1 Oct 60	●	**BUTTON-DOWN MIND OF BOB NEWHART** *Warner Bros. WM 4010* ▲	2	37

Anthony NEWLEY (476 Top 500) *Acclaimed actor / vocalist and composer, b. 24 Sep 1931, London, UK, d. 14 Apr 1999. He appeared in more than 20 films before his singing career started. He was among the most innovative UK acts of the early rock years before moving into musicals and cabaret (Singles: 130 weeks, Albums: 14 weeks)* pos/wks

Date		Title	pos	wks
1 May 59	●	**I'VE WAITED SO LONG** *Decca F 11127*	3	15
8 May 59		**IDLE ON PARADE (EP)** *Decca DFE 6566*	13	4
12 Jun 59	●	**PERSONALITY** *Decca F 11142*	6	12
15 Jan 60	★	**WHY** *Decca F 11194*	1	18
24 Mar 60	★	**DO YOU MIND** *Decca F 11220*	1	15
14 Jul 60	●	**IF SHE SHOULD COME TO YOU** *Decca F 11254*	4	15
24 Nov 60	●	**STRAWBERRY FAIR** *Decca F 11295*	3	11
16 Mar 61	●	**AND THE HEAVENS CRIED** *Decca F 11331*	6	12
15 Jun 61		**POP GOES THE WEASEL / BEE BOM** *Decca F 11362*	12	9
3 Aug 61		**WHAT KIND OF FOOL AM I?** *Decca F 11376*	36	8
25 Jan 62		**D-DARLING** *Decca F 11419*	25	6
26 Jul 62		**THAT NOISE** *Decca F 11486*	34	5
14 May 60		**LOVE IS A NOW AND THEN THING** *Decca LK 4343*	19	2
8 Jul 61	●	**TONY** *Decca LK 4406*	5	12

'Bee Bom' listed together with 'Pop Goes the Weasel' only for weeks of 15 and 22 Jun 1961. It peaked at No.15. Tracks on Idle on Parade (EP): I've Waited So Long / Idle Rock-a-Boogie / Idle on Parade / Saturday Night Rock-a-Boogie

See also Anthony NEWLEY, Peter SELLERS, Joan COLLINS

Anthony NEWLEY, Peter SELLERS, Joan COLLINS *UK, male / female actors (Albums: 10 weeks)* pos/wks

Date		Title	pos	wks
28 Sep 63	●	**FOOL BRITANNIA** *Ember CEL 902*	10	10

See also Anthony NEWLEY; Peter SELLERS

Tara NEWLEY – *See E-ZEE POSSEE*

Brad NEWMAN *UK, male vocalist (Singles: 1 week)* pos/wks

Date		Title	pos	wks
22 Feb 62		**SOMEBODY TO LOVE** *Fontana H 357*	47	1

Dave NEWMAN *UK, male vocalist (Singles: 6 weeks)* pos/wks

Date		Title	pos	wks
15 Apr 72		**THE LION SLEEPS TONIGHT (WIMOWEH) (re)** *Pye 7N 45134*	34	6

Paul NEWMAN – *See CAMISRA; ESCRIMA; PARTIZAN; TALL PAUL; GRIFTERS*

NEWS *UK, male vocal / instrumental group (Singles: 3 weeks)* pos/wks

Date		Title	pos	wks
29 Aug 81		**AUDIO VIDEO** *George GEORGE 1*	52	3

NEWS – *See Huey LEWIS and the NEWS*

NEWTON *UK, male vocalist – William Myers (Singles: 6 weeks)* pos/wks

Date		Title	pos	wks
15 Jul 95		**SKY HIGH** *Bags Of Fun BAGSCD 6*	56	2
15 Feb 97		**SOMETIMES WHEN WE TOUCH** *Dominion CDDMIN 202*	32	3
16 Aug 97		**DON'T WORRY** *Dominion CDDMIN 206*	61	1

Juice NEWTON *US, female vocalist (Singles: 6 weeks)* pos/wks

Date		Title	pos	wks
2 May 81		**ANGEL OF THE MORNING** *Capitol CL 16189*	43	6

Olivia NEWTON-JOHN (157 Top 500) *Top female vocalist in the US in the 1970s, b. 26 Sep 1948, Cambridge, UK. This photogenic Australian-raised singer / actress has won numerous pop and country awards and was the first female to score a dozen US Top 5 singles (Singles: 234 weeks, Albums: 103 weeks)* pos/wks

Date		Title	pos	wks
20 Mar 71	●	**IF NOT FOR YOU** *Pye International 7N 25543*	7	11
23 Oct 71	●	**BANKS OF THE OHIO** *Pye International 7N 25568*	6	17
11 Mar 72		**WHAT IS LIFE** *Pye International 7N 25575*	16	8
13 Jan 73		**TAKE ME HOME COUNTRY ROADS** *Pye International 7N 25599*	15	13
16 Mar 74		**LONG LIVE LOVE** *Pye International 7N 25638*	11	8
12 Oct 74		**I HONESTLY LOVE YOU** *EMI 2216* ▲	22	6
11 Jun 77	●	**SAM** *EMI 2616*	6	11
20 May 78	★	**YOU'RE THE ONE THAT I WANT** *RSO 006* [1] ◆ ▲	1	26
16 Sep 78	★	**SUMMER NIGHTS** *RSO 18* [2] ◆	1	19
4 Nov 78	●	**HOPELESSLY DEVOTED TO YOU** *RSO 17*	2	11
16 Dec 78	●	**A LITTLE MORE LOVE** *EMI 2879*	4	12
30 Jun 79		**DEEPER THAN THE NIGHT** *EMI 2954*	64	3
21 Jun 80	★	**XANADU** *Jet 185* [3]	1	11
23 Aug 80		**MAGIC** *Jet 196* ▲	32	7
25 Oct 80		**SUDDENLY** *Jet 7002* [4]	15	7
10 Oct 81	●	**PHYSICAL** *EMI 5234* ▲	7	16
16 Jan 82		**LANDSLIDE** *EMI 5257*	18	9
17 Apr 82		**MAKE A MOVE ON ME** *EMI 5291*	43	3
23 Oct 82		**HEART ATTACK** *EMI 5347*	46	4
15 Jan 83		**I HONESTLY LOVE YOU (re-issue)** *EMI 5360*	52	4
12 Nov 83		**TWIST OF FATE** *EMI 5438*	57	2
22 Dec 90	●	**THE GREASE MEGAMIX** *Polydor PO 114* [1]	3	10
23 Mar 91		**GREASE – THE DREAM MIX** *PWL / Polydor PO 136* [5]	47	2
4 Jul 92		**I NEED LOVE** *Mercury MER 370*	75	1
9 Dec 95		**HAD TO BE** *EMI CDEMS 410* [6]	22	4
25 Jul 98	●	**YOU'RE THE ONE THAT I WANT (re-issue)** *Polydor 0441332* [1]	4	9
2 Mar 74		**MUSIC MAKES MY DAY** *Pye NSPL 28186*	37	3
29 Jun 74		**LONG LIVE LOVE** *EMI EMC 3028*	40	2
26 Apr 75		**HAVE YOU NEVER BEEN MELLOW** *EMI EMC 3069* ▲	37	2
29 May 76		**COME ON OVER** *EMI EMC 3124*	49	4
27 Aug 77		**MAKING A GOOD THING BETTER** *EMI EMC 3192*	60	1
21 Jan 78		**GREATEST HITS** *EMI EMA 785*	19	9
9 Dec 78		**TOTALLY HOT** *EMI EMA 789*	30	9
31 Oct 81		**PHYSICAL** *EMI EMC 3386*	11	22
23 Oct 82	●	**GREATEST HITS** *EMI EMTV 36*	8	38
8 Mar 86		**SOUL KISS** *Mercury MERH 77*	66	3
25 Jul 92		**BACK TO BASICS – THE ESSENTIAL COLLECTION 1971-1992** *Mercury 5126412*	12	6
4 Feb 95		**GAIA (ONE WOMAN'S JOURNEY)** *D-Sharp DSHLCD 7017*	33	4

[1] John Travolta and Olivia Newton-John [2] John Travolta, Olivia Newton-John and cast [3] Olivia Newton-John and Electric Light Orchestra [4] Olivia Newton-John and Cliff Richard [5] Frankie Valli, John Travolta and Olivia Newton-John [6] Cliff Richard and Olivia Newton-John

Both 'Greatest Hits' albums are different

NEXT *US, male vocal trio (Singles: 8 weeks)* pos/wks

Date		Title	pos	wks
6 Jun 98		**TOO CLOSE** *Arista 74321580672* ▲	24	3
16 Sep 00		**WIFEY** *Arista 74321790912*	19	5

NEXT OF KIN *UK, male vocal / instrumental group (Singles: 6 weeks)* pos/wks

Date		Title	pos	wks
20 Feb 99		**24 HOURS FROM YOU** *Universal MCSTD 40201*	13	4
19 Jun 99		**MORE LOVE** *Universal MCSTD 40207*	33	2

NIAGRA *UK, male / female vocal / DJ / production duo (Singles: 1 week)* pos/wks

Date		Title	pos	wks
27 Sep 97		**CLOUDBURST** *Freeflow FLOW CD2*	65	1

NICE *UK, male instrumental group (Singles: 15 weeks, Albums: 38 weeks)* pos/wks

Date		Title	pos	wks
10 Jul 68		**AMERICA** *Immediate IM 068*	21	15
13 Sep 69	●	**NICE** *Immediate IMSP 026*	3	6
27 Jun 70	●	**FIVE BRIDGES** *Charisma CAS 1014*	2	21
17 Apr 71	●	**ELEGY** *Charisma CAS 1030*	5	11

Hector NICHOL *UK, male comedian (Albums: 1 week)* pos/wks

Date		Title	pos	wks
28 Apr 84		**BRAVO JULIET!** *Klub KLP 42*	92	1

Paul NICHOLAS *UK, male actor / vocalist – Paul Beuselinck (Singles: 31 weeks, Albums: 8 weeks)* pos/wks

Date		Title	pos	wks
17 Apr 76		**REGGAE LIKE IT USED TO BE** *RSO 2090 185*	17	8
9 Oct 76	●	**DANCING WITH THE CAPTAIN** *RSO 2090 206*	8	9
4 Dec 76	●	**GRANDMA'S PARTY** *RSO 2090 216*	9	11

			pos	wks
9 Jul 77		**HEAVEN ON THE 7TH FLOOR** *RSO 2090 249*	40	3
29 Nov 86		**JUST GOOD FRIENDS** *K-Tel ONE 1334*	30	8

Grandma's Party was an EP featuring Grandma's Party / Flat Foot Floyd / Mr Sax and the Girl / Shufflin' Shoes

Sue NICHOLLS

UK, female actor / vocalist (Singles: 8 weeks)

			pos	wks
3 Jul 68		**WHERE WILL YOU BE** *Pye 7N 17565*	17	8

NICKELBACK *Canada, male vocal / instrumental group (Singles: 43 weeks, Albums: 79 weeks)*

			pos	wks
23 Feb 02		**HOW YOU REMIND ME (import)** *Roadrunner 23203323CD*	65	2
9 Mar 02	●	**HOW YOU REMIND ME** *Roadrunner 23203320* ▲	4	21
7 Sep 02	●	**TOO BAD (re)** *Roadrunner 20373*	9	9
7 Dec 02		**NEVER AGAIN** *Roadrunner RR 20253*	30	2
27 Sep 03	●	**SOMEDAY** *Roadrunner RR 20088*	6	9
19 Jan 02	★	**SILVER SIDE UP** *Roadrunner 12084852*	1	67
4 Oct 03	●	**THE LONG ROAD** *Roadrunner RR84002*	5	12

See also Chad KROEGER featuring Josey SCOTT

Stevie NICKS

US, female vocalist (Singles: 30 weeks, Albums: 82 weeks)

			pos	wks
15 Aug 81		**STOP DRAGGIN' MY HEART AROUND** *WEA K 79231* [1]	50	4
25 Jan 86		**I CAN'T WAIT** *Parlophone R 6110*	54	4
29 Mar 86		**TALK TO ME** *Parlophone R 6124*	68	2
6 May 89		**ROOMS ON FIRE** *EMI EM 90*	16	7
12 Aug 89		**LONG WAY TO GO** *EMI EM 97*	60	2
11 Nov 89		**WHOLE LOTTA TROUBLE** *EMI EM 114*	62	2
24 Aug 91		**SOMETIMES IT'S A BITCH** *EMI EM 203*	40	4
9 Nov 91		**I CAN'T WAIT (re-issue)** *EMI EM 214*	47	2
2 Jul 94		**MAYBE LOVE** *EMI CDEMS 328*	42	3
8 Aug 81		**BELLA DONNA** *WEA K 99169* ▲	11	16
2 Jul 83		**THE WILD HEART** *WEA 2500711*	28	19
14 Dec 85		**ROCK A LITTLE** *Modern PCS 7300*	30	22
10 Jun 89	●	**THE OTHER SIDE OF THE MIRROR** *EMI EMD 1008*	3	14
14 Sep 91		**TIMESPACE – THE BEST OF STEVIE NICKS** *EMI EMD 3595*	15	6
4 Jun 94		**STREET ANGEL** *EMI CDEMC 3671*	16	3
12 May 01		**TROUBLE IN SHANGRI-LA** *Reprise 9362473722*	43	2

[1] Stevie Nicks with Tom Petty and the Heartbreakers

See also FLEETWOOD MAC

NICO – *See VELVET UNDERGROUND*

NICOLE *Germany, female vocalist – Nicole Hohloch (Singles: 10 weeks, Albums: 2 weeks)*

			pos	wks
8 May 82	★	**A LITTLE PEACE** *CBS A 2365*	1	9
21 Aug 82		**GIVE ME MORE TIME** *CBS A 2467*	75	1
2 Oct 82		**A LITTLE PEACE** *CBS 85011*	85	2

NICOLE

US, female vocalist – Nicole McLeod (Singles: 9 weeks)

			pos	wks
28 Dec 85		**NEW YORK EYES** *Portrait A 6805* [1]	41	7
26 Dec 92		**ROCK THE HOUSE** *React 12REACT 12* [2]	63	1
6 Jul 96		**RUNNIN' AWAY** *Ore AG 18CD*	69	1

[1] Nicole with Timmy Thomas [2] Source featuring Nicole

NICOLETTE

UK, female vocalist (Singles: 1 week, Albums: 2 weeks)

			pos	wks
23 Dec 95		**NO GOVERNMENT** *Talkin Loud TLCD 1*	67	1
10 Aug 96		**LET NO-ONE LIVE RENT FREE IN YOUR HEAD** *Talkin Loud 5328142*	36	2

See also MASSIVE ATTACK

NIGEL & MARVIN *Trinidad, male vocal duo – Nigel and Marvin Lewis (Singles: 10 weeks)*

			pos	wks
18 May 02	●	**FOLLOW DA LEADER** *Relentless RELENT 19CD*	5	10

NIGHTCRAWLERS featuring John REID

UK, male / female vocal / production group – leader John Reid (Singles: 36 weeks, Albums: 5 weeks)

			pos	wks
15 Oct 94		**PUSH THE FEELING ON** *ffrr FCD 245* [1]	22	5
4 Mar 95	●	**PUSH THE FEELING ON (re-mix)** *ffrr FCD 257*	3	11
27 May 95	●	**SURRENDER YOUR LOVE** *Final Vinyl 74321283982*	7	7
9 Sep 95		**DON'T LET THE FEELING GO** *Final Vinyl 7432129882*	13	4
20 Jan 96		**LET'S PUSH IT** *Final Vinyl 74321328142*	23	4
20 Apr 96		**SHOULD I EVER (FALL IN LOVE)** *Arista 74321358072*	34	2
27 Jul 96		**KEEP ON PUSHING OUR LOVE** *Arista 74321390422* [2]	30	2
3 Jul 99		**NEVER KNEW LOVE** *Riverhorse RIVHCD 1* [1]	59	1
30 Sep 95		**LET'S PUSH IT** *Final Vinyl 74321309702*	14	5

[1] Nightcrawlers [2] Nightcrawlers featuring John Reid and Alysha Warren

Maxine NIGHTINGALE

UK, female vocalist (Singles: 16 weeks)

			pos	wks
1 Nov 75	●	**RIGHT BACK WHERE WE STARTED FROM** *United Artists UP 36015*	8	8
12 Mar 77		**LOVE HIT ME** *United Artists UP 36215*	11	8

NIGHTMARES ON WAX *UK, male producer / vocalist / instrumentalist – George Evelyn (Singles: 6 weeks, Albums: 4 weeks)*

			pos	wks
27 Oct 90		**AFTERMATH / I'M FOR REAL** *Warp WAP 6*	38	5
26 Jun 99		**FINER** *Warp WAP 123CD*	63	1
24 Apr 99		**CAR BOOT SOUL** *Warp WARPCD 61*	71	2
14 Sep 02		**MIND ELEVATION** *Warp WARPCD 95*	47	2

NIGHTWRITERS

US, male vocal / instrumental duo (Singles: 2 weeks)

			pos	wks
23 May 92		**LET THE MUSIC USE YOU** *Ffrreedom TABX 112*	51	2

NIKKE? NICOLE! *US, female rapper (Singles: 1 week)*

			pos	wks
1 Jun 91		**NIKKE DOES IT BETTER** *Love EVOL 5*	73	1

Markus NIKOLAI *Germany, male producer (Singles: 1 week)*

			pos	wks
6 Oct 01		**BUSHES** *Southern Fried ECB 24CD*	74	1

NILSSON *US, male vocalist – Harry Nilsson d. 15 Jan 1994 (Singles: 55 weeks, Albums: 43 weeks)*

			pos	wks
27 Sep 69		**EVERYBODY'S TALKIN' (2re)** *RCA 1876*	23	15
5 Feb 72	★	**WITHOUT YOU** *RCA 2165* ▲	1	20
3 Jun 72		**COCONUT** *RCA 2214*	42	5
16 Oct 76		**WITHOUT YOU (re-issue)** *RCA 2733*	22	8
20 Aug 77		**ALL I THINK ABOUT IS YOU** *RCA PB 9104*	43	3
19 Feb 94		**WITHOUT YOU (2nd re-issue)** *RCA 74321193092*	47	4
29 Jan 72		**THE POINT** *RCA Victor SF 8166*	46	1
5 Feb 72	●	**NILSSON SCHMILSSON** *RCA Victor SF 8242*	4	22
19 Aug 72		**SON OF SCHMILSSON** *RCA Victor SF 8297*	41	1
28 Jul 73		**A LITTLE TOUCH OF SCHMILSSON IN THE NIGHT** *RCA Victor SF 8371*	20	19

'Everybody's Talkin' made No.50 on its first visit, followed by No.23 on first re-entry in Oct 1969 and No.39 on second re-entry in Mar 1970

Charlotte NILSSON *Sweden, female vocalist (Singles: 4 weeks)*

			pos	wks
3 Jul 99		**TAKE ME TO YOUR HEAVEN** *Arista 74321686952*	20	4

NINA and FREDERIK

Denmark, female / male vocal duo – Baroness Nina and Baron Frederik von Pallandt, d. 15 May 1994 (Singles: 29 weeks, Albums: 6 weeks)

			pos	wks
18 Dec 59		**MARY'S BOY CHILD** *Columbia DB 4375*	26	1
10 Mar 60		**LISTEN TO THE OCEAN (re)** *Columbia DB 4332*	46	2
17 Nov 60	●	**LITTLE DONKEY** *Columbia DB 4536*	3	10
28 Sep 61		**LONGTIME BOY** *Columbia DB 4703*	43	3
5 Oct 61		**SUCU-SUCU** *Columbia DB 4632*	23	13
13 Feb 60	●	**NINA AND FREDERICK** *Pye NPT 19023*	9	2
29 Apr 61		**NINA AND FREDERICK** *Columbia COL 1314*	11	4

These two albums, although identically named, are different

9 BELOW ZERO

UK, male vocal / instrumental group (Albums: 12 weeks) pos/wks

14 Mar 81 **DON'T POINT YOUR FINGER** *A&M AMLH 68521* 56 6
20 Mar 82 **AND ALL THAT COULD HAVE BEEN – LIVE** *A&M AMLH 68537* 38 6

NINE INCH NAILS *US, male vocal / instrumental group – leader – Trent Reznor (Singles: 15 weeks, Albums: 13 weeks)* pos/wks

14 Sep 91 **HEAD LIKE A HOLE** *TVT IS 484* 45 4
16 Nov 91 **SIN** *TVT IS 508* 35 2
9 Apr 94 **MARCH OF THE PIGS** *TVT CID 592* 45 3
18 Jun 94 **CLOSER** *TVT CIDX 596* 25 3
13 Sep 97 **THE PERFECT DRUG** *Interscope IND 95542* 43 1
18 Dec 99 **WE'RE IN THIS TOGETHER** *Island 4971402* 39 2
12 Oct 91 **PRETTY HATE MACHINE** *TVT ILPS 9973* 67 1
17 Oct 92 **BROKEN** *Island IMCD 8004* 18 3
19 Mar 94 ● **THE DOWNWARD SPIRAL** *Island CID 8012* 9 4
9 Oct 99 ● **THE FRAGILE** *Island CIDD 8091* ▲ 10 4
16 Mar 02 **AND ALL THAT COULD HAVE BEEN – LIVE** *Nothing CID 8113* 54 1

999 *UK, male vocal / instrumental group (Singles: 13 weeks, Albums: 1 week)* pos/wks

25 Nov 78 **HOMICIDE** *United Artists UP 36467* 40 3
27 Oct 79 **FOUND OUT TOO LATE** *Radar ADA 46* 69 2
16 May 81 **OBSESSED** *Albion ION 1011* 71 1
18 Jul 81 **LIL RED RIDING HOOD** *Albion ION 1017* 59 3
14 Nov 81 **INDIAN RESERVATION** *Albion ION 1023* 51 4
25 Mar 78 **999** *United Artists UAG 30199* 53 1

911 *UK, male vocal trio (Singles: 94 weeks, Albums: 26 weeks)* pos/wks

11 May 96 **NIGHT TO REMEMBER** *Ginga CDGINGA 1* 38 2
10 Aug 96 **LOVE SENSATION** *Ginga CDGINGA 2* 21 4
9 Nov 96 ● **DON'T MAKE ME WAIT (re)** *Ginga VSCDT 1618* 10 8
22 Feb 97 ● **THE DAY WE FIND LOVE** *Virgin VSCDT 1619* 4 8
3 May 97 ● **BODYSHAKIN'** *Virgin VSCDT 1634* 3 7
12 Jul 97 ● **THE JOURNEY** *Virgin VSCDT 1645* 3 7
1 Nov 97 ● **PARTY PEOPLE...FRIDAY NIGHT (re)** *Ginga / Virgin VSCDT 1658* 5 10
4 Apr 98 ● **ALL I WANT IS YOU (re)** *Virgin VSCDT 1681* 4 7
4 Jul 98 ● **HOW DO YOU WANT ME TO LOVE YOU? (re)** *Ginga VSCDT 1686* 10 9
24 Oct 98 ● **MORE THAN A WOMAN (re)** *Virgin VSCDT 1707* 2 13
23 Jan 99 ★ **A LITTLE BIT MORE** *Virgin VSCDT 1719* ■ 1 9
15 May 99 ● **PRIVATE NUMBER** *Virgin VSCDT 1730* 3 7
23 Oct 99 **WONDERLAND** *Virgin VSCDT 1755* 13 3
8 Mar 97 **THE JOURNEY** *Virgin CDV 2820* 13 17
18 Jul 98 ● **MOVING ON** *Virgin CDV 2852* 10 4
6 Feb 99 ● **THERE IT IS** *Virgin CDV 2873* 8 4
6 Nov 99 **THE GREATEST HITS AND A LITTLE MORE** ... *Virgin CDV 2899* 40 1

9.9 *US, female vocal group (Singles: 3 weeks)* pos/wks

6 Jul 85 **ALL OF ME FOR ALL OF YOU** *RCA PB 49951* 53 3

NINE STORIES – *See Lisa LOEB and NINE STORIES*

NINE YARDS *UK, male vocal group (Singles: 3 weeks)* pos/wks

21 Nov 98 **LONELINESS IS GONE** *Virgin VSCDT 1696* 70 1
10 Apr 99 **MATTER OF TIME** *Virgin VSCDT 1723* 59 1
28 Aug 99 **ALWAYS FIND A WAY** *Virgin VSCDT 1746* 50 1

1910 FRUITGUM CO.

US, male vocal / instrumental group (Singles: 16 weeks) pos/wks

20 Mar 68 ● **SIMON SAYS** *Pye International 7N 25447* 2 16

1927 *Australia, male vocal / instrumental group (Singles: 6 weeks)* pos/wks

22 Apr 89 **THAT'S WHEN I THINK OF YOU** *WEA YZ 351* 46 6

98° *US, male vocal group (Singles: 17 weeks)* pos/wks

29 Nov 97 **INVISIBLE MAN** *Motown 8607092* 66 1
31 Oct 98 **TRUE TO YOUR HEART** *Motown 8608832* [1] 51 1
13 Mar 99 **BECAUSE OF YOU** *Motown 8609012* 36 2
11 Mar 00 ● **THANK GOD I FOUND YOU (re)** *Columbia 6690582* [2] ▲ 10 10
11 Mar 00 **THE HARDEST THING** *Universal MCSTD 40228* 29 2
2 Dec 00 **GIVE ME JUST ONE MORE NIGHT (UNA NOCHE)** *Universal MCSTD 40243* 61 1

[1] 98 Degrees featuring Stevie Wonder [2] Mariah Carey featuring Joe and 98 Degrees

99TH FLOOR ELEVATORS

UK, male DJ / production duo (Singles: 5 weeks) pos/wks

12 Aug 95 **HOOKED** *Labello Dance LAD 18CD* [1] 28 2
30 May 96 **I'LL BE THERE** *Labello Dance LAD 25CD1* [1] 37 2
8 Apr 00 **HOOKED (re-mix)** *Tripoli Trax TTRAX 061CD* 66 1

[1] 99th Floor Elevators featuring Tony De Vit

NIO *UK, male vocalist / rapper / producer – Robert Medcalf (Singles: 1 week)* pos/wks

23 Aug 03 **DO YOU THINK YOU'RE SPECIAL** *Echo ECSD 132* 52 1

NIRVANA

Greece / Ireland, male vocal / instrumental duo – Alex Spyropoulos and Patrick Campbell-Lyons (Singles: 6 weeks) pos/wks

15 May 68 **RAINBOW CHASER** *Island WIP 6029* 34 6

NIRVANA (151 Top 500) *Legendary grunge pioneers: Kurt Cobain (g/v) d. 1994, Krist Novoselic (b), Dave Grohl (d) (founder of Foo Fighters). Notorious Seattle superstars topped the US album chart twice before and twice after Cobain's suicide. XFM listeners voted 'Teen Spirit' Greatest Record of All Time (Singles: 36 weeks, Albums: 310 weeks)* pos/wks

30 Nov 91 ● **SMELLS LIKE TEEN SPIRIT** *DGC DGCS 5* 7 6
14 Mar 92 ● **COME AS YOU ARE** *DGC DGCS 7* 9 5
25 Jul 92 **LITHIUM** *DGC DGCS 9* 11 6
12 Dec 92 **IN BLOOM** *Geffen GFS 34* 28 7
6 Mar 93 **OH THE GUILT** *Touch And Go TG 83CD* 12 2
11 Sep 93 ● **HEART-SHAPED BOX** *Geffen GFSTD 54* 5 5
18 Dec 93 **ALL APOLOGIES / RAPE ME** *Geffen GFSTD 66* 32 5
5 Oct 91 ● **NEVERMIND** *DGC DGC 24425* ▲ 7 184
7 Mar 92 **BLEACH** *Tupelo TUPCD 6* 33 7
26 Dec 92 **INCESTICIDE** *Geffen GED 24504* 14 11
25 Sep 93 ★ **IN UTERO** *Geffen GED 24536* ■ ▲ 1 43
12 Nov 94 ★ **UNPLUGGED IN NEW YORK** *Geffen GED 24727* ■ ▲ 1 40
12 Oct 96 ● **FROM THE MUDDY BANKS OF THE WISHKAH** *Geffen GED 25105* ▲ 4 6
9 Nov 02 ● **NIRVANA** *Geffen/Polydor 4935232* 3 19

The listed flip side of 'Oh the Guilt' was 'Puss' by Jesus Lizard

NITRO DELUXE

US, male multi-instrumentalist – Lee Junior (Singles: 16 weeks) pos/wks

14 Feb 87 **THIS BRUTAL HOUSE (re)** *Cooltempo COOL 142* 47 11
6 Feb 88 **LET'S GET BRUTAL (re-mix)** *Cooltempo COOL* 24 5

'Let's Get Brutal' is a re-mixed version of 'This Brutal House'

NITZER EBB

UK, male vocal / instrumental group (Singles: 3 weeks) pos/wks

11 Jan 92 **GODHEAD** *Mute 1MUTE 135T* 56 1
11 Apr 92 **ASCEND** *Mute 110MUTE 145* 52 1
4 Mar 95 **KICK IT** *Mute LCDMUTE 155* 75 1

NIVEA *US, female vocalist – Nivea Hamilton (Singles: 5 weeks)* pos/wks

4 May 02 **RUN AWAY (I WANNA BE WITH U) / DON'T MESS WITH THE RADIO** *Jive 9253362* 48 1
21 Sep 02 **DON'T MESS WITH MY MAN** *Jive 9254082* [1] 41 2
10 May 03 **LAUNDROMAT / DON'T MESS WITH MY MAN (re-mix)** *Jive 9254822* [2] 33 2

[1] Nivea featuring Brian and Brandon Casey [2] Nivea / Nivea featuring Brian and Brandon Casey of Jagged Edge and Mystikal

Review of the Year

JULY 2003

Beyoncé becomes the youngest female act to have a UK No.1 album and single simultaneously. Dangerously in Love, her first solo album, debuts in the top slot on both sides of the Atlantic. **Dido's** No Angel album passes the 2.5 million sales mark – the biggest-selling album in the UK this millennium. **Robbie Williams** scores his 20th Top 20 appearance since leaving Take That with 'Something Beautiful'. **Madonna** clocks up her 11th No.2 single with 'Hollywood', although, oddly, it is her first single to miss the US Hot 100 since she first charted in 1983. **Jim Reeves**, who had only two chart albums in his lifetime, registers his 27th posthumous entry. **Eric Clapton**, **Mick Fleetwood**, **John McVie**, **Mick Taylor** and **Peter Green** help British blues legend **John Mayall** to celebrate his 70th birthday on stage. Disturbing figures from the record industry: two out of every five albums sold around the globe are pirated. **Elton John** reportedly negotiates a three-year $54m deal at Caesar's Palace in Las Vegas, and **Celine Dion** finishes a run of 65 sell-out shows at the same venue, which gross $36m. **The Osmonds**, those 1970s teeny bop idols, celebrate their highest placed chart album with Ultimate Collection. Five thousand fans purchase **Muse's** download-only single 'Stockholm Syndrome' in the first week. Who has now had more than three dozen US Hot 100 entries in less than six years? Answer: **Jay-Z**, who hits the top, with **Beyoncé,** on the single 'Crazy in Love'. **Eminem's** only two US shows of the year draw more than 95,000 fans and gross at least $5.5m. Joining him on stage are **50 Cent** and **Missy Elliott**. **Ashanti's** Chapter II is the last of a record nine albums in a row to enter at US No.1 and to hold that place for only a week. **Duran Duran** take to the stage for their first US show in 18 years at the Roxy in Hollywood. Legendary lurve man **Barry White** dies, as does the man who first recorded **Elvis**, **Johnny Cash** and **Jerry Lee Lewis**: **Sam Phillips**. Sam passes away the day before his studio, Sun, becomes the first recording studio to be named a historic landmark in the US.

'Never Mind the Buzzcocks' team captain **Bill Bailey** slams the current state of pop: 'There's more evil in the charts than in an al-Qa'ida suggestion box'

NO AUTHORITY

US, male vocal group (Singles: 1 week)

Date	Title	pos	wks
14 Mar 98	**DON'T STOP** *EPIC 6655592*	**54**	1

NO DICE

UK, male vocal / instrumental group (Singles: 2 weeks)

Date	Title	pos	wks
5 May 79	**COME DANCING** *EMI 2927*	**65**	2

NO DOUBT

US, male / female vocal / instrumental group – lead vocal Gwen Stefani (Singles: 64 weeks, Albums: 55 weeks)

Date	Title	pos	wks
26 Oct 96	**JUST A GIRL** *Interscope IND 80034*	**38**	2
22 Feb 97 ★	**DON'T SPEAK** *Interscope IND 95515* ■	**1**	18
5 Jul 97 ●	**JUST A GIRL (re-issue)** *Interscope IND 95539*	**3**	7
4 Oct 97	**SPIDERWEBS** *Interscope IND 95551*	**16**	3
20 Dec 97	**SUNDAY MORNING** *Interscope IND 95566*	**50**	3
12 Jun 99	**NEW** *Higher Ground HIGHS 22CD*	**30**	2
25 Mar 00	**EX-GIRLFRIEND** *Interscope 4972992*	**23**	3
7 Oct 00	**SIMPLE KIND OF LIFE** *Interscope 4974162*	**69**	1
16 Feb 02 ●	**HEY BABY** *Interscope 4976682*	**2**	9
15 Jun 02	**HELLA GOOD** *Interscope 4977362*	**12**	7
12 Oct 02	**UNDERNEATH IT ALL** *Interscope 4977792*	**18**	5
6 Dec 03	**IT'S MY LIFE** *Interscope 9813724*	**20**	4+
18 Jan 97 ●	**TRAGIC KINGDOM** *Interscope IND 90003* ▲	**3**	44
22 Apr 00	**RETURN OF SATURN** *Interscope 4906382*	**31**	2
16 Feb 02	**ROCK STEADY** *Interscope 4931582*	**43**	6
13 Dec 03	**THE SINGLES 1992-2003** *Interscope / Polydor 9861382*	**46**	3+

NO MERCY *US / Cuba, male vocal / instrumental trio (Singles: 26 weeks, Albums: 4 weeks)*

Date	Title	pos	wks
18 Jan 97 ●	**WHERE DO YOU GO** *Arista 74321401502*	**2**	15
24 May 97 ●	**PLEASE DON'T GO** *Arista 74321481372*	**4**	7
6 Sep 97	**KISS YOU ALL OVER** *Arista 7432151452*	**16**	4
7 Jun 97	**MY PROMISE** *Arista 74321466902*	**17**	4

NO ONE DRIVING – *See NOVACANE vs NO ONE DRIVING*

NO SWEAT

Ireland, male vocal / instrumental group (Singles: 5 weeks)

Date	Title	pos	wks
13 Oct 90	**HEART AND SOUL** *London LON 274*	**64**	4
2 Feb 91	**TEAR DOWN THE WALLS** *London LON 257*	**61**	1

NO WAY JOSÉ

US, male instrumental group (Singles: 6 weeks)

Date	Title	pos	wks
3 Aug 85	**TEQUILA** *Fourth & Broadway BRW 28*	**47**	6

NO WAY SIS

UK, male vocal / instrumental group (Singles: 4 weeks)

Date	Title	pos	wks
21 Dec 96	**I'D LIKE TO TEACH THE WORLD TO SING** *EMI CDEM 461*	**27**	4

NODDY *Toytown, male animated character / vocalist, and UK, female vocal trio (Singles: 2 weeks)*

Date	Title	pos	wks
20 Dec 03	**MAKE WAY FOR NODDY** *BMG 82876582142*	**29**	2+

NODESHA

US, female vocalist (Singles: 8 weeks)

Date	Title	pos	wks
6 Sep 03 ●	**MISS PERFECT** *BMG 82876556742* [1]	**5**	7
1 Nov 03	**GET IT WHILE IT'S HOT** *Arista 82876559592*	**55**	1

[1] Abs featuring Nodesha

NOFX

US, male vocal / instrumental group (Albums: 4 weeks)

Date	Title	pos	wks
10 Feb 96	**HEAVY PETTING ZOO** *Epitaph 864572*	**60**	1
10 Jun 00	**PUMP UP THE VALUUM** *Epitaph 65842*	**50**	1
23 Mar 02	**SPLIT SERIES – VOL. 3** *BYO BYO 079CD* [1]	**75**	1
17 May 03	**WAR ON ERRORISM** *Fat Wreck FAT657CD*	**48**	1

[1] Rancid / NOFX

NOLANS (385 Top 500)

Dublin-born singing sisters, with considerable MOR / pop appeal. Personnel on most hits: Anne, Maureen, Bernadette (now in 'The Bill'), Linda and Coleen Nolan. First European act to win the Grand Prize at the prestigious Tokyo Music Festival (1981) (Singles: 90 weeks, Albums: 84 weeks)

Date	Title	pos	wks
6 Oct 79	**SPIRIT BODY AND SOUL** *Epic EPC 7796* [1]	**34**	6
22 Dec 79 ●	**I'M IN THE MOOD FOR DANCING** *Epic EPC 8068*	**3**	15
12 Apr 80	**DON'T MAKE WAVES** *Epic EPC 8349*	**12**	11
13 Sep 80 ●	**GOTTA PULL MYSELF TOGETHER** *Epic EPC 8878*	**9**	13
6 Dec 80	**WHO'S GONNA ROCK YOU** *Epic EPC 9325*	**12**	11
14 Mar 81 ●	**ATTENTION TO ME** *Epic EPC 9571*	**9**	13
15 Aug 81	**CHEMISTRY** *Epic EPC A 1485*	**15**	8
20 Feb 82	**DON'T LOVE ME TOO HARD** *Epic EPC A 1927*	**14**	12
1 Apr 95	**I'M IN THE MOOD FOR DANCING (re-recording)** *Living Beat LBECD 31*	**51**	1
20 Jul 78 ●	**20 GIANT HITS** *Target TGS 502* [1]	**3**	12
19 Jan 80	**NOLANS** *Epic EPC 83892*	**15**	13
25 Oct 80	**MAKING WAVES** *Epic EPC 10023*	**11**	33
27 Mar 82 ●	**PORTRAIT** *Epic EPC 10033*	**7**	10
20 Nov 82	**ALTOGETHER** *Epic EPC 10037*	**52**	8
17 Nov 84	**GIRLS JUST WANNA HAVE FUN** *Towerbell TOWLP 10*	**39**	8

[1] Nolan Sisters [1] Nolan Sisters

NOMAD

UK, male / female vocal / instrumental duo – Damon Rochefort and Sharon Dee Clarke (Singles: 22 weeks, Albums: 2 weeks)

Date	Title	pos	wks
2 Feb 91 ●	**(I WANNA GIVE YOU) DEVOTION** *Rumour RUMA 25* [1]	**2**	10
4 May 91	**JUST A GROOVE** *Rumour RUMA 33*	**16**	6
28 Sep 91	**SOMETHING SPECIAL** *Rumour RUMA 35*	**73**	1
25 Apr 92	**YOUR LOVE IS LIFTING ME** *Rumour RUMA 48*	**60**	2
7 Nov 92	**24 HOURS A DAY** *Rumour RUMA 60*	**61**	1
25 Nov 95	**(I WANNA GIVE YOU) DEVOTION (re-mix)** *Rumour RUMACD 75*	**42**	2
22 Jun 91	**CHANGING CABINS** *Rumour RULP 100*	**48**	2

[1] Nomad featuring MC Mikee Freedom

NONCHALANT

US, female vocalist (Singles: 1 week)

Date	Title	pos	wks
29 Jun 96	**5 O'CLOCK** *MCA MCSTD 48011*	**44**	1

Peter NOONE

UK, male vocalist (Singles: 9 weeks)

Date	Title	pos	wks
22 May 71	**OH YOU PRETTY THING** *RAK 114*	**12**	9

See also HERMAN'S HERMITS

NOOTROPIC

UK, male instrumental / production duo (Singles: 1 week)

Date	Title	pos	wks
16 Mar 96	**I SEE ONLY YOU** *Hi-Life 5779832*	**42**	1

Ken NORDENE – *See Billy VAUGHN and His Orchestra*

NOREAGA – *See N.O.R.E.*

Chris NORMAN – *See Suzi QUATRO; SMOKIE*

NORTH AND SOUTH

UK, male vocal / instrumental group (Singles: 16 weeks)

Date	Title	pos	wks
17 May 97 ●	**I'M A MAN NOT A BOY** *RCA 74321461142*	**7**	5
9 Aug 97	**TARANTINO'S NEW STAR** *RCA 74321501242*	**18**	5
8 Nov 97	**BREATHING** *RCA 74321528422*	**27**	2
4 Apr 98	**NO SWEAT '98** *RCA 74321562212*	**29**	4

NORTHERN LINE

UK / South Africa, male vocal group (Singles: 12 weeks)

Date	Title	pos	wks
9 Oct 99	**RUN FOR YOUR LIFE** *Global Talent GTR 002CDS1*	**18**	4
11 Mar 00	**LOVE ON THE NORTHERN LINE** *Global Talent GTR 003CDS1*	**15**	5
17 Jun 00	**ALL AROUND THE WORLD** *Global Talent GTR 004CDS1*	**27**	3

NORTHERN UPROAR *UK, male vocal / instrumental group (Singles: 11 weeks, Albums: 2 weeks)* pos/wks

21 Oct 95 **ROLLERCOASTER / ROUGH BOYS** *Heavenly HVN 047CD* 41 2
3 Feb 96 **FROM A WINDOW / THIS MORNING** *Heavenly HVN 051CD* 17 3
20 Apr 96 **LIVIN' IT UP** *Heavenly HVN 52CD* 24 2
22 Jun 96 **TOWN** *Heavenly HVN 54CD* 48 1
7 Jun 97 **ANY WAY YOU LOOK** *Heavenly HVN 70CD* 36 2
23 Aug 97 **A GIRL I ONCE KNEW** *Heavenly HVN 73CD* 63 1
11 May 96 NORTHERN UPROAR *Heavenly HVNLP 12CD* 22 2

NORTHSIDE *UK, male vocal / instrumental group (Singles: 12 weeks, Albums: 3 weeks)* pos/wks

9 Jun 90 **SHALL WE TAKE A TRIP / MOODY PLACES** *Factory FAC 268* ..50 5
3 Nov 90 **MY RISING STAR** *Factory FAC 2987* 32 3
1 Jun 91 **TAKE 5** *Factory FAC 3087* 40 4
29 Jun 91 CHICKEN RHYTHMS *Factory FACT 310* 19 3

NOT THE 9 O'CLOCK NEWS CAST *UK / New Zealand, male / female comedians (Albums: 51 weeks)* pos/wks

8 Nov 80 ● NOT THE 9 O'CLOCK NEWS *BBC REB 400* 5 23
17 Oct 81 ● HEDGEHOG SANDWICH *BBC REB 421* 5 24
23 Oct 82 THE MEMORY KINDA LINGERS *BBC REF 453* 63 4

See also Mel SMITH; MR. BEAN; SMITH and JONES

Freddie NOTES and the RUDIES *Jamaica, male vocal / instrumental group (Singles: 2 weeks)* pos/wks

10 Oct 70 **MONTEGO BAY** *Trojan TR 7791* 45 2

NOTORIOUS B.I.G. *US, male rapper – Christopher Wallace d. 9 Mar 1997 (Singles: 30 weeks, Albums: 17 weeks)* pos/wks

29 Oct 94 **JUICY** *Bad Boy 74321240102* 72 1
1 Apr 95 **BIG POPPA** *Puff Daddy 74321263412* 63 1
15 Jul 95 **CAN'T YOU SEE** *Tommy Boy TBCD 700* [1] 43 2
19 Aug 95 **ONE MORE CHANCE – STAY WITH ME** *Puff Daddy 74321300782* 34 2
3 May 97 ● **HYPNOTIZE** *Arista 74321466412* ▲ 10 4
9 Aug 97 ● **MO MONEY MO PROBLEMS** *Puff Daddy 74321492492* [2] ▲ 6 10
14 Feb 98 **SKY'S THE LIMIT** *Puff Daddy 74321561992* [3] 35 2
18 Jul 98 **RUNNIN'** *Black Jam BJAM 9005* [4] 15 3
5 Feb 00 **NOTORIOUS B.I.G** *Puff Daddy / Arista 74321737312* [5] 16 5
5 Apr 97 LIFE AFTER DEATH *Puff Daddy 78612730112* ▲ 23 16
18 Dec 99 BORN AGAIN *Puff Daddy 74321717182* ▲ 70 1

[1] Total featuring the Notorious B.I.G. [2] Notorious B.I.G. featuring Puff Daddy and Mase [3] Notorious B.I.G. featuring 112 [4] 2Pac and Notorious B.I.G. [5] Notorious B.I.G. featuring Puff Daddy and Lil' Kim

NOTTING HILLBILLIES *UK, male vocal / instrumental group – leader Mark Knopfler (Albums: 14 weeks)* pos/wks

17 Mar 90 ● MISSING ... PRESUMED HAVING A GOOD TIME *Vertigo 8426711* 2 14

See also DIRE STRAITS; Mark KNOPFLER

NOTTINGHAM FOREST with PAPER LACE *UK, football team with male vocal / instrumental group. (Singles: 6 weeks)* pos/wks

4 Mar 78 **WE GOT THE WHOLE WORLD IN OUR HANDS** *Warner Bros. K 17110* 24 6

Heather NOVA *Bermuda, female vocalist (Singles: 1 week, Albums: 2 weeks)* pos/wks

25 Feb 95 **WALK THIS WORLD** *Butterfly BFLD 19* 69 1
8 Apr 95 OYSTER *Butterfly BFLCD 12* 72 1
20 Jun 98 SIREN *V2 VVR 1001872* 55 1

Nancy NOVA *UK, female vocalist (Singles: 2 weeks)* pos/wks

4 Sep 82 **NO, NO, NO** *EMI 5328* 63 2

NOVACANE vs NO ONE DRIVING *UK, male production group (Singles: 1 week)* pos/wks

15 Jun 02 **LOVE BE MY LOVER (PLAYA SOL)** *Direction 6727792* 69 1

NOVASPACE *Germany, male production / vocal duo – Felix Gauder and Jessi (Singles: 3 weeks)* pos/wks

22 Feb 03 **TIME AFTER TIME** *MOS / Substance SUBS 15CDS* 29 3

Tom NOVY *Germany, male producer – Thomas Reichold (Singles: 8 weeks)* pos/wks

2 May 98 **SUPERSTAR** *D:disco 74321569352* [1] 32 3
3 Jun 00 **PUMPIN** *Positiva CDTIV 132* [1] 19 3
2 Sep 00 **I ROCK** *Rulin RULIN 3CDS* [2] 55 1
4 Aug 01 **NOW OR NEVER** *Rulin RULIN 14CDS* [3] 64 1

[1] Novy vs Eniac [2] Tom Novy featuring Virginia [3] Tom Novy featuring Lima

NU CIRCLES featuring Emma B *UK, male producer – Andy Lysandrou and female vocalist – Emma Blocksage (Singles: 1 week)* pos/wks

8 Feb 03 **WHAT YOU NEED (TONIGHT)** *East West EW 258CD* 46 1

NU COLOURS *UK, male / female vocal / instrumental group (Singles: 11 weeks)* pos/wks

6 Jun 92 **TEARS** *Wild Card CARD 1* 55 2
10 Oct 92 **POWER** *Wild Card CARD 3* 64 1
5 Jun 93 **WHAT IN THE WORLD** *Wild Card CARDD 4* 57 2
27 Nov 93 **POWER (re-mix)** *Wild Card CARDD 5* 40 2
25 May 96 **DESIRE** *Wild Card 5763652* 31 2
24 Aug 96 **SPECIAL KIND OF LOVER** *Wild Card 5752012* 38 2

NU GENERATION *UK, male producer – Aston Harvey (Singles: 9 weeks)* pos/wks

29 Jan 00 ● **IN YOUR ARMS (RESCUE ME)** *Concept CDCON 7* 8 8
21 Oct 00 **NOWHERE TO RUN 2000** *Concept CDCON 16* 66 1

NU MATIC *UK, male instrumental / production duo (Singles: 1 week)* pos/wks

8 Aug 92 **SPRING IN MY STEP** *XL Recordings XLS 31* 58 1

NU SHOOZ *US, male / female vocal duo – John Smith and Valerie Day (Singles: 17 weeks, Albums: 8 weeks)* pos/wks

24 May 86 ● **I CAN'T WAIT** *Atlantic A 9446* 2 14
26 Jul 86 **POINT OF NO RETURN** *Atlantic A 9392* 48 3
14 Jun 86 POOLSIDE *Atlantic WX 60* 32 8

NU SOUL featuring Kelli RICH *US, male / female vocal / instrumental duo – Carnell Newbill and Kelli Richardson (Singles: 2 weeks)* pos/wks

13 Jan 96 **HIDE-A-WAY** *ffrr FCD 269* 27 2

NUANCE featuring Vikki LOVE *US, male / female vocal / instrumental group (Singles: 3 weeks)* pos/wks

19 Jan 85 **LOVERIDE** *Fourth & Broadway BRW 20* 59 3

NUBIAN PRINZ – *See POWERCUT featuring NUBIAN PRINZ*

NU-BIRTH *UK, male production duo (Singles: 2 weeks)* pos/wks

6 Sep 97 **ANYTIME** *XL XLS 85CD* 48 1
6 Jun 98 **ANYTIME (re-issue)** *Locked On LOX 97CD* 41 1

NUCLEAR ASSAULT *US, male vocal / instrumental group (Albums: 1 week)* pos/wks

7 Oct 89 HANDLE WITH CARE *Under One Flag FLAG 35* 60 1

NUCLEUS *UK, male instrumental group (Albums: 1 week)* pos/wks

11 Jul 70 ELASTIC ROCK *Vertigo 6360 006* 46 1

NUFF JUICE – *See D MOB*

Ted NUGENT

US, male vocalist / instrumentalist – guitar (Albums: 14 weeks) pos/wks

Date	Title	pos	wks
4 Sep 76	**TED NUGENT** *Epic EPC 81268*	56	1
30 Oct 76	**FREE FOR ALL** *Epic EPC 81397*	33	2
2 Jul 77	**CAT SCRATCH FEVER** *Epic EPC 82010*	28	5
11 Mar 78	**DOUBLE LIVE GONZO!** *Epic EPC 88282*	47	2
14 Jun 80	**SCREAM DREAM** *Epic EPC 86111*	37	3
25 Apr 81	**IN 10 CITIES** *Epic EPC 84917*	75	1

NUKLEUZ DJ'S

UK, male / female DJs / producers (Singles: 7 weeks) pos/wks

Date	Title	pos	wks
24 Aug 02	**DJ NATION** *Nukleuz NUKF 0440*	40	2
8 Feb 03	**DJ NATION – BOOTLEG EDITION** *Nukleuz 0468 FNUK*	33	2
15 Nov 03	**DJ NATION – HARDER EDITION** *Nukleuz 0572 FNUK*	48	3

All releases in this series contain tracks by various combinations of DJ / producers spread across three chart-eligible 12-inch singles

Gary NUMAN (175 Top 500)

The moody, synthesized sound of London-born Gary Webb (b. 8 Mar 1958) first hit the charts in 1979 under the group name Tubeway Army. Four-times chart hit 'Cars' was also the basis of Armand Van Helden's Top 20 hit 'Koochy' in 2000 (Singles: 169 weeks, Albums: 145 weeks) pos/wks

Date		Title	pos	wks
19 May 79	★	**ARE 'FRIENDS' ELECTRIC?** *Beggars Banquet BEG 18* [1]	1	16
1 Sep 79	★	**CARS** *Beggars Banquet BEG 23*	1	11
24 Nov 79	●	**COMPLEX** *Beggars Banquet BEG 29*	6	9
24 May 80	●	**WE ARE GLASS** *Beggars Banquet BEG 35*	5	7
30 Aug 80	●	**I DIE: YOU DIE** *Beggars Banquet BEG 46*	6	7
20 Dec 80		**THIS WRECKAGE** *Beggars Banquet BEG 50*	20	7
29 Aug 81	●	**SHE'S GOT CLAWS** *Beggars Banquet BEG 62*	6	6
5 Dec 81		**LOVE NEEDS NO DISGUISE** *Beggars Banquet BEG 68* [2]	33	7
6 Mar 82		**MUSIC FOR CHAMELEONS** *Beggars Banquet BEG 70*	19	7
19 Jun 82	●	**WE TAKE MYSTERY (TO BED)** *Beggars Banquet BEG 77*	9	4
28 Aug 82		**WHITE BOYS AND HEROES** *Beggars Banquet BEG 81*	20	4
3 Sep 83		**WARRIORS** *Beggars Banquet BEG 95*	20	5
22 Oct 83		**SISTER SURPRISE** *Beggars Banquet BEG 101*	32	3
3 Nov 84		**BERSERKER** *Numa NU 4*	32	5
22 Dec 84		**MY DYING MACHINE** *Numa NU 6*	66	1
9 Feb 85		**CHANGE YOUR MIND** *Polydor POSP 722* [3]	17	8
25 May 85		**THE LIVE EP** *Numa NUM 7*	27	4
10 Aug 85		**YOUR FASCINATION** *Numa NU 9*	46	5
21 Sep 85		**CALL OUT THE DOGS** *Numa NU 11*	49	2
16 Nov 85		**MIRACLES** *Numa NU 13*	49	3
19 Apr 86		**THIS IS LOVE** *Numa NU 16*	28	3
28 Jun 86		**I CAN'T STOP** *Numa NU 17*	27	4
4 Oct 86		**NEW THING FROM LONDON TOWN** *Numa NU 19* [3]	52	3
6 Dec 86		**I STILL REMEMBER** *Numa NU 21*	74	1
28 Mar 87		**RADIO HEART** *GFM GFM 109* [4]	35	6
13 Jun 87		**LONDON TIMES** *GFM GFM 112* [4]	48	2
19 Sep 87		**CARS (E REG MODEL) / ARE 'FRIENDS' ELECTRIC? (re-mix)** *Beggars Banquet BEG 199*	16	7
30 Jan 88		**NO MORE LIES** *Polydor POSP 894* [3]	34	3
1 Oct 88		**NEW ANGER** *Illegal ILS 1003*	46	2
3 Dec 88		**AMERICA** *Illegal ILS 1004*	49	1
3 Jun 89		**I'M ON AUTOMATIC** *Polydor PO 43* [3]	44	2
16 Mar 91		**HEART** *IRS NUMAN 1*	43	2
21 Mar 92		**THE SKIN GAME** *Numa NU 23*	68	1
1 Aug 92		**MACHINE + SOUL** *Numa NUM 124*	72	1
4 Sep 93		**CARS (2nd re-mix)** *Beggars Banquet BEG 264CD*	53	1
16 Mar 96		**CARS (re-issue) (re-mix)** *PolyGram TV PRMCD 1*	17	4
13 Jul 02		**RIP** *Jagged Halo JHCD 5*	29	2
5 Jul 03		**CRAZIER** *Jagged Halo JHCDV 6* [5]	13	3
9 Jun 79	★	**REPLICAS** *Beggars Banquet BEGA 7* [1]	1	31
25 Aug 79		**TUBEWAY ARMY** *Beggars Banquet BEGA 4* [1]	14	10
22 Sep 79	★	**THE PLEASURE PRINCIPLE** *Beggars Banquet BEGA 10* ■	1	21
13 Sep 80	★	**TELEKON** *Beggars Banquet BEGA 19* ■	1	11
2 May 81		**LIVING ORNAMENTS 1979** *Beggars Banquet BEGA 24*	47	3
2 May 81	●	**LIVING ORNAMENTS 1979-1980** *Beggars Banquet BOX 1*	2	4
2 May 81		**LIVING ORNAMENTS 1980** *Beggars Banquet BEGA 25*	39	3
12 Sep 81	●	**DANCE** *Beggars Banquet BEGA 28*	3	8
18 Sep 82	●	**I ASSASSIN** *Beggars Banquet BEGA 40*	8	6
27 Nov 82		**NEW MAN NUMAN – THE BEST OF GARY NUMAN** *TV TVA 7*	45	7
24 Sep 83		**WARRIORS** *Beggars Banquet BEGA 47*	12	6
6 Oct 84		**THE PLAN 1978** *Beggars Banquet BEGA 55*	29	4
24 Nov 84		**BERSERKER** *Numa NUMA 1001*	45	3
13 Apr 85		**WHITE NOISE – LIVE** *Numa NUMAD 1002*	29	5
28 Sep 85		**THE FURY** *Numa NUMA 1003*	24	5
8 Nov 86		**STRANGE CHARM** *Numa NUMA 1005*	59	2
3 Oct 87		**EXHIBITION** *Beggars Banquet BEGA 88*	43	3
8 Oct 88		**METAL RHYTHM** *Illegal ILP 035*	48	2
8 Jul 89		**AUTOMATIC** *Polydor 8395201* [2]	59	1
28 Oct 89		**SKIN MECHANIC** *IRS EIRSA 1019*	55	1
30 Mar 91		**OUTLAND** *IRS EIRSA 1039*	39	1
22 Aug 92		**MACHINE AND SOUL** *Numa NUMACD 1009*	42	1
2 Oct 93		**BEST OF GARY NUMAN 1978-83** *Beggars Banquet BEGA 150CD*	70	1
30 Mar 96		**THE PREMIER HITS** *PolyGram TV 5311492* [3]	21	3
1 Nov 97		**EXILE** *Eagle EAGCD 008*	48	1
21 Oct 00		**PURE** *Eagle EAGCD 078*	58	1
1 Jun 02		**EXPOSURE – THE BEST OF GARY NUMAN 1977-2002** *Jagged Halo JHCD 2*	44	1

[1] Tubeway Army [2] Gary Numan and Dramatis [3] Sharpe and Numan [4] Radio Heart featuring Gary Numan [5] Gary Numan vs Rico [1] Tubeway Army [2] Sharpe and Numan [3] Gary Numan/Tubeway Army

Tracks on The Live EP: Are 'Friends' Electric? / Berserker / Cars / We Are Glass. 'Cars' in 1996 is a re-issue of the 1987 remix 'Living Ornaments 1979-1980' is a boxed set of 'Living Ornaments 1979' and 'Living Ornaments 1980'

See also Paul GARDINER

NUMBER ONE CUP

US, male vocal / instrumental group (Singles: 1 week) pos/wks

Date	Title	pos	wks
2 Mar 96	**DIVEBOMB** *Blue Rose BRRC 10032*	61	1

Jose NUNEZ featuring OCTAHVIA

US, male DJ / producer (Singles: 2 weeks) pos/wks

Date	Title	pos	wks
5 Sep 98	**IN MY LIFE** *Ministry of Sound MOSCDS 126*	56	1
5 Jun 99	**HOLD ON** *Ministry of Sound MOSCDS 130*	44	1

See also CHOO CHOO PROJECT

Bobby NUNN *US, male vocalist / instrumentalist d. 5 Nov 1986 (Singles: 3 weeks)*

pos/wks

Date	Title	pos	wks
4 Feb 84	**DON'T KNOCK IT (UNTIL YOU TRY IT)** *Motown TMG 1323*	65	3

NUSH *UK, male instrumental / production duo – Danny Matlock and Danny Harrison (Singles: 7 weeks)*

pos/wks

Date	Title	pos	wks
23 Jul 94	**U GIRLS** *Blunted Vinyl BLNCDX 006*	58	1
22 Apr 95	**MOVE THAT BODY** *Blunted Vinyl BLNCD 012*	46	2
16 Sep 95	**U GIRLS (LOOK SO SEXY) (re-mix)** *Blunted Vinyl BLNCD 13*	15	4

NUT *UK, female vocalist (Singles: 4 weeks)*

pos/wks

Date	Title	pos	wks
8 Jun 96	**BRAINS** *Epic NUTCD 2*	64	1
21 Sep 96	**CRAZY** *Epic NUTCD 5*	56	1
11 Jan 97	**SCREAM** *Epic NUTCD 6*	43	2

NUTTIN' NYCE

US, female vocal group (Singles: 2 weeks) pos/wks

Date	Title	pos	wks
10 Jun 95	**DOWN 4 WHATEVA** *Jive JIVECD 365*	62	1
12 Aug 95	**FROGGY STYLE** *Jive JIVECD 381*	68	1

NUYORICAN SOUL *US, male DJ / production group (Singles: 8 weeks, Albums: 2 weeks)*

pos/wks

Date	Title	pos	wks
8 Feb 97	**RUNAWAY** *Talkin Loud TLCD20* [1]	24	4
10 May 97	**IT'S ALRIGHT, I FEEL IT!** *Talkin Loud TLCD 22* [2]	26	2
25 Oct 97	**I AM THE BLACK GOLD OF THE SUN** *Talkin Loud TLCD 26* [2]	31	2
1 Mar 97	**NUYORICAN SOUL** *Talkin Loud 5344602*	25	2

[1] Nuyorican Soul featuring India [2] Nuyorican Soul featuring Jocelyn Brown

See also MASTERS AT WORK

Joe NYE – *See DNA*

NYLON MOON
Italy, male instrumental duo (Singles: 2 weeks) pos/wks

Date		Title	pos	wks
13 Apr 96		**SKY PLUS** *Positiva CDTIV 50*	**43**	2

Michael NYMAN *UK, male instrumentalist – piano (Singles: 2 weeks, Albums: 15 weeks)* pos/wks

Date		Title	pos	wks
19 Mar 94		**THE HEART ASKS PLEASURE FIRST / THE PROMISE** *Virgin VEND 3*	**60**	2
12 Feb 94		**THE PIANO (FILM SOUNDTRACK)** *Venture CDVE 919*	**31**	15

OMC *New Zealand, male vocalist – Paul Fuemana Lawrence (Singles: 17 weeks)* pos/wks

Date		Title	pos	wks
20 Jul 96	●	**HOW BIZARRE** *Polydor 5776202*	**5**	16
18 Jan 97		**ON THE RUN** *Polydor 5732452*	**56**	1

OMD – *See ORCHESTRAL MANOEUVRES IN THE DARK*

OPM *US, male vocal / instrumental group (Singles: 18 weeks, Albums: 8 weeks)* pos/wks

Date		Title	pos	wks
14 Jul 01	●	**HEAVEN IS A HALFPIPE** *Atlantic AT 0107CD*	**4**	14
12 Jan 02		**EL CAPITAN (re)** *Atlantic AT 0118CD*	**20**	4
21 Jul 01		**MENACE TO SOBRIETY** *Atlantic 7567929772*	**31**	8

O.T. QUARTET – *See OUR TRIBE / ONE TRIBE*

O-TOWN
US, male vocal group (Singles: 27 weeks, Albums: 5 weeks) pos/wks

Date		Title	pos	wks
28 Apr 01	●	**LIQUID DREAMS** *J 74321853202*	**3**	10
4 Aug 01	●	**ALL OR NOTHING** *J 74321875822*	**4**	10
3 Nov 01		**WE FIT TOGETHER (re)** *J 74321893692*	**20**	4
23 Feb 02		**LOVE SHOULD BE A CRIME** *J 74321920232*	**38**	2
15 Feb 03		**THESE ARE THE DAYS** *J 82876503052*	**36**	1
18 Aug 01	●	**O-TOWN** *RCA/J Records 74321882992*	**7**	5

OTT
Ireland, male vocal group (Singles: 18 weeks) pos/wks

Date		Title	pos	wks
15 Feb 97		**LET ME IN** *Epic 6642052*	**12**	5
17 May 97		**FOREVER GIRL** *Epic 6645082*	**24**	3
23 Aug 97		**ALL OUT OF LOVE** *Epic 6649152*	**11**	4
24 Jan 98		**THE STORY OF LOVE** *Epic OTT 1CD*	**11**	6

OAKENFOLD *UK, male DJ / producer – Paul Oakenfold (Singles: 16 weeks, Albums: 12 weeks)* pos/wks

Date		Title	pos	wks
25 Aug 01		**PLANET ROCK** *Tommy Boy TBCD2266* [1]	**47**	1
22 Jun 02		**SOUTHERN SUN / READY STEADY GO** *Perfecto PERF 17CDS*	**16**	4
31 Aug 02	●	**STARRY EYED SURPRISE** *Perfecto PERF 27CDS*	**6**	8
22 Feb 03		**THE HARDER THEY COME** *Perfecto PERF 49CDS* [2]	**38**	2
27 Sep 03		**HYPNOTISED** *East West EW 271CD* [3]	**57**	1
6 Jul 02		**BUNKKA** *Perfecto PERFALB 09CD*	**25**	12

[1] Paul Oakenfold presents Afrika Bambaataa [2] Oakenfold, vocals by Keisha White and Tricky [3] Paul Oakenfold

See also VIRUS

Philip OAKEY and Giorgio MORODER *UK, male vocalist / instrumentalist – keyboards (Singles: 14 week, Albums: 5 weeks)* pos/wks

Date		Title	pos	wks
22 Sep 84	●	**TOGETHER IN ELECTRIC DREAMS** *Virgin VS 713* [1]	**3**	13
26Apr 03		**L.A. TODAY** *Xtravaganza XTRAV 37CDS* [2]	**68**	1
10 Aug 85		**PHILIP OAKEY AND GIORGIO MORODER** *Virgin V 2351* [2]	**52**	5

[1] Giorgio Moroder and Phil Oakey [2] Alex Gold featuring Philip Oakey
[2] Philip Oakey and Giorgio Moroder

See also HUMAN LEAGUE

OASIS *UK, male / female vocal / instrumental group – includes Mary Hopkin and Peter Skellern (Albums: 15 weeks)* pos/wks

Date		Title	pos	wks
28 Apr 84		**OASIS** *WEA WX 3*	**23**	15

See also Mary HOPKIN; Peter SKELLERN

OASIS (27 Top 500)
Peerless Manchester-based, Beatles-influenced band: Liam (v) and Noel (g/v) Gallagher, Gem Archer (g), Andy Bell (b), Alan White (d). Tony McCarroll was replaced by Alan White in 1994. In 1999 Paul 'Bonehead' Arthurs was replaced by Gem Archer and Paul McGuigan was replaced by Andy Bell. The often controversial Britpop group smashed the record for most weeks on the chart in one year (134 in 1996). Best-selling single: 'Wonderwall' 966,940 (Singles: 348 weeks, Albums: 483 weeks) pos/wks

Date		Title	pos	wks
23 Apr 94		**SUPERSONIC (5re)** *Creation CRESCD 176*	**31**	14
2 Jul 94		**SHAKERMAKER (5re)** *Creation CRESCD 182*	**11**	15
20 Aug 94	●	**LIVE FOREVER (6re)** *Creation CRESCD 185*	**10**	18
22 Oct 94	●	**CIGARETTES AND ALCOHOL (9re)** *Creation CRESCD 190*	**7**	35
31 Dec 94	●	**WHATEVER (8re)** *Creation CRESCD 195*	**3**	50
6 May 95	★	**SOME MIGHT SAY (6re)** *Creation CRESCD 204* ■	**1**	27
13 May 95		**SOME MIGHT SAY** *Creation CRE 204T*	**71**	1
26 Aug 95	●	**ROLL WITH IT (3re)** *Creation CRESCD 212*	**2**	18
11 Nov 95	●	**WONDERWALL (2re)** *Creation CRESCD 215*	**2**	34
25 Nov 95		**WIBBLING RIVALRY (INTERVIEWS WITH NOEL AND LIAM GALLAGHER)** *Fierce Panda NING 12CD* [1]	**52**	2
2 Mar 96	★	**DON'T LOOK BACK IN ANGER (2re)** *Creation CRESCD 221* ■	**1**	24
19 Jul 97	★	**D'YOU KNOW WHAT I MEAN?** *Creation CRESCD 256* ■	**1**	18
4 Oct 97	●	**STAND BY ME** *Creation CRESCD 278*	**2**	18
24 Jan 98	★	**ALL AROUND THE WORLD (re)** *Creation CRESCD 282* ■	**1**	9
19 Feb 00	★	**GO LET IT OUT (re)** *Big Brother RKIDSCD 001* ■	**1**	12
29 Apr 00	●	**WHO FEELS LOVE? (re)** *Big Brother RKIDSCD 003*	**4**	8
15 Jul 00	●	**SUNDAY MORNING CALL** *Big Brother RKIDSCD004*	**4**	6
27 Apr 02	★	**THE HINDU TIMES** *Big Brother RKIDSCD 23* ■	**1**	11
29 Jun 02	●	**STOP CRYING YOUR HEART OUT** *Big Brother RKIDSCD 24*	**2**	10
5 Oct 02	●	**LITTLE BY LITTLE / SHE IS LOVE** *Big Brother RKIDSCD 26*	**2**	8
15 Feb 03	●	**SONGBIRD** *Big Brother RKIDSCD 27*	**3**	10
10 Sep 94	★	**DEFINITELY MAYBE** *Creation CRECD 169* ■	**1**	177
14 Oct 95	★	**(WHAT'S THE STORY) MORNING GLORY?** *Creation CRECD 189* ■	**1**	145
16 Nov 96		**(WHAT'S THE STORY) MORNING GLORY? SINGLES BOX – GOLD** *Creation CREMG 002*	**24**	3
16 Nov 96		**DEFINITELY MAYBE SINGLES BOX – SILVER** *Creation CREDM 002*	**23**	3
30 Aug 97	★	**BE HERE NOW** *Creation CRECD 219* ■	**1**	37
14 Nov 98	●	**THE MASTERPLAN** *Creation CRECD 241*	**2**	28
11 Mar 00	★	**STANDING ON THE SHOULDER OF GIANTS** *Big Brother RKIDCD 002* ■	**1**	29
17 Jun 00		**(WHAT'S THE STORY) MORNING GLORY? (re-issue)** *Big Brother RKIDCD 008*	**63**	8

25 Nov 00 ● **FAMILIAR TO MILLIONS** *Big Brother RKIDCD 005* 5 10
13 Jul 02 ★ **HEATHEN CHEMISTRY** *Big Brother RKIDCD 25* ■ 1 43

[1] Oas*s

Chart rules allow for a maximum of three formats; the 12-inch of 'Some Might Say' already available on CD, seven-inch and cassette – was therefore listed separately. Oasis had a record number of re-entries between 1995 and 1997 as new releases were accompanied by the regular return of singles from their back catalogue

John OATES – *See Daryl HALL and John OATES*

Sam OBERNIK – *See Tim DELUXE; LINUS LOVES featuring Sam OBERNIK*

OBERNKIRCHEN CHILDREN'S CHOIR

Germany, children's choir (Singles: 26 weeks) pos/wks

22 Jan 54 ● **THE HAPPY WANDERER (re)** *Parlophone R 3799* 2 26

OBI PROJECT featuring HARRY, ASHER D and DJ WHAT?

UK, male vocal / rap / production group (Singles: 1 week) pos/wks

4 Aug 01 **BABY, CAN I GET YOUR NUMBER** *East West EW 235CD* 75 1

OBITUARY *US, male vocal / instrumental group (Albums: 2 weeks)* pos/wks

18 Apr 92 **THE END COMPLETE** *Roadrunner RC 92012* 52 1
17 Sep 94 **WORLD DEMISE** *Roadrunner RR 89955* 65 1

Dermot O'BRIEN and his CLUBMEN

Ireland, male vocal / instrumental group (Singles: 2 weeks) pos/wks

20 Oct 66 **THE MERRY PLOUGHBOY (re)** *Envoy ENV 016* 46 2

Billy OCEAN (198 Top 500)

Top British-based R&B singer / songwriter of the 1980s, b. Leslie Charles, 21 Jan 1950, Trinidad. He waited seven years after scoring his first four UK Top 20 hits before accumulating an impressive run of transatlantic successes, which included three US No.1s (Singles: 153 weeks, Albums: 141 weeks) pos/wks

21 Feb 76 ● **LOVE REALLY HURTS WITHOUT YOU** *GTO GT 52* 2 10
10 Jul 76 **L.O.D. (LOVE ON DELIVERY)** *GTO GT 62* 19 8
13 Nov 76 **STOP ME (IF YOU'VE HEARD IT ALL BEFORE)** *GTO GT 72* 12 11
19 Mar 77 ● **RED LIGHT SPELLS DANGER** *GTO GT 85* 2 10
1 Sep 79 **AMERICAN HEARTS** *GTO GT 244* 54 5
19 Jan 80 **ARE YOU READY** *GTO GT 259* 42 7
13 Oct 84 ● **CARIBBEAN QUEEN (NO MORE LOVE ON THE RUN)** *Jive JIVE 77* ▲ 6 14
19 Jan 85 **LOVERBOY** *Jive JIVE 80* 15 10
11 May 85 ● **SUDDENLY** *Jive JIVE 90* 4 14
17 Aug 85 **MYSTERY LADY** *Jive JIVE 98* 49 4
25 Jan 86 ★ **WHEN THE GOING GETS TOUGH, THE TOUGH GET GOING** *Jive JIVE 114* 1 13
12 Apr 86 **THERE'LL BE SAD SONGS (TO MAKE YOU CRY)** *Jive JIVE 117* ▲ 12 13
9 Aug 86 **LOVE ZONE** *Jive JIVE 124* 49 3
11 Oct 86 **BITTERSWEET** *Jive JIVE 133* 44 4
10 Jan 87 **LOVE IS FOREVER** *Jive JIVE 134* 34 7
6 Feb 88 ● **GET OUTTA MY DREAMS GET INTO MY CAR** *Jive BOS 1* ▲ 3 11
7 May 88 **CALYPSO CRAZY** *Jive BOS 2* 35 4
6 Aug 88 **THE COLOUR OF LOVE** *Jive BOS 3* 65 3
6 Feb 93 **PRESSURE** *Jive BOSCD 6* 55 2
24 Nov 84 ● **SUDDENLY** *Jive JIP 12* 9 59
17 May 86 ● **LOVE ZONE** *Jive HIP 35* 2 32
19 Mar 88 ● **TEAR DOWN THESE WALLS** *Jive HIP 57* 3 13
28 Oct 89 ● **GREATEST HITS** *Jive BOTV 1* 4 15
16 Aug 97 ● **LOVE IS FOR EVER** *Jive BOCD 2* 7 21
15 Feb 03 **LET'S GET BACK TOGETHER – THE LOVE SONGS** *Jive 9225232* 69 1

OCEAN COLOUR SCENE (298 Top 500)

Birmingham-based retro-rockers, formed in 1990 include Simon Fowler (v) and Steve Cradock (g). Publicly championed by Paul Weller and Noel Gallagher, whose brother Liam partnered Cradock on a Top 10 hit. They ended 1990s with nine successive Top 20 singles (Singles: 67 weeks, Albums: 149 weeks) pos/wks

23 Mar 91 **YESTERDAY TODAY** *!Phfft FIT 2* 49 1
17 Feb 96 **THE RIVERBOAT SONG** *MCA MCSTD 40021* 15 5
6 Apr 96 ● **YOU'VE GOT IT BAD** *MCA MCSTD 40036* 7 4
15 Jun 96 ● **THE DAY WE CAUGHT THE TRAIN** *MCA MCSTD 40046* 4 11
28 Sep 96 ● **THE CIRCLE** *MCA MCSTD 40077* 6 6
28 Jun 97 ● **HUNDRED MILE HIGH CITY** *MCA MCSTD 40133* 4 7
6 Sep 97 ● **TRAVELLERS TUNE** *MCA MCSTD 40144* 5 5
22 Nov 97 ● **BETTER DAY** *MCA MCSTD 40151* 9 5
28 Feb 98 **IT'S A BEAUTIFUL THING** *MCA MCSTD 40157* 12 4
4 Sep 99 **PROFIT IN PEACE** *Island CID 757* 13 5
27 Nov 99 **SO LOW** *Island CID 759* 34 2
8 Jul 00 **JULY / I AM THE NEWS** *Island CID 763* 31 2
7 Apr 01 **UP ON THE DOWN SIDE** *Island CID 774* 19 3
14 Jul 01 **MECHANICAL WONDER** *Island CID 779* 49 1
22 Dec 01 **CRAZY LOWDOWN WAYS** *Island CID 787* 64 1
12 Jul 03 **I JUST NEED MYSELF** *Sanctuary SANXD 159* 13 3
6 Sep 03 **MAKE THE DEAL** *Sanctuary SANXD 219* 35 2
20 Apr 96 ● **MOSELEY SHOALS** *MCA MCD 60008* 2 73
21 Sep 96 **OCEAN COLOUR SCENE** *Fontana 5122692* 54 2
15 Mar 97 ● **B-SIDES SEASIDES & FREERIDES** *MCA MCD 60034* 4 14
27 Sep 97 ★ **MARCHIN' ALREADY** *MCA MCD 60048* ■ 1 37
25 Sep 99 ● **ONE FROM THE MODERN** *Island CID 8090* 4 11
21 Apr 01 ● **MECHANICAL WONDER** *Island CID 8104* 7 4
17 Nov 01 **SONGS FOR THE FRONT ROW – THE BEST OF OCEAN COLOUR SCENE** *Island CID 8111* 16 4
19 Jul 03 **NORTH ATLANTIC DRIFT** *Sanctuary SANDP160* 14 3
13 Sep 03 **ANTHOLOGY** *Island 9807210* 75 1

OCEANIA *New Zealand / UK, male / female vocal / instrumental group (Albums: 1 week)* pos/wks

23 Oct 99 **OCEANIA** *Universal TV/Point Music 5367752* 70 1

OCEANIC *UK, male / female vocal / instrumental group (Singles: 26 weeks, Albums: 2 weeks)* pos/wks

24 Aug 91 ● **INSANITY** *Dead Dead Good GOOD 4* 3 15
30 Nov 91 **WICKED LOVE (re)** *Dead Dead Good GOOD 5* 25 5
13 Jun 92 **CONTROLLING ME** *Dead Dead Good GOOD 14* 14 5
14 Nov 92 **IGNORANCE** *Dead Dead Good GOOD 22* [1] 72 1
4 Jul 92 **THAT ALBUM BY OCEANIC** *Dead Dead Good 4509900832* 49 2

[1] Oceanic featuring Siobhan Maher

OCEANLAB featuring Justine SUISSA

UK, male production trio and female vocalist (Singles: 1 week) pos/wks

27 Apr 02 **CLEAR BLUE WATER** *Code Blue BLU 024CD* 48 1

Des O'CONNOR (411 Top 500)

Entertainer, comedian and MOR vocalist, b. 12 Jan 1932. This London-based all-rounder toured with Buddy Holly and Lonnie Donegan in the 1950s, had a series of hits in the 1960s and has been a top-rated TV star for more than 40 years (Singles: 117 weeks, Albums: 47 weeks) pos/wks

1 Nov 67 ● **CARELESS HANDS** *Columbia DB 8275* [1] 6 17
8 May 68 ★ **I PRETEND** *Columbia DB 8397* 1 36
20 Nov 68 ● **ONE, TWO THREE O'LEARY** *Columbia DB 8492* 4 11
7 May 69 **DICK-A-DUM-DUM (KING'S ROAD)** *Columbia DB 8566* 14 10
29 Nov 69 **LONELINESS** *Columbia DB 8632* 18 11
14 Mar 70 **I'LL GO ON HOPING** *Columbia DB 8661* 30 7
26 Sep 70 **THE TIP OF MY FINGERS** *Columbia DB 8713* 15 15
8 Nov 86 ● **THE SKYE BOAT SONG** *Tembo TML119* [2] 10 10
7 Dec 68 ● **I PRETEND** *Columbia SCX 6295* 8 10
5 Dec 70 **WITH LOVE** *Columbia SCX 6417* 40 4
2 Dec 72 **SING A FAVOURITE SONG** *Pye NSPL 18390* 25 6
2 Feb 80 **JUST FOR YOU** *Warwick WW 5071* 17 7
13 Oct 84 **DES O'CONNOR NOW** *Telstar STAR 2245* 24 14
5 Dec 92 **PORTRAIT** *Columbia 4727302* 63 4
17 Nov 01 **A TRIBUTE TO THE CROONERS** *UMTV/Decca 4704702* 51 2

[1] Des O'Connor with the Michael Sammes Singers [2] Roger Whittaker and Des O'Connor

Hazel O'CONNOR

UK, female vocalist (Singles: 46 weeks, Albums: 45 weeks) pos/wks

16 Aug 80 ● **EIGHTH DAY** *A&M AMS 7553* 5 11
25 Oct 80 **GIVE ME AN INCH** *A&M AMS 7569* 41 4

21 Mar 81 ● **D-DAYS** *Albion ION 1009* ...10 9
23 May 81 ● **WILL YOU** *A&M AMS 8131* ...8 10
1 Aug 81 **(COVER PLUS) WE'RE ALL GROWN UP** *Albion ION 1018* ...41 6
3 Oct 81 **HANGING AROUND** *Albion ION 1022* ...45 3
23 Jan 82 **CALLS THE TUNE** *A&M AMS 8203* ...60 3
9 Aug 80 ● **BREAKING GLASS (FILM SOUNDTRACK)** *A&M AMLH 64820* ...5 38
12 Sep 81 **COVER PLUS** *Albion ALB 108*...32 7

Sinead O'CONNOR (435 Top 500)

Distinctive singer / songwriter who never ducked controversy, b.12 Dec 1966, Glenageary, Ireland. The one-time In Tua Nua vocalist is the first Irish woman to top either the UK or US album chart and the first person to refuse to collect Brit or Grammy awards (1991) (Singles: 65 weeks, Albums: 90 weeks) pos/wks

16 Jan 88 **MANDINKA** *Ensign ENY 611* ...17 9
20 Jan 90 ★ **NOTHING COMPARES 2 U** *Ensign ENY 630* ▲ ...1 14
21 Jul 90 **THE EMPEROR'S NEW CLOTHES** *Ensign ENY 633* ...31 5
20 Oct 90 **THREE BABIES** *Ensign ENY 635* ...42 4
8 Jun 91 **MY SPECIAL CHILD** *Ensign ENY 646* ...42 3
14 Dec 91 **SILENT NIGHT** *Ensign ENY 652*...60 4
12 Sep 92 **SUCCESS HAS MADE A FAILURE OF OUR HOME** *Ensign ENY 656* ...18 4
12 Dec 92 **DON'T CRY FOR ME ARGENTINA** *Ensign ENY 657* ...53 4
19 Feb 94 **YOU MADE ME THE THIEF OF YOUR HEART** *Island CID 588* ...42 3
26 Nov 94 **THANK YOU FOR HEARING ME** *Ensign CDENYS 662* ...13 7
29 Apr 95 **HAUNTED** *ZTT ZANG 65CD* [1] ...30 2
26 Aug 95 **FAMINE** *Ensign CDENY 663* ...51 1
17 May 97 **GOSPEL OAK (EP)** *Chrysalis CDCHS 5051* ...28 3
6 Dec 97 **THIS IS A REBEL SONG** *Columbia 6652992* ...60 1
24 Aug 02 **TROY (THE PHOENIX FROM THE FLAME)** *Devolution DEVR 003CDS* ...48 1
23 Jan 88 **THE LION AND THE COBRA** *Ensign CHEN 7* ...27 20
24 Mar 90 ★ **I DO NOT WANT WHAT I HAVEN'T GOT** *Ensign CHEN 14* ■ ▲..1 51
26 Sep 92 ● **AM I NOT YOUR GIRL?** *Ensign CCD 1952* ...6 6
24 Sep 94 **UNIVERSAL MOTHER** *Ensign CDCHEN 34* ...19 8
22 Nov 97 **SO FAR ... THE BEST OF SINEAD O'CONNOR** *Chrysalis 8215812*...28 3
24 Jun 00 **FAITH AND COURAGE** *Atlantic 7567833372* ...61 1
19 Oct 02 **SEAN - NOS NUA** *R & M Entertainment RAMCD 001* ...52 1

[1] Shane MacGowan and Sinead O'Connor

Tracks on Gospel Oak (EP): This Is to Mother You / I Am Enough for Myself / Petit Poulet / 4 My Love

See also MARXMAN; Jah WOBBLE'S INVADERS of the HEART

OCTAHVIA – *See Jose NUNEZ featuring OCTAHVIA; CHOO CHOO PROJECT*

OCTAVE ONE featuring Ann SAUNDERSON

US, male production trio and female vocalist (Singles: 2 weeks) pos/wks

16 Feb 02 **BLACKWATER** *Concept / 430 West CDCON 26* ...47 1
28 Sep 02 **BLACKWATER (REMIX)** *Concept / 430 CDCON 34* ...69 1

OCTOPUS

UK / France, male vocal / instrumental group (Singles: 5 weeks) pos/wks

22 Jun 96 **YOUR SMILE** *Food CDFOOD 78* ...42 2
14 Sep 96 **SAVED** *Food CDFOODS 84* ...40 2
23 Nov 96 **JEALOUSY** *Food CDFOODS 87* ...59 1

Alan O'DAY

US, male vocalist (Singles: 3 weeks) pos/wks

2 Jul 77 **UNDERCOVER ANGEL** *Atlantic K 10926* ▲ ...43 3

ODETTA – *See Harry BELAFONTE*

Daniel O'DONNELL (256 Top 500)

The top country vocalist in Britain who received an MBE in 2002, b. 12 Dec 1961, Co Donegal, Ireland. The popular live performer, who held six of the top seven places on the UK country chart (1991), is the only act with at least one hit album every year since 1988 (Singles: 67 weeks, Albums: 177 weeks) pos/wks

12 Sep 92 **I JUST WANT TO DANCE WITH YOU** *Ritz RITZ 250P* ...20 7
2 Jan 93 **THE THREE BELLS** *Ritz RITZCD 239* ...71 1
8 May 93 **THE LOVE IN YOUR EYES** *Ritz RITZCD 257* ...47 3
7 Aug 93 **WHAT EVER HAPPENED TO OLD FASHIONED LOVE** *Ritz RITZCD 262* ...21 5
16 Apr 94 **SINGING THE BLUES** *Ritz RITZCD 270* ...23 3
26 Nov 94 **THE GIFT** *Ritz RITZCD 275* ...46 3
10 Jun 95 **SECRET LOVE** *Ritz RITZCD 285* [1] ...28 3
9 Mar 96 **TIMELESS** *Ritz RITZCD 293* [1] ...32 3
28 Sep 96 **FOOTSTEPS** *Ritz RITZCD 300* ...25 5
7 Jun 97 **THE LOVE SONGS EP** *Ritz RITZCD 306* ...27 4
11 Apr 98 ● **GIVE A LITTLE LOVE** *Ritz RITZCD 315* ...7 5
17 Oct 98 **THE MAGIC IS THERE** *Ritz RZCD 320* ...16 4
20 Mar 99 **THE WAY DREAMS ARE** *Ritz RZCD 325* ...18 3
24 Jul 99 **UNO MAS** *Ritz RZCD 326* ...25 3
18 Dec 99 **A CHRISTMAS KISS** *Ritz RZCD 330* ...20 4
15 Apr 00 **LIGHT A CANDLE** *Ritz RZCD 335* ...23 4
16 Dec 00 **MORNING HAS BROKEN** *Ritz RZCD 341* ...32 4
13 Dec 03 **YOU RAISE ME UP** *Rosette ROSCD 310* ...22 3+
15 Oct 88 **FROM THE HEART** *Telstar STAR 2327*...56 12
28 Oct 89 **THOUGHTS OF HOME** *Telstar STAR 2372*...43 10
21 Apr 90 **FAVOURITES** *Ritz RITZLP 052* ...61 3
17 Nov 90 **THE LAST WALTZ** *Ritz RITZALP 058*...46 7
9 Nov 91 **THE VERY BEST OF DANIEL O'DONNELL** *Ritz RITZBLD 700* ...34 14
21 Nov 92 **FOLLOW YOUR DREAM** *Ritz RITZBCD 701* ...17 9
6 Nov 93 **A DATE WITH DANIEL O'DONNELL LIVE** *Ritz RITZBCD 702*...21 10
22 Oct 94 **ESPECIALLY FOR YOU** *Ritz RITZBCD 703*...14 11
3 Dec 94 **CHRISTMAS WITH DANIEL** *Ritz RITZBCD 704* ...34 5
11 Nov 95 **THE CLASSIC COLLECTION** *Ritz RITZBCD 705*...34 9
6 Apr 96 **TIMELESS** *Ritz RITZBCD 707* [1] ...13 5
20 Jul 96 **IRISH COLLECTION** *Ritz RITZCD 0080*...35 3
26 Oct 96 **SONGS OF INSPIRATION** *Ritz RITZBCD 709*...11 16
8 Nov 97 **I BELIEVE** *Ritz RITZBCD 710*...11 11
31 Oct 98 ● **LOVE SONGS** *Ritz RZBCD 715* ...9 10
2 Oct 99 ● **GREATEST HITS** *Ritz RZBCD 716*...10 8
28 Oct 00 ● **FAITH & INSPIRATION** *Ritz RZBCD 717* ...4 10
1 Dec 01 **LIVE LAUGH LOVE** *Rosette ROSCD 2002* ...27 5
2 Nov 02 **YESTERDAY'S MEMORIES** *Rosette ROSCD 2020* ...19 3
22 Mar 03 ● **DANIEL IN BLUE JEANS** *DMG DMGTV001* ...3 10
25 Oct 03 **AT THE END OF THE DAY** *Rosette ROSCD2040* ...11 6

[1] Daniel O'Donnell and Mary Duff [1] Daniel O'Donnell and Mary Duff

Tracks on The Love Songs EP: Save the Last Dance for Me / I Can't Stop Loving You / You're the Only Good Thing / Limerick You're a Lady

Ryan and Rachel O'DONNELL

Ireland, male / female vocal / instrumental duo (Albums: 13 weeks) pos/wks

16 Mar 02 **THE CELTIC CHILLOUT ALBUM** *Decadance DECTV 001 / 007* ..17 14
22 Mar 03 **THE CELTIC CHILLOUT ALBUM 2** *Decadance DECTV 009* ...37 3

The first album was released twice with different catalogue numbers and slightly different content

ODYSSEY

US, male / female vocal / instrumental group (Singles: 82 weeks, Albums: 32 weeks) pos/wks

24 Dec 77 ● **NATIVE NEW YORKER** *RCA PC 1129* ...5 11
21 Jun 80 ★ **USE IT UP AND WEAR IT OUT** *RCA PB 1962* ...1 12
13 Sep 80 ● **IF YOU'RE LOOKIN' FOR A WAY OUT** *RCA 5* ...6 15
17 Jan 81 **HANG TOGETHER** *RCA 23* ...36 7
30 May 81 ● **GOING BACK TO MY ROOTS** *RCA 85* ...4 12
19 Sep 81 **IT WILL BE ALRIGHT** *RCA 128*...43 5
12 Jun 82 ● **INSIDE OUT** *RCA 226* ...3 11
11 Sep 82 **MAGIC TOUCH** *RCA 275* ...41 5
17 Aug 85 **(JOY) I KNOW IT** *Mirror BUTCH 12* ...51 4
16 Aug 80 **HANG TOGETHER** *RCA PL 13526*...38 3
4 Jul 81 **I'VE GOT THE MELODY** *RCA RCALP 5028*...29 7
3 Jul 82 **HAPPY TOGETHER** *RCA RCALP 6036* ...21 9
20 Nov 82 **THE MAGIC TOUCH OF ODYSSEY** *Telstar STAR 2223* ...69 5
26 Sep 87 **THE GREATEST HITS** *Stylus SMR 735*...26 8

Esther and Abi OFARIM

Israel, female / male vocal duo – Esther Zaled and Abraham Reichstadt (Singles: 22 weeks, Albums: 24 weeks) pos/wks

14 Feb 68 ★ **CINDERELLA ROCKEFELLA** *Philips BF 1640* ...1 13
19 Jun 68 **ONE MORE DANCE** *Philips BF 1678* ...13 9
24 Feb 68 ● **2 IN 3** *Philips SBL 7825*...6 20
12 Jul 69 **OFARIM CONCERT – LIVE '69** *Philips XL 4*...29 4

Wiston OFFICE – *See Frank K featuring Wiston OFFICE*

Kardinal OFFISHALL – *See TEXAS*

OFF-SHORE *Germany, male instrumental / production duo – Jens Lissat and Peter Harder (Singles: 12 weeks)* pos/wks

22 Dec 90 ● **I CAN'T TAKE THE POWER** *CBS 6565707* 7 11
17 Aug 91 **I GOT A LITTLE SONG** *Dance Pool 6568257* 64 1

OFFSPRING (428 Top 500)

Celebrated California-based punk pop band formed 1984, fronted by 'Dexter' Holland (v) b. 29 Dec 1966. 'Smash' sold more than 11 million worldwide and their No.1 single reportedly had record 22 million downloads – pretty fly for a white group (Singles: 56 weeks, Albums: 101 weeks) pos/wks

25 Feb 95 **SELF ESTEEM** *Golf CDSHOLE 001* 37 3
19 Aug 95 **GOTTA GET AWAY** *Out Of Step WOOS 2CDS* 43 2
1 Feb 97 **ALL I WANT** *Epitaph 64912* 31 2
26 Apr 97 **GONE AWAY** *Epitaph 64982* 42 1
30 Jan 99 ★ **PRETTY FLY (FOR A WHITE GUY)** *Columbia 6668022* ■ 1 11
8 May 99 ● **WHY DON'T YOU GET A JOB?** *Columbia 6673542* 2 8
11 Sep 99 **THE KIDS AREN'T ALRIGHT** *Columbia 6677632* 11 6
4 Dec 99 **SHE'S GOT ISSUES** *Columbia 6683772* 41 2
18 Nov 00 ● **ORIGINAL PRANKSTER** *Columbia 6699972* 6 8
31 Mar 01 **WANT YOU BAD (re)** *Columbia 6709292* 15 9
7 Jul 01 **MILLION MILES AWAY** *Columbia 6714082* 21 4
4 Mar 95 **SMASH** *Epitaph E 864322* 21 34
15 Feb 97 **IXNAY ON THE HOMBRE** *Epitaph 64872* 17 3
28 Nov 98 ● **AMERICANA** *Columbia 4916562* 10 45
25 Nov 00 **CONSPIRACY OF ONE** *Columbia 4984819* 12 18
13 Dec 03 **SPLINTER** *Columbia 5122013* 74 1

OH WELL

Germany, male producer – Ackim Faulker (Singles: 7 weeks) pos/wks

14 Oct 89 **OH WELL** *Parlophone R 6236* 28 6
3 Mar 90 **RADAR LOVE** *Parlophone R 6244* 65 1

Mary O'HARA

UK, female vocalist / instrumentalist – harp (Albums: 12 weeks) pos/wks

8 Apr 78 **MARY O'HARA AT THE ROYAL FESTIVAL HALL** *Chrysalis CHR 1159* 37 3
1 Dec 79 **TRANQUILLITY** *Warwick WW 5072* 12 9

OHIO EXPRESS

US, male vocal / instrumental group (Singles: 15 weeks) pos/wks

5 Jun 68 ● **YUMMY YUMMY YUMMY** *Pye International 7N 25459* 5 15

OHIO PLAYERS

US, male vocal / instrumental group (Singles: 4 weeks) pos/wks

10 Jul 76 **WHO'D SHE COO?** *Mercury PLAY 001* 43 4

David OISTRAKH – *See Herbert VON KARAJAN*

O'JAYS *US, male vocal group (Singles: 72 weeks)* pos/wks

23 Sep 72 **BACK STABBERS** *CBS 8270* 14 9
3 Mar 73 ● **LOVE TRAIN** *CBS 1181* ▲ 9 13
31 Jan 76 **I LOVE MUSIC** *Philadelphia International PIR 3879* 13 9
12 Feb 77 **DARLIN' DARLIN' BABY (SWEET, TENDER, LOVE)** *Philadelphia International PIR 4834* 24 6
8 Apr 78 **I LOVE MUSIC (re-issue)** *Philadelphia International PIR 6093* 36 3
17 Jun 78 **USED TA BE MY GIRL** *Philadelphia International PIR 6332* 12 12
30 Sep 78 **BRANDY** *Philadelphia International PIR 6658* 21 9
29 Sep 79 **SING A HAPPY SONG** *Philadelphia International PIR 7825* 39 6
30 Jul 83 **PUT OUR HEADS TOGETHER** *Philadelphia International A 3642* 45 5

OK GO *US, male vocal / instrumental group (Singles: 3 weeks)* pos/wks

22 Mar 03 **GET OVER IT** *Capitol CDR 6603* 21 3

John O'KANE *UK, male vocalist (Singles: 4 weeks)* pos/wks

9 May 92 **STAY WITH ME** *Circa YR 88* 41 4

OL' DIRTY BASTARD

US, male rapper – Russell Jones (Singles: 25 weeks) pos/wks

27 Jun 98 ● **GHETTO SUPERSTAR (THAT IS WHAT YOU ARE)** *Interscope IND 95593* [1] 2 17
8 Jul 00 **GOT YOUR MONEY** *Elektra E 7077CD* [2] 11 8

[1] Pras Michel featuring Ol' Dirty Bastard introducing Mya [2] Ol' Dirty Bastard featuring Kelis

See also WU-TANG CLAN

OLD SKOOL ORCHESTRA

UK, male DJ / production duo (Singles: 1 week) pos/wks

23 Jan 99 **B-BOY HUMP** *East West EW 186CD1* 55 1

See also STRETCH 'N' VERN present MADDOG

Mike OLDFIELD (46 Top 500)

Composer / producer / multi-instrumentalist, b. 15 May 1953, Reading, UK. His chart-topping 1973 debut album, 'Tubular Bells', spent five years on the chart, and the belated 'Tubular Bells II' also reached UK No.1 (1992) (Singles: 113 weeks, Albums: 551 weeks) pos/wks

13 Jul 74 **MIKE OLDFIELD'S SINGLE (THEME FROM TUBULAR BELLS)** *Virgin VS 101* 31 6
20 Dec 75 ● **IN DULCI JUBILO / ON HORSEBACK** *Virgin VS 131* 4 10
27 Nov 76 ● **PORTSMOUTH** *Virgin VS 163* 3 12
23 Dec 78 **TAKE 4 (EP)** *Virgin VS 238* 72 3
21 Apr 79 **GUILTY** *Virgin VS 245* 22 8
8 Dec 79 **BLUE PETER** *Virgin VS 317* 19 9
20 Mar 82 **FIVE MILES OUT** *Virgin VS 464* 43 5
12 Jun 82 **FAMILY MAN** *Virgin VS 489* [1] 45 6
28 May 83 ● **MOONLIGHT SHADOW** *Virgin VS 586* [2] 4 17
14 Jan 84 **CRIME OF PASSION** *Virgin VS 648* [2] 61 3
30 Jun 84 **TO FRANCE** *Virgin VS 686* [1] 48 7
14 Dec 85 **PICTURES IN THE DARK** *Virgin VS 836* [3] 50 6
3 Oct 92 ● **SENTINEL** *WEA YZ 698* 10 6
19 Dec 92 **TATTOO** *WEA YZ 708* 33 5
17 Apr 93 **THE BELL** *WEA YZ 737CD* 50 2
9 Oct 93 **MOONLIGHT SHADOW (re-issue)** *Virgin VSCDT 1477* 52 2
17 Dec 94 **HIBERNACULUM** *WEA YZ 871CD* 47 3
2 Sep 95 **LET THERE BE LIGHT** *WEA YZ 880CD* 51 1
22 Nov 97 **WOMEN OF IRELAND** *WEA WEA 093CD* 70 1
24 Apr 99 **FAR ABOVE THE CLOUDS** *WEA WEA 206CD1* 53 1
14 Jul 73 ★ **TUBULAR BELLS** *Virgin V 2001* 1279
14 Sep 74 ★ **HERGEST RIDGE** *Virgin V 2013* ■ 1 17
8 Feb 75 **THE ORCHESTRAL TUBULAR BELLS** *Virgin V 2026* [1] 17 7
15 Nov 75 ● **OMMADAWN** *Virgin V 2043* 4 23
20 Nov 76 **BOXED** *Virgin V BOX 1* 22 13
9 Dec 78 **INCANTATIONS** *Virgin VDT 101* 14 17
11 Aug 79 **EXPOSED** *Virgin VD 2511* 16 9
8 Dec 79 **PLATINUM** *Virgin V 2141* 24 9
8 Nov 80 **QE 2** *Virgin V 2181* 27 12
27 Mar 82 ● **FIVE MILES OUT** *Virgin V 2222* 7 27
4 Jun 83 ● **CRISES** *Virgin V 2262* 6 29
7 Jul 84 **DISCOVERY** *Virgin V 2308* 15 16
15 Dec 84 **THE KILLING FIELDS** *Virgin V 2328* 97 1
2 Nov 85 **THE COMPLETE MIKE OLDFIELD** *Virgin MOC 1* 36 17
10 Oct 87 **ISLANDS** *Virgin V 2466* 29 5
22 Jul 89 **EARTH MOVING** *Virgin V 2610* 30 5
9 Jun 90 **AMAROK** *Virgin V 2640* 49 2
12 Sep 92 ★ **TUBULAR BELLS II** *WEA 4509906182* ■ 1 30
25 Sep 93 ● **ELEMENTS – THE BEST OF MIKE OLDFIELD** *Virgin VTCD 18* 5 10
3 Dec 94 **THE SONGS OF DISTANT EARTH** *WEA 4509985812* 24 6
7 Sep 96 **VOYAGER** *WEA 630158962* 12 5
12 Sep 98 ● **TUBULAR BELLS III** *WEA 3984243492* 4 7
5 Jun 99 **GUITARS** *WEA 3984274012* 40 2
16 Jun 01 **THE BEST OF TUBULAR BELLS** *Virgin CDV 2936* 60 2
7 Jun 03 **TUBULAR BELLS 2003** *WEA 0927499212* 51 1

[1] Mike Oldfield featuring Maggie Reilly [2] Mike Oldfield with vocals by Maggie Reilly [3] Mike Oldfield featuring Aled Jones, Anita Hegerland and Barry Palmer
[1] Mike Oldfield with the Royal Philharmonic Orchestra

Tracks on Take 4 (EP): Portsmouth / In Dulci Jubilo / Wrekorder Wrondo / Sailors Hornpipe. 'The Bell' credits Vivian Stanshall. Barry Palmer supplied uncredited vocals on 'Crime of Passion

Sally OLDFIELD *UK, female vocalist (Singles: 13 weeks)* pos/wks

9 Dec 78 MIRRORS *Bronze BRO 66* 19 13

Misty OLDLAND *UK, female vocalist (Singles: 7 weeks)* pos/wks

16 Oct 93 GOT ME A FEELING *Columbia 6597872* 59 2
12 Mar 94 A FAIR AFFAIR (JE T'AIME) *Columbia 6601612* 49 4
9 Jul 94 I WROTE YOU A SONG *Columbia 6603732* 73 1

OLGA *Italy, female vocalist (Singles: 1 week)* pos/wks

1 Oct 94 I'M A BITCH *UMM UMM 144UKCD* 68 1

OLIVE *UK, male / female vocal / instrumental group – vocal Ruth Ann Boyle (Singles: 24 weeks, Albums: 3 weeks)* pos/wks

7 Sep 96 YOU'RE NOT ALONE *RCA 74321406272* 42 4
15 Mar 97 MIRACLE *RCA 74321461242* 41 2
17 May 97 ★ YOU'RE NOT ALONE (re-issue) *RCA 74321473232* ■ 1 13
16 Aug 97 OUTLAW *RCA 74321508372* 14 4
8 Nov 97 MIRACLE (re-mix) *RCA 74321530842* 41 1
31 May 97 EXTRA VIRGIN *RCA 74321392302* 15 3

OLIVER *US, male vocalist – William Swofford (Singles: 18 weeks)* pos/wks

9 Aug 69 ● GOOD MORNING STARSHINE (re) *CBS 4435* 6 18

Frankie OLIVER *UK, male vocalist (Singles: 1 week)* pos/wks

7 Jun 97 GIVE HER WHAT SHE WANTS *Island Jamaica IJCD 2011* 58 1

OLLIE and JERRY *US, male vocal duo – Ollie Brown and Jerry Knight (Singles: 14 weeks)* pos/wks

23 Jun 84 ● BREAKIN' ... THERE'S NO STOPPING US *Polydor POSP 690* 5 11
9 Mar 85 ELECTRIC BOOGALOO *Polydor POSP 730* 57 3

OLYMPIC ORCHESTRA *UK, orchestra (Singles: 15 weeks)* pos/wks

1 Oct 83 REILLY *Red Bus RBUS 82* 26 15

OLYMPIC RUNNERS *UK, male vocal / instrumental group (Singles: 21 weeks)* pos/wks

13 May 78 WHATEVER IT TAKES *RCA PC 5078* 61 2
14 Oct 78 GET IT WHILE YOU CAN *Polydor RUN 7* 35 6
20 Jan 79 SIR DANCEALOT *Polydor POSP 17* 35 6
28 Jul 79 THE BITCH *Polydor POSP 63* 37 7

OLYMPICS *US, male vocal group (Singles: 9 weeks)* pos/wks

3 Oct 58 WESTERN MOVIES *HMV POP 528* 12 8
19 Jan 61 I WISH I COULD SHIMMY LIKE MY SISTER KATE *Vogue V9174* 40 1

OMAR *UK, male vocalist – Omar Hammer (Singles: 18 weeks, Albums: 14 weeks)* pos/wks

22 Jun 91 THERE'S NOTHING LIKE THIS *Talkin Loud TLK 9* 14 7
23 May 92 YOUR LOSS MY GAIN *Talkin Loud TLK 22* 47 2
26 Sep 92 MUSIC *Talkin Loud TLK 28* 53 2
23 Jul 94 OUTSIDE / SATURDAY *RCA 74321213982* 43 2
15 Oct 94 KEEP STEPPIN' *RCA 74321233682* 57 1
2 Aug 97 SAY NOTHIN' *RCA 74321502872* 29 2
18 Oct 97 GOLDEN BROWN *RCA 74321525422* 37 2
14 Jul 90 THERE'S NOTHING LIKE THIS *Kongo Dance KDLP 2* 54 4
27 Jul 91 THERE'S NOTHING LIKE THIS (re-issue) *Talkin Loud 5100211* 19 6
24 Oct 92 MUSIC *Talkin Loud 5124012* 37 2
2 Jul 94 FOR PLEASURE *RCA 74321208532* 50 1
16 Aug 97 THIS IS NOT A LOVE SONG *RCA 74321496262* 50 1

OMNI TRIO *UK, male producer – Rob Haigh (Singles: 4 weeks, Albums: 2 weeks)* pos/wks

7 Jul 01 THE ANGELS & SHADOWS PROJECT *Moving Shadow SHADOW 150CD* 44 3
26 Jul 03 RENEGADE SNARES *Moving Shadow SHADOW 166* 61 1
11 Feb 95 THE DEEPEST CUT VOL.1 *Moving Shadow ASHADOW 1CD* 60 1
24 Aug 96 THE HAUNTED SCIENCE *Moving Shadow ASHADOW 6CD* 43 1

ONE *UK, male vocal group (Singles: 2 weeks)* pos/wks

11 Jan 97 ONE MORE CHANCE *Mercury MERDD 478* 31 2

Michie ONE – *See Louchie LOU and Michie ONE*

ONE DOVE *UK, male / female vocal / instrumental group (Singles: 9 weeks, Albums: 2 weeks)* pos/wks

7 Aug 93 WHITE LOVE *Boy's Own BOICD 14* 43 3
16 Oct 93 BREAKDOWN *Boy's Own BOICD 15* 24 3
15 Jan 94 WHY DON'T YOU TAKE ME *Boy's Own BOICD 16* 30 3
25 Sep 93 MORNING DOVE WHITE *London 8283522* 30 2

See also Dot ALLISON

187 LOCKDOWN *UK, male production duo – Danny Harrison and Julian Jonah (Singles: 16 weeks)* pos/wks

15 Nov 97 GUNMAN *East West EW 140CD* 16 4
25 Apr 98 ● KUNG-FU *East West EW 155CD* 9 5
25 Jul 98 GUNMAN (re-mix) *East West EW 176CD* 17 4
3 Oct 98 THE DON *East West EW 180CD* 29 2
13 Feb 99 ALL 'N' ALL *East West EW 194CD* [1] 43 1

[1] 187 Lockdown (featuring D'Empress)

See also REFLEX featuring MC VIPER

1 GIANT LEAP *UK, male production duo – Jamie Catto and Duncan Bridgeman (Singles: 6 weeks, Albums: 3 weeks)* pos/wks

20 Apr 02 ● MY CULTURE *Palm Pictures PPCD 70732* 9 6
27 Apr 02 ONE GIANT LEAP *Palm Pictures PALMCD 2077* 51 3

Guest vocals on 'My Culture' by Robbie Williams and Maxi Jazz (Faithless)

ONE HUNDRED & ONE STRINGS *Germany, orchestra (Albums: 35 weeks)* pos/wks

26 Sep 59 ● GYPSY CAMPFIRES *Pye GGL 0009* 9 7
26 Mar 60 SOUL OF SPAIN *Pye GGL 0017* 17 1
16 Apr 60 ● GRAND CANYON SUITE *Pye GGL 0048* 10 1
27 Aug 60 ★ DOWN DRURY LANE TO MEMORY LANE *Pye GGL 0061* 1 21
15 Oct 83 MORNING, NOON AND NIGHT *Ronco RTL 2094* 32 5

ONE HUNDRED TON AND A FEATHER – *See Jonathan KING*

ONE MINUTE SILENCE *UK, male vocal / rap / instrumental group (Singles: 2 weeks, Albums: 1 week)* pos/wks

20 Jan 01 FISH OUT OF WATER *V2 VVR 5013213* 56 1
5 Jul 03 I WEAR MY SKIN *Taste Media TMCDS 5005* 44 1
22 Apr 00 BUY NOW ... SAVED LATER *V2 VVR 1012362* 61 1

112 *US, male vocal / instrumental group (Singles: 34 weeks)* pos/wks

28 Jun 97 ★ I'LL BE MISSING YOU *Puff Daddy 74321499102* [1] ◆ ■ ▲ 1 21
10 Jan 98 ALL CRIED OUT *Epic 6652715* [2] 12 5
14 Feb 98 SKY'S THE LIMIT *Puff Daddy 74321561992* [3] 35 2
30 Jun 01 IT'S OVER NOW *Puff Daddy / Arista 74321849912* 22 3
8 Sep 01 PEACHES & CREAM *ARISTA 74321882632* 32 3

[1] Puff Daddy and Faith Evans featuring 112 [2] Allure featuring 112 [3] Notorious B.I.G. featuring 112

ONE THE JUGGLER *UK, male vocal / instrumental group (Singles: 1 week)* pos/wks

19 Feb 83 PASSION KILLER *Regard RG 107* 71 1

1000 CLOWNS *US, male / female vocal / rap group (Singles: 4 weeks)* pos/wks

22 May 99 (NOT THE) GREATEST RAPPER *Elektra E 3759CD* 23 4

ONE TRIBE – *See OUR TRIBE / ONE TRIBE*

ONE TRUE VOICE *UK, male vocal group (Singles: 14 weeks)* pos/wks

28 Dec 02 ● SACRED TRUST / AFTER YOU'RE GONE (I'LL STILL BE LOVING YOU) *Ebul / Jive 9201532* 2 9
14 Jun 03 ● SHAKESPEARE'S WAY WITH WORDS (re) *Ebul / Jive 9201572* 10 5

ONE 2 MANY *Norway, male / female vocal / instrumental group (Singles: 11 weeks)* pos/wks

12 Nov 88 **DOWNTOWN** *A&M AM 476* 65 4
3 Jun 89 **DOWNTOWN (re-issue)** *A&M AM 456* 43 7

ONE WAY
US, male vocal / instrumental group (Singles: 8 weeks) pos/wks

8 Dec 79 **MUSIC** *MCA 542* [1] 56 6
29 Jun 85 **LET'S TALK ABOUT SHHH** *MCA 972* 64 2

[1] One Way featuring Al Hudson

ONE WORLD
UK, male vocal / instrumental group (Albums: 3 weeks) pos/wks

9 Jun 90 **ONE WORLD ONE VOICE** *Virgin V 2632* 27 3

Alexander O'NEAL 222 Top 500
Soulful ex-vocalist with Minneapolis-based Flyte Time (line-up featured star producers Jimmy Jam and Terry Lewis, who worked on most of his hits), b. 15 Nov 1953, Mississippi, US. Co-wrote his biggest hit single and clocked up an impressive five Top 20 albums between 1985 and 1993 (Singles: 110 weeks, Albums: 162 weeks) pos/wks

28 Dec 85 ● **SATURDAY LOVE** *Tabu A 6829* [1] 6 11
15 Feb 86 **IF YOU WERE HERE TONIGHT** *Tabu A 6391* 13 10
5 Apr 86 **A BROKEN HEART CAN MEND** *Tabu A 6244* 53 4
6 Jun 87 **FAKE** *Tabu 650891 7* 33 6
31 Oct 87 ● **CRITICIZE** *Tabu 651211 7* 4 14
6 Feb 88 **NEVER KNEW LOVE LIKE THIS** *Tabu 651382 7* [2] 26 7
28 May 88 **THE LOVERS** *Tabu 6515957* 28 4
23 Jul 88 **(WHAT CAN I SAY) TO MAKE YOU LOVE ME** *Tabu 652852 7* 27 5
24 Sep 88 **FAKE '88 (re-mix)** *Tabu 652949 7* 16 7
10 Dec 88 **CHRISTMAS SONG (CHESTNUTS ROASTING ON AN OPEN FIRE) / THANK YOU FOR A GOOD YEAR** *Tabu 653182 7* 30 5
25 Feb 89 **HEARSAY '89** *Tabu 654667 7* 56 2
2 Sep 89 **SUNSHINE** *Tabu 655191 7* 72 1
9 Dec 89 **HITMIX (OFFICIAL BOOTLEG MEGA-MIX)** *Tabu 655504 7* 19 7
24 Mar 90 **SATURDAY LOVE (re-mix)** *Tabu 655680 7* [1] 55 2
12 Jan 91 **ALL TRUE MAN** *Tabu 6565717* 18 6
23 Mar 91 **WHAT IS THIS THING CALLED LOVE?** *Tabu 6567317* 53 2
11 May 91 **SHAME ON ME** *Tabu 6568737* 71 1
9 May 92 **SENTIMENTAL** *Tabu 6580147* 53 2
30 Jan 93 **LOVE MAKES NO SENSE** *Tabu AMCD 7708* 26 6
3 Jul 93 **IN THE MIDDLE** *Tabu 5877152* 32 3
25 Sep 93 **ALL THAT MATTERS TO ME** *Tabu 6577232* 67 1
2 Nov 96 **LET'S GET TOGETHER** *EMI Premier PRESCD 11* 38 2
2 Aug 97 **BABY COME TO ME** *One World OWECD 1* [2] 56 1
12 Dec 98 **CRITICIZE (re-recording)** *One World OWECD 3* 51 1
1 Jun 85 **ALEXANDER O'NEAL** *Tabu TBU 26485* 19 18
8 Aug 87 ● **HEAR SAY / ALL MIXED UP** *Tabu 4509361* 4 103
17 Dec 88 **MY GIFT TO YOU** *Tabu 463152 1* 53 3
2 Feb 91 ● **ALL TRUE MAN** *Tabu 4658821* 2 16
30 May 92 ● **THIS THING CALLED LOVE – THE GREATEST HITS OF ALEXANDER O'NEAL** *Tabu 4717142* 4 18
20 Feb 93 **LOVE MAKES NO SENSE** *Tabu 5495022* 14 4

[1] Cherrelle with Alexander O'Neal [2] Alexander O'Neal featuring Cherrelle

'All Mixed Up', a re-mix album, was listed with 'Hearsay' from 15 Jul 89

Shaquille O'NEAL *US, male rapper (Singles: 4 weeks)* pos/wks

26 Mar 94 **I'M OUTSTANDING** *Jive JIVECD 349* 70 1
1 Feb 97 **YOU CAN'T STOP THE REIGN** *Interscope IND 95522* 40 2
17 Oct 98 **THE WAY IT'S GOIN' DOWN (T.W.I.S.M. FOR LIFE)** *A&M 5827932* 62 1

Martin O'NEILL – *See LISBON LIONS featuring Martin O'NEILL & CELTIC CHORUS*

ONEPHATDEEVA – *See A.T.F.C. presents ONEPHATDEEVA*

ONES *US, male production trio (Singles: 13 weeks)* pos/wks

20 Oct 01 ● **FLAWLESS (re)** *Positiva CDTIV 164* 7 12
1 Mar 03 **SUPERSTAR** *Positiva CDTIVS 186* 45 1

ONLY ONES *UK, male vocal / instrumental group (Singles: 2 weeks, Albums: 8 weeks)* pos/wks

1 Feb 92 **ANOTHER GIRL – ANOTHER PLANET** *Columbia 6577507* 57 2
3 Jun 78 **THE ONLY ONES** *CBS 82830* 56 1
31 Mar 79 **EVEN SERPENTS SHINE** *CBS 83451* 42 2
3 May 80 **BABY'S GOT A GUN** *CBS 84089* 37 5

Yoko ONO
Japan, female vocalist (Singles: 44 weeks, Albums: 57 weeks) pos/wks

21 Feb 70 ● **INSTANT KARMA** *Apple APPLES 1003* [1] 5 9
9 Dec 72 ● **HAPPY XMAS (WAR IS OVER) (4re)** *Apple R 5970* [2] 2 26
28 Feb 81 **WALKING ON THIN ICE** *Geffen K 79202* 35 5
14 Jun 03 **WALKING ON THIN ICE (re-mix)** *Parlophone CDMINDS 002* [3] 35 2
20 Dec 03 **HAPPY XMAS (WAR IS OVER) (re-issue)** *Parlophone CDR 6627* [4] ....33 2+
14 Oct 72 **SOMETIME IN NEW YORK CITY** *Apple PCSP 716* [1] 11 6
22 Nov 80 ★ **DOUBLE FANTASY** *Geffen K 99131* [2] ▲ 1 36
20 Jun 81 **SEASON OF GLASS** *Geffen K 99164* 47 2
4 Feb 84 ● **MILK AND HONEY** *Polydor POLH 5* [2] 3 13

[1] Lennon, Ono and the Plastic Ono Band [2] John and Yoko and the Plastic Ono Band with the Harlem Community Choir [3] Ono [4] John and Yoko and the Plastic Ono Band [1] John and Yoko Lennon with the Plastic Ono Band and Elephant's Memor [2] John Lennon and Yoko Ono

'Happy Xmas (War Is Over)' peaked at No.4 in Dec 1972, No.48 in Jan 1975, and No.2 in Dec 1980, and the re-entry made No.28 in Dec 1981 and peaked at No.56 in Dec 1982

See also John LENNON

Ben ONONO – *See FUTURESHOCK; Saffron HILL featuring Ben ONONO*

ONSLAUGHT *UK, male vocal / instrumental group (Singles: 3 weeks, Albums: 2 weeks)* pos/wks

6 May 89 **LET THERE BE ROCK** *London LON 224* 50 3
20 May 89 **IN SEARCH OF SANITY** *London 828142 1* 46 2

ONYX *US, male rap group (Singles: 8 weeks, Albums: 3 weeks)* pos/wks

28 Aug 93 **SLAM** *Columbia 6596302* 31 4
27 Nov 93 **THROW YA GUNZ** *Columbia 6598312* 34 3
20 Feb 99 **ROC-IN-IT** *Independiente ISOM 21MS* [1] 59 1
4 Sep 93 **BACDAFUCUP** *Columbia 4729802* 59 3

[1] Deejay Punk-Roc vs Onyx

ONYX STONE – *See ROUND SOUND presents ONYX STONE & MC MALIBU*

OO LA LA *UK, male vocal / instrumental group (Singles: 2 weeks)* pos/wks

5 Sep 92 **OO . . . AH . . . CANTONA** *North Speed OOAH 1* 64 2

OOBERMAN
UK, male / female vocal / instrumental group (Singles: 5 weeks) pos/wks

8 May 99 **BLOSSOMS FALLING** *Independiente ISOM 26MS* 39 2
17 Jul 99 **MILLION SUNS** *Independiente ISOM 30MS* 43 1
23 Oct 99 **TEARS FROM A WILLOW** *Independiente ISOM 37MS* 63 1
8 Apr 00 **SHORLEY WALL** *Independiente ISOM 41MS* 47 1

OOE – *See COLUMBO featuring OOE*

OPEN ARMS featuring ROWETTA
UK, male / female vocal / instrumental group (Singles: 1 week) pos/wks

15 Jun 96 **HEY MR DJ** *All Around the World CDGLOBE 136* 62 1

OPERABABES
UK, female vocal duo (Singles: 1 week, Albums: 6 weeks) pos/wks

6 Jul 02 **ONE FINE DAY** *Sony Classical 6727062* 54 1
8 Jun 02 **BEYOND IMAGINATION** *Sony Classical SK 89916* 24 6

OPTICAL – *See Ed RUSH & OPTICAL / UNIVERSAL PROJECT*

OPTIMYSTIC *UK, male / female vocal group (Singles: 6 weeks)* pos/wks

17 Sep 94	**CAUGHT UP IN MY HEART** *WEA YZ 841CD*	49	3
10 Dec 94	**NOTHING BUT LOVE** *WEA 864CD1*	37	2
13 May 95	**BEST THING IN THE WORLD** *WEA YZ 920CD*	70	1

OPUS *Austria, male vocal / instrumental group (Singles: 15 weeks)* pos/wks

15 Jun 85 ●	**LIVE IS LIFE** *Polydor POSP 743*	6	15

OPUS III
UK, male / female vocal / instrumental group (Singles: 10 weeks) pos/wks

22 Feb 92 ●	**IT'S A FINE DAY** *PWL International PWL 215*	5	8
27 Jun 92	**I TALK TO THE WIND** *PWL International PWL 235*	52	1
11 Jun 94	**WHEN YOU MADE THE MOUNTAIN** *PWL International PWCD 302*	71	1

ORANGE *UK, male vocal / instrumental group (Singles: 1 week)* pos/wks

8 Oct 94	**JUDY OVER THE RAINBOW** *Chrysalis CDCHS 5012*	73	1

ORANGE JUICE *UK, male vocal / instrumental group (Singles: 34 weeks, Albums: 18 weeks)* pos/wks

7 Nov 81	**L.O.V.E. . . . LOVE** *Polydor POSP 357*	65	2
30 Jan 82	**FELICITY** *Polydor POSP 386*	63	3
21 Aug 82	**TWO HEARTS TOGETHER / HOKOYO** *Polydor POSP 470*	60	2
23 Oct 82	**I CAN'T HELP MYSELF** *Polydor POSP 522*	42	3
19 Feb 83 ●	**RIP IT UP** *Polydor POSP 547*	8	11
4 Jun 83	**FLESH OF MY FLESH** *Polydor OJ 4*	41	6
25 Feb 84	**BRIDGE** *Polydor OJ 5*	67	2
12 May 84	**WHAT PRESENCE?** *Polydor OJ 6*	47	4
27 Oct 84	**LEAN PERIOD** *Polydor OJ 7*	74	1
6 Mar 82	**YOU CAN'T HIDE YOUR LOVE FOREVER** *Polydor POLS 1057*	21	6
20 Nov 82	**RIP IT UP** *Holden Caulfield Universal POLS 1076*	39	8
10 Mar 84	**TEXAS FEVER** *Polydor OJMLP 1*	34	4

See also Edwyn COLLINS

ORB *UK, male instrumental / production duo – Dr Alex Paterson and Kris Weston (Singles: 32 weeks, Albums: 28 weeks)* pos/wks

15 Jun 91	**PERPETUAL DAWN (re)** *Big Life BLRD 46*	18	6
20 Jun 92 ●	**BLUE ROOM** *Big Life BLRT 75*	8	6
17 Oct 92	**ASSASSIN** *Big Life BLRT 81*	12	5
13 Nov 93 ●	**LITTLE FLUFFY CLOUDS** *Big Life BLRD 98*	10	5
27 May 95	**OXBOW LAKES** *Island CID 609*	38	2
8 Feb 97 ●	**TOXYGENE** *Island CID 652*	4	4
24 May 97	**ASYLUM** *Island CID 657*	20	2
24 Feb 01	**ONCE MORE** *Island CID 767*	38	2
27 Apr 91	**ORB'S ADVENTURES BEYOND THE ULTRAWORLD** *Big Life BLRDLP 5*	29	5
18 Jul 92 ★	**U.F. ORB** *Big Life BLRCD 18* ■	1	9
4 Dec 93	**LIVE 93** *Island CIDD 8022*	23	2
25 Jun 94 ●	**POMME FRITZ** *Inter-Modo ORBCD 1*	6	4
1 Apr 95	**ORBVS TERRARVM** *Island CIDX 8037*	20	3
8 Mar 97	**ORBLIVION** *Island CID 8055*	19	3
17 Oct 98	**U.F.OFF – THE BEST OF THE ORB** *Island CID 8078*	38	2

'Perpetual Dawn' made No.61 on its original visit to the chart before re-entering in Feb 1994 and making its peak position

Roy ORBISON (57 Top 500) *Unmistakable vocalist, b. 23 Apr 1936, Texas, d. 6 Dec 1988. The 'Big O' recorded for the legendary Sun label in the mid-1950s, and was the most popular US singer in Britain during the Beat Boom era (1963-65), when The Beatles supported him on tour. The performer, whose trademark was his dark glasses, had a hit span of 33 years, and was enjoying a successful comeback, both as a soloist and member of The Traveling Wilburys, when he died. This multi-award-winner is in the Grammy Hall of Fame as well as the Songwriters' and Rock and Roll Halls of Fame (Singles: 345 weeks, Albums: 243 weeks)* pos/wks

28 Jul 60 ★	**ONLY THE LONELY (KNOW HOW I FEEL) (re)** *London HLU 9149*	1	24
27 Oct 60	**BLUE ANGEL** *London HLU 9207*	11	16
25 May 61 ●	**RUNNING SCARED** *London HLU 9342* ▲	9	15
21 Sep 61	**CRYIN'** *London HLU 9405*	25	9
8 Mar 62 ●	**DREAM BABY** *London HLU 9511*	2	14
28 Jun 62	**THE CROWD** *London HLU 9561*	40	4
8 Nov 62	**WORKIN' FOR THE MAN** *London HLU 9607*	50	1
28 Feb 63 ●	**IN DREAMS** *London HLU 9676*	6	23
30 May 63 ●	**FALLING** *London HLU 9727*	9	11
19 Sep 63 ●	**BLUE BAYOU / MEAN WOMAN BLUES** *London HLU 9777*	3	19
20 Feb 64	**BORNE ON THE WIND** *London HLU 9845*	15	10
30 Apr 64 ★	**IT'S OVER** *London HLU 9882*	1	18
10 Sep 64 ★	**OH, PRETTY WOMAN** *London HLU 9919* ▲	1	18
19 Nov 64 ●	**PRETTY PAPER** *London HLU 9930*	6	11
11 Feb 65	**GOODNIGHT** *London HLU 9951*	14	9
22 Jul 65	**(SAY) YOU'RE MY GIRL** *London HLU 9978*	23	8
9 Sep 65	**RIDE AWAY** *London HLU 9986*	34	6
4 Nov 65	**CRAWLING BACK** *London HLU 10000*	19	9
27 Jan 66	**BREAKIN' UP IS BREAKIN' MY HEART** *London HLU 10015*	22	6
7 Apr 66	**TWINKLE TOES** *London HLU 10034*	29	5
16 Jun 66	**LANA** *London HLU 10051*	15	9
18 Aug 66 ●	**TOO SOON TO KNOW** *London HLU 10067*	3	17
1 Dec 66	**THERE WON'T BE MANY COMING HOME** *London HLU 10096*	12	9
23 Feb 67	**SO GOOD** *London HLU 10113*	32	6
24 Jul 68	**WALK ON** *London HLU 10206*	39	10
25 Sep 68	**HEARTACHE** *London HLU 10222*	44	4
30 Apr 69	**MY FRIEND** *London HLU 10261*	35	4
13 Sep 69	**PENNY ARCADE (re)** *London HLU 10285*	27	14
14 Jan 89 ●	**YOU GOT IT** *Virgin VS 1166*	3	10
1 Apr 89	**SHE'S A MYSTERY TO ME** *Virgin VS 1173*	27	5
4 Jul 92 ●	**I DROVE ALL NIGHT** *MCA MCS 1652*	7	10
22 Aug 92	**CRYING** *Virgin America VUS 63* [1]	13	6
7 Nov 92	**HEARTBREAK RADIO** *Virgin America VUS 68*	36	3
13 Nov 93	**I DROVE ALL NIGHT (re-issue)** *Virgin America VUSCD 79*	47	2
8 Jun 63	**LONELY AND BLUE** *London HAU 2342*	15	8
29 Jun 63	**CRYING** *London HAU 2437*	17	3
30 Nov 63 ●	**IN DREAMS** *London HAU 8108*	6	57
25 Jul 64	**THE EXCITING SOUNDS OF ROY ORBISON** *Ember NR 5013*	17	2
5 Dec 64 ●	**OH, PRETTY WOMAN** *London HAU 8207*	4	16
25 Sep 65 ●	**THERE IS ONLY ONE ROY ORBISON** *London HAU 8252*	10	12
26 Feb 66	**THE ORBISON WAY** *London HAU 8279*	11	10
24 Sep 66	**THE CLASSIC ROY ORBISON** *London HAU 8297*	12	8
22 Jul 67	**ORBISONGS** *Monument SMO 5004*	40	1
30 Sep 67	**ROY ORBISON'S GREATEST HITS** *Monument SMO 5007*	40	1
27 Jan 73	**ALL-TIME GREATEST HITS** *Monument MNT 67290*	39	3
29 Nov 75 ★	**THE BEST OF ROY ORBISON** *Arcade ADEP 19*	1	20
18 Jul 81	**GOLDEN DAYS** *CBS 10026*	63	1
4 Jul 87	**IN DREAMS: THE GREATEST HITS** *Virgin VGD 3514*	86	2
29 Oct 88 ★	**THE LEGENDARY ROY ORBISON** *Telstar STAR 2330*	1	38
11 Feb 89 ●	**MYSTERY GIRL** *Virgin V 2576*	2	23
25 Nov 89	**A BLACK AND WHITE NIGHT** *Virgin V 2601*	51	3
2 Nov 90	**BALLADS – 22 CLASSIC LOVE SONGS** *Telstar STAR 2441*	38	10
28 Nov 92	**KING OF HEARTS** *Virgin America CDVUS 58*	23	4
16 Nov 96	**THE VERY BEST OF ROY ORBISON** *Virgin CDV 2804*	18	11
10 Feb 01 ●	**LOVE SONGS** *Virgin VTDCD 360*	4	10

[1] Roy Orbison (duet with kd lang)

See also TRAVELING WILBURYS

William ORBIT *UK, male producer – William Wainwright (Singles: 29 weeks, Albums: 14 weeks)* pos/wks

26 Jun 93	**WATER FROM A VINE LEAF** *Guerilla VSCDT 1465*	59	1
18 Dec 99 ●	**BARBER'S ADAGIO FOR STRINGS (re)** *WEA WEA 247 CD*	4	15
6 May 00	**RAVEL'S PAVANE POUR UNE INFANTE DÉFUNTE** *WEA WEA 269CD*	31	2
19 Jul 03 ●	**FEEL GOOD TIME** *Columbia 6741062* [1]	3	11
29 Jan 00 ●	**PIECES IN A MODERN STYLE** *WEA 3984289572*	2	14

[1] Pink featuring William Orbit

See also BASS-O-MATIC

ORBITAL *UK, male instrumental duo – Paul and Phil Hartnoll (Singles: 56 weeks, Albums: 36 weeks)* pos/wks

24 Mar 90	**CHIME** *ffrr F B5*	17	7
22 Sep 90	**OMEN** *ffrr F 145*	46	3
19 Jan 91	**SATAN** *ffrr FX 149*	31	4
15 Feb 92	**MUTATIONS (EP)** *ffrr FCD 181*	24	3

26 Sep 92	**RADICCIO (EP)** *Internal LIARX 1*	37	2
21 Aug 93	**LUSH** *Internal LIECD 7*	43	2
24 Sep 94	**ARE WE HERE** *Internal LIECD 15*	33	2
27 May 95	**BELFAST** *Volume VOLCD 1*	53	1
27 Apr 96	**THE BOX** *Internal LIECD 30*	11	4
11 Jan 97 ●	**SATAN (re-recording)** *Internal LIECD 37*	3	6
19 Apr 97 ●	**THE SAINT** *ffrr FCD 296*	3	7
20 Mar 99	**STYLE** *ffrr FCD 358*	13	4
17 Jul 99	**NOTHING LEFT** *ffrr FCD 365*	32	2
11 Mar 00	**BEACHED** *ffrr FCD 377* [1]	36	3
28 Apr 01	**FUNNY BREAK (ONE IS ENOUGH)** *ffrr FCD 395*	21	3
8 Jun 02	**REST & PLAY (EP)** *ffrr FCD 407*	33	3
12 Oct 91	**ORBITAL** *ffrr 8282481*	71	1
5 Jun 93	**ORBITAL** *Internal TRUCD 2*	28	2
19 Mar 94	**PEEL SESSIONS** *Internal LIECD 12*	32	2
20 Aug 94 ●	**SNIVILISATION** *Internal TRUCD 5*	4	4
11 May 96 ●	**IN SIDES** *Internal TRUCD 10*	5	12
25 Jan 97	**SATAN LIVE** *Internal LIARX 37*	48	1
17 Apr 99 ●	**THE MIDDLE OF NOWHERE** *ffrr 5560762*	4	7
12 May 01	**THE ALTOGETHER** *ffrr 8573877822*	11	4
15 Jun 02	**WORK 1989-2002** *London 927461902*	36	3

[1] Orbital and Angelo Badalamenti

Tracks on Mutations (EP): Chime Crime / Oolaa / Farenheit 3D 3 / Speed Freak. Tracks on Radiccio (EP): Halcyon / The Naked and the Dead / Sunday. The listed flip side of 'Belfast' was 'Innocent X' by Therapy?. Tracks on Rest & Play (EP): 'Frenetic' / 'Illuminate' (featuring David Gray) / 'Chime' The identically titled albums are different

ORCHESTRA ON THE HALF SHELL

US, male vocal / instrumental group (Singles: 6 weeks) pos/wks

15 Dec 90	**TURTLE RHAPSODY** *SBK SBK 17*	36	6

ORCHESTRAL MANOEUVRES IN THE DARK (102 Top 500)

One of the most regular chart visitors of the 1980s had a nucleus of Andy McCluskey (v/syn/b) and Paul Humphries (syn), who left in 1989. This Liverpool-based synthesizer band had numerous international hits including 'Maid of Orleans', which was Germany's biggest seller in 1982 (Singles: 201 weeks, Albums: 226 weeks) pos/wks

9 Feb 80	**RED FRAME WHITE LIGHT** *Dindisc DIN 6*	67	2
10 May 80	**MESSAGES** *Dindisc DIN 15*	13	11
4 Oct 80 ●	**ENOLA GAY** *Dindisc DIN 22*	8	15
29 Aug 81 ●	**SOUVENIR** *Dindisc DIN 24*	3	12
24 Oct 81 ●	**JOAN OF ARC** *Dindisc DIN 36*	5	14
23 Jan 82 ●	**MAID OF ORLEANS (THE WALTZ JOAN OF ARC)** *Dindisc DIN 40*	4	10
19 Feb 83	**GENETIC ENGINEERING** *Virgin VS 527*	20	8
9 Apr 83	**TELEGRAPH** *Virgin VS 580*	42	4
14 Apr 84 ●	**LOCOMOTION** *Virgin VS 660*	5	11
16 Jun 84	**TALKING LOUD AND CLEAR** *Virgin VS 685*	11	10
8 Sep 84	**TESLA GIRLS** *Virgin VS 705*	21	8
10 Nov 84	**NEVER TURN AWAY** *Virgin VS 727*	70	2
25 May 85	**SO IN LOVE** *Virgin VS 766*	27	7
20 Jul 85	**SECRET** *Virgin VS 796*	34	7
26 Oct 85	**LA FEMME ACCIDENT** *Virgin VS 811*	42	4
3 May 86	**IF YOU LEAVE** *Virgin VS 843*	48	4
6 Sep 86	**(FOREVER) LIVE AND DIE** *Virgin VS 888*	11	10
15 Nov 86	**WE LOVE YOU** *Virgin VS 911*	54	5
2 May 87	**SHAME** *Virgin VS 938*	52	3
6 Feb 88	**DREAMING (re)** *Virgin VS 987*	50	6
30 Mar 91 ●	**SAILING ON THE SEVEN SEAS** *Virgin VS 1310*	3	13
6 Jul 91 ●	**PANDORA'S BOX** *Virgin VS 1331*	7	10
14 Sep 91	**THEN YOU TURN AWAY** *Virgin VS 1368*	50	4
7 Dec 91	**CALL MY NAME** *Virgin VS 1380*	50	2
15 May 93	**STAND ABOVE ME** *Virgin VSCDG 1444*	21	4
17 Jul 93	**DREAM OF ME (BASED ON LOVE'S THEME)** *Virgin VSCDT 1461*	24	5
18 Sep 93	**EVERYDAY** *Virgin VSCDT 1471*	59	2
17 Aug 96	**WALKING ON THE MILKY WAY** *Virgin VSCDT 1599*	17	5
2 Nov 96	**UNIVERSAL** *Virgin VSCDT 1606*	55	1
26 Sep 98	**THE OMD REMIXES (EP)** *Virgin VSCDT 1694*	35	2
1 Mar 80	**ORCHESTRAL MANOEUVRES IN THE DARK** *DinDisc DID 2*	27	29
1 Nov 80 ●	**ORGANISATION** *DinDisc DID 6*	6	25
14 Nov 81 ●	**ARCHITECTURE & MORALITY** *DinDisc DID 12*	3	39
12 Mar 83 ●	**DAZZLE SHIPS** *Telegraph V 2261*	5	13
12 May 84 ●	**JUNK CULTURE** *Virgin V 2310*	9	27
29 Jun 85	**CRUSH** *Virgin V 2349*	13	12
11 Oct 86	**THE PACIFIC AGE** *Virgin V 2398*	15	7
12 Mar 88 ●	**THE BEST OF O.M.D.** *Virgin OMD 1*	2	33
18 May 91 ●	**SUGAR TAX** *Virgin V 2648*	3	29
26 Jun 93	**LIBERATOR** *Virgin CDV 2715*	14	6
14 Sep 96	**UNIVERSAL** *Virgin CDV 2807*	24	2
10 Oct 98	**THE O.M.D. SINGLES** *Virgin CDV 2859*	16	4

Group often known as OMD. Tracks on the OMD Remixes (EP): Enola Gay / Souvenir / Electricity

ORCHESTRE NATIONALE DE LA RADIO DIFFUSION FRANÇAISE – *See Sir Thomas BEECHAM*

Raul ORELLANA

Spain, male producer (Singles: 8 weeks) pos/wks

30 Sep 89	**THE REAL WILD HOUSE** *RCA BCM 322*	29	8

O.R.G.A.N.

Spain, male DJ / producer – Vidana Crespo (Singles: 2 weeks) pos/wks

16 May 98	**TO THE WORLD** *Multiply CDMULTY 34*	33	2

ORIGIN *UK, male production duo (Singles: 1 week)*

pos/wks

12 Aug 00	**WIDE EYED ANGEL** *Lost Language LOST 001CD*	73	1

ORIGIN UNKNOWN

UK, male instrumental / production duo (Singles: 3 weeks) pos/wks

13 Jul 96	**VALLEY OF THE SHADOWS** *Ram RAMM 16CD*	60	1
11 May 02	**TRULY ONE** *Ram RAMM 38CD*	53	1
27 Sep 03	**HOTNESS** *Ram RAMM 45* [1]	66	1

[1] Dynamite MC and Origin Unknown

ORIGINAL *US, male vocal / instrumental duo – Everett Bradley and Walter Taieb (Singles: 14 weeks)*

pos/wks

14 Jan 95	**I LUV U BABY** *Ore AG 8CD*	31	3
19 Aug 95 ●	**I LUV U BABY (re-mix)** *Ore AGR 8CD*	2	9
11 Nov 95	**B 2 GETHER** *Ore AG 12CD*	29	2

See also DIVA SURPRISE featuring Georgia JONES

ORIGINOO GUNN CLAPPAZ – *See HELTAH SKELTAH and ORIGINOO GUNN CLAPPAZ as the FABULOUS FIVE*

ORION *UK, male / female production / vocal / instrumental duo – Darren Tate and Sarah J (Singles: 2 weeks)*

pos/wks

7 Oct 00	**ETERNITY** *Incentive CENT 11CDS*	38	2

ORION TOO

Belgium, male producer and female vocalist (Singles: 1 week) pos/wks

9 Nov 02	**HOPE AND WAIT** *Data DATA 40CDS*	46	1

See also ANGELIC; CITIZEN CANED; Jurgen VRIES

ORLANDO – *See LA's; PRETENDERS*

Tony ORLANDO *US, male vocalist – Michael Anthony Orlando Cassavitis (Singles: 70 weeks)*

pos/wks

5 Oct 61 ●	**BLESS YOU** *Fontana H 330*	5	11
10 Mar 73 ★	**TIE A YELLOW RIBBON ROUND THE OLE OAK TREE** *Bell 1287* [1] ▲	1	40
4 Aug 73	**SAY, HAS ANYBODY SEEN MY SWEET GYPSY ROSE** *Bell 1322* [1]	12	15
9 Mar 74	**WHO'S IN THE STRAWBERRY PATCH WITH SALLY** *Bell 1343* [2]	37	4

[1] Dawn featuring Tony Orlando [2] Tony Orlando and Dawn

See also DAWN

ORLONS *US, female / male vocal group (Singles: 3 weeks)* pos/wks

27 Dec 62	**DON'T HANG UP (re)** *Cameo Parkway C 231*	39	3

ORN *UK, male DJ / producer – Omio Nourizadeh (Singles: 1 week)* pos/wks

1 Mar 97	**SNOW** *Deconstruction 74321447612*	61	1

Cyril ORNADEL – *See LONDON SYMPHONY ORCHESTRA*

Stacie ORRICO
US, female vocalist (Singles: 16 weeks, Albums: 13 weeks) pos/wks

23 Aug 03 ●	**STUCK** *Virgin VUSCD 269*	9	8
1 Nov 03	**(THERE'S GOTTA BE) MORE TO LIFE** *Virgin VUSCD 275*	12	8
4 Oct 03	**STACIE ORRICO** *Virgin CDVUS 238*	37	13+

Claudette ORTIZ – *See Wyclef JEAN*

Beth ORTON
UK, female vocalist (Singles: 13 weeks, Albums: 18 weeks) pos/wks

1 Feb 97	**TOUCH ME WITH YOUR LOVE** *Heavenly HVN 64CD*	60	1
5 Apr 97	**SOMEONE'S DAUGHTER** *Heavenly HVN 65CD*	49	1
14 Jun 97	**SHE CRIES YOUR NAME** *Heavenly HVN 68CD*	40	2
13 Dec 97	**BEST BIT (EP)** *Heavenly HVN 72CD* [1]	36	3
13 Mar 99	**STOLEN CAR** *Heavenly HVN 89CD*	34	2
25 Sep 99	**CENTRAL RESERVATION** *Heavenly HVN 92CD*	37	2
16 Nov 02	**ANYWHERE** *Heavenly HVN 125CDS*	55	1
12 Apr 03	**THINKING ABOUT TOMORROW** *Heavenly HVN 129CD*	57	1
26 Oct 96	**TRAILER PARK** *Heavenly HVNLP 17CD*	68	3
27 Mar 99	**CENTRAL RESERVATION** *Heavenly HVNLP 22CD*	17	8
10 Aug 02 ●	**DAYBREAKER** *Heavenly HVNLP 37CD*	8	5
4 Oct 03	**PASS IN TIME – THE DEFINITIVE COLLECTION** *Heavenly HVNLP 45CD*	45	2

[1] Beth Orton featuring Terry Callier

Tracks on Best Bit (EP): Best Bit / Skimming Stone / Dolphins / Lean on Me

ORVILLE – *See Keith HARRIS and ORVILLE*

Jeffrey OSBORNE
US, male vocalist (Singles: 38 weeks, Albums: 10 weeks) pos/wks

17 Sep 83	**DON'T YOU GET SO MAD** *A&M AM 140*	54	2
14 Apr 84	**STAY WITH ME TONIGHT** *A&M AM 188*	18	11
23 Jun 84	**ON THE WINGS OF LOVE** *A&M AM 198*	11	14
20 Oct 84	**DON'T STOP** *A&M AM 222*	61	2
26 Jul 86	**SOWETO (re)** *A&M AM 334*	44	6
15 Aug 87	**LOVE POWER** *Arista RIS 27* [1]	63	3
5 May 84	**STAY WITH ME TONIGHT** *A&M AMLX 64940*	56	7
13 Oct 84	**DON'T STOP** *A&M AMA 5017*	59	3

[1] Dionne Warwick and Jeffrey Osborne

See also LTD

Joan OSBORNE
US, female vocalist (Singles: 13 weeks, Albums: 18 weeks) pos/wks

10 Feb 96 ●	**ONE OF US** *Blue Gorilla JOACD 1*	6	10
8 Jun 96	**ST TERESA** *Blue Gorilla JOACD 3*	33	3
9 Mar 96 ●	**RELISH** *Blue Gorilla 5266992*	5	18

Tony OSBORNE SOUND *UK, orchestra (Singles: 3 weeks)* pos/wks

23 Feb 61	**THE MAN FROM MADRID** *HMV POP 827* [1]	50	1
3 Feb 73	**THE SHEPHERD'S SONG** *Philips 6006 266*	46	2

[1] Tony Osborne Sound featuring Joanne Brown

Kelly OSBOURNE
UK, female vocalist (Singles: 21 weeks, Albums: 2 weeks) pos/wks

24 Aug 02	**PAPA DON'T PREACH (import)** *Epic 6729152*	65	3
21 Sep 02 ●	**PAPA DON'T PREACH (re)** *Epic 6731602*	3	10
8 Feb 03	**SHUT UP** *Epic 6735552*	12	6
20 Dec 03 ★	**CHANGES** *Sanctuary SANXD 234* [1] ■	1	2+
22 Feb 03	**SHUT UP** *Epic 5094782*	31	2

[1] Ozzy and Kelly Osbourne

Ozzy OSBOURNE
UK, male vocalist (Singles: 50 weeks, Albums: 67 weeks) pos/wks

13 Sep 80	**CRAZY TRAIN** *Jet 197* [1]	49	4
15 Nov 80	**MR CROWLEY** *Jet 7003* [1]	46	3
26 Nov 83	**BARK AT THE MOON** *Epic A 3915*	21	8
2 Jun 84	**SO TIRED** *Epic A 4452*	20	9
1 Feb 86	**SHOT IN THE DARK** *Epic A 6859*	20	6
9 Aug 86	**THE ULTIMATE SIN / LIGHTNING STRIKES** *Epic A 7311*	72	1
20 May 89	**CLOSE MY EYES FOREVER** *Dreamland PB 49409* [2]	47	3
28 Sep 91	**NO MORE TEARS** *Epic 6574407*	32	3
30 Nov 91	**MAMA I'M COMING HOME** *Epic 6576177*	46	2
25 Nov 95	**PERRY MASON** *Epic 6626395*	23	2
31 Aug 96	**I JUST WANT YOU** *Epic 6635702*	43	1
8 Jun 02	**DREAMER / GETS ME THROUGH** *Epic 6724122*	18	6
20 Dec 03 ★	**CHANGES** *Sanctuary SANXD 234* [3] ■	1	2+
20 Sep 80 ●	**OZZY OSBOURNE'S BLIZZARD OF OZZ** *Jet JETLP 234* [1]	7	8
7 Nov 81	**DIARY OF A MADMAN** *Jet JETLP 237*	14	12
27 Nov 82	**TALK OF THE DEVIL** *Jet JETDP 401*	21	6
10 Dec 83	**BARK AT THE MOON** *Epic EPC 25739*	24	7
22 Feb 86 ●	**THE ULTIMATE SIN** *Epic EPC 26404*	8	10
23 May 87	**TRIBUTE** *Epic 450 4751*	13	6
22 Oct 88	**NO REST FOR THE WICKED** *Epic 462581 1*	23	4
17 Mar 90	**JUST SAY OZZY** *Epic 4659401*	69	1
19 Oct 91	**NO MORE TEARS** *Epic 4678591*	17	3
4 Nov 95	**OZZMOSIS** *Epic 4810222*	22	3
15 Nov 97	**THE OZZMAN COMETH – THE BEST OF OZZY OSBOURNE** *Epic 4872602*	68	1
27 Oct 01	**DOWN TO EARTH** *Epic 4984742*	19	3
15 Mar 03	**THE ESSENTIAL OZZY OSBOURNE** *Epic 5108402*	21	3

[1] Ozzy Osbourne Blizzard of Ozz [2] Lita Ford duet with Ozzy Osbourne [3] Ozzy and Kelly Osbourne [1] Ozzy Osbourne's Blizzard of Ozz

See also BLACK SABBATH

OSIBISA *Ghana / Nigeria, male vocal / instrumental group (Singles: 12 weeks, Albums: 17 weeks)* pos/wks

17 Jan 76	**SUNSHINE DAY** *Bronze BRO 20*	17	6
5 Jun 76	**DANCE THE BODY MUSIC** *Bronze BRO 26*	31	6
22 May 71	**OSIBISA** *MCA MDKS 8001*	11	10
5 Feb 72	**WOYAYA** *MCA MDKS 8005*	11	7

Donny OSMOND (267 Top 500) *Teenage teen-idol vocalist, b. 9 Dec 1957, Utah, US. The main focal point of the hitmaking family act The Osmonds, he was one of the most popular pin-ups of the 1970s, had three solo No.1s before his 16th birthday and returned to the album Top 20 in 2002 (Singles: 118 weeks, Albums: 117 weeks)* pos/wks

17 Jun 72 ★	**PUPPY LOVE (3re)** *MGM 2006 104*	1	23
16 Sep 72 ●	**TOO YOUNG (re)** *MGM 2006 113*	5	15
11 Nov 72 ●	**WHY** *MGM 2006 119*	3	20
10 Mar 73 ★	**THE TWELFTH OF NEVER** *MGM 2006 199*	1	14
18 Aug 73 ★	**YOUNG LOVE** *MGM 2006 300*	1	10
10 Nov 73 ●	**WHEN I FALL IN LOVE** *MGM 2006 365*	4	13
9 Nov 74	**WHERE DID ALL THE GOOD TIMES GO** *MGM 2006 468*	18	10
26 Sep 87	**I'M IN IT FOR LOVE** *Virgin VS 994*	70	1
6 Aug 88	**SOLDIER OF LOVE** *Virgin VS 1094*	29	8
12 Nov 88	**IF IT'S LOVE THAT YOU WANT** *Virgin VS 1140*	70	2
9 Feb 91	**MY LOVE IS A FIRE** *Capitol CL 600*	64	2
23 Sep 72 ●	**PORTRAIT OF DONNY** *MGM 2315 108*	5	43
16 Dec 72 ●	**TOO YOUNG** *MGM 2315 113*	7	24
26 May 73 ●	**ALONE TOGETHER** *MGM 2315 210*	6	19
15 Dec 73 ●	**A TIME FOR US** *MGM 2315 273*	4	13
8 Feb 75	**DONNY** *MGM 2315 314*	16	4
2 Oct 76	**DISCOTRAIN** *Polydor 2391 226*	59	1
21 Apr 01 ●	**THIS IS THE MOMENT** *Decca 1587772*	10	3
7 Dec 02	**SOMEWHERE IN TIME** *Decca 0665302*	12	10

See also Donny and Marie OSMOND; OSMONDS

Donny and Marie OSMOND
US, male / female vocal duo (Singles: 37 weeks, Albums: 19 weeks) pos/wks

3 Aug 74 ●	**I'M LEAVING IT (ALL) UP TO YOU** *MGM 2006 446*	2	12
14 Dec 74 ●	**MORNING SIDE OF THE MOUNTAIN** *MGM 2006 474*	5	12

21 Jun 75 **MAKE THE WORLD GO AWAY** *MGM 2006 523* 18 6
17 Jan 76 **DEEP PURPLE** *MGM 2006 561* 25 7
2 Nov 74 I'M LEAVING IT ALL UP TO YOU *MGM 2315 307*....................13 15
26 Jul 75 MAKE THE WORLD GO AWAY *MGM 2315 343* 30 3
5 Jun 76 DEEP PURPLE *Polydor 2391 220*....................48 1

See also Donny OSMOND; Marie OSMOND

Little Jimmy OSMOND
US, male vocalist (Singles: 50 weeks, Albums: 12 weeks) pos/wks

25 Nov 72 ★ **LONG HAIRED LOVER FROM LIVERPOOL (re)** *MGM 2006 109* [1] 1 27
31 Mar 73 ● **TWEEDLEE DEE** *MGM 2006 175* 4 13
23 Mar 74 **I'M GONNA KNOCK ON YOUR DOOR** *MGM 2006 389* [2] 11 10
17 Feb 73 KILLER JOE *MGM 2315 157* 20 12

[1] Little Jimmy Osmond with the Mike Curb Congregation [2] Jimmy Osmond

Marie OSMOND
US, female vocalist (Singles: 15 weeks, Albums: 1 week) pos/wks

17 Nov 73 ● **PAPER ROSES** *MGM 2006 315* 2 15
9 Feb 74 PAPER ROSES *MGM 2315 262* 46 1

See also Donny and Marie OSMOND

OSMOND BOYS *US, male vocal group (Singles: 6 weeks)* pos/wks

9 Nov 91 **BOYS WILL BE BOYS** *Curb 6573847* 65 2
11 Jan 92 **SHOW ME THE WAY** *Curb 6577227* 60 4

OSMONDS (303 Top 500)
Top teeny-bop act, brothers Donny, Alan, Wayne, Merrill and Jay Osmond from Utah, US. Polished pop quintet created hysteria wherever they appeared. Osmond family (including Marie and Little Jimmy) had a record 13 UK hits in 1973 (Singles: 94 weeks, Albums: 119 weeks) pos/wks

25 Mar 72 **DOWN BY THE LAZY RIVER** *MGM 2006 096* 40 5
11 Nov 72 ● **CRAZY HORSES** *MGM 2006 142* 2 18
14 Jul 73 ● **GOIN' HOME** *MGM 2006 288* 4 10
27 Oct 73 ● **LET ME IN** *MGM 2006 321* 2 14
20 Apr 74 **I CAN'T STOP** *MCA 129* 12 10
24 Aug 74 ★ **LOVE ME FOR A REASON** *MGM 2006 458* 1 9
1 Mar 75 **HAVING A PARTY** *MGM 2006 492* 28 8
24 May 75 ● **THE PROUD ONE** *MGM 2006 520* 5 8
15 Nov 75 **I'M STILL GONNA NEED YOU** *MGM 2006 551* 32 4
30 Oct 76 **I CAN'T LIVE A DREAM** *Polydor 2066 726* 37 5
23 Sep 95 **CRAZY HORSES (re-mix)** *Polydor 5793212* 50 1
12 Jun 99 **CRAZY HORSES (re-issue) (re-mix)** *Polydor 5611372* 34 2
18 Nov 72 OSMONDS LIVE *MGM 2315 117* 13 22
16 Dec 72 ● CRAZY HORSES *MGM 2315 123* 9 19
25 Aug 73 ● THE PLAN *MGM 2315 251* 6 25
17 Aug 74 ● OUR BEST TO YOU *MGM 2315 300* 5 20
7 Dec 74 LOVE ME FOR A REASON *MGM 2315 312* 13 9
14 Jun 75 I'M STILL GONNA NEED YOU *MGM 2315 342* 19 7
10 Jan 76 AROUND THE WORLD – LIVE IN CONCERT *MGM 2659 044* 41 1
20 Apr 96 THE VERY BEST OF THE OSMONDS *Polydor 5270722* 17 5
12 Jul 03 ● ULTIMATE COLLECTION *Polydor / Universal TV 9808355* ....4 11+

See also Donny OSMOND; Donny and Marie OSMOND

Gilbert O'SULLIVAN (153 Top 500)
Distinctive Irish singer / songwriter / pianist, b. Raymond O'Sullivan, 1 Dec 1946, Waterford. His unusual image – short trousers, flat cap and pudding-basin haircut – helped to launch the successful international career of the performer voted No.1 UK Male Singer of 1972 (Singles: 145 weeks, Albums: 196 weeks) pos/wks

28 Nov 70 ● **NOTHING RHYMED** *MAM 3* 8 11
3 Apr 71 **UNDERNEATH THE BLANKET GO (re)** *MAM 13* 40 4
24 Jul 71 **WE WILL** *MAM 30* 16 11
27 Nov 71 ● **NO MATTER HOW I TRY** *MAM 53* 5 15
4 Mar 72 ● **ALONE AGAIN (NATURALLY)** *MAM 66* ▲ 3 12
17 Jun 72 ● **OOH-WAKKA-DOO-WAKKA-DAY** *MAM 78* 8 11
21 Oct 72 ★ **CLAIR** *MAM 84* 1 14
17 Mar 73 ★ **GET DOWN** *MAM 96* 1 13
15 Sep 73 **OOH BABY** *MAM 107* 18 7
10 Nov 73 ● **WHY, OH WHY, OH WHY** *MAM 111* 6 14
9 Feb 74 **HAPPINESS IS ME AND YOU** *MAM 114* 19 7
24 Aug 74 **A WOMAN'S PLACE** *MAM 122* 42 3
14 Dec 74 **CHRISTMAS SONG** *MAM 124* 12 6
14 Jun 75 **I DON'T LOVE YOU BUT I THINK I LIKE YOU** *MAM 130* 14 6
27 Sep 80 **WHAT'S IN A KISS** *CBS 8929* 19 9
24 Feb 90 **SO WHAT** *Dover ROJ 3* 70 2
25 Sep 71 ● HIMSELF *MAM 501* 5 82
18 Nov 72 ★ BACK TO FRONT *MAM 502* 1 65
6 Oct 73 ● I'M A WRITER NOT A FIGHTER *MAMS 505* 2 25
26 Oct 74 ● STRANGER IN MY OWN BACK YARD *MAM MAMS 506* 9 8
18 Dec 76 GREATEST HITS *MAM MAMA 2003* 13 11
12 Sep 81 20 GOLDEN GREATS *K-Tel NE 1133* 98 1
11 May 91 NOTHING BUT THE BEST *Castle Communications CTVLP 107* 50 4

The OTHER TWO *UK, male / female vocal / instrumental duo – Stephen Morris and Gillian Gilbert (Singles: 5 weeks)* pos/wks

9 Nov 91 **TASTY FISH** *Factory FAC 3297* 41 3
6 Nov 93 **SELFISH** *London TWOCD 1* 46 2

See also NEW ORDER

Johnny OTIS SHOW
US, band – leader John Veliotes (Singles: 22 weeks) pos/wks

22 Nov 57 ● **MA (HE'S MAKING EYES AT ME)** *Capitol CL 14794* [1] 2 15
10 Jan 58 **BYE BYE BABY** *Capitol CL 14817* [2] 20 7

[1] Johnny Otis and His Orchestra with Marie Adams and the Three Tons of Joy
[2] Johnny Otis Show, vocals by Marie Adams and Johnny Otis

OTTAWAN
France, male / female vocal duo (Singles: 45 weeks) pos/wks

13 Sep 80 ● **D.I.S.C.O.** *Carrere CAR 161* 2 18
13 Dec 80 **YOU'RE OK** *Carrere CAR 168* 56 6
29 Aug 81 ● **HANDS UP (GIVE ME YOUR HEART)** *Carrere CAR 183* 3 15
5 Dec 81 **HELP, GET ME SOME HELP!** *Carrere CAR 215* 49 6

John OTWAY and Wild Willy BARRETT *UK, male vocal / instrumental duo (Singles: 15 weeks, Albums: 1 week)* pos/wks

3 Dec 77 **REALLY FREE** *Polydor 2058 951* 27 8
5 Jul 80 **DK 50-80** *Polydor 2059 250* [1] 45 4
12 Oct 02 ● **BUNSEN BURNER** *U-Vibe OTWAY 02X* [2] 9 3
1 Jul 78 DEEP AND MEANINGLESS *Polydor 2382 501* 44 1

[1] Otway and Barrett [2] John Otway

OUI 3 *UK / US / Switzerland, male / female rap / instrumental group (Singles: 21 weeks, Albums: 3 weeks)* pos/wks

20 Feb 93 **FOR WHAT IT'S WORTH** *MCA MCSTD 1736* 28 6
24 Apr 93 **ARMS OF SOLITUDE** *MCA MCSTD 1759* 54 2
17 Jul 93 **BREAK FROM THE OLD ROUTINE** *MCA MCSTD 1793* 17 6
23 Oct 93 **FOR WHAT IT'S WORTH (re-mix)** *MCA MCSTD 1941* 26 3
29 Jan 94 **FACT OF LIFE** *MCA MCSTD 1939* 38 2
27 May 95 **JOY OF LIVING** *MCA MCSTD 2057* 55 2
7 Aug 93 OUI LOVE YOU *MCA MCD 10833* 39 3

OUR DAUGHTER'S WEDDING
US, male vocal / instrumental group (Singles: 6 weeks) pos/wks

1 Aug 81 **LAWNCHAIRS** *EMI America EA 124* 49 6

OUR HOUSE
Australia, male instrumental production duo (Singles: 1 week) pos/wks

31 Aug 96 **FLOOR SPACE** *Perfecto PERF 125CD* 52 1

OUR KID *UK, male vocal group (Singles: 11 weeks)* pos/wks

29 May 76 ● **YOU JUST MIGHT SEE ME CRY** *Polydor 2058 729* 2 11

OUR LADY PEACE
Canada, male vocal / instrumental group (Singles: 1 week) pos/wks

15 Jan 00 **ONE MAN ARMY** *Epic 6688662* 70 1

OUR TRIBE / ONE TRIBE *UK / US, male / female vocal / instrumental group (Singles: 13 weeks)*

Date	Title / Label	pos	wks
20 Jun 92	**WHAT HAVE YOU DONE (IS THIS ALL)** *Inner Rhythm HEART 03* [1]	52	2
27 Mar 93	**I BELIEVE IN YOU** *Ffrreedom TABCD 117* [2]	42	2
30 Apr 94	**HOLD THAT SUCKER DOWN** *Cheeky CHEKCD 004* [3]	24	3
21 May 94	**LOVE COME HOME** *Triangle BLUESCD 001* [4]	73	1
13 May 95	**HIGH AS A KITE** *ffrr FCD 259* [5]	55	1
30 Sep 95	**HOLD THAT SUCKER DOWN (re-mix)** *Cheeky CHEKCD 009* [3]	26	3
9 Dec 00	**HOLD THAT SUCKER DOWN (re-issue)** *Champion CHAMPCD 786* [3]	45	1

[1] One Tribe featuring Gem [2] Our Tribe [3] OT Quartet [4] Our Tribe with Franke Pharoah and Kristine W [5] One Tribe featuring Roger

See also FAITHLESS; ROLLO; SPHINX; DUSTED

OUT OF MY HAIR *UK, male vocal / instrumental group (Singles: 1 week)*

Date	Title / Label	pos	wks
1 Jul 95	**MISTER JONES** *RCA 74321267812*	73	1

OUTHERE BROTHERS *US, male rap / vocal duo – Lamar Mahone and Craig Simpkins (Singles: 50 weeks, Albums: 9 weeks)*

Date	Title / Label	pos	wks
18 Mar 95 ★	**DON'T STOP (WIGGLE WIGGLE)** *Eternal YZ 917CD*	1	15
17 Jun 95 ★	**BOOM BOOM BOOM** *Eternal YZ 938CD*	1	15
23 Sep 95 ●	**LA LA LA HEY HEY** *Eternal YZ 974CD*	7	7
16 Dec 95 ●	**IF YOU WANNA PARTY** *Eternal WEA 030CD* [1]	9	10
25 Jan 97	**LET ME HEAR YOU SAY 'OLE OLE'** *WEA 089CD*	18	3
27 May 95	**1 POLISH 2 BISCUITS AND A FISH SANDWICH** *Eternal 0630105852*	56	5
30 Dec 95	**THE PARTY ALBUM** *Eternal 0630127812*	41	4

[1] Molella featuring the Outhere Brothers

'The Party Album' is a sanitised version of '1 Polish 2 Biscuits And A Fish Sandwich'

OUTKAST *US, male rap / vocal duo – Andre Benjamin and Antoine Patton (Singles: 36 weeks, Albums: 25 weeks)*

Date	Title / Label	pos	wks
23 Dec 00	**B.O.B (BOMBS OVER BAGHDAD)** *LaFace / Arista 74321822942*	61	1
3 Feb 01	**MS JACKSON (import)** *LaFace 73008245252*	48	4
3 Mar 01 ●	**MS JACKSON** *LaFace / Arista 74321836822* ▲	2	10
9 Jun 01	**SO FRESH, SO CLEAN** *LaFace / Arista 74321863402*	16	8
6 Apr 02	**THE WHOLE WORLD** *LaFace 74321917592* [1]	19	5
27 Jul 02	**LAND OF A MILLION DRUMS** *Atlantic AT 0134CD* [2]	46	1
4 Oct 03	**GHETTO MUSICK** *Arista 82876567232*	55	1
22 Nov 03 ●	**HEY YA!** *Arista 82876579532* ▲	6	6+
20 Jan 01 ●	**STANKONIA** *LaFace 73008260722*	10	13
11 Oct 03	**SPEAKERBOXXX / THE LOVE BELOW** *Arista 82876529052* ▲	44	12+

[1] Outkast featuring Killer Mike [2] Outkast featuring Killer Mike and Sleepy Brown

OUTLANDER *Belgium, male producer – Marcos Salon (Singles: 3 weeks)*

Date	Title / Label	pos	wks
31 Aug 91	**VAMP** *R&S RSUK 1*	51	2
7 Feb 98	**THE VAMP (REVAMPED)** *R&S RS 97113CDX*	62	1

OUTLANDISH *Morocco / Pakistan / Honduras, male rap / production trio (Singles: 2 weeks)*

Date	Title / Label	pos	wks
31 May 03	**GUANTANAMO** *RCA 82876517702*	31	2

OUTLAWS *UK, male instrumental group (Singles: 4 weeks)*

Date	Title / Label	pos	wks
13 Apr 61	**SWINGIN' LOW** *HMV POP 844*	46	2
8 Jun 61	**AMBUSH** *HMV POP 877*	43	2

See also Mike BERRY

OUTLAWZ – *See* 2PAC

OUTRAGE *US, male vocalist (Singles: 2 weeks)*

Date	Title / Label	pos	wks
11 Mar 95	**TALL 'N' HANDSOME** *Effective ECFL 001CD*	57	1
23 Nov 96	**TALL 'N' HANDSOME (re-mix)** *Positiva CDTIV 64*	51	1

OUTSIDAZ featuring Rah DIGGA and Melanie BLATT *US, male rap group with female rapper and UK, female vocalist (Singles: 2 weeks)*

Date	Title / Label	pos	wks
2 Mar 02	**I'M LEAVIN'** *Rufflife RLCDM 03*	41	2

OVERLANDERS *UK, male vocal / instrumental group – lead vocal Paul Arnold (Singles: 10 weeks)*

Date	Title / Label	pos	wks
13 Jan 66 ★	**MICHELLE** *Pye 7N 17034*	1	10

OVERLORD X *UK, male rapper (Albums: 1 week)*

Date	Title / Label	pos	wks
4 Feb 89	**WEAPON IS MY LYRIC** *Mango Street ILPS 9924*	68	1

OVERWEIGHT POOCH featuring Ce Ce PENISTON *US, female rapper and female vocalist (Singles: 2 weeks)*

Date	Title / Label	pos	wks
18 Jan 92	**I LIKE IT** *A&M AM 847*	58	2

Mark OWEN *UK, male vocalist (Singles: 35 weeks, Albums: 12 weeks)*

Date	Title / Label	pos	wks
30 Nov 96 ●	**CHILD (re)** *RCA 74321424422*	3	15
15 Feb 97 ●	**CLEMENTINE** *RCA 74321454982*	3	6
23 Aug 97	**I AM WHAT I AM** *RCA 74321501222*	29	3
16 Aug 03 ●	**FOUR MINUTE WARNING** *Universal MCSTD 40329*	4	9
8 Nov 03	**ALONE WITHOUT YOU** *Universal MCSTD 40342*	26	2
14 Dec 96	**GREEN MAN** *RCA 74321435142*	33	11
15 Nov 03	**IN YOUR OWN TIME** *Universal MCD 60092*	59	1

See also TAKE THAT

Reg OWEN and His ORCHESTRA *UK, orchestra, leader d. 1978 (Singles: 10 weeks)*

Date	Title / Label	pos	wks
27 Feb 59	**MANHATTAN SPIRITUAL** *Pye International 7N 25009*	20	8
27 Oct 60	**OBSESSION** *Palette PG 9004*	43	2

Sid OWEN *UK, male actor / vocalist (Singles: 6 weeks)*

Date	Title / Label	pos	wks
16 Dec 95	**BETTER BELIEVE IT (CHILDREN IN NEED)** *Trinity TDM 001CD* [1]	60	1
8 Jul 00	**GOOD THING GOING** *Mushroom MUSH 74CDS*	14	5

[1] Sid Owen and Patsy Palmer

Robert OWENS *US, male vocalist (Singles: 6 weeks)*

Date	Title / Label	pos	wks
7 Dec 91	**I'LL BE YOUR FRIEND** *Perfecto PB 45161*	75	2
26 Apr 97	**I'LL BE YOUR FRIEND (re-mix)** *Perfecto PERF 137CD1*	25	2
24 Feb 01	**MINE TO GIVE** *Science QEDCD 10* [1]	44	1
15 Feb 03	**LAST NIGHT A DJ BLEW MY MIND** *Illustrious CDILL 013* [2]	34	1

[1] Photek featuring Robert Owens [2] Fab For featuring Robert Owens

OXIDE & NEUTRINO *UK, male production / rap duo – Alex Rivers and Mark Oseitutu (Singles: 45 weeks, Albums: 22 weeks)*

Date	Title / Label	pos	wks
6 May 00 ★	**BOUND 4 DA RELOAD (CASUALTY)** *East West OXIDE 01CD1* ■	1	11
30 Dec 00 ●	**NO GOOD 4 ME** *East West OXIDE 02CD* [1]	6	8
26 May 01 ●	**UP MIDDLE FINGER** *East West OXIDE 03CD*	7	7
28 Jul 01	**DEVIL'S NIGHTMARE** *East West OXIDE 07CD1*	16	5
8 Dec 01	**RAP DIS / ONLY WANNA KNOW U COS URE FAMOUS** *East West OXIDE 08CD*	12	8
28 Sep 02 ●	**DEM GIRLZ (I DON'T KNOW WHY) (re)** *East West OXIDE 09CD1* [2]	10	6
6 May 00	**BOUND 4 DA RELOAD (CASUALTY)** *East West OXIDE 01T*	71	1
9 Jun 01	**EXECUTE** *East West 8573885592*	11	19
12 Oct 02	**2 STEPZ AHEAD** *East West 5046607562*	28	2

[1] Oxide & Neutrino featuring Megaman, Romeo and Lisa Maffia [2] Oxide & Neutrino featuring Kowdean

The double 12-inch vinyl format of the act's No.1 hit was ineligible for the singles chart but sales were sufficient to qualify for a place on the album chart

OXYGEN featuring Andrea BRITTON
UK, male production duo and female vocalist (Singles: 3 weeks)

		pos	wks
11 Jan 03	**AM I ON YOUR MIND** *Innocent SINCD 40*	30	3

See also ASCENSION; CHAKRA; ESSENCE; LUSTRAL; SPACE BROTHERS

OZOMATLI *US, male vocal / instrumental group (Singles: 2 weeks)*

		pos	wks
20 Mar 99	**CUT CHEMIST SUITE** *Almo Sounds CDALM 62*	58	1
22 May 99	**SUPER BOWL SUNDAE** *Almo Sounds CDALM 63*	68	1

OZRIC TENTACLES
UK, male instrumental / vocal group (Albums: 7 weeks)

		pos	wks
31 Aug 91	**STRANGEITUDE** *Dovetail DOVELP 3*	70	1
1 May 93	**JURASSIC SHIFT** *Dovetail DOVECD 6*	11	4
9 Jul 94	**ARBORESCENCE** *Dovetail DOVECD 7*	18	2

Jazzi P *UK, female rapper – Pauline Bennett (Singles: 12 weeks)*

		pos	wks
8 Jul 89	**GET LOOSE** *Breakout USA 659* [1]	25	6
9 Jun 90	**FEEL THE RHYTHM** *A&M USA 691*	51	2
3 Aug 91	**REBEL WOMAN** *DNA 7DNA 001* [2]	42	4

[1] LA Mix featuring Jazzi P [2] DNA featuring Jazzi P

PF PROJECT featuring Ewan McGREGOR
UK, male production duo – Jamie White and Moussa Clarke and UK, male actor (Singles: 11 weeks)

		pos	wks
15 Nov 97 ●	**CHOOSE LIFE** *Positiva CDTIV 84*	6	11

See also TZANT; MUSIQUE vs U2

PhD *UK, male vocal / instrumental trio – leader Jim Diamond (Singles: 14 weeks, Albums: 8 weeks)*

		pos	wks
3 Apr 82 ●	**I WON'T LET YOU DOWN** *WEA K 79209*	3	14
1 May 82	**PHD** *WEA K 99150*	33	8

See also Jim DIAMOND

P.I.L. – See PUBLIC IMAGE LTD

PJ *Canada, male producer – Paul Jacobs (Singles: 2 weeks)*

		pos	wks
20 Sep 97	**HAPPY DAYS** *Deconstruction 74321511822*	72	1
4 Sep 99	**HAPPY DAYS (re-mix)** *Defected DEFECT 6CDS*	57	1

PJ and DUNCAN – See ANT & DEC

PJB featuring HANNAH and her SISTERS *Germany, male production group and US, female vocalists (Singles: 8 weeks)*

		pos	wks
14 Sep 91	**BRIDGE OVER TROUBLED WATER** *Dance Pool 6565467*	21	8

See also Hannah JONES

PKA *UK, male producer – Phil Kelsey (Singles: 2 weeks)*

		pos	wks
20 Apr 91	**TEMPERATURE RISING** *Stress SS 4*	68	1
7 Mar 92	**POWERGEN (ONLY YOUR LOVE)** *Stress PKA 1*	70	1

PM DAWN *US, male vocal / instrumental / rap duo – Attrell and Jarrett Cordes (Singles: 39 weeks, Albums: 17 weeks)*

		pos	wks
8 Jun 91	**A WATCHER'S POINT OF VIEW (DON'T CHA THINK)** *Gee Street GEE 32*	36	5
17 Aug 91 ●	**SET ADRIFT ON MEMORY BLISS** *Gee Street GEE 33* ▲	3	8
19 Oct 91	**PAPER DOLL** *Gee Street GEE 35*	49	3
22 Feb 92	**REALITY USED TO BE A FRIEND OF MINE** *Gee Street GEE 37*	29	4
7 Nov 92	**I'D DIE WITHOUT YOU** *Gee Street GEE 39*	30	5
13 Mar 93	**LOOKING THROUGH PATIENT EYES** *Gee Street GESCD 47*	11	7
12 Jun 93	**MORE THAN LIKELY** *Gee Street GESCD 49* [1]	40	3
30 Sep 95	**DOWNTOWN VENUS** *Gee Street GESCD 63*	58	2
6 Apr 96	**SOMETIMES I MISS YOU SO MUCH** *Gee Street GESCD 65*	58	1
31 Oct 98	**GOTTA BE...MOVIN' ON UP** *Gee Street GEE 5003933* [2]	68	1
14 Sep 91 ●	**OF THE HEART OF THE SOUL AND OF THE CROSS** *Gee Street GEEA 7*	8	12
3 Apr 93 ●	**THE BLISS ALBUM ... ?** *Gee Street GEED 9*	9	5

[1] PM Dawn featuring Boy George [2] PM Dawn featuring Ky-Mani

POB featuring DJ Patrick REID *UK, male producer – Paul Brogden and male DJ (Singles: 1 week)*

		pos	wks
11 Dec 99	**BLUEBOTTLE / FLY** *Platipus PLAT 63CD*	74	1

P.O.D. *US, male vocal / instrumental group (Singles: 9 weeks, Albums: 6 weeks)*

		pos	wks
2 Feb 02	**ALIVE** *Atlantic AT 0119CD*	19	6
18 May 02	**YOUTH OF THE NATION** *Atlantic AT 0127CD*	36	2
7 Jun 03	**SLEEPING AWAKE** *Maverick W 608CD*	42	1
19 Jan 02	**SATELLITE** *Atlantic 7567834752*	16	6

P.O.V. featuring JADE *US, male vocal group and female vocal group (Singles: 3 weeks)*

		pos	wks
5 Feb 94	**ALL THRU THE NITE** *Giant 74321187552*	32	3

PPK *Russia, male production / instrumental duo – Sergey Pimenov and Alexander Polyakov (Singles: 17 weeks)*

		pos	wks
8 Dec 01 ●	**RESURECTION** *Perfecto PERF 32CDS*	3	15
26 Oct 02	**RELOAD** *Perfecto PERF 41CDS*	39	2

PQM featuring CICA
US, male producer and female vocalist (Singles: 1 week)

		pos	wks
9 Dec 00	**THE FLYING SONG** *Renaissance / Yoshitoshi RENCDS 004*	68	1

PSG – See COLOUR GIRL

Petey PABLO *US, male rapper (Singles: 1 week)*

		pos	wks
9 Feb 02	**I** *Jive 9253092*	51	1

Thom PACE *US, male vocalist (Singles: 15 weeks)*

		pos	wks
19 May 79	**MAYBE** *RSO 34*	14	15

PACEMAKERS – See GERRY and the PACEMAKERS

PACIFICA *UK, male production duo (Singles: 1 week)*

		pos	wks
31 Jul 99	**LOST IN THE TRANSLATION** *Wildstar CDWILD 25*	54	1

PACK featuring Nigel BENN *UK, male vocal / instrumental group and boxer / rapper (Singles: 2 weeks)*

		pos	wks
8 Dec 90	**STAND AND FIGHT** *IQ ZB 44237*	61	2

PACKABEATS *UK, male instrumental group (Singles: 1 week)* pos/wks

23 Feb 61 **GYPSY BEAT** *Parlophone R 4729* 49 1

José PADILLA featuring Angela JOHN
Spain, male DJ and UK, female vocalist (Singles: 1 week) pos/wks

8 Aug 98 **WHO DO YOU LOVE** *Manifesto FESCD 45* 59 1

PAFFENDORF *Germany, male production duo – Gottfried Engels and Ramon Zenker (Singles: 8 weeks)* pos/wks

15 Jun 02 ● **BE COOL** *Data DATA 29CDS* 7 7
26 Apr 03 **CRAZY SEXY MARVELLOUS** *Data / MoS DATA 51CDS* 52 1

PAGANINI TRAXX *Italy, male DJ / producer (Singles: 1 week)* pos/wks

1 Feb 97 **ZOE** *Sony S3 DANUCD 18X* 47 1

Jimmy PAGE *UK, male instrumentalist – guitar (Singles: 16 weeks, Albums: 37 weeks)* pos/wks

17 Dec 94 **GALLOWS POLE** *Fontana PPCD 2* [1] 35 3
11 Apr 98 **MOST HIGH** *Mercury 5687512* [2] 26 2
1 Aug 98 **COME WITH ME (import)** *Epic 34K78954* [3] 75 1
8 Aug 98 ● **COME WITH ME** *Epic 6662842* [3] 2 10
27 Feb 82 **DEATH WISH II (FILM SOUNDTRACK)** *Swansong SSK 59415* 40 4
16 Mar 85 **WHATEVER HAPPENED TO JUGULA?** *Beggars Banquet BEGA 60* [1] 44 4
2 Jul 88 **OUTRIDER** *Geffen WX 155* 27 6
19 Nov 94 ● **NO QUARTER** *Fontana 5263622* [2] 7 13
2 May 98 ● **WALKING INTO CLARKSDALE** *Mercury 5580252* [2] 3 6
22 Jul 00 **LIVE AT THE GREEK** *SPV Recordings SPV 09172022* [3] 39 4

[1] Jimmy Page and Robert Plant [2] Page and Plant [3] Puff Daddy featuring Jimmy Page [1] Roy Harper with Jimmy Page [2] Jimmy Page and Robert Plant [3] Jimmy Page and the Black Crowes

See also LED ZEPPELIN; COVERDALE PAGE

Patti PAGE
US, female vocalist – Clara Ann Fowler (Singles: 5 weeks) pos/wks

27 Mar 53 ● **(HOW MUCH IS) THAT DOGGIE IN THE WINDOW** *Oriole CB 1156* ▲ 9 5

Tommy PAGE
US, male vocalist (Singles: 3 weeks) pos/wks

26 May 90 **I'LL BE YOUR EVERYTHING** *Sire W 9959* ▲ 53 3

Wendy PAGE – *See TIN TIN OUT*

PAGLIARO
Canada, male vocalist – Michel Pagliaro (Singles: 6 weeks) pos/wks

19 Feb 72 **LOVING YOU AIN'T EASY** *Pye 7N 45111* 31 6

PAID & LIVE featuring Lauryn HILL *US, male production duo and female rapper / vocalist (Singles: 1 week)* pos/wks

27 Dec 97 **ALL MY TIME** *World Entertainment OWECD 2* 57 1

See also Lauryn HILL

Elaine PAIGE (337 Top 500) *Revered actor / vocalist who has been a West End stage regular for 40 years, b. Elaine Bickerstaff, 5 Mar 1948, London. The entertainer, who will be for ever associated with Lloyd Webber / Rice musicals, had the biggest hit of the 600 recordings of 'Memory' (Singles: 41 weeks, Albums: 155 weeks)* pos/wks

21 Oct 78 **DON'T WALK AWAY TILL I TOUCH YOU** *EMI 2862* 46 5
6 Jun 81 ● **MEMORY (re)** *Polydor POSP 279* 6 15
14 Apr 84 **SOMETIMES (THEME FROM 'CHAMPIONS')** *Island IS 174* 72 1
5 Jan 85 ★ **I KNOW HIM SO WELL** *RCA CHESS 3* [1] 1 16
21 Nov 87 **THE SECOND TIME (THEME FROM 'BILITIS')** *WEA YZ 163* 69 1
21 Jan 95 **HYMNE À L'AMOUR (IF YOU LOVE ME)** *WEA YZ 899CD* 68 1
24 Oct 98 **MEMORY (re-recording)** *WEA WEA 197CD* 36 2
1 May 82 **ELAINE PAIGE** *WEA K 58385* 56 6
5 Nov 83 ● **STAGES** *K-Tel NE 1262* 2 48
20 Oct 84 **CINEMA** *K-Tel NE 1282* 12 25
16 Nov 85 ● **LOVE HURTS** *WEA WX 28* 8 20
29 Nov 86 **CHRISTMAS** *WEA WX 80* 27 6
5 Dec 87 **MEMORIES – THE BEST OF ELAINE PAIGE** *Telstar STAR 2313* 14 15
19 Nov 88 **THE QUEEN ALBUM** *Siren SRNLP 22* 51 8
27 Apr 91 **LOVE CAN DO THAT** *RCA PL 74932* 36 4
28 Nov 92 **THE BEST OF ELAINE PAIGE AND BARBARA DICKSON** *Telstar TCD 2632* [1] 22 9
10 Apr 93 **ROMANCE AND THE STAGE** *RCA 74321136152* 71 1
19 Nov 94 **PIAF** *WEA 4509946412* 46 3
1 Jul 95 **ENCORE** *WEA 0630104762* 20 6
28 Nov 98 **ON REFLECTION – THE VERY BEST OF ELAINE PAIGE** *Telstar TV/WEA TTVCD 2999* 60 4

[1] Elaine Paige and Barbara Dickson [1] Elaine Paige and Barbara Dickson

Hal PAIGE and the WHALERS
US, male vocal / instrumental group (Singles: 1 week) pos/wks

25 Aug 60 **GOING BACK TO MY HOME TOWN** *Melodisc MEL 1553* 50 1

Jennifer PAIGE
US, female vocalist (Singles: 13 weeks, Albums: 1 week) pos/wks

12 Sep 98 ● **CRUSH** *EAR 0039425* 4 12
20 Mar 99 **SOBER** *EAR / Edel 0044185 ERE* 68 1
31 Oct 98 **JENNIFER PAIGE** *E.A.R. 0039842 ERE* 67 1

Orchestre de Chambre Jean-François PAILLARD
France, male conductor and orchestra (Singles: 3 weeks) pos/wks

20 Aug 88 **THEME FROM 'VIETNAM' (CANON IN D)** *Debut DEBT 3053* 61 3

PALE
Ireland, male vocal / instrumental group (Singles: 2 weeks) pos/wks

13 Jun 92 **DOGS WITH NO TAILS** *A&M AM 866* 51 2

PALE FOUNTAINS *UK, male vocal / instrumental group (Singles: 6 weeks, Albums: 3 weeks)* pos/wks

27 Nov 82 **THANK YOU** *Virgin VS 557* 48 6
10 Mar 84 **PACIFIC STREET** *Virgin V 2274* 85 2
16 Feb 85 **FROM ACROSS THE KITCHEN TABLE** *Virgin V 2333* 94 1

PALE SAINTS *UK, male / female vocal / instrumental group (Singles: 1 week, Albums: 3 weeks)* pos/wks

6 Jul 91 **KINKY LOVE** *4AD AD 1009* 72 1
24 Feb 90 **THE COMFORTS OF MADNESS** *4AD CAD 0002* 40 2
4 Apr 92 **IN RIBBONS** *4AD CAD 2004CD* 61 1

PALE X *Holland, male producer (Singles: 1 week)* pos/wks

3 Feb 01 **NITRO** *Nukleuz NUKP 0280* 74 1

PALLAS
UK, male vocal / instrumental group (Albums: 4 weeks) pos/wks

25 Feb 84 **SENTINEL** *Harvest SHSP 2400121* 41 3
22 Feb 86 **THE WEDGE** *Harvest SHVL 850* 70 1

Nerina PALLOT
UK, female vocalist (Singles: 1 week) pos/wks

18 Aug 01 **PATIENCE** *Polydor 5872122* 61 1

Barry PALMER – *See Mike OLDFIELD; KENNY*

Jhay PALMER featuring MC IMAGE
UK, male producer / vocalist and male rapper (Singles: 1 week) pos/wks

27 Apr 02 **HELLO** *Bagatrix CDBTX 002* 69 1

Patsy PALMER – *See Sid OWEN*

Robert PALMER (196 Top 500)

Grammy-winning UK rock-group veteran and former member of Vinegar Joe, b. 19 Jan 1949, Yorkshire, d. 26 Sep 2003. This vocalist's hottest run of transatlantic hits came after he fronted short-lived Anglo-American supergroup Power Station in 1985. He benefited from some striking award-winning videos featuring an all-female backing band (parodied in a 1999 Shania Twain video) (Singles: 129 weeks, Albums: 166 weeks) pos/wks

Date		Title / Label	pos	wks
20 May 78		**EVERY KINDA PEOPLE** *Island WIP 6425*	53	4
7 Jul 79		**BAD CASE OF LOVIN' YOU (DOCTOR DOCTOR)** *Island WIP 6481*	61	2
6 Sep 80		**JOHNNY AND MARY** *Island WIP 6638*	44	8
22 Nov 80		**LOOKING FOR CLUES** *Island WIP 6651*	33	9
13 Feb 82		**SOME GUYS HAVE ALL THE LUCK** *Island WIP 6754*	16	8
2 Apr 83		**YOU ARE IN MY SYSTEM** *Island IS 104*	53	4
18 Jun 83		**YOU CAN HAVE IT (TAKE MY HEART)** *Island IS 121*	66	2
10 May 86	●	**ADDICTED TO LOVE** *Island IS 270* ▲	5	15
19 Jul 86	●	**I DIDN'T MEAN TO TURN YOU ON** *Island IS 283*	9	9
1 Nov 86		**DISCIPLINE OF LOVE** *Island IS 242*	68	1
26 Mar 88		**SWEET LIES** *Island IS 352*	58	3
11 Jun 88		**SIMPLY IRRESISTABLE** *EMI EM 61*	44	4
15 Oct 88	●	**SHE MAKES MY DAY** *EMI EM 65*	6	12
13 May 89		**CHANGE HIS WAYS** *EMI EM 85*	28	7
26 Aug 89		**IT COULD HAPPEN TO YOU** *EMI EM 99*	71	1
3 Nov 90	●	**I'LL BE YOUR BABY TONIGHT** *EMI EM 167* [1]	6	10
5 Jan 91	●	**MERCY MERCY ME – I WANT YOU** *EMI EM 173*	9	9
15 Jun 91		**DREAMS TO REMEMBER** *EMI EM 193*	68	1
7 Mar 92		**EVERY KINDA PEOPLE (re-mix)** *Island IS 498*	43	3
17 Oct 92		**WITCHCRAFT** *EMI EM 251*	50	3
9 Jul 94		**GIRL U WANT** *EMI CDEMS 331*	57	2
3 Sep 94		**KNOW BY NOW** *EMI CDEMS 343*	25	5
24 Dec 94		**YOU BLOW ME AWAY** *EMI CDEMS 350*	38	4
14 Oct 95		**RESPECT YOURSELF** *EMI CDEMS 399*	45	2
18 Jan 03		**ADDICTED TO LOVE** *Serious SER 060CD* [2]	42	1
6 Nov 76		**SOME PEOPLE CAN DO WHAT THEY LIKE** *Island ILPS 9420*	46	1
14 Jul 79		**SECRETS** *Island ILPS 9544*	54	4
6 Sep 80		**CLUES** *Island ILPS 9595*	31	8
3 Apr 82		**MAYBE IT'S LIVE** *Island ILPS 9665*	32	6
23 Apr 83		**PRIDE** *Island ILPS 9720*	37	9
16 Nov 85	●	**RIPTIDE** *Island ILPS 9801*	5	37
9 Jul 88		**HEAVY NOVA** *EMI EMD 1007*	17	25
11 Nov 89	●	**ADDICTIONS VOLUME 1** *Island ILPS 9944*	7	17
17 Nov 90	●	**DON'T EXPLAIN** *EMI EMDX 1018*	9	20
4 Apr 92		**ADDICTIONS VOLUME 2** *Island CIDTV 4*	12	7
31 Oct 92		**RIDIN' HIGH** *EMI CDEMD 1038*	32	3
24 Sep 94		**HONEY** *EMI CDEMD 1069*	25	4
28 Oct 95	●	**THE VERY BEST OF ROBERT PALMER** *EMI CDEMD 1088*	4	21
16 Nov 02		**AT HIS VERY BEST** *Universal TV 697812*	38	4

[1] Robert Palmer and UB40 [2] Shake B4 Use vs Robert Palmer

Suzanne PALMER – *See ABSOLUTE; CLUB 69; DJ TIESTO*

Tyrone 'Visionary' PALMER – *See SLAM*

PAN POSITION

Italy / Venezuela, male instrumental / production group (Singles: 1 week) pos/wks

Date		Title / Label	pos	wks
18 Jun 94		**ELEPHANT PAW (GET DOWN TO THE FUNK)** *Positiva CDTIV 13*	55	1

PANDORA'S BOX

US, male / female vocal / instrumental group (Singles: 3 weeks) pos/wks

Date		Title / Label	pos	wks
21 Oct 89		**IT'S ALL COMING BACK TO ME NOW** *Virgin VS 1216*	51	3

Darryl PANDY

US, male vocalist (Singles: 5 weeks) pos/wks

Date		Title / Label	pos	wks
14 Dec 96		**LOVE CAN'T TURN AROUND** *4 Liberty LIBTCD 27* [1]	40	2
20 Feb 99		**RAISE YOUR HANDS** *VC Recordings VCRD 44* [2]	40	2
2 Oct 99		**SUNSHINE & HAPPINESS** *Azuli AZNYCD 103* [3]	68	1

[1] Farley 'Jackmaster' Funk with Darryl Pandy [2] Big Room Girl featuring Darryl Pandy [3] Darryl Pandy / Nerio's Dubwork

Johnny PANIC and the BIBLE OF DREAMS

UK, male / female vocal / instrumental group (Singles: 2 weeks) pos/wks

Date		Title / Label	pos	wks
2 Feb 91		**JOHNNY PANIC AND THE BIBLE OF DREAMS** *Fontana PANIC 1*	70	2

See also TEARS FOR FEARS

PANJABI MC

UK, male DJ / producer – Rajinder Rai (Singles: 19 weeks) pos/wks

Date		Title / Label	pos	wks
4 Jan 03		**MUNDIAN TO BACH KE (import)** *Big Star BIG CDMO 76*	59	3
25 Jan 03	●	**MUNDIAN TO BACH KE** *Showbiz / Instant Karma KARMA 28CD*	5	13
5 Jul 03		**JOGI / BEWARE OF THE BOYS** *Showbiz / Dharma DHARMA 1 CDS* [1]	25	3

[1] Panjabi MC / Panjabi MC featuring Jay-Z

PANTERA

US, male vocal / instrumental group (Singles: 8 weeks, Albums: 10 weeks) pos/wks

Date		Title / Label	pos	wks
10 Oct 92		**MOUTH FOR WAR** *Atco A 5845T*	73	1
27 Feb 93		**WALK** *Atco B 6076CD*	35	2
19 Mar 94		**I'M BROKEN** *Atco B 5932CD1*	19	2
22 Oct 94		**PLANET CARAVAN** *East West A 5836CD1*	26	3
7 Mar 92		**VULGAR DISPLAY OF POWER** *Atco 7567917582*	64	1
2 Apr 94	●	**FAR BEYOND DRIVEN** *Atco 7567923752* ▲	3	4
18 May 96		**THE GREAT SOUTHERN TRENDKILL** *East West 7559619082*	17	3
30 Aug 97		**OFFICIAL LIVE – 101 PROOF** *East West 7559620682*	54	1
8 Apr 00		**REINVENTING THE STEEL** *Elektra 7559624512*	33	1

PAPA ROACH

US, male vocal / instrumental group (Singles: 25 weeks, Albums: 43 weeks) pos/wks

Date		Title / Label	pos	wks
17 Feb 01	●	**LAST RESORT** *Dreamworks / Polydor 4509212*	3	10
5 May 01		**BETWEEN ANGELS & INSECTS** *Dreamworks / Polydor 4509082*	17	6
22 Jun 02		**SHE LOVES ME NOT** *Dreamworks / Polydor 4508182*	14	8
2 Nov 02		**TIME AND TIME AGAIN** *Dreamworks / Polydor 4508052*	54	1
13 Jan 01	●	**INFEST** *Dreamworks 4502232*	9	36
29 Jun 02	●	**LOVEHATETRAGEDY** *Dreamworks 4503672*	4	7

PAPER DOLLS

UK, female vocal group (Singles: 13 weeks) pos/wks

Date		Title / Label	pos	wks
13 Mar 68		**SOMETHING HERE IN MY HEART (KEEPS A-TELLIN' ME NO)** *Pye 7N 17456*	11	13

PAPER LACE

UK, male vocal / instrumental group – lead vocal Phil Wright (Singles: 41 weeks) pos/wks

Date		Title / Label	pos	wks
23 Feb 74	★	**BILLY DON'T BE A HERO** *Bus Stop BUS 1014*	1	14
4 May 74	●	**THE NIGHT CHICAGO DIED** *Bus Stop BUS 1016* ▲	3	11
24 Aug 74		**THE BLACK EYED BOYS** *Bus Stop BUS 1019*	11	10
4 Mar 78		**WE GOT THE WHOLE WORLD IN OUR HANDS** *Warner Bros. K 17110* [1]	24	6

[1] Nottingham Forest with Paper Lace

PAPERDOLLS

UK, female vocal group (Singles: 1 week) pos/wks

Date		Title / Label	pos	wks
12 Sep 98		**GONNA MAKE YOU BLUSH** *MCA MCSTD 40175*	65	1

PAPPA BEAR featuring VAN DER TOORN

Germany, male rapper and Holland, male vocalist (Singles: 1 week) pos/wks

Date		Title / Label	pos	wks
16 May 98		**CHERISH** *Universal UMD 70316*	47	1

PAR-T-ONE vs INXS

Italy, male production trio and Australia, male vocal / instrumental group (Singles: 6 weeks) pos/wks

Date		Title / Label	pos	wks
3 Nov 01		**I'M SO CRAZY (re)** *Credence CDCRED 016*	19	6

Vanessa PARADIS

France, female vocalist (Singles: 30 weeks, Albums: 2 weeks) pos/wks

Date		Title / Label	pos	wks
13 Feb 88	●	**JOE LE TAXI** *FA Productions POSP 902*	3	10
10 Oct 92	●	**BE MY BABY** *Remark PO 235*	6	15
27 Feb 93		**SUNDAY MONDAYS** *Remark PZCD 251*	49	4
24 Jul 93		**JUST AS LONG AS YOU ARE THERE** *Remark PZCD 272*	57	1
7 Nov 92		**VANESSA PARADIS** *Remark 5139542*	45	2

PARADISE *UK, male vocal / instrumental group (Singles: 4 weeks)* pos/wks

10 Sep 83 **ONE MIND, TWO HEARTS** *Priority P 1* ... **42** 4

PARADISE LOST *UK, male vocal / instrumental group (Singles: 3 weeks, Albums: 6 weeks)* pos/wks

20 May 95 **THE LAST TIME** *Music for Nations CDKUT 165* ... **60** 1
7 Oct 95 **FOREVER FAILURE** *Music for Nations CDKUT 169* ... **66** 1
28 Jun 97 **SAY JUST WORDS** *Music for Nations CDKUT 174* ... **53** 1
24 Jun 95 DRACONIAN TIMES *Music For Nations CDMFNX 184* ... 16 3
26 Jul 97 ONE SECOND *Music For Nations CDMFNX 222* ... 31 2
19 Jun 99 HOST *EMI 5205672* ... 61 1

PARADISE ORGANISATION
UK, male instrumental / production group (Singles: 1 week) pos/wks

23 Jan 93 **PRAYER TOWER** *Cowboy RODEO 13* ... **70** 1

PARADOX *UK, male instrumental duo (Singles: 2 weeks)* pos/wks

24 Feb 90 **JAILBREAK** *Ronin 7R2* ... **66** 2

Norrie PARAMOR
UK, orchestra, leader – d. 9 Sep 1979 (Singles: 8 weeks) pos/wks

17 Mar 60 **THEME FROM 'A SUMMER PLACE'** *Columbia DB 4419* ... **36** 2
22 Mar 62 **THEME FROM 'Z CARS'** *Columbia DB 4789* ... **33** 6

PARAMOUNT JAZZ BAND – See Acker BILK

PARAMOUNTS
UK, male vocal / instrumental group (Singles: 7 weeks) pos/wks

16 Jan 64 **POISON IVY** *Parlophone R 5093* ... **35** 7

PARCHMENT
UK, male / female vocal / instrumental group (Singles: 5 weeks) pos/wks

16 Sep 72 **LIGHT UP THE FIRE** *Pye 7N 45178* ... **31** 5

PARIS *UK, male / female vocal group (Singles: 4 weeks)* pos/wks

19 Jun 82 **NO GETTING OVER YOU** *RCA 222* ... **49** 4

PARIS *US, male vocalist – Oscar Jackson (Singles: 2 weeks)* pos/wks

21 Jan 95 **GUERRILLA FUNK** *Priority PTYCD 100* ... **38** 2

Mica PARIS *UK, female vocalist – Michelle Wallen (Singles: 63 weeks, Albums: 40 weeks)* pos/wks

7 May 88 ● **MY ONE TEMPTATION** *Fourth & Broadway BRW 85* ... **7** 11
30 Jul 88 **LIKE DREAMERS DO** *Fourth & Broadway BRW 108* [1] ... **26** 5
22 Oct 88 **BREATHE LIFE INTO ME** *Fourth & Broadway BRW 115* ... **26** 10
21 Jan 89 **WHERE IS THE LOVE** *Fourth & Broadway BRW 122* [2] ... **19** 7
6 Oct 90 **CONTRIBUTION** *Fourth & Broadway BRW 188* ... **33** 4
1 Dec 90 **SOUTH OF THE RIVER** *Fourth & Broadway BRW 199* ... **50** 2
23 Feb 91 **IF I LOVE U 2 NITE** *Fourth & Broadway BRW 207* ... **43** 3
31 Aug 91 **YOUNG SOUL REBELS** *Big Life BLR 57* ... **61** 3
3 Apr 93 **I NEVER FELT LIKE THIS BEFORE** *Fourth & Broadway BRCD 263* ... **15** 5
5 Jun 93 **I WANNA HOLD ON TO YOU** *Fourth & Broadway BRCD 275* ... **27** 3
7 Aug 93 **TWO IN A MILLION** *Fourth & Broadway BRCD 285* ... **51** 2
4 Dec 93 **WHISPER A PRAYER** *Fourth & Broadway BRCD 287* ... **65** 1
8 Apr 95 **ONE** *Cooltempo CDCOOL 304* ... **29** 4
16 May 98 **STAY** *Cooltempo CDCOOL 334* ... **40** 2
14 Nov 98 **BLACK ANGEL** *Cooltempo CDCOOL 341* ... **72** 1
3 Sep 88 ● SO GOOD *Fourth & Broadway BRLP 525* ... 6 32
27 Oct 90 CONTRIBUTION *Fourth & Broadway BRLP 558* ... 26 3
26 Jun 93 WHISPER A PRAYER *Fourth & Broadway BRCD 591* ... 20 4
22 Aug 98 BLACK ANGEL *Cooltempo 4958132* ... 59 1

[1] Mica Paris featuring Courtney Pine [2] Mica Paris and Will Downing

Ryan PARIS
France, male vocalist – Fabio Roscioli (Singles: 10 weeks) pos/wks

3 Sep 83 ● **DOLCE VITA** *Carrere CAR 289* ... **5** 10

PARIS ANGELS *UK, male / female vocal / instrumental group (Singles: 5 weeks, Albums: 2 weeks)* pos/wks

3 Nov 90 **SCOPE** *Sheer Joy SHEER 0047* ... **75** 1
20 Jul 91 **PERFUME** *Virgin VS 1360* ... **55** 3
21 Sep 91 **FADE** *Virgin VS 1365* ... **70** 1
17 Aug 91 SUNDEW *Virgin V 2667* ... 37 2

PARIS RED *US / Germany, male / female vocal / instrumental duo (Singles: 2 weeks)* pos/wks

29 Feb 92 **GOOD FRIEND** *Columbia 6569417* ... **61** 1
15 May 93 **PROMISES** *Columbia 6592342* ... **59** 1

PARIS & SHARP
UK, male production duo (Singles: 1 week) pos/wks

1 Dec 01 **APHRODITE** *Cream / Parlophone CREAM 16CD* ... **61** 1

John PARISH and Polly Jean HARVEY *US, male producer / instrumentalist and UK, female vocalist (Singles: 1 week)* pos/wks

23 Nov 96 **THAT WAS MY VEIL** *Island CID 648* ... **75** 1

See also PJ HARVEY

Simon PARK ORCHESTRA
UK, orchestra (Singles: 24 weeks) pos/wks

25 Nov 72 ★ **EYE LEVEL (THEME FROM THE TV SERIES 'VAN DER VALK') (re)** *Columbia DB 8946* ◆ ... **1** 24

'Eye Level' made No.41 on its original visit to the chart before re-entering and peaking at No.1 in Sep 1973

Graham PARKER and the RUMOUR *UK, male vocal / instrumental group (Singles: 16 weeks, Albums: 35 weeks)* pos/wks

19 Mar 77 **THE PINK PARKER EP** *Vertigo PARK 001* ... **24** 5
22 Apr 78 **HEY LORD, DON'T ASK ME QUESTIONS** *Vertigo PARK 002* ... **32** 7
20 Mar 82 **TEMPORARY BEAUTY** *RCA PARK 100* [1] ... **50** 4
27 Nov 76 HEAT TREATMENT *Vertigo 6360 137* ... 52 2
12 Nov 77 STICK TO ME *Vertigo 9102 017* ... 19 4
27 May 78 PARKERILLA *Vertigo 6641 797* ... 14 5
7 Apr 79 SQUEEZING OUT SPARKS *Vertigo 9102 030* ... 18 8
7 Jun 80 THE UP ESCALATOR *Stiff SEEZ 23* ... 11 10
27 Mar 82 ANOTHER GREY AREA *RCA RCALP 6029* [1] ... 40 6

[1] Graham Parker [1] Graham Parker

Tracks on The Pink Parker EP: Hold Back the Night / (Let Me Get) Sweet on You / White Honey / Soul Shoes

Ray PARKER Jr
US, male vocalist / instrumentalist – guitar (Singles: 47 weeks, Albums: 7 weeks) pos/wks

25 Aug 84 ● **GHOSTBUSTERS** *Arista ARIST 580* ▲ ... **2** 31
18 Jan 86 **GIRLS ARE MORE FUN** *Arista ARIST 641* ... **46** 4
3 Oct 87 **I DON'T THINK THAT MAN SHOULD SLEEP ALONE** *Geffen GEF 27* ... **13** 10
30 Jan 88 **OVER YOU** *Geffen GEF 33* ... **65** 2
10 Oct 87 AFTER DARK *WEA WX 122* ... 40 7

See also RAYDIO

Robert PARKER
US, male vocalist / instrumentalist – saxophone (Singles: 8 weeks) pos/wks

4 Aug 66 **BAREFOOTIN'** *Island WI 286* ... **24** 8

Sara PARKER *US, female vocalist (Singles: 2 weeks)* pos/wks

12 Apr 97 **MY LOVE IS DEEP** *Manifesto FESCD 22* ... **22** 2

Jimmy PARKINSON
Australia, male vocalist (Singles: 19 weeks) pos/wks

2 Mar 56 ● **THE GREAT PRETENDER** *Columbia DB 3729* ... **9** 13
17 Aug 56 **WALK HAND IN HAND (re)** *Columbia DB 3775* ... **26** 2
9 Nov 56 **IN THE MIDDLE OF THE HOUSE (re)** *Columbia DB 3833* ... **20** 4

Alex PARKS

UK, female vocalist (Singles: 5 weeks, Albums: 4 weeks) pos/wks

29 Nov 03 ● **MAYBE THAT'S WHAT IT TAKES** *Polydor 9814581* ....3 5+
6 Dec 03 ● **INTRODUCTION** *Polydor 9866005* ....5 4+

PARKS & WILSON

UK, male production duo – Michael Parks and Michael Wilson (Singles: 1 week) pos/wks

9 Sep 00 **FEEL THE DRUM (EP)** *Hooj Choons HOOJ 099* 71 1

Tracks on Feel the Drum (EP): My Orbit / The Dragon / My Orbit (remix) / Drum Parade (No UFOs)

PARLIAMENT – *See Scott GROOVES*

John PARR

UK, male vocalist (Singles: 22 weeks, Albums: 2 weeks) pos/wks

14 Sep 85 ● **ST ELMO'S FIRE (MAN IN MOTION)** *London LON 73* ▲ 6 13
18 Jan 86 **NAUGHTY NAUGHTY** *London LON 80* 58 3
30 Aug 86 **ROCK 'N' ROLL MERCENARIES** *Arista ARIST 666* [1] 31 6
2 Nov 85 **JOHN PARR** *London LONLP 12* 60 2

[1] Meat Loaf featuring John Parr

Dean PARRISH

US, male vocalist (Singles: 5 weeks) pos/wks

8 Feb 75 **I'M ON MY WAY** *UK USA 2* 38 5

Man PARRISH

US, male DJ / producer (Singles: 26 weeks) pos/wks

26 Mar 83 **HIP HOP, BE BOP (DON'T STOP)** *Polydor POSP 575* 41 6
23 Mar 85 **BOOGIE DOWN (BRONX)** *Boiling Point POSP 731* 56 4
13 Sep 86 ● **MALE STRIPPER (2re)** *Bolts BOLTS 4* [1] 4 16

[1] Man 2 Man meet Man Parrish

'Male Stripper' made No.64 on its first chart visit followed by No.63 in Jan 1987 and No.4 on its second re-entry in Feb 1987

Karen PARRY – *See PASCAL featuring Karen PARRY*

Bill PARSONS

US, male vocalist (Singles: 2 weeks) pos/wks

10 Apr 59 **THE ALL AMERICAN BOY** *London HL 8798* 22 2

Record erroneously credited to Bill Parsons; actual vocalist is Bobby Bare

Alan PARSONS PROJECT

UK, male vocal / instrumental group (Singles: 4 weeks, Albums: 38 weeks) pos/wks

15 Jan 83 **OLD AND WISE** *Arista ARIST 494* [1] 74 1
10 Mar 84 **DON'T ANSWER ME** *Arista ARIST 553* 58 3
28 Aug 76 **TALES OF MYSTERY AND IMAGINATION** *Charisma CDS 4003* 56 1
13 Aug 77 **I ROBOT** *Arista SPARTY 1016* 30 1
10 Jun 78 **PYRAMID** *Arista SPART 1054* 49 4
29 Sep 79 **EVE** *Arista SPARTY 1100* 74 1
15 Nov 80 **THE TURN OF A FRIENDLY CARD** *Arista DLART 1* 38 4
29 May 82 **EYE IN THE SKY** *Arista 204 666* 27 11
26 Nov 83 **THE BEST OF THE ALAN PARSONS PROJECT** *Arista APP 1* 99 1
3 Mar 84 **AMMONIA AVENUE** *Arista 206 100* 24 8
23 Feb 85 **VULTURE CULTURE** *Arista 206 577* 40 5
14 Feb 87 **GAUDI** *Arista 208 084* 66 2

[1] Alan Parsons Project: Lead vocals by Colin Blunstone

PARTISANS

UK, male vocal / instrumental group (Albums: 1 week) pos/wks

19 Feb 83 **THE PARTISANS** *No Future PUNK 4* 94 1

PARTIZAN

UK, male DJ / production duo – 'Tall Paul' Newman and Craig Daniel-Yefet (Singles: 3 weeks) pos/wks

8 Feb 97 **DRIVE ME CRAZY** *Multiply CDMULTY 17* 36 2
6 Dec 97 **KEEP YOUR LOVE** *Multiply CDMULTY 29* [1] 53 1

[1] Partizan featuring Natalie Robb

See also CAMISRA; ESCRIMA; TALL PAUL; GRIFTERS

PARTNERS – *See Al HUDSON*

PARTNERS IN KRYME

US, male rap duo – James Alpem and Richard Usher (Singles: 10 weeks) pos/wks

21 Jul 90 ★ **TURTLE POWER** *SBK TURTLE 1* 1 10

David PARTON

UK, male vocalist (Singles: 9 weeks) pos/wks

15 Jan 77 ● **ISN'T SHE LOVELY** *Pye 7N 45663* 4 9

Dolly PARTON

US, female vocalist / instrumentalist - guitar (Singles: 34 weeks, Albums: 46 weeks) pos/wks

15 May 76 ● **JOLENE** *RCA 2675* 7 10
21 Feb 81 **9 TO 5** *RCA 25* ▲ 47 5
12 Nov 83 ● **ISLANDS IN THE STREAM** *RCA 378* [1] ▲ 7 15
7 Apr 84 **HERE YOU COME AGAIN** *RCA 395* 75 1
16 Apr 94 **THE DAY I FALL IN LOVE** *Columbia 6600282* [2] 64 2
19 Oct 02 **IF** *Sanctuary SANX 139* 73 1
25 Nov 78 **BOTH SIDES** *Lotus WH 5006* 45 12
7 Sep 85 **GREATEST HITS** *RCA PL 84422* 74 1
14 Mar 87 **TRIO** *Warner Bros. 9254911* [1] 60 4
22 Oct 94 **THE GREATEST HITS** *Telstar TCD 2739* 65 2
8 Nov 97 **A LIFE IN MUSIC – ULTIMATE COLLECTION** *RCA 74321443632* 38 3
26 Sep 98 **HUNGRY AGAIN** *MCA Nashville UMD 80522* 41 3
24 Feb 01 **LITTLE SPARROW** *Sanctuary SANCD 074* 30 6
3 Mar 01 **GOLD – GREATEST HITS** *RCA 74321840202* 23 5
20 Jul 02 **HALOS & HORNS** *Sanctuary SANCD 126* 37 4
2 Aug 03 **ULTIMATE** *RCA 82876542012* 17 6

[1] Kenny Rogers and Dolly Parton [2] Dolly Parton and James Ingram
[1] Dolly Parton / Emmylou Harris / Linda Ronstadt

Stella PARTON

US, female vocalist (Singles: 4 weeks) pos/wks

22 Oct 77 **THE DANGER OF A STRANGER** *Elektra K 12272* 35 4

Alan PARTRIDGE

UK, male comedian – Steve Coogan (Albums: 3 weeks) pos/wks

18 Mar 95 **KNOWING ME KNOWING YOU 3** *BBC Canned Laughter ZBBC 1671CD* 41 3

Don PARTRIDGE

UK, male vocalist / instrumentalist – one-man band (Singles: 32 weeks) pos/wks

7 Feb 68 ● **ROSIE** *Columbia DB 8330* 4 12
29 May 68 ● **BLUE EYES** *Columbia DB 8416* 3 13
19 Feb 69 **BREAKFAST ON PLUTO** *Columbia DB 8538* 26 7

PARTRIDGE FAMILY

US, male / female actor / vocal group (Singles: 53 weeks, Albums: 13 weeks) pos/wks

13 Feb 71 **I THINK I LOVE YOU** *Bell 1130* [1] ▲ 18 9
26 Feb 72 **IT'S ONE OF THOSE NIGHTS (YES LOVE)** *Bell 1203* [1] 11 11
8 Jul 72 ● **BREAKING UP IS HARD TO DO** *Bell MABEL 1* [1] 3 13
3 Feb 73 ● **LOOKING THRU THE EYES OF LOVE** *Bell 1278* [2] 9 9
19 May 73 ● **WALKING IN THE RAIN** *Bell 1293* [2] 10 11
8 Jan 72 **UP TO DATE** *Bell SBLL 143* 46 2
22 Apr 72 **THE PARTRIDGE FAMILY SOUND MAGAZINE** *Bell BELLS 206* 14 7
30 Sep 72 **SHOPPING BAG** *Bell BELLS 212* 28 3
9 Dec 72 **CHRISTMAS CARD** *Bell BELLS 214* 45 1

[1] Partridge Family starring Shirley Jones featuring David Cassidy [2] Partridge Family starring David Cassidy

See also David CASSIDY

PARTY ANIMALS

Holland, male instrumental / production duo (Singles: 3 weeks) pos/wks

1 Jun 96 **HAVE YOU EVER BEEN MELLOW** *Mokum DB 17553* 56 1
19 Oct 96 **HAVE YOU EVER BEEN MELLOW (EP)** *Mokum DB 17413* 43 2

Tracks on Have You Ever Been Mellow (EP): Have You Ever Been Mellow / Hava Naquilla / Aquarius

PARTY FAITHFUL

UK, male / female vocal / instrumental group (Singles: 1 week) pos/wks

22 Jul 95 **BRASS: LET THERE BE HOUSE** *Ore AG 10CD* 54 1

PASADENAS
UK, male vocal group (Singles: 57 weeks, Albums: 32 weeks) pos/wks

Date		Title	pos	wks
28 May 88	●	**TRIBUTE (RIGHT ON)** *CBS PASA 1*	5	14
17 Sep 88		**RIDING ON A TRAIN** *CBS PASA 2*	13	9
26 Nov 88		**ENCHANTED LADY** *CBS PASA 3*	31	6
12 May 90		**LOVE THING** *CBS PASA 4*	22	5
14 Jul 90		**REELING** *CBS PASA 5*	75	1
1 Feb 92	●	**I'M DOING FINE NOW** *Columbia 6577187*	4	10
4 Apr 92		**MAKE IT WITH YOU** *Columbia 6579257*	20	4
6 Jun 92		**I BELIEVE IN MIRACLES** *Columbia 6580567*	34	3
29 Aug 92		**MOVING IN THE RIGHT DIRECTION** *Columbia 6583417*	49	2
21 Nov 92		**LET'S STAY TOGETHER** *Columbia 6587747*	22	3
22 Oct 88	●	**TO WHOM IT MAY CONCERN** *CBS 462877 1*	3	21
7 Mar 92	●	**YOURS SINCERELY** *Columbia 4712642*	6	11

PASCAL featuring Karen PARRY
UK, male producer and female vocalist (Singles: 5 weeks) pos/wks

Date		Title	pos	wks
28 Dec 02		**I THINK WE'RE ALONE NOW** *All Around the World CDGLOBE 267*	23	5

PASSENGERS
Ireland / UK / Italy, male vocal / instrumental group (Singles: 9 weeks, Albums: 5 weeks) pos/wks

Date		Title	pos	wks
2 Dec 95	●	**MISS SARAJEVO** *Island CID 625*	6	9
18 Nov 95		**ORIGINAL SOUNDTRACKS 1** *Island CID 8043*	12	5

PASSION
UK, male vocal / rap group (Singles: 1 week) pos/wks

Date		Title	pos	wks
25 Jan 97		**SHARE YOUR LOVE (NO DIGGITY)** *Charm CRTCDS 269*	62	1

PASSIONS
UK, male / female vocal / instrumental group (Singles: 8 weeks, Albums: 1 week) pos/wks

Date		Title	pos	wks
31 Jan 81		**I'M IN LOVE WITH A GERMAN FILM STAR** *Polydor POSP 222*	25	8
3 Oct 81		**THIRTY THOUSAND FEET OVER CHINA** *Polydor POLS 1041*	92	1

PAT and MICK
UK, male DJ / vocal duo – Pat Sharp and Mick Brown (Singles: 27 weeks) pos/wks

Date		Title	pos	wks
9 Apr 88		**LET'S ALL CHANT / ON THE NIGHT** *PWL PWL 10* [1]	11	9
25 Mar 89	●	**I HAVEN'T STOPPED DANCING YET** *PWL PWL 33*	9	8
14 Apr 90		**USE IT UP AND WEAR IT OUT** *PWL PWL 55*	22	6
23 Mar 91		**GIMME SOME** *PWL PWL 75*	53	2
15 May 93		**HOT HOT HOT** *PWL International PARKCD 1*	47	2

[1] Mick and Pat

'On the Night' listed only from 4 Jun 1988. It peaked at No.70

PATIENCE and PRUDENCE
US, female vocal duo – Patience and Prudence McIntyre (Singles: 8 weeks) pos/wks

Date		Title	pos	wks
2 Nov 56		**TONIGHT YOU BELONG TO ME** *London HLU 8321*	28	3
1 Mar 57		**GONNA GET ALONG WITHOUT YA NOW (re)** *London HLU 8369*	22	5

PATRA
Jamaica, female vocalist – Dorothy Smith (Singles: 11 weeks) pos/wks

Date		Title	pos	wks
25 Dec 93		**FAMILY AFFAIR** *Polydor PZCD 304* [1]	18	8
30 Sep 95		**PULL UP TO THE BUMPER** *Epic 6623942*	50	2
10 Aug 96		**WORK MI BODY** *Heavenly HVN 53CD* [2]	75	1

[1] Shabba Ranks featuring Patra and Terri & Monica [2] Monkey Mafia featuring Patra

PATRIC
UK, male vocalist (Singles: 2 weeks) pos/wks

Date		Title	pos	wks
9 Jul 94		**LOVE ME** *Bell 7432125352*	54	2

Dee PATTEN
UK, male DJ / producer (Singles: 1 week) pos/wks

Date		Title	pos	wks
30 Jan 99		**WHO'S THE BAD MAN?** *Higher Ground HIGHS 15CD*	42	1

Kellee PATTERSON
US, female vocalist (Singles: 7 weeks) pos/wks

Date		Title	pos	wks
18 Feb 78		**IF IT DON'T FIT DON'T FORCE IT** *EMI International INT 544*	44	7

Rahsaan PATTERSON
US, male vocalist (Singles: 2 weeks) pos/wks

Date		Title	pos	wks
26 Jul 97		**STOP BY** *MCA MCSTD 48055*	50	1
21 Mar 98		**WHERE YOU ARE** *MCA MCSTD 48073*	55	1

Lizzy PATTINSON – *See MILK & SUGAR*

Billy PAUL
US, male vocalist – Paul Williams (Singles: 44 weeks) pos/wks

Date		Title	pos	wks
13 Jan 73		**ME AND MRS JONES** *Epic EPC 1055* ▲	12	9
12 Jan 74		**THANKS FOR SAVING MY LIFE** *Philadelphia International PIR 1928*	33	6
22 May 76		**LET'S MAKE A BABY** *Philadelphia International PIR 4144*	30	5
30 Apr 77		**LET 'EM IN** *Philadelphia International PIR 5143*	26	5
16 Jul 77		**YOUR SONG** *Philadelphia International PIR 5391*	37	7
19 Nov 77		**ONLY THE STRONG SURVIVE** *Philadelphia International PIR 5699*	33	7
14 Jul 79		**BRING THE FAMILY BACK** *Philadelphia International PIR 7456*	51	5

Chris PAUL
UK, male producer / instrumentalist – guitar (Singles: 8 weeks) pos/wks

Date		Title	pos	wks
31 May 86		**EXPANSIONS '86 (EXPAND YOUR MIND)** *Fourth & Broadway BRW 48* [1]	58	5
21 Nov 87		**BACK IN MY ARMS** *Syncopate SY 5*	74	2
13 Aug 88		**TURN THE MUSIC UP** *Syncopate SY 13*	73	1

[1] Chris Paul featuring David Joseph

See also ISOTONIK

Frankie PAUL – *See APACHE INDIAN*

Les PAUL and Mary FORD
US, male instrumentalist – guitar, and female vocalist, d. 30 Sep 1977 (Singles: 4 weeks) pos/wks

Date		Title	pos	wks
20 Nov 53	●	**VAYA CON DIOS (MAY GOD BE WITH YOU)** *Capitol CL 13943* ▲	7	4

Lyn PAUL
UK, female vocalist – Lynda Belcher (Singles: 6 weeks) pos/wks

Date		Title	pos	wks
28 Jun 75		**IT OUGHTA SELL A MILLION** *Polydor 2058 602*	37	6

See also NEW SEEKERS

Owen PAUL
UK, male vocalist – Owen McGee (Singles: 14 weeks) pos/wks

Date		Title	pos	wks
31 May 86	●	**MY FAVOURITE WASTE OF TIME** *Epic A 7125*	3	14

Sean PAUL
Jamaica, male vocalist – Sean Paul Henriques (Singles: 65 weeks, Albums: 34 weeks) pos/wks

Date		Title	pos	wks
21 Sep 02		**GIMME THE LIGHT (re)** *VP VPCD 6400*	32	7
15 Feb 03	●	**GIMME THE LIGHT (re-issue)** *VP / Atlantic AT 0146CD*	5	10
24 May 03	●	**GET BUSY** *VP / Atlantic AT 0155CD* ▲	4	7
19 Jul 03		**BREATHE (import)** *Arista 8786509842* [1]	59	3
9 Aug 03	★	**BREATHE** *Arista 82876545722* [1] ■	1	18
6 Sep 03	●	**LIKE GLUE** *VP / Atlantic AT 0162*	3	10
18 Oct 03	●	**BABY BOY** *Columbia 6744082* [2] ▲	2	10
10 May 03	●	**DUTTY ROCK** *Atlantic 7567836202*	2	34+

[1] Blu Cantrell Featuring Sean Paul [2] Beyoncé featuring Sean Paul

PAUL and PAULA
US, male / female vocal duo – Ray Hildebrand and Jill Jackson (Singles: 31 weeks) pos/wks

Date		Title	pos	wks
14 Feb 63	●	**HEY PAULA (re)** *Philips 304012 BF* ▲	8	17
18 Apr 63	●	**YOUNG LOVERS** *Philips 304016 BF*	9	14

Luciano PAVAROTTI (165 Top 500)
The world's best-known opera singer, b. 12 Oct 1935, Modena, Italy. The tenor, who first took opera to the top of the pop charts and on to the world's football terraces, was also the first Italian to score a UK No.1 album (Singles: 30 weeks, Albums: 298 weeks) pos/wks

Date		Title	pos	wks
16 Jun 90	●	**NESSUN DORMA** *Decca PAV 03*	2	11
24 Oct 92		**MISERERE** *London LON 329* [1]	15	5
30 Jul 94		**LIBIAMO / LA DONNA E MOBILE** *Teldec YZ 843CD* [2]	21	4
14 Dec 96	●	**LIVE LIKE HORSES** *Rocket LLHDD 1* [3]	9	6
25 Jul 98		**YOU'LL NEVER WALK ALONE** *Decca 4607982* [4]	35	4

Date		Title / Label	Pos	Wks
15 May 82		**PAVAROTTI'S GREATEST HITS** *Decca D 2362*	95	1
30 Jun 84		**MAMMA** *Decca 411959* [1]	96	1
9 Aug 86		**THE PAVAROTTI COLLECTION** *Stylus SMR 8617*	12	34
16 Jul 88		**THE NEW PAVAROTTI COLLECTION LIVE!** *Stylus SMR 857*	63	8
17 Mar 90	★	**THE ESSENTIAL PAVAROTTI** *Decca 4302101*	1	72
1 Sep 90	★	**IN CONCERT** *Decca 4304331* [2]	1	78
20 Jul 91	★	**ESSENTIAL PAVAROTTI II** *Decca 4304701*	1	28
15 Feb 92		**PAVAROTTI IN HYDE PARK** *Decca 4363202*	19	7
4 Sep 93		**TI AMO – PUCCINI'S GREATEST LOVE SONGS** *Decca 4250992*	23	4
12 Feb 94		**MY HEART'S DELIGHT** *Decca 4432602*	44	4
10 Sep 94	★	**THE THREE TENORS IN CONCERT 1994** *Teldec 4509962002* [3]	1	26
30 Mar 96		**TOGETHER FOR THE CHILDREN OF BOSNIA** *Decca 4521002* [4]	11	6
14 Dec 96		**FOR WAR CHILD** *Decca 4529002* [4]	45	4
25 Oct 97		**THE ULTIMATE COLLECTION** *Decca 4580002*	39	5
29 Aug 98		**THE THREE TENORS IN PARIS 1998** *Decca 4605002* [2]	14	6
19 Jun 99		**LOVE SONGS** *Decca 4664002*	26	6
23 Dec 00		**THE THREE TENORS CHRISTMAS** *Sony Classical SK 89131* [5]	57	2
21 Jul 01		**AMORE – THE LOVE ALBUM** *Decca 4701302*	41	2
15 Nov 03		**TI ADORO** *Decca 4754602*	21	4

[1] Zucchero with Luciano Pavarotti [2] José Carreras featuring Placido Domingo and Luciano Pavarotti with Mehta [3] Elton John and Luciano Pavarotti [4] José Carreras, Placido Domingo and Luciano Pavarotti with Mehta [1] Luciano Pavarotti with the Henry Mancini Orchestra [2] José Carreras Placido Domingo and Luciano Pavarotti [3] José Carreras Placido Domingo and Luciano Pavarotti conducted by Zubin Mehta [4] Pavarotti and Friends [5] José Carreras Placido Domingo and Luciano Pavarotti featuring Zubin Mehta

PAVEMENT *US, male vocal / instrumental group (Singles: 6 weeks, Albums: 13 weeks)*

Date		Title / Label	pos	wks
28 Nov 92		**WATERY, DOMESTIC (EP)** *Big Cat ABB 38T*	58	1
12 Feb 94		**CUT YOUR HAIR** *Big Cat ABB 55SCD*	52	1
8 Feb 97		**STEREO** *Domino RUG 51CD*	48	1
3 May 97		**SHADY LANE** *Domino RUG 53CD*	40	1
22 May 99		**CARROT ROPE** *Domino RUG 90CD1*	27	2
25 Apr 92		**SLANTED AND ENCHANTED** *Big Cat ABB 34CD*	72	1
3 Apr 93		**WESTING (BY MUSKET AND SEXTANT)** *Big Cat ABBCD 40*	30	2
26 Feb 94		**CROOKED RAIN CROOKED RAIN** *Big Cat ABB 56CD*	15	3
22 Apr 95		**WOWEE ZOWEE** *Big Cat ABB 84CD*	18	2
22 Feb 97		**BRIGHTEN THE CORNERS** *Domino Recordings WIGCD 31*	27	2
19 Jun 99		**TERROR TWILIGHT** *Domino Recordings WIGCD 66*	19	3

Tracks on Watery, Domestic (EP): Texas Never Whispers / Frontwards / Feed 'Em / The Linden Lions / Shoot the Singer (1 Sick Verse)

Rita PAVONE *Italy, female vocalist (Singles: 19 weeks)*

Date		Title / Label	pos	wks
1 Dec 66		**HEART** *RCA 1553*	27	12
19 Jan 67		**YOU ONLY YOU** *RCA 1561*	21	7

Tom PAXTON *US, male vocalist (Albums: 11 weeks)*

Date		Title / Label	pos	wks
13 Jun 70		**NO. 6** *Elektra 2469003*	23	5
27 Mar 71		**THE COMPLEAT TOM PAXTON** *Elektra EKD 2003*	18	5
1 Jul 72		**PEACE WILL COME** *Reprise K 44182*	47	1

PAY AS U GO *UK, male rap / production group (Singles: 4 weeks)*

Date		Title / Label	pos	wks
27 Apr 02		**CHAMPAGNE DANCE** *So Urban 6721362*	13	4

Freda PAYNE *US, female vocalist (Singles: 30 weeks)*

Date		Title / Label	pos	wks
5 Sep 70	★	**BAND OF GOLD** *Invictus INV 502*	1	19
21 Nov 70		**DEEPER AND DEEPER** *Invictus INV 505*	33	9
27 Mar 71		**CHERISH WHAT IS DEAR TO YOU (WHILE IT'S NEAR TO YOU)** *Invictus INV 509*	46	2

Tammy PAYNE *UK, female vocalist (Singles: 2 weeks)*

Date		Title / Label	pos	wks
20 Jul 91		**TAKE ME NOW** *Talkin Loud TLK 12*	55	2

Heather PEACE *UK, female vocalist (Singles: 1 week)*

Date		Title / Label	pos	wks
13 May 00		**THE ROSE** *RCA 74321742892*	56	1

PEACE BY PIECE *UK, male vocal group (Singles: 2 weeks)*

Date		Title / Label	pos	wks
21 Sep 96		**SWEET SISTER** *Blanco Y Negro NEG 94CD*	46	1
25 Apr 98		**NOBODY'S BUSINESS** *Blanco Y Negro NEG 110CD1*	50	1

PEACH *UK / Belgium, female / male vocal / production group (Singles: 1 week)*

Date		Title / Label	pos	wks
17 Jan 98		**ON MY OWN** *Mute CDMUTE 215*	69	1

PEACHES *Canada, female producer / vocalist – Merrill Nisker (Singles: 2 weeks)*

Date		Title / Label	pos	wks
15 Jun 02		**SET IT OFF** *Epic 6726862*	36	2

PEACHES and HERB *US, female / male vocal duo – Linda Green and Herbert Feemster (Singles: 23 weeks)*

Date		Title / Label	pos	wks
20 Jan 79		**SHAKE YOUR GROOVE THING** *Polydor 2066 992*	26	10
21 Apr 79	●	**REUNITED** *Polydor POSP 43* ▲	4	13

Mary PEARCE – *See UP YER RONSON featuring Mary PEARCE*

Natasha PEARL – *See TASTE XPERIENCE featuring Natasha PEARL*

PEARL JAM *(413 Top 500)*

Stadium-packing Seattle rock band fronted by Eddie Vedder, b. Edward Mueller, 23 Dec 1966, Illinois. The quintet evolved from revered pioneers Mother Love Bone, and has released more than 50 live albums, with a record 17 of them charting Stateside (Singles: 43 weeks, Albums: 119 weeks)

Date		Title / Label	pos	wks
15 Feb 92		**ALIVE** *Epic 6575727*	16	6
18 Apr 92		**EVEN FLOW** *Epic 6578577*	27	3
26 Sep 92		**JEREMY** *Epic 6582587*	15	4
1 Jan 94		**DAUGHTER** *Epic 6600202*	18	5
28 May 94		**DISSIDENT** *Epic 6604415*	14	4
26 Nov 94	●	**SPIN THE BLACK CIRCLE** *Epic 6610362*	10	3
25 Feb 95		**NOT FOR YOU** *Epic 6612032*	34	2
16 Dec 95		**MERKINBALL** *Epic 6627162*	25	3
17 Aug 96		**WHO YOU ARE** *Epic 6635392*	18	2
31 Jan 98		**GIVEN TO FLY** *Epic 6653942*	12	3
23 May 98		**WISHLIST** *Epic 6657902*	30	2
14 Aug 99		**LAST KISS** *Epic 6674791*	42	1
13 May 00		**NOTHING AS IT SEEMS** *Epic 6693742*	22	2
22 Jul 00		**LIGHT YEARS** *Epic 6696282*	52	1
9 Nov 02		**I AM MINE** *Epic 6733082*	26	2
7 Mar 92		**TEN** *Epic 4688842*	18	65
23 Oct 93	●	**VS** *Epic 4745492* ▲	2	24
3 Dec 94	●	**VITALOGY** *Epic 4778611* ▲	4	11
7 Sep 96	●	**NO CODE** *Epic 4844482* ▲	3	5
14 Feb 98	●	**YIELD** *Epic 4893652*	7	7
5 Dec 98		**LIVE – ON TWO LEGS** *Epic 4928592*	68	1
27 May 00	●	**BINAURAL** *Epic 4945902*	5	4
23 Nov 02		**RIOT ACT** *Epic 5100002*	34	2

'Merkinball' is the title of the single featuring 'I Got Id' and 'Long Road'

PEARLS *UK, female vocal duo (Singles: 24 weeks)*

Date		Title / Label	pos	wks
27 May 72		**THIRD FINGER, LEFT HAND** *Bell 1217*	31	6
23 Sep 72		**YOU CAME, YOU SAW, YOU CONQUERED** *Bell 1254*	32	5
24 Mar 73		**YOU ARE EVERYTHING** *Bell 1284*	41	3
1 Jun 74	●	**GUILTY** *Bell 1352*	10	10

Johnny PEARSON

UK, orchestra – Johnny Pearson – piano (Singles: 15 weeks)

Date		Title / Label	pos	wks
18 Dec 71	●	**SLEEPY SHORES** *Penny Farthing PEN 778*	8	15

David PEASTON *US, male vocalist (Albums: 1 week)*

Date		Title / Label	pos	wks
26 Aug 89		**INTRODUCING ... DAVID PEASTON** *Geffen 924228 1*	66	1

PEBBLES *US, female vocalist – Perri McKissack (Singles: 17 weeks, Albums: 4 weeks)*

Date		Title / Label	pos	wks
19 Mar 88	●	**GIRLFRIEND** *MCA MCA 1233*	8	11
28 May 88		**MERCEDES BOY** *MCA MCA 1248*	42	4

27 Oct 90	**GIVING YOU THE BENEFIT** *MCA MCA 1448*	**73**	2
14 May 88	**PEBBLES** *MCA MCF 3418*	**56**	4

PEDDLERS *UK, male vocal / instrumental group (Singles: 14 weeks, Albums: 16 weeks)*

		pos	wks
7 Jan 65	**LET THE SUNSHINE IN** *Philips BF 1375*	**50**	1
23 Aug 69	**BIRTH** *CBS 4449*	**17**	9
31 Jan 70	**GIRLIE** *CBS 4720*	**34**	4
16 Mar 68	**FREE WHEELERS** *CBS SBPG 63183*	**27**	13
7 Feb 70	**BIRTHDAY** *CBS 63682*	**16**	3

PEE BEE SQUAD *UK, male vocalist – Paul Burnett (Singles: 3 weeks)*

		pos	wks
5 Oct 85	**RUGGED AND MEAN, BUTCH AND ON SCREEN** *Project PRO 3*	**52**	3

Ann PEEBLES *US, female vocalist (Singles: 3 weeks)*

		pos	wks
20 Apr 74	**I CAN'T STAND THE RAIN (re)** *London HLU 10428*	**41**	3

PEECH BOYS *US, male vocal / instrumental group (Singles: 3 weeks)*

		pos	wks
30 Oct 82	**DON'T MAKE ME WAIT** *TMT TMT 7001*	**49**	3

Kevin PEEK *UK, male instrumentalist – guitar (Albums: 8 weeks)*

		pos	wks
21 Mar 81	**AWAKENING** *Ariola ARL 5065*	**52**	2
13 Oct 84	**BEYOND THE PLANETS** *Telstar STAR 2244* [1]	**64**	6

[1] Kevin Peek and Rick Wakeman

'Beyond the Planets' also features Jeff Wayne with narration by Patrick Allen

See also SKY

Donald PEERS *UK, male vocalist d. 9 Aug 1973 (Singles: 28 weeks)*

		pos	wks
29 Dec 66	**GAMES THAT LOVERS PLAY** *Columbia DB 8079*	**46**	1
18 Dec 68 ●	**PLEASE DON'T GO (re)** *Columbia DB 8502*	**3**	21
24 Jun 72	**GIVE ME ONE MORE CHANCE** *Decca F 13302* [1]	**36**	6

[1] Donald Peers with the Les Reed Orchestra and Chorus

PELE *UK, male / female vocal / instrumental group (Singles: 3 weeks)*

		pos	wks
15 Feb 92	**MEGALOMANIA** *M & G MAGS 20*	**73**	1
13 Jun 92	**FAIR BLOWS THE WIND FOR FRANCE** *M & G MAGS 24*	**62**	1
31 Jul 93	**FAT BLACK HEART** *M & G MAGCD 43*	**75**	1

Marti PELLOW *UK, male vocalist (Singles: 9 weeks, Albums: 16 weeks)*

		pos	wks
16 Jun 01 ●	**CLOSE TO YOU** *Mercury MERCD 532*	**9**	6
1 Dec 01	**I'VE BEEN AROUND THE WORLD** *Mercury 5887772*	**28**	2
22 Nov 03	**A LOT OF LOVE** *Universal TV 9813763*	**59**	1
7 Jul 01 ●	**SMILE** *Mercury 5860032*	**7**	7
30 Nov 02	**MARTI PELLOW SINGS THE HITS OF WET WET WET & SMILE** *UMTV TV 0632902*	**34**	8
29 Nov 03	**BETWEEN THE COVERS** *Universal TV 9812067*	**66**	1

See also WET WET WET

Debbie PENDER *US, female vocalist (Singles: 1 week)*

		pos	wks
30 May 98	**MOVIN' ON** *AM:PM 5826492*	**41**	1

Teddy PENDERGRASS *US, male vocalist (Singles: 24 weeks, Albums: 8 weeks)*

		pos	wks
21 May 77	**THE WHOLE TOWN'S LAUGHING AT ME** *Philadelphia International PIR 5116*	**44**	3
28 Oct 78	**ONLY YOU / CLOSE THE DOOR** *Philadelphia International PIR 6713*	**41**	6
23 May 81	**TWO HEARTS** *20th Century TC 2492* [1]	**49**	5
25 Jan 86	**HOLD ME** *Asylum EKR 32* [2]	**44**	5
28 May 88	**JOY** *Elektra EKR 75*	**58**	3
19 Nov 94	**THE MORE I GET THE MORE I WANT** *X-clusive XCLU 011CD* [3]	**35**	2
21 May 88	**JOY** *Elektra 960775 1*	**45**	8

[1] Stephanie Mills featuring Teddy Pendergrass [2] Teddy Pendergrass with Whitney Houston [3] KWS featuring Teddy Pendergrass

See also Harold MELVIN and the BLUENOTES

PENETRATION *UK, male / female vocal / instrumental group (Albums: 8 weeks)*

		pos	wks
28 Oct 78	**MOVING TARGETS** *Virgin V 2109*	**22**	4
6 Oct 79	**COMING UP FOR AIR** *Virgin V 2131*	**36**	4

PENGUIN CAFÉ ORCHESTRA *UK, male instrumental group (Albums: 5 weeks)*

		pos	wks
4 Apr 87	**SIGNS OF LIFE** *Edition EG EGED 50*	**49**	5

Ce Ce PENISTON *US, female vocalist (Singles: 53 weeks, Albums: 21 weeks)*

		pos	wks
12 Oct 91	**FINALLY** *A&M AM 822*	**29**	7
11 Jan 92 ●	**WE GOT A LOVE THANG** *A&M AM 846*	**6**	8
18 Jan 92	**I LIKE IT** *A&M AM 847* [1]	**58**	2
21 Mar 92 ●	**FINALLY (re-issue)** *A&M AM 858*	**2**	8
23 May 92 ●	**KEEP ON WALKIN'** *A&M AM 878*	**10**	6
5 Sep 92	**CRAZY LOVE** *A&M AM 0060*	**44**	3
12 Dec 92	**INSIDE THAT I CRIED** *A&M AM 0121*	**42**	2
15 Jan 94	**I'M IN THE MOOD** *A&M 5804552*	**16**	4
2 Apr 94	**KEEP GIVIN' ME YOUR LOVE** *A&M 5805492*	**36**	2
6 Aug 94	**HIT BY LOVE** *A&M 5806932*	**33**	2
13 Sep 97	**FINALLY (re-mix)** *AM:PM 5823432*	**26**	5
7 Feb 98	**SOMEBODY ELSE'S GUY** *AM:PM 5825112*	**13**	4
8 Feb 92 ●	**FINALLY** *A&M 3971822*	**10**	19
5 Feb 94	**THOUGHT 'YA KNEW** *A&M 5402012*	**31**	2

[1] Overweight Pooch featuring Ce Ce Peniston

Dawn PENN *Jamaica, female vocalist – Dawn Pickering (Singles: 12 weeks, Albums: 2 weeks)*

		pos	wks
11 Jun 94 ●	**YOU DON'T LOVE ME (NO, NO, NO)** *Big Beat A 8295CD*	**3**	12
9 Jul 94	**NO NO NO** *Big Beat 7567923652*	**51**	2

Barbara PENNINGTON *US, female vocalist (Singles: 8 weeks)*

		pos	wks
27 Apr 85	**FAN THE FLAME** *Record Shack SOHO 37*	**62**	3
27 Jul 85	**ON A CROWDED STREET** *Record Shack SOHO 49*	**57**	5

Tricia PENROSE *UK, female vocalist / actor (Singles: 2 weeks)*

		pos	wks
7 Dec 96	**WHERE DID OUR LOVE GO** *RCA 74321428152*	**71**	1
4 Mar 00	**DON'T WANNA BE ALONE** *Doop DP 2001CD*	**44**	1

PENTANGLE *UK, male / female vocal / instrumental group (Singles: 4 weeks, Albums: 39 weeks)*

		pos	wks
28 May 69	**ONCE I HAD A SWEETHEART** *Big T BIG 124*	**46**	1
14 Feb 70	**LIGHT FLIGHT (re)** *Big T BIG 128*	**43**	3
15 Jun 68	**THE PENTANGLE** *Transatlantic TRA 162*	**21**	9
1 Nov 69 ●	**BASKET OF LIGHT** *Transatlantic TRA 205*	**5**	28
12 Dec 70	**CRUEL SISTER** *Transatlantic TRA 228*	**51**	2

PENTHOUSE 4 *UK, male vocal / instrumental duo (Singles: 3 weeks)*

		pos	wks
23 Apr 88	**BUST THIS HOUSE DOWN** *Syncopate SY 10*	**56**	3

PEOPLES CHOICE *US, male vocal / instrumental group (Singles: 9 weeks)*

		pos	wks
20 Sep 75	**DO IT ANY WAY YOU WANNA** *Philadelphia International PIR 3500*	**36**	5
21 Jan 78	**JAM, JAM, JAM (ALL NIGHT LONG)** *Philadelphia International PIR 5891* [1]	**40**	4

[1] People's Choice

THE MISSING HITS

The Best Selling Discs in Britain by British Artists Chart

In the pre-decimal early 1950s, there were 12 pennies in a shilling, 12 inches in a foot and 12 singles in a British chart. When it became clear that American acts were hogging the Top 12, the New Musical Express introduced a UK-artist-only Top 12. The catchily titled 'Best Selling Discs in Britain by British Artists' chart was published alongside the normal chart from 9 April 1954 to 24 September 1954. The NME then decided to enlarge the main chart to a Top 20 – thus increasing the number of British hit artists and ending the need for this separate chart.

Many of the singles that reached the UK-only Top 12 would have made the normal chart had it been extended to a Top 20 earlier and would therefore be listed in this book. So, 50 years on, it is about time these worthy missing hits are name-checked in the bible of British hits although, sadly, few of the artists involved are still alive to see the results.

There are just three artists who did not have a hit on the real chart: one-time cinema organist Jackie Brown and His Orchestra; music-hall comedy legend Max Miller; and Frances and Stella, The Tanner Sisters, who were the UK's No.1 sister act before the Beverleys and were on the bill for Buddy Holly's UK tour. Acts which were at their peak in this period include Indian-born balladeer Tony Brent and UK saxophonist Frank Weir, whose UK-only chart entries include his US Top 10 single 'The Happy Wanderer'. The vast majority of the songs were covers of US hits; however, the list does include Eddie Calvert's original recording of Vera Lynn's chart-topper 'My Son, My Son', and The Johnston Brothers' US success 'The Bandit'.

Comedian Max Miller and (right) The Tanner Sisters accompanied by Max Bygraves are two of three acts which are included in our missing hits list but don't get an entry in our book

Best-Selling Discs in Britain chart entries

ACT / DATE OF ENTRY / SINGLE / LABEL / PEAK POSITION / WEEKS ON CHART

Winifred ATWELL 21/05/54 THE CHARLESTON (re) Decca 5 10
BEVERLEY SISTERS 04/06/54 *CROSS OVER THE BRIDGE (re) Phillips 11 3
Eve BOSWELL 30/04/54 *DON'T EVER LEAVE ME Parlophone 12 1
Tony BRENT 14/05/54 WANTED (re) Columbia 10 2
Tony BRENT 23/07/54 THREE COINS IN THE FOUNTAIN Columbia 4 9
Tony BRENT 24/09/54 SWAY Columbia 5 1
Tony BRENT AND BILLIE ANTHONY 21/05/54 *CROSS OVER THE BRIDGE Columbia 9 1
Jackie BROWN AND HIS ORCHESTRA 09/04/54 *THEME FROM 'THE GLENN MILLER STORY' Columbia 9 2
Max BYGRAVES 09/04/54 *THE JONES BOY (re) HMV 8 2
Max BYGRAVES AND THE TANNER SISTERS 21/05/54 FRIENDS AND NEIGHBOURS HMV 7 4
Eddie CALVERT 14/05/54 *MIDNIGHT (re) Columbia 5 12
Eddie CALVERT 24/09/54 MY SON, MY SON Columbia 12 1
Alma COGAN 11/06/54 THE LITTLE SHOEMAKER HMV 10 3
Diana DECKER 16/04/54 THE HAPPY WANDERER Columbia 9 1
Ted HEATH 09/04/54 *LUSH SLIDE Decca 10 1
JOHNSTON BROTHERS 25/09/54 *THE BANDIT (re) London 6 2
Vera LYNN 23/04/54 *TWO EASTER SUNDAY SWEETHEARTS Decca 9 3
Vera LYNN 14/05/54 *HOMECOMING WALTZ Decca 12 1
MANTOVANI 16/04/54 *LUXEMBOURG POLKA (re) Decca 8 2
MANTOVANI 07/05/54 *BEWITCHED Decca 10 1
Max MILLER 09/04/54 *MARY FROM THE DAIRY Phillips 12 1
Joan REGAN 25/06/54 *JILTED Decca 7 1
Lita ROZA 09/04/54 BELL BOTTOM BLUES (re) Decca 9 4
Lita ROSA 23/04/54 MAKE LOVE TO ME Decca 10 1
Anne SHELTON 23/04/54 *CROSS OVER THE BRIDGE (re) HMV 9 2
SQUADRONAIRES 30/04/54 *WOLF ON THE PROWL Decca 12 1
Cyril STAPLETON 16/07/54 *LESTER LEAPS IN Decca 12 1
Frank WEIR 28/05/54 THE HAPPY WANDERER (re) Decca 12 2
Frank WEIR 25/06/54 THE LITTLE SHOEMAKER (re) Decca 6 3
Frank WEIR 02/07/54 *THE NEVER NEVER LAND Decca 4 11
David WHITFIELD 27/08/54 SMILE Decca Also 11 4
Jimmy YOUNG 16/04/54 WISH YOU WERE HERE Decca 12 1
Jimmy YOUNG 18/06/54 LITTLE THINGS MEAN A LOT (re) Decca 8

* Songs not already in this book

A New Chart!

BEST SELLING DISCS IN BRITAIN (BY BRITISH ARTISTS)

1 I SEE THE MOON
Stargazers (Decca)
2 DON'T LAUGH AT ME
Norman Wisdom (Columbia)
3 BELL BOTTOM BLUES
Alma Cogan (HMV)
4 THE BOOK
David Whitfield (Decca)
5 OH MEIN PAPA
Eddie Calvert (Columbia)
6 HAPPY WANDERER
Stargazers (Decca)
7 HEART OF MY HEART
Max Bygraves (HMV)
8 JONES BOY
Max Bygraves (HMV)
9 BELL BOTTOM BLUES
Lita Roza (Decca)
10 LUSH SLIDE
Ted Heath (Decca)
11 GLENN MILLER THEME
Jackie Brown (Columbia)
12 MARY FROM THE DAIRY
Max Miller (Philips)

These charts are compiled from weekly returns made to us by the largest record retailers throughout the country, based on their actual sales figures.

PEPE DELUXE
Finland, male DJ / production group (Singles: 3 weeks) pos/wks

26 May 01 **BEFORE YOU LEAVE** *Catskills / Incredible 6712392* 20 3

Danny PEPPERMINT and the JUMPING JACKS *US, male vocal / instrumental group, leader – Danny Lamego (Singles: 8 weeks)* pos/wks

18 Jan 62 **THE PEPPERMINT TWIST** *London HLL 9478* 26 8

PEPPERS *France, male instrumental group (Singles: 12 weeks)* pos/wks

26 Oct 74 ● **PEPPER BOX** *Spark SRL 1100* 6 12

PEPSI and SHIRLIE *UK, female vocal duo – Helen DeMacque and Shirley Holliman (Singles: 24 weeks, Albums: 2 weeks)* pos/wks

17 Jan 87 ● **HEARTACHE** *Polydor POSP 837* 2 12
30 May 87 ● **GOODBYE STRANGER** *Polydor POSP 865* 9 7
26 Sep 87 **CAN'T GIVE ME LOVE** *Polydor POSP 885* 58 3
12 Dec 87 **ALL RIGHT NOW** *Polydor POSP 896* 50 2
7 Nov 87 **ALL RIGHT NOW** *Polydor POLH 38* 69 2

PERAN
Holland, male producer – Peran van Dijk (Singles: 2 weeks) pos/wks

23 Mar 02 **GOOD TIME** *Incentive CENT 37CDS* 37 2

PERCEPTION *UK, male vocal group (Singles: 2 weeks)* pos/wks

7 Mar 92 **FEED THE FEELING** *Talkin Loud TLK 17* 58 2

The listed flip side of 'Feed the Feeling' was 'Three Times a Maybe' by K-Creative

Lance PERCIVAL
UK, male vocalist / comedian (Singles: 3 weeks) pos/wks

28 Oct 65 **SHAME AND SCANDAL IN THE FAMILY** *Parlophone R 5335* ..37 3

PERCY FILTH *UK, male production duo – Mark Baker and Gary Little (Singles: 1 week)* pos/wks

9 Aug 03 **SHOW ME YOUR MONKEY** *Southern Fried ECB 53CDS* 72 1

See also LIL' DEVIOUS

PERFECT CIRCLE – See A PERFECT CIRCLE

PERFECT DAY
UK, male vocal / instrumental group (Singles: 4 weeks) pos/wks

21 Jan 89 **LIBERTY TOWN** *London LON 214* 58 3
1 Apr 89 **JANE** *London LON 188* 68 1

PERFECT PHASE *Holland, male production duo – Freek Fontein and Willem Faber (Singles: 7 weeks)* pos/wks

25 Dec 99 **HORNY HORNS** *Positiva CDTIV 123* 21 7

PERFECTLY ORDINARY PEOPLE
UK, male vocal / instrumental group (Singles: 3 weeks) pos/wks

22 Oct 88 **THEME FROM P.O.P.** *Urban URB 25* 61 3

PERFECTO ALLSTARZ *UK, male instrumental / production duo – Paul Oakenfold and Steve Osborne (Singles: 11 weeks)* pos/wks

4 Feb 95 ● **REACH UP (PAPA'S GOT A BRAND NEW PIG BAG)** *Perfecto YZ 892CD* 6 11

See also VIRUS; OAKENFOLD; RISE

PERFUME
UK, male vocal / instrumental group (Singles: 1 week) pos/wks

10 Feb 96 **HAVEN'T SEEN YOU** *Aromasound AROMA 005CDS* 71 1

Emilio PERICOLI *Italy, male vocalist (Singles: 14 weeks)* pos/wks

28 Jun 62 **AL DI LA** *Warner Bros. WB 69* 30 14

Carl PERKINS *US, male vocalist d. 19 Jan 1998 (Singles: 8 weeks, Albums: 3 weeks)* pos/wks

18 May 56 ● **BLUE SUEDE SHOES** *London HLU 8271* 10 8
15 Apr 78 **OL' BLUE SUEDES IS BACK** *Jet UATV 30146* 38 3

PERPETUAL MOTION
UK, male instrumental / production group (Singles: 5 weeks) pos/wks

2 May 98 **KEEP ON DANCIN' (LET'S GO)** *Positiva CDTIV 90* 12 5

Lee 'Scratch' PERRY
Jamaica, male producer / vocalist (Albums: 1 week) pos/wks

26 Jul 97 **ARKOLOGY** *Island Jamaica CRNCD 6* 49 1

'Arkology' was a triple-CD boxset

Steve PERRY
UK, male vocalist (Singles: 1 week, Albums: 3 weeks) pos/wks

4 Aug 60 **STEP BY STEP** *HMV POP 745* 41 1
14 Jul 84 **STREET TALK** *CBS 25967* 59 2
27 Aug 94 **FOR THE LOVE OF STRANGE MEDICINE** *Columbia 4771962* 64 1

Nina PERSSON and David ARNOLD *Sweden, female vocalist and UK, male instrumentalist / producer (Singles: 1 week)* pos/wks

29 Apr 00 **THEME FROM 'RANDALL & HOPKIRK (DECEASED)'** *Island CID 762* 49 1

See also CARDIGANS

Jon PERTWEE
UK, male actor / vocalist d. 20 May 1996 (Singles: 7 weeks) pos/wks

1 Mar 80 **WORZEL'S SONG** *Decca F 13885* 33 7

PESHAY *UK, male DJ / producer – Paul Pesce (Singles: 6 weeks, Albums: 1 week)* pos/wks

9 May 98 **MILES FROM HOME** *Mo Wax MW 092* 75 1
17 Jul 99 **SWITCH** *Island Blue PFACD 1* 59 1
19 Feb 00 **TRULY** *Island Blue PFACD 4* [1] 55 1
4 May 02 **YOU GOT ME BURNING / FUZION** *Cubik Music CUBIKSAMP CD001CD* [2] 41 2
24 Aug 02 **SATISFY MY LOVE** *Cubik Music CUBIK 002CD* [3] 67 1
31 Jul 99 **MILES FROM HOME** *Island Blue PFA 1CD* 63 1

[1] Peshay featuring Kym Mazelle [2] Peshay featuring Co-ordinate [3] Peshay vs Flytronix

PESTALOZZI CHILDREN'S CHOIR
International, male / female vocal group (Albums: 2 weeks) pos/wks

26 Dec 81 **SONGS OF JOY** *K-Tel NE 1140* 65 2

PET SHOP BOYS (59 Top 500)
Critically acclaimed and quintessentially English duo: former assistant editor of Smash Hits, Neil Tennant (v), and Chris Lowe (k). No duo has amassed more chart entries than this act, whose first hit was voted Best British Single at the 1987 Brit Awards (Singles: 240 weeks, Albums: 347 weeks) pos/wks

23 Nov 85 ★ **WEST END GIRLS** *Parlophone R 6115* ▲ 1 15
8 Mar 86 **LOVE COMES QUICKLY** *Parlophone R 6116* 19 9
31 May 86 **OPPORTUNITIES (LET'S MAKE LOTS OF MONEY)** *Parlophone R 6129* 11 8
4 Oct 86 ● **SUBURBIA** *Parlophone R 6140* 8 9
27 Jun 87 ★ **IT'S A SIN** *Parlophone R 6158* 1 11
22 Aug 87 ● **WHAT HAVE I DONE TO DESERVE THIS?** *Parlophone R 6163* [1] 2 9
24 Oct 87 ● **RENT** *Parlophone R 6168* 8 7
12 Dec 87 ★ **ALWAYS ON MY MIND** *Parlophone R 6171* 1 11
2 Apr 88 ★ **HEART** *Parlophone R 6177* 1 10
24 Sep 88 ● **DOMINO DANCING** *Parlophone R 6190* 7 8
26 Nov 88 ● **LEFT TO MY OWN DEVICES** *Parlophone R 6198* 4 8
8 Jul 89 ● **IT'S ALRIGHT** *Parlophone R 6220* 5 8
6 Oct 90 ● **SO HARD** *Parlophone R 6269* 4 6

24 Nov 90 **BEING BORING** *Parlophone R 6275* 20 8
23 Mar 91 ● **WHERE THE STREETS HAVE NO NAME – CAN'T TAKE MY EYES OFF YOU / HOW CAN YOU EXPECT TO BE TAKEN SERIOUSLY** *Parlophone R 6285* 4 8
8 Jun 91 **JEALOUSY** *Parlophone R 6283* 12 5
26 Oct 91 **DJ CULTURE** *Parlophone R 6301* 13 3
23 Nov 91 **DJ CULTURE (re-mix)** *Parlophone 12RX 6301* 40 2
21 Dec 91 **WAS IT WORTH IT?** *Parlophone R 6306* 24 4
12 Jun 93 ● **CAN YOU FORGIVE HER** *Parlophone CDR 6348* 7 7
18 Sep 93 ● **GO WEST** *Parlophone CDR 6356* 2 9
11 Dec 93 **I WOULDN'T NORMALLY DO THIS KIND OF THING** *Parlophone CDR 6370* 13 7
16 Apr 94 **LIBERATION** *Parlophone CDR 6377* 14 5
11 Jun 94 ● **ABSOLUTELY FABULOUS** *Spaghetti CDR 6382* [2] 6 7
10 Sep 94 **YESTERDAY WHEN I WAS MAD** *Parlophone CDR 6386* 13 4
5 Aug 95 **PANINARO** *Parlophone CDR 6414* 15 4
4 May 96 ● **BEFORE** *Parlophone CDR 6431* 7 5
24 Aug 96 ● **SE A VIDEA E (THAT'S THE WAY LIFE IS)** *Parlophone CDR 6443* 8 8
23 Nov 96 **SINGLE** *Parlophone CDR 6452* 14 3
29 Mar 97 ● **A RED LETTER DAY** *Parlophone CDR 6460* 9 3
5 Jul 97 ● **SOMEWHERE** *Parlophone CDR 6470* 9 5
31 Jul 99 **I DON'T KNOW WHAT YOU WANT BUT I CAN'T GIVE IT ANYMORE** *Parlophone CDR 6523* 15 3
9 Oct 99 **NEW YORK CITY BOY** *Parlophone CDR 6525* 14 4
15 Jan 00 ● **YOU ONLY TELL ME YOU LOVE ME WHEN YOU'RE DRUNK** *Parlophone CDR 6533* 8 4
30 Mar 02 **HOME AND DRY** *Parlophone CDRS 6572* 14 6
27 Jul 02 **I GET ALONG** *Parlophone CDRS 6581* 18 3
29 Nov 03 ● **MIRACLES** *Parlophone CDR 6620* 10 4
5 Apr 86 ● **PLEASE** *Parlophone PSB 1* 3 82
29 Nov 86 **DISCO** *EMI PRG 1001* 15 72
19 Sep 87 ● **ACTUALLY** *Parlophone PCSD 104* 2 59
22 Oct 88 ● **INTROSPECTIVE** *Parlophone PCS 7325* 2 39
3 Nov 90 ● **BEHAVIOUR** *Parlophone PCSD 113* 2 14
16 Nov 91 ● **DISCOGRAPHY – THE COMPLETE SINGLES COLLECTION** *Parlophone PMTV 3* 3 30
9 Oct 93 ★ **VERY** *Parlophone CDPCSD 143* ■ 1 22
24 Sep 94 ● **DISCO 2** *Parlophone CDPCSD 159* 6 4
19 Aug 95 ● **ALTERNATIVE** *Parlophone CDPCSD 166* 2 5
14 Sep 96 ● **BILINGUAL** *Parlophone CDPCSD 170* 4 8
23 Oct 99 ● **NIGHTLIFE** *Parlophone 5218572* 7 3
13 Apr 02 ● **RELEASE** *Parlophone 5381502* 7 4
15 Feb 03 **DISCO 3** *Parlophone 5821402* 36 1
6 Dec 03 **POPART – THE HITS** *Parlophone 5950932* ....30 4+

[1] Pet Shop Boys and Dusty Springfield [2] Absolutely Fabulous

'Absolutely Fabulous' featured sampled speech by Jennifer Saunders and Joanna Lumley from the TV series of the same name

PETER and GORDON *UK, male vocal duo – Peter Asher and Gordon Waller (Singles: 77 weeks, Albums: 1 week)* pos/wks

12 Mar 64 ★ **A WORLD WITHOUT LOVE** *Columbia DB 7225* ▲ 1 14
4 Jun 64 ● **NOBODY I KNOW** *Columbia DB 7292* 10 11
8 Apr 65 ● **TRUE LOVE WAYS** *Columbia DB 7524* 2 15
24 Jun 65 ● **TO KNOW YOU IS TO LOVE YOU** *Columbia DB 7617* 5 10
21 Oct 65 **BABY I'M YOURS** *Columbia DB 7729* 19 9
24 Feb 66 **WOMAN** *Columbia DB 7834* 28 7
22 Sep 66 **LADY GODIVA** *Columbia DB 8003* 16 11
20 Jun 64 **PETER AND GORDON** *Columbia 33SX 1630* 18 1

PETER, PAUL and MARY *US, male / female vocal / instrumental group (Singles: 38 weeks, Albums: 26 weeks)* pos/wks

10 Oct 63 **BLOWING IN THE WIND** *Warner Bros. WB 104* 13 16
16 Apr 64 **TELL IT ON THE MOUNTAIN** *Warner Bros. WB 127* 33 4
15 Oct 64 **THE TIMES THEY ARE A-CHANGIN'** *Warner Bros. WB 142* 44 2
17 Jan 70 ● **LEAVING ON A JET PLANE** *Warner Bros. WB 7340* ▲ 2 16
4 Jan 64 **PETER PAUL AND MARY** *Warner Bros. WM 4064* ▲ 18 1
21 Mar 64 **IN THE WIND** *Warner Bros. WM 8142* ▲ 11 19
13 Feb 65 **IN CONCERT VOLUME 1** *Warner Bros. WM 8158* 20 2
5 Sep 70 **TEN YEARS TOGETHER** *Warner Bros. WS 2552* 60 4

PETERS and LEE (286 Top 500) *London-based, Opportunity Knocks-winning MOR duo: Lennie Peters (blind since 16) d. 10 Oct 1992 (age 59) (p/v) and Diane Lee (v). Peters, the uncle of Rolling Stone Charlie Watts, first recorded in 1962 backed by Migil Five. Lee married Wizzard's Rick Price (Singles: 57 weeks, Albums: 166 weeks)* pos/wks

26 May 73 ★ **WELCOME HOME** *Philips 6006 307* 1 24
3 Nov 73 **BY YOUR SIDE** *Philips 6006 339* 39 4
20 Apr 74 ● **DON'T STAY AWAY TOO LONG** *Philips 6006 388* 3 15
17 Aug 74 **RAINBOW** *Philips 6006 406* 17 7
6 Mar 76 **HEY MR MUSIC MAN** *Philips 6006 502* 16 7
30 Jun 73 ★ **WE CAN MAKE IT** *Philips 6308 165* 1 55
22 Dec 73 ● **BY YOUR SIDE** *Philips 6308 192* 9 48
21 Sep 74 ● **RAINBOW** *Philips 6308 208* 6 27
4 Oct 75 ● **FAVOURITES** *Philips 9109 205* 2 32
18 Dec 76 **INVITATION** *Philips 9101 027* 44 4

Jonathan PETERS presents LUMINAIRE *US, male DJ / producer (Singles: 1 week)* pos/wks

24 Jul 99 **FLOWER DUET** *Pelican PELID 001* 75 1

Ray PETERSON *US, male vocalist (Singles: 9 weeks)* pos/wks

4 Sep 59 **THE WONDER OF YOU** *RCA 1131* 23 1
24 Mar 60 **ANSWER ME** *RCA 1175* 47 1
19 Jan 61 **CORINNA, CORINNA (re)** *London HLX 9246* 41 7

Tom PETTY and the HEARTBREAKERS (470 Top 500) *One of America's most popular rock groups of the past 30 years, formed Los Angeles 1975. Petty, b. 20 Oct 1953, Florida, was also a Traveling Wilbury. The Grammy-winning group signed a $20m deal with Warner Brothers in 1993 (Singles: 43 weeks, Albums: 104 weeks)* pos/wks

25 Jun 77 **ANYTHING THAT'S ROCK 'N' ROLL** *Shelter WIP 6396* 36 3
13 Aug 77 **AMERICAN GIRL** *Shelter WIP 6403* 40 5
15 Aug 81 **STOP DRAGGIN' MY HEART AROUND** *WEA K 79231* [1] 50 4
13 Apr 85 **DON'T COME AROUND HERE NO MORE** *MCA MCA 926* 50 4
13 May 89 **I WON'T BACK DOWN** *MCA MCA 1334* [2] 28 10
12 Aug 89 **RUNNIN' DOWN A DREAM** *MCA MCA 1359* [2] 55 4
25 Nov 89 **FREE FALLIN'** *MCA MCA 1381* [2] 64 2
29 Jun 91 **LEARNING TO FLY** *MCA MCS 1555* 46 4
4 Apr 92 **TOO GOOD TO BE TRUE** *MCA MCS 1616* 34 3
30 Oct 93 **SOMETHING IN THE AIR** *MCA MCSTD 1945* [2] 53 2
12 Mar 94 **MARY JANE'S LAST DANCE** *MCA MCSTD 1966* 52 2
4 Jun 77 **TOM PETTY AND THE HEARTBREAKERS** *Shelter ISA 5014* 24 12
1 Jul 78 **YOU'RE GONNA GET IT** *Island ISA 5017* 34 5
17 Nov 79 **DAMN THE TORPEDOES** *MCA MCF 3044* 57 4
23 May 81 **HARD PROMISES** *MCA MCF 3098* 32 5
20 Nov 82 **LONG AFTER DARK** *MCA MCF 3155* 45 4
20 Apr 85 **SOUTHERN ACCENTS** *MCA MCF 3260* 23 6
2 May 87 **LET ME UP (I'VE HAD ENOUGH)** *MCA MCG 6014* 59 2
8 Jul 89 ● **FULL MOON FEVER** *MCA MCG 6034* [1] 8 16
20 Jul 91 ● **INTO THE GREAT WIDE OPEN** *MCA MCA 10317* 3 18
13 Nov 93 ● **GREATEST HITS** *MCA MCD 10964* 10 20
12 Nov 94 **WILDFLOWERS** *Warner Bros. 9362457592* [1] 36 2
24 Aug 96 **SHE'S THE ONE (FILM SOUNDTRACK)** *Warner Bros. 9362462852* 37 2
1 May 99 **ECHO** *Warner Bros. 9362472942* 43 2
16 Jun 01 **ANTHOLOGY – THROUGH THE YEARS** *MCA 1701772* 14 6

[1] Stevie Nicks with Tom Petty and the Heartbreakers [2] Tom Petty [1] Tom Petty

PHANTOMS – *See Johnny BRANDON with The PHANTOMS*

PHARAO *Germany, male / female vocal / instrumental group (Singles: 2 weeks)* pos/wks

4 Mar 95 **THERE IS A STAR** *Epic 6611832* 43 2

PHARAOHS – *See SAM THE SHAM and the PHARAOHS*

PHARCYDE *US, male rap group (Singles: 6 weeks, Albums: 2 weeks)* pos/wks

31 Jul 93 **PASSIN' ME BY** *Atlantic A 8360CD* 55 3

6 Apr 96	**RUNNIN'** *Go.Beat GODCD 142*	**36** 2
10 Aug 96	**SHE SAID** *Go.Beat GODCD 144*	**51** 1
21 Aug 93	**BIZARRE RIDE II THE PHARCYDE** *Atlantic 756792222*	**58** 1
13 Apr 96	**LABCABINCALIFORNIA** *Go! Beat 8287332*	**46** 1

Franke PHAROAH – *See FRANKE*

PHARRELL *US, male producer / vocalist (Singles: 46 weeks)* pos/wks

8 Jun 02	**PASS THE COURVOISIER – PART II** *J 74321937902* [1]	**16** 7
10 Aug 02 ●	**BOYS** *Jive 9253912* [2]	**7** 8
5 Apr 03	**BEAUTIFUL** *Priority CDCL 842* [3]	**23** 20
29 Nov 03	**LIGHT YOUR ASS ON FIRE** *Arista 82876572512* [4]	**62** 1
16 Aug 03	**FRONTIN'** *Arista 82867655332* [5]	**6** 10

[1] Busta Rhymes featuring P Diddy and Pharrell [2] Britney Spears featuring Pharrell Williams [3] Snoop Dogg featuring Pharrell [4] Busta Rhymes featuring Pharrell [4] Pharrell Williams featuring Jay-Z

*See also N*E*R*D; NEPTUNES*

PHASE II *US, male vocal group (Singles: 2 weeks)* pos/wks

18 Mar 89	**REACHIN'** *Republic LICT 006*	**70** 1
21 Dec 91	**REACHIN' (re-mix)** *Republic LIC 160* [1]	**70** 1

[1] Joey Negro presents Phase II

PHAT 'N' PHUNKY *UK, male production duo (Singles: 1 week)* pos/wks

14 Jun 97	**LET'S GROOVE** *Chase CDCHASE 8*	**61** 1

PHATS & SMALL *UK, male DJ / production duo – Jason Hayward and Russell Small (Singles: 36 weeks)* pos/wks

10 Apr 99 ●	**TURN AROUND** *Multiply CDMULTY 49*	**2** 16
14 Aug 99 ●	**FEEL GOOD** *Multiply CDMULTY 54*	**7** 8
4 Dec 99	**TONITE** *Multiply CDMULTY 57*	**11** 6
30 Jun 01	**THIS TIME AROUND** *Multiply CDMULTY 75*	**15** 5
24 Nov 01	**CHANGE** *Multiply CDMULTY 80*	**45** 1

PHATT B
Holland, male DJ / producer – Bernsquil Verndoom (Singles: 1 week) pos/wks

11 Nov 00	**AND DA DRUM MACHINE** *Nulife / Arista 74321801902*	**58** 1

Barrington PHELOUNG
Australia, male conductor (Singles: 2 weeks, Albums: 55 weeks) pos/wks

13 Mar 93	**'INSPECTOR MORSE' THEME** *Virgin VSCDT 1458*	**61** 2
2 Mar 91 ●	**INSPECTOR MORSE MUSIC FROM THE TV SERIES** *Virgin Television VTLP 2*	**4** 30
7 Mar 92	**INSPECTOR MORSE VOLUME 2** *Virgin Television VTCD 14*	**18** 12
16 Jan 93	**INSPECTOR MORSE VOLUME 3** *Virgin Television VTCD 16*	**20** 11
25 Nov 00	**THE MAGIC OF INSPECTOR MORSE** *Virgin VTDCD 353*	**62** 2

PHENOMENA
UK, male vocal / instrumental group (Albums: 2 weeks) pos/wks

6 Jul 85	**PHENOMENA** *Bronze PM 1*	**63** 2

PHILADELPHIA INTERNATIONAL ALL-STARS
US, male / female vocal / instrumental group (Singles: 8 weeks) pos/wks

13 Aug 77	**LET'S CLEAN UP THE GHETTO** *Philadelphia International PIR 5451*	**34** 8

PHILHARMONIA ORCHESTRA, conductor Lorin MAAZEL
UK, orchestra and US, male conductor (Singles: 7 weeks) pos/wks

30 Jul 69	**THUS SPAKE ZARATHUSTRA** *Columbia DB 8607*	**33** 7

Arlene PHILLIPS
UK, female exercise instructor (Albums: 24 weeks) pos/wks

28 Aug 82	**KEEP IN SHAPE SYSTEM** *Supershape SUP 01*	**41** 23
18 Feb 84	**KEEP IN SHAPE SYSTEM VOLUME 2** *Supershape SUP 2*	**100** 1

'Keep in Shape System' features music by Funk Federation

Chynna PHILLIPS
US, female vocalist (Singles: 1 week) pos/wks

3 Feb 96	**NAKED AND SACRED** *EMI CDEM 409*	**62** 1

Esther PHILLIPS *US, female vocalist – Esther Mae Jones d. 7 Aug 1984 (Singles: 8 weeks)* pos/wks

4 Oct 75 ●	**WHAT A DIFFERENCE A DAY MADE** *Kudu 925*	**6** 8

PHIXX *UK, male vocal group (Singles: 4 weeks)* pos/wks

8 Nov 03 ●	**HOLD ON ME** *Concept CDCON 51*	**10** 4

PHOEBE ONE
UK, female rapper – Phoebe Espirit (Singles: 3 weeks) pos/wks

12 Dec 98	**DOIN' OUR THING / ONE MAN'S BITCH** *Mecca Recordings MECX 1020*	**59** 1
15 May 99	**GET ON IT** *Mecca Recordings MECX 1026*	**38** 2

PHOENIX
France, male vocal / instrumental group (Singles: 1 week) pos/wks

3 Feb 01	**IF I EVER FEEL BETTER** *Source DINSD 210*	**65** 1

Paul PHOENIX *UK, male vocalist (Singles: 4 weeks)* pos/wks

3 Nov 79	**NUNC DIMITTIS** *Different HAVE 20*	**56** 4

Full artist credit on hit as follows: Paul Phoenix (treble) with Instrumental Ensemble – James Watson (trumpet), John Scott (organ), conducted by Barry Rose

PHOTEK *UK, male producer – Rupert Parkes (Singles: 4 weeks, Albums: 4 weeks)* pos/wks

22 Mar 97	**NI-TEN-ICHI-RYU (TWO SWORDS TECHNIQUE)** *Science QEDCD 2*	**37** 2
28 Feb 98	**MODUS OPERANDI** *Virgin QEDCD 6*	**66** 1
24 Feb 01	**MINE TO GIVE** *Science QEDCD 10* [1]	**44** 1
15 Jun 96	**THE HIDDEN CAMERA** *Science QEDCD 1*	**39** 1
27 Sep 97	**MODUS OPERANDI** *Science CDQED 1*	**30** 2
26 Sep 98	**FORM & FUNCTION** *Science CDQED 2*	**61** 1

[1] Photek featuring Robert Owens

PHOTOS *UK, male / female vocal / instrumental group (Singles: 4 weeks, Albums: 9 weeks)* pos/wks

17 May 80	**IRENE** *Epic EPC 8517*	**56** 4
21 Jun 80 ●	**THE PHOTOS** *CBS PHOTO 5*	**4** 9

PHUNKY PHANTOM
UK, male producer – Lawrence Nelson (Singles: 3 weeks) pos/wks

16 May 98	**GET UP STAND UP** *Club for Life DISNCD 44*	**27** 3

See also GAT DECOR; REST ASSURED

PHUTURE ASSASSINS
UK, male instrumental / production group (Singles: 1 week) pos/wks

6 Jun 92	**FUTURE SOUND (EP)** *Suburban Base SUBBASE 010*	**64** 1

Tracks on Future Sound (EP): Future Sound / African Sanctus / Rydim Come Foward / Freedom Sound

PIA – *See Pia ZADORA*

Edith PIAF *France, female vocalist – Edith Gassion d. 11 Oct 1963 (Singles: 15 weeks, Albums: 5 weeks)* pos/wks

12 May 60	**MILORD (re)** *Columbia DC 754*	**24** 15
26 Sep 87	**HEART AND SOUL** *Stylus SMR 736*	**58** 5

PIANOHEADZ *US, male DJ / production duo – Erick Morillo and Jose Nunez (Singles: 2 weeks)* pos/wks

11 Jul 98	**IT'S OVER (DISTORTION)** *Incredible Music INCRL 3CD*	**39** 2

See also LIL MO' YIN YANG; Erick 'More' MORILLO presents RAW; REEL 2 REAL

PIANOMAN
UK, male producer – James Sammon (Singles: 8 weeks) pos/wks

15 Jun 96 ● **BLURRED** *Ffrreedom TABCD 243* 6 7
26 Apr 97 **PARTY PEOPLE (LIVE YOUR LIFE BE FREE)** *3 Beat 3 BTCD1* ..43 1

See also BASS BOYZ

Mark PICCHIOTTI presents BASSTOY featuring DANA
US, male / female production / vocal duo (Singles: 5 weeks) pos/wks

19 Jan 02 **RUNNIN' (re-mix)** *Black & White NEOCD 073* 13 5

See also SANDSTORM; BASSTOY

Bobby 'Boris' PICKETT and the CRYPT-KICKERS
US, male vocal / instrumental group (Singles: 13 weeks) pos/wks

1 Sep 73 ● **MONSTER MASH** *London HLU 10320* ▲ 3 13

Wilson PICKETT *US, male vocalist (Singles: 61 weeks)* pos/wks

23 Sep 65 **IN THE MIDNIGHT HOUR** *Atlantic AT 4036* 12 11
25 Nov 65 **DON'T FIGHT IT** *Atlantic AT 4052* 29 8
10 Mar 66 **634-5789** *Atlantic AT 4072* 36 5
1 Sep 66 **LAND OF 1000 DANCES** *Atlantic 584 039* 22 9
15 Dec 66 **MUSTANG SALLY** *Atlantic 584 066* 28 7
27 Sep 67 **FUNKY BROADWAY** *Atlantic 584 130* 43 3
11 Sep 68 **I'M A MIDNIGHT MOVER** *Atlantic 584 203* 38 6
8 Jan 69 **HEY JUDE** *Atlantic 584 236* 16 9
21 Nov 87 **IN THE MIDNIGHT HOUR (re-recording)** *Motown ZB 41583* 62 3

PICKETTYWITCH *UK, male / female vocal / instrumental group – includes Polly Brown (Singles: 34 weeks)* pos/wks

28 Feb 70 ● **THAT SAME OLD FEELING** *Pye 7N 17887* 5 14
4 Jul 70 **(IT'S LIKE A) SAD OLD KINDA MOVIE** *Pye 7N 17951* 16 10
7 Nov 70 **BABY I WON'T LET YOU DOWN** *Pye 7N 45002* 27 10

Mauro PICOTTO *Italy, male producer (Singles: 23 weeks)* pos/wks

12 Jun 99 **LIZARD (GONNA GET YOU)** *VC Recordings VCRD 50* 27 3
20 Nov 99 **LIZARD (GONNA GET YA) (re-mix)** *VC Recordings VCRD 57* 33 2
15 Jul 00 **IGUANA** *VC Recordings VCRD 68* 33 3
13 Jan 01 **KOMODO (SAVE A SOUL)** *VC Recordings VCRD 85* 13 5
11 Aug 01 **LIKE THIS LIKE THAT** *VC Recordings VCRD 92* 21 4
25 Aug 01 **VERDI** *BXR BXRP 0318* 74 1
16 Mar 02 **PULSAR 2002** *BXR BXRC 0162* 35 3
3 Aug 02 **BACK TO CALI** *BXR BXRC 0433* 42 2

See also RAF; CRW

PIGBAG *UK, male instrumental group (Singles: 20 weeks, Albums: 14 weeks)* pos/wks

7 Nov 81 **SUNNY DAY** *Y Records Y 12* 53 3
27 Feb 82 **GETTING UP** *Y Records Y 16* 61 3
3 Apr 82 ● **PAPA'S GOT A BRAND NEW PIGBAG** *Y Records Y 10* 3 11
10 Jul 82 **THE BIG BEAN** *Y Records Y 24* 40 3
13 Mar 82 DR HECKLE AND MR JIVE *Y Y 17* 18 14

PIGEON HED – See LO FIDELITY ALLSTARS

Nelson PIGFORD – See De Etta LITTLE and Nelson PIGFORD

PIGLETS *UK, female vocal group (Singles: 12 weeks)* pos/wks

6 Nov 71 ● **JOHNNY REGGAE** *Bell 1180* 3 12

Dick PIKE – See Ruby WRIGHT

PILOT *UK, male vocal / instrumental group (Singles: 29 weeks, Albums: 1 week)* pos/wks

2 Nov 74 **MAGIC** *EMI 2217* 11 11
18 Jan 75 ★ **JANUARY** *EMI 2255* 1 10
19 Apr 75 **CALL ME ROUND** *EMI 2287* 34 4
27 Sep 75 **JUST A SMILE** *EMI 2338* 31 4
31 May 75 SECOND FLIGHT *EMI EMC 3075* 48 1

PILTDOWN MEN
US, male instrumental group (Singles: 36 weeks) pos/wks

8 Sep 60 **MCDONALD'S CAVE** *Capitol CL 15149* 14 18
12 Jan 61 **PILTDOWN RIDES AGAIN** *Capitol CL 15175* 14 10
9 Mar 61 **GOODNIGHT MRS. FLINTSTONE** *Capitol CL 15186* 18 8

Courtney PINE *UK, male instrumentalist – saxophone (Singles: 6 weeks, Albums: 13 weeks)* pos/wks

30 Jul 88 **LIKE DREAMERS DO** *Fourth & Broadway BRW 108* [1] 26 5
7 Jul 90 **I'M STILL WAITING** *Mango MNG 749* [2] 66 1
25 Oct 86 JOURNEY TO THE URGE WITHIN *Island ILPS 9846* 39 11
6 Feb 88 DESTINY'S SONGS *Antilles AN 8275* 54 2

[1] Mica Paris featuring Courtney Pine [2] Courtney Pine featuring Carroll Thompson

'PING PING' and Al VERLAINE
Belgium, male vocal duo (Singles: 4 weeks) pos/wks

28 Sep 61 **SUCU SUCU** *Oriole CB 1589* 41 4

PINK (287 Top 500)
Brit-winning R&B / pop diva whose hair colour regularly matches her name, b. Alecia Moore, 8 Sep 1979, Pennsylvania, US. Rock-influenced UK million-selling 'M!ssundaztood' was 2002's top-selling album by a female artist in both the US and UK. Seven UK Top 10 hits with her first seven releases is a total unbeaten by any other US female (Singles: 105 weeks, Albums: 117 weeks) pos/wks

10 Jun 00 ● **THERE YOU GO** *LaFace / Arista 74321757602* 6 9
30 Sep 00 ● **MOST GIRLS** *LaFace / Arista 74321792012* 5 8
27 Jan 01 ● **YOU MAKE ME SICK** *LaFace / Arista 74321828702* 9 6
30 Jun 01 ★ **LADY MARMALADE** *Interscope / Polydor 4975612* [1] ■ ▲ 1 16
26 Jan 02 ● **GET THE PARTY STARTED** *LaFace / Arista 74321913372* 2 15
25 May 02 ● **DON'T LET ME GET ME** *Arista 74321939212* 6 11
28 Sep 02 ★ **JUST LIKE A PILL** *Arista 74321959652* ■ 1 11
14 Dec 02 **FAMILY PORTRAIT (import)** *Arista 74321982102* 66 1
21 Dec 02 **FAMILY PORTRAIT** *Arista 74321982052* 11 9
19 Jul 03 ● **FEEL GOOD TIME** *Columbia 6741062* [2] 3 11
8 Nov 03 ● **TROUBLE** *Arista 82876572172* ....7 8+
27 May 00 CAN'T TAKE ME HOME *Arista 73008260622* 13 41
9 Feb 02 ● M!SSUNDAZTOOD *Arista 7822147182* 2 70
22 Nov 03 ● TRY THIS *Arista 82876571852* ....3 6+

[1] Christina Aguilera, Lil' Kim, Mya and Pink [2] William Orbit featuring Pink

PINK FAIRIES
UK, male vocal / instrumental group (Albums: 1 week) pos/wks

29 Jul 72 WHAT A BUNCH OF SWEETIES *Polydor 2383 132* 48 1

PINK FLOYD (21 Top 500)
One of the world's most respected rock groups formed London 1965: David Gilmour (g), Roger Waters (b), Rick Wright (k) and Nick Mason (d). In US, 'The Dark Side of the Moon' has spent a record 27 years on the chart and 'The Wall' sold more than 23 million (Singles: 55 weeks, Albums: 911 weeks) pos/wks

30 Mar 67 **ARNOLD LAYNE** *Columbia DB 8156* 20 8
22 Jun 67 ● **SEE EMILY PLAY** *Columbia DB 8214* 6 12
1 Dec 79 ★ **ANOTHER BRICK IN THE WALL (PART 2)** *Harvest HAR 5194* ▲ 1 12
7 Aug 82 **WHEN THE TIGERS BROKE FREE** *Harvest HAR 5222* 39 5
7 May 83 **NOT NOW JOHN** *Harvest HAR 5224* 30 4
19 Dec 87 **ON THE TURNING AWAY** *EMI EM 34* 55 4
25 Jun 88 **ONE SLIP** *EMI EM 52* 50 3
4 Jun 94 **TAKE IT BACK** *EMI CDEMS 309* 23 4
29 Oct 94 **HIGH HOPES / KEEP TALKING** *EMI CDEMS 342* 26 3
19 Aug 67 ● THE PIPER AT THE GATES OF DAWN *Columbia SCX 6157* 6 14
13 Jul 68 ● A SAUCERFUL OF SECRETS *Columbia SCX 6258* 9 11
28 Jun 69 ● MORE (FILM SOUNDTRACK) *Columbia SCX 6346* 9 5
15 Nov 69 ● UMMAGUMMA *Harvest SHDW 1/2* 5 21
24 Oct 70 ★ ATOM HEART MOTHER *Harvest SHVL 781* ■ 1 18
7 Aug 71 RELICS *Starline SRS 5071* 32 6
20 Nov 71 ● MEDDLE *Harvest SHVL 795* 3 82
17 Jun 72 ● OBSCURED BY CLOUDS (FILM SOUNDTRACK) *Harvest SHSP 4020* 6 14
31 Mar 73 ● THE DARK SIDE OF THE MOON *Harvest SHVL 804* ▲ 2 364

19 Jan 74 **A NICE PAIR (double re-issue)** *Harvest SHDW 403*..........21 20
27 Sep 75 ★ **WISH YOU WERE HERE** *Harvest SHVL 814* ▲..........1 89
19 Feb 77 ● **ANIMALS** *Harvest SHVL 815*..........2 33
8 Dec 79 ● **THE WALL** *Harvest SHDW 411* ▲..........3 56
5 Dec 81 **A COLLECTION OF GREAT DANCE SONGS** *Harvest SHVL 822* 37 10
2 Apr 83 ★ **THE FINAL CUT** *Harvest SHPF 1983* ■..........1 25
19 Sep 87 ● **A MOMENTARY LAPSE OF REASON** *EMI EMD 1003*..........3 34
3 Dec 88 **DELICATE SOUND OF THUNDER** *EMI EQ 5009*..........11 12
9 Apr 94 ★ **THE DIVISION BELL** *EMI CDEMD 1055* ■ ▲..........1 51
10 Jun 95 ★ **PULSE** *EMI CDEMD 1078* ■ ▲..........1 21
9 Mar 96 **RELICS (re-issue)** *EMI CDEMD 1082*..........48 2
16 Aug 97 **THE PIPER AT THE GATES OF DAWN (re-issue)** *EMI CDEMD 1110*..........44 2
8 Apr 00 **IS THERE ANYBODY OUT THERE? – THE WALL LIVE 1980–81** *EMI 5235622*..........15 5
17 Nov 01 ● **ECHOES – THE BEST OF PINK FLOYD** *EMI 5361112*..........2 16

'A Nice Pair' is a double re-issue of the first two albums

See also David GILMOUR; Rick WRIGHT; Roger WATERS; Syd BARRETT

PINKEES *UK, male vocal / instrumental group (Singles: 9 weeks)* pos/wks

18 Sep 82 ● **DANGER GAMES** *Creole CR 39*..........8 9

PINKERTON'S ASSORTED COLOURS

UK, male vocal / instrumental group (Singles: 12 weeks) pos/wks

13 Jan 66 ● **MIRROR MIRROR** *Decca F 12307*..........9 11
21 Apr 66 **DON'T STOP LOVING ME BABY** *Decca F 12377*..........50 1

PINKY and PERKY

UK, male porcine puppet vocal duo (Singles: 3 weeks) pos/wks

29 May 93 **REET PETITE** *Telstar CDPIGGY 1*..........47 3

Lisa PIN-UP

UK, female DJ / producer – Lisa Chilcott (Singles: 4 weeks) pos/wks

25 May 02 **TURN UP THE SOUND** *Nukleuz NUKC 0406*..........60 1
21 Dec 02 **BLOW YOUR MIND (I AM THE WOMAN)** *Nukleuz 0450 FNUK*..60 3

PIONEERS

Jamaica, male vocal / instrumental group (Singles: 34 weeks) pos/wks

18 Oct 69 **LONG SHOT KICK DE BUCKET (re)** *Trojan TR 672*..........21 11
31 Jul 71 ● **LET YOUR YEAH BE YEAH** *Trojan TR 7825*..........5 12
15 Jan 72 **GIVE AND TAKE** *Trojan TR 7846*..........35 6
29 Mar 80 **LONG SHOT KICK DE BUCKET (re-issue)** *Trojan TRO 9063*......42 5

Re-issue of 'Long Shot Kick De Bucket' coupled with re-issue of Liquidator by Harry J All Stars

Billie PIPER

UK, female vocalist (Singles: 87 weeks, Albums: 27 weeks) pos/wks

11 Jul 98 ★ **BECAUSE WE WANT TO** *Innocent SINCD 2* [1] ■..........1 12
17 Oct 98 ★ **GIRLFRIEND (re)** *Innocent SINCD 3* [1] ■..........1 12
19 Dec 98 ● **SHE WANTS YOU (re)** *Innocent SINDXX 6* [1]..........3 13
3 Apr 99 ● **HONEY TO THE BEE (re)** *Innocent SINCD 8* [1]..........3 11
10 Apr 99 ● **THANK ABBA FOR THE MUSIC** *Epic ABCD 1* [2]..........4 13
27 May 00 ★ **DAY & NIGHT (re)** *Innocent SINCD 11* ■..........1 12
30 Sep 00 ● **SOMETHING DEEP INSIDE (re)** *Innocent SINCD 19*..........4 9
23 Dec 00 **WALK OF LIFE** *Innocent SINCD 23*..........25 5
31 Oct 98 **HONEY TO THE B** *Innocent CDSIN 1* [1]..........14 23
14 Oct 00 **WALK OF LIFE** *Innocent CDSINX 3*..........14 4

[1] Billie [2] Steps, Tina Cousins, Cleopatra, B*Witched, Billie [1] Billie

See also H20

PIPKINS *UK, male vocal duo – Roger Greenaway and Tony Burrows (Singles: 10 weeks)* pos/wks

28 Mar 70 ● **GIMME DAT DING** *Columbia DB 8662*..........6 10

See also BLUE MINK; DAVID and JONATHAN; EDISON LIGHTHOUSE; WHITE PLAINS; BROTHERHOOD OF MAN

PIPS – *See Gladys KNIGHT and the PIPS*

PIRANHAS *UK, male vocal / instrumental group (Singles: 21 weeks, Albums: 3 weeks)* pos/wks

2 Aug 80 ● **TOM HARK** *Sire SIR 4044*..........6 12
16 Oct 82 **ZAMBESI** *Dakota DAK 6* [1]..........17 9
20 Sep 80 **PIRANHAS** *Sire SRK 6098*..........69 3

[1] Piranhas featuring Boring Bob Grover

PIRATES *UK, male vocal / instrumental group (Albums: 3 weeks)* pos/wks

19 Nov 77 **OUT OF THEIR SKULLS** *Warner Bros. K 56411*..........57 3

See also Johnny KIDD

PITCHSHIFTER *UK, male vocal / instrumental group (Singles: 4 weeks, Albums: 2 weeks)* pos/wks

28 Feb 98 **GENIUS** *Geffen GFSTD 22324*..........71 1
26 Sep 98 **MICROWAVED** *Geffen GFSTD 22348*..........54 1
21 Oct 00 **DEAD BATTERY** *MCA MCSTD 40241*..........71 1
29 Jun 02 **SHUTDOWN** *Mayan MYNX 008*..........66 1
3 Jun 00 **DEVIANT** *MCA 1122542*..........35 1
11 May 02 **P.SI** *Mayan MYNCD 004*..........54 1

Gene PITNEY (204 Top 500)

Leading US performer in the 1960s, b. 17 Feb 1941, Connecticut. This unmistakable vocalist and songwriter had a longer and more impressive track record in the UK than in his homeland. Nonetheless, it took him 28 years to reach No.1 (Singles: 212 weeks, Albums: 75 weeks) pos/wks

23 Mar 61 **(I WANNA) LOVE MY LIFE AWAY** *London HL 9270*..........26 11
8 Mar 62 **TOWN WITHOUT PITY** *HMV POP 952*..........32 6
5 Dec 63 ● **TWENTY FOUR HOURS FROM TULSA** *United Artists UP 1035*..........5 19
5 Mar 64 ● **THAT GIRL BELONGS TO YESTERDAY** *United Artists UP 1045*..........7 12
15 Oct 64 **IT HURTS TO BE IN LOVE** *United Artists UP 1063*..........36 4
12 Nov 64 ● **I'M GONNA BE STRONG** *Stateside SS 358*..........2 14
18 Feb 65 ● **I MUST BE SEEING THINGS** *Stateside SS 390*..........6 10
10 Jun 65 ● **LOOKING THRU THE EYES OF LOVE** *Stateside SS 420*..........3 12
4 Nov 65 ● **PRINCESS IN RAGS** *Stateside SS 471*..........9 12
17 Feb 66 ● **BACKSTAGE** *Stateside SS 490*..........4 10
9 Jun 66 ● **NOBODY NEEDS YOUR LOVE** *Stateside SS 518*..........2 13
10 Nov 66 ● **JUST ONE SMILE** *Stateside SS 558*..........8 12
23 Feb 67 **(IN THE) COLD LIGHT OF DAY** *Stateside SS 597*..........38 6
15 Nov 67 ● **SOMETHING'S GOTTEN HOLD OF MY HEART** *Stateside SS 2060*..........5 13
3 Apr 68 **SOMEWHERE IN THE COUNTRY** *Stateside SS 2103*..........19 9
27 Nov 68 **YOURS UNTIL TOMORROW** *Stateside SS 2131*..........34 7
5 Mar 69 **MARIA ELENA** *Stateside SS 2142*..........25 6
14 Mar 70 **A STREET CALLED HOPE** *Stateside SS 2164*..........37 5
3 Oct 70 **SHADY LADY** *Stateside SS 2177*..........29 8
28 Apr 73 **24 SYCAMORE** *Pye International 7N 25606*..........34 7
2 Nov 74 **BLUE ANGEL (re)** *Bronze BRO 11*..........39 4
14 Jan 89 ★ **SOMETHING'S GOTTEN HOLD OF MY HEART** *Parlophone R 6201* [1]..........1 12
11 Apr 64 ● **BLUE GENE** *United Artists ULP 1061*..........7 11
6 Feb 65 **GENE PITNEY'S BIG 16** *Stateside SL 10118*..........12 6
20 Mar 65 **I'M GONNA BE STRONG** *Stateside SL 10120*..........15 2
20 Nov 65 **LOOKIN' THRU THE EYES OF LOVE** *Stateside SL 10148*..........15 5
17 Sep 66 **NOBODY NEEDS YOUR LOVE** *Stateside SL 10183*..........13 17
4 Mar 67 **YOUNG WARM AND WONDERFUL** *Stateside SSL 10194*..........39 1
22 Apr 67 **GENE PITNEY'S BIG SIXTEEN** *Stateside SSL 10199*..........40 1
20 Sep 69 ● **BEST OF GENE PITNEY** *Stateside SSL 10286*..........8 9
2 Oct 76 ● **HIS 20 GREATEST HITS** *Arcade ADEP 22*..........6 14
20 Oct 90 **BACKSTAGE – THE GREATEST HITS AND MORE** *Polydor 8471191*..........17 7
22 Sep 01 **THE ULTIMATE COLLECTION** *Sequel NEECD 380*..........40 2

[1] Marc Almond featuring special guest star Gene Pitney

Mario PIU *Italy, male DJ / producer (Singles: 14 weeks)* pos/wks

11 Dec 99 ● **COMMUNICATION (SOMEBODY ANSWER THE PHONE)** *Incentive CENT 2CDS*..........5 9
10 Mar 01 **THE VISION (re)** *BXR BXRC 0253* [1]..........16 5

[1] Mario Piu presents DJ Arabesque

PIXIES
US, male / female vocal / instrumental group (Singles: 13 weeks, Albums: 29 weeks)

Date	Title	pos	wks
1 Apr 89	**MONKEY GONE TO HEAVEN** *4AD AD 904*	60	3
1 Jul 89	**HERE COMES YOUR MAN** *4AD AD 909*	54	1
28 Jul 90	**VELOURIA** *4AD AD 0009*	28	3
10 Nov 90	**DIG FOR FIRE** *4AD AD 0014*	62	1
8 Jun 91	**PLANET OF SOUND** *4AD AD 1008*	27	3
4 Oct 97	**DEBASER** *4AD BAD 7010CD*	23	2
29 Apr 89	● **DOOLITTLE** *4AD CAD 905*	8	9
25 Aug 90	● **BOSSANOVA** *4AD CAD 0010*	3	8
5 Oct 91	● **TROMPE LE MONDE** *4AD CAD 1014*	7	5
18 Oct 97	**DEATH TO THE PIXIES** *4AD DAD 7011CD*	28	3
18 Oct 97	**DEATH TO THE PIXIES – DELUXE EDITION** *4AD DADD 7011CD*	20	2
18 Jul 98	**AT THE BBC** *4AD GAD 8013CD*	45	1
17 Mar 01	**COMPLETE B-SIDES** *4AD GAD 2103CD*	53	1

PIZZAMAN
UK, male producer – Norman Cook (Singles: 18 weeks)

Date	Title	pos	wks
27 Aug 94	**TRIPPIN' ON SUNSHINE** *Cowboy Records CDLOAD 16*	33	2
10 Jun 95	**SEX ON THE STREETS (re)** *Cowboy Records CDLOAD 24*	23	8
18 Nov 95	**HAPPINESS** *Cowboy Records CDLOAD 29*	19	4
1 Jun 96	**TRIPPIN' ON SUNSHINE (re-issue)** *Cowboy Records CDLOAD 32*	18	3
14 Sep 96	**HELLO HONKY TONKS (ROCK YOUR BODY)** *Cowboy Records CDLOAD 39*	41	1

See also BEATS INTERNATIONAL; Norman COOK; FREAKPOWER; HOUSEMARTINS; MIGHTY DUB KATZ

PIZZICATO FIVE
Japan, male / female vocal / instrumental group (Singles: 1 week)

Date	Title	pos	wks
1 Nov 97	**MON AMOUR TOKYO** *Matador OLE 2902*	72	1

Joe PIZZULO – *See Sergio MENDES*

PLACEBO
US / Sweden / UK, male vocal / instrumental group (Singles: 46 weeks, Albums: 46 weeks)

Date	Title	pos	wks
28 Sep 96	**TEENAGE ANGST** *Elevator Music FLOORCD 3*	30	3
1 Feb 97	● **NANCY BOY** *Elevator Music FLOORCD 4*	4	6
24 May 97	**BRUISE PRISTINE** *Elevator Music FLOORCD 5*	14	3
15 Aug 98	● **PURE MORNING** *Hut FLOORCD 6*	4	6
10 Oct 98	● **YOU DON'T CARE ABOUT US** *Hut FLOORCD 7*	5	5
6 Feb 99	**EVERY YOU EVERY ME** *Hut / Virgin FLOORCD 9*	11	5
29 Jul 00	**TASTE IN MEN** *Hut / Virgin FLOORCD 11*	16	6
7 Oct 00	**SLAVE TO THE WAGE** *Hut / Virgin FLOORCD 12*	19	3
22 Mar 03	**THE BITTER END** *Hut / Virgin FLOOR CD 16*	12	5
28 Jun 03	**THIS PICTURE** *Hut / Virgin FLOORCD 18*	23	2
27 Sep 03	**SPECIAL NEEDS** *Hut / Virgin FLOORCD 19*	27	2
29 Jun 96	● **PLACEBO** *Elevator Music CDFLOORX 2*	5	13
24 Oct 98	● **WITHOUT YOU I'M NOTHING** *Hut CDFLOOR 8*	7	17
21 Oct 00	● **BLACK MARKET MUSIC** *Hut CDFLOORX 13*	6	5
5 Apr 03	**SLEEPING WITH GHOSTS** *Hut / Virgin CDFLOORX 17*	11	11

PLANET FUNK
Italy / UK / Finland, male / female vocal / production group (Singles: 12 weeks)

Date	Title	pos	wks
10 Feb 01	● **CHASE THE SUN (re)** *Virgin VSCDT 1794*	5	9
26 Apr 03	**WHO SAID (STUCK IN THE UK)** *Illustrious / Bustin' Loose CDILL 015*	36	2
16 Aug 03	**THE SWITCH** *Illustrious / Bustin' Loose CDILL 017*	52	1

PLANET PATROL
US, male vocal / instrumental group (Singles: 3 weeks)

Date	Title	pos	wks
17 Sep 83	**CHEAP THRILLS** *Polydor POSP 639*	64	3

PLANET PERFECTO
UK, male production group (Singles: 15 weeks)

Date	Title	pos	wks
14 Aug 99	**NOT OVER YET 99** *Code Blue BLU 004CD1* [1]	16	4
13 Nov 99	**BULLET IN THE GUN** *Perfecto PERF 3CDS*	15	4
16 Sep 00	● **BULLET IN THE GUN 2000 (re-mix)** *Perfecto PERF 03CDSX*	7	6
29 Sep 01	**BITES DA DUST** *Perfecto PERF 19CDS*	52	1

[1] Planet Perfecto featuring Grace

PLANETS
UK, male vocal / instrumental group (Singles: 8 weeks, Albums: 13 weeks)

Date	Title	pos	wks
18 Aug 79	**LINES** *Rialto TREB 104*	36	6
25 Oct 80	**DON'T LOOK DOWN** *Rialto TREB 116*	66	2
2 Mar 02	**CLASSICAL GRAFFITI** *EMI / Dramatico CDC 5573162*	34	13

PLANK 15
UK, male producer – Andrew Holt (Singles: 1 week)

Date	Title	pos	wks
2 Feb 02	**STRINGS OF LIFE** *Multiply CDMULTY 82*	60	1

Robert PLANT
UK, male vocalist (Singles: 33 weeks, Albums: 82 weeks)

Date	Title	pos	wks
9 Oct 82	**BURNING DOWN ONE SIDE** *Swansong SSK 19429*	73	1
16 Jul 83	**BIG LOG** *WEA B 9848*	11	10
30 Jan 88	**HEAVEN KNOWS** *Es Paranza A 9373*	33	5
28 Apr 90	**HURTING KIND (I'VE GOT MY EYES ON YOU)** *Es Paranza A 8985*	45	3
8 May 93	**29 PALMS** *Fontana FATEX 1*	21	5
3 Jul 93	**I BELIEVE** *Fontana FATEX 2*	64	2
25 Dec 93	**IF I WERE A CARPENTER** *Fontana FATEX 4*	63	2
17 Dec 94	**GALLOWS POLE** *Fontana PPCD 2* [1]	35	3
11 Apr 98	**MOST HIGH** *Mercury 5687512* [2]	26	2
10 Jul 82	● **PICTURES AT ELEVEN** *Swansong SSK 59418*	2	15
23 Jul 83	● **THE PRINCIPLES OF MOMENTS** *WEA 7901011*	7	14
1 Jun 85	**SHAKEN 'N' STIRRED** *Es Paranza 7902651*	19	4
12 Feb 88	● **NOW AND ZEN** *Es Paranza WX 149*	10	7
31 Mar 90	**MANIC NIRVANA** *Es Paranza WX 339*	15	9
5 Jun 93	● **FATE OF NATIONS** *Es Paranza 5148672*	6	8
19 Nov 94	● **NO QUARTER** *Fontana 5263622* [1]	7	13
2 May 98	● **WALKING INTO CLARKSDALE** *Mercury 5580252* [1]	3	6
6 Jul 02	**DREAMLAND** *Mercury 5869632*	20	3
15 Nov 03	**SIXTY SIX TO TIMBUKTU** *Mercury 9813199*	27	3

[1] Jimmy Page and Robert Plant [2] Page and Plant [1] Jimmy Page and Robert Plant

See also LED ZEPPELIN

PLASMATICS
US, female / male vocal / instrumental group (Singles: 4 weeks, Albums: 3 weeks)

Date	Title	pos	wks
26 Jul 80	**BUTCHER BABY** *Stiff BUY 76*	55	4
11 Oct 80	**NEW HOPE FOR THE WRETCHED** *Stiff SEEZ 24*	55	3

PLASTIC BERTRAND
Belgium, male vocalist – Roger Jouret (Singles: 17 weeks)

Date	Title	pos	wks
13 May 78	● **ÇA PLANE POUR MOI** *Sire 6078 616*	8	12
5 Aug 78	**SHA LA LA LA LEE** *Vertigo 6059 209*	39	5

PLASTIC BOY featuring ROZALLA
Belgium, male producer – Mike Dierickx and Zimbabwe, female vocalist (Singles: 1 week)

Date	Title	pos	wks
22 Nov 03	**LIVE ANOTHER LIFE** *Inferno CDFERN 59*	55	1

PLASTIC JAM – *See BUG KANN and the PLASTIC JAM*

PLASTIC ONO BAND – *See John LENNON*

PLASTIC PENNY
UK, male vocal / instrumental group (Singles: 10 weeks)

Date	Title	pos	wks
3 Jan 68	● **EVERYTHING I AM** *Page One POF 051*	6	10

PLASTIC POPULATION – *See YAZZ*

PLASTIK MAN
Canada, male instrumentalist – keyboards – Richie Hawtin (Albums: 1 week)

Date	Title	pos	wks
19 Nov 94	**MUSIK** *Novamute NOMU 37CD*	58	1

See also FUSE

PLATINUM 45 featuring MORE FIRE CREW
UK, male producer and UK male rap / vocal trio (Singles: 8 weeks) pos/wks

16 Mar 02 ● **OI!** *Go Beat GOBCD 48* 8 8

PLATINUM HOOK
US, male vocal / instrumental group (Singles: 1 week) pos/wks

2 Sep 78 **STANDING ON THE VERGE (OF GETTING IT ON)** *Motown TMG 1115* 72 1

PLATTERS *US, male / female vocal group – leader Tony Williams, b. 5 Apr 1928, d.14 Aug 1992 (Singles: 92 weeks, Albums: 13 weeks)* pos/wks

7 Sep 56 ● **THE GREAT PRETENDER / ONLY YOU (re)** *Mercury MT 117* 5 13
2 Nov 56 ● **MY PRAYER (2re)** *Mercury MT 120* ▲ 4 13
25 Jan 57 **YOU'LL NEVER NEVER KNOW / IT ISN'T RIGHT (2re)** *Mercury MT 130* 23 3
29 Mar 57 **ONLY YOU (AND YOU ALONE)** *Mercury MT 117.* 18 3
17 May 57 **I'M SORRY (2re)** *Mercury MT 145* 18 8
16 May 58 ● **TWILIGHT TIME** *Mercury MT 214* ▲ 3 18
16 Jan 59 ★ **SMOKE GETS IN YOUR EYES** *Mercury AMT 1016* ▲ 1 20
28 Aug 59 **REMEMBER WHEN** *Mercury AMT 1053* 25 2
29 Jan 60 **HARBOUR LIGHTS** *Mercury AMT 1081* 11 12
8 Apr 78 ● **20 CLASSIC HITS** *Mercury 9100 049* 8 13

PLAVKA – *See JAM & SPOON featuring PLAVKA*

PLAYBOY BAND – *See John FRED and the PLAYBOY BAND*

PLAYBOYS – *See Gary LEWIS and the PLAYBOYS*

PLAYER
US / UK, male vocal / instrumental group (Singles: 7 weeks) pos/wks

25 Feb 78 **BABY COME BACK** *RSO 2090 254* ▲ 32 7

PLAYERS ASSOCIATION *US, male vocal / instrumental group (Singles: 17 weeks, Albums: 4 weeks)* pos/wks

10 Mar 79 ● **TURN THE MUSIC UP!** *Vanguard VS 5011* 8 9
5 May 79 **RIDE THE GROOVE** *Vanguard VS 5012* 42 5
9 Feb 80 **WE GOT THE GROOVE** *Vanguard VS 5016* 61 3
17 Mar 79 **TURN THE MUSIC UP** *Vanguard VSD 79421* 54 4

PLAYGROUP
UK, male producer – Trevor Jackson (Singles: 1 week) pos/wks

24 Nov 01 **NUMBER ONE** *Source SOURCD 026* 66 1

PLAYN JAYN
UK, male vocal / instrumental group (Albums: 1 week) pos/wks

1 Sep 84 **FRIDAY THE 13TH (AT THE MARQUEE CLUB)** *A&M JAYN 13* .. 93 1

PLAYTHING *Italy, male production duo – Luca Moretti and Riccardo Romanini (Singles: 6 weeks)* pos/wks

5 May 01 **INTO SPACE** *Manifesto FESCD 81* 48 1
24 Aug 02 **DO YOU SEE THE LIGHT? (re-mix)** *Data MOS DATA 33CDS* [1] 14 5

[1] Snap! vs Plaything

See also TRIPLE X

PLUMMET
US, male DJ / producer – Eric B Muniz (Singles: 10 weeks) pos/wks

26 Apr 03 **DAMAGED** *Serious SER 68CD* 12 10

PLUS ONE featuring SIRRON
UK, male / female vocal / instrumental group (Singles: 4 weeks) pos/wks

19 May 90 **IT'S HAPPENIN'** *MCA MCA 1405* 40 4

PLUTO – *See Pluto SHERVINGTON*

PLUX featuring Georgia JONES
US, male / female vocal / instrumental group (Singles: 2 weeks) pos/wks

4 May 96 **OVER AND OVER** *ffrr FCD 277* 33 2

POETS *UK, male vocal / instrumental group (Singles: 5 weeks)* pos/wks

29 Oct 64 **NOW WE'RE THRU** *Decca F 11995* 31 5

POGUES (450 Top 500)
Irish band which presented an aggressive, compelling collision of folk, punk and rock. Led by Shane MacGowan (v/g) b. 25 Dec, 1957 and originally named Pogue Mahone. 'The Irish Rover' was the final Top 20 hit released by legendary Stiff label (Singles: 70 weeks, Albums: 83 weeks) pos/wks

6 Apr 85 **A PAIR OF BROWN EYES** *Stiff BUY 220* 72 2
22 Jun 85 **SALLY MACLENNANE** *Stiff BUY 224* 51 4
14 Sep 85 **DIRTY OLD TOWN** *Stiff BUY 229* 62 3
8 Mar 86 **POGUETRY IN MOTION (EP)** *Stiff BUY 243* 29 6
30 Aug 86 **HAUNTED** *MCA MCA 1084* 42 4
28 Mar 87 ● **THE IRISH ROVER** *Stiff BUY 258* [1] 8 8
5 Dec 87 ● **FAIRYTALE OF NEW YORK** *Pogue Mahone NY 7* [2] 2 9
5 Mar 88 **IF I SHOULD FALL FROM GRACE WITH GOD** *Pogue Mahone PG 1* 58 3
16 Jul 88 **FIESTA** *Pogue Mahone PG 2* 24 5
17 Dec 88 **YEAH, YEAH, YEAH, YEAH, YEAH** *Pogue Mahone YZ 355* 43 4
8 Jul 89 **MISTY MORNING, ALBERT BRIDGE** *PM YZ 407* 41 3
16 Jun 90 **JACK'S HEROES / WHISKEY IN THE JAR** *PM YZ 500* [1] 63 2
15 Sep 90 **SUMMER IN SIAM** *PM YZ 519* 64 2
21 Sep 91 **A RAINY NIGHT IN SOHO** *PM YZ 603* 67 1
14 Dec 91 **FAIRYTALE OF NEW YORK (re-issue)** *PM YZ 628* [2] 36 5
30 May 92 **HONKY TONK WOMEN** *PM YZ 673* 56 2
21 Aug 93 **TUESDAY MORNING** *PM YZ 758 CD* 18 5
22 Jan 94 **ONCE UPON A TIME** *PM YZ 771CD* 66 2
3 Nov 84 **RED ROSES FOR ME** *Stiff SEEZ 55* 89 1
17 Aug 85 **RUM SODOMY AND THE LASH** *Stiff SEEZ 58* 13 14
30 Jan 88 ● **IF I SHOULD FALL FROM GRACE WITH GOD** *Stiff NYR 1* 3 16
29 Jul 89 ● **PEACE AND LOVE** *WEA WX 247* 5 8
13 Oct 90 **HELL'S DITCH** *Pogue Mahone WX 366* 12 5
12 Oct 91 **THE BEST OF THE POGUES** *PM WX 430* 11 17
11 Sep 93 **WAITING FOR HERB** *PM 4509934632* 20 3
17 Mar 01 **THE VERY BEST OF THE POGUES** *WSM 8573874592* 18 19

[1] Pogues and the Dubliners [2] Pogues featuring Kirsty MacColl

Tracks on Poguetry in Motion (EP): London Girl / The Body of an American / A Rainy Night in Soho / Planxty Noel Hill Group was male / female for first two albums

POINT BREAK
UK, male vocal group (Singles: 21 weeks, Albums: 3 weeks) pos/wks

9 Oct 99 **DO WE ROCK** *Eternal WEA 216CD1* 29 2
22 Jan 00 ● **STAND TOUGH** *Eternal WEA 248CD1* 7 5
22 Apr 00 **FREAKYTIME** *Eternal WEA 265CD1* 13 6
5 Aug 00 **YOU** *Eternal WEA 290CD1* 14 5
2 Dec 00 **WHAT ABOUT US** *Eternal WEA 314CD1* 24 3
19 Aug 00 **APOCADELIC** *Eternal 8573828882* 21 3

POINTER SISTERS (383 Top 500) *Talented sibling vocal quartet formed 1971, Oakland, California, US, whose recordings touched many musical bases. Reduced to trio – June, Anita and Ruth – when Bonnie left in 1978. Soulful sisters surprisingly won a country music Grammy for 'Fairytale' in 1974 (Singles: 87 weeks, Albums: 88 weeks)* pos/wks

3 Feb 79 **EVERYBODY IS A STAR** *Planet K 12324* 61 3
17 Mar 79 **FIRE** *Planet K 12339* 34 8
22 Aug 81 ● **SLOWHAND** *Planet K 12530* 10 11
5 Dec 81 **SHOULD I DO IT?** *Planet K 12578* 50 5
14 Apr 84 ● **AUTOMATIC** *Planet RPS 105* 2 15
23 Jun 84 ● **JUMP (FOR MY LOVE)** *Planet RPS 106* 6 10
11 Aug 84 **I NEED YOU** *Planet RPS 107* 25 9
27 Oct 84 **I'M SO EXCITED** *Planet RPS 108* 11 11
12 Jan 85 **NEUTRON DANCE** *Planet RPS 109* 31 7
20 Jul 85 **DARE ME** *RCA PB 49957* 17 8
29 Aug 81 **BLACK AND WHITE** *Planet K 52300* 21 13
5 May 84 ● **BREAK OUT** *Planet PL 84705* 9 58

27 Jul 85 **CONTACT** *Planet PL 85457* 34 7
29 Jul 89 **JUMP – THE BEST OF THE POINTER SISTERS** *RCA PL 90319*..11 10

POISON *US, male vocal / instrumental group (Singles: 43 weeks, Albums: 37 weeks)* pos/wks

23 May 87 **TALK DIRTY TO ME** *Music For Nations KUT 125* 67 1
7 May 88 **NOTHIN' BUT A GOOD TIME** *Capitol CL 486* 35 3
5 Nov 88 **FALLEN ANGEL** *Capitol CL 500* 59 1
11 Feb 89 **EVERY ROSE HAS ITS THORN** *Capitol CL 520* ▲ 13 9
29 Apr 89 **YOUR MAMA DON'T DANCE** *Capitol CL 523* 13 7
23 Sep 89 **NOTHIN' BUT A GOOD TIME (re-issue)** *Capitol CL 539* 48 3
30 Jun 90 **UNSKINNY BOP** *Capitol CL 582* 15 7
27 Oct 90 **SOMETHING TO BELIEVE IN** *Enigma CL 594* 35 4
23 Nov 91 **SO TELL ME WHY** *Capitol CL 640* 25 2
13 Feb 93 **STAND** *Capitol CDCL 679* 25 3
24 Apr 93 **UNTIL YOU SUFFER SOME (FIRE AND ICE)** *Capitol CDCL 685* 32 3
21 May 88 **OPEN UP AND SAY ... AAH!** *Capitol EST 2059* 18 21
21 Jul 90 ● **FLESH AND BLOOD** *Enigma EST 2126* 3 11
14 Dec 91 **SWALLOW THIS LIVE** *Capitol ESTU 2159* 52 2
6 Mar 93 **NATIVE TONGUE** *Capitol CDSETU 2190* 20 3

POKEMON ALLSTARS – *See 50 GRIND featuring POKEMON ALLSTARS*

POLECATS *UK, male vocal / instrumental group (Singles: 18 weeks, Albums: 2 weeks)* pos/wks

7 Mar 81 **JOHN I'M ONLY DANCING / BIG GREEN CAR** *Mercury POLE 1* 35 8
16 May 81 **ROCKABILLY GUY** *Mercury POLE 2* 35 6
22 Aug 81 **JEEPSTER / MARIE CELESTE** *Mercury POLE 3* 53 4
4 Jul 81 **POLECATS** *Vertigo 6359 057* 28 2

POLICE (63 Top 500) *World-famous Anglo-American rock trio: Sting (b. Gordon Sumner) (v/b), Andy Summers (g/v), Stewart Copeland (d/v). These Brit and Grammy award winners were one of the 1980s' most popular acts. These Rock and Roll Hall of Fame members had five successive albums entering the UK chart at No.1. Their single sales total 5,617,175 (Singles: 153 weeks, Albums: 405 weeks)* pos/wks

7 Oct 78 ● **CAN'T STAND LOSING YOU (re)** *A&M AMS 7381* 2 16
28 Apr 79 **ROXANNE** *A&M AMS 7348* 12 9
22 Sep 79 ★ **MESSAGE IN A BOTTLE** *A&M AMS 7474* 1 11
17 Nov 79 **FALL OUT** *Illegal IL 001* 47 4
1 Dec 79 ★ **WALKING ON THE MOON** *A&M AMS 7494* 1 10
16 Feb 80 ● **SO LONELY** *A&M AMS 7402* 6 10
14 Jun 80 **SIX PACK** *A&M AMPP 6001* 17 4
27 Sep 80 ★ **DON'T STAND SO CLOSE TO ME** *A&M AMS 7564* ■ 1 10
13 Dec 80 ● **DE DO DO DO, DE DA DA DA** *A&M AMS 7578* 5 8
26 Sep 81 ● **INVISIBLE SUN** *A&M AMS 8164* 2 8
24 Oct 81 ★ **EVERY LITTLE THING SHE DOES IS MAGIC** *A&M AMS 8174* 1 13
12 Dec 81 **SPIRITS IN THE MATERIAL WORLD** *A&M AMS 8194* 12 8
28 May 83 ★ **EVERY BREATH YOU TAKE** *A&M AM 117* ▲ 1 11
23 Jul 83 ● **WRAPPED AROUND YOUR FINGER** *A&M AM 127* 7 7
5 Nov 83 **SYNCHRONICITY II** *A&M AM 153* 17 4
14 Jan 84 **KING OF PAIN** *A&M AM 176* 17 5
11 Oct 86 **DON'T STAND SO CLOSE TO ME '86 (re-mix)** *A&M AM 354* 24 4
13 May 95 **CAN'T STAND LOSING YOU (LIVE)** *A&M 5810372* 27 2
20 Dec 97 **ROXANNE '97 (re-mix)** *A&M 5824552* [1] 17 6
5 Aug 00 **WHEN THE WORLD IS RUNNING DOWN** *Pagan PAGAN 039CDS* [2] 28 3
21 Apr 79 ● **OUTLANDOS D'AMOUR** *A&M AMLH 68502* 6 96
13 Oct 79 ★ **REGGATTA DE BLANC** *A&M AMLH 64792* ■ 1 74
11 Oct 80 ★ **ZENYATTA MONDATTA** *A&M AMLH 64831* ■ 1 31
10 Oct 81 ★ **GHOST IN THE MACHINE** *A&M AMLK 63730* ■ 1 27
25 Jun 83 ★ **SYNCHRONICITY** *A&M AMLX 63735* ■ ▲ 1 48
8 Nov 86 ★ **EVERY BREATH YOU TAKE – THE SINGLES** *A&M EVERY 1* ■ 1 55
10 Oct 92 ● **GREATEST HITS** *A&M 5400302* 10 21
10 Jun 95 **LIVE!** *A&M 540222* 25 3
22 Nov 97 ★ **THE VERY BEST OF STING AND THE POLICE** *A&M 5404282* [1] ■ 1 50

[1] Sting and The Police [2] Different Gear vs The Police [1] Sting and the Police

'Can't Stand Losing You' made No.42 on its first visit and peaked at No.2 only on re-entry in Jul 1979. Six Pack consists of six separate Police singles as follows: The Bed's Too Big Without You / Roxanne / Message in a Bottle / Walking on the Moon / So Lonely / Can't Stand Losing You. The last five titles were re-issues. In 1997 'The Very Best of Sting and the Police' orignally peaked at No.11 but on 2 Mar 2002 an updated version containing three new tracks re-entered the chart and sales were combined with the original album

See also STING; Klark KENT

Su POLLARD *UK, female actor / vocalist (Singles: 11 weeks, Albums: 3 weeks)* pos/wks

5 Oct 85 **COME TO ME (I AM WOMAN)** *Rainbow RBR 1* 71 1
1 Feb 86 ● **STARTING TOGETHER** *Rainbow RBR 4* 2 10
22 Nov 86 **SU** *K-Tel NE 1327* 86 3

Jimi POLO *US, male vocalist (Singles: 5 weeks)* pos/wks

9 Nov 91 **NEVER GOIN' DOWN** *MCA MCS 1578* [1] 51 2
1 Aug 92 **EXPRESS YOURSELF** *Perfecto 74321101827* 59 2
9 Aug 97 **EXPRESS YOURSELF (re-issue)** *Perfecto PERF 146CD1* 62 1

[1] Adamski featuring Jimi Polo

The listed flip side of 'Never Goin' Down' was 'Born to Be Alive' by Adamski featuring Soho

POLOROID *UK, male / female production / vocal trio (Singles: 2 weeks)* pos/wks

11 Oct 03 **SO DAMN BEAUTIFUL** *Decode / Telstar CDSTAS 3351* 28 2

POLTERGEIST *UK, male producer – Simon Berry (Singles: 2 weeks)* pos/wks

6 Jul 96 **VICIOUS CIRCLES** *Manifesto FESCD 8* 32 2

See also VICIOUS CIRCLES

Peter POLYCARPOU *UK, male actor / vocalist (Singles: 4 weeks)* pos/wks

20 Feb 93 **LOVE HURTS** *Soundtrack Music CDEM 259* 26 4

POLYGON WINDOW *UK, male producer – Richard James (Singles: 1 week)* pos/wks

3 Apr 93 **QUOTH** *Warp WAP 33CD* 49 1

See also APHEX TWIN; AFX

POLYPHONIC SPREE *US, male / female vocal / instrumental ensemble (Singles: 4 weeks, Albums: 1 week)* pos/wks

2 Nov 02 **HANGING AROUND** *679 Recordings 679L 012CD* 39 1
22 Feb 03 **LIGHT AND DAY** *679 Recordings 679L 015CD1* 40 1
26 Jul 03 **SOLDIER GIRL** *679 Recordings 679L 014CD* 26 2
12 Jul 03 **THE BEGINNING STAGES OF** *679 Recordings 2564603525*....70 1

PONI-TAILS *US, female vocal group (Singles: 14 weeks)* pos/wks

19 Sep 58 ● **BORN TOO LATE** *HMV POP 516* 5 11
10 Apr 59 **EARLY TO BED** *HMV POP 596* 26 3

Brian POOLE and The TREMELOES – *See TREMELOES*

Glyn POOLE *UK, male vocalist (Singles: 8 weeks)* pos/wks

20 Oct 73 **MILLY MOLLY MANDY** *York SYK 565* 35 8

Ian POOLEY *Germany, male DJ / producer (Singles: 3 weeks)* pos/wks

10 Mar 01 **900 DEGREES** *V2 VVR 5015143* 57 1
11 Aug 01 **BALMES** *V2 VVR 5016613* [1] 65 1
23 Nov 02 **PIHA** *Honchos Music HONMO 019CD* [2] 53 1

[1] Ian Pooley featuring Esthero [2] Ian Pooley and Magik J

Iggy POP *US, male vocalist – James Jewel Osterburg (Singles: 28 weeks, Albums: 27 weeks)* pos/wks

13 Dec 86 ● **REAL WILD CHILD (WILD ONE)** *A&M AM 368* 10 11
10 Feb 90 **LIVIN' ON THE EDGE OF THE NIGHT** *Virgin America VUS 18* ..51 4
13 Oct 90 **CANDY** *Virgin America VUS 29* 67 1

		pos	wks
5 Jan 91	**WELL DID YOU EVAH!** *Chrysalis CHS 3646* [1]	**42**	4
4 Sep 93	**WILD AMERICA (EP)** *Virgin America VUSCD 74*	**63**	1
21 May 94	**BESIDE YOU** *Virgin America VUSCD 77*	**47**	2
23 Nov 96	**LUST FOR LIFE** *Virgin America VUSCD 116*	**26**	2
7 Mar 98	**THE PASSENGER** *Virgin VSCDT 1689*	**22**	3
9 Apr 77	**THE IDIOT** *RCA Victor PL 12275*	**30**	3
4 Jun 77	**RAW POWER** *Embassy 31464* [1]	**44**	2
1 Oct 77	**LUST FOR LIFE** *RCA PL 12488*	**28**	5
19 May 79	**NEW VALUES** *Arista SPART 1092*	**60**	4
16 Feb 80	**SOLDIER** *Arista SPART 1117*	**62**	2
11 Oct 86	**BLAH-BLAH-BLAH** *A&M AMA 5145*	**43**	7
2 Jul 88	**INSTINCT** *A&M AMA 5198*	**61**	1
21 Jul 90	**BRICK BY BRICK** *Virgin America VUSLP 19*	**50**	2
25 Sep 93	**AMERICAN CAESAR** *Virgin CDVUS 64*	**43**	1

[1] Deborah Harry and Iggy Pop [1] Iggy and the Stooges

Tracks on Wild America (EP): Wild America / Credit Card / Come Back Tomorrow / My Angel

POP WILL EAT ITSELF *UK, male vocal / instrumental group (Singles: 43 weeks, Albums: 13 weeks)*

		pos	wks
30 Jan 88	**THERE IS NO LOVE BETWEEN US ANYMORE** *Chapter 22 CHAP 20*	**66**	1
23 Jul 88	**DEF CON ONE** *Chapter 22 PWEI 001*	**63**	4
11 Feb 89	**CAN U DIG IT?** *RCA PB 42621*	**38**	4
22 Apr 89	**WISE UP! SUCKER** *RCA PB 42761*	**41**	3
2 Sep 89	**VERY METAL NOISE POLLUTION (EP)** *RCA PB 42883*	**45**	3
9 Jun 90	**TOUCHED BY THE HAND OF CICCIOLINA** *RCA PB 43735*	**28**	4
13 Oct 90	**DANCE OF THE MAD** *RCA PB 44023*	**32**	2
12 Jan 91	**X Y & ZEE** *RCA PB 44243*	**15**	4
1 Jun 91	**92º F** *RCA PB 44555*	**23**	3
6 Jun 92	**KARMADROME / EAT ME DRINK ME LOVE ME** *RCA PB 45467*	**17**	2
29 Aug 92	**BULLETPROOF!** *RCA 74321110137*	**24**	3
16 Jan 93 ●	**GET THE GIRL! KILL THE BADDIES!** *RCA 74321128802*	**9**	4
16 Oct 93	**RSVP / FAMILIUS HORRIBILUS** *Infectious INFECT 1CD*	**27**	2
12 Mar 94	**ICH BIN EIN AUSLANDER** *Infectious INFECT 4CD*	**28**	2
10 Sep 94	**EVERYTHING'S COOL** *Infectious INFECT 9CD*	**23**	2
13 May 89	**THIS IS THE DAY ... THIS IS THE HOUR ... THIS IS THIS!** *RCA PL 74141*	**24**	2
2 Nov 90	**CURE FOR SANITY** *RCA PL 74828*	**33**	3
19 Sep 92	**THE LOOKS OR THE LIFESTYLE** *RCA 74321102652*	**15**	3
6 Mar 93	**WEIRD'S BAR AND GRILL** *RCA 74321133432*	**44**	0
6 Nov 93	**16 DIFFERENT FLAVOURS OF HELL** *RCA 74321153172*	**73**	1
1 Oct 94	**DOS DEDOS MIS AMIGOS** *Infectious INFECT 10CDX*	**11**	2
18 Mar 95	**TWO FINGERS MY FRIENDS** *Infectious INFECT 10CDRX*	**25**	2

Tracks on Very Metal Noise Pollution (EP): Def Con 1989 AD including the Twilight Zone / Preaching to the Perverted / PWEI-zation / 92º F 'Two Fingers My Friends' is a remixed version of 'Dos Dedos Mis Amigos'

POPE JOHN PAUL II *Poland, pontiff (Albums: 8 weeks)*

		pos	wks
3 Jul 82	**JOHN PAUL II – THE PILGRIM POPE** *BBC REB445*	**71**	4
10 Dec 94	**THE ROSARY** *Pure Music PMCD 7009*	**50**	4

'The Rosary' is a double CD or cassette: one with the Rosary in Latin by the Pope and the other featuring its English reading by Father Kilcoyne

POPES – *See Shane MacGOWAN*

POPPERS presents AURA *UK, male production trio and UK, female vocalist (Singles: 1 week)*

		pos	wks
25 Oct 97	**EVERY LITTLE TIME** *VC VCRD 26*	**44**	1

POPPY FAMILY *Canada, male / female vocal / instrumental group – Terry Jacks and Susan Peklevits (Singles: 14 weeks)*

		pos	wks
15 Aug 70 ●	**WHICH WAY YOU GOIN' BILLY?** *Decca F 22976*	**7**	14

See also Terry JACKS

PORN KINGS *UK, male instrumental / production group (Singles: 12 weeks)*

		pos	wks
28 Sep 96	**UP TO NO GOOD** *All Around the World CDGLOBE 145*	**28**	2
21 Jun 97	**AMOUR (C'MON)** *All Around the World CDGLOBE 152*	**17**	3
16 Jan 99 ●	**UP TO THE WILDSTYLE** *All Around the World CDGLOBE 170* [1]	**10**	4
10 Feb 01	**SLEDGER** *All Around the World CDGLOBE 229*	**71**	1
22 Mar 03	**SHAKE YA SHIMMY** *All Around the World CDGLOBE 213* [2]	**28**	2

[1] Porn Kings vs DJ Supreme [2] Porn Kings vs Flip and Fill featuring 740 Boyz

PORNO FOR PYROS *US, male vocal / instrumental group (Singles: 2 weeks, Albums: 5 weeks)*

		pos	wks
5 Jun 93	**PETS** *Warner Bros. W 0177 CD*	**53**	2
8 May 93	**PORNO FOR PYROS** *Warner Bros. 9362452282*	**13**	3
8 Jun 96	**GOOD GOD'S URGE** *Warner Bros. 9362461262*	**40**	2

PORTISHEAD *UK, male / female vocal / instrumental group (Singles: 20 weeks, Albums: 95 weeks)*

		pos	wks
13 Aug 94	**SOUR TIMES (re)** *Go.Beat GODCD 116*	**13**	5
14 Jan 95	**GLORY BOX** *Go.Beat GODCD 120*	**13**	7
20 Sep 97 ●	**ALL MINE** *Go.Beat 5715972*	**8**	4
22 Nov 97	**OVER** *Go.Beat 5719932*	**25**	2
14 Mar 98	**ONLY YOU** *Go.Beat 5694752*	**35**	2
3 Sep 94 ●	**DUMMY** *Go! Beat 8285222*	**2**	71
11 Oct 97 ●	**PORTISHEAD** *Go! Beat 5391892*	**2**	22
14 Nov 98	**PNYC** *Go! Beat 5594242*	**40**	2

'Sour Times' made No.57 on its first visit and peaked at No.13 in Apr 1995

See also Beth GIBBONS & RUSTIN' MAN

Nick PORTLOCK – *See ROYAL PHILHARMONIC ORCHESTRA*

Gary PORTNOY *US, male vocalist (Singles: 3 weeks)*

		pos	wks
25 Feb 84	**THEME FROM 'CHEERS'** *Starblend CHEER 1*	**58**	3

PORTRAIT *US, male vocal group (Singles: 6 weeks)*

		pos	wks
27 Mar 93	**HERE WE GO AGAIN** *Capitol CDCL 683*	**37**	3
8 Apr 95	**I CAN CALL YOU** *Capitol CDCL 740*	**61**	1
8 Jul 95	**HOW DEEP IS YOUR LOVE** *Capitol CDCL 751*	**41**	2

PORTSMOUTH SINFONIA *UK, orchestra (Singles: 4 weeks)*

		pos	wks
12 Sep 81	**CLASSICAL MUDDLY** *Island WIP 6736*	**38**	4

Sandy POSEY *US, female vocalist (Singles: 32 weeks, Albums: 1 week)*

		pos	wks
15 Sep 66	**BORN A WOMAN** *MGM 1321*	**24**	11
5 Jan 67	**SINGLE GIRL** *MGM 1330*	**15**	13
13 Apr 67	**WHAT A WOMAN IN LOVE WON'T DO** *MGM 1335*	**48**	3
6 Sep 75	**SINGLE GIRL (re-issue)** *MGM 2006 533*	**35**	5
11 Mar 67	**BORN A WOMAN** *MGM MGMCS 8035*	**39**	1

POSIES *US, male vocal / instrumental group (Singles: 1 week)*

		pos	wks
19 Mar 94	**DEFINITE DOOR** *Geffen GFSTD 68*	**67**	1

POSITIVE FORCE *US, female vocal duo – Brenda Reynolds and Vicki Drayton (Singles: 9 weeks)*

		pos	wks
22 Dec 79	**WE GOT THE FUNK** *Sugarhill SHL 102*	**18**	9

POSITIVE GANG *UK, male / female instrumental / vocal group (Singles: 5 weeks)*

		pos	wks
17 Apr 93	**SWEET FREEDOM** *PWL Continental PWCD 261*	**34**	4
31 Jul 93	**SWEET FREEDOM PART 2** *PWL Continental PWCD 264*	**67**	1

POSITIVE K *US, male rapper (Singles: 2 weeks)*

		pos	wks
15 May 93	**I GOT A MAN** *Fourth & Broadway BRCD 280*	**43**	2

Mike POST

US, orchestra (Singles: 18 weeks) pos/wks

9 Aug 75 **AFTERNOON OF THE RHINO (re)** *Warner Bros. K 16588* [1] **47** 2
16 Jan 82 **THEME FROM 'HILL STREET BLUES'** *Elektra K 12576* [2] **25** 11
29 Sep 84 **THE A TEAM** *RCA 443* **45** 5

[1] Mike Post Coalition [2] Mike Post featuring Larry Carlton

POTTERS

UK, male Stoke City football supporters vocal group (Singles: 2 weeks) pos/wks

1 Apr 72 **WE'LL BE WITH YOU** *Pye JT 100* **34** 2

Frank POURCEL

France, male orchestra leader d. 12 Dec 2000 (Albums: 7 weeks) pos/wks

20 Nov 71 ● **THIS IS POURCEL** *Studio Two STWO 7* 8 7

POWDER

UK, male / female vocal / instrumental group (Singles: 1 week) pos/wks

24 Jun 95 **AFRODISIAC** *Parkway PARK 002CD* **72** 1

Bryan POWELL

UK, male vocalist (Singles: 3 weeks) pos/wks

13 Mar 93 **IT'S ALRIGHT** *Talkin' Loud TLKCD 34* **73** 1
15 May 93 **I THINK OF YOU** *Talkin' Loud TLKCD 38* **61** 1
7 Aug 93 **NATURAL** *Talkin' Loud TLKCD 41* **73** 1

Cozy POWELL

UK, male instrumentalist – drums – Colin Flooks, d. 5 Apr 1998 (Singles: 38 weeks, Albums: 8 weeks) pos/wks

8 Dec 73 ● **DANCE WITH THE DEVIL** *RAK 164* **3** 15
25 May 74 **THE MAN IN BLACK** *RAK 173* **18** 8
10 Aug 74 ● **NA NA NA** *RAK 180* **10** 10
10 Nov 79 **THEME ONE** *Ariola ARO 189* **62** 2
19 Jun 93 **RESURRECTION** *Parlophone CDRS 6351* [1] **23** 3
26 Jan 80 **OVER THE TOP** *Ariola ARL 5038* 34 3
19 Sep 81 **TILT** *Polydor POLD 5047* 58 4
28 May 83 **OCTOPUSS** *Polydor POLD 5093* 86 1

[1] Brian May with Cozy Powell

See also EMERSON LAKE and POWELL

Kobie POWELL – *See US3*

Peter POWELL

UK, male DJ / exercise instructor (Albums: 13 weeks) pos/wks

20 Mar 82 ● **KEEP FIT AND DANCE** *K-Tel NE 1167* 9 13

POWER CIRCLE – *See CHICANE*

POWER OF DREAMS

Ireland, male vocal / instrumental group (Singles: 2 weeks) pos/wks

19 Jan 91 **AMERICAN DREAM** *Polydor PO 117* **74** 1
11 Apr 92 **THERE I GO AGAIN** *Polydor PO 200* **65** 1

POWER STATION

UK / US, male vocal / instrumental group (Singles: 17 weeks, Albums: 23 weeks) pos/wks

16 Mar 85 **SOME LIKE IT HOT** *Parlophone R 6091* **14** 8
11 May 85 **GET IT ON** *Parlophone R 6096* **22** 7
9 Nov 85 **COMMUNICATION** *Parlophone R 6114* **75** 1
12 Oct 96 **SHE CAN ROCK IT** *Chrysalis CDCHS 5039* **63** 1
6 Apr 85 **THE POWER STATION** *Parlophone POST 1* 12 23

POWERCUT featuring NUBIAN PRINZ

US, male vocal / instrumental group (Singles: 4 weeks) pos/wks

22 Jun 91 **GIRLS** *Eternal YZ 570* **50** 4

POWERHOUSE

UK, male production duo (Singles: 4 weeks) pos/wks

20 Dec 97 **RHYTHM OF THE NIGHT** *Satellite 74321522592* **38** 4

POWERHOUSE featuring Duane HARDEN

US, male producer – Lenny Fontana and male vocalist (Singles: 5 weeks) pos/wks

22 May 99 **WHAT YOU NEED** *Defected DEFECT 3CDS* **13** 5

See also Armand VAN HELDEN

POWERPILL

UK, male instrumental / production group (Singles: 3 weeks) pos/wks

6 Jun 92 **PAC-MAN** *Ffrreedom TABX 110* **43** 3

PJ POWERS – *See LADYSMITH BLACK MAMBAZO*

Will POWERS

US, female vocalist – Lyn Goldsmith (Singles: 9 weeks) pos/wks

1 Oct 83 **KISSING WITH CONFIDENCE** *Island IS 134* **17** 9

Hit features uncredited vocals by Carly Simon

POWERS THAT BE

UK / Sweden, production duo – Giles Goodman and Pierre Jerksten (Singles: 1 week) pos/wks

26 Jul 03 **PLANET ROCK / FUNKY PLANET** *Defected DFTD 074* **63** 1

Perez PRADO and his ORCHESTRA

Cuba, orchestra, leader d. 14 Sep 1989 (Singles: 57 weeks) pos/wks

25 Mar 55 ★ **CHERRY PINK AND APPLE BLOSSOM WHITE** *HMV B 10833* [1] ▲ **1** 17
25 Jul 58 ● **PATRICIA** *RCA 1067* **8** 16
10 Dec 94 ● **GUAGLIONE (2re)** *RCA 74321250192* [2] **2** 24

[1] Perez 'Prez' Prado and his Orchestra, the King of the Mambo [2] Perez 'Prez' Prado and his Orchestra

'Guaglione' did not made its peak position until its second re-entry in May 1995 after first making No.41 in 1994 and No.58 on its first re-entry

PRAISE

UK, male / female vocal / instrumental group (Singles: 7 weeks) pos/wks

2 Feb 91 ● **ONLY YOU** *Epic 6566117* **4** 7

Uncredited vocals by Miriam Stockley

PRAISE CATS

US, male producer – Eric 'E-Smoove' Miller (Singles: 1 week) pos/wks

26 Oct 02 **SHINED ON ME** *Pias PIAS 028CD* **56** 1

See also E-SMOOVE featuring Latanza WATERS; THICK D

PRAS – *See Pras MICHEL; FUGEES*

PRATT and McCLAIN with BROTHERLOVE

US, male vocal duo – Truett Pratt and Jerry McClain with male instrumental group (Singles: 6 weeks) pos/wks

1 Oct 77 **HAPPY DAYS** *Reprise K 14435* **31** 6

PRAXIS featuring KATHY BROWN

UK, male producer – David Shaw and US, female vocalist (Singles: 5 weeks) pos/wks

25 Nov 95 **TURN ME OUT** *Stress CDSTR 40* **44** 2
20 Sep 97 **TURN ME OUT (TURN TO SUGAR) (re-mix)** *ffrr FCD 314* **35** 3

PRAYING MANTIS

UK, male vocal / instrumental group (Singles: 2 weeks, Albums: 2 weeks) pos/wks

31 Jan 81 **CHEATED** *Arista ARIST 378* **69** 2
11 Apr 81 **TIME TELLS NO LIES** *Arista SPART 1153* 60 2

PRECIOUS

UK, female vocal group (Singles: 20 weeks) pos/wks

29 May 99 ● **SAY IT AGAIN (re)** *EMI CDEM 544* **6** 11
1 Apr 00 **REWIND** *EMI CDEM 557* **11** 5
15 Jul 00 **IT'S GONNA BE MY WAY** *EMI CDEM 569* **27** 3
25 Nov 00 **NEW BEGINNING** *EMI CDEM 573* **50** 1

PRECOCIOUS BRATS featuring KEVIN and PERRY

UK, male production duo – Julius O'Riordan (Judge Jules) and Matt Smith with UK, male / female vocal / comedy duo – Harry Enfield and Kathy Burke (Singles: 4 weeks)

			pos	wks
6 May 00		**BIG GIRL** *Virgin / EMI VTSCD 1*	**16**	4

PREFAB SPROUT (406 Top 500)

Critically acclaimed, intelligent, fragile pop band, formed 1978 in Newcastle, England. Named after a phrase from the Sinatra / Hazlewood hit 'Jackson' misheard by leader / songwriter Paddy McAloon (v.g). Stevie Wonder and Pete Townshend guested on 'From Langley Park to Memphis' (Singles: 60 weeks, Albums: 106 weeks)

			pos	wks
28 Jan 84		**DON'T SING** *Kitchenware SK 9*	**62**	2
20 Jul 85		**FARON YOUNG** *Kitchenware SK 22*	**74**	1
9 Nov 85		**WHEN LOVE BREAKS DOWN** *Kitchenware SK 21*	**25**	10
8 Feb 86		**JOHNNY JOHNNY** *Kitchenware SK 24*	**64**	2
13 Feb 88		**CARS AND GIRLS** *Kitchenware SK 35*	**44**	5
30 Apr 88	●	**THE KING OF ROCK 'N' ROLL** *Kitchenware SK 37*	**7**	10
23 Jul 88		**HEY MANHATTAN!** *Kitchenware SK 38*	**72**	2
18 Aug 90		**LOOKING FOR ATLANTIS** *Kitchenware SK 47*	**51**	3
20 Oct 90		**WE LET THE STARS GO** *Kitchenware SK 48*	**50**	3
5 Jan 91		**JORDAN: THE EP** *Kitchenware SK 49*	**35**	4
13 Jun 92		**THE SOUND OF CRYING** *Kitchenware SK 58*	**23**	5
8 Aug 92		**IF YOU DON'T LOVE ME** *Kitchenware SK 60*	**33**	4
3 Oct 92		**ALL THE WORLD LOVES LOVERS** *Kitchenware SK 62*	**61**	2
9 Jan 93		**LIFE OF SURPRISES** *Kitchenware SKCD 63*	**24**	4
10 May 97		**A PRISONER OF THE PAST** *Columbia SKZD 70*	**30**	2
2 Aug 97		**ELECTRIC GUITARS** *Columbia SKZD 71*	**53**	1
17 Mar 84		**SWOON** *Kitchenware KWLP 1*	**22**	7
22 Jun 85		**STEVE MCQUEEN** *Kitchenware KWLP 3*	**21**	35
26 Mar 88	●	**FROM LANGLEY PARK TO MEMPHIS** *Kitchenware KWLP 9*	**5**	24
1 Jul 89		**PROTEST SONGS** *Kitchenware KWLP 4*	**18**	4
8 Sep 90	●	**JORDAN: THE COMEBACK** *Kitchenware KWLP 14*	**7**	17
11 Jul 92	●	**A LIFE OF SURPRISES – THE BEST OF PREFAB SPROUT** *Kitchenware 4718862*	**3**	13
17 May 97	●	**ANDROMEDA HEIGHTS** *Columbia KWCD 30*	**7**	5
30 Jun 01		**THE GUNMAN AND OTHER STORIES** *Liberty 5326132*	**60**	1

Tracks on Jordan: The EP: Carnival 2000 / The Ice Maiden / One of the Broken / Jordan: The Comeback

PRELUDE

UK, male / female vocal group (Singles: 26 weeks)

			pos	wks
26 Jan 74		**AFTER THE GOLDRUSH** *Dawn DNS 1052*	**21**	9
26 Apr 80		**PLATINUM BLONDE** *EMI 5046*	**45**	7
22 May 82		**AFTER THE GOLDRUSH (re-recording)** *After Hours AFT 02*	**28**	7
31 Jul 82		**ONLY THE LONELY** *After Hours AFT 06*	**55**	3

PRESENCE

UK, male / female vocal / production group (Singles: 2 weeks)

			pos	wks
5 Dec 98		**SENSE OF DANGER** *Pagan PAGAN 024CDS* [1]	**61**	1
19 Jun 99		**FUTURE LOVE** *Pagan PAGAN 028CDS*	**66**	1

[1] Presence featuring Shara Nelson

PRESIDENT BROWN – *See SABRE featuring PRESIDENT BROWN*

PRESIDENTS OF THE UNITED STATES OF AMERICA

US, male vocal / instrumental trio (Singles: 21 weeks, Albums: 31 weeks)

			pos	wks
6 Jan 96		**LUMP** *Columbia 6624962*	**15**	7
20 Apr 96	●	**PEACHES** *Columbia 6631072*	**8**	7
20 Jul 96		**DUNE BUGGY** *Columbia 6634892*	**15**	4
2 Nov 96		**MACH 5** *Columbia 6638812*	**29**	2
1 Aug 98		**VIDEO KILLED THE RADIO STAR** *Maverick W 0450CD*	**52**	1
13 Jan 96		**THE PRESIDENTS OF THE UNITED STATES OF AMERICA** *Columbia 4810392*	**14**	29
16 Nov 96		**II** *Columbia 4850922*	**36**	2

Elvis PRESLEY (1 Top 500)

The most important, most influential and most impersonated artist of the 20th century, b. 8 Jan 1935, Mississippi, US, d. 16 Aug 1977. The singer, whose first five US singles failed to reach the pop charts, went from rock 'n' roll rebel to Las Vegas veteran and on the way sold more records than any other performer in history. He holds, or has held, almost every chart-related record including perhaps the most important: more No.1s than any act in chart history. No other solo artist of the rock era can match his number of best-selling singles and albums in the UK or US, nor his collection of platinum and gold records. The 'King of Rock 'n' Roll' was the first artist to enter the UK chart at No.1, and the first to amass US advance orders in excess of one million copies for a single. He now has a 46-year span of UK No.1 albums and also holds the record for most simultaneous UK album chart entries (27 in the Top 100) and held the record for the most entries on the UK singles chart (nine). The most documented entertainer ever has won hundreds of awards, starred in dozens of films, broken numerous box office records in North America (the only continent he ever performed in), made Memphis a major tourist attraction and was the first artist credited with sales of one billion records (20 million of which were reportedly sold the day after his death). In 2002, after a 25-year gap, he returned to top the UK singles chart and his album 'ELV1S' entered at No.1 in 17 countries. He has sold more than 19 million UK singles, his best-seller being 'It's Now or Never' at 1,210,000 (Singles: 1193 Weeks, Albums: 1260 weeks)

			pos	wks
11May 56	●	**HEARTBREAK HOTEL (re)** *HMV POP 182* ▲	**2**	22
25 May 56	●	**BLUE SUEDE SHOES (re)** *HMV POP 213*	**9**	10
13 Jul 56		**I WANT YOU, I NEED YOU, I LOVE YOU (re)** *HMV POP 235* ▲	**14**	11
21 Sep 56	●	**HOUND DOG** *HMV POP 249* ▲	**2**	23
16 Nov 56	●	**BLUE MOON** *HMV POP 272*	**9**	11
23 Nov 56		**I DON'T CARE IF THE SUN DON'T SHINE (re)** *HMV POP 272*	**23**	4
7 Dec 56		**LOVE ME TENDER** *HMV POP 253* ▲	**11**	9
15 Feb 57		**MYSTERY TRAIN** *HMV POP 295*	**25**	5
8 Mar 57		**RIP IT UP** *HMV POP 305*	**27**	1
10 May 57	●	**TOO MUCH (re)** *HMV POP 330* [1] ▲	**6**	9
14 Jun 57	★	**ALL SHOOK UP (re)** *HMV POP 359* [1] ▲	**1**	21
12 Jul 57	●	**(LET ME BE YOUR) TEDDY BEAR** *RCA1013* [1] ▲	**3**	19
30 Aug 57	●	**PARALYZED** *HMV POP 378*	**8**	10
4 Oct 57	●	**PARTY** *RCA 1020* [1]	**2**	15
18 Oct 57		**GOT A LOT O' LIVIN' TO DO** *RCA 1020.* [1]	**17**	4
1 Nov 57		**LOVING YOU** *RCA 1013* [1]	**24**	2
1 Nov 57		**TRYING TO GET TO YOU** *HMV POP 408*	**16**	4
8 Nov 57		**LAWDY MISS CLAWDY** *HMV POP 408*	**15**	5
15 Nov 57	●	**SANTA BRING MY BABY BACK (TO ME)** *RCA 1025*	**7**	8
17 Jan 58		**I'M LEFT, YOU'RE RIGHT, SHE'S GONE (re)** *HMV POP 428*	**21**	3
24 Jan 58	★	**JAILHOUSE ROCK (re)** *RCA 1028* ■ ▲	**1**	20
31 Jan 58		**JAILHOUSE ROCK (EP)** *RCA RCX 106* [1]	**18**	5
28 Feb 58	●	**DON'T** *RCA 1043* [1] ▲	**2**	11
2 May 58	●	**WEAR MY RING AROUND YOUR NECK** *RCA 1058* [1]	**3**	10
25 Jul 58	●	**HARD HEADED WOMAN** *RCA 1070* [1] ▲	**2**	11
3 Oct 58	●	**KING CREOLE** *RCA 1081* [1]	**2**	15
23 Jan 59	★	**ONE NIGHT / I GOT STUNG** *RCA 1100*	**1**	12
24 Apr 59	★	**A FOOL SUCH AS I / I NEED YOUR LOVE TONIGHT** *RCA 1113* [1]	**1**	15
24 Jul 59	●	**A BIG HUNK O' LOVE** *RCA 1136* [1] ▲	**4**	9
12 Feb 60		**STRICTLY ELVIS (EP)** *RCA RCX 175*	**26**	1
7 Apr 60	●	**STUCK ON YOU** *RCA 1187* [1] ▲	**3**	14
28 Jul 60	●	**A MESS OF BLUES** *RCA 1194* [1]	**2**	18
3 Nov 60	★	**IT'S NOW OR NEVER** *RCA 1207* [1] ◆ ■ ▲	**1**	19
19 Jan 61	★	**ARE YOU LONESOME TONIGHT?** *RCA 1216* [1] ▲	**1**	15
9 Mar 61	★	**WOODEN HEART** *RCA 1226*	**1**	27
25 May 61	★	**SURRENDER** *RCA 1227* [1] ▲	**1**	15
7 Sep 61	●	**WILD IN THE COUNTRY / I FEEL SO BAD** *RCA 1244* [1]	**4**	12
2 Nov 61	★	**(MARIE'S THE NAME) HIS LATEST FLAME / LITTLE SISTER** *RCA 1258*	**1**	13
1 Feb 62	★	**ROCK-A-HULA BABY / CAN'T HELP FALLING IN LOVE** *RCA 1270* [1]	**1**	20
10 May 62	★	**GOOD LUCK CHARM** *RCA 1280* [1] ▲	**1**	17
21 Jun 62		**FOLLOW THAT DREAM (EP)** *RCA RCX 211*	**34**	2
30 Aug 62	★	**SHE'S NOT YOU** *RCA 1303* [1]	**1**	14

29 Nov 62 ★ RETURN TO SENDER *RCA 1320* [1] 1 14
28 Feb 63 ONE BROKEN HEART FOR SALE *RCA 1337* [2] 12 9
4 Jul 63 ★ (YOU'RE THE) DEVIL IN DISGUISE *RCA 1355* [1] 1 12
24 Oct 63 BOSSA NOVA BABY *RCA 1374* [1] 13 8
19 Dec 63 KISS ME QUICK *RCA 1375* [1] 14 10
12 Mar 64 VIVA LAS VEGAS *RCA 1390* [1] 17 12
25 Jun 64 ● KISSIN' COUSINS *RCA 1404* [1] 10 11
20 Aug 64 SUCH A NIGHT *RCA 1411* [1] 13 10
29 Oct 64 AIN'T THAT LOVING YOU BABY *RCA 1422* 15 8
3 Dec 64 BLUE CHRISTMAS *RCA 1430* [1] 11 7
11 Mar 65 DO THE CLAM *RCA 1443* [3] 19 8
27 May 65 ★ CRYING IN THE CHAPEL *RCA 1455* [1] 1 15
11 Nov 65 TELL ME WHY *RCA 1489* [1] 15 10
24 Feb 66 BLUE RIVER *RCA 1504* 22 7
7 Apr 66 FRANKIE AND JOHNNY *RCA 1509* 21 9
7 Jul 66 ● LOVE LETTERS *RCA 1526* 6 10
13 Oct 66 ALL THAT I AM *RCA 1545* [1] 18 8
1 Dec 66 ● IF EVERY DAY WAS LIKE CHRISTMAS *RCA 1557* [4] 9 7
9 Feb 67 INDESCRIBABLY BLUE *RCA 1565* [4] 21 5
11 May 67 YOU GOTTA STOP / THE LOVE MACHINE *RCA 1593* 38 5
16 Aug 67 LONG LEGGED GIRL (WITH THE SHORT DRESS ON)
RCA RCA 1616 [1] 49 2
21 Feb 68 GUITAR MAN *RCA 1663* 19 9
15 May 68 U.S. MALE *RCA 1688* [1] 15 8
17 Jul 68 YOUR TIME HASN'T COME YET BABY *RCA 1714* [1] 22 11
16 Oct 68 YOU'LL NEVER WALK ALONE *RCA 1747* [1] 44 3
26 Feb 69 IF I CAN DREAM *RCA 1795* 11 10
11 Jun 69 ● IN THE GHETTO (re) *RCA 1831* 2 17
6 Sep 69 CLEAN UP YOUR OWN BACK YARD *RCA 1869* 21 7
29 Nov 69 ● SUSPICIOUS MINDS *RCA 1900* ▲ 2 14
28 Feb 70 ● DON'T CRY DADDY *RCA 1916* 8 11
16 May 70 KENTUCKY RAIN (re) *RCA 1949* 21 12
11 Jul 70 ★ THE WONDER OF YOU (re) *RCA 1974* 1 21
14 Nov 70 ● I'VE LOST YOU *RCA 1999* 9 12
9 Jan 71 ● YOU DON'T HAVE TO SAY YOU LOVE ME (re) *RCA 2046* 9 10
20 Mar 71 ● THERE GOES MY EVERYTHING *RCA 2060* [5] 6 11
15 May 71 ● RAGS TO RICHES *RCA 2084* [5] 9 11
17 Jul 71 ● HEARTBREAK HOTEL / HOUND DOG (re-issue)
RCA Maximillion 2104 10 12
2 Oct 71 I'M LEAVIN' *RCA 2125* [5] 23 9
4 Dec 71 ● I JUST CAN'T HELP BELIEVING *RCA 2158* [6] 6 16
11 Dec 71 JAILHOUSE ROCK (re-issue) *RCA Maximillion 2153* 42 5
1 Apr 72 ● UNTIL IT'S TIME FOR YOU TO GO *RCA 2188* [5] 5 9
17 Jun 72 ● AN AMERICAN TRILOGY *RCA 2229* 8 11
30 Sep 72 ● BURNING LOVE *RCA 2267* [7] 7 9
16 Dec 72 ● ALWAYS ON MY MIND *RCA 2304* [7] 9 13
26 May 73 POLK SALAD ANNIE *RCA 2359* 23 7
11 Aug 73 FOOL *RCA 2393* [7] 15 10
24 Nov 73 RAISED ON ROCK *RCA 2435* 36 7
16 Mar 74 I'VE GOT A THING ABOUT YOU BABY *RCA APBO 0196* [7] 33 5
13 Jul 74 IF YOU TALK IN YOUR SLEEP *RCA APBO 0280* 40 3
16 Nov 74 ● MY BOY *RCA 2458* 5 13
18 Jan 75 ● PROMISED LAND *RCA PB 10074* 9 8
24 May 75 T.R.O.U.B.L.E. *RCA 2562* 31 4
29 Nov 75 GREEN GREEN GRASS OF HOME *RCA 2635* 29 7
1 May 76 HURT *RCA 2674* 37 5
4 Sep 76 ● THE GIRL OF MY BEST FRIEND *RCA 2729* 9 12
25 Dec 76 ● SUSPICION *RCA 2768* 9 12
5 Mar 77 ● MOODY BLUE *RCA PB 0857* [8] 6 9
13 Aug 77 ★ WAY DOWN *RCA PB 0998* [9] 1 13
3 Sep 77 ALL SHOOK UP (re-issue) *RCA PB 2694* [1] 41 2
3 Sep 77 ARE YOU LONESOME TONIGHT? (re-issue) *RCA PB 2699* [1] 46 1
3 Sep 77 CRYING IN THE CHAPEL (re-issue) *RCA PB 2708* [1] 43 2
3 Sep 77 IT'S NOW OR NEVER (re-issue) *RCA PB 2698* [1] 39 2
3 Sep 77 JAILHOUSE ROCK (2nd re-issue) *RCA PB 2695* [1] 44 2
3 Sep 77 RETURN TO SENDER (re-issue) *RCA PB 2706* [1] 42 3
3 Sep 77 THE WONDER OF YOU (re-issue) *RCA PB 2709* 48 1
3 Sep 77 WOODEN HEART (re-issue) *RCA PB 2700* 49 1
10 Dec 77 ● MY WAY *RCA PB 1165* [10] 9 8
24 Jun 78 DON'T BE CRUEL *RCA PB 9265* 24 12
15 Dec 79 IT WON'T SEEM LIKE CHRISTMAS (WITHOUT YOU)
RCA PB 9464 13 6
30 Aug 80 ● IT'S ONLY LOVE / BEYOND THE REEF *RCA 4* 3 10
6 Dec 80 SANTA CLAUS IS BACK IN TOWN *RCA 16* 41 6
14 Feb 81 GUITAR MAN (re-recording) *RCA 43* 43 4
18 Apr 81 LOVING ARMS *RCA 48* 47 6
13 Mar 82 ARE YOU LONESOME TONIGHT? (LIVE) *RCA 196* [10] 25 7
26 Jun 82 THE SOUND OF YOUR CRY *RCA 232* [5] 59 2
7 May 83 BABY I DON'T CARE *RCA 332* 61 3
3 Dec 83 I CAN HELP *RCA 369* [11] 30 9
10 Nov 84 THE LAST FAREWELL *RCA 459* [8] 48 6
19 Jan 85 THE ELVIS MEDLEY *RCA 476* [1] 51 3
10 Aug 85 ALWAYS ON MY MIND (re-mix) *RCA PB 49943* 59 4
11 Apr 87 AIN'T THAT LOVIN' YOU BABY / BOSSA NOVA BABY
(re-recording) *RCA ARON 1* 47 5
22 Aug 87 LOVE ME TENDER / IF I CAN DREAM (re-issue) *RCA ARON 2* 56 3
16 Jan 88 STUCK ON YOU (re-issue) *RCA PB 49595* [1] 58 2
17 Aug 91 ARE YOU LONESOME TONIGHT (LIVE) (re-issue)
RCA PB 49177 68 2
29 Aug 92 DON'T BE CRUEL (re-issue) *RCA 74321110777* [1] 42 2
11 Nov 95 THE TWELFTH OF NEVER *RCA 74321320122* [11] 21 3
18 May 96 HEARTBREAK HOTEL / I WAS THE ONE
(2nd re-issue) *RCA 74321336862* 45 1
24 May 97 ALWAYS ON MY MIND (re-issue) (re-mix) *RCA 74321485412* 13 6
14 Apr 01 SUSPICIOUS MINDS (LIVE) *RCA 74321855822* 15 4
10 Nov 01 AMERICA THE BEAUTIFUL *RCA 74321904022* 69 1
22 Jun 02 ★ A LITTLE LESS CONVERSATION *RCA 74321943572* [12] ■ 1 12
4 Oct 03 ● RUBBERNECKIN' (re) *RCA 82876543412* 5 8
3 Nov 56 ★ ROCK 'N ROLL *HMV CLP 1093* 1 16
4 May 57 ● ROCK 'N ROLL (NO.2) *HMV CLP 1105* 3 3
31 Aug 57 ★ LOVING YOU (SOUNDTRACK) *RCA RC 24001* ▲ 1 25
26 Oct 57 ● THE BEST OF ELVIS *RCA DLP 1159* 3 7
30 Nov 57 ● ELVIS' CHRISTMAS ALBUM *RCA RD 27052* ▲ 2 6
13 Sep 58 ★ KING CREOLE (FILM SOUNDTRACK) *RCA RD 27086* 1 22
11 Oct 58 ● ELVIS' GOLDEN RECORDS *RCA RB 16069* 2 48
8 Aug 59 ● A DATE WITH ELVIS *RCA RD 27128* 4 15
18 Jun 60 ● ELVIS' GOLDEN RECORDS VOLUME 2 *RCA RD 27159* 4 20
18 Jun 60 ★ ELVIS IS BACK! *RCA RD 27171* 1 27
10 Dec 60 ★ G.I. BLUES (FILM SOUNDTRACK) *RCA RD 27192* ▲ 1 55
20 May 61 ● HIS HAND IN MINE *RCA RD 27211* 3 25
4 Nov 61 ● SOMETHING FOR EVERYBODY *RCA RD 27224* ▲ 2 18
9 Dec 61 ★ BLUE HAWAII (FILM SOUNDTRACK) *RCA RD 27238* ▲ 1 65
7 Jul 62 ★ POT LUCK *RCA RD 27265* 1 25
8 Dec 62 ● ROCK 'N' ROLL NO.2 (re-issue) *RCA RD 7528* 3 17
26 Jan 63 ● GIRLS! GIRLS! GIRLS! (FILM SOUNDTRACK) *RCA RD 7534* 2 21
11 May 63 ● IT HAPPENED AT THE WORLD'S FAIR (FILM SOUNDTRACK)
RCA RD 7565 4 21
28 Dec 63 ● FUN IN ACAPULCO (FILM SOUNDTRACK) *RCA RD 7609* 9 14
11 Apr 64 ● ELVIS' GOLDEN RECORDS VOLUME 3 *RCA RD 7630* 6 13
4 Jul 64 ● KISSIN' COUSINS (FILM SOUNDTRACK) *RCA RD 7645* 5 17
9 Jan 65 ROUSTABOUT (FILM SOUNDTRACK) *RCA RD 7678* ▲ 12 4
1 May 65 ● GIRL HAPPY (FILM SOUNDTRACK) *RCA RD 7714* 8 18
25 Sep 65 FLAMING STAR AND SUMMER KISSES *RCA RD 7723* 11 4
4 Dec 65 ● ELVIS FOR EVERYONE *RCA RD 7782* 8 8
15 Jan 66 HAREM HOLIDAY (FILM SOUNDTRACK) *RCA RD 7767* 11 5
30 Apr 66 FRANKIE AND JOHNNY (FILM SOUNDTRACK) *RCA RD 7793* 11 5
6 Aug 66 ● PARADISE HAWAIIAN STYLE (FILM SOUNDTRACK)
RCA Victor RD 7810 7 9
26 Nov 66 CALIFORNIA HOLIDAY (FILM SOUNDTRACK)
RCA Victor RD 7820 17 5
8 Apr 67 HOW GREAT THOU ART *RCA Victor SF 7867* 11 14
2 Sep 67 DOUBLE TROUBLE (FILM SOUNDTRACK)
RCA Victor SF 7892 34 1
20 Apr 68 CLAMBAKE (FILM SOUNDTRACK) *RCA Victor SD 7917* 39 1
3 May 69 ● ELVIS – NBC TV SPECIAL *RCA RD 8011* 2 26
5 Jul 69 ● FLAMING STAR *RCA International INTS 1012* 2 14
23 Aug 69 ★ FROM ELVIS IN MEMPHIS *RCA SF 8029* 1 13
28 Feb 70 PORTRAIT IN MUSIC (import) *RCA 558* 36 1
14 Mar 70 ● FROM MEMPHIS TO VEGAS – FROM VEGAS TO MEMPHIS
RCA SF 8080/1 3 16
1 Aug 70 ● ON STAGE – FEBRUARY 1970 *RCA SF 8128* 2 18
5 Dec 70 ELVIS' GOLDEN RECORDS VOLUME 1 (re-issue)
RCA SF 8129 21 11
12 Dec 70 WORLDWIDE 50 GOLD AWARD HITS VOLUME 1
RCA LPM 6401 49 2
30 Jan 71 THAT'S THE WAY IT IS *RCA SF 8162* 12 35
10 Apr 71 ● I'M 10000 YEARS OLD – ELVIS COUNTRY *RCA SF 8172* 6 9
24 Jul 71 ● LOVE LETTERS FROM ELVIS *RCA SF 8202* 7 5

7 Aug 71 ● **C'MON EVERYBODY** *RCA International INTS 1286* 5 21
7 Aug 71 **YOU'LL NEVER WALK ALONE** *RCA Camden CDM 1088* 20 4
25 Sep 71 **ALMOST IN LOVE** *RCA International INTS 1206* 38 2
4 Dec 71 ● **ELVIS' CHRISTMAS ALBUM (re-issue)** *RCA International INTS 1126* 7 5
18 Dec 71 **I GOT LUCKY** *RCA International INTS 1322* 26 3
27 May 72 **ELVIS NOW** *RCA Victor SF 8266* 12 8
3 Jun 72 **ELVIS FOR EVERYONE** *RCA Victor SF 8232* 48 1
3 Jun 72 **ROCK AND ROLL (RE-ISSUE OF ROCK 'N' ROLL NO.1)** *RCA Victor SF 8233* 34 4
15 Jul 72 ● **ELVIS AS RECORDED AT MADISON SQUARE GARDEN** *RCA Victor SF 8296* 3 20
12 Aug 72 **HE TOUCHED ME** *RCA Victor SF 8275* 38 3
24 Feb 73 **ALOHA FROM HAWAII VIA SATELLITE** *RCA Victor DPS 2040* ▲ 11 10
15 Sep 73 **ELVIS** *RCA Victor SF 8378* 16 4
2 Mar 74 **ELVIS – A LEGENDARY PERFORMER VOL.1** *RCA Victor CPLI 0341* 20 3
25 May 74 **GOOD TIMES** *RCA Victor APLI 0475* 42 1
7 Sep 74 **ELVIS RECORDED LIVE ON STAGE IN MEMPHIS** *RCA Victor APLI 0606* 44 1
22 Feb 75 **PROMISED LAND** *RCA Victor APLI 0873* 21 4
14 Jun 75 **TODAY** *RCA Victor RS 1011* 48 3
5 Jul 75 ★ **40 GREATEST HITS** *Arcade ADEP 12* 1 38
6 Sep 75 **THE ELVIS PRESLEY SUN COLLECTION** *RCA Starcall HY 1001* 16 13
19 Jun 76 **FROM ELVIS PRESLEY BOULEVARD, MEMPHIS, TENNESSEE** *RCA Victor RS 1060* 29 5
19 Feb 77 **ELVIS IN DEMAND** *RCA Victor PL 42003* 12 11
27 Aug 77 ● **MOODY BLUE** *RCA PL 12428* 3 15
3 Sep 77 ● **WELCOME TO MY WORLD** *RCA PL 12274* 7 9
3 Sep 77 **G.I. BLUES (re-issue)** *RCA SF 5078* 14 10
10 Sep 77 **BLUE HAWAII (re-issue)** *RCA SF 8145* 49 2
10 Sep 77 **ELVIS' GOLDEN RECORDS VOLUME 3 (re-issue)** *RCA SF 7630* 26 6
10 Sep 77 **ELVIS' GOLDEN RECORDS VOLUME 2 (re-issue)** *RCA SF 8151* 27 4
10 Sep 77 **HITS OF THE 70'S** *RCA LPLI 7527* 30 4
10 Sep 77 **PICTURES OF ELVIS** *RCA Starcall HY 1023* 52 1
8 Oct 77 **THE SUN YEARS** *Charly SUN 1001* 31 2
15 Oct 77 **LOVING YOU (re-issue)** *RCA PL 42358* 24 3
19 Nov 77 **ELVIS IN CONCERT** *RCA PL 02578* 13 11
22 Apr 78 **HE WALKS BESIDE ME** *RCA PL 12772* 37 1
3 Jun 78 **THE '56 SESSIONS VOLUME 1** *RCA PL 42101* 47 4
2 Sep 78 **TV SPECIAL** *RCA PL 42370* 50 2
11 Nov 78 **40 GREATEST HITS (re-issue)** *RCA PL 42691* 40 14
3 Feb 79 **A LEGENDARY PERFORMER VOLUME 3** *RCA PL 13082* 43 3
5 May 79 **OUR MEMORIES OF ELVIS** *RCA PL 13279* 72 1
24 Nov 79 ● **LOVE SONGS** *K-Tel NE 1062* 4 13
21 Jun 80 **ELVIS PRESLEY SINGS LEIBER AND STOLLER** *RCA International INTS 5031* 32 5
23 Aug 80 **ELVIS ARON PRESLEY** *RCA ELVIS 25* 21 4
23 Aug 80 **PARADISE HAWAIIAN STYLE (re-issue)** *RCA International INTS 5037* 53 2
29 Nov 80 ● **INSPIRATION** *K-Tel NE 1101* 6 8
14 Mar 81 **GUITAR MAN** *RCA RCALP 5010* 33 5
9 May 81 **THIS IS ELVIS PRESLEY** *RCA RCALP 5029* 47 4
28 Nov 81 **THE ULTIMATE PERFORMANCE** *K-Tel NE 1141* 45 6
13 Feb 82 **THE SOUND OF YOUR CRY** *RCA RCALP 3060* 31 12
6 Mar 82 **ELVIS PRESLEY EP PACK** *RCA EP1* 97 1
21 Aug 82 **ROMANTIC ELVIS / ROCKIN' ELVIS** *RCA RCALP 1000/1* 62 5
18 Dec 82 **IT WON'T SEEM LIKE CHRISTMAS WITHOUT YOU** *RCA INTS 5235* 80 1
30 Apr 83 **JAILHOUSE ROCK / LOVE IN LAS VEGAS** *RCA RCALP 9020* 40 2
20 Aug 83 **I WAS THE ONE** *RCA RCALP 3105* 83 1
3 Dec 83 **A LEGENDARY PERFORMER VOLUME 4** *RCA PL 84848* 91 1
7 Apr 84 **I CAN HELP** *RCA PL 89287* 71 3
21 Jul 84 **THE FIRST LIVE RECORDINGS** *RCA International PG 89387* 69 2
26 Jan 85 **20 GREATEST HITS VOLUME 2** *RCA International NL 89168* 98 1
25 May 85 **RECONSIDER BABY** *RCA PL 85418* 92 1
12 Oct 85 **BALLADS** *Telstar STAR 2264* 23 17
29 Aug 87 ● **PRESLEY – THE ALL TIME GREATEST HITS** *RCA PL 90100* 4 34
28 Jan 89 **STEREO '57 (ESSENTIAL ELVIS VOLUME 2)** *RCA PL 90250* 60 2
21 Jul 90 **HITS LIKE NEVER BEFORE (VOL.3)** *RCA PL 90486* 71 1
1 Sep 90 **THE GREAT PERFORMANCES** *RCA PL 82227* 62 1
24 Aug 91 **COLLECTORS GOLD** *RCA PL 90574* 57 1
22 Feb 92 ● **FROM THE HEART – HIS GREATEST LOVE SONGS** *RCA PD 90642* 4 18
10 Sep 94 ● **THE ESSENTIAL COLLECTION** *RCA 74321228712* 6 25
11 May 96 **ELVIS 56** *RCA 7863668562* 42 3
7 Jun 97 ● **ALWAYS ON MY MIND – ULTIMATE LOVE SONGS** *RCA 74321489842* 3 33
28 Feb 98 **BLUE SUEDE SHOES** *RCA 74321556282* 39 4
2 Dec 00 ● **THE 50 GREATEST HITS** *RCA 74321811022* 8 25
31 Mar 01 **THE LIVE GREATEST HITS** *RCA 74321847082* 50 3
24 Nov 01 **THE 50 GREATEST LOVE SONGS** *RCA 74321900752* 21 9
5 Oct 02 ★ **ELV1S – 30 #1 HITS** *RCA 07863680792* ■ ▲ 1 32
18 Oct 03 ● **2ND TO NONE** *RCA 82876570852* ....4 11+
6 Dec 03 **CHRISTMAS PEACE** *RCA 82876574892* ....41 4+

[1] With The Jordanaires [2] With The Mellomen [3] With The Jordanaires Jubilee Four & Carol Lombard Trio [4] With The Jordanaires and Imperials Quartet [5] Vocal Accompaniment: The Imperial Quartet [6] Vocal acc. The Imperials Quartet & The Sweet Inspirations [7] Vocal acc. J.D. Sumner & The Stamps [8] Vocal acc. J.D. Sumner & the Stamps Qt. Kathy Westmoreland, Myrna Smith [9] Vocal acc. J.D. Sumner & the Stamps Qt. K. Westmoreland, S. Neilson & M. Smith [10] Vocal acc. J.D. Sumner & the Stamps, The Sweet Inspirations and Kathy Westmoreland [11] Vocal accompaniment The Voice [12] Elvis vs JXL

'Jailhouse Rock' re-entry was in Feb 1983 peaking at No.27. Tracks on Jailhouse Rock (EP): Jailhouse Rock / Young and Beautiful / I Want to Be Free / Don't Leave Me Now / Baby I Don't Care. Tracks on Strictly Elvis (EP): Old Shep / Any Place Is Paradise / Paralyzed / Is It So Strange. Tracks on Follow That Dream (EP): Follow That Dream / Angel / What a Wonderful Life / I'm Not the Marrying Kind. On 5 Jul 1962, a note on the Top 50 for that week stated: "Due to difficulties in assessing returns of Follow That Dream EP, it has been decided not to include it in Britain's Top 50. It is of course No.1 in the EP charts." Therefore this EP had only a two-week run on the chart when its sales would certainly have justified a much longer one. 'Beyond the Reef' listed only from 30 Aug to 13 Sep 1980. It peaked at No.7. RCA PB 49177 is a re-issue of RCA 196. 'Can't Help Falling in Love' credited from 1 Mar 1962. Tracks on The Elvis Medley: Jailhouse Rock / Teddy Bear / Hound Dog / Don't Be Cruel / Burning Love / Suspicious Minds. 'Guitar Man' on 14 Feb 1981 is an overdubbed release

Sharp-eyed readers will have counted 17 US No.1 hits listed for 'The King'. However, he actually scored 18 chart-toppers – with 'Don't Be Cruel' which gets an individual top placing in the US in addition to a joint listing with 'Hound Dog'

Lisa Marie PRESLEY

US, female vocalist (Singles: 5 weeks, Albums: 1 week) pos/wks

12 Jul 03 **LIGHTS OUT (re)** *Capitol CDCL 844* 16 5
26 Jul 03 **TO WHOM IT MAY CONCERN** *Capitol 5905220* 52 1

PRESSURE DROP

UK, male vocal / instrumental duo (Singles: 2 weeks) pos/wks

21 Mar 98 **SILENTLY BAD MINDED** *Higher Ground HIGHS6 CD* 53 1
17 Mar 01 **WARRIOR SOUND** *Higher Ground 6697192* 72 1

Billy PRESTON

US, male vocalist / instrumentalist – keyboards (Singles: 51 weeks) pos/wks

23 Apr 69 ★ **GET BACK (2re)** *Apple R 5777* [1] ■ ▲ 1 23
2 Jul 69 **THAT'S THE WAY GOD PLANNED IT** *Apple 12* 11 10
16 Sep 72 **OUTA SPACE** *A&M AMS 7007* 44 3
15 Dec 79 ● **WITH YOU I'M BORN AGAIN** *Motown TMG 1159* [2] 2 11
8 Mar 80 **IT WILL COME IN TIME** *Motown TMG 1175* [2] 47 4

[1] Beatles with Billy Preston [2] Billy Preston and Syreeta

Johnny PRESTON

US, male vocalist – Johnny Courville (Singles: 46 weeks) pos/wks

12 Feb 60 ★ **RUNNING BEAR (re)** *Mercury AMT 1079* ▲ 1 16
21 Apr 60 ● **CRADLE OF LOVE** *Mercury AMT 1092* 2 16
28 Jul 60 **I'M STARTING TO GO STEADY** *Mercury AMT 1104* 49 1
11 Aug 60 **FEEL SO FINE** *Mercury AMT 1104* 18 10
8 Dec 60 **CHARMING BILLY (re)** *Mercury AMT 1114* 34 3

Review of the Year

AUGUST 2003

The first three days of the month see **Robbie Williams** play Knebworth with a total attendance of 375,000 fans. For the record, the support acts are **The Darkness**, **Ash**, **Moby** and **Kelly Osbourne**. Joining Robbie on stage are **Max Beezley** (at the piano) and **Mark Owen**. The gig is broadcast on Channel 4 and Robbie's Escapology album returns to the top of the chart, rising 17 places. While on the subject of huge attendance figures, Molson Canadian Rocks for Toronto draws 489,176 fans to a one-day event headlined by **The Rolling Stones** and featuring, **AC/DC**, **Isley Brothers**, **Justin Timberlake** and Canadian rock bands **Rush** and **The Guess Who**. The Stones attempt to play two days at Twickenham rugby stadium but **Mick Jagger** is told to rest his voice by his doctor and one show is cancelled. UK album sales are at a record high as **Eva Cassidy** becomes the first artist to score three posthumous No.1 albums thanks to American Tune. Rock albums hog half the top slots on the UK chart. The Who's **Roger Daltrey** plays dustman Alfred P Doolittle in a one-off production of My Fair Lady at the Hollywood Bowl. British acts receive eight nominations at the MTV awards. **Radiohead** and **Coldplay** account for seven of them. Coldplay, **Beyoncé** and **Justin Timberlake** are the big winners with three awards apiece and **Johnny Cash** (who has six nominations) is another winner just days before his death. **The Sex Pistols** tour the US and **Sting**, receives the prestigious Billboard Century Award. At the Soul Train Lady of Soul awards, no one betters London's R&B duo **Floetry's** four nominations. The American version of TV's Stars in Their Eyes (Performing As…) is launched by the American Idol TV company, Fox. **Yes** return to the UK Album Top 10 after 12 years away. **Madonna's** first children's book, The English Rose, is published. **Kraftwerk's** first new album in 17 years, Tour de France Soundtracks, enters the German chart at No.1. Kerrang! award winners include **Feeder** (best British act), **Good Charlotte** (best single) and **Metallica** (hall of fame). At times seven of the top nine (including all the top five) tropical Latin albums in the US are by the recently deceased legendary performer **Celia Cruz**.

Knebworth in Hertfordshire is the scene of Robbie Williams' biggest and best live show to date

Feeder's Grant Nicholas with Mark Richardson and the Kerrang! best British act award

Mike PRESTON

UK, male vocalist – Jack Davis (Singles: 33 weeks) pos/wks

30 Oct 59	**MR BLUE** *Decca F 11167*	12	8
25 Aug 60	**I'D DO ANYTHING** *Decca F 11255*	23	10
22 Dec 60	**TOGETHERNESS** *Decca F 11287*	41	5
9 Mar 61	**MARRY ME** *Decca F 11335*	14	10

PRETENDERS (189 Top 500)

Internationally successful, British-based post-punk group with an ever-changing line-up, but with ex-NME journalist Chrissie Hynde (b. 7 Sep 1951, Ohio, US) (v/g) as a common factor. Hynde was briefly married to the lead singer of Simple Minds, Jim Kerr, and had a child with Ray Davies of The Kinks (Singles: 132 weeks, Albums: 171 weeks) pos/wks

10 Feb 79	**STOP YOUR SOBBING** *Real ARE 6*	34	9
14 Jul 79	**KID** *Real ARE 9*	33	7
17 Nov 79 ★	**BRASS IN POCKET** *Real ARE 11*	1	17
5 Apr 80 ●	**TALK OF THE TOWN** *Real ARE 12*	8	8
14 Feb 81	**MESSAGE OF LOVE** *Real ARE 15*	11	7
12 Sep 81	**DAY AFTER DAY** *Real ARE 17*	45	4
14 Nov 81 ●	**I GO TO SLEEP** *Real ARE 18*	7	10
2 Oct 82	**BACK ON THE CHAIN GANG** *Real ARE 19*	17	9
26 Nov 83	**2000 MILES** *Real ARE 20*	15	9
9 Jun 84	**THIN LINE BETWEEN LOVE AND HATE** *Real ARE 22*	49	3
11 Oct 86 ●	**DON'T GET ME WRONG** *Real YZ 85*	10	9
13 Dec 86 ●	**HYMN TO HER** *Real YZ 93*	8	12
15 Aug 87	**IF THERE WAS A MAN** *Real YZ 149* [1]	49	6
23 Apr 94 ●	**I'LL STAND BY YOU** *WEA YZ 815CD*	10	10
2 Jul 94	**NIGHT IN MY VEINS** *WEA YZ 825CD*	25	5
15 Oct 94	**977** *WEA YZ 848CD1*	66	2
14 Oct 95	**KID (re-recording)** *WEA 014CD*	73	1
10 May 97	**FEVER PITCH THE EP** *Blanco Y Negro NEG 104CD* [2]	65	1
15 May 99	**HUMAN** *WEA WEA 207CD*	33	3
19 Jan 80 ★	**PRETENDERS** *Real RAL 3* ■	1	35
15 Aug 81 ●	**PRETENDERS II** *Real SRK 3572*	7	27
21 Jan 84	**LEARNING TO CRAWL** *Real WX 2*	11	16
1 Nov 86 ●	**GET CLOSE** *WEA WX 64*	6	28
7 Nov 87 ●	**THE SINGLES** *WEA WX 135*	6	32
26 May 90	**PACKED!** *WEA WX 346*	19	5
21 May 94 ●	**LAST OF THE INDEPENDENTS** *WEA 4509958222*	8	13
28 Oct 95	**THE ISLE OF VIEW** *WEA 0630120592*	23	4
29 May 99	**VIVA EL AMOR** *WEA 3984271522*	32	2
30 Sep 00	**GREATEST HITS** *Warner.ESP 8573846072*	21	8
31 May 03	**LOOSE SCREW** *Eagle EAGCD256*	55	1

[1] Pretenders for 007 [2] Pretenders, La's, Orlando, Neil MacColl, Nick Hornby

Tracks on Fever Pitch the EP: Goin' Back – Pretenders; There She Goes – La's; How Can We Hang on to a Dream – Orlando; Football – Neil MacColl; Boo Hewerdine – Nick Hornby. 'Kid' in 1995 is a re-recording

See also Chrissie HYNDE

PRETTY BOY FLOYD

US, male vocal / instrumental group (Singles: 1 week) pos/wks

10 Mar 90	**ROCK AND ROLL (IS GONNA SET THE NIGHT ON FIRE)** *MCA MCA 1393*	75	1

PRETTY THINGS *UK, male vocal / instrumental group (Singles: 41 weeks, Albums: 13 weeks)*

pos/wks

18 Jun 64	**ROSALYN** *Fontana TF 469*	41	5
22 Oct 64 ●	**DON'T BRING ME DOWN** *Fontana TF 503*	10	11
25 Feb 65	**HONEY I NEED** *Fontana TF 537*	13	10
15 Jul 65	**CRY TO ME** *Fontana TF 585*	28	7
20 Jan 66	**MIDNIGHT TO SIX MAN** *Fontana TF 647*	46	1
5 May 66	**COME SEE ME** *Fontana TF 688*	43	5
21 Jul 66	**A HOUSE IN THE COUNTRY (re)** *Fontana TF 722*	50	2
27 Mar 65 ●	**PRETTY THINGS** *Fontana TL 5239*	6	10
27 Jun 70	**PARACHUTE** *Harvest SHVL 774*	43	3

Alan PRICE *UK, male vocalist / instrumentalist – keyboards (Singles: 87 weeks, Albums: 10 weeks)*

pos/wks

31 Mar 66 ●	**I PUT A SPELL ON YOU** *Decca F 12367* [1]	9	10
14 Jul 66	**HI LILI, HI LO** *Decca F 12442* [1]	11	12
2 Mar 67 ●	**SIMON SMITH AND HIS AMAZING DANCING BEAR** *Decca F 12570* [1]	4	12
2 Aug 67 ●	**THE HOUSE THAT JACK BUILT** *Decca F 12641* [1]	4	10
15 Nov 67	**SHAME** *Decca F 12691* [1]	45	2
31 Jan 68	**DON'T STOP THE CARNIVAL** *Decca F 12731* [1]	13	8
10 Apr 71	**ROSETTA** *CBS 7108* [2]	11	10
25 May 74 ●	**JARROW SONG** *Warner Bros. K 16372*	6	9
29 Apr 78	**JUST FOR YOU** *Jet UP 36358*	43	7
17 Feb 79	**BABY OF MINE / JUST FOR YOU (re-issue)** *Jet 135*	32	3
30 Apr 88	**CHANGES** *Ariola 109911*	54	4
8 Jun 74 ●	**BETWEEN TODAY AND YESTERDAY** *Warner Bros. K 56032*	9	10

[1] Alan Price Set [2] Fame and Price Together

Kelly PRICE

US, female vocalist (Singles: 10 weeks) pos/wks

7 Nov 98	**FRIEND OF MINE** *Island Black Music CID 723*	25	3
8 May 99	**SECRET LOVE** *Island Black Music CID 739*	26	2
30 Dec 00	**HEARTBREAK HOTEL** *Arista 74321820572* [1]	25	5

[1] Whitney Houston featuring Faith Evans and Kelly Price

Lloyd PRICE

US, male vocalist (Singles: 36 weeks) pos/wks

13 Feb 59 ●	**STAGGER LEE** *HMV POP 580* ▲	7	14
15 May 59	**WHERE WERE YOU (ON OUR WEDDING DAY)?** *HMV POP 598*	15	6
12 Jun 59 ●	**PERSONALITY (re)** *HMV POP 626*	9	10
11 Sep 59	**I'M GONNA GET MARRIED** *HMV POP 650*	23	5
21 Apr 60	**LADY LUCK** *HMV POP 712*	45	1

PRICKLY HEAT

UK, male producer (Singles: 1 week) pos/wks

26 Dec 98	**OOOIE, OOOIE, OOOIE** *Virgin VSCDT 1727*	57	1

Charley PRIDE *US, male vocalist (Albums: 17 weeks)*

pos/wks

10 Apr 71	**CHARLEY PRIDE SPECIAL** *RCA SF 8171*	29	1
28 May 77	**SHE'S JUST AN OLD LOVE TURNED MEMORY** *RCA Victor PL 12261*	34	2
3 Jun 78	**SOMEONE LOVES YOU HONEY** *RCA PL 12478*	48	2
26 Jan 80 ●	**GOLDEN COLLECTION** *K-Tel NE 1056*	6	12

Dickie PRIDE

UK, male vocalist – Richard Knellar d. May 1969 (Singles: 1 week) pos/wks

30 Oct 59	**PRIMROSE LANE** *Columbia DB 4340*	28	1

Maxi PRIEST (497 Top 500)

Popular dancehall reggae star, b. Max Elliott, 10 Jun 1960, London, UK. This internationally acclaimed vocalist is one of only two UK reggae acts to top the US chart ('Close to You', 1990). A duet with Roberta Flack, 'Set the Night to Music', also reached the US Top 10 in 1991 (Singles: 106 weeks, Albums: 35 weeks) pos/wks

29 Mar 86	**STROLLIN' ON** *10 TEN 84*	32	9
12 Jul 86	**IN THE SPRINGTIME** *10 TEN 127*	54	3
8 Nov 86	**CRAZY LOVE** *10 TEN 135*	67	5
4 Apr 87	**LET ME KNOW** *10 TEN 156*	49	4
24 Oct 87	**SOME GUYS HAVE ALL THE LUCK** *10 TEN 198*	12	12
20 Feb 88	**HOW CAN WE EASE THE PAIN** *10 TEN 207*	41	6
4 Jun 88 ●	**WILD WORLD** *10 TEN 221*	5	9
27 Aug 88	**GOODBYE TO LOVE AGAIN** *10 TEN 238*	57	3
9 Jun 90 ●	**CLOSE TO YOU** *10 TEN 294* ▲	7	10
1 Sep 90	**PEACE THROUGHOUT THE WORLD** *10 TEN 317* [1]	41	4
1 Dec 90	**HUMAN WORK OF ART (re)** *10 TEN 328*	71	4
24 Aug 91	**HOUSECALL** *Epic 6573477* [2]	31	7
5 Oct 91	**JUST A LITTLE BIT LONGER (EP)** *Ten TEN 343*	62	3
26 Sep 92	**GROOVIN' IN THE MIDNIGHT** *Ten TEN 412*	50	2
28 Nov 92	**JUST WANNA KNOW / FE' REAL** *Ten TEN 416* [3]	33	3
20 Mar 93	**ONE MORE CHANCE** *Ten TENCD 420*	40	3
8 May 93 ●	**HOUSECALL (re-mix)** *Epic 6592842* [2]	8	8
31 Jul 93	**WAITING IN VAIN** *GRP MCSTD 1921* [4]	65	2
22 Jun 96	**THAT GIRL** *Virgin America VUSCD 106* [5]	15	7
21 Sep 96	**WATCHING THE WORLD GO BY** *Virgin America VUSCD 108*	36	2
6 Dec 86	**INTENTIONS** *10 DIX 32*	96	1

5 Dec 87 **MAXI** *10 DIX 64* ... 25 15
15 Jul 90 **BONAFIDE** *10 DIX 92* ... 11 13
9 Nov 91 **BEST OF ME** *10 DIX 111* ... 23 5
14 Nov 92 **FE REAL** *10 DIXCD 113* ... 60 1

[1] Maxi Priest featuring Jazzie B [2] Shabba Ranks featuring Maxi Priest [3] Maxi Priest / Maxi Priest featuring Apache Indian [4] Lee Ritenour and Maxi Priest [5] Maxi Priest featuring Shaggy

Tracks on Just a Little Bit Longer (EP): Just a Little Bit Longer / Best of Me / Searching / Fever

Louis PRIMA *US, male vocalist d. 24 Aug 1978 (Singles: 1 week)* pos/wks

21 Feb 58 **BUONA SERA** *Capitol CL 14821* ... 25 1

PRIMA DONNA

UK, male / female vocal group (Singles: 4 weeks) pos/wks

26 Apr 80 **LOVE ENOUGH FOR TWO** *Ariola ARO 221* ... 48 4

PRIMAL SCREAM *UK, male vocal / instrumental group (Singles: 54 weeks, Albums: 75 weeks)* pos/wks

3 Mar 90 **LOADED** *Creation CRE 070* ... 16 9
18 Aug 90 **COME TOGETHER** *Creation CRE 078* ... 26 6
22 Jun 91 **HIGHER THAN THE SUN** *Creation CRE 096* ... 40 2
24 Aug 91 **DON'T FIGHT IT FEEL IT** *Creation CRE 110* [1] ... 41 2
8 Feb 92 **DIXIE-NARCO (EP)** *Creation CRE 117* ... 11 6
12 Mar 94 ● **ROCKS / FUNKY JAM** *Creation CRESCD 129* ... 7 5
18 Jun 94 **JAILBIRD** *Creation CRESCD 145* ... 29 2
10 Dec 94 **(I'M GONNA) CRY MYSELF BLIND** *Creation CRESCD 183* ... 49 2
15 Jun 96 **THE BIG MAN AND THE SCREAM TEAM MEET THE BARMY ARMY UPTOWN** *Creation CRESCD 194* [2] ... 17 2
17 May 97 ● **KOWALSKI** *Creation CRESCD 245* ... 8 3
28 Jun 97 **STAR** *Creation CRESCD 263* ... 16 3
25 Oct 97 **BURNING WHEEL** *Creation CRESCD 272* ... 17 2
20 Nov 99 **SWASTIKA EYES** *Creation CRESCD 326* ... 22 2
1 Apr 00 **KILL ALL HIPPIES** *Creation CRESCD 332* ... 24 2
23 Sep 00 **ACCELERATOR** *Creation CRESCD 333* ... 34 1
3 Aug 02 **MISS LUCIFER** *Columbia 6728252* ... 25 2
9 Nov 02 **AUTOBAHN 66** *Columbia 6733122* ... 44 1
29 Nov 03 **SOME VELVET MORNING** *Columbia 6744022* [3] ... 44 2
17 Oct 87 **SONIC FLOWER GROOVE** *Elevation ELV 2* ... 62 1
5 Oct 91 ● **SCREAMADELICA** *Creation CRELP 076* ... 8 30
9 Apr 94 ● **GIVE OUT BUT DON'T GIVE UP** *Creation CRECD 146* ... 2 18
19 Jul 97 ● **VANISHING POINT** *Creation CRECD 178* ... 2 10
8 Nov 97 **ECHO DEK** *Creation CRECD 224* ... 43 1
12 Feb 00 ● **EXTERMINATOR** *Creation CRECD 239* ... 3 10
17 Aug 02 ● **EVIL HEAT** *Columbia 5089232* ... 9 3
15 Nov 03 **DIRTY HITS** *Columbia 5136039* ... 25 2

[1] Primal Scream featuring Denise Johnson [2] Primal Scream, Irvine Welsh and On-U Sound [3] Primal Scream & Kate Moss

Tracks on Dixie-Narco (EP): Movin' On Up / Stone My Soul / Carry Me Home / Screamadelica

PRIME MOVERS

US, male vocal / instrumental group (Singles: 1 week) pos/wks

8 Feb 86 **ON THE TRAIL** *Island IS 263* ... 74 1

PRIMITIVE RADIO GODS

US, male vocalist – Chris O'Connor (Singles: 1 week) pos/wks

30 Mar 96 **STANDING OUTSIDE A BROKEN PHONE BOOTH WITH MONEY IN MY HAND** *Columbia 6627692* ... 74 1

PRIMITIVES *UK, male / female vocal / instrumental group (Singles: 27 weeks, Albums: 13 weeks)* pos/wks

27 Feb 88 ● **CRASH** *Lazy PB 41761* ... 5 10
30 Apr 88 **OUT OF REACH** *Lazy PB 42011* ... 25 4
3 Sep 88 **WAY BEHIND ME** *Lazy PB 42209* ... 36 4
29 Jul 89 **SICK OF IT** *Lazy PB 42947* ... 24 4
30 Sep 89 **SECRETS** *Lazy PB 43173* ... 49 3
3 Aug 91 **YOU ARE THE WAY** *RCA PB 44481* ... 58 2
9 Apr 88 ● **LOVELY** *RCA PL 71688* ... 6 10
2 Sep 89 **LAZY 86-88** *Lazy 15* ... 73 1
28 Oct 89 **PURE** *RCA PL 74252* ... 33 2

PRIMUS *US, male vocal / instrumental group (Albums: 1 week)* pos/wks

8 May 93 **PORK SODA** *Interscope 75679922572* ... 56 1

PRINCE (34 Top 500) *Prolific singer / songwriter / producer / multi-instrumentalist / actor / label and studio owner, b. Prince Rogers Nelson, 7 Jun 1958, Minneapolis, US. This often controversial entertainer has packed stadiums and collected awards worldwide. He has recorded under a variety of monikers including a symbol and 'The Artist Formerly Known As Prince' (Singles: 305 weeks, Albums: 436 weeks)* pos/wks

19 Jan 80 **I WANNA BE YOUR LOVER** *Warner Bros. K 17537* ... 41 3
29 Jan 83 **1999** *Warner Bros. W 9896* ... 25 7
30 Apr 83 **LITTLE RED CORVETTE** *Warner Bros. W 9688* ... 54 6
26 Nov 83 **LITTLE RED CORVETTE (re-issue)** *Warner Bros. W 9436* ... 66 2
30 Jun 84 ● **WHEN DOVES CRY** *Warner Bros. W 9286* ▲ ... 4 15
22 Sep 84 ● **PURPLE RAIN** *Warner Bros. W 9174* [1] ... 8 9
8 Dec 84 **I WOULD DIE 4 U** *Warner Bros. W 9121* [1] ... 58 6
19 Jan 85 ● **1999 / LITTLE RED CORVETTE (re-issue)** *Warner Bros. W 1999* ... 2 10
23 Feb 85 ● **LET'S GO CRAZY / TAKE ME WITH U** *Warner Bros. W 2000* [1] ▲ ... 7 9
25 May 85 **PAISLEY PARK** *WEA W 9052* [1] ... 18 10
27 Jul 85 **RASPBERRY BERET** *WEA W 8929* [1] ... 25 8
26 Oct 85 **POP LIFE** *Paisley Park W 8858* [1] ... 60 2
8 Mar 86 ● **KISS** *Paisley Park W 8751* [1] ▲ ... 6 9
14 Jun 86 **MOUNTAINS** *Paisley Park W 8711* [1] ... 45 4
16 Aug 86 **GIRLS AND BOYS** *Paisley Park W 8586* [1] ... 11 8
1 Nov 86 **ANOTHERLOVERHOLENYOHEAD** *Paisley Park W 8521* [1] ... 36 3
14 Mar 87 ● **SIGN 'O' THE TIMES** *Paisley Park W 8399* ... 10 9
20 Jun 87 **IF I WAS YOUR GIRLFRIEND** *Paisley Park W 8334* ... 20 6
15 Aug 87 **U GOT THE LOOK** *Paisley Park W 8289* ... 11 9
28 Nov 87 **I COULD NEVER TAKE THE PLACE OF YOUR MAN** *Paisley Park W 8288* ... 29 6
7 May 88 ● **ALPHABET STREET** *Paisley Park W 7900* ... 9 6
23 Jul 88 **GLAM SLAM** *Paisley Park W 7806* ... 29 4
5 Nov 88 **I WISH U HEAVEN** *Paisley Park W 7745* ... 24 5
24 Jun 89 ● **BATDANCE** *Warner Bros. W 2924* ▲ ... 2 12
9 Sep 89 **PARTYMAN** *Warner Bros. W 2814* ... 14 6
18 Nov 89 **THE ARMS OF ORION** *Warner Bros. W 2757* [2] ... 27 5
4 Aug 90 ● **THIEVES IN THE TEMPLE** *Paisley Park W 9751* ... 7 6
10 Nov 90 **NEW POWER GENERATION** *Paisley Park W 9525* ... 26 4
31 Aug 91 ● **GETT OFF** *Paisley Park W 0056* [3] ... 4 8
21 Sep 91 **CREAM** *Paisley Park W 0061* [3] ▲ ... 15 7
7 Dec 91 **DIAMONDS AND PEARLS** *Paisley Park W 0075* [3] ... 25 6
28 Mar 92 **MONEY DON'T MATTER 2 NIGHT** *Paisley Park W 0091* [3] ... 19 5
27 Jun 92 **THUNDER** *Paisley Park W 0113* [3] ... 28 3
18 Jul 92 ● **SEXY MF / STROLLIN'** *Paisley Park W 0123* [3] ... 4 7
10 Oct 92 ● **MY NAME IS PRINCE** *Paisley Park W 0132* [3] ... 7 5
14 Nov 92 **MY NAME IS PRINCE (re-mix)** *Paisley Park W 0142T* [3] ... 51 1
5 Dec 92 **7** *Paisley Park W 0147* [3] ... 27 6
13 Mar 93 **THE MORNING PAPERS** *Paisley Park W 0162CD* [3] ... 52 3
16 Oct 93 **PEACH** *Paisley Park W 0210CD* ... 14 5
11 Dec 93 ● **CONTROVERSY** *Paisley Park W 0215CD1* ... 5 5
9 Apr 94 ★ **THE MOST BEAUTIFUL GIRL IN THE WORLD** *NPG NPG 60155* ... 1 12
4 Jun 94 **THE BEAUTIFUL EXPERIENCE (re-mix)** *NPG NPG 60212* ... 18 3
10 Sep 94 **LETITGO** *Warner Bros. W 0260CD* ... 30 4
18 Mar 95 **PURPLE MEDLEY** *Warner Bros. W 0289CD* ... 33 2
23 Sep 95 **EYE HATE U** *Warner Bros. W 0315CD* ... 20 3
9 Dec 95 ● **GOLD** *Warner Bros. W 0325CD* ... 10 9
3 Aug 96 **DINNER WITH DELORES** *Warner Bros. 9362437422* ... 36 2
14 Dec 96 **BETCHA BY GOLLY WOW** *NPG CDEM 463* [4] ... 11 7
8 Mar 97 **THE HOLY RIVER** *EMI CDEM 467* [4] ... 19 3
9 Jan 99 ● **1999 (re) (re-issue)** *Warner Bros. W 467CD* ... 10 9
26 Feb 00 **THE GREATEST ROMANCE EVER SOLD** *NPG / Arista 74321745002* [4] ... 65 1
21 Jul 84 ● **PURPLE RAIN (FILM SOUNDTRACK)** *Warner Bros. 9251101* [1] ▲ ... 7 91
8 Sep 84 **1999** *Warner Bros. 923720* ... 30 21
4 May 85 ● **AROUND THE WORLD IN A DAY** *Warner Bros. 92-5286-1* [1] ▲ ... 5 20

12 Apr 86 ● **PARADE – MUSIC FROM 'UNDER THE CHERRY MOON' (FILM SOUNDTRACK)** *Warner Bros. WX 39* [1] 4 26
11 Apr 87 ● **SIGN 'O' THE TIMES** *Paisley Park WX 88* 4 32
21 May 88 ★ **LOVESEXY** *Paisley Park WX 164* ■ 1 32
1 Jul 89 ★ **BATMAN (FILM SOUNDTRACK)** *Warner Bros. WX 281* ■ ▲....1 20
1 Sep 90 ★ **GRAFFITI BRIDGE** *Paisley Park WX 361* ■....1 8
24 Aug 91 **GETT OFF (import)** *Paisley Park 9401382*....33 3
12 Oct 91 ● **DIAMONDS AND PEARLS** *Paisley Park WX 432* [2] 2 57
17 Oct 92 ★ **SYMBOL** *Paisley Park 9362450372* [2] ■....1 21
25 Sep 93 ● **THE HITS 1** *Paisley Park 9362454312* 5 27
25 Sep 93 ● **THE HITS 2** *Paisley Park 9362454352* 5 28
25 Sep 93 ● **THE HITS / THE B-SIDES** *Paisley Park 9362454402* 4 7
27 Aug 94 ★ **COME** *Warner Bros. 9362457002* ■....1 8
3 Dec 94 **THE BLACK ALBUM** *Warner Bros. 9362457932*....36 3
7 Oct 95 ● **THE GOLD EXPERIENCE** *Warner Bros. 9362459992* [3] 4 5
20 Jul 96 **CHAOS AND DISORDER** *Warner Bros. 9362463172* [4] 14 4
30 Nov 96 **EMANCIPATION** *NPG CDEMD 1102* [5]....18 6
11 Jul 98 **NEWPOWER SOUL** *RCA 74321605982* [5] 38 2
4 Sep 99 **THE VAULT ... OLD FRIENDS 4 SALE** *Warner Bros. 9362475222* 47 1
11 Aug 01 ● **THE VERY BEST OF PRINCE** *Warner Bros. 8122742722* 2 14

[1] Prince and the Revolution [2] Prince with Sheena Easton [3] Prince and the New Power Generation [4] The Artist [1] Prince and the Revolution [2] Prince and the New Power Generation [3] (SYMBOL) [4] T.A.F.K.A.P. [5] Artist

Although uncredited, Sheena Easton also sings on 'U Got the Look'. 'The Beautiful Experience' was a seven-track CD featuring 'The Most Beautiful Girl in the World' and six further mixes of the track. 'Let's Go Crazy' was the track from the double A side single that topped the US chart. Purple Medley comprised re-recordings of Batdance / When Doves Cry / Kiss / Erotic City / Darling Nikki / 1999 / Baby I'm a Star / Diamonds And Pearls / Purple Rain / Let's Go Crazy

See also *NEW POWER GENERATION*

PRINCE BUSTER

Jamaica, male vocalist – Buster Campbell (Singles: 16 weeks) pos/wks

23 Feb 67 **AL CAPONE** *Blue Beat BB 324* 18 13
4 Apr 98 **WHINE AND GRINE** *Island CID 691* 21 3

PRINCE CHARLES and the CITY BEAT BAND *US, male vocal / instrumental group (Singles: 2 weeks, Albums: 1 week)* pos/wks

22 Feb 86 **WE CAN MAKE IT HAPPEN** *PRT 7P 348* 56 2
30 Apr 83 **STONE KILLERS** *Virgin V 2271*....84 1

PRINCE NASEEM – See *KALEEF*

PRINCESS *UK, female vocalist – Desiree Heslop (Singles: 44 weeks, Albums: 14 weeks)* pos/wks

3 Aug 85 ● **SAY I'M YOUR NUMBER ONE** *Supreme SUPE 101* 7 12
9 Nov 85 **AFTER THE LOVE HAS GONE** *Supreme SUPE 103* 28 13
19 Apr 86 **I'LL KEEP ON LOVING YOU** *Supreme SUPE 105* 16 8
5 Jul 86 **TELL ME TOMORROW** *Supreme SUPE 106* 34 5
25 Oct 86 **IN THE HEAT OF A PASSIONATE MOMENT** *Supreme SUPE 109* 74 1
13 Jun 87 **RED HOT** *Polydor POSP 868* 58 5
17 May 86 **PRINCESS** *Supreme SU1*....15 14

PRINCESS IVORI *US, female rapper (Singles: 2 weeks)* pos/wks

17 Mar 90 **WANTED** *Supreme SUPE 163* 69 2

PRINCESS SUPERSTAR

US, female vocalist – Concetta Kirschner (Singles: 7 weeks) pos/wks

2 Mar 02 **BAD BABYSITTER** *Rapster RR 007CDM* 11 7

Patrick PRINZ – See *ARTEMESIA; ETHICS; MOVIN' MELODIES; SUBLIMINAL CUTS*

Maddy PRIOR – See *STATUS QUO; STEELEYE SPAN*

PRIORY OF THE RESURRECTION

UK, male / female choir (Albums: 1 week) pos/wks

31 Mar 01 **ETERNAL LIGHT – MUSIC OF INNER PEACE** *Deutsche Grammophon 4710902* 68 1

PRIVATE LIVES

UK, male vocal / instrumental duo (Singles: 4 weeks) pos/wks

11 Feb 84 **LIVING IN A WORLD (TURNED UPSIDE DOWN)** *EMI PRIV 2* 53 4

PRIZNA featuring DEMOLITION MAN

UK, male vocal / instrumental group (Singles: 2 weeks) pos/wks

29 Apr 95 **FIRE** *Labello Blanco NLBCDX 18* 33 2

PJ PROBY *US, male vocalist – James Marcus Smith (Singles: 91 weeks, Albums: 3 weeks)* pos/wks

28 May 64 ● **HOLD ME** *Decca F 11904* 3 15
3 Sep 64 ● **TOGETHER** *Decca F 11967* 8 11
10 Dec 64 ● **SOMEWHERE** *Liberty LIB 10182* 6 12
25 Feb 65 **I APOLOGISE** *Liberty LIB 10188* 11 8
8 Jul 65 **LET THE WATER RUN DOWN** *Liberty LIB 10206* 19 8
30 Sep 65 **THAT MEANS A LOT** *Liberty LIB 10215* 30 6
25 Nov 65 ● **MARIA** *Liberty LIB 10218* 8 9
10 Feb 66 **YOU'VE COME BACK** *Liberty LIB 10223* 25 7
16 Jun 66 **TO MAKE A BIG MAN CRY** *Liberty LIB 10236* 34 3
27 Oct 66 **I CAN'T MAKE IT ALONE** *Liberty LIB 10250* 37 5
6 Mar 68 **IT'S YOUR DAY TODAY** *Liberty LBF 15046* 32 5
28 Dec 96 **YESTERDAY HAS GONE (re)** *EMI Premier CDPRESX 13* [1] 58 2
27 Feb 65 **I'M PJ PROBY** *Liberty LBY 1235*....16 3

[1] PJ Proby and Marc Almond featuring the My Life Story Orchestra

PROCLAIMERS *UK, male vocal / instrumental duo – Charlie and Craig Reid (Singles: 50 weeks, Albums: 62 weeks)* pos/wks

14 Nov 87 ● **LETTER FROM AMERICA** *Chrysalis CHS 3178* 3 10
5 Mar 88 **MAKE MY HEART FLY** *Chrysalis CLAIM 1* 63 3
27 Aug 88 **I'M GONNA BE (500 MILES)** *Chrysalis CLAIM 2* 11 11
12 Nov 88 **SUNSHINE ON LEITH** *Chrysalis CLAIM 3* 41 5
11 Feb 89 **I'M ON MY WAY** *Chrysalis CLAIM 4* 43 4
24 Nov 90 ● **KING OF THE ROAD (EP)** *Chrysalis CLAIM 5* 9 8
19 Feb 94 **LET'S GET MARRIED** *Chrysalis CDCLAIMS 6* 21 4
16 Apr 94 **WHAT MAKES YOU CRY** *Chrysalis CDCLAIMS 7* 38 3
22 Oct 94 **THESE ARMS OF MINE** *Chrysalis CDCLAIM 8* 51 2
9 May 87 **THIS IS THE STORY** *Chrysalis CHR 1602*....43 21
24 Sep 88 ● **SUNSHINE ON LEITH** *Chrysalis CHR 1668*....6 27
19 Mar 94 ● **HIT THE HIGHWAY** *Chrysalis CDCHR 6066*....8 6
9 Jun 01 **PERSEVERE** *Persevere PERSRECCD 04*....61 1
25 May 02 **THE BEST OF THE PROCLAIMERS** *Chrysalis 5386822* 30 6
27 Sep 03 **BORN INNOCENT** *Persevere PERSRECCD09* 70 1

Tracks on King of the Road (EP): King of the Road / Long Black Veil / Lulu Selling Tea / Not Ever

PROCOL HARUM *UK, male vocal / instrumental group – includes Robin Trower and Gary Brooker (Singles: 56 weeks, Albums: 11 weeks)* pos/wks

25 May 67 ★ **A WHITER SHADE OF PALE** *Deram DM 126* 1 15
4 Oct 67 ● **HOMBURG** *Regal Zonophone RZ 3003* 6 10
24 Apr 68 **QUITE RIGHTLY SO** *Regal Zonophone RZ 3007* 50 1
18 Jun 69 **A SALTY DOG (2re)** *Regal Zonophone RZ 3019* 44 3
22 Apr 72 **A WHITER SHADE OF PALE (re-issue)** *Fly Magnifly ECHO 101* 13 13
5 Aug 72 **CONQUISTADOR** *Chrysalis CHS 2003* 22 7
23 Aug 75 **PANDORA'S BOX** *Chrysalis CHS 2073* 16 7
19 Jul 69 **A SALTY DOG** *Regal Zonophone SLRZ 1009*....27 2
27 Jun 70 **HOME** *Regal Zonophone SLRZ 1014*....49 1
3 Jul 71 **BROKEN BARRICADES** *Island ILPS 9158*....42 1
6 May 72 **PROCOL HARUM IN CONCERT WITH THE EDMONTON SYMPHONY ORCHESTRA** *Chrysalis CHR 1004*....48 1
6 May 72 **A WHITER SHADE OF PALE / A SALTY DOG (re-issue)** *Fly Double Back TOOFA 7/8* 26 4
30 Aug 75 **PROCOL'S NINTH** *Chrysalis CHR 1080* 41 2

'A Whiter Shade of Pale / A Salty Dog' is a double re-issue although 'A Whiter Shade of Pale' was not previously a hit. The Edmonton Symphony Orchestra is a Canadian orchestra

See also *EDMONTON SYMPHONY ORCHESTRA*

Michael PROCTER – See *URBAN BLUES PROJECT presents Michael PROCTER*

PRODIGY 159 Top 500

Confrontational dance-rock collision masterminded by Liam Howlett (k/prog) and featuring charismatic Keith Flint (v). This act has achieved a run of 12 successive Top 20 singles, while their 1997 album, 'Fat of the Land', debuted at No.1 in more than 20 countries, including the UK and the US. MC / dancer Maxim went solo in 2000. Best-selling single 'Breathe' 709,000 (Singles: 145 weeks, Albums: 189 weeks) pos/wks

			pos	wks
24 Aug 91	●	**CHARLY (re)** *XL XL Recordings 21CD*	3	11
4 Jan 92	●	**EVERYBODY IN THE PLACE (EP) (re)** *XL XL Recordings 26CD1*	2	10
26 Sep 92		**FIRE / JERICHO (re)** *XL XL Recordings 30CD*	11	5
21 Nov 92	●	**OUT OF SPACE / RUFF IN THE JUNGLE BIZNESS (re)** *XL XL Recordings 35CD*	5	14
17 Apr 93		**WIND IT UP (REWOUND) (re)** *XL XL Recordings 39CD*	11	8
16 Oct 93	●	**ONE LOVE** *XL XL Recordings 47CD*	8	6
28 May 94	●	**NO GOOD (START THE DANCE) (re)** *XL XL Recordings 51CD*	4	14
24 Sep 94		**VOODOO PEOPLE (re)** *XL XL Recordings 54CD*	13	6
18 Mar 95		**POISON (re)** *XL XL Recordings 58CD*	15	7
30 Mar 96	★	**FIRESTARTER (2re)** *XL XL Recordings 70CD* ■	1	30
23 Nov 96	★	**BREATHE (re)** *XL XL Recordings 80CD* ■	1	18
29 Nov 97	●	**SMACK MY BITCH UP** *XL XL Recordings 90CD*	8	10
13 Jul 02	●	**BABY'S GOT A TEMPER** *XL Recordings XLS 145CD*	5	6
10 Oct 92		EXPERIENCE *XL Recordings XLCD 110*	12	31
16 Jul 94	★	MUSIC FOR THE JILTED GENERATION *XL Recordings XLCD 114* ■	1	98
12 Jul 97	★	THE FAT OF THE LAND *XL Recordings XLCD 121* ■ ▲	1	60

Tracks on Everybody in the Place (EP): Everybody in the Place / Crazy Man / G-Force (Energy Flow) / Rip Up the Sound System. Eight of their singles re-entered the chart in Apr 1996

PRODUCT G&B – *See SANTANA*

PROFESSIONALS

UK, male vocal / instrumental group (Singles: 4 weeks) pos/wks

			pos	wks
11 Oct 80		**1-2-3** *Virgin VS 376*	43	4

PROFESSOR – *See DJ PROFESSOR*

PROFESSOR T – *See SHUT UP AND DANCE*

PROGRAM – *See MR PINK presents The PROGRAM*

PROGRAM 2 BELTRAM – *See BELTRAM*

PROGRESS FUNK *Italy, male production trio (Singles: 1 week)* pos/wks

			pos	wks
11 Oct 97		**AROUND MY BRAIN** *Deconstruction 74321518182*	73	1

PROGRESS presents the BOY WUNDA

UK, male DJ / producer – Robert Webster (Singles: 10 weeks) pos/wks

			pos	wks
18 Dec 99	●	**EVERYBODY** *Manifesto FESCD 65*	7	10

PROJECT D *UK, male instrumental duo – Chris Cozens and Nick Magnus (Albums: 18 weeks)* pos/wks

			pos	wks
17 Feb 90		THE SYNTHESIZER ALBUM *Telstar STAR 2371*	13	11
29 Sep 90		SYNTHESIZED VOL.2 *Telstar STAR 2428*	25	7

See also SYMPHONIQUE

PROJECT featuring GERIDEAU

US, male vocal / instrumental duo (Singles: 1 week) pos/wks

			pos	wks
27 Aug 94		**BRING IT BACK 2 LUV** *Fruittree FTREE 10CD*	65	1

PROJECT 1

UK, male producer – Mark Williams (Singles: 3 weeks) pos/wks

			pos	wks
16 May 92		**ROUGH NECK (EP)** *Rising High RSN 22*	49	2
29 Aug 92		**DON GARGON COMIN'** *Rising High RSN 35*	64	1

Tracks on Roughneck (EP): Come My Selector / Can't Take the Heartbreak / Live Vibe 4 (Summer Vibes)

PRONG *US, male vocal / instrumental group (Singles: 1 week, Albums: 1 week)* pos/wks

			pos	wks
25 Apr 92		**WHOSE FIST IS THIS ANYWAY (EP)** *Epic 6580026*	58	1
12 Feb 94		CLEANSING *Epic 4747962*	71	1

Tracks on Whose Fist Is This Anyway (EP): Prove You Wrong / Hell If I Could / (Get a) Grip (On Yourself) / Prove You Wrong (re-mix)

PROPAGANDA *Germany, male / female vocal / instrumental group (Singles: 35 weeks, Albums: 16 weeks)* pos/wks

			pos	wks
17 Mar 84		**DR MABUSE** *ZTT ZTAS 2*	27	9
4 May 85		**DUEL** *ZTT ZTAS 8*	21	12
10 Aug 85		**P MACHINERY** *ZTT ZTAS 12*	50	5
28 Apr 90		**HEAVEN GIVE ME WORDS** *Virgin VS 1245*	36	5
8 Sep 90		**ONLY ONE WORD** *Virgin VS 1271*	71	4
13 Jul 85		A SECRET WISH *ZTT ZTTIQ 3*	16	12
23 Nov 85		WISHFUL THINKING *ZTT ZTTIQ 20*	82	2
9 Jun 90		1234 *Virgin V 2625*	46	2

PROPELLERHEADS *UK, male instrumental / production duo – Alex Gifford and Will White (Singles: 15 weeks, Albums: 13 weeks)* pos/wks

			pos	wks
7 Dec 96		**TAKE CALIFORNIA** *Wall of Sound WALLD 024*	69	1
17 May 97		**SPYBREAK!** *Wall of Sound WALLD 029X*	40	1
18 Oct 97	●	**ON HER MAJESTY'S SECRET SERVICE** *East West EW 136CD* [1]	7	5
20 Dec 97		**HISTORY REPEATING** *Wall of Sound WALLD 036* [2]	19	7
27 Jun 98		**BANG ON!** *Wall of Sound WALLD 039*	53	1
7 Feb 98	●	DECKSANDRUMSANDROCKANDROLL *Wall of Sound WALLCD 015*	6	13

[1] Propellerheads / David Arnold [2] Propellerheads featuring Miss Shirley Bassey

PROPHETS OF SOUND

UK, male instrumental / production duo (Singles: 2 weeks) pos/wks

			pos	wks
14 Nov 98		**HIGH** *Distinctive DISNCD 47*	73	1
23 Feb 02		**NEW DAWN** *Ink NIBNE 10CD*	51	1

PROSPECT PARK / Carolyn HARDING

UK, male / female vocal / production duo (Singles: 1 week) pos/wks

			pos	wks
8 Aug 98		**MOVIN' ON** *AM:PM 5827312*	55	1

Shaila PROSPERE – *See RIMES featuring Shaila PROSPERE*

Brian PROTHEROE *UK, male vocalist (Singles: 6 weeks)* pos/wks

			pos	wks
7 Sep 74		**PINBALL** *Chrysalis CHS 2043*	22	6

PROUD MARY

UK, male vocal / instrumental group (Singles: 1 week) pos/wks

			pos	wks
25 Aug 01		**VERY BEST FRIEND** *Sour Mash JDNCSCD 004*	75	1

Dorothy PROVINE

US, female actor / vocalist (Singles: 15 weeks, Albums: 49 weeks) pos/wks

			pos	wks
7 Dec 61		**DON'T BRING LULU** *Warner Bros. WB 53*	17	12
28 Jun 62		**CRAZY WORDS, CRAZY TUNE** *Warner Bros. WB 70*	45	3
2 Dec 61	●	THE ROARING TWENTIES – SONGS FROM THE TV SERIES *Warner Bros. WM 4035*	3	42
10 Feb 62	●	VAMP OF THE ROARING TWENTIES *Warner Bros. WM 4053*	9	7

PSEUDO ECHO

Australia, male vocal / instrumental group (Singles: 12 weeks) pos/wks

			pos	wks
18 Jul 87	●	**FUNKY TOWN** *RCA PB 49705*	8	12

PSYCHEDELIC FURS *UK, male vocal / instrumental group (Singles: 31 weeks, Albums: 39 weeks)* pos/wks

			pos	wks
2 May 81		**DUMB WAITERS** *CBS A 1166*	59	2
27 Jun 81		**PRETTY IN PINK** *CBS A 1327*	43	5
31 Jul 82		**LOVE MY WAY** *CBS A 2549*	42	6
31 Mar 84		**HEAVEN** *CBS A 4300*	29	6
16 Jun 84		**GHOST IN YOU** *CBS A 4470*	68	2

23 Aug 86	**PRETTY IN PINK (re-recording)** *CBS A 7242*	18	9
9 Jul 88	**ALL THAT MONEY WANTS** *CBS FURS 4*	75	1
15 Mar 80	**PSYCHEDELIC FURS** *CBS 84084*	18	6
23 May 81	**TALK TALK TALK** *CBS 84892*	30	9
2 Oct 82	**FOREVER NOW** *CBS 85909*	20	6
19 May 84	**MIRROR MOVES** *CBS 25950*	15	9
14 Feb 87	**MIDNIGHT TO MIDNIGHT** *CBS 450 2561*	12	5
13 Aug 88	**ALL OF THIS AND NOTHING** *CBS 461101*	67	2
18 Nov 89	**BOOK OF DAYS** *CBS 465982 1*	74	1
13 Jul 91	**WORLD OUTSIDE** *East West WX 422*	68	1

PSYCHEDELIC WALTONS *UK, male production duo – Nellee Hooper and Fabien Waltmann, and Ireland, female vocalist (Singles: 3 weeks)* pos/wks

19 Jan 02	**WONDERLAND** *Echo ECSCD 120* [1]	37	2
12 Apr 03	**PAYBACK TIME** *Sony Music 6737622* [2]	48	1

[1] Psychedelic Waltons featuring Roisin Murphy [2] Dysfunctional Psychedelic Waltons

See also MOLOKO; SOUL II SOUL

PSYCHIC TV

UK, male / female vocal / instrumental group (Singles: 4 weeks) pos/wks

26 Apr 86	**GODSTAR** *Temple TOPY 009* [1]	67	2
20 Sep 86	**GOOD VIBRATIONS / ROMAN P** *Temple TOPY 23*	65	2

[1] Psychic TV and The Angels of Light

PSYCHO RADIO – *See LC ANDERSON vs PSYCHO RADIO*

PSYCHOTROPIC – *See FREEFALL featuring PSYCHOTROPIC; SALT-N-PEPA*

PUBLIC ANNOUNCEMENT

US, male vocal / instrumental group (Singles: 5 weeks) pos/wks

9 May 92	**SHE'S GOT THAT VIBE** *Jive JIVET 292* [1]	57	2
20 Nov 93	**SEX ME** *Jive JIVECD 346* [1]	75	1
4 Jul 98	**BODY BUMPIN' (YIPPEE-YI-YO)** *A&M 5826972*	38	2

[1] R Kelly and Public Announcement

PUBLIC DEMAND *UK, male vocal group (Singles: 2 weeks)* pos/wks

15 Feb 97	**INVISIBLE** *ZTT ZANG 85CD*	41	2

PUBLIC DOMAIN

UK, male production / vocal group (Singles: 18 weeks) pos/wks

2 Dec 00 ●	**OPERATION BLADE (BASS IN THE PLACE)** *Xtrahard / Xtravaganza X2H 1CDS*	5	13
23 Jun 01	**ROCK DA FUNKY BEATS** *Xtrahard/Xtravaganza X2H 3CDS* [1]	19	3
12 Jan 02	**TOO MANY MC'S / LET ME CLEAR MY THROAT** *Xtrahard/Xtravaganza X2H 8CDS*	34	2

[1] Public Domain featuring Chuck D

PUBLIC ENEMY *US, male rap group – leader – Chuck D (Singles: 53 weeks, Albums: 37 weeks)* pos/wks

21 Nov 87	**REBEL WITHOUT A PAUSE (re)** *Def Jam 651245 7*	37	7
9 Jan 88	**BRING THE NOISE** *Def Jam 651335 7*	32	5
2 Jul 88	**DON'T BELIEVE THE HYPE** *Def Jam 652833 7*	18	5
15 Oct 88	**NIGHT OF THE LIVING BASEHEADS** *Def Jam 6530460*	63	2
24 Jun 89	**FIGHT THE POWER** *Motown ZB 42877*	29	5
20 Jan 90	**WELCOME TO THE TERRORDOME** *Def Jam 655476 0*	18	4
7 Apr 90	**911 IS A JOKE** *Def Jam 655830 7*	41	3
23 Jun 90	**BROTHERS GONNA WORK IT OUT** *Def Jam 656018 1*	46	2
3 Nov 90	**CAN'T DO NUTTIN' FOR YA MAN** *Def Jam 656385 7*	53	2
12 Oct 91	**CAN'T TRUSS IT** *Def Jam 6575307*	22	4
25 Jan 92	**SHUT 'EM DOWN** *Def Jam 6577617*	21	3
11 Apr 92	**NIGHTTRAIN** *Def Jam 6578647*	55	2
13 Aug 94	**GIVE IT UP** *Def Jam DEFCD 1*	18	3
29 Jul 95	**SO WATCHA GONNA DO NOW** *Def Jam DEFCD 5*	50	1
6 Jun 98	**HE GOT GAME** *Def Jam 5689852* [1]	16	4
25 Sep 99	**DO YOU WANNA GO OUR WAY???** *Pias Recordings PIASX 005CDX*	66	1
30 Jul 88 ●	**IT TAKES A NATION OF MILLIONS TO HOLD US BACK** *Def Jam 4624151*	8	9
28 Apr 90 ●	**FEAR OF A BLACK PLANET** *Def Jam 4662811*	4	10
19 Oct 91 ●	**APOCALYPSE 91 – THE ENEMY STRIKES BLACK** *Def Jam 4687511*	8	7
3 Oct 92	**GREATEST MISSES** *Def Jam 4720312*	14	3
3 Sep 94	**MUSE SICK-N-HOUR MESS AGE** *Def Jam 5233622*	12	3
16 May 98	**HE GOT GAME (FILM SOUNDTRACK)** *Def Jam 5581302*	50	4
31 Jul 99	**THERE'S A POISON GOIN ON ...** *PIAS Recordings PIASXCD 004*	55	1

[1] Public Enemy featuring Stephen Stills

PUBLIC IMAGE LTD [PiL] *UK, male vocal / instrumental group (Singles: 61 weeks, Albums: 51 weeks)* pos/wks

21 Oct 78 ●	**PUBLIC IMAGE** *Virgin VS 228*	9	8
7 Jul 79	**DEATH DISCO** *Virgin VS 274*	20	7
20 Oct 79	**MEMORIES** *Virgin VS 299*	60	2
4 Apr 81	**FLOWERS OF ROMANCE** *Virgin VS 397*	24	7
17 Sep 83 ●	**THIS IS NOT A LOVE SONG** *Virgin VS 529*	5	10
19 May 84	**BAD LIFE** *Virgin VS 675*	71	2
1 Feb 86	**RISE** *Virgin VS 841*	11	8
3 May 86	**HOME** *Virgin VS 855*	75	1
22 Aug 87	**SEATTLE** *Virgin VS 988*	47	4
6 May 89	**DISAPPOINTED** *Virgin VS 1181*	38	5
20 Oct 90	**DON'T ASK ME** *Virgin VS 1231*	22	5
22 Feb 92	**CRUEL** *Virgin VS 1390*	49	2
23 Dec 78	**PUBLIC IMAGE** *Virgin V 2114*	22	11
8 Dec 79	**METAL BOX** *Virgin METAL 1*	18	8
8 Mar 80	**SECOND EDITION OF PIL** *Virgin VD 2512*	46	2
22 Nov 80	**PARIS AU PRINTEMPS (PARIS IN THE SPRING)** *Virgin V 2183*	61	2
18 Apr 81	**FLOWERS OF ROMANCE** *Virgin V 2189*	11	5
8 Oct 83	**LIVE IN TOKYO** *Virgin VGD 3508*	28	6
21 Jul 84	**THIS IS WHAT YOU WANT ... THIS IS WHAT YOU GET** *Virgin V 2309*	56	2
15 Feb 86	**ALBUM / CASSETTE / COMPACT DISC** *Virgin V 2366*	14	6
26 Sep 87	**HAPPY?** *Virgin V 2455*	40	2
10 Jun 89	**9** *Virgin V 2588*	36	2
10 Nov 90	**THE GREATEST HITS SO FAR** *Virgin V 2644*	20	3
7 Mar 92	**THAT WHAT IS NOT** *Virgin CDV 2681*	46	2

See also John LYDON

Gary PUCKETT and the UNION GAP *US, male vocal / instrumental group (Singles: 47 weeks, Albums: 4 weeks)* pos/wks

17 Apr 68 ★	**YOUNG GIRL** *CBS 3365* [1]	1	17
7 Aug 68 ●	**LADY WILLPOWER** *CBS 3551* [1]	5	16
28 Aug 68	**WOMAN, WOMAN** *CBS 3110*	48	1
15 Jun 74 ●	**YOUNG GIRL (re-issue)** *CBS 8202*	6	13
29 Jun 68	**UNION GAP** *CBS 63342*	24	4

[1] Union Gap featuring Gary Puckett

PUDDLE OF MUDD *US, male vocal / instrumental group (Singles: 22 weeks, Albums: 36 weeks)* pos/wks

23 Feb 02	**CONTROL (re)** *Flawless / Geffen 4976822*	15	5
15 Jun 02 ●	**BLURRY** *Flawless / Geffen 4977342*	8	9
28 Sep 02	**SHE HATES ME** *Flawless / Geffen 4977982*	14	7
13 Dec 03	**AWAY FROM ME** *Flawless / Geffen 9814810*	55	1
2 Feb 02	**COME CLEAN** *Interscope 4930742*	12	36

Tito PUENTE Jr and The LATIN RHYTHM featuring Tito PUENTE, INDIA and Cali ALEMAN

US, male / female vocal / instrumental group (Singles: 3 weeks) pos/wks

16 Mar 96	**OYE COMO VA** *Media MCSTD 40013*	36	2
19 Jul 97	**OYE COMA VA (re-mix)** *Nukleuz MCSTD 40120*	56	1

PUFF DADDY (401 Top 500) *World Music Award-winning rapper / songwriter / producer and record label owner, now known as P Diddy, b. Sean Combs 1970, New York, US. Only producer to score three successive US No.1 singles in the 1990s. 'I'll Be Missing You', a tribute to (his discovery) Notorious B.I.G., is the most successful rap single of all time and sold 1,409,688 copies in the UK (Singles: 136 weeks, Albums: 31 weeks)* pos/wks

29 Mar 97	**CAN'T NOBODY HOLD ME DOWN** *Arista 74321464552* [1] ▲	19	4

26 Apr 97 **NO TIME** *Atlantic A 5594CD* [2] 45 1
28 Jun 97 ★ **I'LL BE MISSING YOU** *Puff Daddy 74321499102* [3] ◆ ■ ▲ 1 21
9 Aug 97 ● **MO MONEY MO PROBLEMS** *Puff Daddy 74321492492* [4] ▲ 6 10
13 Sep 97 **SOMEONE** *RCA 74321513942* [5] 34 2
1 Nov 97 **BEEN AROUND THE WORLD (re)** *Puff Daddy 74321539442* [6] 20 6
7 Feb 98 **IT'S ALL ABOUT THE BENJAMINS** *Puff Daddy 74321561972* [6] 18 3
1 Aug 98 **COME WITH ME (import)** *Epic 34K78954* [7] 75 1
8 Aug 98 ● **COME WITH ME** *Epic 6662842* [7] 2 10
1 May 99 **ALL NIGHT LONG** *Puff Daddy / Arista 74321665692* [8] 23 3
29 May 99 **HATE ME NOW** *Columbia 6672562* [9] 14 6
21 Aug 99 **P.E. 2000** *Puff Daddy / Arista 74321694972* [10] 13 4
20 Nov 99 **BEST FRIEND** *Puff Daddy / Arista 74321712312* [11] 24 4
5 Feb 00 **NOTORIOUS B.I.G.** *Puff Daddy / Arista 74321737312* [12] 16 5
19 Feb 00 **SATISFY YOU (import) (re)** *Bad Boy / Arista 7928322* [13] 73 2
11 Mar 00 ● **SATISFY YOU** *Puff Daddy / Arista 74321745592* [13] 8 8
6 Oct 01 **BAD BOY FOR LIFE** *Bad Boy / Arista 74321889982* [14] 13 6
26 Jan 02 **DIDDY** *Puff Daddy / Arista 74321911652* [15] 19 4
8 Jun 02 **PASS THE COURVOISIER – PART II** *J 74321937902* [16] 16 7
10 Aug 02 ● **I NEED A GIRL (PART ONE)** *Puff Daddy / Arista 74321947242* [17] 4 11
29 Mar 03 **BUMP, BUMP, BUMP** *Epic 6736452* [18] ▲ 11 8
23 Aug 03 **LET'S GET ILL** *Bad Boy / Universal / Island MCSTD 40331* [19] 25 3
20 Sep 03 ● **SHAKE YA TAILFEATHER** *Bad Boy MCSTD 40337* [20] ▲ 10 7
2 Aug 97 ● **NO WAY OUT** *Puff Daddy 78612730122* [1] ▲ 8 13
4 Sep 99 ● **FOREVER** *Puff Daddy 74321689052* 9 6
8 Jun 02 **WE INVENTED THE REMIX** *Puff Daddy 74321945402* [2] 17 12

[1] Puff Daddy featuring Mase [2] Lil' Kim featuring Puff Daddy [3] Puff Daddy and Faith Evans featuring 112 [4] Notorious B.I.G. featuring Puff Daddy and Mase [5] SWV featuring Puff Daddy [6] Puff Daddy and the Family [7] Puff Daddy featuring Jimmy Page [8] Faith Evans featuring Puff Daddy [9] Nas featuring Puff Daddy [10] Puff Daddy featuring Hurricane G [11] Puff Daddy featuring Mario Winans [12] Notorious B.I.G. featuring Puff Daddy and Lil' Kim [13] Puff Daddy featuring R Kelly [14] P Diddy, Black Rob and Mark Curry [15] P. Diddy featuring The Neptunes [16] Busta Rhymes featuring P Diddy and Pharrell [17] P Diddy featuring Usher and Loon [18] B2K featuring P Diddy [19] P Diddy featuring Kelis [20] Nelly, P Diddy and Murphy Lee
[1] Puff Daddy and the Family [2] P Diddy & the Bad Boy Family

PULP (310 Top 500)

Jarvis Cocker b. 19 Sep 1963, Sheffield, UK, is frontman of Pulp, or Arabacus Pulp as his band was called in 1978. After countless line-up changes and modest commercial success, 17 years passed before No.1 album 'Different Class' and a string of Top 10 singles troubled the charts. Cocker's unique brand of wit and wisdom was then exposed to the wider world culminating in the legendary bottom-wiggling 'protest' at Michael Jackson's 1996 Brit Awards performance (Singles: 74 weeks, Albums: 136 weeks) pos/wks

27 Nov 93 **LIP GLOSS** *Island CID 567* 50 2
2 Apr 94 **DO YOU REMEMBER THE FIRST TIME (re)** *Island CID 574* 33 5
4 Jun 94 **THE SISTERS (EP)** *Island CID 595* 19 4
3 Jun 95 ● **COMMON PEOPLE** *Island CID 613* 2 13
7 Oct 95 ● **MIS-SHAPES / SORTED FOR E'S AND WIZZ (re)** *Island CID 620* 2 11
9 Dec 95 ● **DISCO 2000** *Island CID 623* 7 11
6 Apr 96 ● **SOMETHING CHANGED (2re)** *Island CID 632* 10 7
22 Nov 97 ● **HELP THE AGED (re)** *Island CID 679* 8 9
28 Mar 98 **THIS IS HARDCORE** *Island CID 695* 12 4
20 Jun 98 **A LITTLE SOUL** *Island CID 708* 22 2
19 Sep 98 **PARTY HARD** *Island CID 719* 29 2
20 Oct 01 **SUNRISE / THE TREES** *Island CID 786* 23 2
27 Apr 02 **BAD COVER VERSION** *Island CID 794* 27 2
30 Apr 94 ● **HIS 'N' HERS** *Island CID 8025* 9 43
11 Nov 95 ★ **DIFFERENT CLASS** *Island CID 8041* ■ 1 62
23 Mar 96 ● **COUNTDOWN 1992-1983** *Nectar Masters NTMCDD 521* 10 6
11 Apr 98 ★ **THIS IS HARDCORE** *Island CID 8066* ■ 1 21
3 Nov 01 ● **WE LOVE LIFE** *Island CID 8110* 6 3
30 Nov 02 **HITS** *Island CID 8126* 71 1

Tracks on The Sisters (EP): Babies / Your Sister's Clothes / Seconds / His 'n' Hers

PULSE featuring Antoinette ROBERSON

US, male producer – David Morales with female vocalist (Singles: 3 weeks) pos/wks

25 May 96 **THE LOVER THAT YOU ARE** *ffrr FCD 278* 22 3

See also BOSS; David MORALES

PUNK CHIC

Sweden, male producer – Johan Strandkvist (Singles: 1 week) pos/wks

6 Oct 01 **DJ SPINNIN'** *WEA WEA 333CD* 69 1

PUNX

Germany, male production trio (Singles: 1 week) pos/wks

16 Nov 02 **THE ROCK** *Data / Ministry of Sound DATA 38CDS* 59 1

PURE SUGAR

UK, male / female vocal / instrumental trio (Singles: 1 week) pos/wks

24 Oct 98 **DELICIOUS** *Geffen GFSTD 22355* 70 1

PURESSENCE

UK, male vocal / instrumental group (Singles: 6 weeks, Albums: 2 weeks) pos/wks

23 May 98 **THIS FEELING** *Island CID 688* 33 2
8 Aug 98 **IT DOESN'T MATTER ANYMORE** *Island CID 703* 47 1
21 Nov 98 **ALL I WANT** *Island CID 722* 39 2
5 Oct 02 **WALKING DEAD** *Island CID 803* 40 1
29 Aug 98 **ONLY FOREVER** *Island CID 8064* 36 2

PURETONE

Australia, male producer – Josh Abrahams (Singles: 17 weeks) pos/wks

12 Jan 02 ● **ADDICTED TO BASS** *Gusto CDGUS 6* 2 15
10 May 03 **STUCK IN A GROOVE** *Illustrious CDILL 014* 26 2

James and Bobby PURIFY

US, male vocal duo – James Purify and Robert Dickey (Singles: 16 weeks) pos/wks

24 Apr 76 **I'M YOUR PUPPET** *Mercury 6167 324* 12 10
7 Aug 76 **MORNING GLORY** *Mercury 6167 380* 27 6

PURPLE HEARTS

UK, male vocal / instrumental group (Singles: 5 weeks) pos/wks

22 Sep 79 **MILLIONS LIKE US** *Fiction FICS 003* 57 3
8 Mar 80 **JIMMY** *Fiction FICS 9* 60 2

PURPLE KINGS

UK, male vocal / instrumental duo – Rob Tillen and Glen Williamson (Singles: 3 weeks) pos/wks

15 Oct 94 **THAT'S THE WAY YOU DO IT** *Positiva CDTIV 21* 26 3

PUSH

Belgium, male producer – Dirk Dierickx (Singles: 19 weeks) pos/wks

15 May 99 **UNIVERSAL NATION** *Bonzai / Inferno CDFERN 16* 36 2
9 Oct 99 **UNIVERSAL NATION '99 (re-mix)** *Inferno CDFERN 20* 35 2
23 Sep 00 **TILL WE MEET AGAIN** *Inferno CDFERN 29* 46 1
12 May 01 **STRANGE WORLD** *Inferno CDFERN 38* 21 4
20 Oct 01 **PLEASE SAVE ME** *Inferno / Five AM FAMFERN 1CD* [1] 36 2
3 Nov 01 **THE LEGACY** *Inferno CDFERN 43* 22 4
4 May 02 **TRANZY STATE OF MIND** *Inferno CDFERN 45* 31 2
5 Oct 02 **STRANGE WORLD / THE LEGACY** *Inferno CDFERN 49* 55 1
15 Mar 03 **UNIVERSAL NATION (re-mix)** *Inferno CDFERN 53* 54 1

[1] Sunscreem vs Push

PUSSY 2000

UK, male production duo (Singles: 1 week) pos/wks

3 Nov 01 **IT'S GONNA BE ALRIGHT** *Ink NIBNE 9CD* 70 1

PUSSYCAT

Holland, male / female vocal / instrumental group (Singles: 30 weeks) pos/wks

28 Aug 76 ★ **MISSISSIPPI** *Sonet SON 2077* 1 22
25 Dec 76 **SMILE** *Sonet SON 2096* 24 8

PYRAMIDS

Jamaica, male vocal / instrumental group (Singles: 4 weeks) pos/wks

Date	Title	Pos	Wks
22 Nov 67	**TRAIN TOUR TO RAINBOW CITY** *President PT 161*	35	4

PYTHON LEE JACKSON

Australia, male vocal / instrumental group (Singles: 12 weeks) pos/wks

Date	Title	Pos	Wks
30 Sep 72 ●	**IN A BROKEN DREAM** *Youngblood YB 1002*	3	12

Uncredited lead vocals by Rod Stewart

Q

UK, male instrumental / production duo (Singles: 6 weeks) pos/wks

Date	Title	Pos	Wks
5 Jun 93	**GET HERE** *Arista 74321145972* [1]	37	4
12 Mar 94	**(EVERYTHING I DO) I DO IT FOR YOU** *Bell 74321193062* [2]	47	2

[1] Q featuring Tracy Ackerman [2] Q featuring Tony Jackson

QB FINEST featuring NAS & BRAVEHEARTS

US, male rappers (Singles: 3 weeks) pos/wks

Date	Title	Pos	Wks
21 Apr 01	**OOCHIE WALLY** *Columbia 6710852*	30	3

Q-BASS

UK, male production / instrumental group (Singles: 1 week) pos/wks

Date	Title	Pos	Wks
8 Feb 92	**HARDCORE WILL NEVER DIE** *Suburban Base SUBBASE 007*	64	1

Q-CLUB

Italy, male / female vocal / instrumental group (Singles: 3 weeks) pos/wks

Date	Title	Pos	Wks
6 Jan 96	**TELL IT TO MY HEART** *Manifesto FESCD 5*	28	3

QFX

UK, male vocal / instrumental group (Singles: 18 weeks, Albums: 1 week) pos/wks

Date	Title	Pos	Wks
6 May 95	**FREEDOM (EP)** *Epidemic EPICD 004*	41	3
3 Feb 96	**EVERYTIME YOU TOUCH ME** *Epidemic EPICD 006*	22	4
3 Aug 96	**YOU GOT THE POWER** *Epidemic EPICD 007*	33	3
18 Jan 97	**FREEDOM 2 (re-mix)** *Epidemic EPICD 008*	21	4
20 Mar 99	**SAY YOU'LL BE MINE** *Quality Recordings QUAL 005CD*	34	2
23 Aug 03	**FREEDOM (2nd re-mix)** *Data / MoS DATA 57CDS*	36	2
8 Mar 97	**ALIEN CHILD** *Epidemic EPICD 009*	62	1

Tracks on Freedom (EP): Freedom / Metropolis / Sianora Baby / The Machine

Q-TEE

UK, female rapper – Tatiana Mais (Singles: 7 weeks) pos/wks

Date	Title	Pos	Wks
21 Apr 90	**AFRIKA** *SBK SBK 7008* [1]	42	5
10 Feb 96	**GIMME THAT BODY** *Heavenly HVN 48CD*	40	2

[1] History featuring Q-Tee

Q-TEX

UK, male / female vocal / instrumental group (Singles: 7 weeks) pos/wks

Date	Title	Pos	Wks
9 Apr 94	**THE POWER OF LOVE** *Stoatin' STOAT 002CD*	65	1
26 Nov 94	**BELIEVE** *23rd Precinct THIRD 2CD*	41	2
15 Jun 96	**LET THE LOVE** *23rd Precinct THIRD 4CD*	30	2
30 Nov 96	**DO YOU WANT ME** *23rd Precinct THIRD 5CD*	48	1
28 Jun 97	**POWER OF LOVE '97 (re-mix)** *23rd Precinct THIRD 7CD*	49	1

Q-TIP

US, male rapper – John Davis (Singles: 23 weeks) pos/wks

Date	Title	Pos	Wks
4 Oct 97 ●	**GOT 'TIL IT'S GONE** *Virgin VSCDG 1666* [1]	6	9
19 Jun 99	**GET INVOLVED** *Hollywood 0101185 HWR* [2]	36	2
22 Jan 00	**HOT BOYZ** *Elektra E7002CD* [3]	18	3
12 Feb 00	**BREATHE AND STOP** *Arista 74321727062*	12	7
6 May 00	**VIVRANT THING** *Arista 74321751302*	39	2

[1] Janet featuring Q-Tip and Joni Mitchell [2] Raphael Saadiq and Q-Tip [3] Missy 'Misdemeanor' Elliott featuring Nas, Eve and Q-Tip

See also DEEE-LITE; A TRIBE CALLED QUEST

Q-TIPS

UK, male vocal / instrumental group – includes Paul Young (Albums: 1 week) pos/wks

Date	Title	Pos	Wks
30 Aug 80	**Q-TIPS** *Chrysalis CHR 1255*	50	1

See also Paul YOUNG

Q UNIQUE – *See C & C MUSIC FACTORY*

QATTARA

UK, male production duo – Andy Cato and Alex Whitcombe (Singles: 2 weeks) pos/wks

Date	Title	Pos	Wks
15 Mar 97	**COME WITH ME** *Positiva CDTIV 71*	31	2

See also Alex WHITCOMBE & BIG C

QUAD CITY DJs

US, male rap duo (Singles: 1 week) pos/wks

Date	Title	Pos	Wks
15 Nov 97	**SPACE JAM** *Atlantic EW773*	57	1

See also TAG TEAM

QUADROPHONIA

Belgium, male instrumental / production group (Singles: 15 weeks) pos/wks

Date	Title	Pos	Wks
13 Apr 91	**QUADROPHONIA** *ARS 6567687*	14	9
6 Jul 91	**THE WAVE OF THE FUTURE** *ARS 6569937*	40	3
21 Dec 91	**FIND THE TIME (PART ONE)** *ARS 6576260*	41	3

QUADS

UK, male vocal / instrumental group (Singles: 2 weeks) pos/wks

Date	Title	Pos	Wks
22 Sep 79	**THERE MUST BE THOUSANDS** *Big Bear BB 23*	66	2

QUAKE featuring Marcia RAE

UK, male producer and UK, female vocalist (Singles: 1 week) pos/wks

Date	Title	Pos	Wks
29 Aug 98	**THE DAY WILL COME** *ffrr FCD 344*	53	1

QUANTUM JUMP

UK, male vocal / instrumental group (Singles: 10 weeks) pos/wks

Date	Title	Pos	Wks
2 Jun 79 ●	**THE LONE RANGER** *Electric WOT 33*	5	10

QUARTERFLASH

US, male / female vocal / instrumental group (Singles: 5 weeks) pos/wks

Date	Title	Pos	Wks
27 Feb 82	**HARDEN MY HEART** *Geffen GEF A 1838*	49	5

QUARTZ

UK, male instrumental group (Singles: 19 weeks) pos/wks

Date	Title	Pos	Wks
17 Mar 90	**WE'RE COMIN' AT YA** *Mercury ITMR 2* [1]	65	2
2 Feb 91 ●	**IT'S TOO LATE** *Mercury ITM 3* [2]	8	14
15 Jun 91	**NAKED LOVE (JUST SAY YOU WANT ME)** *Mercury ITM 4* [3]	39	3

[1] Quartz featuring Stepz [2] Quartz introducing Dina Carroll [3] Quartz and Dina Carroll

Jakie QUARTZ

France, female vocalist (Singles: 3 weeks) pos/wks

Date	Title	Pos	Wks
11 Mar 89	**À LA VIE, À L'AMOUR** *PWL PWL 30*	55	3

QUARTZ LOCK featuring Lonnie GORDON

UK, male production / instrumental duo – Mark Andrews and Donald Lynch, and US, female vocalist (Singles: 2 weeks) pos/wks

7 Oct 95 LOVE EVICTION *X:Plode BANG 2CD* 32 2

Suzi QUATRO *US, female vocalist / instrumentalist – Suzi Quatrocchio (Singles: 122 weeks, Albums: 13 weeks)* pos/wks

19 May 73 ★ CAN THE CAN *RAK 150* 1 14
28 Jul 73 ● 48 CRASH *RAK 158* 3 9
27 Oct 73 DAYTONA DEMON *RAK 161* 14 13
9 Feb 74 ★ DEVIL GATE DRIVE *RAK 167* 1 11
29 Jun 74 TOO BIG *RAK 175* 14 6
9 Nov 74 ● THE WILD ONE *RAK 185* 7 10
8 Feb 75 YOUR MAMMA WON'T LIKE ME *RAK 191* 31 5
5 Mar 77 TEAR ME APART *RAK 248* 27 6
18 Mar 78 ● IF YOU CAN'T GIVE ME LOVE *RAK 271* 4 13
22 Jul 78 THE RACE IS ON *RAK 278* 43 5
11 Nov 78 STUMBLIN' IN *RAK 285* [1] 41 8
20 Oct 79 SHE'S IN LOVE WITH YOU *RAK 299* 11 9
19 Jan 80 MAMA'S BOY *RAK 303* 34 5
5 Apr 80 I'VE NEVER BEEN IN LOVE *RAK 307* 56 3
25 Oct 80 ROCK HARD *Dreamland DLSP 6* 68 2
13 Nov 82 HEART OF STONE *Polydor POSP 477* 60 3
13 Oct 73 SUZI QUATRO *RAK SRAK 505* 32 4
26 Apr 80 ● SUZI QUATRO'S GREATEST HITS *RAK EMTV 24* 4 9

[1] Suzi Quatro and Chris Norman

Finley QUAYE *UK, male vocal / instrumentalist – guitar (Singles: 23 weeks, Albums: 59 weeks)* pos/wks

21 Jun 97 SUNDAY SHINING *Epic 6644552* 16 6
13 Sep 97 ● EVEN AFTER ALL *Epic 6649712* 10 5
29 Nov 97 IT'S GREAT WHEN WE'RE TOGETHER *Epic 6653382* 29 3
7 Mar 98 YOUR LOVE GETS SWEETER *Epic 6656065* 16 5
15 Aug 98 ULTRA STIMULATION *Epic 6660792* 51 1
23 Sep 00 SPIRITUALIZED *Epic 6698032* 26 3
4 Oct 97 ● MAVERICK A STRIKE *Epic 4887582* 3 56
14 Oct 00 VANGUARD *Epic 4997102* 35 2
11 Oct 03 MUCH MORE THAN MUCH LOVE *Sony Music 5125492* 56 1

QUEDO BRASS – *See CHAQUITO ORCHESTRA*

QUEEN (4 Top 500)

World-renowned British quartet, second only to The Beatles in chart success when it comes to UK groups: Freddie Mercury (v) (d. 1991), Brian May (g/v), John Deacon (b/v), Roger Taylor (d/v). 'Bohemian Rhapsody' (which in places has 180 vocal overdubs) was recently voted this book's readers' No.1 single of all time. It was the first recording to top the UK singles chart on two occasions (selling more than a million each time) and was No.1 in a record four calendar years. They were also the first act to have chart-topping singles in the 1970s, 1980s, 1990s and 21st century. Front man Mercury was rightfully regarded as one of the greatest entertainers in rock, and the group, which stole the show at Live Aid, has attracted millions to its concerts around the globe. Queen have sold more than 25 million greatest hits albums and are the only act to sell in excess of two million copies of two greatest hits albums in the UK. Additionally they have held the top four places on the UK video chart (1992) and 'We Are the Champions' has become the most-sung song by the world's sporting crowds. The group, which has contributed enormously to Aids awareness, won the Brit Award for Outstanding Contribution to British Music Award (1992) and was inducted into the Rock and Roll Hall of Fame (2000). Queen musical 'We Will Rock You' penned by Ben Elton and backed by Robert De Niro opened in 2002. Of their 10 million singles sold, the best-seller is 'Bohemian Rhapsody' on 2,130,000 (Singles: 423 weeks, Albums: 1271 weeks) pos/wks

9 Mar 74 ● SEVEN SEAS OF RHYE *EMI 2121* 10 10
26 Oct 74 ● KILLER QUEEN *EMI 2229* 2 12
25 Jan 75 NOW I'M HERE *EMI 2256* 11 7
8 Nov 75 ★ BOHEMIAN RHAPSODY *EMI 2375* ◆ 1 17
3 Jul 76 ● YOU'RE MY BEST FRIEND *EMI 2494* 7 8
27 Nov 76 ● SOMEBODY TO LOVE *EMI 2565* 2 9
19 Mar 77 TIE YOUR MOTHER DOWN *EMI 2593* 31 4
4 Jun 77 QUEEN'S FIRST EP *EMI 2623* 17 10
22 Oct 77 ● WE ARE THE CHAMPIONS *EMI 2708* 2 11
25 Feb 78 SPREAD YOUR WINGS *EMI 2757* 34 4
28 Oct 78 BICYCLE RACE / FAT BOTTOMED GIRLS *EMI 2870* 11 12
10 Feb 79 ● DON'T STOP ME NOW *EMI 2910* 9 12
14 Jul 79 LOVE OF MY LIFE *EMI 2959* 63 2
20 Oct 79 ● CRAZY LITTLE THING CALLED LOVE *EMI 5001* ▲ 2 14
2 Feb 80 SAVE ME *EMI 5022* 11 6
14 Jun 80 PLAY THE GAME *EMI 5076* 14 8
6 Sep 80 ● ANOTHER ONE BITES THE DUST *EMI 5102* ▲ 7 9
6 Dec 80 ● FLASH *EMI 5126* 10 13
14 Nov 81 ★ UNDER PRESSURE *EMI 5250* [1] 1 11
1 May 82 BODY LANGUAGE *EMI 5293* 25 6
12 Jun 82 LAS PALABRAS DE AMOR *EMI 5316* 17 8
21 Aug 82 BACKCHAT *EMI 5325* 40 4
4 Feb 84 ● RADIO GAGA *EMI QUEEN 1* 2 9
14 Apr 84 ● I WANT TO BREAK FREE *EMI QUEEN 2* 3 15
28 Jul 84 ● IT'S A HARD LIFE *EMI QUEEN 3* 6 9
22 Sep 84 HAMMER TO FALL *EMI QUEEN 4* 13 7
8 Dec 84 THANK GOD IT'S CHRISTMAS *EMI QUEEN 5* 21 6
16 Nov 85 ● ONE VISION *EMI QUEEN 6* 7 10
29 Mar 86 ● A KIND OF MAGIC *EMI QUEEN 7* 3 11
21 Jun 86 FRIENDS WILL BE FRIENDS *EMI QUEEN 8* 14 8
27 Sep 86 WHO WANTS TO LIVE FOREVER *EMI QUEEN 9* 24 5
13 May 89 ● I WANT IT ALL *Parlophone QUEEN 10* 3 7
1 Jul 89 ● BREAKTHRU' *Parlophone QUEEN 11* 7 7
19 Aug 89 THE INVISIBLE MAN *Parlophone QUEEN 12* 12 6
21 Oct 89 SCANDAL *Parlophone QUEEN 14* 25 4
9 Dec 89 THE MIRACLE *Parlophone QUEEN 15* 21 5
26 Jan 91 ★ INNUENDO *Parlophone QUEEN 16* ■ 1 6
25 May 91 I'M GOING SLIGHTLY MAD *Parlophone QUEEN 17* 22 5
25 May 91 HEADLONG *Parlophone QUEEN 18* 14 4
26 Oct 91 THE SHOW MUST GO ON (re) *Parlophone QUEEN 19* 16 10
21 Dec 91 ★ BOHEMIAN RHAPSODY / THESE ARE THE DAYS OF OUR LIVES (re-issue) *Parlophone QUEEN 20* ◆ ■ 1 14
1 May 93 ★ FIVE LIVE (EP) (re) *Parlophone CDRS 6340* [2] ■ 1 12
4 Nov 95 ● HEAVEN FOR EVERYONE *Parlophone CDQUEEN 21* 2 12
23 Dec 95 ● A WINTER'S TALE *Parlophone CDQUEEN 22* 6 6
9 Mar 96 TOO MUCH LOVE WILL KILL YOU *Parlophone CDQUEEN 23* 15 6
29 Jun 96 ● LET ME LIVE *Parlophone CDQUEEN 24* 9 4
30 Nov 96 YOU DON'T FOOL ME *Parlophone CDQUEEN 25* 17 4
17 Jan 98 NO-ONE BUT YOU / TIE YOUR MOTHER DOWN *Parlophone CDQUEEN 27* 13 4
14 Nov 98 ● ANOTHER ONE BITES THE DUST *Dreamworks DRMCD 22364* [3] 5 6
18 Dec 99 UNDER PRESSURE (re-mix) *Parlophone CDQUEEN 28* [1] 14 7
29 Jul 00 ★ WE WILL ROCK YOU (re) *RCA 74321774022* [4] ■ 1 13
29 Mar 03 FLASH *Nebula NEBCD 041* [5] 15 4
23 Mar 74 ● QUEEN 2 *EMI EMA 767* 5 29
30 Mar 74 QUEEN *EMI EMC 3006* 24 18
23 Nov 74 ● SHEER HEART ATTACK *EMI EMC 3061* 2 42
13 Dec 75 ★ A NIGHT AT THE OPERA *EMI EMTC 103* 1 50
25 Dec 76 ★ A DAY AT THE RACES *EMI EMTC 104* 1 24
12 Nov 77 ● NEWS OF THE WORLD *EMI EMA 784* 4 20
25 Nov 78 ● JAZZ *EMI EMA 788* 2 27
7 Jul 79 ● LIVE KILLERS *EMI EMSP 330* 3 27
12 Jul 80 ★ THE GAME *EMI EMA 795* ▲ 1 18
20 Dec 80 ● FLASH GORDON (FILM SOUNDTRACK) *EMI EMC 3351* 10 15
7 Nov 81 ★ GREATEST HITS *Parlophone EMYV 30* 1 450
15 May 82 ● HOT SPACE *EMI EMA 797* 4 19
10 Mar 84 ● THE WORKS *EMI EMC 240014* 2 93
14 Jun 86 ★ A KIND OF MAGIC *EMI EU 3509* ■ 1 63
13 Dec 86 ● LIVE MAGIC *EMI EMC 3519* 3 43
3 Jun 89 ★ THE MIRACLE *Parlophone PCSD 107* ■ 1 32
16 Dec 89 QUEEN AT THE BEEB *Band Of Joy BOJLP 001* 67 1
16 Feb 91 ★ INNUENDO *Parlophone PCSD 115* ■ 1 37
9 Nov 91 ★ GREATEST HITS II *Parlophone PMTV 2* ■ 1 106
6 Jun 92 ● LIVE AT WEMBLEY '86 *Parlophone CDPCSP 725* 2 15
19 Nov 94 GREATEST HITS I AND II *Parlophone CDPCSD 161* 37 7
18 Nov 95 ★ MADE IN HEAVEN *Parlophone CDPCSD 167* ■ 1 28
15 Nov 97 ● QUEEN ROCKS *Parlophone 8230912* 7 12

20 Nov 99 ● **GREATEST HITS III** *Parlophone 5238942*..........5 19
25 Nov 00 ● **GREATEST HITS I II & III – THE PLATINUM COLLECTION** *Parlophone 5298832*..........2 74
21 Jun 03 **LIVE AT WEMBLEY '86** *Parlophone 5904402*..........38 2

[1] Queen and David Bowie [2] George Michael and Queen with Lisa Stansfield [3] Queen with Wyclef Jean featuring Pras and Free [4] Five and Queen [5] Queen & Vanguard

Tracks on Queen's First EP: Good Old Fashioned Lover Boy / Death on Two Legs (Dedicated to...) / Tenement Funster / White Queen (As it Began). Tracks on Five Live (EP): Somebody to Love / These Are the Days of Our Lives / Calling You / Papa Was a Rolling Stone – Killer (medley). Queen appear only on the first two tracks. The first features George Michael and the second George Michael with Lisa Stansfield 'The Works' changed label number to EMI WORK 1 during its chart run

See also Brian MAY; Freddie MERCURY; Roger TAYLOR

QUEEN LATIFAH

US, female rapper – Dana Owens (Singles: 17 weeks) pos/wks

24 Mar 90 **MAMA GAVE BIRTH TO THE SOUL CHILDREN** *Gee Street GEE 26* [1]..........14 7
26 May 90 **FIND A WAY** *Ahead of Our Time CCUT 8* [2]..........52 2
31 Aug 91 **FLY GIRL** *Gee Street GEE 34*..........67 1
26 Jun 93 **WHAT'CHA GONNA DO** *Epic 6593072* [3]..........21 4
26 Mar 94 **U.N.I.T.Y.** *Motown TMGCD 1422*..........74 1
12 Apr 97 **MR BIG STUFF** *Motown 5736572* [4]..........31 2

[1] Queen Latifah + De La Soul [2] Coldcut featuring Queen Latifah [3] Shabba Ranks featuring Queen Latifah [4] Queen Latifah, Shades and Free

QUEEN PEN

US, female rapper – Lynise Walters (Singles: 10 weeks) pos/wks

7 Mar 98 **MAN BEHIND THE MUSIC** *Interscope IND 95562*..........38 2
9 May 98 **ALL MY LOVE** *Interscope IND 95584* [1]..........11 5
5 Sep 98 **IT'S TRUE** *Interscope IND 95597*..........24 3

[1] Queen Pen featuring Eric Williams

QUEENS OF THE STONE AGE

US, male vocal / instrumental group (Singles: 14 weeks, Albums: 25 weeks) pos/wks

26 Aug 00 **THE LOST ART OF KEEPING A SECRET** *Interscope 4973912*..........31 2
16 Nov 02 **NO ONE KNOWS** *Interscope / Polydor 4978122*..........15 7
19 Apr 03 **GO WITH THE FLOW** *Interscope / Polydor 4978702*..........21 3
30 Aug 03 **FIRST IT GIVETH** *Interscope / Polydor 9810505*..........33 2
2 Sep 00 **R** *Interscope 4906832*..........54 3
7 Sep 02 ● **SONGS FOR THE DEAF** *Interscope / Polydor 4934352*..........4 22

QUEENSRŸCHE *US, male vocal / instrumental group (Singles: 21 weeks, Albums: 12 weeks)*

pos/wks

13 May 89 **EYES OF A STRANGER** *EMI USA MT 65*..........59 1
10 Nov 90 **EMPIRE** *EMI USA MT 90*..........61 1
20 Apr 91 **SILENT LUCIDITY** *EMI USA MT 94*..........34 5
6 Jul 91 **BEST I CAN** *EMI USA MT 97*..........36 3
7 Sep 91 **JET CITY WOMAN** *EMI USA MT 98*..........39 2
8 Aug 92 **SILENT LUCIDITY (re-issue)** *EMI USA MT 104*..........18 4
28 Jan 95 **I AM I** *EMI CDMT 109*..........40 2
25 Mar 95 **BRIDGE** *EMI CDMT 111*..........40 3
29 Sep 84 **THE WARNING** *EMI America EJ 2402201*..........100 1
26 Jul 86 **RAGE FOR ORDER** *EMI America AML 3105*..........66 1
4 Jun 88 **OPERATION MINDCRIME** *Manhattan MTL 1023*..........58 3
22 Sep 90 **EMPIRE** *EMI-USA MTL 1058*..........13 3
22 Oct 94 **PROMISED LAND** *EMI CDMTL 1081*..........13 3
29 Mar 97 **HEAR IN THE NOW FRONTIER** *EMI CDEMC 3764*..........46 1

QUENCH

Australia, male instrumental / production duo (Singles: 1 week) pos/wks

17 Feb 96 **DREAMS** *Infectious INFECT 3CD*..........75 1

QUENTIN and ASH *UK, female actor / vocal duo – Caroline Quentin and Leslie Ash (Singles: 3 weeks)*

pos/wks

6 Jul 96 **TELL HIM** *East West EW 049CD*..........25 3

? (QUESTION MARK) and the MYSTERIANS

US, male vocal / instrumental group (Singles: 4 weeks) pos/wks

17 Nov 66 **96 TEARS** *Cameo Parkway C428* ▲..........37 4

QUESTIONS

UK, male vocal / instrumental group (Singles: 8 weeks) pos/wks

23 Apr 83 **PRICE YOU PAY** *Respond KOB 702*..........56 3
17 Sep 83 **TEAR SOUP** *Respond KOB 705*..........66 1
10 Mar 84 **TUESDAY SUNSHINE** *Respond KOB 707*..........46 4

QUICK *UK, male vocal / instrumental group (Singles: 7 weeks)*

pos/wks

15 May 82 **RHYTHM OF THE JUNGLE** *Epic EPC A 2013*..........41 7

Tommy QUICKLY and The REMO FOUR

UK, male vocalist (Singles: 8 weeks) pos/wks

22 Oct 64 **WILD SIDE OF LIFE** *Pye 7N 15708*..........33 8

QUIET FIVE

UK, male vocal / instrumental group (Singles: 3 weeks) pos/wks

13 May 65 **WHEN THE MORNING SUN DRIES THE DEW** *Parlophone R 5273*..........45 1
21 Apr 66 **HOMEWARD BOUND** *Parlophone R 5421*..........44 2

QUIET RIOT *US, male vocal / instrumental group (Singles: 5 weeks, Albums: 1 week)*

pos/wks

3 Dec 83 **METAL HEALTH / CUM ON FEEL THE NOIZE** *Epic A 3968*..........45 5
4 Aug 84 **CONDITION CRITICAL** *Epic EPC 26075*..........71 1

'Cum on Feel the Noize' credited only from 10 Dec 1983

Eimear QUINN *Ireland, female vocalist (Singles: 2 weeks)*

pos/wks

15 Jun 96 **THE VOICE** *Polydor 5768842*..........40 2

Paul QUINN and EDWYN COLLINS

UK, male vocal / instrumental duo (Singles: 2 weeks) pos/wks

11 Aug 84 **PALE BLUE EYES** *Swamplands SWP 1*..........72 2

See also Edwyn COLLINS

Sinead QUINN

UK, female vocalist (Singles: 15 weeks, Albums: 2 weeks) pos/wks

22 Feb 03 ● **I CAN'T BREAK DOWN** *Mercury 0637282*..........2 12
12 Jul 03 **WHAT YOU NEED IS... (re)** *Fontana 9808971*..........19 3
26 Jul 03 **READY TO RUN** *Fontana 9865367*..........48 2

QUINTESSENCE

UK / Australia, male vocal / instrumental group (Albums: 6 weeks) pos/wks

27 Jun 70 **QUINTESSENCE** *Island ILPS 9128*..........22 4
3 Apr 71 **DIVE DEEP** *Island ILPS 9143*..........43 1
27 May 72 **SELF** *RCA Victor SF 8273*..........50 1

QUIREBOYS *UK, male vocal / instrumental group (Singles: 27 weeks, Albums: 17 weeks)*

pos/wks

4 Nov 89 **7 O'CLOCK** *Parlophone R 6230*..........36 4
6 Jan 90 **HEY YOU** *Parlophone R 6241*..........14 7
7 Apr 90 **I DON'T LOVE YOU ANYMORE** *Parlophone R 6248*..........24 6
8 Sep 90 **THERE SHE GOES AGAIN / MISLED** *Parlophone R 6267*..........37 4
10 Oct 92 **TRAMPS AND THIEVES** *Parlophone RS 6323*..........41 3
20 Feb 93 **BROTHER LOUIE** *Parlophone CDR 6335*..........31 3
10 Feb 90 ● **A BIT OF WHAT YOU FANCY** *Parlophone PCS 7335*..........2 15
27 Mar 93 **BITTER SWEET AND TWISTED** *Parlophone CDPCSD 120*..........31 2

QUIVER – See SUTHERLAND BROTHERS and QUIVVER

QUIVVER

UK, male instrumental / production duo (Singles: 3 weeks) pos/wks

5 Mar 94 **SAXY LADY** *A&M 5805152*..........56 2
18 Nov 95 **BELIEVE IN ME** *Perfecto PERF 111CD*..........56 1

QUO VADIS *UK, male production trio (Singles: 1 week)* pos/wks

16 Dec 00 **SONIC BOOM (LIFE'S TOO SHORT)** *Serious SERR 028CD* 49 1

QWILO – *See FELIX DA HOUSECAT*

RAF *Italy, male producer – Mauro Picotto (Singles: 6 weeks)* pos/wks

14 Mar 92 **WE'VE GOT TO LIVE TOGETHER** *PWL Continental PWL 218* 34 3
5 Mar 94 **TAKE ME HIGHER** *Media MRLCD 0012* 71 1
23 Mar 96 **TAKE ME HIGHER (re-mix)** *Media MCSTD 40026* 59 1
27 Jul 96 **ANGEL'S SYMPHONY** *Media MCSTD 40051* 73 1

R.E.M. 35 Top 500

'America's Best Rock Band', according to Rolling Stone: Michael Stipe (v), Peter Buck (g), Mike Mills (b), Bill Berry (d). This Georgia group went from the US college circuit to packing stadiums worldwide. In 1996, the award-winning, platinum-album-earning quartet signed an $80m record deal (Singles: 171 weeks, Albums: 561 weeks) pos/wks

28 Nov 87 **THE ONE I LOVE** *IRS IRM 46* 51 8
30 Apr 88 **FINEST WORKSONG** *IRS IRM 161* 50 2
4 Feb 89 **STAND** *Warner Bros. W 7577* 51 3
3 Jun 89 **ORANGE CRUSH** *Warner Bros. W 2960* 28 5
12 Aug 89 **STAND (re-issue)** *Warner Bros. W 2833* 48 2
9 Mar 91 **LOSING MY RELIGION** *Warner Bros. W 0015* 19 9
18 May 91 ● **SHINY HAPPY PEOPLE** *Warner Bros. W 0027* 6 11
17 Aug 91 **NEAR WILD HEAVEN** *Warner Bros. W 0055* 27 4
21 Sep 91 **THE ONE I LOVE (re-issue)** *IRS IRM 178* 16 6
16 Nov 91 **RADIO SONG** *Warner Bros. W 0072* 28 3
14 Dec 91 **IT'S THE END OF THE WORLD AS WE KNOW IT** *IRS IRM 180* ..39 4
3 Oct 92 **DRIVE** *Warner Bros. W 0136* 11 5
28 Nov 92 **MAN ON THE MOON** *Warner Bros. W 0143* 18 8
20 Feb 93 **THE SIDEWINDER SLEEPS TONITE** *Warner Bros. W 0152CD1* 17 6
17 Apr 93 ● **EVERYBODY HURTS** *Warner Bros W 0169CD1* 7 12
24 Jul 93 **NIGHTSWIMMING** *Warner Bros. W 0184CD* 27 5
11 Dec 93 **FIND THE RIVER** *Warner Bros. W 0211CD* 54 1
17 Sep 94 ● **WHAT'S THE FREQUENCY, KENNETH** *Warner Bros. W 0265CD* 9 7
12 Nov 94 **BANG AND BLAME** *Warner Bros. W 0275CD* 15 4
4 Feb 95 **CRUSH WITH EYELINER** *Warner Bros. W 0281CD* 23 3
15 Apr 95 ● **STRANGE CURRENCIES** *Warner Bros. W 0290CD* 9 4
29 Jul 95 **TONGUE** *Warner Bros. W 0308CD* 13 5
31 Aug 96 ● **E-BOW THE LETTER** *Warner Bros. W 0369CD* 4 5
2 Nov 96 **BITTERSWEET ME** *Warner Bros. W 0377CD* 19 2
14 Dec 96 **ELECTROLITE** *Warner Bros. W 0383CD* 29 2
24 Oct 98 ● **DAYSLEEPER** *Warner Bros. W 0455CD* 6 6
19 Dec 98 **LOTUS** *Warner Bros. W 466CD* 26 5
20 Mar 99 ● **AT MY MOST BEAUTIFUL** *Warner Bros. W 477CD* 10 4
5 Feb 00 ● **THE GREAT BEYOND** *Warner Bros. W 516CD* 3 10
12 May 01 ● **IMITATION OF LIFE** *Warner Bros. W 559CD* 6 9
4 Aug 01 **ALL THE WAY TO RENO** *Warner Bros. W 568CD* 24 3
1 Dec 01 **I'LL TAKE THE RAIN** *Warner Bros. W 573CD* 44 1
25 Oct 03 ● **BAD DAY** *Warner Bros. W 624CD1* 8 7
28 Apr 84 **RECKONING** *IRS A 7045* 91 2
29 Jun 85 **FABLES OF THE RECONSTRUCTION** *IRS MIRF 1003* 35 4
6 Sep 86 **LIFE'S RICH PAGEANT** *IRS MIRG 1014* 43 4
16 May 87 **DEAD LETTER OFFICE** *IRS SP 70054* 60 2
26 Sep 87 **DOCUMENT** *IRS MIRG 1025* 28 5
29 Oct 88 **EPONYMOUS** *IRS MIRG 1038* 69 3
19 Nov 88 **GREEN** *Warner Bros. WX 234* 27 22
23 Mar 91 ★ **OUT OF TIME** *Warner Bros. WX 404* ■ ▲ 1 183
12 Oct 91 ● **THE BEST OF R.E.M.** *IRS MIRH 1* 7 28
10 Oct 92 ★ **AUTOMATIC FOR THE PEOPLE** *Warner Bros. 9362450552* ■ 1 179
8 Oct 94 ★ **MONSTER** *Warner Bros. 9362457632* ■ ▲ 1 56
21 Sep 96 ★ **NEW ADVENTURES IN HI-FI** *Warner Bros. 9362463202* ■ 1 20
7 Nov 98 ● **UP** *Warner Bros. 9362471122* 2 29
26 May 01 ★ **REVEAL** *Warner Bros. 9362479462* ■ 1 15
8 Nov 03 ★ **IN TIME – THE BEST OF – 1988-2003** *Warner Bros. 9362483812* ■ ....1 8+
8 Nov 03 **IN TIME – THE BEST OF – 1988-2003 - LTD** *Warner Bros. 9362486022* 36 1

REO SPEEDWAGON *US, male vocal / instrumental group (Singles: 38 weeks, Albums: 36 weeks)* pos/wks

11 Apr 81 ● **KEEP ON LOVING YOU** *Epic EPC 9544* ▲ 7 14
27 Jun 81 **TAKE IT ON THE RUN** *Epic EPC A 1207* 19 14
16 Mar 85 **CAN'T FIGHT THIS FEELING** *Epic A 4880* ▲ 16 10
25 Apr 81 ● **HI INFIDELITY** *Epic EPC 84700* ▲ 6 29
17 Jul 82 **GOOD TROUBLE** *Epic EPC 85789* 29 7

RHC *Belgium, male / female vocal / instrumental duo (Singles: 1 week)* pos/wks

11 Jan 92 **FEVER CALLED LOVE** *R&S RSUK 9* 65 1

RIP PRODUCTIONS *UK, production duo (Singles: 1 week)* pos/wks

29 Nov 97 **THE CHANT (WE R) / RIP PRODUCTIONS** *Satellite 74321534022* 58 1

See also CARNIVAL featuring RIP vs RED RAT; DOUBLE 99

RM PROJECT *UK, production group (Singles: 1 week)* pos/wks

3 Jul 99 **GET IT UP** *Inferno CDFERN 15* 49 1

RTE CONCERT ORCHESTRA – *See Bill WHELAN*

Eddie RABBITT

US, male vocalist, d. 7 May 1998 (Singles: 14 weeks) pos/wks

27 Jan 79 **EVERY WHICH WAY BUT LOOSE** *Elektra K 12331* 41 9
28 Feb 81 **I LOVE A RAINY NIGHT** *Elektra K 12498* ▲ 53 5

Harry RABINOWITZ – *See ROYAL PHILHARMONIC ORCHESTRA*

Steve RACE

UK, male instrumentalist – piano (Singles: 9 weeks) pos/wks

28 Feb 63 **PIED PIPER (THE BEEJE)** *Parlophone R 4981* 29 9

RACEY *UK, male vocal / instrumental group (Singles: 44 weeks)* pos/wks

25 Nov 78 ● **LAY YOUR LOVE ON ME** *RAK 284* 3 14
31 Mar 79 ● **SOME GIRLS** *RAK 291* 2 11
18 Aug 79 **BOY OH BOY** *RAK 297* 22 9
20 Dec 80 **RUNAROUND SUE** *RAK 325* 13 10

RACING CARS *UK, male vocal / instrumental group (Singles: 7 weeks, Albums: 6 weeks)* pos/wks

12 Feb 77 **THEY SHOOT HORSES DON'T THEY?** *Chrysalis CHS 2129* 14 7
19 Feb 77 **DOWNTOWN TONIGHT** *Chrysalis CHR 1099* 39 6

RACKETEERS – *See Elbow BONES and the RACKETEERS*

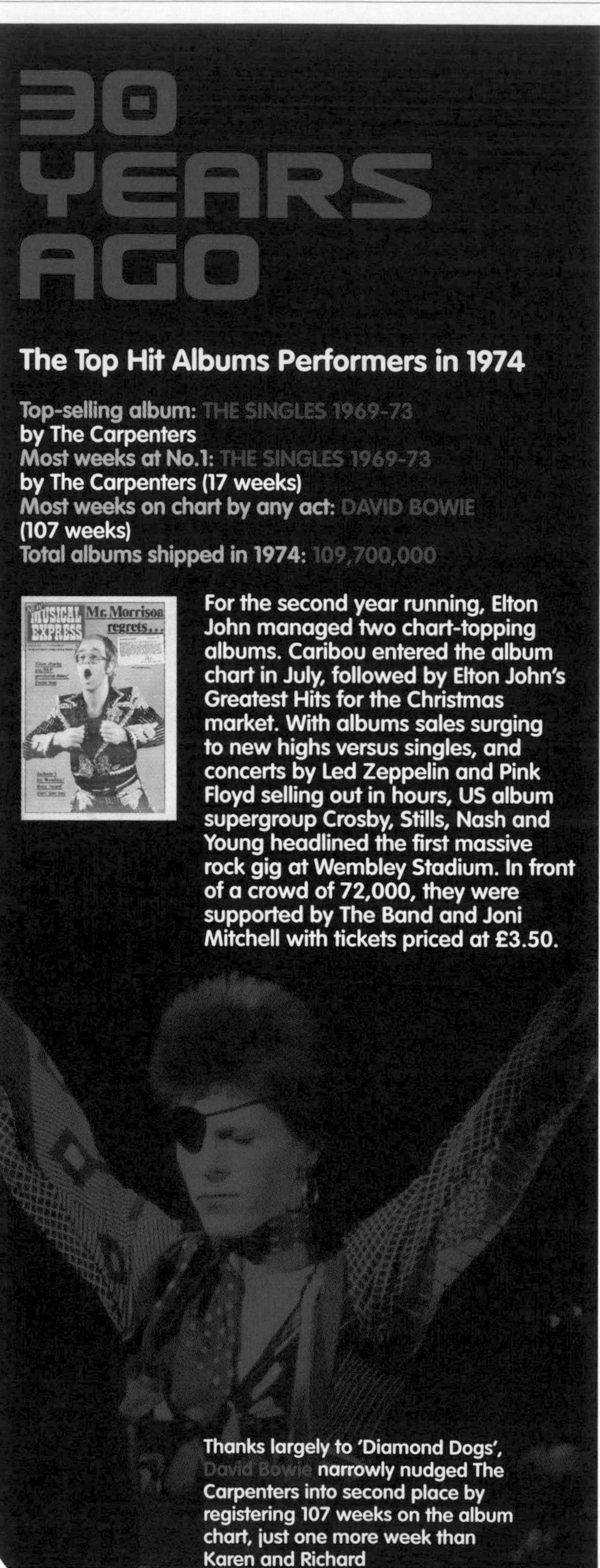

30 YEARS AGO

The Top Hit Albums Performers in 1974

Top-selling album: THE SINGLES 1969-73 by The Carpenters
Most weeks at No.1: THE SINGLES 1969-73 by The Carpenters (17 weeks)
Most weeks on chart by any act: DAVID BOWIE (107 weeks)
Total albums shipped in 1974: 109,700,000

For the second year running, Elton John managed two chart-topping albums. Caribou entered the album chart in July, followed by Elton John's Greatest Hits for the Christmas market. With albums sales surging to new highs versus singles, and concerts by Led Zeppelin and Pink Floyd selling out in hours, US album supergroup Crosby, Stills, Nash and Young headlined the first massive rock gig at Wembley Stadium. In front of a crowd of 72,000, they were supported by The Band and Joni Mitchell with tickets priced at £3.50.

Thanks largely to 'Diamond Dogs', David Bowie narrowly nudged The Carpenters into second place by registering 107 weeks on the album chart, just one more week than Karen and Richard

Jimmy RADCLIFFE
US, male vocalist, d. 27 Jul 1973 (Singles: 2 weeks)

		pos	wks
4 Feb 65	**LONG AFTER TONIGHT IS ALL OVER** *Stateside SS 374*	40	2

RADHA KRISHNA TEMPLE
UK, male / female vocal / instrumental group (Singles: 17 weeks)

		pos	wks
13 Sep 69	**HARE KRISHNA MANTRA** *Apple 15*	12	9
28 Mar 70	**GOVINDA** *Apple 25*	23	8

RADICAL ROB
UK, male producer – Rob McLuan (Singles: 1 week)

		pos	wks
11 Jan 92	**MONKEY WAH** *R&S RSUK 8*	67	1

Jack RADICS – *See Chaka DEMUS and PLIERS; SUPERCAT*

RADIO HEART featuring Gary NUMAN *UK, male instrumental group and male vocalist / instrumentalist (Singles: 8 weeks)*

		pos	wks
28 Mar 87	**RADIO HEART** *GFM GFM 109*	35	6
13 Jun 87	**LONDON TIMES** *GFM GFM 112*	48	2

RADIO 1 DJ POSSE – *See Liz KERSHAW and Bruno BROOKES*

RADIO REVELLERS – *See Anthony STEEL and the RADIO REVELLERS*

RADIO STARS
UK, male vocal / instrumental group (Singles: 3 weeks)

		pos	wks
4 Feb 78	**NERVOUS WRECK** *Chiswick NS 23*	39	3

RADIOHEAD (103 Top 500)
Innovative boundary-bending group is a regular Top 10 album fixture around the globe. This Grammy-winning band formed in Oxford 1991 is fronted by Thom Yorke (g/v/k), and is the only contemporary UK act to top the US chart in the 21st century (Singles: 63 weeks, Albums: 360 weeks)

			pos	wks
13 Feb 93		**ANYONE CAN PLAY GUITAR** *Parlophone CDR 6333*	32	2
22 May 93		**POP IS DEAD** *Parlophone CDR 6345*	42	2
18 Sep 93	●	**CREEP** *Parlophone CDR 6359*	7	6
8 Oct 94		**MY IRON LUNG** *Parlophone CDR 6394*	24	2
11 Mar 95		**HIGH AND DRY / PLANET TELEX** *Parlophone CDR 6405*	17	4
27 May 95		**FAKE PLASTIC TREES** *Parlophone CDR 6411*	20	4
2 Sep 95		**JUST** *Parlophone CDR 6415*	19	3
3 Feb 96	●	**STREET SPIRIT (FADE OUT)** *Parlophone CDR 6419*	5	4
7 Jun 97	●	**PARANOID ANDROID** *Parlophone CDODATA S 01*	3	5
6 Sep 97	●	**KARMA POLICE** *Parlophone CDODATAS 03*	8	4
24 Jan 98	●	**NO SURPRISES (re)** *Parlophone CDODATAS 04*	4	7
2 Jun 01	●	**PYRAMID SONG** *Parlophone CDSFHEIT 45102*	5	5
18 Aug 01		**KNIVES OUT** *Parlophone CDFHEIT 45103*	13	4
7 Jun 03	●	**THERE THERE** *Parlophone CDR 6608*	4	4
30 Aug 03		**GO TO SLEEP** *Parlophone CDR 6613*	12	4
29 Nov 03		**2 + 2 = 5** *Parlophone CDR 6623*	15	3
6 Mar 93		**PABLO HONEY** *Parlophone CDPCS 7360*	22	82
25 Mar 95	●	**THE BENDS** *Parlophone CDPCS 7372*	4	160
28 Jun 97	★	**OK COMPUTER** *Parlophone CDNODATA 02* ■	1	75
14 Oct 00	★	**KID A** *Parlophone CDKIDA 1* ■ ▲	1	15
16 Jun 01	★	**AMNESIAC** *Parlophone CDFHEIT 45101* ■	1	12
24 Nov 01		**I MIGHT BE WRONG** *Parlophone CDFHEIT 45104*	23	2
21 Jun 03	★	**HAIL TO THE THIEF** *Palophone 5845432* ■	1	14

RADISH *US, male vocal / instrumental group (Singles: 3 weeks)*

		pos	wks
30 Aug 97	**LITTLE PINK STARS** *Mercury MERCD 494*	32	2
15 Nov 97	**SIMPLE SINCERITY** *Mercury MERCD 498*	50	1

Fonda RAE *US, female vocalist (Singles: 4 weeks)*

		pos	wks
6 Oct 84	**TUCH ME** *Streetwave KHAN 28*	49	4

Jesse RAE *UK, male vocalist (Singles: 2 weeks)*

		pos	wks
11 May 85	**OVER THE SEA** *Scotland-Video YZ 36*	65	2

Marcia RAE – *See QUAKE featuring Marcia RAE*

RAE & CHRISTIAN

UK, male production duo (Singles: 1 week, Albums: 1 week) pos/wks

Date		Title / Label	pos	wks
6 Mar 99		**ALL I ASK** *Grand Central GCCD 120* [1]	67	1
10 Mar 01		**SLEEPWALKING** *K7 K 7096CD*	57	1

[1] Rae and Christian featuring Veba

Gerry RAFFERTY (473 Top 500)

Mellow folk-rocker and former Humblebum (with Billy Connolly) and Stealers Wheel vocalist / guitarist b. 16 Apr 1947, Paisley, Scotland. Won Ivor Novello award for classic 'Baker Street' (composed in that street) which has been heard on US radio more than three million times (Singles: 47 weeks, Albums: 99 weeks) pos/wks

Date		Title / Label	pos	wks
18 Feb 78	●	**BAKER STREET** *United Artists UP 36346*	3	15
26 May 79	●	**NIGHT OWL** *United Artists UP 36512*	5	13
18 Aug 79		**GET IT RIGHT NEXT TIME** *United Artists BP 301*	30	9
22 Mar 80		**BRING IT ALL HOME** *United Artists BP 340*	54	4
21 Jun 80		**ROYAL MILE** *United Artists BP 354*	67	2
10 Mar 90		**BAKER STREET (re-mix)** *EMI EM 132*	53	4
25 Feb 78	●	**CITY TO CITY** *United Artists UAS 30104* ▲	6	37
2 Jun 79	●	**NIGHT OWL** *United Artists UAK 30238*	9	24
26 Apr 80		**SNAKES AND LADDERS** *United Artists UAK 30298*	15	9
25 Sep 82		**SLEEPWALKING** *Liberty LBG 30352*	39	4
21 May 88		**NORTH AND SOUTH** *London LONLP 55*	43	4
13 Feb 93		**ON A WING & A PRAYER** *A&M 5174952*	73	1
28 Oct 95		**ONE MORE DREAM – THE VERY BEST OF GERRY RAFFERTY** *PolyGram TV 5292792*	17	20

RAGE

UK, male vocal / instrumental group (Singles: 15 weeks) pos/wks

Date		Title / Label	pos	wks
31 Oct 92	●	**RUN TO YOU** *Pulse 8 LOSE 33*	3	11
27 Feb 93		**WHY DON'T YOU** *Pulse 8 CDLOSE 39*	44	2
15 May 93		**HOUSE OF THE RISING SUN** *Pulse 8 CDLOSE 43*	41	2

RAGE AGAINST THE MACHINE

US, male vocal / instrumental group (Singles: 19 weeks, Albums: 53 weeks) pos/wks

Date		Title / Label	pos	wks
27 Feb 93		**KILLING IN THE NAME** *Epic 6584922*	25	4
8 May 93		**BULLET IN THE HEAD** *Epic 6592582*	16	4
4 Sep 93		**BOMBTRACK** *Epic 6594712*	37	2
13 Apr 96	●	**BULLS ON PARADE** *Epic 6631522*	8	3
7 Sep 96		**PEOPLE OF THE SUN** *Epic 6636282*	26	2
6 Nov 99		**GUERRILLA RADIO** *Epic 6683142*	32	2
15 Apr 00		**SLEEP NOW IN THE FIRE** *Epic 6691362*	43	2
13 Feb 93		**RAGE AGAINST THE MACHINE** *Epic 4722242*	17	43
27 Apr 96	●	**EVIL EMPIRE** *Epic 4810262* ▲	4	7
13 Nov 99		**THE BATTLE OF LOS ANGELES** *Epic 4919932* ▲	23	2
9 Dec 00		**RENEGADES** *Epic 4999210*	71	1

RAGGA TWINS

UK, male vocal duo – Flinty Badman and Deman Rocker (Singles: 10 weeks, Albums: 5 weeks) pos/wks

Date		Title / Label	pos	wks
10 Nov 90		**ILLEGAL GUNSHOT / SPLIFFHEAD** *Shut Up and Dance SUAD 7*	51	2
6 Apr 91		**WIPE THE NEEDLE / JUGGLING** *Shut Up and Dance SUAD 12S*	71	2
6 Jul 91		**HOOLIGAN 69** *Shut Up and Dance SUAD 16S*	56	2
7 Mar 92		**MIXED TRUTH / BRING UP THE MIC SOME MORE** *Shut Up and Dance SUAD 27S*	65	2
11 Jul 92		**SHINE EYE** *Shut Up and Dance SUAD 32S* [1]	63	2
1 Jun 91		**REGGAE OWES ME MONEY** *Shut Up and Dance SUADLP 2*	26	5

[1] Ragga Twins featuring Junior Reid

RAGING SPEEDHORN

UK, male vocal / instrumental group (Singles: 2 weeks, Albums: 1 week) pos/wks

Date		Title / Label	pos	wks
16 Jun 01		**THE GUSH** *ZTT GIR 004CD*	47	1
6 Jul 02		**THE HATE SONG** *ZTT RSH 001CD*	69	1
17 Aug 02		**WE WILL BE DEAD TOMORROW** *ZTT RSH 002CD*	63	1

RAGTIMERS

UK, male instrumental group (Singles: 8 weeks) pos/wks

Date		Title / Label	pos	wks
16 Mar 74		**THE STING (re)** *Pye 7N 45323*	31	8

RAH BAND

UK, male / female vocal / instrumental group, leaders – Richard A and Liz Hewson (Singles: 50 weeks, Albums: 6 weeks) pos/wks

Date		Title / Label	pos	wks
9 Jul 77	●	**THE CRUNCH** *Good Earth GD 7*	6	12
1 Nov 80		**FALCON** *DJM DJS 10954*	35	7
7 Feb 81		**SLIDE** *DJM DJS 10964*	50	7
1 May 82		**PERFUMED GARDEN** *KR KR 5*	45	7
9 Jul 83		**MESSAGES FROM THE STARS** *TMT TMT 5*	42	5
19 Jan 85		**ARE YOU SATISFIED? (FUNKA NOVA)** *RCA RCA 470*	70	2
30 Mar 85	●	**CLOUDS ACROSS THE MOON** *RCA PB 40025*	6	10
6 Apr 85		**MYSTERY** *RCA PL 70640*	60	6

See also KEY WEST

RAHSAAN – *See US3*

RAILWAY CHILDREN

UK, male vocal / instrumental group (Singles: 13 weeks, Albums: 3 weeks) pos/wks

Date		Title / Label	pos	wks
24 Mar 90		**EVERY BEAT OF THE HEART (re)** *Virgin VS 1237*	24	8
2 Jun 90		**MUSIC STOP** *Virgin VS 1255*	66	2
20 Oct 90		**SO RIGHT** *Virgin VS 1289*	68	1
20 Apr 91		**SOMETHING SO GOOD** *Virgin VS 1318*	57	2
21 May 88		**RECURRENCE** *Virgin V 2525*	96	1
16 Mar 91		**NATIVE PLACE** *Virgin V 2627*	59	2

'Every Beat of the Heart' debuted on the chart at No.68 before making its peak position after re-entry in Feb 1991

RAIN – *See Stephanie DE SYKES*

RAIN BAND

UK, male vocal / instrumental group (Singles: 2 weeks) pos/wks

Date		Title / Label	pos	wks
1 Mar 03		**EASY RIDER** *Temptation TEMPT CD003*	63	1
19 Jul 03		**KNEE DEEP AND DOWN** *Temptation TEMPTCD 007*	56	1

RAIN PARADE

US, male vocal / instrumental group (Albums: 1 week) pos/wks

Date		Title / Label	pos	wks
29 Jun 85		**BEYOND THE SUNSET** *Island IMA 17*	78	1

RAIN TREE CROW

UK, male vocal / instrumental group (Singles: 1 week, Albums: 3 weeks) pos/wks

Date		Title / Label	pos	wks
30 Mar 91		**BLACKWATER** *Virgin VS 1340*	62	1
20 Apr 91		**RAIN TREE CROW** *Virgin V 2659*	24	3

See also JAPAN

RAINBOW (285 Top 500)

Melodic Anglo-American hard rock band with ever-changing personnel, formed UK, 1975, by ex-Deep Purple guitarist Ritchie Blackmore. Original vocalist Ronnie James Dio replaced by Graham Bonnet (1979), then Joe Lynn Turner (1980). After band split in 1984, Blackmore rejoined Deep Purple (Singles: 62 weeks, Albums: 163 weeks) pos/wks

Date		Title / Label	pos	wks
17 Sep 77		**KILL THE KING** *Polydor 2066 845*	44	3
8 Apr 78		**LONG LIVE ROCK 'N' ROLL** *Polydor 2066 913*	33	3
30 Sep 78		**L.A. CONNECTION** *Polydor 2066 968*	40	4
15 Sep 79	●	**SINCE YOU'VE BEEN GONE** *Polydor POSP 70*	6	10
16 Feb 80	●	**ALL NIGHT LONG** *Polydor POSP 104*	5	11
31 Jan 81	●	**I SURRENDER** *Polydor POSP 221*	3	10
20 Jun 81		**CAN'T HAPPEN HERE** *Polydor POSP 251*	20	8
11 Jul 81		**KILL THE KING (re-issue)** *Polydor POSP 274*	41	4
3 Apr 82		**STONE COLD** *Polydor POSP 421*	34	4
27 Aug 83		**STREET OF DREAMS** *Polydor POSP 631*	52	3
5 Nov 83		**CAN'T LET YOU GO** *Polydor POSP 654*	43	2
13 Sep 75		**RITCHIE BLACKMORE'S RAINBOW** *Oyster OYA 2001* [1]	11	6
5 Jun 76		**RAINBOW RISING** *Polydor 2490 137* [1]	11	33
30 Jul 77	●	**ON STAGE** *Polydor 2657 016*	7	10
6 May 78	●	**LONG LIVE ROCK 'N' ROLL** *Polydor POLD 5002*	7	12
18 Aug 79	●	**DOWN TO EARTH** *Polydor POLD 5023*	6	37
21 Feb 81	●	**DIFFICULT TO CURE** *Polydor POLD 5036*	3	22
8 Aug 81		**RITCHIE BLACKMORE'S RAINBOW (re-issue)** *Polydor 2940141* [1]	91	2
21 Nov 81		**THE BEST OF RAINBOW** *Polydor POLDV 2*	14	17

24 Apr 82 ● **STRAIGHT BETWEEN THE EYES** *Polydor POLD 5056* 5 14
17 Sep 83 **BENT OUT OF SHAPE** *Polydor POLD 5116* 11 6
8 Mar 86 **FINYL VINYL** *Polydor PODV 8* 31 4

1 Ritchie Blackmore's Rainbow

RAINBOW *UK, male puppet rappers, DJ George and MC Zippy (Roy Skelton) (Singles: 6 weeks)* pos/wks

14 Dec 02 **IT'S A RAINBOW** *BBC Music ZIPPCD 1* 15 6

RAINBOW COTTAGE
UK, male vocal / instrumental group (Singles: 4 weeks) pos/wks

6 Mar 76 **SEAGULL** *Penny Farthing PEN 906* 33 4

RAINDANCE *UK, male production / instrumental duo – Stewart and Bradley Palmer (Albums: 7 weeks)* pos/wks

27 Apr 96 **RAINDANCE** *PolyGram TV 5298622* 15 7

See also BLOWING FREE; HARMONIUM; HYPNOSIS; IN TUNE; JAMES BOYS; SCHOOL OF EXCELLENCE

RAINMAKERS
US, male vocal / instrumental group (Singles: 11 weeks) pos/wks

7 Mar 87 **LET MY PEOPLE GO-GO** *Mercury MER 238* 18 11

Marvin RAINWATER
US, male vocalist – Marvin Percy (Singles: 22 weeks) pos/wks

7 Mar 58 ★ **WHOLE LOTTA WOMAN** *MGM 974* 1 15
6 Jun 58 **I DIG YOU BABY** *MGM 980* 19 7

RAISSA *UK, female vocalist – Raissa Khan-Panni (Singles: 1 week)* pos/wks

12 Feb 00 **HOW LONG DO I GET** *Polydor 5616282* 47 1

Bonnie RAITT *US, female vocalist / instrumentalist – guitar (Singles: 9 weeks, Albums: 17 weeks)* pos/wks

14 Dec 91 **I CAN'T MAKE YOU LOVE ME** *Capitol CL 639* 50 4
9 Apr 94 **LOVE SNEAKIN' UP ON YOU** *Capitol CDCL 713* 69 1
18 Jun 94 **YOU** *Capitol CDCLS 718* 31 2
11 Nov 95 **ROCK STEADY** *Capitol CDCL 763* 1 ....50 2
28 Apr 90 **NICK OF TIME** *Capitol EST 2095* ▲ 51 5
6 Jul 91 **LUCK OF THE DRAW** *Capitol EST 2145* 38 3
16 Apr 94 **LONGING IN THEIR HEARTS** *Capitol CDEST 2227* ▲ 26 5
25 Nov 95 **ROAD TESTED** *Capitol CDEST 2274* 69 1
18 Apr 98 **FUNDAMENTAL** *Capitol 8563972* 52 1
24 May 03 **THE BEST OF BONNIE RAITT** *Capitol 5821132* 37 2

1 Bonnie Raitt and Bryan Adams

Dionne RAKEEM *UK, female vocalist (Singles: 2 weeks)* pos/wks

4 Aug 01 **SWEETER THAN WINE** *Virgin VSCDT 1809* 46 2

RAKIM *US, male rapper – William Griffin (Singles: 17 weeks, Albums: 1 week)* pos/wks

27 Dec 97 **GUESS WHO'S BACK** *Universal UND 56151* 32 3
22 Aug 98 **STAY A WHILE** *Universal UND 56203* 53 1
3 Oct 98 **BUFFALO GIRLS STAMPEDE (re-mix)** *Virgin VSCDT 1717* 1 65 1
31 Aug 02 ● **ADDICTIVE** *Aftermath / Interscope 4977782* 2 ....3 12
22 Nov 97 **18TH LETTER** *Universal U 253113* 72 1

1 Malcolm McLaren and the World's Famous Supreme Team plus Rakim and Roger Sanchez 2 Truth Hurts featuring Rakim

See also Eric B and RAKIM

Tony RALLO and the MIDNITE BAND
France / US, male vocal / instrumental group (Singles: 8 weeks) pos/wks

23 Feb 80 **HOLDIN' ON** *Calibre CAB 150* 34 8

Sheryl Lee RALPH *US, female vocalist (Singles: 2 weeks)* pos/wks

26 Jan 85 **IN THE EVENING** *Arista ARIST 595* 64 2

RAM JAM *US, male vocal / instrumental group (Singles: 20 weeks)* pos/wks

10 Sep 77 ● **BLACK BETTY** *Epic EPC 5492* 7 12
17 Feb 90 **BLACK BETTY (re-mix)** *Epic 655430 7* 13 8

RAM JAM BAND – *See Geno WASHINGTON and the RAM JAM BAND*

RAM TRILOGY *UK, male production trio (Singles: 3 weeks)* pos/wks

6 Jul 02 **CHAPTER FOUR** *Ram RAMM 39* 71 1
20 Jul 02 **CHAPTER 5** *Ram RAMM 40* 62 1
3 Aug 02 **CHAPTER 6** *Ram RAMM 41* 60 1

RAMBLERS – *See Perry COMO*

RAMBLERS (from the Abbey Hey Junior School)
UK, children's choir (Singles: 15 weeks) pos/wks

13 Oct 79 **THE SPARROW** *Decca F 13860* 11 15

Karen RAMIREZ *UK, female vocalist – Karen Ramelize (Singles: 15 weeks, Albums: 2 weeks)* pos/wks

28 Mar 98 **TROUBLED GIRL** *Manifesto FESCD 31* 50 1
27 Jun 98 ● **LOOKING FOR LOVE** *Manifesto FESCD 44* 8 11
21 Nov 98 **IF WE TRY** *Manifesto FESCD 50* 23 3
1 Aug 98 **DISTANT DREAMS** *Manifesto 5586742* 45 2

RAMMSTEIN
Germany, male vocal / instrumental group (Singles: 4 weeks) pos/wks

25 May 02 **ICH WILL** *Motor / Universal MCSTD 40280* 30 2
23 Nov 02 **FEUER FREI** *Universal MCSTD 40302* 35 2

RAMONES *US, male vocal / instrumental group (Singles: 32 weeks, Albums: 30 weeks)* pos/wks

21 May 77 **SHEENA IS A PUNK ROCKER** *Sire RAM 001* 22 7
6 Aug 77 **SWALLOW MY PRIDE** *Sire 6078 607* 36 3
30 Sep 78 **DON'T COME CLOSE** *Sire SRE 1031* 39 5
8 Sep 79 **ROCK 'N' ROLL HIGH SCHOOL** *Sire SIR 4021* 67 2
26 Jan 80 ● **BABY, I LOVE YOU** *Sire SIR 4031* 8 9
19 Apr 80 **DO YOU REMEMBER ROCK 'N' ROLL RADIO?** *Sire SIR 4037* 54 3
10 May 86 **SOMEBODY PUT SOMETHING IN MY DRINK / SOMETHING TO BELIEVE IN** *Beggars Banquet BEG 157* 69 1
19 Dec 92 **POISON HEART** *Chrysalis CHS 3917* 69 2
23 Apr 77 **LEAVE HOME** *Philips 9103 254* 45 1
24 Dec 77 **ROCKET TO RUSSIA** *Sire 9103 255* 60 2
7 Oct 78 **ROAD TO RUIN** *Sire SRK 6063* 32 2
16 Jun 79 **IT'S ALIVE** *Sire SRK 26074* 27 8
19 Jan 80 **END OF THE CENTURY** *Sire SRK 6077* 14 8
26 Jan 85 **TOO TOUGH TO DIE** *Beggars Banquet BEGA 59* 63 3
31 May 86 **ANIMAL BOY** *Beggars Banquet BEGA 70* 38 2
10 Oct 87 **HALFWAY TO SANITY** *Beggars Banquet BEGA 89* 78 1
19 Aug 89 **BRAIN DRAIN** *Chrysalis CHR 1725* 75 1
8 Jul 95 **!ADIOS AMIGOS!** *Chrysalis CDCHR 6104* 62 1
9 Jun 01 **HEY HO LET'S GO! – ANTHOLOGY** *Warner Bros. 8122735572* ..74 1

RAMP *UK, male instrumental / production duo – Shem McCauley and Simon Rogers (Singles: 1 week)* pos/wks

8 Jun 96 **ROCK THE DISCOTEK** *Loaded LOADCD 30* 49 1

See also SLACKER

RAMPAGE *UK, male DJ / production group (Singles: 1 week)* pos/wks

25 Nov 95 **THE MONKEES** *Almo Sounds CDALMOS 017* 51 1

RAMPAGE featuring Billy LAWRENCE *US male rapper – Roger McNair and US, male vocalist (Singles: 1 week)* pos/wks

18 Oct 97 **TAKE IT TO THE STREETS** *Elektra E 3914CD* 58 1

RAMRODS
US, male / female instrumental group (Singles: 12 weeks) pos/wks

23 Feb 61 ● **RIDERS IN THE SKY** *London HLU 9282* 8 12

RAMSEY and FEN featuring Lynsey MOORE

UK, male production duo and female vocalist (Singles: 1 week) pos/wks

10 Jun 00	**LOVE BUG** *Nebula VCNEBD 4*	75	1

RANCID *US, male vocal / instrumental group (Singles: 3 weeks, Albums: 7 weeks)* pos/wks

7 Oct 95	**TIME BOMB** *Out of Step WOOS 8CDS*	56	1
27 Sep 03	**FALL BACK DOWN** *Hellcat / WEA W 618CD*	42	2
2 Sep 95	**... AND OUT COME THE WOLVES** *Epitaph 864442*	55	1
4 Jul 98	**LIFE WON'T WAIT** *Epitaph 864972*	32	2
5 Aug 00	**RANCID** *Hellcat 4272*	68	1
23 Mar 02	**SPLIT SERIES – VOL.3** *BYO BYO 079CD* [1]	75	1
6 Sep 03	**INDESCTRUCTIBLE** *Hellcat / WEA 9362485392*	29	2

[1] Rancid / NOFX

RANGE – *See Bruce HORNSBY and the RANGE*

RANGERS FC *UK, male football team vocalists (Singles: 2 weeks)* pos/wks

4 Oct 97	**GLASGOW RANGERS (NINE IN A ROW)** *Gers GERSCD 1*	54	2

RANI – *See DELERIUM*

RANK 1 *Holland, male production duo – Piet Bervoets and Benno de Goeij (Singles: 5 weeks)* pos/wks

15 Apr 00 ●	**AIRWAVE** *Manifesto FESCD 69*	10	5

RANKING ANN – *See SCRITTI POLITTI*

RANKING ROGER – *See Pato BANTON*

Shabba RANKS *Jamaica, male vocalist – Rexton Rawlston Fernando Gordon (Singles: 67 weeks, Albums: 10 weeks)* pos/wks

16 Mar 91	**SHE'S A WOMAN** *Virgin VS 1333* [1]	20	7
18 May 91	**TRAILER LOAD A GIRLS** *Epic 6568747*	63	2
24 Aug 91	**HOUSECALL** *Epic 6573477* [2]	31	7
8 Aug 92	**MR LOVERMAN** *Epic 6582517*	23	7
28 Nov 92	**SLOW AND SEXY** *Epic 6587727* [3]	17	7
6 Mar 93	**I WAS A KING** *Motown TMGCD 1414* [4]	64	1
13 Mar 93 ●	**MR LOVERMAN (re-issue)** *Epic 6590782*	3	11
8 May 93 ●	**HOUSECALL (re-mix)** *Epic 6592842* [2]	8	8
26 Jun 93	**WHAT'CHA GONNA DO** *Epic 6593072* [5]	21	4
25 Dec 93	**FAMILY AFFAIR** *Polydor PZCD 304* [6]	18	8
29 Apr 95	**LET'S GET IT ON** *Epic 6614122*	22	3
5 Aug 95	**SHINE EYE GAL** *Epic 6622332* [7]	46	2
22 Jun 91	**AS RAW AS EVER** *Epic 4681021*	51	2
22 Aug 92	**ROUGH AND READY VOLUME 1** *Epic 4714422*	71	2
24 Apr 93	**X-TRA NAKED** *Epic 4723332*	38	6

[1] Scritti Politti featuring Shabba Ranks [2] Shabba Ranks featuring Maxi Priest [3] Shabba Ranks featuring Johnny Gill [4] Eddie Murphy featuring Shabba Ranks [5] Shabba Ranks featuring Queen Latifah [6] Shabba Ranks featuring Patra and Terri & Monica [7] Shabba Ranks (featuring Mykal Rose)

Bubbler RANX – *See Peter ANDRE*

RAPINATION *Italy, male instrumental / production duo – Marco Sabiu and Charlie Mallozzi (Singles: 12 weeks)* pos/wks

26 Dec 92	**LOVE ME THE RIGHT WAY** *Logic 74321128097* [1]	22	10
10 Jul 93	**HERE'S MY A** *Logic 74321153092* [2]	69	1
28 Sep 96	**LOVE ME THE RIGHT WAY (re-mix)** *Logic 7432140442* [1]	55	1

[1] Rapination featuring Kym Mazelle [2] Rapination featuring Carol Kenyon

RAPPIN' 4-TAY

US, male rapper – Anthony Forte (Singles: 5 weeks) pos/wks

24 Jun 95	**I'LL BE AROUND** *Cooltempo CDCOOL 306* [1]	30	4
30 Sep 95	**PLAYAZ CLUB** *Cooltempo CDCOOL 310*	63	1

[1] Rappin' 4-Tay featuring The Spinners

The Spinners on 'I'll Be Around' are The Detroit Spinners

The RAPTURE

US, male vocal / instrumental group (Singles: 3 weeks, Albums: 2 weeks) pos/wks

6 Sep 03	**HOUSE OF JEALOUS LOVERS** *Vertigo 9810767*	27	2
13 Dec 03	**SISTER SAVIOUR** *DFA / Output / Vertigo 9814181*	51	1
20 Sep 03	**ECHOES** *DFA / Output / Vertigo 9865447*	32	2

RARE

UK, male / female vocal / instrumental group (Singles: 1 week) pos/wks

17 Feb 96	**SOMETHING WILD** *Equator AXISCD 011*	57	1

RARE BIRD

UK, male vocal / instrumental group (Singles: 8 weeks) pos/wks

14 Feb 70	**SYMPATHY** *Charisma CB 120*	27	8

O RASBURY – *See Rahni HARRIS and F.L.O.*

RASHAAN – *See US3*

Roland RAT SUPERSTAR *UK, male rodent vocalist / rapper (Singles: 20 weeks, Albums: 3 weeks)* pos/wks

19 Nov 83	**RAT RAPPING** *Rodent RAT 1*	14	12
28 Apr 84	**LOVE ME TENDER** *Rodent RAT 2*	32	7
2 Mar 85	**NO.1 RAT FAN** *Rodent RAT 4*	72	1
15 Dec 84	**THE CASSETTE OF THE ALBUM** *Rodent RATL 1001*	67	3

RATPACK

UK, male instrumental / production duo (Singles: 3 weeks) pos/wks

6 Jun 92	**SEARCHIN' FOR MY RIZLA** *Big Giant BIGT 02*	58	3

RATT *US, male vocal / instrumental group (Albums: 5 weeks)* pos/wks

13 Jul 85	**INVASION OF YOUR PRIVACY** *Atlantic 7812571*	50	2
25 Oct 86	**DANCING UNDERCOVER** *Atlantic 781 6831*	51	1
12 Nov 88	**REACH FOR THE SKY** *Atlantic 781929*	82	1
8 Sep 90	**DETONATOR** *Atlantic 7567821271*	55	1

RATTLES

Germany, male vocal / instrumental group (Singles: 15 weeks) pos/wks

3 Oct 70 ●	**THE WITCH** *Decca F 23058*	8	15

Mark RATTRAY *UK, male vocalist (Albums: 8 weeks)* pos/wks

8 Dec 90	**SONGS OF THE MUSICALS** *Telstar STAR 2458*	46	7
10 Oct 92	**THE MAGIC OF THE MUSICALS** *Quality Television QTV 013* [1]	55	1

[1] Marti Webb and Mark Rattray

RATTY *Germany, male production group (Singles: 1 week)* pos/wks

24 Mar 01	**SUNRISE (HERE I AM)** *Neo NEOCD 051*	51	1

RAVEN *UK, male vocal / instrumental group (Albums: 3 weeks)* pos/wks

17 Oct 81	**ROCK UNTIL YOU DROP** *Neat NEAT 1001*	63	3

RAVEN MAIZE

UK, male producer – Dave Lee (Singles: 9 weeks) pos/wks

5 Aug 89	**FOREVER TOGETHER** *Republic LIC 014*	67	1
18 Aug 01	**THE REAL LIFE (re)** *Rulin / MoS / Credence RULIN 18CDS*	12	6
17 Aug 02	**FASCINATED** *Ministry of Sound / Rulin RULIN 27CDS*	37	2

See also HED BOYS; Li KWAN; Joey NEGRO; Z FACTOR; JAKATTA; AKABU featuring Linda CLIFFORD; PHASE II; IL PADRINOS featuring Jocelyn BROWN

The RAVEONETTES *Denmark, male / female vocal / instrumental group (Singles: 4 weeks, Albums: 1 week)* pos/wks

21 Dec 02	**ATTACK OF THE GHOSTRIDERS** *Columbia 6733892*	73	1
30 Aug 03	**THAT GREAT LOVE SOUND** *Columbia RAVEON 005*	34	2
20 Dec 03	**HEARTBREAK STROLL** *Columbia RAVEON 008*	49	1
6 Sep 03	**CHAIN GANG OF LOVE** *Columbia 5123782*	43	1

RAVESIGNAL III

Belgium, male producer – Christian Bolland (Singles: 2 weeks) pos/wks

Date		Title / Label	pos	wks
14 Dec 91		**HORSEPOWER** *R&S RSUK 6*	61	2

See also CJ BOLLAND

RAW – *See Erick 'More' MORILLO presents RAW*

RAW SILK

US, female vocal group (Singles: 12 weeks) pos/wks

Date		Title / Label	pos	wks
16 Oct 82		**DO IT TO THE MUSIC** *KR KR 14*	18	9
10 Sep 83		**JUST IN TIME** *West End WEND 2*	49	3

RAW STYLUS

UK, male / female vocal / instrumental duo (Singles: 1 week) pos/wks

Date		Title / Label	pos	wks
26 Oct 96		**BELIEVE IN ME** *Wired WIRED 234*	66	1

Lou RAWLS

US, male vocalist (Singles: 10 weeks) pos/wks

Date		Title / Label	pos	wks
31 Jul 76	●	**YOU'LL NEVER FIND ANOTHER LOVE LIKE MINE** *Philadelphia International PIR 4372*	10	10

Gene Anthony RAY – *See KIDS FROM 'FAME'*

Jimmy RAY

UK, male vocalist – James Edwards (Singles: 6 weeks) pos/wks

Date		Title / Label	pos	wks
25 Oct 97		**ARE YOU JIMMY RAY?** *Sony S2 6650125*	13	5
14 Feb 98		**GOIN' TO VEGAS** *Sony S2 6654652*	49	1

Johnnie RAY (399 Top 500)

A sensation in the 1950s, the heart-wrenching vocal delivery of the 'Cry Guy' (b. 10 Jan 1927, Oregon, US, d. 25 Feb 1990) influenced many acts, including Elvis, and Ray was the prime target for teen hysteria in pre-Presley days (Singles: 168 weeks) pos/wks

Date		Title / Label	pos	wks
14 Nov 52		**WALKIN' MY BABY BACK HOME** *Columbia DB 3060*	12	1
19 Dec 52	●	**FAITH CAN MOVE MOUNTAINS (re)** *Columbia DB 3154* [1]	7	3
3 Apr 53		**MA SAYS, PA SAYS** *Columbia DB3242* [2]	12	1
10 Apr 53	●	**SOMEBODY STOLE MY GAL (3re)** *Philips PB 123*	6	7
17 Apr 53		**FULL TIME JOB** *Columbia DB 3242* [2]	11	1
24 Jul 53	●	**LET'S WALK THAT-A-WAY** *Philips PB 157* [2]	4	14
9 Apr 54	★	**SUCH A NIGHT** *Philips PB 244*	1	18
8 Apr 55	●	**IF YOU BELIEVE (re)** *Philips PB 379*	7	11
20 May 55		**PATHS OF PARADISE** *Philips PB 441*	20	1
7 Oct 55		**HERNANDO'S HIDEAWAY** *Philips PB 495*	11	5
14 Oct 55	●	**HEY THERE** *Philips PB 495*	5	9
28 Oct 55	●	**SONG OF THE DREAMER** *Philips PB 516*	10	5
17 Feb 56		**WHO'S SORRY NOW** *Philips PB 546*	17	2
20 Apr 56		**AIN'T MISBEHAVIN' (re)** *Philips PB 580*	17	7
12 Oct 56	★	**JUST WALKING IN THE RAIN** *Philips PB 624*	1	19
18 Jan 57		**YOU DON'T OWE ME A THING** *Philips PB 655*	12	15
8 Feb 57	●	**LOOK HOMEWARD ANGEL** *Philips PB 655*	7	16
10 May 57	★	**YES TONIGHT JOSEPHINE** *Philips PB 686*	1	16
6 Sep 57		**BUILD YOUR LOVE (ON A STRONG FOUNDATION)** *Philips PB 721*	17	7
4 Oct 57		**GOOD EVENING FRIENDS / UP ABOVE MY HEAD, I HEAR MUSIC IN THE AIR** *Philips PB 708* [3]	25	4
4 Dec 59		**I'LL NEVER FALL IN LOVE AGAIN (2re)** *Philips PB 952*	26	6

[1] Johnnie Ray and The Four Lads [2] Doris Day and Johnnie Ray [3] Frankie Laine and Johnnie Ray

The chart history of 'You Don't Owe Me a Thing / Look Homeward Angel' is complicated and is as follows: 'You Don't Owe Me a Thing' entered the chart by itself on 18 Jan 1957. On 8 and 15 Feb 1957, 'Look Homeward Angel' was coupled with 'You Don't Owe Me a Thing', but from 22 Feb 1957 the two sides went their individual ways on the chart and were listed separately: 'You Don't Owe Me a Thing' for a further 10 weeks and 'Look Homeward Angel' for a further 14 weeks

Nicole RAY

US, female vocalist – Nicole Wray (Singles: 5 weeks) pos/wks

Date		Title / Label	pos	wks
22 Aug 98		**MAKE IT HOT** *East West E 3821CD* [1]	22	4
5 Dec 98		**I CAN'T SEE** *East West E 3801CD*	55	1

[1] Nicole featuring Missy 'Misdemeanor' Elliott and Mocha

RAYDIO

US, male vocal / instrumental group – leader Ray Parker Jr (Singles: 21 weeks) pos/wks

Date		Title / Label	pos	wks
8 Apr 78		**JACK AND JILL** *Arista 161*	11	12
8 Jul 78		**IS THIS A LOVE THING** *Arista 193*	27	9

See also Ray PARKER Jr

Simon RAYMONDE – *See Harold BUDD / Liz FRASER / Robin GUTHRIE / Simon RAYMONDE*

RAYVON

Barbados, male rapper / vocalist – Bruce Brewster (Singles: 26 weeks) pos/wks

Date		Title / Label	pos	wks
8 Jul 95	●	**IN THE SUMMERTIME** *Virgin VSCDT 1542* [1]	5	9
9 Jun 01	★	**ANGEL** *MCA MCSTD 40257* [1] ■ ▲	1	16
3 Aug 02		**2-WAY** *MCA MCSTD 40287*	67	1

[1] Shaggy featuring Rayvon

RAZE

US, male / female vocal / production group (Singles: 48 weeks) pos/wks

Date		Title / Label	pos	wks
1 Nov 86		**JACK THE GROOVE (re)** *Champion CHAMP 23*	20	15
28 Feb 87		**LET THE MUSIC MOVE U** *Champion CHAMP 27*	57	3
31 Dec 88		**BREAK 4 LOVE (re)** *Champion CHAMP 67*	28	16
15 Jul 89		**LET IT ROLL** *Atlantic A 8866* [1]	27	5
27 Jan 90		**ALL 4 LOVE (BREAK 4 LOVE 1990)** *Champion CHAMP 228* [2]	30	5
10 Feb 90		**CAN YOU FEEL IT / CAN YOU FEEL IT** *Champion CHAMP 227* [3]	62	1
24 Sep 94		**BREAK 4 LOVE (re-mix)** *Champion CHAMPCD 314*	44	2
29 Mar 03		**BREAK 4 LOVE (2nd re-mix)** *Champion CHAMPCD 784*	64	1

[1] Raze presents Doug Lazy [2] Raze featuring Lady J and Secretary of Entertainment [3] Raze / Championship Legend

'Can You Feel It' by Championship Legend is a montage of six Raze tracks

RAZORLIGHT

UK, male vocal / instrumental group (Singles: 2 weeks) pos/wks

Date		Title / Label	pos	wks
30 Aug 03		**ROCK 'N' ROLL LIES** *Vertigo 9800413*	56	1
22 Nov 03		**RIP IT UP** *Vertigo 9814045*	42	1

RE-FLEX

UK, male vocal / instrumental group (Singles: 9 weeks) pos/wks

Date		Title / Label	pos	wks
28 Jan 84		**THE POLITICS OF DANCING** *EMI FLEX 2*	28	9

REA – *See JAM & SPOON featuring PLAVKA*

Chris REA (84 Top 500)

One of the most popular UK singer / songwriters of the late 1980s, b. 4 Mar 1951, Middlesbrough. He was already a major European star by the time he finally cracked the UK Top 10 with his 18th chart entry, 'The Road to Hell (Part 2)' (Singles: 120 weeks, Albums: 354 weeks) pos/wks

Date		Title / Label	pos	wks
7 Oct 78		**FOOL (IF YOU THINK IT'S OVER)** *Magnet MAG 111*	30	7
21 Apr 79		**DIAMONDS** *Magnet MAG 144*	44	3
27 Mar 82		**LOVING YOU** *Magnet MAG 215*	65	3
1 Oct 83		**I CAN HEAR YOUR HEARTBEAT** *Magnet MAG 244*	60	2
17 Mar 84		**I DON'T KNOW WHAT IT IS BUT I LOVE IT** *Magnet MAG 255*	65	2
30 Mar 85		**STAINSBY GIRLS** *Magnet MAG 276*	26	10
29 Jun 85		**JOSEPHINE** *Magnet MAG 280*	67	2
29 Mar 86		**IT'S ALL GONE** *Magnet MAG 283*	69	1
31 May 86		**ON THE BEACH (2re)** *Magnet MAG 294*	57	8
6 Jun 87		**LET'S DANCE** *Magnet MAG 299*	12	10
29 Aug 87		**LOVING YOU AGAIN** *Magnet MAG 300*	47	4
5 Dec 87		**JOYS OF CHRISTMAS** *Magnet MAG 314*	67	1
13 Feb 88		**QUE SERA** *Magnet MAG 318*	73	2
13 Aug 88		**ON THE BEACH SUMMER '88** *WEA YZ 195*	12	6
22 Oct 88		**I CAN HEAR YOUR HEARTBEAT** *WEA YZ 320*	74	2
17 Dec 88		**THE CHRISTMAS EP** *WEA YZ 325*	53	3
18 Feb 89		**WORKING ON IT** *WEA YZ 350*	53	3
14 Oct 89	●	**THE ROAD TO HELL (PART 2)** *WEA YZ 431*	10	9
10 Feb 90		**TELL ME THERE'S A HEAVEN** *East West YZ 455*	24	6
5 May 90		**TEXAS** *East West YZ 468*	69	1
16 Feb 91		**AUBERGE** *East West YZ 555*	16	6

Date		Title / Label	Pos	Wks
6 Apr 91		**HEAVEN** *East West YZ 566*	57	2
29 Jun 91		**LOOKING FOR THE SUMMER** *East West YZ 584*	49	3
9 Nov 91		**WINTER SONG** *East West YZ 629*	27	4
24 Oct 92		**NOTHING TO FEAR** *East West YZ 699*	16	4
28 Nov 92		**GOD'S GREAT BANANA SKIN** *East West YZ 706*	31	3
30 Jan 93		**SOFT TOP HARD SHOULDER** *East West YZ 710CD*	53	2
23 Oct 93		**JULIA** *East West YZ 772CD*	18	5
12 Nov 94		**YOU CAN GO YOUR OWN WAY** *East West YZ 835CD*	28	3
24 Dec 94		**TELL ME THERE'S A HEAVEN (re-issue)** *East West YZ 885CD*	70	1
16 Nov 96		**'DISCO' LA PASSIONE** *East West EW 072CD* [1]	41	1
24 May 97		**LET'S DANCE** *Magnet EW 112CD* [2]	44	1
28 Apr 79		**DELTICS** *Magnet MAG 5028*	54	3
12 Apr 80		**TENNIS** *Magnet MAG 5032*	60	1
3 Apr 82		**CHRIS REA** *Magnet MAGL 5040*	52	4
18 Jun 83		**WATER SIGN** *Magnet MAGL 5048*	64	2
21 Apr 84		**WIRED TO THE MOON** *Magnet MAGL 5057*	35	7
25 May 85		**SHAMROCK DIARIES** *Magnet MAGL 5062*	15	14
26 Apr 86		**ON THE BEACH** *Magnet MAGL 5069*	11	37
26 Sep 87	●	**DANCING WITH STRANGERS** *Magnet MAGL 5071*	2	46
13 Aug 88		**ON THE BEACH (re-issue)** *WEA WX 191*	37	10
29 Oct 88	●	**NEW LIGHT THROUGH OLD WINDOWS** *WEA WX 200*	5	51
11 Nov 89	★	**THE ROAD TO HELL** *WEA WX 317* ■	1	76
9 Mar 91	★	**AUBERGE** *East West 9031735801* ■	1	37
14 Nov 92	●	**GOD'S GREAT BANANA SKIN** *East West 4509909952*	4	15
13 Nov 93	●	**ESPRESSO LOGIC** *East West 4509943112*	8	10
5 Nov 94	●	**THE BEST OF CHRIS REA** *East West 4509980402*	3	18
23 Nov 96		**LA PASSIONE (FILM SOUNDTRACK)** *East West 630166952*	43	4
31 Jan 98	●	**THE BLUE CAFÉ** *East West 3984216882*	10	7
20 Nov 99		**THE ROAD TO HELL - PART 2** *East West 8573803992*	54	1
14 Oct 00		**KING OF THE BEACH** *East West 8573850172*	26	3
1 Dec 01		**THE VERY BEST OF CHRIS REA** *East West 927421282*	69	1
28 Sep 02		**DANCING DOWN THE STONY ROAD** *Jazzee Blue JBLUECD 01X*	14	7

[1] Chris Rea and Shirley Bassey [2] Middlesbrough FC featuring Bob Mortimer and Chris Rea

Both 'On the Beach Summer '88' and 'I Can Hear Your Heartbeat' in 1988 are re-recordings. Tracks on Driving Home for Christmas (EP): Driving Home for Christmas / Footsteps in the Snow / Joys of Christmas / Smile

REACT 2 RHYTHM *UK, male production group (Singles: 1 week)*

Date		Title / Label	Pos	Wks
28 Jun 97		**INTOXICATION** *Jackpot WIN 014CD*	73	1

Eileen READ – *See CADETS with Eileen REID*

Eddi READER

UK, female vocalist (Singles: 14 weeks, Albums: 21 weeks)

Date		Title / Label	Pos	Wks
4 Jun 94		**PATIENCE OF ANGELS** *Blanco Y Negro NEG 68CD*	33	5
13 Aug 94		**JOKE (I'M LAUGHING)** *Blanco Y Negro NEG 72CD*	42	3
5 Nov 94		**DEAR JOHN** *Blanco Y Negro NEG 75CD1*	48	2
22 Jun 96		**TOWN WITHOUT PITY** *Blanco Y Negro NEG 90CD1*	26	3
21 Aug 99		**FRAGILE THING** *Track TRACK 0004A* [1]	69	1
7 Mar 92		**MIRMAMA** *RCA PD 75156*	34	2
2 Jul 94	●	**EDDI READER** *Blanco Y Negro 4509961772*	4	12
20 Jul 96		**CANDYFLOSS AND MEDICINE** *Blanco Y Negro 630151202*	24	5
23 May 98		**ANGELS & ELECTRICITY** *Blanco Y Negro 3984228162*	49	2

[1] Big Country featuring Eddi Reader

See also FAIRGROUND ATTRACTION

READY FOR THE WORLD

US, male vocal / instrumental group (Singles: 8 weeks)

Date		Title / Label	Pos	Wks
26 Oct 85		**OH SHEILA** *MCA MCA 1005* ▲	50	5
14 Mar 87		**LOVE YOU DOWN** *MCA MCA 1110*	60	3

REAL & RICHARDSON featuring JOBABE

UK, male production duo and female vocalist (Singles: 1 week)

Date		Title / Label	Pos	Wks
10 May 03		**SUNSHINE ON A RAINY DAY** *Nukleuz 0489 CNUK*	69	1

REAL EMOTION

UK, male / female vocal / instrumental group (Singles: 1 week)

Date		Title / Label	Pos	Wks
1 Jul 95		**BACK FOR GOOD** *Living Beat LBECD 34*	67	1

REAL McCOY

Germany / US, male / female vocal / instrumental duo (Singles: 36 weeks, Albums: 5 weeks)

Date		Title / Label	Pos	Wks
6 Nov 93		**ANOTHER NIGHT** *Logic 74321173732* [1]	61	1
5 Nov 94	●	**ANOTHER NIGHT (re-issue)** *Logic 74321236992* [1]	2	12
28 Jan 95	●	**RUN AWAY** *Logic 74321258822* [1]	6	10
22 Apr 95		**LOVE AND DEVOTION** *Logic 74321272702* [1]	11	8
26 Aug 95		**COME AND GET YOUR LOVE** *Logic 74321301272*	19	4
11 Nov 95		**AUTOMATIC LOVER (CALL FOR LOVE)** *Logic 74321325042*	58	1
20 May 95	●	**ANOTHER NIGHT – U.S. ALBUM** *Logic 74321280972*	6	5

[1] (MC Sar &) the Real McCoy

REAL PEOPLE

UK, male vocal / instrumental group (Singles: 8 weeks, Albums: 1 week)

Date		Title / Label	Pos	Wks
16 Feb 91		**OPEN UP YOUR MIND (LET ME IN)** *CBS 6566127*	70	1
20 Apr 91		**THE TRUTH** *Columbia 6567877*	73	1
6 Jul 91		**WINDOW PANE (EP)** *Columbia 6569327*	60	1
11 Jan 92		**THE TRUTH (re-issue)** *Columbia 6576987*	41	3
23 May 92		**BELIEVER** *Columbia 6580067*	38	2
18 May 91		**THE REAL PEOPLE** *Columbia 4680841*	59	1

Tracks on Window Pane (EP): Window Pane / See Through You / Everything Must Change

REAL ROXANNE

US, female rapper – Joanne Martinez (Singles: 10 weeks)

Date		Title / Label	Pos	Wks
28 Jun 86		**(BANG ZOOM) LET'S GO-GO** *Cooltempo COOL 124* [1]	11	9
12 Nov 88		**RESPECT** *Cooltempo COOL 176*	71	1

[1] Real Roxanne with Hitman Howie Tee

REAL THING

Liverpool vocal quartet comprising brothers Chris and Eddie Amoo, Ray Lake and Dave Smith. They were the UK's best-selling black group of the late 1970s, whose biggest hits returned to the Top 10 (when re-mixed) in the 1980s (Singles: 114 weeks, Albums: 17 weeks)

Date		Title / Label	Pos	Wks
5 Jun 76	★	**YOU TO ME ARE EVERYTHING** *Pye International 7N 25709*	1	11
4 Sep 76	●	**CAN'T GET BY WITHOUT YOU** *Pye 7N 45618*	2	10
12 Feb 77		**YOU'LL NEVER KNOW WHAT YOU'RE MISSING** *Pye 7N 45662*	16	9
30 Jul 77		**LOVE'S SUCH A WONDERFUL THING** *Pye 7N 45701*	33	5
4 Mar 78		**WHENEVER YOU WANT MY LOVE** *Pye 7N 46045*	18	9
3 Jun 78		**LET'S GO DISCO** *Pye 7N 46078*	39	7
12 Aug 78		**RAININ' THROUGH MY SUNSHINE** *Pye 7N 46113*	40	8
17 Feb 79	●	**CAN YOU FEEL THE FORCE?** *Pye 7N 46147*	5	11
21 Jul 79		**BOOGIE DOWN (GET FUNKY NOW)** *Pye 7P 109*	33	6
22 Nov 80		**SHE'S A GROOVY FREAK** *Calibre CAB 105*	52	4
8 Mar 86	●	**YOU TO ME ARE EVERYTHING (THE DECADE REMIX 76-86) (re)** *PRT 7P 349*	5	13
24 May 86	●	**CAN'T GET BY WITHOUT YOU (THE SECOND DECADE REMIX)** *PRT 7P 352*	6	13
2 Aug 86		**CAN YOU FEEL THE FORCE? ('86 REMIX)** *PRT 7P 358*	24	6
25 Oct 86		**STRAIGHT TO THE HEART** *Jive JIVE 129*	71	2
6 Nov 76		**REAL THING** *Pye NSPL 18507*	34	3
7 Apr 79		**CAN YOU FEEL THE FORCE** *Pye NSPH 18601*	73	1
10 May 80		**20 GREATEST HITS** *K-Tel NE 1073*	56	2
12 Jul 86		**BEST OF THE REAL THING** *West Five NRT 1*	24	11

REAL TO REEL

US, male vocal / instrumental group (Singles: 2 weeks)

Date		Title / Label	Pos	Wks
21 Apr 84		**LOVE ME LIKE THIS** *Arista ARIST 565*	68	2

REBEL MC *UK, male rapper – Mike West*

(Singles: 52 weeks, Albums: 11 weeks)

Date		Title / Label	Pos	Wks
27 May 89		**JUST KEEP ROCKIN'** *Desire WANT 9* [1]	11	12
7 Oct 89	●	**STREET TUFF** *Desire WANT 18* [2]	3	14
31 Mar 90		**BETTER WORLD** *Desire WANT 25*	20	6
2 Jun 90		**REBEL MUSIC** *Desire WANT 31*	53	2
6 Apr 91		**WICKEDEST SOUND** *Desire WANT 40* [3]	43	6
15 Jun 91		**TRIBAL BASE** *Desire WANT 44* [4]	20	6

31 Aug 91 **BLACK MEANING GOOD** *Desire WANT 47* 73 1
21 Mar 92 **RICH AH GETTING RICHER** *Big Life BLR 70* [5] 48 4
8 Aug 92 **HUMANITY** *Big Life BLR 78* [6] 62 1
28 Apr 90 **REBEL MUSIC** *Desire LUVLP 5* 18 7
13 Jul 91 **BLACK MEANING GOOD** *Desire LUVLP 12* 23 4

[1] Double Trouble and the Rebel MC [2] Rebel MC and Double Trouble [3] Rebel MC featuring Tenor Fly [4] Rebel MC featuring Tenor Fly and Barrington Levy [5] Rebel MC introducing Little T [6] Rebel MC featuring Lincoln Thompson

REBEL ROUSERS – *See Cliff BENNETT and the REBEL ROUSERS*

REBELETTES – *See Duane EDDY*

REBELS – *See Duane EDDY*

Ivan REBROFF

Russia, male vocalist (Albums: 4 weeks) pos/wks

16 Jun 90 **THE VERY BEST OF IVAN REBROFF** *BBC REB 778* 57 4

Ezz RECO and The LAUNCHERS with Boysie GRANT

Jamaica, male vocal / instrumental group (Singles: 4 weeks) pos/wks

5 Mar 64 **KING OF KINGS** *Columbia DB 7217* 44 4

RECOIL

UK, male vocal / instrumental group (Singles: 1 week) pos/wks

21 Mar 92 **FAITH HEALER** *Mute MUTE 110* 60 1

RED *UK, male production duo – Ian Bland and Paul Fitzpatrick (Singles: 1 week)* pos/wks

20 Jan 01 **HEAVEN & EARTH** *Slinky Music SLINKY 008CD* 41 1

See also DREAM FREQUENCY; BEAT RENEGADES

RED 'N' WHITE MACHINES

UK, football supporters group (Singles: 1 week) pos/wks

24 May 03 **SOUTHAMPTON BOYS** *Centric CEN 008* 16 1

RED BOX *UK, male vocal / instrumental duo – Julian Close and Simon Toulson (Singles: 28 weeks, Albums: 4 weeks)* pos/wks

24 Aug 85 ● **LEAN ON ME (AH-LI-AYO)** *Sire W 8926* 3 14
25 Oct 86 ● **FOR AMERICA** *Sire YZ 84* 10 12
31 Jan 87 **HEART OF THE SUN** *Sire YZ 100* 71 2
6 Dec 86 **THE CIRCLE AND THE SQUARE** *Sire WX 79* 73 4

RED CAR AND THE BLUE CAR

UK, male vocal / instrumental group (Singles: 4 weeks) pos/wks

14 Dec 91 **HOME FOR CHRISTMAS DAY** *Virgin VS 1394* 44 4

RED DRAGON with Brian and Tony GOLD

Jamaica, male vocal group (Singles: 15 weeks) pos/wks

30 Jul 94 ● **COMPLIMENTS ON YOUR KISS (re)** *Mango CIDM 820* 2 15

RED EYE

UK, male instrumental / production duo (Singles: 1 week) pos/wks

3 Dec 94 **KUT IT** *Champion CHAMPCD 315* 62 1

RED 5

Germany, male producer – Thomas Kukula (Singles: 10 weeks) pos/wks

10 May 97 **I LOVE YOU ... STOP!** *Multiply CDMULTY 20* 11 5
20 Dec 97 **LIFT ME UP** *Multiply CDMULTY 30* 26 5

RED HED – *See VINYLGROOVER and The RED HED*

RED HILL CHILDREN

UK, male / female children's choir (Singles: 2 weeks) pos/wks

30 Nov 96 **WHEN CHILDREN RULE THE WORLD** *Really Useful 5797262* ..40 2

RED HOT CHILI PEPPERS (123 Top 500) *Los Angeles-based funk / punk rock quartet formed by high school pals Anthony Kiedis (v) and Michael 'Flea' Balzary (b) (currently featuring John Frusciante (g) and Chad Smith (d)). Their 'By the Way' album sold more than a million copies in both the US and UK in 2002, taking their worldwide album sales tally to more than 30 million (Singles: 91 weeks, Albums: 293 weeks)* pos/wks

10 Feb 90 **HIGHER GROUND** *EMI-USA MT 75* 55 3
23 Jun 90 **TASTE THE PAIN** *EMI-USA MT 85* 29 3
8 Sep 90 **HIGHER GROUND (re-issue)** *EMI-USA MT 88* 54 3
14 Mar 92 **UNDER THE BRIDGE** *Warner Bros. W 0084* 26 4
15 Aug 92 **BREAKING THE GIRL** *Warner Bros. W 0126* 41 3
5 Feb 94 ● **GIVE IT AWAY** *Warner Bros. W 0225CD1* 9 4
30 Apr 94 **UNDER THE BRIDGE (re-issue)** *Warner Bros. W 0237CD* 13 6
2 Sep 95 **WARPED** *Warner Bros. W 0316CD* 31 2
21 Oct 95 **MY FRIENDS** *Warner Bros. W 0317CD* 29 2
17 Feb 96 **AEROPLANE** *Warner Bros. W 0331CD* 11 3
14 Jun 97 ● **LOVE ROLLERCOASTER** *Geffen GFSTD 22188* 7 8
12 Jun 99 **SCAR TISSUE** *Warner Bros. W 490CD* 15 6
4 Sep 99 **AROUND THE WORLD** *Warner Bros. W 500CD1* 35 2
12 Feb 00 **OTHERSIDE** *Warner Bros. W 510CD1* 33 2
19 Aug 00 **CALIFORNICATION** *Warner Bros. W 534CD* 16 5
13 Jan 01 **ROAD TRIPPIN'** *Warner Bros. W 546CD1* 30 2
13 Jul 02 ● **BY THE WAY** *Warner Bros. W 580CD* 2 10
2 Nov 02 **THE ZEPHYR SONG** *Warner Bros. W 592CD* 11 10
22 Feb 03 **CAN'T STOP** *Warner Bros. W 599CD1* 22 6
28 Jun 03 **UNIVERSALLY SPEAKING** *Warner Bros. W 609CD1* 27 2
22 Nov 03 **FORTUNE FADED** *Warner Bros. W 630CD1* 11 5
12 Oct 91 **BLOOD SUGAR SEX MAGIK** *Warner Bros. WX 441* 25 83
17 Oct 92 **WHAT HITS?!** *EMI USA CDMTL 1071* 23 5
19 Nov 94 **OUT IN L.A.** *EMI CDMTL 1082* 61 1
23 Sep 95 ● **ONE HOT MINUTE** *Warner Bros. 9362457332* 2 11
19 Jun 99 ● **CALIFORNICATION** *Warner Bros. 9362473862* 5 121
20 Jul 02 ★ **BY THE WAY** *Warner Bros. 9362481402* ■ 1 67
29 Nov 03 ● **GREATEST HITS** *Warner Bros. 9362485962* ....4 5+

RED HOUSE PAINTERS

US, male vocal / instrumental group (Albums: 2 weeks) pos/wks

5 Jun 93 **RED HOUSE PAINTERS** *4AD DAD 3008CD* 63 1
30 Oct 93 **RED HOUSE PAINTERS** *4AD CAD 3016CD* 68 1

The identically titled albums are different

RED JERRY – *See WESTBAM; LOST TRIBE*

RED NOISE – *See Bill NELSON*

RED RAT – *See CARNIVAL featuring RIP vs RED RAT; Curtis LYNCH Jr featuring Kele LE ROC and RED RAT*

RED RAW featuring 007

UK, male vocal / instrumental duo (Singles: 1 week) pos/wks

28 Oct 95 **OOH LA LA LA** *Media MCSTD 2065* 59 1

RED SNAPPER *UK, male vocal / instrumental / production group (Singles: 1 week, Albums: 2 weeks)* pos/wks

21 Nov 98 **IMAGE OF YOU** *Warp WAP 111CD* 60 1
21 Sep 96 **PRINCE BLIMEY** *Warp WARPCD 45* 60 1
10 Oct 98 **MAKING BONES** *Warp WARPCD 56* 59 1

RED VENOM – *See BIG BOSS STYLUS presents RED VENOM*

REDBONE

US, male vocal / instrumental group (Singles: 12 weeks) pos/wks

25 Sep 71 ● **THE WITCH QUEEN OF NEW ORLEANS** *Epic EPC 7351* 2 12

Sharon REDD *US, female vocalist, d. 1 May 1992 (Singles: 32 weeks, Albums: 5 weeks)* pos/wks

28 Feb 81 **CAN YOU HANDLE IT** *Epic EPC 9572* 31 8
2 Oct 82 **NEVER GIVE YOU UP** *Prelude PRL A2755* 20 9
15 Jan 83 **IN THE NAME OF LOVE** *Prelude PRL A2905* 31 5

22 Oct 83 **LOVE HOW YOU FEEL** *Prelude A3868* 39 5
1 Feb 92 **CAN YOU HANDLE IT (re-recording)** *EMI EM 219* [1] 17 5
23 Oct 82 **REDD HOTT** *Prelude PRL 25056* 59 5

[1] DNA featuring Sharon Redd

REDD KROSS

US, male vocal / instrumental group (Singles: 4 weeks) pos/wks

5 Feb 94 **VISIONARY** *This Way Up WAY 2733* 75 1
10 Sep 94 **YESTERDAY ONCE MORE** *A&M 5807932* 45 2
1 Feb 97 **GET OUT OF MYSELF** *This Way Up WAY 5466* 63 1

The listed flip side of 'Yesterday Once More' was 'Superstar' by Sonic Youth

REDD SQUARE featuring Tiff LACEY

UK, male production group and female vocalist (Singles: 1 week) pos/wks

26 Oct 02 **IN YOUR HANDS** *Inferno CDFERN 50* 64 1

Otis REDDING (138 Top 500)

Peerless singer / songwriter, b. 9 Sep 1941, Georgia, US, d. 10 Dec 1967. He was one of the first and most influential Sixties soul stars. He replaced Elvis as the World's Top Male Singer in a Melody Maker poll shortly before his death in a plane crash (Singles: 124 weeks, Albums: 235 weeks) pos/wks

25 Nov 65 **MY GIRL** *Atlantic AT 4050* 11 16
7 Apr 66 **(I CAN'T GET NO) SATISFACTION** *Atlantic AT 4080* 33 4
14 Jul 66 **MY LOVER'S PRAYER** *Atlantic 584 019* 37 6
25 Aug 66 **I CAN'T TURN YOU LOOSE** *Atlantic 584 030* 29 8
24 Nov 66 **FA FA FA FA FA (SAD SONG)** *Atlantic 584 049* 23 9
26 Jan 67 **TRY A LITTLE TENDERNESS** *Atlantic 584 070* 46 4
23 Mar 67 **DAY TRIPPER** *Stax 601 005* 43 6
4 May 67 **LET ME COME ON HOME** *Stax 601 007* 48 1
15 Jun 67 **SHAKE** *Stax 601 011* 28 10
19 Jul 67 **TRAMP** *Stax 601 012* [1] 18 11
11 Oct 67 **KNOCK ON WOOD** *Stax 601 021* [1] 35 5
14 Feb 68 **MY GIRL (re-issue)** *Atlantic 584 092* 36 9
21 Feb 68 ● **(SITTIN' ON) THE DOCK OF THE BAY** *Stax 601 031* ▲ 3 15
29 May 68 **THE HAPPY SONG (DUM-DUM)** *Stax 601 040* 24 5
31 Jul 68 **HARD TO HANDLE** *Atlantic 584 199* 15 12
9 Jul 69 **LOVE MAN** *Atco 226 001* 43 3
19 Feb 66 ● **OTIS BLUE / OTIS REDDING SINGS SOUL** *Atlantic ATL 5041* 6 21
23 Apr 66 **SOUL BALLADS** *Atlantic ATL 5029* 30 1
23 Jul 66 **THE SOUL ALBUM** *Atlantic 587011* 22 9
21 Jan 67 **OTIS BLUE (re-issue)** *Atlantic 587036* 23 16
21 Jan 67 ● **OTIS REDDING'S DICTIONARY OF SOUL** *Atlantic 588050* 7 54
29 Apr 67 **PAIN IN MY HEART** *Atlantic 587042* 28 9
1 Jul 67 **KING & QUEEN** *Atlantic 589007* [1] 18 17
10 Feb 68 ● **HISTORY OF OTIS REDDING** *Volt S 418* 2 43
30 Mar 68 **OTIS REDDING IN EUROPE** *Stax 589016* 14 16
1 Jun 68 ★ **DOCK OF THE BAY** *Stax 231001* 1 15
12 Oct 68 **THE IMMORTAL OTIS REDDING** *Atlantic 588113* 19 8
11 Sep 93 **DOCK OF THE BAY – THE DEFINITIVE COLLECTION (re-issue)** *Atlantic 9548317092* 44 18
11 Nov 00 **THE VERY BEST OF OTIS REDDING** *Atco 9548380872* 26 8

[1] Otis Redding and Carla Thomas [1] Otis Redding and Carla Thomas

Helen REDDY

Australia, female vocalist (Singles: 18 weeks, Albums: 27 weeks) pos/wks

18 Jan 75 ● **ANGIE BABY** *Capitol CL 15799* ▲ 5 10
28 Nov 81 **I CAN'T SAY GOODBYE TO YOU** *MCA 744* 43 8
8 Feb 75 **FREE AND EASY** *Capitol EST 11348* 17 9
14 Feb 76 ● **THE BEST OF HELEN REDDY** *Capitol EST 11467* 5 18

REDHEAD KINGPIN and the FBI

US, male rapper – David Guppy, and rap group (Singles: 11 weeks, Albums: 3 weeks) pos/wks

22 Jul 89 **DO THE RIGHT THING** *10 TEN 271* 13 10
2 Dec 89 **SUPERBAD SUPERSLICK** *10 TEN 286* 68 1
9 Sep 89 **A SHADE OF RED** *10 DIX 85* 35 3

REDMAN

US, male rapper – Reggie Noble (Singles: 38 weeks, Albums: 7 weeks) pos/wks

25 Apr 98 **RAP SCHOLAR** *East West E 3853CD* [1] 42 1
30 May 98 **MADE IT BACK** *Parlophone Rhythm CDRHYTHM 11* [2] 21 3
24 Oct 98 ● **HOW DEEP IS YOUR LOVE (re)** *Island Black Music CID 725* [3] 9 8
12 Jun 99 **DA GOODNESS** *Def Jam 8709232* 52 1
22 Jul 00 **OOOH** *Tommy Boy TBCD 2102* [4] 29 2
15 Sep 01 **SMASH SUMTHIN'** *Def Jam 5886932* [5] 11 7
31 Aug 02 **SMASH SUMTHIN' (re-mix)** *Kaos KAOSCD 003* [6] 47 2
23 Nov 02 ★ **DIRRTY** *RCA 74321962722* [7] ■ 1 9
11 Jan 03 **REACT** *J 74321988492* [8] 14 5
9 Oct 99 **BLACKOUT!** *Def Jam 5466092* [1] 45 3
9 Jun 01 **MALPRACTICE** *Def Jam 5483812* 57 4

[1] Das EFX featuring Redman [2] Beverley Knight featuring Redman [3] Dru Hill featuring Redman [4] De La Soul featuring Redman [5] Redman featuring Adam F [6] Adam F featuring Redman [7] Christina Aguilera featuring Redman [8] Erick Sermon featuring Redman [1] Method Man and Redman

REDNEX

Sweden, male / female vocal / instrumental group (Singles: 23 weeks) pos/wks

17 Dec 94 ★ **COTTON EYE JOE** *Internal Affairs KGBCD 016* 1 16
25 Mar 95 **OLD POP IN AN OAK** *Internal Affairs KGBD 019* 12 6
21 Oct 95 **WILD 'N FREE** *Internal Affairs KGBD 024* 55 1

REDS UNITED

UK, male vocal group – 40 Manchester United FC fans (Singles: 13 weeks) pos/wks

6 Dec 97 **SING UP FOR THE CHAMPIONS** *Music Collection MANUCDP 2* 12 9
9 May 98 **UNITED CALYPSO '98** *Music Collection MANUCDP 3* 33 4

REDSKINS

UK, male vocal / instrumental trio (Singles: 12 weeks, Albums: 4 weeks) pos/wks

10 Nov 84 **KEEP ON KEEPIN' ON** *Decca F 1* 43 5
22 Jun 85 **BRING IT DOWN (THIS INSANE THING)** *Decca F 2* 33 5
22 Feb 86 **THE POWER IS YOURS** *Decca F 3* 59 2
22 Mar 86 **NEITHER WASHINGTON NOR MOSCOW** *Decca FLP 1* 31 4

Alex REECE

UK, male producer (Singles: 7 weeks, Albums: 5 weeks) pos/wks

16 Dec 95 **FEEL THE SUNSHINE** *Blunted Vinyl BLNCD 016* 69 1
11 May 96 **FEEL THE SUNSHINE (re-mix)** *Fourth & Broadway BRCD 332* 26 3
27 Jul 96 **CANDLES** *Fourth & Broadway BRCD 333* 33 2
18 Nov 96 **ACID LAB** *Fourth & Broadway BRCD 344* 64 1
17 Aug 96 **SO FAR** *Fourth & Broadway BRCD 621* 19 5

Jimmy REED

US, male vocalist / instrumentalist – guitar, d. 29 Aug 1976 (Singles: 2 weeks) pos/wks

10 Sep 64 **SHAME, SHAME, SHAME** *Stateside SS 330* 45 2

Les REED – *See Donald PEERS*

Lou REED

US, male vocalist – Lou Firbank (Singles: 19 weeks, Albums: 95 weeks) pos/wks

12 May 73 ● **WALK ON THE WILD SIDE** *RCA 2303* 10 9
17 Jan 87 **SOUL MAN** *A&M AM 364* [1] 30 10
21 Apr 73 **TRANSFORMER** *RCA Victor LSP 4807* 13 26
20 Oct 73 ● **BERLIN** *RCA Victor RS 1002* 7 5
16 Mar 74 **ROCK 'N' ROLL ANIMAL** *RCA Victor APLI 0472* 26 1
14 Feb 76 **CONEY ISLAND BABY** *RCA Victor RS 1035* 52 1
3 Jul 82 **TRANSFORMER (re-issue)** *RCA INTS 5061* 91 2
9 Jun 84 **NEW SENSATIONS** *RCA PL 84998* 92 1
24 May 86 **MISTRIAL** *RCA PL 87190* 69 1
28 Jan 89 **NEW YORK** *Sire WX 246* 14 22
7 Oct 89 **RETRO** *RCA PL 90389* 29 5
5 May 90 **SONGS FOR DRELLA** *Sire WX 345* [1] 22 5
25 Jan 92 ● **MAGIC AND LOSS** *Sire 7599266622* 6 6
28 Oct 95 **THE BEST OF LOU REED AND THE VELVET UNDERGROUND** *Global Television RADCD 21* [2] 56 4
2 Mar 96 **SET THE TWILIGHT REELING** *Warner Bros. 9362461592* 26 2

7 Feb 98	**TRANSFORMER (2nd re-issue)** *RCA ND 83806*	16	10
15 Apr 00	**ECSTASY** *Reprise 9362474252*	54	1
24 May 03	**NYC MAN** *BMG 74321984012*	31	3

[1] Sam Moore and Lou Reed [1] Lou Reed and John Cale [2] Lou Reed and the Velvet Underground

See also John CALE; VELVET UNDERGROUND

Dan REED NETWORK *US, male vocal / instrumental group (Singles: 16 weeks, Albums: 6 weeks)*

		pos/wks	
20 Jan 90	**COME BACK BABY** *Mercury DRN 2*	51	3
17 Mar 90	**RAINBOW CHILD** *Mercury DRN 3*	60	3
21 Jul 90	**STARDATE 1990 / RAINBOW CHILD (re-issue)** *Mercury DRN 4*	39	4
8 Sep 90	**LOVER / MONEY** *Mercury DRN 5*	45	3
13 Jul 91	**MIX IT UP** *Mercury MER 345*	49	2
21 Sep 91	**BABY NOW I** *Mercury MER 352*	65	1
4 Nov 89	**SLAM** *Mercury 8388681*	66	2
27 Jul 91	**THE HEAT** *Mercury 8488551*	15	4

Michael REED ORCHESTRA – *See Richard HARTLEY / Michael REED ORCHESTRA*

Don REEDMAN – *See Jeff JARRATT and Don REEDMAN*

REEF *UK, male vocal / instrumental group (Singles: 48 weeks, Albums: 55 weeks)*

		pos/wks	
15 Apr 95	**GOOD FEELING** *Sony S2 6613602*	24	4
3 Jun 95	**NAKED** *Sony S2 6620622*	11	5
5 Aug 95	**WEIRD** *Sony S2 6622772*	19	3
2 Nov 96 ●	**PLACE YOUR HANDS** *Sony S2 6635712*	6	7
25 Jan 97 ●	**COME BACK BRIGHTER** *Sony S2 6640972*	8	5
5 Apr 97	**CONSIDERATION** *Sony S2 6643125*	13	4
2 Aug 97	**YER OLD** *Sony S2 6647032*	21	3
10 Apr 99	**I'VE GOT SOMETHING TO SAY** *Sony S2 6669542*	15	6
5 Jun 99	**SWEETY** *Sony S2 6673732*	46	1
11 Sep 99	**NEW BIRD** *Sony S2 6678512*	73	1
12 Aug 00	**SET THE RECORD STRAIGHT** *Sony S2 6695952*	19	5
16 Dec 00	**SUPERHERO** *Sony S2 66999382*	55	1
19 May 01	**ALL I WANT** *Sony S2 6708222*	51	1
25 Jan 03	**GIVE ME YOUR LOVE** *Sony S2 6731645*	44	1
28 Jun 03	**WASTER** *Snapper / Reef SMASCD 051*	56	1
1 Jul 95 ●	**REPLENISH** *Sony S2 4806982*	9	11
8 Feb 97 ★	**GLOW** *Sony S2 4869402* ■	1	32
1 May 99 ●	**RIDES** *Sony S2 4928822*	3	7
2 Sep 00	**GETAWAY** *Sony S2 4988912*	15	4
8 Feb 03	**TOGETHER – THE BEST OF** *Sony S2 5094352*	52	1

REEL *Ireland, male vocal group (Singles: 3 weeks)*

		pos/wks	
24 Nov 01	**LIFT ME UP** *Universal TV 0154632*	39	1
8 Jun 02	**YOU TAKE ME AWAY** *Universal TV 0190172*	31	2

REEL BIG FISH *US, male vocal / instrumental group (Singles: 1 week)*

		pos/wks	
6 Apr 02	**SOLD OUT (EP)** *Jive 9270002*	62	1

Tracks on Sold Out (EP): Sell Out / Take on Me / Hungry Like the Wolf

REEL 2 REAL featuring The MAD STUNTMAN *US, male vocal / production duo – Erick Morillo and Mark 'The Mad Stuntman' Quashie (Singles: 53 weeks, Albums: 8 weeks)*

		pos/wks	
12 Feb 94 ●	**I LIKE TO MOVE IT** *Positiva CDTIV 10*	5	20
2 Jul 94 ●	**GO ON MOVE** *Positiva CDTIV 15*	7	9
1 Oct 94	**CAN YOU FEEL IT** *Positiva CDTIV 22*	13	5
3 Dec 94	**RAISE YOUR HANDS** *Positiva CDTIV 27*	14	6
1 Apr 95	**CONWAY** *Positiva CDTIVS 30*	27	4
6 Jul 96 ●	**JAZZ IT UP** *Positiva CDTIV 59* [1]	7	7
5 Oct 96	**ARE YOU READY FOR SOME MORE** *Positiva CDTIV 56* [1]	24	2
22 Oct 94 ●	**MOVE IT!** *Positiva CDTIVA 1003*	8	8

[1] Reel 2 Real

See also LIL MO' YIN YANG; Erick 'More' MORILLO presents RAW; PIANOHEADS

REELISTS *UK, male vocal / production duo – Kaywan Qazzaz and Saif Naqui (Singles: 13 weeks)*

		pos/wks	
19 Jan 02 ●	**HATERS** *Relentless RELENT 23CD* [1]	8	7
25 May 02	**FREAK MODE (re)** *Go Beat GOBCD 45*	16	6

[1] So Solid Crew presents Mr Shabz featuring MBD and The Reelists

Maureen REES *UK, female TV learner driver / vocalist (Singles: 4 weeks)*

		pos/wks	
20 Dec 97	**DRIVING IN MY CAR** *Eagle EAGXS 014*	49	4

Tony REES and The COTTAGERS *UK, male vocal group of Fulham FC supporters (Singles: 1 week)*

		pos/wks	
10 May 75	**VIVA EL FULHAM** *Sonet SON 2059*	46	1

REESE PROJECT *US, male producer – Kevin Saunderson (Singles: 7 weeks)*

		pos/wks	
8 Aug 92	**THE COLOUR OF LOVE** *Network NWK 51*	52	2
12 Dec 92	**I BELIEVE** *Network NWKT 63*	74	1
13 Mar 93	**SO DEEP** *Network NWKCD 68*	54	2
24 Sep 94	**THE COLOUR OF LOVE (re-mix)** *Network NWKCD 81*	55	1
6 May 95	**DIRECT-ME** *Network NWKCD 87*	44	1

Conner REEVES *UK, male vocalist (Singles: 18 weeks, Albums: 8 weeks)*

		pos/wks	
30 Aug 97	**MY FATHER'S SON** *Wildstar CDWILD 1*	12	5
22 Nov 97	**EARTHBOUND** *Wildstar CDWILD 2*	14	4
11 Apr 98	**READ MY MIND** *Wildstar CXWILD 4*	19	4
3 Oct 98	**SEARCHING FOR A SOUL** *Wildstar CDWILD 6*	28	2
4 Sep 99	**BEST FRIEND** *WEA WEA 221CD1* [1]	23	3
6 Dec 97	**EARTHBOUND** *Wildstar CDWILD 3*	25	8

[1] Mark Morrison and Conner Reeves

Jim REEVES (36 Top 500) *Internationally acclaimed velvet-voiced vocalist b. 20 Aug 1924, Texas, US, d. 31 Jul 1964. 'Gentleman Jim', who managed only two hit LPs in his lifetime, then 27 posthumously, had a record-breaking eight albums simultaneously in the UK chart three months after his death (Singles: 322 weeks, Albums: 405 weeks)*

		pos/wks	
24 Mar 60	**HE'LL HAVE TO GO (re)** *RCA 1168*	12	31
16 Mar 61	**WHISPERING HOPE** *RCA 1223*	50	1
23 Nov 61	**YOU'RE THE ONLY GOOD THING (THAT HAPPENED TO ME)** *RCA 1261*	17	19
28 Jun 62	**ADIOS AMIGO** *RCA 1293*	23	21
22 Nov 62	**I'M GONNA CHANGE EVERYTHING** *RCA 1317*	42	2
13 Jun 63 ●	**WELCOME TO MY WORLD** *RCA 1342*	6	15
17 Oct 63	**GUILTY** *RCA 1364*	29	7
20 Feb 64 ●	**I LOVE YOU BECAUSE** *RCA 1385*	5	39
18 Jun 64 ●	**I WON'T FORGET YOU (re)** *RCA 1400*	3	26
5 Nov 64 ●	**THERE'S A HEARTACHE FOLLOWING ME** *RCA 1423*	6	13
4 Feb 65 ●	**IT HURTS SO MUCH (TO SEE YOU GO)** *RCA 1437*	8	10
15 Apr 65	**NOT UNTIL THE NEXT TIME** *RCA 1446*	13	12
6 May 65	**HOW LONG HAS IT BEEN** *RCA 1445*	45	5
15 Jul 65	**THIS WORLD IS NOT MY HOME** *RCA 1412*	22	9
11 Nov 65	**IS IT REALLY OVER** *RCA 1488*	17	9
18 Aug 66 ★	**DISTANT DRUMS** *RCA 1537*	1	25
2 Feb 67	**I WON'T COME IN WHILE HE'S THERE** *RCA 1563*	12	11
26 Jul 67	**TRYING TO FORGET** *RCA 1611*	33	5
22 Nov 67	**I HEARD A HEART BREAK LAST NIGHT** *RCA 1643*	38	6
27 Mar 68	**PRETTY BROWN EYES** *RCA 1672*	33	5
25 Jun 69	**WHEN TWO WORLDS COLLIDE** *RCA 1830*	17	17
6 Dec 69	**BUT YOU LOVE ME DADDY** *RCA 1899*	15	16
21 Mar 70	**NOBODY'S FOOL** *RCA 1915*	32	5
12 Sep 70	**ANGELS DON'T LIE (re)** *RCA 1997*	32	3
26 Jun 71	**I LOVE YOU BECAUSE (re-issue) / HE'LL HAVE TO GO (re-issue) / MOONLIGHT & ROSES** *RCA Maximillion 2092*	34	8
19 Feb 72	**YOU'RE FREE TO GO** *RCA 2174*	48	2
28 Mar 64 ●	**GOOD 'N' COUNTRY** *RCA Camden CDN 5114*	10	34
9 May 64 ●	**GENTLEMAN JIM** *RCA RD 7541*	3	23
15 Aug 64	**INTERNATIONAL JIM REEVES** *RCA RD 7577*	11	15
15 Aug 64 ●	**A TOUCH OF VELVET** *RCA RD 7521*	8	9

			pos	wks
22 Aug 64		**HE'LL HAVE TO GO** *RCA RD 27176*	16	4
29 Aug 64		**THE INTIMATE JIM REEVES** *RCA RD 27193*	12	4
29 Aug 64	●	**GOD BE WITH YOU** *RCA RD 7636*	10	10
5 Sep 64	●	**MOONLIGHT AND ROSES** *RCA RD 7639*	2	51
19 Sep 64		**COUNTRY SIDE OF JIM REEVES** *RCA Camden CDN 5100*	12	5
26 Sep 64		**WE THANK THEE** *RCA RD 7637*	17	3
28 Nov 64	●	**TWELVE SONGS OF CHRISTMAS** *RCA RD 7663*	3	17
30 Jan 65	●	**THE BEST OF JIM REEVES** *RCA RD 7666*	3	47
10 Apr 65		**HAVE I TOLD YOU LATELY THAT I LOVE YOU** *RCA Camden CDN 5122*	12	5
22 May 65		**THE JIM REEVES WAY** *RCA RD 7694*	16	4
5 Nov 66	●	**DISTANT DRUMS** *RCA Victor RD 7814*	2	34
18 Jan 69		**A TOUCH OF SADNESS** *RCA SF 7978*	15	5
5 Jul 69	★	**ACCORDING TO MY HEART** *RCA International INTS 1013*	1	14
23 Aug 69		**JIM REEVES AND SOME FRIENDS** *RCA SF 8022*	24	4
29 Nov 69		**ON STAGE** *RCA SF 8047*	13	4
26 Dec 70		**MY CATHEDRAL** *RCA SF 8146*	48	2
3 Jul 71		**JIM REEVES WRITES YOU A RECORD** *RCA SF 8176*	47	2
7 Aug 71	●	**JIM REEVES' GOLDEN RECORDS** *RCA International INTS 1070*	9	21
14 Aug 71	●	**THE INTIMATE JIM REEVES (re-issue)** *RCA International INTS 1256*	8	15
21 Aug 71		**GIRLS I HAVE KNOWN** *RCA International INTS 1140*	35	5
27 Nov 71		**A TOUCH OF VELVET (re-issue)** *RCA International INTS 1089*	49	2
27 Nov 71	●	**TWELVE SONGS OF CHRISTMAS (re-issue)** *RCA International INTS 1188*	3	6
15 Apr 72		**MY FRIEND** *RCA SF 8258*	32	5
20 Sep 75	★	**40 GOLDEN GREATS** *Arcade ADEP 16*	1	25
6 Sep 80		**COUNTRY GENTLEMAN** *K-Tel NE 1088*	53	4
8 Aug 92	●	**THE DEFINITIVE JIM REEVES** *Arcade ARC 94982*	9	10
28 Sep 96		**THE ULTIMATE COLLECTION** *RCA Victor 74321410872*	17	6
5 Jul 03		**GENTLEMAN JIM – DEFINITIVE COLLECTION** *RCA 82876530372*	21	10

Martha REEVES and The VANDELLAS

US, female vocal trio (Singles: 85 weeks)

			pos	wks
29 Oct 64		**DANCING IN THE STREET** *Stateside SS 345* [1]	28	8
1 Apr 65		**NOWHERE TO RUN** *Tamla Motown TMG 502* [1]	26	8
1 Dec 66		**I'M READY FOR LOVE** *Tamla Motown TMG 582* [1]	22	8
30 Mar 67		**JIMMY MACK (re)** *Tamla Motown TMG 599* [1]	21	21
17 Jan 68		**HONEY CHILE** *Tamla Motown TMG 636*	30	9
15 Jan 69	●	**DANCING IN THE STREET (re-issue)** *Tamla Motown TMG 684*	4	12
16 Apr 69		**NOWHERE TO RUN (re-issue)** *Tamla Motown TMG 694*	42	3
13 Feb 71		**FORGET ME NOT** *Tamla Motown TMG 762*	11	8
8 Jan 72		**BLESS YOU** *Tamla Motown TMG 794*	33	5
23 Jul 88		**NOWHERE TO RUN (2nd re-issue)** *A&M AM 444*	52	3

[1] Martha and The Vandellas

The listed flip side of 'Nowhere to Run' in 1988 was 'I Got You (I Feel Good)' by James Brown. 'Jimmy Mack' re-entry peaked at No.21 in 1970

Vic REEVES *UK, male comedian / vocalist – Jim Moir (Singles: 29 weeks, Albums: 9 weeks)*

			pos	wks
27 Apr 91	●	**BORN FREE** *Sense SIGH 710* [1]	6	6
26 Oct 91	★	**DIZZY** *Sense SIGH 712* [2]	1	12
14 Dec 91		**ABIDE WITH ME** *Sense SIGH 713*	47	3
8 Jul 95	●	**I'M A BELIEVER** *Parlophone CDR 6412* [3]	3	8
16 Nov 91		**I WILL CURE YOU** *Sense SIGH 111*	16	9

[1] Vic Reeves and The Roman Numerals [2] Vic Reeves and The Wonder Stuff
[3] EMF and Reeves and Mortimer

REFLEX featuring MC VIPER *UK, male production duo – Danny Harrison and Julian Jonah, and male rapper (Singles: 1 week)*

			pos	wks
19 May 01		**PUT YOUR HANDS UP** *Gusto CDGUS 2*	72	1

See also 187 LOCKDOWN

REFUGEE ALLSTARS – *See FUGEES; Wyclef JEAN*

REFUGEE CAMP ALLSTARS – *See Lauryn HILL*

Joan REGAN *UK, female vocalist (Singles: 62 weeks)*

			pos	wks
11 Dec 53	●	**RICOCHET (re)** *Decca F 10193* [1]	8	5
14 May 54	●	**SOMEONE ELSE'S ROSES** *Decca F 10257*	5	8
1 Oct 54	●	**IF I GIVE MY HEART TO YOU (re)** *Decca F 10373*	3	11
5 Nov 54		**WAIT FOR ME, DARLING** *Decca F 10362* [2]	18	1
25 Mar 55	●	**PRIZE OF GOLD** *Decca F 10432*	6	8
6 May 55		**OPEN UP YOUR HEART** *Decca F 10474* [3]	19	1
1 May 59	●	**MAY YOU ALWAYS** *HMV POP 593*	9	16
5 Feb 60		**HAPPY ANNIVERSARY (re)** *Pye 7N 15238*	29	2
28 Jul 60		**PAPA LOVES MAMA** *Pye 7N 15278*	29	8
24 Nov 60		**ONE OF THE LUCKY ONES** *Pye 7N 15310*	47	1
5 Jan 61		**IT MUST BE SANTA** *Pye 7N 15303*	42	1

[1] Joan Regan with The Squadronaires [2] Joan Regan with The Johnston Brothers
[3] Joan and Rusty Regan

REGENTS

UK, male / female vocal / instrumental group (Singles: 14 weeks)

			pos	wks
22 Dec 79		**7 TEEN** *Rialto TREB 111*	11	12
7 Jun 80		**SEE YOU LATER** *Arista ARIST 350*	55	2

REGGAE BOYZ

Jamaica, male vocal / instrumental group (Singles: 1 week)

			pos	wks
27 Jun 98		**KICK IT** *Universal MCSTD 40167*	59	1

REGGAE PHILHARMONIC ORCHESTRA *UK, male / female vocal / instrumental group (Singles: 11 weeks)*

			pos	wks
19 Nov 88		**MINNIE THE MOOCHER** *Mango IS 378*	35	9
28 Jul 90		**LOVELY THING** *Mango MNG 742* [1]	71	2

[1] Reggae Philharmonic Orchestra featuring Jazzy Joyce

REGGAE REVOLUTION – *See Pato BANTON*

REGGIE – *See TECHNOTRONIC*

REGINA *US, female vocalist (Singles: 3 weeks)*

			pos	wks
1 Feb 86		**BABY LOVE** *Funkin' Marvellous MARV 01*	50	3

REID *UK, male vocal group (Singles: 12 weeks)*

			pos	wks
8 Oct 88		**ONE WAY OUT** *Syncopate SY 16*	66	2
11 Feb 89		**REAL EMOTION** *Syncopate SY 24*	65	2
15 Apr 89		**GOOD TIMES** *Syncopate SY 27*	55	6
21 Oct 89		**LOVIN' ON THE SIDE** *Syncopate REID 1*	71	2

Ellen REID – *See CRASH TEST DUMMIES*

John REID – *See NIGHTCRAWLERS featuring John REID*

Junior REID – *See COLDCUT; RAGGA TWINS; SOUP DRAGONS*

Mike REID *UK, male actor / comedian (Singles: 10 weeks)*

			pos	wks
22 Mar 75	●	**THE UGLY DUCKLING** *Pye 7N 45434*	10	8
24 Apr 99		**THE MORE I SEE YOU** *Telstar TV CDSTAS 3049* [1]	46	2

[1] Barbara Windsor and Mike Reid

Neil REID

UK, male vocalist (Singles: 26 weeks, Albums: 18 weeks)

			pos	wks
1 Jan 72	●	**MOTHER OF MINE** *Decca F 13264*	2	20
8 Apr 72		**THAT'S WHAT I WANT TO BE (re)** *Decca F 13300*	45	6
5 Feb 72	★	**NEIL REID** *Decca SKL 5122*	1	16
2 Sep 72		**SMILE** *Decca SKL 5136*	47	2

Patrick REID – *See POB featuring DJ Patrick REID*

Maggie REILLY – *See Mike OLDFIELD*

Keith RELF *UK, male vocalist, d. 14 May 1976 (Singles: 1 week)*

			pos	wks
26 May 66		**MR ZERO** *Columbia DB 7920*	50	1

See also YARDBIRDS

MOST NO.1 ALBUMS

The champion UK chart-toppers, the Fab Four, were even more successful Stateside with 19 No.1 LPs. Ties are decided by weeks at the top spot, then weeks at No.2 if still level.

1. BEATLES – 15 No.1 albums
2. ELVIS PRESLEY – 10 No.1 albums
3. ROLLING STONES – 10 No.1 albums
4. ABBA – 9 No.1 albums
5. QUEEN – 9 No.1 albums
6. MADONNA – 8 No.1 albums
7. DAVID BOWIE – 8 No.1 albums
8. MICHAEL JACKSON – 8 No.1 albums
9. LED ZEPPELIN – 8 No.1 albums
10. U2 – 8 No.1 albums
11. CLIFF RICHARD – 7 No.1 albums
12. ROD STEWART – 7 No.1 albums
13. PAUL McCARTNEY – 7 No.1 albums
14. SHADOWS – 6 No.1 albums
15. ELTON JOHN – 6 No.1 albums
16. BOB DYLAN – 6 No.1 albums
17. POLICE – 6 No.1 albums
18. GENESIS – 6 No.1 albums
19. R.E.M. – 6 No.1 albums
20. SIMPLY RED – 5 No.1 albums

The Beatles in front of the 'Ready Steady Go!' TV cameras. Their product-promoting weekend back in the 1960s could include 'Top of the Pops' (Thursday), 'Ready Steady Go!' (Friday), 'Saturday Club' and 'Juke Box Jury' (Saturday) and 'Thank Your Lucky Stars' (Sunday)

REMBRANDTS *US, male vocal / instrumental group (Singles: 28 weeks, Albums: 5 weeks)* pos/wks

2 Sep 95 ● **I'LL BE THERE FOR YOU (THEME FROM 'FRIENDS') (re)** *East West A 4390CD* 3 27
20 Jan 96 **THIS HOUSE IS NOT A HOME** *East West A 4336CD* 58 1
23 Sep 95 **LP** *East West 7559617522* 14 5

'I'll Be There for You' re-entry made No.5 in May 1997

REMO FOUR – *See Tommy QUICKLY and The REMO FOUR*

REMY ZERO *US, male vocal / instrumental group (Singles: 1 week)* pos/wks

27 Apr 02 **SAVE ME** *Elektra E 7297CD* 55 1

RENAISSANCE *UK, male / female vocal / instrumental group (Singles: 11 weeks, Albums: 10 weeks)* pos/wks

15 Jul 78 ● **NORTHERN LIGHTS** *Warner Bros. K 17177* 10 11
21 Feb 70 **RENAISSANCE** *Island ILPS 9114* 60 1
19 Aug 78 **A SONG FOR ALL SEASONS** *Warner Bros. K 56460* 35 8
2 Jun 79 **AZUR D'OR** *Warner Bros. K 56633* 73 1

RENATO *Italy, male vocalist – Renato Pagliari (Albums: 14 weeks)* pos/wks

25 Dec 82 **SAVE YOUR LOVE** *Lifestyle LEG 9* 26 14

See also RENÉE and RENATO

RENÉ and ANGELA *US, male / female vocal duo – Rene Moore and Angela Winbush (Singles: 15 weeks)* pos/wks

15 Jun 85 **SAVE YOUR LOVE (FOR NUMBER 1)** *Club JAB 14* [1] 66 2
7 Sep 85 **I'LL BE GOOD** *Club JAB 18* 22 10
2 Nov 85 **SECRET RENDEZVOUS** *Champion CHAMP 5* 54 3

[1] René and Angela featuring Kurtis Blow

RENÉ and YVETTE *UK, male / female vocal duo (Singles: 4 weeks)* pos/wks

22 Nov 86 **JE T'AIME ('ALLO 'ALLO) / RENÉ DMC (DEVASTATING MACHO CHARISMA)** *Sedition EDIT 3319* 57 4

Nicole RENEE *US, female vocalist (Singles: 1 week)* pos/wks

12 Dec 98 **STRAWBERRY** *Atlantic AT 0050CD* 55 1

RENÉE and RENATO *UK / Italy, female / male vocal duo – Hilary Lester and Renato Pagliari (Singles: 22 weeks)* pos/wks

30 Oct 82 ★ **SAVE YOUR LOVE** *Hollywood HWD 003* 1 16
12 Feb 83 **JUST ONE MORE KISS** *Hollywood HWD 006* 48 6

See also RENATO

RENEGADE SOUNDWAVE *UK, male vocal / instrumental group (Singles: 7 weeks, Albums: 1 week)* pos/wks

3 Feb 90 **PROBABLY A ROBBERY** *Mute MUTE 102* 38 6
5 Feb 94 **RENEGADE SOUNDWAVE** *Mute CDMUTE 146* 64 1
24 Mar 90 **SOUNDCLASH** *Mute STUMM 63* 74 1

REPARATA and The DELRONS *US, female vocal group (Singles: 12 weeks)* pos/wks

20 Mar 68 **CAPTAIN OF YOUR SHIP** *Bell 1002* 13 10
18 Oct 75 **SHOES** *Dart 2066 562* [1] 43 2

[1] Reparata

REPRAZENT – *See Roni SIZE / REPRAZENT*

REPUBLICA *UK, male / female vocal / instrumental group (Singles: 18 weeks, Albums: 38 weeks)* pos/wks

27 Apr 96 **READY TO GO** *Deconstruction 74321326132* 43 2
1 Mar 97 **READY TO GO (re-issue)** *Deconstruction 74321421332* 13 6
3 May 97 ● **DROP DEAD GORGEOUS** *Deconstruction 74321408442* 7 7
3 Oct 98 **FROM RUSH HOUR WITH LOVE** *Deconstruction 74321610472* 20 3

15 Mar 97 ● **REPUBLICA** *Deconstruction 74321410522* 4 36
17 Oct 98 **SPEED BALLADS** *Deconstruction 74321610462* 37 2

See also SAFFRON

RESONANCE featuring The BURRELLS
US, male producer and male vocal duo (Singles: 1 week) pos/wks

26 May 01 **DJ** *Strictly Rhythm SRUKCD 02* 67 1

RESOURCE
Germany, male production / vocal group (Singles: 2 weeks) pos/wks

31 May 03 **(I JUST) DIED IN YOUR ARMS** *Substance SUBS 17CDS* 42 2

REST ASSURED *UK, male production trio (Singles: 7 weeks)* pos/wks

28 Feb 98 **TREAT INFAMY** *ffrr FCD 333* 14 7

See also GAT DECOR; PHUNKY PHANTOM

REUNION *US, male vocal group (Singles: 4 weeks)* pos/wks

21 Sep 74 **LIFE IS A ROCK (BUT THE RADIO ROLLED ME)** *RCA PB 10056* 33 4

REVELATION
UK, male / female production / vocal group (Singles: 2 weeks) pos/wks

10 May 03 **JUST BE DUB TO ME** *Multiply CDMULTY 99* 36 2

REVILLOS – *See REZILLOS*

REVIVAL 3000 *UK, male DJ / production trio (Singles: 1 week)* pos/wks

1 Nov 97 **THE MIGHTY HIGH** *Hi-Life 5718092* 47 1

REVOLTING COCKS *US, male vocal / instrumental group (Singles: 1 week, Albums: 1 week)* pos/wks

18 Sep 93 **DA YA THINK I'M SEXY** *Devotion CDDVN 111* 61 1
2 Oct 93 **LINGER FICKEN' GOOD** *Devotion CDDVN 22* 39 1

REVOLUTION – *See PRINCE*

Debbie REYNOLDS
US, female actor / vocalist (Singles: 17 weeks) pos/wks

30 Aug 57 ● **TAMMY** *Vogue-Coral Q 72274* ▲ 2 17

Jody REYNOLDS *US, male vocalist (Singles: 1 week)* pos/wks

14 Apr 79 **ENDLESS SLEEP** *Lightning LIG 9015* 66 1

'Endless Sleep' was coupled with 'To Know Him Is to Love Him' by The Teddy Bears as a double A-side

LJ REYNOLDS *US, male vocalist (Singles: 3 weeks)* pos/wks

30 Jun 84 **DON'T LET NOBODY HOLD YOU DOWN** *Club JAB 5* 53 3

REYNOLDS GIRLS *UK, female vocal duo – Linda and Aisling Reynolds (Singles: 12 weeks)* pos/wks

25 Feb 89 ● **I'D RATHER JACK** *PWL PWL 25* 8 12

REZILLOS *UK, male / female vocal / instrumental group (Singles: 21 weeks, Albums: 15 weeks)* pos/wks

12 Aug 78 **TOP OF THE POPS** *Sire SIR 4001* 17 9
25 Nov 78 **DESTINATION VENUS** *Sire SIR 4008* 43 4
18 Aug 79 **I WANNA BE YOUR MAN / I CAN'T STAND MY BABY (re)** *Sensible SAB 1* 71 2
26 Jan 80 **MOTORBIKE BEAT** *Dindisc DIN 5* [1] 45 6
5 Aug 78 **CAN'T STAND THE REZILLOS** *Sire WEA K 56530* 16 10
28 Apr 79 **MISSION ACCOMPLISHED BUT THE BEAT GOES ON** *Sire SRK 6069* 30 5

[1] Revillos

REZONANCE Q *UK, male / female production / vocal duo – Mike Di Scala and Nazene (Singles: 2 weeks)* pos/wks

1 Mar 03 **SOMEDAY** *All Around the World CDGLOBE 266* 28 2

RHIANNA *UK, female vocalist – Rhianna Kelly (Singles: 6 weeks)* pos/wks

1 Jun 02 **OH BABY** *S2 6726232* 18 5
14 Sep 02 **WORD LOVE** *S2 6730112* 41 1

RHODA with the SPECIAL AKA *UK, female vocalist and male vocal / instrumental group (Singles: 5 weeks)* pos/wks

23 Jan 82 **THE BOILER** *2 Tone CHSTT 18* 35 5

See also SPECIALS

Busta RHYMES *US, male rapper – Trevor Smith (Singles: 90 weeks, Albums: 21 weeks)* pos/wks

11 May 96 ● **WOO-HAH!! GOT YOU ALL IN CHECK** *Elektra EKR 220CD* 8 7
21 Sep 96 **IT'S A PARTY** *Elektra EKR 226CD* [1] 23 2
5 Apr 97 ● **HIT EM HIGH (THE MONSTARS' ANTHEM)** *Atlantic A 5449CD* [2] 8 6
3 May 97 **DO MY THING** *Elektra EKR 235CD* 39 1
18 Oct 97 **PUT YOUR HANDS WHERE MY EYES COULD SEE** *Elektra E 3900CD* 16 3
20 Dec 97 **DANGEROUS** *Elektra E 3877CD* 32 4
18 Apr 98 ● **TURN IT UP / FIRE IT UP** *Elektra E 3847CD* 2 10
11 Jul 98 **ONE** *Elektra E 3833CD1* [3] 23 3
30 Jan 99 ● **GIMME SOME MORE** *Elektra E 3782CD* 5 6
1 May 99 ● **WHAT'S IT GONNA BE?!** *Elektra E 3762CD1* [4] 6 7
22 Jul 00 **GET OUT** *Elektra E 7075CD* 57 1
16 Dec 00 **FIRE** *East West E 7136* 60 1
18 Aug 01 ● **ANTE UP (re)** *Epic 6717882* [5] 7 8
16 Mar 02 **BREAK YA NECK** *J 74321922332* 11 6
8 Jun 02 **PASS THE COURVOISIER – PART II** *J 74321937902* [6] 16 7
8 Feb 03 **MAKE IT CLAP** *J 82876502062* [7] 16 4
7 Jun 03 ● **I KNOW WHAT YOU WANT** *J 82876528292* [8] 3 13
29 Nov 03 **LIGHT YOUR ASS ON FIRE** *Arista 82876572512* [9] 62 1
30 Mar 96 **THE COMING** *Elektra 7559617422* 48 4
4 Oct 97 **WHEN DISASTER STRIKES ...** *Elektra 7559621542* 34 5
16 Jan 99 **EXTINCTION LEVEL EVENT/FINAL WORLD FRONT** *Elektra 7559622112* 54 7
1 Jul 00 **ANARCHY** *Elektra 7559625172* 38 1
29 Sep 01 **TURN IT UP! – THE VERY BEST** *Elektra 8122735802* 44 3
23 Mar 02 **GENESIS** *J 80813200092* 58 1

[1] Busta Rhymes featuring Zhane [2] B Real / Busta Rhymes / Coolio / LL Cool J / Method Man [3] Busta Rhymes featuring Erykah Badu [4] Busta Rhymes featuring Janet [5] M.O.P. featuring Busta Rhymes [6] Busta Rhymes featuring P Diddy and Pharrell [7] Busta Rhymes featuring Spliff Star [8] Busta Rhymes and Mariah Carey featuring the Flipmode Squad [9] Busta Rhymes featuring Pharrell

See also Syleena JOHNSON

RHYTHIM IS RHYTHIM
US, male production group (Singles: 1 week) pos/wks

11 Nov 89 **STRINGS OF LIFE** *Kool Kat KOOL 509* 74 1

RHYTHM BANGERS – *See Robbie RIVERA*

RHYTHM ETERNITY
UK, male / female vocal / instrumental group (Singles: 1 week) pos/wks

23 May 92 **PINK CHAMPAGNE** *Dead Dead Good GOOD 15T* 72 1

RHYTHM FACTOR
US, male / female vocal / instrumental group (Singles: 2 weeks) pos/wks

29 Apr 95 **YOU BRING ME JOY** *Multiply CDMULTY 4* 53 2

RHYTHM MASTERS
UK / Malta, male DJ / production duo (Singles: 4 weeks) pos/wks

16 Aug 97 **COME ON Y'ALL** *Faze 2 CDFAZE 37* 49 1
6 Dec 97 **ENTER THE SCENE** *Distinctive DISNCD 40* [1] 49 1
18 Aug 01 **UNDERGROUND** *Black & Blue NEOCD 056* 50 1
30 Mar 02 **GHETTO** *Black & Blue NEOCD 074* [2] 71 1

[1] DJ Supreme vs The Rhythm Masters [2] Rhythm Masters featuring Joe Watson

See also BIG ROOM GIRL featuring Darryl PANDY; RHYTHMATIC JUNKIES

RHYTHM-N-BASS *UK, male vocal group (Singles: 4 weeks)* pos/wks

19 Sep 92	**ROSES** *Epic 6582907*	**56**	2
3 Jul 93	**CAN'T STOP THIS FEELING** *Epic 6592002*	**59**	2

RHYTHM OF LIFE
UK, male DJ / producer – Steve Burgess (Singles: 2 weeks) pos/wks

13 May 00	**YOU PUT ME IN HEAVEN WITH YOUR TOUCH** *Xtravaganza XTRAV 4CDS*	**24**	2

RHYTHM ON THE LOOSE
UK, male producer – Geoff Hibbert (Singles: 2 weeks) pos/wks

19 Aug 95	**BREAK OF DAWN** *Six6 SIXCD 126*	**36**	2

RHYTHM QUEST
UK, male producer – Mark Hadfield (Singles: 2 weeks) pos/wks

20 Jun 92	**CLOSER TO ALL YOUR DREAMS** *Network NWK 40*	**45**	2

RHYTHM SECTION
UK, male vocal / instrumental group (Singles: 1 week) pos/wks

18 Jul 92	**MIDSUMMER MADNESS (EP)** *Rhythm Section RSEC 006*	**66**	1

Tracks on Midsummer Madness (EP): Dreamworld / Burnin' Up / Perfect Love 2am / Perfect Love 8am

RHYTHM SOURCE
UK, male / female vocal / instrumental group (Singles: 1 week) pos/wks

17 Jun 95	**LOVE SHINE** *A&M 5810672*	**74**	1

RHYTHM SPINNERS – *See Rolf HARRIS*

RHYTHMATIC
UK, male instrumental / production duo (Singles: 3 weeks) pos/wks

12 May 90	**TAKE ME BACK (re)** *Network NWK 8*	**71**	2
3 Nov 90	**FREQUENCY** *Network NWK 13*	**62**	1

RHYTHMATIC JUNKIES
UK, male vocal / production group (Singles: 1 week) pos/wks

15 May 99	**THE FEELIN (CLAP YOUR HANDS)** *Sound of Ministry RIDE 2CDS*	**67**	1

RHYTHMKILLAZ *Holland, male production duo – Rene ter Horst and Gaston Steenkist (Singles: 2 weeks)* pos/wks

31 Mar 01	**WACK ASS MF** *Incentive CENT 18 CDS*	**32**	2

See also GOODMEN; JARK PRONGO; CHOCOLATE PUMA; TOMBA VIRA; RIVA featuring Dannii MINOGUE

RIALTO *UK, male vocal / instrumental group (Singles: 8 weeks, Albums: 3 weeks)* pos/wks

8 Nov 97	**MONDAY MORNING 5: 19** *East West EW 116CD*	**37**	2
17 Jan 98	**UNTOUCHABLE** *East West EW 107CD1*	**20**	3
28 Mar 98	**DREAM ANOTHER DREAM** *East West EW 156CD1*	**39**	2
17 Oct 98	**SUMMER'S OVER** *China WOKCDR 2099*	**60**	1
25 Jul 98	**RIALTO** *China WOLCD 1086*	**21**	3

Rosie RIBBONS *UK, female vocalist (Singles: 7 weeks)* pos/wks

2 Nov 02	**BLINK** *T2 / Telstar CDSTAS 3288*	**12**	4
25 Jan 03	**A LITTLE BIT** *T2 / Telstar CDSTAS 3312*	**19**	3

Reva RICE and Greg ELLIS
UK, male / female vocal duo (Singles: 2 weeks) pos/wks

27 Mar 93	**NEXT TIME YOU FALL IN LOVE** *Really Useful RURCD 12*	**59**	2

Damien RICE *Ireland, male vocalist / instrumentalist (Singles: 2 weeks, Albums: 14 weeks)* pos/wks

1 Nov 03	**CANNONBALL** *DRM 14th Floor DR 03CD1*	**32**	2
2 Aug 03	**O** *DRM / 14th Floor 5046647882*	**23**	14

Charlie RICH *US, male vocalist / instrumentalist – keyboards, d. 25 July 1995 (Singles: 29 weeks, Albums: 28 weeks)* pos/wks

16 Feb 74 ●	**THE MOST BEAUTIFUL GIRL** *Epic EPC 1897* ▲	**2**	14
13 Apr 74	**BEHIND CLOSED DOORS** *Epic EPC 1539*	**16**	10
1 Feb 75	**WE LOVE EACH OTHER** *Epic EPC 2868*	**37**	5
23 Mar 74 ●	**BEHIND CLOSED DOORS** *Epic 65716*	**4**	26
13 Jul 74	**VERY SPECIAL LOVE SONGS** *Epic 80031*	**34**	2

Kelli RICH – *See NU SOUL featuring Kelli RICH*

Richie RICH
UK, male DJ / producer (Singles: 16 weeks, Albums: 1 week) pos/wks

16 Jul 88	**TURN IT UP** *Club JAB 68*	**48**	3
22 Oct 88	**I'LL HOUSE YOU** *Gee Street GEE 003* [1]	**22**	5
10 Dec 88	**MY DJ (PUMP IT UP SOME)** *Gee Street GEE 7*	**74**	1
2 Sep 89	**SALSA HOUSE** *ffrr F 113*	**50**	3
9 Mar 91	**YOU USED TO SALSA** *ffrr F 156* [2]	**52**	3
29 Mar 97	**STAY WITH ME** *Castle CATX 1001* [3]	**58**	1
22 Jul 89	**I CAN MAKE YOU DANCE** *Gee St. GEEA 3*	**65**	1

[1] Richie Rich meets The Jungle Brothers [2] Richie Rich featuring Ralphi Rosario [3] Richie Rich and Esera Tuaolo

'You Used to Salsa' is a remix of 'Salsa House'

RICH KIDS *UK, male vocal / instrumental group (Singles: 5 weeks, Albums: 1 week)* pos/wks

28 Jan 78	**RICH KIDS** *EMI 2738*	**24**	5
7 Oct 78	**GHOSTS OF PRINCES IN TOWERS** *EMI EMC 3263*	**51**	1

Rishi RICH PROJECT featuring Jay SEAN & JUGGY D
UK, male production / vocal / rap group – leader Rishpal Rekhi (Singles: 5 weeks) pos/wks

20 Sep 03	**DANCE WITH YOU (NACHNA TERE NAAL)** *Relentless RELCD 1*	**12**	5

Tony RICH PROJECT *US, male vocalist – Antonio Jeffries (Singles: 22 weeks, Albums: 10 weeks)* pos/wks

4 May 96 ●	**NOBODY KNOWS** *LaFace 74321356422*	**4**	17
31 Aug 96	**LIKE A WOMAN** *LaFace 74321401612*	**27**	4
14 Dec 96	**LEAVIN'** *LaFace 74321438382*	**52**	1
25 May 96	**WORDS** *LaFace 73008260222*	**27**	10

Cliff RICHARD (2 Top 500)
'The Peter Pan of Pop' – Britain's most successful solo vocalist, b. Harry Webb, 14 Oct 1940, Lucknow, India. Ex-member of Dick Teague Skiffle Group was instantly successful, and almost overnight became the UK's No.1 rock 'n' roll star despite bad press due to 'too sexy' live performances. Many successes on film, stage, TV, radio and video. He has had hits in every major market around the globe and was named World's No.1 Artist by Billboard in 1963 (with Elvis second and Shadows third). Between 1959 and 2003, Cliff had a staggering 35 Top 10 albums including seven No.1s, and had more Top 10 albums in the 1980s than any other artist. He was seen on the first 'Top of the Pops' and has appeared on the TV show more often than any other artist. He is one of the few performers to top the chart with two different recordings of the same song (Living Doll). This seemingly ageless entertainer's record number of 64 Top 10 entries now spans 43 years, and at times he held the record for being the youngest (1959) and oldest (1999) British singer to top the singles chart. Cliff, who has sold almost 21 million singles in the UK, was awarded the Outstanding Contribution to British Music trophy at the 1989 Brits, was made an OBE in 1980 and was knighted in 1995, and holds the unique achievement of a UK No.1 single in five different decades. Best-selling single: 'The Young Ones' 1,052,000 (Singles: 1154 weeks, Albums: 805 weeks) pos/wks

12 Sep 58 ●	**MOVE IT!** *Columbia DB 4178* [1]	**2**	17
21 Nov 58 ●	**HIGH CLASS BABY** *Columbia DB 4203* [1]	**7**	10
30 Jan 59	**LIVIN' LOVIN' DOLL** *Columbia DB 4249* [1]	**20**	6
8 May 59 ●	**MEAN STREAK** *Columbia DB 4290 A* [1]	**10**	9
15 May 59	**NEVER MIND** *Columbia DB 4290 B* [1]	**21**	2
10 Jul 59 ★	**LIVING DOLL (2re)** *Columbia DB 4306* [1]	**1**	23

9 Oct 59 ★ **TRAVELLIN' LIGHT** *Columbia DB 4351 B* [2] 1 17
9 Oct 59 **DYNAMITE (re)** *Columbia DB 4351 A* [2] 16 4
15 Jan 60 **EXPRESSO BONGO (EP)** *Columbia SEG 7971* [2] 14 7
22 Jan 60 ● **A VOICE IN THE WILDERNESS (re)** *Columbia DB 4398* [2] 2 16
24 Mar 60 ● **FALL IN LOVE WITH YOU** *Columbia DB 4431* [2] 2 15
30 Jun 60 ★ **PLEASE DON'T TEASE** *Columbia DB 4479* [2] 1 18
22 Sep 60 ● **NINE TIMES OUT OF TEN** *Columbia DB 4506* [2] 3 12
1 Dec 60 ★ **I LOVE YOU** *Columbia DB 4547* [2] 1 16
2 Mar 61 ● **THEME FOR A DREAM** *Columbia DB 4593* [2] 3 14
30 Mar 61 ● **GEE WHIZ IT'S YOU** *Columbia DC 756* [2] 4 14
22 Jun 61 ● **A GIRL LIKE YOU** *Columbia DB 4667* [2] 3 14
19 Oct 61 ● **WHEN THE GIRL IN YOUR ARMS IS THE GIRL IN YOUR HEART** *Columbia DB 4716* 3 15
11 Jan 62 ★ **THE YOUNG ONES** *Columbia DB 4761* [2] ◆ ■ 1 21
10 May 62 ● **I'M LOOKING OUT THE WINDOW / DO YOU WANT TO DANCE** *Columbia DB 4828* [3] 2 17
6 Sep 62 ● **IT'LL BE ME** *Columbia DB 4886* [2] 2 12
6 Dec 62 ★ **THE NEXT TIME / BACHELOR BOY** *Columbia DB 4950* [2] 1 18
21 Feb 63 ★ **SUMMER HOLIDAY** *Columbia DB 4977* [2] 1 18
9 May 63 ● **LUCKY LIPS** *Columbia DB 7034* [2] 4 15
22 Aug 63 ● **IT'S ALL IN THE GAME** *Columbia DB 7089* 2 13
7 Nov 63 ● **DON'T TALK TO HIM (re)** *Columbia DB 7150* [2] 2 14
6 Feb 64 ● **I'M THE LONELY ONE** *Columbia DB 7203* [2] 8 10
30 Apr 64 ● **CONSTANTLY** *Columbia DB 7272* 4 13
2 Jul 64 ● **ON THE BEACH** *Columbia DB 7305* [2] 7 13
8 Oct 64 ● **THE TWELFTH OF NEVER** *Columbia DB 7372* 8 11
10 Dec 64 ● **I COULD EASILY FALL** *Columbia DB 7420* [2] 6 11
11 Mar 65 ★ **THE MINUTE YOU'RE GONE** *Columbia DB 7496* 1 14
10 Jun 65 **ON MY WORD** *Columbia DB 7596* 12 10
19 Aug 65 **THE TIME IN BETWEEN** *Columbia DB 7660* [2] 22 8
4 Nov 65 ● **WIND ME UP (LET ME GO)** *Columbia DB 7745* 2 16
24 Mar 66 **BLUE TURNS TO GREY** *Columbia DB 7866* [2] 15 9
21 Jul 66 ● **VISIONS** *Columbia DB 7968* 7 12
13 Oct 66 ● **TIME DRAGS BY** *Columbia DB 8017* [2] 10 12
15 Dec 66 ● **IN THE COUNTRY** *Columbia DB 8094* [2] 6 10
16 Mar 67 ● **IT'S ALL OVER** *Columbia DB 8150* 9 10
8 Jun 67 **I'LL COME RUNNIN'** *Columbia DB 8210* 26 8
16 Aug 67 ● **THE DAY I MET MARIE** *Columbia DB 8245* 10 14
15 Nov 67 ● **ALL MY LOVE** *Columbia DB 8293* 6 12
20 Mar 68 ★ **CONGRATULATIONS** *Columbia DB 8376* 1 13
26 Jun 68 **I'LL LOVE YOU FOREVER TODAY** *Columbia DB 8437* 27 6
25 Sep 68 **MARIANNE** *Columbia DB 8476* 22 8
27 Nov 68 **DON'T FORGET TO CATCH ME** *Columbia DB 8503* [2] 21 10
26 Feb 69 **GOOD TIMES (BETTER TIMES)** *Columbia DB 8548* 12 11
28 May 69 ● **BIG SHIP** *Columbia DB 8581* 8 10
13 Sep 69 ● **THROW DOWN A LINE** *Columbia DB 8615* [4] 7 9
6 Dec 69 **WITH THE EYES OF A CHILD** *Columbia DB 8641* 20 11
21 Feb 70 **THE JOY OF LIVING** *Columbia DB 8657* [4] 25 8
6 Jun 70 ● **GOODBYE SAM, HELLO SAMANTHA** *Columbia DB 8685* 6 15
5 Sep 70 **I AIN'T GOT TIME ANYMORE** *Columbia DB 8708* 21 7
23 Jan 71 **SUNNY HONEY GIRL** *Columbia DB 8747* 19 8
10 Apr 71 **SILVERY RAIN** *Columbia DB 8774* 27 6
17 Jul 71 **FLYING MACHINE** *Columbia DB 8797* 37 7
13 Nov 71 **SING A SONG OF FREEDOM** *Columbia DB 8836* 13 12
11 Mar 72 **JESUS** *Columbia DB 8864* 35 3
26 Aug 72 **LIVING IN HARMONY** *Columbia DB 8917* 12 10
17 Mar 73 ● **POWER TO ALL OUR FRIENDS** *EMI 2012* 4 12
12 May 73 **HELP IT ALONG / TOMORROW RISING** *EMI 2022* 29 6
1 Dec 73 **TAKE ME HIGH** *EMI 2088* 27 12
18 May 74 **(YOU KEEP ME) HANGIN' ON** *EMI 2150* 13 8
7 Feb 76 **MISS YOU NIGHTS** *EMI 2376* 15 10
8 May 76 ● **DEVIL WOMAN** *EMI 2458* 9 8
21 Aug 76 **I CAN'T ASK FOR ANYTHING MORE THAN YOU** *EMI 2499* 17 8
4 Dec 76 **HEY MR DREAM MAKER** *EMI 2559* 31 5
5 Mar 77 **MY KINDA LIFE** *EMI 2584* 15 8
16 Jul 77 **WHEN TWO WORLDS DRIFT APART** *EMI 2633* 46 3
31 Mar 79 **GREEN LIGHT** *EMI 2920* 57 3
21 Jul 79 ★ **WE DON'T TALK ANYMORE** *EMI 2975* 1 14
3 Nov 79 **HOT SHOT** *EMI 5003* 46 5
2 Feb 80 ● **CARRIE** *EMI 5006* 4 10
16 Aug 80 ● **DREAMIN'** *EMI 5095* 8 10
25 Oct 80 **SUDDENLY** *Jet 7002* [5] 15 7
24 Jan 81 **A LITTLE IN LOVE** *EMI 5123* 15 8
29 Aug 81 ● **WIRED FOR SOUND** *EMI 5221* 4 9
21 Nov 81 ● **DADDY'S HOME** *EMI 5251* 2 12
17 Jul 82 ● **THE ONLY WAY OUT** *EMI 5318* 10 9
25 Sep 82 **WHERE DO WE GO FROM HERE** *EMI 5341* 60 3
4 Dec 82 **LITTLE TOWN** *EMI 5348* 11 7
19 Feb 83 ● **SHE MEANS NOTHING TO ME** *Capitol CL 276* [6] 9 9
16 Apr 83 ● **TRUE LOVE WAYS** *EMI 5385* [7] 8 8
4 Jun 83 **DRIFTING** *DJM SHEIL 1* [8] 64 2
3 Sep 83 **NEVER SAY DIE (GIVE A LITTLE BIT MORE)** *EMI 5415* 15 7
26 Nov 83 ● **PLEASE DON'T FALL IN LOVE** *EMI 5437* 7 9
31 Mar 84 **BABY YOU'RE DYNAMITE / OCEAN DEEP (re)** *EMI 5457* 27 7
3 Nov 84 **SHOOTING FROM THE HEART** *EMI RICH 1* 51 4
9 Feb 85 **HEART USER** *EMI RICH 2* 46 3
14 Sep 85 **SHE'S SO BEAUTIFUL** *EMI 5531* 17 9
7 Dec 85 **IT'S IN EVERY ONE OF US** *EMI 5537* 45 6
22 Mar 86 ★ **LIVING DOLL** *WEA YZ 65* [9] 1 11
4 Oct 86 ● **ALL I ASK OF YOU** *Polydor POSP 802* [10] 3 16
29 Nov 86 **SLOW RIVERS** *Rocket EJS 13* [11] 44 8
20 Jun 87 ● **MY PRETTY ONE** *EMI EM 4* 6 10
29 Aug 87 ● **SOME PEOPLE** *EMI EM 18* 3 10
31 Oct 87 **REMEMBER ME** *EMI EM 31* 35 4
13 Feb 88 **TWO HEARTS** *EMI EM 42* 34 3
3 Dec 88 ★ **MISTLETOE AND WINE** *EMI EM 78* 1 8
10 Jun 89 ● **THE BEST OF ME** *EMI EM 92* 2 7
26 Aug 89 ● **I JUST DON'T HAVE THE HEART** *EMI EM 101* 3 8
14 Oct 89 **LEAN ON YOU** *EMI EM 105* 17 6
9 Dec 89 **WHENEVER GOD SHINES HIS LIGHT** *Polydor VANS 2* [12] 20 6
24 Feb 90 **STRONGER THAN THAT** *EMI EM 129* 14 5
25 Aug 90 ● **SILHOUETTES** *EMI EM 152* 10 7
13 Oct 90 **FROM A DISTANCE** *EMI EM 155* 11 6
8 Dec 90 ★ **SAVIOUR'S DAY** *EMI XMAS 90* 1 7
14 Sep 91 **MORE TO LIFE** *EMI EM 205* 23 5
7 Dec 91 ● **WE SHOULD BE TOGETHER** *EMI XMAS 91* 10 6
11 Jan 92 **THIS NEW YEAR** *EMI EMS 218* 30 2
5 Dec 92 ● **I STILL BELIEVE IN YOU** *EMI EM 255* 7 6
27 Mar 93 ● **PEACE IN OUR TIME** *EMI CDEM 265* 8 5
12 Jun 93 **HUMAN WORK OF ART** *EMI CDEM 267* 24 4
2 Oct 93 **NEVER LET GO** *EMI CDEM 281* 32 3
18 Dec 93 **HEALING LOVE** *EMI CDEM 294* 19 5
10 Dec 94 **ALL I HAVE TO DO IS DREAM / MISS YOU NIGHTS (re) (re-issue)** *EMI CDEM 359* [13] 14 9
2 Oct 95 **MISUNDERSTOOD MAN** *EMI CDEM 394* 19 3
9 Dec 95 **HAD TO BE** *EMI CDEM 410* [14] 22 4
30 Mar 96 **THE WEDDING** *EMI CDEM 422* [15] 40 1
25 Jan 97 **BE WITH ME ALWAYS** *EMI CDEM 453* 52 1
24 Oct 98 ● **CAN'T KEEP THIS FEELING IN** *EMI CDEM 526* 10 4
7 Aug 99 **THE MIRACLE** *EMI / Blacknight CDEM 546* 23 2
27 Nov 99 ★ **THE MILLENNIUM PRAYER** *Papillon PROMISECD 01* 1 16
15 Dec 01 **SOMEWHERE OVER THE RAINBOW / WHAT A WONDERFUL WORLD** *Papillon CLIFF CD 1* 11 6
13 Apr 02 **LET ME BE THE ONE** *Papillon CLIFF CD2* 29 3
20 Dec 03 ● **SANTA'S LIST** *EMI SANTA 01* 5 2+
18 Apr 59 ● **CLIFF** *Columbia 33SX 1147* [1] 4 31
14 Nov 59 ● **CLIFF SINGS** *Columbia 33SX 1192* 2 36
15 Oct 60 ● **ME AND MY SHADOWS** *Columbia 33SX 1261* [2] 2 33
22 Apr 61 ● **LISTEN TO CLIFF** *Columbia 33SX 1320* 2 28
21 Oct 61 ★ **21 TODAY** *Columbia 33SX 1368* 1 16
23 Dec 61 ★ **THE YOUNG ONES (FILM SOUNDTRACK)** *Columbia 33SX 1384* [3] 1 42
29 Sep 62 ● **32 MINUTES AND 17 SECONDS** *Columbia 33SX 1431* [2] 3 21
26 Jan 63 ★ **SUMMER HOLIDAY (FILM SOUNDTRACK)** *Columbia 33SX 1472* [2] 1 36
13 Jul 63 ● **CLIFF'S HIT ALBUM** *Columbia 33SX 1512* [2] 2 19
28 Sep 63 ● **WHEN IN SPAIN** *Columbia 33SX 1541* [2] 8 10
11 Jul 64 ● **WONDERFUL LIFE (FILM SOUNDTRACK)** *Columbia 33SX 1628* [2] 2 23
9 Jan 65 **HITS FROM ALADDIN AND HIS WONDERFUL LAMP (PANTOMIME)** *Columbia 33SX 1676* [2] 13 5
17 Apr 65 ● **CLIFF RICHARD** *Columbia 33SX 1709* 9 5
14 Aug 65 **MORE HITS BY CLIFF** *Columbia 33SX 1737* 20 1
8 Jan 66 **LOVE IS FOREVER** *Columbia 33SX 1769* 19 1
21 May 66 ● **KINDA LATIN** *Columbia SX 6039* 9 12

17 Dec 66 ● FINDERS KEEPERS (FILM SOUNDTRACK) *Columbia SX 6079* 2 ....6 18
7 Jan 67 CINDERELLA (PANTOMIME) *Columbia 33SCX 6103* 2 ....30 6
15 Apr 67 DON'T STOP ME NOW ... *Columbia SCX 6133* 23 9
11 Nov 67 GOOD NEWS *Columbia SCX 6167* 37 1
1 Jun 68 CLIFF IN JAPAN *Columbia SCX 6244* 29 2
16 Nov 68 ESTABLISHED 1958 *Columbia SCX 6282* 2 ....30 4
12 Jul 69 ● THE BEST OF CLIFF *Columbia SCX 6343* 5 17
27 Sep 69 SINCERELY *Columbia SCX 6357* 24 3
12 Dec 70 TRACKS 'N' GROOVES *Columbia SCX 6435* 37 2
23 Dec 72 THE BEST OF CLIFF VOLUME 2 *Columbia SCX 6519* 49 2
19 Jan 74 TAKE ME HIGH (FILM SOUNDTRACK) *EMI EMC 3016* 41 4
29 May 76 ● I'M NEARLY FAMOUS *EMI EMC 3122* 5 21
26 Mar 77 ● EVERY FACE TELLS A STORY *EMI EMC 3172* 8 10
22 Oct 77 ★ 40 GOLDEN GREATS *EMI EMTV 6* 1 19
4 Mar 78 SMALL CORNERS *EMI EMC 3219* 33 5
21 Oct 78 GREEN LIGHT *EMI EMC 3231* 25 3
17 Feb 79 ● THANK YOU VERY MUCH – REUNION CONCERT AT THE LONDON PALLADIUM *EMI EMTV 15* 2 ....5 12
15 Sep 79 ● ROCK 'N' ROLL JUVENILE *EMI EMC 3307* 3 22
13 Sep 80 ● I'M NO HERO *EMI EMA 796* 4 12
4 Jul 81 ★ LOVE SONGS *EMI EMTV 27* 1 43
26 Sep 81 ● WIRED FOR SOUND *EMI EMC 3377* 4 25
4 Sep 82 ● NOW YOU SEE ME ... NOW YOU DON'T *EMI EMC 3415* 4 14
21 May 83 ● DRESSED FOR THE OCCASION *EMI EMC 3432* 4 ....7 17
15 Oct 83 ● SILVER *EMI EMC 1077871* 7 24
14 Jul 84 20 ORIGINAL GREATS *EMI CRS 1* 2 ....43 6
1 Dec 84 THE ROCK CONNECTION *EMI CLIF 2* 43 5
26 Sep 87 ● ALWAYS GUARANTEED *EMI EMD 1004* 5 25
19 Nov 88 ★ PRIVATE COLLECTION 1979-1988 *EMI CRTV 30* 1 26
11 Nov 89 ● STRONGER *EMI EMD 1012* 7 21
17 Nov 90 ● FROM A DISTANCE ... THE EVENT *EMI CRTV 31* 3 15
30 Nov 91 ● TOGETHER WITH CLIFF RICHARD *EMI EMD 1028* 10 7
1 May 93 ★ THE ALBUM *EMI CDEMD 1043* ■ 1 15
15 Oct 94 ● THE HIT LIST *EMI CDEMTV 84* 3 21
11 Nov 95 SONGS FROM 'HEATHCLIFF' *EMI CDEMD 1091* 15 9
24 Aug 96 AT THE MOVIES – 1959-1974 *EMI CDEMD 1096* 17 3
2 Aug 97 THE ROCK 'N' ROLL YEARS *EMI CDEMD 1109* 32 3
31 Oct 98 ● REAL AS I WANNA BE *EMI 4974062* 10 9
21 Oct 00 ● THE WHOLE STORY – HIS GREATEST HITS *EMI 5293222* 6 13
17 Nov 01 WANTED *Papillon WANTED 1* 11 8
29 Nov 03 ● CLIFF AT CHRISTMAS *EMI 5934982* ....9 5+

1 Cliff Richard and The Drifters 2 Cliff Richard and the Shadows 3 Cliff Richard / The Shadows 4 Cliff and Hank 5 Olivia Newton-John and Cliff Richard 6 Phil Everly and Cliff Richard 7 Cliff Richard with the London Philharmonic Orchestra 8 Sheila Walsh and Cliff Richard 9 Cliff Richard and The Young Ones featuring Hank B Marvin 10 Cliff Richard and Sarah Brightman 11 Elton John and Cliff Richard 12 Van Morrison with Cliff Richard 13 Cliff Richard with Phil Everly / Cliff Richard 14 Cliff Richard and Olivia Newton-John 15 Cliff Richard featuring Helen Hobson 1 Cliff Richard and The Drifters 2 Cliff Richard and The Shadows 3 Cliff Richard – the Shadows with Grazina Frame 4 Cliff Richard with the London Philharmonic Orchestra

Tracks on Expresso Bongo (EP): Love / A Voice in the Wilderness / The Shrine on the Second Floor / Bongo Blues. 'Bongo Blues' features only The Shadows. 'Bachelor Boy' was listed with 'The Next Time' from 10 Jan 1963. 'Ocean Deep' listed from 28 Apr 1984 onwards. It peaked at No.41. 'Gee Whiz It's You' was an 'export' single.

Wendy RICHARD – *See Mike SARNE*

RICHARD X

UK, male producer (Singles: 16 weeks, Albums: 2 weeks) pos/wks

29 Mar 03 ● BEING NOBODY *Virgin RXCD 1* 1 ....3 11
23 Aug 03 ● FINEST DREAMS *Virgin RXCD 2* 2 ....8 5
6 Sep 03 RICHARD X PRESENTS HIS X-FACTOR VOL.1 *Virgin CDRICH1* 31 2

1 Richard X vs Liberty X 2 Richard X featuring Kelis

Keith RICHARDS

UK, male vocalist / instrumentalist – guitar (Albums: 4 weeks) pos/wks

15 Oct 88 TALK IS CHEAP *Virgin V 2554* 37 3
31 Oct 92 MAIN OFFENDER *Virgin America CDVUS 59* 45 1

See also ROLLING STONES

Lionel RICHIE (52 Top 500)

Singer / composer / producer, b. 20 Jun 1949, Alabama, US. Launched a solo career in 1982 after 12 years fronting The Commodores. Arguably the most successful US songwriter of the 1980s, who composed at least one US chart-topper per year for a record nine successive years (Singles: 186 weeks, Albums: 443 weeks) pos/wks

12 Sep 81 ● ENDLESS LOVE *Motown TMG 1240* 1 ▲ 7 12
20 Nov 82 ● TRULY *Motown TMG 1284* ▲ 6 11
29 Jan 83 YOU ARE *Motown TMG 1290* 43 7
7 May 83 MY LOVE *Motown TMG 1300* 70 3
1 Oct 83 ● ALL NIGHT LONG (ALL NIGHT) *Motown TMG 1319* ▲ 2 16
3 Dec 83 ● RUNNING WITH THE NIGHT *Motown TMG 1324* 9 12
10 Mar 84 ★ HELLO *Motown TMG 1330* ▲ 1 15
23 Jun 84 STUCK ON YOU *Motown TMG 1341* 12 12
20 Oct 84 PENNY LOVER *Motown TMG 1356* 18 7
16 Nov 85 ● SAY YOU, SAY ME *Motown ZB 40421* ▲ 8 11
26 Jul 86 ● DANCING ON THE CEILING *Motown LIO1* 7 11
11 Oct 86 LOVE WILL CONQUER ALL *Motown LIO 2* 45 5
20 Dec 86 BALLERINA GIRL / DEEP RIVER WOMAN *Motown LIO3* 17 8
28 Mar 87 SELA *Motown LIO4* 43 6
9 May 92 DO IT TO ME *Motown TMG 1407* 33 6
22 Aug 92 ● MY DESTINY *Motown TMG 1408* 7 13
28 Nov 92 LOVE OH LOVE (re) *Motown TMG 1413* 52 4
6 Apr 96 DON'T WANNA LOSE YOU *Mercury MERCD 461* 17 5
23 Nov 96 STILL IN LOVE *Mercury MERCD 477* 66 1
27 Jun 98 CLOSEST THING TO HEAVEN *Mercury 5661312* 26 2
21 Oct 00 ANGEL *Mercury 5726702* 18 5
23 Dec 00 DON'T STOP THE MUSIC *Mercury 5688992* 34 5
17 Mar 01 TENDER HEART *Mercury 5728462* 29 3
23 Jun 01 I FORGOT *Mercury 5729922* 34 2
26 Apr 03 TO LOVE A WOMAN *Mercury 0779082* 2 ....19 4
27 Nov 82 ● LIONEL RICHIE *Motown STMA 8037* 9 86
29 Oct 83 ★ CAN'T SLOW DOWN *Motown STMA 8041* ▲ 1 154
23 Aug 86 ● DANCING ON THE CEILING *Motown ZL 72412* ▲ 2 53
6 Jun 92 ★ BACK TO FRONT *Motown 5300182* ■ 1 80
20 Apr 96 LOUDER THAN WORDS *Mercury 5322412* 11 5
31 Jan 98 ● TRULY – THE LOVE SONGS *Motown / PolyGram TV 5308432* 5 21
11 Jul 98 TIME *Mercury 5585182* 31 3
28 Oct 00 ● RENAISSANCE *Island 5482222* 6 24
7 Dec 02 ● ENCORE *Mercury 0633482* 8 11
22 Nov 03 ● THE DEFINITIVE COLLECTION *Universal TV 9861394* 1 ....10 6+

1 Diana Ross and Lionel Richie 2 Lionel Richie featuring Enrique Iglesias
1 Lionel Richie / The Commodores

'Deep River Woman' was listed only from 17 Jan 1987. It has the following credit: background vocal 'Alabama'

Shane RICHIE

UK, male actor / vocalist (Singles: 4 weeks) pos/wks

6 Dec 03 ● I'M YOUR MAN *BMG 82876578582* ....2 4+

Jonathan RICHMAN and the MODERN LOVERS

US, male vocal / instrumental group (Singles: 27 weeks, Albums: 3 weeks) pos/wks

16 Jul 77 ROADRUNNER *Beserkley BZZ 1* 11 9
29 Oct 77 ● EGYPTIAN REGGAE *Beserkley BZZ 2* 5 14
21 Jan 78 THE MORNING OF OUR LIVES *Beserkley BZZ 7* 1 ....29 4
27 Aug 77 ROCK 'N' ROLL WITH THE MODERN LOVERS *Beserkeley BSERK 9* 50 3

1 Modern Lovers

RICHMOND STRINGS / MIKE SAMMES SINGERS

UK, orchestra and male / female vocal group (Albums: 7 weeks) pos/wks

19 Jan 76 MUSIC OF AMERICA *Ronco TRD 2016* 18 7

Sviatoslav RICHTER – *See Herbert VON KARAJAN*

Adam RICKITT

UK, male actor / vocalist (Singles: 19 weeks, Albums: 1 week) pos/wks

26 Jun 99 ● I BREATHE AGAIN *Polydor 5611862* 5 10
16 Oct 99 EVERYTHING MY HEART DESIRES *Polydor 5614392* 15 6
5 Feb 00 BEST THING *Polydor 5616132* 25 3
30 Oct 99 GOOD TIMES *Polydor 5431422* 41 1

RICO – *See Gary NUMAN; SPECIALS*

Frank RICOTTI ALL STARS

UK, male instrumental group (Albums: 1 week)

		pos	wks
26 Jun 93	**THE BEIDERBECKE COLLECTION** *Dormouse DM 20CD*	**73**	1

Album first entered the chart on 24 Dec 88 as a compilation

See also VARIOUS ARTISTS – TV and Radio Soundtracks and Spin-Offs

Nelson RIDDLE ORCHESTRA – *See Shirley BASSEY; Linda RONSTADT; Kiri TE KANAWA*

RIDE *UK, male vocal / instrumental group (Singles: 22 weeks, Albums: 16 weeks)*

		pos	wks
27 Jan 90	**RIDE (EP)** *Creation CRE 072T*	**71**	2
14 Apr 90	**PLAY (EP)** *Creation CRE 075T*	**32**	3
29 Sep 90	**FALL (EP)** *Creation CRE 087T*	**34**	3
16 Mar 91	**TODAY FOREVER (EP)** *Creation CRE 100T*	**14**	4
15 Feb 92 ●	**LEAVE THEM ALL BEHIND** *Creation CRE 123T*	**9**	3
25 Apr 92	**TWISTERELLA** *Creation CRE 150T*	**36**	2
30 Apr 94	**BIRDMAN** *Creation CRESCD 155*	**38**	2
25 Jun 94	**HOW DOES IT FEEL TO FEEL** *Creation CRESCD 184*	**58**	1
8 Oct 94	**I DON'T KNOW WHERE IT COMES FROM** *Creation CRESCD 189R*	**46**	1
24 Feb 96	**BLACK NITE CRASH** *Creation CRESCD 199*	**67**	1
27 Oct 90	**NOWHERE** *Creation CRELP 074*	**11**	5
21 Mar 92 ●	**GOING BLANK AGAIN** *Creation CRECD 124*	**5**	5
2 Jul 94 ●	**CARNIVAL OF LIGHT** *Creation CRECD 147*	**5**	4
23 Mar 96	**TARANTULA** *Creation CRECD 180*	**21**	2

Tracks on Ride (EP): Chelsea Girl / Drive Blind / All I Can See / Close My Eyes. Tracks on Play (EP): Like a Daydream / Silver / Furthest Sense / Perfect Time. Tracks on Fall (EP): Dreams Burn Down / Taste / Hear and Now / Nowhere. Tracks on Today Forever (EP): Unfamiliar / Sennen / Beneath / Today

RIDER & Terry VENABLES *UK, male vocal / instrumental group and soccer-styled vocalist (Singles: 2 weeks)*

		pos	wks
1 Jun 02	**ENGLAND CRAZY** *East West EW 248CD*	**46**	2

Andrew RIDGELEY *UK, male vocalist (Singles: 3 weeks)*

		pos	wks
31 Mar 90	**SHAKE** *Epic AJR 1*	**58**	3

See also WHAM!

Stan RIDGWAY

US, male vocalist (Singles: 12 weeks)

		pos	wks
5 Jul 86 ●	**CAMOUFLAGE** *IRS IRM 114*	**4**	12

André RIEU

Holland, male conductor / instrumentalist – violin (Albums: 2 weeks)

		pos	wks
22 Apr 00	**CELEBRATION!** *Philips 5430692*	**51**	2

RIGHEIRA *Italy, male vocal duo (Singles: 3 weeks)*

		pos	wks
24 Sep 83	**VAMOS A LA PLAYA** *A&M AM 137*	**53**	3

RIGHT SAID FRED *UK, male vocal / instrumental group – lead vocal Richard Fairbrass (Singles: 66 weeks, Albums: 53 weeks)*

		pos	wks
27 Jul 91 ●	**I'M TOO SEXY** *Tug SNOG 1* ▲	**2**	16
7 Dec 91 ●	**DON'T TALK JUST KISS** *Tug SNOG 2* [1]	**3**	11
21 Mar 92 ★	**DEEPLY DIPPY** *Tug SNOG 3*	**1**	14
1 Aug 92	**THOSE SIMPLE THINGS / DAYDREAM** *Tug SNOG 4*	**29**	5
27 Feb 93 ●	**STICK IT OUT** *Tug CDCOMIC 1* [2]	**4**	7
23 Oct 93	**BUMPED** *Tug CDSNOG 7*	**32**	4
18 Dec 93	**HANDS UP (4 LOVERS)** *Tug CDSNOG 8*	**60**	3
19 Mar 94	**WONDERMAN** *Tug CDSNOG 9*	**55**	1
13 Oct 01	**YOU'RE MY MATE** *Kingsize 74321895632*	**18**	5
28 Mar 93 ★	**UP** *Tug SNOGCD 1*	**1**	49
13 Nov 93	**SEX AND TRAVEL** *Tug SNOGCD 2*	**35**	4

[1] Right Said Fred. Guest vocals: Jocelyn Brown [2] Right Said Fred and Friends

RIGHTEOUS BROTHERS

US, male vocal duo – Bill Medley and Bobby Hatfield, d. 5 Nov 2003 (Singles: 86 weeks, Albums: 17 weeks)

		pos	wks
14 Jan 65 ★	**YOU'VE LOST THAT LOVIN' FEELIN'** *London HLU 9943* ▲	**1**	10
12 Aug 65	**UNCHAINED MELODY** *London HL 9975*	**14**	12
13 Jan 66	**EBB TIDE** *London HL 10011*	**48**	2
14 Apr 66	**(YOU'RE MY) SOUL AND INSPIRATION** *Verve VS 535* ▲	**15**	10
10 Nov 66	**THE WHITE CLIFFS OF DOVER** *London HL 10086*	**21**	9
22 Dec 66	**ISLAND IN THE SUN** *Verve VS 547*	**24**	5
12 Feb 69 ●	**YOU'VE LOST THAT LOVIN' FEELIN' (re-issue)** *London HL 10241*	**10**	11
19 Nov 77	**YOU'VE LOST THAT LOVIN' FEELIN' (2nd re-issue)** *Phil Spector International 2010 022*	**42**	4
27 Oct 90 ★	**UNCHAINED MELODY (re-issue)** *Verve / Polydor PO 101*	**1**	14
15 Dec 90 ●	**YOU'VE LOST THAT LOVIN' FEELIN' / EBB TIDE (3rd re-issue)** *Verve / Polydor PO 116*	**3**	9
1 Dec 90	**THE VERY BEST OF THE RIGHTEOUS BROTHERS** *Verve 8472481*	**11**	17

RIKKI and DAZ featuring Glen CAMPBELL

UK, male production duo – John Matthews and Darren Sampson and US, male vocalist (Singles: 8 weeks)

		pos	wks
30 Nov 02	**RHINESTONE COWBOY (GIDDY UP GIDDY UP)** *Serious SER 059CD*	**12**	8

Cheryl Pepsii RILEY *US, female vocalist (Singles: 1 week)*

		pos	wks
28 Jan 89	**THANKS FOR MY CHILD** *CBS 653153 7*	**75**	1

Jeannie C RILEY

US, female vocalist – Jeanne C Stephenson (Singles: 15 weeks)

		pos	wks
16 Oct 68	**HARPER VALLEY P.T.A.** *Polydor 56748* ▲	**12**	15

Teddy RILEY *US, male producer (Singles: 5 weeks)*

		pos	wks
21 Mar 92	**IS IT GOOD TO YOU** *MCA MCS 1611* [1]	**53**	2
19 Jun 93	**BABY BE MINE** *MCA MCSTD 1772* [2]	**37**	3

[1] Teddy Riley featuring Tammy Lucas [2] BLACKstreet featuring Teddy Riley

See also BLACKSTREET

RIMES featuring Shaila PROSPERE

UK, male rapper – Julian Johnson (Singles: 1 week)

		pos	wks
22 May 99	**IT'S OVER** *Universal MCSTD 40199*	**51**	1

LeAnn RIMES

US, female vocalist (Singles: 92 weeks, Albums: 40 weeks)

		pos	wks
7 Mar 98 ●	**HOW DO I LIVE (re)** *Curb CUBCX 30*	**7**	34
12 Sep 98	**LOOKING THROUGH YOUR EYES / COMMITMENT** *Curb CUBC 32*	**38**	2
12 Dec 98	**BLUE** *Curb CUBC 39*	**23**	6
6 Mar 99 ●	**WRITTEN IN THE STARS (re)** *Mercury EJSCD 45* [1]	**10**	8
18 Dec 99	**CRAZY** *Curb CUBC 52*	**36**	3
25 Nov 00 ★	**CAN'T FIGHT THE MOONLIGHT** *Curb CUBC 58* ■	**1**	17
31 Mar 01	**I NEED YOU (re)** *Curb CUBC 60*	**13**	7
23 Feb 02	**BUT I DO LOVE YOU** *London / Curb CUBC 075*	**20**	4
12 Oct 02	**LIFE GOES ON** *Curb CUBC 085*	**11**	8
8 May 03	**SUDDENLY** *Curb / London CUBC 088*	**47**	1
23 Aug 03	**WE CAN** *Curb / London CUBC 092*	**27**	2
6 Jun 98	**SITTIN' ON TOP OF THE WORLD** *Curb / The Hit Label 5560202*	**11**	22
14 Apr 01 ●	**I NEED YOU** *Curb / London 8573876382*	**7**	15
26 Oct 02	**TWISTED ANGEL** *Curb / London 5046611562*	**14**	3

[1] Elton John and LeAnn Rimes

RIMSHOTS

US, male / female instrumental / vocal group (Singles: 5 weeks)

		pos	wks
19 Jul 75	**7-6-5-4-3-2-1 (BLOW YOUR WHISTLE)** *All Platinum 6146 304*	**26**	5

RIO and MARS *France / UK, male / female vocal / instrumental duo (Singles: 3 weeks)* pos/wks

28 Jan 95	**BOY I GOTTA HAVE YOU** *Dome CDDOME 1014*	**43** 2
13 Apr 96	**BOY I GOTTA HAVE YOU (re-issue)** *Feverpitch CDFVR 1007*	**46** 1

Miguel RIOS *Spain, male vocalist (Singles: 12 weeks)* pos/wks

11 Jul 70	**SONG OF JOY** *A&M AMS 790*	**16** 12

Waldo de los RIOS *Argentina, orchestra, leader – Osvaldo Ferraro Guiterrez (Singles: 16 weeks, Albums: 26 weeks)* pos/wks

10 Apr 71 ●	**MOZART SYMPHONY NO.40 IN G MINOR K550 1ST MOVEMENT (ALLEGRO MOLTO)** *A&M AMS 836*	**5** 16
1 May 71 ●	**SYMPHONIES FOR THE SEVENTIES** *A&M AMLS 2014*	**6** 26

RIP RIG AND PANIC *UK / US, male / female vocal / instrumental group (Albums: 3 weeks)* pos/wks

26 Jun 82	**I AM COLD** *Virgin V 2228*	**67** 3

See also Neneh CHERRY

Minnie RIPERTON *US, female vocalist, d. 12 Jul 1979 (Singles: 10 weeks, Albums: 3 weeks)* pos/wks

12 Apr 75 ●	**LOVIN' YOU** *Epic EPC 3121* ▲	**2** 10
17 May 75	**PERFECT ANGEL** *Epic EPC 80426*	**33** 3

Angela RIPPON
UK, female TV newsreader / exercise instructor (Albums: 26 weeks) pos/wks

17 Apr 82 ●	**SHAPE UP AND DANCE (VOLUME II)** *Lifestyle LEG 2*	**8** 26

RISE *UK, male production duo – Paul Oakenfold and Steve Osborne (Singles: 1 week)* pos/wks

3 Sep 94	**THE SINGLE** *East West YZ 839CD*	**70** 1

See also VIRUS; PERFECTO ALL STARZ; OAKENFOLD

RITCHIE FAMILY *US, female vocal group (Singles: 19 weeks)* pos/wks

23 Aug 75	**BRAZIL** *Polydor 2058 625*	**41** 4
18 Sep 76 ●	**THE BEST DISCO IN TOWN** *Polydor 2058 777*	**10** 9
17 Feb 79	**AMERICAN GENERATION** *Mercury 6007 199*	**49** 6

Lee RITENOUR and Maxi PRIEST
US, male instrumentalist – guitar – and UK, male vocalist (Singles: 2 weeks) pos/wks

31 Jul 93	**WAITING IN VAIN** *GRP MCSTD 1921*	**65** 2

RITMO-DYNAMIC
France, male producer – Laurent Wolf (Singles: 1 week) pos/wks

15 Nov 03	**CALINDA** *Xtravaganza XTRAV 42CDS*	**68** 1

Tex RITTER *US, male vocalist, d. 3 Jan 1974 (Singles: 14 weeks)* pos/wks

22 Jun 56 ●	**THE WAYWARD WIND** *Capitol CL 14581*	**8** 14

RIVA featuring Dannii MINOGUE
Holland, male production duo – Rene ter Horst and Gaston Steenkist, and Australia, female vocalist (Singles: 15 weeks) pos/wks

1 Dec 01 ●	**WHO DO YOU LOVE NOW (STRINGER)** *ffrr DFCD 002* [1]	**3** 15

[1] Riva featuring Dannii Minogue

See also GOODMEN; JARK PRONGO; RHYTHMKILLAZ; CHOCOLATE PUMA; TOMBA VIRA

RIVAL SCHOOLS
US, male vocal / instrumental group (Singles: 2 weeks) pos/wks

30 Mar 02	**USED FOR GLUE** *Mercury 5889652*	**42** 1
20 Jul 02	**GOOD THINGS** *Mercury 5829662*	**74** 1

Paco RIVAZ – *See GAMBAFREAKS*

RIVER CITY PEOPLE *UK, male / female vocal / instrumental group (Singles: 27 weeks, Albums: 10 weeks)* pos/wks

12 Aug 89	**(WHAT'S WRONG WITH) DREAMING?** *EMI EM 95*	**70** 3
3 Mar 90	**WALKING ON ICE** *EMI EM 130*	**62** 2
30 Jun 90	**CARRY THE BLAME / CALIFORNIA DREAMIN'** *EMI EM 145*	**13** 10
22 Sep 90	**(WHAT'S WRONG WITH) DREAMING? (re-issue)** *EMI EM 156*	**40** 3
2 Mar 91	**WHEN I WAS YOUNG** *EMI EM 176*	**62** 2
28 Sep 91	**SPECIAL WAY** *EMI EM 207*	**44** 3
22 Feb 92	**STANDING IN THE NEED OF LOVE** *EMI EM 216*	**36** 4
25 Aug 90	**SAY SOMETHING GOOD** *EMI EMCX 3561*	**23** 9
2 Nov 91	**THIS IS THE WORLD** *EMI EMC 3611*	**56** 1

RIVER DETECTIVES *UK, male vocal / instrumental duo (Singles: 4 weeks, Albums: 1 week)* pos/wks

29 Jul 89	**CHAINS** *WEA YZ 383*	**51** 4
23 Sep 89	**SATURDAY NIGHT SUNDAY MORNING** *WEA WX 2955*	**51** 1

RIVER OCEAN featuring INDIA *US, male producer – Louie Vega and female vocalist (Singles: 2 weeks)* pos/wks

26 Feb 94	**LOVE AND HAPPINESS (YEMAYA Y OCHUN)** *Cooltempo CDCOOL 287*	**50** 2

See also INDIA; Louie VEGA

Robbie RIVERA *Puerto Rico, male producer (Singles: 8 weeks)* pos/wks

2 Sep 00	**BANG** *Multiply CDMULTY 64* [1]	**13** 7
12 Oct 02	**SEX** *352 Recordings 352CD 001* [2]	**55** 1

[1] Robbie Rivera presents Rhythm Bangers [2] Robbie Rivera vs Billy Paul W

Sandy RIVERA *US, male producer (Singles: 3 weeks)* pos/wks

18 Jan 03	**CHANGES** *Defected DFTD 059* [1]	**48** 2
5 Apr 03	**I CAN'T STOP** *Defected DFTD 063*	**58** 1

[1] Sandy Rivera featuring Haze

See also KINGS OF TOMORROW

Danny RIVERS *UK, male vocalist (Singles: 3 weeks)* pos/wks

12 Jan 61	**CAN'T YOU HEAR MY HEART** *Decca F 11294*	**36** 3

David ROACH
UK, male vocalist / instrumentalist – saxophone (Albums: 1 week) pos/wks

14 Apr 84	**I LOVE SAX** *Nouveau Music NML 1006*	**73** 1

ROACH MOTEL
UK, male instrumental / production group (Singles: 2 weeks) pos/wks

21 Aug 93	**AFRO SLEEZE / TRANSATLANTIC** *Junior Boy's Own JBO 1412*	**73** 1
10 Dec 94	**HAPPY BIZZNESS / WILD LUV** *Junior Boy's Own JBO 24*	**75** 1

ROACHFORD *UK, male / female vocal / instrumental group, leader – Andrew Roachford (Singles: 61 weeks, Albums: 56 weeks)* pos/wks

18 Jun 88	**CUDDLY TOY** *CBS ROA 2*	**61** 4
14 Jan 89 ●	**CUDDLY TOY (re-issue)** *CBS ROA 4*	**4** 9
18 Mar 89	**FAMILY MAN** *CBS ROA 5*	**25** 6
1 Jul 89	**KATHLEEN** *CBS ROA 6*	**43** 5
13 Apr 91	**GET READY!** *Columbia 6567057*	**22** 8
19 Mar 94	**ONLY TO BE WITH YOU** *Columbia 6601562*	**21** 7
18 Jun 94	**LAY YOUR LOVE ON ME** *Columbia 6603722*	**36** 5
20 Aug 94	**THIS GENERATION** *Columbia 6607452*	**38** 4
3 Dec 94	**CRY FOR ME** *Columbia 6610742*	**46** 2
1 Apr 95	**I KNOW YOU DON'T LOVE ME** *Columbia 6612525*	**42** 2
11 Oct 97	**THE WAY I FEEL** *Columbia 6651042*	**20** 4
14 Feb 98	**HOW COULD I? (INSECURITY)** *Columbia 6653462*	**34** 3
11 Jul 98	**NAKED WITHOUT YOU** *Columbia 6659362*	**53** 2
23 Jul 88	**ROACHFORD** *CBS 460630 1*	**11** 27
18 May 91	**GET READY!** *Columbia 4681361*	**20** 5
16 Apr 94	**PERMANENT SHADE OF BLUE** *Columbia 4758429*	**25** 21
25 Oct 97	**FEEL** *Columbia 4885262*	**19** 3

ROB 'N' RAZ featuring Leila K *Sweden, male production duo and female rapper (Singles: 17 weeks)* pos/wks

25 Nov 89 ● **GOT TO GET** *Arista 112696* 8 14
17 Mar 90 **ROK THE NATION** *Arista 112971* 41 3

ROBBIE – *See SLY and ROBBIE*

Kate ROBBINS and BEYOND

UK, female / male vocal / instrumental group (Singles: 10 weeks) pos/wks

30 May 81 ● **MORE THAN IN LOVE** *RCA 69* 2 10

Marty ROBBINS *US, male vocalist / instrumentalist – guitar – Marty Robinson, d. 8 Nov 1982 (Singles: 33 weeks, Albums: 15 weeks)* pos/wks

29 Jan 60 **EL PASO (re)** *Fontana H 233* ▲ 19 9
26 May 60 **BIG IRON** *Fontana H 229* 48 1
27 Sep 62 ● **DEVIL WOMAN** *CBS AAG 114* 5 17
17 Jan 63 **RUBY ANN** *CBS AAG 128* 24 6
13 Aug 60 **GUNFIGHTER BALLADS AND TRAIL SONGS** *Fontana TFL 5063* 20 1
10 Feb 79 ● **MARTY ROBBINS COLLECTION** *Lotus WH 5009* 5 14

Antoinette ROBERSON – *See PULSE featuring Antoinette ROBERSON*

Austin ROBERTS *US, male vocalist (Singles: 7 weeks)* pos/wks

25 Oct 75 **ROCKY** *Private Stock PVT 33* 22 7

Joe ROBERTS *UK, male vocalist (Singles: 17 weeks)* pos/wks

28 Aug 93 **BACK IN MY LIFE** *ffrr FCD 215* 59 1
29 Jan 94 **LOVER** *ffrr FCD 220* 22 5
14 May 94 **BACK IN MY LIFE (re-issue)** *ffrr FCD 230* 39 3
6 Aug 94 **ADORE** *ffrr FCD 240* 45 3
18 Feb 95 **YOU ARE EVERYTHING** *Columbia 6611755* [1] 28 4
24 Feb 96 **HAPPY DAYS** *Grass Green GRASS 10CD* [2] 63 1

[1] Melanie Williams and Joe Roberts [2] Sweet Mercy featuring Joe Roberts

Juliet ROBERTS

UK, female vocalist (Singles: 34 weeks, Albums: 1 week) pos/wks

31 Jul 93 **CAUGHT IN THE MIDDLE** *Cooltempo CDCOOL 272* 24 6
6 Nov 93 **FREE LOVE** *Cooltempo CDCOOL 281* 25 3
19 Mar 94 **AGAIN / I WANT YOU** *Cooltempo CDCOOL 285* 33 3
2 Jul 94 **CAUGHT IN THE MIDDLE (re-mix)** *Cooltempo CDCOOL 291* 14 5
15 Oct 94 **I WANT YOU (re-issue)** *Cooltempo CDCOOL 297* 28 3
31 Jan 98 **SO GOOD / FREE LOVE 98 (re-mix)** *Delirious 74321554002* 15 4
23 Jan 99 **BAD GIRLS / I LIKE** *Delirious DELICD 11* 17 5
20 Jan 01 **NEEDIN' U II** *Manifesto FESCD 78* [1] 11 5
2 Apr 94 **NATURAL THING** *Cooltempo CTCD 39* 65 1

[1] David Morales presents The Face featuring Juliet Roberts

Malcolm ROBERTS

UK, male vocalist, d. 7 Feb 2003 (Singles: 29 weeks) pos/wks

11 May 67 **TIME ALONE WILL TELL** *RCA 1578* 45 2
30 Oct 68 ● **MAY I HAVE THE NEXT DREAM WITH YOU (re)** *Major Minor MM 581* 8 15
22 Nov 69 **LOVE IS ALL** *Major Minor MM 637* 12 12

Paddy ROBERTS

South Africa, male vocalist d. Sep 1975 (Albums: 6 weeks) pos/wks

26 Sep 59 ● **STRICTLY FOR GROWN-UPS** *Decca LF 1322* 8 5
17 Sep 60 **PADDY ROBERTS TRIES AGAIN** *Decca LK 4358* 16 1

B A ROBERTSON

UK, male vocalist (Singles: 60 weeks, Albums: 10 weeks) pos/wks

28 Jul 79 ● **BANG BANG** *Asylum K 13152* 2 12
27 Oct 79 ● **KNOCKED IT OFF** *Asylum K 12396* 8 12
1 Mar 80 **KOOL IN THE KAFTAN** *Asylum K 12427* 17 12
31 May 80 ● **TO BE OR NOT TO BE** *Asylum K 12449* 9 11
17 Oct 81 **HOLD ME** *Swansong BAM 1* [1] 11 8
17 Dec 83 **TIME** *Epic A 3983* [2] 45 5
29 Mar 80 **INITIAL SUCCESS** *Asylum K 52216* 32 8
4 Apr 81 **BULLY FOR YOU** *Asylum K 52275* 61 2

[1] B A Robertson and Maggie Bell [2] Frida and B A Robertson

Don ROBERTSON

US, male instrumentalist – piano and whistle (Singles: 9 weeks) pos/wks

11 May 56 ● **THE HAPPY WHISTLER** *Capitol CL 14575* 8 9

Robbie ROBERTSON *Canada, male vocalist / instrumentalist (Singles: 11 weeks, Albums: 16 weeks)* pos/wks

23 Jul 88 **SOMEWHERE DOWN THE CRAZY RIVER** *Geffen GEF 40* 15 10
11 Apr 98 **TAKE YOUR PARTNER BY THE HAND** *Polydor 5693272* [1] 74 1
14 Nov 87 **ROBBIE ROBERTSON** *Geffen WX 133* 23 14
12 Oct 91 **STORYVILLE** *Geffen GEF 24303* 30 2

[1] Howie B featuring Robbie Robertson

See also The BAND

Ivo ROBIC *Croatia, male vocalist (Singles: 1 week)* pos/wks

6 Nov 59 **MORGEN** *Polydor 23923* 23 1

Dawn ROBINSON – *See FIRM*

Floyd ROBINSON *US, male vocalist (Singles: 9 weeks)* pos/wks

16 Oct 59 ● **MAKIN' LOVE** *RCA 1146* 9 9

Smokey ROBINSON

US, male vocalist (Singles: 51 weeks, Albums: 19 weeks) pos/wks

23 Feb 74 **JUST MY SOUL RESPONDING** *Tamla Motown TMG 883* 35 6
2 Oct 76 **THE TEARS OF A CLOWN (re-issue)** *Tamla Motown TMG 1048* 34 6
24 Feb 79 **POPS, WE LOVE YOU** *Motown TMG 1136* [1] 66 5
9 May 81 ★ **BEING WITH YOU** *Motown TMG 1223* 1 13
13 Mar 82 **TELL ME TOMORROW** *Motown TMG 1255* 51 4
28 Mar 87 **JUST TO SEE HER** *Motown ZB 41147* 52 6
17 Sep 88 **INDESTRUCTIBLE** *Arista 111717* [2] 55 4
25 Feb 89 **INDESTRUCTIBLE** *Arista 112074* [2] 30 7
20 Jun 81 **BEING WITH YOU** *Motown STML 12151* 17 10
12 Nov 88 **LOVE SONGS** *Telstar STAR 2331* [1] 69 9

[1] Diana Ross, Marvin Gaye, Smokey Robinson and Stevie Wonder [2] Four Tops featuring Smokey Robinson [1] Marvin Gaye and Smokey Robinson

The original US recording of 'Indestructible' was not issued until after the chart run of the UK-only mix

Smokey ROBINSON and the MIRACLES

Motown's first US Top 10 act was fronted, between 1955 and 1972, by William 'Smokey' Robinson, b. 19 Feb 1940, Detroit. He wrote and produced hits for many Motown acts including this quartet. Smokey received coveted Grammy Living Legend Award in 1989 and has a US album chart span covering 36 years (Singles: 81 weeks, Albums: 2 week) pos/wks

24 Feb 66 **GOING TO A GO-GO** *Tamla Motown TMG 547* [1] 44 5
22 Dec 66 **(COME 'ROUND HERE) I'M THE ONE YOU NEED** *Tamla Motown TMG 584* 45 2
27 Dec 67 **I SECOND THAT EMOTION** *Tamla Motown TMG 631* 27 11
3 Apr 68 **IF YOU CAN WANT** *Tamla Motown TMG 648* 50 1
7 May 69 ● **TRACKS OF MY TEARS** *Tamla Motown TMG 696* 9 13
1 Aug 70 ★ **THE TEARS OF A CLOWN** *Tamla Motown TMG 745* ▲ 1 14
30 Jan 71 **(COME 'ROUND HERE) I'M THE ONE YOU NEED (re-issue)** *Tamla Motown TMG 761* 13 9
5 Jun 71 **I DON'T BLAME YOU AT ALL** *Tamla Motown TMG 774* 11 10
10 Jan 76 ● **LOVE MACHINE** *Tamla Motown TMG 1015* ▲ [1] 3 10
2 Oct 76 **THE TEARS OF A CLOWN (re-issue)** *Tamla Motown TMG 1048* 34 6
14 Nov 92 **THE GREATEST HITS** *PolyGram TV 5301212* 65 2

[1] Miracles

1976 re-issue of 'The Tears of a Clown' was a double A-side Motown release with 'Tracks of My Tears'

See also Smokey ROBINSON

Tom ROBINSON BAND *UK, male vocalist / instrumentalist (Singles: 41 weeks, Albums: 23 weeks)* pos/wks

22 Oct 77 ● **2-4-6-8 MOTORWAY** *EMI 2715* 5 9
18 Feb 78 **RISING FREE (EP)** *EMI 2749* 18 6
13 May 78 **UP AGAINST THE WALL** *EMI 2787* 33 6
17 Mar 79 **BULLY FOR YOU** *EMI 2916* 68 2
25 Jun 83 ● **WAR BABY** *Panic NIC 2* [1] 6 9
12 Nov 83 **LISTEN TO THE RADIO: ATMOSPHERICS** *Panic NIC 3* [1] 39 6
15 Sep 84 **RIKKI DON'T LOSE THAT NUMBER** *Castaway TR 2* [1] 58 3
3 Jun 78 ● **POWER IN THE DARKNESS** *EMI EMC 3226* 4 12
24 Mar 79 **TRB2** *EMI EMC 3296* 18 6
29 Sep 84 **HOPE AND GLORY** *Castaway ZL 70483* [1] 21 5

[1] Tom Robinson [1] Tom Robinson

Tracks on Rising Free (EP): Don't Take No for an Answer / Sing If You're Glad to Be Gay / Martin / Right On Sister

Vicki Sue ROBINSON *US, female vocalist, d. 27 Apr 2000 (Singles: 1 week)* pos/wks

27 Sep 97 **HOUSE OF JOY** *Logic 74321511492* 48 1

ROBO BABE – *See SIR KILLALOT vs ROBO BABE*

ROBSON & JEROME *UK, male actors / vocal duo – Robson Green and Jerome Flynn (Singles: 45 weeks, Albums: 53 weeks)* pos/wks

20 May 95 ★ **UNCHAINED MELODY / (THERE'LL BE BLUEBIRDS OVER) THE WHITE CLIFFS OF DOVER (re)** *RCA 74321284362* [1] ◆ ■ 1 17
11 Nov 95 ★ **I BELIEVE / UP ON THE ROOF** *RCA 74321326882* ◆ ■ 1 14
9 Nov 96 ★ **WHAT BECOMES OF THE BROKENHEARTED / SATURDAY NIGHT AT THE MOVIES / YOU'LL NEVER WALK ALONE** *RCA 74321424732* ■ 1 14
25 Nov 95 ★ **ROBSON & JEROME** *RCA 74321323902* ■ 1 31
23 Nov 96 ★ **TAKE TWO** *RCA 74321426252* ■ 1 16
29 Nov 97 **HAPPY DAYS – THE BEST OF ROBSON & JEROME** *RCA 74321542602* 20 6

[1] Robson Green and Jerome Flynn

ROBYN *Sweden, female vocalist – Robyn Carlsson (Singles: 14 weeks)* pos/wks

20 Jul 96 **YOU'VE GOT THAT SOMETHIN'** *RCA 74321393462* 54 1
16 Aug 97 **DO YOU KNOW (WHAT IT TAKES)** *RCA 74321509932* 26 3
7 Mar 98 ● **SHOW ME LOVE** *RCA 74321555032* 8 6
30 May 98 **DO YOU REALLY WANT ME** *RCA 74321582982* 20 4

ROC PROJECT featuring Tina ARENA *US, male producer – Ray Checo and Australia, female vocalist (Singles: 1 week)* pos/wks

12 Apr 03 **NEVER (PAST TENSE)** *Illustrious CDILL 010* 42 1

John ROCCA – *See FREEEZ*

Erin ROCHA *UK, female vocalist (Singles: 1 week)* pos/wks

27 Dec 03 **CAN'T DO RIGHT FOR DOING WRONG** *Flying Sparks TDBCDS 76* ....36 1+

ROCHELLE *US, female vocalist (Singles: 6 weeks)* pos/wks

1 Feb 86 **MY MAGIC MAN** *Warner Bros. W 8838* 27 6

Chubb ROCK *US, male rapper (Singles: 1 week)* pos/wks

19 Jan 91 **TREAT 'EM RIGHT** *Champion CHAMP 272* 67 1

Sir Monti ROCK III – *See DISCO TEX & the SEX-O-LETTES*

The ROCK – *See Wyclef JEAN*

Pete ROCK and CL SMOOTH *US, male rap / DJ duo (Albums: 1 week)* pos/wks

19 Nov 94 **THE MAIN INGREDIENT** *Elektra 7559616612* 69 1

ROCK CANDY *UK, male vocal / instrumental group (Singles: 6 weeks)* pos/wks

11 Sep 71 **REMEMBER** *MCA MK 5069* 32 6

ROCK AID ARMENIA *UK, male vocal / instrumental charity ensemble (Singles: 5 weeks)* pos/wks

16 Dec 89 **SMOKE ON THE WATER** *Life Aid Armenia ARMEN 001* 39 5

ROCK GODDESS *UK, female vocal / instrumental group (Singles: 5 weeks, Albums: 3 weeks)* pos/wks

5 Mar 83 **MY ANGEL** *A&M AMS 8311* 64 2
24 Mar 84 **I DIDN'T KNOW I LOVED YOU (TILL I SAW YOU ROCK 'N' ROLL)** *A&M AMS 185* 57 3
12 Mar 83 **ROCK GODDESS** *A&M AMLH 68554* 65 2
29 Oct 83 **HELL HATH NO FURY** *A&M AMLX 68560* 84 1

ROCKER'S REVENGE featuring Donnie CALVIN *US, male / female vocal / instrumental group (Singles: 20 weeks)* pos/wks

14 Aug 82 ● **WALKING ON SUNSHINE** *London LON 11* 4 13
29 Jan 83 **THE HARDER THEY COME** *London LON 18* 30 7

ROCKET FROM THE CRYPT *US, male vocal / instrumental group (Singles: 7 weeks, Albums: 4 weeks)* pos/wks

27 Jan 96 **BORN IN 69** *Elemental ELM 32CD* 68 1
13 Apr 96 **YOUNG LIVERS** *Elemental ELM 33CDS* 67 1
14 Sep 96 **ON A ROPE** *Elemental ELM 38CDS1* 12 4
29 Aug 98 **LIPSTICK** *Elemental ELM 48CDS1* 64 1
3 Feb 96 **SCREAM DRACULA SCREAM!** *Elemental ELM 34CD* 40 3
18 Jul 98 **RFTC** *Elemental ELM 50CD* 63 1

ROCKETS – *See Tony CROMBIE and His ROCKETS*

ROCKFORD FILES *UK, male instrumental / production duo (Singles: 4 weeks)* pos/wks

11 Mar 95 **YOU SEXY DANCER** *Escapade CDJAPE 7* 34 3
6 Apr 96 **YOU SEXY DANCER (re-issue)** *Escapade CDJAPE 14* 59 1

ROCKIN' BERRIES *UK, male vocal / instrumental group, includes Geoff 'Jefferson' Turton (Singles: 41 weeks, Albums: 1 week)* pos/wks

1 Oct 64 **I DIDN'T MEAN TO HURT YOU** *Piccadilly 7N 35197* 43 1
15 Oct 64 ● **HE'S IN TOWN** *Piccadilly 7N 35203* 3 13
21 Jan 65 **WHAT IN THE WORLD'S COME OVER YOU** *Piccadilly 7N 35217* 23 7
13 May 65 ● **POOR MAN'S SON** *Piccadilly 7N 35236* 5 11
26 Aug 65 **YOU'RE MY GIRL** *Piccadilly 7N 35254* 40 7
6 Jan 66 **THE WATER IS OVER MY HEAD (re)** *Piccadilly 7N 35270* 43 2
19 Jun 65 **IN TOWN** *Pye NPL 38013* 15 1

ROCKNEY – *See CHAS and DAVE*

ROCKPILE *UK, male vocal / instrumental group (Albums: 5 weeks)* pos/wks

18 Oct 80 **SECONDS OF PLEASURE** *F-Beat XXLP 7* 34 5

See also Dave EDMUNDS; Nick LOWE

ROCKSTEADY CREW *US, male / female vocal group (Singles: 16 weeks, Albums: 1 week)* pos/wks

1 Oct 83 ● **(HEY YOU) THE ROCKSTEADY CREW** *Charisma / Virgin RSC 1* ..6 12
5 May 84 **UPROCK** *Charisma / Virgin RSC 2* 64 4
16 Jun 84 **READY FOR BATTLE** *Charisma RSC LP1* 73 1

ROCKWELL *US, male vocalist – Kennedy Gordy (Singles: 11 weeks, Albums: 5 weeks)* pos/wks

4 Feb 84 ● **SOMEBODY'S WATCHING ME** *Motown TMG 1331* 6 11
25 Feb 84 **SOMEBODY'S WATCHING ME** *Motown ZL 72147* 52 5

'Somebody's Watching Me' features uncredited vocal by Michael Jackson

ROCKY V – *See Joey B ELLIS*

ROCOCO *UK / Italy, male / female vocal / instrumental group (Singles: 5 weeks)* pos/wks

16 Dec 89 **ITALO HOUSE MIX** *Mercury MER 314* **54** 5

RODEO JONES *UK / Grenada, male / female vocal / instrumental group (Singles: 2 weeks)* pos/wks

30 Jan 93 **NATURAL WORLD** *A&M AMCD 0165* **75** 1
3 Apr 93 **SHADES OF SUMMER** *A&M AMCD 212* **59** 1

Clodagh RODGERS
Ireland, female vocalist (Singles: 59 weeks, Albums: 1 week) pos/wks

26 Mar 69 ● **COME BACK AND SHAKE ME** *RCA 1792* **3** 14
9 Jul 69 ● **GOODNIGHT MIDNIGHT (re)** *RCA 1852* **4** 12
8 Nov 69 **BILJO** *RCA 1891* **22** 9
4 Apr 70 **EVERYBODY GO HOME THE PARTY'S OVER** *RCA 1930* **47** 2
20 Mar 71 ● **JACK IN THE BOX** *RCA 2066* **4** 10
9 Oct 71 **LADY LOVE BUG** *RCA 2117* **28** 12
13 Sep 69 **CLODAGH RODGERS** *RCA SF 8033* **27** 1

Jimmie RODGERS *US, male vocalist (Singles: 37 weeks)* pos/wks

1 Nov 57 **HONEYCOMB** *Columbia DB 3986* ▲ **30** 1
20 Dec 57 ● **KISSES SWEETER THAN WINE** *Columbia DB 4052* **7** 11
28 Mar 58 **OH-OH, I'M FALLING IN LOVE AGAIN** *Columbia DB 4078* **18** 6
19 Dec 58 **WOMAN FROM LIBERIA** *Columbia DB 4206* **18** 6
14 Jun 62 ● **ENGLISH COUNTRY GARDEN** *Columbia DB 4847* **5** 13

Paul RODGERS
UK, male vocalist (Singles: 2 weeks, Albums: 11 weeks) pos/wks

12 Feb 94 **MUDDY WATER BLUES** *Victory ROGCD 1* **45** 2
3 Jul 93 ● **MUDDY WATER BLUES** *London 8284242* **9** 7
15 Feb 97 **NOW** *SPV Recordings SPV 08544662* **30** 4

See also BAD COMPANY; FREE

RODRIGUEZ – *See SASH!*

RODS *UK, male vocal / instrumental group (Albums: 4 weeks)* pos/wks

24 Jul 82 **WILD DOGS** *Arista SPART 1196* **75** 4

See also EDDIE and the HOT RODS

Tommy ROE *UK, male vocalist (Singles: 74 weeks)* pos/wks

6 Sep 62 ● **SHEILA** *HMV POP 1060* ▲ **3** 14
6 Dec 62 **SUSIE DARLIN'** *HMV POP 1092* **37** 5
21 Mar 63 ● **THE FOLK SINGER** *HMV POP 1138* **4** 13
26 Sep 63 ● **EVERYBODY (re)** *HMV POP 1207* **9** 14
16 Apr 69 ★ **DIZZY** *Stateside SS 2143* ▲ **1** 19
23 Jul 69 **HEATHER HONEY** *Stateside SS 2152* **24** 9

ROFO
UK, male instrumental / production duo (Singles: 3 weeks) pos/wks

1 Aug 92 **ROFO'S THEME** *PWL Continental PWLT 236* **44** 3

ROGER *US, male vocalist – Roger Troutman, d. 24 Apr 1999 (Singles: 8 weeks)* pos/wks

17 Oct 87 **I WANT TO BE YOUR MAN** *Reprise W 8229* **61** 4
12 Nov 88 **BOOM! THERE SHE WAS** *Virgin VS 1143* **55** 3
13 May 95 **HIGH AS A KITE** *ffrr FCD 259* [1] **55** 1

[1] One Tribe featuring Roger

See also ZAPP

Julie ROGERS
UK, female vocalist – Julie Rolls (Singles: 38 weeks) pos/wks

13 Aug 64 ● **THE WEDDING** *Mercury MF 820* [1] **3** 23
10 Dec 64 **LIKE A CHILD** *Mercury MF 838* **20** 9
25 Mar 65 **HAWAIIAN WEDDING SONG** *Mercury MF 849* **31** 6

[1] Julie Rogers with Johnny Arthey and his Orchestra and Chorus

Kenny ROGERS (292 Top 500) *Celebrated crossover country vocalist / actor, who was one of the US's top-selling artists of the past 30 years, b. 21 Aug 1938, Houston. This Grammy-winning ex-New Christy Minstrel has collected more than 20 US gold albums and is a household name in many countries (Singles: 109 weeks, Albums: 111 weeks)* pos/wks

18 Oct 69 ● **RUBY, DON'T TAKE YOUR LOVE TO TOWN** *Reprise RS 20829* [1] **2** 23
7 Feb 70 ● **SOMETHING'S BURNING** *Reprise RS 20888* [1] **8** 14
30 Apr 77 ★ **LUCILLE** *United Artists UP 36242* **1** 14
17 Sep 77 **DAYTIME FRIENDS** *United Artists UP 36289* **39** 4
2 Jun 79 **SHE BELIEVES IN ME** *United Artists UP 36533* **42** 7
26 Jan 80 ★ **COWARD OF THE COUNTY** *United Artists UP 614* **1** 12
15 Nov 80 **LADY** *United Artists UP 635* ▲ **12** 12
12 Feb 83 **WE'VE GOT TONIGHT** *Liberty UP 658* [2] **28** 7
22 Oct 83 **EYES THAT SEE IN THE DARK** *RCA 358* **61** 1
12 Nov 83 ● **ISLANDS IN THE STREAM** *RCA 378* [3] ▲ **7** 15
18 Jun 77 **KENNY ROGERS** *United Artists UAS 30046* **14** 7
6 Oct 79 **THE KENNY ROGERS SINGLES ALBUM** *United Artists UAK 30263* **12** 22
9 Feb 80 ● **KENNY ROGERS** *United Artists UAG 30273* **7** 10
31 Jan 81 **LADY** *Liberty LBG 30334* **40** 5
1 Oct 83 **EYES THAT SEE IN THE DARK** *RCA RCALP 6088* **53** 19
27 Oct 84 **WHAT ABOUT ME?** *RCA PL 85043* **97** 1
27 Jul 85 ● **THE KENNY ROGERS STORY** *Liberty EMTV 39* **4** 29
25 Sep 93 **DAYTIME FRIENDS – THE VERY BEST OF KENNY ROGERS** *EMI CDEMTV 79* **16** 5
22 Nov 97 **LOVE SONGS** *Virgin KENNYCD 1* **27** 7
29 May 99 **ALL THE HITS & ALL NEW LOVE SONGS** *EMI 5207782* **14** 6

[1] Kenny Rogers and the First Edition [2] Kenny Rogers and Sheena Easton
[3] Kenny Rogers and Dolly Parton

ROKOTTO *UK, male vocal / instrumental group (Singles: 10 weeks)* pos/wks

22 Oct 77 **BOOGIE ON UP** *State STAT 62* **40** 4
10 Jun 78 **FUNK THEORY** *State STAT 80* **49** 6

ROLLERGIRL
Germany, female vocalist – Nicci Juice (Singles: 3 weeks) pos/wks

16 Sep 00 **DEAR JESSIE** *Neo NEOCD 038* **22** 3

ROLLING STONES (16 Top 500) *'World's No.1 rock group': Sir Mick Jagger (v), Keith Richards (g), Brian Jones (g, d. 1969), Bill Wyman (b) (left 1991), Charlie Watts (d) – Ron Wood (g) joined 1975 replacing Mick Taylor. No group has accumulated more UK or US Top 10 albums (they have a record 30 US platinum and nine US gold albums) or grossed more income from touring than this legendary British band which has broken box-office records on every continent and is still the world's highest-earning live band. Transportation of the 300-person entourage and 350 tons of stage set during the 2003 40 Licks tour required 10 buses, 53 trucks and a tour jet. They played in front of a word record paying crowd of 489,176 when they topped the bill at a 2003 Toronto gig. Jagger and Richards, nicknamed The Glimmer Twins, were inducted into the Songwriters' Hall of Fame and the group, early members of the Rock and Roll Hall of Fame, received a Grammy Lifetime Achievement award (1986). Jagger was awarded a knighthood in 2002 (Singles: 374 weeks, Albums: 799 weeks)* pos/wks

25 Jul 63 **COME ON** *Decca F 11675* **21** 14
14 Nov 63 **I WANNA BE YOUR MAN** *Decca F 11764* **12** 16
27 Feb 64 ● **NOT FADE AWAY** *Decca F 11845* **3** 15
2 Jul 64 ★ **IT'S ALL OVER NOW** *Decca F 11934* **1** 15
19 Nov 64 ★ **LITTLE RED ROOSTER** *Decca F 12014* **1** 12
4 Mar 65 ★ **THE LAST TIME** *Decca F 12104* **1** 13
26 Aug 65 ★ **(I CAN'T GET NO) SATISFACTION** *Decca F 12220* ▲ **1** 12
28 Oct 65 ★ **GET OFF OF MY CLOUD** *Decca F 12263* ▲ **1** 12
10 Feb 66 ● **NINETEENTH NERVOUS BREAKDOWN** *Decca F 12331* **2** 8
19 May 66 ★ **PAINT IT BLACK** *Decca F 12395* ▲ **1** 10
29 Sep 66 ● **HAVE YOU SEEN YOUR MOTHER BABY STANDING IN THE SHADOW** *Decca F 12497* **5** 8
19 Jan 67 ● **LET'S SPEND THE NIGHT TOGETHER / RUBY TUESDAY** *Decca F 12546* ▲ **3** 10
23 Aug 67 ● **WE LOVE YOU / DANDELION** *Decca F 12654* **8** 8
29 May 68 ★ **JUMPIN' JACK FLASH** *Decca F 12782* **1** 11

9 Jul 69 ★ **HONKY TONK WOMEN** *Decca F 12952* ▲ 1 17
24 Apr 71 ● **BROWN SUGAR / BITCH / LET IT ROCK**
Rolling Stones RS 19100 ▲ 2 13
3 Jul 71 **STREET FIGHTING MAN** *Decca F 13195* 21 8
29 Apr 72 ● **TUMBLING DICE** *Rolling Stones RS 19103* 5 8
1 Sep 73 ● **ANGIE** *Rolling Stones RS 19105* ▲ 5 10
3 Aug 74 ● **IT'S ONLY ROCK AND ROLL** *Rolling Stones RS 19114* 10 7
20 Sep 75 **OUT OF TIME** *Decca F 13597* 45 2
1 May 76 ● **FOOL TO CRY** *Rolling Stones RS 19121* 6 10
3 Jun 78 ● **MISS YOU / FARAWAY EYES** *Rolling Stones EMI 2802* ▲ 3 13
30 Sep 78 **RESPECTABLE** *Rolling Stones EMI 2861* 23 9
5 Jul 80 ● **EMOTIONAL RESCUE** *Rolling Stones RSR 105* 9 8
4 Oct 80 **SHE'S SO COLD** *Rolling Stones RSR 106* 33 6
29 Aug 81 ● **START ME UP** *Rolling Stones RSR 108* 7 9
12 Dec 81 **WAITING ON A FRIEND** *Rolling Stones RSR 109* 50 6
12 Jun 82 **GOING TO A GO GO** *Rolling Stones RSR 110* 26 6
2 Oct 82 **TIME IS ON MY SIDE** *Rolling Stones RSR 111* 62 2
12 Nov 83 **UNDERCOVER OF THE NIGHT** *Rolling Stones RSR 113* 11 9
11 Feb 84 **SHE WAS HOT** *Rolling Stones RSR 114* 42 4
21 Jul 84 **BROWN SUGAR (re-issue)** *Rolling Stones SUGAR 1* 58 2
15 Mar 86 **HARLEM SHUFFLE** *Rolling Stones A 6864* 13 7
2 Sep 89 **MIXED EMOTIONS** *Rolling Stones 655193 7* 36 5
2 Dec 89 **ROCK AND A HARD PLACE** *Rolling Stones 655422 7* 63 1
23 Jun 90 **PAINT IT BLACK (re-issue)** *London LON 264* 61 3
30 Jun 90 **ALMOST HEAR YOU SIGH** *Rolling Stones 656065 7* 31 5
30 Mar 91 **HIGHWIRE** *Rolling Stones 6567567* 29 4
1 Jun 91 **RUBY TUESDAY (LIVE)** *Rolling Stones 6568927* 59 2
16 Jul 94 **LOVE IS STRONG** *Virgin VSCDT 1503* 14 5
8 Oct 94 **YOU GOT ME ROCKING** *Virgin VSCDG 1518* 23 3
10 Dec 94 **OUT OF TEARS** *Virgin VSCDT 1524* 36 4
15 Jul 95 **I GO WILD** *Virgin VSCDX 1539* 29 3
11 Nov 95 **LIKE A ROLLING STONE** *Virgin VSCDT 1562* 12 5
4 Oct 97 **ANYBODY SEEN MY BABY?** *Virgin VSCDT 1653* 22 3
7 Feb 98 **SAINT OF ME** *Virgin VSCDT 1667* 26 2
22 Aug 98 **OUT OF CONTROL** *Virgin VSCDT 1700* 51 1
28 Dec 02 **DON'T STOP** *Virgin VCSDT 1838* 36 2
13 Sep 03 **SYMPATHY FOR THE DEVIL** *Mercury 9810612* 14 6
25 Apr 64 ★ **THE ROLLING STONES** *Decca LK 4605* 1 51
23 Jan 65 ★ **ROLLING STONES NO.2** *Decca LK 4661* 1 37
2 Oct 65 ● **OUT OF OUR HEADS** *Decca LK 4733* ▲ 2 24
23 Apr 66 ★ **AFTERMATH** *Decca LK 4786* 1 28
12 Nov 66 ● **BIG HITS (HIGH TIDE AND GREEN GRASS)** *Decca TXS 101* 3 43
28 Jan 67 ● **BETWEEN THE BUTTONS** *Decca SKL 4852* 3 22
23 Dec 67 ● **THEIR SATANIC MAJESTIES REQUEST** *Decca TXS 103* 3 13
21 Dec 68 ● **BEGGARS BANQUET** *Decca SKL 4955* 3 12
27 Sep 69 ● **THROUGH THE PAST DARKLY (BIG HITS VOL.2)**
Decca SKL 5019 ....2 37
20 Dec 69 ★ **LET IT BLEED** *Decca SKL 5025* ■ 1 29
19 Sep 70 ★ **GET YER YA-YA'S OUT!** *Decca SKL 5065* ■ 1 15
27 Mar 71 ● **STONE AGE** *Decca SKL 5084* 4 8
8 May 71 ★ **STICKY FINGERS** *Rolling Stones COC 59100* ■ ▲ 1 25
18 Sep 71 **GIMME SHELTER** *Decca SKL 5101* 19 5
11 Mar 72 **MILESTONES** *Decca SKL 5098* 14 8
10 Jun 72 ★ **EXILE ON MAIN STREET** *Rolling Stones COC 69100* ■ ▲ 1 16
11 Nov 72 **ROCK 'N' ROLLING STONES** *Decca SKL 5149* 41 1
22 Sep 73 ★ **GOAT'S HEAD SOUP** *Rolling Stones COC 59101* ■ ▲ 1 14
2 Nov 74 ● **IT'S ONLY ROCK 'N' ROLL** *Rolling Stones COC 59103* ▲ 2 9
28 Jun 75 **MADE IN THE SHADE** *Rolling Stones COC 59104* 14 12
28 Jun 75 **METAMORPHOSIS** *Decca SKL 5212* 45 1
29 Nov 75 ● **ROLLED GOLD – THE VERY BEST OF THE ROLLING STONES** *Decca ROST 1/2* 7 50
8 May 76 ● **BLACK AND BLUE** *Rolling Stones COC 59106* ▲ 2 14
8 Oct 77 ● **LOVE YOU LIVE** *Rolling Stones COC 89101* 3 8
5 Nov 77 ● **GET STONED** *Arcade ADEP 32* 8 15
24 Jun 78 ● **SOME GIRLS** *Rolling Stones CUN 39108* ▲ 2 25
5 Jul 80 ★ **EMOTIONAL RESCUE** *Rolling Stones CUN 39111* ■ ▲ 1 18
12 Sep 81 ● **TATTOO YOU** *Rolling Stones CUNS 39114* ▲ 2 29
12 Jun 82 ● **STILL LIFE (AMERICAN CONCERTS 1981)**
Rolling Stones CUN 39115 ....4 18
31 Jul 82 **IN CONCERT (import)** *Decca (Holland) 6640 037* 94 3
11 Dec 82 **STORY OF THE STONES** *K-Tel NE 1201* 24 12
19 Nov 83 ● **UNDERCOVER** *Rolling Stones CUN 1654361* 3 18
7 Jul 84 **REWIND 1971-1984 (THE BEST OF THE ROLLING STONES)** *Rolling Stones 4501991* 23 18
5 Apr 86 ● **DIRTY WORK** *Rolling Stones CUN 86321* 4 10
23 Sep 89 ● **STEEL WHEELS** *CBS 4657521* 2 18
7 Jul 90 ● **HOT ROCKS 1964-1971** *London 8201401* 3 24
20 Apr 91 ● **FLASHPOINT** *Rolling Stones 4681351* 6 7
4 Dec 93 **JUMP BACK – THE BEST OF THE ROLLING STONES '71-'93** *Virgin CDV 2726* 16 28
2 Jul 94 **STICKY FINGERS (re-issue)** *Virgin CDVX 2730* 74 1
23 Jul 94 ★ **VOODOO LOUNGE** *Virgin CDV 2750* ■ 1 24
25 Nov 95 ● **STRIPPED** *Virgin CDV 2801* 9 13
11 Oct 97 ● **BRIDGES TO BABYLON** *Virgin CDV 2840* 6 6
14 Nov 98 **NO SECURITY** *Virgin CDV 2880* 67 1
12 Oct 02 ● **FORTY LICKS** *Virgin/Decca CDVDX 2964* 2 29

US No.1 symbol on F 12546 applies to Ruby Tuesday which hit the top spot in 1967

'Faraway Eyes' was listed from 15 July 1978, with a peak position of No.10

See also Mick JAGGER; Bill WYMAN; Keith RICHARDS

ROLLINS BAND *US, male vocal / instrumental group (Singles: 4 weeks, Albums: 2 weeks)* pos/wks

12 Sep 92 **TEARING** *Imago 72787250187* 54 2
10 Sep 94 **LIAR / DISCONNECTED** *Imago 74321213052* 27 2
23 Apr 94 **WEIGHT** *Imago 72787210342* 22 2

ROLLO *UK, male producer – Roland Armstrong (Singles: 8 weeks)* pos/wks

29 Jan 94 **GET OFF YOUR HIGH HORSE (re)** *Cheeky CHEKCD 003* [1] 43 4
10 Jun 95 **LOVE LOVE LOVE – HERE I COME** *Cheeky CHEKCD 007* [2] 32 2
8 Jun 96 **LET THIS BE A PRAYER** *Cheeky CHEKCD 013* [3] 26 2

[1] Rollo Goes Camping [2] Rollo Goes Mystic [3] Rollo Goes Spiritual with Pauline Taylor

See also FAITHLESS; OUR TRIBE / ONE TRIBE; SPHINX; DUSTED

ROMAN HOLLIDAY *UK, male vocal / instrumental group (Singles: 19 weeks, Albums: 3 weeks)* pos/wks

2 Apr 83 **STAND BY** *Jive JIVE 31* 61 3
2 Jul 83 **DON'T TRY TO STOP IT** *Jive JIVE 39* 14 9
24 Sep 83 **MOTORMANIA** *Jive JIVE 49* 40 7
22 Oct 83 **COOKIN' ON THE ROOF** *Jive HIP 9* 31 3

ROMAN NUMERALS – *See Vic REEVES*

ROMANTICS – *See RUBY and The ROMANTICS*

ROMEO *UK, male rapper – Marvin Dawkins (Singles: 24 weeks, Albums: 2 weeks)* pos/wks

30 Dec 00 ● **NO GOOD 4 ME** *East West OXIDE 02CD* [1] 6 8
24 Aug 02 ● **ROMEO DUNN** *Relentless RELENT 29CD* 3 9
9 Nov 02 ● **IT'S ALL GRAVY** *Relentless RELENT 32CD* [2] 9 6
6 Dec 03 **I SEE GIRLS (CRAZY)** *Multiply CDMULTY 109* [3] 52 1
23 Nov 02 **SOLID LOVE** *Relentless RELEN 006CD* 46 2

[1] Oxide & Neutrino featuring Megaman, Romeo and Lisa Maffia [2] Romeo featuring Christina Milian [3] Studio B / Romeo and Harry Brooks

See also SO SOLID CREW

Max ROMEO *Jamaica, male vocalist – Maxie Smith (Singles: 25 weeks)* pos/wks

28 May 69 ● **WET DREAM (re)** *Unity UN 503* 10 25

Harry 'Choo-Choo' ROMERO *US, male producer (Singles: 3 weeks)* pos/wks

22 May 99 **JUST CAN'T GET ENOUGH** *AM:PM CDAMPM 121* [1] 39 2
1 Sep 01 **I WANT OUT (I CAN'T BELIEVE)** *Perfecto PERF 22CDS* 51 1

[1] Harry 'Choo Choo' Romero presents Inaya Day

See also CHOO CHOO PROJECT

RONALDO'S REVENGE *UK, male production duo – Mike Gray and Jon Pearn (Singles: 2 weeks)* pos/wks

1 Aug 98 **MAS QUE MANCADA** *AM:PM 5827532* 37 2

See also FULL INTENTION

RONDO VENEZIANO

Italy, orchestra (Singles: 3 weeks, Albums: 33 weeks)

Date	Title	pos	wks
22 Oct 83	**LA SERENISSIMA (THEME FROM 'VENICE IN PERIL')** *Ferroway 7 RON 1*	58	3
5 Nov 83	**VENICE IN PERIL** *Ferroway RON 1*	39	13
10 Nov 84	**THE GENIUS OF VENICE** *Ferroway RON 2*	60	13
9 Jul 88	**VENICE IN PERIL (re-issue)** *Fanfare RON 1*	34	7

RONETTES *US, female vocal group (Singles: 34 weeks)*

Date	Title	pos	wks
17 Oct 63	● **BE MY BABY** *London HLU 9793*	4	13
9 Jan 64	**BABY, I LOVE YOU** *London HLU 9826*	11	14
27 Aug 64	**(THE BEST PART OF) BREAKIN' UP** *London HLU 9905*	43	3
8 Oct 64	**DO I LOVE YOU** *London HLU 9922*	35	4

RONNETTE – *See FIDELFATTI featuring RONNETTE*

Mark RONSON featuring GHOSTFACE KILLAH & Nate DOGG

UK, male DJ / producer and US, male rapper and vocalist (Singles: 7 weeks)

Date	Title	pos	wks
1 Nov 03	**OOH WEE** *Elektra E 7490CD*	15	7

Mick RONSON *UK male vocalist / instrumentalist – guitar, d. 29 Apr 1993 (Albums: 10 weeks)*

Date	Title	pos	wks
7 May 94	**DON'T LOOK DOWN** *Epic 6603582*	55	1
16 Mar 74	● **SLAUGHTER ON TENTH AVENUE** *RCA Victor APL1 0353*	9	7
8 Mar 75	**PLAY DON'T WORRY** *RCA Victor APL1 0681*	29	3

[1] Mick Ronson with Joe Elliott

See also MOTT THE HOOPLE

Linda RONSTADT

US, female vocalist (Singles: 34 weeks, Albums: 46 weeks)

Date	Title	pos	wks
8 May 76	**TRACKS OF MY TEARS** *Asylum K 13034*	42	3
28 Jan 78	**BLUE BAYOU** *Asylum K 13106*	35	4
26 May 79	**ALISON** *Asylum K 13149*	66	2
11 Jul 87	● **SOMEWHERE OUT THERE** *MCA MCA 1132* [1]	8	13
11 Nov 89	● **DON'T KNOW MUCH** *Elektra EKR 101* [2]	2	12
4 Sep 76	**HASTEN DOWN THE WIND** *Asylum K 53045*	32	8
25 Dec 76	**GREATEST HITS** *Asylum K 53055*	37	9
1 Oct 77	**SIMPLE DREAMS** *Asylum K 53065* ▲	15	5
14 Oct 78	**LIVING IN THE USA** *Asylum K 53085* ▲	39	2
8 Mar 80	**MAD LOVE** *Asylum K 52210*	65	1
28 Jan 84	**WHAT'S NEW** *Asylum 96 0260* [1]	31	5
19 Jan 85	**LUSH LIFE** *Asylum 9603871* [1]	100	1
14 Mar 87	**TRIO** *Warner Bros. 9254911* [2]	60	4
11 Nov 89	**CRY LIKE A RAINSTORM – HOWL LIKE THE WIND** *Elektra EKT 76*	43	8
11 Oct 03	**THE VERY BEST OF LINDA RONSTADT** *Elektra 8122736052*	46	3

[1] Linda Ronstadt and James Ingram [2] Linda Ronstadt featuring Aaron Neville
[1] Linda Ronstadt with the Nelson Riddle Orchestra [2] Dolly Parton / Emmylou Harris / Linda Ronstadt

ROOFTOP SINGERS

US, male / female vocal group (Singles: 12 weeks)

Date	Title	pos	wks
31 Jan 63	● **WALK RIGHT IN** *Fontana 271700 TF* ▲	10	12

ROOM 5 featuring Oliver CHEATHAM

Italy, male producer – Vito Lucente and US, male vocalist (Singles: 17 weeks)

Date	Title	pos	wks
5 Apr 03	★ **MAKE LUV** *Positiva CDTIV 187* ■	1	15
6 Dec 03	**MUSIC & YOU** *Positiva CDTIV 197*	38	2

ROOTJOOSE *UK, male vocal / instrumental group (Singles: 3 weeks, Albums: 1 week)*

Date	Title	pos	wks
17 May 97	**CAN'T KEEP LIVING THIS WAY** *Rage RAGECD 2*	73	1
2 Aug 97	**MR FIXIT** *Rage RAGECDX 3*	54	1
4 Oct 97	**LONG WAY** *Rage RAGECD 5*	68	1
18 Oct 97	**RHUBARB** *Rage RAGECD 6*	58	1

ROOTS *US, male rap / production group (Singles: 6 weeks)*

Date	Title	pos	wks
3 May 97	**WHAT THEY DO** *Geffen GFSTD 22240*	49	1
6 Mar 99	**YOU GOT ME** *MCA MCSTD 48110* [1]	31	2
12 Apr 03	**THE SEED (2.0)** *MCA MCSTD 40316* [2]	33	2
16 Aug 03	**BREAK YOU OFF** *MCA MCSTD 40330* [3]	59	1

[1] Roots featuring Erykah Badu [2] Roots featuring Cody Chesnutt [3] Roots featuring Musiq

Ralphi ROSARIO – *See Richie RICH*

Mykal ROSE – *See Shabba RANKS*

ROSE OF ROMANCE ORCHESTRA

UK, orchestra (Singles: 1 week)

Date	Title	pos	wks
9 Jan 82	**TARA'S THEME FROM 'GONE WITH THE WIND'** *BBC RESL 108*	71	1

ROSE ROYCE (382 Top 500)

The best-selling nine-piece soul / dance combo from Los Angeles, whose biggest hits featured vocalist Gwen Dickey, started as a backing band for Motown acts and topped the UK album chart with their Greatest Hits collection in 1980 (Singles: 113 weeks, Albums: 62 weeks)

Date	Title	pos	wks
25 Dec 76	● **CAR WASH** *MCA 267* ▲	9	12
22 Jan 77	**PUT YOUR MONEY WHERE YOUR MOUTH IS** *MCA 259*	44	5
2 Apr 77	**I WANNA GET NEXT TO YOU** *MCA 278*	14	8
24 Sep 77	**DO YOUR DANCE** *Whitfield K 17006*	30	6
14 Jan 78	● **WISHING ON A STAR** *Warner Bros. K 17060*	3	14
6 May 78	**IT MAKES YOU FEEL LIKE DANCIN'** *Warner Bros. K 17148*	16	10
16 Sep 78	● **LOVE DON'T LIVE HERE ANYMORE** *Whitfield K 17236*	2	10
3 Feb 79	**I'M IN LOVE (AND I LOVE THE FEELING)** *Whitfield K 17291*	51	4
17 Nov 79	**IS IT LOVE YOU'RE AFTER** *Whitfield K 17456*	13	13
8 Mar 80	**OOH BOY** *Whitfield K 17575*	46	7
21 Nov 81	**R.R. EXPRESS** *Warner Bros. K 17875*	52	3
1 Sep 84	**MAGIC TOUCH** *Streetwave KHAN 21*	43	8
6 Apr 85	**LOVE ME RIGHT NOW** *Streetwave KHAN 39*	60	3
11 Jun 88	**CAR WASH / IS IT LOVE YOU'RE AFTER (re-issue)** *MCA MCA 1253*	20	7
31 Oct 98	**CAR WASH (re-recording)** *MCA MCSTD 48096* [1]	18	3
22 Oct 77	**IN FULL BLOOM** *Warner Bros. K 56394*	18	13
30 Sep 78	● **STRIKES AGAIN** *Whitfield 56257*	7	11
22 Sep 79	**RAINBOW CONNECTION IV** *Atlantic K 56714*	72	2
1 Mar 80	★ **GREATEST HITS** *Whitfield K RRTV 1*	1	34
13 Oct 84	**MUSIC MAGIC** *Streetwave MKL 2*	69	2

[1] Rose Royce featuring Gwen Dickey

ROSE TATTOO *Australia, male vocal / instrumental group (Singles: 4 weeks, Albums: 4 weeks)*

Date	Title	pos	wks
11 Jul 81	**ROCK 'N' ROLL OUTLAW** *Carrere CAR 200*	60	4
26 Sep 81	**ASSAULT AND BATTERY** *Carrere CAL 127*	40	4

Jimmy ROSELLI *US, male vocalist (Singles: 8 weeks)*

Date	Title	pos	wks
5 Mar 83	**WHEN YOUR OLD WEDDING RING WAS NEW** *A1 282*	51	5
20 Jun 87	**WHEN YOUR OLD WEDDING RING WAS NEW (re-issue)** *First Night SCORE 9*	52	3

ROSIE – *See G NATION featuring ROSIE*

Diana ROSS (13 Top 500)

Perennially popular ex-leader of The Supremes, the most successful girl group of all time, b. Diane Earle, 26 Mar 1944, Detroit, US. Ross continued to clock up worldwide hits after leaving the trio in 1970 and sang lead on at least one hit every year for a record 33 years (1964-1996). The classy vocalist has also had more albums on the UK chart than any other American female artist. Diana, who starred in the movies 'Lady Sings the Blues' (1972), 'Mahogany' (1976) and 'The Wiz' (1978), moved from Motown to RCA in 1981 for a (female) record $20m. In 1994, she was the star of the opening ceremony of football's World Cup, and in 1998 was sampled on US chart-topping singles by Puff Daddy and Monica. In her homeland this supreme song stylist has collected a staggering 22 Top 5 entries during her career, *even though she has not had a major hit there since 1984. She has been inducted into the Soul Train and Songwriters' Hall of Fame and was the recipient of a Lifetime Achievement trophy at the World Music Awards in 1996 (Singles: 560 weeks, Albums: 740 weeks)* pos/wks

30 Aug 67 ● **REFLECTIONS** *Tamla Motown TMG 616* [1] 5 14
29 Nov 67 **IN AND OUT OF LOVE** *Tamla Motown TMG 632* [1] 13 13
10 Apr 68 **FOREVER CAME TODAY** *Tamla Motown TMG 650* [1] 28 8
3 Jul 68 **SOME THINGS YOU NEVER GET USED TO**
Tamla Motown TMG 662 [1] 34 6
20 Nov 68 **LOVE CHILD** *Tamla Motown TMG 677* [1] ▲ 15 14
29 Jan 69 ● **I'M GONNA MAKE YOU LOVE ME** (re)
Tamla Motown TMG 685 [2] 3 12
23 Apr 69 **I'M LIVIN' IN SHAME** (re) *Tamla Motown TMG 695* [1] 14 10
16 Jul 69 **NO MATTER WHAT SIGN YOU ARE**
Tamla Motown TMG 704 [1] 37 7
20 Sep 69 **I SECOND THAT EMOTION** *Tamla Motown TMG 709* [2] 18 8
13 Dec 69 **SOMEDAY WE'LL BE TOGETHER**
Tamla Motown TMG 721 [1] ▲ 13 13
21 Mar 70 **WHY (MUST WE FALL IN LOVE)**
Tamla Motown TMG 730 [2] 31 7
18 Jul 70 **REACH OUT AND TOUCH** *Tamla Motown TMG 743* 33 5
12 Sep 70 ● **AIN'T NO MOUNTAIN HIGH ENOUGH**
Tamla Motown TMG 751 ▲ 6 12
3 Apr 71 ● **REMEMBER ME** *Tamla Motown TMG 768* 7 12
31 Jul 71 ★ **I'M STILL WAITING** *Tamla Motown TMG 781* 1 14
30 Oct 71 ● **SURRENDER** *Tamla Motown TMG 792* 10 11
13 May 72 **DOOBEDOOD'NDOOBE DOOBEDOOD'NDOOBE**
Tamla Motown TMG 812 12 9
14 Jul 73 ● **TOUCH ME IN THE MORNING** (re)
Tamla Motown TMG 861 ▲ 9 13
5 Jan 74 ● **ALL OF MY LIFE** *Tamla Motown TMG 880* 9 13
23 Mar 74 ● **YOU ARE EVERYTHING** *Tamla Motown TMG 890* [3] 5 12
4 May 74 **LAST TIME I SAW HIM** *Tamla Motown TMG 893* 35 4
20 Jul 74 **STOP LOOK LISTEN (TO YOUR HEART)**
Tamla Motown TMG 906 [3] 25 8
24 Aug 74 **BABY LOVE** (re-issue) *Tamla Motown TMG 915* [1] 12 10
28 Sep 74 **LOVE ME** *Tamla Motown TMG 917* 38 5
29 Mar 75 **SORRY DOESN'T ALWAYS MAKE IT RIGHT**
Tamla Motown TMG 941 23 9
3 Apr 76 ● **THEME FROM 'MAHOGANY' (DO YOU KNOW WHERE YOU'RE GOING TO)** *Tamla Motown TMG 1010* ▲ 5 8
24 Apr 76 ● **LOVE HANGOVER** *Tamla Motown TMG 1024* ▲ 10 10
10 Jul 76 **I THOUGHT IT TOOK A LITTLE TIME (BUT TODAY I FELL IN LOVE)** *Tamla Motown TMG 1032* 32 5
16 Oct 76 **I'M STILL WAITING** (re-issue) *Tamla Motown TMG 1041* 41 4
19 Nov 77 **GETTIN' READY FOR LOVE** *Motown TMG 1090* 23 7
22 Jul 78 **LOVIN' LIVIN' AND GIVIN'** *Motown TMG 1112* 54 6
18 Nov 78 **EASE ON DOWN THE ROAD** *MCA 396* [4] 45 4
24 Feb 79 **POPS, WE LOVE YOU** *Motown TMG 1136* [5] 66 5
21 Jul 79 **THE BOSS** *Motown TMG 1150* 40 7
6 Oct 79 **NO ONE GETS THE PRIZE** *Motown TMG 1160* 59 3
24 Nov 79 **IT'S MY HOUSE** *Motown TMG 1169* 32 10
19 Jul 80 ● **UPSIDE DOWN** *Motown TMG 1195* ▲ 2 12
20 Sep 80 ● **MY OLD PIANO** *Motown TMG 1202* 5 9
15 Nov 80 **I'M COMING OUT** *Motown TMG 1210* 13 10
17 Jan 81 **IT'S MY TURN** *Motown TMG 1217* 16 8
28 Mar 81 **ONE MORE CHANCE** *Motown TMG 1227* 49 5
13 Jun 81 **CRYIN' MY HEART OUT FOR YOU** *Motown TMG 1233* 58 3
12 Sep 81 ● **ENDLESS LOVE** *Motown TMG 1240* [6] ▲ 7 12
7 Nov 81 ● **WHY DO FOOLS FALL IN LOVE** *Capitol CL 226* 4 12
23 Jan 82 **TENDERNESS** (re) *Motown TMG 1248* 73 2
30 Jan 82 **MIRROR MIRROR** *Capitol CL 234* 36 5
29 May 82 ● **WORK THAT BODY** *Capitol CL 241* 7 11
7 Aug 82 **IT'S NEVER TOO LATE** *Capitol CL 256* 41 4
23 Oct 82 **MUSCLES** *Capitol CL 268* 15 9
15 Jan 83 **SO CLOSE** *Capitol CL 277* 43 4
23 Jul 83 **PIECES OF ICE** *Capitol CL 298* 46 3
7 Jul 84 **ALL OF YOU** *CBS A 4522* [7] 43 8
15 Sep 84 **TOUCH BY TOUCH** *Capitol CL 337* 47 6
28 Sep 85 **EATEN ALIVE** *Capitol CL 372* 71 1
25 Jan 86 ★ **CHAIN REACTION** *Capitol CL 386* 1 17
3 May 86 **EXPERIENCE** *Capitol CL 400* 47 3
13 Jun 87 **DIRTY LOOKS** *EMI EM 2* 49 3
8 Oct 88 **MR LEE** *EMI EM 73* 58 2
26 Nov 88 **LOVE HANGOVER** (re-mix) *Motown ZB 42307* 75 1
18 Feb 89 **STOP! IN THE NAME OF LOVE** (re-issue)
Motown ZB 41963 [1] 62 1
6 May 89 **WORKIN' OVERTIME** *EMI EM 91* 32 5
29 Jul 89 **PARADISE** *EMI EM 94* 61 2
7 Jul 90 **I'M STILL WAITING** (re-mix) *Motown ZB 43781* 21 6
30 Nov 91 ● **WHEN YOU TELL ME THAT YOU LOVE ME** *EMI EM 217* 2 11
15 Feb 92 **THE FORCE BEHIND THE POWER** *EMI EM 221* 27 3
20 Jun 92 ● **ONE SHINING MOMENT** *EMI EM 239* 10 8
28 Nov 92 **IF WE HOLD ON TOGETHER** *EMI EM 257* 11 10
13 Mar 93 **HEART (DON'T CHANGE MY MIND)** *EMI CDEM 261* 31 3
9 Oct 93 **CHAIN REACTION** (re-issue) *EMI CDEM 290* 20 5
11 Dec 93 **YOUR LOVE** *EMI CDEM 299* 14 8
2 Apr 94 **THE BEST YEARS OF MY LIFE** *EMI CDEM 305* 28 4
9 Jul 94 **WHY DO FOOLS FALL IN LOVE / I'M COMING OUT**
(re-issue) (re-mix) *EMI CDEM 332* 36 4
2 Sep 95 **TAKE ME HIGHER** *EMI CDEM 388* 32 4
25 Nov 95 **I'M GONE** *EMI CDEM 402* 36 3
17 Feb 96 **I WILL SURVIVE** *EMI CDEM 415* [8] 14 4
21 Dec 96 **IN THE ONES YOU LOVE** *EMI CDEM 457* 34 4
6 Nov 99 ● **NOT OVER YOU YET** (re) *EMI CDEMS 553* 9 7
20 Jan 68 ★ **GREATEST HITS** *Tamla Motown STML 11063* [1] ▲ 1 60
30 Mar 68 ● **LIVE AT THE TALK OF THE TOWN**
Tamla Motown STML 11070 [1] 6 18
20 Jul 68 **REFLECTIONS** *Tamla Motown STML 11073* [1] 30 2
25 Jan 69 ★ **DIANA ROSS AND THE SUPREMES JOIN THE TEMPTATIONS**
Tamla Motown STML 11096 [2] ▲ 1 15
1 Feb 69 ● **LOVE CHILD** *Tamla Motown STML 11095* [1] 8 6
28 Jun 69 **TCB** *Tamla Motown STML 11110* [2] 11 12
14 Feb 70 **TOGETHER** *Tamla Motown STML 11122* [2] 28 4
24 Oct 70 **DIANA ROSS** *Tamla Motown SFTML 11159* 14 5
19 Jun 71 **EVERYTHING IS EVERYTHING** *Tamla Motown STML 11178* 31 3
9 Oct 71 **I'M STILL WAITING** *Tamla Motown STML 11193* 43 1
9 Oct 71 ● **DIANA** *Tamla Motown STMA 8001* 10 11
11 Nov 72 **GREATEST HITS** *Tamla Motown STMA 8006* 34 10
1 Sep 73 ● **TOUCH ME IN THE MORNING**
Tamla Motown STML 11239 7 35
27 Oct 73 **LADY SINGS THE BLUES** *Tamla Motown TMSP 1131* ▲ 50 1
19 Jan 74 ● **DIANA AND MARVIN** *Tamla Motown STMA 8015* [3] 6 43
2 Mar 74 **LAST TIME I SAW HIM** *Tamla Motown STML 11255* 41 1
8 Jun 74 **LIVE** *Tamla Motown STML 11248* 21 8
27 Mar 76 ● **DIANA ROSS** *Tamla Motown STML 12022* 4 26
7 Aug 76 ● **GREATEST HITS 2** *Tamla Motown STML 12036* 2 29
19 Mar 77 **AN EVENING WITH DIANA ROSS** *Motown TMSP 6005* 52 1
4 Aug 79 **THE BOSS** *Motown STML 12118* 52 2
17 Sep 77 ★ **20 GOLDEN GREATS** *Motown EMTV 5* [1] ■ 1 34
17 Nov 79 ● **20 GOLDEN GREATS** *Motown EMTV 21* 2 29
21 Jun 80 **DIANA** *Motown STMA 8033* 12 32
28 Mar 81 **TO LOVE AGAIN** *Motown STML 12152* 26 10
29 Aug 81 **DIANA AND MARVIN** (re-issue) *Motown STMS 5001* [3] 78 2
7 Nov 81 **WHY DO FOOLS FALL IN LOVE** *Capitol EST 26733* 17 24
21 Nov 81 **ALL THE GREAT HITS** *Motown STMA 8036* 21 31
13 Feb 82 **DIANA'S DUETS** *Motown STML 12163* 43 6
23 Oct 82 **SILK ELECTRIC** *Capitol EAST 27313* 33 12
4 Dec 82 ● **LOVE SONGS** *K-Tel NE 1200* 5 17
19 Jul 83 **ROSS** *Capitol EST 1867051* 44 5
24 Dec 83 ● **PORTRAIT** *Telstar STAR 2238* 8 31
6 Oct 84 **SWEPT AWAY** *Capitol ROSS 1* 40 5
28 Sep 85 **EATEN ALIVE** *Capitol ROSS 2* 11 19
15 Nov 86 **DIANA ROSS. MICHAEL JACKSON. GLADYS KNIGHT. STEVIE WONDER. THEIR VERY BEST BACK TO BACK**
Priority TV PTVR 2 [4] 21 10
30 May 87 **RED HOT RHYTHM 'N' BLUES** *EMI EMC 3532* 47 4
31 Oct 87 **LOVE SONGS** *Telstar STAR 2298* [5] 12 24
21 Jan 89 ● **LOVE SUPREME** *Motown ZL 72701* [1] 10 9
27 May 89 **WORKIN' OVERTIME** *EMI EMD 1009* 23 4
25 Nov 89 **GREATEST HITS LIVE** *EMI EMDC 1001* 34 6
14 Dec 91 **THE FORCE BEHIND THE POWER** *EMI EMD 1023* 11 31
29 Feb 92 **MOTOWN'S GREATEST HITS** *Motown 5300132* 20 11
24 Apr 93 **LIVE STOLEN MOMENTS** *EMI CDEMD 1044* 45 2
30 Oct 93 ★ **ONE WOMAN – THE ULTIMATE COLLECTION**
EMI CDONE 1 1 67
25 Dec 93 **CHRISTMAS IN VIENNA** *Sony Classical SK 53358* [6] 71 2
23 Apr 94 **DIANA EXTENDED – THE REMIXES** *EMI CDDREX 1* 58 1
26 Nov 94 **A VERY SPECIAL SEASON** *EMI CDEMD 1075* 37 6

16 Sep 95 ● **TAKE ME HIGHER** *EMI CDEMD 1085* 10 3
23 Nov 96 **VOICE OF LOVE** *EMI CDEMD 1100* 42 7
31 Oct 98 **40 GOLDEN MOTOWN GREATS** *Motown / PolyGram TV 5309612* [1] 35 4
20 Nov 99 **EVERY DAY IS A NEW DAY** *EMI 5214762* 71 1
17 Nov 01 **LOVE & LIFE – THE VERY BEST OF DIANA ROSS** *EMI / Universal TV 5358622* 28 7

[1] Diana Ross and the Supremes [2] Diana Ross and the Supremes and the Temptations [3] Diana Ross and Marvin Gaye [4] Diana Ross and Michael Jackson [5] Diana Ross, Marvin Gaye, Smokey Robinson and Stevie Wonder [6] Diana Ross and Lionel Richie [7] Julio Iglesias and Diana Ross [8] Diana [1] Diana Ross and the Supremes [2] Diana Ross and the Supremes with the Temptations [3] Diana Ross and Marvin Gaye [4] Diana Ross / Michael Jackson / Gladys Knight / Stevie Wonder [5] Diana Ross and Michael Jackson [6] Placido Domingo, Diana Ross and José Carreras

The two 'Diana' albums and both 'Diana Ross' titles are different. From 14 Jan 89 when multi-artist albums were excluded from the main chart, 'Love Songs' by Diana Ross and Michael Jackson was listed in the compilation albums chart

See also SUPREMES

Ricky ROSS

UK, male vocalist (Singles: 3 weeks, Albums: 1 week) pos/wks

18 May 96 **RADIO ON** *Epic 6631352* 35 2
10 Aug 96 **GOOD EVENING PHILADELPHIA** *Epic 6635335* 58 1
15 Jun 96 **WHAT YOU ARE** *Epic 4839982* 36 1

See also DEACON BLUE

Francis ROSSI

UK, male vocalist (Singles: 6 weeks) pos/wks

11 May 85 **MODERN ROMANCE (I WANT TO FALL IN LOVE AGAIN)** *Vertigo FROS 1* [1] 54 4
3 Aug 96 **GIVE MYSELF TO LOVE** *Virgin VSCDT 1594* [2] 42 2

[1] Francis Rossi and Bernard Frost [2] Francis Rossi of Status Quo

See also STATUS QUO

Natalie ROSSI – *See FOUNDATION featuring Natalie ROSSI*

Nini ROSSO

Italy, male instrumentalist – trumpet (Singles: 14 weeks) pos/wks

26 Aug 65 ● **IL SILENZIO** *Durium DRS 54000* 8 14

ROSTAL and SCHAEFER

UK, male instrumental duo (Albums: 2 weeks) pos/wks

14 Jul 79 **BEATLES CONCERTO** *Parlophone PAS 10014* 61 2

Mstilav ROSTROPOVICH – *See Herbert VON KARAJAN*

David Lee ROTH

US, male vocalist (Singles: 15 weeks, Albums: 32 weeks) pos/wks

23 Feb 85 **CALIFORNIA GIRLS** *Warner Bros. W 9102* 68 2
5 Mar 88 **JUST LIKE PARADISE** *Warner Bros. W 8119* 27 7
3 Sep 88 **DAMN GOOD / STAND UP** *Warner Bros. W 7753* 72 1
12 Jan 91 **A LIL' AIN'T ENOUGH** *Warner Bros. W 0002* 32 3
19 Feb 94 **SHE'S MY MACHINE** *Reprise W 0229CD* 64 1
28 May 94 **NIGHT LIFE** *Reprise W 0249CD* 72 1
2 Mar 85 **CRAZY FROM THE HEAT** *Warner Bros. 9252221* 91 2
19 Jul 86 **EAT 'EM AND SMILE** *Warner Bros. WX 56* 28 9
6 Feb 88 **SKYSCRAPER** *Warner Bros. 925671 1* 11 12
26 Jan 91 ● **A LITTLE AIN'T ENOUGH** *Warner Bros. WX 403* 4 7
19 Mar 94 **YOUR FILTHY LITTLE MOUTH** *Reprise 9362453912* 28 2

See also VAN HALEN

Uli Jon ROTH and ELECTRIC SUN

Germany, male vocal / instrumental group (Albums: 2 weeks) pos/wks

23 Feb 85 **BEYOND THE ASTRAL SKIES** *EMI ROTH 1* 64 2

ROTTERDAM TERMINATION SOURCE

Holland, male instrumental / production duo – Maurice Steenbergen and Danny Scholte (Singles: 6 weeks) pos/wks

7 Nov 92 **POING** *SEP EDGE 74* 27 4
25 Dec 93 **MERRY X-MESS** *React CDREACT 33* 73 2

ROULA – *See 20 FINGERS*

ROULETTES – *See Adam FAITH*

Thomas ROUND – *See June BRONHILL and Thomas ROUND*

ROUND SOUND presents ONYX STONE & MC MALIBU

UK, male production trio and male rappers (Singles: 1 week) pos/wks

16 Mar 02 **WHADDA WE LIKE?** *Cooltempo CDCOOL 358* 69 1

Demis ROUSSOS (344 Top 500)

Unmistakable Greek MOR vocalist / multi-instrumentalist and entertainer, b. 15 Jun 1947, Egypt. He was in Aphrodite's Child (with Vangelis) before starting successful solo career. The Roussos Phenomenon was the first four-track EP to top the singles chart (Singles: 44 weeks, Albums: 147 weeks) pos/wks

22 Nov 75 ● **HAPPY TO BE ON AN ISLAND IN THE SUN** *Philips 6042 033* 5 10
28 Feb 76 **CAN'T SAY HOW MUCH I LOVE YOU** *Philips 6042 114* 35 5
26 Jun 76 ★ **THE ROUSSOS PHENOMENON (EP)** *Philips DEMIS 001* 1 12
2 Oct 76 ● **WHEN FOREVER HAS GONE** *Philips 6042 186* 2 10
19 Mar 77 **BECAUSE** *Philips 6042 245* 39 4
18 Jun 77 **KYRILA (EP)** *Philips Demis 002* 33 3
22 Jun 74 ● **FOREVER AND EVER** *Philips 6325 021* 2 68
19 Apr 75 **SOUVENIRS** *Philips 6325 201* 25 18
24 Apr 76 ● **HAPPY TO BE** *Philips 9101 027* 4 34
3 Jul 76 **MY ONLY FASCINATION** *Philips 6325 094* 39 6
16 Apr 77 **THE MAGIC OF DEMIS ROUSSOS** *Philips 9101 131* 29 6
28 Oct 78 **LIFE AND LOVE** *Philips 9199 873* 36 11
16 Mar 02 **FOREVER AND EVER – THE DEFINITIVE COLLECTION** *Philips 5867702* 17 4

Tracks on The Roussos Phenomenon (EP): Forever and Ever / Sing an Ode to Love / So Dreamy / My Friend the Wind. Tracks on Kyrila (EP): Kyrila / I'm Gonna Fall in Love / I Dig You / Sister Emilyne

ROUTERS

US, male instrumental group (Singles: 7 weeks) pos/wks

27 Dec 62 **LET'S GO** *Warner Bros. WB 77* 32 7

Maria ROWE

UK, female vocalist (Singles: 2 weeks) pos/wks

20 May 95 **SEXUAL** *ffrr FCD 248* 67 2

ROWETTA – *See OPEN ARMS featuring ROWETTA*

Kelly ROWLAND

US, female vocalist (Singles: 54 weeks, Albums: 26 weeks) pos/wks

26 Oct 02 ★ **DILEMMA** *Universal MCSTD 40299* [1] ■ ▲ 1 21
28 Dec 02 **STOLE (import)** *Columbia 6732122* 57 5
8 Feb 03 ● **STOLE (re)** *Columbia 6735182* 2 14
10 May 03 ● **CAN'T NOBODY** *Columbia 6738142* 5 10
16 Aug 03 **TRAIN ON A TRACK** *Columbia 6742155* 20 4
15 Feb 03 ★ **SIMPLY DEEP** *Columbia 5096042* ■ 1 26

[1] Nelly featuring Kelly Rowland

See also DESTINY'S CHILD

Kevin ROWLAND – *See DEXY'S MIDNIGHT RUNNERS*

John ROWLES

New Zealand, male vocalist (Singles: 28 weeks) pos/wks

13 Mar 68 ● **IF I ONLY HAD TIME** *MCA MU 1000* 3 18
19 Jun 68 **HUSH ... NOT A WORD TO MARY** *MCA MU 1023* 12 10

Lisa ROXANNE

UK, female vocalist – Lisa Roxanne Naraine (Singles: 2 weeks) pos/wks

9 Jun 01 **NO FLOW** *Palm Pictures PPCD 70542* 18 2

The 706 No.1 Albums

NO.1 ALBUMS OF THE 90S

Here is the complete chronological list of every UK chart-topping album from the 90s. All dates given are for an album's first week at No.1, not its first entry into the chart. The run at the top of the chart in weeks follows in brackets, followed by the US peak position of the album.

1990

27 Jan COLOUR Christians (1 week)
3 Feb ...BUT SERIOUSLY Phil Collins (7 weeks) US 1
24 Mar I DO NOT WANT WHAT I HAVEN'T GOT Sinead O'Connor (1 week) US 1
31 Mar CHANGESBOWIE David Bowie (1 week) US 39
7 Apr ONLY YESTERDAY Carpenters (2 weeks)
21 Apr BEHIND THE MASK Fleetwood Mac (1 week) US 18
28 Apr ONLY YESTERDAY Carpenters (5 weeks)
2 Jun VOL II (1990 A NEW DECADE) Soul II Soul (3 weeks) US 21
23 Jun THE ESSENTIAL PAVAROTTI Luciano Pavarotti (1 week)
30 Jun STEP BY STEP New Kids on the Block (1 week) US 1
7 Jul THE ESSENTIAL PAVAROTTI Luciano Pavarotti (3 weeks)
28 Jul SLEEPING WITH THE PAST Elton John (5 weeks) US 23
1 Sep GRAFFITI BRIDGE Prince (1 week) US 6
8 Sep IN CONCERT Luciano Pavarotti / Placido Domingo / José Carreras (1 week)
15 Sep LISTEN WITHOUT PREJUDICE VOL. 1 George Michael (1 week) US 2
22 Sep IN CONCERT Luciano Pavarotti / Placido Domingo / José Carreras (4 weeks)
20 Oct SOME FRIENDLY Charlatans (1 week) US 73
27 Oct THE RHYTHM OF THE SAINTS Paul Simon (2 weeks) US 4
10 Nov THE VERY BEST OF ELTON JOHN Elton John (2 weeks)
24 Nov THE IMMACULATE COLLECTION Madonna (9 weeks) US 3

1991

26 Jan MCMXC A.D. Enigma (1 week) US 6
2 Feb THE SOUL CAGES Sting (1 week) US 2
9 Feb DOUBT Jesus Jones (1 week) US 25
16 Feb INNUENDO Queen (2 weeks) US 30
2 Mar CIRCLE OF ONE Oleta Adams (1 week) US 20
9 Mar AUBERGE Chris Rea (1 week) US 176
16 Mar SPARTACUS Farm (1 week)
23 Mar OUT OF TIME R.E.M. (1 week) US 1
30 Mar GREATEST HITS Eurythmics (9 weeks) US 72
1 Jun SEAL Seal (3 weeks) US 15
22 Jun GREATEST HITS Eurythmics (1 week) US 72
29 Jun LOVE HURTS Cher (6 weeks) US 48
10 Aug ESSENTIAL PAVAROTTI II Luciano Pavarotti (2 weeks)
24 Aug METALLICA Metallica (1 week) US 1
31 Aug JOSEPH AND THE AMAZING TECHNICOLOR DREAM COAT Jason Donovan/Cast (2 weeks)
14 Sep FROM TIME TO TIME – THE SINGLES COLLECTION Paul Young (1 week)
21 Sep ON EVERY STREET Dire Straits (1 week) US 12
28 Sep USE YOUR ILLUSION II Guns N' Roses (1 week) US 2
5 Oct WAKING UP THE NEIGHBOURS Bryan Adams (1 week) US 6
12 Oct STARS Simply Red (2 weeks) US 76
26 Oct CHORUS Erasure (1 week) US 29
2 Nov STARS Simply Red (1 week) US 76
9 Nov QUEEN'S GREATEST HITS II Queen (1 week)
16 Nov SHEPHERD MOONS Enya (1 week) US 17
23 Nov WE CAN'T DANCE Genesis (1 week) US 4
30 Nov DANGEROUS Michael Jackson (1 week) US 1
7 Dec QUEEN'S GREATEST HITS II Queen (4 weeks)

1992

4 Jan STARS Simply Red (5 weeks) US 76
8 Feb HIGH ON THE HAPPY SIDE Wet Wet Wet (2 weeks)
22 Feb STARS Simply Red (3 weeks) US 76
14 Mar DIVINE MADNESS Madness (3 weeks)
4 Apr HUMAN TOUCH Bruce Springsteen (1 week) US 2
11 Apr ADRENALIZE Def Leppard (1 week) US 1
18 Apr DIVA Annie Lennox (1 week) US 23
25 Apr UP Right Said Fred (1 week) US 46
2 May WISH Cure (1 week) US 2
9 May STARS Simply Red (1 week) US 76
16 May 1992 – THE LOVE ALBUM Carter – the Unstoppable Sex Machine (1 week)
23 May FEAR OF THE DARK Iron Maiden (1 week) US 12
30 May MICHAEL BALL Michael Ball (1 week)
6 Jun BACK TO FRONT Lionel Richie (6 weeks) US 19
18 Jul U.F.ORB Orb (1 week)
25 Jul THE GREATEST HITS 1966-1992 Neil Diamond (3 weeks) US 90
15 Aug WELCOME TO WHEREVER YOU ARE INXS (1 week) US 16
22 Aug WE CAN'T DANCE Genesis (1 week) US 4
29 Aug BEST...1 Smiths (1 week) US 139
5 Sep GREATEST HITS Kylie Minogue (1 week)
12 Sep TUBULAR BELLS II Mike Oldfield (2 weeks)
26 Sep THE BEST OF BELINDA VOL. I Belinda Carlisle (1 week)
3 Oct GOLD – GREATEST HITS Abba (1 week) US 63
10 Oct AUTOMATIC FOR THE PEOPLE R.E.M. (1 week) US 2
17 Oct SYMBOL Prince (1 week) US 5
24 Oct GLITTERING PRIZE 81-92 Simple Minds (3 weeks)
14 Nov KEEP THE FAITH Bon Jovi (1 week) US 5
21 Nov CHER'S GREATEST HITS: 1965-1992 Cher (1 week)
28 Nov POP! – THE FIRST 20 HITS Erasure (2 weeks) US 112
12 Dec CHER'S GREATEST HITS: 1965-1992 Cher (6 weeks)

1993

23 Jan LIVE – THE WAY WE WALK VOLUME II – THE LONGS Genesis (2 weeks) US 20
6 Feb JAM Little Angels (1 week)
13 Feb PURE CULT Cult (1 week)
20 Feb WORDS OF LOVE Buddy Holly and the Crickets (1 week)
27 Feb WALTHAMSTOW East 17 (1 week)
6 Mar DIVA Annie Lennox (1 week) US 23
13 Mar ARE YOU GONNA GO MY WAY Lenny Kravitz (2 weeks) US 12
27 Mar THEIR GREATEST HITS Hot Chocolate (1 week)
3 Apr SONGS OF FAITH AND DEVOTION Depeche Mode (1 week) US 1
10 Apr SUEDE Suede (1 week)
17 Apr BLACK TIE WHITE NOISE David Bowie (1 week) US 93
24 Apr AUTOMATIC FOR THE PEOPLE R.E.M. (1 week) US 2

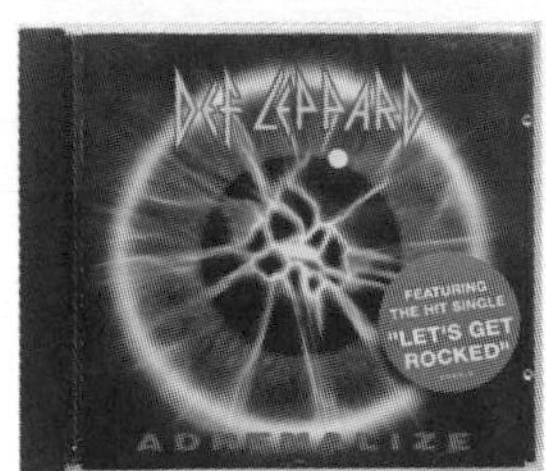

1992: ADRENALIZE Def Leppard's follow-up to the hugely successful 'Hysteria' and the first album recorded after the death of guitarist Steve Clark

1995: THE GREAT ESCAPE Blur's great pop album topped the charts three weeks before the mega-seller from their Britpop rivals Oasis, '(What's the Story) Morning Glory', made No.1. 'The Great Escape' includes 'The Universal', 'Charmless Man' and 'Country House'

1 May THE ALBUM Cliff Richard (1 week)
8 May AUTOMATIC FOR THE PEOPLE R.E.M. (1 week) US 2
15 May REPUBLIC New Order (1 week) US 11
22 May AUTOMATIC FOR THE PEOPLE R.E.M. (1 week) US 2
29 May JANET Janet Jackson (2 weeks) US 1
12 Jun NO LIMITS 2 Unlimited (1 week)
19 Jun WHAT'S LOVE GOT TO DO WITH IT Tina Turner (1 week) US 17
26 Jun EMERGENCY ON PLANET EARTH Jamiroquai (3 weeks)
17 Jul ZOOROPA U2 (1 week) US 1
24 Jul PROMISES AND LIES UB40 (7 weeks) US 6
11 Sep MUSIC BOX Mariah Carey (1 week) US 1
18 Sep BAT OUT OF HELL II – BACK INTO HELL Meat Loaf (1 week) US 1
25 Sep IN UTERO Nirvana (1 week) US 1
2 Oct BAT OUT OF HELL II – BACK INTO HELL Meat Loaf (1 week) US 1
9 Oct VERY Pet Shop Boys (1 week) US 20
16 Oct BAT OUT OF HELL II – BACK INTO HELL Meat Loaf (1 week) US 1
23 Oct EVERYTHING CHANGES Take That (1 week)
30 Oct BAT OUT OF HELL II – BACK INTO HELL Meat Loaf (1 week) US 1
20 Nov BOTH SIDES Phil Collins (1 week) US 13
27 Nov BAT OUT OF HELL II – BACK INTO HELL Meat Loaf (5 weeks) US 1

1994

1 Jan ONE WOMAN – THE ULTIMATE COLLECTION Diana Ross (1 week)
8 Jan EVERYTHING CHANGES Take That (1 week)
15 Jan SO FAR SO GOOD Bryan Adams (1 week) US 6
22 Jan ONE WOMAN – THE ULTIMATE COLLECTION Diana Ross (1 week)
29 Jan TEASE ME Chaka Demus and Pliers (2 weeks)
12 Feb UNDER THE PINK Tori Amos (1 week) US 12
19 Feb CROSS OF CHANGES Enigma (1 week) US 9
26 Feb MUSIC BOX Mariah Carey (4 weeks) US 1
26 Mar VAUXHALL AND I Morrissey (1 week) US 18
2 Apr MUSIC BOX Mariah Carey (1 week) US 1
9 Apr THE DIVISION BELL Pink Floyd (4 weeks) US 1
7 May PARKLIFE Blur (1 week)
14 May OUR TOWN – GREATEST HITS Deacon Blue (2 weeks)
28 May I SAY I SAY I SAY Erasure (1 week) US 18
4 Jun SEAL Seal (2 weeks) US 15
18 Jun REAL THINGS 2 Unlimited (1 week)
25 Jun EVERYBODY ELSE IS DOING IT, SO WHY CAN'T WE Cranberries (1 week) US 18
2 Jul HAPPY NATION Ace of Base (2 weeks) US 1
16 Jul MUSIC FOR THE JILTED GENERATION Prodigy (1 week) US 198
23 Jul VOODOO LOUNGE Rolling Stones (1 week) US 2
30 Jul END OF PART ONE (THEIR GREATEST HITS) Wet Wet Wet (4 weeks)
27 Aug COME Prince (1 week) US 15
3 Sep END OF PART ONE (THEIR GREATEST HITS) Wet Wet Wet (1 week)
10 Sep DEFINITELY MAYBE Oasis (1 week) US 58
17 Sep THE 3 TENORS IN CONCERT 1994 José Carreras, Placido Domingo and Luciano Pavarotti (1 week) US 4
24 Sep FROM THE CRADLE Eric Clapton (1 week) US 1
1 Oct SONGS Luther Vandross (1 week) US 5
8 Oct MONSTER R.E.M. (2 weeks) US 1
22 Oct CROSSROAD – THE BEST OF Bon Jovi (3 weeks) US 8
12 Nov UNPLUGGED IN NEW YORK Nirvana (1 week) US 1
19 Nov CROSSROAD – THE BEST OF Bon Jovi (2 weeks) US 8
3 Dec CARRY ON UP THE CHARTS – THE BEST OF Beautiful South (1 week)
10 Dec LIVE AT THE BBC Beatles (1 week) US 3
17 Dec CARRY ON UP THE CHARTS – THE BEST OF Beautiful South (6 weeks)

1995

28 Jan THE COLOUR OF MY LOVE Celine Dion (6 weeks) US 4
11 Mar GREATEST HITS Bruce Springsteen (1 week) US 1
18 Mar MEDUSA Annie Lennox (1 week) US 11
25 Mar ELASTICA Elastica (1 week) US 66
1 Apr THE COLOUR OF MY LOVE Celine Dion (1 week) US 4
8 Apr WAKE UP! Boo Radleys (1 week)
15 Apr GREATEST HITS Bruce Springsteen (1 week) US 1
22 Apr PICTURE THIS Wet Wet Wet (3 weeks)
13 May NOBODY ELSE Take That (2 weeks) US 69
27 May STANLEY ROAD Paul Weller (1 week)
3 Jun SINGLES Alison Moyet (1 week)
10 Jun PULSE Pink Floyd (2 weeks) US 1
24 Jun HISTORY-PAST, PRESENT AND FUTURE, BOOK I Michael Jackson (1 week) US 1
1 Jul THESE DAYS Bon Jovi (4 weeks) US 9
29 Jul I SHOULD COCO Supergrass (3 weeks)
19 Aug IT'S GREAT WHEN YOUR'RE STRAIGHT … YEAH! Black Grape (2 weeks)
2 Sep SAID AND DONE Boyzone (1 week)
9 Sep THE CHARLATANS Charlatans (1 week)
16 Sep ZEITGEIST Levellers (1 week)
23 Sep THE GREAT ESCAPE Blur (2 weeks) US 150
7 Oct DAYDREAM Mariah Carey (1 week) US 1
14 Oct (WHAT'S THE STORY) MORNING GLORY Oasis (1 week) US 4
21 Oct LIFE Simply Red (3 weeks) US 75
11 Nov DIFFERENT CLASS Pulp (1 week)
18 Nov MADE IN HEAVEN Queen (1 week) US 58
25 Nov ROBSON & JEROME Robson & Jerome (7 weeks)

1996

13 Jan (WHAT'S THE STORY) MORNING GLORY Oasis (6 weeks) US 4
24 Feb EXPECTING TO FLY Bluetones (1 week)
2 Mar (WHAT'S THE STORY) MORNING GLORY Oasis (3 weeks) US 4
23 Mar FALLING INTO YOU Celine Dion (1 week) US 1
30 Mar ANTHOLOGY 2 Beatles (1 week) US 1
6 Apr GREATEST HITS Take That (4 weeks)
4 May JAGGED LITTLE PILL Alanis Morissette (2 weeks) US 1
18 May 1977 Ash (1 week)
25 May OLDER George Michael (3 weeks) US 6
15 Jun LOAD Metallica (1 week) US 1
22 Jun 18 TIL I DIE Bryan Adams (1 week) US 31
29 Jun JAGGED LITTLE PILL Alanis Morissette (1 week)

NO.1 ALBUMS OF THE 90S CONTINUED

1998: LIFE THRU A LENS
The first of five consecutive solo No.1 albums for Robbie Williams. 'Life Thru a Lens' has clocked up 123 weeks on chart in total up to the end of 2003

6 Jul RECURRING DREAM – THE VERY BEST OF **Crowded House** (2 weeks)
20 Jul JAGGED LITTLE PILL **Alanis Morissette** (8 weeks) US 1
14 Sep COMING UP **Suede** (1 week)
21 Sep NEW ADVENTURES IN HI-FI **R.E.M.** (1 week) US 2
28 Sep K **Kula Shaker** (2 weeks) US 200
12 Oct NATURAL **Peter Andre** (1 week)
19 Oct GREATEST HITS **Simply Red** (2 weeks) US 116
2 Nov BLUE IS THE COLOUR **Beautiful South** (1 week)
9 Nov A DIFFERENT BEAT **Boyzone** (1 week)
16 Nov SPICE **Spice Girls** (1 week) US 1
23 Nov TAKE TWO **Robson & Jerome** (2 weeks)
7 Dec SPICE **Spice Girls** (8 weeks) US 1

1997

1 Feb EVITA Soundtrack **Various / Madonna** (1 week) US 2
8 Feb GLOW **Reef** (1 week)
15 Feb WHITE ON BLONDE **Texas** (1 week)
22 Feb BLUR **Blur** (1 week) US 61
1 Mar ATTACK OF THE GREY LANTERN **Mansun** (1 week)
8 Mar SPICE **Spice Girls** (1 week) US 1
15 Mar POP **U2** (1 week) US 1
22 Mar SPICE **Spice Girls** (4 weeks) US 1
19 Apr DIG YOUR OWN HOLE **Chemical Brothers** (1 week) US 14
26 Apr ULTRA **Depeche Mode** (1 week) US 5
3 May TELLIN' STORIES **Charlatans** (2 weeks)
17 May SPICE **Spice Girls** (1 week) US 1
24 May BLOOD ON THE DANCE FLOOR **Michael Jackson** (2 weeks) US 24
7 Jun OPEN ROAD **Gary Barlow** (1 week)
14 Jun WU-TANG FOREVER **Wu-Tang Clan** (1 week) US 1
21 Jun MIDDLE OF NOWHERE **Hanson** (1 week) US 2
28 Jun OK COMPUTER **Radiohead** (2 weeks) US 21
12 Jul THE FAT OF THE LAND **Prodigy** (6 weeks) US 1
23 Aug WHITE ON BLONDE **Texas** (1 week)
30 Aug BE HERE NOW **Oasis** (4 weeks) US 2
27 Sep MARCHIN' ALREADY **Ocean Colour Scene** (1 week)
4 Oct BE HERE NOW **Oasis** (1 week)
11 Oct URBAN HYMNS **Verve** (5 weeks) US 23
15 Nov SPICEWORLD **Spice Girls** (2 weeks) US 3
29 Nov LET'S TALK ABOUT LOVE **Celine Dion** (2 weeks) US 1
13 Dec SPICEWORLD **Spice Girls** (1 week) US 3
20 Dec LET'S TALK ABOUT LOVE **Celine Dion** (2 weeks) US 1

1998

3 Jan URBAN HYMNS **Verve** (6 weeks) US 23
14 Feb TITANIC Soundtrack **James Horner** (1 week) US 1
21 Feb URBAN HYMNS **Verve** (1 week) US 23
28 Feb TITANIC Soundtrack **James Horner** (2 weeks) US 1
14 Mar RAY OF LIGHT **Madonna** (2 weeks) US 2
28 Mar LET'S TALK ABOUT LOVE **Celine Dion** (1 week) US 1
4 Apr THE BEST OF **James** (1 week)
11 Apr THIS IS HARDCORE **Pulp** (1 week) US 114
18 Apr LIFE THRU A LENS **Robbie Williams** (2 weeks)
2 May MEZZANINE **Massive Attack** (2 weeks) US 60
16 May INTERNATIONAL VELVET **Catatonia** (1 week)
23 May VERSION 2.0 **Garbage** (1 week) US 13
30 May BLUE **Simply Red** (1 week) US 145
6 Jun WHERE WE BELONG **Boyzone** (1 week) US 167
13 Jun BLUE **Simply Red** (1 week) US 145
20 Jun THE GOOD WILL OUT **Embrace** (1 week)
27 Jun TALK ON CORNERS **Corrs** (1 week) US 72
4 Jul FIVE **Five** (1 week) US 27
11 Jul TALK ON CORNERS **Corrs** (1 week) US 72
18 Jul HELLO NASTY **Beastie Boys** (1 week) US 1
25 Jul JANE McDONALD **Jane McDonald** (3 weeks)
15 Aug TALK ON CORNERS **Corrs** (3 weeks) US 72
5 Sep WHERE WE BELONG **Boyzone** (2 weeks) US 167
19 Sep TALK ON CORNERS **Corrs** (1 week) US 72
26 Sep THIS IS MY TRUTH TELL ME YOURS **Manic Street Preachers** (3 weeks)
17 Oct HITS **Phil Collins** (1 week) US 18
24 Oct QUENCH **Beautiful South** (2 weeks)
7 Nov I'VE BEEN EXPECTING YOU **Robbie Williams** (1 week)
14 Nov THE BEST OF 1980-1990 & B-SIDES **U2** (1 week) US 2
21 Nov LADIES & GENTLEMEN – THE BEST OF **George Michael** (8 weeks) US 24

1999

16 Jan I'VE BEEN EXPECTING YOU **Robbie Williams** (1 week)
23 Jan YOU'VE COME A LONG WAY, BABY **Fatboy Slim** (4 weeks) US 34
20 Feb I'VE BEEN EXPECTING YOU **Robbie Williams** (1 week)
27 Feb TALK ON CORNERS **Corrs** (3 weeks) US 72
20 Mar PERFORMANCE AND COCKTAILS **Stereophonics** (1 week)
27 Mar 13 **Blur** (2 weeks) US 80
10 Apr TALK ON CORNERS **Corrs** (1 week) US 72
17 Apr GOLD – GREATEST HITS **Abba** (1 week) US 63
24 Apr EQUALLY CURSED AND BLESSED **Catatonia** (1 week)
1 May GOLD – GREATEST HITS **Abba** (2 weeks) US 63
15 May HEAD MUSIC **Suede** (1 week)
22 May THE HUSH **Texas** (1 week)
29 May GOLD – GREATEST HITS **Abba** (2 weeks) US 63
12 Jun BY REQUEST **Boyzone** (2 weeks)
26 Jun SYNKRONIZED **Jamiroquai** (1 week) US 28
3 Jul SURRENDER **Chemical Brothers** (1 week) US 32
10 Jul BY REQUEST **Boyzone** (7 weeks)
28 Aug THE MAN WHO **Travis** (2 weeks) US 135
11 Sep COME ON OVER **Shania Twain** (3 weeks) US 2
2 Oct RHYTHM AND STEALTH **Leftfield** (1 week)
9 Oct RELOAD **Tom Jones** (1 week)
16 Oct COME ON OVER **Shania Twain** (3 weeks) US 2
6 Nov STEPTACULAR **Steps** (3 weeks)
27 Nov ALL THE WAY… A DECADE OF SONG **Celine Dion** (1 week) US 1
4 Dec STEPTACULAR **Steps** (1 week)
11 Dec COME ON OVER **Shania Twain** (5 weeks) US 2

ROXETTE 187 Top 500

The most successful Scandinavian act in the US singles chart: Marie Fredriksson (v), Per Gessle (v/g). The duo, who have even appeared on postage stamps in their homeland, can claim total worldwide sales in excess of 40 million. Gesle scored solo No.1 album in homeland in 2003. (Singles: 143 weeks, Albums: 162 weeks)

Date		Title / Label	pos	wks
22 Apr 89	●	**THE LOOK** *EMI EM 87* ▲	7	10
15 Jul 89		**DRESSED FOR SUCCESS** *EMI EM 96*	48	5
28 Oct 89		**LISTEN TO YOUR HEART** *EMI EM 108* ▲	62	3
2 Jun 90	●	**IT MUST HAVE BEEN LOVE** *EMI EM 141* ▲	3	14
11 Aug 90	●	**LISTEN TO YOUR HEART / DANGEROUS (re-issue)** *EMI EM 149*	6	9
27 Oct 90		**DRESSED FOR SUCCESS (re-issue)** *EMI EM 162*	18	7
9 Mar 91	●	**JOYRIDE** *EMI EM 177* ▲	4	10
11 May 91		**FADING LIKE A FLOWER (EVERY TIME YOU LEAVE)** *EMI EM 190*	12	6
7 Sep 91		**THE BIG L** *EMI EM 204*	21	6
23 Nov 91		**SPENDING MY TIME** *EMI EM 215*	22	4
28 Mar 92		**CHURCH OF YOUR HEART** *EMI EM 227*	21	4
1 Aug 92		**HOW DO YOU DO!** *EMI EM 241*	13	7
7 Nov 92		**QUEEN OF RAIN** *EMI EM 253*	28	4
24 Jul 93	●	**ALMOST UNREAL** *EMI CDEM 268*	7	9
18 Sep 93	●	**IT MUST HAVE BEEN LOVE (re-issue)** *EMI CDEM 285*	10	8
26 Mar 94		**SLEEPING IN MY CAR** *EMI CDEM 314*	14	6
4 Jun 94		**CRASH! BOOM! BANG!** *EMI CDEM 324*	26	5
17 Sep 94		**FIREWORKS** *EMI CDEM 345*	30	4
3 Dec 94		**RUN TO YOU** *EMI CDEM 360*	27	6
8 Apr 95		**VULNERABLE** *EMI CDEM 369*	44	2
25 Nov 95		**THE LOOK (re-mix)** *EMI CDEM 406*	28	3
30 Mar 96		**YOU DON'T UNDERSTAND ME** *EMI CDEM 418*	42	2
20 Jul 96		**JUNE AFTERNOON** *EMI CDEM 437*	52	1
20 Mar 99		**WISH I COULD FLY** *EMI CDEM 537*	11	7
9 Oct 99		**STARS** *EMI CDEM 550*	56	1
17 Jun 89	●	**LOOK SHARP!** *EMI EMC 3557*	4	53
13 Apr 91	●	**JOYRIDE** *EMI EMD 1019*	2	48
12 Sep 92	●	**TOURISM** *EMI CDEMD 1036*	2	17
23 Apr 94	●	**CRASH BOOM BANG** *EMI CDEMD 1056*	3	16
4 Nov 95	●	**DON'T BORE US – GET TO THE CHORUS! – ROXETTE'S GREATEST HITS** *EMI CDXEMTV 98*	5	20
10 Apr 99		**HAVE A NICE DAY** *EMI 4994612*	28	3
15 Feb 03		**THE BALLAD HITS** *Capitol 5427982*	11	4

ROXY MUSIC 60 Top 500

Stylish art-rock group regarded as highly influential pioneers. Nucleus of oft-changing group line-up: Bryan Ferry (v), Andy Mackay (sax), Phil Manzanera (g). A major act of its time, this group amassed 11 Top 10 albums (Singles: 155 weeks, Albums: 426 weeks)

Date		Title / Label	pos	wks
19 Aug 72	●	**VIRGINIA PLAIN** *Island WIP 6144*	4	12
10 Mar 73	●	**PYJAMARAMA** *Island WIP 6159*	10	12
17 Nov 73	●	**STREET LIFE** *Island WIP 6173*	9	12
12 Oct 74		**ALL I WANT IS YOU** *Island WIP 6208*	12	8
11 Oct 75	●	**LOVE IS THE DRUG** *Island WIP 6248*	2	10
27 Dec 75		**BOTH ENDS BURNING** *Island WIP 6262*	25	7
22 Oct 77		**VIRGINIA PLAIN (re-issue)** *Polydor 2001 739*	11	6
3 Mar 79		**TRASH** *Polydor POSP 32*	40	6
28 Apr 79	●	**DANCE AWAY** *Polydor POSP 44*	2	14
11 Aug 79	●	**ANGEL EYES** *Polydor POSP 67*	4	11
17 May 80	●	**OVER YOU** *Polydor POSP 93*	5	9
2 Aug 80	●	**OH YEAH (ON THE RADIO)** *Polydor 2001 972*	5	8
8 Nov 80		**THE SAME OLD SCENE** *Polydor ROXY 1*	12	7
21 Feb 81	★	**JEALOUS GUY** *EG ROXY 2*	1	11
3 Apr 82	●	**MORE THAN THIS** *EG ROXY 3*	6	8
19 Jun 82		**AVALON** *EG ROXY 4*	13	6
25 Sep 82		**TAKE A CHANCE WITH ME** *EG ROXY 5*	26	6
27 Apr 96		**LOVE IS THE DRUG (re-mix)** *EG VSCDT 1580*	33	2
29 Jul 72	●	**ROXY MUSIC** *Island ILPS 9200*	10	16
7 Apr 73	●	**FOR YOUR PLEASURE** *Island ILPS 9232*	4	27
1 Dec 73	★	**STRANDED** *Island ILPS 9252*	1	17
30 Nov 74	●	**COUNTRY LIFE** *Island ILPS 9303*	3	10
8 Nov 75	●	**SIREN** *Island ILPS 9344*	4	17
31 Jul 76	●	**VIVA! ROXY MUSIC** *Island ILPS 9400*	6	12
19 Nov 77		**GREATEST HITS** *Polydor 2302 073*	20	11
24 Mar 79	●	**MANIFESTO** *Polydor POLH 001*	7	34
31 May 80	★	**FLESH AND BLOOD** *Polydor POLH 002*	1	60
5 Jun 82	★	**AVALON** *EG EGLP 50* ■	1	57
19 Mar 83		**THE HIGH ROAD (import)** *EG EGMLP 1*	26	7
12 Nov 83		**ATLANTIC YEARS 1973-1980** *EG EGLP 54*	23	25
26 Apr 86	★	**STREET LIFE – 20 GREAT HITS** *EG EGTV 1* [1] ■	1	77
19 Nov 88	●	**THE ULTIMATE COLLECTION** *EG EGTV 2* [1]	6	35
4 Nov 95		**MORE THAN THIS – THE BEST OF BRYAN FERRY AND ROXY MUSIC** *Virgin CDV 2791* [1]	15	15
23 Jun 01		**THE BEST OF ROXY MUSIC** *Virgin CDV 2939*	12	6

[1] Bryan Ferry and Roxy Music

See also Bryan FERRY; Phil MANZANERA

Billy Joe ROYAL

US, male vocalist (Singles: 4 weeks)

Date		Title / Label	pos	wks
7 Oct 65		**DOWN IN THE BOONDOCKS** *CBS 201802*	38	4

Central Band of the ROYAL AIR FORCE, Conductor W/Cdr AE SIMS OBE

UK, military band (Singles: 1 week)

Date		Title / Label	pos	wks
21 Oct 55		**THE DAM BUSTERS MARCH** *HMV B 10877*	18	1

ROYAL CHORAL SOCIETY – *See LONDON SYMPHONY ORCHESTRA*

ROYAL GUARDSMEN

US, male vocal / instrumental group (Singles: 17 weeks)

Date		Title / Label	pos	wks
19 Jan 67	●	**SNOOPY VS THE RED BARON** *Stateside SS 574*	8	13
6 Apr 67		**RETURN OF THE RED BARON** *Stateside SS 2010*	37	4

ROYAL HOUSE

US, male DJ / producer – Todd Terry (Singles: 18 weeks)

Date		Title / Label	pos	wks
10 Sep 88		**CAN YOU PARTY** *Champion CHAMP 79*	14	14
7 Jan 89		**YEAH! BUDDY** *Champion CHAMP 91*	35	4

ROYAL LIVERPOOL PHILHARMONIC ORCHESTRA – *See Carl DAVIS and the ROYAL LIVERPOOL PHILHARMONIC ORCHESTRA*

ROYAL PHILHARMONIC ORCHESTRA 420 Top 500

Formed in 1946 by Sir Thomas Beecham, who wanted a first-rate ensemble that would attract the country's top musicians. Since his death (1961), it has come under various maestros including André Previn and Louis Clark (who was behind its biggest sellers) (Singles: 19 weeks, Albums: 140 weeks)

Date		Title / Label	pos	wks
25 Jul 81	●	**HOOKED ON CLASSICS** *RCA 109* [1]	2	11
24 Oct 81		**HOOKED ON CAN-CAN** *RCA 151* [1]	47	3
10 Jul 82		**BBC WORLD CUP GRANDSTAND** *BBC RESL 116*	61	3
7 Aug 82		**IF YOU KNEW SOUSA (AND FRIENDS)** *RCA 256* [1]	71	2
8 Jan 77		**CLASSICAL GOLD** *Ronco RTD 42020*	24	13
23 Dec 78		**CLASSIC GOLD VOLUME 2** *Ronco RTD 42032*	31	4
19 Sep 81	●	**HOOKED ON CLASSICS** *K-Tel ONE 1146*	4	43
31 Jul 82		**CAN'T STOP THE CLASSICS – HOOKED ON CLASSICS 2** *K-Tel ONE 1173*	13	26
9 Apr 83		**JOURNEY THROUGH THE CLASSICS – HOOKED ON CLASSICS 3** *K-Tel ONE 1266*	19	15
8 Oct 83		**LOVE CLASSICS** *Nouveau Music NML 1003* [1]	30	9
10 Dec 83		**THE BEST OF HOOKED ON CLASSICS** *K-Tel ONE 1266*	51	6
11 Feb 84		**SERENADE** *K-Tel ONE 1267* [2]	21	9
26 May 84		**AS TIME GOES BY** *Telstar STAR 2240* [3]	95	2
26 Nov 88		**RHYTHM AND CLASSICS** *Telstar STAR 2344*	96	1
22 Sep 90		**MUSIC FOR THE LAST NIGHT OF THE PROMS** *Cirrus TVLP 501* [4]	39	4
5 Oct 91		**SERIOUSLY ORCHESTRAL** *Virgin RPOLP 1*	31	6
30 Jul 94		**BIG SCREEN CLASSICS** *Quality Television GIGSCD 1*	49	2

[1] Royal Philharmonic Orchestra arranged and conducted by Louis Clark

[1] Royal Philharmonic Orchestra conducted by Nick Portlock [2] Juan Martin and the Royal Philharmonic Orchestra [3] Royal Philharmonic Orchestra conducted by Harry Rabinowitz [4] Sir Charles Groves Royal Philharmonic Orchestra and Chorus with Sarah Walker

See also Elvis COSTELLO; Harry RABINOWITZ; Louis CLARK; Nick PORTLOCK; Sir Charles GROVES; Elkie BROOKS; Richard CLAYDERMAN; Julian LLOYD WEBBER; Juan MARTIN; Andy WILLIAMS; Michael CRAWFORD

Pipes and Drums and Military Band of the ROYAL SCOTS DRAGOON GUARDS *UK, military band (Singles: 43 weeks)* pos/wks

1 Apr 72 ★ **AMAZING GRACE (re)** *RCA 2191* 1 27
19 Aug 72 **HEYKENS SERENADE (STANDCHEN) / THE DAY IS ENDED (THE DAY THOU GAVE US LORD, IS ENDED)** *RCA 2251* 30 7
2 Dec 72 **LITTLE DRUMMER BOY** *RCA 2301* 13 9

ROYALLE DELITE *US, female vocal group (Singles: 6 weeks)* pos/wks

14 Sep 85 **(I'LL BE A) FREAK FOR YOU** *Streetwave KHAN 51* 45 6

ROYCE DA 5'9" – *See BAD MEETS EVIL featuring EMINEM & ROYCE DA 5'9*

RÖYKSOPP *Norway, male production duo (Singles: 10 weeks, Albums: 41 weeks)* pos/wks

15 Dec 01 **POOR LENO** *Wall of Sound WALLD 073* 59 1
17 Aug 02 **REMIND ME / SO EASY** *Wall of Sound WALLD 074X* 21 3
30 Nov 02 **POOR LENO (re-issue)** *Wall of Sound WALLD 079CD* 38 2
8 Mar 03 **EPLE** *Wall of Sound WALLD 080* 16 3
28 Jun 03 **SPARKS** *Wall of Sound WALLD 084* 41 1
24 Aug 02 ● **MELODY A.M.** *Wall Of Sound WALLCD 027* 9 41

Lita ROZA *UK, female vocalist (Singles: 18 weeks)* pos/wks

13 Mar 53 ★ **(HOW MUCH IS) THAT DOGGIE IN THE WINDOW** *Decca F 10070* 1 11
7 Oct 55 **HEY THERE** *Decca F 10611* 17 2
23 Mar 56 **JIMMY UNKNOWN** *Decca F 10679* 15 5

ROZALLA *Zimbabwe, female vocalist – Rozalla Miller (Singles: 49 weeks, Albums: 4 weeks)* pos/wks

27 Apr 91 **FAITH (IN THE POWER OF LOVE)** *Pulse 8 LOSE 7* 65 2
7 Sep 91 ● **EVERYBODY'S FREE (TO FEEL GOOD)** *Pulse 8 LOSE 13* 6 11
16 Nov 91 **FAITH (IN THE POWER OF LOVE) (re-issue)** *Pulse 8 LOSE 15* 11 6
22 Feb 92 **ARE YOU READY TO FLY** *Pulse 8 LOSE 21* 14 6
9 May 92 **LOVE BREAKDOWN** *Pulse 8 LOSE 25* 65 2
15 Aug 92 **IN 4 CHOONS LATER** *Pulse 8 LOSE 29* 50 2
30 Oct 93 **DON'T PLAY WITH ME** *Pulse 8 CDLOSE 52* 50 1
5 Feb 94 **I LOVE MUSIC** *Epic 6598932* 18 5
6 Aug 94 **THIS TIME I FOUND LOVE** *Epic 6603742* 33 3
29 Oct 94 **YOU NEVER LOVE THE SAME WAY TWICE** *Epic 6609052* 16 5
4 Mar 95 **BABY** *Epic 6611955* 26 3
31 Aug 96 **EVERYBODY'S FREE (re-mix)** *Pulse 8 CDLOSE 110* 30 2
22 Nov 03 **LIVE ANOTHER LIFE** *Inferno CDFERN 59* [1] 55 1
4 Apr 92 **EVERYBODY'S FREE** *Pulse 8 PULSECD 3* 20 4

[1] Plastic Boy featuring Rozalla

RUBBADUBB *UK, male / female vocal / instrumental group (Singles: 1 week)* pos/wks

18 Jul 98 **TRIBUTE TO OUR ANCESTORS** *Perfecto PERF 165CD* 56 1

RUBETTES *UK, male vocal / instrumental group – leader Alan Williams (Singles: 68 weeks, Albums: 1 week)* pos/wks

4 May 74 ★ **SUGAR BABY LOVE** *Polydor 2058 442* 1 10
13 Jul 74 **TONIGHT** *Polydor 2058 499* 12 9
16 Nov 74 ● **JUKE BOX JIVE** *Polydor 2058 529* 3 12
8 Mar 75 ● **I CAN DO IT** *State STAT 1* 7 9
21 Jun 75 **FOE-DEE-O-DEE** *State STAT 7* 15 6
22 Nov 75 **LITTLE DARLING** *State STAT 13* 30 5
1 May 76 **YOU'RE THE REASON WHY** *State STAT 20* 28 4
25 Sep 76 **UNDER ONE ROOF** *State STAT 27* 40 3
12 Feb 77 ● **BABY I KNOW** *State STAT 37* 10 10
10 May 75 **WE CAN DO IT** *State ETAT 001* 41 1

Maria RUBIA *UK, female vocalist (Singles: 2 weeks)* pos/wks

19 May 01 **SAY IT** *Neo NEOCD 055* 40 2

See also FRAGMA

Paulina RUBIO *Mexico, female vocalist (Singles: 1 week)* pos/wks

28 Sep 02 **DON'T SAY GOODBYE** *Universal MCSTD 40291* 68 1

RUBY and The ROMANTICS *US, female / male vocal group (Singles: 6 weeks)* pos/wks

28 Mar 63 **OUR DAY WILL COME** *London HLR 9679* ▲ 38 6

RUDE BOY OF HOUSE – *See HOUSEMASTER BOYZ and the RUDE BOY OF HOUSE*

RUDIES – *See Freddie NOTES and the RUDIES*

RUFF DRIVERZ *UK, male / female vocal / production trio (Singles: 21 weeks)* pos/wks

7 Feb 98 **DON'T STOP** *Inferno CDFERN 003* 30 2
23 May 98 **DEEPER LOVE** *Inferno CDFERN 006* 19 3
24 Oct 98 **SHAME** *Inferno CXFERN 9* 51 2
28 Nov 98 ● **DREAMING** *Inferno CXFERN 11* [1] 10 8
24 Apr 99 **LA MUSICA** *Inferno CDFERN 14* [1] 14 4
2 Oct 99 **WAITING FOR THE SUN** *Inferno CDFERN 19* 37 2

[1] Ruff Driverz presents Arrola

RUFF ENDZ *US, male vocal duo – David Chance and Dante Jordan (Singles: 5 weeks)* pos/wks

19 Aug 00 **NO MORE** *Epic 6696202* 11 5

Frances RUFFELLE *UK, female vocalist (Singles: 6 weeks)* pos/wks

16 Apr 94 **LONELY SYMPHONY** *Virgin VSCDT 1499* 25 6

Bruce RUFFIN *Jamaica, male vocalist – Bernard Downer (Singles: 23 weeks)* pos/wks

1 May 71 **RAIN** *Trojan TR 7814* 19 11
24 Jun 72 ● **MAD ABOUT YOU** *Rhino RNO 101* 9 12

David RUFFIN *US, male vocalist, d. 1 Jun 1991 (Singles: 10 weeks)* pos/wks

17 Jan 76 ● **WALK AWAY FROM LOVE** *Tamla Motown TMG 1017* 10 8
21 Sep 85 **A NIGHT AT THE APOLLO LIVE!** *RCA PB 49935* [1] 58 2

[1] Daryl Hall and John Oates featuring David Ruffin and Eddie Kendrick

See also Daryl HALL and John OATES; TEMPTATIONS

Jimmy RUFFIN *US, male vocalist (Singles: 106 weeks, Albums: 10 weeks)* pos/wks

27 Oct 66 ● **WHAT BECOMES OF THE BROKENHEARTED** *Tamla Motown TMG 577* 8 15
9 Feb 67 **I'VE PASSED THIS WAY BEFORE** *Tamla Motown TMG 593* 29 7
20 Apr 67 **GONNA GIVE HER ALL THE LOVE I'VE GOT** *Tamla Motown TMG 603* 26 6
9 Aug 69 **I'VE PASSED THIS WAY BEFORE (re-issue)** *Tamla Motown TMG 703* 33 6
28 Feb 70 ● **FAREWELL IS A LONELY SOUND** *Tamla Motown TMG 726* 8 16
4 Jul 70 ● **I'LL SAY FOREVER MY LOVE** *Tamla Motown TMG 740* 7 12
17 Oct 70 ● **IT'S WONDERFUL (TO BE LOVED BY YOU)** *Tamla Motown TMG 753* 6 14
27 Jul 74 ● **WHAT BECOMES OF THE BROKENHEARTED (re-issue)** *Tamla Motown TMG 911* 4 12
2 Nov 74 **FAREWELL IS A LONELY SOUND (re-issue)** *Tamla Motown TMG 922* 30 5
16 Nov 74 **TELL ME WHAT YOU WANT** *Polydor 2058 433* 39 4
3 May 80 ● **HOLD ON TO MY LOVE** *RSO 57* 7 8
26 Jan 85 **THERE WILL NEVER BE ANOTHER YOU** *EMI 5541* 68 1
13 May 67 **THE JIMMY RUFFIN WAY** *Tamla Motown STML 11048* 32 6
1 Jun 74 **GREATEST HITS** *Tamla Motown STML 11259* 41 4

Kim RUFFIN – *See Chubby CHUNKS*

RUFFNECK featuring YAVAHN *US, male production group featuring US female vocalist (Singles: 6 weeks)* pos/wks

11 Nov 95 **EVERYBODY BE SOMEBODY** *Positiva CDTIV 46* 13 4
7 Sep 96 **MOVE YOUR BODY** *Positiva CDTIV 61* 60 1
1 Dec 01 **EVERYBODY BE SOMEBODY (re-mix)** *Strictly Rhythm SRUKCD 08* 66 1

RUFUS *US, male / female vocal / instrumental group – includes Chaka Khan (Albums: 7 weeks)*

Date		Title / Label	pos	wks
12 Apr 75		**RUFUSIZED** *ABC ABCL 5063*	48	2
21 Apr 84		**STOMPIN' AT THE SAVOY** *Warner Bros. 923679* [1]	64	5

[1] Rufus and Chaka Khan

See also Chaka KHAN

RUKMANI – *See SNAP!*

Dick RULES – *See SCOOTER*

RUMOUR – *See Graham PARKER and the RUMOUR*

RUMPLE-STILTS-SKIN *US, male / female vocal / instrumental group (Singles: 4 weeks)*

Date		Title / Label	pos	wks
24 Sep 83		**I THINK I WANT TO DANCE WITH YOU** *Polydor POSP 649*	51	4

RUN-DMC *US, male rap group (Singles: 62 weeks, Albums: 44 weeks)*

Date		Title / Label	pos	wks
19 Jul 86		**MY ADIDAS / PETER PIPER** *London LON 101*	62	2
6 Sep 86	●	**WALK THIS WAY** *London LON 104*	8	10
7 Feb 87		**YOU BE ILLIN'** *Profile LON 118*	42	4
30 May 87		**IT'S TRICKY** *Profile LON 130*	16	7
12 Dec 87		**CHRISTMAS IN HOLLIS** *Profile LON 163*	56	4
21 May 88		**RUN'S HOUSE** *London LON 177*	37	4
2 Sep 89		**GHOSTBUSTERS** *MCA 1360*	65	2
1 Dec 90		**WHAT'S IT ALL ABOUT** *Profile PROF 315*	48	3
27 Mar 93		**DOWN WITH THE KING** *Profile PROFCD 39*	69	2
21 Feb 98		**IT'S LIKE THAT (German import)** *Columbia 6652932* [1]	63	3
14 Mar 98		**IT'S LIKE THAT (US import)** *Columbia 6652932* [1]	65	1
21 Mar 98	★	**IT'S LIKE THAT** *Sm:)e Communications SM 90652* [1] ◆ ■	1	16
18 Apr 98		**IT'S TRICKY (re-mix) (import)** *Epidrome EPD 6656982* [1]	74	1
19 Apr 03		**IT'S TRICKY (2nd re-mix)** *Arista 82876513712* [2]	20	3
26 Jul 86		**RAISING HELL** *Profile LONLP 21*	41	26
4 Jun 88		**TOUGHER THAN LEATHER** *Profile LONLP 38*	13	5
15 May 93		**DOWN WITH THE KING** *Profile FILECD 440*	44	2
6 Jun 98		**TOGETHER FOREVER – GREATEST HITS 1983-1998** *Profile FILECD 474*	31	3
26 Apr 03		**GREATEST HITS** *Arista 74321980602*	15	8

[1] Run-DMC vs Jason Nevins [2] Run-DMC featuring Jacknife Lee

'Walk This Way' featured Steve Tyler and Joe Perry of Aerosmith

RUN TINGS *UK, male instrumental / production duo (Singles: 1 week)*

Date		Title / Label	pos	wks
16 May 92		**FIRES BURNING** *Suburban Base SUBBASE 009*	58	1

Todd RUNDGREN *US, male vocalist / instrumentalist (Singles: 8 weeks, Albums: 9 weeks)*

Date		Title / Label	pos	wks
30 Jun 73		**I SAW THE LIGHT** *Bearsville K 15506*	36	6
14 Dec 85		**LOVING YOU'S A DIRTY JOB BUT SOMEBODY'S GOTTA DO IT** *CBS A 6662* [1]	73	2
29 Jan 77		**RA** *Bearsville K 55514*	27	6
6 May 78		**HERMIT OF MINK HOLLOW** *Bearsville K 55521*	42	3

[1] Bonnie Tyler, guest vocals Todd Rundgren

See also UTOPIA

RUNRIG *UK, male vocal / instrumental group (Singles: 28 weeks, Albums: 50 weeks)*

Date		Title / Label	pos	wks
29 Sep 90		**CAPTURE THE HEART (EP)** *Chrysalis CHS 3594*	49	2
7 Sep 91		**HEARTHAMMER (EP)** *Chrysalis CHS 3754*	25	4
9 Nov 91		**FLOWER OF THE WEST** *Chrysalis CHS 3805*	43	2
6 Mar 93		**WONDERFUL** *Chrysalis CDCHS 3952*	29	3
15 May 93		**THE GREATEST FLAME** *Chrysalis CDCHS 3975*	36	3
7 Jan 95		**THIS TIME OF YEAR** *Chrysalis CDCHS 5018*	38	2
6 May 95		**AN UBHAL AS AIRDE (THE HIGHEST APPLE)** *Chrysalis CDCHS 5021*	18	5
4 Nov 95		**THINGS THAT ARE** *Chrysalis CDCHS 5029*	40	2
12 Oct 96		**RHYTHM OF MY HEART** *Chrysalis CDCHS 5035*	24	2
11 Jan 97		**THE GREATEST FLAME (re-issue)** *Chrysalis CDCHSS 5045*	30	3
26 Nov 88		**ONCE IN A LIFETIME** *Chrysalis CHR 1695*	61	2
7 Oct 89		**SEARCHLIGHT** *Chrysalis CHR 1713*	11	4
22 Jun 91	●	**THE BIG WHEEL** *Chrysalis CHR 1858*	4	15
27 Mar 93	●	**AMAZING THINGS** *Chrysalis CDCHR 2000*	2	6
26 Nov 94		**TRANSMITTING LIVE** *Chrysalis CDCHR 6090*	41	3
20 May 95		**THE CUTTER AND THE CLAN** *Chrysalis CCD 1669*	45	2
18 Nov 95		**MARA** *Chrysalis CDCHR 6111*	24	4
19 Oct 96		**LONG DISTANCE – THE BEST OF RUNRIG** *Chrysalis CDCHRS 6116*	13	10
23 May 98		**THE GAELIC COLLECTION 1973-1995** *Ridge RR 009*	71	1
13 Mar 99		**IN SEARCH OF ANGELS** *Ridge RR 010*	29	2
26 May 01		**THE STAMPING GROUND** *Ridge RR 016*	64	1

Tracks on Capture the Heart (EP): Stepping Down the Glory Road / Satellite Flood / Harvest Moon / The Apple Came Down. Tracks on Hearthammer (EP): Hearthammer / Pride of the Summer (Live) / Loch Lomond (Live) / Solus Na Madain

RuPAUL *US, male (female impersonator) vocalist – Rupaul Charles (Singles: 19 weeks)*

Date		Title / Label	pos	wks
26 Jun 93		**SUPERMODEL (YOU BETTER WORK)** *Union City UCRD 21*	39	4
18 Sep 93		**HOUSE OF LOVE / BACK TO MY ROOTS** *Union City UCRD 23*	40	2
22 Jan 94		**SUPERMODEL / LITTLE DRUMMER BOY (re-mix)** *Union City UCRD 25*	61	2
26 Feb 94	●	**DON'T GO BREAKING MY HEART** *Rocket EJCD 33* [1]	7	7
21 May 94		**HOUSE OF LOVE** *Union City UCRDG 29*	68	1
28 Feb 98		**IT'S RAINING MEN…THE SEQUEL** *Logic 74321555412* [2]	21	3

[1] Elton John with RuPaul [2] Martha Wash featuring RuPaul

Kate RUSBY *UK, female vocalist / instrumentalist – guitar (Albums: 1 week)*

Date		Title / Label	pos	wks
9 Jun 01		**LITTLE LIGHTS** *Pure PRCD 07*	75	1

RUSH (481 Top 500)

Enduring Canadian pomp rockers Geddy Lee (v/b), Alex 'Lifeson (g) and Neil Peart (d), who were hailed Ambassadors of Music by the Canadian government in the late 70s and honoured as officers of the Order of Canada in 1997 (Singles: 43 weeks, Albums: 100 weeks)

Date		Title / Label	pos	wks
11 Feb 78		**CLOSER TO THE HEART** *Mercury RUSH 7*	36	3
15 Mar 80		**THE SPIRIT OF RADIO** *Mercury RADIO 7*	13	7
28 Mar 81		**VITAL SIGNS / A PASSAGE TO BANGKOK** *Mercury VITAL7*	41	4
31 Oct 81		**TOM SAWYER** *Mercury EXIT 7*	25	6
4 Sep 82		**NEW WORLD MAN** *Mercury RUSH 8*	42	3
30 Oct 82		**SUBDIVISIONS** *Mercury RUSH 9*	53	2
7 May 83		**COUNTDOWN / NEW WORLD MAN (LIVE)** *Mercury RUSH 10*	36	5
26 May 84		**THE BODY ELECTRIC** *Vertigo RUSH 11*	56	3
12 Oct 85		**THE BIG MONEY** *Vertigo RUSH 12*	46	3
31 Oct 87		**TIME STAND STILL** *Vertigo RUSH 13* [1]	42	3
23 Apr 88		**PRIME MOVER** *Vertigo RUSH 14*	43	3
7 Mar 92		**ROLL THE BONES** *Atlantic A 7524*	49	1
8 Oct 77		**FAREWELL TO KINGS** *Mercury 9100 042*	22	4
25 Nov 78		**HEMISPHERES** *Mercury 9100 059*	14	6
26 Jan 80	●	**PERMANENT WAVES** *Mercury 9100 071*	3	16
21 Feb 81	●	**MOVING PICTURES** *Mercury 6337 160*	3	11
7 Nov 81	●	**EXIT STAGE LEFT** *Mercury 6619 053*	6	14
18 Sep 82	●	**SIGNALS** *Mercury 6337 243*	3	9
28 Apr 84	●	**GRACE UNDER PRESSURE** *Vertigo VERH 12*	5	12
9 Nov 85	●	**POWER WINDOWS** *Vertigo VERH 31*	9	4
21 Nov 87	●	**HOLD YOUR FIRE** *Vertigo VERH 47*	10	4
28 Jan 89		**A SHOW OF HANDS** *Vertigo 836346*	12	4
9 Dec 89		**PRESTO** *Atlantic WX 327*	27	2
13 Oct 90		**CHRONICLES** *Vertigo CBTV 1*	42	2
14 Sep 91	●	**ROLL THE BONES** *Atlantic WX 436*	10	4
30 Oct 93		**COUNTERPARTS** *Atlantic 7567825282*	14	3
21 Sep 96		**TEST FOR ECHO** *Atlantic 7567829252*	25	3
25 May 02		**VAPOR TRAILS** *Atlantic 7567835312*	38	2

[1] Rush with Aimee Mann

Donell RUSH *US, male vocalist (Singles: 1 week)*

Date		Title / Label	pos	wks
5 Dec 92		**SYMPHONY** *ID 6587977*	66	1

Ed RUSH & OPTICAL

UK, male production duo (Singles: 1 week) pos/wks

Date		Title	pos	wks
1 Jun 02		**PACMAN / VESSEL** *Virus VRS 010*	61	1

'Pacman' shared chart billing with 'Vessel' by Universal Project

Jennifer RUSH

US, female vocalist (Singles: 58 weeks, Albums: 43 weeks) pos/wks

Date		Title	pos	wks
29 Jun 85	★	**THE POWER OF LOVE (re)** *CBS A 5003* ◆	1	36
14 Dec 85		**RING OF ICE** *CBS A 4745*	14	10
20 Jun 87		**FLAMES OF PARADISE** *CBS 650865 7* [1]	59	3
27 May 89		**TILL I LOVED YOU** *CBS 654843 7* [2]	24	9
16 Nov 85	●	**JENNIFER RUSH** *CBS 26488*	7	35
3 May 86		**MOVIN'** *CBS 26710*	32	5
18 Apr 87		**HEART OVER MIND** *CBS 450 4701*	48	3

[1] Jennifer Rush and Elton John [2] Placido Domingo and Jennifer Rush

'The Power of Love' re-entry, peaking at No.55, was in Dec 1986

Patrice RUSHEN *US, female vocalist / instrumentalist*

keyboards (Singles: 25 weeks, Albums: 17 weeks) pos/wks

Date		Title	pos	wks
1 Mar 80		**HAVEN'T YOU HEARD** *Elektra K 12414*	62	3
24 Jan 81		**NEVER GONNA GIVE YOU UP (WON'T LET YOU BE)** *Elektra K 12494*	66	3
24 Apr 82	●	**FORGET ME NOTS** *Elektra K 13173*	8	11
10 Jul 82		**I WAS TIRED OF BEING ALONE** *Elektra K 13184*	39	5
9 Jun 84		**FEELS SO REAL (WON'T LET GO)** *Elektra E 9742*	51	3
1 May 82		**STRAIGHT FROM THE HEART** *Elektra K 52352*	24	14
16 Jun 84		**NOW** *Elektra 960360*	73	3

RUSSELL

US, male vocalist – Russell Taylor (Singles: 1 week) pos/wks

Date		Title	pos	wks
27 May 00		**FOOL FOR LOVE** *Rulin RULIN 1CDS*	52	1

Brenda RUSSELL *US, female vocalist / instrumentalist*

– keyboards – Brenda Gordon (Singles: 17 weeks, Albums: 4 weeks) pos/wks

Date		Title	pos	wks
19 Apr 80		**SO GOOD SO RIGHT / IN THE THICK OF IT** *A&M AM 7515*	51	5
12 Mar 88		**PIANO IN THE DARK** *Breakout USA 623*	23	12
23 Apr 88		**GET HERE** *A&M AMA 5178*	77	4

Leon RUSSELL *US, male vocalist (Albums: 1 week)* pos/wks

Date		Title	pos	wks
3 Jul 71		**LEON RUSSELL AND THE SHELTER PEOPLE** *A&M AMLS 65003*	29	1

Patti RUSSO – *See MEAT LOAF*

RUSTIN' MAN – *See Beth GIBBONS & RUSTIN' MAN; TALK TALK*

RUTH *UK, male vocal / instrumental group (Singles: 1 week)* pos/wks

Date		Title	pos	wks
12 Apr 97		**I DON'T KNOW** *Arc 5737812*	66	1

Mike RUTHERFORD

UK, male vocalist / instrumentalist – guitar (Albums: 11 weeks) pos/wks

Date		Title	pos	wks
23 Feb 80		**SMALLCREEP'S DAY** *Charisma CAS 1149*	13	7
18 Sep 82		**ACTING VERY STRANGE** *WEA K 99249*	23	4

See also MIKE and the MECHANICS; GENESIS

Paul RUTHERFORD *UK, male vocalist (Singles: 6 weeks)* pos/wks

Date		Title	pos	wks
8 Oct 88		**GET REAL** *Fourth & Broadway BRW 113*	47	3
19 Aug 89		**OH WORLD** *Fourth & Broadway BRW 136*	61	3

See also FRANKIE GOES TO HOLLYWOOD

RUTHLESS RAP ASSASSINS

UK, male rappers (Singles: 2 weeks) pos/wks

Date		Title	pos	wks
9 Jun 90		**JUST MELLOW** *Syncopate SY 35*	75	1
1 Sep 90		**AND IT WASN'T A DREAM** *Syncopate SY 38* [1]	75	1

[1] Ruthless Rap Assassins featuring Tracey Carmen

RUTLES

UK, male vocal group (Singles: 5 weeks, Albums: 11 weeks) pos/wks

Date		Title	pos	wks
15 Apr 78		**I MUST BE IN LOVE (re)** *Warner Bros. K 17125*	39	4
16 Nov 96		**SHANGRI-LA** *Virgin America VUSCD 117*	68	1
15 Apr 78		**THE RUTLES** *Warner Bros. K 56459*	12	11

RUTS *UK, male vocal / instrumental*

group (Singles: 28 weeks, Albums: 10 weeks) pos/wks

Date		Title	pos	wks
16 Jun 79	●	**BABYLON'S BURNING** *Virgin VS 271*	7	11
8 Sep 79		**SOMETHING THAT I SAID** *Virgin VS 285*	29	5
19 Apr 80		**STARING AT THE RUDE BOYS** *Virgin VS 327*	22	8
30 Aug 80		**WEST ONE (SHINE ON ME)** *Virgin VS 370*	43	4
13 Oct 79		**THE CRACK** *Virgin V 2132*	16	6
18 Oct 80		**GRIN AND BEAR IT** *Virgin V 2188* [1]	28	4

[1] Ruts D.C.

John RUTTER

UK, male composer / arranger (Albums: 1 week) pos/wks

Date		Title	pos	wks
2 Nov 02		**THE JOHN RUTTER COLLECTION** *UCJ 4726222*	75	1

'The John Rutter Collection' features The Cambridge Singers and the City of London Sinfonia

Barry RYAN

UK, male vocalist – Barry Sapherson (Singles: 33 weeks) pos/wks

Date		Title	pos	wks
23 Oct 68	●	**ELOISE** *MGM 1442*	2	12
19 Feb 69		**LOVE IS LOVE** *MGM 1464*	25	4
4 Oct 69		**THE HUNT** *Polydor 56 348*	34	5
21 Feb 70		**MAGICAL SPIEL** *Polydor 56 370*	49	1
16 May 70		**KITSCH** *Polydor 2001 035* [1]	37	6
15 Jan 72		**CAN'T LET YOU GO** *Polydor 2001 256*	32	5

[1] Barry Ryan with the Paul Ryan Orchestra

See also Paul and Barry RYAN

Joshua RYAN *US, male producer (Singles: 3 weeks)* pos/wks

Date		Title	pos	wks
27 Jan 01		**PISTOL WHIP** *Nulife/Arista 74321825482*	29	3

Marion RYAN *UK, female vocalist – Marion*

Sapherson, d. 15 Jan 1999 (Singles: 11 weeks) pos/wks

Date		Title	pos	wks
24 Jan 58	●	**LOVE ME FOREVER** *Pye Nixa N 15121*	5	11

With the Peter Knight Orchestra and the Beryl Stott Chorus

Paul and Barry RYAN *UK, male vocal duo – Paul*

(d. 29 Nov 1992) and Barry Sapherson (Singles: 43 weeks) pos/wks

Date		Title	pos	wks
11 Nov 65		**DON'T BRING ME YOUR HEARTACHES** *Decca F 12260*	13	9
3 Feb 66		**HAVE PITY ON THE BOY** *Decca F 12319*	18	6
12 May 66		**I LOVE HER** *Decca F 12391*	17	8
14 Jul 66		**I LOVE HOW YOU LOVE ME** *Decca F 12445*	21	7
29 Sep 66		**HAVE YOU EVER LOVED SOMEBODY** *Decca F 12494*	49	1
8 Dec 66		**MISSY MISSY** *Decca F 12520*	43	4
2 Mar 67		**KEEP IT OUT OF SIGHT** *Decca F 12567*	30	6
29 Jun 67		**CLAIRE** *Decca F 12633*	47	2

See also Barry RYAN

Rebekah RYAN *UK, female vocalist (Singles: 5 weeks)* pos/wks

Date		Title	pos	wks
18 May 96		**YOU LIFT ME UP** *MCA MCSTD 40022*	26	3
7 Sep 96		**JUST A LITTLE BIT OF LOVE** *MCA MCSTD 40063*	51	1
17 May 97		**WOMAN IN LOVE** *MCA MCSTD 40109*	64	1

Bobby RYDELL

US, male vocalist – Robert Ridarelli (Singles: 60 weeks) pos/wks

Date		Title	pos	wks
10 Mar 60	●	**WILD ONE (re)** *Columbia DB 4429*	7	15
30 Jun 60		**SWINGIN' SCHOOL** *Columbia DB 4471*	44	1
1 Sep 60		**VOLARE (re)** *Columbia DB 4495*	22	6
15 Dec 60		**SWAY** *Columbia DB 4545*	12	13
23 Mar 61		**GOOD TIME BABY** *Columbia DB 4600*	42	7
19 Apr 62		**TEACH ME TO TWIST** *Columbia DB 4802* [1]	45	1

20 Dec 62 JINGLE BELL ROCK *Cameo Parkway C 205* [1] 40 3
23 May 63 FORGET HIM *Cameo Parkway C 108* 13 14

[1] Chubby Checker and Bobby Rydell

Mitch RYDER and the DETROIT WHEELS
US, male vocal / instrumental group (Singles: 5 weeks) pos/wks

10 Feb 66 JENNY TAKE A RIDE (re) *Stateside SS 481* 33 5

Mark RYDER
UK, male producer – Mark Rydquist (Singles: 2 weeks) pos/wks

31 Mar 01 JOY *Relentless Public Demand RELENT 9CDS* 34 2

See also M-D-EMM

Shaun RYDER – *See BLACK GRAPE; HAPPY MONDAYS; HEADS with Shaun RYDER; Russell WATSON*

RYTHM SYNDICATE
US, male vocal / instrumental group (Singles: 5 weeks) pos/wks

27 Jul 91 P.A.S.S.I.O.N. *Impact American EM 197* 58 5

RYZE *UK, male vocal trio (Singles: 1 week)* pos/wks

2 Nov 02 IN MY LIFE *Inferno Cool CDFERN 48* 46 1

RZA
US, male producer / rapper (Albums: 1 week) pos/wks

28 Nov 98 BOBBY DIGITAL IN STEREO *Gee Street GEE 1003802* 70 1

See also WU TANG CLAN; GRAVEDIGGAZ

Robin S *US, female vocalist – Robin Stone (Singles: 38 weeks, Albums: 3 weeks)* pos/wks

16 Jan 93 ● SHOW ME LOVE (re) *Champion CHAMPCD 300* 6 17
31 Jul 93 LUV 4 LUV *Champion CHAMPCD 301* 11 7
4 Dec 93 WHAT I DO BEST *Champion CHAMPCD 307* 43 2
19 Mar 94 I WANT TO THANK YOU *Champion CHAMPCD 310* 48 1
5 Nov 94 BACK IT UP *Champion CHAMPCD 312* 43 2
8 Mar 97 ● SHOW ME LOVE (re-mix) *Champion CHAMPCD 326* 9 5
12 Jul 97 IT MUST BE LOVE *Atlantic A 5596CD* 37 2
4 Oct 97 YOU GOT THE LOVE *Champion CHAMPCD 330* 62 1
7 Dec 02 SHOW ME LOVE (2nd re-mix) *Champion CHAMPCD 796* 61 1
4 Sep 93 SHOW ME LOVE *Champion CHAMPCD 1028* 34 3

S CLUB JUNIORS *UK, male / female vocal group (Singles: 70 weeks, Albums: 17 weeks)* pos/wks

4 May 02 ● ONE STEP CLOSER *Polydor 5707322* 2 16
3 Aug 02 ● AUTOMATIC HIGH *Polydor 5708922* 2 13
19 Oct 02 ● NEW DIRECTION *Polydor 0659692* 2 13
21 Dec 02 ● PUPPY LOVE / SLEIGH RIDE (re) *Polydor 0658442* 6 10
12 Jul 03 ● FOOL NO MORE *Polydor 9808753* [1] 4 8
11 Oct 03 ● SUNDOWN *Polydor 9811790* [1] 4 10
2 Nov 02 ● TOGETHER *Polydor 0652502* 5 13
25 Oct 03 SUNDOWN *Polydor 9865703* [1] 13 4

[1] S Club 8 [1] S Club 8

S CLUB 7 (172 Top 500) *Made-for-TV act (series seen in more than 100 countries) had the best start to its career of any mixed vocal group, with nine Top 3 hits from first nine releases, including four No.1s. Award-winning septet is the largest vocal group ever to top the chart, comprising Jo O'Meara, Tina Barrett, Hannah Spearritt, Rachel Stevens, Paul Cattermole, Bradley McIntosh and Jon Lee. When Cattermole left in 2002, the sextet became S Club, then disbanded in 2003. Best-selling single: 'Don't Stop Movin' – 709,198 (Singles: 166 weeks, Albums: 149 weeks)* pos/wks

19 Jun 99 ★ BRING IT ALL BACK *Polydor 5610852* ■ 1 15
2 Oct 99 ● S CLUB PARTY (re) *Polydor 5614172* 2 14
25 Dec 99 ● TWO IN A MILLION / YOU'RE MY NUMBER ONE *Polydor 5615962* 2 11
3 Jun 00 ● REACH *Polydor 5618302* 2 17
23 Sep 00 ● NATURAL (re) *Polydor 5877602* 3 16
9 Dec 00 ★ NEVER HAD A DREAM COME TRUE (re) *Polydor 5879032* ■ 1 18
5 May 01 ★ DON'T STOP MOVIN' *Polydor 5870832* ■ 1 19
1 Dec 01 ★ HAVE YOU EVER *Polydor 5705002* ■ 1 14
23 Feb 02 ● YOU *Polydor 5705812* 2 14
30 Nov 02 ● ALIVE (2re) *Polydor 0658912* [1] 5 16
7 Jun 03 ● SAY GOODBYE / LOVE AIN'T GONNA WAIT FOR YOU *Polydor 9807139* [1] 2 12
16 Oct 99 ● S CLUB *Polydor 5431032* 2 46
24 Jun 00 ★ 7 *Polydor 5438572* 1 61
8 Dec 01 ● SUNSHINE *Polydor 5894092* 3 24
7 Dec 02 SEEING DOUBLE *Polydor 0654962* [1] 17 5
14 Jun 03 ● BEST – THE GREATEST HITS OF S CLUB 7 *Polydor 9807374* 2 13

[1] S Club [1] S Club

See also Rachel STEVENS

S EXPRESS *UK, male / female vocal / instrumental group, leader – Mark Moore (Singles: 50 weeks, Albums: 9 weeks)* pos/wks

16 Apr 88 ★ THEME FROM S-EXPRESS *Rhythm King LEFT 21* 1 13
23 Jul 88 ● SUPERFLY GUY *Rhythm King LEFT 28* 5 9
18 Feb 89 ● HEY MUSIC LOVER *Rhythm King LEFT 30* 6 10
16 Sep 89 MANTRA FOR A STATE OF MIND *Rhythm King LEFT 35* 21 8
15 Sep 90 NOTHING TO LOSE *Rhythm King SEXY 01* 32 4
30 May 92 FIND 'EM, FOOL 'EM, FORGET 'EM *Rhythm King 6580137* 43 2
11 May 96 THEME FROM S.EXPRESS (re-mix) *Rhythm King SEXY 9CD* [1] 14 4
1 Apr 89 ● ORIGINAL SOUNDTRACK *Rhythm King LEFTLP 8* 5 9

[1] Mark Moore presents S Express

SFX *UK, male instrumental / production duo (Singles: 3 weeks)* pos/wks

15 May 93 LEMMINGS *Parlophone CDR 6343* 51 3

S-J
UK, female vocalist – Sarah James Jiminez-Heany (Singles: 4 weeks) pos/wks

11 Jan 97 FEVER *React CDREACT 93* 46 1
24 Jan 98 I FEEL DIVINE *React CDREACT 113* 30 2
7 Nov 98 SHIVER *React CDREACT 138* 59 1

SL2 *UK, male DJ / production duo – Matt 'Slipmatt' Nelson and John 'Lime' Fernandez (Singles: 25 weeks)* pos/wks

2 Nov 91 DJS TAKE CONTROL / WAY IN MY BRAIN (re) *XL Recordings XLS 24* 11 6
18 Apr 92 ● ON A RAGGA TIP *XL Recordings XLS 29* 2 11

19 Dec 92 **WAY IN MY BRAIN (re-mix) / DRUMBEATS** *XL Recordings XLS 36* 26 6
15 Feb 97 **ON A RAGGA TIP (re-mix)** *XL Recordings XLSR 29CD* 31 2

See also SLIPMATT

S.O.S. BAND *US, male / female vocal / instrumental group (Singles: 46 weeks, Albums: 19 weeks)*

		pos/wks
19 Jul 80	**TAKE YOUR TIME (DO IT RIGHT) PART 1** *Tabu TBU 8564*	51 4
26 Feb 83	**GROOVIN' (THAT'S WHAT WE'RE DOIN')** *Tabu TBU A3120*	72 1
7 Apr 84	**JUST BE GOOD TO ME** *Tabu A 3626*	13 11
4 Aug 84	**JUST THE WAY YOU LIKE IT** *Tabu A 4621*	32 7
13 Oct 84	**WEEKEND GIRL** *Tabu A 4785*	51 5
29 Mar 86	**THE FINEST** *Tabu A 6997*	17 10
5 Jul 86	**BORROWED LOVE** *Tabu A 7241*	50 5
2 May 87	**NO LIES** *Tabu 650444 7*	64 3
1 Sep 84	**JUST THE WAY YOU LIKE IT** *Tabu TBU 26058*	29 10
17 May 86	**SANDS OF TIME** *Tabu TBU 26863*	15 9

SWV
US, female vocal trio (Singles: 43 weeks, Albums: 27 weeks)

		pos/wks
1 May 93	**I'M SO INTO YOU** *RCA 74321144972*	17 6
26 Jun 93	**WEAK** *RCA 74321153352* ▲	33 3
28 Aug 93 ●	**RIGHT HERE** *RCA 74321160482*	3 12
26 Feb 94	**DOWNTOWN** *RCA 74321189012*	19 5
11 Jun 94	**ANYTHING** *RCA 74321212212*	24 3
25 May 96	**YOU'RE THE ONE** *RCA 74321383312*	13 3
21 Dec 96	**IT'S ALL ABOUT U** *RCA 74321442152*	36 5
12 Apr 97	**CAN WE** *Jive JIVECD 423*	18 4
13 Sep 97	**SOMEONE** *RCA 74321513942* [1]	34 2
17 Jul 93	**IT'S ABOUT TIME** *RCA 7863660742*	17 17
4 May 96	**NEW BEGINNING** *RCA 7863664872*	26 5
16 Aug 97	**RELEASE SOME TENSION** *RCA 74321493162*	19 5

[1] SWV featuring Puff Daddy

Raphael SAADIQ
US, male vocalist – Raphael Wiggins (Singles: 4 weeks)

		pos/wks
23 Nov 96	**STRESSED OUT** *Jive JIVECD 404* [1]	33 2
19 Jun 99	**GET INVOLVED** *Hollywood 0101185 HWR* [2]	36 2

[1] A Tribe Called Quest featuring Faith Evans and Raphael Saadiq [2] Raphael Saadiq and Q-Tip

See also TONY TONI TONÉ; LUCY PEARL

SABRE featuring PRESIDENT BROWN
Jamaica, male vocal duo (Singles: 1 week)

		pos/wks
19 Aug 95	**WRONG OR RIGHT** *Greensleeves GRECD 485*	71 1

SABRES – *See Denny SEYTON and the SABRES*

SABRES OF PARADISE
UK, male production group (Singles: 8 weeks, Albums: 3 weeks)

		pos/wks
2 Oct 93	**SMOKEBELCH II** *Sabres of Paradise PT 009CD*	55 3
9 Apr 94	**THEME** *Sabres of Paradise PT 014CD*	56 3
17 Sep 94	**WILMOT** *Warp WAP 50CD*	36 2
23 Oct 93	**SABRESONIC** *Warp WARPCD 16*	29 2
10 Dec 94	**HAUNTED DANCEHALL** *Warp WARPCD 26*	57 1

SABRINA
Italy, female vocalist – Sabrina Salerno (Singles: 22 weeks)

		pos/wks
6 Feb 88 ●	**BOYS (SUMMERTIME LOVE) (re)** *IBIZA IBIZ 1*	3 14
1 Oct 88	**ALL OF ME** *PWL PWL 19*	25 7
1 Jul 89	**LIKE A YO-YO** *Videogram DCUP 1*	72 1

'Boys' peaked during re-entry in Jun 1988

SACARIO – *See Angie MARTINEZ featuring Lil' MO & SACARIO*

SACRED SPIRIT *Germany, male producer – Claus Zundel, utilising Native American chants (Singles: 5 weeks, Albums: 30 weeks)*

		pos/wks
15 Apr 95	**YEHA-NOHA (WISHES OF HAPPINESS AND PROSPERITY)** *Virgin VSCDT 1514*	71 1
18 Nov 95	**WISHES OF HAPPINESS AND PROSPERITY (YEHA-NOHA) (re-issue)** *Virgin VSC 1568*	37 2
16 Mar 96	**WINTER CEREMONY (TOR-CHENEY-NAHANA)** *Virgin VSCDT 1574*	45 2
1 Apr 95 ●	**CHANTS AND DANCES OF THE NATIVE AMERICANS** *Virgin CDV 2753*	9 27
26 Apr 97	**SACRED SPIRIT VOLUME 2 – CULTURE CLASH** *Virgin CDV 2827*	24 3

See also DIVINE WORKS

SAD CAFÉ *UK, male vocal / instrumental group – leader Paul Young, d. 15 Jul 2000 (Singles: 44 weeks, Albums: 36 weeks)*

		pos/wks
22 Sep 79 ●	**EVERY DAY HURTS** *RCA PB 5180*	3 12
19 Jan 80	**STRANGE LITTLE GIRL** *RCA PB 5202*	32 5
15 Mar 80	**MY OH MY** *RCA SAD 3*	14 11
21 Jun 80	**NOTHING LEFT TOULOUSE** *RCA SAD 4*	62 4
27 Sep 80	**LA-DI-DA** *RCA SAD 5*	41 6
20 Dec 80	**I'M IN LOVE AGAIN** *RCA SAD 6*	40 6
1 Oct 77	**FANX TA RA** *RCA PL 25101*	56 1
29 Apr 78	**MISPLACED IDEALS** *RCA PL 25133*	50 1
29 Sep 79 ●	**FAÇADES** *RCA PL 25249*	8 23
25 Oct 80	**SAD CAFÉ** *RCA SADLP 4*	46 5
21 Mar 81	**LIVE** *RCA SAD LP 5*	37 4
24 Oct 81	**OLE** *Polydor POLD 5045*	72 2

SADE (211 Top 500) *Popular, jazz-styled vocalist, b. Helen Folasade Adu, 16 Jan 1959, Nigeria. The UK-based Brit and Grammy winner, who received OBE in 2002, is the only African artist to top the album chart in the UK or US (where all her albums have reached the Top 10) (Singles: 69 weeks, Albums: 213 weeks)*

		pos/wks
25 Feb 84 ●	**YOUR LOVE IS KING (re)** *Epic A 4137*	6 12
26 May 84	**WHEN AM I GONNA MAKE A LIVING** *Epic A 4437*	36 5
15 Sep 84	**SMOOTH OPERATOR** *Epic A 4655*	19 10
12 Oct 85	**THE SWEETEST TABOO** *Epic A 6609*	31 5
11 Jan 86	**IS IT A CRIME** *Epic A 6742*	49 3
2 Apr 88	**LOVE IS STRONGER THAN PRIDE** *Epic SADE 1*	44 3
4 Jun 88	**PARADISE** *Epic SADE 2*	29 7
10 Oct 92	**NO ORDINARY LOVE (re)** *Epic 6583562*	14 11
28 Nov 92	**FEEL NO PAIN** *Epic 6588297*	56 2
8 May 93	**KISS OF LIFE** *Epic 6591162*	44 3
31 Jul 93	**CHERISH THE DAY** *Epic 6594812*	53 2
18 Nov 00	**BY YOUR SIDE** *Epic 6699992*	17 5
24 Mar 01	**KING OF SORROW** *Epic 6708672*	59 1
28 Jul 84 ●	**DIAMOND LIFE** *Epic EPC 26044*	2 99
16 Nov 85 ★	**PROMISE** *Epic EPC 86318* ■ ▲	1 31
14 May 88 ●	**STRONGER THAN PRIDE** *Epic 460497 1*	3 17
7 Nov 92 ●	**LOVE DELUXE** *Epic 4726262*	10 27
12 Nov 94 ●	**THE BEST OF SADE** *Epic 4777932*	6 16
25 Nov 00	**LOVERS ROCK** *Epic 5007662*	18 21
2 Mar 02	**LOVERS LIVE** *Epic 5061252*	51 2

'No Ordinary Love' first peaked at No.26 and did not reach its peak position until re-entering in Jun 1993

Staff Sergeant Barry SADLER
US, male vocalist, d. 5 Nov 1989 (Singles: 8 weeks)

		pos/wks
24 Mar 66	**THE BALLAD OF THE GREEN BERETS** *RCA 1506* ▲	24 8

SAFFRON
UK, female vocalist (Singles: 2 weeks)

		pos/wks
16 Jan 93	**CIRCLES** *WEA SAFF 9CD*	60 2

See also REPUBLICA

SAFFRON HILL featuring Ben ONONO
UK, male DJ / producer and male vocalist (Singles: 3 weeks)

		pos/wks
17 May 03	**MY LOVE IS ALWAYS** *Illustrious CDILL 016*	28 3

See also TIM DELUXE

SAFFRONS – *See CINDY and the SAFFRONS*

TRIBUTE ALBUMS

This chronological list of compilation albums features various artists paying tribute to the stars who created the original masterpieces. This is the place where Ol' Dirty Bastard gets to cover Phil Collins' 'Sussudio'; The Tremeloes have a go at Dylan's 'I Shall Be Released' and R.E.M. give Leonard Cohen's 'First We Take Manhattan' their best shot.

CHART ENTRY DATE / **ALBUM TITLE** / LABEL / **PEAK POSITION / WEEKS ON CHART**

29 Feb 1964 **BEATLEMANIA** Top Six **19 2**
9 Nov 1985 **OVATION – THE BEST OF ANDREW LLOYD WEBBER** K-Tel **34 12**
7 Dec 1985 **PERFORMANCE – THE VERY BEST OF TIM RICE AND ANDREW LLOYD WEBBER** Telstar **33 7**
24 Oct 1987 **THE HIT FACTORY – THE BEST OF STOCK AITKEN WATERMAN** Stylus **18 17**
9 Apr 1988 **SERGEANT PEPPER KNEW MY FATHER** NME **37 8**
12 Nov 1988 **ANDREW LLOYD WEBBER – THE PREMIERE COLLECTION** Polydor **1 64**
15 Apr 1989 **THE SONGS OF BOB DYLAN** Start **13 5**
24 Nov 1990 **A TON OF HITS – THE BEST OF STOCK AITKEN WATERMAN** Dover **7 8**
29 Dec 1990 **BACHARACH AND DAVID – THEY WRITE THE SONGS** Dino **6 3**
13 Jul 1991 **PURPLE RAINBOWS (Deep Purple and Rainbow Tribute)** Polydor/EMI **1 13**
9 Feb 1991 **TRACKS OF MY TEARS (SMOKEY ROBINSON – WRITER AND PERFORMER)** Dino **6 8**
12 Oct 1991 **I'M YOUR FAN – THE SONGS OF LEONARD COHEN** East West **16 2**
26 Oct 1991 **TWO ROOMS – ELTON JOHN AND BERNIE TAUPIN** Mercury **1 21**
28 Nov 1992 **THE PREMIERE COLLECTION ENCORE – ANDREW LLOYD WEBBER** Really Useful **2 11**
19 Mar 1994 **I KNOW THEM SO WELL – TIM RICE** PolyGram TV **2 7**
5 Nov 1994 **THE VERY BEST OF ANDREW LLOYD WEBBER** Really Useful **3 13**
14 Sep 1996 **TRIBUTE TO THE SMALL FACES – LONG AGOS / WORLDS APART** Nice **20 1**
20 Feb 1999 **THE LOVE SONGS OF BURT BACHARACH** Universal Music TV **5 3**
13 Nov 1999 **FIRE & SKILL – THE SONGS OF THE JAM** Ignition **12 1**
20 Nov 1999 **ABBAMANIA** Polydor/Universal Music TV **2 7**
28 Oct 2000 **THE HIT FACTORY – PETE WATERMAN'S GREATEST HITS** Universal Music TV **3 5**
19 May 2001 **THE LOOK OF LOVE – THE BURT BACHARACH COLLECTION** WSM/Universal Music TV **4 17**
30 Jun 2001 **URBAN RENEWAL FEATURING THE SONGS OF PHIL COLLINS** WEA **16 1**
8 Dec 2001 **ANDREW LLOYD WEBBER – GOLD** Really Useful/Polydor **5 4**

Ol' Dirty Bastard was just one of the 'Urban Renewal' artists let loose on the Phil Collins back catalogue in 2001

Alessandro SAFINA *Italy, male vocalist (Albums: 2 weeks)* pos/wks

27 Jul 02 ● **YOUR SONG (re)** *Mercury 639972* [1] 4 10
30 Mar 02 **SAFINA** *Mercury 167432* 27 2

[1] Elton John & Alessandro Safina

SAFRI DUO *Denmark, male instrumental / production duo – Uffe Savery and Morten Friis (Singles: 10 weeks)* pos/wks

3 Feb 01 ● **PLAYED-A-LIVE (THE BONGO SONG)** *AM:PM CDAMPM 141* 6 9
5 Oct 02 **SWEET FREEDOM** *Serious SERR 55CD* [1] 54 1

[1] Safri Duo featuring Michael McDonald

Mike SAGAR and the CRESTERS
UK, male vocalist (Singles: 5 weeks) pos/wks

8 Dec 60 **DEEP FEELING** *HMV POP 819* 44 5

SAGAT *US, male rapper – Faustin Lenon (Singles: 6 weeks)* pos/wks

4 Dec 93 **FUNK DAT** *ffrr FCD 224* 25 5
3 Dec 94 **LUVSTUFF** *ffrr FCD 250* 71 1

Carole Bayer SAGER *US, female vocalist (Singles: 9 weeks)* pos/wks

28 May 77 ● **YOU'RE MOVING OUT TODAY** *Elektra K 12257* 6 9

Bally SAGOO *India, male producer / instrumentalist (Singles: 8 weeks, Albums: 1 week)* pos/wks

3 Sep 94 **CHURA LIYA** *Columbia 6607092* 64 1
22 Apr 95 **CHOLI KE PEECHE** *Columbia 6613352* 45 1
19 Oct 96 **DIL CHEEZ (MY HEART...)** *Higher Ground 6634882* 12 3
1 Feb 97 **TUM BIN JIYA** *Higher Ground 6641372* 21 3
9 Nov 96 **RISING FROM THE EAST** *Higher Ground 4850162* 63 1

SAILOR *UK, male vocal / instrumental group (Singles: 24 weeks, Albums: 8 weeks)* pos/wks

6 Dec 75 ● **GLASS OF CHAMPAGNE** *Epic EPC 3770* 2 12
27 Mar 76 ● **GIRLS GIRLS GIRLS** *Epic EPC 3858* 7 8
19 Feb 77 **ONE DRINK TOO MANY** *Epic EPC 4804* 35 4
7 Feb 76 **TROUBLE** *Epic EPC 69192* 45 8

SAINT featuring Suzanna DEE *UK, male production duo – Mark Smith and Dave Pickard, and female vocalist (Singles: 2 weeks)* pos/wks

12 Apr 03 **SHOW ME HEAVEN** *Inferno CDFERN 52* 36 2

ST ANDREWS CHORALE *UK, church choir (Singles: 5 weeks)* pos/wks

14 Feb 76 **CLOUD 99** *Decca F 13617* 31 5

ST CECILIA
UK, male vocal / instrumental group (Singles: 17 weeks) pos/wks

19 Jun 71 **LEAP UP AND DOWN (WAVE YOUR KNICKERS IN THE AIR)** *Polydor 2058 104* 12 17

SAINT ETIENNE *UK, male / female vocal / instrumental group – lead vocal Sarah Cracknell (Singles: 54 weeks, Albums: 31 weeks)* pos/wks

18 May 91 **NOTHING CAN STOP US / SPEEDWELL** *Heavenly HVN 009* 54 3
7 Sep 91 **ONLY LOVE CAN BREAK YOUR HEART / FILTHY** *Heavenly HVN 12* 39 4
16 May 92 **JOIN OUR CLUB / PEOPLE GET REAL** *Heavenly HVN 15* 21 3
17 Oct 92 **AVENUE** *Heavenly HVN 2312* 40 2
13 Feb 93 **YOU'RE IN A BAD WAY** *Heavenly HVN 25CD* 12 5
22 May 93 **HOBART PAVING / WHO DO YOU THINK YOU ARE** *Heavenly HVN 29CD* 23 5
18 Dec 93 **I WAS BORN ON CHRISTMAS DAY** *Heavenly HVN 36CD* [1] 37 5
19 Feb 94 **PALE MOVIE** *Heavenly HVN 37CD* 28 3
28 May 94 **LIKE A MOTORWAY** *Heavenly HVN 40CD* 47 2
1 Oct 94 **HUG MY SOUL** *Heavenly HVN 42CD* 32 2
11 Nov 95 **HE'S ON THE PHONE** *Heavenly HVN 50CDR* [2] 11 5
7 Feb 98 **SYLVIE** *Creation CRESCD 279* 12 3
2 May 98 **THE BAD PHOTOGRAPHER** *Creation CRESCD 290* 27 2
20 May 00 ● **TELL ME WHY (THE RIDDLE)** *Deviant DVNT 36CDS* [3] 7 5
24 Jun 00 **HEART FAILED (IN THE BACK OF A TAXI)** *Mantra / Beggars Banquet MNT 54CD* 50 1
20 Jan 01 **BOY IS CRYING** *Mantra / Beggars Banquet MNT 60CD* 34 2
7 Sep 02 **ACTION** *Mantra / Beggars Banquet MNT 73CD* 41 1
29 Mar 03 **SOFT LIKE ME** *Mantra MNT 78CD* 40 1
26 Oct 91 **FOXBASE ALPHA** *Heavenly HVNLP 1* 34 3
6 Mar 93 ● **SO TOUGH** *Heavenly HVNLP 6CD* 7 7
12 Mar 94 ● **TIGER BAY** *Heavenly HVNLP 8CD* 8 4
25 Nov 95 **TOO YOUNG TO DIE – THE SINGLES** *Heavenly HVNLP 10CD* 17 9
27 Jan 96 **RESERECTION** *Virgin DINSD 150* [1] 50 1
19 Oct 96 **CASINO CLASSICS** *Heavenly HVNLP 16CD* 34 2
16 May 98 **GOOD HUMOR** *Creation CRECD 225* 18 3
3 Jun 00 **SOUND OF WATER** *Mantra MNTCD 1018* 33 1
19 Oct 02 **FINISTERRE** *Mantra / Beggars Banquet MNTCD 1033* 55 1

[1] Saint Etienne co-starring Tim Burgess [2] Saint Etienne featuring Etienne Daho
[3] Paul Van Dyk featuring Saint Etienne [1] Saint Etienne Daho

See also Sarah CRACKNELL

ST GERMAIN
France, male producer (Singles: 3 weeks, Albums: 1 week) pos/wks

31 Aug 96 **ALABAMA BLUES (REVISITED)** *F Communications F 050CD* ..50 1
10 Mar 01 **ROSE ROUGE** *Blue Note CDROSE 001* 54 2
20 May 00 **TOURIST** *Blue Note 5262012* 73 1

Barry ST JOHN *UK, female vocalist (Singles: 1 week)* pos/wks

9 Dec 65 **COME AWAY MELINDA** *Columbia DB 7783* 47 1

ST JOHN'S COLLEGE SCHOOL CHOIR and the Band of the GRENADIER GUARDS
UK, school choir and military band (Singles: 3 weeks) pos/wks

3 May 86 **THE QUEEN'S BIRTHDAY SONG** *Columbia Q1* 40 3

ST LOUIS UNION
UK, male vocal / instrumental group (Singles: 10 weeks) pos/wks

13 Jan 66 **GIRL** *Decca F 12318* 11 10

ST LUNATICS – *See NELLY*

Crispian ST PETERS
UK, male vocalist – Peter Smith (Singles: 31 weeks) pos/wks

6 Jan 66 ● **YOU WERE ON MY MIND** *Decca F 12287* 2 14
31 Mar 66 ● **THE PIED PIPER** *Decca F 12359* 5 13
15 Sep 66 **CHANGES (re)** *Decca F 12480* 47 4

ST PHILIPS CHOIR *UK, choir (Singles: 4 weeks)* pos/wks

12 Dec 87 **SING FOR EVER** *BBC RESL 222* 49 4

ST THOMAS MORE SCHOOL CHOIR – *See Scott FITZGERALD*

ST WINIFRED'S SCHOOL CHOIR
UK, school choir – lead vocal Dawn Ralph (Singles: 11 weeks) pos/wks

22 Nov 80 ★ **THERE'S NO ONE QUITE LIKE GRANDMA** *MFP FP 900* 1 11

Buffy SAINTE-MARIE
Canada, female vocalist (Singles: 29 weeks, Albums: 2 weeks) pos/wks

17 Jul 71 ● **SOLDIER BLUE** *RCA 2081* 7 18
18 Mar 72 **I'M GONNA BE A COUNTRY GIRL AGAIN** *Vanguard VRS 35143* 34 5
8 Feb 92 **THE BIG ONES GET AWAY** *Ensign ENY 650* 39 5
4 Jul 92 **FALLEN ANGELS** *Ensign ENY 655* 57 1
21 Mar 92 **COINCIDENCE (AND LIKELY STORIES)** *Ensign CCD 1920* 39 2

SAINTS
Australia, male vocal / instrumental group (Singles: 4 weeks) pos/wks

16 Jul 77 **THIS PERFECT DAY** *Harvest HAR 5130* 34 4

Kyu SAKAMOTO

Japan, male vocalist. d. 12 Aug 1985 (Singles: 13 weeks) pos/wks

27 Jun 63 ● **SUKIYAKI** *HMV POP 1171* ▲ 6 13

Ryuichi SAKAMOTO *Japan, male instrumentalist – keyboards (Singles: 15 weeks, Albums: 9 weeks)* pos/wks

7 Aug 82 **BAMBOO HOUSES / BAMBOO MUSIC** *Virgin VS 510* [1] 30 4
2 Jul 83 **FORBIDDEN COLOURS** *Virgin VS 601* [2] 16 8
13 Jun 92 **HEARTBEAT (TAINAI KAIKI II) RETURNING TO THE WOMB** *Virgin America VUS 57* [3] 58 3
3 Sep 83 **MERRY CHRISTMAS MR LAWRENCE (FILM SOUNDTRACK)** *Virgin V 2276* 36 9

[1] Sylvian Sakamoto [2] David Sylvian and Riuichi Sakamoto [4] David Sylvian / Riuichi Sakamoto featuring Ingrid Chavez

SAKKARIN – *See Jonathan KING*

SALAD *UK / Holland, male / female vocal / instrumental group (Singles: 5 weeks, Albums: 2 weeks)* pos/wks

11 Mar 95 **DRINK THE ELIXIR** *Island Red CIRD 104* 66 1
13 May 95 **MOTORBIKE TO HEAVEN** *Island Red CIRD 106* 42 1
16 Sep 95 **GRANITE STATUE** *Island Red CIRD 108* 50 1
26 Oct 96 **I WANT YOU** *Island CID 646* 60 1
17 May 97 **CARDBOY KING** *Island CID 654* 65 1
27 May 95 **DRINK ME** *Island Red CIRDX 1002* 16 2

SALFORD JETS

UK, male vocal / instrumental group (Singles: 2 weeks) pos/wks

31 May 80 **WHO YOU LOOKING AT?** *RCA PB 5239* 72 2

SALIVA *US, male vocal / instrumental group (Singles: 1 week)* pos/wks

15 Mar 03 **ALWAYS** *Mercury 0637082* 47 1

SALSOUL ORCHESTRA – *See CHARO and the SALSOUL ORCHESTRA*

SALT TANK

UK, male production duo – Malcolm Stanners and David Gates (Singles: 4 weeks) pos/wks

11 May 96 **EUGINA** *Internal LIECD 29* 40 2
3 Jul 99 **DIMENSION** *Hooj Choons HOOJ 74CD* 52 1
9 Dec 00 **EUGINA (re-mix)** *Lost Language LOST 004CD* 58 1

SALT-N-PEPA (371 Top 500)

Rappers Cheryl 'Salt' James (b. 28 Mar 1969, Brooklyn, US) and Sandra 'Pepa' Denton (b. 9 Nov 1969, Kingston, Jamaica), backed up by DJ Dee Dee 'Spinderella' Roper, are the most commercially successful female rap troupe of all time (Singles: 123 weeks, Albums: 57 weeks) pos/wks

26 Mar 88 **PUSH IT / I AM DOWN** *ffrr FFR 2* 41 6
25 Jun 88 ● **PUSH IT / TRAMP** *Champion CHAMP 51 & ffrr FFR 2* 2 13
3 Sep 88 **SHAKE YOUR THANG (IT'S YOUR THING)** *ffrr FFR 11* [1] 22 8
12 Nov 88 ● **TWIST AND SHOUT** *ffrr FFR 16* 4 9
14 Apr 90 **EXPRESSION** *ffrr F 127* 40 6
25 May 91 ● **DO YOU WANT ME** *ffrr F 151* 5 12
31 Aug 91 ● **LET'S TALK ABOUT SEX** *ffrr F 162* 2 13
30 Nov 91 **YOU SHOWED ME** *ffrr F 174* [2] 15 9
28 Mar 92 **EXPRESSION (re-mix)** *ffrr F 182* 23 6
3 Oct 92 **START ME UP** *ffrr F 196* 39 3
9 Oct 93 **SHOOP** *ffrr FCD 219* 29 3
19 Mar 94 ● **WHATTA MAN** *ffrr FCD 222* [3] 7 10
28 May 94 **SHOOP (re-mix)** *ffrr FCD 234* 13 8
12 Nov 94 **NONE OF YOUR BUSINESS (re)** *ffrr FCD 244* 19 5
21 Dec 96 **CHAMPAGNE** *MCA MCSTD 48025* 23 6
29 Nov 97 **R U READY** *ffrr FCDP 322* 24 2
11 Dec 99 **THE BRICK TRACK VERSUS GITTY UP** *ffrr FCD 373* [4] 22 4
6 Aug 88 **A SALT WITH A DEADLY PEPA** *ffrr FFRLP 3* 19 27
12 May 90 **BLACKS' MAGIC** *ffrr 8281641* 70 1
6 Jul 91 **A BLITZ OF SALT-N-PEPA HITS – THE HITS REMIXED** *ffrr 8282491* 70 2
19 Oct 91 ● **GREATEST HITS** *ffrr 8282911* 6 20
25 Apr 92 **RAPPED IN REMIXES** *ffrr 8282972* 37 2
23 Apr 94 **VERY NECESSARY** *ffrr 8284542* 36 5

[1] Salt-N-Pepa featuring EU [2] Additional vocals Joyce Martin & Cari Linger [3] Salt-N-Pepa with En Vogue [4] Saltnpepa

'I Am Down' listed only from 2 Apr 1988. The disc re-entered on 25 Jun when it was made available on Champion with a different flip side. Sales for both discs were amalgamated

SALVATION ARMY

UK, brass band (Albums: 5 weeks) pos/wks

24 Dec 77 **BY REQUEST** *Warwick WW 5038* 16 5

SAM and DAVE *US, male vocal duo – Sam Moore and Dave Prater d. 9 Apr 1998 (Singles: 39 weeks, Albums: 20 weeks)* pos/wks

16 Mar 67 **SOOTHE ME (re)** *Stax 601 004* 35 8
1 Nov 67 **SOUL MAN** *Stax 601 023* 24 14
13 Mar 68 **I THANK YOU** *Stax 601 030* 34 9
29 Jan 69 **SOUL SISTER, BROWN SUGAR** *Atlantic 584 237* 15 8
21 Jan 67 **HOLD ON I'M COMIN'** *Atlantic 588045* 35 7
22 Apr 67 **DOUBLE DYNAMITE** *Stax 589003* 28 5
23 Mar 68 **SOUL MEN** *Stax 589015* 32 8

See also Lou REED

SAM THE SHAM and the PHARAOHS

US, male vocal / instrumental group (Singles: 18 weeks) pos/wks

24 Jun 65 **WOOLY BULLY** *MGM 1269* 11 15
4 Aug 66 **LIL' RED RIDING HOOD (re)** *MGM 1315* 46 3

Richie SAMBORA *US, male vocalist / instrumentalist – guitar (Singles: 4 weeks, Albums: 5 weeks)* pos/wks

7 Sep 91 **BALLAD OF YOUTH** *Mercury MER 350* 59 1
7 Mar 98 **HARD TIMES COME EASY** *Mercury 5686972* 37 2
1 Aug 98 **IN IT FOR LOVE** *Mercury 5660632* 58 1
14 Sep 91 **STRANGER IN THIS TOWN** *Mercury 8488951* 20 3
14 Mar 98 **UNDISCOVERED SOUL** *Mercury 5369722* 24 2

See also BON JOVI

Mike SAMMES SINGERS *UK, male female vocal group – leader d. 19 May 2001 (Singles: 38 weeks)* pos/wks

15 Sep 66 **SOMEWHERE MY LOVE (re)** *HMV POP 1546* 14 38
19 Jan 76 **MUSIC OF AMERICA** *Ronco TRD 2016* [1] 18 7

[1] Richmond Strings / Mike Sammes Singers

'Somewhere My Love' first peaked at No.22 and reached No.14 after re-entry in 1967

See also Michael FLANDERS; Michael HOLLIDAY; Des O'CONNOR; Andy STEWART; Malcolm VAUGHAN; Jimmy YOUNG

Dave SAMPSON *UK, male vocalist (Singles: 6 weeks)* pos/wks

19 May 60 **SWEET DREAMS (re)** *Columbia DB 4449* 29 6

SAMSON *UK, male vocal / instrumental group (Singles: 6 weeks, Albums: 6 weeks)* pos/wks

4 Jul 81 **RIDING WITH THE ANGELS** *RCA 67* 55 3
24 Jul 82 **LOSING MY GRIP** *Polydor POSP 471* 63 2
5 Mar 83 **RED SKIES** *Polydor POSP 554* 65 1
26 Jul 80 **HEAD ON** *Gem GEMLP 108* 34 6

SAN JOSE featuring Rodriguez ARGENTINA

UK, male instrumental group (Singles: 8 weeks) pos/wks

17 Jun 78 **ARGENTINE MELODY (CANCION DE ARGENTINA)** *MCA 369* 14 8

Rodriguez Argentina is Rod Argent

See also ARGENT; SILSOE

SAN REMO STRINGS *US, orchestra (Singles: 8 weeks)* pos/wks

18 Dec 71 **FESTIVAL TIME** *Tamla Motown TMG 795* 39 8

David SANBORN

UK, male instrumentalist – saxophone (Albums: 1 week) pos/wks

14 Mar 87 A CHANGE OF HEART *Warner Bros. 925 4791* 86 1

Junior SANCHEZ featuring DAJAE *US, male DJ / producer and female vocalist – Karen Gordon (Singles: 2 weeks)* pos/wks

16 Oct 99 B WITH U *Manifesto FESCD 62* 31 2

Roger SANCHEZ

US, male producer (Singles: 21 weeks, Albums: 2 weeks) pos/wks

3 Oct 98 BUFFALO GALS STAMPEDE (re-mix) *Virgin VSCDT 1717* [1] 65 1
20 Feb 99 I WANT YOUR LOVE *Perpetual PERPCDS 001* [2] 31 2
29 Jan 00 I NEVER KNEW *INCredible INCS 4CDS* [3] 24 2
14 Jul 01 ★ ANOTHER CHANCE *Defected DFECT 35CDS* ■ 1 12
15 Dec 01 YOU CAN'T CHANGE ME *Defected DFECT 41CDS* [4] 25 4
11 Aug 01 FIRST CONTACT *Defected SMAN 01CD* 34 2

[1] Malcolm McLaren and the World's Famous Supreme Team plus Rakim and Roger Sanchez [2] Roger Sanchez presents Twilight [3] Roger Sanchez featuring Cooly's Hot Box [4] Roger Sanchez featuring Armand Van Helden and N'Dea Davenport

See also EL MARIACHI; FUNK JUNKEEZ; TRANSATLANTIC SOUL

Chris SANDFORD *UK, male actor / vocalist (Singles: 9 weeks)* pos/wks

12 Dec 63 NOT TOO LITTLE NOT TOO MUCH *Decca F 11778* 17 9

SANDPIPERS *US, male vocal group (Singles: 33 weeks)* pos/wks

15 Sep 66 ● GUANTANAMERA *Pye International 7N 25380* 7 17
5 Jun 68 QUANDO M'INNAMORO (A MAN WITHOUT LOVE) *A&M AMS 723* 33 6
26 Mar 69 KUMBAYA (re) *A&M AMS 744* 38 2
27 Nov 76 HANG ON SLOOPY *Satril SAT 114* 32 8

SANDRA *Germany, female vocalist (Singles: 8 weeks)* pos/wks

17 Dec 88 EVERLASTING LOVE *Siren SRN 85* 45 8

Jodie SANDS *US, female vocalist (Singles: 10 weeks)* pos/wks

17 Oct 58 SOMEDAY (YOU'LL WANT ME TO WANT YOU) *HMV POP 533* 14 10

Tommy SANDS *US, male vocalist (Singles: 7 weeks)* pos/wks

4 Aug 60 THE OLD OAKEN BUCKET *Capitol CL 15143* 25 7

SANDSTORM *US, male producer – Mark Picchiotti (Singles: 1 week)* pos/wks

13 May 00 THE RETURN OF NOTHING *Renaissance Recordings RENCDS 001* 54 1

See also Mark PICCHIOTTI presents BASSTOY featuring DANA

Samantha SANG

Australia, female vocalist – Cheryl Gray (Singles: 13 weeks) pos/wks

4 Feb 78 EMOTION *Private Stock PVT 128* 11 13

SANTA CLAUS and the CHRISTMAS TREES

UK, male vocal / instrumental group (Singles: 10 weeks) pos/wks

11 Dec 82 SINGALONG-A-SANTA *Polydor IVY 1* 19 5
10 Dec 83 SINGALONG-A-SANTA AGAIN *Polydor IVY 2* 39 5

SANTA ESMERALDA and Leroy GOMEZ *US / France, male / female vocal / instrumental group (Singles: 5 weeks)* pos/wks

12 Nov 77 DON'T LET ME BE MISUNDERSTOOD *Philips 6042 325* 41 5

SANTANA (148 Top 500)

Latin rock band from the 1960s which peaked in the 21st century, formed in San Francisco in 1966 by Carlos Santana, b. 20 Jul 1947, Mexico. Their first US No.1 for 28 years, 'Supernatural', won record eight Grammy awards (2000) and sold in excess of 21 million worldwide (Singles: 53 weeks, Albums: 298 weeks) pos/wks

28 Sep 74 SAMBA PA TI *CBS 2561* 27 7
15 Oct 77 SHE'S NOT THERE *CBS 5671* 11 12
25 Nov 78 WELL ALL RIGHT *CBS 6755* 53 3
22 Mar 80 ALL I EVER WANTED *CBS 8160* 57 3
23 Oct 99 SMOOTH *Arista 74321709492* [1] ▲ 75 1
1 Apr 00 ● SMOOTH (re-issue) *Arista 74321748762* [1] 3 10
5 Aug 00 ● MARIA MARIA *Arista 74321769372* [2] ▲ 6 9
23 Nov 02 THE GAME OF LOVE *Arista 74321959442* [3] 16 8
2 May 70 SANTANA *CBS 63815* 26 11
28 Nov 70 ● ABRAXAS *CBS 64807* ▲ 7 52
13 Nov 71 ● SANTANA III *CBS 69015* ▲ 6 14
26 Aug 72 CARLOS SANTANA AND BUDDY MILES LIVE *CBS 65142* [1] 29 4
25 Nov 72 ● CARAVANSERAI *CBS 65299* 6 11
28 Jul 73 ● LOVE DEVOTION AND SURRENDER *CBS 69037* [2] 7 9
8 Dec 73 ● WELCOME *CBS 69040* 8 6
21 Sep 74 GREATEST HITS *CBS 69081* 14 15
2 Nov 74 ILLUMINATIONS *CBS 69063* [3] 40 1
30 Nov 74 BARBOLETTA *CBS 69084* 18 5
10 Apr 76 AMIGOS *CBS 86005* 21 9
8 Jan 77 FESTIVAL *CBS 86020* 27 3
5 Nov 77 ● MOONFLOWER *CBS 88272* 7 27
11 Nov 78 INNER SECRETS *CBS 86075* 17 16
24 Mar 79 ONENESS – SILVER DREAMS GOLDEN REALITY *CBS 86037* [4] 55 4
27 Oct 79 MARATHON *CBS 86098* 28 5
20 Sep 80 THE SWING OF DELIGHT *CBS 22075* [4] 65 2
18 Apr 81 ZEBOP! *CBS 84946* 33 4
14 Aug 82 SHANGO *CBS 85914* 35 7
30 Apr 83 HAVANA MOON *CBS 25350* [4] 84 3
23 Mar 85 BEYOND APPEARANCES *CBS 86307* 58 3
15 Nov 86 VIVA! SANTANA – THE VERY BEST *K-Tel NE 1338* 50 8
14 Jul 90 SPIRITS DANCING IN THE FLESH *CBS 4669131* 68 1
15 Aug 98 THE ULTIMATE COLLECTION *Columbia SONYTV 47CD* 12 26
4 Sep 99 ★ SUPERNATURAL *Arista 7822190802* ▲ 1 47
2 Nov 02 SHAMAN *RCA 74321959382* ▲ 15 5

[1] Santana featuring Rob Thomas [2] Santana featuring the Product G&B [3] Santana featuring Michelle Branch [1] Carlos Santana and Buddy Miles [2] Carlos Santana and Mahavishnu John McLaughlin [3] Carlos Santana and Alice Coltrane [4] Carlos Santana

Juelz SANTANA – *See CAM'RON*

SANTO and JOHNNY *US, male instrumental duo – steel and electric guitars – Santo and Johnny Farina (Singles: 5 weeks)* pos/wks

16 Oct 59 SLEEP WALK *Pye International 7N 25037* ▲ 22 4
31 Mar 60 TEARDROP *Parlophone R 4619* 50 1

SANTOS

Italy, male producer – Sante Pucello (Singles: 6 weeks) pos/wks

20 Jan 01 ● CAMELS *Incentive CENT 15CDS* 9 6

Mike SARNE

UK, male vocalist – Mike Scheuer (Singles: 43 weeks) pos/wks

10 May 62 ★ COME OUTSIDE *Parlophone R 4902* [1] 1 19
30 Aug 62 WILL I WHAT *Parlophone R 4932* [2] 18 10
10 Jan 63 JUST FOR KICKS *Parlophone R 4974* 22 7
28 Mar 63 CODE OF LOVE *Parlophone R 5010* 29 7

[1] Mike Sarne with Wendy Richard [2] Mike Sarne with Billie Davis

Joy SARNEY

UK, female vocalist (Singles: 6 weeks) pos/wks

7 May 77 NAUGHTY NAUGHTY NAUGHTY *Alaska ALA 2005* 26 6

SARR BAND *Italy / UK / France, male / female vocal / instrumental group (Singles: 1 week)* pos/wks

16 Sep 78 MAGIC MANDRAKE *Calendar DAY 111* 68 1

Peter SARSTEDT

UK, male vocalist (Singles: 25 weeks, Albums: 4 weeks) pos/wks

5 Feb 69 ★ WHERE DO YOU GO TO (MY LOVELY) *United Artists UP 2262* 1 16
4 Jun 69 ● FROZEN ORANGE JUICE *United Artists UP 35021* 10 9
15 Mar 69 ● PETER SARSTEDT *United Artists SULP 1219* 8 4

Robin SARSTEDT

UK, male vocalist (Singles: 9 weeks) pos/wks

8 May 76 ● **MY RESISTANCE IS LOW** *Decca F 13624* 3 9

SARTORELLO

Italy, male / female vocal / instrumental duo (Singles: 1 week) pos/wks

10 Aug 96 **MOVE BABY MOVE** *Multiply CDMULTY 12* 56 1

SASH! (400 Top 500)

German pop / dance act named after instrumentalist / producer Sascha (aka Sasha) Lappessen, featuring programmers Thomas Alisson and Ralf Kappmeier. First four hits uniquely featured vocals in different languages (French, Spanish, English, Italian) (Singles: 103 weeks, Albums: 65 weeks) pos/wks

1 Mar 97 ● **ENCORE UNE FOIS** *Multiply CDMULTY 18* 2 15
5 Jul 97 ● **ECUADOR** *Multiply CDMULTY 23* [1] 2 12
18 Oct 97 ● **STAY** *Multiply CDMULTY 26* [2] 2 14
4 Apr 98 ● **LA PRIMAVERA** *Multiply CXMULTY 32* 3 12
15 Aug 98 ● **MYSTERIOUS TIMES** *Multiply CXMULTY 40* [3] 2 12
28 Nov 98 ● **MOVE MANIA** *Multiply CDMULTY 45* [4] 8 10
3 Apr 99 **COLOUR THE WORLD** *Multiply CDMULTY 48* 15 6
12 Feb 00 ● **ADELANTE** *Multiply CDMULTY 60* 2 10
22 Apr 00 ● **JUST AROUND THE HILL** *Multiply CDMULTY 62* [3] 8 7
23 Sep 00 ● **WITH MY OWN EYES** *Multiply CDMULTY 67* 10 5
19 Jul 97 ● **IT'S MY LIFE – THE ALBUM** *Multiply MULTYCD 1* 6 38
5 Sep 98 ● **LIFE GOES ON** *Multiply MULTYCD 2* 5 19
29 Apr 00 **TRILENIUM** *Multiply MULTYCD 7* 13 5
11 Nov 00 **ENCORE UNE FOIS – THE GREATEST HITS** *Multiply MULTYCD 10* 33 3

[1] Sash! featuring Rodriguez [2] Sash! featuring La Trec [3] Sash! featuring Tina Cousins [4] Sash! featuring Shannon

SASHA

UK, male producer – Alexander Coe (Singles: 16 weeks, Albums: 8 weeks) pos/wks

31 Jul 93 **TOGETHER** *ffrr FCD 212* [1] 57 1
19 Feb 94 **HIGHER GROUND** *Deconstruction 74321189002* [2] 19 3
27 Aug 94 **MAGIC** *Deconstruction 74321221862* [2] 32 4
9 Mar 96 **BE AS ONE** *Deconstruction 74321342962* [3] 17 4
23 Sep 00 **SCORCHIO** *Arista 74321788222* [4] 23 3
31 Aug 02 **WAVY GRAVY** *Arista 74321960602* 64 1
12 Mar 94 **THE QAT COLLECTION** *Deconstruction 74321191962* 55 2
17 Jul 99 **EXPANDER (EP)** *Deconstruction 74321681992* 18 3
17 Aug 02 **AIRDRAWNDAGGER** *Arista 74321947862* 18 3

[1] Danny Campbell and Sasha [2] Sasha with Sam Mollison [3] Sasha and Maria [4] Sasha / Emerson

Joe SATRIANI

US, male instrumentalist – guitar (Singles: 1 week, Albums: 13 weeks) pos/wks

13 Feb 93 **THE SATCH EP** *Relativity 6589532* 53 1
15 Aug 92 **THE EXTREMIST** *Epic 4716722* 13 6
6 Nov 93 **TIME MACHINE** *Relativity 4745152* 32 2
14 Oct 95 **JOE SATRIANI** *Relativity 4811022* 21 3
14 Mar 98 **CRYSTAL PLANET** *Epic 4894732* 32 2

Tracks on The Satch EP: The Extremist / Cryin / Banana Bongo / Crazy

SATURDAY NIGHT BAND

US, male vocal / instrumental group (Singles: 9 weeks) pos/wks

1 Jul 78 **COME ON, DANCE DANCE** *CBS 6367* 16 9

Deion SAUNDERS – *See MC HAMMER*

Ann SAUNDERSON – *See OCTAVE ONE featuring Ann SAUNDERSON*

Kevin SAUNDERSON – *See INNER CITY*

Anne SAVAGE

UK, female DJ / producer (Singles: 1 week) pos/wks

19 Apr 03 **HELLRAISER** *Tidy Trax TIDY 186T* 74 1

Chantay SAVAGE

US, female vocalist (Singles: 9 weeks, Albums: 1 week) pos/wks

4 May 96 **I WILL SURVIVE** *RCA 74321377682* 12 8
8 Nov 97 **REMINDING ME (OF SEF)** *Relativity 6560762* [1] 59 1
25 May 96 **I WILL SURVIVE (DOIN' IT MY WAY)** *RCA 74321381622* 66 1

[1] Common featuring Chantay Savage

Edna SAVAGE

UK, female vocalist, d. 31 Dec 2000 (Singles: 1 week) pos/wks

13 Jan 56 **ARRIVEDERCI DARLING** *Parlophone R 4097* 19 1

SAVAGE GARDEN (270 Top 500)

Australian pop vocal / instrumental duo: Daniel Jones and Darren Hayes. Eponymous debut album sold more than 11 million copies worldwide and huge critical acclaim followed with a record-breaking 10 Arias at the 1997 Australian music industry awards. Duo went separate ways in 2001 and Hayes had solo success. Best-selling single: 'Truly, Madly, Deeply' 657,500 (Singles: 101 weeks, Albums: 132 weeks) pos/wks

21 Jun 97 **I WANT YOU** *Columbia 6645452* 11 7
27 Sep 97 **TO THE MOON AND BACK** *Columbia 6648932* 55 1
28 Feb 98 ● **TRULY MADLY DEEPLY** *Columbia 6656022* ▲ 4 23
22 Aug 98 ● **TO THE MOON AND BACK (re-issue)** *Columbia 6662882* 3 16
12 Dec 98 **I WANT YOU '98 (re-mix)** *Columbia 6667332* 12 10
10 Jul 99 **THE ANIMAL SONG** *Columbia 6675882* 16 6
13 Nov 99 ● **I KNEW I LOVED YOU** *Columbia 6683102* ▲ 10 12
1 Apr 00 **CRASH AND BURN** *Columbia 6690442* 14 6
29 Jul 00 ● **AFFIRMATION** *Columbia 6696882* 8 10
25 Nov 00 **HOLD ME (re)** *Columbia 6706032* 16 7
31 Mar 01 **THE BEST THING (re)** *Columbia 6709852* 35 3
14 Mar 98 ● **SAVAGE GARDEN** *Columbia 4871612* 2 68
20 Nov 99 ● **AFFIRMATION** *Columbia 4949352* 7 64

Telly SAVALAS

US, male actor / vocalist, d. 22 Jan 1994 (Singles: 12 weeks, Albums: 10 weeks) pos/wks

22 Feb 75 ★ **IF** *MCA 174* 1 9
31 May 75 **YOU'VE LOST THAT LOVIN' FEELIN'** *MCA 189* 47 3
22 Mar 75 **TELLY** *MCA MCF 2699* 12 10

SAVANNA

UK, male vocal group (Singles: 4 weeks) pos/wks

10 Oct 81 **I CAN'T TURN AWAY** *R & B RBS 203* 61 4

SAVOY BROWN

UK, male vocal / instrumental group (Albums: 1 week) pos/wks

28 Nov 70 **LOOKIN' IN** *Decca SKL 5066* 50 1

SAVUKA – *See Johnny CLEGG and SAVUKA*

SAW DOCTORS

Ireland, male vocal / instrumental group (Singles: 10 weeks, Albums: 12 weeks) pos/wks

12 Nov 94 **SMALL BIT OF LOVE** *Shamtown SAW 001CD* 24 3
27 Jan 96 **WORLD OF GOOD** *Shamtown SAW 002CD* 15 3
13 Jul 96 **TO WIN JUST ONCE** *Shamtown SAW 004CD* 14 2
6 Dec 97 **SIMPLE THINGS** *Shamtown SAW 006CD* 56 1
1 Jun 02 **THIS IS ME** *Shamtown SAW 012CD* 31 1
8 Jun 91 **IF THIS IS ROCK AND ROLL I WANT MY OLD JOB BACK** *Solid ROCK 7* 69 2
31 Oct 92 **ALL THE WAY FROM TUAM** *Solid 4509911462* 33 2
24 Feb 96 ● **SAME OUL' TOWN** *Shamtown SAWDOC 004CD* 6 5
24 Oct 98 **SONGS FROM SUN STREET** *Shamtown SAWDOC 006CD* 24 2
13 Oct 01 **VILLAINS?** *Shamtown SAWDOC 008CD* 58 1

Nitin SAWHNEY

UK, male instrumentalist / producer (Singles: 1 week, Albums: 4 weeks) pos/wks

28 Jul 01 **SUNSET** *V2 VVR 5016763* [1] 65 1
25 Sep 99 **BEYOND SKIN** *Outcaste CASTE 9CD* 44 2
30 Jun 01 **PROPHESY** *V2 VVR 1015912* 40 1
26 Jul 03 **HUMAN** *V2 VVR1021852* 54 1

[1] Nitin Sawhney featuring Eska

SAXON (425) Top 500

Key band on the early 1980s British New Wave of Heavy Metal scene, formed in Barnsley (originally as Son of a Bitch) 1977, and fronted by Peter 'Biff' Byford. In the 1980s, the group's 15 hit singles all missed the Top 10 (Singles: 61 weeks, Albums: 97 weeks) pos/wks

Date		Title / Label	pos	wks
22 Mar 80		**WHEELS OF STEEL** *Carrere CAR 143*	20	11
21 Jun 80		**747 (STRANGERS IN THE NIGHT)** *Carrere CAR 151*	13	9
28 Jun 80		**BACKS TO THE WALL** *Carrere HM 6*	64	2
28 Jun 80		**BIG TEASER / RAINBOW THEME – FROZEN RAINBOW** *Carrere HM 5*	66	2
29 Nov 80		**STRONG ARM OF THE LAW** *Carrere CAR 170*	63	3
11 Apr 81		**AND THE BANDS PLAYED ON** *Carrere CAR 180*	12	8
18 Jul 81		**NEVER SURRENDER** *Carrere CAR 204*	18	6
31 Oct 81		**PRINCESS OF THE NIGHT** *Carrere CAR 208*	57	3
23 Apr 83		**POWER AND THE GLORY** *Carrere SAXON 1*	32	5
30 Jul 83		**NIGHTMARE** *Carrere CAR 284*	50	3
31 Aug 85		**BACK ON THE STREETS** *Parlophone R 6103*	75	1
29 Mar 86		**ROCK 'N' ROLL GYPSY** *Parlophone R 6112*	71	1
30 Aug 86		**WAITING FOR THE NIGHT** *EMI EMI 5575*	66	2
5 Mar 88		**RIDE LIKE THE WIND** *EMI EM 43*	52	4
30 Apr 88		**I CAN'T WAIT ANYMORE** *EMI EM 54*	71	1
12 Apr 80	●	**WHEELS OF STEEL** *Carrere CAL 115*	5	29
15 Nov 80		**STRONG ARM OF THE LAW** *Carrere CAL 120*	11	13
3 Oct 81	●	**DENIM AND LEATHER** *Carrere CAL 128*	9	11
22 May 82	●	**THE EAGLE HAS LANDED** *Carrere CAL 157*	5	19
26 Mar 83		**POWER AND THE GLORY** *Carrere CAL 147*	15	9
11 Feb 84		**CRUSADER** *Carrere CAL 200*	18	7
14 Sep 85		**INNOCENCE IS NO EXCUSE** *Parlophone SAXON 2*	36	4
27 Sep 86		**ROCK THE NATIONS** *EMI EMC 3515*	34	3
9 Apr 88		**DESTINY** *EMI EMC 3543*	49	2

Al SAXON *UK, male vocalist – Allan Fowler (Singles: 10 weeks)* pos/wks

Date		Title / Label	pos	wks
16 Jan 59		**YOU'RE THE TOP CHA** *Fontana H 164*	17	4
28 Aug 59		**ONLY SIXTEEN** *Fontana H 205*	24	3
22 Dec 60		**BLUE-EYED BOY** *Fontana H 278*	39	2
7 Sep 61		**THERE I'VE SAID IT AGAIN** *Piccadilly 7N 35011*	48	1

Leo SAYER (120) Top 500

Distinctive singer / songwriter (b. 21 May 1948, Sussex, UK) who was a top singles and album act on both sides of the Atlantic in the late 1970s. His first seven hits all reached the Top 10 – a feat first achieved by his manager, Adam Faith (Singles: 151 weeks, Albums: 238 weeks) pos/wks

Date		Title / Label	pos	wks
15 Dec 73	●	**THE SHOW MUST GO ON** *Chrysalis CHS 2023*	2	13
15 Jun 74	●	**ONE MAN BAND** *Chrysalis CHS 2045*	6	9
14 Sep 74	●	**LONG TALL GLASSES** *Chrysalis CHS 2052*	4	9
30 Aug 75	●	**MOONLIGHTING** *Chrysalis CHS 2076*	2	8
30 Oct 76	●	**YOU MAKE ME FEEL LIKE DANCING** *Chrysalis CHS 2119* ▲	2	12
29 Jan 77	★	**WHEN I NEED YOU** *Chrysalis CHS 2127* ▲	1	13
9 Apr 77	●	**HOW MUCH LOVE** *Chrysalis CHS 2140*	10	8
10 Sep 77		**THUNDER IN MY HEART** *Chrysalis CHS 2163*	22	8
16 Sep 78	●	**I CAN'T STOP LOVING YOU (THOUGH I TRY)** *Chrysalis CHS 2240*	6	11
25 Nov 78		**RAINING IN MY HEART** *Chrysalis CHS 2277*	21	10
5 Jul 80	●	**MORE THAN I CAN SAY** *Chrysalis CHS 2442*	2	11
13 Mar 82	●	**HAVE YOU EVER BEEN IN LOVE** *Chrysalis CHS 2596*	10	9
19 Jun 82		**HEART (STOP BEATING IN TIME)** *Chrysalis CHS 2616*	22	10
12 Mar 83		**ORCHARD ROAD** *Chrysalis CHS 2677*	16	8
15 Oct 83		**TILL YOU COME BACK TO ME** *Chrysalis LEO 01*	51	3
8 Feb 86		**UNCHAINED MELODY** *Chrysalis LEO 3*	54	4
13 Feb 93		**WHEN I NEED YOU (re-issue)** *Chrysalis CDCHS 3926*	65	2
8 Aug 98		**YOU MAKE ME FEEL LIKE DANCING** *Brothers Org. CDBRUV 8* [1]	32	3
5 Jan 74	●	**SILVER BIRD** *Chrysalis CHR 1050*	2	22
26 Oct 74	●	**JUST A BOY** *Chrysalis CHR 1068*	4	14
20 Sep 75	●	**ANOTHER YEAR** *Chrysalis CHR 1087*	8	9
27 Nov 76	●	**ENDLESS FLIGHT** *Chrysalis CHR 1125*	4	66
22 Oct 77	●	**THUNDER IN MY HEART** *Chrysalis CDL 1154*	8	16
2 Sep 78		**LEO SAYER** *Chrysalis CDL 1198*	15	25
31 Mar 79	★	**THE VERY BEST OF LEO SAYER** *Chrysalis CDL 1222*	1	37
13 Oct 79		**HERE** *Chrysalis CDL 1240*	44	4
23 Aug 80		**LIVING IN A FANTASY** *Chrysalis CDL 1297*	15	9
8 May 82		**WORLD RADIO** *Chrysalis CDL 1345*	30	12
12 Nov 83		**HAVE YOU EVER BEEN IN LOVE** *Chrysalis LEOTV 1*	15	18
6 Mar 93		**ALL THE BEST** *Chrysalis CDCHR 1980*	26	4
20 Feb 99		**THE DEFINITIVE HITS COLLECTION** *PolyGram TV 5471152*	35	2

[1] Groove Generation featuring Leo Sayer

Alexei SAYLE

UK, male comedian / vocalist (Singles: 8 weeks, Albums: 5 weeks) pos/wks

Date		Title / Label	pos	wks
25 Feb 84		**'ULLO JOHN GOT A NEW MOTOR?** *Island IS 162*	15	8
17 Mar 84		**THE FISH PEOPLE TAPES** *Island IMA 9*	62	5

SCAFFOLD *UK, male vocal group (Singles: 62 weeks)* pos/wks

Date		Title / Label	pos	wks
22 Nov 67	●	**THANK U VERY MUCH** *Parlophone R 5643*	4	12
27 Mar 68		**DO YOU REMEMBER** *Parlophone R 5679*	34	5
6 Nov 68	★	**LILY THE PINK** *Parlophone R 5734*	1	24
1 Nov 69		**GIN GAN GOOLIE (re)** *Parlophone R 5812*	38	12
1 Jun 74	●	**LIVERPOOL LOU** *Warner Bros. K 16400*	7	9

See also Mike McGEAR

Boz SCAGGS *US, male vocalist – William Royce Scaggs (Singles: 31 weeks, Albums: 29 weeks)* pos/wks

Date		Title / Label	pos	wks
30 Oct 76		**LOWDOWN** *CBS 4563*	28	4
22 Jan 77	●	**WHAT CAN I SAY** *CBS 4869*	10	10
14 May 77		**LIDO SHUFFLE** *CBS 5136*	13	9
10 Dec 77		**HOLLYWOOD** *CBS 5836*	33	8
12 Mar 77		**SILK DEGREES** *CBS 81193*	37	24
17 Dec 77		**DOWN TWO THEN LEFT** *CBS 86036*	55	1
3 May 80		**MIDDLE MAN** *CBS 86094*	52	4

SCANTY SANDWICH

UK, male DJ / producer – Richard Marshall (Singles: 8 weeks) pos/wks

Date		Title / Label	pos	wks
29 Jan 00	●	**BECAUSE OF YOU** *Southern Fried ECB 18CDS*	3	8

SCARFACE *US, male rapper – Brad Jordan (Singles: 6 weeks)* pos/wks

Date		Title / Label	pos	wks
11 Mar 95		**HAND OF THE DEAD BODY** *Virgin America VUSCD 88* [1]	41	2
5 Aug 95		**I SEEN A MAN DIE** *Virgin America VUSCD 94*	55	2
5 Jul 97		**GAME OVER** *Virgin VUSCD 121*	34	2

[1] Scarface featuring Ice Cube

SCARFO *UK, male vocal / instrumental group (Singles: 2 weeks)* pos/wks

Date		Title / Label	pos	wks
19 Jul 97		**ALKALINE** *Deceptive BLUFF 044CD*	61	1
18 Oct 97		**COSMONAUT NO.7** *Deceptive BLUFF 053CD*	67	1

SCARLET *UK, female vocal / instrumental duo – Cheryl Parker and Joe Youle (Singles: 18 weeks, Albums: 2 weeks)* pos/wks

Date		Title / Label	pos	wks
21 Jan 95		**INDEPENDENT LOVE SONG** *WEA YZ 820CD*	12	12
29 Apr 95		**I WANNA BE FREE (TO BE WITH HIM)** *WEA YZ 913CD*	21	4
5 Aug 95		**LOVE HANGOVER** *WEA YZ 969CD*	54	1
6 Jul 96		**BAD GIRL** *WEA WEA 046CD*	54	1
11 Mar 95		**NAKED** *WEA 4509976432*	59	2

SCARLET FANTASTIC

UK, male / female vocal / instrumental group (Singles: 12 weeks) pos/wks

Date		Title / Label	pos	wks
3 Oct 87		**NO MEMORY** *Arista RIS 36*	24	10
23 Jan 88		**PLUG ME IN (TO THE CENTRAL LOVE LINE)** *Arista 109693*	67	2

SCARLET PARTY

UK, male vocal / instrumental group (Singles: 5 weeks) pos/wks

Date		Title / Label	pos	wks
16 Oct 82		**101 DAM-NATIONS** *Parlophone R 6058*	44	5

SCARS *UK, male vocal / instrumental group (Albums: 3 weeks)* pos/wks

Date		Title / Label	pos	wks
18 Apr 81		**AUTHOR! AUTHOR!** *Pre PREX 5*	67	3

SCATMAN JOHN

US, male vocalist – John Larkin, d. 3 Dec 1999 (Singles: 19 weeks) pos/wks

Date		Title / Label	pos	wks
13 May 95	●	**SCATMAN (SKI-BA-BOP-BA-DOP-BOP)** *RCA 74321281712*	3	12
2 Sep 95	●	**SCATMAN'S WORLD** *RCA 74321289952*	10	7

SCHAEFER – *See ROSTAL and SCHAEFER*

Michael SCHENKER GROUP *Germany / UK, male vocal / instrumental group (Singles: 9 weeks, Albums: 44 weeks)*

Date		Title	pos	wks
13 Sep 80		**ARMED AND READY** *Chrysalis CHS 2455*	53	3
8 Nov 80		**CRY FOR THE NATIONS** *Chrysalis CHS 2471*	56	3
11 Sep 82		**DANCER** *Chrysalis CHS 2636*	52	3
6 Sep 80	●	**MICHAEL SCHENKER GROUP** *Chrysalis CHR 1302*	8	8
19 Sep 81		**MICHAEL SCHENKER GROUP (re-issue)** *Chrysalis CHR 1336*	14	8
13 Mar 82	●	**ONE NIGHT AT BUDOKAN** *Chrysalis CTY 1375*	5	11
23 Oct 82		**ASSAULT ATTACK** *Chrysalis CHR 1393*	19	5
10 Sep 83		**BUILT TO DESTROY** *Chrysalis CHR 1441*	23	5
23 Jun 84		**ROCK WILL NEVER DIE** *Chrysalis CUX 1470*	24	5
24 Oct 87		**PERFECT TIMING** *EMI EMC 3539* [1]	65	2

[1] MSG

Lalo SCHIFRIN *Argentina, male conductor and US, orchestra (Singles: 11 weeks)*

Date		Title	pos	wks
9 Oct 76		**JAWS** *CTI CTSP 005*	14	9
25 Oct 97		**BULLITT** *Warner.esp WESP 002CD*	36	2

SCHILLER *Germany, male production duo – Christopher von Deylen and Mirko von Schlieffen (Singles: 3 weeks)*

Date		Title	pos	wks
28 Apr 01		**DAS GLOCKENSPIEL** *Data DATA 22CDS*	17	3

Peter SCHILLING *Germany, male vocalist (Singles: 6 weeks)*

Date		Title	pos	wks
5 May 84		**MAJOR TOM (COMING HOME) (re)** *PSP/WEA X 9438*	42	6

Phillip SCHOFIELD *UK, male TV presenter / actor / vocalist (Singles: 6 weeks)*

Date		Title	pos	wks
5 Dec 92		**CLOSE EVERY DOOR** *Really Useful RUR 11*	27	6

SCHOOL OF EXCELLENCE *UK, male instrumental / production duo – Bradley and Stewart Palmer (Albums: 2 weeks)*

Date		Title	pos	wks
28 Oct 95		PIANO MOODS *Dino DINCD 114*	47	2

See also HYPNOSIS; HARMONIUM; IN TUNE; JAMES BOYS; RAINDANCE; SCHOOL OF EXCELLENCE

SCIENCE DEPARTMENT featuring ERIRE *UK, male production duo and female vocalist (Singles: 1 week)*

Date		Title	pos	wks
10 Nov 01		**BREATHE** *Renaissance Recordings RENCDS 010*	64	1

SCIENTIST *UK, male producer – Phil Sebastiane (Singles: 13 weeks)*

Date		Title	pos	wks
6 Oct 90		**THE EXORCIST** *Kickin KICK 1*	62	3
1 Dec 90		**THE EXORCIST (re-mix)** *Kickin KICK 1TR*	46	3
15 Dec 90		**THE BEE (re)** *Kickin KICK 3S*	47	6
11 May 91		**SPIRAL SYMPHONY** *Kickin KICK 5*	74	1

SCISSOR SISTERS *US, male / female vocal / instrumental group (Singles: 2 weeks)*

Date		Title	pos	wks
8 Nov 03		**LAURA** *Polydor 9812788*	54	2

SCOOBIE *UK, male / female vocal / production / Celtic FC supporters group (Singles: 3 weeks)*

Date		Title	pos	wks
22 Dec 01		**THE MAGNIFICENT 7** *Big Tongue BTR 001CDS*	58	2
1 Jun 02		**THE MAGNIFICENT 7 (re-mix)** *Big Tongue BTR 001CDSX*	71	1

SCOOCH *UK, male / female vocal group (Singles: 20 weeks, Albums: 2 weeks)*

Date		Title	pos	wks
6 Nov 99		**WHEN MY BABY** *Accolade CDAC 002*	29	4
22 Jan 00	●	**MORE THAN I NEEDED TO KNOW** *Accolade CDAC 003*	5	5
6 May 00		**THE BEST IS YET TO COME (re)** *Accolade CDAC 004*	12	5
5 Aug 00		**FOR SURE** *Accolade CDAS 005*	15	6
19 Aug 00		**FOUR SURE** *Accolade 5278190*	41	2

SCOOTER *UK / Germany, male vocal / instrumental group (Singles: 64 weeks, Albums: 23 weeks)*

Date		Title	pos	wks
21 Oct 95		**THE MOVE YOUR ASS EP** *Club Tools 0061675 CLU*	23	4
17 Feb 96		**BACK IN THE UK** *Club Tools 0061955 CLU*	18	3
25 May 96		**REBEL YELL** *Club Tools 0062575 CLU*	30	2
19 Oct 96		**I'M RAVING** *Club Tools 0063015 CLU*	33	3
17 May 97		**FIRE** *Club Tools 006005 CLU*	45	2
22 Jun 02	●	**THE LOGICAL SONG** *Sheffield Tunes 0139295STU*	2	15
21 Sep 02	●	**NESSAJA** *Sheffield Tunes 0142165STU*	4	9
7 Dec 02		**POSSE (I NEED YOU ON THE FLOOR)** *Sheffield Tunes 0143775STU*	15	7
5 Apr 03		**WEEKEND!** *Sheffield Tunes 0147315 STU*	12	10
5 Jul 03		**THE NIGHT** *Sheffield Tunes 0149005 STU*	16	5
18 Oct 03		**MARIA (I LIKE IT LOUD)** *Sheffield Tunes 051135 STU* [1]	16	4
13 Apr 96		OUR HAPPY HARDCORE *Club Tools 0062282 CLU*	24	5
10 Aug 02	●	PUSH THE BEAT FOR THIS JAM (THE SINGLES '94-'02) *Sheffield Tunes 0141172 STU*	6	14
26 Apr 03		THE STADIUM TECHNO EXPERIENCE *Sheffield Tunes / Edel UK STU00147112CD*	20	4

[1] Scooter vs Marc Acardipane and Dick Rules

Tracks on The Move Your Ass EP: Move Your Ass / Friends / Endless Summer / Move Your Ass (remix)

SCORPIONS *Germany, male vocal / instrumental group (Singles: 35 weeks, Albums: 56 weeks)*

Date		Title	pos	wks
26 May 79		**IS THERE ANYBODY THERE? / ANOTHER PIECE OF MEAT** *Harvest HAR 5185*	39	4
25 Aug 79		**LOVEDRIVE** *Harvest HAR 5188*	69	2
31 May 80		**MAKE IT REAL** *Harvest HAR 5206*	72	2
20 Sep 80		**THE ZOO** *Harvest HAR 5212*	75	1
3 Apr 82		**NO ONE LIKE YOU (re)** *Harvest HAR 5219*	64	4
17 Jul 82		**CAN'T LIVE WITHOUT YOU** *Harvest HAR 5221*	63	2
4 Jun 88		**RHYTHM OF LOVE** *Harvest HAR 5240*	59	2
18 Feb 89		**PASSION RULES THE GAME** *Harvest 5242*	74	1
1 Jun 91		**WIND OF CHANGE** *Vertigo VER 54*	53	3
28 Sep 91	●	**WIND OF CHANGE (re-issue)** *Vertigo VER 58*	2	9
30 Nov 91		**SEND ME AN ANGEL (re)** *Vertigo VER 60*	27	5
21 Apr 79		LOVE DRIVE *Harvest SHSP 4097*	36	11
3 May 80		ANIMAL MAGNETISM *Harvest SHSP 4113*	23	6
10 Apr 82		BLACKOUT *Harvest SHVL 823*	11	11
24 Mar 84		LOVE AT FIRST STING *Harvest SHSP 2400071*	17	6
29 Jun 85		WORLD WIDE LIVE *Harvest SCORP 1*	18	8
14 May 88		SAVAGE AMUSEMENT *Harvest SHSP 4125*	18	6
17 Nov 90		CRAZY WORLD *Vertigo 8469081*	27	7
25 Sep 93		FACE THE HEAT *Mercury 5182802*	51	1

SCOTLAND WORLD CUP SQUAD *UK, male football team vocalists (Singles: 27 weeks, Albums: 9 weeks)*

Date		Title	pos	wks
22 Jun 74		**EASY EASY** *Polydor 2058 452*	20	4
27 May 78	●	**OLE OLA (MULHER BRASILEIRA)** *Riva 15* [1]	4	6
1 May 82	●	**WE HAVE A DREAM** *WEA K 19145* [2]	5	9
9 Jun 90		**SAY IT WITH PRIDE** *RCA PB 43791* [2]	45	3
15 Jun 96		**PURPLE HEATHER** *Warner Bros. W 0354CD* [3]	16	5
25 May 74	●	EASY EASY *Polydor 2383 282*	3	9

[1] Rod Stewart featuring the Scottish World Cup Squad '78 [2] Scottish World Cup Squad [3] Rod Stewart with the Scottish Euro '96 Squad

Band of the SCOTS GUARDS *UK, military band (Albums: 2 weeks)*

Date		Title	pos	wks
28 Jun 69		BAND OF THE SCOTS GUARDS *Fontana SFXL 54*	25	2

Jack SCOTT *Canada, male vocalist – Jack Scafone Jr (Singles: 28 weeks, Albums: 12 weeks)*

Date		Title	pos	wks
10 Oct 58	●	**MY TRUE LOVE** *London HLU 8626*	9	10
25 Sep 59		**THE WAY I WALK** *London HLL 8912*	30	1
10 Mar 60		**WHAT IN THE WORLD'S COME OVER YOU** *Top Rank JAR 280*	11	15
2 Jun 60		**BURNING BRIDGES** *Top Rank JAR 375*	32	2
7 May 60	●	I REMEMBER HANK WILLIAMS *Top Rank BUY 034*	7	11
3 Sep 60		WHAT IN THE WORLD'S COME OVER YOU *Top Rank 25/024*	11	1

Jill SCOTT
US, female vocalist (Singles: 4 weeks, Albums: 3 weeks)

		Title	pos	wks
4 Nov 00		GETTIN' IN THE WAY *Epic 6705272*	30	3
7 Apr 01		A LONG WALK *Epic 6710382*	54	1
29 Jul 00		WHO IS JILL SCOTT? – WORDS AND SOUNDS VOL. 1 *Epic 4986252*	69	3

Josey SCOTT – *See Chad KROEGER featuring Josey SCOTT*

Linda SCOTT
US, female vocalist – Linda Sampson (Singles: 14 weeks)

		Title	pos	wks
18 May 61	●	I'VE TOLD EVERY LITTLE STAR *Columbia DB 4638*	7	13
14 Sep 61		DON'T BET MONEY HONEY *Columbia DB 4692*	50	1

Mike SCOTT
UK, male vocalist / instrumentalist (Singles: 4 weeks, Albums: 4 weeks)

		Title	pos	wks
16 Sep 95		BRING 'EM ALL IN *Chrysalis CDCHS 5025*	56	1
11 Nov 95		BUILDING THE CITY OF LIGHT *Chrysalis CDCHS 5026*	60	1
27 Sep 97		LOVE ANYWAY *Chrysalis CDCHS 5064*	50	1
14 Feb 98		RARE, PRECIOUS AND GONE *Chrysalis CDCHSS 5073*	74	1
30 Sep 95		BRING 'EM ALL IN *Chrysalis CDCHR 6108*	23	2
11 Oct 97		STILL BURNING *Chrysalis CDCHR 6122*	34	2

Millie SCOTT
US, female vocalist (Singles: 11 weeks)

		Title	pos	wks
12 Apr 86		PRISONER OF LOVE *Fourth & Broadway BRW 45*	52	4
23 Aug 86		AUTOMATIC *Fourth & Broadway BRW 51*	56	3
21 Feb 87		EV'RY LITTLE BIT *Fourth & Broadway BRW 58*	63	4

Simon SCOTT
UK, male vocalist (Singles: 8 weeks)

		Title	pos	wks
13 Aug 64		MOVE IT BABY *Parlophone R 5164*	37	8

Tony SCOTT
Holland, male rapper (Singles: 6 weeks)

		Title	pos	wks
15 Apr 89		THAT'S HOW I'M LIVING / THE CHIEF *Champion CHAMP 97* [1]	48	4
10 Feb 90		GET INTO IT / THAT'S HOW I'M LIVING (re-issue) *Champion CHAMP 232*	63	2

[1] Toni Scott

'The Chief' listed only from 22 Apr 1989

SCOTT & LEON
UK, male production duo – Scott Anderson and Leon McCormack (Singles: 6 weeks)

		Title	pos	wks
30 Sep 00		YOU USED TO HOLD ME *AM:PM CDAMPM 137*	19	4
19 May 01		SHINE ON *AM:PM CDAMPM 143*	34	2

Lisa SCOTT-LEE
UK, female vocalist (Singles: 12 weeks)

		Title	pos	wks
24 May 03	●	LATELY *Fontana 9800295*	6	8
20 Sep 03		TOO FAR GONE *Fontana 9811642*	11	4

See also STEPS

SCOTTISH RUGBY TEAM with Ronnie BROWNE
UK, male rugby team vocalists (Singles: 1 week)

		Title	pos	wks
2 Jun 90		FLOWER OF SCOTLAND *Greentrax STRAX 1001*	73	1

SCREAMING BLUE MESSIAHS
US / UK, male vocal / instrumental group (Singles: 6 weeks, Albums: 1 week)

		Title	pos	wks
16 Jan 88		I WANNA BE A FLINTSTONE *WEA YZ 166*	28	6
17 May 86		GUN-SHY *WEA WX 41*	90	1

SCREAMING TREES
US, male vocal / instrumental group (Singles: 2 weeks, Albums: 4 weeks)

		Title	pos	wks
6 Mar 93		NEARLY LOST YOU *Epic 6582372*	50	1
1 May 93		DOLLAR BILL *Epic 6591792*	52	1
20 Jul 96		DUST *Epic 4839802*	32	4

Tracks on 'Nearly Lost You': E.S.K. / Song of a Baker / Winter Song (acoustic)

SCREEN II
UK, male vocal / instrumental group (Albums: 1 week)

		Title	pos	wks
9 Apr 94		LET THE RECORD SPIN *Cleveland City CLE 13015*	36	1

SCRITTI POLITTI
UK, male vocal / instrumental group – leader Green Gartside (Singles: 78 weeks, Albums: 39 weeks)

		Title	pos	wks
21 Nov 81		THE SWEETEST GIRL *Rough Trade RT 091*	64	3
22 May 82		FAITHLESS *Rough Trade RT 101*	56	4
7 Aug 82		ASYLUMS IN JERUSALEM / JACQUES DERRIDA *Rough Trade RT 111*	43	5
10 Mar 84	●	WOOD BEEZ (PRAY LIKE ARETHA FRANKLIN) *Virgin VS 657*	10	12
9 Jun 84		ABSOLUTE *Virgin VS 680*	17	9
17 Nov 84		HYPNOTIZE *Virgin VS 725*	68	2
11 May 85	●	THE WORD GIRL *Virgin VS 747*	6	12
7 Sep 85		PERFECT WAY *Virgin VS 780*	48	5
7 May 88		OH PATTI (DON'T FEEL SORRY FOR LOVERBOY) *Virgin VS 1006*	13	9
27 Aug 88		FIRST BOY IN THIS TOWN (LOVE SICK) *Virgin VS 1082*	63	3
12 Nov 88		BOOM! THERE SHE WAS *Virgin VS 1143*	55	3
16 Mar 91		SHE'S A WOMAN *Virgin VS 1333* [1]	20	7
3 Aug 91		TAKE ME IN YOUR ARMS AND LOVE ME *Virgin VS 1346* [2]	47	3
31 Jul 99		TINSELTOWN TO THE BOOGIEDOWN *Virgin VSCDT 1731*	46	1
11 Sep 82		SONGS TO REMEMBER *Rough Trade ROUGH 20*	12	7
22 Jun 85	●	CUPID AND PSYCHE 85 *Virgin V 2350*	5	19
18 Jun 88	●	PROVISION *Virgin V 2515*	8	11
7 Aug 99		ANOMIE & BONHOMIE *Virgin CDV 2884*	33	2

[1] Scritti Politti featuring Shabba Ranks [2] Scritti Politti and Sweetie Irie

Earl SCRUGGS – *See Lester FLATT and Earl SCRUGGS*

SCUMFROG
Holland, male producer – Jesse Houk and UK, male vocalist (Singles: 3 weeks)

		Title	pos	wks
11 May 02		LOVING THE ALIEN (re-mix) *Positiva CDTIV 172* [1]	41	1
31 May 03		MUSIC REVOLUTION *Positiva CDTIV 191*	46	2

[1] Scumfrog vs Bowie

SEA FRUIT
UK, male vocal / instrumental group (Singles: 1 week)

		Title	pos	wks
24 Jul 99		HELLO WORLD *Electric Canyon ECCD 3055*	59	1

SEA LEVEL
US, male instrumental group (Singles: 4 weeks)

		Title	pos	wks
17 Feb 79		FIFTY-FOUR *Capricorn POSP 28*	63	4

SEAFOOD
UK, male / female vocal / instrumental group (Singles: 1 week)

		Title	pos	wks
28 Jul 01		CLOAKING *Infectious INFEC 103CDS*	71	1

SEAHORSES
UK, male vocal / instrumental group (Singles: 26 weeks, Albums: 38 weeks)

		Title	pos	wks
10 May 97	●	LOVE IS THE LAW *Geffen GFSTD 22243*	3	7
26 Jul 97	●	BLINDED BY THE SUN *Geffen GFSTD 22266*	7	7
11 Oct 97		LOVE ME AND LEAVE ME *Geffen GFSTD 22282*	16	4
13 Dec 97		YOU CAN TALK TO ME *Geffen GFSTD 22297*	15	8
7 Jun 97	●	DO IT YOURSELF *Geffen GED 25134*	2	38

See also John SQUIRE

SEAL
291 Top 500 *Golden-voiced soul artist, b. Sealhenry Samuel 19 Feb 1963, London, UK. Found fame in 1990 thanks to his Adamski collaboration 'Killer'. Seal proceeded to record and perform with an impressive array of artists: Queen, Joni Mitchell, Jeff Beck and The Rolling Stones (Singles: 82 weeks, Albums: 138 weeks)*

		Title	pos	wks
8 Dec 90	●	CRAZY *ZTT ZANG 8*	2	15
4 May 91		FUTURE LOVE (EP) *ZTT ZANG 11*	12	6
20 Jul 91		THE BEGINNING *ZTT ZANG 21*	24	6
16 Nov 91	●	KILLER (EP) *ZTT ZANG 23*	8	8
29 Feb 92		VIOLET *ZTT ZANG 27*	39	2
21 May 94		PRAYER FOR THE DYING *ZTT ZANG 51CD*	14	5
30 Jul 94		KISS FROM A ROSE *ZTT ZANG 52CD1*	20	5
5 Nov 94		NEWBORN FRIEND *ZTT ZANG 58CD*	45	2
15 Jul 95	●	KISS FROM A ROSE / I'M ALIVE (re-issue) *ZTT ZANG 70CD* ▲	4	13

9 Dec 95 **DON'T CRY / PRAYER FOR THE DYING (re-issue)** *ZTT ZANG 75CD* 51 2
29 Mar 97 **FLY LIKE AN EAGLE** *ZTT ZEAL 1CD* 13 5
14 Nov 98 **HUMAN BEINGS** *Warner Brothers W 464CD* 50 1
12 Oct 02 ● **MY VISION** *Rulin RULIN 26CDS* [1] 6 8
20 Sep 03 **GET IT TOGETHER** *Warner W 620CD1* 25 3
22 Nov 03 **LOVE'S DIVINE** *Warner W 629CD* 68 1
1 Jun 91 ★ **SEAL** *ZTT ZTT 9* ■ 1 65
4 Jun 94 ★ **SEAL** *ZTT 4509962562* ■ 1 65
28 Nov 98 **HUMAN BEING** *Warner Bros. 9362468282* 44 2
27 Sep 03 ● **IV** *Warner Bros. 9362485412* 4 6

[1] Jakatta featuring Seal

Tracks on Future Love (EP): Future Love Paradise / A Minor Groove / Violet. Tracks on Killer (EP): Killer / Hey Joe / Come See What Love Has Done. The US No.1 symbol on ZTT ZANG 70CD refers only to 'Kiss from a Rose' The identically titled albums are different

See also ADAMSKI

Jay 'Sinister' SEALEE – *See Louie VEGA*

Jay SEAN – *See Rishi RICH PROJECT featuring Jay SEAN & JUGGY D*

SEARCHERS
301 Top 500 *Merseybeat combo, named after the 1956 movie starring John Wayne. Initially tipped to be as big as The Beatles, formed 1960: Mike Pender (v/g), John McNally (g/v), Tony Jackson, d. 2003, (v/b) (left 1964 – replaced by Frank Allen), Chris Curtis (d). Unlike The Beatles, however, most of this influential act's early hits were cover versions of US originals (Singles: 128 weeks, Albums: 87 weeks)* pos/wks

27 Jun 63 ★ **SWEETS FOR MY SWEET** *Pye 7N 15533* 1 16
10 Oct 63 **SWEET NOTHINS** *Philips BF 1274* 48 2
24 Oct 63 ● **SUGAR AND SPICE** *Pye 7N 15566* 2 13
16 Jan 64 ★ **NEEDLES AND PINS** *Pye 7N 15594* 1 15
16 Apr 64 ★ **DON'T THROW YOUR LOVE AWAY** *Pye 7N 15630* 1 11
16 Jul 64 **SOMEDAY WE'RE GONNA LOVE AGAIN** *Pye 7N 15670* 11 8
17 Sep 64 ● **WHEN YOU WALK IN THE ROOM** *Pye 7N 15694* 3 12
3 Dec 64 **WHAT HAVE THEY DONE TO THE RAIN** *Pye 7N 15739* 13 11
4 Mar 65 ● **GOODBYE MY LOVE** *Pye 7N 15794* 4 11
8 Jul 65 **HE'S GOT NO LOVE** *Pye 7N 15878* 12 10
14 Oct 65 **WHEN I GET HOME** *Pye 7N 15950* 35 3
16 Dec 65 **TAKE ME FOR WHAT I'M WORTH** *Pye 7N 15992* 20 8
21 Apr 66 **TAKE IT OR LEAVE IT** *Pye 7N 17094* 31 6
13 Oct 66 **HAVE YOU EVER LOVED SOMEBODY** *Pye 7N 17170* 48 2
10 Aug 63 ● **MEET THE SEARCHERS** *Pye NPL 18086* 2 44
16 Nov 63 ● **SUGAR AND SPICE** *Pye NPL 18089* 5 21
30 May 64 ● **IT'S THE SEARCHERS** *Pye NPL 18092* 4 17
27 Mar 65 ● **SOUNDS LIKE THE SEARCHERS** *Pye NPL 18111* 8 5

SEASHELLS
UK, female vocal group (Singles: 5 weeks) pos/wks

9 Sep 72 **MAYBE I KNOW** *CBS 8218* 32 5

SEB
UK, male instrumentalist – keyboards (Singles: 1 week) pos/wks

18 Feb 95 **SUGAR SHACK** *React CDREACT 50* 61 1

SEBADOH
US, male vocal / instrumental group (Singles: 4 weeks, Albums: 5 weeks) pos/wks

27 Jul 96 **BEAUTY OF THE RIDE** *Domino RUG 47CD* 74 1
30 Jan 99 **FLAME** *Domino RUG 80CD1* 30 3
8 May 93 **BUBBLE AND SCRAPE** *Domino WIGCD 4* 63 1
3 Sep 94 **BAKESALE** *Domino WIGCD 11* 40 2
31 Aug 96 **HARMACY** *Domino Recordings WIGCD 26* 38 1
6 Mar 99 **THE SEBADOH** *Domino Recordings WIGCD 57* 45 1

Jon SECADA
Cuba, male vocalist (Singles: 42 weeks, Albums: 16 weeks) pos/wks

18 Jul 92 ● **JUST ANOTHER DAY** *SBK SBK 35* 5 15
31 Oct 92 **DO YOU BELIEVE IN US** *SBK SBK 37* 30 4
6 Feb 93 **ANGEL** *SBK CDSBK 39* 23 5
17 Jul 93 **DO YOU REALLY WANT ME** *SBK CDSBK 41* 30 4
16 Oct 93 **I'M FREE** *SBK CDSBK 44* 50 2
14 May 94 **IF YOU GO (re)** *SBK CDSBK 51* 39 5
4 Feb 95 **MENTAL PICTURE** *SBK CDSBK 54* 44 2
16 Dec 95 **IF I NEVER KNEW YOU (LOVE THEME FROM 'POCAHONTAS')** *Walt Disney WD 7023C* [1] 51 4
14 Jun 97 **TOO LATE, TOO SOON** *SBK CDSBK 57* 43 1
5 Sep 92 **JON SECADA** *SBK SBKCD 19* 20 11
4 Jun 94 **HEART SOUL AND A VOICE** *SBK SBKCD 29* 17 5

[1] Jon Secada and Shanice

SECCHI featuring Orlando JOHNSON
Italy / US, male vocal / instrumental duo (Singles: 3 weeks) pos/wks

4 May 91 **I SAY YEAH** *Epic 6568467* 46 3

Harry SECOMBE
UK, male vocalist / comedian, d. 12 Apr 2001 (Singles: 35 weeks, Albums: 61 weeks) pos/wks

9 Dec 55 **ON WITH THE MOTLEY (VESTA LA GIUBBA)** *Philips PB 523* 16 3
3 Oct 63 **IF I RULED THE WORLD (re)** *Philips BF 1261* 18 17
23 Feb 67 ● **THIS IS MY SONG** *Philips BF 1539* 2 15
31 Mar 62 **SACRED SONGS** *Philips RBL 7501* 16 1
22 Apr 67 ● **SECOMBE'S PERSONAL CHOICE** *Philips BETS 707* 6 13
7 Aug 71 **IF I RULED THE WORLD** *Contour 6870 501* 17 20
16 Dec 78 ● **20 SONGS OF JOY** *Warwick WW 5052* 8 12
5 Dec 81 **GOLDEN MEMORIES** *Warwick WW 5107* [1] 46 5
13 Dec 86 **HIGHWAY OF LIFE** *Telstar STAR 2289* 45 5
30 Nov 91 **YOURS SINCERELY** *Philips 5107321* 46 5

[1] Harry Secombe and Moira Anderson

See also Harry SECOMBE Peter SELLERS and Spike MILLIGAN; GOONS

Harry SECOMBE Peter SELLERS and Spike MILLIGAN
UK, male comedy group (Albums: 1 week) pos/wks

18 Apr 64 **HOW TO WIN AN ELECTION** *Philips AL 3464* 20 1

See also Harry SECOMBE; Peter SELLERS; Spike MILLIGAN; GOONS

SECOND CITY SOUND
UK, male instrumental group (Singles: 8 weeks) pos/wks

20 Jan 66 **TCHAIKOVSKY ONE** *Decca F 12310* 22 7
2 Apr 69 **DREAM OF OLWEN** *Major Minor MM 600* 43 1

SECOND IMAGE
UK, male vocal / instrumental group (Singles: 11 weeks, Albums: 1 week) pos/wks

24 Jul 82 **STAR** *Polydor POSP 457* 60 2
2 Apr 83 **BETTER TAKE TIME** *Polydor POSP 565* 67 2
26 Nov 83 **DON'T YOU** *MCA 848* 68 2
11 Aug 84 **SING AND SHOUT** *MCA 882* 53 3
2 Feb 85 **STARTING AGAIN** *MCA 936* 65 2
30 Mar 85 **STRANGE REFLECTIONS** *MCA MCF 3255* 100 1

SECOND PHASE
US, male producer – Joey Beltram (Singles: 2 weeks) pos/wks

21 Sep 91 **MENTASM** *R&S RSUK 2* 48 2

SECOND PROTOCOL
UK, male production duo (Singles: 2 weeks) pos/wks

23 Sep 00 **BASSLICK** *East West EW 216CD* 58 2

SECRET AFFAIR
UK, male vocal / instrumental group (Singles: 34 weeks, Albums: 15 weeks) pos/wks

1 Sep 79 **TIME FOR ACTION** *I-Spy SEE 1* 13 10
10 Nov 79 **LET YOUR HEART DANCE** *I-Spy SEE 3* 32 6
8 Mar 80 **MY WORLD** *I-Spy SEE 5* 16 9
23 Aug 80 **SOUND OF CONFUSION** *I-Spy SEE 8* 45 5
17 Oct 81 **DO YOU KNOW** *I-Spy SEE 10* 57 4
1 Dec 79 **GLORY BOYS** *I-Spy 1* 41 8
20 Sep 80 **BEHIND CLOSED DOORS** *I-Spy 2* 48 4
13 Mar 82 **BUSINESS AS USUAL** *I-Spy 3* 84 3

SECRET KNOWLEDGE
UK / US, male / female vocal / instrumental duo (Singles: 2 weeks) pos/wks

Date		Title / Label	pos	wks
27 Apr 96		**LOVE ME NOW** *Deconstruction 74321342432*	**66**	1
24 Aug 96		**SUGAR DADDY** *Deconstruction 74321400242*	**75**	1

SECRET LIFE
UK, male vocal / production group (Singles: 10 weeks) pos/wks

Date		Title / Label	pos	wks
12 Dec 92		**AS ALWAYS** *Cowboy 7RODEO 9*	**45**	4
7 Aug 93		**LOVE SO STRONG** *Cowboy RODEO 18CD*	**38**	2
7 May 94		**SHE HOLDS THE KEY** *Pulse 8 CDLOSE 58*	**63**	1
29 Oct 94		**I WANT YOU** *Pulse 8 CDLOSE 71*	**70**	1
28 Jan 95		**LOVE SO STRONG (re-mix)** *Pulse 8 CDLOSE 79*	**37**	2

SECRETARY OF ENTERTAINMENT – *See RAZE*

SECTION-X *France, male instrumental duo (Singles: 1 week)* pos/wks

Date		Title / Label	pos	wks
8 Mar 97		**ATLANTIS** *Perfecto PERF 136*	**42**	1

Neil SEDAKA (225 Top 500)
The man who put the 'Tra-La-La' into 1960s pop, b. 13 Mar 1939, New York, US. The ultra-commercial singer / songwriter / pianist enjoyed two separate chart runs as an artist and wrote many hits for numerous other acts (Singles: 190 weeks, Albums: 80 weeks) pos/wks

Date		Title / Label	pos	wks
24 Apr 59	●	**I GO APE** *RCA 1115*	**9**	13
13 Nov 59	●	**OH! CAROL** *RCA 1152*	**3**	17
14 Apr 60	●	**STAIRWAY TO HEAVEN** *RCA 1178*	**8**	15
1 Sep 60		**YOU MEAN EVERYTHING TO ME** *RCA 1198*	**45**	3
2 Feb 61	●	**CALENDAR GIRL** *RCA 1220*	**8**	14
18 May 61	●	**LITTLE DEVIL** *RCA 1236*	**9**	12
21 Dec 61	●	**HAPPY BIRTHDAY, SWEET SIXTEEN** *RCA 1266*	**3**	18
19 Apr 62		**KING OF CLOWNS** *RCA 1282*	**23**	11
19 Jul 62	●	**BREAKING UP IS HARD TO DO** *RCA 1298* ▲	**7**	16
22 Nov 62		**NEXT DOOR TO AN ANGEL** *RCA 1319*	**29**	4
30 May 63		**LET'S GO STEADY AGAIN (re)** *RCA 1343*	**42**	3
7 Oct 72		**OH CAROL / BREAKING UP IS HARD TO DO / LITTLE DEVIL (re-issue)** *RCA Maximillion 2259*	**19**	14
4 Nov 72		**BEAUTIFUL YOU** *RCA 2269*	**43**	3
24 Feb 73		**THAT'S WHEN THE MUSIC TAKES ME** *RCA 2310*	**18**	10
2 Jun 73		**STANDING ON THE INSIDE** *MGM 2006 267*	**26**	9
25 Aug 73		**OUR LAST SONG TOGETHER** *MGM 2006 307*	**31**	8
9 Feb 74		**A LITTLE LOVIN'** *Polydor 2058 434*	**34**	6
22 Jun 74		**LAUGHTER IN THE RAIN** *Polydor 2058 494* ▲	**15**	9
22 Mar 75		**THE QUEEN OF 1964** *Polydor 2058 546*	**35**	5
1 Sep 73		THE TRA-LA DAYS ARE OVER *MGM 2315 248*	**13**	10
22 Jun 74		LAUGHTER IN THE RAIN *Polydor 2383 265*	**17**	10
23 Nov 74		LIVE AT THE ROYAL FESTIVAL HALL *Polydor 2383 299*	**48**	1
1 Mar 75		OVERNIGHT SUCCESS *Polydor 2442 131*	**31**	6
10 Jul 76	●	LAUGHTER AND TEARS – THE BEST OF NEIL SEDAKA TODAY *Polydor 2383399*	**2**	25
2 Nov 91	●	TIMELESS – THE VERY BEST OF NEIL SEDAKA *Polydor 5114421*	**10**	16
4 Nov 95		CLASSICALLY SEDAKA *Vision VISCD 5*	**23**	9
19 Jun 99		THE VERY BEST OF NEIL SEDAKA *Universal Music TV 5646452*	**33**	3

SEDUCTION *US, female vocal group (Singles: 1 week)* pos/wks

Date		Title / Label	pos	wks
21 Apr 90		**HEARTBEAT** *Breakout USA 685*	**75**	1

SEEKERS (116 Top 500)
First Australian act to top the UK single or album chart: Judith Durham (v), Keith Potger (g), Bruce Woodley (g), Athol Guy (b). Their unique harmony vocals were displayed on many of their hits, which were penned and produced by Tom Springfield. Durham went solo in 1967, and Potger later went on to form The New Seekers. Best-selling single: 'The Carnival Is Over' 1,400,000 (Singles: 120 weeks, Albums: 275 weeks) pos/wks

Date		Title / Label	pos	wks
7 Jan 65	★	**I'LL NEVER FIND ANOTHER YOU** *Columbia DB 7431*	**1**	23
15 Apr 65	●	**A WORLD OF OUR OWN** *Columbia DB 7532*	**3**	18
28 Oct 65	★	**THE CARNIVAL IS OVER** *Columbia DB 7711* ◆	**1**	17
24 Mar 66		**SOMEDAY ONE DAY** *Columbia DB 7867*	**11**	11
8 Sep 66	●	**WALK WITH ME** *Columbia DB 8000*	**10**	12
24 Nov 66	●	**MORNINGTOWN RIDE** *Columbia DB 8060*	**2**	15
23 Feb 67	●	**GEORGY GIRL** *Columbia DB 8134*	**3**	11
20 Sep 67		**WHEN WILL THE GOOD APPLES FALL** *Columbia DB 8273*	**11**	12
13 Dec 67		**EMERALD CITY** *Columbia DB 8313*	**50**	1
3 Jul 65	●	A WORLD OF OUR OWN *Columbia 33SX 1722*	**5**	37
3 Jul 65		THE SEEKERS *Decca LK 4694*	**16**	1
19 Nov 66	●	COME THE DAY *Columbia SX 6093*	**2**	67
25 Nov 67		SEEKERS – SEEN IN GREEN *Columbia SCX 6193*	**15**	10
14 Sep 68	●	LIVE AT THE TALK OF THE TOWN *Columbia SCX 6278*	**2**	29
16 Nov 68	★	THE BEST OF THE SEEKERS *Columbia SCX 6268*	**1**	117
23 Apr 94	●	A CARNIVAL OF HITS *EMI CDEMTV 83* [1]	**7**	14

[1] Judith Durham and the Seekers

SEELENLUFT featuring Michael SMITH *Switzerland, male producer – Beat Soler and US, male rapper (Singles: 1 week)* pos/wks

Date		Title / Label	pos	wks
4 Oct 03		**MANILA** *Back Yard BACK 10CSC1*	**70**	1

Bob SEGER and the SILVER BULLET BAND *US, male vocal / instrumental group (Singles: 30 weeks, Albums: 52 weeks)* pos/wks

Date		Title / Label	pos	wks
30 Sep 78		**HOLLYWOOD NIGHTS** *Capitol CL 16004*	**42**	6
3 Feb 79		**WE'VE GOT TONITE** *Capitol CL 16028*	**41**	6
24 Oct 81		**HOLLYWOOD NIGHTS** *Capitol CL 223*	**49**	3
6 Feb 82		**WE'VE GOT TONITE** *Capitol CL 235*	**60**	4
9 Apr 83		**EVEN NOW** *Capitol CL 284*	**73**	2
28 Jan 95		**WE'VE GOT TONIGHT (re-issue)** *Capitol CDCL 734*	**22**	5
29 Apr 95		**NIGHT MOVES** *Capitol CDCL 741*	**45**	2
29 Jul 95		**HOLLYWOOD NIGHTS (re-issue)** *Capitol CDCL 749*	**52**	1
10 Feb 96		**LOCK AND LOAD** *Parlophone CDCL 765*	**57**	1
3 Jun 78		STRANGER IN TOWN *Capitol EAST 11698*	**31**	6
15 Mar 80		AGAINST THE WIND *Capitol EAST 12041* ▲	**26**	6
26 Sep 81		NINE TONIGHT *Capitol ESTSP 23*	**24**	10
8 Jan 83		THE DISTANCE *Capitol EST 12254*	**45**	10
26 Apr 86		LIKE A ROCK *Capitol EST 2011*	**35**	6
21 Sep 91		THE FIRE INSIDE *Capitol EST 2149*	**54**	2
18 Feb 95	●	GREATEST HITS *Capitol CDEST 2241*	**6**	12

Capitol CL 223 and CL 235 were live versions of earlier studio hits

Shea SEGER *US, female vocalist (Singles: 1 week)* pos/wks

Date		Title / Label	pos	wks
5 May 01		**CLUTCH** *RCA 74321828142*	**47**	1

SEIKO and Donnie WAHLBERG
Japan / US, female / male vocal duo (Singles: 5 weeks) pos/wks

Date		Title / Label	pos	wks
18 Aug 90		**THE RIGHT COMBINATION** *Epic 656203 7*	**44**	5

See also NEW KIDS ON THE BLOCK

SELECTER *UK, male / female vocal / instrumental group (Singles: 28 weeks, Albums: 17 weeks)* pos/wks

Date		Title / Label	pos	wks
13 Oct 79	●	**ON MY RADIO** *2 Tone CHSTT 4*	**8**	9
2 Feb 80		**THREE MINUTE HERO** *2 Tone CHSTT 8*	**16**	6
29 Mar 80		**MISSING WORDS** *2 Tone CHSTT 10*	**23**	8
23 Aug 80		**THE WHISPER** *Chrysalis CHSS 1*	**36**	5
23 Feb 80	●	TOO MUCH PRESSURE *2-Tone CDL TT 5002*	**5**	13
7 Mar 81		CELEBRATE THE BULLET *Chrysalis CHR 1306*	**41**	4

SELENA vs X MEN
UK, female vocalist and male production duo (Singles: 1 week) pos/wks

Date		Title / Label	pos	wks
14 Jul 01		**GIVE IT UP** *GO Beat BOBCD 40*	**61**	1

Peter SELLERS (493 Top 500)
Revered British actor / comedian and Goons mainstay, b. 8 Sep 1952, London, d. 24 Jul 1980. He helped to change the face of British comedy, became a world star in the 'Pink Panther' films and has a rock music connection in that his Surrey home was also owned by Ringo Starr and Stephen Stills (Singles: 39 weeks, Albums: 102 weeks) pos/wks

Date		Title / Label	pos	wks
2 Aug 57		**ANY OLD IRON (re)** *Parlophone R 4337* [1]	**17**	11
10 Nov 60	●	**GOODNESS GRACIOUS ME** *Parlophone R 4702* [2]	**4**	14
12 Jan 61		**BANGERS AND MASH** *Parlophone R 4724* [2]	**22**	5
23 Dec 65		**A HARD DAY'S NIGHT** *Parlophone R 5393*	**14**	7

27 Nov 93 **A HARD DAY'S NIGHT (re-issue)** *EMI CDEMS 293* 52 2
14 Feb 59 ● **THE BEST OF SELLERS** *Parlophone PMD 1069* 3 47
12 Dec 59 ● **SONGS FOR SWINGING SELLERS** *Parlophone PMC 1111* 3 37
3 Dec 60 ● **PETER AND SOPHIA** *Parlophone PMC 1131* [1] 5 18

[1] Peter Sellers presents Mate's Skiffle Group featuring Fred Spoons E.P.N.S.
[2] Peter Sellers and Sophia Loren [1] Peter Sellers and Sophia Loren

See also Harry SECOMBE Peter SELLERS and Spike MILLIGAN; GOONS

Michael SEMBELLO *US, male vocalist (Singles: 6 weeks)* pos/wks

20 Aug 83 **MANIAC** *Casablanca CAN 1017* ▲ 43 6

SEMISONIC *US, male vocal / instrumental group (Singles: 20 weeks, Albums: 41 weeks)* pos/wks

10 Jul 99 **SECRET SMILE** *MCA MCSTD 40210* 13 11
6 Nov 99 **CLOSING TIME** *MCA MCSTD 40221* 25 5
1 Apr 00 **SINGING IN MY SLEEP** *MCA MCSTD 40227* 39 2
3 Mar 01 **CHEMISTRY** *MCA MCSTD 40248* 35 2
24 Jul 99 **FEELING STRANGELY FINE** *MCA MCD 11733* 16 37
17 Mar 01 **ALL ABOUT CHEMISTRY** *MCA 1125012* 13 4

SEMPRINI *UK, male pianist – Fernando Riccardo Alberto Semprini d. 19 Jan 1990, and orchestra (Singles: 8 weeks)* pos/wks

16 Mar 61 **MAIN THEME FROM 'EXODUS'** *HMV POP 842* 25 8

SENSATIONAL ALEX HARVEY BAND *UK, male vocal / instrumental group, leader d. 4 Feb 1982 (Singles: 25 weeks, Albums: 42 weeks)* pos/wks

26 Jul 75 ● **DELILAH** *Vertigo ALEX 001* 7 7
22 Nov 75 **GAMBLIN' BAR ROOM BLUES** *Vertigo ALEX 002* 38 8
19 Jun 76 **THE BOSTON TEA PARTY** *Mountain TOP 12* 13 10
26 Oct 74 **THE IMPOSSIBLE DREAM** *Vertigo 6360 112* 16 4
10 May 75 ● **TOMORROW BELONGS TO ME** *Vertigo 9102 003* 9 10
23 Aug 75 **NEXT** *Vertigo 6360 103* 37 5
27 Sep 75 **SENSATIONAL ALEX HARVEY BAND LIVE** *Vertigo 6360 122* 14 7
10 Apr 76 **PENTHOUSE TAPES** *Vertigo 9102 007* 14 7
31 Jul 76 **SAHB STORIES** *Mountain TOPS 112* 11 9

SENSELESS THINGS *UK, male vocal / instrumental group (Singles: 19 weeks, Albums: 2 weeks)* pos/wks

22 Jun 91 **EVERYBODY'S GONE** *Epic 6569807* 73 1
28 Sep 91 **GOT IT AT THE DELMAR** *Epic 6574497* 50 3
11 Jan 92 **EASY TO SMILE** *Epic 6576957* 18 4
11 Apr 92 **HOLD IT DOWN** *Epic 6579267* 19 4
5 Dec 92 **HOMOPHOBIC ASSHOLE** *Epic 6588337* 52 2
13 Feb 93 **PRIMARY INSTINCT** *Epic 6589402* 41 2
12 Jun 93 **TOO MUCH KISSING** *Epic 6592502* 69 1
5 Nov 94 **CHRISTINE KEELER** *Epic 6609572* 56 1
28 Jan 95 **SOMETHING TO MISS** *Epic 6611162* 57 1
26 Oct 91 **THE FIRST OF TOO MANY** *Epic 4691571* 66 1
13 Mar 93 **EMPIRE OF THE SENSELESS** *Epic 4735252* 37 1

SENSER *UK, male / female vocal / instrumental group (Singles: 5 weeks, Albums: 6 weeks)* pos/wks

25 Sep 93 **THE KEY** *Ultimate TOPP 019CD* 47 1
19 Mar 94 **SWITCH** *Ultimate TOPP 022CD* 39 2
23 Jul 94 **AGE OF PANIC** *Ultimate TOPP 027CD* 52 1
17 Aug 96 **CHARMING DEMONS** *Ultimate TOPP 045CD* 42 1
7 May 94 ● **STACKED UP** *Ultimate TOPPCD 008* 4 5
2 May 98 **ASYLUM** *Ultimate TOPPCD 064* 73 1

Nick SENTIENCE – *See BK*

SEPULTURA *Brazil, male vocal / instrumental group (Singles: 12 weeks, Albums: 12 weeks)* pos/wks

2 Oct 93 **TERRITORY** *Roadrunner RR 23823* 66 2
26 Feb 94 **REFUSE-RESIST** *Roadrunner RR 23773* 51 2
4 Jun 94 **SLAVE NEW WORLD** *Roadrunner RR 23745* 46 2
24 Feb 96 **ROOTS BLOODY ROOTS** *Roadrunner RR 23205* 19 2
17 Aug 96 **RATAMAHATTA** *Roadrunner RR 23145* 23 2
14 Dec 96 **ATTITUDE** *Roadrunner RR 22995* 46 2
6 Apr 91 **ARISE** *Roadracer RO 93281* 40 2
23 Oct 93 **CHAOS A.D.** *Roadrunner RR 90002* 11 4
9 Mar 96 ● **ROOTS** *Roadrunner RR 89002* 4 5
17 Oct 98 **AGAINST** *Roadrunner RR 87002* 40 1

SERAFIN *UK, male vocal / instrumental group (Singles: 2 weeks)* pos/wks

17 May 03 **THINGS FALL APART** *Taste Media TMCDS 5003* 49 1
16 Aug 03 **DAY BY DAY** *Taste Media TMCDS 5006* 49 1

SERIAL DIVA *UK, male / female production group (Singles: 3 weeks)* pos/wks

18 Jan 97 **KEEP HOPE ALIVE** *Sound Of Ministry SOMCD 26* 57 1
15 May 99 **PEARL RIVER** *Low Sense SENSECD 24* [1] 32 2

[1] Three 'N One presents Johnny Shaker featuring Serial Diva

SERIOUS DANGER *UK, male producer – Richard Phillips (Singles: 4 weeks)* pos/wks

20 Dec 97 **DEEPER** *Fresh FRSHD 68* 40 3
2 May 98 **HIGH NOON** *Fresh FRSHD 69* 54 1

SERIOUS INTENTION *US, male vocal / instrumental group (Singles: 6 weeks)* pos/wks

16 Nov 85 **YOU DON'T KNOW (OH-OH-OH)** *Important TAN 8* 75 1
5 Apr 86 **SERIOUS** *Pow Wow LON 93* 51 5

SERIOUS ROPE *UK, male / female vocal / production group (Singles: 3 weeks)* pos/wks

22 May 93 **HAPPINESS** *Rumour RUMACD 64* [1] 54 2
1 Oct 94 **HAPPINESS – YOU MAKE ME HAPPY (re-mix)** *Mercury MERCD 407* 70 1

[1] Serious Rope presents Sharon Dee Clarke

Erick SERMON *US, male rapper (Singles: 8 weeks)* pos/wks

6 Oct 01 **MUSIC** *Polydor 4976222* [1] 36 2
11 Jan 03 **REACT** *J 74321988492* [2] 14 5
19 Apr 03 **LOVE IZ** *J 82876510971* 72 1

[1] Erick Sermon featuring Marvin Gaye [2] Erick Sermon featuring Redman

Eric SERRA *France, male conductor (Albums: 2 weeks)* pos/wks

28 Jun 97 **THE FIFTH ELEMENT (FILM SOUNDTRACK)** *Virgin CDVIRX 63* 58 2

SERTAB *Turkey, female vocalist – Sertab Erener (Singles: 1 week)* pos/wks

21 Jun 03 **EVERYWAY THAT I CAN** *Columbia 6739621* 72 1

SET THE TONE *UK, male vocal / instrumental group (Singles: 4 weeks)* pos/wks

22 Jan 83 **DANCE SUCKER** *Island WIP 6836* 62 2
26 Mar 83 **RAP YOUR LOVE** *Island IS 110* 67 2

SETTLERS *UK, male / female vocal / instrumental group (Singles: 5 weeks)* pos/wks

16 Oct 71 **THE LIGHTNING TREE** *York SYK 505* 36 5

Brian SETZER ORCHESTRA *US, male vocal / instrumental group (Singles: 3 weeks)* pos/wks

3 Apr 99 **JUMP JIVE AN' WAIL** *Interscope IND 95601* 34 3

See also STRAY CATS

Taja SEVELLE *US, female vocalist (Singles: 13 weeks, Albums: 4 weeks)* pos/wks

20 Feb 88 ● **LOVE IS CONTAGIOUS** *Paisley Park W 8257* 7 9
14 May 88 **WOULDN'T YOU LOVE TO LOVE ME?** *Paisley Park W 8127* 59 4
26 Mar 88 **TAJA SEVELLE** *Paisley Park WX 165* 48 4

Review of the Year

SEPTEMBER 2003

Staff at Tesco, the first supermarket to import the giant avocado, have nicknamed the watermelon-sized fruit "J-Lo" after **Jennifer Lopez's** best known anatomical feature. In what is turning into a very strange month, the first Junior Eurovision Song Contest takes place. Fifty-six-year-old **Elton John** tops the chart with a remix of his Philly-style No.42 hit from 1979, 'Are You Ready for Love'. **The Rolling Stones** world tour trundles into Wembley Arena comprising, at times, a reported 53 trucks, 10 buses and just the one tour jet. Mick and the boys return to the singles Top 20 after an eight-year absence with a remix of 'Sympathy for the Devil', which also tops the dance charts. Jamaican dancehall star **Sean Paul** has two singles simultaneously in the Top 3 (the first act to do so since **Madonna** in 1985), and **Beyoncé** has two entries in the US Top 4. After 35 years of chart hits and 60 albums, German band leader **James Last** scores his first No.1 – albeit on the classical chart. Suffolk sensations **The Darkness** top the chart with their acclaimed and over-the-top 'Permission to Land' album. The music industry gets tough as 261 people including a 12-year-old girl are reportedly due to be sued for downloading songs on the net by the Recording Industry Association of America. In an attempt to boost sales, the world's No.1 record company, Universal, reduces US album prices by a third and EMI launches the two-track CD single, which retails at £1.99. One of the first releases, 'Superstar' by **Jamelia**, surprises chart-watchers by going up the chart on two separate weeks. **Black Eyed Peas'** single 'Where Is the Love?' becomes the first single this century to spend more than four weeks at the top. Murder suspect **Phil Spector** returns to the Top 10 as producer of Starsailor's 'Silence Is Easy' single and album. **James Taylor's** 'You've Got a Friend' album peaks at No. 4, equalling his highest placing. **Enrique Iglesias** signs a sponsorship deal with Pepsi which could earn him up to $80m. **Neil Young** has five albums in the internet Top 20 bestsellers and nine tracks in the US digital download Top 20. **Cher's** farewell tour reaches the end of the road having grossed a staggering $118m since June 2002. London rapper **Dizzee Rascal** wins the Mercury Music Prize for his album 'Boy in Da Corner', and a couple of weeks later Ireland's **Damien Rice's** 'O' album wins the Shortlist Music Prize (the US version of the Mercury Music prize). **David Bowie** enjoys his first Top 3 album for 10 years with 'Reality', and 50,000 of his fans in 86 cinemas in 26 countries watch his gig at Hammersmith, the first live 5.1 broadcast beamed by satellite in widescreen. **George Martin's** son **Giles** produces 16-year-old New Zealand operatic vocalist **Hayley Westenra**, whose album goes Top 10. **Rachel Stevens** scores her first solo hit since the demise of **S Club** and **Christina Aguilera's** 'Stripped' passes the million mark in the UK. **Radiohead's** 'Go to Sleep' makes the Top 10 US bestsellers. British groups The Sex Pistols, Traffic and Black Sabbath are among the acts nominated for the Rock and Roll Hall of Fame. He has had one of his most successful years on record but sadly the 'Man in Black', **Johnny Cash**, dies. Other obituaries: 'Pub with No Beer' singer **Slim Dusty**, who released 91 albums in his native Australia; US rocker **Warren Zevon**, whose last album, 'The Wind', tops the internet chart and gives him his first UK chart entry; and 'Purple People Eater' hitmaker **Sheb Wooley**, who at his request was buried at High Noon, the title of the award-winning western movie he appeared in.

Mick Jagger is supported on tour by 350 tons of stage sets transported by 53 trucks. Stones PR Bernard Doherty nixes the reported rumour that Keith Richards' culinary demands included 392 shepherd's pies

Dizzee Rascal wins the much-coveted Mercury Music Prize

702 *US, female vocal group (Singles: 10 weeks)* pos/wks

14 Dec 96 **STEELO** *Motown 8606072* 41 2
29 Nov 97 **NO DOUBT** *Motown 8607052* 59 1
7 Aug 99 **WHERE MY GIRLS AT?** *Motown TMGCD 1500* 22 4
27 Nov 99 **YOU DON'T KNOW** *Motown TMGCD 1502* 36 3

740 BOYZ *US, male vocal / instrumental duo (Singles: 3 week)* pos/wks

4 Nov 95 **SHIMMY SHAKE** *MCA MCSTD 40002* 54 1
22 Mar 03 **SHAKE YA SHIMMY** *All Around the World CDGLOBE 213* 2 ..28 2

2 Porn Kings vs Flip and Fill featuring 740 Boyz

SEVEN GRAND HOUSING AUTHORITY
UK, male producer – Terence Parker (Singles: 1 week) pos/wks

23 Oct 93 **THE QUESTION** *Olympic ELYCD 010* 70 1

7669 *US, female rap group (Singles: 1 week)* pos/wks

18 Jun 94 **JOY** *Motown TMGCD 1429* 60 1

7TH HEAVEN *UK, male vocal group (Singles: 5 weeks)* pos/wks

14 Sep 85 **HOT FUN** *Mercury MER 199* 47 5

SÉVERINE *France, female vocalist (Singles: 11 weeks)* pos/wks

24 Apr 71 ● **UN BANC, UN ARBRE, UNE RUE** *Philips 6009 135* 9 11

David SEVILLE *US, male vocalist – Ross Bagdasarian, d. 16 Jan 1972 (Singles: 6 weeks)* pos/wks

23 May 58 **WITCH DOCTOR** *London HLU 8619* ▲ 11 6

See also ALFI and HARRY; CHIPMUNKS

Janette SEWELL – *See DOUBLE TROUBLE*

SEX CLUB featuring BROWN SUGAR
US, male / female vocal / instrumental duo (Singles: 1 week) pos/wks

28 Jan 95 **BIG DICK MAN** *Club Tools CLU 60775* 67 1

SEX-O-LETTES – *See DISCO TEX & the SEX-O-LETTES*

SEX-O-SONIQUE *UK, male production / instrumental duo – Mike Gray and Jon Pearn (Singles: 3 weeks)* pos/wks

6 Dec 97 **I THOUGHT IT WAS YOU** *ffrr FCD 321* 32 3

See also FULL INTENTION; HUSTLERS CONVENTION featuring Dave LAUDAT and Ondrea DUVERNEY; RONALDO'S REVENGE

SEX PISTOLS (325 Top 500) *Provocative and influential quartet which popularised punk. Formed 1975 in London UK, split 1978: Johnny Rotten (v), Steve Jones (g), Paul Cook (d) and Glen Matlock (b) – replaced 1977 by Sid Vicious (d. 1979). Notorious group reunited for brief and profitable tours in 1996 and 2003 (Singles: 91 weeks, Albums: 112 weeks)* pos/wks

18 Dec 76 **ANARCHY IN THE UK** *EMI 2566* 38 4
4 Jun 77 ● **GOD SAVE THE QUEEN** *Virgin VS 181* 2 9
9 Jul 77 ● **PRETTY VACANT** *Virgin VS 184* 6 8
22 Oct 77 ● **HOLIDAYS IN THE SUN** *Virgin VS 191* 8 6
8 Jul 78 ● **NO ONE IS INNOCENT (A PUNK PRAYER BY RONALD BIGGS) / MY WAY** *Virgin VS 220* 1 ....7 10
3 Mar 79 ● **SOMETHING ELSE / FRIGGIN' IN THE RIGGIN'** *Virgin VS 240* 2 ....3 12
7 Apr 79 ● **SILLY THING** *Virgin VS 256* 6 8
30 Jun 79 ● **C'MON EVERYBODY** *Virgin VS 272* 3 ....3 9
13 Oct 79 **THE GREAT ROCK 'N' ROLL SWINDLE** *Virgin VS 290* 21 6
14 Jun 80 **(I'M NOT YOUR) STEPPING STONE** *Virgin VS 339* 21 8
3 Oct 92 **ANARCHY IN THE UK (re-issue)** *Virgin VS 1431* 33 3
5 Dec 92 **PRETTY VACANT (re-issue)** *Virgin VS 1448* 56 2
27 Jul 96 **PRETTY VACANT (LIVE)** *Virgin America VUSCD 113* 18 3
8 Jun 02 **GOD SAVE THE QUEEN (re-issue)** *Virgin VSCDT 1832* 15 3
12 Nov 77 ★ **NEVER MIND THE BOLLOCKS HERE'S THE SEX PISTOLS** *Virgin V 2086* ■ 1 54
10 Mar 79 ● **THE GREAT ROCK 'N' ROLL SWINDLE (FILM SOUNDTRACK)** *Virgin VD 2410* 7 33
11 Aug 79 ● **SOME PRODUCT – CARRI ON SEX PISTOLS** *Virgin VR 2* 6 10
16 Feb 80 **FLOGGING A DEAD HORSE** *Virgin V 2142* 23 6
17 Oct 92 ● **KISS THIS** *Virgin CDV 2702* 10 4
10 Aug 96 **FILTHY LUCRE LIVE** *Virgin CDVUS 116* 26 2
15 Jun 02 **JUBILEE** *Virgin CDV 2961* 29 3

1 Uncredited vocal by Ronald Biggs 2 Sex Pistols: vocals, Sid Vicious / Sex Pistols: vocals, Steve Jones 3 Sex Pistols, vocals: Sid Vicious

The listed flip side of 'Silly Thing' was 'Who Killed Bambi' by Ten Pole Tudor. The listed flip side of 'The Great Rock 'n' Roll Swindle' was 'Rock Around the Clock', also by Ten Pole Tudor

See also Sid VICIOUS; John LYDON, PUBLIC IMAGE LIMITED

Denny SEYTON and the SABRES
UK, male vocal / instrumental group (Singles: 1 week) pos/wks

17 Sep 64 **THE WAY YOU LOOK TONIGHT** *Mercury MF 824* 48 1

SHABOOM
UK, male instrumental / production group (Singles: 1 week) pos/wks

31 Jul 99 **SWEET SENSATION** *WEA WEA 218CD1* 64 1

SHACK *UK, male vocal / instrumental group (Singles: 4 weeks, Albums: 3 weeks)* pos/wks

26 Jun 99 **COMEDY** *London LONCD 427* 44 1
14 Aug 99 **NATALIE'S PARTY** *London LONCD 436* 63 1
11 Mar 00 **OSCAR** *London LONCD 445* 67 1
4 Oct 03 **BYRDS TURN TO STONE** *North Country NCCDA 002* 63 1
3 Jul 99 **H.M.S. FABLE** *London 5561132* 25 2
23 Aug 03 **HERE'S TOM WITH THE WEATHER** *North County NCCD 002* 55 1

SHADES
US, female vocal group (Singles: 3 weeks) pos/wks

12 Apr 97 **MR BIG STUFF** *Motown 5736572* 1 ....31 2
20 Sep 97 **SERENADE** *Motown 8606892* 75 1

1 Queen Latifah, Shades and Free

SHADES OF LOVE
US, male instrumental / production duo (Singles: 1 week) pos/wks

22 Apr 95 **KEEP IN TOUCH (BODY TO BODY)** *Vicious Muzik MUZCD 102* ..64 1

SHADES OF RHYTHM *UK, male instrumental / production group (Singles: 25 weeks, Albums: 3 weeks)* pos/wks

2 Feb 91 **HOMICIDE / EXORCIST** *ZTT ZANG 13* 53 3
13 Apr 91 **SWEET SENSATION** *ZTT ZANG 18* 54 4
20 Jul 91 **THE SOUND OF EDEN** *ZTT ZANG 22* 35 5
30 Nov 91 **EXTACY** *ZTT ZANG 24* 16 7
20 Feb 93 **SWEET REVIVAL (KEEP IT COMIN')** *ZTT ZANG 40CD* 61 1
11 Sep 93 **SOUND OF EDEN (re-issue)** *ZTT ZANG 44CD* 37 3
5 Nov 94 **THE WANDERING DRAGON** *Public Demand PPDCD 5* 55 1
21 Jun 97 **PSYCHO BASE** *Coalition CRUM 002CD* 57 1
17 Aug 91 **SHADES** *ZTT ZTT 8* 51 3

SHADOWS (7 Top 500) *Headliners for five decades and Britain's most successful instrumental group: Hank Marvin (born Brian Rankin, 28 Oct 1941, Newcastle-upon-Tyne) (g), Bruce Welch (b. Bruce Cripps, 2 Nov 1941, Bognor Regis) (g), Terence 'Jet' Harris (b. Terence Hawkins, 6 Jul 1939, London) (b), Tony Meehan (b. Daniel Meehan, 2 Mar 1943, London) (d). Bespectacled Marvin and Welch, who started together in The Railroaders skiffle group, first recorded with The Five Chesternuts (1958) before joining Cliff Richard's backing band, The Drifters. The group (with the above line-up) released its first single, 'Feelin' Fine', in early 1959. After another couple of unsuccessful releases and a name change, they started a staggering run of successive hit singles and albums, and clocked up dozens of hits with Cliff Richard. They were Britain's most influential and imitated act before The Beatles. 'The 'Shadows walk' (which they say they borrowed from R&B band The Treniers) was aped by hundreds of UK groups. They won awards* *during the 1960s, and were named the world's third most successful recording act of 1963 (behind Cliff and Elvis) by Billboard. In addition, they were the first group to top the UK album charts (a feat they managed before Cliff) and were the first to have a 40-year span of hit albums (Singles: 771 weeks, Albums: 691 weeks)*

Date		Title	pos	wks
12 Sep 58	●	**MOVE IT!** *Columbia DB 4178* [1]	2	17
21 Nov 58	●	**HIGH CLASS BABY** *Columbia DB 4203* [1]	7	10
30 Jan 59		**LIVIN' LOVIN' DOLL** *Columbia DB 4249* [1]	20	6
8 May 59	●	**MEAN STREAK** *Columbia DB 4290 A* [1]	10	9
15 May 59		**NEVER MIND** *Columbia DB 4290 B* [1]	21	2
10 Jul 59	★	**LIVING DOLL (2re)** *Columbia DB 4306* [1]	1	23
9 Oct 59	★	**TRAVELLIN' LIGHT** *Columbia DB 4351 B* [2]	1	17
9 Oct 59		**DYNAMITE (re)** *Columbia DB 4351 A* [2]	16	4
15 Jan 60		**EXPRESSO BONGO (EP)** *Columbia SEG 7971* [2]	14	7
22 Jan 60	●	**A VOICE IN THE WILDERNESS (re)** *Columbia DB 4398* [2]	2	16
24 Mar 60	●	**FALL IN LOVE WITH YOU** *Columbia DB 4431* [2]	2	15
30 Jun 60	★	**PLEASE DON'T TEASE** *Columbia 4479* [2]	1	18
21 Jul 60	★	**APACHE** *Columbia DB 4484*	1	21
22 Sep 60	●	**NINE TIMES OUT OF TEN** *Columbia DB 4506* [2]	3	12
10 Nov 60	●	**MAN OF MYSTERY / THE STRANGER** *Columbia DB 4530*	5	15
1 Dec 60	★	**I LOVE YOU** *Columbia DB 4547* [2]	1	16
9 Feb 61	●	**F.B.I.** *Columbia DB 4580*	6	19
2 Mar 61	●	**THEME FOR A DREAM** *Columbia DB 4593* [2]	3	14
30 Mar 61	●	**GEE WHIZ IT'S YOU** *Columbia DC 756* [2]	4	14
11 May 61	●	**THE FRIGHTENED CITY** *Columbia DB 4637*	3	20
22 Jun 61	●	**A GIRL LIKE YOU** *Columbia DB 4667* [2]	3	14
7 Sep 61	★	**KON-TIKI (re)** *Columbia DB 4698*	1	12
16 Nov 61	●	**THE SAVAGE** *Columbia DB 4726*	10	8
11 Jan 62	★	**THE YOUNG ONES** *Columbia DB 4761* [2] ◆ ■	1	21
1 Mar 62	★	**WONDERFUL LAND** *Columbia DB 4790*	1	19
10 May 62	●	**I'M LOOKING OUT THE WINDOW / DO YOU WANT TO DANCE** *Columbia DB 4828* [3]	2	17
2 Aug 62	●	**GUITAR TANGO** *Columbia DB 4870*	4	15
6 Sep 62	●	**IT'LL BE ME** *Columbia DB 4886* [2]	2	12
6 Dec 62	★	**THE NEXT TIME / BACHELOR BOY** *Columbia DB 4950* [2]	1	18
13 Dec 62	★	**DANCE ON!** *Columbia DB 4948*	1	15
21 Feb 63	★	**SUMMER HOLIDAY** *Columbia DB 4977* [2]	1	18
7 Mar 63	★	**FOOT TAPPER** *Columbia DB 4984*	1	16
9 May 63	●	**LUCKY LIPS** *Columbia DB 7034* [2]	4	15
6 Jun 63	●	**ATLANTIS** *Columbia DB 7047*	2	17
19 Sep 63	●	**SHINDIG** *Columbia DB 7106*	6	12
7 Nov 63	●	**DON'T TALK TO HIM (re)** *Columbia DB 7150* [2]	2	14
5 Dec 63		**GERONIMO** *Columbia DB 7163*	11	12
6 Feb 64	●	**I'M THE LONELY ONE** *Columbia DB 7203* [2]	8	10
5 Mar 64		**THEME FOR YOUNG LOVERS** *Columbia DB 7231*	12	10
7 May 64	●	**THE RISE AND FALL OF FLINGEL BUNT** *Columbia DB 7261*	5	14
2 Jul 64	●	**ON THE BEACH** *Columbia DB 7305* [2]	7	13
3 Sep 64		**RHYTHM AND GREENS** *Columbia DB 7342*	22	7
3 Dec 64		**GENIE WITH THE LIGHT BROWN LAMP** *Columbia DB 7416*	17	10
10 Dec 64	●	**I COULD EASILY FALL** *Columbia DB 7420* [2]	6	11
11 Feb 65		**MARY ANNE** *Columbia DB 7476*	17	10
10 Jun 65		**STINGRAY** *Columbia DB 7588*	19	7
5 Aug 65	●	**DON'T MAKE MY BABY BLUE** *Columbia DB 7650*	10	10
19 Aug 65		**THE TIME IN BETWEEN** *Columbia DB 7660* [2]	22	8
25 Nov 65		**THE WAR LORD** *Columbia DB 7769*	18	9
17 Mar 66		**I MET A GIRL** *Columbia DB 7853*	22	5
24 Mar 66		**BLUE TURNS TO GREY** *Columbia DB 7866* [2]	15	9
7 Jul 66		**A PLACE IN THE SUN** *Columbia DB 7952*	24	6
13 Oct 66	●	**TIME DRAGS BY** *Columbia DB 8017* [2]	10	12
3 Nov 66		**THE DREAMS I DREAM** *Columbia DB 8034*	42	6
15 Dec 66	●	**IN THE COUNTRY** *Columbia DB 8094* [2]	6	10
13 Apr 67		**MAROC 7** *Columbia DB 8170*	24	8
27 Nov 68		**DON'T FORGET TO CATCH ME** *Columbia DB 8503* [2]	21	10
8 Mar 75		**LET ME BE THE ONE** *EMI 2269*	12	9
16 Dec 78	●	**DON'T CRY FOR ME ARGENTINA** *EMI 2890*	5	14
28 Apr 79	●	**THEME FROM 'THE DEER HUNTER' (CAVATINA)** *EMI 2939*	9	14
26 Jan 80		**RIDERS IN THE SKY** *EMI 5027*	12	12
23 Aug 80		**EQUINOXE (PART V)** *Polydor POSP 148*	50	3
2 May 81		**THE THIRD MAN** *Polydor POSP 255*	44	4
15 Oct 60	●	**ME AND MY SHADOWS** *Columbia 33SX 1261* [1]	2	33
16 Sep 61	★	**THE SHADOWS** *Columbia 33SX 1374*	1	57
23 Dec 61	★	**THE YOUNG ONES (FILM SOUNDTRACK)** *Columbia 33SX 1384* [2]	1	42
29 Sep 62	●	**32 MINUTES AND 17 SECONDS** *Columbia 33SX 1431* [1]	3	21
13 Oct 62	★	**OUT OF THE SHADOWS** *Columbia 33SX 1458*	1	38
26 Jan 63	★	**SUMMER HOLIDAY (FILM SOUNDTRACK)** *Columbia 33SX 1472* [1]	1	36
22 Jun 63	●	**GREATEST HITS** *Columbia 33SX 1522*	2	49
28 Sep 63	●	**WHEN IN SPAIN** *Columbia 33SX 1541* [1]	8	10
9 May 64	●	**DANCE WITH THE SHADOWS** *Columbia 33SX 1619*	2	27
11 Jul 64	●	**WONDERFUL LIFE (FILM SOUNDTRACK)** *Columbia 33SX 1628* [1]	2	23
9 Jan 65		**HITS FROM ALADDIN AND HIS WONDERFUL LAMP (PANTOMIME)** *Columbia 33SX 1676* [1]	13	5
17 Jul 65	●	**THE SOUND OF THE SHADOWS** *Columbia 33SX 1736*	4	17
21 May 66	●	**SHADOW MUSIC** *Columbia SX 6041*	5	17
17 Dec 66	●	**FINDERS KEEPERS (FILM SOUNDTRACK)** *Columbia SX 6079* [1]	6	18
7 Jan 67		**CINDERELLA (PANTOMIME)** *Columbia 33SCX 6103* [1]	30	6
15 Jul 67	●	**JIGSAW** *Columbia SCX 6148*	8	16
16 Nov 68		**ESTABLISHED 1958** *Columbia SCX 6282* [1]	30	4
24 Oct 70		**SHADES OF ROCK** *Columbia SCX 6420*	30	4
13 Apr 74		**ROCKIN' WITH CURLY LEADS** *EMI EMA 762*	45	1
11 May 74		**GREATEST HITS (re-issue)** *Columbia SCX 1522*	48	6
29 Mar 75		**SPECS APPEAL** *EMI EMC 3066*	30	5
12 Feb 77	★	**20 GOLDEN GREATS** *EMI EMTV 3*	1	43
17 Feb 79	●	**THANK YOU VERY MUCH – REUNION CONCERT AT THE LONDON PALLADIUM** *EMI EMTV 15* [1]	5	12
15 Sep 79	★	**STRING OF HITS** *EMI EMC 3310*	1	43
26 Jul 80		**ANOTHER STRING OF HITS** *EMI EMC 3339*	16	8
13 Sep 80		**CHANGE OF ADDRESS** *Polydor 2442 179*	17	6
19 Sep 81		**HITS RIGHT UP YOUR STREET** *Polydor POLD 5046*	15	16
25 Sep 82		**LIFE IN THE JUNGLE / LIVE AT ABBEY ROAD** *Polydor SHADS 1*	24	6
22 Oct 83		**XXV** *Polydor POLD 5120*	34	6
14 Jul 84		**20 ORIGINAL GREATS** *EMI CRS 1* [1]	43	6
17 Nov 84		**GUARDIAN ANGEL** *Polydor POLD 5169*	98	1
24 May 86	●	**MOONLIGHT SHADOWS** *Polydor PROLP 8*	6	19
24 Oct 87		**SIMPLY SHADOWS** *Polydor SHAD 1*	11	17
20 May 89		**STEPPIN' TO THE SHADOWS** *Polydor SHAD 30*	11	9
16 Dec 89		**AT THEIR VERY BEST** *Polydor 8415201*	12	9
13 Oct 90	●	**REFLECTION** *Roll Over 8471201*	5	15
16 Nov 91		**THEMES AND DREAMS** *Polydor 5113741*	21	11
15 May 93		**SHADOWS IN THE NIGHT – 16 CLASSIC TRACKS** *PolyGram TV 8437982*	22	4
22 Oct 94		**THE BEST OF HANK MARVIN AND THE SHADOWS** *PolyGram TV 5238212* [3]	19	11
22 Nov 97		**PLAY ANDREW LLOYD WEBBER AND TIM RICE** *PolyGram TV 5394792* [3]	41	6
14 Nov 98		**VERY BEST OF HANK MARVIN AND THE SHADOWS – THE FIRST 40 YEARS** *PolyGram TV 5592112* [3]	56	5
12 Aug 00		**50 GOLDEN GREATS** *EMI 5275862*	35	3

[1] Cliff Richard and The Drifters [2] Cliff Richard and the Shadows [3] Cliff Richard / The Shadows [1] Cliff Richard and the Shadows [2] Cliff Richard – The Shadows with Grazina Frame [3] Hank Marvin and the Shadows

All the Shadows hits without Cliff Richard were instrumentals except for 'Mary Anne', 'Don't Make My Baby Blue', 'I Met a Girl', 'The Dreams I Dream' and 'Let Me Be the One'. Tracks on Expresso Bongo (EP): Love / A Voice in the Wilderness / The Shrine on the Second Floor / Bongo Blues. Last track featured Shadows only

See also Jet HARRIS and Tony MEEHAN; Hank MARVIN; Cliff RICHARD; MARVIN, WELCH and FARRAR

Only albums where The Shadows are credited on the front sleeve are included in associations with Cliff Richard are concerned, however they were involved in a number of albums without a front of sleeve credit including three more No.1s

SHAFT

UK, male producer – Mark Pritchard (Singles: 9 weeks)

Date		Title	pos	wks
21 Dec 91	●	**ROOBARB AND CUSTARD** *Ffrreedom TAB 100*	7	8
25 Jul 92		**MONKEY** *Ffrreedom TAB 114*	61	1

SHAFT

UK, male production duo – Elliot Ireland and Alex Rizzo (Singles: 19 weeks)

Date		Title	pos	wks
4 Sep 99	●	**(MUCHO MAMBO) SWAY** *Wonderboy WBOYD 015*	2	12
20 May 00		**MAMBO ITALIANO** *Wonderboy WBDD 017*	12	6
21 Jul 01		**KIKI RIRI BOOM** *Wonderboy WBOYD 026*	62	1

SHAG – *See Jonathan KING*

SHAGGY 319 Top 500

World's top selling Jamaican artist, born Orville Burrell, 22 Oct 1968. He has had more UK and US No.1s than any other West Indian-born act. The US-based artist sold 345,000 copies of 'It Wasn't Me' in the first week in the UK (then 1,180,700 in total), and his album 'Hotshot' sold more than 11 million globally (Singles: 143 weeks, Albums: 61 weeks)

Date		Title / Label	pos	wks
6 Feb 93	★	**OH CAROLINA** *Greensleeves GRECD 361*	1	19
10 Jul 93		**SOON BE DONE** *Greensleeves GRECD 380*	46	3
8 Jul 95	●	**IN THE SUMMERTIME** *Virgin VSCDT 1542* [1]	5	9
23 Sep 95	★	**BOOMBASTIC** *Virgin VSCDT 1536* ■	1	12
13 Jan 96		**WHY YOU TREAT ME SO BAD** *Virgin VSCDT 1566* [2]	11	5
23 Mar 96		**SOMETHING DIFFERENT / THE TRAIN IS COMING** *Virgin VSCDT 1581* [3]	21	5
22 Jun 96		**THAT GIRL** *Virgin America VUSCDX 106* [4]	15	7
19 Jul 97	●	**PIECE OF MY HEART** *Virgin VSCDT 1647* [5]	7	6
17 Feb 01		**IT WASN'T ME (IMPORT)** *MCA 1558032* [6]	31	3
10 Mar 01	★	**IT WASN'T ME** *MCA 1558022* [6] ◆ ■ ▲	1	20
9 Jun 01	★	**ANGEL** *MCA MCSTD 40257* [1] ■ ▲	1	16
29 Sep 01	●	**LUV ME LUV ME** *MCA MCSTD 40263*	5	10
1 Dec 01		**DANCE AND SHOUT / HOPE** *MCA MCSTD 40272*	19	7
23 Mar 02	●	**ME JULIE** *Island CID 793* [7]	2	14
9 Nov 02	●	**HEY SEXY LADY (re)** *MCA MCSTD 40304* [8]	10	7
24 Jul 93		**PURE PLEASURE** *Greensleeves GRELCD 184*	67	1
14 Oct 95		**BOOMBASTIC** *Virgin CDV 2782*	37	6
17 Feb 01	★	**HOT SHOT** *MCA 1122932* ▲	1	47
16 Feb 02		**MR LOVER LOVER – THE BEST OF SHAGGY – PART 1** *Virgin VTCD 429*	20	5
16 Nov 02		**LUCKY DAY** *MCA 1131192*	54	2

[1] Shaggy featuring Rayvon [2] Shaggy featuring Grand Puba [3] Shaggy featuring Wayne Wonder / Shaggy [4] Maxi Priest featuring Shaggy [5] Shaggy featuring Marsha [6] Shaggy featuring Ricardo "Rikrok" Ducent [7] Ali G and Shaggy [8] Shaggy featuring Brian and Tony Gold

SHAH

UK, female vocalist (Singles: 1 week)

Date		Title / Label	pos	wks
6 Jun 98		**SECRET LOVE** *Evocative EVOKE 5CDS*	69	1

SHAI

US, male vocal group (Singles: 6 weeks)

Date		Title / Label	pos	wks
19 Dec 92		**IF I EVER FALL IN LOVE** *MCA MCS 1727*	36	6

SHAKATAK 424 Top 500

London-based pop / jazz / funk ensemble which was big in Japan. Sound was typified by tinkling piano of Bill Sharpe and Jill Saward's soothing vocals. Sharpe later hit with Gary Numan, while Nigel Wright (k) produced hits for Madonna, Take That, Robson and Jerome, Barbra Streisand, Cliff Richard and Boyzone (Singles: 85 weeks, Albums: 73 weeks)

Date		Title / Label	pos	wks
8 Nov 80		**FEELS LIKE THE RIGHT TIME** *Polydor POSP 188*	41	5
7 Mar 81		**LIVING IN THE UK** *Polydor POSP 230*	52	4
25 Jul 81		**BRAZILIAN DAWN** *Polydor POSP 282*	48	3
21 Nov 81		**EASIER SAID THAN DONE** *Polydor POSP 375*	12	17
3 Apr 82	●	**NIGHT BIRDS** *Polydor POSP 407*	9	8
19 Jun 82		**STREETWALKIN'** *Polydor POSP 452*	38	6
4 Sep 82		**INVITATIONS** *Polydor POSP 502*	24	7
6 Nov 82		**STRANGER** *Polydor POSP 530*	43	3
4 Jun 83		**DARK IS THE NIGHT** *Polydor POSP 595*	15	8
27 Aug 83		**IF YOU COULD SEE ME NOW** *Polydor POSP 635*	49	4
7 Jul 84	●	**DOWN ON THE STREET** *Polydor POSP 688*	9	11
15 Sep 84		**DON'T BLAME IT ON LOVE** *Polydor POSP 699*	55	3
16 Nov 85		**DAY BY DAY** *Polydor POSP 770* [1]	53	3
24 Oct 87		**MR MANIC AND SISTER COOL** *Polydor MANIC 1*	56	3
30 Jan 82		**DRIVIN' HARD** *Polydor POLS 1030*	35	17
15 May 82	●	**NIGHT BIRDS** *Polydor POLS 1059*	4	28
27 Nov 82		**INVITATIONS** *Polydor POLD 5068*	30	11
22 Oct 83		**OUT OF THIS WORLD** *Polydor POLD 5115*	30	4
25 Aug 84		**DOWN ON THE STREET** *Polydor POLD 5148*	17	9
23 Feb 85		**LIVE!** *Polydor POLH 21*	82	3
22 Oct 88		**THE COOLEST CUTS** *K-Tel NE 1422*	73	1

[1] Shakatak featuring Al Jarreau

SHAKE B4 USE featuring Robert PALMER

UK, male production trio and male vocalist (Singles: 1 week)

Date		Title / Label	pos	wks
18 Jan 03		**ADDICTED TO LOVE** *Serious SER 060CD*	42	1

SHAKEDOWN

Switzerland, male DJ / production duo – Stephan and Sebastien Kohler (Singles: 10 weeks)

Date		Title / Label	pos	wks
11 May 02	●	**AT NIGHT** *Defected DFECT 50CDS*	6	8
28 Jun 03		**DROWSY WITH HOPE** *Defected DFTD 071CDS*	46	2

Johnny SHAKER – *See THREE 'N ONE*

SHAKESPEAR'S SISTER

UK / US, female vocal / instrumental duo – Siobhan Fahey and Marcella (Detroit) Levy (Singles: 52 weeks, Albums: 63 weeks)

Date		Title / Label	pos	wks
29 Jul 89	●	**YOU'RE HISTORY** *ffrr F 112*	7	9
14 Oct 89		**RUN SILENT** *ffrr F 119*	54	3
10 Mar 90		**DIRTY MIND** *ffrr F 128*	71	1
12 Oct 91		**GOODBYE CRUEL WORLD** *London LON 309*	59	2
25 Jan 92	★	**STAY** *London LON 314*	1	16
16 May 92	●	**I DON'T CARE** *London LON 318*	7	7
18 Jul 92		**GOODBYE CRUEL WORLD (re-issue)** *London LON 322*	32	4
7 Nov 92		**HELLO (TURN YOUR RADIO ON)** *London LON 330*	14	6
27 Feb 93		**MY 16TH APOLOGY (EP)** *London LONCD 337*	61	1
22 Jun 96		**I CAN DRIVE** *London LONCD 383*	30	3
2 Sep 89	●	**SACRED HEART** *London 828131 1*	9	8
29 Feb 92	●	**HORMONALLY YOURS** *London 8282262*	3	55

Tracks on My 16th Apology (EP): My 16th Apology / Catwoman / Dirty Mind (live re-recording) / Hot Love. From 1996 Shakespear's Sister was essentially just vocalist Siobhan Fahey

See also BANANARAMA; Marcella DETROIT

SHAKIN' PYRAMIDS

UK, male vocal / instrumental group (Albums: 4 weeks)

Date		Title / Label	pos	wks
4 Apr 81		**SKIN 'EM UP** *Cuba Libra V 2199*	48	4

SHAKIRA

Colombia, female vocalist (Singles: 42 weeks, Albums: 47 weeks)

Date		Title / Label	pos	wks
9 Mar 02	●	**WHENEVER, WHEREVER** *Epic 6724262*	2	19
3 Aug 02	●	**UNDERNEATH YOUR CLOTHES** *Epic 6729532*	3	15
23 Nov 02		**OBJECTION (TANGO)** *Epic 6733402*	17	8
23 Mar 02	●	**LAUNDRY SERVICE** *Epic 4987202*	2	47

SHAKY – *See Shakin' STEVENS*

SHAKY and BONNIE – *See Shakin' STEVENS; Bonnie TYLER*

SHALAMAR 239 Top 500

Influential US dance-music vocal trio masterminded by 'Soul Train' TV producer Don Cornelius. Line-up 1979-1983: Jeffrey Daniel, Jody Watley, Howard Hewett. Regarded as fashion icons and trendsetters, they helped to introduce 'body-popping' to Britain (Singles: 134 weeks, Albums: 121 weeks)

Date		Title / Label	pos	wks
14 May 77		**UPTOWN FESTIVAL** *Soul Train FB 0885*	30	5
9 Dec 78		**TAKE THAT TO THE BANK** *RCA FB 1379*	20	12
24 Nov 79		**THE SECOND TIME AROUND** *Solar FB 1709*	45	9
9 Feb 80		**RIGHT IN THE SOCKET** *Solar SO 2*	44	6
30 Aug 80		**I OWE YOU ONE** *Solar SO 11*	13	10
28 Mar 81		**MAKE THAT MOVE** *Solar SO 17*	30	10
27 Mar 82	●	**I CAN MAKE YOU FEEL GOOD** *Solar K 12599*	7	11
12 Jun 82	●	**A NIGHT TO REMEMBER** *Solar K 13162*	5	12
4 Sep 82	●	**THERE IT IS** *Solar K 13194*	5	10
27 Nov 82		**FRIENDS** *Solar CHUM 1*	12	10
11 Jun 83	●	**DEAD GIVEAWAY** *Solar E 9819*	8	10
13 Aug 83		**DISAPPEARING ACT** *Solar E 9807*	18	8
15 Oct 83		**OVER AND OVER** *Solar E 9792*	23	6
24 Mar 84		**DANCING IN THE SHEETS** *CBS A 4171*	41	3
31 Mar 84		**DEADLINE USA** *MCA MCA 866*	52	3
24 Nov 84		**AMNESIA** *Solar/MCA SHAL 1*	61	2
2 Feb 85		**MY GIRL LOVES ME** *MCA SHAL 2*	45	3
26 Apr 86		**A NIGHT TO REMEMBER (re-mix)** *MCA SHAL 3*	52	4

			pos	wks
27 Mar 82	●	**FRIENDS** *Solar K 52345*	6	72
11 Sep 82		**GREATEST HITS** *Solar SOLA 3001*	71	5
30 Jul 83	●	**THE LOOK** *Solar 960239*	7	20
12 Apr 86	●	**THE GREATEST HITS** *Stylus SMR 8615*	5	24

The two 'Greatest Hits' albums are different

See also BABYFACE

SHAM ROCK *Ireland, male / female vocal / instrumental group (Singles: 11 weeks)*

			pos	wks
7 Nov 98		**TELL ME MA** *Jive 0522352*	13	11

SHAM 69 *UK, male vocal / instrumental group (Singles: 53 weeks, Albums: 27 weeks)*

			pos	wks
13 May 78		**ANGELS WITH DIRTY FACES** *Polydor 2059 023*	19	10
29 Jul 78	●	**IF THE KIDS ARE UNITED** *Polydor 2059 050*	9	9
14 Oct 78	●	**HURRY UP HARRY** *Polydor POSP 7*	10	8
24 Mar 79		**QUESTIONS AND ANSWERS** *Polydor POSP 27*	18	9
4 Aug 79	●	**HERSHAM BOYS** *Polydor POSP 64*	6	9
27 Oct 79		**YOU'RE A BETTER MAN THAN I** *Polydor POSP 82*	49	5
12 Apr 80		**TELL THE CHILDREN** *Polydor POSP 136*	45	3
11 Mar 78		**TELL US THE TRUTH** *Polydor 2383 491*	25	8
2 Dec 78		**THAT'S LIFE** *Polydor POLD 5010*	27	11
29 Sep 79	●	**THE ADVENTURES OF THE HERSHAM BOYS** *Polydor POLD 5025*	8	8

SHAMEN *UK, male vocal / instrumental duo (Singles: 77 weeks, Albums: 54 weeks)*

			pos	wks
7 Apr 90		**PRO-GEN** *One Little Indian 36 TP7*	55	4
22 Sep 90		**MAKE IT MINE** *One Little Indian 46 TP7*	42	5
6 Apr 91		**HYPERREAL** *One Little Indian 48 TP7*	29	5
27 Jul 91	●	**MOVE ANY MOUNTAIN (re-mix)** *One Little Indian 52 TP7*	4	10
18 Jul 92	●	**L.S.I.** *One Little Indian 68 TP7*	6	8
5 Sep 92	★	**EBENEEZER GOODE** *One Little Indian 78 TP7*	1	10
7 Nov 92	●	**BOSS DRUM** *One Little Indian 88 TP7*	4	7
7 Nov 92		**BOSS DRUM (re-mix)** *One Little Indian 88 TP12*	58	1
19 Dec 92	●	**PHOREVER PEOPLE** *One Little Indian 98 TP7*	5	10
6 Mar 93		**RE: EVOLUTION** *One Little Indian 118 TP7CD* [1]	18	2
6 Nov 93		**THE SOS EP** *One Little Indian 108 TP7CD*	14	4
19 Aug 95		**DESTINATION ESCHATON** *One Little Indian 128 TP7CDL*	15	4
21 Oct 95		**TRANSAMAZONIA** *One Little Indian 138 TP7CD*	28	2
10 Feb 96		**HEAL (THE SEPARATION)** *One Little Indian 158 TP7CDL*	31	2
21 Dec 96		**MOVE ANY MOUNTAIN '96 (2nd re-mix)** *One Little Indian 169 TP7CD*	35	3
2 Nov 90		**EN-TACT** *One Little Indian TPLP 22*	31	10
28 Sep 91		**PROGENY** *One Little Indian TPLP 32*	23	2
26 Sep 92	●	**BOSS DRUM / DIFFERENT DRUM** *One Little Indian TPLP 42CD*	3	35
20 Nov 93		**ON AIR** *Band Of Joy BOJCD 006*	61	1
4 Nov 95		**AXIS MUTATIS** *One Little Indian TPLP 52CDL*	27	2
2 May 98		**THE SHAMEN COLLECTION** *One Little Indian TPLP 72CDE*	26	4

[1] Shamen with Terence McKenna

'Move Any Mountain' is a re-mix of 'Pro-Gen'. Tracks on The SOS EP: Comin' On / Make It Mine / Possible Worlds (re-mix) From 18 Dec 93 sales of 'Boss Drum' and the remix album 'Different Drum' were amalgamated

SHAMPOO *UK, female vocal duo – Jacqui Blake and Carrie Askew (Singles: 28 weeks, Albums: 2 weeks)*

			pos	wks
30 Jul 94		**TROUBLE** *Food CDFOOD 51*	11	12
15 Oct 94		**VIVA LA MEGABABES** *Food CDFOOD 54*	27	4
18 Feb 95		**DELICIOUS** *Food CDFOOD 58*	21	4
5 Aug 95		**TROUBLE (re-issue)** *Food CDFOOD 66*	36	3
13 Jul 96		**GIRL POWER** *Food CDFOOD 76*	25	4
21 Sep 96		**I KNOW WHAT BOYS LIKE** *Food CDFOOD 83*	42	1
5 Nov 94		**WE ARE SHAMPOO** *Food FOODCD 12*	45	2

Jimmy SHAND BAND
UK, male dance band, leader d. 23 Dec 2000 (Singles: 2 weeks)

			pos	wks
23 Dec 55		**BLUEBELL POLKA** *Parlophone F 3436*	20	2
24 Dec 83		**FIFTY YEARS ON WITH JIMMY SHAND** *Ross WGR 062* [1]	97	2

[1] Jimmy Shand his Band and Guests

Paul SHANE and the YELLOWCOATS
UK, male actor / vocalist with male / female vocal group (Singles: 5 weeks)

			pos	wks
16 May 81		**HI-DE-HI (HOLIDAY ROCK)** *EMI 5180*	36	5

SHANGRI-LAS *US, female vocal group (Singles: 47 weeks)*

			pos	wks
8 Oct 64		**REMEMBER (WALKIN' IN THE SAND)** *Red Bird RB 10008*	14	12
14 Jan 65		**LEADER OF THE PACK** *Red Bird RB 10014* ▲	11	9
14 Oct 72	●	**LEADER OF THE PACK (re-issue)** *Kama Sutra 2013 024*	3	14
5 Jun 76	●	**LEADER OF THE PACK (2nd re-issue)** *Charly CS 1009*	7	12

From 19 Jun 1976 until 14 Aug 1976, the last week of the disc's chart run, the Charly and another Contempo release of 'Leader of the Pack' were bracketed together on the chart

SHANICE *US, female vocalist – Shanice Wilson (Singles: 24 weeks, Albums: 4 weeks)*

			pos	wks
23 Nov 91		**I LOVE YOUR SMILE** *Motown ZB 44907*	55	4
22 Feb 92	●	**I LOVE YOUR SMILE (re-mix)** *Motown TMG 1401*	2	10
14 Nov 92		**LOVIN' YOU** *Motown TMG 1409*	54	1
16 Jan 93		**SAVING FOREVER FOR YOU** *Giant W 0148CD*	42	3
13 Aug 94		**I LIKE** *Motown TMGCD 1427*	49	2
16 Dec 95		**IF I NEVER KNEW YOU (LOVE THEME FROM 'POCAHONTAS')** *Walt Disney WD 7023CD* [1]	51	4
21 Mar 92		**INNER CHILD** *Motown 5300082*	21	4

[1] Jon Secada and Shanice

SHANKS & BIGFOOT *UK, male production duo – Stephen Meade and Daniel Langsman (Singles: 24 weeks)*

			pos	wks
29 May 99	★	**SWEET LIKE CHOCOLATE (re)** *Pepper / Jive / Chocolate Boy 0530352* ■	1	16
29 Jul 00		**SING-A-LONG (re)** *Pepper 9230232*	12	8

See also DOOLALLY

SHANNON *US, female vocalist – Brenda Shannon Greene (Singles: 54 weeks, Albums: 12 weeks)*

			pos	wks
19 Nov 83		**LET THE MUSIC PLAY (re)** *Club LET 1*	14	15
7 Apr 84		**GIVE ME TONIGHT** *Club JAB 1*	24	7
30 Jun 84		**SWEET SOMEBODY** *Club JAB 3*	25	8
20 Jul 85		**STRONGER TOGETHER** *Club JAB 15*	46	6
6 Dec 97		**IT'S OVER LOVE** *Manifesto FESCD 37* [1]	16	8
28 Nov 98	●	**MOVE MANIA** *Multiply CDMULTY 45* [2]	8	10
10 Mar 84		**LET THE MUSIC PLAY** *Club JABL 1*	52	12

[1] Todd Terry presents Shannon [2] Sash! featuring Shannon

Del SHANNON (394 Top 500)
Early 1960s chart regular, b. Charles Westover, 30 Dec 1934, Michigan, US, d. 8 Feb 1990. This unmistakable singer / songwriter who used a falsetto vocal on most hits topped both the UK and US charts with the first of his many hits (Singles: 147 weeks, Albums: 23 weeks)

			pos	wks
27 Apr 61	★	**RUNAWAY** *London HLX 9317* ▲	1	22
14 Sep 61	●	**HATS OFF TO LARRY** *London HLX 9402*	6	12
7 Dec 61	●	**SO LONG BABY** *London HLX 9462*	10	11
15 Mar 62	●	**HEY! LITTLE GIRL** *London HLX 9515*	2	15
6 Sep 62		**CRY MYSELF TO SLEEP** *London HLX 9587*	29	6
11 Oct 62	●	**THE SWISS MAID** *London HLX 9609*	2	17
17 Jan 63	●	**LITTLE TOWN FLIRT** *London HLX 9653*	4	13
25 Apr 63	●	**TWO KINDS OF TEARDROPS** *London HLX 9710*	5	13
22 Aug 63		**TWO SILHOUETTES** *London HLX 9761*	23	8
24 Oct 63		**SUE'S GOTTA BE MINE** *London HLU 9800*	21	8
12 Mar 64		**MARY JANE** *Stateside SS 269*	35	5
30 Jul 64		**HANDY MAN** *Stateside SS 317*	36	4
14 Jan 65	●	**KEEP SEARCHIN' (WE'LL FOLLOW THE SUN)** *Stateside SS 368*	3	11
18 Mar 65		**STRANGER IN TOWN** *Stateside SS 395*	40	2
11 May 63	●	**HATS OFF TO DEL SHANNON** *London HAX 8071*	9	17
2 Nov 63		**LITTLE TOWN FLIRT** *London HAX 8091*	15	6

The Oct 1963 hit 'Sue's Gotta Be Mine' is the correct title although a label printing error shows 'Sue's Gonna Be Mine' on copies of the record

Roxanne SHANTE *US, female rapper (Singles: 11 weeks)* pos/wks

Date		Title / Label	pos	wks
1 Aug 87		HAVE A NICE DAY *Breakout USA 612*	58	3
4 Jun 88		GO ON GIRL *Breakout USA 633*	55	3
29 Oct 88		SHARP AS A KNIFE *Club JAB 73* [1]	45	3
14 Apr 90		GO ON GIRL (re-mix) *Breakout USA 689*	74	1
23 Sep 00		WHAT'S GOING ON *Wall of Sound WALLD 064* [2]	43	1

[1] Brandon Cooke featuring Roxanne Shante [2] Mekon featuring Roxanne Shante

Helen SHAPIRO (475 Top 500) *Youngest female chart-topper, b. 28 Sep 1946, London. Before she was 16 years old, she amassed four Top 5 hits (including two No.1s) and had been voted Britain's Top Female Singer. She headlined the first UK tour on which The Beatles appeared (as her support act) (Singles: 119 weeks, Albums: 25 weeks)* pos/wks

Date		Title / Label	pos	wks
23 Mar 61	●	DON'T TREAT ME LIKE A CHILD *Columbia DB 4589*	3	20
29 Jun 61	★	YOU DON'T KNOW *Columbia DB 4670*	1	23
28 Sep 61	★	WALKIN' BACK TO HAPPINESS *Columbia DB 4715*	1	19
15 Feb 62	●	TELL ME WHAT HE SAID *Columbia DB 4782*	2	15
3 May 62		LET'S TALK ABOUT LOVE *Columbia DB 4824*	23	7
12 Jul 62	●	LITTLE MISS LONELY *Columbia DB 4869*	8	11
18 Oct 62		KEEP AWAY FROM OTHER GIRLS *Columbia DB 4908*	40	6
7 Feb 63		QUEEN FOR TONIGHT *Columbia DB 4966*	33	5
25 Apr 63		WOE IS ME *Columbia DB 7026*	35	6
24 Oct 63		LOOK WHO IT IS *Columbia DB 7130*	47	3
23 Jan 64		FEVER *Columbia DB 7190*	38	4
10 Mar 62	●	'TOPS' WITH ME *Columbia 33SX 1397*	2	25

SHARADA HOUSE GANG *Italy, male / female vocal / instrumental group (Singles: 4 weeks)* pos/wks

Date		Title / Label	pos	wks
12 Aug 95		KEEP IT UP *Media MCSTD 2071*	36	2
11 May 96		LET THE RHYTHM MOVE YOU *Media MCSTD 40035*	50	1
18 Oct 97		GYPSY BOY, GYPSY GIRL *Gut CXGUT 12*	52	1

SHARKEY *UK, male DJ / producer / instrumentalist – Jonathan Sharkey (Singles: 1 week)* pos/wks

Date		Title / Label	pos	wks
8 Mar 97		REVOLUTIONS (EP) *React CDREACT 95*	53	1

Tracks on Revolutions (EP): Revolution Part One / Revolution Part Two / Revolution Part Two (remix)

Feargal SHARKEY *UK, male vocalist (Singles: 58 weeks, Albums: 24 weeks)* pos/wks

Date		Title / Label	pos	wks
13 Oct 84		LISTEN TO YOUR FATHER *Zarjazz JAZZ 1*	23	7
29 Jun 85		LOVING YOU *Virgin VS 770*	26	10
12 Oct 85	★	A GOOD HEART *Virgin VS 808*	1	16
4 Jan 86	●	YOU LITTLE THIEF *Virgin VS 840*	5	9
5 Apr 86		SOMEONE TO SOMEBODY *Virgin VS 828*	64	3
16 Jan 88		MORE LOVE *Virgin VS 992*	44	5
16 Mar 91		I'VE GOT NEWS FOR YOU *Virgin VS 1294*	12	8
23 Nov 85		FEARGAL SHARKEY *Virgin V 2360*	12	20
20 Apr 91		SONGS FROM THE MARDI GRAS *Virgin V 2642*	27	4

See also ASSEMBLY; UNDERTONES

SHARONETTES *US, female vocal group (Singles: 8 weeks)* pos/wks

Date		Title / Label	pos	wks
26 Apr 75		PAPA OOM MOW MOW *Black Magic BM 102*	26	5
12 Jul 75		GOING TO A GO-GO *Black Magic BM 104*	46	3

Debbie SHARP – *See DREAM FREQUENCY*

Dee Dee SHARP *US, female vocalist (Singles: 2 weeks)* pos/wks

Date		Title / Label	pos	wks
25 Apr 63		DO THE BIRD *Cameo Parkway C 244*	46	2

Barrie K SHARPE – *See Diana BROWN and Barrie K SHARPE*

SHARPE and NUMAN – *See Gary NUMAN; SHAKATAK*

Rocky SHARPE and The REPLAYS *UK, male / female vocal group (Singles: 41 weeks)* pos/wks

Date		Title / Label	pos	wks
16 Dec 78		RAMA LAMA DING DONG *Chiswick CHIS 104*	17	10
24 Mar 79		IMAGINATION *Chiswick CHIS 110*	39	6
25 Aug 79		LOVE WILL MAKE YOU FAIL IN SCHOOL *Chiswick CHIS 114* [1]	60	4
9 Feb 80		MARTIAN HOP *Chiswick CHIS 121* [1]	55	4
17 Apr 82		SHOUT SHOUT (KNOCK YOURSELF OUT) *Chiswick DICE 3*	19	9
7 Aug 82		CLAP YOUR HANDS *RAK 345*	54	3
26 Feb 83		IF YOU WANNA BE HAPPY *Polydor POSP 560*	46	5

[1] Rocky Sharpe and the Replays featuring the Top Liners

Ben SHAW featuring Adele HOLNESS *UK, male producer and female vocalist (Singles: 1 week)* pos/wks

Date		Title / Label	pos	wks
14 Jul 01		SO STRONG *Fire Recordings ERIF 009CDS*	72	1

Mark SHAW *UK, male vocalist (Singles: 1 week)* pos/wks

Date		Title / Label	pos	wks
17 Nov 90		LOVE SO BRIGHT *EMI EM 161*	54	1

See also THEN JERICHO

Roland SHAW – *See MANTOVANI*

Sandie SHAW (372 Top 500) *Barefoot pop princess of the Sixties, b. Sandra Goodrich, 26 Feb 1947, Essex, UK. This distinctive vocalist, who has a 30-year chart span, was the first UK act to win the Eurovision Song Contest (with 'Puppet on a String' in 1967) (Singles: 165 weeks, Albums: 14 weeks)* pos/wks

Date		Title / Label	pos	wks
8 Oct 64	★	(THERE'S) ALWAYS SOMETHING THERE TO REMIND ME *Pye 7N 15704*	1	11
10 Dec 64	●	GIRL DON'T COME *Pye 7N 15743*	3	12
18 Feb 65	●	I'LL STOP AT NOTHING *Pye 7N 15783*	4	11
13 May 65	★	LONG LIVE LOVE *Pye 7N 15841*	1	14
23 Sep 65	●	MESSAGE UNDERSTOOD *Pye 7N 15940*	6	10
18 Nov 65		HOW CAN YOU TELL *Pye 7N 15987*	21	9
27 Jan 66	●	TOMORROW *Pye 7N 17036*	9	9
19 May 66		NOTHING COMES EASY *Pye 7N 17086*	14	9
8 Sep 66		RUN *Pye 7N 17163*	32	5
24 Nov 66		THINK SOMETIMES ABOUT ME *Pye 7N 17212*	32	4
19 Jan 67		I DON'T NEED ANYTHING *Pye 7N 17239*	50	1
16 Mar 67	★	PUPPET ON A STRING *Pye 7N 17272*	1	18
12 Jul 67		TONIGHT IN TOKYO *Pye 7N 17346*	21	6
4 Oct 67		YOU'VE NOT CHANGED *Pye 7N 17378*	18	12
7 Feb 68		TODAY *Pye 7N 17441*	27	7
12 Feb 69	●	MONSIEUR DUPONT *Pye 7N 17675*	6	15
14 May 69		THINK IT ALL OVER *Pye 7N 17726*	42	4
21 Apr 84		HAND IN GLOVE *Rough Trade RT 130*	27	5
14 Jun 86		ARE YOU READY TO BE HEARTBROKEN? *Polydor POSP 793*	68	1
12 Nov 94		NOTHING LESS THAN BRILLIANT *Virgin VSCDT 1521*	66	2
6 Mar 65	●	SANDIE *Pye NPL 18110*	3	13
19 Nov 94		NOTHING LESS THAN BRILLIANT *Virgin VTCD 34*	64	1

Tracy SHAW *UK, female actor / vocalist (Singles: 1 week)* pos/wks

Date		Title / Label	pos	wks
4 Jul 98		HAPPENIN' ALL OVER AGAIN *Recognition CDREC 2*	46	1

Winifred SHAW *US, female vocalist, d. 2 May 1982 (Singles: 4 weeks)* pos/wks

Date		Title / Label	pos	wks
14 Aug 76		LULLABY OF BROADWAY *United Artists UP 36131*	42	4

SHE – *See URBAN DISCHARGE featuring SHE*

SHE ROCKERS *UK, female rap duo (Singles: 2 weeks)* pos/wks

Date		Title / Label	pos	wks
13 Jan 90		JAM IT JAM *Jive JIVE 233*	58	2

George SHEARING *UK / US, male instrumentalist – piano (Singles: 15 weeks, Albums: 13 weeks)* pos/wks

Date		Title / Label	pos	wks
19 Jul 62		LET THERE BE LOVE *Capitol CL 15257* [1]	11	14
4 Oct 62		BAUBLES, BANGLES AND BEADS *Capitol CL 15269* [2]	49	1
11 Jun 60		BEAUTY AND THE BEAT *Capitol T 1219* [1]	16	6
20 Oct 62	●	NAT 'KING' COLE SINGS / GEORGE SHEARING PLAYS WITH THE QUINTET AND STRING CHOIR *Capitol W 1675* [2]	8	7

[1] Nat 'King' Cole with George Shearing [2] George Shearing Quintet [1] Peggy Lee and George Shearing [2] Nat 'King' Cole and the George Shearing Quintet

Gary SHEARSTON *Australia, male vocalist (Singles: 8 weeks)* pos/wks

5 Oct 74 ● **I GET A KICK OUT OF YOU** *Charisma CB 234* 7 8

SHED SEVEN *UK, male vocal / instrumental group (Singles: 49 weeks, Albums: 46 weeks)* pos/wks

25 Jun 94 **DOLPHIN** *Polydor YORCD 2* 28 4
27 Aug 94 **SPEAKEASY** *Polydor YORCD 3* 24 3
12 Nov 94 **OCEAN PIE** *Polydor YORCD 4* 33 2
13 May 95 **WHERE HAVE YOU BEEN TONIGHT** *Polydor YORCD 5* 23 2
27 Jan 96 **GETTING BETTER** *Polydor 5778912* 14 3
23 Mar 96 ● **GOING FOR GOLD** *Polydor 5762152* 8 5
18 May 96 **BULLY BOY** *Polydor 5765972* 22 3
31 Aug 96 **ON STANDBY** *Polydor 5752732* 12 4
23 Nov 96 **CHASING RAINBOWS** *Polydor 5759292* 17 5
14 Mar 98 **SHE LEFT ME ON FRIDAY** *Polydor 5695412* 11 4
23 May 98 **THE HEROES** *Polydor 5699172* 18 3
22 Aug 98 **DEVIL IN YOUR SHOES (WALKING ALL OVER)** *Polydor 5672072* 37 2
5 Jun 99 **DISCO DOWN** *Polydor 5638752* 13 6
5 May 01 **CRY FOR HELP** *Artful CD 35ARTFUL* 30 2
24 May 03 **WHY CAN'T I BE YOU?** *Taste Media TMCDS 5004* 23 2
17 Sep 94 **CHANGE GIVER** *Polydor 5236152* 16 2
13 Apr 96 ● **A MAXIMUM HIGH** *Polydor 5310392* 8 26
13 Jun 98 ● **LET IT RIDE** *Polydor 5573592* 9 7
12 Jun 99 ● **GOING FOR GOLD – THE GREATEST HITS** *Polydor 5474422* 7 10
19 May 01 **TRUTH BE TOLD** *Artful ARTFULCD 38* 42 1

SHEEP ON DRUGS *UK, male vocal / instrumental duo – Duncan Gil-Rodriguez and Lee Fraser (Singles: 5 weeks, Albums: 1 week)* pos/wks

27 Mar 93 **15 MINUTES OF FAME** *Transglobal CID 564* 44 2
30 Oct 93 **FROM A TO H AND BACK AGAIN** *Transglobal CID 575* 40 2
14 May 94 **LET THE GOOD TIMES ROLL** *Transglobal CID 576* 56 1
10 Apr 93 **GREATEST HITS** *Transglobal CID 8006* 55 1

SHEER BRONZE featuring Lisa MILLETT *UK, male / female vocal / instrumental duo (Singles: 1 week)* pos/wks

3 Sep 94 **WALKIN' ON** *Go.Beat GODCD 115* 63 1

SHEER ELEGANCE *UK, male vocal group (Singles: 23 weeks)* pos/wks

20 Dec 75 **MILKY WAY** *Pye International 7N 25697* 18 10
3 Apr 76 ● **LIFE IS TOO SHORT GIRL** *Pye International 7N 25703* 9 9
24 Jul 76 **IT'S TEMPTATION** *Pye International 7N 25715* 41 4

SHEILA B DEVOTION *France, female vocalist – Anny Chancel – and male vocal trio (Singles: 33 weeks)* pos/wks

11 Mar 78 **SINGIN' IN THE RAIN PART 1** *Carrere EMI 2751* 11 13
22 Jul 78 **YOU LIGHT MY FIRE** *Carrere EMI 2828* 44 6
24 Nov 79 **SPACER** *Carrere CAR 128* [1] 18 14

[1] Sheila & B. Devotion (Some pressings still credited Sheila B. Devotion)

Shade SHEIST featuring Nate DOGG and KURUPT *US, male rappers – leader Tremayne Thompson (Singles: 7 weeks)* pos/wks

25 Aug 01 **WHERE I WANNA BE (re)** *London LONCD461* 14 7

Doug SHELDON *UK, male vocalist (Singles: 15 weeks)* pos/wks

9 Nov 61 **RUNAROUND SUE** *Decca F 11398* 36 3
4 Jan 62 **YOUR MA SAID YOU CRIED IN YOUR SLEEP LAST NIGHT** *Decca F 11416* 29 6
7 Feb 63 **I SAW LINDA YESTERDAY** *Decca F 11564* 36 6

Michelle SHELLERS – *See SOUL PROVIDERS featuring Michelle SHELLERS*

Pete SHELLEY *UK, male vocalist (Singles: 1 week, Albums: 4 weeks)* pos/wks

12 Mar 83 **TELEPHONE OPERATOR** *Genetic XX1* 66 1
2 Jul 83 **XL-1** *Genetic XL 1* 42 4

See also BUZZCOCKS

Peter SHELLEY *UK, male vocalist (Singles: 20 weeks)* pos/wks

14 Sep 74 ● **GEE BABY** *Magnet MAG 12* 4 10
22 Mar 75 ● **LOVE ME LOVE MY DOG** *Magnet MAG 22* 3 10

Anne SHELTON *UK, female vocalist – Patricia Sibley, d. 31 Jul 1994 (Singles: 31 weeks)* pos/wks

16 Dec 55 **ARRIVEDERCI DARLING** *HMV POP 146* 17 4
13 Apr 56 **SEVEN DAYS** *Philips PB 567* 20 4
24 Aug 56 ★ **LAY DOWN YOUR ARMS** *Philips PB 616* 1 14
20 Nov 59 **THE VILLAGE OF ST BERNADETTE** *Philips PB 969* 27 1
26 Jan 61 ● **SAILOR** *Philips PB 1096* 10 8

SHENA *UK, female vocalist – Shena McSween (Singles: 6 weeks)* pos/wks

2 Aug 97 **LET THE BEAT HIT 'EM** *VC VCRD 24* 28 2
1 Sep 01 **I'LL BE WAITING** *Rulin RULIN 17CDS* [1] 44 1
4 Oct 03 **WILDERNESS** *Direction 6742692* [2] 20 3

[1] Full Intention presents Shena [2] Jurgen Vries featuring Shena

Vikki SHEPARD – *See SLEAZESISTERS*

Vonda SHEPARD *US, female vocalist / instrumentalist – piano (Singles: 9 weeks, Albums: 49 weeks)* pos/wks

5 Dec 98 ● **SEARCHIN' MY SOUL** *Epic 6666332* 10 9
17 Oct 98 ● **SONGS FROM ALLY MCBEAL** *Epic 4911242* 3 34
12 Jun 99 **BY 7:30** *Epic 4945792* 39 2
20 Nov 99 ● **HEART & SOUL – NEW SONGS FROM ALLY MCBEAL** *Epic 4950912* 9 13

SHEPHERD SISTERS *US, female vocal group (Singles: 6 weeks)* pos/wks

15 Nov 57 **ALONE (WHY MUST I BE) (re)** *HMV POP 411* 14 6

SHERBET *Australia, male vocal / instrumental group (Singles: 10 weeks)* pos/wks

25 Sep 76 ● **HOWZAT** *Epic EPC 4574* 4 10

Tony SHERIDAN and The BEATLES *UK, male vocalist / instrumental group (Singles: 1 week)* pos/wks

6 Jun 63 **MY BONNIE** *Polydor NH 66833* 48 1

Allan SHERMAN *US, male vocalist / comedian – Allan Copelon, d. 21 Nov 1973 (Singles: 10 weeks)* pos/wks

12 Sep 63 **HELLO MUDDAH! HELLO FADDAH!** *Warner Bros. WB 106* 14 10

Bobby SHERMAN *US, male vocalist (Singles: 4 weeks)* pos/wks

31 Oct 70 **JULIE DO YA LOVE ME** *CBS 5144* 28 4

SHERRICK *US, male vocalist – F Lamonte-Smith (Singles: 10 weeks, Albums: 6 weeks)* pos/wks

1 Aug 87 **JUST CALL** *Warner Bros. W 8380* 23 8
21 Nov 87 **LET'S BE LOVERS TONIGHT** *Warner Bros. W 8146* 63 2
29 Aug 87 **SHERRICK** *Warner Bros. WX 118* 27 6

Pluto SHERVINGTON *Jamaica, male vocalist (Singles: 20 weeks)* pos/wks

7 Feb 76 ● **DAT** *Opal Pal 5* 6 8
10 Apr 76 **RAM GOAT LIVER** *Trojan TR 7978* 43 4
6 Mar 82 **YOUR HONOUR** *KR KR 4* [1] 19 8

[1] Pluto

Holly SHERWOOD *US, female vocalist (Singles: 7 weeks)* pos/wks

5 Feb 72 **DAY BY DAY** *Bell 1182* 29 7

Tony SHEVETON *UK, male vocalist (Singles: 1 week)* pos/wks

13 Feb 64 **A MILLION DRUMS** *Oriole CB 1895* 49 1

SHIMMON & WOOLFSON

UK, male DJ / production duo (Singles: 1 week) pos/wks

10 Jan 98 **WELCOME TO THE FUTURE** *React CDREACT 119* 69 1

See also SUNDANCE

SHIMON & Andy C *UK, male production duo (Singles: 5 weeks)* pos/wks

15 Sep 01 **BODY ROCK (re)** *Ram RAMM 34CD* 28 5

Brendan SHINE *Ireland, male vocalist (Albums: 29 weeks)* pos/wks

12 Nov 83 **THE BRENDON SHINE COLLECTION** *Play PLAYTV 1* 51 12
3 Nov 84 **WITH LOVE** *Play PLAYTV 2* 74 4
16 Nov 85 **MEMORIES** *Play PLAYTV 3* 81 7
18 Nov 89 **MAGIC MOMENTS** *Stylus SMR 991* 62 6

SHINEHEAD

Jamaica, male vocalist – Edmund Aiken (Singles: 6 weeks) pos/wks

3 Apr 93 **JAMAICAN IN NEW YORK** *Elektra EKR 161CD* 30 5
26 Jun 93 **LET 'EM IN** *Elektra EKR 168CD* 70 1

SHINING *UK, male vocal / instrumental group (Singles: 2 weeks, Albums: 1 week)* pos/wks

6 Jul 02 **I WONDER HOW** *Zuma ZUMAD 002* 58 1
14 Sep 02 **YOUNG AGAIN** *Zuma ZUMASCD 003* 52 1
28 Sep 02 **TRUE SKIES** *Zuma ZUMACD 001* 73 1

Mike SHINODA – *See X-ECUTIONERS featuring Mike SHINODA and Mr HAHN of LINKIN PARK*

SHIREHORSES

UK, male vocal instrumental group – includes Mark Radcliffe and Marc 'Lard' Riley (Albums: 8 weeks) pos/wks

15 Nov 97 **THE WORST ALBUM IN THE WORLD EVER ... EVER!** *East West 3984208512* 22 4
26 May 01 **OUR KID EH** *Columbia 5030492* 20 4

SHIRELLES *US, female vocal group (Singles: 29 weeks)* pos/wks

9 Feb 61 ● **WILL YOU LOVE ME TOMORROW** *Top Rank JAR 540* ▲ 4 15
31 May 62 **SOLDIER BOY** *HMV POP 1019* ▲ 23 9
23 May 63 **FOOLISH LITTLE GIRL** *Stateside SS 181* 38 5

SHIRLEY and COMPANY *US, female vocalist and male vocal / instrumental backing group (Singles: 9 weeks)* pos/wks

8 Feb 75 ● **SHAME SHAME SHAME** *All Platinum 6146 301* 6 9

SHIRLIE – *See PEPSI and SHIRLIE*

SHIVA

UK, male / female vocal / instrumental group (Singles: 5 weeks) pos/wks

13 May 95 **WORK IT OUT** *ffrr FCD 261* 36 2
19 Aug 95 **FREEDOM** *ffrr FCD 263* 18 3

SHIVAREE

US, female / male vocal / instrumental group (Singles: 1 week) pos/wks

17 Feb 01 **GOODNIGHT MOON** *Capitol CDCL 825* 63 1

SHO NUFF *US, male vocal / instrumental group (Singles: 4 weeks)* pos/wks

24 May 80 **IT'S ALRIGHT** *Ensign ENY 37* 53 4

Michelle SHOCKED

US, female vocalist (Singles: 10 weeks, Albums: 24 weeks) pos/wks

8 Oct 88 **ANCHORAGE** *Cooking Vinyl LON 193* 60 4
14 Jan 89 **IF LOVE WAS A TRAIN** *Cooking Vinyl LON 212* 63 3
11 Mar 89 **WHEN I GROW UP** *Cooking Vinyl LON 219* 67 3
10 Sep 88 **SHORT SHARP SHOCKED** *Cooking Vinyl CVLP 1* 33 19
18 Nov 89 **CAPTAIN SWING** *Cooking Vinyl 838878 1* 31 3
11 Apr 92 **ARKANSAS TRAVELER** *London 5121892* 46 2

SHOCKING BLUE *Holland, male / female vocal / instrumental group (Singles: 14 weeks)* pos/wks

17 Jan 70 ● **VENUS** *Penny Farthing PEN 702* ▲ 8 11
25 Apr 70 **MIGHTY JOE** *Penny Farthing PEN 713* 43 3

SHOLAN

Germany, male / female production / vocal trio (Singles: 1 week) pos/wks

5 Apr 03 **CAN YOU FEEL (WHAT I'M GOING THRU)** *Data / Ministry of Sound DATA 39CDS* 47 1

Troy SHONDELL

US, male vocalist – Gary Schelton (Singles: 11 weeks) pos/wks

2 Nov 61 **THIS TIME** *London HLG 9432* 22 11

SHONDELLS – *See Tommy JAMES and the SHONDELLS*

SHOOTING PARTY *UK, male vocal duo (Singles: 2 weeks)* pos/wks

31 Mar 90 **LET'S HANG ON** *Lisson DOLE 15* 66 2

SHOP ASSISTANTS

UK, male / female vocal / instrumental group (Albums: 1 week) pos/wks

29 Nov 86 **SHOP ASSISTANTS** *Blue Guitar AZLP 2* 100 1

Howard SHORE *US, male conductor (Albums: 24 weeks)* pos/wks

5 Jan 02 ● **THE LORD OF THE RINGS: THE FELLOWSHIP OF THE RING (FILM SOUNDTRACK)** *Reprise 9362481102* 10 14
11 Jan 03 **THE LORD OF THE RINGS: THE TWO TOWERS (FILM SOUNDTRACK)** *Reprise 936248212* 28 9
27 Dec 03 **THE LORD OF THE RINGS: RETURN OF THE KING (FILM SOUNDTRACK)** *Reprise 9362486092* ....66 1+

Mike SHOREY – *See FABOLOUS*

SHORTIE vs BLACK LEGEND

Italy, male production duo and male vocalist (Singles: 2 weeks) pos/wks

4 Aug 01 **SOMEBODY** *WEA WEA 328 CD* 37 2

SHOWADDYWADDY (158 Top 500)

Rock 'n' roll revival male vocal / instrumental octet from Leicester, UK, which included vocalists Dave Bartram and Buddy Gask. At the peak of their career, they had seven successive Top 5 entries with rousing revivals of old US rock 'n' roll songs. Best-selling single: 'Under the Moon of Love' 985,000 (Singles: 209 weeks, Albums: 126 weeks) pos/wks

18 May 74 ● **HEY ROCK AND ROLL** *Bell 1357* 2 14
17 Aug 74 **ROCK 'N' ROLL LADY** *Bell 1374* 15 9
30 Nov 74 **HEY MR CHRISTMAS** *Bell 1387* 13 8
22 Feb 75 **SWEET MUSIC** *Bell 1403* 14 9
17 May 75 ● **THREE STEPS TO HEAVEN** *Bell 1426* 2 11
6 Sep 75 ● **HEARTBEAT** *Bell 1450* 7 7
15 Nov 75 **HEAVENLY** *Bell 1460* 34 6
29 May 76 **TROCADERO** *Bell 1476* 32 3
6 Nov 76 ★ **UNDER THE MOON OF LOVE** *Bell 1495* 1 15
5 Mar 77 ● **WHEN** *Arista 91* 3 11
23 Jul 77 ● **YOU GOT WHAT IT TAKES** *Arista 126* 2 10
5 Nov 77 ● **DANCIN' PARTY** *Arista 149* 4 11
25 Mar 78 ● **I WONDER WHY** *Arista 174* 2 11
24 Jun 78 ● **A LITTLE BIT OF SOAP** *Arista 191* 5 12
4 Nov 78 ● **PRETTY LITTLE ANGEL EYES** *Arista ARIST 222* 5 12
31 Mar 79 **REMEMBER THEN** *Arista 247* 17 8
28 Jul 79 **SWEET LITTLE ROCK 'N' ROLLER** *Arista 278* 15 9
10 Nov 79 **A NIGHT AT DADDY GEES** *Arista 314* 39 5
27 Sep 80 **WHY DO LOVERS BREAK EACH OTHERS' HEARTS** *Arista ARIST 359* 22 10
29 Nov 80 **BLUE MOON** *Arista ARIST 379* 32 9
13 Jun 81 **MULTIPLICATION** *Arista ARIST 416* 39 4
28 Nov 81 **FOOTSTEPS** *Bell BELL 1499* 31 9
28 Aug 82 **WHO PUT THE BOMP (IN THE BOMP-A-BOMP-A-BOMP)** *RCA 236* 37 6
7 Dec 74 ● **SHOWADDYWADDY** *Bell BELLS 248* 9 19

12 Jul 75 ● **STEP TWO** *Bell BELLS 256* 7 17
29 May 76 **TROCADERO** *Bell SYBEL 8003* 41 3
25 Dec 76 ● **GREATEST HITS** *Arista ARTY 145* 4 26
3 Dec 77 **RED STAR** *Arista SPARTY 1023* 20 10
9 Dec 78 ★ **GREATEST HITS (1976-1978)** *Arista ARTV 1* 1 17
10 Nov 79 ● **CREPES AND DRAPES** *Arista ARTV 3* 8 14
20 Dec 80 **BRIGHT LIGHTS** *Arista SPART 1142* 54 8
7 Nov 81 **THE VERY BEST OF SHOWADDYWADDY** *Arista SPART 1178* 33 11
5 Dec 87 **THE BEST STEPS TO HEAVEN** *Tiger SHTV 1* 90 1

SHOWDOWN
US, male vocal / instrumental group (Singles: 3 weeks) pos/wks

17 Dec 77 **KEEP DOIN' IT** *State STAT 63* 41 3

SHOWDOWN – *See Garry LEE and SHOWDOWN*

SHOWSTOPPERS *US, male vocal group (Singles: 25 weeks)* pos/wks

13 Mar 68 **AIN'T NOTHING BUT A HOUSEPARTY** *Beacon 3-100* 11 15
13 Nov 68 **EENY MEENY** *MGM 1436* 33 7
30 Jan 71 **AIN'T NOTHING BUT A HOUSEPARTY (2re) (re-issue)** *Beacon BEA 100* 33 3

SHRIEKBACK *UK, male vocal / instrumental group (Singles: 4 weeks, Albums: 1 week)* pos/wks

28 Jul 84 **HAND ON MY HEART** *Arista SHRK 1* 52 4
11 Aug 84 **JAM SCIENCE** *Arista 206 416* 85 1

SHRINK *Holland, male DJ / production trio (Singles: 4 weeks)* pos/wks

10 Oct 98 **NERVOUS BREAKDOWN** *VC Recordings VCRD42* 42 2
19 Aug 00 **ARE YOU READY TO PARTY** *Nulife 74321783772* 39 2

SHUT UP AND DANCE *UK, male vocal / production group (Singles: 14 weeks, Albums: 2 weeks)* pos/wks

21 Apr 90 **£20 TO GET IN** *Shut Up and Dance SUAD 3* 56 3
28 Jul 90 **LAMBORGHINI** *Shut Up and Dance SUAD 4* 55 2
8 Feb 92 **AUTOBIOGRAPHY OF A CRACKHEAD / THE GREEN MAN** *Shut Up and Dance SUAD 21* 43 2
30 May 92 ● **RAVING I'M RAVING** *Shut Up and Dance SUAD 30S* [1] 2 2
15 Aug 92 **THE ART OF MOVING BUTTS** *Shut Up and Dance SUAD 34S* [2] 69 1
1 Apr 95 **SAVE IT 'TIL THE MOURNING AFTER** *Pulse 8 PULS 84CD* 25 3
8 Jul 95 **I LOVE U** *Pulse 8 PULS 90CD* [3] 68 1
27 Jun 92 **DEATH IS NOT THE END** *Shut Up and Dance SUADCD 005* 38 2

[1] Shut Up and Dance featuring Peter Bouncer [2] Shut Up and Dance featuring Erin [3] Shut Up and Dance featuring Richie Davis and Professor T

SHY *UK, male vocal / instrumental group (Singles: 3 weeks, Albums: 2 weeks)* pos/wks

19 Apr 80 **GIRL (IT'S ALL I HAVE)** *Gallery GA 1* 60 3
11 Apr 87 **EXCESS ALL AREAS** *RCA PL 71221* 74 2

SHY FX *UK, male / producer – Andre Williams (Singles: 22 weeks)* pos/wks

1 Oct 94 **ORIGINAL NUTTAH** *Sound of Underground SOUR 008CD* [1] 39 3
20 Mar 99 **BAMBAATA 2012** *Ebony EBR 020CD* 60 1
6 Apr 02 ● **SHAKE UR BODY** *Positiva CDTIV 171* [2] 7 11
23 Nov 02 **DON'T WANNA KNOW** *ffrr FCD 408* [3] 19 4
28 Dec 02 **WOLF** *Ebony Dubs EBD 001* 60 1
7 Jun 03 **FEELIN' U** *London FCD 409* [4] 34 2

[1] UK Apachi with Shy FX [2] Shy FX and T-Power featuring Di [3] Shy FX and T-Power featuring Di and Skibadee [4] Shy FX and T-Power featuring Kele Le Roc

SHYHEIM *US, male rapper (Singles: 1 week)* pos/wks

8 Jun 96 **THIS IZ REAL** *Noo Trybe VUSCD 105* 61 1

SIA *Australia, female vocalist – Sia Furler (Singles: 9 weeks)* pos/wks

3 Jun 00 ● **TAKEN FOR GRANTED** *Long Lost Brother S 002CD1* 10 5
18 Aug 01 **DESTINY** *Ultimate Dilemma UDRCDS 043* [1] 30 3
30 Mar 02 **DISTRACTIONS** *Ultimate Dilemma UDRCDS046* [2] 45 1

[1] Zero 7 featuring Sia & Sophie [2] Zero 7 featuring Sia

Labi SIFFRE *UK, male vocalist / instrumentalist – guitar (Singles: 44 weeks, Albums: 2 weeks)* pos/wks

27 Nov 71 **IT MUST BE LOVE** *Pye International 7N 25572* 14 12
25 Mar 72 **CRYING LAUGHING LOVING LYING** *Pye International 7N 25576* 11 9
29 Jul 72 **WATCH ME** *Pye International 7N 25586* 29 6
4 Apr 87 ● **(SOMETHING INSIDE) SO STRONG** *China WOK 12* 4 13
21 Nov 87 **NOTHIN'S GONNA CHANGE** *China WOK 16* 52 4
24 Jul 71 **SINGER AND THE SONG** *Pye NSPL 28147* 47 1
14 Oct 72 **CRYING LAUGHING LOVING LYING** *Pye NSPL 28163* 46 1

SIGNUM *Holland, male production duo – Ronald Hagen and Pascal Minnard (Singles: 6 weeks)* pos/wks

28 Nov 98 **WHAT YA GOT 4 ME** *Tidy Trax TIDY 118CD* 70 1
31 Jul 99 **COMING ON STRONG** *Tidy Trax TIDY 128T* [1] 66 1
9 Feb 02 **WHAT YA GOT 4 ME (re-mix)** *Tidy Trax TIDY 163CD* 35 3
29 Jun 02 **COMING ON STRONG (re-mix)** *Tidy Two TIDYTWO 104CD* [1] 50 1

[1] Signum featuring Scott Mac

SIGUE SIGUE SPUTNIK *UK, male vocal / instrumental group (Singles: 20 weeks, Albums: 7 weeks)* pos/wks

1 Mar 86 ● **LOVE MISSILE F1-11** *Parlophone SSS 1* 3 9
7 Jun 86 **21ST CENTURY BOY** *Parlophone SSS 2* 20 5
19 Nov 88 **SUCCESS** *Parlophone SSS 3* 31 3
1 Apr 89 **DANCERAMA** *Parlophone SSS 5* 50 2
20 May 89 **ALBINONI VS STAR WARS** *Parlophone SSS 4* 75 1
9 Aug 86 ● **FLAUNT IT** *Parlophone PCS 7305* 10 6
15 Apr 89 **DRESS FOR EXCESS** *Parlophone PCS 7328* 53 1

SIGUR ROS *Iceland, male vocal / instrumental group (Singles: 1 week, Albums: 2 weeks)* pos/wks

24 May 03 **()** *PIAS CD 10FAT02* 72 1
26 Aug 00 **AGAETIS BYRJUN** *Fat Cat/PIAS FATCD 11* 52 1
9 Nov 02 **()** *Fat Cat FATCD 22* 49 1

SIL *Holland, male DJ / production duo (Singles: 1 week)* pos/wks

11 Apr 98 **WINDOWS '98** *Hooj Choons HOOJCD 60* 58 1

SILENCERS *UK, male vocal / instrumental group (Singles: 7 weeks, Albums: 3 weeks)* pos/wks

25 Jun 88 **PAINTED MOON** *RCA HUSH 1* 57 4
27 May 89 **SCOTTISH RAIN** *RCA PB 42701* 71 2
15 May 93 **I CAN FEEL IT** *RCA 74321147112* 62 1
23 Mar 91 **DANCE TO THE HOLY MAN** *RCA PL 74924* 39 2
5 Jun 93 **SECONDS OF PLEASURE** *RCA 74321141132* 52 1

SILENT UNDERDOG
UK, male instrumentalist – Paul Hardcastle (Singles: 1 week) pos/wks

16 Feb 85 **PAPA'S GOT A BRAND NEW PIGBAG** *Kaz KAZ 50* 73 1

See also Paul HARDCASTLE

SILICONE SOUL featuring Louise Clare MARSHALL
UK, male production duo and female vocalist (Singles: 5 weeks) pos/wks

6 Oct 01 **RIGHT ON! (re)** *VC Recordings / Soma VCRD 96* 15 5

SILJE *Norway, female vocalist (Singles: 6 weeks)* pos/wks

15 Dec 90 **TELL ME WHERE YOU'RE GOING** *EMI EM 159* 55 6

SILK *US, male vocal group (Singles: 10 weeks)* pos/wks

24 Apr 93 **FREAK ME (re)** *Elektra EKR 165CD* ▲ 46 6
5 Jun 93 **GIRL U FOR ME** *Elektra EKR 167CD* 67 2
9 Oct 93 **BABY IT'S YOU** *Elektra EKR 173CD* 44 2

SILKIE
UK, male / female vocal / instrumental group (Singles: 6 weeks) pos/wks

23 Sep 65 **YOU'VE GOT TO HIDE YOUR LOVE AWAY** *Fontana TF 603* 28 6

SILKK THE SHOCKER – *See Montell JORDAN*

SILSOE
UK, male instrumentalist – Rod Argent (Singles: 4 weeks) pos/wks

21 Jun 86	**AZTEC GOLD** *CBS A 7231*	48	4

'Aztec Gold' was the ITV theme to the 1986 World Cup

See also ARGENT; SAN JOSE featuring Rodriguez ARGENTINA

Luci SILVAS *UK, female vocalist (Singles: 1 week)* pos/wks

17 Jun 00	**IT'S TOO LATE** *EMI CDEM 565*	62	1

John SILVER *Switzerland / Italy, male production / vocal duo – Dimitri Derisiotis and Gabriel Rizzo (Singles: 2 weeks)* pos/wks

25 Jan 03	**COME ON OVER** *Cream CREAM 20CD*	35	2

SILVER BULLET *UK, male rapper – Richard Brown (Singles: 20 weeks, Albums: 2 weeks)* pos/wks

2 Sep 89	**BRING FORTH THE GUILLOTINE (re)** *Tam Tam TTT 013*	45	6
9 Dec 89	**20 SECONDS TO COMPLY** *Tam Tam 7TTT 019*	11	10
13 Apr 91	**UNDERCOVER ANARCHIST** *Parlophone R 6284*	33	4
4 May 91	**BRING DOWN THE WALLS NO LIMIT SQUAD** *Parlophone PCS 7350*	38	2

'Bring Forth the Guillotine' reached its peak position on re-entry during Mar 1990

SILVER BULLET BAND – *See Bob SEGER and the SILVER BULLET BAND*

SILVER CITY
UK, male / female vocal / instrumental duo (Singles: 1 week) pos/wks

30 Oct 93	**LOVE INFINITY** *Silver City GFJMCD 1*	62	1

SILVER CONVENTION *Germany / US, female vocal group (Singles: 35 weeks, Albums: 3 weeks)* pos/wks

5 Apr 75	**SAVE ME** *Magnet MAG 26*	30	7
15 Nov 75	**FLY ROBIN FLY** *Magnet MAG 43* ▲	28	8
3 Apr 76 ●	**GET UP AND BOOGIE** *Magnet MAG 55*	7	11
19 Jun 76	**TIGER BABY / NO NO JOE** *Magnet MAG 69*	41	4
29 Jan 77	**EVERYBODY'S TALKIN' 'BOUT LOVE** *Magnet MAG 81*	25	5
25 Jun 77	**SILVER CONVENTION: GREATEST HITS** *Magnet MAG 6001*	34	3

SILVER SUN *UK, male vocal / instrumental group (Singles: 13 weeks, Albums: 2 weeks)* pos/wks

2 Nov 96	**LAVA** *Polydor 5756872*	54	1
22 Feb 97	**LAST DAY** *Polydor 5732432*	48	1
3 May 97	**GOLDEN SKIN** *Polydor 5738272*	32	2
5 Jul 97	**JULIA** *Polydor 5711752*	51	1
18 Oct 97	**LAVA (re-issue)** *Polydor 5714242*	35	2
20 Jun 98	**TOO MUCH, TOO LITTLE, TOO LATE** *Polydor 5699152*	20	4
26 Sep 98	**I'LL SEE YOU AROUND** *Polydor 5674532*	26	2
24 May 97	**SILVER SUN** *Polydor 5372082*	30	1
17 Oct 98	**NEO WAVE** *Polydor 5590852*	74	1

SILVERCHAIR *Australia, male vocal / instrumental group (Singles: 8 weeks, Albums: 5 weeks)* pos/wks

29 Jul 95	**PURE MASSACRE** *Murmur 6622642*	71	1
9 Sep 95	**TOMORROW** *Murmur 6623952*	59	2
5 Apr 97	**FREAK** *Murmur 6640765*	34	2
19 Jul 97	**ABUSE ME** *Murmur 6647907*	40	2
15 May 99	**ANA'S SONG** *Columbia 6673452*	45	1
23 Sep 95	**FROGSTOMP** *Murmur 4803402*	49	1
15 Feb 97	**FREAK SHOW** *Columbia 4871032*	38	2
27 Mar 99	**NEON BALLROOM** *Columbia 4933092*	29	2

SILVERFISH *US, male vocal / instrumental group (Albums: 1 week)* pos/wks

27 Jun 92	**ORGAN FAN** *Creation CRECD 118*	65	1

Dooley SILVERSPOON *US, male vocalist (Singles: 3 weeks)* pos/wks

31 Jan 76	**LET ME BE THE NUMBER 1 (LOVE OF YOUR LIFE)** *Seville SEV 1020*	44	3

Harry SIMEONE CHORALE *US, choir (Singles: 14 weeks)* pos/wks

13 Feb 59	**LITTLE DRUMMER BOY** *Top Rank JAR 101*	13	7
22 Dec 60	**ONWARD CHRISTIAN SOLDIERS (2re)** *Ember EMBS 118*	35	5
20 Dec 62	**ONWARD CHRISTIAN SOLDIERS (re-issue)** *Ember EMBS 144*	38	2

SIMIAN *UK, male vocal / instrumental group (Singles: 1 week)* pos/wks

14 Jun 03	**LA BREEZE** *Source SOURCD 069*	55	1

Gene SIMMONS *US, male vocalist (Singles: 4 weeks)* pos/wks

27 Jan 79	**RADIOACTIVE** *Casablanca CAN 134*	41	4

See also KISS

SIMON *UK, male producer – Simon Pearson (Singles: 2 weeks)* pos/wks

31 Mar 01	**FREE AT LAST** *Positiva CDTIV 152*	36	2

Carly SIMON (455 Top 500) *First charted in the US in 1964 as half of folk duo Simon Sisters with sister Lucy, b. 25 Jun 1945, New York. Winner of 1971's Best New Artist Grammy was married to fellow singer / songwriter James Taylor (1972-1983). Elected to Songwriters Hall of Fame 1994 (Singles: 85 weeks, Albums: 67 weeks)* pos/wks

16 Dec 72 ●	**YOU'RE SO VAIN** *Elektra K 12077* ▲	3	15
31 Mar 73	**THE RIGHT THING TO DO** *Elektra K 12095*	17	9
16 Mar 74	**MOCKINGBIRD** *Elektra K 12134*	34	5
6 Aug 77 ●	**NOBODY DOES IT BETTER** *Elektra K 12261*	7	12
21 Aug 82 ●	**WHY** *WEA K 79300*	10	13
24 Jan 87 ●	**COMING AROUND AGAIN** *Arista ARIST 687*	10	12
10 Jun 89	**WHY (re-issue)** *WEA U 7501*	56	5
20 Apr 91	**YOU'RE SO VAIN (re-issue)** *Elektra EKR 123*	41	5
22 Dec 01	**SON OF A GUN (I BETCHA THINK THIS SONG IS ABOUT YOU) (re)** *Virgin VUSCD 232* [1]	13	9
20 Jan 73 ●	**NO SECRETS** *Elektra K 42127* ▲	3	26
16 Mar 74	**HOT CAKES** *Elektra K 52005*	19	9
9 May 87	**COMING AROUND AGAIN** *Arista 208 140*	25	20
3 Sep 88	**GREATEST HITS LIVE** *Arista 209196*	49	6
20 Mar 99	**NOBODY DOES IT BETTER – THE VERY BEST OF CARLY SIMON** *Warner.ESP / Global TV RADCD 103*	22	6

[1] Janet with Carly Simon featuring Missy Elliott

'Mockingbird' was a duet with uncredited vocals by James Taylor

See also Will POWERS

Joe SIMON *US, male vocalist (Singles: 10 weeks)* pos/wks

16 Jun 73	**STEP BY STEP** *Mojo 2093 030*	14	10

Paul SIMON (129 Top 500) *Acclaimed award-winning singer / songwriter b. 13 Oct 1941, New Jersey, US. Recorded under various names in early 1960s before forming top duo Simon and Garfunkel. Married to actress Carrie Fisher (1983-85) and later Edie Brickell. Also helped to popularise world music (Singles: 85 weeks, Albums: 291 weeks)* pos/wks

19 Feb 72 ●	**MOTHER AND CHILD REUNION** *CBS 7793*	5	12
29 Apr 72	**ME AND JULIO DOWN BY THE SCHOOLYARD** *CBS 7964*	15	9
16 Jun 73 ●	**TAKE ME TO THE MARDI GRAS** *CBS 1578*	7	11
22 Sep 73	**LOVES ME LIKE A ROCK** *CBS 1700*	39	5
10 Jan 76	**50 WAYS TO LEAVE YOUR LOVER** *CBS 3887* ▲	23	6
3 Dec 77	**SLIP SLIDIN' AWAY** *CBS 5770*	36	5
6 Sep 80	**LATE IN THE EVENING** *Warner Bros. K 17666*	58	4
13 Sep 86 ●	**YOU CAN CALL ME AL** *Warner Bros. W 8667*	4	13
13 Dec 86	**THE BOY IN THE BUBBLE** *Warner Bros. W 8509*	26	8
6 Oct 90	**THE OBVIOUS CHILD** *Warner Bros. W 9549*	15	10
9 Dec 95	**SOMETHING SO RIGHT** *RCA 74321332392* [1]	44	2
26 Feb 72 ★	**PAUL SIMON** *CBS 69007*	1	26
2 Jun 73 ●	**THERE GOES RHYMIN' SIMON** *CBS 69035*	4	22
1 Nov 75 ●	**STILL CRAZY AFTER ALL THESE YEARS** *CBS 86001* ▲	6	31
3 Dec 77 ●	**GREATEST HITS ETC.** *CBS 10007*	6	15
30 Aug 80	**ONE-TRICK PONY** *Warner Bros. K 56846*	17	12
12 Nov 83	**HEARTS AND BONES** *Warner Bros. 9239421*	34	8
13 Sep 86 ★	**GRACELAND** *Warner Bros. WX 52*	1	115
24 Jan 87	**GREATEST HITS ETC. (re-issue)** *CBS 450 1661*	73	2
5 Nov 88	**NEGOTIATIONS AND LOVE SONGS 1971-1986** *Warner Bros. WX 223*	17	15

27 Oct 90 ★	**THE RHYTHM OF THE SAINTS** *Warner Bros. WX 340* ■	1	28
23 Nov 91	**PAUL SIMON'S CONCERT IN THE PARK – AUGUST 15TH 1991** *Warner Bros. WX 448*	60	1
27 May 00 ●	**GREATEST HITS – SHINING LIKE A NATIONAL GUITAR** *Warner Bros. 9362477212*	6	12
14 Oct 00	**YOU'RE THE ONE** *Warner Bros. 9362478442*	20	4

1 Annie Lennox featuring Paul Simon

See also SIMON and GARFUNKEL

Ronni SIMON *UK, male vocalist (Singles: 2 weeks)* pos/wks

13 Aug 94	**B GOOD 2 ME** *Network NWKCD 80*	73	1
10 Jun 95	**TAKE YOU THERE** *Network NWKCD 85*	58	1

Tito SIMON *Jamaica, male vocalist (Singles: 4 weeks)* pos/wks

8 Feb 75	**THIS MONDAY MORNING FEELING** *Horse HOSS 57*	45	4

SIMON and GARFUNKEL (15 Top 500)

The most successful recording duo ever: singer / songwriter / guitarist Paul Simon, b. 13 Oct 1941, New Jersey, and vocalist Art Garfunkel b. 5 Nov 1941, New York. The pair met at high school and joined doo-wop group The Peptones. Their first US hit came as Tom & Jerry in 1957. They then both recorded solo with Simon charting in the US as both Jerry Landis and Tico and The Triumphs. The duo reunited and released 'Wednesday Morning: 3AM'. When this album flopped, Simon went on a solo UK folk club tour (when he penned 'Homeward Bound'). Producer Tom Wilson remixed album track, 'The Sound of Silence', transforming it into a folk rock track that quickly took off. Paul rushed home, reunited with Art and the rest is history. Before splitting in 1971, they won numerous Grammy awards, became the first duo to top either the UK and US album chart, and at times had three of America's Top 5 albums (1968). 'Greatest Hits' is the world's biggest seller by a duo (13m in the US alone) and 'Bridge Over Troubled Water' (surely the most performed song on reality TV pop shows) was voted Best Single of All Time at the Brits (1977), while its parent LP, the UK's top seller in 1970 and 1971, was named Best Album. The duo, who reunite occasionally for tours (the latest being 2003), were inducted into the Rock and Roll Hall of Fame (1990) and received a Lifetime Achievement Grammy (2003) (Singles: 87 weeks, Albums: 1103 weeks) pos/wks

24 Mar 66 ●	**HOMEWARD BOUND** *CBS 202045*	9	12
16 Jun 66	**I AM A ROCK** *CBS 202303*	17	10
10 Jul 68 ●	**MRS ROBINSON** *CBS 3443* ▲	4	12
8 Jan 69 ●	**MRS ROBINSON (EP)** *CBS EP 6400*	9	5
30 Apr 69 ●	**THE BOXER** *CBS 4162*	6	14
21 Feb 70 ★	**BRIDGE OVER TROUBLED WATER (re)** *CBS 4790* 1 ▲	1	20
7 Oct 72	**AMERICA** *CBS 8336*	25	7
7 Dec 91	**A HAZY SHADE OF WINTER / SILENT NIGHT – SEVEN O'CLOCK NEWS** *Columbia 6576537*	30	6
15 Feb 92	**THE BOXER (re-issue)** *Columbia 6578067*	75	1
16 Apr 66	**SOUNDS OF SILENCE** *CBS 62690*	13	104
3 Aug 68 ★	**BOOKENDS** *CBS 63101* ▲	1	77
31 Aug 68	**PARSLEY SAGE ROSEMARY AND THYME** *CBS 62860*	13	58
26 Oct 68 ●	**THE GRADUATE (FILM SOUNDTRACK)** *CBS 70042* ▲	3	71
9 Nov 68	**WEDNESDAY MORNING 3 A.M.** *CBS 63370*	24	6
21 Feb 70 ★	**BRIDGE OVER TROUBLED WATER** *CBS 63699* ■ ▲	1	307
22 Jul 72 ●	**SIMON AND GARFUNKEL'S GREATEST HITS** *CBS 69003*	2	283
4 Apr 81	**SOUNDS OF SILENCE (re-issue)** *CBS 32020*	68	1
21 Nov 81 ●	**THE SIMON AND GARFUNKEL COLLECTION** *CBS 10029*	4	80
20 Mar 82 ●	**THE CONCERT IN CENTRAL PARK** *Geffen GEF 96008*	6	43
30 Nov 91 ●	**THE DEFINITIVE SIMON AND GARFUNKEL** *Columbia MOODCD 21*	8	57
5 Feb 00 ●	**TALES FROM NEW YORK – THE VERY BEST OF SIMON AND GARFUNKEL** *Columbia SONYTV 81CD*	8	12
6 Dec 03	**THE ESSENTIAL SIMON AND GARFUNKEL** *Columbia 5134702*	25	4+

1 Keyboard: Larry Knechtel

Tracks on Mrs Robinson (EP): Mrs Robinson / Scarborough Fair – Canticle / The Sound of Silence / April Come She Will. This EP would have stayed more than five weeks on chart had a decision to exclude EPs from the chart in Feb 1969 not been taken

See also Art GARFUNKEL; Paul SIMON

SIMONE *US, female vocalist (Singles: 1 week)* pos/wks

23 Nov 91	**MY FAMILY DEPENDS ON ME** *Strictly Rhythm A 8678*	75	1

Nina SIMONE *US, female vocalist / instrumentalist – keyboards – Eunice Waymon, d. 21 Apr 2003 (Singles: 46 weeks, Albums: 33 weeks)* pos/wks

5 Aug 65	**I PUT A SPELL ON YOU** *Philips BF 1415*	49	1
16 Oct 68 ●	**AIN'T GOT NO – I GOT LIFE / DO WHAT YOU GOTTA DO** *RCA 1743*	2	18
15 Jan 69 ●	**TO LOVE SOMEBODY** *RCA 1779*	5	9
15 Jan 69	**I PUT A SPELL ON YOU (re-issue)** *Philips BF 1736*	28	4
31 Oct 87 ●	**MY BABY JUST CARES FOR ME** *Charly CYZ 7112*	5	11
9 Jul 94	**FEELING GOOD** *Mercury MERCD 403*	40	3
24 Jul 65	**I PUT A SPELL ON YOU** *Philips BL 7671*	18	3
15 Feb 69	**NUFF SAID** *RCS SF 7979*	11	1
14 Nov 87	**MY BABY JUST CARES FOR ME** *Charly CR 30217*	56	8
16 Jul 94 ●	**FEELING GOOD – THE VERY BEST OF NINA SIMONE** *PolyGram TV 5226692*	9	8
7 Feb 98	**BLUE FOR YOU – THE VERY BEST OF NINA SIMONE** *Global Television RADCD 84*	12	10
21 Jun 03	**GOLD** *UCJ 9808087*	27	3

'Do What You Gotta Do' was listed only for the first eight weeks of the record's chart run. It peaked at No.7

Victor SIMONELLI presents SOLUTION

US, male producer (Singles: 1 week) pos/wks

2 Nov 96	**FEELS SO RIGHT** *Soundproof MCSTD 40068*	63	1

SIMPLE KID *UK, male vocalist – Phil Nicholls (Singles: 1 week)* pos/wks

13 Sep 03	**THE AVERAGE MAN** *2M 2M 005CD*	72	1

SIMPLE MINDS (66 Top 500)

Most successful Scottish band of the 1980s, fronted by Jim Kerr (b. 9 Jul 1959, Glasgow), who married Chrissie Hynde, lead singer of Pretenders. Five of the quintet's albums entered the UK chart at No.1, and world sales topped 30 million (Singles: 190 weeks, Albums: 354 weeks) pos/wks

12 May 79	**LIFE IN A DAY** *Zoom ZUM 10*	62	2
23 May 81	**THE AMERICAN** *Virgin VS 410*	59	3
15 Aug 81	**LOVE SONG** *Virgin VS 434*	47	4
7 Nov 81	**SWEAT IN BULLET** *Virgin VS 451*	52	3
10 Apr 82	**PROMISED YOU A MIRACLE** *Virgin VS 488*	13	11
28 Aug 82	**GLITTERING PRIZE** *Virgin VS 511*	16	11
13 Nov 82	**SOMEONE SOMEWHERE (IN SUMMERTIME)** *Virgin VS 538*	36	5
26 Nov 83	**WATERFRONT** *Virgin VS 636*	13	10
28 Jan 84	**SPEED YOUR LOVE TO ME** *Virgin VS 649*	20	4
24 Mar 84	**UP ON THE CATWALK** *Virgin VS 661*	27	5
20 Apr 85 ●	**DON'T YOU (FORGET ABOUT ME) (4re)** *Virgin VS 749* ▲	7	24
12 Oct 85 ●	**ALIVE AND KICKING (re)** *Virgin VS 817*	7	11
1 Feb 86 ●	**SANCTIFY YOURSELF** *Virgin SM 1*	10	7
12 Apr 86 ●	**ALL THE THINGS SHE SAID (re)** *Virgin VS 860*	9	9
15 Nov 86	**GHOSTDANCING (re)** *Virgin VS 907*	13	8
20 Jun 87	**PROMISED YOU A MIRACLE** *Virgin SM 2*	19	7
18 Feb 89 ★	**BELFAST CHILD** *Virgin SMX 3*	1	11
22 Apr 89	**THIS IS YOUR LAND** *Virgin SMX4*	13	4
29 Jul 89	**KICK IT IN** *Virgin SM 5*	15	5
9 Dec 89	**THE AMSTERDAM EP** *Virgin SMX 6*	18	6
23 Mar 91 ●	**LET THERE BE LOVE** *Virgin VS 1332*	6	7
25 May 91	**SEE THE LIGHTS** *Virgin VS 1343*	20	4
31 Aug 91	**STAND BY LOVE** *Virgin VS 1358*	13	4
26 Oct 91	**REAL LIFE** *Virgin VS 1382*	34	3
10 Oct 92 ●	**LOVE SONG / ALIVE AND KICKING (re-issue)** *Virgin VS 1440*	6	6
28 Jan 95 ●	**SHE'S A RIVER** *Virgin VSCDX 1509*	9	5
8 Apr 95	**HYPNOTISED** *Virgin VSCDX 1534*	18	5
14 Mar 98	**GLITTERBALL** *Chrysalis CDCHSS 5078*	18	2
30 May 98	**WAR BABIES** *Chrysalis CDCHS 5088*	43	1
2 Feb 02	**BELFAST TRANCE** *Nebula BELFCD 001* 1	74	1
30 Mar 02	**CRY** *Eagle EAGXS 218*	47	1
20 Jul 02	**MONSTER** *Defected DFECT 49* 2	67	1
5 May 79	**A LIFE IN THE DAY** *Zoom ZULP 1*	30	6
27 Sep 80	**EMPIRES AND DANCE** *Arista SPART 1140*	41	3
12 Sep 81	**SONS AND FASCINATIONS / SISTERS FEELINGS CALL** *Virgin V 2207*	11	7

27 Feb 82	**CELEBRATION** *Arista SPART 1183*	45	7
25 Sep 82 ●	**NEW GOLD DREAM (81 82 83 84)** *Virgin V 2230*	3	52
18 Feb 84 ★	**SPARKLE IN THE RAIN** *Virgin V 2300* ■	1	57
2 Nov 85 ★	**ONCE UPON A TIME** *Virgin V 2364* ■	1	83
6 Jun 87 ★	**LIVE IN THE CITY OF LIGHT** *Virgin V SMDL 1* ■	1	26
13 May 89 ★	**STREET FIGHTING YEARS** *Virgin MINDS 1* ■	1	28
20 Apr 91 ●	**REAL LIFE** *Virgin V 2660*	2	25
24 Oct 92 ★	**GLITTERING PRIZE 81/92** *Virgin SMTVD 1* ■	1	39
11 Feb 95 ●	**GOOD NEWS FROM THE NEXT WORLD** *Virgin CDV 2760*	2	14
28 Mar 98	**NEAPOLIS** *Chrysalis 4937122*	19	3
17 Nov 01	**THE BEST OF SIMPLE MINDS** *Virgin CDVD 2953*	34	4

[1] John 'OO' Fleming vs Simple Minds [2] Liquid People vs Simple Minds

The 1987 version of 'Promised You a Miracle' was a live recording. Tracks on The Amsterdam EP: Let It All Come Down / Jerusalem / Sign of the Times

SIMPLE PLAN

US, male vocal / instrumental group (Singles: 9 weeks) pos/wks

5 Jul 03	**ADDICTED** *Lava / Atlantic AT 0158 CD*	63	1

SIMPLICIOUS *US, male vocal group (Singles: 9 weeks)* pos/wks

29 Sep 84	**LET HER FEEL IT** *Fourth & Broadway BRW 13*	65	3
2 Feb 85	**LET HER FEEL IT (re-issue)** *Fourth & Broadway BRW 18*	34	6

The re-issue of 'Let Her Feel It' was listed with 'Personality' by Eugene Wilde

SIMPLY RED (28 Top 500)

The unmistakable Mick Hucknall (b. 8 Jun 1960, Manchester, UK) quickly became the representative face and voice of this internationally popular outfit. Their 'Stars' album sold more than two million in the UK and was the biggest British seller in 1991 and 1992. Best-selling single 'Fairground' 783,000 (Singles: 232 weeks, Albums: 597 weeks) pos/wks

15 Jun 85	**MONEY'S TOO TIGHT (TO MENTION)** *Elektra EKR 9*	13	12
21 Sep 85	**COME TO MY AID** *Elektra EKR 19*	66	2
16 Nov 85	**HOLDING BACK THE YEARS** *Elektra EKR 29* ▲	51	4
8 Mar 86	**JERICHO** *WEA YZ 63*	53	3
17 May 86 ●	**HOLDING BACK THE YEARS (re-issue)** *WEA YZ 70*	2	13
9 Aug 86	**OPEN UP THE RED BOX** *WEA YZ 75*	61	4
14 Feb 87	**THE RIGHT THING** *WEA YZ 103*	11	10
23 May 87	**INFIDELITY** *Elektra YZ 114*	31	5
28 Nov 87	**EV'RY TIME WE SAY GOODBYE** *Elektra YZ 161*	11	9
12 Mar 88	**I WON'T FEEL BAD** *Elektra YZ 172*	68	3
28 Jan 89	**IT'S ONLY LOVE** *Elektra YZ 349*	13	8
8 Apr 89 ●	**IF YOU DON'T KNOW ME BY NOW** *Elektra YZ 377* ▲	2	10
8 Jul 89	**A NEW FLAME** *WEA YZ 404*	17	8
28 Oct 89	**YOU'VE GOT IT** *Elektra YZ 424*	46	3
21 Sep 91	**SOMETHING GOT ME STARTED** *East West YZ 614*	11	8
30 Nov 91 ●	**STARS** *East West YZ 626*	8	10
8 Feb 92 ●	**FOR YOUR BABIES** *East West YZ 642*	9	8
2 May 92	**THRILL ME** *East West YZ 671*	33	5
25 Jul 92	**YOUR MIRROR** *East West YZ 689*	17	4
21 Nov 92	**MONTREUX (EP)** *East West YZ 716*	11	10
30 Sep 95 ★	**FAIRGROUND** *East West EW 001CD1* ■	1	14
16 Dec 95	**REMEMBERING THE FIRST TIME** *East West EW 015CD1*	22	6
24 Feb 96	**NEVER NEVER LOVE** *East West EW 029CD1*	18	4
22 Jun 96	**WE'RE IN THIS TOGETHER** *East West EW 046CD1*	11	6
9 Nov 96 ●	**ANGEL** *East West EW 074CD1*	4	13
20 Sep 97	**NIGHT NURSE** *East West EW 129CD1* [1]	13	8
16 May 98 ●	**SAY YOU LOVE ME** *East West EW 164CD*	7	7
22 Aug 98 ●	**THE AIR THAT I BREATHE** *East West EW 3821CD*	6	7
12 Dec 98	**GHETTO GIRL** *East West EW 191CD1*	34	2
30 Oct 99	**AIN'T THAT A LOT OF LOVE** *East West EW 208CD1*	14	6
19 Feb 00	**YOUR EYES** *East West EW 212CD1*	26	2
29 Mar 03 ●	**SUNRISE** *Simplyred.com SRS 001CD1*	7	11
19 Jul 03	**FAKE** *Simplyred.com SRS 002CD1*	21	4
13 Dec 03 ●	**YOU MAKE ME FEEL BRAND NEW** *Simplyred.com SRS 003CD1*	7	3+
26 Oct 85 ●	**PICTURE BOOK** *Elektra EKT 27*	2	130
21 Mar 87 ●	**MEN AND WOMEN** *WEA WX 85*	2	60
25 Feb 89 ★	**A NEW FLAME** *Elektra WX 242* ■	1	84
12 Oct 91 ★	**STARS** *East West WX 427* ■	1	134
21 Oct 95 ★	**LIFE** *East West 0630120692* ■	1	47
24 Feb 96	**A NEW FLAME (re-issue)** *East West K 2446892*	28	6
24 Feb 96	**PICTURE BOOK (re-issue)** *East West 9031769932*	33	5
2 Mar 96	**MEN AND WOMEN (re-issue)** *East West K 2420712*	50	3
19 Oct 96 ★	**GREATEST HITS** *East West 630165522* ■	1	52
30 May 98 ★	**BLUE** *East West 3984230972* ■	1	26
13 Nov 99 ●	**LOVE AND THE RUSSIAN WINTER** *East West 3984299422*	6	17
25 Nov 00	**IT'S ONLY LOVE** *East West 8573855372*	27	6
5 Apr 03 ●	**HOME** *Simplyred.com SRA001CD*	2	27+

[1] Sly and Robbie featuring Simply Red

Tracks on Montreux (EP): Drowning In My Own Tears / Grandma's Hands / Lady Godiva's Room / Love for Sale

SIMPLY RED AND WHITE

UK, male Sunderland FC supporters vocal group (Singles: 4 weeks) pos/wks

6 Apr 96	**DAYDREAM BELIEVER (CHEER UP PETER REID) (re)** *Ropery SHAYISGOD 1D*	41	4

SIMPLY SMOOTH

US, male / female vocal group (Singles: 1 week) pos/wks

17 Oct 98	**LADY (YOU BRING ME UP)** *Big Bang CDBANG 07*	70	1

Jessica SIMPSON

US, female vocalist (Singles: 24 weeks, Albums: 2 weeks) pos/wks

22 Apr 00 ●	**I WANNA LOVE YOU FOREVER (re)** *Columbia 6691272*	7	11
15 Jul 00	**I THINK I'M IN LOVE WITH YOU** *Columbia 6695942*	15	7
14 Jul 01	**IRRESISTIBLE** *Columbia 6714102*	11	6
6 May 00	**SWEET KISSES** *Columbia 4949332*	36	2

Paul SIMPSON featuring ADEVA *US, producer / instrumentalist with female vocalist (Singles: 8 weeks)* pos/wks

25 Mar 89	**MUSICAL FREEDOM (MOVING ON UP)** *Cooltempo CDCOOL 182*	22	8

Vida SIMPSON

US, female vocalist (Singles: 1 week) pos/wks

18 Feb 95	**OOHHH BABY** *Hi-Life HICD 6*	70	1

SIMPSONS *US, male / female cartoon group, lead vocal – Bart Simpson (Nancy Cartwright) (Singles: 19 weeks, Albums: 30 weeks)* pos/wks

26 Jan 91 ★	**DO THE BARTMAN** *Geffen GEF 87*	1	12
6 Apr 91 ●	**DEEP DEEP TROUBLE** *Geffen GEF 88* [1]	7	7
2 Feb 91 ●	**THE SIMPSONS SING THE BLUES** *Geffen 7599243081*	6	30

[1] Simpsons featuring Bart and Homer

Joyce SIMS

US, female vocalist (Singles: 36 weeks, Albums: 25 weeks) pos/wks

19 Apr 86	**ALL AND ALL** *London LON 94*	16	10
13 Jun 87	**LIFETIME LOVE** *London LON 137*	34	6
9 Jan 88 ●	**COME INTO MY LIFE** *London LON 161*	7	9
23 Apr 88	**WALK AWAY** *London LON 176*	24	6
17 Jun 89	**LOOKING FOR A LOVE** *ffrr F 109*	39	4
27 May 95	**COME INTO MY LIFE (re-mix)** *Club Tools 0060435 CLU*	72	1
9 Jan 88 ●	**COME INTO MY LIFE** *London LONLP 47*	5	24
16 Sep 89	**ALL ABOUT LOVE** *London 828129 1*	64	1

Kym SIMS

US, female vocalist (Singles: 23 weeks, Albums: 2 weeks) pos/wks

7 Dec 91 ●	**TOO BLIND TO SEE IT** *Atco B 8667*	5	12
28 Mar 92	**TAKE MY ADVICE** *Atco B 8591*	13	7
27 Jun 92	**A LITTLE BIT MORE** *Atco B 8528*	30	3
8 Jun 96	**WE GOTTA LOVE** *Pulse 8 CDLOSE 104*	58	1
18 Apr 92	**TOO BLIND TO SEE IT** *Atco 7567921042*	39	2

SIN WITH SEBASTIAN

Germany, male vocalist – Sebastian Roth (Singles: 2 weeks) pos/wks

16 Sep 95	**SHUT UP (AND SLEEP WITH ME)** *Sing Sing 74321253592*	44	1
27 Jan 96	**SHUT UP (AND SLEEP WITH ME) (re-mix)** *Sing Sing 74321337972*	46	1

Frank SINATRA (12) Top 500

Legendary entertainer regarded by many as the greatest song stylist of the 20th century, b. 12 Dec 1915, New Jersey, d. 14 May 1998. The vocalist (with Tommy Dorsey Orchestra) on first US No.1 'I'll Never Smile Again' (1940) was the first teen idol. 'Songs for Swingin' Lovers' is the only album to reach the UK Top 20 singles chart, and is one of 26 US gold albums amassed by the influential vocalist who has scored more US Top 10 LPs than any other soloist. Sinatra, the first recipient of a Grammy Lifetime Achievement award (1965), holds the UK chart longevity record with 'My Way' (Singles: 440 weeks, Albums: 889 weeks) pos/wks

9 Jul 54 **YOUNG-AT-HEART** *Capitol CL 14064* 12 1
16 Jul 54 ★ **THREE COINS IN THE FOUNTAIN** *Capitol CL 14120* 1 19
10 Jun 55 **YOU MY LOVE (2re)** *Capitol CL 14240* 13 7
5 Aug 55 ● **LEARNIN' THE BLUES** *Capitol CL 14296* 2 13
2 Sep 55 **NOT AS A STRANGER** *Capitol CL 14326* 18 1
13 Jan 56 ● **LOVE AND MARRIAGE** *Capitol CL 14503* 3 8
20 Jan 56 ● **(LOVE IS) THE TENDER TRAP** *Capitol CL 14511* 2 9
15 Jun 56 **SONGS FOR SWINGIN' LOVERS (LP)** *Capitol LCT 6106* 12 8
22 Nov 57 ● **ALL THE WAY / CHICAGO (3re)** *Capitol CL 14800* 3 20
7 Feb 58 **WITCHCRAFT** *Capitol CL 14819* 12 8
14 Nov 58 **MR SUCCESS (2re)** *Capitol CL 14956* 25 4
10 Apr 59 **FRENCH FOREIGN LEGION** *Capitol CL 14997* 18 5
15 May 59 **COME DANCE WITH ME! (LP)** *Capitol LCT 6179* [1] 30 1
28 Aug 59 ● **HIGH HOPES (2re)** *Capitol CL 15052* [2] 6 15
7 Apr 60 **IT'S NICE TO GO TRAV'LING** *Capitol CL 15116* 48 2
16 Jun 60 **RIVER STAY 'WAY FROM MY DOOR** *Capitol CL 15135* 18 9
8 Sep 60 **NICE 'N' EASY** *Capitol CL 15150* 15 12
24 Nov 60 **OL' MACDONALD** *Capitol CL 15168* 11 8
20 Apr 61 **MY BLUE HEAVEN** *Capitol CL 15193* 33 7
28 Sep 61 **GRANADA** *Reprise R 20010* 15 8
23 Nov 61 **THE COFFEE SONG** *Reprise R 20035* 39 3
5 Apr 62 **EV'RYBODY'S TWISTING** *Reprise R 20063* 22 12
13 Dec 62 **ME AND MY SHADOW (re)** *Reprise R 20128* [3] 20 9
7 Mar 63 **MY KIND OF GIRL** *Reprise R 20148* [4] 35 6
24 Sep 64 **HELLO DOLLY** *Reprise R 20351* [4] 47 1
12 May 66 ★ **STRANGERS IN THE NIGHT** *Reprise R 23052* ▲ 1 20
29 Sep 66 **SUMMER WIND** *Reprise RS 20509* 36 5
15 Dec 66 **THAT'S LIFE** *Reprise RS 20531* 44 5
23 Mar 67 ★ **SOMETHIN' STUPID** *Reprise RS 23166* [5] ▲ 1 18
23 Aug 67 **THE WORLD WE KNEW (OVER AND OVER)** *Reprise RS 20610* 33 11
2 Apr 69 ● **MY WAY (8re)** *Reprise RS 20817* 8 122
4 Oct 69 ● **LOVE'S BEEN GOOD TO ME** *Reprise RS 20852* 8 18
6 Mar 71 **I WILL DRINK THE WINE** *Reprise RS 23487* 16 12
20 Dec 75 **I BELIEVE I'M GONNA LOVE YOU** *Reprise K 14400* 34 7
9 Aug 80 ● **THEME FROM 'NEW YORK, NEW YORK' (re)** *Reprise K 14502* ..4 14
4 Dec 93 ● **I'VE GOT YOU UNDER MY SKIN** *Island CID 578* [6] 4 9
16 Apr 94 **MY WAY (re-issue)** *Reprise W 0163CD* 45 2
30 Jan 99 **THEY ALL LAUGHED** *Reprise W 469CD* 41 1
27 Aug 56 ★ **SONGS FOR SWINGIN' LOVERS** *Capitol LCT 6106* 1 34
16 Feb 57 ★ **THIS IS SINATRA!** *Capitol LCT 6123* 1 13
25 May 57 ● **CLOSE TO YOU** *Capitol LCT 6130* 2 9
20 Jul 57 ● **FRANKIE** *Philips BBL 7168* 3 7
7 Sep 57 ★ **A SWINGIN' AFFAIR!** *Capitol LCT 6135* 1 19
1 Mar 58 ● **WHERE ARE YOU?** *Capitol LCT 6152* 3 5
21 Jun 58 ● **THIS IS SINATRA (VOL.2)** *Capitol LCT 6155* 3 12
13 Sep 58 ● **COME FLY WITH ME** *Capitol LCT 6154* ▲ 2 18
29 Nov 58 ● **FRANK SINATRA STORY** *Fontana TFL 5030* 8 1
13 Dec 58 ● **FRANK SINATRA SINGS FOR ONLY THE LONELY** *Capitol LCT 6168* 5 13
16 May 59 ● **COME DANCE WITH ME!** *Capitol LCT 6179* 2 30
22 Aug 59 ● **LOOK TO YOUR HEART** *Capitol LCT 6181* 5 8
11 Jun 60 ● **COME BACK TO SORRENTO** *Fontana TFL 5082* 6 9
29 Oct 60 ● **SWING EASY** *Capitol W 587* 5 17
21 Jan 61 ● **NICE 'N EASY** *Capitol W 1417* ▲ 4 27
15 Jul 61 **SINATRA SOUVENIR** *Fontana TFL 5138* 18 1
19 Aug 61 ● **WHEN YOUR LOVER HAS GONE** *Encore ENC 101* 6 10
23 Sep 61 ● **SINATRA'S SWINGIN' SESSION!!! AND MORE** *Capitol W 1491* ..6 8
28 Oct 61 ● **SINATRA SWINGS** *Reprise R 1002* 8 8
25 Nov 61 ● **SINATRA PLUS** *Fontana SET 303* 7 9
16 Dec 61 ● **RING-A-DING-DING** *Reprise R 1001* 8 9
17 Feb 62 **COME SWING WITH ME** *Capitol W 1594* 13 4
7 Apr 62 ● **I REMEMBER TOMMY ...** *Reprise R 1003* 10 12
9 Jun 62 ● **SINATRA AND STRINGS** *Reprise R 1004* 6 20
27 Oct 62 **GREAT SONGS FROM GREAT BRITAIN** *Reprise R 1006* 12 9
29 Dec 62 **SINATRA WITH SWINGING BRASS** *Reprise R 1005* 14 11
23 Feb 63 ● **SINATRA – BASIE** *Reprise R 1008* [1] 2 23
27 Jul 63 ● **CONCERT SINATRA** *Reprise R 1009* 8 18
5 Oct 63 ● **SINATRA'S SINATRA** *Reprise R 1010* 9 24
19 Sep 64 **IT MIGHT AS WELL BE SWING** *Reprise R 1012* 17 4
20 Mar 65 **SOFTLY AS I LEAVE YOU** *Reprise R 1013* 20 1
22 Jan 66 ● **A MAN AND HIS MUSIC** *Reprise R 1016* 9 19
21 May 66 **MOONLIGHT SINATRA** *Reprise R 1018* 18 8
2 Jul 66 ● **STRANGERS IN THE NIGHT** *Reprise R 1017* ▲ 4 18
1 Oct 66 ● **SINATRA AT 'THE SANDS'** *Reprise RLP 1019* 7 18
3 Dec 66 **FRANK SINATRA SINGS SONGS FOR PLEASURE** *MFP 1120*....26 2
25 Feb 67 **THAT'S LIFE** *Reprise RSLP 1020* 22 12
7 Oct 67 **FRANK SINATRA** *Reprise RSLP 1022* 28 5
19 Oct 68 ● **GREATEST HITS** *Reprise RSLP 1025* 8 38
7 Dec 68 **BEST OF FRANK SINATRA** *Capitol ST 21140* 17 10
7 Jun 69 ● **MY WAY** *Reprise RSLP 1029* 2 51
4 Oct 69 **A MAN ALONE – THE WORDS & MUSIC OF ROD MCKUEN** *Reprise RSLP 1030* 18 7
9 May 70 **WATERTOWN** *Reprise RSLP 1031* 14 9
12 Dec 70 ● **GREATEST HITS VOLUME 2** *Reprise RSLP 1032* 6 39
5 Jun 71 ● **SINATRA AND COMPANY** *Reprise RSLP 1033* 9 9
27 Nov 71 **FRANK SINATRA SINGS RODGERS AND HART** *Starline SRS 5083* 35 1
8 Jan 72 **GREATEST HITS VOLUME 2 (re-issue)** *Reprise K 44018* 29 3
8 Jan 72 **MY WAY (re-issue)** *Reprise K 44015* 35 1
1 Dec 73 **OL' BLUE EYES IS BACK** *Warner Bros. K 44249* 12 13
17 Aug 74 **SOME NICE THINGS I'VE MISSED** *Reprise K 54020* 35 3
15 Feb 75 **THE MAIN EVENT (TV SOUNDTRACK)** *Reprise K 54031* 30 2
14 Jun 75 **THE BEST OF OL' BLUE EYES** *Reprise K 54042* 30 3
19 Mar 77 ★ **PORTRAIT OF SINATRA** *Reprise K 64039* 1 18
13 May 78 ● **20 GOLDEN GREATS** *Capitol EMTV 10* 4 11
18 Aug 84 **L.A. IS MY LADY** *Qwest 925145* 41 8
22 Mar 86 **NEW YORK NEW YORK (GREATEST HITS)** *Warner Bros. WX 32* 13 12
4 Oct 86 **THE FRANK SINATRA COLLECTION** *Capitol EMTV 41* 40 5
6 Nov 93 ● **DUETS** *Capitol CDEST 2218* 5 14
26 Nov 94 **DUETS II** *Capitol CDEST 2245* 29 6
11 Mar 95 **THIS IS FRANK SINATRA 1953-1957** *Music For Pleasure CDDL 1275* 56 1
2 Dec 95 **SINATRA 80TH – ALL THE BEST** *Capitol CDESTD 2* 49 5
16 Aug 97 ● **MY WAY – THE BEST OF FRANK SINATRA** *Reprise 9362467122* 7 129
24 Jun 00 ● **CLASSIC SINATRA – HIS GREAT PERFORMANCES 1953-1960** *Capitol 5235022* 10 7
9 Feb 02 ● **A FINE ROMANCE – THE LOVE SONGS OF FRANK SINATRA** *Reprise 8122735892* 6 9

[1] Frank Sinatra with Billy May and His Orchestra [2] Frank Sinatra with a bunch of kids [3] Frank Sinatra and Sammy Davis Jr [4] Frank Sinatra with Count Basie [5] Nancy Sinatra and Frank Sinatra [6] Frank Sinatra with Bono [1] Frank Sinatra and Count Basie

As a re-entry 'My Way' peaked at No.49, No.30, No.33, No.28 and No.18 in 1970, No.22 and No.39 in 1971 and No.50 in 1972. 'Theme From 'New York, New York' reached its peak position only on re-entry in Feb 1996. Tracks on Songs for Swingin' Lovers (LP): You Make Me Feel So Young / It Happened In Monterey / You're Getting to Be a Habit with Me / You Brought a New Kind of Love to Me / Too Marvellous for Words / Old Devil Moon / Pennies from Heaven / Love Is Here to Stay / I've Got You Under My Skin / I Thought About You / We'll Be Together Again / Makin' Whoopee / Swingin' Down the Lane / Anything Goes / How About You. Tracks on Come Dance With Me (LP): Come Dance With Me / Something's Gotta Give / Just in Time / Dancing in the Dark / Too Close for Comfort / I Could Have Danced All Night / Saturday Night Is the Loneliest Night of the week / Day In Day Out / Cheek to Cheek / Baubles Bangles and Beads / The Song Is You / The Last Dance. 'All the Way' and 'Chicago', Capitol CL 14800, were at first billed separately, then together for one week, then 'All the Way' on its own. 'I've Got You Under My Skin' was the flip side of 'Stay (Faraway So Close)' by U2 'Songs For Swingin' Lovers' was re-released in 98 with a new catalogue number Capitol CDP7465702

Nancy SINATRA

US, female vocalist (Singles: 99 weeks, Albums: 32 weeks) pos/wks

27 Jan 66 ★ **THESE BOOTS ARE MADE FOR WALKIN'** *Reprise R 20432* ▲ ..1 14
28 Apr 66 **HOW DOES THAT GRAB YOU DARLIN'** *Reprise R 20461* 19 8
19 Jan 67 ● **SUGAR TOWN** *Reprise RS 20527* 8 10

23 Mar 67 ★	**SOMETHIN' STUPID** *Reprise RS 23166* 1 ▲	**1** 18
5 Jul 67	**YOU ONLY LIVE TWICE / JACKSON** *Reprise RS 20595* 2	**11** 19
8 Nov 67	**LADYBIRD** *Reprise RS 20629* 3	**47** 1
29 Nov 69	**THE HIGHWAY SONG** *Reprise RS 20869*	**21** 10
21 Aug 71 ●	**DID YOU EVER** *Reprise K 14093* 4	**2** 19
16 Apr 66	**BOOTS** *Reprise R 6202*	**12** 9
18 Jun 66	**HOW DOES THAT GRAB YOU** *Reprise R 6207*	**17** 3
29 Jun 68	**NANCY AND LEE** *Reprise RSLP 6273* 1	**17** 12
10 Oct 70	**NANCY'S GREATEST HITS** *Reprise RSLP 6409*	**39** 3
25 Sep 71	**NANCY AND LEE (re-issue)** *Reprise K 44126* 1	**42** 1
29 Jan 72	**DID YOU EVER** *RCA Victor SF 8240* 1	**31** 4

1 Nancy Sinatra and Frank Sinatra 2 Nancy Sinatra / Nancy Sinatra and Lee Hazlewood 3 Nancy Sinatra and Lee Hazlewood 4 Nancy and Lee 1 Nancy Sinatra and Lee Hazlewood

'Jackson' listed with 'You Only Live Twice' from 12 Jul 1967

SINCLAIR

UK, male vocalist – Mike Sinclair (Singles: 8 weeks) pos/wks

21 Aug 93	**AIN'T NO CASANOVA** *Dome CDDOME 1004*	**28** 5
26 Feb 94	**(I WANNA KNOW) WHY** *Dome CDDOME 1009*	**58** 2
6 Aug 94	**DON'T LIE** *Dome CDDOME 1010*	**70** 1

Bob SINCLAR

France, male DJ / Producer (Singles: 10 weeks) pos/wks

20 Mar 99	**MY ONLY LOVE** *East West EW 196CD* 1	**56** 1
19 Aug 00 ●	**I FEEL FOR YOU** *Defected DEFECT 18CDS*	**9** 5
7 Apr 01	**DARLIN'** *Defected DFECT 30CDS* 2	**46** 1
25 Jan 03	**THE BEAT GOES ON** *Defected DFTD 062CDS*	**33** 2
2 Aug 03	**KISS MY EYES** *Defected DFTD 070CDS*	**67** 1

1 Bob Sinclar featuring Lee A Genesis 2 Bob Sinclar featuring James Williams

SINDY *UK, female doll vocalist (Singles: 1 week)* pos/wks

5 Oct 96	**SATURDAY NIGHT** *Love This LUVTHISCD 13*	**70** 1

SINE

US, male / female vocal / instrumental group (Singles: 9 weeks) pos/wks

10 Jun 78	**JUST LET ME DO MY THING** *CBS 6351*	**33** 9

SINFONIA OF LONDON – See Peter AUTY and the SINFONIA OF LONDON conducted by Howard BLAKE

Talvin SINGH

UK, male multi-instrumentalist / producer (Albums: 5 weeks) pos/wks

18 Sep 99	**OK** *Island CID 8075*	**41** 4
7 Apr 01	**HA** *Island CID 8103*	**57** 1

SINGING CORNER meets DONOVAN

UK, male vocal group and male vocalist (Singles: 1 week) pos/wks

1 Dec 90	**JENNIFER JUNIPER** *Fontana SYP 1*	**68** 1

SINGING DOGS *Denmark, canine vocal group (Singles: 4 weeks)* pos/wks

25 Nov 55	**THE SINGING DOGS (MEDLEY)** *Nixa N 15009* 1	**13** 4

1 Don Carlos presents The Singing Dogs

Medley songs: Pat-a-Cake / Three Blind Mice / Jingle Bells / Oh Susanna

SINGING NUN (Soeur Sourire) *Belgium, female vocalist – Jeanine Deckers, d. 31 Mar 1985 (Singles: 14 weeks)* pos/wks

5 Dec 63 ●	**DOMINIQUE** *Philips BF 1293* ▲	**7** 14

SINGING SHEEP

UK, computerised sheep noises (Singles: 5 weeks) pos/wks

18 Dec 82	**BAA BAA BLACK SHEEP** *Sheep BAA 1*	**42** 5

Maxine SINGLETON *US, female vocalist (Singles: 3 weeks)* pos/wks

2 Apr 83	**YOU CAN'T RUN FROM LOVE** *Creole CR 50*	**57** 3

SINITTA *US, female vocalist – Sinitta Malone (Singles: 104 weeks, Albums: 23 weeks)* pos/wks

8 Mar 86 ●	**SO MACHO / CRUISING (re)** *Fanfare FAN 7*	**2** 28
11 Oct 86	**FEELS LIKE THE FIRST TIME** *Fanfare FAN 8*	**45** 5
25 Jul 87 ●	**TOY BOY** *Fanfare FAN 12*	**4** 14
12 Dec 87	**G.T.O.** *Fanfare FAN 14*	**15** 9
19 Mar 88 ●	**CROSS MY BROKEN HEART** *Fanfare FAN 15*	**6** 9
24 Sep 88	**I DON'T BELIEVE IN MIRACLES** *Fanfare FAN 16*	**22** 8
3 Jun 89 ●	**RIGHT BACK WHERE WE STARTED FROM** *Fanfare FAN 18*	**4** 10
7 Oct 89	**LOVE ON A MOUNTAIN TOP** *Fanfare FAN 21*	**20** 6
21 Apr 90	**HITCHIN' A RIDE** *Fanfare FAN 24*	**24** 6
22 Sep 90	**LOVE AND AFFECTION** *Fanfare FAN 31*	**62** 3
4 Jul 92	**SHAME SHAME SHAME** *Arista 74321100327*	**28** 4
17 Apr 93	**THE SUPREME EP** *Arista 74321139592*	**49** 2
26 Dec 87	**SINITTA!** *Fanfare BOYLP 1*	**34** 19
9 Dec 89	**WICKED!** *Fanfare FARE 2*	**52** 4

Tracks on The Supreme EP: Where Did Our Love Go / Stop! In the Name of Love / You Can't Hurry Love / Remember Me

SINNAMON

US, male vocal / instrumental group (Singles: 1 week) pos/wks

28 Sep 96	**I NEED YOU NOW** *Worx WORXCD 003*	**70** 1

SIOUXSIE and the BANSHEES (227 Top 500)

Long-running commercially successful UK punk band included Susan 'Siouxsie' Ballion (v), Steve Severin (b) (also recorded as The Glove), Siouxsie's husband, Peter 'Budgie' Clark (d) (who recorded with Siouxsie as The Creatures) and, at times, Cure front man Robert Smith (g) (Singles: 150 weeks, Albums: 119 weeks) pos/wks

26 Aug 78 ●	**HONG KONG GARDEN** *Polydor 2059 052*	**7** 10
31 Mar 79	**THE STAIRCASE (MYSTERY)** *Polydor POSP 9*	**24** 8
7 Jul 79	**PLAYGROUND TWIST** *Polydor POSP 59*	**28** 6
29 Sep 79	**MITTAGEISEN (METAL POSTCARD)** *Polydor 2059 151*	**47** 3
15 Mar 80	**HAPPY HOUSE** *Polydor POSP 117*	**17** 8
7 Jun 80	**CHRISTINE** *Polydor 2059 249*	**22** 8
6 Dec 80	**ISRAEL** *Polydor POSP 205*	**41** 8
30 May 81	**SPELLBOUND** *Polydor POSP 273*	**22** 8
1 Aug 81	**ARABIAN KNIGHTS** *Polydor POSP 309*	**32** 7
29 May 82	**FIRE WORKS** *Polydor POSPG 450*	**22** 6
9 Oct 82	**SLOWDIVE** *Polydor POSP 510*	**41** 4
4 Dec 82	**MELT / IL EST NÉ LE DIVIN ENFANT** *Polydor POSP 539*	**49** 5
1 Oct 83 ●	**DEAR PRUDENCE** *Wonderland SHE 4*	**3** 8
24 Mar 84	**SWIMMING HORSES** *Wonderland SHE 6*	**28** 4
2 Jun 84	**DAZZLE** *Wonderland SHE 7*	**33** 3
27 Oct 84	**THE THORN EP** *Wonderland SHEEP 8*	**47** 3
26 Oct 85	**CITIES IN DUST** *Wonderland SHE 9*	**21** 6
8 Mar 86	**CANDYMAN** *Wonderland SHE 10*	**34** 5
17 Jan 87	**THIS WHEEL'S ON FIRE** *Wonderland SHE 11*	**14** 6
28 Mar 87	**THE PASSENGER** *Wonderland SHE 12*	**41** 6
25 Jul 87	**SONG FROM THE EDGE OF THE WORLD** *Wonderland SHE 13*	**59** 3
30 Jul 88	**PEEK-A-BOO** *Wonderland SHE 14*	**16** 6
8 Oct 88	**THE KILLING JAR** *Wonderland SHE 15*	**41** 3
3 Dec 88	**THE LAST BEAT OF MY HEART** *Wonderland SHE 16*	**44** 1
25 May 91	**KISS THEM FOR ME** *Wonderland SHE 19*	**32** 4
13 Jul 91	**SHADOWTIME** *Wonderland SHE 20*	**57** 1
25 Jul 92	**FACE TO FACE** *Wonderland SHE 21*	**21** 4
20 Aug 94	**INTERLUDE** *Parlophone CDR 6365* 1	**25** 2
7 Jan 95	**O BABY** *Wonderland SHECD 22*	**34** 3
18 Feb 95	**STARGAZER** *Wonderland SHECD 23*	**64** 1
2 Dec 78	**THE SCREAM** *Polydor POLD 5009*	**12** 11
22 Sep 79	**JOIN HANDS** *Polydor POLD 5024*	**13** 5
16 Aug 80 ●	**KALEIDOSCOPE** *Polydor 2442 177*	**5** 6
27 Jun 81 ●	**JU JU** *Polydor POLS 1034*	**7** 17
12 Dec 81	**ONCE UPON A TIME – THE SINGLES** *Polydor POLS 1056*	**21** 26
13 Nov 82	**A KISS IN THE DREAMHOUSE** *Polydor POLD 5064*	**11** 11
3 Dec 83	**NOCTURNE** *Wonderland SHAH 1*	**29** 10
16 Jun 84	**HYAENA** *Wonderland SHELP 2*	**15** 6
26 Apr 86	**TINDERBOX** *Wonderland SHELP 3*	**13** 6
14 Mar 87	**THROUGH THE LOOKING GLASS** *Wonderland SHELP 4*	**15** 8
17 Sep 88	**PEEPSHOW** *Wonderland SHELP 5*	**20** 5

22 Jun 91 **SUPERSTITION** *Wonderland 8477311* 25 4
17 Oct 92 **TWICE UPON A TIME – THE SINGLES** *Wonderland 5171602* 26 2
28 Jan 95 **THE RAPTURE** *Wonderland 5237252* 33 2

1 Morrissey and Siouxsie

Tracks on The Thorn EP: Overground / Voices / Placebo Effect / Red Over White

See also GLOVE

SIR DOUGLAS QUINTET *US, male vocal / instrumental group – leader Doug Sahm, d. 18 Nov 1999 (Singles: 10 weeks)* pos/wks

17 Jun 65 **SHE'S ABOUT A MOVER** *London HLU 9964* 15 10

SIR KILLALOT vs ROBO BABE
UK, male robot rapper with female vocalist (Singles: 3 weeks) pos/wks

30 Dec 00 **ROBOT WARS (ANDROID LOVE)** *Polydor 5879362* 51 3

SIR MIX-A-LOT *US, male rapper (Singles: 2 weeks)* pos/wks

8 Aug 92 **BABY GOT BACK** *Def American DEFA 20* ▲ 56 2

SIRRON – *See PLUS ONE featuring SIRRON*

SISQO *US, male vocalist – Mark Andrews (Singles: 43 weeks, Albums: 41 weeks)* pos/wks

12 Feb 00 **GOT TO GET IT** *Def Soul 5626442* 14 4
22 Apr 00 ● **THONG SONG** *Def Soul 5688902* 3 14
30 Sep 00 ● **UNLEASH THE DRAGON** *Def Soul 5726422* 6 7
16 Dec 00 **INCOMPLETE** *Def Soul 5727542* ▲ 13 8
28 Jul 01 ● **DANCE FOR ME** *Def Soul 5887002* 6 10
26 Feb 00 **UNLEASH THE DRAGON** *Def Soul 5469392* 15 36
4 Aug 01 **RETURN OF DRAGON** *Def Soul 5864182* 22 5

See also DRU HILL

SISSEL
Norway, female vocalist (Singles: 7 weeks, Albums: 56 weeks) pos/wks

10 Jan 98 **PRINCE IGOR** *Def Jam 5749652* 1 ..... 15 7
20 May 95 **DEEP WITHIN MY SOUL** *Mercury 5267752* 58 1
31 Jan 98 ★ **TITANIC (FILM SOUNDTRACK)** *Sony Classical SK 63213* 1 ..... 1 55

1 Warren G featuring Sissel 1 James Horner - vocals by Sissel

See also Warren G ; James HORNER

SISTER BLISS *UK, female DJ / producer / instrumentalist – Ayalah Ben-Tovim (Singles: 11 weeks)* pos/wks

15 Oct 94 **CANTGETAMAN CANTGETAJOB (LIFE'S A BITCH)** *Go.Beat GODCD 124* 1 ..... 31 4
15 Jul 95 **OH! WHAT A WORLD** *Go.Beat GODCD 126* 1 ..... 40 2
29 Jun 96 **BAD MAN** *Junk Dog JDOGCD 1* 51 1
7 Oct 00 **SISTER SISTER** *Multiply CDMULTY 68* 34 2
24 Mar 01 **DELIVER ME** *Multiply CDMULTY 72* 2 ..... 31 2

1 Sister Bliss featuring Collette 2 Sister Bliss featuring John Martyn

SISTER SLEDGE 398 Top 500 *Successful US family group from Philadelphia: Kathy, Debra, Joni and Kim Sledge. They found more fame in the UK than in the US, and recorded some of the best-known disco records with noted producers / songwriters Nile Rodgers and Bernard Edwards (Singles: 111 weeks, Albums: 58 weeks)* pos/wks

21 Jun 75 **MAMA NEVER TOLD ME** *Atlantic K 10619* 20 6
17 Mar 79 ● **HE'S THE GREATEST DANCER** *Atlantic / Cotillion K 11257* 6 11
26 May 79 ● **WE ARE FAMILY** *Atlantic / Cotillion K 11293* 8 10
11 Aug 79 **LOST IN MUSIC** *Atlantic / Cotillion K 11337* 17 10
19 Jan 80 **GOT TO LOVE SOMEBODY** *Atlantic / Cotillion K 11404* 34 4
28 Feb 81 **ALL AMERICAN GIRLS** *Atlantic K 11656* 41 5
26 May 84 **THINKING OF YOU** *Cotillion / Atlantic B 9744* 11 13
8 Sep 84 ● **LOST IN MUSIC (re-mix)** *Cotillion / Atlantic B 9718* 4 12
17 Nov 84 **WE ARE FAMILY (re-mix)** *Cotillion / Atlantic B 9692* 33 4
1 Jun 85 ★ **FRANKIE** *Atlantic A 9547* 1 16
31 Aug 85 **DANCING ON THE JAGGED EDGE** *Atlantic A 9520* 50 3
23 Jan 93 ● **WE ARE FAMILY (2nd re-mix)** *Atlantic A 4508CD* 5 8
13 Mar 93 **LOST IN MUSIC (2nd re-mix)** *Atlantic A 4509CD* 14 5
12 Jun 93 **THINKING OF YOU (re-mix)** *Atlantic A 4515CD* 17 4
12 May 79 ● **WE ARE FAMILY** *Atlantic K 50587* 7 39
22 Jun 85 **WHEN THE BOYS MEET THE GIRLS** *Atlantic 7812551* 19 11
5 Dec 87 **FREAK OUT** *Telstar STAR 2319* 1 ..... 72 3
20 Feb 93 **THE VERY BEST OF SISTER SLEDGE 1973-1993** *Atlantic 9548318132* 19 5

1 Chic and Sister Sledge

SISTER 2 SISTER *Australia, female vocal duo – Christine and Sharon Muscat (Singles: 5 weeks)* pos/wks

22 Apr 00 **SISTER** *Mushroom MUSH 70CDS* 18 4
28 Oct 00 **WHAT'S A GIRL TO DO** *Mushroom MUSH 76CDS* 61 1

SISTERHOOD
UK, male vocal / instrumental group (Albums: 1 week) pos/wks

26 Jul 86 **GIFT** *Merciful Release SIS 020* 90 1

SISTERS OF MERCY *UK, male / female vocal / instrumental group – leader Andrew Eldritch (Singles: 40 weeks, Albums: 42 weeks)* pos/wks

16 Jun 84 **BODY AND SOUL / TRAIN** *Merciful Release MR 029* 46 3
20 Oct 84 **WALK AWAY** *Merciful Release MR 033* 45 3
9 Mar 85 **NO TIME TO CRY** *Merciful Release MR 035* 63 2
3 Oct 87 ● **THIS CORROSION** *Merciful Release MR 39* 7 6
27 Feb 88 **DOMINION** *Merciful Release MR 43* 13 6
18 Jun 88 **LUCRETIA MY REFLECTION** *Merciful Release MR 45* 20 4
13 Oct 90 **MORE** *Merciful Release MR 47* 14 4
22 Dec 90 **DOCTOR JEEP** *Merciful Release MR 51* 37 4
2 May 92 ● **TEMPLE OF LOVE** *Merciful Release MR 53* 3 5
28 Aug 93 **UNDER THE GUN** *Merciful Release MR 59CDX* 19 3
23 Mar 85 **FIRST AND LAST AND ALWAYS** *Merciful Release MR 337 L* 14 8
28 Nov 87 ● **FLOODLAND** *Merciful Release MR 441 L* 9 20
2 Nov 90 **VISION THING** *Merciful Release* 11 4
9 May 92 ● **SOME GIRLS WANDER BY MISTAKE** *Merciful Release 9031764762* 5 5
4 Sep 93 **GREATEST HITS VOLUME 1** *Merciful Release 4509935792* 14 5

Act was male only for first album

SIVUCA
Brazil, male instrumentalist (Singles: 3 weeks) pos/wks

28 Jul 84 **AIN'T NO SUNSHINE** *London LON 51* 56 3

SIX BY SEVEN *UK, male vocal / instrumental group (Singles: 2 weeks, Albums: 1 week)* pos/wks

9 May 98 **CANDLELIGHT** *Mantra MNT 34CD* 70 1
2 Mar 02 **I.O.U. LOVE** *Mantra MNT 68CD* 48 1
23 Mar 02 **THE WAY I FEEL TODAY** *Mantra MNTCD 1027* 69 1

6 BY SIX
UK, male instrumental / production duo (Singles: 1 week) pos/wks

4 May 96 **INTO YOUR HEART** *Six6 SIXCD 130* 51 1

SIX CHIX *UK, female vocal group (Singles: 1 week)* pos/wks

26 Feb 00 **ONLY THE WOMEN KNOW** *EMI CDCHIX 001* 72 1

666 *Germany, male / female vocal / instrumental group (Singles: 1 week)* pos/wks

3 Oct 98 **ALARMA** *Danceteria CDDAN 001* 58 1

666 *Holland, male production duo (Singles: 4 weeks)* pos/wks

25 Nov 00 **DEVIL** *Echo ECSCD 102* 18 4

SIXPENCE NONE THE RICHER *US, male / female vocal / instrumental group (Singles: 17 weeks, Albums: 3 weeks)* pos/wks

29 May 99 ● **KISS ME** *Elektra E 3750CD* 4 12
18 Sep 99 **THERE SHE GOES** *Elektra E 3728CD* 14 5
26 Jun 99 **SIXPENCE NONE THE RICHER** *Elektra 7559624202* 27 3

60FT DOLLS *UK, male vocal / instrumental group (Singles: 4 weeks, Albums: 2 weeks)*

			pos	wks
3 Feb 96		**STAY** *Indolent DOLLS 002CD*	**48**	1
11 May 96		**TALK TO ME** *Indolent DOLLS 003CD*	**37**	1
20 Jul 96		**HAPPY SHOPPER** *Indolent DOLLS 005CD*	**38**	1
9 May 98		**ALISON'S ROOM** *Indolent DOLLS 007CD1*	**61**	1
8 Jun 96		**THE BIG 3** *Indolent DOLLSCD 004*	**36**	2

SIZE 9 *US, male producer – Josh Wink (Singles: 4 weeks)*

			pos	wks
17 Jun 95		**I'M READY** *Virgin America VUSCD 92*	**52**	1
11 Nov 95		**I'M READY (re-issue)** *VC VCRD 2* [1]	**30**	3

[1] Josh Wink's Size 9

See also Josh WINK

Roni SIZE / REPRAZENT
UK, male producer – Ryan Williams with male / female vocal / instrumental group (Singles: 24 weeks, Albums: 39 weeks)

			pos	wks
14 Jun 97		**SHARE THE FALL** *Talkin Loud TLCD 21*	**37**	2
13 Sep 97		**HEROES** *Talkin Loud TLCD 25*	**31**	2
15 Nov 97		**BROWN PAPER BAG** *Talkin Loud TLCD 28*	**20**	3
14 Mar 98		**WATCHING WINDOWS** *Talkin Loud TLCD 31*	**28**	2
7 Oct 00		**WHO TOLD YOU** *Talkin Loud TLCD 61*	**17**	3
24 Mar 01		**DIRTY BEATS** *Talkin Loud TLCDD 63*	**32**	3
23 Jun 01		**LUCKY PRESSURE** *Talkin Loud TLCD 64*	**58**	1
19 Oct 02		**SOUND ADVICE** *Full Cycle FCY 044* [1]	**69**	1
9 Nov 02		**PLAYTIME** *Full Cycle FCY 045* [1]	**53**	2
7 Dec 02		**SCRAMBLED EGGS / SWINGS & ROUNDABOUTS** *Full Cycle FCY 046* [1]	**57**	1
18 Jan 03		**FEEL THE HEAT** *Full Cycle FCY 048*	**55**	1
22 Feb 03		**SNAPSHOT 3 / SORRY FOR YOU** *Full Cycle FCY 033* [1]	**61**	1
12 Jul 03		**SIREN SOUNDS / AT THE MOVIES** *Full Cycle FCY 054* [1]	**67**	1
6 Sep 03		**SOUND ADVICE (re-mix)/ FORGET ME KNOTS** *Full Cycle FCY 056*	**61**	1
5 Jul 97	●	**NEW FORMS** *Talkin Loud 5349332*	**8**	34
21 Oct 00		**IN THE MODE** *Talkin Loud 5481762*	**15**	4
2 Nov 02		**TOUCHING DOWN** *Full Cycle FCYCDLP 010* [1]	**72**	1

[1] Roni Size [1] Roni Size

SIZZLA
Jamaica, male rapper – Miguel Collins (Singles: 2 weeks)

			pos	wks
17 Apr 99		**RAIN SHOWERS** *Xterminator EXTCDS 76*	**51**	2

SKANDAL *UK, male vocal group (Singles: 1 week)*

			pos	wks
14 Oct 00		**CHAMPAGNE HIGHWAY** *Prestige Management CDGING 1*	**53**	1

SKATALITES
Jamaica, male instrumental group (Singles: 6 weeks)

			pos	wks
20 Apr 67		**GUNS OF NAVARONE** *Island WI 168*	**36**	6

SKEE-LO
US, male rapper – Antoine Roundtree (Singles: 10 weeks)

			pos	wks
9 Dec 95		**I WISH** *Wild Card 5777752*	**15**	8
27 Apr 96		**TOP OF THE STAIRS** *Wild Card 5763352*	**38**	2

Beverli SKEETE – *See DE-CODE featuring Beverli SKEETE*

Peter SKELLERN *UK, male vocalist / instrumentalist – keyboards (Singles: 24 weeks, Albums: 31 weeks)*

			pos	wks
23 Sep 72	●	**YOU'RE A LADY** *Decca F 13333*	**3**	11
29 Mar 75		**HOLD ON TO LOVE** *Decca F 13568*	**14**	9
28 Oct 78		**LOVE IS THE SWEETEST THING** *Mercury 6008 603* [1]	**60**	4
9 Sep 78		**SKELLERN** *Mercury 9109 701*	**48**	3
8 Dec 79		**ASTAIRE** *Mercury 9102 702*	**23**	20
4 Dec 82		**A STRING OF PEARLS** *Mercury MERL 10*	**67**	5
1 Apr 95		**STARDUST MEMORIES** *WEA 4509981322*	**50**	3

[1] Peter Skellern featuring The Grimethorpe Colliery Band

See also OASIS

SKIBADEE – *See SHY FX; T-POWER; DILLINJA*

SKID ROW *UK, male vocal / instrumental group (Albums: 3 weeks)*

			pos	wks
17 Oct 70		**SKID** *CBS 63965*	**30**	3

SKID ROW *US, male vocal / instrumental group (Singles: 27 weeks, Albums: 28 weeks)*

			pos	wks
18 Nov 89		**YOUTH GONE WILD** *Atlantic A 8935*	**42**	3
3 Feb 90		**18 AND LIFE** *Atlantic A 8883*	**12**	6
31 Mar 90		**I REMEMBER YOU** *East West A 8886*	**36**	4
15 Jun 91		**MONKEY BUSINESS** *Atlantic A 7673*	**19**	3
14 Sep 91		**SLAVE TO THE GRIND** *Atlantic A 7603*	**43**	2
23 Nov 91		**WASTED TIME** *Atlantic A 7570*	**20**	3
29 Aug 92		**YOUTH GONE WILD / DELIVERING THE GOODS (re-issue)** *Atlantic A 7444*	**22**	4
18 Nov 95		**BREAKIN' DOWN** *Atlantic A 7135CD1*	**48**	2
2 Sep 89		**SKID ROW** *Atlantic 781936 1*	**30**	16
22 Jun 91	●	**SLAVE TO THE GRIND** *Atlantic WX 423* ▲	**5**	9
8 Apr 95	●	**SUBHUMAN RACE** *Atlantic 7567827302*	**8**	3

SKIDS *UK, male vocal / instrumental group (Singles: 60 weeks, Albums: 21 weeks)*

			pos	wks
23 Sep 78		**SWEET SUBURBIA (re)** *Virgin VS 227*	**70**	3
4 Nov 78		**THE SAINTS ARE COMING** *Virgin VS 232*	**48**	3
17 Feb 79	●	**INTO THE VALLEY** *Virgin VS 241*	**10**	11
26 May 79		**MASQUERADE** *Virgin VS 262*	**14**	9
29 Sep 79		**CHARADE** *Virgin VS 288*	**31**	6
24 Nov 79		**WORKING FOR THE YANKEE DOLLAR** *Virgin VS 306*	**20**	11
1 Mar 80		**ANIMATION** *Virgin VS 323*	**56**	3
16 Aug 80		**CIRCUS GAMES** *Virgin VS 359*	**32**	7
18 Oct 80		**GOODBYE CIVILIAN** *Virgin VS 373*	**52**	4
6 Dec 80		**WOMAN IN WINTER** *Virgin VSK 101*	**49**	3
17 Mar 79		**SCARED TO DANCE** *Virgin V 2116*	**19**	10
27 Oct 79		**DAYS IN EUROPA** *Virgin V 2138*	**32**	5
27 Sep 80	●	**THE ABSOLUTE GAME** *Virgin V 2174*	**9**	5
8 Jun 02		**THE GREATEST HITS OF BIG COUNTRY AND THE SKIDS – THE BEST OF STUART ADAMSON** *UMTV 5869892* [1]	**71**	1

[1] Big Country and the Skids

SKIN *UK / Germany, male vocal / instrumental group (Singles: 19 weeks Albums: 5 weeks)*

			pos	wks
25 Dec 93		**THE SKIN UP EP** *Parlophone CDR 6363*	**67**	2
12 Mar 94		**HOUSE OF LOVE** *Parlophone CDR 6374*	**45**	2
30 Apr 94		**THE MONEY EP** *Parlophone CDR 6381*	**18**	3
23 Jul 94		**TOWER OF STRENGTH** *Parlophone CDR 6387*	**19**	3
15 Oct 94		**LOOK BUT DON'T TOUCH (EP)** *Parlophone CDRS 6391*	**33**	3
20 May 95		**TAKE ME DOWN TO THE RIVER** *Parlophone CDR 6409*	**26**	2
23 Mar 96		**HOW LUCKY YOU ARE** *Parlophone CDR 6426*	**32**	2
18 May 96		**PERFECT DAY** *Parlophone CDR 6433*	**33**	2
14 May 94	●	**SKIN** *Parlophone CDPCSD 151*	**9**	3
6 Apr 96		**LUCKY** *Parlophone CDPCSD 168*	**38**	1
13 Sep 97		**EXPERIENCE ELECTRIC** *Reef Recordings SRECD 705*	**72**	1

Tracks on The Skin Up (EP): Look But Don't Touch / Shine Your Light / Monkey. Tracks on The Money EP: Money / Unbelievable / Express Yourself / Funktified. Tracks on Look But Don't Touch (EP): Look But Don't Touch / Should I Stay or Should I Go / Pump It Up / Monkey (re-issue).

SKIN *UK, female vocalist – Deborah Dyer (Singles: 4 weeks, , Albums: 2 weeks)*

			pos	wks
20 Jul 02		**GOOD TIMES** *Columbia 6727672* [1]	**49**	1
7 Jun 03		**TRASHED** *EMI CDEM 622*	**30**	2
20 Sep 03		**FAITHFULNESS** *EMI CDEM 624*	**64**	1
14 Jun 03		**FLESHWOUNDS** *EMI 5841592*	**43**	2

[1] Ed Case featuring Skin

See also SKUNK ANANSIE; MAXIM

SKIN UP *UK, male producer – Jason Cohen (Singles: 9 weeks)*

			pos	wks
7 Sep 91		**IVORY** *Love EVOL 4*	**48**	3
14 Mar 92		**A JUICY RED APPLE** *Love EVOL 11*	**32**	4
18 Jul 92		**ACCELERATE** *Love EVOL 17*	**45**	2

TOP 100

Our annual list of the Top 100 most successful acts in previous editions of British Hit Singles been ranked by weeks on the singles chart alone. In this, the first edition to combine singles and albums chart data, we now calculate the top 100 chart acts even more thoroughly taking into account the entire chart history of the acts in our database adding together their weeks spent on chart from both Hit Singles and Hit Albums. Elvis still rules the roost but a number of acts with moderate singles action but highly successful album chart careers, such as Dire Straits, Pink Floyd and Led Zeppelin, now take their rightful positions in the pantheon of popular music gods.

1 **ELVIS PRESLEY** 2,453
2 **CLIFF RICHARD** 1,959
3 **BEATLES** 1,740
4 **QUEEN** 1,694
5 **MADONNA** 1,637
6 **ELTON JOHN** 1,593
7 **SHADOWS** 1,462
8 **DAVID BOWIE** 1,441
9 **MICHAEL JACKSON** 1,425
10 **U2** 1,380
11 **ROD STEWART** 1,352
12 **FRANK SINATRA** 1,329
13 **DIANA ROSS** 1,300
14 **DIRE STRAITS** 1,252
15 **SIMON AND GARFUNKEL** 1,190
16 **ROLLING STONES** 1,173
17 **ABBA** 1,119
18 **FLEETWOOD MAC** 1,102
19 **PHIL COLLINS** 1,038
20 **PAUL McCARTNEY** 980
21 **PINK FLOYD** 966
22 **UB40** 949
23 **MEAT LOAF** 936
24 **TOM JONES** 903
25 **STATUS QUO** 881
26 **BEACH BOYS** 844
27 **OASIS** 831
28 **SIMPLY RED** 829
29 **STEVIE WONDER** 789
30 **CARPENTERS** 776

Diana Ross and **Madonna** (right), the most successful female solo artists in the history of popular music at positions No.13 and No.5 respectively in our Top 100 all time greats

ACTS

Any tied positions are decided according to the weeks acts have spent at No.1, then No.2 and so on.

Use the Top 500 symbol 500 Top 500 to check out an even larger ranking list of the most successful acts throughout the A-Z by Artist section

31 **BEE GEES** 760
32 **BOB DYLAN** 751
33 **TINA TURNER** 745
34 **PRINCE** 741
35 **R.E.M.** 732
36 **JIM REEVES** 727
37 **NEIL DIAMOND** 709
38 **BOB MARLEY AND THE WAILERS** 703
39 **ERIC CLAPTON** 693
40 **WHITNEY HOUSTON** 692
41 **ANDY WILLIAMS** 685
42 **EURYTHMICS** 684
43 **MADNESS** 682
44 **GENESIS** 678
45 **BRUCE SPRINGSTEEN** 667
46 **MIKE OLDFIELD** 664
47 **BON JOVI** 659
48 **CELINE DION** 651
49 **ELECTRIC LIGHT ORCHESTRA** 648
50 **ROBBIE WILLIAMS** 647
51 **BRYAN ADAMS** 641
52 **LIONEL RICHIE** 629
53 **BARBRA STREISAND** 623
54 **DURAN DURAN** 623
55 **SHIRLEY BASSEY** 620
56 **KYLIE MINOGUE** 612
57 **ROY ORBISON** 588
58 **MARIAH CAREY** 588
59 **PET SHOP BOYS** 587
60 **ROXY MUSIC** 581
61 **GEORGE MICHAEL** 577
62 **FOUR TOPS** 574
63 **POLICE** 558
64 **JANET JACKSON** 556
65 **STING** 552
66 **SIMPLE MINDS** 544
67 **JOHN LENNON** 536
68 **ERASURE** 535
69 **SUPREMES** 532
70 **CHER** 529
71 **BUDDY HOLLY** 529
72 **PERRY COMO** 525
73 **BLONDIE** 521
74 **LED ZEPPELIN** 497
75 **DONNA SUMMER** 497
76 **BILLY JOEL** 495
77 **ENGELBERT HUMPERDINCK** 494
78 **SLADE** 491
79 **EAGLES** 489
80 **WET WET WET** 487
81 **GUNS N' ROSES** 486
82 **BARRY MANILOW** 479
83 **EVERLY BROTHERS** 474
84 **CHRIS REA** 474
85 **HOLLIES** 472
86 **T. REX** 470
87 **WHO** 469
88 **BRYAN FERRY** 458
89 **BLUR** 453
90 **JAMES LAST** 450
91 **KATE BUSH** 449
92 **MOODY BLUES** 449
93 **STEREOPHONICS** 448
94 **LUTHER VANDROSS** 447
95 **BEAUTIFUL SOUTH** 443
96 **GEORGE BENSON** 441
97 **CORRS** 439
98 **HOT CHOCOLATE** 436
99 **SHAKIN' STEVENS** 435
100 **SPANDAU BALLET** 433

SKINNY *UK, male vocal / instrumental / production duo – Matt Benbrook and Paul Herman (Singles: 2 weeks)*

			pos	wks
11 Apr 98		**FAILURE** *Cheeky CHEKCD 023*	31	2

SKIP RAIDERS featuring JADA
UK, male production duo and female vocalist (Singles: 1 week)

			pos	wks
15 Jul 00		**ANOTHER DAY** *Perfecto PERF 4CDS*	46	1

SKIPWORTH & TURNER *US, male vocal duo – Rodney Skipworth and Phil Turner (Singles: 12 weeks)*

			pos	wks
27 Apr 85		**THINKING ABOUT YOUR LOVE** *Fourth & Broadway BRW 23*	24	10
21 Jan 89		**MAKE IT LAST** *Fourth & Broadway BRW 118*	60	2

Nick SKITZ – *See FUNKY CHOAD featuring Nick SKITZ*

SKUNK ANANSIE (491 Top 500) *British rock quartet fusing punk rock intensity with issue-led, polemic lyrics from shaven-headed singer Skin, b. Deborah Anne Dyer, 3 Aug 1967, London. The Brit-nominated and Kerrang! double award winners' (1997) debut album went gold. Skin had solo success in 2003 (Singles: 41 weeks, Albums: 101 weeks)*

			pos	wks
25 Mar 95		**SELLING JESUS** *One Little Indian 101 TP7CD*	46	1
17 Jun 95		**I CAN DREAM** *One Little Indian 121 TP7CD*	41	2
2 Sep 95		**CHARITY** *One Little Indian 131 TP7CD*	40	2
27 Jan 96		**WEAK** *One Little Indian 141 TP7CD*	20	5
27 Apr 96		**CHARITY (re-issue)** *One Little Indian 151 TP7CD*	20	3
28 Sep 96		**ALL I WANT** *One Little Indian 161 TP7CD*	14	4
30 Nov 96		**TWISTED (EVERYDAY HURTS)** *One Little Indian 171 TP7CD*	26	4
1 Feb 97		**HEDONISM (JUST BECAUSE YOU FEEL GOOD)** *One Little Indian 181TP7CD*	13	6
14 Jun 97		**BRAZEN 'WEEP'** *One Little Indian 191TP7CD1*	11	5
13 Mar 99		**CHARLIE BIG POTATO** *Virgin VSCDT 1725*	17	3
22 May 99		**SECRETLY** *Virgin VSCDT 1733*	16	4
7 Aug 99		**LATELY** *Virgin VSCDT 1738*	33	2
30 Sep 95	●	**PARANOID & SUNBURNT** *One Little Indian TPLP 55CD*	8	32
19 Oct 96	●	**STOOSH** *One Little Indian TPLP 85CD*	9	55
3 Apr 99		**POST ORGASMIC CHILL** *Virgin CDV 2881*	16	14

See also SKIN

SKY (305 Top 500) *Anglo-Australian jazz-rock fusion quintet with a progressive element. Classical guitarist John Williams OBE was joined by similarly accomplished instrumentalists including Herbie Flowers (b), Kevin Peek (g) and Tristan Fry (d). In Feb 1981, they gave the only concert ever held in Westminster Abbey (Singles: 11 weeks, Albums: 202 weeks)*

			pos	wks
5 Apr 80	●	**TOCCATA** *Ariola ARO 300*	5	11
2 Jun 79	●	**SKY** *Ariola ARLH 5022*	9	56
26 Apr 80	★	**SKY 2** *Ariola ADSKY 2*	1	53
28 Mar 81	●	**SKY 3** *Ariola ASKY 3*	3	23
3 Apr 82	●	**SKY 4 – FORTHCOMING** *Ariola ASKY 4*	7	22
22 Jan 83		**SKY FIVE LIVE** *Ariola 302 171*	14	14
3 Dec 83		**CADMIUM** *Ariola 205 885*	44	10
12 May 84		**MASTERPIECES – THE VERY BEST OF SKY** *Telstar STAR 2241*	15	18
13 Apr 85		**THE GREAT BALLOON RACE** *Epic EPC 26419*	63	6

SKYE – *See LANGE*

SKYHOOKS
Australia, male vocal / instrumental group (Singles: 1 week)

			pos	wks
9 Jun 79		**WOMEN IN UNIFORM** *United Artists UP 36508*	73	1

SKYY – *See NEW YORK SKYY*

SLACKER *UK, male production duo – Shem McCauley and Simon Rogers (Singles: 4 weeks)*

			pos	wks
26 Apr 97		**SCARED** *XL XLS 84CD*	36	2
30 Aug 97		**YOUR FACE** *XL XLS 87CD*	33	2

See also RAMP

SLADE (78 Top 500) *Top group of the 1970s with a total of 6,520,171 single sales to their credit: Noddy Holder (v/g), Dave Hill (g), Jimmy Lea (b/p), Don Powell (d). They were the first act to have three singles enter at No.1. All six of the Wolverhampton band's chart-topping stompers were penned by Holder and Lea. Noddy, who is now a popular TV personality, was made an MBE in 2000. Best-selling single: 'Merry Xmas Everybody' 1,006,500 (Singles: 279 weeks, Albums: 212 weeks)*

			pos	wks
19 Jun 71		**GET DOWN AND GET WITH IT** *Polydor 2058 112*	16	14
30 Oct 71	★	**COZ I LUV YOU** *Polydor 2058 155*	1	15
5 Feb 72	●	**LOOK WOT YOU DUN** *Polydor 2058 195*	4	10
3 Jun 72	★	**TAKE ME BAK 'OME** *Polydor 2058 231*	1	13
2 Sep 72	★	**MAMA WEER ALL CRAZEE NOW** *Polydor 2058 274*	1	10
25 Nov 72	●	**GUDBUY T'JANE** *Polydor 2058 312*	2	13
3 Mar 73	★	**CUM ON FEEL THE NOIZE** *Polydor 2058 339* ■	1	12
30 Jun 73	★	**SKWEEZE ME PLEEZE ME** *Polydor 2058 377* ■	1	10
6 Oct 73	●	**MY FRIEND STAN** *Polydor 2058 407*	2	8
15 Dec 73	★	**MERRY XMAS EVERYBODY (4re)** *Polydor 2058 422* ◆ ■	1	25
6 Apr 74	●	**EVERYDAY** *Polydor 2058 453*	3	7
6 Jul 74	●	**THE BANGIN' MAN** *Polydor 2058 492*	3	7
19 Oct 74	●	**FAR FAR AWAY** *Polydor 2058 522*	2	6
15 Feb 75		**HOW DOES IT FEEL?** *Polydor 2058 547*	15	7
17 May 75	●	**THANKS FOR THE MEMORY (WHAM BAM THANK YOU MAM)** *Polydor 2058 585*	7	7
22 Nov 75		**IN FOR A PENNY** *Polydor 2058 663*	11	8
7 Feb 76		**LET'S CALL IT QUITS** *Polydor 2058 690*	11	7
5 Feb 77		**GYPSY ROADHOG** *Barn 2014 105*	48	2
29 Oct 77		**MY BABY LEFT ME – THAT'S ALL RIGHT** *Barn 2014 114*	32	4
18 Oct 80		**SLADE – ALIVE AT READING (EP)** *Cheapskate CHEAP 5*	44	5
27 Dec 80		**MERRY XMAS EVERYBODY (re-recording)** *Cheapskate CHEAP 11* [1]	70	2
31 Jan 81	●	**WE'LL BRING THE HOUSE DOWN** *Cheapskate CHEAP 16*	10	9
4 Apr 81		**WHEELS AIN'T COMING DOWN** *Cheapskate CHEAP 21*	60	3
19 Sep 81		**LOCK UP YOUR DAUGHTERS** *RCA 124*	29	8
27 Mar 82		**RUBY RED** *RCA 191*	51	3
27 Nov 82		**(AND NOW – THE WALTZ) C'EST LA VIE** *RCA 291*	50	6
19 Nov 83	●	**MY OH MY** *RCA 373*	2	11
4 Feb 84	●	**RUN RUNAWAY** *RCA 385*	7	10
17 Nov 84		**ALL JOIN HANDS** *RCA 455*	15	9
26 Jan 85		**7 YEAR BITCH** *RCA 475*	60	3
23 Mar 85		**MYZSTERIOUS MIZSTER JONES** *RCA PB 40027*	50	5
30 Nov 85		**DO YOU BELIEVE IN MIRACLES** *RCA PB 40449*	54	6
21 Dec 85		**MERRY XMAS EVERYBODY (re) (re-issue)** *Polydor POSP 780*	48	4
21 Feb 87		**STILL THE SAME** *RCA PB 41137*	73	2
19 Oct 91		**RADIO WALL OF SOUND** *Polydor PO 180*	21	5
26 Dec 98		**MERRY XMAS EVERYBODY '98 (re-mix)** *Polydor 5633532* [2]	30	3
8 Apr 72	●	**SLADE ALIVE!** *Polydor 2383 101*	2	58
9 Dec 72	★	**SLAYED?** *Polydor 2383 163*	1	34
6 Oct 73	★	**SLADEST** *Polydor 2442 119* ■	1	24
23 Feb 74	★	**OLD NEW BORROWED AND BLUE** *Polydor 2383 261*	1	16
14 Dec 74	●	**SLADE IN FLAME** *Polydor 2442 126*	6	18
27 Mar 76		**NOBODY'S FOOL** *Polydor 2383 377*	14	4
22 Nov 80		**SLADE SMASHES** *Polydor POLTV 13*	21	15
21 Mar 81		**WE'LL BRING THE HOUSE DOWN** *Cheapskate SKATE 1*	25	4
28 Nov 81		**TILL DEAF US DO PART** *RCA RCALP 6021*	68	2
18 Dec 82		**SLADE ON STAGE** *RCA RCALP 3107*	58	3
24 Dec 83		**THE AMAZING KAMIKAZE SYNDROME** *RCA PL 70116*	49	13
9 Jun 84		**SLADE'S GREATS** *Polydor SLAD 1*	89	1
6 Apr 85		**ROGUES GALLERY** *RCA PL 70604*	60	2
30 Nov 85		**CRACKERS – THE CHRISTMAS PARTY ALBUM** *Telstar STAR 2271*	34	7
9 May 87		**YOU BOYZ MAKE BIG NOIZE** *RCA PL 71260*	98	1
23 Nov 91		**WALL OF HITS** *Polydor 5116121*	34	5
25 Jan 97		**GREATEST HITS – FEEL THE NOIZE** *Polydor 5371052*	19	5

[1] Slade and the Reading Choir [2] Slade vs Flush

'Merry Xmas Everybody' re-entries peaked at No.32 in 1981, No.67 in 1982, No.20 in 1983, No.47 in 1984 and the re-entry of the 1985 re-issue made No.71 in 1986. Tracks on Slade – Alive at Reading (EP): When I'm Dancin' I Ain't Fightin' / Born to Be Wild / Somethin' Else / Pistol Packin' Mama / Keep a Rollin'

SLAM *UK, male production duo – Orde Meikle and Stuart McMillan (Singles: 4 weeks)*

			pos	wks
17 Feb 01		**POSITIVE EDUCATION** *VC Recordings VCRD 84*	44	2

17 Mar 01 **NARCO TOURISTS** *Soma SOMA 100CD* [1] 66 1
7 Jul 01 **LIFETIMES** *Soma SOMA 107CDS* [2] 61 1

[1] Slam vs Unkle [2] Slam featuring Tyrone 'Visionary' Palmer

SLAMM *UK, male vocal / instrumental group (Singles: 6 weeks)* pos/wks

17 Jul 93 **ENERGIZE** *PWL International PWCD 266* 57 2
23 Oct 93 **VIRGINIA PLAIN** *PWL International PWCD 274* 60 1
22 Oct 94 **THAT'S WHERE MY MIND GOES** *PWL International PWCD 310* 68 1
4 Feb 95 **CAN'T GET BY** *PWL International PWCD 316* 47 2

SLARTA JOHN – *See HATIRAS featuring SLARTA JOHN*

SLASH'S SNAKEPIT *US, male vocal / instrumental group (Albums: 4 weeks)* pos/wks

25 Feb 95 **IT'S FIVE O'CLOCK SOMEWHERE** *Geffen GED 24730* 15 4

See also GUNS 'N ROSES

Luke SLATER *UK, male producer (Singles: 2 weeks)* pos/wks

16 Sep 00 **ALL EXHALE** *Novamute CDNOMU 79* 74 1
6 Apr 02 **NOTHING AT ALL** *Mute CDMUTE 261* 70 1

SLAUGHTER *US, male vocal / instrumental group (Singles: 2 weeks, Albums: 1 week)* pos/wks

29 Sep 90 **UP ALL NIGHT** *Chrysalis CHS 3556* 62 1
2 Feb 91 **FLY TO THE ANGELS** *Chrysalis CHS 3634* 55 1
23 May 92 **THE WILD LIFE** *Chrysalis CCD 1911* 64 1

SLAVE *US, male vocal / instrumental group (Singles: 3 weeks)* pos/wks

8 Mar 80 **JUST A TOUCH OF LOVE** *Atlantic / Cotillion K 11442* 64 3

SLAYER *US, male vocal / instrumental group (Singles: 3 weeks, Albums: 21 weeks)* pos/wks

13 Jun 87 **CRIMINALLY INSANE** *Def Jam LON 133* 64 1
26 Oct 91 **SEASONS IN THE ABYSS** *Def American DEFA 9* 51 1
9 Sep 95 **SERENITY IN MURDER** *American 74321312482* 50 1
2 May 87 **REIGN IN BLOOD** *Def Jam LONLP 34* 47 3
23 Jul 88 **SOUTH OF HEAVEN** *London LONLP 63* 25 4
6 Oct 90 **SEASONS IN THE ABYSS** *Def American 8468711* 18 3
2 Nov 91 **DECADE OF AGGRESSION – LIVE** *Def American 5106051* 29 2
15 Oct 94 **DIVINE INTERVENTION** *American 74321236772* 15 4
1 Jun 96 **UNDISPUTED ATTITUDE** *American Recordings 74321357592* ..31 2
20 Jun 98 **DIABOLUS IN MUSICA** *Columbia 4913022* 27 2
22 Sep 01 **GOD HATES US ALL** *Mercury 5863312* 31 1

SLEAZESISTERS *UK, male producer – Paul Masterson (Singles: 3 weeks)* pos/wks

29 Jul 95 **SEX** *Pulse 8 CDLOSE 92* [1] 53 1
30 Mar 96 **LET'S WHIP IT UP (YOU GO GIRL)** *Pulse 8 CDLOSE 102* [1] 46 1
26 Sep 98 **WORK IT UP** *Logic 74321616622* [2] 74 1

[1] Sleazesisters with Vikki Shepard [2] Sleaze Sisters

See also CANDY GIRLS; DOROTHY; YOMANDA; HI-GATE; CLERGY; Paul MASTERSON presents SUSHI

Kathy SLEDGE *US, female vocalist (Singles: 7 weeks)* pos/wks

16 May 92 **TAKE ME BACK TO LOVE AGAIN** *Epic 6579837* 62 2
18 Feb 95 **ANOTHER STAR** *NRC DEACD 002* 54 1
29 Nov 97 **FREEDOM** *Deconstruction 74321536952* [1] 15 4

[1] Robert Miles featuring Kathy Sledge

See also SISTER SLEDGE

Percy SLEDGE *US, male vocalist (Singles: 34 weeks, Albums: 4 weeks)* pos/wks

12 May 66 ● **WHEN A MAN LOVES A WOMAN** *Atlantic 584 001* ▲ 4 17
4 Aug 66 **WARM AND TENDER LOVE** *Atlantic 584 034* 34 7
14 Feb 87 ● **WHEN A MAN LOVES A WOMAN (re-issue)** *Atlantic YZ 96* 2 10
14 Mar 87 **WHEN A MAN LOVES A WOMAN (THE ULTIMATE COLLECTION)** *Atlantic WX 89* 36 4

SLEEPER *UK, female / male vocal / instrumental group (Singles: 29 weeks, Albums: 48 weeks)* pos/wks

21 May 94 **DELICIOUS** *Indolent SLEEP 003CD* 75 1
21 Jan 95 **INBETWEENER** *Indolent SLEEP 006CD* 16 4
8 Apr 95 **VEGAS** *Indolent SLEEP 008CD* 33 3
7 Oct 95 **WHAT DO I DO NOW** *Indolent SLEEP 009CD1* 14 4
4 May 96 ● **SALE OF THE CENTURY** *Indolent SLEEP 011CD* 10 5
13 Jul 96 ● **NICE GUY EDDIE** *Indolent SLEEP 013CD* 10 5
5 Oct 96 **STATUESQUE** *Indolent SLEEP 014CD1* 17 3
4 Oct 97 **SHE'S A GOOD GIRL** *Indolent SLEEP 015CD* 28 2
6 Dec 97 **ROMEO ME** *Indolent SLEEP 17CD1* 39 2
25 Feb 95 ● **SMART** *Indolent SLEEPCD 007* 5 11
18 May 96 ● **THE IT GIRL** *Indolent SLEEPCD 012* 5 34
25 Oct 97 ● **PLEASED TO MEET YOU** *Indolent SLEEPCD 016* 7 3

SLEEPY JACKSON *Australia, male vocal / instrumental trio (Singles: 2 weeks, Albums: 1 week)* pos/wks

19 Jul 03 **VAMPIRE RACECOURSE** *Virgin DINSD 261* 50 1
25 Oct 03 **GOOD DANCERS** *Virgin DINSD 265* 71 1
26 Jul 03 **LOVERS** *Virgin CDVIR208* 69 1

SLEIGHRIDERS *UK, male vocal / instrumental group (Albums: 1 week)* pos/wks

17 Dec 83 **A VERY MERRY DISCO** *Warwick WW 5136* 100 1

SLICK *US, male / female vocal / instrumental group (Singles: 15 weeks)* pos/wks

16 Jun 79 **SPACE BASS** *Fantasy FTC 176* 16 10
15 Sep 79 **SEXY CREAM** *Fantasy FTC 182* [1] 47 5

[1] Slick featuring Doris James

Grace SLICK *US, female vocalist – Grace Wing (Singles: 4 weeks, Albums: 6 weeks)* pos/wks

24 May 80 **DREAMS** *RCA PB 9534* 50 4
31 May 80 **DREAMS** *RCA PL 13544* 28 6

See also JEFFERSON AIRPLANE

SLICK RICK – *See Montell JORDAN; Al B SURE!*

SLIK *UK, male vocal / instrumental group – lead vocal Midge Ure (Singles: 18 weeks, Albums: 1 week)* pos/wks

17 Jan 76 ★ **FOREVER AND EVER** *Bell 1464* 1 9
8 May 76 **REQUIEM** *Bell 1478* 24 9
12 Jun 76 **SLIK** *Bell SYBEL 8004* 58 1

SLIM CHANCE – *See Ronnie LANE*

SLIPKNOT *US, male vocal / instrumental group (Singles: 11 weeks, Albums: 12 weeks)* pos/wks

11 Mar 00 **WAIT AND BLEED** *Roadrunner RR 21125* 27 3
16 Sep 00 **SPIT IT OUT** *Roadrunner RR20903* 28 2
10 Nov 01 **LEFT BEHIND** *Roadrunner 23203355* 24 4
20 Jul 02 **MY PLAGUE** *Roadrunner RR 20453* 43 2
10 Jul 99 **SLIPKNOT** *Roadrunner RR 86552* 37 5
8 Sep 01 ★ **IOWA** *Roadrunner 12085642* ■ 1 7

SLIPMATT *UK, male producer – Matt Nelson (Singles: 2 weeks)* pos/wks

19 Apr 03 **SPACE** *Concept CDCON 37* 41 2

See also SL2

SLIPSTREEM *UK, male vocal group (Singles: 7 weeks)* pos/wks

19 Dec 92 **WE ARE RAVING – THE ANTHEM** *Boogie Food 7BF 1* 18 7

SLITS

UK, female vocal / instrumental group (Singles: 3 weeks, Albums: 5 weeks) pos/wks

13 Oct 79	**TYPICAL GIRLS / I HEARD IT THROUGH THE GRAPEVINE** *Island WIP 6505*	60	3
22 Sep 79	**CUT** *Island ILPS 9573*	30	5

PF SLOAN

US, male vocalist – Philip 'Flip' Sloan (Singles: 3 weeks) pos/wks

4 Nov 65	**SINS OF THE FAMILY** *RCA 1482*	38	3

SLO-MOSHUN

UK / US, male / female production / vocal trio (Singles: 4 weeks) pos/wks

5 Feb 94	**BELLS OF NY** *Six6 SIXCD 108*	29	3
30 Jul 94	**HELP MY FRIEND** *Six6 SIXCD 117*	52	1

SLOWDIVE

UK, male / female vocal / instrumental group (Singles: 2 weeks, Albums: 3 weeks) pos/wks

15 Jun 91	**CATCH THE BREEZE / SHINE** *Creation CRE 112*	52	1
29 May 93	**OUTSIDE YOUR ROOM (EP)** *Creation CRESCD 119*	69	1
14 Sep 91	**JUST FOR A DAY** *Creation CRELP 094*	32	2
12 Jun 93	**SOUVLAKI** *Creation CRECD 139*	51	1

Tracks on Outside Your Room (EP): Outside Your Room / Alison / So Tired / Souvlaki Space Station

SLUSNIK LUNA

Finland, male producer – Niko Nyman (Singles: 2 weeks) pos/wks

1 Sep 01	**SUN** *Incentive CENT 29CDS*	40	2

SLY and the FAMILY STONE

US, male / female vocal / instrumental / production group – includes Sly Stone and Larry Graham (Singles: 42 weeks, Albums: 2 weeks) pos/wks

10 Jul 68 ●	**DANCE TO THE MUSIC** *Direction 58 3568*	7	14
2 Oct 68	**M'LADY** *Direction 58 3707*	32	7
19 Mar 69	**EVERYDAY PEOPLE (re)** *Direction 58 3938* ▲	36	5
8 Jan 72	**FAMILY AFFAIR** *Epic EPC 7632* ▲	15	8
15 Apr 72	**RUNNIN' AWAY** *Epic EPC 7810*	17	8
5 Feb 72	**THERE'S A RIOT GOIN' ON** *Epic EPC 64613* ▲	31	2

SLY and ROBBIE

Jamaica, male vocal / instrumental duo – Sly Dunbar and Robbie Shakespeare (Singles: 23 weeks, Albums: 5 weeks) pos/wks

4 Apr 87	**BOOPS (HERE TO GO)** *Fourth & Broadway BRW 61*	12	11
25 Jul 87	**FIRE** *Fourth & Broadway BRW 71*	60	4
20 Sep 97	**NIGHT NURSE** *East West EW 129CD1* [1]	13	8
9 May 87	**RHYTHM KILLERS** *Fourth & Broadway BRLP 512*	35	5

[1] Sly and Robbie featuring Simply Red

SLY FOX

US, male vocal / instrumental duo – Gary Cooper and Michael Camacho (Singles: 16 weeks) pos/wks

31 May 86 ●	**LET'S GO ALL THE WAY** *Capitol CL 403*	3	16

Heather SMALL

UK, female vocalist (Singles: 9 weeks, Albums: 4 weeks) pos/wks

20 May 00	**PROUD** *Arista 74321748902*	16	5
19 Aug 00	**HOLDING ON** *Arista 74321781332*	58	1
18 Nov 00	**YOU NEED LOVE LIKE I DO** *GUT CDGUT 36* [1]	24	3
10 Jun 00	**PROUD** *Arista 74321765482*	12	4

[1] Tom Jones and Heather Small

See also M PEOPLE

SMALL ADS

UK, male vocal / instrumental group (Singles: 3 weeks) pos/wks

18 Apr 81	**SMALL ADS** *Bronze BRO 115*	63	3

SMALL FACES (312 Top 500)

Revered London-based mod quartet: Steve Marriott (v/g) (d. 1991), Ronnie Lane (b) (d. 1997), Ian McLagan (k), Kenney Jones (d). Marriott and Lane penned most of the act's UK hits. Further international fame came when Marriott formed Humble Pie and the other members formed The Faces (Singles: 137 weeks, Albums: 71 weeks) pos/wks

2 Sep 65	**WHATCHA GONNA DO ABOUT IT?** *Decca F 12208*	14	12
10 Feb 66 ●	**SHA-LA-LA-LA-LEE** *Decca F 12317*	3	11
12 May 66 ●	**HEY GIRL** *Decca F 12393*	10	9
11 Aug 66 ★	**ALL OR NOTHING** *Decca F 12470*	1	12
17 Nov 66 ●	**MY MIND'S EYE** *Decca F 12500*	4	11
9 Mar 67	**I CAN'T MAKE IT** *Decca F 12565*	26	7
8 Jun 67	**HERE COME THE NICE** *Immediate IM 050*	12	10
9 Aug 67 ●	**ITCHYCOO PARK** *Immediate IM 057*	3	14
6 Dec 67 ●	**TIN SOLDIER** *Immediate IM 062*	9	12
17 Apr 68 ●	**LAZY SUNDAY** *Immediate IM 064*	2	11
10 Jul 68	**UNIVERSAL** *Immediate IM 069*	16	11
19 Mar 69	**AFTERGLOW OF YOUR LOVE** *Immediate IM 077*	36	1
13 Dec 75 ●	**ITCHYCOO PARK (re-issue)** *Immediate IMS 102*	9	11
20 Mar 76	**LAZY SUNDAY (re-issue)** *Immediate IMS 106*	39	5
14 May 66 ●	**SMALL FACES** *Decca LK 4790*	3	25
17 Jun 67	**FROM THE BEGINNING** *Decca LK 4879*	17	5
1 Jul 67	**SMALL FACES** *Immediate IMSP 008*	12	17
15 Jun 68 ★	**OGDEN'S NUT GONE FLAKE** *Immediate IMLP 012*	1	19
11 May 96	**THE DECCA ANTHOLOGY 1965-1967** *Deram 8445832*	66	1
7 Jun 03	**ULTIMATE COLLECTION** *Sanctuary TDSAN004*	24	4

The two albums titled 'Small Faces' are different

SMALLER

UK, male vocal / instrumental group (Singles: 2 weeks) pos/wks

28 Sep 96	**WASTED** *Better BETSCD 006*	72	1
29 Mar 97	**IS** *Better BETSCD 008*	55	1

SMART E'S

UK, male instrumental / production group (Singles: 9 weeks) pos/wks

11 Jul 92 ●	**SESAME'S TREET** *Suburban Base SUBBASE 12S*	2	9

S*M*A*S*H

UK, male vocal / instrumental group (Singles: 1 week, Albums: 4 weeks) pos/wks

6 Aug 94	**(I WANT TO) KILL SOMEBODY** *Hi-Rise FLATSCD 5*	26	1
2 Apr 94	**S*M*A*S*H** *Hi-Rise FLATMCD 2*	28	3
17 Sep 94	**SELF ABUSED** *Hi-Rise FLATCD 6*	59	1

SMASH MOUTH

US, male vocal / instrumental group (Singles: 9 weeks) pos/wks

25 Oct 97	**WALKIN' ON THE SUN** *Interscope IND 95555*	19	4
31 Jul 99	**ALL STAR** *Interscope 4971172*	24	5

SMASHING PUMPKINS

US, male / female vocal / instrumental group (Singles: 36 weeks, Albums: 71 weeks) pos/wks

5 Sep 92	**I AM ONE** *Hut HUTT 18*	73	1
3 Jul 93	**CHERUB ROCK** *Hut HUTCD 31*	31	2
25 Sep 93	**TODAY** *Hut HUTCD 37*	44	2
5 Mar 94	**DISARM** *Hut HUTCD 43*	11	3
28 Oct 95	**BULLET WITH BUTTERFLY WINGS** *Hut HUTCD 63*	20	3
10 Feb 96	**1979** *Hut HUTCD 67*	16	3
18 May 96 ●	**TONIGHT TONIGHT** *Hut HUTDX 69*	7	6
23 Nov 96	**THIRTY THREE** *Hut HUTCD 78*	21	2
14 Jun 97 ●	**THE END IS THE BEGINNING IS THE END** *Warner Bros. W 0404CD*	10	4
23 Aug 97	**THE END IS THE BEGINNING IS THE END (re-mix)** *Warner Bros. W 0410CD*	72	1
30 May 98	**AVA ADORE** *Hut HUTCD 101*	11	4
19 Sep 98	**PERFECT** *Hut HUTCD 106*	24	2
4 Mar 00	**STAND INSIDE YOUR LOVE** *Hut HUTCD 127*	23	2
23 Sep 00	**TRY TRY TRY** *Hut HUTCD 140*	73	1
31 Jul 93 ●	**SIAMESE DREAM** *Hut CDHUT 11*	4	15
4 Nov 95 ●	**MELLON COLLIE AND THE INFINITE SADNESS** *Hut CDHUTD 30* ▲	4	37

13 Jun 98 ●	**ADORE** *Hut CDHUTX 51*	5	12
11 Mar 00 ●	**MACHINA / THE MACHINES OF GOD** *Hut CDHUT 59*	7	4
1 Dec 01	**ROTTEN APPLES – THE SMASHING PUMPKINS GREATEST HITS** *Hut CDHUTD 70*	28	3

SMEAR CAMPAIGN – *See MR BEAN and SMEAR CAMPAIGN featuring Bruce DICKINSON*

SMELLS LIKE HEAVEN

Italy, male producer – Fabio Paras (Singles: 1 week) pos/wks

10 Jul 93	**LONDRES STRUTT** *Deconstruction 74321154312*	57	1

Ann-Marie SMITH *UK, female vocalist (Singles: 5 weeks)* pos/wks

23 Jan 93	**MUSIC** *Synthetic CDR 6334* [1]	34	2
18 Mar 95	**ROCKIN' MY BODY** *Media MCSTD 2021* [2]	31	2
15 Jul 95	**(YOU'RE MY ONE AND ONLY) TRUE LOVE** *Media MCSTD 2060*	46	1

[1] Fargetta and Anne-Marie Smith [2] 49ers featuring Ann-Marie Smith

Brian SMITH and his HAPPY PIANO

UK, male instrumentalist – piano (Albums: 1 week) pos/wks

19 Sep 81	**PLAY IT AGAIN** *Deram DS 047*	97	1

Elliott SMITH *US, male vocalist / instrumentalist (Singles: 3 weeks, Albums: 2 weeks)* pos/wks

19 Dec 98	**WALTZ #2 (XO)** *DreamWorks DRMCD 22347*	52	1
1 May 99	**BABY BRITAIN** *DreamWorks DRMDM 50950*	55	1
8 Jul 00	**SON OF SAM** *DreamWorks DRMCD 4509492*	55	1
29 Apr 00	**FIGURE 8** *Dreamworks 4502252*	37	2

'Fast' Eddie SMITH – *See DJ 'FAST' EDDIE*

Hurricane SMITH

UK, male vocalist – Norman Smith (Singles: 35 weeks) pos/wks

12 Jun 71 ●	**DON'T LET IT DIE** *Columbia DB 8785*	2	12
29 Apr 72 ●	**OH BABE, WHAT WOULD YOU SAY?** *Columbia DB 8878*	4	16
2 Sep 72	**WHO WAS IT** *Columbia DB 8916*	23	7

Jimmy SMITH *US, male instrumentalist – organ (Singles: 3 weeks, Albums: 3 weeks)* pos/wks

28 Apr 66	**GOT MY MOJO WORKING (re)** *Verve VS 536*	48	3
18 Jun 66	GOT MY MOJO WORKING *Verve VLP 912*	19	3

Keely SMITH

US, female vocalist (Singles: 10 weeks, Albums: 9 weeks) pos/wks

18 Mar 65	**YOU'RE BREAKIN' MY HEART** *Reprise R 20346*	14	10
16 Jan 65	LENNON-MCCARTNEY SONGBOOK *Reprise R 6142*	12	9

Mandy SMITH

UK, female vocalist (Singles: 2 weeks) pos/wks

20 May 89	**DON'T YOU WANT ME BABY** *PWL PWL 37*	59	2

Mark E SMITH – *See FALL; INSPIRAL CARPETS*

Mel SMITH

UK, male vocalist / comedian (Singles: 10 weeks) pos/wks

5 Dec 87 ●	**ROCKIN' AROUND THE CHRISTMAS TREE** *10 TEN 2* [1]	3	7
21 Dec 91	**ANOTHER BLOOMING CHRISTMAS** *Epic 6576877*	59	3

[1] Mel and Kim [Kim is Kim Wilde]

See also SMITH and JONES; NOT THE NINE O'CLOCK NEWS CAST

Michael SMITH – *See SEELENLUFT featuring Michael SMITH*

Muriel SMITH *US, female vocalist, d. 1985, with Wally Stott and his Orchestra (Singles: 17 weeks)* pos/wks

15 May 53 ●	**HOLD ME, THRILL ME, KISS ME** *Philips PB 122*	3	17

OC SMITH *US, male vocalist, d. 23 Nov 2001 (Singles: 23 weeks, Albums: 1 week)* pos/wks

29 May 68 ●	**THE SON OF HICKORY HOLLER'S TRAMP** *CBS 3343*	2	15
26 Mar 77	**TOGETHER** *Caribou CRB 4910*	25	8
17 Aug 68	HICKORY HOLLER REVISITED *CBS 63362*	40	1

Patti SMITH GROUP *US, female / male vocal / instrumental group (Singles: 16 weeks, Albums: 23 weeks)* pos/wks

29 Apr 78 ●	**BECAUSE THE NIGHT** *Arista 181*	5	12
19 Aug 78	**PRIVILEGE (SET ME FREE)** *Arista 197*	72	1
2 Jun 79	**FREDERICK** *Arista 264*	63	3
1 Apr 78	EASTER *Arista SPART 1043*	16	14
19 May 79	WAVE *Arista SPART 1086*	41	6
16 Jul 88	DREAM OF LIFE *Arista 209172* [1]	70	1
13 Jul 96	GONE AGAIN *Arista 7822187472* [1]	44	2

[1] Patti Smith

Rex SMITH and Rachel SWEET

US, male / female vocal duo (Singles: 7 weeks) pos/wks

22 Aug 81	**EVERLASTING LOVE** *CBS A 1405*	35	7

Richard Jon SMITH

South Africa, male vocalist (Singles: 2 weeks) pos/wks

16 Jul 83	**SHE'S THE MASTER OF THE GAME** *Jive JIVE 38*	63	2

Rose SMITH – *See DELAKOTA*

Sheila SMITH – *See Cevin FISHER*

Simon SMITH – *See DRUMSOUND & Simon 'BASSLINE' SMITH*

Steven SMITH and FATHER

UK, male instrumental duo (Albums: 3 weeks) pos/wks

13 May 72	STEVEN SMITH AND FATHER AND 16 GREAT SONGS *Decca SKL 5128*	17	3

Whistling Jack SMITH

UK, male whistler – Billy Moeller (Singles: 12 weeks) pos/wks

2 Mar 67 ●	**I WAS KAISER BILL'S BATMAN** *Deram DM 112*	5	12

Will SMITH (335 Top 500) *Artist formerly known as The Fresh Prince was not only one of the 1990s most successful rap stars, but also a top TV personality and Oscar-nominated movie actor, b. 25 Sep 1968, Philadelphia, US. The quadruple World Music Award winner (1999) helped to make rap accessible to all ages. Best-selling single 'Men in Black' 883,000 (Singles: 110 weeks, Albums: 87 weeks)* pos/wks

16 Aug 97 ★	**MEN IN BLACK** *Columbia 6648682* ■	1	16
13 Dec 97	**JUST CRUISIN'** *Columbia 6653482*	23	6
7 Feb 98 ●	**GETTIN' JIGGY WIT IT** *Columbia 6655605* ▲	3	10
1 Aug 98 ●	**JUST THE TWO OF US** *Columbia 6662092*	2	10
5 Dec 98 ●	**MIAMI** *Columbia 6666782*	3	14
13 Feb 99 ●	**BOY YOU KNOCK ME OUT (re)** *MJJ / Epic 6669372* [1]	3	9
10 Jul 99 ●	**WILD WILD WEST** *Columbia 6675962* [2] ▲	2	16
20 Nov 99 ●	**WILL 2K** *Columbia 6684452*	2	11
25 Mar 00	**FREAKIN' IT (re)** *Columbia 6691052*	15	8
10 Aug 02 ●	**BLACK SUITS COMIN' (NOD YA HEAD)** *Columbia 6730132* [3]	3	10
6 Dec 97 ●	BIG WILLIE STYLE *Columbia 4886622*	9	70
27 Nov 99 ●	WILLENNIUM *Columbia 4949392*	10	15
24 Aug 02	BORN TO REIGN *Columbia 5079552*	24	2

[1] Tatyana Ali featuring Will Smith [2] Will Smith featuring Dru Hill – additional vocals Kool Moe Dee [3] Will Smith featuring Tra-Knox

See also DJ JAZZY JEFF and The FRESH PRINCE

SMITH and JONES *UK, male comedy duo – Mel Smith and Griff Rhys Jones (Albums: 8 weeks)* pos/wks

15 Nov 86	SCRATCH AND SNIFF *10 DIX 51*	62	8

See also Mel SMITH

SMITHS (179 Top 500) *Mancunian quartet with loyal fan base: Morrissey (b. Stephen Morrissey) (v), Johnny Marr (g), Andy Rourke (b), Mike Joyce (d). Their achievements include monopolising the Top 3 indie chart placings (Feb 1984) and having seven albums simultaneously in the UK chart (Mar 1995) (Singles: 105 weeks, Albums: 206 weeks)*

		pos	wks
12 Nov 83	THIS CHARMING MAN *Rough Trade RT 136*	25	12
28 Jan 84	WHAT DIFFERENCE DOES IT MAKE *Rough Trade RT 146*	12	9
2 Jun 84	● HEAVEN KNOWS I'M MISERABLE NOW *Rough Trade RT 156*	10	8
1 Sep 84	WILLIAM, IT WAS REALLY NOTHING *Rough Trade RT 166*	17	6
9 Feb 85	HOW SOON IS NOW? *Rough Trade RT 176*	24	6
30 Mar 85	SHAKESPEARE'S SISTER *Rough Trade RT 181*	26	4
13 Jul 85	THAT JOKE ISN'T FUNNY ANYMORE *Rough Trade RT 186*	49	3
5 Oct 85	THE BOY WITH THE THORN IN HIS SIDE *Rough Trade RT 191*	23	5
31 May 86	BIG MOUTH STRIKES AGAIN *Rough Trade RT 192*	26	4
2 Aug 86	PANIC *Rough Trade RT 193*	11	8
1 Nov 86	ASK *Rough Trade RT 194*	14	5
7 Feb 87	SHOPLIFTERS OF THE WORLD UNITE *Rough Trade RT 195*	12	4
25 Apr 87	● SHEILA TAKE A BOW *Rough Trade RT 196*	10	5
22 Aug 87	GIRLFRIEND IN A COMA *Rough Trade RT 197*	13	5
14 Nov 87	I STARTED SOMETHING I COULDN'T FINISH *Rough Trade RT 198*	23	4
19 Dec 87	LAST NIGHT I DREAMT THAT SOMEBODY LOVED ME *Rough Trade RT 200*	30	4
15 Aug 92	● THIS CHARMING MAN (re-issue) *WEA YZ 0001*	8	5
12 Sep 92	HOW SOON IS NOW (re-issue) *WEA YZ 0002*	16	4
24 Oct 92	THERE IS A LIGHT THAT NEVER GOES OUT *WEA YZ 0003*	25	3
18 Feb 95	ASK (re-issue) *WEA YZ 0004CDX*	62	1
3 Mar 84	● THE SMITHS *Rough Trade ROUGH 61*	2	33
24 Nov 84	● HATFUL OF HOLLOW *Rough Trade ROUGH 76*	7	46
23 Feb 85	★ MEAT IS MURDER *Rough Trade ROUGH 81* ■	1	13
28 Jun 86	● THE QUEEN IS DEAD *Rough Trade ROUGH 96*	2	22
7 Mar 87	● THE WORLD WON'T LISTEN *Rough Trade ROUGH 101*	2	15
30 May 87	LOUDER THAN BOMBS (import) *Rough Trade ROUGH 255*	38	5
10 Oct 87	● STRANGEWAYS HERE WE COME *Rough Trade ROUGH 106*	2	17
17 Sep 88	● RANK *Rough Trade ROUGH 126*	2	7
29 Aug 92	★ BEST ... I *WEA 4509903272* ■	1	9
14 Nov 92	BEST ... II *WEA 4509904062*	29	5
4 Mar 95	HATFUL OF HOLLOW (re-issue) *WEA 4509918932*	26	3
4 Mar 95	MEAT IS MURDER (re-issue) *WEA 4509918952*	39	2
4 Mar 95	● SINGLES *WEA 4509990902*	5	9
4 Mar 95	STRANGEWAYS HERE WE COME (re-issue) *WEA 4509918992*	38	4
4 Mar 95	THE QUEEN IS DEAD (re-issue) *WEA 4509918962*	30	4
4 Mar 95	THE SMITHS (re-issue) *WEA 4509918922*	42	4
4 Mar 95	THE WORLD WON'T LISTEN (re-issue) *WEA 4509918982*	52	2
14 Oct 00	LOUDER THAN BOMBS (re-issue) *WEA 4509938332*	52	2
16 Jun 01	THE VERY BEST OF THE SMITHS *WEA 8573889482*	30	4

SMOKE *UK, male vocal / instrumental group (Singles: 3 weeks)*

		pos	wks
9 Mar 67	MY FRIEND JACK *Columbia DB 8115*	45	3

SMOKE CITY *UK / Brazil, male / female vocal / instrumental group (Singles: 5 weeks)*

		pos	wks
12 Apr 97	● UNDERWATER LOVE *Jive JIVECD 422*	4	5

SMOKE 2 SEVEN *UK, female vocal trio (Singles: 2 weeks)*

		pos	wks
16 Mar 02	BEEN THERE DONE THAT *Curb / London CUBC 077*	26	2

SMOKED – *See Oliver LIEB presents SMOKED*

SMOKIE (396 Top 500) *British group which became European superstars, fronted by vocalist Chris Norman. Especially popular in Germany, many of their hits were penned by Mike Chapman and Nicky Chinn (Singles: 125 weeks, Albums: 45 weeks)*

		pos	wks
19 Jul 75	● IF YOU THINK YOU KNOW HOW TO LOVE ME *RAK 206* [1]	3	9
4 Oct 75	● DON'T PLAY YOUR ROCK 'N ROLL TO ME *RAK 217* [1]	8	7
31 Jan 76	SOMETHING'S BEEN MAKING ME BLUE *RAK 227*	17	8
25 Sep 76	I'LL MEET YOU AT MIDNIGHT *RAK 241*	11	9
4 Dec 76	● LIVING NEXT DOOR TO ALICE *RAK 244*	5	11
19 Mar 77	LAY BACK IN THE ARMS OF SOMEONE *RAK 251*	12	9
16 Jul 77	● IT'S YOUR LIFE *RAK 260*	5	9
15 Oct 77	● NEEDLES AND PINS *RAK 263*	10	9
28 Jan 78	FOR A FEW DOLLARS MORE *RAK 267*	17	6
20 May 78	● OH CAROL *RAK 276*	5	13
23 Sep 78	MEXICAN GIRL *RAK 283*	19	9
19 Apr 80	TAKE GOOD CARE OF MY BABY *RAK 309*	34	7
13 May 95	● LIVING NEXT DOOR TO ALICE (WHO THE F**K IS ALICE) (re) *NOW CDWAG 245* [2]	3	19
1 Nov 75	SMOKIE / CHANGING ALL THE TIME *RAK SRAK 517*	18	5
30 Apr 77	● GREATEST HITS *RAK SRAK 526*	6	22
4 Nov 78	THE MONTREUX ALBUM *RAK SRAK 6757*	52	2
11 Oct 80	SMOKIE'S HITS *RAK SRAK 540*	23	13
17 Mar 01	UNCOVERED – THE VERY BEST OF SMOKIE *Universal Music TV 138172*	63	3

[1] Smokey [2] Smokie featuring Roy 'Chubby' Brown

*'Living Next Door to Alice (Who The F**k Is Alice)' is a re-recorded version of 'Living Next Door to Alice' which peaked on re-entry in Aug 1995*

SMOKIN BEATS featuring Lyn EDEN
UK, male DJ / production duo – Neil Rumney and Paul Landon, and UK, female vocalist (Singles: 3 weeks)

		pos	wks
17 Jan 98	DREAMS *AM:PM 5824711*	23	3

SMOKIN' MOJO FILTERS *UK / US, male / female vocal / instrumental charity group (Singles: 5 weeks)*

		pos	wks
23 Dec 95	COME TOGETHER (WAR CHILD) *Go! Discs GODCD 136*	19	5

SMOOTH
US, female vocalist – Juanita Stokes (Singles: 7 weeks)

		pos	wks
22 Jul 95	MIND BLOWIN' *Jive JIVECD 379*	36	2
7 Oct 95	IT'S SUMMERTIME (LET IT GET INTO YOU) *Jive JIVECD 383*	46	1
16 Mar 96	WE GOT IT *MCA MCSTD 48009* [1]	26	2
16 Mar 96	LOVE GROOVE (GROOVE WITH YOU) *Jive JIVECD 390*	46	1
6 Jul 96	UNDERCOVER LOVER *Jive JIVECD 397*	41	1

[1] Immature featuring Smooth

CL SMOOTH – *See Pete ROCK and CL SMOOTH*

Joe SMOOTH *US, male producer (Singles: 4 weeks)*

		pos	wks
4 Feb 89	PROMISED LAND *DJ International DJIN 6*	56	4

SMOOTH TOUCH
US, male instrumental / production duo (Singles: 1 week)

		pos	wks
2 Apr 94	HOUSE OF LOVE (IN MY HOUSE) *Six6 SIXCD 112*	58	1

Jean Jacques SMOOTHIE
UK, male DJ / producer – Steve Robson (Singles: 7 weeks)

		pos	wks
13 Oct 01	2 PEOPLE *Echo ECSCD 112*	12	7

SMURFS *Holland, small blue creatures vocal group (Singles: 52 weeks, Albums: 77 weeks)*

		pos	wks
3 Jun 78	● THE SMURF SONG *Decca F 13759* [1]	2	17
30 Sep 78	DIPPETY DAY *Decca F 13798* [1]	13	12
2 Dec 78	CHRISTMAS IN SMURFLAND *Decca F 13819*	19	7
7 Sep 96	● I'VE GOT A LITTLE PUPPY *EMI TV CDSMURF 100*	4	10
21 Dec 96	● YOUR CHRISTMAS WISH *EMI TV CDSMURF 102*	8	6
25 Nov 78	FATHER ABRAHAM IN SMURFLAND *Decca SMURF 1* [1]	19	11
6 Jul 96	● THE SMURFS GO POP! *EMI TV CDEMTV 121*	2	33
16 Nov 96	● SMURF'S CHRISTMAS PARTY *EMI TV CDEMTV 140*	8	9
22 Feb 97	● THE SMURFS HITS '97 – VOLUME 1 *EMI TV CDEMTV 150*	2	11
6 Sep 97	GO POP! AGAIN *EMI CDEMTV 155*	15	7
18 Apr 98	GREATEST HITS *EMI 4941972*	28	6

[1] Father Abraham and the Smurfs [1] Father Abraham and the Smurfs

Patty SMYTH with Don HENLEY
US, female / male vocal duo (Singles: 6 weeks)

		pos	wks
3 Oct 92	SOMETIMES LOVE JUST AIN'T ENOUGH *MCA MCS 1692*	22	6

SNAKEBITE *Italy, male production trio (Singles: 2 weeks)* pos/wks

9 Aug 97 **THE BIT GOES ON** *Multiply CDMULTY 22* 25 2

SNAP! 363 Top 500 *German-based producers Benito Benites (b. Michael Munzing) and John Garrett Virgo III (b. Luca Anzilotti) masterminded a string of worldwide dance hits for this act, which featured a host of mostly US vocalists and rappers including Turbo B, Jackie Harris, Penny Ford and Thea Austin. Best-selling single 'Rhythm Is a Dancer' 582,700 (Singles: 126 weeks, Albums: 56 weeks)* pos/wks

24 Mar 90 ★ **THE POWER** *Arista 113133* 1 15
16 Jun 90 ● **OOOPS UP** *Arista 113296* 5 12
22 Sep 90 ● **CULT OF SNAP!** *Arista 113596* 8 7
8 Dec 90 ● **MARY HAD A LITTLE BOY** *Arista 113831* 8 10
30 Mar 91 ● **SNAP! MEGAMIX** *Arista 114169* 10 6
21 Dec 91 **THE COLOUR OF LOVE** *Arista 114678* 54 3
4 Jul 92 ★ **RHYTHM IS A DANCER** *Arista 115309* 1 19
9 Jan 93 ● **EXTERMINATE!** *Arista 74321106962* [1] 2 11
12 Jun 93 ● **DO YOU SEE THE LIGHT (LOOKING FOR)** *Arista 74321147622* [1] 10 8
17 Sep 94 ● **WELCOME TO TOMORROW (re)** *Arista 74321223852* [2] 6 14
1 Apr 95 **THE FIRST THE LAST ETERNITY (TIL THE END)** *Arista 74321254672* [2] 15 7
28 Oct 95 **THE WORLD IN MY HANDS** *Arista 74321314792* [2] 44 1
13 Apr 96 **RAME** *Arista 74321368902* [3] 50 1
24 Aug 96 **THE POWER 96** *Arista 74321398672* [4] 42 1
24 Aug 02 **DO YOU SEE THE LIGHT? (re-mix)** *Data MOS DATA 33CDS* [5] 14 5
17 May 03 **RHYTHM IS A DANCER (re-mix)** *Data / Mos DATA 47CDS* 17 4
6 Sep 03 **THE POWER (OF BHANGRA) (re-mix)** *Data / MoS DATA 60CDS* [6] 34 2
26 May 90 ● **WORLD POWER** *Arista 210682* 10 39
8 Aug 92 ● **THE MADMAN'S RETURN** *Logic 262552* 8 15
15 Oct 94 **WELCOME TO TOMORROW** *Ariola 74321223842* 69 1
7 Sep 96 **SNAP! ATTACK – THE BEST OF SNAP! / THE REMIXES** *Ariola 74321395192* 47 1

[1] Snap! featuring Niki Haris [2] Snap! featuring Summer [3] Snap! featuring Rukmani [4] Snap! featuring Einstein [5] Snap! vs Plaything [6] Snap! vs Motivo

'The Madman's Return' changed catalogue number to 74321128512 during its chart run

SNEAKER PIMPS *UK, male / female vocal / instrumental group (Singles: 19 weeks, Albums: 7 weeks)* pos/wks

19 Oct 96 **6 UNDERGROUND** *Clean Up CUP 023CDS* 15 4
15 Mar 97 **SPIN SPIN SUGAR** *Clean Up CUP 033CDS* 21 3
7 Jun 97 ● **6 UNDERGROUND (re-mix)** *Clean Up CUP 036CDM* 9 4
30 Aug 97 **POST MODERN SLEAZE** *Clean Up CUP 038CDM* 22 3
7 Feb 98 **SPIN SPIN SUGAR (re-mix)** *Clean Up CUP 037X* 46 2
21 Aug 99 **LOW FIVE** *Clean Up CUP 052CDM* 39 2
30 Oct 99 **TEN TO TWENTY** *Clean Up CUP 054CDS* 56 1
31 Aug 96 **BECOMING X** *Clean Up CUP 020CD* 27 7

David SNEDDON
UK, male vocalist (Singles: 33 weeks, Albums: 5 weeks) pos/wks

25 Jan 03 ★ **STOP LIVING THE LIE** *Mercury 0637292* ■ 1 18
3 May 03 ● **DON'T LET GO** *Mercury 9800044* 3 10
23 Aug 03 **BEST OF ORDER** *Fontana 9810276* 19 3
8 Nov 03 **BABY GET HIGHER** *Fontana 9813421* 38 2
10 May 03 ● **SEVEN YEARS – TEN WEEKS** *Mercury 9800063* 5 5

SNIFF 'N' THE TEARS
UK, male vocal / instrumental group (Singles: 5 weeks) pos/wks

23 Jun 79 **DRIVER'S SEAT** *Chiswick CHIS 105* 42 5

SNOOP DOGG 495 Top 500
Ground-breaking g-funk rapper, b. Calvin Broadus, 20 Oct 1972, Long Beach, California. Discovered by Dr Dre, he was the first artist to enter the US album chart at No.1 with a debut album. The distinctive rapper, who has had various brushes with the law, now fronts a successful MTV comedy show (Singles: 91 weeks, Albums: 50 weeks) pos/wks

4 Dec 93 **WHAT'S MY NAME?** *Death Row A 8337CD* [1] 20 8
12 Feb 94 **GIN AND JUICE** *Death Row A 8316CD* [1] 39 3
20 Aug 94 **DOGGY DOGG WORLD** *Death Row A 8289CD* [1] 32 3
14 Dec 96 **SNOOP'S UPSIDE YA HEAD** *Interscope IND 95520* [2] 12 7
26 Apr 97 **WANTED DEAD OR ALIVE** *Def Jam 5744052* [3] 16 3
3 May 97 **VAPORS** *Interscope IND 95530* [1] 18 2
20 Sep 97 **WE JUST WANNA PARTY WITH YOU** *Columbia 6649902* [4] 21 2
24 Jan 98 **THA DOGGFATHER** *Interscope IND 95550* [1] 36 2
12 Dec 98 **COME AND GET WITH ME** *Elektra E 3787CD* [5] 58 1
25 Mar 00 ● **STILL D.R.E.** *Interscope 4972742* [6] 6 10
3 Feb 01 ● **THE NEXT EPISODE** *Interscope 4974762* [6] 3 10
17 Mar 01 **X** *Epic 6709072* [7] 14 7
28 Apr 01 **SNOOP DOGG** *Priority PTYCD 134* 13 5
30 Nov 02 **FROM THA CHUUUCH TO DA PALACE** *Priority / Capitol 5516102* 27 6
1 Mar 03 **THE STREETS** *Def Jam 0779852* [8] 48 2
5 Apr 03 **BEAUTIFUL** *Priority CDCL 842* [9] 23 20
11 Dec 93 **DOGGYSTYLE** *Death Row 6544922792* [1] ▲ 38 27
23 Nov 96 **THA DOGGFATHER** *Interscope INTD 90038* [1] ▲ 15 11
15 Aug 98 **DA GAME IS TO BE SOLD NOT TO BE TOLD** *Priority CDPTY 153* ▲ 28 3
5 Jun 99 **TOP DOGG** *Priority CDPTY 171* 48 1
5 May 01 **THA LAST MEAL** *Priority CDPTY 199* 62 2
10 May 03 **PAID THA COST TO BE DA BO$$** *Priority 5391572* 64 6

[1] Snoop Doggy Dogg [2] Snoop Doggy Dogg featuring Charlie Wilson [3] 2Pac and Snoop Doggy Dogg [4] Snoop Doggy Dogg featuring JD [5] Keith Sweat featuring Snoop Dogg [6] Dr Dre featuring Snoop Dogg [7] Xzibit featuring Snoop Dogg [8] WC featuring Snoop Dogg and Nate Dogg [9] Snoop Dogg featuring Pharrell, Uncle Charlie Wilson [1] Snoop Doggy Dogg

SNOW *Canada, male rapper – Darrin O'Brien (Singles: 18 weeks, Albums: 4 weeks)* pos/wks

13 Mar 93 ● **INFORMER** *East West America A 8436CD* ▲ 2 15
5 Jun 93 **GIRL I'VE BEEN HURT** *East West America A 8417CD* 48 2
4 Sep 93 **UHH IN YOU** *Atlantic A 8378CD* 67 1
17 Apr 93 **12 INCHES OF SNOW** *East West America 7567922072* 41 4

Mark SNOW *US, male instrumentalist – keyboards (Singles: 15 weeks, Albums: 2 weeks)* pos/wks

30 Mar 96 ● **THE X-FILES** *Warner Bros. W 0341CD* 2 15
12 Oct 96 **THE TRUTH AND THE LIGHT – MUSIC FROM THE X-FILES** *Warner Bros. 9362464482* 42 2

Phoebe SNOW *US, female vocalist / instrumentalist – guitar – Phoebe Laub (Singles: 7 weeks)* pos/wks

6 Jan 79 **EVERY NIGHT** *CBS 6842* 37 7

SNOW PATROL
UK, male vocal / instrumental group (Singles: 1 week) pos/wks

27 Sep 03 **SPITTING GAMES** *Polydor 9809350* 54 1

SNOWMAN – *See Peter AUTY and the SINFONIA OF LONDON conducted by Howard BLAKE*

SNOWMEN
UK, male vocal / instrumental group (Singles: 12 weeks) pos/wks

12 Dec 81 **HOKEY COKEY** *Stiff ODB 1* 18 8
18 Dec 82 **XMAS PARTY** *Solid STOP 006* 44 4

SNUG *UK, male vocal / instrumental group (Singles: 1 week)* pos/wks

18 Apr 98 **BEATNIK GIRL** *WEA WEA 151CDX* 55 1

SO *UK, male vocal / instrumental group (Singles: 3 weeks)* pos/wks

13 Feb 88 **ARE YOU SURE** *Parlophone R 6173* 62 3

SO SOLID CREW
UK, male / female vocal / rap / production collective – includes Asher D, Lisa Maffia, Romeo (Singles: 42 weeks, Albums: 25 weeks) pos/wks

18 Aug 01 ★ **21 SECONDS (re)** *Relentless RELENT 16CD* ■ 1 15

17 Nov 01 ● **THEY DON'T KNOW** *Relentless RELENT 26CD* 3 9
19 Jan 02 ● **HATERS** *Relentless RELENT 23CD* [1] 8 7
20 Apr 02 **RIDE WID US** *Relentless / Independiente ISOM 55MS* 19 6
27 Sep 03 ● **BROKEN SILENCE** *Independiente ISOM 71MS* 9 5
1 Dec 01 ● **THEY DON'T KNOW** *Relentless / Independiente ISOM 27CD* 6 20
26 Jan 02 ● **FUCK IT** *Relentless Rel 004CD* 3 4
11 Oct 03 **2ND VERSE** *Independiente ISOM35CD* 70 1

[1] So Solid Crew presents Mr Shabz featuring MBD and The Reelists

'Fuck It' appeared only on the UK Compilation Chart and not on the standard Top 75

S.O.A.P. *Denmark, female vocal duo – Heidi and Line Sorensen (Singles: 2 weeks)* pos/wks

25 Jul 98 **THIS IS HOW WE PARTY** *Columbia 6661295* 36 2

SOAPY *UK, male instrumental / production duo – Jak Kaleniuk and Dan Bewick (Singles: 2 weeks)* pos/wks

14 Sep 96 **HORNY AS FUNK** *WEA WEA 074CD* 35 2

Gino SOCCIO

Canada, male instrumentalist – keyboards (Singles: 5 weeks) pos/wks

28 Apr 79 **DANCER** *Warner Bros. K 17357* 46 5

SODA CLUB

UK, male production duo – Andy and Pete Lee (Singles: 10 weeks) pos/wks

9 Nov 02 **TAKE MY BREATH AWAY** *Concept CDCON 33* 16 4
8 Mar 03 **HEAVEN IS A PLACE ON EARTH** *Concept CDCON 39* [1] 13 4
23 Aug 03 **KEEP LOVE TOGETHER** *Concept CDCON 44* [2] 31 2

[1] Soda Club featuring Hannah Alethea [2] Soda Club featuring Andrea Anatola

SOEUR SOURIRE – *See SINGING NUN (Soeur Sourire)*

SOFT CELL (304 Top 500) *Successful synth-driven duo from Leeds: Marc Almond (v), David Ball (k). The visually striking pair's revival of northern soul classic 'Tainted Love' was the Top UK single of 1981 and went on to sell 1,135,000 and also broke the longevity record in the US Top 100 (Singles: 110 weeks, Albums: 103 weeks)* pos/wks

1 Aug 81 ★ **TAINTED LOVE (3re)** *Some Bizzare BZS 2* ◆ 1 36
14 Nov 81 ● **BEDSITTER** *Some Bizzare BZS 6* 4 12
6 Feb 82 ● **SAY HELLO WAVE GOODBYE** *Some Bizzare BZS 7* 3 9
29 May 82 ● **TORCH** *Some Bizzare BZS 9* 2 9
21 Aug 82 ● **WHAT** *Some Bizzare BZS 11* 3 8
4 Dec 82 **WHERE THE HEART IS** *Some Bizzare BZS 16* 21 7
5 Mar 83 **NUMBERS / BARRIERS** *Some Bizzare BZS 17* 25 4
24 Sep 83 **SOUL INSIDE** *Some Bizzare BZS 20* 16 5
25 Feb 84 **DOWN IN THE SUBWAY** *Some Bizzare BZS 22* 24 6
23 Mar 91 **SAY HELLO WAVE GOODBYE '91 (re-recording)** *Mercury SOFT 1* [1] 38 3
18 May 91 ● **TAINTED LOVE (re-issue)** *Mercury SOFT 2* [1] 5 8
28 Sep 02 **MONOCULTURE** *Cooking Vinyl FRYCD 132* 52 1
8 Feb 03 **THE NIGHT** *Cooking Vinyl FRYCD 135* 39 2
5 Dec 81 ● **NON-STOP EROTIC CABARET** *Some Bizzare BZLP 2* 5 46
26 Jun 82 ● **NON-STOP ECSTATIC DANCING** *Some Bizzare BZX 1012* 6 18
22 Jan 83 ● **THE ART OF FALLING APART** *Some Bizzare BIZL 3* 5 10
31 Mar 84 **THIS LAST NIGHT IN SODOM** *Some Bizzare BIZL 6* 12 5
20 Dec 86 **THE SINGLES ALBUM** *Some Bizzare BZLP 3* 58 9
1 Jun 91 ● **MEMORABILIA – THE SINGLES** *Mercury 8485121* 8 13
13 Apr 02 **THE VERY BEST OF SOFT CELL** *UMTV 5868342* 37 2

[1] Soft Cell / Marc Almond

'Tainted Love' re-entries made No.43 in Jan 1982, No.50 in Jul 1982 and No.43 in Feb 1985

SOFT MACHINE

UK, male vocal / instrumental group (Albums: 8 weeks) pos/wks

4 Jul 70 **THIRD** *CBS 66246* 18 6
3 Apr 71 **FOURTH** *CBS 64280* 32 2

See also Robert WYATT

SOFT PARADE – *See ELECTRIC SOFT PARADE*

SOHO

UK, male / female vocal / instrumental group (Singles: 11 weeks) pos/wks

5 May 90 ● **HIPPY CHICK (re)** *Savage 7SAV 106* 8 9
9 Nov 91 **BORN TO BE ALIVE** *MCA MCS 1578* [1] 51 2

[1] Adamski featuring Soho

'Hippy Chick' originally peaked at No.67 and made its peak position only on re-entry to the chart in Jan 1991. The listed flip side of 'Born to Be Alive' was 'Never Goin' Down' by Adamski featuring Jimi Polo

SOIL *US, male vocal / instrumental group (Singles: 1 week)* pos/wks

9 Nov 02 **HALO** *J 74321970132* 74 1

SOLAR STONE *UK, male DJ / production trio (Singles: 5 weeks)* pos/wks

21 Feb 98 **THE IMPRESSIONS EP** *Hooj Choons HOOJCD 57* 75 1
6 Nov 99 **7 CITIES** *Hooj Choons HOOJ 85CD* 39 2
28 Sep 02 **7 CITIES (re-mix)** *Lost Language LOST 018CD* 44 2

Tracks on The Impressions EP: The Calling / Day By Day / The Calling / Day By Day / So Clear

SOLID GOLD CHARTBUSTERS

UK, male / female production / vocal group (Singles: 1 week) pos/wks

25 Dec 99 **I WANNA 1-2-1 WITH YOU** *Virgin VSCDT 1765* 62 1

SOLID HARMONIE

UK / US, female vocal group (Singles: 11 weeks) pos/wks

31 Jan 98 **I'LL BE THERE FOR YOU** *Jive JIVECD 437* 18 3
18 Apr 98 **I WANT YOU TO WANT ME** *Jive JIVECD 452* 16 3
15 Aug 98 **I WANNA LOVE YOU** *Jive 0521742* 20 4
21 Nov 98 **TO LOVE ONCE AGAIN** *Jive 0522472* 55 1

SOLID SENDERS

UK, male vocal / instrumental group (Albums: 3 weeks) pos/wks

23 Sep 78 **SOLID SENDERS** *Virgin V 2105* 42 3

SOLID SESSIONS *Holland, male production duo (Singles: 1 week)* pos/wks

14 Sep 02 **JANEIRO** *Positiva CDTIV 175* 47 1

SOLITAIRE *UK, male production duo (Singles: 2 weeks)* pos/wks

29 Nov 03 **I LIVE LOVE (I LOVE LOVE)** *Susu CDSUSU 21* 57 2

SOLO *UK, male producer – Stuart Crichton (Singles: 4 weeks)* pos/wks

20 Jul 91 **RAINBOW (SAMPLE FREE)** *Reverb RVBT 003* 59 2
18 Jan 92 **COME ON!** *Reverb RVBT 008* 75 1
11 Sep 93 **COME ON! (re-mix)** *Stoatin' STOAT 003CD* 63 1

Sal SOLO *UK, male vocalist (Singles: 13 weeks)* pos/wks

15 Dec 84 **SAN DAMIANO (HEART AND SOUL)** *MCA MCA 930* 15 10
6 Apr 85 **MUSIC AND YOU** *MCA MCA 946* [1] 52 3

[1] Sal Solo with the London Community Gospel Choir

See also CLASSIX NOUVEAUX

SOLO (US) *US, male vocal group (Singles: 3 weeks)* pos/wks

3 Feb 96 **HEAVEN** *Perspective 5875212* 35 2
30 Mar 96 **WHERE DO U WANT ME TO PUT IT** *Perspective 5875312* 45 1

Diane SOLOMON *UK, female vocalist (Albums: 6 weeks)* pos/wks

9 Aug 75 **TAKE TWO** *Philips 6308 236* 26 6

Sir George SOLTI – *See Dudley MOORE*

SOLUTION – *See Victor SIMONELLI presents SOLUTION*

Belouis SOME

UK, male vocalist – Neville Keighley (Singles: 26 weeks) pos/wks

27 Apr 85 **IMAGINATION** *Parlophone R 6097* 50 7

18 Jan 86 **IMAGINATION (re-issue)** *Parlophone R 1986* 17 10
12 Apr 86 **SOME PEOPLE** *Parlophone R 6130* 33 7
16 May 87 **LET IT BE WITH YOU** *Parlophone R 6154* 53 2

Jimmy SOMERVILLE

UK, male vocalist (Singles: 53 weeks, Albums: 46 weeks) pos/wks

11 Nov 89 **COMMENT TE DIRE ADIEU** *London LON 241* [1] 14 9
13 Jan 90 ● **YOU MAKE ME FEEL (MIGHTY REAL)** *London LON 249* 5 8
17 Mar 90 **READ MY LIPS (ENOUGH IS ENOUGH)** *London LON 254* 26 6
3 Nov 90 ● **TO LOVE SOMEBODY** *London LON 281* 8 11
2 Feb 91 **SMALLTOWN BOY (re-mix)** *London LON 287* [2] 32 4
10 Aug 91 **RUN FROM LOVE** *London LON 301* 52 2
28 Jan 95 **HEARTBEAT** *London LONCD 358* 24 4
27 May 95 **HURT SO GOOD** *London LONCD 364* 15 6
28 Oct 95 **BY YOUR SIDE** *London LONCD 372* 41 2
13 Sep 97 **DARK SKY** *Gut CXGUT 11* 66 1
9 Dec 89 **READ MY LIPS** *London 8281661* 29 14
24 Nov 90 ● **THE SINGLES COLLECTION 1984/1990** *London 8282261* 4 26
24 Jun 95 **DARE TO LOVE** *London 8285402* 38 2
22 Sep 01 **THE VERY BEST OF JIMMY SOMERVILLE, BRONSKI BEAT AND THE COMMUNARDS** *London 927412582* [1] 29 4

[1] Jimmy Somerville featuring June Miles-Kingston [2] Jimmy Somerville with Bronski Beat [1] Jimmy Somerville, Bronski Beat and the Communards

See also BRONSKI BEAT; COMMUNARDS

SOMETHIN' FOR THE PEOPLE featuring TRINA and TAMARA

US, male vocal / instrumental group and female vocal duo (Singles: 1 week) pos/wks

7 Feb 98 **MY LOVE IS THE SHHH!** *Warner Bros W 0427CD* 64 1

SOMETHING CORPORATE

US, male vocal / instrumental group (Singles: 3 weeks) pos/wks

29 Mar 03 **PUNK ROCK PRINCESS** *MCA MCSTD 40315* 33 2
12 Jul 03 **IF YOU C JORDAN** *MCA MCSTD 40324* 68 1

SOMORE featuring Damon TRUEITT

US, male production group and male vocalist (Singles: 2 weeks) pos/wks

24 Jan 98 **I REFUSE (WHAT YOU WANT)** *XL Recordings XLS 93CD* 21 2

SONGSTRESS

US, male production / vocal duo (Singles: 1 week) pos/wks

27 Feb 99 **SEE LINE WOMAN '99** *Locked On LOX 106CD* 64 1

SONIA

UK, female vocalist (Singles: 78 weeks, Albums: 14 weeks) pos/wks

24 Jun 89 ★ **YOU'LL NEVER STOP ME LOVING YOU** *Chrysalis CHS 3385* 1 13
7 Oct 89 **CAN'T FORGET YOU** *Chrysalis CHS 3419* 17 6
9 Dec 89 ● **LISTEN TO YOUR HEART** *Chrysalis CHS 3465* 10 10
7 Apr 90 **COUNTING EVERY MINUTE** *Chrysalis CHS 3492* 16 7
23 Jun 90 **YOU'VE GOT A FRIEND** *Jive CHILD 90* [1] 14 6
25 Aug 90 **END OF THE WORLD** *Chrysalis/PWL CHS 3557* 18 7
1 Jun 91 ● **ONLY FOOLS (NEVER FALL IN LOVE)** *IQ ZB 44613* 10 8
31 Aug 91 **BE YOUNG BE FOOLISH BE HAPPY** *IQ ZB 44935* 22 5
16 Nov 91 **YOU TO ME ARE EVERYTHING** *IQ ZB 45121* 13 5
12 Sep 92 **BOOGIE NIGHTS** *Arista 74321113467* 30 3
1 May 93 **BETTER THE DEVIL YOU KNOW** *Arista 74321146872* 15 7
30 Jul 94 **HOPELESSLY DEVOTED TO YOU** *Cockney COCCD 2* 61 1
5 May 90 ● **EVERYBODY KNOWS** *Chrysalis CHR 1734* 7 10
19 Oct 91 **SONIA** *IQ ZL 751675* 33 2
29 May 93 **BETTER THE DEVIL YOU KNOW** *Arista 74321149802* 32 2

[1] Big Fun and Sonia featuring Gary Barnacle

SONIC BOOM

UK, male vocal / instrumental group (Albums: 1 week) pos/wks

17 Mar 90 **SPECTRUM** *Silvertone ORELP 56* 65 1

SONIC SOLUTION

Belgium, male production duo – CJ Bolland and Steve Cop (Singles: 1 week) pos/wks

4 Apr 92 **BEATSTIME** *R&S RSUK 11* 59 1

WORLD'S BEST-SELLING ALBUMS

Accepting that it is notoriously difficult to pin down accurate figures for album sales worldwide, we still think it is worth printing here the results of our research from figures we have collected over the years. The results may be hotly disputed but are nonetheless fascinating, dominated as they are by the largest record-buying market on earth, the US.

> THRILLER – Michael Jackson – 47 million*
> THEIR GREATEST HITS 1971-1975 – Eagles – 31 million
> SATURDAY NIGHT FEVER – Soundtrack – 30 million
> COME ON OVER – Shania Twain – 30 million
> JAGGED LITTLE PILL – Alanis Morissette – 29 million
> RUMOURS – Fleetwood Mac – 26 million
> LED ZEPPELIN (Untitled fourth album) – Led Zeppelin – 26 million
> BAT OUT OF HELL – Meat Loaf – 24 million
> DARK SIDE OF THE MOON – Pink Floyd – 23 million
> 1 – Beatles – 23 million
> HOTEL CALIFORNIA – Eagles – 23 million
> BACK IN BLACK – AC/DC – 23 million

* 47 to 51.2 million depending on the sources of information used.

Madonna's True Blue is another real contender for our Top 12, with estimates varying between 17 and 25 million

The UK's best-seller is Sgt. Pepper's Lonely Hearts Club Band by The Beatles with 4.5 million sales and 21 million worldwide.

The world's best-selling debut album is Boston by Boston, released in 1976 and with sales to date of more than 16 million.

Track listing for the world's best-selling album:

Wanna Be Startin' Somethin'
Baby Be Mine
The Girl Is Mine
Thriller
Beat It
Billie Jean
Human Nature
PYT (Pretty Young Thing)
The Lady in My Life

SONIC SURFERS
Holland, male instrumental / production duo (Singles: 2 weeks) pos/wks

20 Mar 93	TAKE ME UP *A&M AMCD 210* [1]	61	1
30 Jul 94	DON'T GIVE IT UP *Brilliant CDBRIL 6*	54	1

[1] Sonic Surfers featuring Jocelyn Brown

SONIC THE HEDGEHOG – *See HWA featuring SONIC THE HEDGEHOG*

SONIC YOUTH *US, male / female vocal / instrumental group (Singles: 14 weeks, Albums: 14 weeks)* pos/wks

11 Jul 92	100% *DGC DGCS 11*	28	4
7 Nov 92	YOUTH AGAINST FASCISM *Geffen GFS 26*	52	2
3 Apr 93	SUGAR KANE *Geffen GFSTD 37*	26	3
7 May 94	BULL IN THE HEATHER *Geffen GFSTD 72*	24	2
10 Sep 94	SUPERSTAR *A&M 5807932*	45	2
11 Jul 98	SUNDAY *Geffen GFSTD 22332*	72	1
29 Oct 88	DAYDREAM NATION *Blast First BFFP 34*	99	1
4 Feb 89	THE WHITEY ALBUM *Blast First BFFP 28* [1]	63	1
7 Jul 90	GOO *DGC 7599242971*	32	2
4 May 91	DIRTY BOOTS – PLUS 5 LIVE TRACKS *DGC DGC 21634*	69	1
1 Aug 92 ●	DIRTY *DGC DGCD 24485*	6	5
21 May 94 ●	EXPERIMENTAL JET SET TRASH AND NO STAR *Geffen GED 24632*	10	2
14 Oct 95	WASHING MACHINE *Geffen GED 24825*	39	1
23 May 98	A THOUSAND LEAVES *Geffen GED 25203*	38	1

[1] Ciccone Youth

The listed flip side of 'Superstar' was 'Yesterday Once More' by Redd Kross

SONIQUE *UK, female vocalist / DJ – Sonia Clarke (Singles: 47 weeks, Albums: 37 weeks)* pos/wks

13 Jun 98	I PUT A SPELL ON YOU *Serious SERR 001CD*	36	2
5 Dec 98	IT FEELS SO GOOD *Serious SERR 004CD*	24	3
3 Jun 00 ★	IT FEELS SO GOOD (re-mix) *Universal MCSTD 40233* ■	1	17
16 Sep 00 ●	SKY *Universal MCSTD 40240*	2	10
9 Dec 00 ●	I PUT A SPELL ON YOU (re-issue) *Universal MCSTD 40245*	8	10
31 May 03	CAN'T MAKE UP MY MIND *Serious 9807217*	17	4
13 Sep 03	ALIVE *Serious 9811500*	70	1
24 Jun 00 ●	HEAR MY CRY *Universal 1592302*	6	37

SONNY
US, male vocalist – Salvatore Bono, d. 5 Jan 1998 (Singles: 11 weeks) pos/wks

19 Aug 65 ●	LAUGH AT ME *Atlantic AT 4038*	9	11

See also SONNY and CHER

SONNY and CHER
US, male / female vocal / instrumental duo – Salvatore Bono d. 5 Jan 1998, and Cherilyn LaPierre (Singles: 78 weeks, Albums: 20 weeks) pos/wks

12 Aug 65 ★	I GOT YOU BABE *Atlantic AT 4035* ▲	1	12
16 Sep 65	BABY DON'T GO *Reprise R 20309*	11	9
21 Oct 65	BUT YOU'RE MINE *Atlantic AT 4047*	17	8
17 Feb 66	WHAT NOW MY LOVE *Atlantic AT 4069*	13	11
30 Jun 66	HAVE I STAYED TOO LONG *Atlantic 584 018*	42	3
8 Sep 66 ●	LITTLE MAN *Atlantic 584 040*	4	10
17 Nov 66	LIVING FOR YOU *Atlantic 584 057*	44	4
2 Feb 67	THE BEAT GOES ON *Atlantic 584 078*	29	8
15 Jan 72 ●	ALL I EVER NEED IS YOU (2re) *MCA MU 1145*	8	12
22 May 93	I GOT YOU BABE (re-issue) *Epic 6592402*	66	1
16 Oct 65 ●	LOOK AT US *Atlantic ATL 5036*	7	13
14 May 66	THE WONDROUS WORLD OF SONNY AND CHER *Atlantic 587006*	15	7

See also CHER; SONNY

SONO *Germany, male production duo (Singles: 1 week)* pos/wks

16 Jun 01	KEEP CONTROL *Code Blue BLU 020CD1*	66	1

SON'Z OF A LOOP DA LOOP ERA
UK, male producer – Danny Breaks (Singles: 4 weeks) pos/wks

15 Feb 92	FAR OUT *Suburban Base SUBBASE 008*	36	3
17 Oct 92	PEACE + LOVEISM *Suburban Base SUBBASE 14*	60	1

SOOZY Q – *See BIG TIME CHARLIE*

SOPHIE – *See ZERO 7*

SORROWS
UK, male vocal / instrumental group (Singles: 8 weeks) pos/wks

16 Sep 65	TAKE A HEART *Piccadilly 7N 35260*	21	8

Aaron SOUL *UK, male vocalist – Aaron Anyia (Singles: 4 weeks)* pos/wks

2 Jun 01	RING RING RING *Def Soul 5689042*	14	4

David SOUL *US, male actor / vocalist – David Solberg (Singles: 56 weeks, Albums: 51 weeks)* pos/wks

18 Dec 76 ★	DON'T GIVE UP ON US *Private Stock PVT 84* ◆ ▲	1	16
26 Mar 77 ●	GOING IN WITH MY EYES OPEN *Private Stock PVT 99*	2	8
27 Aug 77 ★	SILVER LADY *Private Stock PVT 115*	1	14
17 Dec 77 ●	LET'S HAVE A QUIET NIGHT IN *Private Stock PVT 130*	8	9
27 May 78	IT SURE BRINGS OUT THE LOVE IN YOUR EYES *Private Stock PVT 137*	12	9
27 Nov 76 ●	DAVID SOUL *Private Stock PVLP 1012*	2	28
17 Sep 77 ●	PLAYING TO AN AUDIENCE OF ONE *Private Stock PVLP 1026*	8	23

Jimmy SOUL *US, male vocalist – James McCleese, d. 25 Jun 1988 (Singles: 5 weeks)* pos/wks

11 Jul 63	IF YOU WANNA BE HAPPY *Stateside SS 178* ▲	39	2
15 Jun 91	IF YOU WANNA BE HAPPY (re-issue) *Epic 6569647*	68	3

SOUL ASYLUM *US, male vocal / instrumental group (Singles: 33 weeks, Albums: 29 weeks)* pos/wks

19 Jun 93 ●	RUNAWAY TRAIN (re) *Columbia 6593902*	7	19
4 Sep 93	SOMEBODY TO SHOVE *Columbia 6596492*	34	3
22 Jan 94	BLACK GOLD *Columbia 6598442*	26	4
26 Mar 94	SOMEBODY TO SHOVE (re-issue) *Columbia 6602245*	32	3
15 Jul 95	MISERY *Columbia 6621092*	30	3
2 Dec 95	JUST LIKE ANYONE *Columbia 6624785*	52	1
31 Jul 93	GRAVE DANCERS UNION *Columbia 4722532*	27	25
1 Jul 95	LET YOUR DIM LIGHT SHINE *Columbia 4803202*	22	4

'Runaway Train' peaked during re-entry in Nov 1993

SOUL BROTHERS
UK, male vocal / instrumental group (Singles: 3 weeks) pos/wks

22 Apr 65	I KEEP RINGING MY BABY *Decca F 12116*	42	3

SOUL CITY ORCHESTRA
UK, male instrumental / production group (Singles: 1 week) pos/wks

11 Dec 93	IT'S JURASSIC *London JURCD 1*	70	1

SOUL CITY SYMPHONY – *See Van McCOY*

SOUL FAMILY SENSATION *UK / US, male / female vocal / instrumental group (Singles: 4 weeks)* pos/wks

11 May 91	I DON'T EVEN KNOW IF I SHOULD CALL YOU BABY *One Little Indian 47 TP7*	49	4

SOUL FOR REAL *US, male vocal group (Singles: 4 weeks)* pos/wks

8 Jul 95	CANDY RAIN *Uptown MCSTD 2052*	23	2
23 Mar 96	EVERY LITTLE THING I DO *Uptown MCSTD 48005*	31	2

SOUL II SOUL (334 Top 500)
Enormously influential dance music project led by entrepreneurial producer / DJ Jazzie B, b. Beresford Romeo, 16 Jan 1963, London. Act featured Nellee Hooper's innovative arrangements and was fronted by a succession of vocalists, most notably Caron Wheeler. Unlike UK contemporaries they were equally successful in US (Singles: 89 weeks, Albums: 108 weeks) pos/wks

21 May 88	FAIRPLAY *10 TEN 228* [1]	63	3
17 Sep 88	FEEL FREE *10 TEN 236* [2]	64	2
18 Mar 89 ●	KEEP ON MOVING *10 TEN 263* [3]	5	12

10 Jun 89 ★ **BACK TO LIFE (HOWEVER DO YOU WANT ME)** *10 TEN 265* [3] ..1 14
9 Dec 89 ● **GET A LIFE** *10 TEN 284* 3 13
5 May 90 ● **A DREAM'S A DREAM** *10 TEN 300* 6 6
24 Nov 90 **MISSING YOU** *10 TEN 345* [4] 22 7
4 Apr 92 ● **JOY** *Ten TEN 350* 4 7
13 Jun 92 **MOVE ME NO MOUNTAIN** *Ten TEN 400* [5] 31 4
26 Sep 92 **JUST RIGHT** *Ten TEN 410* 38 2
6 Nov 93 **WISH** *Virgin VSCDG 1480* 24 4
22 Jul 95 **LOVE ENUFF** *Virgin VSCDT 1527* 12 6
21 Oct 95 **I CARE (SOUL II SOUL)** *Virgin VSCDT 1560* 17 4
19 Oct 96 **KEEP ON MOVIN' (re-mix)** *Virgin VSCDT 1612* 31 2
30 Aug 97 **REPRESENT** *Island CID 668* 39 2
8 Nov 97 **PLEASURE DOME** *Island CID 669* 51 1
22 Apr 89 ★ **CLUB CLASSICS VOL. ONE** *10 DIX 82* 1 60
2 Jun 90 ★ **VOLUME II (1990 A NEW DECADE)** *10 DIX 90* ■ 1 20
25 Apr 92 ● **VOLUME III JUST RIGHT** *Ten DIXCD 100* 3 11
27 Nov 93 ● **VOLUME IV THE CLASSIC SINGLES 88-93** *Virgin CDV 2724* 10 13
12 Aug 95 **VOLUME V – BELIEVE** *Virgin CDV 2739* 13 4

[1] Soul II Soul featuring Rose Windross [2] Soul II Soul featuring Do'reen [3] Soul II Soul featuring Caron Wheeler [4] Soul II Soul featuring Kym Mazelle [5] Soul II Soul, lead vocals Kofi

See also PSYCHEDELIC WALTONS

SOUL PROVIDERS featuring Michelle SHELLERS
UK, male production duo and US, female vocalist (Singles: 1 week) pos/wks

14 Jul 01 **RISE** *AM:PM CDAMPM 147* 59 1

SOUL SONIC FORCE – *See Afrika BAMBAATAA; OAKENFOLD*

S.O.U.L. S.Y.S.T.E.M. introducing Michelle VISAGE
US, male / female vocal / instrumental group (Singles: 5 weeks) pos/wks

16 Jan 93 **IT'S GONNA BE A LOVELY DAY** *Arista 74321125692* 17 5

See also C & C MUSIC FACTORY

SOUL U*NIQUE
UK, male / female vocal group (Singles: 2 weeks) pos/wks

19 Feb 00 **BE MY FRIEND** *M&J MAJCD 2* 53 1
29 Jul 00 **3IL (THRILL)** *M&J MAJCD 3X* 66 1

SOUL VISION – *See EVERYTHING BUT THE GIRL*

SOULED OUT *Italy / US / UK, male / female vocal / instrumental group (Singles: 1 week)* pos/wks

9 May 92 **IN MY LIFE** *Columbia 6578367* 75 1

SOULFLY
Brazil / US, male vocal / instrumental group (Albums: 4 weeks) pos/wks

2 May 98 **SOULFLY** *Roadrunner RR 87482* 16 2
7 Oct 00 **PRIMITIVE** *Roadrunner RR 85652* 45 1
6 Jul 02 **3** *Roadrunner RR 84552* 61 1

SOULSEARCHER
US, male / female production / vocal group (Singles: 9 weeks) pos/wks

13 Feb 99 ● **CAN'T GET ENOUGH** *Defected DEFECT 1CDS* 8 7
8 Apr 00 **DO IT TO ME AGAIN** *Defected DFECT 15CDS* 32 2

SOULWAX *Belgium, male vocal / instrumental duo – Stephen and David Dewaele (Singles: 5 weeks)* pos/wks

25 Mar 00 **CONVERSATION INTERCOM** *Pias Recordings PIASB 018CD* 65 1
24 Jun 00 **MUCH AGAINST EVERYONE'S ADVICE** *Pias Recordings PIASB 026CD* 56 1
30 Sep 00 **TOO MANY DJ'S** *Pias Recordings PIASB 036CD* 40 2
3 Mar 01 **CONVERSATION INTERCOM (re-mix)** *Pias Recordings PIASB 046CD* 50 1

SOUND BLUNTZ
Germany, male production / vocal group (Singles: 2 weeks) pos/wks

30 Nov 02 **BILLIE JEAN** *Incentive CENT 51CDS* 32 2

SOUND-DE-ZIGN
Holland, male DJ / production duo – Adri Blok and Arjen Rietvink (Singles: 5 weeks) pos/wks

14 Apr 01 **HAPPINESS** *Nulife / Arista 74321844002* 19 5

SOUND FACTORY
Sweden, male vocal / instrumental duo (Singles: 1 week) pos/wks

5 Jun 93 **2 THE RHYTHM** *Logic 74321149422* 72 1

SOUND 5
UK, male vocal / instrumental group (Singles: 1 week) pos/wks

24 Apr 99 **ALA KABOO** *Gut CDGUT 23* 69 1

SOUND 9418 – *See Jonathan KING*

SOUND OF ONE featuring GLADEZZ
US, male / female vocal / instrumental duo (Singles: 1 week) pos/wks

20 Nov 93 **AS I AM** *Cooltempo CDCOOL 280* 65 1

SOUNDGARDEN
US, male vocal / instrumental group (Singles: 24 weeks, Albums: 32 weeks) pos/wks

11 Apr 92 **JESUS CHRIST POSE** *A&M AM 862* 30 3
20 Jun 92 **RUSTY CAGE** *A&M AM 874* 41 1
21 Nov 92 **OUTSHINED** *A&M AM 0102* 50 1
26 Feb 94 **SPOONMAN** *A&M 5805392* 20 3
30 Apr 94 **THE DAY I TRIED TO LIVE** *A&M 5805952* 42 2
20 Aug 94 **BLACK HOLE SUN** *A&M 5807532* 12 5
28 Jan 95 **FELL ON BLACK DAYS** *A&M 5809472* 24 2
18 May 96 **PRETTY NOOSE** *A&M 5816202* 14 3
28 Sep 96 **BURDEN IN MY HAND** *A&M 5818552* 33 2
28 Dec 96 **BLOW UP THE OUTSIDE WORLD** *A&M 5819862* 40 2
25 Apr 92 **BADMOTORFINGER** *A&M 3953742* 39 2
19 Mar 94 ● **SUPERUNKNOWN** *A&M 5402152* ▲ 4 24
1 Jun 96 ● **DOWN ON THE UPSIDE** *A&M 5405262* 7 6

SOUNDMAN and Don LLOYDIE with Elisabeth TROY
UK, male / female vocal / production group (Singles: 2 weeks) pos/wks

25 Feb 95 **GREATER LOVE** *Sound of Underground SOURCD 016* 49 2

SOUNDS INCORPORATED
UK, male instrumental group (Singles: 11 weeks) pos/wks

23 Apr 64 **THE SPARTANS** *Columbia DB 7239* 30 6
30 Jul 64 **SPANISH HARLEM** *Columbia DB 7321* 35 5

See also Gene VINCENT

SOUNDS NICE featuring Tim MYCROFT
UK, male instrumental group (Singles: 11 weeks) pos/wks

6 Sep 69 **LOVE AT FIRST SIGHT (JE T'AIME . . . MOI NON PLUS)** *Parlophone R 5797* 18 11

SOUNDS OF BLACKNESS *US, male / female gospel choir (Singles: 32 weeks, Albums: 6 weeks)* pos/wks

22 Jun 91 **OPTIMISTIC** *Perspective PERSS 786* 45 4
28 Sep 91 **THE PRESSURE PART 1** *Perspective PERSS 816* 71 1
15 Feb 92 **OPTIMISTIC (re-issue)** *Perspective PERSS 849* 28 4
25 Apr 92 **THE PRESSURE PART 1 (re-mix)** *Perspective PERSS 867* 49 2
8 May 93 **I'M GOING ALL THE WAY** *Perspective 5874252* 27 3
26 Mar 94 **I BELIEVE** *A&M 5874512* 17 4
2 Jul 94 **GLORYLAND** *Mercury MERCD 404* [1] 36 4
20 Aug 94 **EVERYTHING IS GONNA BE ALRIGHT** *A&M 5874672* 29 3
14 Jan 95 **I'M GOING ALL THE WAY (re-issue)** *A&M 5874832* 14 4
7 Jun 97 **SPIRIT** *A&M 5822292* [2] 35 2
14 Feb 98 **THE PRESSURE (2nd re-mix)** *AM:PM 5824872* 46 1
30 Apr 94 **AFRICA TO AMERICA: THE JOURNEY OF THE DRUM** *A&M 5490092* 28 6

[1] Daryl Hall and the Sounds of Blackness [2] Sounds of Blackness / Craig Mack

SOUNDS ORCHESTRAL *UK, orchestra (Singles: 18 weeks, Albums: 1 week)* pos/wks

Date	Title / Label	pos	wks
3 Dec 64 ●	**CAST YOUR FATE TO THE WIND** *Piccadilly 7N 35206*	5	16
8 Jul 65	**MOONGLOW** *Piccadilly 7N 35248*	43	2
12 Jun 65	**CAST YOUR FATE TO THE WIND** *Piccadilly NPL 38041*	17	1

SOUNDSATION *UK, male producer (Singles: 1 week)* pos/wks

Date	Title / Label	pos	wks
14 Jan 95	**PEACE AND JOY** *Ffrreedom TABCD 224*	48	1

SOUNDSCAPE *UK, male DJ / production group (Singles: 1 week)* pos/wks

Date	Title / Label	pos	wks
14 Feb 98	**DUBPLATE CULTURE** *Satellite 74321552002*	61	1

SOUNDSOURCE *Sweden / UK, male instrumental / production group (Singles: 1 week)* pos/wks

Date	Title / Label	pos	wks
11 Jan 92	**TAKE ME UP** *ffrr FX 177*	62	1

SOUNDTRACKS – *See VARIOUS ARTISTS (EPs and LPs)*

SOUP DRAGONS *UK, male vocal / instrumental group (Singles: 23 weeks, Albums: 17 weeks)* pos/wks

Date	Title / Label	pos	wks
20 Jun 87	**CAN'T TAKE NO MORE** *Raw TV RTV 3*	65	1
5 Sep 87	**SOFT AS YOUR FACE** *Raw TV RTV 4*	66	2
14 Jul 90 ●	**I'M FREE** *Raw TV RTV 9* [1]	5	12
20 Oct 90	**MOTHER UNIVERSE** *Big Life BLR 30*	26	5
11 Apr 92	**DIVINE THING** *Big Life BLR 68*	53	3
7 May 88	**THIS IS OUR ART** *Sire WX 169*	60	1
5 May 90 ●	**LOVEGOD** *Raw TV SOUPLP 2*	7	15
16 May 92	**HOTWIRED** *Big Life BLRCD 15*	74	1

[1] Soup Dragons featuring Junior Reid

SOURCE *UK, male producer – John Truelove (Singles: 22 weeks)* pos/wks

Date	Title / Label	pos	wks
2 Feb 91 ●	**YOU GOT THE LOVE** *Truelove TLOVE 7001* [1]	4	11
26 Dec 92	**ROCK THE HOUSE** *React 12REACT 12* [2]	63	1
1 Mar 97 ●	**YOU GOT THE LOVE (re-mix)** *React CDREACT 89* [1]	3	8
23 Aug 97	**CLOUDS** *XL Recordings XLS 83CD*	38	2

[1] Source featuring Candi Staton [2] Source featuring Nicole

SOURMASH *UK, male production trio (Singles: 1 week)* pos/wks

Date	Title / Label	pos	wks
23 Dec 00	**PILGRIMAGE / MESCALITO** *Hooj Choons HOOJ 102*	73	1

SOUTH *UK, male vocal / instrumental group (Singles: 2 weeks)* pos/wks

Date	Title / Label	pos	wks
17 Mar 01	**PAINT THE SILENCE** *Mo Wax MWR 134CD*	69	1
23 Aug 03	**LOOSEN YOUR HOLD** *Double Dragon DD 2010CD*	73	1

Joe SOUTH *US, male vocalist – Joe Souter (Singles: 11 weeks)* pos/wks

Date	Title / Label	pos	wks
5 Mar 69 ●	**GAMES PEOPLE PLAY** *Capitol CL 15579*	6	11

SOUTH BANK ORCHESTRA *UK, orchestra (Albums: 6 weeks)* pos/wks

Date	Title / Label	pos	wks
2 Dec 78	**LILLIE** *Sounds MOR 516*	47	6

Album was conducted by Joseph Morovitz and Laurie Holloway

SOUTH ST PLAYER *US, male vocalist / producer – Roland Clark (Singles: 1 week)* pos/wks

Date	Title / Label	pos	wks
2 Sep 00	**WHO KEEPS CHANGING YOUR MIND** *Cream CREAM 4CD*	49	1

Jeri SOUTHERN *US, female vocalist – Genevieve Hering, d. 4 Aug 1991 (Singles: 3 weeks)* pos/wks

Date	Title / Label	pos	wks
21 Jun 57	**FIRE DOWN BELOW** *Brunswick 05665*	22	3

SOUTHERN DEATH CULT – *See CULT*

SOUTHLANDERS *Jamaica / UK, male vocal group (Singles: 10 weeks)* pos/wks

Date	Title / Label	pos	wks
22 Nov 57	**ALONE** *Decca F 10946*	17	10

SOUTHSIDE SPINNERS *Holland, male production duo – Marco Verkuylen and Benjamin Kuyten (Singles: 7 weeks)* pos/wks

Date	Title / Label	pos	wks
27 May 00 ●	**LUVSTRUCK** *AM:PM CDAMPM 132*	9	7

SOUVERNANCE *Holland, male production duo (Singles: 1 week)* pos/wks

Date	Title / Label	pos	wks
31 Aug 02	**HAVIN' A GOOD TIME** *Positiva CDTIV 174*	63	1

SOUVLAKI *UK, male producer – Mark Summers (Singles: 4 weeks)* pos/wks

Date	Title / Label	pos	wks
15 Feb 97	**INFERNO** *Wonderboy WBOYD 003*	24	3
8 Aug 98	**MY TIME** *Wonderboy WBOYD 009*	63	1

See also Mark SUMMERS

SOVEREIGN COLLECTION *UK, orchestra (Singles: 6 weeks)* pos/wks

Date	Title / Label	pos	wks
3 Apr 71	**MOZART 40** *Capitol CL 15676*	27	6

Red SOVINE *US, male vocalist – Woodrow Wilson Sovine, d. 4 Apr 1980 (Singles: 8 weeks)* pos/wks

Date	Title / Label	pos	wks
13 Jun 81 ●	**TEDDY BEAR** *Starday SD 142*	4	8

SOX *UK, female vocal / instrumental group – lead vocal Samantha Fox (Singles: 1 week)* pos/wks

Date	Title / Label	pos	wks
15 Apr 95	**GO FOR THE HEART** *Living Beat LBECD 33*	47	1

Bob B SOXX and the BLUE JEANS *US, male / female vocal group (Singles: 2 weeks)* pos/wks

Date	Title / Label	pos	wks
31 Jan 63	**ZIP-A-DEE-DOO-DAH** *London HLU 9646*	45	2

SPACE *France, male instrumental group (Singles: 12 weeks, Albums: 9 weeks)* pos/wks

Date	Title / Label	pos	wks
13 Aug 77 ●	**MAGIC FLY** *Pye International 7N 25746*	2	12
17 Sep 77	**MAGIC FLY** *Pye NSPL 28232*	11	9

SPACE *UK, male vocal / instrumental group (Singles: 51 weeks, Albums: 67 weeks)* pos/wks

Date	Title / Label	pos	wks
6 Apr 96	**NEIGHBOURHOOD** *Gut CDGUT 1*	56	1
8 Jun 96	**FEMALE OF THE SPECIES** *Gut CDGUT 2*	14	10
7 Sep 96 ●	**ME AND YOU VERSUS THE WORLD** *Gut CDGUT 4*	9	6
2 Nov 96	**NEIGHBOURHOOD (re-issue)** *Gut CDGUT 5*	11	6
22 Feb 97	**DARK CLOUDS** *Gut CDGUT 6*	14	4
10 Jan 98 ●	**AVENGING ANGELS** *Gut CDGUT 16*	6	8
7 Mar 98 ●	**THE BALLAD OF TOM JONES** *Gut CDGUT 018* [1]	4	8
4 Jul 98	**BEGIN AGAIN** *Gut CDGUT 19*	21	4
5 Dec 98	**THE BAD DAYS (EP)** *Gut CDGUT 22*	20	3
8 Jul 00	**DIARY OF A WIMP** *Gut CDGUT 34*	49	1
28 Sep 96 ●	**SPIDERS** *Gut GUTCD 1*	5	42
21 Mar 98 ●	**TIN PLANET** *Gut GUTCD 5*	3	25

[1] Space with Cerys of Catatonia

Tracks on The Bad Days (EP): Bad Days / We Gotta Get Out of This Place / The Unluckiest Man in the World

SPACE BABY *UK, male producer – Matt Darey (Singles: 1 week)* pos/wks

Date	Title / Label	pos	wks
8 Jul 95	**FREE YOUR MIND** *Hooj Choons HOOJ 34CD*	55	1

SPACE BROTHERS *UK, male production duo – Ricky Simmonds and Stephen Jones (Singles: 19 weeks)* pos/wks

Date	Title / Label	pos	wks
17 May 97	**SHINE** *Manifesto FESCD 23*	23	3
13 Dec 97	**FORGIVEN (I FEEL YOUR LOVE)** *Manifesto FESCD 36*	27	7
10 Jul 99	**LEGACY (SHOW ME LOVE)** *Manifesto FESCD 55*	31	3
9 Oct 99	**HEAVEN WILL COME** *Manifesto FESCD 61*	25	2
5 Feb 00	**SHINE 2000 (re-mix)** *Manifesto FESCD 67*	18	4

See also ASCENSION; CHAKRA; ESSENCE; LUSTRAL; OXYGEN featuring Andrea BRITTON

SPACE COWBOY
France, male producer – Nick Dresti (Singles: 3 weeks) pos/wks

6 Jul 02 **I WOULD DIE 4 U** *Southern Fried ECB 29CD* 55 2
2 Aug 03 **JUST PUT YOUR HAND IN MINE** *Southern Fried ECB 37CD* 71 1

SPACE FROG
Germany, male production duo (Singles: 1 week) pos/wks

16 Mar 02 **(X RAY) FOLLOW ME** *Tripoli Trax TTRAX 082CD* 70 1

SPACE KITTENS
UK, male instrumental / production group (Singles: 1 week) pos/wks

13 Apr 96 **STORM** *Hooj Choons HOOJCD 41* 58 1

SPACE MANOEUVRES
UK, male producer – John Graham (Singles: 2 weeks) pos/wks

29 Jan 00 **STAGE ONE** *Hooj Choons HOOJ 79CD* 25 2

SPACE MONKEY
UK, male producer – Paul Goodchild (Singles: 4 weeks) pos/wks

8 Oct 83 **CAN'T STOP RUNNING** *Innervision A 3742* 53 4

SPACE MONKEYZ vs GORILLAZ
UK, male production / instrumental duo (Singles: 1 week) pos/wks

3 Aug 02 **LIL' DUB CHEFIN'** *Parlophone CDR 6584* 73 1

SPACE RAIDERS
UK, male production trio (Singles: 1 week) pos/wks

28 Mar 98 **GLAM RAID** *Skint SKINT 32CD* 68 1

SPACE 2000
UK, male vocal / instrumental duo (Singles: 1 week) pos/wks

12 Aug 95 **DO U WANNA FUNK** *Wired WIRED 218* 50 1

SPACECORN
Sweden, male DJ / producer – Daniel Ellenson (Singles: 1 week) pos/wks

28 Apr 01 **AXEL F** *69 SN 069CD* 74 1

SPACEDUST
UK, male production duo – Paul Glancey and Duncan Glasson (Singles: 12 weeks) pos/wks

24 Oct 98 ★ **GYM AND TONIC (re)** *East West EW 188CD* ■ 1 10
27 Mar 99 **LET'S GET DOWN** *East West EW 195CD* 20 2

SPACEHOG
UK, male vocal / instrumental group (Singles: 8 weeks, Albums: 2 weeks) pos/wks

11 May 96 **IN THE MEANTIME (re)** *Sire 7559643162* 29 7
7 Feb 98 **CARRY ON** *Sire W 0428CD* 43 1
15 Feb 97 **RESIDENT ALIEN** *Sire 7559618342* 40 2

'In the Meantime' peaked during re-entry in Dec 1996

SPACEMAID
UK, male vocal / instrumental group (Singles: 1 week) pos/wks

5 Apr 97 **BABY COME ON** *Big Star STARC 105* 70 1

SPACEMEN 3
UK, male instrumental group (Albums: 1 week) pos/wks

9 Mar 91 **RECURRING** *Fire FIRELP 23* 46 1

SPAGHETTI SURFERS
UK, male instrumental / production duo (Singles: 1 week) pos/wks

22 Jul 95 **MISIRLOU (THE THEME TO THE MOTION PICTURE 'PULP FICTION')** *Tempo Toons CDTOON 4* 55 1

SPAGNA
Italy, female vocalist – Ivana Spagna (Singles: 23 weeks) pos/wks

25 Jul 87 ● **CALL ME** *CBS 650279 7* 2 12
17 Oct 87 **EASY LADY** *CBS 651169 7* 62 3
20 Aug 88 **EVERY GIRL AND BOY** *CBS SPAG 1* 23 8

SPANDAU BALLET (100) (Top 500)
Kilt-clad New Romantic revolutionaries. This London band went on to become smart-suited Top 10 regulars: Tony Hadley (v), Gary Kemp (g), Martin Kemp (b), Steve Norman (g/sax/prc), John Keeble (d). The Kemp brothers later went into the movies and TV, including lead roles in 'The Krays' (1990) and Martin, who starred in 'EastEnders' and other TV programmes, was voted Best Actor and Sexiest Male in the 2002 Soap Awards. Hadley won 2003 reality TV pop show 'Reborn in the USA' (Singles: 159 weeks, Albums: 274 weeks) pos/wks

15 Nov 80 ● **TO CUT A LONG STORY SHORT** *Reformation CHS 2473* 5 11
24 Jan 81 **THE FREEZE** *Reformation CHS 2486* 17 8
4 Apr 81 ● **MUSCLEBOUND / GLOW** *Reformation CHS 2509* 10 10
18 Jul 81 ● **CHANT NO.1 (I DON'T NEED THIS PRESSURE ON)** *Reformation CHS 2528* 3 10
14 Nov 81 **PAINT ME DOWN** *Chrysalis CHS 2560* 30 5
30 Jan 82 **SHE LOVED LIKE DIAMOND** *Chrysalis CHS 2585* 49 4
10 Apr 82 ● **INSTINCTION** *Chrysalis CHS 2602* 10 11
2 Oct 82 ● **LIFELINE** *Chrysalis CHS 2642* 7 9
12 Feb 83 **COMMUNICATION** *Reformation CHS 2662* 12 10
23 Apr 83 ★ **TRUE** *Reformation SPAN 1* 1 12
13 Aug 83 ● **GOLD** *Reformation SPAN 2* 2 9
9 Jun 84 ● **ONLY WHEN YOU LEAVE (re)** *Reformation SPAN 3* 3 10
25 Aug 84 ● **I'LL FLY FOR YOU** *Reformation SPAN 4* 9 9
20 Oct 84 **HIGHLY STRUNG** *Reformation SPAN 5* 15 5
8 Dec 84 **ROUND AND ROUND** *Reformation SPAN 6* 18 8
26 Jul 86 **FIGHT FOR OURSELVES** *Reformation A 7264* 15 7
8 Nov 86 ● **THROUGH THE BARRICADES** *Reformation SPANS 1* 6 10
14 Feb 87 **HOW MANY LIES** *Reformation SPANS 2* 34 4
3 Sep 88 **RAW** *CBS SPANS 3* 47 3
26 Aug 89 **BE FREE WITH YOUR LOVE** *CBS SPANS 4* 42 4
14 Mar 81 ● **JOURNEYS TO GLORY** *Reformation CHR 1331* 5 29
20 Mar 82 **DIAMOND** *Reformation CDL 1353* 15 18
12 Mar 83 ★ **TRUE** *Reformation CDL 1403* 1 90
7 Jul 84 ● **PARADE** *Reformation CDL 1473* 2 39
16 Nov 85 ● **THE SINGLES COLLECTION** *Chrysalis SBTV 1* 3 53
29 Nov 86 ● **THROUGH THE BARRICADES** *Reformation CBS 450 2591* 7 19
30 Sep 89 **HEART LIKE A SKY** *CBS 4633181* 31 3
28 Sep 91 **THE BEST OF SPANDAU BALLET** *Chrysalis CHR 1894* 44 3
16 Sep 00 ● **GOLD – THE BEST OF SPANDAU BALLET** *Chrysalis 5267002* 7 20

SPARKLE
US, female vocalist (Singles: 10 weeks, Albums: 1 week) pos/wks

18 Jul 98 ● **BE CAREFUL (re)** *Jive 0521452* [1] 7 7
7 Nov 98 **TIME TO MOVE ON** *Jive 0522032* 40 2
28 Aug 99 **LOVIN' YOU** *Jive 0523450* 65 1
1 Aug 98 **SPARKLE** *Jive 521462* 57 1

[1] Sparkle featuring R Kelly

SPARKLEHORSE
US, male vocal / instrumental group (Singles: 2 weeks, Albums: 4 weeks) pos/wks

31 Aug 96 **RAINMAKER** *Capitol CDCL 777* 61 1
17 Oct 98 **SICK OF GOODBYES** *Parlophone CDCLS 808* 57 1
18 May 96 **VIVADIXIESUBMARINETRANSMISSIONPLOT** *Parlophone CDP 8328162* 58 1
1 Aug 98 **GOOD MORNING SPIDER** *Parlophone 4960142* 30 2
23 Jun 01 **IT'S A WONDERFUL LIFE** *Capitol 5256162* 49 1

SPARKS
US / UK, male vocal / instrumental duo – Russell and Ron Mael (Singles: 81 weeks, Albums: 42 weeks) pos/wks

4 May 74 ● **THIS TOWN AIN'T BIG ENOUGH FOR BOTH OF US** *Island WIP 6193* 2 10
20 Jul 74 ● **AMATEUR HOUR** *Island WIP 6203* 7 9
19 Oct 74 **NEVER TURN YOUR BACK ON MOTHER EARTH** *Island WIP 6211* 13 7
18 Jan 75 **SOMETHING FOR THE GIRL WITH EVERYTHING** *Island WIP 6221* 17 7
19 Jul 75 **GET IN THE SWING** *Island WIP 6236* 27 7
4 Oct 75 **LOOKS, LOOKS, LOOKS** *Island WIP 6249* 26 4
21 Apr 79 **THE NUMBER ONE SONG IN HEAVEN** *Virgin VS 244* 14 12
21 Jul 79 ● **BEAT THE CLOCK** *Virgin VS 270* 10 9
27 Oct 79 **TRYOUTS FOR THE HUMAN RACE** *Virgin VS 289* 45 5

29 Oct 94 **WHEN DO I GET TO SING 'MY WAY'** *Logic 74321234472* **38** 3
11 Mar 95 **WHEN I KISS YOU (I HEAR CHARLIE PARKER PLAYING)** *Logic 74321264272* **36** 2
20 May 95 **WHEN DO I GET TO SING 'MY WAY' (re-issue)** *Logic 74321274002* **32** 2
9 Mar 96 **NOW THAT I OWN THE BBC** *Logic 74321348672* **60** 1
25 Oct 97 **THE NUMBER ONE SONG IN HEAVEN (re-recording)** *Roadrunner RR 22692* **70** 1
13 Dec 97 **THIS TOWN AIN'T BIG ENOUGH FOR BOTH OF US** *Roadrunner RR 22513* [1] **40** 2
1 Jun 74 ● KIMONO MY HOUSE *Island ILPS 9272* 4 24
23 Nov 74 ● PROPAGANDA *Island ILPS 9312* 9 13
18 Oct 75 INDISCREET *Island ILPS 9345* 18 4
8 Sep 79 NUMBER ONE IN HEAVEN *Virgin V 2115* 73 1

[1] Sparks vs Faith No More

Group was a UK / US group for first six hits

Bubba SPARXXX

US, male rapper – Warren Mathis (Singles: 12 weeks) pos/wks

24 Nov 01 ● **UGLY** *Interscope / Polydor 4976542* **7** 10
9 Mar 02 **LOVELY** *Interscope 4976752* **24** 2

SPEAR OF DESTINY *UK, male vocal / instrumental group (Singles: 43 weeks, Albums: 35 weeks)* pos/wks

21 May 83 **THE WHEEL** *Epic A 3372* **59** 5
21 Jan 84 **PRISONER OF LOVE** *Epic A 4068* **59** 3
14 Apr 84 **LIBERATOR** *Epic A 4310* **67** 2
15 Jun 85 **ALL MY LOVE (ASK NOTHING)** *Epic A 6333* **61** 3
10 Aug 85 **COME BACK** *Epic A 6445* **55** 3
7 Feb 87 **STRANGERS IN OUR TOWN** *10 TEN 148* **49** 4
4 Apr 87 **NEVER TAKE ME ALIVE** *10 TEN 162* **14** 11
25 Jul 87 **WAS THAT YOU?** *10 TEN 173* **55** 4
3 Oct 87 **THE TRAVELLER** *10 TEN 189* **44** 3
24 Sep 88 **SO IN LOVE WITH YOU** *Virgin VS 1123* **36** 5
23 Apr 83 GRAPES OF WRATH *Epic EPC 25318* 62 2
28 Apr 84 ONE EYED JACKS *Burning Rome EPC 25836* 22 7
7 Sep 85 WORLD SERVICE *Burning Rome EPC 26514* 11 7
2 May 87 OUTLAND *10 DIX 59* 16 13
16 May 87 S.O.D. – THE EPIC YEARS *Epic 450 8721* 53 3
22 Oct 88 THE PRICE YOU PAY *Virgin V 2549* 37 3

SPEARHEAD *US, male vocal / instrumental group (Singles: 5 weeks, Albums: 1 week)* pos/wks

17 Dec 94 **OF COURSE YOU CAN** *Capitol CDCL 733* **74** 1
22 Apr 95 **HOLE IN THE BUCKET** *Capitol CDCL 742* **55** 1
15 Jul 95 **PEOPLE IN THA MIDDLE** *Capitol CDCLS 752* **49** 2
15 Mar 97 **WHY OH WHY** *Capital CDCL 785* **45** 1
29 Mar 97 CHOCOLATE SUPA HIGHWAY *Capitol CDEST 2293* 68 1

Billie Jo SPEARS

US, female vocalist (Singles: 40 weeks, Albums: 28 weeks) pos/wks

12 Jul 75 ● **BLANKET ON THE GROUND** *United Artists UP 35805* **6** 13
17 Jul 76 ● **WHAT I'VE GOT IN MIND** *United Artists UP 36118* **4** 13
11 Dec 76 **SING ME AN OLD FASHIONED SONG** *United Artists UP 36179* **34** 9
21 Jul 79 **I WILL SURVIVE** *United Artists UP 601* **47** 5
11 Sep 76 WHAT I'VE GOT IN MIND *United Artists UAS 29955* 47 2
19 May 79 ● THE BILLIE JO SPEARS SINGLES ALBUM *United Artists UAK 30231* 7 17
21 Nov 81 COUNTRY GIRL *Warwick WW 5109* 17 9

Britney SPEARS (166 Top 500)

World's top-selling teenager with album sales exceeding 40 million, b. 2 Dec 1981, Louisiana, US. Broke debut-act first-week UK sales record with 464,000 for 'Baby One More Time' (going on to 1,450,154 in total) and is the youngest million-selling female in the history of the UK singles chart (Singles: 162 weeks, Albums: 166 weeks) pos/wks

27 Feb 99 ★ **...BABY ONE MORE TIME** *Jive 0522752* ◆ ■ ▲ **1** 22
26 Jun 99 ● **SOMETIMES** *Jive 0523202* **3** 16
2 Oct 99 ● **(YOU DRIVE ME) CRAZY** *Jive 0550582* **5** 11
29 Jan 00 ★ **BORN TO MAKE YOU HAPPY** *Jive 9250022* ■ **1** 12
13 May 00 ★ **OOPS!...I DID IT AGAIN** *Jive 9250542* ■ **1** 14
26 Aug 00 ● **LUCKY** *Jive 9251022* **5** 11
16 Dec 00 ● **STRONGER** *Jive 9251502* **7** 10
7 Apr 01 **DON'T LET ME BE THE LAST TO KNOW** *Jive 9251982* **12** 8
27 Oct 01 ● **I'M A SLAVE 4 U** *Jive 9252892* **4** 14
2 Feb 02 ● **OVERPROTECTED** *Jive 9253072* **4** 12
13 Apr 02 ● **I'M NOT A GIRL, NOT YET A WOMAN** *Jive 9253472* **2** 10
10 Aug 02 ● **BOYS** *Jive 9253912* [1] **7** 8
16 Nov 02 **I LOVE ROCK 'N' ROLL (re)** *Jive 9254202* **13** 8
22 Nov 03 ● **ME AGAINST THE MUSIC** *Jive 82876576432* [2] ....**2** 6+
20 Mar 99 ● ... BABY ONE MORE TIME *Jive 522172* ▲ 2 82
27 May 00 ● OOPS! ... I DID IT AGAIN *Jive 9220392* ▲ 2 45
17 Nov 01 ● BRITNEY *Jive 9222532* ▲ 4 34
29 Nov 03 IN THE ZONE *Jive 82876576442* ▲ ....14 5+

[1] Britney Spears featuring Pharrell Williams [2] Britney Spears featuring Madonna

SPECIALS (360 Top 500)

Midlands-based septet which led the early 1980s ska revival and, under Jerry Dammers (k), founded the trailblazing indie label 2-Tone. In 1981, Terry Hall (v), Neville Staples (v) and Lynval Golding (g) broke away to form Fun Boy Three (Singles: 101 weeks, Albums: 82 weeks) pos/wks

28 Jul 79 ● **GANGSTERS** *2-Tone CHSTT 1* [1] **6** 12
27 Oct 79 ● **A MESSAGE TO YOU RUDY / NITE KLUB** *2-Tone CHSTT 5* [2] **10** 14
26 Jan 80 ★ **THE SPECIAL A.K.A. LIVE! EP** *2-Tone CHSTT 7* **1** 10
24 May 80 ● **RAT RACE / RUDE BUOYS OUTA JAIL** *2-Tone CHSTT 11* **5** 9
20 Sep 80 ● **STEREOTYPE / INTERNATIONAL JET SET** *2-Tone CHSTT 13* **6** 8
13 Dec 80 ● **DO NOTHING / MAGGIE'S FARM** *2-Tone CHSTT 16* [3] **4** 11
20 Jun 81 ★ **GHOST TOWN** *2-Tone CHSTT 17* **1** 14
23 Jan 82 **THE BOILER** *2-Tone CHSTT 18* [4] **35** 5
3 Sep 83 **RACIST FRIEND / BRIGHT LIGHTS** *2-Tone CHSTT 25* [1] **60** 3
17 Mar 84 ● **NELSON MANDELA** *2-Tone CHSTT 26* [1] **9** 10
8 Sep 84 **WHAT I LIKE MOST ABOUT YOU IS YOUR GIRLFRIEND** *2-Tone CHSTT 27* [1] **51** 4
10 Feb 96 **HYPOCRITE** *Kuff KUFFD 3* **66** 1
3 Nov 79 ● SPECIALS *2-Tone CDL TT 5001* 4 45
4 Oct 80 ● MORE SPECIALS *2-Tone CHRTT 5003* 5 19
23 Jun 84 IN THE STUDIO *2-Tone CHRTT 5008* [1] 34 6
7 Sep 91 ● THE SPECIALS SINGLES *2-Tone CHRTT 5010* 10 9
7 Jul 01 SPECIALS (re-issue) *Chrysalis CCD 5001* 22 3

[1] Special AKA [2] Specials featuring Rico + [3] Specials featuring Rico with the Ice Rink String Sounds / Specials [4] Rhoda with the Special AKA [1] Special AKA

Tracks on The Special AKA Live EP: Too Much Too Young / Guns of Navarone / Longshot Kick De Bucket / The Liquidator / Skinhead Moonstomp. 'Maggie's Farm' listed with 'Do Nothing' only from 10 Jan 1981. Group was male / female for last four hits

Group was male / female for the third and fourth albums

See also Terry HALL

Phil SPECTOR

US, male producer (Albums: 29 weeks) pos/wks

23 Dec 72 PHIL SPECTOR'S CHRISTMAS ALBUM *Apple SAPCOR 24* 21 3
15 Oct 77 PHIL SPECTOR'S ECHOES OF THE 60'S *Phil Spector International 2307 013* 21 10
25 Dec 82 PHIL SPECTOR'S CHRISTMAS ALBUM (re-issue) *Phil Spector International 2307 005* 96 2
10 Dec 83 PHIL SPECTOR'S GREATEST HITS / PHIL SPECTOR'S CHRISTMAS ALBUM (re-issue) *Impression PSLP 1/2* 19 8
12 Dec 87 PHIL SPECTOR'S CHRISTMAS ALBUM (re-issue) *Chrysalis CDL 1625* 69 6

SPECTRUM

UK, male instrumental / production group (Singles: 1 week) pos/wks

26 Sep 92 **TRUE LOVE WILL FIND YOU IN THE END** *Silvertone ORE 44* ..**70** 1

Chris SPEDDING

UK, male vocalist / instrumentalist – guitar (Singles: 8 weeks) pos/wks

23 Aug 75 **MOTOR BIKIN'** *RAK 210* **14** 8

SPEECH *US, male vocalist – Todd Thomas (Singles: 2 weeks)* pos/wks

17 Feb 96	**LIKE MARVIN GAYE SAID (WHAT'S GOING ON)** *Cooltempo CDCOOL 314*	35	2

SPEEDWAY *UK, male / female vocal / instrumental duo – Jill Jackson and Jim Duguid (Singles: 4 weeks)* pos/wks

6 Sep 03 ●	**GENIE IN A BOTTLE / SAVE YOURSELF** *Innocent SINCD 47*	10	4

SPEEDY
UK, male / female vocal / instrumental group (Singles: 1 week) pos/wks

9 Nov 96	**BOY WONDER** *Boiler House! BOIL 2CD*	56	1

SPEEDY J
Holland, male producer – Jochem Paap (Albums: 1 week) pos/wks

10 Jul 93	**GINGER** *Warp WARPCD 14*	68	1

SPELLBOUND *India, female vocal duo (Singles: 1 week)* pos/wks

31 May 97	**HEAVEN ON EARTH** *East West EW 098CD*	73	1

Johnnie SPENCE *UK, orchestra (Singles: 15 weeks)* pos/wks

1 Mar 62	**THE 'DR KILDARE' THEME** *Parlophone R 4872*	15	15

Don SPENCER *UK, male vocalist (Singles: 12 weeks)* pos/wks

21 Mar 63	**FIREBALL (re)** *HMV POP 1087*	32	12

Jon SPENCER BLUES EXPLOSION *US, male vocal / instrumental group (Singles: 3 weeks, Albums: 2 weeks)* pos/wks

10 May 97	**WAIL** *Mute CDMUTE 204*	66	1
6 Apr 02	**SHE SAID** *Mute LCDMUTE 263*	58	1
6 Jul 02	**SWEET N SOUR** *Mute LCDMUTE 271*	66	1
12 Oct 96	**NOW I GOT WORRY** *Mute CDSTUMM 132*	50	1
31 Oct 98	**ACME** *Mute CDSTUMM 154*	72	1

Tracie SPENCER *US, female vocalist (Singles: 3 weeks)* pos/wks

4 May 91	**THIS HOUSE** *Capitol CL 612*	65	2
6 Nov 99	**IT'S ALL ABOUT YOU (NOT ABOUT ME)** *Parlophone Rhythm Series CDCL 815*	65	1

SPHINX
UK / US, male vocal / instrumental group (Singles: 2 weeks) pos/wks

25 Mar 95	**WHAT HOPE HAVE I** *Champion CHAMPCD 318*	43	2

See also FAITHLESS; OUR TRIBE / ONE TRIBE; ROLLO; DUSTED

SPICE GIRLS 173 Top 500
Britain's most successful and influential female vocal group: Geri Halliwell (Ginger Spice – left 1998), Melanie Chisholm (Mel C / Sporty Spice), Emma Bunton (Baby Spice), Victoria Adams – then Beckham (Posh Spice), Melanie Brown (Mel B / Mel G / Scary Spice). The ground-breaking girl-power group which made it a Spiceworld was the first act to put its first six singles at No.1 and the only group to spawn five solo hitmakers. Their total UK single sales amounted to 7,507,213 with 'Wannabe' their biggest seller on 1,269,841 (Singles: 179 weeks, Albums: 135 weeks) pos/wks

20 Jul 96 ★	**WANNABE** *Virgin VSCDX 1588* ◆ ▲	1	26
26 Oct 96 ★	**SAY YOU'LL BE THERE** *Virgin VSCDT 1601* ■	1	17
28 Dec 96 ★	**2 BECOME 1 (re)** *Virgin VSCDT 1607* ◆ ■	1	23
15 Mar 97 ★	**MAMA / WHO DO YOU THINK YOU ARE** *Virgin VSCDT 1623* ■	1	15
25 Oct 97 ★	**SPICE UP YOUR LIFE** *Virgin VSCDT 1660* ■	1	15
27 Dec 97 ★	**TOO MUCH** *Virgin VSCDR 1669* ■	1	15
21 Mar 98 ●	**STOP (re)** *Virgin VSCDT 1679*	2	17
1 Aug 98 ★	**VIVA FOREVER** *Virgin VSCDT 1692* ■	1	13
26 Dec 98 ★	**GOODBYE** *Virgin VSCDT 1721* ■	1	21
4 Nov 00 ★	**HOLLER / LET LOVE LEAD THE WAY** *Virgin VSCDT 1788* ■	1	17
16 Nov 96 ★	**SPICE** *Virgin CDV 2812* ■ ▲	1	72
15 Nov 97 ★	**SPICEWORLD** *Virgin CDV 2850* ■	1	55
18 Nov 00 ●	**FOREVER** *Virgin CDVX 2928*	2	8

See also Melanie B; Melanie C; Geri HALLIWELL; Emma BUNTON; Victoria BECKHAM

SPIDER *UK, male vocal / instrumental group (Singles: 5 weeks, Albums: 2 weeks)* pos/wks

5 Mar 83	**WHY D'YA LIE TO ME** *RCA 313*	65	2
10 Mar 84	**HERE WE GO ROCK 'N' ROLL** *A&M AM 180*	57	3
23 Oct 82	**ROCK 'N' ROLL GYPSIES** *RCA RCALP 3101*	75	1
7 Apr 84	**ROUGH JUSTICE** *A&M AMLX 68563*	96	1

SPIKEY TEE – *See BOMB THE BASS*

SPILLER
Italy, male producer – Cristiano Spiller (Singles: 26 weeks) pos/wks

26 Aug 00 ★	**GROOVEJET (IF THIS AIN'T LOVE)** *Positiva CDTIV 137* ■ [1]	1	24
2 Feb 02	**CRY BABY** *Positiva CDTIV 167*	40	2

[1] Spiller, lead vocals by Sophie Ellis-Bextor

See also LAGUNA

SPIN CITY
UK / Ireland, male vocal group (Singles: 3 weeks) pos/wks

26 Aug 00	**LANDSLIDE** *Epic 6696132*	30	3

SPIN DOCTORS *US, male vocal / instrumental group (Singles: 28 weeks, Albums: 57 weeks)* pos/wks

15 May 93 ●	**TWO PRINCES** *Epic 6591452*	3	15
14 Aug 93	**LITTLE MISS CAN'T BE WRONG** *Epic 6584892*	23	5
9 Oct 93	**JIMMY OLSEN'S BLUES** *Epic 6597582*	40	2
4 Dec 93	**WHAT TIME IS IT** *Epic 6599552*	56	1
25 Jun 94	**CLEOPATRA'S CAT** *Epic 6604192*	29	2
30 Jul 94	**YOU LET YOUR HEART GO TOO FAST** *Epic 6606612*	66	1
29 Oct 94	**MARY JANE** *Epic 6609772*	55	1
8 Jun 96	**SHE USED TO BE MINE** *Epic 6632682*	55	1
20 Mar 93 ●	**POCKET FULL OF KRYPTONITE** *Epic 4682502*	2	48
9 Jul 94 ●	**TURN IT UPSIDE DOWN** *Epic 4768862*	3	9

SPINAL TAP
US / UK, male vocal / instrumental group (Singles: 3 weeks, Albums: 2 weeks) pos/wks

28 Mar 92	**BITCH SCHOOL** *MCA MCS 1624*	35	2
2 May 92	**THE MAJESTY OF ROCK** *MCA MCS 1629*	61	1
11 Apr 92	**BREAK LIKE THE WIND** *MCA MCAD 10514*	51	2

SPINNERS
UK, male vocal / instrumental group (Albums: 24 weeks) pos/wks

5 Sep 70	**THE SPINNERS ARE IN TOWN** *Fontana 6309 014*	40	5
7 Aug 71	**SPINNERS LIVE PERFORMANCE** *Contour 6870 502*	14	12
13 Nov 71	**THE SWINGING CITY** *Philips 6382 002*	20	3
8 Apr 72	**LOVE IS TEASING** *Columbia SCX 6493*	33	4

SPINNERS – *See DETROIT SPINNERS*

SPIRAL TRIBE
UK, male / female vocal / instrumental group (Singles: 2 weeks) pos/wks

29 Aug 92	**BREACH THE PEACE (EP)** *Butterfly BLRT 79*	66	1
21 Nov 92	**FORWARD THE REVOLUTION** *Butterfly BLRT 85*	70	1

Tracks on Breach the Peace (EP): Breach the Peace / Do It / Seven / 25 Minute Warning

SPIRIT
US, male vocal / instrumental group (Albums: 3 week) pos/wks

13 Mar 71	**THE TWELVE DREAMS OF DR SARDONICUS** *Epic EPC 64191*	29	1
18 Apr 81	**POTATO LAND** *Beggars Banquet BEGA 23*	40	2

SPIRITS *UK, male / female vocal duo – Beverly Thomas and Osmond Wright (Singles: 5 weeks)* pos/wks

19 Nov 94	**DON'T BRING ME DOWN** *MCA MCSTD 2018*	31	3
8 Apr 95	**SPIRIT INSIDE** *MCA MCSTD 2045*	39	2

SPIRITUAL COWBOYS – *See David A STEWART*

SPIRITUALIZED *UK, male / female vocal / instrumental group (Singles: 19 weeks, Albums: 26 weeks)*

Date		Title / Label	pos	wks
30 Jun 90		ANYWAY THAT YOU WANT ME / STEP INTO THE BREEZE *Dedicated ZB 43783*	75	1
17 Aug 91		RUN *Dedicated SPIRT 002*	59	1
25 Jul 92		MEDICATION *Dedicated SPIRT 005T*	55	1
23 Oct 93		ELECTRIC MAINLINE *Dedicated SPIRT 007CD*	49	1
4 Feb 95		LET IT FLOW *Dedicated SPIRT 009CD* [1]	30	2
9 Aug 97		ELECTRICITY *Dedicated SPIRT 012CD1*	32	2
14 Feb 98		I THINK I'M IN LOVE *Dedicated SPIRT 014CD*	27	2
6 Jun 98		THE ABBEY ROAD EP *Dedicated SPIRT 015CD*	39	2
15 Sep 01		STOP YOUR CRYING *Spaceman / Arista OPM 002*	18	3
8 Dec 01		OUT OF SIGHT *Spaceman / Arista OPM 005*	65	1
23 Feb 02		DO IT ALL OVER AGAIN *Spaceman / Arista OPM 004*	31	2
13 Sep 03		SHE KISSED ME (IT FELT LIKE A HIT) *Sanctuary SANXD 222*	38	1
11 Apr 92		LAZER GUIDED MELODIES *Dedicated DEDCD 004*	27	2
18 Feb 95		PURE PHASE *Dedicated DEDCD 0175* [1]	20	2
28 Jun 97	●	LADIES & GENTLEMEN WE ARE FLOATING IN SPACE *Dedicated DEDCD 034*	4	15
7 Nov 98		LIVE AT THE ROYAL ALBERT HALL *Dedicated 74321622852*	38	1
29 Sep 01	●	LET IT COME DOWN *Arista OPM 001CD*	3	4
20 Sep 03		AMAZING GRACE *Spaceman / Sanctuary SANDCD214X*	25	2

[1] Spiritualized Electric Mainline [1] Spiritualized Electric Mainline

Tracks on The Abbey Road EP: Come Together / Broken Heart / Broken Heart (instrumental)

SPIRO and WIX *UK, male instrumental duo – Steve Spiro and Paul Wickens (Singles: 2 weeks)*

Date		Title / Label	pos	wks
10 Aug 96		TARA'S THEME *EMI Premier PRESCD 4*	29	2

SPITTING IMAGE *UK, male / female latex puppets (Singles: 18 weeks, Albums: 3 weeks)*

Date		Title / Label	pos	wks
10 May 86	★	THE CHICKEN SONG (re) *Virgin SPIT 1*	1	11
6 Dec 86		SANTA CLAUS IS ON THE DOLE / FIRST ATHEIST TABERNACLE CHOIR *Virgin VS 921*	22	7
18 Oct 86		SPIT IN YOUR EAR *Virgin V 2403*	55	3

SPLIFF STAR – *See Busta RHYMES*

SPLINTER *UK, male vocal / instrumental duo – Bill Elliott and Bob Purvis (Singles: 10 weeks)*

Date		Title / Label	pos	wks
2 Nov 74		COSTAFINE TOWN *Dark Horse AMS 7135*	17	10

SPLINTER GROUP – *See Peter GREEN*

SPLIT ENZ *New Zealand / UK, male vocal / instrumental group (Singles: 15 weeks, Albums: 9 weeks)*

Date		Title / Label	pos	wks
16 Aug 80		I GOT YOU *A&M AMS 7546*	12	11
23 May 81		HISTORY NEVER REPEATS *A&M AMS 8128*	63	4
30 Aug 80		TRUE COLOURS *A&M AMLH 64822*	42	8
8 May 82		TIME AND TIDE *A&M AMLH 64894*	71	1

A SPLIT SECOND *Belgium / Italy, male instrumental / production group (Singles: 1 week)*

Date		Title / Label	pos	wks
14 Dec 91		FLESH *ffrr FX 178*	68	1

SPLODGENESSABOUNDS *UK, male vocal / instrumental group (Singles: 17 weeks)*

Date		Title / Label	pos	wks
14 Jun 80	●	SIMON TEMPLER / TWO PINTS OF LAGER AND A PACKET OF CRISPS PLEASE *Deram BUM 1*	7	8
6 Sep 80		TWO LITTLE BOYS / HORSE *Deram ROLF 1*	26	7
13 Jun 81		COWPUNK MEDLUM *Deram BUM 3*	69	2

SPOILED & ZIGO *Israel, male DJ / production duo – Elad Avnon and Ziv Goland (Singles: 3 weeks)*

Date		Title / Label	pos	wks
12 Aug 00		MORE & MORE *Manifesto FESCD 72*	31	3

SPONGE *US, male vocal / instrumental group (Singles: 1 week)*

Date		Title / Label	pos	wks
19 Aug 95		PLOWED *Work 6623162*	74	1

SPOOKS *US, male / female vocal / rap group (Singles: 17 weeks, Albums: 12 weeks)*

Date		Title / Label	pos	wks
27 Jan 01	●	THINGS I'VE SEEN *Epic 6706722*	6	10
5 May 01		KARMA HOTEL *Epic 6709012*	15	6
15 Sep 01		SWEET REVENGE *Epic 6718072*	67	1
17 Feb 01		S.I.O.S.O.S. – VOLUME ONE *Epic 4982612*	25	12

SPOOKY *UK, male vocal / instrumental duo (Singles: 1 week)*

Date		Title / Label	pos	wks
13 Mar 93		SCHMOO *Guerilla GRRR 45CD*	72	1

SPORTY THIEVZ *US, male rap / vocal group (Singles: 6 weeks)*

Date		Title / Label	pos	wks
10 Jul 99		NO PIGEONS *Columbia / Roc-a-Blok / Ruffhouse 6676022*	21	6

SPOTNICKS *Sweden, male instrumental group (Singles: 37 weeks, Albums: 1 week)*

Date		Title / Label	pos	wks
14 Jun 62		ORANGE BLOSSOM SPECIAL *Oriole CB 1724*	29	10
6 Sep 62		ROCKET MAN *Oriole CB 1755*	38	9
31 Jan 63		HAVA NAGILA *Oriole CB 1790*	13	12
25 Apr 63		JUST LISTEN TO MY HEART *Oriole CB 1818*	36	6
9 Feb 63		OUT-A-SPACE *Oriole PS 40036*	20	1

Dusty SPRINGFIELD (152 Top 500)

One of Britain's leading female vocalists of the 1960s, b. Mary O'Brien, 16 Apr 1939, London, d. 2 Mar 1999. After leaving The Springfields in 1963, she had numerous transatlantic solo hits, and during the Sixties was regularly voted UK's Top Female Singer (Singles: 211 weeks, Albums: 134 weeks)

Date		Title / Label	pos	wks
21 Nov 63	●	I ONLY WANT TO BE WITH YOU *Philips BF 1292*	4	18
20 Feb 64		STAY AWHILE *Philips BF 1313*	13	10
2 Jul 64	●	I JUST DON'T KNOW WHAT TO DO WITH MYSELF *Philips BF 1348*	3	12
22 Oct 64	●	LOSING YOU *Philips BF 1369*	9	13
18 Feb 65		YOUR HURTIN' KINDA LOVE *Philips BF 1396*	37	4
1 Jul 65	●	IN THE MIDDLE OF NOWHERE *Philips BF 1418*	8	10
16 Sep 65	●	SOME OF YOUR LOVIN' *Philips BF 1430*	8	12
27 Jan 66		LITTLE BY LITTLE *Philips BF 1466*	17	9
31 Mar 66	★	YOU DON'T HAVE TO SAY YOU LOVE ME *Philips BF 1482*	1	13
7 Jul 66	●	GOIN' BACK *Philips BF 1502*	10	10
15 Sep 66	●	ALL I SEE IS YOU *Philips BF 1510*	9	12
23 Feb 67		I'LL TRY ANYTHING *Philips BF 1553*	13	9
25 May 67		GIVE ME TIME *Philips BF 1577*	24	6
10 Jul 68	●	I CLOSE MY EYES AND COUNT TO TEN *Philips BF 1682*	4	12
4 Dec 68	●	SON-OF-A PREACHER MAN *Philips BF 1730*	9	9
20 Sep 69		AM I THE SAME GIRL (re) *Philips BF 1811*	43	4
19 Sep 70		HOW CAN I BE SURE *Philips 6006 045*	36	4
20 Oct 79		BABY BLUE *Mercury DUSTY 4*	61	5
22 Aug 87	●	WHAT HAVE I DONE TO DESERVE THIS? *Parlophone R 6163* [1]	2	9
25 Feb 89		NOTHING HAS BEEN PROVED *Parlophone R 6207*	16	7
2 Dec 89		IN PRIVATE *Parlophone R 6234*	14	10
26 May 90		REPUTATION *Parlophone R 6253*	38	6
24 Nov 90		ARRESTED BY YOU *Parlophone R 6266*	70	2
30 Oct 93		HEART AND SOUL *Columbia 6598562* [2]	75	1
10 Jun 95		WHEREVER WOULD I BE *Columbia 6620592* [3]	44	3
4 Nov 95		ROLL AWAY *Columbia 6623682*	68	1
25 Apr 64	●	A GIRL CALLED DUSTY *Philips BL 7594*	6	23
23 Oct 65	●	EV'RYTHING'S COMING UP DUSTY *Philips RBL 1002*	6	12
22 Oct 66	●	GOLDEN HITS *Philips BL 7737*	2	36
11 Nov 67		WHERE AM I GOING *Philips SBL 7820*	40	1
21 Dec 68		DUSTY ... DEFINITELY *Philips SBL 7864*	30	6
2 May 70		FROM DUSTY ... WITH LOVE *Philips SBL 7927*	35	2
4 Mar 78		IT BEGINS AGAIN *Mercury 9109 607*	41	2
30 Jan 88		DUSTY – THE SILVER COLLECTION *Phonogram DUSTV 1*	14	10
7 Jul 90		REPUTATION *Parlophone PCSD 111*	18	6
14 May 94	●	GOIN' BACK – THE VERY BEST OF DUSTY SPRINGFIELD 1962-1994 *Philips 8487892*	5	11
8 Jul 95		A VERY FINE LOVE *Columbia 4785082*	43	1
7 Nov 98		THE BEST OF DUSTY SPRINGFIELD *Mercury / PolyGram TV 5383452*	19	24

[1] Pet Shop Boys and Dusty Springfield [2] Cilla Black with Dusty Springfield
[3] Dusty Springfield and Daryl Hall

From 27 Mar 99 'The Best of Dusty Springfield' changed label to Mercury / Universal Music TV

See also SPRINGFIELDS

Rick SPRINGFIELD

Australia, male vocalist / actor – Richard Springthorpe (Singles: 13 weeks, Albums: 8 weeks) pos/wks

14 Jan 84	**HUMAN TOUCH / SOULS** *RCA RICK 1*	23	7
24 Mar 84	**JESSIE'S GIRL** *RCA RICK 2* ▲	43	6
11 Feb 84	**LIVING IN OZ** *RCA PL 84660*	41	4
25 May 85	**TAO** *RCA PL 85370*	68	3
26 Mar 88	**ROCK OF LIFE** *RCA PL 86620*	80	1

'Souls' listed only from 11 Feb 1984. It peaked at No.24

SPRINGFIELDS

UK, male / female vocal / instrumental group (Singles: 66 weeks) pos/wks

31 Aug 61	**BREAKAWAY** *Philips BF 1168*	31	8
16 Nov 61	**BAMBINO** *Philips BF 1178*	16	11
13 Dec 62 ●	**ISLAND OF DREAMS** *Philips 326557 BF*	5	26
28 Mar 63 ●	**SAY I WON'T BE THERE** *Philips 326577 BF*	5	15
25 Jul 63	**COME ON HOME** *Philips BF 1263*	31	6

See also Dusty SPRINGFIELD

Bruce SPRINGSTEEN (45 Top 500)

'The Boss', b. 23 Sep 1949, New Jersey, US. Singer / songwriter / guitarist / rock superstar, whose legendary four-hour stage performances have packed stadiums worldwide for 25 years. An insurance valuation of $3m was once placed on Springsteen's voice. He released the biggest-selling box set (Singles: 146 weeks, Albums: 521 weeks) pos/wks

22 Nov 80	**HUNGRY HEART** *CBS 9309*	44	4
13 Jun 81	**THE RIVER** *CBS A 1179*	35	6
26 May 84 ●	**DANCING IN THE DARK (re)** *CBS A 4436*	4	23
6 Oct 84	**COVER ME (re)** *CBS A 4662*	16	13
15 Jun 85 ●	**I'M ON FIRE / BORN IN THE USA** *CBS A 6342*	5	12
3 Aug 85	**GLORY DAYS** *CBS A 6375*	17	6
14 Dec 85 ●	**SANTA CLAUS IS COMIN' TO TOWN / MY HOMETOWN** *CBS A 6773*	9	5
29 Nov 86	**WAR** *CBS 650193 7* [1]	18	7
7 Feb 87	**FIRE** *CBS 650381 7* [1]	54	2
23 May 87	**BORN TO RUN** *CBS BRUCE 2*	16	4
3 Oct 87	**BRILLIANT DISGUISE** *CBS 651141 7*	20	5
12 Dec 87	**TUNNEL OF LOVE** *CBS 651295 7*	45	4
18 Jun 88	**TOUGHER THAN THE REST** *CBS BRUCE 3*	13	8
24 Sep 88	**SPARE PARTS** *CBS BRUCE 4*	32	3
21 Mar 92	**HUMAN TOUCH** *Columbia 6578727*	11	5
23 May 92	**BETTER DAYS** *Columbia 6578907*	34	3
25 Jul 92	**57 CHANNELS (AND NOTHIN' ON)** *Columbia 6581387*	32	4
24 Oct 92	**LEAP OF FAITH** *Columbia 6583697*	46	3
10 Apr 93	**LUCKY TOWN (LIVE)** *Columbia 6592282*	48	3
19 Mar 94 ●	**STREETS OF PHILADELPHIA** *Columbia 6600652*	2	12
22 Apr 95	**SECRET GARDEN** *Columbia 6612955*	44	3
11 Nov 95	**HUNGRY HEART (re-issue)** *Columbia 6626252*	28	3
4 May 96	**THE GHOST OF TOM JOAD** *Columbia 6630315*	26	2
19 Apr 97	**SECRET GARDEN (re-issue)** *Columbia 6643245*	17	4
14 Dec 02	**LONESOME DAY** *Columbia 6734082*	39	2
1 Nov 75	**BORN TO RUN** *CBS 69170*	17	50
17 Jun 78	**DARKNESS ON THE EDGE OF TOWN** *CBS 86061*	16	40
25 Oct 80 ●	**THE RIVER** *CBS 88510* ▲	2	88
2 Oct 82 ●	**NEBRASKA** *CBS 25100*	3	19
16 Jun 84 ★	**BORN IN THE U.S.A.** *CBS 86304* ▲	1	129
15 Jun 85	**GREETINGS FROM ASBURY PARK N.J.** *CBS 32210*	41	10
15 Jun 85	**THE WILD THE INNOCENT & THE E STREET SHUFFLE** *CBS 32363*	33	12
22 Nov 86 ●	**LIVE 1975–85** *CBS 450 2271* [1] ▲	4	9
17 Oct 87 ★	**TUNNEL OF LOVE** *CBS 460 2701* ■ ▲	1	33
4 Apr 92 ●	**LUCKY TOWN** *Columbia 4714242*	2	11
4 Apr 92 ★	**HUMAN TOUCH** *Columbia 4714232* ■	1	17
24 Apr 93 ●	**IN CONCERT – MTV PLUGGED** *Columbia 4738602*	4	7
11 Mar 95 ★	**GREATEST HITS** *Columbia 4785552* ■ ▲	1	44
25 Nov 95	**THE GHOST OF TOM JOAD** *Columbia 4816502*	16	14
21 Nov 98	**TRACKS** *Columbia 4926052*	50	1
24 Apr 99	**18 TRACKS** *Columbia 4942002*	23	7
14 Apr 01	**LIVE IN NEW YORK CITY** *Columbia 5000002* [1]	12	6
10 Aug 02 ★	**THE RISING** *Columbia 5080002* ■ ▲	1	16
22 Nov 03	**THE ESSENTIAL** *Columbia 5137009*	28	2
22 Nov 03	**THE ESSENTIAL** *Columbia 5137002*	32	6+

[1] Bruce Springsteen and the E Street Band

[1] Bruce Springsteen and the E Street Band

'Dancing in the Dark' debuted at No.28 before making its peak position on re-entry in Jan 1985. 'Cover Me' debuted at No.38 before making its peak position on re-entry in Mar 1985 The Essential (Columbia 5137009) is a three CD set and The Essential (Columbia 5137002) is a double CD

See also E STREET BAND

SPRINGWATER

UK, male instrumentalist - Phil Cordell (Singles: 12 weeks) pos/wks

23 Oct 71 ●	**I WILL RETURN** *Polydor 2058 141*	5	12

SPRINKLER

UK / US, male / female vocal / rap group (Singles: 2 weeks) pos/wks

11 Jul 98	**LEAVE 'EM SOMETHING TO DESIRE** *Island CID 706*	45	2

[SPUNGE]

UK, male vocal / instrumental group (Singles: 3 weeks, Albums: 1 week) pos/wks

15 Jun 02	**JUMP ON DEMAND** *Rough Trade RTRADESCD 054*	37	2
24 Aug 02	**ROOTS** *B Unique BUN 030CDS*	52	1
7 Sep 02	**THE STORY SO FAR ...** *B Unique 0927487452*	48	1

SPYRO GYRA

US, male instrumental group (Singles: 10 weeks, Albums: 23 weeks) pos/wks

21 Jul 79	**MORNING DANCE** *Infinity INF 111*	17	10
14 Jul 79	**MORNING DANCE** *Infinity INS 2003*	11	16
23 Feb 80	**CATCHING THE SUN** *MCA MCG 4009*	31	7

SQUADRONAIRES – *See Joan REGAN*

SQUEEZE (240 Top 500)

Critically acclaimed London band, which had several UK / US best sellers. Featured noted singer / songwriters Glenn Tilbrook (g/v) and Chris Difford (v/g). Fluctuating line-up included Jools Holland (k) and Paul Carrack (v/k – also of Ace, and Mike and the Mechanics fame) (Singles: 123 weeks, Albums: 130 weeks) pos/wks

8 Apr 78	**TAKE ME I'M YOURS** *A&M AMS 7335*	19	9
10 Jun 78	**BANG BANG** *A&M AMS 7360*	49	5
18 Nov 78	**GOODBYE GIRL** *A&M AMS 7398*	63	2
24 Mar 79 ●	**COOL FOR CATS** *A&M AMS 7426*	2	11
2 Jun 79 ●	**UP THE JUNCTION** *A&M AMS 7444*	2	11
8 Sep 79	**SLAP & TICKLE** *A&M AMS 7466*	24	8
1 Mar 80	**ANOTHER NAIL IN MY HEART** *A&M AMS 7507*	17	9
10 May 80	**PULLING MUSSELS (FROM THE SHELL)** *A&M AMS 7523*	44	6
16 May 81	**IS THAT LOVE** *A&M AMS 8129*	35	8
25 Jul 81	**TEMPTED** *A&M AMS 8147*	41	5
10 Oct 81 ●	**LABELLED WITH LOVE** *A&M AMS 8166*	4	10
24 Apr 82	**BLACK COFFEE IN BED** *A&M AMS 8219*	51	4
23 Oct 82	**ANNIE GET YOUR GUN** *A&M AMS 8259*	43	4
15 Jun 85	**LAST TIME FOREVER** *A&M AM 255*	45	5
8 Aug 87	**HOURGLASS** *A&M AM 400*	16	10
17 Oct 87	**TRUST ME TO OPEN MY MOUTH** *A&M AM 412*	72	1
25 Apr 92	**COOL FOR CATS (re-issue)** *A&M AM 860*	62	2
24 Jul 93	**THIRD RAIL** *A&M 5803372*	39	3
11 Sep 93	**SOME FANTASTIC PLACE** *A&M 5803792*	73	1
9 Sep 95	**THIS SUMMER** *A&M 5811912*	36	3
18 Nov 95	**ELECTRIC TRAINS** *A&M 5812692*	44	2
15 Jun 96	**HEAVEN KNOWS** *A&M 5816052*	27	2
24 Aug 96	**THIS SUMMER (re-mix)** *A&M 5818372*	32	2
28 Apr 79	**COOL FOR CATS** *A&M AMLH 68503*	45	11
16 Feb 80	**ARGY BARGY** *A&M AMLH 64802*	32	15
23 May 81	**EAST SIDE STORY** *A&M AMLH 64854*	19	26
15 May 82	**SWEETS FROM A STRANGER** *A&M AMLH 64899*	20	7
6 Nov 82 ●	**SINGLES – 45'S AND UNDER** *A&M AMLH 68552*	3	29
7 Sep 85	**COSI FAN TUTTI FRUTTI** *A&M AMA 5085*	31	7
19 Sep 87	**BABYLON AND ON** *A&M AMA 5161*	14	8
23 Sep 89	**FRANK** *A&M AMA 5278*	58	1
7 Apr 90	**A ROUND AND A BOUT** *IRS DFCLP 1*	50	1

7 Sep 91	PLAY *Reprise WX 428*	41 1
23 May 92 ●	GREATEST HITS *A&M 3971812*	6 13
25 Sep 93	SOME FANTASTIC PLACE *A&M 5401402*	26 4
25 Nov 95	RIDICULOUS *A&M 5404402*	50 1
22 Jun 02 ●	BIG SQUEEZE – THE VERY BEST OF SQUEEZE *UMTV 4932532*	8 6

See also DIFFORD and TILBROOK; Jools HOLLAND; Paul CARRACK

Billy SQUIER
US, male vocalist / instrumentalist – guitar (Singles: 3 weeks) pos/wks

3 Oct 81	THE STROKE *Capitol CL 214*	52 3

Chris SQUIRE
UK, male vocalist / instrumentalist – bass (Albums: 7 weeks) pos/wks

6 Dec 75	FISH OUT OF WATER *Atlantic K 50203*	25 7

See also YES

John SQUIRE *UK, male vocalist / instrumentalist – guitar (Singles: 1 week, Albums: 2 weeks)* pos/wks

2 Nov 02	JOE LOUIS *North Country NCCDA 001*	43 1
28 Sep 02	TIME CHANGES EVERYTHING *North Country NCCDS 001*	17 2

See also SEAHORSES; STONE ROSES

Dorothy SQUIRES
UK, female vocalist, d. 14 Apr 1998 (Singles: 56 weeks) pos/wks

5 Jun 53	I'M WALKING BEHIND YOU *Polygon P 1068*	12 1
24 Aug 61	SAY IT WITH FLOWERS *Columbia DB 4665* [1]	23 10
20 Sep 69	FOR ONCE IN MY LIFE (re) *President PT 267*	24 11
21 Feb 70	TILL (re) *President PT 281*	25 11
8 Aug 70	MY WAY (2re) *President PT 305*	25 23

[1] Dorothy Squires and Russ Conway

ST PAUL'S BOYS' CHOIR *UK, choir (Albums: 8 weeks)* pos/wks

29 Nov 80	REJOICE *K-Tel NE 1064*	36 8

STABBS *Finland / US / Cameroon, male instrumental / production group (Singles: 1 week)* pos/wks

24 Dec 94	JOY AND HAPPINESS *Hi-Life HICD 3*	65 1

STACCATO *UK / Holland, male / female vocal / instrumental duo (Singles: 1 week)* pos/wks

20 Jul 96	I WANNA KNOW *Multiply CDMULTY 11*	65 1

Warren STACEY *UK, male vocalist (Singles: 3 weeks)* pos/wks

23 Mar 02	MY GIRL MY GIRL *Def Soul 5889932*	26 3

Jim STAFFORD *US, male vocalist (Singles: 16 weeks)* pos/wks

27 Apr 74	SPIDERS & SNAKES *MGM 2006 374*	14 8
6 Jul 74	MY GIRL BILL *MGM 2006 423*	20 8

Jo STAFFORD *US, female vocalist (Singles: 28 weeks)* pos/wks

14 Nov 52 ★	YOU BELONG TO ME *Columbia DB 3152* ▲	1 19
19 Dec 52	JAMBALAYA *Columbia DB 3169*	11 2
7 May 54 ●	MAKE LOVE TO ME! *Philips PB 233* ▲	8 1
9 Dec 55	SUDDENLY THERE'S A VALLEY (re) *Philips PB 509*	12 6

Terry STAFFORD
US, male vocalist, d. 17 Mar 1996 (Singles: 9 weeks) pos/wks

7 May 64	SUSPICION *London HLU 9871*	31 9

STAGECOACH featuring Penny FOSTER
UK, male / female vocal ensemble (Singles: 1 week) pos/wks

18 Oct 03	ANGEL LOOKING THROUGH *Stagecoach Theatre SCR 001*	59 1

STAIFFI and his MUSTAFAS
France, male vocal / instrumental group (Singles: 1 week) pos/wks

28 Jul 60	MUSTAFA CHA CHA CHA *Pye International 7N 25057*	43 1

STAIND *US, male vocal / instrumental group (Singles: 11 weeks, Albums: 29 weeks)* pos/wks

15 Sep 01	IT'S BEEN AWHILE *Elektra E 7252CD*	15 6
1 Dec 01	OUTSIDE *Elektra E 7277CD*	33 2
23 Feb 02	FOR YOU *Elektra E 7281CD*	55 1
24 May 03	PRICE TO PAY *Elektra E 7417CD*	36 2
1 Sep 01 ★	BREAK THE CYCLE *Elektra 7559626642* ■ ▲	1 26
31 May 03	14 SHADES OF GREY *Elektra 7559628822* ▲	16 3

STAKKA BO *Sweden, male rap / DJ duo – Johan Renck and Oscar Franzen (Singles: 12 weeks)* pos/wks

25 Sep 93	HERE WE GO *Polydor PZCD 280*	13 8
18 Dec 93	DOWN THE DRAIN *Polydor PZCD 301*	64 4

Frank STALLONE *US, male vocalist (Singles: 2 weeks)* pos/wks

22 Oct 83	FAR FROM OVER *RSO 95*	68 2

STAMFORD AMP
UK, male vocal / instrumental group (Singles: 2 weeks) pos/wks

12 Oct 02	ANYTHING FOR YOU *Mercury 638972*	33 2

STAMFORD BRIDGE
UK, male Chelsea FC supporters vocal group (Singles: 1 week) pos/wks

16 May 70	CHELSEA *Penny Farthing PEN 715*	47 1

STAMINA MC – See DJ MARKY & XRS; D KAY & EPSILON featuring STAMINA MC

STAMPS QUARTET – See Elvis PRESLEY

STAN *UK, male vocal / instrumental duo – Simon Andrew and Kevin Stagg (Singles: 3 weeks)* pos/wks

31 Jul 93	SUNTAN *Hug CDBUM 1*	40 3

The STANDS
UK, male vocal / instrumental group (Singles: 3 weeks) pos/wks

16 Aug 03	WHEN THE RIVER ROLLS OVER YOU *Echo ECSCD 142*	32 1
25 Oct 03	I NEED YOU *Echo ECSCD 146*	39 2

Lisa STANSFIELD (241 Top 500)
Only UK act to have three US R&B No.1 hits, b. 11 Apr 1966, Lancashire. Like Yazz, she was featured vocalist on a Coldcut single before achieving a No.1 in her own right. This multi-Brit award winner has sold millions of records all around the world (Singles: 127 weeks, Albums: 125 weeks) pos/wks

25 Mar 89	PEOPLE HOLD ON *Ahead of Our Time CCUT 5* [1]	11 9
12 Aug 89	THIS IS THE RIGHT TIME *Arista 112512*	13 8
28 Oct 89 ★	ALL AROUND THE WORLD *Arista 112693*	1 14
10 Feb 90 ●	LIVE TOGETHER *Arista 112914*	10 6
12 May 90	WHAT DID I DO TO YOU (EP) *Arista 113168*	25 4
19 Oct 91 ●	CHANGE *Arista 114820*	10 7
21 Dec 91	ALL WOMAN *Arista 115000*	20 8
14 Mar 92	TIME TO MAKE YOU MINE *Arista 115113*	14 8
6 Jun 92	SET YOUR LOVING FREE *Arista 74321100587*	28 4
19 Dec 92 ●	SOMEDAY (I'M COMING BACK) *Arista 74321123567*	10 9
1 May 93 ★	FIVE LIVE (EP) (re) *Parlophone CDRS 6340* [2] ■	1 12
5 Jun 93 ●	IN ALL THE RIGHT PLACES *MCA MCSTD 1780*	8 11
23 Oct 93	SO NATURAL *Arista 74321169132*	15 5
11 Dec 93	LITTLE BIT OF HEAVEN *Arista 74321178202*	32 4
18 Jan 97 ●	PEOPLE HOLD ON (THE BOOTLEG MIXES) *Arista 74321452012* [3]	4 6
22 Mar 97 ●	THE REAL THING *Arista 74321463222*	9 7
21 Jun 97	NEVER, NEVER GONNA GIVE YOU UP *Arista 74321490392*	25 3
4 Oct 97	THE LINE *RCA 74321511372*	64 1
23 Jun 01	LET'S JUST CALL IT LOVE *Arista 74321863422*	48 1
2 Dec 89 ●	AFFECTION *Arista 210379*	2 31

23 Nov 91 ● **REAL LOVE** *Arista 212300* 3 51
20 Nov 93 ● **SO NATURAL** *Arista 74321172312* 6 14
5 Apr 97 ● **LISA STANSFIELD** *Arista 74321458512* 2 18
7 Jul 01 **FACE UP** *Arista 74321863462* 38 2
15 Feb 03 ● **BIOGRAPHY – THE GREATEST HITS** *Arista 74321989542* 4 9

[1] Coldcut featuring Lisa Stansfield [2] George Michael and Queen with Lisa Stansfield [3] Lisa Stansfield vs The Dirty Rotten Scoundrels

Tracks on What Did I Do to You (EP): What Did I Do to You / My Apple Heart / Lay Me Down / Something's Happenin'. Tracks on Five Live (EP): Somebody to Love / These Are the Days of Our Lives / Calling You / Papa Was a Rolling Stone – Killer (medley). Lisa Stansfield appears only on the second track

Vivian STANSHALL – *See Mike OLDFIELD; BONZO DOG DOO-DAH BAND*

STANTON WARRIORS

UK, male production duo (Singles: 1 week) pos/wks

22 Sep 01 **DA ANTIDOTE** *Mob MOBCD 006* 69 1

STAPLE SINGERS

US, male / female vocal group (Singles: 14 weeks) pos/wks

10 Jun 72 **I'LL TAKE YOU THERE** *Stax 2025 110* ▲ 30 8
8 Jun 74 **IF YOU'RE READY (COME GO WITH ME)** *Stax 2025 224* 34 6

Cyril STAPLETON and his ORCHESTRA

UK, orchestra, leader d. 25 Feb 1974 (Singles: 27 weeks) pos/wks

27 May 55 **ELEPHANT TANGO (2re)** *Decca F 10488* 19 4
23 Sep 55 ● **BLUE STAR (THE MEDIC THEME)** *Decca F 10559* [1] 2 12
6 Apr 56 **THE ITALIAN THEME** *Decca F 10703* 18 2
1 Jun 56 **THE HAPPY WHISTLER** *Decca F 10735* [2] 22 4
19 Jul 57 **FORGOTTEN DREAMS** *Decca F 10912* 27 5

[1] Cyril Stapleton Orchestra featuring Julie Dawn [2] Cyril Stapleton Orchestra featuring Desmond Lane, penny whistle

STAR INC – *See Ed STARINK*

STAR SPANGLES

UK, male vocal / instrumental group (Singles: 1 week) pos/wks

19 Apr 03 **STAY AWAY FROM ME** *Parlophone CDR 6604* 52 1
12 Jul 03 **I LIVE FOR SPEED** *Parlophone CDR 6609* 60 1

STAR TURN ON 45 (PINTS)

UK, male vocalist – Steve O'Donnell, d. 4 Aug 1997 (Singles: 9 weeks) pos/wks

24 Oct 81 **STARTURN ON 45 (PINTS)** *V Tone V TONE 003* 45 4
30 Apr 88 **PUMP UP THE BITTER** *Pacific DRINK 1* 12 5

STARCHASER *Italy, male DJ / production trio (Singles: 4 weeks)* pos/wks

22 Jun 02 **LOVE WILL SET YOU FREE (JAMBE MYTH)** *Rulin RULIN 23CDS* 24 4

STARDUST *Sweden, male / female vocal / instrumental group (Singles: 3 weeks)* pos/wks

8 Oct 77 **ARIANA** *Satril SAT 120* 42 3

STARDUST

France, male vocal / production group (Singles: 26 weeks) pos/wks

1 Aug 98 **MUSIC SOUNDS BETTER WITH YOU (import)** *Roule ROULE 305* 55 3
22 Aug 98 ● **MUSIC SOUNDS BETTER WITH YOU** *Virgin DINSD 175* 2 23

Alvin STARDUST *UK, male vocalist – Bernard Jewry (Singles: 119 weeks, Albums: 17 weeks)* pos/wks

3 Nov 73 ● **MY COO-CA-CHOO** *Magnet MAG 1* 2 21
16 Feb 74 ★ **JEALOUS MIND** *Magnet MAG 5* 1 11
4 May 74 ● **RED DRESS** *Magnet MAG 8* 7 8
31 Aug 74 ● **YOU YOU YOU** *Magnet MAG 13* 6 10
30 Nov 74 **TELL ME WHY** *Magnet MAG 19* 16 8
1 Feb 75 **GOOD LOVE CAN NEVER DIE** *Magnet MAG 21* 11 9
12 Jul 75 **SWEET CHEATIN' RITA** *Magnet MAG 32* 37 4
5 Sep 81 ● **PRETEND** *Stiff BUY 124* 4 10
21 Nov 81 **A WONDERFUL TIME UP THERE** *Stiff BUY 132* 56 8
5 May 84 ● **I FEEL LIKE BUDDY HOLLY** *Chrysalis CHS 2784* 7 11
27 Oct 84 ● **I WON'T RUN AWAY** *Chrysalis CHS 2829* 7 13
15 Dec 84 **SO NEAR TO CHRISTMAS** *Chrysalis CHS 2835* 29 4
23 Mar 85 **GOT A LITTLE HEARTACHE** *Chrysalis CHS 2856* 55 2
16 Mar 74 ● **THE UNTOUCHABLE** *Magnet MAG 5001* 4 12
21 Dec 74 **ALVIN STARDUST** *Magnet MAG 5004* 37 3
4 Oct 75 **ROCK WITH ALVIN** *Magnet MAG 5007* 52 2

STARFIGHTER

Belgium, male producer – Philip Dirix (Singles: 3 weeks) pos/wks

5 Feb 00 **APACHE** *Sound of Ministry MOSCDS 136* 31 3

STARGARD *US, female vocal group (Singles: 14 weeks)* pos/wks

28 Jan 78 **THEME SONG FROM 'WHICH WAY IS UP'** *MCA 346* 19 7
15 Apr 78 **LOVE IS SO EASY** *MCA 354* 45 1
9 Sep 78 **WHAT YOU WAITIN' FOR** *MCA 382* 39 6

STARGATE *Norway / US, male / female production / vocal / rap group (Singles: 1 week)* pos/wks

7 Sep 02 **EASIER SAID THAN DONE** *Telstar CDSTAS 3269* 55 1

STARGAZERS

UK / Australia, male / female vocal group (Singles: 68 weeks) pos/wks

13 Feb 53 ★ **BROKEN WINGS (re)** *Decca F 10047* 1 12
19 Feb 54 ★ **I SEE THE MOON** *Decca F 10213* 1 15
9 Apr 54 **THE HAPPY WANDERER** *Decca F 10259* 12 1
17 Dec 54 ★ **THE FINGER OF SUSPICION** *Decca F 10394* [1] 1 15
4 Mar 55 **SOMEBODY** *Decca F 10437* 20 1
3 Jun 55 **THE CRAZY OTTO RAG** *Decca F 10523* 18 3
9 Sep 55 ● **CLOSE THE DOOR** *Decca F 10594* 6 9
11 Nov 55 ● **TWENTY TINY FINGERS** *Decca F 10626* 4 11
22 Jun 56 **HOT DIGGITY (DOG ZIGGITY BOOM)** *Decca F 10731* 28 1

[1] Dickie Valentine with The Stargazers

STARGAZERS

UK, male vocal / instrumental group (Singles: 3 weeks) pos/wks

6 Feb 82 **GROOVE BABY GROOVE (EP)** *Epic EPC A 1924* 56 3

Tracks on Groove Baby Groove (EP): Groove Baby Groove / Jump Around / La Rock 'n' Roll (Quelques Uns à la Lune) / Red Light Green Light

Ed STARINK *Holland, male instrumentalist (Albums: 11 weeks)* pos/wks

27 Oct 90 **SYNTHESIZER GREATEST** *Arcade ARC 938101* [1] 22 5
9 Jan 93 **SYNTHESIZER GOLD** *Arcade ARC 3100012* 29 6

[1] Star Inc

STARJETS

UK, male vocal / instrumental group (Singles: 5 weeks) pos/wks

8 Sep 79 **WAR STORIES** *Epic EPC 7770* 51 5

STARLAND VOCAL BAND

US, male / female vocal group (Singles: 10 weeks) pos/wks

7 Aug 76 **AFTERNOON DELIGHT** *RCA 2716* ▲ 18 10

STARLIGHT

Italy, male instrumental / production group (Singles: 11 weeks) pos/wks

19 Aug 89 ● **NUMERO UNO** *Citybeat CBE 742* 9 11

STARLITERS – *See Joey DEE and the STARLITERS*

STARPARTY *Holland, male production duo – Ferry Corsten and Robert Smit (Singles: 2 weeks)* pos/wks

26 Feb 00 **I'M IN LOVE** *Incentive CENT 5CDS* 26 2

See also MOONMAN; SYSTEM F; VERACOCHA; GOURYELLA; ALBION; Ferry CORSTEN

TOP 20 SINGLES ACTS

The Top 20 singles acts by weeks on chart still show the big two – Elvis and Cliff - dominating proceedings. The boys from Memphis, Tennessee, and Cheshunt, Hertfordshire, continued to add a trickle of hit singles chart weeks to their considerable totals in 2003. Oasis enter the Top 20 all-time great singles acts for the first time, with the Everly Brothers slipping down to make way.

POSITION / ACT / TOTAL WEEKS ON THE SINGLES CHART

1. ELVIS PRESLEY 1,193
2. CLIFF RICHARD 1,154
3. SHADOWS 771
4. ELTON JOHN 623
5. MADONNA 611
6. DIANA ROSS 560
7. MICHAEL JACKSON 512
8. ROD STEWART 477
9. BEATLES 456
10. DAVID BOWIE 452
11. FRANK SINATRA 440
12. QUEEN 423
13. STATUS QUO 417
14. STEVIE WONDER 416
15. PAUL McCARTNEY 410
16. TOM JONES 394
17. ROLLING STONES 374
18. BEE GEES 354
19. OASIS 348
20. ROY ORBISON 345

TOP 20 ALBUMS ACTS

The Top 20 Album acts by weeks on chart show British groups at one and two in the rankings. Perhaps it is no surprise to see The Beatles and Queen battling it out for Top Albums act but Dire Straits are worthy of note in fourth spot, particularly as their 1,133 chart weeks were achieved from the comparatively small number of just 11 hit albums.

POSITION / ACT / TOTAL WEEKS ON THE ALBUMS CHART

1. BEATLES 1,284
2. QUEEN 1,271
3. ELVIS PRESLEY 1,260
4. DIRE STRAITS 1,133
5. U2 1,110
6. SIMON AND GARFUNKEL 1,103
7. MADONNA 1,026
8. DAVID BOWIE 989
9. ELTON JOHN 970
10. MICHAEL JACKSON 913
11. PINK FLOYD 911
12. FRANK SINATRA 889
13. FLEETWOOD MAC 879
14. ROD STEWART 875
15. ABBA 867
16. CLIFF RICHARD 805
17. PHIL COLLINS 803
18. ROLLING STONES 799
19. MEAT LOAF 784
20. DIANA ROSS 740

Cliff Richard Top UK act in the top singles performers list and 16th in the albums rankings. Pictured in the early days of a career spanning five decades, Sir Cliff has a grand total of 190 hit singles and albums to his credit

Edwin STARR *US, male vocalist, d. 2 Apr 2003 (Singles: 70 weeks)* pos/wks

12 May 66		**STOP HER ON SIGHT (SOS)** *Polydor BM 56 702*	35	8
18 Aug 66		**HEADLINE NEWS** *Polydor 56 717*	39	3
11 Dec 68		**STOP HER ON SIGHT (SOS) / HEADLINE NEWS (re-issue)** *Polydor 56 753*	11	11
13 Sep 69		**25 MILES** *Tamla Motown TMG 672*	36	6
24 Oct 70	●	**WAR** *Tamla Motown TMG 754* ▲	3	12
20 Feb 71		**STOP THE WAR NOW** *Tamla Motown TMG 764*	33	1
27 Jan 79	●	**CONTACT** *20th Century BTC 2396*	6	12
26 May 79	●	**H.A.P.P.Y. RADIO** *RCA TC 2408*	9	11
1 Jun 85		**IT AIN'T FAIR** *Hippodrome HIP 101*	56	4
30 Oct 93		**WAR** *weekend CDWEEK 103* [1]	69	2

[1] Edwin Starr and Shadow

'Headline News' not listed with 'SOS' from 22 Jan 1969 to 19 Feb 1969. It therefore peaked at No.16. 'War' in 1993 was a re-recording and was listed with the flip side 'Wild Thing' by The Troggs and Wolf

See also UTAH SAINTS

Freddie STARR *UK, male vocalist / comedian – Fred Smith (Singles: 14 weeks, Albums: 16 weeks)* pos/wks

23 Feb 74	●	**IT'S YOU** *Tiffany 6121 501*	9	10
20 Dec 75		**WHITE CHRISTMAS** *Thunderbird THE 102*	41	4
18 Nov 89	●	**AFTER THE LAUGHTER** *Dover ADD 10*	10	9
17 Nov 90		**THE WANDERER** *Dover ADD 17*	33	7

Kay STARR *US, female vocalist – Katherine Starks (Singles: 58 weeks, Albums: 1 week)* pos/wks

5 Dec 52	★	**COMES A-LONG A-LOVE** *Capitol CL 13808*	1	16
24 Apr 53	●	**SIDE BY SIDE** *Capitol CL 13871*	7	4
19 Mar 54	●	**CHANGING PARTNERS** *Capitol CL 14050*	4	14
15 Oct 54		**AM I A TOY OR TREASURE (re)** *Capitol CL 14151*	17	4
17 Feb 56	★	**ROCK AND ROLL WALTZ** *HMV POP 168* ▲	1	20
26 Mar 60		**MOVIN'** *Capitol 1254*	16	1

Ringo STARR *UK, male vocalist / instrumentalist – drums – Richard Starkey (Singles: 56 weeks, Albums: 28 weeks)* pos/wks

17 Apr 71	●	**IT DON'T COME EASY** *Apple R 5898*	4	11
1 Apr 72	●	**BACK OFF BOOGALOO** *Apple R 5944*	2	10
27 Oct 73	●	**PHOTOGRAPH** *Apple R 5992* ▲	8	13
23 Feb 74	●	**YOU'RE SIXTEEN** *Apple R 5995* ▲	4	10
30 Nov 74		**ONLY YOU** *Apple R 6000*	28	11
6 Jun 92		**WEIGHT OF THE WORLD** *Private Music 115392*	74	1
18 Apr 70	●	**SENTIMENTAL JOURNEY** *Apple PCS 7101*	7	6
8 Dec 73	●	**RINGO** *Apple PCTC 252*	7	20
7 Dec 74		**GOODNIGHT VIENNA** *Apple PMC 7168*	30	2

See also BEATLES

STARS ON 54 *US, female vocal trio (Singles: 3 weeks)* pos/wks

28 Nov 98		**IF YOU COULD READ MY MIND** *Tommy Boy TBCD 7497*	23	3

STARSAILOR *UK, male vocal / instrumental group (Singles: 32 weeks, Albums: 49 weeks)* pos/wks

17 Feb 01		**FEVER** *Chrysalis CDCHSS 5123*	18	3
5 May 01		**GOOD SOULS** *Chrysalis CDCHS 5125*	12	6
29 Sep 01	●	**ALCOHOLIC** *Chrysalis CDCHSS 5130*	10	6
22 Dec 01		**LULLABY** *Chrysalis CDCHS 5131*	36	4
30 Mar 02		**POOR MISGUIDED FOOL** *Chrysalis CDCHS 5136*	23	3
13 Sep 03	●	**SILENCE IS EASY** *EMI CDEM 625*	6	8
29 Nov 03		**BORN AGAIN** *EMI CDEM 632*	40	2
20 Oct 01	●	**LOVE IS HERE** *Chrysalis 5353502*	2	41
27 Sep 03	●	**SILENCE IS EASY** *EMI 5900072*	2	8

STARSHIP – *See JEFFERSON AIRPLANE*

STARSOUND *Holland, male producer – Jaap Eggermont with male / female session singers (Singles: 37 weeks, Albums: 28 weeks)* pos/wks

18 Apr 81	●	**STARS ON 45** *CBS A 1102* ▲	2	14
4 Jul 81	●	**STARS ON 45 VOL2** *CBS A 1407*	2	10
19 Sep 81		**STARS ON 45 VOL3** *CBS A 1521*	17	6
27 Feb 82		**STARS ON STEVIE** *CBS A 2041*	14	7
16 May 81	★	**STARS ON 45** *CBS 86132*	1	21
19 Sep 81		**STARS ON 45 VOLUME 2** *CBS 85181*	18	6
3 Apr 82		**STARS MEDLEY** *CBS 85651*	94	1

STARTRAX
UK, male / female vocal group (Singles: 8 weeks, Albums: 7 weeks) pos/wks

1 Aug 81		**STARTRAX CLUB DISCO** *Picksy KSY 1001*	18	8
1 Aug 81		**STARTRAX CLUB DISCO** *Picksy KSYA 1001*	26	7

STARVATION *Multinational, male / female vocal / instrumental charity assembly (Singles: 6 weeks)* pos/wks

9 Mar 85		**STARVATION / TAM-TAM POUR L'ÉTHIOPIE** *Zarjazz JAZZ 3*	33	6

STARVING SOULS
UK, male vocal / instrumental group (Singles: 1 week) pos/wks

21 Oct 95		**I BE THE PROPHET** *Durban Poison DPCD 1*	66	1

STATE OF MIND
UK, male / female vocal / production group (Singles: 3 weeks) pos/wks

18 Apr 98		**THIS IS IT** *Ministry of Sound MOSCDS 123*	30	2
25 Jul 98		**TAKE CONTROL** *Ministry of Sound MOSCDS 124*	46	1

STATE OF THE HEART *UK, male instrumental group featuring Dave Lewis – saxophone (Albums: 9 weeks)* pos/wks

16 Mar 96		**PURE SAX** *Virgin VTCD 78*	18	7
12 Oct 96		**SAX AT THE MOVIES** *Virgin VTCD 98*	62	2

STATE ONE
UK / Germany, male production group (Singles: 1 week) pos/wks

27 Sep 03		**FOREVER AND A DAY** *Incentive CENT 54CDS*	62	1

STATIC REVENGER
US, male producer – Dennis White (Singles: 3 weeks) pos/wks

7 Jul 01		**HAPPY PEOPLE** *Incentive / Rulin CENRUL 1CDS*	23	3

STATIC-X *US, male vocal / instrumental group (Singles: 1 week, Albums: 2 weeks)* pos/wks

6 Oct 01		**BLACK AND WHITE** *Warner Bros. W 560CD*	65	1
23 Jun 01		**MACHINE** *Warner Bros. 9362479482*	56	2

STATLER BROTHERS
US, male vocal group (Singles: 4 weeks) pos/wks

24 Feb 66		**FLOWERS ON THE WALL** *CBS 201976*	38	4

Candi STATON
US, female vocalist (Singles: 71 weeks, Albums: 3 weeks) pos/wks

29 May 76	●	**YOUNG HEARTS RUN FREE** *Warner Bros. K 16730*	2	13
18 Sep 76		**DESTINY** *Warner Bros. K 16806*	41	3
23 Jul 77	●	**NIGHTS ON BROADWAY** *Warner Bros. K 16972*	6	12
3 Jun 78		**HONEST I DO LOVE YOU** *Warner Bros. K 17164*	48	5
24 Apr 82		**SUSPICIOUS MINDS** *Sugarhill SH 112*	31	9
31 May 86		**YOUNG HEARTS RUN FREE (re-mix)** *Warner Bros. W 8680*	47	5
2 Feb 91	●	**YOU GOT THE LOVE** *Truelove TLOVE 7001* [1]	4	11
1 Mar 97	●	**YOU GOT THE LOVE (re-mix)** *React CDREACT 89* [1]	3	8
17 Apr 99		**LOVE ON LOVE** *React CDREACT 143*	27	3
7 Aug 99		**YOUNG HEARTS RUN FREE (re-recording)** *React CDREACT 158*	29	2
24 Jul 76		**YOUNG HEARTS RUN FREE** *Warner Bros. K 56259*	34	3

[1] Source featuring Candi Staton

STATUS IV *US, male vocal group (Singles: 3 weeks)* pos/wks

9 Jul 83		**YOU AIN'T REALLY DOWN** *TMT TMT 4*	56	3

STATUS QUO (25 Top 500) *Ever popular London-based three-chord boogie band: Francis Rossi (g/v), Rick Parfitt (g/v), Alan Lancaster (b), John Coghlan (d). These long-time festival favourites recorded as The Spectres and Traffic Jam before their psychedelic-sounding debut hit introduced them to the UK and US Top 20 (their only major American hit). No group has accumulated more UK hits or has a wider Top 20 chart span and only The Beatles and Rolling Stones can better their tally of Top 20 albums. These heroes of the head-banging set who were chosen to open Live Aid in 1985 have been rockin' all over the world for more than 35 years (Singles: 417 weeks, Albums: 464 weeks)* pos/wks

24 Jan 68 ● **PICTURES OF MATCHSTICK MEN** *Pye 7N 17449* ... 7 12
21 Aug 68 ● **ICE IN THE SUN** *Pye 7N 17581* ... 8 12
28 May 69 **ARE YOU GROWING TIRED OF MY LOVE (re)** *Pye 7N 17728* ... 46 3
2 May 70 **DOWN THE DUSTPIPE** *Pye 7N 17907* ... 12 17
7 Nov 70 **IN MY CHAIR** *Pye 7N 17998* ... 21 14
13 Jan 73 ● **PAPER PLANE** *Vertigo 6059 071* ... 8 11
14 Apr 73 **MEAN GIRL** *Pye 7N 45229* ... 20 11
8 Sep 73 ● **CAROLINE** *Vertigo 6059 085* ... 5 13
4 May 74 ● **BREAK THE RULES** *Vertigo 6059 101* ... 8 8
7 Dec 74 ★ **DOWN DOWN** *Vertigo 6059 114* ... 1 11
17 May 75 ● **LIVE! (EP)** *Vertigo QUO 13* ... 9 8
14 Feb 76 ● **RAIN** *Vertigo 6059 133* ... 7 7
10 Jul 76 **MYSTERY SONG** *Vertigo 6059 146* ... 11 9
11 Dec 76 ● **WILD SIDE OF LIFE** *Vertigo 6059 163* ... 9 12
8 Oct 77 ● **ROCKIN' ALL OVER THE WORLD** *Vertigo 6059 184* ... 3 16
2 Sep 78 **AGAIN AND AGAIN** *Vertigo QUO 1* ... 13 9
25 Nov 78 **ACCIDENT PRONE** *Vertigo QUO 2* ... 36 8
22 Sep 79 ● **WHATEVER YOU WANT** *Vertigo 6059 242* ... 4 9
24 Nov 79 **LIVING ON AN ISLAND** *Vertigo 6059 248* ... 16 10
11 Oct 80 ● **WHAT YOU'RE PROPOSING** *Vertigo QUO 3* ... 2 11
6 Dec 80 **LIES / DON'T DRIVE MY CAR** *Vertigo QUO 4* ... 11 10
28 Feb 81 ● **SOMETHING 'BOUT YOU BABY I LIKE** *Vertigo QUO 5* ... 9 7
28 Nov 81 ● **ROCK 'N' ROLL** *Vertigo QUO 6* ... 8 11
27 Mar 82 ● **DEAR JOHN** *Vertigo QUO 7* ... 10 8
12 Jun 82 **SHE DON'T FOOL ME** *Vertigo QUO 8* ... 36 5
30 Oct 82 **CAROLINE (LIVE AT THE NEC)** *Vertigo QUO 10* ... 13 7
10 Sep 83 ● **OL' RAG BLUES** *Vertigo QUO 11* ... 9 8
5 Nov 83 **A MESS OF BLUES** *Vertigo QUO 12* ... 15 6
10 Dec 83 ● **MARGUERITA TIME** *Vertigo QUO 14* ... 3 11
19 May 84 **GOING DOWN TOWN TONIGHT** *Vertigo QUO 15* ... 20 6
27 Oct 84 ● **THE WANDERER** *Vertigo QUO 16* ... 7 11
17 May 86 ● **ROLLIN' HOME** *Vertigo QUO 18* ... 9 6
26 Jul 86 **RED SKY** *Vertigo QUO 19* ... 19 8
4 Oct 86 ● **IN THE ARMY NOW** *Vertigo QUO 20* ... 2 14
6 Dec 86 **DREAMIN'** *Vertigo QUO 21* ... 15 8
26 Mar 88 **AIN'T COMPLAINING** *Vertigo QUO 22* ... 19 6
21 May 88 **WHO GETS THE LOVE?** *Vertigo QUO 23* ... 34 4
20 Aug 88 **RUNNING ALL OVER THE WORLD** *Vertigo QUAID 1* ... 17 6
3 Dec 88 ● **BURNING BRIDGES (ON AND OFF AND ON AGAIN)** *Vertigo QUO 25* ... 5 10
28 Oct 89 **NOT AT ALL** *Vertigo QUO 26* ... 50 2
29 Sep 90 ● **THE ANNIVERSARY WALTZ – PART ONE** *Vertigo QUO 28* ... 2 9
15 Dec 90 **THE ANNIVERSARY WALTZ – PART TWO** *Vertigo QUO 29* ... 16 7
7 Sep 91 **CAN'T GIVE YOU MORE** *Vertigo QUO 30* ... 37 3
18 Jan 92 **ROCK 'TIL YOU DROP** *Vertigo QUO 32* ... 38 3
10 Oct 92 **ROADHOUSE MEDLEY (ANNIVERSARY WALTZ PART 25)** *Polydor QUO 33* ... 21 4
6 Aug 94 **I DIDN'T MEAN IT** *Polydor QUOCD 34* ... 21 4
22 Oct 94 **SHERRI DON'T FAIL ME NOW** *Polydor QUOCD 35* ... 38 2
3 Dec 94 **RESTLESS** *Polydor QUOCD 36* ... 39 2
4 Nov 95 **WHEN YOU WALK IN THE ROOM** *PolyGram TV 5775122* ... 34 2
2 Mar 96 **FUN FUN FUN** *PolyGram TV 5762632* [1] ... 24 4
13 Apr 96 **DON'T STOP** *PolyGram TV 5766352* ... 35 2
9 Nov 96 **ALL AROUND MY HAT** *PolyGram TV 5759452* [2] ... 47 1
20 Mar 99 **THE WAY IT GOES** *Eagle EAGXS 075* ... 39 2
12 Jun 99 **LITTLE WHITE LIES** *Eagle EAGXS 101* ... 47 1
2 Oct 99 **TWENTY WILD HORSES** *Eagle EAGXS 105* ... 53 1
13 May 00 **MONY MONY** *Universal TV 1580132* ... 48 1
17 Aug 02 **JAM SIDE DOWN** *Universal TV 192342* ... 17 3
9 Nov 02 **ALL STAND UP (NEVER SAY NEVER)** *Universal TV 0194872* ... 51 1
20 Jan 73 ● **PILEDRIVER** *Vertigo 6360 082* ... 5 37
9 Jun 73 **THE BEST OF STATUS QUO** *Pye NSPL 18402* ... 32 7
6 Oct 73 ★ **HELLO** *Vertigo 6360 098* ... 1 28
18 May 74 ● **QUO** *Vertigo 9102 001* ... 2 16
1 Mar 75 ★ **ON THE LEVEL** *Vertigo 9102 002* ■ ... 1 27
8 Mar 75 **DOWN THE DUSTPIPE** *Golden Hour CH 604* ... 20 6
20 Mar 76 ★ **BLUE FOR YOU** *Vertigo 9102 006* ■ ... 1 30
12 Mar 77 ● **LIVE** *Vertigo 6641 580* ... 3 14
26 Nov 77 ● **ROCKIN' ALL OVER THE WORLD** *Vertigo 9102 014* ... 5 15
11 Nov 78 ● **IF YOU CAN'T STAND THE HEAT** *Vertigo 9102 027* ... 3 14
20 Oct 79 ● **WHATEVER YOU WANT** *Vertigo 9102 037* ... 3 14
22 Mar 80 ● **12 GOLD BARS** *Vertigo QUO TV 1* ... 3 48
25 Oct 80 ● **JUST SUPPOSIN'** *Vertigo 6302 057* ... 4 18
28 Mar 81 ● **NEVER TOO LATE** *Vertigo 6302 104* ... 2 13
10 Oct 81 **FRESH QUOTA** *PRT DOW 2* ... 74 1
24 Apr 82 ★ **1982** *Vertigo 6302 169* ■ ... 1 20
13 Nov 82 ● **FROM THE MAKERS OF ...** *Vertigo PROLP 1* ... 4 18
3 Dec 83 ● **BACK TO BACK** *Vertigo VERH 10* ... 9 22
4 Aug 84 **LIVE AT THE N.E.C.** *Vertigo (Holland) 8189 471* ... 83 3
1 Dec 84 **12 GOLD BARS VOLUME 2 (AND 1)** *Vertigo QUO TV 2* ... 12 18
6 Sep 86 ● **IN THE ARMY NOW** *Vertigo VERH 36* ... 7 23
18 Jun 88 **AIN'T COMPLAINING** *Vertigo VERH 58* ... 12 5
2 Dec 89 **PERFECT REMEDY** *Vertigo 842098 1* ... 49 2
20 Oct 90 ● **ROCKING ALL OVER THE YEARS** *Vertigo 8467971* ... 2 25
5 Oct 91 ● **ROCK 'TIL YOU DROP** *Vertigo 5103411* ... 10 7
14 Nov 92 **LIVE ALIVE QUO** *Polydor 5173672* ... 37 1
3 Sep 94 **THIRSTY WORK** *Polydor 5236072* ... 13 3
17 Feb 96 ● **DON'T STOP – THE 30TH ANNIVERSARY ALBUM** *PolyGram TV 5310352* ... 2 11
25 Oct 97 **WHATEVER YOU WANT – THE VERY BEST OF STATUS QUO** *Mercury / PolyGram TV 5535072* ... 13 6
10 Apr 99 **UNDER THE INFLUENCE** *Eagle EAGCD 076* ... 26 2
29 Apr 00 **FAMOUS IN THE LAST CENTURY** *Universal Music TV 1578142* ... 19 5
5 Oct 02 **HEAVY TRAFFIC** *Universal TV 0187902* ... 15 3
29 Nov 03 **RIFFS** *Universal TV 9813909* ... 44 2

[1] Status Quo with The Beach Boys
[2] Status Quo with Maddy Prior from Steeleye Span

'Don't Drive My Car' listed from 20 Dec 1980 only. 'Running All Over the World' is a re-recorded version of 'Rockin' All Over the World', with a slightly changed lyric, released to promote the Race Against Time of 28 Aug 1988. The 'Live!' EP from 1975 featured three tracks: Roll Over Lay Down (Live) / Gerundula / Junior's Wailing (Live). The Anniversary Waltz – Part One was a medley consisting of Let's Dance / Red River Rock / No Particular Place to Go / The Wanderer / I Hear You Knocking / Lucille / Great Balls of Fire. The Anniversary Waltz – Part Two consisted of Rock & Roll Music / Lover Please / That'll Be the Day / Singing the Blues / When Will I Be Loved / Let's Work Together / Keep a Knockin' / Long Tall Sally. Roadhouse Medley consisted of The Wanderer / Marguerita Time / Living on a Island / Break the Rules / Something 'Bout You Baby I Like

STAXX featuring Carol LEEMING *UK, male / female vocal / instrumental group (Singles: 11 weeks)* pos/wks

2 Oct 93 **JOY** *Champion CHAMPCD 303* ... 25 6
20 May 95 **YOU** *Champion CHAMPCD 316* ... 50 1
13 Sep 97 **JOY (re-mix)** *Champion CHAMPCD 328* ... 14 4

STEALERS WHEEL *UK, male vocal / instrumental group – includes Gerry Rafferty (Singles: 22 weeks)* pos/wks

26 May 73 ● **STUCK IN THE MIDDLE WITH YOU** *A&M AMS 7036* ... 8 10
1 Sep 73 **EVERYTHING WILL TURN OUT FINE** *A&M AMS 7079* ... 33 6
26 Jan 74 **STAR** *A&M AMS 7094* ... 25 6

STEAM *US, male vocal / instrumental group (Singles: 14 weeks)* pos/wks

31 Jan 70 ● **NA NA HEY HEY KISS HIM GOODBYE** *Fontana TF 1058* ▲ ... 9 14

STEEL – *See UNITONE ROCKERS featuring STEEL*

Anthony STEEL and the RADIO REVELLERS *UK, male actor / vocalist, d. 21 Mar 2001 and male vocal group (Singles: 6 weeks)* pos/wks

10 Sep 54 **WEST OF ZANZIBAR** *Polygon P 1114* ... 11 6

Act name also credits 'With Jackie Brown and his Music'

STEEL HORSES – *See TRUMAN & WOLFF featuring STEEL HORSES*

STEEL PULSE *UK, male vocal / instrumental group (Singles: 12 weeks, Albums: 18 weeks)* pos/wks

1 Apr 78 **KU KLUX KLAN** *Island WIP 6428* 41 4
8 Jul 78 **PRODIGAL SON** *Island WIP 6449* 35 6
23 Jun 79 **SOUND SYSTEM** *Island WIP 6490* 71 2
5 Aug 78 ● **HANDSWORTH REVOLUTION** *Island EMI ILPS 9502* 9 12
14 Jul 79 **TRIBUTE TO MARTYRS** *Island ILPS 9568* 42 6

Tommy STEELE 366 Top 500

Britain's first home-grown rock 'n' roll star, b. Thomas Hicks, 17 Dec 1936, London. Just four months after his chart debut he was filming his life story. The singer / songwriter / guitarist, who was the first UK act to have a No.1 album and who topped the singles chart before Elvis, starred in many other movies and musicals (Singles: 147 weeks, Albums: 34 weeks) pos/wks

26 Oct 56 **ROCK WITH THE CAVEMAN (re)** *Decca F 10795* [1] 13 5
14 Dec 56 ★ **SINGING THE BLUES (2re)** *Decca F 10819* [1] 1 15
15 Feb 57 **KNEE DEEP IN THE BLUES** *Decca F 10849* [1] 15 9
3 May 57 ● **BUTTERFINGERS (re)** *Decca F 10877* [1] 8 18
16 Aug 57 ● **WATER WATER / A HANDFUL OF SONGS (re)** *Decca F 10923* [1] 5 17
30 Aug 57 **SHIRALEE** *Decca F 10896* [1] 11 4
22 Nov 57 **HEY YOU!** *Decca F 10941* [1] 28 1
7 Mar 58 ● **NAIROBI** *Decca F 10991* 3 11
25 Apr 58 **HAPPY GUITAR** *Decca F 10976* 20 5
18 Jul 58 **THE ONLY MAN ON THE ISLAND** *Decca F 11041* [1] 16 8
14 Nov 58 ● **COME ON, LET'S GO** *Decca F 11072* 10 13
14 Aug 59 **TALLAHASSEE LASSIE (re)** *Decca F 11152* 16 5
28 Aug 59 **GIVE! GIVE! GIVE!** *Decca F 11152X* 28 2
4 Dec 59 ● **LITTLE WHITE BULL (re)** *Decca F 11177* 6 17
23 Jun 60 ● **WHAT A MOUTH (WHAT A NORTH AND SOUTH)** *Decca F 11245* 5 11
29 Dec 60 **MUST BE SANTA** *Decca F 11299* 40 1
17 Aug 61 **THE WRITING ON THE WALL** *Decca F 11372* 30 5
27 Apr 57 ● **TOMMY STEELE STAGE SHOW** *Decca LF 1287* 5 1
8 Jun 57 ★ **THE TOMMY STEELE STORY** *Decca LF 1288* 1 21
12 Apr 58 ★ **THE DUKE WORE JEANS (SOUNDTRACK)** *Decca LF 1308* 1 12

[1] Tommy Steele and The Steelmen

'Handful of Songs' listed together with 'Water Water' from week of 23 Aug 1957

STEELEYE SPAN *UK, male / female vocal / instrumental group (Singles: 18 weeks, Albums: 48 weeks)* pos/wks

8 Dec 73 **GAUDETE** *Chrysalis CHS 2007* 14 9
15 Nov 75 ● **ALL AROUND MY HAT** *Chrysalis CHS 2078* 5 9
10 Apr 71 **PLEASE TO SEE THE KING** *B & C CAS 1029* 45 2
14 Oct 72 **BELOW THE SALT** *Chrysalis CHR 1008* 43 1
28 Apr 73 **PARCEL OF ROGUES** *Chrysalis CHR 1046* 26 5
23 Mar 74 **NOW WE ARE SIX** *Chrysalis CHR 1053* 13 13
15 Feb 75 **COMMONER'S CROWN** *Chrysalis CHR 1071* 21 4
25 Oct 75 ● **ALL AROUND MY HAT** *Chrysalis CHR 1091* 7 20
16 Oct 76 **ROCKET COTTAGE** *Chrysalis CHR 1123* 41 3

STEELY DAN *US, male vocal / instrumental group – led by Donald Fagen and Walter Becker (Singles: 21 weeks, Albums: 91 weeks)* pos/wks

30 Aug 75 **DO IT AGAIN** *ABC 4075* 39 4
11 Dec 76 **HAITIAN DIVORCE** *ABC 4152* 17 9
29 Jul 78 **FM (NO STATIC AT ALL) (re)** *MCA 374* 49 5
10 Mar 79 **RIKKI DON'T LOSE THAT NUMBER** *ABC 4241* 58 3
30 Mar 74 **PRETZEL LOGIC** *Probe SPBA 6282* 37 2
3 May 75 **KATY LIED** *ABC ABCL 5094* 13 6
20 Sep 75 **CAN'T BUY A THRILL** *ABC ABCL 5024* 38 1
22 May 76 **THE ROYAL SCAM** *ABC ABCL 5161* 11 13
8 Oct 77 ● **AJA** *ABC ABCL 5225* 5 10
2 Dec 78 **GREATEST HITS** *ABC BLD 616* 41 18
29 Nov 80 **GAUCHO** *MCA MCF 3090* 27 12
3 Jul 82 **GOLD** *MCA MCF 3145* 44 6
26 Oct 85 **REELIN' IN THE YEARS – THE VERY BEST OF STEELY DAN** *MCA DANTV 1* 43 5
10 Oct 87 **DO IT AGAIN – THE VERY BEST OF STEELY DAN** *Telstar STAR 2297* 64 4
20 Nov 93 **REMASTERED – THE BEST OF STEELY DAN** *MCA MCD 10967* 42 5
28 Oct 95 **ALIVE IN AMERICA** *Giant 74321286912* 62 1
11 Mar 00 **TWO AGAINST NATURE** *Giant 74321621902* 11 5
21 Jun 03 **EVERYTHING MUST GO** *Reprise 9362484352* 21 3

Wout STEENHUIS *Holland, male instrumentalist – guitar, d. 12 Oct 1996 (Albums: 7 weeks)* pos/wks

21 Nov 81 **HAWAIIAN PARADISE/CHRISTMAS** *Warwick WW 5106* 28 7

STEFY – *See DJH featuring STEFY*

Jim STEINMAN *US, male producer (Singles: 9 weeks, Albums: 25 weeks)* pos/wks

4 Jul 81 **ROCK AND ROLL DREAMS COME THROUGH** *Epic EPC A 1236* [1] 52 7
23 Jun 84 **TONIGHT IS WHAT IT MEANS TO BE YOUNG** *MCA MCA 889* [2] 67 2
9 May 81 ● **BAD FOR GOOD** *Epic EPC 84361* 7 25

[1] Jim Steinman, vocals by Rory Dodd [2] Jim Steinman and Fire Inc

STEINSKI and MASS MEDIA *US, male / female production group (Singles: 2 weeks)* pos/wks

31 Jan 87 **WE'LL BE RIGHT BACK** *Fourth & Broadway BRW 59* 63 2

Mike STEIPHENSON – *See BURUNDI STEIPHENSON BLACK*

STELLA BROWNE *UK, male production duo (Singles: 3 weeks)* pos/wks

20 May 00 **EVERY WOMAN NEEDS LOVE** *Perfecto PERF 06* 55 1
9 Feb 02 **NEVER KNEW LOVE** *Perfecto PERF 26CDS* 42 2

STELLASTARR* *US, male / female vocal / instrumental group (Singles: 2 weeks)* pos/wks

31 May 03 **SOMEWHERE ACROSS FOREVER** *Twenty-20 TWENTYCDS 001* 73 1
27 Sep 03 **JENNY** *Twenty-20 TWENTYCDS 002* 61 1

Doreen STEPHENS – *See Billy COTTON and His BAND*

Richie STEPHENS *Jamaica, male vocalist (Singles: 3 weeks)* pos/wks

15 May 93 **LEGACY** *Columbia 6592852* [1] 64 2
9 Aug 97 **COME GIVE ME YOUR LOVE** *Delirious 74321450442* [2] 61 1

[1] Mad Cobra featuring Richie Stephens [2] Richie Stephens and General Degree

Martin STEPHENSON and the DAINTEES *UK, male vocal / instrumental group (Singles: 7 weeks, Albums: 11 weeks)* pos/wks

8 Nov 86 **BOAT TO BOLIVIA** *Kitchenware SL 27* 70 2
17 Jan 87 **TROUBLE TOWN** *Kitchenware SK 13* [1] 58 3
27 Jun 92 **BIG SKY NEW LIGHT** *Kitchenware SK 57* 71 2
17 May 86 **BOAT TO BOLIVIA** *Kitchenware KWLP 5* 85 3
16 Apr 88 **GLADSOME HUMOUR AND BLUE** *Kitchenware KWLP 8* 39 4
19 May 90 **SALUTATION ROAD** *Kitchenware 8281981* 35 3
25 Jul 92 **THE BOY'S HEART** *Kitchenware 8283242* 68 1

[1] Daintees

STEPPENWOLF *US / Canada, male vocal / instrumental group (Singles: 14 weeks, Albums: 20 weeks)* pos/wks

11 Jun 69 **BORN TO BE WILD (re)** *Stateside SS 8017* 30 9
27 Feb 99 **BORN TO BE WILD (re-issue)** *MCA MCSTD 48104* 18 5
28 Feb 70 **MONSTER** *Stateside SSL 5021* 43 4
25 Apr 70 **STEPPENWOLF** *Stateside SSL 5020* 59 2
4 Jul 70 **STEPPENWOLF LIVE** *Stateside SSL 5029* 16 14

STEPS 118 Top 500

Steptacular pop vocal quintet: Lisa Scott-Lee, Claire Richards, Faye Tozer, Lee Latchford-Evans, Ian Watkins (aka H). The hard-working live act's 1999 tour was reportedly the biggest pop arena tour ever in the UK. The first UK mixed quintet to top the chart twice, they bagged 14 consecutive Top 5 singles (a feat bettered only by The Beatles), sold more than 12 million records and announced their split on Boxing Day 2001. Best-selling single: 'Heartbeat / Tragedy' 1,150,285 (Singles: 217 weeks, Albums: 172 weeks) pos/wks

22 Nov 97 **5, 6, 7, 8** *Jive JIVECD 438* 14 17
2 May 98 ● **LAST THING ON MY MIND** *Jive 0518492* 6 14
5 Sep 98 ● **ONE FOR SORROW** *Jive 0519092* 2 11
21 Nov 98 ★ **HEARTBEAT / TRAGEDY** *Jive 0519142* ◆ 1 30
20 Mar 99 ● **BETTER BEST FORGOTTEN (re)** *Ebul / Jive 0519242* 2 17
10 Apr 99 ● **THANK ABBA FOR THE MUSIC** *Epic ABCD 1* [1] 4 13
24 Jul 99 ● **LOVE'S GOT A HOLD ON MY HEART (re)** *Ebul / Jive 0519372* 2 12
23 Oct 99 ● **AFTER THE LOVE HAS GONE (re)** *Ebul / Jive 0519462* 5 11
25 Dec 99 ● **SAY YOU'LL BE MINE / BETTER THE DEVIL YOU KNOW** *Ebul / Jive 9201008* 4 17
15 Apr 00 ● **DEEPER SHADE OF BLUE** *Ebul / Jive 9201022* 4 9
15 Jul 00 ● **WHEN I SAID GOODBYE / SUMMER OF LOVE** *Ebul / Jive 9201162* 5 11
28 Oct 00 ★ **STOMP** *Ebul / Jive 9201212* ■ 1 11
6 Jan 01 ● **IT'S THE WAY YOU MAKE ME FEEL / TOO BUSY THINKING 'BOUT MY BABY** *Ebul / Jive 9201232* 2 11
16 Jun 01 ● **HERE AND NOW / YOU'LL BE SORRY** *Ebul / Jive 9201322* 4 10
6 Oct 01 ● **CHAIN REACTION / ONE FOR SORROW (re-mix)** *Ebul / Jive 9201422* 2 12
15 Dec 01 ● **WORDS ARE NOT ENOUGH / I KNOW HIM SO WELL** *Ebul / Jive 9201452* 5 11
26 Sep 98 ● **STEP ONE** *Jive 519112* 2 62
6 Nov 99 ★ **STEPTACULAR** *Jive 519442* ■ 1 62
11 Nov 00 ● **BUZZ** *Jive 9201172* 4 26
27 Oct 01 ★ **GOLD – THE GREATEST HITS** *Jive 9201412* ■ 1 21
7 Dec 02 **THE LAST DANCE** *Jive 9201522* 57 1

[1] Steps, Tina Cousins, Cleopatra, B*Witched, Billie

See also Lisa SCOTT-LEE; H and CLAIRE

STEREO MC's

UK, male / female vocal / rap group (Singles: 37 weeks, Albums: 55 weeks) pos/wks

29 Sep 90 **ELEVATE MY MIND** *Fourth & Broadway BRW 186* 74 1
9 Mar 91 **LOST IN MUSIC** *Fourth & Broadway BRW 198* 46 3
26 Sep 92 **CONNECTED** *Fourth & Broadway BRW 262* 18 6
5 Dec 92 **STEP IT UP** *Fourth & Broadway BRW 266* 12 12
20 Feb 93 **GROUND LEVEL** *Fourth & Broadway BRCD 268* 19 5
29 May 93 **CREATION** *Fourth & Broadway BRCD 276* 19 4
26 May 01 **DEEP DOWN & DIRTY (re)** *Island CID 777* 17 5
1 Sep 01 **WE BELONG IN THIS WORLD TOGETHER** *Island CID 782* 59 1
17 Oct 92 ● **CONNECTED** *Fourth & Broadway BRCD 589* 2 52
9 Jun 01 **DEEP DOWN & DIRTY** *Island CID 8106* 17 3

STEREO NATION

UK, male vocal / instrumental duo (Singles: 3 weeks) pos/wks

17 Aug 96 **I'VE BEEN WAITING** *EMI Premier PRESCD 5* 53 1
27 Oct 01 **LAILA** *Wizard WIZ 015* [1] 44 2

[1] Taz & Stereo Nation

STEREOLAB

UK / France / Australia, male / female vocal / instrumental group (Singles: 6 weeks, Albums: 11 weeks) pos/wks

8 Jan 94 **JENNY ONDIOLINE / FRENCH DISCO** *Duophonic UHF DUHFCD 01* 75 1
30 Jul 94 **PING PONG** *Duophonic UHF DUHFCD 04* 45 2
12 Nov 94 **WOW AND FLUTTER** *Duophonic UHF DUHFCD 07* 70 1
2 Mar 96 **CYBELE'S REVERIE** *Duophonic UHF DUHFCD 10* 62 1
13 Sep 97 **MISS MODULAR** *Duophonic DUHFCD 16* 60 1
18 Sep 93 **TRANSIENT RANDOM NOISE BURSTS** *Duophonic UHF DUHFCD 02* 62 1
20 Aug 94 **MARS AUDIAC QUINTET** *Duophonic UHF DUHFCD 05X* 16 3
29 Apr 95 **MUSIC FOR AMORPHOUS BODY STUDY CENTRE** *Duophonic UHF DUHFCD 08* 59 1
16 Sep 95 **REFRIED ECTOPLASM (SWITCHED ON VOLUME 2)** *Duophonic UHF DUHFCD 09* 30 2
30 Mar 96 **EMPEROR TOMATO KETCHUP** *Duophonic UHF DUHFCD 11* 27 2
4 Oct 97 **DOTS AND LOOPS** *Duophonic UHF DUHFCD 17* 19 2

STEREOPHONICS 93 Top 500

1998 Best Newcomer Brit award-winning rock trio – Kelly Jones (v,g), Richard Jones (b) and Stuart Cable (d, left 2003) – from Cwmaman, Wales, UK. Their 14 hit singles and two chart-topping albums of new material between 1997 and 2001 cannot be bettered by any other group (Singles: 124 weeks, Albums: 324 weeks) pos/wks

29 Mar 97 **LOCAL BOY IN THE PHOTOGRAPH** *V2 SPHD 2* 51 1
31 May 97 **MORE LIFE IN A TRAMP'S VEST** *V2 SPHD 4* 33 2
23 Aug 97 **A THOUSAND TREES** *V2 VVR 5000443* 22 3
8 Nov 97 **TRAFFIC** *V2 VVR 5000948* 20 3
21 Feb 98 **LOCAL BOY IN THE PHOTOGRAPH (re-issue)** *V2 VVR 5001263* 14 4
21 Nov 98 ● **THE BARTENDER AND THE THIEF** *V2 VVR 5004653* 3 12
6 Mar 99 ● **JUST LOOKING (re)** *V2 VVR 5005303* 4 9
15 May 99 ● **PICK A PART THAT'S NEW** *V2 VVR 5006778* 4 9
4 Sep 99 **I WOULDN'T BELIEVE YOUR RADIO (re)** *V2 VVR 5008823* 11 7
20 Nov 99 **HURRY UP AND WAIT (re)** *V2 VVR 5009323* 11 8
18 Mar 00 ● **MAMA TOLD ME NOT TO COME** *Gut CDGUT 031* [1] 4 7
31 Mar 01 ● **MR WRITER** *V2 VVR 5015933* 5 12
23 Jun 01 ● **HAVE A NICE DAY** *V2 VVR 5016243* 5 9
6 Oct 01 **STEP ON MY OLD SIZE NINES** *V2 VVR 5016253* 16 5
15 Dec 01 ● **HANDBAGS AND GLADRAGS (re)** *V2 VVR 5017753* 4 15
13 Apr 02 **VEGAS TWO TIMES** *V2 VVR 5019173* 23 2
31 May 03 ● **MADAME HELGA** *V2 VVR 5021743* 4 4
2 Aug 03 ● **MAYBE TOMORROW** *V2 VVR 5021893* 3 8
22 Nov 03 **SINCE I TOLD YOU IT'S OVER** *V2 VVR 5022623* 16 4
6 Sep 97 ● **WORD GETS AROUND** *V2 VVR 1000432* 6 115
20 Mar 99 ★ **PERFORMANCE AND COCKTAILS** *V2 VVR 1004498* ■ 1 97
21 Apr 01 ★ **JUST ENOUGH EDUCATION TO PERFORM** *V2 VVR 1015832* ■ 1 86
14 Jun 03 ★ **YOU GOTTA GO THERE TO COME BACK** *V2 VVR 1021902* ■ ......1 26+

[1] Tom Jones and Stereophonics

STEREOPOL featuring NEVADA

Sweden / UK, male production / vocal group and UK, male vocalist (Singles: 2 weeks) pos/wks

29 Mar 03 **DANCIN' TONIGHT** *Rulin' 28 CDS* 36 2

STETSASONIC

US, male rap group (Singles: 3 weeks) pos/wks

24 Sep 88 **TALKIN' ALL THAT JAZZ** *Breakout USA 640* 73 2
7 Nov 98 **TALKIN ALL THAT JAZZ (re-mix)** *Tommy Boy TBCD 7310A* 54 1

STEVE and EYDIE – *See Eydie GORME; Steve LAWRENCE*

April STEVENS – *See Nino TEMPO and April STEVENS*

Cat STEVENS 137 Top 500

Critically acclaimed folk-pop singer / songwriter, b. Steven Georgiou, 21 Jul 1947, London, UK, whose songs have been recorded by many top acts. One of the world's biggest album sellers in 1970s. Semi-retired in 1979, converted to Islam and changed his name to Yusuf Islam. Gave royalties for Boyzone version of 'Father and Son' to charity (Singles: 96 weeks, Albums: 267 weeks) pos/wks

20 Oct 66 **I LOVE MY DOG** *Deram DM 102* 28 7
12 Jan 67 ● **MATTHEW AND SON** *Deram DM 110* 2 10
30 Mar 67 ● **I'M GONNA GET ME A GUN** *Deram DM 118* 6 10
2 Aug 67 **A BAD NIGHT** *Deram DM 140* 20 8
20 Dec 67 **KITTY** *Deram DM 156* 47 1
27 Jun 70 ● **LADY D'ARBANVILLE** *Island WIP 6086* 8 13
28 Aug 71 **MOON SHADOW** *Island WIP 6092* 22 11
1 Jan 72 ● **MORNING HAS BROKEN** *Island WIP 6121* 9 13
9 Dec 72 **CAN'T KEEP IT IN** *Island WIP 6152* 13 12
24 Aug 74 **ANOTHER SATURDAY NIGHT** *Island WIP 6206* 19 8
2 Jul 77 **(REMEMBER THE DAYS OF THE) OLD SCHOOL YARD** *Island WIP 6387* 44 3
25 Mar 67 ● **MATTHEW AND SON** *Deram SML 1004* 7 16
11 Jul 70 **MONA BONE JAKON** *Island ILPS 9118* 63 4
28 Nov 70 **TEA FOR THE TILLERMAN** *Island ILPS 9135* 20 31
2 Oct 71 ● **TEASER AND THE FIRECAT** *Island ILPS 9154* 3 93
7 Oct 72 ● **CATCH BULL AT FOUR** *Island ILPS 9206* ▲ 2 27
21 Jul 73 ● **FOREIGNER** *Island ILPS 9240* 3 10

6 Apr 74 ●	BUDDAH AND THE CHOCOLATE BOX *Island ILPS 9274*	3 15
19 Jul 75 ●	GREATEST HITS *Island ILPS 9310*	2 24
14 May 77	IZITSO *Island ILPS 9451*	18 15
3 Feb 90 ●	THE VERY BEST OF CAT STEVENS *Island CATV 1*	4 16
27 Nov 99	REMEMBER CAT STEVENS – THE ULTIMATE COLLECTION *Island CID 8079*	31 6
25 Oct 03 ●	THE VERY BEST OF CAT STEVENS *Universal TV 9811208*	6 10+

Both 'Very Best Of's are different

Connie STEVENS

US, female vocalist / actor – Concetta Ingolia (Singles: 20 weeks) pos/wks

5 May 60 ●	SIXTEEN REASONS (re) *Warner Bros. WB 3*	9 12
5 May 60	KOOKIE KOOKIE (LEND ME YOUR COMB) *Warner Bros. WB 5* [1]	27 8

[1] Edward Byrnes and Connie Stevens

Rachel STEVENS

UK, female vocalist (Singles: 12 weeks, Albums: 6 weeks) pos/wks

27 Sep 03 ●	SWEET DREAMS MY L.A. EX *19 / Polydor 9811874*	2 10
20 Dec 03	FUNKY DORY *Polydor 9614984*	26 2+
11 Oct 03 ●	FUNKY DORY *19 / Polydor 9865702*	9 6

See also S CLUB 7

Ray STEVENS *US, male vocalist – Ray Ragsdale (Singles: 64 weeks, Albums: 8 weeks)* pos/wks

16 May 70 ●	EVERYTHING IS BEAUTIFUL *CBS 4953* ▲	6 16
13 Mar 71 ●	BRIDGET THE MIDGET (THE QUEEN OF THE BLUES) *CBS 7070*	2 14
25 Mar 72	TURN YOUR RADIO ON *CBS 7634*	33 4
25 May 74 ★	THE STREAK *Janus 6146 201* ▲	1 12
21 Jun 75 ●	MISTY *Janus 6146 204*	2 10
27 Sep 75	INDIAN LOVE CALL *Janus 6146 205*	34 4
5 Mar 77	IN THE MOOD *Warner Bros. K 16875*	31 4
26 Sep 70	EVERYTHING IS BEAUTIFUL *CBS 64074*	62 1
13 Sep 75	MISTY *Janus 9109 401*	23 7

'In the Mood' features Ray Stevens not as a conventional vocalist, but as a group of chickens

Ricky STEVENS *UK, male vocalist (Singles: 7 weeks)* pos/wks

14 Dec 61	I CRIED FOR YOU *Columbia DB 4739*	34 7

Shakin' STEVENS (99 Top 500)

With single sales of 7,108,336, Shaky performs and records under a broad umbrella of styles from rock and country blues to cajun, b. Michael Barratt, 4 Mar 1948, Glamorgan, Wales. Shares with The Beatles (60s) and Elton John (70s) the distinction of being the most successful UK singles chart performer of a decade (80s) (Singles: 277 weeks, Albums: 158 weeks) pos/wks

16 Feb 80	HOT DOG *Epic EPC 8090*	24 9
16 Aug 80	MARIE MARIE *Epic EPC 8725*	19 10
28 Feb 81 ★	THIS OLE HOUSE *Epic EPC 9555*	1 17
2 May 81 ●	YOU DRIVE ME CRAZY *Epic A 1165*	2 12
25 Jul 81 ★	GREEN DOOR *Epic A 1354*	1 12
10 Oct 81 ●	IT'S RAINING *Epic A 1643*	10 9
16 Jan 82 ★	OH JULIE *Epic EPC A 1742*	1 10
24 Apr 82 ●	SHIRLEY *Epic EPC A 2087*	6 6
21 Aug 82	GIVE ME YOUR HEART TONIGHT *Epic EPC A 2656*	11 10
16 Oct 82 ●	I'LL BE SATISFIED *Epic EPC A 2846*	10 8
11 Dec 82 ●	THE SHAKIN' STEVENS EP *Epic SHAKY 1*	2 7
23 Jul 83	IT'S LATE *Epic A 3565*	11 7
5 Nov 83 ●	CRY JUST A LITTLE BIT *Epic A 3774*	3 12
7 Jan 84 ●	A ROCKIN' GOOD WAY *Epic A 4071* [1]	5 9
24 Mar 84 ●	A LOVE WORTH WAITING FOR *Epic A 4291*	2 10
15 Sep 84 ●	A LETTER TO YOU *Epic A 4677*	10 8
24 Nov 84 ●	TEARDROPS *Epic A 4882*	5 9
2 Mar 85	BREAKING UP MY HEART *Epic A 6072*	14 7
12 Oct 85	LIPSTICK POWDER AND PAINT *Epic A 6610*	11 9
7 Dec 85 ★	MERRY CHRISTMAS EVERYONE (re) *Epic A 6769*	1 11
8 Feb 86	TURNING AWAY *Epic A 6819*	15 7
1 Nov 86	BECAUSE I LOVE YOU *Epic SHAKY 2*	14 10
27 Jun 87	A LITTLE BOOGIE WOOGIE (IN THE BACK OF MY MIND) *Epic SHAKY 3*	12 10
19 Sep 87	COME SEE ABOUT ME *Epic SHAKY 4*	24 6
28 Nov 87 ●	WHAT DO YOU WANT TO MAKE THOSE EYES AT ME FOR *Epic SHAKY 5*	5 8
23 Jul 88	FEEL THE NEED IN ME *Epic SHAKY 6*	26 5
15 Oct 88	HOW MANY TEARS CAN YOU HIDE *Epic SHAKY 7*	47 4
10 Dec 88	TRUE LOVE *Epic SHAKY 8*	23 6
18 Feb 89	JEZEBEL *Epic SHAKY 9*	58 2
13 May 89	LOVE ATTACK *Epic SHAKY 10*	28 4
24 Feb 90	I MIGHT *Epic SHAKY 11*	18 6
12 May 90	YES I DO *Epic SHAKY 12*	60 2
18 Aug 90	PINK CHAMPAGNE *Epic SHAKY 13*	59 2
13 Oct 90	MY CUTIE CUTIE *Epic SHAKY 14*	75 1
15 Dec 90	THE BEST CHRISTMAS OF THEM ALL *Epic SHAKY 15*	19 4
7 Dec 91	I'LL BE HOME THIS CHRISTMAS *Epic 6576507*	34 5
10 Oct 92	RADIO *Epic 6584367* [2]	37 3
15 Mar 80	TAKE ONE! *Epic EPC 83978*	62 2
4 Apr 81 ●	THIS OLE HOUSE *Epic EPC 84985*	2 28
8 Aug 81	SHAKIN' STEVENS *Hallmark/Pickwick SHM 3065*	34 5
19 Sep 81 ★	SHAKY *Epic EPC 10027*	1 28
9 Oct 82 ●	GIVE ME YOUR HEART TONIGHT *Epic EPC 10035*	3 18
26 Nov 83	THE BOP WON'T STOP *Epic EPC 86301*	21 27
17 Nov 84 ●	GREATEST HITS *Epic EPC 10047*	8 22
16 Nov 85	LIPSTICK POWDER AND PAINT *Epic EPC 26646*	37 9
31 Oct 87	LET'S BOOGIE *Epic 460 1261*	59 7
19 Nov 88	A WHOLE LOTTA SHAKY *Epic MOOD 5*	42 8
20 Oct 90	THERE'S TWO KINDS OF MUSIC: ROCK 'N' ROLL *Telstar STAR 2454*	65 2
31 Oct 92	THE EPIC YEARS *Epic 4724222* [1]	57 2

[1] Shaky and Bonnie [2] Shaky featuring Roger Taylor [1] Shaky

Tracks on The Shakin' Stevens EP: Blue Christmas / Que Sera Sera / Josephine / Lawdy Miss Clawdy. 'Merry Christmas Everyone' re-entered peaking at No.58 in Dec 1986

See also Bonnie TYLER

STEVENSON'S ROCKET

UK, male vocal / instrumental group (Singles: 5 weeks) pos/wks

29 Nov 75	ALRIGHT BABY (re) *Magnet MAG 47*	37 5

Al STEWART

UK, male vocalist (Singles: 6 weeks, Albums: 20 weeks) pos/wks

29 Jan 77	YEAR OF THE CAT *RCA 2771*	31 6
11 Apr 70	ZERO SHE FLIES *CBS 63848*	40 4
5 Feb 77	YEAR OF THE CAT *RCA RS 1082*	38 7
21 Oct 78	TIME PASSAGES *RCA PL 25173*	39 1
6 Sep 80	24 CARAT *RCA PL 25306*	55 6
9 Jun 84	RUSSIANS AND AMERICANS *RCA PL 70307*	83 2

Amii STEWART *US, female vocalist (Singles: 61 weeks)* pos/wks

7 Apr 79 ●	KNOCK ON WOOD *Atlantic / Hansa K 11214* ▲	6 12
16 Jun 79 ●	LIGHT MY FIRE / 137 DISCO HEAVEN (MEDLEY) *Atlantic / Hansa K 11278*	5 11
3 Nov 79	JEALOUSY *Atlantic / Hansa K 11386*	58 3
19 Jan 80	THE LETTER / PARADISE BIRD *Atlantic / Hansa K 11424*	39 4
19 Jul 80	MY GUY – MY GIRL (MEDLEY) *Atlantic / Hansa K 11550* [1]	39 5
29 Dec 84	FRIENDS *RCA 471*	12 11
17 Aug 85 ●	KNOCK ON WOOD / LIGHT MY FIRE (re-mix) *Sedition EDIT 3303*	7 12
25 Jan 86	MY GUY – MY GIRL (MEDLEY) *Sedition EDIT 3310* [2]	63 3

[1] Amii Stewart and Johnny Bristol [2] Amii Stewart and Deon Estus

Andy STEWART *UK, male vocalist, d. 11 Oct 1993 (Singles: 67 weeks, Albums: 2 weeks)* pos/wks

15 Dec 60	DONALD WHERE'S YOUR TROOSERS *Top Rank JAR 427* [1]	37 1
12 Jan 61	A SCOTTISH SOLDIER (re) *Top Rank JAR 512* [1]	19 40
1 Jun 61	THE BATTLE'S O'ER *Top Rank JAR 565* [1]	28 13
12 Aug 65	DR FINLAY (re) *HMV POP 1454*	43 5
9 Dec 89 ●	DONALD WHERE'S YOUR TROOSERS (re-issue) *Stone SON 2353* [1]	4 8
3 Feb 62	ANDY STEWART *Top Rank 35116*	13 2

[1] Andy Stewart with the Michael Sammes Singers

Billy STEWART

US, male vocalist, d. 17 Jan 1970 (Singles: 2 weeks) pos/wks

8 Sep 66 **SUMMERTIME** *Chess CRS 8040* 39 2

Dave STEWART

UK, male instrumentalist – keyboards (Singles: 30 weeks) pos/wks

14 Mar 81 **WHAT BECOMES OF THE BROKEN HEARTED** *Stiff BROKEN 1* [1] 13 10
19 Sep 81 ★ **IT'S MY PARTY** *Stiff BROKEN 2* [2] 1 13
13 Aug 83 **BUSY DOING NOTHING** *Broken BROKEN 5* [2] 49 4
14 Jun 86 **THE LOCOMOTION** *Broken BROKEN 8* [2] 70 3

[1] Dave Stewart. Guest vocals: Colin Blunstone [2] Dave Stewart with Barbara Gaskin

David A STEWART *UK, male instrumentalist – guitar (Singles: 19 weeks, Albums: 7 weeks)* pos/wks

24 Feb 90 ● **LILY WAS HERE** *RCA ZB 43045* [1] 6 12
18 Aug 90 **JACK TALKING** *RCA PB 43907* [2] 69 2
3 Sep 94 **HEART OF STONE** *East West YZ 845CD* [3] 36 5
7 Apr 90 **LILY WAS HERE (FILM SOUNDTRACK)** *Anxious ZL 74233* 35 5
15 Sep 90 **DAVE STEWART AND THE SPIRITUAL COWBOYS** *RCA OB 74710* [1] 38 2

[1] David A Stewart featuring Candy Dulfer [2] Dave Stewart and the Spiritual Cowboys [3] Dave Stewart [1] Dave Stewart and the Spiritual Cowboys

See also EURYTHMICS; VEGAS; TOURISTS

Jermaine STEWART *US, male vocalist, b.7 Sep 1957, d.17 Mar 1997 (Singles: 42 weeks, Albums: 12 weeks)* pos/wks

9 Aug 86 ● **WE DON'T HAVE TO … TAKE OUR CLOTHES OFF TO HAVE A GOOD TIME** *10 TEN 96* 2 14
1 Nov 86 **JODY** *10 TEN 143* 50 4
16 Jan 88 ● **SAY IT AGAIN** *10 TEN 188* 7 12
2 Apr 88 **GET LUCKY** *Siren SRN 82* 13 9
24 Sep 88 **DON'T TALK DIRTY TO ME** *Siren SRN 86* 61 3
4 Oct 86 **FRANTIC ROMANTIC** *10 DIX 26* 49 4
5 Mar 88 **SAY IT AGAIN** *Siren SRNLP 14* 32 8

John STEWART *US, male vocalist (Singles: 6 weeks)* pos/wks

30 Jun 79 **GOLD** *RSO 35* 43 6

Rod STEWART (11 Top 500)

World-renowned rock superstar b. 10 Jan 1945, London, UK, of Scottish parents. In the 1960s 'Rod the Mod' recorded solo singles for Decca, EMI and Immediate, but is best remembered in that period as a member of The Five Dimensions, Hoochie Coochie Men, Steampacket, Shotgun Express and The Jeff Beck Group. Between 1969 and 1975, the gravel-voiced vocalist fronted The Faces as well as having a successful solo career. Over the past 30 years, Stewart has played to packed stadiums worldwide and amassed a vast collection of platinum and gold albums. In the US, he is one of the top-selling UK artists of all time with 10 Top 10 albums and 16 Top 10 singles. In Britain, he has scored 23 Top 10 LPs including seven solo No.1s. His song-writing skills have earned him a Lifetime Ivor Novello Award in the UK, while in the US he has recently been nominated for the prestigious Songwriters' Hall of Fame. The football mad Stewart, whose love life also attracts much media attention, earned a Grammy Living Legend Award in 1989 (Singles: 477 weeks, Albums: 875 weeks) pos/wks

4 Sep 71 **REASON TO BELIEVE** *Mercury 6052 097* 19 2
18 Sep 71 ★ **MAGGIE MAY** *Mercury 6052 097* ▲ 1 19
12 Aug 72 ★ **YOU WEAR IT WELL** *Mercury 6052 171* 1 12
18 Nov 72 ● **ANGEL / WHAT MADE MILWAUKEE FAMOUS (HAS MADE A LOSER OUT OF ME)** *Mercury 6052 198* 4 11
5 May 73 **I'VE BEEN DRINKING** *RAK RR 4* [1] 27 6
8 Sep 73 ● **OH! NO NOT MY BABY** *Mercury 6052 371* 6 9
5 Oct 74 ● **FAREWELL – BRING IT ON HOME TO ME / YOU SEND ME** *Mercury 6167 033* 7 7
7 Dec 74 **YOU CAN MAKE ME DANCE SING OR ANYTHING (EVEN TAKE THE DOG FOR A WALK, MEND A FUSE, FOLD AWAY THE IRONING BOARD, OR ANY OTHER DOMESTIC SHORT COMINGS)** *Warner Bros. K 16494* [2] 12 9
16 Aug 75 ★ **SAILING (2re)** *Warner Bros. K 16600* 1 34
15 Nov 75 ● **THIS OLD HEART OF MINE** *Riva 1* 4 9
5 Jun 76 ● **TONIGHT'S THE NIGHT** *Riva 3* ▲ 5 9
21 Aug 76 ● **THE KILLING OF GEORGIE** *Riva 4* 2 10
20 Nov 76 **GET BACK** *Riva 6* 11 9
4 Dec 76 **MAGGIE MAY (re-issue)** *Mercury 6160 006* 31 7
23 Apr 77 ★ **I DON'T WANT TO TALK ABOUT IT / FIRST CUT IS THE DEEPEST** *Riva 7* 1 13
15 Oct 77 ● **YOU'RE IN MY HEART** *Riva 11* 3 10
28 Jan 78 ● **HOT LEGS / I WAS ONLY JOKING** *Riva 10* 5 8
27 May 78 ● **OLE OLA (MULHER BRASILEIRA)** *Riva 15* [3] 4 6
18 Nov 78 ★ **DA YA THINK I'M SEXY?** *Riva 17* ▲ 1 13
3 Feb 79 **AIN'T LOVE A BITCH** *Riva 18* 11 8
5 May 79 **BLONDES (HAVE MORE FUN)** *Riva 19* 63 3
31 May 80 **IF LOVING YOU IS WRONG (I DON'T WANT TO BE RIGHT)** *Riva 23* 23 9
8 Nov 80 **PASSION** *Riva 26* 17 10
20 Dec 80 **MY GIRL** *Riva 28* 32 7
17 Oct 81 ● **TONIGHT I'M YOURS (DON'T HURT ME)** *Riva 33* 8 13
12 Dec 81 **YOUNG TURKS** *Riva 34* 11 9
27 Feb 82 **HOW LONG** *Riva 35* 41 4
4 Jun 83 ★ **BABY JANE** *Warner Bros. W 9608* 1 14
27 Aug 83 ● **WHAT AM I GONNA DO (I'M SO IN LOVE WITH YOU)** *Warner Bros. W 9564* 3 8
10 Dec 83 **SWEET SURRENDER** *Warner Bros. W 9440* 23 9
26 May 84 **INFATUATION** *Warner Bros. W 9256* 27 7
28 Jul 84 **SOME GUYS HAVE ALL THE LUCK** *Warner Bros. W 9204* 15 10
24 May 86 **LOVE TOUCH (re)** *Warner Bros. W 8668* 27 8
12 Jul 86 ● **EVERY BEAT OF MY HEART** *Warner Bros. W 8625* 2 9
20 Sep 86 **ANOTHER HEARTACHE** *Warner Bros. W 8631* 54 2
28 May 88 **LOST IN YOU** *Warner Bros. W 7927* 21 6
13 Aug 88 **FOREVER YOUNG** *Warner Bros. W 7796* 57 3
6 May 89 **MY HEART CAN'T TELL YOU NO** *Warner Bros. W 7729* 49 4
11 Nov 89 **THIS OLD HEART OF MINE** *Warner Bros. W 2686* [4] 51 3
13 Jan 90 ● **DOWNTOWN TRAIN** *Warner Bros. W 2647* 10 12
24 Nov 90 ● **IT TAKES TWO** *Warner Bros. ROD 1* [5] 5 8
16 Mar 91 ● **RHYTHM OF MY HEART** *Warner Bros. W 0017* 3 11
15 Jun 91 ● **THE MOTOWN SONG** *Warner Bros. W 0030* [6] 10 8
7 Sep 91 **BROKEN ARROW** *Warner Bros. W 0059* 54 3
7 Mar 92 **PEOPLE GET READY** *Epic 6577567* [1] 49 3
18 Apr 92 **YOUR SONG / BROKEN ARROW (re-issue)** *Warner Bros. W 0104* 41 4
5 Dec 92 ● **TOM TRAUBERT'S BLUES (WALTZING MATILDA)** *Warner Bros. W 0144* 6 9
20 Feb 93 **RUBY TUESDAY** *Warner Bros. W 0158CD* 11 6
17 Apr 93 **SHOTGUN WEDDING** *Warner Bros. W 0171CD* 21 4
26 Jun 93 ● **HAVE I TOLD YOU LATELY** *Warner Bros. W 0185CD* 5 9
21 Aug 93 **REASON TO BELIEVE** *Warner Bros. W 0198CD1* 51 3
18 Dec 93 **PEOPLE GET READY** *Warner Bros. W 0226CD1* 45 4
15 Jan 94 ● **ALL FOR LOVE** *A&M 5804772* [7] ▲ 2 13
20 May 95 **YOU'RE THE STAR** *Warner Bros. W 0296CD* 19 5
19 Aug 95 **LADY LUCK** *Warner Bros. W 0310CD1* 56 1
15 Jun 96 **PURPLE HEATHER** *Warner Bros. W 0354CD* [8] 16 5
14 Dec 96 **IF WE FALL IN LOVE TONIGHT** *Warner Bros. W 0380CD* 58 1
1 Nov 97 ● **DA YA THINK I'M SEXY?** *All Around the World CDGLOBE 150* [9] 7 10
30 May 98 **OOH LA LA** *Warner Brothers W 0446CD* 16 5
5 Sep 98 **ROCKS** *Warner Brothers W 0452CD1* 55 1
17 Apr 99 **FAITH OF THE HEART** *Universal UND 56235* 60 1
24 Mar 01 **I CAN'T DENY IT** *Atlantic AT 0096CD* 26 2
3 Oct 70 **GASOLINE ALLEY** *Vertigo 6360 500* 62 7
24 Jul 71 ★ **EVERY PICTURE TELLS A STORY** *Mercury 6338 063* ▲ 1 81
5 Aug 72 ★ **NEVER A DULL MOMENT** *Philips 6499 153* 1 36
25 Aug 73 ★ **SING IT AGAIN ROD** *Mercury 6499 484* 1 30
26 Jan 74 ● **OVERTURE AND BEGINNERS** *Mercury 9100 001* [1] 3 7
19 Oct 74 ★ **SMILER** *Mercury 9104 011* ■ 1 20
30 Aug 75 ★ **ATLANTIC CROSSING** *Warner Bros. K 56151* ■ 1 88
3 Jul 76 ★ **A NIGHT ON THE TOWN** *Riva RVLP 1* 1 47
16 Jul 77 **THE BEST OF ROD STEWART** *Mercury 6643 030* 18 22
19 Nov 77 ● **FOOT LOOSE & FANCY FREE** *Riva RVLP 5* 3 26
21 Jan 78 **ATLANTIC CROSSING (re-issue)** *Riva RVLP 4* 60 1
9 Dec 78 ● **BLONDES HAVE MORE FUN** *Riva RVLP 8* ▲ 3 31
10 Nov 79 ★ **GREATEST HITS** *Riva ROD TV 1* 1 74
22 Nov 80 ● **FOOLISH BEHAVIOUR** *Riva RVLP 11* 4 13
14 Nov 81 ● **TONIGHT I'M YOURS** *Riva RVLP 14* 8 21

13 Nov 82 ABSOLUTELY LIVE *Riva RVLP 17* 35 5
18 Jun 83 ● BODY WISHES *Warner Bros. K 923 8771* 5 27
23 Jun 84 ● CAMOUFLAGE *Warner Bros. 925095* 8 17
5 Jul 86 ● EVERY BEAT OF MY HEART *Warner Bros. WX 53* 5 17
4 Jun 88 OUT OF ORDER *Warner Bros. WX 152* 11 8
25 Nov 89 ● THE BEST OF ROD STEWART *Warner Bros. WX 314* 3 127
6 Apr 91 ● VAGABOND HEART *Warner Bros. WX 408* 2 27
7 Nov 92 THE BEST OF ROD STEWART AND THE FACES 1971–1975 *Mercury 5141802* [1] 58 1
6 Mar 93 ● ROD STEWART LEAD VOCALIST *Warner Bros. 9362452582* 3 9
5 Jun 93 ● UNPLUGGED ... AND SEATED *Warner Bros. 9362452892* 2 27
10 Jun 95 ● A SPANNER IN THE WORKS *Warner Bros. 9362458672* 4 12
16 Nov 96 ● IF WE FALL IN LOVE TONIGHT *Warner Bros. 9362464672* 8 19
13 Jun 98 ● WHEN WE WERE THE NEW BOYS *Warner Bros. 9362467922* 2 11
7 Apr 01 ● HUMAN *Atlantic 7567929742* 9 8
24 Nov 01 ● THE STORY SO FAR – THE VERY BEST OF ROD STEWART *Warner Bros. 8122735812* ....7 24+
9 Nov 02 ● IT HAD TO BE YOU – THE GREAT AMERICAN SONGBOOK *J 74321968672* 8 18
1 Nov 03 ● AS TIME GOES BY – THE GREAT AMERICAN SONGBOOK VOL.2 *J 82876574842* ....4 9+
1 Nov 03 CHANGING FACES – THE VERY BEST OF ROD STEWART AND THE FACES *Universal TV 9812604* [1] ....13 5+

[1] Jeff Beck and Rod Stewart [2] Faces / Rod Stewart [3] Rod Stewart featuring the Scottish World Cup Squad '78 [4] Rod Stewart featuring Ronald Isley [5] Rod Stewart and Tina Turner [6] Rod Stewart with backing vocals by The Temptations [7] Bryan Adams, Rod Stewart and Sting [8] Rod Stewart with the Scottish Euro '96 Squad [9] N-Trance featuring Rod Stewart [1] Rod Stewart and the Faces

'Reason to Believe' and 'People Get Ready' in 1993 were re-recordings. 'Reason to Believe' additionally credits Ronnie Wood on the sleeve. 'Sailing' re-entries peaked at No.3 in 1976 and No.41 in 1987 'Greatest Hits' changed label / number to Warner Bros. K 56744 during its chart run

See also FACES; GLASS TIGER; PYTHON LEE JACKSON

STEX

UK, male / female vocal / instrumental group (Singles: 2 weeks) pos/wks

19 Jan 91 STILL FEEL THE RAIN *Some Bizarre SBZ 7002* 63 2

STICKY featuring MS DYNAMITE *UK, male producer – Richard Forbes and UK, female rapper (Singles: 6 weeks)* pos/wks

23 Jun 01 BOOO! *ffrr / Public Demand / Social Circles FCD 399* 12 6

STIFF LITTLE FINGERS *UK, male vocal / instrumental group (Singles: 39 weeks, Albums: 57 weeks)* pos/wks

29 Sep 79 STRAW DOGS *Chrysalis CHS 2368* 44 4
16 Feb 80 AT THE EDGE *Chrysalis CHS 2406* 15 9
24 May 80 NOBODY'S HERO / TIN SOLDIERS *Chrysalis CHS 2424* 36 5
2 Aug 80 BACK TO FRONT *Chrysalis CHS 2447* 49 4
28 Mar 81 JUST FADE AWAY *Chrysalis CHS 2510* 47 6
30 May 81 SILVER LINING *Chrysalis CHS 2517* 68 3
23 Jan 82 LISTEN (EP) *Chrysalis CHS 2580* 33 6
18 Sep 82 BITS OF KIDS *Chrysalis CHS 2637* 73 2
3 Mar 79 INFLAMMABLE MATERIAL *Rough Trade ROUGH 1* 14 19
15 Mar 80 ● NOBODY'S HEROES *Chrysalis CHR 1270* 8 10
20 Sep 80 ● HANX *Chrysalis CHR 1300* 9 5
25 Apr 81 GO FOR IT *Chrysalis CHX 1339* 14 8
2 Oct 82 NOW THEN *Chrysalis CHR 1400* 24 6
12 Feb 83 ALL THE BEST *Chrysalis CTY 1414* 19 9

Tracks on Listen (EP): That's When Your Blood Bumps / Two Guitars Clash / Listen / Sad–Eyed People

Curtis STIGERS

US, male vocalist (Singles: 34 weeks, Albums: 52 weeks) pos/wks

18 Jan 92 ● I WONDER WHY *Arista 114716* 5 10
28 Mar 92 ● YOU'RE ALL THAT MATTERS TO ME *Arista 115273* 6 12
11 Jul 92 SLEEPING WITH THE LIGHTS ON *Arista 74321102307* 53 4
17 Oct 92 NEVER SAW A MIRACLE *Arista 74321117257* 34 4
3 Jun 95 THIS TIME *Arista 74321286962* 28 3
2 Dec 95 KEEP ME FROM THE COLD *Arista 74321319162* 57 1
29 Feb 92 ● CURTIS STIGERS *Arista 261953* 7 50
1 Jul 95 TIME WAS *Arista 74321282792* 34 2

The STILLS

Canada, male vocal / instrumental group (Singles: 1 week) pos/wks

6 Sep 03 REMEMBERESE *679 Recordings 679L 026CD* 75 1

Stephen STILLS *US, male vocalist / instrumentalist (Singles: 8 weeks, Albums: 27 weeks)* pos/wks

13 Mar 71 LOVE THE ONE YOU'RE WITH *Atlantic 2091 046* 37 4
6 Jun 98 HE GOT GAME *Def Jam 5689852* [1] 16 4
19 Dec 70 ● STEPHEN STILLS *Atlantic 2401 004* 8 9
14 Aug 71 STEPHEN STILLS 2 *Atlantic 2401 013* 22 3
20 May 72 MANASSAS *Atlantic K 60021* [1] 30 5
19 May 73 DOWN THE ROAD *Atlantic K 40440* [1] 33 2
26 Jul 75 STILLS *CBS 69146* 31 1
29 May 76 ILLEGAL STILLS *CBS 81330* 54 2
9 Oct 76 LONG MAY YOU RUN *Reprise K 54081* [2] 12 5

[1] Public Enemy featuring Stephen Stills [1] Manassas [2] Stills-Young Band

1972 and 1973 albums were both by the US, male vocal instrumental group Manassas led by Stephen Stills

See also CROSBY, STILLS, NASH and YOUNG

STILTSKIN *UK, male vocal / instrumental group – lead vocal Ray Wilson (Singles: 15 weeks, Albums: 4 weeks)* pos/wks

7 May 94 ★ INSIDE *White Water LEV 1CD* 1 13
24 Sep 94 FOOTSTEPS *White Water WWRD 2* 34 2
29 Oct 94 THE MIND'S EYE *White Water WWD 1* 17 4

See also Armin VAN BUUREN featuring Ray WILSON

STING (65 Top 500)

World's best-known ex-Police-man, b. Gordon Sumner, 2 Oct 1951, Newcastle, UK. This singer / songwriter / bass player has amassed more solo hits than as front man of that top-selling trio. As a soloist, he has won both Brit and Grammy awards and reportedly earns £1 a second from touring and royalties (Singles: 165 weeks, Albums: 387 weeks) pos/wks

14 Aug 82 SPREAD A LITTLE HAPPINESS *A&M AMS 8242* 16 8
8 Jun 85 IF YOU LOVE SOMEBODY SET THEM FREE *A&M AM 258* 26 7
24 Aug 85 LOVE IS THE SEVENTH WAVE *A&M AM 272* 41 5
19 Oct 85 FORTRESS AROUND YOUR HEART *A&M AM 286* 49 3
7 Dec 85 RUSSIANS (re) *A&M AM 292* 12 12
15 Feb 86 MOON OVER BOURBON STREET *A&M AM 305* 44 4
7 Nov 87 WE'LL BE TOGETHER *A&M AM 410* 41 4
20 Feb 88 ENGLISHMAN IN NEW YORK *A&M AM 431* 51 3
9 Apr 88 FRAGILE *A&M AM 439* 70 2
11 Aug 90 ENGLISHMAN IN NEW YORK (re-mix) *A&M AM 580* 15 7
12 Jan 91 ALL THIS TIME *A&M AM 713* 22 4
9 Mar 91 MAD ABOUT YOU *A&M AM 721* 56 2
4 May 91 THE SOUL CAGES *A&M AM 759* 57 1
29 Aug 92 IT'S PROBABLY ME *A&M AM 883* [1] 30 5
13 Feb 93 IF I EVER LOSE MY FAITH IN YOU *A&M AMCD 0172* 14 6
24 Apr 93 SEVEN DAYS *A&M 5802232* 25 4
19 Jun 93 FIELDS OF GOLD *A&M 5803012* 16 6
4 Sep 93 SHAPE OF MY HEART *A&M 5803532* 57 1
20 Nov 93 DEMOLITION MAN *A&M 5804512* 21 4
15 Jan 94 ● ALL FOR LOVE *A&M 5804772* [2] ▲ 2 13
26 Feb 94 NOTHING 'BOUT ME *A&M 5805292* 32 3
29 Oct 94 ● WHEN WE DANCE *A&M 5808612* 9 7
11 Feb 95 THIS COWBOY SONG *A&M 5809652* [3] 15 6
20 Jan 96 SPIRITS IN THE MATERIAL WORLD *MCA MCSTD 2113* [4] 36 2
2 Mar 96 LET YOUR SOUL BE YOUR PILOT *A&M 5813312* 15 4
11 May 96 YOU STILL TOUCH ME *A&M 5815472* 27 3
22 Jun 96 LIVE AT TFI FRIDAY (EP) *A&M 5817652* 53 2
14 Sep 96 I WAS BROUGHT TO MY SENSES *A&M 5818912* 31 2
30 Nov 96 I'M SO HAPPY I CAN'T STOP CRYING *A&M 5820312* 54 1
20 Dec 97 ROXANNE '97 (re-mix) *A&M 5824552* [5] 17 6
25 Sep 99 BRAND NEW DAY *A&M / Polydor 4971522* 13 5
29 Jan 00 DESERT ROSE *A&M / Mercury 4972402* [6] 15 6
22 Apr 00 AFTER THE RAIN HAS FALLEN *A&M / Mercury 4973252* 31 4
10 May 03 ● RISE & FALL *Wildstar CDWILD 45* [7] 2 10
27 Sep 03 SEND YOUR LOVE *A&M 9810103* 30 2
20 Dec 03 WHENEVER I SAY YOUR NAME *A&M 9815394* [8] 60 1
29 Jun 85 ● THE DREAM OF THE BLUE TURTLES *A&M DREAM 1* 3 64

28 Jun 86 **BRING ON THE NIGHT** *A&M BRING 1* 16 12
24 Oct 87 ★ **... NOTHING LIKE THE SUN** *A&M AMA 6402* ■ 1 47
2 Feb 91 ★ **THE SOUL CAGES** *A&M 3964051* ■.....1 16
13 Mar 93 ● **TEN SUMMONER'S TALES** *A&M 5400752*.....2 60
19 Nov 94 ● **FIELDS OF GOLD – THE BEST OF STING 1984-1994** *A&M 5403072*.....2 41
16 Mar 96 ● **MERCURY FALLING** *A&M 5404862* 4 27
22 Nov 97 ★ **THE VERY BEST OF STING AND THE POLICE** *A&M 5404282* [1].....1 50
9 Oct 99 ● **BRAND NEW DAY** *A&M 4904512* 5 44
17 Nov 01 ● **ALL THIS TIME** *A&M 4931802*.....3 15
4 Oct 03 ● **SACRED LOVE** *A&M 9860535*.....3 11+

[1] Sting with Eric Clapton [2] Bryan Adams, Rod Stewart and Sting [3] Sting featuring Pato Banton [4] Pato Banton with Sting [5] Sting and The Police [6] Sting featuring Cheb Mami [7] Craig David featuring Sting [8] Sting and Mary J Blige
[1] Sting and the Police

Tracks on Live at TFI Friday (EP): You Still Touch Me / Lithium Sunset / Message in a Bottle. In 1997 'The Very Best of Sting and the Police' orignally peaked at No.11 but on 2 Mar 2002 an updated version containing three new tracks re-entered the chart and sales were combined with the original album

See also POLICE

STINGERS – *See B BUMBLE and the STINGERS*

Byron STINGILY *US, male vocalist (Singles: 14 weeks)* pos/wks

25 Jan 97 **GET UP (EVERYBODY)** *Manifesto FESCD 19* 14 5
1 Nov 97 **SING A SONG** *Manifesto FESCD 35* 38 2
31 Jan 98 **YOU MAKE ME FEEL (MIGHTY REAL)** *Manifesto FESCD 38* 13 4
13 Jun 98 **TESTIFY** *Manifesto FESCD 42* 48 1
12 Feb 00 **THAT'S THE WAY LOVE IS** *Manifesto FESCD 66* 32 2

See also TEN CITY

STINX *UK, female vocal duo (Singles: 3 weeks)* pos/wks

24 Mar 01 **WHY DO YOU KEEP ON RUNNING** *HEBS HEBS 1* 49 3

STIX 'N' STONED *UK, male instrumental / production duo – Julius O'Riordan and Jon Kelly (Singles: 2 weeks)* pos/wks

20 Jul 96 **OUTRAGEOUS** *Positiva CDTIV 52* 39 2

Catherine STOCK *UK, female vocalist (Singles: 6 weeks)* pos/wks

18 Oct 86 **TO HAVE AND TO HOLD** *Sierra FED 29* 17 6

STOCK AITKEN WATERMAN
UK, male production trio (Singles: 36 weeks) pos/wks

25 Jul 87 **ROADBLOCK** *Breakout USA 611* 13 9
24 Oct 87 ● **MR SLEAZE** *London NANA14* 3 10
12 Dec 87 **PACKJAMMED (WITH THE PARTY POSSE)** *Breakout USA 620* 41 6
21 May 88 **ALL THE WAY** *MCA GOAL 1* [1] 64 2
3 Dec 88 **SS PAPARAZZI** *PWL PWL 22* 68 2
20 May 89 ★ **FERRY 'CROSS THE MERSEY** *PWL PWL 41* [2] ■ 1 7

[1] England Football Team and the 'sound' of Stock, Aitken and Waterman
[2] Christians, Holly Johnson, Paul McCartney, Gerry Marsden and Stock Aitken Waterman

The listed flip side of 'Mr Sleaze' was 'Love in the First Degree' by Bananarama

See also 2 IN A TENT; 14-18

Miriam STOCKLEY – *See PRAISE; ATLANTIS vs AVATAR*

Rhet STOLLER
UK, male instrumentalist – guitar (Singles: 8 weeks) pos/wks

12 Jan 61 **CHARIOT** *Decca F 11302* 26 8

Morris STOLOFF
US, orchestra, leader d. 16 Apr 1980 (Singles: 11 weeks) pos/wks

1 Jun 56 ● **MOONGLOW AND THE THEME FROM 'PICNIC'** *Brunswick 05553* 7 11

Angie STONE
US, female vocalist (Singles: 12 weeks, Albums: 3 weeks) pos/wks

15 Apr 00 **LIFE STORY** *Arista 74321748492* 22 3
16 Dec 00 **KEEP YOUR WORRIES** *Virgin VUSCD 177* [1] 57 1
9 Mar 02 **BROTHA PART II** *J 74321922142* [2] 37 2
27 Jul 02 **WISH I DIDN'T MISS YOU** *J 74321939182* 30 5
27 Dec 03 **SIGNED, SEALED, DELIVERED, I'M YOURS** *Innocent SINCD 54* [3] .....11 1+
11 Mar 00 **BLACK DIAMOND** *Arista 74321727752* 62 3

[1] Guru's Jazzmatazz featuring Angie Stone [2] Angie Stone featuring Alicia Keys and Eve [3] Blue featuring Stevie Wonder and Angie Stone

R & J STONE *UK / US, male / female vocal duo – Russell and Joanne Stone (Singles: 9 weeks)* pos/wks

10 Jan 76 ● **WE DO IT** *RCA 2616* 5 9

STONE ROSES (271 Top 500)
'Madchester', 'Baggy' pioneers who successfully combined rock guitar and acid house attitude, inspiring a massive return to guitar-based bands in northern Britain in the 1990s. Ian Brown (v), John Squire (g), Mani (aka Gary Mountfield) (b), Reni (aka Alan Wren) (d/v), all from Manchester. Their eponymous debut album, which peaked no higher than No.19 in 1989, continues to register in the top five of best all-time album surveys (Singles: 77 weeks, Albums: 156 weeks) pos/wks

29 Jul 89 **SHE BANGS THE DRUMS (re)** *Silvertone ORE 6* 34 6
25 Nov 89 ● **WHAT THE WORLD IS WAITING FOR / FOOL'S GOLD (re)** *Silvertone ORE 13*.....8 19
6 Jan 90 **SALLY CINNAMON (re)** *Revolver REV 36* 46 5
3 Mar 90 ● **ELEPHANT STONE** *Silvertone ORE 1* 8 6
17 Mar 90 **MADE OF STONE** *Silvertone ORE 2* 20 4
14 Jul 90 ● **ONE LOVE** *Silvertone ORE 17* 4 7
14 Sep 91 **I WANNA BE ADORED** *Silvertone ORE 31* 20 3
11 Jan 92 **WATERFALL** *Silvertone ORE 35* 27 4
11 Apr 92 **I AM THE RESURRECTION** *Silvertone ORE 40* 33 2
30 May 92 **FOOL'S GOLD (re-issue)** *Silvertone ORET 13* 73 1
3 Dec 94 ● **LOVE SPREADS** *Geffen GFSTD 84* 2 8
11 Mar 95 **TEN STOREY LOVE SONG** *Geffen GFSTD 87* 11 3
29 Apr 95 **FOOL'S GOLD (2nd re-issue)** *Silvertone ORECD 71* 25 3
11 Nov 95 **BEGGING YOU** *Geffen GFSTD 22060* 15 3
6 Mar 99 **FOOL'S GOLD (re-mix)** *Jive Electro 0523092* 25 3
13 May 89 **THE STONE ROSES** *Silvertone ORELP 502*.....19 86
1 Aug 92 **TURNS INTO STONE** *Silvertone ORECD 521*.....32 3
17 Dec 94 ● **SECOND COMING** *Geffen GED 24503*.....4 28
27 May 95 ● **THE COMPLETE STONE ROSES** *Silvertone ORECD 535* 4 25
7 Dec 96 **GARAGE FLOWER** *Silvertone GARAGECD 1*.....58 1
16 Oct 99 **STONE ROSES – 10TH ANNIVERSARY EDITION** *Silvertone 591242* 26 3
11 Nov 00 **THE REMIXES** *Silvertone 9260152*.....41 2
16 Nov 02 **THE VERY BEST OF THE STONE ROSES** *Silvertone 9260382* 19 8

'She Bangs the Drums' made No.36 on its chart debut and reached its peak position only on re-entry in Mar 1990. 'What the World Is Waiting For' / 'Fool's Gold' made No.22 on re-entry in Sep 1990

See also Ian BROWN; SEAHORSES; John SQUIRE

STONE SOUR *US, male vocal / instrumental group (Singles: 3 weeks, Albums: 1 week)* pos/wks

15 Mar 03 **BOTHER** *Roadrunner RR 20243* 28 2
19 Jul 03 **INHALE** *Roadrunner RR 20093* 63 1
7 Sep 02 **STONE SOUR** *Roadrunner RR 84252*.....41 1

STONE TEMPLE PILOTS *US, male vocal / instrumental group (Singles: 11 weeks, Albums: 19 weeks)* pos/wks

27 Mar 93 **SEX TYPE THING** *Atlantic A 5769CD* 60 2
4 Sep 93 **PLUSH** *Atlantic A 7349CD* 23 4
27 Nov 93 **SEX TYPE THING (re-issue)** *Atlantic A 7293CD* 55 2
20 Aug 94 **VASOLINE** *Atlantic A 5650CD* 48 2
10 Dec 94 **INTERSTATE LOVE SONG** *Atlantic A 7192CD* 53 1
4 Sep 93 **CORE** *Atlantic 7567824182* 27 8
18 Jun 94 ● **PURPLE** *Atlantic 7567826072* ▲ 10 9
6 Apr 96 **TINY MUSIC ... SONGS FROM THE VATICAN GIFT SHOP** *Atlantic 7567828712* 31 2

Review of the Year

OCTOBER 2003

'I've had a good year and I know what I want to do with my life. Being a pop star isn't it'

David Sneddon (BBC 2002 Fame Academy winner)

Dido's Life for Rent album enters charts at No.1 in 10 countries. **Alex Parks** from Cornwall wins the final of BBC TV's Fame Academy. **Gareth Gates's** second album Go Your Own Way fails to break into the Top 10. However, he does sing the title song on the compilation chart-topper Greasemania. **Sean Paul** scores his fifth Top 5 single in eight months with 'Baby Boy', which also gives co-performer Beyoncé her 11th Top 10 entry in a row. **Robbie Williams's** album Live at Knebworth sells 117,000 in week one, smashing the live album record set by The Beatles 26 years earlier. A 22-CD box set of **Stephen Fry** reading Harry Potter (which costs £75) reaches the UK Top 200 album chart. **Elvis Presley** achieves his first back-to-back Top 5 hits since 1962, thanks to the **Paul Oakenfold** remix of 'Rubberneckin'' (a song Oakenfold knew nothing about before he was given the job). On the US sales chart this 34-year-old **Elvis** single is dethroned at No.1 by the 35-year-old **Rolling Stones** single 'Sympathy for the Devil'. **Muse's** new album Absolution reaches the Top 10 in 10 countries and Sting's Sacred Love enters the Top 5 in the same number of territories. Take That's **Gary Barlow** is 'Guilty' of co-writing Blue's latest hit. **Simon and Garfunkel** start their first tour for 20 years, supported by the duo that first influenced them, **The Everly Brothers**. **50 Cent** walks away with five trophies at the World Music Awards. A duet between late rap legends and rivals **Tupac** and **The Notorious B.I.G.**, 'Runnin' (Dying to Live)', runs up the US charts several years after both performers were killed. Fifty-nine years after his death, **Glenn Miller** returns to the UK album chart. **David Beckham** gets a name-check in the US rap hit 'Gigolo' by **Nick Cannon** and **R Kelly**. **Barbra Streisand** scores her 60th US hit and 49th gold album with The Movie Album. The record for most new entries in the US Top 10 album chart is broken when seven enter from nowhere, led by **Outkast's** 'Speakerboxxx/The Love Below' with sales of more than 500,000. **DMX** becomes the only artist in history to reach No.1 with his first five albums in the US; like the previous four, the aptly titled Grand Champ also makes its first chart appearance in pole position. **Madonna** manages her 50th US chart entry with her first duet hit, 'Me Against the Music' with **Britney Spears**. **Blur's** not so aptly titled 'A Good Song' became their first single for 10 years not to breach the Top 20. **Craig David** misses the Top 10 for the first time with 'World Filled With Love'. Napster is relaunched and charges downloaders $9.95 a month, and another internet music purveyor, Kazaa, says that at any moment of the night or day it has at least five million users. The TV series Martin Scorsese Presents the Blues starts Stateside, sparking 11 albums from the series to enter the top 15 places in the US blues chart. Canadian Pop Idol winner **Malcolm Ryan** enters the Canadian chart at No.1 with 'Something More' and 'Rise Up' by the Australian Idol Final 12 is a chart-topper down under. Leaving us this month are the award-winning **Robert Palmer** and **Tony** "The Sheffield Grinder" **Capstick**.

Rod Stewart, with girlfriend Penny Lancaster, who publicly and wittily manages to slag off Sting, Sir Paul and Sir Elton in October

STONE THE CROWS *UK, female / male vocal / instrumental group – includes Maggie Bell (Albums: 3 weeks)*

Date		Title	pos	wks
7 Oct 72		ONTINUOUS PERFORMANCE *Polydor 2391 043*	33	3

See also Maggie BELL

STONEBRIDGE McGUINNESS *UK, male vocal / instrumental duo (Singles: 2 weeks)*

Date		Title	pos	wks
14 Jul 79		OO-EEH BABY *RCA PB 5163*	54	2

STONEFREE *UK, male vocalist (Singles: 1 week)*

Date		Title	pos	wks
23 May 87		CAN'T SAY 'BYE *Ensign ENY 607*	73	1

STONEPROOF *UK, male producer – John Graham (Singles: 1 week)*

Date		Title	pos	wks
15 May 99		EVERYTHING'S NOT YOU *VC Recordings VCRD 47*	68	1

STONKERS – *See HALE and PACE and the STONKERS*

STOOGES – *See Iggy POP*

STOP THE VIOLENCE MOVEMENT *US, male / female rap charity ensemble (Singles: 1 week)*

Date		Title	pos	wks
18 Feb 89		SELF DESTRUCTION *Jive BDPST 1*	75	1

Axel STORDAHL – *See June HUTTON*

STORM *UK, male / female vocal / instrumental group (Singles: 10 weeks)*

Date		Title	pos	wks
17 Nov 79		IT'S MY HOUSE *Scope SC 10*	36	10

STORM *Germany, male production duo – Rolf Ellmer and Markus Loffel (Singles: 19 weeks)*

Date		Title	pos	wks
29 Aug 98		STORM *Positiva CDTIV 94*	32	2
12 Aug 00	●	TIME TO BURN *Data DATA 16CDS*	3	10
23 Dec 00		STORM ANIMAL *Data DATA 20CDS*	21	5
26 May 01		STORM (re-mix) *Positiva CDTIV 154*	32	2

See also DANCE 2 TRANCE; JAM & SPOON; TOKYO GHETTO PUSSY

Danny STORM *UK, male vocalist (Singles: 4 weeks)*

Date		Title	pos	wks
12 Apr 62		HONEST I DO *Piccadilly 7N 35025*	42	4

Rebecca STORM *UK, female vocalist (Singles: 13 weeks)*

Date		Title	pos	wks
13 Jul 85		THE SHOW (THEME FROM 'CONNIE') *Towerbell TVP 3*	22	13

STORYVILLE JAZZ BAND – *See Bob WALLIS and his STORYVILLE JAZZ BAND*

Izzy STRADLIN *US, male vocalist / instrumentalist – guitar and male vocal / instrumental group (Singles: 2 weeks, Albums: 1 week)*

Date		Title	pos	wks
26 Sep 92		PRESSURE DROP *Geffen GFS 25*	45	2
24 Oct 92		IZZY STRADLIN AND THE JU JU HOUNDS *Geffen GED 24490* [1]	52	1

[1] Izzy Stradlin and the Ju Ju Hounds

See also GUNS N' ROSES

Nick STRAKER BAND *UK, male vocal / instrumental group (Singles: 15 weeks)*

Date		Title	pos	wks
2 Aug 80		A WALK IN THE PARK *CBS 8525*	20	12
15 Nov 80		LEAVING ON THE MIDNIGHT TRAIN *CBS 9088*	61	3

Peter STRAKER and the HANDS OF DR TELENY *UK, male vocalist and male vocal / instrumental group (Singles: 4 weeks)*

Date		Title	pos	wks
19 Feb 72		THE SPIRIT IS WILLING *RCA 2163*	40	4

STRANGE BEHAVIOUR – *See Jane KENNAWAY and STRANGE BEHAVIOUR*

STRANGE FRUIT – *See Jimmy NAIL*

STRANGELOVE *UK, male vocal / instrumental group (Singles: 8 weeks, Albums: 3 weeks)*

Date		Title	pos	wks
20 Apr 96		LIVING WITH THE HUMAN MACHINES *Food CDFOOD 70*	53	1
15 Jun 96		BEAUTIFUL ALONE *Food CDFOOD 81*	35	2
19 Oct 96		SWAY *Food CDFOOD 82*	47	1
26 Jul 97		THE GREATEST SHOW ON EARTH *Food CDFOODS 97*	36	2
11 Oct 97		FREAK *Food CDFOOD 105*	43	1
21 Feb 98		ANOTHER NIGHT IN *Food CDFOOD 110*	46	1
13 Aug 94		TIME FOR THE REST OF YOUR LIFE *Food FOODCD 11*	69	1
29 Jun 96		LOVE AND OTHER DEMONS *Food FOODCD 15*	44	1
18 Oct 97		STRANGELOVE *Food FOODCD 24*	67	1

STRANGLERS (108 Top 500) *The most commercially successful and long-lasting group to emerge from the punk / new wave scene: Hugh Cornwell (v/g), Jean-Jacques Burnel (b/v), Dave Greenfield (k), Jet Black (d). This London-based band had at least one hit every year between 1977 and 1992 (Singles: 194 weeks, Albums: 222 weeks)*

Date		Title	pos	wks
19 Feb 77		(GET A) GRIP (ON YOURSELF) *United Artists UP 36211*	44	4
21 May 77	●	PEACHES / GO BUDDY GO *United Artists UP 36248*	8	14
30 Jul 77	●	SOMETHING BETTER CHANGE / STRAIGHTEN OUT *United Artists UP 36277*	9	8
24 Sep 77	●	NO MORE HEROES *United Artists UP 36300*	8	9
4 Feb 78		5 MINUTES *United Artists UP 36350*	11	9
6 May 78		NICE 'N' SLEAZY *United Artists UP 36379*	18	8
12 Aug 78		WALK ON BY *United Artists UP 36429*	21	8
18 Aug 79		DUCHESS *United Artists BP 308*	14	9
20 Oct 79		NUCLEAR DEVICE (THE WIZARD OF AUS) *United Artists BP 318*	36	4
1 Dec 79		DON'T BRING HARRY (EP) *United Artists STR 1*	41	3
22 Mar 80		BEAR CAGE *United Artists BP 344*	36	5
7 Jun 80		WHO WANTS THE WORLD *United Artists BP 355*	39	4
31 Jan 81		THROWN AWAY *Liberty BP 383*	42	4
14 Nov 81		LET ME INTRODUCE YOU TO THE FAMILY *Liberty BP 405*	42	3
9 Jan 82	●	GOLDEN BROWN *Liberty BP 407*	2	12
24 Apr 82		LA FOLIE *Liberty BP 410*	47	3
24 Jul 82	●	STRANGE LITTLE GIRL *Liberty BP 412*	7	9
8 Jan 83	●	EUROPEAN FEMALE *Epic EPC A 2893*	9	6
26 Feb 83		MIDNIGHT SUMMER DREAM *Epic EPC A 3167*	35	4
6 Aug 83		PARADISE *Epic A 3387*	48	3
6 Oct 84		SKIN DEEP *Epic A 4738*	15	7
1 Dec 84		NO MERCY *Epic A 4921*	37	7
16 Feb 85		LET ME DOWN EASY *Epic A 6045*	48	4
23 Aug 86		NICE IN NICE *Epic 6500557*	30	5
18 Oct 86		ALWAYS THE SUN *Epic SOLAR 1*	30	5
13 Dec 86		BIG IN AMERICA *Epic HUGE 1*	48	6
7 Mar 87		SHAKIN' LIKE A LEAF *Epic SHEIK 1*	58	4
9 Jan 88	●	ALL DAY AND ALL OF THE NIGHT *Epic VICE 1*	7	7
28 Jan 89		GRIP '89 (GET A) GRIP (ON YOURSELF) (re-mix) *EMI EM 84*	33	3
17 Feb 90		96 TEARS *Epic TEARS 1*	17	6
21 Apr 90		SWEET SMELL OF SUCCESS *Epic TEARS 2*	65	2
5 Jan 91		ALWAYS THE SUN (re-mix) *Epic 6564307*	29	5
30 Mar 91		GOLDEN BROWN (RE-RELEASE) *Epic 6567617*	68	2
22 Aug 92		HEAVEN OR HELL *Psycho WOK 2025*	46	2
30 Apr 77	●	STRANGLERS IV (RATTUS NORVEGICUS) *United Artists UAG 30045*	4	34
8 Oct 77	●	NO MORE HEROES *United Artists UAG 30200*	2	19
3 Jun 78	●	BLACK AND WHITE *United Artists UAK 30222*	2	18
10 Mar 79	●	LIVE (X CERT) *United Artists UAG 30224*	7	10
6 Oct 79	●	THE RAVEN *United Artists UAG 30262*	4	8
21 Feb 81	●	THEMENINBLACK *Liberty LBG 30313*	8	5
21 Nov 81		LA FOLIE *Liberty LBG 30342*	11	18
25 Sep 82		THE COLLECTION 1977-1982 *Liberty LBS 30353*	12	16
22 Jan 83	●	FELINE *Epic EPC 25237*	4	11
17 Nov 84		AURAL SCULPTURE *Epic EPC 26220*	14	10
20 Sep 86		OFF THE BEATEN TRACK *Liberty LBG 5001*	80	2
8 Nov 86		DREAMTIME *Epic EPC 26648*	16	6
20 Feb 88		ALL LIVE AND ALL OF THE NIGHT *Epic 465259*	12	6
18 Feb 89		THE SINGLES *EMI EM 1314*	57	2
17 Mar 90		10 *Epic 4664831*	15	4
1 Dec 90	●	GREATEST HITS 1977-1990 *Epic 4675411*	4	47
19 Sep 92		STRANGLERS IN THE NIGHT *Psycho WOLCD 1030*	33	1

27 May 95 **ABOUT TIME** *When! WENCD 001* 31 1
8 Feb 97 **WRITTEN IN RED** *When! WENCD 009* 52 1
22 Jun 02 **PEACHES – THE VERY BEST OF THE STRANGLERS** *EMI 5402022* 21 3

'Go Buddy Go' credited with 'Peaches' from 11 Jun 1977. 'Straighten Out' credited with 'Something Better Change' from 13 Aug 1977. Tracks on Don't Bring Harry (EP): Don't Bring Harry / Wired / Crabs (Live) / In the Shadows (Live)

STRAW

UK, male vocal / instrumental group (Singles: 4 weeks) pos/wks

6 Feb 99 **THE AEROPLANE SONG** *WEA WEA 196CD* 37 2
24 Apr 99 **MOVING TO CALIFORNIA** *WEA WEA 205CD1* 50 1
3 Mar 01 **SAILING OFF THE EDGE OF THE WORLD** *Columbia 6708452* ..52 1

STRAWBERRY SWITCHBLADE *UK, female vocal duo – Rose McDowell and Jill Bryson (Singles: 26 weeks, Albums: 4 weeks)* pos/wks

17 Nov 84 ● **SINCE YESTERDAY** *Korova KOW 38* 5 17
23 Mar 85 **LET HER GO** *Korova KOW 39* 59 5
21 Sep 85 **JOLENE** *Korova KOW 42* 53 4
13 Apr 85 **STRAWBERRY SWITCHBLADE** *Korova KODE 11* 25 4

STRAWBS *UK, male vocal / instrumental group (Singles: 27 weeks, Albums: 31 weeks)* pos/wks

28 Oct 72 **LAY DOWN** *A&M AMS 7035* 12 13
27 Jan 73 ● **PART OF THE UNION** *A&M AMS 7047* 2 11
6 Oct 73 **SHINE ON SILVER SUN** *A&M AMS 7082* 34 3
21 Nov 70 **JUST A COLLECTION OF ANTIQUES AND CURIOS** *A&M AMLS 994* 27 2
17 Jul 71 **FROM THE WITCHWOOD** *A&M AMLH 64304* 39 2
26 Feb 72 **GRAVE NEW WORLD** *A&M AMLH 68078* 11 12
24 Feb 73 ● **BURSTING AT THE SEAMS** *A&M AMLH 68144* 2 12
27 Apr 74 **HERO AND HEROINE** *A&M AMLH 63607* 35 3

STRAY CATS *US, male vocal / instrumental group – includes Brian Setzer (Singles: 49 weeks, Albums: 32 weeks)* pos/wks

29 Nov 80 ● **RUNAWAY BOYS** *Arista SCAT 1* 9 10
7 Feb 81 ● **ROCK THIS TOWN** *Arista SCAT 2* 9 8
25 Apr 81 **STRAY CAT STRUT** *Arista SCAT 3* 11 10
20 Jun 81 **THE RACE IS ON** *Swansong SSK 19425* [1] 34 6
7 Nov 81 **YOU DON'T BELIEVE ME** *Arista SCAT 4* 57 3
6 Aug 83 **(SHE'S) SEXY AND 17** *Arista SCAT 6* 29 9
4 Mar 89 **BRING IT BACK AGAIN** *EMI USA MT 62* 64 3
28 Feb 81 ● **STRAY CATS** *Arista STRAY 1* 6 22
21 Nov 81 **GONNA BALL** *Arista STRAY 2* 48 4
3 Sep 83 **RANT 'N' RAVE WITH THE STRAY CATS** *Arista STRAY 3* 51 5
8 Apr 89 **BLAST OFF** *EMI MTL 1040* 58 1

[1] Dave Edmunds and the Stray Cats

STRAY MOB – *See MC SKAT KAT and the STRAY MOB*

STREETBAND

UK, male vocal / instrumental group (Singles: 6 weeks) pos/wks

4 Nov 78 **TOAST / HOLD ON** *Logo GO 325* 18 6

See also Paul YOUNG

The STREETS *UK, male producer / vocalist – Mike Skinner (Singles: 14 weeks, Albums: 44 weeks)* pos/wks

20 Oct 01 **HAS IT COME TO THIS (re)** *Locked On / 679 Recordings 679L 001CD* 18 5
27 Apr 02 **LET'S PUSH THINGS FORWARD** *Locked On / 679 Recordings 679L 005CD* 30 3
3 Aug 02 **WEAK BECOME HEROES** *Locked On / 679 Recordings 679L 007CD* 27 3
2 Nov 02 **DON'T MUG YOURSELF** *Locked On / 679 Recordings 679L 008CDX* 21 3
6 Apr 02 **ORIGINAL PIRATE MATERIAL** *Locked On / 679 927435682* 12 44

See also GRAFITI

STREETWALKERS

UK, male vocal / instrumental group (Albums: 6 weeks) pos/wks

12 Jun 76 **RED CARD** *Vertigo 9102 010* 16 6

Barbra STREISAND (53 Top 500)

Acclaimed song stylist who has more gold albums than any other female, b. 24 Apr 1942, Brooklyn, US. This world-renowned MOR vocalist / actress has collected countless awards for her recordings and her stage and film work, and is a recipient of both Grammy Living Legend and Lifetime Achievement awards (Singles: 155 weeks, Albums: 468 weeks) pos/wks

20 Jan 66 **SECOND HAND ROSE** *CBS 202025* 14 13
30 Jan 71 **STONEY END (re)** *CBS 5321* 27 11
30 Mar 74 **THE WAY WE WERE** *CBS 1915* ▲ 31 6
9 Apr 77 ● **LOVE THEME FROM 'A STAR IS BORN' (EVERGREEN)** *CBS 4855* ▲ 3 19
25 Nov 78 ● **YOU DON'T BRING ME FLOWERS** *CBS 6803* [1] ▲ 5 12
3 Nov 79 ● **NO MORE TEARS (ENOUGH IS ENOUGH)** *Casablanca CAN 174/ CBS 8000* [2] ▲ 3 13
4 Oct 80 ★ **WOMAN IN LOVE** *CBS 8966* ▲ 1 16
6 Dec 80 **GUILTY** *CBS 9315* [3] 34 10
30 Jan 82 **COMIN' IN AND OUT OF YOUR LIFE** *CBS A 1789* 66 3
20 Mar 82 **MEMORY** *CBS A 1903* 34 6
5 Nov 88 **TILL I LOVED YOU (LOVE THEME FROM 'GOYA')** *CBS BARB 2* [4] 16 7
7 Mar 92 **PLACES THAT BELONG TO YOU** *Columbia 6577947* 17 5
5 Jun 93 **WITH ONE LOOK** *Columbia 6593422* 30 3
15 Jan 94 **THE MUSIC OF THE NIGHT** *Columbia 6597382* [5] 54 3
30 Apr 94 **AS IF WE NEVER SAID GOODBYE** *Columbia 6603572* 20 3
8 Feb 97 ● **I FINALLY FOUND SOMEONE** *A&M 5820832* [6] 10 7
15 Nov 97 ● **TELL HIM** *Epic 6653052* [7] 3 15
30 Oct 99 **IF YOU EVER LEAVE ME** *Columbia 6681242* [8] 26 3
22 Jan 66 ● **MY NAME IS BARBRA TWO** *CBS BPG 62603* 6 22
4 Apr 70 **BARBRA STREISAND'S GREATEST HITS** *CBS 63921* 44 2
17 Apr 71 **STONEY END** *CBS 64269* 28 2
15 Jun 74 **THE WAY WE WERE** *CBS 69057* ▲ 49 1
23 Jul 77 **STREISAND SUPERMAN** *CBS 86030* 32 9
15 Jul 78 **SONGBIRD** *CBS 86060* 50 1
17 Mar 79 ★ **BARBRA STREISAND'S GREATEST HITS VOLUME 2** *CBS 10012* ▲ 1 30
17 Nov 79 **WET** *CBS 86104* 25 13
11 Oct 80 ★ **GUILTY** *CBS 86122* ▲ 1 82
16 Jan 82 ★ **LOVE SONGS** *CBS 10031* 1 129
19 Nov 83 **YENTL (FILM SOUNDTRACK)** *CBS 86302* 21 35
27 Oct 84 **EMOTION** *CBS 86309* 15 12
18 Jan 86 ● **THE BROADWAY ALBUM** *CBS 86322* ▲ 3 16
30 May 87 **ONE VOICE** *CBS 450 8901* 27 7
3 Dec 88 **TILL I LOVED YOU** *CBS 462943 1* 29 13
25 Nov 89 **A COLLECTION – GREATEST HITS ... AND MORE** *CBS 465845 1* 22 23
10 Jul 93 ● **BACK TO BROADWAY** *Columbia 4738802* ▲ 4 17
29 Oct 94 **THE CONCERT** *Columbia 4775992* 63 1
22 Nov 97 **HIGHER GROUND** *Columbia 4885322* ▲ 12 12
2 Oct 99 **A LOVE LIKE OURS** *Columbia 4949342* 12 9
30 Sep 00 **TIMELESS – LIVE IN CONCERT** *Columbia 4974352* 54 1
9 Mar 02 ★ **THE ESSENTIAL BARBRA STREISAND** *Columbia 5062572* 1 22
30 Nov 02 **DUETS** *Columbia 5098129* 30 6
8 Nov 03 **THE MOVIE ALBUM** *Columbia 5134213* 25 3

[1] Barbra and Neil [2] Donna Summer and Barbra Streisand [3] Barbra Streisand and Barry Gibb [4] Barbra Streisand and Don Johnson [5] Barbra Streisand (duet with Michael Crawford) [6] Barbra Streisand and Bryan Adams [7] Barbra Streisand and Celine Dion [8] Barbra Streisand / Vince Gill

Neil was Neil Diamond. 'No More Tears (Enough Is Enough)' was released simultaneously on two different labels, a seven-inch single on Casablanca and a 12-inch on CBS

STRESS *UK, male vocal / instrumental group (Singles: 1 week)* pos/wks

13 Oct 90 **BEAUTIFUL PEOPLE** *Eternal YZ 495* 74 1

STRETCH *UK, male vocal / instrumental group (Singles: 9 weeks)* pos/wks

8 Nov 75 **WHY DID YOU DO IT** *Anchor ANC 1021* 16 9

STRETCH 'N' VERN present MADDOG

UK, male instrumental / production duo – Stuart Collins and Julian Peake (Singles: 14 weeks) pos/wks

14 Sep 96 ● **I'M ALIVE** *ffrr FCD 284* 6 9
9 Aug 97 **GET UP! GO INSANE!** *ffrr FCD 304* 17 5

STRICT INSTRUCTOR

Russia, female vocalist (Singles: 1 week) pos/wks

24 Oct 98 **STEP-TWO-THREE-FOUR** *All Around the World CDGLOBE 155* 49 1

STRIKE *UK / Australia, male / female vocal / instrumental group (Singles: 24 weeks)* pos/wks

24 Dec 94 ● **U SURE DO (re)** *Fresh FRSHD 19* 4 14
23 Sep 95 **THE MORNING AFTER (FREE AT LAST)** *Fresh FRSHD 37* 38 1
29 Jun 96 **INSPIRATION** *Fresh FRSHD 45* 27 2
16 Nov 96 **MY LOVE IS FOR REAL** *Fresh FRSHD 46* 35 2
31 May 97 **I HAVE PEACE** *Fresh FRSHCD 58* 17 4
25 Sep 99 **U SURE DO (re-mix)** *Fresh FRSHD 78* 53 1

'U Sure Do' debuted at No.31 and made its peak position only on re-entry in Apr 1995

STRIKERS

US, male vocal / instrumental group (Singles: 5 weeks) pos/wks

6 Jun 81 **BODY MUSIC** *Epic EPC A 1290* 45 5

STRING-A-LONGS

US, male instrumental group (Singles: 16 weeks) pos/wks

23 Feb 61 ● **WHEELS** *London HLU 9278* 8 16

STRINGS FOR PLEASURE *UK, orchestra (Albums: 1 week)* pos/wks

4 Dec 71 **THE BEST OF BACHARACH** *MFP 1334* 49 1

STRINGS OF LOVE

Italy, male / female vocal / instrumental group (Singles: 2 weeks) pos/wks

3 Mar 90 **NOTHING HAS BEEN PROVED** *Breakout USA 688* 59 2

The STROKES *US, male vocal / instrumental group (Singles: 19 weeks, Albums: 48 weeks)* pos/wks

7 Jul 01 **HARD TO EXPLAIN / NEW YORK CITY COPS** *Rough Trade RTRADESCD 023* 16 5
7 Jul 01 **MODERN AGE (2re)** *Rough Trade RTRADESCD 010* 68 3
17 Nov 01 **LAST NITE** *Rough Trade RTRADESCD 041* 14 5
5 Oct 02 **SOMEDAY** *Rough Trade RTRADESCD 063* 27 2
18 Oct 03 ● **12:51** *Rough Trade RTRADESCD 140* 7 4
8 Sep 01 ● **IS THIS IT** *Rough Trade RTRADECD 030* 2 39
1 Nov 03 ● **ROOM ON FIRE** *Rough Trade RTRADECD130* 2 9+

Modern Age is a three-track CD featuring 'Modern Age', 'Last Nite' (later re-recorded and released as the band's next single in 2001) and 'Barely Legal'

Joe STRUMMER *UK, male vocalist – John Mellor, d. 23 Dec 2002 (Singles: 16 weeks, Albums: 4 weeks)* pos/wks

2 Aug 86 **LOVE KILLS** *CBS A 7244* 69 1
23 Dec 95 **JUST THE ONE** *China WOKCD 2076* [1] 12 8
29 Jun 96 ● **ENGLAND'S IRIE** *Radioactive RAXTD 25* [2] 6 4
18 Oct 03 **COMA GIRL** *Hellcat 11352* [3] 33 2
27 Dec 03 **REDEMPTION SONG / ARMS ALOFT** *Hellcat 11472* [3] 46 1+
14 Oct 89 **EARTHQUAKE WEATHER** *Epic 465347 1* 58 1
30 Oct 99 **ROCK ART AND THE X-RAY STYLE** *Mercury 5466542* [1] 71 1
28 Jul 01 **GLOBAL A GO GO** *Hellcat 4402* [1] 68 1
1 Nov 03 **STREETCORE** *Hellcat 04542* [1] 50 1

[1] Levellers, special guest Joe Strummer [2] Black Grape featuring Joe Strummer and Keith Allen [3] Joe Strummer and the Mescaleros
[1] Joe Strummer and the Mescaleros

See also CLASH

STRYKER – *See MANCHESTER UNITED FOOTBALL CLUB*

STUART

Holland, male producer – Sjoerd Wijdoogen (Singles: 2 weeks) pos/wks

5 Apr 03 **FREE (LET IT BE)** *Product / Incentive PDT 07CDS* 41 2

Chad STUART and Jeremy CLYDE

UK, male vocal duo (Singles: 7 weeks) pos/wks

28 Nov 63 **YESTERDAY'S GONE** *Ember EMB S 180* 37 7

STUDIO 2

Jamaica, male vocalist – Errol Jones (Singles: 1 week) pos/wks

27 Jun 98 **TRAVELLING MAN** *Multiply CDMULTY 35* 40 1

STUDIO B / ROMEO and Harry BROOKS

UK, male production / vocal / rap trio (Singles: 1 week) pos/wks

6 Dec 03 **I SEE GIRLS (CRAZY)** *Multiply CDMULTY 109* 52 1

See also SO SOLID CREW

STUDIO 45 *Germany, male DJ / production duo – Tilo Cielsa and Jens Brachvogel (Singles: 2 weeks)* pos/wks

20 Feb 99 **FREAK IT!** *Azuli AZNYCD 090* 36 2

Amy STUDT

UK, female vocalist (Singles: 22 weeks, Albums: 11 weeks) pos/wks

13 Jul 02 **JUST A LITTLE GIRL** *Polydor 5708802* 14 6
21 Jun 03 ● **MISFIT** *Polydor 9800107* 6 10
11 Oct 03 ● **UNDER THE THUMB** *Polydor 9811793* 10 6
12 Jul 03 **FALSE SMILES** *Polydor 9801074* 18 11

STUMP *UK, male vocal / instrumental group (Singles: 1 week)* pos/wks

13 Aug 88 **CHARLTON HESTON** *Ensign ENY 614* 72 1

STUNTMASTERZ *UK, male production duo – Steve Harris and Pete Cook (Singles: 9 weeks)* pos/wks

3 Mar 01 ● **THE LADYBOY IS MINE** *East West EW 226CD* 10 9

STUTZ BEARCATS and The Denis KING ORCHESTRA

UK, male / female vocal group with orchestra (Singles: 6 weeks) pos/wks

24 Apr 82 **THE SONG THAT I SING (THEME FROM 'WE'LL MEET AGAIN')** *Multi-Media Tapes MMT 6* 36 6

STYLE COUNCIL 324 Top 500

Eighties chart regulars: Paul Weller (v/g), Mick Talbot (k) and sometimes Dee C Lee (v – former Wham! backing vocalist and Weller's wife). As with Weller's previous band, The Jam, most of this London act's hits were in their homeland (Singles: 103 weeks, Albums: 100 weeks) pos/wks

19 Mar 83 ● **SPEAK LIKE A CHILD** *Polydor TSC 1* 4 8
28 May 83 **MONEY GO ROUND (PART 1) (re)** *Polydor TSC 2* 11 7
13 Aug 83 ● **LONG HOT SUMMER** *Polydor TSC 3* 3 9
19 Nov 83 **SOLID BOND IN YOUR HEART** *Polydor TSC 4* 11 8
18 Feb 84 ● **MY EVER CHANGING MOODS** *Polydor TSC 5* 5 7
26 May 84 ● **GROOVIN' (YOU'RE THE BEST THING / THE BIG BOSS GROOVE)** *Polydor TSC 6* 5 8
13 Oct 84 ● **SHOUT TO THE TOP** *Polydor TSC 7* 7 8
11 May 85 ● **WALLS COME TUMBLING DOWN!** *Polydor TSC 8* 6 7
6 Jul 85 **COME TO MILTON KEYNES** *Polydor TSC 9* 23 5
28 Sep 85 **THE LODGERS** *Polydor TSC 10* 13 6
5 Apr 86 **HAVE YOU EVER HAD IT BLUE** *Polydor CINE 1* 14 6
17 Jan 87 ● **IT DIDN'T MATTER** *Polydor TSC 12* 9 5
14 Mar 87 **WAITING** *Polydor TSC 13* 52 3
31 Oct 87 **WANTED** *Polydor TSC 14* 20 4
28 May 88 **LIFE AT A TOP PEOPLE'S HEALTH FARM** *Polydor TSC 15* 28 3
23 Jul 88 **HOW SHE THREW IT ALL AWAY (EP)** *Polydor TSC 16* 41 2
18 Feb 89 **PROMISED LAND** *Polydor TSC 17* 27 5
27 May 89 **LONG HOT SUMMER 89 (re-mix)** *Polydor LHS 1* 48 2
24 Mar 84 ● **CAFÉ BLEU** *Polydor TSCLP 1* 2 38
8 Jun 85 ★ **OUR FAVOURITE SHOP** *Polydor TSCLP 2* ■ 1 22
17 May 86 ● **HOME AND ABROAD** *Polydor TSCLP 3* 8 8

14 Feb 87 ● **THE COST OF LOVING** *Polydor TSCLP 4*..........2 7
2 Jul 88 **CONFESSIONS OF A POP GROUP** *Polydor TSCMC 5*..........15 3
18 Mar 89 ● **THE SINGULAR ADVENTURES OF THE STYLE COUNCIL – GREATEST HITS VOL.1** *Polydor TSCTV 1*..........3 15
10 Jul 93 **HERE'S SOME THAT GOT AWAY** *Polydor 5193722*..........39 1
2 Mar 96 **THE STYLE COUNCIL COLLECTION** *Polydor 5294832*..........60 1
2 Sep 00 **GREATEST HITS** *Polydor / Universal TV 5579002*..........28 5

'Paris Match' was listed with 'Long Hot Summer' from 3 Sep 1983. It peaked at No.7. Tracks on How She Threw It All Away (EP): How She Threw It All Away / Love the First Time / Long Hot Summer / I Do Like to Be B-Side the A-Side. The version of 'Long Hot Summer' on the EP is a re-recording of their third hit

Darren STYLES & Mark BREEZE present INFEXTIOUS

UK, male production duo (Singles: 1 week) pos/wks

5 Apr 03 **LET ME FLY** *Nukleuz 0432 CNUK*..........59 1

STYLES & Pharoahe MONCH

US, male rap duo (Singles: 1 week) pos/wks

14 Sep 02 **THE LIFE** *MCA MCSTD 40292*..........50 1

STYLISTICS

206 Top 500 *Stylish and smooth vocal group from Philadelphia, US, fronted by falsetto-voiced Russell Thompkins Jr (b. 21 Mar 1951), whose UK hits continued after success in their homeland diminished. The quintet's Greatest Hits album topped the UK album chart in 1975 (Singles: 143 weeks, Albums: 142 weeks)* pos/wks

24 Jun 72 **BETCHA BY GOLLY WOW** *Avco 6105 011*..........13 12
4 Nov 72 ● **I'M STONE IN LOVE WITH YOU** *Avco 6105 015*..........9 10
17 Mar 73 **BREAK UP TO MAKE UP** *Avco 6105 020*..........34 5
30 Jun 73 **PEEK-A-BOO** *Avco 6105 023*..........35 6
19 Jan 74 ● **ROCKIN' ROLL BABY** *Avco 6105 026*..........6 9
13 Jul 74 ● **YOU MAKE ME FEEL BRAND NEW** *Avco 6105 028*..........2 14
19 Oct 74 ● **LET'S PUT IT ALL TOGETHER** *Avco 6105 032*..........9 9
25 Jan 75 **STAR ON A TV SHOW** *Avco 6105 035*..........12 8
10 May 75 ● **SING BABY SING** *Avco 6105 036*..........3 10
26 Jul 75 ★ **CAN'T GIVE YOU ANYTHING (BUT MY LOVE)** *Avco 6105 039*..........1 11
15 Nov 75 ● **NA-NA IS THE SADDEST WORD** *Avco 6105 041*..........5 10
14 Feb 76 ● **FUNKY WEEKEND** *Avco 6105 044*..........10 7
24 Apr 76 ● **CAN'T HELP FALLING IN LOVE** *H & L 6105 050*..........4 7
7 Aug 76 ● **SIXTEEN BARS** *H & L 6105 059*..........7 9
27 Nov 76 **YOU'LL NEVER GET TO HEAVEN (EP)** *H & L STYL 001*..........24 9
26 Mar 77 **$7000 AND YOU** *H & L 6105 073*..........24 7
24 Aug 74 **ROCKIN' ROLL BABY** *Avco 6466 012*..........42 3
21 Sep 74 **LET'S PUT IT ALL TOGETHER** *Avco 6466 013*..........26 14
1 Mar 75 **FROM THE MOUNTAIN** *Avco 9109 002*..........36 1
5 Apr 75 ★ **THE BEST OF THE STYLISTICS** *Avco 9109 003*..........1 63
5 Jul 75 ● **THANK YOU BABY** *Avco 9109 005*..........5 23
6 Dec 75 **YOU ARE BEAUTIFUL** *Avco 9109 006*..........26 9
12 Jun 76 **FABULOUS** *Avco 9109 008*..........21 5
18 Sep 76 ★ **BEST OF THE STYLISTICS VOLUME 2** *H & L 9109 010*..........1 21
17 Oct 92 **THE GREATEST HITS OF THE STYLISTICS – LET'S PUT IT ALL TOGETHER** *Mercury 5129852*..........34 3

Tracks on You'll Never Get to Heaven (EP): You'll Never Get to Heaven / Country Living / You Are Beautiful / The Miracle

STYLUS TROUBLE

UK, male producer – Pete Heller (Singles: 1 week) pos/wks

23 Jun 01 **SPUTNIK** *Junior London BRG 014*..........63 1

See also FIRE ISLAND; HELLER & FARLEY PROJECT; Pete HELLER

STYX *US, male vocal / instrumental group (Singles: 18 weeks, Albums: 24 weeks)*

pos/wks

5 Jan 80 ● **BABE** *A&M AMS 7489* ▲..........6 10
24 Jan 81 **THE BEST OF TIMES** *A&M AMS 8102*..........42 5
18 Jun 83 **DON'T LET IT END** *A&M AM 120*..........56 3
3 Nov 79 **CORNERSTONE** *A&M AMLK 63711*..........36 8
24 Jan 81 ● **PARADISE THEATER** *A&M AMLH 63719* ▲..........8 8
12 Mar 83 **KILROY WAS HERE** *A&M AMLX 63734*..........67 6
5 May 84 **CAUGHT IN THE ACT** *A&M AMLM 66704*..........44 2

SUB SUB

UK, male instrumental / production group (Singles: 12 weeks) pos/wks

10 Apr 93 ● **AIN'T NO LOVE (AIN'T NO USE)** *Rob's CDROB 9* [1]..........3 11
19 Feb 94 **RESPECT** *Rob's CDROB 19*..........49 1

[1] Sub Sub featuring Melanie Williams

SUBCIRCUS

Denmark / UK, male vocal / instrumental group (Singles: 2 weeks) pos/wks

26 Apr 97 **YOU LOVE YOU** *Echo ECSCD 34*..........61 1
12 Jul 97 **86'D** *Echo ECSCX 43*..........56 1

SUBLIME *US, male vocal / instrumental group (Singles: 1 week)*

pos/wks

5 Jul 97 **WHAT I GOT** *Gasoline Alley MCSTD 48045*..........71 1

SUBLIMINAL CUTS

Holland, male producer – Patrick Prinz (Singles: 3 weeks) pos/wks

15 Oct 94 **LE VOIE LE SOLEIL** *XL XLS 53CD*..........69 1
20 Jul 96 **LE VOIE LE SOLEIL (re-mix)** *XL XLSR 53CD*..........23 2

See also ARTEMESIA; ETHICS; MOVIN' MELODIES

SUBMERGE featuring Jan JOHNSTON

US, male producer / instrumentalist – Victor Imbres – and US, female vocalist (Singles: 2 weeks) pos/wks

8 Feb 97 **TAKE ME BY THE HAND** *AM:PM 5821012*..........28 2

SUBSONIC 2 *UK, male rap duo (Singles: 3 weeks)*

pos/wks

13 Jul 91 **THE UNSUNG HEROES OF HIP HOP** *Unity 6577947*..........63 3

SUBTERRANIA featuring Ann CONSUELO

Sweden, male / female vocal / instrumental duo (Singles: 1 week) pos/wks

5 Jun 93 **DO IT FOR LOVE** *Champion CHAMPCD 297*..........68 1

SUEDE

368 Top 500 *London-based, Britpop pioneers include photogenic front man Brett Anderson (v) and co-writer Bernard Butler (g) who left in 1994. MM's 'Best Band in Britain' won the Mercury Music Prize for their 1993 self-titled debut album, which sold more than 100,000 in its first week (Singles: 75 weeks, Albums: 105 weeks)* pos/wks

23 May 92 **THE DROWNERS / TO THE BIRDS** *Nude NUD 1S*..........49 2
26 Sep 92 **METAL MICKEY** *Nude NUD 3S*..........17 3
6 Mar 93 ● **ANIMAL NITRATE** *Nude NUD 4CD*..........7 7
29 May 93 **SO YOUNG** *Nude NUD 5CD*..........22 3
26 Feb 94 ● **STAY TOGETHER** *Nude NUD 9CD*..........3 6
24 Sep 94 **WE ARE THE PIGS** *Nude NUD 10CD*..........18 3
19 Nov 94 **THE WILD ONES** *Nude NUD 11CD1*..........18 4
11 Feb 95 **NEW GENERATION (re)** *Nude NUD 12CD1*..........21 4
10 Aug 96 ● **TRASH** *Nude NUD 21CD1*..........3 6
26 Oct 96 ● **BEAUTIFUL ONES** *Nude NUD 23CD1*..........8 5
25 Jan 97 ● **SATURDAY NIGHT** *Nude NUD 24CD1*..........6 4
19 Apr 97 ● **LAZY** *Nude NUD 27CD1*..........9 3
23 Aug 97 ● **FILMSTAR** *Nude NUD 30CD1*..........9 4
24 Apr 99 ● **ELECTRICITY** *Nude NUD 43CD1*..........5 5
3 Jul 99 **SHE'S IN FASHION** *Nude NUD 44CD1*..........13 5
18 Sep 99 **EVERYTHING WILL FLOW** *Nude NUD 45CD1*..........24 2
20 Nov 99 **CAN'T GET ENOUGH** *Nude NUD 47CD1*..........23 2
28 Sep 02 **POSITIVITY** *Epic 6729492*..........16 2
30 Nov 02 **OBSESSIONS** *Epic 6732942*..........29 2
18 Oct 03 **ATTITUDE / GOLDEN GUN** *Sony Music 6743582*..........14 3
10 Apr 93 ★ **SUEDE** *Nude NUDE 1CD* ■..........1 22
22 Oct 94 ● **DOG MAN STAR** *Nude 4778112*..........3 16
14 Sep 96 ★ **COMING UP** *Nude NUDE 6CD* ■..........1 44
18 Oct 97 ● **SCI-FI LULLABIES** *Nude NUDE 9CD*..........9 3
15 May 99 ★ **HEAD MUSIC** *Nude NUDE 14CD* ■..........1 16
12 Oct 02 **A NEW MORNING** *Epic 5089569*..........24 2
1 Nov 03 **SINGLES** *Sony Music 5136042*..........31 2

SUENO LATINO *Italy, male production duo (Singles: 6 weeks)*

pos/wks

23 Sep 89 **SUENO LATINO** *BCM BCM 323* [1]..........47 5
11 Nov 00 **SUENO LATINO (re-mix)** *Distinctive DISNCD 64*..........68 1

[1] Sueno Latino featuring Carolina Damas

SUGABABES (462 Top 500) *Internationally successful soulful pop trio: Londoners Keisha Buchanan and Mutya Buena and Liverpudlian Heidi Range (replaced Siobhan Donaghy after act was dropped by London Records). At 18, these chart-toppers were the youngest all-girl group to reach No.1 (Singles: 86 weeks, Albums: 63 weeks)*

Date		Title / Label	pos	wks
23 Sep 00	●	OVERLOAD *London LONCD 449*	6	8
30 Dec 00		NEW YEAR *London LONCD 455*	12	9
21 Apr 01		RUN FOR COVER *London LONCD 459*	13	7
28 Jul 01		SOUL SOUND *London LONCD 460*	30	2
4 May 02	★	FREAK LIKE ME (re) *Island CID 798* ■	1	14
24 Aug 02	★	ROUND ROUND *Island CID 804* ■	1	13
23 Nov 02	●	STRONGER / ANGELS WITH DIRTY FACES *Island CID 813*	7	13
22 Mar 03		SHAPE *Island CID 817*	11	9
25 Oct 03	★	HOLE IN THE HEAD *Island CID 836* ■	1	10+
27 Dec 03	●	TOO LOST IN YOU *Island CID 844*	10	1+
23 Dec 00		ONE TOUCH *London 8573861072*	26	15
7 Sep 02	●	ANGELS WITH DIRTY FACES *Island / Uni-Island CID 8122*	2	40
8 Nov 03	●	THREE *Island / Uni-Island CID 8137*	3	8+

SUGAR *US, male vocal / instrumental group (Singles: 7 weeks, Albums: 19 weeks)*

Date		Title / Label	pos	wks
31 Oct 92		A GOOD IDEA *Creation CRE 143*	65	1
30 Jan 93		IF I CAN'T CHANGE YOUR MIND *Creation CRESCD 149*	30	2
21 Aug 93		TILTED *Creation CRECD 156*	48	1
3 Sep 94		YOUR FAVORITE THING *Creation CRESCD 186*	40	2
29 Oct 94		BELIEVE WHAT YOU'RE SAYING *Creation CRESCD 193*	73	1
19 Sep 92	●	COPPER BLUE *Creation CRECD 129*	10	11
17 Apr 93	●	BEASTER *Creation CRECD 153*	3	5
17 Sep 94	●	FILE UNDER EASY LISTENING *Creation CRECD 172*	7	3

See also Bob MOULD

SUGAR CANE
US, male / female vocal group (Singles: 5 weeks)

Date		Title / Label	pos	wks
30 Sep 78		MONTEGO BAY *Ariola Hansa AHA 524*	54	5

SUGAR RAY *US, male vocal / instrumental group (Singles: 12 weeks, Albums: 1 week)*

Date		Title / Label	pos	wks
31 Jan 98		FLY *Atlantic AT 0008CD*	58	1
29 May 99	●	EVERY MORNING *Lava / Atlantic AT 0065CD*	10	9
20 Oct 01		WHEN IT'S OVER *Atlantic AT 0114CD*	32	2
19 Jun 99		14:59 *Atlantic 7567831512*	60	1

SUGARCOMA
UK, male / female vocal / instrumental group (Singles: 1 week)

Date		Title / Label	pos	wks
13 Apr 02		YOU DRIVE ME CRAZY / WINDINGS *Music for Nations CDKUT 190*	57	1

SUGARCUBES *Iceland, female / male vocal / instrumental group (Singles: 22 weeks, Albums: 14 weeks)*

Date		Title / Label	pos	wks
14 Nov 87		BIRTHDAY *One Little Indian 7TP 7*	65	3
30 Jan 88		COLD SWEAT *One Little Indian 7TP 9*	56	4
16 Apr 88		DEUS *One Little Indian 7TP 10*	51	3
3 Sep 88		BIRTHDAY (re-recording) *One Little Indian 7TP 11*	65	3
16 Sep 89		REGINA *One Little Indian 26TP7*	55	2
11 Jan 92		HIT *One Little Indian 62 TP7*	17	6
3 Oct 92		BIRTHDAY (re-mix) *One Little Indian 104 TP12*	64	1
7 May 88		LIFE'S TOO GOOD *One Little Indian TPLP 5*	14	6
14 Oct 89		HERE TODAY TOMORROW NEXT WEEK *One Little Indian TPLP 15*	15	3
22 Feb 92		STICK AROUND FOR JOY *One Little Indian TPLP 30CD*	16	4
17 Oct 92		IT'S IT *One Little Indian TPLP 40CD*	47	1

See also BJÖRK

SUGARHILL GANG
US, male rap group (Singles: 16 weeks)

Date		Title / Label	pos	wks
1 Dec 79	●	RAPPER'S DELIGHT *Sugarhill SHL 101*	3	11
11 Sep 82		THE LOVER IN YOU *Sugarhill SH 116*	54	3
25 Nov 89		RAPPER'S DELIGHT (re-mix) *Sugarhill SHRD 0007*	58	2

SUGGS *UK, male vocalist – Graham McPherson (Singles: 46 weeks, Albums: 5 weeks)*

Date		Title / Label	pos	wks
12 Aug 95	●	I'M ONLY SLEEPING / OFF ON HOLIDAY *WEA YZ 975CD*	7	6
14 Oct 95		CAMDEN TOWN *WEA WEA 019CD*	14	6
16 Dec 95		THE TUNE *WEA WEA 031CD*	33	3
13 Apr 96	●	CECILIA (2re) *WEA WEA 042CD1* [1]	4	19
21 Sep 96		NO MORE ALCOHOL *WEA WEA 065CD1* [1]	24	4
17 May 97		BLUE DAY *WEA WEA 112CD* [2]	22	5
5 Sep 98		I AM *WEA WEA 174CD*	38	3
28 Oct 95		THE LONE RANGER *WEA 0630124782*	14	5

[1] Suggs featuring Louchie Lou and Michie One [2] Suggs & Co featuring Chelsea Team

See also MADNESS

SUICIDAL TENDENCIES
US, male vocal / instrumental band (Albums: 2 weeks)

Date		Title / Label	pos	wks
9 May 87		JOIN THE ARMY *Virgin V 2424*	81	1
21 Jul 90		LIGHTS ... CAMERA ... REVOLUTION *Epic 4665691*	59	1

Justine SUISSA – *See OCEANLAB featuring Justine SUISSA*

SULTANA
Italy, male instrumental / production group (Singles: 1 week)

Date		Title / Label	pos	wks
26 Mar 94		TE AMO *Union City UCRD 28*	57	1

SULTANS OF PING *Ireland, male vocal / instrumental group (Singles: 12 weeks, Albums: 3 weeks)*

Date		Title / Label	pos	wks
8 Feb 92		WHERE'S ME JUMPER? *Divine ATHY 01* [1]	67	2
9 May 92		STUPID KID *Divine ATHY 02* [1]	67	1
10 Oct 92		VERONICA *Divine ATHY 03* [1]	69	1
9 Jan 93		YOU TALK TOO MUCH *Rhythm King 6588872* [1]	26	3
11 Sep 93		TEENAGE PUNKS *Epic 6595792*	49	2
30 Oct 93		MICHIKO *Epic 6598222*	43	2
19 Feb 94		WAKE UP AND SCRATCH ME *Epic 6601122*	50	1
13 Feb 93		CASUAL SEX IN THE CINEPLEX *Rhythm King 4724952* [1]	26	2
5 Mar 94		TEENAGE DRUG *Epic 4747162*	57	1

[1] Sultans of Ping FC [1] Sultans Of Ping FC

SUM 41 *Canada, male vocal / instrumental group (Singles: 40 weeks, Albums: 49 weeks)*

Date		Title / Label	pos	wks
13 Oct 01	●	FAT LIP *Mercury 5888012*	8	9
15 Dec 01		IN TOO DEEP *Mercury 5888982*	13	11
6 Apr 02		MOTIVATION *Mercury 5889452*	21	7
29 Jun 02		IT'S WHAT WE'RE ALL ABOUT *Columbia 6728642*	32	3
30 Nov 02		STILL WAITING *Mercury 0638312*	16	7
22 Feb 03		THE HELL SONG *Mercury 0637202*	35	3
11 Aug 01	●	ALL KILLER NO FILLER *Mercury 5486622*	7	43
7 Dec 02		DOES THIS LOOK INFECTED? *Mercury 0634832*	39	6

SUMMER – *See SNAP!*

Donna SUMMER (75 Top 500) *'Queen of disco music', b. LaDonna Gaines, 31 Dec 1948, Massachusetts, US. Germany was the launching pad for this diva, who had eight successive US Top 5 singles in the late 1970s. She was also the first female to score three consecutive US No.1 albums (Singles: 299 weeks, Albums: 198 weeks)*

Date		Title / Label	pos	wks
17 Jan 76	●	LOVE TO LOVE YOU BABY *GTO GT 17*	4	9
29 May 76		COULD IT BE MAGIC *GTO GT 60*	40	7
25 Dec 76		WINTER MELODY *GTO GT 76*	27	6
9 Jul 77	★	I FEEL LOVE *GTO GT 100*	1	11
20 Aug 77	●	DOWN DEEP INSIDE (THEME FROM 'THE DEEP') *Casablanca CAN 111*	5	10
24 Sep 77		I REMEMBER YESTERDAY *GTO GT 107*	14	7
3 Dec 77	●	LOVE'S UNKIND *GTO GT 113*	3	13
10 Dec 77	●	I LOVE YOU *Casablanca CAN 114*	10	9
25 Feb 78		RUMOUR HAS IT *Casablanca CAN 122*	19	8
22 Apr 78		BACK IN LOVE AGAIN *GTO GT 117*	29	7
10 Jun 78		LAST DANCE (re) *Casablanca TGIF 2*	51	9
14 Oct 78	●	MACARTHUR PARK *Casablanca CAN 131* ▲	5	10

Date		Title / Label	pos	wks
17 Feb 79		**HEAVEN KNOWS** *Casablanca CAN 141*	**34**	8
12 May 79		**HOT STUFF** *Casablanca CAN 151* ▲	**11**	10
7 Jul 79		**BAD GIRLS** *Casablanca CAN 155* ▲	**14**	10
1 Sep 79		**DIM ALL THE LIGHTS** *Casablanca CAN 162*	**29**	9
3 Nov 79	●	**NO MORE TEARS (ENOUGH IS ENOUGH)** *Casablanca CAN 174 / CBS 8000* [1] ▲	**3**	13
16 Feb 80		**ON THE RADIO** *Casablanca NB 2236*	**32**	6
21 Jun 80		**SUNSET PEOPLE** *Casablanca CAN 198*	**46**	5
27 Sep 80		**THE WANDERER** *Geffen K 79180*	**48**	6
17 Jan 81		**COLD LOVE** *Geffen K 79193*	**44**	3
10 Jul 82		**LOVE IS IN CONTROL (FINGER ON THE TRIGGER)** *Warner Bros. K 79302*	**18**	11
6 Nov 82		**STATE OF INDEPENDENCE** *Warner Bros. K 79344*	**14**	11
4 Dec 82		**I FEEL LOVE (re-mix)** *Casablanca FEEL 7*	**21**	10
5 Mar 83		**THE WOMAN IN ME** *Warner Bros. U 9983*	**62**	2
18 Jun 83		**SHE WORKS HARD FOR THE MONEY** *Mercury DONNA 1*	**25**	8
24 Sep 83		**UNCONDITIONAL LOVE** *Mercury DONNA 2*	**14**	12
21 Jan 84		**STOP LOOK AND LISTEN** *Mercury DONNA 3*	**57**	2
24 Oct 87		**DINNER WITH GERSHWIN** *Warner Bros. U 8237*	**13**	11
23 Jan 88		**ALL SYSTEMS GO** *WEA U 8122*	**54**	3
25 Feb 89	●	**THIS TIME I KNOW IT'S FOR REAL** *Warner Bros. U 7780*	**3**	14
27 May 89	●	**I DON'T WANNA GET HURT** *Warner Bros. U 7567*	**7**	9
26 Aug 89		**LOVE'S ABOUT TO CHANGE MY HEART** *Warner Bros. U 7494*	**20**	6
25 Nov 89		**WHEN LOVE TAKES OVER YOU** *WEA U 7361*	**72**	1
17 Nov 90		**STATE OF INDEPENDENCE (re-issue)** *Warner Bros. U 2857*	**45**	3
12 Jan 91		**BREAKAWAY** *Warner Bros. U 3308*	**49**	4
30 Nov 91		**WORK THAT MAGIC** *Warner Bros. U 5937*	**74**	1
12 Nov 94		**MELODY OF LOVE (WANNA BE LOVED)** *Mercury MERCD 418*	**21**	3
9 Sep 95	●	**I FEEL LOVE (re-recording)** *Manifesto FESCD 1*	**8**	5
6 Apr 96		**STATE OF INDEPENDENCE (re-mix)** *Manifesto FESCD 7* [2]	**13**	5
11 Jul 98		**CARRY ON** *Almighty CDALMY 120* [3]	**65**	1
30 Oct 99		**I WILL GO WITH YOU (CON TE PARTIRO)** *Epic 6682092*	**44**	1
31 Jan 76		**LOVE TO LOVE YOU BABY** *GTO GTLP 008*	**16**	9
22 May 76		**A LOVE TRILOGY** *GTO GTLP 010*	**41**	10
25 Jun 77	●	**I REMEMBER YESTERDAY** *GTO GTLP 025*	**3**	23
26 Nov 77		**ONCE UPON A TIME** *Casablanca CALD 5003*	**24**	13
7 Jan 78	●	**GREATEST HITS** *GTO GTLP 028*	**4**	18
21 Oct 78		**LIVE AND MORE** *Casablanca CALD 5006* ▲	**16**	16
2 Jun 79		**BAD GIRLS** *Casablanca CALD 5007* ▲	**23**	23
10 Nov 79		**ON THE RADIO – GREATEST HITS VOLUMES 1 & 2** *Casablanca CALD 5008* ▲	**24**	22
1 Nov 80		**THE WANDERER** *Geffen K 99124*	**55**	2
31 Jul 82		**DONNA SUMMER** *Warner Bros. K 99163*	**13**	16
16 Jul 83		**SHE WORKS HARD FOR THE MONEY** *Mercury MERL 21*	**28**	5
15 Sep 84		**CATS WITHOUT CLAWS** *Warner Bros. 250806*	**69**	2
25 Mar 89		**ANOTHER PLACE AND TIME** *Warner Bros. WX 219*	**17**	28
24 Nov 90		**THE BEST OF DONNA SUMMER** *Warner Bros. WX 397*	**24**	9
26 Nov 94		**ENDLESS SUMMER – GREATEST HITS** *Mercury 5262172*	**37**	2

[1] Donna Summer and Barbra Streisand [2] Donna Summer featuring the All Star Choir [3] Donna Summer and Giorgio Moroder

'No More Tears (Enough Is Enough)' was released simultaneously on two different labels, a seven-inch single on Casablanca and a 12-inch on CBS. 'Unconditional Love' features the additional vocals of Musical Youth

SUMMER DAZE

UK, male instrumental / production duo (Singles: 1 week) pos/wks

Date	Title / Label	pos	wks
26 Oct 96	**SAMBA MAGIC** *VC VCRD 14*	**61**	1

Mark SUMMERS *UK, male producer (Singles: 6 weeks)* pos/wks

Date	Title / Label	pos	wks
26 Jan 91	**SUMMER'S MAGIC** *Fourth & Broadway BRW 205*	**27**	6

See also SOUVLAKI

J D SUMNER – *See Elvis PRESLEY*

SUNBURST *UK, male producer – Matt Darey (Singles: 1 week)* pos/wks

Date	Title / Label	pos	wks
8 Jul 00	**EYEBALL (EYEBALL PAUL'S THEME)** *Virgin / EMI VTSCD 4*	**48**	1

See also LOST TRIBE; Matt DAREY; MELT featuring Little Ms MARCIE; MDM

SUNCLUB – *See UD PROJECT vs SUNCLUB*

SUNDANCE *UK, male production duo – Nick Woolfson and Mark Shimmon (Singles: 7 weeks)* pos/wks

Date	Title / Label	pos	wks
8 Nov 97	**SUNDANCE** *React CDREACT 109*	**33**	2
3 Oct 98	**SUNDANCE '98 (re-mix)** *React CDREACTX 136*	**37**	2
27 Feb 99	**THE LIVING DREAM** *React CDREACT 134*	**56**	1
5 Feb 00	**WON'T LET THIS FEELING GO** *Inferno CDFERN 23*	**40**	2

See also SHIMMON & WOOLFSON;

SUNDANCE – *See DJ 'FAST' EDDIE*

SUNDAYS *UK, male / female vocal / instrumental group (Singles: 12 weeks, Albums: 15 weeks)* pos/wks

Date		Title / Label	pos	wks
11 Feb 89		**CAN'T BE SURE** *Rough Trade RT 218*	**45**	5
3 Oct 92		**GOODBYE** *Parlophone R 6319*	**27**	2
20 Sep 97		**SUMMERTIME** *Parlophone CDRS 6475*	**15**	4
22 Nov 97		**CRY** *Parlophone CDR 6487*	**43**	1
27 Jan 90	●	**READING, WRITING AND ARITHMETIC** *Rough Trade ROUGH 148*	**4**	8
31 Oct 92		**BLIND** *Parlophone CDPCSD 121*	**15**	3
4 Oct 97	●	**STATIC & SILENCE** *Parlophone CDEST 2300*	**10**	4

SUNDRAGON

UK, male vocal / instrumental duo (Singles: 1 week) pos/wks

Date	Title / Label	pos	wks
21 Feb 68	**GREEN TAMBOURINE** *MGM 1380*	**50**	1

SUNFIRE *US, male vocal / instrumental group (Singles: 11 weeks)* pos/wks

Date	Title / Label	pos	wks
12 Mar 83	**YOUNG, FREE AND SINGLE** *Warner Bros. W 9897*	**20**	11

SUNKIDS featuring CHANCE

US, male production duo and female vocalist (Singles: 2 weeks) pos/wks

Date	Title / Label	pos	wks
13 Nov 99	**RESCUE ME** *AM:PM CDAMPM 126*	**50**	2

SUNNY *UK, female vocalist – Sunny Leslie (Singles: 10 weeks)* pos/wks

Date		Title / Label	pos	wks
30 Mar 74	●	**DOCTOR'S ORDERS** *CBS 2068*	**7**	10

SUNSCREEM *UK, male / female vocal / instrumental group (Singles: 36 weeks, Albums: 6 weeks)* pos/wks

Date	Title / Label	pos	wks
29 Feb 92	**PRESSURE** *Sony S2 6578017*	**60**	2
18 Jul 92	**LOVE U MORE** *Sony S2 6581727*	**23**	6
17 Oct 92	**PERFECT MOTION** *Sony S2 6584057*	**18**	5
9 Jan 93	**BROKEN ENGLISH** *Sony S2 6589032*	**13**	5
27 Mar 93	**PRESSURE US (re-mix)** *Sony S2 6591102*	**19**	5
2 Sep 95	**WHEN** *Sony S2 6623222*	**47**	2
18 Nov 95	**EXODUS** *Sony S2 6625342*	**40**	2
20 Jan 96	**WHITE SKIES** *Sony S2 6627425*	**25**	3
23 Mar 96	**SECRETS** *Sony S2 6629342*	**36**	2
6 Sep 97	**CATCH** *Pulse-8 CDLOSE 117*	**55**	1
20 Oct 01	**PLEASE SAVE ME** *Inferno / Five AM FAMFERN 1CD* [1]	**36**	2
16 Nov 02	**PERFECT MOTION (re-mix)** *Five AM FAM 15CD*	**71**	1
13 Feb 93	**03** *Sony S2 4722182*	**33**	5
30 Mar 96	**CHANGE OR DIE** *Sony S2 4813132*	**53**	1

[1] Sunscreem vs Push

Monty SUNSHINE – *See Chris BARBER*

SUNSHINE BAND – *See KC & THE SUNSHINE BAND*

SUNSHIP featuring MCRB

UK, male producer and male vocalist (Singles: 1 week) pos/wks

Date	Title / Label	pos	wks
1 Apr 00	**CHEQUE ONE-TWO** *Filter FILT 044*	**75**	1

SUPER FURRY ANIMALS *UK, male vocal / instrumental group (Singles: 43 weeks, Albums: 32 weeks)* pos/wks

Date	Title / Label	pos	wks
9 Mar 96	**HOMETOWN UNICORN** *Creation CRESCD 222*	**47**	1
11 May 96	**GOD! SHOW ME MAGIC** *Creation CRESCD 231*	**33**	2
13 Jul 96	**SOMETHING 4 THE WEEKEND** *Creation CRESCD 235*	**18**	3
12 Oct 96	**IF YOU DON'T WANT ME TO DESTROY YOU** *Creation CRESCD 243*	**18**	2

Date	Title / Label	Pos	Wks
14 Dec 96	**THE MAN DON'T GIVE A FUCK** *Creation CRESCD 247*	22	2
24 May 97	**HERMANN LOVES PAULINE** *Creation CRESCD 252*	26	2
26 Jul 97	**THE INTERNATIONAL LANGUAGE OF SCREAMING** *Creation CRESCD 269*	24	2
4 Oct 97	**PLAY IT COOL** *Creation CRESCD 275*	27	2
6 Dec 97	**DEMONS** *Creation CRESCD 283*	27	2
6 Jun 98	**ICE HOCKEY HAIR** *Creation CRESCD 288*	12	3
22 May 99	**NORTHERN LITES** *Creation CRESCD 314*	11	4
21 Aug 99	**FIRE IN MY HEART** *Creation CRESCD 323*	25	3
29 Jan 00	**DO OR DIE** *Creation CRESCD 329*	20	2
21 Jul 01	**JUXTAPOZED WITH U** *Epic 6712242*	14	4
20 Oct 01	**(DRAWING) RINGS AROUND THE WORLD** *Epic 6719082*	28	2
26 Jan 02	**IT'S NOT THE END OF THE WORLD?** *Epic 6721752*	30	2
26 Jul 03	**GOLDEN RETRIEVER** *Epic 6739062*	13	3
1 Nov 03	**HELLO SUNSHINE** *Epic 6743602*	31	2
1 Jun 96	**FUZZY LOGIC** *Creation CRECD 190*	23	6
6 Sep 97 ●	**RADIATOR** *Creation CRECD 214*	8	3
5 Dec 98	**OUT SPACED** *Creation CRECD 229*	44	1
26 Jun 99 ●	**GUERRILLA** *Creation CRECD 242*	10	9
27 May 00	**MWNG** *Placid Casual PLC 03CD*	11	2
4 Aug 01 ●	**RINGS AROUND THE WORLD** *Epic 5024132*	3	7
2 Aug 03 ●	**PHANTOM POWER** *Epic 5123752*	4	4

SUPERCAR
Italy, male DJ production duo – Alberto Pizarelli and Ricki Pagano (Singles: 6 weeks) pos/wks

Date	Title / Label	Pos	Wks
13 Feb 99	**TONITE** *Pepper 0530202*	15	5
21 Aug 99	**COMPUTER LOVE** *Pepper 0530392* [1]	67	1

[1] Supercar featuring Mikaela

SUPERCAT
Jamaica, male vocalist – William Maragh (Singles: 5 weeks) pos/wks

Date	Title / Label	Pos	Wks
1 Aug 92	**IT FE DONE** *Columbia 6582737*	66	1
6 May 95	**MY GIRL JOSEPHINE** *Columbia 6614702* [1]	22	4

[1] Supercat featuring Jack Radics

SUPERFUNK
France, male production trio (Singles: 2 weeks) pos/wks

Date	Title / Label	Pos	Wks
4 Mar 00	**LUCKY STAR** *Virgin DINSD 198* [1]	42	1
10 Jun 00	**THE YOUNG MC** *Virgin DINSD 206*	62	1

[1] Superfunk featuring Ron Carroll

SUPERGRASS (441 Top 500)
Acclaimed power-pop group, formed in Oxford in 1994: Gaz Coombes (g/v), Danny Goffey (d/v), Mick Quinn (b/v) and in 1995 Gaz's brother Rob (k). Popular live band was voted Best British Newcomers at 1996 Brit awards. Their first three albums achieved platinum status (Singles: 62 weeks, Albums: 92 weeks) pos/wks

Date	Title / Label	Pos	Wks
29 Oct 94	**CAUGHT BY THE FUZZ** *Parlophone CDR 6396*	43	2
18 Feb 95	**MANSIZE ROOSTER** *Parlophone CDR 6402*	20	3
25 Mar 95	**LOSE IT** *Sub Pop SP 281*	75	1
13 May 95 ●	**LENNY** *Parlophone CDR 6410*	10	3
15 Jul 95 ●	**ALRIGHT / TIME** *Parlophone CDR 6413*	2	10
9 Mar 96 ●	**GOING OUT** *Parlophone CDR 6428*	5	6
12 Apr 97 ●	**RICHARD III** *Parlophone CDR 6461*	2	5
21 Jun 97 ●	**SUN HITS THE SKY** *Parlophone CDR 6469*	10	4
18 Oct 97	**LATE IN THE DAY** *Parlophone CDR 6484*	18	4
5 Jun 99	**PUMPING ON YOUR STEREO (re)** *Parlophone CDR 6518*	11	7
18 Sep 99 ●	**MOVING** *Parlophone CDR 6524*	9	5
4 Dec 99	**MARY (re)** *Parlophone CDR 6531*	36	4
13 Jul 02	**NEVER DONE NOTHING LIKE THAT BEFORE** *Parlophone CDR 6563*	75	1
28 Sep 02	**GRACE** *Parlophone CDR 6586*	13	4
8 Feb 03	**SEEN THE LIGHT** *Parlophone CDR 6592*	22	3
27 May 95 ★	**I SHOULD COCO** *Parlophone CDPCS 7373*	1	36
3 May 97 ●	**IN IT FOR THE MONEY** *Parlophone CDPCS 7388*	2	25
2 Oct 99 ●	**SUPERGRASS** *Parlophone 5220562*	3	25
12 Oct 02 ●	**LIFE ON OTHER PLANETS** *Parlophone 5418002*	9	6

SUPERMEN LOVERS featuring Mani HOFFMAN
France, male producer – Guillaume Atlan and male vocalist (Singles: 16 weeks) pos/wks

Date	Title / Label	Pos	Wks
15 Sep 01 ●	**STARLIGHT (re)** *Independiente ISOM 53MS*	2	16

SUPERNATURALS
UK, male vocal / instrumental group (Singles: 15 weeks, Albums: 7 weeks) pos/wks

Date	Title / Label	Pos	Wks
26 Oct 96	**LAZY LOVER** *Food CDFOOD 85*	34	2
8 Feb 97	**THE DAY BEFORE YESTERDAY'S MAN** *Food CDFOODS 88*	25	3
26 Apr 97	**SMILE** *Food CDFOOD 92*	23	2
12 Jul 97	**LOVE HAS PASSED AWAY** *Food CDFOOD 99*	38	2
25 Oct 97	**PREPARE TO LAND** *Food CDFOODS 106*	48	1
1 Aug 98	**I WASN'T BUILT TO GET UP** *Food CDFOOD 112*	25	3
24 Oct 98	**SHEFFIELD SONG** *Food CDFOODS 115*	45	1
13 Mar 99	**EVEREST** *Food CDFOOD 119*	52	1
17 May 97 ●	**IT DOESN'T MATTER ANYMORE** *Food FOODCD 21*	9	4
22 Aug 98	**A TUNE A DAY** *Food 4960662*	21	3

SUPERNOVA
UK, male / female vocal / instrumental duo (Singles: 1 week) pos/wks

Date	Title / Label	Pos	Wks
11 May 96	**SOME MIGHT SAY** *Sing Sing 74321369442*	55	1

SUPERSISTER
UK, female vocal group (Singles: 8 weeks) pos/wks

Date	Title / Label	Pos	Wks
14 Oct 00	**COFFEE** *Gut CDGUT 35*	16	5
25 Aug 01	**SHOPPING** *Gut CDGUT 37*	36	2
17 Nov 01	**SUMMER GONNA COME AGAIN** *Gut CDGUT 38*	51	1

SUPERSTAR
UK, male vocal / instrumental group (Singles: 2 weeks) pos/wks

Date	Title / Label	Pos	Wks
7 Feb 98	**EVERY DAY I FALL APART** *Camp Fabulous CFAB 003 CD*	66	1
25 Apr 98	**SUPERSTAR** *Camp Fabulous CFAB 007CD*	49	1

SUPERTRAMP (272 Top 500)
Acclaimed Anglo-American group formed in 1969 by UK musicians Rick Davies (v/k) and Roger Hodgson (v/g). A change of sound from progressive rock to more focused pop in the mid-70s was internationally successful: 'Breakfast In America', their biggest seller, shifted 18 million albums (Singles: 52 weeks, Albums: 181 weeks) pos/wks

Date	Title / Label	Pos	Wks
15 Feb 75	**DREAMER** *A&M AMS 7132*	13	10
25 Jun 77	**GIVE A LITTLE BIT** *A&M AMS 7293*	29	7
31 Mar 79 ●	**THE LOGICAL SONG** *A&M AMS 7427*	7	11
30 Jun 79 ●	**BREAKFAST IN AMERICA** *A&M AMS 7451*	9	10
27 Oct 79	**GOODBYE STRANGER** *A&M AMS 7481*	57	3
30 Oct 82	**IT'S RAINING AGAIN** *A&M AMS 8255* [1]	26	11
23 Nov 74 ●	**CRIME OF THE CENTURY** *A&M AMLS 68258*	4	22
6 Dec 75	**CRISIS? WHAT CRISIS?** *A&M AMLH 68347*	20	15
23 Apr 77	**EVEN IN THE QUIETEST MOMENTS** *A&M AMLK 64634*	12	22
31 Jan 79 ●	**BREAKFAST IN AMERICA** *A&M AMLK 63708* ▲	3	53
4 Oct 80 ●	**PARIS** *A&M AMLM 66702*	7	17
6 Nov 82 ●	**FAMOUS LAST WORDS** *A&M AMLK 63732*	6	16
25 May 85	**BROTHER WHERE YOU BOUND** *A&M AMA 5014*	20	5
18 Oct 86 ●	**THE AUTOBIOGRAPHY OF SUPERTRAMP** *A&M TRAMP 1*	9	19
31 Oct 87	**FREE AS A BIRD** *A&M AMA 5181*	93	1
15 Aug 92	**THE VERY BEST OF SUPERTRAMP** *A&M TRACD 1992*	24	4
3 May 97	**SOME THINGS NEVER CHANGE** *EMI CDCHR 6121*	74	1
27 Sep 97 ●	**THE VERY BEST OF SUPERTRAMP (re-issue)** *PolyGram TV 3970912*	8	6

[1] Supertramp featuring vocals by Roger Hodgson

SUPREMES (69 Top 500)
World's most successful female group: Diana Ross, Mary Wilson, Florence Ballard (d. 1976). Before Ross went solo in 1969, this Detroit-based trio had amassed a dozen US No.1s and became the first female trio to top the UK singles chart. They were inducted into the Rock and Roll Hall of Fame in 1988 (Singles: 306 weeks, Albums: 226 weeks) pos/wks

Date	Title / Label	Pos	Wks
3 Sep 64 ●	**WHERE DID OUR LOVE GO** *Stateside SS 327* ▲	3	14
22 Oct 64 ★	**BABY LOVE** *Stateside SS 350* ▲	1	15
21 Jan 65	**COME SEE ABOUT ME** *Stateside SS 376* ▲	27	6
25 Mar 65 ●	**STOP! IN THE NAME OF LOVE** *Tamla Motown TMG 501* ▲	7	12
10 Jun 65	**BACK IN MY ARMS AGAIN** *Tamla Motown TMG 516* ▲	40	5
9 Dec 65	**I HEAR A SYMPHONY (re)** *Tamla Motown TMG 543* ▲	39	5
8 Sep 66 ●	**YOU CAN'T HURRY LOVE** *Tamla Motown TMG 575* ▲	3	12
1 Dec 66 ●	**YOU KEEP ME HANGIN' ON** *Tamla Motown TMG 585* ▲	8	10
2 Mar 67	**LOVE IS HERE AND NOW YOU'RE GONE** *Tamla Motown TMG 597* ▲	17	10

11 May 67 ● **THE HAPPENING** *Tamla Motown TMG 607* ▲ 6 12
30 Aug 67 ● **REFLECTIONS** *Tamla Motown TMG 616* [1] 5 14
29 Nov 67 **IN AND OUT OF LOVE** *Tamla Motown TMG 632* [1] 13 13
10 Apr 68 **FOREVER CAME TODAY** *Tamla Motown TMG 650* [1] 28 8
3 Jul 68 **SOME THINGS YOU NEVER GET USED TO** *Tamla Motown TMG 662* [1] 34 6
20 Nov 68 **LOVE CHILD** *Tamla Motown TMG 677* [1] ▲ 15 14
29 Jan 69 ● **I'M GONNA MAKE YOU LOVE ME (re)** *Tamla Motown TMG 685* [2] 3 12
23 Apr 69 **I'M LIVIN' IN SHAME (re)** *Tamla Motown TMG 695* [1] 14 10
16 Jul 69 **NO MATTER WHAT SIGN YOU ARE** *Tamla Motown TMG 704* [1] 37 7
20 Sep 69 **I SECOND THAT EMOTION** *Tamla Motown TMG 709* [2] 18 8
13 Dec 69 **SOMEDAY WE'LL BE TOGETHER** *Tamla Motown TMG 721* [1] ▲ 13 13
21 Mar 70 **WHY (MUST WE FALL IN LOVE)** *Tamla Motown TMG 730* [2] ..31 7
2 May 70 ● **UP THE LADDER TO THE ROOF** *Tamla Motown TMG 735* 6 15
16 Jan 71 ● **STONED LOVE** *Tamla Motown TMG 760* 3 13
26 Jun 71 **RIVER DEEP MOUNTAIN HIGH** *Tamla Motown TMG 777* [3] 11 10
21 Aug 71 ● **NATHAN JONES** *Tamla Motown TMG 782* 5 11
20 Nov 71 **YOU GOTTA HAVE LOVE IN YOUR HEART** *Tamla Motown TMG 793* [3] 25 10
4 Mar 72 ● **FLOY JOY** *Tamla Motown TMG 804* 9 10
15 Jul 72 ● **AUTOMATICALLY SUNSHINE** *Tamla Motown TMG 821* 10 9
21 Apr 73 **BAD WEATHER** *Tamla Motown TMG 847* 37 4
24 Aug 74 **BABY LOVE (re-issue)** *Tamla Motown TMG 915* [1] 12 10
18 Feb 89 **STOP! IN THE NAME OF LOVE (re-issue)** *Motown ZB 41963* [1] 62 1
5 Dec 64 ● **MEET THE SUPREMES** *Stateside SL 10109* 8 6
17 Dec 66 **SUPREMES A GO-GO** *Tamla Motown STML 11039* ▲ 15 21
13 May 67 **THE SUPREMES SING MOTOWN** *Tamla Motown STML 11047*..15 16
30 Sep 67 **THE SUPREMES SING RODGERS & HART** *Tamla Motown STML 11054*....25 7
20 Jan 68 ★ **GREATEST HITS** *Tamla Motown STML 11063* [1] ▲ 1 60
30 Mar 68 ● **LIVE AT THE TALK OF THE TOWN** *Tamla Motown STML 11070* [1] 6 18
20 Jul 68 **REFLECTIONS** *Tamla Motown STML 11073* [1] 30 2
25 Jan 69 ★ **DIANA ROSS AND THE SUPREMES JOIN THE TEMPTATIONS** *Tamla Motown STML 11096* [2] ▲ 1 15
1 Feb 69 ● **LOVE CHILD** *Tamla Motown STML 11095* [1] 8 6
28 Jun 69 **TCB** *Tamla Motown STML 11110* [2] 11 12
14 Feb 70 **TOGETHER** *Tamla Motown STML 11122* [2]....28 4
29 May 71 ● **MAGNIFICENT SEVEN** *Tamla Motown STML 11179* [3] 6 11
25 Sep 71 **TOUCH** *Tamla Motown STML 11189* 40 1
17 Sep 77 ★ **20 GOLDEN GREATS** *Motown EMTV 5* [1] 1 34
21 Jan 89 ● **LOVE SUPREME** *Motown ZL 72701* [1] 10 9
31 Oct 98 **40 GOLDEN MOTOWN GREATS** *Motown / PolyGram TV 5309612* [1] 35 4

[1] Diana Ross and The Supremes [2] Diana Ross and the Supremes and the Temptations [3] Supremes and The Four Tops [1] Diana Ross and the Supremes [2] Diana Ross and the Supremes with the Temptations [3] Supremes and the Four Tops

Al B SURE! *US, male vocalist – Al Brown (Singles: 13 weeks)* pos/wks

16 Apr 88 **NITE AND DAY** *Uptown W 8192* 44 5
30 Jul 88 **OFF ON YOUR OWN (GIRL)** *Uptown W 7870* 70 2
10 Jun 89 **IF I'M NOT YOUR LOVER** *Uptown W 2908* [1] 54 3
31 Mar 90 **SECRET GARDEN** *Qwest W 9992* [2] 67 1
12 Jun 93 **BLACK TIE WHITE NOISE** *Arista 74321148682* [3] 36 2

[1] Al B Sure featuring Slick Rick [2] Quincy Jones featuring Al B Sure!, James Ingram, El DeBarge and Barry White [3] David Bowie featuring Al B Sure!

SUREAL
UK, male / female production / vocal group (Singles: 4 weeks) pos/wks

7 Oct 00 **YOU TAKE MY BREATH AWAY** *Cream CREAM 7CD* 15 4

SURFACE *US, male vocal / instrumental duo (Singles: 14 weeks)* pos/wks

23 Jul 83 **FALLING IN LOVE** *Salsoul SAL 104* 67 3
23 Jun 84 **WHEN YOUR 'EX' WANTS YOU BACK** *Salsoul SAL 106* 52 4
28 Feb 87 **HAPPY** *CBS 650393 7* 56 5
12 Jan 91 **THE FIRST TIME** *Columbia 6564767* ▲ 60 2

SURFACE NOISE
UK, male instrumental group (Singles: 11 weeks) pos/wks

31 May 80 **THE SCRATCH** *WEA K 18291* 26 8
30 Aug 80 **DANCIN' ON A WIRE** *Groove Production GP102* 59 3

SURFARIS *US, male instrumental group (Singles: 14 weeks)* pos/wks

25 Jul 63 ● **WIPE OUT** *London HLD 9751* 5 14

SURPRISE SISTERS
Australia, female vocal group (Singles: 3 weeks) pos/wks

13 Mar 76 **LA BOOGA ROOGA** *Good Earth GD 1* 38 3

SURVIVOR *US, male vocal / instrumental group – lead vocal Dave Bickler (Singles: 26 weeks, Albums: 10 weeks)* pos/wks

31 Jul 82 ★ **EYE OF THE TIGER** *Scotti Brothers SCT A 2411* ▲ 1 15
1 Feb 86 ● **BURNING HEART** *Scotti Brothers A 6708* 5 11
21 Aug 82 **EYE OF THE TIGER** *Scotti Bros SCT 85845* 12 10

SUSHI – *See Paul MASTERSON presents SUSHI*

Walter SUSSKIND – *See LONDON PHILHARMONIC CHOIR*

SUTHERLAND BROTHERS and QUIVVER *UK, male vocal / instrumental group (Singles: 20 weeks, Albums: 11 weeks)* pos/wks

3 Apr 76 ● **ARMS OF MARY** *CBS 4001* 5 12
20 Nov 76 **SECRETS** *CBS 4668* 35 4
2 Jun 79 **EASY COME, EASY GO** *CBS 7121* [1] 50 4
15 May 76 **REACH FOR THE SKY** *CBS 69191*....26 8
9 Oct 76 **SLIPSTREAM** *CBS 81593* 49 3

[1] Sutherland Brothers

Pat SUZUKI *US, female vocalist (Singles: 1 week)* pos/wks

14 Apr 60 **I ENJOY BEING A GIRL** *RCA 1171* 49 1

SVENSON and GIELEN *Belgium, male production duo – Sven Maes and Johan Gielen (Singles: 2 weeks)* pos/wks

22 Sep 01 **THE BEAUTY OF SILENCE** *Xtrahard / Xtravaganza* 41 2

See also AIRSCAPE; BLUE BAMBOO; CUBIC 22; TRANSFORMER 2; Johan GIELEN presents ABNEA

Billy SWAN *US, male vocalist (Singles: 13 weeks)* pos/wks

14 Dec 74 ● **I CAN HELP** *Monument MNT 2752* ▲ 6 9
24 May 75 **DON'T BE CRUEL** *Monument MNT 3244* 42 4

SWAN LAKE *US, male producer – Todd Terry (Singles: 4 weeks)* pos/wks

17 Sep 88 **IN THE NAME OF LOVE** *Champion CHAMP 86* 53 4

SWANS WAY *UK, male / female vocal / instrumental group (Singles: 12 weeks, Albums: 1 week)* pos/wks

4 Feb 84 **SOUL TRAIN** *Exit EXT 3* 20 7
26 May 84 **ILLUMINATIONS** *Balgier PH 5* 57 5
3 Nov 84 **THE FUGITIVE KIND** *Balgier SWAN 1* 88 1

Patrick SWAYZE featuring Wendy FRASER
US, male / female vocal / actor duo (Singles: 11 weeks) pos/wks

26 Mar 88 **SHE'S LIKE THE WIND** *RCA PB 49565* 17 11

Keith SWEAT
US, male vocalist (Singles: 23 weeks, Albums: 32 weeks) pos/wks

20 Feb 88 **I WANT HER** *Vintertainment EKR 68* 26 10
14 May 88 **SOMETHING JUST AIN'T RIGHT** *Vintertainment EKR 72* 55 3
14 May 94 **HOW DO YOU LIKE IT** *Elektra EKR 185CD* 71 1
22 Jun 96 **TWISTED** *Elektra EKR 223CD* 39 2
23 Nov 96 **JUST A TOUCH** *Elektra EKR 227CD* 35 2
3 May 97 **NOBODY** *Elektra EKR 233CD* [1] 30 2
6 Dec 97 **I WANT HER (re-mix)** *Elektra E 3887CD* 44 1

12 Dec 98 **COME AND GET WITH ME** *Elektra E 3787CD* [2] 58 1
27 Mar 99 **I'M NOT READY** *Elektra E 3767CD* 53 1
16 Jan 88 **MAKE IT LAST FOREVER** *Elektra 960763 1* 41 21
23 Jun 90 **I'LL GIVE ALL MY LOVE TO YOU** *Vintertainment EKT 60* 47 4
9 Jul 94 **GET UP ON IT** *Elektra 7559615502* 20 4
29 Jun 96 **KEITH SWEAT** *Elektra 7559617072* 36 2
3 Oct 98 **STILL IN THE GAME** *Elektra 7559622622* 62 1

[1] Keith Sweat featuring Athena Cage [2] Keith Sweat featuring Snoop Dogg

Claire SWEENEY

UK, female actor / vocalist (Albums: 3 weeks) pos/wks

27 Jul 02 **CLAIRE** *T2 TCD 3254* 15 3

Michelle SWEENEY *US, female vocalist (Singles: 1 week)* pos/wks

29 Oct 94 **THIS TIME** *Big Beat A 8229CD* 57 1

SWEET (387 Top 500)

Glam-rock giants: Brian Connolly (v) (d. 1997), Andy Scott (g), Steve Priest (b), Mick Tucker (d) (d. 2002). The flamboyantly attired UK quartet was very popular in Europe and the US. Despite topping the chart only once, they achieved five No.2 hits (Singles: 159 weeks, Albums: 14 weeks) pos/wks

13 Mar 71 **FUNNY FUNNY** *RCA 2051* 13 14
12 Jun 71 ● **CO-CO** *RCA 2087* 2 15
16 Oct 71 **ALEXANDER GRAHAM BELL** *RCA 2121* 33 5
5 Feb 72 **POPPA JOE** *RCA 2164* 11 12
10 Jun 72 ● **LITTLE WILLY** *RCA 2225* 4 14
9 Sep 72 ● **WIG-WAM BAM** *RCA 2260* 4 13
13 Jan 73 ★ **BLOCKBUSTER!** *RCA 2305* 1 15
5 May 73 ● **HELL RAISER** *RCA 2357* 2 11
22 Sep 73 ● **THE BALLROOM BLITZ** *RCA 2403* 2 9
19 Jan 74 ● **TEENAGE RAMPAGE** *RCA LPBO 5004* 2 8
13 Jul 74 ● **THE SIX TEENS** *RCA LPBO 5037* 9 7
9 Nov 74 **TURN IT DOWN** *RCA 2480* 41 2
15 Mar 75 ● **FOX ON THE RUN** *RCA 2524* 2 10
12 Jul 75 **ACTION** *RCA 2578* 15 6
24 Jan 76 **THE LIES IN YOUR EYES** *RCA 2641* 35 4
28 Jan 78 ● **LOVE IS LIKE OXYGEN** *Polydor POSP 1* 9 9
26 Jan 85 **IT'S... IT'S... THE SWEET MIX** *Anagram ANA 28* 45 5
18 May 74 SWEET FANNY ADAMS *RCA LPI 5038* 27 2
22 Sep 84 SWEET 16 IT'S ... IT'S ... SWEET'S HITS *Anagram GRAM 16* 49 6
20 Jan 96 BALLROOM HITZ – THE VERY BEST OF SWEET *PolyGram TV 5350012* 15 6

It's... It's... the Sweet Mix is a medley of the following songs: Blockbuster / Fox on the Run / Teenage Rampage / Hell Raiser / Ballroom Blitz

Rachel SWEET

US, female vocalist (Singles: 15 weeks) pos/wks

9 Dec 78 **B-A-B-Y** *Stiff BUY 39* 35 8
22 Aug 81 **EVERLASTING LOVE** *CBS A 1405* [1] 35 7

[1] Rex Smith and Rachel Sweet

SWEET DREAMS *UK, male / female vocal duo – Polly Brown and Tony Jackson (Singles: 12 weeks)* pos/wks

20 Jul 74 ● **HONEY HONEY** *Bradley's BRAD 7408* 10 12

SWEET DREAMS

UK, male / female vocal trio (Singles: 7 weeks) pos/wks

9 Apr 83 **I'M NEVER GIVING UP** *Ariola ARO 333* 21 7

SWEET FEMALE ATTITUDE *UK, female vocal duo – Leanne Brown and Catherine Cassidy (Singles: 14 weeks)* pos/wks

15 Apr 00 ● **FLOWERS** *WEA WEA 267CD* 2 12
7 Oct 00 **8 DAYS A WEEK** *WEA WEA 296CD* 43 2

SWEET MERCY featuring Joe ROBERTS *UK, male production / instrumental duo and male vocalist (Singles: 1 week)* pos/wks

24 Feb 96 **HAPPY DAYS** *Grass Green GRASS 10CD* 63 1

SWEET PEOPLE

France, male vocal / instrumental group (Singles: 10 weeks) pos/wks

4 Oct 80 ● **ET LES OISEAUX CHANTAIENT (AND THE BIRDS WERE SINGING) (re)** *Polydor POSP 179* 4 10

Re-entry made No.73 in Aug 1987

SWEET PUSSY PAULINE – *See CANDY GIRLS*

SWEET SENSATION

UK, male vocal group – lead vocal Marcel King (Singles: 17 weeks) pos/wks

14 Sep 74 ★ **SAD SWEET DREAMER** *Pye 7N 45385* 1 10
18 Jan 75 **PURELY BY COINCIDENCE** *Pye 7N 45421* 11 7

SWEET TEE *US, female rapper – Toi Jackson (Singles: 8 weeks)* pos/wks

16 Jan 88 **IT'S LIKE THAT Y'ALL / I GOT DA FEELIN'** *Cooltempo COOL 160* 31 6
13 Aug 94 **THE FEELING** *Deep Distraxion OILYCD 029* [1] 32 2

[1] Tin Tin Out featuring Sweet Tee

SWEETBACK

UK, male vocal / instrumental group (Singles: 1 week) pos/wks

29 Mar 97 **YOU WILL RISE** *Epic 6643155* 64 1

SWEETBOX *Germany / US, male / female vocal / production duo – Rosan Roberto and Tina Harris (Singles: 12 weeks)* pos/wks

22 Aug 98 ● **EVERYTHING'S GONNA BE ALRIGHT** *RCA 74321606842* 5 12

Sally SWEETLAND – *See Eddie FISHER*

SWERVEDRIVER *UK, male vocal / instrumental group (Singles: 3 weeks, Albums: 2 weeks)* pos/wks

10 Aug 91 **SANDBLASTED (EP)** *Creation CRE 102* 67 1
30 May 92 **NEVER LOSE THAT FEELING** *Creation CRE 120* 62 1
14 Aug 93 **DUEL** *Creation CRESCD 136* 60 1
12 Oct 91 RAISE *Creation CRELP 093* 44 1
9 Oct 93 MEZCAL HEAD *Creation CCRE 143* 55 1

Tracks on Sandblasted (EP): Sandblaster / Flawed / Out / Laze It Up

SWIMMING WITH SHARKS

Germany, female vocal duo (Singles: 3 weeks) pos/wks

7 May 88 **CARELESS LOVE** *WEA YZ 173* 63 3

SWING featuring DR ALBAN

US, male rapper and Nigeria, male vocalist (Singles: 1 week) pos/wks

29 Apr 95 **SWEET DREAMS** *Logic 74321251552* 59 1

SWING 52 *US, male vocal / instrumental group (Singles: 1 week)* pos/wks

25 Feb 95 **COLOR OF MY SKIN** *ffrr FCD 256* 60 1

SWING KIDS – *See K7*

SWING OUT SISTER *UK, male / female vocal / instrumental trio (Singles: 55 weeks, Albums: 36 weeks)* pos/wks

25 Oct 86 ● **BREAKOUT** *Mercury SWING 2* 4 14
10 Jan 87 ● **SURRENDER** *Mercury SWING 3* 7 8
18 Apr 87 **TWILIGHT WORLD** *Mercury SWING 4* 32 6
11 Jul 87 **FOOLED BY A SMILE** *Mercury SWING 5* 43 4
8 Apr 89 **YOU ON MY MIND** *Fontana SWING 6* 28 9
8 Jul 89 **WHERE IN THE WORLD** *Fontana SWING 7* 47 4
11 Apr 92 **AM I THE SAME GIRL** *Fontana SWING 9* 21 6
20 Jun 92 **NOTGONNACHANGE** *Fontana SWING 10* 49 2
27 Aug 94 **LA LA (MEANS I LOVE YOU)** *Fontana SWIDD 11* 37 2
23 May 87 ★ IT'S BETTER TO TRAVEL *Mercury OUTLP 1* ■ 1 21
20 May 89 ● KALEIDOSCOPE WORLD *Fontana 838293 1* 3 11
16 May 92 GET IN TOUCH WITH YOURSELF *Fontana 5122412* 27 4

Act became male / female duo in 1989

SWINGING BLUE JEANS
UK, male vocal / instrumental group (Singles: 57 weeks) pos/wks

20 Jun 63 IT'S TOO LATE NOW (re) *HMV POP 1170* 30 9
12 Dec 63 ● HIPPY HIPPY SHAKE *HMV POP 1242* 2 17
19 Mar 64 GOOD GOLLY MISS MOLLY *HMV POP 1273* 11 10
4 Jun 64 ● YOU'RE NO GOOD *HMV POP 1304* 3 13
20 Jan 66 DON'T MAKE ME OVER *HMV POP 1501* 31 8

SWINGLE SISTERS
US / France, male / female vocal group (Albums: 18 weeks) pos/wks

1 Feb 64 JAZZ SEBASTIAN BACH *Philips BL 7572* 13 18

SWIRL 360 *US, male vocal duo (Singles: 1 week)* pos/wks

14 Nov 98 HEY NOW NOW *Mercury 5665352* 61 1

SWITCH *US, male vocal / instrumental group (Singles: 3 weeks)* pos/wks

10 Nov 84 KEEPING SECRETS *Total Experience RCA XE 502* 61 3

SYBIL *US, female vocalist – Sybil Lynch*
(Singles: 69 weeks, Albums: 12 weeks) pos/wks

1 Nov 86 FALLING IN LOVE *Champion CHAMP 22* 68 3
25 Apr 87 LET YOURSELF GO *Champion CHAMP 42* 32 6
29 Aug 87 MY LOVE IS GUARANTEED *Champion CHAMPX 55* 42 5
22 Jul 89 DON'T MAKE ME OVER (re) *Champion CHAMP 213* 19 11
27 Jan 90 ● WALK ON BY *PWL PWL 48* 6 9
21 Apr 90 CRAZY FOR YOU *PWL PWL 53* 71 1
16 Jan 93 ● THE LOVE I LOST *PWL Sanctuary PWCD 253* [1] 3 13
20 Mar 93 ● WHEN I'M GOOD AND READY *PWL International PWCD 260* 5 13
26 Jun 93 BEYOND YOUR WILDEST DREAMS *PWL International PWCD 265* 41 2
11 Sep 93 STRONGER TOGETHER *PWL International PWCD 269* 41 2
11 Dec 93 MY LOVE IS GUARANTEED (re-mix) *PWL International PWCD 277* 48 1
9 Mar 96 SO TIRED OF BEING ALONE *PWL International PWL 324CD* 53 1
8 Mar 97 WHEN I'M GOOD AND READY (re-mix) *Next Plateau NP 14183* 66 1
26 Jul 97 STILL A THRILL *Coalition COLA 007CD* 55 1
5 Sep 87 LET YOURSELF GO *Champion CHAMP 1009* 92 1
24 Feb 90 WALK ON BY *PWL HF 10* 21 5
12 Jun 93 GOOD 'N' READY *PWL International HFCD 28* 13 6

[1] West End featuring Sybil

SYLK 130 *US, male production duo – King Britt and John Wicks (Singles: 2 weeks)* pos/wks

25 Apr 98 LAST NIGHT A DJ SAVED MY LIFE *Sony S2 SYLK 1CD* 33 2

SYLVER *Belgium, male / female DJ / production / vocal duo (Singles: 1 week)* pos/wks

1 Jun 02 TURN THE TIDE *Pepper 9230562* 56 1

SYLVESTER *US, male vocalist – Sylvester James, d. 16 Dec 1988 (Singles: 45 weeks, Albums: 3 weeks)* pos/wks

19 Aug 78 ● YOU MAKE ME FEEL (MIGHTY REAL) *Fantasy FTC 160* 8 15
18 Nov 78 DANCE (DISCO HEAT) *Fantasy FTC 163* 29 12
31 Mar 79 I (WHO HAVE NOTHING) *Fantasy FTC 171* 46 5
7 Jul 79 STARS *Fantasy FTC 177* 47 3
11 Sep 82 DO YOU WANNA FUNK *London LON 13* [1] 32 8
3 Sep 83 BAND OF GOLD *London LON 33* 67 2
23 Jun 79 MIGHTY REAL *Fantasy FTA 3009* 62 3

[1] Sylvester with Patrick Cowley

SYLVIA *US, female vocalist – Sylvia Vanderpool (Singles: 11 weeks)* pos/wks

23 Jun 73 PILLOW TALK *London HL 10415* 14 11

SYLVIA
Sweden, female vocalist – Sylvia Vrethammer (Singles: 33 weeks) pos/wks

10 Aug 74 ● Y VIVA ESPAÑA (re) *Sonet SON 2037* 4 28
26 Apr 75 HASTA LA VISTA *Sonet SON 2055* 38 5

David SYLVIAN
UK, male vocalist – David Batt (Singles: 36 weeks, Albums: 27 weeks) pos/wks

7 Aug 82 BAMBOO HOUSES / BAMBOO MUSIC *Virgin VS 510* [1] 30 4
2 Jul 83 FORBIDDEN COLOURS *Virgin VS 601* [2] 16 8
2 Jun 84 RED GUITAR *Virgin VS 633* 17 5
18 Aug 84 THE INK IN THE WELL *Virgin VS 700* 36 3
3 Nov 84 PULLING PUNCHES *Virgin VS 717* 56 2
14 Dec 85 WORDS WITH THE SHAMAN *Virgin VS 835* 72 1
9 Aug 86 TAKING THE VEIL *Virgin VS 815* 53 3
17 Jan 87 BUOY *Virgin VS 910* [3] 63 2
10 Oct 87 LET THE HAPPINESS IN *Virgin VS 1001* 66 1
13 Jun 92 HEARTBEAT (TAINAI KAIKI II) RETURNING TO THE WOMB *Virgin America VUS 57* [4] 58 3
28 Aug 93 JEAN THE BIRDMAN *Virgin VSCDG 1462* [5] 68 2
27 Mar 99 I SURRENDER *Virgin VSCDT 1722* 40 2
7 Jul 84 ● BRILLIANT TREES *Virgin V 2290* 4 14
13 Sep 86 GONE TO EARTH *Virgin VDL 1* 24 5
7 Nov 87 SECRETS OF THE BEEHIVE *Virgin V 2471* 37 2
2 Apr 88 PLIGHT AND PREMONITION *Virgin VE 11* [1] 71 1
17 Jul 93 THE FIRST DAY *Virgin CDVX 2712* [2] 21 2
10 Apr 99 DEAD BEES ON A CAKE *Virgin CDV 2876* 31 2
21 Oct 00 EVERYTHING AND NOTHING *Virgin CDVD 2897* 57 1

[1] Sylvian Sakamoto [2] David Sylvian and Riuichi Sakamoto [3] Mick Karn featuring David Sylvian [4] David Sylvian / Riuichi Sakamoto featuring Ingrid Chavez [5] David Sylvian and Robert Fripp [1] David Sylvian and Holgar Czukay [2] David Sylvian and Robert Fripp

See also JAPAN

SYMARIP
UK, male vocal / instrumental group (Singles: 3 weeks) pos/wks

2 Feb 80 SKINHEAD MOONSTOMP *Trojan TRO 9062* 54 3

SYMBOLS
UK, male vocal / instrumental group (Singles: 15 weeks) pos/wks

2 Aug 67 BYE BYE BABY *President PT 144* 44 3
3 Jan 68 (THE BEST PART OF) BREAKING UP *President PT 173* 25 12

Terri SYMON *UK, female vocalist (Singles: 1 week)* pos/wks

10 Jun 95 I WANT TO KNOW WHAT LOVE IS *A&M 5810592* 54 1

SYMPHONIQUE *UK, male instrumentalist – keyboards – Chris Cozens (Albums: 4 weeks)* pos/wks

1 Apr 95 MOODS SYMPHONIQUE 95 *Vision VISCD 10* 21 4

See also PROJECT D

SYMPOSIUM *UK, male vocal / instrumental group (Singles: 10 weeks, Albums: 3 weeks)* pos/wks

22 Mar 97 FAREWELL TO TWILIGHT *Infectious INFECT 34CD* 25 2
31 May 97 THE ANSWER TO WHY I HATE YOU *Infectious INFECT 37CD* 32 2
30 Aug 97 FAIRWEATHER FRIEND *Infectious INFECT 44CD* 25 3
14 Mar 98 AVERAGE MAN *Infectious INFECT 52CD* 45 1
16 May 98 BURY YOU *Infectious INFECT 55CDS* 41 1
18 Jul 98 BLUE *Infectious INFECT 57CD* 48 1
8 Nov 97 ONE DAY AT A TIME *Infectious INFECT 49CD* 29 2
30 May 98 ON THE OUTSIDE *Infectious INFECT 56CD* 32 1

See also HELL IS FOR HEROES

SYNTAX *UK, male producer – Mike Tournier (Singles: 3 weeks)* pos/wks

8 Feb 03 PRAY *Illustrious CDILL 012* 28 3

SYNTHPHONIC VARIATIONS
UK, session musicians (Albums: 1 week) pos/wks

1 Nov 86 SEASONS *CBS 450 1491* 84 1

SYREETA *US, female vocalist – Rita Wright (Singles: 30 weeks)* pos/wks

21 Sep 74 SPINNIN' AND SPINNIN' *Tamla Motown TMG 912* 49 3
1 Feb 75 YOUR KISS IS SWEET *Tamla Motown TMG 933* 12 8

12 Jul 75		**HARMOUR LOVE** *Tamla Motown TMG 954*	**32**	4
15 Dec 79	●	**WITH YOU I'M BORN AGAIN** *Motown TMG 1159* [1]	**2**	11
8 Mar 80		**IT WILL COME IN TIME** *Motown TMG 1175* [1]	**47**	4

[1] Billy Preston and Syreeta

Stanislas SYREWICZ – *See Anthony WAY*

SYSTEM *US, male vocal / instrumental duo (Singles: 2 weeks)* pos/wks

9 Jun 84		**I WANNA MAKE YOU FEEL GOOD** *Polydor POSP 685*	**73**	2

SYSTEM F
Holland, male producer – Ferry Corsten (Singles: 10 weeks) pos/wks

3 Apr 99		**OUT OF THE BLUE** *Essential Recordings ESCD 1*	**14**	6
6 May 00		**CRY** *Essential Recordings ESCD 14*	**19**	4

See also MOONMAN; VERACOCHA; GOURYELLA; STARPARTY; ALBION; Ferry CORSTEN

SYSTEM OF A DOWN *US, male vocal / instrumental group (Singles: 9 weeks, Albums: 28 weeks)* pos/wks

3 Nov 01		**CHOP SUEY!** *Columbia 6720342*	**17**	4
23 Mar 02		**TOXICITY** *Columbia 6725022*	**25**	3
27 Jul 02		**AERIALS** *Columbia 6728692*	**34**	2
8 Sep 01		TOXICITY *Columbia 5015346* ▲	13	27
7 Dec 02		STEAL THIS ALBUM *American Recordings 5102489*	56	1

SYSTEM presents Kerri B
UK, male production group and female vocalist (Singles: 1 week) pos/wks

8 Nov 03		**IF YOU LEAVE ME NOW** *All Around The World CDGLOBE 288*	**55**	1

SYSTEM 7 *UK / France, male / female instrumental duo – Steve Hillage and Miquette Giraudy (Singles: 2 weeks, Albums: 3 weeks)* pos/wks

13 Feb 93		**7:7 EXPANSION** *Butterfly BFLD 2*	**39**	1
17 Jul 93		**SINBAD / QUEST** *Butterfly BFLD 8*	**74**	1
20 Jun 92		ALTITUDE *Ten TENG 403*	75	1
20 Mar 93		777 *Big Life BFLCD 1*	30	2

T-BOZ *US, female vocalist (Singles: 2 weeks)* pos/wks

23 Nov 96		**TOUCH MYSELF** *LaFace 74321422882*	**48**	1
14 Apr 01		**MY GETAWAY** *Maverick W 549CD* [1]	**44**	1

[1] Tionne 'T-Boz' Watkins

See also TLC

TC *Italy, male instrumental / production group (Singles: 5 weeks)* pos/wks

14 Mar 92		**BERRY** *Union City UCRT 1* [1]	**73**	1
21 Nov 92		**FUNKY GUITAR** *Union City UCRT 13* [2]	**40**	2
10 Jul 93		**HARMONY** *Union UCRD 20* [3]	**51**	2

[1] TC 1991 [2] TC 1992 [3] TC 1993

T-CONNECTION
US, male vocal / instrumental group (Singles: 27 weeks) pos/wks

18 Jun 77		**DO WHAT YOU WANNA DO** *TK XC 9109*	**11**	8
14 Jan 78		**ON FIRE** *TK TKR 6006*	**16**	5
10 Jun 78		**LET YOURSELF GO** *TK TKR 6024*	**52**	3
24 Feb 79		**AT MIDNIGHT** *TK TKR 7517*	**53**	5
5 May 79		**SATURDAY NIGHT** *TK TKR 7536*	**41**	6

T-COY – *See VARIOUS ARTISTS (EPs and LPs)*

T-EMPO
UK, male / female vocal / instrumental group (Singles: 4 weeks) pos/wks

7 May 94		**SATURDAY NIGHT SUNDAY MORNING** *ffrr FCD 232*	**19**	3
9 Nov 96		**THE LOOK OF LOVE / THE BLUE ROOM** *ffrr FCD 281*	**71**	1

T-FACTORY *Italy, male production group (Singles: 2 weeks)* pos/wks

13 Apr 02		**MESSAGE IN A BOTTLE** *Inferno CDFERN 44*	**51**	2

THS – THE HORN SECTION
US, male / female vocal / instrumental group (Singles: 3 weeks) pos/wks

18 Aug 84		**LADY SHINE (SHINE ON)** *Fourth & Broadway BRW 10*	**54**	3

TJR featuring XAVIER
UK, male instrumental / production group (Singles: 2 weeks) pos/wks

27 Sep 97		**JUST GETS BETTER** *Multiply CDMULTY 25*	**28**	2

TLC (365 Top 500) *Multi-award-winning 1990s female trio: Tionne 'T-Boz' Watkins, Lisa 'Left Eye' Lopes (d. 25 Apr 2002) and Rozonda 'Chilli' Thomas. They have nine US gold singles, and The Supremes are the only female group with more US No.1s. Best-selling single: 'No Scrubs' 553,200 (Singles: 85 weeks, Albums: 97 weeks)* pos/wks

20 Jun 92		**AIN'T 2 PROUD 2 BEG** *Arista 115265*	**13**	5
22 Aug 92		**BABY-BABY-BABY** *LaFace 74321111297*	**55**	3
24 Oct 92		**WHAT ABOUT YOUR FRIENDS** *LaFace 74321118177*	**59**	2
21 Jan 95		**CREEP** *LaFace 74321254212* ▲	**22**	4
22 Apr 95		**RED LIGHT SPECIAL** *LaFace 74321273662*	**18**	4
5 Aug 95	●	**WATERFALLS** *LaFace 74321298812* ▲	**4**	14
4 Nov 95		**DIGGIN' ON YOU** *LaFace 74321319252*	**18**	5
13 Jan 96	●	**CREEP (re-issue)** *LaFace 74321340942*	**6**	7
3 Apr 99	●	**NO SCRUBS** *LaFace 74321660952* ▲	**3**	19
28 Aug 99	●	**UNPRETTY** *LaFace 74321695842* ▲	**6**	11
18 Dec 99		**DEAR LIE** *LaFace 74321724012*	**31**	9
14 Dec 02		**GIRL TALK** *Arista 74321983482*	**30**	2
20 May 95	●	CRAZYSEXYCOOL *LaFace 73008260092*	4	39
6 Mar 99	●	FANMAIL *LaFace 73008260552* ▲	7	57
23 Nov 02		3D *LaFace 74321981502*	45	1

See also T-BOZ; Lisa 'Left Eye' LOPES

T99
Belgium, male instrumental / production group (Singles: 10 weeks) pos/wks

11 May 91		**ANASTHASIA** *XL XLS 19*	**14**	6
19 Oct 91		**NOCTURNE** *Emphasis 6574097*	**33**	4

T-POWER *UK, male producer – Mark Royal (Singles: 18 weeks)* pos/wks

13 Apr 96		**POLICE STATE** *Sound of Underground TPOWCD 001*	**63**	1
6 Apr 02	●	**SHAKE UR BODY** *Positiva CDTIV 171* [1]	**7**	11
23 Nov 02		**DON'T WANNA KNOW** *ffrr FCD 408* [2]	**19**	4
7 Jun 03		**FEELIN' U** *London FCD 409* [3]	**34**	2

[1] Shy FX and T-Power featuring Di [2] Shy FX and T-Power featuring Di and Skibadee [3] Shy FX and T-Power featuring Kele Le Roc

TQ *US, male rapper – Terrance Quaites (Singles: 35 weeks, Albums: 9 weeks)* pos/wks

30 Jan 99 ● **WESTSIDE** *Epic 6668102* 4 9
1 May 99 ● **BYE BYE BABY** *Epic 6672372* 7 7
21 Aug 99 **BETTER DAYS** *Epic 6677532* 32 2
4 Sep 99 ● **SUMMERTIME** *Northwestside 74321694672* [1] 7 7
29 Apr 00 **DAILY** *Epic 6692752* 14 5
13 Oct 01 **LET'S GET BACK TO BED ... BOY** *Epic 6718662* [2] 16 5
8 May 99 **THEY NEVER SAW ME COMING** *Epic 4914032* 27 7
20 May 00 **THE SECOND COMING** *Epic 4977602* 32 2

[1] Another Level featuring TQ [2] Sarah Connor featuring TQ

T. REX (86 Top 500)
Highly influential acoustic act turned superstar glam rock boogie duo; singer / songwriter / guitarist Marc Bolan (b. Mark Feld, 30 Sep 1947, London, UK; d. 16 Sep 1977), and percussionist Steve Peregrin Took (d. 27 Oct 1980) – replaced by Mickey Finn in 1969 (d. 12 Jan 2003) (Singles: 236 weeks, Albums: 234 weeks) pos/wks

8 May 68 **DEBORA** *Regal Zonophone RZ 3008* [1] 34 7
4 Sep 68 **ONE INCH ROCK** *Regal Zonophone RZ 3011* [1] 28 7
9 Aug 69 **KING OF THE RUMBLING SPIRES** *Regal Zonophone RZ 3022* [1] 44 1
24 Oct 70 ● **RIDE A WHITE SWAN** *Fly BUG 1* 2 20
27 Feb 71 ★ **HOT LOVE** *Fly BUG 6* 1 17
10 Jul 71 ★ **GET IT ON** *Fly BUG 10* 1 13
13 Nov 71 ● **JEEPSTER** *Fly BUG 16* 2 15
29 Jan 72 ★ **TELEGRAM SAM (re)** *T. Rex 101* 1 14
1 Apr 72 ● **DEBORA / ONE INCH ROCK (re-issue)** *Magnifly ECHO 102* [1] ..7 10
13 May 72 ★ **METAL GURU** *EMI MARC 1* 1 14
16 Sep 72 ● **CHILDREN OF THE REVOLUTION** *EMI MARC 2* 2 10
9 Dec 72 ● **SOLID GOLD EASY ACTION** *EMI MARC 3* 2 11
10 Mar 73 ● **20TH CENTURY BOY** *EMI MARC 4* 3 9
16 Jun 73 ● **THE GROOVER** *EMI MARC 5* 4 9
24 Nov 73 **TRUCK ON (TYKE)** *EMI MARC 6* 12 11
9 Feb 74 **TEENAGE DREAM** *EMI MARC 7* [2] 13 5
13 Jul 74 **LIGHT OF LOVE** *EMI MARC 8* 22 5
16 Nov 74 **ZIP GUN BOOGIE** *EMI MARC 9* 41 3
12 Jul 75 **NEW YORK CITY** *EMI MARC 10* 15 8
11 Oct 75 **DREAMY LADY** *EMI MARC 11* [3] 30 5
6 Mar 76 **LONDON BOYS** *EMI MARC 13* 40 3
19 Jun 76 **I LOVE TO BOOGIE** *EMI MARC 14* 13 9
2 Oct 76 **LASER LOVE** *EMI MARC 15* 41 4
2 Apr 77 **THE SOUL OF MY SUIT** *EMI MARC 16* 42 3
9 May 81 **RETURN OF THE ELECTRIC WARRIOR (EP)** *Rarn MBSF 001* [4] 50 4
19 Sep 81 **YOU SCARE ME TO DEATH** *Cherry Red CHERRY 29* [4] 51 4
18 May 85 **MEGAREX** *Marc on Wax TANX 1* [2] 72 2
9 May 87 **GET IT ON (re-mix)** *Marc on Wax MARC 10* [2] 54 4
24 Aug 91 **20TH CENTURY BOY (re-issue)** *Marc on Wax MARC 501* [2] 13 8
7 Oct 00 **GET IT ON** *All Around the World CDGLOBE 225* [5] 59 1
13 Jul 68 **MY PEOPLE WERE FAIR AND HAD SKY IN THEIR HAIR BUT NOW THEY'RE CONTENT TO WEAR STARS ON THEIR BROWS** *Regal Zonophone SLRZ 1003* [1] 15 9
7 Jun 69 **UNICORN** *Regal Zonophone S 1007* [1] 12 3
14 Mar 70 **A BEARD OF STARS** *Regal Zonophone SLRZ 1013* [1] 21 6
16 Jan 71 ● **T. REX** *Fly HIFLY 2* 7 25
27 Mar 71 **THE BEST OF T. REX** *Flyback TON 2* 21 8
9 Oct 71 ★ **ELECTRIC WARRIOR** *Fly HIFLY 6* 1 44
29 Mar 72 ★ **PROPHETS SEERS & SAGES THE ANGELS OF THE AGES / MY PEOPLE WERE FAIR ...** *Fly Double Back TOOFA 3/4* [1] 1 12
20 May 72 ★ **BOLAN BOOGIE** *Fly HIFLY 8* ■ 1 19
5 Aug 72 ● **THE SLIDER** *EMI BLN 5001* 4 18
9 Dec 72 **A BEARD OF STARS / UNICORN (re-issue)** *Cube TOOFA 9/10* [1] 44 2
31 Mar 73 ● **TANX** *EMI BLN 5002* 4 12
10 Nov 73 **GREAT HITS** *EMI BLN 5003* 32 3
16 Mar 74 **ZINC ALLOY AND THE HIDDEN RIDERS OF TOMORROW** *EMI BLNA 7751* [2] 12 3
21 Feb 76 **FUTURISTIC DRAGON** *EMI BLN 5004* 50 1
9 Apr 77 **DANDY IN THE UNDERWORLD** *EMI BLN 5005* 26 3
30 Jun 79 **SOLID GOLD** *EMI NUT 5* 51 3
12 Sep 81 **T. REX IN CONCERT** *Marc ABOLAN 1* 35 6
7 Nov 81 **YOU SCARE ME TO DEATH** *Cherry Red ERED 20* [3] 88 1
24 Sep 83 **DANCE IN THE MIDNIGHT** *Marc On Wax MARCL 501* [3] 83 3
4 May 85 ● **BEST OF THE 20TH CENTURY BOY** *K-Tel NE 1297* [2] 5 21
28 Sep 91 ● **THE ULTIMATE COLLECTION** *Telstar TCD 2539* [2] 4 16
7 Oct 95 **THE ESSENTIAL COLLECTION** *PolyGram TV 5259612* [2] 24 8
28 Sep 02 **THE ESSENTIAL COLLECTION – 25TH ANNIVERSARY EDITION** *Universal TV 4934882* [2] 18 8

[1] Tyrannosaurus Rex [2] Marc Bolan and T. Rex [3] T. Rex Disco Party [4] Marc Bolan [5] Bus Stop featuring T. Rex
[1] Tyrannosaurus Rex [2] Marc Bolan and T. Rex [3] Marc Bolan

'Telegram Sam' re-entered making No.69 in Mar 1982. Tracks on Return of the Electric Warrior (EP): Sing Me a Song / Endless Sleep Extended / The Lilac Hand of Menthol Dan. Megarex is a medley of extracts from the following T. Rex hits: Truck On (Tyke) / The Groover / Telegram Sam / Shock Rock / Metal Guru / 20th Century Boy / Children of the Revolution / Hot Love 'Prophets ...'/'My People ...' is a double re-issue although 'Prophets ...' had not previously been a hit

TSD *UK, female vocal group (Singles: 2 weeks)* pos/wks

17 Feb 96 **HEART AND SOUL** *Avex UK AVEXCD 21* 69 1
30 Mar 96 **BABY I LOVE YOU** *Avex UK AVEXCD 34* 64 1

T-SHIRT *UK, female vocal duo (Singles: 1 week)* pos/wks

13 Sep 97 **YOU SEXY THING** *Eternal WEA 122CD* 63 1

T-SPOON *Holland, male / female vocal / instrumental group (Singles: 15 weeks)* pos/wks

19 Sep 98 ● **SEX ON THE BEACH** *Control 0042395 CON* 2 13
23 Jan 99 **TOM'S PARTY** *Control 0043505 CON* 27 2

T2 featuring Robin S
US, male production duo with female vocalist (Singles: 1 week) pos/wks

4 Oct 97 **YOU GOT THE LOVE** *Champion CHAMPCD 330* 62 1

TWA
UK, male instrumental / production group (Singles: 1 week) pos/wks

16 Sep 95 **NASTY GIRLS** *Mercury MERCD 441* 51 1

TABERNACLE
UK, male instrumental / production group (Singles: 2 weeks) pos/wks

4 Mar 95 **I KNOW THE LORD** *Good Groove CDGG 1* 62 1
3 Feb 96 **I KNOW THE LORD (re-mix)** *Good Groove CDGGX 1* 55 1

TACKHEAD
US / UK, male vocal / production / rap group (Singles: 3 weeks) pos/wks

30 Jun 90 **DANGEROUS SEX** *SBK SBK 7014* 48 3

TAFFY
UK, female vocalist – Catherine Quaye (Singles: 14 weeks) pos/wks

10 Jan 87 ● **I LOVE MY RADIO (MY DEE JAY'S RADIO)** *Transglobal TYPE 1* ..6 10
18 Jul 87 **STEP BY STEP** *Transglobal TYPE 5* 59 4

TAG TEAM
US, male rap duo – Cecil Glenn and Steve Gibson (Singles: 8 weeks) pos/wks

8 Jan 94 **WHOOMP! (THERE IT IS)** *Club Tools SHXCD 1* 34 5
29 Jan 94 **ADDAMS FAMILY (WHOOMP!)** *Atlas PZCD 305* 53 1
10 Sep 94 **WHOOMP! (THERE IT IS) (re-mix)** *Club Tools SHXR 1* 48 2

See also QUAD CITY DJs

Caddillac TAH – *See JA RULE; Jennifer LOPEZ*

TAIKO *Germany, male DJ / production duo – Oliver Huntemann and Stephan Bodzin (Singles: 1 week)* pos/wks

29 Jun 02 **SILENCE** *Nukleuz NUKC 0330* 72 1

TAK TIX
US, male / female vocal / production group (Singles: 2 weeks) pos/wks

20 Jan 96 **FEEL LIKE SINGING** *A&M 5813212* 33 2

TAKE 5 *US, male vocal group (Singles: 4 weeks)*

Date		Title / Label	pos	wks
7 Nov 98		I GIVE *Edel 0039635 ERE*	70	1
27 Mar 99		NEVER HAD IT SO GOOD *Edel 0039355 ERE*	34	3

TAKE THAT (122 Top 500)

Record-breaking British boy band: Robbie Williams (v), Gary Barlow (v), Jason Orange (v), Howard Donald (v), Mark Owen (v). They were the first artists since The Beatles to score four consecutive chart-toppers, and the first act to release eight singles entering at No.1. Robbie Williams departed in July 1995 and Gary Barlow dissolved the band in Feb 1996 having sold nine million albums and 10 million singles. Best-selling single: 'Back for Good' 959,582 (Singles: 158 weeks, Albums: 228 weeks)

Date		Title / Label	pos	wks
23 Nov 91		PROMISES *RCA PB 45085*	38	2
8 Feb 92		ONCE YOU'VE TASTED LOVE *RCA PB 45257*	47	3
6 Jun 92	●	IT ONLY TAKES A MINUTE *RCA 74321101007*	7	8
15 Aug 92		I FOUND HEAVEN *RCA 74321108137*	15	6
10 Oct 92	●	A MILLION LOVE SONGS *RCA 74321116307*	7	9
12 Dec 92	●	COULD IT BE MAGIC *RCA 74321123137*	3	12
20 Feb 93	●	WHY CAN'T I WAKE UP WITH YOU *RCA 74321133102*	2	10
17 Jul 93	★	PRAY *RCA 74321154502* ■	1	11
9 Oct 93	★	RELIGHT MY FIRE *RCA 74321167722* [1] ■	1	14
18 Dec 93	★	BABE *RCA 74321182122* ■	1	10
9 Apr 94	★	EVERYTHING CHANGES *RCA 74321167732* ■	1	10
9 Jul 94	●	LOVE AIN'T HERE ANYMORE (re) *RCA 74321214832*	3	12
15 Oct 94	★	SURE *RCA 74321236622* ■	1	15
8 Apr 95	★	BACK FOR GOOD *RCA 74321271462* ■	1	13
5 Aug 95	★	NEVER FORGET *RCA 74321299572* ■	1	9
9 Mar 96	★	HOW DEEP IS YOUR LOVE (re) *RCA 74321355592* ■	1	14
5 Sep 92	●	TAKE THAT & PARTY *RCA 74321109232*	2	73
23 Oct 93	★	EVERYTHING CHANGES *RCA 74321169262* ■	1	78
13 May 95	★	NOBODY ELSE *RCA 74321279092* ■	1	33
26 Aug 95		NOBODY ELSE (import) *Arista 07822188002*	26	4
6 Apr 96	★	GREATEST HITS *RCA 74321355582* ■	1	40

[1] Take That featuring Lulu

Billy TALBOT – *See Ian McNABB*

TALI

New Zealand, female DJ / producer (Singles: 1 week)

Date		Title / Label	pos	wks
10 Aug 02		LYRIC ON MY LIP *Full Cycle FCY 042*	75	1

TALISMAN P featuring Barrington LEVY

UK, male producer and Jamaica, male vocalist (Singles: 2 weeks)

Date		Title / Label	pos	wks
13 Oct 01		HERE I COME (SING DJ) *Nulife / Arista 74321895622*	37	2

TALK TALK (416 Top 500)

London-based synth-pop band which rapidly evolved into organic, reflective rock group; Mark Hollis (v/g/k), Paul Webb (b) and Lee Harris (d). Act, who had several legal wrangles with EMI, also scored four Top 20 singles in Italy (Singles: 74 weeks, Albums: 86 weeks)

Date		Title / Label	pos	wks
24 Apr 82		TALK TALK *EMI 5284*	52	4
24 Jul 82		TODAY *EMI 5314*	14	13
13 Nov 82		TALK TALK (re-mix) *EMI 5352*	23	10
19 Mar 83		MY FOOLISH FRIEND *EMI 5373*	57	3
14 Jan 84		IT'S MY LIFE *EMI 5443*	46	5
7 Apr 84		SUCH A SHAME *EMI 5433*	49	6
11 Aug 84		DUM DUM GIRL *EMI 5480*	74	1
18 Jan 86		LIFE'S WHAT YOU MAKE IT *EMI EMI 5540*	16	9
15 Mar 86		LIVING IN ANOTHER WORLD *EMI EMI 5551*	48	4
17 May 86		GIVE IT UP *Parlophone R 6131*	59	3
19 May 90		IT'S MY LIFE (re-issue) *Parlophone R 6254*	13	9
1 Sep 90		LIFE'S WHAT YOU MAKE IT (re-issue) *Parlophone R 6264*	23	6
21 Jun 03		IT'S MY LIFE (re-mix) *Nebula NEBCD 045* [1]	64	1
24 Jul 82		THE PARTY'S OVER *EMI EMC 3413*	21	25
25 Feb 84		IT'S MY LIFE *EMI EMC 2400021*	35	8
1 Mar 86	●	THE COLOUR OF SPRING *EMI EMC 3506*	8	21
24 Sep 88		SPIRIT OF EDEN *Parlophone PCSD 105*	19	5
9 Jun 90	●	THE VERY BEST OF TALK TALK – NATURAL HISTORY *Parlophone PCSD 109*	3	21
6 Apr 91		HISTORY REVISITED – THE REMIXES *Parlophone PCS 7349*	35	2
28 Sep 91		LAUGHING STOCK *Verve 8477171*	26	2
8 Feb 97		THE VERY BEST OF TALK TALK *EMI CDEMC 3763*	54	2

[1] Liquid People vs Talk Talk

See also Beth GIBBONS & RUSTIN' MAN

TALKING HEADS (205 Top 500)

Unorthodox US 'punk funk' eccentrics, formed 1974, New York. Tina Weymouth (b) and husband Chris Frantz (d) had successful side project, Tom Tom Club, while Scottish-born front man David Byrne (v,g) went solo and won an Oscar for his soundtrack to The Last Emperor (Singles: 54 weeks, Albums: 232 weeks)

Date		Title / Label	pos	wks
7 Feb 81		ONCE IN A LIFETIME *Sire SIR 4048*	14	10
9 May 81		HOUSES IN MOTION *Sire SIR 4050*	50	3
21 Jan 84		THIS MUST BE THE PLACE *Sire W 9451*	51	3
3 Nov 84		SLIPPERY PEOPLE *EMI 5504*	68	2
12 Oct 85	●	ROAD TO NOWHERE *EMI EMI 5530*	6	16
8 Feb 86		AND SHE WAS *EMI EMI 5543*	17	8
6 Sep 86		WILD WILD LIFE *EMI EMI 5567*	43	4
16 May 87		RADIO HEAD *EMI EM 1*	52	2
13 Aug 88		BLIND *EMI EM 68*	59	3
10 Oct 92		LIFETIME PILING UP *EMI EM 250*	50	3
25 Feb 78		TALKING HEADS '77 *Sire 9103 328*	60	1
29 Jul 78		MORE SONGS ABOUT BUILDINGS AND FOOD *Sire K 56531*	21	3
15 Sep 79		FEAR OF MUSIC *Sire SRK 6076*	33	5
1 Nov 80		REMAIN IN LIGHT *Sire SRK 6095*	21	17
10 Apr 82		THE NAME OF THIS BAND IS TALKING HEADS *Sire SRK 23590*	22	5
18 Jun 83		SPEAKING IN TONGUES *Sire K 923 8831*	21	12
27 Oct 84		STOP MAKING SENSE *EMI TAH 1*	24	84
29 Jun 85	●	LITTLE CREATURES *EMI TAH 2*	10	65
27 Sep 86	●	TRUE STORIES *EMI EU 3511*	7	9
26 Mar 88	●	NAKED *EMI EMD 1005*	3	15
24 Oct 92	●	ONCE IN A LIFETIME – THE BEST OF TALKING HEADS / SAND IN THE VASELINE *EMI CDEQ 5010*	7	16

See also HEADS with Shaun RYDER; David BYRNE

TALL PAUL

UK, male DJ / producer – Paul Newman (Singles: 15 weeks)

Date		Title / Label	pos	wks
29 Mar 97		ROCK DA HOUSE *VC Recordings VCRD 18*	12	4
29 May 99		BE THERE *Duty Free DF 009CD*	45	1
8 Apr 00		FREEBASE *Duty Free DF 015CD*	43	2
2 Jun 01		ROCK DA HOUSE (re-mix) *VC Recordings VCRD 89*	29	2
18 Aug 01		PRECIOUS HEART (re) *Duty Free / Decode DFTELCD 001* [1]	14	5
13 Apr 02		EVERYBODY'S A ROCKSTAR *Duty Free / Decode DFTELCD 003*	60	1

[1] Tall Paul vs Inxs

See also CAMISRA; ESCRIMA; PARTIZAN; GRIFTERS; Paul NEWMAN

TAMBA TRIO

Argentina, male vocal / instrumental group (Singles: 2 weeks)

Date		Title / Label	pos	wks
18 Jul 98		MAS QUE NADA *Talkin Loud TLCD 34*	34	2

TAMIA – *See FABOLOUS*

TAMPERER featuring MAYA

Italy, male production duo – Alex Farolfi and Mario Fargetta – and female vocalist (Singles: 38 weeks)

Date		Title / Label	pos	wks
25 Apr 98	★	FEEL IT *Pepper 0530032*	1	17
14 Nov 98	●	IF YOU BUY THIS RECORD YOUR LIFE WILL BE BETTER *Pepper 0530082*	3	14
12 Feb 00	●	HAMMER TO THE HEART (re) *Pepper 9230032*	6	7

See also FARGETTA

TAMS *US, male vocal group – lead vocal Joseph Pope (Singles: 31 weeks)*

Date		Title / Label	pos	wks
14 Feb 70		BE YOUNG, BE FOOLISH, BE HAPPY *Stateside SS 2123*	32	7
31 Jul 71	★	HEY GIRL DON'T BOTHER ME *Probe PRO 532*	1	17
21 Nov 87		THERE AIN'T NOTHING LIKE SHAGGIN' *Virgin VS 1029*	21	7

Norma TANEGA

US, female vocalist (Singles: 8 weeks) pos/wks

			pos	wks
7 Apr 66		**WALKIN' MY CAT NAMED DOG** *Stateside SS 496*	22	8

TANGERINE DREAM

Germany, male instrumental group (Albums: 77 weeks) pos/wks

			pos	wks
20 Apr 74		**PHAEDRA** *Virgin V 2010*	15	15
5 Apr 75		**RUBYCON** *Virgin V 2025*	12	14
20 Dec 75		**RICOCHET** *Virgin V 2044*	40	2
13 Nov 76		**STRATOSFEAR** *Virgin V 2068*	39	4
23 Jul 77		**SORCERER (FILM SOUNDTRACK)** *MCA MCF 2806*	25	7
19 Nov 77		**ENCORE** *Virgin VD 2506*	55	1
1 Apr 78		**CYCLONE** *Virgin V 2097*	37	4
17 Feb 79		**FORCE MAJEURE** *Virgin V 2111*	26	7
7 Jun 80		**TANGRAM** *Virgin V 2147*	36	5
18 Apr 81		**THIEF (FILM SOUNDTRACK)** *Virgin V 2198*	43	3
19 Sep 81		**EXIT** *Virgin V 2212*	43	5
10 Apr 82		**WHITE EAGLE** *Virgin V 2226*	57	5
5 Nov 83		**HYPERBOREA** *Virgin V 2292*	45	2
10 Nov 84		**POLAND** *Jive Electro HIP 22*	90	1
26 Jul 86		**UNDERWATER SUNLIGHT** *Jive Electro HIP 40*	97	1
27 Jun 87		**TYGER** *Jive Electro HIP 47*	88	1

TANK

UK, male vocal / instrumental group (Albums: 5 weeks) pos/wks

			pos	wks
13 Mar 82		**FILTH HOUNDS OF HADES** *Kamaflage KAMLP 1*	33	5

Children of TANSLEY SCHOOL

UK, children's choir (Singles: 4 weeks) pos/wks

			pos	wks
28 Mar 81		**MY MUM IS ONE IN A MILLION** *EMI 5151*	27	4

Jimmy TARBUCK

UK, male comedian / vocalist (Singles: 2 weeks) pos/wks

			pos	wks
16 Nov 85		**AGAIN (re)** *Safari SAFE 68*	68	2

TARLISA – *See CO-RO featuring TARLISA*

Bill TARMEY

UK, male actor / vocalist (Singles: 9 weeks, Albums: 25 weeks) pos/wks

			pos	wks
3 Apr 93		**ONE VOICE** *Arista 74321140852*	16	4
19 Feb 94		**WIND BENEATH MY WINGS** *EMI CDEM 304*	40	3
19 Nov 94		**IOU** *EMI CDEM 361*	55	2
27 Nov 93		**A GIFT OF LOVE** *EMI CDEMC 3665*	15	14
5 Nov 94		**TIME FOR LOVE** *EMI CDEMTV 85*	28	9
18 May 96		**AFTER HOURS** *EMI Premier PRMTVCD 2*	61	2

'One Voice' features backing vocals by St Winifred's School Choir

TARRIERS *US, male vocal / instrumental group (Singles: 6 weeks)* pos/wks

			pos	wks
14 Dec 56		**CINDY, OH CINDY** *London HLN 8340* [1]	26	1
1 Mar 57		**THE BANANA BOAT SONG** *Columbia DB 3891*	15	5

[1] Vince Martin and The Tarriers

TARTAN ARMY *UK, male vocal ensemble (Singles: 4 weeks)* pos/wks

			pos	wks
6 Jun 98		**SCOTLAND BE GOOD** *The Precious JWLCD 33*	54	4

TASTE

Ireland, male vocal / instrumental group (Albums: 16 weeks) pos/wks

			pos	wks
7 Feb 70		**ON THE BOARDS** *Polydor 583083*	18	11
6 Mar 71		**LIVE TASTE** *Polydor 2310 082*	14	4
9 Sep 72		**LIVE AT THE ISLE OF WIGHT** *Polydor 2383 120*	41	1

See also Rory GALLAGHER

A TASTE OF HONEY *US, female vocal duo – Janice Marie Johnson and Hazel Payne (Singles: 19 weeks)* pos/wks

			pos	wks
17 Jun 78	●	**BOOGIE OOGIE OOGIE** *Capitol CL 15988* ▲	3	16
18 May 85		**BOOGIE OOGIE OOGIE (re-mix)** *Capitol CL 357*	59	3

TASTE XPERIENCE featuring Natasha PEARL

UK, male instrumental / production group and UK, female vocalist (Singles: 1 week) pos/wks

			pos	wks
6 Nov 99		**SUMMERSAULT** *Manifesto FESCD 64*	66	1

TATA BOX INHIBITORS

Holland, male production duo (Singles: 1 week) pos/wks

			pos	wks
3 Feb 01		**FREET** *Hooj Choons HOOJ 103CD*	67	1

Jeffrey TATE – *See Nigel KENNEDY*

TATJANA

Croatia, female vocalist – Tatjana Simic (Singles: 2 weeks) pos/wks

			pos	wks
21 Sep 96		**SANTA MARIA** *Love This LUVTHISCDX 4*	40	2

t.A.T.u. *Russia, female vocal duo – Julia Volkova and Lena Katina (Singles: 25 weeks, Albums: 15 weeks)* pos/wks

			pos	wks
25 Jan 03		**ALL THE THINGS SHE SAID (import)** *Interscope 0193332*	44	2
8 Feb 03	★	**ALL THE THINGS SHE SAID** *Interscope 0196972* ■	1	15
31 May 03	●	**NOT GONNA GET US** *Interscope 9806961*	7	8
25 Jan 03		**200 KMH IN THE WRONG LANE** *Interscope / Polydor 0674562*	12	15

TAVARES

US, male vocal group – Antone, 'Chubby', Ralph, Feliciano, Arthur Lee and Perry Lee Tavares (Singles: 77 weeks, Albums: 15 weeks) pos/wks

			pos	wks
10 Jul 76	●	**HEAVEN MUST BE MISSING AN ANGEL** *Capitol CL 15876*	4	11
9 Oct 76	●	**DON'T TAKE AWAY THE MUSIC** *Capitol CL 15886*	4	10
5 Feb 77		**THE MIGHTY POWER OF LOVE** *Capitol CL 15905*	25	6
9 Apr 77	●	**WHODUNIT** *Capitol CL 15914*	5	10
2 Jul 77		**ONE STEP AWAY** *Capitol CL 15930*	16	7
18 Mar 78		**THE GHOST OF LOVE** *Capitol CL 15968*	29	6
6 May 78	●	**MORE THAN A WOMAN** *Capitol CL 15977*	7	11
12 Aug 78		**SLOW TRAIN TO PARADISE** *Capitol CL 15996*	62	3
22 Feb 86		**HEAVEN MUST BE MISSING AN ANGEL (re-mix)** *Capitol TAV 1*	12	9
3 May 86		**IT ONLY TAKES A MINUTE** *Capitol TAV 2*	46	4
21 Aug 76		**SKY HIGH** *Capitol EST 11533*	22	13
1 Apr 78		**THE BEST OF TAVARES** *Capitol EST 11701*	39	2

TAXMAN – *See KICKING BACK with TAXMAN*

TAYLOR – *See LIBRA presents TAYLOR*

Andy TAYLOR *UK, male vocalist / instrumentalist – guitar (Singles: 2 weeks, Albums: 1 week)* pos/wks

			pos	wks
20 Oct 90		**LOLA** *A&M AM 596*	60	2
30 May 87		**THUNDER** *MCA MCG 6018*	61	1

See also DURAN DURAN

Becky TAYLOR

UK, female vocalist (Singles: 1 week, Albums: 1 week) pos/wks

			pos	wks
16 Jun 01		**SONG OF DREAMS** *EMI Classics 8794880*	60	1
23 Jun 01		**A DREAM COME TRUE** *EMI Classics CDC 5571422*	67	1

Dina TAYLOR – *See BBG*

Felice TAYLOR *US, female vocalist (Singles: 13 weeks)* pos/wks

			pos	wks
25 Oct 67		**I FEEL LOVE COMIN' ON** *President PT 155*	11	13

James TAYLOR (500 Top 500) *Legendary US singer / songwriter / guitarist, b. 12 Mar 1948, Boston. First American on Beatles' Apple label has a Top 10 album span of 33 years. Inducted into the Songwriters and Rock and Roll Halls of Fame in 2000 (Singles: 18 weeks, Albums: 122 weeks)* pos/wks

			pos	wks
21 Nov 70		**FIRE AND RAIN** *Warner Bros. WB 6104*	42	3
28 Aug 71	●	**YOU'VE GOT A FRIEND** *Warner Bros. WB 16085* ▲	4	15
21 Nov 70	●	**SWEET BABY JAMES** *Warner Bros. ES 1843*	6	53
29 May 71	●	**MUD SLIDE SLIM AND THE BLUE HORIZON** *Warner Bros. WS 2561*	4	41

8 Jan 72	**SWEET BABY JAMES (re-issue)** *Warner Bros. K 46043*	34	6
18 Mar 72	**MUD SLIDE SLIM AND THE BLUE HORIZON (re-issue)** *Warner Bros. K 46085*	49	1
9 Dec 72	**ONE MAN DOG** *Warner Bros. K 46185*	27	5
4 Apr 87	**CLASSIC SONGS** *CBS/WEA JTV 1*	53	5
21 Jun 97	**HOURGLASS** *Columbia 4877482*	46	1
24 Aug 02	**OCTOBER ROAD** *Columbia 5032922*	39	3
13 Sep 03 ●	**YOU'VE GOT A FRIEND – THE BEST OF JAMES TAYLOR** *Warner Bros. 8122738372*	4	7

JAMES TAYLOR QUARTET *See JTQ*

John TAYLOR *UK, male vocalist (Singles: 4 weeks)* pos/wks

15 Mar 86	**I DO WHAT I DO . . . THEME FOR '9 1/2 WEEKS'** *Parlophone R 6125*	42	4

See also DURAN DURAN

Johnnie TAYLOR *US, male vocalist, d. 13 May 2000 (7 weeks)* pos/wks

24 Apr 76	**DISCO LADY** *CBS 4044* ▲	25	7

JT TAYLOR *US, male vocalist (Singles: 5 weeks)* pos/wks

24 Aug 91	**LONG HOT SUMMER NIGHT** *MCA MCS 1567*	63	2
30 Nov 91	**FEEL THE NEED** *MCA MCS 1592*	57	1
18 Apr 92	**FOLLOW ME** *MCA MCS 1617*	59	2

See also KOOL and the GANG

Pauline TAYLOR *UK, female vocalist (Singles: 3 weeks)* pos/wks

8 Jun 96	**LET THIS BE A PRAYER** *Cheeky CHEKCD 013* [1]	26	2
9 Nov 96	**CONSTANTLY WAITING** *Cheeky CHEKCD 015*	51	1

[1] Rollo Goes Spiritual with Pauline Taylor

R Dean TAYLOR *Canada, male vocalist (Singles: 48 weeks)* pos/wks

19 Jun 68	**GOTTA SEE JANE** *Tamla Motown TMG 656*	17	12
3 Apr 71 ●	**INDIANA WANTS ME** *Tamla Motown TMG 763*	2	15
11 May 74 ●	**THERE'S A GHOST IN MY HOUSE** *Tamla Motown TMG 896*	3	12
31 Aug 74	**WINDOW SHOPPING** *Polydor 2058 502*	36	5
21 Sep 74	**GOTTA SEE JANE (re-issue)** *Tamla Motown TMG 918*	41	4

Rob TAYLOR – *See Mathias WARE featuring Rob TAYLOR*

Roger TAYLOR *UK, male vocalist / instrumentalist – drums (Singles: 18 weeks, Albums: 11 weeks)* pos/wks

18 Apr 81	**FUTURE MANAGEMENT** *EMI 5157*	49	4
16 Jun 84	**MAN ON FIRE** *EMI 5478*	66	2
10 Oct 92	**RADIO** *Epic 6584367* [1]	37	3
14 May 94	**NAZIS** *Parlophone CDR 6379*	22	2
1 Oct 94	**FOREIGN SAND** *Parlophone CDR 6389* [2]	26	2
26 Nov 94	**HAPPINESS** *Parlophone CDR 6399*	32	2
10 Oct 98	**PRESSURE ON** *Parlophone CDR 6507*	45	1
10 Apr 99	**SURRENDER** *Parlophone CDR 6517*	38	2
18 Apr 81	**FUN IN SPACE** *EMI EMC 3369*	18	5
7 Jul 84	**STRANGE FRONTIER** *EMI RTA 1*	30	4
17 Sep 94	**HAPPINESS?** *Parlophone CDPCSD 157*	22	1
10 Oct 98	**ELECTRIC FIRE** *Parlophone 4967242*	53	1

[1] Shaky featuring Roger Taylor [2] Roger Taylor and Yoshiki

See also QUEEN

TAZ – *STEREO NATION*

Kiri TE KANAWA *New Zealand, female vocalist (Singles: 11 weeks, Albums: 53 weeks)* pos/wks

28 Sep 91 ●	**WORLD IN UNION** *Columbia 6574817*	4	11
2 Apr 83	**CHANTS D'AUVERGNE VOLUME 1** *Decca SXDL 7604* [1]	57	1
26 Oct 85	**BLUE SKIES** *London KTKT 1* [2]	40	29
13 Dec 86	**CHRISTMAS WITH KIRI** *Decca PROLP 12*	47	4
17 Dec 88	**KIRI** *K-Tel NE 1424*	70	3
29 Feb 92	**THE ESSENTIAL KIRI** *Decca 4362862*	23	10
23 May 92	**KIRI SIDETRACKS THE JAZZ ALBUM** *Philips 4340922*	73	1
9 Apr 94	**KIRI!** *PolyGram 4436002*	16	4
10 Nov 01	**KIRI – THE DEFINITIVE COLLECTION** *EMI Classics CDC 5572312*	73	1

[1] Kiri Te Kanawa with the English Chamber Orchestra [2] Kiri Te Kanawa with the Nelson Riddle Orchestra

TEACH-IN *Holland, male / female vocal / instrumental group (Singles: 7 weeks)* pos/wks

12 Apr 75	**DING-A-DONG** *Polydor 2058 570*	13	7

TEAM *UK, male vocal / instrumental group (Singles: 5 weeks)* pos/wks

1 Jun 85	**WICKI WACKY HOUSE PARTY** *EMI 5519*	55	5

TEAM DEEP *Belgium, male production duo (Singles: 1 week)* pos/wks

17 May 97	**MORNINGLIGHT** *Multiply CDMULTY 19*	42	1

TEARDROP EXPLODES *UK, male vocal / instrumental group (Singles: 50 weeks, Albums: 45 weeks)* pos/wks

27 Sep 80	**WHEN I DREAM** *Mercury TEAR 1*	47	6
31 Jan 81 ●	**REWARD** *Vertigo TEAR 2*	6	13
2 May 81	**TREASON (IT'S JUST A STORY)** *Mercury TEAR 3*	18	8
29 Aug 81	**PASSIONATE FRIEND** *Zoo / Mercury TEAR 5*	25	10
21 Nov 81	**COLOURS FLY AWAY** *Mercury TEAR 6*	54	3
19 Jun 82	**TINY CHILDREN** *Mercury TEAR 7*	44	7
19 Mar 83	**YOU DISAPPEAR FROM VIEW** *Mercury TEAR 8*	41	3
18 Oct 80	**KILIMANJARO** *Mercury 6359 035*	24	35
5 Dec 81	**WILDER** *Mercury 6359 056*	29	6
14 Apr 90	**EVERYBODY WANTS TO SHAG ... THE TEARDROP EXPLODES** *Fontana 8424391 72*	72	1
15 Aug 92	**FLOORED GENIUS – THE BEST OF JULIAN COPE AND THE TEARDROP EXPLODES** *Island CID 8000* [1]	22	3

[1] Julian Cope and the Teardrop Explodes

See also Julian COPE

TEARS FOR FEARS (143 Top 500) *Bath-based band at the forefront of the mid-1980s 'British Invasion' of the US: Roland Orzabal (v/g/k), Curt Smith (v/b; left in 1991). The first of their two US No.1s, 'Everybody Wants to Rule the World', also won the 1986 Brit award for Best Single. Duo reunited in 2003 (Singles: 143 weeks, Albums: 210 weeks)* pos/wks

2 Oct 82 ●	**MAD WORLD** *Mercury IDEA 3*	3	16
5 Feb 83 ●	**CHANGE** *Mercury IDEA 4*	4	9
30 Apr 83 ●	**PALE SHELTER** *Mercury IDEA 5*	5	8
3 Dec 83	**THE WAY YOU ARE** *Mercury IDEA 6*	24	8
18 Aug 84	**MOTHER'S TALK** *Mercury IDEA 7*	14	8
1 Dec 84 ●	**SHOUT** *Mercury IDEA 8* ▲	4	16
30 Mar 85 ●	**EVERYBODY WANTS TO RULE THE WORLD (re)** *Mercury IDEA 9* ▲	2	15
22 Jun 85	**HEAD OVER HEELS** *Mercury IDEA 10*	12	9
31 Aug 85	**SUFFER THE CHILDREN** *Mercury IDEA 1*	52	4
7 Sep 85	**PALE SHELTER (re-issue)** *Mercury IDEA 2*	73	2
12 Oct 85	**I BELIEVE (A SOULFUL RE-RECORDING)** *Mercury IDEA 11*	23	4
31 May 86 ●	**EVERYBODY WANTS TO RUN THE WORLD (re)** *Mercury RACE 1*	5	7
2 Sep 89 ●	**SOWING THE SEEDS OF LOVE** *Fontana IDEA 12*	5	9
18 Nov 89	**WOMAN IN CHAINS** *Fontana IDEA 13*	26	8
3 Mar 90	**ADVICE FOR THE YOUNG AT HEART** *Fontana IDEA 14*	36	4
22 Feb 92	**LAID SO LOW (TEARS ROLL DOWN)** *Fontana IDEA 17*	17	5
25 Apr 92	**WOMAN IN CHAINS (re-issue)** *Fontana IDEA 16* [1]	57	1
29 May 93	**BREAK IT DOWN AGAIN** *Mercury IDECD 18*	20	5
31 Jul 93	**COLD** *Mercury IDECD 19*	72	1
7 Oct 95	**RAOUL AND THE KINGS OF SPAIN** *Epic 6624765*	31	3
29 Jun 96	**GOD'S MISTAKE** *Epic 6634185*	61	1
19 Mar 83 ★	**THE HURTING** *Mercury MERS 17*	1	65
9 Mar 85 ●	**SONGS FROM THE BIG CHAIR** *Mercury MERH 58* ▲	2	81
7 Oct 89 ★	**THE SEEDS OF LOVE** *Fontana 838730 1* ■	1	30
14 Mar 92 ●	**TEARS ROLL DOWN (GREATEST HITS 1982-1992)** *Fontana 5109392*	2	26

		pos	wks
19 Jun 93	● **ELEMENTAL** *Mercury 5148752*	5	7
28 Oct 95	**RAOUL AND THE KINGS OF SPAIN** *Epic 4809822*	41	1

[1] Tears for Fears featuring Oleta Adams

Mercury RACE 1 was a slightly changed version of Mercury IDEA 9, released to promote the Race Against Time of 15 May 1986. Oleta Adams is given no label credit on the original release of 'Woman in Chains'. From 1992 Tears for Fears was essentially a male vocalist / multi-instrumentalist Roland Orzabal

See also Johnny PANIC and the BIBLE OF DREAMS

TECHNATION *UK, male production duo (Singles: 1 week)*

		pos	wks
7 Apr 01	**SEA OF BLUE** *Slinky Music SLINKY 012CD*	56	1

TECHNICIAN 2
UK, male instrumental / production group (Singles: 1 week)

		pos	wks
14 Nov 92	**PLAYING WITH THE BOY** *MCA MCS 1710*	70	1

TECHNIQUE
UK, female vocal / instrumental duo (Singles: 2 weeks)

		pos	wks
10 Apr 99	**SUN IS SHINING** *Creation CRESCD 306*	64	1
28 Aug 99	**YOU + ME** *Creation CRESCD 315*	56	1

TECHNO TWINS *UK, male / female vocal duo (Singles: 2 weeks)*

		pos	wks
16 Jan 82	**FALLING IN LOVE AGAIN (re)** *PRT 7P 224*	70	2

TECHNOCAT featuring Tom WILSON
UK, male producer – Tom Wilson (Singles: 3 weeks)

		pos	wks
2 Dec 95	**TECHNOCAT** *Pukka CDPUKKA 4*	33	3

TECHNOHEAD *UK, male / female vocal / instrumental duo – Michael Wells and Lee Newman (Singles: 20 weeks)*

		pos	wks
3 Feb 96	● **I WANNA BE A HIPPY** *Mokum DB 17703*	6	14
27 Apr 96	**HAPPY BIRTHDAY** *Mokum DB 17593*	18	5
12 Oct 96	**BANANA-NA-NA (DUMB DI DUMB)** *Mokum DB 17473*	64	1

See also GTO; TRICKY DISCO

TECHNOTRONIC *Belgium, male producer – Jo Bogaert (Singles: 66 weeks, Albums: 62 weeks)*

		pos	wks
2 Sep 89	● **PUMP UP THE JAM** *Swanyard SYR 4* [1]	2	15
3 Feb 90	● **GET UP (BEFORE THE NIGHT IS OVER)** *Swanyard SYR 8* [2]	2	10
7 Apr 90	**THIS BEAT IS TECHNOTRONIC** *Swanyard SYR 9* [3]	14	7
14 Jul 90	● **ROCKIN' OVER THE BEAT** *Swanyard SYR 14* [2]	9	9
6 Oct 90	● **MEGAMIX** *Swanyard SYR 19*	6	8
15 Dec 90	**TURN IT UP** *Swanyard SYD 9* [4]	42	4
25 May 91	**MOVE THAT BODY** *ARS 6568377* [5]	12	7
3 Aug 91	**WORK** *ARS 6573317* [5]	40	4
14 Dec 96	**PUMP UP THE JAM (re-mix)** *Worx WORXCD 004*	36	2
6 Jan 90	● **PUMP UP THE JAM** *Swanyard SYRLP 1*	2	44
2 Nov 90	● **TRIP ON THIS – REMIXES** *Telstar STAR 2461*	7	14
15 Jun 91	**BODY TO BODY** *ARS 4683421*	27	4

[1] Technotronic featuring Felly [2] Technotronic featuring Ya Kid K
[3] Technotronic featuring MC Eric [4] Technotronic featuring Melissa and Einstein
[5] Technotronic featuring Reggie

See also HI-TEK 3 featuring YA KID K

TEDDY BEARS *US, male / female vocal trio (Singles: 17 weeks)*

		pos	wks
19 Dec 58	● **TO KNOW HIM IS TO LOVE HIM** *London HLN 8733* ▲	2	16
14 Apr 79	**TO KNOW HIM IS TO LOVE HIM (re-issue)** *Lightning LIG 9015*	66	1

'To Know Him Is to Love Him' re-issue was coupled with 'Endless Sleep' by Jody Reynolds as a double A-side. Act was a trio plus Phil Spector

TEEBONE featuring MC KIE and MC SPARKS *UK, male producer – Leon Thompson – and UK, male rap duo (Singles: 2 weeks)*

		pos	wks
5 Aug 00	**FLY BI** *East West EW 217CD*	43	2

TEENAGE FANCLUB *UK, male vocal / instrumental group (Singles: 22 weeks, Albums: 24 weeks)*

		pos	wks
24 Aug 91	**STAR SIGN** *Creation CRE 105*	44	2
2 Nov 91	**THE CONCEPT** *Creation CRE 111*	51	1
8 Feb 92	**WHAT YOU DO TO ME (EP)** *Creation CRE 115*	31	2
26 Jun 93	**RADIO** *Creation CRESCD 130*	31	2
2 Oct 93	**NORMAN 3** *Creation CRESCD 142*	50	1
2 Apr 94	**FALLIN'** *Epic 6602622* [1]	59	1
8 Apr 95	**MELLOW DOUBT** *Creation CRESCD 175*	34	2
27 May 95	**SPARKY'S DREAM** *Creation CRESCD 201*	40	2
2 Sep 95	**NEIL JUNG** *Creation CRESCD 210*	62	1
16 Dec 95	**HAVE LOST IT (EP)** *Creation CRESCD 216*	53	1
12 Jul 97	**AIN'T THAT ENOUGH** *Creation CRESCD 228*	17	3
30 Aug 97	**I DON'T WANT CONTROL OF YOU** *Creation CRESCD 238*	43	1
29 Nov 97	**START AGAIN** *Creation CRESCD 280*	54	1
28 Oct 00	**I NEED DIRECTION** *Columbia 6699512*	48	1
2 Mar 02	**NEAR TO YOU (re-mix)** *Geographic GEOG 013CD* [2]	68	1
7 Sep 91	**THE KING** *Creation CRELP 096*	53	2
16 Nov 91	**BANDWAGONESQUE** *Creation CRELP 106*	22	7
16 Oct 93	**THIRTEEN** *Creation CRECD 144*	14	3
10 Jun 95	● **GRAND PRIX** *Creation CRECD 173*	7	4
2 Aug 97	● **SONGS FROM NORTHERN BRITAIN** *Creation CRECD 196*	3	5
4 Nov 00	**HOWDY!** *Columbia 5006222*	33	2
8 Feb 03	**FOUR THOUSAND SEVEN HUNDRED & SIXTY-SIX** *Poolside POOLS3CDX*	47	1

[1] Teenage Fanclub and De La Soul [2] Teenage Fanclub and Jad Fair

Tracks on What You Do to Me (EP): What You Do to Me / B-Side / Life's a Gas / Filler. Tracks on Have Lost It (EP): Don't Look Back / Everything Flows / Star Sign (re-recorded version of the band's first hit) / 120 mins

TEENAGERS – *See Frankie LYMON and the TEENAGERS*

Towa TEI featuring Kylie MINOGUE *Japan, male DJ / producer and Australia, female vocalist (Singles: 1 week)*

		pos	wks
31 Oct 98	**GBI** *Athrob ART 021CD*	63	1

TEKNO TOO
UK, male instrumental / production duo (Singles: 2 weeks)

		pos	wks
13 Jul 91	**JET-STAR** *D-Zone DANCE 012*	56	2

TELEPOPMUSIK *France, male instrumental / production trio and UK, female vocalist (Singles: 1 week)*

		pos	wks
2 Mar 02	**BREATHE** *Chrysalis CDCHS 5133*	42	1

TELETUBBIES *UK, male / female cuddly alien vocal group (Singles: 32 weeks, Albums: 4 weeks)*

		pos	wks
13 Dec 97	★ **TELETUBBIES SAY EH-OH! (2re)** *BBC Worldwide WMXS 00092* ◆ ■	1	32
4 Apr 98	**THE ALBUM** *BBC Worldwide Music WMXU 00142*	31	4

TELEVISION *US, male vocal / instrumental group (Singles: 10 weeks, Albums: 17 weeks)*

		pos	wks
16 Apr 77	**MARQUEE MOON** *Elektra K 12252*	30	4
30 Jul 77	**PROVE IT** *Elektra K 12262*	25	4
22 Apr 78	**FOXHOLE** *Elektra K 12287*	36	2
26 Mar 77	**MARQUEE MOON** *Elektra K 52046*	28	13
29 Apr 78	● **ADVENTURE** *Elektra K 52072*	7	4

TELEX *Belgium, male vocal / instrumental trio (Singles: 7 weeks)*

		pos	wks
21 Jul 79	**ROCK AROUND THE CLOCK** *Sire SIR 4020*	34	7

Sylvia TELLA – *See BLOW MONKEYS*

TEMPERANCE SEVEN *UK, male vocal / instrumental group – lead vocal Paul MacDowell (Singles: 45 weeks, Albums: 10 weeks)*

		pos	wks
30 Mar 61	★ **YOU'RE DRIVING ME CRAZY** *Parlophone R 4757*	1	16
15 Jun 61	● **PASADENA** *Parlophone R 4781*	4	17
28 Sep 61	**HARD HEARTED HANNAH / CHILI BOM BOM** *Parlophone R 4823*	28	4

7 Dec 61	THE CHARLESTON *Parlophone R 4851*	22	8
13 May 61	TEMPERANCE SEVEN PLUS ONE *Argo RG 11*	19	1
25 Nov 61	● TEMPERANCE SEVEN 1961 *Parlophone PMC 1152*	8	9

'Chili Bom Bom' listed with 'Hard Hearted Hannah' only for the weeks of 12 and 19 Oct 1961

TEMPLE CHURCH CHOIR

UK, male vocal / instrumental group (Albums: 3 weeks) pos/wks

16 Dec 61	● CHRISTMAS CAROLS *HMV CLP 1309*	8	3

TEMPLE OF THE DOG

US, male vocal / instrumental group (Singles: 2 weeks) pos/wks

24 Oct 92	HUNGER STRIKE *A&M AM 0091*	51	2

Nino TEMPO and April STEVENS

US, male / female vocal duo – Antonio and Carol Lo Tempio (Singles: 19 weeks) pos/wks

7 Nov 63	DEEP PURPLE *London HLK 9782* ▲	17	11
16 Jan 64	WHISPERING *London HLK 9829*	20	8

TEMPTATIONS (150 Top 500)

The world's most successful R&B vocal group: Eddie Kendricks (d. 1992), Otis Williams, Paul Williams (d. 1973), Melvin Franklin (d. 1995), David Ruffin (d. 1991). The Detroit quintet's biggest UK hit, 'My Girl', was a 27-year-old US No.1. The current line-up of the group is still doing well Stateside (Singles: 211 weeks, Albums: 137 weeks) pos/wks

18 Mar 65	MY GIRL *Stateside SS 378* ▲	43	1
1 Apr 65	IT'S GROWING (re) *Tamla Motown TMG 504*	45	2
14 Jul 66	AIN'T TOO PROUD TO BEG *Tamla Motown TMG 565*	21	11
6 Oct 66	BEAUTY IS ONLY SKIN DEEP *Tamla Motown TMG 578*	18	10
15 Dec 66	(I KNOW) I'M LOSING YOU *Tamla Motown TMG 587*	19	9
6 Sep 67	YOU'RE MY EVERYTHING *Tamla Motown TMG 620*	26	15
6 Mar 68	I WISH IT WOULD RAIN *Tamla Motown TMG 641*	45	1
12 Jun 68	I COULD NEVER LOVE ANOTHER *Tamla Motown TMG 658*	47	1
29 Jan 69	● I'M GONNA MAKE YOU LOVE ME (re) *Tamla Motown TMG 685* [1]	3	12
5 Mar 69	● GET READY *Tamla Motown TMG 688*	10	9
23 Aug 69	CLOUD NINE *Tamla Motown TMG 707*	15	10
20 Sep 69	I SECOND THAT EMOTION *Tamla Motown TMG 709* [1]	18	8
17 Jan 70	I CAN'T GET NEXT TO YOU *Tamla Motown TMG 722* ▲	13	9
21 Mar 70	WHY (MUST WE FALL IN LOVE) *Tamla Motown TMG 730* [1]	31	7
13 Jun 70	PSYCHEDELIC SHACK *Tamla Motown TMG 741*	33	7
19 Sep 70	● BALL OF CONFUSION (THAT'S WHAT THE WORLD IS TODAY) (re) *Tamla Motown TMG 749*	7	15
22 May 71	● JUST MY IMAGINATION (RUNNING AWAY WITH ME) *Tamla Motown TMG 773* ▲	8	16
5 Feb 72	SUPERSTAR (REMEMBER HOW YOU GOT WHERE YOU ARE) *Tamla Motown TMG 800*	32	5
15 Apr 72	TAKE A LOOK AROUND *Tamla Motown TMG 808*	13	10
13 Jan 73	PAPA WAS A ROLLIN' STONE *Tamla Motown TMG 839* ▲	14	8
29 Sep 73	LAW OF THE LAND *Tamla Motown TMG 866*	41	4
12 Jun 82	STANDING ON THE TOP (PART 1) *Motown TMG 1263* [2]	53	3
17 Nov 84	TREAT HER LIKE A LADY *Motown TMG 1365*	12	10
15 Aug 87	PAPA WAS A ROLLIN' STONE (re-mix) *Motown ZB 41431*	31	6
6 Feb 88	LOOK WHAT YOU STARTED *Motown ZB 41733*	63	2
21 Oct 89	ALL I WANT FROM YOU *Motown ZB 43233*	71	1
15 Jun 91	● THE MOTOWN SONG *Warner Bros. W 0030* [3]	10	8
15 Feb 92	● MY GIRL (re-issue) *Epic 6576767*	2	10
22 Feb 92	THE JONES' *Motown TMG 1403*	69	1
24 Dec 66	GETTING READY *Tamla Motown STML 11035*	40	1
11 Feb 67	TEMPTATIONS GREATEST HITS *Tamla Motown STML 11042*	17	40
22 Jul 67	TEMPTATIONS LIVE! *Tamla Motown STML 11053*	20	4
18 Nov 67	TEMPTATIONS WITH A LOT OF SOUL *Tamla Motown STML 11057*	19	18
25 Jan 69	★ DIANA ROSS AND THE SUPREMES JOIN THE TEMPTATIONS *Tamla Motown STML 11096* [1]	1	15
28 Jun 69	TCB *Tamla Motown STML 11110* [1]	11	12
20 Sep 69	CLOUD NINE *Tamla Motown STML 11109*	32	1
14 Feb 70	PUZZLE PEOPLE *Tamla Motown STML 11133*	20	4
14 Feb 70	TOGETHER *Tamla Motown STML 11122* [1]	28	4
11 Jul 70	PSYCHEDELIC SHACK *Tamla Motown STML 11147*	56	1
26 Dec 70	GREATEST HITS VOLUME 2 *Tamla Motown STML 11170*	28	5
29 Apr 72	SOLID ROCK *Tamla Motown STML 11202*	34	2
20 Jan 73	ALL DIRECTIONS *Tamla Motown STML 11218*	19	7
7 Jul 73	MASTERPIECE *Tamla Motown STML 11229*	28	3
8 Dec 84	TRULY FOR YOU *Motown ZL 72342*	75	5
11 Apr 92	● MOTOWN'S GREATEST HITS *Motown 5300152*	8	9
27 Jan 01	AT THEIR VERY BEST *Universal Music TV 135782*	28	5
30 Mar 02	AT THEIR VERY BEST – TEMPTATIONS / FOUR TOPS *Universal TV 5830142*	18	1

[1] Diana Ross and The Supremes and The Temptations [2] Temptations featuring Rick James [3] Rod Stewart with backing vocals by The Temptations [1] Diana Ross and the Supremes with the Temptations

2002 'At Their Very Best' album appeared only in the UK Compilation Chart and not in the standard Top 75

10cc (144 Top 500)

Multi-talented Manchester supergroup: Graham Gouldman (previously penned hits for Hollies, Yardbirds and Herman's Hermits), Eric Stewart (ex-Mindbenders, Hotlegs), and Lol Creme and Kevin Godley (both ex-Hotlegs). Godley and Creme went on to have hits as a duo and produced award-winning videos (Singles: 133 weeks, Albums: 219 weeks) pos/wks

23 Sep 72	● DONNA *UK 6*	2	13
19 May 73	★ RUBBER BULLETS *UK 36*	1	15
25 Aug 73	● THE DEAN AND I *UK 48*	10	8
15 Jun 74	● THE WALL STREET SHUFFLE *UK 69*	10	10
14 Sep 74	SILLY LOVE *UK 77*	24	7
5 Apr 75	● LIFE IS A MINESTRONE *Mercury 6008 010*	7	8
31 May 75	★ I'M NOT IN LOVE *Mercury 6008 014*	1	11
29 Nov 75	● ART FOR ART'S SAKE *Mercury 6008 017*	5	10
20 Mar 76	● I'M MANDY FLY ME *Mercury 6008 019*	6	9
11 Dec 76	● THE THINGS WE DO FOR LOVE *Mercury 6008 022*	6	11
16 Apr 77	● GOOD MORNING JUDGE *Mercury 6008 025*	5	12
12 Aug 78	★ DREADLOCK HOLIDAY *Mercury 6008 035*	1	13
7 Aug 82	RUN AWAY *Mercury MER 113*	50	4
18 Mar 95	I'M NOT IN LOVE (re-recording) *Avex UK AVEXCD 2*	29	2
1 Sep 73	10 C.C. *UK UKAL 1005*	36	5
15 Jun 74	● SHEET MUSIC *UK UKAL 1007*	9	24
22 Mar 75	● THE ORIGINAL SOUNDTRACK *Mercury 9102 50Q*	4	40
7 Jun 75	● GREATEST HITS OF 10cc *Decca UKAL 1012*	9	18
31 Jan 76	● HOW DARE YOU! *Mercury 9102 501*	5	31
14 May 77	● DECEPTIVE BENDS *Mercury 9102 502*	3	21
10 Dec 77	LIVE AND LET LIVE *Mercury 6641 698*	14	15
23 Sep 78	● BLOODY TOURISTS *Mercury 9102 503*	3	15
6 Oct 79	● GREATEST HITS 1972-1978 *Mercury 9102 504*	5	21
5 Apr 80	LOOK HERE *Mercury 9102 505*	35	5
15 Oct 83	WINDOW IN THE JUNGLE *Mercury MERL 28*	70	2
29 Aug 87	● CHANGING FACES – THE VERY BEST OF 10cc AND GODLEY AND CREME *ProTV TGCLP 1* [1]	4	18
5 Apr 97	THE VERY BEST OF 10cc *Mercury / PolyGram TV 5346122*	37	4

[1] 10cc and Godley and Creme

From 'Things We Do For Love' 10cc were a male vocal / instrumental duo

See also Graham GOULDMAN; WAX; GODLEY and CREME

TEN CITY

US, male vocal / instrumental group – includes Byron Stingily (Singles: 21 weeks, Albums: 12 weeks) pos/wks

21 Jan 89	● THAT'S THE WAY LOVE IS *Atlantic A 8963*	8	10
8 Apr 89	DEVOTION *Atlantic A 8916*	29	4
22 Jul 89	WHERE DO WE GO? *Atlantic A 8864*	60	1
27 Oct 90	WHATEVER MAKES YOU HAPPY *Atlantic A 7819*	60	2
15 Aug 92	ONLY TIME WILL TELL / MY PEACE OF HEAVEN *East West America A 8516*	63	2
11 Sep 93	FANTASY *Columbia 6595042*	45	2
18 Feb 89	FOUNDATION *Atlantic WX 249*	22	12

10 REVOLUTIONS

UK, male production group (Singles: 1 week) pos/wks

30 Aug 03	TIME FOR THE REVOLUTION *Incentive CENT 53CDS*	59	1

TEN SHARP

Holland, male vocal / instrumental duo (Singles: 15 weeks, Albums: 2 weeks) pos/wks

21 Mar 92	● YOU *Columbia 6566647*	10	13

20 Jun 92 **AIN'T MY BEATING HEART** *Columbia 6580947* 63 2
9 May 92 **UNDER THE WATER-LINE** *Columbia 4690702* 46 2

10,000 MANIACS *US, female / male vocal / instrumental group – includes Natalie Merchant (Singles: 7 weeks, Albums: 12 weeks)* pos/wks

12 Sep 92 **THESE ARE DAYS** *Elektra EKR 156* 58 3
10 Apr 93 **CANDY EVERYBODY WANTS** *Elektra EKR 160CD1* 47 3
23 Oct 93 **BECAUSE THE NIGHT** *Elektra EKR 175CD* 65 1
27 May 89 **BLIND MAN'S ZOO** *Elektra EKT 57* 18 8
10 Oct 92 **OUR TIME IN EDEN** *Elektra 7559613852* 33 2
6 Nov 93 **UNPLUGGED** *Elektra 7559615692* 40 2

TEN YEARS AFTER *UK, male vocal / instrumental group (Singles: 18 weeks, Albums: 70 weeks)* pos/wks

6 Jun 70 ● **LOVE LIKE A MAN** *Deram DM 299* 10 18
21 Sep 68 **UNDEAD** *Deram SML 1023* 26 7
22 Feb 69 ● **STONEDHENGE** *Deram SML 1029* 6 5
4 Oct 69 ● **SSSSH** *Deram SML 1052* 4 18
2 May 70 ● **CRICKLEWOOD GREEN** *Deram SML 1065* 4 27
9 Jan 71 ● **WATT** *Deram SML 1078* 5 9
13 Nov 71 **A SPACE IN TIME** *Chrysalis CHR 1001* 36 1
7 Oct 72 **ROCK & ROLL MUSIC TO THE WORLD** *Chrysalis CHR 1009* 27 1
28 Jul 73 **RECORDED LIVE** *Chrysalis CHR 1049* 36 2

TENACIOUS D *US, male vocal / instrumental duo – Jack Black and Kyle Gass (Singles: 2 weeks, Albums: 31 weeks)* pos/wks

23 Nov 02 **WONDERBOY** *Epic 6733512* 34 2
13 Jul 02 **TENACIOUS D** *Epic 5077352* 38 31

Danny TENAGLIA *US, male DJ / producer (Singles: 5 weeks)* pos/wks

5 Sep 98 **MUSIC IS THE ANSWER (DANCIN' AND PRANCIN')** *Twisted UK TWCD 10038* [1] 36 3
10 Apr 99 **TURN ME ON** *Twisted UK TWCD 10045* [2] 53 1
23 Oct 99 **MUSIC IS THE ANSWER (re-mix)** *Twisted UK TWCD 10052* [1] 50 1

[1] Danny Tenaglia and Celeda [2] Danny Tenaglia featuring Liz Torres

TENNESSEE THREE – *See Johnny CASH*

TENOR FLY *UK, male vocalist – Jonathan Sutter (Singles: 17 weeks)* pos/wks

6 Apr 91 **WICKEDEST SOUND** *Desire WANT 40* [1] 43 6
15 Jun 91 **TRIBAL BASE** *Desire WANT 44* [2] 20 6
7 Jan 95 **BRIGHT SIDE OF LIFE** *Mango CIDM 825* 51 2
7 Feb 98 **B-BOY STANCE** *Freskanova FND 7* [3] 23 3

[1] Rebel MC featuring Tenor Fly [2] Rebel MC featuring Tenor Fly and Barrington Levy [3] Freestylers featuring Tenor Fly

TENPOLE TUDOR *UK, male vocal / instrumental group (Singles: 40 weeks, Albums: 8 weeks)* pos/wks

7 Apr 79 ● **WHO KILLED BAMBI** *Virgin VS 256* [1] 6 8
13 Oct 79 **ROCK AROUND THE CLOCK** *Virgin VS 290* 21 6
25 Apr 81 ● **SWORDS OF A THOUSAND MEN** *Stiff BUY 109* 6 12
1 Aug 81 **WUNDERBAR** *Stiff BUY 120* 16 9
14 Nov 81 **THROWING MY BABY OUT WITH THE BATHWATER** *Stiff BUY 129* 49 5
9 May 81 **EDDIE, OLD BOB, DICK & GARRY** *Stiff SEEZ 31* 44 8

[1] Ten Pole Tudor

The listed flip side of 'Who Killed Bambi' was 'Silly Thing' by The Sex Pistols. The listed flip side of 'Rock Around the Clock' was 'The Great Rock 'n' Roll Swindle', also by The Sex Pistols

TENTH PLANET *UK, male / female vocal / production group (Singles: 1 week)* pos/wks

14 Apr 01 **GHOSTS** *Nebula NEBCD 015* 59 1

Bryn TERFEL *UK, male vocalist (Singles: 3 week, Albums: 21 weeks)* pos/wks

23 Oct 99 **WORLD IN UNION** *Universal TV 4669402* [4] 35 3
16 Nov 96 **SOMETHING WONDERFUL** *Deutsche Grammophon 4491632* 72 1
28 Oct 00 **WE'LL KEEP A WELCOME – THE WELSH ALBUM** *Deutsche Grammophon 4635932* 33 10
3 Nov 01 **SOME ENCHANTED EVENING** *Deutsche Grammophon 4714252* 49 2
8 Nov 03 ● **BRYN** *Deutsche Grammophon 4747032* 6 8

[1] Shirley Bassey / Bryn Terfel

TERMINATERS – *See ARNEE and the TERMINATERS*

TERRA DEVA – *See WHO DA FUNK*

TERRA FIRMA *Italy, male producer – Claudio Giussani (Singles: 1 week)* pos/wks

18 May 96 **FLOATING** *Platipus PLAT 21CD* 64 1

TERRAPLANE *UK, male vocal / instrumental group (Albums: 1 week)* pos/wks

25 Jan 86 **BLACK AND WHITE** *Epic EPC 26439* 74 1

Tammi TERRELL – *See Marvin GAYE*

TERRIS *UK, male vocal / instrumental group (Singles: 1 week)* pos/wks

17 Mar 01 **FABRICATED LUNACY** *Blanco Y Negro NEG 130CD* 62 1

TERRORIZE *UK, male producer – Shaun Imrei (Singles: 6 weeks)* pos/wks

2 May 92 **IT'S JUST A FEELING** *Hamster STER 1* 52 3
22 Aug 92 **FEEL THE RHYTHM** *Hamster 12STER 2* 69 1
14 Nov 92 **IT'S JUST A FEELING (re-issue)** *Hamster STER 8* 47 2

TERRORVISION *UK, male vocal / instrumental group (Singles: 55 weeks, Albums: 41 weeks)* pos/wks

19 Jun 93 **AMERICAN TV** *Total Vegas CDVEGAS 3* 63 1
30 Oct 93 **NEW POLICY ONE** *Total Vegas CDVEGAS 4* 42 2
8 Jan 94 **MY HOUSE** *Total Vegas CDVEGAS 5* 29 4
9 Apr 94 **OBLIVION** *Total Vegas CDVEGAS 6* 21 5
25 Jun 94 **MIDDLEMAN** *Total Vegas CDVEGAS 7* 25 4
3 Sep 94 **PRETEND BEST FRIEND** *Total Vegas CDVEGAS 8* 25 3
29 Oct 94 **ALICE WHAT'S THE MATTER** *Total Vegas CDVEGAS 9* 24 4
18 Mar 95 **SOME PEOPLE SAY** *Total Vegas CDVEGAS 10* 22 3
2 Mar 96 ● **PERSEVERANCE** *Total Vegas CDVEGAS 11* 5 4
4 May 96 **CELEBRITY HIT LIST** *Total Vegas CDVEGAS 12* 20 3
20 Jul 96 ● **BAD ACTRESS** *Total Vegas CDVEGAS 13* 10 3
11 Jan 97 **EASY** *Total Vegas CDVEGASS 14* 12 4
3 Oct 98 **JOSEPHINE** *EMI CDVEGAS 15* 23 2
30 Jan 99 ● **TEQUILA** *Total Vegas CDVEGAS 16* 2 10
15 May 99 **III WISHES** *Total Vegas CDVEGAS 17* 42 1
27 Jan 01 **D'YA WANNA GO FASTER** *Papillion BTFLYS 0007* 28 2
15 May 93 **FORMALDEHYDE** *Total Vegas VEGASCD 1* 75 1
30 Apr 94 **HOW TO MAKE FRIENDS AND INFLUENCE PEOPLE** *Total Vegas VEGASCD 2* 18 25
23 Mar 96 ● **REGULAR URBAN SURVIVORS** *Total Vegas VEGASCD 3* 8 12
17 Oct 98 **SHAVING PEACHES** *Total Vegas 4961322* 34 2
17 Feb 01 **GOOD TO GO** *Papillon BTFLYCD 0011* 48 1

Helen TERRY *UK, female vocalist (Singles: 6 weeks)* pos/wks

12 May 84 **LOVE LIES LOST** *Virgin VS 678* 34 6

Todd TERRY *US, male producer (Albums: 1 week)* pos/wks

5 Aug 95 **A DAY IN THE LIFE OF TODD TERRY** *Sound Of Ministry SOMCD 2* 73 1

Tony TERRY *US, male vocalist (Singles: 6 weeks)* pos/wks

27 Feb 88 **LOVEY DOVEY** *Epic TONY 2* 44 6

Todd TERRY PROJECT

US, male producer (Singles: 33 weeks, Albums: 1 week)

		pos	wks
12 Nov 88	**WEEKEND** *Sleeping Bag SBUK 1T*	**56**	3
14 Oct 95	**WEEKEND (re-mix)** *Ore AG 13CD*	**28**	3
13 Jul 96 ●	**KEEP ON JUMPIN'** *Manifesto FESCD 11* [1]	**8**	6
12 Jul 97 ●	**SOMETHING GOIN' ON** *Manifesto FESCD 25* [1]	**5**	10
6 Dec 97	**IT'S OVER LOVE** *Manfiesto FESCD 37* [2]	**16**	8
11 Apr 98	**READY FOR A NEW DAY** *Manifesto FESCD 40* [3]	**20**	2
3 Jul 99	**LET IT RIDE** *Innocent RESTCD 1*	**58**	1
5 Aug 95	**A DAY IN THE LIFE OF TODD TERRY** *Sound of Ministry SOMCD 2* [1]	**73**	1

[1] Todd Terry featuring Martha Wash and Jocelyn Brown [2] Todd Terry presents Shannon [3] Todd Terry featuring Martha Wash [1] Todd Terry

See also BLACK RIOT; ROYAL HOUSE; SWAN LAKE; GYPSYMEN

TESLA *US, male vocal / instrumental group (Singles: 1 week, Albums: 6 weeks)*

		pos	wks
27 Apr 91	**SIGNS** *Geffen GFS 3*	**70**	1
11 Feb 89	**THE GREAT RADIO CONTROVERSY** *Geffen WX 244*	**34**	2
2 Mar 91	**FIVE MAN ACOUSTICAL JAM** *Geffen 9243111*	**59**	1
21 Sep 91	**PSYCHOTIC SUPPER** *Geffen GEF 24424*	**44**	2
3 Sep 94	**BUST A NUT** *Geffen GED 24713*	**51**	1

TESTAMENT

US, male vocal / instrumental group (Albums: 6 weeks)

		pos	wks
28 May 88	**THE NEW ORDER** *Megaforce 781849 1*	**81**	1
19 Aug 89	**PRACTICE WHAT YOU PREACH** *Atlantic WX 297*	**40**	2
6 Oct 90	**SOULS OF BLACK** *Megaforce 7567821431*	**35**	2
30 May 92	**THE RITUAL** *Atlantic 7567823922*	**48**	1

Joe TEX

US, male vocalist – Joe Arlington, d. 13 Aug 1982 (Singles: 11 weeks)

		pos	wks
23 Apr 77 ●	**AIN'T GONNA BUMP NO MORE (WITH NO BIG FAT WOMAN)** *Epic EPC 5035*	**2**	11

TEXAS (131 Top 500)

Named after Wim Wenders' movie 'Paris, Texas', the Scots blues turned pop-chart mainstays are: Sharleen Spiteri (v), Ally McErlaine (g), Johnny McElhone (b), Eddie Campbell (k), all from Glasgow. Stuart Kerr, Richard Hynde and Mykey Wilson have all contributed on drums with Tony McGovern (g) the most recent recruit to a band now well established among the multi-million-selling album elite (Singles: 134 weeks, Albums: 236 weeks)

		pos	wks
4 Feb 89 ●	**I DON'T WANT A LOVER** *Mercury TEX 1*	**8**	11
6 May 89	**THRILL HAS GONE** *Mercury TEX 2*	**60**	3
5 Aug 89	**EVERYDAY NOW** *Mercury TEX 3*	**44**	5
2 Dec 89	**PRAYER FOR YOU** *Mercury TEX 4*	**73**	1
7 Sep 91	**WHY BELIEVE IN YOU** *Mercury TEX 5*	**66**	1
26 Oct 91	**IN MY HEART** *Mercury TEX 6*	**74**	1
8 Feb 92	**ALONE WITH YOU** *Mercury TEX 7*	**32**	4
25 Apr 92	**TIRED OF BEING ALONE** *Mercury TEX 8*	**19**	6
11 Sep 93	**SO CALLED FRIEND** *Vertigo TEXCD 9*	**30**	3
30 Oct 93	**YOU OWE IT ALL TO ME** *Vertigo TEXCD 10*	**39**	3
12 Feb 94	**SO IN LOVE WITH YOU** *Vertigo TEXCD 11*	**28**	2
18 Jan 97 ●	**SAY WHAT YOU WANT** *Mercury MERCD 480*	**3**	10
19 Apr 97 ●	**HALO** *Mercury MERCD 482*	**10**	7
9 Aug 97 ●	**BLACK EYED BOY** *Mercury MERCD 490*	**5**	6
15 Nov 97 ●	**PUT YOUR ARMS AROUND ME (2re)** *Mercury MERCD 497*	**10**	8
21 Mar 98 ●	**INSANE / SAY WHAT YOU WANT (ALL DAY EVERY DAY) (re-mix)** *Mercury MERCD 499* [1]	**4**	7
1 May 99 ●	**IN OUR LIFETIME** *Mercury MERCD 517*	**4**	9
28 Aug 99 ●	**SUMMER SON** *Mercury MERCD 520*	**5**	9
27 Nov 99	**WHEN WE ARE TOGETHER** *Mercury MERCD 525*	**12**	9
14 Oct 00 ●	**IN DEMAND (re)** *Mercury MERCD 528*	**6**	10
20 Jan 01 ●	**INNER SMILE** *Mercury MERCD 531*	**6**	8
21 Jul 01	**I DON'T WANT A LOVER (re-mix)** *Mercury MERCD 533*	**16**	4
18 Oct 03 ●	**CARNIVAL GIRL** *Mercury 9812253* [2]	**9**	5
20 Dec 03	**I'LL SEE IT THROUGH** *Mercury 9815221*	**40**	2+
25 Mar 89 ●	**SOUTHSIDE** *Mercury 8381711*	**3**	30
5 Oct 91	**MOTHERS HEAVEN** *Mercury 8485781*	**32**	4
13 Nov 93	**RICKS ROAD** *Vertigo 5182522*	**18**	2
15 Feb 97 ★	**WHITE ON BLONDE** *Mercury 5343152* ■	**1**	102
22 May 99 ★	**THE HUSH** *Mercury 5389722* ■	**1**	47
4 Nov 00 ★	**THE GREATEST HITS** *Mercury 5482622* ■	**1**	47
1 Nov 03 ●	**CAREFUL WHAT YOU WISH FOR** *Mercury 9865712*	**5**	4

[1] Texas featuring The Wu-Tang Clan [2] Texas featuring Kardinal Offishall

'Say What You Want (All Day Every Day)' is a new mix of the hit from 18 Jan 97 with rap by Method Man and The RZA

THA DOGG POUND

US, male rap group (Albums: 2 weeks)

		pos	wks
11 Nov 95	**DOGG FOOD** *Death Row 5241772* ▲	**66**	2

See also SNOOP DOGG

THAT KID CHRIS

US, male DJ / producer – Chris Staropoli (Singles: 1 week)

		pos	wks
22 Feb 97	**FEEL THA VIBE** *Manifesto FESCD 16*	**52**	1

THAT PETROL EMOTION *UK / US, male vocal / instrumental group (Singles: 24 weeks, Albums: 8 weeks)*

		pos	wks
11 Apr 87	**BIG DECISION** *Polydor TPE 1*	**43**	7
11 Jul 87	**DANCE** *Polydor TPE 2*	**64**	2
17 Oct 87	**GENIUS MOVE** *Virgin VS 1002*	**65**	2
31 Mar 90	**ABANDON** *Virgin VS 1242*	**73**	1
1 Sep 90	**HEY VENUS** *Virgin VS 1290*	**49**	4
9 Feb 91	**TINGLE** *Virgin VS 1312*	**49**	4
27 Apr 91	**SENSITIZE** *Virgin VS 1261*	**55**	4
10 May 86	**MANIC POP THRILL** *Demon FIEND 70*	**84**	2
23 May 87	**BABBLE** *Polydor TPE LP 1*	**30**	3
24 Sep 88	**END OF MILLENNIUM PSYCHOSIS BLUES** *Virgin V 2550*	**53**	2
21 Apr 90	**CHEMICRAZY** *Virgin V 2618*	**62**	1

The THE *UK, male vocalist / multi-instrumentalist – Matt Johnson and backing musicians (Singles: 52 weeks, Albums: 53 weeks)*

		pos	wks
4 Dec 82	**UNCERTAIN SMILE** *Epic EPC A 2787*	**68**	3
17 Sep 83	**THIS IS THE DAY** *Epic A 3710*	**71**	3
9 Aug 86	**HEARTLAND** *Some Bizarre TRUTH 2*	**29**	10
25 Oct 86	**INFECTED** *Some Bizarre TRUTH 3*	**48**	5
24 Jan 87	**SLOW TRAIN TO DAWN** *Some Bizarre TENSE 1*	**64**	2
23 May 87	**SWEET BIRD OF TRUTH** *Epic TENSE 2*	**55**	2
1 Apr 89	**THE BEAT(EN) GENERATION** *Epic EMU 8*	**18**	5
22 Jul 89	**GRAVITATE TO ME** *Epic EMU 9*	**63**	3
7 Oct 89	**ARMAGEDDON DAYS ARE HERE (AGAIN)** *Epic EMU 10*	**70**	2
2 Mar 91	**SHADES OF BLUE (EP)** *Epic 6557968*	**54**	1
16 Jan 93	**DOGS OF LUST** *Epic 6584572*	**25**	4
17 Apr 93	**SLOW EMOTION REPLAY** *Epic 6590772*	**35**	3
19 Jun 93	**LOVE IS STRONGER THAN DEATH** *Epic 6593712*	**39**	3
15 Jan 94	**DIS-INFECTED (EP)** *Epic 6598112*	**17**	4
4 Feb 95	**I SAW THE LIGHT** *Epic 6610912*	**31**	2
29 Oct 83	**SOUL MINING** *Some Bizzare EPC 25525*	**27**	5
29 Nov 86	**INFECTED** *Some Bizzare EPC 26770*	**14**	30
27 May 89 ●	**MIND BOMB** *Epic 463319 1*	**4**	9
6 Feb 93 ●	**DUSK** *Epic 4724682*	**2**	4
19 Jun 93	**BURNING BLUE SOUL** *4AD HAD 113CD*	**65**	1
25 Feb 95	**HANKY PANKY** *Epic 4781392*	**28**	2
11 Mar 00	**NAKED SELF** *Nothing 4905102*	**45**	1
1 Jun 02	**45 RPM – THE SINGLES OF THE THE** *Epic 5044699*	**60**	1

Tracks on Shades of Blue (EP): Jealous of Youth / Another Boy Drowning (Live) / Solitude / Dolphins.
Tracks on Dis-Infected (EP): This Was The Day / Dis-Infected / Helpline Operator (sickboy remix) / Dogs of Lust (germicide remix). 'That Was the Day' and 'Dis-Infected' on the EP are re-recordings of earlier hits. 'Dogs of Lust' is a re-mix

THEATRE OF HATE *UK, male vocal / instrumental group (Singles: 9 weeks, Albums: 9 weeks)*

		pos	wks
23 Jan 82	**DO YOU BELIEVE IN THE WESTWORLD** *Burning Rome BRR 2*	**40**	7
29 May 82	**THE HOP** *Burning Rome BRR 3*	**70**	2
13 Mar 82	**WESTWORLD** *Burning Rome TOH 1*	**17**	6
18 Aug 84	**REVOLUTION** *Burning Rome TOH 2*	**67**	3

THEAUDIENCE *UK, male / female, vocal / instrumental group – lead vocal – Sophie Ellis-Bextor (Singles: 5 weeks, Albums: 2 weeks)* pos/wks

Date		Title	pos	wks
7 Mar 98		IF YOU CAN'T DO IT WHEN YOU'RE YOUNG, WHEN CAN YOU DO IT? *Mercury AUDCD 2*	48	1
23 May 98		A PESSIMIST IS NEVER DISAPPOINTED *Mercury AUDCD 3*	27	2
8 Aug 98		I KNOW ENOUGH (I DON'T GET ENOUGH) *Elleffe AUDC 4*	25	2
29 Aug 98		THEAUDIENCE *Mercury 5587712*	22	2

THEM *UK, male vocal / instrumental group, leader – Van Morrison (Singles: 23 weeks)* pos/wks

Date		Title	pos	wks
7 Jan 65	●	BABY PLEASE DON'T GO *Decca F 12018*	10	9
25 Mar 65	●	HERE COMES THE NIGHT *Decca F 12094*	2	12
9 Feb 91		BABY PLEASE DON'T GO (re-issue) *London LON 292*	65	2

THEN JERICO *UK, male vocal / instrumental group – includes Mark Shaw (Singles: 36 weeks, Albums: 24 weeks)* pos/wks

Date		Title	pos	wks
31 Jan 87		LET HER FALL *London LON 97*	65	3
25 Jul 87		THE MOTIVE (LIVING WITHOUT YOU) *London LON 145*	18	12
24 Oct 87		MUSCLE DEEP *London LON 156*	48	4
28 Jan 89		BIG AREA *London LON 204*	13	7
8 Apr 89		WHAT DOES IT TAKE? *London LON 223*	33	4
12 Aug 89		SUGAR BOX *London LON 235*	22	6
3 Oct 87		FIRST (THE SOUND OF MUSIC) *London LONLP 26*	35	7
4 Mar 89	●	THE BIG AREA *London 828122 1*	4	17

THERAPY? *UK, male vocal / instrumental group (Singles: 33 weeks, Albums: 24 weeks)* pos/wks

Date		Title	pos	wks
31 Oct 92		TEETHGRINDER *A&M AM 0097*	30	2
20 Mar 93	●	SHORTSHARPSHOCK (EP) *A&M AMCD 208*	9	4
12 Jun 93		FACE THE STRANGE (EP) *A&M 5803052*	18	3
28 Aug 93		OPAL MANTRA *A&M 5803612*	13	3
29 Jan 94		NOWHERE *A&M 5805052*	18	4
12 Mar 94		TRIGGER INSIDE *A&M 5805352*	22	3
11 Jun 94		DIE LAUGHING *A&M 5805892*	29	2
27 May 95		INNOCENT X *Volume VOLCD 1*	53	1
3 Jun 95		STORIES *A&M 5811052*	14	3
29 Jul 95		LOOSE *A&M 5811652*	25	3
18 Nov 95		DIANE *A&M 5812912*	26	2
14 Mar 98		CHURCH OF NOISE *A&M 5825392*	29	2
30 May 98		LONELY, CRYIN' ONLY *A&M 0441212*	32	1
8 Feb 92		PLEASURE DEATH *Wiiija WIJ 11*	52	1
14 Nov 92		NURSE *A&M 5400442*	38	3
19 Feb 94	●	TROUBLEGUM *A&M 5401962*	5	11
24 Jun 95	●	INFERNAL LOVE *A&M 5403792*	9	7
11 Apr 98		SEMI-DETACHED *A&M 5408912*	21	1
30 Oct 99		SUICIDE PACT – YOU FIRST *Ark 21 1539722*	61	1

Tracks on Shortsharpshock (EP): Screamager / Auto Surgery / Totally Random Man / Accelerator. Tracks on Face the Strange (EP): Turn / Speedball / Bloody Blue / Neckfreak. The listed flip side of 'Innocent X' was 'Belfast' by Orbital

THESE ANIMAL MEN *UK, male vocal / instrumental group (Singles: 3 weeks, Albums: 4 weeks)* pos/wks

Date		Title	pos	wks
24 Sep 94		THIS IS THE SOUND OF YOUTH *Hi-Rise FLATSCD 7*	72	1
8 Feb 97		LIFE SUPPORT MACHINE *Hut HUTCD 76*	62	1
12 Apr 97		LIGHT EMITTING ELECTRICAL WAVE *Hut HUTCD 81*	72	1
2 Jul 94		TOO SUSSED *Hi-Rise FLATMCD 4*	39	2
8 Oct 94		(COME ON JOIN) THE HIGH SOCIETY *Hi-Rise FLATCD 8*	62	1
25 Mar 95		TAXI FOR THESE ANIMAL MEN *Hi-Rise FLATMCD 14*	64	1

THEY MIGHT BE GIANTS
US, male vocal / instrumental duo – John Flansburgh and John Linnell (Singles: 18 weeks, Albums: 12 weeks) pos/wks

Date		Title	pos	wks
3 Mar 90	●	BIRDHOUSE IN YOUR SOUL *Elektra EKR 104*	6	11
2 Jun 90		ISTANBUL (NOT CONSTANTINOPLE) *Elektra EKR 110*	61	2
28 Jul 01		BOSS OF ME *Pias / Restless PIASREST 001 CD*	21	5
7 Apr 90		FLOOD *Elektra EKT 68*	14	12

THICK D *US, male producer – Eric 'E-Smoove' Miller (Singles: 3 weeks)* pos/wks

Date		Title	pos	wks
12 Oct 02		INSATIABLE *Multiply CDMULTY 88*	35	3

See also E-SMOOVE featuring Latanza WATERS; PRAISE CATS

THIN LIZZY (126 Top 500) *Accomplished Irish hard-rock group (which at times included noted guitarists Gary Moore, Snowy White and Midge Ure) was built around distinctive singer / bass guitarist Phil Lynott (d. 1986). After a slow start, they wrote their own chapter in British rock history (Singles: 128 weeks, Albums: 250 weeks)* pos/wks

Date		Title	pos	wks
20 Jan 73	●	WHISKY IN THE JAR *Decca F 13355*	6	12
29 May 76	●	THE BOYS ARE BACK IN TOWN *Vertigo 6059 139*	8	10
14 Aug 76		JAILBREAK *Vertigo 6059 150*	31	4
15 Jan 77		DON'T BELIEVE A WORD *Vertigo Lizzy 001*	12	7
13 Aug 77		DANCIN' IN THE MOONLIGHT (IT'S CAUGHT ME IN ITS SPOTLIGHT) *Vertigo 6059 177*	14	8
13 May 78		ROSALIE - (COWGIRLS' SONG) (MEDLEY) *Vertigo LIZZY 2*	20	13
3 Mar 79	●	WAITING FOR AN ALIBI *Vertigo LIZZY 003*	9	8
16 Jun 79		DO ANYTHING YOU WANT TO *Vertigo LIZZY 004*	14	9
20 Oct 79		SARAH *Vertigo LIZZY 5*	24	13
24 May 80		CHINATOWN *Vertigo LIZZY 6*	21	9
27 Sep 80	●	KILLER ON THE LOOSE *Vertigo LIZZY 7*	10	7
2 May 81		KILLERS LIVE (EP) *Vertigo LIZZY 8*	19	7
8 Aug 81		TROUBLE BOYS *Vertigo LIZZY 9*	53	4
6 Mar 82		HOLLYWOOD (DOWN ON YOUR LUCK) *Vertigo LIZZY 10*	53	3
12 Feb 83		COLD SWEAT *Vertigo LIZZY 11*	27	5
7 May 83		THUNDER AND LIGHTNING *Vertigo LIZZY 12*	39	2
6 Aug 83		THE SUN GOES DOWN *Vertigo LIZZY 13*	52	3
26 Jan 91		DEDICATION *Vertigo LIZZY 14*	35	3
23 Mar 91		THE BOYS ARE BACK IN TOWN (re-issue) *Vertigo LIZZY 15*	63	1
27 Sep 75		FIGHTING *Vertigo 6360 121*	60	1
10 Apr 76	●	JAILBREAK *Vertigo 9102 008*	10	50
6 Nov 76		JOHNNY THE FOX *Vertigo 9102 012*	11	24
1 Oct 77	●	BAD REPUTATION *Vertigo 9102 016*	4	9
17 Jun 78	●	LIVE AND DANGEROUS *Vertigo 6641 807*	2	62
5 May 79	●	BLACK ROSE (A ROCK LEGEND) *Vertigo 9102 032*	2	21
18 Oct 80	●	CHINATOWN *Vertigo 6359 030*	7	7
11 Apr 81	●	THE ADVENTURES OF THIN LIZZY *Vertigo LIZTV 1*	6	13
5 Dec 81		RENEGADE *Vertigo 6359 083*	38	8
12 Mar 83	●	THUNDER AND LIGHTNING *Vertigo VERL 3*	4	11
26 Nov 83		LIFE – LIVE *Vertigo VERD 6*	29	6
14 Nov 87		SOLDIER OF FORTUNE – THE BEST OF PHIL LYNOTT AND THIN LIZZY *Telstar STAR 2300* [1]	55	10
16 Feb 91	●	DEDICATION – THE VERY BEST OF THIN LIZZY *Vertigo 8481921*	8	17
13 Jan 96		WILD ONE – THE VERY BEST OF THIN LIZZY *Vertigo 5281132*	18	11

[1] Phil Lynott and Thin Lizzy

Tracks on Killers Live (EP): Bad Reputation / Are You Ready / Dear Miss Lonely Hearts

3RD BASS
US, male rap group (Singles: 5 weeks, Albums: 1 week) pos/wks

Date		Title	pos	wks
10 Feb 90		THE GAS FACE *Def Jam 655627 0*	71	1
7 Apr 90		BROOKLYN-QUEENS *Def Jam 655830 7*	61	2
22 Jun 91		POP GOES THE WEASEL *Def Jam 6569547*	64	2
20 Jul 91		DERELICTS OF DIALECT *Def Jam 4683171*	46	1

THIRD DIMENSION featuring Julie McDERMOTT
UK, male / female vocal / instrumental group (Singles: 2 weeks) pos/wks

Date		Title	pos	wks
12 Oct 96		DON'T GO *Soundproof MCSTD 40082*	34	2

THIRD EAR BAND
UK, male instrumental group (Albums: 2 weeks) pos/wks

Date		Title	pos	wks
27 Jun 70		AIR EARTH FIRE WATER *Harvest SHVL 773*	49	2

3RD EDGE
UK, male vocal trio (Singles: 9 weeks) pos/wks

Date		Title	pos	wks
31 Aug 02		IN AND OUT (re) *Q Zone / Parlophone CDR 6568*	15	5
8 Feb 03		KNOW YA WANNA (re) *Parlophone CDRS 6596*	17	4

THIRD EYE BLIND
US, male vocal / instrumental group (Singles: 6 weeks) pos/wks

27 Sep 97	**SEMI-CHARMED LIFE** *Elektra E 3907CD*	**33** 5
21 Mar 98	**HOW'S IT GOING TO BE** *Elektra E 3863CD*	**51** 1

3RD STOREE *US, male vocal group (Singles: 1 week)* pos/wks

5 Jun 99	**IF EVER** *Yab Yum / Elektra E 3752CD*	**53** 1

THIRD WORLD *Jamaica, male vocal / instrumental group (Singles: 53 weeks, Albums: 18 weeks)* pos/wks

23 Sep 78 ●	**NOW THAT WE'VE FOUND LOVE** *Island WIP 6457*	**10** 9
6 Jan 79	**COOL MEDITATION** *Island WIP 6469*	**17** 10
16 Jun 79	**TALK TO ME** *Island WIP 6496*	**56** 5
6 Jun 81 ●	**DANCING ON THE FLOOR (HOOKED ON LOVE)** *CBS A 1214*	**10** 15
17 Apr 82	**TRY JAH LOVE** *CBS A 2063*	**47** 6
9 Mar 85	**NOW THAT WE'VE FOUND LOVE (re-issue)** *Island IS 219*	**22** 8
21 Oct 78	JOURNEY TO ADDIS *Island ILPS 9554*	30 6
11 Jul 81	ROCKS THE WORLD *CBS 85027*	37 9
15 May 82	YOU'VE GOT THE POWER *CBS 85563*	87 3

THIRST
UK, male vocal / instrumental group (Singles: 2 weeks) pos/wks

6 Jul 91	**THE ENEMY WITHIN** *Ten TEN 379*	**61** 2

1300 DRUMS featuring the UNJUSTIFIED ANCIENTS OF MU
UK, male instrumental / production group (Singles: 4 weeks) pos/wks

18 May 96	**OOH! AAH! CANTONA** *Dynamo DYND 5*	**11** 4

THIS ISLAND EARTH
UK, male / female vocal / instrumental group (Singles: 5 weeks) pos/wks

5 Jan 85	**SEE THAT GLOW** *Magnet MAG 266*	**47** 5

THIS MORTAL COIL *UK, male / female vocal / instrumental group (Singles: 3 weeks, Albums: 10 weeks)* pos/wks

22 Oct 83	**SONG TO THE SIREN (re)** *4AD AD 310*	**66** 3
20 Oct 84	IT'LL END IN TEARS *4AD CAD 411*	38 4
11 Oct 86	FILIGREE AND SHADOW *4AD DAD 609*	53 3
4 May 91	BLOOD *4AD DAD 1005*	65 3

THIS WAY UP
UK, male vocal / instrumental duo (Singles: 2 weeks) pos/wks

22 Aug 87	**TELL ME WHY** *Virgin VS 954*	**72** 2

THIS YEAR'S BLONDE
UK, male / female vocal / instrumental group (Singles: 8 weeks) pos/wks

10 Oct 81	**PLATINUM POP** *Creole CR 19*	**46** 5
14 Nov 87	**WHO'S THAT MIX** *Debut DEBT 3034*	**62** 3

BJ THOMAS *US, male vocalist (Singles: 4 weeks)* pos/wks

21 Feb 70	**RAINDROPS KEEP FALLIN' ON MY HEAD (re)** *Wand WN1* ▲	**38** 4

Carla THOMAS – *See Otis REDDING*

Dante THOMAS featuring PRAS *US, male vocalist – Darin Espinoza – and US, male rapper (Singles: 3 weeks)* pos/wks

1 Sep 01	**MISS CALIFORNIA** *Elektra E7192CD*	**25** 3

Evelyn THOMAS *US, female vocalist (Singles: 29 weeks)* pos/wks

24 Jan 76	**WEAK SPOT** *20th Century BTC 1014*	**26** 7
17 Apr 76	**DOOMSDAY (re)** *20th Century BTC 1017*	**41** 2
21 Apr 84 ●	**HIGH ENERGY** *Record Shack SOHO 18*	**5** 17
25 Aug 84	**MASQUERADE** *Record Shack SOHO 25*	**60** 3

Jamo THOMAS and his PARTY BROTHERS ORCHESTRA
US, male vocalist (Singles: 2 weeks) pos/wks

26 Feb 69	**I SPY (FOR THE FBI) (re)** *Polydor 56755*	**44** 2

Kenny THOMAS
UK, male vocalist (Singles: 54 weeks, Albums: 28 weeks) pos/wks

26 Jan 91	**OUTSTANDING** *Cooltempo COOL 227*	**12** 10
1 Jun 91 ●	**THINKING ABOUT YOUR LOVE** *Cooltempo COOL 235*	**4** 13
5 Oct 91	**BEST OF YOU** *Cooltempo COOL 243*	**11** 7
30 Nov 91	**TENDER LOVE** *Cooltempo COOL 247*	**26** 6
10 Jul 93	**STAY** *Cooltempo CDCOOL 271*	**22** 6
4 Sep 93	**TRIPPIN' ON YOUR LOVE** *Cooltempo CDCOOL 277*	**17** 5
6 Nov 93	**PIECE BY PIECE** *Cooltempo CDCOOL 283*	**36** 3
14 May 94	**DESTINY** *Cooltempo CDCOOL 289*	**59** 1
2 Sep 95	**WHEN I THINK OF YOU** *Cooltempo CDCOOL 309*	**27** 3
26 Oct 91 ●	VOICES *Cooltempo CTLP 24*	3 23
25 Sep 93 ●	WAIT FOR ME *Cooltempo CTCD 36*	10 5

Lillo THOMAS
US, male vocalist (Singles: 10 weeks, Albums: 7 weeks) pos/wks

27 Apr 85	**SETTLE DOWN** *Capitol CL 356*	**66** 2
21 Mar 87	**SEXY GIRL** *Capitol CL 445*	**23** 5
30 May 87	**I'M IN LOVE** *Capitol CL 450*	**54** 3
2 May 87	LILLO *Capitol EST 2031*	43 7

Mickey THOMAS – *See Elvin BISHOP; STARSHIP*

Millard THOMAS – *See Harry BELAFONTE*

Nicky THOMAS
Jamaica, male vocalist (Singles: 14 weeks) pos/wks

13 Jun 70 ●	**LOVE OF THE COMMON PEOPLE** *Trojan TR 7750*	**9** 14

Ray THOMAS *UK, male vocalist (Albums: 3 weeks)* pos/wks

26 Jul 75	FROM MIGHTY OAKS *Threshold THS 16*	23 3

See also MOODY BLUES

Rob THOMAS – *See MATCHBOX TWENTY; SANTANA*

Rufus THOMAS
US, male vocalist, d. 15 Dec 2001 (Singles: 12 weeks) pos/wks

11 Apr 70	**DO THE FUNKY CHICKEN** *Stax 144*	**18** 12

Tasha THOMAS
US, female vocalist – d. 8 Nov 1984 (Singles: 3 weeks) pos/wks

20 Jan 79	**SHOOT ME (WITH YOUR LOVE)** *Atlantic LV 4*	**59** 3

Timmy THOMAS *US, male vocalist (Singles: 20 weeks)* pos/wks

24 Feb 73	**WHY CAN'T WE LIVE TOGETHER** *Mojo 2027 012*	**12** 11
28 Dec 85	**NEW YORK EYES** *Portrait A 6805* [1]	**41** 7
14 Jul 90	**WHY CAN'T WE LIVE TOGETHER (re-mix)** *TK TKR 1*	**54** 2

[1] Nicole with Timmy Thomas

THOMAS and TAYLOR
US, male / female vocal duo (Singles: 5 weeks) pos/wks

17 May 86	**YOU CAN'T BLAME LOVE** *Cooltempo COOL 123*	**53** 5

Amanda THOMPSON – *See Lesley GARRETT*

Carroll THOMPSON – *See MOVEMENT 98 featuring Carroll THOMPSON; Courtney PINE*

Chris THOMPSON
UK, male vocalist (Singles: 5 weeks) pos/wks

27 Oct 79	**IF YOU REMEMBER ME** *Planet K 12389*	**42** 5

Danny THOMPSON – *See Richard THOMPSON*

Gina THOMPSON – *See MC LYTE*

Lincoln THOMPSON – *See REBEL MC*

Richard THOMPSON

UK, male vocalist / instrumentalist – guitar (Albums: 16 weeks) pos/wks

27 Apr 85 **ACROSS A CROWDED ROOM** *Polydor POLD 5175* 80 2
18 Oct 86 **DARING ADVENTURES** *Polydor POLD 5202* 92 1
29 Oct 88 **AMNESIA** *Capitol EST 2075* 89 1
25 May 91 **RUMOR AND SIGH** *Capitol EST 2142* 32 3
29 Jan 94 **MIRROR BLUE** *Capitol CDEST 2207* 23 3
20 Apr 96 **YOU? ME? US?** *Capitol CDEST 2282* 32 2
24 May 97 **INDUSTRY** *Parlophone CDPCS 7383* [1] 69 1
4 Sep 99 **MOCK TUDOR** *Capitol 4988602* 28 2
15 Feb 03 **THE OLD KIT BAG** *Cooking Vinyl COOKCD251* 52 1

[1] Richard and Danny Thompson

Sue THOMPSON

US, female vocalist – Eva Sue McKee (Singles: 9 weeks) pos/wks

2 Nov 61 **SAD MOVIES (MAKE ME CRY) (re)** *Polydor NH 66967* 46 2
21 Jan 65 **PAPER TIGER (re)** *Hickory 1284* 30 7

THOMPSON TWINS (263 Top 500)

British-based synth-rock trio: Tom Bailey (v/syn), New Zealand-born Alannah Currie (v/prc/s), Joe Leeway (prc). Named after characters in a Tin Tin cartoon, they were joined on stage at Live Aid by Madonna and were at the forefront of the second so-called 'British Invasion' (Singles: 110 weeks, Albums: 128 weeks) pos/wks

6 Nov 82 **LIES** *Arista ARIST 486* 67 3
29 Jan 83 ● **LOVE ON YOUR SIDE** *Arista ARIST 504* 9 12
16 Apr 83 ● **WE ARE DETECTIVE** *Arista ARIST 526* 7 9
16 Jul 83 **WATCHING** *Arista TWINS 1* 33 6
19 Nov 83 ● **HOLD ME NOW** *Arista TWINS 2* 4 15
4 Feb 84 ● **DOCTOR DOCTOR** *Arista TWINS 3* 3 10
31 Mar 84 ● **YOU TAKE ME UP** *Arista TWINS 4* 2 9
7 Jul 84 **SISTER OF MERCY (re)** *Arista TWINS 5* 11 9
8 Dec 84 **LAY YOUR HANDS ON ME** *Arista TWINS 6* 13 9
31 Aug 85 **DON'T MESS WITH DOCTOR DREAM** *Arista TWINS 9* 15 6
19 Oct 85 **KING FOR A DAY** *Arista TWINS 7* 22 6
7 Dec 85 **REVOLUTION (re)** *Arista TWINS 10* 56 4
21 Mar 87 **GET THAT LOVE (re)** *Arista TWINS 12* 66 3
15 Oct 88 **IN THE NAME OF LOVE '88** *Arista 111808* 46 3
28 Sep 91 **COME INSIDE** *Warner Bros. W 0058* 56 4
25 Jan 92 **THE SAINT** *Warner Bros. W 0080* 53 2
13 Mar 82 **SET** *Tee TELP 2* 48 3
26 Feb 83 ● **QUICK STEP & SIDE KICK** *Arista 204 924* 2 56
25 Feb 84 ★ **INTO THE GAP** *Arista 205 971* ■ 1 51
28 Sep 85 ● **HERE'S TO FUTURE DAYS** *Arista 207 164* 5 9
2 May 87 **CLOSE TO THE BONE** *Arista 208 143* 90 1
10 Mar 90 **GREATEST HITS** *Stylus SMR 92* 23 8

Tracey THORN – *See EVERYTHING BUT THE GIRL; MASSIVE ATTACK*

David THORNE

US, male vocalist (Singles: 8 weeks) pos/wks

24 Jan 63 **THE ALLEY CAT SONG** *Stateside SS 141* 21 8

Ken THORNE

UK, orchestra (Singles: 15 weeks) pos/wks

18 Jul 63 ● **THEME FROM THE FILM 'THE LEGION'S LAST PATROL'** *HMV POP 1176* 4 15

Trumpet solo by Ray Davies

THORNS

US male vocal / instrumental trio (Albums: 1 week) pos/wks

14 Jun 03 **THE THORNS** *Columbia 5113732* 68 1

George THOROGOOD and the DESTROYERS

US, male vocal / instrumental group (Albums: 1 week) pos/wks

2 Dec 78 **GEORGE THOROGOOD AND THE DESTROYERS** *Sonet SNTF 781* 67 1

THOSE 2 GIRLS

UK, female vocal duo – Denise Van Outen and Cathy Warwick (Singles: 4 weeks) pos/wks

5 Nov 94 **WANNA MAKE YOU GO . . . UUH!** *Final Vinyl 74321233782* 74 1
4 Mar 95 **ALL I WANT** *Final Vinyl 74321254202* 36 3

See also DENISE and JOHNNY; Andy WILLIAMS

THOUSAND YARD STARE

UK, male vocal / instrumental group (Singles: 5 weeks, Albums: 2 weeks) pos/wks

26 Oct 91 **SEASONSTREAM (EP)** *Stifled Aardvark AARD 5T* 65 1
8 Feb 92 **COMEUPPANCE** *Stifled Aardvark AARD 007* 37 2
11 Jul 92 **SPINDRIFT (EP)** *Stifled Aardvark AARDT 010* 58 1
8 May 93 **VERSION OF ME** *Polydor AARDC 012* 57 1
7 Mar 93 **HANDS ON** *Polydor 5130012* 38 2

Tracks on Seasonstream (EP): O-O AET / Village End / Keepsake / Worse for Wear
Tracks on Spindrift (EP): Wideshire Two / Hand, Son / Happenstance / Mocca Pune

THRASHING DOVES

UK, male vocal / instrumental group (Singles: 3 weeks) pos/wks

24 Jan 87 **BEAUTIFUL IMBALANCE** *A&M TDOVE 1* 50 3

THREE AMIGOS

UK, male production trio (Singles: 8 weeks) pos/wks

3 Jul 99 **LOUIE LOUIE** *Inferno CDFERN 17* 15 6
24 Mar 01 **25 MILES 2001** *Wonderboy WBOYD 25* 30 2

3 COLOURS RED

UK, male vocal / instrumental group (Singles: 17 weeks, Albums: 4 weeks) pos/wks

18 Jan 97 **NUCLEAR HOLIDAY** *Creation CRESCD 250* 22 2
15 Mar 97 **SIXTY MILE SMILE** *Creation CRESCD 254* 20 3
10 May 97 **PURE** *Creation CRESCD 265* 28 1
12 Jul 97 **COPPER GIRL** *Creation CRESCD 270* 30 2
8 Nov 97 **THIS IS MY HOLLYWOOD** *Creation CRESCD 277* 48 1
23 Jan 99 **BEAUTIFUL DAY** *Creation CRESCD 308* 11 6
29 May 99 **THIS IS MY TIME** *Creation CRESCD 313* 36 2
24 May 97 **PURE** *Creation CRECD 208* 16 2
20 Feb 99 **REVOLT** *Creation CRECD 227* 17 2

THREE DEGREES (321 Top 500)

US R&B vocal group, which became top UK stars in the 1970s: Sheila Ferguson, Valerie Holiday, Fayette Pinkney. The trio, tagged by the media as 'Prince Charles's favourites', was the first girl group to top the UK chart since The Supremes in 1964 (Singles: 113 weeks, Albums: 91 weeks) pos/wks

13 Apr 74 **YEAR OF DECISION** *Philadelphia International PIR 2073* 13 10
27 Apr 74 **TSOP (THE SOUND OF PHILADELPHIA)** *Philadelphia International PIR 2289* [1] ▲ 22 9
13 Jul 74 ★ **WHEN WILL I SEE YOU AGAIN** *Philadelphia International PIR 2155* 1 16
2 Nov 74 **GET YOUR LOVE BACK** *Philadelphia International PIR 2737* 34 4
12 Apr 75 ● **TAKE GOOD CARE OF YOURSELF** *Philadelphia International PIR 3177* 9 9
5 Jul 75 **LONG LOST LOVER** *Philadelphia International PIR 3352* 40 4
1 May 76 **TOAST OF LOVE** *Epic EPC 4215* 36 4
7 Oct 78 **GIVING UP, GIVING IN** *Ariola ARO 130* 12 10
13 Jan 79 ● **WOMAN IN LOVE** *Ariola ARO 141* 3 11
24 Mar 79 ● **THE RUNNER** *Ariola ARO 154* 10 10
23 Jun 79 **THE GOLDEN LADY** *Ariola ARO 170* 56 3
29 Sep 79 **JUMP THE GUN** *Ariola ARO 183* 48 5
24 Nov 79 ● **MY SIMPLE HEART** *Ariola ARO 202* 9 11
5 Oct 85 **THE HEAVEN I NEED** *Supreme SUPE 102* 42 5
26 Dec 98 **LAST CHRISTMAS** *Wildstar CDWILD 15* [2] 54 2
10 Aug 74 **THREE DEGREES** *Philadelphia International 65858* 12 22
17 May 75 ● **TAKE GOOD CARE OF YOURSELF** *Philadelphia International PIR 69137* 6 16
24 Feb 79 **NEW DIMENSIONS** *Ariola ARLH 5012* 34 13
3 Mar 79 ● **A COLLECTION OF THEIR 20 GREATEST HITS** *Epic EPC 10013* ..8 18
15 Dec 79 **3D** *Ariola 3D 1* 61 7
27 Sep 80 ● **GOLD** *Ariola 3D 2* 9 15

[1] MFSB featuring the Three Degrees [2] Alien Voices featuring The Three Degrees

THREE DOG NIGHT

US, male vocal / instrumental group (Singles: 23 weeks) pos/wks

8 Aug 70 ● **MAMA TOLD ME NOT TO COME** *Stateside SS 8052* ▲ 3 14
29 May 71 **JOY TO THE WORLD** *Probe PRO 523* ▲ 24 9

THREE DRIVES

Holland, male vocal / instrumental group (Singles: 8 weeks) pos/wks

27 Jun 98 **GREECE 2000** *Hooj Choons HOOJCD 63* [1] 44 1

30 Jan 99	**GREECE 2000 (re-mix)** *Hooj Choons HOOJ 70CD* [1]	12	4
17 Nov 01	**SUNSET ON IBIZA** *Xtravaganza XTRAV 27CDS* [2]	44	2
7 Jun 03	**CARERRA 2** *Nebula NEBCD 043*	57	1

[1] Three Drives [2] Three Drives on a Vinyl

THREE GOOD REASONS *UK, male vocal / instrumental group (Singles: 3 weeks)*

		pos	wks
10 Mar 66	**NOWHERE MAN** *Mercury MF 899*	47	3

3 JAYS *UK, male production / vocal trio (Singles: 5 weeks)*

		pos	wks
31 Jul 99	**FEELING IT TOO** *Multiply CDMULTY 53*	17	5

THREE KAYES – *See KAYE SISTERS*

3LW *US, female vocal group (Singles: 13 weeks, Albums: 1 week)*

		pos	wks
2 Jun 01 ●	**NO MORE (BABY I'MA DO RIGHT) (re)** *Epic 6712722*	6	9
8 Sep 01	**PLAYAS GON' PLAY** *Epic 6717932*	21	3
19 Oct 02	**FEELS GOOD (DON'T WORRY BOUT A THING)** *Island CID 806* [1]	44	1
16 Jun 01	**3LW** *Epic 4989142*	75	1

[1] Naughty By Nature featuring 3LW

THREE 'N ONE *Germany, male production duo – Sharam Khososi and Andre Straesser (Singles: 3 weeks)*

		pos	wks
7 Jun 97	**REFLECT** *ffrr FCD 301*	66	1
15 May 99	**PEARL RIVER** *Low Sense SENSECD 24* [1]	32	2

[1] Three 'N One presents Johnny Shaker featuring Serial Diva

See also Billy HENDRIX

3SL *UK, male vocal trio (Singles: 10 weeks)*

		pos	wks
20 Apr 02	**TAKE IT EASY (re)** *Epic 6724042*	11	6
7 Sep 02	**TOUCH ME TEASE ME (re)** *Epic 6727872*	16	4

3T *US, male vocal trio (Singles: 45 weeks, Albums: 15 weeks)*

		pos	wks
27 Jan 96 ●	**ANYTHING** *MJJ 6627152*	2	14
4 May 96	**24 / 7** *MJJ 6631995*	11	7
24 Aug 96 ●	**WHY** *MJJ 6636482* [1]	2	9
7 Dec 96 ●	**I NEED YOU** *Epic 6639912*	3	10
5 Apr 97 ●	**GOTTA BE YOU** *Epic 6643645* [2]	10	5
24 Feb 96	**BROTHERHOOD** *Epic 4816942*	11	15

[1] 3T featuring Michael Jackson [2] 3T: rap by Herbie

THREE TONS OF JOY – *See Johnny OTIS SHOW*

THRICE *US, male vocal / instrumental group (Singles: 1 week)*

		pos	wks
18 Oct 03	**ALL THAT'S LEFT** *Island / Mercury 9811957*	69	1

The THRILLS *Ireland, male vocal / instrumental group (Singles: 10 weeks, Albums: 18 weeks)*

		pos	wks
22 Mar 03	**ONE HORSE TOWN** *Virgin VSCDT 1845*	18	3
21 Jun 03	**BIG SUR** *Virgin VSCDT 1852*	17	4
6 Sep 03	**SANTA CRUZ (YOU'RE NOT THAT FAR)** *Virgin VSCDT 1862*	33	2
6 Dec 03	**DON'T STEAL OUR SUN** *Virgin VSCDT 1864*	45	1
12 Jul 03 ●	**SO MUCH FOR THE CITY** *Virgin CDV2974*	3	18

THRILLSEEKERS *UK, male producer / instrumentalist – Steve Helstrip (Singles: 3 weeks)*

		pos	wks
17 Feb 01	**SYNAESTHESIA (FLY AWAY)** *Neo NEOCD 050* [1]	28	2
7 Sep 02	**DREAMING OF YOU** *Ministry of Sound / Data DATA 36CDS*	48	1

[1] Thrillseekers featuring Sheryl Deane

THROWING MUSES *US, male / female vocal / instrumental group – leader Kristin Hersh (Singles: 6 weeks, Albums: 14 weeks)*

		pos	wks
9 Feb 91	**COUNTING BACKWARDS** *4AD AD 1001*	70	2
1 Aug 92	**FIREPILE (EP)** *4AD BAD 2012*	46	1
24 Dec 94	**BRIGHT YELLOW GUN** *4AD BAD 4018CD*	51	2
10 Aug 96	**SHARK** *4AD BAD 6016CD*	53	1
4 Feb 89	**HUNKPAPA** *4AD CAD 901*	59	1
2 Mar 91	**THE REAL RAMONA** *4AD CAD 1002*	26	4
22 Aug 92	**RED HEAVEN** *4AD CAD 2013CD*	13	3
28 Nov 92	**THE CURSE** *4AD TAD 2019CD*	74	1
28 Jan 95 ●	**UNIVERSITY** *4AD CADD 5002CD*	10	3
31 Aug 96	**LIMBO** *4AD CAD 6014CD*	36	1
29 Mar 03	**THROWING MUSES** *4AD CAD 2301CD*	75	1

Tracks on Firepile (EP): Firepile / Manic Depression / Snailhead / City of the Dead

Harry THUMANN *Germany, male instrumentalist – keyboards (Singles: 6 weeks)*

		pos	wks
21 Feb 81	**UNDERWATER** *Decca F 13901*	41	6

See also WONDER DOG

THUNDER *UK, male vocal / instrumental group (Singles: 53 weeks, Albums: 39 weeks)*

		pos	wks
17 Feb 90	**DIRTY LOVE** *EMI EM 126*	32	4
12 May 90	**BACKSTREET SYMPHONY** *EMI EM 137*	25	4
14 Jul 90	**GIMME SOME LOVIN'** *EMI EM 148*	36	3
29 Sep 90	**SHE'S SO FINE** *EMI EM 158*	34	3
23 Feb 91	**LOVE WALKED IN** *EMI EM 175*	21	4
15 Aug 92	**LOW LIFE IN HIGH PLACES** *EMI EM 242*	22	5
10 Oct 92	**EVERYBODY WANTS HER** *EMI EM 249*	36	4
13 Feb 93	**A BETTER MAN** *EMI CDBETTER 1*	18	4
19 Jun 93	**LIKE A SATELLITE (EP)** *EMI CDEM 272*	28	2
7 Jan 95	**STAND UP** *EMI CDEM 365*	23	4
25 Feb 95	**RIVER OF PAIN** *EMI CDEM 367*	31	2
6 May 95	**CASTLES IN THE SAND** *EMI CDEM 372*	30	3
23 Sep 95	**IN A BROKEN DREAM** *EMI CDEM 384*	26	2
25 Jan 97	**DON'T WAIT UP** *Raw Power RAWX 1020*	27	2
5 Apr 97	**LOVE WORTH DYING FOR** *Raw Power RAWX 1043*	60	1
7 Feb 98	**THE ONLY ONE** *Eagle EAGXA 016*	31	2
27 Jun 98	**PLAY THAT FUNKY MUSIC** *Eagle EAGXS 030*	39	2
20 Mar 99	**YOU WANNA KNOW** *Eagle EAGXA 037*	49	1
31 May 03	**LOSER** *STC Recordings STC 20032*	48	1
17 Mar 90	**BACK STREET SYMPHONY** *EMI EMC 3570*	21	16
5 Sep 92 ●	**LAUGHING ON JUDGEMENT DAY** *EMI CDEMD 1035*	2	10
4 Feb 95 ●	**BEHIND CLOSED DOORS** *EMI CDEMD 1076*	5	5
7 Oct 95	**BEST OF THUNDER – THEIR FINEST HOUR (AND A BIT)** *EMI CDEMD 1086*	22	3
15 Feb 97	**THE THRILL OF IT ALL** *Raw Power RAWCD 115*	14	3
28 Feb 98	**LIVE** *Eagle EDGCD 016*	35	1
27 Mar 99	**GIVING THE GAME AWAY** *Eagle EAGCD 046*	49	1

Tracks on Like a Satellite (EP): Like a Satellite / The Damage Is Done / Like a Satellite (Live) / Gimme Shelter

THUNDERBIRDS – *See Chris FARLOWE*

THUNDERBUGS *UK / France / Germany, female vocal / instrumental group (Singles: 15 weeks)*

		pos	wks
18 Sep 99 ●	**FRIENDS FOREVER (re)** *First Avenue / Epic 6676932*	5	10
18 Dec 99	**IT'S ABOUT TIME YOU WERE MINE** *First Avenue / Epic 6683972*	43	5

THUNDERCLAP NEWMAN *UK, male vocal / instrumental group – lead vocal John 'Speedy' Keen (Singles: 13 weeks)*

		pos	wks
11 Jun 69 ★	**SOMETHING IN THE AIR** *Track 604-031*	1	12
27 Jun 70	**ACCIDENTS** *Track 2094 001*	46	1

THUNDERTHIGHS *UK, female vocal group (Singles: 5 weeks)*

		pos	wks
22 Jun 74	**CENTRAL PARK ARREST** *Philips 6006 386*	30	5

THURSDAY *US, male vocal / instrumental group (Singles: 1 weeks, Albums: 1 week)*

		pos	wks
25 Oct 03	**SIGNALS OVER THE AIR** *Island US / Mercury 9812292*	62	1
27 Sep 03	**WAR ALL THE TIME** *Island US / Mercury 9860874*	62	1

Bobby THURSTON *US, male vocalist (Singles: 10 weeks)* pos/wks

29 Mar 80 ● **CHECK OUT THE GROOVE** *Epic EPC 8348* 10 10

TIFFANY *US, female vocalist – Tiffany Darwish (Singles: 45 weeks, Albums: 27 weeks)* pos/wks

16 Jan 88 ★ **I THINK WE'RE ALONE NOW** *MCA MCA 1211* ▲ 1 13
19 Mar 88 ● **COULD'VE BEEN** *MCA TIFF 2* ▲ 4 9
4 Jun 88 ● **I SAW HIM STANDING THERE** *MCA TIFF 3* 8 7
6 Aug 88 **FEELINGS OF FOREVER** *MCA TIFF 4* 52 2
12 Nov 88 **RADIO ROMANCE** *MCA TIFF 5* 13 11
11 Feb 89 **ALL THIS TIME** *MCA TIFF 6* 47 3
27 Feb 88 ● **TIFFANY** *MCA MCF 3415* ▲ 5 21
17 Dec 88 **HOLD AN OLD FRIEND'S HAND** *MCA MCF 3437* 56 6

TIGA *Canada, male producer – Tiga Sontag (Singles: 5 weeks)* pos/wks

11 May 02 **SUNGLASSES AT NIGHT** *City Rockers ROCKERS 15CD* [1] 25 3
6 Sep 03 **HOT IN HERRE** *Skint SKINT 90CD* 46 2

[1] Tiga and Zyntherius

TIGER *UK / Ireland, male / female vocal / instrumental group (Singles: 5 weeks)* pos/wks

31 Aug 96 **RACE** *Trade 2 TRDCD 004* 37 2
16 Nov 96 **MY PUPPET PAL** *Trade 2 TRDCD 005* 62 1
22 Feb 97 **ON THE ROSE** *Trade 2 TRDCD 008* 57 1
22 Aug 98 **FRIENDS** *Trade 2 TRDCD 013* 72 1

TIGERTAILZ *US, male vocal / instrumental group (Singles: 2 weeks, Albums: 2 weeks)* pos/wks

24 Jun 89 **LOVE BOMB BABY** *Music for Nations KUT 132* 75 1
16 Feb 91 **HEAVEN** *Music for Nations KUT 137* 71 1
7 Apr 90 **BEZERK** *Music For Nations MFN 96* 36 2

TIGHT FIT *UK, male / female vocal group (Singles: 49 weeks, Albums: 6 weeks)* pos/wks

18 Jul 81 ● **BACK TO THE SIXTIES** *Jive JIVE 002* 4 11
26 Sep 81 **BACK TO THE SIXTIES PART 2** *Jive JIVE 005* 33 5
23 Jan 82 ★ **THE LION SLEEPS TONIGHT** *Jive JIVE 9* 1 15
1 May 82 ● **FANTASY ISLAND** *Jive JIVE 13* 5 12
31 Jul 82 **SECRET HEART** *Jive JIVE 20* 41 6
26 Sep 81 **BACK TO THE SIXTIES** *Jive HIP 1* 38 4
4 Sep 82 **TIGHT FIT** *Jive HIP 2* 87 2

TIJUANA BRASS – *See Herb ALPERT and the TIJUANA BRASS*

TIK and TOK *UK, male vocal duo (Singles: 2 weeks, Albums: 2 weeks)* pos/wks

8 Oct 83 **COOL RUNNING** *Survival SUR 016* 69 2
4 Aug 84 **INTOLERANCE** *Survival SUR LP 008* 89 2

Tanita TIKARAM *UK, female vocalist (Singles: 31 weeks, Albums: 62 weeks)* pos/wks

30 Jul 88 ● **GOOD TRADITION** *WEA YZ 196* 10 10
22 Oct 88 **TWIST IN MY SOBRIETY** *WEA YZ 321* 22 8
14 Jan 89 **CATHEDRAL SONG** *WEA YZ 331* 48 3
18 Mar 89 **WORLD OUTSIDE YOUR WINDOW** *WEA YZ 363* 58 2
13 Jan 90 **WE ALMOST GOT IT TOGETHER** *WEA YZ 443* 52 3
9 Feb 91 **ONLY THE ONES WE LOVE** *East West YZ 558* 69 1
4 Feb 95 **I MIGHT BE CRYING** *East West YZ 879CD* 64 2
6 Jun 98 **STOP LISTENING** *Mother MUMCD 102* 67 1
29 Aug 98 **I DON'T WANNA LOSE AT LOVE** *Mother MUMCD 105* 73 1
24 Sep 88 ● **ANCIENT HEART** *WEA WX 210* 3 49
10 Feb 90 ● **THE SWEET KEEPER** *East West WX 330* 3 7
16 Feb 91 **EVERYBODY'S ANGEL** *East West WX 401* 19 4
25 Feb 95 **LOVERS IN THE CITY** *East West 4509988042* 75 1
19 Sep 98 **THE CAPPUCCINO SONGS** *Mother MUMCD 9801* 69 1

TILLMANN and REIS *Germany, male production duo – Tillmann Uhrmacher and Peter Reis (Singles: 1 week)* pos/wks

16 Sep 00 **BASSFLY** *Liquid Asset ASSET CD004* 70 1

See also Tillmann UHRMACHER

Johnny TILLOTSON *US, male vocalist (Singles: 50 weeks)* pos/wks

1 Dec 60 ★ **POETRY IN MOTION** *London HLA 9231* 1 15
2 Feb 61 **JIMMY'S GIRL (re)** *London HLA 9275* 43 2
12 Jul 62 **IT KEEPS RIGHT ON A HURTIN'** *London HLA 9550* 31 10
4 Oct 62 **SEND ME THE PILLOW YOU DREAM ON** *London HLA 9598* 21 10
27 Dec 62 **I CAN'T HELP IT (2re)** *London HLA 9642* 41 6
9 May 63 **OUT OF MY MIND** *London HLA 9695* 34 5
14 Apr 79 **POETRY IN MOTION / PRINCESS PRINCESS (re-issue)** *Lightning LIG 9016* 67 2

TILT *UK, male instrumental / production group (Singles: 8 weeks)* pos/wks

2 Dec 95 **I DREAM** *Perfecto PERF 112CD* 69 1
10 May 97 **MY SPIRIT** *Perfecto PERF 139CD* 61 1
13 Sep 97 **PLACES** *Perfecto PERF 149CD* 64 1
7 Feb 98 **BUTTERFLY** *Perfecto PERF 154CD1* [1] 41 1
27 Mar 99 **CHILDREN** *Deconstruction 74321648172* 51 1
8 May 99 **INVISIBLE** *Hooj Choons HOOJ 73CD* 20 2
12 Feb 00 **DARK SCIENCE (EP)** *Hooj Choons HOOJ 87* 55 1

[1] Tilt featuring Zee

Tracks on Dark Science (EP): 36 (two mixes) / Seduction of Orphheus (two mixes)

TIMBALAND *US, male producer / rapper – Tim Mosley (Singles: 13 weeks)* pos/wks

23 Jan 99 **GET ON THE BUS** *East West E3780CD* [1] 15 5
13 Mar 99 **HERE WE COME** *Virgin DINSD 179* [2] 43 1
19 Jun 99 **LOBSTER & SCRIMP** *Virgin DINSD 186* [3] 48 1
21 Jul 01 **WE NEED A RESOLUTION (re)** *Blackground VUSCD 206* [4] 20 6

[1] Destiny's Child featuring Timbaland [2] Timbaland / Missy Elliott and Magoo [3] Timbaland featuring Jay-Z [4] Aaliyah featuring Timbaland

Justin TIMBERLAKE *US, male vocalist (Singles: 61 weeks, Albums: 59 weeks)* pos/wks

2 Nov 02 ● **LIKE I LOVE YOU** *Jive 9254342* 2 16
15 Feb 03 ● **CRY ME A RIVER** *Jive 9254612* 2 12
15 Mar 03 ● **WORK IT** *Universal MCSCD 40312* [1] 7 11
24 May 03 **ROCK YOUR BODY (import)** *Jive 9254962* 46 1
31 May 03 ● **ROCK YOUR BODY** *Jive 9254952* 2 13
27 Sep 03 **SENORITA** *Jive 82876563442* 13 8
16 Nov 02 ★ **JUSTIFIED** *Jive 9224772* ....1 59+

[1] Nelly featuring Justin Timberlake

See also 'N SYNC

TIMBUK 3 *US, male / female vocal / instrumental duo – Pat and Barbara Kooyman MacDonald (Singles: 7 weeks, Albums: 4 weeks)* pos/wks

31 Jan 87 **THE FUTURE'S SO BRIGHT I GOTTA WEAR SHADES** *IRS IRM 126* 21 7
14 Feb 87 **GREETINGS FROM TIMBUK 3** *IRS MIRF 1015* 51 4

TIME *US, male vocal / instrumental group (Albums: 1 week)* pos/wks

28 Jul 90 **PANDEMONIUM** *Paisley Park WX 336* 66 1

TIME FREQUENCY *UK, male instrumental / production group (Singles: 34 weeks, Albums: 4 weeks)* pos/wks

6 Jun 92 **REAL LOVE** *Jive JIVET 307* 60 1
9 Jan 93 **NEW EMOTION** *Internal Affairs KGBCD 009* 36 6
12 Jun 93 **THE POWER ZONE (EP)** *Internal Affairs KGBD 010* 17 11
6 Nov 93 ● **REAL LOVE (re) (re-mix)** *Internal Affairs KGBCD 011* 8 8
28 May 94 **SUCH A PHANTASY** *Internal Affairs KGBD 013* 25 4
8 Oct 94 **DREAMSCAPE '94** *Internal Affairs KGBD 015* 32 3
31 Aug 02 **REAL LOVE (2nd re-mix)** *Jive 9253782* 43 1
18 Jun 94 **DOMINATOR** *Internal Affairs KGBD 500* 23 4

Tracks on The Power Zone (EP): The Ultimate High / The Ultimate High (full length) / The Power Zone / Take Me Away

TIME OF THE MUMPH *UK, male producer – Mark Mumford (Singles: 1 week)* pos/wks

11 Feb 95 **CONTROL** *Fresh FRSHD 24* 69 1

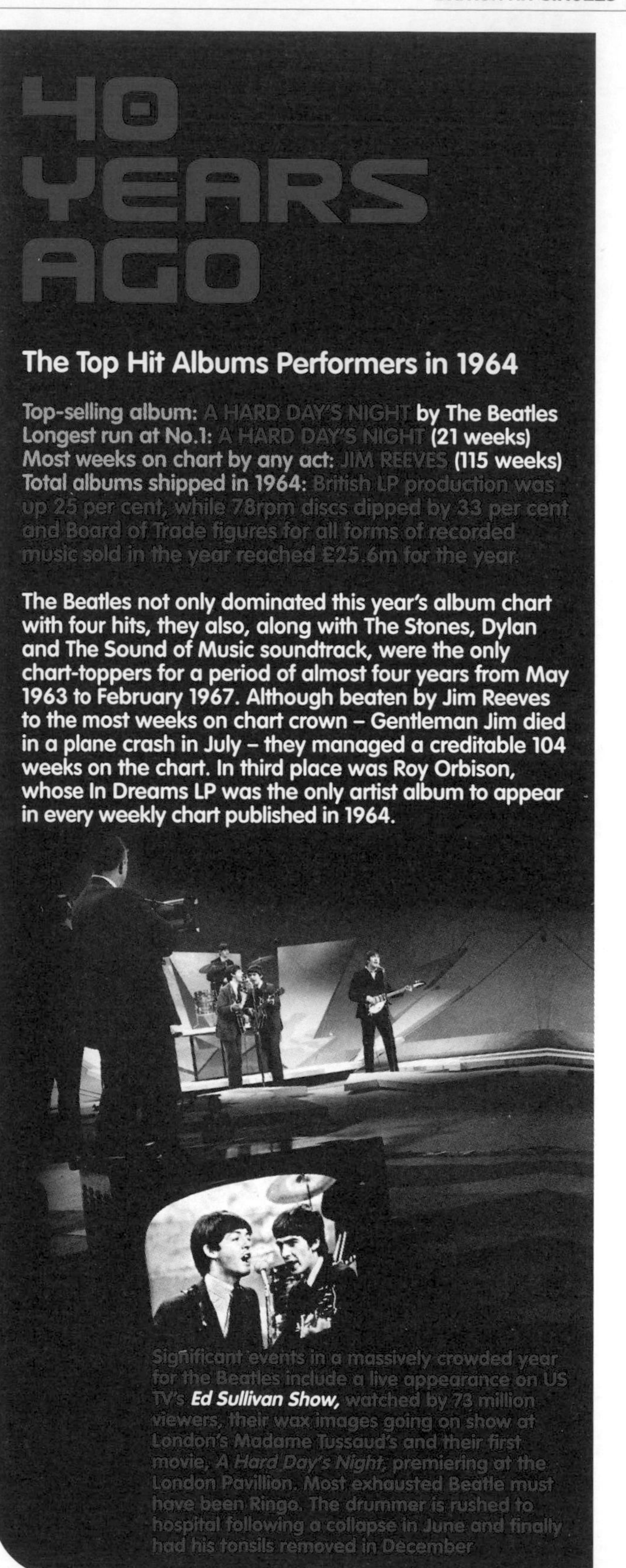

40 YEARS AGO

The Top Hit Albums Performers in 1964

Top-selling album: A HARD DAY'S NIGHT by The Beatles
Longest run at No.1: A HARD DAY'S NIGHT (21 weeks)
Most weeks on chart by any act: JIM REEVES (115 weeks)
Total albums shipped in 1964: British LP production was up 25 per cent, while 78rpm discs dipped by 33 per cent and Board of Trade figures for all forms of recorded music sold in the year reached £25.6m for the year.

The Beatles not only dominated this year's album chart with four hits, they also, along with The Stones, Dylan and The Sound of Music soundtrack, were the only chart-toppers for a period of almost four years from May 1963 to February 1967. Although beaten by Jim Reeves to the most weeks on chart crown – Gentleman Jim died in a plane crash in July – they managed a creditable 104 weeks on the chart. In third place was Roy Orbison, whose In Dreams LP was the only artist album to appear in every weekly chart published in 1964.

Significant events in a massively crowded year for the Beatles include a live appearance on US TV's *Ed Sullivan Show,* watched by 73 million viewers, their wax images going on show at London's Madame Tussaud's and their first movie, *A Hard Day's Night,* premiering at the London Pavillion. Most exhausted Beatle must have been Ringo. The drummer is rushed to hospital following a collapse in June and finally had his tonsils removed in December

TIME UK *UK, male vocal / instrumental group (Singles: 3 weeks)* pos/wks

8 Oct 83	**THE CABARET** *Red Bus / Aroadia TIM 123*	63	3

TIME ZONE
UK / US, male vocal / instrumental duo (Singles: 9 weeks) pos/wks

19 Jan 85	**WORLD DESTRUCTION** *Virgin VS 743*	44	9

TIMEBOX *UK, male vocal / instrumental group (Singles: 4 weeks)* pos/wks

24 Jul 68	**BEGGIN'** *Deram DM 194*	38	4

TIMELORDS
UK, male vocal / instrumental group (Singles: 9 weeks) pos/wks

4 Jun 88 ★	**DOCTORIN' THE TARDIS** *KLF Communications KLF 003*	1	9

See also JUSTIFIED ANCIENTS OF MU MU; KLF; 2K

TIMEX SOCIAL CLUB
US, male vocal / instrumental group (Singles: 9 weeks) pos/wks

13 Sep 86	**RUMORS** *Cooltempo COOL 133*	13	9

TIN MACHINE *US / UK, male vocal / instrumental group (Singles: 10 weeks, Albums: 12 weeks)* pos/wks

1 Jul 89	**UNDER THE GOD** *EMI-USA MT 68*	51	2
9 Sep 89	**TIN MACHINE / MAGGIE'S FARM (LIVE)** *EMI-USA MT 73*	48	2
24 Aug 91	**YOU BELONG IN ROCK 'N' ROLL** *London LON 305*	33	3
2 Nov 91	**BABY UNIVERSAL** *London LON 310*	48	3
3 Jun 89 ●	**TIN MACHINE** *EMI-USA MTLS 1044*	3	9
14 Sep 91	**TIN MACHINE II** *London 8282721*	23	3

See also David BOWIE

TIN TIN – *See Stephen 'Tin Tin' DUFFY*

TIN TIN OUT *UK, male instrumental / production duo – Lindsay Edwards and Darren Stokes (Singles: 42 weeks, Albums: 1 week)* pos/wks

13 Aug 94	**THE FEELING** *Deep Distraxion OILYCD 029* [1]	32	2
25 Mar 95	**ALWAYS SOMETHING THERE TO REMIND ME** *WEA YZ 911CD* [2]	14	5
8 Feb 97	**ALL I WANNA DO** *VC VCRD 15*	31	2
10 May 97	**DANCE WITH ME** *VC VCRD 17* [3]	35	2
20 Sep 97	**STRINGS FOR YASMIN** *VC VCRD 20*	31	3
28 Mar 98 ●	**HERE'S WHERE THE STORY ENDS** *VC Recordings VCRD 30* [4]	7	10
12 Sep 98	**SOMETIMES** *VC Recordings VCRD 34* [4]	20	4
11 Sep 99	**ELEVEN TO FLY** *VC Recordings VCRDX 52* [5]	26	2
13 Nov 99 ●	**WHAT I AM** *VC Recordings VCRD 53* [6]	2	12
5 Oct 96	**ADVENTURES IN TIN TIN OUT LAND** *VC Recordings VCRLPX 1*	65	1

[1] Tin Tin Out featuring Sweet Tee [2] Tin Tin Out featuring Espiritu [3] Tin Tin Out featuring Tony Hadley [4] Tin Tin Out featuring Shelley Nelson [5] Tin Tin Out featuring Wendy Page [6] Tin Tin Out featuring Emma Bunton

TINA – *See Tina TURNER*

TINDERSTICKS *UK, male vocal / instrumental group (Singles: 7 weeks, Albums: 9 weeks)* pos/wks

5 Feb 94	**KATHLEEN (EP)** *This Way Up WAY 2833CD*	61	1
18 Mar 95	**NO MORE AFFAIRS** *This Way Up WAY 3833*	58	1
12 Aug 95	**TRAVELLING LIGHT** *This Way Up WAY 4533*	51	1
7 Jun 97	**BATHTIME** *This Way Up WAY 6166*	38	1
1 Nov 97	**RENTED ROOMS** *This Way Up WAY 6566*	56	1
4 Sep 99	**CAN WE START AGAIN?** *Island CID 756*	54	1
2 Aug 03	**SOMETIMES IT HURTS** *Beggars Banquet BBQ 369CD*	60	1
23 Oct 93	**TINDERSTICKS** *This Way Up 5183064*	56	1
15 Apr 95	**THE SECOND TINDERSTICKS ALBUM** *This Way Up 5263032*	13	3
28 Oct 95	**THE BLOOMSBURY THEATRE 12.3.95** *This Way Up 5285972*	32	1
21 Jun 97	**CURTAINS** *This Way Up 5243442*	37	2
18 Sep 99	**SIMPLE PLEASURE** *Island CID 8085*	36	1
2 Jun 01	**CAN OUR LOVE ...** *Beggars Banquet BBQCD 222*	47	1

Tracks on Kathleen (EP): Kathleen / Summat Moon / A Sweet Sweet Man / E-Type Joe

TINGO TANGO *UK, male instrumental group (Singles: 2 weeks)* pos/wks

21 Jul 90 **IT IS JAZZ** *Champion CHAMP 250* 68 2

TINMAN *UK, male producer – Paul Dakeyne (Singles: 9 weeks)* pos/wks

20 Aug 94 ● **EIGHTEEN STRINGS** *ffrr FCD 242* 9 8
3 Jun 95 **GUDVIBE** *ffrr FCD 262* 49 1

TINY TIM *US, male vocalist / instrumentalist – banjo – Herbert Khaury, d. 30 Nov 1996 (Singles: 1 week)* pos/wks

5 Feb 69 **GREAT BALLS OF FIRE** *Reprise RS 20802* 45 1

TITANIC
Norway / UK, male instrumental group (Singles: 12 weeks) pos/wks

25 Sep 71 ● **SULTANA** *CBS 5365* 5 12

TITIYO *Sweden, female vocalist (Singles: 6 weeks)* pos/wks

3 Mar 90 **AFTER THE RAIN** *Arista 112722* 60 3
6 Oct 90 **FLOWERS** *Arista 113212* 71 1
5 Feb 94 **TELL ME I'M NOT DREAMING** *Arista 74321185622* 45 2

Cara TIVEY – *See Billy BRAGG*

TOADS – *See Stan FREBERG*

Art and Dotty TODD *US, male / female vocal duo, Dotty Todd d. 12 Dec 2000 (Singles: 7 weeks)* pos/wks

13 Feb 53 ● **BROKEN WINGS** *HMV B 10399* 6 7

TOGETHER
UK, male vocal / instrumental group (Singles: 8 weeks) pos/wks

4 Aug 90 **HARDCORE UPROAR** *ffrr F 143* 12 8

TOGETHER *France, male production duo – Thomas Bangalter and Martial Weiss (Singles: 1 week)* pos/wks

4 Jan 03 **SO MUCH LOVE TO GIVE (import)** *Roule TOGETHER2* 71 1

See also DAFT PUNK

TOI – *See Warren G*

TOKENS *US, male vocal group (Singles: 12 weeks)* pos/wks

21 Dec 61 **THE LION SLEEPS TONIGHT (WIMOWEH)** *RCA 1263* ▲ 11 12

TOKYO GHETTO PUSSY *Germany, male instrumental / production duo – Rolf Ellmer and Markus Loeffel (Singles: 4 weeks)* pos/wks

16 Sep 95 **EVERYBODY ON THE FLOOR (PUMP IT)** *Epic 6611132* 26 2
16 Mar 96 **I KISS YOUR LIPS** *Epic 6623212* 55 2

See also JAM & SPOON featuring PLAVKA; STORM

TOL and TOL
Holland, male vocal / instrumental duo (Singles: 2 weeks) pos/wks

14 Apr 90 **ELENI** *Dover ROJ 5* 73 2

TOM TOM CLUB *US, female / male vocal / instrumental group (Singles: 20 weeks, Albums: 1 week)* pos/wks

20 Jun 81 ● **WORDY RAPPINGHOOD** *Island WIP 6694* 7 9
10 Oct 81 **GENIUS OF LOVE** *Island WIP 6735* 65 2
7 Aug 82 **UNDER THE BOARDWALK** *Island WIP 6762* 22 9
24 Oct 81 **TOM TOM CLUB** *Island ILPS 9686* 78 1

See also TALKING HEADS

TOMBA VIRA *Holland, male production duo – Rene ter Horst and Gaston Steenkist (Singles: 1 week)* pos/wks

16 Jun 01 **THE SOUND OF: OH YEAH** *VC Recordings VCRD 88* 51 1

See also GOODMEN; JARK PRONGO; RHYTHMKILLAZ; CHOCOLATE PUMA; RIVA featuring Dannii MINOGUE

TOMCAT
UK, male vocal / instrumental group (Singles: 1 week) pos/wks

14 Oct 00 **CRAZY** *Virgin VSCDT 1785* 48 1

TOMCRAFT *Germany, male producer – Thomas Bruckner (Singles: 15 weeks)* pos/wks

10 May 03 ★ **LONELINESS** *Data / Ministry of Sound DATA 52CDS* ■ 1 13
25 Oct 03 **BRAINWASHED (CALL YOU)** *Data DATA 63CDS* 43 2

Satoshi TOMIIE – *See Frankie KNUCKLES*

TOMITA *Japan, male instrumentalist – synthesizer – Isao Tomita (Albums: 33 weeks)* pos/wks

7 Jun 75 **SNOWFLAKES ARE DANCING** *RCA Red Seal ARL 10488* 17 20
16 Aug 75 **PICTURES AT AN EXHIBITION** *RCA Red Seal ARL 10838* 42 5
7 May 77 **HOLST: THE PLANETS** *RCA Red Seal RL 11919* 41 6
9 Feb 80 **TOMITA'S GREATEST HITS** *RCA Red Seal RL 43076* 66 2

Ricky TOMLINSON
UK, male actor / vocalist (Singles: 3 weeks) pos/wks

10 Nov 01 **ARE YOU LOOKIN' AT ME?** *All Around the World CDRICKY 1* ..28 3

TOMSKI
UK, male producer – Tom Jankiewicz (Singles: 3 weeks) pos/wks

18 Apr 98 **14 HOURS TO SAVE THE EARTH** *Xtravaganza 0091515 EXT* 42 1
12 Feb 00 **LOVE WILL COME** *Xtravaganza XTRAV6CDS* [1] 31 2

[1] Tomski featuring Jan Johnston

TONE LOC *US, male rapper – Anthony Smith (Singles: 19 weeks, Albums: 16 weeks)* pos/wks

11 Feb 89 **WILD THING / LOC'ED AFTER DARK** *Fourth & Broadway BRW 121* 21 8
20 May 89 **FUNKY COLD MEDINA / ON FIRE** *Fourth & Broadway BRW 129* 13 9
5 Aug 89 **I GOT IT GOIN' ON** *Fourth & Broadway BRW 140* 55 2
25 Mar 89 **LOC'ED AFTER DARK** *Delicious BRLP 526* ▲ 22 16

TONGUE 'N' CHEEK *UK, male / female vocal / instrumental group (Singles: 28 weeks, Albums: 3 weeks)* pos/wks

27 Feb 88 **NOBODY (CAN LOVE ME)** *Criminal BUS 6* [1] 59 6
25 Nov 89 **ENCORE** *Syncopate SY 33* 41 4
14 Apr 90 **TOMORROW** *Syncopate SY 34* 20 7
4 Aug 90 **NOBODY (re-recording)** *Syncopate SY 37* 37 5
19 Jan 91 **FORGET ME NOTS** *Syncopate SY 39* 26 6
22 Sep 90 **THIS IS TONGUE 'N' CHEEK** *Syncopate SYLP 6006* 45 3

[1] Tongue in Cheek

TONICS – *See Adrian BAKER and the TONICS*

TONIGHT
UK, male vocal / instrumental group (Singles: 10 weeks) pos/wks

28 Jan 78 **DRUMMER MAN** *Target TDS 1* 14 8
20 May 78 **MONEY THAT'S YOUR PROBLEM** *Target TDS 2* 66 2

TONY! TONI! TONÉ!
US, male vocal group (Singles: 12 weeks, Albums: 1 week) pos/wks

30 Jun 90 **OAKLAND STROKE** *Wing WING 7* [1] 50 5
9 Mar 91 **IT NEVER RAINS (IN SOUTHERN CALIFORNIA)** *Wing WING 10* [1] 69 2
4 Sep 93 **IF I HAD NO LOOT** *Polydor PZCD 292* 44 3
3 May 97 **LET'S GET DOWN** *Mercury MERCD 485* [2] 33 2
2 Oct 93 **SONS OF SOUL** *Polydor 5149332* 66 1

[1] Tony! Toni! Toné! [2] Tony Toni Toné featuring DJ Quick

See also Raphael SAADIQ

TOO TOUGH TEE – *See DYNAMIX II featuring TOO TOUGH TEE*

TOOL *US, male vocal / instrumental group (Albums: 3 weeks)* pos/wks

26 May 01 **LATERALUS** *Tool Dissectional 9210132* ▲ 16 3

TOON TRAVELLERS – See MUNGO JERRY

TOP *UK, male vocal / instrumental group (Singles: 2 weeks)* pos/wks

20 Jul 91 **NUMBER ONE DOMINATOR** *Island IS 496* 67 2

TOP LINERS – See Rocky SHARPE and The REPLAYS

Martina TOPLEY-BIRD *UK, female vocalist (Albums: 1 week)* pos/wks

26 Jul 03 **QUIXOTIC** *Independiente ISOM 34CD* 70 1

TOPLOADER *UK, male vocal / instrumental group (Singles: 56 weeks, Albums: 66 weeks)* pos/wks

22 May 99 **ACHILLES HEEL** *Sony S2 6671612* 64 1
7 Aug 99 **LET THE PEOPLE KNOW** *Sony S2 6677132* 52 1
4 Mar 00 **DANCING IN THE MOONLIGHT** *Sony S2 6689412* 19 7
13 May 00 ● **ACHILLES HEEL (re-issue)** *Sony S2 6691872* 8 7
2 Sep 00 **JUST HOLD ON** *Sony S2 6696242* 20 4
25 Nov 00 ● **DANCING IN THE MOONLIGHT (re-issue)** *Sony S2 6699852* 7 25
21 Apr 01 **ONLY FOR A WHILE** *Sony S2 S2 6708612* 19 4
17 Aug 02 **TIME OF MY LIFE** *Sony S2 S26728862* 18 7
3 Jun 00 ● **ONKA'S BIG MOKA** *Sony S2 4947802* 4 61
31 Aug 02 ● **MAGIC HOTEL** *Sony S2 5084712* 3 5

TOPOL *Israel, male vocalist / actor – Chaim Topol (Singles: 20 weeks, Albums: 1 week)* pos/wks

20 Apr 67 ● **IF I WERE A RICH MAN** *CBS 202651* 9 20
11 May 85 **TOPOL'S ISRAEL** *BBC REH 529* 80 1

Bernie TORME *Ireland male vocalist / instrumentalist – guitar (Albums: 3 weeks)* pos/wks

3 Jul 82 **TURN OUT THE LIGHTS** *Kamaflage KAMLP 2* 50 3

See also GILLAN

Mel TORME *US, male vocalist, d. 5 Jun 1999 (Singles: 32 weeks, Albums: 8 weeks)* pos/wks

27 Apr 56 ● **MOUNTAIN GREENERY (re)** *Vogue / Coral Q 72150* 4 24
3 Jan 63 **COMIN' HOME BABY** *London HLK 9643* 13 8
28 Jul 56 ● **MEL TORME AT THE CRESCENDO** *Vogue-Coral LVA 9004*....3 4
18 Aug 56 ● **MEL TORME WITH THE MARTY PAICH DEK-TETTE** *London Jazz LTZ N 15009* 3 4

TORNADOS
UK, male instrumental group – includes Heinz (Singles: 59 weeks) pos/wks

30 Aug 62 ★ **TELSTAR** *Decca F 11494* ▲ 1 25
10 Jan 63 ● **GLOBETROTTER** *Decca F 11562* 5 11
21 Mar 63 **ROBOT** *Decca F 11606* 17 12
6 Jun 63 **THE ICE CREAM MAN** *Decca F 11662* 18 9
10 Oct 63 **DRAGONFLY** *Decca F 11745* 41 2

See also HEINZ

Mitchell TOROK *US, male vocalist (Singles: 19 weeks)* pos/wks

28 Sep 56 ● **WHEN MEXICO GAVE UP THE RHUMBA (re)** *Brunswick 05586* 6 18
11 Jan 57 **RED LIGHT, GREEN LIGHT** *Brunswick 05626* 29 1

Liz TORRES – See Danny TENAGLIA

Emiliana TORRINI *Iceland, female vocalist (Singles: 3 weeks)* pos/wks

10 Jun 00 **EASY** *One Little Indian 274 TP7CD* 63 1
9 Sep 00 **UNEMPLOYED IN SUMMERTIME** *One Little Indian 275 TP7CDL* 63 1
3 Feb 01 **TO BE FREE** *One Little Indian 276 TP7CD* 44 1

Peter TOSH *Jamaica, male vocalist, d. 11 Sep 1987 (Singles: 12 weeks, Albums: 1 week)* pos/wks

21 Oct 78 **(YOU GOTTA WALK) DON'T LOOK BACK** *Rolling Stones 2859* 43 7
2 Apr 83 **JOHNNY B GOODE** *EMI RIC 115* 48 5
25 Sep 76 **LEGALIZE IT** *Virgin V 2061* 54 1

TOTAL *US, female vocal group (Singles: 11 weeks)* pos/wks

15 Jul 95 **CAN'T YOU SEE** *Tommy Boy TBCD 700* [1] 43 2
14 Sep 96 **KISSIN' YOU** *Arista 74321404172* 29 2
15 Feb 97 **DO YOU THINK ABOUT US** *Puff Daddy 74321458492* 49 1
18 Apr 98 **WHAT YOU WANT** *Puff Daddy 74321578772* [2] 15 5
30 Sep 00 **I WONDER WHY HE'S THE GREATEST DJ** *Tommy Boy TBCD 2100* [3] 68 1

[1] Total featuring the Notorious B.I.G. [2] Mase featuring Total [3] Tony Touch featuring Total

TOTAL CONTRAST
UK, male vocal / instrumental duo – Robin Achampong and Delroy Murray (Singles: 22 weeks, Albums: 3 weeks) pos/wks

3 Aug 85 **TAKES A LITTLE TIME** *London LON 71* 17 10
19 Oct 85 **HIT AND RUN** *London LON 76* 41 5
1 Mar 86 **THE RIVER** *London LON 83* 44 3
10 May 86 **WHAT YOU GONNA DO ABOUT IT** *London LON 95* 63 4
8 Mar 86 **TOTAL CONTRAST** *London LONLP 15* 66 3

TOTO *US, male vocal / instrumental group (Singles: 35 weeks, Albums: 39 weeks)* pos/wks

10 Feb 79 **HOLD THE LINE** *CBS 6784* 14 11
5 Feb 83 ● **AFRICA** *CBS A 2510* ▲ 3 10
9 Apr 83 **ROSANNA** *CBS A 2079* 12 8
18 Jun 83 **I WON'T HOLD YOU BACK** *CBS A 3392* 37 5
18 Nov 95 **I WILL REMEMBER** *Columbia 6626552* 64 1
31 Mar 79 **TOTO** *CBS 83148*....37 5
26 Feb 83 ● **TOTO IV** *CBS 85529* 4 30
17 Nov 84 **ISOLATION** *CBS 86305* 67 2
20 Sep 86 **FAHRENHEIT** *CBS 57091* 99 1
9 Apr 88 **THE SEVENTH ONE** *CBS 460465 1*....73 1

TOTO COELO *UK, female vocal group (Singles: 14 weeks)* pos/wks

7 Aug 82 ● **I EAT CANNIBALS PART 1** *Radialchoice TIC 10* 8 10
13 Nov 82 **DRACULA'S TANGO / MUCHO MACHO** *Radialchoice TIC 11* 54 4

TOTTENHAM HOTSPUR FA CUP FINAL SQUAD
UK, male football team vocalists (Singles: 23 weeks) pos/wks

9 May 81 ● **OSSIE'S DREAM (SPURS ARE ON THEIR WAY TO WEMBLEY)** *Shelf SHELF 1* 5 8
1 May 82 **TOTTENHAM TOTTENHAM** *Shelf SHELF 2* 19 7
9 May 87 **HOT SHOT TOTTENHAM!** *Rainbow RBR 16* 18 5
11 May 91 **WHEN THE YEAR ENDS IN 1** *A1 A 1324* 44 3

All hits feature the vocal and instrumental talents of Chas and Dave

See also COCKEREL CHORUS

TOUCH & GO
UK, male / female vocal / production group (Singles: 12 weeks) pos/wks

7 Nov 98 ● **WOULD YOU...?** *Oval VVR 5003083* 3 12

TOUCH OF SOUL
UK, male / female vocal / instrumental group (Singles: 3 weeks) pos/wks

19 May 90 **WE GOT THE LOVE** *Cooltempo COOL 204* 46 3

Tony TOUCH featuring TOTAL *US, male producer – Anthony Hernandez and US, female vocal group (Singles: 1 week)* pos/wks

30 Sep 00 **I WONDER WHY HE'S THE GREATEST DJ** *Tommy Boy TBCD 2100* 68 1

TOUR DE FORCE
UK, male production trio (Singles: 1 week) pos/wks

16 May 98 **CATALAN** *East West EW 161CD* 71 1

Ali Farka TOURE – See Ry COODER

TOURISTS *UK, male / female vocal / instrumental group (Singles: 40 weeks, Albums: 18 weeks)* pos/wks

9 Jun 79 **BLIND AMONG THE FLOWERS** *Logo GO 350* 52 5
8 Sep 79 **THE LONELIEST MAN IN THE WORLD** *Logo GO 360* 32 7
10 Nov 79 ● **I ONLY WANT TO BE WITH YOU** *Logo GO 370* 4 14
9 Feb 80 ● **SO GOOD TO BE BACK HOME AGAIN** *Logo TOUR 1* 8 9
18 Oct 80 **DON'T SAY I TOLD YOU SO** *RCA TOUR 2* 40 5
14 Jul 79 **THE TOURISTS** *Logo GO 1018* 72 1
3 Nov 79 **REALITY EFFECT** *Logo GO 1019* 23 16
22 Nov 80 **LUMINOUS BASEMENT** *RCA RCALP 5001* 75 1

See also EURYTHMICS; VEGAS; David A STEWART; ANNIE LENNOX

TOUTES LES FILLES *UK, female vocal group (Singles: 1 week)* pos/wks

4 Sep 99 **THAT'S WHAT LOVE CAN DO** *London LONCD 434* 44 1

Carol Lynn TOWNES *US, female vocalist (Singles: 7 weeks)* pos/wks

4 Aug 84 **99 1/2** *Polydor POSP 693* 47 4
19 Jan 85 **BELIEVE IN THE BEAT** *Polydor POSP 720* 56 3

Fuzz TOWNSHEND *UK, male producer (Singles: 1 week)* pos/wks

6 Sep 97 **HELLO DARLIN** *Echo ECSCD 46* 51 1

Pete TOWNSHEND *UK, male vocalist / instrumentalist – guitar (Singles: 17 weeks, Albums: 28 weeks)* pos/wks

5 Apr 80 **ROUGH BOYS** *Atco K 11460* 39 6
21 Jun 80 **LET MY LOVE OPEN YOUR DOOR** *Atco K 11486* 46 6
21 Aug 82 **UNIFORMS (CORPS D'ESPRIT)** *Atco K 11751* 48 5
21 Oct 72 **WHO CAME FIRST** *Track 2408 201* 30 2
15 Oct 77 **ROUGH MIX** *Polydor 2442147* [1] 44 3
3 May 80 **EMPTY GLASS** *Atco K 50699* 11 14
3 Jul 82 **ALL THE BEST COWBOYS HAVE CHINESE EYES** *Atco K 50889* 32 8
30 Nov 85 **WHITE CITY** *Atco 2523921* 70 1

[1] Pete Townshend and Ronnie Lane

See also The WHO

TOXIC TWO *US, male instrumental / production duo – Ray Love and Damon Wild (Singles: 6 weeks)* pos/wks

7 Mar 92 **RAVE GENERATOR** *PWL International PWL 223* 13 6

TOY DOLLS *UK, male vocal / instrumental group (Singles: 12 weeks, Albums: 1 week)* pos/wks

1 Dec 84 ● **NELLIE THE ELEPHANT** *Volume VOL 11* 4 12
25 May 85 **A FAR OUT DISC** *Volume VOLP 2* 71 1

TOYAH (359 Top 500) *Visually striking punk / pop vocalist, b. Toyah Willcox 16 May 1958, Birmingham, UK. Came to prominence through acting – first major role in 1977 movie 'Jubilee'. Married King Crimson guitarist Robert Fripp in 1986. One of the first acts to chart regularly with EPs (Singles: 87 weeks, Albums: 97 weeks)* pos/wks

14 Feb 81 ● **FOUR FROM TOYAH (EP)** *Safari TOY 1* 4 14
16 May 81 ● **I WANT TO BE FREE** *Safari SAFE 34* 8 11
3 Oct 81 ● **THUNDER IN THE MOUNTAINS** *Safari SAFE 38* 4 9
28 Nov 81 **FOUR MORE FROM TOYAH (EP)** *Safari TOY 2* 14 9
22 May 82 **BRAVE NEW WORLD** *Safari SAFE 45* 21 8
17 Jul 82 **IEYA** *Safari SAFE 28* 48 5
9 Oct 82 **BE LOUD BE PROUD (BE HEARD)** *Safari SAFE 52* 30 7
24 Sep 83 **REBEL RUN** *Safari SAFE 56* 24 5
19 Nov 83 **THE VOW** *Safari SAFE 58* 50 5
27 Apr 85 **DON'T FALL IN LOVE (I SAID)** *Portrait A 6160* 22 6
29 Jun 85 **SOUL PASSING THROUGH SOUL** *Portrait A 6359* 57 3
25 Apr 87 **ECHO BEACH** *EG EGO 31* 54 5
14 Jun 80 **THE BLUE MEANING** *Safari IEYA 666* 40 4
17 Jan 81 **TOYAH! TOYAH! TOYAH!** *Safari LIVE 2* 22 14
30 May 81 ● **ANTHEM** *Safari VOOR 1* 2 46
19 Jun 82 ● **THE CHANGELING** *Safari VOOR 9* 6 12
13 Nov 82 **WARRIOR ROCK – TOYAH ON TOUR** *Safari TNT 1* 20 6
5 Nov 83 **LOVE IS THE LAW** *Safari VOOR 10* 28 7
25 Feb 84 **TOYAH! TOYAH! TOYAH!** *K-Tel NE 1268* 43 4
3 Aug 85 **MINX** *Portrait PRT 26415* 24 4

Tracks on Four From Toyah (EP): It's a Mystery / Revelations / War Boys / Angels and Demons. Tracks on Four More From Toyah (EP): Good Morning Universe / Urban Tribesman / In the Fairground / The Furious Futures

TOY-BOX *Denmark, male / female vocal duo (Singles: 2 weeks)* pos/wks

18 Sep 99 **BEST FRIEND** *Edel 0058245 ERE* 41 2

TOYS *US, female vocal group (Singles: 17 weeks)* pos/wks

4 Nov 65 ● **A LOVER'S CONCERTO** *Stateside SS 460* 5 13
27 Jan 66 **ATTACK** *Stateside SS 483* 36 4

Faye TOZER – *See STEPS; Russell WATSON*

T'PAU (412 Top 500) *Shropshire lads and a lass whose No.1 hit in 1987 had the distinction of being the 600th chart-topper. T'Pau (Mr Spock's Vulcan friend in 'Star Trek') comprised writers Carol Decker (v) and Ron Rogers (g), plus Michael Chetwood (k), Paul Jackson (b), Tim Burgess (d) and Taj Wyzgowski (g) (Singles: 77 weeks, Albums: 85 weeks)* pos/wks

8 Aug 87 ● **HEART AND SOUL** *Siren SRN 41* 4 13
24 Oct 87 ★ **CHINA IN YOUR HAND** *Siren SRN 64* 1 15
30 Jan 88 ● **VALENTINE** *Siren SRN 69* 9 8
2 Apr 88 **SEX TALK (LIVE)** *Siren SRN 80* 23 7
25 Jun 88 **I WILL BE WITH YOU** *Siren SRN 87* 14 6
1 Oct 88 **SECRET GARDEN** *Siren SRN 93* 18 7
3 Dec 88 **ROAD TO OUR DREAM** *Siren SRN 100* 42 6
25 Mar 89 **ONLY THE LONELY** *Siren SRN 107* 28 6
18 May 91 **WHENEVER YOU NEED ME** *Siren SRN 140* 16 6
27 Jul 91 **WALK ON AIR** *Siren SRN 142* 62 2
20 Feb 93 **VALENTINE (re-issue)** *Virgin VALEG 1* 53 1
26 Sep 87 ★ **BRIDGE OF SPIES** *Siren SIRENLP 8* 1 59
5 Nov 88 ● **RAGE** *Siren SRNLP 20* 4 17
22 Jun 91 ● **THE PROMISE** *Siren SRNLP 32* 10 7
27 Feb 93 **HEART AND SOUL – THE VERY BEST OF T'PAU** *Virgin TPAUD 1* 35 2

TRA-KNOX – *See Will SMITH*

Ian TRACEY / LIVERPOOL CATHEDRALS' CHOIRS *UK, conductor and male / female choirs (Albums: 3 weeks)* pos/wks

21 Mar 92 **YOUR FAVOURITE HYMNS** *Virgin Classics 7912092* 62 3

TRACIE *UK, female vocalist – Tracie Young (Singles: 24 weeks, Albums: 2 weeks)* pos/wks

26 Mar 83 ● **THE HOUSE THAT JACK BUILT** *Respond KOB 701* 9 8
16 Jul 83 **GIVE IT SOME EMOTION** *Respond KOB 704* 24 9
14 Apr 84 **SOUL'S ON FIRE** *Respond KOB 708* 73 2
9 Jun 84 **(I LOVE YOU) WHEN YOU SLEEP** *Respond KOB 710* 59 3
17 Aug 85 **I CAN'T LEAVE YOU ALONE** *Respond SBS 1* [1] 60 2
30 Jun 84 **FAR FROM THE HURTING KIND** *Respond RRL 502* 64 2

[1] Tracie Young

Gordon TRACKS – *See AIR*

TRACY – *See MASSIVO featuring TRACY*

Jeanie TRACY *US, female vocalist (Singles: 3 weeks)* pos/wks

11 Jun 94 **IF THIS IS LOVE** *Pulse 8 CDLOSE 63* 73 1
5 Nov 94 **DO YOU BELIEVE IN THE WONDER** *Pulse 8 CDLOSE 74* 57 1
13 May 95 **IT'S A MAN'S MAN'S MAN'S WORLD** *Pulse 8 CDLOSE 89* [1] 73 1

[1] Jeanie Tracy and Bobby Womack

TRAFFIC *UK, male vocal / instrumental group (Singles: 40 weeks, Albums: 41 weeks)* pos/wks

1 Jun 67 ● **PAPER SUN** *Island WIP 6002* 5 10
6 Sep 67 ● **HOLE IN MY SHOE** *Island WIP 6017* 2 14

29 Nov 67 ● **HERE WE GO ROUND THE MULBERRY BUSH** *Island WIP 6025* 8 12
6 Mar 68 **NO FACE, NO NAME, NO NUMBER** *Island WIP 6030* 40 4
30 Dec 67 ● **MR FANTASY** *Island ILP 9061* 8 16
26 Oct 68 ● **TRAFFIC** *Island ILPS 9081 T* 9 8
8 Aug 70 **JOHN BARLEYCORN MUST DIE** *Island ILPS 9116* 11 9
24 Nov 73 **ON THE ROAD** *Island ISLD 2* 40 3
28 Sep 74 **WHEN THE EAGLE FLIES** *Island ILPS 9273* 31 1
21 May 94 **FAR FROM HOME** *Virgin CDV 2727* 29 4

TRAIN *US, male vocal / instrumental group (Singles: 10 weeks, Albums: 9 weeks)* pos/wks

11 Aug 01 ● **DROPS OF JUPITER (TELL ME)** *Columbia 6714472* 10 8
2 Mar 02 **SHE'S ON FIRE** *Columbia 6722812* 49 2
18 Aug 01 ● **DROPS OF JUPITER** *Columbia 5023069* 8 9

TRAMAINE *US, female vocalist (Singles: 2 weeks)* pos/wks

5 Oct 85 **FALL DOWN (SPIRIT OF LOVE)** *A&M AM 281* 60 2

TRAMMPS *US, male vocal group (Singles: 55 weeks)* pos/wks

23 Nov 74 **ZING WENT THE STRINGS OF MY HEART** *Buddah BDS 405* 29 10
1 Feb 75 **SIXTY MINUTE MAN** *Buddah BDS 415* 40 4
11 Oct 75 ● **HOLD BACK THE NIGHT** *Buddah BDS 437* 5 8
13 Mar 76 **THAT'S WHERE THE HAPPY PEOPLE GO** *Atlantic K 10703* 35 8
24 Jul 76 **SOUL SEARCHING TIME** *Atlantic K 10797* 42 3
14 May 77 **DISCO INFERNO** *Atlantic K 10914* 16 7
24 Jun 78 **DISCO INFERNO (re-issue)** *Atlantic K 11135* 47 10
12 Dec 92 **HOLD BACK THE NIGHT** *Network NWK 65* [1] 30 5

[1] KWS features guest vocal from The Trammps

TRANCESETTERS *Holland, male production duo (Singles: 2 weeks)* pos/wks

4 Mar 00 **ROACHES** *Hooj Choons HOOJ 89CD* 55 1
9 Jun 01 **SYNERGY** *Hooj Choons 107* 72 1

TRANSA *UK, male DJ / production duo (Singles: 2 weeks)* pos/wks

30 Aug 97 **PROPHASE** *Perfecto PERF 147CD* 65 1
21 Feb 98 **ENERVATE** *Perfecto PERF 155CD* 42 1

TRANSATLANTIC SOUL *US, male producer – Roger Sanchez (Singles: 1 week)* pos/wks

22 Mar 97 **RELEASE YO SELF** *Deconstruction 74321459102* 43 1

TRANSFER *UK, male producer (Singles: 1 week)* pos/wks

3 Nov 01 **POSSESSION** *Mulitply CDMULTY 76* 54 1

TRANSFORMER 2 *Belgium / Holland, male / female vocal / instrumental group (Singles: 1 week)* pos/wks

24 Feb 96 **JUST CAN'T GET ENOUGH** *Positiva CDTIV 49* 45 1

See also CONVERT

TRANSGLOBAL UNDERGROUND *UK, male / female vocal / instrumental group (Albums: 3 weeks)* pos/wks

30 Oct 93 **DREAM OF 100 NATIONS** *Nation NR 021CD* 45 1
29 Oct 94 **INTERNATIONAL TIMES** *Nation NATCD 38* 40 1
25 May 96 **PSYCHIC KARAOKE** *Nation NRCD 1067* 62 1

TRANSISTER *UK / US, male / female vocal / instrumental group (Singles: 1 week)* pos/wks

28 Mar 98 **LOOK WHO'S PERFECT NOW** *Virgin VSCDT 1678* 56 1

TRANSPLANTS *US, male vocal / instrumental group (Singles: 3 weeks)* pos/wks

19 Apr 03 **DIAMONDS AND GUNS** *Hellcat 11082* 27 2
19 Jul 03 **DJ DJ** *Hellcat 11122* 49 1

TRANSVISION VAMP *UK, female / male vocal / instrumental group (Singles: 59 weeks, Albums: 58 weeks)* pos/wks

16 Apr 88 **TELL THAT GIRL TO SHUT UP** *MCA TVV 2* 45 3
25 Jun 88 ● **I WANT YOUR LOVE** *MCA TVV 3* 5 13
17 Sep 88 **REVOLUTION BABY** *MCA TVV 4* 30 5
19 Nov 88 **SISTER MOON** *MCA TVV 5* 41 5
1 Apr 89 ● **BABY I DON'T CARE** *MCA TVV 6* 3 11
10 Jun 89 **THE ONLY ONE** *MCA TVV 7* 15 6
5 Aug 89 **LANDSLIDE OF LOVE** *MCA TVV 8* 14 5
4 Nov 89 **BORN TO BE SOLD** *MCA TVV 9* 22 4
13 Apr 91 **(I JUST WANNA) B WITH U** *MCA TVV 10* 30 4
22 Jun 91 **IF LOOKS COULD KILL** *MCA TVV 11* 41 3
15 Oct 88 ● **POP ART** *MCA MCF 3421* 4 32
8 Jul 89 ★ **VELVETEEN** *MCA MCG 6050* ■ 1 26

TRANS-X *Canada, female / male vocal / instrumental group (Singles: 9 weeks)* pos/wks

13 Jul 85 ● **LIVING ON VIDEO** *Boiling Point POSP 650* 9 9

TRASH *UK, male vocal / instrumental group (Singles: 3 weeks)* pos/wks

25 Oct 69 **GOLDEN SLUMBERS / CARRY THAT WEIGHT** *Apple 17* 35 3

TRASH CAN SINATRAS *UK, male vocal / instrumental group (Singles: 1 week, Albums: 2 weeks)* pos/wks

24 Apr 93 **HAYFEVER** *Go! Discs GODCD 98* 61 1
7 Jul 90 **CAKE** *Go! Discs 82820211* 74 1
15 May 93 **I'VE SEEN EVERYTHING** *Go! Discs 8284082* 50 1

TRAVEL *France, male producer – Laurent Gutbier (Singles: 2 weeks)* pos/wks

24 Apr 99 **BULGARIAN** *Tidy Trax TIDY 121CD* 67 2

TRAVELING WILBURYS *UK / US, male vocal / instrumental group (Singles: 19 weeks, Albums: 44 weeks)* pos/wks

29 Oct 88 **HANDLE WITH CARE** *Wilbury W 7732* 21 13
11 Mar 89 **END OF THE LINE** *Wilbury W 7637* 52 4
30 Jun 90 **NOBODY'S CHILD** *Wilbury W 9773* 44 2
5 Nov 88 **THE TRAVELING WILBURYS VOLUME 1** *Wilbury WX 224* 16 35
10 Nov 90 **THE TRAVELING WILBURYS VOLUME 3** *Wilbury WX 384* 14 9

See also Bob DYLAN; George HARRISON; Jeff LYNNE; Roy ORBISON; Tom PETTY and the HEARTBREAKERS

Pat TRAVERS *Canada, male instrumentalist – guitar (Albums: 3 weeks)* pos/wks

2 Apr 77 **MAKIN' MAGIC** *Polydor 2383 436* 40 3

TRAVIS (230 Top 500)

Scottish melodic rock merchants named after a character from the 1984 movie 'Paris, Texas', consisting of English-born Fran Healy (v,g) and native Glaswegians Andy Dunlop (g), Dougie Payne (b) and Neil Primrose (d). Their Brit award-winning 'The Man Who' was the best-selling album by a British act in the UK in 1999 (Singles: 84 weeks, Albums: 182 weeks) pos/wks

12 Apr 97 **U16 GIRLS** *Independiente ISOM 1MS* 40 2
28 Jun 97 **ALL I WANT TO DO IS ROCK** *Independiente ISOM 3MS* 39 2
23 Aug 97 **TIED TO THE 90'S** *Independiente ISOM 5MS* 30 2
25 Oct 97 **HAPPY** *Independiente ISOM 6MS* 38 2
11 Apr 98 **MORE THAN US (EP)** *Independiente ISOM 11MS* 16 3
20 Mar 99 **WRITING TO REACH YOU** *Independiente ISOM 22MS* 14 5
29 May 99 **DRIFTWOOD** *Independiente ISOM 27MS* 13 5
14 Aug 99 ● **WHY DOES IT ALWAYS RAIN ON ME?** *Independiente ISOM 33MS* 10 8
20 Nov 99 ● **TURN** *Independiente ISOM 39MS* 8 11
17 Jun 00 ● **COMING AROUND (2re)** *Independiente ISOM 45MS* 5 10
9 Jun 01 ● **SING** *Independiente ISOM 49MS* 3 14
29 Sep 01 **SIDE** *Independiente ISOM 54MS* 14 8
6 Apr 02 **FLOWERS IN THE WINDOW** *Independiente ISOM 56MS* 18 7
11 Oct 03 ● **RE-OFFENDER** *Independiente ISOM 78SMS* 7 4

27 Dec 03 **THE BEAUTIFUL OCCUPATION** *Independiente ISOM 81MS* ......48 1+
20 Sep 97 ● **GOOD FEELING** *Independiente ISOM 1CD*......9 16
5 Jun 99 ★ **THE MAN WHO** *Independiente ISOM 9CD*......1 102
23 Jun 01 ★ **THE INVISIBLE BAND** *Independiente ISOM 25CD* ■......1 54
25 Oct 03 ● **12 MEMORIES** *Independiente ISOM 40CD*......3 10+

Tracks on More Than Us (EP): More Than Us / Give Me Some Truth / All I Want to Do Is Rock / Funny Thing

Randy TRAVIS *US, male vocalist / instrumentalist – guitar (Singles: 6 weeks, Albums: 2 weeks)* pos/wks

21 May 88 **FOREVER AND EVER, AMEN** *Warner Bros. W 8384* 55 6
6 Aug 88 **OLD 8X10** *Warner Bros. WX 162* 64 2

John TRAVOLTA
US, male actor / vocalist (Singles: 90 weeks, Albums: 6 weeks) pos/wks

20 May 78 ★ **YOU'RE THE ONE THAT I WANT** *RSO 006* [1] ◆ ▲ 1 26
16 Sep 78 ★ **SUMMER NIGHTS** *RSO 18* [2] ◆ 1 19
7 Oct 78 ● **SANDY** *Polydor POSP 6* 2 15
2 Dec 78 **GREASED LIGHTNING** *Polydor POSP 14* 11 9
22 Dec 90 ● **THE GREASE MEGAMIX** *Polydor PO 114* [1] 3 10
23 Mar 91 **GREASE – THE DREAM MIX** *PWL / Polydor PO 136* [3] 47 2
25 Jul 98 ● **YOU'RE THE ONE THAT I WANT (re-issue)** *Polydor 0441332* [1] 4 9
23 Dec 78 **SANDY** *Polydor POLD 5014* 40 6

[1] John Travolta and Olivia Newton-John [2] John Travolta, Olivia Newton-John and cast [3] Frankie Valli, John Travolta and Olivia Newton-John

TREMELOES (277 Top 500)
Brian Poole and the Tremeloes were formed in 1959 and signed by Decca in preference to The Beatles (auditioned same day). First south of England group to top the chart in the Beat Boom era. Poole, b. 2 Nov 1941, Essex, UK, went solo in 1966. Poole's daughters hit in the late 90s as Alisha's Attic. After supporting Brian Poole on his many hits, the Tremeloes – Len 'Chip' Hawkes (v/b), Rick West (g), Alan Blakely (g), Dave Munden (d) – went on to score even more hits in their own right. Hawkes is the father of 1991 chart-topper Chesney Hawkes (Singles: 222 weeks, Albums: 7 weeks) pos/wks

4 Jul 63 ● **TWIST AND SHOUT** *Decca F 11694* [1] 4 14
12 Sep 63 ★ **DO YOU LOVE ME** *Decca F 11739* [1] 1 14
28 Nov 63 **I CAN DANCE** *Decca F 11771* [1] 31 8
30 Jan 64 ● **CANDY MAN** *Decca F 11823* [1] 6 13
7 May 64 ● **SOMEONE, SOMEONE** *Decca F 11893* [1] 2 17
20 Aug 64 **TWELVE STEPS TO LOVE** *Decca F 11951* [1] 32 7
31 Dec 64 **THREE BELLS** *Decca F 12037* [1] 17 10
22 Jul 65 **I WANT CANDY** *Decca F 12197* [1] 25 8
2 Feb 67 ● **HERE COMES MY BABY** *CBS 202519* 4 11
27 Apr 67 ★ **SILENCE IS GOLDEN** *CBS 2723* 1 15
2 Aug 67 ● **EVEN THE BAD TIMES ARE GOOD** *CBS 2930* 4 13
8 Nov 67 **BE MINE** *CBS 3043* 39 2
17 Jan 68 ● **SUDDENLY YOU LOVE ME** *CBS 3234* 6 11
8 May 68 **HELULE HELULE** *CBS 2889* 14 9
18 Sep 68 ● **MY LITTLE LADY** *CBS 3680* 6 12
11 Dec 68 **I SHALL BE RELEASED** *CBS 3873* 29 5
19 Mar 69 **HELLO WORLD** *CBS 4065* 14 8
1 Nov 69 ● **(CALL ME) NUMBER ONE** *CBS 4582* 2 14
21 Mar 70 **BY THE WAY** *CBS 4815* 35 6
12 Sep 70 ● **ME AND MY LIFE** *CBS 5139* 4 18
10 Jul 71 **HELLO BUDDY** *CBS 7294* 32 7
3 Jun 67 **HERE COME THE TREMELOES – THE COMPLETE 1967 SESSIONS** *CBS SBPG 63017* 15 7

[1] Brian Poole & The Tremeloes

Jackie TRENT
UK, female vocalist – Yvonne Burgess (Singles: 17 weeks) pos/wks

22 Apr 65 ★ **WHERE ARE YOU NOW** *Pye 7N 15776* 1 11
1 Jul 65 **WHEN THE SUMMERTIME IS OVER** *Pye 7N 15865* 39 2
2 Apr 69 **I'LL BE THERE** *Pye 7N 17693* 38 4

Ralph TRESVANT
US, male vocalist (Singles: 21 weeks, Albums: 3 weeks) pos/wks

12 Jan 91 **SENSITIVITY** *MCA MCS 1462* 18 8
15 Aug 92 ● **THE BEST THINGS IN LIFE ARE FREE** *Perspective PERSS 7400* [1] 2 13
23 Feb 91 **RALPH TRESVANT** *MCA MCG 6120* 37 3

[1] Luther Vandross and Janet Jackson with special guests BBD and Ralph Tresvant

See also NEW EDITION

TREVOR & SIMON *UK, male production duo – Trevor Reilly and Simon Foy (Singles: 5 weeks)* pos/wks

10 Jun 00 **HANDS UP** *Substance SUBS 1CDS* 12 5

TRI *UK, male vocal / instrumental group (Singles: 1 week)* pos/wks

2 Sep 95 **WE GOT THE LOVE** *Epic 6623642* 61 1

TRIBAL HOUSE
US, male vocal / instrumental group (Singles: 2 weeks) pos/wks

3 Feb 90 **MOTHERLAND-A-FRI-CA** *Cooltempo COOL 198* 57 2

Tony TRIBE *Jamaica, male vocalist (Singles: 2 weeks)* pos/wks

16 Jul 69 **RED RED WINE (re)** *Downtown DT 419* 46 2

A TRIBE CALLED QUEST
US, male rap group (Singles: 18 weeks, Albums: 9 weeks) pos/wks

18 Aug 90 **BONITA APPLEBUM** *Jive JIVE 256* 47 3
19 Jan 91 **CAN I KICK IT?** *Jive JIVE 265* 15 7
11 Jun 94 **OH MY GOD** *Jive JIVECD 355* 68 1
13 Jul 96 **1NCE AGAIN** *Jive JIVECD 399* 34 2
23 Nov 96 **STRESSED OUT** *Jive JIVECD 404* [1] 33 2
23 Aug 97 **THE JAM EP** *Jive JIVECD 427* 61 1
29 Aug 98 **FIND A WAY** *Jive 0518982* 41 2
19 May 90 **PEOPLE'S INSTINCTIVE TRAVELS AND THE PATHS OF RHYTHM** *Jive HIP 96* 54 2
12 Oct 91 **THE LOW END THEORY** *Jive HIP 117* 58 1
27 Nov 93 **MIDNIGHT MARAUDERS** *Jive CHIP 143* 70 1
10 Aug 96 **BEATS RHYMES AND LIFE** *Jive CHIP 170* ▲......28 4
10 Oct 98 **THE LOVE MOVEMENT** *Jive 521032* 38 1

[1] A Tribe Called Quest featuring Faith Evans and Raphael Saadiq

Tracks on The Jam EP: Jam / Get a Hold / Mardi Gras at Midnight / Same Ol' Thing

See also Q-TIP

TRIBE OF TOFFS
UK, male vocal / instrumental group (Singles: 5 weeks) pos/wks

24 Dec 88 **JOHN KETTLEY (IS A WEATHERMAN)** *Completely Different DAFT 1* 21 5

Obie TRICE *US, male rapper (Singles: 8 weeks, Albums: 8 weeks)* pos/wks

1 Nov 03 ● **GOT SOME TEETH** *Interscope 9813061* 8 8
11 Oct 03 **CHEERS** *Interscope / Polydor 9860986* 11 8

TRICKBABY
UK, female vocal / instrumental group (Singles: 2 weeks) pos/wks

12 Oct 96 **INDIE-YARN** *Logic 74321423152* 47 2

TRICKSTER *UK, male producer – Liam Sullivan (Singles: 3 weeks)* pos/wks

4 Apr 98 **MOVE ON UP** *AM:PM 5825812* 19 3

TRICKY *UK, male vocalist / multi-instrumentalist – Adrian Thaws (Singles: 29 weeks, Albums: 43 weeks)* pos/wks

5 Feb 94 **AFTERMATH** *Fourth & Broadway BRCD 288* 69 1
28 Jan 95 **OVERCOME** *Fourth & Broadway BRCD 304* 34 3
15 Apr 95 **BLACK STEEL** *Fourth & Broadway BRCD 320* 28 3
5 Aug 95 **THE HELL (EP)** *Fourth & Broadway BRCD 326* [1] 12 3
11 Nov 95 **PUMPKIN** *Fourth & Broadway BRCD 330* 26 2
9 Nov 96 **CHRISTIANSANDS** *Fourth & Broadway BRCD 340* 36 2
23 Nov 96 ● **MILK (re)** *Mushroom D 1494* [2] 10 8
11 Jan 97 **TRICKY KID** *Fourth & Broadway BRCD 341* 28 2
3 May 97 **MAKES ME WANNA DIE** *Fourth & Broadway BRCD 348* 29 2

		pos	wks
30 May 98	**MONEY GREEDY / BROKEN HOMES** *Island CID 701*	**25**	2
21 Aug 99	**FOR REAL** *Island CID 753*	**45**	1
4 Mar 95 ●	**MAXINQUAYE** *Fourth & Broadway BRCD 610*	**3**	35
23 Nov 96	**PRE-MILLENNIUM TENSION** *Fourth & Broadway BRCDX 623*	**30**	2
6 Jun 98	**ANGELS WITH DIRTY FACES** *Island CID 8071*	**23**	2
28 Aug 99	**JUXTAPOSE** *Island CID 8087* [1]	**22**	2
14 Jul 01	**BLOWBACK** *Anti 65962*	**34**	2

[1] Tricky vs The Gravediggaz [2] Garbage featuring Tricky [1] Tricky with DJ Muggs and Grease

Tracks on The Hell (EP): Hell Is Round the Corner (original) / Hell Is Round the Corner (Hell and Water mix) / Psychosis / Tonite Is a Special Nite (Chaos mass confusion mix)

See also NEARLY GOD

TRICKY DISCO *UK, male instrumental / production duo – Lee Newman and Michael Wells (Singles: 10 weeks)*

		pos	wks
28 Jul 90	**TRICKY DISCO** *Warp WAP 7*	**14**	8
20 Apr 91	**HOUSE FLY** *Warp 7WAP 11*	**55**	2

See also GTO; TECHNOHEAD

TRIFFIDS *Australia, male vocal / instrumental group (Singles: 1 week, Albums: 1 week)*

		pos	wks
6 Feb 88	**A TRICK OF THE LIGHT** *Island IS 350*	**73**	1
22 Apr 89	**THE BLACK SWAN** *Island ILPS 9928*	**63**	1

TRINA
US, female vocalist (Singles: 1 week)

		pos	wks
19 Oct 02	**NO PANTIES** *Atlantic AT 0141CD*	**45**	1

TRINA and TAMARA *US, female vocal duo (Singles: 3 weeks)*

		pos	wks
7 Feb 98	**MY LOVE IS THE SHHH!** *Warner Bros W 0427CD*	**64**	1
12 Jun 99	**WHAT'D YOU COME HERE FOR?** *Columbia 6673382*	**46**	2

TRINIDAD OIL COMPANY *Trinidad, male / female vocal / instrumental group (Singles: 5 weeks)*

		pos	wks
21 May 77	**THE CALENDAR SONG (JANUARY, FEBRUARY, MARCH, APRIL, MAY)** *Harvest HAR 5122*	**34**	5

TRINITY – *See Julie DRISCOLL, Brian AUGER and the TRINITY*

TRINITY-X
UK, male / female production / vocal trio (Singles: 3 weeks)

		pos	wks
19 Oct 02	**FOREVER** *All Around the World CDGLOBE 255*	**19**	3

TRIO
Germany, male vocal / instrumental group (Singles: 10 weeks)

		pos	wks
3 Jul 82 ●	**DA DA DA** *Mobile Suit Corporation CORP 5*	**2**	10

TRIPLE 8
UK, male vocal group (Singles: 9 weeks)

		pos	wks
3 May 03 ●	**KNOCK OUT** *Polydor 9800048*	**8**	4
2 Aug 03 ●	**GIVE ME A REASON (re)** *Polydor 9809136*	**9**	5

TRIPLE X *Italy, male production duo – Lucia Moretti and Ricky Romanini (Singles: 2 weeks)*

		pos	wks
30 Oct 99	**FEEL THE SAME** *Sound of Ministry MOSCDS 135*	**32**	2

See also PLAYTHING

TRIPPING DAISY
US, male vocal / instrumental group (Singles: 1 week)

		pos	wks
30 Mar 96	**PIRANHA** *Island CID 638*	**72**	1

TRISCO *UK, male production duo – Harvey Dawson and Rupert Edwards (Singles: 2 weeks)*

		pos	wks
30 Jun 01	**MUSAK** *Positiva CDTIV 155*	**28**	2

TRIUMPH *Canada, male vocal / instrumental group (Singles: 2 weeks, Albums: 8 weeks)*

		pos	wks
22 Nov 80	**I LIVE FOR THE WEEKEND** *RCA 13*	**59**	2
10 May 80	**PROGRESSIONS OF POWER** *RCA PL 13524*	**61**	5
3 Oct 81	**ALLIED FORCES** *RCA RCALP 6002*	**64**	3

TROGGS *UK, male vocal / instrumental quartet – leader – Reg Presley (Singles: 87 weeks, Albums: 35 weeks)*

		pos	wks
5 May 66 ●	**WILD THING** *Fontana TF 689* ▲	**2**	12
14 Jul 66 ★	**WITH A GIRL LIKE YOU** *Fontana TF 717*	**1**	12
29 Sep 66 ●	**I CAN'T CONTROL MYSELF** *Page One POF 001*	**2**	14
15 Dec 66 ●	**ANY WAY THAT YOU WANT ME** *Page One POF 010*	**8**	10
16 Feb 67	**GIVE IT TO ME** *Page One POF 015*	**12**	10
1 Jun 67	**NIGHT OF THE LONG GRASS** *Page One POF 022*	**17**	6
26 Jul 67	**HI HI HAZEL** *Page One POF 030*	**42**	3
18 Oct 67 ●	**LOVE IS ALL AROUND** *Page One POF 040*	**5**	14
28 Feb 68	**LITTLE GIRL** *Page One POF 056*	**37**	4
30 Oct 93	**WILD THING** *weekend CDWEEK 103* [1]	**69**	2
30 Jul 66 ●	**FROM NOWHERE ... THE TROGGS** *Fontana TL 5355*	**6**	16
25 Feb 67 ●	**TROGGLODYNAMITE** *Page One POL 001*	**10**	11
5 Aug 67	**THE BEST OF THE TROGGS** *Page One FOR 001*	**24**	5
16 Jul 94	**GREATEST HITS** *PolyGram TV 5227392*	**27**	3

[1] Troggs and Wolf

'Wild Thing' in 1993 is a re-recording and was listed with the flip side, 'War', by Edwin Starr and Shadow

TRONIKHOUSE
US, male producer – Kevin Saunderson (Singles: 1 week)

		pos	wks
14 Mar 92	**UP TEMPO** *KMS UK KMSUK 1*	**68**	1

TROUBADOURS DU ROI BAUDOUIN *Zaire, male / female vocal group (Singles: 11 weeks, Albums: 1 week)*

		pos	wks
19 Mar 69	**SANCTUS (MISSA LUBA) (re)** *Philips BF 1732*	**28**	11
22 May 76	**MISSA LUBA** *Philips SBL 7592*	**59**	1

TROUBLE FUNK *US, male vocal / instrumental group (Singles: 3 weeks, Albums: 4 weeks)*

		pos	wks
27 Jun 87	**WOMAN OF PRINCIPLE** *Fourth & Broadway BRW 70*	**65**	3
8 Nov 86	**SAY WHAT!** *Fourth & Broadway DCLP 101*	**75**	2
5 Sep 87	**TROUBLE OVER HERE TROUBLE OVER THERE** *Fourth & Broadway BRLP 513*	**54**	2

Roger TROUTMAN – *See ZAPP; ROGER*

Robin TROWER
UK, male instrumentalist – guitar (Albums: 16 weeks)

		pos	wks
1 Mar 75	**FOR EARTH BELOW** *Chrysalis CHR 1073*	**26**	4
13 Mar 76	**LIVE!** *Chrysalis CHR 1089*	**15**	6
30 Oct 76	**LONG MISTY DAYS** *Chrysalis CHR 1107*	**31**	1
29 Oct 77	**IN CITY DREAMS** *Chrysalis CHR 1148*	**58**	1
16 Feb 80	**VICTIMS OF THE FURY** *Chrysalis CHR 1215*	**61**	4

See also PROCOL HARUM

Doris TROY *US, female vocalist – Doris Higginson, d. 16 Feb 2004 (Singles: 12 weeks)*

		pos	wks
19 Nov 64	**WHATCHA GONNA DO ABOUT IT (re)** *Atlantic AT 4011*	**37**	12

Elisabeth TROY – *See MJ COLE; SOUNDMAN and Don LLOYDIE with Elisabeth TROY; Y-TRIBE featuring Elisabeth TROY; 4 VINI featuring Elisabeth TROY*

TRU FAITH & DUB CONSPIRACY
UK, male production groups (Singles: 5 weeks)

		pos	wks
9 Sep 00	**FREAK LIKE ME** *Public Demand / Positiva CDTIV 138*	**12**	5

TRUBBLE
UK, male / female production / vocal trio (Singles: 5 weeks)

		pos	wks
26 Dec 98	**DANCING BABY (OOGA-CHAKA)** *Island YYCD 1*	**21**	5

TRUCE *UK, female vocal group (Singles: 6 weeks)* pos/wks

2 Sep 95	**THE FINEST** *Big Life BLRD 118*	**54**	1
30 Mar 96	**CELEBRATION OF LIFE** *Big Life BLRD 126*	**51**	1
29 Nov 97	**NOTHIN' BUT A PARTY** *Big Life BLRD 138*	**71**	1
5 Sep 98	**EYES DON'T LIE** *Big Life BLRD 146*	**20**	3

TRUCKIN' CO – *See Garnet MIMMS and TRUCKIN' CO*

TRUCKS *UK / Norway, male vocal / instrumental group (Singles: 2 weeks)* pos/wks

5 Oct 02	**IT'S JUST PORN MUM** *Gut CDGUT 43*	**35**	2

Andrea TRUE CONNECTION *US, female vocalist and male instrumental group (Singles: 16 weeks)* pos/wks

17 Apr 76 ●	**MORE, MORE, MORE** *Buddah BDS 442*	**5**	10
4 Mar 78	**WHAT'S YOUR NAME, WHAT'S YOUR NUMBER** *Buddah BDS 467*	**34**	6

TRUE FAITH and Bridgette GRACE with FINAL CUT *US, male / female vocal / instrumental group (Singles: 4 weeks)* pos/wks

2 Mar 91	**TAKE ME AWAY** *Network NWK 20*	**51**	4

TRUE IMAGE – *See Monie LOVE*

TRUE PARTY *UK, male production / vocal group (Singles: 6 weeks)* pos/wks

2 Dec 00	**WHAZZUP** *Positiva CDBUD 001*	**13**	6

TRUE STEPPERS *UK, male production / instrumental duo – Jonny Linders and Andy Lysandrou (Singles: 31 weeks)* pos/wks

29 Apr 00 ●	**BUGGIN** *Nulife 74321753342* [1]	**6**	8
26 Aug 00 ●	**OUT OF YOUR MIND (re)** *Nulife 74321782942* [2]	**2**	20
2 Dec 00	**TRUE STEP TONIGHT** *Nulife 74321811312* [3]	**25**	3

[1] True Steppers featuring Dane Bowers [2] True Steppers and Dane Bowers featuring Victoria Beckham [3] True Steppers featuring Brian Harvey and Donell Jones

Damon TRUEITT – *See SOMORE featuring Damon TRUEITT*

TRUMAN & WOLFF featuring STEEL HORSES *UK, male production duo and male rap group (Singles: 1 week)* pos/wks

22 Aug 98	**COME AGAIN** *Multiply CDMULTY 38*	**57**	1

TRUMPET MAN – *See MONTANO vs THE TRUMPET MAN*

TRUSSEL *US, male vocal / instrumental group (Singles: 4 weeks)* pos/wks

8 Mar 80	**LOVE INJECTION** *Elektra K 12412*	**43**	4

TRUTH *UK, male vocal duo – Stephen 'Nosmo King' Gold and Francis Aiello (Singles: 6 weeks)* pos/wks

3 Feb 66	**GIRL** *Pye 7N 17035*	**27**	6

See also JAVELLS featuring Nosmo KING

TRUTH *UK, male vocal / instrumental group (Singles: 16 weeks)* pos/wks

11 Jun 83	**CONFUSION (HITS US EVERY TIME)** *Formation TRUTH 1*	**22**	7
27 Aug 83	**A STEP IN THE RIGHT DIRECTION** *Formation TRUTH 2*	**32**	7
4 Feb 84	**NO STONE UNTURNED** *Formation TRUTH 3*	**66**	2

TRUTH HURTS *US, female vocalist – Shari Watson (Singles: 12 weeks, Albums: 4 weeks)* pos/wks

31 Aug 02 ●	**ADDICTIVE** *Aftermath / Interscope 4977782* [1]	**3**	12
24 Aug 02	**TRUTHFULLY SPEAKING** *Interscope 4934592*	**61**	4

[1] Truth Hurts featuring Rakim

Esera TUAOLO – *See Richie RICH*

TUBBY T *UK, male vocalist – Anthony Robinson (Singles: 3 weeks)* pos/wks

21 Sep 02	**TALES OF THE HOOD** *Go! Beat GOBCD 51*	**47**	1
24 May 03	**BIG N BASHY** *Virgin VSCDT 1847* [1]	**45**	2

[1] Fallacy featuring Tubby T

TUBES *US, male vocal / instrumental group (Singles: 18 weeks, Albums: 7 weeks)* pos/wks

19 Nov 77	**WHITE PUNKS ON DOPE** *A&M AMS 7323*	**28**	4
28 Apr 79	**PRIME TIME** *A&M AMS 7423*	**34**	10
12 Sep 81	**DON'T WANT TO WAIT ANYMORE** *Capitol CL 208*	**60**	4
4 Mar 78	**WHAT DO YOU WANT FROM LIFE** *A&M AMS 68460*	**38**	1
2 Jun 79	**REMOTE CONTROL** *A&M AMLH 64751*	**40**	5
4 Jun 83	**OUTSIDE INSIDE** *Capitol EST 12260*	**77**	1

TUBEWAY ARMY – *See Gary NUMAN*

Barbara TUCKER *US, female vocalist (Singles: 12 weeks)* pos/wks

5 Mar 94	**BEAUTIFUL PEOPLE** *Positiva CDTIV 11*	**23**	3
26 Nov 94	**I GET LIFTED** *Positiva CDTIV 23*	**33**	2
23 Sep 95	**STAY TOGETHER** *Positiva CDTIV 39*	**46**	1
8 Aug 98	**EVERYBODY DANCE (THE HORN SONG)** *Positiva CDTIV 96*	**28**	2
18 Mar 00	**STOP PLAYING WITH MY MIND** *Positiva CDTIV 127* [1]	**17**	4

[1] Barbara Tucker featuring Darryl D'Bonneau

Junior TUCKER *UK, male vocalist (Singles: 2 weeks)* pos/wks

2 Jun 90	**DON'T TEST** *10 TEN 299*	**54**	2

Louise TUCKER *UK, female vocalist (Singles: 5 weeks)* pos/wks

9 Apr 83	**MIDNIGHT BLUE** *Ariola ARO 289*	**59**	5

Tommy TUCKER *US, male vocalist – Robert Higginbotham, d. 22 Jan 1982 (Singles: 10 weeks)* pos/wks

26 Mar 64	**HI-HEEL SNEAKERS** *Pye International 7N 25238*	**23**	10

TUFF JAM *UK, male production duo (Singles: 1 week)* pos/wks

10 Oct 98	**NEED GOOD LOVE** *Locked On LOX 99CD*	**44**	1

TUKAN *Denmark, male production duo – Soren Weile and Lars Fredriksen (Singles: 3 weeks)* pos/wks

15 Dec 01	**LIGHT A RAINBOW** *Incentive CENT 33CDS*	**38**	3

TURIN BRAKES *UK, male vocal / instrumental duo – Gale Paridjanian and Olly Knight (Singles: 15 weeks, Albums: 29 weeks)* pos/wks

3 Mar 01	**THE DOOR** *Source SOURCDS 024*	**67**	1
12 May 01	**UNDERDOG (SAVE ME)** *Source SOURCDSE 101*	**39**	2
11 Aug 01	**MIND OVER MONEY** *Source SOURCD 038*	**31**	2
27 Oct 01	**72** *Source SOURCD 041*	**41**	1
2 Nov 02	**LONG DISTANCE** *Source SOURCD 064*	**22**	2
1 Mar 03 ●	**PAIN KILLER** *Source SOURCD 068*	**5**	3
7 Jun 03	**AVERAGE MAN** *Source SOURCD 85*	**35**	2
11 Oct 03	**5 MILE (THESE ARE THE DAYS)** *Source SOURCD 089*	**31**	2
17 Mar 01	**THE OPTIMIST LP** *Source SOURCD 023*	**27**	18
15 Mar 03 ●	**ETHER SONG** *Source CDSOURX054*	**4**	11

Ike and Tina TURNER *US, male / female vocal instrumental duo (Singles: 44 weeks, Albums: 1 week)* pos/wks

9 Jun 66 ●	**RIVER DEEP – MOUNTAIN HIGH** *London HLU 10046*	**3**	13
28 Jul 66	**TELL HER I'M NOT HOME** *Warner Bros. WB 5753*	**48**	1
27 Oct 66	**A LOVE LIKE YOURS** *London HLU 10083*	**16**	10
12 Feb 69	**RIVER DEEP MOUNTAIN HIGH (re-issue)** *London HLU 10242*	**33**	7
8 Sep 73 ●	**NUTBUSH CITY LIMITS** *United Artists UP 35582*	**4**	13
1 Oct 66	**RIVER DEEP – MOUNTAIN HIGH** *London HAU 8298*	**27**	1

See also Tina TURNER

Ruby TURNER *UK, female vocalist (Singles: 31 weeks, Albums: 19 weeks)* pos/wks

25 Jan 86	**IF YOU'RE READY (COME GO WITH ME)** *Jive JIVE 109* [1]	**30**	7

29 Mar 86 I'M IN LOVE *Jive JIVE 118* 61 4
13 Sep 86 BYE BABY *Jive JIVE 126* 52 3
14 Mar 87 I'D RATHER GO BLIND *Jive RTS 1* 24 8
16 May 87 I'M IN LOVE (re-issue) *Jive RTS 2* 57 2
13 Jan 90 IT'S GONNA BE ALRIGHT *Jive RTS 7* 57 3
5 Feb 94 STAY WITH ME BABY *M & G MAGCD 53* 39 3
9 Dec 95 SHAKABOOM! *Telstar HUNTCD 1* [2] 64 1
18 Oct 86 WOMEN HOLD UP HALF THE SKY *Jive HIP 36* 47 11
8 Oct 88 THE MOTOWN SONGBOOK *Jive HIP 58* 22 6
17 Feb 90 PARADISE *Jive HIP 89* 74 2

[1] Ruby Turner featuring Jonathan Butler [2] Hunter featuring Ruby Turner

Sammy TURNER

US, male vocalist – Samuel Black (Singles: 2 weeks) pos/wks

13 Nov 59 ALWAYS *London HLX 8963* 26 2

Tina TURNER

(33 Top 500) *Supreme soul singer cum rock legend, b. Anna Mae Bullock, 26 Nov 1939, Tennessee, US. After a successful, if stormy, partnership with husband Ike, she reached greater heights as a Grammy-winning soloist and is one of the world's most popular live acts (Singles: 224 weeks, Albums: 521 weeks)* pos/wks

19 Nov 83 ● LET'S STAY TOGETHER *Capitol CL 316* 6 13
25 Feb 84 HELP *Capitol CL 325* 40 6
16 Jun 84 ● WHAT'S LOVE GOT TO DO WITH IT *Capitol CL 334* ▲ 3 16
15 Sep 84 BETTER BE GOOD TO ME *Capitol CL 338* 45 5
17 Nov 84 PRIVATE DANCER *Capitol CL 343* 26 9
2 Mar 85 I CAN'T STAND THE RAIN *Capitol CL 352* 57 3
20 Jul 85 ● WE DON'T NEED ANOTHER HERO (THUNDERDOME) *Capitol CL 364* 3 12
12 Oct 85 ONE OF THE LIVING *Capitol CL 376* 55 2
2 Nov 85 IT'S ONLY LOVE *A&M AM 285* [1] 29 6
23 Aug 86 TYPICAL MALE *Capitol CL 419* 33 6
8 Nov 86 TWO PEOPLE *Capitol CL 430* 43 4
14 Mar 87 WHAT YOU GET IS WHAT YOU SEE *Capitol CL 439* 30 7
13 Jun 87 BREAK EVERY RULE *Capitol CL 452* 43 3
20 Jun 87 TEARING US APART *Duck W 8299* [2] 56 3
19 Mar 88 ADDICTED TO LOVE (LIVE) *Capitol CL 484* 71 2
2 Sep 89 ● THE BEST *Capitol CL 543* 5 12
18 Nov 89 ● I DON'T WANNA LOSE YOU *Capitol CL 553* 8 11
17 Feb 90 STEAMY WINDOWS *Capitol CL 560* 13 6
11 Aug 90 LOOK ME IN THE HEART *Capitol CL 584* 31 6
13 Oct 90 BE TENDER WITH ME BABY *Capitol CL 593* 28 4
24 Nov 90 ● IT TAKES TWO *Warner Bros. ROD 1* [3] 5 8
21 Sep 91 NUTBUSH CITY LIMITS (re-recording) *Capitol CL 630* 23 5
23 Nov 91 WAY OF THE WORLD *Capitol CL 637* 13 7
15 Feb 92 LOVE THING *Capitol CL 644* 29 4
6 Jun 92 I WANT YOU NEAR ME *Capitol CL 659* 22 4
22 May 93 ● I DON'T WANNA FIGHT *Parlophone CDRS 6346* 7 9
28 Aug 93 DISCO INFERNO *Parlophone CDR 6357* 12 6
30 Oct 93 WHY MUST WE WAIT UNTIL TONIGHT *Parlophone CDR 6366* 16 4
18 Nov 95 ● GOLDENEYE *Parlophone CDR 0071001* 10 9
23 Mar 96 WHATEVER YOU WANT *Parlophone CDR 6429* 23 6
8 Jun 96 ON SILENT WINGS *Parlophone CDR 6434* 13 6
27 Jul 96 MISSING YOU *Parlophone CDR 6441* [4] 12 5
19 Oct 96 SOMETHING BEAUTIFUL REMAINS *Parlophone CDR 6448* 27 2
21 Dec 96 IN YOUR WILDEST DREAMS *Parlophone CDR 6451* [5] 32 3
30 Oct 99 ● WHEN THE HEARTACHE IS OVER *Parlophone CDR 6529* [4] ..10 7
12 Feb 00 WHATEVER YOU NEED *Parlophone CDR 6532* [4] 27 3
30 Jun 84 ● PRIVATE DANCER *Capitol TINA 1* 2 147
20 Sep 86 ● BREAK EVERY RULE *Capitol EST 2018* 2 49
2 Apr 88 ● LIVE IN EUROPE *Capitol ESTD 1* 8 13
30 Sep 89 ★ FOREIGN AFFAIR *Capitol ESTU 2103* ■ 1 78
12 Oct 91 ● SIMPLY THE BEST *Capitol ESTV 1* 2 141
19 Jun 93 ★ WHAT'S LOVE GOT TO DO WITH IT (FILM SOUNDTRACK) *Parlophone CDPCSD 128* ■ 1 33
13 Apr 96 ● WILDEST DREAMS *Parlophone CDEST 2279* 4 41
13 Nov 99 ● TWENTY FOUR SEVEN *Parlophone 5231802* 9 19

[1] Bryan Adams and Tina Turner [2] Eric Clapton and Tina Turner [3] Rod Stewart and Tina Turner [4] Tina [5] Tina Turner featuring Barry White

See also Ike and Tina TURNER

TURNTABLE ORCHESTRA

US, male vocal / instrumental duo (Singles: 4 weeks) pos/wks

21 Jan 89 YOU'RE GONNA MISS ME *Republic LIC 012* 52 4

TURTLES

US, male vocal / instrumental group (Singles: 39 weeks, Albums: 9 weeks) pos/wks

23 Mar 67 HAPPY TOGETHER *London HLU 10115* ▲ 12 12
15 Jun 67 ● SHE'D RATHER BE WITH ME *London HLU 10135* 4 15
30 Oct 68 ● ELENORE *London HLU 10223* 7 12
22 Jul 67 HAPPY TOGETHER *London HAU 8330* 18 9

TUXEDOS – *See Bobby ANGELO and the TUXEDOS*

Shania TWAIN

(167 Top 500) *Pop and country music queen, b. Eileen Regina Edwards 28 Aug 1965, Ontario, Canada. Self-penned 'Come On Over' album sold more than 34 million, including two million in the UK and a record-breaking 19 million in the US. Her tours in 1999 grossed $36.6m. Best-selling single 'That Don't Impress Me Much' 763,000 (Singles: 116 weeks, Albums: 210 weeks)* pos/wks

28 Feb 98 ● YOU'RE STILL THE ONE *Mercury 5684932* 10 10
13 Jun 98 WHEN *Mercury 5661192* 18 4
28 Nov 98 ● FROM THIS MOMENT ON *Mercury 5665632* 9 8
22 May 99 ● THAT DON'T IMPRESS ME MUCH *Mercury 8708032* 3 21
2 Oct 99 ● MAN! I FEEL LIKE A WOMAN! *Mercury 5623242* 3 18
26 Feb 00 ● DON'T BE STUPID (YOU KNOW I LOVE YOU) (re) *Mercury 1721492* 5 11
16 Nov 02 ● I'M GONNA GETCHA GOOD! *Mercury 1722702* 4 15
22 Mar 03 ● KA-CHING! *Mercury 1722862* 8 8
14 Jun 03 ● FOREVER AND FOR ALWAYS *Mercury 9807733* 6 10
6 Sep 03 THANK YOU BABY (FOR MAKIN' SOMEDAY COME SO SOON) *Mercury 9810627* 11 7
29 Nov 03 WHEN YOU KISS ME / UP! *Mercury 9814003* 21 4
21 Mar 98 ★ COME ON OVER *Mercury 5580002* 1 138
18 Mar 00 ● THE WOMAN IN ME *Mercury 1701292* 7 25
15 Jul 00 WILD & WICKED *RWP RWPCD 1123* 62 2
30 Nov 02 ● UP! *Mercury 1703442* ▲ 4 45

TWEENIES

UK, male / female children's TV characters (Singles: 58 weeks, Albums: 9 weeks) pos/wks

11 Nov 00 ● NUMBER 1 (2re) *BBC Music WMSS 60332* 5 27
31 Mar 01 BEST FRIENDS FOREVER (re) *BBC Music WMSS 60382* 12 10
4 Aug 01 DO THE LOLLIPOP *BBC Music WMSS 60452* 17 8
15 Dec 01 ● I BELIEVE IN CHRISTMAS *BBC Music WMSS 60502* 9 6
14 Sep 02 HAVE FUN GO MAD *BBC Music WMSS 60572* 20 7
25 Nov 00 FRIENDS FOREVER *BBC Music WMSF 60362* 56 4
1 Dec 01 THE CHRISTMAS ALBUM *BBC Music WMSF 60482* 34 5

TWEET

US, female vocalist – Charlene Keys (Singles: 10 weeks, Albums: 5 weeks) pos/wks

11 May 02 ● OOPS (OH MY) *Elektra E 7306CD* 5 8
7 Sep 02 CALL ME *Elektra E 7326CD* 35 2
25 May 02 SOUTHERN HUMMINGBIRD *Elektra 7559627772* 15 5

TWEETS

UK, male feathered vocal / instrumental group (Singles: 34 weeks) pos/wks

12 Sep 81 ● THE BIRDIE SONG (BIRDIE DANCE) (re) *PRT 7P 219* 2 28
5 Dec 81 LET'S ALL SING LIKE THE BIRDIES SING *PRT 7P 226* 44 6

'The Birdie Song (Birdie Dance)' re-entered in Dec 1982 peaking at No.48

TWELFTH NIGHT

UK, male vocal / instrumental group (Albums: 2 weeks) pos/wks

27 Oct 84 ART AND ILLUSION *Music for Nations MFN 36* 83 2

20 FINGERS

US, male instrumental / production duo – Charles Babie and Manfred Mohr (Singles: 14 weeks) pos/wks

26 Nov 94 SHORT DICK MAN *Multiply CDMULT 12* [1] 21 4
30 Sep 95 SHORT SHORT MAN (re-mix) *Multiply CXMULTY 7* [1] 11 7
30 Sep 95 LICK IT *Zyx ZYX 75908* [2] 48 3

[1] 20 Fingers featuring Gillette [2] 20 Fingers featuring Roula

21ST CENTURY GIRLS
UK, female vocal / instrumental group (Singles: 4 weeks) pos/wks

Date	Title	pos	wks
12 Jun 99	21ST CENTURY GIRLS *EMI NTNCDS 001*	16	4

TWENTY 4 SEVEN Featuring CAPTAIN HOLLYWOOD
US / Germany, male / female vocal / instrumental group (Singles: 20 weeks, Albums: 2 weeks) pos/wks

Date	Title	pos	wks
22 Sep 90 ●	I CAN'T STAND IT *BCM BCMR 395*	7	10
24 Nov 90	ARE YOU DREAMING *BCM BCM 07504*	17	10
19 Jan 91	STREET MOVES *BCM BCM 3124* [1]	69	2

[1] Twenty 4 Seven

See also CAPTAIN HOLLYWOOD PROJECT

29 PALMS *UK, male producer – Pete Lorimar (Singles: 1 week)* pos/wks

Date	Title	pos	wks
25 May 02	TOUCH THE SKY *Perfecto PERF 35CDS*	51	1

TWICE AS MUCH *UK, male vocal duo – David Skinner and Stephen Rose (Singles: 9 weeks)* pos/wks

Date	Title	pos	wks
16 Jun 66	SITTIN' ON A FENCE *Immediate IM 033*	25	9

TWIGGY *UK, female model / vocalist – Lesley Hornby (Singles: 10 weeks, Albums: 11 weeks)* pos/wks

Date	Title	pos	wks
14 Aug 76	HERE I GO AGAIN *Mercury 6007 100*	17	10
21 Aug 76	TWIGGY *Mercury 9102 600*	33	8
30 Apr 77	PLEASE GET MY NAME RIGHT *Mercury 9102 601*	35	3

TWILIGHT – *See* Roger SANCHEZ

TWIN HYPE *US, male rap duo (Singles: 2 weeks)* pos/wks

Date	Title	pos	wks
15 Jul 89	DO IT TO THE CROWD *Profile PROF 255*	65	2

TWINKLE *UK, female vocalist – Lynn Ripley (Singles: 20 weeks)* pos/wks

Date	Title	pos	wks
26 Nov 64 ●	TERRY *Decca F 12013*	4	15
25 Feb 65	GOLDEN LIGHTS *Decca F 12076*	21	5

TWISTED INDIVIDUAL
UK, male producer – Lee Greenaway (Singles: 1 week) pos/wks

Date	Title	pos	wks
9 Aug 03	BANDWAGON BLUES *Formation FORM 12102*	51	1

TWISTED SISTER *US, male vocal / instrumental group (Singles: 28 weeks, Albums: 20 weeks)* pos/wks

Date	Title	pos	wks
26 Mar 83	I AM (I'M ME) *Atlantic A 9854*	18	9
28 May 83	THE KIDS ARE BACK *Atlantic A 9827*	32	6
20 Aug 83	YOU CAN'T STOP ROCK 'N' ROLL *Atlantic A 9792*	43	4
2 Jun 84	WE'RE NOT GONNA TAKE IT *Atlantic A 9657*	58	6
18 Jan 86	LEADER OF THE PACK *Atlantic A 9478*	47	3
25 Sep 82	UNDER THE BLADE *Secret SECX 9*	70	3
7 May 83	YOU CAN'T STOP ROCK 'N' ROLL *Atlantic A 0074*	14	9
16 Jun 84	STAY HUNGRY *Atlantic 780156*	34	5
14 Dec 85	COME OUT AND PLAY *Atlantic 7812751*	95	1
25 Jul 87	LOVE IS FOR SUCKERS *Atlantic WX 120*	57	2

Conway TWITTY *US, male vocalist – Harold Jenkins, d. 5 Jun 1993 (Singles: 36 weeks)* pos/wks

Date	Title	pos	wks
14 Nov 58 ★	IT'S ONLY MAKE BELIEVE *MGM 992* ▲	1	15
27 Mar 59	THE STORY OF MY LOVE *MGM 1003*	30	1
21 Aug 59 ●	MONA LISA *MGM 1029*	5	14
21 Jul 60	IS A BLUE BIRD BLUE *MGM 1082*	43	3
23 Feb 61	C'EST SI BON *MGM 1118*	40	3

2 BAD MICE
UK, male instrumental / production group (Singles: 4 weeks) pos/wks

Date	Title	pos	wks
15 Feb 92	HOLD IT DOWN (re) *Moving Shadow SHADOW 14*	48	3
7 Sep 96	BOMBSCARE *Arista 74321397662*	46	1

TWO COWBOYS *Italy, male instrumental / production duo – Roberto Sagotto and Maurizio Braccagni (Singles: 11 weeks)* pos/wks

Date	Title	pos	wks
9 Jul 94 ●	EVERYBODY GONFI-GON *3 Beat TABCD 221*	7	11

2 EIVISSA *Germany, female vocal duo – Pascale Jean Louis and Ellen Helbig (Singles: 6 weeks)* pos/wks

Date	Title	pos	wks
4 Oct 97	OH LA LA LA *Club Tools 0063475 CLU*	13	6

2 FOR JOY *UK, male instrumental / production duo (Singles: 3 weeks)* pos/wks

Date	Title	pos	wks
1 Dec 90	IN A STATE *Mercury MER 333*	61	1
9 Nov 91	LET THE BASS KICK *All Around the World GLOBE 102*	67	2

2-4 FAMILY
UK / US / Korea, male / female rap / vocal group (Singles: 1 week) pos/wks

Date	Title	pos	wks
29 May 99	LEAN ON ME (WITH THE FAMILY) *Epic 6670132*	69	1

2 FUNKY 2 starring Kathryn DION
UK, male / female vocal / instrumental group (Singles: 4 weeks) pos/wks

Date	Title	pos	wks
6 Nov 93	BROTHERS AND SISTERS *Logic 74321170772*	56	2
30 Nov 96	BROTHERS AND SISTERS (re-mix) *All Around the World CDGLOBE 138*	36	2

2 HOUSE *US, male instrumental / production duo (Singles: 1 week)* pos/wks

Date	Title	pos	wks
21 Mar 92	GO TECHNO *Atlantic A 7519*	65	1

2 IN A ROOM *US, male vocal duo – Roger Pauletta and Rafael Vargas (Singles: 15 weeks, Albums: 1 week)* pos/wks

Date	Title	pos	wks
18 Nov 89	SOMEBODY IN THE HOUSE SAY YEAH! *Big Life BLR 12*	66	1
26 Jan 91 ●	WIGGLE IT *SBK SBK 19*	3	8
6 Apr 91	SHE'S GOT ME GOING CRAZY *SBK SBK 23*	54	2
22 Oct 94	EL TRAGO (THE DRINK) *Positiva CDTIV 18*	34	2
8 Apr 95	AHORA ES (NOW IS THE TIME) *Positiva CDTIV 32*	43	1
17 Aug 96	GIDDY-UP *Encore CDCOR 008*	74	1
2 Mar 91	WIGGLE IT *SBK SBKLP 11*	73	1

2 IN A TENT *UK, male instrumental / production duo – Mike Stock and Matt Aitken (Singles: 7 weeks)* pos/wks

Date	Title	pos	wks
17 Dec 94	WHEN I'M CLEANING WINDOWS (TURNED OUT NICE AGAIN) (re) *Love This SPONCD 1*	25	6
13 May 95	BOOGIE WOOGIE BUGLE BOY (DON'T STOP) *Bald Cat BALDCD 1* [1]	48	1

[1] 2 In a Tank

First hit which features the sampled vocals of George Formby re-entered and peaked at No.62 in Jan 1996

See also STOCK AITKEN WATERMAN

2K *UK, male production duo – Bill Drummond and Jimmy Cauty (Singles: 2 weeks)* pos/wks

Date	Title	pos	wks
25 Oct 97	***K THE MILLENNIUM *Blast First BFFP 146CDK*	28	2

See also JUSTIFIED ANCIENTS OF MU MU; KLF; TIMELORDS

2 MAD *UK, male vocal / instrumental duo (Singles: 4 weeks)* pos/wks

Date	Title	pos	wks
9 Feb 91	THINKIN' ABOUT YOUR BODY *Big Life BLR 37*	43	4

TWO MAN SOUND
Belgium, male vocal / instrumental group (Singles: 7 weeks) pos/wks

Date	Title	pos	wks
20 Jan 79	QUE TAL AMERICA *Miracle M 1*	46	7

TWO MEN, A DRUM MACHINE AND A TRUMPET *UK, male instrumental duo – Andy Cox and David Steele (Singles: 17 weeks)* pos/wks

Date	Title	pos	wks
9 Jan 88	TIRED OF GETTING PUSHED AROUND *London LON 141*	18	8
25 Jun 88	HEAT IT UP *Jive JIVE 174* [1]	21	9

[1] Wee Papa Girl Rappers featuring Two Men and a Drum Machine

See also FINE YOUNG CANNIBALS

TWO NATIONS
UK, male vocal / instrumental group (Singles: 1 week) pos/wks

Date	Title	pos	wks
20 Jun 87	THAT'S THE WAY IT FEELS *10 TEN 168*	74	1

Review of the Year

NOVEMBER 2003

Dido's album Life for Rent becomes the fastest UK million-selling album by a female and passes the five-million mark worldwide. It's a good month for The Beatles as the Let It Be album is released minus the Phil Spector arrangements and enters the Japanese chart at No.1. John Lennon's single-sheet, handwritten, tea-stained lyrics for 'Nowhere Man' fetches an auction record of almost £270,000 at Christies, New York. Pink Floyd's Dave Gilmour picks up a CBE and Jools Holland receives an OBE. Christina Aguilera hosts the MTV awards in Edinburgh; among the winners are Justin Timberlake, Coldplay, Sean Paul and Christina herself. Acts appearing include The White Stripes, whose guitarist Jack White has Scottish blood and pays a nice tribute: "We'd like to thank Scotland's Lonnie Donegan for everything he has done for rock and roll." The Andi Peters-produced All New Top of the Pops is launched with an hour-long live show. Westlife perform their revival of the Scott English/Barry Manilow song 'Mandy', which gives them a record 12 No.1s from 16 releases. A Kylie Minogue show at the Hammersmith Apollo is broadcast worldwide by AOL, and is the subject of a one-hour TV documentary. Kylie's seventh chart-topper, 'Slow', is the first one she had a hand in writing. Blue become the first UK boy band to notch up three successive No.1 albums thanks to Guilty, and R.E.M. become the first American band to amass six No.I UK albums as In Time goes top. MPs criticise the Pop Idol jury for being too harsh on contestants. Epic Records announces that Michael Jackson's world sales are now in excess of 140 million, and on the day he releases his Number Ones album he is arrested. His fanbase still ensures that it is his eighth UK No.1 album and sells more than 118,000 in its first week. Ronan Keating's 'Lost For Words' becomes his record 25th successive Top 10 entry and Melanie C's run of 28 successive Top 20 entries ends with 'Melt/Yeh Yeh'. Surprise of the month: George Michael rejoins Sony Records after leaving acrimoniously in 1994. Veteran 1950s rocker Johnny Hallyday's latest album tops the French chart. Johnny Cash posthumously receives three Country Music Association awards – his first for 34 years. Figures show that the sales of country albums in the US in 2003 is down a third on 2002. Britney Spears becomes the world's youngest singer to be given a star on the Hollywood Walk of Fame as about 2,000 fans turn up for the ceremony. Kiss-and-tell couple Britney and Madonna's 'Me Against the Music' is the subject of a $1.75m video. Chart-topping pianist Floyd Cramer ('On the Rebound') is inducted into the Country Music Hall of Fame. American Idol runner-up Clay Aiken's debut LP Measure of a Man enters at No.1 in the US with first-week sales of more than 600,000. (Only Snoop Dogg has sold more with a debut album in its first week.) Tom Jones returns to the US LP chart after 22 years away. Both Apple and Napster report legitimate downloads into the millions in the first few weeks of their operations going live. In the US, for the first time, the top-selling digital download outsells the top-selling CD single – Outkast's 'Hey Ya!' (8,500 downloads) to MercyMe's 'I Can Only Imagine' (7,500 physical sales). Charlie Chaplin's composition 'Smile' is currently on two US Top 10 albums by Barbra Streisand and Rod Stewart. Rod's 'As Time Goes By' sells more than 212,000 in its first week and misses the top slot Stateside by only 500 sales. Rapper Ludacris has two singles simultaneously in the US top three: 'Stand Up' and 'Holidae In'. Coldplay Live 2003 enters the US Music Video chart at No.1. The Rock and Roll Hall of Fame announces its new inductees: George Harrison, Prince, Traffic, ZZ Top, Jackson Browne, Bob Seger and The Dells. Simon Cowell signs up for three more series of American Idol. Chubby Checker returns to the US charts with a remix of his 41-year-old 'Limbo Rock'. Obituaries: Righteous Brother Bobby Hatfield (who sang lead on 'Unchained Melody'); Arthur 'Sweet Soul Music' Conley; four-time Grammy winner Michael Kamen, whose compositions include Bryan Adams' 16-week chart-topper '(Everything I Do) I Do It for You'; Chic and Power Station member Tony Thompson; 50s US rock star Teddy Randazzo (composer of 'Yesterday Has Gone', 'Going Out of My Head', Pretty Blue Eyes' and 'Better Use Your Head'); critically acclaimed singer/songwriter Elliott Smith; country singer/songwriter Don Gibson, who penned the chart-topper 'I Can't Stop Loving You' and had a hit with 'Sea of Heartbreak'.

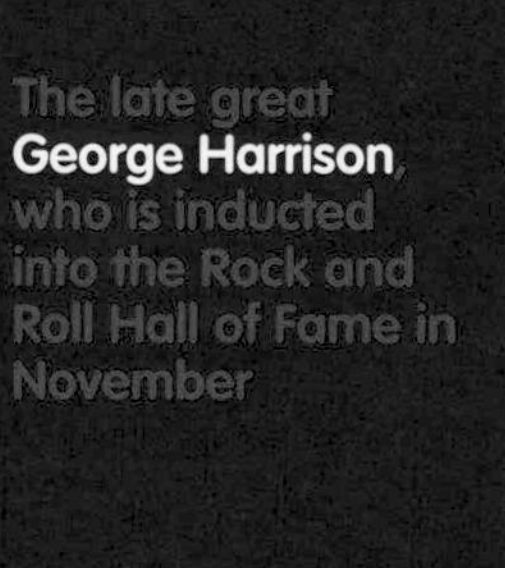

The late great **George Harrison**, who is inducted into the Rock and Roll Hall of Fame in November

2PAC (472 Top 500)
Legendary rapper / actor, born Tupac Amaru Shakur, New York City, 16 Jun 1971 (d.13 Sep 1998), who achieved more UK and US single and album hits after his death (in a Las Vegas shooting incident) than before. In his homeland, no rapper has sold more albums and no artist has had more posthumous chart success (Singles: 81 weeks, Albums: 65 weeks) pos/wks

13 Apr 96 ● **CALIFORNIA LOVE** *Death Row DRWCD 3* [1] 6 8
27 Jul 96 **HOW DO YOU WANT IT** *Death Row DRWCD 4* [2] ▲ 17 4
30 Nov 96 **I AIN'T MAD AT CHA** *Death Row DRWCD 5* 13 9
12 Apr 97 ● **TO LIVE & DIE IN LA** *Interscope IND 95529* [3] 10 4
26 Apr 97 **WANTED DEAD OR ALIVE** *Def Jam 5744052* [4] 16 3
9 Aug 97 **TOSS IT UP** *Interscope IND 95521* [3] 15 3
10 Jan 98 **I WONDER IF HEAVEN GOT A GHETTO** *Jive JIVECD 446* 21 4
14 Feb 98 **HAIL MARY** *Interscope IND 95575* [3] 43 1
13 Jun 98 **DO FOR LOVE** *Jive 0518512* [5] 12 4
18 Jul 98 **RUNNIN'** *Black Jam BJAM 9005* [6] 15 3
28 Nov 98 **HAPPY HOME** *Eagle EAGXS 058* 17 2
20 Feb 99 ● **CHANGES** *Jive 0522832* 3 12
3 Jul 99 **DEAR MAMA** *Jive 0523702* 27 3
23 Jun 01 ● **UNTIL THE END OF TIME** *Interscope / Polydor 4975812* 4 11
10 Nov 01 **LETTER 2 MY UNBORN** *Interscope / Polydor 4976142* 21 5
22 Feb 03 **THUGZ MANSION** *Interscope / Polydor 4978542* 24 5
9 Mar 96 **ALL EYEZ ON ME** *Death Row 5242042* ▲ 32 7
16 Nov 96 **THE DON KILLUMINATI – THE 7 DAY THEORY** *Death Row IND 90039* [1] 53 1
6 Dec 97 **R U STILL DOWN? (REMEMBER ME)** *Jive CHIP 195* 44 1
8 Aug 98 **IN HIS OWN WORDS** *Eagle EAGCD 050* 65 1
12 Dec 98 **GREATEST HITS** *Jive 522662* 17 35
8 Jan 00 **STILL I RISE** *Interscope 4904172* [2] 75 1
21 Apr 01 **UNTIL THE END OF TIME** *Interscope 4908402* ▲ 31 17
14 Dec 02 **BETTER DAYZ** *Interscope 4970702* 68 1
22 Nov 03 **RESURRECTION (OST)** *Interscope / Polydor 9861159* 62 1

[1] 2Pac featuring Dr Dre [2] 2Pac featuring K-Ci and JoJo [3] Makaveli [4] 2Pac and Snoop Doggy Dogg [5] 2Pac featuring Eric Williams [6] 2Pac and Notorious B.I.G.
[1] Makaveli [2] 2Pac and Outlawz

TWO PEOPLE
UK, male vocal / instrumental group (Singles: 2 weeks) pos/wks

31 Jan 87 **HEAVEN** *Polydor POSP 844* 63 2

2WO THIRD3
UK, male vocal / instrumental group (Singles: 15 weeks) pos/wks

19 Feb 94 **HEAR ME CALLING** *Epic 6600642* 48 3
11 Jun 94 **EASE THE PRESSURE** *Epic 6604782* 45 2
8 Oct 94 **I WANT THE WORLD** *Epic 6608542* 20 5
17 Dec 94 **I WANT TO BE ALONE** *Epic 6610852* 29 5

2 UNLIMITED (459 Top 500)
The brainchild of Jean-Paul de Coster and Phil Wilde, fronted by the minimalist vocals / chants / raps of Dutch duo Ray Slijngaard and Anita Dels. Their youth-aimed, infectious dance tracks sold millions around Europe and gave them 11 successive UK Top 20 hits. Best-selling UK single: 'No Limit' 531,9000 (Singles: 112 weeks, Albums: 38 weeks) pos/wks

5 Oct 91 ● **GET READY FOR THIS** *PWL Continental PWL 206* 2 15
25 Jan 92 ● **TWILIGHT ZONE** *PWL Continental PWL 211* 2 10
2 May 92 ● **WORKAHOLIC** *PWL Continental PWL 228* 4 7
15 Aug 92 **THE MAGIC FRIEND** *PWL Continental PWL 240* 11 7
30 Jan 93 ★ **NO LIMIT** *PWL Continental PWCD 256* 1 16
8 May 93 ● **TRIBAL DANCE** *PWL Continental PWCD 262* 4 11
4 Sep 93 ● **FACES** *PWL Continental PWCD 268* 8 7
20 Nov 93 **MAXIMUM OVERDRIVE** *PWL Continental PWCD 276* 15 8
19 Feb 94 ● **LET THE BEAT CONTROL YOUR BODY** *PWL Continental PWCD 280* 6 9
21 May 94 ● **THE REAL THING** *PWL Continental PWCD 306* 6 7
1 Oct 94 **NO ONE** *PWL Continental PWCD 314* 17 6
25 Mar 95 **HERE I GO** *PWL Continental PWCD 317* 22 3
21 Oct 95 **DO WHAT'S GOOD FOR ME** *PWL Continental PWL 322CD1* 16 4
11 Jul 98 **WANNA GET UP** *Big Life BLRD 143* 38 2
7 Mar 92 **GET READY** *PWL Continental HFCD 23* 37 3
22 May 93 ★ **NO LIMITS** *PWL Continental HFCD 27* 1 21
18 Jun 94 ★ **REAL THINGS** *PWL Continental HFCD 38* ■ 1 9
11 Nov 95 **HITS UNLIMITED** *PWL Continental HF 47CD* 27 5

In 1995 both Ray Slijngaard and Anita Dels left the act which was fronted by a Dutch female duo for 'Wanna Get Up'

Tommy TYCHO – *See David GRAY and Tommy TYCHO*

TYGERS OF PAN TANG *UK, male vocal / instrumental group (Singles: 15 weeks, Albums: 20 weeks)* pos/wks

14 Feb 81 **HELLBOUND** *MCA 672* 48 3
27 Mar 82 **LOVE POTION NO. 9** *MCA 769* 45 6
10 Jul 82 **RENDEZVOUS** *MCA 777* 49 4
11 Sep 82 **PARIS BY AIR** *MCA 790* 63 2
30 Aug 80 **WILD CAT** *MCA MCF 3075* 18 5
18 Apr 81 **SPELLBOUND** *MCA MCF 3104* 33 4
21 Nov 81 **CRAZY NIGHTS** *MCA MCF 3123* 51 3
28 Aug 82 **THE CAGE** *MCA MCF 3150* 13 8

Bonnie TYLER (415 Top 500) *Raspy-voiced vocalist b. Gaynor Hopkins, 8 Jun 1953, Swansea, Wales. Made the US country Top 10 with 'It's a Heartache', and 'Total Eclipse of the Heart' was the first record by a Welsh artist to top the US pop chart (Singles: 81 weeks, Albums: 79 weeks)* pos/wks

30 Oct 76 ● **LOST IN FRANCE** *RCA 2734* 9 10
19 Mar 77 **MORE THAN A LOVER** *RCA PB 5008* 27 6
3 Dec 77 ● **IT'S A HEARTACHE** *RCA PB 5057* 4 12
30 Jun 79 **MARRIED MEN** *RCA PB 5164* 35 6
19 Feb 83 ★ **TOTAL ECLIPSE OF THE HEART** *CBS TYLER 1* ▲ 1 12
7 May 83 **FASTER THAN THE SPEED OF NIGHT** *CBS A 3338* 43 4
25 Jun 83 **HAVE YOU EVER SEEN THE RAIN** *CBS A 3517* 47 3
7 Jan 84 ● **A ROCKIN' GOOD WAY** *Epic A 4071* [1] 5 9
31 Aug 85 ● **HOLDING OUT FOR A HERO** *CBS A 4251* 2 13
14 Dec 85 **LOVING YOU'S A DIRTY JOB BUT SOMEBODY'S GOTTA DO IT** *CBS A 6662* [2] 73 2
28 Dec 91 **HOLDING OUT FOR A HERO (re-issue)** *Total TYLER 10* 69 2
27 Jan 96 **MAKING LOVE (OUT OF NOTHING AT ALL)** *East West EW 010CD* 45 2
16 Apr 83 ★ **FASTER THAN THE SPEED OF NIGHT** *CBS 25304* ■ 1 45
17 May 86 **SECRET DREAMS AND FORBIDDEN FIRE** *CBS 86319* 24 12
29 Nov 86 **THE GREATEST HITS** *Telstar STAR 2291* 24 17
21 May 88 **HIDE YOUR HEART** *CBS 460125 1* 78 1
14 Jul 01 **THE GREATEST HITS** *Sanctuary / Sony TV SANCD 082* 18 4

[1] Shaky and Bonnie [2] Bonnie Tyler, guest vocals Todd Rundgren

The two 'The Greatest Hits' albums are different

See also SHAKIN' STEVENS

TYMES *US, male vocal group – lead vocal George Williams (Singles: 41 weeks)* pos/wks

25 Jul 63 **SO MUCH IN LOVE** *Cameo Parkway P 871* ▲ 21 8
15 Jan 69 **PEOPLE** *Direction 58 3903* 16 10
21 Sep 74 **YOU LITTLE TRUSTMAKER** *RCA 2456* 18 9
21 Dec 74 ★ **MS GRACE** *RCA 2493* 1 11
17 Jan 76 **GOD'S GONNA PUNISH YOU** *RCA 2626* 41 3

TYMES 4 *UK, female vocal group (Singles: 5 weeks)* pos/wks

25 Aug 01 **BODYROCK** *Edel 0118635 ERE* 23 3
15 Dec 01 **SHE GOT GAME** *Blacklist 0133135 ERE* 40 2

TYPE O NEGATIVE
US, male vocal / instrumental group (Albums: 2 weeks) pos/wks

14 Sep 96 **OCTOBER RUST** *Roadrunner RR 88742* 26 1
2 Oct 99 **WORLD COMING DOWN** *Roadrunner RR 86602* 49 1

TYPICALLY TROPICAL *UK, male vocal / instrumental duo – Jeff Calvert and Max West (Singles: 11 weeks)* pos/wks

5 Jul 75 ★ **BARBADOS** *Gull GULS 14* 1 11

TYREE *US, male producer – Tyree Cooper (Singles: 10 weeks)* pos/wks

25 Feb 89 **TURN UP THE BASS** *ffrr FFR 24* [1] 12 7

			pos	wks
6 May 89		**HARDCORE HIP HOUSE** *DJ International DJIN 11*	70	2
2 Dec 89		**MOVE YOUR BODY** *CBS 655470 7* [2]	72	1

[1] Tyree featuring Kool Rock Steady [2] Tyree featuring JMD

TYRELL CORPORATION *UK, male vocal / instrumental duo – Joe Watson and Tony Barry (Singles: 9 weeks)*

			pos	wks
14 Mar 92		**THE BOTTLE** *Volante TYR 1*	71	1
15 Aug 92		**GOING HOME** *Volante TYR 2*	58	2
10 Oct 92		**WAKING WITH A STRANGER / ONE DAY** *Volante TYRS 3*	59	1
24 Sep 94		**YOU'RE NOT HERE** *Cooltempo CDCOOL 292*	42	2
14 Jan 95		**BETTER DAYS AHEAD** *Cooltempo CDCOOL 303*	29	3

TYRESE *US, male vocalist – Tyrese Gibson (Singles: 6 weeks)*

			pos	wks
31 Jul 99		**NOBODY ELSE** *RCA 74321688282*	59	1
25 Sep 99		**SWEET LADY** *RCA 74321700842*	55	1
26 Jul 03		**HOW YOU GONNA ACT LIKE THAT** *J 82876544892*	30	4

TZANT *UK, male rap / instrumental duo – Jamie White and Marcus Thomas (aka ODC MC) (Singles: 10 weeks)*

			pos	wks
7 Sep 96		**HOT AND WET (BELIEVE IT)** *Logic 74321376832*	36	2
25 Apr 98		**SOUNDS OF WICKEDNESS** *Logic 74321568842*	11	6
22 Aug 98		**BOUNCE WITH THE MASSIVE** *Logic 74321602102*	39	2

Judie TZUKE

UK, female vocalist (Singles: 10 weeks, Albums: 61 weeks)

			pos	wks
14 Jul 79		**STAY WITH ME TILL DAWN** *Rocket XPRES 17*	16	10
4 Aug 79		**WELCOME TO THE CRUISE** *Rocket TRAIN 7*	14	17
10 May 80	●	**SPORTS CAR** *Rocket TRAIN 9*	7	11
16 May 81		**I AM PHOENIX** *Rocket TRAIN 15*	17	10
17 Apr 82		**SHOOT THE MOON** *Chrysalis CDL 1382*	19	10
30 Oct 82		**ROAD NOISE – THE OFFICIAL BOOTLEG** *Chrysalis CTY 1405*	39	4
1 Oct 83		**RITMO** *Chrysalis CDL 1442*	26	5
15 Jun 85		**THE CAT IS OUT** *Legacy LLP 102*	35	3
29 Apr 89		**TURNING STONES** *Polydor 839087 1*	57	1

UB40 (22 Top 500) *Reggae's most successful transatlantic group: includes brothers Ali (v/g) and Robin (v/g) Campbell, and Earl Falconer (b). Only three groups can claim more chart hits than this Birmingham act, named after the number of the UK unemployment benefit form (Singles: 339 weeks, Albums: 610 weeks)*

			pos	wks
8 Mar 80	●	**KING / FOOD FOR THOUGHT** *Graduate GRAD 6* [1]	4	13
14 Jun 80	●	**MY WAY OF THINKING / I THINK IT'S GOING TO RAIN** *Graduate GRAD 8* [1]	6	10
1 Nov 80	●	**THE EARTH DIES SCREAMING / DREAM A LIE** *Graduate GRAD 10*	10	12
23 May 81		**DON'T LET IT PASS YOU BY / DON'T SLOW DOWN** *DEP International DEP 1*	16	9
8 Aug 81	●	**ONE IN TEN** *DEP International DEP 2*	7	10
13 Feb 82		**I WON'T CLOSE MY EYES** *DEP International DEP 3*	32	6
15 May 82		**LOVE IS ALL IS ALRIGHT** *DEP International DEP 4*	29	7
28 Aug 82		**SO HERE I AM** *DEP International DEP 5*	25	9
5 Feb 83		**I'VE GOT MINE** *DEP International 7 DEP 6*	45	4
20 Aug 83	★	**RED RED WINE** *DEP International 7 DEP 7* ▲	1	14
15 Oct 83	●	**PLEASE DON'T MAKE ME CRY** *DEP International 7 DEP 8*	10	8
10 Dec 83		**MANY RIVERS TO CROSS** *DEP International 7 DEP 9*	16	8
17 Mar 84		**CHERRY OH BABY** *DEP International DEP 10*	12	8
22 Sep 84	●	**IF IT HAPPENS AGAIN** *DEP International DEP 11*	9	8
1 Dec 84		**RIDDLE ME** *DEP International DEP 15*	59	2
3 Aug 85	★	**I GOT YOU BABE** *DEP International DEP 20* [2]	1	13
26 Oct 85	●	**DON'T BREAK MY HEART** *DEP International DEP 22*	3	13
12 Jul 86	●	**SING OUR OWN SONG** *DEP International DEP 23*	5	9
27 Sep 86		**ALL I WANT TO DO** *DEP International DEP 24*	41	4
17 Jan 87		**RAT IN MI KITCHEN** *DEP International DEP 25*	12	7
9 May 87		**WATCHDOGS** *DEP International DEP 26*	39	4
10 Oct 87		**MAYBE TOMORROW** *DEP International DEP 27*	14	8
27 Feb 88		**RECKLESS** *EMI EM 41* [3]	17	8
18 Jun 88	●	**BREAKFAST IN BED** *DEP International DEP 29* [2]	6	11
20 Aug 88		**WHERE DID I GO WRONG** *DEP International DEP 30*	26	6
17 Jun 89		**I WOULD DO FOR YOU** *DEP International DEP 32*	45	4
18 Nov 89	●	**HOMELY GIRL** *DEP International DEP 33*	6	10
27 Jan 90		**HERE I AM (COME AND TAKE ME)** *DEP International DEP 34*	46	3
31 Mar 90	●	**KINGSTON TOWN** *DEP International DEP 35*	4	12
28 Jul 90		**WEAR YOU TO THE BALL** *DEP International DEP 36*	35	6
3 Nov 90	●	**I'LL BE YOUR BABY TONIGHT** *EMI EM 167* [4]	6	10
1 Dec 90		**IMPOSSIBLE LOVE** *DEP International DEP 37*	47	2
2 Feb 91		**THE WAY YOU DO THE THINGS YOU DO** *DEP International DEP 38*	49	3
12 Dec 92		**ONE IN TEN (re-mix)** *ZTT ZANG 39* [5]	17	8
22 May 93	★	**(I CAN'T HELP) FALLING IN LOVE WITH YOU** *DEP International DEPDG 40* ▲	1	16
21 Aug 93	●	**HIGHER GROUND** *DEP International DEPD 41*	8	9
11 Dec 93		**BRING ME YOUR CUP** *DEP International DEPD 42*	24	6
2 Apr 94		**C'EST LA VIE** *DEP International DEPD 43*	37	3
27 Aug 94		**REGGAE MUSIC** *DEP International DEPDG 44*	28	2
4 Nov 95		**UNTIL MY DYING DAY** *DEP International DEPD 45*	15	6
30 Aug 97		**TELL ME IT IS TRUE** *DEP International DEP 48*	14	4
15 Nov 97		**ALWAYS THERE** *DEP International DEPD 49*	53	1
10 Oct 98	●	**COME BACK DARLING** *DEP International DEPD 50*	10	6
19 Dec 98		**HOLLY HOLY** *DEP International DEPD 51*	31	3
1 May 99		**THE TRAIN IS COMING** *DEP International DEPD 52*	30	2
9 Dec 00		**LIGHT MY FIRE** *DEP International DEPD 53*	63	1
20 Oct 01		**SINCE I MET YOU LADY / SPARKLE OF MY EYES** *DEP International DEPD 55* [6]	40	2
2 Mar 02		**COVER UP** *DEP International DEPD 56*	54	1
8 Nov 03		**SWING LOW** *Dep International DEPD 58* [7]	17	8+
6 Sep 80	●	**SIGNING OFF** *Graduate GRAD LP 2*	2	71
6 Jun 81	●	**PRESENT ARMS** *DEP International LPDEP 1*	2	38
10 Oct 81		**PRESENT ARMS IN DUB** *DEP International LPDEP 2*	38	7
28 Aug 82		**THE SINGLES ALBUM** *Graduate GRADLSP 3*	17	8
9 Oct 82	●	**UB 44** *DEP International LPDEP 3*	4	8
26 Feb 83		**UB40 LIVE** *DEP International LPDEP 4*	44	5
24 Sep 83	★	**LABOUR OF LOVE** *DEP International LPDEP 5* ■	1	76
20 Oct 84	●	**GEFFERY MORGAN** *DEP International DEP 6*	3	14
14 Sep 85		**BAGGARIDDIM** *DEP International LPDEP 10*	14	23
9 Aug 86	●	**RAT IN THE KITCHEN** *DEP International LPDEP 11*	8	20
7 Nov 87	●	**THE BEST OF UB40 VOLUME ONE** *Virgin UBTV 1*	3	132
23 Jul 88		**UB40** *DEP International LPDEP 13*	12	12
9 Dec 89	●	**LABOUR OF LOVE II** *DEP International LPDEP 14*	3	69
24 Jul 93	★	**PROMISES AND LIES** *DEP International DEPCD 15* ■	1	37
12 Nov 94	●	**LABOUR OF LOVE VOLUMES I AND II (re-issue)** *DEP International DEPDD 1*	5	15
11 Nov 95		**THE BEST OF UB40 -VOLUME TWO** *DEP International DUBTV2*	12	11
12 Jul 97	●	**GUNS IN THE GHETTO** *DEP International DEPCD 16*	7	9
24 Oct 98	●	**LABOUR OF LOVE III** *DEP International DEPCD 18*	8	12
4 Nov 00	●	**THE VERY BEST OF UB40 – 1980-2000** *Virgin DUBTVX 3*	7	23
3 Nov 01		**COVER UP** *Virgin DEPCD 19*	29	2
14 Jun 03	●	**LABOUR OF LOVE – VOL I., II & III** *Virgin 5847242*	7	16
15 Nov 03		**HOMEGROWN** *DEP International DEPCD22*	49	2

[1] U.B.40 [2] UB40 featuring Chrissie Hynde [3] Afrika Bambaataa and Family featuring UB40 [4] Robert Palmer and UB40 [5] 808 State vs UB40 [6] UB40 featuring Lady Saw [7] UB40 featuring United Colours of Sound

UBM
Germany, male / female vocal / instrumental group (Singles: 1 week) pos/wks

Date	Title	pos	wks
23 May 98	**LOVIN' YOU** *Logic 74321571692*	46	1

UCC – *See URBAN COOKIE COLLECTIVE*

UD PROJECT vs SUNCLUB
Germany, male producer – Vick Krishna (Singles: 6 weeks) pos/wks

Date	Title	pos	wks
4 Oct 03	**SUMMER JAM** *Free 2 Air / Kontor 0150345KON*	14	6

UFO *UK / Germany, male vocal / instrumental group (Singles: 31 weeks, Albums: 48 weeks)* pos/wks

Date	Title	pos	wks
5 Aug 78	**ONLY YOU CAN ROCK ME** *Chrysalis CHS 2241*	50	4
27 Jan 79	**DOCTOR DOCTOR** *Chrysalis CHS 2287*	35	6
31 Mar 79	**SHOOT, SHOOT** *Chrysalis CHS 2318*	48	5
12 Jan 80	**YOUNG BLOOD** *Chrysalis CHS 2399*	36	5
17 Jan 81	**LONELY HEART** *Chrysalis CHS 2482*	41	5
30 Jan 82	**LET IT RAIN** *Chrysalis CHS 2576*	62	3
19 Mar 83	**WHEN IT'S TIME TO ROCK** *Chrysalis CHS 2672*	70	3
4 Jun 77	LIGHTS OUT *Chrysalis CHR 1127*	54	2
15 Jul 78	OBSESSION *Chrysalis CDL 1182*	26	7
10 Feb 79 ●	STRANGERS IN THE NIGHT *Chrysalis CJT 5*	8	11
19 Jan 80	NO PLACE TO RUN *Chrysalis CDL 1239*	11	7
24 Jan 81	THE WILD THE WILLING AND THE INNOCENT *Chrysalis CHR 1307*	19	5
20 Feb 82 ●	MECHANIX *Chrysalis CHR 1360*	8	6
12 Feb 83	MAKING CONTACT *Chrysalis CHR 1402*	32	4
3 Sep 83	HEADSTONE – THE BEST OF UFO *Chrysalis CTY 1437*	39	4
16 Nov 85	MISDEMEANOUR *Chrysalis CHR 1518*	74	2

U4EA featuring BERRI – *See NEW ATLANTIC*

UHF *US, male instrumental / production group (Singles: 4 weeks)* pos/wks

Date	Title	pos	wks
14 Dec 91	**UHF / EVERYTHING** *XL Recordings XLS 25*	46	4

U.T.F.O. *US, male vocal group (Albums: 1 week)* pos/wks

Date	Title	pos	wks
16 Mar 85	ROXANNE ROXANNE (6 TRACK VERSION) *Streetwave 6 Track XKHAN 506*	72	1

UGLY DUCKLING *US, male production / rap (Singles: 1 week)* pos/wks

Date	Title	pos	wks
13 Oct 01	**A LITTLE SAMBA** *XL Recordings XLS 135CD*	70	1

UGLY KID JOE *US, male vocal / instrumental group (Singles: 28 weeks, Albums: 42 weeks)* pos/wks

Date	Title	pos	wks
16 May 92 ●	**EVERYTHING ABOUT YOU** *Mercury MER 367*	3	9
22 Aug 92	**NEIGHBOR** *Mercury MER 374*	28	4
31 Oct 92	**SO DAMN COOL** *Mercury MER 383*	44	2
13 Mar 93 ●	**CATS IN THE CRADLE** *Mercury MERCD 385*	7	9
19 Jun 93	**BUSY BEE** *Mercury MERCD 389*	39	2
8 Jul 95	**MILKMAN'S SON** *Mercury MERCD 435*	39	2
13 Jun 92 ●	AS UGLY AS THEY WANNA BE *Mercury 8688232*	9	13
12 Sep 92	AMERICA'S LEAST WANTED *Vertigo 5125712*	11	24
17 Jun 95	MENACE TO SOBRIETY *Mercury 5282622*	25	5

Tillmann UHRMACHER
Germany, male producer (Singles: 3 weeks) pos/wks

Date	Title	pos	wks
23 Mar 02	**ON THE RUN** *Direction 6721352*	16	3

See also TILLMANN AND REIS

UK *UK, male vocal / instrumental group (Singles: 2 weeks, Albums: 3 weeks)* pos/wks

Date	Title	pos	wks
30 Jun 79	**NOTHING TO LOSE** *Polydor POSP 55*	67	2
27 May 78	U.K. *Polydor 2302 080*	43	3

UK *Canada / Spain, male vocal / instrumental group (Singles: 1 week)* pos/wks

Date	Title	pos	wks
3 Aug 96	**SMALL TOWN BOY** *Media MCSTD 400*	74	1

UK APACHI / APACHE *UK, male vocalist / rapper – Lafta Wahab (Singles: 4 weeks)* pos/wks

Date	Title	pos	wks
1 Oct 94	**ORIGINAL NUTTAH** *Sound of Underground SOUR 008CD* [1]	39	3
28 Jul 01	**SIGNS** *Outcaste OUT 38CD1* [2]	63	1

[1] UK Apachi with Shy FX [2] DJ Badmarsh and Shri featuring UK Apache

UK MIXMASTERS
UK, male producer – Nigel Wright (Singles: 15 weeks) pos/wks

Date	Title	pos	wks
2 Feb 91	**THE NIGHT FEVER MEGAMIX** *IQ ZB 44339* [1]	23	5
27 Jul 91	**LUCKY 7 MEGAMIX** *IQ ZB 44731*	43	3
14 Dec 91	**THE BARE NECESSITIES MEGAMIX** *Connect ZB 35135*	14	7

[1] Mixmasters

UK PLAYERS
UK, male vocal / instrumental group (Singles: 3 weeks) pos/wks

Date	Title	pos	wks
14 May 83	**LOVE'S GONNA GET YOU** *RCA 326*	52	3

UK SUBS *UK, male vocal / instrumental group (Singles: 39 weeks, Albums: 26 weeks)* pos/wks

Date	Title	pos	wks
23 Jun 79	**STRANGLEHOLD** *Gem GEMS 5*	26	8
8 Sep 79	**TOMORROW'S GIRLS** *Gem GEMS 10*	28	6
1 Dec 79	**SHE'S NOT THERE / KICKS (EP)** *Gem GEMS 14*	36	7
8 Mar 80	**WARHEAD** *Gem GEMS 23*	30	4
17 May 80	**TEENAGE** *Gem GEMS 30*	32	5
25 Oct 80	**PARTY IN PARIS** *Gem GEMS 42*	37	4
18 Apr 81	**KEEP ON RUNNIN' (TILL YOU BURN)** *Gem GEMS 45*	41	5
13 Oct 79	ANOTHER KIND OF BLUES *Gem GEMLP 100*	21	6
19 Apr 80	BRAND NEW AGE *Gem GEMLP 106*	18	9
27 Sep 80 ●	CRASH COURSE *Gem GEMLP 111*	8	6
21 Feb 81	DIMINISHED RESPONSIBILITY *Gem GEMLP 112*	18	5

Tracks on She's Not There / Kicks (EP): She's Not There / Kicks / Victim / The Same Thing

UKNY – *See Jason NEVINS*

Tracey ULLMAN
UK, female vocalist / actor (Singles: 49 weeks, Albums: 22 weeks) pos/wks

Date	Title	pos	wks
19 Mar 83 ●	**BREAKAWAY** *Stiff BUY 168*	4	11
24 Sep 83 ●	**THEY DON'T KNOW** *Stiff BUY 180*	2	11
3 Dec 83 ●	**MOVE OVER DARLING** *Stiff BUY 195*	8	9
3 Mar 84	**MY GUY** *Stiff BUY 197*	23	6
28 Jul 84	**SUNGLASSES** *Stiff BUY 205*	18	9
27 Oct 84	**HELPLESS** *Stiff BUY 211*	61	3
3 Dec 83	YOU BROKE MY HEART IN 17 PLACES *Stiff SEEZ 51*	14	20
8 Dec 84	YOU CAUGHT ME OUT *Stiff SEEZ 56*	92	2

ULTIMATE KAOS
UK, male vocal group (Singles: 28 weeks, Albums: 1 week) pos/wks

Date	Title	pos	wks
22 Oct 94 ●	**SOME GIRLS (re)** *Wild Card CARDD 12*	9	9
21 Jan 95	**HOOCHIE BOOTY** *Wild Card CARDW 14*	17	4
1 Apr 95	**SHOW A LITTLE LOVE** *Wild Card CARDW 18*	23	5
1 Jul 95	**RIGHT HERE** *Wild Card 5795832*	18	4
8 Mar 97	**CASANOVA** *Polydor 5759312*	24	3
18 Jul 98	**CASANOVA (re-issue)** *Mercury MERCD 505*	29	2
5 Jun 99	**ANYTHING YOU WANT (I'VE GOT IT)** *Mercury MERCD 510*	52	1
29 Apr 95	ULTIMATE KAOS *Polydor 5274442*	51	1

ULTRA *UK, male vocal / instrumental group (Singles: 22 weeks, Albums: 2 weeks)* pos/wks

Date	Title	pos	wks
18 Apr 98	**SAY YOU DO** *East West EW 124CD*	11	7
4 Jul 98	**SAY IT ONCE** *East West EW 171CD1*	16	6
10 Oct 98	**THE RIGHT TIME (re)** *East West EW 182CD*	28	3
16 Jan 99 ●	**RESCUE ME** *East West EW 193CD1*	8	6
6 Feb 99	ULTRA *East West 3984222452*	37	2

ULTRA HIGH
UK, male vocalist – Michael McCloud (Singles: 3 weeks) pos/wks

Date	Title	pos	wks
2 Dec 95	**STAY WITH ME** *MCA MCSTD 40007*	36	2
20 Jul 96	**ARE YOU READY FOR LOVE** *MCA MCSTD 40039*	45	1

ULTRA VIVID SCENE *US, male vocalist (Albums: 1 week)* pos/wks

Date	Title	pos	wks
19 May 90	JOY 1967-1990 *4AD CAD 005*	58	1

ULTRABEAT
UK, male DJ / production / vocal trio (Singles: 15 weeks) pos/wks

Date	Title	pos	wks
16 Aug 03 ●	**PRETTY GREEN EYES** *All Around the World CDGLOBE 281*	2	14
27 Dec 03	**FEELIN' FINE** *All Around the World CDGLOBE 320*	12	1+

ULTRACYNIC

UK, male / female vocal / instrumental group (Singles: 3 weeks) pos/wks

Date		Title / Label	pos	wks
29 Aug 92		**NOTHING IS FOREVER** *380 PEW 2*	50	2
19 Apr 97		**NOTHING IS FOREVER (re-mix)** *All Around the World CDGLOBE 139*	47	1

ULTRAMARINE

UK, male instrumental duo (Singles: 4 weeks, Albums: 1 week) pos/wks

Date		Title / Label	pos	wks
24 Jul 93		**KINGDOM** *Blanco Y Negro NEG 65CD*	46	2
29 Jan 94		**BAREFOOT (EP)** *Blanco Y Negro NEG 67CD*	61	1
27 Apr 96		**HYMN** *Blanco Y Negro NEG 87CD* [1]	65	1
4 Sep 93		**UNITED KINGDOMS** *Blanco Y Negro 4509934252*	49	1

[1] Ultramarine featuring David McAlmont

Tracks on Barefoot (EP): Hooter / The Badger / Urf / Happy Land

ULTRA-SONIC

UK, male instrumental / production duo (Singles: 2 weeks, Albums: 1 week) pos/wks

Date		Title / Label	pos	wks
3 Sep 94		**OBSESSION** *Clubscene DCSRT 027*	75	1
21 Sep 96		**DO YOU BELIEVE IN LOVE** *Clubscene DCSRT 070*	47	1
11 Nov 95		**GLOBAL TEKNO** *Cluscene DCSR 007*	58	1

ULTRASOUND

UK, male / female vocal / instrumental group (Singles: 5 weeks, Albums: 1 week) pos/wks

Date		Title / Label	pos	wks
7 Mar 98		**BEST WISHES** *Nude NUD 33CD*	68	1
13 Jun 98		**STAY YOUNG** *Nude NUD 35CD1*	30	2
10 Apr 99		**FLOODLIT WORLD** *Nude NUD 41CD1*	39	2
1 May 99		**EVERYTHING PICTURE** *Nude NUDE 12CD*	23	1

ULTRAVOX

133 Top 500 *Ground-breaking British electro-rock quartet: Midge Ure (v/g) (replaced John Foxx in 1979), Billy Currie (k/syn), Chris Cross (b/syn), Warren Cann (d). Ex-Slik and Visage vocalist Ure was a driving force behind Band Aid hits, Live Aid and Nelson Mandela birthday concerts (Singles: 142 weeks, Albums: 227 weeks)* pos/wks

Date		Title / Label	pos	wks
5 Jul 80		**SLEEPWALK** *Chrysalis CHS 2441*	29	11
18 Oct 80		**PASSING STRANGERS** *Chrysalis CHS 2457*	57	4
17 Jan 81	●	**VIENNA** *Chrysalis CHS 2481*	2	14
28 Mar 81		**SLOW MOTION** *Island WIP 6691*	33	4
6 Jun 81	●	**ALL STOOD STILL** *Chrysalis CHS 2522*	8	10
22 Aug 81		**THE THIN WALL** *Chrysalis CHS 2540*	14	8
7 Nov 81		**THE VOICE** *Chrysalis CHS 2559*	16	12
25 Sep 82		**REAP THE WILD WIND** *Chrysalis CHS 2639*	12	9
27 Nov 82		**HYMN** *Chrysalis CHS 2657*	11	11
19 Mar 83		**VISIONS IN BLUE** *Chrysalis CHS 2676*	15	6
4 Jun 83		**WE CAME TO DANCE** *Chrysalis VOX 1*	18	7
11 Feb 84		**ONE SMALL DAY** *Chrysalis VOX 2*	27	6
19 May 84	●	**DANCING WITH TEARS IN MY EYES (re)** *Chrysalis UV 1*	3	11
7 Jul 84		**LAMENT (re)** *Chrysalis UV 2*	22	7
20 Oct 84		**LOVE'S GREAT ADVENTURE** *Chrysalis UV 3*	12	9
27 Sep 86		**SAME OLD STORY** *Chrysalis UV 4*	31	4
22 Nov 86		**ALL FALL DOWN** *Chrysalis UV 5*	30	5
6 Feb 93		**VIENNA (re-issue)** *Chrysalis CDCHSS 3936*	13	4
19 Jul 80	●	**VIENNA** *Chrysalis CHR 1296*	3	72
19 Sep 81	●	**RAGE IN EDEN** *Chrysalis CDL 1338*	4	23
23 Oct 82	●	**QUARTET** *Chrysalis CDL 1394*	6	30
22 Oct 83	●	**MONUMENT – THE SOUNDTRACK** *Chrysalis CUX 1452*	9	15
14 Apr 84	●	**LAMENT** *Chrysalis CDL 1459*	8	26
10 Nov 84	●	**THE COLLECTION** *Chrysalis UTV 1*	2	53
25 Oct 86	●	**U-VOX** *Chrysalis CDL 1545*	9	6
10 Nov 01		**THE VERY BEST OF MIDGE URE & ULTRAVOX** *EMI 5358112* [1]	45	2

[1] Midge URE and Ultravox

See also Midge URE

UMBOZA

UK, male instrumental / production duo – Bryan Chamberlyn and Stuart Crichton (Singles: 9 weeks) pos/wks

Date		Title / Label	pos	wks
23 Sep 95		**CRY INDIA** *Positiva CDTIV 43*	19	4
20 Jul 96		**SUNSHINE** *Positiva CDTIV 47*	14	5

See also MUKKAA; EYE TO EYE featuring Taka BOOM

Piero UMILIANI

Italy, orchestra and chorus, leader d. Feb 2001 (Singles: 8 weeks) pos/wks

Date		Title / Label	pos	wks
30 Apr 77	●	**MAH-NA, MAH-NA** *EMI International INT 530*	8	8

UNA MAS

UK, male production duo (Singles: 1 week) pos/wks

Date		Title / Label	pos	wks
6 Apr 02		**I WILL FOLLOW** *Defected DFECT 47CDS*	55	1

UNATION

UK, male / female vocal / instrumental group (Singles: 3 weeks) pos/wks

Date		Title / Label	pos	wks
5 Jun 93		**HIGHER AND HIGHER** *MCA MCSTD 1773*	42	2
7 Aug 93		**DO YOU BELIEVE IN LOVE** *MCA MCSTD 1796*	75	1

UNBELIEVABLE TRUTH

UK, male vocal / instrumental group (Singles: 5 weeks, Albums: 2 weeks) pos/wks

Date		Title / Label	pos	wks
14 Feb 98		**HIGHER THAN REASON** *Virgin VSCDT 1676*	38	2
9 May 98		**SOLVED** *Virgin VSCDT 1684*	39	2
18 Jul 98		**SETTLE DOWN / DUNE SEA** *Virgin VSCDT 1697*	46	1
23 May 98		**ALMOST HERE** *Virgin CDV 2849*	21	2

UNCANNY ALLIANCE

US, male / female vocal / instrumental duo – Brinsley Evans and EV Mystique (Singles: 5 weeks) pos/wks

Date		Title / Label	pos	wks
19 Dec 92		**I GOT MY EDUCATION** *A&M AM 0128*	39	5

UNCLE KRACKER

US, male vocalist – Matt Shafer (Singles: 18 weeks, Albums: 3 weeks) pos/wks

Date		Title / Label	pos	wks
8 Sep 01	●	**FOLLOW ME** *Atlantic AT 0108CD*	3	18
22 Sep 01		**DOUBLE WIDE** *Atlantic 7567832792*	40	3

UNCLE SAM

US, male vocalist – Sam Turner (Singles: 2 weeks) pos/wks

Date		Title / Label	pos	wks
16 May 98		**I DON'T EVER WANT TO SEE YOU AGAIN** *Epic 6656382*	30	2

UN-CUT

UK, male production duo and female vocalist (Singles: 4 weeks) pos/wks

Date		Title / Label	pos	wks
29 Mar 03		**MIDNIGHT** *WEA WEA 364CD1*	26	3
28 Jun 03		**FALLIN'** *WEA WEA 368CD1*	63	1

UNDERCOVER

UK, male vocal / instrumental group (Singles: 29 weeks, Albums: 9 weeks) pos/wks

Date		Title / Label	pos	wks
15 Aug 92	●	**BAKER STREET** *PWL International PWL 239*	2	14
14 Nov 92	●	**NEVER LET HER SLIP AWAY** *PWL International PWL 255*	5	11
6 Feb 93		**I WANNA STAY WITH YOU** *PWL International PWCD 258*	28	3
14 Aug 93		**LOVESICK** *PWL International PWCD 271* [1]	62	1
5 Dec 92		**CHECK OUT THE GROOVE** *PWL International HFCD 26*	26	9

[1] Undercover featuring John Matthews

UNDERTAKERS

UK, male vocal / instrumental group (Singles: 1 week) pos/wks

Date		Title / Label	pos	wks
9 Apr 64		**JUST A LITTLE BIT** *Pye 7N 15607*	49	1

UNDERTONES

UK, male vocal / instrumental group (Singles: 67 weeks, Albums: 52 weeks) pos/wks

Date		Title / Label	pos	wks
21 Oct 78		**TEENAGE KICKS** *Sire SIR 4007*	31	6
3 Feb 79		**GET OVER YOU** *Sire SIR 4010*	57	4
28 Apr 79		**JIMMY JIMMY** *Sire SIR 4015*	16	10
21 Jul 79		**HERE COMES THE SUMMER** *Sire SIR 4022*	34	6
20 Oct 79		**YOU'VE GOT MY NUMBER (WHY DON'T YOU USE IT!)** *Sire SIR 4024*	32	6
5 Apr 80	●	**MY PERFECT COUSIN** *Sire SIR 4038*	9	10
5 Jul 80		**WEDNESDAY WEEK** *Sire SIR 4042*	11	9
2 May 81		**IT'S GOING TO HAPPEN!** *Ardeck ARDS 8*	18	9
25 Jul 81		**JULIE OCEAN** *Ardeck ARDS 9*	41	5
9 Jul 83		**TEENAGE KICKS (re-issue)** *Ardeck ARDS 1*	60	2
19 May 79		**THE UNDERTONES** *Sire SRK 6071*	13	21
26 Apr 80	●	**HYPNOTISED** *Sire SRK 6088*	6	10
16 May 81		**POSITIVE TOUCH** *Ardeck ARD 103*	17	6
19 Mar 83		**THE SIN OF PRIDE** *Ardeck ARD 104*	43	5
10 Dec 83		**ALL WRAPPED UP** *Ardeck ARD 1654281/3*	67	4

14 Jun 86 **CHER O'BOWLIES – PICK OF THE UNDERTONES** *Ardeck EMS 1172* 96 1
25 Sep 93 **THE BEST OF THE UNDERTONES – TEENAGE KICKS** *Castle Communications CTVCD 121* 45 3
13 Sep 03 **TEENAGE KICKS – THE BEST OF THE UNDERTONES** *Sanctuary / Sony TV TVSAN005* 35 2

See also Feargal SHARKEY

UNDERWORLD

UK, male instrumental / vocal group (Singles: 49 weeks, Albums: 54 weeks) pos/wks

18 Dec 93 **SPIKEE / DOGMAN GO** *Junior Boy's Own JBO 17CD* 63 1
25 Jun 94 **DARK AND LONG** *Junior Boy's Own JBO 19CDS* 57 1
13 May 95 **BORN SLIPPY** *Junior Boy's Own JBO 29CDS* 52 2
18 May 96 **PEARL'S GIRL** *Junior Boy's Own JBO 38CDS1* 24 2
13 Jul 96 ● **BORN SLIPPY (re) (re-mix)** *Junior Boy's Own JBO 44CDS* 2 21
9 Nov 96 **PEARL'S GIRL (re-issue)** *Junior Boy's Own JBO 45CDS1* 22 3
27 Mar 99 **PUSH UPSTAIRS** *Junior Boy's Own JBO 5005443* 12 4
5 Jun 99 **JUMBO** *Junior Boy's Own JBO 5007193* 21 2
28 Aug 99 **KING OF SNAKE** *Junior Boy's Own JBO 5008793* 17 3
2 Sep 00 **COWGIRL** *Junior Boy's Own JBO 5012513* 24 2
14 Sep 02 **TWO MONTHS OFF** *Junior Boy's Own JBO 5020093* 12 4
1 Feb 03 **DINOSAUR ADVENTURE 3D** *Junior Boy's Own JBO 5020523* 34 1
8 Nov 03 **BORN SLIPPY NUXX (2nd re-mix)** *Junior Boy's Own JBO 5024703* 27 3
5 Feb 94 **DUBNOBASSWITHMYHEADMAN** *Junior Boy's Own JBOCD 1* 12 6
23 Mar 96 ● **SECOND TOUGHEST IN THE INFANTS** *Junior Boy's Own JBOCD 4* 9 28
13 Mar 99 ● **BEAUCOUP FISH** *JBO JBO 1005438* 3 12
16 Sep 00 **EVERYTHING EVERYTHING** *JBO JBO 1012542* 22 3
28 Sep 02 **A HUNDRED DAYS OFF** *JBO JBO 1020102* 16 3
15 Nov 03 **1992-2002** *JBO VVR 1024692* 43 2

UNDISPUTED TRUTH

US, male / female vocal group (Singles: 4 weeks) pos/wks

22 Jan 77 **YOU + ME = LOVE** *Warner Bros. K 16804* 43 4

U96

Germany, male producer – Alex Christiansen (Singles: 7 weeks) pos/wks

29 Aug 92 **DAS BOOT** *M & G MAGS 28* 18 5
4 Jun 94 **INSIDE YOUR DREAMS** *Logic 74321209722* 44 1
29 Jun 96 **CLUB BIZARRE** *Urban 5750152* 70 1

UNION featuring the ENGLAND WORLD CUP SQUAD

UK / Holland, male instrumental group and UK, rugby team vocalists (Singles: 7 weeks, Albums: 6 weeks) pos/wks

12 Oct 91 **SWING LOW (RUN WITH THE BALL)** *Columbia 6575317* 16 7
26 Oct 91 **WORLD IN UNION** *Columbia 4690471* [1] 17 6

[1] Union

UNION GAP – *See Gary PUCKETT and the UNION GAP*

UNION STATION – *See Alison KRAUSS and UNION STATION*

UNIQUE

US, male / female vocal / instrumental group (Singles: 7 weeks) pos/wks

10 Sep 83 **WHAT I GOT IS WHAT YOU NEED** *Prelude A 3707* 27 7

UNIQUE 3

UK, male rap / DJ group (Singles: 12 weeks) pos/wks

4 Nov 89 **THE THEME** *10 TEN 285* 61 3
14 Apr 90 **MUSICAL MELODY / WEIGHT FOR THE BASS** *10 TEN 298* 29 5
10 Nov 90 **RHYTHM TAKES CONTROL** *10 TEN 327* [1] 41 3
16 Nov 91 **NO MORE** *10 TEN 387* 74 1

[1] Unique 3 featuring Karin

UNIT FOUR PLUS TWO *UK, male vocal / instrumental group – lead vocal Peter Moules (Singles: 29 weeks)* pos/wks

13 Feb 64 **GREEN FIELDS** *Decca F 11821* 48 2
25 Feb 65 ★ **CONCRETE AND CLAY** *Decca F 12071* 1 15
13 May 65 **(YOU'VE) NEVER BEEN IN LOVE LIKE THIS BEFORE** *Decca F 12144* 14 11
17 Mar 66 **BABY NEVER SAY GOODBYE** *Decca F 12333* 49 1

UNITED CITIZEN FEDERATION featuring Sarah BRIGHTMAN

UK, male production duo and female vocalist (Singles: 1 week) pos/wks

14 Feb 98 **STARSHIP TROOPERS** *Coalition COLA 040CD* 58 1

UNITED COLOURS OF SOUND – *See UB40*

UNITED KINGDOM SYMPHONY

UK, orchestra (Singles: 4 weeks) pos/wks

27 Jul 85 **SHADES (THEME FROM THE CROWN PAINT TELEVISION COMMERCIAL)** *Food for Thought YUM 108* 68 4

UNITONE – *See Laurel AITKEN and the UNITONE*

UNITONE ROCKERS featuring STEEL

UK, male vocal / instrumental group (Singles: 1 week) pos/wks

26 Jun 93 **CHILDREN OF THE REVOLUTION** *The Hit Label HLC 4* 60 1

UNITY

UK, male / female vocal / instrumental group (Singles: 2 weeks) pos/wks

31 Aug 91 **UNITY** *Cardiac CNY 6* 64 2

UNIVERSAL

Australia, male vocal group (Singles: 6 weeks) pos/wks

2 Aug 97 **ROCK ME GOOD** *London LONCD 397* 19 4
18 Oct 97 **MAKE IT WITH YOU** *London LONCD 404* 33 2

UNIVERSAL PROJECT – *See Ed RUSH & OPTICAL / UNIVERSAL PROJECT*

UNIVERSAL PROJECT

UK, male production group (Singles: 1 week) pos/wks

1 Jun 02 **VESSEL** *Virus VRS 010* 61 1

'Vessel' shared chart billing with 'Pacman' by Ed Rush & Optical

UNJUSTIFIED ANCIENTS OF M U – *See 1300 DRUMS featuring the UNJUSTIFIED ANCIENTS OF M U*

UNKLE *US / UK, male DJ / production duo – Josh Davis and James Lavelle (Singles: 11 weeks, Albums: 12 weeks)* pos/wks

20 Feb 99 ● **BE THERE** *Mo Wax MW 108CD1* [1] 8 6
17 Mar 01 **NARCO TOURISTS** *Soma SOMA 100CD* [2] 66 1
6 Sep 03 **EYE FOR AN EYE** *Mo Wax CID 826* 31 2
15 Nov 03 **IN A STATE** *Mo Wax CID 839* 44 2
21 Jan 95 **THE TIME HAS COME (EP)** *Mo Wax MW 028P* [1] 73 1
5 Sep 98 ● **PSYENCE FICTION** *Mo Wax MW 085CD* 4 9
4 Oct 03 **NEVER, NEVER LAND** *Mo Wax MWU 001CD* 24 2

[1] Unkle featuring Ian Brown [2] Slam vs Unkle [1] U.N.K.L.E.

UNO CLIO featuring Martine McCUTCHEON

UK, male instrumental group with female vocalist (Singles: 1 week) pos/wks

18 Nov 95 **ARE YOU MAN ENOUGH** *Avex UK AVEX CD 14* 62 1

UNTOUCHABLES *US, male vocal / instrumental group (Singles: 16 weeks, Albums: 7 weeks)* pos/wks

6 Apr 85 **FREE YOURSELF** *Stiff BUY 221* 26 11
27 Jul 85 **I SPY FOR THE FBI** *Stiff BUY 227* 59 5
13 Jul 85 **WILD CHILD** *Stiff SEEZ 57* 51 7

UP YER RONSON featuring Mary PEARCE

UK, male / female vocal / instrumental group (Singles: 7 weeks) pos/wks

5 Aug 95 **LOST IN LOVE** *Hi-Life 5795572* 27 3
30 Mar 96 **ARE YOU GONNA BE THERE** *Hi-Life 5763272* 27 2
19 Apr 97 **I WILL BE RELEASED** *Hi-Life 5737352* 32 2

Phil UPCHURCH COMBO *US, male instrumental group – Phil Upchurch – bass guitar (Singles: 2 weeks)* pos/wks

5 May 66 **YOU CAN'T SIT DOWN** *Sue WI 4005* 39 2

UPSETTERS
Jamaica, male instrumental group (Singles: 15 weeks) pos/wks

4 Oct 69 ● **RETURN OF DJANGO / DOLLAR IN THE TEETH** *Upsetter US 301* 5 15

Dawn UPSHAW (soprano) / LONDON SINFONIETTA / David ZINMAN (conductor)
US, female vocalist, UK, orchestra and US, conductor (Albums: 18 weeks) pos/wks

23 Jan 93 ● **GORECKI SYMPHONY NO.3** *Elektra Nonsuch 7559792822* 6 18

UPSIDE DOWN
UK, male vocal group (Singles: 16 weeks) pos/wks

20 Jan 96 **CHANGE YOUR MIND** *World CDWORLD 1A* 11 7
13 Apr 96 **EVERY TIME I FALL IN LOVE (re)** *World CDWORLD 2A* 18 4
29 Jun 96 **NEVER FOUND A LOVE LIKE THIS BEFORE** *World CDWORLD 3A* 19 3
23 Nov 96 **IF YOU LEAVE ME NOW** *World CDWORLD 4A* 27 2

URBAN ALL STARS
UK, male producer – Norman Cook – and US, male / female vocal / instrumental group (Singles: 2 weeks) pos/wks

27 Aug 88 **IT BEGAN IN AFRICA** *Urban URB 23* 64 2

URBAN BLUES PROJECT presents Michael PROCTER
US, male vocal / instrumental group (Singles: 1 week) pos/wks

10 Aug 96 **LOVE DON'T LIVE** *AM:PM 5817932* 55 1

URBAN COOKIE COLLECTIVE
UK, male / female vocal / instrumental group (Singles: 37 weeks, Albums: 2 weeks) pos/wks

10 Jul 93 ● **THE KEY THE SECRET** *Pulse 8 CDLOSE 48* 2 16
13 Nov 93 ● **FEELS LIKE HEAVEN** *Pulse 8 CDLOSE 55* 5 9
19 Feb 94 **SAIL AWAY** *Pulse 8 CDLOSE 56* 18 4
23 Apr 94 **HIGH ON A HAPPY VIBE** *Pulse 8 CDLOSE 60* 31 3
15 Oct 94 **BRING IT ON HOME** *Pulse 8 CDLOSE 73* 56 1
27 May 95 **SPEND THE DAY** *Pulse 8 CDLOSE 85* 59 1
9 Sep 95 **REST OF MY LOVE** *Pulse 8 CDLOSE 93* 67 1
16 Dec 95 **SO BEAUTIFUL** *Pulse 8 CDLOSE 100* 68 1
24 Aug 96 **THE KEY THE SECRET (re-mix)** *Pulse 8 CDLOSE 109* [1] 52 1
26 Mar 94 HIGH ON A HAPPY VIBE *Pulse 8 PULSE 13CD* 28 2

[1] UCC

URBAN DISCHARGE featuring SHE
US, male / female vocal / instrumental group (Singles: 1 week) pos/wks

27 Jan 96 **WANNA DROP A HOUSE (ON THAT BITCH)** *MCA MCSTD 40020* 51 1

URBAN HYPE
UK, male production / instrumental group – Robert Dibden and Mark Chitty (Singles: 12 weeks) pos/wks

11 Jul 92 ● **A TRIP TO TRUMPTON** *Faze 2 FAZE 5* 6 8
17 Oct 92 **THE FEELING** *Faze 2 FAZE 10* 67 1
9 Jan 93 **LIVING IN A FANTASY** *Faze 2 CDFAZE 13* 57 3

URBAN SHAKEDOWN
UK / Italy, male DJ / production duo – Michael Hearn and Gavin King (Singles: 8 weeks) pos/wks

27 Jun 92 **SOME JUSTICE** *Urban Shakedown URBST 1* 23 5
12 Sep 92 **BASS SHAKE** *Urban Shakedown URBST 2* [1] 59 2
10 Jun 95 **SOME JUSTICE (re-recording)** *Urban Shakedown URBCD 3* [2] 49 1

[1] Urban Shakedown featuring Mickey Finn
[2] Urban Shakedown featuring DBO General

URBAN SOUL
UK / US, male / female vocal / production group (Singles: 11 weeks) pos/wks

30 Mar 91 **ALRIGHT** *Cooltempo COOL 231* 60 4
21 Sep 91 **ALRIGHT (re-mix)** *Cooltempo COOL 244* 43 3
28 Mar 92 **ALWAYS** *Cooltempo COOL 251* 41 3
13 Jun 98 **LOVE IS SO NICE** *VC Recordings VCRD 33* 75 1

URBAN SPECIES
UK, male vocal / instrumental group (Singles: 10 weeks, Albums: 2 weeks) pos/wks

12 Feb 94 **SPIRITUAL LOVE** *Talkin Loud TLKCD 45* 35 4
16 Apr 94 **BROTHER** *Talkin Loud TLKCD 47* 40 3
20 Aug 94 **LISTEN** *Talkin Loud TLKCD 50* [1] 47 2
6 Mar 99 **BLANKET** *Talkin Loud TLDD 39* [2] 56 1
7 May 94 LISTEN *Talkin Loud 5186482* 43 2

[1] Urban Species featuring MC Solaar
[2] Urban Species featuring Imogen Heap

Midge URE
UK, male vocalist (Singles: 56 weeks, Albums: 28 weeks) pos/wks

12 Jun 82 ● **NO REGRETS** *Chrysalis CHS 2618* 9 10
9 Jul 83 **AFTER A FASHION** *Musicfest FEST 1* [1] 39 4
14 Sep 85 ★ **IF I WAS** *Chrysalis URE 1* 1 11
16 Nov 85 **THAT CERTAIN SMILE** *Chrysalis URE 2* 28 4
8 Feb 86 **WASTELANDS** *Chrysalis URE 3* 46 3
7 Jun 86 **CALL OF THE WILD** *Chrysalis URE 4* 27 8
20 Aug 88 **ANSWERS TO NOTHING** *Chrysalis URE 5* 49 4
19 Nov 88 **DEAR GOD** *Chrysalis URE 6* 55 4
17 Aug 91 **COLD COLD HEART** *Arista 114555* 17 7
25 May 96 **BREATHE** *Arista 74321371172* 70 1
19 Oct 85 ● THE GIFT *Chrysalis CHR 1508* 2 15
10 Sep 88 ANSWERS TO NOTHING *Chrysalis CHR 1649* 30 3
28 Sep 91 PURE *Arista 211922* 36 2
6 Mar 93 ● IF I WAS: THE VERY BEST OF MIDGE URE & ULTRAVOX *Chrysalis CDCHR 1987* 10 6
10 Nov 01 THE VERY BEST OF MIDGE URE & ULTRAVOX *EMI 5358112* [1] 45 2

[1] Midge Ure and Mick Karn [1] Midge Ure and Ultravox

See also RICH KIDS; SLIK; ULTRAVOX; VISAGE

URGE OVERKILL
US, male vocal / instrumental group (Singles: 6 weeks) pos/wks

21 Aug 93 **SISTER HAVANA** *Geffen GFSTD 51* 67 1
16 Oct 93 **POSITIVE BLEEDING** *Geffen GFSTD 57* 61 1
19 Nov 94 **GIRL YOU'LL BE A WOMAN SOON** *MCA MCSTD 2024* 37 4

URIAH HEEP
UK, male vocal / instrumental group (Albums: 51 weeks) pos/wks

13 Nov 71 LOOK AT YOURSELF *Island ILPS 9169* 39 1
10 Jun 72 DEMONS AND WIZARDS *Bronze ILPS 9193* 20 11
2 Dec 72 THE MAGICIAN'S BIRTHDAY *Bronze ILPS 9213* 28 3
19 May 73 LIVE *Island ISLD 1* 23 8
29 Sep 73 SWEET FREEDOM *Island ILPS 9245* 18 3
29 Jun 74 WONDERWORLD *Bronze ILPS 9280* 23 3
5 Jul 75 ● RETURN TO FANTASY *Bronze ILPS 9335* 7 6
12 Jun 76 HIGH AND MIGHTY *Island ILPS 9384* 55 1
22 Mar 80 CONQUEST *Bronze BRON 524* 37 3
17 Apr 82 ABOMINOG *Bronze BRON 538* 34 6
18 Jun 83 HEAD FIRST *Bronze BRON 545* 46 4
6 Apr 85 EQUATOR *Portrait PRT 261414* 79 2

URUSEI YATSURA
UK, male / female vocal / instrumental group (Singles: 4 weeks, Albums: 1 week) pos/wks

22 Feb 97 **STRATEGIC HAMLETS** *Che CHE 67CD* 64 1
28 Jun 97 **FAKE FUR** *Che CHE 70CD* 58 1
21 Feb 98 **HELLO TIGER** *Che CHE 75CD1* 40 1
6 Jun 98 **SLAIN BY ELF** *Che CHE 80CD1* 63 1
14 Mar 98 SLAIN BY *Che CHE 76CD* 64 1

USA FOR AFRICA
US, male / female vocal charity ensemble, producer – Quincy Jones (Singles: 9 weeks, Albums: 5 weeks) pos/wks

13 Apr 85 ★ **WE ARE THE WORLD** *CBS USAID 1* ▲ 1 9
25 May 85 WE ARE THE WORLD *CBS USAID F1* ▲ 31 5

Soloists: Lionel Richie, Stevie Wonder, Paul Simon, Kenny Rogers, James Ingram, Tina Turner, Billy Joel, Michael Jackson, Diana Ross, Dionne Warwick, Willie Nelson, Al Jarreau, Bruce Springsteen, Kenny Loggins, Steve Perry, Daryl Hall, Huey Lewis, Cyndi Lauper, Kim Carnes, Bob Dylan, Ray Charles. Also credited: Dan Aykroyd, Harry Belafonte, Lindsey Buckingham, Sheila E, Bob Geldof, John Oates, Jackie Jackson, La Toya Jackson, Marlon Jackson, Randy Jackson, Tito Jackson, Waylon Jennings, The News, Bette Midler, Jeffrey Osborne, The Pointer Sisters, Smokey Robinson

Album contains tracks by various artists in addition to the title track

The USED
US, male vocal / instrumental group (Singles: 1 week) pos/wks

22 Mar 03 **THE TASTE OF INK** *Reprise W 601CD* 52 1

USHER

US, male vocalist – Usher Raymond
(Singles: 62 weeks, Albums: 56 weeks)

Date		Title / Label	pos	wks
18 Mar 95		**THINK OF YOU** *LaFace 74321269252*	70	1
31 Jan 98	★	**YOU MAKE ME WANNA... (re)** *LaFace 74321560652* ■	1	13
2 May 98		**NICE & SLOW** *LaFace 74321579102* ▲	24	5
3 Feb 01	●	**POP YA COLLAR** *LaFace 74321828692*	2	9
7 Jul 01	●	**U REMIND ME** *LaFace 74321863382* ▲	3	9
20 Oct 01	●	**U GOT IT BAD** *LaFace 74321898552* ▲	5	8
20 Apr 02		**U-TURN** *LaFace 74321934072*	16	6
10 Aug 02	●	**I NEED A GIRL (PART ONE)** *Puff Daddy / Arista 74321947242* [1]	4	11
17 Jan 98		**MY WAY** *LaFace 73008260432*	16	18
21 Jul 01	★	**8701** *Arista 74321874712* ■	1	38

[1] P Diddy featuring Usher and Loon

US3

UK, male instrumental / production / vocal trio
(Singles: 15 weeks, Albums: 6 weeks)

Date		Title / Label	pos	wks
10 Jul 93		**RIDDIM** *Blue Note CDCL 686* [1]	34	6
25 Sep 93		**CANTALOOP** *Blue Note CDCL 696* [2]	23	5
28 May 94		**I GOT IT GOIN' ON** *Blue Note CDCL 708* [3]	52	2
1 Mar 97		**COME ON EVERYBODY (GET DOWN)** *Blue Note CDCL 784*	38	2
31 Jul 93		**HAND ON THE TORCH** *Capitol CDEST 2195*	40	6

[1] Us3 featuring Tukka Yoot [2] Us3 featuring Rahsaan [3] Us3 featuring Kobie Powell and Rahsaan

USURA *Italy, male / female vocal / instrumental group (Singles: 15 weeks)*

Date		Title / Label	pos	wks
23 Jan 93	●	**OPEN YOUR MIND** *Deconstruction 74321128042*	7	9
10 Jul 93		**SWEAT** *Deconstruction 74321154602*	29	3
6 Dec 97		**OPEN YOUR MIND 97 (re-mix)** *Malarky MLKD 4* [1]	21	3

[1] U.S.U.R.A.

UTAH SAINTS

UK, male instrumental / production duo – Jez Willis and Tim Garbutt (Singles: 39 weeks, Albums: 15 weeks)

Date		Title / Label	pos	wks
24 Aug 91	●	**WHAT CAN YOU DO FOR ME** *ffrr F 164*	10	11
6 Jun 92	●	**SOMETHING GOOD** *ffrr F 187*	4	9
8 May 93	●	**BELIEVE IN ME** *ffrr FCD 209*	8	6
17 Jul 93		**I WANT YOU** *ffrr FCD 213*	25	5
25 Jun 94		**I STILL THINK OF YOU** *ffrr FCD 225*	32	2
2 Sep 95		**OHIO** *ffrr FCD 264*	42	2
5 Feb 00		**LOVE SONG** *Echo ECSCD 83*	37	2
20 May 00		**FUNKY MUSIC (SHO NUFF TURNS ME ON)** *Echo ECSCD 96*	23	2
5 Jun 93	●	**UTAH SAINTS** *ffrr 8283792*	10	15

'Funky Music (Sho Nuff Turns Me On) features the uncredited vocals by Edwin Starr

UTOPIA

UK, male vocal / instrumental group – includes Todd Rundgren (Albums: 3 weeks)

Date		Title / Label	pos	wks
1 Oct 77		**OOPS! SORRY WRONG PLANET** *Bearsville K 53517*	59	1
16 Feb 80		**ADVENTURES IN UTOPIA** *Island ILPS 9602*	57	2

U2 (10 *Top 500*)

The most successful group of the past 20 years: Paul (Bono) Hewson, b. 10 May 1960, Dublin (v), David (The Edge) Evans, b. 8 Aug 1961, Essex (g), Adam Clayton, b. 13 Mar 1960, Oxfordshire (b) and Larry Mullen Jr, b. 31 Oct 1961, Dublin (d). The Ireland-based act, named after an American spy plane, has come a long way since winning a Guinness-sponsored talent contest in 1978 in Limerick. Their first release, the EP, 'U2:2', reportedly topped the Irish charts but success overseas came slower: their first London show drew nine people, and their first few UK releases sold poorly. However, in 1981 they made their UK and US chart debuts, and since then have set standards for record sales and concert crowds that few, if any, can come close to. They have won every music-related award and broken countless attendance, sales and concert-grossing records. These stadium-packing giants of contemporary rock, whose humanitarian work is legendary, have the ear of many top politicians. They regularly enter the world's charts at No.1 and sales of 10 million albums are commonplace. The first act to sell a million CDs (with 'The Joshua Tree') has had seven albums simultaneously on both the US and UK charts and scored five consecutive US No. 1s. The only non-UK act to receive a Brits Outstanding Contribution to British Music award is also the only musical act in 70 years to receive the Freedom of Dublin
(Singles: 270 weeks, Albums: 1110 weeks)

Date		Title / Label	pos	wks
8 Aug 81		**FIRE** *Island WIP 6679*	35	6
17 Oct 81		**GLORIA** *Island WIP 6733*	55	4
3 Apr 82		**A CELEBRATION** *Island WIP 6770*	47	4
22 Jan 83	●	**NEW YEARS DAY** *Island WIP 6848*	10	8
2 Apr 83		**TWO HEARTS BEAT AS ONE** *Island IS 109*	18	5
15 Sep 84	●	**PRIDE (IN THE NAME OF LOVE)** *Island IS 202*	3	11
4 May 85	●	**THE UNFORGETTABLE FIRE** *Island IS 220*	6	6
28 Mar 87	●	**WITH OR WITHOUT YOU** *Island IS 319* ▲	4	11
6 Jun 87	●	**I STILL HAVEN'T FOUND WHAT I'M LOOKING FOR** *Island IS 328* ▲	6	11
12 Sep 87	●	**WHERE THE STREETS HAVE NO NAME** *Island IS 340*	4	6
26 Dec 87		**IN GOD'S COUNTRY (import)** *Island 7-99385*	48	4
1 Oct 88	★	**DESIRE** *Island IS 400*	1	8
17 Dec 88	●	**ANGEL OF HARLEM** *Island IS 402*	9	6
15 Apr 89	●	**WHEN LOVE COMES TO TOWN** *Island IS 411* [1]	6	7
24 Jun 89	●	**ALL I WANT IS YOU** *Island IS 422*	4	6
2 Nov 91	★	**THE FLY (re)** *Island IS 500* ■	1	6
14 Dec 91		**MYSTERIOUS WAYS** *Island IS 509*	13	7
7 Mar 92	●	**ONE** *Island IS 515*	7	6
20 Jun 92		**EVEN BETTER THAN THE REAL THING** *Island IS 525*	12	7
11 Jul 92	●	**EVEN BETTER THAN THE REAL THING (re-mix)** *Island REALU 2*	8	7
5 Dec 92		**WHO'S GONNA RIDE YOUR WILD HORSES** *Island IS 550*	14	8
4 Dec 93	●	**STAY (FARAWAY, SO CLOSE)** *Island CID 578*	4	9
17 Jun 95	●	**HOLD ME THRILL ME KISS ME KILL ME** *Atlantic A 7131CD*	2	14
15 Feb 97	★	**DISCOTHEQUE (re)** *Island CID 649* ■	1	11
26 Apr 97	●	**STARING AT THE SUN** *Island CID 658*	3	6
2 Aug 97	●	**LAST NIGHT ON EARTH (re)** *Island CID 664*	10	5
4 Oct 97	●	**PLEASE** *Island CID 673*	7	4
20 Dec 97		**IF GOD WILL SEND HIS ANGELS** *Island CID 684*	12	6
31 Oct 98	●	**SWEETEST THING** *Island CID 727*	3	13
21 Oct 00	★	**BEAUTIFUL DAY** *Island CID 766* ■	1	16
10 Feb 01	●	**STUCK IN A MOMENT YOU CAN'T GET OUT OF** *Island CID 770*	2	8
2 Jun 01		**NEW YEAR'S DUB (re)** *Serious SERR 030CD* [2]	15	5
28 Jul 01	●	**ELEVATION** *Island CID 780*	3	8
1 Dec 01	●	**WALK ON** *Island CID 788*	5	8
2 Nov 02	●	**ELECTRICAL STORM** *Island CID 808*	5	13
29 Aug 81		**BOY** *Island ILPS 9646*	52	31
24 Oct 81		**OCTOBER** *Island ILPS 9680*	11	42
12 Mar 83	★	**WAR** *Island ILPS 9733* ■	1	147
3 Dec 83	●	**LIVE: UNDER A BLOOD RED SKY** *Island IMA 3*	2	203
13 Oct 84	★	**THE UNFORGETTABLE FIRE** *Island U 25* ■	1	130
27 Jul 85		**WIDE AWAKE IN AMERICA (import)** *Island 902791 A*	11	16
21 Mar 87	★	**THE JOSHUA TREE** *Island U 26* ■ ▲	1	156
20 Feb 88		**THE JOSHUA TREE SINGLES** *Island U2PK 1*	100	1
22 Oct 88	★	**RATTLE AND HUM** *Island U 27* ■ ▲	1	61
30 Nov 91	●	**ACHTUNG BABY** *Island U 28* ▲	2	87
17 Jul 93	★	**ZOOROPA** *Island CIDU 29* ■ ▲	1	31
15 Mar 97	★	**POP** *Island CIDU 210* ■ ▲	1	35
14 Nov 98	★	**THE BEST OF – 1980-1990 & B-SIDES** *Island CIDDU 211* ■	1	12
21 Nov 98	●	**THE BEST OF – 1980-1990** *Island CIDU 211*	4	64
11 Nov 00	★	**ALL THAT YOU CAN'T LEAVE BEHIND** *Island CIDU 212* ■	1	62
16 Nov 02	●	**THE BEST OF – 1990-2000 & B-SIDES** *Island CIDTU 213*	2	21
23 Nov 02		**THE BEST OF – 1990-2000** *Island CIDU 213*	37	11

[1] U2 with B B King

[2] Musique vs U2

1993's 'Stay (Faraway, So Close)' was listed with 'I've Got You Under My Skin' by Frank Sinatra with Bono, which was featured on many but not all formats of this single

Verna V – *See HELIOTROPIC featuring Verna V*

VDC – *See BLAST featuring VDC*

V.I.P.'s *UK, male vocal / instrumental group (Singles: 4 weeks)* pos/wks

6 Sep 80		**THE QUARTER MOON** *Gem GEMS 39*	**55**	4

VAGABONDS – *See Jimmy JAMES and the VAGABONDS*

Steve VAI *US, male instrumentalist – guitar (Albums: 21 weeks)* pos/wks

2 Jun 90	●	**PASSION AND WARFARE** *Food For Thought GRUB 17*	**8**	10
7 Aug 93		**SEX AND RELIGION** *Relativity 4729472* [1]	**17**	6
15 Apr 95		**ALIEN LOVE SECRETS** *Relativity 4785862*	**39**	3
28 Sep 96		**FIRE GARDEN** *Epic 4850622*	**41**	2

[1] Vai

Holly VALANCE *Australia, female vocalist – Holly Vukadinovic (Singles: 47 weeks, Albums: 12 weeks)* pos/wks

11 May 02	★	**KISS KISS** *London LONCD 464* ■	**1**	16
12 Oct 02	●	**DOWN BOY (re)** *London LONCD 469*	**2**	14
21 Dec 02		**NAUGHTY GIRL** *London LONCD 472*	**16**	9
8 Nov 03	●	**STATE OF MIND** *London LONCD 482*	**8**	8+
26 Oct 02	●	**FOOTPRINTS** *London 0927493722*	**9**	11
22 Nov 03		**STATE OF MIND** *London 5046701625*	**60**	1+

Ricky VALANCE *UK, male vocalist – David Spencer (Singles: 16 weeks)* pos/wks

25 Aug 60	★	**TELL LAURA I LOVE HER** *Columbia DB 4493*	**1**	16

Ritchie VALENS *US, male vocalist / instrumentalist – guitar – Ritchie Valenzuela, d. 3 Feb 1959 (Singles: 5 weeks)* pos/wks

6 Mar 59		**DONNA** *London HL 8803*	**29**	1
1 Aug 87		**LA BAMBA** *RCA PB 41435*	**49**	4

Caterina VALENTE with Werner MULLER and the RIAS DANCE ORCHESTRA *France, female vocalist and Germany Orchestra(Singles: 14 weeks)* pos/wks

19 Aug 55	●	**THE BREEZE AND I** *Polydor BM 6002*	**5**	14

Dickie VALENTINE *UK male vocalist – Richard Brice (92 weeks)* pos/wks

20 Feb 53		**BROKEN WINGS** *Decca F 9954*	**12**	1
13 Mar 53	●	**ALL THE TIME AND EVERYWHERE** *Decca F 10038*	**9**	3
5 Jun 53	●	**IN A GOLDEN COACH (THERE'S A HEART OF GOLD)** *Decca F 10098*	**7**	1
5 Nov 54		**ENDLESS** *Decca F 10346*	**19**	1
17 Dec 54	●	**MISTER SANDMAN** *Decca F 10415*	**5**	12
17 Dec 54	★	**THE FINGER OF SUSPICION** *Decca F 10394* [1]	**1**	15
18 Feb 55	●	**A BLOSSOM FELL (re)** *Decca F 10430*	**9**	10
3 Jun 55	●	**I WONDER** *Decca F 10493*	**4**	15
25 Nov 55	★	**CHRISTMAS ALPHABET** *Decca F 10628*	**1**	7
16 Dec 55		**THE OLD PI-ANNA RAG** *Decca F 10645*	**15**	5
7 Dec 56	●	**CHRISTMAS ISLAND** *Decca F 10798*	**8**	5
27 Dec 57		**SNOWBOUND FOR CHRISTMAS** *Decca F 10950*	**28**	1
13 Mar 59		**VENUS (4re)** *Pye Nixa 7N 15192*	**20**	8
23 Oct 59		**ONE MORE SUNRISE (MORGEN)** *Pye 7N 15221*	**14**	8

[1] Dickie Valentine with The Stargazers

VALENTINE BROTHERS *US, male vocal duo and Germany, orchestra – leader, d. 28 Dec 1998 (Singles: 1 week)* pos/wks

23 Apr 83		**MONEY'S TOO TIGHT (TO MENTION)** *Energy NRG 1*	**73**	1

Joe VALINO *US, male vocalist – Joseph Paolino, d. 26 Dec 1996 (Singles: 2 weeks)* pos/wks

18 Jan 57		**THE GARDEN OF EDEN** *HMV POP 283*	**23**	2

Frankie VALLI *US, male vocalist – Frankie Castellucio (Singles: 52 weeks)* pos/wks

12 Dec 70		**YOU'RE READY NOW** *Philips 320226 BF*	**11**	13
1 Feb 75	●	**MY EYES ADORED YOU** *Private Stock PVT 1* ▲	**5**	11
21 Jun 75		**SWEARIN' TO GOD** *Private Stock PVT 21*	**31**	5
17 Apr 76		**FALLEN ANGEL** *Private Stock PVT 51*	**11**	7
26 Aug 78	●	**GREASE** *RSO 012* ▲	**3**	14
23 Mar 91		**GREASE – THE DREAM MIX** *PWL / Polydor PO 136* [1]	**47**	2

[1] Frankie Valli, John Travolta and Olivia Newton-John

See also FOUR SEASONS

Armin VAN BUUREN featuring Ray WILSON *Belgium, male producer and UK, male vocalist (Singles: 1 week)* pos/wks

10 May 03		**YET ANOTHER DAY** *Nebula NEBCD 042*	**70**	1

See also STILTSKIN

VAN DAHL – *See IAN VAN DAHL*

Mark VAN DALE with ENRICO *Belgium, male production duo (Singles: 1 week)* pos/wks

3 Oct 98		**WATER WAVE** *Club Tools 0065815 CLU*	**71**	1

David VAN DAY *UK, male vocalist (Singles: 3 weeks)* pos/wks

14 May 83		**YOUNG AMERICANS TALKING** *WEA DAY 1*	**43**	3

See also DOLLAR; GUYS 'N' DOLLS

VAN DER GRAAF GENERATOR *UK, male vocal / instrumental group (Albums: 2 weeks)* pos/wks

25 Apr 70		**THE LEAST WE CAN DO IS WAVE TO EACH OTHER** *Charisma CAS 1007*	**47**	2

VAN DER TOORN – *See PAPPA BEAR featuring VAN DER TOORN*

George VAN DUSEN *UK, male vocalist – George Harrington, d. 1992 (Singles: 4 weeks)* pos/wks

17 Dec 88		**IT'S PARTY TIME AGAIN** *Bri-Tone 7BT 001*	**43**	4

Paul VAN DYK *Germany, male DJ / producer (Singles: 31 weeks, Albums: 3 weeks)* pos/wks

17 May 97		**FORBIDDEN FRUIT** *Deviant DVNT 18CDR*	**69**	1
15 Nov 97		**WORDS** *Deviant DVNT 26CDS* [1]	**54**	1
5 Sep 98		**FOR AN ANGEL** *Deviant DVT 24CDS*	**28**	4
20 Nov 99		**ANOTHER WAY / AVENUE (re)** *Deviant DVNT 35CDS*	**13**	7
20 May 00	●	**TELL ME WHY (THE RIDDLE)** *Deviant DVNT 36CDS* [2]	**7**	5
2 Dec 00		**WE ARE ALIVE** *Deviant DVNT 38CDS*	**15**	6

12 Jul 03	NOTHING BUT YOU *Positiva CDTIVS 192* [3]	14 5
18 Oct 03	TIME OUT OF LIVES / CONNECTED *Positiva CDTIVS 196* [4]	28 2
17 Jun 00	OUT THERE AND BACK *Deviant DVNT 37CD*	12 3

[1] Paul Van Dyk featuring Toni Halliday [2] Paul Van Dyk featuring Saint Etienne [3] Paul Van Dyk featuring Hemstock [4] Paul Van Dyk featuring Vega 4

Leroy VAN DYKE *US, male vocalist (Singles: 20 weeks)* pos/wks

4 Jan 62 ●	WALK ON BY *Mercury AMT 1166*	5 17
26 Apr 62	BIG MAN IN A BIG HOUSE *Mercury AMT 1173*	34 3

Niels VAN GOGH *Germany, male producer (Singles: 1 week)* pos/wks

10 Apr 99	PULVERTURM *Logic 74321649192*	75 1

VAN HALEN (457 Top 500) *Hard-rock heroes, formed 1974, California. Members included Dutch-born Eddie (g) and Alex Van Halen (d), David Lee Roth (v), Sammy Hagar (v) and Gary Cherone (ex-Extreme) (v). Their first 12 albums each topped two million sales Stateside (with two passing 10 million) (Singles: 51 weeks, Albums: 101 weeks)* pos/wks

28 Jun 80	RUNNIN' WITH THE DEVIL *Warner Bros. HM 10*	52 3
4 Feb 84 ●	JUMP *Warner Bros. W 9384* ▲	7 13
19 May 84	PANAMA *Warner Bros. W 9273*	61 2
5 Apr 86 ●	WHY CAN'T THIS BE LOVE *Warner Bros. W 8740*	8 14
12 Jul 86	DREAMS *Warner Bros. W 8642*	62 2
6 Aug 88	WHEN IT'S LOVE *Warner Bros. W 7816*	28 7
1 Apr 89	FEELS SO GOOD *Warner Bros. W 7565*	63 1
22 Jun 91	POUNDCAKE *Warner Bros. W 0045*	74 1
19 Oct 91	TOP OF THE WORLD *Warner Bros. W 0066*	63 1
27 Mar 93	JUMP (LIVE) *Warner Bros. W 0155CD*	26 3
21 Jan 95	DON'T TELL ME *Warner Bros. W 0280CD*	27 2
1 Apr 95	CAN'T STOP LOVIN' YOU *Warner Bros. W 0288CD*	33 2
27 May 78	VAN HALEN *Warner Bros. K 56470*	34 11
14 Apr 79	VAN HALEN II *Warner Bros. K 566116*	23 7
5 Apr 80	WOMEN AND CHILDREN FIRST *Warner Bros. K 56793*	15 7
23 May 81	FAIR WARNING *Warner Bros. K 56899*	49 4
1 May 82	DIVER DOWN *Warner Bros. K 57003*	36 5
4 Feb 84	1984 *Warner Bros. 923985*	15 24
5 Apr 86	5150 *Warner Bros. WS 5150* ▲	16 18
4 Jun 88	OU812 *Warner Bros. WX 177* ▲	16 12
29 Jun 91	FOR UNLAWFUL CARNAL KNOWLEDGE *Warner Bros. WX 420* ▲	12 5
6 Mar 93	LIVE: RIGHT HERE RIGHT NOW *Warner Bros. 9362451982*	24 3
4 Feb 95 ●	BALANCE *Warner Bros. 9362457602* ▲	8 3
9 Nov 96	THE BEST OF VAN HALEN – VOLUME 1 *Warner Bros. 9362464742* ▲	45 1
28 Mar 98	VAN HALEN 3 *Warner Bros. 9362466622*	43 1

Armand VAN HELDEN *US, male DJ / producer (Singles: 33 weeks, Albums: 7 weeks)* pos/wks

8 Mar 97	THE FUNK PHENOMENA *ZYX ZYX 8523U8*	38 2
8 Nov 97	ULTRAFUNKULA *ffrr FCD 317*	46 1
6 Feb 99 ★	YOU DON'T KNOW ME (re) *ffrr FCD 357* [1] ■	1 12
1 May 99	FLOWERZ *ffrr FCD 361* [2]	18 5
20 May 00 ●	KOOCHY *ffrr FCD 379*	4 7
3 Nov 01	WHY CAN'T YOU FREE SOME TIME *ffrr FCD 402*	34 2
15 Dec 01	YOU CAN'T CHANGE ME *Defected DFECT 41CDS* [3]	25 4
10 Apr 99	2 FUTURE 4 U *ffrr 5560902*	22 6
10 Jun 00	KILLING PURITANS *ffrr 8573833192*	38 1

[1] Armand Van Helden featuring Duane Harden
[2] Armand Van Helden featuring Roland Clark
[3] Roger Sanchez featuring Armand Van Helden and N'Dea Davenport

Denise VAN OUTEN *UK, female actor / vocalist (Albums: 2 weeks)* pos/wks

29 Jun 02	CAN'T TAKE MY EYES OFF YOU *Columbia 6721052* [1]	23 4
26 Apr 03	TELL ME ON A SUNDAY *Really Useful / Polydor 4932922*	34 2

[1] Andy Williams and Denise Van Outen

See also DENISE and JOHNNY; THOSE 2 GIRLS

VAN TWIST *Zaire / Belgium, male / female vocal / instrumental group (Singles: 2 weeks)* pos/wks

16 Feb 85	SHAFT *Polydor POSP 729*	57 2

VANDELLAS – *See Martha REEVES and The VANDELLAS*

Luther VANDROSS (94 Top 500) *Superior soul singer / songwriter and producer, b. 20 Apr 1951, New York, US. Former David Bowie backing vocalist fronted chart group Change before embarking on a solo career that earned him 10 successive US platinum albums and a stack of awards (Singles: 148 weeks, Albums: 299 weeks)* pos/wks

19 Feb 83	NEVER TOO MUCH *Epic EPC A 3101*	44 6
26 Jul 86	GIVE ME THE REASON *Epic A 7288*	60 3
21 Feb 87	GIVE ME THE REASON (re-issue) *Epic 650216 7*	71 2
28 Mar 87	SEE ME *Epic LUTH 1*	60 4
11 Jul 87	I REALLY DIDN'T MEAN IT *Epic LUTH 3*	16 10
5 Sep 87	STOP TO LOVE *Epic LUTH 2*	24 7
7 Nov 87	SO AMAZING *Epic LUTH 4*	33 6
23 Jan 88	GIVE ME THE REASON (2nd re-issue) *Epic LUTH 5*	26 6
16 Apr 88	I GAVE IT UP (WHEN I FELL IN LOVE) *Epic LUTH 6*	28 5
9 Jul 88	THERE'S NOTHING BETTER THAN LOVE *Epic LUTH 7* [1]	72 1
8 Oct 88	ANY LOVE *Epic LUTH 8*	31 4
4 Feb 89	SHE WON'T TALK TO ME *Epic LUTH 9*	34 4
22 Apr 89	COME BACK *Epic LUTH 10*	53 3
28 Oct 89	NEVER TOO MUCH (re-mix) *Epic LUTH 12*	13 7
6 Jan 90	HERE AND NOW *Epic LUTH 13*	43 3
27 Apr 91	POWER OF LOVE – LOVE POWER *Epic 6568227*	46 5
18 Jan 92	THE RUSH *Epic 6577237*	53 3
15 Aug 92 ●	THE BEST THINGS IN LIFE ARE FREE *Perspective PERSS 7400* [2]	2 13
22 May 93	LITTLE MIRACLES (HAPPEN EVERY DAY) *Epic 6590442*	28 3
18 Sep 93	HEAVEN KNOWS *Epic 6596522*	34 3
4 Dec 93	LOVE IS ON THE WAY *Epic 6599592*	38 2
17 Sep 94 ●	ENDLESS LOVE (2re) *Epic 6608062* [3]	3 16
26 Nov 94	LOVE THE ONE YOU'RE WITH *Epic 6610612*	31 4
4 Feb 95	ALWAYS AND FOREVER *Epic 6611942*	20 5
15 Apr 95	AIN'T NO STOPPING US NOW *Epic 6614242*	22 3
11 Nov 95	POWER OF LOVE – LOVE POWER (re-mix) *Epic 6625902*	31 3
16 Dec 95 ●	THE BEST THINGS IN LIFE ARE FREE (re-mix) *A&M 5813092* [4]	7 7
23 Dec 95	EVERY YEAR EVERY CHRISTMAS *Epic 6627762*	43 2
12 Oct 96	YOUR SECRET LOVE *Epic 6638385*	14 5
28 Dec 96	I CAN MAKE IT BETTER *Epic 6640632*	44 2
20 Oct 01	TAKE YOU OUT *J 74321899442*	59 1
21 Jan 84	BUSY BODY *Epic EPC 25608*	42 8
6 Apr 85	THE NIGHT I FELL IN LOVE *Epic EPC 26387*	19 10
1 Nov 86 ●	GIVE ME THE REASON *Epic EPC 4501341*	3 99
21 Feb 87	NEVER TOO MUCH *Epic EPC 32807*	41 30
4 Jul 87	FOREVER FOR ALWAYS FOR LOVE *Epic EPC 25013*	23 16
16 Apr 88	BUSY BODY (RE-ISSUE) *Epic 460183 1*	78 4
29 Oct 88 ●	ANY LOVE *Epic 462908 1*	3 22
11 Nov 89	BEST OF LUTHER VANDROSS – BEST OF LOVE *Epic 4658011*	14 23
25 May 91 ●	POWER OF LOVE *Epic 4680121*	9 9
12 Jun 93	NEVER LET ME GO *Epic 4735982*	11 5
1 Oct 94 ★	SONGS *Epic 4766562* ■	1 28
28 Oct 95	GREATEST HITS 1981–1995 *Epic 4811002*	12 14
19 Oct 96	YOUR SECRET LOVE *Epic 4843832*	14 4
11 Oct 97	ONE NIGHT WITH YOU – THE BEST OF LOVE *Epic 4888882*	56 2
22 Aug 98	I KNOW *EMI 8460892*	42 1
16 Feb 02	THE ESSENTIAL LUTHER VANDROSS *Epic 5050252*	72 2
5 Jul 03	DANCE WITH MY FATHER *J 82876540732* ▲	41 15
23 Aug 03	THE ESSENTIAL LUTHER VANDROSS *Epic 5133532*	18 7

[1] Luther Vandross, duet with Gregory Hines [2] Luther Vandross and Janet Jackson with special guests BBD and Ralph Tresvant [3] Luther Vandross and Mariah Carey [4] Luther Vandross and Janet Jackson

VANESSA-MAE *Singapore, female instrumentalist – violin – Vanessa-Mae Vanakorn Nicholson (Singles: 21 weeks, Albums: 33 weeks)* pos/wks

28 Jan 95	TOCCATA AND FUGUE *EMI Classics MAE 8816812*	16 10
20 May 95	RED HOT *EMI CDMAE 2*	37 2
18 Nov 95	CLASSICAL GAS *EMI CDEM 404*	41 2

		pos	wks
26 Oct 96	**I'M A DOUN FOR LACK O' JOHNNIE (A LITTLE SCOTTISH FANTASY)** *EMI CDMAE 3*	28	2
25 Oct 97	**STORM** *EMI CDEM 497*	54	1
20 Dec 97	**I FEEL LOVE** *EMI CDEM 553*	41	2
5 Dec 98	**DEVIL'S TRILL / REFLECTION** *EMI CDEM 530*	53	1
28 Jul 01	**WHITE BIRD** *EMI CDVAN 002*	66	1
25 Feb 95	**THE VIOLIN PLAYER** *EMI Classics CDC 5550892*	11	21
2 Nov 96	**THE CLASSICAL ALBUM 1** *EMI Classics CDC 5553952*	47	2
8 Nov 97	**STORM** *EMI 8218002*	27	5
7 Feb 98	**CHINA GIRL – THE CLASSICAL ALBUM 2** *EMI Classics CDC 5564832*	56	3
26 May 01	**SUBJECT TO CHANGE** *EMI 5331002*	58	2

VANGELIS (347 Top 500) *Synthesised soundtrack whizzkid*

(b. Evangelos Papathanassiou, 29 Mar 1943, Volos, Greece). Grammy nominated artist, whose 'Conquest of Paradise' is one of Germany's biggest-selling singles, also had hits in Aphrodite's Child and Jon and Vangelis (Singles: 25 weeks, Albums: 165 weeks)

		pos	wks
9 May 81	**CHARIOTS OF FIRE – TITLES (re)** *Polydor POSP 246* ▲	12	17
11 Jul 81	**HEAVEN AND HELL, THIRD MOVEMENT (THEME FROM THE BBC-TV SERIES 'THE COSMOS')** *BBC 1*	48	6
31 Oct 92	**CONQUEST OF PARADISE** *East West YZ 704*	60	2
10 Jan 76	**HEAVEN AND HELL** *RCA Victor RS 1025*	31	7
9 Oct 76	**ALBEDO 0.39** *RCA Victor RS 1080*	18	6
18 Apr 81 ●	**CHARIOTS OF FIRE (FILM SOUNDTRACK)** *Polydor POLS 1026*	5	97
5 May 84	**CHARIOTS OF FIRE (FILM SOUNDTRACK) (RE-ISSUE)** *Polydor POLD 5160*	39	10
13 Oct 84	**SOIL FESTIVITIES** *Polydor POLH 11*	55	4
30 Mar 85	**MASK** *Polydor POLH 19*	69	2
22 Jul 89	**THEMES** *Polydor VGTV 1*	11	13
24 Oct 92	**1492 – THE CONQUEST OF PARADISE (FILM SOUNDTRACK)** *East West 4509910142*	33	6
18 Jun 94	**BLADERUNNER (FILM SOUNDTRACK)** *East West 4509965742*	20	6
2 Mar 96	**VOICES** *East West 630127862*	58	1
20 Apr 96	**PORTRAIT (SO LONG AGO SO CLEAR)** *Polydor 5311512*	14	6
8 Nov 03	**ODYSSEY – THE DEFINITIVE COLLECTION** *Universal TV 9813149*	20	7

'Chariots of Fire – Titles' re-entered in Apr 1982 peaking at No.41

See also JON and VANGELIS; APHRODITE'S CHILD

VANGUARD – See QUEEN

VANILLA

UK, female vocal group (Singles: 10 weeks)

		pos	wks
22 Nov 97	**NO WAY NO WAY (re)** *EMI CDEM 487*	14	8
23 May 98	**TRUE TO US** *EMI CDEM 509*	36	2

VANILLA FUDGE *US, male vocal / instrumental group (Singles: 11 weeks, Albums: 3 weeks)*

		pos	wks
9 Aug 67	**YOU KEEP ME HANGIN' ON** *Atlantic 584 123*	18	11
4 Nov 67	**VANILLA FUDGE** *Atlantic 588086*	31	3

VANILLA ICE *US, male rapper – Robert Van Winkle (Singles: 32 weeks, Albums: 23 weeks)*

		pos	wks
24 Nov 90 ★	**ICE ICE BABY** *SBK SBK 18* ▲	1	13
2 Feb 91 ●	**PLAY THAT FUNKY MUSIC** *SBK SBK 20*	10	6
30 Mar 91	**I LOVE YOU** *SBK SBK 22*	45	5
29 Jun 91	**ROLLIN' IN MY 5.0** *SBK SBK 27*	27	4
10 Aug 91	**SATISFACTION** *SBK SBK 29*	22	4
15 Dec 90 ●	**TO THE EXTREME** *SBK SBKLP 9* ▲	4	20
6 Jul 91	**EXTREMELY LIVE** *SBK SBKLP 12*	35	3

VANITY FARE

UK, male vocal / instrumental group (Singles: 34 weeks)

		pos	wks
28 Aug 68	**I LIVE FOR THE SUN** *Page One POF 075*	20	9
23 Jul 69 ●	**EARLY IN THE MORNING** *Page One POF 142*	8	12
27 Dec 69	**HITCHIN' A RIDE** *Page One POF 158*	16	13

Joe T VANNELLI PROJECT

Italy, male producer (Singles: 2 weeks)

		pos	wks
17 Jun 95	**SWEETEST DAY OF MAY** *Positiva CDTIV 36*	45	2

Randy VANWARMER

US, male vocalist – Randall Van Wormer d. 12 Jan 2004 (Singles: 11 weeks)

		pos	wks
4 Aug 79 ●	**JUST WHEN I NEEDED YOU MOST** *Bearsville WIP 6516*	8	11

VAPORS *UK, male vocal / instrumental group (Singles: 23 weeks, Albums: 6 weeks)*

		pos	wks
9 Feb 80 ●	**TURNING JAPANESE** *United Artists BP 334*	3	13
5 Jul 80	**NEWS AT TEN** *United Artists BP 345*	44	4
11 Jul 81	**JIMMIE JONES** *Liberty BP 401*	44	6
7 Jun 80	**NEW CLEAR DAYS** *United Artists UAG 30300*	44	6

VARDIS *UK, male vocal / instrumental group (Singles: 4 weeks, Albums: 1 week)*

		pos	wks
27 Sep 80	**LET'S GO** *Logo VAR 1*	59	4
1 Nov 80	**100 MPH** *Logo MOGO 4012*	52	1

Halo VARGA *US, male producer (Singles: 1 week)*

		pos	wks
9 Dec 00	**FUTURE** *Hooj Choons HOOJ 101CD*	67	1

VARIOUS ARTISTS (EPs and LPs) *(Singles: 74 weeks)*

		pos	wks
15 Jun 56	**CAROUSEL – ORIGINAL SOUNDTRACK (LP) (re)** *Capitol LCT 6105*	26	2
29 Jun 56 ●	**ALL STAR HIT PARADE** *Decca F 10752*	2	9
26 Jul 57	**ALL STAR HIT PARADE NO.2** *Decca F 10915*	15	7
9 Dec 89	**THE FOOD CHRISTMAS EP** *Food FOOD 23*	63	1
20 Jan 90	**THE FURTHER ADVENTURES OF NORTH (EP)** *Deconstruction PT 43372*	64	2
2 Nov 91	**THE APPLE EP** *Apple APP 1*	60	1
11 Jul 92	**FOURPLAY (EP)** *XL XLFP 1*	45	2
7 Nov 92	**THE FRED EP** *Heavenly HVN 19*	26	3
24 Apr 93	**GIMME SHELTER (EP)** *Food CDORDERA 1*	23	4
5 Jun 93	**SUBPLATES VOLUME 1 (EP)** *Suburban Base SUBBASE 24CD*	69	1
9 Oct 93	**THE TWO TONE EP** *2 Tone CHSTT 31*	30	3
4 Nov 95	**HELP (EP)** *Go! Discs GODCD 135*	51	2
16 Mar 96	**NEW YORK UNDERCOVER (EP)** *Uptown MCSTD 48002*	39	1
30 Mar 96	**DANGEROUS MINDS (EP)** *MCA MCSTD 48007*	35	1
29 Nov 97 ★	**PERFECT DAY (re)** *Chrysalis CDNEED 01* ◆ ■	1	21
12 Sep 98	**THE FULL MONTY – MONSTER MIX** *RCA Victor 74321602582*	62	1
26 Sep 98	**TRADE (EP) (DISC 2)** *Tidy Trax TREP2*	75	1
25 Dec 99	**IT'S ONLY ROCK 'N' ROLL (re)** *Universal TV 1566012*	19	10
17 Jun 00	**PERFECT DAY (re-recording)** *Chrysalis 8887840*	69	1
10 Nov 01	**HARD BEAT EP 19** *Nukleuz NUKP 0369*	71	1

Tracks and artists on Carousel are as follows: Carousel Waltz – Orchestra conducted by Alfred Newman; You're a Queer One Julie Jordan – Barbara Ruick and Shirley Jones; Mister Snow – Barbara Ruick; If I Loved You – Shirley Jones and Gordon MacRae; June Is Busting Out All Over – Claramae Turner; Soliloquy – Gordon MacRae; Blow High Blow Low – Cameron Mitchell; When the Children Are Asleep – Robert Rounseville and Barbara Ruick; This Was a Real Nice Clambake – Barbara Ruick, Claramae Turner, Robert Rounseville and Cameron Mitchell; Stonecutters Cut It on Stone (There's Nothing So Bad for a Woman) – Cameron Mitchell; What's the Use of Wonderin' – Shirley Jones; You'll Never Walk Alone – Claramae Turner; If I Loved You – Gordon MacRae; You'll Never Walk Alone – Shirley Jones; Tracks on All Star Hit Parade: Theme from The Threepenny Opera – Winifred Atwell; No Other Love – Dave King; My September Love – Joan Regan; A Tear Fell – Lita Roza; Out of Town – Dickie Valentine; It's Almost Tomorrow – David Whitfield. Tracks on All Star Hit Parade No.2: Around the World – Johnston Brothers; Puttin' On the Style – Billy Cotton; When I Fall In Love – Jimmy Young; A White Sport Coat – Max Bygraves; Freight Train – Beverley Sisters; Butterfly – Tommy Steele. Tracks on The Food Christmas EP: Like Princes Do – Crazyhead; I Don't Want That Kind of Love – Jesus Jones; Info Freako – Diesel Park West. Tracks on The Further Adventures of North (EP): Dream 17 – Annette; Carino 90 – T-Coy; The Way I Feel – Frequency 9; Stop This Thing – Dynasty of Two featuring Rowetta. Tracks on The Apple EP: Those Were the Days – Mary Hopkin; That's the Way God Planned It – Billy Preston; Sour Milk Sea – Jackie Lomax; Come and Get It – Badfinger. Tracks on Fourplay (EP): DJs Unite; Alright – Glide; Be Free – Noisy Factory; True Devotion – EQ. Tracks on The Fred EP: Deeply Dippy – Rockingbirds; Don't Talk Just Kiss – Flowered Up; I'm Too

*Sexy – Saint Etienne. Gimme Shelter EP was available on all four formats, each featuring an interview with the featured artist plus the following artists performing versions of Gimme Shelter: (cassette) Jimmy Somerville and Voice of the Beehive; Heaven 17; (12") Blue Pearl, 808 State and Robert Owens; Pop Will Eat Itself vs Gary Clail; Ranking Roger and the Mighty Diamonds; (CD) Thunder; Little Angels; Hawkwind and Sam Fox; (2nd CD) Cud with Sandie Shaw; Kingmaker; New Model Army and Tom Jones. Tracks on Subplates Volume 1 (EP): Style Warz – Son'z of a Loop Da Loop Era; Funky Dope Track – Q–Bass; The Chopper – DJ Hype; Look No Further – Run Tings. Tracks on The Two Tone EP: Gangsters – Special AKA; The Prince –Madness; On My Radio – Selecter; Tears of a Clown – Beat. Tracks on Help (EP): Lucky – Radiohead; 50ft Queenie (Live) – PJ Harvey; Momentum – Guru featuring Big Shug; an untitled piece of incidental music. Tracks on New York Undercover (EP): Tell Me What You Like – Guy; Dom Perignon – Little Shawn; I Miss You – Monifah; Jeeps, Lex Coups, Bimax & Menz – Lost Boys. Tracks on Dangerous Minds (EP): Curiosity – Aaron Hall; Gin & Dance – De Vante; It's Alright – Sista featuring Craig Mack. Artists on Perfect Day are as follows: BBC Symphony Orchestra and Andrew Davis, Bono (U2), Boyzone, Brett Anderson (Suede), Brodsky Quartet, Burning Spear, Courtney Pine, David Bowie, Dr John, Elton John, Emmylou Harris, Evan Dando (Lemonheads), Gabrielle, Heather Small (M People), Huey (Fun Lovin' Criminals), Ian Broudie (Lightning Seeds), Joan Armatrading, Laurie Anderson, Lesley Garrett, Lou Reed, Robert Cray, Shane MacGowan, Sheona White, Skye (Morcheeba), Suzanne Vega, Tammy Wynette, Thomas Allen, Tom Jones, Visual Ministry Orchestra. Tracks on The Full Monty – Monster Mix (medley): You Sexy Thing – Hot Chocolate; Hot Stuff – Donna Summer; You Can Leave Your Hat On – Tom Jones. CD also has a full version of 'You Can Leave Your Hat On' by Tom Jones and 'The Stripper' by David Rose. Tracks on Trade (EP) (disc 2): Put Your House in Order – Steve Thomas; The Dawn – Tony De Vit. Artists on 'It's Only Rock 'n' Roll': Keith Richards, Kid Rock, Mary J Blige, Kelly Jones of Stereophonics, Jon Bon Jovi, Kéllé Bryan, Jay Kay of Jamiroquai, Ozzy Osbourne, Womack and Womack, Lionel Richie, Bonnie Raitt, Dolores O'Riordan of The Cranberries, James Brown, Spice Girls (minus Geri), Mick Jagger, Robin Williams, Jackson Browne, Iggy Pop, Chrissie Hynde, Skin of Skunk Anansie, Annie Lennox, Mark Owen, Natalie Imbruglia, Huey of Fun Lovin' Criminals, Dina Carroll, Gavin Rossdale of Bush, BB King, Joe Cocker, The Corrs, Steve Cradock and Simon Fowler of Ocean Colour Scene, Ronan Keating, Ray Barretto, Herbie Hancock, Francis Rossi and Rick Parfitt of Status Quo, S Club 7 and Eric Idle. Tracks on 'Hard Beat EP 19': 'Eternal '99' by Eternal Rhythm and 'Tragic', 'F**k Me' and 'Don't Give Up' all by BK*

See also COMPILATION ALBUMS; SOUNDTRACKS (films, TV etc); STUDIO CAST RECORDINGS

VARIOUS ARTISTS (MONTAGES) *(Singles: 31 weeks)*

Date		Title / Label	pos	wks
17 May 80		**CALIBRE CUTS** *Calibre CAB 502*	**75**	2
25 Nov 89		**DEEP HEAT '89** *Deep Heat DEEP 10*	**12**	11
3 Mar 90	●	**THE BRITS 1990** *RCA PB 43565*	**2**	7
28 Apr 90		**THE SIXTH SENSE** *Deep Heat DEEP 12*	**49**	2
10 Nov 90		**TIME TO MAKE THE FLOOR BURN** *Megabass MEGAX 1*	**16**	9

The following tracks are sampled: Calibre Cuts: Big Apples Rock – Black Ivory; Don't Hold Back – Chanson; The River Drive – Jupiter Beyond; Dancing in the Disco – LAX; Mellow Mellow Right On – Lowrell; Pata Pata – Osibisa; I Like It – Players Association; We Got the Funk – Positive Force; Holdin' On – Tony Rallo and the Midnite Band; Can You Feel the Force – Real Thing; Miami Heatwave – Seventh Avenue; Rapper's Delight – Sugarhill Gang; Que Tal America – Two Man Sound; Remakes by session musicians: Ain't No Stoppin' Us Now, Bad Girls, We Are Family. Deep Heat '89 (credited to Latino Rave): Pump Up the Jam – Technotronics; Stakker Humanoid – Humanoid; A Day in the Life – Black Riot; Work it to the Bone – LNR; I Can Make U Dance – DJ 'Fast' Eddie; Voodoo Ray – A Guy Called Gerald; Numero Uno – Starlight; Bango (To the Batmobile) – Todd Terry; Break 4 Love – Raze; Don't Scandalize Mine – Sugar Bear. The Brits 1990: Street Tuff – Double Trouble and the Rebel MC; Voodoo Ray – A Guy Called Gerald; Theme From S–Express – S–Express; Hey DJ I Can't Dance to That Music You're Playing – Beatmasters; Eve of the War – Jeff Wayne; Pacific State – 808 State; We Call It Acieed – D Mob; Got to Keep On – Cookie Crew. The Sixth Sense (credited to Latino Rave): Get Up – Technotronic; The Magic Number – De La Soul; G'Ding G'Ding (Do Wanna Wanna) – Anna G; Show 'M the Bass – MC Miker G; Turn It Out (Go Base) – Rob Base; Eve of the War (War of the Worlds) – Project D; Moments In Love – 2 to the Power.Time to Make the Floor Burn (credited to Megabass): Do This My Way – Kid 'N' Play; Street Tuff – Double Trouble and the Rebel MC; Sex 4 Daze – Lake Eerie; Ride On Time – Black Box; Make My Body Rock – Jomanda; Don't Miss the Partyline – Bizz Nizz; Pump Pump It Up – Hypnotek; Big Fun – Inner City; Pump That Body – Mr Lee; Pump Up the Jam – Technotronic; This Beat Is Technotronic – Technotronic; Get Busy – Mr Lee; Touch Me – 49ers; Thunderbirds Are Go – FAB

Junior VASQUEZ

US, male DJ / producer – Donald Martin (Singles: 5 weeks)

Date	Title / Label	pos	wks
15 Jul 95	**GET YOUR HANDS OFF MY MAN!** *Positiva CDTIV 37*	**22**	3
31 Aug 96	**IF MADONNA CALLS** *Multiply CDMULTY 13*	**24**	2

Elaine VASSELL – *See BEATMASTERS*

VAST

Australia, male vocal / instrumental group (Singles: 1 week)

Date	Title / Label	pos	wks
16 Sep 00	**FREE** *Mushroom MUSH 79CDS*	**55**	1

Sven VATH

Germany, male DJ / producer (Singles: 5 weeks)

Date	Title / Label	pos	wks
24 Jul 93	**L'ESPERANZA** *Eye Q YZ 757*	**63**	2
6 Nov 93	**AN ACCIDENT IN PARADISE** *Eye Q YZ 778CD*	**57**	2
22 Oct 94	**HARLEQUIN – THE BEAUTY AND THE BEAST** *Eye Q YZ 857*	**72**	1

Frankie VAUGHAN (242 Top 500)

High-kicking 1950s heart-throb vocalist, b. Frank Abelson, 3 Feb 1928, Liverpool, UK, d. 17 Sep 1999. This variety-show veteran was made an OBE in 1965 for his charity work, and was one of the most popular performers of the 1950s (Singles: 232 weeks, Albums: 20 weeks)

Date		Title / Label	pos	wks
29 Jan 54		**ISTANBUL (NOT CONSTANTINOPLE)** *HMV B 10599* [1]	**11**	1
28 Jan 55		**HAPPY DAYS AND LONELY NIGHTS** *HMV B 10783*	**12**	3
22 Apr 55		**TWEEDLE DEE** *Philips PB 423*	**17**	1
2 Dec 55		**SEVENTEEN** *Philips PB 511*	**18**	3
3 Feb 56		**MY BOY FLAT TOP** *Philips PB 544*	**20**	2
9 Nov 56	●	**THE GREEN DOOR** *Philips PB 640*	**2**	15
11 Jan 57	★	**THE GARDEN OF EDEN** *Philips PB 660*	**1**	13
4 Oct 57	●	**MAN ON FIRE / WANDERIN' EYES** *Philips PB 729*	**6**	12
1 Nov 57	●	**GOT-TA HAVE SOMETHING IN THE BANK, FRANK** *Philips PB 751* [2]	**8**	11
20 Dec 57	●	**KISSES SWEETER THAN WINE** *Philips PB 775*	**8**	11
7 Mar 58		**CAN'T GET ALONG WITHOUT YOU / WE ARE NOT ALONE** *Philips PB 793*	**11**	6
9 May 58	●	**KEWPIE DOLL** *Philips PB 825*	**10**	12
1 Aug 58		**WONDERFUL THINGS (re)** *Philips PB 834*	**22**	6
10 Oct 58		**AM I WASTING MY TIME ON YOU (re)** *Philips PB 865*	**25**	4
30 Jan 59		**THAT'S MY DOLL** *Philips PB 895*	**28**	2
1 May 59	●	**COME SOFTLY TO ME** *Philips PB 913* [2]	**9**	9
24 Jul 59	●	**THE HEART OF A MAN** *Philips PB 930*	**5**	14
18 Sep 59		**WALKIN' TALL (re)** *Philips PB 931*	**28**	2
29 Jan 60		**WHAT MORE DO YOU WANT** *Philips PB 985*	**25**	2
22 Sep 60		**KOOKIE LITTLE PARADISE** *Philips PB 1054*	**31**	5
27 Oct 60		**MILORD** *Philips PB 1066*	**34**	6
9 Nov 61	★	**TOWER OF STRENGTH** *Philips PB 1195*	**1**	13
1 Feb 62		**DON'T STOP – TWIST!** *Philips BF 1219*	**22**	7
27 Sep 62		**HERCULES** *Philips 326542 BF*	**42**	4
24 Jan 63	●	**LOOP DE LOOP** *Philips 326566 BF*	**5**	12
20 Jun 63		**HEY MAMA** *Philips BF 1254*	**21**	9
4 Jun 64		**HELLO, DOLLY!** *Philips BF 1339*	**18**	11
11 Mar 65		**SOMEONE MUST HAVE HURT YOU A LOT** *Philips BF 1394*	**46**	1
23 Aug 67	●	**THERE MUST BE A WAY** *Columbia DB 8248*	**7**	21
15 Nov 67		**SO TIRED** *Columbia DB 8298*	**21**	9
28 Feb 68		**NEVERTHELESS** *Columbia DB 8354*	**29**	5
5 Sep 59	●	**FRANKIE VAUGHAN AT THE LONDON PALLADIUM** *Philips BDL 7330*	**6**	2
4 Nov 67		**FRANKIE VAUGHAN SONGBOOK** *Philips DBL 001*	**40**	1
25 Nov 67		**THERE MUST BE A WAY** *Columbia SCX 6200*	**22**	8
12 Nov 77		**100 GOLDEN GREATS** *Ronco RTDX 2021*	**24**	9

[1] Frankie Vaughan with The Peter Knight Singers [2] Frankie Vaughan and The Kaye Sisters

Malcolm VAUGHAN

UK, male vocalist – Malcolm Thomas (Singles: 106 weeks)

Date		Title / Label	pos	wks
1 Jul 55	●	**EV'RY DAY OF MY LIFE** *HMV B 10874*	**5**	16
27 Jan 56		**WITH YOUR LOVE (2re)** *HMV POP 130* [1]	**18**	3
26 Oct 56	●	**ST THERESE OF THE ROSES (re)** *HMV POP 250*	**3**	20
12 Apr 57		**THE WORLD IS MINE (2re)** *HMV POP 303*	**26**	4
10 May 57		**CHAPEL OF THE ROSES** *HMV POP 325*	**13**	8
29 Nov 57	●	**MY SPECIAL ANGEL** *HMV POP 419*	**3**	14
21 Mar 58		**TO BE LOVED** *HMV POP 459* [2]	**14**	12
17 Oct 58	●	**MORE THAN EVER (COME PRIMA)** *HMV POP 538* [2]	**5**	14
27 Feb 59		**WAIT FOR ME / WILLINGLY (re)** *HMV POP 590*	**13**	15

[1] Malcolm Vaughan with the Peter Knight Singers [2] Malcolm Vaughan with the Michael Sammes Singers

The 706 No.1 Albums

NO.1 ALBUMS OF THE 00S

Here is the complete chronological list of every UK chart-topping album stretching back to 2000. All dates given are for an album's first week at No.1, not its first entry into the chart.

The run at the top of the chart in weeks follows in brackets, followed by the US peak position of the album.

2000

15 Jan **THE MAN WHO Travis** (5 weeks) US 135
19 Feb **RISE Gabrielle** (3 weeks)
11 Mar **STANDING ON THE SHOULDER OF GIANTS Oasis** (1 week) US 24
18 Mar **THE MAN WHO Travis** (2 weeks) US 135
1 Apr **SUPERNATURAL Santana** (2 weeks) US 1
15 Apr **PLAY Moby** (5 weeks) US 38
20 May **RELOAD Tom Jones** (1 week)
27 May **THE GREATEST HITS Whitney Houston** (2 weeks) US 5
10 Jun **CRUSH Bon Jovi** (1 week) US 9
17 Jun **RELOAD Tom Jones** (1 week)
24 Jun **7 S Club 7** (1 week)
1 Jul **THE MARSHALL MATHERS LP Eminem** (1 week) US 1
8 Jul **ALONE WITH EVERBODY Richard Ashcroft** (1 week) US 127
15 Jul **THE MARSHALL MATHERS LP Eminem** (1 week) US 1
22 Jul **PARACHUTES Coldplay** (1 week) US 51
29 Jul **IN BLUE Corrs** (2 weeks) US 21
12 Aug **RONAN Ronan Keating** (2 weeks)
26 Aug **BORN TO DO IT Craig David** (2 weeks) US 11
9 Sep **SING WHEN YOU'RE WINNING Robbie Williams** (3 weeks) US 110
30 Sep **MUSIC Madonna** (2 weeks) US 1
14 Oct **KID A Radiohead** (2 weeks) US 1
28 Oct **SAINTS & SINNERS All Saints** (1 week)
4 Nov **THE GREATEST HITS Texas** (1 week)
11 Nov **ALL THAT YOU CAN'T LEAVE BEHIND U2** (1 week) US 3
18 Nov **COAST TO COAST Westlife** (1 week)
25 Nov **1 Beatles** (9 weeks) US 1

2001

27 Jan **THE GREATEST HITS Texas** (1 week)
3 Feb **CHOCOLATE STARFISH AND THE HOT DOG FLAVORED WATER Limp Bizkit** (1 week) US 1
10 Feb **NO ANGEL Dido** (6 weeks) US 4
24 Mar **SONGBIRD Eva Cassidy** (2 weeks)
7 Apr **POPSTARS Hear'Say** (2 weeks)
21 Apr **JUST ENOUGH EDUCATION TO PERFORM Stereophonics** (2 weeks) US 188
5 May **FREE ALL ANGELS Ash** (1 week)
12 May **SURVIVOR Destiny's Child** (2 weeks) US 1
26 May **REVEAL R.E.M.** (2 weeks) US 6
9 Jun **HOT SHOT Shaggy** (1 week) US 1
16 Jun **AMNESIAC Radiohead** (1 week) US 2
23 Jun **THE INVISIBLE BAND Travis** (4 weeks) US 39
21 Jul **8701 Usher** (1 week) US 4
28 Jul **SURVIVOR Destiny's Child** (2 weeks) US 1
11 Aug **WHITE LADDER David Gray** (1 week) US 35
18 Aug **RIGHT NOW Atomic Kitten** (1 week)
25 Aug **WHITE LADDER David Gray** (1 week) US 35
1 Sep **BREAK THE CYCLE Staind** (1 week) US 1
8 Sep **IOWA Slipknot** (1 week) US 3
15 Sep **A FUNK ODYSSEY Jamiroquai** (2 weeks) US 44
29 Sep **THE ID Macy Gray** (1 week) US 11
6 Oct **NO ANGEL Dido** (1 week) US 4
13 Oct **FEVER Kylie Minogue** (2 weeks)
27 Oct **GOLD – THE GREATEST HITS Steps** (2 weeks)
10 Nov **INVINCIBLE Michael Jackson** (1 week) US 1
17 Nov **GOLD – THE GREATEST HITS Steps** (1 week)
24 Nov **WORLD OF OUR OWN Westlife** (1 week)
1 Dec **SWING WHEN YOU'RE WINNING Robbie Williams** (7 weeks)

2002

19 Jan **JUST ENOUGH EDUCATION TO PERFORM Stereophonics** (3 weeks) US 188
9 Feb **COME WITH US Chemical Brothers** (1 week) US 32
16 Feb **ESCAPE Enrique Iglesias** (2 weeks) US 2
2 Mar **THE VERY BEST OF Sting / Police** (2 weeks)
16 Mar **THE ESSENTIAL Barbra Streisand** (1 week) US 15
23 Mar **SILVER SIDE UP Nickelback** (2 weeks) US 2
6 Apr **A NEW DAY HAS COME Celine Dion** (4 weeks) US 1
4 May **ALL RISE Blue** (1 week)
11 May **THE LAST BROADCAST Doves** (2 weeks) US 83
25 May **18 Moby** (1 week) US 4
1 Jun **DESTINATION Ronan Keating** (1 week)
8 Jun **THE EMINEM SHOW Eminem** (5 weeks) US 1
13 Jul **HEATHEN CHEMISTRY Oasis** (1 week) US 23
20 Jul **BY THE WAY Red Hot Chili Peppers** (3 weeks) US 2
10 Aug **THE RISING Bruce Springsteen** (1 week) US 1
17 Aug **BY THE WAY Red Hot Chili Peppers** (2 weeks) US 2
31 Aug **IMAGINE Eva Cassidy** (1 week) US 32
7 Sep **A RUSH OF BLOOD TO THE HEAD Coldplay** (2 weeks) US 5
21 Sep **FEELS SO GOOD Atomic Kitten** (1 week)
28 Sep **ILLUMINATION Paul Weller** (1 week)
5 Oct **ELVIS – 30 #1 HITS Elvis Presley** (2 weeks) US 1
19 Oct **FROM NOW ON Will Young** (2 weeks)
2 Nov **ONE BY ONE Foo Fighters** (1 week) US 3
9 Nov **A NEW DAY AT MIDNIGHT David Gray** (1 week) US 17
16 Nov **ONE LOVE Blue** (1 week)
23 Nov **UNBREAKABLE – THE BIGGEST HITS VOL.1 Westlife** (1 week)
30 Nov **ESCAPOLOGY Robbie Williams** (6 weeks) US 43

2003

11 Jan **LET GO Avril Lavigne** (3 weeks) US 2
1 Feb **JUSTIFIED Justin Timberlake** (2 weeks) US 2
15 Feb **SIMPLY DEEP Kelly Rowland** (1 week) US 12
22 Feb **100TH WINDOW Massive Attack** (1 week)
1 Mar **JUSTIFIED Justin Timberlake** (1 week) US 2
8 Mar **COME AWAY WITH ME Norah Jones** (4 weeks) US 1
5 Apr **METEORA Linkin Park** (1 week) US 1
12 Apr **ELEPHANT The White Stripes** (2 weeks) US 6
26 Apr **A RUSH OF BLOOD TO THE HEAD Coldplay** (1 week) US 5
3 May **AMERICAN LIFE Madonna** (1 week) US 1
10 May **JUSTIFIED Justin Timberlake** (1 week) US 2
17 May **THINK TANK Blur** (1 week) US 56
24 May **JUSTIFIED Justin Timberlake** (3 weeks) US 2
14 Jun **YOU GOTTA GO THERE TO COME BACK Stereophonics** (1 week)
21 Jun **HAIL TO THE THIEF Radiohead** (1 week) US 3
28 Jun **FALLEN Evanescence** (1 week) US 3
5 Jul **DANGEROUSLY IN LOVE Beyoncé** (5 weeks) US 1

09 Aug MAGIC AND MEDICINE Coral (1 week)
16 Aug ESCAPOLOGY Robbie Williams (1 week) US 43
23 Aug AMERICAN TUNE Eva Cassidy (2 weeks) US 112
06 Sep PERMISSION TO LAND Darkness (4 weeks)
04 Oct ABSOLUTION Muse (1 week)
11 Oct LIFE FOR RENT Dido (4 weeks) US 4
08 Nov IN TIME – THE BEST OF – 1998-2003 R.E.M. (1 week) US 16
15 Nov GUILTY Blue (1 week)
22 Nov LIFE FOR RENT Dido (1 week) US 4
29 Nov NUMBER ONES Michael Jackson (1 week) US 13
06 Dec TURNAROUND Westlife (1 week)
13 Dec FRIDAY'S CHILD Will Young (1 week)
20 Dec LIFE FOR RENT Dido (2 weeks) US 4

2001: A FUNK ODYSSEY Jamiroquai's disco/funk fusion chart-topper with stand-out track 'Love Foolosophy'

2003: ABSOLUTION Muse made their major breakthrough to the big time with 'Absolution' which went straight in at No.1 in October 2003

Norman VAUGHAN

UK, male vocalist / comedian (Singles: 5 weeks) pos/wks

17 May 62 **SWINGING IN THE RAIN** *Pye 7N 15438* **34** 5

Sarah VAUGHAN *US, female vocalist, d. 3 Apr 1990 (Singles: 34 weeks, Albums: 1 week)* pos/wks

27 Sep 57 **PASSING STRANGERS** *Mercury MT 164* [1] **22** 2
11 Sep 59 ● **BROKEN HEARTED MELODY** *Mercury AMT 1057* **7** 13
29 Dec 60 **LET'S / SERENATA (re)** *Columbia DB 4542* **37** 4
12 Mar 69 **PASSING STRANGERS (re-issue)** *Mercury MF 1082* [1] **20** 15
26 Mar 60 **NO COUNT – SARAH** *Mercury MMC 14021* **19** 1

[1] Billy Eckstine and Sarah Vaughan

Stevie Ray VAUGHAN and DOUBLE TROUBLE *US, male vocal / instrumental group – leader d. 27 Aug 1990 (Albums: 1 week)* pos/wks

15 Jul 89 **IN STEP** *Epic 463395 1* **63** 1

VAUGHAN BROTHERS

US, male vocal / instrumental group (Albums: 1 week) pos/wks

20 Oct 90 **FAMILY STYLE** *Epic 4670141* **63** 1

Billy VAUGHN and His ORCHESTRA

US, orchestra and chorus, leader d. 26 Sep 1991 (Singles: 8 weeks) pos/wks

27 Jan 56 **THE SHIFTING WHISPERING SANDS PART 1** *London HLD 8205* [1] **20** 1
23 Mar 56 **THEME FROM "THE THREEPENNY OPERA"** *London HLD 8238* **12** 7

[1] Billy Vaughn Orchestra and Chorus, narration by Ken Nordene

VBIRDS

UK / Planet V, female robot cartoon vocal / rap group (Singles: 3 weeks) pos/wks

3 May 03 **VIRTUALITY** *EMI / Liberty CDSVIRT 001* **21** 3

VEBA – *See RAE & CHRISTIAN*

Bobby VEE (313 Top 500)

Early 1960s teen idol, b. Robert Velline, 30 Apr 1943, North Dakota, US. This photogenic, Buddy Holly-influenced teenaged vocalist (whose backing band once included Bob Dylan) was rarely away from the UK or US charts in the pre-Beat Boom years (Singles: 134 weeks, Albums: 73 weeks) pos/wks

19 Jan 61 ● **RUBBER BALL** *London HLG 9255* **4** 11
13 Apr 61 ● **MORE THAN I CAN SAY / STAYIN' IN** *London HLG 9316* **4** 16
3 Aug 61 ● **HOW MANY TEARS** *London HLG 9389* **10** 13
26 Oct 61 ● **TAKE GOOD CARE OF MY BABY** *London HLG 9438* ▲ **3** 16
21 Dec 61 ● **RUN TO HIM** *London HLG 9470* **6** 15
8 Mar 62 **PLEASE DON'T ASK ABOUT BARBARA** *Liberty LIB 55419* **29** 9
7 Jun 62 ● **SHARING YOU** *Liberty LIB 55451* **10** 13
27 Sep 62 **A FOREVER KIND OF LOVE** *Liberty LIB 10046* **13** 19
7 Feb 63 ● **THE NIGHT HAS A THOUSAND EYES** *Liberty LIB 10069* **3** 12
20 Jun 63 **BOBBY TOMORROW** *Liberty LIB 55530* **21** 10
24 Feb 62 ● **TAKE GOOD CARE OF MY BABY** *London HAG 2428* **7** 8
31 Mar 62 **HITS OF THE ROCKIN' 50'S** *London HAG 2406* **20** 1
27 Oct 62 ● **BOBBY VEE MEETS THE CRICKETS** *Liberty LBY 1086* [1] **2** 27
12 Jan 63 ● **A BOBBY VEE RECORDING SESSION** *Liberty LBY 1084* **10** 11
20 Apr 63 ● **BOBBY VEE'S GOLDEN GREATS** *Liberty LBY 1112* **10** 14
5 Oct 63 **THE NIGHT HAS A THOUSAND EYES** *Liberty LIB 1139* **15** 2
19 Apr 80 ● **THE BOBBY VEE SINGLES ALBUM** *United Artists UAG 30253* **5** 10

[1] Bobby Vee and the Crickets

'Stayin' In' listed with 'More Than I Can Say' from 13 Apr to 4 May 1961. It peaked at No.13

Louie VEGA *US, male producer (Singles: 5 weeks)* pos/wks

5 Oct 91 **RIDE ON THE RHYTHM** *Atlantic A 7602* [1] **71** 1
23 May 92 **RIDE ON THE RHYTHM (re-issue)** *Atlantic A 7486* **70** 1
31 Jan 98 **RIDE ON THE RHYTHM (re-mix)** *Perfecto PERF 151CD1* [2] **36** 2
23 Nov 02 **DIAMOND LIFE** *Distance DI 2409* [3] **52** 1

[1] Little Louie Vega and Marc Anthony [2] Little Louie and Mark Anthony [3] Louie Vega and Jay 'Sinister' Sealee starring Julie McKnight

See also LIL MO' YIN YANG; MASTERS AT WORK

Suzanne VEGA 358 Top 500 *Award-winning singer / songwriter / guitarist, who started as a fragile folk-pop performer, was educated at New York's High School for Performing Arts, b. 11 Jul 1959, Santa Monica, California. First artist to chart with accompanied and unaccompanied version of the same song ('Tom's Diner' – inspired by her brother's restaurant) (Singles: 52 weeks, Albums: 132 weeks)* pos/wks

		pos	wks
18 Jan 86	SMALL BLUE THING *A&M AM 294*	65	3
22 Mar 86	MARLENE ON THE WALL *A&M AM 309*	21	9
7 Jun 86	LEFT OF CENTER *A&M AM 320* [1]	32	9
23 May 87	LUKA *A&M VEGA 1*	23	8
18 Jul 87	TOM'S DINER *A&M VEGA 2*	58	3
19 May 90	BOOK OF DREAMS *A&M AM 559*	66	1
28 Jul 90 ●	TOM'S DINER (re-mix) *A&M AM 592* [2]	2	10
22 Aug 92	IN LIVERPOOL *A&M AM 0029*	52	2
24 Oct 92	99.9°F *A&M AM 0085*	46	2
19 Dec 92	BLOOD MAKES NOISE *A&M AM 0112*	60	3
6 Mar 93	WHEN HEROES GO DOWN *A&M AMCD 0158*	58	1
22 Feb 97	NO CHEAP THRILL *A&M 5818692*	40	1
19 Oct 85	SUZANNE VEGA *A&M AMA 5072*	11	71
9 May 87 ●	SOLITUDE STANDING *A&M SUZLP 2*	2	39
28 Apr 90 ●	DAYS OF OPEN HAND *A&M 3952931*	7	7
19 Sep 92	99.9°F *A&M 5400122*	20	4
8 Mar 97	NINE OBJECTS OF DESIRE *A&M 5405832*	43	3
31 Oct 98	TRIED AND TRUE – THE BEST OF SUZANNE VEGA *A&M 5409452*	46	3
19 Jul 03	RETROSPECTIVE – THE BEST OF *Universal TV 9808884*	27	5

[1] Suzanne Vega featuring Joe Jackson [2] DNA featuring Suzanne Vega

Tata VEGA
US, female vocalist (Singles: 4 weeks) pos/wks

		pos	wks
26 May 79	GET IT UP FOR LOVE / I JUST KEEP THINKING ABOUT YOU BABY *Motown TMG 1140*	52	4

VEGA 4 – *See Paul VAN DYK*

VEGAS *UK, male vocal / instrumental duo – David A Stewart and Terry Hall (Singles: 10 weeks)* pos/wks

		pos	wks
19 Sep 92	POSSESSED *RCA 74321110437*	32	4
28 Nov 92	SHE *RCA 74321124657*	43	4
3 Apr 93	WALK INTO THE WIND *RCA 74321122462*	65	2

See also EURYTHMICS; FUN BOY THREE; Terry HALL; SPECIALS; David A STEWART; TOURISTS

Rosie VELA
US, female vocalist (Singles: 7 weeks, Albums: 11 weeks) pos/wks

		pos	wks
17 Jan 87	MAGIC SMILE *A&M AM 369*	27	7
31 Jan 87	ZAZU *A&M AMA 5016*	20	11

Wil VELOZ – *See LOS DEL MAR featuring Wil VELOZ*

VELVELETTES *US, female vocal group (Singles: 7 weeks)* pos/wks

		pos	wks
31 Jul 71	THESE THINGS WILL KEEP ME LOVING YOU *Tamla Motown TMG 780*	34	7

VELVET UNDERGROUND *UK / US, male / female vocal / instrumental group (Singles: 1 week, Albums: 10 weeks)* pos/wks

		pos	wks
12 Mar 94	VENUS IN FURS *Sire W 0224CD*	71	1
23 Feb 85	V.U. *Polydor POLD 5167*	47	4
13 Nov 93	LIVE MCMXCIII *Sire 9362454642*	70	1
28 Oct 95	THE BEST OF LOU REED AND THE VELVET UNDERGROUND *Global Television RADCD 21* [1]	56	4
6 Jul 02	VELVET UNDERGROUND & NICO *Polydor 8232902* [2]	59	1

[1] Lou Reed and the Velvet Underground [2] Velvet Underground & Nico

See also NICO; Lou REED; John CALE

VELVETS *US, male vocal group (Singles: 2 weeks)* pos/wks

		pos	wks
11 May 61	THAT LUCKY OLD SUN *London HLU 9328*	46	1
17 Aug 61	TONIGHT (COULD BE THE NIGHT) *London HLU 9372*	50	1

Terry VENABLES – *See RIDER & Terry VENABLES*

VENGABOYS 379 Top 500
Hungary / Trinidad / Brazil / Holland, male / female vocal / production dance-pop troupe formed in 1992 by Spanish DJs Danski and Delmundo. In 1996 they added singers / dancers Kim, Robin (replaced by Yorick in 1999), Roy and Denice to front group. First Netherlands-based act to score six successive Top 5 singles. Best-selling single: 'Boom, Boom, Boom, Boom!!' 578,900 (Singles: 99 weeks, Albums: 77 weeks) pos/wks

		pos	wks
28 Nov 98 ●	UP AND DOWN *Positiva CDTIV 105*	4	15
13 Mar 99 ●	WE LIKE TO PARTY! (THE VENGABUS) *Positiva CDTIV 108*	3	14
26 Jun 99 ★	BOOM, BOOM, BOOM, BOOM!! *Positiva CDTIV 114* ■	1	15
11 Sep 99	WE'RE GOING TO IBIZA (import) *Jive 550422*	69	1
18 Sep 99 ★	WE'RE GOING TO IBIZA! *Positiva CDTIV 119* ■	1	12
18 Dec 99 ●	KISS (WHEN THE SUN DON'T SHINE) *Positiva CDTIV 122*	3	18
11 Mar 00 ●	SHALALA LALA *Positiva CDTIV 126*	5	10
8 Jul 00 ●	UNCLE JOHN FROM JAMAICA *Positiva CDTIV 135*	6	7
14 Oct 00	CHEEKAH BOW BOW (THAT COMPUTER SONG) *Positiva CDTIV 142*	19	5
24 Feb 01	FOREVER AS ONE *Positiva CDTIV 148*	28	2
3 Apr 99 ●	THE PARTY ALBUM! *Positiva 4993472*	6	49
25 Mar 00 ●	THE PLATINUM ALBUM *Positiva 5259530*	9	28

VENOM *UK, male vocal / instrumental group (Albums: 2 weeks)* pos/wks

		pos	wks
21 Apr 84	AT WAR WITH SATAN *Neat NEAT 1015*	64	1
13 Apr 85	POSSESSED *Neat NEAT 1024*	99	1

VENT 414 *UK, male vocal / instrumental group (Singles: 1 week)* pos/wks

		pos	wks
28 Sep 96	FIXER *Polydor 5753292*	71	1

Anthony VENTURA ORCHESTRA
Switzerland, orchestra (Albums: 4 weeks) pos/wks

		pos	wks
20 Jan 79	DREAM LOVER *Lotus WH 5007*	44	4

VENTURES *US, male instrumental group (Singles: 31 weeks)* pos/wks

		pos	wks
8 Sep 60 ●	WALK DON'T RUN *Top Rank JAR 417*	8	13
1 Dec 60 ●	PERFIDIA *London HLG 9232*	4	13
9 Mar 61	RAM-BUNK-SHUSH *London HLG 9292*	45	1
11 May 61	LULLABY OF THE LEAVES *London HLG 9344*	43	4

VERACOCHA *Holland, male production duo – Vincent de Moor and Ferry Corsten (Singles: 4 weeks)* pos/wks

		pos	wks
15 May 99	CARTE BLANCHE *Positiva CDTIV 110*	22	4

See also MOONMAN; SYSTEM F; GOURYELLA; STARPARTY; ALBION; Ferry CORSTEN

Al VERLAINE – *See 'PING PING' and AL VERLAINE*

Tom VERLAINE
US, male vocalist / instrumentalist – guitar (Albums: 1 week) pos/wks

		pos	wks
14 Mar 87	FLASH LIGHT *Fontana SFLP 1*	99	1

VERNONS GIRLS *UK, female vocal group (Singles: 31 weeks)* pos/wks

		pos	wks
17 May 62	LOVER PLEASE / YOU KNOW WHAT I MEAN (3re) *Decca F 11450*	16	20
6 Sep 62	LOCO-MOTION *Decca F 11495*	47	1
3 Jan 63	FUNNY ALL OVER *Decca F 11549*	31	8
18 Apr 63	DO THE BIRD (re) *Decca F 11629*	44	2

For the initial chart run of Decca F 11450, during which it peaked, and the first week of its Aug re-entry, the chart listed only 'Lover Please'. 'You Know What I Mean' was listed jointly for the remainder of the first re-entry and in its own right for subsequent re-entries in Oct and Nov 1962, peaking at No.37

VERNON'S WONDERLAND
Germany, male producer – Matthias Hoffmann (Singles: 1 week) pos/wks

		pos	wks
25 May 96	VERNON'S WONDERLAND *Eye-Q Classics EYECL 004CD*	59	1

VERONIKA – *See CRW*

VERTICAL HORIZON
US, male vocal / instrumental group (Singles: 2 weeks) pos/wks

26 Aug 00 **EVERYTHING YOU WANT** *RCA 74321748692* ▲ 42 2

VERUCA SALT
US, male / female vocal / instrumental group (Singles: 5 weeks, Albums: 2 weeks) pos/wks

2 Jul 94 **SEETHER** *Scared Hitless FRET 003CD* 61 1
3 Dec 94 **SEETHER (re-issue)** *Hi-Rise FLATSDG 12* 73 1
4 Feb 95 **NUMBER ONE BLIND** *Hi-Rise FLATSCD 16* 68 1
22 Feb 97 **VOLCANO GIRLS** *Outpost OPRCD 22197* 56 1
30 Aug 97 **BENJAMIN** *Outpost OPRCD 22261* 75 1
15 Oct 94 **AMERICAN THIGHS** *Hi-Rise FLATCD 9* 47 2

The VERVE
(408 Top 500) *Anthemic UK indie-rock band, formed 1991, Wigan, fronted by Richard Ashcroft (v/g). Double Brit winners' swan song, 'Urban Hymns', went gold in 17 countries, and was the first album to sell a million in UK in two successive years (1997/98). Ashcroft went solo when group split in 1999 (Singles: 50 weeks, Albums: 115 weeks)* pos/wks

4 Jul 92 **SHE'S A SUPERSTAR** *Hut HUT 16* 66 1
22 May 93 **BLUE** *Hut HUTCD 29* 69 1
13 May 95 **THIS IS MUSIC** *Hut HUTCD 54* 35 3
24 Jun 95 **ON YOUR OWN** *Hut HUTCD 55* 28 2
30 Sep 95 **HISTORY** *Hut HUTCD 59* 24 3
28 Jun 97 ● **BITTER SWEET SYMPHONY (re)** *Hut HUTDG 82* 2 13
13 Sep 97 ★ **THE DRUGS DON'T WORK (re)** *Hut HUTDG 88* ■ 1 13
6 Dec 97 ● **LUCKY MAN** *Hut HUTDG 92* 7 13
30 May 98 **SONNET (import)** *Hut 8950752* 74 1
3 Jul 93 **A STORM IN HEAVEN** *Hut CDHUT 10* [1] 27 2
15 Jul 95 **A NORTHERN SOUL** *Hut DGHUT 27* 13 11
11 Oct 97 ★ **URBAN HYMNS** *Hut CDHUT 45* ■ 1 102

[1] Verve

See also Richard ASHCROFT

A VERY GOOD FRIEND OF MINE
Italy, male / female vocal / production / instrumental group (Singles: 1 week) pos/wks

3 Jul 99 **JUST ROUND** *Positiva CDTIV 109* 55 1

VEX RED
UK, male vocal / instrumental group (Singles: 1 week, Albums: 1 week) pos/wks

2 Mar 02 **CAN'T SMILE** *Virgin VUSCD 237* 45 1
16 Mar 02 **START WITH A STRONG AND PERSISTENT DESIRE** *Virgin CDVUS 215* 48 1

VIBRATIONS – *See Tony JACKSON and the VIBRATIONS*

VIBRATORS
UK, male vocal / instrumental group (Singles: 8 weeks, Albums: 7 weeks) pos/wks

18 Mar 78 **AUTOMATIC LOVER** *Epic EPC 6137* 35 5
17 Jun 78 **JUDY SAYS (KNOCK YOU IN THE HEAD)** *Epic EPC 6393* 70 3
25 Jun 77 **THE VIBRATORS** *Epic EPC 82907* 49 5
29 Apr 78 **V2** *Epic EPC 82495* 33 2

VICE SQUAD
UK, male / female vocal / instrumental group (Singles: 1 week, Albums: 10 weeks) pos/wks

13 Feb 82 **OUT OF REACH** *Zonophone Z 26* 68 1
24 Oct 81 **NO CAUSE FOR CONCERN** *Zonophone ZEM 103* 32 5
22 May 82 **STAND STRONG STAND PROUD** *Zonophone ZEM 104* 47 5

Sid VICIOUS
UK, male vocalist – John Beverley, d. 2 Feb 1979 (Albums: 8 weeks) pos/wks

15 Dec 79 **SID SINGS** *Virgin V 2144* 30 8

See also SEX PISTOLS

VICIOUS CIRCLES
UK, male producer – Simon Berry (Singles: 1 week) pos/wks

16 Dec 00 **VICIOUS CIRCLES** *Platipus PLATCD 82* 68 1

See also POLTERGEIST

VICIOUS PINK
UK, male / female vocal / instrumental duo (Singles: 4 weeks) pos/wks

15 Sep 84 **CCCAN'T YOU SEE** *Parlophone R 6074* 67 4

Mike VICKERS – *See Kenny EVERETT*

Maria VIDAL
US, female vocalist (Singles: 13 weeks) pos/wks

24 Aug 85 **BODY ROCK** *EMI America EA 189* 11 13

VIDEO KIDS
Holland, male / female vocal duo (Singles: 1 week) pos/wks

5 Oct 85 **WOODPECKERS FROM SPACE** *Epic A 6504* 72 1

VIDEO SYMPHONIC
UK, orchestra (Singles: 3 weeks) pos/wks

24 Oct 81 **THE FLAME TREES OF THIKA** *EMI EMI 5222* 42 3

VIENNA PHILHARMONIC ORCHESTRA
Austria, orchestra – conducted by Aram Khachaturian (Singles: 14 weeks) pos/wks

18 Dec 71 **THE 'ONEDIN LINE' THEME** *Decca F 13259* 15 14

VIENNA SYMPHONY ORCHESTRA
Austria, orchestra (Albums: 4 weeks) pos/wks

4 Apr 87 **SYMPHONIC ROCK WITH THE VIENNA SYMPHONY ORCHESTRA** *Stylus SMR 730* 43 4

VIEW FROM THE HILL
UK, male / female vocal / instrumental group (Singles: 6 weeks) pos/wks

19 Jul 86 **NO CONVERSATION** *EMI EMI 5565* 58 3
21 Feb 87 **I'M NO REBEL** *EMI EM 5580* 59 3

VIKKI
UK, female vocalist (Singles: 3 weeks) pos/wks

4 May 85 **LOVE IS . . .** *PRT 7P 326* 49 3

VILLAGE PEOPLE
US, male vocal group (Singles: 66 weeks, Albums: 29 weeks) pos/wks

3 Dec 77 **SAN FRANCISCO (YOU'VE GOT ME)** *DJM DJS 10817* 45 5
25 Nov 78 ★ **Y.M.C.A.** *Mercury 6007 192* ◆ 1 16
17 Mar 79 ● **IN THE NAVY** *Mercury 6007 209* 2 9
16 Jun 79 **GO WEST** *Mercury 6007 221* 15 8
9 Aug 80 **CAN'T STOP THE MUSIC** *Mercury MER 16* 11 11
9 Feb 85 **SEX OVER THE PHONE** *Record Shack SOHO 34* 59 5
4 Dec 93 **Y.M.C.A. (re-mix)** *Bell 74321177182* 12 7
28 May 94 **IN THE NAVY (re-mix)** *Bell 74321198192* 36 2
27 Nov 99 **Y.M.C.A. (2nd re-mix)** *Wrasse WRASX 002* 35 3
27 Jan 79 **CRUISIN'** *Mercury 9109 614* 24 9
12 May 79 **GO WEST** *Mercury 9109 621* 14 19
18 Dec 93 **THE BEST OF THE VILLAGE PEOPLE** *Bell 4321178312* 72 1

V.I.M.
UK, male instrumental / production group (Singles: 1 week) pos/wks

26 Jan 91 **MAGGIE'S LAST PARTY** *F2 BOZ 1* 68 1

Gene VINCENT
US, male vocalist – Eugene Craddock, d. 12 Oct 1971 (Singles: 51 weeks, Albums: 2 weeks) pos/wks

13 Jul 56 **BE-BOP-A-LULA (2re)** *Capitol CL 14599* [1] 16 7
12 Oct 56 **RACE WITH THE DEVIL** *Capitol CL 14628* [1] 28 1
19 Oct 56 **BLUE JEAN BOP** *Capitol CL 14637* [1] 16 5
8 Jan 60 **WILD CAT (re)** *Capitol CL 15099* 21 6
10 Mar 60 **MY HEART (2re)** *Capitol CL 15115* [1] 16 8
16 Jun 60 **PISTOL PACKIN' MAMA** *Capitol CL 15136* [2] 15 9
1 Jun 61 **SHE SHE LITTLE SHEILA (re)** *Capitol CL 15202* 22 11
31 Aug 61 **I'M GOING HOME (TO SEE MY BABY)** *Capitol CL 15215* [3] 36 4
16 Jul 60 **CRAZY TIMES** *Capitol T 1342* 12 2

[1] Gene Vincent and The Blue Caps [2] Gene Vincent with The Beat Boys [3] Gene Vincent with Sounds Incorporated

Vinnie VINCENT
US, male vocalist / instrumentalist – guitar (Albums: 2 weeks) pos/wks

28 May 88 **ALL SYSTEMS GO** *Chrysalis CHR 1626* **51** 2

See also KISS

VINDALOO SUMMER SPECIAL
UK, male / female vocal / instrumental group (Singles: 3 weeks) pos/wks

19 Jul 86 **ROCKIN' WITH RITA (HEAD TO TOE)** *Vindaloo UGH 13* **56** 3

VINES *Australia, male vocal / instrumental group (Singles: 7 weeks, Albums: 7 weeks)* pos/wks

20 Apr 02 **HIGHLY EVOLVED** *Heavenly HVN 112CD* **32** 2
29 Jun 02 **GET FREE** *Heavenly HVN 113CD* **24** 3
19 Oct 02 **OUTTATHAWAY** *Heavenly HVN 120CDS* **20** 2
20 Jul 02 ● **HIGHLY EVOLVED** *Heavenly HVNLP 36CD* **3** 7

Bobby VINTON
US, male vocalist (Singles: 29 weeks, Albums: 2 weeks) pos/wks

2 Aug 62 **ROSES ARE RED (MY LOVE)** *Columbia DB 4878* ▲ **15** 8
19 Dec 63 **THERE! I'VE SAID IT AGAIN** *Columbia DB 7179* ▲ **34** 10
29 Sep 90 ● **BLUE VELVET** *Epic 6505240* ▲ **2** 10
17 Nov 90 **ROSES ARE RED (MY LOVE) (re-issue)** *Epic 6564677* **71** 1
17 Nov 90 **BLUE VELVET** *Epic 4675701* **67** 2

VINYLGROOVER and The RED HED
UK, male production duo (Singles: 1 week) pos/wks

27 Jan 01 **ROK DA HOUSE** *Nukleuz NUKP 0285* **72** 1

VIOLENT DELIGHT
UK, male vocal / instrumental group (Singles: 4 weeks) pos/wks

1 Mar 03 **I WISH I WAS A GIRL** *WEA WEA 362CD* **25** 2
21 Jun 03 **ALL YOU EVER DO** *WEA WEA 367CD1* **38** 1
13 Sep 03 **TRANSMISSION** *WEA WEA 370 CD1* **64** 1

VIOLENT FEMMES
US, male / female vocal / instrumental group (Albums: 1 week) pos/wks

1 Mar 86 **THE BLIND LEADING THE NAKED** *Slash SLAP 10* **81** 1

VIOLINSKI
UK, male instrumental group (Singles: 9 weeks, Albums: 1 week) pos/wks

17 Feb 79 **CLOG DANCE** *Jet 136* **17** 9
26 May 79 **NO CAUSE FOR ALARM** *Jet JETLU 219* **49** 1

VIPER *Belgium, male production group (Singles: 1 week)* pos/wks

7 Feb 98 **THE TWISTER** *Hooj Choons HOOJCD 59* **55** 1

VIPERS SKIFFLE GROUP
UK, male vocal / instrumental group (Singles: 18 weeks) pos/wks

25 Jan 57 ● **DON'T YOU ROCK ME DADDY-O** *Parlophone R 4261* **10** 9
22 Mar 57 ● **THE CUMBERLAND GAP** *Parlophone R 4289* **10** 6
31 May 57 **STREAMLINE TRAIN** *Parlophone R 4308* **23** 3

VIRGINIA – *See Tom NOVY*

VIRUS *UK, male instrumental / production duo – Paul Oakenfold and Steve Osborne (Singles: 3 weeks)* pos/wks

26 Aug 95 **SUN** *Perfecto PERF 107CD* **62** 1
25 Jan 97 **MOON** *Perfecto PERF 134CD* **36** 2

See also OAKENFOLD; PERFECTO ALL STARZ

VISAGE *UK, male vocal / instrumental group (Singles: 56 weeks, Albums: 58 weeks)* pos/wks

20 Dec 80 ● **FADE TO GREY** *Polydor POSP 194* **8** 15
14 Mar 81 **MIND OF A TOY** *Polydor POSP 236* **13** 8
11 Jul 81 **VISAGE** *Polydor POSP 293* **21** 7
13 Mar 82 **DAMNED DON'T CRY** *Polydor POSP 390* **11** 8
26 Jun 82 **NIGHT TRAIN** *Polydor POSP 441* **12** 10
13 Nov 82 **PLEASURE BOYS** *Polydor POSP 523* **44** 3
1 Sep 84 **LOVE GLOVE** *Polydor POSP 691* **54** 3
28 Aug 93 **FADE TO GREY (re-mix)** *Polydor PZCD 282* **39** 2
24 Jan 81 **VISAGE** *Polydor 2490 157* **13** 29
3 Apr 82 ● **THE ANVIL** *Polydor POLD 5050* **6** 16
19 Nov 83 **FADE TO GREY – THE SINGLES COLLECTION** *Polydor POLD 5117* **38** 11
3 Nov 84 **BEAT BOY** *Polydor POLH 12* **79** 2

See also Midge URE

Michelle VISAGE – *See S.O.U.L. S.Y.S.T.E.M. introducing Michelle VISAGE*

VISCOUNTS *UK, male vocal group (Singles: 18 weeks)* pos/wks

13 Oct 60 **SHORT'NIN' BREAD** *Pye 7N 15287* **16** 8
14 Sep 61 **WHO PUT THE BOMP (IN THE BOMP, BOMP, BOMP)** *Pye 7N 15379* **21** 10

VISION *UK, male vocal / instrumental group (Singles: 1 week)* pos/wks

9 Jul 83 **LOVE DANCE** *MVM MVM 2886* **74** 1

VISIONMASTERS with Tony KING and Kylie MINOGUE
UK, male DJ / production duo, UK, male DJ / producer and Australia, female vocalist (Singles: 1 week) pos/wks

30 Nov 91 **KEEP ON PUMPIN' IT** *PWL PWL 207* **49** 1

VITA – *See N*E*R*D; Irv GOTTI presents JA RULE, ASHANTI, Charli BALTIMORE & VITA*

VITAMIN C
US, female vocalist – Colleen Fitzpatrick (Singles: 1 week) pos/wks

19 Jul 03 **LAST NITE** *V2 VVR 5023283* **70** 1

Soraya VIVIAN *UK, female vocalist (Singles: 1 week)* pos/wks

16 Mar 02 **WHEN YOU'RE GONE** *Activ 8 ACT 501* **59** 1

VIXEN *US, female vocal / instrumental group (Singles: 21 weeks, Albums: 5 weeks)* pos/wks

3 Sep 88 **EDGE OF A BROKEN HEART** *Manhattan MT 48* **51** 4
4 Mar 89 **CRYIN'** *EMI Manhattan MT 60* **27** 4
3 Jun 89 **LOVE MADE ME** *EMI-USA MT 66* **36** 4
2 Sep 89 **EDGE OF A BROKEN HEART (re-issue)** *EMI-USA MT 48* **59** 2
28 Jul 90 **HOW MUCH LOVE** *EMI-USA MT 87* **35** 3
20 Oct 90 **LOVE IS A KILLER** *EMI-USA MT 91* **41** 2
16 Mar 91 **NOT A MINUTE TOO SOON** *EMI-USA MT 93* **37** 2
8 Oct 88 **VIXEN** *Manhattan MTL 1028* **66** 1
18 Aug 90 **REV IT UP** *EMI USA MTL 1054* **20** 4

VOGGUE
Canada, male / female production / vocal group (Singles: 6 weeks) pos/wks

18 Jul 81 **DANCIN' THE NIGHT AWAY** *Mercury MER 76* **39** 6

VOICE OF THE BEEHIVE *US / UK, male / female vocal / instrumental group (Singles: 51 weeks, Albums: 26 weeks)* pos/wks

14 Nov 87 **I SAY NOTHING** *London LON 151* **45** 5
5 Mar 88 **I WALK THE EARTH** *London LON 169* **42** 4
14 May 88 **DON'T CALL ME BABY** *London LON 175* **15** 10
23 Jul 88 **I SAY NOTHING (re-issue)** *London LON 190* **22** 6
22 Oct 88 **I WALK THE EARTH (re-issue)** *London LON 206* **46** 4
13 Jul 91 **MONSTERS AND ANGELS** *London LON 302* **17** 10
28 Sep 91 **I THINK I LOVE YOU** *London LON 308* **25** 6
11 Jan 92 **PERFECT PLACE** *London LON 312* **37** 6
2 Jul 88 **LET IT BEE** *London LONLP 57* **13** 13
24 Aug 91 **HONEY LINGERS** *London 8282591* **17** 13

VOICES OF LIFE *US, male / female vocal / production duo – Sharon Pass and Steve 'Silk' Hurley (Singles: 2 weeks)* pos/wks

21 Mar 98 **THE WORD IS LOVE (SAY THE WORD)** *AM:PM 5825272* **26** 2

See also Steve 'Silk' HURLEY

Sterling VOID
UK, male instrumentalist / vocalist (Singles: 3 weeks) pos/wks

4 Feb 89	**RUNAWAY GIRL / IT'S ALL RIGHT** *ffrr FFR 21*	**53**	3

VOLATILE AGENTS featuring Simone BENN
UK, male production duo and female vocalist (Singles: 3 weeks) pos/wks

15 Dec 01	**HOOKED ON YOU** *Melting Pot MPRCD 10*	**54**	3

VOLCANO *Norway / UK, male / female vocal / instrumental group (Singles: 4 weeks)* pos/wks

23 Jul 94	**MORE TO LOVE** *Deconstruction 74321221832*	**32**	3
18 Nov 95	**THAT'S THE WAY LOVE IS** *EXP EXPCD 002* [1]	**72**	1

[1] Volcano with Sam Cartwright

Herbert VON KARAJAN
Austria, male conductor d. 16 Jul 1989 (Albums: 18 weeks) pos/wks

26 Sep 70	**BEETHOVEN TRIPLE CONCERTO** *HMV ASD 2582*	**51**	2
16 Apr 88	**THE ESSENTIAL KARAJAN** *Deutsche Grammophon HVKTV 1*	**51**	5
3 Aug 91	**HOLST: THE PLANETS** *Deutsche Grammophon 4352891*	**52**	2
7 Oct 95	**KARAJAN: ADAGIO** *Deutsche Grammophon 4452822*	**30**	8
13 Apr 96	**ADAGIO 2** *Deutsche Grammophon 4495152* [1]	**63**	1

[1] Berlin Philharmonic Orchestra / Herbert von Karajan

On 'Beethoven Triple Concerto' the soloists were David Oistrakh (violin), Mstislav Rostropovich (cello) and Sviatoslav Richter (piano)

Anne Sofie VON OTTER
Sweden, female vocalist (Albums: 1 week) pos/wks

31 Mar 01	**FOR THE STARS** *Deutsche Grammophon 4695302* [1]	**67**	1

[1] Anne Sofie Von Otter Meets Elvis Costello

VOODOO & SERANO *Germany, male production duo – Reinhard Raith and Tommy Serano (Singles: 6 weeks)* pos/wks

3 Feb 01	**BLOOD IS PUMPIN'** *Xtrahard / Xtravaganza X2H2 CDS*	**19**	4
16 Aug 03	**OVERLOAD** *All Around The World CDGLOBE 284*	**30**	2

VOW WOW
Japan / US, male vocal / instrumental group (Albums: 1 week) pos/wks

18 Mar 89	**HELTER SKELTER** *Arista 209691*	**75**	1

VOYAGE
UK / France, disco aggregation (Singles: 27 weeks, Albums: 1 week) pos/wks

17 Jun 78	**FROM EAST TO WEST / SCOTS MACHINE** *GTO GT 224*	**13**	13
25 Nov 78	**SOUVENIRS** *GTO GT 241*	**56**	7
24 Mar 79	**LET'S FLY AWAY** *GTO GT 245*	**38**	7
9 Sep 78	**VOYAGE** *GTO GTLP 030*	**59**	1

'Scots Machine' credited from 24 Jun 1978 until end of record's chart run

VOYAGER
UK, male vocal / instrumental group (Singles: 8 weeks) pos/wks

26 May 79	**HALFWAY HOTEL** *Mountain VOY 001*	**33**	8

Jurgen VRIES
UK, male DJ / producer – Darren Tate (Singles: 17 weeks) pos/wks

14 Sep 02	**THE THEME** *Direction 6730952*	**13**	4
1 Feb 03 ●	**THE OPERA SONG (BRAVE NEW WORLD) (re)** *Direction 6734642* [1]	**3**	10
4 Oct 03	**WILDERNESS** *Direction 6742692* [2]	**20**	3

[1] Jurgen Vries featuirng CMC [2] Jurgen Vries featuring Shena

See also ANGELIC; ORION; CITIZEN CANED; DT8 featuring Roxanne WILDE

VYBE
US, female vocal group (Singles: 1 week) pos/wks

7 Oct 95	**WARM SUMMER DAZE** *Fourth & Broadway BRCD 315*	**60**	1

Billy Paul W – *See Robbie RIVERA*

Kristine W *US, female vocalist – Kristine Weitz (Singles: 8 weeks)* pos/wks

21 May 94	**LOVE COME HOME** *Triangle BLUESCD 001* [1]	**73**	1
25 Jun 94	**FEEL WHAT YOU WANT** *Champion CHAMPCD 304*	**33**	3
25 May 96	**ONE MORE TRY** *Champion CHAMPCD 317*	**41**	1
21 Dec 96	**LAND OF THE LIVING** *Champion CHAMPCD 324*	**57**	1
5 Jul 97	**FEEL WHAT YOU WANT (re-issue)** *Champion CHAMPCD 329*	**40**	2

[1] Our Tribe with Franke Pharoah and Kristine W

WC featuring SNOOP DOGG & Nate DOGG
US, male rap / vocal trio (WC is William Calhoun) (Singles: 2 weeks) pos/wks

1 Mar 03	**THE STREETS** *Def Jam 0779852*	**48**	2

See also SNOOP DOGG; Nate DOGG

W.I.P. featuring EMMIE
UK, male production duo and female vocalist (Singles: 1 week) pos/wks

16 Feb 02	**I WON'T LET YOU DOWN** *Decode / Telstar CDSTAS 3210*	**53**	1

Andrew W.K. *US, male vocalist / producer – Andrew Wilkes-Krier (Singles: 5 weeks, Albums: 1 week)* pos/wks

10 Nov 01	**PARTY HARD** *Mercury 5888132*	**19**	4
9 Mar 02	**SHE IS BEAUTIFUL** *Mercury 5889522*	**55**	1
24 Nov 01	**I GET WET** *Mercury 5865882*	**71**	1

W.O.S.P.
UK, male / female production / vocal duo (Singles: 1 week) pos/wks

17 Nov 01	**GETTIN' INTO U** *Data DATA 26CDS*	**48**	1

WWF SUPERSTARS *US / UK, male wrestling vocalists (Singles: 15 weeks, Albums: 5 weeks)* pos/wks

12 Dec 92 ●	**SLAM JAM (re)** *Arista 74321124887*	**4**	9
3 Apr 93	**WRESTLEMANIA** *Arista 74321136832*	**14**	5
10 Jul 93	**USA** *Arista 74321153092* [1]	**71**	1
17 Apr 93 ●	**WRESTLEMANIA – THE ALBUM** *Arista 74321138062*	**10**	5

[1] WWF Superstars featuring Hacksaw Jim Duggan

Bill WADDINGTON – *See CORONATION STREET CAST featuring Bill WADDINGTON*

Adam WADE *US, male vocalist (Singles: 6 weeks)* pos/wks

8 Jun 61	**TAKE GOOD CARE OF HER (re)** *HMV POP 843*	**38**	6

With the George Paxton Orchestra and Chorus

WAG YA TAIL

UK, male vocal / instrumental group (Singles: 1 week) pos/wks

			pos	wks
3 Oct 92		**XPAND YA MIND (EXPANSIONS)** *PWL International PWL 238*	**49**	1

WAH!

UK, male vocal / instrumental group – leader Pete Wylie (Singles: 26 weeks, Albums: 11 weeks) pos/wks

			pos	wks
25 Dec 82	●	**THE STORY OF THE BLUES** *Eternal JF 1*	**3**	12
19 Mar 83		**HOPE (I WISH YOU'D BELIEVE ME)** *WEA X 9880*	**37**	5
30 Jun 84		**COME BACK** *Beggars Banquet BEG 111* [1]	**20**	9
18 Jul 81		**NAH-POO = THE ART OF BLUFF** *Eternal CLASSIC 1*	**33**	5
4 Aug 84		**A WORD TO THE WISE GUY** *Beggars Banquet BEGA 54* [1]	**28**	6

[1] Mighty Wah! [1] Mighty Wah!

See also Pete WYLIE

Donnie WAHLBERG – *See NEW KIDS ON THE BLOCK; SEIKO and Donnie WAHLBERG*

WAIKIKIS

Belgium, male instrumental group (Singles: 2 weeks) pos/wks

			pos	wks
11 Mar 65		**HAWAII TATTOO** *Pye International 7N 25286*	**41**	2

WAILERS – *See Bob MARLEY and the WAILERS*

John WAITE

UK, male vocalist (Singles: 13 weeks, Albums: 3 weeks) pos/wks

			pos	wks
29 Sep 84	●	**MISSING YOU** *EMI America EA 182* ▲	**9**	11
13 Feb 93		**MISSING YOU (re-issue)** *Chrysalis CDCHS 3938*	**56**	2
10 Nov 84		**NO BRAKES** *EMI America WAIT 1*	**64**	3

See also BABYS

WAITRESSES

US, male / female vocal intstrumental group (Singles: 4 weeks) pos/wks

			pos	wks
18 Dec 82		**CHRISTMAS WRAPPING** *Ze / Island WIP 6821*	**45**	4

Tom WAITS

US, male vocalist / instrumentalist – guitar (Albums: 29 weeks) pos/wks

			pos	wks
8 Oct 83		**SWORDFISHTROMBONES** *Island ILPS 9762*	**62**	3
19 Oct 85		**RAIN DOGS** *Island ILPS 9803*	**29**	5
5 Sep 87		**FRANKS WILD YEARS** *Island ITW 3*	**20**	5
8 Oct 88		**BIG TIME** *Island ITW 4*	**84**	1
19 Sep 92		**BONE MACHINE** *Island CID 9993*	**26**	3
20 Nov 93		**THE BLACK RIDER** *Island CID 8021*	**47**	2
27 Jun 98		**BEAUTIFUL MALADIES – THE ISLAND YEARS** *Island 5245192*	**63**	1
1 May 99	●	**MULE VARIATIONS** *Epitaph 65472*	**9**	5
18 May 02		**ALICE** *Anti 66322*	**20**	2
18 May 02		**BLOOD MONEY** *Anti 66292*	**21**	2

Johnny WAKELIN

UK, male vocalist (Singles: 20 weeks) pos/wks

			pos	wks
18 Jan 75	●	**BLACK SUPERMAN (MUHAMMAD ALI)** *Pye 7N 45420* [1]	**7**	10
24 Jul 76	●	**IN ZAIRE** *Pye 7N 45595*	**4**	10

[1] Johnny Wakelin and The Kinshasa Band

Rick WAKEMAN

UK, male instrumentalist – keyboards (Albums: 131 weeks) pos/wks

			pos	wks
24 Feb 73	●	**THE SIX WIVES OF HENRY VIII** *A&M AMLH 64361*	**7**	22
18 May 74	★	**JOURNEY TO THE CENTRE OF THE EARTH** *A&M AMLH 63621*	**1**	30
12 Apr 75	●	**THE MYTHS AND LEGENDS OF KING ARTHUR & THE KNIGHTS OF THE ROUND TABLE** *A&M AMLH 645150022*	**2**	28
24 Apr 76	●	**NO EARTHLY CONNECTION** *A&M AMLK 64583*	**9**	9
12 Feb 77		**WHITE ROCK** *A&M AMLH 64614*	**14**	9
3 Dec 77		**RICK WAKEMAN'S CRIMINAL RECORD** *A&M AMLK 64660*	**25**	5
2 Jun 79		**RHAPSODIES** *A&M AMLX 68508*	**25**	10
27 Jun 81		**1984** *Charisma CDS 4022*	**24**	9
13 Oct 84		**BEYOND THE PLANETS** *Telstar STAR 2244* [1]	**64**	6
16 May 87		**THE GOSPELS** *Stylus SMR 729*	**94**	1
27 Mar 99		**RETURN TO THE CENTRE OF THE EARTH** *EMI Classics CDC 5567632*	**34**	2

[1] Kevin Peek and Rick Wakeman

See also YES; ANDERSON BRUFORD WAKEMAN HOWE; STRAWBS

Narada Michael WALDEN

US, male vocalist / producer (Singles: 28 weeks, Albums: 109 weeks) pos/wks

			pos	wks
23 Feb 80		**TONIGHT I'M ALRIGHT** *Atlantic K 11437*	**34**	9
26 Apr 80	●	**I SHOULDA LOVED YA** *Atlantic K 11413*	**8**	9
23 Apr 88	●	**DIVINE EMOTIONS** *Reprise W 7967* [1]	**8**	10
14 May 88		**DIVINE EMOTION** *Reprise WX 172* [1]	**60**	5

[1] Narada [1] Narada

Gary WALKER

US, male vocalist / instrumentalist – drums – Gary Leeds (Singles: 12 weeks) pos/wks

			pos	wks
24 Feb 66		**YOU DON'T LOVE ME** *CBS 202036*	**26**	6
26 May 66		**TWINKIE-LEE** *CBS 202081*	**26**	6

See also WALKER BROTHERS

John WALKER

US, male vocalist / instrumentalist – guitar – John Maus (Singles: 6 weeks) pos/wks

			pos	wks
5 Jul 67		**ANNABELLA (re)** *Philips BF 1593*	**24**	6

See also WALKER BROTHERS

Scott WALKER

US, male vocalist – Scott Engel (Singles: 30 weeks, Albums: 58 weeks) pos/wks

			pos	wks
6 Dec 67		**JACKIE** *Philips BF 1628*	**22**	9
1 May 68	●	**JOANNA** *Philips BF 1662*	**7**	11
11 Jun 69		**LIGHTS OF CINCINNATI** *Philips BF 1793*	**13**	10
16 Sep 67	●	**SCOTT** *Philips SBL 7816*	**3**	17
20 Apr 68	★	**SCOTT 2** *Philips SBL 7840*	**1**	18
5 Apr 69	●	**SCOTT 3** *Philips S 7882*	**3**	4
5 Jul 69	●	**SONGS FROM HIS TV SERIES** *Philips SBL 7900*	**7**	3
31 Mar 84		**CLIMATE OF HUNTER** *Virgin V 2303*	**60**	2
25 Jan 92	●	**NO REGRETS – THE BEST OF SCOTT WALKER AND THE WALKER BROTHERS 1965-1976** *Fontana 5108312* [1]	**4**	13
20 May 95		**TILT** *Fontana 5268592*	**27**	1

[1] Scott Walker and the Walker Brothers

See also WALKER BROTHERS

Terri WALKER

UK, female vocalist (Singles: 3 weeks) pos/wks

			pos	wks
1 Mar 03		**GUESS YOU DIDN'T LOVE ME** *Def Soul 779962*	**60**	1
17 May 03		**CHING CHING (LOVIN' YOU STILL)** *Def Soul 9800075*	**38**	2

Jr WALKER & The ALL-STARS

US, male instrumental / vocal group, leader d. 23 Nov 1995 (Singles: 59 weeks) pos/wks

			pos	wks
18 Aug 66		**HOW SWEET IT IS (TO BE LOVED BY YOU)** *Tamla Motown TMG 571*	**22**	10
2 Apr 69		**ROAD RUNNER** *Tamla Motown TMG 691*	**12**	12
18 Oct 69		**WHAT DOES IT TAKE (TO WIN YOUR LOVE)** *Tamla Motown TMG 712*	**13**	12
26 Aug 72		**WALK IN THE NIGHT** *Tamla Motown TMG 824*	**16**	11
27 Jan 73		**TAKE ME GIRL, I'M READY** *Tamla Motown TMG 840*	**16**	9
30 Jun 73		**WAY BACK HOME** *Tamla Motown TMG 857*	**35**	5

WALKER BROTHERS

(326 Top 500) *Unrelated US trio, who were top UK teen idols in the mid-60s. Members Scott Walker (Engel) (v/b/k), John Walker (Maus) (v/g), Gary Walker (Leeds) (d) all had solo hits after trio split in 1967, with Scott (who first recorded solo in 1957) creating a large cult following (Singles: 93 weeks, Albums: 109 weeks)* pos/wks

			pos	wks
29 Apr 65		**LOVE HER** *Philips BF 1409*	**20**	13
19 Aug 65	★	**MAKE IT EASY ON YOURSELF** *Philips BF 1428*	**1**	14
2 Dec 65	●	**MY SHIP IS COMING IN** *Philips BF 1454*	**3**	12
3 Mar 66	★	**THE SUN AIN'T GONNA SHINE ANYMORE** *Philips BF 1473*	**1**	11
14 Jul 66		**(BABY) YOU DON'T HAVE TO TELL ME** *Philips BF 1497*	**13**	8

22 Sep 66 **ANOTHER TEAR FALLS** *Philips BF 1514* 12 8
15 Dec 66 **DEADLIER THAN THE MALE** *Philips BF 1537* 34 6
9 Feb 67 **STAY WITH ME BABY** *Philips BF 1548* 26 6
18 May 67 **WALKING IN THE RAIN** *Philips BF 1576* 26 6
17 Jan 76 ● **NO REGRETS** *GTO GT 42* 7 9
18 Dec 65 ● **TAKE IT EASY WITH THE WALKER BROTHERS** *Philips BL 7691* 3 36
3 Sep 66 ● **PORTRAIT** *Philips SBL 7732* 3 23
18 Mar 67 ● **IMAGES** *Philips SBL 7770*....................6 15
16 Sep 67 ● **THE WALKER BROTHERS' STORY** *Philips DBL 002* 9 19
21 Feb 76 **NO REGRETS** *GTO GTLP 007* 49 3
25 Jan 92 ● **NO REGRETS – THE BEST OF SCOTT WALKER AND THE WALKER BROTHERS 1965-1976** *Fontana 5108312* [1]....................4 13

[1] Scott Walker and the Walker Brothers

See also Gary WALKER; John WALKER; Scott WALKER

WALL OF SOUND featuring Gerald LETHAN
US, male vocal / instrumental group (Singles: 1 week) pos/wks

31 Jul 93 **CRITICAL (IF YOU ONLY KNEW)** *Positiva CDTIV 4* 73 1

WALL OF VOODOO
US, male vocal / instrumental group (Singles: 3 weeks) pos/wks

19 Mar 83 **MEXICAN RADIO** *Illegal ILS 36* 64 3

Jerry WALLACE *US, male vocalist (Singles: 1 week)* pos/wks

23 Jun 60 **YOU'RE SINGING OUR LOVE SONG TO SOMEBODY ELSE** *London HLH 9110* 46 1

Rik WALLER *UK, male vocalist (Singles: 12 weeks)* pos/wks

16 Mar 02 ● **I WILL ALWAYS LOVE YOU (re)** *EMI / Liberty CDRIK 001* 6 8
6 Jul 02 **(SOMETHING INSIDE) SO STRONG** *EMI / Liberty CDRIK 002*....25 4

WALLFLOWERS *US, male vocal / instrumental group (Singles: 1 week, Albums: 2 weeks)* pos/wks

12 Jul 97 **ONE HEADLIGHT** *Interscope IND 95532* 54 1
21 Jun 97 **BRINGING DOWN THE HORSE** *Interscope IND 90055*....................58 2

Bob WALLIS and his STORYVILLE JAZZ BAND
UK, vocalist / instrumentalist – trumpet d. 10 Jan 1991, and male jazz band (Singles: 7 weeks, Albums: 1 week) pos/wks

6 Jul 61 **I'M SHY MARY ELLEN, I'M SHY** *Pye Jazz 7NJ 2043* 44 2
4 Jan 62 **COME ALONG PLEASE** *Pye Jazz 7NJ 2048* 33 5
11 Jun 60 **EVERYBODY LOVES SATURDAY NIGHT** *Top Rank BUY 023* 20 1

Joe WALSH *US, male vocalist / instrumentalist – guitar (Singles: 15 weeks, Albums: 20 weeks)* pos/wks

16 Jul 77 **ROCKY MOUNTAIN WAY (EP)** *ABC ABE 12002* 39 4
8 Jul 78 **LIFE'S BEEN GOOD** *Asylum K 13129* 14 11
17 Apr 76 **YOU CAN'T ARGUE WITH A SICK MIND** *Anchor ABCL 5156*......28 3
10 Jun 78 **BUT SERIOUSLY FOLKS** *Asylum K 53081*....................16 17

Tracks on Rocky Mountain Way (EP): Rocky Mountain Way / Turn to Stone / Meadows / Walk Away

See also EAGLES

Maureen WALSH – *See MAUREEN*

Sheila WALSH and Cliff RICHARD
UK, female / male vocal duo (Singles: 2 weeks) pos/wks

4 Jun 83 **DRIFTING** *DJM SHEIL 1* 64 2

Steve WALSH
UK, male DJ / vocalist, d. 3 July 1988 (Singles: 18 weeks) pos/wks

18 Jul 87 ● **I FOUND LOVIN' (re)** *A1 A1 299* 9 13
12 Dec 87 **LET'S GET TOGETHER TONITE** *A1 A1 303* 74 1
30 Jul 88 **AIN'T NO STOPPING US NOW (PARTY FOR THE WORLD)** *A1 A1 304* 44 4

Trevor WALTERS
UK, male vocalist (Singles: 22 weeks) pos/wks

24 Oct 81 **LOVE ME TONIGHT** *Magnet MAG 198* 27 8
21 Jul 84 ● **STUCK ON YOU** *Sanity IS 002* 9 12
1 Dec 84 **NEVER LET HER SLIP AWAY** *Polydor POSP 716* 73 2

WAMDUE PROJECT
US, male producer – Chris Brann (Singles: 19 weeks) pos/wks

20 Nov 99 **KING OF MY CASTLE (import)** *Orange ORCDM 53584CD* 61 1
27 Nov 99 ★ **KING OF MY CASTLE (re)** *AM:PM CDAMPM 127*■ 1 16
15 Apr 00 **YOU'RE THE REASON** *AM:PM CDAMPM 130* 39 2

WANG CHUNG *UK, male vocal / instrumental group (Singles: 12 weeks, Albums: 5 weeks)* pos/wks

28 Jan 84 **DANCE HALL DAYS** *Geffen A 3837* 21 12
21 Apr 84 **POINTS ON THE CURVE** *Geffen GEF 25589*....................34 5

WANNADIES *Sweden, male / female vocal / instrumental group (Singles: 12 weeks, Albums: 4 weeks)* pos/wks

18 Nov 95 **MIGHT BE STARS** *Indolent DIE 003CD1* 51 2
24 Feb 96 **HOW DOES IT FEEL** *Indolent DIE 004CD1* 53 1
20 Apr 96 **YOU AND ME SONG** *Indolent DIE 005CD* 18 3
7 Sep 96 **SOMEONE SOMEWHERE** *Indolent DIE 006CD* 38 1
26 Apr 97 **HIT** *Indolent DIE 009CD1* 20 2
5 Jul 97 **SHORTY** *Indolent DIE 010CD1* 41 2
4 Mar 00 **YEAH** *RCA 74321745552* 56 1
17 May 97 **BAGSY ME** *Indolent DIECD 008* 37 3
18 Mar 00 **YEAH** *RCA 74321687022* 73 1

Dexter WANSELL
US, male instrumentalist – keyboards (Singles: 3 weeks) pos/wks

20 May 78 **ALL NIGHT LONG** *Philadelphia International PIR 6255* 59 3

WAR *US / Canada / Denmark, male vocal / instrumental group (Singles: 32 weeks)* pos/wks

24 Jan 76 **LOW RIDER** *Island WIP 6267* 12 7
26 Jun 76 **ME AND BABY BROTHER** *Island WIP 6303* 21 7
14 Jan 78 **GALAXY** *MCA 339* 14 7
15 Apr 78 **HEY SENORITA** *MCA 359* 40 2
10 Apr 82 **YOU GOT THE POWER** *RCA 201* 58 4
6 Apr 85 **GROOVIN'** *Bluebird BR 16* 43 5

See Eric BURDON and WAR

Stephen WARBECK *UK, male conductor (Albums: 5 weeks)* pos/wks

19 May 01 **CAPTAIN CORELLI'S MANDOLIN (FILM SOUNDTRACK)** *Decca 4676782* 30 5

Anita WARD *US, female vocalist (Singles: 11 weeks)* pos/wks

2 Jun 79 ★ **RING MY BELL** *TK TKR 7543* ▲ 1 11

Chrissy WARD
US, female vocalist (Singles: 2 weeks) pos/wks

24 Jun 95 **RIGHT AND EXACT** *Ore AG 6CD* 62 1
8 Feb 97 **RIGHT AND EXACT (re-mix)** *Ore AG 21CD* 59 1

Clifford T WARD *UK, male vocalist / instrumentalist – keyboards, d. 18 Dec 2001 (Singles: 16 weeks, Albums: 5 weeks)* pos/wks

30 Jun 73 ● **GAYE** *Charisma CB 205* 8 11
26 Jan 74 **SCULLERY** *Charisma CB 221* 37 5
21 Jul 73 **HOME THOUGHTS** *Charisma CAS 1066*....................40 3
16 Feb 74 **MANTLE PIECES** *Charisma CAS 1077*....................42 2

Michael WARD
UK, male vocalist (Singles: 13 weeks, Albums: 3 weeks) pos/wks

29 Sep 73 **LET THERE BE PEACE ON EARTH (LET IT BEGIN WITH ME) (re)** *Philips 6006 340* 15 13
5 Jan 74 **INTRODUCING MICHAEL WARD** *Philips 6308 189* 26 3

Billy WARD and his DOMINOES

US, male vocal group, leader d. 15 Feb 2002 (Singles: 13 weeks) pos/wks

Date	Title / Label	pos	wks
13 Sep 57	**STARDUST (re)** *London HLU 8465*	13	12
29 Nov 57	**DEEP PURPLE** *London HLU 8502*	30	1

WARD BROTHERS

UK, male vocal / instrumental group (Singles: 8 weeks) pos/wks

Date	Title / Label	pos	wks
10 Jan 87	**CROSS THAT BRIDGE** *Siren SIREN 37*	32	8

Mathias WARE featuring Rob TAYLOR

Germany, male producer and male vocalist (Singles: 1 week) pos/wks

Date	Title / Label	pos	wks
9 Mar 02	**HEY LITTLE GIRL** *Manifesto FESCD 91*	42	1

Justin WARFIELD – *See BOMB THE BASS*

WARLOCK *Germany, male / female vocal / instrumental group (Albums: 2 weeks)*

pos/wks

Date	Title / Label	pos	wks
14 Nov 87	**TRIUMPH AND AGONY** *Vertigo VERH 50*	54	2

WARM JETS *UK / Canada, male vocal / instrumental group (Singles: 4 weeks, Albums: 1 week)*

pos/wks

Date	Title / Label	pos	wks
14 Feb 98	**NEVER NEVER** *Island WAY 6766*	37	2
25 Apr 98	**HURRICANE** *Island CID 697*	34	2
7 Mar 98	**FUTURE SIGNS** *Island 5243542*	40	1

WARM SOUNDS *UK, male vocal duo – Barry Husband and Denver Gerrard (Singles: 6 weeks)*

pos/wks

Date	Title / Label	pos	wks
4 May 67	**BIRDS AND BEES** *Deram DM 120*	27	6

Toni WARNE *UK, female vocalist (Singles: 4 weeks)*

pos/wks

Date	Title / Label	pos	wks
25 Apr 87	**BEN** *Mint CHEW 110*	50	4

Jennifer WARNES

US, female vocalist (Singles: 37 weeks, Albums: 12 weeks) pos/wks

Date	Title / Label	pos	wks
15 Jan 83 ●	**UP WHERE WE BELONG** *Island WIP 6830* [1] ▲	7	13
25 Jul 87	**FIRST WE TAKE MANHATTAN** *Cypress PB 49709*	74	1
31 Oct 87 ●	**(I'VE HAD) THE TIME OF MY LIFE (re)** *RCA PB 49625* [2] ▲	6	23
18 Jul 87	**FAMOUS BLUE RAINCOAT** *RCA PL 90048*	33	12

[1] Joe Cocker and Jennifer Warnes [2] Bill Medley and Jennifer Warnes

'(I've Had) The Time of My Life' re-entered in Dec 1990 peaking at No.8

WARP BROTHERS

Germany, male DJ / production group (Singles: 18 weeks) pos/wks

Date	Title / Label	pos	wks
11 Nov 00	**PHATT BASS (IMPORT)** *Dos or Die BMSCDM 40009*	58	3
9 Dec 00 ●	**PHATT BASS** *Nulife / Arista 74321817102* [1]	9	8
17 Feb 01	**WE WILL SURVIVE** *Nulife / Arista 74321832722*	19	4
29 Dec 01	**BLAST THE SPEAKERS** *Nulife 74321899162*	40	3

[1] Warp Brothers vs Aquagen

WARRANT *US, male vocal / instrumental group (Singles: 7 weeks, Albums: 1 week)*

pos/wks

Date	Title / Label	pos	wks
17 Nov 90	**CHERRY PIE** *CBS 6562587*	59	2
9 Mar 91	**CHERRY PIE (re-issue)** *Columbia 6566867*	35	5
19 Sep 92	**DOG EAT DOG** *Columbia 4720332*	74	1

Alysha WARREN *UK, female vocalist (Singles: 4 weeks)*

pos/wks

Date	Title / Label	pos	wks
24 Sep 94	**I'M SO IN LOVE** *Wild Card CARDD 10*	61	1
25 Mar 95	**I THOUGHT I MEANT THE WORLD TO YOU** *Wild Card CARDD 16*	40	1
27 Jul 96	**KEEP ON PUSHING OUR LOVE** *Arista 74321390422* [1]	30	2

[1] Nightcrawlers featuring John Reid and Alysha Warren

Ann WARREN – *See Ruby MURRAY*

Nikita WARREN *Italy, female vocalist (Singles: 1 week)*

pos/wks

Date	Title / Label	pos	wks
13 Jul 96	**I NEED YOU** *VC VCRD 12*	48	1

WARRIOR *UK, male vocal / production / instrumental duo – Stacey Charles and Michael Woods (Singles: 7 weeks)*

pos/wks

Date	Title / Label	pos	wks
21 Oct 00	**WARRIOR** *Incentive CENT 12CDS*	19	4
30 Jun 01	**VOODOO** *Incentive CENT 26CDS*	37	2
4 Oct 03	**X** *Incentive CENT 56CDS*	64	1

Dionne WARWICK (238 Top 500) *Super-stylish soul diva, b. 12 Dec 1940, New Jersey, US, whose classy and unmistakable vocals on songs written by Burt Bacharach and Hal David produced more than 30 US hits for her between 1962 and 1972. She is a cousin of Whitney Houston (Singles: 101 weeks, Albums: 154 weeks)*

pos/wks

Date	Title / Label	pos	wks
13 Feb 64	**ANYONE WHO HAD A HEART** *Pye International 7N 25234*	42	3
16 Apr 64 ●	**WALK ON BY** *Pye International 7N 25241*	9	14
30 Jul 64	**YOU'LL NEVER GET TO HEAVEN (IF YOU BREAK MY HEART)** *Pye International 7N 25256*	20	8
8 Oct 64	**REACH OUT FOR ME** *Pye International 7N 25265*	23	7
1 Apr 65	**YOU CAN HAVE HIM** *Pye International 7N 25290*	37	5
13 Mar 68	**(THEME FROM) VALLEY OF THE DOLLS** *Pye International 7N 25445*	28	8
15 May 68 ●	**DO YOU KNOW THE WAY TO SAN JOSE** *Pye International 7N 25457*	8	10
19 Oct 74	**THEN CAME YOU** *Atlantic K 10495* [1] ▲	29	6
23 Oct 82 ●	**HEARTBREAKER** *Arista ARIST 496*	2	13
11 Dec 82 ●	**ALL THE LOVE IN THE WORLD** *Arista ARIST 507*	10	10
26 Feb 83	**YOURS** *Arista ARIST 518*	66	2
28 May 83	**I'LL NEVER LOVE THIS WAY AGAIN** *Arista ARIST 530*	62	3
9 Nov 85	**THAT'S WHAT FRIENDS ARE FOR** *Arista ARIST 638* [2] ▲	16	9
15 Aug 87	**LOVE POWER** *Arista RIS 27* [3]	63	3
23 May 64	**PRESENTING DIONNE WARWICK** *Pye NPL 28037*	14	10
7 May 66 ●	**BEST OF DIONNE WARWICK** *Pye NPL 28078*	8	11
4 Feb 67	**HERE WHERE THERE IS LOVE** *Pye NPL 28096*	39	2
18 May 68 ●	**VALLEY OF THE DOLLS** *Pye NSPL 28114*	10	13
23 May 70	**GREATEST HITS VOLUME 1** *Wand WNS 1*	31	26
6 Jun 70	**GREATEST HITS VOLUME 2** *Wand WNS 2*	28	14
30 Oct 82 ●	**HEARTBREAKER** *Arista 204 974*	3	33
21 May 83	**THE COLLECTION – HER ALL-TIME GREATEST HITS** *Arista DIONE 1*	11	17
29 Oct 83	**SO AMAZING** *Arista 205 755*	60	3
23 Feb 85	**WITHOUT YOUR LOVE** *Arista 206 571*	86	2
6 Jan 90 ●	**LOVE SONGS** *Arista 410441*	6	13
10 Dec 94	**CHRISTMAS IN VIENNA II** *Sony Classical SK 64304* [1]	60	2
14 Dec 96	**THE ESSENTIAL COLLECTION** *Global Television RADCD 48*	58	4
3 Aug 02	**HEARTBREAKER – THE VERY BEST OF DIONNE WARWICK** *BMG TV/WSM WSMCD 101*	32	4

[1] Dionne Warwicke and The Detroit Spinners [2] Dionne Warwick and Friends featuring Elton John, Stevie Wonder and Gladys Knight [3] Dionne Warwick and Jeffrey Osborne [1] Dionne Warwick and Placido Domingo

WAS (NOT WAS) *US, male vocal / instrumental duo – Don Fagenson and David Weiss (Singles: 58 weeks, Albums: 15 weeks)*

pos/wks

Date	Title / Label	pos	wks
3 Mar 84	**OUT COME THE FREAKS** *Ze / Geffen A 4178*	41	5
18 Jul 87	**SPY IN THE HOUSE OF LOVE (re)** *Fontana WAS 2*	21	15
3 Oct 87 ●	**WALK THE DINOSAUR** *Fontana WAS 3*	10	10
7 May 88	**OUT COME THE FREAKS (AGAIN)** *Fontana WAS 4*	44	3
16 Jul 88	**ANYTHING CAN HAPPEN** *Fontana WAS 5*	67	3
26 May 90	**PAPA WAS A ROLLING STONE** *Fontana WAS 7*	12	7
11 Aug 90	**HOW THE HEART BEHAVES** *Fontana WAS 8*	53	3
23 May 92	**LISTEN LIKE THIEVES** *Fontana WAS 10*	58	2
11 Jul 92 ●	**SHAKE YOUR HEAD** *Fontana WAS 11*	4	9
26 Sep 92	**SOMEWHERE IN AMERICA (THERE'S A STREET NAMED AFTER MY DAD)** *Fontana WAS 12*	57	1
9 Apr 88	**WHAT UP DOG?** *Fontana SFLP 4*	47	6
21 Jul 90	**ARE YOU OKAY?** *Fontana 8463511*	35	6
13 Jun 92	**HELLO DAD ... I'M IN JAIL** *Fontana 5124642*	61	3

'Spy in the House of Love' first peaked at No.51 and made its peak position only on re-entry in Feb 1988. Fontana WAS 4 was a re-recorded version of their first hit. 'Shake Your Head' features uncredited vocals by Ozzy Osbourne and Kim Basinger. The group dropped the brackets from their name during the chart run of 'Papa Was a Rolling Stone'

Martha WASH *US, female vocalist (Singles: 34 weeks)* pos/wks

28 Nov 92	**CARRY ON** *RCA 74321125457*	74	1
6 Mar 93	**GIVE IT TO YOU** *RCA 74321136562*	37	4
10 Jul 93	**RUNAROUND / CARRY ON (re-mix)** *RCA 74321153702*	49	2
18 Feb 95	**I FOUND LOVE** *Columbia 6612112* 1	26	2
13 Jul 96 ●	**KEEP ON JUMPIN'** *Manifesto FESCD 11* 2	8	6
12 Jul 97 ●	**SOMETHING GOIN' ON** *Manifesto FESCD 25* 2	5	10
25 Oct 97	**CARRY ON (2nd re-mix)** *Delirious DELICD 6*	49	1
28 Feb 98	**IT'S RAINING MEN...THE SEQUEL** *Logic 74321555412* 3	21	3
11 Apr 98	**READY FOR A NEW DAY** *Manifesto FESCD 40* 4	20	2
15 Aug 98	**CATCH THE LIGHT** *Logic 74321587912*	45	1
3 Jul 99	**COME** *Logic 74321653942*	64	1
5 Feb 00	**IT'S RAINING MEN (re-recording)** *Logic 74321726282*	56	1

1 C & C Music Factory featuring Martha Wash 2 Todd Terry featuring Martha Wash and Jocelyn Brown 3 Martha Wash featuring RuPaul 4 Todd Terry featuring Martha Wash

The listed flip side of 'I Found Love' was 'Take a Toke' by C & C Music Factory

See also WEATHER GIRLS

Dinah WASHINGTON
US, female vocalist – Ruth Jones, d. 14 Dec 1963 (Singles: 8 weeks) pos/wks

30 Nov 61	**SEPTEMBER IN THE RAIN (re)** *Mercury AMT 1162*	35	4
4 Apr 92	**MAD ABOUT THE BOY** *Mercury DINAH 1*	41	4

Geno WASHINGTON and the RAM JAM BAND
US, male vocalist and UK, male instrumental backing group (Singles: 20 weeks, Albums: 51 weeks) pos/wks

19 May 66	**WATER** *Piccadilly 7N 35312*	39	8
21 Jul 66	**HI HI HAZEL (re)** *Piccadilly 7N 35329*	45	4
6 Oct 66	**QUE SERA SERA** *Piccadilly 7N 35346*	43	3
2 Feb 67	**MICHAEL (HE'S A LOVER)** *Piccadilly 7N 35359*	39	5
10 Dec 66 ●	**HAND CLAPPIN' – FOOT STOMPIN' – FUNKY-BUTT – LIVE!** *Piccadilly NPL 38026* 1	5	38
23 Sep 67 ●	**HIPSTERS FLIPSTERS AND FINGER-POPPIN' DADDIES** *Piccadilly NSPL 38032* 1	8	13

1 Geno Washington

Grover WASHINGTON Jr *US, male instrumentalist – saxophone, d. 17 Dec 1999 (Singles: 7 weeks, Albums: 10 weeks)* pos/wks

16 May 81	**JUST THE TWO OF US** *Elektra K 12514*	34	7
9 May 81	**WINELIGHT** *Elektra K 52262*	34	9
19 Dec 81	**COME MORNING** *Elektra K 52337*	98	1

Although uncredited, Bill Withers sings on 'Just the Two of Us'

Keith WASHINGTON – *See Kylie MINOGUE*

Sarah WASHINGTON *UK, female vocalist (Singles: 13 weeks)* pos/wks

14 Aug 93	**I WILL ALWAYS LOVE YOU** *Almighty CDALMY 33*	12	7
27 Nov 93	**CARELESS WHISPER** *Almighty CDALMY 43*	45	2
25 May 96	**HEAVEN** *AM:PM 5815352*	28	2
12 Oct 96	**EVERYTHING** *AM:PM 5818872*	30	2

W.A.S.P. *US, male vocal / instrumental group (Singles: 38 weeks, Albums: 24 weeks)* pos/wks

31 May 86	**WILD CHILD** *Capitol CL 388*	71	2
11 Oct 86	**95 – NASTY** *Capitol CL 432*	70	1
29 Aug 87	**SCREAM UNTIL YOU LIKE IT** *Capitol CL 458*	32	5
31 Oct 87	**I DON'T NEED NO DOCTOR (LIVE)** *Capitol CL 469*	31	5
20 Feb 88	**ANIMAL (F**K LIKE A BEAST)** *Music for Nations KUT 109*	61	3
4 Mar 89	**MEAN MAN** *Capitol CL 521*	21	5
27 May 89	**THE REAL ME** *Capitol CL 534*	23	5
9 Sep 89	**FOREVER FREE** *Capitol CL 546*	25	5
4 Apr 92	**CHAINSAW CHARLIE (MURDERS IN THE NEW MORGUE)** *Parlophone RS 6308*	17	2
6 Jun 92	**THE IDOL** *Parlophone RPD 6314*	41	2
31 Oct 92	**I AM ONE** *Parlophone 10RG 6324*	56	1
23 Oct 93	**SUNSET AND BABYLON** *Capitol CDCL 698*	38	2
8 Sep 84	**W.A.S.P.** *Capitol EJ 2401951*	51	2
9 Nov 85	**THE LAST COMMAND** *Capitol WASP 2*	48	1
8 Nov 86	**INSIDE THE ELECTRIC CIRCUS** *Capitol EST 2025*	53	3
26 Sep 87	**LIVE ... IN THE RAW** *Capitol EST 2040*	23	4
15 Apr 89 ●	**THE HEADLESS CHILDREN** *Capitol EST 2087*	8	10
20 Jun 92	**THE CRIMSON IDOL** *Parlophone CDPCSD 118*	21	2
6 Nov 93	**FIRST BLOOD ... LAST CUTS** *Capitol CDESTFG 2217*	69	1
1 Jul 95	**STILL NOT BLACK ENOUGH** *Raw Power RAWCD 103*	52	1

WASP STAR – *See XTC*

WATERBOYS *UK / Ireland, male vocal / instrumental group (Singles: 33 weeks, Albums: 72 weeks)* pos/wks

2 Nov 85	**THE WHOLE OF THE MOON** *Ensign ENY 520*	26	7
14 Jan 89	**FISHERMAN'S BLUES** *Ensign ENY 621*	32	6
1 Jul 89	**AND A BANG ON THE EAR** *Ensign ENY 624*	51	4
6 Apr 91 ●	**THE WHOLE OF THE MOON (re-issue)** *Ensign ENY 642*	3	9
8 Jun 91	**FISHERMAN'S BLUES (re-issue)** *Ensign ENY 645*	75	1
15 May 93	**THE RETURN OF PAN** *Geffen GFSTD 42*	24	3
24 Jul 93	**GLASTONBURY SONG** *Geffen GFSTD 49*	29	3
16 Jun 84	**A PAGAN PLACE** *Ensign ENCL 3*	100	1
28 Sep 85	**THIS IS THE SEA** *Ensign ENCL 5*	37	18
29 Oct 88	**FISHERMAN'S BLUES** *Ensign CHEN 5*	13	19
22 Sep 90 ●	**ROOM TO ROAM** *Ensign CHEN 16*	5	6
11 May 91 ●	**THE BEST OF THE WATERBOYS '81-'90** *Ensign CHEN 19*	2	16
5 Jun 93 ●	**DREAM HARDER** *Geffen GED 24476*	5	10
7 Oct 00	**A ROCK IN THE WEARY LAND** *RCA 74321783052*	47	1
21 Jun 03	**UNIVERSAL HALL** *Puck PUCK1*	74	1

WATERFRONT *UK, male vocal / instrumental duo - Phil Cilia and Chris Duffy (Singles: 19 weeks, Albums: 3 weeks)* pos/wks

15 Apr 89	**BROKEN ARROW** *Polydor WON 3*	63	2
27 May 89	**CRY** *Polydor WON 1*	17	13
9 Sep 89	**NATURE OF LOVE** *Polydor WON 2*	63	4
12 Aug 89	**WATERFRONT** *Polydor 837970 1*	45	3

WATERGATE
Turkey, male DJ / producer - Orhan Terzi (Singles: 10 weeks) pos/wks

13 May 00 ●	**HEART OF ASIA** *Positiva CDTIV 129*	3	10

See also DJ QUICKSILVER

Dennis WATERMAN
UK, male actor / vocalist (Singles: 17 weeks) pos/wks

25 Oct 80 ●	**I COULD BE SO GOOD FOR YOU** *EMI 5009* 1	3	12
17 Dec 83	**WHAT ARE WE GONNA GET 'ER INDOORS** *EMI MIN 101* 2	21	5

1 Dennis Waterman with The Dennis Waterman Band 2 Dennis Waterman and George Cole

Crystal WATERS
US, female vocalist (Singles: 35 weeks) pos/wks

18 May 91 ●	**GYPSY WOMAN (LA DA DEE)** *A&M AM 772*	2	10
7 Sep 91	**MAKIN' HAPPY** *A&M AM 790*	18	6
11 Jan 92	**MEGAMIX** *A&M AM 843*	39	3
3 Oct 92	**GYPSY WOMAN (re-mix)** *Epic 6584377*	35	2
23 Apr 94	**100% PURE LOVE** *A&M 8586692*	15	7
2 Jul 94	**GHETTO DAY** *A&M 8589592*	40	2
25 Nov 95	**RELAX** *Manifesto FESCD 4*	37	2
24 Aug 96	**IN DE GHETTO** *Manifesto FESCD 12* 1	35	2
19 Apr 97	**SAY ... IF YOU FEEL ALRIGHT** *Mercury 5742912*	45	1

1 David Morales and the Bad Yard Club featuring Crystal Waters and Delta

The listed flip side of 'Gypsy Woman' (re-mix) was 'Peace' (re-mix) by Sabrina Johnston

LATANZA WATERS – *See E-SMOOVE featuring Latanza WATERS*

Muddy WATERS *US, male vocalist / instrumentalist – guitar, d. 30 Apr 1983 (Singles: 6 weeks)* pos/wks

16 Jul 88	**MANNISH BOY** *Epic MUD 1*	51	6

Roger WATERS *UK, male vocalist / instrumentalist – bass (Singles: 8 weeks, Albums: 25 weeks)*

		pos/wks	
30 May 87	**RADIO WAVES** *Harvest EM 6*	**74**	1
26 Dec 87	**THE TIDE IS TURNING (AFTER LIVE AID)** *Harvest EM 37*	**54**	4
5 Sep 92	**WHAT GOD WANTS PART 1** *Columbia 6581390*	**35**	3
12 May 84	**THE PROS AND CONS OF HITCH-HIKING** *Harvest SHVL 240105*	**13**	11
27 Jun 87	**RADIO K.A.O.S.** *EMI KAOS 1*	**25**	7
22 Sep 90	**THE WALL – LIVE IN BERLIN** *Mercury 8466111*	**27**	3
19 Sep 92 ●	**AMUSED TO DEATH** *Columbia 4687612*	**8**	4

See also PINK FLOYD

Lauren WATERWORTH
UK, female vocalist (Singles: 3 weeks)

		pos/wks	
1 Jun 02	**BABY NOW THAT I'VE FOUND YOU** *Jive 9253622*	**24**	3

Michael WATFORD *US, male vocalist (Singles: 2 weeks)*

		pos/wks	
26 Feb 94	**SO INTO YOU** *East West A 8309CD*	**53**	2

Tionne 'T-Boz' WATKINS – *See* T-BOZ; TLC

Adam WATKISS *UK, male vocalist (Albums: 3 weeks)*

		pos/wks	
15 Dec 01	**THIS IS THE MOMENT** *UMTV/Decca 166082*	**65**	3

Jody WATLEY
US, female vocalist (Singles: 35 weeks, Albums: 4 weeks)

		pos/wks	
9 May 87	**LOOKING FOR A NEW LOVE** *MCA MCA 1107*	**13**	11
17 Oct 87	**DON'T YOU WANT ME** *MCA MCA 1198*	**55**	3
8 Apr 89	**REAL LOVE** *MCA MCA 1324*	**31**	7
12 Aug 89	**FRIENDS** *MCA MCA 1352* [1]	**21**	6
10 Feb 90	**EVERYTHING** *MCA MCA 1395*	**74**	2
11 Apr 92	**I'M THE ONE YOU NEED** *MCA MCS 1608*	**50**	3
21 May 94	**WHEN A MAN LOVES A WOMAN** *MCA MCSTD 1964*	**33**	2
25 Apr 98	**OFF THE HOOK** *Atlantic AT 0024CD1*	**51**	1
5 Sep 87	**JODY WATLEY** *MCA MCG 6024*	**62**	2
27 May 89	**LARGER THAN LIFE** *MCA MCG 6044*	**39**	2

[1] Jody Watley with Eric B and Rakim

See also SHALAMAR

Joe WATSON – *See* RHYTHM MASTERS

Johnny 'Guitar' WATSON *US, male vocalist / instrumentalist – guitar, d. 17 May 1996 (Singles: 8 weeks)*

		pos/wks	
28 Aug 76	**I NEED IT** *DJM DJS 10694*	**35**	5
23 Apr 77	**A REAL MOTHER FOR YA** *DJM DJS 10762*	**44**	3

Nigel WATSON – *See* Peter GREEN

Russell WATSON
UK, male vocalist (Singles: 12 weeks, Albums: 65 weeks)

		pos/wks	
30 Oct 99	**SWING LOW '99** *Decca / Universal TV 4669502*	**38**	2
22 Jul 00	**BARCELONA (FRIENDS UNTIL THE END)** *Decca 4672772* [1]	**68**	1
18 May 02 ●	**SOMEONE LIKE YOU** *Decca 4730002* [2]	**10**	4
21 Dec 02	**NOTHING SACRED – A SONG FOR KIRSTY** *Decca 4737402*	**17**	5
7 Oct 00 ●	**THE VOICE** *Decca 4672512*	**5**	36
10 Nov 01 ●	**THE VOICE – ENCORE** *Decca 4703002*	**6**	21
30 Nov 02	**THE VOICE – REPRISE** *Decca 4731002*	**13**	8

[1] Russell Watson and Shaun Ryder [2] Russell Watson and Faye Tozer

Barrett WAUGH *UK, male vocalist (Singles: 1 week)*

		pos/wks	
26 Jul 03	**SKIP A BEAT** *White Elephant BNWCD 02*	**56**	1

WAVELENGTH
UK, male vocal group (Singles: 12 weeks)

		pos/wks	
10 Jul 82	**HURRY HOME** *Ariola ARO 281*	**17**	12

WAVES – *See* KATRINA and the WAVES

WAX *US / UK, male vocal / instrumental duo – Andrew Gold and Graham Gouldman (Singles: 16 weeks, Albums: 3 weeks)*

		pos/wks	
12 Apr 86	**RIGHT BETWEEN THE EYES** *RCA PB 40509*	**60**	5
1 Aug 87	**BRIDGE TO YOUR HEART** *RCA PB 41405*	**12**	11
12 Sep 87	**AMERICAN ENGLISH** *RCA PL 71430*	**59**	3

See also Andrew GOLD; Graham GOULDMAN; 10cc

Anthony WAY
UK, male vocalist (Singles: 2 weeks, Albums: 19 weeks)

		pos/wks	
15 Apr 95	**PANIS ANGELICUS** *Decca 4481642*	**55**	2
8 Apr 95 ●	**THE CHOIR – MUSIC FROM THE BBC TV SERIES** *Decca 4481652* [1]	**3**	12
9 Dec 95	**THE CHOIRBOY** *Permanent PERMCD 41*	**61**	3
14 Dec 96	**THE CHOIRBOY'S CHRISTMAS** *Decca 4550502*	**59**	3
15 Mar 97	**WINGS OF A DOVE** *Decca 4556452*	**69**	1

[1] Anthony Way and Stanislas Syrewicz

A WAY OF LIFE
US, male / female vocal / instrumental group (Singles: 3 weeks)

		pos/wks	
21 Apr 90	**TRIPPIN' ON YOUR LOVE** *Eternal YZ 464*	**55**	3

WAY OF THE WEST
UK, male vocal / instrumental group (Singles: 5 weeks)

		pos/wks	
25 Apr 81	**DON'T SAY THAT'S JUST FOR WHITE BOYS** *Mercury MER 66*	**54**	5

WAY OUT WEST *UK, male instrumental / production duo – Nick Warren and Jody Wisternoff (Singles: 17 weeks, Albums: 2 weeks)*

		pos/wks	
3 Dec 94	**AJARE** *Deconstruction 74321243802*	**52**	1
2 Mar 96	**DOMINATION** *Deconstruction 74321342822*	**38**	2
14 Sep 96	**THE GIFT** *Deconstruction 74321401912* [1]	**15**	5
30 Aug 97	**BLUE** *Deconstruction 74321477512*	**41**	2
29 Nov 97	**AJARE (re-mix)** *Deconstruction 74321521352*	**36**	2
9 Dec 00	**THE FALL** *Wow WOW 005CD*	**61**	1
18 Aug 01	**INTENSIFY** *Distinctive Breaks DISNCD 74*	**46**	1
30 Mar 02	**MINDCIRCUS** *Distinctive Breaks DISNCD 80* [2]	**39**	2
21 Sep 02	**STEALTH** *Distinctive Breaks DISNCD 90* [3]	**67**	1
13 Sep 97	**WAY OUT WEST** *Deconstruction 74321501952*	**42**	1
1 Sep 01	**INTENSIFY** *Distinctive Breaks DISNCD 76*	**61**	1

[1] Way Out West featuring Miss Joanna Law [2] Way Out West featuring Tricia Lee Kelshall [3] Way Out West featuring Kirsty Hawkshaw

Bruce WAYNE
Germany, male DJ / producer (Singles: 2 weeks)

		pos/wks	
13 Dec 97	**READY** *Logic 74321527012*	**44**	1
4 Jul 98	**NO GOOD FOR ME** *Logic 74321587052*	**70**	1

Jan WAYNE
Germany, male producer – Jan Christiansen (Singles: 8 weeks)

		pos/wks	
9 Nov 02	**BECAUSE THE NIGHT** *Product / Incentive PDT 02CDS*	**14**	5
29 Mar 03	**TOTAL ECLIPSE OF THE HEART** *Product / Incentive PDT 10CDS*	**28**	3

Jeff WAYNE'S 'WAR OF THE WORLDS' (213 Top 500)
Talented New York-born producer / songwriter / arranger and keyboard player, who was educated at the prestigious Julliard School of Music. Before unveiling his epic all-star concept album 'War of the Worlds' (more than four years on the chart) he produced a string of David Essex hits (Singles: 21 weeks, Albums: 261 weeks)

		pos/wks	
9 Sep 78	**THE EVE OF THE WAR** *CBS 6496*	**36**	8
10 Jul 82	**MATADOR** *CBS A 2493* [1]	**57**	3
25 Nov 89 ●	**EVE OF THE WAR (re-mix)** *CBS 6551267*	**3**	10
1 Jul 78 ●	**JEFF WAYNE'S MUSICAL VERSION OF THE WAR OF THE WORLDS** *CBS 96000*	**5**	235
3 Oct 92	**JEFF WAYNE'S MUSICAL VERSION OF SPARTACUS** *Columbia 4720302*	**36**	2
6 Jul 96	**JEFF WAYNE'S MUSICAL VERSION OF THE WAR OF THE WORLDS (re-issue)** *Columbia CDX 96000*	**23**	21

19 Oct 96 **HIGHLIGHTS FROM JEFF WAYNE'S MUSICAL VERSION OF THE WAR OF THE WORLDS** *Columbia CD 32356*.....64 2
22 Apr 00 **JEFF WAYNE'S MUSICAL VERSION OF THE WAR OF THE WORLDS – ULLADUBULLA – THE REMIX ALBUM** *Columbia SONYTV 74CD*.....64 1

[1] Jeff Wayne

All albums feature various artists but are commonly credited to Jeff Wayne the creator and producer

WAYSTED *UK, male vocal / instrumental group (Albums: 5 weeks)* pos/wks

8 Oct 83 **VICES** *Chrysalis CHR 1438*.....78 3
22 Sep 84 **WAYSTED** *Music For Nations MFN 31*.....73 2

WEATHER GIRLS *US, female vocal duo – Martha Wash and Izora Redman (Singles: 14 weeks)* pos/wks

27 Aug 83 ● **IT'S RAINING MEN (re)** *CBS A 2924*.....2 14

'It's Raining Men' first peaked at No.73 in 1983 and reached its peak position only on re-entry in Mar 1984

See also Martha WASH

WEATHER PROPHETS *UK, male vocal / instrumental group (Singles: 2 weeks, Albums: 2 weeks)* pos/wks

28 Mar 87 **SHE COMES FROM THE RAIN** *Elevation ACID 1*.....62 2
9 May 87 **MAYFLOWER** *Elevation ELV 1*.....67 2

WEATHER REPORT *US, male instrumental group (Albums: 12 weeks)* pos/wks

23 Apr 77 **HEAVY WEATHER** *CBS 81775*.....43 6
11 Nov 78 **MR GONE** *CBS 82775*.....47 3
27 Feb 82 **WEATHER REPORT** *CBS 85326*.....88 2
24 Mar 84 **DOMINO THEORY** *CBS 25839*.....54 1

WEATHERMEN – *See Jonathan KING*

Marti WEBB *UK, female vocalist (Singles: 42 weeks, Albums: 33 weeks)* pos/wks

9 Feb 80 ● **TAKE THAT LOOK OFF YOUR FACE** *Polydor POSP 100*.....3 12
19 Apr 80 **TELL ME ON A SUNDAY** *Polydor POSP 111*.....67 2
20 Sep 80 **YOUR EARS SHOULD BE BURNING NOW** *Polydor POSP 166*..61 4
8 Jun 85 ● **BEN** *Starblend STAR 6*.....5 11
20 Sep 86 **ALWAYS THERE** *BBC RESL 190* [1].....13 12
6 Jun 87 **I CAN'T LET GO** *Rainbow RBR 12*.....65 1
16 Feb 80 ● **TELL ME ON A SUNDAY** *Polydor POLD 5031*.....2 23
28 Sep 85 **ENCORE** *Starblend BLEND 1*.....55 4
6 Dec 86 **ALWAYS THERE** *BBC REB 619*.....65 5
10 Oct 92 **THE MAGIC OF THE MUSICALS** *Quality Television QTV 013* [1].....55 1

[1] Marti Webb and the Simon May Orchestra [1] Marti Webb and Mark Rattray

WEBB BROTHERS *US, male vocal / instrumental duo (Singles: 1 week)* pos/wks

17 Feb 01 **I CAN'T BELIEVE YOU'RE GONE** *WEA WEA 320CD*.....69 1

Joan WEBER *US, female vocalist d. 13 May 1981 (Singles: 1 week)* pos/wks

18 Feb 55 **LET ME GO LOVER** *Philips PB 389* ▲.....16 1

Ben WEBSTER – *See Gerry MULLIGAN and Ben WEBSTER*

Nikki WEBSTER *Australia, female vocalist (Singles: 1 week)* pos/wks

8 Jun 02 **STRAWBERRY KISSES** *Gotham 74321943642*.....64 1

WEDDING PRESENT *UK, male vocal / instrumental group (Singles: 38 weeks, Albums: 20 weeks)* pos/wks

5 Mar 88 **NOBODY'S TWISTING YOUR ARM** *Reception REC 009*.....46 2
1 Oct 88 **WHY ARE YOU BEING SO REASONABLE NOW?** *Reception REC 011*.....42 2
7 Oct 89 **KENNEDY** *RCA PB 43117*.....33 3
17 Feb 90 **BRASSNECK** *RCA PB 43403*.....24 3
29 Sep 90 **3 SONGS (EP)** *RCA PB 44021*.....25 4
11 May 91 **DALLIANCE** *RCA PB 44495*.....29 3
27 Jul 91 **LOVENEST** *RCA PT 44750*.....58 1
18 Jan 92 **BLUE EYES** *RCA PB 45185*.....26 2
15 Feb 92 **GO-GO DANCER** *RCA PB 45183*.....20 1
14 Mar 92 **THREE** *RCA PB 45181*.....14 2
18 Apr 92 **SILVER SHORTS** *RCA PB 45311*.....14 1
16 May 92 ● **COME PLAY WITH ME** *RCA PB 45313*.....10 2
13 Jun 92 **CALIFORNIA** *RCA PB 45315*.....16 1
18 Jul 92 **FLYING SAUCER** *RCA 74321101157*.....22 1
15 Aug 92 **BOING!** *RCA 74321101177*.....19 1
19 Sep 92 **LOVE SLAVE** *RCA 743211101167*.....17 1
17 Oct 92 **STICKY** *RCA 74321116917*.....17 1
14 Nov 92 **THE QUEEN OF OUTER SPACE** *RCA 74321116927*.....23 1
19 Dec 92 **NO CHRISTMAS** *RCA 74321116937*.....25 1
10 Sep 94 **YEAH YEAH YEAH YEAH YEAH** *Island CID 585*.....51 2
26 Nov 94 **IT'S A GAS** *Island CID 591*.....71 1
31 Aug 96 **2, 3, GO** *Cooking Vinyl FRYCD 048*.....67 1
25 Jan 97 **MONTREAL** *Cooking Vinyl FRYCD 053*.....40 1
24 Oct 87 **GEORGE BEST** *Reception LEEDS 001*.....47 2
23 Jul 88 **TOMMY** *Reception LEEDS 2*.....42 3
29 Apr 89 **UKRAINSKI VISTUIP V JOHNA PEELA** *RCA PL 74104*.....22 3
4 Nov 89 **BIZARRO** *RCA PL 74302*.....22 3
8 Jun 91 **SEA MONSTERS** *RCA PL 75012*.....13 3
20 Jun 92 **HIT PARADE 1** *RCA PD 75343*.....22 2
16 Jan 93 **HIT PARADE 2** *RCA 74321127752*.....19 2
24 Sep 94 **WATUSI** *Island CID 8014*.....47 1
21 Sep 96 **SATURNALIA** *Cooking Vinyl COOKCD 099*.....36 1

Tracks on 3 Songs (EP): Corduroy / Crawl / Make Me Smile (Come Up and See Me)

Fred WEDLOCK *UK, male vocalist (Singles: 10 weeks)* pos/wks

31 Jan 81 ● **OLDEST SWINGER IN TOWN** *Rocket XPRES 46*.....6 10

WEE PAPA GIRL RAPPERS *UK, female rap / vocal duo – Samantha and Sandra Lawrence (Singles: 27 weeks, Albums: 3 weeks)* pos/wks

12 Mar 88 **FAITH** *Jive JIVE 164*.....60 4
25 Jun 88 **HEAT IT UP** *Jive JIVE 174* [1].....21 9
1 Oct 88 ● **WEE RULE** *Jive JIVE 185*.....6 9
24 Dec 88 **SOULMATE** *Jive JIVE 193*.....45 4
25 Mar 89 **BLOW THE HOUSE DOWN** *Jive JIVE 197*.....65 1
5 Nov 88 **THE BEAT THE RHYME AND THE NOISE** *Jive HIP 67*.....39 3

[1] Wee Papa Girl Rappers featuring Two Men and a Drum Machine

Bert WEEDON *UK, male instrumentalist – guitar (Singles: 38 weeks, Albums: 26 weeks)* pos/wks

15 May 59 ● **GUITAR BOOGIE SHUFFLE** *Top Rank JAR 117*.....10 9
20 Nov 59 **NASHVILLE BOOGIE** *Top Rank JAR 221*.....29 2
10 Mar 60 **BIG BEAT BOOGIE (re)** *Top Rank JAR 300*.....37 4
9 Jun 60 **TWELFTH STREET RAG** *Top Rank JAR 360*.....47 2
28 Jul 60 **APACHE (re)** *Top Rank JAR 415*.....24 4
27 Oct 60 **SORRY ROBBIE** *Top Rank JAR 517*.....28 11
2 Feb 61 **GINCHY** *Top Rank JAR 537*.....35 5
4 May 61 **MR GUITAR** *Top Rank JAR 559*.....47 1
16 Jul 60 **KING SIZE GUITAR** *Top Rank BUY 026*.....18 1
23 Oct 76 ★ **22 GOLDEN GUITAR GREATS** *Warwick WW 5019*.....1 25

WEEKEND *International, male / female vocal / instrumental group (Singles: 5 weeks)* pos/wks

14 Dec 85 **CHRISTMAS MEDLEY / AULD LANG SYNE** *Lifestyle XY 1*.....47 5

WEEKEND PLAYERS *UK, male / female production / vocal duo – Rachel Foster and Andy Cato (Singles: 5 weeks)* pos/wks

8 Sep 01 **21ST CENTURY** *Multiply CDMULTY 78*.....22 4
16 Mar 02 **INTO THE SUN** *Multiply CDMULTY 84*.....42 1

See also GROOVE ARMADA

Michelle WEEKS *US, female vocalist (Singles: 7 weeks)* pos/wks

2 Aug 97 **MOMENT OF MY LIFE** *Ministry of Sound MOSCDS 1* [1].....23 3
8 Nov 97 **DON'T GIVE UP** *Ministry of Sound MOSCDS 2*.....28 2

11 Jul 98 **GIVE ME LOVE** *VC Recordings VCRD 37* [2] 59 1
3 May 03 **THE LIGHT** *Defected DFTD 064* 69 1

[1] Bobby D'Ambrosio featuring Michelle Weeks [2] DJ Dado vs Michelle Weeks

WEEN – *See FOO FIGHTERS*

WEEZER *US, male vocal / instrumental group (Singles: 19 weeks, Albums: 19 weeks)* pos/wks

11 Feb 95 **UNDONE – THE SWEATER SONG** *Geffen GFSTD 85* 35 2
6 May 95 **BUDDY HOLLY** *Geffen GFSTD 88* 12 7
22 Jul 95 **SAY IT AIN'T SO** *Geffen GFSTD 95* 37 2
5 Oct 96 **EL SCORCHO** *Geffen GFSTD 22167* 50 1
14 Jul 01 **HASH PIPE** *Geffen 4975642* 21 3
3 Nov 01 **ISLAND IN THE SUN** *Geffen 4976102* 31 2
14 Sep 02 **KEEP FISHIN'** *Geffen 4977912* 29 2
4 Mar 95 **WEEZER** *Geffen GED 24629* 23 11
12 Oct 96 **PINKERTON** *Geffen GED 25007* 43 1
26 May 01 **THE GREEN ALBUM** *Geffen 4930612* 31 4
25 May 02 **MALADROIT** *Geffen 4933252* 16 3

Frank WEIR and His ORCHESTRA *UK, orchestra – leader, d. 12 May 1981 (Singles: 18 weeks)* pos/wks

15 Oct 54 ★ **MY SON, MY SON** *Decca F 10372* [1] 1 14
15 Sep 60 **CARIBBEAN HONEYMOON** *Oriole CB 1559* 42 4

[1] Vera Lynn with Frank Weir, his saxophone, his Orchestra and Chorus

WEIRD SCIENCE *UK, male DJ / production duo (Singles: 1 week)* pos/wks

1 Jul 00 **FEEL THE NEED** *Nulife 74321751982* 62 1

Eric WEISSBERG – *See 'DELIVERANCE' SOUNDTRACK*

Denise WELCH *UK, female actor / vocalist (Singles: 3 weeks)* pos/wks

4 Nov 95 **YOU DON'T HAVE TO SAY YOU LOVE ME / CRY ME A RIVER** *Virgin VSCDT 1569* 23 3

Gillian WELCH *US, female vocalist / instrumentalist - guitar (Albums: 1 week)* pos/wks

14 Jun 03 **SOUL JOURNEY** *WEA 5046668682* 65 1

Paul WELLER (209 Top 500) *Angry young man reinvented as Britpop's elder statesman, b. John Weller, 25 May 1958, Surrey. Vocalist, guitarist and songwriter, 'The Modfather' achieved No.1 albums both solo and as leader of The Jam and Style Council. Won Best Male Solo Brit 1995 and 1996 (Singles: 67 weeks, Albums: 216 weeks)* pos/wks

18 May 91 **INTO TOMORROW** *Freedom High FHP 1* [1] 36 3
15 Aug 92 **UH HUH OH YEH** *Go! Discs GOD 86* 18 5
10 Oct 92 **ABOVE THE CLOUDS** *Go! Discs GOD 91* 47 2
17 Jul 93 **SUNFLOWER** *Go! Discs GODCD 102* 16 5
4 Sep 93 **WILD WOOD** *Go! Discs GODCD 104* 14 3
13 Nov 93 **THE WEAVER (EP)** *Go! Discs GODCD 107* 18 3
9 Apr 94 **HUNG UP** *Go! Discs GODCD 111* 11 3
5 Nov 94 **OUT OF THE SINKING** *Go! Discs GODCD 121* 20 3
6 May 95 ● **THE CHANGINGMAN** *Go! Discs GODCD 127* 7 4
22 Jul 95 ● **YOU DO SOMETHING TO ME** *Go! Discs GODCD 130* 9 6
30 Sep 95 **BROKEN STONES** *Go! Discs GODCD 132* 20 4
9 Mar 96 **OUT OF THE SINKING** *Go! Discs GODCD 143* 16 2
17 Aug 96 ● **PEACOCK SUIT** *Go! Discs GODCD 149* 5 5
9 Aug 97 **BRUSHED** *Island CID 666* 14 3
11 Oct 97 **FRIDAY STREET** *Island CID 676* 21 2
6 Dec 97 **MERMAIDS** *Island CID 683* 30 2
14 Nov 98 **BRAND NEW START** *Island CID 711* 16 3
9 Jan 99 **WILDWOOD (re-issue)** *Island CID 734* 22 3
2 Sep 00 **SWEET PEA, MY SWEET PEA** *Island CID 764* 44 1
14 Sep 02 ● **IT'S WRITTEN IN THE STARS** *Independiente ISOM 63SMS* 7 3
30 Nov 02 **LEAFY MYSTERIES** *Independiente ISOM 65MS* 23 2
12 Sep 92 ● **PAUL WELLER** *Go! Discs 8283432* 8 7
18 Sep 93 ● **WILD WOOD** *Go! Discs 8284352* 2 51
24 Sep 94 **LIVE WOOD** *Go! Discs 8285612* 13 5
27 May 95 ★ **STANLEY ROAD** *Go! Discs / Island 8286192* ■ 1 87
5 Jul 97 ● **HEAVY SOUL** *Go! Discs / Island CID 8058* 2 13
21 Nov 98 ● **MODERN CLASSICS – THE GREATEST HITS** *Island CID 8080* 7 19
22 Apr 00 ● **HELIOCENTRIC** *Island CID 8093* 2 8
20 Oct 01 ● **DAYS OF SPEED** *Independiente ISOM 26CD* 3 16
28 Sep 02 ★ **ILLUMINATION** *Independiente ISOM 33CDL* ■ 1 7
6 Sep 03 **FLY ON THE WALL – B SIDES & RARITIES** *Island 0635272* 22 3

[1] Paul Weller Movement

Tracks on The Weaver (EP): The Weaver / This Is No Time / Another New Day / Ohio (live). 'Out of the Sinking' in 1996 is a re-recording of the 1994 hit and both versions feature uncredited vocals by Carleen Anderson

See also JAM; STYLE COUNCIL; COUNCIL COLLECTIVE

Brandi WELLS *US, female vocalist – Marguerite J. Pinder, d. 25 Mar 2003 (Singles: 1 week)* pos/wks

20 Feb 82 **WATCH OUT** *Virgin VS 479* 74 1

Houston WELLS and the MARKSMEN *UK, male vocalist – Andrew Smith, and instrumental group (Singles: 10 weeks)* pos/wks

1 Aug 63 **ONLY THE HEARTACHES** *Parlophone R 5031* 22 10

Mary WELLS *US, female vocalist, d. 26 Jul 1992 (Singles: 25 weeks)* pos/wks

21 May 64 ● **MY GUY** *Stateside SS 288* ▲ 5 14
30 Jul 64 **ONCE UPON A TIME** *Stateside SS 316* [1] 50 1
8 Jul 72 **MY GUY (re-issue)** *Tamla Motown TMG 820* 14 10

[1] Marvin Gaye and Mary Wells

Terri WELLS *US, female vocalist (Singles: 9 weeks)* pos/wks

2 Jul 83 **YOU MAKE IT HEAVEN** *Phillyworld PWS 111* 53 2
5 May 84 **I'LL BE AROUND** *Phillyworld LON 48* 17 7

Alex WELSH BAND *UK, male instrumentalist – trumpet, d. 25 Jun 1982 (Singles: 4 weeks)* pos/wks

10 Aug 61 **TANSY** *Columbia DB 4686* 45 4

Irvine WELSH – *See PRIMAL SCREAM*

WENDY and LISA *US, female vocal duo – Wendy Melvoin and Lisa Coleman (Singles: 31 weeks, Albums: 7 weeks)* pos/wks

5 Sep 87 **WATERFALL** *Virgin VS 999* 66 4
16 Jan 88 **SIDESHOW** *Virgin VS 1012* 49 5
18 Feb 89 **ARE YOU MY BABY** *Virgin VS 1156* 70 3
29 Apr 89 **LOLLY LOLLY** *Virgin VS 1175* 64 3
8 Jul 89 **SATISFACTION** *Virgin VS 1194* 27 8
18 Nov 89 **WATERFALL (re-mix)** *Virgin VS 1223* 69 2
30 Jun 90 **STRUNG OUT** *Virgin VS 1272* 44 5
10 Nov 90 **RAINBOW LAKE** *Virgin VS 1280* 70 1
10 Oct 87 **WENDY AND LISA** *Virgin V 2444* 84 2
28 Mar 89 **FRUIT AT THE BOTTOM** *Virgin V 2580* 45 2
4 Aug 90 **EROICA** *Virgin V 2633* 33 3

WES *France, male vocalist – Wes Madiko (Singles: 7 weeks)* pos/wks

14 Feb 98 **ALANE** *Epic 6654682* 11 6
27 Jun 98 **I LOVE FOOTBALL** *Epic 6660772* 75 1

Dodie WEST *UK, female vocalist (Singles: 4 weeks)* pos/wks

14 Jan 65 **GOING OUT OF MY HEAD** *Decca F 12046* 39 4

Keith WEST *UK, male vocalist – Keith Hopkins, (Singles: 18 weeks)* pos/wks

9 Aug 67 ● **EXCERPT FROM A TEENAGE OPERA** *Parlophone R 5623* 2 15
22 Nov 67 **SAM** *Parlophone R 5651* 38 3

Kit WEST – *See DEGREES OF MOTION featuring BITI*

WEST END *UK, female vocal group (Singles: 2 weeks)* pos/wks

19 Aug 95 **LOVE RULES** *RCA 74321292702* 44 2

TOP 10 NORTHERN SOUL

Top of our northern soul chart: The Tams, so named due to their liking for the Tam O'Shanter head gear they favoured on stage

Northern soul was the name given to the Motown-like 100mph dance music that was produced mainly in the northern part of the US in the 1960s and 1970s, and which initially became popular in the North of England clubs in the 1970s.

Unlike other soul musical trends it was a uniquely English phenomenon, and the majority of the records concerned had never been successful in their homeland. In fact, several of the most popular tracks were B-sides of unsuccessful singles. The clubs that pioneered the music, and the amazing dances that went with it, included the Twisted Wheel in Manchester, the Golden Torch in Stoke, the Blackpool Mecca and Wigan Casino.

Here are discs that were big on the northern soul scene before they gained a wider audience in the charts.

Title Act (Peak/Weeks on chart)

1. HEY GIRL DON'T BOTHER ME – Tams (1/17)
2. THERE'S A GHOST IN MY HOUSE – R Dean Taylor (1/12)
3. HEAVEN MUST HAVE SENT YOU – Elgins (3/13)
4. I'M GONNA RUN AWAY FROM YOU – Tami Lynn (4/14)
5. HOLD BACK THE NIGHT – Trammps (5/8)
6. HARLEM SHUFFLE – Bob and Earl (7/13)
7. THE NIGHT – Frankie Valli and the Four Seasons (7/9)
8. I GET THE SWEETEST FEELING – Jackie Wilson (9/13)
9. FOOTSEE – Wigan's Chosen Few (9/11)
10. LOVE ON A MOUNTAIN TOP – Robert Knight (10/16)

WEST END featuring SYBIL

UK, male production duo and female vocalist (Singles: 13 weeks) pos/wks

16 Jan 93 ● **THE LOVE I LOST** *PWL Sanctuary PWCD253* 3 13

WEST HAM UNITED CUP SQUAD

UK, male football team vocalists (Singles: 2 weeks) pos/wks

10 May 75 **I'M FOREVER BLOWING BUBBLES** *Pye 7N 45470* 31 2

WEST STREET MOB

US, male DJs / producers (Singles: 3 weeks) pos/wks

8 Oct 83 **BREAK DANCIN' – ELECTRIC BOOGIE (re)** *Sugarhill SH 128* 64 3

WESTBAM

Germany, male producer – Maximillian Lenz (Singles: 9 weeks) pos/wks

9 Jul 94 **CELEBRATION GENERATION** *Low Spirit PQCD 5* 48 2
19 Nov 94 **BAM BAM BAM** *Low Spirit PZCD 329* 57 1
3 Jun 95 **WIZARDS OF THE SONIC** *Urban PZCD 344* 32 2
23 Mar 96 **ALWAYS MUSIC** *Low Spirit 5779152* [1] 51 1
13 Jun 98 **WIZARDS OF THE SONIC (re-mix)** *Wonderboy WBOYD 010* [2] 43 2
28 Nov 98 **ROOF IS ON FIRE** *Logic 74321633162* 58 1

[1] Westbam / Koon + Stephenson [2] Westbam vs Red Jerry

Hayley WESTENRA

New Zealand, female vocalist (Albums: 14 weeks) pos/wks

27 Sep 03 ● **PURE** *Decca 4753302* ....7 14+

WESTLIFE (139 Top 500)

Record-shattering Irish boy band: Bryan McFadden (left 2004), Kian Egan, Mark Feehily, Nicky Byrne and Shane Filan. Only act to reach No.1 with their first seven releases or enter the chart at No.1 11 times out of their first 13. They are also the first UK-based act to amass four No.1 singles in a calendar year and average album sales of 1.5 million for each release (Singles: 193 weeks, Albums: 163 weeks) pos/wks

1 May 99 ★ **SWEAR IT AGAIN (re)** *RCA 74321662062* ■ 1 13
21 Aug 99 ★ **IF I LET YOU GO** *RCA74321692352* ■ 1 11
30 Oct 99 ★ **FLYING WITHOUT WINGS** *RCA 74321709162* ■ 1 13
25 Dec 99 ★ **I HAVE A DREAM / SEASONS IN THE SUN** *RCA 74321726012* ■ 1 17
8 Apr 00 ★ **FOOL AGAIN (re)** *RCA 74321751562* ■ 1 12
30 Sep 00 ★ **AGAINST ALL ODDS (re)** *Columbia 6698872* [1] ■ 1 12
11 Nov 00 ★ **MY LOVE** *RCA 74321802792* ■ 1 10
30 Dec 00 ● **WHAT MAKES A MAN** *RCA 74321826252* 2 13
17 Mar 01 ★ **UPTOWN GIRL** *RCA 74321841682* ■ 1 16
17 Nov 01 ★ **QUEEN OF MY HEART** *RCA 74321899132* ■ 1 15
2 Mar 02 ★ **WORLD OF OUR OWN** *S 74321918802* ■ 1 13
1 Jun 02 ● **BOP BOP BABY** *S 74321940452* 5 10
16 Nov 02 ★ **UNBREAKABLE (re)** *S 74321975182* ■ 1 16
5 Apr 03 ● **TONIGHT / MISS YOU NIGHTS** *S 74321986792* 3 10
27 Sep 03 ● **HEY WHATEVER** *S 82876560822* 4 7
29 Nov 03 ★ **MANDY** *S 82876570832* ■ ....1 5+
13 Nov 99 ● **WESTLIFE** *RCA 74321713212* 2 69
18 Nov 00 ★ **COAST TO COAST** *RCA 74321808312* ■ 1 28
24 Nov 01 ★ **WORLD OF OUR OWN** *RCA 74321903082* ■ 1 35
23 Nov 02 ★ **UNBREAKABLE – THE GREATEST HITS VOL.1** *S 74321975902* ■ 1 27
6 Dec 03 ★ **TURNAROUND** *S 82876557412* ■ ....1 4+

[1] Mariah [Carey] featuring Westlife

WESTMINSTER ABBEY CHOIR

UK, male / female choir - Choirmaster Dr. Martin Neary (Albums: 7 weeks) pos/wks

20 Sep 97	**JOHN TAVERNER: INNOCENCE** *Sony Classical SK 6661*	**34**	4
12 Sep 98	**PERFECT PEACE** *Sony Classical SONYTV 49CD*	**58**	3

WESTMINSTER CATHEDRAL CHOIR – *See Martin NEARY*

Kim WESTON – *See Marvin GAYE*

WESTWORLD

UK / US, male / female vocal / instrumental group (Singles: 23 weeks, Albums: 2 weeks) pos/wks

21 Feb 87	**SONIC BOOM BOY** *RCA BOOM 1*	**11**	7
2 May 87	**BA-NA-NA-BAM-BOO** *RCA BOOM 2*	**37**	5
25 Jul 87	**WHERE THE ACTION IS** *RCA BOOM 3*	**54**	4
17 Oct 87	**SILVERMAC** *RCA BOOM 4*	**42**	5
15 Oct 88	**EVERYTHING GOOD IS BAD** *RCA PB 42243*	**72**	2
5 Sep 87	**WHERE THE ACTION IS** *RCA PL 71429*	**49**	2

WET WET WET

(80 Top 500) *Glasgow quartet fronted by vocalist Marti Pellow (b. Mark McLoughlin, 23 Mar 1966). They were voted Best British Newcomers at the 1988 Brit Awards and they hold the record for most weeks at No.1 by a UK act – 15 consecutive weeks. Best-selling single: 'Love Is All Around' 1,783,827 (Singles: 209 weeks, Albums: 278 weeks)* pos/wks

11 Apr 87 ●	**WISHING I WAS LUCKY** *Precious JEWEL 3*	**6**	14
25 Jul 87 ●	**SWEET LITTLE MYSTERY** *Precious JEWEL 4*	**5**	12
5 Dec 87 ●	**ANGEL EYES (HOME AND AWAY)** *Precious JEWEL 6*	**5**	12
19 Mar 88	**TEMPTATION** *Precious JEWEL 7*	**12**	8
14 May 88 ★	**WITH A LITTLE HELP FROM MY FRIENDS** *Childline CHILD 1*	**1**	11
30 Sep 89 ●	**SWEET SURRENDER** *Precious JEWEL 9*	**6**	8
9 Dec 89	**BROKE AWAY** *Precious JEWEL 10*	**19**	7
10 Mar 90	**HOLD BACK THE RIVER** *Precious JEWEL 11*	**31**	4
11 Aug 90	**STAY WITH ME HEARTACHE / I FEEL FINE** *Precious JEWEL 13*	**30**	4
14 Sep 91	**MAKE IT TONIGHT** *Precious JEWEL 15*	**37**	3
2 Nov 91	**PUT THE LIGHT ON** *Precious JEWEL 16*	**56**	2
4 Jan 92 ★	**GOODNIGHT GIRL** *Precious JEWEL 17*	**1**	11
21 Mar 92	**MORE THAN LOVE** *Precious JEWEL 18*	**19**	5
11 Jul 92	**LIP SERVICE (EP)** *Precious JEWEL 19*	**15**	5
8 May 93	**BLUE FOR YOU / THIS TIME (LIVE)** *Precious JWLCD 20*	**38**	2
6 Nov 93	**SHED A TEAR** *Precious JWLCD 21*	**22**	5
8 Jan 94	**COLD COLD HEART** *Precious JWLCD 22*	**20**	4
21 May 94 ★	**LOVE IS ALL AROUND** *Precious JWLCD 23* ◆	**1**	37
25 Mar 95 ●	**JULIA SAYS** *Precious JWLDD 24*	**3**	9
17 Jun 95 ●	**DON'T WANT TO FORGIVE ME NOW** *Precious JWLDD 25*	**7**	8
30 Sep 95 ●	**SOMEWHERE SOMEHOW** *Precious JWLDD 26*	**7**	7
2 Dec 95	**SHE'S ALL ON MY MIND** *Precious JWLDD 27*	**17**	7
30 Mar 96	**MORNING** *Precious JWLDD 28*	**16**	4
22 Mar 97 ●	**IF I NEVER SEE YOU AGAIN (re)** *Precious JWLCD 29*	**3**	9
14 Jun 97	**STRANGE (re)** *Precious JWLCD 30*	**13**	5
16 Aug 97 ●	**YESTERDAY** *Precious JWLCD 31*	**4**	6
3 Oct 87 ★	**POPPED IN SOULED OUT** *Precious JWWWL 1*	**1**	72
19 Nov 88 ●	**THE MEMPHIS SESSIONS** *Precious JWWWL 2*	**3**	13
11 Nov 89 ●	**HOLDING BACK THE RIVER** *Precious 842011 1*	**2**	26
8 Feb 92 ★	**HIGH ON THE HAPPY SIDE** *Precious 5104272* ■	**1**	25
29 May 93 ●	**LIVE AT THE ROYAL ALBERT HALL** *Precious 5147742* [1]	**10**	4
20 Nov 93 ★	**END OF PART ONE (THEIR GREATEST HITS)** *Precious 5184772*	**1**	67
22 Apr 94 ★	**PICTURE THIS** *Precious 5268512* ■	**1**	45
12 Apr 97 ●	**10** *Precious Organisation 5345852*	**2**	26

[1] Wet Wet Wet with the Wren Orchestra

The listed A-side of 'With a Little Help from My Friends' was 'She's Leaving Home' by Billy Bragg with Cara Tivey. Tracks on Lip Service (EP): Lip Service / High on the Happy Side / Lip Service (Live) / More than Love (Live)

WE'VE GOT A FUZZBOX AND WE'RE GONNA USE IT

UK, female vocal / instrumental group (Singles: 39 weeks, Albums: 6 weeks) pos/wks

26 Apr 86	**XX SEX / RULES AND REGULATIONS** *Vindaloo UGH 11*	**41**	7
15 Nov 86	**LOVE IS THE SLUG** *Vindaloo UGH 14*	**31**	4
7 Feb 87	**WHAT'S THE POINT** *Vindaloo YZ 101* [1]	**51**	2
25 Feb 89	**INTERNATIONAL RESCUE** *WEA YZ 347*	**11**	10
20 May 89	**PINK SUNSHINE** *WEA YZ 401* [1]	**14**	10
5 Aug 89	**SELF!** *WEA YZ 408* [1]	**24**	6
26 Aug 89 ●	**BIG BANG** *WEA WX 282*	**5**	6

[1] Fuzzbox

WHALE

Sweden, male / female vocal / instrumental group (Singles: 8 weeks, Albums: 2 weeks) pos/wks

19 Mar 94	**HOBO HUMPIN' SLOBO BABE** *East West YZ 798CD*	**46**	2
15 Jul 95	**I'LL DO YA** *Hut HUTDG 51*	**53**	1
25 Nov 95	**HOBO HUMPIN' SLOBO BABE (re-issue)** *Hut HUTCD 64*	**15**	4
4 Jul 98	**FOUR BIG SPEAKERS** *Hut HUTCD 96* [1]	**69**	1
12 Aug 95	**WE CARE** *Hut DGHUT 25*	**42**	2

[1] Whale featuring Bus 75

WHALERS – *See Hal PAIGE and the WHALERS*

WHAM!

(115 Top 500) *Teen-dream duo with a feel-good, pure pop sound: George Michael (v), Andrew Ridgeley (g). With total single sales of 5,298,431, they were the only British group to have three chart-toppers in the UK and the US during the 1980s, a feat George later equalled as a solo artist. Best-selling single: 'Last Christmas' / 'Everything She Wants' 1,420,000 (Singles: 137 weeks, Albums: 259 weeks)* pos/wks

16 Oct 82 ●	**YOUNG GUNS (GO FOR IT)** *Innervision IVL A2766*	**3**	17
15 Jan 83 ●	**WHAM RAP!** *Innervision IVL A2442*	**8**	11
14 May 83 ●	**BAD BOYS** *Innervision A 3143*	**2**	14
30 Jul 83 ●	**CLUB TROPICANA** *Innervision A 3613*	**4**	11
3 Dec 83	**CLUB FANTASTIC MEGAMIX** *Innervision A 3586*	**15**	8
26 May 84 ★	**WAKE ME UP BEFORE YOU GO GO** *Epic A 4440* ▲	**1**	16
13 Oct 84 ★	**FREEDOM** *Epic A 4743*	**1**	14
15 Dec 84 ●	**LAST CHRISTMAS / EVERYTHING SHE WANTS** *Epic GA / QA 4949* ◆ ▲	**2**	13
23 Nov 85 ★	**I'M YOUR MAN** *Epic A 6716*	**1**	12
14 Dec 85 ●	**LAST CHRISTMAS (re-issue)** *Epic WHAM 1*	**6**	7
21 Jun 86 ★	**THE EDGE OF HEAVEN / WHERE DID YOUR HEART GO** *Epic FIN 1*	**1**	10
20 Dec 86	**LAST CHRISTMAS (2nd re-issue)** *Epic 650269 7*	**45**	4
9 Jul 83 ★	**FANTASTIC** *Inner Vision IVL 25328* ■	**1**	116
17 Nov 84 ★	**MAKE IT BIG** *Epic EPC 86311* ■ ▲	**1**	72
19 Jul 86 ●	**THE FINAL** *Epic EPC 88681*	**2**	47
6 Dec 97 ●	**THE BEST OF WHAM!** *Epic 4890202*	**4**	24

Chart entry dated 21 June 1986 was a double record set. 'The Edge of Heaven'/ 'Wham Rap 86 (remix)' on disc one and 'Battlestations' / 'Where Did Your Heart Go' on disc two. Where Did Your Heart Go' listed only from 2 Aug 1986, peaking at No.28. Chart entry 15 Dec 1984 was first catalogued as GA 4949 but from 5 Jan 1985 the special remix of 'Everything She Wants' (QA 4949) was listed as the A-side and this was the track that topped the US charts

Sarah WHATMORE

UK, female vocalist (Singles: 17 weeks) pos/wks

21 Sep 02 ●	**WHEN I LOST YOU** *RCA 74321965952*	**6**	9
22 Feb 03	**AUTOMATIC** *RCA 82876504612*	**11**	8

WHATNAUTS – *See MOMENTS*

Rebecca WHEATLEY

UK, female actor / vocalist (Singles: 8 weeks) pos/wks

26 Feb 00 ●	**STAY WITH ME (BABY) (re)** *BBC Music WMSS 60222*	**10**	8

WHEATUS

US, male vocal / instrumental group (Singles: 37 weeks, Albums: 30 weeks) pos/wks

17 Feb 01 ●	**TEENAGE DIRTBAG** *Columbia 6707962*	**2**	20
14 Jul 01 ●	**A LITTLE RESPECT** *Columbia 6714282*	**3**	12
26 Jan 02	**WANNABE GANGSTAR / LEROY** *Columbia 6721272*	**22**	5
6 Sep 03	**AMERICAN IN AMSTERDAM** *Columbia 6741072*	**59**	1
3 Mar 01 ●	**WHEATUS** *Columbia 4996052*	**7**	30

Caron WHEELER

UK, female vocalist (Singles: 42 weeks, Albums: 5 weeks) pos/wks

18 Mar 89 ●	**KEEP ON MOVING** *10 TEN 263* [1]	**5**	12
10 Jun 89 ★	**BACK TO LIFE (HOWEVER DO YOU WANT ME)** *10 TEN 265* [1]	**1**	14

8 Sep 90 **LIVIN' IN THE LIGHT** *RCA PB 43939* 14 6
10 Nov 90 **UK BLAK** *RCA PB 43719* 40 4
9 Feb 91 **DON'T QUIT** *RCA PB 44259* 53 3
7 Nov 92 **I ADORE YOU** *Perspective PERSS 7407* 59 2
11 Sep 93 **BEACH OF THE WAR GODDESS** *EMI CDEM 282* 75 1
13 Oct 90 **UK BLAK** *RCA PL 74751* 14 5

[1] Soul II Soul featuring Caron Wheeler

Bill WHELAN

Ireland, male composer (Singles: 16 weeks, Albums: 38 weeks) pos/wks

17 Dec 94 ● **RIVERDANCE** *Son RTEBUACD 1* [1] 9 16
25 Mar 95 **MUSIC FROM RIVERDANCE – THE SHOW** *Celtic Heartbeat 75678061112* 31 38

[1] Bill Whelan and Anuna featuring the RTE Concert Orchestra

WHEN IN ROME

UK, male vocal / instrumental group (Singles: 3 weeks) pos/wks

28 Jan 89 **THE PROMISE** *10 TEN 244* 58 3

WHIGFIELD *Denmark, female vocalist – Sannia Carlson (Singles: 52 weeks, Albums: 7 weeks)* pos/wks

17 Sep 94 ★ **SATURDAY NIGHT** *Systematic SYSCD 3* ◆ ■ 1 18
10 Dec 94 ● **ANOTHER DAY** *Systematic SYSCD 4* 7 10
10 Jun 95 ● **THINK OF YOU** *Systematic SYSCDP 10* 7 11
9 Sep 95 **CLOSE TO YOU** *Systematic SYCDP 18* 13 7
16 Dec 95 **LAST CHRISTMAS / BIG TIME** *Systematic SYSCD 24* 21 5
10 Oct 98 **SEXY EYES – REMIXES** *ZYX ZYX 8085R8* 68 1
1 Jul 95 **WHIGFIELD** *Systematic 8286512* 13 7

WHIPPING BOY

Ireland, male vocal / instrumental group (Singles: 4 weeks) pos/wks

14 Oct 95 **WE DON'T NEED NOBODY ELSE** *Columbia 6622205* 51 1
3 Feb 96 **WHEN WE WERE YOUNG** *Columbia 6628062* 46 2
25 May 96 **TWINKLE** *Columbia 6632272* 55 1

Nancy WHISKEY – *See Charles McDEVITT SKIFFLE GROUP featuring Nancy WHISKEY*

WHISPERS

US, male vocal group (Singles: 52 weeks, Albums: 9 weeks) pos/wks

2 Feb 80 ● **AND THE BEAT GOES ON** *Solar SO 1* 2 12
10 May 80 **LADY** *Solar SO 4* 55 3
12 Jul 80 **MY GIRL** *Solar SO 8* 26 6
14 Mar 81 ● **IT'S A LOVE THING** *Solar SO 16* 9 11
13 Jun 81 **I CAN MAKE IT BETTER** *Solar SO 19* 44 5
19 Jan 85 **CONTAGIOUS** *MCA MCA 937* 56 3
28 Mar 87 **AND THE BEAT GOES ON (re-issue)** *Solar MCA 1126* 45 4
23 May 87 **ROCK STEADY** *Solar MCA 1152* 38 6
15 Aug 87 **SPECIAL F/X** *Solar MCA 1178* 69 2
14 Mar 81 **IMAGINATION** *Solar SOLA 7* 42 5
6 Jun 87 **JUST GETS BETTER WITH TIME** *Solar MCF 3381* 63 4

WHISTLE

US, male rap group (Singles: 8 weeks) pos/wks

1 Mar 86 ● **(NOTHIN' SERIOUS) JUST BUGGIN'** *Champion CHAMP 12* 7 8

Alex WHITCOMBE & BIG C

UK, male production duo (Singles: 1 week) pos/wks

23 May 98 **ICE RAIN** *Xtravaganza 0091075 EXT* 44 1

See also QATTARA

Alan WHITE

UK, male instrumentalist – drums (Albums: 4 weeks) pos/wks

13 Mar 76 **RAMSHACKLED** *Atlantic K 50217* 41 4

See also YES

Barry WHITE (125 Top 500)

Seventies soul and disco icon, b. 12 Sep 1944, Texas, US, d. 5 Jul 2003. This singer / songwriter / pianist / producer / arranger was behind best-sellers by Love Unlimited and Love Unlimited Orchestra. Lovingly named the 'Walrus of Love', his unmistakable deep voice had been heard in the charts for four decades (Singles: 138 weeks, Albums: 242 weeks) pos/wks

9 Jun 73 **I'M GONNA LOVE YOU JUST A LITTLE MORE BABY** *Pye International 7N 25610* 23 7
26 Jan 74 **NEVER NEVER GONNA GIVE YA UP** *Pye International 7N 25633* 14 11
17 Aug 74 ● **CAN'T GET ENOUGH OF YOUR LOVE, BABE** *Pye International 7N 25661* ▲ 8 12
2 Nov 74 ★ **YOU'RE THE FIRST, THE LAST, MY EVERYTHING** *20th Century BTC 2133* 1 14
8 Mar 75 ● **WHAT AM I GONNA DO WITH YOU** *20th Century BTC 2177* 5 8
24 May 75 **(FOR YOU) I'LL DO ANYTHING YOU WANT ME TO** *20th Century BTC 2208* 20 6
27 Dec 75 ● **LET THE MUSIC PLAY** *20th Century BTC 2265* 9 8
6 Mar 76 ● **YOU SEE THE TROUBLE WITH ME** *20th Century BTC 2277* 2 10
21 Aug 76 **BABY, WE BETTER TRY TO GET IT TOGETHER** *20th Century BTC 2298* 15 7
13 Nov 76 **DON'T MAKE ME WAIT TOO LONG** *20th Century BTC 2309* 17 8
5 Mar 77 **I'M QUALIFIED TO SATISFY YOU** *20th Century BTC 2328* 37 5
15 Oct 77 **IT'S ECSTASY WHEN YOU LAY DOWN NEXT TO ME** *20th Century BTC 2350* 40 3
16 Dec 78 **JUST THE WAY YOU ARE** *20th Century BTC 2380* 12 12
24 Mar 79 **SHA LA LA MEANS I LOVE YOU** *20th Century BTC 1041* 55 6
7 Nov 87 **SHO' YOU RIGHT** *Breakout USA 614* 14 7
16 Jan 88 **NEVER NEVER GONNA GIVE YOU UP (re-mix)** *Club JAB 59* 63 2
31 Mar 90 **SECRET GARDEN** *Qwest W 9992* [1] 67 1
21 Jan 95 **PRACTICE WHAT YOU PREACH / LOVE IS THE ICON** *A&M 5808992* 20 4
8 Apr 95 **I ONLY WANT TO BE WITH YOU** *A&M 5810252* 36 2
21 Dec 96 **IN YOUR WILDEST DREAMS** *Parlophone CDR 6451* [2] 32 3
4 Nov 00 **LET THE MUSIC PLAY (re-mix)** *Wonderboy WBOYD 020* 45 2
9 Mar 74 **STONE GON'** *Pye NSPL 28186* 18 17
6 Apr 74 **RHAPSODY IN WHITE** *Pye NSPL 28191* 50 1
2 Nov 74 ● **CAN'T GET ENOUGH** *20th Century BT 444* ▲ 4 34
26 Apr 75 **JUST ANOTHER WAY TO SAY I LOVE YOU** *20th Century BT 466* 12 15
22 Nov 75 **GREATEST HITS** *20th Century BTH 8000* 18 12
21 Feb 76 **LET THE MUSIC PLAY** *20th Century BT 502* 22 14
9 Apr 77 **BARRY WHITE'S GREATEST HITS VOLUME 2** *20th Century BTH 8001* 17 7
10 Feb 79 **THE MAN** *20th Century BT 571* 46 4
21 Dec 85 **HEART AND SOUL** *K-Tel NE 1316* 34 10
17 Oct 87 **THE RIGHT NIGHT AND BARRY WHITE** *Breakout AMA 5154* 74 6
2 Jul 88 ● **THE COLLECTION** *Mercury BWTV 1* 5 116
11 Feb 95 **THE ICON IS LOVE** *A&M 5402802* 44 3
15 Feb 03 **LOVE SONGS** *Universal TV 0686422* 21 3

[1] Quincy Jones featuring Al B Sure!, James Ingram, El DeBarge and Barry White
[2] Tina Turner featuring Barry White

Chris WHITE

UK, male vocalist (Singles: 4 weeks) pos/wks

20 Mar 76 **SPANISH WINE** *Charisma CB 272* 37 4

Karyn WHITE

US, female vocalist (Singles: 38 weeks, Albums: 30 weeks) pos/wks

5 Nov 88 **THE WAY YOU LOVE ME** *Warner Bros. W 7773* 42 5
18 Feb 89 **SECRET RENDEZVOUS** *Warner Bros. W 7562* 52 3
10 Jun 89 **SUPERWOMAN** *Warner Bros. W 2920* 11 13
9 Sep 89 **SECRET RENDEZVOUS (re-issue)** *Warner Bros. W 2855* 22 9
17 Aug 91 **ROMANTIC** *Warner Bros. W 0028* ▲ 23 5
18 Jan 92 **THE WAY I FEEL ABOUT YOU** *Warner Bros. W 0073* 65 2
24 Sep 94 **HUNGAH** *Warner Bros. W 0264CD* 69 1
11 Mar 89 **KARYN WHITE** *Warner Bros. WX 235* 20 27
21 Sep 91 **RITUAL OF LOVE** *Warner Bros. WX 411* 31 3

Keisha WHITE – *See OAKENFOLD; DESERT EAGLE DISCS featuring Keisha WHITE*

Snowy WHITE *UK, male vocalist / instrumentalist – guitar (Singles: 12 weeks, Albums: 5 weeks)* pos/wks

24 Dec 83 ●	**BIRD OF PARADISE** *Towerbell TOW 42*	6 10
28 Dec 85	**FOR YOU (re)** *R4 FOR 3*	65 2
11 Feb 84	**WHITE FLAMES** *Towerbell TOWLP 3*	21 4
9 Feb 85	**SNOWY WHITE** *Towerbell TOWLP 8*	88 1

Tam WHITE *UK, male vocalist (Singles: 4 weeks)* pos/wks

15 Mar 75	**WHAT IN THE WORLD'S COME OVER YOU** *RAK 193*	36 4

Tony Joe WHITE *US, male vocalist / instrumentalist – guitar (Singles: 10 weeks, Albums: 1 week)* pos/wks

6 Jun 70	**GROUPIE GIRL** *Monument MON 1043*	22 10
26 Sep 70	**TONY JOE** *CBS 63800*	63 1

WHITE and TORCH
UK, male vocal / instrumental duo (Singles: 4 weeks) pos/wks

2 Oct 82	**PARADE** *Chrysalis CHS 2641*	54 4

WHITE LION
US, male vocal / instrumental group (Albums: 3 weeks) pos/wks

1 Jul 89	**BIG GAME** *Atlantic WX 277*	47 1
20 Apr 91	**MANE ATTRACTION** *Atlantic WX 415*	31 2

WHITE PLAINS *UK, male vocal / instrumental group – lead vocal – Tony Burrows (Singles: 56 weeks)* pos/wks

7 Feb 70 ●	**MY BABY LOVES LOVIN'** *Deram DM 280*	9 11
18 Apr 70	**I'VE GOT YOU ON MY MIND** *Deram DM 291*	17 11
24 Oct 70 ●	**JULIE DO YA LOVE ME** *Deram DM 315*	8 14
12 Jun 71	**WHEN YOU ARE A KING** *Deram DM 333*	13 11
17 Feb 73	**STEP INTO A DREAM** *Deram DM 371*	21 9

WHITE STRIPES *US, male / female vocal / instrumental duo – Jack and Meg White (Singles: 18 weeks, Albums: 51 weeks)* pos/wks

24 Nov 01	**HOTEL YORBA** *XL Recordings XLS 139CD*	26 2
9 Mar 02	**FELL IN LOVE WITH A GIRL** *XL Recordings XLS 142CD*	21 2
14 Sep 02	**DEAD LEAVES AND THE DIRTY GROUND** *XL Recordings XLS 148CD*	25 2
3 May 03 ●	**7 NATION ARMY** *XL Recordings XLS 162CD*	7 4
13 Sep 03	**I JUST DON'T KNOW WHAT TO DO WITH MYSELF** *XL Recordings XLS 166CD*	13 5
29 Nov 03	**THE HARDEST BUTTON TO BUTTON** *XL Recordings XLS 173CD*	23 3
18 Aug 01	**WHITE BLOOD CELLS** *Sympathy for the Record Industry SFTRI 660CD*	55 17
12 Apr 03 ★	**ELEPHANT** *XL Recordings XLCD162* ■	1 34+

WHITE TOWN *UK, male vocalist / producer – Jyoti Mishra (Singles: 10 weeks)* pos/wks

25 Jan 97 ★	**YOUR WOMAN** *Chrysalis CDCHS 5052* ■	1 9
24 May 97	**UNDRESSED** *Chrysalis CDCHS 5058*	57 1

WHITE ZOMBIE *US, male vocal / instrumental group (Singles: 4 weeks, Albums: 6 weeks)* pos/wks

20 May 95	**MORE HUMAN THAN HUMAN** *Geffen GFSTD 92*	51 2
18 May 96	**ELECTRIC HEAD PART 2 (THE ECSTASY)** *Geffen GFSXD 22140*	31 2
27 May 95	**ASTRO CREEP 2000 / SUPERSEXY SWINGIN' SOUNDS** *Geffen GED 24806*	25 6

'Supersexy Swingin' Sounds', a remix album, was listed with 'Astro Creep 2000' from 31 Aug 96 and sales were combined

See also Rob ZOMBIE

WHITEHEAD BROS *US, male vocal duo – Kenny and Johnny Whitehead (Singles: 5 weeks)* pos/wks

14 Jan 95	**YOUR LOVE IS A 187** *Motown TMGCD 1434*	32 3
13 May 95	**FORGET I WAS A G** *Motown TMGCD 1441*	40 2

WHITEHOUSE *US / UK, male vocal / instrumental / production duo (Singles: 1 week)* pos/wks

15 Aug 98	**AIN'T NO MOUNTAIN HIGH ENOUGH** *Beautiful Noise BNOISE 2CD*	60 1

WHITEOUT *UK, male vocal / instrumental group (Singles: 2 weeks, Albums: 1 week)* pos/wks

24 Sep 94	**DETROIT** *Silvertone ORECD 66*	73 1
18 Feb 95	**JACKIE'S RACING** *Silvertone ORECD 68*	72 1
1 Jul 95	**BITE IT** *Silvertone ORECD 536*	71 1

WHITESNAKE (218 Top 500) *Leading 1980s British rock group founded by ex-Deep Purple vocalist David Coverdale (b. 22 Sep 1949, North Yorkshire, UK), but with an ever-changing line-up. 'Whitesnake' (1987), their most successful album, shifted more than 10 million copies worldwide (Singles: 112 weeks, Albums: 162 weeks)* pos/wks

24 Jun 78	**SNAKE BITE (EP)** *EMI International INEP 751* [1]	61 3
10 Nov 79	**LONG WAY FROM HOME** *United Artists BP 324*	55 2
26 Apr 80	**FOOL FOR YOUR LOVING** *United Artists BP 352*	13 9
12 Jul 80	**READY AN' WILLING (SWEET SATISFACTION)** *United Artists BP 363*	43 4
22 Nov 80	**AIN'T NO LOVE IN THE HEART OF THE CITY** *Sunburst / Liberty BP 381*	51 4
11 Apr 81	**DON'T BREAK MY HEART AGAIN** *Liberty BP 395*	17 9
6 Jun 81	**WOULD I LIE TO YOU** *Liberty BP 399*	37 6
6 Nov 82	**HERE I GO AGAIN / BLOODY LUXURY** *Liberty BP 416* ▲	34 10
13 Aug 83	**GUILTY OF LOVE** *Liberty BP 420*	31 5
14 Jan 84	**GIVE ME MORE TIME** *Liberty BP 422*	29 4
28 Apr 84	**STANDING IN THE SHADOW** *Liberty BP 423*	62 2
9 Feb 85	**LOVE AIN'T NO STRANGER** *Liberty BP 424*	44 4
28 Mar 87	**STILL OF THE NIGHT** *EMI EMI 5606*	16 8
6 Jun 87 ●	**IS THIS LOVE** *EMI EM 3*	9 11
31 Oct 87 ●	**HERE I GO AGAIN (re-mix)** *EMI EM 35*	9 11
6 Feb 88	**GIVE ME ALL YOUR LOVE** *EMI EM 23*	18 6
2 Dec 89	**FOOL FOR YOUR LOVING** *EMI EM 123*	43 2
10 Mar 90	**THE DEEPER THE LOVE** *EMI EM 128*	35 3
25 Aug 90	**NOW YOU'RE GONE** *EMI EM 150*	31 4
6 Aug 94	**IS THIS LOVE / SWEET LADY LUCK (re-issue)** *EMI CDEM 329*	25 4
7 Jun 97	**TOO MANY TEARS** *EMI CDEM 471* [2]	46 1
18 Nov 78	**TROUBLE** *EMI International INS 3022*	50 2
13 Oct 79	**LOVE HUNTER** *United Artists UAG 30264*	29 7
7 Jun 80 ●	**READY AND WILLING** *United Artists UAG 30302*	6 15
8 Nov 80 ●	**LIVE IN THE HEART OF THE CITY** *United Artists SNAKE 1*	5 15
18 Apr 81 ●	**COME AND GET IT** *Liberty LBG 30327*	2 23
27 Nov 82 ●	**SAINTS 'N' SINNERS** *Liberty LBG 30354*	9 9
11 Feb 84 ●	**SLIDE IT IN** *Liberty LBG 2400001*	9 7
11 Apr 87 ●	**WHITESNAKE 1987** *EMI EMC 3528*	8 57
25 Nov 89 ●	**SLIP OF THE TONGUE** *EMI EMD 1013*	10 10
16 Jul 94 ●	**GREATEST HITS** *EMI CDEMD 1065*	4 12
21 Jun 97	**RESTLESS HEART** *EMI CDEMD 1104* [1]	34 2
5 Apr 03	**BEST OF WHITESNAKE** *EMI 5812452*	44 3

[1] David Coverdale's Whitesnake [2] David Coverdale and Whitesnake
[1] David Coverdale and Whitesnake

Tracks on Snake Bite (EP): Bloody Mary / Steal Away / Ain't No Love in the Heart of the City / Come On. EM 123 is a re-recording of their third hit

See also COVERDALE / PAGE; Bernie MARSDEN

David WHITFIELD (346 Top 500) *Most successful UK male singer in the US during the pre-rock years, b. 2 Feb 1925, Yorkshire, d. 16 Jan 1980. This operatic-style tenor had a formidable and predominantly female fan following in the 1950s (Singles: 190 weeks)* pos/wks

2 Oct 53 ●	**THE BRIDGE OF SIGHS** *Decca F 10129*	9 1
16 Oct 53 ★	**ANSWER ME (re)** *Decca F 10192*	1 14
11 Dec 53 ●	**RAGS TO RICHES (re)** *Decca F 10207* [1]	3 11
19 Feb 54 ●	**THE BOOK (re)** *Decca F 10242*	5 15
18 Jun 54 ★	**CARA MIA** *Decca F 10327*	1 25
12 Nov 54 ●	**SANTO NATALE (MERRY CHRISTMAS)** *Decca F 10399*	2 10
11 Feb 55 ●	**BEYOND THE STARS** *Decca F 10458*	8 9
27 May 55	**MAMA (2re)** *Decca F 10515*	12 11
8 Jul 55 ●	**EV'RYWHERE** *Decca F 10515* [2]	3 20

25 Nov 55 ● **WHEN YOU LOSE THE ONE YOU LOVE** *Decca F 10627* [3] 7 11
2 Mar 56 ● **MY SEPTEMBER LOVE (3re)** *Decca F 10690* 3 24
24 Aug 56 **MY SON JOHN** *Decca F 10769* 22 4
31 Aug 56 **MY UNFINISHED SYMPHONY** *Decca F 10769* 29 1
25 Jan 57 ● **THE ADORATION WALTZ** *Decca F 10833* [2] 9 11
5 Apr 57 **I'LL FIND YOU (re)** *Decca F 10864* 27 4
14 Feb 58 **CRY MY HEART** *Decca F 10978* [4] 22 3
16 May 58 **ON THE STREET WHERE YOU LIVE** *Decca F 11018* [5] 16 14
8 Aug 58 **THE RIGHT TO LOVE** *Decca F 11039* 30 1
24 Nov 60 **I BELIEVE** *Decca F 11289* 49 1

[1] David Whitfield with Stanley Black and his Orchestra [2] David Whitfield with the Roland Shaw Orchestra [3] David Whitfield with Mantovani His Orchestra and Chorus [4] David Whitfield with chorus and Mantovani and his Orchestra [5] David Whitfield with Cyril Stapleton and his Orchestra

Slim WHITMAN *US, male vocalist / instrumentalist – guitar (Singles: 77 weeks, Albums: 61 weeks)* pos/wks

15 Jul 55 ★ **ROSE MARIE** *London HL 8061* 1 19
29 Jul 55 ● **INDIAN LOVE CALL** *London L 1149* 7 12
23 Sep 55 **CHINA DOLL** *London L 1149* 15 2
9 Mar 56 **TUMBLING TUMBLEWEEDS** *London HLU 8230* 19 2
13 Apr 56 **I'M A FOOL (re)** *London HLU 8252* 16 4
22 Jun 56 ● **SERENADE (re)** *London HLU 8287* 8 15
12 Apr 57 ● **I'LL TAKE YOU HOME AGAIN KATHLEEN** *London HLP 8403* 7 13
5 Oct 74 **HAPPY ANNIVERSARY** *United Artists UP 35728* 14 10
14 Dec 74 **HAPPY ANNIVERSARY** *United Artists UAS 29670* 44 2
31 Jan 76 ★ **THE VERY BEST OF SLIM WHITMAN** *United Artists UAS 29898* 1 17
15 Jan 77 ★ **RED RIVER VALLEY** *United Artists UAS 29993* 1 14
15 Oct 77 ● **HOME ON THE RANGE** *United Artists UATV 30102* 2 13
13 Jan 79 **GHOST RIDERS IN THE SKY** *United Artists UATV 30202* 27 6
22 Dec 79 **SLIM WHITMAN'S 20 GREATEST LOVE SONGS** *United Artists UAG 30270* 18 7
27 Sep 97 **THE VERY BEST OF SLIM WHITMAN – 50TH ANNIVERSARY COLLECTION** *EMI CDEMC 3772* 54 2

Roger WHITTAKER (338 Top 500) *World-renowned vocalist and whistler, b. 22 Mar 1936, Nairobi, Kenya. Easy-listening legend and popular live performer had more than 10 million albums sold in his home base of Germany (Singles: 85 weeks, Albums: 111 weeks)* pos/wks

8 Nov 69 **DURHAM TOWN (THE LEAVIN')** *Columbia DB 8613* 12 18
11 Apr 70 ● **I DON'T BELIEVE IN IF ANYMORE** *Columbia DB 8664* 8 18
10 Oct 70 **NEW WORLD IN THE MORNING** *Columbia DB 8718* 17 14
3 Apr 71 **WHY** *Columbia DB 8752* 47 1
2 Oct 71 **MAMMY BLUE** *Columbia DB 8822* 31 10
26 Jul 75 ● **THE LAST FAREWELL** *EMI 2294* 2 14
8 Nov 86 ● **THE SKYE BOAT SONG** *Tembo TML 119* [1] 10 10
27 Jun 70 **I DON'T BELIEVE IN IF ANYMORE** *Columbia SCX 6404* 23 1
3 Apr 71 **NEW WORLD IN THE MORNING** *Columbia SCX 6456* 45 2
6 Sep 75 ● **THE VERY BEST OF ROGER WHITTAKER** *Columbia SCX 6560* 5 42
15 May 76 **THE SECOND ALBUM OF THE VERY BEST OF ROGER WHITTAKER** *EMI EMC 3117* 27 7
9 Dec 78 **ROGER WHITTAKER SINGS THE HITS** *Columbia SCX 6601* 52 5
4 Aug 79 **20 ALL TIME GREATS** *Polydor POLTV 8* 24 9
7 Feb 81 **THE ROGER WHITTAKER ALBUM** *K-Tel NE 1105* 18 14
27 Dec 86 **SKYE BOAT SONG AND OTHER GREAT SONGS** *Tembo TMB 113* 89 1
23 May 87 **HIS FINEST COLLECTION** *Tembo RWTV 1* 15 19
23 Sep 89 **HOME LOVIN' MAN** *Tembo RWTV 2* 20 10
11 May 96 **A PERFECT DAY - HIS GREATEST HITS & MORE** *RCA 74321371562* 74 1

[1] Roger Whittaker and Des O'Connor

WHO (87 Top 500)

Legendary live band from London, whose 'Tommy' album (1969) popularised rock opera: Roger Daltrey (v), Pete Townshend (g), John Entwistle (The Ox), (b) d. 27 Jun 2002, Keith Moon (d) (d. 1978). These gold-record collectors have spent five decades breaking both guitars and box-office records (Singles: 247 weeks, Albums: 222 weeks) pos/wks

18 Feb 65 ● **I CAN'T EXPLAIN** *Brunswick 05926* 8 13
27 May 65 ● **ANYWAY ANYHOW ANYWHERE** *Brunswick 05935* 10 12
4 Nov 65 ● **MY GENERATION** *Brunswick 05944* 2 13
10 Mar 66 ● **SUBSTITUTE** *Reaction 591 001* 5 13
24 Mar 66 **A LEGAL MATTER** *Brunswick 05956* 32 6
1 Sep 66 ● **I'M A BOY** *Reaction 591 004* 2 13
1 Sep 66 **THE KIDS ARE ALRIGHT (re)** *Brunswick 05965* 41 3
15 Dec 66 ● **HAPPY JACK** *Reaction 591 010* 3 11
27 Apr 67 ● **PICTURES OF LILY** *Track 604 002* 4 10
26 Jul 67 **THE LAST TIME / UNDER MY THUMB** *Track 604 006* 44 3
18 Oct 67 ● **I CAN SEE FOR MILES** *Track 604 011* 10 12
19 Jun 68 **DOGS** *Track 604 023* 25 5
23 Oct 68 **MAGIC BUS** *Track 604 024* 26 6
19 Mar 69 ● **PINBALL WIZARD** *Track 604 027* 4 13
4 Apr 70 **THE SEEKER** *Track 604 036* 19 11
8 Aug 70 **SUMMERTIME BLUES** *Track 2094 002* 38 4
10 Jul 71 ● **WON'T GET FOOLED AGAIN** *Track 2094 009* 9 12
23 Oct 71 **LET'S SEE ACTION** *Track 2094 012* 16 12
24 Jun 72 ● **JOIN TOGETHER** *Track 2094 102* 9 9
13 Jan 73 **RELAY** *Track 2094 106* 21 5
13 Oct 73 **5.15** *Track 2094 115* 20 6
24 Jan 76 ● **SQUEEZE BOX** *Polydor 2121 275* 10 9
30 Oct 76 ● **SUBSTITUTE (re-issue)** *Polydor 2058 803* 7 7
22 Jul 78 **WHO ARE YOU** *Polydor WHO 1* 18 12
28 Apr 79 **LONG LIVE ROCK** *Polydor WHO 2* 48 5
7 Mar 81 ● **YOU BETTER YOU BET** *Polydor WHO 004* 9 8
9 May 81 **DON'T LET GO THE COAT** *Polydor WHO 005* 47 4
2 Oct 82 **ATHENA** *Polydor WHO 6* 40 4
26 Nov 83 **READY STEADY WHO (EP)** *Polydor WHO 7* 58 2
20 Feb 88 **MY GENERATION (re-issue)** *Polydor POSP 907* 68 2
27 Jul 96 **MY GENERATION (2nd re-issue)** *Polydor 8546372* 31 2
25 Dec 65 ● **MY GENERATION** *Brunswick LAT 8616* 5 11
17 Dec 66 ● **A QUICK ONE** *Reaction 593002* 4 17
13 Jan 68 **THE WHO SELL-OUT** *Track 613002* 13 11
7 Jun 69 ● **TOMMY** *Track 613013/4* 2 9
6 Jun 70 ● **LIVE AT LEEDS** *Track 2406001* 3 21
11 Sep 71 ★ **WHO'S NEXT** *Track 2408102* 1 13
18 Dec 71 ● **MEATY BEATY BIG AND BOUNCY** *Track 2406006* 9 8
17 Nov 73 ● **QUADROPHENIA** *Track 2647013* 2 13
26 Oct 74 ● **ODDS AND SODS** *Track 2406116* 10 4
23 Aug 75 **TOMMY (FILM SOUNDTRACK)** *Track 2657 007* 30 2
18 Oct 75 ● **THE WHO BY NUMBERS** *Polydor 2490129* 7 6
9 Oct 76 ● **THE STORY OF THE WHO** *Polydor 2683069* 2 18
9 Sep 78 ● **WHO ARE YOU** *Polydor WHOD 5004* 6 9
30 Jun 79 **THE KIDS ARE ALRIGHT** *Polydor 2675 174* 26 13
25 Oct 80 **MY GENERATION (re-issue)** *Virgin V 2179* 20 7
28 Mar 81 ● **FACE DANCES** *Polydor WHOD 5037* 2 9
11 Sep 82 **IT'S HARD** *Polydor WHOD 5066* 11 6
17 Nov 84 **WHO'S LAST** *MCA WHO 1* 48 4
12 Oct 85 **THE WHO COLLECTION** *Impression IMDP 4* 44 6
19 Mar 88 ● **WHO'S BETTER WHO'S BEST** *Polydor WTV 1* 10 11
19 Nov 88 **THE WHO COLLECTION** *Stylus SMR 570* 71 4
24 Mar 90 **JOIN TOGETHER** *Virgin VDT 102* 59 1
16 Jul 94 **30 YEARS OF MAXIMUM R&B** *Polydor 5217512* 48 1
4 Mar 95 **LIVE AT LEEDS (re-issue)** *Polydor 5271692* 59 1
6 Jul 96 **QUADROPHENIA (re-issue)** *Polydor 5319712* 47 2
24 Aug 96 **MY GENERATION – THE VERY BEST OF THE WHO** *Polydor 5331502* 11 6
26 Feb 00 **BBC SESSIONS** *BBC Music / Polydor 5477272* 24 2
21 Sep 02 **MY GENERATION (2ND re-issue)** *MCA / Uni-Island 1129262* 47 1
2 Nov 02 **THE ULTIMATE COLLECTION** *Polydor / Universal TV 0653002* 17 5
12 Jul 03 **LIVE AT THE ROYAL ALBERT HALL** *SPV Recordings SPV09374882* 72 1

Tracks on Ready Steady Who (EP): Disguises / Circles / Batman / Bucket 'T' / Barbara Ann The second re-issue of 'My Generation' contains a bonus disc of out-takes and rarities. The two albums titled 'The Who Collection' are different. 'The Ultimate Collection' is a three-CD boxed set

See also HIGH NUMBERS; Pete TOWNSHEND; Roger DALTREY

WHO DA FUNK

US, male production duo and female vocalist (Singles: 8 weeks) pos/wks

26 Oct 02 **SHINY DISCO BALLS (import)** *White Label SSA 03* [1] 69 1
2 Nov 02 **SHINY DISCO BALLS** *Cream CREAM 22CD* [1] 15 5
15 Feb 03 **STING ME RED (YOU THINK YOU'RE SO CLEVER)** *Cream CREAM 19CDS* [2] 32 2

[1] Who Da Funk featuring Jessica Eve [2] Who Da Funk featuring Terra Deva

WHODINI *US, male rap / DJ duo (Singles: 10 weeks)* pos/wks

25 Dec 82	**MAGIC'S WAND** *Jive JIVE 28*	47	6
17 Mar 84	**MAGIC'S WAND (THE WHODINI ELECTRIC EP)** *Jive JIVE 61*	63	4

Tracks on The Whodini Electric EP: Jive Magic Wand / Nasty Lady / Rap Machine / The Haunted House of Rock

WHOOLIGANZ
US, male rap duo (Singles: 2 weeks) pos/wks

13 Aug 94	**PUT YOUR HANDZ UP** *Positiva CDTIV 17*	53	2

WHOOSH *UK, male production trio (Singles: 1 week)* pos/wks

13 Sep 97	**WHOOSH** *Wonderboy WBOYD 006*	72	1

WHYCLIFFE *UK, male vocalist (Singles: 2 weeks)* pos/wks

20 Nov 93	**HEAVEN** *MCA MCSTD 1944*	56	1
2 Apr 94	**ONE MORE TIME** *MCA MCSTD 1955*	72	1

WIDEBOYS featuring Dennis G
UK, male production duo and male vocalist (Singles: 6 weeks) pos/wks

27 Oct 01	**SAMBUCA** *Locked On / 679 Recordings 679L 002CD*	15	6

Jane WIEDLIN
US, female vocalist (Singles: 14 weeks, Albums: 3 weeks) pos/wks

6 Aug 88	**RUSH HOUR** *Manhattan MT 36*	12	11
29 Oct 88	**INSIDE A DREAM** *Manhattan MT 55*	64	3
24 Sep 88	**FUR** *Manhattan MTL 1029*	48	3

See also GO-GO'S

WIGAN'S CHOSEN FEW *Canada, male vocal / instrumental group and UK, crowd chants (Singles: 11 weeks)* pos/wks

18 Jan 75 ●	**FOOTSEE** *Pye Disco Demand DDS 111*	9	11

WIGAN'S OVATION
UK, male vocal / instrumental group (Singles: 19 weeks) pos/wks

15 Mar 75	**SKIING IN THE SNOW** *Spark SRL 1122*	12	10
28 Jun 75	**PER-SO-NAL-LY** *Spark SRL 1129*	38	6
29 Nov 75	**SUPER LOVE** *Spark SRL 1133*	41	3

WILCO *US, male vocal / instrumental group (Singles: 1 week, Albums: 6 weeks)* pos/wks

17 Apr 99	**CAN'T STAND IT** *Reprise W 475CD1*	67	1
11 Jul 98	**MERMAID AVENUE** *Elektra 7559622042* [1]	34	2
20 Mar 99	**SUMMERTEETH** *Reprise 9362472822*	38	2
10 Jun 00	**MERMAID AVENUE – VOL. 2** *Elektra 7559625222* [1]	61	1
4 May 02	**YANKEE HOTEL FOXTROT** *Nonesuch 7559796692*	40	1

[1] Billy Bragg and Wilco

Jack WILD
UK, male actor / vocalist (Singles: 2 weeks) pos/wks

2 May 70	**SOME BEAUTIFUL** *Capitol CL 15635*	46	2

WILD CHERRY
US, male vocal / instrumental group (Singles: 11 weeks) pos/wks

9 Oct 76 ●	**PLAY THAT FUNKY MUSIC** *Epic EPC 4593* ▲	7	11

WILD COLOUR
UK, male / female vocal / instrumental group (Singles: 2 weeks) pos/wks

14 Oct 95	**DREAMS** *Perfecto PERF 105CD*	25	2

WILD HORSES
UK, male vocal / instrumental group (Albums: 4 weeks) pos/wks

26 Apr 80	**WILD HORSES** *EMI EMC 3324*	38	4

WILD PAIR – *See Paula ABDUL*

WILD WEEKEND
UK, male vocal / instrumental group (Singles: 2 weeks) pos/wks

29 Apr 89	**BREAKIN' UP** *Parlophone R 6204*	74	1
5 May 90	**WHO'S AFRAID OF THE BIG BAD LOVE?** *Parlophone R 6249*	70	1

WILDCHILD
UK, male producer – Roger McKenzie (Singles: 20 weeks) pos/wks

22 Apr 95	**LEGENDS OF THE DARK BLACK PART 2** *Hi-Life HICD 9*	34	3
21 Oct 95	**RENEGADE MASTER (re-issue)** *Hi-Life 5771312*	11	4
23 Nov 96	**JUMP TO MY BEAT** *Hi-Life 5757372*	30	2
17 Jan 98 ●	**RENEGADE MASTER '98 (re-mix)** *Hi-Life 5692792*	3	10
25 Apr 98	**BAD BOY** *Polydor 5716072* [1]	38	1

[1] Wildchild featuring Jomalski

Although titled differently, first two hits are identical

Eugene WILDE *US, male vocalist – Ron Broomfield (Singles: 15 weeks, Albums: 4 weeks)* pos/wks

13 Oct 84	**GOTTA GET YOU HOME TONIGHT** *Fourth & Broadway BRW 15*	18	9
2 Feb 85	**PERSONALITY** *Fourth & Broadway BRW 18*	34	6
8 Dec 84	**EUGENE WILDE** *Fourth & Broadway BRLP 502*	67	4

'Personality' was coupled with 'Let Her Feel It' by Simplicious, which also features Wilde's vocals

Kim WILDE (212 Top 500)
Most charted British female vocalist in the 1980s, b. Kim Smith, 18 Nov 1960, London. Neither Kim nor her father, rock 'n' roll star Marty Wilde, managed a UK No.1, but Kim did top the US chart. Returned with major Continental hit, duetting with Nena, 'Any place, Any time, Anywhere' in 2003 and is now a celebrity gardener (Singles: 194 weeks, Albums: 88 weeks) pos/wks

21 Feb 81 ●	**KIDS IN AMERICA** *RAK 327*	2	13
9 May 81 ●	**CHEQUERED LOVE** *RAK 330*	4	9
1 Aug 81	**WATER ON GLASS / BOYS** *RAK 334*	11	8
14 Nov 81	**CAMBODIA** *RAK 336*	12	12
17 Apr 82	**VIEW FROM A BRIDGE** *RAK 342*	16	7
16 Oct 82	**CHILD COME AWAY** *RAK 352*	43	4
30 Jul 83	**LOVE BLONDE** *RAK 360*	23	8
12 Nov 83	**DANCING IN THE DARK** *RAK 365*	67	2
13 Oct 84	**THE SECOND TIME** *MCA KIM 1*	29	6
8 Dec 84	**THE TOUCH** *MCA KIM 2*	56	3
27 Apr 85	**RAGE TO LOVE** *MCA KIM 3*	19	8
25 Oct 86 ●	**YOU KEEP ME HANGIN' ON** *MCA KIM 4* ▲	2	14
4 Apr 87 ●	**ANOTHER STEP (CLOSER TO YOU)** *MCA KIM 5* [1]	6	11
8 Aug 87	**SAY YOU REALLY WANT ME** *MCA KIM 6*	29	5
5 Dec 87 ●	**ROCKIN' AROUND THE CHRISTMAS TREE** *10 TEN 2* [2]	3	7
14 May 88	**HEY MISTER HEARTACHE** *MCA KIM 7*	31	5
16 Jul 88 ●	**YOU CAME** *MCA KIM 8*	3	11
1 Oct 88 ●	**NEVER TRUST A STRANGER** *MCA KIM 9*	7	9
3 Dec 88 ●	**FOUR LETTER WORD** *MCA KIM 10*	6	12
4 Mar 89	**LOVE IN THE NATURAL WAY** *MCA KIM 11*	32	6
14 Apr 90	**IT'S HERE** *MCA KIM 12*	42	4
16 Jun 90	**TIME** *MCA KIM 13*	71	3
15 Dec 90	**I CAN'T SAY GOODBYE** *MCA KIM 14*	51	3
2 May 92	**LOVE IS HOLY** *MCA KIM 15*	16	6
27 Jun 92	**HEART OVER MIND** *MCA KIM 16*	34	3
12 Sep 92	**WHO DO YOU THINK YOU ARE** *MCA KIM 17*	49	3
10 Jul 93	**IF I CAN'T HAVE YOU** *MCA KIMTD 18*	12	8
13 Nov 93	**IN MY LIFE** *MCA KIMTD 19*	54	1
14 Oct 95	**BREAKIN' AWAY** *MCA KIMTD 21*	43	2
10 Feb 96	**THIS I SWEAR** *MCA KIMTD 22*	46	1
11 Jul 81 ●	**KIM WILDE** *RAK SRAK 544*	3	14
22 May 82	**SELECT** *RAK SRAK 548*	19	11
26 Nov 83	**CATCH AS CATCH CAN** *RAK SRAK 165408*	90	1
17 Nov 84	**TEASES AND DARES** *MCA MCF 3250*	66	2
18 May 85	**THE VERY BEST OF KIM WILDE** *RAK WILDE 1*	78	4
15 Nov 86	**ANOTHER STEP** *MCA MCF 3339*	73	5
25 Jun 88 ●	**CLOSE** *MCA MCG 6030*	8	38
26 May 90	**LOVE MOVES** *MCA MCG 6088*	37	3

			pos	wks
30 May 92		**LOVE IS** *MCA MCAD 10625*	21	3
25 Sep 93		**THE SINGLES COLLECTION 1981-1993** *MCA MCD 10921*	11	7

[1] Kim Wilde and Junior [2] Mel and Kim

Mel was Mel Smith 'Another Step' changed label number to MCA KIML 1 during its chart run

Marty WILDE *UK, male vocalist (Singles: 117 weeks)*

			pos	wks
11 Jul 58	●	**ENDLESS SLEEP** *Philips PB 835*	4	14
6 Mar 59	●	**DONNA (re)** *Philips PB 902*	3	18
5 Jun 59	●	**A TEENAGER IN LOVE** *Philips PB 926*	2	17
25 Sep 59	●	**SEA OF LOVE** *Philips PB 959*	3	12
11 Dec 59	●	**BAD BOY** *Philips PB 972*	7	8
10 Mar 60		**JOHNNY ROCCO** *Philips PB 1002*	30	4
19 May 60		**THE FIGHT** *Philips PB 1022*	47	1
22 Dec 60		**LITTLE GIRL** *Philips PB 1078*	16	9
26 Jan 61	●	**RUBBER BALL** *Philips PB 1101*	9	9
27 Jul 61		**HIDE AND SEEK** *Philips PB 1161*	47	2
9 Nov 61		**TOMORROW'S CLOWN** *Philips PB 1191*	33	5
24 May 62		**JEZEBEL** *Philips PB 1240*	19	11
25 Oct 62		**EVER SINCE YOU SAID GOODBYE** *Philips 326546 BF*	31	7

Roxanne WILDE – *See DT8 featuring Roxanne WILDE*

Matthew WILDER *US, male vocalist (Singles: 11 weeks)*

			pos	wks
21 Jan 84	●	**BREAK MY STRIDE** *Epic A 3908*	4	11

WILDFLOWER – *See APHRODITE featuring WILDFLOWER*

WILDHEARTS *UK, male vocal / instrumental group (Singles: 32 weeks, Albums: 9 weeks)*

			pos	wks
20 Nov 93		**TV TAN** *Bronze YZ 784CD*	53	2
19 Feb 94		**CAFFEINE BOMB** *Bronze YZ 794CD*	31	3
9 Jul 94		**SUCKERPUNCH** *Bronze YZ 828CD*	38	2
28 Jan 95		**IF LIFE IS LIKE A LOVE BANK I WANT AN OVERDRAFT / GEORDIE IN WONDERLAND** *East West YZ 874CD*	31	3
6 May 95		**I WANNA GO WHERE THE PEOPLE GO** *East West YZ 923CD*	16	3
29 Jul 95		**JUST IN LUST** *East West YZ 967CD*	28	2
20 Apr 96		**SICK OF DRUGS** *Round WILD 1CD*	14	3
29 Jun 96		**RED LIGHT – GREEN LIGHT (EP)** *Round WILD 2CD*	30	2
16 Aug 97		**ANTHEM** *Mushroom MUSH 6CD*	21	2
18 Oct 97		**URGE** *Mushroom MUSH 14CD*	26	2
12 Oct 02		**VANILLA RADIO** *Round / Snapper SMACD 048S*	26	2
1 Feb 03		**STORMY IN THE NORTH – KARMA IN THE SOUTH** *Round SMASCD 049*	17	2
24 May 03		**SO INTO YOU** *Gut / Round CDGUT 49*	22	2
15 Nov 03		**TOP OF THE WORLD** *Gut CDGUT 54*	26	2
11 Sep 93		**EARTH VS THE WILDHEARTS** *East West 4509932871*	46	1
3 Jun 95	●	**P.H.U.Q.** *East West 0630104372*	6	4
1 Jun 96		**FISHING FOR LUCKIES** *Round 630148552*	16	2
8 Nov 97		**ENDLESS NAMELESS** *Mushroom MUSH 13CD*	41	1
6 Sep 03		**THE WILDHEARTS MUST BE DESTROYED!** *Gut GUTCD 25*	54	1

Tracks on Red Light – Green Light (EP): Red Light – Green Light / Got It On Tuesday / Do Anything / The British All-American Homeboy Crowd

Jonathan WILKES *UK, male vocalist (Singles: 2 weeks)*

			pos	wks
17 Mar 01		**JUST ANOTHER DAY** *Innocent SINCD 25*	24	2

Colm WILKINSON *Ireland, male vocalist (Albums: 6 weeks)*

			pos	wks
10 Jun 89		**STAGE HEROES** *RCA BL 74105*	27	6

Sue WILKINSON *UK, female vocalist (Singles: 8 weeks)*

			pos	wks
2 Aug 80		**YOU GOTTA BE A HUSTLER IF YOU WANNA GET ON** *Cheapskate CHEAP 2*	25	8

WILL TO POWER *US, male / female vocal / instrumental duo – Bob Rosenberg and Suzi Carr (Singles: 18 weeks)*

			pos	wks
7 Jan 89	●	**BABY I LOVE YOUR WAY – FREEBIRD** *Epic 6530947* ▲	6	9
22 Dec 90		**I'M NOT IN LOVE** *Epic 6565377*	29	9

Alyson WILLIAMS *US, female vocalist (Singles: 28 weeks, Albums: 21 weeks)*

			pos	wks
4 Mar 89		**SLEEP TALK** *Def Jam 654656 7*	17	9
6 May 89		**MY LOVE IS SO RAW** *Def Jam 654898 7* [1]	34	5
19 Aug 89	●	**I NEED YOUR LOVIN'** *Def Jam 655143 7*	8	11
18 Nov 89		**I SECOND THAT EMOTION** *Def Jam 655456 7* [2]	44	3
25 Mar 89		**RAW** *Def Jam 463293 1*	29	21

[1] Alyson Williams featuring Nikki D [2] Alyson Williams with Chuck Stanley

Andy WILLIAMS (41 Top 500) *Leading MOR vocalist, who hosted a top-rated 1960s TV series, b. 3 Dec 1928, Iowa, US. He left the noted family act The Williams Brothers in 1951 and had an enviable portfolio of smooth UK and US hit singles and albums in the 1950s and 1960s. Had a surprise 1999 re-entry for 'Music to Watch Girls By' following its use in a TV car commercial (Singles: 238 weeks, Albums: 447 weeks)*

			pos	wks
19 Apr 57	★	**BUTTERFLY (re)** *London HLA 8399*	1	16
21 Jun 57		**I LIKE YOUR KIND OF LOVE** *London HLA 8437*	16	10
14 Jun 62		**STRANGER ON THE SHORE** *CBS AAG 103*	30	10
21 Mar 63	●	**CAN'T GET USED TO LOSING YOU** *CBS AAG 138*	2	18
27 Feb 64		**A FOOL NEVER LEARNS** *CBS AAG 182*	40	4
16 Sep 65	●	**ALMOST THERE** *CBS 201813*	2	17
24 Feb 66		**MAY EACH DAY** *CBS 202042*	19	8
22 Sep 66		**IN THE ARMS OF LOVE** *CBS 202300*	33	7
4 May 67		**MUSIC TO WATCH GIRLS BY** *CBS 2675*	33	6
2 Aug 67		**MORE AND MORE** *CBS 2886*	45	1
13 Mar 68	●	**CAN'T TAKE MY EYES OFF YOU** *CBS 3298*	5	18
7 May 69		**HAPPY HEART (re)** *CBS 4062*	19	10
14 Mar 70	●	**CAN'T HELP FALLING IN LOVE** *CBS 4818*	3	17
1 Aug 70		**IT'S SO EASY (re)** *CBS 5113*	13	14
21 Nov 70	●	**HOME LOVIN' MAN** *CBS 5267*	7	12
20 Mar 71	●	**(WHERE DO I BEGIN) LOVE STORY (re)** *CBS 7020*	4	18
5 Aug 72		**LOVE THEME FROM 'THE GODFATHER' (SPEAK SOFTLY LOVE) (2re)** *CBS 8166*	42	9
8 Dec 73	●	**SOLITAIRE** *CBS 1824*	4	18
18 May 74		**GETTING OVER YOU** *CBS 2181*	35	5
31 May 75		**YOU LAY SO EASY ON MY MIND** *CBS 3167*	32	7
6 Mar 76		**THE OTHER SIDE OF ME** *CBS 3903*	42	3
27 Mar 99	●	**MUSIC TO WATCH GIRLS BY (re-issue)** *Columbia 6671322*	9	6
29 Jun 02		**CAN'T TAKE MY EYES OFF YOU** *Columbia 6721052* [1]	23	4
26 Jun 65	●	**ALMOST THERE** *CBS BPG 62533*	4	46
7 Aug 65		**CAN'T GET USED TO LOSING YOU** *CBS BPG 62146*	16	1
19 Mar 66		**MAY EACH DAY** *CBS BPG 62658*	11	6
30 Apr 66		**GREAT SONGS FROM MY FAIR LADY** *CBS BPG 62430*	30	1
23 Jul 66		**SHADOW OF YOUR SMILE** *CBS 62633*	24	4
29 Jul 67		**BORN FREE** *CBS SBPG 63027*	22	11
11 May 68	★	**LOVE ANDY** *CBS 63167*	1	22
6 Jul 68	●	**HONEY** *CBS 63311*	4	17
26 Jul 69		**HAPPY HEART** *CBS 63614*	22	9
27 Dec 69		**GET TOGETHER WITH ANDY WILLIAMS** *CBS 63800*	13	12
24 Jan 70		**ANDY WILLIAMS' SOUND OF MUSIC** *CBS 63920*	22	10
11 Apr 70	★	**GREATEST HITS** *CBS 63920*	1	116
20 Jun 70	●	**CAN'T HELP FALLING IN LOVE** *CBS 64067*	7	40
5 Dec 70	●	**ANDY WILLIAMS SHOW** *CBS 64127*	10	6
27 Mar 71	★	**HOME LOVIN' MAN** *CBS 64286* ■	1	26
31 Jul 71		**LOVE STORY** *CBS 64467*	11	11
29 Apr 72		**THE IMPOSSIBLE DREAM** *CBS 67236*	26	3
29 Jul 72		**LOVE THEME FROM 'THE GODFATHER'** *CBS 64869*	11	16
16 Dec 72		**GREATEST HITS VOLUME 2** *CBS 65151*	23	10
22 Dec 73	●	**SOLITAIRE** *CBS 65638*	3	26
15 Jun 74	●	**THE WAY WE WERE** *CBS 80152*	7	11
11 Oct 75		**THE OTHER SIDE OF ME** *CBS 69152*	60	1
28 Jan 78	●	**REFLECTIONS** *CBS 10006*	2	17
27 Oct 84		**GREATEST LOVE CLASSICS** *EMI ANDY 1* [1]	22	10
7 Nov 92		**THE BEST OF ANDY WILLIAMS** *Dino DINCD 50*	51	3
10 Apr 99		**IN THE LOUNGE WITH ... ANDY WILLIAMS** *Columbia 4916182*	39	3
19 Feb 00		**THE VERY BEST OF ANDY WILLIAMS** *Columbia SONYTV 78CD*	27	7
6 Jul 02		**THE ESSENTIAL ANDY WILLIAMS** *Columbia 5084142*	32	2

[1] Andy Williams and Denise Van Outen [1] Andy Williams and the Royal Philharmonic Orchestra

Andy and David WILLIAMS

US, male vocal duo (Singles: 5 weeks)

Date		Title	pos	wks
24 Mar 73		I DON'T KNOW WHY (I JUST DO) *MCA MUS 1183*	37	5

Do not see Andy Williams. This Andy is the nephew of the other Andy

Billy WILLIAMS

US, male vocalist, d. 17 Oct 1972 (Singles: 9 weeks)

Date		Title	pos	wks
2 Aug 57		I'M GONNA SIT RIGHT DOWN AND WRITE MYSELF A LETTER (re) *Vogue Coral Q 72266*	22	9

Danny WILLIAMS

Velvet-voiced, British-based, easy-listening vocalist; b. 7 Jan 1942, South Africa. Johnny Mathis-styled singer who won the UK 'Moon River' battle was first seen on rock 'n' roll TV show 'Drumbeat'. Had US Top 10 hit with 1964 UK flop 'White on White' (Singles: 74 weeks)

Date		Title	pos	wks
25 May 61		WE WILL NEVER BE AS YOUNG AS THIS AGAIN *HMV POP 839*	44	3
6 Jul 61		THE MIRACLE OF YOU *HMV POP 885*	41	8
2 Nov 61	★	MOON RIVER *HMV POP 932*	1	19
18 Jan 62		JEANNIE *HMV POP 968*	14	14
12 Apr 62	●	THE WONDERFUL WORLD OF THE YOUNG *HMV POP 1002*	8	13
5 Jul 62		TEARS *HMV POP 1035*	22	7
28 Feb 63		MY OWN TRUE LOVE *HMV POP 1112*	45	3
30 Jul 77		DANCIN' EASY *Ensign ENY 3*	30	7

Deniece WILLIAMS

US, female vocalist – Deniece Chandler (Singles: 59 weeks, Albums: 23 weeks)

Date		Title	pos	wks
2 Apr 77	★	FREE *CBS 4978*	1	10
30 Jul 77	●	THAT'S WHAT FRIENDS ARE FOR *CBS 5432*	8	11
12 Nov 77		BABY, BABY MY LOVE'S ALL FOR YOU *CBS 5779*	32	5
25 Mar 78	●	TOO MUCH, TOO LITTLE, TOO LATE *CBS 6164* [1] ▲	3	14
29 Jul 78		YOU'RE ALL I NEED TO GET BY *CBS 6483* [1]	45	6
5 May 84	●	LET'S HEAR IT FOR THE BOY (re) *CBS A 4319* ▲	2	13
21 May 77		THIS IS NIECEY *CBS 81869*	31	12
26 Aug 78		THAT'S WHAT FRIENDS ARE FOR *CBS 86068* [1]	16	11

[1] Johnny Mathis and Deniece Williams [1] Johnny Mathis and Deniece Williams

Diana WILLIAMS

US, female vocalist (Singles: 3 weeks)

Date		Title	pos	wks
25 Jul 81		TEDDY BEAR'S LAST RIDE *Capitol CL 207*	54	3

Don WILLIAMS

454 Top 500 *Easy-on-the-ear country singer / songwriter and guitarist, b. 27 May 1939, Floydada, Texas. Member of Pozo-Seco Singers (1964-71), who amassed 17 US country No.1s between 1974 and 1986 and was named Country Music Association Vocalist of the Year in 1978 (Singles: 16 weeks, Albums: 136 weeks)*

Date		Title	pos	wks
19 Jun 76		I RECALL A GYPSY WOMAN *ABC 4098*	13	10
23 Oct 76		YOU'RE MY BEST FRIEND *ABC 4144*	35	6
10 Jul 76		GREATEST HITS VOLUME 1 *ABC ABCL 5147*	29	15
19 Feb 77		VISIONS *ABC ABCL 5200*	13	20
15 Oct 77		COUNTRY BOY *ABC ABCL 5233*	27	5
5 Aug 78	●	IMAGES *K-Tel NE 1033*	2	38
5 Aug 78		YOU'RE MY BEST FRIEND *ABC ABCD 5127*	58	1
4 Nov 78		EXPRESSIONS *ABC ABCL 5253*	28	8
22 Sep 79		NEW HORIZONS *K-Tel NE 1048*	29	12
15 Dec 79		PORTRAIT *MCA MCS 3045*	58	4
6 Sep 80		I BELIEVE IN YOU *MCA MCF 3077*	36	5
18 Jul 81		ESPECIALLY FOR YOU *MCA MCF 3114*	33	7
17 Apr 82		LISTEN TO THE RADIO *MCA MCF 3135*	69	3
23 Apr 83		YELLOW MOON *MCA MCF 3159*	52	1
15 Oct 83		LOVE STORIES *K-Tel NE 1252*	22	13
26 May 84		CAFE CAROLINA *MCA MCF 3225*	65	4

Eric WILLIAMS – *See QUEEN PEN; 2PAC*

Freedom WILLIAMS

US, male rapper (Singles: 31 weeks)

Date		Title	pos	wks
15 Dec 90	●	GONNA MAKE YOU SWEAT (EVERYBODY DANCE NOW) *CBS 6564540* [1] ▲	3	12
30 Mar 91		HERE WE GO *Columbia 6567537* [1]	20	7
6 Jul 91	●	THINGS THAT MAKE YOU GO HMMM... *Columbia 6566907* [1]	4	11
5 Jun 93		VOICE OF FREEDOM *Columbia 6593342*	62	1

[1] C & C Music Factory (featuring Freedom Williams)

Geoffrey WILLIAMS

UK, male vocalist (Singles: 8 weeks)

Date		Title	pos	wks
11 Apr 92		IT'S NOT A LOVE THING *EMI EM 228*	63	2
22 Aug 92		SUMMER BREEZE *EMI EM 245*	56	3
18 Jan 97		DRIVE *Hands On CDHOR 11*	52	2
19 Apr 97		SEX LIFE *Hands On CDHOR 12*	71	1

Iris WILLIAMS

UK, female vocalist (Singles: 8 weeks, Albums: 4 weeks)

Date		Title	pos	wks
27 Oct 79		HE WAS BEAUTIFUL (CAVATINA) (THE THEME FROM 'THE DEER HUNTER') *Columbia DB 9070*	18	8
22 Dec 79		HE WAS BEAUTIFUL *Columbia SCX 6627*	69	4

James WILLIAMS – *See D TRAIN; Bob SINCLAR*

John WILLIAMS

UK, male instrumentalist – guitar (Singles: 11 weeks, Albums: 65 weeks)

Date		Title	pos	wks
19 May 79		CAVATINA *Cube BUG 80*	13	11
3 Oct 70		PLAYS SPANISH MUSIC *CBS 72860*	46	1
8 Feb 76		RODRIGO: CONCERTO DE ARANJUEZ *CBS 79369* [1]	20	9
7 Jan 78		BEST OF FRIENDS *RCA RS 1094* [2]	18	22
17 Jun 78		TRAVELLING *Cube HIFLY 27*	23	5
30 Jun 79	●	BRIDGES *Lotus WH 5015*	5	22
4 Aug 79		CAVATINA *Cube HIFLY 32*	64	3
26 Oct 96		JOHN WILLIAMS PLAYS THE MOVIES *Sony Classical S2K 62784*	54	3

[1] John Williams with the English Chamber Orchestra conducted by Daniel Barenboim [2] Cleo Laine and John Williams

'Star Wars – The Phantom Menace' and 'Star Wars Episode II – Attack of the Clones' are performed by the London Symphony Orchestra

John WILLIAMS

US, male orchestra leader (Singles: 12 weeks, Albums: 46 weeks)

Date		Title	pos	wks
18 Dec 82		THEME FROM 'E.T.' (THE EXTRA-TERRESTRIAL) *MCA 800*	17	10
14 Aug 93		THEME FROM 'JURASSIC PARK' *MCA MCSTD 1927*	45	2
25 Dec 82		E.T. – THE EXTRATERRESTRIAL (FILM SOUNDTRACK) *MCA MCF 3160*	47	10
31 Jul 93		JURASSIC PARK (FILM SOUNDTRACK) *MCA MCD 10859*	42	5
2 Apr 94		SCHINDLER'S LIST (FILM SOUNDTRACK) *MCA MCD 10969*	59	2
15 May 99	●	STAR WARS – THE PHANTOM MENACE (FILM SOUNDTRACK) *Sony Classical SK 61816*	8	17
10 Nov 01		HARRY POTTER AND THE PHILOSOPHER'S STONE (FILM SOUNDTRACK) *Atlantic 7567930865*	19	7
11 May 02		STAR WARS EPISODE II – ATTACK OF THE CLONES (FILM SOUNDTRACK) *Sony Classical SK 89932*	15	5

Kathryn WILLIAMS

UK, female vocalist (Albums: 3 weeks)

Date		Title	pos	wks
15 Sep 01		LITTLE BLACK NUMBERS *East West 8573899242*	70	1
12 Oct 02		OLD LOW LIGHT *East West 0927475522*	56	2

Kenny WILLIAMS

US, male vocalist (Singles: 7 weeks)

Date		Title	pos	wks
19 Nov 77		(YOU'RE) FABULOUS BABE *Decca FR 13731*	35	7

Larry WILLIAMS

US, male vocalist / instrumentalist – keyboards, d. 7 Jan 1980 (Singles: 18 weeks)

Date		Title	pos	wks
20 Sep 57		SHORT FAT FANNIE *London HLN 8472*	21	8
17 Jan 58		BONY MORONIE *London HLU 8532*	11	10

Lenny WILLIAMS

US, male vocalist (Singles: 7 weeks)

Date		Title	pos	wks
5 Nov 77		SHOO DOO FU FU OOH! *ABC 4194*	38	4
16 Sep 78		YOU GOT ME BURNING *ABC 4228*	67	3

Lucinda WILLIAMS

US, female vocalist / instrumentalist – guitar (Albums: 2 weeks)

Date		Title	pos	wks
16 Jun 01		ESSENCE *Lost Highway 1701972*	63	1
19 Apr 03		WORLD WITHOUT TEARS *Lost Highway 1703552*	48	1

Mark WILLIAMS – *See Karen BODDINGTON and Mark WILLIAMS*

Mason WILLIAMS
US, male instrumentalist – guitar (Singles: 13 weeks) pos/wks

28 Aug 68 ● **CLASSICAL GAS** *Warner Bros. WB 7190* 9 13

Maurice WILLIAMS and the ZODIACS
US, male vocal group (Singles: 9 weeks) pos/wks

5 Jan 61 **STAY** *Top Rank JAR 526* ▲ 14 9

Melanie WILLIAMS *UK, female vocalist (Singles: 21 weeks)* pos/wks

10 Apr 93 ● **AIN'T NO LOVE (AIN'T NO USE)** *Rob's CDROB 9* [1] 3 11
9 Apr 94 **ALL CRIED OUT** *Columbia 6601872* 60 2
11 Jun 94 **EVERYDAY THANG** *Columbia 6604712* 38 3
17 Sep 94 **NOT ENOUGH?** *Columbia 6607752* 65 1
18 Feb 95 **YOU ARE EVERYTHING** *Columbia 6611755* [2] 28 4

[1] Sub Sub featuring Melanie Williams [2] Melanie Williams and Joe Roberts

Pharrell WILLIAMS – *See PHARRELL, N*E*R*D, NEPTUNES*

Robbie WILLIAMS (50 Top 500)
Former Take That teen idol who became a multi-award winning vocalist / songwriter and multi-millionaire after a UK record-breaking 2002 deal with EMI reportedly worth up to £80m, b. 13 Feb 1974, Stoke-on-Trent, UK. This energetic and humorous showman has won more Brits (14) than any other artist, has amassed 20 solo Top 20 hits and attracted record-breaking crowds of 375,000 to Knebworth in 2003. Best-selling single 'Angels' 828,000 (Singles: 265 weeks, Albums: 382 weeks) pos/wks

10 Aug 96 ● **FREEDOM (re)** *Chrysalis CDFREE 1* 2 14
26 Apr 97 ● **OLD BEFORE I DIE (2re)** *Chrysalis CDCHS 5055* 2 11
26 Jul 97 ● **LAZY DAYS** *Chrysalis CDCHS 5063* 8 5
27 Sep 97 **SOUTH OF THE BORDER** *Chrysalis CDCHS 5068* 14 4
13 Dec 97 ● **ANGELS (4re)** *Chrysalis CDCHS 5072* 4 27
28 Mar 98 ● **LET ME ENTERTAIN YOU** *Chrysalis CDCHS 5080* 3 12
19 Sep 98 ★ **MILLENNIUM (re)** *Chrysalis CDCHS 5099* ■ 1 21
12 Dec 98 ● **NO REGRETS** *Chrysalis CDCHS 5100* 4 13
27 Mar 99 ● **STRONG** *Chrysalis CDCHS 5107* 4 9
20 Nov 99 ★ **SHE'S THE ONE / IT'S ONLY US (re)** *Chrysalis CDCHS 5112* ■ 1 20
12 Aug 00 ★ **ROCK DJ (re)** *Chrysalis CDCHS 5118* ■ 1 20
21 Oct 00 ● **KIDS (2re)** *Chrysalis CHCHS 5119* [1] 2 19
23 Dec 00 ● **SUPREME** *Chrysalis CDCHS 5120* 4 10
21 Mar 01 ● **LET LOVE BE YOUR ENERGY (re)** *Chrysalis CDCHS 5124* 10 11
21 Jul 01 ★ **ETERNITY / THE ROAD TO MANDALAY** *Chrysalis CDCHS 5126* ■ 1 16
22 Dec 01 ★ **SOMETHIN' STUPID** *Chrysalis CDCHS 5132* [2] ■ 1 12
14 Dec 02 ● **FEEL (re)** *Chrysalis CDCHS 5150* 4 15
26 Apr 03 ● **COME UNDONE** *Chrysalis CDCHS 5151* 4 11
9 Aug 03 ● **SOMETHING BEAUTIFUL** *Chrysalis CDCHS 5152* 3 8
15 Nov 03 ● **SEXED UP** *Chrysalis CDCHS 5153* ....10 7+
11 Oct 97 ★ **LIFE THRU A LENS** *Chrysalis CDCHR 6127* 1 123
7 Nov 98 ★ **I'VE BEEN EXPECTING YOU** *Chrysalis 4978372* ■ 1 98
9 Sep 00 ★ **SING WHEN YOU'RE WINNING** *Chrysalis 5281252* ■ 1 62
1 Dec 01 ★ **SWING WHEN YOU'RE WINNING** *Chrysalis 5368262* ■ 1 37
30 Nov 02 ★ **ESCAPOLOGY** *EMI 5439942* ■ 1 50
11 Oct 03 ● **LIVE AT KNEBWORTH** *Chrysalis 5946372* ....2 12+

[1] Robbie Williams / Kylie Minogue [2] Robbie Williams and Nicole Kidman

'Angels' re-entered the chart in Jan, Feb and Mar 1999 and again in Jan 2000. 'Millennium' re-entered in Jan 2000

Saul WILLIAMS – *See KRUST*

Vanessa WILLIAMS
US, female vocalist (Singles: 24 weeks, Albums: 4 weeks) pos/wks

20 Aug 88 **THE RIGHT STUFF** *Wing WING 3* 71 1
25 Mar 89 **DREAMIN'** *Wing WING 4* 74 2
19 Aug 89 **THE RIGHT STUFF (re-mix)** *Wing WINR 3* 62 2
21 Mar 92 ● **SAVE THE BEST FOR LAST** *Polydor PO 192* ▲ 3 11
8 Apr 95 **THE SWEETEST DAYS** *Mercury MERCD 422* 41 2
8 Jul 95 **THE WAY THAT YOU LOVE** *Mercury MERCD 439* 52 1
18 Sep 95 **COLOURS OF THE WIND** *Walt Disney WD 7677CD* 21 5
25 Apr 92 **THE COMFORT ZONE** *Polydor 5112672* 24 4

Vesta WILLIAMS *US, female vocalist (Singles: 13 weeks)* pos/wks

20 Dec 86 **ONCE BITTEN TWICE SHY** *A&M AM 362* 14 13

Wendell WILLIAMS *US, male rapper (Singles: 6 weeks)* pos/wks

6 Oct 90 **EVERYBODY (RAP)** *Deconstruction PB 44701* [1] 30 4
18 May 91 **SO GROOVY** *Deconstruction PB 44567* 74 2

[1] Criminal Element Orchestra and Wendell Williams

Wendy O WILLIAMS
US, female vocalist, d. 6 Apr 1998 (Albums: 1 week) pos/wks

30 Jun 84 **W.O.W.** *Music for Nations MFN 24* 100 1

See also PLASMATICS

Ann WILLIAMSON *UK, female vocalist (Albums: 13 weeks)* pos/wks

15 Feb 86 **PRECIOUS MEMORIES** *Emerald Gem ERTV 1* 16 9
6 Feb 88 **COUNT YOUR BLESSINGS** *Emerald Gem ERTV 2* 58 4

Sonny Boy WILLIAMSON *US male vocalist / instrumentalist – Rice Miller – guitar, d. 25 May 1965 (Albums: 1 week)* pos/wks

20 Jun 64 **DOWN AND OUT BLUES** *Pye NPL 28036* 20 1

WILLING SINNERS – *See Marc ALMOND*

Bruce WILLIS
US, male actor / vocalist (Singles: 30 weeks, Albums: 28 weeks) pos/wks

7 Mar 87 ● **RESPECT YOURSELF** *Motown ZB 41117* 7 10
30 May 87 ● **UNDER THE BOARDWALK** *Motown ZB 41349* 2 15
12 Sep 87 **SECRET AGENT MAN – JAMES BOND IS BACK** *Motown ZB 41437* 43 4
23 Jan 88 **COMIN' RIGHT UP** *Motown ZB 41453* 73 1
18 Apr 87 ● **THE RETURN OF BRUNO** *Motown ZL 72571* 4 28

Chris WILLIS – *See David GUETTA featuring Chris WILLIS*

Chill WILLS – *See LAUREL and HARDY with the AVALON BOYS featuring Chill WILLS*

Viola WILLS
US, female vocalist (Singles: 16 weeks) pos/wks

6 Oct 79 ● **GONNA GET ALONG WITHOUT YOU NOW** *Ariola / Hansa AHA 546* 8 10
15 Mar 86 **BOTH SIDES NOW / DARE TO DREAM** *Streetwave KHAN 66* ..35 6

Maria WILLSON *UK, female vocalist (Singles: 3 weeks)* pos/wks

9 Aug 03 **CHOOZA LOOZA** *Telstar CDSTAS 3343* 29 2
1 Nov 03 **MR ALIBI** *Telstar CDSTAS 3355* 43 1

Al WILSON *US, male vocalist (Singles: 5 weeks)* pos/wks

23 Aug 75 **THE SNAKE** *Bell 1436* 41 5

Brian WILSON *US, male vocalist / producer / instrumentalist – keyboards (Albums: 3 weeks)* pos/wks

16 Sep 95 **I JUST WASN'T MADE FOR THESE TIMES** *MCA MCD 11270* 59 1
27 Jun 98 **IMAGINATION** *Giant 74321573032* 30 2

See also BEACH BOYS

Charlie WILSON – *See GAP BAND; SNOOP DOGG*

Dooley WILSON
US, male vocalist, d. 30 May 1953 (Singles: 9 weeks) pos/wks

3 Dec 77 **AS TIME GOES BY** *United Artists UP 36331* 15 9

Disc has credit: 'With the voices of Humphrey Bogart and Ingrid Bergman'

Jackie WILSON
US, male vocalist, d. 21 Jan 1984 (Singles: 97 weeks) pos/wks

15 Nov 57 ● **REET PETITE (THE SWEETEST GIRL IN TOWN)** *Coral Q 72290* ..6 14

14 Mar 58 **TO BE LOVED (2re)** *Coral Q 72306* 23 8
15 Sep 60 **(YOU WERE MADE FOR) ALL MY LOVE (re)** *Coral Q 72407* 33 7
22 Dec 60 **ALONE AT LAST** *Coral Q 72412* 50 1
14 May 69 **(YOUR LOVE KEEPS LIFTING ME) HIGHER AND HIGHER** *MCA BAG 2* 11 11
29 Jul 72 ● **I GET THE SWEETEST FEELING** *MCA MU 1160* 9 13
3 May 75 **I GET THE SWEETEST FEELING / (YOUR LOVE KEEPS LIFTING ME) HIGHER AND HIGHER (re-issue)** *Brunswick BR 18* 25 8
29 Nov 86 ★ **REET PETITE (THE SWEETEST GIRL IN TOWN) (re-issue)** *SMP SKM 3* 1 17
28 Feb 87 ● **I GET THE SWEETEST FEELING (2nd re-issue)** *SMP SKM 1* 3 11
4 Jul 87 **(YOUR LOVE KEEPS LIFTING ME) HIGHER AND HIGHER (2nd re-issue)** *SMP SKM 10* 15 7

'Higher and Higher' was not listed together with 'I Get the Sweetest Feeling' on Brunswick until 17 May 1975

Mari WILSON

UK, female vocalist (Singles: 34 weeks, Albums: 9 weeks) pos/wks

6 Mar 82 **BEAT THE BEAT** *Compact PINK 2* 59 3
8 May 82 **BABY IT'S TRUE** *Compact PINK 3* 42 6
11 Sep 82 ● **JUST WHAT I ALWAYS WANTED** *Compact PINK 4* 8 10
13 Nov 82 **(BEWARE) BOYFRIEND** *Compact PINK 5* 51 4
19 Mar 83 **CRY ME A RIVER** *Compact PINK 6* 27 7
11 Jun 83 **WONDERFUL** *Compact PINK 7* [1] 47 4
26 Feb 83 **SHOW PEOPLE** *Compact COMP 2* [1] 24 9

[1] Mari Wilson and the Wilsations [1] Mari Wilson and the Wilsations

Meri WILSON

US, female vocalist, d. 28 Dec 2002 (Singles: 10 weeks) pos/wks

27 Aug 77 ● **TELEPHONE MAN** *Pye International 7N 25747* 6 10

Mike 'Hitman' WILSON *US, male producer (Singles: 1 week)* pos/wks

22 Sep 90 **ANOTHER SLEEPLESS NIGHT** *Arista 113506* 74 1

Precious WILSON – *See ERUPTION; MESSIAH*

Ray WILSON – *See STILTSKIN; Armin VAN BUUREN featuring Ray WILSON*

Tom WILSON *UK, male producer (Singles: 4 weeks)* pos/wks

2 Dec 95 **TECHNOCAT** *Pukka CDPUKKA 4* [1] 33 3
16 Mar 96 **LET YOUR BODY GO** *Clubscene DCSRT 050* 60 1

[1] Technocat featuring Tom Wilson

Victoria WILSON JAMES *US, female vocalist (Singles: 1 week)* pos/wks

9 Aug 97 **REACH 4 THE MELODY** *Sony S3 VWJCD1* 72 1

WILSON PHILLIPS

US, female vocal group (Singles: 33 weeks, Albums: 38 weeks) pos/wks

26 May 90 ● **HOLD ON** *SBK SBK 6* ▲ 6 12
18 Aug 90 **RELEASE ME** *SBK SBK 11* ▲ 36 5
10 Nov 90 **IMPULSIVE** *SBK SBK 16* 42 3
11 May 91 **YOU'RE IN LOVE** *SBK SBK 25* ▲ 29 5
23 May 92 **YOU WON'T SEE ME CRY** *SBK SBK 34* 18 5
22 Aug 92 **GIVE IT UP** *SBK SBK 36* 36 3
30 Jun 90 ● **WILSON PHILLIPS** *SBK SBKLP 5* 7 32
13 Jun 92 ● **SHADOWS AND LIGHT** *SBK SBKCD 18* 6 6

WILT *Ireland, male vocal / instrumental group (Singles: 3 weeks)* pos/wks

8 Apr 00 **RADIO DISCO** *Mushroom MUSH 71CDS* 56 1
8 Jul 00 **OPEN ARMS** *Mushroom MUSH 75CDS* 59 1
13 Jul 02 **DISTORTION** *Mushroom MUSH 103CDS* 66 1

Chris WILTSHIRE – *See CLASS ACTION featuring Chris WILTSHIRE*

WIMBLEDON CHORAL SOCIETY

UK, choral group (Singles: 8 weeks) pos/wks

4 Jul 98 **WORLD CUP '98 – PAVANE** *Telstar CDSTAS 2979* 20 5
12 Dec 98 **IF – READ TO FAURÉ'S 'PAVANE'** *BBC Worldwide WMSS60062* [1] 45 3

[1] Des Lynam featuring Wimbledon Choral Society

WIN *UK, male vocal / instrumental group (Singles: 3 weeks, Albums: 1 week)* pos/wks

4 Apr 87 **SUPER POPOID GROOVE** *Swamplands LON 128* 63 3
25 Apr 87 **UH! TEARS BABY** *Swampland LONLP 31* 51 1

WINANS *US, male vocal group (Singles: 1 week)* pos/wks

30 Nov 85 **LET MY PEOPLE GO (PART 1)** *Qwest W 8874* 71 1

BeBe WINANS – *See ETERNAL*

CeCe WINANS – *See Whitney HOUSTON*

Mario WINANS – *See PUFF DADDY*

WINCHESTER CATHEDRAL CHOIR – *See Andrew LLOYD WEBBER*

WINDJAMMER *US, male vocal / instrumental group (Singles: 12 weeks, Albums: 1 week)* pos/wks

30 Jun 84 **TOSSING AND TURNING** *MCA MCA 897* 18 12
25 Aug 84 **WINDJAMMER II** *MCA MCF 3231* 82 1

Rose WINDROSS – *See SOUL II SOUL*

Barbara WINDSOR

UK, female actor / vocalist (Singles: 2 weeks, Albums: 2 weeks) pos/wks

24 Apr 99 **THE MORE I SEE YOU** *Telstar CDSTAS 3049* [1] 46 2
3 Apr 99 **YOU'VE GOT A FRIEND** *Telstar TV TTVCD 3034* 45 2

[1] Barbara Windsor and Mike Reid

Amy WINEHOUSE *UK, female vocalist / instrumentalist – guitar (Singles: 1 week, Albums: 1 week)* pos/wks

18 Oct 03 **STRONGER THAN ME** *Island CID 830* 71 1
1 Nov 03 **FRANK** *Island 9812918* 60 1

WING AND A PRAYER FIFE AND DRUM CORPS

US, male / female vocal / instrumental group (Singles: 7 weeks) pos/wks

24 Jan 76 **BABY FACE** *Atlantic K 10705* 12 7

WINGER

US, male vocal / instrumental group (Singles: 3 weeks) pos/wks

19 Jan 91 **MILES AWAY** *Atlantic A 7802* 56 3

Pete WINGFIELD

UK, male vocalist / instrumentalist – piano (Singles: 7 weeks) pos/wks

28 Jun 75 ● **EIGHTEEN WITH A BULLET** *Island WIP 6231* 7 7

WINGS – *See Linda McCARTNEY; Paul McCARTNEY*

Josh WINK *US, male producer – Joshua Winkelman (Singles: 29 weeks, Albums: 1 week)* pos/wks

6 May 95 **DON'T LAUGH** *XL XLS 62CD* [1] 38 2
21 Oct 95 ● **HIGHER STATE OF CONSCIOUSNESS (re)** *Manifesto FESCD 3* ..8 12
2 Mar 96 **HYPNOTIZIN'** *XL XLS 71CD* [1] 35 2
27 Jul 96 ● **HIGHER STATE OF CONSCIOUSNESS (re-mix)** *Manifesto FESCD 9* [1] 7 10
12 Aug 00 **HOW'S YOUR EVENING SO FAR** *ffrr FCD 384* [2] 23 3
21 Sep 96 **LEFT ABOVE THE CLOUDS** *XL Recordings XLCD 119* 43 1

[1] Winx [2] Josh Wink and Lil' Louis

See also SIZE 9

Kate WINSLET *UK, female actor / vocalist (Singles: 14 weeks)* pos/wks

8 Dec 01 ● **WHAT IF** *EMI / Liberty CDKATE 001* 6 14

Edgar WINTER GROUP

US, male instrumental group (Singles: 9 weeks)

		pos	wks
26 May 73	**FRANKENSTEIN** *Epic EPC 1440* ▲	**18**	9

Johnny WINTER

US, male vocal / instrumental group (Albums: 12 weeks)

		pos	wks
16 May 70	**SECOND WINTER** *CBS 66321*	**59**	2
31 Oct 70	**JOHNNY WINTER AND ...** *CBS 64117*	**29**	4
15 May 71	**JOHNNY WINTER AND LIVE** *CBS 64289*	**20**	6

Ruby WINTERS

US, female vocalist (Singles: 35 weeks, Albums: 17 weeks)

		pos	wks
5 Nov 77 ●	**I WILL!** *Creole CR 141*	**4**	13
29 Apr 78	**COME TO ME!** *Creole CR 153*	**11**	12
26 Aug 78	**I WON'T MENTION IT AGAIN** *Creole CR 160*	**45**	5
16 Jun 79	**BABY LAY DOWN** *Creole CR 171*	**43**	5
10 Jun 78	**RUBY WINTERS** *Creole CRLP 512*	**27**	7
23 Jun 79	**SONGBIRD** *K-Tel NE 1045*	**31**	10

Steve WINWOOD (439 Top 500)

R&B vocalist / instrumentalist – keyboards, b. 12 May 1948, Birmingham, UK, whose prodigious talent in the Spencer Davis Group led to supergroup Blind Faith in 1969 and the more enduring Traffic from 1967 to 1974. This Grammy winner became one of the most successful UK acts Stateside in the late 1980s (Singles: 33 weeks, Albums: 122 weeks)

		pos	wks
17 Jan 81	**WHILE YOU SEE A CHANCE** *Island WIP 6655*	**45**	5
9 Oct 82	**VALERIE** *Island WIP 6818*	**51**	4
28 Jun 86	**HIGHER LOVE** *Island IS 288* ▲	**13**	9
13 Sep 86	**FREEDOM OVERSPILL** *Island IS 294*	**69**	1
24 Jan 87	**BACK IN THE HIGH LIFE AGAIN** *Island IS 303*	**53**	2
19 Sep 87	**VALERIE (re-mix)** *Island IS 336*	**19**	8
11 Jun 88	**ROLL WITH IT** *Virgin VS 1085* ▲	**53**	4
9 Jul 77	**STEVE WINWOOD** *Island ILPS 9494*	**12**	9
10 Jan 81	**ARC OF A DIVER** *Island ILPS 9576*	**13**	20
14 Aug 82 ●	**TALKING BACK TO THE NIGHT** *Island ILPS 9777*	**6**	13
12 Jul 86 ●	**BACK IN THE HIGH LIFE** *Island ILPS 9844*	**8**	42
7 Nov 87	**CHRONICLES** *Island SSW 1*	**12**	17
2 Jul 88 ●	**ROLL WITH IT** *Virgin V 2532* ▲	**4**	16
17 Nov 90	**REFUGEES OF THE HEART** *Virgin V 2650*	**26**	3
14 Jun 97	**JUNCTION SEVEN** *Virgin CDV 2832*	**32**	2

See also Spencer DAVIS GROUP; BLIND FAITH

WIRE

UK, male vocal / instrumental group (Singles: 4 weeks, Albums: 3 weeks)

		pos	wks
27 Jan 79	**OUTDOOR MINER** *Harvest HAR 5172*	**51**	3
13 May 89	**EARDRUM BUZZ** *Mute MUTE 87*	**68**	1
7 Oct 78	**CHAIRS MISSING** *Harvest SHSP 4093*	**48**	1
13 Oct 79	**154** *Harvest SHSP 4105*	**39**	1
9 May 87	**THE IDEAL COPY** *Mute STUMM 42*	**87**	1

WIRED

Holland / Finland, male production / instrumental duo (Singles: 1 week)

		pos	wks
20 Feb 99	**TRANSONIC** *Future Groove CDFGR 001*	**73**	1

WIRELESS

UK, male vocal / instrumental group (Singles: 2 weeks)

		pos	wks
28 Jun 97	**I NEED YOU** *Chrysalis CDCHS 5059*	**68**	1
7 Feb 98	**IN LOVE WITH THE FAMILIAR** *Chrysalis CDCHS 5075*	**69**	1

Norman WISDOM

UK, male actor / vocalist (Singles: 20 weeks)

		pos	wks
19 Feb 54 ●	**DON'T LAUGH AT ME ('CAUSE I'M A FOOL)** *Columbia DB 3133*	**3**	15
15 Mar 57	**THE WISDOM OF A FOOL** *Columbia DB 3903*	**13**	5

WISDOME

Italy, male / female production / vocal group (Singles: 2 weeks)

		pos	wks
11 Mar 00	**OFF THE WALL** *Positiva CDTIV 125*	**33**	2

WISEGUYS

UK, male DJ / producer – Theo Keating (Singles: 13 weeks)

		pos	wks
6 Jun 98	**OOH LA LA** *Wall of Sound WALLD 038*	**55**	1
12 Sep 98	**START THE COMMOTION** *Wall of Sound WALLD 044*	**66**	1
5 Jun 99 ●	**OOH LA LA (re-issue)** *Wall of Sound WALLD 038X*	**2**	10
11 Sep 99	**START THE COMMOTION (re-issue)** *Wall of Sound WALLD 059*	**47**	1

WISHBONE ASH

UK, male vocal / instrumental group (Albums: 76 weeks)

		pos	wks
23 Jan 71	**WISHBONE ASH** *MCA MKPS 2014*	**29**	3
9 Oct 71	**PILGRIMAGE** *MCA MDKS 8004*	**14**	9
20 May 72 ●	**ARGUS** *MCA MDKS 8006*	**3**	20
26 May 73	**WISHBONE FOUR** *MCA MDKS 8011*	**12**	10
30 Nov 74	**THERE'S THE RUB** *MCA MCF 2585*	**16**	5
3 Apr 76	**LOCKED IN** *MCA MCF 2750*	**36**	2
27 Nov 76	**NEW ENGLAND** *MCA MCG 3523*	**22**	3
29 Oct 77	**FRONT PAGE NEWS** *MCA MCG 3524*	**31**	4
28 Oct 78	**NO SMOKE WITHOUT FIRE** *MCA MCG 3528*	**43**	3
2 Feb 80	**JUST TESTING** *MCA MCF 3052*	**41**	4
1 Nov 80	**LIVE DATES II** *MCA MCG 4012*	**40**	3
25 Apr 81	**NUMBER THE BRAVE** *MCA MCF 3103*	**61**	5
16 Oct 82	**BOTH BARRELS BURNING** *A&M ASH 1*	**22**	5

Bill WITHERS

US, male vocalist / instrumentalist – guitar (Singles: 29 weeks, Albums: 10 weeks)

		pos	wks
12 Aug 72	**LEAN ON ME** *A&M AMS 7004* ▲	**18**	9
14 Jan 78 ●	**LOVELY DAY** *CBS 5773*	**7**	8
25 May 85	**OH YEAH!** *CBS A 6154*	**60**	3
10 Sep 88 ●	**LOVELY DAY (re-mix)** *CBS 6530017*	**4**	9
11 Feb 78	**MENAGERIE** *CBS 82265*	**27**	5
15 Jun 85	**WATCHING YOU WATCHING ME** *CBS 26200*	**60**	1
17 Sep 88	**GREATEST HITS** *CBS 32343*	**90**	4

See also Grover WASHINGTON Jr

WITNESS

UK, male vocal / instrumental group (Singles: 2 weeks, Albums: 2 weeks)

		pos	wks
13 Mar 99	**SCARS** *Island CID 740*	**71**	1
19 Jun 99	**AUDITION** *Island CID 749*	**71**	1
24 Jul 99	**BEFORE THE CALM** *Island CID 8084*	**59**	1
4 Aug 01	**UNDER A SUN** *Island CID 8107*	**62**	1

WIX – *See SPIRO and WIX*

WIZZARD

UK, male vocal / instrumental group – leader Roy Wood (Singles: 77 weeks, Albums: 11 weeks)

		pos	wks
9 Dec 72 ●	**BALL PARK INCIDENT** *Harvest HAR 5062*	**6**	12
21 Apr 73 ★	**SEE MY BABY JIVE** *Harvest HAR 5070* [1]	**1**	17
1 Sep 73 ★	**ANGEL FINGERS (A TEEN BALLAD)** *Harvest HAR 5076* [2]	**1**	10
8 Dec 73 ●	**I WISH IT COULD BE CHRISTMAS EVERYDAY** *Harvest HAR 5079* [3]	**4**	9
27 Apr 74 ●	**ROCK 'N' ROLL WINTER (LOONY'S TUNE)** *Warner Bros. K16497*	**6**	7
10 Aug 74	**THIS IS THE STORY OF MY LOVE (BABY)** *Warner Bros. K 16434*	**34**	4
21 Dec 74 ●	**ARE YOU READY TO ROCK** *Warner Bros. K 16357*	**8**	10
19 Dec 81	**I WISH IT COULD BE CHRISTMAS EVERYDAY (re) (re-issue)** *Harvest HAR 5173* [3]	**23**	8
19 May 73	**WIZZARD BREW** *Harvest SHSP 4025*	**29**	7
17 Aug 74	**INTRODUCING EDDY AND THE FALCONS** *Warner Bros. K 52029*	**19**	4

[1] Vocal backing by the Suedettes [2] Vocal backing: The Suedettes and The Bleach Boys [3] Wizzard featuring vocal backing by the Suedettes plus the Stockland Green Bilateral School First Year Choir with additional noises by Miss Snob and Class 3C

The 'I Wish It Could Be Christmas Everyday' re-issue debuted and made No.41 in Dec 1981 before re-entering and peaking at No.23 in Dec 1984

Jah WOBBLE'S INVADERS of the HEART

UK, male vocal / multi-instrumental group, leader – John Wardle (Singles: 10 weeks, Albums: 6 weeks) pos/wks

1 Feb 92	VISIONS OF YOU *Oval OVAL 103*	35	5
30 Apr 94	BECOMING MORE LIKE GOD *Island CID 571*	36	2
25 Jun 94	THE SUN DOES RISE *Island CIDX 587*	41	3
28 May 94	TAKE ME TO GOD *Island CID 8017*	13	5
14 Oct 95	SPINNER *All Saints ASCD 023* 1	71	1

1 Brian Eno and Jah Wobble

First hit features the uncredited vocals of Sinead O'Connor

Terry WOGAN

Ireland, male TV / radio presenter / vocalist (Singles: 5 weeks) pos/wks

7 Jan 78	THE FLORAL DANCE *Philips 6006 592*	21	5

WOLF – *See TROGGS*

WOLFGANG PRESS

UK, male vocal / instrumental duo (Albums: 1 week) pos/wks

4 Feb 95	FUNKY LITTLE DEMONS *4AD CADD 4016CD*	75	1

WOLFSBANE *UK, male vocal / instrumental group (Singles: 1 week, Albums: 3 weeks)* pos/wks

5 Oct 91	EZY *Def American DEFA 11*	68	1
5 Aug 89	LIVE FAST DIE FAST *Def American 838486 1*	48	1
20 Oct 90	ALL HELL'S BREAKING LOOSE ... *Def American 8469671*	48	1
19 Oct 91	DOWN FALL THE GOOD GUYS *Def American 5104131*	53	1

Bobby WOMACK *US, male vocalist / instrumentalist – guitar (Singles: 21 weeks, Albums: 15 weeks)* pos/wks

16 Jun 84	TELL ME WHY *Motown TMG 1339*	60	3
5 Oct 85	I WISH HE DIDN'T TRUST ME SO MUCH *MCA MCA 994*	64	2
26 Sep 87	SO THE STORY GOES *Chrysalis LIB 3* 1	34	8
7 Nov 87	LIVING IN A BOX *MCA MCA 1210*	70	2
3 Apr 93	I'M BACK FOR MORE *Dome CDDOME 1002* 2	27	5
13 May 95	IT'S A MAN'S MAN'S MAN'S WORLD *Pulse 8 CDLOSE 89* 3	73	1
28 Apr 84	THE POET II *Motown ZL 72205*	31	8
28 Sep 85	SO MANY RIVERS *MCA MCF 3282*	28	7

1 Living in a Box featuring Bobby Womack 2 Lulu and Bobby Womack 3 Jeanie Tracy and Bobby Womack

See also Wilton FELDER

Lee Ann WOMACK *US, female vocalist (Singles: 2 weeks)* pos/wks

9 Jun 01	I HOPE YOU DANCE *MCA Nashville MCSTD 40254*	40	2

WOMACK and WOMACK *US, male / female vocal duo – Linda and Cecil Womack (Singles: 51 weeks, Albums: 52 weeks)* pos/wks

28 Apr 84	LOVE WARS *Elektra E 9799*	14	10
30 Jun 84	BABY I'M SCARED OF YOU *Elektra E 9733*	72	2
6 Dec 86	SOUL LOVE – SOUL MAN *Manhattan MT 16*	58	6
6 Aug 88 ●	TEARDROPS *Fourth & Broadway BRW 101*	3	17
12 Nov 88	LIFE'S JUST A BALLGAME *Fourth & Broadway BRW 116*	32	5
25 Feb 89	CELEBRATE THE WORLD *Fourth & Broadway BRW 125*	19	8
5 Feb 94	SECRET STAR *Warner Bros. W 0222CD* 1	46	3
21 Apr 84	LOVE WARS *Elektra 960293*	45	13
22 Jun 85	RADIO M.U.S.I.C. MAN *Elektra EKT 6*	56	2
27 Aug 88 ●	CONSCIENCE *Fourth & Broadway BRLP 519*	4	37

1 House of Zekkariyas aka Womack and Womack

WOMBLES (432 Top 500) *Furriest (and possibly the tidiest) act in the Top 500 are natives of Wimbledon Common, London, and come under the musical guidance of songwriter and producer Mike Batt, b. 6 Feb 1950, Southampton, UK (Singles: 98 weeks, Albums: 58 weeks)* pos/wks

26 Jan 74 ●	THE WOMBLING SONG *CBS 1794*	4	23
6 Apr 74 ●	REMEMBER YOU'RE A WOMBLE *CBS 2241*	3	16
22 Jun 74 ●	BANANA ROCK *CBS 2465*	9	13
12 Oct 74	MINUETTO ALLEGRETTO *CBS 2710*	16	9
7 Dec 74 ●	WOMBLING MERRY CHRISTMAS *CBS 2842*	2	8
10 May 75	WOMBLING WHITE TIE AND TAILS (FOXTROT) *CBS 3266*	22	7
9 Aug 75	SUPER WOMBLE *CBS 3480*	20	6
13 Dec 75	LET'S WOMBLE TO THE PARTY TONIGHT *CBS 3794*	34	5
21 Mar 98	REMEMBER YOU'RE A WOMBLE (re-issue) *Columbia 6656202*	13	5
13 Jun 98	THE WOMBLING SONG (UNDERGROUND OVERGROUND) (re-issue) *Columbia 6660412*	27	3
30 Dec 00	I WISH IT COULD BE A WOMBLING MERRY CHRISTMAS EVERYDAY *Dramatico DRAMCDS 0001* 1	22	3
2 Mar 74	WOMBLING SONGS *CBS 65803*	19	17
13 Jul 74	REMEMBER YOU'RE A WOMBLE *CBS 80191*	18	31
21 Dec 74	KEEP ON WOMBLING *CBS 80526*	17	6
8 Jan 77	20 WOMBLING GREATS *Warwick PR 5022*	29	1
18 Apr 98	THE BEST WOMBLES ALBUM SO FAR – VOLUME 1 *Columbia 4895622*	26	3

1 Wombles with Roy Wood

See also Mike BATT

Stevie WONDER (29 Top 500)

Multi-award-winner born Steveland Judkins, 13 May 1950, Michigan, is one of the most successful singer / songwriters of all time. The youngest artist to top the US singles and album chart (aged 13) also recorded Motown's biggest UK seller, 'I Just Called to Say I Love You'. This very popular live performer has recorded with many of the biggest names in music, and has had his songs sung and sampled by countless acts. No one has amassed more No.1 US R&B hits than the blind entertainer who helped to turn Martin Luther King's birthday into a US holiday, and whose charitable work is legendary. Best-selling single: 'I Just Called to Say I Love You' 1,775,000 (Singles: 416 weeks, Albums: 373 weeks) pos/wks

3 Feb 66	UPTIGHT (EVERYTHING'S ALRIGHT) *Tamla Motown TMG 545*	14	10
18 Aug 66	BLOWIN' IN THE WIND *Tamla Motown TMG 570*	36	5
5 Jan 67	A PLACE IN THE SUN *Tamla Motown TMG 588*	20	5
26 Jul 67 ●	I WAS MADE TO LOVE HER *Tamla Motown TMG 613*	5	15
25 Oct 67	I'M WONDERING *Tamla Motown TMG 626*	22	8
8 May 68	SHOO BE DOO BE DOO DA DAY *Tamla Motown TMG 653*	46	4
18 Dec 68 ●	FOR ONCE IN MY LIFE *Tamla Motown TMG 679*	3	13
19 Mar 69	I DON'T KNOW WHY (I LOVE YOU) (re) *Tamla Motown TMG 690*	14	11
16 Jul 69 ●	MY CHERIE AMOUR *Tamla Motown TMG 690*	4	15
15 Nov 69 ●	YESTER-ME, YESTER-YOU, YESTERDAY *Tamla Motown TMG 717*	2	13
28 Mar 70 ●	NEVER HAD A DREAM COME TRUE *Tamla Motown TMG 731*	6	12
18 Jul 70	SIGNED SEALED DELIVERED I'M YOURS (re) *Tamla Motown TMG 744*	15	10
21 Nov 70	HEAVEN HELP US ALL *Tamla Motown TMG 757*	29	11
15 May 71	WE CAN WORK IT OUT *Tamla Motown TMG 772*	27	7
22 Jan 72	IF YOU REALLY LOVE ME *Tamla Motown TMG 798*	20	7
3 Feb 73	SUPERSTITION *Tamla Motown TMG 841* ▲	11	9
19 May 73 ●	YOU ARE THE SUNSHINE OF MY LIFE *Tamla Motown TMG 852* ▲	7	11
13 Oct 73	HIGHER GROUND *Tamla Motown TMG 869*	29	5
12 Jan 74	LIVING FOR THE CITY *Tamla Motown TMG 881*	15	9
13 Apr 74 ●	HE'S MISSTRA KNOW-IT-ALL *Tamla Motown TMG 892*	10	9
19 Oct 74	YOU HAVEN'T DONE NOTHIN' *Tamla Motown TMG 921* ▲	30	5
11 Jan 75	BOOGIE ON REGGAE WOMAN *Tamla Motown TMG 928*	12	8
18 Dec 76 ●	I WISH *Motown TMG 1054* ▲	5	10
9 Apr 77 ●	SIR DUKE *Motown TMG 1068* ▲	2	9
10 Sep 77	ANOTHER STAR *Motown TMG 1083*	29	5
24 Feb 79	POPS, WE LOVE YOU *Motown TMG 1136* 1	66	5
24 Nov 79	SEND ONE YOUR LOVE *Motown TMG 1149*	52	3
26 Jan 80	BLACK ORCHID *Motown TMG 1173*	63	3
29 Mar 80	OUTSIDE MY WINDOW *Motown TMG 1179*	52	4
13 Sep 80 ●	MASTERBLASTER (JAMMIN') *Motown TMG 1204*	2	10
27 Dec 80 ●	I AIN'T GONNA STAND FOR IT *Motown TMG 1215*	10	10
7 Mar 81 ●	LATELY *Motown TMG 1226*	3	13
25 Jul 81 ●	HAPPY BIRTHDAY *Motown TMG 1235*	2	11
23 Jan 82	THAT GIRL *Motown TMG 1254*	39	6
10 Apr 82 ★	EBONY AND IVORY *Parlophone R 6054* 2 ▲	1	10
5 Jun 82 ●	DO I DO *Motown TMG 1269*	10	7

25 Sep 82 **RIBBON IN THE SKY** *Motown TMG 1280* 45 4
25 Aug 84 ★ **I JUST CALLED TO SAY I LOVE YOU (re)** *Motown TMG 1349* ◆ ▲ 1 26
1 Dec 84 **LOVE LIGHT IN FLIGHT** *Motown TMG 1364* 44 5
29 Dec 84 **DON'T DRIVE DRUNK (re)** *Motown TMG 1372* 62 3
7 Sep 85 ● **PART-TIME LOVER** *Motown ZB 40351* ▲ 3 12
9 Nov 85 **THAT'S WHAT FRIENDS ARE FOR** *Arista ARIST 638* [3] ▲ 16 9
23 Nov 85 **GO HOME** *Motown ZB 40501* 67 2
8 Mar 86 **OVERJOYED** *Motown ZB 40567* 17 8
17 Jan 87 **STRANGER ON THE SHORE OF LOVE** *Motown WOND 2* 55 3
31 Oct 87 **SKELETONS** *Motown ZB 41439* 59 3
28 May 88 **GET IT** *Motown ZB 41883* [4] 37 4
6 Aug 88 ● **MY LOVE** *CBS JULIO 2* [5] 5 11
20 May 89 **FREE** *Motown ZB 42855* 49 5
12 Oct 91 **FUN DAY** *Motown ZB 44957* 63 1
25 Feb 95 **FOR YOUR LOVE** *Motown TMGCD 1437* 23 4
22 Jul 95 **TOMORROW ROBINS WILL SING** *Motown 8603732* 71 1
19 Jul 97 ● **HOW COME, HOW LONG** *Epic 6646202* [6] 10 5
31 Oct 98 **TRUE TO YOUR HEART** *Motown 8608832* [7] 51 1
27 Dec 03 **SIGNED, SEALED, DELIVERED, I'M YOURS** *Innocent SINCD 54* [8] .... 11 1+
7 Sep 68 **STEVIE WONDER'S GREATEST HITS** *Tamla Motown STML 11075* 25 10
13 Dec 69 **MY CHERIE AMOUR** *Tamla Motown STML 11128* 17 2
12 Feb 72 **GREATEST HITS VOLUME 2** *Tamla Motown STML 11196* 30 4
3 Feb 73 **TALKING BOOK** *Tamla Motown STMA 8007* 16 48
1 Sep 73 ● **INNERVISIONS** *Tamla Motown STMA 8011* 8 55
17 Aug 74 ● **FULFILLINGNESS' FIRST FINALE** *Tamla Motown STMA 8019* 5 16
16 Oct 76 ● **SONGS IN THE KEY OF LIFE** *Tamla Motown TMSP 6002* 2 54
10 Nov 79 ● **JOURNEY THROUGH THE SECRET LIFE OF PLANTS** *Motown TMSP 6009* 8 15
8 Nov 80 ● **HOTTER THAN JULY** *Motown STMA 8035* 2 55
22 May 82 ● **ORIGINAL MUSIQUARIUM 1** *Motown TMSP 6012* 8 17
22 Sep 84 ● **THE WOMAN IN RED (FILM SOUNDTRACK)** *Motown ZL 72285* 2 19
24 Nov 84 **LOVE SONGS – 16 CLASSIC HITS** *Telstar STAR 2251* 20 10
28 Sep 85 ● **IN SQUARE CIRCLE** *Motown ZL 72005* 5 16
15 Nov 86 **DIANA ROSS, MICHAEL JACKSON, GLADYS KNIGHT, STEVIE WONDER. THEIR VERY BEST BACK TO BACK** *Priority TV PTVR 2* [1] 21 10
28 Nov 87 **CHARACTERS** *RCA ZL 72001* 33 4
8 Jun 91 **JUNGLE FEVER (FILM SOUNDTRACK)** *Motown ZL 71750* 56 1
25 Mar 95 ● **CONVERSATION PEACE** *Motown 5302382* 8 4
23 Nov 96 **SONG REVIEW – A GREATEST HITS COLLECTION** *Motown 5307572* 19 12
23 Aug 97 **SONGS IN THE KEY OF LIFE (RE-ISSUE)** *Motown 5300342* 66 1
9 Nov 02 **THE DEFINITIVE COLLECTION** *Universal TV 0665022* .... 16 20+

[1] Diana Ross, Marvin Gaye, Smokey Robinson and Stevie Wonder [2] Paul McCartney with Stevie Wonder [3] Dionne Warwick and Friends featuring Elton John, Stevie Wonder and Gladys Knight [4] Stevie Wonder and Michael Jackson [5] Julio Iglesias featuring Stevie Wonder [6] Babyface featuring Stevie Wonder [7] 98 Degrees featuring Stevie Wonder [8] Blue featuring Stevie Wonder and Angie Stone [1] Diana Ross / Michael Jackson / Gladys Knight / Stevie Wonder

'You Haven't Done Nothin' included an additional credit on the label: 'Doo Doo Wopsssss by The Jackson 5'. 'I Just Called to Say I Loved You' re-entered in Dec 1985

Wayne WONDER *Jamaica, male vocalist – DeWayne Charles (Singles: 14 weeks, Albums: 7 weeks)* pos/wks

28 Jun 03 ● **NO LETTING GO** *VP / Atlantic AT 0154CD* 3 8
8 Nov 03 **BOUNCE ALONG** *Atlantic AT 0165CD* 19 6
28 Jun 03 **NO HOLDING BACK** *VP / Atlantic 7567836282* 40 7

WONDER DOG

Germany, canine vocalist – Harry Thumann (Singles: 7 weeks) pos/wks

21 Aug 82 **RUFF MIX** *Flip FLIP 001* 31 7

See also Harry THUMANN

WONDER STUFF *UK, male vocal / instrumental group (Singles: 66 weeks, Albums: 48 weeks)* pos/wks

30 Apr 88 **GIVE GIVE GIVE ME MORE MORE MORE** *Polydor GONE 3* 72 2
16 Jul 88 **A WISH AWAY** *Polydor GONE 4* 43 5
24 Sep 88 **IT'S YER MONEY I'M AFTER BABY** *Polydor GONE 5* 40 3
11 Mar 89 **WHO WANTS TO BE THE DISCO KING?** *Polydor GONE 6* 28 3
23 Sep 89 **DON'T LET ME DOWN GENTLY** *Polydor GONE 7* 19 4
11 Nov 89 **GOLDEN GREEN / GET TOGETHER** *Polydor GONE 8* 33 3
12 May 90 **CIRCLESQUARE** *Polydor GONE 10* 20 4
13 Apr 91 ● **THE SIZE OF A COW** *Polydor GONE 11* 5 7
25 May 91 **CAUGHT IN MY SHADOW** *Polydor GONE 12* 18 3
7 Sep 91 **SLEEP ALONE** *Polydor GONE 13* 43 2
26 Oct 91 ★ **DIZZY** *Sense SIGH 712* [1] 1 12
25 Jan 92 ● **WELCOME TO THE CHEAP SEATS (EP)** *Polydor GONE 14* 8 5
25 Sep 93 ● **ON THE ROPES (EP)** *Polydor GONCD 15* 10 4
27 Nov 93 **FULL OF LIFE (HAPPY NOW)** *Polydor GONCD 16* 28 3
26 Mar 94 **HOT LOVE NOW! (EP)** *Polydor GONCD 17* 19 3
10 Sep 94 **UNBEARABLE** *Polydor GONCD 18* 16 3
27 Aug 88 **THE EIGHT LEGGED GROOVE MACHINE** *Polydor GONLP 1* 18 7
14 Oct 89 ● **HUP** *Polydor 841187 1* 5 8
8 Jun 91 ● **NEVER LOVED ELVIS** *Polydor 8472521* 3 23
16 Oct 93 ● **CONSTRUCTION FOR THE MODERN IDIOT** *Polydor 5198942* 4 5
8 Oct 94 ● **IF THE BEATLES HAD READ HUNTER … THE SINGLES** *Polydor 5213972* 8 4
29 Jul 95 **LIVE IN MANCHESTER** *Windsong WINCD 074X* 74 1

[1] Vic Reeves and The Wonder Stuff

Tracks on Welcome to the Cheap Seats (EP): Welcome to the Cheap Seats / Me, My Mom, My Dad and My Brother / Will the Circle Be Unbroken / That's Entertainment. Tracks on On the Ropes (EP): On the Ropes / Professional Disturber of the Peace / Hank and John / Whites. Tracks on Hot Love Now (EP): Hot Love Now! / I Think I Must've Had Something Really Useful to Say / Room 512 / All the News That's Fit to Print

WONDERS *US, male vocal / instrumental group (Singles: 3 weeks)* pos/wks

22 Feb 97 **THAT THING YOU DO!** *Play-Tone 6640552* 22 3

WONDRESS – *See MANTRONIX*

Brenton WOOD

US, male vocalist – Alfred Smith (Singles: 14 weeks) pos/wks

27 Dec 67 ● **GIMME LITTLE SIGN** *Liberty LBF 15021* 8 14

Roy WOOD *UK, male vocalist / multi-instrumentalist – Ulysses Adrian Wood (Singles: 44 weeks, Albums: 14 weeks)* pos/wks

11 Aug 73 **DEAR ELAINE** *Harvest HAR 5074* 18 8
1 Dec 73 ● **FOREVER** *Harvest HAR 5078* 8 13
15 Jun 74 **GOIN' DOWN THE ROAD (A SCOTTISH REGGAE SONG)** *Harvest HAR 5083* 13 7
31 May 75 **OH WHAT A SHAME** *Jet 754* 13 7
22 Nov 86 **WATERLOO** *IRS IRM 125* [1] 45 4
23 Dec 95 **I WISH IT COULD BE CHRISTMAS EVERYDAY** *Woody WOODY 001CD* [2] 59 2
30 Dec 00 **I WISH IT COULD BE A WOMBLING MERRY CHRISTMAS EVERYDAY** *Dramatico DRAMCDS 0001* [3] 22 3
18 Aug 73 **BOULDERS** *Harvest SHVL 803* 15 8
24 Jul 82 **THE SINGLES** *Speed SPEED 1000* 37 6

[1] Doctor and the Medics featuring Roy Wood [2] Roy Wood Big Band [3] Wombles with Roy Wood

See also ELECTRIC LIGHT ORCHESTRA; MOVE; WIZZARD

WOODENTOPS *UK, male vocal / instrumental group (Singles: 1 week, Albums: 6 weeks)* pos/wks

11 Oct 86 **EVERYDAY LIVING** *Rough Trade RT 178* 72 1
12 Jul 86 **GIANT** *Rough Trade ROUGH 87* 35 4
5 Mar 88 **WOODENFOOT COPS ON THE HIGHWAY** *Rough Trade ROUGH 127* 48 2

Marcella WOODS – *See Matt DAREY; MELT featuring Little Ms MARCIE; LIQUID STATE featuring Marcella WOODS*

Michael WOODS *UK, male producer (Singles: 2 weeks)* pos/wks

21 Jun 03 **IF YOU WANT ME** *Incentive CENT 48CDS* [1] 46 1
29 Nov 03 **SOLEX (CLOSE TO THE EDGE)** *Free 2 Air 0150355F2A* 52 1

[1] Michael Woods featuring Imogen Bailey

See also M3; WARRIOR; M1

Edward WOODWARD

UK, male actor / vocalist (Singles: 2 weeks, Albums: 12 weeks) pos/wks

Date	Title	pos	wks
16 Jan 71	**THE WAY YOU LOOK TONIGHT (re)** *DJM DJS 232*	**42**	2
6 Jun 70	**THE MAN ALONE** *DJM DJLPS 405*	**53**	2
19 Aug 72	**THE EDWARD WOODWARD ALBUM** *Jam JAL 103*	**20**	10

WOOKIE

UK, male producer / vocalist – Jason Chue (Singles: 11 weeks) pos/wks

Date	Title	pos	wks
3 Jun 00	**WHAT'S GOING ON** *Soul II Soul S2SCD 001*	**45**	1
12 Aug 00 ●	**BATTLE** *Soul II Soul / Pias S2SPCD001* [1]	**10**	7
12 May 01	**BACK UP (TO ME)** *Soul II Soul S2SPCD 003* [1]	**38**	3

[1] Wookie featuring Lain

Sheb WOOLEY

US, male vocalist / actor d. 16 Sep 2003 (Singles: 8 weeks) pos/wks

Date	Title	pos	wks
20 Jun 58	**THE PURPLE PEOPLE EATER** *MGM 981* ▲	**12**	8

WOOLPACKERS

UK, male vocal group (Singles: 24 weeks, Albums: 13 weeks) pos/wks

Date	Title	pos	wks
16 Nov 96 ●	**HILLBILLY ROCK HILLBILLY ROLL** *RCA 74321425412*	**5**	14
29 Nov 97	**LINE DANCE PARTY** *RCA 74321512262*	**25**	10
14 Dec 96	**EMMERDANCE** *RCA 74321444052*	**26**	10
29 Nov 97	**THE GREATEST LINE DANCING PARTY ALBUM** *RCA 74321512272*	**48**	3

WORKING WEEK *UK, male / female vocal / instrumental group (Singles: 2 weeks, Albums: 10 weeks)* pos/wks

Date	Title	pos	wks
9 Jun 84	**VENCEREMOS – WE WILL WIN** *Virgin VS 684*	**64**	2
4 Jun 85	**WORKING NIGHTS** *Virgin V 2343*	**23**	9
27 Sep 86	**COMPANEROS** *Virgin V 2397*	**72**	1

WORLD – *See LIL' LOUIS*

WORLD OF TWIST *UK, male / female vocal / instrumental group (Singles: 12 weeks, Albums: 1 week)* pos/wks

Date	Title	pos	wks
24 Nov 90	**THE STORM (re)** *Circa YR 55*	**42**	5
23 Mar 91	**SONS OF THE STAGE** *Circa YR 62*	**47**	3
12 Oct 91	**SWEETS** *Circa YR 72*	**58**	2
22 Feb 92	**SHE'S A RAINBOW** *Circa YR 82*	**62**	2
9 Nov 91	**QUALITY STREET** *Circa CIRCA 17*	**50**	1

WORLD PARTY *UK / Ireland, male vocal / instrumental group (Singles: 29 weeks, Albums: 25 weeks)* pos/wks

Date	Title	pos	wks
14 Feb 87	**SHIP OF FOOLS** *Ensign ENY 606*	**42**	6
16 Jun 90	**MESSAGE IN THE BOX** *Ensign ENY 631*	**39**	6
15 Sep 90	**WAY DOWN NOW** *Ensign ENY 634*	**66**	2
18 May 91	**THANK YOU WORLD** *Ensign ENY 643*	**68**	1
10 Apr 93	**IS IT LIKE TODAY** *Ensign CDENY 658*	**19**	6
10 Jul 93	**GIVE IT ALL AWAY** *Ensign CDENY 659*	**43**	3
2 Oct 93	**ALL I GAVE** *Ensign CDENYS 660*	**37**	3
7 Jun 97	**BEAUTIFUL DREAM** *Chrysalis CDCHS 5053*	**31**	2
21 Mar 87	**PRIVATE REVOLUTION** *Chrysalis CHEN 4*	**56**	4
19 May 90	**GOODBYE JUMBO** *Ensign CHEN 10*	**36**	10
8 May 93 ●	**BANG!** *Ensign CDCHEN 33*	**2**	8
28 Jun 97	**EGYPTOLOGY** *Chrysalis CDCHR 6124*	**34**	2
2 Sep 00	**DUMBING UP** *Papillon BTFLYCD 0006*	**64**	1

WORLD PREMIERE

US, male vocal / instrumental group (Singles: 4 weeks) pos/wks

Date	Title	pos	wks
28 Jan 84	**SHARE THE NIGHT** *Epic A 4133*	**64**	4

WORLD WARRIOR

UK, male producer – Simon Harris (Singles: 1 week) pos/wks

Date	Title	pos	wks
16 Apr 94	**STREET FIGHTER II** *Living Beat LBECD 27*	**70**	1

See also Simon HARRIS

WORLDS APART *UK, male vocal group (Singles: 17 weeks)* pos/wks

Date	Title	pos	wks
27 Mar 93	**HEAVEN MUST BE MISSING AN ANGEL** *Arista 74321139362*	**29**	3
3 Jul 93	**WONDERFUL WORLD** *Arista 74321153402*	**51**	1
25 Sep 93	**EVERLASTING LOVE** *Bell 74321164802*	**20**	4
26 Mar 94	**COULD IT BE I'M FALLING IN LOVE** *Bell 74321189952*	**15**	6
4 Jun 94	**BEGGIN' TO BE WRITTEN** *Bell 74321211982*	**29**	3

WORLD'S FAMOUS SUPREME TEAM

US, male vocal / DJ group (Singles: 19 weeks) pos/wks

Date	Title	pos	wks
4 Dec 82 ●	**BUFFALO GALS** *Charisma MALC 1* [1]	**9**	12
25 Feb 84	**HEY DJ** *Charisma TEAM 1*	**52**	5
8 Dec 90	**OPERAA HOUSE** *Virgin VS 1273* [2]	**75**	1
3 Oct 98	**BUFFALO GALS STAMPEDE (re-mix)** *Virgin VSCDT 1717* [3]	**65**	1

[1] Malcolm McLaren and the World's Famous Supreme Team [2] World Famous Supreme Team Show [3] Malcolm McLaren and the World's Famous Supreme Team plus Rakim and Roger Sanchez

WRECKLESS ERIC

UK, male vocalist – Eric Goulden (Albums: 5 weeks) pos/wks

Date	Title	pos	wks
1 Apr 78	**WRECKLESS ERIC** *Stiff SEEZ 6*	**46**	1
8 Mar 80	**BIG SMASH** *Stiff SEEZ 21*	**30**	4

WRECKX-N-EFFECT *US, male vocal group (Singles: 18 weeks)* pos/wks

Date	Title	pos	wks
13 Jan 90	**JUICY** *Motown ZB 43295* [1]	**29**	7
5 Dec 92	**RUMP SHAKER** *MCA MCS 1725*	**24**	7
7 May 94	**WRECKX SHOP** *MCA MCSTD 1969* [2]	**26**	2
13 Aug 94	**RUMP SHAKER (re-issue)** *MCA MCSTD 1989*	**40**	2

[1] Wrecks-N-Effect [2] Wreckx-N-Effect featuring Apache Indian

WREN ORCHESTRA – *See WET WET WET*

Betty WRIGHT *US, female vocalist (Singles: 23 weeks)* pos/wks

Date	Title	pos	wks
25 Jan 75	**SHOORAH! SHOORAH!** *RCA 2491*	**27**	7
19 Apr 75	**WHERE IS THE LOVE** *RCA 2548*	**25**	7
8 Feb 86	**PAIN** *Cooltempo COOL 117*	**42**	6
9 Sep 89	**KEEP LOVE NEW** *Sure Delight SD 11*	**71**	3

See also Peter BROWN

Ian WRIGHT *UK, male footballer / vocalist (Singles: 2 weeks)* pos/wks

Date	Title	pos	wks
28 Aug 93	**DO THE RIGHT THING** *M & G MAGCD 45*	**43**	2

Linda WRIGHT – *See NEW ATLANTIC*

Rick WRIGHT

UK, male vocal / instrumentalist – keyboards (Albums: 1 week) pos/wks

Date	Title	pos	wks
19 Oct 96	**BROKEN CHINA** *EMI CDEMD 1098*	**61**	1

See also PINK FLOYD

Ruby WRIGHT *US, female vocalist (Singles: 15 weeks)* pos/wks

Date	Title	pos	wks
16 Apr 54 ●	**BIMBO (re)** *Parlophone R 3816*	**7**	5
22 May 59	**THREE STARS** *Parlophone R 4556*	**19**	10

'Three Stars' is narrated by Dick Pike

Steve WRIGHT *UK, male DJ / vocalist (Singles: 10 weeks)* pos/wks

Date	Title	pos	wks
27 Nov 82	**I'M ALRIGHT** *RCA 296* [1]	**40**	6
15 Oct 83	**GET SOME THERAPY** *RCA 362* [2]	**75**	1
1 Dec 84	**THE GAY CAVALIEROS (THE STORY SO FAR)** *MCA 925*	**61**	3

[1] Young Steve and The Afternoon Boys [2] Steve Wright and The Sisters of Soul

WUBBLE-U *UK, male production group (Singles: 1 week)* pos/wks

Date	Title	pos	wks
7 Mar 98	**PETAL** *Indolent DGOL 003CD1*	**55**	1

Klaus WUNDERLICH *Germany, male instrumentalist – organ, d. 28 Oct 1997 (Albums: 19 weeks)* pos/wks

Date	Title	pos	wks
30 Aug 75	**THE HIT WORLD OF KLAUS WUNDERLICH** *Decca SPA 434*	**27**	8
20 May 78	**THE UNIQUE KLAUS WUNDERLICH SOUND** *Decca DBC 5/5*	**28**	4
26 May 79	**THE FANTASTIC SOUND OF KLAUS WUNDERLICH** *Lotus LH 5013*	**43**	5
17 Mar 84	**ON THE SUNNY SIDE OF THE STREET** *Polydor POLD 5133*	**81**	2

Review of the Year

DECEMBER 2003

A Nelson Mandela-inspired concert to mark World Aids Day attracts a 40,000-strong crowd in Cape Town. The concert – named 46664 after Mandela's prisoner number on Robben Island – features performances by **Beyoncé**, **Peter Gabriel**, **Bob Geldof** and members of **Eurythmics**, **Queen** and **U2**. **Will Young's** second album, Friday's Child, surprises many by selling more than 200,000 in its first week and more than a million before the end of the year. Also, Pop Idol Will's 'Leave Right Now' gives him his fourth No.1 from five releases – a record for a solo act. Scottish singer **Michelle McManus** becomes the second UK Pop Idol winner and the final attracts a record 10.2 million votes. Norway, for so long the butt of Eurovision jokes, celebrates as its Pop Idol **Kurt Nilsen** wins the first ever World Idol show. The much-tipped 'Happy Xmas (War is Over)' by the last 12 Pop Idol finalists manages only a No.5 position. **Westlife** become the first act in the 21st century to notch up four No.1 albums when Turnaround hits the top. The group's revival of 'Mandy' comes top in a public vote on ITV1's Record of the Year. The second Fame Academy winner, **Alex Parks**, sells more than 96,000 copies in the first week of her debut album, Introduction – more than the total sale of first winner **David Sneddon's** debut CD. Miss Ireland, **Chris de Burgh's** daughter Rosanna Davison, wins the Miss World competition. **Ozzy Osbourne** is badly injured in a quad bike accident: he suffers a fractured vertebra in his neck, a broken collarbone and eight broken ribs. He also breaks the record for the longest chart span before a No.1 (33 years), when 'Changes', with daughter Kelly, becomes the first father/daughter duo to top the chart since Frank and Nancy Sinatra in 1967. EastEnder **Shane Richie** narrowly misses the top with his update of Wham!'s 'I'm Your Man'. Not only do the proceeds of the record go to Children in Need but so do **George Michael's** composer's royalties. **Elvis Costello** marries jazz star **Diana Krall**. **Mick Jagger** is knighted and **Gerry Marsden** (leader of the Pacemakers) and **Gary Brooker** (Procol Harum) receive MBEs. As the year closes, it is announced that **Eric Clapton**, **Ray Davies** and top 1950s and 60s producer **Norman Newell** are on the Queen's New Year's honours list. Coca-Cola signs a deal to sponsor the official UK charts. **Robbie Williams's** Live at Knebworth tops the German charts and his What We Did Last Summer breaks the music DVD sales record set earlier in the year by **Led Zeppelin** when it sells 46,000 in week one. **Michael Jackson's** comeback single, 'One More Chance', gives him his 31st UK Top 5 entry and Iron Maiden score their 31st Top 40 entry with 'Rainmaker', which tops the chart in Spain, Portugal and Finland. You know it must nearly be Christmas as **Cliff Richard** notches up his 26th Top 10 album, Cliff at Christmas, and 'Santa's List' gives him a record 65th Top 10 single. Thanks to England's World Cup rugby win, **UB40's** 'Swing Low' reaches the Top 20 in its seventh chart week – the slowest climb since the 1980s. In the tightest Christmas No.1 race for years, **Michael Andrews** and **Gary Jules'** 'Mad World' just pips 'Christmas Time (Don't Let the Bells End)' by **The Darkness**. And for the first time ever it's a pop-free Christmas Top 3 with the Osbournes taking third position with pop offerings from **The Idols**, **Sugababes**, **Atomic Kitten** and **Blue** all falling by the wayside. The Jules single reportedly was recorded in 90 minutes at a cost of £50 and sells more than 440,00 in its first 20 days. As the year draws to a close Now 56! passes the million sales mark; **Culture Club** issue a writ against Virgin Records for alleged accounting discrepancies; **The Darkness** sign a reported £2m publishing deal with Universal Music; and **Liberty X** and **Lulu** perform as themselves in an EastEnders Christmas special.

In one of the most keenly fought battles for the Christmas No.1 spot, the understated Michael Andrews and Gary Jules offering 'Mad World' pips the wonderfully extravagant Darkness single 'Christmas Time (Don't Let the Bells End)'

WURZELS *UK, male vocal / instrumental group (Singles: 31 weeks, Albums: 29 weeks)* pos/wks

2 Feb 67 DRINK UP THY ZIDER *Columbia DB 8081* 1 ....45 1
15 May 76 ★ THE COMBINE HARVESTER (BRAND NEW KEY) *EMI 2450* 1 13
11 Sep 76 ● I AM A CIDER DRINKER (PALOMA BLANCA) *EMI 2520* 3 9
25 Jun 77 FARMER BILL'S COWMAN (I WAS KAISER BILL'S BATMAN) *EMI 2637* 32 5
11 Aug 01 COMBINE HARVESTER 2001 (re-mix) *EMI Gold CDWURZ 001* ..39 2
12 Oct 02 DON'T LOOK BACK IN ANGER *EMI Gold 5515082* 59 1
11 Mar 67 ADGE CUTLER AND THE WURZELS *Columbia SX 6126* 1 ....38 4
3 Jul 76 COMBINE HARVESTER *One Up OU 2138* 15 20
2 Apr 77 GOLDEN DELICIOUS *EMI Note NTS 122* 32 5

1 Adge Cutler and The Wurzels 1 Adge Cutler and The Wurzels

WU-TANG CLAN *US, male rap / instrumental group (Singles: 21 weeks, Albums: 23 weeks)* pos/wks

16 Aug 97 TRIUMPH *Loud 74321510212* 1 ....46 1
21 Mar 98 ● SAY WHAT YOU WANT / INSANE *Mercury MERC 499* 2 ....4 7
25 Nov 00 ● GRAVEL PIT *Loud / Epic 67015182* 6 13
14 Jun 97 ★ WU-TANG FOREVER *Loud 74321457682* ■ ▲ 1 10
2 Dec 00 THE W *Epic 4995762* 19 13

1 Wu-Tang Clan featuring Cappadonna 2 Texas featuring Wu-Tang Clan (rap by Method Man and RZA)

See also GZA / GENIUS; METHOD MAN; OL' DIRTY BASTARD (DIRT MCGIRT); RAEKWON; GHOSTFACE KILLAH; RZA

Robert WYATT *UK, male vocalist – Robert Wyatt-Ellidge (Singles: 11 weeks)* pos/wks

28 Sep 74 I'M A BELIEVER *Virgin VS 114* 29 5
7 May 83 SHIPBUILDING *Rough Trade RT 115* 35 6

See also SOFT MACHINE

Michael WYCOFF *US, male vocalist (Singles: 2 weeks)* pos/wks

23 Jul 83 (DO YOU REALLY LOVE ME) TELL ME LOVE *RCA 348* 60 2

Pete WYLIE *UK, male vocalist (Singles: 18 weeks)* pos/wks

3 May 86 SINFUL *Eternal MDM 7* 13 10
13 Sep 86 DIAMOND GIRL *Eternal MDM 12* 57 3
13 Apr 91 SINFUL! (SCARY JIGGIN' WITH DR LOVE) *Siren SRN 138* 1 ..28 5

1 Pete Wylie with The Farm

See also WAH!

Bill WYMAN *UK, male vocalist / instrumentalist – bass – William Perks (Singles: 13 weeks, Albums: 8 weeks)* pos/wks

25 Jul 81 (SI SI) JE SUIS UN ROCK STAR *A&M AMS 8144* 14 9
20 Mar 82 A NEW FASHION *A&M AMS 8209* 37 4
8 Jun 74 MONKEY GRIP *Rolling Stones COC 59102* 39 1
10 Apr 82 BILL WYMAN *A&M AMLH 68540* 55 6
27 May 00 GROOVIN' *Papillon BTFLYCD 003* 1 ....52 1

1 Bill Wyman's Rhythm Kings

See also ROLLING STONES

Jane WYMAN – *See Bing CROSBY*

Tammy WYNETTE *US, female vocalist – Virginia Wynette Pugh, d. 6 Apr 1998 (Singles: 35 weeks, Albums: 49 weeks)* pos/wks

26 Apr 75 ★ STAND BY YOUR MAN *Epic EPC 7137* 1 12
28 Jun 75 D.I.V.O.R.C.E. *Epic EPC 3361* 12 7
12 Jun 76 I DON'T WANNA PLAY HOUSE *Epic EPC 4091* 37 4
7 Dec 91 ● JUSTIFIED AND ANCIENT *KLF Communications KLF 099* 1 ..2 12
17 May 75 ● THE BEST OF TAMMY WYNETTE *Epic EPC 63578* 4 23
21 Jun 75 STAND BY YOUR MAN *Epic EPC 69141* 13 7
17 Dec 77 ● 20 COUNTRY CLASSICS *CBS PR 5040* 3 11
4 Feb 78 COUNTRY GIRL MEETS COUNTRY BOY *Warwick PR 5039* 43 3
6 Jun 87 ANNIVERSARY – 20 YEARS OF HITS *Epic 450 3931* 45 5

1 KLF guest vocals: Tammy Wynette

Mark WYNTER *UK, male vocalist – Terence Lewis (Singles: 80 weeks)* pos/wks

25 Aug 60 IMAGE OF A GIRL *Decca F 11263* 11 10
10 Nov 60 KICKIN' UP THE LEAVES *Decca F 11279* 24 10
9 Mar 61 DREAM GIRL *Decca F 11323* 27 5
8 Jun 61 EXCLUSIVELY YOURS *Decca F 11354* 32 7
4 Oct 62 ● VENUS IN BLUE JEANS *Pye 7N 15466* 4 15
13 Dec 62 ● GO AWAY LITTLE GIRL *Pye 7N 15492* 6 11
6 Jun 63 SHY GIRL *Pye 7N 15525* 28 6
14 Nov 63 IT'S ALMOST TOMORROW *Pye 7N 15577* 12 12
9 Apr 64 ONLY YOU (AND YOU ALONE) *Pye 7N 15626* 38 4

Malcolm X *US, male orator, d. 21 Feb 1965 (Singles: 4 weeks)* pos/wks

7 Apr 84 NO SELL OUT *Tommy Boy IS 165* 60 4

Hit features credit: 'Music by Keith Le Blanc'

X-ECUTIONERS featuring Mike SHINODA and Mr HAHN of LINKIN PARK *US, male DJ / production / rap group and male DJ / vocal duo (Singles: 9 weeks)* pos/wks

13 Apr 02 ● IT'S GOIN' DOWN *Epic 6725642* 7 9

X MAL DEUTSCHLAND *UK / Germany, male / female vocal / instrumental group (Albums: 1 week)* pos/wks

7 Jul 84 TOCSIN *4AD CAD 407* 86 1

X MEN – *See SELENA vs X MEN*

XAVIER – *See TJR featuring XAVIER*

XAVIER *US, male / female vocal / instrumental group (Singles: 3 weeks)* pos/wks

20 Mar 82 WORK THAT SUCKER TO DEATH / LOVE IS ON THE ONE *Liberty UP 651* 53 3

XPANSIONS *UK, male producer – Richie Malone (Singles: 21 weeks)* pos/wks

6 Oct 90 ELEVATION *Optimism 113683* 49 5
23 Feb 91 ● MOVE YOUR BODY (ELEVATION) *Arista 113 683* 7 9
15 Jun 91 WHAT YOU WANT *Arista 114 246* 1 ....55 2
26 Aug 95 MOVE YOUR BODY (re-mix) *Arista 74321294982* 2 ....14 4
30 Nov 02 ELEVATION (MOVE YOUR BODY) 2002 (re-mix) *RM RMRCD 10* 70 1

1 Xpansions featuring Dale Joyner 2 Xpansions 95

'Move Your Body' is a re-mix of 'Elevation'

X-PRESS 2 *UK, male instrumental / production group (Singles: 24 weeks, Albums: 3 weeks)*

		pos	wks
5 Jun 93	**LONDON X-PRESS** *Junior Boy's Own JBO 12*	**59**	1
16 Oct 93	**SAY WHAT!** *Junior Boy's Own JBO 16CD*	**32**	2
30 Jul 94	**ROCK 2 HOUSE / HIP HOUSIN'** *Junior Boy's Own JBO 21CD* [1]	**55**	2
9 Mar 96	**THE SOUND** *Junior Boy's Own JBO 36*	**38**	1
12 Oct 96	**TRANZ EURO XPRESS** *Junior Boy's Own JBO 42CD*	**45**	1
30 Sep 00	**AC / DC** *Skint SKINT 57*	**60**	1
28 Apr 01	**MUZIKIZUM** *Skint SKINT 65*	**52**	1
20 Oct 01	**SMOKE MACHINE** *Skint SKINT 69*	**43**	1
20 Apr 02 ●	**LAZY** *Skint SKINT 74CD* [2]	**2**	13
21 Sep 02	**I WANT YOU BACK** *Skint SKINT 81CD*	**50**	1
4 May 02	**MUZIKIZUM** *Skint BRASSIC 23CD*	**15**	3

[1] X-Press 2 featuring Lo-Pro [2] X-Press 2 featuring David Byrne

'I Want You Back' features Dieter Meier

X-RAY SPEX *UK, male / female vocal / instrumental group (Singles: 33 weeks, Albums: 14 weeks)*

		pos	wks
29 Apr 78	**THE DAY THE WORLD TURNED DAYGLO** *EMI International INT 553*	**23**	8
22 Jul 78	**IDENTITY** *EMI International INT 563*	**24**	10
4 Nov 78	**GERM FREE ADOLESCENCE** *EMI International INT 573*	**19**	11
21 Apr 79	**HIGHLY INFLAMMABLE** *EMI International INT 583*	**45**	4
9 Dec 78	**GERM FREE ADOLESCENTS** *EMI International INS 3023*	**30**	14

XRS – *See DJ MARKY & XRS*

XSCAPE *US, female vocal group (Singles: 15 weeks)*

		pos	wks
20 Nov 93	**JUST KICKIN' IT** *Columbia 6598622*	**49**	2
5 Nov 94	**JUST KICKIN' IT (re-issue)** *Columbia 6608642*	**54**	2
7 Oct 95	**FEELS SO GOOD** *Columbia 6625022*	**34**	2
27 Jan 96	**WHO CAN I RUN TO** *Columbia 6628112*	**31**	3
29 Jun 96	**KEEP ON KEEPIN' ON** *East West A 4287CD* [1]	**39**	2
19 Apr 97	**KEEP ON KEEPIN' ON (re-issue)** *East West A 3950CD1* [1]	**27**	2
22 Aug 98	**THE ARMS OF THE ONE WHO LOVES YOU** *Columbia 6662522*	**46**	2

[1] MC Lyte featuring Xscape

XSTASIA
UK, male / female vocal / production duo (Singles: 1 week)

		pos	wks
17 Mar 01	**SWEETNESS** *Liquid Asset ASSETCD 005*	**65**	1

X-STATIC
Italy, male / female vocal / instrumental group (Singles: 2 weeks)

		pos	wks
4 Feb 95	**I'M STANDING (HIGHER)** *Positiva CDTIV 25*	**41**	2

XTC *UK, male vocal / instrumental group (Singles: 70 weeks, Albums: 51 weeks)*

		pos	wks
12 May 79	**LIFE BEGINS AT THE HOP** *Virgin VS 259*	**54**	4
22 Sep 79	**MAKING PLANS FOR NIGEL** *Virgin VS 282*	**17**	11
6 Sep 80	**GENERALS AND MAJORS / DON'T LOSE YOUR TEMPER** *Virgin VS 365*	**32**	8
18 Oct 80	**TOWERS OF LONDON** *Virgin VS 372*	**31**	5
24 Jan 81	**SGT ROCK (IS GOING TO HELP ME)** *Virgin VS 384*	**16**	9
23 Jan 82 ●	**SENSES WORKING OVERTIME** *Virgin VS 462*	**10**	9
27 Mar 82	**BALL AND CHAIN** *Virgin VS 482*	**58**	4
15 Oct 83	**LOVE ON A FARMBOY'S WAGES** *Virgin VS 613*	**50**	4
29 Sep 84	**ALL YOU PRETTY GIRLS** *Virgin VS 709*	**55**	5
28 Jan 89	**MAYOR OF SIMPLETON** *Virgin VS 1158*	**46**	5
4 Apr 92	**THE DISAPPOINTED** *Virgin VS 1404*	**33**	5
13 Jun 92	**THE BALLAD OF PETER PUMPKINHEAD** *Virgin VS 1415*	**71**	1
11 Feb 78	**WHITE MUSIC** *Virgin V 2095*	**38**	4
28 Oct 78	**GO 2** *Virgin V 2108*	**21**	3
1 Sep 79	**DRUMS AND WIRES** *Virgin V 2129*	**34**	7
20 Sep 80	**BLACK SEA** *Virgin V 2173*	**16**	7
20 Feb 82 ●	**ENGLISH SETTLEMENT** *Virgin V 2223*	**5**	11
13 Nov 82	**WAXWORKS – SOME SINGLES (1977-1982)** *Virgin V 2251*	**54**	3
10 Sep 83	**MUMMER** *Virgin V 2264*	**51**	4
27 Oct 84	**THE BIG EXPRESS** *Virgin V 2325*	**38**	2
8 Nov 86	**SKYLARKING** *Virgin V 2399*	**90**	1
11 Mar 89	**ORANGES AND LEMONS** *Virgin V 2581*	**28**	3
9 May 92	**NONSUCH** *Virgin CDV 2699*	**28**	2
28 Sep 96	**FOSSIL FUEL – THE XTC SINGLES 1977-92** *Virgin CDVD 2811*	**33**	2
6 Mar 99	**APPLE VENUS – VOLUME 1** *Cooking Vinyl COOKCD 172*	**42**	1
3 Jun 00	**APPLE VENUS – VOLUME 2** *Cooking Vinyl COOKCD 194* [1]	**40**	1

[1] XTC and Wasp Star

XTM & DJ CHUCKY presents ANNIA *Spain / Japan, male DJ / production trio and female vocalist (Singles: 19 weeks)*

		pos	wks
7 Jun 03 ●	**FLY ON THE WINGS OF LOVE** *Serious SER 62CD*	**8**	19

XZIBIT *US, male rapper – Alvin Joiner (Singles: 9 weeks, Albums: 13 weeks)*

		pos	wks
17 Mar 01	**X** *Epic 6709072* [1]	**14**	7
16 Nov 02	**MULTIPLY** *Epic / Loud 6731552*	**39**	2
10 Feb 01	**RESTLESS** *Epic 4989132*	**27**	11
12 Oct 02	**MAN VS MACHINE** *Epic 5047539*	**43**	2

[1] Xzibit featuring Snoop Dogg

Y?N-VEE *US, female vocal group (Singles: 1 week)*

		pos	wks
17 Dec 94	**CHOCOLATE** *RAL RALCD 2*	**65**	1

Y & T *US, male vocal / instrumental group (Singles: 4 weeks, Albums: 15 weeks)*

		pos	wks
13 Aug 83	**MEAN STREAK** *A&M AM 135*	**41**	4
11 Sep 82	**BLACK TIGER** *A&M AMLH 64910*	**53**	8
10 Sep 83	**MEAN STREAK** *A&M AMLX 64960*	**35**	4
18 Aug 84	**IN ROCK WE TRUST** *A&M AMLX 65007*	**33**	3

Y-TRAXX
Belgium, male producer – Frédérique de Backer (Singles: 2 weeks)

		pos	wks
24 May 97	**MYSTERY LAND (EP)** *ffrr FCD 292*	**63**	1
20 Sep 03	**MYSTERY LAND (re-mix)** *Nebula NEBT 047* [1]	**70**	1

[1] Y-Traxx featuring Neve

Tracks on Mystery Land (EP): Mystery Land (radio edit) / Trance Piano / Kiss the Sound / Mystery Land

Y-TRIBE featuring Elisabeth TROY *UK, male instrumental / production duo with female vocalist (Singles: 3 weeks)*

		pos	wks
18 Dec 99	**ENOUGH IS ENOUGH (re)** *Northwest 10 NORTHCD 002*	**49**	3

FILM SOUNDTRACKS

A list of all the film soundtrack albums dating back to the 1950s when these collections dominated the LP charts. Soundtrack albums recorded by one act only appear in the main A-Z by artist section.

CHART ENTRY DATE / **ALBUM TITLE** / LABEL / **PEAK POSITION / WEEKS ON CHART**

28 Jul 1956 **OKLAHOMA!** Capitol **1 162**
28 Jul 1956 **CAROUSEL** Capitol **1 40**
25 Aug 1956 **THE EDDY DUCHIN STORY** Brunswick **3 4**
22 Sep 1956 **THE KING AND I** Capitol **1 200**
22 Dec 1956 **HIGH SOCIETY** Capitol **2 25**
18 Jan 1958 **PAL JOEY** Capitol **1 23**
8 Feb 1958 **THE PYJAMA GAME** Philips **3 10**
3 May 1958 **SOUTH PACIFIC** RCA **1 313**
31 Jan 1959 **GIGI** MGM **2 88**
10 Oct 1959 **PORGY AND BESS** Philips **7 5**
23 Jan 1960 **THE FIVE PENNIES** London **2 15**
7 May 1960 **CAN CAN** Capitol **2 31**
23 Jul 1960 **HIGH SOCIETY** Capitol **16 1**
5 Nov 1960 **BEN HUR** MGM **15 3**
21 Jan 1961 **NEVER ON SUNDAY** London **17 1**
18 Feb 1961 **SONG WITHOUT END** Pye **9 10**
29 Apr 1961 **SEVEN BRIDES FOR SEVEN BROTHERS** MGM **6 22**
3 Jun 1961 **EXODUS** RCA **17 1**
11 Nov 1961 **THE GLENN MILLER STORY (re-issue)** Ace of Hearts **12 7**
10 Mar 1962 **GREAT MOTION PICTURE THEMES** His Master's Voice **19 1**
24 Mar 1962 **WEST SIDE STORY** Philips **1 175**
28 Apr 1962 **IT'S TRAD DAD** Columbia **3 21**
22 Sep 1962 **THE MUSIC MAN** Warner Bros. **14 9**
3 Nov 1962 **PORGY AND BESS (re-issue)** CBS **14 7**
15 Jun 1963 **JUST FOR FUN** Decca **20 2**
31 Oct 1964 **MY FAIR LADY** CBS **9 51**
31 Oct 1964 **GOLDFINGER** United Artists **14 5**
16 Jan 1965 **MARY POPPINS** HMV **2 82**
10 Apr 1965 **THE SOUND OF MUSIC** RCA **1 381**
30 Apr 1966 **FUNNY GIRL** Capitol **19 3**
11 Sep 1966 **DOCTOR ZHIVAGO** MGM **3 106**
22 Jul 1967 **CASINO ROYALE** RCA Victor **35 1**
29 Jul 1967 **A MAN AND A WOMAN** United Artists **31 11**
28 Oct 1967 **THOROUGHLY MODERN MILLIE** Brunswick **9 19**
9 Mar 1968 **THE JUNGLE BOOK** Disney **5 51**
21 Sep 1968 **STAR** Stateside **36 1**
12 Oct 1968 **THE GOOD, THE BAD AND THE UGLY** United Artists **2 18**
23 Nov 1968 **OLIVER!** RCA Victor **4 107**
23 Nov 1968 **CAMELOT** Warner Bros. **37 1**
8 Feb 1969 **CHITTY CHITTY BANG BANG** United Artists **10 4**
10 May 1969 **FUNNY GIRL** CBS **11 22**
14 Jun 1969 **2001 – A SPACE ODYSSEY** MGM **3 67**
20 Dec 1969 **EASY RIDER** Stateside **2 67**
24 Jan 1970 **JUNGLE BOOK (re-issue)** Disney **25 26**
7 Feb 1970 **PAINT YOUR WAGON** Paramount **2 102**
14 Mar 1970 **HELLO DOLLY** Stateside **45 2**
18 Jul 1970 **WOODSTOCK** Atlantic **35 19**
24 Apr 1971 **LOVE STORY** Paramount **10 33**
12 Feb 1972 **A CLOCKWORK ORANGE** Warner Bros. **4 46**
8 Apr 1972 **FIDDLER ON THE ROOF** United Artists **26 2**
13 May 1972 **2001 – A SPACE ODYSSEY** (re-issue) MGM **20 2**
29 Nov 1972 **SOUTH PACIFIC (re-issue)** RCA Victor **25 2**
31 Mar 1973 **CABARET** Probe **13 22**
14 Apr 1973 **LOST HORIZON** Bell **36 3**
22 Sep 1973 **JESUS CHRIST SUPERSTAR** MCA **23 18**
23 Mar 1974 **THE STING** MCA **7 35**
27 Apr 1974 **AMERICAN GRAFFITI** MCA **37 1**
8 Jun 1974 **A TOUCH OF CLASS** Philips **32 1**
5 Oct 1974 **SUNSHINE** MCA **47 3**
5 Apr 1975 **TOMMY** Polydor **21 9**
31 Jan 1976 **JAWS** MCA **55 1**
5 Mar 1977 **MOSES** Pye **43 2**
9 Apr 1977 **A STAR IS BORN** CBS **1 54**
2 Jul 1977 **THE BEST OF CAR WASH** MCA **59 1**
11 Mar 1978 **SATURDAY NIGHT FEVER** RSO **1 65**
22 Apr 1978 **THE STUD** Ronco **2 19**
29 Apr 1978 **CLOSE ENCOUNTERS OF THE THIRD KIND** Arista **40 6**
6 May 1978 **THE LAST WALTZ** Warner Bros. **39 4**
20 May 1978 **THANK GOD IT'S FRIDAY** Casablanca **40 5**
27 May 1978 **FM** MCA **37 7**
8 Jul 1978 **GREASE** RSO **1 47**
12 Aug 1978 **SGT. PEPPER'S LONELY HEARTS CLUB BAND** A & M **38 2**
7 Oct 1978 **CONVOY** Capitol **52 1**
30 Jun 1979 **THE WORLD IS FULL OF MARRIED MEN** Ronco **25 9**
14 Jul 1979 **THE WARRIORS** A & M **53 7**
6 Oct 1979 **QUADROPHENIA** Polydor **23 16**
10 Nov 1979 **20 SMASH DISCO HITS (THE BITCH)** Warner Bros. **42 5**
5 Jan 1980 **THE SECRET POLICEMAN'S BALL** Island **33 6**
9 Feb 1980 **SUNBURN** Warwick **45 7**

16 Feb 1980 **GOING STEADY** Warwick **25 10**
8 Mar 1980 **THE ROSE** Atlantic **68 1**
19 Jul 1980 **XANADU** Jet **2 17**
16 Aug 1980 **CAN'T STOP THE MUSIC** Mercury **9 8**
6 Sep 1980 **FAME** RSO **1 25**
14 Feb 1981 **DANCE CRAZE** 2-Tone **5 15**
12 Dec 1981 **THE SECRET POLICEMAN'S OTHER BALL** Springtime **69 4**
20 Mar 1982 **THE SECRET POLICEMAN'S OTHER BALL (THE MUSIC)** Springtime **29 5**
27 Mar 1982 **JAMES BOND'S GREATEST HITS** Liberty **4 13**
17 Jul 1982 **THE SOUND OF MUSIC (re-issue)** RCA **98 1**
4 Sep 1982 **ROCKY III** Liberty **42 7**
4 Sep 1982 **ANNIE** CBS **83 2**
11 Sep 1982 **BRIMSTONE AND TREACLE** A & M **67 3**
12 Feb 1983 **AN OFFICER AND A GENTLEMAN** Island **40 14**
25 Jun 1983 **RETURN OF THE JEDI** RSO **85 5**
2 Jul 1983 **FLASHDANCE** Casablanca **9 30**
1 Oct 1983 **STAYING ALIVE** RSO **14 8**
21 Apr 1984 **FOOTLOOSE** CBS **7 25**
21 Apr 1984 **AGAINST ALL ODDS** Virgin **29 10**
16 Jun 1984 **BREAKDANCE** Polydor **6 29**
7 Jul 1984 **BEAT STREET** Atlantic **30 13**
18 Aug 1984 **ELECTRIC DREAMS** Virgin **46 7**
29 Sep 1984 **GHOSTBUSTERS** Arista **24 25**
16 Feb 1985 **BEVERLY HILLS COP** MCA **24 32**
22 Jun 1985 **A VIEW TO A KILL** Parlophone **81 1**
11 Jan 1986 **BACK TO THE FUTURE** MCA **66 8**
1 Feb 1986 **ROCKY IV** Scotti Bros. **3 22**
1 Feb 1986 **MISTRAL'S DAUGHTER** Carrere **53 3**
15 Mar 1986 **THE CINEMA HITS ALBUM** Towerbell **44 9**
5 Apr 1986 **ABSOLUTE BEGINNERS** Virgin **19 9**
26 Apr 1986 **OUT OF AFRICA** MCA **81 2**
5 Jul 1986 **LABYRINTH** EMI America **38 2**
11 Oct 1986 **TOP GUN*** CBS **4 46**
11 Apr 1987 **THE BLUES BROTHERS*** Atlantic **59 26**
2 May 1987 **PLATOON** WEA **90 2**
18 Jul 1987 **BEVERLY HILLS COP 2** MCA **71 5**
1 Aug 1987 **WHO'S THAT GIRL** Sire **4 25**
1 Aug 1987 **THE LIVING DAYLIGHTS** Warner Bros. **57 6**
22 Aug 1987 **LA BAMBA** London **24 15**
3 Oct 1987 **FULL METAL JACKET** Warner Bros. **60 4**
31 Oct 1987 **DIRTY DANCING*** RCA **4 63**
16 Jan 1988 **FLASHDANCE (re-issue)** Mercury **93 2**
20 Feb 1988 **CRY FREEDOM** MCA **73 2**
14 May 1988 **MORE DIRTY DANCING*** RCA **3 27**
24 Sep 1988 **BUSTER*** Virgin **6 16**
22 Oct 1988 **GOOD MORNING VIETNAM*** A & M **50 9**

The new compilations Top 20 chart is used from this point in 1988 except where an album's peak position is listed as lower than 20, indicating that it is taken from the main official albums chart. Records marked* appeared on both charts.

14 Jan 1989 **DIRTY DANCING*** RCA **1 148**
14 Jan 1989 **BUSTER*** Virgin **2 36**
21 Jan 1989 **THE BLUES BROTHERS*** Atlantic **4 80**
21 Jan 1989 **GOOD MORNING VIETNAM*** A & M **7 29**
28 Jan 1989 **THE LOST BOYS** Atlantic **1 61**
4 Feb 1989 **COCKTAIL** Elektra **2 15**
4 Feb 1989 **MORE DIRTY DANCING*** RCA **14 17**
18 Mar 1989 **SCANDAL** Parlophone **13 3**
22 Apr 1989 **TOP GUN*** CBS **4 34**
13 May 1989 **DIRTY DANCING – LIVE IN CONCERT** RCA **19 2**
15 Jul 1989 **LICENCE TO KILL** MCA **17 2**
22 Jul 1989 **GHOSTBUSTERS 2** MCA **15 4**
10 Mar 1990 **THE DELINQUENTS** PWL **16 1**
26 May 1990 **PRETTY WOMAN** EMI USA **2 72**
23 Jun 1990 **TEENAGE MUTANT NINJA TURTLES** SBK **6 18**
11 Aug 1990 **DAYS OF THUNDER** Epic **4 15**
27 Oct 1990 **GHOST** Milan **15 4**
1 Dec 1990 **THE BEST FROM THE MGM MUSICALS** EMI **12 4**
2 Feb 1991 **ROCKY V** Capitol **9 9**
2 Mar 1991 **GREASE (re-issue)** Polydor **8 11**
23 Mar 1991 **THE GODFATHER III** Columbia **19 1**
27 Apr 1991 **NEW JACK CITY** Giant **16 5**
1 Jun 1991 **MERMAIDS** Epic **6 15**
27 Jul 1991 **ROBIN HOOD – PRINCE OF THIEVES** Polydor **3 14**
23 Nov 1991 **LOVE AT THE MOVIES** Telstar **6 14**
18 Jan 1992 **BILL AND TED'S BOGUS JOURNEY** Interscope **3 8**
29 Feb 1992 **MY GIRL** Epic **13 7**
30 May 1992 **WAYNE'S WORLD** Reprise **5 11**
12 Sep 1992 **THE BEST OF JAMES BOND – 30TH ANNIVERSARY** EMI **2 11**
19 Sep 1992 **MO' MONEY** Perspective **16 1**
14 Nov 1992 **BOOMERANG** LaFace **17 2**
28 Nov 1992 **THE BODYGUARD** Arista **1 78**
23 Jan 1993 **MOVIE HITS** Telstar **19 2**
30 Jan 1993 **SISTER ACT** Hollywood **14 4**
13 Feb 1993 **BRAM STOKER'S DRACULA** Columbia **10 6**
20 Mar 1993 **RESERVOIR DOGS** MCA **16 3**
5 Jun 1993 **INDECENT PROPOSAL** MCA **13 3**
24 Jul 1993 **THE LAST ACTION HERO** Columbia **16 6**
18 Sep 1993 **SLIVER** Virgin **20 1**
16 Oct 1993 **SLEEPLESS IN SEATTLE** Epic **10 6**
16 Oct 1993 **JUDGEMENT NIGHT** Epic **16 3**
20 Nov 1993 **THE VERY BEST OF DISNEY** Pickwick **4 13**
8 Jan 1994 **ALADDIN** Pickwick **11 5**
19 Feb 1994 **THE MOVIES' GREATEST LOVE SONGS** PolyGram TV **4 6**
5 Mar 1994 **WAYNE'S WORLD 2** Warner Bros. **17 1**
12 Mar 1994 **PHILADELPHIA** Epic **5 14**

FILM SOUNDTRACKS CONTINUED

7 May 1994 ABOVE THE RIM Interscope 18 1
28 May 1994 FOUR WEDDINGS AND A FUNERAL Vertigo 5 21
25 Jun 1994 THE CROW Atlantic 13 5
6 Aug 1994 THE FLINTSTONES MCA 18 1
22 Oct 1994 THE LION KING Mercury 4 20
22 Oct 1994 FORREST GUMP Epic 5 13
5 Nov 1994 PULP FICTION MCA 5 56
5 Nov 1994 THE LION KING SING-ALONG Pickwick/Disney 16 3
19 Nov 1994 THE VERY BEST OF DISNEY 2 Disney 9 4
11 Mar 1995 NATURAL BORN KILLERS Interscope 10 6
8 Jul 1995 BAD BOYS Work 19 1
29 Jul 1995 BATMAN FOREVER Atlantic 11 4
3 Feb 1996 WAITING TO EXHALE Arista 8 5
3 Feb 1996 DANGEROUS MINDS MCA 13 2
2 Mar 1996 TRAINSPOTTING EMI Premier 2 66
29 Jun 1996 MOVIE KILLERS Telstar 4 16
20 Jul 1996 MISSION: IMPOSSIBLE Mother 18 1
19 Oct 1996 THE NUTTY PROFESSOR Def Jam 20 1
7 Dec 1996 LOVE AT THE MOVIES ... THE ALBUM EMI TV/Sony TV 16 3
29 Mar 1997 SPACE JAM Atlantic 5 10
5 Apr 1997 WILLIAM SHAKESPEARE'S ROMEO + JULIET Premier Soundtracks 3 24
3 May 1997 THE SAINT Virgin 15 1
2 Aug 1997 MEN IN BLACK – THE ALBUM Columbia 5 13
9 Aug 1997 SPRAWN – THE ALBUM Epic 18 1
13 Sep 1997 THE FULL MONTY RCA Victor 1 43
27 Sep 1997 TRAINSPOTTING #2 Premier Soundtracks 11 5
31 Jan 1998 BOOGIE NIGHTS Premier Soundtracks 19 1
21 Feb 1998 MOVIE LOVERS Telstar 17 1
18 Apr 1998 JACKIE BROWN Maverick 11 7
27 Jun 1998 THE WEDDING SINGER Maverick 15 4
4 Jul 1998 CITY OF ANGELS Reprise 18 3
18 Jul 1998 GREASE (2nd re-issue) Polydor 2 15
25 Jul 1998 GODZILLA – THE ALBUM Epic 13 4
12 Sep 1998 LOCK, STOCK AND TWO SMOKING BARRELS Island 7 23
26 Sep 1998 ARMAGEDDON Columbia 19 2
10 Apr 1999 ESSENTIAL SOUNDTRACKS Telstar TV 4 10
5 Jun 1999 NOTTING HILL Island 4 19
19 Jun 1999 HUMAN TRAFFIC London 14 3
26 Jun 1999 THE MATRIX (ORIGINAL SOUNDTRACK) Maverick 16 5
17 Jul 1999 AUSTIN POWERS – THE SPY WHO SHAGGED ME Maverick 6 11
11 Sep 1999 SOUTH PARK: BIGGER, LONGER & UNCUT Atlantic 9 5
2 Oct 1999 MANUMISSION – THE MOVIE Telstar TV 17 1
13 Nov 1999 THE BEST OF BOND ... JAMES BOND Capitol 6 10
4 Mar 2000 THE BEACH (ORIGINAL SOUNDTRACK) London 1 8
25 Mar 2000 THE MILLION DOLLAR HOTEL Island 13 1
8 Apr 2000 POKEMON – THE FIRST MOVIE Atlantic 8 5
8 Apr 2000 THE ARISTOCATS – READ ALONG Walt Disney 60 1
15 Apr 2000 ESSENTIAL SOUNDTRACKS – 40 TRACKS – THE NEW MOVIE COLLECTION Telstar TV 8 3
29 Apr 2000 KEVIN & PERRY GO LARGE Virgin/EMI 4 7
1 Jul 2000 MISSION: IMPOSSIBLE 2 Hollywood 12 8
16 Sep 2000 SNATCH Universal Soundtracks 11 3
21 Oct 2000 BILLY ELLIOT Polydor 10 4
4 Nov 2000 COYOTE UGLY Curb/London 16 3
14 Apr 2001 SAVE THE LAST DANCE Hollywood 5 8
28 Apr 2001 BRIDGET JONES'S DIARY Mercury 1 30
23 Jun 2001 MUSIC TO WATCH MOVIES BY Columbia 18 1
21 Jul 2001 LARA CROFT – TOMB RAIDER Elektra 13 2
15 Sep 2001 MOULIN ROUGE Twentieth Century Fox Film Corp/Interscope 2 12
29 Sep 2001 THE FAST AND THE FURIOUS Murder Inc/Def Jam 20 2
27 Oct 2001 AMERICAN PIE 2 Republic/Universal 17 2
10 Nov 2001 BRIDGET JONES'S DIARY 2 Mercury 8 2
10 Nov 2001 THE ULTIMATE MOVIE ALBUM Decca 16 1
26 Feb 2002 O BROTHER, WHERE ART THOU? Mercury 20 1
2 Mar 2002 OCEAN'S ELEVEN Warner 15 1
16 Mar 2002 MOULIN ROUGE – COLLECTOR'S EDITION Interscope 9 7
30 Mar 2002 ALI G INDAHOUSE – DA SOUNDTRACK Island 5 7
20 Apr 2002 24 HOUR PARTY PEOPLE London 15 2
1 Jun 2002 SPIDERMAN Columbia 14 6
10 Aug 2002 AUSTIN POWERS IN GOLDMEMBER Maverick/Warner 14 2
9 Nov 2002 8 MILE Interscope/Polydor 1 23
25 Jan 2003 CHICAGO Epic 5 10
17 May 2003 THE MATRIX RELOADED (ORIGINAL SOUNDTRACK) Maverick/Warner 2 7
19 Jul 2003 CHARLIE'S ANGELS – FULL THROTTLE Columbia 12 2
18 Oct 2003 BAD BOYS II Bad Boy 17 1
25 Oct 2003 KILL BILL – VOL.1 (ORIGINAL SOUNDTRACK) Maverick/Warner 6 4
29 Nov 2003 LOVE ACTUALLY 2 6*

*Still on chart

YA KID K – *See HI-TEK 3 featuring YA KID K; TECHNOTRONIC*

Weird Al YANKOVIC *US, male vocalist (Singles: 8 weeks)* pos/wks

7 Apr 84 **EAT IT** *Scotti Bros. / Epic A 4257* **36** 7
4 Jul 92 **SMELLS LIKE NIRVANA** *Scotti Bros PO 219* **58** 1

YANNI
Greece, male instrumentalist – keyboards – Yiannis Chryssolmalis (Albums: 2 weeks) pos/wks

4 Apr 98 **TRIBUTE** *Virgin CDVUS 135* **40** 2

YANOU – *See DJ SAMMY*

YARBROUGH and PEOPLES *US, male / female vocal / instrumental duo – Calvin Yarbrough and Alisa Peoples (Singles: 20 weeks)* pos/wks

27 Dec 80 ● **DON'T STOP THE MUSIC** *Mercury MER 53* **7** 12
5 May 84 **DON'T WASTE YOUR TIME** *Total Experience XE 501* **60** 3
11 Jan 86 **GUILTY** *Total Experience FB 49905* **53** 3
5 Jul 86 **I WOULDN'T LIE** *Total Experience FB 49841* **61** 2

YARDBIRDS *UK, male vocal / instrumental group (Singles: 62 weeks, Albums: 8 weeks)* pos/wks

12 Nov 64 **GOOD MORNING LITTLE SCHOOLGIRL** *Columbia DB 7391* **44** 4
18 Mar 65 ● **FOR YOUR LOVE** *Columbia DB 7499* **3** 12
17 Jun 65 ● **HEART FULL OF SOUL** *Columbia DB 7594* **2** 13
14 Oct 65 ● **EVIL HEARTED YOU / STILL I'M SAD** *Columbia DB 7706* **3** 10
3 Mar 66 ● **SHAPES OF THINGS** *Columbia DB 7848* **3** 9
2 Jun 66 ● **OVER UNDER SIDEWAYS DOWN** *Columbia DB 7928* **10** 9
27 Oct 66 **HAPPENINGS TEN YEARS TIME AGO** *Columbia DB 8024* **43** 5
23 Jul 66 **YARDBIRDS** *Columbia SX 6063* **20** 8

See also Jeff BECK; Eric CLAPTON; Keith RELF

YAVAHN – *See RUFFNECK featuring YAVAHN*

YAZOO (492 Top 500) *Former Depeche Mode member Vince Clarke, b. 3 July 1960 (k) and Alison Moyet, b. 18 June 1961 (both from Basildon, Essex) (v), were voted best British Newcomers at 1983 Brits. The Flying Pickets' a capella version of the distinctive duo's debut hit topped the chart in 1983 (Singles: 55 weeks, Albums: 86 weeks)* pos/wks

17 Apr 82 ● **ONLY YOU** *Mute MUTE 020* **2** 14
17 Jul 82 ● **DON'T GO** *Mute YAZ 001* **3** 11
20 Nov 82 **THE OTHER SIDE OF LOVE** *Mute YAZ 002* **13** 9
21 May 83 ● **NOBODY'S DIARY** *Mute YAZ 003* **3** 11
8 Dec 90 **SITUATION** *Mute YAZ 4* **14** 8
4 Sep 99 **ONLY YOU (re-mix)** *Mute CDYAZ 5* **38** 2
4 Sep 82 ● **UPSTAIRS AT ERIC'S** *Mute STUMM 7* **2** 63
16 Jul 83 ★ **YOU AND ME BOTH** *Mute STUMM 12* **1** 20
18 Sep 99 **ONLY YAZOO – THE BEST OF YAZOO** *Mute CDMUTEL 6* **22** 3

See also ASSEMBLY; ERASURE; Alison MOYET

YAZZ *UK, female vocalist – Yasmin Evans (Singles: 69 weeks, Albums: 32 weeks)* pos/wks

20 Feb 88 ● **DOCTORIN' THE HOUSE** *Ahead of Our Time CCUT 27* [1] **6** 9
23 Jul 88 ★ **THE ONLY WAY IS UP** *Big Life BLR 4* [2] **1** 15
29 Oct 88 ● **STAND UP FOR YOUR LOVE RIGHTS** *Big Life BLR 5* **2** 12
4 Feb 89 ● **FINE TIME** *Big Life BLR 6* **9** 8
29 Apr 89 **WHERE HAS ALL THE LOVE GONE** *Big Life BLR 8* **16** 6
23 Jun 90 **TREAT ME GOOD** *Big Life BLR 24* **20** 5
28 Mar 92 **ONE TRUE WOMAN** *Polydor PO 198* **60** 2
31 Jul 93 **HOW LONG** *Polydor PZCD 252* [3] **31** 5
2 Apr 94 **HAVE MERCY** *Polydor PZCD 309* **42** 3
9 Jul 94 **EVERYBODY'S GOT TO LEARN SOMETIME** *Polydor PZCD 316* **56** 2
28 Sep 96 **GOOD THING GOING** *East West EW 062CD* **53** 1
22 Mar 97 **NEVER CAN SAY GOODBYE** *East West EW 081CD* **61** 1
26 Nov 88 ● **WANTED** *Big Life YAZZLP 1* **3** 32

[1] Coldcut featuring Yazz and the Plastic Population [2] Yazz and the Plastic Population [3] Yazz and Aswad

The YEAH YEAH YEAHS *US, male / female vocal / instrumental group (Singles: 8 weeks, Albums: 6 weeks)* pos/wks

16 Nov 02 **MACHINE** *Wichita WEBB 036SCD* **37** 2
26 Apr 03 **DATE WITH THE NIGHT** *Dress Up / Polydor 0657442* **16** 2
5 Jul 03 **PIN** *Dress Up / Polydor 9808085* **29** 2
4 Oct 03 **MAPS** *Dress Up / Polydor 9811413* **26** 2
10 May 03 **FEVER TO TELL** *Dress Up / Polydor 0760612* **13** 6

Trisha YEARWOOD
US, female vocalist (Singles: 1 week, Albums: 2 weeks) pos/wks

9 Aug 97 **HOW DO I LIVE** *MCA MCSTD 48064* **66** 1
25 Jul 98 **WHERE YOUR ROAD LEADS** *MCA Nashville UMD 80513* **36** 2

YELL! *UK, male vocal duo – Paul Varney and Daniel James (Singles: 8 weeks)* pos/wks

20 Jan 90 ● **INSTANT REPLAY** *Fanfare FAN 22* **10** 8

YELLO *Switzerland, male vocal / instrumental duo – Dieter Meier and Boris Blank (Singles: 42 weeks, Albums: 15 weeks)* pos/wks

25 Jun 83 **I LOVE YOU** *Stiff BUY 176* **41** 4
26 Nov 83 **LOST AGAIN** *Stiff BUY 191* **73** 1
9 Aug 86 **GOLDRUSH** *Mercury MER 218* **54** 3
22 Aug 87 **THE RHYTHM DIVINE** *Mercury MER 253* [1] **54** 2
27 Aug 88 ● **THE RACE** *Mercury YELLO 1* **7** 11
17 Dec 88 **TIED UP** *Mercury YELLO 2* **60** 5
25 Mar 89 **OF COURSE I'M LYING** *Mercury YELLO 3* **23** 8
22 Jul 89 **BLAZING SADDLES** *Mercury YELLO 4* **47** 2
8 Jun 91 **RUBBERBANDMAN** *Mercury YELLO 5* **58** 2
5 Sep 92 **JUNGLE BILL** *Mercury MER 376* **61** 2
7 Nov 92 **THE RACE / BOSTICH (re-issue)** *Mercury MER 382* **55** 1
15 Oct 94 **HOW HOW** *Mercury MERCD 414* **59** 1
21 May 83 **YOU GOTTA SAY YES TO ANOTHER EXCESS** *Stiff SEEZ 48* **65** 2
6 Apr 85 **STELLA** *Elektra EKT 1* **92** 1
4 Jul 87 **ONE SECOND** *Mercury MERH 100* **48** 3
10 Dec 88 **FLAG** *Mercury 836778 1* **56** 7
29 Jun 91 **BABY** *Mercury 8487911* **37** 2

[1] Yello featuring Shirley Bassey

YELLOW DOG
US / UK, male vocal / instrumental group (Singles: 13 weeks) pos/wks

4 Feb 78 ● **JUST ONE MORE NIGHT** *Virgin VS 195* **8** 9
22 Jul 78 **WAIT UNTIL MIDNIGHT** *Virgin VS 217* **54** 4

YELLOW MAGIC ORCHESTRA
Japan, male instrumental group (Singles: 11 weeks) pos/wks

14 Jun 80 **COMPUTER GAME (THEME FROM 'THE INVADERS')** *A&M AMS 7502* **17** 11

YELLOWCOATS – *See Paul SHANE and the YELLOWCOATS*

Bryn YEMM *UK, male vocalist (Albums: 14 weeks)* pos/wks

9 Jun 84 **HOW DO I LOVE THEE** *Lifestyle LEG 17* **57** 2
7 Jul 84 **HOW GREAT THOU ART** *Lifestyle LEG 15* **67** 8
22 Dec 84 **THE BRYN YEMM CHRISTMAS COLLECTION** *Bay BAY 104* **95** 2
26 Oct 85 **MY TRIBUTE – BRYN YEMM INSPIRATIONAL ALBUM** *Word WSTR 9665* [1] **85** 2

[1] Bryn Yemm and the Gwent Chorale

YES (236 Top 500) *Seventies progressive rock giants, who later flirted successfully with AOR, formed London 1968. Noted Yes-men include Jon Anderson (v), Bill Bruford (d), Steve Howe (g), Rick Wakeman (k), Patrick Moraz (k) and ex-Buggle Trevor Horn (v/g), who masterminded their 1980s comeback (Singles: 31 weeks, Albums: 226 weeks)* pos/wks

17 Sep 77 ● **WONDROUS STORIES** *Atlantic K 10999* **7** 9
26 Nov 77 **GOING FOR THE ONE** *Atlantic K 11047* **24** 4
9 Sep 78 **DON'T KILL THE WHALE** *Atlantic K 11184* **36** 4
12 Nov 83 **OWNER OF A LONELY HEART** *Atco B 9817* ▲ **28** 9

31 Mar 84 LEAVE IT *Atco B 9787* 56 4
3 Oct 87 LOVE WILL FIND A WAY *Atco A 9449* 73 1
1 Aug 70 TIME AND A WORD *Atlantic 2400006* 45 3
27 Feb 71 ● THE YES ALBUM *Atlantic 2400101* 4 34
4 Dec 71 ● FRAGILE *Atlantic 2409019* 7 17
23 Sep 72 ● CLOSE TO THE EDGE *Atlantic K 50012* 4 13
26 May 73 ● YESSONGS *Atlantic K 60045* 7 13
22 Dec 73 ★ TALES FROM TOPOGRAPHIC OCEANS *Atlantic K 80001* 1 15
21 Dec 74 ● RELAYER *Atlantic K 50096* 4 11
29 Mar 75 YESTERDAYS *Atlantic K 50048* 27 7
30 Jul 77 ★ GOING FOR THE ONE *Atlantic K 50379* 1 28
7 Oct 78 ● TORMATO *Atlantic K 50518* 8 11
30 Aug 80 ● DRAMA *Atlantic K 50736* 2 8
10 Jan 81 YESSHOWS *Atlantic K 60142* 22 9
26 Nov 83 90125 *Atco 790125* 16 28
29 Mar 86 9012 LIVE: THE SOLOS *Atco 790 4741* 44 3
10 Oct 87 BIG GENERATOR *Atco WEX 70* 17 5
11 May 91 ● UNION *Arista 211558* 7 6
2 Apr 94 TALK *London 8284892* 20 4
9 Nov 96 KEYS TO ASCENSION *Essential! EDFCD 417* 48 1
15 Nov 97 KEYS TO ASCENSION 2 *Essential! EDFCD 457* 62 1
2 Oct 99 THE LADDER *Eagle EAGCD 088* 36 1
22 Sep 01 MAGNIFICATION *Eagle EAGCD 189* 71 1
9 Aug 03 ● THE ULTIMATE YES – 35TH ANNIVERSARY *WSM 8122737022* 10 7

See also ANDERSON BRUFORD WAKEMAN HOWE; Rick WAKEMAN; Alan WHITE; Chris SQUIRE; Jon ANDERSON

Melissa YIANNAKOU – *See DESIYA featuring Melissa YIANNAKOU*

YIN and YAN *UK, male vocal duo – Chris Sanford and Bill Mitchell (Singles: 5 weeks)* pos/wks

29 Mar 75 IF *EMI 2282* 25 5

Dwight YOAKAM
US, male vocalist / instrumentalist – guitar (Singles: 2 weeks, Albums: 4 weeks) pos/wks

10 Jul 99 CRAZY LITTLE THING CALLED LOVE *Reprise W 497CD* 43 2
9 May 87 HILLBILLY DELUXE *Reprise WX 106* 51 3
13 Aug 88 BUENAS NOCHES FROM A LONELY ROOM *Reprise WX 193* 87 1

YO-HANS – *See JODE featuring YO-HANS*

YOMANDA
UK, male DJ / producer – Paul Masterson (Singles: 21 weeks) pos/wks

24 Jul 99 ● SYNTH & STRINGS *Manifesto FESCD 59* 8 10
11 Mar 00 SUNSHINE *Manifesto FESCD 68* 16 6
2 Sep 00 ON THE LEVEL *Manifesto FESCD 73* 28 2
26 Jul 03 YOU'RE FREE *Incentive CENT 55CDS* 22 3

See also CANDY GIRLS; DOROTHY; SLEAZESISTERS; HI-GATE; CLERGY; Paul MASTERSON presents SUSHI

Tukka YOOT – *See US3*

YORK *Germany, male production / instrumental duo – Torsten and Jorg Stenzel (Singles: 21 weeks)* pos/wks

9 Oct 99 THE AWAKENING *Manifesto FESCD 60* 11 5
10 Jun 00 ● ON THE BEACH *Manifesto FESCD 70* 4 10
18 Nov 00 FAREWELL TO THE MOON *Manifesto FESCD 76* 37 2
27 Jan 01 THE FIELDS OF LOVE *Club Tools / Edel 0124095 CLU* [1] 16 4

[1] ATB featuring York

YOSH presents LOVEDEEJAY AKEMI
Holland, male producer – Yoshida Rosenboom (Singles: 5 weeks) pos/wks

29 Jul 95 IT'S WHAT'S UPFRONT THAT COUNTS *Limbo LIMB 46CD* 69 1
2 Dec 95 IT'S WHAT'S UPFRONT THAT COUNTS (re-mix) *Limbo LIMB 50CD* 31 2
20 Apr 96 THE SCREAMER *Limbo LIMB 54CD* 38 2

YOSHIKI – *See Roger TAYLOR*

YOTHU YINDI
Australia, male vocal / instrumental group (Singles: 1 week) pos/wks

15 Feb 92 TREATY *Hollywood HWD 116* 72 1

Faron YOUNG *US, male vocalist, d. 10 Dec 1996 (Singles: 23 weeks, Albums: 5 weeks)* pos/wks

15 Jul 72 ● IT'S FOUR IN THE MORNING *Mercury 6052 140* 3 23
28 Oct 72 IT'S FOUR IN THE MORNING *Mercury 6338 095* 27 5

Jimmy YOUNG *UK, male vocalist (Singles: 88 weeks)* pos/wks

9 Jan 53 FAITH CAN MOVE MOUNTAINS *Decca F 9986* 11 1
21 Aug 53 ● ETERNALLY *Decca F 10130* 8 9
6 May 55 ★ UNCHAINED MELODY *Decca F 10502* 1 19
16 Sep 55 ★ THE MAN FROM LARAMIE *Decca F 10597* 1 12
23 Dec 55 SOMEONE ON YOUR MIND *Decca F 10640* 13 5
16 Mar 56 ● CHAIN GANG *Decca F 10694* 9 6
8 Jun 56 WAYWARD WIND *Decca F 10736* 27 1
22 Jun 56 RICH MAN POOR MAN *Decca F 10736* 25 1
28 Sep 56 ● MORE *Decca F 10774* 4 17
3 May 57 ROUND AND ROUND *Decca F 10875* 30 1
10 Oct 63 MISS YOU *Columbia DB 7119* 15 13
26 Mar 64 UNCHAINED MELODY (re-recording) *Columbia DB 7234* 43 3

'Unchained Melody' on Columbia and 'Round and Round' are with The Michael Sammes Singers

John Paul YOUNG *Australia, male vocalist (Singles: 19 weeks)* pos/wks

29 Apr 78 ● LOVE IS IN THE AIR *Ariola ARO 117* 5 13
14 Nov 92 LOVE IS IN THE AIR (re-mix) *Columbia 6587697* 49 3
12 Jan 02 LOVE IS IN THE AIR (2nd re-mix) *Positiva CDTIV 166* [1] 25 3

[1] Milk and Sugar vs John Paul Young

Karen YOUNG *UK, female vocalist (Singles: 21 weeks)* pos/wks

6 Sep 69 ● NOBODY'S CHILD *Major Minor MM 625* 6 21

Karen YOUNG
US, female vocalist, d. 26 Jan 1991 (Singles: 9 weeks) pos/wks

19 Aug 78 HOT SHOT *Atlantic K 11180* 34 7
24 Feb 79 HOT SHOT (re-issue) *Atlantic LV 8* 75 1
15 Nov 97 HOT SHOT '97 (re-recording) *Distinctive DISNCD 37* 68 1

Neil YOUNG (215 Top 500) *Single-minded vocalist, guitarist, singer-songwriter, b. 12 Nov 1945, Toronto, Ontario, Canada. Constantly changing musical direction, with country rock as a member of the Buffalo Springfield and Crosby, Stills, Nash and Young, 'Shakey's' solo activity (and with support bands such as The International Harvesters, The Stray Gators and Crazy Horse) has embraced country, punk, rock and resulted in his oft-used title 'The Godfather of Grunge' (Singles: 22 weeks, Albums: 254 weeks)* pos/wks

11 Mar 72 ● HEART OF GOLD *Reprise K 14140* ▲ 10 11
6 Jan 79 FOUR STRONG WINDS *Reprise K 14493* 57 4
27 Feb 93 HARVEST MOON *Reprise W 0139CD* 36 3
17 Jul 93 THE NEEDLE AND THE DAMAGE DONE *Reprise W 0191CD* 75 1
30 Oct 93 LONG MAY YOU RUN (LIVE) *Reprise W 0207CD* 71 1
9 Apr 94 PHILADELPHIA *Reprise W 0242CD* 62 2
31 Oct 70 ● AFTER THE GOLD RUSH *Reprise RSLP 6383* 7 66
4 Mar 72 ★ HARVEST *Reprise K 54005* ▲ 1 34
27 Oct 73 TIME FADES AWAY *Warner Bros. K 54010* 20 2
10 Aug 74 ON THE BEACH *Reprise K 54014* 42 2
5 Jul 75 TONIGHT'S THE NIGHT *Reprise K 54040* 48 1
27 Dec 75 ZUMA *Reprise K 54057* 44 2
9 Oct 76 LONG MAY YOU RUN *Reprise K 54081* [1] 12 5
9 Jul 77 AMERICAN STARS 'N' BARS *Reprise K 54088* 17 8
17 Dec 77 DECADE *Reprise K 64037* 46 4
28 Oct 78 COMES A TIME *Reprise K 54099* 42 3
14 Jul 79 RUST NEVER SLEEPS *Reprise K 54105* [2] 13 13
1 Dec 79 LIVE RUST *Reprise K 64041* [2] 55 3
15 Nov 80 HAWKS AND DOVES *Reprise K 54109* 34 3
14 Nov 81 RE-AC-TOR *Reprise K 54116* [2] 69 3
5 Feb 83 TRANS *Geffen GEF 25019* 29 5
3 Sep 83 EVERYBODY'S ROCKIN' *Geffen GEF 25590* [3] 50 3

14 Sep 85 **OLD WAYS** *Geffen GEF 26377* 39 3
2 Aug 86 **LANDING ON WATER** *Geffen 924 1091* 52 2
4 Jul 87 **LIFE** *Geffen WX 109* [2] 71 1
30 Apr 88 **THIS NOTE'S FOR YOU** *WEA WX 168* [4] 56 3
21 Oct 89 **FREEDOM** *Reprise WX 257* 17 5
22 Sep 90 **RAGGED GLORY** *Reprise WX 374* 15 5
2 Nov 91 **WELD** *Reprise 7599266711* 20 3
14 Nov 92 ● **HARVEST MOON** *Reprise 9362450572* 9 18
23 Jan 93 **LUCKY THIRTEEN** *Geffen GED 24452* 69 1
26 Jun 93 ● **UNPLUGGED** *Reprise 9362453102* 4 13
27 Aug 94 ● **SLEEPS WITH ANGELS** *Reprise 9362457492* [2] 2 7
8 Jul 95 ● **MIRROR BALL** *Reprise 9362459342* 4 9
6 Jul 96 **BROKEN ARROW** *Reprise 9362462912* [2] 17 5
28 Jun 97 **YEAR OF THE HORSE** *Reprise 9362466522* [2] 36 2
6 May 00 ● **SILVER AND GOLD** *Reprise 9362473052* 10 4
20 Apr 02 **ARE YOU PASSIONATE?** *Reprise 9362481112* 24 3
27 Jul 02 **DECADE** *Reprise 7599272332* 15 9
26 Jul 03 **ON THE BEACH (re-issue)** *Reprise 9362484972* 42 1
30 Aug 03 **GREENDALE** *Reprise 9362485432* [2] 24 3

[1] Stills-Young Band [2] Neil Young and Crazy Horse [3] Neil Young and the Shocking Pinks [4] Neil Young and the Blue Notes

See also CROSBY, STILLS, NASH and YOUNG; CRAZY HORSE

Paul YOUNG (134 Top 500) *Soulful-sounding pop singer / songwriter (b. 17 Jan 1956, Bedfordshire, UK) who earlier fronted The Q-Tips and chart act Streetband. This multi-Brit Award winner sold seven million copies of his 'No Parlez' album (including more than one million in the UK) (Singles: 134 weeks, Albums: 232 weeks)* pos/wks

18 Jun 83 ★ **WHEREVER I LAY MY HAT (THAT'S MY HOME)** *CBS A 3371* [1] 1 15
10 Sep 83 ● **COME BACK AND STAY** *CBS A 3636* 4 9
19 Nov 83 ● **LOVE OF THE COMMON PEOPLE** *CBS A 3585* 2 13
13 Oct 84 ● **I'M GONNA TEAR YOUR PLAYHOUSE DOWN** *CBS A 4786* 9 7
8 Dec 84 ● **EVERYTHING MUST CHANGE** *CBS A 4972* 9 11
9 Mar 85 ● **EVERYTIME YOU GO AWAY** *CBS A 6300* ▲ 4 11
22 Jun 85 **TOMB OF MEMORIES (re)** *CBS A 6321* 16 8
4 Oct 86 **WONDERLAND** *CBS YOUNG 1* 24 5
29 Nov 86 **SOME PEOPLE** *CBS YOUNG 2* 56 3
7 Feb 87 **WHY DOES A MAN HAVE TO BE STRONG?** *CBS YOUNG 3* 63 2
12 May 90 **SOFTLY WHISPERING I LOVE YOU** *CBS YOUNG 4* 21 6
7 Jul 90 **OH GIRL** *CBS YOUNG 5* 25 6
6 Oct 90 **HEAVEN CAN WAIT** *CBS YOUNG 6* 71 2
12 Jan 91 **CALLING YOU** *CBS YOUNG 7* 57 2
30 Mar 91 ● **SENZA UNA DONNA (WITHOUT A WOMAN)** *London LON 294* [2] 4 12
10 Aug 91 **BOTH SIDES NOW** *MCA MCS 1546* [3] 74 1
26 Oct 91 **DON'T DREAM IT'S OVER** *Columbia 6574117* 20 5
25 Sep 93 **NOW I KNOW WHAT MADE OTIS BLUE** *Columbia 6596412* 14 7
27 Nov 93 **HOPE IN A HOPELESS WORLD** *Columbia 6598652* 42 3
23 Apr 94 **IT WILL BE YOU** *Columbia 6602812* 34 4
17 May 97 **I WISH YOU LOVE** *East West EW 100CD1* 33 2
30 Jul 83 ★ **NO PARLEZ** *CBS 25521* 1 119
6 Apr 85 ★ **THE SECRET OF ASSOCIATION** *CBS 26234* ■ 1 49
1 Nov 86 ● **BETWEEN TWO FIRES** *CBS 450 1501* 4 17
16 Jun 90 ● **OTHER VOICES** *CBS 4669171* 4 11
14 Sep 91 ★ **FROM TIME TO TIME – THE SINGLES COLLECTION** *Columbia 4688251* ■ 1 27
23 Oct 93 **THE CROSSING** *Columbia 4739282* 27 2
26 Nov 94 **REFLECTIONS** *Vision VISCD 1* 64 2
31 May 97 **PAUL YOUNG** *East West 630186192* 39 2
21 Jun 03 **THE ESSENTIAL** *Sony Music 5122992* 27 3

[1] Paul Young and the Family [2] Zucchero and Paul Young [3] Clannad and Paul Young

Retta YOUNG *US, female vocalist (Singles: 7 weeks)* pos/wks

24 May 75 **SENDING OUT AN S.O.S.** *All Platinum 6146 305* 28 7

Tracie YOUNG – *See TRACIE*

Will YOUNG *UK, male vocalist (Singles: 71 weeks, Albums: 22 weeks)* pos/wks

9 Mar 02 ★ **EVERGREEN / ANYTHING IS POSSIBLE** *S 74321926142* ◆ ■ 1 16
8 Jun 02 ★ **LIGHT MY FIRE (re)** *S 74321943002* ■ 1 20
5 Oct 02 ★ **THE LONG AND WINDING ROAD / SUSPICIOUS MINDS** *S 74321965972* [1] ■ 1 18
30 Nov 02 ● **DON'T LET ME DOWN / YOU AND I (re)** *S 74321981262* 2 13
6 Dec 03 ★ **LEAVE RIGHT NOW** *S 82876578562* ■ .... 1 4+
19 Oct 02 ★ **FROM NOW ON** *S 74321969592* ■ 1 19
13 Dec 03 ★ **FRIDAY'S CHILD** *S 82876557462* ■ .... 1 3+

[1] Will Young and Gareth Gates / Gareth Gates

YOUNG and COMPANY *US, male / female vocal / instrumental group (Singles: 12 weeks)* pos/wks

1 Nov 80 **I LIKE (WHAT YOU'RE DOING TO ME)** *Excalibur EXC 501* 20 12

YOUNG and MOODY BAND *UK, male vocal / instrumental group (Singles: 4 weeks)* pos/wks

10 Oct 81 **DON'T DO THAT** *Bronze BRO 130* 63 4

YOUNG BLACK TEENAGERS *US, male rap group (Singles: 3 weeks)* pos/wks

9 Apr 94 **TAP THE BOTTLE** *MCA MCSTD 1967* 39 3

YOUNG DISCIPLES *UK / US, male / female vocal / instrumental group (Singles: 17 weeks, Albums: 5 weeks)* pos/wks

13 Oct 90 **GET YOURSELF TOGETHER** *Talkin Loud TLK 2* 68 1
23 Feb 91 **APPARENTLY NOTHIN' (re)** *Talkin Loud TLK 5* 13 11
5 Oct 91 **GET YOURSELF TOGETHER (re-issue)** *Talkin Loud TLK 15* 65 2
5 Sep 92 **YOUNG DISCIPLES (EP)** *Talkin Loud TLKX 18* 48 3
31 Aug 91 **ROAD TO FREEDOM** *Talkin Loud 5100971* 21 5

'Apparently Nothin' first peaked at No.46 in Feb 1991 making its peak position only on re-entry in Aug 1991. Tracks on Young Disciples (EP): Move On / Freedom / All I Have In Me / Move On (re-mix)

YOUNG GODS *Switzerland, male vocal / instrumental group (Albums: 1 week)* pos/wks

15 Feb 92 **TV SKY** *Play It Again Sam BIAS 201CD* 54 1

YOUNG VOICES CHOIR – *See DECLAN*

YOUNG IDEA *UK, male vocal duo – Tony Cox and Douglas MacCrae-Brown (Singles: 6 weeks)* pos/wks

29 Jun 67 ● **WITH A LITTLE HELP FROM MY FRIENDS** *Columbia DB 8205* 10 6

YOUNG MC *US, male rapper – Marvin Young (Singles: 7 weeks)* pos/wks

15 Jul 89 **BUST A MOVE** *Delicious Vinyl BRW 137* 73 2
17 Feb 90 **PRINCIPAL'S OFFICE** *Delicious Vinyl BRW 161* 54 3
17 Aug 91 **THAT'S THE WAY LOVE GOES** *Capitol CL 623* 65 2

YOUNG OFFENDERS *Ireland, male vocal / instrumental group (Singles: 1 week)* pos/wks

7 Mar 98 **THAT'S WHY WE LOSE CONTROL** *Columbia 6651942* 60 1

YOUNG ONES – *See Cliff RICHARD*

YOUNG RASCALS *US, male vocal / instrumental group (Singles: 17 weeks)* pos/wks

25 May 67 ● **GROOVIN'** *Atlantic 584 111* ▲ 8 13
16 Aug 67 **A GIRL LIKE YOU** *Atlantic 584 128* 37 4

Leon YOUNG STRING CHORALE – *See Acker BILK*

Sydney YOUNGBLOOD *US, male vocalist – Sydney Ford (Singles: 31 weeks, Albums: 17 weeks)* pos/wks

26 Aug 89 ● **IF ONLY I COULD** *Circa YR 34* 3 14
9 Dec 89 **SIT AND WAIT** *Circa YR 40* 16 8
31 Mar 90 **I'D RATHER GO BLIND** *Circa YR 43* 44 5
29 Jun 91 **HOOKED ON YOU** *Circa YR 65* 72 2
20 Mar 93 **ANYTHING** *RCA 74321138672* 48 2
28 Oct 89 **FEELING FREE** *Circa CIRCA 9* 23 17

YOUNGER YOUNGER 28'S
UK, male / female vocal / instrumental group (Singles: 1 week) pos/wks

5 Jun 99	**WE'RE GOING OUT** *V2 VVR 5006943*	61	1

Z FACTOR *UK, male DJ / producer – Dave Lee (Singles: 2 weeks)* pos/wks

21 Feb 98	**GOTTA KEEP PUSHIN'** *ffrr FCD 329*	47	1
17 Nov 01	**RIDE THE RHYTHM** *Direction 6718482*	52	1

See also HED BOYS; Li KWAN; RAVEN MAIZE; Joey NEGRO; JAKATTA; AKABU featuring Linda CLIFFORD; PHASE II; IL PADRINOS featuring Jocelyn BROWN

Z2 *UK, male production duo (Singles: 1 week)* pos/wks

26 Feb 00	**I WANT YOU** *Platipus PLATCD 67*	61	1

Helmut ZACHARIAS ORCHESTRA
Germany, orchestra leader, d. 28 Feb 2002 (Singles: 11 weeks) pos/wks

29 Oct 64 ●	**TOKYO MELODY** *Polydor NH 52341*	9	11

Pia ZADORA *US, female vocalist / actor (Singles: 6 weeks)* pos/wks

27 Oct 84	**WHEN THE RAIN BEGINS TO FALL** *Arista ARIST 584* [1]	68	2
12 Nov 88	**DANCE OUT OF MY HEAD** *Epic 6528867* [2]	65	4

[1] Jermaine Jackson and Pia Zadora [2] Pia

ZAGER and EVANS *US, male vocal duo – Denny Zager and Rick Evans (Singles: 13 weeks)* pos/wks

9 Aug 69 ★	**IN THE YEAR 2525 (EXORDIUM AND TERMINUS)** *RCA 1860* ▲	1	13

Michael ZAGER BAND
US, male / female vocal / instrumental group (Singles: 12 weeks) pos/wks

1 Apr 78 ●	**LET'S ALL CHANT** *Private Stock PVT 143*	8	12

Gheorghe ZAMFIR
Romania, male instrumentalist – pipes (Singles: 9 weeks) pos/wks

21 Aug 76 ●	**LIGHT OF EXPERIENCE 'DOINA DE JALE'** *Epic EPC 4310*	4	9

Tommy ZANG *US, male vocalist (Singles: 1 week)* pos/wks

16 Feb 61	**HEY GOOD LOOKING** *Polydor NH 66957*	45	1

ZAPP *US, male vocal / instrumental group – includes Roger Troutman (Singles: 6 weeks)* pos/wks

25 Jan 86	**IT DOESN'T REALLY MATTER** *Warner Bros. W 8879*	57	3
24 May 86	**COMPUTER LOVE (PART 1)** *Warner Bros. W 8805*	64	3

Frank ZAPPA *US, male vocalist / multi-instrumentalist, d. 4 Dec 1993 (Albums: 57 weeks)* pos/wks

28 Feb 70 ●	**HOT RATS** *Reprise RSLP 6356*	9	27
19 Dec 70	**CHUNGA'S REVENGE** *Reprise RSLP 2030*	43	1
6 May 78	**ZAPPA IN NEW YORK** *Discreet K 69204*	55	1
10 Mar 79	**SHEIK YERBOUTI** *CBS 88339*	32	7
13 Oct 79	**JOE'S GARAGE ACT I** *CBS 86101*	62	3
19 Jan 80	**JOE'S GARAGE ACTS II & III** *CBS 88475*	75	1
16 May 81	**TINSEL TOWN REBELLION** *CBS 88516*	55	4
24 Oct 81	**YOU ARE WHAT YOU IS** *CBS 88560*	51	2
19 Jun 82	**SHIP ARRIVING TOO LATE TO SAVE A DROWNING WITCH** *CBS 85804*	61	4
18 Jun 83	**THE MAN FROM UTOPIA** *CBS 25251*	87	1
27 Oct 84	**THEM OR US** *EMI FZD 1*	53	2
30 Apr 88	**GUITAR** *Zappa ZAPPA 6*	82	2
2 Sep 95	**STRICTLY COMMERCIAL – THE BEST OF FRANK ZAPPA** *Rykodisc RCD 40600*	45	2

See also MOTHERS OF INVENTION

Francesco ZAPPALA
Italy, male producer (Singles: 3 weeks) pos/wks

10 Aug 91	**WE GOTTA DO IT** *Fourth & Broadway BRW 225* [1]	57	2
2 May 92	**NO WAY OUT** *PWL Continental PWL 230*	69	1

[1] DJ Professor featuring Francesco Zappala

Lena ZAVARONI *UK, female vocalist, d. 1 Oct 1999 (Singles: 14 weeks, Albums: 5 weeks)* pos/wks

9 Feb 74 ●	**MA! (HE'S MAKING EYES AT ME)** *Philips 6006 367*	10	11
1 Jun 74	**(YOU'VE GOT) PERSONALITY** *Philips 6006 391*	33	3
23 Mar 74 ●	**MA** *Philips 6308 201*	8	5

ZED BIAS *UK, male vocal / production group (Singles: 4 weeks)* pos/wks

15 Jul 00	**NEIGHBOURHOOD** *Locked On / XL Recordings LOX 122CD*	25	4

ZEE *UK, female vocalist – Lesley Cowling (Singles: 4 weeks)* pos/wks

6 Jul 96	**DREAMTIME** *Perfecto PERF 122CD*	31	2
22 Mar 97	**SAY MY NAME** *Perfecto PERF 135CD*	36	1
7 Feb 98	**BUTTERFLY** *Perfecto PERF 154CD1* [1]	41	1

[1] Tilt featuring Zee

ZENA *UK, female vocalist – Zena McNally (Singles: 1 week)* pos/wks

19 Jul 03	**LET'S GET THIS PARTY STARTED** *Serious Ser 69CD*	69	1

See also MIS-TEEQ

ZEPHYRS *UK, male vocal / instrumental group (Singles: 1 week)* pos/wks

18 Mar 65	**SHE'S LOST YOU** *Columbia DB 7481*	48	1

ZERO B *UK, male instrumentalist – keyboards – Peter Riding (Singles: 6 weeks)* pos/wks

22 Feb 92	**THE EP (BRAND NEW MIXES)** *Ffrreedom TAB 102*	32	4
24 Jul 93	**RECONNECTION (EP)** *Internal LIECD 6*	54	2

Tracks on The EP: Lock Up / Spinning Wheel / Module / Tracks on Reconnection (EP): Love to Be in Love (2 mixes)/ Lock Up (remix) / Ou Est Le Spoon.

ZERO 7 *UK, male production duo – Henry Binns and Sam Hardaker (Singles: 5 weeks, Albums: 43 weeks)* pos/wks

18 Aug 01	**DESTINY** *Ultimate Dilemma UDRCDS043* [1]	30	3
17 Nov 01	**IN THE WAITING LINE** *Ultimate Dilemma UDRCDS045*	47	1
30 Mar 02	**DISTRACTIONS** *Ultimate Dilemma UDRCDS046* [2]	45	1
5 May 01	**SIMPLE THINGS** *Ultimate Dilemma UDRCD 016*	28	43

[1] Zero 7 featuring Sia and Sophie [2] Zero 7 featuring Sia

ZERO VU featuring Lorna B
UK, male / female vocal / production group (Singles: 1 week) pos/wks

15 Mar 97	**FEELS SO GOOD** *Avex UK AVEXCD 53*	69	1

ZERO ZERO

UK, male instrumental / production duo (Singles: 1 week)

Date	Title	pos	wks
10 Aug 91	**ZEROXED** *Kickin KICK 9*	71	1

Warren ZEVON

US, male vocalist / instrumentalist – keyboards, d. 7 Sep 2003 (Albums: 1 week)

Date	Title	pos	wks
27 Sep 03	**THE WIND** *Rykodisc RCD17001*	57	1

ZHANÉ

US, female vocal duo – Renee Neufville and Jean Norris (Singles: 18 weeks, Albums: 1 week)

Date	Title	pos	wks
11 Sep 93	**HEY MR DJ (re)** *Epic 6596102*	26	5
19 Mar 94	**GROOVE THANG** *Motown TMGCD 1423*	34	3
20 Aug 94	**VIBE** *Motown TMGCD 1430*	67	1
25 Feb 95	**SHAME** *Jive JIVECD 372*	66	1
21 Sep 96	**IT'S A PARTY** *Elektra EKR 226CD* [1]	23	2
8 Mar 97	**4 MORE** *Tommy Boy TBCD 7779A* [2]	52	1
26 Apr 97	**REQUEST LINE** *Motown 8606452*	22	3
30 Aug 97	**CRUSH** *Motown 5716712*	44	1
11 Sep 99	**JAMBOREE** *Arista 74321692882* [3]	51	1
10 May 97	**SATURDAY NIGHT** *Motown 5305882*	52	1

[1] Busta Rhymes featuring Zhané [2] De La Soul featuring Zhané [3] Naughty By Nature featuring Zhané

ZIG and ZAG

Zog / Ireland, male puppet duo (Singles: 12 weeks)

Date	Title	pos	wks
24 Dec 94 ●	**THEM GIRLS THEM GIRLS** *RCA 74321251042*	5	9
1 Jul 95	**HANDS UP! HANDS UP!** *RCA 74321284392*	21	3

ZIGZAG JIVE FLUTES – *See ELIAS and his ZIG-ZAG JIVE FLUTES*

Hans ZIMMER

Germany, male conductor (Albums: 20 weeks)

Date	Title	pos	wks
27 May 00	**GLADIATOR (FILM SOUNDTRACK)** *Decca 4670942* [1]	17	16
3 Mar 01	**HANNIBAL (FILM SOUNDTRACK)** *Decca 4676962*	74	2
16 Jun 01	**PEARL HARBOR (FILM SOUNDTRACK)** *Hollywood / Warner Bros. 9362481132* [2]	50	2

[1] Hans Zimmer and Lisa Gerrard [2] Hans Zimmer with orchestra conducted by Gavin Greenaway

ZION TRAIN

UK, male / female vocal / instrumental group (Singles: 1 week, Albums: 1 week)

Date	Title	pos	wks
27 Jul 96	**RISE** *China WOKCD 2085*	61	1
13 Jul 96	**GROW TOGETHER** *China WOLCD 1071*	56	1

ZODIAC MINDWARP and the LOVE REACTION

UK, male / female vocal / instrumental group (Singles: 11 weeks, Albums: 5 weeks)

Date	Title	pos	wks
9 May 87	**PRIME MOVER** *Mercury ZOD 1*	18	6
14 Nov 87	**BACKSEAT EDUCATION** *Mercury ZOD 2*	49	3
2 Apr 88	**PLANET GIRL** *Mercury ZOD 3*	63	2
5 Mar 88	**TATTOOED BEAT MESSIAH** *Mercury ZODLP 1*	20	5

ZODIACS – *See Maurice WILLIAMS and the ZODIACS*

ZOE

UK, female vocalist – Zoe Pollock (Singles: 22 weeks, Albums: 1 week)

Date	Title	pos	wks
10 Nov 90	**SUNSHINE ON A RAINY DAY** *M & G MAGS 6*	53	5
24 Aug 91 ●	**SUNSHINE ON A RAINY DAY (re-mix)** *M & G MAGS 14*	4	11
2 Nov 91	**LIGHTNING** *M & G MAGS 18*	37	4
29 Feb 92	**HOLY DAYS** *M & G MAGS 21*	72	2
7 Dec 91	**SCARLET RED AND BLUE** *M & G 5114431*	67	1

ZOMBIE NATION

Germany, male production duo – Florian 'Splank' Senfter and Emanuel 'Mooner' Gunther (Singles: 16 weeks)

Date	Title	pos	wks
2 Sep 00	**KERNKRAFT 400 (IMPORT)** *TRANSK TRANSK 002*	61	1
30 Sep 00 ●	**KERNKRAFT 400** *Data DATA 11CDS*	2	15

Rob ZOMBIE

US, male vocalist – Robert Cummings (Singles: 2 weeks, Albums: 2 weeks)

Date	Title	pos	wks
26 Dec 98	**DRAGULA** *Geffen GFSTD 22367*	44	2
5 Sep 98	**HELLBILLY DELUXE** *Geffen GED 25212*	37	2

See also WHITE ZOMBIE

ZOMBIES

UK, male vocal / instrumental group – includes Rod Argent and Colin Blundstone (Singles: 16 weeks)

Date	Title	pos	wks
13 Aug 64	**SHE'S NOT THERE** *Decca F 11940*	12	11
11 Feb 65	**TELL HER NO** *Decca F 12072*	42	5

ZOO EXPERIENCE featuring DESTRY

UK, male production group and US, male vocalist (Singles: 1 week)

Date	Title	pos	wks
22 Aug 92	**LOVE'S GOTTA HOLD ON ME** *Cooltempo COOL 261*	66	1

ZUCCHERO

Italy, male vocalist / instrumentalist – guitar – Adelmo Fornaciari (Singles: 24 weeks, Albums: 4 weeks)

Date	Title	pos	wks
30 Mar 91 ●	**SENZA UNA DONNA (WITHOUT A WOMAN)** *London LON 294* [1]	4	12
18 Jan 92	**DIAMANTE** *London LON 313* [2]	44	7
24 Oct 92	**MISERERE** *London LON 329* [3]	15	5
18 May 91	**ZUCCHERO** *A&M EVERY 1*	29	4

[1] Zucchero and Paul Young [2] Zucchero with Randy Crawford [3] Zucchero with Luciano Pavarotti

ZWAN

US, male vocal / instrumental group – leader Billy Corgan (Singles: 3 weeks, Albums: 2 weeks)

Date	Title	pos	wks
8 Mar 03	**HONESTLY** *Reprise W 600CD*	28	2
14 Jun 03	**LYRIC** *Reprise W 607*	44	1
22 Feb 03	**MARY STAR OF THE SEA** *Reprise WB484252*	33	2

ZZ TOP (185 Top 500)

Low-slung, guitar-driven blues-rock trio formed 1969 in Houston, Texas, US; long-bearded duo Billy Gibbons (v/g) and Dusty Hill (v/b) plus clean-shaven Frank Beard (d). Hugely popular stadium-packing festival headliners in the 1980s. Named to ensure they would be the last act in record racks and hit books (Singles: 94 weeks, Albums: 211 weeks)

Date	Title	pos	wks
3 Sep 83 ●	**GIMME ALL YOUR LOVIN' (re)** *Warner Bros. W 9693*	10	18
26 Nov 83	**SHARP DRESSED MAN (re)** *Warner Bros. W 9576*	22	13
31 Mar 84	**TV DINNERS** *Warner Bros. W 9334*	67	3
23 Feb 85	**LEGS** *Warner Bros. W 9272*	16	7
13 Jul 85	**THE ZZ TOP SUMMER HOLIDAY (EP)** *Warner Bros. W 8946*	51	5
19 Oct 85	**SLEEPING BAG** *Warner Bros. W 2001*	27	5
15 Feb 86	**STAGES** *Warner Bros. W 2002*	43	3
19 Apr 86	**ROUGH BOY** *Warner Bros. W 2003*	23	9
4 Oct 86	**VELCRO FLY** *Warner Bros. W 8650*	54	3
21 Jul 90	**DOUBLEBACK** *Warner Bros. W 9812*	29	6
13 Apr 91	**MY HEAD'S IN MISSISSIPPI** *Warner Bros W 0009*	37	5
11 Apr 92 ●	**VIVA LAS VEGAS** *Warner Bros. W 0098*	10	7
20 Jun 92	**ROUGH BOY (re-issue)** *Warner Bros. W 0111*	49	3
29 Jan 94	**PINCUSHION** *RCA 74321184732*	15	3
7 May 94	**BREAKAWAY** *RCA 74321192282*	60	1
29 Jun 96	**WHAT'S UP WITH THAT** *RCA 74321394822*	58	1
16 Oct 99	**GIMME ALL YOUR LOVIN' 2000** *Riverhorse RIVHCD 2* [1]	28	2
12 Jul 75	**FANDANGO!** *London SHU 8482*	60	1
8 Aug 81	**EL LOCO** *Warner Bros. K 56929*	88	2
30 Apr 83 ●	**ELIMINATOR** *Warner Bros. W 3774*	3	137
9 Nov 85 ●	**AFTERBURNER** *Warner Bros. WX 27*	2	40
27 Oct 90 ●	**RECYCLER** *Warner Bros. WX 390*	8	7
25 Apr 92 ●	**GREATEST HITS** *Warner Bros. 7599268462*	5	17
5 Feb 94 ●	**ANTENNA** *RCA 74321152602*	3	5
21 Sep 96	**RHYTHMEEN** *RCA 74321394662*	32	2

[1] Martay featuring ZZ Top

'Gimme All Your Lovin' debuted at No.61 in 1983 only hitting its peak position on re-entry in Oct 1984. 'Sharp Dressed Man' debuted at No.53 in Nov 1983 only hitting its peak position in Dec 1984. Tracks on Summer Holiday (EP): Tush / Got Me Under Pressure / Beer Drinkers and Hell Raisers / I'm Bad, I'm Nationwide

US NO.1 ALBUMS

Here's a complete list of all US No.1 albums listed alphabetically by artist from 4 January 1955. Check out US album chart-toppers Crazy Otto, Jackie Gleason and Kenny Chesney, just some of the acts that failed to chart at all in the UK.

Source for US No.1 albums is the Billboard charts. For further information, check out the Billboard range of chart books.

AALIYAH
15 Sep 01 **Aaliyah**

Paula ABDUL
7 Oct 89 **Forever Your Girl**
8 Jun 91 **Spellbound**

AC/DC
26 Dec 81 **For Those About to Rock We Salute You**

ACE OF BASE
2 Apr 94 **The Sign**

Bryan ADAMS
10 Aug 85 **Reckless**

AEROSMITH
8 May 93 **Get a Grip**
5 Apr 97 **Nine Lives**

Christina AGUILERA
11 Sep 99 **Christina Aguilera**

CLAY AIKEN
1 Nov 03 **Measure of a Man**

ALICE IN CHAINS
12 Dec 94 **Jar of Flies**
25 Nov 95 **Alice in Chains**

ALLMAN BROTHERS BAND
8 Sep 73 **Brothers and Sisters**

Herb ALPERT & THE TIJUANA BRASS
27 Nov 65 **Whipped Cream & Other Delights**
5 Mar 66 **Going Places**
28 May 66 **What Now My Love**
17 Jun 67 **Sounds Like**
27 Jul 68 **The Beat of the Brass**

AMERICA
25 Mar 72 **America**

Louis ARMSTRONG
13 Jun 64 **Hello, Dolly!**

ASHANTI
13 Apr 02 **Ashanti**
19 Jul 03 **Chapter II**

ASIA
15 May 82 **Asia**

AVERAGE WHITE BAND
22 Feb 75 **AWB**

BACHMAN-TURNER OVERDRIVE
19 Oct 74 **Not Fragile**

BACKSTREET BOYS
5 Jun 99 **Millennium**
9 Dec 00 **Black & Blue**

BAD COMPANY
28 Sep 74 **Bad Company**

Anita BAKER
24 Dec 88 **Giving You the Best That I Got**

BEACH BOYS
5 Dec 64 **Beach Boys Concert**
5 Oct 74 **Endless Summer**

BEASTIE BOYS
7 Mar 87 **Licensed to Ill**
18 Jun 94 **Ill Communication**
1 Aug 98 **Hello Nasty**

BEATLES
15 Feb 64 **Meet the Beatles**
2 May 64 **The Beatles' Second Album**
25 Jul 64 **A Hard Day's Night**
9 Jan 65 **Beatles '65**
10 Jul 65 **Beatles VI**
11 Sep 65 **Help!**
8 Jan 66 **Rubber Soul**
30 Jul 66 **'Yesterday' … and Today**
10 Sep 66 **Revolver**
1 Jul 67 **Sgt. Pepper's Lonely Hearts Club Band**
6 Jan 68 **Magical Mystery Tour**
28 Dec 68 **The Beatles (White Album)**
1 Nov 69 **Abbey Road**
3 Jun 70 **Let It Be**
26 May 73 **The Beatles/1967-1970**
9 Dec 95 **Anthology I**
6 Apr 96 **Anthology 2**
16 Nov 96 **Anthology 3**
2 Dec 00 **1**

BEE GEES
3 Mar 79 **Spirits Having Flown**
12 Jan 80 **Bee Gees Greatest**
21 Jan 78 **Soundtrack: Saturday Night Fever**

Harry BELAFONTE
24 Mar 56 **Belafonte**
8 Sep 56 **Calypso**

Pat BENATAR
15 Aug 81 **Precious Time**

George BENSON
31 Jul 76 **Breezin'**

BEYONCÉ
12 Jul 03 **Dangerously in Love**

BIG BROTHER & THE HOLDING COMPANY
12 Oct 68 **Cheap Thrills**

BIG TYMERS
18 May 02 **Hood Rich**

BLACK CROWES
30 May 92 **The Southern Harmony and Musical Companion**

Mary J BLIGE
10 May 97 **Share My World**
13 Sep 03 **Love & Life**

BLIND FAITH
20 Sep 69 **Blind Faith**

BLINK-182
30 Jun 01 **Take Off Your Pants and Jacket**

BLOOD, SWEAT & TEARS
29 Mar 69 **Blood Sweat & Tears**
8 Aug 70 **Blood, Sweat & Tears 3**

BLUES BROTHERS
3 Feb 79 **Briefcase Full of Blues**

Michael BOLTON
25 May 91 **Time, Love and Tenderness**
21 Nov 92 **Timeless (The Classics)**

BON JOVI
25 Oct 86 **Slippery When Wet**
15 Oct 88 **New Jersey**

BONE THUGS N HARMONY
12 Aug 95 **E 1900 Eternal**
16 Aug 97 **The Art of War**

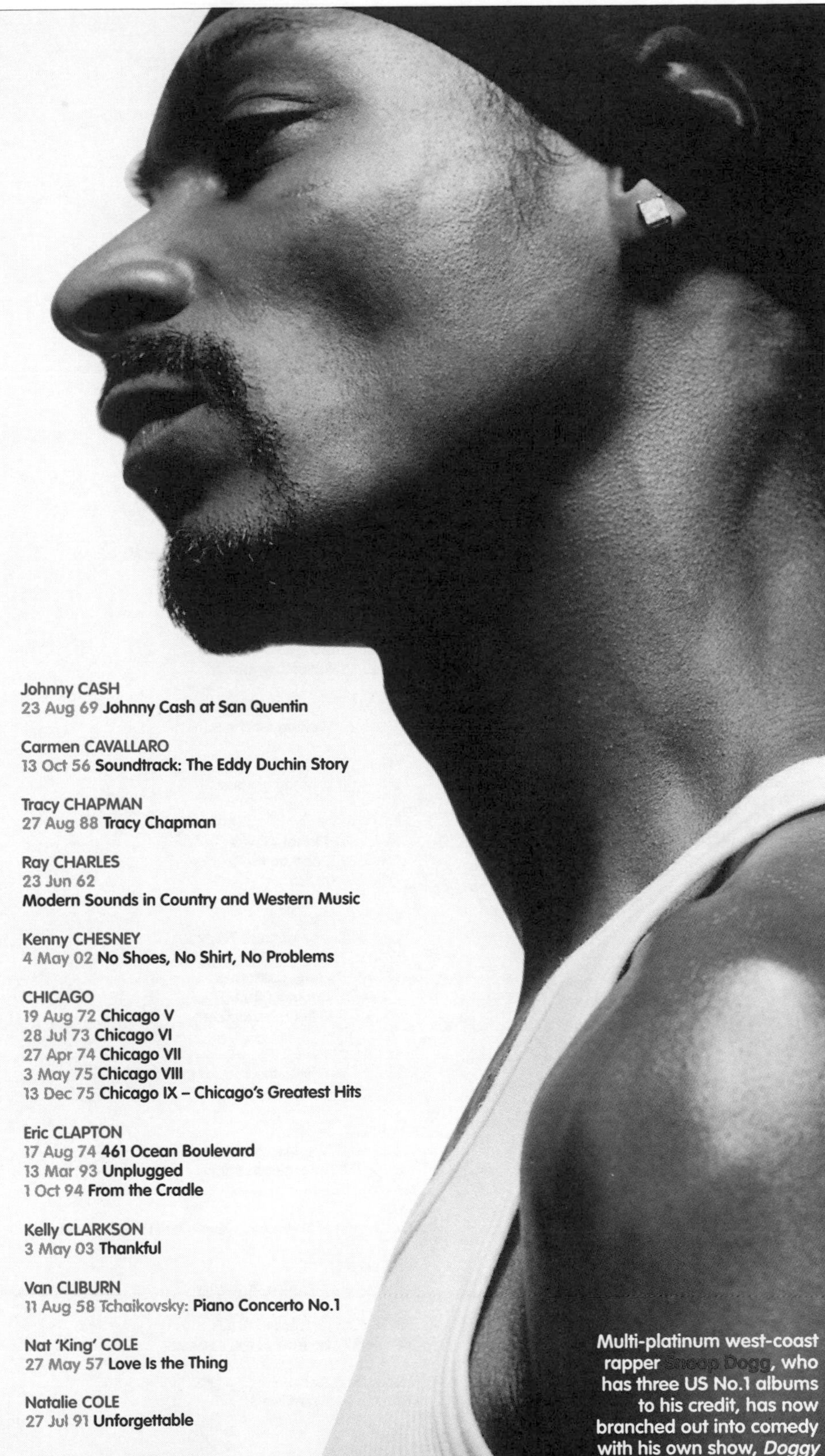

BOSTON
16 Sep 78 **Don't Look Back**
1 Nov 86 **Third Stage**

BOYZ II MEN
17 Sep 94 **II**
11 Oct 97 **Evolution**

Toni BRAXTON
26 Feb 94 **Toni Braxton**

Garth BROOKS
28 Sep 91 **Ropin' the Wind**
10 Oct 92 **The Chase**
18 Sep 93 **In Pieces**
7 Jan 95 **The Hits**
13 Dec 97 **Sevens**
23 May 98 **The Limited Series**
5 Dec 98 **Double Live**
1 Dec 01 **Scarecrow**

Bobby BROWN
21 Jan 89 **Don't Be Cruel**

Foxy BROWN
13 Feb 99 **Chyna Doll**

Jackson BROWNE
13 Sep 80 **Hold Out**

BUSH
7 Dec 96 **Razorblade Suitcase**

Glen CAMPBELL
21 Dec 68 **Wichita Lineman**

Mariah CAREY
2 Mar 91 **Mariah Carey**
25 Dec 93 **Music Box**
21 Oct 95 **Daydream**
4 Oct 97 **Butterfly**

Bob CARLISLE
28 Jun 97 **Butterfly Kisses (Shades of Grace)**

Kim CARNES
27 Jun 81 **Mistaken Identity**

CARPENTERS
5 Jan 74 **The Singles 1969-1973**

Johnny CASH
23 Aug 69 **Johnny Cash at San Quentin**

Carmen CAVALLARO
13 Oct 56 **Soundtrack: The Eddy Duchin Story**

Tracy CHAPMAN
27 Aug 88 **Tracy Chapman**

Ray CHARLES
23 Jun 62
Modern Sounds in Country and Western Music

Kenny CHESNEY
4 May 02 **No Shoes, No Shirt, No Problems**

CHICAGO
19 Aug 72 **Chicago V**
28 Jul 73 **Chicago VI**
27 Apr 74 **Chicago VII**
3 May 75 **Chicago VIII**
13 Dec 75 **Chicago IX – Chicago's Greatest Hits**

Eric CLAPTON
17 Aug 74 **461 Ocean Boulevard**
13 Mar 93 **Unplugged**
1 Oct 94 **From the Cradle**

Kelly CLARKSON
3 May 03 **Thankful**

Van CLIBURN
11 Aug 58 Tchaikovsky: **Piano Concerto No.1**

Nat 'King' COLE
27 May 57 **Love Is the Thing**

Natalie COLE
27 Jul 91 **Unforgettable**

Multi-platinum west-coast rapper Snoop Dogg, who has three US No.1 albums to his credit, has now branched out into comedy with his own show, *Doggy Fizzle Televizzle* on MTV

US NO.1 ALBUMS CONTINUED

Phil COLLINS
30 Mar 85 **No Jacket Required**
6 Jan 90 **...But Seriously**

Alice COOPER
21 Apr 73 **Billion Dollar Babies**

COUNTING CROWS
2 Nov 96 **Recovering the Satellites**

CRAZY OTTO
28 May 55 **Crazy Otto**

CREAM
10 Aug 68 **Wheels of Fire**

CREED
16 Oct 99 **Human Clay**
8 Dec 01 **Weathered**

CREEDENCE CLEARWATER REVIVAL
4 Oct 69 **Green River**
22 Aug 70 **Cosmo's Factory**

Jim CROCE
12 Jan 74 **You Don't Mess Around with Jim**

Bing CROSBY
30 Dec 57 **Merry Christmas**

CROSBY, STILLS, NASH & YOUNG
16 May 70 **Déjà Vu**
15 May 71 **4 Way Street**
2 Nov 74 **So Far**

CYPRESS HILL
7 Aug 93 **Black Sunday**

Billy Ray CYRUS
13 Jun 92 **Some Gave All**

D'ANGELO
12 Feb 00 **Voodoo**

D12
7 Jul 01 **Devil's Night**

Sammy DAVIS JR
11 Jun 55 **Starring Sammy Davis Jr**

DORIS DAY
6 Aug 55 **Love Me or Leave Me**

DEF LEPPARD
23 Jul 88 **Hysteria**
18 Apr 92 **Adrenalize**

Martin DENNY
22 Jun 59 **Exotica**

John DENVER
30 Mar 74 **John Denver's Greatest Hits**
10 Aug 74 **Back Home Again**
18 Oct 75 **Windsong**

DEPECHE MODE
10 Apr 93 **(Songs of Faith and Devotion)**

DESTINY'S CHILD
19 May 01 **Survivor**

Celine DION
5 Oct 96 **Falling into You**
17 Jan 98 **Let's Talk about Love**
11 Dec 99 **All the Way ... A Decade of Song**
13 Apr 02 **A New Day Has Come**

DIRE STRAITS
31 Aug 85 **Brothers in Arms**

DISTURBED
5 Oct 02 **Believe**

DIXIE CHICKS
18 Sep 99 **Fly**
14 Sep 02 **Home**

DMX
6 Jun 98 **It's Dark and Hell Is Hot**
9 Jan 99 **Flesh of My Flesh Blood of My Blood**
8 Jan 00 **...And Then There Was X**
10 Nov 01 **The Great Depression**
4 Oct 03 **Grand Champ**

DOOBIE BROTHERS
7 Apr 79 **Minute by minute**

DOORS
7 Sep 68 **Waiting for the Sun**

Hilary DUFF
20 Sep 03 **Metamorphosis**

Bob DYLAN
16 Feb 74 **Planet Waves**
1 Mar 75 **Blood on the Tracks**
7 Feb 76 **Desire**

EAGLES
26 Jul 75 **One of these Nights**
13 Mar 76 **Eagles/Their Greatest Hits 1971-1975**
15 Jan 77 **Hotel California**
3 Nov 79 **The Long Run**
26 Nov 94 **Hell Freezes Over**

EARTH, WIND & FIRE
17 May 75 **That's the Way of the World (Soundtrack)**
17 Jan 76 **Gratitude**

EMINEM
10 Jun 00 **The Marshall Mathers LP**
8 Jun 02 **The Eminem Show**

EVE
2 Oct 99 **Let There Be ... Eve – Ruff Ryders' First Lady**

50 CENT
22 Feb 03 **Get Rich or Die Tryin'**

FINE YOUNG CANNIBALS
3 Jun 89 **The Raw & the Cooked**

Roberta FLACK
29 Apr 72 **First Take**

FLEETWOOD MAC
4 Sep 76 **Fleetwood Mac**
2 Apr 77 **Rumours**
7 Aug 82 **Mirage**
6 Sep 97 **The Dance**

John FOGERTY
23 Mar 85 **Centerfield**

Frank FONTAINE
16 Mar 63 **Songs I Sing on the Jackie Gleason Show**

FOREIGNER
22 Aug 81 **4**

Peter FRAMPTON
10 Apr 76 **Frampton Comes Alive!**

FUGEES
25 May 96 **Score**

Kenny G
10 Dec 94 **Miracles The Holiday Album**

Judy GARLAND
11 Sep 61 **Judy at Carnegie Hall**

J GEILS BAND
6 Feb 82 **Freeze Frame**

Bobbie GENTRY
14 Oct 67 **Ode to Billy Joe**

Debbie GIBSON
11 Mar 89 **Electric Youth**

Jackie GLEASON
23 Jul 55 **Lonesome Echo**

GO-GO'S
6 Mar 82 **Beauty and the Beat**

GODSMACK
26 Apr 03 **Faceless**

GUNS N' ROSES
6 Aug 88 **Appetite for Destruction**
5 Oct 91 **Use Your Illusion II**

Marvin HAMLISCH
4 May 74 **The Sting (Soundtrack)**

MC HAMMER
9 Jun 90 **Please Hammer Don't Hurt 'Em**

George HARRISON
2 Jan 71 **All Things Must Pass**
23 Jun 73 **Living in the Material World**

Isaac HAYES
6 Nov 71 **Shaft (Soundtrack)**

HEART
21 Dec 85 **Heart**

Jimi HENDRIX EXPERIENCE
16 Nov 68 **Electric Ladyland**

Faith HILL
27 Nov 99 **Breathe**
2 Nov 02 **Cry**

Lauryn HILL
12 Sep 98 **The Miseducation of Lauryn Hill**

HOOTIE & THE BLOWFISH
27 May 95 **Cracked Rear View**
11 May 96 **Fairweather Johnson**

Whitney HOUSTON
8 Mar 86 **Whitney Houston**
27 Jun 87 **Whitney**

Janis IAN
20 Sep 75 **Between the Lines**

ICE CUBE
5 Dec 92 **The Predator**

ISLEY BROTHERS
13 Sep 75 **The Heat Is On**

ISLEY BROTHERS featuring Ronald Isley
24 May 03 **Body Kiss**

JA RULE
28 Oct 00 **Rule 3:36**
20 Oct 01 **Pain Is Love**

Alan JACKSON
2 Feb 02 **Drive**
30 Aug 03 **Alan Jackson Greatest Hits Volume II and Some Other Stuff**

Janet JACKSON
5 Jul 86 **Control**
28 Oct 89 **Janet Jackson's Rhythm Nation 1814**
5 Jun 93 **Janet**
25 Oct 97 **The Velvet Rope**
12 May 01 **All for You**

Michael JACKSON
26 Feb 83 **Thriller**
26 Sep 87 **Bad**
14 Dec 91 **Dangerous**
8 Jul 95 **History: Past, Present and Future Book 1**
17 Nov 01 **Invincible**

JAY-Z
17 Oct 98 **Vol 2 … Hard Knock Life**
15 Jan 00 **Vol. 3 … Life and Times Of S. Carter**
18 Nov 00 **The Dynasty Roc La Familia (2000-)**
29 Sep 01 **The Blueprint**
30 Nov 02 **The Blueprint 2: The Gift and the Curse**
29 Nov 03 **The Black Album**

JEFFERSON STARSHIP
6 Sep 75 **Red Octopus**

JETHRO TULL
3 Jun 72 **Thick as a Brick**
18 Aug 73 **A Passion Play**

Billy JOEL
18 Nov 78 **52nd Street**
14 Jun 80 **Glass Houses**
16 Dec 89 **Storm Front**
28 Aug 93 **River of Dreams**

Elton JOHN
15 Jul 72 **Honky Chateau**
3 Mar 73 **Don't Shoot Me I'm Only the Piano Player**
10 Nov 73 **Goodbye Yellow Brick Road**
13 Jul 74 **Caribou**
30 Nov 74 **Elton John – Greatest Hits**
7 Jun 75 **Captain Fantastic and the Brown Dirt Cowboy**
8 Nov 75 **Rock of the Westies**

Norah JONES
25 Jan 03 **Come Away with Me**

Janis JOPLIN
27 Feb 71 **Pearl**

JOURNEY
12 Sep 81 **Escape**

Bert KAEMPFERT
16 Jan 61 **Wonderland by Night**

Toby KEITH
10 Aug 02 **Unleashed**
22 Nov 03 **Shock'n Y'All**

R KELLY
2 Dec 95 **R Kelly**
25 Nov 00 **Tp-2.Com**
8 Mar 03 **Chocolate Factory**

Alicia KEYS
14 Jul 01 **Songs in A Minor**
20 Dec 03 **The Diary of Alicia Keys**

Carole KING
19 Jun 71 **Tapestry**
1 Jan 72 **Music**
9 Nov 74 **Wrap Around Joy**

KINGSTON TRIO
24 Nov 58 **The Kingston Trio**
27 Jul 59 **The Kingston Trio at Large**
14 Dec 59 **Here We Go Again!**
9 May 60 **Sold Out**
19 Sep 60 **String Along**

KNACK
11 Aug 79 **Get the Knack**

KORN
5 Sep 98 **Follow the Leader**
4 Dec 99 **Issues**

KRIS KROSS
23 May 92 **Totally Krossed Out**

LL COOL J
30 Sep 00 **G.O.A.T. Featuring James T. Smith: the Greatest of All Time**

Patti LABELLE
19 Jul 86 **Winner in You**

Mario LANZA
1 Aug 55 **The Student Prince**

LED ZEPPELIN
27 Dec 69 **Led Zeppelin II**
31 Oct 70 **Led Zeppelin III**
12 May 73 **Houses of the Holy**
22 Mar 75 **Physical Graffiti**
1 May 76 **Presence**
15 Sep 79 **In Through the Out Door**
14 Jun 03 **How the West Was Won**

John LENNON
30 Oct 71 **Imagine**
16 Nov 74 **Walls And Bridges**
27 Dec 80 **Double Fantasy**

Huey LEWIS AND THE NEWS
30 Jun 84 **Sports**
18 Oct 86 **Fore!**

Gordon LIGHTFOOT
22 Jun 74 **Sundown**

LIMP BIZKIT
10 Jul 99 **Significant Other**
4 Nov 00 **Chocolate Starfish and the Hot Dog Flavored Water**

LINKIN PARK
12 Apr 03 **Meteora**

LIVE
6 May 95 **Throwing Copper**
8 Mar 97 **Secret Samadhi**

Jennifer LOPEZ
10 Feb 01 **J.Lo**
23 Feb 02 **J To the L-O! The Remixes**

LUDACRIS
25 Oct 03 **Chicken 'n' Beer**

MADONNA
9 Feb 85 **Like a Virgin**
16 Aug 86 **True Blue**
22 Apr 89 **Like a Prayer**
7 Oct 00 **Music**
10 May 03 **American Life**

MAKAVELI (aka 2PAC)
23 Nov 96 **The Don Killuminati – The 7 Day Theory**

MAMAS & THE PAPAS
21 May 66 **If You Can Believe Your Eyes and Ears**

Henry MANCINI
23 Feb 59 **The Music from Peter Gunn**

Barry MANILOW
16 Jul 77 **Barry Manilow Live**

Marilyn MANSON
3 Oct 98 **Mechanical Animals**
31 May 03 **The Golden Age of Grotesque**

US NO.1 ALBUMS CONTINUED

Ricky MARTIN
29 May 99 **Ricky Martin**

Richard MARX
2 Sep 89 **Repeat Offender**

MASE
15 Nov 97 **Harlem World**

MASTER P
20 Sep 97 **Ghetto D**
20 Jun 98 **MP Da Last Don**

Johnny MATHIS
9 Jun 58 **Johnny's Greatest Hits**
9 Nov 59 **Heavenly**

Dave MATTHEWS BAND
16 May 98 **Before These Crowded Streets**
17 Mar 01 **Everyday**
3 Aug 02 **Busted Stuff**

Paul MAURIAT
2 Mar 68 **Blooming Hits**

MAXWELL
8 Sep 01 **Now**

John MAYER
27 Sep 03 **Heavier Things**

Curtis MAYFIELD
21 Oct 72 **Superfly (Soundtrack)**

Paul McCARTNEY/WINGS
23 May 70 **McCartney**
2 Jun 73 **Red Rose Speedway**
13 Apr 74 **Band on the Run**
19 Jul 75 **Venus and Mars**
24 Apr 76 **Wings at the Speed of Sound**
22 Jan 77 **Wings over America**
29 May 82 **Tug of War**

Tim MCGRAW
21 May 94 **Not a Moment Too Soon**
22 May 99 **A Place in the Sun**

Don MCLEAN
22 Jan 72 **American Pie**

Vaughn MEADER
15 Dec 62 **The First Family**

MEAT LOAF
30 Oct 93 **Bat Out of Hell II: Back into Hell**

John Cougar MELLENCAMP
11 Sep 82 **American Fool**

MEN AT WORK
13 Nov 82 **Business as Usual**

METALLICA
31 Aug 91 **Metallica**
22 Jun 96 **Load**
6 Dec 97 **Reload**
21 Jun 03 **St Anger**

George MICHAEL
16 Jan 88 **Faith**

Mitch MILLER
6 Oct 58 **Sing Along with Mitch**
29 Dec 58 **Christmas Sing-Along with Mitch**

MILLI VANILLI
23 Sep 89 **Girl You Know It's True**

MR MISTER
1 Mar 86 **Welcome to the Real World**

MONICA
5 Jul 03 **After the Storm**

MONKEES
12 Nov 66 **The Monkees**
11 Feb 67 **More of The Monkees**
24 Jun 67 **Headquarters**
9 Dec 67 **Pisces, Aquarius, Capricorn & Jones Ltd**

John Michael MONTGOMERY
19 Feb 94 **Kickin' It Up**

MOODY BLUES
9 Dec 72 **Seventh Sojourn**
25 Jul 81 **Long Distance Voyager**

Alanis MORISSETTE
7 Oct 95 **Jagged Little Pill**
21 Nov 98 **Supposed Former Infatuation Junkie**
16 Mar 02 **Under Rug Swept**

MÖTLEY CRÜE
14 Oct 89 **Dr. Feelgood**

MUSIQ
25 May 02 **Juslisen (Just Listen)**

MYSTIKAL
14 Oct 00 **Let's Get Ready**

'N SYNC
8 Apr 00 **No Strings Attached**
11 Aug 01 **Celebrity**

N.W.A.
22 Jun 91 **Efil4zaggin**

NAS
20 Jul 96 **It Was Written**
24 Apr 99 **I Am…**

NAS ESCOBAR, FOXY BROWN, AZ AND NATURE
8 Nov 97 **The Firm – The Album**

NELLY
26 Aug 00 **Country Grammar**
13 Jul 02 **Nellyville**

Ricky NELSON
20 Jan 58 **Ricky**

NEW EDITION
28 Sep 96 **Home Again**

NEW KIDS ON THE BLOCK
9 Sep 89 **Hangin' Tough**
30 Jun 90 **Step by Step**

Bob NEWHART
25 Jul 60 **The Button Down Mind of Bob Newhart**
2 Jan 61 **The Button Down Mind Strikes Back!**

Olivia NEWTON-JOHN
12 Oct 74 **If You Love Me, Let Me Know**
15 Mar 75 **Have You Never Been Mellow**
29 Jul 78 **Grease (Soundtrack)**

Stevie NICKS
5 Sep 81 **Bella Donna**

NINE INCH NAILS
9 Oct 99 **The Fragile**

NIRVANA
11 Jan 92 **Nevermind**
9 Oct 93 **In Utero**
19 Nov 94 **MTV Unplugged in New York**
19 Oct 96 **From the Muddy Banks of the Wishkah**

NO DOUBT
21 Dec 96 **Tragic Kingdom**

NOTORIOUS B.I.G.
12 Apr 97 **Life After Death**
25 Dec 99 **Born Again**

Sinead O'CONNOR
28 Apr 90 **I Do Not Want What I Haven't Got**

OHIO PLAYERS
8 Feb 75 **Fire**

OUTKAST
11 Oct 03 **Speakerboxxx/The Love Below**

PANTERA
9 Apr 94 **Far Beyond Driven**

PEARL JAM
6 Nov 93 **Vs.**
24 Dec 94 **Vitalogy**
14 Sep 96 **No Code**

PETER, PAUL AND MARY
20 Oct 62 **Peter, Paul and Mary**
2 Nov 63 **In the Wind**

PINK FLOYD
28 Apr 73 **Dark Side of the Moon**
4 Oct 75 **Wish You Were Here**
19 Jan 80 **The Wall**
23 Apr 94 **The Division Bell**
24 Jun 95 **Pulse**

POLICE
23 Jul 83 **Synchronicity**

Elvis PRESLEY
5 May 56 **Elvis Presley**
8 Dec 56 **Elvis**
29 Jul 57 **Loving You**

30 Dec 57 **Elvis' Christmas Album**
5 Dec 60 **G.I. Blues**
21 Aug 61 **Something for Everybody**
11 Dec 61 **Blue Hawaii**
2 Jan 65 **Roustabout**
5 May 73 **Aloha from Hawaii via Satellite**
12 Oct 02 **Elv1s - 30 #1 Hits**

PRINCE
4 Aug 84 **Purple Rain**
1 Jun 85 **Around the World in a Day**
22 Jul 89 **Batman (Soundtrack)**

PRODIGY
19 Jul 97 **The Fat of the Land**

PUFF DADDY & FAMILY
9 Aug 97 **No Way Out**

QUEEN
20 Sep 80 **The Game**

QUIET RIOT
26 Nov 83 **Metal Health**

R.E.M.
18 May 91 **Out of Time**
15 Oct 94 **Monster**

RADIOHEAD
21 Oct 00 **Kid A**

Gerry RAFFERTY
8 Jul 78 **City to City**

RAGE AGAINST THE MACHINE
4 May 96 **Evil Empire**
20 Nov 99 **The Battle of Los Angeles**

Bonnie RAITT
7 Apr 90 **Nick of Time**
16 Apr 94 **Longing in Their Hearts**

RASCALS
28 Sep 68 **Time Peace/The Rascals' Greatest Hits**

REO SPEEDWAGON
21 Feb 81 **Hi Infidelity**

Lionel RICHIE
03 Dec 83 **Can't Slow Down**
27 Sep 86 **Dancing on the Ceiling**

LeAnn RIMES
1 Mar 97 **Unchained Melody/The Early Years**
27 Sep 97 **You Light Up My Life – Inspirational Songs**

Kenny ROGERS
13 Dec 80 **Kenny Rogers' Greatest Hits**

ROLLING STONES
21 Aug 65 **Out of Our Heads**
22 May 71 **Sticky Fingers**
17 Jun 72 **Exile on Main Street**
13 Oct 73 **Goat's Head Soup**
23 Nov 74 **It's Only Rock 'n' Roll**
15 May 76 **Black and Blue**
15 Jul 78 **Some Girls**
19 Sep 81 **Tattoo You**

Linda RONSTADT
15 Feb 75 **Heart Like a Wheel**
3 Dec 77 **Simple Dreams**
4 Nov 78 **Living in the USA**

Diana ROSS
7 Apr 73 **Lady Sings the Blues**

SADE
15 Feb 86 **Promise**

SSGT Barry SADLER
12 Mar 66 **Ballads of the Green Berets**

SANTANA
24 Oct 70 **Abraxas**
13 Nov 71 **Santana III**
30 Oct 99 **Supernatural**
9 Nov 02 **Shaman**

SCARFACE
29 Mar 97 **The Untouchable**

Bob SEGER AND THE SILVER BULLET BAND
3 May 80 **Against the Wind**

SELENA
5 Aug 95 **Dreaming of You**

SHAGGY
17 Feb 01 **Hotshot**

Allan SHERMAN
1 Dec 62 **My Son, the Folk Singer**
31 Aug 63 **My Son, the Nut**

SILKK THE SHOCKER
6 Feb 99 **Made Man**

Carly SIMON
13 Jan 73 **No Secrets**

Paul SIMON
6 Dec 75 Still **Crazy After All These Years**

SIMON AND GARFUNKEL
6 Apr 68 **The Graduate (Soundtrack)**
25 May 68 **Bookends**
7 Mar 70 **Bridge Over Troubled Water**

Frank SINATRA
10 Feb 58 **Come Fly with Me**
13 Oct 58 **Frank Sinatra Sings for Only the Lonely**
24 Oct 60 **Nice 'n' Easy**
23 Jul 66 **Strangers in the Night**

SINGING NUN
7 Dec 63 **The Singing Nun**

SKID ROW
29 Jun 91 **Slave to the Grind**

SLY & THE FAMILY STONE
18 Dec 71 **There's a Riot Goin' On**

SMASHING PUMPKINS
11 Nov 95 **Mellon Collie and the Infinite Sadness**

SNOOP DOGG
11 Dec 93 **Doggy Style**
30 Nov 96 **Tha Doggfather**
22 Aug 98 **Da Game Is to Be Sold, Not to Be Told**

SOUNDGARDEN
26 Mar 94 **Superunknown**

Britney SPEARS
30 Jan 99 **... Baby One More Time**
3 Jun 00 **Oops! I Did It Again**
24 Nov 01 **Britney**
6 Dec 03 **In the Zone**

SPICE GIRLS
24 May 97 **Spice**

Bruce SPRINGSTEEN
8 Nov 80 **The River**
7 Jul 84 **Born in the U.S.A.**
29 Nov 86 **Bruce Springsteen & The E Street Band Live/1975-1985**
7 Nov 87 **Tunnel of Love**
18 Mar 95 **Greatest Hits**
17 Aug 02 **The Rising**

STAIND
9 Jun 01 **Break the Cycle**
7 Jun 03 **14 Shades of Grey**

Cat STEVENS
18 Nov 72 **Catch Bull at Four**

Rod STEWART
2 Oct 71 **Every Picture Tells a Story**
10 Feb 79 **Blondes Have More Fun**

STONE TEMPLE PILOTS
25 Jun 94 **Purple**

George STRAIT
17 May 97 **Carrying Your Love with Me**

Barbra STREISAND
31 Oct 64 **People**
16 Mar 74 **The Way We Were**
12 Feb 77 **A Star Is Born (Soundtrack)**
6 Jan 79 **Barbra Streisand's Greatest Hits, Volume 2**
25 Oct 80 **Guilty**
25 Jan 86 **The Broadway Album**
17 Jul 93 **Back to Broadway**
29 Nov 97 **Higher Ground**

Ruben STUDDARD
27 Dec 03 **Soulful**

STYX
4 Apr 81 **Paradise Theater**

Donna SUMMER
11 Nov 78 **Live and More**
16 Jun 79 **Bad Girls**
5 Jan 80 **On the Radio – Greatest Hits – Volumes I & 2**

US NO.1 ALBUMS CONTINUED

SUPERTRAMP
19 May 79 **Breakfast in America**

SUPREMES
22 Oct 66 **The Supremes a Go-Go**

Diana ROSS & THE SUPREMES
28 Oct 67 **Diana Ross & The Supremes Greatest Hits**

SUPREMES & TEMPTATIONS
8 Feb 69 **TCB**

SYSTEM OF A DOWN
22 Sep 01 **Toxicity**

TEARS FOR FEARS
13 Jul 85 **Songs from the Big Chair**

THA DOGG POUND
18 Nov 95 **Dogg Food**

TIFFANY
23 Jan 88 **Tiffany**

TLC
13 Mar 99 **Fanmail**

TONE LOC
15 Apr 89 **Loc-Ed After Dark**

TOOL
2 Jun 01 **Lateralus**

A TRIBE CALLED QUEST
17 Aug 96 **Beats, Rhymes and Life**

Shania TWAIN
7 Dec 02 **Up!**

2PAC (aka Makaveli)
1 Apr 95 **Me Against the World**
2 Mar 96 **All Eyez on Me**
14 Apr 01 **Until the End of Time**

USA FOR AFRICA
27 Apr 85 **We Are the World**

U2
25 Apr 87 **The Joshua Tree**
12 Nov 88 **Rattle and Hum**
7 Dec 91 **Achtung Baby**
24 Jul 93 **Zooropa**
22 Mar 97 **Pop**

VAN HALEN
26 Apr 86 **5150**
25 Jun 88 **OU812**
6 Jul 91 **For Unlawful Carnal Knowledge**
11 Feb 95 **Balance**
9 Nov 96 **Best Of – Volume I**

Luther VANDROSS
28 Jun 03 **Dance with My Father**

VANGELIS
17 Apr 82 **Chariots of Fire (Soundtrack)**

VANILLA ICE
10 Nov 90 **To the Extreme**

VARIOUS ARTISTS
24 Jul 61 **Stars for a Summer Night**
11 Jul 70 **Woodstock**
15 May 99 **Ruff Ryders: Ryde or Die Vol. 1**
5 Aug 00 **Now 4**
21 Apr 01 **Now 6**
18 Aug 01 **Now 7**
3 Nov 01 **God Bless America**
6 Apr 02 **Now 9**
1 Jun 02 **P Diddy & Bad Boy Records Present … We Invented the Remix**
6 Sep 03 **The Neptunes Present … Clones**

Billy VAUGHN
2 May 60 **Theme from 'A Summer Place'**

WAR
17 Feb 73 **The World Is a Ghetto**

Eric WEISSBERG
17 Mar 73 **Dueling Banjos/Deliverance (Soundtrack)**

Lawrence WELK
13 Mar 61 **Calcutta!**

WHAM!
2 Mar 85 **Make It Big**

Barry WHITE
26 Oct 74 **Can't Get Enough**

Andy WILLIAMS
4 May 63 **Days of Wine and Roses**

Steve WINWOOD
20 Aug 88 **Roll with It**

Stevie WONDER
24 Aug 63 Little **Stevie Wonder/The 12 Year Old Genius**
14 Sep 74 **Fulfillingness' First Finale**
16 Oct 76 **Songs in the Key of Life**

WU-TANG-CLAN
21 Jun 97 **Wu-Tang Forever**

NEIL YOUNG
11 Mar 72 **Harvest**

SOUNDTRACK – TV
2 Nov 85 **Miami Vice**

SOUNDTRACK – FILM
28 Jan 56 **Oklahoma**
6 Oct 56 **The King and I**
22 Jul 57 **Around the World in 80 Days**
19 May 58 **South Pacific**
21 Jul 58 **Gigi**
6 Feb 61 **Exodus**
5 May 62 **West Side Story**
13 Mar 65 **Mary Poppins**
20 Mar 65 **Goldfinger**
13 Nov 65 **The Sound of Music**
5 Nov 66 **Doctor Zhivago**
20 Feb 71 **Jesus Christ Superstar**
21 Jan 78 **Saturday Night Fever**
29 Jul 78 **Grease**
25 Jun 83 **Flashdance**
21 Apr 84 **Footloose**
22 Jun 85 **Beverly Hills Cop**
26 Jul 86 **Top Gun**
12 Sep 87 **La Bamba**
14 Nov 87 **Dirty Dancing**
4 Apr 92 **Wayne's World**
12 Dec 92 **The Bodyguard**
21 Aug 93 **Sleepless in Seattle**
4 Jun 94 **The Crow**
16 Jul 94 **The Lion King**
5 Nov 94 **Murder Was the Case**
13 May 95 **Friday**
22 Jul 95 **Pocahontas**
2 Sep 95 **Dangerous Minds**
20 Jan 96 **Waiting to Exhale**
15 Feb 97 **Gridlock'd**
15 Mar 97 **Howard Stern Private Parts: The Album**
26 Jul 97 **Men in Black – The Album**
23 Jan 98 **Titanic**
13 Jun 98 **City of Angels**
18 Jul 98 **Armageddon – The Album**
23 Mar 02 **O Brother, Where Art Thou?**
16 Nov 02 **8 Mile**
2 Aug 03 **Bad Boys II**

ORIGINAL STAGE CAST RECORDINGS
14 Jul 56 **My Fair Lady**
17 Mar 58 **The Music Man**
2 Feb 59 **Flower Drum Song**
8 Feb 60 **The Sound of Music**
5 Jun 61 **Camelot**
17 Jul 61 **Carnival**
6 Jun 64 **Hello, Dolly!**
26 Apr 69 **Hair**

A-Z BY SONG TITLE

A late 1950s Multi-Horn High Fidelity jukebox capable of storing a tiny fraction of the 28,725 hits listed in the index on the following pages. Disc jockey Pete Murray and actress, stage producer and compère Josephine Douglas model the very grooviest knitwear

The complete list of every song that has ever made the singles chart. This handy index is what you turn to when you know the song but can't recall which act was responsible for it.

HOW TO USE THE SONG TITLE INDEX

This section contains an alphabetical index of every hit single since 1952 in order of title, act name, highest position the hit reached on the chart and the year(s) in which it charted

Covers: Different songs with the same title are differentiated by a letter in brackets after the song title: [A], [B], etc. Cover versions of the same song share the same letter. For example, there are eight versions of the song 'Around the World'. Four of these titles share the letter [A], which indicates that they are all covers of the same song (recorded individually by Bing Crosby, Ronnie Hilton, Gracie Fields and Mantovani). However, the fifth version is followed by the letter [B], which indicates that it is a different song (recorded by East 17). If the original version of a cover was never a chart hit, it will not be listed here.

Non-singles: In most cases, individual titles of songs on EP, LP, medley or megamix singles that made the chart are not listed here in this index of songs, although full track listings of EPs are included in the artist entries in the main A-Z by Artist section.

Duets: Most duets list both artists involved (eg. 'We've Got Tonight' by Ronan Keating and Lulu), but some hits are credited only to the main artist. For example, 'Zing a Little Zong' is credited to Bing Crosby but if you look up his entry in the A-Z by Artist section, a footnote for the hit explains that it was, in fact, a duet with Jane Wyman, who has her own cross-reference entry in 'W'.

Act names: Bold capital letters indicate where to look up act names alphabetically in the A-Z by Artist section. Groups, bands, orchestras and ensembles are alphabetised according to the whole act name, while individual artists are ordered according to their surnames. Therefore, note that DANNY WILSON is a group and appears under 'D', while Danny WILLIAMS is an individual and appears under 'W'.

different letters denote that songs are unique; the same letter indicates different versions of the same song ˅

highest position reached on chart ˅

song title ›

MONEY [A] — **Bern ELLIOTT and the FENMEN** (14) ....63 ‹ year of chart entry
MONEY [A] — **FLYING LIZARDS** (5) 79
MONEY [A] — **BACKBEAT BAND** (48) 94
MONEY [B] — **Dan REED NETWORK** (45) 90
MONEY [C] — **SKIN** (18) 94
MONEY [D] — **Charli BALTIMORE** (12) 98
MONEY [E] — **JAMELIA** (5) 00
(MONEY CAN'T) BUY ME LOVE — **BLACKSTREET** (18) 97
MONEY DON'T MATTER 2 NIGHT — **PRINCE and the NEW POWER GENERATION** (19) 92

˄ artist

˄ bold capital letters are used to indicate where to look for an artist alphabetically in the A-Z by Artist section, except where multi-artist collaborations occur

AM I WRONG [A] – **Etienne DE CRECY** (44) ..01
AM I WRONG [B] – **MULL HISTORICAL SOCIETY** (51) 03
AM I WRY? NO – **MEW** (47) 03
AM TO PM – **Christina MILIAN** (3) 02
AMANDA [A] – **Stuart GILLIES** (13) 73
AMANDA [B] – **Craig McLACHLAN** (19) 90
AMATEUR HOUR – **SPARKS** (7) 74
AMAZED – **LONESTAR** (21) 00
AMAZING – **AEROSMITH** (57) 93
AMAZING GRACE [A] – **Judy COLLINS** (5) 70,71,72
AMAZING GRACE [A] – **The Pipes and Drums and Military Band of the ROYAL SCOTS DRAGOON GUARDS** (1)..72
THE AMAZING SPIDER-MAN – **MC SPY-D + FRIENDS** (37) 95
AMAZON CHANT – **AIRSCAPE** (46) 98
AMBUSH – **OUTLAWS** (43) 61
AMERICA [A] – **NICE** (21) 68
AMERICA [A] – **KING KURT** (73) 86
AMERICA [B] – **SIMON and GARFUNKEL** (25) 72
AMERICA [C] – **David ESSEX** (32)..................74
AMERICA [E] – **Gary NUMAN** (49)..................88
AMERICA (I LOVE AMERICA) – **FULL INTENTION** (32) 96,97
AMERICA THE BEAUTIFUL – **Elvis PRESLEY** (69) 01
AMERICA: WHAT TIME IS LOVE – **KLF** (4) 92
AMERICA – WORLD CUP THEME 1994 – **Leonard BERNSTEIN, ORCHESTRA and CHORUS** (44) 94
THE AMERICAN – **SIMPLE MINDS** (59) 81
AMERICAN BAD ASS – **KID ROCK** (25)..........00
AMERICAN DREAM [A] – **CROSBY, STILLS, NASH and YOUNG** (55) ..89
AMERICAN DREAM [B] – **POWER OF DREAMS** (74) 91
AMERICAN DREAM [C] – **JAKATTA** (3) 01
AMERICAN ENGLISH – **IDLEWILD** (15) 02
AMERICAN GENERATION – **RITCHIE FAMILY** (49) 79
AMERICAN GIRL – **Tom PETTY and the HEARTBREAKERS** (40) 77
AMERICAN GIRLS – **COUNTING CROWS** (33) 02
AMERICAN HEARTS – **Billy OCEAN** (54) 79
AMERICAN IN AMSTERDAM – **WHEATUS** (59) 03
AMERICAN LIFE – **MADONNA** (2) 03
AMERICAN PIE [A] – **Don McLEAN** (2) 72,91
AMERICAN PIE [A] – **CHUPITO** (54) 95
AMERICAN PIE [A] – **JUST LUIS** (31) 95,96
AMERICAN PIE [A] – **MADONNA** (1) 00
AN AMERICAN TRILOGY [A] – **Elvis PRESLEY** (8)...72
AMERICAN TRILOGY [A] – **Mickey NEWBURY** (42)...............................72
AMERICAN TRILOGY [B] – **DELGADOS** (61) 00
AMERICAN TV – **TERRORVISION** (63) 93
AMERICAN WOMAN – **GUESS WHO** (19)........70
AMERICANOS – **Holly JOHNSON** (4) 89
AMIGO – **BLACK SLATE** (9)............................80
AMIGOS PARA SIEMPRE (FRIENDS FOR LIFE) – **José CARRERAS and Sarah BRIGHTMAN** (11)...............................92
AMITYVILLE (THE HOUSE ON THE HILL) – **LOVEBUG STARSKI** (12) 86
AMNESIA [A] – **SHALAMAR** (61) 84
AMNESIA [B] – **CHUMBAWAMBA** (10)............98
AMONG MY SOUVENIRS – **Connie FRANCIS** (11)...................................59
AMOR – **Julio IGLESIAS** (32).........................82
AMOR AMOR – **Ben E KING** (38) 61
AMOUR AMOUR – **MOBILES** (45) 82
AMOUR (C'MON) – **PORN KINGS** (17)............97
AMOUREUSE – **Kiki DEE** (13)....................73,76
THE AMSTERDAM EP – **SIMPLE MINDS** (18) 89
AN ACCIDENT IN PARADISE – **Sven VATH** (57) 93
AN AFFAIR TO REMEMBER – **Vic DAMONE** (29) 57,58
AN ANGEL – **KELLY FAMILY** (69) 95
AN EVERLASTING LOVE – **Andy GIBB** (10) 78
AN INNOCENT MAN – **Billy JOEL** (8).............84
AN OLYMPIC RECORD – **BARRON KNIGHTS** (35) 68
AN UBHAL AS AIRDE (THE HIGHEST APPLE) – **RUNRIG** (18) 95
ANARCHY IN THE UK [A] – **SEX PISTOLS** (33) 76,92
ANARCHY IN THE UK [A] – **MEGADETH** (45)..88
ANARCHY IN THE UK [A] – **GREEN JELLY** (27)...93
ANA'S SONG – **SILVERCHAIR** (45) 99
ANASTHASIA – **T99** (14) 91
ANCHOR – **CAVE IN** (53) 03
ANCHORAGE – **Michelle SHOCKED** (60) 88
AND A BANG ON THE EAR – **WATERBOYS** (51) 89
AND DA DRUM MACHINE – **PHATT B** (58) 00
AND I LOVE YOU SO – **Perry COMO** (3) ..73,74
AND I WISH – **DOOLEYS** (52) 81
AND I'M TELLING YOU I'M NOT GOING [A] – **Jennifer HOLLIDAY** (32) 82
AND I'M TELLING YOU I'M NOT GOING [A] – **Donna GILES** (27) 94,96
AND IT HURTS – **DAYEENE** (63) 99
AND IT WASN'T A DREAM – **RUTHLESS RAP ASSASSINS** (75) 90
(AND NOW – THE WALTZ) C'EST LA VIE – **SLADE** (50)...82
AND SHE WAS – **TALKING HEADS** (17)..........86
AND SO I WILL WAIT FOR YOU – **Dee FREDRIX** (56)...93
AND SO IS LOVE – **Kate BUSH** (26) 94
... AND STONES – **BLUE AEROPLANES** (63)..............................90
... AND THAT'S BEFORE ME TEA! – **MR FOOD** (62) 90
... (AND THAT'S NO LIE) – **HEAVEN 17** (52) ..85
AND THE BAND PLAYED ON (DOWN AMONG THE DEAD MEN) – **FLASH and the PAN** (54) 78
AND THE BANDS PLAYED ON – **SAXON** (12) 81
AND THE BEAT GOES ON – **WHISPERS** (2) 80,87
AND THE HEAVENS CRIED – **Anthony NEWLEY** (6) 61
AND THE LEADER ROCKS ON – **Gary GLITTER** (58) 92
(AND THE) PICTURES IN THE SKY – **MEDICINE HEAD** (22) 71
AND THE SUN WILL SHINE – **José FELICIANO** (25)...69
AND THEN SHE KISSED ME – **Gary GLITTER** (39) 81
AND THEN SHE SMILES – **MOCK TURTLES** (44).....................................91
AND THEN THE RAIN FALLS – **BLUE AMAZON** (53) 97
... AND THEY OBEY – **KINESIS** (63) 03
AND YOU SMILED – **Matt MONRO** (28) 73
ANDRES – **L7** (34) 94
ANDROGYNY – **GARBAGE** (24) 01
ANFIELD RAP (RED MACHINE IN FULL EFFECT) – **LIVERPOOL FC** (3) 88
ANGEL [A] – **Rod STEWART** (4) 72
ANGEL [B] – **Aretha FRANKLIN** (37) 73
ANGEL [B] – **SIMPLY RED** (4)........................96
ANGEL [C] – **MADONNA** (5) 85
ANGEL [D] – **AEROSMITH** (69) 88
ANGEL [E] – **EURYTHMICS** (23)......................90
ANGEL [F] – **Jon SECADA** (23) 93
ANGEL [G] – **A-HA** (41) 93
ANGEL [H] – **GOLDIE** (41) 95
ANGEL [I] – **MASSIVE ATTACK** (30) 98
ANGEL [J] – **Tina COUSINS** (46) 99
ANGEL [K] – **Ralph FRIDGE** (20) 00
ANGEL [L] – **Lionel RICHIE** (18).....................00
ANGEL [M] – **SHAGGY featuring RAYVON** (1) 01
ANGEL [N] – **Sarah McLACHLAN** (36) 02
THE ANGEL AND THE GAMBLER – **IRON MAIDEN** (18) 98
ANGEL EYES – **ROXY MUSIC** (4)....................79
ANGEL EYES (HOME AND AWAY) – **WET WET WET** (5) 87
ANGEL FACE – **GLITTER BAND** (4) 74
ANGEL FINGERS (A TEEN BALLAD) – **WIZZARD** (1) 73
ANGEL IN BLUE – **J GEILS BAND** (55)............82
ANGEL INTERCEPTOR – **ASH** (14) 95
ANGEL (LADADI O-HEYO) – **JAM & SPOON featuring PLAVKA** (26) 95
ANGEL LOOKING THROUGH – **STAGECOACH featuring Penny FOSTER** (59) 03
ANGEL OF HARLEM – **U2** (9) 88
ANGEL OF MINE [A] – **ETERNAL** (4) 97
ANGEL OF MINE [A] – **MONICA** (55) 99
ANGEL OF THE MORNING [A] – **PP ARNOLD** (29) 68
ANGEL OF THE MORNING [A] – **Juice NEWTON** (43)......................................81
ANGEL OF THE MORNING – ANY WAY THAT YOU WANT ME (MEDLEY) – **Mary MASON** (27) 77
ANGEL STREET – **M PEOPLE** (8)....................98
ANGELA JONES – **Michael COX** (7) 60
ANGELEYES – **ABBA** (3) 79
ANGELIA – **Richard MARX** (45)......................89
ANGELO – **BROTHERHOOD OF MAN** (1) 77
ANGELS – **Robbie WILLIAMS** (4) 97,99,00
THE ANGELS AND SHADOWS PROJECT – **OMNI TRIO** (44) 01
ANGELS DON'T LIE – **Jim REEVES** (32)..........70
ANGELS GO BALD: TOO – **Howie B** (36) 97
ANGEL'S HEAP – **FINN** (41)............................95
ANGELS OF THE SILENCES – **COUNTING CROWS** (41) 96
ANGEL'S SYMPHONY – **RAF** (73) 96
ANGELS WITH DIRTY FACES [A] – **SHAM 69** (19)...78
ANGELS WITH DIRTY FACES [B] – **SUGABABES** (7) 02
ANGIE – **ROLLING STONES** (5) 73
ANGIE BABY – **Helen REDDY** (5) 75
ANGRY AT THE BIG OAK TREE – **Frank IFIELD** (25) 64
ANGRY CHAIR – **ALICE IN CHAINS** (33) 93
ANGRY SKIES – **Maria NAYLER** (42)..............00
ANIMAL [A] – **DEF LEPPARD** (6) 87
ANIMAL [B] – **LOST IT.COM** (70)....................01
ANIMAL ARMY – **BABYLON ZOO** (17) 96
ANIMAL CANNABUS – **MULL HISTORICAL SOCIETY** (53) 01
ANIMAL INSTINCT [A] – **COMMODORES** (74) 85
ANIMAL INSTINCT [B] – **CRANBERRIES** (54)..99
ANIMAL NITRATE – **SUEDE** (7) 93
THE ANIMAL SONG – **SAVAGE GARDEN** (16) 99
ANIMATION – **SKIDS** (56)...............................80
ANITINA (THE FIRST TIME I SEE SHE DANCE) – **M/A/R/R/S** (1) 87
ANNABELLA – **John WALKER** (24) 67
ANNIE GET YOUR GUN – **SQUEEZE** (43)........82
ANNIE I'M NOT YOUR DADDY – **Kid CREOLE and the COCONUTS** (2) 82
ANNIE'S SONG [A] – **John DENVER** (1) 74
ANNIE'S SONG [A] – **James GALWAY** (3) 78
ANNIVERSARY WALTZ – **Anita HARRIS** (21) ..68
THE ANNIVERSARY WALTZ – PART 1 – **STATUS QUO** (2) 90
THE ANNIVERSARY WALTZ – PART 2 – **STATUS QUO** (16)...90
ANOMALY – CALLING YOUR NAME – **LIBRA presents TAYLOR** (43) 96,00
ANOTHER BLOOMING CHRISTMAS – **Mel SMITH** (59)..91
ANOTHER BODY MURDERED – **FAITH NO MORE and BOO-YAA T.R.I.B.E.** (26) 93
ANOTHER BRICK IN THE WALL (PART 2) – **PINK FLOYD** (1) 79
ANOTHER CHANCE – **Roger SANCHEZ** (1) 01
ANOTHER CUP OF COFFEE – **MIKE and the MECHANICS** (51) 95
ANOTHER DAY [A] – **Paul McCARTNEY** (2) 71
ANOTHER DAY [B] – **WHIGFIELD** (7)..............94
ANOTHER DAY [C] – **BUCKSHOT LEFONQUE** (65) 97
ANOTHER DAY [D] – **SKIP RAIDERS featuring JADA** (46) 00
ANOTHER DAY (ANOTHER GIRL) – **LAMBRETTAS** (49) 80
ANOTHER DAY IN PARADISE [A] – **Phil COLLINS** (2)..89
ANOTHER DAY IN PARADISE [A] – **JAM TRONIK** (19) 90
ANOTHER DAY IN PARADISE [A] – **BRANDY and RAY J** (5) 01
ANOTHER FUNNY HONEYMOON – **David DUNDAS** (29) 77
ANOTHER GIRL – ANOTHER PLANET – **ONLY ONES** (57)..92
ANOTHER HEARTACHE – **Rod STEWART** (54)..86
ANOTHER KIND OF LOVE – **Hugh CORNWELL** (71) 88
ANOTHER LONELY NIGHT IN NEW YORK – **Robin GIBB** (71) 84
ANOTHER LOVER – **DANE** (9) 01
ANOTHER MAN – **Barbara MASON** (45) 84
ANOTHER MONSTERJAM – **Simon HARRIS featuring EINSTEIN** (65)......89

AROUND THE WORLD [A] — Gracie FIELDS (8) 57
AROUND THE WORLD [A] — MANTOVANI (20) 57
AROUND THE WORLD [A] — Ronnie HILTON (4) 57
AROUND THE WORLD [B] — EAST 17 (3) 94
AROUND THE WORLD [C] — DAFT PUNK (5) 97
AROUND THE WORLD [D] — RED HOT CHILI PEPPERS (35) 99
AROUND THE WORLD [E] — AQUA (26) 00
AROUND THE WORLD (LA LA LA LA LA) — ATC (15) 02
ARRANGED MARRIAGE — APACHE INDIAN (16) 93
ARRESTED BY YOU — Dusty SPRINGFIELD (70) 90
ARRIVEDERCI DARLING [A] — Anne SHELTON (17) 55
ARRIVEDERCI DARLING [A] — Edna SAVAGE (19) 56
ARSENAL NUMBER ONE — ARSENAL FC (46) 00
ART FOR ART'S SAKE — 10cc (5) 75
THE ART OF DRIVING — BLACK BOX RECORDER (53) 00
THE ART OF LOSING — AMERICAN HI-FI (75) 03
ART OF LOVE — ART OF NOISE (67) 90
THE ART OF MOVING BUTTS — SHUT UP AND DANCE (69) 92
THE ART OF PARTIES — JAPAN (48) 81
ARTHUR DALEY ('E'S ALRIGHT) — FIRM (14) ..82
ARTHUR'S THEME (BEST THAT YOU CAN DO) — Christopher CROSS (7) 81,82
AS — George MICHAEL and Mary J BLIGE (4) 99
AS ALWAYS [A] — Farley 'Jackmaster' FUNK (49) 89
AS ALWAYS [A] — SECRET LIFE (45) 92
AS GOOD AS IT GETS — GENE (23) 99
AS I AM — SOUND OF ONE featuring GLADEZZ (65) 93
AS I LAY ME DOWN — Sophie B HAWKINS (24) 95
AS I LOVE YOU — Shirley BASSEY (1) 58,59
AS IF WE NEVER SAID GOODBYE — Barbra STREISAND (20) 94
AS LONG AS HE NEEDS ME — Shirley BASSEY (2) 60
AS LONG AS THE PRICE IS RIGHT — DR FEELGOOD (40) 79
AS LONG AS YOU FOLLOW — FLEETWOOD MAC (66) 88
AS LONG AS YOU LOVE ME — BACKSTREET BOYS (3) 97
AS LONG AS YOU'RE GOOD TO ME — Judy CHEEKS (30) 95
AS TEARS GO BY — Marianne FAITHFULL (9) 64
AS THE TIME GOES BY — FUNKAPOLITAN (41) 81
AS TIME GOES BY [A] — Richard ALLAN (44) 60
AS TIME GOES BY [A] — Dooley WILSON (15) 77
AS TIME GOES BY [A] — Jason DONOVAN (26) 92
AS (UNTIL THE DAY) — KNOWLEDGE (70) 97
AS USUAL — Brenda LEE (5) 64
AS WE DO — DJ ZINC (72) 02
AS YOU LIKE IT — Adam FAITH (5) 62
ASCEND — NITZER EBB (52) 92
ASCENSION DON'T EVER WONDER — MAXWELL (28) 96,97
ASHES AND DIAMONDS — Zaine GRIFF (68) 80
ASHES TO ASHES [A] — MINDBENDERS (14) 66
ASHES TO ASHES [B] — David BOWIE (1) 80
ASHES TO ASHES [C] — FAITH NO MORE (15) 97,98
ASIA MINOR — KOKOMO (35) 61
ASK — SMITHS (14) 86,95
ASK THE LORD — HIPSWAY (50) 85,86
ASLEEP IN THE BACK — ELBOW (19) 02
ASSASSIN — ORB (12) 92
ASSASSINATOR 13 — CHIKINKI (72) 03
ASSASSING — MARILLION (22) 84
ASSHOLE — Denis LEARY (58) 96
ASTOUNDED — BRAN VAN 3000 featuring Curtis MAYFIELD (40) 01
ASTRAL AMERICA — APOLLO FOUR FORTY (36) 94
ASYLUM — ORB (20) 97
ASYLUMS IN JERUSALEM — SCRITTI POLITTI (43) 82
AT HOME HE'S A TOURIST — GANG OF FOUR (58) 79
AT MIDNIGHT — T-CONNECTION (53) 79
AT MY MOST BEAUTIFUL — R.E.M. (10) 99
AT NIGHT — SHAKEDOWN (6) 02
AT THE CLUB — DRIFTERS (3) 65,72
AT THE EDGE — STIFF LITTLE FINGERS (15) ..80
AT THE END — IIO (20) 03
AT THE HOP — DANNY and the JUNIORS (3) 58,76
AT THE MOVIES — Roni SIZE (67) 03
AT THE RIVER — GROOVE ARMADA (19) 99
AT THE TOP OF THE STAIRS — FORMATIONS (28) 71
AT THIS TIME OF YEAR — CRAIG (14) 00,01
(AT YOUR BEST) YOU ARE LOVE — AALIYAH (27) 94
ATHEAMA — NEBULA II (55) 92
ATHENA — WHO (40) 82
ATLANTIS [A] — SHADOWS (2) 63
ATLANTIS [B] — DONOVAN (23) 68
ATLANTIS [C] — SECTION-X (42) 97
ATLANTIS IS CALLING (S.O.S. FOR LOVE) — MODERN TALKING (55) 86
ATMOSPHERE [A] — Russ ABBOT (7) 84
ATMOSPHERE [B] — JOY DIVISION (34) 88
ATMOSPHERE [C] — KAYESTONE (55) 00
ATMOSPHERIC ROAD — FAMILY CAT (69) 93
ATOM BOMB — FLUKE (20) 96
ATOM POWERED ACTION (EP) — BIS (54) 96
ATOMIC — BLONDIE (1) 80,94
ATOMIC CITY — Holly JOHNSON (18) 89
ATTACK [A] — TOYS (36) 66
ATTACK [B] — EXPLOITED (50) 82
ATTACK OF THE GHOSTRIDERS — RAVEONETTES (73) 02
ATTACK ME WITH YOUR LOVE — CAMEO (65) 85
ATTENTION TO ME — NOLANS (9) 81
ATTITUDE [A] — SEPULTURA (46) 96
ATTITUDE [B] — ALIEN ANT FARM (66) 02
ATTITUDE [C] — SUEDE (14) 03
AUBERGE — Chris REA (16) 91
AUDIO VIDEO — NEWS (52) 81
AUDITION — WITNESS (71) 99
AUF WIEDERSEH'N SWEETHEART — Vera LYNN (10) 52
AUGUST OCTOBER — Robin GIBB (45) 70
AULD LANG SYNE — WEEKEND (47) 85
AUSLANDER — LIVING COLOUR (53) 93
AUSTRALIA — MANIC STREET PREACHERS (7) 96
AUTOBAHN — KRAFTWERK (11) 75
AUTOBAHN 66 — PRIMAL SCREAM (44) 02
AUTOBIOGRAPHY OF A CRACKHEAD — SHUT UP AND DANCE (43) 92
AUTODRIVE — Herbie HANCOCK (33) 83
AUTOMATIC [A] — POINTER SISTERS (2) 84
AUTOMATIC [B] — Millie SCOTT (56) 86
AUTOMATIC [C] — FLOORPLAY (50) 96
AUTOMATIC [D] — Sarah WHATMORE (11) 03
AUTOMATIC HIGH — S CLUB JUNIORS (2) 02
AUTOMATIC LOVER [A] — Dee D JACKSON (4) 78
AUTOMATIC LOVER [B] — VIBRATORS (35) 78
AUTOMATIC LOVER (CALL FOR LOVE) — REAL McCOY (58) 95
AUTOMATICALLY SUNSHINE — SUPREMES (10) 72
AUTOMATIK — BEAT RENEGADES (73) 01
AUTOPHILIA — BLUETONES (18) 00
AUTUMN ALMANAC — KINKS (3) 67
AUTUMN CONCERTO — George MELACHRINO ORCHESTRA (18) 56
AUTUMN LEAVES — COLDCUT (50) 94
AUTUMN LOVE — ELECTRA (51) 89
AUTUMN TACTICS — CHICANE (44) 00
AVA ADORE — SMASHING PUMPKINS (11) 98
AVALON — ROXY MUSIC (13) 82
AVE MARIA [A] — Shirley BASSEY (31) 62
AVE MARIA [A] — Lesley GARRETT and Amanda THOMPSON (16) 93
AVE MARIA [A] — Andrea BOCELLI (65) 99
AVENGING ANGELS — SPACE (6) 98
AVENUE [A] — SAINT ETIENNE (40) 92
AVENUE [B] — Paul VAN DYK (13) 99,00
AVENUES AND ALLEYWAYS — Tony CHRISTIE (37) 73
AVERAGE MAN [A] — SYMPOSIUM (45) 98
AVERAGE MAN [B] — TURIN BRAKES (35) 03
THE AVERAGE MAN [C] — SIMPLE KID (72) ..03
THE AWAKENING — YORK (11) 99
AWAY FROM HOME — DR ALBAN (42) 94
AWAY FROM ME — PUDDLE OF MUDD (55) ..03
AWFUL — HOLE (42) 99
AXEL F [A] — Harold FALTERMEYER (2) 85
AXEL F [A] — CLOCK (7) 95
AXEL F [A] — SPACECORN (74) 01
AY AY AY AY MOOSEY — MODERN ROMANCE (10) 81
AYLA — AYLA (22) 99
AZTEC GOLD — SILSOE (48) 86
AZTEC LIGHTNING (THEME FROM BBC WORLD CUP GRANDSTAND) — HEADS (45) 86
B-BOY HUMP — OLD SKOOL ORCHESTRA (55) 99
B-BOY STANCE — FREESTYLERS featuring TENOR FLY (23) 98
B GOOD 2 ME — Ronni SIMON (73) 94
B LINE — LAMB (52) 99
B O B BOMBS OVER BAGHDAD — OUTKAST (61) 00
B 2 GETHER — ORIGINAL (29) 95
B WITH ME — MIS-TEEQ (29) 95
B WITH U — Junior SANCHEZ featuring DAJAE (31) 99
BAA BAA BLACK SHEEP — SINGING SHEEP (42) 82
BAAL'S HYMN (EP) — David BOWIE (29) 82
BA-BA-BANKROBBERY (ENGLISH VERSION) — EAV (63) 86
BABALON A.D. (SO GLAD FOR THE MADNESS) — CRADLE OF FILTH (35) 03
BABARABATIRI — GYPSYMEN (32) 01
BABE [A] — STYX (6) 80
BABE [B] — TAKE THAT (1) 93
BABES IN THE WOOD — MATCHBOX (46) 81
BABETTE — Tommy BRUCE and the BRUISERS (50) 62
BABIES — ASHFORD and SIMPSON (56) 85
BABOOSHKA — Kate BUSH (5) 80
B-A-B-Y — Rachel SWEET (35) 78
BABY [A] — HALO JAMES (43) 90
BABY [B] — ROZALLA (26) 95
THE BABY — HOLLIES (26) 72
BABY BABY [A] — Frankie LYMON and the TEENAGERS (4) 57
BABY BABY [B] — EIGHTH WONDER (65) 88
BABY BABY [C] — Amy GRANT (2) 91
BABY BABY [D] — CORONA (5) 95
BABY-BABY-BABY — TLC (55) 92
BABY BABY BYE BYE — Jerry Lee LEWIS (47) 60
BABY, BABY MY LOVE'S ALL FOR YOU — Deniece WILLIAMS (32) 77
BABY BE MINE — BLACKSTREET featuring Teddy RILEY (37) 93
BABY BLUE — Dusty SPRINGFIELD (61) 79
BABY BOY [A] — BIG BROVAZ (4) 03
BABY BOY [B] — BEYONCÉ featuring Sean PAUL (2) 03
BABY BRITAIN — Elliott SMITH (55) 99
BABY CAN I HOLD YOU — BOYZONE (2) 97
BABY, CAN I GET YOUR NUMBER — OBI PROJECT featuring HARRY, ASHER D & DJ WHAT? (75) 01
BABY COME BACK [A] — EQUALS (1) 68
BABY COME BACK [A] — Pato BANTON (1) 94
BABY COME BACK [B] — PLAYER (32) 78
BABY COME ON — SPACEMAID (70) 97
BABY COME ON OVER — Samantha MUMBA (5) 01
BABY COME TO ME [A] — Patti AUSTIN and James INGRAM (11) 83
BABY COME TO ME [A] — Alexander O'NEAL featuring CHERELLE (56) 97
BABY DID A BAD BAD THING — Chris ISAAK (44) 99
BABY DON'T CHANGE YOUR MIND — Gladys KNIGHT and the PIPS (4) 77
BABY DON'T CRY [A] — Lalah HATHAWAY (54) 91
BABY DON'T CRY [B] — INXS (20) 92
BABY DON'T FORGET MY NUMBER — MILLI VANILLI (16) 88
BABY DON'T GET HOOKED ON ME — Mac DAVIS (29) 72
BABY DON'T GO [A] — SONNY and CHER (11) 65
BABY DON'T GO [B] — 4MANDU (47) 96
BABY FACE [A] — LITTLE RICHARD (2) 59
BABY FACE [A] — Bobby DARIN (40) 62

BALL PARK INCIDENT – WIZZARD (6) 72
BALLAD OF A LANDLORD – Terry HALL (50) 97
BALLAD OF BONNIE AND CLYDE – Georgie FAME (1) 67
THE BALLAD OF CHASEY LAIN – BLOODHOUND GANG (15) 00
BALLAD OF DAVY CROCKETT [A] – Dick JAMES (14) 56
THE BALLAD OF DAVY CROCKETT [A] – Bill HAYES (2) 56
THE BALLAD OF DAVY CROCKETT [A] – Max BYGRAVES (20) 56
THE BALLAD OF DAVY CROCKETT [A] – Tennessee Ernie FORD (3) 56
THE BALLAD OF JAYNE – L.A. GUNS (53) 91
BALLAD OF JOHN AND YOKO – BEATLES (1) 69
THE BALLAD OF LUCY JORDAN – Marianne FAITHFULL (48) 79
BALLAD OF PALADIN – Duane EDDY and the REBELS (10) 62
THE BALLAD OF PETER PUMPKINHEAD [A] – CRASH TEST DUMMIES (30) 95
THE BALLAD OF PETER PUMPKINHEAD [A] – XTC (71) 92
THE BALLAD OF SPOTTY MULDOON – Peter COOK (34) 65
THE BALLAD OF THE GREEN BERETS – Staff Sergeant Barry SADLER (24) 66
THE BALLAD OF TOM JONES – SPACE with Cerys of CATATONIA (4) 98
BALLAD OF YOUTH – Richie SAMBORA (59) 91
BALLERINA GIRL – Lionel RICHIE (17) 86
BALLERINA (PRIMA DONNA) – Steve HARLEY and COCKNEY REBEL (51) 83
BALLOON – CATHERINE WHEEL (59) 92
THE BALLROOM BLITZ [A] – SWEET (2) 73
BALLROOM BLITZ [A] – Tia CARRERE (26) 92
THE BALLROOM OF ROMANCE – Chris DE BURGH (40) 86
BALMES – Ian POOLEY featuring ESTHERO (65) 01
BAM BAM BAM – WESTBAM (57) 94
BAMA BOOGIE WOOGIE – Cleveland EATON (35) 78
BAMA LAMA BAMA LOO – LITTLE RICHARD (20) 64
BAMBAATA 2012 – SHY FX (60) 99
BAMBINO – SPRINGFIELDS (16) 61
BAMBOO HOUSES – David SYLVIAN (30) 82
BAMBOO MUSIC – David SYLVIAN (30) 82
BAMBOOGIE – BAMBOO (2) 98
BANANA BANANA – KING KURT (54) 84
BANANA BOAT SONG [A] – Harry BELAFONTE (2) 57
BANANA BOAT SONG [A] – TARRIERS (15) 57
THE BANANA BOAT SONG [A] – Shirley BASSEY (8) 57
BANANA REPUBLIC – BOOMTOWN RATS (3) 80
BANANA ROCK – WOMBLES (9) 74
THE BANANA SONG – GSP (37) 92
BANANA SPLITS (THE TRA LA LA SONG) – DICKIES (7) 79
BA-NA-NA-BAM-BOO – WESTWORLD (37) 87
BANANA-NA-NA (DUMB DI DUMB) – TECHNOHEAD (64) 96
BAND OF GOLD [A] – Don CHERRY (6) 56
BAND OF GOLD [B] – Freda PAYNE (1) 70
BAND OF GOLD [B] – SYLVESTER (67) 83
BAND ON THE RUN – Paul McCARTNEY (3) 74
THE BAND PLAYED THE BOOGIE – CCS (36) 73
BANDAGES – HOT HOT HEAT (25) 03
BANDWAGON BLUES – TWISTED INDIVIDUAL (51) 03
BANG [A] – BLUR (24) 91
BANG [B] – Robbie RIVERA presents RHYTHM BANGERS (13) 00
BANG AND BLAME – R.E.M. (15) 94
BANG BANG [A] – SQUEEZE (49) 78
BANG BANG [B] – B.A. ROBERTSON (2) 79
BANG BANG (MY BABY SHOT ME DOWN) – CHER (3) 66
BANG ON! – PROPELLERHEADS (53) 98
BANG ZOOM (LET'S GO GO) – REAL ROXANNE (11) 86
BANGERS AND MASH – Peter SELLERS (22) 61
BANGIN' BASS – DA TECHNO BOHEMIAN (63) 97
THE BANGIN' MAN – SLADE (3) 74
BANGLA-DESH – George HARRISON (10) 71
BANJO BOY [A] – JAN and KJELD (36) 60
BANJO BOY [A] – George FORMBY (40) 60
THE BANJO'S BACK IN TOWN – Alma COGAN (17) 55
BANKROBBER [A] – AUDIOWEB (19) 97
BANKROBBER [A] – CLASH (12) 80
BANKS OF THE OHIO – Olivia NEWTON-JOHN (6) 71
BANNER MAN – BLUE MINK (3) 71
BARBADOS – TYPICALLY TROPICAL (1) 75
BARBARA ANN – BEACH BOYS (3) 66
BARBARELLA – ALISHA'S ATTIC (34) 99
BARBER'S ADAGIO FOR STRINGS – William ORBIT (4) 99,00
BARBIE GIRL – AQUA (1) 97,98
BARCELONA [A] – Freddie MERCURY (2) 87,92
BARCELONA [B] – D KAY & EPSILON featuring STAMINA MC (14) 03
BARCELONA (FRIENDS UNTIL THE END) – Russell WATSON (68) 00
BARE NECESSITIES MEGAMIX – UK MIXMASTERS (14) 91
BAREFOOT (EP) – ULTRAMARINE (61) 94
BAREFOOT IN THE HEAD – A MAN CALLED ADAM (60) 90
BAREFOOTIN' – Robert PARKER (24) 66
BARK AT THE MOON – Ozzy OSBOURNE (21) 83
BARMY LONDON ARMY – Charlie HARPER (68) 80
BARNEY (... & ME) – BOO RADLEYS (48) 94
BARREL OF A GUN – DEPECHE MODE (4) 97
BARRIERS – SOFT CELL (25) 83
THE BARTENDER AND THE THIEF – STEREOPHONICS (3) 98
BASEMENT TRACK – HIGH CONTRAST (65) 03
BASKET CASE – GREEN DAY (7) 94,95
THE BASS EP – FERGIE (47) 02
BASS (HOW LOW CAN YOU GO) – Simon HARRIS (12) 88
BASS SHAKE – URBAN SHAKEDOWN (59) 92
BASSCAD – AUTECHRE (56) 94
BASSFLY – TILLMAN AND REIS (70) 00
BASSLICK – SECOND PROTOCOL (58) 00
BASSLINE – MANTRONIX (34) 86
BAT OUT OF HELL – MEAT LOAF (8) 79,93
BATTER UP – NELLY and ST LUNATICS (28) 01
BATDANCE – PRINCE (2) 89
BATHTIME – TINDERSTICKS (38) 97
BATMAN THEME – Neal HEFTI (55) 88
BATTLE – WOOKIE (10) 00
BATTLE OF NEW ORLEANS [A] – Johnny HORTON (16) 59
BATTLE OF NEW ORLEANS [A] – Lonnie DONEGAN (2) 59
BATTLE OF THE SEXES – FAITH, HOPE AND CHARITY (53) 90
BATTLE OF WHO COULD CARE LESS – Ben FOLDS FIVE (26) 97
BATTLEFLAG – LO FIDELITY ALLSTARS (36) 98
THE BATTLE'S O'ER – Andy STEWART (28) 61
BATTLESHIP CHAINS – GEORGIA SATELLITES (44) 87
BAUBLES BANGLES AND BEADS – George SHEARING (49) 62
BAUHAUS – CAPPELLA (60) 88
BAWITABA – KID ROCK (41) 01
BBC WORLD CUP GRANDSTAND – ROYAL PHILHARMONIC ORCHESTRA arranged and conducted by Louis CLARK (61) 82
BE AGGRESSIVE – FAITH NO MORE (3) 93
BE ALONE NO MORE – ANOTHER LEVEL (6) 98,99
BE ANGELED – JAM & SPOON featuring REA (31) 02
BE AS ONE – Maria NAYLER (17) 96
BE-BOP-A-LULA – Gene VINCENT (16) 56
BE CAREFUL – SPARKLE featuring R Kelly (7) 98
BE COOL – PAFFENDORF (7) 02
BE FAITHFUL – FATMAN SCOOP featuring the CROOKLYN CLAN (1) 03
BE FREE – LIVE ELEMENT (26) 02
BE FREE WITH YOUR LOVE – SPANDAU BALLET (42) 89
BE GOOD TO YOURSELF – Frankie MILLER (27) 77
BE HAPPY – Mary J BLIGE (30) 94
BE MINE [A] – Lance FORTUNE (4) 60
BE MINE [B] – TREMELOES (39) 67
BE MINE [C] – CHARLOTTE (59) 98
BE MINE [D] – David GRAY (23) 03
BE MINE TONIGHT – JAMMERS (65) 83
BE MY BABY [A] – RONETTES (4) 63
BE MY BABY [B] – Vanessa PARADIS (6) 92
BE MY BABY [C] – CAPPELLA (53) 97
BE MY DOWNFALL – DEL AMITRI (30) 92
BE MY FRIEND – SOUL U*NIQUE (53) 00
BE MY GIRL [A] – Jim DALE (2) 57
BE MY GIRL [B] – DENNISONS (46) 63
BE MY GUEST – Fats DOMINO (11) 59,60
BE MY LIGHT BE MY GUIDE – GENE (54) 94
BE MY LOVER – LA BOUCHE (25) 95,96
BE MY NUMBER TWO – Joe JACKSON (70) 84
BE MY TWIN – BROTHER BEYOND (14) 89
BE NEAR ME – ABC (26) 85
BE PROUD BE LOUD (BE HEARD) – TOYAH (30) 82
BE QUICK OR BE DEAD – IRON MAIDEN (2) 92
BE QUIET AND DRIVE (FAR AWAY) – DEFTONES (50) 98
BE STIFF – DEVO (71) 78
BE TENDER WITH ME BABY – Tina TURNER (28) 90
BE THANKFUL FOR WHAT YOU'VE GOT – William DE VAUGHN (31) 74,80
BE THE FIRST TO BELIEVE – A1 (6) 99
BE THERE [A] – TALL PAUL (45) 99
BE THERE [B] – Ian BROWN (8) 99
BE WITH ME ALWAYS – Cliff RICHARD (52) 97
BE WITH YOU [A] – BANGLES (23) 89
BE WITH YOU [A] – ATOMIC KITTEN (2) 02
BE YOUNG, BE FOOLISH, BE HAPPY – TAMS (32) [A] 70
BE YOUNG BE FOOLISH BE HAPPY – SONIA (22) [A] 91
BE YOURSELF – CELEDA (61) 99
BEACH BABY – FIRST CLASS (13) 74
BEACH BOY GOLD – GIDEA PARK (11) 81
BEACH BOYS MEDLEY – BEACH BOYS (47) 81
BEACH BUMP – BABY FORD (68) 90
BEACH OF THE WAR GODDESS – Caron WHEELER (75) 93
BEACHBALL – NALIN & KANE (17) 97,98
BEACHED – ORBITAL (36) 00
BEACON LIGHT – WEEN (20) 98
BEAR CAGE – STRANGLERS (36) 80
BEAT BOX – ART OF NOISE (51) 85
A BEAT CALLED LOVE – GRID (64) 90
BEAT DIS – BOMB THE BASS (2) 88
BEAT FOR BEATNIKS – John BARRY ORCHESTRA (40) 60
THE BEAT GOES ON [A] – SONNY and CHER (29) 67
BEAT GOES ON [A] – THE ALL SEEING I (11) 98
THE BEAT GOES ON [B] – Bob SINCLAR (33) 03
BEAT IT – Michael JACKSON (3) 83
BEAT MAMA – CAST (9) 99
BEAT STREET BREAKDOWN – GRANDMASTER FLASH, Melle MEL and the FURIOUS FIVE (42) 84
BEAT SURRENDER – JAM (1) 82
BEAT THE BEAT – Mari WILSON (59) 82
BEAT THE CLOCK – SPARKS (10) 79
THE BEAT(EN) GENERATION – The THE (18) 89
BEATIN' THE HEAT – JACK 'N' CHILL (42) 88
BEATLES AND THE STONES – HOUSE OF LOVE (36) 90
BEATLES MOVIE MEDLEY – BEATLES (10) 82
BEATNIK FLY – JOHNNY and the HURRICANES (8) 60
BEATNIK GIRL – SNUG (55) 98
BEATSTIME – SONIC SOLUTION (59) 92
BEAUTIFUL [A] – MARILLION (29) 95
BEAUTIFUL [B] – Matt DAREY (21) 00
BEAUTIFUL [B] – Matt DAREY featuring Marcella WOODS (10) 02
BEAUTIFUL [C] – ATHLETE (41) 02
BEAUTIFUL [D] – LEMONESCENT (70) 02
BEAUTIFUL [E] – BIGFELLA featuring Noel MCCALLA (52) 02
BEAUTIFUL [F] – SNOOP DOGG featuring PHARRELL, uncle Charlie WILSON (23) 03
BEAUTIFUL [G] – Christina AGUILERA (1) 03
BEAUTIFUL ALONE – STRANGELOVE (35) 96
BEAUTIFUL CHILD (A DEEPER LOVE) – MADELYNE (63) 02
BEAUTIFUL DAY [A] – 3 COLOURS RED (11) 99
BEAUTIFUL DAY [B] – U2 (1) 00
BEAUTIFUL DREAM – WORLD PARTY (31) 97
THE BEAUTIFUL EXPERIENCE – PRINCE (18) 94
BEAUTIFUL GIRL – INXS (23) 93

BOILER — **LIMP BIZKIT** (18) ... 01
THE BOILER — **RHODA with the SPECIAL AKA** (35) ... 82
BOING! — **WEDDING PRESENT** (19) ... 92
BOLL WEEVIL SONG — **Brook BENTON** (30) .. 61
BOM DIGI BOM (THINK ABOUT THE WAY) — **ICE MC** (38) ... 96
THE BOMB — **LOVE CONNECTION** (53) ... 00
BOMB DIGGY — **ANOTHER LEVEL** (6) ... 99
THE BOMB! (THESE SOUNDS FALL INTO MY MIND) — **BUCKETHEADS** (5) ... 95
BOMBADIN — **808 STATE** (67) ... 94
BOMBER — **MOTÖRHEAD** (34) ... 79
BOMBSCARE — **2 BAD MICE** (46) ... 96
BOMBTRACK — **RAGE AGAINST THE MACHINE** (37) ... 93
BON BON VIE — **TS MONK** (63) ... 81
BOND — **808 STATE** (57) ... 96
BONE DRIVEN — **BUSH** (49) ... 97
BONEY M MEGAMIX — **BONEY M** (7) ... 92
BONEYARD — **LITTLE ANGELS** (33) ... 91
BONITA APPLEBUM — **A TRIBE CALLED QUEST** (47) ... 90
BONITA MANANA — **ESPIRITU** (50) ... 94
'03 BONNIE & CLYDE — **JAY-Z featuring Beyoncé KNOWLES** (2) ... 03
BONNIE CAME BACK — **Duane EDDY and the REBELS** (12) ... 60
BONY MORONIE — **Larry WILLIAMS** (11) ... 58
BOO! FOREVER — **BOO RADLEYS** (67) ... 92
BOOGALOO PARTY — **FLAMINGOS** (26) ... 69
BOOGIE — **DIVE** (35) ... 98
BOOGIE AT RUSSIAN HILL — **John Lee HOOKER** (53) ... 93
BOOGIE DOWN [A] — **Eddie KENDRICKS** (39) 74
BOOGIE DOWN [B] — **Al JARREAU** (63) ... 83
BOOGIE DOWN (BRONX) — **Man PARRISH** (56) ... 85
BOOGIE DOWN (GET FUNKY NOW) — **REAL THING** (33) ... 79
BOOGIE MAN — **MATCH** (48) ... 79
BOOGIE NIGHTS [A] — **HEATWAVE** (2) ... 77
BOOGIE NIGHTS [A] — **La FLEUR** (51) ... 83
BOOGIE NIGHTS [A] — **SONIA** (30) ... 92
BOOGIE ON REGGAE WOMAN — **Stevie WONDER** (12) ... 75
BOOGIE ON UP — **ROKOTTO** (40) ... 77
BOOGIE OOGIE OOGIE — **A TASTE OF HONEY** (3) ... 78,85
BOOGIE SHOES — **KC and the SUNSHINE BAND** (34) ... 78
BOOGIE TOWN — **FAT LARRY'S BAND** (46) ... 79
BOOGIE WONDERLAND — **EARTH WIND AND FIRE with the EMOTIONS** (4) ... 79
BOOGIE WOOGIE BUGLE BOY (DON'T STOP) — **2 IN A TENT** (48) ... 95
THE BOOK — **David WHITFIELD** (5) ... 54
BOOK OF DAYS — **ENYA** (10) ... 92
BOOK OF DREAMS — **Suzanne VEGA** (66) ... 90
BOOK OF LOVE — **MUDLARKS** (8) ... 58
BOOM BANG-A-BANG — **LULU** (2) ... 69
BOOM BOOM [A] — **BLACK SLATE** (51) ... 80
BOOM BOOM [B] — **John Lee HOOKER** (16) .. 92
BOOM BOOM [C] — **DEFINITION OF SOUND** (59) ... 95
BOOM BOOM [D] — **N-TYCE** (18) ... 98
BOOM BOOM [E] — **Basil BRUSH featuring India BEAU** (44) ... 03
BOOM BOOM BOOM — **OUTHERE BROTHERS** (1) ... 95
BOOM, BOOM, BOOM, BOOM!! — **VENGABOYS** (1) ... 99
BOOM BOOM (LET'S GO BACK TO MY ROOM) — **Paul LEKAKIS** (60) ... 87
THE BOOM BOOM ROOM — **NATASHA** (44) .. 82
BOOM ROCK SOUL — **BENZ** (62) ... 95
BOOM SELECTION — **GENIUS CRU** (12) ... 01
BOOM! SHAKE THE ROOM — **JAZZY JEFF & the FRESH PRINCE** (1) ... 93,95
BOOM! THERE SHE WAS — **ROGER** (55) ... 88
BOOMBASTIC — **SHAGGY** (1) ... 95
BOOO! — **STICKY featuring MS DYNAMITE** (12) ... 01
BOOPS (HERE TO GO) — **SLY and ROBBIE** (12) ... 87
BOOTI CALL — **BLACKSTREET** (56) ... 94
BOOTIE CALL — **ALL SAINTS** (1) ... 98
BOOTYLICIOUS — **DESTINY'S CHILD** (2) ... 01
BOOTZILLA — **BOOTSY'S RUBBER BAND** (43) 78
BOP BOP BABY — **WESTLIFE** (5) ... 02
BOP GUN (ONE NATION) — **ICE CUBE featuring George CLINTON** (22) .. 94
BORA BORA — **DA HOOL** (35) ... 98
BORDERLINE — **MADONNA** (2) ... 84,86
BORN A WOMAN — **Sandy POSEY** (24) ... 66
BORN AGAIN [A] — **CHRISTIANS** (25) ... 88
BORN AGAIN [B] — **BADLY DRAWN BOY** (16) 03
BORN AGAIN [C] — **STARSAILOR** (40) ... 03
BORN DEAD — **BODY COUNT** (28) ... 94
BORN FREE — **Vic REEVES** (6) ... 91
BORN IN 69 — **ROCKET FROM THE CRYPT** (68) ... 96
BORN IN THE GHETTO — **FUNKY POETS** (72) 94
BORN IN THE USA — **Bruce SPRINGSTEEN** (5) ... 85
BORN OF FRUSTRATION — **JAMES** (13) ... 92
BORN ON THE 5TH OF NOVEMBER — **CARTER — THE UNSTOPPABLE SEX MACHINE** (35) .. 95
BORN SLIPPY — **UNDERWORLD** (2) ... 95,96,03
BORN THIS WAY (LET'S DANCE) — **COOKIE CREW** (23) ... 89
BORN TO BE ALIVE [A] — **Patrick HERNANDEZ** (10) ... 79
BORN TO BE ALIVE [B] — **ADAMSKI featuring SOHO** (51) ... 91
BORN TO BE MY BABY — **BON JOVI** (22) ... 88
BORN TO BE SOLD — **TRANSVISION VAMP** (22) ... 89
BORN TO BE WILD — **STEPPENWOLF** (18) 69,99
BORN TO BE WITH YOU [A] — **CHORDETTES** (8) ... 56
BORN TO BE WITH YOU [A] — **Dave EDMUNDS** (5) ... 73
BORN TO LIVE AND BORN TO DIE — **FOUNDATIONS** (46) ... 69
BORN TO LOSE — **KING ADORA** (68) ... 03
BORN TO MAKE YOU HAPPY — **Britney SPEARS** (1) ... 00
BORN TO RAISE HELL — **MOTÖRHEAD / ICE-T / Whitfield CRANE** (47) ... 94
BORN TO RUN — **Bruce SPRINGSTEEN** (16) .. 87
BORN TO TRY — **Delta GOODREM** (3) ... 03
BORN TOO LATE — **PONI-TAILS** (5) ... 58
BORN 2 B.R.E.E.D. — **Monie LOVE** (18) ... 93
BORN WITH A SMILE ON MY FACE — **Stephanie DE SYKES** (2) ... 74
BORNE ON THE WIND — **Roy ORBISON** (15) .. 64
BORROWED LOVE — **S.O.S. BAND** (50) ... 86
BORROWED TIME — **John LENNON** (32) ... 84
BORSALINO — **Bobby CRUSH** (37) ... 72
THE BOSS [A] — **Diana ROSS** (40) ... 79
THE BOSS [A] — **BRAXTONS** (31) ... 97
BOSS DRUM — **SHAMEN** (4) ... 92
BOSS GUITAR — **Duane EDDY and the REBELS** (27) ... 63
BOSS OF ME — **THEY MIGHT BE GIANTS** (21) 01
BOSSA NOVA BABY — **Elvis PRESLEY** (13) 63,87
BOSTICH — **YELLO** (55) ... 92
THE BOSTON TEA PARTY — **SENSATIONAL ALEX HARVEY BAND** (13) ... 76
BOTH ENDS BURNING — **ROXY MUSIC** (25) .. 75
BOTH SIDES NOW [A] — **CLANNAD and Paul YOUNG** (74) ... 91
BOTH SIDES NOW [A] — **Judy COLLINS** (14) .. 70
BOTH SIDES NOW [A] — **Viola WILLS** (35) ... 86
BOTH SIDES OF THE STORY — **Phil COLLINS** (7) ... 93,94
BOTHER — **STONE SOUR** (28) ... 03
THE BOTTLE [A] — **TYRREL CORPORATION** (71) ... 92
THE BOTTLE [B] — **CHRISTIANS** (39) ... 93
BOTTLE LIVING — **Dave GAHAN** (36) ... 03
BOULEVARD OF BROKEN DREAMS — **BEATMASTERS** (62) ... 91
BOUNCE ALONG — **Wayne WONDER** (19) ... 03
BOUNCE, ROCK, SKATE, ROLL — **BABY DC featuring IMAJIN** (45) ... 99
BOUNCE WITH THE MASSIVE — **TZANT** (39) .. 98
THE BOUNCER — **KICKS LIKE A MULE** (7) ... 92
BOUNCIN' BACK (BUMPIN' ME AGAINST THE WALL) — **MYSTIKAL** (45) ... 02
BOUNCING FLOW — **K2 FAMILY** (27) ... 01
BOUND 4 DA RELOAD (CASUALTY) — **OXIDE & NEUTRINO** (1) ... 00
BOUNDARIES — **Leena CONQUEST and HIP HOP FINGER** (67) ... 94
BOURGIE, BOURGIE — **Gladys KNIGHT and the PIPS** (32) ... 80
BOUT — **JAMELIA featuring Rah DIGGA** (37) .. 03
BOW DOWN MISTER — **JESUS LOVES YOU** (27) ... 91
BOW WOW (THAT'S MY NAME) — **LIL BOW WOW** (6) ... 01
BOW WOW WOW — **FUNKDOOBIEST** (34) ... 94
THE BOX — **ORBITAL** (11) ... 96
BOX SET GO — **HIGH** (28) ... 91
THE BOXER — **SIMON and GARFUNKEL** (6) ... 69,92
BOXER BEAT — **JOBOXERS** (3) ... 83
BOXERS — **MORRISSEY** (23) ... 95
BOY — **LULU** (15) ... 68
THE BOY DONE GOOD — **Billy BRAGG** (55) .. 97
BOY FROM NEW YORK CITY [A] — **Alison JORDAN** (23) ... 92
THE BOY FROM NEW YORK CITY [A] — **DARTS** (2) ... 78
A BOY FROM NOWHERE — **Tom JONES** (2) ... 87
BOY I GOTTA HAVE YOU — **RIO and MARS** (43) ... 95,96
BOY (I NEED YOU) — **Mariah CAREY featuring CAM'RON** (17) ... 03
THE BOY IN THE BUBBLE — **Paul SIMON** (26) ... 86
BOY IS CRYING — **SAINT ETIENNE** (34) ... 01
THE BOY IS MINE — **BRANDY and MONICA** (2) ... 98
A BOY NAMED SUE — **Johnny CASH** (4) ... 69
BOY NEXT DOOR — **JAMELIA** (42) ... 00
BOY OH BOY — **RACEY** (22) ... 79
BOY ON TOP OF THE NEWS — **DIESEL PARK WEST** (58) ... 92
BOY OR A GIRL — **IMPERIAL DRAG** (54) ... 96
THE BOY RACER — **MORRISSEY** (36) ... 95
THE BOY WHO CAME BACK — **Marc ALMOND** (52) ... 84
THE BOY WITH THE THORN IN HIS SIDE — **SMITHS** (23) ... 85
THE BOY WITH THE X-RAY EYES — **BABYLON ZOO** (32) ... 96
BOY WONDER — **SPEEDY** (56) ... 96
BOY YOU KNOCK ME OUT — **Tatyana ALI featuring Will SMITH** (3) ... 99
BOYS [A] — **Kim WILDE** (11) ... 81
BOYS [B] — **MARY JANE GIRLS** (74) ... 83
BOYS [C] — **BON** (15) ... 01
BOYS [D] — **Britney SPEARS** (7) ... 02
BOYS AND GIRLS — **HUMAN LEAGUE** (48) ... 81
THE BOYS ARE BACK IN TOWN [A] — **THIN LIZZY** (8) ... 76,91
THE BOYS ARE BACK IN TOWN [A] — **GLADIATORS** (70) ... 96
THE BOYS ARE BACK IN TOWN [A] — **HAPPY MONDAYS** (24) ... 99
BOYS BETTER — **DANDY WARHOLS** (36) ... 98
BOYS CRY — **Eden KANE** (8) ... 64
BOYS DON'T CRY — **CURE** (22) ... 86
THE BOYS IN THE OLD BRIGHTON BLUE — **BRIGHTON AND HOVE ALBION FC** (65) ... 83
BOYS KEEP SWINGING — **David BOWIE** (7) .. 79
THE BOYS OF SUMMER [A] — **Don HENLEY** (12) ... 85,98
THE BOYS OF SUMMER [A] — **DJ SAMMY** (2) 03
THE BOYS OF SUMMER [A] — **The ATARIS** (49) ... 03
BOYS (SUMMERTIME LOVE) — **SABRINA** (3) .. 88
BOYS WILL BE BOYS — **OSMOND BOYS** (65) ... 91
BOZOS — **LEVELLERS** (44) ... 98
BRACKISH — **KITTIE** (46) ... 00
BRAIN — **JUNGLE BROTHERS** (52) ... 97
BRAIN STEW — **GREEN DAY** (28) ... 96
BRAINS — **NUT** (64) ... 96
BRAINWASHED (CALL YOU) — **TOMCRAFT** (43) ... 03
BRAND NEW — **FINITRIBE** (69) ... 94
BRAND NEW DAY [A] — **DARKMAN** (74) ... 95
BRAND NEW DAY [B] — **MINDS OF MEN** (41) 96
BRAND NEW DAY [C] — **STING** (13) ... 99
BRAND NEW FRIEND — **Lloyd COLE** (19) ... 85
BRAND NEW KEY — **MELANIE** (4) ... 72
BRAND NEW LOVER — **DEAD OR ALIVE** (31) .. 86
BRAND NEW START — **Paul WELLER** (16) ... 98
BRANDY [A] — **Scott ENGLISH** (12) ... 71
BRANDY [B] — **O'JAYS** (21) ... 78
BRAS ON 45 (FAMILY VERSION) — **Ivor BIGGUN** (50) ... 81
BRASS IN POCKET — **PRETENDERS** (1) ... 79
BRASS: LET THERE BE HOUSE — **PARTY FAITHFUL** (54) ... 95
BRASSNECK — **WEDDING PRESENT** (24) ... 90
BRAVE NEW WORLD [A] — **David ESSEX** (55) 78
BRAVE NEW WORLD [B] — **TOYAH** (21) ... 82

BROWN SUGAR [B] – D'ANGELO (24) ... 95
BRUISE PRISTINE – PLACEBO (14) ... 97
BRUSHED – Paul WELLER (14) ... 97
BRUTAL-8-E – ALTERN 8 (43) ... 92
BUBBLE – FLUKE (37) ... 94
BUBBLING HOT – Pato BANTON (15) ... 95
BUCCI BAG – Andrea DORIA (57) ... 03
BUCK ROGERS – FEEDER (5) ... 01
THE BUCKET OF WATER SONG – FOUR BUCKETEERS (26) ... 80
BUDDHA OF SUBURBIA – David BOWIE featuring Lenny KRAVITZ (35) ... 93
BUDDY – DE LA SOUL (7) ... 89
BUDDY HOLLY – WEEZER (12) ... 95
BUDDY X [A] – Neneh CHERRY (35) ... 93
BUDDY X 99 [A] – DREEM TEEM vs Neneh CHERRY (15) ... 99
BUFFALO BILL'S LAST SCRATCH – BARRON KNIGHTS (49) ... 83
BUFFALO GALS [A] – Malcolm McLAREN and the WORLD'S FAMOUS SUPREME TEAM (9) ... 82
BUFFALO GALS STAMPEDE [A] – Malcolm McLAREN (65) ... 98
BUFFALO SOLDIER – Bob MARLEY and the WAILERS (4) ... 83
BUFFALO STANCE – Neneh CHERRY (3) ... 88
THE BUG – DIRE STRAITS (67) ... 92
BUG A BOO – DESTINY'S CHILD (9) ... 99
BUG IN THE BASSBIN – INNERZONE ORCHESTRA (68) ... 96
BUG POWDER DUST – BOMB THE BASS (24) ... 94
BUGGIN – TRUE STEPPERS (6) ... 00
BUGS – HEPBURN (14) ... 99
BUILD [A] – HOUSEMARTINS (15) ... 87
BUILD [B] – INNOCENCE (72) ... 92
BUILD ME UP BUTTERCUP – FOUNDATIONS (2) ... 68,98
BUILD YOUR LOVE – Johnnie RAY (17) ... 57
BUILDING THE CITY OF LIGHT – Mike SCOTT (60) ... 95
BULGARIAN – TRAVEL (67) ... 99
BULL IN THE HEATHER – SONIC YOUTH (24) ... 94
BULLDOG NATION – Kevin KENNEDY (70) ... 00
BULLET – FLUKE (23) ... 95
BULLET COMES – CHARLATANS (32) ... 95
BULLET IN THE GUN – PLANET PERFECTO (7) ... 99,00
BULLET IN THE HEAD – RAGE AGAINST THE MACHINE (16) ... 93
BULLET WITH BUTTERFLY WINGS – SMASHING PUMPKINS (20) ... 95
BULLETPROOF! – POP WILL EAT ITSELF (24) 92
BULLETS – CREED (47) ... 02
BULLFROG – GTO (72) ... 91
BULLITPROOF – BREAKBEAT ERA (65) ... 00
BULLITT – Lalo SCHIFRIN (36) ... 97
BULLS ON PARADE – RAGE AGAINST THE MACHINE (8) ... 96
BULLY BOY – SHED SEVEN (22) ... 96
BULLY FOR YOU – Tom ROBINSON (68) ... 79
BUMP – FUN LOVIN' CRIMINALS (50) ... 01
THE BUMP – KENNY (3) ... 74
BUMP, BUMP, BUMP – B2K featuring P DIDDY (11) ... 03
BUMP 'N' GRIND – R KELLY (8) ... 95
BUMP N GRIND (I AM FEELING HOT TONIGHT) – M DUBS featuring LADY SAW (59) ... 00
BUMPED – RIGHT SAID FRED (32) ... 93
A BUNCH OF THYME – FOSTER and ALLEN (18) ... 82
BUNSEN BURNER – John OTWAY (9) ... 02
BUONA SERA [A] – Louis PRIMA (25) ... 58
BUONA SERA [A] – Mr Acker BILK and his PARAMOUNT JAZZ BAND (7) ... 60
BUONA SERA [A] – BAD MANNERS (34) ... 81
BUOY – Mick KARN featuring David SYLVIAN (63) ... 87
BURDEN IN MY HAND – SOUNDGARDEN (33) ... 96
BURIAL – LEVITICUS (66) ... 95
BURIED ALIVE BY LOVE – HIM (30) ... 03
BURLESQUE – FAMILY (13) ... 72
BURN [A] – DOCTOR and the MEDICS (29) ... 86
BURN [B] – Tina ARENA (47) ... 99
BURN BABY BURN [A] – HUDSON-FORD (15) ... 74
BURN BABY BURN [B] – ASH (13) ... 01
BURN BURN – LOSTPROPHETS (17) ... 03
BURN IT UP – BEATMASTERS with PP ARNOLD (14) ... 88
BURN RUBBER ON ME (WHY YOU WANNA HURT ME) – GAP BAND (22) ... 80
BURNIN' [A] – DAFT PUNK (30) ... 97
BURNIN' [B] – K-KLASS (45) ... 98
BURNIN' [C] – MIRRORBALL (47) ... 00
BURNIN' HOT – Jermaine JACKSON (32) ... 80
BURNIN' LOVE – CON FUNK SHUN (68) ... 86
BURNING '95 [A] – MK featuring ALANA (44) ... 95
BURNING [B] – BABY BUMPS (17) ... 98
BURNING BRIDGES – Jack SCOTT (32) ... 60
BURNING BRIDGES (ON AND OFF AND ON AGAIN) – STATUS QUO (5) ... 88
BURNING CAR – John FOXX (35) ... 80
BURNING DOWN ONE SIDE – Robert PLANT (73) ... 82
BURNING DOWN THE HOUSE – Tom JONES and the CARDIGANS (7) ... 99
BURNING HEART – SURVIVOR (5) ... 86
BURNING LOVE – Elvis PRESLEY (7) ... 72
BURNING OF THE MIDNIGHT LAMP – Jimi HENDRIX EXPERIENCE (18) ... 67
BURNING THE GROUND – DURAN DURAN (31) ... 89
BURNING UP [A] – Tony DE VIT (25) ... 95
BURNING UP [B] – BINI & MARTINI (65) ... 01
BURNING WHEEL – PRIMAL SCREAM (17) ... 97
BURST – DARLING BUDS (50) ... 88
BURUCHACCA – MUKKAA (74) ... 93
BURUNDI BLACK – BURUNDI STEIPHENSON BLACK (31) ... 71
BURUNDI BLUES – BEATS INTERNATIONAL (51) ... 90
BURY YOU – SYMPOSIUM (41) ... 98
BUS STOP – HOLLIES (5) ... 66
BUSHEL AND A PECK – Vivian BLAINE (12) ... 53
BUSINESS – EMINEM (6) ... 03
THE BUSINESS – Brian MAY (51) ... 98
BUST A MOVE – YOUNG MC (73) ... 89
BUST THIS HOUSE DOWN – PENTHOUSE 4 (56) ... 88
BUSTED – Ray CHARLES (21) ... 63
BUSY BEE – UGLY KID JOE (39) ... 93
BUSY DOING NOTHING – Dave STEWART (49) ... 83
BUT I DO – Clarence 'Frogman' HENRY (3) ... 61
BUT I DO LOVE YOU – LeAnn RIMES (20) ... 02
BUT I FEEL GOOD – GROOVE ARMADA (50) 03
BUT NOT FOR ME [A] – Ella FITZGERALD (25) ... 59
BUT NOT FOR ME [A] – Ketty LESTER (45) ... 62
BUT YOU LOVE ME DADDY – Jim REEVES (15) ... 69
BUT YOU'RE MINE – SONNY and CHER (17) 65
BUTCHER BABY – PLASMATICS (55) ... 80
BUTTERCUP – Carl ANDERSON (49) ... 85
BUTTERFINGERS – Tommy STEELE (8) ... 57
BUTTERFLY [A] – Andy WILLIAMS (1) ... 57
BUTTERFLY [A] – Charlie GRACIE (12) ... 57
BUTTERFLY [B] – Danyel GERARD (11) ... 71
BUTTERFLY [C] – Mariah CAREY (22) ... 97
BUTTERFLY [D] – TILT featuring ZEE (41) ... 98
BUTTERFLY [E] – CRAZY TOWN (3) ... 01
BUTTERFLY KISSES – Bob CARLISLE (56) ... 97
BUTTERFLY ON A WHEEL – MISSION (12) ... 90
BUY IT IN BOTTLES – Richard ASHCROFT (26) ... 03
BUZZ BUZZ A DIDDLE IT – MATCHBOX (22) ... 80
BUZZIN' – ASIAN DUB FOUNDATION (31) ... 98
BY MY SIDE – INXS (42) ... 91
BY THE DEVIL (I WAS TEMPTED) – BLUE MINK (26) ... 73
BY THE FOUNTAINS OF ROME [A] – David HUGHES (27) ... 56
BY THE FOUNTAINS OF ROME [A] – Edmund HOCKRIDGE (17) ... 56
BY THE LIGHT OF THE SILVERY MOON – LITTLE RICHARD (17) ... 59
BY THE TIME THIS NIGHT IS OVER – Kenny G with Peabo BRYSON (56) ... 93
BY THE WAY [A] – BIG THREE (22) ... 63
BY THE WAY [B] – TREMELOES (35) ... 70
BY THE WAY [C] – RED HOT CHILI PEPPERS (2) ... 02
BY YOUR SIDE [A] – PETERS and LEE (39) ... 73
BY YOUR SIDE [B] – Jimmy SOMERVILLE (41) ... 95
BY YOUR SIDE [C] – SADE (17) ... 00
BYE BABY – Ruby TURNER (52) ... 86
BYE BYE BABY [A] – Johnny OTIS SHOW (20) ... 58
BYE BYE BABY [B] – SYMBOLS (44) ... 67
BYE BYE BABY [B] – BAY CITY ROLLERS (1) 75
BYE BYE BABY [C] – Tony JACKSON and the VIBRATIONS (38) ... 64
BYE BYE BABY [D] – TQ (7) ... 99
BYE BYE BLUES – Bert KAEMPFERT (24) ... 65
BYE BYE BYE – 'N SYNC (3) ... 00
BYE BYE LOVE – EVERLY BROTHERS (6) ... 57
B.Y.O.F. (BRING YOUR OWN FUNK) – FANTASTIC FOUR (62) ... 79
BYRDS TURN TO STONE – SHACK (63) ... 03
C MOON – Paul McCARTNEY (5) ... 72
C U WHEN U GET THERE – COOLIO (3) ... 97
C'MON PEOPLE (WE'RE MAKING IT NOW) – Richard ASHCROFT (21) ... 00
ÇA PLANE POUR MOI [A] – PLASTIC BERTRAND (8) ... 78
ÇA PLANE POUR MOI [A] – Leila K (69) ... 93
CABARET – Louis ARMSTRONG (1) ... 68
THE CABARET – TIME UK (63) ... 83
CACHARPAYA (ANDES PUMPSA DAESI) – INCANTATION (12) ... 82
CAFE DEL MAR – ENERGY 52 (12) ... 97,98,02
CAFFEINE BOMB – WILDHEARTS (31) ... 94
CALEDONIA – Frankie MILLER (45) ... 92
CALENDAR GIRL – Neil SEDAKA (8) ... 61
THE CALENDAR SONG (JANUARY, FEBRUARY, MARCH, APRIL, MAY) – TRINIDAD OIL COMPANY (34) ... 77
CALIBRE CUTS – VARIOUS ARTISTS (MONTAGES) (75) ... 80
CALIFORNIA [A] – WEDDING PRESENT (16) ... 92
CALIFORNIA [B] – Belinda CARLISLE (31) ... 97
CALIFORNIA DREAMIN' [A] – MAMAS and the PAPAS (9) ... 66,97
CALIFORNIA DREAMING [A] – COLORADO (45) ... 78
CALIFORNIA DREAMIN' [A] – RIVER CITY PEOPLE (13) ... 90
CALIFORNIA GIRLS [A] – BEACH BOYS (26) ... 65
CALIFORNIA GIRLS [A] – David Lee ROTH (68) ... 85
CALIFORNIA HERE I COME [A] – Freddy CANNON (25) ... 60
CALIFORNIA HERE I COME [B] – Sophie B HAWKINS (53) ... 92
CALIFORNIA LOVE – 2PAC featuring Dr DRE (6) ... 96
CALIFORNIA MAN – MOVE (7) ... 72
CALIFORNIA SAGA – CALIFORNIA – BEACH BOYS (37) ... 73
CALIFORNIA SCREAMIN' – CARRIE (55) ... 98
CALIFORNICATION – RED HOT CHILI PEPPERS (16) ... 00
CALINDA – RITMO-DYNAMIC (68) ... 03
THE CALL – BACKSTREET BOYS (8) ... 01
CALL AND ANSWER – BARENAKED LADIES (52) ... 99
CALL HER YOUR SWEETHEART – Frank IFIELD (24) ... 66
CALL IT FATE – Richie DAN (34) ... 00
CALL IT LOVE – DEUCE (11) ... 95
CALL IT ROCK 'N' ROLL – GREAT WHITE (67) ... 91
CALL IT WHAT YOU WANT [A] – NEW KIDS ON THE BLOCK (12) ... 91
CALL IT WHAT YOU WANT [B] – CREDIT TO THE NATION (57) ... 93
CALL ME [A] – BLONDIE (1) ... 80,89
CALL ME [B] – GO WEST (12) ... 85
CALL ME [C] – SPAGNA (2) ... 87
CALL ME [D] – LE CLICK (38) ... 97
CALL ME [E] – JAMELIA (11) ... 00
CALL ME [F] – TWEET (35) ... 02
(CALL ME) NUMBER ONE – TREMELOES (2) 69
CALL ME ROUND – PILOT (34) ... 75
CALL MY NAME – ORCHESTRAL MANOEUVRES IN THE DARK (50) ... 91
CALL OF THE WILD – Midge URE (27) ... 86
CALL OUT THE DOGS – Gary NUMAN (49) ... 85
CALL ROSIE ON THE PHONE – Guy MITCHELL (17) ... 57
CALL THE MAN – Celine DION (11) ... 97
THE CALL UP – CLASH (40) ... 80
CALL UP THE GROUPS – BARRON KNIGHTS (3) ... 64
CALLING – Geri HALLIWELL (7) ... 01
CALLING ALL THE HEROES – IT BITES (6) ... 86

CAN'T TRUSS IT – **PUBLIC ENEMY** (22) 91
CAN'T WAIT ANOTHER MINUTE – **FIVE STAR** (7) 86
CAN'T WAIT TO BE WITH YOU – **JAZZY JEFF & the FRESH PRINCE** (29) 94
CAN'T YOU HEAR MY HEART – **Danny RIVERS** (36) 61
CAN'T YOU HEAR MY HEART BEAT? – **GOLDIE and the GINGERBREADS** (25) 65
CAN'T YOU HEAR THE BEAT OF A BROKEN HEART – **Iain GREGORY** (39) 62
CAN'T YOU SEE – **TOTAL featuring the NOTORIOUS B.I.G.** (43) 95
CAN'T YOU SEE THAT SHE'S MINE – **Dave CLARK FIVE** (10) 64
(CAN'T YOU) TRIP LIKE I DO – **FILTER and the CRYSTAL METHOD** (39) 97
CANTALOOP – **US3** (23) 93
CANTGETAMAN CANTGETAJOB (LIFE'S A BITCH) – **SISTER BLISS** (31) 94
CANTO DELLA TERRA – **Andrea BOCELLI** (24) 99,00
CANTON (LIVE) – **JAPAN** (42) 83
CANTONESE BOY – **JAPAN** (24) 82
CAPOIERA – **INFRARED vs Gil FELIX** (67) 03
CAPSTICK COMES HOME – **Tony CAPSTICK and the CARLTON MAIN / FRICKLEY COLLIERY BAND** (3) 81
CAPTAIN BEAKY – **Keith MICHELL** (5) 80
CAPTAIN DREAD – **DREADZONE** (49) 95
CAPTAIN KREMMEN (RETRIBUTION) – **Kenny EVERETT** (32) 77
THE CAPTAIN OF HER HEART – **DOUBLE** (8) 86
CAPTAIN OF YOUR SHIP – **REPARATA and the DELRONS** (13) 68
CAPTAIN SCARLET THEME – **Barry GRAY ORCHESTRA** (53) 86
CAPTURE THE HEART (EP) – **RUNRIG** (49) 90
CAR BOOT SALE – **BILL** (73) 93
CAR 67 – **DRIVER 67** (7) 78
CAR SONG – **MADDER ROSE** (68) 94
CAR WASH [A] – **ROSE ROYCE** (9) 76,88
CAR WASH [A] – **Gwen DICKEY** (72) 90
CAR WASH [A] – **ROSE ROYCE featuring Gwen DICKEY** (18) ..98
CARA MIA – **David WHITFIELD** (1) 54
CARAMEL – **CITY HIGH featuring EVE** (9) 02
CARAVAN [A] – **Duane EDDY and the REBELS** (42) 61
CARAVAN [B] – **INSPIRAL CARPETS** (30) 91
CARAVAN OF LOVE [A] – **ISLEY JASPER ISLEY** (52) 85
CARAVAN OF LOVE [A] – **HOUSEMARTINS** (1)86
CARAVAN SONG – **Barbara DICKSON** (41) 80
CARBON KID – **ALPINESTARS featuring Brian MOLKO** (63) 02
CARDBOY KING – **SALAD** (65) 97
CARDIAC ARREST – **MADNESS** (14) 82
CAREFUL – **HORSE** (44) 90,97
CARELESS HANDS – **Des O'CONNOR** (6) 67
CARELESS LOVE – **SWIMMING WITH SHARKS** (63) 88
CARELESS MEMORIES – **DURAN DURAN** (37)81
CARELESS WHISPER [A] – **George MICHAEL** (1) 84
CARELESS WHISPER [A] – **Sarah WASHINGTON** (45) 93

CARIBBEAN BLUE – **ENYA** (13) 91
THE CARIBBEAN DISCO SHOW – **LOBO** (8) ..81
CARIBBEAN HONEYMOON – **Frank WEIR** (42) 60
CARIBBEAN QUEEN (NO MORE LOVE ON THE RUN) – **Billy OCEAN** (6) 84
CARMEN QUEASY – **MAXIM** (33) 00
CARNATION – **Liam GALLAGHER and Steve CRADOCK** (6) 99
CARNAVAL DE PARIS – **DARIO G** (5) 98,02
CARNIVAL [A] – **LIONROCK** (34) 93
CARNIVAL [B] – **CARDIGANS** (35) 95
CARNIVAL GIRL – **TEXAS featuring Kardinal OFFISHALL** (9) 03
CARNIVAL IN HEAVEN – **Malandra BURROWS** (49) 97
THE CARNIVAL IS OVER – **SEEKERS** (1) 65
CAROLINA MOON – **Connie FRANCIS** (1) 58
CAROLINE [A] – **STATUS QUO** (5) 73,82
CAROLINE [B] – **Kirsty MacCOLL** (58) 95
CAROUSEL – ORIGINAL SOUNDTRACK (LP) – **VARIOUS ARTISTS (EPs and LPs)** (26) 56
THE CAROUSEL WALTZ – **Ray MARTIN** (24) ..56
CARRERA 2 – **THREE DRIVES** (57) 03
CARRIE [A] – **Cliff RICHARD** (4) 80
CARRIE [B] – **EUROPE** (22) 87
CARRIE-ANNE – **HOLLIES** (3) 67
CARRION – **BRITISH SEA POWER** (36) 03
CARROT ROPE – **PAVEMENT** (27) 99
CARRY ME HOME – **GLOWORM** (9) 94
CARRY ON [A] – **Martha WASH** (49) 92,93,97
CARRY ON [B] – **SPACEHOG** (43) 98
CARRY ON [C] – **Donna SUMMER and Giorgio MORODER** (65) 98
CARRY ON WAYWARD SON – **KANSAS** (51) ..78
CARRY THAT WEIGHT – **TRASH** (35) 69
CARRY THE BLAME – **RIVER CITY PEOPLE** (13) 90
CARRYING A TORCH – **Tom JONES** (57) 91
CARS [A] – **Gary NUMAN** (1) 79,96
CARS [A] – **FEAR FACTORY** (57) 99
CARS (E REG MODEL) – **Gary NUMAN** (16) 87
CARS AND GIRLS – **PREFAB SPROUT** (44) 88
CARS (2ND RE-MIX) – **Gary NUMAN** (53) 93
CARTE BLANCHE – **VERACOCHA** (22) 99
CARTOON HEROES – **AQUA** (7) 00
CARTROUBLE – **ADAM and the ANTS** (33) 81
CASABLANCA – **Kenny BALL and his JAZZMEN** (21) 63
CASANOVA [A] – **Petula CLARK** (39) 63
CASANOVA [B] – **COFFEE** (13) 80
CASANOVA [B] – **BABY D** (67) 94
CASANOVA [C] – **LEVERT** (9) 87
CASANOVA [C] – **ULTIMATE KAOS** (24) 97,98
CASCADE – **FUTURE SOUND OF LONDON** (27) 93
CASE OF THE EX – **MYA** (3) 01
CASINO ROYALE – **Herb ALPERT** (27) 67
CASINO ROYALE – **DJ Zinc** (58) 01
CASSIUS 1999 – **CASSIUS** (7) 99
CAST YOUR FATE TO THE WIND – **SOUNDS ORCHESTRAL** (5) 64
CASTLE ROCK – **BLUETONES** (7) 96
CASTLES IN SPAIN – **ARMOURY SHOW** (69) 84
CASTLES IN THE AIR [A] – **Don McLEAN** (47)82
CASTLES IN THE AIR [B] – **COLOUR FIELD** (51) 85
CASTLES IN THE SAND – **THUNDER** (30) 95

CASTLES IN THE SKY – **IAN VAN DAHL** (5) 01
CASUAL SUB (BURNING SPEAR) – **ETA** (28) 97,98
CAT AMONG THE PIGEONS – **BROS** (2) 88
THE CAT CAME BACK – **Sonny JAMES** (30) ..56
THE CAT CREPT IN – **MUD** (2) 74
CAT PEOPLE (PUTTING OUT FIRE) – **David BOWIE** (26) 82
CATALAN – **TOUR DE FORCE** (71) 98
CATCH [A] – **CURE** (27) 87
CATCH [B] – **SUNSCREEM** (55) 97
CATCH [C] – **KOSHEEN** (15) 01
CATCH A FALLING STAR – **Perry COMO** (9) ..58
CATCH A FIRE – **HADDAWAY** (39) 95
CATCH ME – **ABSOLUTE** (69) 98
CATCH MY FALL – **Billy IDOL** (63) 88
CATCH THE BREEZE – **SLOWDIVE** (52) 91
CATCH THE FIRE – **DRIZABONE** (54) 91
CATCH THE LIGHT – **Martha WASH** (45) 98
CATCH THE SUN – **DOVES** (32) 00
CATCH THE WIND – **DONOVAN** (4) 65
CATCH UP TO MY STEP – **JUNKIE XL featuring Solomon BURKE** (63) ..03
CATCH US IF YOU CAN – **Dave CLARK FIVE** (5) 65
CATERINA – **Perry COMO** (37) 62
THE CATERPILLAR – **CURE** (14) 84
CATH – **BLUEBELLS** (38) 83,84
CATHEDRAL PARK – **DUBSTAR** (41) 97
CATHEDRAL SONG – **Tanita TIKARAM** (48) ..89
CATHY'S CLOWN – **EVERLY BROTHERS** (1) 60
CATS IN THE CRADLE [A] – **UGLY KID JOE** (7) 93
CATS IN THE CRADLE [A] – **Jason DOWNS featuring MILK** (65) 01
CAUGHT A LITE SNEEZE – **Tori AMOS** (20) ..96
CAUGHT BY THE FUZZ – **SUPERGRASS** (43) 94
CAUGHT BY THE RIVER – **DOVES** (29) 02
CAUGHT IN MY SHADOW – **WONDER STUFF** (18) 91
CAUGHT IN THE MIDDLE [A] – **Juliet ROBERTS** (14) 93,94
CAUGHT IN THE MIDDLE [B] – **A1** (2) 02
CAUGHT IN THE MIDDLE [C] – **Cerys MATTHEWS** (47) 03
CAUGHT OUT THERE – **KELIS** (4) 00
CAUGHT UP IN MY HEART – **OPTIMYSTIC** (49) 94
CAUGHT UP IN THE RAPTURE – **Anita BAKER** (51) 87
CAUSING A COMMOTION – **MADONNA** (4) 87
CAVATINA – **John WILLIAMS** (13) 79
CAVE – **MUSE** (52) 99
CCCAN'T YOU SEE – **VICIOUS PINK** (67) 84
CECILIA – **SUGGS featuring Louchie LOU and Michie ONE** (4) 96
THE CEDAR ROOM – **DOVES** (33) 00
CELEBRATE [A] – **AN EMOTIONAL FISH** (46) 90
CELEBRATE [B] – **HORSE** (49) 94
CELEBRATE [C] – **LEVELLERS** (28) 97
CELEBRATE OUR LOVE – **ALICE DEEJAY** (17) ..01
(CELEBRATE) THE DAY AFTER YOU – **BLOW MONKEYS with Curtis MAYFIELD** (52) 87
CELEBRATE THE WORLD – **WOMACK and WOMACK** (19) 89
CELEBRATE YOUR MOTHER – **EIGHTIES MATCHBOX B-LINE DISASTER** (66) 02

CELEBRATION [A] – **KOOL and the GANG** (7) 80,88
CELEBRATION [A] – **Kylie MINOGUE** (20) 92
A CELEBRATION – **U2** (47) 82
CELEBRATION GENERATION – **WESTBAM** (48) 94
CELEBRATION OF LIFE – **TRUCE** (51) 96
CELEBRITY HIT LIST – **TERRORVISION** (20) ..96
CELEBRITY SKIN – **HOLE** (19) 98
CELL 151 – **Steve HACKETT** (66) 83
THE CELTIC SOUL BROTHERS – **DEXY'S MIDNIGHT RUNNERS** (20) 82,83
THE CELTS – **ENYA** (29) 92
CEMENT – **FEEDER** (53) 97
CEMENTED SHOES – **MY VITRIOL** (65) 00
CENTER CITY – **FAT LARRY'S BAND** (31) 77
CENTERFOLD [A] – **J GEILS BAND** (3) 82
CENTERFOLD [A] – **Adam AUSTIN** (41) 99
CENTRAL PARK ARREST – **THUNDERTHIGHS** (30) 74
CENTRAL RESERVATION – **Beth ORTON** (37) 99
CENTURY – **INTASTELLA** (70) 91
CEREMONY – **NEW ORDER** (34) 81
CERTAIN PEOPLE I KNOW – **MORRISSEY** (35) 92
A CERTAIN SMILE – **Johnny MATHIS** (4) 58
THE CERTAINTY OF CHANCE – **DIVINE COMEDY** (49) 98
C'EST LA VIE [A] – **Robbie NEVIL** (3) 86
C'EST LA VIE [B] – **UB40** (37) 94
C'EST LA VIE [C] – **B*WITCHED** (1) 98
C'EST LA VIE [D] – **Jean-Michel JARRE** (40) ..00
C'EST SI BON – **Conway TWITTY** (40) 61
CHA CHA CHA – **FLIPMODE SQUAD** (54) 98
CHA CHA HEELS – **Eartha KITT and BRONSKI BEAT** (32) 89
CHAIN GANG [A] – **Jimmy YOUNG** (9) 56
CHAIN GANG [B] – **Sam COOKE** (9) 60
CHAIN-GANG SMILE – **BROTHER BEYOND** (57) 87
CHAIN OF FOOLS – **Aretha FRANKLIN** (37) 67,68
CHAIN REACTION [A] – **Diana ROSS** (1) 86,93
CHAIN REACTION [A] – **STEPS** (2) 01
CHAIN REACTION [B] – **HURRICANE #1** (30) ..97
CHAINS [A] – **COOKIES** (50) 63
CHAINS [B] – **RIVER DETECTIVES** (51) 89
CHAINS [C] – **Tina ARENA** (6) 95
CHAINS AROUND MY HEART – **Richard MARX** (29) 92
CHAINS OF LOVE – **ERASURE** (11) 88
CHAINSAW CHARLIE (MURDERS IN THE NEW MORGUE) – **W.A.S.P.** (17) 92
CHAIRMAN OF THE BOARD – **CHAIRMEN OF THE BOARD** (48) 71
CHALK DUST – THE UMPIRE STRIKES BACK – **BRAT** (19) 82
THE CHAMP – **MOHAWKS** (58) 87
CHAMPAGNE – **SALT-N-PEPA** (23) 96
CHAMPAGNE DANCE – **PAY AS U GO** (13) 02
CHAMPAGNE HIGHWAY – **SKANDAL** (53) 00
THE CHAMPION – **Willie MITCHELL** (47) 76
CHANCE – **BIG COUNTRY** (9) 83
CHANCES – **HOT CHOCOLATE** (32) 82
CHANGE [A] – **TEARS FOR FEARS** (4) 83
CHANGE [B] – **David GRANT** (55) 87
CHANGE [C] – **Lisa STANSFIELD** (10) 91
CHANGE [D] – **INCOGNITO** (52) 92

COOL BABY — **Charlie GRACIE** (26) ... 58
COOL FOR CATS — **SQUEEZE** (2) ... 79,92
COOL JERK — **GO-GO's** (60) ... 91
COOL MEDITATION — **THIRD WORLD** (17) ... 79
COOL OUT TONIGHT — **David ESSEX** (23) ... 77
COOL RUNNING — **TIK and TOK** (69) ... 83
COOL WATER — **Frankie LAINE** (2) ... 55
COPACABANA (AT THE COPA) — **Barry MANILOW** (42) ... 78,93
COPPER GIRL — **3 COLOURS RED** (30) ... 97
COPPERHEAD ROAD — **Steve EARLE** (45) ... 88
CORNER OF THE EARTH — **JAMIROQUAI** (31) 02
CORNFLAKE GIRL — **Tori AMOS** (4) ... 94
CORONATION RAG — **Winifred ATWELL** (5) ... 53
CORPSES — **Ian BROWN** (14) ... 98
CORRINE, CORRINA — **Ray PETERSON** (41) ... 61
COSMIC GIRL — **JAMIROQUAI** (6) ... 96
COSMONAUT NO.7 — **SCARFO** (67) ... 97
THE COST OF LIVING (EP) — **CLASH** (22) ... 79
COSTAFINE TOWN — **SPLINTER** (17) ... 74
COTTON EYE JOE — **REDNEX** (1) ... 94
COTTONFIELDS — **BEACH BOYS** (5) ... 70
COULD HAVE TOLD YOU SO — **HALO JAMES** (6) ... 89
COULD HEAVEN EVER BE LIKE THIS — **Idris MUHAMMAD** (42) ... 77
COULD I HAVE THIS KISS FOREVER — **Whitney HOUSTON and Enrique IGLESIAS** (7) ... 00
COULD IT BE — **JAHEIM** (33) ... 01
COULD IT BE FOREVER [A] — **David CASSIDY** (2) ... 72
COULD IT BE FOREVER [A] — **GEMINI** (38) ... 96
COULD IT BE I'M FALLING IN LOVE [A] — **DETROIT SPINNERS** (11) ... 73
COULD IT BE I'M FALLING IN LOVE (EP) [A] — **DETROIT SPINNERS** (32) ... 77
COULD IT BE I'M FALLING IN LOVE [A] — **David GRANT and Jaki GRAHAM** (5) ... 85
COULD IT BE I'M FALLING IN LOVE [A] — **WORLDS APART** (15) ... 94
COULD IT BE MAGIC [A] — **Donna SUMMER** (40) ... 76
COULD IT BE MAGIC [A] — **Barry MANILOW** (25) ... 78,93
COULD IT BE MAGIC [A] — **TAKE THAT** (3) ... 92
COULD YOU BE LOVED — **Bob MARLEY and the WAILERS** (5) ... 80,84
COULDN'T GET IT RIGHT — **CLIMAX BLUES BAND** (10) ... 76
COULDN'T HAVE SAID IT BETTER — **MEAT LOAF** (31) ... 03
COULDN'T SAY GOODBYE — **Tom JONES** (51) 91
COULD'VE BEEN — **TIFFANY** (4) ... 88
COULD'VE BEEN ME — **Billy Ray CYRUS** (24) 92
COULD'VE BEEN YOU — **CHER** (31) ... 92
COUNT ON ME [A] — **Julie GRANT** (24) ... 63
COUNT ON ME [B] — **Whitney HOUSTON** (12) 96
COUNT YOUR BLESSINGS — **Bing CROSBY** (11) ... 55
COUNTDOWN — **RUSH** (36) ... 83
COUNTERFEIT — **LOWGOLD** (52) ... 01
COUNTING BACKWARDS — **THROWING MUSES** (70) ... 91
COUNTING EVERY MINUTE — **SONIA** (16) ... 90
COUNTING SHEEP — **AIRHEAD** (35) ... 91
COUNTING TEARDROPS — **Emile FORD and the CHECKMATES** (4) ... 60
COUNTING THE DAYS — **ABI** (44) ... 98

COUNTRY BOY [A] — **Fats DOMINO** (19) ... 60
COUNTRY BOY [B] — **HEINZ** (26) ... 63
COUNTRY BOY [C] — **Jimmy NAIL** (25) ... 96
COUNTRY HOUSE — **BLUR** (1) ... 95
THE COUNTRY OF THE BLIND — **FAITH BROTHERS** (63) ... 85
COUNTRY ROADS — **HERMES HOUSE BAND** (7) ... 01
COURSE BRUV — **GENIUS CRU** (39) ... 01
COUSIN NORMAN — **MARMALADE** (6) ... 71
COVER FROM THE SKY — **DEACON BLUE** (31) 91
COVER GIRL — **NEW KIDS ON THE BLOCK** (4) ... 90
COVER ME — **Bruce SPRINGSTEEN** (16) ... 84,85
COVER MY EYES (PAIN AND HEAVEN) — **MARILLION** (34) ... 91
(COVER PLUS) WE'RE ALL GROWN UP — **Hazel O'CONNOR** (41) ... 81
COVER UP — **UB40** (54) ... 02
COVERS (EP) — **EVERYTHING BUT THE GIRL** (13) ... 92
COWARD OF THE COUNTY — **Kenny ROGERS** (1) ... 80
COWBOY — **KID ROCK** (36) ... 99
COWBOY DREAMS — **Jimmy NAIL** (13) ... 95
COWBOY JIMMY JOE — **Alma COGAN** (37) ... 61
COWBOYS AND ANGELS — **George MICHAEL** (45) ... 91
COWBOYS AND INDIANS — **CROSS** (74) ... 87
COWBOYS & KISSES — **ANASTACIA** (28) ... 01
COWGIRL — **UNDERWORLD** (24) ... 00
COWPUNCHER'S CANTATA — **Max BYGRAVES** (6) ... 52,53
COWPUNK MEDLUM — **SPLODGENESSABOUNDS** (69) ... 81
COZ I LUV YOU — **SLADE** (1) ... 71
CRACKERS INTERNATIONAL (EP) — **ERASURE** (2) ... 88
CRACKIN' UP [A] — **Tommy HUNT** (39) ... 75
CRACKING UP [B] — **Nick LOWE** (34) ... 79
CRACKING UP — **JESUS AND MARY CHAIN** (35) ... 98
CRACKLIN' ROSIE — **Neil DIAMOND** (3) ... 70
CRADLE OF LOVE [A] — **Johnny PRESTON** (2) 60
CRADLE OF LOVE [B] — **Billy IDOL** (34) ... 90
CRANK — **CATHERINE WHEEL** (66) ... 93
CRASH [A] — **PRIMITIVES** (5) ... 88
CRASH [B] — **FEEDER** (48) ... 97
CRASH AND BURN — **SAVAGE GARDEN** (14) .. 00
CRASH! BOOM! BANG! — **ROXETTE** (26) ... 94
CRASHED THE WEDDING — **BUSTED** (1) ... 03
CRASHIN' A PARTY — **LUMIDEE featuring N.O.R.E.** (55) ... 03
CRASHIN' IN — **CHARLATANS** (31) ... 95
CRAWL — **HEADSWIM** (64) ... 95
CRAWL HOME — **DESERT SESSIONS** (41) ... 03
CRAWLIN' BACK — **Roy ORBISON** (19) ... 65
CRAWLING — **LINKIN PARK** (16) ... 01
CRAWLING FROM THE WRECKAGE — **Dave EDMUNDS** (59) ... 79
CRAWLING IN THE DARK — **HOOBASTANK** (47) ... 02
CRAYZY MAN — **BLAST featuring VDC** (22) ... 94
CRAZIER — **Gary NUMAN vs RICO** (13) ... 03
CRAZY [A] — **MUD** (12) ... 73
CRAZY [B] — **MANHATTANS** (63) ... 83
CRAZY [C] — **ICEHOUSE** (38) ... 87,88
CRAZY [D] — **BOYS** (57) ... 90

CRAZY [E] — **Patsy CLINE** (14) ... 90
CRAZY [E] — **Julio IGLESIAS** (43) ... 94
CRAZY [E] — **LeAnn RIMES** (36) ... 99
CRAZY [F] — **SEAL** (2) ... 90
CRAZY [G] — **Bob GELDOF** (65) ... 94
CRAZY [H] — **AEROSMITH** (23) ... 94
CRAZY [I] — **ETERNAL** (15) ... 94
CRAZY [J] — **Mark MORRISON** (6) ... 95,96
CRAZY [K] — **NUT** (56) ... 96
CRAZY [L] — **AWESOME** (63) ... 98
CRAZY [M] — **MOFFATTS** (16) ... 99
CRAZY [N] — **LUCID** (14) ... 99
CRAZY [O] — **TOMCAT** (48) ... 00
CRAZY [P] — **K-CI & JOJO** (35) ... 01
CRAZY BEAT — **BLUR** (18) ... 03
CRAZY CHANCE — **KAVANA** (16) ... 96,97
CRAZY CRAZY NIGHTS — **KISS** (4) ... 87
CRAZY CUTS — **GRANDMIXER DST** (71) ... 83,84
CRAZY DREAM — **Jim DALE** (24) ... 58
CRAZY (FOR ME) — **Freddie JACKSON** (41) ... 88
CRAZY FOR YOU [A] — **MADONNA** (2) ... 85,91
CRAZY FOR YOU [B] — **SYBIL** (71) ... 90
CRAZY FOR YOU [C] — **INCOGNITO** (59) ... 91
CRAZY FOR YOU [D] — **LET LOOSE** (2) ... 93,94
CRAZY HORSES — **OSMONDS** (2) ... 72,95,99
CRAZY IN LOVE — **BEYONCÉ** (1) ... 03
CRAZY LITTLE PARTY GIRL — **Aaron CARTER** (7) ... 98
CRAZY LITTLE THING CALLED LOVE [A] — **QUEEN** (2) ... 79
CRAZY LITTLE THING CALLED LOVE [A] — **Dwight YOAKAM** (43) ... 99
CRAZY LOVE [A] — **Paul ANKA** (26) ... 58
CRAZY LOVE [B] — **Maxi PRIEST** (67) ... 86
CRAZY LOVE [C] — **Ce Ce PENISTON** (44) ... 92
CRAZY LOVE [D] — **MJ COLE** (10) ... 00
CRAZY LOWDOWN WAYS — **OCEAN COLOUR SCENE** (64) ... 01
THE CRAZY OTTO RAG — **STARGAZERS** (18) .. 55
THE CRAZY PARTY MIXES — **JIVE BUNNY and the MASTERMIXERS** (13) .. 90
CRAZY RAP — **AFROMAN** (10) ... 02
CRAZY SEXY MARVELLOUS — **PAFFENDORF** (52) ... 03
CRAZY TRAIN — **Ozzy OSBOURNE** (49) ... 80
CRAZY WATER — **Elton JOHN** (27) ... 77
CRAZY WORDS CRAZY TUNE — **Dorothy PROVINE** (45) ... 62
CRAZY YOU — **GUN** (21) ... 97
CREAM [A] — **PRINCE and the NEW POWER GENERATION** (15) ... 91
CREAM [B] — **BLANK & JONES** (24) ... 99
CREAM (ALWAYS RISES TO THE TOP) — **Gregg DIAMOND BIONIC BOOGIE** (61) ... 79
CREATION — **STEREO MC's** (19) ... 93
CREATURES OF THE NIGHT — **KISS** (34) ... 83
CREDO — **FISH** (38) ... 92
THE CREEP [A] — **Ken MACKINTOSH** (10) ... 54
CREEP [B] — **RADIOHEAD** (7) ... 93
CREEP [C] — **TLC** (6) ... 95,96
CREEQUE ALLEY — **MAMAS and the PAPAS** (9) ... 67
CREOLE JAZZ — **Mr Acker BILK and his PARAMOUNT JAZZ BAND** (22) ... 61
CRESCENT MOON — **Lynden David HALL** (45) ... 98
CRIME OF PASSION — **Mike OLDFIELD** (61) .. 84
CRIMINALLY INSANE — **SLAYER** (64) ... 87

CRIMSON AND CLOVER — **Joan JETT and the BLACKHEARTS** (60) ... 82
CRISPY BACON — **Laurent GARNIER** (60) ... 97
CRITICAL (IF YOU ONLY KNEW) — **WALL OF SOUND featuring Gerald LETHAN** (73) ... 93
CRITICIZE — **Alexander O'NEAL** (4) ... 87,98
CROCKETT'S THEME — **Jan HAMMER** (2) .. 87,91
CROCODILE ROCK — **Elton JOHN** (5) ... 72
CROCODILE SHOES — **Jimmy NAIL** (4) ... 94,95
CROCODILES — **ECHO and the BUNNYMEN** (37) ... 81
CROSS MY BROKEN HEART — **SINITTA** (6) ... 88
CROSS MY HEART — **EIGHTH WONDER** (13) .. 88
CROSS THAT BRIDGE — **WARD BROTHERS** (32) ... 87
CROSS THE TRACK (WE BETTER GO BACK) — **MACEO & THE MACKS** (54) ... 87
CROSSROADS [A] — **Tracy CHAPMAN** (61) ... 89
CROSSROADS [B] — **BLAZIN' SQUAD** (1) ... 89
CROSSTOWN TRAFFIC — **Jimi HENDRIX EXPERIENCE** (37) ... 69,90
THE CROWD — **Roy ORBISON** (40) ... 62
THE CROWN — **Gary BYRD and the GB EXPERIENCE** (6) ... 83
CRUCIAL — **NEW EDITION** (70) ... 89
CRUCIFIED — **ARMY OF LOVERS** (31) ... 91,92
CRUCIFY — **Tori AMOS** (15) ... 92
CRUEL — **PUBLIC IMAGE LTD** (49) ... 92
THE CRUEL SEA — **DAKOTAS** (18) ... 63
CRUEL SUMMER [A] — **BANANARAMA** (8) ... 83,89
CRUEL SUMMER [A] — **ACE OF BASE** (8) ... 98
CRUEL TO BE KIND — **Nick LOWE** (12) ... 79
CRUISE INTO CHRISTMAS MEDLEY — **Jane McDONALD** (10) ... 98
CRUISIN' — **D'ANGELO** (31) ... 96
CRUISING — **SINITTA** (2) ... 86
THE CRUNCH — **RAH BAND** (6) ... 77
CRUSH [A] — **ZHANE** (44) ... 97
CRUSH [B] — **Jennifer PAIGE** (4) ... 98
CRUSH ME — **HOUSE OF LOVE** (67) ... 92
CRUSH (1980 ME) [C] — **Darren HAYES** (19) .. 03
CRUSH ON YOU [A] — **JETS** (5) ... 87
CRUSH ON YOU [A] — **Aaron CARTER** (9) ... 97
CRUSH ON YOU [B] — **LIL' KIM** (23) ... 97
CRUSH TONIGHT — **FAT JOE featuring GINUWINE** (42) ... 02
CRUSH WITH EYELINER — **R.E.M.** (23) ... 95
CRUSHED BY THE WHEELS OF INDUSTRY — **HEAVEN 17** (17) ... 83
CRUSHED LIKE FRUIT — **INME** (25) ... 03
CRY [A] — **Gerry MONROE** (38) ... 70
CRY [B] — **GODLEY and CREME** (19) ... 85,86
CRY [C] — **WATERFRONT** (17) ... 89
CRY [D] — **SUNDAYS** (43) ... 97
CRY [E] — **SYSTEM F** (19) ... 00
CRY [F] — **Michael JACKSON** (25) ... 01
CRY [G] — **SIMPLE MINDS** (47) ... 02
CRY [H] — **Faith HILL** (25) ... 02
CRY [I] — **Kym MARSH** (2) ... 03
CRY AND BE FREE — **MARILYN** (31) ... 84
CRY BABY [A] — **SPILLER** (40) ... 02
CRY BABY [B] — **JEMINI** (15) ... 03
CRY BOY CRY — **BLUE ZOO** (13) ... 82
CRY DIGNITY — **DUB WAR** (59) ... 96
CRY FOR HELP [A] — **Rick ASTLEY** (7) ... 91
CRY FOR HELP [B] — **SHED SEVEN** (30) ... 01
CRY FOR ME — **ROACHFORD** (46) ... 94

DISCOBUG '97 – FREAKYMAN (68) 97
DISCOHOPPING – KLUBBHEADS (35)...........97
DISCONNECT – ROLLINS BAND (27) 94
DISCO'S REVENGE – GUSTO (9)....................96
DISCOTHEQUE – U2 (1) 97
DISCRETION GLOVE –
Stephen MALKMUS (60) 01
DISEASE – MATCHBOX TWENTY (50)............03
DISENCHANTED – COMMUNARDS (29) 86
DISILLUSION – BADLY DRAWN BOY (26)......00
DIS-INFECTED (EP) – The THE (17) 94
DISPOSABLE TEENS –
MARILYN MANSON (12) 00
DISREMEMBRANCE – Dannii MINOGUE (21)..98
DISSIDENT – PEARL JAM (14).........................94
THE DISTANCE – CAKE (22) 97
DISTANT DRUMS – Jim REEVES (1)................66
DISTANT STAR – Anthony HOPKINS (75)......86
DISTANT SUN – CROWDED HOUSE (19)........93
DISTORTION – WILT (66) 02
DISTRACTIONS – ZERO 7 featuring SIA (45) 02
DIVA – DANA INTERNATIONAL (11)...............98
DIVE! DIVE! DIVE! – Bruce DICKINSON (45)..90
DIVE IN – CATCH (44) 98
DIVE TO PARADISE – EUROGROOVE (31)......95
DIVEBOMB – NUMBER ONE CUP (61) 96
DIVINE EMOTIONS –
Narada Michael WALDEN (8) 88
DIVINE HAMMER – BREEDERS (59) 93
DIVINE THING – SOUP DRAGONS (53)..........92
DIVING – 4 STRINGS (38)..............................02
DIVING FACES – LIQUID CHILD (25).............99
D.I.V.O.R.C.E. [A] – Tammy WYNETTE (12) 75
D.I.V.O.R.C.E. [A] – Billy CONNOLLY (1) 75
DIXIE-NARCO (EP) – PRIMAL SCREAM (11)....92
DIZZY [A] – Tommy ROE (1) 69
DIZZY [A] –
Vic REEVES and the WONDER STUFF(1) 91
DJ [A] – David BOWIE (29)............................79
DJ [B] –
RESONANCE featuring The BURRELLS (67) 01
DJ [C] – H & CLAIRE (3) 02
DJ CULTURE – PET SHOP BOYS (13).............91
DJ, DJ – TRANSPLANTS (49)..........................03
DJ NATION – NUKLEUZ DJS (40)....................02
DJ NATION - BOOTLEG EDITION –
NUKLEUZ DJS (33) 03
DJ NATION - HARDER EDITION –
VARIOUS (48)..03
DJ SPINNIN' – PUNK CHIC (69)......................01
DJS FANS & FREAKS – BLANK & JONES (45) 02
DJS TAKE CONTROL – SL2 (11).................91,92
DK 50-80 –
John OTWAY and Wild Willy BARRETT (45) 80
DO AND DON'T FOR LOVE – KIOKA (66) 02
DO ANYTHING – NATURAL SELECTION (69) ..91
DO ANYTHING YOU WANNA DO –
EDDIE and the HOT RODS (9) 77
DO ANYTHING YOU WANT TO –
THIN LIZZY (14) 79
DO FOR LOVE – 2PAC (12)............................98
DO FRIES GO WITH THAT SHAKE –
George CLINTON (57)...................................86
DO I – GIFTED (60) 97
DO I DO – Stevie WONDER (10)....................82
DO I HAVE TO SAY THE WORDS –
Bryan ADAMS (30) 92
DO I LOVE YOU – RONETTES (35) 64
DO I QUALIFY? – Lynden David HALL (26)....98
DO IT – Tony DI BART (21) 94
DO IT ALL OVER AGAIN –
SPIRITUALIZED (31) 02
DO IT AGAIN [A] – BEACH BOYS (1)..........68,91
DO IT AGAIN [B] – STEELY DAN (39) 75
DO IT AGAIN – BILLIE JEAN (MEDLEY) –
CLUBHOUSE (11)..83
DO IT ANY WAY YOU WANNA –
PEOPLES CHOICE (36) 75
DO IT, DO IT AGAIN – Raffaella CARRA (9) ..78
DO IT FOR LOVE [A] – Danni'elle GAHA (52) 93
DO IT FOR LOVE [B] – SUBTERRANIA
featuring Ann CONSUELO (68) 93
DO IT FOR LOVE [C] – 4MANDU (45) 96
DO IT NOW – BRAIN BASHERS (64).............00
DO IT PROPERLY ('NO WAY BACK') –
ADONIS featuring 2 PUERTO RICANS,
A BLACK MAN AND A DOMINICAN (47) 87
DO IT TO ME – Lionel RICHIE (33)................92
DO IT TO ME AGAIN – SOULSEARCHER (32) 00
DO IT TO THE CROWD – TWIN HYPE (65) 89
DO IT TO THE MUSIC – RAW SILK (18) 82
DO IT WITH MADONNA – ANDROIDS (15) 03
DO ME – BELL BIV DEVOE (56) 90
DO ME RIGHT – INNER CITY (47).................96
DO ME WRONG – Mel BLATT (18) 03
DO MY THING – Busta RHYMES (39)............97
DO NOT DISTURB – BANANARAMA (31)........85
DO NOT PASS ME BY – HAMMER (14) 92
DO NOTHING – SPECIALS (4)........................80
DO OR DIE – SUPER FURRY ANIMALS (20) ..00
DO RE ME SO FAR SO GOOD – CARTER –
THE UNSTOPPABLE SEX MACHINE (22)........92
DO SOMETHING – Macy GRAY (51) 99
DO THAT THING – MASAI (42).......................03
DO THAT TO ME –
LISA MARIE EXPERIENCE (33) 96
DO THAT TO ME ONE MORE TIME –
CAPTAIN and TENNILLE (7) 80
DO THE BARTMAN – SIMPSONS (1) 91
DO THE BIRD [A] – Dee Dee SHARP (46)......63
DO THE BIRD [A] – VERNONS GIRLS (44) 63
DO THE CLAM – Elvis PRESLEY (19) 65
DO THE CONGA – BLACK LACE (10) 84
DO THE FUNKY CHICKEN –
Rufus THOMAS (18) 70
(DO) THE HUCKLEBUCK –
COAST TO COAST (5) 81
DO THE LOLLIPOP – TWEENIES (17) 01
DO THE RIGHT THING [A] –
REDHEAD KINGPIN and the FBI (13) 89
DO THE RIGHT THING [B] –
Ian WRIGHT (43) 93
(DO THE) SPANISH HUSTLE –
FATBACK BAND (10).....................................76
DO THEY KNOW IT'S CHRISTMAS? –
BAND AID (1) 84,85,89
DO THIS MY WAY – KID 'N' PLAY (48)..........88
DO U FEEL 4 ME – EDEN (51) 93
DO U KNOW WHERE YOU'RE COMING FROM –
M-BEAT featuring JAMIROQUAI (12) 96
DO U STILL – EAST 17 (7) 96
DO U WANNA FUNK – SPACE 2000 (50) 95
DO WAH DIDDY DIDDY [A] –
MANFRED MANN (1) 64
DO WAH DIDDY DIDDY [A] –
BLUE MELONS (70) 96
DO WAH DIDDY [A] – DJ OTZI (9) 01
DO WATCHA DO –
HYPER GO GO and ADEVA (54) 96,97
DO WE ROCK – POINT BREAK (29) 99
DO WHAT YOU DO [A] –
Jermaine JACKSON (6) 85
DO WHAT YOU DO [B] –
Annabella LWIN (61)....................................95
DO WHAT YOU DO DO WELL –
Ned MILLER (48) 65
DO WHAT YOU DO (EARWORM SONG) –
Clint BOON EXPERIENCE (63).......................00
DO WHAT YOU FEEL [A] – Joey NEGRO (36)..91
DO WHAT YOU FEEL [B] – JOHNNA (43)........96
DO WHAT YOU GOTTA DO [A] –
FOUR TOPS (11) 69
DO WHAT YOU GOTTA DO [A] –
Nina SIMONE (2) 68
DO WHAT YOU WANNA DO –
T-CONNECTION (11) 77
DO WHAT WE WOULD – ACZESS (65) 01
DO WHAT'S GOOD FOR ME –
2 UNLIMITED (16) 95
DO YA – INNER CITY (44)............................94
DO YA DO YA (WANNA PLEASE ME) –
Samantha FOX (10) 86
DO YA WANNA GET FUNKY WITH ME –
Peter BROWN (43) 78
DO YOU BELIEVE IN LOVE [A] –
Huey LEWIS and the NEWS (9) 86
DO YOU BELIEVE IN LOVE [B] –
UNATION (75)..93
DO YOU BELIEVE IN LOVE [C] –
ULTRA-SONIC (47) 96
DO YOU BELIEVE IN MIRACLES –
SLADE (54)..85
DO YOU BELIEVE IN SHAME –
DURAN DURAN (30) 89
DO YOU BELIEVE IN THE WESTWORLD –
THEATRE OF HATE (40) 82
DO YOU BELIEVE IN THE WONDER –
Jeanie TRACY (57) 94
DO YOU BELIEVE IN US – Jon SECADA (30)..92
DO YOU DREAM IN COLOUR? –
Bill NELSON (52)..80
DO YOU FEEL LIKE I FEEL –
Belinda CARLISLE (29) 91
DO YOU FEEL LIKE WE DO –
Peter FRAMPTON (39) 76
DO YOU FEEL ME? (...FREAK YOU) –
MEN OF VIZION (36) 99
DO YOU FEEL MY LOVE? [A] –
Eddy GRANT (8) 80,83
DO YOU KNOW [A] – SECRET AFFAIR (57) 81
DO YOU KNOW [B] – Michelle GAYLE (6)......97
DO YOU KNOW THE WAY TO SAN JOSE –
Dionne WARWICK (8) 68
DO YOU KNOW (WHAT IT TAKES) –
ROBYN (26) 97
DO YOU LIKE IT – KINGDOM COME (73) 89
DO YOU LOVE ME [A] –
Brian POOLE and the TREMELOES (1) 63
DO YOU LOVE ME [A] –
Dave CLARK FIVE (30) 63
DO YOU LOVE ME [A] – DEEP FEELING (34) 70
DO YOU LOVE ME [A] – DUKE BAYSEE (46)..95
DO YOU LOVE ME [B] –
MADEMOISELLE (56).....................................01
DO YOU LOVE ME [C] –
Nick CAVE and the BAD SEEDS (68) 94
DO YOU LOVE ME BOY? – KERRI-ANN (58) ..98
DO YOU LOVE ME LIKE YOU SAY –
Terence Trent D'ARBY (14)..........................93
DO YOU LOVE WHAT YOU FEEL –
INNER CITY (16) 89
DO YOU MIND – Anthony NEWLEY (1) 60
DO YOU REALIZE?? – FLAMING LIPS (32) 02
DO YOU REALLY LIKE IT – DJ PIED PIPER
and the MASTERS OF CEREMONIES (1) 01
(DO YOU REALLY LOVE ME) TELL ME LOVE –
Michael WYCOFF (60)..................................83
DO YOU REALLY LOVE ME TOO –
Billy FURY (13) 64
DO YOU REALLY WANT ME [A] –
Jon SECADA (30) 93
DO YOU REALLY WANT ME [B] –
ROBYN (20) 98
DO YOU REALLY (WANT MY LOVE) –
JUNIOR (47)...85
DO YOU REALLY WANT TO HURT ME –
CULTURE CLUB (1) 82
DO YOU REMEMBER – SCAFFOLD (34) 68
DO YOU REMEMBER HOUSE – BLAZE (55) ..02
DO YOU REMEMBER (LIVE) –
Phil COLLINS (57)...90
DO YOU REMEMBER ROCK 'N' ROLL RADIO? –
RAMONES (54) 80
DO YOU REMEMBER THE FIRST TIME –
PULP (33) 94,96
DO YOU SEE – Warren G (29) 95
DO YOU SEE THE LIGHT (LOOKING FOR) –
SNAP (10) 93
DO YOU SLEEP? –
Lisa LOEB and NINE STORIES (45) 95
DO YOU THINK ABOUT US – TOTAL (49)......97
DO YOU THINK YOU'RE SPECIAL – NIO (52) 03
DO YOU UNDERSTAND – ALMIGHTY (38)......96
DO YOU WANNA DANCE – Barry BLUE (7)....73
DO YOU WANNA FUNK – SYLVESTER (32)....82
DO YOU WANNA GET FUNKY – C&C MUSIC
FACTORY / CLIVILLES & COLE (27) 94
DO YOU WANNA GO OUR WAY??? –
PUBLIC ENEMY (66) 99
DO YOU WANNA HOLD ME –
BOW WOW WOW (47) 83
DO YOU WANNA PARTY –
DJ SCOTT featuring Lorna B (36) 95
DO YOU WANNA TOUCH ME? (OH YEAH) –
Gary GLITTER (2) 73
DO YOU WANT IT RIGHT NOW – DEGREES
OF MOTION featuring BITI (26)..............92,94
DO YOU WANT ME [A] – SALT-N-PEPA (5) 91
DO YOU WANT ME [B] – Q-TEX (48) 96
DO YOU WANT ME? [C] – LEILANI (40)..........99
DO YOU WANT ME TO –
FOUR PENNIES (47) 64
DO YOU WANT TO DANCE –
Cliff RICHARD and the SHADOWS (2) 62
DO YOU WANT TO KNOW A SECRET? –
Billy J KRAMER and the DAKOTAS (2) 63
DO YOUR DANCE – ROSE ROYCE (30) 77
THE DOCTOR – DOOBIE BROTHERS (73)......89
DR BEAT – MIAMI SOUND MACHINE (6) 84
DOCTOR DOCTOR [A] – UFO (35) 79
DOCTOR DOCTOR [B] –
THOMPSON TWINS (3)..................................84

DRIP FED FRED – Ian DURY and the BLOCKHEADS (55) 00
DRIVE [A] – CARS (4) 84,85
DRIVE [B] – R.E.M. (11) 92
DRIVE [C] – Geoffrey WILLIAMS (52) 97
DRIVE [D] – INCUBUS (40) 01
DRIVE-IN SATURDAY (SEATTLE – PHOENIX) – David BOWIE (3) 73
DRIVE ME CRAZY – PARTIZAN (36) 97
DRIVE ON – BROTHER BEYOND (39) 89
DRIVE SAFELY DARLIN' – Tony CHRISTIE (35) 76
DRIVEN BY YOU – Brian MAY (6) 91
DRIVER'S SEAT – SNIFF 'N' THE TEARS (42) 79
DRIVIN' HOME – Duane EDDY and the REBELS (30) 61
DRIVING – EVERYTHING BUT THE GIRL (36)............90,96
DRIVING AWAY FROM HOME (JIM'S TUNE) – IT'S IMMATERIAL (18) 86
DRIVING HOME FOR CHRISTMAS (EP) – Chris REA (53) 88
DRIVING IN MY CAR [A] – MADNESS (4) 82
DRIVING IN MY CAR [A] – Maureen REES (49) 97
DRIVING WITH THE BRAKES ON – DEL AMITRI (18) 95
DROP DEAD GORGEOUS – REPUBLICA (7)....97
DROP SOME DRUMS – [LOVE] TATTOO (58) 01
DROP THE BOY – BROS (2) 88
DROP THE PILOT – Joan ARMATRADING (11) 83
DROP THE ROCK (EP) – D-TEK (70) 93
DROPS OF JUPITER (TELL ME) – TRAIN (10)..01
DROWNED WORLD (SUBSTITUTE FOR LOVE) – MADONNA (10) 98
THE DROWNERS – SUEDE (49) 92
DROWNING [A] – BEAT (22) 81
DROWNING [B] – BACKSTREET BOYS (4) 02
DROWNING IN BERLIN – MOBILES (9) 82
DROWNING IN THE SEA OF LOVE – ADVENTURES (44) 88
DROWSY WITH HOPE – SHAKEDOWN (46) ..03
THE DRUGS DON'T WORK – VERVE (1)....97,98
DRUMBEATS – SL2 (26) 92
DRUMMER MAN – TONIGHT (14) 78
DRUMMIN' UP A STORM – Sandy NELSON (39) 62
DRUMS ARE MY BEAT – Sandy NELSON (30) 62
THE DRUMSTRUCK (EP) – N-JOI (33) 93
DRUNK ON LOVE – BASIA (41).......................95
DRUNKARD LOGIC – FAT LADY SINGS (56) ..93
DRUNKEN FOOL – BURN (54).........................03
DRY COUNTY [A] – BLACKFOOT (43) 82
DRY COUNTY [B] – BON JOVI (9) 94
DRY LAND – MARILLION (34) 91
DRY RISER – KERBDOG (60) 94
DUB BE GOOD TO ME – BEATS INTERNATIONAL featuring Lindy LAYTON (1) 90
DUB WAR – DANCE CONSPIRACY (72)..........92
DUBPLATE CULTURE – SOUNDSCAPE (61) 98
DUCHESS [A] – STRANGLERS (14) 79
DUCHESS [A] – MY LIFE STORY (39) 97
DUCHESS [B] – GENESIS (46)........................80
DUCK FOR THE OYSTER – Malcolm McLAREN (54) 83
DUCK TOY – HAMPENBERG (30) 02
DUDE DESCENDING A STAIRCASE – APOLLO FOUR FORTY featuring the BEATNUTS (58)..03
DUDE (LOOKS LIKE A LADY) – AEROSMITH (20).......................................87,90
DUEL [A] – PROPAGANDA (21) 85
DUEL [B] – SWERVEDRIVER (60) 93
DUELLING BANJOS – 'DELIVERANCE' SOUNDTRACK (17) 73
DUKE OF EARL – DARTS (6)..........................79
DUM DUM – Brenda LEE (22).........................61
DUM DUM GIRL – TALK TALK (74)................84
DUMB – BEAUTIFUL SOUTH (16).............98,99
DUMB WAITERS – PSYCHEDELIC FURS (59)..81
DUMMY CRUSHER – KERBDOG (37)..............94
DUNE BUGGY – PRESIDENTS OF THE UNITED STATES OF AMERICA (15) 96
DUNE SEA – UNBELIEVABLE TRUTH (46)......98
DUNNO WHAT IT IS (ABOUT YOU) – BEATMASTERS (43) 92
DURHAM TOWN (THE LEAVIN') – Roger WHITTAKER (12)................................69
DUSTED – LEFTFIELD (28).......................99,00
DW WASHBURN – MONKEES (17) 68
D'YA WANNA GO FASTER – TERRORVISION (28) 01
DYNAMITE [A] – Cliff RICHARD and the SHADOWS (16)........59
DYNAMITE [B] – Stacy LATTISAW (51) 80
DYNA-MITE – MUD (4) 73
DYNOMITE (PART 1) – Tony CAMILLO'S BAZUKA (28) 75
DY-NA-MI-TEE – MS DYNAMITE (5) 02
D'YOU KNOW WHAT I MEAN? – OASIS (1) 97
E – DRUNKEN MUNKY (41)............................03
E=MC2 – BIG AUDIO DYNAMITE (11) 86
E SAMBA – JUNIOR JACK (34) 03
EACH AND EVERY ONE – EVERYTHING BUT THE GIRL (28) 84
EACH TIME – EAST 17 (2).............................98
EACH TIME YOU BREAK MY HEART – Nick KAMEN (5) 86
EARDRUM BUZZ – WIRE (68) 89
EARLY IN THE MORNING [A] – Buddy HOLLY (17)...58
EARLY IN THE MORNING [B] – VANITY FARE (8) 69
EARLY IN THE MORNING [C] – GAP BAND (55) 82
EARLY TO BED – PONI-TAILS (26) 59
EARTH ANGEL [A] – CREW CUTS (4)..............55
EARTH ANGEL [B] – DREADZONE (51) 97
THE EARTH DIES SCREAMING – UB40 (10) ..80
EARTH SONG – Michael JACKSON (1)............95
EARTHBOUND – Conner REEVES (14) 97
EARTHSHAKER – Paul MASTERSON presents SUSHI (35)......02
EASE MY MIND – ARRESTED DEVELOPMENT (33) 94
EASE ON BY – BASS-O-MATIC (61) 90
EASE ON DOWN THE ROAD – Diana ROSS and Michael JACKSON (45) 78
EASE THE PRESSURE [A] – 2WO THIRD3 (45)...94
EASE THE PRESSURE [B] – BELOVED (43)....96
EASE YOUR MIND – GALLIANO (45)..............96
EASIER SAID THAN DONE [A] – ESSEX (41) ..63
EASIER SAID THAN DONE [B] – SHAKATAK (12) 81
EASIER SAID THAN DONE [C] – STARGATE (55)...02
EASIER TO WALK AWAY – Elton JOHN (63) ..90
EAST COAST / WEST COAST KILLAS – GROUP THERAPY (51) 96
EAST EASY RIDER – Julian COPE (51)............91
EAST OF EDEN – BIG COUNTRY (17) 84
EAST RIVER – BRECKER BROTHERS (34)......78
EAST WEST – HERMAN'S HERMITS (37) 66
EASTER – MARILLION (34)...........................90
EASY [A] – COMMODORES (9) 77,88
EASY [B] – LOUD (67) 92
EASY [C] – TERRORVISION (12) 97
EASY [D] – Emiliana TORRINI (63) 00
EASY [E] – GROOVE ARMADA (31) 03
EASY COME EASY GO – SUTHERLAND BROTHERS and QUIVER (50) 79
EASY EASY – SCOTLAND WORLD CUP SQUAD (20) 74
EASY GOING ME – Adam FAITH (12) 61
EASY LADY – SPAGNA (62) 87
EASY LIFE [A] – BODYSNATCHERS (50) 80
EASY LIFE [B] – CABARET VOLTAIRE (61)......90
EASY LIVIN' – FASTWAY (74)........................83
EASY LOVER – Philip BAILEY (duet with Phil COLLINS) (1) 85
EASY RIDER – RAIN BAND (63) 03
EASY TO SMILE – SENSELESS THINGS (18) ..92
EAT IT – Weird Al YANKOVIC (36) 84
EAT ME DRINK ME LOVE ME – POP WILL EAT ITSELF (17) 92
EAT MY GOAL – COLLAPSED LUNG (31) ..96,98
EAT THE RICH – AEROSMITH (34) 93
EAT YOU ALIVE – LIMP BIZKIT (10) 03
EAT YOUR HEART OUT – Paul HARDCASTLE (59) 84
EAT YOURSELF WHOLE – KINGMAKER (15) ..92
EATEN ALIVE – Diana ROSS (71) 85
EATING ME ALIVE – Diana BROWN and Barrie K SHARPE (53) ..92
EBB TIDE [A] – Frank CHACKSFIELD (9)........54
EBB TIDE [A] – RIGHTEOUS BROTHERS (3) 66,90
EBENEEZER GOODE – SHAMEN (1) 92
EBONY AND IVORY – Paul McCARTNEY with Stevie WONDER (1) 82
EBONY EYES – EVERLY BROTHERS (1)..........61
E-BOW THE LETTER – R.E.M. (4) 96
ECHO BEACH [A] – MARTHA and the MUFFINS (10)....................80
ECHO BEACH [A] – TOYAH (54) 87
ECHO CHAMBER – BEATS INTERNATIONAL (60).........................91
ECHO MY HEART – Lindy LAYTON (42) 91
ECHO ON MY MIND PART II – EARTHLING (61) 95
ECHOES IN A SHALLOW BAY (EP) – COCTEAU TWINS (65).................................85
ECUADOR – SASH! (2) 97
ED'S FUNKY DINER (FRIDAY NIGHT, SATURDAY MORNING) – IT'S IMMATERIAL (65) 86
EDDY VORTEX – Steve GIBBONS BAND (56) 78
EDELWEISS – Vince HILL (2) 67
EDEN – Sarah BRIGHTMAN (68)....................99
EDGE OF A BROKEN HEART – VIXEN (51) 88,89
EDGE OF DARKNESS – Eric CLAPTON (65)....86
THE EDGE OF HEAVEN – WHAM! (1) 86
EDIE (CIAO BABY) – CULT (32) 89
EENY MEENY – SHOWSTOPPERS (33) 68
EGG RUSH – FLOWERED UP (38) 91
EGO – Elton JOHN (34) 78
EGYPTIAN REGGAE – Jonathan RICHMAN and the MODERN LOVERS (5) 77
EIGHT BY TEN – Ken DODD (22) 64
8 DAYS A WEEK – SWEET FEMALE ATTITUDE (43)....................00
EIGHT MILES HIGH – BYRDS (24) 66
808 – BLAQUE IVORY (31)............................99
18 AND LIFE – SKID ROW (12) 90
18 CARAT LOVE AFFAIR – ASSOCIATES (21)..82
EIGHTEEN STRINGS – TINMAN (9) 94
18 TIL I DIE – Bryan ADAMS (22)..................97
EIGHTEEN WITH A BULLET – Pete WINGFIELD (7) 75
EIGHTEEN YELLOW ROSES – Bobby DARIN (37)...63
EIGHTH DAY – Hazel O'CONNOR (5) 80
EIGHTIES – KILLING JOKE (60).....................84
80S ROMANCE – BELLE STARS (71)..............84
86'D – SUBCIRCUS (56) 97
EI – NELLY (11) 01
EINSTEIN A GO-GO – LANDSCAPE (5) 81
EL BIMBO – BIMBO JET (12).........................75
EL CAMINOS IN THE WEST – GRANDADDY (48) 03
EL CAPITAN – OPM (20) 02
EL LUTE – BONEY M (12) 79
EL NINO – AGNELLI & NELSON (21)..............98
EL PARAISO RICO – DEETAH (39) 99
EL PASO – Marty ROBBINS (19)....................60
EL PRESIDENT – DRUGSTORE (20) 98
EL SALVADOR – ATHLETE (31) 03
EL SCORCHO – WEEZER (50) 96
EL TRAGO (THE DRINK) – 2 IN A ROOM (34) 94
EL VINO COLLAPSO – BLACK LACE (42) 85
ELDORADO – DRUM THEATRE (44) 87
ELEANOR RIGBY [A] – BEATLES (1) 66,86
ELEANOR RIGBY [A] – Ray CHARLES (36) 68
ELECTED – Alice COOPER (4) 72
ELECTION DAY – ARCADIA (7) 85
ELECTRIC AVENUE – Eddy GRANT (2) 83,01
ELECTRIC BARBARELLA – DURAN DURAN (23) 99
ELECTRIC BLUE – ICEHOUSE (53).................88
ELECTRIC BOOGALOO – OLLIE and JERRY (57)..................................85
ELECTRIC GUITAR – FLUKE (58) 93
ELECTRIC GUITARS – PREFAB SPROUT (53)..97
ELECTRIC HEAD PART 2 (THE ECSTASY) – WHITE ZOMBIE (31) 96
ELECTRIC LADY – GEORDIE (32) 73
ELECTRIC MAINLINE – SPIRITUALIZED (49) ..93
ELECTRIC MAN – MANSUN (23) 00
ELECTRIC TRAINS – SQUEEZE (44)................95
ELECTRIC YOUTH – Debbie GIBSON (14) 89
ELECTRICAL STORM – U2 (5) 02
ELECTRICITY [A] – SPIRITUALIZED (32) 97
ELECTRICITY [B] – SUEDE (5) 99
ELECTROLITE – R.E.M. (29) 96
ELECTRONIC PLEASURE – N-TRANCE (11)......96
ELEGANTLY AMERICAN: ONE NIGHT IN HEAVEN – M PEOPLE (31) 94
ELEGANTLY WASTED – INXS (20)...................97
ELEKTROBANK – CHEMICAL BROTHERS (17) 97
ELENI – TOL and TOL (73) 90

EVERY KINDA PEOPLE [A] – Chaka DEMUS and PLIERS (47) 96
EVERY LITTLE BIT HURTS – Spencer DAVIS GROUP (41) 65
EVERY LITTLE STEP – Bobby BROWN (6) 89,96
EVERY LITTLE TEARDROP – GALLAGHER and LYLE (32) 77
EVERY LITTLE THING – Jeff LYNNE (59) 90
EVERY LITTLE THING HE DOES IS MAGIC – Shawn COLVIN (65) 94
EVERY LITTLE THING I DO – SOUL FOR REAL (31) 96
EVERY LITTLE THING SHE DOES IS MAGIC [A] – POLICE (1) 81
EVERY LITTLE THING SHE DOES IS MAGIC [A] – Chaka DEMUS and PLIERS (51) 97
EVERY LITTLE TIME – POPPERS presents AURA (44) 97
EVERY LOSER WINS – Nick BERRY (1) 86
EVERY MAN MUST HAVE A DREAM – LIVERPOOL EXPRESS (17) 76
EVERY MORNING – SUGAR RAY (10) 99
EVERY NIGHT – Phoebe SNOW (37) 79
EVERY NITE'S A SATURDAY NIGHT WITH YOU – DRIFTERS (29) 76
EVERY 1'S A WINNER – HOT CHOCOLATE (12) 78,87
EVERY OTHER TIME – LYTE FUNKIE ONES (24) 02
EVERY ROSE HAS ITS THORN – POISON (13) 89
EVERY SINGLE DAY – DODGY (32) 98
EVERY TIME – Janet JACKSON (46) 98
EVERY TIME I FALL – Gina G (52) 97
EVERY TIME I FALL IN LOVE – UPSIDE DOWN (18) 96
EVERY TIME YOU TOUCH ME – MOBY (28) ..95
EVERY WHICH WAY BUT LOOSE – Eddie RABBITT (41) 79
EVERY WOMAN KNOWS – LULU (44) 94
EVERY WOMAN NEEDS LOVE – STELLA BROWNE (55) 00
EVERY YEAR EVERY CHRISTMAS – Luther VANDROSS (43) 95
EVERY YOU EVERY ME – PLACEBO (11) 99
EVERYBODY [A] – Tommy ROE (9) 63
EVERYBODY [B] – CAPPELLA (66) 91
EVERYBODY [C] – ALTERN 8 (58) 93
EVERYBODY [D] – DJ BOBO (47) 94
EVERYBODY [E] – CLOCK (6) 95
EVERYBODY [F] – KINKY (71) 96
EVERYBODY [G] – PROGRESS presents the BOY WUNDA (7) ..99
EVERYBODY [H] – HEAR'SAY (4) 01
EVERYBODY (ALL OVER) – FPI PROJECT (67) 99
EVERYBODY (ALL OVER THE WORLD) – FPI PROJECT (65) 91
EVERYBODY (BACKSTREET'S BACK) – BACKSTREET BOYS (3) 97
EVERYBODY BE SOMEBODY – RUFFNECK featuring YAVAHN (13) 95,01
EVERYBODY COME ON (CAN U FEEL IT) – MR REDS vs DJ SKRIBBLE (13) 03
EVERYBODY DANCE [A] – CHIC (9) 78
EVERYBODY DANCE [A] – EVOLUTION (19) ..93
EVERYBODY DANCE (THE HORN SONG) – Barbara TUCKER (28) 98
EVERYBODY EVERYBODY – BLACK BOX (16) 90
(EVERYBODY) GET DANCIN' – BOMBERS (37) 79
EVERYBODY GET TOGETHER – Dave CLARK FIVE (8) 70
EVERYBODY GET UP [A] – FIVE (2) 98
EVERYBODY GET UP [B] – CAPRICCIO (44) ..99
EVERYBODY GETS A SECOND CHANCE – MIKE and the MECHANICS (56) 92
EVERYBODY GO HOME THE PARTY'S OVER – Clodagh RODGERS (47) 70
EVERYBODY GONFI-GON – TWO COWBOYS (7) 94
EVERYBODY HAVE A GOOD TIME – Archie BELL and the DRELLS (43) 77
EVERYBODY HERE WANTS YOU – Jeff BUCKLEY (43) 98
EVERYBODY HURTS – R.E.M. (7) 93
EVERYBODY IN THE PLACE (EP) – PRODIGY (2) 92,96
EVERYBODY IS A STAR – POINTER SISTERS (61) 79
EVERYBODY KNOWS [A] – Dave CLARK FIVE (37) 65
EVERYBODY KNOWS [B] – Dave CLARK FIVE (2) 67
EVERYBODY KNOWS [C] – FREE ASSOCIATION (74) 03
EVERYBODY KNOWS (EXCEPT YOU) – DIVINE COMEDY (14) 97
EVERYBODY LET'S SOMEBODY LOVE – Frank K featuring Wiston OFFICE (61) 91
EVERYBODY LOVES A LOVER – Doris DAY (25) 58
EVERYBODY LOVES SOMEBODY – Dean MARTIN (11) 64
EVERYBODY MOVE – Cathy DENNIS (25) 91
EVERYBODY (MOVE YOUR BODY) – DIVA (44) 96
EVERYBODY MUST PARTY – GEORGIE PORGIE (61) 95
EVERYBODY NEEDS A 303 – FATBOY SLIM (34) 97
EVERYBODY NEEDS SOMEBODY [A] – BIRDLAND (44) 91
EVERYBODY NEEDS SOMEBODY [B] – Nick HOWARD (64) 95
EVERYBODY NEEDS SOMEBODY TO LOVE – BLUES BROTHERS (12) 90
EVERYBODY ON THE FLOOR (PUMP IT) – TOKYO GHETTO PUSSY (26) 95
EVERYBODY PUMP – DJ POWER (46) 92
EVERYBODY (RAP) – Wally JUMP Jr and the CRIMINAL ELEMENT (30) 90
EVERYBODY SALSA – MODERN ROMANCE (12) 81
EVERYBODY SAY EVERYBODY DO – LET LOOSE (29) 95,96
EVERYBODY THINKS THAT THEY'RE GOING TO GET THEIRS – BIS (64) 97
EVERYBODY UP! – GLAM METAL DETECTIVES (29) 95
EVERYBODY WANTS HER – THUNDER (36) ..92
EVERYBODY WANTS TO RULE THE WORLD – TEARS FOR FEARS (2) 85,86
EVERYBODY WANTS TO RUN THE WORLD – TEARS FOR FEARS (5) 86
EVERYBODY'S A ROCKSTAR – TALL PAUL (60) 02
EVERYBODY'S FREE – ROZALLA (6) 91,96
EVERYBODY'S FREE (TO WEAR SUNSCREEN) – THE SUNSCREEN SONG (CLASS OF '99) – Baz LUHRMANN (1) 99
EVERYBODY'S GONE – SENSELESS THINGS (73) 91
EVERYBODY'S GONNA BE HAPPY – KINKS (17) 65
EVERYBODY'S GOT SUMMER – ATLANTIC STARR (36) 94
EVERYBODY'S GOT TO LEARN SOMETIME [A] – KORGIS (5) 80
EVERYBODY'S GOT TO LEARN SOMETIME [A] – YAZZ (56) 94
(EVERYBODY'S GOT TO LEARN SOMETIME) I NEED YOUR LOVING [A] – BABY D (3) 95
EVERYBODY'S HAPPY NOWADAYS – BUZZCOCKS (29) 79
EVERYBODY'S LAUGHING – Phil FEARON (10) 84
EVERYBODY'S SOMEBODY'S FOOL – Connie FRANCIS (5) 60
EVERYBODY'S TALKIN' [A] – NILSSON (23) 69,70
EVERYBODY'S TALKIN' [A] – BEAUTIFUL SOUTH (12) 94
EVERYBODY'S TALKIN' 'BOUT LOVE – SILVER CONVENTION (25) 77
EVERYDAY [A] – MOODY BLUES (44) 65
EVERYDAY [B] – Don McLEAN (38) 73
EVERYDAY [C] – SLADE (3) 74
EVERYDAY [D] – JAM MACHINE (68) 89
EVERYDAY [E] – ORCHESTRAL MANOEUVRES IN THE DARK (59) 93
EVERYDAY [F] – Phil COLLINS (15) 94
EVERYDAY [G] – INCOGNITO (23) 95
EVERYDAY [H] – Craig McLACHLAN (65) 95
EVERYDAY [I] – AGNELLI & NELSON (17) 99,02
EVERYDAY [J] – BON JOVI (5) 02
EVERYDAY GIRL – DJ RAP (47) 99
EVERYDAY I WRITE THE BOOK – Elvis COSTELLO (28) 83
EVERYDAY IS A WINDING ROAD – Sheryl CROW (12) 96
EVERYDAY IS LIKE SUNDAY – MORRISSEY (9) 88
EVERYDAY LIVING – WOODENTOPS (72) 86
EVERYDAY NOW – TEXAS (44) 89
EVERYDAY PEOPLE [A] – SLY and the FAMILY STONE (36) 69
EVERYDAY PEOPLE [A] – Aretha FRANKLIN (69) 91
EVERYDAY SUNSHINE – FISHBONE (60) 92
EVERYDAY THANG – Melanie WILLIAMS (38) 94
EVERYONE SAYS "HI" – David BOWIE (20) ..02
EVERYONE SAYS YOU'RE SO FRAGILE – IDLEWILD (47) 98
EVERYONE'S GONE TO THE MOON – Jonathan KING (4) 65
EVERYTHING [A] – Jody WATLEY (74) 90
EVERYTHING [B] – KICKING BACK with TAXMAN (54) 90
EVERYTHING [C] – UHF (46) 91
EVERYTHING [D] – HYSTERIX (65) 95
EVERYTHING [E] – Sarah WASHINGTON (30) 96
EVERYTHING [F] – INXS (71) 97
EVERYTHING [G] – Mary J BLIGE (6) 97
EVERYTHING [H] – DUM DUMS (21) 00
EVERYTHING A MAN COULD EVER NEED – Glen CAMPBELL (32) 70
EVERYTHING ABOUT YOU – UGLY KID JOE (3) 92
EVERYTHING CHANGES – TAKE THAT (1) 94
EVERYTHING COUNTS – DEPECHE MODE (6) 83,89
EVERYTHING EVENTUALLY – APPLETON (38) 03
EVERYTHING GOOD IS BAD – WESTWORLD (72) 88
EVERYTHING I AM – PLASTIC PENNY (6) 68
(EVERYTHING I DO) I DO IT FOR YOU [A] – Bryan ADAMS (1) 91
(EVERYTHING I DO) I DO IT FOR YOU [A] – FATIMA MANSIONS (7) 92
(EVERYTHING I DO) I DO IT FOR YOU [A] – Q (47) 94
EVERYTHING I HAVE IS YOURS – Eddie FISHER (8) 53
EVERYTHING I OWN [A] – BREAD (32) 72
EVERYTHING I OWN [A] – Ken BOOTHE (1) ..74
EVERYTHING I OWN [A] – BOY GEORGE (1) ..87
EVERYTHING I WANTED – Dannii MINOGUE (15) 97
EVERYTHING IS ALRIGHT (UPTIGHT) – CJ LEWIS (10) 94
EVERYTHING IS BEAUTIFUL – Ray STEVENS (6) 70
EVERYTHING IS EVERYTHING – Lauryn HILL (19) 99
EVERYTHING IS GONNA BE ALRIGHT – SOUNDS OF BLACKNESS (29) 94
EVERYTHING IS GREAT – INNER CIRCLE (37) 79
EVERYTHING MUST CHANGE – Paul YOUNG (9) 84
EVERYTHING MUST GO – MANIC STREET PREACHERS (5) 96
EVERYTHING MY HEART DESIRES – Adam RICKITT (15) 99
EVERYTHING SHE WANTS – WHAM! (2) 84
EVERYTHING STARTS WITH AN 'E' – E-ZEE POSSEE (15) 89,90
EVERYTHING TO EVERYONE – EVERCLEAR (41) 98
EVERYTHING WILL FLOW – SUEDE (24) 99
EVERYTHING YOU NEED – MADISON AVENUE (33) 01
EVERYTHING YOU WANT – VERTICAL HORIZONS (42) 00
EVERYTHING WILL TURN OUT FINE – STEALER'S WHEEL (33) 73
EVERYTHING'S ALRIGHT – MOJOS (9) 64
EVERYTHING'S COOL – POP WILL EAT ITSELF (23) 94
EVERYTHING'S GONE GREEN – NEW ORDER (38) 81
EVERYTHING'S GONNA BE ALRIGHT – SWEETBOX (5) 98
EVERYTHING'S NOT YOU – STONEPROOF (68) 99
EVERYTHING'S RUINED – FAITH NO MORE (28) 92
EVERYTHING'S TUESDAY – CHAIRMEN OF THE BOARD (12) 71
EVERYTIME [A] – LUSTRAL (30) 97,99
EVERYTIME [B] – Tatyana ALI (20) 99
EVERYTIME [C] – A1 (3) 99

FAMINE – **Sinead O'CONNOR** (51) 95
FAN MAIL – **DICKIES** (57) 80
FAN THE FLAME – **Barbara PENNINGTON** (62) 85
FANCY PANTS – **KENNY** (4) 75
FAN'DABI'DOZI – **KRANKIES** (46) 81
FANFARE FOR THE COMMON MAN – **EMERSON, LAKE and PALMER** (2) 77
FANLIGHT FANNY – **Clinton FORD** (22) 62
FANTASTIC DAY – **HAIRCUT 100** (9) 82
FANTASTIC VOYAGE – **COOLIO** (41) 94
FANTASY [A] – **EARTH WIND AND FIRE** (14) ..78
FANTASY [A] – **BLACK BOX** (5) 90
FANTASY [B] – **Gerard KENNY** (34) 80
FANTASY [C] – **FANTASY UFO** (56) 90
FANTASY [D] – **TEN CITY** (45) 93
FANTASY [E] – **Mariah CAREY** (4) 95
FANTASY [F] – **LEVELLERS** (16) 95
FANTASY [G] – **APPLETONS** (2) 02
FANTASY ISLAND [A] – **TIGHT FIT** (5) 82
FANTASY ISLAND [B] – **M PEOPLE** (33) 97,98
FANTASY REAL – **Phil FEARON** (41) 83
FAR – **LONGPIGS** (37) 96
FAR ABOVE THE CLOUDS – **Mike OLDFIELD** (53) 99
FAR AND AWAY – **AIDA** (58) 00
FAR AWAY – **Shirley BASSEY** (24) 62
FAR FAR AWAY – **SLADE** (2) 74
FAR FROM HOME – **LEVELLERS** (71) 91
FAR FROM OVER – **Frank STALLONE** (68) 83
FAR GONE AND OUT – **JESUS AND MARY CHAIN** (23) 92
FAR OUT [A] – **SON'Z OF A LOOP DA LOOP ERA** (36) 92
FAR OUT [B] – **DEEJAY PUNK-ROC** (43) 98
FAR-OUT SON OF LUNG AND THE RAMBLINGS OF A MADMAN – **FUTURE SOUND OF LONDON** (22) 95
FARAWAY EYES – **ROLLING STONES** (3) 78
FARAWAY PLACES – **BACHELORS** (36) 63
FAREWELL – **Rod STEWART** (7) 74
FAREWELL ANGELINA – **Joan BAEZ** (35) ..65,66
FAREWELL IS A LONELY SOUND – **Jimmy RUFFIN** (8) 70,74
FAREWELL MR SORROW – **ALL ABOUT EVE** (36) 91
FAREWELL MY SUMMER LOVE [A] – **CHAOS** (55) 92
FAREWELL MY SUMMER LOVE [A] – **Michael JACKSON** (7) 84
FAREWELL TO THE MOON – **YORK** (37) 00
FAREWELL TO TWILIGHT – **SYMPOSIUM** (25) 97
FARMER BILL'S COWMAN (I WAS KAISER BILL'S BATMAN) – **WURZELS** (32) 77
FARON YOUNG – **PREFAB SPROUT** (74) 85
FASCINATED [A] – **Lisa B** (35) 93
FASCINATED [A] – **RAVEN MAIZE** (37) 02
FASCINATING RHYTHM – **BASS-O-MATIC** (9) 90
FASHION – **David BOWIE** (5) 80
FASHION CRISIS HITS NEW YORK – **FRANK AND WALTERS** (42) 93
FASHION '98 – **GLAMMA KID** (49) 98
FAST AS YOU CAN – **Fiona APPLE** (33) 00
FAST BOY – **BLUETONES** (25) 03
FAST CAR [A] – **Tracy CHAPMAN** (5) 88
FAST CAR [B] – **DILLINJA** (56) 03
FAST FOOD SONG – **FAST FOOD ROCKERS** (2) 03
FASTER – **MANIC STREET PREACHERS** (16) ..94
FASTER THAN THE SPEED OF NIGHT – **Bonnie TYLER** (43) 83
FASTLOVE – **George MICHAEL** (1) 96
FAT BASTARD – **MEDWAY** (69) 00
FAT BLACK HEART – **PELE** (75) 93
FAT BOTTOMED GIRLS – **QUEEN** (11) 78
FAT LIP – **SUM 41** (8) 01
FAT NECK – **BLACK GRAPE** (10) 96
FATAL HESITATION – **Chris DE BURGH** (44) ..86
FATHER [A] – **CHRISTIANS** (55) 92
FATHER [B] – **LL COOL J** (10) 98
FATHER AND SON – **BOYZONE** (2) 95
FATHER CHRISTMAS DO NOT TOUCH ME – **GOODIES** (7) 74
FATHER FIGURE – **George MICHAEL** (11) 88
FATTIE BUM BUM [A] – **Carl MALCOLM** (8) 75
FATTIE BUM BUM [A] – **DIVERSIONS** (34) 75
FAVOURITE SHIRTS (BOY MEETS GIRL) – **HAIRCUT 100** (4) 81
FAVOURITE THINGS – **BIG BROVAZ** (2) 03
FBI – **SHADOWS** (6) 61
FE' REAL – **Maxi PRIEST featuring APACHE INDIAN** (33) 92
F.E.A.R. – **Ian BROWN** (13) 01
FEAR LOVES THIS PLACE – **Julian COPE** (42) 92
FEAR OF THE DARK [A] – **Gordon GILTRAP** (58) 79
FEAR OF THE DARK (LIVE) [B] – **IRON MAIDEN** (8) 93
FEAR SATAN – **MOGWAI** (57) 98
FEAR: THE MINDKILLER – **EON** (63) 91
FED UP – **HOUSE OF PAIN** (68) 96
FEDORA (I'LL BE YOUR DAWG) – **CARAMBA** (56) 83
FEE FI FO FUM – **CANDY GIRLS** (23) 95
FEED MY FRANKENSTEIN – **Alice COOPER** (27) 92
FEED THE FEELING – **PERCEPTION** (58) 92
FEED THE TREE – **BELLY** (32) 93
FEED YOUR ADDICTION – **EASTERN LANE** (72) 03
FEEDING TIME – **LOOK** (50) 81
FEEL [A] – **Ruth JOY** (67) 92
FEEL [B] – **HOUSE OF LOVE** (45) 92
FEEL [C] – **Robbie WILLIAMS** (4) 02
FEEL EVERY BEAT – **ELECTRONIC** (39) 91
FEEL FREE – **SOUL II SOUL** (64) 88
FEEL GOOD [A] – **PHATS & SMALL** (7) 99
FEEL GOOD [B] – **MADASUN** (29) 00
FEEL GOOD TIME – **PINK featuring William ORBIT** (3) 03
FEEL IT [A] – **HI-LUX** (41) 95
FEEL IT [B] – **Carol BAILEY** (41) 95
FEEL IT [C] – **Neneh CHERRY** (68) 97
FEEL IT [D] – **TAMPERER featuring MAYA** (1) 98
FEEL IT [E] – **Inaya DAY** (51) 00
FEEL IT BOY – **BEENIE MAN** (9) 02
FEEL LIKE CALLING HOME – **MR BIG** (35) 77
FEEL LIKE CHANGE – **BLACK** (56) 91
FEEL LIKE MAKIN' LOVE [A] – **Roberta FLACK** (34) 74
FEEL LIKE MAKIN' LOVE [A] – **George BENSON** (28) 83
FEEL LIKE MAKIN' LOVE [B] – **BAD COMPANY** (20) 75
FEEL LIKE MAKING LOVE [B] – **Pauline HENRY** (12) 93
FEEL LIKE SINGIN' – **Sandy B** (60) 93
FEEL LIKE SINGING – **TAK TIX** (33) 96
FEEL ME – **BLANCMANGE** (46) 82
FEEL ME FLOW – **NAUGHTY BY NATURE** (23) 95
FEEL MY BODY – **Frank'o MOIRAGHI featuring AMNESIA** (39) 96
FEEL NO PAIN – **SADE** (56) 92
FEEL SO FINE – **Johnny PRESTON** (18) 60
FEEL SO GOOD [A] – **MASE** (10) 97
FEEL SO GOOD [B] – **JON THE DENTIST vs Ollie JAYE** (72) 00
FEEL SO HIGH – **DES'REE** (13) 91,92
FEEL SO REAL [A] – **Steve ARRINGTON** (5) ..85
FEEL SO REAL [B] – **DREAM FREQUENCY** (23) 92
FEEL SURREAL – **FREEFALL featuring PSYCHOTROPIC** (63) 91
FEEL THA VIBE – **THAT KID CHRIS** (52) 97
FEEL THE BEAT [A] – **CAMISRA** (32) 98
FEEL THE BEAT [B] – **DARUDE** (5) 00
FEEL THE DRUM (EP) – **PARKS & WILSON** (71) 00
FEEL THE DRUMS – **NATIVE** (46) 01
FEEL THE HEAT – **Roni SIZE** (55) 03
FEEL THE MUSIC – **GURU** (34) 95
FEEL THE NEED [A] – **Leif GARRETT** (38) 79
FEEL THE NEED [A] – **G NATION featuring ROSIE** (58) 97
FEEL THE NEED [B] – **JT TAYLOR** (57) 91
FEEL THE NEED [C] – **WEIRD SCIENCE** (62) ..00
FEEL THE NEED IN ME [A] – **DETROIT EMERALDS** (4) 73,77
FEEL THE NEED IN ME [A] – **FORREST** (17) 83
FEEL THE NEED IN ME [A] – **Shakin' STEVENS** (26) 88
FEEL THE PAIN – **DINOSAUR JR** (25) 94
FEEL THE RAINDROPS – **ADVENTURES** (58) ..85
FEEL THE REAL – **David BENDETH** (44) 79
FEEL THE RHYTHM [A] – **Jazzi P** (51) 90
FEEL THE RHYTHM [B] – **TERRORIZE** (69) 92
FEEL THE RHYTHM [C] – **JINNY** (74) 93
FEEL THE SAME – **TRIPLE X** (32) 99
FEEL THE SUNSHINE – **Alex REECE** (26) ..95,96
FEEL TOO BUSY THINKING 'BOUT MY BABY – **STEPS** (2) 01
FEEL WHAT YOU WANT – **Kristine W** (33) 94,97
FEELIN' – **LA's** (43) 91
FEELIN' ALRIGHT – **EYC** (16) 93
THE FEELIN' (CLAP YOUR HANDS) – **RHYTHMATIC JUNKIES** (67) 99
FEELIN' FINE – **ULTRABEAT** (12) 03
FEELIN' INSIDE – **Bobby BROWN** (40) 97
FEELIN' SO GOOD – **Jennifer LOPEZ** (15) 00
FEELIN' THE SAME WAY – **Norah JONES** (72) 02
FEELIN' U – **SHY FX & T-POWER featuring Kele LE ROC** (34) 03
FEELIN' YOU – **ALI** (63) 98
THE FEELING [A] – **URBAN HYPE** (67) 92
THE FEELING [B] – **TIN TIN OUT featuring SWEET TEE** (32) 94
FEELING FOR YOU – **CASSIUS** (16) 99
FEELING GOOD [A] – **Nina SIMONE** (40) 94
FEELING GOOD [A] – **HUFF & HERB** (31) ..97,98
FEELING GOOD [A] – **MUSE** (24) 01
FEELING IT TOO – **3 JAYS** (17) 99
FEELING SO REAL – **MOBY** (30) 94
FEELING THIS – **BLINK-182** (15) 03
FEELING THIS WAY – **CONDUCTOR & THE COWBOY** (35) 00
FEELINGS – **Morris ALBERT** (4) 75
FEELINGS OF FOREVER – **TIFFANY** (52) 88
FEELS GOOD (DON'T WORRY BOUT A THING) – **NAUGHTY BY NATURE featuring 3LW** (44) ..02
(FEELS LIKE) HEAVEN – **FICTION FACTORY** (6) 84
FEELS LIKE HEAVEN – **URBAN COOKIE COLLECTIVE** (5) 93
FEELS LIKE I'M IN LOVE – **Kelly MARIE** (1) ..80
FEELS LIKE THE FIRST TIME [A] – **FOREIGNER** (39) 78
FEELS LIKE THE FIRST TIME [B] – **SINITTA** (45) 86
FEELS LIKE THE RIGHT TIME – **SHAKATAK** (41) 80
FEELS SO GOOD [A] – **VAN HALEN** (63) 89
FEELS SO GOOD [B] – **XSCAPE** (34) 95
FEELS SO GOOD [C] – **Lorna B** (69) 97
FEELS SO GOOD [D] – **Melanie B** (5) 01
FEELS SO REAL (WON'T LET GO) – **Patrice RUSHEN** (51) 84
FEELS SO RIGHT – **Victor SIMONELLI presents SOLUTION** (63) 96
FEENIN' – **JODECI** (18) 94
FEET UP! – **Guy MITCHELL** (2) 52
FELICITY – **ORANGE JUICE** (63) 82
FELL IN LOVE WITH A GIRL – **WHITE STRIPES** (21) 02
FELL ON BLACK DAYS – **SOUNDGARDEN** (24) 95
FEMALE INTUITION – **MAI TAI** (54) 86
FEMALE OF THE SPECIES – **SPACE** (14) 96
FERGUS SINGS THE BLUES – **DEACON BLUE** (14) 89
FERNANDO – **ABBA** (1) 76
FERRIS WHEEL – **EVERLY BROTHERS** (22) 64
FERRY ACROSS THE MERSEY [A] – **GERRY and the PACEMAKERS** (8) 64
FERRY 'CROSS THE MERSEY [A] – **CHRISTIANS, Holly JOHNSON, Paul McCARTNEY, Gerry MARSDEN and STOCK AITKEN WATERMAN** (1) 89
FESTIVAL TIME – **SAN REMO STRINGS** (39) ..71
FEUER FREI – **RAMMSTEIN** (35) 02
FEVER [A] – **Peggy LEE** (5) 58,92
FEVER [A] – **Helen SHAPIRO** (38) 64
FEVER [A] – **McCOYS** (44) 65
FEVER [A] – **MADONNA** (6) 93
FEVER [B] – **S-J** (46) 97
FEVER [C] – **STARSAILOR** (18) 01
FEVER CALLED LOVE – **RHC** (65) 92
FEVER FOR THE FLAVA – **HOT ACTION COP** (41) 03
FEVER PITCH THE EP – **PRETENDERS, LA'S, ORLANDO, Nick HORNBY** (65) 97
FICTION OF LIFE – **CHINA DRUM** (65) 97
FIELD OF DREAMS – **FLIP & FILL featuring Jo JAMES** (28) 03
FIELDS OF FIRE (400 MILES) – **BIG COUNTRY** (10) 83
FIELDS OF GOLD – **STING** (16) 93

FLIRT! – Jonathan KING (22) 72
FLIRTATION WALTZ – Winifred ATWELL (10)..53
F.L.M. – MEL and KIM (7)..............................87
FLOAT ON – FLOATERS (1) 77
FLOATATION – GRID (60) 90
FLOATING – TERRA FIRMA (64) 96
FLOATING IN THE WIND – HUDSON-FORD (35) 74
FLOBBADANCE – BILL & BEN (23) 02
FLOETIC – FLOETRY (73) 03
FLOODLIT WORLD – ULTRASOUND (39)........99
THE FLOOR – Johnny GILL (53) 93
FLOOR-ESSENCE – MAN WITH NO NAME (68) 95
FLOOR SPACE – OUR HOUSE (52) 96
THE FLORAL DANCE [A] – BRIGHOUSE and RASTRICK BRASS BAND (2) 77
FLORAL DANCE [A] – Terry WOGAN (21) 78
FLORIBUNDA – MOTHER'S PRIDE (42)..........98
FLOWER DUET (FROM 'LAKMÉ') [A] – Mady MESPLE and Danielle MILLET with the PARIS OPÉRA-COMIQUE ORCHESTRA conducted by Alain LOMBARD (47)..............85
FLOWER DUET [A] – Jonathan PETERS presents LUMINAIRE (75) 99
FLOWER OF SCOTLAND – SCOTTISH RUGBY TEAM with Ronnie BROWNE (73)................90
FLOWER OF THE WEST – RUNRIG (43)..........91
FLOWERS [A] – TITIYO (71)...........................90
FLOWERS [B] – SWEET FEMALE ATTITUDE (2) 00
FLOWERS IN DECEMBER – MAZZY STAR (40) 96
FLOWERS IN THE RAIN – MOVE (2) 67
FLOWERS IN THE WINDOW – TRAVIS (18) 02
FLOWERS OF ROMANCE – PUBLIC IMAGE LTD (24)...............................81
FLOWERS ON THE WALL – STATLER BROTHERS (38)............................66
FLOWERZ – Armand VAN HELDEN (18) 99
FLOWTATION – Vincent DE MOOR (54) 97
FLOY JOY – SUPREMES (9)............................72
FLY [A] – SUGAR RAY (58) 98
FLY [B] – POB featuring DJ Patrick REID (74) 99
FLY [C] – Mark JOSEPH (28) 03
THE FLY – U2 (1)...91
FLY AWAY [A] – HADDAWAY (20) 95
FLY AWAY [B] – Lenny KRAVITZ (1) 99
FLY AWAY [C] – Vincent DE MOOR (30) 01
FLY AWAY (BYE BYE) – EYES CREAM (53) 99
FLY BI – TEEBONE featuring MC KIE and MC SPARKS (43) 00
FLY BY II – BLUE (6)......................................02
FLY GIRL – QUEEN LATIFAH (67) 91
FLY LIFE – BASEMENT JAXX (19) 97
FLY LIKE AN EAGLE – SEAL (13)....................97
FLY ON THE WINGS OF LOVE – XTM & DJ CHUCKY presents ANNIA (8) 03
FLY ROBIN FLY – SILVER CONVENTION (28) 75
FLY TO THE ANGELS – SLAUGHTER (55) 91
FLY TOO HIGH – Janis IAN (44) 79
FLY WITH ME – COLOURSOUND (49)............02
FLYING – CAST (4) 96
FLYING ELVIS – LEILANI (73) 00
FLYING HIGH [A] – COMMODORES (37) 78
FLYING HIGH [B] – FREEEZ (35) 81
FLYING HIGH [C] – CAPTAIN HOLLYWOOD PROJECT (58)..........95
FLYING MACHINE – Cliff RICHARD (37)..........71
FLYING SAUCER – WEDDING PRESENT (22)..92
THE FLYING SONG – PQM featuring CICA (68) 00
FLYING WITHOUT WINGS – WESTLIFE (1)......99
FLYSWATTER – EELS (55)..............................00
FM (NO STATIC AT ALL) – STEELY DAN (49) 78
FOE-DEE-O-DEE – RUBETTES (15) 75
FOG ON THE TYNE (REVISITED) – GAZZA and LINDISFARNE (2) 90
FOGGY MOUNTAIN BREAKDOWN – Lester FLATT and Earl SCRUGGS (39) 67
FOGHORN – A (63)..98
THE FOLK SINGER – Tommy ROE (4)............63
FOLLOW DA LEADER – NIGEL & MARVIN (5) 02
FOLLOW ME [A] – JT TAYLOR (59) 92
FOLLOW ME [B] – ALY-US (43) 92,02
FOLLOW ME [C] – ATOMIC KITTEN (20) 00
FOLLOW ME [D] – UNCLE KRACKER (3) 01
FOLLOW THAT DREAM (EP) – Elvis PRESLEY (34) 62
FOLLOW THE LEADER – Eric B and RAKIM (21) 88
FOLLOW THE LEADERS – KILLING JOKE (55) 81
FOLLOW THE RULES – LIVIN' JOY (9)...........96
FOLLOW YOU DOWN – GIN BLOSSOMS (30) 96
FOLLOW YOU FOLLOW ME [A] – GENESIS (7) 78
FOLLOW YOU FOLLOW ME [A] – Sonny JONES featuring Tara CHASE (42)....00
FOLLOWING – BANGLES (55) 87
THE FOOD CHRISTMAS EP – VARIOUS ARTISTS (EPs and LPs) (63)........89
FOOD FOR THOUGHT [A] – BARRON KNIGHTS (46) 79
FOOD FOR THOUGHT [B] – UB40 (4) 80
FOOL [A] – Elvis PRESLEY (15)......................73
FOOL [B] – Al MATTHEWS (16)........................75
FOOL [C] – MANSUN (28) 01
FOOL AGAIN – WESTLIFE (1) 00
A FOOL AM I – Cilla BLACK (13).....................66
FOOL FOR LOVE – RUSSELL (52) 00
FOOL FOR YOUR LOVING – WHITESNAKE (13) 80,89
FOOL (IF YOU THINK IT'S OVER) [A] – Chris REA (30) 78
FOOL IF YOU THINK IT'S OVER [A] – Elkie BROOKS (17) 82
A FOOL NEVER LEARNS – Andy WILLIAMS (40) 64
FOOL NO MORE – S CLUB 8 (4).....................03
FOOL NUMBER ONE – Brenda LEE (38) 61
THE FOOL ON THE HILL – Shirley BASSEY (48) 71
A FOOL SUCH AS I – Elvis PRESLEY (1) 59
FOOL TO CRY – ROLLING STONES (6) 76
FOOLED AROUND AND FELL IN LOVE – Elvin BISHOP (34) 76
FOOLED BY A SMILE – SWING OUT SISTER (43) 87
FOOLIN' YOURSELF – Paul HARDCASTLE (51)................................86
FOOLISH – ASHANTI (68) 02
FOOLISH BEAT – Debbie GIBSON (9)............88
FOOLISH LITTLE GIRL – SHIRELLES (38) 63
FOOL'S GOLD – STONE ROSES (8) 89,90,92,95,99
FOOL'S PARADISE – Meli'sa MORGAN (41) ..86
FOOLS RUSH IN [A] – Brook BENTON (50)....61
FOOLS RUSH IN [A] – Ricky NELSON (12) 63
FOOT STOMPIN' MUSIC – Hamilton BOHANNON (23) 75
FOOT TAPPER – SHADOWS (1).......................63
FOOTLOOSE – Kenny LOGGINS (6) 84
FOOTPRINT – DISCO CITIZENS (34) 97
FOOTPRINTS IN THE SNOW – Johnny DUNCAN and the BLUE GRASS BOYS (27) 57,58
FOOTSEE – WIGAN'S CHOSEN FEW (9) 75
FOOTSTEPS [A] – Ronnie CARROLL (36) 60
FOOTSTEPS [A] – Steve LAWRENCE (4) 60
FOOTSTEPS [A] – SHOWADDYWADDY (31) 81
FOOTSTEPS [B] – STILTSKIN (34)...................94
FOOTSTEPS [C] – Daniel O'DONNELL (25) 96
FOOTSTEPS FOLLOWING ME – Frances NERO (17)..91
FOR A FEW DOLLARS MORE – SMOKIE (17) 78
FOR A FRIEND – COMMUNARDS (28)............88
FOR A PENNY – Pat BOONE (19) 59
FOR A LIFETIME – ASCENCION featuring Erin LORDAN (19) 59
FOR ALL THAT YOU WANT – Gary BARLOW (24).......................................99
FOR ALL THE COWS – FOO FIGHTERS (28) ..95
FOR ALL TIME – Catherine Zeta JONES (36) 92
FOR ALL WE KNOW [A] – Nicki FRENCH (42) 95
FOR ALL WE KNOW [A] – Shirley BASSEY (6) 71
FOR ALL WE KNOW [A] – CARPENTERS (18)..71
FOR AMERICA – RED BOX (10).......................86
FOR AN ANGEL – Paul VAN DYK (28) 98
FOR BRITAIN ONLY – Alice COOPER (66)......82
(FOR GOD'S SAKE) GIVE MORE POWER TO THE PEOPLE – CHI-LITES (32)..............71
FOR HER LIGHT – FIELDS OF THE NEPHILIM (54) 90
FOR LOVE (EP) – LUSH (35)...........................92
FOR MAMA – Matt MONRO (36) 64
4 MY PEOPLE – Missy 'Misdemeanor' ELLIOTT (36) 64
FOR OLD TIME'S SAKE – MILLICAN and NESBITT (38) 74
FOR ONCE IN MY LIFE [A] – Stevie WONDER (3) 68
FOR ONCE IN MY LIFE [A] – Dorothy SQUIRES (24)................................69
FOR REAL – TRICKY (45) 99
FOR SPACIOUS LIES – Norman COOK (48) ..89
FOR SURE – SCOOCH (15) 00
FOR THE DEAD – GENE (14)..........................96
FOR THE GOOD TIMES – Perry COMO (7) 73
FOR THOSE ABOUT TO ROCK (WE SALUTE YOU) – AC/DC (15) 82
FOR TOMORROW – BLUR (28) 93
FOR WHAT IT'S WORTH [A] – OUI 3 (26)......93
FOR WHAT IT'S WORTH [B] – CARDIGANS (31)...03
FOR WHAT YOU DREAM OF – BEDROCK (25) 96
FOR WHOM THE BELL TOLLS [A] – Simon DUPREE and the BIG SOUND (43) ..68
FOR WHOM THE BELL TOLLS [B] – BEE GEES (4) 93
FOR YOU [A] – Ricky NELSON (14)................64
FOR YOU [B] – FARMERS BOYS (66) 83
FOR YOU [C] – Snowy WHITE (65) 85,86
FOR YOU [D] – ELECTRONIC (16) 96
FOR YOU [E] – STAIND (55) 02
FOR YOU FOR LOVE – AVERAGE WHITE BAND (46) 80
FOR YOU I WILL – MONICA (27) 97
FOR YOU I'LL DO ANYTHING YOU WANT ME TO – Barry WHITE (20) 75
FOR YOUR BABIES – SIMPLY RED (9) 92
FOR YOUR BLUE EYES ONLY – Tony HADLEY (67)...92
FOR YOUR EYES ONLY – Sheena EASTON (8) 81
FOR YOUR LOVE [A] – YARDBIRDS (3)..........65
FOR YOUR LOVE [B] – Stevie WONDER (23) 95
FORBIDDEN CITY – ELECTRONIC (14)...........96
FORBIDDEN COLOURS – David SYLVIAN (16) 83
FORBIDDEN FRUIT – Paul VAN DYK (69) 97
FORBIDDEN ZONE – BEDROCK (71) 97
THE FORCE BEHIND THE POWER – Diana ROSS (27) 92
FOREIGN SAND – Roger TAYLOR (26) 94
FORERUNNER – NATURAL BORN GROOVES (64) 96
A FOREST – CURE (31)..................................80
FOREST FIRE – Lloyd COLE (41)....................84
FOREVER [A] – Roy WOOD (8) 73
FOREVER [B] – KISS (65) 90
FOREVER [C] – DAMAGE (6) 96
FOREVER [D] – CHARLATANS (12) 99
FOREVER [E] – Tina COUSINS (45)................99
FOREVER [F] – TRINITY-X (19) 02
FOREVER [G] – N-TRANCE (6).......................02
FOREVER [H] – DEE DEE (12) 02
FOREVER AND A DAY [A] – BROTHERS IN RHYTHM (51).........................94
FOREVER AND A DAY [B] – STATE ONE (62) 03
FOREVER AND EVER – SLIK (1) 76
FOREVER AND EVER, AMEN – Randy TRAVIS (55)..88
FOREVER AND FOR ALWAYS – Shania TWAIN (6)...03
FOREVER AS ONE – VENGABOYS (28) 01
FOREVER AUTUMN – Justin HAYWARD (5)....78
FOREVER CAME TODAY – Diana ROSS and the SUPREMES (28) 68
FOREVER FAILURE – PARADISE LOST (66)....95
FOREVER FREE – W.A.S.P. (25) 89
FOREVER GIRL – OTT (24) 97
FOREVER IN BLUE JEANS – Neil DIAMOND (16).......................................79
FOREVER IN LOVE – Kenny G (47)................93
FOREVER J – Terry HALL (67)........................94
A FOREVER KIND OF LOVE – Bobby VEE (13) 62
(FOREVER) LIVE AND DIE – ORCHESTRAL MANOEUVRES IN THE DARK (11) 86
FOREVER LOVE – Gary BARLOW (1) 96
FOREVER MAN [A] – Eric CLAPTON (51)........85
FOREVER MAN (HOW MANY TIMES) [A] – BEATCHUGGERS featuring Eric CLAPTON (26) 00
FOREVER MORE [A] – Puff JOHNSON (29) 97
FOREVER MORE [B] – MOLOKO (17) 03
FOREVER NOW – LEVEL 42 (19)....................94
FOREVER REELING – KINESIS (65)................03
FOREVER TOGETHER – Raven MAIZE (67) 89

GIMME HOPE JO'ANNA — Eddy GRANT (7)....88
GIMME LITTLE SIGN [A] — Brenton WOOD (8)....67
GIMME LITTLE SIGN [A] — Danielle BRISEBOIS (75)....95
GIMME LOVE — ALEXIA (17)....98
GIMME LUV (EENIE MEENIE MINY MO) — David MORALES (37)....93
GIMME SHELTER (EP) — VARIOUS ARTISTS (EPs and LPs) (23)....93
GIMME SOME [A] — BRENDON (14)....77
GIMME SOME [A] — PAT and MICK (53)....91
GIMME SOME LOVE — Gina G (25)....97
GIMME SOME LOVIN' — THUNDER (36)....90
GIMME SOME LOVING — Spencer DAVIS GROUP (2)....66
GIMME SOME MORE — Busta RHYMES (5)....99
GIMME THE LIGHT — Sean PAUL (32)....02
GIMME THAT BODY — HISTORY featuring Q-TEE (40)....96
GIMME THE LIGHT — Sean PAUL (5)....03
GIMME THE SUNSHINE — CURIOSITY (73)....93
GIMME YOUR LUVIN' — ATLANTIC STARR (66)....78
GIMMIX! PLAY LOUD — John Cooper CLARKE (39)....79
GIN AND JUICE — SNOOP DOGGY DOGG (39)94
GIN GAN GOOLIE — SCAFFOLD (38)....69,70
GIN HOUSE BLUES — AMEN CORNER (12)....67
GIN SOAKED BOY — DIVINE COMEDY (38)....99
GINCHY — Bert WEEDON (35)....61
GINGER — David DEVANT & his SPIRIT WIFE (54)....97
GINGERBREAD — Frankie AVALON (30)....58
GINNY COME LATELY — Brian HYLAND (5)....62
GIRL [A] — ST LOUIS UNION (11)....66
GIRL [A] — TRUTH (27)....66
GIRL ALL THE BAD GUYS WANT — BOWLING FOR SOUP (8)....02
GIRL / BOY (EP) — APHEX TWIN (64)....96
THE GIRL CAN'T HELP IT — LITTLE RICHARD (9)....57
GIRL CRAZY — HOT CHOCOLATE (7)....82
GIRL DON'T COME — Sandie SHAW (3)....64
THE GIRL FROM IPANEMA — Stan GETZ (29)....64,84
GIRL FROM MARS — ASH (11)....95
A GIRL I ONCE KNEW — NORTHERN UPROAR (63)....97
THE GIRL I USED TO KNOW — BROTHER BEYOND (48)....91
GIRL I'M GONNA MISS YOU — MILLI VANILLI (2)....89
GIRL IN THE MOON — DARIUS (21)....03
THE GIRL IN THE WOOD — Frankie LAINE (11)....53
THE GIRL IS MINE — Michael JACKSON and Paul McCARTNEY (8)....82,83
GIRL (IT'S ALL I HAVE) — SHY (60)....80
GIRL I'VE BEEN HURT — SNOW (48)....93
A GIRL LIKE YOU [A] — Cliff RICHARD and the SHADOWS (3)....61
A GIRL LIKE YOU [B] — YOUNG RASCALS (37)....67
A GIRL LIKE YOU [C] — Edwyn COLLINS (4)....94,95
THE GIRL OF MY BEST FRIEND [A] — Elvis PRESLEY (9)....76
GIRL OF MY BEST FRIEND [A] — Bryan FERRY (57)....93
GIRL OF MY DREAMS [A] — Tony BRENT (16)....58
GIRL OF MY DREAMS [A] — Gerry MONROE (43)....72
GIRL ON TV — LYTE FUNKIE ONES (6)....00
GIRL POWER — SHAMPOO (25)....96
THE GIRL SANG THE BLUES — EVERLY BROTHERS (25)....63
GIRL TALK — TLC (30)....02
GIRL TO GIRL — 49ers (31)....90
GIRL U FOR ME — SILK (67)....93
GIRL U WANT — Robert PALMER (57)....94
THE GIRL WITH THE LONELIEST EYES — HOUSE OF LOVE (58)....91
GIRL YOU KNOW IT'S TRUE [A] — MILLI VANILLI (3)....88
GIRL YOU KNOW IT'S TRUE [A] — KEITH 'N' SHANE (36)....00
GIRL YOU'LL BE A WOMAN SOON — URGE OVERKILL (37)....94
GIRL YOU'RE SO TOGETHER — Michael JACKSON (33)....84
GIRLFRIEND [A] — Michael JACKSON (41)....80
GIRLFRIEND [B] — PEBBLES (8)....88
GIRLFRIEND [C] — Billie PIPER (1)....98,99
GIRLFRIEND [D] — 'N SYNC featuring NELLY (2)....02
GIRLFRIEND [E] — Alicia KEYS (24)....02
GIRLFRIEND [F] — B2K (10)....03
GIRLFRIEND / BOYFRIEND — BLACKSTREET (11)....99
GIRLFRIEND IN A COMA — SMITHS (13)....87
GIRLIE — PEDDLERS (34)....70
GIRLIE GIRLIE — Sophia GEORGE (7)....85
GIRLS [A] — Johnny BURNETTE (37)....61
GIRLS [B] — MOMENTS (3)....75
GIRLS [C] — POWERCUT featuring NUBIAN PRINZ (50)....91
GIRLS [C] — BEASTIE BOYS (34)....87
GIRLS AIN'T NOTHING BUT TROUBLE — JAZZY JEFF & the FRESH PRINCE (21)....86
GIRLS AND BOYS [A] — PRINCE (11)....86
GIRLS AND BOYS [B] — BLUR (5)....94
GIRLS + BOYS [C] — HED BOYS (21)....94,95
GIRLS AND BOYS [D] — GOOD CHARLOTTE (6)....03
GIRLS ARE MORE FUN — Ray PARKER Jr (46)....86
GIRLS ARE OUT TO GET YOU — FASCINATIONS (32)....71
GIRLS CAN GET IT — DR HOOK (40)....80
GIRLS DEM SUGAR — BEENIE MAN featuring MYA (13)....01
GIRLS GIRLS GIRLS [A] — Steve LAWRENCE (49)....60
GIRLS GIRLS GIRLS [B] — FOURMOST (33)....65
GIRLS GIRLS GIRLS [C] — SAILOR (7)....76
GIRLS GIRLS GIRLS [D] — KANDIDATE (34)....79
GIRLS, GIRLS, GIRLS [E] — MÖTLEY CRÜE (26)....87
GIRLS, GIRLS, GIRLS [F] — JAY-Z (11)....02
GIRLS JUST WANT TO HAVE FUN [A] — Cyndi LAUPER (2)....84
GIRLS JUST WANNA HAVE FUN [A] — LOLLY (14)....00
GIRL'S LIFE — GIRLFRIEND (68)....93
GIRLS LIKE US — B15 featuring Chrissy D & Lady G (7)....00
(GIRLS GIRLS GIRLS) MADE TO LOVE — Eddie HODGES (37)....62
GIRLS NIGHT OUT — ALDA (20)....98
GIRL'S NOT GREY — AFI (22)....03
THE GIRLS OF SUMMER (EP) — ARAB STRAP (74)....97
GIRLS ON FILM — DURAN DURAN (5)....81
GIRLS ON MY MIND — FATBACK BAND (69)..85
GIRLS ON TOP — GIRL THING (25)....00
GIRLS TALK — Dave EDMUNDS (4)....79
GIRLS' SCHOOL — Paul McCARTNEY (1)....77
GIT DOWN (SHAKE YOUR THANG) — GAYE BYKERS ON ACID (54)....87
GIT DOWN — CENOGINERZ (75)....02
GIT ON UP — DJ 'FAST' EDDIE (49)....89
GITTIN' FUNKY — KID 'N' PLAY (55)....88
GIV ME LUV — ALCATRAZ (12)....96
GIVE A LITTLE BIT — SUPERTRAMP (29)....77
GIVE A LITTLE LOVE [A] — BAY CITY ROLLERS (1)....75
GIVE A LITTLE LOVE [B] — ASWAD (11)....88
GIVE A LITTLE LOVE [C] — Daniel O'DONNELL (7)....98
GIVE A LITTLE LOVE [D] — INVISIBLE MAN (48)....99
GIVE A LITTLE LOVE BACK TO THE WORLD — EMMA (33)....90
GIVE AND TAKE [A] — PIONEERS (35)....72
GIVE AND TAKE [B] — BRASS CONSTRUCTION (62)....85
GIVE GIVE GIVE — Tommy STEELE (28)....59
GIVE GIVE GIVE ME MORE MORE MORE — WONDER STUFF (72)....88
GIVE HER MY LOVE — JOHNSTON BROTHERS (27)....57
GIVE HER WHAT SHE WANTS — Frankie OLIVER (58)....97
GIVE IN TO ME — Michael JACKSON (2)....93
GIVE IRELAND BACK TO THE IRISH — Paul McCARTNEY (16)....72
GIVE IT ALL AWAY — WORLD PARTY (43)....93
GIVE IT AWAY — RED HOT CHILI PEPPERS (9)....94
GIVE IT SOME EMOTION — TRACIE (24)....83
GIVE IT TO ME [A] — TROGGS (12)....67
GIVE IT TO ME [B] — BAM BAM (65)....88
GIVE IT TO ME BABY — Rick JAMES (47)....81
GIVE IT TO ME NOW — KENNY (38)....73
GIVE IT TO YOU [A] — Martha WASH (37)....93
GIVE IT TO YOU [B] — Jordan KNIGHT (5) 99,00
GIVE IT UP [A] — KC and the SUNSHINE BAND (1)....83
GIVE IT UP [A] — CUT 'N' MOVE (61)....93
GIVE IT UP [B] — TALK TALK (59)....86
GIVE IT UP [C] — HOTHOUSE FLOWERS (30) 90
GIVE IT UP [D] — WILSON PHILLIPS (36)....92
GIVE IT UP [E] — GOODMEN (5)....93
GIVE IT UP [F] — PUBLIC ENEMY (18)....94
GIVE IT UP [G] — SELENA vs X.MEN (61)....01
GIVE IT UP TURN IT LOOSE — EN VOGUE (22)....93
GIVE ME A LITTLE MORE TIME — GABRIELLE (5)....96
GIVE ME A REASON [A] — CORRS (27)....01
GIVE ME A REASON [B] — Tony DE VIT featuring Niki MAK (53)....03
GIVE ME A REASON [C] — TRIPLE EIGHT (9)..03
GIVE ME ALL YOUR LOVE [A] — WHITESNAKE (18)....88
GIVE ME ALL YOUR LOVE [B] — MAGIC AFFAIR (30)....94
GIVE ME AN INCH — Hazel O'CONNOR (41)..80
GIVE ME BACK ME BRAIN — DUFFO (60)....79
GIVE ME BACK MY HEART — DOLLAR (4)....82
GIVE ME BACK MY MAN — B-52's (61)....80
GIVE ME FIRE — GBH (69)....82
GIVE ME JUST A LITTLE MORE TIME [A] — CHAIRMEN OF THE BOARD (3)....70
GIVE ME JUST A LITTLE MORE TIME [A] — Kylie MINOGUE (2)....92
GIVE ME JUST ONE MORE NIGHT (UNA NOCHE) — 98° (61)....00
GIVE ME LIFE — MR V (40)....94
GIVE ME LOVE [A] — DIDDY (23)....94,97
GIVE ME LOVE [B] — DJ DADO vs Michelle WEEKS (59)....98
GIVE ME LOVE (GIVE ME PEACE ON EARTH) — George HARRISON (8)....73
GIVE ME MORE TIME [A] — NICOLE (75)....82
GIVE ME MORE TIME [B] — WHITESNAKE (29)....84
GIVE ME ONE MORE CHANCE [A] — Donald PEERS (36)....72
GIVE ME ONE MORE CHANCE [B] — Luke GOSS and the BAND OF THIEVES (68)....93
GIVE ME RHYTHM — BLACK CONNECTION (32)....98
GIVE ME SOME KINDA MAGIC — DOLLAR (34)....82
GIVE ME SOME MORE — DJ GERT (50)....01
GIVE ME STRENGTH — JON OF THE PLEASED WIMMIN (30)....96
GIVE ME THE NIGHT [A] — George BENSON (7)....80
GIVE ME THE NIGHT [A] — MIRAGE (49)....84
GIVE ME THE NIGHT [A] — Randy CRAWFORD (60)....97
GIVE ME THE REASON — Luther VANDROSS (26)....86,87,88
GIVE ME TIME — Dusty SPRINGFIELD (24)....67
GIVE ME TONIGHT — SHANNON (24)....84
GIVE ME YOU — Mary J BLIGE (19)....00
GIVE ME YOUR BODY — CHIPPENDALES (28)92
GIVE ME YOUR HEART TONIGHT — Shakin' STEVENS (11)....82
GIVE ME YOUR LOVE — REEF (44)....03
GIVE ME YOUR WORD [A] — Tennessee Ernie FORD (1)....55
GIVE ME YOUR WORD [A] — Billy FURY (27) 66
GIVE MYSELF TO LOVE — Francis ROSSI (42)96
GIVE PEACE A CHANCE — John LENNON (2)....69,81
GIVE UP THE FUNK (LET'S DANCE) — BT EXPRESS (52)....80
GIVE YOU — DJAIMIN (45)....92
GIVE YOU ALL THE LOVE — MISHKA (34)....99
GIVEN TO FLY — PEARL JAM (12)....98
GIVEN UP — MIRRORBALL (12)....99
GIVIN' IT UP — INCOGNITO (12)....93
GIVING HIM SOMETHING HE CAN FEEL — EN VOGUE (16)....92
GIVING IN — ADEMA (62)....02
GIVING IT ALL AWAY — Roger DALTREY (5)..73
GIVING IT BACK — Phil HURTT (36)....78

HANDBAGS AND GLADRAGS — **STEREOPHONICS** (72) ...02
HAND A HANDKERCHIEF TO HELEN — **Susan MAUGHAN** (41) ...63
HAND HELD IN BLACK AND WHITE — **DOLLAR** (19) ...81
HAND IN GLOVE — **Sandie SHAW** (27) ...84
HAND IN HAND — **GRACE** (38) ...97
HAND IN MY POCKET — **Alanis MORISSETTE** (26) ...95
HAND IN YOUR HEAD — **MONEY MARK** (40) 98
HAND OF THE DEAD BODY — **SCARFACE featuring ICE CUBE** (41) ...95
HAND ON MY HEART — **SHRIEKBACK** (52) ...84
HAND ON YOUR HEART — **Kylie MINOGUE** (1) ...89
HANDBAGS AND GLADRAGS [A] — **Chris FARLOWE** (33) ...67
HANDBAGS AND GLADRAGS [A] — **STEREOPHONICS** (4) ...01
HANDFUL OF PROMISES — **BIG FUN** (21) ...90
HANDFUL OF SONGS — **Tommy STEELE** (5) ..57
HANDLE WITH CARE — **TRAVELING WILBURYS** (21) ...88
HANDS — **JEWEL** (41) ...98
HANDS ACROSS THE OCEAN — **MISSION** (28) ...90
HANDS AROUND MY THROAT — **DEATH IN VEGAS** (36) ...02
HANDS CLEAN — **Alanis MORISSETTE** (12) ...02
HANDS DOWN — **DASHBOARD CONFESSIONAL** (60) ...03
HANDS OFF — SHE'S MINE — **BEAT** (9) ...80
HANDS TO HEAVEN — **BREATHE** (4) ...88
HANDS UP [A] — **CLUBZONE** (50) ...94
HANDS UP [B] — **TREVOR & SIMON** (12) ...00
HANDS UP (4 LOVERS) — **RIGHT SAID FRED** (60) ...93
HANDS UP (GIVE ME YOUR HEART) — **OTTAWAN** (3) ...81
HANDS UP! HANDS UP! — **ZIG and ZAG** (21) 95
HANDY MAN [A] — **Jimmy JONES** (3) ...60
HANDY MAN [A] — **Del SHANNON** (36) ...64
HANG 'EM HIGH — **Hugo MONTENEGRO** (50) 69
HANG IN LONG ENOUGH — **Phil COLLINS** (34) ...90
HANG MYSELF ON YOU — **CANDYSKINS** (65) 97
HANG ON IN THERE BABY [A] — **Johnny BRISTOL** (3) ...74
HANG ON IN THERE BABY [A] — **CURIOSITY** (3) ...92
HANG ON NOW — **KAJAGOOGOO** (13) ...83
HANG ON SLOOPY [A] — **McCOYS** (5) ...65
HANG ON SLOOPY [A] — **SANDPIPERS** (32) ..76
HANG ON TO A DREAM — **Tim HARDIN** (50) 67
HANG ON TO YOUR LOVE — **Jason DONOVAN** (8) ...90
HANG TOGETHER — **ODYSSEY** (36) ...81
HANG YOUR HEAD — **DEACON BLUE** (21) ...93
HANGAR 18 — **MEGADETH** (26) ...91
HANGIN' — **CHIC** (64) ...83
HANGIN' ON A STRING — **LOOSE ENDS** (13) ...85,92
HANGIN' OUT — **KOOL and the GANG** (52) ...80
HANGIN' TOUGH — **NEW KIDS ON THE BLOCK** (1) ...89,90
HANGING AROUND [A] — **Hazel O'CONNOR** (45) ...81
HANGING AROUND [B] — **ME ME ME** (19) ...96
HANGING AROUND [C] — **CARDIGANS** (17) ...99
HANGING AROUND [D] — **Gemma HAYES** (62) ...02
HANGING AROUND [E] — **POLYPHONIC SPREE** (62) ...02
HANGING AROUND WITH THE BIG BOYS — **BLOOMSBURY SET** (56) ...83
HANGING BY A MOMENT — **LIFEHOUSE** (25) 01
HANGING GARDEN — **CURE** (34) ...82
HANGING ON THE TELEPHONE — **BLONDIE** (5) ...78
HANGINAROUND — **COUNTING CROWS** (46) ..99
HANGOVER — **Betty BOO** (50) ...93
HANKY PANKY [A] — **Tommy JAMES and the SHONDELLS** (38) ..66
HANKY PANKY [B] — **MADONNA** (2) ...90
HANNA HANNA — **CHINA CRISIS** (44) ...84
HAPPENIN' ALL OVER AGAIN [A] — **Lonnie GORDON** (4) ...90
HAPPENIN' ALL OVER AGAIN [A] — **Tracy SHAW** (46) ...98
THE HAPPENING — **SUPREMES** (6) ...67
HAPPENINGS TEN YEARS TIME AGO — **YARDBIRDS** (43) ...66
HAPPINESS [A] — **Ken DODD** (31) ...64
HAPPINESS [B] — **SERIOUS ROPE** (54) ...93
HAPPINESS [C] — **Roger TAYLOR** (32) ...94
HAPPINESS [D] — **PIZZAMAN** (19) ...95
HAPPINESS [E] — **KAMASUTRA featuring Jocelyn BROWN** (45) ...97
HAPPINESS [F] — **SOUND-DE-ZIGN** (19) ...01
HAPPINESS HAPPENING — **LOST WITNESS** (18) ...99
HAPPINESS IS JUST AROUND THE BEND — **Cuba GOODING** (72) ...83
HAPPINESS IS ME AND YOU — **Gilbert O'SULLIVAN** (19) ...74
HAPPINESS (MY VISION IS CLEAR) — **BINI & MARTINI** (53) ...00
HAPPINESS — YOU MAKE ME HAPPY — **SERIOUS ROPE** (70) ...94
HAPPY [A] — **SURFACE** (56) ...87
HAPPY [A] — **MN8** (8) ...95
HAPPY [A] — **Pauline HENRY** (46) ...96
HAPPY [B] — **NED'S ATOMIC DUSTBIN** (16) ...91
HAPPY [C] — **TRAVIS** (38) ...97
HAPPY [D] — **ASHANTI** (13) ...02
HAPPY [E] — **LIGHTHOUSE FAMILY** (51) ...02
HAPPY ANNIVERSARY [A] — **Joan REGAN** (29) ...60
HAPPY ANNIVERSARY [B] — **Slim WHITMAN** (14) ...74
HAPPY BIRTHDAY [A] — **Stevie WONDER** (2) ...81
HAPPY BIRTHDAY [B] — **ALTERED IMAGES** (2) ...81
HAPPY BIRTHDAY [C] — **TECHNOHEAD** (18) ..96
HAPPY BIRTHDAY REVOLUTION — **LEVELLERS** (57) ...00
HAPPY BIRTHDAY SWEET SIXTEEN — **Neil SEDAKA** (3) ...61
HAPPY BIZZNESS — **ROACH MOTEL** (75) ...94
HAPPY BUSMAN — **FRANK AND WALTERS** (49) ...92
HAPPY DAY — **BLINK** (57) ...94
HAPPY DAYS [A] — **PRATT and McCLAIN with BROTHERLOVE** (31) ...77
HAPPY DAYS [B] — **SWEET MERCY featuring Joe ROBERTS** (63) ...96
HAPPY DAYS [C] — **PJ** (57) ...97,99
HAPPY DAYS AND LONELY NIGHTS [A] — **Frankie VAUGHAN** (12) ...55
HAPPY DAYS AND LONELY NIGHTS [A] — **JOHNSTON BROTHERS** (14) ...55
HAPPY DAYS AND LONELY NIGHTS [A] — **Ruby MURRAY** (6) ...55
HAPPY ENDING — **Joe JACKSON** (58) ...84
HAPPY ENDINGS (GIVE YOURSELF A PINCH) — **Lionel BART** (68) ...89
HAPPY EVER AFTER — **Julia FORDHAM** (27) ..88
HAPPY FEELING — **Hamilton BOHANNON** (49) ...75
HAPPY GO LUCKY ME — **George FORMBY** (40) ...60
HAPPY GUITAR — **Tommy STEELE** (20) ...58
HAPPY HEART — **Andy WILLIAMS** (19) ...69
HAPPY HOME — **2PAC** (17) ...98
HAPPY HOUR — **HOUSEMARTINS** (3) ...86
HAPPY HOUSE — **SIOUXSIE and the BANSHEES** (17) ...80
HAPPY JACK — **WHO** (3) ...66
HAPPY JUST TO BE WITH YOU — **Michelle GAYLE** (11) ...95
HAPPY (LOVE THEME FROM 'LADY SINGS THE BLUES') — **Michael JACKSON** (52) ...83
THE HAPPY MAN — **Thomas LANG** (67) ...88
HAPPY NATION — **ACE OF BASE** (40) ...93,94
HAPPY PEOPLE — **STATIC REVENGER** (23) ...01
H.A.P.P.Y. RADIO [A] — **Edwin STARR** (9) ...79
H-A-P-P-Y RADIO [A] — **MICHAELA** (62) ...89
HAPPY SHOPPER — **60FT DOLLS** (38) ...96
HAPPY SONG — **Otis REDDING** (24) ...68
HAPPY TALK — **CAPTAIN SENSIBLE** (1) ...82
HAPPY TO BE ON AN ISLAND IN THE SUN — **Demis ROUSSOS** (5) ...75
HAPPY TO MAKE YOUR ACQUAINTANCE — **Sammy DAVIS Jr** (46) ...60
HAPPY TOGETHER [A] — **TURTLES** (12) ...67
HAPPY TOGETHER [A] — **Jason DONOVAN** (10) ...91
THE HAPPY WANDERER [A] — **OBERNKIRCHEN CHILDREN'S CHOIR** (2) ...54
THE HAPPY WANDERER [A] — **STARGAZERS** (12) ...54
HAPPY WHEN IT RAINS — **JESUS AND MARY CHAIN** (25) ...87
THE HAPPY WHISTLER [A] — **Cyril STAPLETON and his ORCHESTRA** (22) ...56
THE HAPPY WHISTLER [A] — **Don ROBERTSON** (8) ...56
HAPPY XMAS (WAR IS OVER) [A] — **JOHN and YOKO and the PLASTIC ONO BAND with the HARLEM COMMUNITY CHOIR** (2) 72,75,80,81,82,88,03
HAPPY XMAS (WAR IS OVER) [A] — **The IDOLS** (5) ...03
HARBOUR LIGHTS — **PLATTERS** (11) ...60
HARD AS A ROCK — **AC/DC** (33) ...95
HARD BEAT EP 19 — **VARIOUS ARTISTS (EPs and LPs)** (71) ...01
A HARD DAY'S NIGHT [A] — **BEATLES** (1)..64,84
A HARD DAY'S NIGHT [A] — **Peter SELLERS** (14) ...65,93
HARD HABIT TO BREAK — **CHICAGO** (8) ...84
HARD HEADED WOMAN — **Elvis PRESLEY** (2)58
HARD HEARTED HANNAH — **TEMPERANCE SEVEN** (28) ...61
HARD HOUSE MUSIC — **MELT featuring LITTLE MS MARCIE** (59) ...00
HARD KNOCK LIFE (GHETTO ANTHEM) — **JAY-Z** (2) ...98
A HARD RAIN'S A-GONNA FALL — **Bryan FERRY** (10) ...73
HARD ROAD — **BLACK SABBATH** (33) ...78
HARD TIMES COME EASY — **Richie SAMBORA** (37) ...98
HARD TO EXPLAIN — **STROKES** (16) ...01
HARD TO HANDLE [A] — **Otis REDDING** (15) ..68
HARD TO HANDLE [A] — **BLACK CROWES** (39) ...90,91
HARD TO MAKE A STAND — **Sheryl CROW** (22) ...97
HARD TO SAY I'M SORRY [A] — **CHICAGO** (4) 82
HARD TO SAY I'M SORRY [A] — **AZ YET featuring Peter CETERA** (7) ...97
HARD TO SAY I'M SORRY [A] — **AQUAGEN** (33) ...03
HARD UP — **AWESOME 3** (55) ...90
THE HARD WAY — **NASHVILLE TEENS** (45) ...66
THE HARDCORE EP — **HYPNOTIST** (68) ...91
HARDCORE HEAVEN — **DJ SEDUCTION** (26) ..92
HARDCORE HIP HOUSE — **TYREE** (70) ...89
HARDCORE — THE FINAL CONFLICT — **HARDCORE RHYTHM TEAM** (69) ...92
HARDCORE UPROAR — **TOGETHER** (12) ...90
HARDCORE WILL NEVER DIE — **Q-BASS** (64) 92
HARDEN MY HEART — **QUARTERFLASH** (49)..82
HARDER — **KOSHEEN** (53) ...02
HARDER BETTER FASTER STRONGER — **DAFT PUNK** (25) ...01
THE HARDER I TRY — **BROTHER BEYOND** (2) 88
THE HARDER THEY COME [A] — **ROCKER'S REVENGE featuring Donnie CALVIN** (30) ...83
THE HARDER THEY COME [A] — **MADNESS** (44) ...92
THE HARDER THEY COME [B] — **OAKENFOLD** (38) ...03
THE HARDEST BUTTON TO BUTTON — **The WHITE STRIPES** (23) ...03
HARDEST PART IS THE NIGHT — **BON JOVI** (68) ...85
THE HARDEST THING — **98°** (29) ...00
HARDROCK — **Herbie HANCOCK** (65) ...84
HARDTRANCE ACPERIENCE — **HARDFLOOR** (56) ...92
HARE KRISHNA MANTRA — **RADHA KRISHNA TEMPLE** (12) ...69
HARLEM DESIRE — **LONDON BOYS** (17) ...89
HARLEM SHUFFLE [A] — **BOB and EARL** (7) ..69
HARLEM SHUFFLE [A] — **ROLLING STONES** (13) ...86
HARLEQUIN — THE BEAUTY AND THE BEAST — **Sven VATH** (72) ...94
HARMONIC GENERATOR — **THE DATSUNS** (33) ...03
HARMONICA MAN — **BRAVADO** (37) ...94
HARMONY — **TC** (51) ...93
HARMONY IN MY HEAD — **BUZZCOCKS** (32)..79
HARMOUR LOVE — **SYREETA** (32) ...75
HARPER VALLEY P.T.A. — **Jeannie C RILEY** (12) ...68
HARVEST FOR THE WORLD [A] — **ISLEY BROTHERS** (10) ...76

HEARTBREAK STROLL – The RAVEONETTES (49) 03
HEARTBREAKER [A] – Dionne WARWICK (2) 82
HEARTBREAKER [B] – MUSICAL YOUTH (44) 83
HEARTBREAKER [C] – COLOR ME BADD (58) 92
HEARTBREAKER [D] – Mariah CAREY featuring JAY-Z (5) 99
HEARTBROKE AND BUSTED – MAGNUM (49)90
HEARTHAMMER (EP) – RUNRIG (25) 91
HEARTLAND – The THE (29) 86
THE HEARTLESS THEME AKA "THE SUPERGLUE RIDDIM" – HEARTLESS CREW (21) 02
HEARTLIGHT – Neil DIAMOND (47) 82
HEARTLINE – Robin GEORGE (68) 85
THE HEART'S FILTHY LESSON – David BOWIE (35) 95
THE HEART'S LONE DESIRE – Matthew MARSDEN (13) 98
HEARTS ON FIRE [A] – Sam HARRIS (67)....85
HEARTS ON FIRE [B] – Bryan ADAMS (57)....87
HEART-SHAPED BOX – NIRVANA (5) 93
HEARTSONG – Gordon GILTRAP (21) 78
HEARTSPARK DOLLARSIGN – EVERCLEAR (48) 96
THE HEAT IS ON [A] – Agnetha FALTSKOG (35) 83
THE HEAT IS ON [B] – Glenn FREY (12) 85
HEAT IT UP – TWO MEN, A DRUM MACHINE AND A TRUMPET (21) 88
HEAT OF THE BEAT – Roy AYERS (43)....79
HEAT OF THE MOMENT – ASIA (46)....82
HEAT OF THE NIGHT – Bryan ADAMS (50)....87
HEATHER HONEY – Tommy ROE (24) 69
HEATSEEKER – AC/DC (12) 88
HEAVEN [A] – Bryan ADAMS (38)....85
HEAVEN [A] – DJ SAMMY & YANOU featuring DO (1) 02
HEAVEN [B] – TWO PEOPLE (63) 87
HEAVEN [C] – CHIMES (24) 89,90
HEAVEN [D] – Chris REA (57) 91
HEAVEN [E] – TIGERTAILZ (71) 91
HEAVEN [F] – WHYCLIFFE (56) 93
HEAVEN [G] – FITS OF GLOOM (47) 94
HEAVEN [H] – Sarah WASHINGTON (28) 96
HEAVEN [I] – KINANE (49) 98
HEAVEN [J] – PSYCHEDELIC FURS (29) 84
HEAVEN [K] – SOLO U.S. (35) 96
HEAVEN & EARTH – RED (41) 01
HEAVEN AND HELL, THIRD MOVEMENT (THEME FROM THE BBC-TV SERIES 'THE COSMOS') – VANGELIS (48) 81
HEAVEN BESIDE YOU – ALICE IN CHAINS (35) 96
HEAVEN CAN WAIT – Paul YOUNG (71) 90
HEAVEN FOR EVERYONE – QUEEN (2) 95
HEAVEN GIVE ME WORDS – PROPAGANDA (36) 90
HEAVEN HELP – Lenny KRAVITZ (20)....93
HEAVEN HELP ME – Deon ESTUS (41) 89
HEAVEN HELP MY HEART – Tina ARENA (25) 95
HEAVEN HELP US ALL – Stevie WONDER (29) 70
THE HEAVEN I NEED – THREE DEGREES (42) 85
HEAVEN IN MY HANDS – LEVEL 42 (12) 88
HEAVEN IS – DEF LEPPARD (13) 93
HEAVEN IS A HALFPIPE – OPM (4) 01
HEAVEN IS A PLACE ON EARTH [A] – Belinda CARLISLE (1) 87
HEAVEN IS A PLACE ON EARTH [A] – SODA CLUB featuring Hannah ALETHEA (13) 03
HEAVEN IS CLOSER (FEELS LIKE HEAVEN) – DARIO G (39) 03
HEAVEN IS HERE – Julie FELIX (22) 70
HEAVEN IS IN THE BACK SEAT OF MY CADILLAC – HOT CHOCOLATE (25) 76
HEAVEN IS MY WOMAN'S LOVE – Val DOONICAN (34) 73
HEAVEN IS WAITING – DANSE SOCIETY (60) 83
HEAVEN KNOWS [A] – Donna SUMMER (34) 79
HEAVEN KNOWS [B] – Jaki GRAHAM (59) 85
HEAVEN KNOWS [B] – Lalah HATHAWAY (66) 90
HEAVEN KNOWS [C] – Robert PLANT (33) 88
HEAVEN KNOWS [D] – COOL DOWN ZONE (52) 90
HEAVEN KNOWS [E] – Luther VANDROSS (34) 93
HEAVEN KNOWS [F] – SQUEEZE (27) 96
HEAVEN KNOWS – DEEP DEEP DOWN – Angel MORAES (72) 96
HEAVEN KNOWS I'M MISERABLE NOW – SMITHS (10) 84
HEAVEN MUST BE MISSING AN ANGEL [A] – TAVARES (4) 76,86
HEAVEN MUST BE MISSING AN ANGEL [A] – WORLDS APART (29) 93
HEAVEN MUST HAVE SENT YOU – ELGINS (3) 71
HEAVEN MUST HAVE SENT YOU BACK – CICERO (70) 92
HEAVEN ON EARTH – SPELLBOUND (73) 97
HEAVEN ON THE 7TH FLOOR – Paul NICHOLAS (40) 77
HEAVEN OR HELL – STRANGLERS (46) 92
HEAVEN SCENT – BEDROCK (35) 99
HEAVEN SENT [A] – Paul HAIG (74) 83
HEAVEN SENT [B] – INXS (31) 92
HEAVEN SENT [C] – M1 (72) 03
HEAVEN WILL COME – SPACE BROTHERS (25) 99
HEAVENLY – SHOWADDYWADDY (34) 75
HEAVEN'S EARTH – DELERIUM (44) 00
HEAVEN'S HERE – Holly JOHNSON (62) 89
HEAVEN'S ON FIRE – KISS (43) 84
HEAVEN'S WHAT I FEEL – Gloria ESTEFAN (17) 98
HEAVY FUEL – DIRE STRAITS (55) 91
HEAVY MAKES YOU HAPPY – Bobby BLOOM (31) 71
HEAVY VIBES – MONTANA SEXTET (59) 83
HEDONISM (JUST BECAUSE YOU FEEL GOOD) – SKUNK ANANSIE (13) 97
HELEN WHEELS – Paul McCARTNEY (12) 73
HELICOPTER TUNE – DEEP BLUE (68) 94
HELIUM – DALLAS SUPERSTARS (64) 03
HELL HATH NO FURY – Frankie LAINE (28) ..56
HE'LL HAVE TO GO [A] – Jim REEVES (12) 60,71
HE'LL HAVE TO GO [A] – Bryan FERRY (63) ..89
HE'LL HAVE TO STAY – Jeanne BLACK (41) ..60
HELL RAISER – SWEET (2) 73
HELL YEAH – GINUWINE (27) 03
THE HELL EP – TRICKY vs the GRAVEDIGGAZ (12) 95
THE HELL SONG – SUM 41 (35) 03
HELLA GOOD – NO DOUBT (12) 02
HELLBOUND – TYGERS OF PAN TANG (48) ..81
HELLO [A] – Lionel RICHIE (1) 84
HELLO [A] – Jhay PALMER featuring MC IMAGE (69) 02
HELLO [B] – BELOVED (19) 90
HELLO AGAIN – Neil DIAMOND (51) 81
HELLO AMERICA – DEF LEPPARD (45) 80
HELLO BUDDY – TREMELOES (32) 71
HELLO DARLIN – Fuzz TOWNSHEND (51)....97
HELLO DARLING – Tippa IRIE (22) 86
HELLO DOLLY! [A] – BACHELORS (38) 66
HELLO DOLLY! [A] – Frank SINATRA (47) 64
HELLO DOLLY! [A] – Frankie VAUGHAN (18)..64
HELLO DOLLY! [A] – Kenny BALL and his JAZZMEN (30) 64
HELLO DOLLY! [A] – Louis ARMSTRONG (4)..64
HELLO GOODBYE – BEATLES (1) 67,87
HELLO HAPPINESS – DRIFTERS (12) 76
HELLO HEARTACHE GOODBYE LOVE – Little Peggy MARCH (29) 63
HELLO HELLO I'M BACK AGAIN – Gary GLITTER (2) 73,95
HELLO HONKY TONKS (ROCK YOUR BODY) – PIZZAMAN (41) 96
HELLO HOW ARE YOU – EASYBEATS (20) 68
HELLO HURRAY – Alice COOPER (6) 73
HELLO I AM YOUR HEART – Bette BRIGHT (50) 80
HELLO I LOVE YOU – DOORS (15)....68,79
HELLO JOSEPHINE – Wayne FONTANA and the MINDBENDERS (46) 63
HELLO LITTLE GIRL – FOURMOST (9)....63
HELLO MARY LOU – Ricky NELSON (2) 61,91
HELLO MUDDAH HELLO FADDAH – Allan SHERMAN (14) 63
HELLO STRANGER – Yvonne ELLIMAN (26) ..77
HELLO SUMMERTIME – Bobby GOLDSBORO (14) 74
HELLO SUNSHINE – SUPER FURRY ANIMALS (31) 03
HELLO SUZIE – AMEN CORNER (4) 69
HELLO, THIS IS JOANNIE (THE TELEPHONE ANSWERING MACHINE SONG) – Paul EVANS (6) 78
HELLO TIGER – URUSEI YATSURA (40) 98
HELLO (TURN YOUR RADIO ON) – SHAKESPEAR'S SISTER (14) 92
HELLO WORLD [A] – TREMELOES (14) 69
HELLO WORLD [B] – SEA FRUIT (59) 99
HELLO YOUNG LOVERS – Paul ANKA (44) 60
HELLRAISER – Anne SAVAGE (74) 03
HELL'S PARTY – GLAM (42) 93
HELP! [A] – BEATLES (1) 65,76
HELP [A] – Tina TURNER (40) 84
HELP [A] – BANANARAMA (3) 89
HELP (EP) – VARIOUS ARTISTS (EPs and LPs) (51) 95
HELP, GET ME SOME HELP! – OTTAWAN (49) 81
HELP! I'M A FISH – LITTLE TREES (11) 01
HELP IT ALONG – Cliff RICHARD (29)....73
HELP ME [A] – Timo MAAS featuring KELIS (65) 02
HELP ME [B] – Nick CARTER (17) 02
HELP ME FIND A WAY TO YOUR HEART – Daryl HALL (70) 94
HELP ME GIRL – ANIMALS (14) 66
HELP ME MAKE IT – HUFF AND PUFF (31) 96,97
HELP ME MAKE IT THROUGH THE NIGHT [A] – Gladys KNIGHT and the PIPS (11) 72
HELP ME MAKE IT THROUGH THE NIGHT [A] – John HOLT (6) 74
HELP ME MAMA – LEMONESCENT (36) 03
HELP ME RHONDA – BEACH BOYS (27)....65
HELP MY FRIEND – SLO-MOSHUN (52) 94
HELP THE AGED – PULP (8) 97,98
HELP YOURSELF [A] – Tom JONES (5) 68
HELP YOURSELF [A] – Tony FERRINO (42)....96
HELP YOURSELF [B] – Julian LENNON (53)....91
HELPLESS – Tracey ULLMAN (61) 84
HELULE HELULE – TREMELOES (14) 68
HELYOM HALIB – CAPPELLA (11) 89
HENRY LEE – Nick CAVE and the BAD SEEDS and P J HARVEY (36) 96
HENRY VIII SUITE (EP) – EARLY MUSIC CONSORT directed by David MUNROW (49) 71
HER – GUY (58) 91
HER ROYAL MAJESTY – James DARREN (36) 62
HERCULES – Frankie VAUGHAN (42) 62
HERE – LUSCIOUS JACKSON (59) 95
HERE AND NOW [A] – Luther VANDROSS (43) 90
HERE AND NOW [B] – DEL AMITRI (21) 95
HERE AND NOW [C] – STEPS (4) 01
HERE COME THE GOOD TIMES – A HOUSE (37) 94
HERE COMES THE NICE – SMALL FACES (12) 67
HERE COMES MY BABY – TREMELOES (4)....67
HERE COMES SUMMER [A] – Jerry KELLER (1) 59
HERE COMES SUMMER [A] – Dave CLARK FIVE (44) 70
HERE COMES THAT FEELING – Brenda LEE (5) 62
HERE COMES THAT SOUND – Simon HARRIS (38) 88
HERE COMES THE BIG RUSH – ECHOBELLY (56) 97
HERE COMES THE HAMMER – HAMMER (15) 91
HERE COMES THE HOTSTEPPER – Ini KAMOZE (4) 95
HERE COMES THE JUDGE [A] – Shorty LONG (30) 68
HERE COMES THE JUDGE [B] – Pigmeat MARKHAM (19) 68
HERE COMES THE MAN – BOOM BOOM ROOM (74) 86
HERE COMES THE NIGHT [A] – LULU (50) 64
HERE COMES THE NIGHT [A] – THEM (2)....65
HERE COMES THE NIGHT [B] – BEACH BOYS (37) 79
HERE COMES THE RAIN AGAIN – EURYTHMICS (8) 84
HERE COMES THE STAR – HERMAN'S HERMITS (33) 69
HERE COMES THE SUMMER – UNDERTONES (34) 79
HERE COMES THE SUN – Steve HARLEY and COCKNEY REBEL (10)....76
HERE COMES THE WAR – NEW MODEL ARMY (25) 93
HERE COMES YOUR MAN – PIXIES (54) 89

HIGHER THAN HEAVEN [B] – **Kéllé BRYAN** (14) 99
HIGHER THAN REASON – **UNBELIEVABLE TRUTH** (38) 98
HIGHER THAN THE SUN – **PRIMAL SCREAM** (40) 91
HIGHFLY – **John MILES** (17) 75
HIGHLIFE – **CYPRESS HILL** (35) 00
HIGHLY EVOLVED – **The VINES** (32) 02
HIGHLY INFLAMMABLE – **X-RAY SPEX** (45) ..79
HIGHLY STRUNG – **SPANDAU BALLET** (15) 84
HIGHRISE TOWN – **LANTERNS** (50) 99
HIGHWAY CODE – **MASTER SINGERS** (25) 66
HIGHWAY 5 – **BLESSING** (30) 91,92
HIGHWAY SONG – **Nancy SINATRA** (21) 69
HIGHWAY TO HELL – **AC/DC** (14) 79,92
HIGHWAYS OF MY LIFE – **ISLEY BROTHERS** (25) 74
HIGHWIRE [A] – **Linda CARR** (15) 75
HIGHWIRE [B] – **ROLLING STONES** (29) 91
HI-HEEL SNEAKERS – **Tommy TUCKER** (23)..64
HI-HO SILVER LINING – **Jeff BECK** (14) 67,72,82
HI-LILI HI-LO – **Richard CHAMBERLAIN** (20)..63
HILLBILLY ROCK HILLBILLY ROLL – **WOOLPACKERS** (5) 96
HIM [A] – **Rupert HOLMES** (31) 80
HIM [B] – **Sarah BRIGHTMAN** (55) 83
THE HINDU TIMES – **OASIS** (1) 02
HIP HOP – **DEAD PREZ** (41) 00
HIP HOP, BE BOP (DON'T STOP) – **Man PARRISH** (41) 83
HIP HOP DON'T YA DROP – **HONKY** (70) 96
HIP HOP HOORAY – **NAUGHTY BY NATURE** (20) 93
HIP HOUSE – **DJ 'FAST' EDDIE** (47) 89
HIP HOUSIN' – **X-PRESS 2** (55) 94
HIP TO BE SQUARE – **Huey LEWIS and the NEWS** (41) 86
HIP TODAY – **EXTREME** (44) 95
HIPPY CHICK – **SOHO** (8) 90,91
HIPPY HIPPY SHAKE [A] – **SWINGING BLUE JEANS** (2) 63
HIPPY HIPPY SHAKE [A] – **GEORGIA SATELLITES** (63) 89
HIS GIRL – **GUESS WHO** (45) 67
HISTORY [A] – **MAI TAI** (8) 85
HISTORY [B] – **VERVE** (24) 95
HISTORY [C] – **Michael JACKSON** (5) 97
HISTORY NEVER REPEATS – **SPLIT ENZ** (63) 81
HISTORY OF THE WORLD (PART 1) – **DAMNED** (51) 80
HISTORY REPEATING – **PROPELLERHEADS featuring Miss Shirley BASSEY** (19) 97
HIT [A] – **SUGARCUBES** (17) 92
HIT [B] – **WANNADIES** (20) 97
HIT AND MISS – **John BARRY ORCHESTRA** (10) 60
HIT AND RUN [A] – **GIRLSCHOOL** (32) 81
HIT AND RUN [B] – **TOTAL CONTRAST** (41) ..85
HIT BY LOVE – **Ce Ce PENISTON** (33) 94
HIT 'EM HIGH (MONSTARS' ANTHEM) – **B REAL / BUSTA RHYMES / COOLIO / LL COOL J / METHOD MAN** (8) 97
HIT 'EM UP STYLE (OOPS!) – **BLU CANTRELL** (12) 01
HIT 'EM WIT DA HEE – **Missy 'Misdemeanor' ELLIOTT featuring LIL' KIM** (25) 98
HIT IT – **BEAT** (70) 81
HIT ME OFF – **NEW EDITION** (20) 96
HIT ME WITH YOUR RHYTHM STICK – **Ian DURY and the BLOCKHEADS** (1) 78,85,91
HIT OR MISS (WAITED TOO LONG) – **NEW FOUND GLORY** (58) 01
HIT THAT PERFECT BEAT – **BRONSKI BEAT** (3) 85
HIT THE FREEWAY – **Toni BRAXTON featuring LOON** (29) 03
HIT THE GROUND – **DARLING BUDS** (27) 89
HIT THE GROUND RUNNING – **Tim FINN** (50)93
HIT THE NORTH – **FALL** (57) 87
HIT THE ROAD JACK – **Ray CHARLES** (6) 61
HITCHIN' A RIDE [A] – **VANITY FARE** (16) 69
HITCHIN' A RIDE [A] – **SINITTA** (24) 90
HITCHIN' A RIDE [B] – **GREEN DAY** (25) 97
HITMIX (OFFICIAL BOOTLEG MEGA-MIX) – **Alexander O'NEAL** (19) 89
HITS MEDLEY – **GIPSY KINGS** (53) 94
HITSVILLE UK – **CLASH** (56) 81
HOBART PAVING – **SAINT ETIENNE** (23) 93
HOBO HUMPIN' SLOBO BABE – **WHALE** (15) 94,95
HOCUS POCUS – **FOCUS** (20) 73
HOGWASH FARM (THE DIESEL HANDS EP) – **DAWN OF THE REPLICANTS** (65) 98
HOKEY COKEY [A] – **JUDGE DREAD** (59) 78
HOKEY COKEY [A] – **SNOWMEN** (18) 81
HOKEY COKEY [A] – **BLACK LACE** (31) 85
THE HOKEY COKEY [A] – **CAPTAIN SENSIBLE** (71) 94
HOKOYO – **ORANGE JUICE** (60) 82
HOKUS POKUS – **INSANE CLOWN POSSE** (53) 98
HOLD BACK THE NIGHT [A] – **TRAMMPS** (5) 75
HOLD BACK THE NIGHT [A] – **KWS features guest vocal from the TRAMMPS** (30) 92
HOLD BACK THE RIVER – **WET WET WET** (31) 90
HOLD BACK TOMORROW – **MIKI and GRIFF** (26) 59
HOLD IT – **Stephen 'Tin Tin' DUFFY** (55) 83
HOLD IT DOWN [A] – **SENSELESS THINGS** (19) 92
HOLD IT DOWN [B] – **2 BAD MICE** (48) 92
HOLD ME [A] – **Teddy PENDERGRASS with Whitney HOUSTON** (44) 86
HOLD ME [B] – **PJ PROBY** (3) 64
HOLD ME [B] – **B.A. ROBERTSON** (11) 81
HOLD ME [C] – **SAVAGE GARDEN** (16) 00,01
HOLD ME CLOSE – **David ESSEX** (1) 75
HOLD ME IN YOUR ARMS – **Rick ASTLEY** (10) 89
HOLD ME NOW [A] – **THOMPSON TWINS** (4) 83
HOLD ME NOW [B] – **Johnny LOGAN** (2) 87
HOLD ME THRILL ME KISS ME [A] – **Muriel SMITH** (3) 53
HOLD ME THRILL ME KISS ME [A] – **Gloria ESTEFAN** (11) 94,95
HOLD ME THRILL ME KISS ME KILL ME – **U2** (2) 95
HOLD ME TIGHT – **Johnny NASH** (5) 68
HOLD ME TIGHTER IN THE RAIN – **Billy GRIFFIN** (17) 83
HOLD MY BODY TIGHT – **EAST 17** (12) 95
HOLD MY HAND [A] – **Don CORNELL** (1) 54
HOLD MY HAND [B] – **Ken DODD** (44) 81
HOLD MY HAND [C] – **HOOTIE & THE BLOWFISH** (50) 95
HOLD ON [A] – **STREETBAND** (18) 78
HOLD ON [B] – **EN VOGUE** (5) 90,98
HOLD ON [C] – **WILSON PHILLIPS** (6) 90
HOLD ON [D] – **CB MILTON** (62) 95
HOLD ON [E] – **HAPPY CLAPPERS** (27) 95
HOLD ON (EP) [F] – **Ann NESBY** (75) 97
HOLD ON [G] – **José NUNEZ featuring OCTAHVIA** (44) 99
HOLD ON [H] – **GOOD CHARLOTTE** (34) 03
HOLD ON ME – **PHIXX** (10) 03
HOLD ON MY HEART – **GENESIS** (16) 92
HOLD ON TIGHT [A] – **ELECTRIC LIGHT ORCHESTRA** (4) 81
HOLD ON TIGHT [B] – **Samantha FOX** (26) ..86
HOLD ON TO LOVE [A] – **Peter SKELLERN** (14) 75
HOLD ON TO LOVE [B] – **Gary MOORE** (65)..84
HOLD ON TO ME – **MJ COLE** (35) 00
HOLD ON TO MY LOVE – **Jimmy RUFFIN** (7) 80
HOLD ON TO THE NIGHTS – **Richard MARX** (60) 90
HOLD ON TO WHAT YOU'VE GOT – **Evelyn 'Champagne' KING** (47) 88
HOLD ON TO YOUR FRIENDS – **MORRISSEY** (47) 94
HOLD THAT SUCKER DOWN – **OUR TRIBE / ONE TRIBE** (24) 00,94,95
HOLD THE HEART – **BIG COUNTRY** (55) 86
HOLD THE LINE – **TOTO** (14) 79
HOLD TIGHT [A] – **Dave DEE, DOZY, BEAKY, MICK and TICH** (4) 66
HOLD TIGHT [B] – **LIVERPOOL EXPRESS** (46) 76
HOLD YOU TIGHT – **Tara KEMP** (69) 91
HOLD YOUR HEAD UP – **ARGENT** (5) 72
HOLD YOUR HEAD UP HIGH – **Boris DLUGOSCH presents BOOOM** (23) 97
HOLD YOUR HORSES, BABE – **Celi BEE and the BUZZY BUNCH** (72) 78
HOLDIN' ON – **Tony RALLO and the MIDNITE BAND** (34) ..80
HOLDING BACK THE YEARS – **SIMPLY RED** (2) 85,86
HOLDING ON [A] – **Beverley CRAVEN** (32) 91
HOLDING ON [B] – **CLOCK** (66) 93
HOLDING ON [C] – **DJ MANTA** (47) 99
HOLDING ON [D] – **Heather SMALL** (58) 00
HOLDING ON 4 U [A] – **CLOCK** (27) 96
HOLDING ON FOR U [B] – **LIBERTY X** (5) 02
HOLDING ON TO YOU – **Terence Trent D'ARBY** (20) 95
HOLDING ON (WHEN LOVE IS GONE) – **L.T.D.** (70) 78
HOLDING OUT FOR A HERO – **Bonnie TYLER** (2) 85,91
HOLE HEARTED – **EXTREME** (12) 91
HOLE IN MY SHOE [A] – **TRAFFIC** (2) 67
HOLE IN MY SHOE [A] – **neil** (2) 84
HOLE IN MY SOUL – **AEROSMITH** (29) 97
HOLE IN THE BUCKET [B] – **SPEARHEAD** (55) 95
HOLE IN THE GROUND – **Bernard CRIBBINS** (9) 62
HOLE IN THE HEAD – **SUGABABES** (1) 03
HOLE IN THE ICE – **Neil FINN** (43) 01
HOLE IN THE WORLD – **EAGLES** (69) 03
HOLIDAY [A] – **MADONNA** (2) 84,85,91
HOLIDAY [A] – **MAD'HOUSE** (24) 02
HOLIDAY 80 – **HUMAN LEAGUE** (46) 80,82
HOLIDAY RAP – **MC MIKER 'G' and Deejay SVEN** (6) 86
HOLIDAYS IN THE SUN – **SEX PISTOLS** (8) ..77
HOLLER [A] – **GINUWINE** (13) 98
HOLLER [B] – **SPICE GIRLS** (1) 00
HOLLIEDAZE (MEDLEY) – **HOLLIES** (28) 81
THE HOLLOW – **A PERFECT CIRCLE** (72) 00
HOLLOW HEART – **BIRDLAND** (70) 89
THE HOLLOW MAN – **MARILLION** (30) 94
HOLLY HOLY – **UB40** (31) 98
HOLLYWOOD [A] – **Boz SCAGGS** (33) 77
HOLLYWOOD [B] – **MADONNA** (2) 03
HOLLYWOOD (DOWN ON YOUR LUCK) – **THIN LIZZY** (53) 82
HOLLYWOOD NIGHTS – **Bob SEGER and the SILVER BULLET BAND** (42) ..78,81,95
HOLLYWOOD TEASE – **GIRL** (50) 80
THE HOLY CITY – **Moira ANDERSON** (43) 69
HOLY COW – **Lee DORSEY** (6) 66
HOLY DAYS – **ZOE** (72) 92
HOLY DIVER – **DIO** (72) 83
HOLY JOE – **HAYSI FANTAYZEE** (51) 82
THE HOLY RIVER – **PRINCE** (19) 97
HOLY ROLLER – **NAZARETH** (36) 75
HOLY ROLLER NOVOCAINE – **KINGS OF LEON** (53) 03
HOLY SMOKE – **IRON MAIDEN** (3) 90
HOLY WARS ... THE PUNISHMENT DUE – **MEGADETH** (24) 90
HOMBURG – **PROCOL HARUM** (6) 67
HOME [A] – **PUBLIC IMAGE LTD** (75) 86
HOME [B] – **GOD MACHINE** (65) 93
HOME [C] – **DEPECHE MODE** (23) 97
HOME [D] – **CHAKRA** (46) 97,00
HOME [E] – **Sheryl CROW** (25) 97
HOME [F] – **COAST 2 COAST featuring DISCOVERY** (44) 01
HOME [G] – **Julie MCKNIGHT** (61) 02
HOME [H] – **BONE THUGS-N-HARMONY featuring Phil COLLINS** (19) 03
HOME ALONE – **R KELLY featuring Keith MURRAY** (17) 98
HOME AND AWAY – **Karen BODDINGTON and Mark WILLIAMS** (73) 89
HOME AND DRY – **PET SHOP BOYS** (14) 02
HOME FOR CHRISTMAS DAY – **RED CAR AND THE BLUE CAR** (44) 91
HOME IS WHERE THE HEART IS – **Gladys KNIGHT and the PIPS** (35) 77
HOME LOVIN' MAN – **Andy WILLIAMS** (7) 70
HOME OF THE BRAVE – **Jody MILLER** (49) 65
HOME SWEET HOME – **MÖTLEY CRÜE** (37) 86,92
HOMELY GIRL [A] – **CHI-LITES** (5) 74
HOMELY GIRL [A] – **UB40** (6) 89
HOMETOWN UNICORN – **SUPER FURRY ANIMALS** (47) 96
HOMEWARD BOUND [A] – **SIMON and GARFUNKEL** (9) 66
HOMEWARD BOUND [A] – **QUIET FIVE** (44) ..66
HOMICIDE [A] – **999** (40) 78
HOMICIDE [B] – **SHADES OF RHYTHM** (53) ..91
THE HOMING WALTZ – **Vera LYNN** (9) 52
HOMOPHOBIC ASSHOLE – **SENSELESS THINGS** (52) 92
HONALOOCHIE BOOGIE – **MOTT THE HOOPLE** (12) 73

HOW DO YOU LIKE IT — **Keith SWEAT** (71)....94
HOW DO YOU SAY ... LOVE — **DEEE-LITE** (52) 91
HOW DO YOU SPEAK TO AN ANGEL — **Dean MARTIN** (15) 54
HOW DO YOU WANT IT — **2PAC** (17) 96
HOW DO YOU WANT ME TO LOVE YOU? — **911** (10) 98
HOW DOES IT FEEL? [A] — **SLADE** (15) 75
HOW DOES IT FEEL [B] — **ELECTROSET** (27)..92
HOW DOES IT FEEL [C] — **WANNADIES** (53) ..96
(HOW DOES IT FEEL TO BE) ON TOP OF THE WORLD — **ENGLAND UNITED** (9) 98
HOW DOES IT FEEL TO FEEL — **RIDE** (58) 94
HOW DOES THAT GRAB YOU DARLIN' — **Nancy SINATRA** (19) 66
HOW GEE — **BLACK MACHINE** (17) 94
HOW HIGH — **CHARLATANS** (6)....97
HOW HIGH THE MOON [A] — **Ella FITZGERALD** (46)....60
HOW HIGH THE MOON [A] — **Gloria GAYNOR** (33) 76
HOW HOW — **YELLO** (59) 94
HOW I WANNA BE LOVED — **Dana DAWSON** (42) 96
HOW I'M COMIN' — **LL COOL J** (37) 93
HOW IT IS — **BIOHAZARD** (62) 94
HOW IT SHOULD BE — **INSPIRAL CARPETS** (49)....93
HOW LONG [A] — **ACE** (20) 74
HOW LONG [A] — **Rod STEWART** (41) 82
HOW LONG [A] — **YAZZ and ASWAD** (31) 93
HOW LONG [A] — **Paul CARRACK** (32)....96
HOW LONG DO I GET — **RAISSA** (47) 00
HOW LONG HAS IT BEEN — **Jim REEVES** (45) 65
HOW LONG'S A TEAR TAKE TO DRY? — **BEAUTIFUL SOUTH** (12) 99
HOW LUCKY YOU ARE — **SKIN** (32)....96
HOW MANY LIES — **SPANDAU BALLET** (34) ..87
HOW MANY TEARS — **Bobby VEE** (10) 61
HOW MANY TEARS CAN YOU HIDE — **Shakin' STEVENS** (47) 88
HOW MANY TIMES — **BROTHER BEYOND** (62) 87
HOW MEN ARE — **AZTEC CAMERA** (25)....88
HOW MUCH I FEEL — **ALIBI** (58) 98
(HOW MUCH IS) THAT DOGGIE IN THE WINDOW [A] — **Lita ROZA** (1)....53
(HOW MUCH IS) THAT DOGGIE IN THE WINDOW [A] — **Patti PAGE** (9) 53
HOW MUCH LOVE [A] — **Leo SAYER** (10)....77
HOW MUCH LOVE [B] — **VIXEN** (35) 90
HOW MUSIC CAME ABOUT (BOP B DA B DA DA) — **GAP BAND** (61) 87
HOW SHE THREW IT ALL AWAY (EP) — **STYLE COUNCIL** (41)....88
HOW SOON — **Henry MANCINI** (10)....64
HOW SOON IS NOW [A] — **SMITHS** (16)....85,92
HOW SOON IS NOW [A] — **INNER SANCTUM** (75)....98
HOW SOON WE FORGET — **Colonel ABRAMS** (75) 87
HOW SWEET IT IS [A] — **Marvin GAYE** (49)....64
HOW SWEET IT IS [A] — **Junior WALKER and the ALL-STARS** (22) 66
HOW THE HEART BEHAVES — **WAS (NOT WAS)** (53)....90
HOW TO BE A MILLIONAIRE — **ABC** (49)....84
HOW TO FALL IN LOVE PART 1 — **BEE GEES** (30) 94
HOW TO WIN YOUR LOVE — **Engelbert HUMPERDINCK** (59) 00
HOW U LIKE BASS — **Norman BASS** (17) 01
HOW WAS IT FOR YOU — **JAMES** (32)....90
HOW WILL I KNOW — **Whitney HOUSTON** (5) 86
HOW WILL I KNOW (WHO YOU ARE) — **JESSICA** (47)....99
HOW WONDERFUL TO KNOW — **Pearl CARR and Teddy JOHNSON** (23) 61
HOW WONDERFUL YOU ARE — **Gordon HASKELL** (2)....01
HOW YOU GONNA ACT LIKE THAT — **TYRESE** (30) 03
HOW YOU GONNA SEE ME NOW — **Alice COOPER** (61) 78
HOW YOU REMIND ME — **NICKELBACK** (4) 02
HOW'D I DO DAT — **BENTLEY RHYTHM ACE** (57)....00
HOW'S IT GOING TO BE — **THIRD EYE BLIND** (51) 98
HOW'S YOUR EVENING SO FAR — **Josh WINK and Lil' LOUIS** (23)....00
HOWARD'S WAY — **Simon MAY** (21) 85
HOWZAT — **SHERBET** (4)....76
HUBBLE BUBBLE TOIL AND TROUBLE — **MANFRED MANN** (11) 64
HUDSON STREET — **AGNELLI & NELSON** (29) 00
HUG MY SOUL — **SAINT ETIENNE** (32) 94
HUMAN [A] — **HUMAN LEAGUE** (8) 86
HUMAN [B] — **PRETENDERS** (33) 99
HUMAN BEHAVIOUR — **BJÖRK** (36)....93
HUMAN BEING — **BETA BAND** (57) 01
HUMAN BEINGS — **SEAL** (50) 98
HUMAN NATURE [A] — **Gary CLAIL ON-U SOUND SYSTEM** (10)....91
HUMAN NATURE [B] — **MADONNA** (8)....95
HUMAN RACING — **Nik KERSHAW** (19) 84
HUMAN TOUCH [A] — **Rick SPRINGFIELD** (23)84
HUMAN TOUCH [B] — **Bruce SPRINGSTEEN** (11) 92
HUMAN WORK OF ART [A] — **Maxi PRIEST** (71) 90
HUMAN WORK OF ART [A] — **Cliff RICHARD** (24) 93
HUMANISTIC — **KAWALA** (68) 00
HUMANITY — **REBEL MC** (62) 92
HUMMING BIRD — **Frankie LAINE** (16) 55
HUMPIN' — **GAP BAND** (36) 81
HUMPIN' AROUND — **Bobby BROWN** (8) ..92,95
HUNDRED MILE HIGH CITY — **OCEAN COLOUR SCENE** (4) 97
A HUNDRED POUNDS OF CLAY — **Craig DOUGLAS** (9) 61
HUNG UP — **Paul WELLER** (11) 94
HUNGAH — **Karyn WHITE** (69) 94
HUNGER STRIKE — **TEMPLE OF THE DOG** (51) 92
HUNGRY — **KOSHEEN** (13)....02
HUNGRY FOR HEAVEN — **DIO** (56)....85,86
HUNGRY FOR LOVE — **Johnny KIDD and the PIRATES** (20) 63
HUNGRY HEART — **Bruce SPRINGSTEEN** (28) 80,95
HUNGRY LIKE THE WOLF — **DURAN DURAN** (5) 82
HUNT — **Barry RYAN** (34) 69
HUNTER [A] — **BJÖRK** (44) 98
HUNTER [B] — **DIDO** (17) 01
HUNTING HIGH AND LOW — **A-HA** (5)....86
HURDY GURDY MAN — **DONOVAN** (4) 68
HURRICANE [A] — **Bob DYLAN** (43)....76
HURRICANE [B] — **WARM JETS** (34)....98
HURRY HOME — **WAVELENGTH** (17) 82
HURRY UP AND WAIT — **STEREOPHONICS** (11) 99,00
HURRY UP HARRY — **SHAM 69** (10) 78
HURT [A] — **Elvis PRESLEY** (37) 76
HURT [A] — **MANHATTANS** (4)....76
HURT [B] — **Johnny CASH** (39) 03
HURT BY LOVE — **Inez FOXX** (40) 64
HURT ME SO BAD — **LULU** (42) 99
HURT SO GOOD [A] — **Susan CADOGAN** (4) ..75
HURT SO GOOD [A] — **Jimmy SOMERVILLE** (15)....95
HURTING KIND (I'VE GOT MY EYES ON YOU) — **Robert PLANT** (45) 90
HUSAN — **BHANGRA KNIGHTS vs HUSAN** (7) 03
HUSBAND — **FLUFFY** (58) 96
HUSH [A] — **DEEP PURPLE** (62) 88
HUSH [A] — **KULA SHAKER** (2) 97
HUSH... NOT A WORD TO MARY — **John ROWLES** (12) 68
THE HUSTLE — **Van McCOY** (3)....75
HUSTLE! (TO THE MUSIC ...) — **FUNKY WORM** (13) 88
HYBRID — **EAT STATIC** (41)....97
HYMN [A] — **ULTRAVOX** (11) 82
HYMN [B] — **MOBY** (31)....94
HYMN [C] — **ULTRAMARINE featuring David McALMONT** (65) 96
HYMN TO HER — **PRETENDERS** (8)....86
HYMNE À L'AMOUR (IF YOU LOVE ME) — **Elaine PAIGE** (68)....95
HYPER MUSIC — **MUSE** (24) 01
HYPERACTIVE — **Thomas DOLBY** (17) 84,94
HYPERBALLAD — **BJÖRK** (8) 96
HYPERREAL — **SHAMEN** (29)....91
HYPNOSIS — **MUD** (16) 73
HYPNOTIC ST-8 — **ALTERN 8** (16) 92
HYPNOTISED [A] — **CABARET VOLTAIRE** (66) 89
HYPNOTISED [B] — **SIMPLE MINDS** (18) 95
HYPNOTISED [C] — **Paul OAKENFOLD** (57) 03
HYPNOTISING — **KID CREME featuring CHARLISE** (31) 03
HYPNOTIZE [A] — **SCRITTI POLITTI** (68) 84
HYPNOTIZE [B] — **D'INFLUENCE** (33)....97
HYPNOTIZE [C] — **NOTORIOUS B.I.G.** (10) 97
HYPNOTIZIN' — **Josh WINK** (35) 96
HYPOCRITE [A] — **LUSH** (52)....94
HYPOCRITE [B] — **SPECIALS** (66) 96
HYSTERIA [A] — **DEF LEPPARD** (26)....87,88
HYSTERIA [B] — **MUSE** (17) 03
I — **Petey PABLO** (51) 02
I ADORE MI AMOR — **COLOR ME BADD** (44)..91
I ADORE YOU — **Caron WHEELER** (59) 92
I AIN'T GOIN' OUT LIKE THAT — **CYPRESS HILL** (15)....93
I AIN'T GONNA CRY — **LITTLE ANGELS** (26) ..91
I AIN'T GONNA STAND FOR IT — **Stevie WONDER** (10) 80
I AIN'T GOT TIME ANYMORE — **Cliff RICHARD** (21) 70
I AIN'T LYIN' — **George McCRAE** (12) 75
I AIN'T MAD AT CHA — **2PAC** (13)....96
I AIN'T MOVIN' — **DES'REE** (44) 94
I AIN'T NEW TA THIS — **ICE-T** (62) 93
I ALMOST FELT LIKE CRYING — **Craig McLACHLAN** (50)....90
I ALMOST LOST MY MIND — **Pat BOONE** (14) 56
I ALONE — **LIVE** (48)....95
I AM [A] — **CHAKRA** (24) 97
I AM [B] — **SUGGS** (38)....98
I AM A CIDER DRINKER (PALOMA BLANCA) — **WURZELS** (3) 76
I AM A CLOWN — **David CASSIDY** (3) 73
I AM A ROCK — **SIMON and GARFUNKEL** (17)66
I AM BLESSED — **ETERNAL** (7) 95
I AM DOWN — **SALT-N-PEPA** (41) 88
I AM I — **QUEENSRYCHE** (40) 95
I AM I FEEL — **ALISHA'S ATTIC** (14) 96
I AM ... I SAID — **Neil DIAMOND** (4) 71
I AM (I'M ME) — **TWISTED SISTER** (18)....83
I AM IN LOVE WITH THE WORLD — **CHICKEN SHED THEATRE** (15) 97
I AM MINE — **PEARL JAM** (26)....02
I AM LV — **LV** (64)....96
I AM ONE [A] — **SMASHING PUMPKINS** (73)..92
I AM ONE [B] — **W.A.S.P.** (56)....92
I AM THE BEAT — **LOOK** (6) 80
I AM THE BLACK GOLD OF THE SUN — **NUYORICAN SOUL featuring Jocelyn BROWN** (31) 97
I AM THE LAW — **ANTHRAX** (32)....87
I AM THE MOB — **CATATONIA** (40) 97
I AM THE MUSIC HEAR ME! — **MILLIONAIRE HIPPIES** (52)....93
I AM THE MUSIC MAN — **BLACK LACE** (52) ..89
I AM THE NEWS — **OCEAN COLOUR SCENE** (31)....00
I AM THE ONE — **CRACKOUT** (72) 02
I AM THE RESURRECTION — **STONE ROSES** (33) 92
I AM THE SUN — **DARK STAR** (31) 00
I AM WHAT I AM [A] — **GREYHOUND** (20)....72
I AM WHAT I AM [B] — **Mark OWEN** (29) 97
I AM WHAT I AM (FROM 'LA CAGE AUX FOLLES') — **Gloria GAYNOR** (13) 83
I APOLOGISE — **PJ PROBY** (11) 65
I BE THE PROPHET — **STARVING SOULS** (66)95
I BEG YOUR PARDON — **KON KAN** (5) 89
I BEGIN TO WONDER — **Dannii MINOGUE** (2) 03
I BELIEVE [A] — **Frankie LAINE** (1)....53
I BELIEVE [A] — **David WHITFIELD** (49)....60
I BELIEVE [A] — **BACHELORS** (2) 64
I BELIEVE [A] — **ROBSON and JEROME** (1) 95
I BELIEVE [B] — **EMF** (6) 91
I BELIEVE [C] — **REESE PROJECT** (74) 92
I BELIEVE [D] — **BON JOVI** (11) 93
I BELIEVE [E] — **Robert PLANT** (64) 93
I BELIEVE [F] — **Marcella DETROIT** (11) 94
I BELIEVE [G] — **SOUNDS OF BLACKNESS** (17)....94
I BELIEVE [H] — **BLESSID UNION OF SOULS** (29)....95
I BELIEVE [I] — **HAPPY CLAPPERS** (7) 95,97
I BELIEVE [J] — **BOOTH and the BAD ANGEL** (25)....96
I BELIEVE [K] — **ABSOLUTE** (38) 97
I BELIEVE [L] — **LANGE featuring SARAH DWYER** (68) 99

I DON'T KNOW [A] – **RUTH** (66) 97
I DON'T KNOW [B] – **HONEYZ** (28) 01
I DON'T KNOW ANYBODY ELSE – **BLACK BOX** (4) 90
I DON'T KNOW HOW TO LOVE HIM [A] – **Petula CLARK** (47) 72
I DON'T KNOW HOW TO LOVE HIM [A] – **Yvonne ELLIMAN** (47) 72
I DON'T KNOW IF IT'S RIGHT – **Evelyn 'Champagne' KING** (67) 79
I DON'T KNOW WHAT IT IS BUT I LOVE IT – **Chris REA** (65) 84
I DON'T KNOW WHAT YOU WANT BUT I CAN'T GIVE IT ANYMORE – **PET SHOP BOYS** (15) 99
I DON'T KNOW WHERE IT COMES FROM – **RIDE** (46) 94
I DON'T KNOW WHY [A] – **Eden KANE** (7) 62
I DON'T KNOW WHY [B] – **Shawn COLVIN** (52)...............................93,95
I DON'T KNOW WHY (I JUST DO) – **Andy and David WILLIAMS** (37)...................73
(I DON'T KNOW WHY) BUT I DO – **Clarence 'Frogman' HENRY** (65)..................93
I DON'T KNOW WHY I LOVE YOU – **HOUSE OF LOVE** (41) 89
I DON'T KNOW WHY (I LOVE YOU) – **Stevie WONDER** (14) 69
I DON'T LIKE MONDAYS – **BOOMTOWN RATS** (1) 79,94
I DON'T LOVE YOU ANYMORE – **QUIREBOYS** (24)..90
I DON'T LOVE YOU BUT I THINK I LIKE YOU – **Gilbert O'SULLIVAN** (14) 75
I DON'T MIND – **BUZZCOCKS** (55) 78
I DON'T MIND AT ALL – **BOURGEOIS TAGG** (35) 88
I DON'T NEED ANYTHING – **Sandie SHAW** (50) 67
I DON'T NEED NO DOCTOR (LIVE) – **W.A.S.P.** (31) 87
I DON'T NEED TO TELL HER – **LURKERS** (49)..78
I DON'T REALLY CARE – **K-GEE** (22)..............00
I DON'T REMEMBER – **Peter GABRIEL** (62) ..83
I DON'T SMOKE – **DJ DEE KLINE** (11) 00
I DON'T THINK SO – **DINOSAUR JR** (67) 95
I DON'T THINK THAT MAN SHOULD SLEEP ALONE – **Ray PARKER Jr** (13) 87
I DON'T WANNA BE A STAR – **CORONA** (22) 95
I DON'T WANNA DANCE – **Eddy GRANT** (1) ..82
I DON'T WANNA FIGHT – **Tina TURNER** (7) ..93
I DON'T WANNA GET HURT – **Donna SUMMER** (7) 89
I DON'T WANNA GO ON WITH YOU LIKE THAT – **Elton JOHN** (30).......................................88
I DON'T WANNA LOSE AT LOVE – **Tanita TIKARAM** (73) 98
I DON'T WANNA LOSE MY WAY – **DREAMCATCHER** (14) 02
I DON'T WANNA LOSE YOU [A] – **KANDIDATE** (11) 79
I DON'T WANNA LOSE YOU [B] – **Tina TURNER** (8) 89
I DON'T WANNA LOSE YOUR LOVE – **EMOTIONS** (40) 77
I DON'T WANNA PLAY HOUSE – **Tammy WYNETTE** (37) 76
I DON'T WANNA TAKE THIS PAIN – **Dannii MINOGUE** (40) 91
I DON'T WANT A LOVER – **TEXAS** (8) 89,01
I DON'T WANT CONTROL OF YOU – **TEENAGE FANCLUB** (43).............................97
I DON'T WANT NOBODY (TELLIN' ME WHAT TO DO) – **Cherie AMORE** (33) 00
I DON'T WANT OUR LOVING TO DIE – **HERD** (5) 68
I DON'T WANT TO – **Toni BRAXTON** (9) 97
I DON'T WANT TO BE A FREAK (BUT I CAN'T HELP MYSELF) – **DYNASTY** (20) 79
I DON'T WANT TO BE A HERO – **JOHNNY HATES JAZZ** (11) 87
I DON'T WANT TO GO ON WITHOUT YOU – **MOODY BLUES** (33) 65
(I DON'T WANT TO GO TO) CHELSEA – **Elvis COSTELLO** (16)....................................78
I DON'T WANT TO HURT YOU (EVERY SINGLE TIME) – **Frank BLACK** (63).........................96
I DON'T WANT TO MISS A THING – **AEROSMITH** (4) 98
I DON'T WANT TO PUT A HOLD ON YOU – **Berni FLINT** (3)..77
I DON'T WANT TO TALK ABOUT IT [A] – **Rod STEWART** (1) 77
I DON'T WANT TO TALK ABOUT IT [A] – **EVERYTHING BUT THE GIRL** (3) 88
I DON'T WANT TO WAIT – **Paula COLE** (43)..98
I DON'T WANT YOUR LOVE – **DURAN DURAN** (14) 88
I DREAM – **TILT** (69).......................................95
I DREAMED – **BEVERLEY SISTERS** (24) 57
I DROVE ALL NIGHT [A] – **Cyndi LAUPER** (7) 89
I DROVE ALL NIGHT [A] – **Roy ORBISON** (7) 92,93
I EAT CANNIBALS PART 1 – **TOTO COELO** (8)82
I ENJOY BEING A GIRL – **Pat SUZUKI** (49) 60
I FEEL A CRY COMING ON – **Hank LOCKLIN** (29) 66
I FEEL DIVINE – **S-J** (30).....................................98
I FEEL FINE [A] – **BEATLES** (1)..................64,84
I FEEL FINE [A] – **WET WET WET** (30) 90
I FEEL FOR YOU [A] – **Chaka KHAN** (1) 84,89
I FEEL FOR YOU [B] – **Bob SINCLAR** (9)........00
I FEEL FREE – **CREAM** (11) 66
I FEEL GOOD THINGS FOR YOU – **DADDY'S FAVOURITE** (44)......................98,99
I FEEL IT – **MOBY** (38) 93
I FEEL LIKE BUDDY HOLLY – **Alvin STARDUST** (7) 84
I FEEL LIKE WALKIN' IN THE RAIN – **Millie JACKSON** (55) 84
I FEEL LOVE [A] – **Donna SUMMER** (1) 77,82,95
I FEEL LOVE (MEDLEY) [A] – **BRONSKI BEAT and Marc ALMOND** (3) 85
I FEEL LOVE [A] – **MESSIAH** (19) 92
I FEEL LOVE [A] – **VANESSA-MAE** (41) 97
I FEEL LOVE [B] – **CRW** (15) 00
I FEEL LOVE COMIN' ON [A] – **Felice TAYLOR** (11) 67
I FEEL LOVE COMIN' ON [A] – **DANA** (66) 82
I FEEL LOVED – **DEPECHE MODE** (12)............01
I FEEL SO – **BOX CAR RACER** (41) 02
I FEEL SO BAD – **Elvis PRESLEY** (4) 61
I FEEL SO FINE – **KMC featuring DHANY** (33) 02
I FEEL SOMETHING IN THE AIR – **CHER** (43) 66
I FEEL STEREO – **Dino LENNY** (60) 02
I FEEL THE EARTH MOVE – **MARTIKA** (7) 89
I FEEL YOU [A] – **LOVE DECADE** (34) 92
I FEEL YOU [B] – **DEPECHE MODE** (8) 93
I FEEL YOU [C] – **Peter ANDRE** (1)............96,97
I FINALLY FOUND SOMEONE – **Barbra STREISAND and Bryan ADAMS** (10) 97
I FORGOT [A] – **COOLNOTES** (63)..................84
I FORGOT [B] – **Lionel RICHIE** (34) 01
I FOUGHT THE LAW [A] – **Bobby FULLER FOUR** (33) 66
I FOUGHT THE LAW [A] – **CLASH** (29) 88
I FOUND HEAVEN – **TAKE THAT** (15) 92
I FOUND LOVE [A] – **Darlene DAVIS** (55) 87
I FOUND LOVE [B] – **LONE JUSTICE** (45) 87
I FOUND LOVE [C] – **C & C MUSIC FACTORY / CLIVILLES & COLE featuring Martha WASH**(26) 95
I FOUND LOVIN' [A] – **FATBACK BAND** (7)..........................84,86,87
I FOUND LOVIN' [A] – **Steve WALSH** (9)........87
I FOUND OUT – **CHRISTIANS** (56) 90
I FOUND OUT THE HARD WAY – **FOUR PENNIES** (14) 64
I FOUND SOMEONE [A] – **CHER** (5) 87
I FOUND SOMEONE [B] – **Billy and Sarah GAINES** (48) 97
I FOUND SUNSHINE – **CHI-LITES** (35) 74
I (FRIDAY NIGHT) – **DUBSTAR** (37) 00
I GAVE IT UP (WHEN I FELL IN LOVE) – **Luther VANDROSS** (28) 88
I GAVE YOU EVERYTHING – **CODE RED** (50) 96
I GAVE YOU MY HEART (DIDN'T I) – **HOT CHOCOLATE** (13)..................................84
I GET A KICK OUT OF YOU – **Gary SHEARSTON** (7)...................................74
I GET A LITTLE SENTIMENTAL OVER YOU – **NEW SEEKERS** (5) 74
I GET ALONG – **PET SHOP BOYS** (18) 02
I GET AROUND – **BEACH BOYS** (7)................64
I GET LIFTED – **Barbara TUCKER** (33) 94
I GET LONELY – **Janet JACKSON** (5) 98
I GET SO EXCITED – **EQUALS** (44) 68
I GET THE SWEETEST FEELING – **Jackie WILSON** (3) 72,75,87
I GET WEAK – **Belinda CARLISLE** (10) 88
I GIVE – **TAKE 5** (70) 98
I GIVE IT ALL TO YOU – **Mary KIANI** (35)......95
I GIVE YOU MY HEART – **MR PRESIDENT** (52)...................................97
I GO APE – **Neil SEDAKA** (9) 59
I GO TO EXTREMES – **Billy JOEL** (70)............90
I GO TO PIECES (EVERYTIME) – **Gerri GRANGER** (50) 78
I GO TO SLEEP – **PRETENDERS** (7)................81
I GO WILD – **ROLLING STONES** (29) 95
I GOT A FEELING – **Ricky NELSON** (27) 58
I GOT A GIRL – **Lou BEGA** (55) 99
I GOT A LITTLE SONG – **OFF-SHORE** (64)......91
I GOT A MAN – **POSITIVE K** (43) 93
I GOT DA FEELIN' – **SWEET TEE** (31) 88
I GOT 5 ON IT – **LUNIZ** (3) 96,98
I GOT ID – **PEARL JAM** (25) 95
I GOT IT GOIN' ON [A] – **Tone LOC** (55)........89
I GOT IT GOIN' ON [B] – **US3** (52) 94
I GOT MINE – **MOTÖRHEAD** (46) 83
I GOT MY EDUCATION – **UNCANNY ALLIANCE** (39) 92
I GOT RHYTHM – **HAPPENINGS** (28) 67
I GOT SOMEBODY ELSE – **CHANGING FACES** (42) 97
I GOT STUNG – **Elvis PRESLEY** (1) 59
I GOT THE VIBRATION – **BLACK BOX** (21) 96
I GOT THIS FEELING – **BABY BUMPS** (22) 00
I GOT TO SING – **J.A.L.N. BAND** (40) 77
I GOT YOU [A] – **James BROWN** (29) ..66,88,92
I GOT YOU [B] – **SPLIT ENZ** (12)....................80
I GOT YOU BABE [A] – **SONNY and CHER** (1) 65,93
I GOT YOU BABE [A] – **UB40 featuring Chrissie HYNDE** (1) 85
I GOT YOU BABE [A] – **CHER** (35) 94
I GUESS I'LL ALWAYS LOVE YOU – **ISLEY BROTHERS** (11) 66,69
I GUESS THAT'S WHY THEY CALL IT THE BLUES – **Elton JOHN** (5) 83
I HAD TOO MUCH TO DREAM LAST NIGHT – **ELECTRIC PRUNES** (49) 67
I HATE MYSELF FOR LOVING YOU – **Joan JETT and the BLACKHEARTS** (46)........88
I HATE ... PEOPLE – **ANTI-NOWHERE LEAGUE** (46) 82
I HATE ROCK 'N' ROLL – **JESUS AND MARY CHAIN** (61).......................95
I HAVE A DREAM [A] – **ABBA** (2) 79
I HAVE A DREAM [A] – **WESTLIFE** (1) 99
I HAVE NOTHING – **Whitney HOUSTON** (3) ..93
I HAVE PEACE – **STRIKE** (17) 97
I HAVEN'T STOPPED DANCING YET – **PAT and MICK** (9)..89
I HEAR A SYMPHONY – **SUPREMES** (39) 65
I HEAR TALK – **BUCKS FIZZ** (34)....................84
I HEAR YOU KNOCKING – **Dave EDMUNDS** (1) 70
I HEAR YOU NOW – **JON and VANGELIS** (8)..80
I HEAR YOUR NAME – **INCOGNITO** (42) 95
I HEARD A HEART BREAK LAST NIGHT – **Jim REEVES** (38)..67
I HEARD A RUMOUR – **BANANARAMA** (14)...87
I HEARD IT THROUGH THE GRAPEVINE [A] – **Gladys KNIGHT and the PIPS** (47) 67
I HEARD IT THROUGH THE GRAPEVINE [A] – **Marvin GAYE** (1) 69,86
I HEARD IT THROUGH THE GRAPEVINE [A] – **SLITS** (60) 79
I HONESTLY LOVE YOU – **Olivia NEWTON-JOHN** (22)......................74,83
I HOPE YOU DANCE – **Lee Ann WOMACK** (40).................................01
I IMAGINE – **Mary KIANI** (35) 95
I JUST CALLED TO SAY I LOVE YOU – **Stevie WONDER** (1) 84,85
I JUST CAN'T BE HAPPY TODAY – **DAMNED** (46) 79
I JUST CAN'T (FORGIVE AND FORGET) – **BLUE ZOO** (60) 83
I JUST CAN'T HELP BELIEVING – **Elvis PRESLEY** (6)..71
I JUST CAN'T STOP LOVING YOU – **Michael JACKSON** (1) 87
(I JUST) DIED IN YOUR ARMS [A] – **CUTTING CREW** (4)..86
(I JUST) DIED IN YOUR ARMS [A] – **RESOURCE** (42) 03
I JUST DON'T HAVE THE HEART – **Cliff RICHARD** (3) 89

I ONLY WANT TO BE WITH YOU [A] – **TOURISTS** (4) 79
I ONLY WANT TO BE WITH YOU [B] – **Barry WHITE** (36) 95
I OWE YOU NOTHING – **BROS** (1) 88
I OWE YOU ONE – **SHALAMAR** (13) 80
I PRETEND – **Des O'CONNOR** (1) 68
I PROMISE YOU (GET READY) – **Samantha FOX** (58) 87
I PROMISED MYSELF – **Nick KAMEN** (50) 90
I PRONOUNCE YOU – **MADNESS** (44) 88
I PUT A SPELL ON YOU [A] – **Alan PRICE** (9) 66
I PUT A SPELL ON YOU [A] – **Nina SIMONE** (28) 65,69
I PUT A SPELL ON YOU [A] – **Bryan FERRY** (18) 93
I PUT A SPELL ON YOU [A] – **SONIQUE** (8) 98,00
I QUIT [A] – **BROS** (4) 88
I QUIT [B] – **HEPBURN** (8) 99
I RAN – **A FLOCK OF SEAGULLS** (43) 82
I REALLY DIDN'T MEAN IT – **Luther VANDROSS** (16) 87
I RECALL A GYPSY WOMAN – **Don WILLIAMS** (13) 76
I REFUSE – **HUE AND CRY** (47) 88
I REFUSE (WHAT YOU WANT) – **SOMORE featuring DAMON TRUEITT** (21) ..98
I REMEMBER – **COOLIO** (73) 94
I REMEMBER ELVIS PRESLEY (THE KING IS DEAD) – **Danny MIRROR** (4) 77
I REMEMBER YESTERDAY – **Donna SUMMER** (14) 77
I REMEMBER YOU [A] – **Frank IFIELD** (1) 62
I REMEMBER YOU [B] – **SKID ROW** (36) 90
I ROCK – **Tom NOVY** (55) 00
I SAID I LOVE YOU – **Raul MALO** (57) 02
I SAVED THE WORLD TODAY – **EURYTHMICS** (11) 99
I SAW HER AGAIN – **MAMAS and the PAPAS** (11) 66
I SAW HER STANDING THERE [A] – **Elton JOHN BAND featuring John LENNON and the MUSCLE SHOALS HORNS** (40) 81
I SAW HIM STANDING THERE [A]– **TIFFANY** (8) 88
I SAW LINDA YESTERDAY – **Doug SHELDON** (36) 63
I SAW MOMMY KISSING SANTA CLAUS [A] – **BEVERLEY SISTERS** (6) 53
I SAW MOMMY KISSING SANTA CLAUS [A] – **Billy COTTON and his BAND** (11) 53
I SAW MOMMY KISSING SANTA CLAUS [A] – **Jimmy BOYD** (3) 53
I SAW THE LIGHT [A] – **Todd RUNDGREN** (36) 73
I SAW THE LIGHT [B] – **The THE** (31) 95
I SAY A LITTLE PRAYER [A] – **Aretha FRANKLIN** (4) 68
I SAY A LITTLE PRAYER [A] – **Diana KING** (17) 97
I SAY NOTHING – **VOICE OF THE BEEHIVE** (22) 87,88
I SAY YEAH – **SECCHI featuring Orlando JOHNSON** (46) 91
I SCARE MYSELF – **Thomas DOLBY** (46) 84
I SECOND THAT EMOTION [A] – **MIRACLES** (27) 67
I SECOND THAT EMOTION [A] – **Diana ROSS and the SUPREMES and the TEMPTATIONS** (18) 69
I SECOND THAT EMOTION [A] – **JAPAN** (9) 82
I SECOND THAT EMOTION [A] – **Alyson WILLIAMS** (44) 89
I SEE A STAR – **MOUTH and MACNEAL** (8) ..74
I SEE GIRLS (CRAZY) – **STUDIO B / ROMEO and Harry BROOKS** (52) 03
I SEE ONLY YOU – **NOOTROPIC** (42) 96
I SEE THE MOON – **STARGAZERS** (1) 54
I SEE YOU BABY – **GROOVE ARMADA** (17) 99,00
I SEE YOUR SMILE – **Gloria ESTEFAN** (48) 93
I SEEN A MAN DIE – **SCARFACE** (55) 95
I SHALL BE RELEASED – **TREMELOES** (29) ..68
I SHALL BE THERE – **B*WITCHED featuring LADYSMITH BLACK MAMBAZO** (13) 99
I SHOT THE SHERIFF [A] – **Eric CLAPTON** (9) 74,82
I SHOT THE SHERIFF [A] – **LIGHT OF THE WORLD** (40) 81
I SHOT THE SHERIFF [A] – **Warren G** (2) 97
I SHOULD BE SO LUCKY – **Kylie MINOGUE** (1) 88
I SHOULD CARE – **Frank IFIELD** (33) 64
I SHOULD HAVE KNOWN BETTER [A] – **NATURALS** (24) 64
I SHOULD HAVE KNOWN BETTER [B] – **Jim DIAMOND** (1) 84
I SHOULDA LOVED YA – **Narada Michael WALDEN** (8) 80
I SHOULD'VE KNOWN – **Aimee MANN** (45) 93,94
I SINGS – **MARY MARY** (32) 00
I SLEEP ALONE AT NIGHT – **Jim DIAMOND** (72) 85
I SPEAKA DA LINGO – **BLACK LACE** (49) 85
I SPECIALIZE IN LOVE [A] – **Sharon BROWN** (38) 82,94
I SPECIALIZE IN LOVE [A] – **ARIZONA featuring ZEITIA** (74) 94
I SPY FOR THE FBI [A] – **Jamo THOMAS** (44) 69
I SPY FOR THE FBI [A] – **UNTOUCHABLES** (59) 85
I STAND ACCUSED – **MERSEYBEATS** (38) 66
I STAND ALONE – **E-MOTION** (60) 96
I STARTED A JOKE – **FAITH NO MORE** (49) ..98
I STARTED SOMETHING I COULDN'T FINISH – **SMITHS** (23) 87
I STILL BELIEVE [A] – **Ronnie HILTON** (3) 54
I STILL BELIEVE [B] – **Mariah CAREY** (16) 99
I STILL BELIEVE IN YOU – **Cliff RICHARD** (7) 92
I STILL HAVEN'T FOUND WHAT I'M LOOKING FOR [A] – **U2** (6) 87
I STILL HAVEN'T FOUND WHAT I'M LOOKING FOR [A] – **CHIMES** (6) 90
I STILL LOVE YOU ALL – **Kenny BALL and his JAZZMEN** (24) 61
I STILL REMEMBER – **Gary NUMAN** (74) 86
I STILL THINK ABOUT YOU – **DANGER DANGER** (46) 92
I STILL THINK OF YOU – **UTAH SAINTS** (32) 94
I SURRENDER [A] – **RAINBOW** (3) 81
I SURRENDER [B] – **Rosie GAINES** (39) 97
I SURRENDER [C] – **David SYLVIAN** (40) 99
I SURRENDER (TO THE SPIRIT OF THE NIGHT) – **Samantha FOX** (25) 87
I SURRENDER TO YOUR LOVE – **BY ALL MEANS** (65) 88
I SWEAR – **ALL-4-ONE** (2) 94
I TALK TO THE TREES – **Clint EASTWOOD** (18) 70
I TALK TO THE WIND – **OPUS III** (52) 92
I THANK YOU [A] – **SAM and DAVE** (34) 68
I THANK YOU [B] – **ADEVA** (17) 89,96
I THINK I LOVE YOU [A] – **PARTRIDGE FAMILY** (18) 71
I THINK I LOVE YOU [A] – **VOICE OF THE BEEHIVE** (25) 91
I THINK I LOVE YOU [A] – **KACI** (10) 02
I THINK I WANT TO DANCE WITH YOU – **RUMPLE-STILTS-SKIN** (51) 83
I THINK I'M IN LOVE – **SPIRITUALIZED** (27) ..98
I THINK I'M IN LOVE WITH YOU – **Jessica SIMPSON** (15) 00
I THINK I'M PARANOID – **GARBAGE** (9) 98
I THINK IT'S GOING TO RAIN TODAY – **UB40** (6) 80
I THINK OF YOU [A] – **MERSEYBEATS** (5) 64
I THINK OF YOU [B] – **Perry COMO** (14) 71
I THINK OF YOU [C] – **DETROIT EMERALDS** (27) 73
I THINK OF YOU [D] – **Bryan POWELL** (61) 93
I THINK WE'RE ALONE NOW [A] – **TIFFANY** (1) 88
I THINK WE'RE ALONE NOW [A] – **PASCAL featuring Karen PARRY** (1) 88
I THOUGHT I MEANT THE WORLD TO YOU – **Alysha WARREN** (40) 95
I THOUGHT IT TOOK A LITTLE TIME (BUT TODAY I FELL IN LOVE) – **Diana ROSS** (32) 76
I THOUGHT IT WAS YOU [A] – **Herbie HANCOCK** (15) 78
I THOUGHT IT WAS YOU [A] – **SEX-O-SONIQUE** (32) 97
I THOUGHT IT WAS YOU [B] – **Julia FORDHAM** (45) 91,92
I THREW IT ALL AWAY – **Bob DYLAN** (30) 69
I TOLD YOU SO – **Jimmy JONES** (33) 61
I TOUCH MYSELF – **DIVINYLS** (10) 91
I TRY – **Macy GRAY** (6) 99
I TURN TO YOU [A] – **Melanie C** (1) 00
I TURN TO YOU [B] – **Christina AGUILERA** (19) 00
I UNDERSTAND [A] – **G-CLEFS** (17) 61
I UNDERSTAND [A] – **FREDDIE and the DREAMERS** (5) 64
I WALK THE EARTH – **VOICE OF THE BEEHIVE** (42) 88
I WANNA BE A FLINTSTONE – **SCREAMING BLUE MESSIAHS** (28) 88
I WANNA BE A HIPPY – **TECHNOHEAD** (6) 96
I WANNA BE A WINNER – **BROWN SAUCE** (15) 81
I WANNA BE ADORED – **STONE ROSES** (20) 91
I WANNA BE DOWN – **BRANDY** (36) 94,95
I WANNA BE FREE – **MINTY** (67) 99
I WANNA BE FREE (TO BE WITH HIM) – **SCARLET** (21) 95
I WANNA BE IN LOVE AGAIN – **BEIJING SPRING** (43) 93
I WANNA BE LOVED [A] – **Ricky NELSON** (30) 60
I WANNA BE LOVED [B] – **Elvis COSTELLO** (25) 84
I WANNA BE THE ONLY ONE – **ETERNAL** (1) 97
I WANNA BE WITH YOU [A] – **COFFEE** (57) ..80
I WANNA BE WITH YOU [B] – **MAZE featuring Frankie BEVERLY** (55) 86
I WANNA BE WITH YOU [C] – **Mandy MOORE** (21) 00
I WANNA BE U – **CHOCOLATE PUMA** (6) 01
I WANNA BE YOUR LADY – **Hinda HICKS** (14) 98
I WANNA BE YOUR LOVER – **PRINCE** (41) 80
I WANNA BE YOUR MAN [A] – **ROLLING STONES** (12) 63
I WANNA BE YOUR MAN [A] – **REZILLOS** (71) 79
I WANNA BE YOUR MAN [B] – **Chaka DEMUS and PLIERS** (19) 94
I WANNA DANCE WIT' CHOO (DOO DAT DANCE) – PART 1 – **DISCO TEX and the SEX-O-LETTES** (6) 75
I WANNA DANCE WITH SOMEBODY (WHO LOVES ME) [A] – **Whitney HOUSTON** (1) 87
I WANNA DANCE WITH SOMEBODY [A] – **FLIP & FILL** (13) 03
I WANNA DO IT WITH YOU – **Barry MANILOW** (8) 82
I WANNA GET NEXT TO YOU – **ROSE ROYCE** (14) 77
(I WANNA GIVE YOU) DEVOTION – **NOMAD** (2) 91,95
I WANNA GO BACK – **NEW SEEKERS** (25) 77
I WANNA GO HOME – **Lonnie DONEGAN** (5) 60
I WANNA GO WHERE THE PEOPLE GO – **WILDHEARTS** (16) 95
I WANNA HAVE SOME FUN – **Samantha FOX** (63) 89
I WANNA HOLD ON TO YOU – **Mica PARIS** (27) 93
I WANNA HOLD YOUR HAND – **DOLLAR** (9) ..79
I WANNA KNOW [A] – **STACCATO** (65) 96
I WANNA KNOW [B] – **JOE** (37) 01
(I WANNA KNOW) WHY – **SINCLAIR** (58) 94
(I WANNA) LOVE MY LIFE AWAY – **Gene PITNEY** (26) 61
I WANNA LOVE YOU [A] – **JADE** (13) 93
I WANNA LOVE YOU [B] – **SOLID HARMONIE** (20) 98
I WANNA LOVE YOU FOREVER – **Jessica SIMPSON** (7) 00
I WANNA MAKE YOU FEEL GOOD – **SYSTEM** (73) 84
I WANNA 1-2-1 WITH YOU – **SOLID GOLD CHARTBUSTERS** (62) 99
I WANNA SEX YOU UP – **COLOR ME BADD** (1) 91
I WANNA SING – **Sabrina JOHNSTON** (46) 92
I WANNA STAY HOME – **JELLYFISH** (59) 91
I WANNA STAY WITH YOU [A] – **GALLAGHER and LYLE** (6) 76
I WANNA STAY WITH YOU [A] – **UNDERCOVER** (28) 93
I WANT AN ALIEN FOR CHRISTMAS – **FOUNTAINS OF WAYNE** (36) 97
I WANT CANDY [A] – **Brian POOLE and the TREMELOES** (25) 65
I WANT CANDY [A] – **BOW WOW WOW** (9) ..82
I WANT CANDY [A] – **CANDY GIRLS** (30) 96

I'D LIKE TO TEACH THE WORLD TO SING [A] – Demi HOLBORN (27) ... 02
I'D LOVE YOU TO WANT ME – LOBO (5) ... 74
I'D NEVER FIND ANOTHER YOU – Billy FURY (5) ... 61
I'D RATHER GO BLIND [A] – CHICKEN SHACK (14) ... 69
I'D RATHER GO BLIND [A] – Ruby TURNER (24) ... 87
I'D RATHER GO BLIND [A] – Sydney YOUNGBLOOD (44) ... 90
I'D RATHER JACK – REYNOLDS GIRLS (8) ... 89
I'D REALLY LOVE TO SEE YOU TONIGHT – ENGLAND DAN and John Ford COLEY (26) .. 76
THE IDEAL HEIGHT – BIFFY CLYRO (46) ... 03
IDEAL WORLD – CHRISTIANS (14) ... 87
IDENTITY – X-RAY SPEX (24) ... 78
IDIOTS AT THE WHEEL (EP) – KINGMAKER (30) ... 92
IDLE GOSSIP – Perry COMO (3) ... 54
IDLE ON PARADE (EP) – Anthony NEWLEY (13) ... 59
IDOL – Amanda GHOST (63) ... 00
THE IDOL [A] – W.A.S.P. (41) ... 92
THE IDOL [B] – Marc ALMOND (44) ... 95
IEYA – TOYAH (48) ... 82
IF [A] – Telly SAVALAS (1) ... 75
IF [A] – Dolly PARTON (73) ... 02
IF [A] – YIN and YAN (25) ... 75
IF [A] – John ALFORD (24) ... 96
IF [B] – Janet JACKSON (14) ... 93
IF... [C] – BLUETONES (13) ... 98
IF – READ TO FAURÉ'S 'PAVANE' [D] – WIMBLEDON CHORAL SOCIETY (45) ... 98
IF A MAN ANSWERS – Bobby DARIN (24) ... 62
IF ANYONE FINDS THIS, I LOVE YOU – Ruby MURRAY (4) ... 55
IF DREAMS CAME TRUE – Pat BOONE (16) .. 58
IF EVER – 3RD STOREE (53) ... 99
IF EVERY DAY WAS LIKE CHRISTMAS – Elvis PRESLEY (9) ... 66
IF EVERYBODY LOOKED THE SAME – GROOVE ARMADA (25) ... 99
IF EYE LOVE U 2 NIGHT – MAYTE (67) ... 95
IF GOD WILL SEND HIS ANGELS – U2 (12) ... 97
IF HE TELLS YOU – Adam FAITH (25) ... 64
IF I CAN DREAM – Elvis PRESLEY (11) ... 69,87
IF I CAN DREAM (EP) – Michael BALL (51) ... 92
IF I CAN'T CHANGE YOUR MIND – SUGAR (30) ... 93
IF I CAN'T HAVE YOU [A] – Yvonne ELLIMAN (4) ... 78
IF I CAN'T HAVE YOU [A] – Kim WILDE (12) .. 93
IF I COULD [A] – David ESSEX (13) ... 75
IF I COULD [B] – HUNDRED REASONS (19) .. 02
IF I COULD BUILD MY WHOLE WORLD AROUND YOU – Marvin GAYE (41) ... 68
IF I COULD (EL CONDOR PASA) – Julie FELIX (19) ... 70
IF I COULD FLY – GRACE (29) ... 96
IF I COULD GIVE ALL MY LOVE – COUNTING CROWS (50) ... 03
IF I COULD GO! – Angie MARTINEZ featuring LIL' MO & SACARIO (61) ... 03
IF I COULD ONLY MAKE YOU CARE – Mike BERRY (37) ... 80
IF I COULD ONLY SAY GOODBYE – David HASSELHOFF (35) ... 93
IF I COULD TALK I'D TELL YOU – LEMONHEADS (39) ... 96
IF I COULD TURN BACK THE HANDS OF TIME – R KELLY (2) ... 99
IF I COULD TURN BACK TIME – CHER (6) ... 89
IF I DIDN'T CARE – David CASSIDY (9) ... 74
IF I EVER FALL IN LOVE – SHAI (36) ... 92
IF I EVER LOSE MY FAITH IN YOU – STING (14) ... 93
IF I FALL – Alice MARTINEAU (45) ... 02
IF I GIVE MY HEART TO YOU [A] – Doris DAY (4) ... 54
IF I GIVE MY HEART TO YOU [A] – Joan REGAN (3) ... 54
IF I GIVE YOU MY NUMBER – ANT & DEC (15) ... 94
IF I HAD A HAMMER – Trini LOPEZ (4) ... 63
IF I HAD NO LOOT – TONY TONI TONÉ (44) 93
IF I HAD WORDS – Scott FITZGERALD (3) ... 78
IF I HAD YOU – KORGIS (13) ... 79
IF I HAVE TO GO AWAY – JIGSAW (36) ... 77
IF I HAVE TO STAND ALONE – Lonnie GORDON (68) ... 90
IF I KNEW THEN WHAT I KNOW NOW – Val DOONICAN (14) ... 68
IF I LET YOU GO – WESTLIFE (1) ... 99
IF I LOVE U 2 NITE – Mica PARIS (43) ... 91
IF I LOVE YA THEN I NEED YA IF I NEED YA THEN I WANT YOU AROUND – Eartha KITT (43) ... 94
IF I LOVED YOU – Richard ANTHONY (18) ... 64
IF I NEEDED SOMEONE – HOLLIES (20) ... 65
IF I NEVER FEEL BETTER – PHOENIX (65) ... 01
IF I NEVER KNEW YOU (LOVE THEME FROM 'POCAHONTAS') – Jon SECADA and SHANICE (51) ... 95
IF I NEVER SEE YOU AGAIN – WET WET WET (3) ... 97
IF I ONLY HAD TIME – John ROWLES (3) ... 68
IF I ONLY KNEW – Tom JONES (11) ... 94
IF I REMEMBER – BENZ (59) ... 97
IF I RULED THE WORLD [A] – Harry SECOMBE (18) ... 63
IF I RULED THE WORLD [A] – Tony BENNETT (40) ... 65
IF I RULED THE WORLD [B] – Kurtis BLOW (24) ... 86
IF I RULED THE WORLD [B] – NAS (12) ... 96
IF I SAID YOU HAVE A BEAUTIFUL BODY WOULD YOU HOLD IT AGAINST ME – BELLAMY BROTHERS (3) ... 79
IF I SAY YES – FIVE STAR (15) ... 86
IF I SHOULD FALL FROM GRACE WITH GOD – POGUES (58) ... 88
IF I SHOULD LOVE AGAIN – Barry MANILOW (66) ... 82
IF I SURVIVE – HYBRID featuring Julee CRUISE (52) ... 99
IF I THOUGHT YOU'D EVER CHANGE YOUR MIND – Cilla BLACK (20) ... 69
IF I TOLD YOU THAT – Whitney HOUSTON / George MICHAEL (9) .. 00
IF I WAS [A] – Midge URE (1) ... 85
IF I WAS [B] – ASWAD (58) ... 95
IF I WAS A RIVER – Tina ARENA (43) ... 98
IF I WAS YOUR GIRLFRIEND – PRINCE (20) .. 87
IF I WERE A CARPENTER [A] – Bobby DARIN (9) ... 66
IF I WERE A CARPENTER [A] – FOUR TOPS (7) ... 68
IF I WERE A CARPENTER [A] – Robert PLANT (63) ... 93
IF I WERE A RICH MAN – TOPOL (9) ... 67
IF I WERE YOU – kd lang (53) ... 95
IF I'M NOT YOUR LOVER – Al B SURE! (54) .. 89
IF IT DON'T FIT DON'T FORCE IT – Kellee PATTERSON (44) ... 78
IF IT HAPPENS AGAIN – UB40 (9) ... 84
IF IT MAKES YOU HAPPY – Sheryl CROW (9) 96
IF IT WASN'T FOR THE REASON THAT I LOVE YOU – Miki ANTHONY (27) ... 73
IF IT'S ALRIGHT WITH YOU BABY – KORGIS (56) ... 80
IF IT'S LOVE THAT YOU WANT – Donny OSMOND (70) ... 88
IF LEAVING ME IS EASY – Phil COLLINS (17) 81
IF LIFE IS LIKE A LOVE BANK I WANT AN OVERDRAFT – WILDHEARTS (31) ... 95
IF LOOKS COULD KILL – TRANSVISION VAMP (41) ... 91
IF LOVE WAS A TRAIN – Michelle SHOCKED (63) ... 89
IF LOVE WAS LIKE GUITARS – Ian McNABB (67) ... 93
IF LOVING YOU IS WRONG (I DON'T WANT TO BE RIGHT) – Rod STEWART (23) ... 80
IF MADONNA CALLS – Junior VASQUEZ (24) 96
IF MY FRIENDS COULD SEE ME NOW – Linda CLIFFORD (50) ... 78
IF NOT FOR YOU – Olivia NEWTON-JOHN (7) 71
IF NOT YOU – DR HOOK (5) ... 76
IF ONLY – HANSON (15) ... 00
IF ONLY I COULD – Sydney YOUNGBLOOD (3) ... 89
IF ONLY I COULD LIVE MY LIFE AGAIN – Jane MORGAN (27) ... 59
IF ONLY TOMORROW – Ronnie CARROLL (33) ... 62
(IF PARADISE IS) HALF AS NICE – AMEN CORNER (1) ... 69,76
IF SHE KNEW WHAT SHE WANTS – BANGLES (31) ... 86
IF SHE SHOULD COME TO YOU – Anthony NEWLEY (4) ... 60
IF 60S WERE 90S – BEAUTIFUL PEOPLE (74) ... 94
IF THAT WERE ME – Melanie C (18) ... 00,01
IF THAT'S YOUR BOYFRIEND (HE WASN'T LAST NIGHT) – Me'Shell NDEGEOCELLO (74) ... 94
IF THE KIDS ARE UNITED – SHAM 69 (9) ... 78
IF THE RIVER CAN BEND – Elton JOHN (32) 98
IF THE WHOLE WORLD STOPPED LOVING – Val DOONICAN (3) ... 67
IF THERE WAS A MAN – PRETENDERS (49) .. 87
IF THIS IS IT – Huey LEWIS and the NEWS (39) ... 84
IF THIS IS LOVE [A] – JJ (55) ... 91
IF THIS IS LOVE [B] – Jeanie TRACY (73) ... 94
IF TOMORROW NEVER COMES – Ronan KEATING (1) ... 02
IF U WANT ME – Michael WOODS featuring Imogen BAILEY (46) ... 03
IF WE FALL IN LOVE TONIGHT – Rod STEWART (58) ... 96
IF WE HOLD ON TOGETHER – Diana ROSS (11) ... 92
IF WE TRY – Karen RAMIREZ (23) ... 98
IF WE WERE LOVERS – Gloria ESTEFAN (40) ... 93
IF YA GETTIN' DOWN – FIVE (2) ... 99
IF YOU ASKED ME TO – Celine DION (57) ... 92
IF YOU BELIEVE – Johnnie RAY (7) ... 55
IF YOU BUY THIS RECORD YOUR LIFE WILL BE BETTER – TAMPERER featuring MAYA (3) ... 98
IF YOU C JORDAN – SOMETHING CORPORATE (68) ... 03
IF YOU CAN WANT – Smokey ROBINSON and the MIRACLES (50) ... 68
IF YOU CAN'T DO IT WHEN YOU'RE YOUNG, WHEN CAN YOU DO IT? – THEAUDIENCE (48) ... 98
IF YOU CAN'T GIVE ME LOVE – Suzi QUATRO (4) ... 78
IF YOU CAN'T SAY NO – Lenny KRAVITZ (48) ... 98
IF YOU CAN'T STAND THE HEAT – BUCKS FIZZ (10) ... 82
IF YOU CARED – Kim APPLEBY (44) ... 91
IF YOU COME BACK – BLUE (1) ... 01
IF YOU COME TO ME – ATOMIC KITTEN (3) .. 03
IF YOU COULD READ MY MIND [A] – Gordon LIGHTFOOT (30) ... 71
IF YOU COULD READ MY MIND [A] – STARS ON 54 (23) ... 98
IF YOU COULD SEE ME NOW – SHAKATAK (49) ... 83
IF YOU DON'T KNOW ME BY NOW [A] – Harold MELVIN and the BLUENOTES (9) ... 73
IF YOU DON'T KNOW ME BY NOW [A] – SIMPLY RED (2) ... 89
IF YOU DON'T LOVE ME – PREFAB SPROUT (33) ... 92
IF YOU DON'T WANT ME TO DESTROY YOU – SUPER FURRY ANIMALS (18) ... 96
IF YOU DON'T WANT MY LOVE – Robert JOHN (42) ... 68
IF YOU EVER – EAST 17 featuring GABRIELLE (2) ... 96
IF YOU EVER LEAVE ME – Barbra STREISAND (26) ... 99
IF YOU FEEL IT – Thelma HOUSTON (48) ... 81
IF YOU GO – Jon SECADA (39) ... 94
IF YOU GO AWAY [A] – Terry JACKS (8) ... 74
IF YOU GO AWAY [B] – NEW KIDS ON THE BLOCK (9) ... 91
IF YOU GOTTA GO GO NOW – MANFRED MANN (2) ... 65
IF YOU GOTTA MAKE A FOOL OF SOMEBODY – FREDDIE and the DREAMERS (3) ... 63
IF YOU HAD MY LOVE – Jennifer LOPEZ (4) ... 99
IF YOU HAVE TO GO – GENEVA (69) ... 00
IF YOU KNEW SOUSA (AND FRIENDS) – ROYAL PHILHARMONIC ORCHESTRA arranged and conducted by Louis CLARK (71) ... 82
IF YOU KNOW WHAT I MEAN – Neil DIAMOND (35) ... 76
IF YOU LEAVE – ORCHESTRAL MANOEUVRES IN THE DARK (48) ... 86
IF YOU LEAVE ME NOW [A] – CHICAGO (1) ... 76
IF YOU LEAVE ME NOW [A] – UPSIDE DOWN (27) ... 96

I'M A MIDNIGHT MOVER — Wilson PICKETT (38) ... 68
I'M A MOODY GUY — Shane FENTON and the FENTONES (22) ... 61
I'M A SLAVE 4 U — Britney SPEARS (4) ... 01
I'M A SUCKER FOR YOUR LOVE — Teena MARIE, co-lead vocals Rick JAMES (43) ... 79
I'M A TIGER — LULU (9) ... 68
I'M A WONDERFUL THING, BABY — Kid CREOLE and the COCONUTS (4) ... 82,93
I'M ALIVE [A] — HOLLIES (1) ... 65
I'M ALIVE [B] — ELECTRIC LIGHT ORCHESTRA (20) ... 80
I'M ALIVE [C] — CUT 'N' MOVE (49) ... 95
I'M ALIVE [D] — SEAL (4) ... 95
I'M ALIVE [E] — STRETCH 'N' VERN present MADDOG (6) ... 96
I'M ALIVE [F] — Celine DION (17) ... 02
I'M ALL ABOUT YOU — DJ LUCK & MC NEAT featuirng Ari GOLD (18) ... 01
I'M ALL YOU NEED — Samantha FOX (41) ... 86
I'M ALRIGHT [A] — Steve WRIGHT (40) ... 82
I'M ALRIGHT [B] — Katherine E (41) ... 91
(I'M ALWAYS HEARING) WEDDING BELLS — Eddie FISHER (5) ... 55
(I'M ALWAYS TOUCHED BY YOUR) PRESENCE DEAR — BLONDIE (10) ... 78
I'M AN UPSTART — ANGELIC UPSTARTS (31) 79
I'M BACK FOR MORE — LULU and Bobby WOMACK (27) ... 93
I'M BAD — LL COOL J (71) ... 87
I'M BORN AGAIN — BONEY M (35) ... 79
I'M BROKEN — PANTERA (19) ... 94
I'M CHILLIN' — Kurtis BLOW (64) ... 86
I'M COMIN' HARDCORE — M.A.N.I.C. (60) ... 92
I'M COMING HOME — Tom JONES (2) ... 67
I'M COMING HOME CINDY — Trini LOPEZ (28) ... 66
I'M COMING OUT — Diana ROSS (13) ... 80,94
I'M COMING WITH YA — Matt GOSS (22) ... 03
I'M COUNTING ON YOU — Petula CLARK (41) 62
I'M CRYING — ANIMALS (8) ... 64
I'M DOIN' FINE — DAY ONE (68) ... 99
I'M DOING FINE — Jason DONOVAN (22) ... 90
I'M DOIN' FINE NOW [A] — NEW YORK CITY (20) ... 73
I'M DOING FINE NOW [A] — PASADENAS (4) 92
I'M EASY — FAITH NO MORE (3) ... 93
I'M EVERY WOMAN [A] — Chaka KHAN (8) ... 78,89
I'M EVERY WOMAN [A] — Whitney HOUSTON (4) ... 93
I'M FALLING — BLUEBELLS (11) ... 84
I'M FOR REAL — NIGHTMARES ON WAX (38) 90
I'M FOREVER BLOWING BUBBLES [A] — WEST HAM UNITED CUP SQUAD (31) ... 75
I'M FOREVER BLOWING BUBBLES [A] — COCKNEY REJECTS (35) ... 80
I'M FREE [A] — Roger DALTREY (13) ... 73
I'M FREE [B] — SOUP DRAGONS (5) ... 90
I'M FREE [C] — Jon SECADA (50) ... 93
I'M GLAD — Jennifer LOPEZ (11) ... 03
I'M GOIN' DOWN — Mary J BLIGE (12) ... 95
I'M GOING ALL THE WAY — SOUNDS OF BLACKNESS (14) ... 93,95
I'M GOING HOME — Gene VINCENT (36) ... 61
I'M GOING SLIGHTLY MAD — QUEEN (22) ... 91
I'M GONE — Diana ROSS (36) ... 95
I'M GONNA BE A COUNTRY GIRL AGAIN — Buffy SAINTE-MARIE (34) ... 72
I'M GONNA BE ALRIGHT — Jennifer LOPEZ (3) ... 02
I'M GONNA BE (500 MILES) — PROCLAIMERS (11) ... 88
I'M GONNA BE STRONG [A] — Gene PITNEY (2) ... 64
I'M GONNA BE STRONG [A] — Cyndi LAUPER (37) ... 95
I'M GONNA BE WARM THIS WINTER — Connie FRANCIS (48) ... 62
I'M GONNA CHANGE EVERYTHING — Jim REEVES (42) ... 62
(I'M GONNA) CRY MYSELF BLIND — PRIMAL SCREAM (49) ... 94
I'M GONNA GET MARRIED — Lloyd PRICE (23) ... 59
I'M GONNA GET ME A GUN — Cat STEVENS (6) ... 67
I'M GONNA GET THERE SOMEHOW — Val DOONICAN (25) ... 65
I'M GONNA GET YA BABY — BLACK CONNECTION (62) ... 98
I'M GONNA GET YOU — BIZARRE INC (3) ... 92,93
I'M GONNA GETCHA GOOD! — Shania TWAIN (4) ... 02
I'M GONNA GIT YOU SUCKA — GAP BAND (63) ... 89
I'M GONNA KNOCK ON YOUR DOOR [A] — Eddie HODGES (37) ... 61
I'M GONNA KNOCK ON YOUR DOOR [A] — Little Jimmy OSMOND (11) ... 74
I'M GONNA LOVE HER FOR BOTH OF US — MEAT LOAF (62) ... 81
I'M GONNA LOVE YOU FOREVER — CROWN HEIGHTS AFFAIR (47) ... 78
I'M GONNA LOVE YOU A LITTLE BIT MORE BABY — Barry WHITE (23) ... 73
I'M GONNA MAKE YOU LOVE ME — Diana ROSS and the SUPREMES and the TEMPTATIONS (3) ... 69
I'M GONNA MAKE YOU MINE [A] — Lou CHRISTIE (2) ... 69
I'M GONNA MAKE YOU MINE [B] — Tanya BLOUNT (69) ... 94
I'M GONNA MISS YOU FOREVER — Aaron CARTER (24) ... 98
I'M GONNA RUN AWAY FROM YOU — Tami LYNN (4) ... 71,75
I'M GONNA SIT RIGHT DOWN AND WRITE MYSELF A LETTER [A] — Billy WILLIAMS (22) ... 57
I'M GONNA SIT RIGHT DOWN AND WRITE MYSELF A LETTER [A] — Barry MANILOW (36) ... 82
I'M GONNA SOOTHE YOU — Maria McKEE (35) ... 93
I'M GONNA TEAR YOUR PLAYHOUSE DOWN — Paul YOUNG (9) ... 84
I'M IN A DIFFERENT WORLD — FOUR TOPS (27) ... 68
I'M IN A PHILLY MOOD — Daryl HALL (52) ... 93,94
I'M IN FAVOUR OF FRIENDSHIP — FIVE SMITH BROTHERS (20) ... 55
I'M IN HEAVEN — Jason NEVINS presents UKNY / Holly JAMES (9) ... 03
I'M IN IT FOR LOVE — Donny OSMOND (70) 87
I'M IN LOVE [A] — FOURMOST (17) ... 63
I'M IN LOVE [B] — Evelyn 'Champagne' KING (27) ... 81
I'M IN LOVE [C] — Ruby TURNER (57) ... 86,87
I'M IN LOVE [D] — Lillo THOMAS (54) ... 87
I'M IN LOVE [E] — STARPARTY (26) ... 00
I'M IN LOVE AGAIN [A] — Fats DOMINO (12) 56
I'M IN LOVE AGAIN [B] — SAD CAFE (40) ... 80
I'M IN LOVE (AND I LOVE THE FEELING) — ROSE ROYCE (51) ... 79
I'M IN LOVE WITH A GERMAN FILM STAR — PASSIONS (25) ... 81
I'M IN LOVE WITH THE GIRL ON A CERTAIN MANCHESTER MEGASTORE CHECKOUT DESK — FRESHIES (54) ... 81
I'M IN LUV — JOE (22) ... 94
I'M IN THE MOOD — Ce Ce PENISTON (16) ... 94
I'M IN THE MOOD FOR DANCING — NOLANS (3) ... 79,95
I'M IN THE MOOD FOR LOVE [A] — LORD TANAMO (58) ... 90
I'M IN THE MOOD FOR LOVE [A] — Jools HOLLAND and JAMIROQUAI (29) ... 01
I'M IN YOU — Peter FRAMPTON (41) ... 77
I'M INTO SOMETHING GOOD — HERMAN'S HERMITS (1) ... 64
I'M JUST A BABY — Louise CORDET (13) ... 62
I'M JUST A SINGER (IN A ROCK & ROLL BAND) — MOODY BLUES (36) ... 73
I'M JUST YOUR PUPPET ON A ... (STRING) — LONDONBEAT (55) ... 95
I'M LEAVIN' — Elvis PRESLEY (23) ... 71
I'M LEAVIN' — OUTSIDAZ featuring Rah DIGGA & Melanie BLATT (41) ... 02
I'M LEAVING — LODGER (40) ... 98
I'M LEAVING IT UP TO YOU [A] — DALE and GRACE (42) ... 64
I'M LEAVING IT (ALL) UP TO YOU [A] — Donny and Marie OSMOND (2) ... 74
I'M LEFT, YOU'RE RIGHT, SHE'S GONE — Elvis PRESLEY (21) ... 58
I'M LIKE A BIRD — Nelly FURTADO (5) ... 01
I'M LIVING IN SHAME — Diana ROSS and the SUPREMES (14) ... 69
I'M LONELY — Hollis P MONROE (51) ... 99
I'M LOOKING FOR THE ONE (TO BE WITH ME) — JAZZY JEFF & the FRESH PRINCE (24) ... 93
I'M LOOKING OUT THE WINDOW — Cliff RICHARD (2) ... 62
I'M LOST WITHOUT YOU — Billy FURY (16) ... 65
I'M LUCKY — Joan ARMATRADING (46) ... 81
I'M MANDY FLY ME — 10cc (6) ... 76
I'M NEVER GIVING UP — SWEET DREAMS (21) ... 83
IM NIN'ALU — Ofra HAZA (15) ... 88
I'M NO ANGEL — Marcella DETROIT (33) ... 94
I'M NO REBEL — VIEW FROM THE HILL (59) ... 87
I'M NOT A FOOL — COCKNEY REJECTS (65) ... 79
I'M NOT A JUVENILE DELINQUENT — Frankie LYMON and the TEENAGERS (12) ... 57
I'M NOT ANYBODY'S GIRL — KACI (55) ... 03
I'M NOT ASHAMED — BIG COUNTRY (69) ... 95
I'M NOT FEELING YOU — Yvette MICHELLE (36) ... 97
I'M NOT GIVING YOU UP — Gloria ESTEFAN (28) ... 96
I'M NOT GONNA LET YOU (GET THE BEST OF ME) — Colonel ABRAMS (24) ... 86
I'M NOT IN LOVE [A] — 10cc (1) ... 75,95
I'M NOT IN LOVE [A] — Johnny LOGAN (51) ... 87
I'M NOT IN LOVE [A] — WILL TO POWER (29) ... 90
I'M NOT IN LOVE [A] — FUN LOVIN' CRIMINALS (12) ... 97
I'M NOT PERFECT (BUT I'M PERFECT FOR YOU) — Grace JONES (56) ... 86
I'M NOT READY — Keith SWEAT (53) ... 99
I'M NOT SATISFIED — FINE YOUNG CANNIBALS (46) ... 90
I'M NOT SCARED — EIGHTH WONDER (7) ... 88
I'M NOT THE MAN I USED TO BE — FINE YOUNG CANNIBALS (20) ... 89
I'M NOT TO BLAME — ALIBI (51) ... 97
I'M NOT A GIRL, NOT YET A WOMAN — Britney SPEARS (2) ... 02
(I'M NOT YOUR) STEPPING STONE — SEX PISTOLS (21) ... 80
I'M ON AUTOMATIC — Gary NUMAN (44) ... 89
I'M ON FIRE [A] — 5000 VOLTS (4) ... 75
I'M ON FIRE [B] — Bruce SPRINGSTEEN (5) ... 85
I'M ON MY WAY [A] — Dean PARRISH (38) ... 75
I'M ON MY WAY [B] — PROCLAIMERS (43) ... 89
I'M ON MY WAY [C] — Betty BOO (44) ... 92
I'M ON MY WAY TO A BETTER PLACE — CHAIRMEN OF THE BOARD (30) ... 72,73
I'M ONLY SLEEPING — SUGGS (7) ... 95
I'M OUT OF YOUR LIFE — ARNIE'S LOVE (67) ... 83
I'M OUTSTANDING — Shaquille O'NEAL (70) 94
I'M OUTTA LOVE — ANASTACIA (6) ... 00
I'M OVER YOU — Martine McCUTCHEON (2) ... 00
I'M QUALIFIED TO SATISFY YOU — Barry WHITE (37) ... 77
I'M RAVING — SCOOTER (33) ... 96
I'M READY [A] — CAVEMAN (65) ... 91
I'M READY [B] — SIZE 9 (30) ... 95
I'M READY [C] — Bryan ADAMS (20) ... 98
I'M READY FOR LOVE — Martha REEVES and the VANDELLAS (29) ... 66
I'M REAL [A] — James BROWN featuring FULL FORCE (31) ... 88
I'M REAL [B] — Jennifer LOPEZ featuring JA RULE (4) ... 01
I'M RIFFIN (ENGLISH RASTA) — MC DUKE (75) ... 89
I'M RIGHT HERE — Samantha MUMBA (5) ... 02
I'M RUSHING — BUMP (40) ... 92,95
I'M SHY MARY ELLEN I'M SHY — Bob WALLIS and his STORYVILLE JAZZ BAND (44) ... 61
I'M SICK OF YOU — GOODBYE MR MACKENZIE (49) ... 89
I'M SO BEAUTIFUL — DIVINE (52) ... 84
I'M SO CRAZY ('BOUT YOU) — KC and the SUNSHINE BAND (34) ... 75
I'M SO CRAZY — PAR-T-ONE vs INXS (19) ... 01
I'M SO EXCITED — POINTER SISTERS (11) ... 84
I'M SO GLAD I'M STANDING HERE TODAY — CRUSADERS, featured vocalist Joe COCKER (61) ... 81
I'M SO HAPPY [A] — LIGHT OF THE WORLD (35) ... 81
I'M SO HAPPY [B] — JULIA and COMPANY (56) ... 85
I'M SO HAPPY [C] — Walter BEASLEY (70) ... 88

IT'S ALRIGHT [D] – Bryan POWELL (73)........93
IT'S ALRIGHT [E] – Deni HINES (35).............97
IT'S ALRIGHT [F] – ECHO and the BUNNYMEN (41) 01
IT'S ALRIGHT (BABY'S COMING BACK) – EURYTHMICS (12) 86
IT'S ALRIGHT, I FEEL IT! – NUYORICAN SOUL featuring Jocelyn BROWN (26) 97
IT'S ALRIGHT NOW – BELOVED (48) 90
IT'S AN OPEN SECRET – JOY STRINGS (32)..64
IT'S BEEN AWHILE – STAIND (15)..................01
IT'S BEEN NICE – EVERLY BROTHERS (26) ..63
IT'S BEEN SO LONG – George McCRAE (4) ..75
IT'S BETTER TO HAVE (AND DON'T NEED) – Don COVAY (29)..74
IT'S CALLED A HEART – DEPECHE MODE (18) 85
IT'S DIFFERENT FOR GIRLS – Joe JACKSON (5)..80
IT'S ECSTASY WHEN YOU LAY DOWN NEXT TO ME – Barry WHITE (40) 77
IT'S FOR YOU – Cilla BLACK (7)....................64
IT'S FOUR IN THE MORNING – Faron YOUNG (3) 72
IT'S GETTING BETTER – MAMA CASS (8)......69
IT'S GOIN DOWN – X-ECUTIONERS featuring Mike SHINODA & Mr HAHN of LINKIN PARK (7)..02
IT'S GOING TO HAPPEN! – UNDERTONES (18) 81
IT'S GONNA BE A COLD COLD CHRISTMAS – DANA (4) 75
IT'S GONNA BE A LOVELY DAY – S.O.U.L. S.Y.S.T.E.M. introducing Michelle VISAGE (17) 93
IT'S GONNA BE ... (A LOVELY DAY) – BRANCACCIO & AISHER (40) 02
IT'S GONNA BE ALL RIGHT – GERRY and the PACEMAKERS (24) 64
IT'S GONNA BE ALRIGHT [A] – Ruby TURNER (57)......................................90
IT'S GONNA BE ALRIGHT [B] – PUSSY 2000 (70) 01
IT'S GONNA BE ME – 'N SYNC (9) 00
IT'S GONNA BE MY WAY – PRECIOUS (27) ..00
IT'S GOOD NEWS WEEK – HEDGEHOPPERS ANONYMOUS (5)..............65
IT'S GREAT WHEN WE'RE TOGETHER – Finley QUAYE (29) 97
IT'S GRIM UP NORTH – JUSTIFIED ANCIENTS OF MU MU (10) 91,92
IT'S GROWING – TEMPTATIONS (45) 65
IT'S HAPPENIN' – PLUS ONE featuring SIRRON (40) 90
IT'S HARD SOMETIMES – Frankie KNUCKLES (67) 91
IT'S HARD TO BE HUMBLE – Mac DAVIS (27) 80
IT'S HERE – Kim WILDE (42) 90
IT'S IMPOSSIBLE – Perry COMO (4) 71
IT'S IN EVERY ONE OF US – Cliff RICHARD (45) 85
IT'S IN HIS KISS [A] – Betty EVERETT (34) ..68
IT'S IN HIS KISS [A] – Linda LEWIS (6) 75
IT'S IN OUR HANDS – BJÖRK (37) 02
IT'S IN YOUR EYES – Phil COLLINS (30) 96
IT'S... IT'S... THE SWEET MIX – SWEET (45) 85
IT'S JURASSIC – SOUL CITY ORCHESTRA (70) 93
IT'S JUST A FEELING – TERRORIZE (47)........92
IT'S JUST PORN MUM – TRUCKS (35) 02
(IT'S JUST) THE WAY THAT YOU LOVE ME – Paula ABDUL (74) 89
IT'S LATE [A] – Ricky NELSON (3) 59
IT'S LATE [A] – Shakin' STEVENS (11) 83
(IT'S LIKE A) SAD OLD KINDA MOVIE – PICKETTYWITCH (16) 70
IT'S LIKE THAT – RUN-DMC vs Jason NEVINS (1) 98
IT'S LIKE THAT Y'ALL – SWEET TEE (31) 88
IT'S LOVE – Ken DODD (36) 66
IT'S LOVE THAT REALLY COUNTS – MERSEYBEATS (24) 63
IT'S LOVE (TRIPPIN') – GOLDTRIX presents Andrea BROWN (6) 02
IT'S LULU – BOO RADLEYS (25)....................95
IT'S ME – Alice COOPER (34)........................94
IT'S MY HOUSE [A] – Diana ROSS (32) 79
IT'S MY HOUSE [A] – STORM (36) 79
IT'S MY LIFE [A] – ANIMALS (7)....................65
IT'S MY LIFE [B] – TALK TALK (13) 84,90
IT'S MY LIFE [B] – LIQUID PEOPLE vs TALK TALK (64) 03
IT'S MY LIFE [B] – NO DOUBT (20) 03
IT'S MY LIFE [C] – DR ALBAN (2) 92
IT'S MY LIFE [D] – BON JOVI (3) 00
IT'S MY PARTY [A] – Lesley GORE (9) 63
IT'S MY PARTY [A] – Dave STEWART (1) 81
IT'S MY PARTY [B] – Chaka KHAN (71) 89
IT'S MY TIME – EVERLY BROTHERS (39)......68
IT'S MY TURN [A] – Diana ROSS (16)...........81
IT'S MY TURN [B] – ANGELIC (11)..................00
IT'S NATURE'S WAY (NO PROBLEM) – DOLLAR (58) 88
IT'S NEVER TOO LATE – Diana ROSS (41) 82
IT'S NICE TO GO TRAV'LING – Frank SINATRA (48) 60
IT'S NO GOOD – DEPECHE MODE (5) 97
IT'S NOT A LOVE THING – Geoffrey WILLIAMS (63)................................92
IT'S NOT RIGHT BUT (IT'S OK) – Whitney HOUSTON (3)................................99
IT'S NOT THE END OF THE WORLD? – SUPER FURRY ANIMALS (30) 02
IT'S NOT UNUSUAL – Tom JONES (1) 65,87
IT'S NOW OR NEVER – Elvis PRESLEY (1) 60,77
IT'S OH SO QUIET – BJÖRK (4) 95
IT'S OK [A] – DELIRIOUS? (18) 00
IT'S OK [B] – ATOMIC KITTEN (3) 02
IT'S OKAY – DES'REE (67) 03
IT'S ON [A] – FLOWERED UP (38) 90,91
IT'S ON [B] – NAUGHTY BY NATURE (48) 93
IT'S ON YOU (SCAN ME) – EUROGROOVE (25).......................................95
IT'S ONE OF THOSE NIGHTS (YES LOVE) – PARTRIDGE FAMILY (11) 72
IT'S ONLY LOVE [A] – Tony BLACKBURN (42)................................69
IT'S ONLY LOVE [A] – Elvis PRESLEY (3) 80
IT'S ONLY LOVE [B] – Gary 'US' BONDS (43) 81
IT'S ONLY LOVE [C] – Bryan ADAMS (29) 85
IT'S ONLY LOVE [C] – Tina TURNER (29) 85
IT'S ONLY LOVE [D] – SIMPLY RED (13)........89
IT'S ONLY MAKE BELIEVE [A] – Billy FURY (10) 64
IT'S ONLY MAKE BELIEVE [A] – CHILD (10) ..78
IT'S ONLY MAKE BELIEVE [A] – Conway TWITTY (1) 58
IT'S ONLY MAKE BELIEVE [A] – Glen CAMPBELL (4) 70
IT'S ONLY NATURAL – CROWDED HOUSE (24) 92
IT'S ONLY ROCK AND ROLL [A] – ROLLING STONES (10) 74
IT'S ONLY ROCK 'N' ROLL [A] – VARIOUS ARTISTS (EPs and LPs) (19) ..99,00
IT'S ONLY US – Robbie WILLIAMS (1)......99,00
IT'S 'ORRIBLE BEING IN LOVE (WHEN YOU'RE 8 1/2) – CLAIRE and FRIENDS (13) 86
IT'S OVER [A] – Roy ORBISON (1) 64
IT'S OVER [B] – FUNK MASTER (8) 83
IT'S OVER [C] – LEVEL 42 (10) 87
IT'S OVER [B] – CLOCK (10) 97
IT'S OVER [D] – RIMES featuring Shaila PROSPERE (51)......99
IT'S OVER [E] – KURUPT (21) 01
IT'S OVER (DISTORTION) – PIANOHEADZ (39) 98
IT'S OVER LOVE – Todd TERRY PROJECT presents SHANNON (16) 97
IT'S OVER NOW [A] – Ultra NATÉ (62) 89
IT'S OVER NOW [B] – Deborah COX (49) 99
IT'S OVER NOW [C] – 112 (22) 01
IT'S PARTY TIME AGAIN – George VAN DUSEN (43) 88
IT'S PROBABLY ME – STING with Eric CLAPTON (30)......................92
IT'S RAINING [A] – DARTS (2) 78
IT'S RAINING [B] – Shakin' STEVENS (10) 81
IT'S RAINING AGAIN – SUPERTRAMP (26) 82
IT'S RAINING MEN [A] – WEATHER GIRLS (2) 83,84
IT'S RAINING MEN [A] – Martha WASH (21)................................98,00
IT'S RAINING MEN [A] – Geri HALLIWELL (1) 01
IT'S SO EASY – Andy WILLIAMS (13)............70
IT'S SO HIGH – Matt FRETTON (50)..............83
IT'S SO NICE (TO HAVE YOU HOME) – NEW SEEKERS (44) 76
IT'S STILL ROCK AND ROLL TO ME – Billy JOEL (14) 80
IT'S STILL YOU – Michael BALL (58) 91
IT'S SUMMERTIME (LET IT GET INTO YOU) – SMOOTH (46)..95
IT'S TEMPTATION – SHEER ELEGANCE (41) ..76
IT'S THE END OF THE WORLD AS WE KNOW IT – R.E.M. (39) 91
IT'S THE SAME OLD SONG [A] – FOUR TOPS (34)...65
IT'S THE SAME OLD SONG [A] – Jonathan KING (19) 71
IT'S THE SAME OLD SONG [A] – KC and the SUNSHINE BAND (47) 78
IT'S THE WAY YOU MAKE ME FEEL – STEPS (2) 01
IT'S TIME – Elvis COSTELLO (58)..................96
IT'S TIME FOR LOVE – CHI-LITES (5) 75
IT'S TIME TO CRY – Paul ANKA (28) 60
IT'S TOO LATE [A] – Carole KING (6) 71
IT'S TOO LATE [A] – QUARTZ introducing Dina CARROLL (8) 91
IT'S TOO LATE [B] – Luci SILVAS (62) 00
IT'S TOO LATE NOW [A] – SWINGING BLUE JEANS (30)........................63
IT'S TOO LATE NOW [B] – Long John BALDRY (21) 69
IT'S TOO SOON TO KNOW – Pat BOONE (7) 58
IT'S TRICKY [A] – RUN-DMC (16) 87,98
IT'S TRICKY 2003 [A] – RUN-DMC featuring Jacknife LEE (20) 03
IT'S TRUE – QUEEN PEN (24).........................98
IT'S UP TO YOU – Ricky NELSON (22)..........63
IT'S UP TO YOU PETULA – EDISON LIGHTHOUSE (49) 71
IT'S UP TO YOU (SHINING THROUGH) – LAYO & BUSHWACKA! (25) 03
IT'S WHAT'S UPFRONT THAT COUNTS – YOSH presents LOVEDEEJAY AKEMI (31) 95
IT'S WHAT WE'RE ALL ABOUT – SUM 41 (32) 02
IT'S WONDERFUL (TO BE LOVED BY YOU) – Jimmy RUFFIN (6) 70
IT'S WRITTEN IN THE STARS – Paul WELLER (7) 02
IT'S WRITTEN ON YOUR BODY – Ronnie BOND (52) 80
IT'S YER MONEY I'M AFTER BABY – WONDER STUFF (40) 88
IT'S YOU [A] – Freddie STARR (9) 74
IT'S YOU [B] – MANHATTANS (43)................77
IT'S YOU [C] – EMF (23)................................92
IT'S YOU ONLY YOU (MEIN SCHMERZ) – Lene LOVICH (68)..82
IT'S YOUR DAY TODAY – PJ PROBY (32) 68
IT'S YOUR DESTINY – ELECTRA (51) 89
IT'S YOUR LIFE – SMOKIE (5) 77
IT'S YOUR THING – ISLEY BROTHERS (30) ..69
IT'S YOUR TIME – Arthur BAKER (64) 89
IT'S YOURS – Jon CUTLER featuring E-MAN (38) 02
ITSY BITSY TEENIE WEENIE YELLOW POLKA DOT BIKINI [A] – Brian HYLAND (8) 60
ITSY BITSY TEENIE WEENIE YELLOW POLKA DOT BIKINI [A] – BOMBALURINA (1)..........90
ITZA TRUMPET THING – MONTANO vs THE TRUMPET MAN (46) 99
I'VE BEEN A BAD BAD BOY – Paul JONES (5) 67
I'VE BEEN AROUND THE WORLD – Marti PELLOW (28) 01
I'VE BEEN DRINKING – Jeff BECK and Rod STEWART (27) 73
I'VE BEEN HURT – Guy DARRELL (12) 73
I'VE BEEN IN LOVE BEFORE – CUTTING CREW (24) 86,87
I'VE BEEN LONELY SO LONG – Frederick KNIGHT (22) 72
I'VE BEEN LOSING YOU – A-HA (8) 86
I'VE BEEN THINKING ABOUT YOU – LONDONBEAT (2) 90
I'VE BEEN TO A MARVELLOUS PARTY – DIVINE COMEDY (28) 98
I'VE BEEN WAITING – STEREO NATION (53) 96
I'VE BEEN WATCHIN' – JOE PUBLIC (75) 92
I'VE BEEN WRONG BEFORE – Cilla BLACK (17) 65
I'VE DONE EVERYTHING FOR YOU – Sammy HAGAR (36) 80
I'VE GOT A LITTLE PUPPY – SMURFS (4)......96

JOHN WAYNE IS BIG LEGGY – **HAYSI FANTAYZEE** (11) 82
JOHNNY AND MARY – **Robert PALMER** (44) ..80
JOHNNY ANGEL [A] – **Shelley FABARES** (41) 62
JOHNNY ANGEL [A] – **Patti LYNN** (37) 62
JOHNNY B GOODE [A] – **Jimi HENDRIX EXPERIENCE** (35) 72
JOHNNY B GOODE [A] – **Peter TOSH** (48) 83
JOHNNY B GOODE [A] – **JUDAS PRIEST** (64) 88
JOHNNY COME HOME – **FINE YOUNG CANNIBALS** (8) 85
JOHNNY COME LATELY – **Steve EARLE** (75) ..88
JOHNNY DAY – **Rolf HARRIS** (44) 63
JOHNNY FRIENDLY – **JOBOXERS** (31) 83
JOHNNY GET ANGRY – **Carol DEENE** (32) 62
JOHNNY JOHNNY – **PREFAB SPROUT** (64) 86
JOHNNY MATHIS' FEET – **AMERICAN MUSIC CLUB** (58) 93
JOHNNY PANIC AND THE BIBLE OF DREAMS –**Johnny PANIC and the BIBLE OF DREAMS** (70) 91
JOHNNY REGGAE – **PIGLETS** (3) 71
JOHNNY REMEMBER ME [A] – **John LEYTON** (1) 61
JOHNNY REMEMBER ME [A] – **METEORS** (66) 83
JOHNNY ROCCO – **Marty WILDE** (30) 60
JOHNNY THE HORSE – **MADNESS** (44) 99
JOHNNY WILL – **Pat BOONE** (4) 61
JOIN IN AND SING AGAIN – **JOHNSTON BROTHERS** (9) 55
JOIN IN AND SING (NO.3) – **JOHNSTON BROTHERS** (24) 56
JOIN ME – **LIGHTFORCE** (53) 00
JOIN OUR CLUB – **SAINT ETIENNE** (21) 92
JOIN THE PARTY – **HONKY** (28) 77
JOIN TOGETHER – **WHO** (9) 72
JOINING YOU – **Alanis MORISSETTE** (28) 99
JOINTS & JAMS – **BLACK EYED PEAS** (53) 98
JOJO ACTION – **MR PRESIDENT** (73) 98
JOKE (I'M LAUGHING) – **Eddi READER** (42) ..94
THE JOKER – **Steve MILLER BAND** (1) 90
THE JOKER (THE WIGAN JOKER) – **ALLNIGHT BAND** (50) 79
JOLE BLON – **Gary 'US' BONDS** (51) 81
JOLENE [A] – **Dolly PARTON** (7) 76
JOLENE [A] – **STRAWBERRY SWITCHBLADE** (53) 85
JONAH – **BREATHE** (60) 88
JONATHAN DAVID – **BELLE & SEBASTIAN** (31) 01
THE JONES' – **TEMPTATIONS** (69) 92
JONES VS JONES – **KOOL and the GANG** (17)81
JONESTOWN MIND – **ALMIGHTY** (26) 95
JORDAN: THE EP – **PREFAB SPROUT** (35) 91
JOSEPH MEGA REMIX – **Jason DONOVAN** (13) 91
JOSEPHINE [A] – **Chris REA** (67) 85
JOSEPHINE [B] – **TERRORVISION** (23) 98
JOSEY – **DEEP BLUE SOMETHING** (27) 96
JOURNEY – **Duncan BROWNE** (23) 72
THE JOURNEY [A] – **911** (3) 97
THE JOURNEY [B] – **CITIZEN CANED** (41) 01
JOURNEY TO THE MOON – **BIDDU** (41) 78
JOURNEY TO THE PAST – **AALIYAH** (22) 98
JOY [A] – **BAND AKA** (24) 83
JOY [B] – **Teddy PENDERGRASS** (58) 88
JOY [C] – **SOUL II SOUL** (4) 92
JOY [D] – **STAXX featuring Carol LEEMING** (14) 93,97
JOY [E] – **7669** (60) 94
JOY [F] – **BLACKSTREET** (56) 95
JOY [G] – **Deni HINES** (47) 98
JOY [H] – **Kathy BROWN** (63) 99
JOY! [I] – **GAY DAD** (22) 99
JOY [J] – **Mark RYDER** (34) 01
JOY AND HAPPINESS – **STABBS** (65) 94
JOY AND HEARTBREAK – **MOVEMENT 98 featuring Carroll THOMPSON** (27) 90
JOY AND PAIN [A] – **Donna ALLEN** (10) 89
JOY AND PAIN [[B] – **MAZE featuring Frankie BEVERLY** (57) 89
JOY AND PAIN [A] – **Rob BASE and DJ E-Z ROCK** (47) 89
JOY AND PAIN [C] – **ANGELLE** (43) 02
(JOY) I KNOW IT – **ODYSSEY** (51) 85
JOY OF LIVING [A] – **Cliff RICHARD** (25) 70
JOY OF LIVING [B] – **OUI 3** (55) 95
JOY TO THE WORLD – **THREE DOG NIGHT** (24) 71
JOYBRINGER – **MANFRED MANN** (9) 73
JOYENERGIZER – **Joy KITIKONTI** (57) 01
JOYRIDE – **ROXETTE** (4) 91
JOYRIDER (YOU'RE PLAYING WITH FIRE) – **COLOUR GIRL** (51) 00
JOYS OF CHRISTMAS – **Chris REA** (67) 87
JOYS OF LIFE – **David JOSEPH** (61) 84
JUDGE FUDGE – **HAPPY MONDAYS** (24) 91
THE JUDGEMENT IS THE MIRROR – **DALI'S CAR** (66) 84
JUDY IN DISGUISE (WITH GLASSES) – **John FRED and the PLAYBOY BAND** (3) 68
JUDY OVER THE RAINBOW – **ORANGE** (73) ..94
JUDY SAYS (KNOCK YOU IN THE HEAD) – **VIBRATORS** (70) 78
JUDY TEEN – **Steve HARLEY and COCKNEY REBEL** (5) 74
JUGGLING – **RAGGA TWINS** (71) 91
JUICY [A] – **WRECKX-N-EFFECT** (29) 90
JUICY [A] – **NOTORIOUS B.I.G.** (72) 94
JUICY FRUIT – **MTUME** (34) 83
A JUICY RED APPLE – **SKIN UP** (32) 92
JUKE BOX BABY – **Perry COMO** (22) 56
JUKE BOX GYPSY – **LINDISFARNE** (56) 78
JUKE BOX HERO – **FOREIGNER** (48) 81
JUKE BOX JIVE – **RUBETTES** (3) 74
JULIA [A] – **EURYTHMICS** (44) 85
JULIA [B] – **Chris REA** (18) 93
JULIA [C] – **SILVER SUN** (51) 97
JULIA SAYS – **WET WET WET** (3) 95
JULIE ANNE – **KENNY** (10) 75
JULIE DO YA LOVE ME [A] – **Bobby SHERMAN** (28) 70
JULIE DO YA LOVE ME [A] – **WHITE PLAINS** (8) 70
JULIE (EP) – **LEVELLERS** (17) 94
JULIE OCEAN – **UNDERTONES** (41) 81
JULIET – **FOUR PENNIES** (1) 64
JULIET (KEEP THAT IN MIND) – **Thea GILMORE** (35) 03
JULY – **OCEAN COLOUR SCENE** (31) 00
JUMBO [A] – **BEE GEES** (25) 68
JUMBO [B] – **UNDERWORLD** (21) 99
JUMP [A] – **VAN HALEN** (7) 84,93
JUMP [A] – **AZTEC CAMERA** (34) 84
JUMP [A] – **BUS STOP** (23) 99
JUMP [B] – **KRIS KROSS** (2) 92
JUMP! [C] – **MOVEMENT** (57) 92
JUMP (FOR MY LOVE) [D] – **POINTER SISTERS** (6) 84
JUMP [D] – **GIRLS ALOUD** (2) 03
JUMP AROUND – **HOUSE OF PAIN** (8) 92,93
JUMP BACK (SET ME FREE) – **Dhar BRAXTON** (32) 86
JUMP DOWN – **B*WITCHED** (16) 00
JUMP JIVE AN' WAIL – **Brian SETZER ORCHESTRA** (34) 99
JUMP 'N SHOUT – **BASEMENT JAXX** (12) 99
THE JUMP OFF – **LIL' KIM featuring MR. CHEEKS** (16) 03
JUMP ON DEMAND – **[SPUNGE]** (39) 02
JUMP START – **Natalie COLE** (36) 87,88
JUMP THE GUN – **THREE DEGREES** (48) 79
JUMP THEY SAY – **David BOWIE** (9) 93
JUMP TO IT – **Aretha FRANKLIN** (42) 82
JUMP TO MY BEAT – **WILDCHILD** (30) 96
JUMP TO MY LOVE – **INCOGNITO** (29) 96
JUMP TO THE BEAT [A] – **Stacy LATTISAW** (3) 80
JUMP TO THE BEAT [A] – **Dannii MINOGUE** (8) 91
JUMP UP – **JUST 4 JOKES featuring MC RB** (67) 02
JUMPIN' – **LIBERTY X** (6) 03
JUMPIN' JACK FLASH [A] – **ROLLING STONES** (1) 68
JUMPIN' JACK FLASH [A] – **Aretha FRANKLIN** (58) 86
JUMPIN' JIVE – **Joe JACKSON** (43) 81
JUMPIN' JUMPIN' – **DESTINY'S CHILD** (5) 00
JUNE AFTERNOON – **ROXETTE** (52) 96
JUNEAU – **FUNERAL FOR A FRIEND** (19) 03
JUNGLE BILL – **YELLO** (61) 92
THE JUNGLE BOOK GROOVE – **JUNGLE BOOK** (14) 93
JUNGLE BROTHER – **JUNGLE BROTHERS** (18) 97,98
JUNGLE FEVER – **CHAKACHAS** (29) 72
JUNGLE HIGH – **JUNO REACTOR** (45) 97
JUNGLE ROCK – **Hank MIZELL** (3) 76
JUNGLIST – **DRUMSOUND & Simon Bassline SMITH** (67) 03
JUNIOR'S FARM – **Paul McCARTNEY** (16) 74
JUNKIES – **EASYWORLD** (40) 03
JUPITER – **EARTH WIND AND FIRE** (41) 78
JUS' A RASCAL – **DIZZEE RASCAL** (30) 03
JUS' COME – **COOL JACK** (44) 96
JUS 1 KISS – **BASEMENT JAXX** (23) 01
JUS' REACH (RECYCLED) – **GALLIANO** (66) 92
JUST – **RADIOHEAD** (19) 95
JUST A DAY – **FEEDER** (12) 01
JUST A DAY AWAY – **BARCLAY JAMES HARVEST** (68) 83
JUST A DREAM [A] – **NENA** (70) 84
JUST A DREAM [B] – **Donna DE LORY** (71) 93
JUST A FEELING – **BAD MANNERS** (13) 81
JUST A FEW THINGS THAT I AIN'T – **BEAUTIFUL SOUTH** (30) 03
JUST A FRIEND [A] – **Biz MARKIE** (55) 90
JUST A FRIEND [B] – **MARIO** (18) 03
JUST A GIRL – **NO DOUBT** (3) 96,97
JUST A GROOVE – **NOMAD** (16) 91
JUST A LITTLE – **LIBERTY X** (1) 02
JUST A LITTLE BIT – **UNDERTAKERS** (49) 64
JUST A LITTLE BIT BETTER – **HERMAN'S HERMITS** (15) 65
JUST A LITTLE BIT OF LOVE – **Rebekah RYAN** (51) 96
JUST A LITTLE BIT TOO LATE – **Wayne FONTANA and the MINDBENDERS** (20) 65
JUST A LITTLE MISUNDERSTANDING – **CONTOURS** (31) 70
JUST A LITTLE GIRL – **Amy STUDT** (14) 02
JUST A LITTLE MORE – **DELUXE** (74) 89
JUST A LITTLE MORE LOVE – **David GUETTA featuring Chris WILLIS** (19) 03
JUST A LITTLE TOO MUCH – **Ricky NELSON** (11) 59
JUST A MIRAGE – **JELLYBEAN** (13) 88
JUST A SHADOW – **BIG COUNTRY** (26) 85
JUST A SMILE – **PILOT** (31) 75
JUST A STEP FROM HEAVEN – **ETERNAL** (8) 94
JUST A TOUCH – **Keith SWEAT** (35) 96
JUST A TOUCH OF LOVE – **SLAVE** (64) 80
JUST A TOUCH OF LOVE (EVERYDAY) – **C & C MUSIC FACTORY / CLIVILLES & COLE** (31) ..91
JUST AN ILLUSION – **IMAGINATION** (2) 82
JUST ANOTHER BROKEN HEART – **Sheena EASTON** (33) 81
JUST ANOTHER DAY [A] – **Jon SECADA** (5) 92
JUST ANOTHER DAY [B] – **Jonathan WILKES** (24) 01
JUST ANOTHER DREAM – **Cathy DENNIS** (13) 91
JUST ANOTHER GROOVE – **MIGHTY DUB KATZ** (43) 96
JUST ANOTHER ILLUSION – **HURRICANE #1** (35) 97
JUST ANOTHER NIGHT – **Mick JAGGER** (32) ..85
JUST AROUND THE HILL – **SASH!** (8) 00
JUST AS LONG AS YOU ARE THERE – **Vanessa PARADIS** (57) 93
JUST AS MUCH AS EVER – **Nat 'King' COLE** (18) 60
JUST BE DUB TO ME [A] – **REVELATION** (36) 03
JUST BE GOOD TO ME [A] – **S.O.S. BAND** (13) 84
JUST BE TONIGHT – **BBG** (45) 97
JUST BECAUSE – **JANE'S ADDICTION** (14) 03
JUST BEFORE YOU LEAVE – **DEL AMITRI** (37) 02
JUST BETWEEN YOU AND ME – **APRIL WINE** (52) 81
JUST BORN – **Jim DALE** (27) 58
JUST CALL – **SHERRICK** (23) 87
JUST CALL ME – **GOOD GIRLS** (75) 93
JUST CAN'T GET ENOUGH [A] – **DEPECHE MODE** (8) 81
JUST CAN'T GET ENOUGH [B] – **TRANSFORMER 2** (45) 96
JUST CAN'T GET ENOUGH [C] – **Harry 'Choo Choo' ROMERO presents Inaya DAY** (39) ..99
JUST CAN'T GET ENOUGH (NO NO NO NO) – **EYE TO EYE featuring Taka BOOM** (36) 01
JUST CAN'T GIVE YOU UP – **MYSTIC MERLIN** (20) 80
JUST CAN'T STAND IT – **MATT BIANCO** (66) ..86
JUST CHECKIN' – **BEAUTIFUL SOUTH** (59) 00
JUST CRUISIN' – **Will SMITH** (23) 97
JUST DON'T WANT TO BE LONELY [A] – **MAIN INGREDIENT** (27) 74

KEEP YOUR WORRIES — **GURU'S JAZZMATAZZ featuring Angie STONE** (57) ...00
KEEPER OF THE CASTLE — **FOUR TOPS** (18) 72
KEEPIN' LOVE NEW — **Howard JOHNSON** (45) ...82
KEEPIN' THE FAITH — **DE LA SOUL** (50) ...91
KEEPING A RENDEZVOUS — **BUDGIE** (71) ...81
KEEPING SECRETS — **SWITCH** (61) ...84
KEEPING THE DREAM ALIVE — **FREIHEIT** (14) 88
KEEPS ME WONDERING WHY — **Steve MILLER BAND** (52) ...82
KELLY — **Wayne GIBSON** (48) ...64
KELLY WATCH THE STARS — **AIR** (18) ...98
KELLY'S HEROES — **BLACK GRAPE** (17) ...95
KENNEDY — **WEDDING PRESENT** (33) ...89
KENTUCKY RAIN — **Elvis PRESLEY** (21) ...70
KERNKRAFT 400 — **ZOMBIE NATION** (2) ...00
KERRY KERRY — **CINERAMA** (71) ...98
THE KETCHUP SONG (ASEREJE) — **LAS KETCHUP** (1) ...02
KEVIN CARTER — **MANIC STREET PREACHERS** (9) ...96
KEWPIE DOLL [A] — **Frankie VAUGHAN** (10) ...58
KEWPIE DOLL [A] — **Perry COMO** (9) ...58
THE KEY [A] — **SENSER** (47) ...93
THE KEY [B] — **Matt GOSS** (40) ...95
KEY LARGO — **Bertie HIGGINS** (60) ...82
THE KEY THE SECRET — **URBAN COOKIE COLLECTIVE** (2) ...93,96
KEY TO MY LIFE — **BOYZONE** (3) ...95
KICK IN THE EYE — **BAUHAUS** (59) ...81
KICK IN THE EYE (EP) — **BAUHAUS** (45) ...82
KICK IT [A] — **NITZER EBB** (75) ...95
KICK IT [B] — **REGGAE BOYZ** (59) ...98
KICK IT IN — **SIMPLE MINDS** (15) ...89
KICKIN' HARD — **KLUBBHEADS** (36) ...98
KICKIN' IN THE BEAT — **Pamela FERNANDEZ** (43) ...94,95
KICKIN' UP DUST — **LITTLE ANGELS** (46) ...90
KICKING MY HEART AROUND — **BLACK CROWES** (55) ...98
KICKIN' UP THE LEAVES — **Mark WYNTER** (24) ...60
KICKS (EP) — **UK SUBS** (36) ...79
KID [A] — **PRETENDERS** (33) ...79,95
KID 2000 [A] — **HYBRID featuring Chrissie HYNDE** (32) ...00
KIDDIO — **Brook BENTON** (41) ...60
KIDS — **Robbie WILLIAMS / Kylie MINOGUE** (2) ...00,01
THE KIDS ARE ALRIGHT — **WHO** (41) ...66
THE KIDS ARE BACK — **TWISTED SISTER** (32) ...83
THE KIDS AREN'T ALRIGHT — **OFFSPRING** (11) ...99
KIDS IN AMERICA — **Kim WILDE** (2) ...81
THE KID'S LAST FIGHT — **Frankie LAINE** (3) ...54
KIDS OF THE CENTURY — **HELLOWEEN** (56) ...91
KIDS ON THE STREET — **ANGELIC UPSTARTS** (57) ...81
KILL ALL HIPPIES — **PRIMAL SCREAM** (24) ...00
KILL THE KING — **RAINBOW** (41) ...77,81
KILL THE POOR — **DEAD KENNEDYS** (49) ...80
KILL YOUR TELEVISION — **NED'S ATOMIC DUSTBIN** (53) ...90
KILLED BY DEATH — **MOTÖRHEAD** (51) ...84
KILLER [A] — **ADAMSKI** (1) ...90
KILLER [A] — **ATB** (4) ...00
KILLER (EP) [A] — **SEAL** (8) ...91
KILLER ON THE LOOSE — **THIN LIZZY** (10) ...80
KILLER QUEEN — **QUEEN** (2) ...74
KILLERS LIVE (EP) — **THIN LIZZY** (19) ...81
KILLIN' TIME — **Tina COUSINS** (15) ...99
KILLING IN THE NAME — **RAGE AGAINST THE MACHINE** (25) ...93
THE KILLING JAR — **SIOUXSIE and the BANSHEES** (41) ...88
KILLING ME SOFTLY WITH HIS SONG [A] — **Roberta FLACK** (6) ...73
KILLING ME SOFTLY [A] — **FUGEES** (1) ...96
THE KILLING MOON — **ECHO and the BUNNYMEN** (9) ...84
THE KILLING OF GEORGIE — **Rod STEWART** (2) ...76
A KIND OF CHRISTMAS CARD — **Morten HARKET** (53) ...95
A KIND OF MAGIC — **QUEEN** (3) ...86
KINETIC — **GOLDEN GIRLS** (38) ...98
KINETIC '99 — **GOLDEN GIRLS** (56) ...99
KING — **UB40** (4) ...80
THE KING AND QUEEN OF AMERICA — **EURYTHMICS** (29) ...90
KING CREOLE — **Elvis PRESLEY** (2) ...58
KING FOR A DAY [A] — **THOMPSON TWINS** (22) ...85
KING FOR A DAY [B] — **JAMIROQUAI** (20) ...99
KING IN A CATHOLIC STYLE (WAKE UP) — **CHINA CRISIS** (19) ...85
THE KING IS DEAD — **GO WEST** (67) ...87
THE KING IS HALF UNDRESSED — **JELLYFISH** (39) ...91
THE KING IS HERE — **45 KING** (60) ...89,90
KING KONG — **Terry LIGHTFOOT and his NEW ORLEANS JAZZMEN** (29) ...61
KING MIDAS IN REVERSE — **HOLLIES** (18) ...67
KING OF CLOWNS — **Neil SEDAKA** (23) ...62
KING OF DREAMS — **DEEP PURPLE** (70) ...90
KING OF EMOTION — **BIG COUNTRY** (16) ...88
KING OF KINGS — **Ezz RECO and the LAUNCHERS with Boysie GRANT** (44) ...64
THE KING OF KISSINGDOM — **MY LIFE STORY** (35) ...97
KING OF LOVE — **Dave EDMUNDS** (68) ...90
KING OF MISERY — **HONEYCRACK** (32) ...96
KING OF MY CASTLE — **WAMDUE PROJECT** (1) ...99,00
KING OF NEW YORK — **FUN LOVIN' CRIMINALS** (28) ...97
KING OF PAIN — **POLICE** (17) ...84
THE KING OF ROCK 'N' ROLL — **PREFAB SPROUT** (7) ...88
KING OF SNAKE — **UNDERWORLD** (17) ...99
KING OF SORROW — **SADE** (59) ...01
KING OF THE COPS — **Billy HOWARD** (6) ...75
KING OF THE KERB — **ECHOBELLY** (25) ...95
KING OF THE NEW YORK STREET — **DION** (74) ...89
KING OF THE ROAD — **Roger MILLER** (1) ...65
KING OF THE ROAD (EP) — **PROCLAIMERS** (9) ...90
KING OF THE RUMBLING SPIRES — **T. REX** (44) ...69
THE KING OF WISHFUL THINKING — **GO WEST** (18) ...90
KING ROCKER — **GENERATION X** (11) ...79
KING WITHOUT A CROWN — **ABC** (44) ...87
KINGDOM — **ULTRAMARINE** (46) ...93
KINGS AND QUEENS — **KILLING JOKE** (58) ...85
KING'S CALL — **Philip LYNOTT** (35) ...80,87
KINGS OF THE WILD FRONTIER — **ADAM and the ANTS** (2) ...80,81
KINGSTON TOWN — **UB40** (4) ...90
KINKY AFRO — **HAPPY MONDAYS** (5) ...90
KINKY BOOTS — **Patrick MacNEE and Honor BLACKMAN** (5) ...90
KINKY LOVE — **PALE SAINTS** (72) ...91
KIKI RIRI BOOM — **SHAFT** (62) ...01
KISS [A] — **Dean MARTIN** (5) ...53
KISS [B] — **PRINCE** (6) ...86
KISS [B] — **AGE OF CHANCE** (50) ...87
KISS [B] — **ART OF NOISE featuring Tom JONES** (5) ...88
KISS AND SAY GOODBYE — **MANHATTANS** (4) ...76
KISS AND TELL [A] — **Bryan FERRY** (41) ...88
KISS AND TELL [B] — **BROWNSTONE** (21) ...97
KISS FROM A ROSE — **SEAL** (4) ...94,95
KISS KISS — **Holly VALANCE** (1) ...02
KISS LIKE ETHER — **Claudia BRUCKEN** (63) ...91
KISS ME [A] — **Stephen 'Tin Tin' DUFFY** (4) ...85
KISS ME [B] — **SIXPENCE NONE THE RICHER** (4) ...99
KISS ME ANOTHER — **Georgia GIBBS** (24) ...56
KISS ME DEADLY — **Lita FORD** (75) ...88
KISS ME GOODBYE — **Petula CLARK** (50) ...68
KISS ME HONEY HONEY, KISS ME — **Shirley BASSEY** (3) ...58
KISS ME QUICK — **Elvis PRESLEY** (14) ...63
KISS MY EYES — **Bob SINCLAR** (67) ...03
KISS OF LIFE — **SADE** (44) ...93
KISS ON MY LIST — **Daryl HALL and John OATES** (33) ...80
KISS THAT FROG — **Peter GABRIEL** (46) ...93
KISS THE BRIDE — **Elton JOHN** (20) ...83
KISS THE DIRT (FALLING DOWN THE MOUNTAIN) — **INXS** (54) ...86
KISS THE GIRL — **Peter ANDRE** (9) ...98
KISS THE RAIN — **Billie MYERS** (4) ...98
KISS THEM FOR ME — **SIOUXSIE and the BANSHEES** (32) ...91
KISS THIS THING GOODBYE — **DEL AMITRI** (43) ...89,90
KISS (WHEN THE SUN DON'T SHINE) — **VENGABOYS** (3) ...99
KISS YOU ALL OVER [A] — **EXILE** (6) ...78
KISS YOU ALL OVER [A] — **NO MERCY** (16) ...97
KISSES IN THE MOONLIGHT — **George BENSON** (60) ...86
KISSES ON THE WIND — **Neneh CHERRY** (20) ...89
KISSES SWEETER THAN WINE [A] — **Jimmie RODGERS** (7) ...57
KISSES SWEETER THAN WINE [A] — **Frankie VAUGHAN** (8) ...57
KISSIN' COUSINS — **Elvis PRESLEY** (10) ...64
KISSIN' IN THE BACK ROW OF THE MOVIES — **DRIFTERS** (2) ...74
KISSIN' YOU — **TOTAL** (29) ...96
KISSING A FOOL — **George MICHAEL** (18) ...88
KISSING GATE — **Sam BROWN** (23) ...90
KISSING WITH CONFIDENCE — **Will POWERS** (17) ...83
KITE — **Nick HEYWARD** (44) ...93
KITES — **Simon DUPREE and the BIG SOUND** (9) ...67
KITSCH — **Barry RYAN** (37) ...70
KITTY — **Cat STEVENS** (47) ...67
KLACTOVEESEDSTEIN — **BLUE RONDO A LA TURK** (50) ...82
KLUB KOLLABORATIONS — **BK** (43) ...03
KLUBBHOPPING — **KLUBBHEADS** (10) ...96
KNEE DEEP AND DOWN — **RAIN BAND** (56) ...03
KNEE DEEP IN THE BLUES [A] — **Guy MITCHELL** (3) ...57
KNEE DEEP IN THE BLUES [A] — **Tommy STEELE** (15) ...57
KNIFE EDGE — **ALARM** (43) ...86
KNIVES OUT — **RADIOHEAD** (13) ...01
KNOCK KNOCK WHO'S THERE — **Mary HOPKIN** (2) ...70
KNOCK ME OUT — **GARY'S GANG** (45) ...82
KNOCK ON WOOD [A] — **Eddie FLOYD** (19) ...67
KNOCK ON WOOD [A] — **Otis REDDING** (35) ...67
KNOCK ON WOOD [A] — **David BOWIE** (10) ...74
KNOCK ON WOOD [A] — **Amii STEWART** (6) ...79,85
KNOCK OUT — **TRIPLE 8** (8) ...03
KNOCK THREE TIMES — **DAWN** (1) ...71
KNOCKED IT OFF — **B.A. ROBERTSON** (8) ...79
KNOCKED OUT — **Paula ABDUL** (21) ...89,90
KNOCKIN' ON HEAVEN'S DOOR [A] — **Bob DYLAN** (14) ...73
KNOCKIN' ON HEAVEN'S DOOR [A] — **Eric CLAPTON** (38) ...75
KNOCKIN' ON HEAVEN'S DOOR [A] — **GUNS N' ROSES** (2) ...92
KNOCKIN' ON HEAVEN'S DOOR [A] — **DUNBLANE** (1) ...96
KNOCKING AT YOUR BACK DOOR — **DEEP PURPLE** (68) ...85
KNOCKS ME OFF MY FEET — **Donell JONES** (58) ...97
KNOW BY NOW — **Robert PALMER** (25) ...94
KNOW YOU WANNA — **3RD EDGE** (17) ...03
KNOW YOUR RIGHTS — **CLASH** (43) ...82
KNOWING ME, KNOWING YOU — **ABBA** (1) ...77
KOKOMO — **BEACH BOYS** (25) ...88
KOMMOTION — **Duane EDDY and the REBELS** (13) ...60
KON-TIKI — **SHADOWS** (1) ...61
KOOCHIE RYDER — **FREAKY REALISTIC** (52) ...93
KOOCHY — **Armand VAN HELDEN** (4) ...00
KOOKIE KOOKIE (LEND ME YOUR COMB) — **Connie STEVENS** (27) ...60
KOOKIE LITTLE PARADISE — **Frankie VAUGHAN** (31) ...60
KOOL IN THE KAFTAN — **B.A. ROBERTSON** (17) ...80
KOOTCHI — **Neneh CHERRY** (38) ...96
KOREAN BODEGA — **FUN LOVIN' CRIMINALS** (15) ...99
KOWALSKI — **PRIMAL SCREAM** (8) ...97
KRUPA — **APOLLO FOUR FORTY** (23) ...96
KU KLUX KLAN — **STEEL PULSE** (41) ...78
KUMBAYA — **SANDPIPERS** (38) ...69
KUNG FU — **ASH** (57) ...95
KUNG FU FIGHTING [A] — **Carl DOUGLAS** (1) ...74
KUNG FU FIGHTING [A] — **BUS STOP featuring Carl DOUGLAS** (8) ...98
KUNG-FU — **187 LOCKDOWN** (9) ...98
KUT IT — **RED EYE** (62) ...94

LAZARUS — BOO RADLEYS (50) 94
LAZY [A] — SUEDE (9) 97
LAZY [B] — X-PRESS 2 featuring David BYRNE (2) 02
LAZY BONES — Jonathan KING (23) 71
LAZY DAYS — Robbie WILLIAMS (8) 97
LAZY LINE PAINTER JANE — BELLE & SEBASTIAN (41) 97
LAZY LOVER — SUPERNATURALS (34) 96
LAZY RIVER — Bobby DARIN (2) 61
LAZY SUNDAY — SMALL FACES (2) 68,76
LAZYITIS — ONE ARMED BOXER — HAPPY MONDAYS and Karl DENVER (46) ..90
LE DISC JOCKEY — ENCORE (12) 98
LE FREAK — CHIC (7) 78
LE VOIE LE SOLEIL — SUBLIMINAL CUTS (23) 94,96
LEADER OF THE PACK [A] — SHANGRI-LAS (3) 65,72,76
LEADER OF THE PACK [A] — TWISTED SISTER (47) 86
LEADER OF THE PACK [A] — JOAN COLLINS FAN CLUB (60) 88
LEAFY MYSTERIES — Paul WELLER (23) 02
LEAN ON ME [A] — Bill WITHERS (18) 72
LEAN ON ME [A] — MUD (7) 76
LEAN ON ME [A] — CLUB NOUVEAU (3) 87
LEAN ON ME [A] — Michael BOLTON (14) 94
LEAN ON ME (WITH THE FAMILY) — 2-4 FAMILY (69) 99
LEAN ON ME (AH-LI-AYO) — RED BOX (3) 85
LEAN ON ME I WON'T FALL OVER — CARTER — THE UNSTOPPABLE SEX MACHINE (16) 93
LEAN ON YOU — Cliff RICHARD (17) 89
LEAN PERIOD — ORANGE JUICE (74) 84
LEAP OF FAITH — Bruce SPRINGSTEEN (46)..92
LEAP UP AND DOWN (WAVE YOUR KNICKERS IN THE AIR) — ST CECILIA (12) 71
LEARN TO FLY — FOO FIGHTERS (21) 99
LEARNIN' THE BLUES — Frank SINATRA (2) ..55
LEARNIN' THE GAME — Buddy HOLLY (36) ..60
LEARNING TO FLY [A] — Tom PETTY and the HEARTBREAKERS (46) 91
LEARNING TO FLY [B] — MOTHER'S PRIDE (54) 99
LEAVE A LIGHT ON — Belinda CARLISLE (4)..89
LEAVE A LITTLE LOVE — LULU (8) 65
LEAVE A TENDER MOMENT ALONE — Billy JOEL (29) 84
LEAVE 'EM SOMETHING TO DESIRE — SPRINKLER (45) 98
LEAVE HOME — CHEMICAL BROTHERS (17) ..95
LEAVE IN SILENCE — DEPECHE MODE (18)....82
LEAVE IT [A] — Mike McGEAR (36) 74
LEAVE IT [B] — YES (56) 84
LEAVE IT ALONE — LIVING COLOUR (34) 93
LEAVE IT UP TO ME — Aaron CARTER (22)....02
LEAVE ME ALONE — Michael JACKSON (2) 89
LEAVE RIGHT NOW — Will YOUNG (1) 03
LEAVE THEM ALL BEHIND — RIDE (9) 92
LEAVIN' [A] — Tony RICH PROJECT (52) 96
LEAVIN' [B] — Shelby LYNNE (73) 00
LEAVIN' ON A JET PLANE — PETER, PAUL and MARY (2) 70
LEAVING HERE — BIRDS (45) 65
LEAVING LAS VEGAS — Sheryl CROW (66) 94
LEAVING ME NOW — LEVEL 42 (15) 85
LEAVING ON A JET PLANE — Chantal KREVIAZUK (59) 99
LEAVING ON THE MIDNIGHT TRAIN — Nick STRAKER BAND (61) 80
THE LEAVING SONG PT.2 — AFI (43) 03
THE LEBANON — HUMAN LEAGUE (11) 84
LEEDS, LEEDS, LEEDS — LEEDS UNITED FC (54) 92
LEEDS UNITED — LEEDS UNITED FC (10) 72
LEFT BANK — Winifred ATWELL (14) 56
LEFT BEHIND — SLIPKNOT (24) 01
LEFT OF CENTER — Suzanne VEGA featuring Joe JACKSON (32) 86
LEFT TO MY OWN DEVICES — PET SHOP BOYS (4) 88
LEGACY — Mad COBRA featuring Richie STEPHENS (64) 93
THE LEGACY — PUSH (22) 01,02
LEGACY (EP) — MANSUN (7) 98
LEGACY (SHOW ME LOVE) — SPACE BROTHERS (31) 99
LEGAL MAN — BELLE & SEBASTIAN (15) 00
A LEGAL MATTER — WHO (32) 66
LEGEND OF A COWGIRL — Imani COPPOLA (32) 98
LEGEND OF THE GOLDEN SNAKE — DEPTH CHARGE (75) 95
LEGEND OF XANADU — Dave DEE, DOZY, BEAKY, MICK and TICH (1) 68
LEGENDS OF THE DARK BLACK PART 2 — WILDCHILD (34) 95
LEGO SKANGA — Rupie EDWARDS (32) 75
LEGS [A] — ART OF NOISE (69) 85
LEGS [B] — ZZ TOP (16) 85
LEMMINGS — SFX (51) 93
LEMON TREE — FOOL'S GARDEN (26) 96
LENINGRAD — Billy JOEL (53) 89
LENNY — SUPERGRASS (10) 95
LENNY AND TERENCE — CARTER — THE UNSTOPPABLE SEX MACHINE (40) 93
LENNY VALENTINO — AUTEURS (41) 93
LEONARD NIMOY — FREAKY REALISTIC (71)..93
LEROY — WHEATUS (22) 02
LES BICYCLETTES DE BELSIZE — Engelbert HUMPERDINCK (5) 68
LES FLEUR — 4 HERO (53) 01
L'ESPERANZA [A] — Sven VATH (63) 93
L'ESPERANZA [B] — AIRSCAPE (33) 99
LESS TALK MORE ACTION — Tim DELUXE (45) 03
LESSON ONE — Russ CONWAY (21) 62
LESSONS IN LOVE [A] — ALLISONS (30) 62
LESSONS IN LOVE [B] — LEVEL 42 (3) 86
LESSONS LEARNED FROM ROCKY I TO ROCKY III — CORNERSHOP (37) 02
LET A BOY CRY — GALA (11) 97
LET A GOOD THING GO — Gemma HAYES (54) 02
LET 'EM IN [A] — Paul McCARTNEY (2) 76
LET 'EM IN [A] — Billy PAUL (26) 77
LET 'EM IN [A] — SHINEHEAD (70) 93
LET FOREVER BE — CHEMICAL BROTHERS (9) 99
LET GO WITH THE FLOW — BEAUTIFUL SOUTH (47) 03
LET HER CRY — HOOTIE & THE BLOWFISH (75) 95
LET HER DOWN EASY — Terence Trent D'ARBY (18) 93
LET HER FALL — THEN JERICO (65) 87
LET HER FEEL IT — SIMPLICIOUS (34) 84,85
LET HER GO — STRAWBERRY SWITCHBLADE (59) 85
LET IT ALL BLOW — DAZZ BAND (12) 84
LET IT ALL HANG OUT — Jonathan KING (26) 70
LET IT BE [A] — BEATLES (2) 70
LET IT BE [A] — FERRY AID (1) 87
LET IT BE ME [A] — EVERLY BROTHERS (13) 60
LET IT BE ME [A] — JUSTIN (15) 00
LET IT BE WITH YOU — BELOUIS SOME (53) 87
LET IT FLOW — SPIRITUALIZED (30) 95
LET IT LAST — Carleen ANDERSON (16) 95
LET IT LIVE — HAVEN (72) 01
LET IT LOOSE — LEMON TREES (55) 93
LET IT RAIN [A] — UFO (62) 82
LET IT RAIN [B] — EAST 17 (10) 95
LET IT RAIN [C] — 4 STRINGS (49) 03
LET IT REIGN — INNER CITY (51) 91
LET IT RIDE — Todd TERRY PROJECT (58) 99
LET IT ROCK [A] — Chuck BERRY (6) 63
LET IT ROCK [A] — ROLLING STONES (2) 71
LET IT ROLL — RAZE presents Doug LAZY (27) 89
LET IT SLIDE [A] — MUDHONEY (60) 91
LET IT SLIDE [B] — ARIEL (57) 93
LET IT SWING — BOBBYSOCKS (44) 85
LET LOVE BE THE LEADER — FM (71) 87
LET LOVE BE YOUR ENERGY — Robbie WILLIAMS (10) 01
LET LOVE LEAD THE WAY — SPICE GIRLS (1) 00
LET LOVE RULE — Lenny KRAVITZ (39) 90
LET LOVE SHINE — AMOS (31) 95
LET LOVE SPEAK UP ITSELF — BEAUTIFUL SOUTH (51) 91
LET ME BE — BLACK DIAMOND (56) 94
LET ME BE THE NUMBER 1 (LOVE OF YOUR LIFE) — Dooley SILVERSPOON (44) 76
LET ME BE THE ONE [A] — SHADOWS (12)....75
LET ME BE THE ONE [B] — FIVE STAR (18)....85
LET ME BE THE ONE [C] — BLESSID UNION OF SOULS (74) 96
LET ME BE THE ONE [D] — MINT CONDITION (63) 97
LET ME BE THE ONE [E] — Cliff RICHARD (29) 02
LET ME BE YOUR FANTASY — BABY D (1) 94,00
(LET ME BE YOUR) TEDDY BEAR — Elvis PRESLEY (3) 57
LET ME BE YOUR UNDERWEAR — CLUB 69 (33) 92
LET ME BE YOUR WINGS — Barry MANILOW (73) 94
LET ME BE YOURS — FIVE STAR (51) 88
LET ME BLOW YA MIND — EVE featuring Gwen STEFANI (4) 01
LET ME CLEAR MY THROAT [A] — DJ KOOL (8) 97
LET ME CLEAR MY THROAT [A] — PUBLIC DOMAIN (34) 02
LET ME COME ON HOME — Otis REDDING (48) 67
LET ME CRY ON YOUR SHOULDER — Ken DODD (11) 67
LET ME DOWN EASY — STRANGLERS (48) 85
LET ME ENTERTAIN YOU — Robbie WILLIAMS (3) 98
LET ME FLY — Darren STYLES & Mark BREEZE present INFEXTIOUS (59) 03
LET ME GO — HEAVEN 17 (41) 82
LET ME GO LOVER [A] — Teresa BREWER (9) 55
LET ME GO LOVER [A] — Dean MARTIN (3) ..55
LET ME GO LOVER [A] — Ruby MURRAY (5) ..55
LET ME GO LOVER [A] — Joan WEBER (16)....55
LET ME GO LOVER [A] — Kathy KIRBY (10)....64
LET ME HEAR YOU SAY 'OLE OLE' — OUTHERE BROTHERS (18) 97
LET ME IN [A] — OSMONDS (2) 73
LET ME IN [A] — OTT (12) 97
LET ME INTRODUCE YOU TO THE FAMILY — STRANGLERS (42) 81
LET ME KNOW [A] — JUNIOR (53) 82
LET ME KNOW [B] — Maxi PRIEST (49) 87
LET ME KNOW (I HAVE A RIGHT) — Gloria GAYNOR (32) 79
LET ME LET GO — Faith HILL (72) 99
LET ME LIVE — QUEEN (9) 96
LET ME LOVE YOU FOR TONIGHT — KARIYA (44) 89
LET ME RIDE — DR DRE (31) 94
LET ME ROCK YOU — KANDIDATE (58) 80
LET ME SEE — MORCHEEBA (46) 98
LET ME SHOW YOU [A] — K-KLASS (13) 93
LET ME SHOW YOU [B] — CAMISRA (5) 98
LET ME SHOW YOU [C] — Tony MOMRELLE (67) 98
LET ME TAKE YOU THERE — Betty BOO (12) 92
LET ME TALK — EARTH WIND AND FIRE (29) 80
LET ME TRY AGAIN — Tammy JONES (5) 75
LET ME WAKE UP IN YOUR ARMS — LULU (51) 93
LET MY LOVE OPEN YOUR DOOR — Pete TOWNSHEND (46) 80
LET MY NAME BE SORROW — Mary HOPKIN (46) 71
LET MY PEOPLE GO (PART 1) — WINANS (71) 85
LET MY PEOPLE GO-GO — RAINMAKERS (18) 87
LET ROBESON SING — MANIC STREET PREACHERS (19) 01
LET SOMEBODY LOVE YOU — Keni BURKE (59) 81
LET THE BASS KICK — 2 FOR JOY (67) 91
LET THE BEAT CONTROL YOUR BODY — 2 UNLIMITED (6) 94
LET THE BEAT HIT 'EM [A] — LISA LISA (17) ..91
LET THE BEAT HIT 'EM [A] — SHENA (28) 97
LET THE DAY BEGIN — CALL (42) 89
LET THE DRUMS SPEAK — MIGHTY DUB KATS (73) 02
LET THE FLAME BURN BRIGHTER — Graham KENDRICK (55) 89
LET THE FREAK — BIG RON (57) 00
LET THE GOOD TIMES ROLL — SHEEP ON DRUGS (56) 94
LET THE HAPPINESS IN — David SYLVIAN (66) 87
LET THE HEALING BEGIN — Joe COCKER (32) 94
LET THE HEARTACHES BEGIN — Long John BALDRY (1) 67
LET THE LITTLE GIRL DANCE — Billy BLAND (15) 60
LET THE LOVE — Q-TEX (30) 96

THE LETTER [A] – LONG AND THE SHORT (35) 64
THE LETTER [B] – BOX TOPS (5) 67
THE LETTER [B] – MINDBENDERS (42)..........67
THE LETTER [B] – Joe COCKER (39) 70
THE LETTER [B] – Amii STEWART (39)..........80
LETTER FROM AMERICA – PROCLAIMERS (3) 87
LETTER FULL OF TEARS – Billy FURY (32) 62
LETTER TO A SOLDIER – Barbara LYON (27) 56
A LETTER TO ELISE – CURE (28) 92
LETTER TO LUCILLE – Tom JONES (31) 73
LETTER 2 MY UNBORN – 2PAC (4)................01
A LETTER TO YOU – Shakin' STEVENS (10)................................84
LETTERS TO YOU – FINCH (39) 03
LETTIN' YA MIND GO – DESERT (74) 01
LETTING GO – Paul McCARTNEY (41)............75
LETTING THE CABLES SLEEP – BUSH (51) 00
LEVI STUBBS' TEARS – Billy BRAGG (29) 86
LFO – LFO (12) 90
LIAR [A] – Graham BONNET (51)....................81
LIAR [B] – ROLLINS BAND (27) 94
LIAR LIAR – CREDIT TO THE NATION (60) 95
LIARS' BAR – BEAUTIFUL SOUTH (43) 97
LIBERATION [A] – LIBERATION (28) 92
LIBERATION [B] – PET SHOP BOYS (14)........94
LIBERATION [C] – Lippy LOU (57) 95
LIBERATION (TEMPTATION – FLY LIKE AN EAGLE) – Matt DAREY (19) 99
LIBERATOR – SPEAR OF DESTINY (67) 84
LIBERIAN GIRL – Michael JACKSON (13)........89
LIBERTY TOWN – PERFECT DAY (58) 89
LIBIAMO – José CARRERAS featuring Placido DOMINGO and Luciano PAVAROTTI with MEHTA (21).........................94
LICENCE TO KILL – Gladys KNIGHT and the PIPS (6) 89
LICK A SHOT – CYPRESS HILL (20) 94
LICK A SMURP FOR CHRISTMAS (ALL FALL DOWN) – Jonathan KING (58) 78
LICK IT – 20 FINGERS (48)............................95
LICK IT UP – KISS (31) 83
LIDO SHUFFLE – Boz SCAGGS (13) 77
LIE TO ME – BON JOVI (10) 95
LIES [A] – STATUS QUO (11)..........................80
LIES [B] – THOMPSON TWINS (67) 82
LIES [C] – Jonathan BUTLER (18) 87
LIES [D] – EN VOGUE (44) 90
LIES [E] – EMF (28)..91
THE LIES IN YOUR EYES – SWEET (35) 76
LIFE [A] – HADDAWAY (6) 93
LIFE [B] – BLAIR (44) 96
LIFE [C] – DES'REE (8) 98
THE LIFE [D] – STYLES & Pharoahe MONCH (60) 02
LIFE AIN'T EASY – CLEOPATRA (4)................98
LIFE AT A TOP PEOPLE'S HEALTH FARM – STYLE COUNCIL (28) 88
LIFE BECOMING A LANDSLIDE – MANIC STREET PREACHERS (36) 94
LIFE BEGINS AT THE HOP – XTC (54) 79
LIFE FOR RENT – DIDO (8) 03
LIFE GOES ON – GEORGIE PORGIE (54)........00
LIFE GOES ON – LeAnn RIMES (11) 02
LIFE GOT COLD – GIRLS ALOUD (3) 03
LIFE IN A DAY [A] – SIMPLE MINDS (62) 79
LIFE IN A DAY [B] – I AM KLOOT (43) 03
LIFE IN A NORTHERN TOWN – DREAM ACADEMY (15) 85
LIFE IN MONO – MONO (60) 98
LIFE IN ONE DAY – Howard JONES (14) 85
LIFE IN TOKYO – JAPAN (28) 82
LIFE IS A FLOWER – ACE OF BASE (5) 98
LIFE IS A HIGHWAY – Tom COCHRANE (62)..92
LIFE IS A LONG SONG – JETHRO TULL (11)....71
LIFE IS A MINESTRONE – 10cc (7) 75
LIFE IS A ROCK (BUT THE RADIO ROLLED ME) – REUNION (33) 74
LIFE IS A ROLLERCOASTER – Ronan KEATING (1)..00
LIFE IS FOR LIVING – BARCLAY JAMES HARVEST (61) 80
LIFE IS SWEET – CHEMICAL BROTHERS (25) 95
LIFE IS TOO SHORT GIRL – SHEER ELEGANCE (9) 76
A LIFE LESS ORDINARY – ASH (10) 97
LIFE, LOVE AND HAPPINESS – Brian KENNEDY (27) 96
LIFE LOVE AND UNITY – DREADZONE (56) ..96
THE LIFE OF RILEY – LIGHTNING SEEDS (28) 92
LIFE OF SURPRISES – PREFAB SPROUT (24) 93
LIFE ON MARS? – David BOWIE (3) 73
LIFE ON YOUR OWN – HUMAN LEAGUE (16) 84
LIFE STORY – Angie STONE (22) 00
LIFE SUPPORT MACHINE – THESE ANIMAL MEN (62)............................97
LIFEBOAT – Terry NEASON (72) 94
THE LIFEBOAT PARTY – Kid CREOLE and the COCONUTS (49) 83
LIFEFORMS – FUTURE SOUND OF LONDON (14) 94
LIFELINE – SPANDAU BALLET (7)..................82
LIFE'S A CINCH – MUNDY (75)......................96
LIFE'S BEEN GOOD – Joe WALSH (14) 78
LIFE'S JUST A BALLGAME – WOMACK and WOMACK (32) 88
LIFE'S TOO SHORT [A] – HOLE IN ONE (36)..97
LIFE'S TOO SHORT [B] – LIGHTNING SEEDS (27)............................99,00
LIFE'S WHAT YOU MAKE IT – TALK TALK (16) 86,90
LIFESAVER – GURU (61) 96
LIFESTYLES OF THE RICH AND FAMOUS – GOOD CHARLOTTE (8) 03
LIFETIME LOVE – Joyce SIMS (34) 87
LIFETIME PILING UP – TALKING HEADS (50) 92
LIFETIMES – SLAM featuring Tyrone PALMER (61) 01
LIFT – 808 STATE (38) 91
LIFT EVERY VOICE (TAKE ME AWAY) – MASS ORDER (35) 92
LIFT IT HIGH (ALL ABOUT BELIEF) – MANCHESTER UNITED FOOTBALL CLUB (11) 99
LIFT ME UP [A] – Howard JONES (52) 92
LIFT ME UP [B] – RED 5 (26) 97
LIFT ME UP [C] – Geri HALLIWELL (1) 99,00
LIFT ME UP [D] – REEL (39) 01
LIFTED – LIGHTHOUSE FAMILY (4) 95,96
LIFTING ME HIGHER – GEMS FOR JEM (28) ..95
LIGHT – Pharoahe MONCH (72) 00
THE LIGHT [A] – COMMON (56) 00
THE LIGHT [B] – Michelle WEEKS (69)..........03
LIGHT A CANDLE – Daniel O'DONNELL (23)..00
LIGHT A RAINBOW – TUKAN (38) 01
LIGHT AIRCRAFT ON FIRE – AUTEURS (58) ..96
LIGHT AND DAY – POLYPHONIC SPREE (40) 03
THE LIGHT COMES FROM WITHIN – Linda McCARTNEY (56) 99
LIGHT EMITTING ELECTRICAL WAVE – THESE ANIMAL MEN (72) 97
LIGHT FLIGHT – PENTANGLE (43) 70
LIGHT MY FIRE [A] – DOORS (7) 67,91
LIGHT MY FIRE [A] – José FELICIANO (6) 68
LIGHT MY FIRE – 137 DISCO HEAVEN (MEDLEY) [A] – Amii STEWART (5)......79,85
LIGHT MY FIRE [A] – Mike FLOWERS POPS (39) 96
LIGHT MY FIRE [A] – UB40 (63) 00
LIGHT MY FIRE [A] – Will YOUNG (1) 02
LIGHT MY FIRE [B] – CLUBHOUSE (7) 93,94
(LIGHT OF EXPERIENCE) DOINA DE JALE – Gheorghe ZAMFIR (4)..................................76
LIGHT OF LOVE – T. REX (22) 74
LIGHT OF MY LIFE – LOUISE (8)....................95
LIGHT OF THE WORLD – Kim APPLEBY (41) 93
LIGHT UP THE FIRE – PARCHMENT (31)........72
LIGHT UP THE NIGHT – BROTHERS JOHNSON (47) 80
LIGHT UP THE WORLD FOR CHRISTMAS – LAMPIES (48) 01
LIGHT YEARS – PEARL JAM (52) 00
LIGHT YOUR ASS ON FIRE – Busta RHYMES featuring PHARRELL (62) 03
LIGHTER – DJ SS (63)......................................02
LIGHTNIN' STRIKES – Lou CHRISTIE (11) 66
LIGHTNING – ZOE (37) 91
LIGHTNING CRASHES – LIVE (33)..................96
LIGHTNING FLASH – BROTHERHOOD OF MAN (67) 82
LIGHTNING STRIKES – Ozzy OSBOURNE (72)..................................86
THE LIGHTNING TREE – SETTLERS (36) 71
LIGHTS OF CINCINNATI – Scott WALKER (13) 69
LIGHTS OUT – Lisa Marie PRESLEY (16) 03
LIKE A BABY – Len BARRY (10) 66
LIKE A BUTTERFLY – Mac and Katie KISSOON (18)........................75
LIKE A CAT – CRW featuring VERONIKA (57) 02
LIKE A CHILD – Julie ROGERS (21) 64
LIKE A CHILD AGAIN – MISSION (30)............92
LIKE A FEATHER – Nikka COSTA (53) 01
LIKE A HURRICANE – MISSION (49) 86
LIKE A MOTORWAY – SAINT ETIENNE (47) ..94
LIKE A PLAYA – LA GANZ (75) 96
LIKE A PRAYER [A] – MADONNA (1) 89
LIKE A PRAYER [A] – MAD'HOUSE (3) 02
LIKE A ROLLING STONE [A] – Bob DYLAN (4) 65
LIKE A ROLLING STONE [A] – ROLLING STONES (12) 95
LIKE A ROSE – A1 (6) 00
LIKE A SATELLITE (EP) – THUNDER (28) 93
LIKE A VIRGIN – MADONNA (3) 84
LIKE A WOMAN – Tony RICH PROJECT (27)..96
LIKE A YO-YO – SABRINA (72) 89
LIKE AN ANIMAL – GLOVE (52) 83
LIKE AN OLD TIME MOVIE – Scott McKENZIE (50) 67
LIKE CLOCKWORK – BOOMTOWN RATS (6) ..78
LIKE DREAMERS DO [A] – APPLEJACKS (20) 64
LIKE DREAMERS DO [B] – Mica PARIS featuring Courtney PINE (26) ..88
LIKE FLAMES – BERLIN (47)..........................87
LIKE GLUE – Sean PAUL (3) 03
LIKE I DO [A] – Maureen EVANS (3)..............62
LIKE I DO [B] – FOR REAL (45)......................97
LIKE I LIKE IT – AURRA (43) 85,86
LIKE I LOVE YOU – Justin TIMBERLAKE (2) ..02
LIKE I'VE NEVER BEEN GONE – Billy FURY (3) 63
LIKE LOVERS DO – Lloyd COLE (24) 95
LIKE MARVIN GAYE SAID (WHAT'S GOING ON) – SPEECH (35) 96
LIKE PRINCES DO – DIESEL PARK WEST (58) 89
LIKE SISTER AND BROTHER – DRIFTERS (7) 73
LIKE STRANGERS – EVERLY BROTHERS (11) 60
LIKE THIS AND LIKE THAT [A] – MONICA (33) 96
LIKE THIS AND LIKE THAT [B] – LaKiesha BERRI (54) 97
LIKE THIS LIKE THAT – Mauro PICOTTO (21) 01
LIKE TO GET TO KNOW YOU WELL – Howard JONES (4) 84
LIKE WE USED TO BE – Georgie FAME (33)..65
A LIL' AIN'T ENOUGH – David Lee ROTH (32) 91
LIL' BIG MAN – Omera MUMBA (42) 02
LIL' DEVIL – CULT (11) 87
LIL' DUB – SPACE MONKEYZ vs GORILLAZ (73)............02
LIL' RED RIDING HOOD [A] – SAM THE SHAM and the PHARAOHS (46) ..66
LIL RED RIDING HOOD [A] – 999 (59) 81
LILAC WINE – Elkie BROOKS (16)..................78
LILY THE PINK – SCAFFOLD (1) 68
LILY WAS HERE – Candy DULFER (6) 90
LIMBO ROCK – Chubby CHECKER (32)..........62
LINDA LU – Johnny KIDD and the PIRATES (47) 61
THE LINE – Lisa STANSFIELD (64) 97
LINE DANCE PARTY – WOOLPACKERS (25) ..97
LINE UP – ELASTICA (20) 94
LINES – PLANETS (36) 79
LINGER – CRANBERRIES (14)....................93,94
THE LION SLEEPS TONIGHT (WIMOWEH) [A] – TOKENS (11) 61
THE LION SLEEPS TONIGHT [A] – Dave NEWMAN (34) 72
THE LION SLEEPS TONIGHT [A] – TIGHT FIT (1) 82
LIONROCK – LIONROCK (63) 92
THE LION'S MOUTH – KAJAGOOGOO (25) 84
LIP GLOSS – PULP (50) 93
LIP SERVICE (EP) – WET WET WET (15)........92
LIP UP FATTY – BAD MANNERS (15) 80
LIPS LIKE SUGAR – ECHO and the BUNNYMEN (36)....................87
LIPSMACKIN' ROCK 'N' ROLLIN' – Peter BLAKE (40)..77
LIPSTICK – ROCKET FROM THE CRYPT (64)..98
LIPSTICK ON YOUR COLLAR – Connie FRANCIS (3) 59
LIPSTICK POWDER AND PAINT – Shakin' STEVENS (11)..................................85
LIQUID COOL – APOLLO FOUR FORTY (35) ..94
LIQUID DREAMS – O-TOWN (3) 01
LIQUID LIPS – BLUETONES (25)....................03

LIZARD (GONNA GET YOU) – Mauro PICOTTO (27) 99
LK (CAROLINA CAROL BELA) – DJ MARKY & XRS featuring STAMINA MC (17) 02
L'L'LUCY – MUD (10) 75
LOADED [A] – PRIMAL SCREAM (16) 90
LOADED [B] – Ricky MARTIN (19) 01
LOADSAMONEY (DOIN' UP THE HOUSE) – Harry ENFIELD (4) 88
LOBSTER & SCRIMP – TIMBALAND featuring JAY-Z (48) 99
LOC'ED AFTER DARK – Tone LOC (21) 89
LOCAL BOY IN THE PHOTOGRAPH – STEREOPHONICS (14) 97,98
LOCK AND LOAD – Bob SEGER and the SILVER BULLET BAND (57) 96
LOCK UP YOUR DAUGHTERS – SLADE (29) ..81
LOCKED OUT – CROWDED HOUSE (12) 94
LOCO – FUN LOVIN' CRIMINALS (5) 01
LOCO IN ACAPULCO – FOUR TOPS (7) 88
LOCOMOTION – ORCHESTRAL MANOEUVRES IN THE DARK (5) 84
LOCO-MOTION [A] – VERNONS GIRLS (47) 62
THE LOCO-MOTION [A] – LITTLE EVA (2) 62,72
THE LOCOMOTION [A] – Dave STEWART (70) 86
THE LOCO-MOTION [A] – Kylie MINOGUE (2) 88
L.O.D. (LOVE ON DELIVERY) – Billy OCEAN (19) 76
THE LODGERS – STYLE COUNCIL (13) 85
THE LOGICAL SONG [A] – SUPERTRAMP (7) 79
THE LOGICAL SONG [A] – SCOOTER (2) 02
L'OISEAU ET L'ENFANT – Marie MYRIAM (42) 77
LOLA [A] – KINKS (2) 70
LOLA [A] – Andy TAYLOR (60) 90
LOLLIPOP [A] – CHORDETTES (6) 58
LOLLIPOP [A] – MUDLARKS (2) 58
LOLLY LOLLY – WENDY and LISA (64) 89
LONDINIUM – CATATONIA (20) 99
LONDON BOYS – T. REX (40) 76
LONDON CALLING – CLASH (11) 79,88,91
LONDON GIRLS – CHAS and DAVE (63) 83
LONDON KID – Jean-Michel JARRE featuring Hank MARVIN (52) 89
LONDON NIGHTS – LONDON BOYS (2) 89
A LONDON THING – Scott GARCIA featuring MC STYLES (29) 97
LONDON TIMES – RADIO HEART featuring Gary NUMAN (48) ..87
LONDON TONIGHT – COLLAPSED LUNG (31) 96
LONDON TOWN [A] – Paul McCARTNEY (60) 78
LONDON TOWN [B] – LIGHT OF THE WORLD (41) 80
LONDON TOWN [C] – BUCKS FIZZ (34) 83
LONDON TOWN [D] – JDS (49) 98
LONDON X-PRESS – X-PRESS 2 (59) 93
LONDON'S BRILLIANT – Wendy JAMES (62) 93
LONDON'S BRILLIANT PARADE – Elvis COSTELLO (48) 94
LONDRES STRUTT – SMELLS LIKE HEAVEN (57) 93
THE LONE RANGER – QUANTUM JUMP (5) 79
LONE RIDER – John LEYTON (40) 62
THE LONELIEST MAN IN THE WORLD – TOURISTS (32) 79
LONELINESS [A] – Des O'CONNOR (18) 69
LONELINESS [B] – TOMCRAFT (1) 03
LONELINESS IS GONE – NINE YARDS (70) 98
LONELY [A] – Eddie COCHRAN (41) 60
LONELY [B] – Mr Acker BILK and his PARAMOUNT JAZZ BAND (14) 62
LONELY [C] – Peter ANDRE (6) 97,98
LONELY BALLERINA – MANTOVANI (16) 55
LONELY BOY [A] – Paul ANKA (3) 59
LONELY BOY [B] – Andrew GOLD (11) 77
LONELY BOY LONELY GUITAR – Duane EDDY and the REBELS (35) 63
THE LONELY BULL – Herb ALPERT (22) 63
LONELY CITY – John LEYTON (14) 62
LONELY, CRYIN' ONLY – THERAPY? (32) 98
LONELY DAYS – BEE GEES (33) 70
LONELY DAYS, LONELY NIGHTS – Don DOWNING (32) 73
LONELY (HAVE WE LOST OUR LOVE) – Lance ELLINGTON (57) 93
LONELY HEART – UFO (41) 81
THE LONELY MAN THEME – Cliff ADAMS ORCHESTRA (39) 60
LONELY NIGHT – MAGNUM (70) 86
THE LONELY ONE – ALICE DEEJAY (16) 00
LONELY PUP (IN A CHRISTMAS SHOP) – Adam FAITH (4) 60
LONELY STREET – Clarence 'Frogman' HENRY (42) 61
LONELY SYMPHONY – Frances RUFFELLE (25) 94
LONELY TEENAGER – DION (47) 61
LONELY THIS CHRISTMAS – MUD (1) 74,85
LONELY TOGETHER – Barry MANILOW (21) ..80
THE LONER – Gary MOORE (53) 87
LONESOME – Adam FAITH (12) 62
LONESOME DAY – Bruce SPRINGSTEEN (39) 02
LONESOME NUMBER ONE – Don GIBSON (47) 62
LONESOME (SI TU VOIS MA MÈRE) – Chris BARBER'S JAZZ BAND (27) 59
LONESOME TRAVELLER – Lonnie DONEGAN (28) 58
LONG AFTER TONIGHT IS ALL OVER – Jimmy RADCLIFFE (40) 65
LONG AND LASTING LOVE (ONCE IN A LIFETIME) – Glenn MEDEIROS (42) 88
THE LONG AND WINDING ROAD [A] – Ray MORGAN (32) 70
THE LONG AND WINDING ROAD [A] – Will YOUNG and Gareth GATES (1) 02
LONG AS I CAN SEE THE LIGHT [A] – CREEDENCE CLEARWATER REVIVAL (20) 70
LONG AS I CAN SEE THE LIGHT [A] – MONKEY MAFIA (51) 98
LONG COOL WOMAN IN A BLACK DRESS – HOLLIES (32) 72
A LONG DECEMBER – COUNTING CROWS (62) 96,97
LONG DISTANCE – TURIN BRAKES (22) 02
THE LONG GOODBYE – Ronan KEATING (3) 03
LONG HAIRED LOVER FROM LIVERPOOL – Little Jimmy OSMOND (1) 72,73
LONG HOT SUMMER – STYLE COUNCIL (3) 83,89
LONG HOT SUMMER NIGHT – JT TAYLOR (63) 91
LONG LEGGED GIRL (WITH THE SHORT DRESS ON) – Elvis PRESLEY (49) 67
LONG LEGGED WOMAN DRESSED IN BLACK – MUNGO JERRY (13) 74
LONG LIVE LOVE [A] – Sandie SHAW (1) 65
LONG LIVE LOVE [A] – Nick BERRY (47) 92
LONG LIVE LOVE [B] – Olivia NEWTON-JOHN (11) 74
LONG LIVE ROCK – WHO (48) 79
LONG LIVE ROCK 'N' ROLL – RAINBOW (33) 78
LONG LIVE THE UK MUSIC SCENE – Helen LOVE (65) 98
LONG LONG WAY TO GO – DEF LEPPARD (40) 03
LONG LOST LOVER – THREE DEGREES (40) ..75
LONG MAY YOU RUN (LIVE) – Neil YOUNG (71) 93
THE LONG RUN – EAGLES (66) 79
LONG SHOT KICK DE BUCKET – PIONEERS (21) 69,70,80
LONG TALL GLASSES – Leo SAYER (4) 74
LONG TALL SALLY [A] – Pat BOONE (18) 56
LONG TALL SALLY [A] – LITTLE RICHARD (3) 57
LONG TERM LOVERS OF PAIN (EP) – HUE AND CRY (48) 91
LONG TIME – ARROW (30) 85
LONG TIME COMING – BUMP & FLEX (73) 98
LONG TIME GONE – GALLIANO (15) 94
LONG TRAIN RUNNING [A] – BANANARAMA (30) 91
LONG TRAIN RUNNIN' [A] – DOOBIE BROTHERS (7) 93
A LONG WALK – Jill SCOTT (54) 01
LONG WAY – ROOTJOOSE (68) 97
LONG WAY AROUND – Eagle-Eye CHERRY featuring Neneh CHERRY (48) 00
LONG WAY FROM HOME – WHITESNAKE (55) 79
LONG WAY SOUTH – JJ72 (68) 00
LONG WAY TO GO – Stevie NICKS (60) 89
LONG WHITE CAR – HIPSWAY (55) 86
LONGER – Dan FOGELBERG (59) 80
THE LONGEST TIME – Billy JOEL (25) 84
LONGTIME BOY – NINA and FREDERICK (43) 61
LONGVIEW – GREEN DAY (30) 95
LONNIE DONEGAN SHOWCASE (LP) – Lonnie DONEGAN (26) 56
LONNIE'S SKIFFLE PARTY – Lonnie DONEGAN (23) 58
LOO-BE-LOO – CHUCKS (22) 63
THE LOOK – ROXETTE (7) 89,95
LOOK AROUND – Vince HILL (12) 71
LOOK AT ME – Geri HALLIWELL (2) 99
LOOK AT ME (I'M IN LOVE) – MOMENTS (42) 75
LOOK AT ME NOW – JESSY (29) 03
LOOK AT THAT GIRL – Guy MITCHELL (1) 53
LOOK AT YOURSELF – David McALMONT (40) 97
LOOK AWAY – BIG COUNTRY (7) 86
LOOK BEFORE YOU LEAP – Dave CLARK FIVE (50) 66
LOOK BUT DON'T TOUCH (EP) – SKIN (33) ..94
LOOK FOR A STAR – Garry MILLS (7) 60
LOOK HOMEWARD ANGEL – Johnnie RAY (7) 57
LOOK INTO MY EYES – BONE THUGS-N-HARMONY (16) 97
LOOK MAMA – Howard JONES (10) 85
LOOK ME IN THE HEART – Tina TURNER (31) 90
THE LOOK OF LOVE [A] – Gladys KNIGHT and the PIPS (21) 73
THE LOOK OF LOVE [A] – T-EMPO (71) 96
THE LOOK OF LOVE [B] – ABC (4) 82,83,90
THE LOOK OF LOVE [C] – MADONNA (9) 87
LOOK THROUGH ANY WINDOW – HOLLIES (4) 65
LOOK THROUGH MY EYES – Phil COLLINS (61) 03
LOOK UP TO THE LIGHT – EVOLUTION (55) 95
LOOK WHAT YOU DONE FOR ME – Al GREEN (44) 72
LOOK WHAT YOU STARTED – TEMPTATIONS (63) 88
LOOK WHO IT IS – Helen SHAPIRO (47) 63
LOOK WHO'S DANCING – Ziggy MARLEY and the MELODY MAKERS (65) 89
LOOK WHO'S PERFECT NOW – TRANSISTER (56) 98
LOOK WHO'S TALKING – DR ALBAN (55) 94
LOOK WOT YOU DUN – SLADE (4) 72
LOOKIN' AT YOU – Warren G featuring TOI (60) 02
LOOKIN' THROUGH THE WINDOWS – JACKSONS (9) 72
LOOKING AFTER NO.1 – BOOMTOWN RATS (11) 77
LOOKING AT MIDNIGHT – IMAGINATION (29) 83
LOOKING FOR A LOVE – Joyce SIMS (39) 89
LOOKING FOR A NEW LOVE – Jody WATLEY (13) 87
LOOKING FOR A SONG – BIG AUDIO DYNAMITE (68) 94
LOOKING FOR ATLANTIS – PREFAB SPROUT (51) 90
LOOKING FOR CLUES – Robert PALMER (33) 80
LOOKING FOR LEWIS AND CLARK – LONG RYDERS (59) 85
LOOKING FOR LINDA – HUE AND CRY (15) ..89
LOOKING FOR LOVE – Karen RAMIREZ (8) 98
LOOKING FOR LOVE TONIGHT – FAT LARRY'S BAND (46) 79
LOOKING FOR THE SUMMER – Chris REA (49) 91
LOOKING HIGH HIGH HIGH – Bryan JOHNSON (20) 60
LOOKING THROUGH PATIENT EYES – PM DAWN (11) 93
LOOKING THROUGH THE EYES OF LOVE [A] – Gene PITNEY (3) 65
LOOKING THRU THE EYES OF LOVE [A] – PARTRIDGE FAMILY (9) 73
LOOKING THROUGH YOUR EYES – LeAnn RIMES (38) 98
LOOKING UP – Michelle GAYLE (11) 93
LOOKS LIKE I'M IN LOVE AGAIN – ERIK (46) 93
LOOKS, LOOKS, LOOKS – SPARKS (26) 75
LOOP-DE-LOOP – Frankie VAUGHAN (5) 63
LOOP DI LOVE – Jonathan KING (4) 72
LOOPS OF FURY (EP) – CHEMICAL BROTHERS (13) 96
LOOPS OF INFINITY – COSMIC BABY (70) 94
LOOPZILLA – George CLINTON (57) 82
LOOSE – THERAPY? (25) 95
LOOSE CANNON – KILLING JOKE (25) 03
LOOSE FIT – HAPPY MONDAYS (17) 91
LOOSEN YOUR HOLD – SOUTH (73) 03

MAYBE I'M AMAZED [A] – **Paul McCARTNEY** (28) 77
MAYBE I'M AMAZED [A] – **Carleen ANDERSON** (24) 98
MAYBE I'M DEAD – **MONEY MARK** (45) 98
MAYBE LOVE – **Stevie NICKS** (42) 94
MAYBE THAT'S WHAT IT TAKES – **Alex PARKS** (3) 03
MAYBE TOMORROW [A] – **Billy FURY** (18) 59
MAYBE TOMORROW [B] – **CHORDS** (40) 80
MAYBE TOMORROW [C] – **UB40** (14) 87
MAYBE TOMORROW [D] – **STEREOPHONICS** (3) 03
MAYBE (WE SHOULD CALL IT A DAY) – **Hazell DEAN** (15) 88
MAYOR OF SIMPLETON – **XTC** (46) 89
McDONALD'S CAVE – **PILTDOWN MEN** (14) ..60
ME AGAINST THE MUSIC – **Britney SPEARS featuring MADONNA** (2) 03
ME AND BABY BROTHER – **WAR** (21) 76
ME AND JULIO DOWN BY THE SCHOOLYARD – **Paul SIMON** (15) 72
ME AND MR SANCHEZ – **BLUE RONDO A LA TURK** (40) 81
ME AND MRS JONES [A] – **Billy PAUL** (12) 73
ME AND MRS JONES [A] – **Freddie JACKSON** (32) 92
ME AND MY GIRL (NIGHT-CLUBBING) – **David ESSEX** (13) 82
ME AND MY LIFE – **TREMELOES** (4) 70
ME AND MY SHADOW – **Frank SINATRA and Sammy DAVIS Jr** (20) 62,63
ME AND THE FARMER – **HOUSEMARTINS** (15) 87
ME AND YOU AND A DOG NAMED BOO – **LOBO** (4) 71
ME AND YOU VERSUS THE WORLD – **SPACE** (9) 96
ME. IN TIME – **CHARLATANS** (28) 91
ME' ISRAELITES – **CHOPS-EMC + EXTENSIVE** (60) 92
ME JULIE – **Ali G & SHAGGY** (2) 02
ME MYSELF AND I – **DE LA SOUL** (22) 89
ME MYSELF I – **Joan ARMATRADING** (21) 80
ME NO POP I – **Kid CREOLE and the COCONUTS** (32) 81
ME OR YOU? – **KILLING JOKE** (57) 83
ME THE PEACEFUL HEART – **LULU** (9) 68
MEA CULPA PART II – **ENIGMA** (55) 91
MEAN GIRL – **STATUS QUO** (20) 73
MEAN MAN – **W.A.S.P.** (21) 89
MEAN MEAN MAN – **Wanda JACKSON** (40) ..61
MEAN STREAK [A] – **Cliff RICHARD** (10) 59
MEAN STREAK [B] – **Y & T** (41) 83
MEAN TO ME – **Shaye COGAN** (40) 60
MEAN WOMAN BLUES – **Roy ORBISON** (3) ..63
THE MEANING OF CHRISTMAS – **Boris GARDINER** (69) 86
THE MEANING OF LOVE – **DEPECHE MODE** (12) 82
MEAT PIE SAUSAGE ROLL – **GRANDAD ROBERTS AND HIS SON ELVIS** (67) 98
MECCA – **CHEETAHS** (36) 64
MECHANICAL WONDER – **OCEAN COLOUR SCENE** (49) 01
THE MEDAL SONG – **CULTURE CLUB** (32) 84,85
MEDICATION – **SPIRITUALIZED** (55) 92
MEDICINE SHOW – **BIG AUDIO DYNAMITE** (29) 86
THE MEDICINE SONG – **Stephanie MILLS** (29) 84
MEET EL PRESIDENTE – **DURAN DURAN** (24) 87
MEET HER AT THE LOVE PARADE – **DA HOOL** (01) 98,01
MEET ME ON THE CORNER [A] – **Max BYGRAVES** (2) 55
MEET ME ON THE CORNER [B] – **LINDISFARNE** (5) 72
(MEET) THE FLINTSTONES – **B-52's** (3) 94
MEGABLAST – **BOMB THE BASS** (6) 88
MEGACHIC – CHIC MEDLEY – **CHIC** (58) 90
MEGALOMANIA – **PELE** (73) 92
MEGAMIX [A] – **TECHNOTRONIC** (6) 90
MEGAMIX [B] – **Crystal WATERS** (39) 92
MEGAMIX [C] – **CORONA** (36) 97
MEGAMIX [D] – **BONEY M** (52) 88
MEGAREX – **T. REX** (72) 85
MEISO – **DJ KRUSH** (52) 96
MELANCHOLY ROSE – **Marc ALMOND** (71) 87
MELLOW DOUBT – **TEENAGE FANCLUB** (34) 95
MELLOW MELLOW RIGHT ON – **LOWRELL** (37) 79
MELLOW YELLOW – **DONOVAN** (8) 67
THE MELOD-EP – **DODGY** (53) 94
MELODY OF LOVE – **INK SPOTS** (10) 55
MELODY OF LOVE (WANNA BE LOVED) – **Donna SUMMER** (21) 94
MELT [A] – **SIOUXSIE and the BANSHEES** (49) 82
MELT [B] – **MELANIE C** (27) 03
MELTING POT – **BLUE MINK** (3) 69
MEMO FROM TURNER – **Mick JAGGER** (32) ..70
MEMORIES [A] – **PUBLIC IMAGE LTD** (60) 79
MEMORIES [B] – **Mike BERRY** (55) 81
MEMORIES [C] – **Beverley CRAVEN** (68) 91
MEMORIES ARE MADE OF THIS [A] – **Dave KING** (5) 56
MEMORIES ARE MADE OF THIS [A] – **Dean MARTIN** (1) 56
MEMORIES ARE MADE OF THIS [A] – **Val DOONICAN** (11) 67
MEMORY [A] – **Elaine PAIGE** (6) 81,82,98
MEMORY [A] – **Barbra STREISAND** (34) 82
MEMORY [A] – **Aled JONES** (42) 85
THE MEMORY REMAINS – **METALLICA** (13) ..97
MEMPHIS – **Lonnie MACK** (47) 79
MEMPHIS TENNESSEE [A] – **Chuck BERRY** (6) 63
MEMPHIS TENNESSEE [A] – **Dave BERRY** (19) 63
MEN IN BLACK [A] – **Frank BLACK** (37) 96
MEN IN BLACK [B] – **Will SMITH** (1) 97
MENTAL – **MANIC MCs featuring Sara CARLSON** (30) 89
MENTAL PICTURE – **Jon SECADA** (44) 95
MENTASM – **SECOND PHASE** (48) 91
MERCEDES BOY – **PEBBLES** (42) 88
MERCI CHERI – **Vince HILL** (36) 66
MERCURY – **LOWGOLD** (48) 01
MERCURY AND SOLACE – **BT** (38) 99
MERCY MERCY ME – I WANT YOU – **Robert PALMER** (9) 91
MERMAIDS – **Paul WELLER** (30) 97
MERRY CHRISTMAS DARLING – **CARPENTERS** (25) 72,90
MERRY CHRISTMAS EVERYONE – **Shakin' STEVENS** (1) 85,86
MERRY GENTLE POPS – **BARRON KNIGHTS** (9) 65
A MERRY JINGLE – **GREEDIES** (28) 79
THE MERRY PLOUGHBOY – **Dermot O'BRIEN** (46) 66
MERRY XMAS EVERYBODY [A] – **SLADE** (1) 73,80,81,82,83,84,85,86,98
MERRY XMAS EVERYBODY [A] – **METAL GURUS** (55) 90
MERRY X-MESS – **ROTTERDAM TERMINATION SOURCE** (73) ..93
MERSEYBEAST – **Ian McNABB** (74) 96
MESCALITO – **SOURMASH** (73) 00
MESMERISE – **CHAPTERHOUSE** (60) 91
MESMERIZE – **JA RULE featuring ASHANTI** (12) 03
A MESS OF BLUES [A] – **Elvis PRESLEY** (2) ..60
A MESS OF BLUES [A] – **STATUS QUO** (15) ..83
THE MESSAGE [A] – **GRANDMASTER FLASH, Melle MEL and the FURIOUS FIVE** (8) 82
THE MESSAGE [B] – **49ers** (68) 92
MESSAGE IN A BOTTLE [A] – **POLICE** (1) 79
MESSAGE IN A BOTTLE [A] – **DANCE FLOOR VIRUS** (49) 95
MESSAGE IN A BOTTLE [A] – **T-FACTORY** (51) 02
MESSAGE IN THE BOX – **WORLD PARTY** (39) 90
THE MESSAGE IS LOVE – **Arthur BAKER and the BACKBEAT DISCIPLES featuring Al GREEN** (38) 89
MESSAGE OF LOVE [A] – **PRETENDERS** (11) ..81
MESSAGE OF LOVE [B] – **LOVEHAPPY** (37) 95,96
MESSAGE TO MARTHA (KENTUCKY BLUEBIRD) [A] – **Adam FAITH** (12) 64
MESSAGE TO MARTHA [A] – **Lou JOHNSON** (36) 64
A MESSAGE TO YOU RUDY – **SPECIALS** (10) 79
A MESSAGE TO YOUR HEART – **Samantha JANUS** (30) 91
MESSAGE II (SURVIVAL) – **GRANDMASTER FLASH, Melle MEL and the FURIOUS FIVE** (74) 83
MESSAGE UNDERSTOOD – **Sandie SHAW** (6) 65
MESSAGES – **ORCHESTRAL MANOEUVRES IN THE DARK** (13) 80
MESSAGES FROM THE STARS – **RAH BAND** (42) 83
MESSIN' – **LADIES FIRST** (30) 01
METAFORCE – **ART OF NOISE** (53) 99
METAL GURU – **T. REX** (1) 72
METAL HEALTH – **QUIET RIOT** (45) 83
METAL MICKEY – **SUEDE** (17) 92
METEOR MAN – **Dee D JACKSON** (48) 78
METHOD OF MODERN LOVE – **Daryl HALL and John OATES** (21) 85
METROSOUND – **Adam F & J MAJIK** (54) 02
METROPOLIS – **Oliver LIEB presents SMOKED** (72) 00
MEXICALI ROSE – **Karl DENVER** (8) 61
THE MEXICAN – **FENTONES** (41) 62
MEXICAN GIRL – **SMOKIE** (19) 78
MEXICAN RADIO – **WALL OF VOODOO** (64) ..83
MEXICAN WAVE – **KERBDOG** (49) 97
MEXICO – **Long John BALDRY** (15) 68
MF FROM HELL – **The DATSUNS** (55) 03
MFEO – **KAVANA** (8) 97
MI CHICO LATINO – **Geri HALLIWELL** (1) 99
MI TIERRA – **Gloria ESTEFAN** (36) 93
MIAMI – **Will SMITH** (3) 98
MIAMI HIT MIX – **Gloria ESTEFAN** (8) 92
MIAMI VICE THEME – **Jan HAMMER** (5) 85
MICHAEL [A] – **HIGHWAYMEN** (1) 61
MICHAEL [B] – **Geno WASHINGTON and the RAM JAM BAND** (39) 67
MICHAEL AND THE SLIPPER TREE – **EQUALS** (24) 69
MICHAEL CAINE – **MADNESS** (11) 84
MICHAEL JACKSON MEDLEY – **ASHAYE** (45) 83
MICHAEL ROW THE BOAT – **Lonnie DONEGAN** (6) 61
MICHELLE [A] – **DAVID and JONATHAN** (11) ..66
MICHELLE [A] – **OVERLANDERS** (1) 66
MICHIKO – **SULTANS OF PING** (43) 93
MICKEY [A] – **Toni BASIL** (2) 82
MICKEY [A] – **LOLLY** (4) 99
MICRO KID – **LEVEL 42** (37) 83
THE MICROPHONE FIEND – **Eric B and RAKIM** (74) 88
MICROWAVED – **PITCH SHIFTER** (54) 98
MIDAS TOUCH – **MIDNIGHT STAR** (8) 86
THE MIDDLE – **JIMMY EAT WORLD** (26) 02
MIDDLE OF THE NIGHT – **BROTHERHOOD OF MAN** (41) 78
MIDDLEMAN – **TERRORVISION** (25) 94
MIDLIFE CRISIS – **FAITH NO MORE** (10) 92
MIDNIGHT [A] – **Paul ANKA** (26) 58
MIDNIGHT [B] – **UN-CUT** (26) 03
MIDNIGHT AT THE LOST AND FOUND – **MEAT LOAF** (17) 83
MIDNIGHT AT THE OASIS [A] – **Maria MULDAUR** (21) 74
MIDNIGHT AT THE OASIS [A] – **BRAND NEW HEAVIES** (13) 94
MIDNIGHT BLUE – **Louise TUCKER** (59) 83
MIDNIGHT COWBOY – **MIDNIGHT COWBOY SOUNDTRACK** (47) 80
MIDNIGHT FLYER – **Nat 'King' COLE** (23) 59
MIDNIGHT GROOVIN' – **LIGHT OF THE WORLD** (72) 79
MIDNIGHT IN A PERFECT WORLD – **DJ SHADOW** (54) 96
MIDNIGHT IN CHELSEA – **Jon BON JOVI** (4) ..97
MIDNIGHT IN MOSCOW – **Kenny BALL and his JAZZMEN** (2) 61
MIDNIGHT RIDER – **Paul DAVIDSON** (10) 75
MIDNIGHT SHIFT – **Buddy HOLLY** (26) 59
MIDNIGHT SUMMER DREAM – **STRANGLERS** (35) 83
MIDNIGHT TO SIX MAN – **PRETTY THINGS** (46) 66
MIDNIGHT TRAIN TO GEORGIA – **Gladys KNIGHT and the PIPS** (10) 76
MIDNITE – **D'INFLUENCE** (58) 95
MIDNITE DYNAMOS – **MATCHBOX** (14) 80
MIDNITE SPECIAL – **Paul EVANS** (41) 60
MIDSUMMER MADNESS (EP) – **RHYTHM SECTION** (66) 92
MIGHT BE STARS – **WANNADIES** (51) 95
THE MIGHTY HIGH – **REVIVAL 3000** (47) 97

MONEY [A] – **Bern ELLIOTT and the FENMEN** (14) ...63
MONEY [A] – **FLYING LIZARDS** (5) ...79
MONEY [A] – **BACKBEAT BAND** (48) ...94
MONEY [B] – **Dan REED NETWORK** (45) ...90
MONEY [C] – **SKIN** (18) ...94
MONEY [D] – **Charli BALTIMORE** (12) ...98
MONEY [E] – **JAMELIA** (5) ...00
(MONEY CAN'T) BUY ME LOVE – **BLACKSTREET** (18) ...97
MONEY DON'T MATTER 2 NIGHT – **PRINCE and the NEW POWER GENERATION** (19) ...92
MONEY (EVERYBODY LOVES HER) – **GUN** (73) ...89
MONEY FOR NOTHING – **DIRE STRAITS** (4) ..85
MONEY GO ROUND (PART 1) – **STYLE COUNCIL** (11) ...83
MONEY GREEDY – **TRICKY** (25) ...98
MONEY HONEY – **BAY CITY ROLLERS** (3) ...75
MONEY IN MY POCKET – **Dennis BROWN** (14) ...79
MONEY LOVE – **Neneh CHERRY** (23) ...92
MONEY, MONEY, MONEY – **ABBA** (3) ...76
MONEY THAT'S YOUR PROBLEM – **TONIGHT** (66) ...78
MONEY TO BURN – **Richard ASHCROFT** (17) 00
MONEY'S TOO TIGHT (TO MENTION) [A] – **VALENTINE BROTHERS** (73) ...83
MONEY'S TOO TIGHT (TO MENTION) [A] – **SIMPLY RED** (13) ...85
MONEYTALKS – **AC/DC** (36) ...90
MONIE IN THE MIDDLE – **Monie LOVE** (46) ..90
THE MONKEES – **RAMPAGE** (51) ...95
THE MONKEES EP – **MONKEES** (33) ...80,89
MONKEY [A] – **George MICHAEL** (13) ...88
MONKEY [B] – **SHAFT** (61) ...92
MONKEY BUSINESS [A] – **SKID ROW** (19) ...91
MONKEY BUSINESS [B] – **DANGER DANGER** (42) ...92
MONKEY CHOP – **DAN-I** (30) ...79
MONKEY GONE TO HEAVEN – **PIXIES** (60) ...89
MONKEY MAN [A] – **MAYTALS** (47) ...70
MONKEY MAN [A] – **GENERAL LEVY** (75) ...93
MONKEY SPANNER – **Dave and Ansil COLLINS** (7) ...71
MONKEY WAH – **RADICAL ROB** (67) ...92
MONKEY WRENCH – **FOO FIGHTERS** (12) ...97
MONOCULTURE – **SOFT CELL** (52) ...02
MONSIEUR DUPONT – **Sandie SHAW** (6) ...69
MONSTER – **L7** (33) ...92
MONSTER – **LIQUID PEOPLE vs SIMPLE MINDS** (67) ...02
MONSTER MASH – **Bobby 'Boris' PICKETT and the CRYPT-KICKERS** (3) ...73
MONSTERS AND ANGELS – **VOICE OF THE BEEHIVE** (17) ...91
MONTEGO BAY [A] – **Freddie NOTES and the RUDIES** (45) ...70
MONTEGO BAY [A] – **Bobby BLOOM** (3) ..70,71
MONTEGO BAY [A] – **SUGAR CANE** (54) ...78
MONTEGO BAY [A] – **AMAZULU** (16) ...86
MONTREAL – **WEDDING PRESENT** (40) ...97
MONTREUX (EP) – **SIMPLY RED** (11) ...92
MONTUNO – **Gloria ESTEFAN** (55) ...93
MONY MONY [A] – **Tommy JAMES and the SHONDELLS** (1) ...68
MONY MONY [A] – **AMAZULU** (38) ...87
MONY MONY [A] – **Billy IDOL** (7) ...87
MONY MONY [A] – **STATUS QUO** (48) ...00
THE MOOD CLUB – **FIRSTBORN** (69) ...99
MOODSWINGS – **MY VITRIOL** (39) ...02
MOODY BLUE – **Elvis PRESLEY** (6) ...77
MOODY PLACES – **NORTHSIDE** (50) ...90
MOODY RIVER – **Pat BOONE** (18) ...61
MOOG ERUPTION – **DIGITAL ORGASM** (62) ..92
MOON – **VIRUS** (36) ...97
MOON HOP – **Derrick MORGAN** (49) ...70
MOON OVER BOURBON STREET – **STING** (44) ...86
MOON RIVER [A] – **Henry MANCINI** (44) ...61
MOON RIVER [A] – **Danny WILLIAMS** (1) ...61
MOON RIVER [A] – **GREYHOUND** (12) ...72
MOON SHADOW – **Cat STEVENS** (22) ...71
MOON TALK – **Perry COMO** (17) ...58
MOONCHILD – **FIELDS OF THE NEPHILIM** (28) ...88
MOONGLOW [A] – **Morris STOLOFF** (7) ...56
MOONGLOW [A] – **SOUNDS ORCHESTRAL** (43) ...65
MOONLIGHT AND MUZAK – **M** (33) ...79
MOONLIGHT & ROSES – **Jim REEVES** (34) ...71
MOONLIGHT GAMBLER – **Frankie LAINE** (13) ...56,57
MOONLIGHT SERENADE – **Glenn MILLER** (12) ...54,76
MOONLIGHT SHADOW – **Mike OLDFIELD** (4) ...83,93
MOONLIGHTING – **Leo SAYER** (2) ...75
'MOONLIGHTING' THEME – **Al JARREAU** (8) ..87
MOONSHINE SALLY – **MUD** (10) ...75
MOR – **BLUR** (15) ...97
MORE [A] – **Jimmy YOUNG** (4) ...56
MORE [A] – **Perry COMO** (10) ...56
MORE [B] – **SISTERS OF MERCY** (14) ...90
MORE ... [C] – **HIGH** (67) ...91
MORE & MORE – **SPOILED & ZIGO** (31) ...00
MORE AND MORE [A] – **Andy WILLIAMS** (45) ...67
MORE AND MORE [B] – **CAPTAIN HOLLYWOOD PROJECT** (23) ...93
MORE AND MORE PARTY POPS – **Russ CONWAY** (5) ...59
MORE BEATS & PIECES – **COLDCUT** (37) ...97
MORE GOOD OLD ROCK 'N' ROLL – **Dave CLARK FIVE** (34) ...70
MORE HUMAN THAN HUMAN – **WHITE ZOMBIE** (51) ...95
THE MORE I GET THE MORE I WANT – **KWS featuring Teddy PENDERGRASS** (35) ..94
THE MORE I SEE (THE LESS I BELIEVE) – **FUN BOY THREE** (68) ...83
THE MORE I SEE YOU [A] – **Joy MARSHALL** (34) ...66
THE MORE I SEE YOU [A] – **Chris MONTEZ** (3) ...66
THE MORE I SEE YOU [A] – **Barbara WINDSOR and Mike REID** (46) ...99
MORE LIFE IN A TRAMP'S VEST – **STEREOPHONICS** (33) ...97
MORE LIKE THE MOVIES – **DR HOOK** (14) ...78
MORE LOVE [A] – **Feargal SHARKEY** (44) ...88
MORE LOVE [B] – **NEXT OF KIN** (33) ...99
MORE MONEY FOR YOU AND ME (MEDLEY) – **FOUR PREPS** (39) ...61
MORE, MORE, MORE [A] – **Andrea TRUE CONNECTION** (5) ...76
MORE MORE MORE [A] – **BANANARAMA** (24) ...93
MORE, MORE, MORE [B] – **CARMEL** (23) ...84
MORE PARTY POPS – **Russ CONWAY** (10) ...58
MORE THAN A FEELING – **BOSTON** (22) ...77
MORE THAN A LOVER – **Bonnie TYLER** (27) 77
MORE THAN A WOMAN [A] – **TAVARES** (7) ..78
MORE THAN A WOMAN [A] – **911** (2) ...98,99
MORE THAN A WOMAN [B] – **AALIYAH** (1) ...02
MORE THAN EVER (COME PRIMA) [A] – **Malcolm VAUGHAN** (5) ...58
MORE THAN EVER (COME PRIMA) [A] – **Robert EARL** (26) ...58
MORE THAN I CAN BEAR – **MATT BIANCO** (50) ...85
MORE THAN I CAN SAY [A] – **CRICKETS** (42) 60
MORE THAN I CAN SAY [A] – **Bobby VEE** (4) 61
MORE THAN I CAN SAY [A] – **Leo SAYER** (2) 80
MORE THAN I NEEDED TO KNOW – **SCOOCH** (5) ...00
MORE THAN IN LOVE – **Kate ROBBINS and BEYOND** (2) ...81
MORE THAN LIKELY – **PM DAWN featuring BOY GEORGE** (40) ...93
MORE THAN LOVE [A] – **Ken DODD** (14) ...66
MORE THAN LOVE [B] – **WET WET WET** (19) 92
MORE THAN ONE KIND OF LOVE – **Joan ARMATRADING** (75) ...90
MORE THAN PHYSICAL – **BANANARAMA** (41) ...86
MORE THAN THAT – **BACKSTREET BOYS** (12) ...01
MORE THAN THIS [A] – **ROXY MUSIC** (6) ...82
MORE THAN THIS [A] – **EMMIE** (5) ...99
MORE THAN THIS [B] – **Peter GABRIEL** (47) 03
MORE THAN US (EP) – **TRAVIS** (16) ...98
MORE THAN WORDS – **EXTREME** (2) ...91
MORE THAN YOU KNOW – **MARTIKA** (15) ...90
THE MORE THEY KNOCK, THE MORE I LOVE YOU – **Gloria D BROWN** (57) ...85
MORE TO LIFE – **Cliff RICHARD** (23) ...91
MORE TO LOVE – **VOLCANO** (32) ...94
MORE TO THIS WORLD – **BAD BOYS INC** (8) ...94
THE MORE YOU IGNORE ME THE CLOSER I GET – **MORRISSEY** (8) ...94
THE MORE YOU LIVE, THE MORE YOU LOVE – **A FLOCK OF SEAGULLS** (26) ...84
MORGEN – **Ivo ROBIC** (23) ...59
MORNIN' – **Al JARREAU** (28) ...83
MORNING [A] – **Val DOONICAN** (12) ...71
MORNING [B] – **WET WET WET** (16) ...96
THE MORNING AFTER (FREE AT LAST) – **STRIKE** (38) ...95
MORNING AFTERGLOW – **ELECTRASY** (19) ...98
MORNING DANCE – **SPYRO GYRA** (17) ...79
MORNING GLORY – **James and Bobby PURIFY** (27) ...76
MORNING HAS BROKEN [A] – **Cat STEVENS** (9) ...72
MORNING HAS BROKEN [A] – **Neil DIAMOND** (36) ...92
MORNING HAS BROKEN [A] – **Daniel O'DONNELL** (32) ...00
THE MORNING OF OUR LIVES – **Jonathan RICHMAN and the MODERN LOVERS** (29) ..78
THE MORNING PAPERS – **PRINCE and the NEW POWER GENERATION** (52) ...93
MORNING SIDE OF THE MOUNTAIN – **Donny and Marie OSMOND** (5) ...74
MORNINGLIGHT – **TEAM DEEP** (42) ...97
MORNINGTOWN RIDE – **SEEKERS** (2) ...66
THE MOST BEAUTIFUL GIRL – **Charlie RICH** (2) ...74
THE MOST BEAUTIFUL GIRL IN THE WORLD – **PRINCE** (1) ...94
MOST GIRLS – **PINK** (5) ...00
MOST HIGH – **Jimmy PAGE** (26) ...98
THE MOST TIRING DAY – **CECIL** (69) ...98
MOTHER – **DANZIG** (62) ...94
MOTHER – **M FACTOR** (18) ...02
MOTHER AND CHILD REUNION – **Paul SIMON** (5) ...72
MOTHER DAWN – **BLUE PEARL** (50) ...92
MOTHER FIXATION – **MINUTEMAN** (45) ...03
MOTHER NATURE AND FATHER TIME – **Nat 'King' COLE** (7) ...53
MOTHER OF MINE – **Neil REID** (2) ...72
MOTHER UNIVERSE – **SOUP DRAGONS** (26) 90
MOTHER-IN-LAW – **Ernie K-DOE** (29) ...61
MOTHERLAND-A-FRI-CA – **TRIBAL HOUSE** (57) ...90
MOTHERLESS CHILD – **Eric CLAPTON** (63) ...94
MOTHER'S TALK – **TEARS FOR FEARS** (14) ...84
MOTHERSHIP RECONNECTION – **Scott GROOVES featuring PARLIAMENT / FUNKADELIC** (55) ...98,99
THE MOTION OF LOVE – **GENE LOVES JEZEBEL** (56) ...87
THE MOTIVE (LIVING WITHOUT YOU) – **THEN JERICO** (18) ...87
MOTIVATION – **SUM 41** (21) ...02
MOTOR BIKIN' – **Chris SPEDDING** (14) ...75
MOTORBIKE BEAT – **REZILLOS** (45) ...80
MOTORBIKE TO HEAVEN – **SALAD** (42) ...95
MOTORCYCLE EMPTINESS – **MANIC STREET PREACHERS** (17) ...92,97
MOTORCYCLE MICHAEL – **Jo Ann CAMPBELL** (41) ...61
MOTORCYCLE RIDER – **ICICLE WORKS** (73) ..90
MOTÖRHEAD LIVE – **MOTÖRHEAD** (6) ...81
MOTORMANIA – **ROMAN HOLLIDAY** (40) ...83
MOTORTOWN – **KANE GANG** (45) ...87
THE MOTOWN SONG – **Rod STEWART** (10) ..91
MOTOWNPHILLY – **BOYZ II MEN** (23) ...92
MOULDY OLD DOUGH – **LIEUTENANT PIGEON** (1) ...72
MOUNTAIN GREENERY – **Mel TORME** (4) ...56
MOUNTAIN OF LOVE – **Kenny LYNCH** (33) ...60
MOUNTAINS – **PRINCE** (45) ...86
THE MOUNTAIN'S HIGH – **DICK and DEEDEE** (37) ...61
MOUSE IN A HOLE – **HEAVY STEREO** (53) ...96
MOUTH – **Merril BAINBRIDGE** (51) ...96
MOUTH FOR WAR – **PANTERA** (73) ...92
MOVE [A] – **INSPIRAL CARPETS** (49) ...89
MOVE [B] – **MOBY** (21) ...93
MOVE ANY MOUNTAIN – **SHAMEN** (4) ...91,96
MOVE AWAY – **CULTURE CLUB** (7) ...86
MOVE AWAY JIMMY BLUE – **DEL AMITRI** (36) ...90
MOVE BABY MOVE – **SARTORELLO** (56) ...96
MOVE CLOSER [A] – **Phyllis NELSON** (1) ..85,94
MOVE CLOSER [A] – **Tom JONES** (49) ...89
MOVE IN A LITTLE CLOSER – **HARMONY GRASS** (24) ...69

MY FATHER'S EYES — **Eric CLAPTON** (33)......98
MY FATHER'S SHOES — **LEVEL 42** (55)..........92
MY FATHER'S SON — **Conner REEVES** (12)....97
MY FAVORITE MISTAKE — **Sheryl CROW** (9) ..98
MY FAVOURITE GAME — **CARDIGANS** (14)......98
MY FAVOURITE WASTE OF TIME — **Owen PAUL** (3) 86
MY FEELING — **JUNIOR JACK** (31) 00
MY FEET KEEP DANCING — **CHIC** (21)..........79
MY FIRST NIGHT WITHOUT YOU — **Cyndi LAUPER** (53)..........89
MY FOOLISH FRIEND — **TALK TALK** (57)........83
MY FORBIDDEN LOVER [A] — **CHIC** (15) 79
MY FORBIDDEN LOVER [A] — **Romina JOHNSON** (59)..........00
MY FRIEND [A] — **Frankie LAINE** (3) 54
MY FRIEND [B] — **Roy ORBISON** (35) 69
MY FRIEND [C] — **GROOVE ARMADA** (36) 01
MY FRIEND JACK [A] — **SMOKE** (45) 67
MY FRIEND JACK [A] — **BONEY M** (57) 80
MY FRIEND STAN — **SLADE** (2) 73
MY FRIEND THE SEA — **Petula CLARK** (7) 61
MY FRIENDS — **RED HOT CHILI PEPPERS** (29) 95
MY FRIENDS OVER YOU — **NEW FOUND GLORY** (30) 02
MY GENERATION [A] — **WHO** (2)..........65,88,96
MY GENERATION [B] — **LIMP BIZKIT** (15) ..00,01
MY GETAWAY — **T-BOZ** (44)..........01
MY GIRL [A] — **Otis REDDING** (11) 65,68
MY GIRL [A] — **TEMPTATIONS** (2) 65,92
MY GIRL [A] — **WHISPERS** (26) 80
MY GIRL [B] — **MADNESS** (3)..........80,92
MY GIRL [C] — **Rod STEWART** (32) 80
MY GIRL BILL — **Jim STAFFORD** (20)..........74
MY GIRL JOSEPHINE [A] — **Fats DOMINO** (32)61
MY GIRL JOSEPHINE [A] — **SUPERCAT** (22)....95
MY GIRL LOLLIPOP (MY BOY LOLLIPOP) — **BAD MANNERS** (9) 82
MY GIRL LOVES ME — **SHALAMAR** (45) 85
MY GIRL MY GIRL — **Warren STACEY** (26) 02
MY GUY [A] — **Mary WELLS** (5) 64,72
MY GUY [B] — **Tracey ULLMAN** (23) 84
MY GUY – MY GIRL (MEDLEY) [A] — **Amii STEWART and Johnny BRISTOL** (39) ..80
MY GUY – MY GIRL (MEDLEY) [A] — **Amii STEWART and Deon ESTUS** (63) 86
MY HAND OVER MY HEART — **Marc ALMOND** (33) 92
MY HAPPINESS — **Connie FRANCIS** (4)..........59
MY HEAD'S IN MISSISSIPPI — **ZZ TOP** (37) ..91
MY HEART — **Gene VINCENT** (16) 60
MY HEART CAN'T TELL YOU NO — **Rod STEWART** (49)..........89
MY HEART GOES BANG (GET ME TO THE DOCTOR) — **DEAD OR ALIVE** (23) 85
MY HEART GOES BOOM — **FRENCH AFFAIR** (44) 00
MY HEART HAS A MIND OF ITS OWN — **Connie FRANCIS** (3) 60
MY HEART THE BEAT — **D-SHAKE** (42) 91
MY HEART WILL GO ON — **Celine DION** (1)....98
MY HEART'S BEATING WILD (TIC TAC TIC TAC) — **GIBSON BROTHERS** (56) 83
MY HEART'S SYMPHONY — **Gary LEWIS and the PLAYBOYS** (36) 75
MY HERO — **FOO FIGHTERS** (21)..........98
MY HOMETOWN — **Bruce SPRINGSTEEN** (9)..85
MY HOUSE — **TERRORVISION** (29) 94
MY HOUSE IS YOUR HOUSE — **MAXTREME** (66) 02
MY IRON LUNG — **RADIOHEAD** (24) 94
MY JAMAICAN GUY — **Grace JONES** (56)........83
MY KIND OF GIRL [A] — **Matt MONRO** (5) 61
MY KIND OF GIRL [A] — **Frank SINATRA** (35) 63
MY KINDA LIFE — **Cliff RICHARD** (15) 77
MY KINGDOM — **FUTURE SOUND OF LONDON** (13)..........96
MY LAST NIGHT WITH YOU — **ARROWS** (25) 75
MY LIFE — **Billy JOEL** (12) 78
MY LIFE IS IN YOUR HANDS — **MELTDOWN** (44) 96
MY LITTLE BABY — **Mike BERRY** (34) 63
MY LITTLE CORNER OF THE WORLD — **Anita BRYANT** (48)..........60
MY LITTLE GIRL [A] — **CRICKETS** (17) 63
MY LITTLE GIRL [B] — **AUTUMN** (37)..........71
MY LITTLE LADY — **TREMELOES** (6) 68
MY LITTLE ONE — **MARMALADE** (15)..........71
MY LOVE [A] — **Petula CLARK** (4) 66
MY LOVE [B] — **Paul McCARTNEY** (9) 73
MY LOVE [C] — **Lionel RICHIE** (70) 83
MY LOVE [D] — **Julio IGLESIAS featuring Stevie WONDER** (5) 88
MY LOVE [E] — **LONDON BOYS** (46) 89
MY LOVE [F] — **Mary J BLIGE** (29)..........94
MY LOVE [G] — **Kele LE ROC** (8) 99
MY LOVE [H] — **WESTLIFE** (1) 00
MY LOVE [I] — **KLUSTER featuring Ron CARROLL** (73) 01
MY LOVE AND DEVOTION [A] — **Doris DAY** (10) 52
MY LOVE AND DEVOTION [A] — **Matt MONRO** (29) 62
MY LOVE FOR YOU — **Johnny MATHIS** (9) 60
MY LOVE IS A FIRE — **Donny OSMOND** (64)..91
MY LOVE IS ALWAYS — **SAFFRON HILL featuring Ben ONONO** (28) 03
MY LOVE IS DEEP — **Sara PARKER** (22) 97
MY LOVE IS FOR REAL [A] — **Paula ABDUL featuring Ofra HAZA** (28) 95
MY LOVE IS FOR REAL [A] — **STRIKE** (35)......96
MY LOVE IS GUARANTEED — **SYBIL** (42) ..87,93
MY LOVE IS LIKE ... WO — **MYA** (33) 03
MY LOVE IS MAGIC — **BAS NOIR** (73)..........89
MY LOVE IS SO RAW — **Alyson WILLIAMS featuring Nikki D** (34) 89
MY LOVE IS THE SHHH! — **SOMETHIN' FOR THE PEOPLE featuring TRINA and TAMARA** (64) 98
MY LOVE IS WAITING — **Marvin GAYE** (34)....83
MY LOVE IS YOUR LOVE — **Whitney HOUSTON** (2) 99
MY LOVE LIFE — **MORRISSEY** (29) 91
MY LOVER'S PRAYER — **Otis REDDING** (37) ..66
MY LOVIN' — **EN VOGUE** (4) 92
MY MAGIC MAN — **ROCHELLE** (27) 86
MY MAMMY — **HAPPENINGS** (34)..........67
MY MAN, A SWEET MAN — **Millie JACKSON** (50) 72
MY MAN AND ME — **Lynsey DE PAUL** (40)....75
MY MARIE — **Engelbert HUMPERDINCK** (31)..70
MY MATE PAUL — **David HOLMES** (39)..........98
MY MELANCHOLY BABY [A] — **Tommy EDWARDS** (29) 59
MY MELANCHOLY BABY [A] — **CHAS and DAVE** (51) 83
MY MIND'S EYE — **SMALL FACES** (4) 66
MY MUM IS ONE IN A MILLION — **Children of TANSLEY SCHOOL** (27) 81
MY NAME IS — **EMINEM** (2) 99
MY NAME IS JACK — **MANFRED MANN** (8) 68
MY NAME IS NOT SUSAN — **Whitney HOUSTON** (29) 91
MY NAME IS PRINCE — **PRINCE and the NEW POWER GENERATION** (7) 92
MY OH MY [A] — **SAD CAFE** (14)..........80
MY OH MY [B] — **SLADE** (2) 83
MY OH MY [C] — **AQUA** (6) 98
MY OLD MAN'S A DUSTMAN — **Lonnie DONEGAN** (1) 60
MY OLD PIANO — **Diana ROSS** (5) 80
MY ONE SIN — **Nat 'King' COLE** (17) 55
MY ONE TEMPTATION — **Mica PARIS** (7) 88
MY ONE TRUE FRIEND — **Bette MIDLER** (58) 98
MY ONLY LOVE — **Bob SINCLAR** (56) 99
MY OWN SUMMER (SHOVE IT) — **DEFTONES** (29) 98
MY OWN TRUE LOVE — **Danny WILLIAMS** (45) 63
MY OWN WAY — **DURAN DURAN** (14) 81
MY OWN WORST ENEMY — **LIT** (16) 99
MY PEACE OF HEAVEN — **TEN CITY** (63)........92
MY PERFECT COUSIN — **UNDERTONES** (9) 80
MY PERSONAL POSSESSION — **Nat 'King' COLE** (21)..........57
MY PHILOSOPHY — **BOOGIE DOWN PRODUCTIONS** (69)..........88
MY PLAGUE — **SLIPKNOT** (43) 02
MY PRAYER [A] — **PLATTERS** (4) 56,57
MY PRAYER [A] — **Gerry MONROE** (9)..........70
MY PREROGATIVE — **Bobby BROWN** (6) ..88,95
MY PRETTY ONE — **Cliff RICHARD** (6)..........87
MY PUPPET PAL — **TIGER** (62) 96
MY REMEDY — **Hinda HICKS** (61) 00
MY RESISTANCE IS LOW — **Robin SARSTEDT** (3) 76
MY RISING STAR — **NORTHSIDE** (32) 90
MY SACRIFICE — **CREED** (18)..........02
MY SALT HEART — **HUE AND CRY** (47) 91
MY SENTIMENTAL FRIEND — **HERMAN'S HERMITS** (2)..........69
MY SEPTEMBER LOVE — **David WHITFIELD** (3) 56
MY SHARONA — **KNACK** (6) 79
MY SHIP IS COMING IN — **WALKER BROTHERS** (3) 65
MY SIDE OF THE BED — **Susanna HOFFS** (44) 91
MY SIMPLE HEART — **THREE DEGREES** (9)....79
MY SISTER — **Juliana HATFIELD** (71)..........93
MY 16TH APOLOGY (EP) — **SHAKESPEAR'S SISTER** (61)..........93
MY SON JOHN — **David WHITFIELD** (22)........56
MY SON, MY SON — **Vera LYNN** (1) 54
MY SPECIAL ANGEL [A] — **Bobby HELMS** (22)..........57
MY SPECIAL ANGEL [A] — **Malcolm VAUGHAN** (3)..........57
MY SPECIAL CHILD — **Sinead O'CONNOR** (42) 91
MY SPECIAL DREAM — **Shirley BASSEY** (32) 64
MY SPIRIT — **TILT** (61) 97
MY STAR — **Ian BROWN** (5) 98
MY SUNDAY BABY — **DALE SISTERS** (36) 61
MY SUPERSTAR — **DIMESTARS** (72) 01
MY SWEET JANE — **GUN** (51)..........97
MY SWEET LORD — **George HARRISON** (1) 71,02
MY SWEET ROSALIE — **BROTHERHOOD OF MAN** (30) 76
MY TELEPHONE — **COLDCUT** (52)..........89
MY TIME — **SOUVLAKI** (63)..........98
MY TOOT TOOT — **Denise LA SALLE** (6) 85
MY TOWN — **GLASS TIGER** (33)..........91
MY TRUE LOVE — **Jack SCOTT** (9)..........58
MY UKULELE — **Max BYGRAVES** (19) 59
MY UNFINISHED SYMPHONY — **David WHITFIELD** (29) 56
MY UNKNOWN LOVE — **COUNT INDIGO** (59)..96
MY VISION — **JAKATTA featuring SEAL** (6) 02
MY WAY [A] — **Eddie COCHRAN** (23)..........63
MY WAY [B] — **Frank SINATRA** (5) 69,70,71,72,94
MY WAY [B] — **Dorothy SQUIRES** (25) 70
MY WAY [B] — **Elvis PRESLEY** (9) 77
MY WAY [B] — **SEX PISTOLS** (7) 78
MY WAY [B] — **Shane MacGOWAN** (29) 96
MY WAY [C] — **LIMP BIZKIT** (6) 01
MY WAY OF GIVING IN — **Chris FARLOWE** (48)..........67
MY WAY OF THINKING — **UB40** (6)..........80
MY WEAKNESS IS NONE OF YOUR BUSINESS — **EMBRACE** (9)..........98
MY WHITE BICYCLE — **NAZARETH** (14) 75
MY WOMAN'S MAN — **Dave DEE** (42)..........70
MY WORLD [A] — **CUPID'S INSPIRATION** (33)68
MY WORLD [B] — **BEE GEES** (16) 72
MY WORLD [C] — **SECRET AFFAIR** (16) 80
MY WORLD OF BLUE — **Karl DENVER** (29) 64
MYFANWY — **David ESSEX** (41)..........87
MYSTERIES OF LOVE — **LA MIX** (46) 91
MYSTERIES OF THE WORLD — **MFSB** (41)......81
MYSTERIOUS GIRL — **Peter ANDRE** (2) 95,96
MYSTERIOUS TIMES — **SASH! featuring Tina COUSINS** (2)..........98
MYSTERIOUS WAYS — **U2** (13) 92
MYSTERY [A] — **DIO** (34)..........84
MYSTERY [B] — **MYSTERY** (56) 01
MYSTERY GIRL [A] — **Jess CONRAD** (18) 61
MYSTERY GIRL [B] — **DUKES** (47) 81
MYSTERY LADY — **Billy OCEAN** (49) 85
MYSTERY LAND (EP) [A] — **Y-TRAXX** (63) 97
MYSTERY LAND [B] — **Y-TRAXX featuring NEVE** (70)..........03
MYSTERY SONG — **STATUS QUO** (11) 76
MYSTERY TRAIN — **Elvis PRESLEY** (25) 57
MYSTICAL MACHINE GUN — **KULA SHAKER** (14) 99
MYSTIFY — **INXS** (14) 89
MYZSTERIOUS MIZSTER JONES — **SLADE** (50)..........85
NA NA HEY HEY KISS HIM GOODBYE [A] — **STEAM** (9) 70
NA NA HEY HEY KISS HIM GOODBYE [A] — **BANANARAMA** (5)..........83
NA NA IS THE SADDEST WORD — **STYLISTICS** (5) 75
NA NA NA — **Cozy POWELL** (10) 74
NADINE (IS IT YOU) — **Chuck BERRY** (27) 64
NAGASAKI BADGER — **DISCO CITIZENS** (56)..98

NEVER SAY DIE (GIVE A LITTLE BIT MORE) — Cliff RICHARD (15) 83
NEVER SAY GOODBYE — BON JOVI (21) 87
NEVER STOP [A] — ECHO and the BUNNYMEN (15) 83
NEVER STOP [B] -- BRAND NEW HEAVIES (43) 91
NEVER SURRENDER — SAXON (18) 81
NEVER TAKE ME ALIVE — SPEAR OF DESTINY (14) 87
NEVER TEAR US APART — INXS (24) 88
NEVER THERE — CAKE (66) 99
NEVER TOO FAR — Mariah CAREY (32) 01
NEVER TOO LATE — Kylie MINOGUE (4) 89
NEVER TOO MUCH — Luther VANDROSS (13) 83,89
NEVER TRUST A STRANGER — Kim WILDE (7) 88
NEVER TURN AWAY — ORCHESTRAL MANOEUVRES IN THE DARK (70) 84
NEVER TURN YOUR BACK ON MOTHER EARTH — SPARKS (13) 74
NEVER UNDERSTAND — JESUS AND MARY CHAIN (47) 85
NEVERENDING — HALO (56) 02
NEVERTHELESS — Frankie VAUGHAN (29) 68
NEVERTHELESS (I'M IN LOVE WITH YOU) — NEW SEEKERS (34) 73
NEW — NO DOUBT (30) 99
NEW AMSTERDAM — Elvis COSTELLO (36) 80
NEW ANGER — Gary NUMAN (46) 88
NEW BEGINNING [A] — Stephen GATELY (3) 00
NEW BEGINNING [B] — PRECIOUS (50) 00
NEW BEGINNING (MAMBA SEYRA) — BUCKS FIZZ (8) 86
NEW BIRD — REEF (73) 99
NEW BORN — MUSE (12) 01
NEW DAWN — PROPHETS OF SOUND (51) 02
NEW DAY [A] — Wyclef JEAN featuring BONO (23) 99
A NEW DAY [B] — KILLING JOKE (56) 84
A NEW DAY HAS COME — Celine DION (7) 02
NEW DIMENSION — IMAGINATION (56) 83
NEW DIRECTION — FREAKPOWER (60) 96
NEW DIRECTION — S CLUB JUNIORS (2) 02
NEW EMOTION — TIME FREQUENCY (36) 93
A NEW ENGLAND — Kirsty MacCOLL (7) 85
A NEW FASHION — Bill WYMAN (37) 82
A NEW FLAME — SIMPLY RED (17) 89
NEW GENERATION — SUEDE (21) 95
NEW GRANGE — CLANNAD (65) 83
NEW GUITAR IN TOWN — LURKERS (72) 79
NEW KICKS — JOHANN (54) 96
NEW KID IN TOWN — EAGLES (20) 77
NEW KIND OF MEDICINE — Ultra NATÉ (14) 98
NEW LIFE — DEPECHE MODE (11) 81
NEW LIVE AND RARE (EP) — DEEP PURPLE (31) 77
NEW LIVE AND RARE II (EP) — DEEP PURPLE (45) 78
NEW LIVE AND RARE III (EP) — DEEP PURPLE (48) 80
NEW MISTAKE — JELLYFISH (55) 93
NEW MOON ON MONDAY — DURAN DURAN (9) 84
NEW ORLEANS [A] — Gary 'US' BONDS (16) 61
NEW ORLEANS [A] — Bern ELLIOTT and the FENMEN (24) 64
NEW ORLEANS [A] — HARLEY QUINNE (19) 72
NEW ORLEANS [A] — GILLAN (17) 81
NEW POLICY ONE — TERRORVISION (42) 93
THE NEW POLLUTION — BECK (14) 97
NEW POWER GENERATION — PRINCE (26) 90
NEW SENSATION — INXS (25) 88
NEW SONG — Howard JONES (3) 83,84
A NEW SOUTH WALES — ALARM (31) 89
NEW THING FROM LONDON TOWN — Gary NUMAN (52) 86
NEW TOY — Lene LOVICH (53) 81
NEW WAY, NEW LIFE — ASIAN DUB FOUNDATION (49) 00
NEW WORLD IN THE MORNING — Roger WHITTAKER (17) 70
NEW WORLD MAN — RUSH (42) 82
NEW WORLD MAN (LIVE) — RUSH (36) 83
NEW YEAR — SUGABABES (12) 00
NEW YEARS DAY [A] — U2 (10) 83
NEW YEAR'S DUB [A] — MUSIQUE vs U2 (15) 01
NEW YORK AFTERNOON — MONDO KANE (70) 86
NEW YORK CITY — T. REX (15) 75
NEW YORK CITY BOY — PET SHOP BOYS (14) 99
NEW YORK CITY COPS — STROKES (16) 01
NEW YORK EYES — NICOLE with Timmy THOMAS (41) 85
NEW YORK GROOVE — HELLO (9) 75
NEW YORK MINING DISASTER 1941 — BEE GEES (12) 67
NEW YORK, NEW YORK [A] — Gerard KENNY (43) 78
NEW YORK NEW YORK [B] — Ryan ADAMS (53) 01
NEW YORK UNDERCOVER (EP) — VARIOUS ARTISTS (EPs and LPs) (39) 96
NEWBORN — ELBOW (42) 01
NEWBORN FRIEND — SEAL (45) 94
NEWS AT TEN — VAPORS (44) 80
NEWS OF THE WORLD — JAM (27) 78,80,83
THE NEXT BIG THING — JESUS JONES (49) 97
NEXT DOOR TO AN ANGEL — Neil SEDAKA (29) 62
THE NEXT EPISODE — DR DRE featuring SNOOP DOGG (3) 01
NEXT LEVEL — ILS (75) 02
NEXT LIFETIME — Erykah BADU (30) 97
THE NEXT TIME — Cliff RICHARD and the SHADOWS (1) 62
NEXT TIME YOU FALL IN LOVE — Reva RICE and Greg ELLIS (59) 93
NEXT TO YOU — ASWAD (24) 90
NEXT YEAR — FOO FIGHTERS (42) 00
NHS (EP) — DJ Doc SCOTT (64) 92
NIALL QUINN'S DISCO PANTS — A LOVE SUPREME (59) 99
NICE GUY EDDIE — SLEEPER (10) 96
NICE IN NICE — STRANGLERS (30) 86
NICE LEGS SHAME ABOUT HER FACE — MONKS (19) 79
NICE 'N' EASY — Frank SINATRA (15) 60
NICE 'N SLEAZY — STRANGLERS (18) 78
NICE 'N' SLOW — Freddie JACKSON (56) 88
NICE ONE CYRIL — COCKEREL CHORUS (14) 73
NICE AND SLOW [A] — Jesse GREEN (17) 76
NICE & SLOW [B] — USHER (24) 98
NICE WEATHER FOR DUCKS — LEMON JELLY (16) 03
NIGHT [A] — FOUR SEASONS (7) [A] 75
THE NIGHT [A] — INTASTELLA (60) 95
THE NIGHT [B] — SCOOTER (16) 03
THE NIGHT [C] — SOFT CELL (39) 03
A NIGHT AT DADDY GEE'S — SHOWADDYWADDY (39) 79
A NIGHT AT THE APOLLO LIVE! — Daryl HALL and John OATES featuring David RUFFIN and Eddie KENDRICK (58) 85
NIGHT BIRDS — SHAKATAK (9) 82
NIGHT BOAT TO CAIRO — MADNESS (56) 93
THE NIGHT CHICAGO DIED — PAPER LACE (3) 74
NIGHT CRAWLER — JUDAS PRIEST (63) 93
NIGHT DANCING — Joe FARRELL (57) 78
NIGHT FEVER [A] — FATBACK BAND (38) 76
NIGHT FEVER [B] — BEE GEES (1) 78
NIGHT FEVER [B] — Carol DOUGLAS (66) 78
NIGHT FEVER [B] — Adam GARCIA (15) 98
THE NIGHT FEVER MEGAMIX — UK MIXMASTERS (23) 91
THE NIGHTFLY — BLANK & JONES (55) 00
NIGHT GAMES — Graham BONNET (6) 81
THE NIGHT HAS A THOUSAND EYES — Bobby VEE (3) 63
NIGHT IN MOTION — CUBIC 22 (15) 91
NIGHT IN MY VEINS — PRETENDERS (25) 94
A NIGHT IN NEW YORK — Elbow BONES and the RACKETEERS (33) 84
THE NIGHT IS YOUNG — Gary MILLER (29) 61,62
NIGHT LADIES — CRUSADERS (55) 84
NIGHT LIFE — David Lee ROTH (72) 94
NIGHT LINE — Randy CRAWFORD (51) 83
NIGHT MOVES — Bob SEGER and the SILVER BULLET BAND (45) 95
NIGHT NURSE — SLY and ROBBIE featuring SIMPLY RED (13) 97
NIGHT OF FEAR — MOVE (2) 67
NIGHT OF THE LIVING BASEHEADS — PUBLIC ENEMY (63) 88
NIGHT OF THE LONG GRASS — TROGGS (17) 67
NIGHT OF THE VAMPIRE — MOONTREKKERS (50) 61
NIGHT OWL — Gerry RAFFERTY (5) 79
NIGHT PORTER — JAPAN (29) 82
THE NIGHT THE EARTH CRIED — GRAVEDIGGAZ (44) 98
THE NIGHT THE WINE AND THE ROSES — LIQUID GOLD (32) 80
THE NIGHT THEY DROVE OLD DIXIE DOWN — Joan BAEZ (6) 71
A NIGHT TO REMEMBER [A] — SHALAMAR (5) 82,86
NIGHT TO REMEMBER [A] — 911 (38) 96
NIGHT TRAIN [A] — Buddy MORROW (12) 53
NIGHT TRAIN [B] — VISAGE (12) 82
NIGHT VISION — HELL IS FOR HEROES (38) 02
THE NIGHT YOU MURDERED LOVE — ABC (31) 87
NIGHTBIRD — CONVERT (39) 92,98
NIGHTLIFE — KENICKIE (27) 97
NIGHTMARE [A] — GILLAN (36) 81
NIGHTMARE [B] — SAXON (50) 83
NIGHTMARE [C] — KID UNKNOWN (64) 92
NIGHTMARE [D] — BRAINBUG (11) 97
NIGHTMARES — A FLOCK OF SEAGULLS (53) 83
NIGHTRAIN — GUNS N' ROSES (17) 88, 89
NIGHTS IN WHITE SATIN [A] — MOODY BLUES (9) 67,72,79
NIGHTS IN WHITE SATIN [A] — DICKIES (39) 79
NIGHTS IN WHITE SATIN [A] — Elkie BROOKS (33) 82
NIGHTS OF PLEASURE — LOOSE ENDS (42) 86
NIGHTS ON BROADWAY — Candi STATON (6) 77
NIGHTS OVER EGYPT — INCOGNITO (56) 99
NIGHTSHIFT — COMMODORES (3) 85
NIGHTSWIMMING — R.E.M. (27) 93
NIGHTTRAIN — PUBLIC ENEMY (55) 92
THE NIGHTTRAIN — KADOC (14) 96
NIKITA — Elton JOHN (3) 85
NIKKE DOES IT BETTER — NIKKE? NICOLE! (73) 91
NIMBUS — 808 STATE (59) 92
9 AM (THE COMFORT ZONE) — LONDONBEAT (19) 88
900 NUMBER — 45 KING (60) 89,90
911 — Wyclef JEAN featuring Mary J BLIGE (9) 00
911 IS A JOKE — PUBLIC ENEMY (41) 90
9PM (TILL I COME) — ATB (1) 99
977 — PRETENDERS (66) 94
NINE TIMES OUT OF TEN — Cliff RICHARD and the SHADOWS (3) 60
9 TO 5 [A] — Sheena EASTON (3) 80
9 TO 5 [B] — Dolly PARTON (47) 81
NINE WAYS — JDS (61) 97,01
19 — Paul HARDCASTLE (1) 85
1998 — BINARY FINARY (24) 98
1999 [A] — PRINCE (10) 83,99
1999 [B] — BINARY FINARY (11) 99
1979 — SMASHING PUMPKINS (16) 96
NINETEEN63 — NEW ORDER (21) 95
1962 — GRASS-SHOW (53) 97
19/2000 — GORILLAZ (6) 01
NINETEENTH NERVOUS BREAKDOWN — ROLLING STONES (2) 66
90S GIRL — BLACKGIRL (23) 94
95 — NASTY — W.A.S.P. (70) 86
98.6 [A] — BYSTANDERS (45) 67
98.6 [A] — KEITH (24) 67
99 1/2 — Carol Lynn TOWNES (47) 84
99 RED BALLOONS — NENA (1) 84
NINETY-NINE WAYS — Tab HUNTER (5) 57
99.9°F — Suzanne VEGA (46) 92
96 TEARS [A] — ? (QUESTION MARK) and the MYSTERIANS (37) 66
96 TEARS [A] — STRANGLERS (17) 90
92°F — POP WILL EAT ITSELF (23) 91
'92 TOUR (EP) — MOTÖRHEAD (63) 92
NIPPLE TO THE BOTTLE — Grace JONES (50) 82
NITE AND DAY — Al B SURE! (44) 88
NITE AND FOG — MERCURY REV (47) 01
NITE KLUB — SPECIALS (10) 79
NITE LIFE — Kim ENGLISH (35) 94,96
NI-TEN-ICHI-RYU (TWO SWORDS TECHNIQUE) — PHOTEK (37) 97
NITRO — PALE X (74) 01
N-N-NINETEEN NOT OUT — COMMENTATORS (13) 85
NO — Chuck D (55) 96
NO ALIBIS — Eric CLAPTON (53) 90

NOT NOW JOHN – **PINK FLOYD** (30) 83
NOT OVER YET [A] – **GRACE** (6) 95
NOT OVER YET 99 [A] – **Planet PERFECTO featuring GRACE** (16)......99
NOT OVER YOU YET – **Diana ROSS** (9) 99,00
NOT RESPONSIBLE – **Tom JONES** (18) 66
NOT SLEEPING AROUND – **NED'S ATOMIC DUSTBIN** (19) 92
NOT SO MANIC NOW – **DUBSTAR** (18) 96
NOT SUCH AN INNOCENT GIRL – **Victoria BECKHAM** (6) 01,02
NOT THAT KIND – **ANASTACIA** (11) 01
NOT THE GIRL YOU THINK YOU ARE – **CROWDED HOUSE** (20) 96
(NOT THE) GREATEST RAPPER – **1000 CLOWNS** (23).....................................99
NOT TODAY – **Mary J. BLIGE featuring EVE** (40) 03
NOT TONIGHT – **LIL' KIM** (11)........................97
NOT TOO LITTLE NOT TOO MUCH – **Chris SANDFORD** (17) 63
NOT UNTIL THE NEXT TIME – **Jim REEVES** (13) 65
NOT WHERE IT'S AT – **DEL AMITRI** (21)........97
NOTGONNACHANGE – **SWING OUT SISTER** (49) 92
NOTHIN' – **N.O.R.E.** (11) 02
NOTHIN' AT ALL – **HEART** (38)......................88
NOTHIN' BUT A GOOD TIME – **POISON** (35) 88,89
NOTHIN' BUT A PARTY – **TRUCE** (71) 97
NOTHIN' MY LOVE CAN'T FIX – **Joey LAWRENCE** (13) 93
NOTHIN' PERSONAL – **DUST JUNKYS** (62) 98
(NOTHIN' SERIOUS) JUST BUGGIN' – **WHISTLE** (7) 86
NOTHIN' (THAT COMPARES 2 U) – **JACKSONS** (33)...89
NOTHIN' TO DO – **Michael HOLLIDAY** (20)....56
NOTHING [A] – **FRAZIER CHORUS** (51) 90
NOTHING [B] – **FLUFFY** (52) 96
NOTHING [C] – **A** (9).......................................02
NOTHING [D] – **HOLDEN & THOMPSON** (51) 03
NOTHING AS IT SEEMS – **PEARL JAM** (22)....00
NOTHING AT ALL – **Luke SLATER** (70) 02
NOTHING 'BOUT ME – **STING** (32) 94
NOTHING BUT LOVE – **OPTIMYSTIC** (37) 94
NOTHING CAN CHANGE THIS LOVE – **Bitty McLEAN** (55) 95
NOTHING CAN DIVIDE US – **Jason DONOVAN** (5) 88
NOTHING CAN STOP ME – **Gene CHANDLER** (41) 68
NOTHING CAN STOP US – **SAINT ETIENNE** (54) 91
NOTHING COMES EASY – **Sandie SHAW** (14) 66
NOTHING COMPARES 2 U [A] – **MXM** (68) 90
NOTHING COMPARES 2 U [A] – **Sinead O'CONNOR** (1) 90
NOTHING ELSE MATTERS – **METALLICA** (6) ..92
NOTHING EVER HAPPENS – **DEL AMITRI** (11) 90
NOTHING HAS BEEN PROVED [A] – **Dusty SPRINGFIELD** (16).............................89
NOTHING HAS BEEN PROVED [A] – **STRINGS OF LOVE** (59) 90
NOTHING IN PARTICULAR – **BROTHERHOOD** (55) 96
NOTHING IS FOREVER – **ULTRACYNIC** (47)....................................92,97
NOTHING IS REAL BUT THE GIRL – **BLONDIE** (26) 99
NOTHING LASTS FOREVER – **ECHO and the BUNNYMEN** (8) 97
NOTHING LEFT – **ORBITAL** (32) 99
NOTHING LEFT TOULOUSE – **SAD CAFE** (62) 80
NOTHING LESS THAN BRILLIANT – **Sandie SHAW** (66) 94
NOTHING NATURAL – **LUSH** (43) 91
NOTHING REALLY MATTERS – **MADONNA** (7)..99
NOTHING RHYMED – **Gilbert O'SULLIVAN** (8) 70
NOTHING SACRED – A SONG FOR KIRSTY – **RUSSELL WATSON** (17) 02
NOTHING TO DECLARE – **LAPTOP** (74) 99
NOTHING TO FEAR – **Chris REA** (16).............92
NOTHING TO LOSE [A] – **UK** (67) 79
NOTHING TO LOSE [B] – **S EXPRESS** (32) 90
NOTHING WITHOUT ME – **MANCHILD** (40) 01
NOTHING'S GONNA CHANGE MY LOVE FOR YOU – **Glenn MEDEIROS** (1) 88
NOTHING'S GONNA STOP ME NOW – **Samantha FOX** (8) 87
NOTHING'S GONNA STOP US NOW – **STARSHIP** (1) 87
NOTHIN'S GONNA CHANGE – **Labi SIFFRE** (52)..87
NOTORIOUS – **DURAN DURAN** (7)...........86,87
NOTORIOUS B.I.G. – **NOTORIOUS B.I.G.** (16) 00
NOVELTY WAVES – **BIOSPHERE** (51) 95
NOVEMBER RAIN – **GUNS N' ROSES** (4) 92
NOVEMBER SPAWNED A MONSTER – **MORRISSEY** (12)...90
NOVOCAINE FOR THE SOUL – **EELS** (10) 97
NOW [A] – **Al MARTINO** (3) 53
NOW [B] – **Val DOONICAN** (43) 68
NOW [C] – **DEF LEPPARD** (23) 02
NOW ALWAYS AND FOREVER – **GAY DAD** (41) 01
NOW AND FOREVER – **Richard MARX** (13) 94
NOW I KNOW WHAT MADE OTIS BLUE – **Paul YOUNG** (14) 93
NOW I'M HERE – **QUEEN** (11) 75
NOW IS THE TIME – **Jimmy JAMES and the VAGABONDS** (5) 76
NOW IS TOMORROW – **DEFINITION OF SOUND** (46).........................91
NOW IT'S GONE – **CHORDS** (63) 79
NOW IT'S ON – **GRANDADDY** (23) 03
NOW I'VE FOUND YOU – **Sean MAGUIRE** (22) 95
NOW OR NEVER – **Tom NOVY featuring LIMA** (64) 01
NOW THAT I OWN THE BBC – **SPARKS** (60) 96
NOW THAT THE MAGIC HAS GONE – **Joe COCKER** (28)..92
NOW THAT WE'VE FOUND LOVE [A] – **THIRD WORLD** (10) 78,85
NOW THAT WE FOUND LOVE [A] – **HEAVY D and the BOYZ** (2) 91
NOW THAT YOU LOVE ME – **ALICE BAND** (44) 02
NOW THAT YOU'VE GONE – **MIKE and the MECHANICS** (35) 99
NOW THEY'LL SLEEP – **BELLY** (28) 95
NOW THOSE DAYS ARE GONE – **BUCKS FIZZ** (8)..82
NOW WE'RE THRU – **POETS** (31) 64
NOW YOU'RE GONE [A] – **BLACK** (66) 89
NOW YOU'RE GONE [B] – **WHITESNAKE** (31)..90
NOW YOU'RE IN HEAVEN – **Julian LENNON** (59) 89
NOWHERE [A] – **THERAPY?** (18) 94
NOWHERE [B] – **LONGVIEW** (72) 03
NOWHERE FAST – **MEAT LOAF** (67) 84
NOWHERE GIRL – **B-MOVIE** (67) 82
NOWHERE LAND – **CLUBHOUSE** (56) 95
NOWHERE MAN – **THREE GOOD REASONS** (47) 66
NOWHERE TO RUN [A] – **Martha REEVES and the VANDELLAS** (26) 65,69,88
NOWHERE TO RUN 2000 [A] – **NU GENERATION** (66).................................00
N-R-G – **ADAMSKI** (12) 90
NU FLOW – **BIG BROVAZ** (3) 02
NUCLEAR – **Ryan ADAMS** (37) 02
NUCLEAR DEVICE (THE WIZARD OF AUS) – **STRANGLERS** (36) 79
NUCLEAR HOLIDAY – **3 COLOURS RED** (22)..97
NUFF VIBES EP – **APACHE INDIAN** (5) 93
NUMB – **LINKIN PARK** (14)............................03
#9 DREAM – **John LENNON** (23) 75
THE NUMBER OF THE BEAST – **IRON MAIDEN** (18)..82
NUMBER ONE [A] – **EYC** (27) 94
NUMBER ONE [B] – **A** (47) 98
NUMBER ONE [C] – **PLAYGROUP** (66)............01
NUMBER 1 [D] – **TWEENIES** (5) 00,01
NUMBER ONE BLIND – **VERUCA SALT** (68) ..95
NUMBER ONE DEE JAY – **GOODY GOODY** (55).....................................78
NUMBER ONE DOMINATOR – **TOP** (67) 91
NUMBER ONE RAT FAN – **Roland RAT SUPERSTAR** (72)......................85
THE NUMBER ONE SONG IN HEAVEN – **SPARKS** (14) 79,97
NUMBERS – **SOFT CELL** (25) 83
NUMERO UNO – **STARLIGHT** (9)....................89
NUNC DIMITTIS – **Paul PHOENIX** (56) 79
NURSERY RHYMES – **ICEBERG SLIMM** (37) ..00
NURTURE – **LFO** (47) 91
NUT ROCKER – **B BUMBLE and the STINGERS** (1) 62,72
NUTBUSH CITY LIMITS [A] – **Ike and Tina TURNER** (4) 73
NUTBUSH CITY LIMITS [A] – **Tina TURNER** (23)..91
NUTHIN' BUT A 'G' THANG – **DR DRE** (31)....94
NWO – **MINISTRY** (49) 92
NYC – **INTERPOL** (65)......................................03
N.Y.C. (CAN YOU BELIEVE THIS CITY) – **CHARLES and EDDIE** (33).............................93
O BABY – **SIOUXSIE and the BANSHEES** (34) 95
O L'AMOUR [A] – **DOLLAR** (7).........................87
OH L'AMOUR [A] – **ERASURE** (13)..................03
O' MY FATHER HAD A RABBIT – **Ray MOORE** (24) 86
O-O-O – **ADRENALIN M.O.D.** (49)..................88
O SUPERMAN – **Laurie ANDERSON** (2)..........81
OAKLAND STROKE – **TONY TONI TONÉ** (50) 90
OBJECTION (TANGO) – **SHAKIRA** (17) 02
OBJECTS IN THE REAR VIEW MIRROR MAY APPEAR CLOSER THAN THEY ARE – **MEAT LOAF** (26)..94
OB-LA-DI OB-LA-DA [A] – **BEDROCKS** (20) 68
OB-LA-DI OB-LA-DA [A] – **MARMALADE** (1)....68
OBLIVION – **TERRORVISION** (21) 94
OBLIVION (HEAD IN THE CLOUDS) (EP) – **MANIX** (43)..92
OBLIVIOUS – **AZTEC CAMERA** (18) 83
THE OBOE SONG – **CLERGY** (50) 02
OBSESSED – **999** (71)......................................81
OBSESSION [A] – **Reg OWEN** (43) 60
OBSESSION [B] – **ANIMOTION** (5) 85
OBSESSION [C] – **ARMY OF LOVERS** (67)......91
OBSESSION [D] – **ULTRA-SONIC** (75) 94
OBSESSION [E] – **TIESTO & JUNKIE XL** (56)..02
OBSESSIONS – **SUEDE** (29) 02
OBSTACLE 1 – **INTERPOL** (41) 02,03
THE OBVIOUS CHILD – **Paul SIMON** (15) 90
OCEAN BLUE – **ABC** (51)................................86
OCEAN DEEP – **Cliff RICHARD** (27)................84
OCEAN DRIVE – **LIGHTHOUSE FAMILY** (11) 95,96
OCEAN OF ETERNITY – **FUTURE BREEZE** (46) 02
OCEAN PIE – **SHED SEVEN** (33) 94
OCEAN SPRAY – **MANIC STREET PREACHERS** (15) 01
OCTOBER SWIMMER – **JJ72** (29) 00
ODE TO BILLY JOE – **Bobbie GENTRY** (13) 67
ODE TO BOY – **Alison MOYET** (59) 94
ODE TO JOY (FROM BEETHOVEN'S SYMPHONY NO.9) – **BBC CONCERT ORCHESTRA, BBC SYMPHONY CHORUS cond. Stephen JACKSON** (36)......................96
ODE TO MY FAMILY – **CRANBERRIES** (26) 94
OF COURSE I'M LYING – **YELLO** (23) 89
OF COURSE YOU CAN – **SPEARHEAD** (74) 94
OFF ON HOLIDAY – **SUGGS** (7) 95
OFF ON YOUR OWN (GIRL) – **Al B SURE!** (70) 88
OFF THE HOOK – **Jody WATLEY** (51) 98
OFF THE WALL [A] – **Michael JACKSON** (7)....79
OFF THE WALL [A] – **WISDOME** (33) 00
OFFICIAL SECRETS – **M** (64)............................80
OFFSHORE – **CHICANE** (14) 96,97
OFFSHORE BANKING BUSINESS – **MEMBERS** (31) 79
OH BABE, WHAT WOULD YOU SAY? – **Hurricane SMITH** (4)....................................72
OH BABY – **RHIANNA** (18) 02
OH BABY I ... – **ETERNAL** (4) 94
(OH BABY MINE) I GET SO LONELY – **FOUR KNIGHTS** (5) 54
OH BOY [A] – **CRICKETS** (3) 57
OH BOY [A] – **MUD** (1) 75
OH BOY [B] – **FABULOUS BAKER BOYS** (34) 97
OH BOY [C] – **CAM'RON** (13) 02
OH BOY (THE MOOD I'M IN) – **BROTHERHOOD OF MAN** (8) 77
OH CAROL [A] – **Neil SEDAKA** (3) 59,72
OH CAROL! [A] – **Clint EASTWOOD and General SAINT** (54) ..94
OH CAROL [B] – **SMOKIE** (5) 78
OH CAROLINA – **SHAGGY** (1) 93
OH DIANE – **FLEETWOOD MAC** (9)................82
OH FATHER – **MADONNA** (16) 96

OVER MY HEAD – **LIT** (37) 00
OVER MY SHOULDER – **MIKE and the MECHANICS** (12) 95
OVER RISING – **CHARLATANS** (15) 91
OVER THE EDGE – **ALMIGHTY** (38) 93
OVER THE HILLS AND FAR AWAY – **Gary MOORE** (20) 86
OVER THE RAINBOW [A] – YOU BELONG TO ME – **MATCHBOX** (15) 80
OVER THE RAINBOW [A] – **Sam HARRIS** (67) 85
OVER THE RAINBOW [A] – **Eva CASSIDY** (42) 01
OVER THE RIVER – **Bitty McLEAN** (27) 95
OVER THE SEA – **Jesse RAE** (65) 85
OVER THE WEEKEND – **Nick HEYWARD** (43) 86
OVER THERE – **BABE TEAM** (45) 02
OVER THERE (I DON'T CARE) – **HOUSE OF PAIN** (20) 95
OVER TO YOU JOHN (HERE WE GO AGAIN) – **JIVE BUNNY and the MASTERMIXERS** (28) ..91
OVER UNDER SIDEWAYS DOWN – **YARDBIRDS** (10) 66
OVER YOU [A] – **FREDDIE and the DREAMERS** (13) 64
OVER YOU [B] – **ROXY MUSIC** (5) 80
OVER YOU [C] – **Ray PARKER Jr** (65) 88
OVER YOU [D] – **JUSTIN** (11) 99
OVER YOU [E] – **Warren CLARKE featuring Kathy BROWN** (42) 01
OVERCOME – **TRICKY** (34) 95
OVERDRIVE – **DJ SANDY vs HOUSETRAP** (32) 00
OVERJOYED – **Stevie WONDER** (17) 86
OVERKILL [A] – **MOTÖRHEAD** (39) 79
OVERKILL [B] – **MEN AT WORK** (21) 83
OVERLOAD [A] – **SUGABABES** (6) 00
OVERLOAD [B] – **VOODOO & SERANO** (30) ..03
OVERPROTECTED – **Britney SPEARS** (4) 02
OVERRATED – **Siobhan DONAGHY** (19) 03
OVERTHROWN – **LIBIDO** (53) 98
OVERTIME – **LEVEL 42** (62) 91
OWNER OF A LONELY HEART – **YES** (28) 83
OXBOW LAKES – **ORB** (38) 95
OXYGEN [A] – **BLAGGERS I.T.A.** (51) 93
OXYGEN [B] – **JJ72** (23) 00
OXYGENE 8 – **Jean-Michel JARRE** (17) 97
OXYGENE PART IV – **Jean-Michel JARRE** (4) 77,89
OXYGENE 10 – **Jean-Michel JARRE** (21) 97
OYE – **Gloria ESTEFAN** (33) 98
OYE COMA VA – **Tito PUENTE Jr and the LATIN RHYTHM featuring Tito PUENTE, INDIA and Cali ALEMAN** (56) 96,97
OYE MI CANTO (HEAR MY VOICE) – **Gloria ESTEFAN** (16) 89
P MACHINERY – **PROPAGANDA** (50) 85
PABLO – **Russ CONWAY** (45) 61
PACIFIC – **808 STATE** (10) 89,98
PACIFIC MELODY – **AIRSCAPE** (27) 97
PACK UP YOUR SORROWS – **Joan BAEZ** (50) 66
PACKET OF PEACE – **LIONROCK** (32) 93
PACKJAMMED (WITH THE PARTY POSSE) – **STOCK AITKEN WATERMAN** (41) 87
PAC-MAN – **POWERPILL** (43) 92
PACMAN – **Ed RUSH & OPTICAL** (61) 02
PAGAN POETRY – **BJÖRK** (38) 01
PAID IN FULL – **Eric B and RAKIM** (15) 87
PAID MY DUES – **ANASTACIA** (14) 01
PAIN – **Betty WRIGHT** (42) 86
THE PAIN INSIDE – **COSMIC ROUGH RIDERS** (36) 01
PAIN KILLER [A] – **TURIN BRAKES** (5) 03
PAINKILLER [B] – **JUDAS PRIEST** (74) 90
PAINT A PICTURE – **MAN WITH NO NAME** (42) 96
PAINT IT BLACK [A] – **ROLLING STONES** (1) 66,90
PAINT IT BLACK [A] – **MODETTES** (42) 80
PAINT ME DOWN – **SPANDAU BALLET** (30) ..81
PAINT THE SILENCE – **SOUTH** (69) 01
PAINTED MOON – **SILENCERS** (57) 88
PAINTER MAN [A] – **CREATION** (36) 66
PAINTER MAN [A] – **BONEY M** (10) 79
A PAIR OF BROWN EYES – **POGUES** (72) 85
PAISLEY PARK – **PRINCE** (18) 85
PAL OF MY CRADLE DAYS – **Ann BREEN** (69) 83,84
PALE BLUE EYES – **Paul QUINN and Edwyn COLLINS** (72) 84
PALE MOVIE – **SAINT ETIENNE** (28) 94
PALE RED – **Jerry BURNS** (64) 92
PALE SHELTER – **TEARS FOR FEARS** (5) ..83,85
PALISADES PARK – **Freddy CANNON** (20) 62
PALOMA BLANCA – **George BAKER SELECTION** (10) 75
PAMELA PAMELA – **Wayne FONTANA** (11) 66
PANAMA – **VAN HALEN** (61) 84
THE PANDEMONIUM SINGLE – **KILLING JOKE** (28) 94
PANDORA'S BOX [A] – **PROCOL HARUM** (16) 75
PANDORA'S BOX [B] – **ORCHESTRAL MANOEUVRES IN THE DARK** (7) 91
PANDORA'S KISS – **LOUISE** (5) 03
PANIC – **SMITHS** (11) 86
PANIC ON – **MADDER ROSE** (65) 94
PANINARO – **PET SHOP BOYS** (15) 95
PANIS ANGELICUS – **Anthony WAY** (55) 95
PANTHER PARTY – **MAD MOSES** (50) 97
PAPA DON'T PREACH [A] – **MADONNA** (1) 86
PAPA DON'T PREACH [A] – **Kelly OSBOURNE** (3) 02
PAPA LOVES MAMA – **Joan REGAN** (29) 60
PAPA LOVES MAMBO – **Perry COMO** (16) 54
PAPA OOM MOW MOW [A] – **Gary GLITTER** (38) 75
PAPA OOM MOW MOW [A] – **SHARONETTES** (26) 75
PAPA WAS A ROLLIN' STONE [A] – **TEMPTATIONS** (14) 73,87
PAPA WAS A ROLLING STONE [A] – **WAS (NOT WAS)** (12) 90
PAPA'S GOT A BRAND NEW BAG – **James BROWN** (25) 65
PAPA'S GOT A BRAND NEW PIGBAG [A] – **PIGBAG** (3) 82
PAPA'S GOT A BRAND NEW PIGBAG [A] – **SILENT UNDERDOG** (73) 85
PAPER DOLL [A] – **Windsor DAVIES and Don ESTELLE** (41) 75
PAPER DOLL [B] – **PM DAWN** (49) 91
PAPER PLANE – **STATUS QUO** (8) 73
PAPER ROSES [A] – **Anita BRYANT** (24) 60
PAPER ROSES [A] – **Maureen EVANS** (40) 60
PAPER ROSES [A] – **KAYE SISTERS** (7) 60
PAPER ROSES [A] – **Marie OSMOND** (2) 73
PAPER SUN – **TRAFFIC** (5) 67
PAPER TIGER – **Sue THOMPSON** (30) 65
PAPERBACK WRITER – **BEATLES** (1) 66,76
PAPERCUT – **LINKIN PARK** (14) 01
PAPERFACES – **FEEDER** (41) 99
PAPILLON – **N-JOI** (70) 94
PAPUA NEW GUINEA – **FUTURE SOUND OF LONDON** (22) 92,01
PARA MI – **MOTIVATION** (71) 01
PARADE – **WHITE and TORCH** (54) 82
PARADISE [A] – **Frank IFIELD** (26) 65
PARADISE [B] – **STRANGLERS** (48) 83
PARADISE [C] – **BLACK** (38) 88
PARADISE [D] – **SADE** (29) 88
PARADISE [E] – **BIRDLAND** (70) 89
PARADISE [F] – **Diana ROSS** (61) 89
PARADISE [G] – **Ralph FRIDGE** (68) 99
PARADISE [H] – **KACI** (11) 01
PARADISE [I] – **LL COOL J featuring AMERIE** (18) 03
PARADISE BIRD – **Amii STEWART** (39) 80
PARADISE CITY [A] – **GUNS N' ROSES** (6) 89
PARADISE CITY [A] – **N-TRANCE** (28) 98
PARADISE LOST – **HERD** (15) 67
PARADISE SKIES – **MAX WEBSTER** (43) 79
PARALYZED – **Elvis PRESLEY** (8) 57
PARANOID [A] – **BLACK SABBATH** (4) 70,80
PARANOID [A] – **DICKIES** (45) 79
PARANOID ANDROID – **RADIOHEAD** (3) 97
PARANOIMIA – **ART OF NOISE** (12) 86
PARDON ME – **INCUBUS** (61) 00
PARIS BY AIR – **TYGERS OF PAN TANG** (63) 82
PARIS IS ONE DAY AWAY – **MOOD** (42) 82
PARIS MATCH – **STYLE COUNCIL** (3) 83
PARISIENNE GIRL – **INCOGNITO** (73) 80
PARISIENNE WALKWAYS – **Gary MOORE** (8) 79,93
PARKLIFE – **BLUR** (10) 94
PART OF THE PROCESS – **MORCHEEBA** (38) 98
PART OF THE UNION – **STRAWBS** (2) 73
PART TIME LOVE [A] – **Gladys KNIGHT and the PIPS** (30) 75
PART TIME LOVE [B] – **Elton JOHN** (15) 78
PART-TIME LOVER – **Stevie WONDER** (3) 85
PARTAY FEELING – **B-CREW** (45) 97
PARTY – **Elvis PRESLEY** (2) 57
THE PARTY – **KRAZE** (29) 88
PARTY ALL NIGHT [A] – **KREUZ** (75) 95
PARTY ALL NIGHT [B] – **MYTOWN** (22) 99
PARTY DOLL [A] – **Buddy KNOX** (29) 57
PARTY DOLL [A] – **JETS** (72) 84
PARTY FEARS TWO – **ASSOCIATES** (9) 82
PARTY FOUR (EP) – **MAD JOCKS featuring JOCKMASTER B.A.** (57) 93
PARTY FREAK – **CA$HFLOW** (15) 86
PARTY HARD [A] – **PULP** (29) 98
PARTY HARD [B] – **Andrew WK** (19) 01
PARTY IN PARIS – **UK SUBS** (37) 80
PARTY LIGHTS – **GAP BAND** (30) 80
PARTY PARTY – **Elvis COSTELLO** (48) 82
PARTY PEOPLE (LIVE YOUR LIFE BE FREE) – **PIANOMAN** (43) 97
PARTY PEOPLE...FRIDAY NIGHT – **911** (5) 97,98
PARTY POPS – **Russ CONWAY** (24) 57
PARTY TIME – **FATBACK BAND** (41) 76
PARTY TIME (THE GO-GO EDIT) – **Kurtis BLOW** (67) 85
PARTY UP THE WORLD – **D:REAM** (20) 95
PARTY ZONE – **DAFFY DUCK featuring the GROOVE GANG** (58) 91
PARTYLINE – **BRASS CONSTRUCTION** (56) 84
PARTYMAN – **PRINCE** (14) 89
THE PARTY'S OVER – **Lonnie DONEGAN** (9) 62
PASADENA – **TEMPERANCE SEVEN** (4) 61
PASILDA – **AFRO MEDUSA** (31) 00
PASS AND MOVE (IT'S THE LIVERPOOL GROOVE) – **LIVERPOOL FC** (4) 96
PASS IT ON [A] – **Bitty McLEAN** (35) 93
PASS IT ON [B] – **The CORAL** (5) 03
PASS THAT DUTCH – **MISSY ELLIOTT** (10) 03
PASS THE COURVOISIER – PART II – **Busta RHYMES featuring P DIDDY & PHARRELL** (16) 02
PASS THE DUTCHIE – **MUSICAL YOUTH** (1) 82,83
PASS THE MIC – **BEASTIE BOYS** (47) 92
PASS THE VIBES – **DEFINITION OF SOUND** (23) 95
A PASSAGE TO BANGKOK – **RUSH** (41) 81
THE PASSENGER [A] – **SIOUXSIE and the BANSHEES** (41) 87
THE PASSENGER [A] – **Iggy POP** (22) 98
PASSENGERS – **Elton JOHN** (5) 84
PASSIN' ME BY – **PHARCYDE** (55) 93
PASSING BREEZE – **Russ CONWAY** (16) 60
PASSING STRANGERS [A] – **Billy ECKSTINE and Sarah VAUGHAN** (20) 57,69
PASSING STRANGERS [A] – **Joe LONGTHORNE** (34) 94
PASSING STRANGERS [B] – **ULTRAVOX** (57) 80
PASSION [A] – **Rod STEWART** (17) 80
PASSION [B] – **GAT DECOR** (6) 92,96
PASSION [C] – **JON OF THE PLEASED WIMMIN** (27) 95
PASSION [D] – **AMEN! UK** (15) 97,03
P.A.S.S.I.O.N. – **RYTHM SYNDICATE** (58) 91
PASSION IN DARK ROOMS – **MOOD** (74) 82
PASSION KILLER – **ONE THE JUGGLER** (71) ..83
THE PASSION OF LOVERS – **BAUHAUS** (56) ..81
PASSION RULES THE GAME – **SCORPIONS** (74) 89
PASSIONATE FRIEND – **TEARDROP EXPLODES** (25) 81
PAST, PRESENT AND FUTURE – **CINDY and the SAFFRONS** (56) 83
PAST THE MISSION – **Tori AMOS** (31) 94
PATCHES – **Clarence CARTER** (2) 70
PATHS – **Robert MILES featuring Nina MIRANDA** (74) 01
PATHS OF PARADISE – **Johnnie RAY** (20) 55
PATHWAY TO THE MOON – **MN8** (25) 96
PATIENCE [A] – **GUNS N' ROSES** (10) 89
PATIENCE [B] – **Nerina PALLOT** (61) 01
PATIENCE OF ANGELS – **Eddi READER** (33) ..94
PATIO SONG – **GORKY'S ZYGOTIC MYNCI** (41) 96
PATRICIA – **Perez PRADO** (8) 58
THE PAY OFF – **Kenny BALL and his JAZZMEN** (23) 62
PAY TO THE PIPER – **CHAIRMEN OF THE BOARD** (34) 71
PAYBACK TIME – **DYSFUNCTIONAL PSYCHEDELIC WALTONS** (48) 03
THE PAYBACK MIX – **James BROWN** (12) 88
PAYING THE PRICE OF LOVE – **BEE GEES** (23) 93

THE PURPLE PEOPLE EATER [A] — **Sheb WOOLEY** (12) 58
PURPLE PILLS — **D12** (2) 01
PURPLE RAIN — **PRINCE** (8) 84
PUSH [A] — **MOIST** (20) 94,95
PUSH [B] — **MATCHBOX 20** (38) 98
PUSH IT [A] — **SALT-N-PEPA** (2) 88
PUSH IT [B] — **GARBAGE** (9) 98
PUSH IT ALL ASIDE — **ALISHA'S ATTIC** (24) ..01
PUSH THE BEAT [A] — **CAPPELLA** (60) 88
PUSH THE BEAT [A] — **MIRAGE** (67) 88
PUSH THE FEELING ON — **NIGHTCRAWLERS featuring John REID** (3) 94,95
PUSH UPSTAIRS — **UNDERWORLD** (12) 99
THE PUSHBIKE SONG — **MIXTURES** (2) 71
PUSS — **JESUS LIZARD** (12) 93
PUSS 'N BOOTS — **Adam ANT** (5) 83
PUSSYCAT — **MULU** (50) 97
PUT A LIGHT IN THE WINDOW — **KING BROTHERS** (25) 58
PUT A LITTLE LOVE IN YOUR HEART [A] — **Dave CLARK FIVE** (31) 69
PUT A LITTLE LOVE IN YOUR HEART [A] — **Annie LENNOX and Al GREEN** (28) 88
PUT HIM OUT — **MS DYNAMITE** (19) 02
PUT HIM OUT OF YOUR MIND — **DR FEELGOOD** (73) 79
PUT IT THERE — **Paul McCARTNEY** (32) 90
PUT MY ARMS AROUND YOU — **Kevin KITCHEN** (64) 85
PUT OUR HEADS TOGETHER — **O'JAYS** (45) ..83
PUT THE LIGHT ON — **WET WET WET** (56) 91
PUT THE MESSAGE IN THE BOX — **Brian KENNEDY** (37) 97
PUT THE NEEDLE ON IT — **Dannii MINOGUE** (7) 02
PUT THE NEEDLE TO THE RECORD — **Wally JUMP Jr and the CRIMINAL ELEMENT** (63) ..87
PUT YOUR ARMS AROUND ME [A] — **TEXAS** (10) 97,98
PUT YOUR ARMS AROUND ME [B] — **NATURAL** (32) 02
PUT YOUR FAITH IN ME — **Alison LIMERICK** (42) 97
PUT YOUR HANDS TOGETHER — **D MOB** (7) 90
PUT YOUR HANDS WHERE MY EYES COULD SEE — **Busta RHYMES** (16) 97
PUT YOUR HANDS UP — **REFLEX featuring MC VIPER** (72) 01
PUT YOUR HANDZ UP — **WHOOLIGANZ** (53)..94
PUT YOUR HEAD ON MY SHOULDER — **Paul ANKA** (7) 59
PUT YOUR LOVE IN ME — **HOT CHOCOLATE** (10) 77
PUT YOUR MONEY WHERE YOUR MOUTH IS — **ROSE ROYCE** (44) 77
PUT YOURSELF IN MY PLACE [A] — **ISLEY BROTHERS** (13) 69
PUT YOURSELF IN MY PLACE [A] — **ELGINS** (28) 71
PUT YOURSELF IN MY PLACE [B] — **Kylie MINOGUE** (11) 94
PUTTING ON THE STYLE — **Lonnie DONEGAN** (1) 57
PYJAMARAMA — **ROXY MUSIC** (10) 73
PYRAMID SONG — **RADIOHEAD** (5) 01
P.Y.T. (PRETTY YOUNG THING) — **Michael JACKSON** (11) 84

QUADROPHONIA — **QUADROPHONIA** (14) 91
QUANDO M'INNAMORO (A MAN WITHOUT LOVE) — **SANDPIPERS** (33) 68
QUANDO QUANDO QUANDO [A] — **Pat BOONE** (41) 62
QUANDO QUANDO QUANDO [A] — **Engelbert HUMPERDINCK** (40) 99
THE QUARTER MOON — **VIPs** (55) 80
QUARTER TO THREE — **Gary 'US' BONDS** (7) 61
QUE SERA — **Chris REA** (73) 88
QUE SERA MI VIDA (IF YOU SHOULD GO) — **GIBSON BROTHERS** (5) 79
QUE SERA SERA [A] — **Doris DAY** (1) 56
QUE SERA SERA [A] — **Geno WASHINGTON and the RAM JAM BAND** (43) 66
QUE SERA SERA [A] — **HERMES HOUSE BAND** (53) 02
QUE TAL AMERICA — **TWO MAN SOUND** (46) 79
QUEEN FOR TONIGHT — **Helen SHAPIRO** (33) 63
QUEEN JANE — **KINGMAKER** (29) 93
QUEEN OF CLUBS — **KC and the SUNSHINE BAND** (7) 74
QUEEN OF HEARTS [A] — **Dave EDMUNDS** (11) 79
QUEEN OF HEARTS [B] — **CHARLOTTE** (54)....94
QUEEN OF MY HEART — **WESTLIFE** (1) 01
QUEEN OF MY SOUL — **AVERAGE WHITE BAND** (23) 76
QUEEN OF NEW ORLEANS — **Jon BON JOVI** (10) 97
THE QUEEN OF 1964 — **Neil SEDAKA** (35) 75
THE QUEEN OF OUTER SPACE — **WEDDING PRESENT** (23) 92
QUEEN OF RAIN — **ROXETTE** (28) 92
QUEEN OF THE HOP — **Bobby DARIN** (24) 59
QUEEN OF THE NEW YEAR — **DEACON BLUE** (21) 90
QUEEN OF THE NIGHT — **Whitney HOUSTON** (14) 93
QUEEN OF THE RAPPING SCENE (NOTHING EVER GOES THE WAY YOU PLAN) — **MODERN ROMANCE** (37) 82
THE QUEEN'S BIRTHDAY SONG — **ST JOHN'S COLLEGE SCHOOL CHOIR and the Band of the GRENADIER GUARDS** (40) 86
QUEEN'S FIRST EP — **QUEEN** (17) 77
QUEER — **GARBAGE** (13) 95
QUEST — **SYSTEM 7** (74) 93
QUESTION — **MOODY BLUES** (2) 70
THE QUESTION — **SEVEN GRAND HOUSING AUTHORITY** (70)..93
QUESTION OF FAITH — **LIGHTHOUSE FAMILY** (21) 98
A QUESTION OF LUST — **DEPECHE MODE** (28) 86
A QUESTION OF TIME — **DEPECHE MODE** (17) 86
QUESTIONS AND ANSWERS [A] — **SHAM 69** (18) 79
QUESTIONS & ANSWERS [B] — **BIFFY CLYRO** (26) 03
QUESTIONS I CAN'T ANSWER — **HEINZ** (39)..64
QUESTIONS (MUST BE ASKED) — **David FORBES** (57) 01
QUICK JOEY SMALL (RUN JOEY RUN) — **KASENETZ-KATZ SINGING ORCHESTRAL CIRCUS** (19) 68

QUIEREME MUCHO (YOURS) — **Julio IGLESIAS** (3) 82
QUIET LIFE — **JAPAN** (19) 81
QUIT PLAYING GAMES (WITH MY HEART) — **BACKSTREET BOYS** (2) 97
QUIT THIS TOWN — **EDDIE and the HOT RODS** (36) 78
QUITE A PARTY — **FIREBALLS** (29) 61
QUITE RIGHTLY SO — **PROCOL HARUM** (50)..68
QUOTE GOODBYE QUOTE — **Carolyne MAS** (71) 80
QUOTH — **POLYGON WINDOW** (49) 93

R.R. EXPRESS — **ROSE ROYCE** (52) 81
R TO THE A — **CJ LEWIS** (34) 95
R U READY — **SALT-N-PEPA** (24) 97
R U SLEEPING — **INDO** (31) 98
RABBIT — **CHAS and DAVE** (8) 80
THE RACE [A] — **YELLO** (7) 88,92
RACE [B] — **TIGER** (37) 96
RACE [C] — **THE LEAVES** (66) 02
RACE FOR THE PRIZE — **FLAMING LIPS** (39)..99
THE RACE IS ON [A] — **Suzi QUATRO** (43) 78
THE RACE IS ON [B] — **Dave EDMUNDS and the STRAY CATS** (34) 81
RACE WITH THE DEVIL [A] — **Gene VINCENT** (28) 56
RACE WITH THE DEVIL [B] — **GIRLSCHOOL** (49) 80
RACE WITH THE DEVIL [B] — **GUN** (8) 68
RACHEL — **Al MARTINO** (10) 53
RACHMANINOFF'S 18TH VARIATION ON A THEME BY PAGANINI (THE STORY OF THREE LOVES) — **Winifred ATWELL** (9) 54
RACIST FRIEND — **SPECIALS** (60) 83
RADANCER — **MARMALADE** (6) 72
RADAR LOVE [A] — **GOLDEN EARRING** (7) 73,77
RADAR LOVE [A] — **OH WELL** (65) 90
RADIATION VIBE — **FOUNTAINS OF WAYNE** (32) 97
RADICAL YOUR LOVER — **LITTLE ANGELS** (34) 90
RADICCIO (EP) — **ORBITAL** (37) 92
RADIO [A] — **Roger TAYLOR** (37) 92
RADIO [B] — **TEENAGE FANCLUB** (31) 93
RADIO [C] — **CORRS** (18) 99
RADIO AFRICA — **LATIN QUARTER** (19) 86
RADIO DISCO — **WILT** (56) 00
RADIO GAGA — **QUEEN** (2) 84
RADIO HEAD — **TALKING HEADS** (52) 87
RADIO HEART — **RADIO HEART featuring Gary NUMAN** (35) 87
RADIO MUSICOLA — **Nik KERSHAW** (43) 86
RADIO #1 — **AIR** (31) 01
RADIO ON — **Ricky ROSS** (35) 96
RADIO RADIO — **Elvis COSTELLO** (29) 78
RADIO ROMANCE — **TIFFANY** (13) 88
RADIO SONG — **R.E.M.** (28) 91
RADIO WALL OF SOUND — **SLADE** (21) 91
RADIO WAVES — **Roger WATERS** (74) 87
RADIOACTIVE — **Gene SIMMONS** (41) 79
RADIOACTIVITY — **KRAFTWERK** (43) 91
RAG DOLL [A] — **FOUR SEASONS** (2) 64
RAG DOLL [B] — **AEROSMITH** (42) 90
RAG MAMA RAG — **BAND** (16) 70
RAGAMUFFIN MAN — **MANFRED MANN** (8)....69
RAGE HARD — **FRANKIE GOES TO HOLLYWOOD** (4) 86
RAGE TO LOVE — **Kim WILDE** (19) 85
RAGGA HOUSE (ALL NIGHT LONG) — **Simon HARRIS** (56) 90
RAGGAMUFFIN GIRL — **APACHE INDIAN** (31)..95
RAGING (EP) [A] — **BEYOND** (68) 91
RAGING [B] — **COSMIC GATE** (48) 03
RAGS TO RICHES [A] — **David WHITFIELD** (3) 53,54
RAGS TO RICHES [A] — **Elvis PRESLEY** (9) 71
RAGTIME COWBOY JOE — **CHIPMUNKS** (11) ..59
RAIN [A] — **Bruce RUFFIN** (19) 71
RAIN [B] — **STATUS QUO** (7) 76
RAIN [C] — **CULT** (17) 85
RAIN [D] — **MADONNA** (7) 93
RAIN [E] — **GROOVE CORPORATION** (71) 94
THE RAIN — **Oran 'Juice' JONES** (4) 86
THE RAIN (SUPA DUPA FLY) — **Missy 'Misdemeanor' ELLIOTT** (16) 97
RAIN AND TEARS — **APHRODITE'S CHILD** (29) 68
RAIN FALLS — **Frankie KNUCKLES** (48) 92
RAIN FOREST [A] — **BIDDU** (39) 76
RAIN FOREST [B] — **Paul HARDCASTLE** (41) 84,85
RAIN IN THE SUMMERTIME — **ALARM** (18) 87
RAIN KING — **COUNTING CROWS** (49) 94
RAIN ON ME — **ASHANTI** (19) 03
RAIN OR SHINE — **FIVE STAR** (2) 86
RAIN RAIN RAIN — **Frankie LAINE and the FOUR LADS** (8) 54
RAIN SHOWERS — **SIZZLA** (51) 99
RAINBOW [A] — **MARMALADE** (3) 70
RAINBOW [B] — **PETERS and LEE** (17) 74
RAINBOW CHASER — **NIRVANA** (34) 68
RAINBOW CHILD — **Dan REED NETWORK** (39) 90
RAINBOW COUNTRY — **Bob MARLEY and the WAILERS** (11) 00
RAINBOW IN THE DARK — **DIO** (46) 83
RAINBOW LAKE — **WENDY and LISA** (70) 90
RAINBOW PEOPLE — **MANIX** (57) 92
RAINBOW (SAMPLE FREE) — **SOLO** (59) 91
RAINBOW THEME – FROZEN RAINBOW — **SAXON** (66) 80
RAINBOW VALLEY — **LOVE AFFAIR** (5) 68
RAINBOWS OF COLOUR — **GROOVERIDER** (40) 98
RAINCLOUD — **LIGHTHOUSE FAMILY** (6) 97
THE RAINDANCE — **DARE** (62) 89
RAINDROPS KEEP FALLIN' ON MY HEAD [A] — **Bobbie GENTRY** (40) 70
RAINDROPS KEEP FALLIN' ON MY HEAD [A] — **BJ THOMAS** (38) 70
RAINDROPS KEEP FALLING ON MY HEAD [A] — **Sacha DISTEL** (10) 70
RAININ' THROUGH MY SUNSHINE — **REAL THING** (40) 78
RAINING ALL OVER THE WORLD — **ADVENTURES** (68) 92
RAINING IN MY HEART — **Leo SAYER** (21) 78
RAINMAKER [A] — **SPARKLEHORSE** (61) 96
RAINMAKER [B] — **IRON MAIDEN** (13) 03
RAINY DAY WOMEN NOS. 12 & 35 — **Bob DYLAN** (7) 66
RAINY DAYS AND MONDAYS — **CARPENTERS** (63) 93
RAINY DAYZ — **Mary J. BLIGE** (17) 02
RAINY NIGHT IN GEORGIA — **Randy CRAWFORD** (18) 81

REGGAE TUNE –
Andy FAIRWEATHER-LOW (10) 74
REGINA – SUGARCUBES (55) 89
REGRET – NEW ORDER (4)............................93
REGULATE – Warren G (5) 94
REIGNS – JA RULE (9) 03
REILLY – OLYMPIC ORCHESTRA (26) 83
RELAX [A] –
FRANKIE GOES TO HOLLYWOOD (1)..83,85,93
RELAX [B] – Crystal WATERS (37) 95
RELAX [C] – DEETAH (11) 98
RELAY – WHO (21) 73
RELEASE [A] –
AFRO CELT SOUND SYSTEM (71) 00
RELEASE [B] – MEDWAY (67) 01
RELEASE ME [A] –
Engelbert HUMPERDINCK (1) 67
RELEASE ME [B] – WILSON PHILLIPS (36)....90
RELEASE THE PRESSURE – LEFTFIELD (13) ..96
RELEASE YO' SELF [A] – METHOD MAN (46) 95
RELEASE YO SELF [B] –
TRANSATLANTIC SOUL (43) 97
RELIGHT MY FIRE –
TAKE THAT featuring LULU (1) 93
RELIGION – FRONT 242 (46) 93
RELOAD – PPK (39) 02
REMEDY – BLACK CROWES (24) 92
REMEMBER [A] –
Jimi HENDRIX EXPERIENCE (35) 71
REMEMBER [B] – ROCK CANDY (32)..............71
REMEMBER [C] – BT (27) 98
REMEMBER [D] – DISTURBED (56)................02
REMEMBER I LOVE YOU –
Jim DIAMOND (42) 85
REMEMBER ME [A] – Diana ROSS (7)............71
REMEMBER ME [B] – Cliff RICHARD (35) 87
REMEMBER ME [C] – BLUE BOY (8) 97
REMEMBER ME [D] – JORIO (54) 01
REMEMBER ME [E] –
BRITISH SEA POWER (30) 03
REMEMBER ME THIS WAY –
Gary GLITTER (3) 74
REMEMBER ME WITH LOVE –
Gloria ESTEFAN (22)......................................91
REMEMBER (SHA-LA-LA) –
BAY CITY ROLLERS (6)..................................74
REMEMBER THE DAY – INNOCENCE (56) 91
(REMEMBER THE DAYS OF THE) OLD SCHOOL
YARD – Cat STEVENS (44) 77
REMEMBER THE RAIN – Bob LIND (46) 66
REMEMBER THE TIME –
Michael JACKSON (3) 92
REMEMBER THEN –
SHOWADDYWADDY (17)................................79
REMEMBER (WALKIN' IN THE SAND) –
SHANGRI-LAS (14) 64
REMEMBER WHEN – PLATTERS (25) 59
REMEMBER YESTERDAY – John MILES (32)..76
REMEMBER YOU'RE A WOMBLE –
WOMBLES (3) 74,98
REMEMBER YOU'RE MINE – Pat BOONE (5) 57
REMEMBERESE – The STILLS (75) 03
REMEMBERING CHRISTMAS –
EXETER BRAMDEAN BOYS' CHOIR (46) 93
REMEMBERING THE FIRST TIME –
SIMPLY RED (22) 95
REMEMBRANCE DAY – B-MOVIE (61) 81
REMIND ME – RÖYKSOPP (21)......................02
REMINDING ME (OF SEF) –
COMMON featuring Chantay SAVAGE (59)..97
REMINISCE [A] – Mary J BLIGE (31) 93
REMINISCE [B] – BLAZIN' SQUAD (8) 03
REMINISCING – Buddy HOLLY (17) 62
REMOTE CONTROL – BEASTIE BOYS (21)......99
RENAISSANCE – M PEOPLE (5) 94
RENDEZVOUS [A] – Tina CHARLES (27) 77
RENDEZVOUS [B] –
TYGERS OF PAN TANG (49) 82
RENDEZVOUS [C] – Craig DAVID (8) 01
RENDEZ-VOUS '98 –
APOLLO FOUR FORTY (12) 98
RENDEZ-VU – BASEMENT JAXX (4)................99
RENÉ DMC (DEVASTATING MACHO CHARISMA)
– RENÉ and YVETTE (57) 86
RENEGADE MASTER – WILDCHILD (3)......95,98
RENEGADE SNARES – OMNI TRIO (61)..........03
RENEGADE SOUNDWAVE –
RENEGADE SOUNDWAVE (64) 94
RENEGADES OF FUNK –
Afrika BAMBAATAA (30)..............................84
RENT – PET SHOP BOYS (8) 87
RENTA SANTA – Chris HILL (10) 75
RENTED ROOMS – TINDERSTICKS (56) 97
RE-OFFENDER – TRAVIS (7) 03
REPEAT – MANIC STREET PREACHERS (26) ..91
REPEATED LOVE – ATGOC (38) 98
REPORT TO THE DANCEFLOOR –
ENERGISE (69) 91
REPRESENT – SOUL II SOUL (39) 97
REPUBLICAN PARTY REPTILE (EP) –
BIG COUNTRY (37) 91
REPUTATION – Dusty SPRINGFIELD (38) 90
REPUTATIONS (JUST BE GOOD TO ME) –
Andrea GRANT (75) 98
REQUEST LINE [A] – ZHANE (22) 97
REQUEST LINE [B] – BLACK EYED
PEAS featuring Macy GRAY (31) 01
REQUIEM [A] – SLIK (24) 76
REQUIEM [B] – LONDON BOYS (4) 88,89
RESCUE – ECHO and the BUNNYMEN (62) ..80
RESCUE ME [A] – Fontella BASS (11) 65
RESCUE ME [B] – ALARM (48) 87
RESCUE ME [C] – MADONNA (3)....................91
RESCUE ME [D] –
BELL BOOK & CANDLE (63) 98
RESCUE ME [E] – ULTRA (8)..........................99
RESCUE ME [F] –
SUNKIDS featuring CHANCE (50) 99
RESPECT [A] – Aretha FRANKLIN (10)............67
RESPECT [A] – REAL ROXANNE (71) 88
RESPECT [A] – ADEVA (17) 89,93
RESPECT [B] – SUB SUB (49)........................94
RESPECT [C] – Judy CHEEKS (23)..................95
RESPECT YOURSELF [A] –
KANE GANG (21) 84,85
RESPECT YOURSELF [A] – Bruce WILLIS (7)..87
RESPECT YOURSELF [A] –
Robert PALMER (45) 95
RESPECTABLE [A] – ROLLING STONES (23) ..78
RESPECTABLE [B] – MEL and KIM (1)............87
RESPECTABLE [B] – GIRLS @ PLAY (29) 01
REST & PLAY EP – ORBITAL (33)....................02
REST IN PEACE – EXTREME (13) 92
REST OF MY LOVE –
URBAN COOKIE COLLECTIVE (67)................95
REST OF THE NIGHT – Natalie COLE (56) 89
RESTLESS [A] –
Johnny KIDD and the PIRATES (22).............60
RESTLESS [B] – GILLAN (25) 82
RESTLESS [C] – STATUS QUO (39)................94
RESTLESS DAYS (SHE CRIES OUT LOUD) –
AND WHY NOT? (38) 89
RESTLESS (I KNOW YOU KNOW) –
NEJA (47) 98
RESURECTION – PPK (3)..............................01
RESURRECTION –
Brian MAY with Cozy POWELL (23) 93
RESURRECTION JOE – CULT (74) 84
THE RESURRECTION SHUFFLE –
ASHTON, GARDNER AND DYKE (3)..............71
RETOX – FATBOY SLIM (73)..........................02
RETREAT – HELL IS FOR HEROES (39)..........03
RETURN OF DJANGO – UPSETTERS (5) 69
THE RETURN OF EVIL BILL – CLINIC (70)......00
THE RETURN OF NOTHING –
SANDSTORM (54)..00
THE RETURN OF PAN – WATERBOYS (24) 93
RETURN OF THE ELECTRIC WARRIOR (EP) –
T. REX (50) 81
THE RETURN OF THE LOS PALMAS SEVEN –
MADNESS (7) 81
RETURN OF THE MACK –
Mark MORRISON (1)......................................96
RETURN OF THE RED BARON –
ROYAL GUARDSMEN (37)..............................67
THE RETURN (TIME TO SAY GOODBYE) –
DJ VISAGE featuring CLARISSA (58)............00
RETURN TO BRIXTON – CLASH (57)..............90
RETURN TO INNOCENCE – ENIGMA (3) 94
RETURN TO ME – Dean MARTIN (2)..............58
RETURN TO REALITY – ANTARTICA (53)........00
RETURN TO SENDER – Elvis PRESLEY (1) 62,77
REUNITED – PEACHES and HERB (4) 79
REVEILLE ROCK –
JOHNNY and the HURRICANES (14) 59
REVELATION – ELECTRIQUE BOUTIQUE (37) 00
REVERENCE [A] –
JESUS AND MARY CHAIN (10)......................92
REVERENCE [B] – FAITHLESS (10) 97
REVEREND BLACK GRAPE –
BLACK GRAPE (9) 95
REVIVAL [A] –
Chris BARBER'S JAZZ BAND (43) 62
REVIVAL [B] – EURYTHMICS (26) 89
REVIVAL [C] – Martine GIRAULT (37) ..92,93,97
REVOL – MANIC STREET PREACHERS (22)....94
REVOLT INTO STYLE – Bill NELSON (69) 79
REVOLUTION [A] – CULT (30) 85
REVOLUTION [B] –
THOMPSON TWINS (56) 85,86
REVOLUTION [C] –
ARRESTED DEVELOPMENT (4) 93
REVOLUTION [D] – COLDCUT (67)..................01
REVOLUTION [E] – BK (42) 02
REVOLUTION (IN THE SUMMERTIME) –
COSMIC ROUGH RIDERS (35) 01
REVOLUTION BABY –
TRANSVISION VAMP (30)..............................88
REVOLUTION 909 – DAFT PUNK (47)............98
REVOLUTIONS – Jean-Michel JARRE (52) 88
REVOLUTIONS (EP) – SHARKEY (53) 97
REWARD – TEARDROP EXPLODES (6) 81
REWIND [A] – CELETIA (29) 98
REWIND [B] – PRECIOUS (11) 00
REWIND (FIND A WAY) –
Beverley KNIGHT (40) 98
RHAPSODY – FOUR SEASONS (37) 77
RHAPSODY IN THE RAIN –
Lou CHRISTIE (37) 66
RHIANNON – FLEETWOOD MAC (46) 78
RHINESTONE COWBOY –
Glen CAMPBELL (4) 75
RHINESTONE COWBOY
(GIDDY UP GIDDY UP) – RIKKI &
DAZ featuring Glen CAMPBELL (12) 02
THE RHYME – Keith MURRAY (59)................96
THE RHYTHM – CLOCK (28) 94
RHYTHM & BLUES ALIBI – GOMEZ (18) 99
RHYTHM AND GREENS – SHADOWS (22) 64
RHYTHM BANDITS – JUNIOR SENIOR (22) 03
RHYTHM DIVINE – Enrique IGLESIAS (45) 99
THE RHYTHM DIVINE –
YELLO featuring Shirley BASSEY (54) 87
RHYTHM IS A DANCER – SNAP! (1)..........92,03
RHYTHM IS A MYSTERY – K-KLASS (3) 91
RHYTHM IS GONNA GET YOU –
Gloria ESTEFAN and
MIAMI SOUND MACHINE (16)......................88
RHYTHM NATION – Janet JACKSON (23) 89
RHYTHM OF LIFE –
Oleta ADAMS (38) 90,,91,95
RHYTHM OF LOVE – SCORPIONS (59) 88
RHYTHM OF MY HEART [A] –
Rod STEWART (3) 91
RHYTHM OF MY HEART [A] – RUNRIG (24) ..96
RHYTHM OF THE BEAST –
Nicko McBRAIN (72) 91
RHYTHM OF THE JUNGLE – QUICK (41) 82
RHYTHM OF THE NIGHT [A] – DeBARGE (4)..85
RHYTHM OF THE NIGHT [A] –
POWERHOUSE (38) 97
THE RHYTHM OF THE NIGHT [C] –
CORONA (2) 94
RHYTHM OF THE RAIN [A] – CASCADES (5) ..63
RHYTHM OF THE RAIN [A] –
Jason DONOVAN (9)......................................90
RHYTHM TAKES CONTROL – UNIQUE 3 (41)..90
RHYTHM TALK – JOCKO (56) 80
RIBBON IN THE SKY – Stevie WONDER (45) 82
RICE IS NICE – LEMON PIPERS (41)..............68
RICH AH GETTING RICHER – REBEL MC (48) 92
RICH AND STRANGE – CUD (24) 92
RICH IN PARADISE – FPI PROJECT (9) 89
RICH KIDS – RICH KIDS (24) 78
RICH MAN POOR MAN – Jimmy YOUNG (25) 56
RICHARD III – SUPERGRASS (2)....................97
RICCOCHET – B B and Q BAND (71) 87
RICOCHET [A] – Joan REGAN (8) 53,54
RICOCHET [B] – FAITH NO MORE (27) 95
RIDDIM – US3 (34)..93
RIDDLE – EN VOGUE (33)..............................00
THE RIDDLE – Nik KERSHAW (3) 84
RIDDLE ME – UB40 (59)..................................84
RIDE – Ana ANN (24) 02
RIDE (EP) – RIDE (71)....................................90
RIDE A ROCKET –
LITHIAM and Sonya MADAN (40) 97
RIDE A WHITE SWAN – T. REX (2) 70
RIDE A WILD HORSE – Dee CLARK (16) 75
RIDE AWAY – Roy ORBISON (34) 65
RIDE LIKE THE WIND [A] –
Christopher CROSS (69)................................80

ROCK 'N' ROLL (I GAVE YOU THE BEST YEARS OF MY LIFE) – **Kevin JOHNSON** (23)..........75
ROCK 'N' ROLL IS KING – **ELECTRIC LIGHT ORCHESTRA** (13) 83
ROCK 'N' ROLL LADY – **SHOWADDYWADDY** (15)..............................74
ROCK 'N' ROLL LIES – **RAZORLIGHT** (56)......03
ROCK 'N' ROLL MERCENARIES – **MEAT LOAF featuring John PARR** (31) 86
ROCK 'N' ROLL NIGGER – **BIRDLAND** (47) 90
ROCK 'N' ROLL OUTLAW – **ROSE TATTOO** (60).......................................81
ROCK 'N ROLL STAGE SHOW (LP) – **Bill HALEY and his COMETS** (30) 56
ROCK 'N' ROLL SUICIDE – **David BOWIE** (22) 74
ROCK 'N' ROLL WINTER (LOONY'S TUNE) – **WIZZARD** (6)...74
ROCK OF AGES – **DEF LEPPARD** (41) 83
ROCK ON – **David ESSEX** (3) 73
ROCK ON BROTHER – **CHEQUERS** (21)..........75
THE ROCK SHOW – **BLINK-182** (14) 01
ROCK STAR – **N*E*R*D** (15) 02
ROCK STEADY [A] – **WHISPERS** (38) 87
ROCK STEADY [B] – **Bonnie RAITT and Bryan ADAMS** (50) 95
(ROCK) SUPERSTAR – **CYPRESS HILL** (13) 00
ROCK THE BELLS – **KADOC** (34).....................97
ROCK THE BOAT [A] – **HUES CORPORATION** (6) 74
ROCK THE BOAT [A] – **FORREST** (4)..............83
ROCK THE BOAT [A] – **DELAGE** (63)..............90
ROCK THE BOAT [B] – **AALIYAH** (12) 02
ROCK THE CASBAH – **CLASH** (15) 82,91
ROCK THE DISCOTEK – **RAMP** (49) 96
ROCK THE FUNKY BEATS – **NATURAL BORN CHILLERS** (30) 97
ROCK THE HOUSE [A] – **SOURCE featuring NICOLE** (63) 92
ROCK THE HOUSE [B] – **GORILLAZ** (18) 01
ROCK THE JOINT – **Bill HALEY and his COMETS** (20)..................57
ROCK THE MIDNIGHT – **David GRANT** (46) ..83
ROCK THE NIGHT – **EUROPE** (12)..................87
ROCK THIS TOWN – **STRAY CATS** (9) 81
ROCK 'TIL YOU DROP – **STATUS QUO** (38) ..92
ROCK 2 HOUSE – **X-PRESS 2** (55) 94
ROCK WIT U (AWWW BABY) – **ASHANTI** (7)..03
ROCK WIT'CHA – **Bobby BROWN** (33) 89
ROCK WITH THE CAVEMAN – **Tommy STEELE** (13) 56
ROCK WITH YOU [A] – **D'INFLUENCE** (30) 98
ROCK WITH YOU [A] – **Michael JACKSON** (7) 80
ROCK YOUR BABY [A] – **George McCRAE** (1) 74
ROCK YOUR BABY [A] – **KWS** (8) 92
ROCK YOUR BODY [A] – **CLOCK** (30) 98
ROCK YOUR BODY [B] – **Justin TIMBERLAKE** (2)..................................03
ROCK-A-BEATIN' BOOGIE – **Bill HALEY and his COMETS** (4)..................55
ROCK-A-BILLY – **Guy MITCHELL** (1)................57
ROCKABILLY BOB – **COLUMBO featuring OOE** (59)......................99
ROCKABILLY GUY – **POLECATS** (35) 81
ROCKABILLY REBEL – **MATCHBOX** (18)..........79
ROCK-A-BYE YOUR BABY (WITH A DIXIE MELODY) – **Jerry LEWIS** (12)......................57
CK-A-DOODLE-DOO – **Linda LEWIS** (15)....73

THE ROCKAFELLER SKANK – **FATBOY SLIM** (6) 98
ROCKALL – **MEZZOFORTE** (75) 83
ROCKARIA! – **ELECTRIC LIGHT ORCHESTRA** (9) 77
ROCKET [A] – **MUD** (6) 74
ROCKET [B] – **DEF LEPPARD** (15) 89
ROCKET MAN – **SPOTNICKS** (38) 62
ROCKET MAN (I THINK IT'S GOING TO BE A LONG LONG TIME) [A] – **Elton JOHN** (2) 72
ROCKET MAN (I THINK IT'S GOING TO BE A LONG LONG TIME) [A] – **Kate BUSH** (12) ..91
ROCKET 2 U – **JETS** (69)...................................88
ROCKIN' ALL OVER THE WORLD – **STATUS QUO** (3) 77
ROCKIN' ALONE – **MIKI and GRIFF** (44) 60
ROCKIN' AROUND THE CHRISTMAS TREE [A] – **Brenda LEE** (6) 62
ROCKIN' AROUND THE CHRISTMAS TREE [A] – **JETS** (62) 83
ROCKIN' AROUND THE CHRISTMAS TREE [A] – **Kim WILDE** (3) 87
ROCKIN' BACK INSIDE MY HEART – **Julee CRUISE** (66) 91
ROCKIN' CHAIR – **MAGNUM** (27) 90
ROCKIN' FOR MYSELF – **MOTIV 8** (18) 93,94
ROCKIN' GOOD CHRISTMAS – **Roy 'Chubby' BROWN** (51)..........................96
A ROCKIN' GOOD WAY – **Bonnie TYLER** (5) ..84
ROCKIN' ME – **DJ PROFESSOR** (56) 94
ROCKIN' MY BODY – **49ers featuring Ann-Marie SMITH** (31)........95
ROCKIN' OVER THE BEAT – **TECHNOTRONIC** (9) 90
ROCKIN' RED WING – **Sammy MASTERS** (36) 60
ROCKIN' ROBIN [A] – **Bobby DAY** (29) 58
ROCKIN' ROBIN [A] – **Michael JACKSON** (3) ..72
ROCKIN' ROBIN [A] – **LOLLY** (10) 99
ROCKIN' ROLL BABY – **STYLISTICS** (6)..........74
ROCKIN' SOUL – **HUES CORPORATION** (24)..74
ROCKIN' THE SUBURBS – **Ben FOLDS** (53) ..01
ROCKIN' THROUGH THE RYE – **Bill HALEY and his COMETS** (3) 56,57
ROCKIN' TO THE MUSIC – **BLACK BOX** (39)..93
ROCKIN' TO THE RHYTHM – **CONVERT** (42)..93
ROCKIN' WITH RITA (HEAD TO TOE) – **VINDALOO SUMMER SPECIAL** (56)..............86
ROCKING GOOSE – **JOHNNY and the HURRICANES** (3) 60
ROCKIT – **Herbie HANCOCK** (8) 83
ROCKS [A] – **PRIMAL SCREAM** (7) 94
ROCKS [A] – **Rod STEWART** (55) 98
ROCKS ON THE ROAD – **JETHRO TULL** (47) ..92
ROCKY – **Austin ROBERTS** (22) 75
ROCKY MOUNTAIN WAY (EP) – **Joe WALSH** (39) 77
THE RODEO SONG – **Garry LEE and SHOWDOWN** (44) 93
RODRIGO'S GUITAR CONCERTO DE ARANJUEZ (THEME FROM 2ND MOVEMENT) – **MANUEL and his MUSIC OF THE MOUNTAINS** (3) 76
ROFO'S THEME – **ROFO** (44) 92
ROK DA HOUSE [A] – **BEATMASTERS featuring the COOKIE CREW** (5)..................88
ROK DA HOUSE [B] – **VINYLGROOVER and the RED HED** (72) 01

ROK THE NATION – **ROB 'N' RAZ featuring Leila K** (41) 90
ROLL AWAY – **Dusty SPRINGFIELD** (68) 95
ROLL AWAY THE STONE – **MOTT THE HOOPLE** (8) 73
ROLL ON – **MIS-TEEQ** (7) 02
ROLL ON DOWN THE HIGHWAY – **BACHMAN-TURNER OVERDRIVE** (22) 75
ROLL OVER BEETHOVEN – **ELECTRIC LIGHT ORCHESTRA** (6) 73
ROLL OVER LAY DOWN – **STATUS QUO** (9) ..75
ROLL THE BONES – **RUSH** (49) 92
ROLL TO ME – **DEL AMITRI** (22)....................95
ROLL WITH IT [A] – **Steve WINWOOD** (53)....88
ROLL WITH IT [B] – **OASIS** (2) 95,96,97
A ROLLER SKATING JAM NAMED 'SATURDAYS' – **DE LA SOUL** (22) 91
ROLLERBLADE [A] – **Nick HEYWARD** (37)......96
ROLLERBLADE [B] – **MOVIN' MELODIES** (71) 97
ROLLERCOASTER [A] – **GRID** (19) 94
ROLLERCOASTER [B] – **NORTHERN UPROAR** (41) 95
ROLLERCOASTER [C] – **B*WITCHED** (1)..........98
ROLLERCOASTER (EP) – **JESUS AND MARY CHAIN** (46) 90
ROLLERCOASTER (EP) – **EVERYTHING BUT THE GIRL** (65) 94
ROLLIN' – **LIMP BIZKIT** (1) 01
ROLLIN' HOME – **STATUS QUO** (9)................86
ROLLIN' IN MY 5.0 – **VANILLA ICE** (27) 91
ROLLIN' ON – **CIRRUS** (62)...........................78
ROLLING STONE – **David ESSEX** (5)..............75
ROLLOUT (MY BUSINESS) – **LUDACRIS** (20)..02
ROLLOVER DJ – **JET** (34)...............................03
ROLODEX PROPAGANDA – **AT THE DRIVE-IN** (54) 00
ROMAN P – **PSYCHIC TV** (65).........................86
ROMANCE (LET YOUR HEART GO) – **David CASSIDY** (54) 85
ROMANCING THE STONE – **Eddy GRANT** (52) 84
ROMANTIC – **Karyn WHITE** (23) 91
ROMANTICA – **Jane MORGAN** (39) 60
ROME WASN'T BUILT IN A DAY – **MORCHEEBA** (34)...00
ROMEO [A] – **Petula CLARK** (3).......................61
ROMEO [B] – **MR BIG** (4) 77
ROMEO [C] – **BASEMENT JAXX** (6) 01
ROMEO AND JULIET – **DIRE STRAITS** (8) 81
ROMEO DUNN – **ROMEO** (3) 02
ROMEO ME – **SLEEPER** (39)..........................97
ROMEO WHERE'S JULIET? – **COLLAGE** (46) ..85
RONDO – **Kenny BALL and his JAZZMEN** (24) 63
RONI – **Bobby BROWN** (21) 89
ROOBARB AND CUSTARD – **SHAFT** (7) 91
ROOF IS ON FIRE – **WESTBAM** (58) 98
ROOFTOP SINGING – **NEW WORLD** (50)........73
ROOM AT THE TOP – **Adam ANT** (13) 90
ROOM ELEVEN – **DAISY CHAINSAW** (65) 92
ROOM IN YOUR HEART – **LIVING IN A BOX** (5)..................................89
ROOMS ON FIRE – **Stevie NICKS** (16) 89
ROOTS – **SPONGE** (52).................................02
ROOTS BLOODY ROOTS – **SEPULTURA** (19) ..96
ROSALIE – COWGIRLS' SONG (MEDLEY) – **THIN LIZZY** (20) 78
ROSALYN – **PRETTY THINGS** (41) 64

ROSANNA – **TOTO** (12)..................................83
THE ROSE [A] – **Heather PEACE** (56) 00
THE ROSE [A] – **Michael BALL** (42) 95
ROSE GARDEN [A] – **Lynn ANDERSON** (3) 71
ROSE GARDEN [A] – **NEW WORLD** (15)..........71
A ROSE HAS TO DIE – **DOOLEYS** (11)............78
A ROSE IS STILL A ROSE – **Aretha FRANKLIN** (22) 98
ROSE MARIE – **Slim WHITMAN** (1) 55
ROSE ROUGE – **ST GERMAIN** (54) 01
ROSEABILITY – **IDLEWILD** (38).......................00
ROSES [A] – **HAYWOODE** (11) 85,86
ROSES [A] – **RHYTHM-N-BASS** (56) 92
ROSES [B] – **dEUS** (56) 97
ROSES ARE RED [A] – **Ronnie CARROLL** (3)..62
ROSES ARE RED [B] – **Bobby VINTON** (15)...............................62,90
ROSES ARE RED [C] – **MAC BAND featuring the McCAMPBELL BROTHERS** (8) 88
ROSES IN THE HOSPITAL – **MANIC STREET PREACHERS** (15) 93
ROSES OF PICARDY – **Vince HILL** (13) 67
ROSETTA – **Alan PRICE** (11)..............................71
ROSIE [A] – **Don PARTRIDGE** (4) 68
ROSIE [B] – **Joan ARMATRADING** (49) 80
ROTATION – **Herb ALPERT** (46) 80
ROTTERDAM – **BEAUTIFUL SOUTH** (5) 96
ROUGH BOY – **ZZ TOP** (23) 86,92
ROUGH BOYS [A] – **Pete TOWNSHEND** (39)..80
ROUGH BOYS [B] – **NORTHERN UPROAR** (41) 95
ROUGH JUSTICE – **BANANARAMA** (23) 84
ROUGH WITH THE SMOOTH – **Shara NELSON** (30) 95
ROUGH NECK (EP) – **PROJECT 1** (49) 92
ROULETTE – **Russ CONWAY** (1) 59
ROUND AND ROUND [A] – **Jimmy YOUNG** (30)......................................57
ROUND AND ROUND [B] – **SPANDAU BALLET** (18) 84
ROUND AND ROUND [C] – **Jaki GRAHAM** (9) 85
ROUND AND ROUND [D] – **NEW ORDER** (21) 89
ROUND & ROUND [E] – **HI-TEK featuring JONELL** (73) 01
ROUND EVERY CORNER – **Petula CLARK** (43) 65
ROUND HERE – **COUNTING CROWS** (70) 94
ROUND HERE – **COUNTING CROWS** (70) 94
ROUND ROUND – **SUGABABES** (1) 02
THE ROUSSOS PHENOMENON (EP) – **Demis ROUSSOS** (1)....................................76
ROXANNE – **POLICE** (12) 79,97
ROYAL EVENT – **Russ CONWAY** (15)..............60
ROYAL MILE – **Gerry RAFFERTY** (67)..............80
ROY'S KEEN – **MORRISSEY** (42)....................97
RSVP [A] – **FIVE STAR** (45)............................85
RSVP [B] – **Jason DONOVAN** (17) 91
RSVP [C] – **POP WILL EAT ITSELF** (27) 93
RUB A DUB DUB – **EQUALS** (34) 69
RUB-A-DUB – **DOUBLE TROUBLE** (66) 91
RUBBER BALL [A] – **AVONS** (30)....................61
RUBBER BALL [A] – **Bobby VEE** (4) 61
RUBBER BALL [A] – **Marty WILDE** (9) 61
RUBBER BULLETS – **10cc** (1)..........................73
RUBBERBAND GIRL – **Kate BUSH** (12) 93
THE RUBBERBAND MAN – **DETROIT SPINNERS** (16) 76
RUBBERBANDMAN – **YELLO** (58) 91

THE SHOW – **Doug E FRESH and the GET FRESH CREW** (7) 85
SHOW A LITTLE LOVE – **ULTIMATE KAOS** (23) 95
SHOW ME [A] – **DEXY'S MIDNIGHT RUNNERS** (16) 81
SHOW ME [B] – **Lindy LAYTON** (47) 93
SHOW ME [C] – **Ultra NATÉ** (62) 94
SHOW ME [D] – **Dana DAWSON** (28) 96
SHOW ME A SIGN – **KONTAKT** (19) 03
SHOW ME GIRL – **HERMAN'S HERMITS** (19) 64
SHOW ME HEAVEN [A] – **Maria McKEE** (1) 90
SHOW ME HEAVEN [A] – **Tina ARENA** (29) 95
SHOW ME HEAVEN [A] – **CHIMIRA** (70) 97
SHOW ME HEAVEN [A] – **SAINT featuring Suzanna DEE** (36) 03
SHOW ME LOVE [A] – **Robin S** (6) 93,97,02
SHOW ME LOVE [B] – **ROBYN** (8) 98
SHOW ME LOVE [C] – **INDIEN** (69) 03
SHOW ME MARY – **CATHERINE WHEEL** (62) 93
SHOW ME THE MEANING OF BEING LONELY – **BACKSTREET BOYS** (3) 00
SHOW ME THE MONEY – **ARCHITECHS** (20) ..01
SHOW ME THE WAY [A] – **Peter FRAMPTON** (10) 76
SHOW ME THE WAY [B] – **OSMOND BOYS** (60) 92
SHOW ME YOUR MONKEY – **PERCY FILTH** (72) 03
SHOW ME YOU'RE A WOMAN – **MUD** (8) 75
THE SHOW MUST GO ON [A] – **Leo SAYER** (2) 73
THE SHOW MUST GO ON [B] – **QUEEN** (16) ..91
THE SHOW (THEME FROM 'CONNIE') – **Rebecca STORM** (22) 85
SHOW YOU THE WAY TO GO [A] – **Dannii MINOGUE** (30) 92
SHOW YOU THE WAY TO GO [A] – **JACKSONS** (1) 77
SHOWDOWN [A] – **ELECTRIC LIGHT ORCHESTRA** (12) 73
SHOWDOWN [B] – **Jody LEI** (34) 03
SHOWER YOUR LOVE – **KULA SHAKER** (14) ..99
SHOWING OUT (GET FRESH AT THE WEEKEND) – **MEL and KIM** (3) 86
SHOWROOM DUMMIES – **KRAFTWERK** (25) ..82
THE SHUFFLE – **Van McCOY** (4) 77
SHUT 'EM DOWN – **PUBLIC ENEMY** (21) 92
SHUT UP [A] – **MADNESS** (7) 81
SHUT UP [B] – **Kelly OSBOURNE** (12) 03
SHUT UP [C] – **BLACK EYED PEAS** (2) 03
SHUT UP AND DANCE – **AEROSMITH** (24) 94
SHUT UP AND FORGET ABOUT IT – **DANE** (9) 01
SHUT UP AND KISS ME – **Mary-Chapin CARPENTER** (35) 95
SHUT UP (AND SLEEP WITH ME) – **SIN WITH SEBASTIAN** (44) 95,96
SHUT YOUR MOUTH [A] – **MADE IN LONDON** (74) 00
SHUT YOUR MOUTH [A] – **GARBAGE** (20) 02
SHY BOY – **BANANARAMA** (4) 82
SHY GIRL – **Mark WYNTER** (28) 63
SHY GUY [A] – **Diana KING** (2) 95
SHY GUY [A] – **ASWAD** (62) 02
(SI SI) JE SUIS UN ROCK STAR – **Bill WYMAN** (14) 81
SI TU DOIS PARTIR – **FAIRPORT CONVENTION** (21) 69
SICK AND TIRED [A] – **Fats DOMINO** (26) 58
SICK AND TIRED [B] – **CARDIGANS** (34) 95
SICK MAN BLUES – **GOODIES** (4) 75
SICK OF DRUGS – **WILDHEARTS** (14) 96
SICK OF GOODBYES – **SPARKLEHORSE** (57) 98
SICK OF IT – **PRIMITIVES** (24) 89
SIDE – **TRAVIS** (14) 01
SIDE BY SIDE – **Kay STARR** (7) 53
SIDE SADDLE – **Russ CONWAY** (1) 59
THE SIDEBOARD SONG (GOT MY BEER IN THE SIDEBOARD HERE) – **CHAS and DAVE** (55) 79
SIDESHOW [A] – **CHANTER SISTERS** (43) 76
SIDESHOW [A] – **Barry BIGGS** (3) 76
SIDEWALK TALK – **JELLYBEAN** (47) 86
SIDEWALKING – **JESUS AND MARY CHAIN** (30) 88
THE SIDEWINDER SLEEPS TONITE – **R.E.M.** (17) 93
SIGHT FOR SORE EYES – **M PEOPLE** (6) 94
THE SIGN – **ACE OF BASE** (2) 94
SIGN 'O' THE TIMES – **PRINCE** (10) 87
SIGN OF THE TIMES [A] – **Bryan FERRY** (37) 78
SIGN OF THE TIMES [B] – **BELLE STARS** (3) 83
SIGN OF THE TIMES [C] – **GRANDMASTER FLASH, Melle MEL and the FURIOUS FIVE** (72) 85
A SIGN OF THE TIMES – **Petula CLARK** (49) 66
SIGN YOUR NAME – **Terence Trent D'ARBY** (2) 88
SIGNAL [A] – **JD aka 'DREADY'** (64) 03
SIGNAL [B] – **FRESH BC** (58) 03
SIGNALS OVER THE AIR – **THURSDAY** (62) ..03
THE SIGNATURE TUNE OF 'THE ARMY GAME' – **Michael MEDWIN, Bernard BRESSLAW, Alfie BASS and Leslie FYSON** (5) 58
SIGNED SEALED DELIVERED I'M YOURS [A] – **Stevie WONDER** (15) 70
SIGNED SEALED DELIVERED (I'M YOURS) [A] – **BOYSTOWN GANG** (50) 82
SIGNED, SEALED, DELIVERED, I'M YOURS [A] – **BLUE featuring Stevie WONDER & Angie STONE** (11) 03
SIGNS... – **BLAMELESS** (49) 96
SIGNS [A] – **TESLA** (70) 91
SIGNS [B] – **DJ BADMARSH & SHRI featuring UK APACHE** (63) 01
SILENCE – **DELERIUM** (73) 99,00
THE SILENCE – **Mike KOGLIN** (20) 98
SILENCE IS EASY – **STARSAILOR** (6) 03
SILENCE IS GOLDEN – **TREMELOES** (1) 67
SILENT ALL THESE YEARS – **Tori AMOS** (26) 91,92
SILENT LUCIDITY – **QUEENSRŸCHE** (18)....91,92
SILENT NIGHT [A] – **Bing CROSBY** (8) 52
SILENT NIGHT [A] – **DICKIES** (47) 78
SILENT NIGHT [A] – **BROS** (2) 88
SILENT NIGHT [A] – **Sinead O'CONNOR** (60) 91
SILENT NIGHT – SEVEN O'CLOCK NEWS [A] – **SIMON and GARFUNKEL** (30) 91
SILENT RUNNING – **MIKE and the MECHANICS** (61) 86,96
SILENT SCREAM – **Richard MARX** (32) 94
SILENT VOICE – **INNOCENCE** (37) 90
SILENT WORDS – **Jan JOHNSTON** (57) 01
SILENTLY BAD MINDED – **PRESSURE DROP** (53) 98
SILHOUETTES [A] – **HERMAN'S HERMITS** (3) 65
SILHOUETTES [A] – **Cliff RICHARD** (10) 90
SILK PYJAMAS – **Thomas DOLBY** (62) 92
SILLY GAMES [A] – **Janet KAY** (2) 79,90
SILLY GAMES [A] – **Lindy LAYTON featuring Janet KAY** (22) 90
SILLY LOVE – **10cc** (24) 74
SILLY LOVE SONGS – **Paul McCARTNEY** (2) ..76
SILLY THING – **SEX PISTOLS** (6) 79
SILVER [A] – **ECHO and the BUNNYMEN** (30) 84
SILVER [B] – **MOIST** (50) 95
SILVER [C] – **HUNDRED REASONS** (15) 02
SILVER AND GOLD – **ASAP** (60) 89
SILVER DREAM MACHINE (PART 1) – **David ESSEX** (4) 80
SILVER LADY – **David SOUL** (1) 77
SILVER LINING – **STIFF LITTLE FINGERS** (68) 81
SILVER MACHINE – **HAWKWIND** (3) 72,78,83
SILVER SCREEN SHOWER SCENE – **FELIX DA HOUSECAT** (39) 01,02
SILVER SHADOW – **ATLANTIC STARR** (41) 85
SILVER SHORTS – **WEDDING PRESENT** (14) ..92
SILVER STAR – **FOUR SEASONS** (3) 76
SILVER THUNDERBIRD – **Marc COHN** (54) 91
SILVERMAC – **WESTWORLD** (42) 87
SILVERY RAIN – **Cliff RICHARD** (27) 71
SIMBA GROOVE – **HI POWER** (73) 90
SIMON SAYS [A] – **Pharoahe MONCH** (24)....00
SIMON SAYS [B] – **1910 FRUITGUM CO** (2) ..68
SIMON SMITH AND HIS AMAZING DANCING BEAR – **Alan PRICE** (4) 67
SIMON TEMPLER – **SPLODGENESSABOUNDS** (7) 80
SIMPLE AS THAT – **Huey LEWIS and the NEWS** (47) 87
SIMPLE GAME – **FOUR TOPS** (3) 71
SIMPLE KIND OF LIFE – **NO DOUBT** (69) 00
SIMPLE LIFE – **Elton JOHN** (44) 93
SIMPLE SIMON (YOU GOTTA REGARD) – **MANTRONIX** (72) 88
SIMPLE SINCERITY – **RADISH** (50) 97
SIMPLE THINGS – **SAW DOCTORS** (56) 97
THE SIMPLE THINGS – **Joe COCKER** (17) 94
THE SIMPLE TRUTH (A CHILD IS BORN) – **Chris DE BURGH** (36) 87,88,91
SIMPLY IRRESISTABLE – **Robert PALMER** (44) 88
SIN – **NINE INCH NAILS** (35) 91
SINBAD – **SYSTEM 7** (74) 93
SINCE DAY ONE – **Teena MARIE** (69) 90
SINCE I DON'T HAVE YOU [A] – **Art GARFUNKEL** (38) 79
SINCE I DON'T HAVE YOU [A] – **GUNS N' ROSES** (10) 94
SINCE I LEFT YOU – **AVALANCHES** (16) 01
SINCE I MET YOU BABY [A] – **Gary MOORE and BB KING** (59) 92
SINCE I MET YOU BABY [B] – **UB40 and LADY SAW** (40) 01
SINCE I TOLD YOU IT'S OVER – **STEREOPHONICS** (16) 03
SINCE YESTERDAY – **STRAWBERRY SWITCHBLADE** (5) 84
SINCE YOU'RE GONE – **CARS** (37) 82
SINCE YOU'VE BEEN GONE [A] – **Aretha FRANKLIN** (47) 68
SINCE YOU'VE BEEN GONE [B] – **RAINBOW** (6) 79
SINCERE – **MJ COLE** (13) 98,00
SINCERELY – **McGUIRE SISTERS** (14) 55
SINFUL – **Pete WYLIE** (13) 86,91
SING – **TRAVIS** (3) 01
SING A HAPPY SONG [A] – **George McCRAE** (38) 75
SING A HAPPY SONG [B] – **O'JAYS** (39) 79
SING A LITTLE SONG – **Desmond DEKKER and the ACES** (16) 75
SING-A-LONG [A] – **A** (57) 98
SING-A-LONG [B] – **SHANKS & BIGFOOT** (12) 00
SING A SONG – **Byron STINGILY** (38) 97
SING A SONG (BREAK IT DOWN) – **MANTRONIX** (61) 88
SING A SONG OF FREEDOM – **Cliff RICHARD** (13) 71
SING AND SHOUT – **SECOND IMAGE** (53) 84
SING BABY SING – **STYLISTICS** (3) 75
SING DON'T SPEAK – **BLACKFOOT SUE** (36) 72
SING FOR EVER – **ST PHILIPS CHOIR** (49) 87
SING FOR THE MOMENT – **EMINEM** (6) 03
SING HALLELUJAH! – **DR ALBAN** (16) 93
SING IT AGAIN WITH JOE – **Joe 'Mr Piano' HENDERSON** (18) 55
SING IT BACK – **MOLOKO** (4) 99
SING IT (THE HALLELUJAH SONG) – **MOZAIC** (14) 95
SING IT TO YOU (DEE-DOOB-DEE-DOO) – **Lavinia JONES** (45) 95
SING IT WITH JOE – **Joe 'Mr Piano' HENDERSON** (14) 55
SING LIKE AN ANGEL – **Jerry LORDAN** (36) ..60
SING LITTLE BIRDIE – **Pearl CARR and Teddy JOHNSON** (12) 59
SING ME – **BROTHERS** (8) 77
SING ME AN OLD FASHIONED SONG – **Billie Jo SPEARS** (34) 76
SING (OOH-EE-OOH) – **Vivienne McKONE** (47) 92
SING OUR OWN SONG – **UB40** (5) 86
SING SING – **GAZ** (60) 79
SING UP FOR THE CHAMPIONS – **REDS UNITED** (12) 97
SING YOUR LIFE – **MORRISSEY** (33) 91
SINGALONG-A-SANTA – **SANTA CLAUS and the CHRISTMAS TREES** (19) 82
SINGALONG-A-SANTA AGAIN – **SANTA CLAUS and the CHRISTMAS TREES** (39) 83
THE SINGER SANG HIS SONG – **BEE GEES** (25) 68
SINGIN' IN THE RAIN PART 1 – **Sheila B DEVOTION** (11) 78
THE SINGING DOGS (MEDLEY) – **SINGING DOGS** (13) 55
SINGING IN MY SLEEP – **SEMISONIC** (39) 00
SINGING THE BLUES [A] – **Guy MITCHELL** (1) 56
SINGING THE BLUES [A] – **Tommy STEELE** (1) 56,57
SINGING THE BLUES [A] – **Dave EDMUNDS** (28) 80
SINGING THE BLUES [A] – **Daniel O'DONNELL** (23) 94

SON OF HICKORY HOLLER'S TRAMP – OC SMITH (2) 68
SON OF MARY – Harry BELAFONTE (18) 58
SON OF MY FATHER – CHICORY TIP (1) 72
SON OF SAM – Elliott SMITH (55) 00
SON OF THREE – BREEDERS (72) 02
SON THIS IS SHE – John LEYTON (15) 61
THE SONG FROM THE MOULIN ROUGE – MANTOVANI (1) 53
(SONG FOR A) FUTURE GENERATION – B-52's (63) 83
SONG FOR GUY – Elton JOHN (4) 78
SONG FOR LOVE – EXTREME (12) 92
A SONG FOR MAMA – BOYZ II MEN (34) 97
SONG FOR SHELTER – FATBOY SLIM (30) 01
A SONG FOR THE LOVERS – Richard ASHCROFT (3) 00
SONG FOR WHOEVER – BEAUTIFUL SOUTH (2) 89
SONG FROM THE EDGE OF THE WORLD – SIOUXSIE and the BANSHEES (59) 87
SONG OF DREAMS – Becky TAYLOR (60) 01
SONG OF JOY – Miguel RIOS (16) 70
SONG OF LIFE – LEFTFIELD (59) 92
SONG OF MEXICO – Tony MEEHAN COMBO (39) 64
THE SONG OF MY LIFE – Petula CLARK (32) 71
SONG OF THE DREAMER – Johnnie RAY (10) 55
SONG SUNG BLUE – Neil DIAMOND (14) 72
THE SONG THAT I SING (THEME FROM 'WE'LL MEET AGAIN') – STUTZ BEARCATS and the Denis KING ORCHESTRA (36) 82
SONG TO THE SIREN – THIS MORTAL COIL (66) 83
SONG 2 – BLUR (2) 97
SONGBIRD [A] – Kenny G (22) 87
SONGBIRD [B] – OASIS (3) 03
SONGS FOR CHRISTMAS '87 (EP) – MINI POPS (39) 87
SONGS FOR SWINGING LOVERS (LP) – Frank SINATRA (12) 56
SONIC BOOM BOY – WESTWORLD (11) 87
SONIC BOOM (LIFE'S TOO SHORT) – QUO VADIS (49) 00
SONNET – VERVE (74) 98
'SONS AND DAUGHTERS' THEME – KERRI and MICK (68) 84
SONS OF THE STAGE – WORLD OF TWIST (47) 91
SOON – MY BLOODY VALENTINE (41) 90
SOON BE DONE – SHAGGY (46) 93
SOONER OR LATER – Larry GRAHAM (54) 82
SOOTHE ME – SAM and DAVE (35) 67
SORRENTO MOON (I REMEMBER) – Tina ARENA (22) 96
SORROW [A] – MERSEYS (4) 66
SORROW [A] – David BOWIE (3) 73
SORRY BUT I'M GONNA HAVE TO PASS – COASTERS (41) 94
SORRY DOESN'T ALWAYS MAKE IT RIGHT – Diana ROSS (23) 75
SORRY FOR YOU – Roni SIZE (61) 03
SORRY (I DIDN'T KNOW) – MONSTA BOY featuring DENZIE (25) 00
SORRY (I RAN ALL THE WAY HOME) – IMPALAS (28) 59
SORRY I'M A LADY – BACCARA (8) 78
SORRY ROBBIE – Bert WEEDON (28) 60
SORRY SEEMS TO BE THE HARDEST WORD [A] – Elton JOHN (11) 76
SORRY SEEMS TO BE THE HARDEST WORD [A] – BLUE featuring Elton JOHN (1) 02
SORRY SUZANNE – HOLLIES (3) 69
SORTED FOR E'S AND WIZZ – PULP (2) 95
S.O.S. [A] – ABBA (6) 75
S.O.S. [B] – ABC (39) 84
THE SOS EP – SHAMEN (14) 93
SOUL BEAT CALLING – I KAMANCHI (69) 03
SOUL BOSSA NOVA – COOL, the FAB, and the GROOVY present Quincy JONES (47) 98
THE SOUL CAGES – STING (57) 91
SOUL CHA CHA – Van McCOY (34) 77
THE SOUL CITY WALK – Archie BELL and the DRELLS (13) 76
SOUL CLAP '69 – BOOKER T and the MG's (35) 69
SOUL COAXING – Raymond LEFEVRE (46) 68
SOUL DEEP [A] – BOX TOPS (22) 69
SOUL DEEP [A] – Gary 'US' BONDS (59) 82
SOUL DEEP (PART 1) – COUNCIL COLLECTIVE (24) 84
SOUL DRACULA – HOT BLOOD (32) 76
SOUL FINGER – BAR-KAYS (33) 67
SOUL FREEDOM – FREE YOUR SOUL – DEGREES OF MOTION featuring BITI (64) ..92
SOUL HEAVEN – GOODFELLAS featuring Lisa MILLETT (27) ..01
SOUL INSIDE – SOFT CELL (16) 83
SOUL INSPIRATION – Simon CLIMIE (60) 92
SOUL LIMBO – BOOKER T and the MG's (30) 68
SOUL LOVE – BLESSING (73) 94
SOUL LOVE – SOUL MAN – WOMACK and WOMACK (58) 86
SOUL MAN [A] – SAM and DAVE (24) 67
SOUL MAN [A] – Sam MOORE and Lou REED (30) 87
SOUL OF MY SOUL – Michael BOLTON (32) 94
THE SOUL OF MY SUIT – T. REX (42) 77
SOUL PASSING THROUGH SOUL – TOYAH (57) 85
SOUL PROVIDER – Michael BOLTON (35) 96
SOUL SEARCHIN' TIME – TRAMMPS (42) 76
SOUL SERENADE – Willie MITCHELL (43) 68
SOUL SISTER, BROWN SUGAR – SAM and DAVE (15) 69
SOUL SOUND – SUGABABES (30) 01
SOUL TRAIN – SWANS WAY (20) 84
SOULJACKER PART 1 – EELS (30) 01
SOULMATE – WEE PAPA GIRL RAPPERS (45) 88
SOULS – Rick SPRINGFIELD (23) 84
THE SOULSHAKER – MAX LINEN (55) 01
SOUL'S ON FIRE – TRACIE (73) 84
SOUND – JAMES (9) 91
THE SOUND – X-PRESS 2 (38) 96
SOUND ADVICE – Roni SIZE (61) 03
SOUND AND VISION – David BOWIE (3) 77
SOUND BWOY BURIAL – GANT (67) 97
SOUND CLASH (CHAMPION SOUND) – KICK SQUAD (59) 90
THE SOUND OF BAMBOO – FLICKMAN (11) ..00
SOUND OF CONFUSION – SECRET AFFAIR (45) 80
THE SOUND OF CRYING – PREFAB SPROUT (23) 92
SOUND OF DRUMS – KULA SHAKER (3) 98
SOUND OF EDEN [A] – SHADES OF RHYTHM (35) 91,93
SOUND OF EDEN [A] – CASINO (52) 97
THE SOUND OF MUSIC – DAYTON (75) 83
THE SOUND OF MUSIK – FALCO (61) 86
THE SOUND OF: OH YEAH – TOMBA VIRA (51) 01
THE SOUND OF SILENCE – BACHELORS (3) ..66
SOUND OF SOUNDS – GOMEZ (48) 02
SOUND OF SPEED (EP) – JESUS AND MARY CHAIN (30) 93
THE SOUND OF THE CROWD – HUMAN LEAGUE (12) 81
THE SOUND OF THE SUBURBS – MEMBERS (12) 79
SOUND OF THE UNDERGROUND – GIRLS ALOUD (1) 02
THE SOUND OF VIOLENCE – CASSIUS (49) ..02
THE SOUND OF YOUR CRY – Elvis PRESLEY (59) 82
SOUND SYSTEM [A] – STEEL PULSE (71) 79
SOUND SYSTEM [B] – DRUM CLUB (62) 93
SOUND YOUR FUNKY HORN – KC and the SUNSHINE BAND (17) 74
SOUNDS OF WICKEDNESS – TZANT (11) 98
SOUR TIMES – PORTISHEAD (13) 94,95
SOUTH AFRICAN MAN – Hamilton BOHANNON (22) 75
SOUTH MANZ – DILLINJA (53) 02
SOUTH OF THE BORDER – Robbie WILLIAMS (14) 97
SOUTH OF THE RIVER – Mica PARIS (50) 90
SOUTHAMPTON BOYS – RED 'N' WHITE MACHINES (16) 03
SOUTHERN COMFORT – Berni FLINT (48) 77
SOUTHERN FREEEZ – FREEEZ (8) 81,87
SOUTHERN NIGHTS – Glen CAMPBELL (28) 77
SOUTHERN SUN – OAKENFOLD (16) 02
SOUTHSIDE – Dave CLARKE (34) 96
SOUVENIR – ORCHESTRAL MANOEUVRES IN THE DARK (3) 81
SOUVENIRS – VOYAGE (56) 78
SOWETO [A] – Malcolm McLAREN (32) 83
SOWETO [B] – Jeffrey OSBORNE (44) 86
SOWING THE SEEDS OF HATRED – CREDIT TO THE NATION (72) 94
SOWING THE SEEDS OF LOVE – TEARS FOR FEARS (5) 89
SPACE [A] – NEW MODEL ARMY (39) 91
SPACE [B] – SLIPMATT (41) 03
SPACE AGE LOVE SONG – A FLOCK OF SEAGULLS (34) 82
SPACE BASS – SLICK (16) 79
THE SPACE BETWEEN – Dave MATTHEWS BAND (35) 01
SPACE COWBOY – JAMIROQUAI (17) 94
SPACE JAM – QUAD CITY DJs (57) 97
THE SPACE JUNGLE – ADAMSKI (7) 90
SPACE LORD – MONSTER MAGNET (45) 99
SPACE OASIS – Billie Ray MARTIN (66) 96
SPACE ODDITY – David BOWIE (1) 69,75
SPACE RIDER – Shaun ESCOFFERY (52) 01
SPACE STATION NO.5 [A] – Sammy HAGAR (52) 79
SPACE STATION NUMBER 5 [A] – MONTROSE (71) 80
SPACE WALK – LEMON JELLY (36) 02
SPACED INVADER – HATIRAS featuring SLARTA JOHN (14) 01
SPACEHOPPER – BAD COMPANY (56) 02
SPACEMAN [A] – 4 NON BLONDES (53) 93
SPACEMAN [B] – BABYLON ZOO (1) 96
A SPACEMAN CAME TRAVELLING – Chris DE BURGH (40) 86
SPACER – Sheila B DEVOTION (18) 79
SPANISH – Craig DAVID (8) 03
SPANISH DANCE TROUPE – GORKY'S ZYGOTIC MYNCI (47) 99
SPANISH EYES – Al MARTINO (5) 70,73
SPANISH FLEA – Herb ALPERT (3) 65
SPANISH HARLEM [A] – Jimmy JUSTICE (20) 62
SPANISH HARLEM [A] – SOUNDS INCORPORATED (35) 64
SPANISH HARLEM [A] – Aretha FRANKLIN (14) 71
SPANISH HORSES – AZTEC CAMERA (52) 92
SPANISH STROLL – MINK DeVILLE (20) 77
SPANISH WINE – Chris WHITE (37) 76
SPARE PARTS – Bruce SPRINGSTEEN (32) 88
SPARK – Tori AMOS (16) 98
SPARKLE – MY LIFE STORY (34) 96
SPARKLE OF MY EYES – UB40 and LADY SAW (40) 01
SPARKS – RÖYKSOPP (41) 03
SPARKY'S DREAM – TEENAGE FANCLUB (40) 95
THE SPARROW – RAMBLERS (from the Abbey Hey Junior School) (11) 79
THE SPARTANS – SOUNDS INCORPORATED (30) 64
SPEAK LIKE A CHILD – STYLE COUNCIL (4) ..83
SPEAK TO ME PRETTY – Brenda LEE (3) 62
SPEAK TO ME SOMEONE – GENE (30) 97
SPEAKEASY – SHED SEVEN (24) 94
SPECIAL [A] – GARBAGE (15) 98
SPECIAL 2003 [B] – LEE-CABRERA (45) 03
THE SPECIAL AKA LIVE EP – SPECIALS (1) ..80
SPECIAL BREW – BAD MANNERS (3) 80
SPECIAL CASES – MASSIVE ATTACK (15) 03
SPECIAL F/X – WHISPERS (69) 87
SPECIAL KIND OF LOVE – Dina CARROLL (16) 92
SPECIAL KIND OF LOVER – NU COLOURS (38) 96
SPECIAL KIND OF SOMETHING – KAVANA (13) 98
SPECIAL NEEDS – PLACEBO (27) 03
SPECIAL WAY – RIVER CITY PEOPLE (44) 91
THE SPECIAL YEARS – Val DOONICAN (7) 65
SPEECHLESS – D-SIDE (9) 03
SPEED – Billy IDOL (47) 94
SPEED AT THE SOUND OF LONELINESS – ALABAMA 3 (72) 97
SPEED YOUR LOVE TO ME – SIMPLE MINDS (20) 84
SPEEDWELL – SAINT ETIENNE (54) 91
SPEEDY GONZALES – Pat BOONE (2) 62
THE SPELL! – FUNKY WORM (61) 88
SPELLBOUND – SIOUXSIE and the BANSHEES (22) 81
SPEND SOME TIME – BRAND NEW HEAVIES (26) 94

SUDDENLY THERE'S A VALLEY [A] – Petula CLARK (7) 55
SUDDENLY YOU LOVE ME – TREMELOES (6) 68
SUEDEHEAD – MORRISSEY (5)....88
SUENO LATINO – SUENO LATINO (47) 89,00
SUEPERMAN'S BIG SISTER – Ian DURY and the BLOCKHEADS (51) 80
SUE'S GOTTA BE MINE – Del SHANNON (21) 63
SUFFER NEVER – FINN (29) 95
SUFFER THE CHILDREN – TEARS FOR FEARS (52) 85
SUFFOCATE [A] – FEEDER (37) 98
SUFFOCATE [B] – KING ADORA (39) 01
SUGAH – Ruby AMANFU (32)....03
SUGAR AND SPICE – SEARCHERS (2) 63
SUGAR BABY LOVE – RUBETTES (1)....74
SUGAR BEE – CANNED HEAT (49) 70
SUGAR BOX – THEN JERICO (22) 89
SUGAR BRIDGE (IT WILL STAND) – BLUEBELLS (72)....83
SUGAR CANDY KISSES – Mac and Katie KISSOON (3) 75
SUGAR COATED ICEBERG – LIGHTNING SEEDS (12) 97
SUGAR DADDY – SECRET KNOWLEDGE (75) 96
SUGAR DOLL – JETS (55) 81
SUGAR FREE [A] – JUICY (45) 86
SUGAR FREE [A] – Pauline HENRY (57) 95
SUGAR HONEY ICE TEA – GOODFELLAZ (25) 97
SUGAR IS SWEETER – CJ BOLLAND (11)....96
SUGAR KANE – SONIC YOUTH (26) 93
SUGAR ME – Lynsey DE PAUL (5) 72
SUGAR MICE – MARILLION (22) 87
SUGAR MOON – Pat BOONE (6) 58
SUGAR RUSH – MAN WITH NO NAME (55) ..96
SUGAR SHACK [A] – FIREBALLS (45) 63
SUGAR SHACK [B] – SEB (61)....95
SUGAR SUGAR [A] – ARCHIES (1) 69
SUGAR SUGAR [A] – Jonathan KING (12) 71
SUGAR SUGAR [A] – DUKE BAYSEE (30) 94
SUGAR TOWN – Nancy SINATRA (8) 67
SUGARBUSH – Doris DAY and Frankie LAINE (8) 52
SUGARHILL – AZ (67)....96
SUGARMAN – FREE ASSOCIATION (53) 03
SUGARTIME [A] – Alma COGAN (16)....58
SUGARTIME [A] – Jim DALE (25) 58
SUGARTIME [A] – McGUIRE SISTERS (14)....58
SUICIDE BLONDE – INXS (11) 90
SUKIYAKI [A] – Kenny BALL and his JAZZMEN (10) 63
SUKIYAKI [A] – Kyu SAKAMOTO (6) 63
SULKY GIRL – Elvis COSTELLO (22) 94
SULTANA – TITANIC (5)....71
SULTANS OF SWING – DIRE STRAITS (8) 79,88
SUMAHAMA – BEACH BOYS (45) 79
SUMATRAN – SOFT PARADE (65) 01
SUMERLAND (DREAMED) – FIELDS OF THE NEPHILIM (37)....90
SUMMER BREEZE [A] – ISLEY BROTHERS (16) 74
SUMMER BREEZE [A] – Geoffrey WILLIAMS (56) 92
SUMMER BUNNIES – R KELLY (23) 94
SUMMER EDITION – DJ NATION (59) 03
SUMMER '89 – CALIFORNIA SUNSHINE (56) 97
SUMMER FUN – BARRACUDAS (37) 80
SUMMER GIRLS – LYTE FUNKIE ONES (16) ..99
SUMMER GONNA COME AGAIN – SUPERSISTER (51)....01
SUMMER HOLIDAY [A] – Cliff RICHARD and the SHADOWS (1)....63
SUMMER HOLIDAY [A] – KEVIN THE GERBIL (50) 84
SUMMER HOLIDAY (EP) – ZZ TOP (51)....85
SUMMER HOLIDAY MEDLEY – Darren DAY (17) 96
SUMMER IN SIAM – POGUES (64) 90
SUMMER IN SPACE – COSMOS (49)....99
SUMMER IN THE CITY – LOVIN' SPOONFUL (8) 66
THE SUMMER IS MAGIC – EXOTICA featuring Itsy FOSTER (68) 95
SUMMER IS OVER – Frank IFIELD (25) 64
SUMMER JAM – UD PROJECT vs SUNCLUB (14) 03
SUMMER MADNESS – KOOL and the GANG (17) 81
SUMMER MOVED ON – A-HA (33) 00
SUMMER NIGHT CITY – ABBA (5) 78
SUMMER NIGHTS [A] – Marianne FAITHFULL (10) 65
SUMMER NIGHTS [B] – John TRAVOLTA and Olivia NEWTON-JOHN (1)....78
SUMMER OF '42 – BIDDU (14) 75
SUMMER OF LOVE [A] – LONYO – COMME CI COMME ÇA (8)....00
SUMMER OF LOVE [B] – STEPS (5) 00
THE SUMMER OF MY LIFE – Simon MAY (7) 76
SUMMER OF '69 – Bryan ADAMS (42)....85
SUMMER OF THE SEVENTEENTH DOLL – Winifred ATWELL (24) 59
SUMMER ON THE UNDERGROUND – A (72)..98
SUMMER RAIN – Belinda CARLISLE (23) 90
SUMMER SET – Mr Acker BILK and his PARAMOUNT JAZZ BAND (5) 60
SUMMER SON – TEXAS (5) 99
SUMMER SONG – BEDAZZLED (73) 92
SUMMER (THE FIRST TIME) – Bobby GOLDSBORO (9) 73
SUMMER WIND – Frank SINATRA (36)....66
SUMMERLANDS – BEIJING SPRING (53)....93
SUMMERLOVE SENSATION – BAY CITY ROLLERS (3) 74
SUMMER'S MAGIC – Mark SUMMERS (27) 91
SUMMER'S OVER – RIALTO (60) 98
SUMMERSAULT – TASTE XPERIENCE featuring NATASHA PEARL (66) 99
SUMMERTIME [A] – Al MARTINO (49) 60
SUMMERTIME [A] – MARCELS (46)....61
SUMMERTIME [A] – Billy STEWART (39) 66
SUMMERTIME [A] – FUN BOY THREE (18) 82
SUMMERTIME [B] – JAZZY JEFF & the FRESH PRINCE (8) 91,94
SUMMERTIME [C] – SUNDAYS (15)....97
SUMMERTIME [D] – ANOTHER LEVEL featuring TQ (7) 99
SUMMERTIME BLUES [A] – Eddie COCHRAN (18)....58,68
SUMMERTIME BLUES [A] – WHO (38) 70
SUMMERTIME CITY – Mike BATT with the NEW EDITION (4)....75
SUMMERTIME HEALING – EUSEBE (32) 95
SUMMERTIME OF OUR LIVES – A1 (5) 99
SUMTHIN' SUMTHIN' THE MANTRA – MAXWELL (27) 97
SUN [A] – VIRUS (62) 95
SUN [B] – John LYDON (42) 97
SUN [C] – SLUSNIK LUNA (40) 01
THE SUN AIN'T GONNA SHINE ANYMORE [A] – WALKER BROTHERS (1) 66
THE SUN AIN'T GONNA SHINE ANYMORE [A] – CHER (26)....96
THE SUN ALWAYS SHINES ON TV [A] – A-HA (1) 85
THE SUN ALWAYS SHINES ON TV [A] – DIVA (53) 95
THE SUN AND THE RAIN – MADNESS (5) 83
SUN ARISE – Rolf HARRIS (3) 62,97
SUN CITY – ARTISTS UNITED AGAINST APARTHEID (21) 85
THE SUN DOES RISE – Jah WOBBLE'S INVADERS of the HEART (41)....94
THE SUN DOESN'T SHINE – BEATS INTERNATIONAL (66)....91
THE SUN GOES DOWN – THIN LIZZY (52) 83
THE SUN GOES DOWN (LIVING IT UP) – LEVEL 42 (10)....83
SUN HITS THE SKY – SUPERGRASS (10) 97
SUN IS SHINING [A] – TECHNIQUE (64) 99
SUN IS SHINING [B] – Bob MARLEY vs FUNKSTAR DE LUXE (3) 99
SUN KING – CULT (39) 89
THE SUN MACHINE – E-ZEE POSSEE (62) 90
SUN OF JAMAICA – GOOMBAY DANCE BAND (50) 82
THE SUN RISING – BELOVED (26)....89,97
SUN SHINING DOWN – CIRCA featuring DESTRY (70) 99
SUN STREET – KATRINA and the WAVES (22) 86
SUN WORSHIPPERS (POSITIVE THINKING) – Diana BROWN and Barrie K SHARPE (61) ..90
SUNBURN [A] – Graham GOULDMAN (52) 79
SUNBURN [B] – Michelle COLLINS (28) 99
SUNBURN [C] – MUSE (22)....00
SUNCHYME – DARIO G (2) 97
SUNDANCE – SUNDANCE (33)....97,98
SUNDAY [A] – BUSTER (49) 76
SUNDAY [B] – SONIC YOUTH (72) 98
SUNDAY GIRL – BLONDIE (1) 79
SUNDAY MONDAYS – Vanessa PARADIS (49)....93
SUNDAY MORNING – NO DOUBT (50) 97
SUNDAY MORNING CALL – OASIS (4) 00
SUNDAY SHINING – Finley QUAYE (16) 97
SUNDAY SHOUTIN' – JOHNNY CORPORATE (45) 00
SUNDAY SUNDAY – BLUR (26)....93
SUNDOWN [A] – Gordon LIGHTFOOT (33) 74
SUNDOWN [A] – ELWOOD (72)....00
SUNDOWN [B] – S CLUB 8 (4) 03
SUNFLOWER – Paul WELLER (16)....93
SUNGLASSES – Tracey ULLMAN (18) 84
SUNLIGHT – DJ SAMMY (8) 03
SUNMACHINE – Dario G (17) 98
SUNNY [A] – CHER (32) 66
SUNNY [A] – Georgie FAME (13)....66
SUNNY [A] – Bobby HEBB (12)....66
SUNNY [A] – BONEY M (3) 77
SUNNY [B] – MORRISSEY (42) 95
SUNNY AFTERNOON – KINKS (1) 66
SUNNY CAME HOME – Shawn COLVIN (29)..98
SUNNY DAY – PIGBAG (53) 81
SUNNY HONEY GIRL – Cliff RICHARD (19) 71
SUNRISE [A] – GOLDENSCAN (52) 00
SUNRISE [B] – MOVEMENT 98 featuring Carroll THOMPSON (58) 90
SUNRISE [C] – PULP (23) 01
SUNRISE [D] – SIMPLY RED (7) 03
SUNSET – Nitin SAWHNEY featuring ESKA (65) 01
SUNSET AND BABYLON – W.A.S.P. (38) 93
SUNSET (BIRD OF PREY) – FATBOY SLIM (9) 00
SUNSET BOULEVARD – Michael BALL (72) ..93
SUNRISE (HERE I AM) – RATTY (51) 01
SUNSET NOW – HEAVEN 17 (24) 84
SUNSET ON IBIZA – THREE DRIVES ON A VINYL (44) 01
SUNSET PEOPLE – Donna SUMMER (46)....80
SUNSHINE [A] – Warren MILLS (74) 85
SUNSHINE [B] – JAY-Z featuring BABYFACE and Foxy BROWN (25) 97
SUNSHINE [C] – GABRIELLE (9) 99
SUNSHINE [D] – UMBOZA (14) 96
SUNSHINE [E] – Alexander O'NEAL (72)....89
SUNSHINE [F] – YOMANDA (16) 00
SUNSHINE [G] – Gareth GATES (3) 03
SUNSHINE AFTER THE RAIN [A] – Elkie BROOKS (10)....77
THE SUNSHINE AFTER THE RAIN [A] – BERRI (4) 94,95
SUNSHINE & HAPPINESS – Darryl PANDY (68) 99
SUNSHINE AND LOVE – HAPPY MONDAYS (62)....92
SUNSHINE DAY [A] – OSIBISA (17)....76
SUNSHINE DAY [A] – CLOCK (58)....99
SUNSHINE GIRL – HERMAN'S HERMITS (8) ..68
SUNSHINE OF LOVE – Louis ARMSTRONG (41) 68
SUNSHINE OF YOUR LOVE – CREAM (25) 68
THE SUNSHINE OF YOUR SMILE – Mike BERRY (9) 80
SUNSHINE ON A RAINY DAY [A] – ZOE (4) 90,91
SUNSHINE ON A RAINY DAY [A] – REAL & RICHARDSON featuring JOBABE (69) 03
SUNSHINE ON LEITH – PROCLAIMERS (41) ..88
SUNSHINE PLAYROOM – Julian COPE (64)....83
SUNSHINE SUPERMAN – DONOVAN (2)....66
SUNSTORM – HURLEY & TODD (38) 00
SUNSTROKE – CHICANE (21) 97
SUNTAN – STAN (40) 93
SUPER BOWL SUNDAE – OZOMATLI (68)....99
SUPER DJ – DILLINJA (47) 03
SUPER GRAN – Billy CONNOLLY (32)....85
SUPER LOVE – WIGAN'S OVATION (41) 75
SUPER POPOID GROOVE – WIN (63) 87
SUPER TROUPER [A] – ABBA (1) 80
SUPER TROUPER [A] – A TEENS (21) 99
SUPER WOMBLE – WOMBLES (20) 75
SUPERBAD SUPERSLICK – REDHEAD KINGPIN and the FBI (68) 89
SUPERFLY GUY – S EXPRESS (5) 88
SUPERFLY 1990 – Curtis MAYFIELD and ICE-T (48)....90
SUPERFREAKON – Missy 'Misdemeanor' ELLIOTT (72) 01
SUPERGIRL – Graham BONNEY (19)....66
SUPERHERO – REEF (55) 00

SWING MY HIPS (SEX DANCE) – **LEMONESCENT** (48) 02
SWING, SWING – **ALL-AMERICAN REJECTS** (13) 03
SWING THAT HAMMER – **Mike COTTON'S JAZZMEN** (36) 63
SWING THE MOOD – **JIVE BUNNY and the MASTERMIXERS** (1) 89
SWING YOUR DADDY – **Jim GILSTRAP** (4) 75
SWINGIN' – **LIGHT OF THE WORLD** (45) 79
SWINGIN' LOW – **OUTLAWS** (46) 61
SWINGIN' SHEPHERD BLUES [A] – **Ella FITZGERALD** (15) 58
SWINGIN' SHEPHERD BLUES [A] – **Moe KOFFMAN QUARTETTE** (23) 58
SWINGIN' SHEPHERD BLUES [A] – **Ted HEATH** (3) 58
SWINGING IN THE RAIN – **Norman VAUGHAN** (34) 62
SWINGING ON A STAR – **Big Dee IRWIN** (7) 63
SWINGING SCHOOL – **Bobby RYDELL** (44) 60
SWINGS AND ROUNDABOUTS – **Roni SIZE** (57) 02
SWISS MAID – **Del SHANNON** (2) 62
SWITCH [A] – **BENELUX and Nancy DEE** (52) 79
SWITCH [B] – **SENSER** (39) 94
SWITCH [C] – **Howie B** (62) 97
SWITCH [D] – **PESHAY** (59) 99
THE SWITCH – **PLANET FUNK** (52) 03
SWITCHED ON SWING – **KINGS OF SWING ORCHESTRA** (48) 82
SWOON – **MISSION** (73) 95
SWORDS OF A THOUSAND MEN – **TEN POLE TUDOR** (6) 81
SYLVIA – **FOCUS** (4) 73
SYLVIA'S MOTHER – **DR HOOK** (2) 72
SYLVIE – **SAINT ETIENNE** (12) 98
SYMMETRY C – **BRAINCHILD** (31) 99
SYMPATHY [A] – **RARE BIRD** (27) 70
SYMPATHY [B] – **MARILLION** (17) 92
SYMPATHY FOR THE DEVIL [A] – **GUNS N' ROSES** (9) 95
SYMPATHY FOR THE DEVIL [A] – **ROLLING STONES** (14) 03
SYMPHONY – **Donell RUSH** (66) 92
SYMPHONY OF DESTRUCTION – **MEGADETH** (15) 92
SYNAESTHESIA (FLY AWAY) – **THRILLSEEKERS featuring SHERYL DEANE** (28) 01
SYNCHRONICITY II – **POLICE** (17) 83
SYNERGY – **TRANCESETTERS** (72) 01
SYNTH & STRINGS – **YOMANDA** (8) 99
SYSTEM ADDICT – **FIVE STAR** (3) 86
SYSTEM OF SURVIVAL – **EARTH WIND AND FIRE** (54) 87
THE TABLE – **BEAUTIFUL SOUTH** (47) 99
TABOO – **GLAMMA KID featuring Shola AMA** (10) 99
TACKY LOVE SONG – **CREDIT TO THE NATION** (60) 98
TAHITI (FROM 'MUTINY ON THE BOUNTY') – **David ESSEX** (8) 83
TAINTED LOVE [A] – **SOFT CELL** (1) 81,82,85,91
TAINTED LOVE [A] – **IMPEDANCE** (54) 89
TAINTED LOVE [A] – **ICON** (51) 96
TAINTED LOVE [A] – **MARILYN MANSON** (5) 02
TAKE – **COLOUR FIELD** (70) 84
TAKE A BOW – **MADONNA** (16) 94
TAKE A CHANCE ON ME – **ABBA** (1) 78
TAKE A CHANCE WITH ME – **ROXY MUSIC** (26) 82
TAKE A FREE FALL – **DANCE 2 TRANCE** (36) 93
TAKE A HEART – **SORROWS** (21) 65
(TAKE A LITTLE) PIECE OF MY HEART – **Erma FRANKLIN** (9) 92
TAKE A LITTLE TIME – **Gary MOORE** (75) 87
TAKE A LOOK – **LEVEL 42** (32) 88
TAKE A LOOK AROUND – **TEMPTATIONS** (13) 72
TAKE A LOOK AROUND (THEME FROM 'MI:2') – **LIMP BIZKIT** (3) 00
TAKE A LOOK AT YOURSELF – **COVERDALE PAGE** (43) 93
TAKE A MESSAGE TO MARY – **EVERLY BROTHERS** (20) 59
TAKE A PICTURE – **FILTER** (25) 00
TAKE A REST – **GANG STARR** (63) 91
TAKE A RUN AT THE SUN – **DINOSAUR JR** (53) 97
TAKE A TOKE – **C & C MUSIC FACTORY / CLIVILLES & COLE** (26) 95
TAKE CALIFORNIA – **PROPELLERHEADS** (69) 96
TAKE CARE OF YOURSELF – **LEVEL 42** (39) 89
TAKE CONTROL [A] – **STATE OF MIND** (46) 98
TAKE CONTROL [B] – **John B** (58) 02
TAKE CONTROL OF THE PARTY – **BG THE PRINCE OF RAP** (71) 92
TAKE DOWN THE UNION JACK – **Billy BRAGG and the BLOKES** (22) 02
TAKE FIVE [A] – **Dave BRUBECK QUARTET** (6) 61
TAKE 5 [B] – **NORTHSIDE** (40) 91
TAKE 4 (EP) – **Mike OLDFIELD** (72) 78
TAKE GOOD CARE OF HER – **Adam WADE** (38) 61
TAKE GOOD CARE OF MY BABY [A] – **Bobby VEE** (3) 61
TAKE GOOD CARE OF MY BABY [A] – **SMOKIE** (34) 80
TAKE GOOD CARE OF MY HEART – **MICHAELA** (66) 90
TAKE GOOD CARE OF YOURSELF – **THREE DEGREES** (9) 75
TAKE IT – **FLOWERED UP** (34) 91
TAKE IT AND RUN – **The BANDITS** (32) 03
TAKE IT AWAY – **Paul McCARTNEY** (15) 82
TAKE IT BACK – **PINK FLOYD** (23) 94
TAKE IT EASY [A] – **LET LOOSE** (25) 96
TAKE IT EASY [B] – **MINT ROYALE** (66) 00
TAKE IT EASY [C] – **3SL** (64) 02
TAKE IT EASY ON ME – **A HOUSE** (55) 92
TAKE IT FROM ME [A] – **Roger CHRISTIAN** (63) 89
TAKE IT FROM ME [B] – **GIRLFRIEND** (47) 93
TAKE IT OFF – **DONNAS** (38) 03
TAKE IT ON THE RUN – **REO SPEEDWAGON** (19) 81
TAKE IT OR LEAVE IT – **SEARCHERS** (31) 66
TAKE IT SATCH (EP) – **Louis ARMSTRONG** (29) 56
TAKE IT TO THE LIMIT – **EAGLES** (12) 76
TAKE IT TO THE STREETS – **RAMPAGE featuring Billy LAWRENCE** (58) 97
TAKE IT TO THE TOP [A] – **KOOL and the GANG** (15) 81
TAKE IT TO THE TOP [B] – **CLOUD** (72) 81
TAKE ME – **DREAM FREQUENCY** (39) 92
TAKE ME AWAY [A] – **TRUE FAITH with FINAL CUT** (51) 91
TAKE ME AWAY [A] – **CAPPELLA featuring Loleatta HOLLOWAY** (25) 92
TAKE ME AWAY [B] – **D:REAM** (18) 94
TAKE ME AWAY [C] – **CULTURE BEAT** (52) 96
TAKE ME AWAY (I'LL FOLLOW YOU) – **BAD BOYS INC** (15) 94
TAKE ME AWAY (INTO THE NIGHT) – **4 STRINGS** (15) 02
TAKE ME AWAY (PARADISE) – **MIX FACTORY** (51) 93
TAKE ME BACK – **RHYTHMATIC** (71) 90
TAKE ME BACK TO LOVE AGAIN – **Kathy SLEDGE** (62) 92
TAKE ME BAK 'OME – **SLADE** (1) 72
TAKE ME BY THE HAND – **SUBMERGE featuring Jan JOHNSTON** (28) 97
TAKE ME DOWN TO THE RIVER – **SKIN** (26) 95
TAKE ME FOR A LITTLE WHILE – **COVERDALE PAGE** (29) 93
TAKE ME FOR WHAT I'M WORTH – **SEARCHERS** (20) 65
TAKE ME GIRL I'M READY – **Junior WALKER and the ALL-STARS** (16) 73
TAKE ME HIGH – **Cliff RICHARD** (27) 73
TAKE ME HIGHER [A] – **RAF** (59) 94,96
TAKE ME HIGHER [B] – **Diana ROSS** (32) 95
TAKE ME HIGHER [C] – **GEORGIE PORGIE** (61) 96
TAKE ME HOME [A] – **Phil COLLINS** (19) 85
TAKE ME HOME [B] – **Joe COCKER** (41) 94
TAKE ME HOME (A GIRL LIKE ME) – **Sophie ELLIS-BEXTOR** (2) 01
TAKE ME HOME COUNTRY ROADS – **Olivia NEWTON-JOHN** (15) 73
TAKE ME I'M YOURS – **SQUEEZE** (19) 78
TAKE ME IN YOUR ARMS (ROCK ME A LITTLE WHILE) – **DOOBIE BROTHERS** (29) 75
TAKE ME IN YOUR ARMS AND LOVE ME [A] – **Gladys KNIGHT and the PIPS** (13) 67
TAKE ME IN YOUR ARMS AND LOVE ME [A] – **SCRITTI POLITTI** (47) 91
TAKE ME NOW – **Tammy PAYNE** (55) 91
TAKE ME OVER – **McKAY** (65) 03
TAKE ME THERE – **BLACKSTREET and MYA featuring MASE and BLINKY BLINK** (7) 98
TAKE ME TO HEAVEN – **BABY D** (15) 96
TAKE ME TO THE MARDI GRAS – **Paul SIMON** (7) 73
TAKE ME TO THE NEXT PHASE – **ISLEY BROTHERS** (50) 78
TAKE ME TO YOUR HEART – **Rick ASTLEY** (8) 88
TAKE ME TO YOUR HEART AGAIN – **Vince HILL** (13) 66
TAKE ME TO YOUR HEAVEN – **Charlotte NILSSON** (20) 99
TAKE ME UP [A] – **SOUNDSOURCE** (62) 92
TAKE ME UP [B] – **SONIC SURFERS featuring Jocelyn BROWN** (61) 93
TAKE ME WITH U [A] – **PRINCE** (7) 85
TAKE ME WITH U [B] – **COSMOS** (32) 02
TAKE MY ADVICE – **Kym SIMS** (13) 92
TAKE MY BREATH AWAY [A] – **BERLIN** (1) 86,88,90
TAKE MY BREATH AWAY [A] – **SODA CLUB featuring Hannah ALETHEA** (16) 02
TAKE MY BREATH AWAY [B] – **Emma BUNTON** (5) 01
TAKE MY HEART – **Al MARTINO** (9) 52
TAKE MY HEART (YOU CAN HAVE IT IF YOU WANT IT) – **KOOL and the GANG** (29) 82
TAKE MY SCARS – **MACHINE HEAD** (73) 97
TAKE MY TIME – **Sheena EASTON** (44) 81
TAKE OFF SOME TIME – **NEW ATLANTIC** (64) 93
TAKE ON ME [A] – **A-HA** (2) 85
TAKE ON ME [A] – **A1** (1) 00
TAKE ON THE WORLD – **JUDAS PRIEST** (14) 79
TAKE THAT LOOK OFF YOUR FACE – **Marti WEBB** (3) 80
TAKE THAT SITUATION – **Nick HEYWARD** (11) 83
TAKE THAT TO THE BANK – **SHALAMAR** (20) 78
TAKE THE LONG ROAD AND WALK IT – **THE MUSIC** (14) 02
TAKE THE LONG WAY HOME – **FAITHLESS** (15) 98
TAKE THESE CHAINS FROM MY HEART – **Ray CHARLES** (5) 63
TAKE THIS HEART – **Richard MARX** (13) 92
TAKE THIS TIME – **Sean MAGUIRE** (27) 94
TAKE TO THE MOUNTAINS – **Richard BARNES** (35) 70
TAKE YOU OUT – **Luther VANDROSS** (59) 01
TAKE YOU THERE – **Ronni SIMON** (58) 95
TAKE YOUR MAMA FOR A RIDE – **LULU** (37) 75
TAKE YOUR PARTNER BY THE HAND – **Howie B featuring Robbie ROBERTSON** (74) 98
TAKE YOUR SHOES OFF – **CHEEKY GIRLS** (3) 03
TAKE YOUR TIME [A] – **HIGH** (56) 90
TAKE YOUR TIME [B] – **MANTRONIX** (10) 90
TAKE YOUR TIME [C] – **LOVE BITE** (56) 00
TAKE YOUR TIME (DO IT RIGHT) PART 1 – **S.O.S. BAND** (51) 80
TAKEN FOR GRANTED – **SIA** (10) 00
TAKES A LITTLE TIME – **TOTAL CONTRAST** (17) 85
TAKES TWO TO TANGO – **Louis ARMSTRONG** (6) 52
TAKIN' A CHANCE ON YOU – **DOLLAR** (62) 80
TAKIN' HOLD – **Sam LA MORE** (70) 03
TAKING ON THE WORLD – **GUN** (50) 90
TAKING THE VEIL – **David SYLVIAN** (53) 86
TALES FROM A DANCEOGRAPHIC OCEAN EP – **JAM & SPOON featuring PLAVKA** (49) 92
TALES FROM THE HARD SIDE – **BIOHAZARD** (47) 94
TALES OF THE HOOD – **TUBBY T** (47) 02
TALK ABOUT IT IN THE MORNING – **Martyn JOSEPH** (43) 95
TALK BACK – **DOUBLE TROUBLE** (71) 90
TALK DIRTY TO ME – **POISON** (67) 87
TALK OF THE TOWN – **PRETENDERS** (8) 80
TALK TALK [A] – **TALK TALK** (23) 82
TALK TO ME [A] – **THIRD WORLD** (56) 79
TALK TO ME [B] – **Stevie NICKS** (68) 86
TALK TO ME [C] – **Anita BAKER** (68) 90
TALK TO ME [D] – **6oFT DOLLS** (37) 96
TALKIN ALL THAT JAZZ – **STETSASONIC** (54) 88,98

TEMPORARY BEAUTY – **Graham PARKER and the RUMOUR** (50) ... 82
TEMPTATION [A] – **EVERLY BROTHERS** (1) ... 61
TEMPTATION [B] – **NEW ORDER** (29) ... 82
TEMPTATION [C] – **HEAVEN 17** (2) ... 83,92
TEMPTATION [D] – **Joan ARMATRADING** (65) 85
TEMPTATION [E] – **WET WET WET** (12) ... 88
TEMPTED – **SQUEEZE** (41) ... 81
10538 OVERTURE – **ELECTRIC LIGHT ORCHESTRA** (9) ... 72
10 IN 01 – **MEMBERS OF MAYDAY** (31) ... 01
TEN MILES HIGH – **LITTLE ANGELS** (18) ... 94
10 SECOND BIONIC MAN – **KINKY MACHINE** (66) ... 94
TEN STOREY LOVE SONG – **STONE ROSES** (11) ... 95
TEN THOUSAND MILES – **Michael HOLLIDAY** (24) ... 56
10 X 10 – **808 STATE** (67) ... 93
TEN TO TWENTY – **SNEAKER PIMPS** (56) ... 99
10 YEARS ASLEEP – **KINGMAKER** (15) ... 93
TENDER – **BLUR** (2) ... 99
TENDER HANDS – **Chris DE BURGH** (43) ... 89
TENDER HEART – **Lionel RICHIE** (29) ... 01
TENDER LOVE [A] – **FORCE M.D.s** (23) ... 86
TENDER LOVE [A] – **Kenny THOMAS** (26) ... 91
TENDERLY – **Nat 'King' COLE** (10) ... 54
TENDERNESS – **Diana ROSS** (73) ... 82
TENNESSEE – **ARRESTED DEVELOPMENT** (18) ... 92,93
TENNESSEE WIG WALK – **Bonnie LOU** (4) ... 54
TENSHI – **GOURYELLA** (45) ... 00
THE TENTH PLANET – **DISTORTED MINDS** (43) ... 03
TEQUILA [A] – **CHAMPS** (5) ... 58
TEQUILA [A] – **Ted HEATH** (21) ... 58
TEQUILA [A] – **NO WAY JOSÉ** (47) ... 85
TEQUILA [B] – **TERRORVISION** (2) ... 99
TEQUILA SUNRISE – **CYPRESS HILL** (23) ... 98
TERESA – **Joe DOLAN** (20) ... 69
TERRITORY – **SEPULTURA** (66) ... 93
TERRY – **TWINKLE** (4) ... 64
TERRY'S THEME FROM 'LIMELIGHT' [A] – **Frank CHACKSFIELD** (2) ... 53
TERRY'S THEME FROM 'LIMELIGHT' [A] – **Ron GOODWIN** (3) ... 53
TESLA GIRLS – **ORCHESTRAL MANOEUVRES IN THE DARK** (21) ... 84
THE TEST – **CHEMICAL BROTHERS** (14) ... 02
TEST OF TIME [A] – **Will DOWNING** (67) ... 89
TEST OF TIME [A] – **CRESCENT** (60) ... 02
TEST THE THEORY – **AUDIOWEB** (56) ... 99
TESTAMENT 4 – **Chubby CHUNKS** (52) ... 94
TESTIFY [A] – **M PEOPLE** (12) ... 98
TESTIFY [B] – **Byron STINGILY** (48) ... 98
TETRIS – **DOCTOR SPIN** (6) ... 92
TEXAS – **Chris REA** (69) ... 90
TEXAS COWBOYS – **GRID** (17) ... 93,94
THA CROSSROADS – **BONE THUGS-N-HARMONY** (8) ... 96
THA DOGGFATHER – **SNOOP DOGG** (36) ... 98
THA HORNS OF JERICHO – **DJ SUPREME** (29) ... 98
THA WILD STYLE – **DJ SUPREME** (24) ... 96,97
THANK ABBA FOR THE MUSIC – **VARIOUS ARTISTS (EPs and LPs)** (4) ... 99
THANK GOD I FOUND YOU – **98°** (10) ... 00
THANK GOD IT'S CHRISTMAS – **QUEEN** (21) 84
THANK GOD IT'S FRIDAY – **R KELLY** (14) ... 96
THANK U – **Alanis MORISSETTE** (5) ... 98
THANK U VERY MUCH – **SCAFFOLD** (4) ... 67
THANK YOU [A] – **PALE FOUNTAINS** (48) ... 82
THANK YOU [B] – **BOYZ II MEN** (26) ... 95
THANK YOU [C] – **DIDO** (3) ... 01
THANK YOU BABY (FOR MAKIN' SOMEDAY COME SO SOON) – **Shania TWAIN** (11) ... 03
THANK YOU FOR A GOOD YEAR – **Alexander O'NEAL** (30) ... 88
THANK YOU FOR BEING A FRIEND – **Andrew GOLD** (42) ... 78
THANK YOU FOR HEARING ME – **Sinead O'CONNOR** (13) ... 94
THANK YOU FOR LOVING ME – **BON JOVI** (12) ... 00
THANK YOU FOR THE MUSIC – **ABBA** (33) ... 83
THANK YOU FOR THE PARTY – **DUKES** (53) .. 82
THANK YOU MY LOVE – **IMAGINATION** (22) .. 84
THANK YOU WORLD – **WORLD PARTY** (68) .. 91
THANKS A LOT – **Brenda LEE** (41) ... 65
THANKS FOR MY CHILD – **Cheryl Pepsii RILEY** (75) ... 89
THANKS FOR SAVING MY LIFE – **Billy PAUL** (33) ... 74
THANKS FOR THE MEMORY (WHAM BAM THANK YOU MAM) – **SLADE** (7) ... 75
THANKS FOR THE NIGHT – **DAMNED** (43) ... 84
THAT CERTAIN SMILE – **Midge URE** (28) ... 85
THAT DAY – **Natalie IMBRUGLIA** (11) ... 01
THAT DON'T IMPRESS ME MUCH – **Shania TWAIN** (3) ... 99
THAT FEELING – **DJ CHUS presents GROOVE FOUNDATION** (65) ... 02
THAT GIRL [A] – **Stevie WONDER** (39) ... 82
THAT GIRL [B] – **Maxi PRIEST featuring SHAGGY** (15) ... 96
THAT GIRL BELONGS TO YESTERDAY – **Gene PITNEY** (7) ... 64
THAT GIRL (GROOVY SITUATION) – **Freddie McGREGOR** (47) ... 87
THAT GREAT LOVE SOUND – **The RAVEONETTES** (34) ... 03
THAT JOKE ISN'T FUNNY ANYMORE – **SMITHS** (49) ... 85
THAT LADY – **ISLEY BROTHERS** (14) ... 73
THAT LOOK – **DE'LACY** (19) ... 96
THAT LOOK IN YOUR EYE – **Ali CAMPBELL** (5) ... 95
THAT LOVING FEELING – **CICERO** (46) ... 92
THAT LUCKY OLD SUN – **VELVETS** (46) ... 61
THAT MAN (HE'S ALL MINE) – **INNER CITY** (42) ... 90
THAT MEANS A LOT – **PJ PROBY** (30) ... 65
THAT NOISE – **Anthony NEWLEY** (34) ... 62
THAT OLD BLACK MAGIC – **Sammy DAVIS Jr** (16) ... 55
THAT OLE DEVIL CALLED LOVE – **Alison MOYET** (2) ... 85
THAT SAME OLD FEELING – **PICKETTYWITCH** (5) ... 70
THAT SOUND – **Michael MOOG** (32) ... 99
THAT SOUNDS GOOD TO ME – **JIVE BUNNY and the MASTERMIXERS** (4) ... 90
THAT THING YOU DO! – **WONDERS** (22) ... 97
THAT WAS MY VEIL – **John PARISH and Polly Jean HARVEY** (75) ... 96
THAT WAS THEN THIS IS NOW [A] – **ABC** (18) ... 83
THAT WAS THEN, THIS IS NOW [B] – **MONKEES** (68) ... 86
THAT WAS YESTERDAY – **FOREIGNER** (28) .. 85
THAT WOMAN'S GOT ME DRINKING – **Shane MacGOWAN** (34) ... 94
THAT ZIPPER TRACK – **DJ DAN presents NEEDLE DAMAGE** (53) ... 01
THAT'LL BE THE DAY [A] – **CRICKETS** (1) 57,58
THAT'LL BE THE DAY [A] – **EVERLY BROTHERS** (30) ... 65
THAT'LL DO NICELY – **BAD MANNERS** (49) .. 83
THAT'S ALL – **GENESIS** (16) ... 83
THAT'S AMORE – **Dean MARTIN** (2) ... 54,96
THAT'S ENTERTAINMENT – **JAM** (21) ... 81,83,91
THAT'S HOW A LOVE SONG WAS BORN – **Ray BURNS with the CORONETS** (14) ... 55
THAT'S HOW GOOD YOUR LOVE IS – **IL PADRINOS featuring JOCELYN BROWN** (69) 92
THAT'S HOW I FEEL ABOUT YOU – **LONDONBEAT** (69) ... 92
THAT'S HOW I'M LIVING [A] – **Tony SCOTT** (48) ... 89,90
THAT'S HOW I'M LIVIN' [B] – **ICE-T** (21) ... 93
THAT'S HOW STRONG MY LOVE IS – **IN CROWD** (48) ... 65
THAT'S JUST THE WAY IT IS – **Phil COLLINS** (26) ... 90
THAT'S LIFE – **Frank SINATRA** (46) ... 66
THAT'S LIVIN' ALRIGHT – **Joe FAGIN** (3) ... 84
THAT'S LOVE – **Billy FURY** (19) ... 60
THAT'S LOVE, THAT IT IS – **BLANCMANGE** (33) ... 83
THAT'S MY DOLL – **Frankie VAUGHAN** (28) .. 59
THAT'S MY HOME – **Mr Acker BILK and his PARAMOUNT JAZZ BAND** (7) ... 61
THAT'S NICE – **Neil CHRISTIAN** (14) ... 66
THAT'S RIGHT – **DEEP RIVER BOYS** (29) ... 56
THAT'S THE WAY – **HONEYCOMBS** (12) ... 65
THAT'S THE WAY GOD PLANNED IT – **Billy PRESTON** (11) ... 69
THAT'S THE WAY I LIKE IT [A] – **KC and the SUNSHINE BAND** (4) ... 75,91
THAT'S THE WAY (I LIKE IT) [A] – **DEAD OR ALIVE** (22) ... 84
THAT'S THE WAY (I LIKE IT) [A] – **CLOCK** (11) ... 98
THAT'S THE WAY I WANNA ROCK 'N' ROLL – **AC/DC** (22) ... 88
THAT'S THE WAY IT FEELS – **TWO NATIONS** (74) ... 87
THAT'S THE WAY IT IS [A] – **MEL and KIM** (10) ... 88
THAT'S THE WAY IT IS [B] – **Celine DION** (12) ... 99
THAT'S THE WAY LOVE GOES [A] – **Charles DICKENS** (37) ... 65
THAT'S THE WAY LOVE GOES [B] – **YOUNG MC** (65) ... 91
THAT'S THE WAY LOVE GOES [C] – **Janet JACKSON** (2) ... 93
THAT'S THE WAY LOVE IS [A] – **TEN CITY** (8) ... 89
THAT'S THE WAY LOVE IS [A] – **VOLCANO** (72) ... 95
THAT'S THE WAY LOVE IS [A] – **Byron STINGILY** (32) ... 00
THAT'S THE WAY LOVE IS [B] – **Bobby BROWN** (56) ... 93
THAT'S THE WAY OF THE WORLD – **D MOB with Cathy DENNIS** (48) ... 90
THAT'S THE WAY THE MONEY GOES – **M** (45) ... 80
THAT'S THE WAY YOU DO IT – **PURPLE KINGS** (26) ... 94
THAT'S WHAT FRIENDS ARE FOR [A] – **Deniece WILLIAMS** (8) ... 77
THAT'S WHAT FRIENDS ARE FOR [B] – **Dionne WARWICK and FRIENDS featuring Elton JOHN, Stevie WONDER and Gladys KNIGHT** (16) ... 85
THAT'S WHAT I LIKE – **JIVE BUNNY and the MASTERMIXERS** (1) ... 89
THAT'S WHAT I THINK – **Cyndi LAUPER** (31) 93
THAT'S WHAT I WANT – **MARAUDERS** (43) .. 63
THAT'S WHAT I WANT TO BE – **Neil REID** (45) ... 72
THAT'S WHAT LIFE IS ALL ABOUT – **Bing CROSBY** (41) ... 75
THAT'S WHAT LOVE CAN DO – **TOUTES LES FILLES** (44) ... 99
THAT'S WHAT LOVE IS FOR – **Amy GRANT** (60) ... 91
THAT'S WHAT LOVE WILL DO – **Joe BROWN and the BRUVVERS** (3) ... 63
THAT'S WHEN I REACH FOR MY REVOLVER – **MOBY** (50) ... 96
THAT'S WHEN I THINK OF YOU – **1927** (46) 89
THAT'S WHEN THE MUSIC TAKES ME – **Neil SEDAKA** (18) ... 73
THAT'S WHERE MY MIND GOES – **SLAMM** (68) ... 94
THAT'S WHERE THE HAPPY PEOPLE GO – **TRAMMPS** (35) ... 76
THAT'S WHY I LIE – **Ray J** (71) ... 98
THAT'S WHY I'M CRYING – **IVY LEAGUE** (22) 65
THAT'S WHY WE LOSE CONTROL – **YOUNG OFFENDERS** (60) ... 98
THAT'S YOU – **Nat 'King' COLE** (10) ... 60
THEM BONES – **ALICE IN CHAINS** (26) ... 93
THEM GIRLS THEM GIRLS – **ZIG and ZAG** (5) ... 94
THEM THERE EYES – **Emile FORD and the CHECKMATES** (18) ... 60
THEME – **SABRES OF PARADISE** (56) ... 94
THE THEME [A] – **UNIQUE 3** (61) ... 89
THE THEME [B] – **Tracey LEE** (51) ... 97
THE THEME [C] – **DREEM TEEM** (34) ... 97
THE THEME [D] – **Jurgen VRIES** (13) ... 02
THEME FOR A DREAM – **Cliff RICHARD and the SHADOWS** (3) ... 61
THEME FOR YOUNG LOVERS – **SHADOWS** (12) ... 64
THEME FROM 'A SUMMER PLACE' [A] – **Norrie PARAMOR** (36) ... 60
THE THEME FROM 'A SUMMER PLACE' [A] – **Percy FAITH** (2) ... 60
THEME FROM 'CADE'S COUNTY' – **Henry MANCINI** (42) ... 72
THEME FROM 'CHEERS' – **Gary PORTNOY** (58) ... 84
THEME FROM 'COME SEPTEMBER' – **Bobby DARIN** (50) ... 61
THEME FROM DIXIE – **Duane EDDY and the REBELS** (7) ... 61

THE THINGS THE LONELY DO – AMAZULU (43) 86
THINGS THAT GO BUMP IN THE NIGHT – ALLSTARS (12) 01
THE THINGS WE DO FOR LOVE [A] – 10cc (6) 76
THINGS WE DO FOR LOVE [B] – Horace BROWN (27) 96
THINK [A] – Brenda LEE (26) 64
THINK [B] – Chris FARLOWE (37) 66
THINK [C] – Aretha FRANKLIN (26) 68,90
THINK ABOUT ... – DJH featuring STEFY (22) 91
THINK ABOUT ME – ARTFUL DODGER featuring Michelle ESCOFFERY (11) 01
THINK ABOUT THAT – Dandy LIVINGSTONE (26) 73
THINK ABOUT THE WAY (BOM DIGI DIGI BOM...) – ICE MC (42) 94
THINK ABOUT YOUR CHILDREN – Mary HOPKIN (19) 70,71
THINK FOR A MINUTE – HOUSEMARTINS (18) 86
THINK I'M GONNA FALL IN LOVE WITH YOU – DOOLEYS (13) 77
THINK IT ALL OVER – Sandie SHAW (42) 69
THINK IT OVER – CRICKETS (11) 58
THINK OF ME (WHEREVER YOU ARE) – Ken DODD (21) 75
THINK OF YOU [A] – USHER (70) 95
THINK OF YOU [B] – WHIGFIELD (7) 95
THINK SOMETIMES ABOUT ME – Sandie SHAW (32) 66
THINK TWICE – Celine DION (1) 94
THINKIN' ABOUT YOUR BODY – Bobby McFERRIN (46) 88
THINKIN' AIN'T FOR ME – Paul JONES (32) ..67
THINKING ABOUT TOMORROW – Beth ORTON (57) 03
THINKING ABOUT YOUR BODY – 2 MAD (43)91
THINKING ABOUT YOUR LOVE [A] – SKIPWORTH and TURNER (24) 85
THINKING ABOUT YOUR LOVE [A] – Phillip LEO (64) 95
THINKING ABOUT YOUR LOVE [B] – Kenny THOMAS (4) 91
THINKING IT OVER – LIBERTY (5) 01
THINKING OF YOU [A] – SISTER SLEDGE (11) 84,93
THINKING OF YOU [A] – MAUREEN (11) 90
THINKING OF YOU [A] – Curtis LYNCH Jr featuring Kele LE ROC and RED RAT (70) ..00
THINKING OF YOU [B] – COLOUR FIELD (12) 85
THINKING OF YOU [C] – HANSON (23) 98
THINKING OF YOU BABY – Dave CLARK FIVE (26) 64
THINKING OVER – Dana GLOVER (38) 03
THIRD FINGER, LEFT HAND – PEARLS (31)....72
THE THIRD MAN – SHADOWS (44) 81
THIRD RAIL – SQUEEZE (39) 93
13 STEPS LEAD DOWN – Elvis COSTELLO (59) 94
THE 13TH – CURE (15) 96
13TH DISCIPLE – FIVE THIRTY (67) 91
30 CENTURY MAN – CATHERINE WHEEL (47) 93
36D – BEAUTIFUL SOUTH (46) 92
THIRTY THREE – SMASHING PUMPKINS (21) 96
THIS AIN'T A LOVE SONG – BON JOVI (6) 95
THIS AND THAT – Tom JONES (44) 66
THIS BEAT IS MINE – Vicky D (42) 82
THIS BEAT IS TECHNOTRONIC – TECHNOTRONIC (14) 90
THIS BOY – JUSTIN (34) 98
THIS BRUTAL HOUSE – NITRO DELUXE (47) 87
THIS CAN BE REAL – CANDY FLIP (60) 90
THIS CHARMING MAN – SMITHS (8) 83,92
THIS CORROSION – SISTERS OF MERCY (7) 87
THIS COWBOY SONG – STING featuring Pato BANTON (15) 95
THIS DJ – Warren G (12) 94
THIS DOOR SWINGS BOTH WAYS – HERMAN'S HERMITS (18) 66
THIS FEELIN' – Frank HOOKER and POSITIVE PEOPLE (48) 80
THIS FEELING – PURESSENCE (33) 98
THIS FLIGHT TONIGHT – NAZARETH (11) 73
THIS GARDEN – LEVELLERS (12) 93
THIS GENERATION – ROACHFORD (38) 94
THIS GIVEN LINE – ELECTRIC SOFT PARADE (39) 02
THIS GOLDEN RING – FORTUNES (15) 66
THIS GUY'S IN LOVE WITH YOU – Herb ALPERT (3) 68,69
THIS HERE GIRAFFE – FLAMING LIPS (72) 96
THIS HOUSE [A] – Tracie SPENCER (65) 91
THIS HOUSE [B] – Alison MOYET (40) 91
THIS HOUSE IS NOT A HOME – REMBRANDTS (58) 96
THIS HOUSE (IS WHERE YOUR LOVE STANDS) – BIG SOUND AUTHORITY (21) 85
THIS I PROMISE YOU – 'N SYNC (21) 00
THIS I SWEAR [A] – Richard DARBYSHIRE (50) 93
THIS I SWEAR [B] – Kim WILDE (46) 96
THIS IS A CALL – FOO FIGHTERS (5) 95
THIS IS A REBEL SONG – Sinead O'CONNOR (60) 97
THIS IS A WARNING – DILLINJA (47) 03
THIS IS ENGLAND – CLASH (24) 85
THIS IS FOR REAL – David DEVANT & HIS SPIRIT WIFE (61) 97
THIS IS FOR THE LOVER IN YOU – BABYFACE (12) 96
THIS IS GOODBYE – Lucy CARR (41) 03
THIS IS HARDCORE – PULP (12) 98
THIS IS HOW IT FEELS – INSPIRAL CARPETS (14) 90
THIS IS HOW WE DO IT [A] – Montell JORDAN (11) 95
THIS IS HOW WE DO IT [A] – MIS-TEEQ (7) ..02
THIS IS HOW WE PARTY – S.O.A.P. (36) 98
THIS IS IT! [A] – Adam FAITH (5) 61
THIS IS IT [B] – Melba MOORE (9) 76
THIS IS IT [B] – Dannii MINOGUE (10) 93
THIS IS IT [C] – Dan HARTMAN (17) 79
THIS IS IT [D] – 4MANDU (45) 95
THIS IS IT [E] – STATE OF MIND (30) 98
THIS IS IT (YOUR SOUL) – HOTHOUSE FLOWERS (67) 93
THIS IS LOVE [A] – Gary NUMAN (28) 86
THIS IS LOVE [B] – George HARRISON (55) ..88
THIS IS LOVE [C] – PJ HARVEY (41) 01
THIS IS ME – CLIMIE FISHER (22) 88
THIS IS MINE – HEAVEN 17 (23) 84
THIS IS MUSIC – VERVE (35) 95
THIS IS MY HOLLYWOOD – 3 COLOURS RED (48) 97
THIS IS MY LIFE – Eartha KITT (73) 86
THIS IS MY NIGHT – Chaka KHAN (14) 85
THIS IS MY SONG [A] – Harry SECOMBE (2) 67
THIS IS MY SONG [A] – Petula CLARK (1) 67
THIS IS MY SOUND – DJ SHOG (40) 02
THIS IS MY TIME – 3 COLOURS RED (36) 99
THIS IS NOT A LOVE SONG – PUBLIC IMAGE LTD (5) 83
THIS IS NOT A SONG – FRANK AND WALTERS (46) 92
THIS IS NOT AMERICA (THE THEME FROM 'THE FALCON AND THE SNOWMAN') – David BOWIE (14) 85
THIS IS OUR SONG – CODE RED (59) 96
THIS IS RADIO CLASH – CLASH (47) 81
THIS IS SKA – Longsy D (56) 89
THIS IS THE DAY – The THE (71) 83
THIS IS THE NEW *HIT – Marilyn MANSON (29) 03
THIS IS THE PLACE – Zeitia MASSIAH (62) ..94
THIS IS THE RIGHT TIME – Lisa STANSFIELD (13) 89
THIS IS THE SOUND OF YOUTH – THESE ANIMAL MEN (72) 94
THIS IS THE STORY OF MY LOVE (BABY) – WIZZARD (34) 74
THIS IS THE WAY [A] – Bruce FOXTON (56)..83
THIS IS THE WAY [B] – Dannii MINOGUE (27) 93
THIS IS THE WAY [C] – FKW (63) 94
THIS IS THE WAY [D] – E-TYPE (53) 95
THIS IS THE WORLD CALLING – Bob GELDOF (25) 86
THIS IS TOMORROW – Bryan FERRY (9) 77
THIS IS WHERE I CAME IN – BEE GEES (18)..01
THIS IS YOUR LAND – SIMPLE MINDS (13) ..89
THIS IS YOUR LIFE [A] – BLOW MONKEYS (32) 88,89
THIS IS YOUR LIFE [B] – BANDERAS (16) 91
THIS IS YOUR LIFE [C] – DUST BROTHERS (60) 99
THIS IS YOUR NIGHT [A] – HEAVY D and the BOYZ (30) 94
THIS IS YOUR NIGHT [B] – ANOTHERSIDE (41) 03
THIS IZ REAL – SHYHEIM (61) 96
THIS KIND OF LOVE – Phil FEARON (70) 85
THIS KISS – Faith HILL (13) 98
THIS LITTLE BIRD [A] – Marianne FAITHFULL (6) 65
THIS LITTLE BIRD [A] – NASHVILLE TEENS (38) 65
THIS LITTLE GIRL – Gary 'US' BONDS (43)....81
THIS LOVE AFFAIR – Stefan DENNIS (67) 89
THIS LOVE I HAVE FOR YOU – Lance FORTUNE (26) 60
THIS MONDAY MORNING FEELING – Tito SIMON (45) 75
THIS MORNING – NORTHERN UPROAR (17)..96
THIS MUST BE THE PLACE – TALKING HEADS (51) 84
THIS NEW YEAR – Cliff RICHARD (30) 92
THIS OLD HEART OF MINE [A] – ISLEY BROTHERS (3) 66,68
THIS OLD HEART OF MINE [A] – Rod STEWART (4) 75,89
THIS OLE HOUSE [A] – Billie ANTHONY (4) ..54
THIS OLE HOUSE [A] – Rosemary CLOONEY (1) 54
THIS OLE HOUSE [A] – Shakin' STEVENS (1) 81
THIS ONE – Paul McCARTNEY (18) 89
THIS ONE'S FOR THE CHILDREN – NEW KIDS ON THE BLOCK (9) 90
THIS PARTY SUCKS! – FUSED (64) 99
THIS PERFECT DAY – SAINTS (34) 77
THIS PICTURE – PLACEBO (23) 03
THIS PLANET'S ON FIRE (BURN IN HELL) – Sammy HAGAR (52) 79
THIS STRANGE EFFECT – Dave BERRY (37)..65
THIS SUMMER – SQUEEZE (32) 95,96
THIS TIME [A] – Troy SHONDELL (22) 61
THIS TIME [B] – Bryan ADAMS (41) 86
THIS TIME [C] – Dina CARROLL (23) 93
THIS TIME [D] – Michelle SWEENEY (57) 94
THIS TIME [E] – Judy CHEEKS (23) 95
THIS TIME [F] – Curtis STIGERS (28) 95
THIS TIME (LIVE) [G] – WET WET WET (38) ..93
THIS TIME AROUND – PHATS & SMALL (15) 01
THIS TIME (WE'LL GET IT RIGHT) – ENGLAND WORLD CUP SQUAD (2) 82
THIS TIME BABY – Jackie MOORE (49) 79
THIS TIME I FOUND LOVE – ROZALLA (33) ..94
THIS TIME I KNOW IT'S FOR REAL – Donna SUMMER (3) 89
THIS TIME OF YEAR – RUNRIG (38) 95
THIS TOWN AIN'T BIG ENOUGH FOR BOTH OF US – SPARKS (2) 74,97
THIS USED TO BE MY PLAYGROUND – MADONNA (3) 92
THIS WAITING HEART – Chris DE BURGH (59) 89
THIS WHEEL'S ON FIRE [A] – Julie DRISCOLL, Brian AUGER and the TRINITY (5) 68
THIS WHEEL'S ON FIRE [A] – SIOUXSIE and the BANSHEES (14) 87
THIS WILL BE – Natalie COLE (32) 75
THIS WOMAN'S WORK – Kate BUSH (25) 89
THIS WORLD IS NOT MY HOME – Jim REEVES (22) 65
THIS WORLD OF WATER – NEW MUSIK (31) 80
THIS WRECKAGE – Gary NUMAN (20) 80
THIS YEAR'S LOVE – David GRAY (20) 01
THOIA THOING – R KELLY (14) 03
THONG SONG – SISQO (3) 00
THE THORN EP – SIOUXSIE and the BANSHEES (47) 84
THORN IN MY SIDE – EURYTHMICS (5) 86
THOSE FIRST IMPRESSIONS – ASSOCIATES (43) 84
THOSE SIMPLE THINGS – RIGHT SAID FRED (29) 92
THOSE WERE THE DAYS – Mary HOPKIN (1) 68
THOU SHALT NOT STEAL – FREDDIE and the DREAMERS (44) 65
THOUGHT I'D DIED AND GONE TO HEAVEN – Bryan ADAMS (8) 92
THE THOUGHT OF IT – Louie LOUIE (34) 92
THOUGHT U WERE THE ONE FOR ME – Joey B ELLIS (58) 91
THOUGHTLESS – KORN (37) 02
A THOUSAND MILES – Vanessa CARLTON (6) 02
A THOUSAND STARS – Billy FURY (14) 61

UNDERSTANDING JANE – ICICLE WORKS (52) ... 86
UNDERWATER [A] – Harry THUMANN (41) ... 81
UNDERWATER [B] – DELERIUM featuring RANI (33) ... 01
UNDERWATER LOVE – SMOKE CITY (4) ... 97
UNDIVIDED LOVE – LOUISE (5) ... 96
UNDONE – THE SWEATER SONG – WEEZER (35) ... 95
UNDRESSED – WHITE TOWN (57) ... 97
UNEMPLOYED IN SUMMERTIME – Emiliana TORRINI (63) ... 00
UNEXPLAINED – GRAVEDIGGAZ (48) ... 98
UNEXPLAINED (EP) – EMF (18) ... 92
UNFINISHED SYMPATHY – MASSIVE ATTACK (13) ... 91
UNFORGETTABLE – Natalie COLE (19) ... 91
THE UNFORGETTABLE FIRE – U2 (6) ... 85
UNFORGIVABLE SINNER – Lene MARLIN (13) 00
UNFORGIVEN – D:REAM (29) ... 93
THE UNFORGIVEN – METALLICA (15) ... 91
THE UNFORGIVEN II – METALLICA (15) ... 98
UNHOLY – KISS (26) ... 92
UNIFORM – INSPIRAL CARPETS (51) ... 94
UNIFORMS (CORPS D'ESPRIT) – Pete TOWNSHEND (48) ... 82
UNINTENDED – MUSE (20) ... 00
UNINVITED GUEST – MARILLION (53) ... 89
UNION CITY BLUE – BLONDIE (13) ... 79,95
UNION OF THE SNAKE – DURAN DURAN (3) 83
UNITED – JUDAS PRIEST (26) ... 80
UNITED CALYPSO '98 – REDS UNITED (33) .. 98
UNITED COLOURS – BEST SHOT (64) ... 94
UNITED STATES OF WHATEVER – Liam LYNCH (10) ... 02
UNITED (WE LOVE YOU) – MANCHESTER UNITED FOOTBALL CLUB (37) ... 93
UNITED WE STAND – BROTHERHOOD OF MAN (10) ... 70
UNITY – UNITY (64) ... 91
U.N.I.T.Y. – QUEEN LATIFAH (74) ... 94
UNITY (PART 1 – THE THIRD COMING) – Afrika BAMBAATAA and James BROWN (49) ... 84
UNIVERSAL [A] – SMALL FACES (16) ... 68
UNIVERSAL [B] – ORCHESTRAL MANOEUVRES IN THE DARK (55) ... 96
THE UNIVERSAL [C] – BLUR (5) ... 95
UNIVERSAL HEART-BEAT – Juliana HATFIELD (65) ... 95
UNIVERSAL MUSIC – METEOR SEVEN (71) ... 02
UNIVERSAL NATION – PUSH (35) ... 99,03
UNIVERSALLY SPEAKING – RED HOT CHILI PEPPERS (27) ... 03
THE UNKNOWN – Mark B & BLADE (49) ... 01
UNLEASH THE DRAGON – SISQO (6) ... 00
UNLOCK THE FUNK – LOCKSMITH (42) ... 80
UNO – MUSE (73) ... 99
UNO MAS – Daniel O'DONNELL (25) ... 99
UNPRETTY – TLC (6) ... 99
UNSAFE BUILDING 1990 – ALARM (54) ... 90
UNSKINNY BOP – POISON (15) ... 90
UNSQUARE DANCE – Dave BRUBECK QUARTET (14) ... 62
UNSTABLE – ADEMA (46) ... 03
THE UNSUNG HEROES OF HIP HOP – SUBSONIC 2 (63) ... 91
UNTIL IT SLEEPS – METALLICA (5) ... 96
UNTIL IT'S TIME FOR YOU TO GO [A] – FOUR PENNIES (19) ... 65
UNTIL IT'S TIME FOR YOU TO GO [A] – Elvis PRESLEY (5) ... 72
UNTIL MY DYING DAY – UB40 (15) ... 95
UNTIL THE DAY – FUNKY GREEN DOGS (75) 98
UNTIL THE END OF TIME – 2PAC (4) ... 01
UNTIL THE NIGHT – Billy JOEL (50) ... 79
UNTIL THE TIME IS THROUGH – FIVE (2) ... 98
UNTIL YOU COME BACK TO ME – ADEVA (45) ... 92
UNTIL YOU COME BACK TO ME (THAT'S WHAT I'M GONNA DO) [A] – Aretha FRANKLIN (26) ... 74
UNTIL YOU COME BACK TO ME (THAT'S WHAT I'M GONNA DO) [A] – Miki HOWARD (67) 90
UNTIL YOU FIND OUT – NED'S ATOMIC DUSTBIN (51) ... 90
UNTIL YOU LOVED ME – MOFFATTS (36) ... 99
UNTIL YOU SUFFER SOME (FIRE AND ICE) – POISON (32) ... 93
UNTOUCHABLE – RIALTO (20) ... 98
UP! – Shania TWAIN (21) ... 03
UP ABOVE MY HEAD I HEAR MUSIC IN THE AIR – Frankie LAINE and Johnnie RAY (25) 57
UP AGAINST THE WALL – Tom ROBINSON (33) ... 78
UP ALL NIGHT [A] – SLAUGHTER (62) ... 90
UP ALL NIGHT [A] – John B (58) ... 02
UP AND DOWN [A] – HIGH (53) ... 90
UP AND DOWN [B] – VENGABOYS (4) ... 98
UP & DOWN [C] – BOYSTEROUS (53) ... 03
UP AROUND THE BEND [A] – CREEDENCE CLEARWATER REVIVAL (3) ... 70
UP AROUND THE BEND [A] – HANOI ROCKS (61) ... 84
UP IN A PUFF OF SMOKE – Polly BROWN (43) ... 74
UP MIDDLE FINGER – OXIDE & NEUTRINO (7) ... 01
UP ON THE CATWALK – SIMPLE MINDS (27) 84
UP ON THE DOWN SIDE – OCEAN COLOUR SCENE (19) ... 01
UP ON THE ROOF [A] – Kenny LYNCH (10) .. 62
UP ON THE ROOF [A] – Julie GRANT (33) ... 63
UP ON THE ROOF [A] – ROBSON and JEROME (1) ... 95
UP ROCKING BEATS – BOMFUNK MC'S (11) .. 00
UP TEMPO – TRONIKHOUSE (68) ... 92
UP THE BRACKET – LIBERTINES (29) ... 02
UP THE HILL BACKWARDS – David BOWIE (32) ... 81
UP THE JUNCTION – SQUEEZE (2) ... 79
UP THE LADDER TO THE ROOF – SUPREMES (6) ... 70
UP THE POOL – JETHRO TULL (11) ... 71
UP TO NO GOOD – PORN KINGS (28) ... 96
UP TO THE WILDSTYLE – PORN KINGS vs DJ SUPREME (10) ... 99
UP, UP AND AWAY – Johnny MANN SINGERS (6) ... 67
UP WHERE WE BELONG – Joe COCKER and Jennifer WARNES (7) ... 83
UP WITH PEOPLE – LAMBCHOP (66) ... 00
UP WITH THE COCK – JUDGE DREAD (49) 78
UPFIELD – Billy BRAGG (46) ... 96
UPROCK – ROCKSTEADY CREW (64) ... 84
UPSIDE DOWN [A] – Diana ROSS (2) ... 80
UPSIDE DOWN [B] – A TEENS (10) ... 01
UPTIGHT – Shara NELSON (19) ... 94
UPTIGHT (EVERYTHING'S ALRIGHT) – Stevie WONDER (14) ... 66
UPTOWN DOWNTOWN – FULL INTENTION (61) ... 96
UPTOWN FESTIVAL – SHALAMAR (30) ... 77
UPTOWN GIRL [A] – Billy JOEL (1) ... 83
UPTOWN GIRL [A] – WESTLIFE (1) ... 01
UPTOWN TOP RANKING [A] – ALTHIA and DONNA (1) ... 77
UPTOWN TOP RANKING [A] – ALI and FRAZIER (33) ... 93
UPTOWN UPTEMPO WOMAN – Randy EDELMAN (25) ... 76
URBAN CITY GIRL – BENZ (31) ... 96
URBAN GUERRILLA – HAWKWIND (39) ... 73
URBAN PRESSURE – GRIM NORTHERN SOCIAL (60) ... 03
URBAN TRAIN – DJ TIESTO featuring Kirsty HAWKSHAW (22) ... 01
URGE – WILDHEARTS (26) ... 97
THE URGE – Freddy CANNON (18) ... 60
URGENT – FOREIGNER (45) ... 81,82
URGENTLY IN LOVE – Billy CRAWFORD (48) 98
US MALE – Elvis PRESLEY (15) ... 68
USA – WWF SUPERSTARS (71) ... 93
USE IT UP AND WEAR IT OUT [A] – ODYSSEY (1) ... 80
USE IT UP AND WEAR IT OUT [A] – PAT and MICK (22) ... 90
USED FOR GLUE – RIVAL SCHOOLS (42) ... 02
USED TA BE MY GIRL – O'JAYS (12) ... 78
USELESS – DEPECHE MODE (28) ... 97
USELESS (I DON'T NEED YOU NOW) – Kym MAZELLE (48) ... 88,90
U16 GIRLS – TRAVIS (40) ... 97
UTOPIA – GOLDFRAPP (62) ... 01
V THIRTEEN – BIG AUDIO DYNAMITE (49) 87
VACATION – Connie FRANCIS (10) ... 62
VADO VIA – DRUPI (17) ... 73
VAGABONDS – NEW MODEL ARMY (37) ... 89
VALENTINE – T'PAU (9) ... 88,93
VALENTINO – Connie FRANCIS (27) ... 60
VALERIE – Steve WINWOOD (19) ... 82,87
VALLERI – MONKEES (12) ... 68
VALLEY OF TEARS [A] – Fats DOMINO (25) .. 57
VALLEY OF TEARS [A] – Buddy HOLLY (12) .. 61
VALLEY OF THE DOLLS – GENERATION X (23) ... 79
VALLEY OF THE SHADOWS – ORIGIN UNKNOWN (60) ... 96
THE VALLEY ROAD – Bruce HORNSBY and the RANGE (44) ... 88
VALOTTE – Julian LENNON (55) ... 84
VAMOS A LA PLAYA – RIGHEIRA (53) ... 83
VAMP – OUTLANDER (51) ... 91,98
VAMPIRE RACECOURSE – SLEEPY JACKSON (50) ... 03
VANESSA – Ted HEATH (11) ... 53
VANILLA RADIO – WILDHEARTS (26) ... 02
VANITY KILLS – ABC (70) ... 85
VAPORIZER – LUPINE HOWL (68) ... 00
VAPORS – SNOOP DOGG (18) ... 97
VASOLINE – STONE TEMPLE PILOTS (48) 94
VAVOOM! – MAN WITH NO NAME (43) ... 98
VAYA CON DIOS (MAY GOD BE WITH YOU) [A] – Les PAUL and Mary FORD (7) ... 53
VAYA CON DIOS (MAY GOD BE WITH YOU) [A] – MILLICAN and NESBITT (20) ... 73
VEGAS [A] – SLEEPER (33) ... 95
VEGAS [B] – AGNELLI & NELSON (48) ... 01
VEGAS TWO TIMES – STEREOPHONICS (23) 02
VEHICLE – IDES OF MARCH (31) ... 70
VELCRO FLY – ZZ TOP (54) ... 86
VELOURIA – PIXIES (28) ... 90
VELVET MOODS – Johan GIELEN presents ABNEA (74) ... 01
VENCEREMOS – WE WILL WIN – WORKING WEEK (64) ... 84
VENI VIDI VICI – Ronnie HILTON (12) ... 54
VENTOLIN – APHEX TWIN (49) ... 95
VENTURA HIGHWAY – AMERICA (43) ... 72
VENUS [A] – Dickie VALENTINE (20) ... 59
VENUS [A] – Frankie AVALON (16) ... 59
VENUS [B] – SHOCKING BLUE (8) ... 70
VENUS [B] – BANANARAMA (8) ... 86
VENUS [B] – DON PABLO'S ANIMALS (4) ... 90
VENUS AND MARS – Jo BREEZER (27) ... 01
VENUS AS A BOY – BJÖRK (29) ... 93
VENUS IN BLUE JEANS – Mark WYNTER (4) .. 62
VENUS IN FURS – VELVET UNDERGROUND (71) ... 94
VERNON'S WONDERLAND – VERNON'S WONDERLAND (59) ... 96
VERONICA [A] – Elvis COSTELLO (31) ... 89
VERONICA [B] – SULTANS OF PING (69) ... 92
VERDI – Mauro PICOTTO (74) ... 01
VERSION OF ME – THOUSAND YARD STARE (57) ... 93
VERY BEST FRIEND – PROUD MARY (75) ... 01
VERY METAL NOISE POLLUTION (EP) – POP WILL EAT ITSELF (45) ... 89
A VERY PRECIOUS LOVE – Doris DAY (16) 58
THE VERY THOUGHT OF YOU [A] – Tony BENNETT (21) ... 65
THE VERY THOUGHT OF YOU [A] – Natalie COLE (71) ... 92
VESSEL – Ed RUSH & OPTICAL / UNIVERSAL PROJECT (61) ... 02
VIBE – ZHANÉ (67) ... 94
VIBEOLOGY – Paula ABDUL (19) ... 92
VIBRATOR – Terence Trent D'ARBY (57) ... 95
VICIOUS CIRCLES [A] – POLTERGEIST (32) 96
VICIOUS CIRCLES [A] – VICIOUS CIRCLES (68) ... 00
VICTIM OF LOVE [A] – ERASURE (7) ... 87
VICTIM OF LOVE [B] – Bryan ADAMS (68) 87
VICTIMS – CULTURE CLUB (3) ... 83
VICTIMS OF SUCCESS – DOGS D'AMOUR (36) ... 90
VICTORIA [A] – KINKS (33) ... 70
VICTORIA [A] – FALL (35) ... 88
VICTORY – KOOL and the GANG (30) ... 86
VIDEO – india.arie (32) ... 01
VIDEO KILLED THE RADIO STAR [A] – BUGGLES (1) ... 79
VIDEO KILLED THE RADIO STAR [A] – PRESIDENTS OF THE UNITED STATES OF AMERICA (52) ... 98
VIDEOTHEQUE – DOLLAR (17) ... 82
VIENNA – ULTRAVOX (2) ... 81,93
VIENNA CALLING – FALCO (10) ... 86
VIETNAM – Jimmy CLIFF (46) ... 70
VIEW FROM A BRIDGE – Kim WILDE (16) ... 82
A VIEW TO A KILL – DURAN DURAN (2) ... 85

WALKING DEAD – **PURESSENCE** (40)..............02
WALKING DOWN MADISON – **Kirsty MacCOLL** (23)..............91
WALKING DOWN YOUR STREET – **BANGLES** (16)..............87
WALKING IN MEMPHIS [A] – **Marc COHN** (22)..............91
WALKING IN MEMPHIS [A] – **CHER** (11)..............95
WALKING IN MY SHOES – **DEPECHE MODE** (14)..............93
WALKING IN MY SLEEP – **Roger DALTREY** (56)..............84
WALKING IN RHYTHM – **BLACKBYRDS** (23)..75
WALKING IN THE AIR [A] – **Aled JONES** (5)..85
WALKING IN THE AIR [A] – **Peter AUTY and the SINFONIA OF LONDON conducted by Howard BLAKE** (37)........85,87
WALKING IN THE AIR [A] – **DIGITAL DREAM BABY** (49)..............91
WALKING IN THE RAIN [A] – **WALKER BROTHERS** (26)..............67
WALKING IN THE RAIN [A] – **PARTRIDGE FAMILY** (10)..............73
WALKING IN THE RAIN [B] – **MODERN ROMANCE** (7)..............83
WALKING IN THE SUNSHINE – **BAD MANNERS** (10)..............81
WALKING INTO SUNSHINE – **CENTRAL LINE** (42)..............81
WALKING MY BABY BACK HOME – **Johnnie RAY** (12)..............52
WALKING MY CAT NAMED DOG – **Norma TANEGA** (22)..............66
WALKING ON AIR [A] – **FRAZIER CHORUS** (60)..............91
WALKING ON AIR [B] – **BAD BOYS INC** (24)..93
WALKING ON BROKEN GLASS – **Annie LENNOX** (8)..............92
WALKING ON ICE – **RIVER CITY PEOPLE** (62)90
WALKING ON SUNSHINE [A] – **ROCKER'S REVENGE featuring Donnie CALVIN** (4)........82
WALKING ON SUNSHINE [A] – **Eddy GRANT** (57)..............89,01
WALKING ON SUNSHINE [A] – **KRUSH** (71)..92
WALKING ON SUNSHINE [B] – **KATRINA and the WAVES** (8)..............85,96
WALKING ON THE CHINESE WALL – **Philip BAILEY** (34)..............85
WALKING ON THE MILKY WAY – **ORCHESTRAL MANOEUVRES IN THE DARK** (17)..............96
WALKING ON THE MOON – **POLICE** (1)........79
WALKING ON THIN ICE – **Yoko ONO** (35) 81,03
WALKING ON WATER – **MADASUN** (14)........00
WALKING THE FLOOR OVER YOU – **Pat BOONE** (39)..............60
WALKING TO NEW ORLEANS – **Fats DOMINO** (19)..............60
WALKING WITH THEE – **CLINIC** (65)..............02
WALKING WOUNDED – **EVERYTHING BUT THE GIRL** (6)..............96
THE WALL STREET SHUFFLE – **10cc** (10)......74
WALLFLOWER – **MEGA CITY FOUR** (69)........93
WALLS COME TUMBLING DOWN! – **STYLE COUNCIL** (6)..............85
THE WALLS FELL DOWN – **MARBLES** (28)....69
WALTZ AWAY DREAMING – **George MICHAEL** (10)..............97
WALTZ DARLING – **Malcolm McLAREN** (31)..89
WALTZ #2 (XO) – **Elliott SMITH** (52)..............98
WALTZING ALONG – **JAMES** (23)..............97
WAM BAM [A] – **HANDLEY FAMILY** (30)........73
WAM BAM [B] – **NT GANG** (71)..............88
THE WANDERER [A] – **DION** (10)..............62,76
THE WANDERER [A] – **STATUS QUO** (7)........84
THE WANDERER [B] – **Donna SUMMER** (48) 80
WANDERIN' EYES [A] – **Charlie GRACIE** (6)..57
WANDERIN' EYES [A] – **Frankie VAUGHAN** (6)..............57
THE WANDERING DRAGON – **SHADES OF RHYTHM** (55)..............94
WAND'RIN' STAR – **Lee MARVIN** (1)..............70
WANNA BE STARTIN' SOMETHIN' – **Michael JACKSON** (8)..............83
WANNA BE WITH YOU – **JINNY** (30)..............95
WANNA BE YOUR LOVER – **GAYLE & GILLIAN** (62)..............94
WANNA DROP A HOUSE (ON THAT BITCH) – **URBAN DISCHARGE featuring SHE** (51)......96
WANNA GET UP – **2 UNLIMITED** (38)..............98
WANNA MAKE YOU GO ... UUH! – **THOSE 2 GIRLS** (74)..............94
WANNABE – **SPICE GIRLS** (1)..............96
WANNABE GANGSTAR – **WHEATUS** (22)........02
WANT LOVE – **HYSTERIC EGO** (28)..............96
WANT YOU BAD – **OFFSPRING** (15)..............01
WANTED [A] – **Perry COMO** (4)..............54
WANTED [A] – **Al MARTINO** (4)..............54
WANTED [B] – **DOOLEYS** (3)..............79
WANTED [C] – **STYLE COUNCIL** (20)..............87
WANTED [D] – **HALO JAMES** (45)..............89
WANTED [E] – **PRINCESS IVORI** (69)..............90
WANTED DEAD OR ALIVE [A] – **BON JOVI** (13)..............87
WANTED DEAD OR ALIVE [B] – **2PAC and SNOOP DOGG** (16)..............97
WANTED IT ALL – **CLAYTOWN TROUPE** (74) 92
WAP-BAM-BOOGIE – **MATT BIANCO** (11)..88,89
WAR [A] – **Edwin STARR** (3)..............70,93
WAR [A] – **Bruce SPRINGSTEEN** (18)..............86
WAR BABIES – **SIMPLE MINDS** (43)..............98
WAR BABY – **Tom ROBINSON** (6)..............83
WAR CHILD – **BLONDIE** (39)..............82
WAR LORD – **SHADOWS** (18)..............65
WAR OF NERVES – **ALL SAINTS** (7)..............98
WAR PARTY – **Eddy GRANT** (42)..............83
THE WAR SONG – **CULTURE CLUB** (2)..........84
WAR STORIES – **STARJETS** (51)..............79
WARFAIR – **CLAWFINGER** (54)..............94
WARHEAD – **UK SUBS** (30)..............80
WARLOCK – **BLACK RIOT** (68)..............88
WARM AND TENDER LOVE – **Percy SLEDGE** (34)..............66
WARM IT UP – **KRIS KROSS** (16)..............92
WARM LOVE – **BEATMASTERS** (51)..............89
WARM MACHINE – **BUSH** (45)..............00
WARM SUMMER DAZE – **VYBE** (60)..............95
WARM WET CIRCLES – **MARILLION** (22)........87
WARMED OVER KISSES – **Brian HYLAND** (28) 62
WARNING [A] – **ADEVA** (17)..............89
WARNING [B] – **AKA** (43)..............96
WARNING [C] – **FREESTYLERS** (68)..............98
WARNING [D] – **GREEN DAY** (27)..............00
WARNING SIGN – **Nick HEYWARD** (25)......84,85
WARPAINT – **BROOK BROTHERS** (5)..............61
WARPED – **RED HOT CHILI PEPPERS** (31)....95
WARRIOR [A] – **MC WILDSKI** (49)..............90
WARRIOR [B] – **DANCE 2 TRANCE** (56)..........95
WARRIOR [C] – **WARRIOR** (19)..............00
WARRIOR GROOVE – **DSM** (68)..............85
WARRIOR SOUND – **PRESSURE DROP** (72)..01
WARRIORS [A] – **Gary NUMAN** (20)..............83
WARRIORS [B] – **ASWAD** (33)..............94
WARRIORS (OF THE WASTELAND) – **FRANKIE GOES TO HOLLYWOOD** (19)..........86
WAS IT WORTH IT – **PET SHOP BOYS** (24)..91
WAS THAT ALL IT WAS – **Kym MAZELLE** (33)..............90
WAS THAT YOU – **SPEAR OF DESTINY** (55)..87
WASH YOUR FACE IN MY SINK – **DREAM WARRIORS** (16)..............90
WASSUUP – **DA MUTTZ** (11)..............00
WASTED [A] – **DEF LEPPARD** (61)..............79
WASTED [B] – **SMALLER** (72)..............96
WASTED IN AMERICA – **LOVE / HATE** (38)....92
WASTED TIME [A] – **SKID ROW** (20)..............91
WASTED TIME [B] – **KINGS OF LEON** (51)......03
WASTED YEARS – **IRON MAIDEN** (18)..........86
WASTELAND – **MISSION** (11)..............87
WASTELANDS – **Midge URE** (46)..............86
WASTER – **REEF** (56)..............03
WASTING MY TIME [A] – **DEFAULT** (73)........03
WASTING MY TIME [B] – **KOSHEEN** (49)......03
WATCH ME – **Labi SIFFRE** (29)..............72
WATCH OUT – **Brandi WELLS** (74)..............82
WATCH THE MIRACLE START – **Pauline HENRY** (54)..............94
WATCH WHAT YOU SAY – **GURU featuring Chaka KHAN** (28)..............95
WATCHDOGS – **UB40** (39)..............87
A WATCHER'S POINT OF VIEW – **PM DAWN** (36)..............91
WATCHING – **THOMPSON TWINS** (33)..........83
WATCHING THE DETECTIVES – **Elvis COSTELLO** (15)..............77
WATCHING THE RIVER FLOW – **Bob DYLAN** (24)..............71
WATCHING THE WHEELS – **John LENNON** (30)..............81
WATCHING THE WILDLIFE – **FRANKIE GOES TO HOLLYWOOD** (28)........87
WATCHING THE WORLD GO BY – **Maxi PRIEST** (36)..............96
WATCHING WINDOWS – **Roni SIZE / REPRAZENT** (28)..............98
WATCHING YOU – **ETHER** (74)..............98
WATCHING YOU WATCHING ME – **David GRANT** (10)..............83
WATER [A] – **Geno WASHINGTON and the RAM JAM BAND** (39)..............66
WATER [B] – **MARTIKA** (59)..............90
WATER FROM A VINE LEAF – **William ORBIT** (59)..............93
THE WATER IS OVER MY HEAD – **ROCKIN' BERRIES** (43)..............66
THE WATER MARGIN – **GODIEGO** (37)..........77
WATER ON GLASS – **Kim WILDE** (11)..............81
WATER RUNS DRY – **BOYZ II MEN** (24)........95
WATER WATER – **Tommy STEELE** (5)..............57
WATER WAVE – **Mark VAN DALE with ENRICO** (71)..............98
WATERFALL [A] – **WENDY and LISA** (66)..87,89
WATERFALL [B] – **STONE ROSES** (27)..........92
WATERFALL [C] – **ATLANTIC OCEAN** (21)..94,96
WATERFALLS [A] – **Paul McCARTNEY** (9)......80
WATERFALLS [B] – **TLC** (4)..............95
WATERFRONT – **SIMPLE MINDS** (13)..............83
WATERLOO [A] – **Stonewall JACKSON** (24)....59
WATERLOO [B] – **ABBA** (1)..............74
WATERLOO [B] – **DOCTOR and the MEDICS featuring Roy WOOD** (45)..............86
WATERLOO SUNSET [A] – **KINKS** (2)..............67
WATERLOO SUNSET [A] – **Cathy DENNIS** (11)97
WATERY, DOMESTIC (EP) – **PAVEMENT** (58) 92
THE WAVE – **COSMIC GATE** (48)..............03
THE WAVE OF THE FUTURE – **QUADROPHONIA** (40)..............91
WAVES – **BLANCMANGE** (19)..............83
WAVY GRAVY – **SASHA** (64)..............83
WAX THE VAN – **LOLA** (65)..............87
THE WAY [A] – **FUNKY GREEN DOGS** (43)....97
THE WAY [B] – **GLOBAL COMMUNICATION** (51)..............97
THE WAY [C] – **FASTBALL** (21)..............98
WAY BACK HOME – **Junior WALKER and the ALL-STARS** (35)....73
WAY BEHIND ME – **PRIMITIVES** (36)..............88
WAY DOWN – **Elvis PRESLEY** (1)..............77
WAY DOWN NOW – **WORLD PARTY** (66)......90
WAY DOWN YONDER IN NEW ORLEANS – **Freddy CANNON** (3)..............60
THE WAY DREAMS ARE – **Daniel O'DONNELL** (18)..............99
THE WAY I AM – **EMINEM** (8)..............00
THE WAY I FEEL [A] – **LEMON TREES** (62)....92
THE WAY I FEEL [B] – **ROACHFORD** (20)......97
THE WAY I FEEL ABOUT YOU – **Karyn WHITE** (65)..............92
THE WAY I WALK – **Jack SCOTT** (30)..............59
THE WAY I WANT TO TOUCH YOU – **CAPTAIN and TENNILLE** (28)..............76
WAY IN MY BRAIN – **SL2** (11)..............91,92
THE WAY IT GOES – **STATUS QUO** (39)........99
THE WAY IT IS [A] – **Bruce HORNSBY and the RANGE** (15)........86
THE WAY IT IS [A] – **CHAMELEON** (34)..........96
THE WAY IT USED TO BE – **Engelbert HUMPERDINCK** (3)..............69
THE WAY IT'S GOIN' DOWN (T.W.I.S.M. FOR LIFE) – **Shaquille O'NEAL** (62)..........98
WAY OF LIFE [A] – **FAMILY DOGG** (6)..............69
WAY OF LIFE [B] – **Dave CLARKE** (59)..........03
WAY OF THE WORLD [A] – **CHEAP TRICK** (73)..............80
WAY OF THE WORLD [B] – **Tina TURNER** (13)91
THE WAY (PUT YOUR HAND IN MY HAND) – **DIVINE INSPIRATION** (5)..............03
THE WAY SHE LOVES ME – **Richard MARX** (38)..............94
THE WAY THAT YOU FEEL – **ADEVA** (54)......97
THE WAY THAT YOU LOVE – **Vanessa WILLIAMS** (52)..............95
THE WAY TO YOUR LOVE – **HEAR'SAY** (1)....01
THE WAY WE WERE – **Barbra STREISAND** (31)..............74
THE WAY WE WERE – TRY TO REMEMBER – **Gladys KNIGHT and the PIPS** (4)..............75
THE WAY YOU ARE – **TEARS FOR FEARS** (24)..............83
THE WAY YOU DO THE THINGS YOU DO – **UB40** (49)..............91
THE WAY YOU LIKE IT – **ADEMA** (61)..............02

WE'RE ALL IN LOVE – BLACK REBEL MOTORCYCLE CLUB (45) 03
WE'RE ALMOST THERE – Michael JACKSON (46) 81
WE'RE COMIN' AT YA – QUARTZ (65) 90
WE'RE COMING OVER – MR SMASH & FRIENDS (67) 02
WE'RE GOING OUT – YOUNGER YOUNGER 28'S (61) 99
WE'RE GOING TO IBIZA! – VENGABOYS (1) 99
WE'RE GOING TO MISS YOU – JAMES (48) 99
WE'RE GONNA DO IT AGAIN – MANCHESTER UNITED FOOTBALL CLUB (6) 95
WE'RE GONNA GO FISHIN' – Hank LOCKLIN (18) 62
WE'RE IN THIS LOVE TOGETHER – Al JARREAU (55) 81
WE'RE IN THIS TOGETHER [A] – SIMPLY RED (11) 96
WE'RE IN THIS TOGETHER [B] – NINE INCH NAILS (39) 99
WE'RE NOT ALONE – HHC (44) 97
WE'RE NOT GONNA SLEEP TONIGHT – Emma BUNTON (20) 01
WE'RE NOT GONNA TAKE IT – TWISTED SISTER (58) 84
WE'RE ON THE BALL – ANT & DEC (3) 02
WE'RE ONLY YOUNG ONCE – AVONS (45) 60
WE'RE REALLY SAYING SOMETHING – BUFFALO G (17) 00
WE'RE THROUGH – HOLLIES (7) 64
WEST END GIRLS [A] – PET SHOP BOYS (1) 85
WEST END GIRLS [A] – EAST 17 (11) 93
WEST END PAD – Cathy DENNIS (25) 96
WEST OF ZANZIBAR – Anthony STEEL and the RADIO REVELLERS (11) 54
WEST ONE (SHINE ON ME) – RUTS (43) 80
WESTERN MOVIES – OLYMPICS (12) 58
WESTSIDE [A] – TQ (4) 99
WESTSIDE [B] – ATHLETE (42) 03
WET DREAM – Max ROMEO (10) 69
WET MY WHISTLE – MIDNIGHT STAR (60) 87
WE'VE GOT IT GOIN' ON – BACKSTREET BOYS (3) 95,96
WE'VE GOT THE JUICE – Derek B (56) 88
WE'VE GOT THE WHOLE WORLD AT OUR FEET – ENGLAND WORLD CUP SQUAD (66) 86
WE GOT THE WHOLE WORLD IN OUR HANDS – NOTTINGHAM FOREST FC with PAPER LACE (24) 78
WE'VE GOT TO LIVE TOGETHER – RAF (34) 92
WE'VE GOT TO WORK IT OUT – BEL CANTO (65) 95
WE'VE GOT TONITE [A] – Bob SEGER and the SILVER BULLET BAND (41) 79,82
WE'VE GOT TONIGHT [A] – Kenny ROGERS and Sheena EASTON (28) 83
WE'VE GOT TONIGHT [A] – Elkie BROOKS (69) 87
WE'VE GOT TONIGHT [A] – Bob SEGER and the SILVER BULLET BAND (22) 95
WE'VE GOT TONIGHT [A] – Ronan KEATING featuring LULU (4) 02
WE'VE HAD ENOUGH – ALKALINE TRIO (50) 03
WE'VE ONLY JUST BEGUN [A] – CARPENTERS (28) 71
WE'VE ONLY JUST BEGUN [A] – Bitty McLEAN (23) 95
WFL – HAPPY MONDAYS (68) 89
WHADDA U WANT (FROM ME) – Frankie KNUCKLES featuring ADEVA (36) 95
WHADDA WE LIKE? – ROUND SOUND presents ONYX STONE & MC MALIBU (69) 02
WHAM BAM – CANDY GIRLS (20) 96
WHAM RAP! – WHAM! (8) 83
WHAT – SOFT CELL (3) 82
WHAT A BEAUTIFUL DAY – LEVELLERS (13) 97
WHAT A CRAZY WORLD WE'RE LIVING IN – Joe BROWN and the BRUVVERS (37) 62
WHAT A DIFFERENCE A DAY MADE – Esther PHILLIPS (6) 75
WHAT A FOOL BELIEVES [A] – DOOBIE BROTHERS (31) 79,87
WHAT A FOOL BELIEVES [A] – Aretha FRANKLIN (46) 80
WHAT A FOOL BELIEVES [A] – Peter COX (39) 98
WHAT A GIRL WANTS – Christina AGUILERA (3) 00
WHAT A MOUTH – Tommy STEELE (5) 60
WHAT A NIGHT – CITY BOY (39) 78
WHAT A PARTY – Fats DOMINO (43) 61
WHAT A WASTE! – Ian DURY and the BLOCKHEADS (9) 78
WHAT A WASTER – LIBERTINES (37) 02
WHAT A WOMAN IN LOVE WON'T DO – Sandy POSEY (48) 67
WHAT A WONDERFUL WORLD [A] – Louis ARMSTRONG (1) 68,88
WHAT A WONDERFUL WORLD [A] – Nick CAVE and the BAD SEEDS (72) 92
WHAT A WONDERFUL WORLD [A] – Cliff RICHARD (11) 01
(WHAT A) WONDERFUL WORLD – Johnny NASH (25) 76
WHAT ABOUT LOVE – HEART (14) 88
WHAT ABOUT THIS LOVE – MR FINGERS (74) 90
WHAT ABOUT US [A] – POINT BREAK (24) 00
WHAT ABOUT US? [B] – BRANDY (4) 02
WHAT ABOUT YOUR FRIENDS – TLC (59) 92
WHAT AM I GONNA DO – Emile FORD and the CHECKMATES (33) 61
WHAT AM I GONNA DO (I'M SO IN LOVE WITH YOU) – Rod STEWART (3) 83
WHAT AM I GONNA DO WITH YOU – Barry WHITE (5) 75
WHAT AM I TO YOU – Kenny LYNCH (37) 64
WHAT ARE WE GONNA DO ABOUT IT? – MERCY MERCY (59) 85
WHAT ARE WE GONNA GET 'ER INDOORS – Dennis WATERMAN (21) 83
WHAT ARE YOU DOING SUNDAY – DAWN (3) 71
WHAT BECOMES OF THE BROKENHEARTED [A] – Jimmy RUFFIN (4) 66,74
WHAT BECOMES OF THE BROKEN HEARTED [A] – Dave STEWART guest vocals: Colin BLUNSTONE (13) 81
WHAT BECOMES OF THE BROKENHEARTED [A] – ROBSON and JEROME (1) 96
WHAT CAN I DO – CORRS (3) 98
WHAT CAN I SAY – Boz SCAGGS (10) 77
(WHAT CAN I SAY) TO MAKE YOU LOVE ME – Alexander O'NEAL (27) 88
WHAT CAN YOU DO FOR ME [A] – UTAH SAINTS (10) 91
WHAT CAN YOU DO 4 ME? [B] – Lisa LASHES (52) 03
WHAT 'CHA GONNA DO – ETERNAL (16) 99
WHAT DID I DO TO YOU (EP) – Lisa STANSFIELD (25) 90
WHAT DIFFERENCE DOES IT MAKE – SMITHS (12) 84
WHAT DO I DO – Phil FEARON (5) 84
WHAT DO I DO NOW – SLEEPER (14) 95
WHAT DO I GET? – BUZZCOCKS (37) 78
WHAT DO I HAVE TO DO – Kylie MINOGUE (6) 91
WHAT DO YA SAY – Chubby CHECKER (37) 63
WHAT DO YOU WANT – Adam FAITH (1) 59
WHAT DO YOU WANT FROM ME? – MONACO (11) 97
WHAT DO YOU WANT TO MAKE THOSE EYES AT ME FOR? [A] – Emile FORD and the CHECKMATES (1) 59
WHAT DO YOU WANT TO MAKE THOSE EYES AT ME FOR [A] – Shakin' STEVENS (5) 87
WHAT DOES IT FEEL LIKE? – FELIX DA HOUSECAT (66) 02
WHAT DOES IT TAKE – THEN JERICO (33) 89
WHAT DOES IT TAKE (TO WIN YOUR LOVE) [A] – Junior WALKER and the ALL-STARS (13) 69
WHAT DOES IT TAKE (TO WIN YOUR LOVE) [A] – Kenny G (64) 86
WHAT DOES YOUR SOUL LOOK LIKE – DJ SHADOW (59) 95,98
WHAT EVER HAPPENED TO OLD FASHIONED LOVE – Daniel O'DONNELL (21) 93
WHAT GOD WANTS PART 1 – Roger WATERS (35) 92
WHAT GOES AROUND [A] – Bitty McLEAN (36) 94
WHAT GOES AROUND [B] – LUCIANA (67) 94
WHAT GOES AROUND COMES AROUND – Bob MARLEY and the WAILERS (42) 96
WHAT GOES ON – Bryan FERRY (67) 78
WHAT GOOD AM I – Cilla BLACK (24) 67
WHAT HAPPENED TO THE MUSIC – Joey NEGRO (51) 93
WHAT HAVE I DONE TO DESERVE THIS – PET SHOP BOYS and Dusty SPRINGFIELD (2) 87
WHAT HAVE THEY DONE TO MY SONG MA [A] – NEW SEEKERS (44) 70
WHAT HAVE THEY DONE TO MY SONG MA [A] – MELANIE (39) 71
WHAT HAVE THEY DONE TO THE RAIN – SEARCHERS (13) 64
WHAT HAVE YOU DONE FOR ME LATELY – Janet JACKSON (3) 86
WHAT HAVE YOU DONE (IS THIS ALL) – OUR TRIBE / ONE TRIBE (52) 92
WHAT HOPE HAVE I – SPHINX (43) 95
WHAT I AM [A] – Edie BRICKELL and the NEW BOHEMIANS (31) 89
WHAT I AM [A] – TIN TIN OUT featuring Emma BUNTON (2) 99
WHAT I CAN DO FOR YOU – Sheryl CROW (43) 95
WHAT I DO BEST – Robin S (43) 93
WHAT I GO TO SCHOOL FOR – BUSTED (3) 02
WHAT I GOT – SUBLIME (71) 97
WHAT I GOT IS WHAT YOU NEED – UNIQUE (27) 83
WHAT I LIKE MOST ABOUT YOU IS YOUR GIRLFRIEND – SPECIALS (51) 84
WHAT I MEAN – MODJO (59) 01
WHAT I MISS THE MOST – ALOOF (70) 98
WHAT I SAW – KINGS OF LEON (22) 03
WHAT IF ... – LIGHTNING SEEDS (14) 96,97
WHAT IF – Kate WINSLET (6) 01
WHAT IF A WOMAN – JOE (53) 02
WHAT IN THE WORLD – NU COLOURS (57) 93
WHAT IN THE WORLD'S COME OVER YOU [A] – Jack SCOTT (11) 60
WHAT IN THE WORLD'S COME OVER YOU [A] – ROCKIN' BERRIES (23) 65
WHAT IN THE WORLD'S COME OVER YOU [A] – Tam WHITE (36) 75
WHAT IS A MAN – FOUR TOPS (16) 69
WHAT IS HOUSE (EP) – LFO (62) 92
WHAT IS LIFE [A] – Olivia NEWTON-JOHN (16) 72
WHAT IS LIFE [A] – Shawn MULLINS (62) 99
WHAT IS LIFE? [B] – BLACK UHURU (56) 84
WHAT IS LOVE [A] – Howard JONES (2) 83
WHAT IS LOVE [B] – DEEE-LITE (2) 90
WHAT IS LOVE [C] – HADDAWAY (2) 93
WHAT IS THE PROBLEM? – GRAFITI (37) 03
WHAT IS THIS THING CALLED LOVE – Alexander O'NEAL (53) 91
WHAT IS TRUTH – Johnny CASH (21) 70
WHAT IT FEELS LIKE FOR A GIRL – MADONNA (7) 01
WHAT IT IS [A] – Garnet MIMMS and TRUCKIN' CO (44) 77
WHAT IT IS [B] – Freddy FRESH (63) 99
WHAT IT'S LIKE – EVERLAST (34) 99
WHAT I'VE GOT IN MIND – Billie Jo SPEARS (4) 76
WHAT KIND OF FOOL – ALL ABOUT EVE (29) 88
WHAT KIND OF FOOL AM I? [A] – Anthony NEWLEY (36) 61
WHAT KIND OF FOOL AM I? [A] – Sammy DAVIS Jr (26) 62
WHAT KIND OF FOOL AM I? [A] – Shirley BASSEY (47) 63
WHAT KIND OF FOOL (HEARD IT ALL BEFORE) – Kylie MINOGUE (14) 92
WHAT KIND OF MAN WOULD I BE – MINT CONDITION (38) 97
WHAT KINDA BOY YOU LOOKING FOR (GIRL) – HOT CHOCOLATE (10) 83

WHO YOU ARE – **PEARL JAM** (18) 96
WHO YOU LOOKING AT – **SALFORD JETS** (72) 80
WHO YOU WIT – **JAY-Z** (65) 97
WHO'S THE BAD MAN? – **Dee PATTEN** (42)..99
WHO'S THE DADDY – **LOVEBUG** (35)............03
WHO'S THE MAN – **HOUSE OF PAIN** (23) 93
WHOA – **BLACK ROB** (44) 00
WHO'D SEE COO – **OHIO PLAYERS** (43) 76
WHODUNIT – **TAVARES** (5) 77
WHOLE AGAIN – **ATOMIC KITTEN** (1) 01
WHOLE LOTTA LOVE [A] – **CCS** (13) 70
WHOLE LOTTA LOVE [A] – **GOLDBUG** (3) 96
WHOLE LOTTA LOVE [A] – **LED ZEPPELIN** (21) 97
WHOLE LOTTA ROSIE – **AC/DC** (36) 80
WHOLE LOTTA SHAKIN' GOIN' ON – **Jerry Lee LEWIS** (8) 57
WHOLE LOTTA TROUBLE – **Stevie NICKS** (62)................89
WHOLE LOTTA WOMAN – **Marvin RAINWATER** (1)................58
WHOLE NEW WORLD – **IT BITES** (54) 86
A WHOLE NEW WORLD (ALADDIN'S THEME) – **Regina BELLE and Peabo BRYSON** (12)......93
THE WHOLE OF THE MOON [A] – **WATERBOYS** (3)................85,91
THE WHOLE OF THE MOON [A] – **LITTLE CAESAR** (68) 90
THE WHOLE TOWN'S LAUGHING AT ME – **Teddy PENDERGRASS** (44)................77
THE WHOLE WORLD – **OUTKAST featuring KILLER MIKE** (19) 02
THE WHOLE WORLD LOST ITS HEAD – **GO-GO's** (29) 95
WHOOMP! (THERE IT IS) [A] – **TAG TEAM** (34)................94
WHOOMPH! (THERE IT IS) [A] – **CLOCK** (4)................95
WHOOMP THERE IT IS [A] – **BM DUBS present MR RUMBLE** (32) 01
WHOOPS NOW – **Janet JACKSON** (9) 95
WHOOSH – **WHOOSH** (72)................97
WHO'S AFRAID OF THE BIG BAD LOVE – **WILD WEEKEND** (70) 90
WHO'S AFRAID OF THE BIG BAD NOISE! – **AGE OF CHANCE** (65) 87
WHO'S COMING ROUND – **5050** (54) 01
WHO'S CRYING NOW – **JOURNEY** (46) 82
WHO'S GONNA LOVE ME – **IMPERIALS** (17)................77
WHO'S GONNA RIDE YOUR WILD HORSES – **U2** (14) 92
WHO'S GONNA ROCK YOU – **NOLANS** (12) ..80
WHO'S IN THE HOUSE – **BEATMASTERS** (8) 89
WHO'S IN THE STRAWBERRY PATCH WITH SALLY – **DAWN** (37) 74
WHO'S JOHNNY ('SHORT CIRCUIT' THEME) – **El DeBARGE** (60) 86
WHO'S LEAVING WHO – **Hazell DEAN** (4) 88
WHO'S LOVING MY BABY – **Shola AMA** (13) 97
WHO'S SORRY NOW [A] – **Johnnie RAY** (17) 56
WHO'S SORRY NOW [A] – **Connie FRANCIS** (1) 58
WHO'S THAT GIRL? [A] – **EURYTHMICS** (3)....83
WHO'S THAT GIRL [A] – **FLYING PICKETS** (71) 84
WHO'S THAT GIRL [B] – **MADONNA** (1) 87
WHO'S THAT GIRL [C] – **EVE** (6) 01
WHO'S THAT GIRL (SHE'S GOT IT) – **A FLOCK OF SEAGULLS** (66)................85
WHO'S THAT MIX – **THIS YEAR'S BLONDE** (62) 87
WHO'S THE DARKMAN – **DARKMAN** (46)......94
WHO'S THE MACK! – **Mark MORRISON** (13)................97
WHO'S ZOOMIN' WHO – **Aretha FRANKLIN** (11)................85
WHOSE FIST IS THIS ANYWAY (EP) – **PRONG** (58) 92
WHOSE LAW (IS IT ANYWAY) – **GURU JOSH** (26) 90
WHOSE PROBLEM? – **MOTELS** (42) 80
WHY [A] – **Anthony NEWLEY** (1)................60
WHY [A] – **Frankie AVALON** (20) 60
WHY [A] – **Donny OSMOND** (3) 72
WHY [B] – **Roger WHITTAKER** (47) 71
WHY [C] – **Carly SIMON** (10) 82,89
WHY [C] – **GLAMMA KID** (10) 99
WHY? [D] – **BRONSKI BEAT** (6)................84
WHY [E] – **Annie LENNOX** (5) 92
WHY [F] – **D MOB with Cathy DENNIS** (23) ..94
WHY [G] – **Ricardo DA FORCE** (58)................96
WHY [H] – **3T** (2) 96
WHY [I] – **MIS-TEEQ** (8) 01
WHY? [J] – **AGENT SUMO** (40) 02
WHY ARE PEOPLE GRUDGEFUL – **FALL** (43)..93
WHY ARE YOU BEING SO REASONABLE NOW – **WEDDING PRESENT** (42) 88
WHY BABY WHY – **Pat BOONE** (17) 57
WHY BELIEVE IN YOU – **TEXAS** (66)..............91
WHY CAN'T YOU – **Clarence 'Frogman' HENRY** (42)................61
WHY CAN'T I BE YOU [A] – **CURE** (21) 87
WHY CAN'T I BE YOU? [B] – **SHED SEVEN** (23) 03
WHY CAN'T I WAKE UP WITH YOU – **TAKE THAT** (2) 93
WHY CAN'T THIS BE LOVE – **VAN HALEN** (8)................86
WHY CAN'T WE BE LOVERS – **HOLLAND-DOZIER featuring Lamont DOZIER** (29)................72
WHY CAN'T WE LIVE TOGETHER – **Timmy THOMAS** (12) 73,90
WHY CAN'T YOU FREE SOME TIME – **Armand VAN HELDEN** (34) 01
WHY DID YA – **Tony DI BART** (46) 95
WHY DID YOU DO IT – **STRETCH** (16) 75
WHY DIDN'T YOU CALL ME – **Macy GRAY** (38) 00
WHY DO FOOLS FALL IN LOVE [A] – **Alma COGAN** (22)................56
WHY DO FOOLS FALL IN LOVE [A] – **Frankie LYMON and the TEENAGERS** (1) 56
WHY DO FOOLS FALL IN LOVE [A] – **Diana ROSS** (4) 81,94
WHY DO I ALWAYS GET IT WRONG – **LIVE REPORT** (73) 89
WHY DO LOVERS BREAK EACH OTHER'S HEARTS – **SHOWADDYWADDY** (22)............80
WHY DO YOU KEEP ON RUNNING – **STINX** (49) 01
WHY DOES A MAN HAVE TO BE STRONG – **Paul YOUNG** (63) 87
WHY DOES IT ALWAYS RAIN ON ME? – **TRAVIS** (10) 99
WHY DOES MY HEART FEEL SO BAD? – **MOBY** (16) 99,00
WHY DON'T THEY UNDERSTAND – **George HAMILTON IV** (22) 58
WHY DON'T WE FALL IN LOVE – **AMERIE featuring LUDACRIS** (40)................02
WHY DON'T WE TRY AGAIN – **Brian MAY** (44)................98
WHY DON'T YOU – **RAGE** (44) 93
WHY DON'T YOU BELIEVE ME – **Joni JAMES** (11)................53
WHY DON'T YOU DANCE WITH ME – **FUTURE BREEZE** (50) 97
WHY DON'T YOU GET A JOB? – **OFFSPRING** (2) 99
WHY DON'T YOU TAKE ME – **ONE DOVE** (30) 94
WHY D'YA LIE TO ME – **SPIDER** (65) 83
WHY (LOOKING BACK) – **HEARTLESS CREW** (50) 03
WHY ME [A] – **Linda MARTIN** (59) 92
WHY ME [B] – **A HOUSE** (52) 94
WHY ME [C] – **ANT & DEC** (27) 94
WHY ME [D] – **ASHER D** (43) 02
WHY (MUST WE FALL IN LOVE) – **Diana ROSS and the SUPREMES and the TEMPTATIONS** (31) 70
WHY MUST WE WAIT UNTIL TONIGHT – **Tina TURNER** (16)................93
WHY NOT NOW – **Matt MONRO** (24) 61
WHY NOT TONIGHT – **MOJOS** (25) 64
WHY OH WHY – **SPEARHEAD** (45) 97
WHY, OH WHY, OH WHY – **Gilbert O'SULLIVAN** (6) 73
WHY SHE'S A GIRL FROM THE CHAINSTORE – **BUZZCOCKS** (61)................80
WHY SHOULD I – **Bob MARLEY and the WAILERS** (42)......92,93
WHY SHOULD I BE LONELY – **Tony BRENT** (24) 59
WHY SHOULD I CRY – **Nona HENDRYX** (60) 87
WHY SHOULD I LOVE YOU – **DES'REE** (44) 92
WHY WHY BYE BYE – **Bob LUMAN** (46)........60
WHY WHY WHY – **DEJA VU** (57)................94
WHY YOU FOLLOW ME – **Eric BENET** (48) 00
WHY YOU TREAT ME SO BAD – **SHAGGY featuring GRAND PUBA** (11) 96
WHY'D YOU LIE TO ME – **ANASTACIA** (25) ..02
WHY'S EVERYBODY ALWAYS PICKIN' ON ME? – **BLOODHOUND GANG** (56) 97
WIBBLING RIVALRY (INTERVIEWS WITH NOEL AND LIAM GALLAGHER) – **OASIS** (52) 95
WICHITA LINEMAN – **Glen CAMPBELL** (7) 69
WICKED – **ICE CUBE** (62) 93
WICKED GAME – **Chris ISAAK** (10) 90
WICKED LOVE – **OCEANIC** (25)................91
WICKED WAYS – **BLOW MONKEYS** (60) 86
WICKEDEST SOUND – **REBEL MC featuring TENOR FLY** (43) 91
THE WICKER MAN – **IRON MAIDEN** (9) 00
WICKI WACKY HOUSE PARTY – **TEAM** (55) 85
WIDE AWAKE IN A DREAM – **Barry BIGGS** (44) 81
WIDE BOY – **Nik KERSHAW** (9) 85
WIDE EYED AND LEGLESS – **Andy FAIRWEATHER-LOW** (6) 75
WIDE EYED ANGEL – **ORIGIN** (73) 00
WIDE OPEN SKY – **GOLDRUSH** (70) 02
WIDE OPEN SPACE – **MANSUN** (15) 96
WIDE PRAIRIE – **Linda McCARTNEY** (74) 98
WIFEY – **NEXT** (19) 00
WIG WAM BAM [A] – **BLACK LACE** (63) 86
WIG WAM BAM [A] – **DAMIAN** (49) 89
WIGGLE IT – **2 IN A ROOM** (3) 91
WIGGLY WORLD – **MR JACK** (32) 97
WIG-WAM BAM – **SWEET** (4) 72
WIKKA WRAP – **EVASIONS** (20) 81
THE WILD AMERICA (EP) – **Iggy POP** (63)....93
WILD AND WONDERFUL – **ALMIGHTY** (50)....90
WILD AS ANGELS EP – **LEVELLERS** (34) 03
THE WILD BOYS – **DURAN DURAN** (2) 84
WILD CAT – **Gene VINCENT** (21)................60
WILD CHILD [A] – **W.A.S.P.** (71) 86
WILD CHILD [B] – **ENYA** (72) 01
WILD FLOWER – **CULT** (24) 87
WILD FRONTIER – **Gary MOORE** (35) 87
WILD HEARTED SON – **CULT** (40)................91
WILD HEARTED WOMAN – **ALL ABOUT EVE** (33) 88
WILD HONEY – **BEACH BOYS** (29) 67
WILD IN THE COUNTRY – **Elvis PRESLEY** (4) 61
WILD IS THE WIND – **David BOWIE** (24)................81
WILD LOVE – **MUNGO JERRY** (32) 73
WILD LUV – **ROACH MOTEL** (75) 94
WILD 'N FREE – **REDNEX** (55) 95
WILD NIGHT – **John Cougar MELLENCAMP** (34) 94
WILD ONE – **Bobby RYDELL** (7) 60
THE WILD ONE – **Suzi QUATRO** (7) 74
THE WILD ONES – **SUEDE** (18)................94
WILD SIDE – **MÖTLEY CRÜE** (23) 88
WILD SIDE OF LIFE [A] – **Tommy QUICKLY** (33)................64
WILD SIDE OF LIFE [A] – **STATUS QUO** (9)....76
WILD SURF – **ASH** (31)................98
WILD THING [A] – **TROGGS** (2) 66,93
WILD THING [A] – **GOODIES** (21) 75
WILD THING [B] – **Tone LOC** (21) 89
WILD WEST HERO – **ELECTRIC LIGHT ORCHESTRA** (6) 78
WILD WILD LIFE – **TALKING HEADS** (43) 86
WILD WILD WEST [A] – **GET READY** (65) 95
WILD WILD WEST [B] – **Will SMITH featuring DRU HILL – additional vocals Kool Moe DEE** (2) 99
WILD WIND – **John LEYTON** (2) 61
WILD WOMEN DO – **Natalie COLE** (16)..........90
WILD WOOD – **Paul WELLER** (14)................93
WILD WORLD [A] – **Jimmy CLIFF** (8) 70
WILD WORLD [A] – **Maxi PRIEST** (5) 88
WILD WORLD [A] – **MR BIG** (59) 93
WILDERNESS – **Jurgen VRIES featuring SHENA** (20)............03
WILDEST DREAMS – **IRON MAIDEN** (6) 03
WILDLIFE (EP) – **GIRLSCHOOL** (58) 82

WOMAN TO WOMAN – **Beverley CRAVEN** (40) ... 91
WOMAN TROUBLE – **ARTFUL DODGER and Robbie CRAIG featuring Craig DAVID** (6) ... 00
WOMAN WOMAN – **UNION GAP featuring Gary PUCKETT** (48) ... 68
WOMANKIND – **LITTLE ANGELS** (12) ... 93
A WOMAN'S PLACE – **Gilbert O'SULLIVAN** (42) ... 74
A WOMAN'S STORY – **Marc ALMOND** (41) ... 86
WOMAN'S WORLD – **JAGS** (75) ... 80
A WOMAN'S WORTH – **Alicia KEYS** (18) ... 02
WOMBLING MERRY CHRISTMAS – **WOMBLES** (2) ... 74
THE WOMBLING SONG – **WOMBLES** (4) ... 74,98
WOMBLING WHITE TIE AND TAILS (FOX TROT) – **WOMBLES** (22) ... 75
WOMEN BEAT THEIR MEN – **Junior CARTIER** (70) ... 99
WOMEN IN UNIFORM [A] – **SKYHOOKS** (73) ... 79
WOMEN IN UNIFORM [A] – **IRON MAIDEN** (35) ... 80
WOMEN OF IRELAND – **Mike OLDFIELD** (70) ... 97
WON – **BETA BAND** (30) ... 01
WONDER – **EMBRACE** (14) ... 01
WONDERBOY – **TENACIOUS D** (34) ... 02
THE WONDER OF LOVE – **LOVELAND featuring the voice of Rachel McFARLANE** (53) ... 95
THE WONDER OF YOU [A] – **Ronnie HILTON** (22) ... 59
THE WONDER OF YOU [A] – **Ray PETERSON** (23) ... 59
THE WONDER OF YOU [A] – **Elvis PRESLEY** (1) ... 70,71,77
WONDERBOY – **KINKS** (36) ... 68
WONDERFUL [A] – **Mari WILSON** (47) ... 83
WONDERFUL [B] – **RUNRIG** (29) ... 93
WONDERFUL [C] – **Adam ANT** (32) ... 95
WONDERFUL [D] – **EVERCLEAR** (36) ... 00
WONDERFUL CHRISTMASTIME – **Paul McCARTNEY** (6) ... 79
WONDERFUL COPENHAGEN – **Danny KAYE** (5) ... 53
WONDERFUL DREAM – **Anne-Marie DAVID** (13) ... 73
WONDERFUL EXCUSE – **FAMILY CAT** (48) ... 94
WONDERFUL LAND – **SHADOWS** (1) ... 62
WONDERFUL LIFE [A] – **BLACK** (8) ... 86,87,94
WONDERFUL LIFE [A] – **TJ DAVIS** (42) ... 01
THE WONDERFUL SECRET OF LOVE – **Robert EARL** (17) ... 59
WONDERFUL THINGS – **Frankie VAUGHAN** (22) ... 58
A WONDERFUL TIME UP THERE [A] – **Pat BOONE** (2) ... 58
A WONDERFUL TIME UP THERE [A] – **Alvin STARDUST** (56) ... 81
WONDERFUL TONIGHT [A] – **DAMAGE** (3) ... 97
WONDERFUL TONIGHT (LIVE) [A] – **Eric CLAPTON** (30) ... 91

WONDERFUL! WONDERFUL! [A] – **Ronnie HILTON** (27) ... 57
WONDERFUL, WONDERFUL [A] – **Gary MILLER** (29) ... 57
WONDERFUL WORLD [A] – **Sam COOKE** (2) ... 60,86
WONDERFUL WORLD [A] – **HERMAN'S HERMITS** (7) ... 65
WONDERFUL WORLD [B] – **WORLDS APART** (51) ... 93
WONDERFUL WORLD BEAUTIFUL PEOPLE – **Jimmy CLIFF** (6) ... 69
WONDERFUL WORLD OF THE YOUNG – **Danny WILLIAMS** (8) ... 62
WONDERING WHY – **MJ COLE** (30) ... 03
WONDERLAND [A] – **COMMODORES** (40) ... 80
WONDERLAND [B] – **BIG COUNTRY** (8) ... 84
WONDERLAND [C] – **Paul YOUNG** (24) ... 86
WONDERLAND [D] – **911** (13) ... 99
WONDERLAND [E] – **PSYCHEDELIC WALTONS featuring Roisin MURPHY** (37) ... 02
WONDERMAN – **RIGHT SAID FRED** (55) ... 94
WONDERWALL [A] – **OASIS** (2) ... 95,96
WONDERWALL [A] – **Mike FLOWERS POPS** (2) ... 95,96
WONDERWALL [A] – **DE-CODE featuring Beverli SKEETE** (69) ... 96
WONDROUS PLACE – **Billy FURY** (25) ... 60
WONDROUS STORIES – **YES** (7) ... 77
WON'T GET FOOLED AGAIN – **WHO** (9) ... 71
WON'T LET THIS FEELING GO – **SUNDANCE** (40) ... 00
WON'T SOMEBODY DANCE WITH ME – **Lynsey DE PAUL** (14) ... 73
WON'T STOP LOVING YOU – **A CERTAIN RATIO** (55) ... 90
WON'T TALK ABOUT IT [A] – **Billy BRAGG** (29) ... 89
WON'T TALK ABOUT IT [A] – **Norman COOK** (29) ... 89
WON'T TALK ABOUT IT [A] – **BEATS INTERNATIONAL** (9) ... 90
WON'T YOU HOLD MY HAND NOW – **KING** (24) ... 85
WON'T YOU SAY – **Christian FRY** (48) ... 99
WOOD BEEZ (PRAY LIKE ARETHA FRANKLIN) – **SCRITTI POLITTI** (10) ... 84
WOODEN HEART – **Elvis PRESLEY** (1) ... 61,77
WOODPECKERS FROM SPACE – **VIDEO KIDS** (72) ... 85
WOODSTOCK – **MATTHEWS' SOUTHERN COMFORT** (1) ... 70
WOO-HAH!! GOT YOU ALL IN CHECK – **Busta RHYMES** (8) ... 96
WOOLY BULLY – **SAM THE SHAM and the PHARAOHS** (11) ... 65
WOPBABALUBOP – **FUNKDOOBIEST** (37) ... 93
THE WORD – **DOPE SMUGGLAZ** (62) ... 98
THE WORD GIRL – **SCRITTI POLITTI** (6) ... 85
A WORD IN YOUR EAR – **ALFIE** (66) ... 02
THE WORD IS LOVE (SAY THE WORD) – **VOICES OF LIFE** (26) ... 98
WORD IS OUT – **Kylie MINOGUE** (16) ... 91
WORD OF MOUTH – **MIKE and the MECHANICS** (13) ... 91
WORD PERFECT – **KRS ONE** (70) ... 97
WORD UP [A] – **CAMEO** (3) ... 86

WORD UP [A] – **GUN** (8) ... 94
WORD UP [A] – **Melanie B** (14) ... 99
WORDS [A] – **ALLISONS** (34) ... 61
WORDS [B] – **BEE GEES** (8) ... 68
WORDS [B] – **Rita COOLIDGE** (25) ... 78
WORDS [B] – **BOYZONE** (1) ... 96
WORDS [C] – **FR DAVID** (2) ... 83
WORDS [D] – **CHRISTIANS** (18) ... 89
WORDS [E] – **Paul VAN DYK** (54) ... 97
WORDS ARE NOT ENOUGH – **STEPS** (5) ... 01
WORDS LOVE – **RHIANNA** (41) ... 02
WORDS OF LOVE – **MAMAS and the PAPAS** (47) ... 67
WORDS THAT SAY – **MEGA CITY FOUR** (66) ... 91
WORDS WITH THE SHAMAN – **David SYLVIAN** (72) ... 85
WORDY RAPPINGHOOD – **TOM TOM CLUB** (7) ... 81
WORK [A] – **TECHNOTRONIC** (40) ... 91
WORK [B] – **Barrington LEVY** (65) ... 94
WORK ALL DAY – **Barry BIGGS** (38) ... 76
WORK IT [A] – **Missy ELLIOTT** (6) ... 02
WORK IT [B] – **NELLY featuring Justin TIMBERLAKE** (7) ... 03
WORK IT OUT [A] – **SHIVA** (36) ... 95
WORK IT OUT [B] – **DEF LEPPARD** (22) ... 96
WORK IT OUT [C] – **BEYONCÉ** (7) ... 02
WORK IT TO THE BONE – **LNR** (64) ... 89
WORK IT UP – **SLEAZESISTERS** (74) ... 98
WORK MI BODY – **MONKEY MAFIA featuring PATRA** (75) ... 96
W.O.R.K. (N.O. NAH NO NO MY DADDY DON'T) – **BOW WOW WOW** (62) ... 81
WORK REST AND PLAY (EP) – **MADNESS** (6) ... 80
WORK THAT BODY – **Diana ROSS** (7) ... 82
WORK THAT MAGIC – **Donna SUMMER** (74) ... 91
WORK THAT SUCKER TO DEATH – **XAVIER** (53) ... 82
WORKAHOLIC – **2 UNLIMITED** (4) ... 92
THE WORKER – **FISCHER-Z** (53) ... 79
WORKIN' FOR THE MAN – **Roy ORBISON** (50) ... 62
WORKIN' MY WAY BACK TO YOU – **FOUR SEASONS** (50) ... 66
WORKIN' OVERTIME – **Diana ROSS** (32) ... 89
WORKIN' UP A SWEAT – **FULL CIRCLE** (41) ... 87
WORKING FOR THE YANKEE DOLLAR – **SKIDS** (20) ... 79
WORKING IN A GOLDMINE – **AZTEC CAMERA** (31) ... 88
WORKING IN THE COALMINE – **Lee DORSEY** (8) ... 66
WORKING MAN – **Rita MacNEIL** (11) ... 90
WORKING MOTHER – **Martyn JOSEPH** (65) ... 92
WORKING MY WAY BACK TO YOU – FORGIVE ME GIRL (MEDLEY) – **DETROIT SPINNERS** (1) ... 80
WORKING ON A BUILDING OF LOVE – **CHAIRMEN OF THE BOARD** (20) ... 72
WORKING ON IT – **Chris REA** (53) ... 89
WORKING WITH FIRE AND STEEL – **CHINA CRISIS** (48) ... 83
WORLD – **BEE GEES** (9) ... 67
THE WORLD – **Nick HEYWARD** (47) ... 95
WORLD CUP '98 – PAVANE – **WIMBLEDON CHORAL SOCIETY** (20) ... 98

WORLD DESTRUCTION – **TIME ZONE** (44) ... 85
WORLD FILLED WITH LOVE – **Craig DAVID** (15) ... 03
WORLD OF OUR OWN – **WESTLIFE** (1) ... 02
WORLD IN MOTION... – **ENGLAND WORLD CUP SQUAD** (1) ... 90
THE WORLD IN MY ARMS – **Nat 'King' COLE** (36) ... 61
WORLD IN MY EYES – **DEPECHE MODE** (17) ... 90
THE WORLD IN MY HANDS – **SNAP** (44) ... 95
WORLD IN UNION [A] – **Kiri TE KANAWA** (4) ... 91
WORLD IN UNION [A] – **Shirley BASSEY** (35) ... 99
WORLD IN UNION '95 – **LADYSMITH BLACK MAMBAZO** (47) ... 95
WORLD IN YOUR HANDS – **CULTURE BEAT** (20) ... 94
THE WORLD IS A GHETTO – **GETO BOYS featuring FLAJ** (49) ... 96
THE WORLD IS FLAT – **ECHOBELLY** (31) ... 97
THE WORLD IS MINE [A] – **Malcolm VAUGHAN** (26) ... 57
THE WORLD IS MINE [B] – **ICE CUBE** (60) ... 97
THE WORLD IS NOT ENOUGH – **GARBAGE** (11) ... 99
THE WORLD IS STONE – **Cyndi LAUPER** (15) ... 92
THE WORLD IS WHAT YOU MAKE IT – **Paul BRADY** (67) ... 96
WORLD LOOKING AWAY – **MORCHEEBA** (48) ... 01
WORLD OF BROKEN HEARTS – **AMEN CORNER** (24) ... 67
WORLD OF GOOD – **SAW DOCTORS** (15) ... 96
A WORLD OF OUR OWN – **SEEKERS** (3) ... 65
THE WORLD OUTSIDE [A] – **Russ CONWAY** (24) ... 59
THE WORLD OUTSIDE [A] – **Ronnie HILTON** (18) ... 59
THE WORLD OUTSIDE [A] – **FOUR ACES** (18) ... 59
WORLD OUTSIDE YOUR WINDOW – **Tanita TIKARAM** (58) ... 89
THE WORLD SHE KNOWS – **DMAC** (33) ... 02
WORLD SHUT YOUR MOUTH – **Julian COPE** (19) ... 86,92
WORLD (THE PRICE OF LOVE) – **NEW ORDER** (13) ... 93
THE WORLD TONIGHT – **Paul McCARTNEY** (23) ... 97
THE WORLD WE KNEW (OVER AND OVER) – **Frank SINATRA** (33) ... 67
A WORLD WITHOUT HEROES – **KISS** (55) ... 82
A WORLD WITHOUT LOVE – **PETER and GORDON** (1) ... 64
WORLD WITHOUT YOU – **Belinda CARLISLE** (34) ... 88
WORLDS APART – **CACTUS WORLD NEWS** (58) ... 86
THE WORLD'S GREATEST – **R KELLY** (4) ... 02
WORST COMES TO WORST – **DILATED PEOPLES** (29) ... 02
WORZEL'S SONG – **Jon PERTWEE** (33) ... 80
WOT! – **CAPTAIN SENSIBLE** (26) ... 82
WOT'S IT TO YA – **Robbie NEVIL** (43) ... 87
WOULD – **ALICE IN CHAINS** (19) ... 93

YOU BRING ME JOY [A] – **MEECHIE** (74)........95
YOU BRING ME JOY [A] – **RHYTHM FACTOR** (53) 95
YOU BRING ME UP – **K-CI & JOJO** (21) 97
YOU BRING ON THE SUN – **LONDONBEAT** (32) 92
YOU CAME – **Kim WILDE** (3) 88
YOU CAME, YOU SAW, YOU CONQUERED – **PEARLS** (32)........72
YOU CAN CALL ME AL – **Paul SIMON** (4)......86
YOU CAN COUNT ON ME – **Jaki GRAHAM** (62) 95
YOU CAN DANCE (IF YOU WANT TO) – **GO GO LORENZO and the DAVIS PINCKNEY PROJECT** (46) 86
YOU CAN DO IT – **Al HUDSON** (15) 79
YOU CAN DO MAGIC [A] – **LIMMIE and the FAMILY COOKIN'** (3)..........73
YOU CAN DO MAGIC [B] – **AMERICA** (59)......82
YOU CAN GET IT – **MAXX** (21) 94
YOU CAN GET IT IF YOU REALLY WANT – **Desmond DEKKER and the ACES** (2) 70
YOU CAN GO YOUR OWN WAY – **Chris REA** (28) 94
YOU CAN HAVE HIM – **Dionne WARWICK** (37) 65
YOU CAN HAVE IT ALL [A] – **George McCRAE** (23)........74
YOU CAN HAVE IT ALL [B] – **Eve GALLAGHER** (43) 95
YOU CAN HAVE IT (TAKE MY HEART) – **Robert PALMER** (66) 83
YOU CAN LOVE ME NOW – **HOTHOUSE FLOWERS** (65)........98
YOU CAN MAKE ME DANCE SING OR ANYTHING (EVEN TAKE THE DOG FOR A WALK, MEND A FUSE, FOLD AWAY THE IRONING BOARD, OR ANY OTHER DOMESTIC SHORT COMINGS) – **FACES / Rod STEWART** (12) 74
YOU CAN NEVER STOP ME LOVING YOU – **Kenny LYNCH** (10) 63
YOU CAN TALK TO ME – **SEAHORSES** (15)....97
YOU CAN WIN IF YOU WANT – **MODERN TALKING** (70) 85
YOU CAN'T BE TRUE TO TWO – **Dave KING** (11)........56
YOU CAN'T BLAME LOVE – **THOMAS and TAYLOR** (53) 86
YOU CAN'T CHANGE ME – **Roger SANCHEZ featuring Armand VAN HELDEN and N'Dea DAVENPORT** (25) 01
YOU CAN'T GO HOME AGAIN – **DJ SHADOW** (13)........83
YOU CAN'T HIDE (YOUR LOVE FROM ME) – **David JOSEPH** (13) 83
YOU CAN'T HURRY LOVE [A] – **SUPREMES** (3) 66
YOU CAN'T HURRY LOVE [A] – **Phil COLLINS** (1)........82
YOU CAN'T RUN FROM LOVE – **Maxine SINGLETON** (57)........83
YOU CAN'T SIT DOWN – **Phil UPCHURCH COMBO** (39)........66
YOU CAN'T STOP ROCK 'N' ROLL – **TWISTED SISTER** (43)........83
YOU CAN'T STOP THE REIGN – **Shaquille O'NEAL** (40) 97
YOU CAUGHT MY EYE – **Judy BOUCHER** (18) 87
YOU COME FROM EARTH – **Lena FIAGBE** (69)........93
YOU COULD BE MINE – **GUNS N' ROSES** (3) 91
YOU COULD BE MY EVERYTHING – **Mikey GRAHAM** (62)........01
YOU COULD HAVE BEEN A LADY – **HOT CHOCOLATE** (22)........71
YOU COULD HAVE BEEN WITH ME – **Sheena EASTON** (54) 81
YOU DID CUT ME – **CHINA CRISIS** (54) 85
YOU DIDN'T EXPECT THAT – **Billy CRAWFORD** (35)........03
YOU DISAPPEAR FROM VIEW – **TEARDROP EXPLODES** (41) 83
YOU DO – **Bernard BUTLER** (17) 95
YOU DO SOMETHING TO ME [A] – **Paul WELLER** (9) 95
YOU DO SOMETHING TO ME [B] – **DUM DUMS** (27) 00
YOU DON'T BELIEVE ME – **STRAY CATS** (57) 81
YOU DON'T BRING ME FLOWERS – **Barbra STREISAND** (5) 78
YOU DON'T CARE ABOUT US – **PLACEBO** (5)........98
YOU DON'T FOOL ME – **QUEEN** (17) 96
YOU DON'T HAVE TO BE A BABY TO CRY – **CARAVELLES** (6)........63
YOU DON'T HAVE TO BE A STAR (TO BE IN MY SHOW) – **Marilyn McCOO and Billy DAVIS Jr** (7) 77
YOU DON'T HAVE TO BE IN THE ARMY TO FIGHT IN THE WAR – **MUNGO JERRY** (13) ..71
YOU DON'T HAVE TO GO – **CHI-LITES** (3) 76
YOU DON'T HAVE TO SAY YOU LOVE ME [A] – **Dusty SPRINGFIELD** (1)........66
YOU DON'T HAVE TO SAY YOU LOVE ME [A] – **Elvis PRESLEY** (9)........71
YOU DON'T HAVE TO SAY YOU LOVE ME [A] – **GUYS n' DOLLS** (5)........76
YOU DON'T HAVE TO SAY YOU LOVE ME [A] – **Denise WELCH** (23) 95
YOU DON'T HAVE TO WORRY – **Mary J BLIGE** (36) 93
YOU DON'T KNOW [A] – **Helen SHAPIRO** (1) 61
YOU DON'T KNOW [B] – **BERLIN** (39)...........87
YOU DON'T KNOW [C] – **Cyndi LAUPER** (27)........97
YOU DON'T KNOW [D] – **MASS SYNDICATE featuring Su Su BOBIEN** (71) 98
YOU DON'T KNOW [E] – **702** (36) 99
(YOU DONT KNOW) HOW GLAD I AM – **Kiki DEE** (33) 75
YOU DON'T KNOW ME [A] – **Ray CHARLES** (9) 62
YOU DON'T KNOW ME [B] – **Armand VAN HELDEN** (1) 99
YOU DON'T KNOW MY NAME – **Alicia KEYS** (19) 03
YOU DON'T KNOW NOTHIN' – **FOR REAL** (54) 95
YOU DON'T KNOW (OH-OH-OH) – **SERIOUS INTENTION** (75)........85
YOU DON'T KNOW WHAT YOU'VE GOT (UNTIL YOU LOSE IT) – **Ral DONNER** (25) 61
YOU DON'T LOVE ME [A] – **Gary WALKER** (26) 66
YOU DON'T LOVE ME [B] – **MARILYN** (40) 84
YOU DON'T LOVE ME [C] – **JAGGED EDGE** (66) 90
YOU DON'T LOVE ME (NO, NO, NO) – **Dawn PENN** (3) 94
YOU DON'T NEED A REASON – **Phil FEARON** (42)........85
YOU DON'T NEED SOMEONE NEW – **LOTUS EATERS** (53)........83
YOU DON'T OWE ME A THING – **Johnnie RAY** (12) 57
YOU DON'T UNDERSTAND – **HOUSE OF LOVE** (46) 92
YOU DON'T UNDERSTAND ME – **ROXETTE** (42)........96
YOU DREAMER – **BIG COUNTRY** (68) 95
YOU DRIVE ME CRAZY [A] – **Shakin' STEVENS** (2) 81
(YOU DRIVE ME) CRAZY [B] – **Britney SPEARS** (5) 99
YOU DRIVE ME CRAZY [B] – **SUGARCOMA** (57)........02
YOU DROVE ME TO IT – **HELL IS FOR HEROES** (63) 02,03
YOU GAVE ME LOVE – **CROWN HEIGHTS AFFAIR** (10) 80
YOU GAVE ME SOMEBODY TO LOVE – **MANFRED MANN** (36)........66
YOU GET THE BEST FROM ME (SAY, SAY, SAY) – **Alicia MYERS** (58) 84
YOU GET WHAT YOU GIVE – **NEW RADICALS** (5)........99
YOU GIVE LOVE A BAD NAME – **BON JOVI** (14)........86
YOU GIVE ME SOMETHING – **JAMIROQUAI** (16)........01
YOU GO TO MY HEAD – **Bryan FERRY** (33) ..75
YOU GOT IT – **Roy ORBISON** (3) 89
YOU GOT IT (THE RIGHT STUFF) – **NEW KIDS ON THE BLOCK** (1) 89
YOU GOT ME [A] – **Christian FRY** (45) 98
YOU GOT ME [B] – **ROOTS featuring Erykah BADU** (31) 99
YOU GOT ME BURNING [A] – **Lenny WILLIAMS** (67)........78
YOU GOT ME BURNING [B] – **PESHAY featuring CO-ORDINATE** (41) 02
(YOU GOT ME) BURNING UP – **Cevin FISHER / Loleatta HOLLOWAY** (14)....99
YOU GOT ME ROCKING – **ROLLING STONES** (23) 94
YOU GOT SOUL – **Johnny NASH** (6) 69
YOU GOT THE FLOOR – **Arthur ADAMS** (38)........81
YOU GOT THE LOVE [A] – **SOURCE featuring Candi STATON** (3) 91,97
YOU GOT THE LOVE [B] – **Robin S** (62) 97
YOU GOT THE POWER [A] – **WAR** (58) 82
YOU GOT THE POWER [B] – **QFX** (33) 96
YOU GOT THE STYLE – **ATHLETE** (37)......02,03
YOU GOT TO BE THERE – **KADOC** (45)..........96
YOU GOT WHAT IT TAKES [A] – **Marv JOHNSON** (7)........60
YOU GOT WHAT IT TAKES [A] – **Johnny KIDD and the PIRATES** (25) 60
YOU GOT WHAT IT TAKES [A] – **Dave CLARK FIVE** (28) 67
YOU GOT WHAT IT TAKES [A] – **SHOWADDYWADDY** (2) 77
YOU GOTTA BE – **DES'REE** (10) 94,95,99
YOU GOTTA BE A HUSTLER IF YOU WANNA GET ON – **Sue WILKINSON** (25) ..80
YOU GOTTA BELIEVE – **MARKY MARK and the FUNKY BUNCH** (54) 92
(YOU GOTTA) FIGHT FOR YOUR RIGHT (TO PARTY) – **BEASTIE BOYS** (11)........87
YOU GOTTA HAVE LOVE IN YOUR HEART – **SUPREMES and the FOUR TOPS** (25)..........71
YOU GOTTA LOVE SOMEONE – **Elton JOHN** (33) 90
YOU GOTTA STOP – **Elvis PRESLEY** (38) 67
(YOU GOTTA WALK) DON'T LOOK BACK – **Peter TOSH** (43)........78
YOU HAVE – **Marc ALMOND** (57) 84
YOU HAVE BEEN LOVED – **George MICHAEL** (2)........97
YOU HAVE PLACED A CHILL IN MY HEART – **EURYTHMICS** (16)........88
YOU HAVEN'T DONE NOTHIN' – **Stevie WONDER** (30) 74
YOU HELD THE WORLD IN YOUR ARMS – **IDLEWILD** (9) 02
YOU JUST MIGHT SEE ME CRY – **OUR KID** (2) 76
YOU KEEP IT ALL IN – **BEAUTIFUL SOUTH** (8) 89
YOU KEEP ME HANGIN' ON [A] – **SUPREMES** (8) 66
YOU KEEP ME HANGIN' ON [A] – **VANILLA FUDGE** (18)........67
(YOU KEEP ME) HANGIN' ON [A] – **Cliff RICHARD** (13) 74
YOU KEEP ME HANGIN' ON [A] – **Kim WILDE** (2) 86
YOU KEEP ME HANGIN' ON – STOP IN THE NAME OF LOVE – **Roni HILL** (36) 77
YOU KEEP RUNNING AWAY – **FOUR TOPS** (26)........67
YOU KNOW HOW TO LOVE ME – **Phyllis HYMAN** (47) 80
YOU KNOW HOW WE DO IT – **ICE CUBE** (41)........94
YOU KNOW I LOVE YOU...DON'T YOU? – **Howard JONES** (43) 86
YOU KNOW THAT I LOVE YOU – **Donell JONES** (41) 02
YOU KNOW WHAT I MEAN – **VERNONS GIRLS** (16) 62
(YOU KNOW) YOU CAN DO IT – **CENTRAL LINE** (67)........81
YOU LAY SO EASY ON MY MIND – **Andy WILLIAMS** (32) 75
YOU LEARN – **Alanis MORISSETTE** (24) 96
YOU LET YOUR HEART GO TOO FAST – **SPIN DOCTORS** (66)........94
YOU LIED TO ME – **Cathy DENNIS** (34) 92
YOU LIFT ME UP – **Rebekah RYAN** (26) 96
YOU LIGHT MY FIRE – **Sheila B DEVOTION** (44) 78

YOUNG DISCIPLES (EP) – **YOUNG DISCIPLES** (48) 92
YOUNG EMOTIONS – **Ricky NELSON** (48)......60
YOUNG, FREE AND SINGLE – **SUNFIRE** (20) 83
YOUNG FRESH N' NEW – **KELIS** (32) 01
YOUNG, GIFTED AND BLACK – **BOB and MARCIA** (5) 70
YOUNG GIRL [A] – **UNION GAP featuring Gary PUCKETT** (1) 68,74
YOUNG GIRL [A] – **Darren DAY** (42) 94
YOUNG GIRL [A] – **Joe LONGTHORNE** (61) 94
YOUNG GIRLS & HAPPY ENDINGS – **GORKY'S ZYGOTIC MYNCI** (49) 97
YOUNG GODS – **LITTLE ANGELS** (34) 91
YOUNG GUNS (GO FOR IT) – **WHAM!** (3) 82
YOUNG HEARTS – **KINGS OF TOMORROW** (36) 02
YOUNG HEARTS RUN FREE [A] – **Candi STATON** (2) 76,86,99
YOUNG HEARTS RUN FREE [A] – **Kym MAZELLE** (20) 97
YOUNG LIVERS – **ROCKET FROM THE CRYPT** (67) 96
YOUNG LOVE [A] – **Tab HUNTER** (1) 57
YOUNG LOVE [A] – **Sonny JAMES** (11) 57
YOUNG LOVE [A] – **Donny OSMOND** (1) 73
YOUNG LOVERS – **PAUL and PAULA** (9) 63
THE YOUNG MC – **SUPERFUNK** (62) 00
THE YOUNG NEW MEXICAN PUPPETEER – **Tom JONES** (6) 72
THE YOUNG OFFENDER'S MUM – **CARTER – THE UNSTOPPABLE SEX MACHINE** (34) 95
THE YOUNG ONES – **Cliff RICHARD and the SHADOWS** (1) 62
YOUNG PARISIANS – **ADAM and the ANTS** (9) 80
YOUNG SOUL REBELS – **Mica PARIS** (61) 91
YOUNG TURKS – **Rod STEWART** (11) 81
YOUNG WORLD – **Ricky NELSON** (19) 62
YOUNGER GIRL – **CRITTERS** (38) 66
YOUR BABY AIN'T YOUR BABY ANYMORE – **Paul DA VINCI** (20) 74
YOUR BABY'S GONE SURFIN' – **Duane EDDY and the REBELS** (49) 63
YOUR BODY'S CALLIN' – **R KELLY** (19) 94
YOUR CARESS (ALL I NEED) – **DJ FLAVOURS** (19) 97
YOUR CASSETTE PET – **BOW WOW WOW** (58) 80
YOUR CHEATING HEART – **Ray CHARLES** (13) 62
YOUR CHRISTMAS WISH – **SMURFS** (8) 96
YOUR DREAM – **Adrian GURVITZ** (61) 82
YOUR DRESS – **John FOXX** (61) 83
YOUR EARS SHOULD BE BURNING NOW – **Marti WEBB** (61) 80
YOUR EYES – **SIMPLY RED** (26) 00
YOUR FACE – **SLACKER** (33) 97
YOUR FASCINATION – **Gary NUMAN** (46) 85
YOUR FAVORITE THING – **SUGAR** (40) 94
YOUR GENERATION – **GENERATION X** (36) ..77
YOUR GHOST – **Kristin HERSH** (45) 94
YOUR HONOUR – **Pluto SHERVINGTON** (19) 82
YOUR HURTIN' KIND OF LOVE – **Dusty SPRINGFIELD** (37) 65
YOUR KISS IS SWEET – **SYREETA** (12) 75
YOUR KISSES ARE CHARITY – **CULTURE CLUB** (25) 99
YOUR LATEST TRICK – **DIRE STRAITS** (26) 86
YOUR LOSS MY GAIN – **OMAR** (47) 92
YOUR LOVE [A] – **HIPSWAY** (66) 89
YOUR LOVE [B] – **Frankie KNUCKLES** (59) 89
YOUR LOVE [C] – **Diana ROSS** (14) 93
YOUR LOVE [D] – **INNER CITY** (28) 96
YOUR LOVE GETS SWEETER – **Finley QUAYE** (16) 98
(YOUR LOVE HAS LIFTED ME) HIGHER AND HIGHER – **Rita COOLIDGE** (48) 77
YOUR LOVE IS A 187 – **WHITEHEAD BROS** (32) 95
YOUR LOVE IS CALLING – **EVOLUTION** (60) ..96
YOUR LOVE IS KING – **SADE** (6) 84
YOUR LOVE IS LIFTING ME – **NOMAD** (60) 92
(YOUR LOVE KEEPS LIFTING ME) HIGHER AND HIGHER – **Jackie WILSON** (11) 69,75
YOUR LOVE TAKES ME HIGHER – **BELOVED** (39) 90
YOUR LOVING ARMS – **Billie Ray MARTIN** (6) 94,95
YOUR LUCKY DAY IN HELL – **EELS** (35) 97
YOUR MA SAID YOU CRIED IN YOUR SLEEP LAST NIGHT – **Doug SHELDON** (29) 62
YOUR MAGIC PUT A SPELL ON ME – **LJ JOHNSON** (27) 76
YOUR MAMA DON'T DANCE – **POISON** (13) ..89
YOUR MAMMA WON'T LIKE ME – **Suzi QUATRO** (31) 75
YOUR MIRROR – **SIMPLY RED** (17) 92
YOUR MUSIC – **INTENSO PROJECT featuring Laura JAYE** (32) 03
YOUR NEW CUCKOO – **CARDIGANS** (35) 97
YOUR OWN SPECIAL WAY – **GENESIS** (43) 77
YOUR PAINTED SMILE – **Bryan FERRY** (52) 94
YOUR PERSONAL TOUCH – **Evelyn 'Champagne' KING** (37) 85
YOUR SECRET LOVE – **Luther VANDROSS** (14) 96
YOUR SMILE – **OCTOPUS** (42) 96
YOUR SONG [A] – **Elton JOHN** (7) 71,02
YOUR SONG [A] – **Billy PAUL** (37) 77
YOUR SONG [A] – **Rod STEWART** (41) 92
YOUR SWAYING ARMS – **DEACON BLUE** (23) 91
YOUR TENDER LOOK – **Joe BROWN and the BRUVVERS** (31) 62
YOUR TIME HASN'T COME YET BABY – **Elvis PRESLEY** (22) 68
YOUR TIME IS GONNA COME – **DREAD ZEPPELIN** (59) 90
YOUR TOWN – **DEACON BLUE** (14) 92
YOUR WOMAN – **WHITE TOWN** (1) 97
YOU'RE A BETTER MAN THAN I – **SHAM 69** (49) 79
YOU'RE A LADY – **Peter SKELLERN** (3) 72
YOU'RE A STAR – **AQUARIAN DREAM** (67) 79
YOU'RE A SUPERSTAR – **LOVE INC.** (7) 02
YOU'RE ALL I NEED – **MÖTLEY CRÜE** (23) 88
YOU'RE ALL I NEED TO GET BY [A] – **Marvin GAYE** (19) 68
YOU'RE ALL I NEED TO GET BY [A] – **Johnny MATHIS and Deniece WILLIAMS** (45) 78
YOU'RE ALL THAT MATTERS TO ME – **Curtis STIGERS** (6) 92
YOU'RE BREAKIN' MY HEART – **Keely SMITH** (14) 65
YOU'RE DRIVING ME CRAZY – **TEMPERANCE SEVEN** (1) 61
YOU'RE EVERYTHING TO ME – **Boris GARDINER** (11) 86
(YOU'RE) FABULOUS BABE – **Kenny WILLIAMS** (35) 77
YOU'RE FREE – **YOMANDA** (22) 03
YOU'RE FREE TO GO – **Jim REEVES** (48) 72
YOU'RE GONNA GET NEXT TO ME – **Bo KIRKLAND and Ruth DAVIS** (12) 77
YOU'RE GONNA MISS ME – **TURNTABLE ORCHESTRA** (52) 89
YOU'RE GORGEOUS – **BABYBIRD** (3) 96
(YOU'RE) HAVING MY BABY – **Paul ANKA** (6) 74
YOU'RE HISTORY – **SHAKESPEAR'S SISTER** (7) 89
YOU'RE IN A BAD WAY – **SAINT ETIENNE** (12) 93
YOU'RE IN LOVE – **WILSON PHILLIPS** (29) 91
YOU'RE IN MY HEART [A] – **Rod STEWART** (3) 77
YOU'RE IN MY HEART [B] – **David ESSEX** (59) 83
YOU'RE INVITED (BUT YOUR FRIEND CAN'T COME) – **Vince NEIL** (63) 92
YOU'RE LOOKING HOT TONIGHT – **Barry MANILOW** (47) 83
YOU'RE LYING – **LINX** (15) 80
YOU'RE MAKIN' ME HIGH – **Toni BRAXTON** (7) 96
YOU'RE MORE THAN A NUMBER IN MY LITTLE RED BOOK – **DRIFTERS** (5) 76
YOU'RE MOVING OUT TODAY – **Carole Bayer SAGER** (6) 77
YOU'RE MY ANGEL – **Mikey GRAHAM** (13) 00
YOU'RE MY BEST FRIEND [A] – **QUEEN** (7) 76
YOU'RE MY BEST FRIEND [B] – **Don WILLIAMS** (35) 76
YOU'RE MY EVERYTHING [A] – **TEMPTATIONS** (26) 67
YOU'RE MY EVERYTHING [B] – **Max BYGRAVES** (34) 69
YOU'RE MY EVERYTHING [C] – **EAST SIDE BEAT** (65) 93
YOU'RE MY EVERYTHING [C] – **Lee GARRETT** (15) 76
YOU'RE MY GIRL – **ROCKIN' BERRIES** (40) ..65
YOU'RE MY HEART, YOU'RE MY SOUL – **MODERN TALKING** (56) 85
YOU'RE MY LAST CHANCE – **52ND STREET** (49) 86
YOU'RE MY LIFE – **Barry BIGGS** (36) 77
YOU'RE MY MATE – **RIGHT SAID FRED** (18) ..01
YOU'RE MY NUMBER ONE – **S CLUB 7** (2) 99
(YOU'RE MY ONE AND ONLY) TRUE LOVE – **Ann-Marie SMITH** (46) 95
(YOU'RE MY) SOUL AND INSPIRATION – **RIGHTEOUS BROTHERS** (15) 66
YOU'RE MY WORLD [A] – **Cilla BLACK** (1) 64
YOU'RE MY WORLD [B] – **Nick HEYWARD** (67) 88
YOU'RE NEVER TOO YOUNG – **COOLNOTES** (42) 84
YOU'RE NO GOOD [A] – **SWINGING BLUE JEANS** (3) 64
YOU'RE NO GOOD [B] – **ASWAD** (35) 95
YOU'RE NOT ALONE [A] – **OLIVE** (1) 96,97
YOU'RE NOT ALONE [B] – **EMBRACE** (14) 00
YOU'RE NOT HERE – **TYRREL CORPORATION** (42) 94
YOU'RE OK [A] – **OTTAWAN** (56) 80
YOU'RE OK [B] – **kd LANG** (44) 96
YOU'RE ONE – **IMPERIAL TEEN** (69) 96
(YOU'RE PUTTIN') A RUSH ON ME – **Stephanie MILLS** (62) 87
YOU'RE READY NOW – **Frankie VALLI** (11) 70
YOU'RE SINGING OUR LOVE SONG TO SOMEBODY ELSE – **Jerry WALLACE** (46) 60
YOU'RE SIXTEEN [A] – **Johnny BURNETTE** (3) 61
YOU'RE SIXTEEN [A] – **Ringo STARR** (4) 74
YOU'RE SO RIGHT FOR ME – **EASTSIDE CONNECTION** (44) 78
YOU'RE SO VAIN – **Carly SIMON** (3) 72,91
YOU'RE STILL THE ONE – **Shania TWAIN** (10) 98
YOU'RE SUCH A GOOD LOOKING WOMAN – **Joe DOLAN** (17) 70
YOU'RE THE BEST THING – **STYLE COUNCIL** (5) 84
(YOU'RE THE) DEVIL IN DISGUISE – **Elvis PRESLEY** (1) 63
YOU'RE THE FIRST, THE LAST, MY EVERYTHING – **Barry WHITE** (1) 74
YOU'RE THE GREATEST LOVER – **Jonathan KING** (67) 79
YOU'RE THE INSPIRATION – **CHICAGO** (14) ..85
YOU'RE THE ONE [A] – **Kathy KIRBY** (17) 64
YOU'RE THE ONE [B] – **Petula CLARK** (23) 65
YOU'RE THE ONE [C] – **BANG** (74) 89
YOU'RE THE ONE [D] – **SWV** (13) 96
YOU'RE THE ONE FOR ME – **D TRAIN** (15) 82,85
YOU'RE THE ONE FOR ME – DAYBREAK – AM – **Paul HARDCASTLE** (41) 84
YOU'RE THE ONE FOR ME, FATTY – **MORRISSEY** (19) 92
YOU'RE THE ONE I LOVE – **Shola AMA** (3) 97
YOU'RE THE ONE THAT I WANT [A] – **John TRAVOLTA and Olivia NEWTON-JOHN** (1) 78,98
YOU'RE THE ONE THAT I WANT [A] – **Hylda BAKER and Arthur MULLARD** (22) 78
YOU'RE THE ONE THAT I WANT [A] – **Craig McLACHLAN and Debbie GIBSON** (13) 93
YOU'RE THE ONLY GOOD THING – **Jim REEVES** (17) 61
YOU'RE THE ONLY ONE – **Val DOONICAN** (37) 68
YOU'RE THE REASON – **WAMDUE PROJECT** (39) 00
YOU'RE THE REASON WHY – **RUBETTES** (28) 76
YOU'RE THE STAR – **Rod STEWART** (19) 95
YOU'RE THE STORM – **CARDIGANS** (74) 03

PICTURE CREDITS

page 1 IDOLS
page 3 Betty Halvagi
page 6 Mirropix
page 7 Ann Ronan Picture Library
Apple
page 9 Rex Features
page 22 Corbis
page 35 Rex Features
page 47 Sean Spencer (2)
page 59 Rex Features
page 64 Cover Art
page 70 London Features International
page 83 Corbis
NME
page 92 Redferns
page 93 Redferns
Getty Images/Hulton Archive
page 106 Rex Features
page 117 Sean Spencer
page 131 Scott Gries/Getty Images
page 142 Melody Maker
Rex Features
page 154 Getty Images/Hulton Archive
page 165 Rex Features
page 192 London Features International
page 203 Sean Spencer (2)
page 213 Kevin Winter/Getty Images
Betty Halvagi
page 227 Rex Features
page 237 Rex Features
Mirrorpix
page 248 IDOLS
Universal Music
page 259 Liverpool Daily Post and Echo
page 293 MBC PR
page 302 Betty Halvagi
London Features International
page 316 Mirrorpix
page 333 Mirrorpix
page 345 Sean Spencer (2)
page 346 Sean Spencer
page 351 London Features International
Betty Halvagi
page 362 Cover Art (2)
page 375 Rex Features (2)
page 386 Betty Halvagi
page 397 IDOLS
page 420 Rex Features
page 421 Getty Images/Hulton Archive
NME
page 435 Rex Features
IDOLS
page 446 NME
Rex Features
page 456 Mirrorpix
page 471 Sean Spencer (2)
page 472 Sean Spencer
page 479 London Features International (2)
page 490 Rex Features
London Features International
page 506 Rex Features
page 507 MBC PR
page 515 Sean Spencer
page 526 Rex Features
page 535 Mercury Records
Rex Features
page 560 Mirrorpix
page 570 Mirrorpix
page 583 Sean Spencer
Betty Halvagi
page 595 Redferns
page 609 Mirrorpix
IDOLS
page 621 Zzonked
page 627 Mirrorpix
page 767 Yeung Poon
page 768 Betty Halvagi
Yeung Poon (2)

Forward
Stop
Refresh
Home
http://www.bibleofpop.com/
BRITISH
HIT
SINGLES
& ALBUMS
VISIT:
www.bibleofpop.com
Our website has been going from strength to strength since its launch in 2002. Put together by the editorial team of this very book, with the assistance of Guinness World Records web boffins, we aim to give our readers the opportunity to stay in touch all year round, and get lots of new and interesting stats and facts on a daily basis.
Every day we bring you the best in pop facts from the past six decades with our chart consultant Dave McAleer's BACKTRACK and DAILY RECORD columns, and each week we give you an in-depth look at the current No.1 hit single. The best of the current crop of album releases are reviewed in our FUTURE CLASSICS section, and there's Matthew White's weekly POP GENIUS quiz which starts every Friday with a prize for the lucky player who gets the best score against the clock. Also, check out the FORUM where you can contact like-minded fans of the book to exchange information.
As if all that wasn't enough, you can calculate what was No.1 on the day you were born.
Finally, we want YOU to help us to develop the site. If you put together your own charts and stories, send them to us. If we like them we'll put them online. And if you have other ideas for features you would like to see on bibleofpop.com, then we would like to hear from you.
Email us at editor@bibleofpop.com

EVER WANTED
TO OWN YOUR
OWN GOLD DISC?

QUEEN
To
PAUL COLEMAN
10-01-2004
QUEEN
The Miracle
1989